KU-401-709

Annual Abstract
of Statistics

Warwickshire
County Council

LOVE
YOUR
LIBRARY

No 152
2016 Edition
Compiled by: Dandy Booksellers

Contacts

For information about the content of this publication, contact
Dandy Booksellers: Tel 020 7624 2993
Email: dandybooksellers@btconnect.com

Publications orders

To obtain the print version of this publication, please contact
Dandy Booksellers
Tel: 0207 624 2993
Email: dandybooksellers@btconnect.com
Fax: 0207 624 5049
Post: Unit 3&4, 31-33 Priory Park Road, London, NW6 7UP
Web: www.dandybooksellers.com

Contents

5: Social Protection

6: External trade and investment

7: Research and development

8: Personal income, expenditure & wealth

9: Lifestyles

12: Banking and Finance

13: Service industry

14: Defence

15: Population and vital statistics

16: Health

17: Prices

18: Production

19: National Accounts

20: Education

22: Transport

23:Government Finance

24:Agriculture

Sources:

Units of measurement

Length

1 millimetre (mm)	= 0.03937 inch	
1 centimetre (cm)	= 10 millimetres	= 0.3937 inch
1 metre (m)	= 1,000 millimetres	= 1.094 yards
1 kilometre (km)	= 1,000 metres	= 0.6214 mile
1 inch (in.)		= 25.40 millimetres or 2.540 centimetres
1 foot (ft.)	= 12 inches	= 0.3048 metre
1 yard (yd.)	= 3 feet	= 0.9144 metre
1 mile	= 1,760 yards	= 1.609 kilometres

Area

1 square millimetre (mm2)		= 0.001550 square inch
1 square metre (m2)	= one million square millimetres	= 1.196 square yards
1 hectare (ha)	= 10,000 square metres	= 2.471 acres
1 square kilometre (km2)	= one million square metres	= 247.1 acres
1 square inch (sq. in.)		= 645.2 square millimetres or 6.452 square centimetres
1 square foot (sq. ft.)	= 144 square inches	= 0.09290 square metre or 929.0 square centimetres
1 square yard (sq. yd.)	= 9 square feet	= 0.8361 square metre
1 acre	= 4,840 square yards	= 4,046 square metres or 0.4047 hectare
1 square mile (sq. mile)	= 640 acres	= 2.590 square kilometres or 259.0 hectares

Volume

1 cubic centimetre (cm3)		= 0.06102 cubic inch
1 cubic decimetre (dm3)	= 1,000 cubic centimetres	= 0.03531 cubic foot
1 cubic metre (m3)	= one million cubic centimetres	= 1.308 cubic yards
1 cubic inch (cu.in.)		=16.39 cubic centimetres
1 cubic foot (cu. ft.)	= 1,728 cubic inches	= 0.02832 cubic metre or 28.32 cubic decimetres
1 cubic yard (cu. yd.)	= 27 cubic feet	= 0.7646 cubic metre

Capacity

1 litre (l)	= 1 cubic decimetre	= 0.2200 gallon
1 hectolitre (hl)	= 100 litres	= 22.00 gallons
1 pint		= 0.5682 litre
1 quart	= 2 pints	= 1.137 litres
1 gallon	= 8 pints	= 4.546 litres
1 bulk barrel	= 36 gallons (gal.)	= 1.637 hectolitres

Weight

1 gram (g)		= 0.03527 ounce avoirdupois
1 hectogram (hg)	= 100 grams	= 3.527 ounces or 0.2205 pound
1 kilogram (kg)	= 1,000 grams or 10 hectograms	= 2.205 pounds
1 tonne (t)	= 1,000 kilograms	= 1.102 short tons or 0.9842 long ton
1 ounce avoirdupois (oz.)	= 437.5 grains	= 28.35 grams
1 pound avoirdupois (lb.)	= 16 ounces	= 0.4536 kilogram
1 hundredweight (cwt.)	= 112 pounds	= 50.80 kilograms
1 short ton	= 2,000 pounds	= 907.2 kilograms or 0.9072 tonne
1 long ton (referred to as ton)	= 2,240 pounds	= 1,016 kilograms or 1.016 tonnes
1 ounce troy	= 480 grains	= 31.10 grams

Energy

British thermal unit (Btu)	= 0.2520 kilocalorie (kcal) = 1.055 kilojoule (kj)
Therm	= 105 British thermal units = 25,200 kcal = 105,506 kj
Megawatt hour (MWh)	= 106 watt hours (Wh)
Gigawatt hour (GWh)	= 106 kilowatt hours = 34,121 therms

Food and drink

Butter	23,310 litres milk	= 1 tonne butter (average)
Cheese	10,070 litres milk	= 1 tonne cheese
Condensed milk	2,550 litres milk	= 1 tonne full cream condensed milk
	2,953 litres skimmed milk	= 1 tonne skimmed condensed milk
Milk	1 million litres	= 1,030 tonnes
Milk powder	8,054 litres milk	= 1 tonne full cream milk powder
	10,740 litres skimmed milk	= 1 tonne skimmed milk powder
Eggs	17,126 eggs	= 1 tonne (approximate)
Sugar	100 tonnes sugar beet	= 92 tonnes refined sugar
	100 tonnes cane sugar	= 96 tonnes refined sugar

Shipping

Gross tonnage	= The total volume of all the enclosed spaces of a vessel, the unit of measurement being a 'ton' of 100 cubic feet.
Deadweight tonnage	= Deadweight tonnage is the total weight in tons of 2,240 lb. that a ship can legally carry, that is the total weight of cargo, bunkers, stores and crew.

Introduction

Welcome to the 2016 edition of the Annual Abstract of Statistics. This compendium draws together statistics from a wide range of official and other authoritative sources.

Dandy Booksellers have sourced and formatted these tables under instruction from various government departments/ organisations

Current data for many of the series appearing in this Annual Abstract are contained in other ONS publications, such as Economic & Labour Market Review, Population Trends, Health Statistics Quarterly and Financial Statistics. These titles can be purchased through Dandy Booksellers.

The name (and telephone number, where this is available) of the organisation providing the statistics are shown under each table. In addition, a list of Sources is given at the back of the book, which sets out the official publications or other sources to which further reference can be made.

Identification codes

The four-letter identification code at the top of each data column, or at the side of each row is the ONS reference for this series of data on their database. Please quote the relevant code if you contact them requiring any further information about the data. On some tables it is not possible to include these codes, so please quote the table number in these cases.

Definitions and classification

Time series
So far as possible annual totals are given throughout, but quarterly or monthly figures are given where these are more suitable to the type of series.

Standard Industrial Classification

A Standard Industrial Classification (SIC) was first introduced into the UK in 1948 for use in classifying business establishments and other statistical units by the type of economic activity in which they are engaged. The classification provides a framework for the collection, tabulation, presentation and analysis of data about economic activities. Its use promotes uniformity of data collected by various government departments and agencies.

Since 1948 the classification has been revised in 1958, 1968, 1980, 1992, 2003 and 2007. One of the principal objectives of the 1980 revision was to eliminate differences from the activity classification issued by the Statistical Office of the European Communities (Eurostat) and entitled 'Nomenclature générale des activités économiques dans les Communautés Européennes', usually abbreviated to NACE.

In 1990 the European Communities introduced a new statistical classification of economic activities (NACE Rev 1) by regulation. The regulation made it obligatory for the UK to introduce a new Standard Industrial Classification SIC(92), based on NACE Rev 1. UK SIC(92) was based exactly on NACE Rev 1 but, where it was thought necessary or helpful, a fifth digit was added to form subclasses of the NACE 1 four digit system. Classification systems need to be revised periodically because, over time, new products, processes and industries emerge. In January 2003 a minor revision of NACE Rev 1, known as NACE Rev 1.1, was published in the Official Journal of the European Communities.

Consequently, the UK was obliged to introduce a new Standard Industrial Classification, SIC(2003) consistent with NACE Rev 1.1. The UK took the opportunity of the 2003 revision also to update the national Subclasses. Full details are available in UK Standard Industrial Classification of Economic Activities 2003 and the Indexes to the UK Standard Industrial Classification of Economic Activities 2003. These are the most recent that are currently used. The most up to date version is the UK Standard Industrial Classification of Economic activities 2007 (SIC2007). It will be implemented in five stages and came into effect on 1 January 2008.

- For reference year 2008, the Annual Business Inquiry (parts 1 & 2) will be based on SIC 2007

- PRODCOM will also be based on SIC 2007 from reference year 2008

- Other annual outputs will be based on SIC 2007 from reference year 2009, unless otherwise determined by regulation

- Quarterly and monthly surveys will be based on SIC 2007 from the first reference period in 2010, unless otherwise determined by regulation

- National Accounts will move to SIC 2007 in September 2011

Symbols and conventions used

Change of basis
Where consecutive figures have been compiled on different bases and are not strictly comparable, a footnote is added indicating the nature of the difference.

Geographic coverage
Statistics relate mainly to the UK. Where figures relate to other areas, this is indicated on the table.

Units of measurement
The various units of measurement used are listed after the Contents.

Rounding of figures
In tables where figures have been rounded to the nearest final digit, the constituent items may not add up exactly to the total.

Symbols
The following symbols have been used throughout:

.. = not available or not applicable (also information supressed to avoid disclosure)

- = nil or less than half the final digit shown

Office for National Statistics online:
www.ons.gov.uk
Web-based access to time series, cross-sectional data and metadata from across the Government Statistical Service (GSS), is available using the site search function from the homepage. Download many datasets, in whole or in part, or consult directory information for all GSS statistical resources, including censuses, surveys, periodicals and enquiry services. Information is posted as PDF electronic documents or in XLS and CSV formats, compatible with most spreadsheet packages.

Contact point
Dandy Booksellers welcomes any feedback on the content of the Annual Abstract, including comments on the format of the data and the selection of topics. Comments and requests for general information should be addressed to:

Dandy Booksellers
Unit 3&4
31-33 Priory Park Road
London
NW6 7UP
or
enquiries@dandybooksellers.com

this page is intentionally blank

Area

Chapter 1

Area

The United Kingdom (UK) comprises Great Britain and Northern Ireland. Great Britain comprises England, Wales and Scotland.

Physical Features

The United Kingdom (UK) constitutes the greater part of the British Isles. The largest of the islands is Great Britain. The next largest comprises Northern Ireland and the Irish Republic. Western Scotland is fringed by the large island chain known as the Hebrides, and to the north east of the Scottish mainland are the Orkney and Shetland Islands. All these, along with the Isle of Wight, Anglesey and the Isles of Scilly, form part of the UK, but the Isle of Man, in the Irish Sea and the Channel Islands, between Great Britain and France are largely self-governing and are not part of the UK. The UK is currently one of the 28 member states of the European Union. With an area of about 243 000 sq km (about 94 000 sq miles), the UK is just under 1 000 km (about 600 miles) from the south coast to the extreme north of Scotland and just under 500 km (around 300 miles) across at the widest point.

- Highest mountain: Ben Nevis, in the highlands of Scotland, at 1 343 m (4 406 ft)
- Longest river: the Severn, 354 km (220 miles) long, which rises in central Wales and flows through Shrewsbury, Worcester and Gloucester in England to the Bristol Channel
- Largest lake: Lough Neagh, Northern Ireland, at 396 sq km (153 sq miles)
- Deepest lake: Loch Morar in the Highlands of Scotland, 310 m (1 017 ft) deep
- Highest waterfall: Eas a'Chual Aluinn, from Glas Bheinn, in the highlands of Scotland, with a drop of 200 m (660 ft)
- Deepest cave: Ogof Ffynnon Ddu, Wales, at 308 m (1 010 ft) deep
- Most northerly point on the British mainland: Dunnet Head, north-east Scotland
- Most southerly point on the British mainland: Lizard Point, Cornwall
- Closest point to mainland continental Europe: Dover, Kent. The Channel Tunnel, which links England and France, is a little over 50 km (31 miles) long, of which nearly 38 km (24 miles) are actually under the Channel

Area Measurements

I'd like to get area figures for all the local authorities in the UK. Where do I look?

UK Standard Area Measurements (SAM) are now available to download free of charge from the Open Geography portal in both MS Excel and CSV formats for a variety of administrative areas (countries, counties, local authority districts, electoral wards/divisions, regions, output areas, super output areas and workplace zones). The two questions below show some statistics taken from SAM 2015 (Extent of the Realm figures).

Which is the largest local authority in the UK?

- The largest anywhere in the UK is Highland (Scotland), at 2,648,436.54 hectares (ha).
- The largest in England is Northumberland, at 507,835.00 ha.
- The largest in Wales is Powys, at 519,545.63 ha.
- The largest in Northern Ireland is Fermanagh, at 187,125.95 ha.

Which is the smallest local authority in the UK?

- The smallest anywhere in the UK is the City of London, at 314.94 ha
- The smallest in Scotland is Dundee City, at 6,222.59 ha.
- The smallest in Wales is Blaenau Gwent, at 10,872.80 ha
- The smallest in Northern Ireland is North Down, at 8,150.19 ha.

UK Standard Area Measurements (SAM)

About UK Standard Area Measurements (SAM)

The SAM product provides a definitive list of measurements for administrative, health, Census, electoral and other geographic areas in the UK. SAM will change annually for some geographies, but for others it will be 'frozen' for several years.

The land measurement figures provided are defined by topographic boundaries (coastline and inland water), where available.

Measurements are reviewed annually and include information up to the end of December.

The measurements have been produced in conjunction with the following UK government statistical organisations and independent mapping agencies: National Records of Scotland (NRS), Northern Ireland Statistics and Research Agency (NISRA), Ordnance Survey®(OS) and Land & Property Services (LPS).

The SAM User Guide explains differences in methodology and base mapping between these agencies.

Product details

If you have any queries about this dataset, please contact:

ONS Geography Customer Services
Office for National Statistics
Segensworth Road
Titchfield
Fareham
Hampshire
PO15 5RR

Tel: 01329 444 971
Email: ons.geography@ons.gov.uk

1.1 Standard Area Measurement for Local Authority Districts at at 31/12/2015

Local Authority Name	Code	Extent of the realm (Km^2)	Area to mean high water (Km^2)	Inland water (Km^2)	Land only (Km^2)
United Kingdom	**K02000001**	248532	244186	1643	242542
Great Britain	**K03000001**	234399	230052	1098	228954
England	**E92000001**	132948	130459	152	130308
Hartlepool	E06000001	98	94	0	94
Middlesbrough	E06000002	55	54	0	54
Redcar and Cleveland	E06000003	254	245	0	245
Stockton-on-Tees	E06000004	210	205	0	205
Darlington	E06000005	197	197	0	197
Halton	E06000006	90	79	0	79
Warrington	E06000007	182	181	0	181
Blackburn with Darwen	E06000008	137	137	0	137
Blackpool	E06000009	43	35	0	35
Kingston upon Hull, City of	E06000010	81	71	0	71
East Riding of Yorkshire	E06000011	2495	2406	1	2405
North East Lincolnshire	E06000012	204	192	0	192
North Lincolnshire	E06000013	876	846	0	846
York	E06000014	272	272	0	272
Derby	E06000015	78	78	0	78
Leicester	E06000016	73	73	0	73
Rutland	E06000017	394	394	12	382
Nottingham	E06000018	75	75	0	75
Herefordshire, County of	E06000019	2180	2180	0	2180
Telford and Wrekin	E06000020	290	290	0	290
Stoke-on-Trent	E06000021	93	93	0	93
Bath and North East Somerset	E06000022	351	351	5	346
Bristol, City of	E06000023	235	110	0	110
North Somerset	E06000024	391	375	1	374
South Gloucestershire	E06000025	537	497	0	497
Plymouth	E06000026	84	80	0	80
Torbay	E06000027	119	63	0	63
Bournemouth	E06000028	47	46	0	46
Poole	E06000029	75	65	0	65
Swindon	E06000030	230	230	0	230
Peterborough	E06000031	343	343	0	343
Luton	E06000032	43	43	0	43
Southend-on-Sea	E06000033	68	42	0	42
Thurrock	E06000034	184	163	0	163
Medway	E06000035	269	194	0	194
Bracknell Forest	E06000036	109	109	0	109
West Berkshire	E06000037	704	704	0	704
Reading	E06000038	40	40	0	40
Slough	E06000039	33	33	0	33
Windsor and Maidenhead	E06000040	198	198	2	197
Wokingham	E06000041	179	179	0	179
Milton Keynes	E06000042	309	309	0	309
Brighton and Hove	E06000043	85	83	0	83
Portsmouth	E06000044	60	40	0	40
Southampton	E06000045	56	50	0	50
Isle of Wight	E06000046	395	380	0	380
County Durham	E06000047	2233	2232	6	2226
Cheshire East	E06000049	1166	1166	0	1166
Cheshire West and Chester	E06000050	941	917	0	917
Shropshire	E06000051	3197	3197	0	3197
Cornwall	E06000052	3613	3550	4	3546
Isles of Scilly	E06000053	23	16	0	16
Wiltshire	E06000054	3255	3255	0	3255
Bedford	E06000055	476	476	0	476
Central Bedfordshire	E06000056	716	716	0	716
Northumberland	E06000057	5078	5026	12	5014
Aylesbury Vale	E07000004	903	903	0	903
Chiltern	E07000005	196	196	0	196
South Bucks	E07000006	141	141	0	141

1.1 Standard Area Measurement for Local Authority Districts at at 31/12/2015

Local Authority Name	Code	Extent of the realm (Km^2)	Area to mean high water (Km^2)	Inland water (Km^2)	Land only (Km^2)
Wycombe	E07000007	325	325	0	325
Cambridge	E07000008	41	41	0	41
East Cambridgeshire	E07000009	652	651	0	651
Fenland	E07000010	547	546	0	546
Huntingdonshire	E07000011	913	912	6	906
South Cambridgeshire	E07000012	902	902	0	902
Allerdale	E07000026	1321	1258	16	1242
Barrow-in-Furness	E07000027	132	78	0	78
Carlisle	E07000028	1054	1039	0	1039
Copeland	E07000029	776	738	6	732
Eden	E07000030	2156	2156	14	2142
South Lakeland	E07000031	1743	1553	19	1534
Amber Valley	E07000032	265	265	0	265
Bolsover	E07000033	160	160	0	160
Chesterfield	E07000034	66	66	0	66
Derbyshire Dales	E07000035	795	795	3	792
Erewash	E07000036	110	110	0	110
High Peak	E07000037	540	540	1	539
North East Derbyshire	E07000038	276	276	0	276
South Derbyshire	E07000039	338	338	0	338
East Devon	E07000040	824	814	0	814
Exeter	E07000041	48	47	0	47
Mid Devon	E07000042	913	913	0	913
North Devon	E07000043	1105	1086	0	1086
South Hams	E07000044	905	886	0	886
Teignbridge	E07000045	681	674	0	674
Torridge	E07000046	996	985	1	984
West Devon	E07000047	1165	1161	1	1160
Christchurch	E07000048	52	50	0	50
East Dorset	E07000049	354	354	0	354
North Dorset	E07000050	609	609	0	609
Purbeck	E07000051	428	404	0	404
West Dorset	E07000052	1087	1081	0	1081
Weymouth and Portland	E07000053	43	42	0	42
Eastbourne	E07000061	46	44	0	44
Hastings	E07000062	31	30	0	30
Lewes	E07000063	294	292	0	292
Rother	E07000064	518	512	2	509
Wealden	E07000065	836	835	2	833
Basildon	E07000066	110	110	0	110
Braintree	E07000067	612	612	0	612
Brentwood	E07000068	153	153	0	153
Castle Point	E07000069	64	45	0	45
Chelmsford	E07000070	343	342	3	339
Colchester	E07000071	347	333	4	329
Epping Forest	E07000072	339	339	0	339
Harlow	E07000073	31	31	0	31
Maldon	E07000074	427	359	0	359
Rochford	E07000075	263	169	0	169
Tendring	E07000076	366	338	0	338
Uttlesford	E07000077	641	641	0	641
Cheltenham	E07000078	47	47	0	47
Cotswold	E07000079	1165	1165	0	1165
Forest of Dean	E07000080	561	526	0	526
Gloucester	E07000081	41	41	0	41
Stroud	E07000082	476	461	0	461
Tewkesbury	E07000083	415	414	0	414
Basingstoke and Deane	E07000084	634	634	0	634
East Hampshire	E07000085	514	514	0	514
Eastleigh	E07000086	85	80	0	80
Fareham	E07000087	78	74	0	74
Gosport	E07000088	28	25	0	25
Hart	E07000089	215	215	0	215
Havant	E07000090	79	55	0	55
New Forest	E07000091	777	753	0	753
Rushmoor	E07000092	39	39	0	39

1.1 Standard Area Measurement for Local Authority Districts at at 31/12/2015

Local Authority Name	Code	Extent of the realm (Km²)	Area to mean high water (Km²)	Inland water (Km²)	Land only (Km²)
Test Valley	E07000093	628	628	0	628
Winchester	E07000094	661	661	0	661
Broxbourne	E07000095	51	51	0	51
Dacorum	E07000096	212	212	0	212
Hertsmere	E07000098	101	101	0	101
North Hertfordshire	E07000099	375	375	0	375
Three Rivers	E07000102	89	89	0	89
Watford	E07000103	21	21	0	21
Ashford	E07000105	581	581	0	581
Canterbury	E07000106	321	309	0	309
Dartford	E07000107	76	73	0	73
Dover	E07000108	321	315	0	315
Gravesham	E07000109	105	99	0	99
Maidstone	E07000110	393	393	0	393
Sevenoaks	E07000111	370	370	1	369
Shepway	E07000112	365	357	0	357
Swale	E07000113	422	374	0	374
Thanet	E07000114	112	103	0	103
Tonbridge and Malling	E07000115	241	240	0	240
Tunbridge Wells	E07000116	331	331	0	331
Burnley	E07000117	111	111	0	111
Chorley	E07000118	203	203	0	203
Fylde	E07000119	183	166	0	166
Hyndburn	E07000120	73	73	0	73
Lancaster	E07000121	654	576	0	576
Pendle	E07000122	169	169	0	169
Preston	E07000123	143	142	0	142
Ribble Valley	E07000124	584	584	1	583
Rossendale	E07000125	138	138	0	138
South Ribble	E07000126	115	113	0	113
West Lancashire	E07000127	381	347	0	347
Wyre	E07000128	329	283	0	283
Blaby	E07000129	130	130	0	130
Charnwood	E07000130	279	279	0	279
Harborough	E07000131	593	593	1	592
Hinckley and Bosworth	E07000132	297	297	0	297
Melton	E07000133	481	481	0	481
North West Leicestershire	E07000134	279	279	0	279
Oadby and Wigston	E07000135	24	24	0	24
Boston	E07000136	398	365	0	365
East Lindsey	E07000137	1831	1765	0	1765
Lincoln	E07000138	36	36	0	36
North Kesteven	E07000139	922	922	0	922
South Holland	E07000140	816	751	0	751
South Kesteven	E07000141	943	943	0	943
West Lindsey	E07000142	1158	1156	0	1156
Breckland	E07000143	1305	1305	0	1305
Broadland	E07000144	553	552	0	552
Great Yarmouth	E07000145	182	174	0	174
King's Lynn and West Norfolk	E07000146	1528	1438	0	1438
North Norfolk	E07000147	991	965	2	963
Norwich	E07000148	41	39	0	39
South Norfolk	E07000149	909	908	0	908
Corby	E07000150	80	80	0	80
Daventry	E07000151	666	666	3	663
East Northamptonshire	E07000152	510	510	0	510
Kettering	E07000153	233	233	0	233
Northampton	E07000154	81	81	0	81
South Northamptonshire	E07000155	634	634	0	634
Wellingborough	E07000156	163	163	0	163
Craven	E07000163	1179	1179	1	1177
Hambleton	E07000164	1311	1311	0	1311
Harrogate	E07000165	1309	1309	1	1308
Richmondshire	E07000166	1319	1319	0	1319
Ryedale	E07000167	1507	1507	0	1507
Scarborough	E07000168	827	817	0	817

1.1 Standard Area Measurement for Local Authority Districts at at 31/12/2015

Local Authority Name	Code	Extent of the realm (Km^2)	Area to mean high water (Km^2)	Inland water (Km^2)	Land only (Km^2)
Selby	E07000169	602	599	0	599
Ashfield	E07000170	110	110	0	110
Bassetlaw	E07000171	639	638	0	638
Broxtowe	E07000172	80	80	0	80
Gedling	E07000173	120	120	0	120
Mansfield	E07000174	77	77	0	77
Newark and Sherwood	E07000175	652	651	0	651
Rushcliffe	E07000176	409	409	0	409
Cherwell	E07000177	589	589	0	589
Oxford	E07000178	46	46	0	46
South Oxfordshire	E07000179	679	679	0	679
Vale of White Horse	E07000180	579	579	1	578
West Oxfordshire	E07000181	714	714	0	714
Mendip	E07000187	739	739	0	739
Sedgemoor	E07000188	606	564	0	564
South Somerset	E07000189	959	959	0	959
Taunton Deane	E07000190	463	462	0	462
West Somerset	E07000191	747	727	1	725
Cannock Chase	E07000192	79	79	0	79
East Staffordshire	E07000193	390	390	3	387
Lichfield	E07000194	331	331	0	331
Newcastle-under-Lyme	E07000195	211	211	0	211
South Staffordshire	E07000196	407	407	0	407
Stafford	E07000197	598	598	0	598
Staffordshire Moorlands	E07000198	576	576	0	576
Tamworth	E07000199	31	31	0	31
Babergh	E07000200	612	595	1	594
Forest Heath	E07000201	378	378	0	378
Ipswich	E07000202	40	39	0	39
Mid Suffolk	E07000203	871	871	0	871
St Edmundsbury	E07000204	657	657	0	657
Suffolk Coastal	E07000205	921	892	0	892
Waveney	E07000206	375	370	0	370
Elmbridge	E07000207	96	96	1	95
Epsom and Ewell	E07000208	34	34	0	34
Guildford	E07000209	271	271	0	271
Mole Valley	E07000210	258	258	0	258
Reigate and Banstead	E07000211	129	129	0	129
Runnymede	E07000212	78	78	0	78
Spelthorne	E07000213	51	51	6	45
Surrey Heath	E07000214	95	95	0	95
Tandridge	E07000215	248	248	0	248
Waverley	E07000216	345	345	0	345
Woking	E07000217	64	64	0	64
North Warwickshire	E07000218	284	284	0	284
Nuneaton and Bedworth	E07000219	79	79	0	79
Rugby	E07000220	354	354	2	351
Stratford-on-Avon	E07000221	978	978	0	978
Warwick	E07000222	283	283	0	283
Adur	E07000223	44	42	0	42
Arun	E07000224	224	221	0	221
Chichester	E07000225	812	786	0	786
Crawley	E07000226	45	45	0	45
Horsham	E07000227	531	530	0	530
Mid Sussex	E07000228	334	334	0	334
Worthing	E07000229	34	32	0	32
Bromsgrove	E07000234	217	217	0	217
Malvern Hills	E07000235	577	577	0	577
Redditch	E07000236	54	54	0	54
Worcester	E07000237	33	33	0	33
Wychavon	E07000238	664	664	0	664
Wyre Forest	E07000239	195	195	0	195
St Albans	E07000240	161	161	0	161
Welwyn Hatfield	E07000241	130	130	0	130
East Hertfordshire	E07000242	476	476	0	476
Stevenage	E07000243	26	26	0	26

1.1 Standard Area Measurement for Local Authority Districts at at 31/12/2015

Local Authority Name	Code	Extent of the realm (Km²)	Area to mean high water (Km²)	Inland water (Km²)	Land only (Km²)
Bolton	E08000001	140	140	0	140
Bury	E08000002	99	99	0	99
Manchester	E08000003	116	116	0	116
Oldham	E08000004	142	142	0	142
Rochdale	E08000005	158	158	0	158
Salford	E08000006	97	97	0	97
Stockport	E08000007	126	126	0	126
Tameside	E08000008	103	103	0	103
Trafford	E08000009	106	106	0	106
Wigan	E08000010	188	188	0	188
Knowsley	E08000011	87	87	0	87
Liverpool	E08000012	134	112	0	112
St. Helens	E08000013	136	136	0	136
Sefton	E08000014	205	153	0	153
Wirral	E08000015	256	157	0	157
Barnsley	E08000016	329	329	0	329
Doncaster	E08000017	569	568	0	568
Rotherham	E08000018	287	287	0	287
Sheffield	E08000019	368	368	0	368
Newcastle upon Tyne	E08000021	115	113	0	113
North Tyneside	E08000022	85	82	0	82
South Tyneside	E08000023	67	64	0	64
Sunderland	E08000024	140	137	0	137
Birmingham	E08000025	268	268	0	268
Coventry	E08000026	99	99	0	99
Dudley	E08000027	98	98	0	98
Sandwell	E08000028	86	86	0	86
Solihull	E08000029	178	178	0	178
Walsall	E08000030	104	104	0	104
Wolverhampton	E08000031	69	69	0	69
Bradford	E08000032	366	366	0	366
Calderdale	E08000033	364	364	0	364
Kirklees	E08000034	409	409	0	409
Leeds	E08000035	552	552	0	552
Wakefield	E08000036	339	339	0	339
Gateshead	E08000037	144	142	0	142
City of London	E09000001	3	3	0	3
Barking and Dagenham	E09000002	38	36	0	36
Barnet	E09000003	87	87	0	87
Bexley	E09000004	64	61	0	61
Brent	E09000005	43	43	0	43
Bromley	E09000006	150	150	0	150
Camden	E09000007	22	22	0	22
Croydon	E09000008	86	86	0	86
Ealing	E09000009	56	56	0	56
Enfield	E09000010	82	82	1	81
Greenwich	E09000011	50	47	0	47
Hackney	E09000012	19	19	0	19
Hammersmith and Fulham	E09000013	17	16	0	16
Haringey	E09000014	30	30	0	30
Harrow	E09000015	50	50	0	50
Havering	E09000016	114	112	0	112
Hillingdon	E09000017	116	116	0	116
Hounslow	E09000018	57	56	0	56
Islington	E09000019	15	15	0	15
Kensington and Chelsea	E09000020	12	12	0	12
Kingston upon Thames	E09000021	37	37	0	37
Lambeth	E09000022	27	27	0	27
Lewisham	E09000023	35	35	0	35
Merton	E09000024	38	38	0	38
Newham	E09000025	39	36	0	36
Redbridge	E09000026	56	56	0	56
Richmond upon Thames	E09000027	59	57	0	57
Southwark	E09000028	30	29	0	29
Sutton	E09000029	44	44	0	44
Tower Hamlets	E09000030	22	20	0	20

1.1 Standard Area Measurement for Local Authority Districts at at 31/12/2015

Local Authority Name	Code	Extent of the realm (Km²)	Area to mean high water (Km²)	Inland water (Km²)	Land only (Km²)
Waltham Forest	E09000031	39	39	0	39
Wandsworth	E09000032	35	34	0	34
Westminster	E09000033	22	21	0	21
Northern Ireland	**N92000002**	14133	14133	545	13588
Antrim and Newtownabbey	N09000001	728	728	156	572
Armagh City, Banbridge and Craigavon	N09000002	1436	1436	99	1337
Belfast	N09000003	132	132	0	132
Causeway Coast and Glens	N09000004	1980	1980	0	1980
Derry City and Strabane	N09000005	1239	1239	0	1238
Fermanagh and Omagh	N09000006	3006	3006	149	2857
Lisburn and Castlereagh	N09000007	510	510	5	505
Mid and East Antrim	N09000008	1049	1049	2	1046
Mid Ulster	N09000009	1955	1955	128	1827
Newry, Mourne and Down	N09000010	1637	1637	5	1633
Ards and North Down	N09000011	461	461	0	461
Scotland	**S92000003**	80226	78811	900	77910
Clackmannanshire	S12000005	164	159	0	159
Dumfries and Galloway	S12000006	6676	6438	11	6427
East Ayrshire	S12000008	1270	1270	8	1262
East Lothian	S12000010	701	679	0	679
East Renfrewshire	S12000011	174	174	0	174
Na h-Eileanan Siar	S12000013	3269	3101	41	3060
Falkirk	S12000014	315	297	0	297
Fife	S12000015	1374	1325	0	1325
Highland	S12000017	26473	26163	506	25657
Inverclyde	S12000018	174	162	2	160
Midlothian	S12000019	355	355	2	354
Moray	S12000020	2257	2238	0	2238
North Ayrshire	S12000021	904	885	0	885
Orkney Islands	S12000023	1086	1013	25	989
Perth and Kinross	S12000024	5419	5384	98	5286
Scottish Borders	S12000026	4743	4739	7	4732
Shetland Islands	S12000027	1657	1468	1	1467
South Ayrshire	S12000028	1235	1224	2	1222
South Lanarkshire	S12000029	1774	1774	2	1772
Stirling	S12000030	2255	2253	66	2187
Aberdeen City	S12000033	206	186	0	186
Aberdeenshire	S12000034	6338	6318	5	6313
Argyll and Bute	S12000035	7164	7008	99	6909
City of Edinburgh	S12000036	273	263	0	263
Renfrewshire	S12000038	269	261	0	261
West Dunbartonshire	S12000039	183	177	19	159
West Lothian	S12000040	432	429	1	428
Angus	S12000041	2203	2185	4	2182
Dundee City	S12000042	62	60	0	60
North Lanarkshire	S12000044	472	472	2	470
East Dunbartonshire	S12000045	174	174	0	174
Glasgow City	S12000046	176	175	0	175
Wales	**W92000004**	21224	20782	46	20736
Isle of Anglesey	W06000001	749	714	3	711
Gwynedd	W06000002	2622	2548	13	2535
Conwy	W06000003	1153	1130	4	1126
Denbighshire	W06000004	846	839	2	837
Flintshire	W06000005	489	437	0	437
Wrexham	W06000006	504	504	0	504
Ceredigion	W06000008	1806	1789	3	1786
Pembrokeshire	W06000009	1650	1619	0	1619
Carmarthenshire	W06000010	2439	2371	1	2370
Swansea	W06000011	421	380	0	380
Neath Port Talbot	W06000012	452	442	1	441
Bridgend	W06000013	255	251	0	251
Vale of Glamorgan	W06000014	340	331	0	331
Cardiff	W06000015	150	142	1	141

1.1 Standard Area Measurement for Local Authority Districts at at 31/12/2015

Local Authority Name	Code	Extent of the realm (Km^2)	Area to mean high water (Km^2)	Inland water (Km^2)	Land only (Km^2)
Rhondda Cynon Taf	W06000016	424	424	0	424
Caerphilly	W06000018	277	277	0	277
Blaenau Gwent	W06000019	109	109	0	109
Torfaen	W06000020	126	126	1	126
Monmouthshire	W06000021	886	850	1	849
Newport	W06000022	218	191	0	191
Powys	W06000023	5195	5195	15	5181
Merthyr Tydfil	W06000024	112	112	1	111

Source: ONS Geography Codes
Standard Area Measurement for UK Local Authority District

Parliamentary elections

Chapter 2

Parliamentary elections

This chapter covers parliamentary elections, by-elections and devolved assembly elections in the UK, Wales, Scotland and Northern Ireland.

Parliamentary elections (Table 2.1)

Information is supplied on the total electorate, average electorate and valid votes as a percentage of electorate. The number of seats by party is also listed.

Parliamentary by-elections (Table 2.2)

Information can be found on the votes recorded for each party and General Elections and subsequent by-elections between General Elections.

Devolved assembly elections (Tables 2.3 and 2.4)

Table 2.3 provides information on the devolved assembly elections in Wales and Scotland, listing information on the number of votes, percentage share and number of seats per party.

Table 2.4 provides information on the devolved assembly elections in Northern Ireland, listing information the number of seats by party and percentage share of the vote.

2.1 Parliamentary elections[1]

United Kingdom

Thousands and percentages

		15-Oct 1964	31-Mar 1966	18-Jun 1970[1]	28-Feb 1974		10-Oct 1974	03-May 1979	09-Jun 1983	11-Jun 1987	09-Apr 1992	01-May 1997	07-Jun 2001	05-May 2005	06-May 2010	07-May 2015	08-Jun 2017
United Kingdom																	
Electorate	DZ5P	35894	35957	39615	40256	DZ6V	40256	41573	42704	43666	43719	43846	44403	44246	45597	46354	46844
Average-electors per seat	DZ5T	57	57.1	62.9	63.4	DZ6R	63.4	65.5	66.7	67.2	67.2	66.5	67.4	68.5	70.1	71.3	72.1
Valid votes counted	DZ5X	27657	27265	28345	31340	DZ6N	29189	31221	30671	32530	33614	31286	26367	27149	29688	30698	32204
As percentage of electorate	DZ63	77.1	75.8	71.5	77.9	DZ6J	72.5	75.1	71.8	74.5	76.7	71.4	59.4	61.4	65.1	66.2	68.7
England and Wales																	
Electorate	DZ5Q	31610	31695	34931	35509	DZ6W	35509	36695	37708	38568	38648	38719	39228	39266	40565	40968	41613
Average-electors per seat	DZ5U	57.8	57.9	63.9	64.3	DZ6S	64.3	66.5	67.2	68.8	68.8	68	68.9	69	70.8	71.6	72.7
Valid votes counted	DZ5Y	24384	24116	24877	27735	DZ6O	25729	27609	27082	28832	29897	27679	23243	24097	26548	27034	28732
As percentage of electorate	DZ64	77.1	76.1	71.2	78.1	DZ6K	72.5	75.2	71.8	74.8	77.5	71.5	59.3	61.4	65.4	66.0	69.0
Scotland																	
Electorate	DZ5R	3393	3360	3659	3705	DZ6X	3705	3837	3934	3995	3929	3949	3984	3840	3863	4100	3988
Average-electors per seat	DZ5V	47.8	47.3	51.5	52.2	DZ6T	52.2	54	54.6	55.5	54.6	54.8	55.3	65.1	65.5	69.5	67.6
Valid votes counted	DZ5Z	2635	2553	2688	2887	DZ6P	2758	2917	2825	2968	2931	2817	2313	2334	2466	2910	2650
As percentage of electorate	DZ65	77.6	76	73.5	77.9	DZ6L	74.5	76	71.8	74.3	74.2	71.3	58.1	60.8	63.8	71.0	66.4
Northern Ireland																	
Electorate	DZ5S	891	902	1025	1027	DZ6Y	1037	1028	1050	1090	1141	1178	1191	1140	1169	1237	1243
Average-electors per seat	DZ5W	74.2	75.2	85.4	85.6	DZ6U	86.4	85.6	61.8	64.1	67.1	65.4	66.2	63.3	65.0	68.7	69
Valid votes counted	DZ62	638	596	779	718	DZ6Q	702	696	765	730	785	791	810	718	674	718	857
As percentage of electorate	DZ66	71.7	66.1	76	69.9	DZ6M	67.7	67.7	72.9	67	68.8	67.1	68	62.9	57.6	58.1	65.4
Members of Parliament elected: (numbers)	DZV7	630	630	630	635	DZV8	635	635	650	650	651	659	659	646	650	650	650
Conservative	DZ67	303	253	330	296	DZ6D	276	339	396	375	336	165	166	198	306	331	317
Labour	DZ68	317	363	287	301	DZ6E	319	268	209	229	271	418	412	355	258	232	262
Liberal Democrat[2]	DZ69	9	12	6	14	DZ6F	13	11	23	22	20	46	52	62	57	8	12
Scottish National Party	DZ6A	–	–	1	7	DZ6G	11	2	2	3	3	6	5	6	6	56	35
Plaid Cymru	DZ6B	–	–	–	2	DZ6H	3	2	2	3	4	4	4	3	3	3	4
Other[3]	DZ6C	1	2	6	15	DZ6I	13	13	18	18	17	20	20	22	20	20	20

The Representation of the People Act 1969 lowered the minimum voting age from 21 to 18 years with effect from 16 February 1970.
Liberal before 1992. The figures for 1983 and 1987 include six and five MPs respectively who were elected for the Social Democratic Party.
Including the Speaker.

Source: British Electoral Facts 1832-2012
Plymouth University for the Electoral Commission: 01752 233207

13

2.2a Summary of parliamentary by-elections in Great Britain (excluding Northern Ireland), 1945-2017

	Number of by-elections	Net Seat Gains and Losses						Average change in share of vote since previous election					Average turnout
		CON	LAB	LD	SNP/PC	Other	No change	CON	LAB	LD	SNP/PC	Other	
1945-50	50	+4	-1	...		-3	45	3.7%	-2.3%	-1.1%	1.4%	-1.0%	67.3%
1950-51	14	...	...	...	...	...	14	+6.8%	-2.0%	-4.6%		-0.2%	68.8%
1951-55	44	+1	-1	...	...	...	43	-0.6%	+0.3%	-0.6%	+0.6%	+0.3%	58.6%
1955-59	49	-2	+4	...		-2	34	-8.7%	+1.3%	+6.2%	+0.3%	+0.9%	63.5%
1959-64	61	-5	+4	+1	...	...	54	-14.1%	-2.1%	+13.7%	+1.2%	+1.5%	62.9%
1964-66	13	...	-1	+1	...	...	11	+1.3%	-1.8%	+0.5%	+0.3%	+0.4%	58.2%
1966-70	37	+11	-15	+1	+2	+1	22	+6.8%	-17.3%	+3.3%	+5.5%	+1.7%	62.1%
1970-74	30	-5	...	+5	+1	-1	20	-10.7%	-4.2%	+9.0%	+4.0%	+1.9%	56.5%
1974	1	...	...	...	...	...	1	-1.1%	-3.4%	-2.3%	...	+6.8%	25.9%
1974-79	30	+6	-6	+1	...	-1	23	+9.9%	-9.3%	-4.9%	-0.3%	+4.6%	57.5%
1979-83	17	-3	+1	+4	...	-2	11	-11.4%	-10.2%	+18.6%	+1.6%	+1.4%	56.7%
1983-87	16	-4	...	+4	...	...	11	-14.0%	+0.4%	+12.3%	+0.1%	+1.2%	63.5%
1987-92	23	-7	+3	+3	+1	...	15	-11.0%	-0.8%	-0.6%	+5.7%	+6.6%	57.4%
1992-97	17	-8	+3	+4	+1	...	9	-19.9%	+7.4%	+5.2%	+2.4%	+4.9%	52.7%
1997-2001	15	-2	+1	+2	...	-1	14	-0.6%	-11.1%	+5.0%	+3.1%	+3.6%	42.4%
2001-05	6	...	-2	+2	...	...	4	-4.2%	-19.8%	+15.8%	+1.1%	+7.0%	39.3%
2005-10	14	...	-1	+1	...	...	9	+2.6%	-10.4%	+2.0%	+4.3%	+5.3%	48.8%
2010-15	19	-3	...	...		+3	13	-6.4%	+5.4%	-7.6%	+1.1%	+17.9%	39.6%
2015-17	10	...	-1	+1	...	...	8	-4.7%	+3.9%	+7.7%	+5.7%	-6.6%	44.1%

Updated on 21 August 2017

Sources

F.W.S. Craig, *Chronology of British Parliamentary By-elections 1833-1987*

Colin Rallings and Michael Thrasher, *British Electoral Facts 1832-2006*

House of Commons Library, RP10/50 *By-election results 2005-10*; SN05833 *By-elections since 2010 General Election*

2.2b Parliamentary by-elections in Northern Ireland, 1974-2015[5]

Date	Constituency	Result	Change in share of the vote since previous election:					Turnout
			DUP	UUP	SF	SDLP	Other	
GENERAL ELECTION 1974 (FEB)								
None								
GENERAL ELECTION 1974 (OCT)								
None								
GENERAL ELECTION 1979								
09/04/81	Fermanagh and South Tyrone	Anti-H Block gain from Ind Rep	...	+41.0%	...	...	+51.2%	82.4%
20/08/81	Fermanagh and South Tyrone	Anti-H Block hold	...	-3.2%	...	...	+3.2%	87.5%
04/03/82	Belfast South	UUP hold	+22.6%	-22.4%	...	+0.9%	+29.3%	65.7%
GENERAL ELECTION 1983[6]								
23/01/86	East Antrim	UUP hold	...	+47.5%	...	...	-4.8%	58.9%
23/01/86	North Antrim	DUP hold	+43.2%	...	...	...	...	53.5%
23/01/86	South Antrim	UUP hold	...	+48.5%	...	...	...	52.2%
23/01/86	Belfast East	DUP hold	+35.6%	...	...	...	-6.1%	63.6%
23/01/86	Belfast North	UUP hold	...	+35.3%	...	...	+13.7%	54.7%
23/01/86	Belfast South	UUP hold	...	+21.4%	...	...	+2.4%	56.6%
23/01/86	North Down	UPU hold	...	...	...	...	+21.9%	60.5%
23/01/86	South Down	UUP hold	...	+8.1%	-2.2%	+5.6%	-0.6%	73.8%
23/01/86	Fermanagh and South Tyrone	UUP hold	...	+2.1%	-7.6%	+5.0%	+0.5%	80.4%
23/01/86	Lagan Valley	UUP hold	...	+31.5%	...	...	+7.3%	81.4%
23/01/86	East Londonderry	UUP hold	...	+56.0%	...	...	...	47.0%
23/01/86	Mid Ulster	DUP hold	+16.1%	...	-2.6%	+3.0%	-0.1%	77.0%
23/01/86	Newry and Armagh	SDLP gain from UUP	...	+0.2%	-7.7%	+8.7%	-1.2%	76.6%
23/01/86	Strangford	UUP hold	...	+45.4%	...	...	...	55.1%
23/01/86	Upper Bann	UUP hold	...	+23.9%	...	...	+13.8%	57.2%
GENERAL ELECTION 1987								
17/05/90	Upper Bann	UUP hold	...	-3.5%	-1.7%	-1.6%	-4.8%	53.4%
GENERAL ELECTION 1992								
15/06/95	North Down	UKU gain from UPU	...	...	...	...	-19.3%	38.6%
GENERAL ELECTION 1997								
21/09/00	South Antrim	DUP gain from UUP	...	-22.2%	+3.0%	-4.7%	-5.0%	43.0%
GENERAL ELECTION 2001								
None								
GENERAL ELECTION 2005								
None								
GENERAL ELECTION 2010 (up to July 2011)								
09/06/11	Belfast West	SF hold	-1.5%	-1.4%	-0.4%	-2.9%	+6.3%	37.4%
07/03/13	Mid Ulster	SF hold	...	...	-5.1%	+3.1%	+1.9%	55.4%
GENERAL ELECTION 2015								
None								
GENERAL ELECTION 2017 (as at August 2017)								
None								

2.2b Parliamentary by-elections in Northern Ireland, 1974-2015[5]

Notes for table 2.2b

5. The formation of new parties in the early 1970s altered the pattern of party competition at Westminster elections. The SDLP (formed 1970) and the DUP (formed 1971) are included in this table. The Ulster Unionist Party (UUP) took the Conservative whip at Westminster until 1972, prior to this were listed under Conservatives.

6. Multiple by-elections were held in January 1986 after fifteen unionist Members resigned their seats in protest at the Anglo-Irish Agreement.

Party descriptions:

DUP	Democratic Unionist Party	SDLP	Social Democratic and Labour Party
UUP	Ulster Unionist Party	UPU	Ulster Popular Unionist Party
SF	Sinn Fein	UKU	United Kingdom Unionist

Sources
F.W.S. Craig, *British Parliamentary Election Results 1918-1949*
F.W.S. Craig, *British Parliamentary Election Results 1950-1973*
F.W.S. Craig, *British Parliamentary Election Results 1974-1983*
Colin Rallings and Michael Thrasher, British Parliamentary Election Results 1983-1997
House of Commons Library RP01/36, *By-election results 1997-2000*; RP05/34, *By-election results 2001-05*;
RP10/50, *By-election results 2005-10*; SN05833, *By-elections since 2010 General Election*

2.3a National Assembly for Wales elections, 1999-2016

	Number of Votes					% share				
	1999	2003	2007	2011	2016	1999	2003	2007	2011	2016
Constituency votes										
LAB	384,671	340,515	314,925	401,677	353,865	37.6%	40.0%	32.2%	42.3%	34.7%
PC	290,565	180,185	219,121	182,907	209,374	28.4%	21.2%	22.4%	19.3%	20.5%
CON	162,133	169,832	218,730	237,389	215,597	15.8%	20.0%	22.4%	25.0%	21.1%
UKIP		19,795	18,047		127,038		2.3%	1.8%		12.5%
LD	137,657	120,250	144,410	100,259	78,165	13.5%	14.1%	14.8%	10.6%	7.7%
Others	47,992	20,266	62,859	27,021	35,341	4.7%	2.4%	6.4%	2.8%	3.5%
Total	1,023,018	850,843	978,092	949,253	1,019,380	100%	100%	100%	100%	100%
Constituency seats										
LAB	27	30	24	28	27	67.5%	75.0%	60.0%	70.0%	67.5%
PC	9	5	7	5	6	22.5%	12.5%	17.5%	12.5%	15.0%
CON	1	1	5	6	6	2.5%	2.5%	12.5%	15.0%	15.0%
UKIP	0	0	0	0	0	0.0%	0.0%	0.0%	0.0%	0.0%
LD	3	3	3	1	1	7.5%	7.5%	7.5%	2.5%	2.5%
Others	0	1	1	0	0	0.0%	2.5%	2.5%	0.0%	0.0%
Total:	**40**	**40**	**40**	**40**	**40**	**100%**	**100%**	**100%**	**100%**	**100%**
Regional votes										
LAB	361,657	310,658	288,955	349,935	319,196	35.4%	36.6%	29.6%	36.9%	31.5%
PC	312,048	167,653	204,757	169,799	211,548	30.5%	19.7%	21.0%	17.9%	20.8%
CON	168,206	162,725	209,154	213,773	190,846	16.5%	19.2%	21.5%	22.5%	18.8%
UKIP		29,427	38,349	43,256	132,138		3.5%	3.9%	4.6%	13.0%
LD	128,008	108,013	114,500	76,349	65,504	12.5%	12.7%	11.7%	8.0%	6.5%
Others	51,938	71,076	119,071	95,776	95,511	5.1%	8.4%	12.2%	10.1%	9.4%
Total	1,021,857	849,552	974,786	948,888	1,014,743	100%	100%	100%	100%	100%
Regional seats										
LAB	1	0	2	2	2	5.0%	0.0%	10.0%	10.0%	10.0%
PC	8	7	8	6	6	40.0%	35.0%	40.0%	30.0%	30.0%
CON	8	10	7	8	5	40.0%	50.0%	35.0%	40.0%	25.0%
UKIP	0	0	0	0	7	0.0%	0.0%	0.0%	0.0%	35.0%
LD	3	3	3	4	0	15.0%	15.0%	15.0%	20.0%	0.0%
Others	0	0	0	0	0	0.0%	0.0%	0.0%	0.0%	0.0%
Total:	**20**	**20**	**20**	**20**	**20**	**100%**	**100%**	**100%**	**100%**	**100%**
Total seats										
LAB	28	30	26	30	29	46.7%	50.0%	43.3%	50.0%	48.3%
PC	17	12	15	11	12	28.3%	20.0%	25.0%	18.3%	20.0%
CON	9	11	12	14	11	15.0%	18.3%	20.0%	23.3%	18.3%
UKIP	0	0	0	0	7	0.0%	0.0%	0.0%	0.0%	11.7%
LD	6	6	6	5	1	10.0%	10.0%	10.0%	8.3%	1.7%
Others	0	1	1	0	0	0.0%	1.7%	1.7%	0.0%	0.0%
Total:	**60**	**60**	**60**	**60**	**60**	**100%**	**100%**	**100%**	**100%**	**100%**
Constituency turnout										
	46.4%	38.2%	43.5%	41.5%	45.5%					
Regional turnout										
	46.3%	38.1%	43.4%	41.4%	45.3%					

Source: House of Commons Library Briefing Paper CBP7594, National Assembly for Wales Elections: 2016

The next National Assembly for Wales election is expected in 2021

2.3b Scottish Parliament elections, 1999-2016

	Number of votes and seats					% Share				
	1999	2003	2007	2011	2016	1999	2003	2007	2011	2016
Constituency votes										
SNP	672,768	455,742	664,227	902,915	1,059,898	28.7%	23.8%	32.9%	45.4%	46.5%
CON	364,425	318,279	334,742	276,652	501,844	15.6%	16.6%	16.6%	13.9%	22.0%
LAB	908,346	663,585	648,374	630,461	514,261	38.8%	34.6%	32.1%	31.7%	22.6%
LD	333,179	294,347	326,232	157,714	178,238	14.2%	15.4%	16.2%	7.9%	7.8%
GRN			2,971		13,172			0.1%		0.6%
Other	63,770	184,641	43,402	21,534	11,741	2.7%	9.6%	2.2%	1.1%	0.5%
Total	2,342,488	1,916,594	2,016,977	1,989,276	2,279,154	100%	100%	100%	100%	100.0%
Constituency seats										
SNP	7	9	21	53	59	9.6%	12.3%	28.8%	72.6%	80.8%
CON	0	3	4	3	7	0.0%	4.1%	5.5%	4.1%	9.6%
LAB	53	46	37	15	3	72.6%	63.0%	50.7%	20.5%	4.1%
LD	12	13	11	2	4	16.4%	17.8%	15.1%	2.7%	5.5%
GRN										
Other	1	2	0	0	0	1.4%	2.7%	0.0%	0.0%	0.0%
Total	73	73	73	73	73	100%	100%	100%	100%	100%
Regional votes										
SNP	638,644	399,659	633,401	876,421	953,587	27.3%	20.9%	31.0%	44.0%	41.7%
CON	359,109	296,929	284,005	245,967	524,220	15.4%	15.5%	13.9%	12.4%	22.9%
LAB	786,818	561,375	595,415	523,469	435,919	33.6%	29.3%	29.2%	26.3%	19.1%
LD	290,760	225,774	230,671	103,472	119,284	12.4%	11.8%	11.3%	5.2%	5.2%
GRN	84,023	132,138	82,584	86,939	150,426	3.6%	6.9%	4.0%	4.4%	6.6%
Other	179,560	299,976	215,973	154,568	102,315	7.7%	15.7%	10.6%	7.8%	4.5%
Total	2,338,914	1,915,851	2,042,049	1,990,836	2,285,751	100%	100%	100%	100%	100%
Regional Seats										
SNP	28	18	26	16	4	50.0%	32.1%	46.4%	28.6%	7.1%
CON	18	15	13	12	24	32.1%	26.8%	23.2%	21.4%	42.9%
LAB	3	4	9	22	21	5.4%	7.1%	16.1%	39.3%	37.5%
LD	5	4	5	3	1	8.9%	7.1%	8.9%	5.4%	1.8%
GRN	1	7	2	2	6	1.8%	12.5%	3.6%	3.6%	10.7%
Other	1	8	1	1	0	1.8%	14.3%	1.8%	1.8%	0.0%
Total	56	56	56	56	56	100%	100%	100%	100%	100%
Total seats										
SNP	35	27	47	69	63	62.5%	48.2%	83.9%	123.2%	112.5%
CON	18	18	17	15	31	32.1%	32.1%	30.4%	26.8%	55.4%
LAB	56	50	46	37	24	100.0%	89.3%	82.1%	66.1%	42.9%
LD	17	17	16	5	5	30.4%	30.4%	28.6%	8.9%	8.9%
GRN	1	7	2	2	6	1.8%	12.5%	3.6%	3.6%	10.7%
Other	2	10	1	1		3.6%	17.9%	1.8%	1.8%	0.0%
Total	129	129	129	129	129	100%	100%	100%	100%	100%
Constituency Turnout										
	58.8%	49.4%	51.7%	50.4%	55.6%					
Regional Turnout										
	58.7%	49.4%	52.4%	50.4%	55.7%					

Sources:

1. Colin Rallings and Michael Thrasher, British Electoral Facts 1832-2006
2. Electoral Commission, Report on the Scottish Parliament election on 5 May 2016
3. House of Commons Library Briefing Paper CBP7599, Scottish Parliament Elections: 2016
4. House of Commons Library Research Paper RP07/46, Scottish Parliament Elections: 3 May 2007
5. House of Commons Library Research Paper RP11/41, Scottish Parliament Elections: 2011
6. House of Commons Library Briefing Paper CBP-7529, Scottish Parliament Elections: 2016

The next Scottish Parliament election is expected in 2021

2.4 Northern Ireland Assembly elections: 1998-2017

	1st Pref Votes and seats won						% of votes and seats won					
	1998	2003	2007	2011	2016	2017	1998	2003	2007	2011	2016	2017
Votes												
DUP	146,917	177,944	207,721	198,436	202,567	225,413	18.1%	25.3%	30.1%	30.0%	29.2%	28.1%
Sinn Féin	142,858	162,758	180,573	178,222	166,785	224,245	17.6%	23.2%	26.2%	26.9%	24.0%	27.9%
UUP	172,225	156,931	103,145	87,531	87,302	103,314	21.3%	22.3%	14.9%	13.2%	12.6%	12.9%
SDLP	177,963	117,547	105,164	94,286	83,364	95,958	22.0%	16.7%	15.2%	14.2%	12.0%	11.9%
Alliance	52,636	25,372	36,139	50,875	48,447	72,717	6.5%	3.6%	5.2%	7.7%	7.0%	9.1%
UK Unionists	36,541	5,700	10,452	...	...	...	4.5%	0.8%	1.5%	...	...	...
PUP	20,634	8,032	3,822	1,493	5,955	5,590	2.5%	1.1%	0.6%	0.2%	0.9%	0.7%
People before Profit Alliance	...	...	774	5,438	13,761	14,100	...	...	0.1%	0.8%	2.0%	1.8%
TUV	...	...	...	16,480	23,776	20,523	...	...	...	2.5%	3.4%	2.6%
UKIP	...	...	...	4,152	10,109	1,579	...	...	...	0.6%	1.5%	0.2%
Green Party	510	2,688	11,985	6,031	18,718	18,527	0.1%	0.4%	1.7%	0.9%	2.7%	2.3%
Others	59,961	45,277	30,538	18,790	33,526	21,349	7.4%	6.4%	4.4%	2.8%	4.8%	2.7%
Total	810,245	702,249	690,313	661,734	694,310	803,315	100.0%	100.0%	100.0%	100.0%	100.0%	100.0%
Seats von												
DUP	20	30	36	38	38	28	18.5%	27.8%	33.3%	35.2%	35.2%	31.1%
Sinn Féin	18	24	28	29	28	27	16.7%	22.2%	25.9%	26.9%	25.9%	30.0%
UUP	28	27	18	16	16	10	25.9%	25.0%	16.7%	14.8%	14.8%	11.1%
SDLP	24	18	16	14	12	12	22.2%	16.7%	14.8%	13.0%	11.1%	13.3%
Alliance	6	6	7	8	8	8	5.6%	5.6%	6.5%	7.4%	7.4%	8.9%
UK Unionists	5	1	0	...	...	...	4.6%	0.9%	0.0%	...	...	...
PUP	2	1	1	0	0	0	1.9%	0.9%	0.9%	0.0%	0.0%	0.0%
People before Profit Alliance	...	...	0	0	2	1	...	...	0.0%	0.0%	1.9%	1.1%
TUV	...	...	...	1	1	1	...	...	...	0.9%	0.9%	1.1%
UKIP	...	...	...	0	0	0	...	...	...	0.0%	0.0%	0.0%
Green Party	0	0	1	1	2	2	0.0%	0.0%	0.9%	0.9%	1.9%	2.2%
Others	5	1	1	1	1	1	4.6%	0.9%	0.9%	0.9%	0.9%	1.1%
Total	108	108	108	108	108	90	100.0%	100.0%	100.0%	100.0%	100.0%	100.0%
Electorate	1,178,556	1,097,526	1,107,904	1,210,009	1,281,595	1,254,709						
Turnout	68.7%	64.0%	62.3%	54.7%	54.2%	64.0%						

Sources:
Colin Rallings and Michael Thrasher, *British Electoral Facts 1832-2006*
Electoral Office for Northern Ireland, www.eoni.org.uk

19

this page is intentionally blank

International development

Chapter 3

International development

Overseas development assistance

The Department for International Development (DFID) is the UK Government Department with lead responsibility for overseas development. DFID's aim is to eliminate poverty in poorer countries through achievement of the Millennium Development Goals (MDG's). Statistics relating to international development are published on a financial year basis and on a calendar year basis. Statistics on a calendar year basis allow comparisons of aid expenditure with other donor countries. Aid flows can be measured before (gross) or after (net) deductions of repayments of principal on past loans. These tables show only the gross figures.

Aid is provided in two main ways: Bilateral funding is provided directly to partner countries while multilateral funding is provided through international organisations.

Funds can only be classified as multilateral if they are channelled through an organisation on a list in the OECD –

Development Assistance Committee (DAC) Statistical Reporting Directives – which identifies all multilateral organisations. This list also highlights some bodies that might appear to be multilateral but are actually bilateral (in particular this latter category includes some international non-governmental organisations such as the International Committee of the Red Cross and some Public-Private Partnerships). The DAC list of multilaterals is updated annually based on members nominations; organisations must be engaged in development work to be classified as multilateral aid channels although money may be classified as bilateral while a case is being made for a new multilateral organisation to be recognised.

While core funding to multilateral organisations is always classified as multilateral expenditure, additional funding channelled through multilaterals is often classified as bilateral expenditure. This would be the case in circumstances where a DFID country office transfers some money to a multilateral organisation (for example UN agency) for a particular programme in that country (or region). That is where DFID has control over what the money is being spent on and/or where it is being spent. Likewise, if DFID responds to an emergency appeal from an agency for a particular country or area, the funds will be allocated as bilateral spend to that country or region. As a result, some organisations, such as UN agencies have some of their DFID funding classified as bilateral and some as multilateral.

Bilateral assistance takes various forms:

Financial Aid – Poverty Reduction Budget Support (PRBS) – Funds provided to developing countries for them to spend in support of their expenditure programmes whose long-term objective is to reduce poverty; funds are spent using the overseas governments' own financial management, procurement and accountability systems to increase ownership and long term sustainability. PRBS can take the form of a general contribution to the overall budget – general budget support – or support with a more restricted focus which is earmarked for a specific sector – sector budget support.

Other Financial Aid – Funding of projects and programmes such as Sector Wide Programmes not classified as PRBS. Financial aid in its broader sense covers all bilateral aid expenditure other than technical cooperation and administrative costs but in SID we separately categorise this further.

Technical Co-operation – Activities designed to enhance the knowledge, intellectual skills, technical expertise or the productive capability of people in recipient countries. It also covers funding of services which contribute to the design or implementation of development projects and programmes.

This assistance is mainly delivered through research and development, the use of consultants, training (generally overseas partners visiting the UK or elsewhere for a training programme) and employment of 'other Personnel' (non-DFID experts on fixed term contracts). This latter category is growing less significant over time as existing contracted staff reach the end of their assignments.

Bilateral Aid Delivered Through a Multilateral Organisation – This category covers funding that is channelled through a multilateral organisation and DFID has control over the country, sector or theme that the funds will be spent on. For example, where a DFID country office transfers money to a multilateral organisation for a particular piece of work in that country. This also includes aid delivered through multi donor funds such as the United Nations Central Emergency Response Fund (CERF).

Bilateral Aid Delivered Through a Non-Governmental Organisation (NGO) – This category covers support to the international development work of UK and international not for profit organisations such as NGOs or Civil Society Organisations. This covers Partnership Programme Arrangements (PPAs), the Civil Society Challenge Fund and other grants.

Other Bilateral Aid – This category includes any aid not elsewhere classified such as funding to other donors for shared development purposes. More information on all of the above aid types is provided in the Glossary.

Humanitarian Assistance – Provides food, aid and other humanitarian assistance including shelter, medical care and advice in emergency situations and their aftermath. Work of the conflict pools is also included.

DFID Debt Relief – This includes sums for debt relief on DFID aid loans and cancellation of debt under the Commonwealth Debt Initiative (CDI). The non-CDI DFID debt relief is reported on the basis of the 'benefit to the recipient country'. This means that figures shown represent the money available to the country in the year in question that would otherwise have been spent on debt servicing. The CDI debt cancellation is reported on a 'lump sum' basis where all outstanding amounts on a loan are shown at the time the agreement to cancel is made.

CDC Gross Investments – **CDC Group PLC** is wholly government owned. Its investments must have a clear development objective. The net amount (that is equity purchase less equity sales) of

CDC investments in official development assistance (ODA)-eligible countries is reported as ODA and the gross amount (that is equity purchase only) is reported in GPEX.

Non-DFID Debt Relief – Comprises CDC Debt and ECGD Debt. CDC has a portfolio of loans to governments which can become eligible for debt relief under the Heavily Indebted Poor Countries (HIPC) or other debt relief deals. In 2005/06 £90 million of debts owed to CDC were reorganised. Export Credit Guarantee Department (ECGD) is the UK's official export credit agency providing insurance for exporters against the main risks in selling overseas and guarantees to banks providing export finance. It also negotiates debt relief arrangements on commercial debt.

The Foreign and Commonwealth Office (FCO) contributes to UK GPEX in a number of ways:

The FCO Strategic Programme Fund supports a range of the UK government's international goals. Where the programme funds projects which meet the required OECD definition these projects are included in UK GPEX statistics.

The FCO supports the British Council through grant-in-aid funding. This funding goes to support a range of initiatives including building the capacity and quality of English language teaching; supporting education systems; and using cultural exchange to improve economic welfare. UK GPEX statistics include the proportion of this work which is clearly focussed on delivering economic welfare and development in ODA eligible countries.

The British Council also manages, on behalf of the FCO, the Chevening Scholarships programme, which provides funding for postgraduate students or researchers from developing countries to study in UK universities. Funding from this scheme to students from ODA eligible countries are included in UK ODA and GPEX statistics.

The FCO makes annual contributions to UN and Commonwealth organisations. A proportion of these contributions are allowed to score as ODA in line with Annex 2 of the DAC Statistical Reporting Directives.

In addition to contributing directly to the Conflict Pool (see below) the FCO is also responsible for the UK contribution to the UN Department for Peacekeeping Operations (UNDPKO). In line with DAC rules 6 per cent of donor funding to UNDPKO is allowed to score as ODA. FCO also funds other bilateral peacekeeping missions including the Organisation for Security and Cooperation in Europe (OSCE) and the European Security and Defence Policy (ESDP) civilian missions; a proportion of which is reported as bilateral GPEX.

The Conflict Pool (CP) –is governed and jointly managed by DFID, the FCO and the Ministry of Defence (MoD) to bring together the UK government's development, diplomatic and defence interest and expertise to ensure a coherent response to conflict prevention. Some of the CP's expenditure is ODA eligible. All CP funds disbursed through DFID are included in GPEX and appear in these statistics as part of DFID expenditure. The remaining figures comprise the aggregate of FCO and MOD spending. Data on the ODA eligible CP funds disbursed by the FCO and MOD are collected by DFID in liaison with programme officers in the relevant departments.

Other –includes contributions from other government departments including: Department of Energy and Climate Change; Department of Health; Department for Environment, Food & Rural

Affairs; Department for Culture, Media and Sport; Scottish Government; and the Welsh Assembly Government. It also includes estimates of the UK Border Agency's costs of supporting refugees in the UK; as well as estimates of gift aid to NGOs and other official funding to NGOs.

Further details on the UK's development assistance can be found in the Department for International Developments publication Statistics on International Development which can be found on the website www.dfid.gov.uk

Comparisons are available in the OECD Development Assistance Committee's annual report.

3.1. DFID Gross Public Expenditure 2010/11 - 2014/15

£ thousands

	2010/11	2011/12	2012/13	2013/14	2014/15
DFID Bilateral Programme[1]					
Poverty Reduction Budget Support	643,671	536,662	410,133	567,073	434,844
of which					
General Budget Support	360,467	242,290	167,343	106,600	49,698
Sector Budget Support	283,204	294,372	242,790	460,474	385,146
Other Financial Aid	550,728	544,778	685,571	601,174	468,481
Technical Co-operation	467,939	527,907	638,258	901,383	1,003,205
Bilateral Aid Delivered through a Multilateral Organisation[2]	1,465,789	1,404,592	1,074,957	1,436,580	1,286,186
Bilateral Aid Delivered through a NGO	626,752	739,558	747,302	999,809	1,029,908
of which:					
Partnership Programme Agreements	119,097	119,625	110,347	124,309	24,000
Other CSO's	507,655	619,933	636,955	875,500	1,005,908
Other Bilateral Aid[3]	76,009	81,372	119,120	142,378	143,084
Humanitarian Assistance	350,669	354,293	476,878	866,485	1,071,957
DFID Debt Relief	66,460	14,954	17,169	9,172	11,384
Total DFID Bilateral Programme	**4,248,018**	**4,204,114**	**4,169,389**	**5,524,054**	**5,449,049**
DFID Multilateral Programme					
European Commission	1,268,563	1,220,076	1,085,769	1,095,770	701,140
World Bank	926,713	1,038,568	1,025,431	1,206,227	1,407,938
UN Agencies	355,337	376,708	360,304	441,269	392,631
Other Multilateral	671,061	622,373	809,804	1,563,745	1,416,051
Total DFID Multilateral Programme	**3,221,673**	**3,257,724**	**3,281,308**	**4,307,012**	**3,917,760**
Total DFID Programme (excl. Total Operating Costs)	**7,469,691**	**7,461,839**	**7,450,696**	**9,831,066**	**9,366,809**
DFID Total Operating Costs[4]	219,457	220,352	220,220	226,743	231,973
Total DFID Programme	**7,689,149**	**7,682,191**	**7,670,916**	**10,057,810**	**9,598,783**

Source: Department for International Development (DFID)

1.   Descriptions of aid types given in Technical Note 1.

2.   This covers earmarked funding provided through multilateral organisations where the recipient country, region, sector, theme or specific project are known. This figure does not include all bilateral aid spent through a multilateral organisation – other types of aid such as humanitarian assistance or debt relief also include aid spent through a multilateral organisation. In total in 2013/14 £2,015 million of bilateral aid was spent through multilateral organisations.
3.   Other Bilateral Aid covers bilateral aid that does not fit into any other category.
4.   Includes Front Line Delivery costs and Administration spend.

3.2 DFID Bilateral Gross Public Expenditure by Region and Country Groupings 2010/11 - 2014/15

£ thousands

	Year	Financial Aid — General Poverty Reduction Budget Support	Financial Aid — Sector Poverty Reduction Budget Support	Financial Aid — Other Financial Aid[4]	Technical Co-operation	Bilateral aid delivered through a Multilateral	Bilateral aid Delivered through an NGO	Other Bilateral Aid[2]	Humanitarian Assistance	DFID Debt Relief	Total DFID Bilateral Programme[5]
TOTAL ALL COUNTRIES	2010/11	360,467	283,204	550,728	467,939	1,465,789	626,752	76,009	350,669	66,460	4,248,018
	2011/12	242,290	294,372	544,778	527,907	1,404,592	739,558	81,372	354,293	14,954	4,204,115
	2012/13	167,343	242,790	685,571	638,258	1,074,957	747,302	119,120	476,878	17,169	4,169,389
	2013/14	106,600	460,474	601,174	901,383	1,436,580	999,809	142,378	866,485	9,172	5,524,054
	2014/15	49,698	385,146	468,481	1,003,205	1,286,186	1,029,908	143,084	1,071,957	11,384	5,449,049
Africa	2010/11	310,467	185,454	211,960	248,588	437,496	158,238	47,869	211,732	55,358	1,867,162
	2011/12	222,290	242,372	222,158	298,059	386,727	213,000	45,046	260,329	1,713	1,891,694
	2012/13	167,343	213,090	297,050	368,762	316,222	207,660	76,600	317,865	1,124	1,965,716
	2013/14	106,600	301,524	255,996	491,619	419,387	308,233	48,176	379,607	-	2,311,141
	2014/15	49,698	266,896	159,625	530,160	397,398	291,669	45,574	642,456	0	2,383,476
of which: Africa: South of Sahara	2010/11	310,467	185,454	205,460	242,213	393,112	135,751	47,445	184,984	55,358	1,760,245
	2011/12	222,290	242,372	222,158	285,327	356,386	190,709	38,047	248,159	1,713	1,807,161
	2012/13	167,343	213,090	297,050	340,240	265,232	180,258	70,965	266,401	1,124	1,801,704
	2013/14	106,600	301,524	255,996	461,636	369,362	274,171	45,601	328,780	-	2,143,668
	2014/15	49,698	266,896	159,623	480,926	316,186	258,450	34,758	574,999	0	2,141,536
Americas	2010/11	-	-	20,103	3,170	29,618	1,624	3,170	7,442	1,706	66,833
	2011/12	-	-	26,576	3,932	14,004	2,215	526	2,537	-	49,789
	2012/13	-	-	30,440	2,552	11,979	1,947	364	6,383	-	53,665
	2013/14	-	-	26,857	1,028	8,503	1,522	154	7,273	3,535	48,872
	2014/15	0	0	23,231	2,905	5,059	1,509	841	3,945		37,490
Asia	2010/11	50,000	95,250	313,750	135,553	257,527	110,479	13,349	109,028	8,508	1,093,443
	2011/12	20,000	52,000	293,140	142,103	413,386	130,578	15,342	88,841	9,218	1,164,608
	2012/13	-	29,700	349,146	158,565	230,559	154,291	17,503	147,882	9,781	1,097,428
	2013/14	-	158,950	308,699	207,705	357,438	180,964	54,985	439,868	-	1,708,610
	2014/15	0	118,250	275,918	208,528	221,946	178,572	63,097	391,541	0	1,457,853

3.2 DFID Bilateral Gross Public Expenditure by Region and Country Groupings 2010/11 - 2014/15

£ thousands

	Financial Aid			Technical Co-operation	Bilateral aid delivered through a Multilateral	Bilateral aid Delivered through an NGO	Other Bilateral Aid[2]	Humanitarian Assistance	DFID Debt Relief	Total DFID Bilateral Programme[5]
	General Poverty Reduction Budget Support	Sector Poverty Reduction Budget Support	Other Financial Aid[4]							
Europe										
2010/11	-	2,500	2,239	7,030	4,703	937	68	26	365	17,868
2011/12	-	-	-	3,230	244	344	-14	425	378	4,607
2012/13	-	-	6,746	2,305	782	193	12	7	-	10,046
2013/14	-	-	6,340	25	66	-	12	129	-	6,573
2014/15	0	0	5,915	261	1,389	0	500	6,410	-	14,475
Pacific										
2010/11	-	-	2,235	212	-	-	-	-	191	2,638
2011/12	-	-	2,738	36	-	-	-	-	212	2,986
2012/13	-	-	2,883	11	-	-	-	150	166	3,210
2013/14	-	-	2,839	-	-	-	-	-	44	2,883
2014/15	0	0	3,070	106	570	218	0	1,300	-	5,264
Non Region Specific										
2010/11	-	-	442	73,386	736,445	355,473	11,553	22,442	332	1,200,074
2011/12	-	-	167	80,546	590,230	393,421	20,473	2,161	3,433	1,090,431
2012/13	-	-	-695	106,063	515,415	383,211	24,640	4,591	6,097	1,039,323
2013/14	-	-	441	201,007	651,186	509,090	39,051	39,608	5,593	1,445,976
2014/15	0	0	722	261,245	659,824	557,940	33,072	26,305	11,384	1,550,492
Total Developing Countries[3]										
2010/11	360,467	283,204	550,728	467,358	1,464,655	626,506	76,009	349,290	66,460	4,244,679
2011/12	242,290	294,372	541,881	525,763	1,404,592	739,319	81,372	354,131	14,954	4,198,672
2012/13	167,343	242,790	685,571	638,258	1,074,957	747,302	119,120	476,878	17,169	4,169,389
2013/14	106,600	460,474	601,174	901,264	1,436,580	999,557	171,970	866,485	9,172	5,553,275
2014/15	49,698	385,146	467,759	741,960	626,362	471,968	110,013	1,045,652	0	3,898,558
Least Developed Countries										
2010/11	274,467	167,454	248,317	165,797	396,371	164,974	36,065	199,400	19,896	1,672,742
2011/12	210,000	210,372	196,839	160,589	408,071	221,335	36,995	147,398	4,612	1,596,211
2012/13	153,235	203,090	329,843	220,994	273,248	232,812	66,016	282,805	4,857	1,766,900
2013/14	93,668	299,024	302,854	295,780	426,444	298,523	59,634	344,688	44	2,120,659
2014/15	49,698	287,403	237,567	316,108	330,156	286,036	49,313	613,048	-	2,169,329

3.2 DFID Bilateral Gross Public Expenditure by Region and Country Groupings 2010/11 - 2014/15

£ thousands

		Financial Aid				Bilateral aid delivered through a Multilateral	Bilateral aid Delivered through an NGO	Other Bilateral Aid[2]	Humanitarian Assistance	DFID Debt Relief	Total DFID Bilateral Programme[5]
		General Poverty Reduction Budget Support	Sector Poverty Reduction Budget Support	Other Financial Aid[4]	Technical Co-operation						
Commonwealth[7]	2010/11	340,467	169,254	362,725	250,728	247,917	139,987	35,191	96,664	1,111	1,644,044
	2011/12	222,290	147,539	441,137	278,081	305,734	191,852	30,273	94,825	1,135	1,712,866
	2012/13	167,343	114,290	487,666	329,497	204,792	208,203	52,367	80,472	1,291	1,645,921
	2013/14	-	-	-	1,546	-	252	117,901	-	-	119,699
	2014/15	0	0	94,294	2,572	0	216	0	0	0	97,083
of which											
Overseas Territories	2010/11	-	-	45,882	7,142	-	242	-	-	-	53,267
	2011/12	-	-	88,269	4,232	-	90	-	-	-	92,591
	2012/13	-	-	130,123	3,581	-	201	-	-	-	133,905
	2013/14	-	-	117,901	1,546	-	252	-	-	-	119,699
	2014/15	0	0	87,204	1,722	0	0	0	0	0	88,926
HIPC Countries[6]	2010/11	310,467	185,454	193,421	115,476	318,635	88,733	26,442	184,608	55,564	1,478,800
	2011/12	222,290	242,372	154,929	114,231	290,711	122,120	29,698	132,324	-	1,308,676
	2012/13	167,343	213,090	171,428	303,951	190,153	122,886	59,125	245,884	-	1,473,861
	2013/14	106,600	301,524	254,558	234,391	266,066	187,735	39,630	302,209	-	1,692,713
	2014/15	49,698	266,896	187,047	277,856	250,065	191,153	30,810	570,905	0	1,824,430

Source: Department for International Development (DFID)

1. Descriptions of aid types given in Technical Note 1.
2. Other Bilateral Aid covers bilateral aid not elsewhere classified
3. Developing Countries are those countries and regions in the DAC List of Recipients of Official Development Assistance.
   Since the 2008 edition of SID, Turks and Caicos,Barbados and Trinidad & Tobago and Saudi Arabia have been removed from the DAC list.
4. Pension payments have been reclassified from "Other Financial Aid" to "Aid from other UK Official Sources". This is consistent with the classification of spending under Department Expenditure Limits (DEL) agreed with Treasury.
5. Includes Non Region Specific
6. Highly Indebted Poor Countries
7. Dependant countries

3.3: DFID Bilateral Expenditure by Input Sector Code 2010/11 to 2014/15

£ thousand

Input Sector Code	2010/11	2011/12	2012/13	2013/14	2014/15
Education:					
11010 Education Poverty Reduction Budget Support	152,581	90,301	135,395	181,996	123,328
11020 Education Unallocable/Unspecified	8,718	51,403	6,399	15,311	22,056
11110 Education Policy and Administrative Management	68,527	122,537	63,369	116,728	59,170
11120 Facilities and Training Education	31,044	44,756	25,531	8,609	15,555
11130 Teacher Training	17,775	15,879	24,181	24,727	41,289
11220 Primary Education	210,797	231,124	143,204	242,755	187,509
11230 Basic Life Skills for Youth and Adults Education	10,933	11,426	25,215	29,378	38,899
11240 Pre-School	4,337	3,717	2,123	849	252
11320 Secondary Education	27,059	28,089	58,090	119,432	138,908
11330 Vocational Training	8,588	6,609	7,028	7,241	8,955
11420 Higher Education	20,237	19,267	21,146	26,990	32,252
11430 Advanced Technical and Managerial Training	312	281	562	738	427
Education Total	**560,907**	**625,389**	**512,243**	**774,754**	**668,599**
Health:					
12010 Health Poverty Reduction Budget Support	100,327	57,306	48,440	46,270	27,216
12020 Health Unallocable/Unspecified	3,712	13,504	8,346	12,944	12,711
12110 Health Policy and Administrative Management	58,667	43,590	56,090	79,308	72,531
12220 Basic Health Care	74,650	105,712	144,027	151,359	140,901
12240 Basic Nutrition	23,715	37,505	49,433	64,363	56,893
12250 Infectious Disease Control	73,853	146,612	105,375	187,174	93,728
12261 Health Education	26,392	31,717	34,434	39,817	34,022
12262 Malaria Control	101,393	86,181	111,521	166,897	115,262
12263 Tuberculosis Control	44,187	10,051	12,735	12,455	12,895
12281 Health Personnel Development	7,773	12,295	12,611	19,825	19,360
13010 Population Policy and Administrative Management	7,092	6,063	5,463	11,535	4,312
13021 Reproductive Health Care	47,962	108,852	36,746	49,428	55,384
13022 Maternal and Neonatal Health	49,987	121,362	125,862	163,402	207,024
13030 Family Planning	31,082	43,767	109,727	127,019	124,451
13041 HIV/AIDS including STD Prevention	119,094	69,002	50,271	37,459	25,546
13042 HIV/AIDS including STD Treatment and Care	52,717	27,331	40,160	10,942	8,126
13081 Personnel Development for Population and Reproductive Health	7,506	8,332	7,543	9,274	12,927
Health Total	**830,109**	**929,182**	**958,785**	**1,189,468**	**1,023,290**
Social Infrastructure and Services:					
16011 Social Protection	186,531	103,647	104,931	138,082	118,343
16012 Social Other	48,714	83,879	53,237	88,583	60,441
16020 Employment Policy & Admin Management	2,956	2,924	4,271	7,459	102
16030 Housing Policy and Admin Management	73	594	566	943	616
16040 Low-cost Housing	1,706	5,693	7,867	3,403	4,311
16070 Poverty Reduction Budget Support-Social infrastructure and services	18,273	12,940	7,078	12,392	6,965
52010 Food Aid and Food Security Programmes	52,145	50,622	47,148	54,806	18,570
Social Infrastructure and Services Total	**310,396**	**260,300**	**225,098**	**305,667**	**209,349**
Water Supply and Sanitation:					
14010 Water Resources Policy and Administrative Management	14,317	20,655	14,926	29,139	31,131
14015 Water Resources Protection	2,335	5,216	5,192	6,541	5,935
14020 Water Supply and Sanitation Large Systems	4,869	9,175	10,934	13,458	14,148
14021 Water Supply – Large Systems	4,039	5,100	-	-730	452
14022 - Sanitation - large systems, (MDG Water and Sanitation)	-	-	-	-	651
14030 Basic Drinking Water	63,219	73,031	55,664	400	74,721
14031 Basic drinking water supply	964	891	2,581	51,941	18,404
14032 Basic sanitation	1,466	7,605	17,237	3,084	30,267
14040 River Development	3,688	1,360	29	25,430	249
14050 Waste Management and Disposal	2,669	2,519	3,737	3,328	4,552
14060 Water Poverty Reduction Budget Support	13,271	8,255	9,134	10,539	7,493
14070 Water Unallocable/Unspecified	868	6,976	9,623	14,315	8,915
14081 Education and Training	354	1,408	962	5,651	8,219
Water Supply and Sanitation Total	**112,061**	**142,191**	**130,020**	**163,096**	**205,138**
Government and Civil Society:					
15010 Government Poverty Reduction Budget Support	115,004	58,494	37,665	25,034	12,581
15020 Government Unallocated/ Unspecified	52,166	37,876	42,945	57,967	36,134
15110 Economic and Development Policy/Planning	121,076	90,314	86,146	111,772	69,181
15121 Public Sector Financial Management	105,996	132,449	126,422	83,940	65,849
15122 Corruption - Public Sector Financial Management	17,719	18,010	16,677	24,254	22,294
15130 Legal and Judicial Development	17,351	18,158	15,623	23,218	22,433
15141 National Government Administration	30,876	33,736	49,375	43,878	59,110
15142 Local Government Administration	36,266	57,607	53,882	28,903	41,413
15150 Strengthening Civil Society	116,792	121,683	102,697	111,472	87,071
15152 Legislatures and political parties (Governance and Security)	-	-	-	-	4,882
15161 Elections	33,880	28,920	1,877	33,212	22,379
15162 Human Rights	10,688	10,284	27,490	12,991	21,441

3.3: DFID Bilateral Expenditure by Input Sector Code 2010/11 to 2014/15

£ thousand

Input Sector Code	2010/11	2011/12	2012/13	2013/14	2014/15
15163 Free Flow of Information	9,997	10,144	9,369	17,971	15,641
15164 Women's Equality Organisations and Institutions	12,306	11,742	13,170	21,999	31,477
15171 Culture and Recreation	82	-	-	-	-
15172 Statistical Capacity Building	40,395	31,102	15,752	37,682	14,032
15173 Narcotics Control	53	24	21,880	63	393
15210 Security System Management and Reform	19,285	27,065	34,429	29,462	33,476
15220 Civilian Peace-Building, Conflict Prevention and Resolution	20,497	21,597	38,480	49,842	33,622
15230 Post-Conflict Peace-Building (UN)	6,520	5,719	9,257	9,130	4,638
15240 Reintegration and SALW Control	4,683	754	269	696	1029
15250 Land Mine Clearance	9,902	11,720	10,586	8,955	6,773
15261 Child Soldiers (Prevention and Demobilisation)	141	159	14	-	-
Government and Civil Society Total	**781,674**	**727,557**	**714,004**	**736,329**	**605,849**
Economic:					
Economic Infrastructure					
21010 Transport Policy and Administrative Management	65,697	42,208	53,921	52,833	47,200
21021 Road Transport: Excluding Rural Feeder Roads	37,096	26,548	24,630	31,739	21,733
21022 Road Transport: Rural Feeder Roads	15,224	17,222	9,427	26,326	34,526
21031 Other Transport	5,755	22,965	45,652	50,437	35,865
22010 Communications Policy and Administrative Management	6,065	1,680	1,649	1,998	1,402
22020 Telecommunications	8,596	8,892	1,444	364	311
22030 Radio/Television/Print Media: Communications	64	38	1	-	247
22040 Information and Communication Technology (ICT)	2,055	655	135	407	304
23010 Energy Policy and Administrative Management	35,208	12,887	14,973	26,779	11,695
23020 Power Generation/Non-Renewable Sources: Energy	11,809	9,760	3,628	5,924	9,729
23030 Power Generation/Renewable Sources: Energy	30,633	3,956	13,090	22,751	39,441
23040 Energy Access for Households, Enterprises and Communities: Energy (Wealth Creation)	-	-	-	17	232
24010 Financial Policy and Administrative Management	26,098	27,913	26,940	38,290	53,817
24020 Monetary Institutions	1,319	3,111	1,409	634	1898
24030 Formal Sector Financial Intermediaries	10,968	12,825	14,092	48,896	31,048
24040 Informal/Semi-Formal Financial Intermediaries	7,449	6,764	10,277	26,203	10,818
24081 Education/Training in Banking and Financial Services	2,471	4,877	3,518	5,868	4,316
25010 Business Support Services and Institutions	29,087	25,071	29,458	45,966	42,926
25020 Privatisation	7,896	5,479	4,626	4,853	3,228
Production Sectors					
31110 Agriculture Policy and Administrative Management	38,879	34,080	19,891	35,408	19,728
31120 Agricultural Development	18,023	37,625	18,877	39,261	56,095
31130 Agricultural Land Resources	11,033	4,115	3,639	5,972	8,490
31163 Livestock: Agriculture	2,281	2,895	5,133	5,967	5,632
31191 Agricultural Services	865	2,766	4,617	10,101	14,329
31210 Forestry Policy and Administrative Management	30,650	4,910	15,936	14,683	19,343
31220 Forestry Development	28,989	4,351	865	419	295
31310 Fishing Policy and Administrative Management	3,046	1,838	1,496	1,469	328
31320 Fishery Development	265	0	9	99	112
32110 Industrial Policy and Administrative Management	1,068	1,632	2,054	1,223	639
32120 Industrial Development	2,034	2,816	1,901	4,458	2,815
32130 Small and Medium-Sized Enterprises (SME): Development	30,011	25,575	20,686	36,225	56,607
32210 Mineral/Mining Policy and Administrative Management	369	8,663	5,287	3,229	6,003
32310 Construction Policy and Administrative Management	939	2,503	1,430	1,228	253
32350 Production Poverty Reduction Budget Support	30,984	18,803	15,905	7,718	6,268
33110 Trade Policy and Administrative Management	30,713	19,204	18,423	19,172	20,897
33120 Trade Facilitation	40,024	11,613	16,343	22,318	-25,043
33130 Regional Trade Agreements (RTAs)	6,792	4,191	6,031	13,192	7,131
33140 Multilateral Trade Negotiations	120	273	1,742	3,676	5,198
33181 Trade Education/Training	613	838	400	676	1641
33210 Tourism Policy and Administrative Management	1,272	2,215	1,345	429	458
43050 Non-Agricultural Alternative Development	818	1,692	2,132	2,283	3,915
Development Planning					
43020 Poverty Reduction Budget Support for Econ. Infrastructure & Dev. Planning	67,825	42,162	26,009	42,885	11,050
43030 Urban Development and Management	30,362	19,907	28,356	26,378	23,928
43040 Rural Development	68,083	55,302	53,854	91,862	55,393
Economic Total	**749,546**	**542,821**	**531,231**	**780,618**	**652,239**
Environment Protection:					
41010 Environmental Policy and Administrative Management	16,512	9,506	7,029	8,402	8,911
41031 Bio-Diversity	198	3,264	963	1,245	278
41032 Climate Change	2,191	30,997	59,724	113,595	145,572
41033 Desertification	101,790	-	1,711	-	-
41040 Site Preservation	242	-	-	-	-
41050 Flood Prevention/Control	22	898	-	6,113	3,499
41060 Environment: Poverty Reduction Budget Support	377	1,418	627	210	65
41070 Environment Unallocable/Unspecified	1,846	3,104	6,011	7,864	7,377
41081 Environmental Education/ Training	1,905	2,591	2,302	2,213	2,981
41090 Climate Change - Low Carbon Emissions	-	55,772	12,688	16,858	28,898

3.3: DFID Bilateral Expenditure by Input Sector Code 2010/11 to 2014/15

£ thousand

Input Sector Code	2010/11	2011/12	2012/13	2013/14	2014/15
41092 Climate Change - Cross Cutting	-	2,811	4,319	51	51
41093 Climate Change - Adaptation	-	99,048	141,088	63,644	88,073
Environment Protection Total	**135,226**	**217,304**	**238,246**	**220,196**	**285,706**
Research:					
80010 Economic Research	12,651	16,350	20,533	30,275	30,193
80011 Education Research	1,775	2,884	5,121	15,597	19,429
80012 Health Research	46,997	49,312	49,412	58,734	71,441
80013 Water Supply and Sanitation Research	2,064	1,502	1,748	2,600	2,686
80014 Governance Research	6,825	11,836	9,781	11,054	13,444
80015 Social Research	12,257	8,327	11,248	12,850	11,054
80016 Humanitarian Research	1,185	1,163	1,486	6,354	7,572
80017 Renewable Natural Resources Research	7,603	6,139	1,596	1,246	2,962
80018 Environment Research	6,883	8,968	11,375	13,483	16,348
80019 Energy Research	817	1,037	2,553	6,346	7,956
80020 Agricultural Research	19,624	22,073	33,287	37,356	40,353
80021 Forestry Research	269	54	-	-	46
80022 Fishery Research	169	-	-	23	-
80023 Technological Research and Development	1,541	1,210	1,670	4,486	4,404
80024 Unspecified/Unallocated Research	7,442	9,253	17,182	31,160	38,520
Research Total	**128,103**	**140,109**	**166,994**	**231,566**	**266,408**
Humanitarian Assistance:					
72010 Material Relief Assistance and Services	198,368	157,678	243,333	407,196	504,606
72040 Emergency Food Aid	68,862	106,548	145,762	259,547	223,742
72050 Relief Coordination, Protection and Support Services	61,763	38,336	69,742	128,549	266,246
73010 Reconstruction Relief and Rehabilitation	27,996	47,043	14,345	36,124	50,610
74010 Disaster Prevention and Preparedness	-	-	-	-	31,871
Humanitarian Assistance Total	**356,989**	**349,604**	**473,182**	**866,440**	**1,077,075**
Non Sector Allocable:					
Core Contributions to Multilateral Institutions - Global Partnerships	-	-	-	200	360
Core Contributions to Multilateral Institutions - Governance & Security	-	-	-	3,214	292
Core Contributions to Multilateral Institutions - MDG Humanitarian	-	-	-	10,014	2,667
Core Contributions to Multilateral Institutions - MDG Other Health	-	-	-	1,875	4,375
Core Contributions to Multilateral Institutions - MDG Water & Sanitation	-	-	-	2,700	5,306
Core Contributions to Multilateral Institutions - Wealth Creation	-	-	-	-	3,663
Core Contributions to Multilateral Institutions - Climate Change ICF	-	-	-	-	1,000
88889 Multilateral Capacity Building and Administration	17,850	42,463	2,675	2,940	2,520
88890 Multilateral Institutions: Secondees to & Staffing of	1,838	4,673	5,264	4,794	7,389
60010 Action Relating to Debt	66,483	15,110	17,440	9,172	11,384
90010 Programme Partnership Agreements	116,100	91,508	124,808	124,401	122,893
91010 Administrative Costs of Donors	1,236	-	-	-	-
91020 Front Line Delivery Costs	-	-	-	-	18821
92000 Support to Non-Governmental Organisations (NGOs)	50,815	101,785	62,436	136,946	178,081
93020 Aid to Refugees in Recipient Countries	9,164	2,344	2,882	3,035	2,441
88888 Multilateral Core Contribution	-	-	-14,249	10,797	85,822
99820 Promotion of Development Awareness	19,300	11,775	16,008	9,352	8,382
Others	-	-	-684	-63,516	-
Non Sector Allocable Total	**283,006**	**269,658**	**219,589**	**255,922**	**455,397**

Source: Department for International Development (DFID)

1. '-' means nil
   '0' means less than half the final digit shown
   '..' means not available
   'n/a' means not applicable
2. Figures are rounded to the nearest unit, therefore they may not add exactly to the rounded totals.
3. Negative amounts reflect accounting adjustments.

Labour market

Chapter 4

Labour Market

Labour Force Survey

Background

The Labour Force Survey (LFS) is the largest regular household survey in the UK. LFS interviews are conducted continuously throughout the year. In any three-month period, nationally representative samples of approximately 110,000 people aged 16 and over in around 50,000 households are interviewed. Each household is interviewed five times, at three-monthly intervals. The initial interview is done face-to-face by an interviewer visiting the address, except for residents north of the Caledonian Canal in Scotland. The other interviews are done by telephone wherever possible. The survey asks a series of questions about respondents' personal circumstances and their labour market activity. Most questions refer to activity in the week before the interview.

The LFS collects information on a sample of the population. To convert this information to give estimates for the population, the data must be grossed. This is achieved by calculating weighting factors (often referred to simply as weights) which can be applied to each sampled individual in such a way that the weighted-up results match estimates or projections of the total population in terms of age distribution, sex, and region of residence. There is a considerable amount of ongoing research to improve methodologies. Whenever methodologies are implemented the estimates may be revised.

The concepts and definitions used in the LFS are agreed by the International Labour Organisation (ILO) – an agency of the United Nations. The definitions are used by European Union member countries and members of the Organisation for Economic Co-operation and Development (OECD). The LFS was carried out every two years from 1973 to 1983. The ILO definition was first used in 1984. This was also the first year in which the survey was conducted on an annual basis with results available for every spring quarter (representing an average of the period from March to May). The survey moved to a continuous basis in spring 1992 in Great Britain and in winter 1994/95 in Northern Ireland, with average quarterly results published four times a year for seasonal quarters: spring (March to May), summer (June to August), autumn (September to November) and winter (December to February). From April 1998, results are published 12 times a year for the average of three consecutive months.

Strengths and limitations of the LFS

The LFS produces coherent labour market information on the basis of internationally standard concepts and definitions. It is a rich source of data on a wide variety of labour market and personal characteristics. It is the most suitable source for making comparisons between countries. The LFS is designed so that households interviewed in each three month period constitute a representative sample of UK households. The survey covers those living in private households and nurses in

National Health Service accommodation. Students living in halls of residence have been included since 1992, as information about them is collected at their parents' address.

However the LFS has its limitations. It is a sample survey and is therefore subject to sampling variability. The survey does not include people living in institutions such as hostels, hotels, boarding houses, mobile home sites or residential homes. 'Proxy' reporting (when members of the household are not present at the interview, another member of the household answers the questions on their behalf) can affect the quality of information on topics such as earnings, hours worked, benefit receipt and qualifications. Around a third of interviews are conducted 'by proxy', usually by a spouse or partner but sometimes by a parent or other near relation. LFS estimates are also potentially affected by non-response.

Sampling Variability

Survey estimates are prone to sampling variability. The easiest way to explain this concept is by example. In the September to November 1997 period, ILO unemployment in Great Britain (seasonally adjusted) stood at 1,847,000. If we drew another sample for the same period we could get a different result, perhaps 1,900,000 or 1,820,000.

In theory, we could draw many samples, and each would give a different result. This is because each sample would be made up of different people who would give different answers to the questions. The spread of these results is the sampling variability. Sampling variability is determined by a number of factors including the sample size, the variability of the population from which the sample is drawn and the sample design. Once we know the sampling variability we can calculate a range of values about the sample estimate that represents the expected variation with a given level of assurance. This is called a confidence interval. For a 95 per cent confidence interval we expect that in 95 per cent of the samples (19 times out of 20) the confidence interval will contain the true value that would be obtained by surveying the entire population. For the example given above, we can be 95 per cent confident that the true value was in the range 1,791,000 to 1,903,000.

Unreliable estimates

Estimates of small numbers have relatively wide confidence intervals making them unreliable. For this reason, the Office for National Statistics (ONS) does not currently publish LFS estimates below 10,000.

Non-response

All surveys are subject to non-response – that is respondents in the sample who either refuse to take part in the survey or who cannot be contacted. Non-response can introduce bias to a survey, particularly if the people not responding have characteristics that are different from those who do respond.

The LFS has a response rate of around 65 per cent to the first interview, and over 90 per cent of those who are interviewed once go on to complete all five interviews. These are relatively high levels for a household survey.

Any bias from non-response is minimised by weighting the results. Weighting (or grossing) converts sample data to represent the full population. In the LFS, the data are weighted separately by age, sex and area of residence to population estimates based on the census. Weighting also adjusts for people not in the survey and thus minimises non-response bias.

LFS concepts and definitions

Discouraged worker - A sub-group of the economically inactive population who said although they would like a job their main reason for not seeking work was because they believed there were no jobs available.

Economically active – People aged 16 and over who are either in employment or unemployed.

Economic activity rate – The number of people who are in employment or unemployed expressed as a percentage of the relevant population.

Economically inactive – People who are neither in employment nor unemployed. These include those who want a job but have not been seeking work in the last four weeks, those who want a job and are seeking work but not available to start, and those who do not want a job.

Employment – People aged 16 and over who did at least one hour of paid work in the reference week (as an employee or self-employed), those who had a job that they were temporarily away from, those on government-supported training and employment programmes, and those doing unpaid family work.

Employees – The division between employees and self employed is based on survey respondents' own assessment of their employment status.

Full Time – The classification of employees, self-employed and unpaid family workers in their main job as full-time or part-time is on the basis of self-assessment. However, people on government supported employment and training programmes that are at college in the reference week are classified, by convention, as part-time.

Government -supported training and employment programmes – Comprise all people aged 16 and over participating in one of the government's employment and training programmes (Youth Training, Training for Work and Community Action), together with those on similar programmes administered by Training and Enterprise Councils in England and Wales, or Local Enterprise Companies in Scotland.

Hours worked – Respondents to the LFS are asked a series of questions enabling the identification of both their usual hours and their actual hours. Total hours include overtime (paid and unpaid) and exclude lunch breaks.

Actual Hours Worked – Actual hours worked statistics measure how many hours were actually worked. These statistics are directly affected by changes in the number of people in employment and in the number of hours that individual works.

Usual Hours Worked – Usual hours worked statistics measure how many hours people usually work per week. Compared with actual hours worked, they are not affected by absences and so can provide a better measure of normal working patterns.

Unemployment – The number of unemployed people in the UK is measured through the LFS following the internationally agreed definition recommended by the International Labour Organisation (ILO), an agency of the United Nations.

Unemployed people are:

Without a job, have actively sought work in the last four weeks and are available to start work in the next two weeks, or

Out of work, have found a job and are waiting to start in the next two weeks

Unemployment (rate) – The number of unemployed people expressed as a percentage of the relevant economically active population.

Unemployment (duration) – The duration of respondents unemployment is defined as the shorter of the following two periods:

Duration of active search for work

Length of time since employment

Part-time – see full-time.

Second jobs – Jobs which LFS respondents hold in addition to a main full-time or part-time job.

Self-employment – See Employees.

Temporary employees – In the LFS these are defined as those employees who say that their main job is non permanent in one of the following ways: fixed period contract, agency temping, casual work, seasonal work or other temporary work.

Unpaid family workers – Persons doing unpaid work for a business they own or for a business that a relative owns.

International Employment Comparisons

All employment rates for European Union (EU) countries published by Eurostat (including the rate for the UK) are based on the population aged 15–64. The rates for Canada and Japan are also based on the population aged 15–64, but the rate for the US is for those aged 16–64. The employment rate for the UK published by ONS is based on the working age population aged 16–64 (men) and 16–59 (women) and therefore takes into account both the current school leaving age and state pension ages.

The unemployment rate published by Eurostat for most EU countries (but not for the UK), are calculated by extrapolating from the most recent LFS data using monthly registered unemployment data. A standard population basis (15–74) is used by Eurostat except for Spain and the UK (16–74). The unemployment rate for the US is based on those aged 16 and over, but the rates for Canada and Japan are for those aged 15 and over. All unemployment rates are seasonally adjusted.

The unemployment rate for the UK published by Eurostat is based on the population aged 16–74 while the unemployment rate for the UK published by ONS is based on those aged 16 and over. There are other minor definitional differences.

Jobseekers allowance claimant count

This is a count of all those people who are claiming Jobseeker's Allowance (JSA) at Jobcentre Plus local offices. People claiming JSA must declare that they are:

- out of work
- capable of work
- available for work
- actively seeking work

during the week in which the claim is made.

All people claiming JSA on the day of the monthly count are included in the claimant count, irrespective of whether they are actually receiving benefits. Also see table 5.6 in Social protection chapter.

Annual Survey of Hours and Earnings

The Annual Survey of Hours and Earnings (ASHE) is based on a one per cent sample of employee jobs taken from HM Revenue & Customs (HMRC) PAYE records. Information on earnings and paid hours worked is obtained from employers and treated confidentially. ASHE does not cover the self-employed nor does it cover employees not paid during the reference period.

The headline statistics for ASHE are based on the median rather than the mean. The median is the value below which 50 per cent of employees fall. It is ONS's preferred measure of average earnings as it is less affected by a relatively small number of very high earners and the skewed distribution of earnings. It therefore gives a better indication of typical pay than the mean.

The earnings information presented relates to gross pay before tax, National Insurance or other deductions, and excludes payments in kind. With the exception of annual earnings, the results are restricted to earnings relating to the survey pay period and so exclude payments of arrears from another period made during the survey period; any payments due as a result of a pay settlement but not yet paid at the time of the survey will also be excluded.

Average Weekly Earnings

The Average Weekly Earnings (AWE) indicator measures changes in the level of earnings in Great Britain. Average earnings are calculated as the total wages and salaries paid by firms, divided by the number of employees paid. It is given as a level, in pounds per employee per week. Annual growth rates are derived from the level of average weekly earnings.

The AWE data are now published on a SIC 2007 basis, and the historic time series have been re-estimated as a result.

AWE is based on the Monthly wages and Salaries Survey (MWSS). As such, it is a timely indicator of changes in the level of earnings. The survey does not cover businesses with fewer than 20 employees; an adjustment is made to AWE to reflect these businesses. Note that the survey does not include Northern Ireland.

Unlike the previous measure of average earnings (the Average Earnings Index), changes in the composition of the workforce have an impact on AWE. If a high-paying sector of the economy employs more people, other things staying the same, average earnings will increase.

Average Weekly Earnings, like AEI before it, is a measure based on earnings per employee. If the number of paid hours worked per employee change, average earnings will also change.

Trade unions

The statistics relate to all organisations of workers known to the Certification Officer with head offices in Great Britain that fall within the appropriate definition of a trade union in the Trade Union and Labour Relations (Consolidation) Act 1992. Included in the data are home and overseas membership figures of contributory and non-contributory members. Employment status of members is not provided and the figures may therefore include some people who are self-employed, unemployed or retired.

4.1 Labour Force Summary by Sex: United Kingdom

United Kingdom
(thousands) seasonally
adjusted

		LFS household population		Headline indicators						
				Employment		Unemployment			Inactivity	
				Level	Rate	Level	Rate		Level	Rate
		All aged 16 & over	All aged 16 to 64	All aged 16 & over	All aged 16 to 64	All aged 16 & over	All aged 16 & over		All aged 16 to 64	All aged 16 to 64
People		**MGSL**	**LF2O**	**MGRZ**	**LF24**	**MGSC**	**MGSX**		**LF2M**	**LF2S**
	Aug-Oct 2012	51,045	40,508	29,740	71.0	2,539	7.9		9,215	22.7
	Aug-Oct 2013	51,378	40,564	30,208	71.8	2,412	7.4		9,047	22.3
	Aug-Oct 2014	51,718	40,649	30,796	73.0	1,958	6.0		9,056	22.3
	Nov-Jan 2015	51,801	40,673	30,939	73.3	1,856	5.7		9,026	22.2
	Feb-Apr 2015	51,884	40,697	31,053	73.4	1,813	5.5		9,016	22.2
	May-Jul 2015	51,967	40,722	31,095	73.5	1,823	5.5		8,993	22.1
	Aug-Oct 2015	**52,048**	**40,748**	**31,302**	**73.9**	**1,713**	**5.2**		**8,930**	**21.9**
	Change on quarter	*81*	*26*	*207*	*0.4*	*-110*	*-0.3*		*-63*	*-0.2*
	Change %	*0.2*	*0.1*	*0.7*		*-6.0*			*-0.7*	
	Change on year	*330*	*99*	*506*	*0.9*	*-245*	*-0.8*		*-126*	*-0.4*
	Change %	*0.6*	*0.2*	*1.6*		*-12.5*			*-1.4*	
Men		**MGSM**	**YBTG**	**MGSA**	**MGSV**	**MGSD**	**MGSY**		**YBSO**	**YBTM**
	Aug-Oct 2012	24,849	20,082	15,904	76.2	1,436	8.3		3,352	16.7
	Aug-Oct 2013	25,039	20,122	16,095	76.8	1,355	7.8		3,335	16.6
	Aug-Oct 2014	25,228	20,178	16,384	77.9	1,092	6.2		3,391	16.8
	Nov-Jan 2015	25,274	20,193	16,458	78.1	1,024	5.9		3,405	16.9
	Feb-Apr 2015	25,321	20,208	16,524	78.3	1,002	5.7		3,398	16.8
	May-Jul 2015	25,367	20,224	16,542	78.3	989	5.6		3,414	16.9
	Aug-Oct 2015	**25,413**	**20,241**	**16,697**	**79.0**	**939**	**5.3**		**3,332**	**16.5**
	Change on quarter	*46*	*17*	*155*	*0.7*	*-50*	*-0.3*		*-82*	*-0.4*
	Change %	*0.2*	*0.1*	*0.9*		*-5.1*			*-2.4*	
	Change on year	*185*	*63*	*313*	*1.1*	*-153*	*-0.9*		*-59*	*-0.3*
	Change %	*0.7*	*0.3*	*1.9*		*-14.0*			*-1.7*	
Women		**MGSN**	**LF2P**	**MGSB**	**LF25**	**MGSE**	**MGSZ**		**LF2N**	**LF2T**
	Aug-Oct 2012	26,196	20,426	13,836	65.9	1,103	7.4		5,863	28.7
	Aug-Oct 2013	26,340	20,441	14,113	66.9	1,058	7.0		5,712	27.9
	Aug-Oct 2014	26,490	20,471	14,412	68.1	866	5.7		5,666	27.7
	Nov-Jan 2015	26,527	20,480	14,481	68.5	831	5.4		5,621	27.4
	Feb-Apr 2015	26,563	20,489	14,528	68.6	811	5.3		5,618	27.4
	May-Jul 2015	26,600	20,498	14,553	68.8	834	5.4		5,579	27.2
	Aug-Oct 2015	**26,635**	**20,507**	**14,605**	**69.0**	**774**	**5.0**		**5,598**	**27.3**
	Change on quarter	*35*	*9*	*52*	*0.2*	*-60*	*-0.4*		*19*	*0.1*
	Change %	*0.1*	*0.0*	*0.4*		*-7.2*			*0.3*	
	Change on year	*145*	*36*	*193*	*0.9*	*-92*	*-0.7*		*-68*	*-0.4*
	Change %	*0.5*	*0.2*	*1.3*		*-10.6*			*-1.2*	

Source: Labour Force Survey
Labour market statistics enquiries: labour.market@ons.gsi.gov.uk

Note: When comparing quarterly changes ONS recommends comparing with the previous non-overlapping 3-month average time period (eg, compare Apr-Jun with Jan-Mar, not with Mar-May).

The headline employment rate is the number of people aged 16 to 64 in employment divided by the population aged 16 to 64.
The headline unemployment rate is the number of unemployed people (aged 16+) divided by the economically active population (aged 16+).
The economically active population is defined as those in employment plus those who are unemployed.
The headline inactivity rate is the number of economically inactive people aged 16 to 64 divided by the population aged 16 to 64.

Note on headline employment, unemployment and inactivity rates
The headline employment and inactivity rates are based on the population aged 16 to 64 but the headline unemployment rate is based on the economically active population aged 16 and over. The employment and inactivity rates for those aged 16 and over are affected by the inclusion of the retired population in the denominators and are therefore less meaningful than the rates for those aged from 16 to 64. However, for the unemployment rate for those aged 16 and over, no such effect occurs as the denominator for the unemployment rate is the economically active population which only includes people in work or actively seeking and able to work.

Note on headline employment, unemployment and inactivity levels
The headline employment and unemployment levels are for those aged 16 and over; they measure all people in work or actively seeking and able to work. However, the headline inactivity level is for those aged 16 to 64. The inactivity level for those aged 16 and over is less meaningful as it includes elderly people who have retired from the labour force.

4.2 Full-time, part-time and temporary workers

United Kingdom (thousands) seasonally adjusted

	All in employment					Full-time and part-time workers[1]						
	Total	Employees	Self employed	Unpaid family workers	Government supported training & employment programmes[2]	Total people working full-time	Total people working part-time	Employees working full-time	Employees working part-time	Self-employed people working full-time	Self-employed people working part-time	Total workers with second jobs
People (16+)	MGRZ	MGRN	MGRQ	MGRT	MGRW	YCBE	YCBH	YCBK	YCBN	YCBQ	YCBT	YCBW
Nov-Jan 2005	28,726	24,903	3,603	98	123	21,430	7,296	18,571	6,332	2,783	819	1,067
Dec-Feb 2005	28,794	24,944	3,619	105	126	21,510	7,284	18,633	6,312	2,799	820	1,065
Jan-Mar 2005	28,789	24,949	3,608	105	127	21,509	7,280	18,630	6,319	2,798	810	1,061
Feb-Apr 2005	28,759	24,926	3,609	103	121	21,472	7,287	18,595	6,331	2,797	812	1,067
Mar-May 2005	28,780	24,926	3,637	102	114	21,452	7,327	18,551	6,375	2,820	817	1,084
Apr-Jun 2005	28,802	24,974	3,617	99	112	21,469	7,333	18,581	6,393	2,807	810	1,078
May-Jul 2005	28,855	25,023	3,626	95	111	21,520	7,335	18,625	6,398	2,818	809	1,071
Jun-Aug 2005	28,906	25,077	3,638	85	107	21,595	7,311	18,715	6,362	2,810	827	1,066
Jul-Sep 2005	28,928	25,066	3,666	90	106	21,625	7,303	18,722	6,345	2,831	835	1,071
Aug-Oct 2005	28,913	25,073	3,646	92	102	21,625	7,288	18,742	6,331	2,813	833	1,062
Sep-Nov 2005	28,880	25,006	3,680	92	102	21,604	7,276	18,701	6,305	2,831	849	1,036
Oct-Dec 2005	28,880	24,999	3,683	90	108	21,623	7,257	18,719	6,280	2,833	850	1,032
Nov-Jan 2006	28,934	25,046	3,692	92	104	21,660	7,274	18,746	6,300	2,842	851	1,038
Dec-Feb 2006	28,988	25,092	3,714	88	94	21,678	7,309	18,761	6,331	2,851	863	1,047
Jan-Mar 2006	29,048	25,143	3,724	89	93	21,704	7,344	18,774	6,369	2,865	859	1,029
Feb-Apr 2006	29,085	25,170	3,738	85	92	21,757	7,328	18,818	6,352	2,874	865	1,035
Mar-May 2006	29,063	25,179	3,703	86	95	21,745	7,319	18,833	6,347	2,852	850	1,025
Apr-Jun 2006	29,106	25,210	3,711	91	94	21,745	7,360	18,831	6,379	2,853	858	1,048
May-Jul 2006	29,140	25,226	3,726	99	90	21,769	7,371	18,847	6,379	2,858	869	1,053
Jun-Aug 2006	29,224	25,283	3,749	105	87	21,821	7,402	18,875	6,408	2,880	869	1,060
Jul-Sep 2006	29,183	25,211	3,771	104	98	21,763	7,421	18,817	6,394	2,877	895	1,068
Aug-Oct 2006	29,189	25,195	3,795	98	101	21,709	7,480	18,755	6,440	2,888	908	1,067
Sep-Nov 2006	29,204	25,200	3,788	101	115	21,745	7,459	18,779	6,421	2,895	893	1,059
Oct-Dec 2006	29,214	25,217	3,789	102	106	21,749	7,466	18,787	6,431	2,896	893	1,081
Nov-Jan 2007	29,202	25,186	3,809	100	107	21,753	7,449	18,762	6,424	2,924	885	1,072
Dec-Feb 2007	29,175	25,155	3,816	99	105	21,748	7,427	18,760	6,394	2,922	894	1,076
Jan-Mar 2007	29,194	25,169	3,821	103	100	21,756	7,438	18,782	6,387	2,908	914	1,074
Feb-Apr 2007	29,232	25,211	3,821	101	100	21,797	7,435	18,829	6,382	2,905	915	1,095
Mar-May 2007	29,314	25,310	3,801	99	104	21,896	7,419	18,926	6,384	2,907	894	1,100
Apr-Jun 2007	29,322	25,310	3,803	98	111	21,902	7,420	18,935	6,375	2,907	896	1,107
May-Jul 2007	29,352	25,319	3,811	104	118	21,921	7,431	18,965	6,355	2,897	914	1,118
Jun-Aug 2007	29,376	25,330	3,830	102	113	21,947	7,428	18,983	6,347	2,904	926	1,117
Jul-Sep 2007	29,420	25,380	3,832	97	111	21,989	7,431	19,026	6,354	2,902	930	1,103
Aug-Oct 2007	29,470	25,422	3,841	97	111	22,038	7,433	19,067	6,355	2,911	930	1,115
Sep-Nov 2007	29,527	25,471	3,843	103	110	22,054	7,472	19,086	6,385	2,901	942	1,116
Oct-Dec 2007	29,576	25,521	3,834	106	114	22,075	7,501	19,104	6,417	2,899	936	1,126
Nov-Jan 2008	29,614	25,546	3,847	109	112	22,083	7,531	19,108	6,438	2,901	947	1,112
Dec-Feb 2008	29,676	25,557	3,892	110	117	22,130	7,546	19,100	6,457	2,955	937	1,125
Jan-Mar 2008	29,684	25,582	3,878	109	115	22,134	7,549	19,123	6,459	2,946	932	1,103
Feb-Apr 2008	29,706	25,623	3,851	115	117	22,160	7,546	19,150	6,473	2,939	911	1,121
Mar-May 2008	29,749	25,657	3,856	116	119	22,227	7,522	19,216	6,441	2,941	915	1,116
Apr-Jun 2008	29,722	25,641	3,859	111	110	22,189	7,533	19,176	6,465	2,947	912	1,130
May-Jul 2008	29,696	25,629	3,854	101	112	22,170	7,526	19,166	6,463	2,942	912	1,131
Jun-Aug 2008	29,612	25,591	3,826	90	105	22,081	7,531	19,117	6,473	2,913	913	1,120
Jul-Sep 2008	29,580	25,566	3,818	90	107	22,061	7,519	19,097	6,469	2,915	903	1,126
Aug-Oct 2008	29,535	25,545	3,794	91	105	22,010	7,525	19,075	6,469	2,886	908	1,127
Sep-Nov 2008	29,556	25,532	3,830	91	103	21,959	7,597	19,016	6,516	2,900	930	1,145
Oct-Dec 2008	29,528	25,507	3,828	94	100	21,951	7,578	19,007	6,499	2,898	930	1,142
Nov-Jan 2009	29,539	25,508	3,845	88	99	21,952	7,587	18,994	6,514	2,918	927	1,152
Dec-Feb 2009	29,429	25,416	3,826	85	102	21,843	7,586	18,867	6,549	2,919	907	1,155
Jan-Mar 2009	29,366	25,335	3,844	87	101	21,768	7,598	18,794	6,540	2,918	926	1,161
Feb-Apr 2009	29,272	25,220	3,860	88	103	21,715	7,557	18,747	6,474	2,911	949	1,156
Mar-May 2009	29,155	25,096	3,856	101	102	21,585	7,570	18,641	6,455	2,892	964	1,143
Apr-Jun 2009	29,087	25,043	3,843	98	104	21,479	7,609	18,553	6,490	2,869	974	1,126
May-Jul 2009	29,018	24,962	3,858	91	107	21,412	7,606	18,462	6,500	2,895	963	1,121
Jun-Aug 2009	29,076	24,987	3,894	84	110	21,446	7,630	18,466	6,521	2,923	971	1,139
Jul-Sep 2009	29,069	25,002	3,881	78	109	21,388	7,681	18,434	6,568	2,903	978	1,143
Aug-Oct 2009	29,084	25,019	3,881	83	102	21,349	7,734	18,392	6,627	2,909	971	1,146
Sep-Nov 2009	29,092	25,013	3,896	76	107	21,344	7,748	18,401	6,611	2,898	998	1,129
Oct-Dec 2009	29,102	24,988	3,912	87	115	21,349	7,753	18,382	6,606	2,917	995	1,129
Nov-Jan 2010	29,057	24,947	3,906	86	119	21,291	7,766	18,335	6,612	2,906	999	1,094
Dec-Feb 2010	29,024	24,902	3,909	92	122	21,281	7,743	18,320	6,583	2,913	996	1,081
Jan-Mar 2010	29,013	24,844	3,954	90	124	21,234	7,778	18,247	6,598	2,940	1,014	1,067
Feb-Apr 2010	29,048	24,857	3,973	91	126	21,221	7,827	18,221	6,635	2,949	1,024	1,097
Mar-May 2010	29,144	24,960	3,959	93	131	21,265	7,878	18,278	6,683	2,932	1,027	1,134
Apr-Jun 2010	29,192	25,019	3,949	90	133	21,301	7,891	18,315	6,704	2,928	1,021	1,136
May-Jul 2010	29,325	25,094	3,989	103	139	21,335	7,991	18,323	6,771	2,949	1,040	1,134
Jun-Aug 2010	29,339	25,105	3,993	109	132	21,314	8,025	18,291	6,814	2,962	1,031	1,121
Jul-Sep 2010	29,385	25,106	4,046	105	129	21,341	8,044	18,294	6,812	2,990	1,055	1,121
Aug-Oct 2010	29,308	25,101	3,980	99	127	21,289	8,019	18,306	6,795	2,932	1,048	1,114
Sep-Nov 2010	29,284	25,056	4,003	94	131	21,282	8,001	18,285	6,771	2,944	1,059	1,114

4.2 Full-time, part-time and temporary workers

United Kingdom (thousands) seasonally adjusted

| | All in employment | | | | | Full-time and part-time workers[1] | | | | | | |
	Total	Employees	Self employed	Unpaid family workers	Government supported training & employment programmes[2]	Total people working full-time	Total people working part-time	Employees working full-time	Employees working part-time	Self-employed people working full-time	Self-employed people working part-time	Total workers with second jobs
People (16+)	MGRZ	MGRN	MGRQ	MGRT	MGRW	YCBE	YCBH	YCBK	YCBN	YCBQ	YCBT	YCBW
Oct-Dec 2010	29,324	25,098	4,009	93	125	21,326	7,999	18,337	6,761	2,938	1,071	1,121
Nov-Jan 2011	29,391	25,138	4,025	100	129	21,387	8,004	18,406	6,732	2,929	1,096	1,151
Dec-Feb 2011	29,442	25,192	4,026	98	126	21,433	8,009	18,472	6,720	2,916	1,109	1,174
Jan-Mar 2011	29,441	25,235	3,983	98	125	21,437	8,005	18,507	6,728	2,883	1,100	1,166
Feb-Apr 2011	29,436	25,217	4,009	93	117	21,414	8,021	18,474	6,743	2,893	1,116	1,153
Mar-May 2011	29,466	25,249	4,022	91	104	21,451	8,016	18,519	6,731	2,891	1,131	1,151
Apr-Jun 2011	29,447	25,247	4,008	96	96	21,476	7,971	18,527	6,720	2,906	1,102	1,136
May-Jul 2011	29,345	25,162	4,001	94	88	21,452	7,893	18,502	6,660	2,915	1,086	1,142
Jun-Aug 2011	29,299	25,066	4,051	100	81	21,441	7,858	18,451	6,615	2,952	1,099	1,123
Jul-Sep 2011	29,277	24,967	4,122	105	84	21,406	7,871	18,384	6,583	2,980	1,142	1,142
Aug-Oct 2011	29,297	24,944	4,156	110	88	21,397	7,900	18,323	6,622	3,022	1,133	1,141
Sep-Nov 2011	29,324	24,967	4,148	112	96	21,376	7,947	18,308	6,659	3,006	1,142	1,145
Oct-Dec 2011	29,340	25,019	4,114	110	97	21,364	7,976	18,320	6,698	2,989	1,126	1,127
Nov-Jan 2012	29,351	25,009	4,125	111	105	21,366	7,985	18,321	6,689	2,992	1,133	1,118
Dec-Feb 2012	29,386	25,014	4,152	100	120	21,346	8,041	18,303	6,712	2,987	1,165	1,147
Jan-Mar 2012	29,460	25,049	4,186	97	128	21,374	8,085	18,322	6,728	2,992	1,193	1,152
Feb-Apr 2012	29,495	25,068	4,194	99	133	21,415	8,079	18,344	6,724	3,010	1,184	1,149
Mar-May 2012	29,559	25,113	4,187	111	149	21,477	8,083	18,380	6,733	3,021	1,166	1,141
Apr-Jun 2012	29,663	25,180	4,225	112	147	21,521	8,142	18,405	6,775	3,035	1,189	1,124
May-Jul 2012	29,746	25,218	4,255	119	154	21,537	8,209	18,405	6,813	3,039	1,217	1,126
Jun-Aug 2012	29,780	25,278	4,235	112	156	21,565	8,216	18,460	6,818	3,014	1,220	1,117
Jul-Sep 2012	29,753	25,248	4,233	110	162	21,561	8,192	18,448	6,800	3,017	1,216	1,110
Aug-Oct 2012	29,740	25,240	4,225	108	166	21,554	8,186	18,435	6,805	3,025	1,201	1,121
Sep-Nov 2012	29,846	25,341	4,231	111	163	21,659	8,188	18,537	6,805	3,029	1,202	1,122
Oct-Dec 2012	29,910	25,380	4,251	112	166	21,738	8,171	18,601	6,779	3,042	1,209	1,147
Nov-Jan 2013	29,895	25,425	4,202	106	163	21,755	8,140	18,651	6,773	3,004	1,198	1,142
Dec-Feb 2013	29,827	25,355	4,215	102	154	21,703	8,124	18,599	6,756	3,006	1,209	1,121
Jan-Mar 2013	29,851	25,411	4,182	104	153	21,740	8,110	18,630	6,781	3,017	1,165	1,109
Feb-Apr 2013	29,889	25,408	4,214	106	161	21,734	8,155	18,623	6,785	3,026	1,188	1,098
Mar-May 2013	29,856	25,403	4,187	104	163	21,730	8,126	18,639	6,764	3,015	1,172	1,121
Apr-Jun 2013	29,935	25,454	4,201	115	165	21,786	8,149	18,682	6,773	3,020	1,181	1,124
May-Jul 2013	29,999	25,516	4,207	111	165	21,865	8,134	18,740	6,777	3,035	1,171	1,133
Jun-Aug 2013	30,028	25,502	4,244	116	165	21,891	8,137	18,727	6,775	3,068	1,176	1,158
Jul-Sep 2013	30,098	25,572	4,241	113	172	21,933	8,165	18,777	6,796	3,063	1,178	1,162
Aug-Oct 2013	30,208	25,629	4,296	117	167	21,982	8,226	18,802	6,827	3,093	1,203	1,165
Sep-Nov 2013	30,288	25,633	4,397	112	146	22,096	8,192	18,853	6,780	3,165	1,232	1,183
Oct-Dec 2013	30,288	25,627	4,413	107	141	22,137	8,151	18,873	6,754	3,182	1,230	1,177
Nov-Jan 2014	30,322	25,589	4,493	110	131	22,159	8,162	18,840	6,749	3,240	1,253	1,180
Dec-Feb 2014	30,491	25,719	4,524	116	132	22,240	8,252	18,894	6,825	3,260	1,265	1,156
Jan-Mar 2014	30,534	25,715	4,572	126	122	22,281	8,253	18,926	6,788	3,269	1,303	1,176
Feb-Apr 2014	30,629	25,817	4,564	127	121	22,382	8,247	19,029	6,788	3,264	1,300	1,179
Mar-May 2014	30,717	25,879	4,599	119	121	22,446	8,271	19,093	6,786	3,271	1,328	1,187
Apr-Jun 2014	30,680	25,831	4,608	115	127	22,413	8,268	19,062	6,769	3,269	1,339	1,210
May-Jul 2014	30,682	25,864	4,564	120	133	22,376	8,305	19,048	6,816	3,248	1,316	1,201
Jun-Aug 2014	30,763	25,986	4,523	126	128	22,483	8,281	19,149	6,837	3,255	1,268	1,223
Jul-Sep 2014	30,793	26,027	4,520	123	123	22,523	8,270	19,203	6,824	3,250	1,271	1,208
Aug-Oct 2014	30,796	26,029	4,535	115	117	22,542	8,254	19,223	6,807	3,253	1,282	1,204
Sep-Nov 2014	30,801	26,066	4,520	102	112	22,524	8,277	19,239	6,827	3,220	1,300	1,198
Oct-Dec 2014	30,896	26,181	4,501	102	113	22,597	8,299	19,337	6,843	3,197	1,304	1,197
Nov-Jan 2015	30,939	26,193	4,526	114	106	22,640	8,299	19,362	6,831	3,212	1,315	1,200
Dec-Feb 2015	31,049	26,302	4,523	114	110	22,688	8,361	19,429	6,872	3,192	1,331	1,215
Jan-Mar 2015	31,098	26,370	4,504	119	105	22,735	8,362	19,472	6,898	3,194	1,311	1,214
Feb-Apr 2015	31,053	26,361	4,472	112	107	22,743	8,309	19,482	6,880	3,181	1,291	1,212
Mar-May 2015	30,982	26,307	4,468	107	100	22,718	8,264	19,474	6,832	3,160	1,308	1,196
Apr-Jun 2015	31,035	26,316	4,512	102	104	22,764	8,270	19,484	6,832	3,198	1,314	1,195
May-Jul 2015	31,095	26,369	4,513	103	110	22,737	8,358	19,491	6,878	3,173	1,340	1,188
Jun-Aug 2015	31,122	26,427	4,497	92	106	22,773	8,349	19,545	6,882	3,159	1,338	1,162
Jul-Sep 2015	31,211	26,462	4,551	95	104	22,796	8,416	19,516	6,945	3,207	1,344	1,169
Aug-Oct 2015	31,302	26,515	4,607	84	95	22,880	8,421	19,571	6,944	3,248	1,358	1,162
Sep-Nov 2015	31,389	26,587	4,618	96	89	22,960	8,428	19,655	6,931	3,243	1,375	1,164
Oct-Dec 2015	31,417	26,561	4,655	99	101	22,984	8,433	19,636	6,925	3,284	1,371	1,142

Source: Labour Force Survey
Inquiries: Email: labour.market@ons.gsi.gov.uk
Tel: 01633 455400

Note: When comparing quarterly changes ONS recommends comparing with the previous non-overlapping 3-month average time period (eg, compare Apr-Jun with Jan-Mar, not with Mar-May).

1. The split between full-time and part-time employment is based on respondents' self-classification.
2. This series does not include all people on these programmes; it only includes those engaging in any form of work, work experience or work-related training.
3. These series cover Employees and Self-employed only. These series include some temporary employees.
4. The total includes those who did not give a reason for working part-time and it therefore does not equal the sum of the other columns in this section of the table.

4.2 Full-time, part-time and temporary workers

United Kingdom (thousands) seasonally adjusted

	Temporary employees (reasons for temporary working)							Part-time workers (reasons for working part-time)[3]					
	Total	Total as % of all employees	Could not find permanent job	% that could not find permanent job	Did not want permanent job	Had a contract with period of training	Some other reason	Total[4]	Could not find full-time job	% that could not find full-time job	Did not want full-time job	Ill or disabled	Student or at school
People (16+)	YCBZ	YCCC	YCCF	YCCI	YCCL	YCCO	YCCR	YCCU	YCCX	YCDA	YCDD	YCDG	YCDJ
Nov-Jan 2005	1,499	6.0	357	23.8	426	113	603	7,152	539	7.5	5,248	167	1,170
Dec-Feb 2005	1,502	6.0	357	23.8	417	114	614	7,132	549	7.7	5,237	166	1,148
Jan-Mar 2005	1,466	5.9	357	24.4	403	102	603	7,129	568	8.0	5,220	166	1,141
Feb-Apr 2005	1,444	5.8	356	24.7	383	104	600	7,143	563	7.9	5,236	176	1,133
Mar-May 2005	1,445	5.8	357	24.7	380	105	603	7,193	585	8.1	5,271	168	1,138
Apr-Jun 2005	1,450	5.8	356	24.6	385	99	610	7,202	588	8.2	5,255	165	1,160
May-Jul 2005	1,473	5.9	355	24.1	401	107	609	7,207	592	8.2	5,246	162	1,173
Jun-Aug 2005	1,471	5.9	378	25.7	396	100	597	7,189	589	8.2	5,247	167	1,149
Jul-Sep 2005	1,481	5.9	393	26.5	394	104	590	7,181	598	8.3	5,248	169	1,139
Aug-Oct 2005	1,434	5.7	387	27.0	387	100	559	7,165	594	8.3	5,241	170	1,129
Sep-Nov 2005	1,421	5.7	371	26.1	378	102	569	7,154	614	8.6	5,227	168	1,112
Oct-Dec 2005	1,390	5.6	347	25.0	377	94	571	7,129	606	8.5	5,221	169	1,099
Nov-Jan 2006	1,432	5.7	364	25.4	388	105	575	7,150	612	8.6	5,226	169	1,107
Dec-Feb 2006	1,451	5.8	364	25.1	401	102	584	7,194	620	8.6	5,233	177	1,125
Jan-Mar 2006	1,486	5.9	374	25.2	410	114	588	7,227	620	8.6	5,256	175	1,133
Feb-Apr 2006	1,484	5.9	369	24.9	416	115	584	7,216	618	8.6	5,245	172	1,142
Mar-May 2006	1,478	5.9	369	25.0	412	115	582	7,197	610	8.5	5,228	171	1,147
Apr-Jun 2006	1,462	5.8	370	25.3	417	110	565	7,237	623	8.6	5,243	170	1,163
May-Jul 2006	1,439	5.7	359	24.9	414	99	566	7,247	632	8.7	5,233	176	1,170
Jun-Aug 2006	1,469	5.8	363	24.7	432	96	577	7,277	644	8.9	5,236	186	1,183
Jul-Sep 2006	1,466	5.8	367	25.0	433	94	573	7,290	646	8.9	5,228	186	1,197
Aug-Oct 2006	1,479	5.9	385	26.1	428	88	577	7,349	660	9.0	5,259	188	1,203
Sep-Nov 2006	1,495	5.9	391	26.2	437	94	573	7,313	662	9.1	5,240	190	1,177
Oct-Dec 2006	1,512	6.0	392	25.9	450	92	579	7,322	664	9.1	5,242	194	1,179
Nov-Jan 2007	1,529	6.1	399	26.1	442	105	583	7,309	668	9.1	5,235	198	1,166
Dec-Feb 2007	1,522	6.0	397	26.1	440	105	579	7,288	646	8.9	5,255	192	1,158
Jan-Mar 2007	1,534	6.1	405	26.4	435	112	583	7,300	660	9.0	5,257	189	1,162
Feb-Apr 2007	1,514	6.0	403	26.6	426	104	581	7,297	671	9.2	5,264	178	1,152
Mar-May 2007	1,513	6.0	407	26.9	422	101	584	7,278	685	9.4	5,246	176	1,140
Apr-Jun 2007	1,507	6.0	417	27.7	409	97	583	7,271	682	9.4	5,251	174	1,131
May-Jul 2007	1,501	5.9	411	27.4	412	92	586	7,270	697	9.6	5,228	181	1,131
Jun-Aug 2007	1,491	5.9	406	27.2	417	87	582	7,274	698	9.6	5,248	165	1,128
Jul-Sep 2007	1,485	5.9	393	26.4	421	84	587	7,285	694	9.5	5,259	169	1,127
Aug-Oct 2007	1,462	5.8	385	26.3	422	84	571	7,286	701	9.6	5,257	168	1,123
Sep-Nov 2007	1,478	5.8	380	25.7	432	83	583	7,326	698	9.5	5,286	173	1,136
Oct-Dec 2007	1,495	5.9	380	25.4	449	81	585	7,351	729	9.9	5,260	170	1,152
Nov-Jan 2008	1,473	5.8	367	24.9	440	78	588	7,385	739	10.0	5,273	174	1,160
Dec-Feb 2008	1,445	5.7	363	25.1	428	83	572	7,394	728	9.8	5,276	177	1,170
Jan-Mar 2008	1,430	5.6	363	25.4	426	83	558	7,391	705	9.5	5,290	184	1,168
Feb-Apr 2008	1,439	5.6	358	24.9	431	86	564	7,385	696	9.4	5,275	187	1,183
Mar-May 2008	1,420	5.5	357	25.1	404	85	574	7,356	671	9.1	5,281	193	1,165
Apr-Jun 2008	1,396	5.4	348	24.9	404	85	560	7,376	679	9.2	5,283	203	1,168
May-Jul 2008	1,385	5.4	351	25.3	391	88	555	7,376	689	9.3	5,268	215	1,162
Jun-Aug 2008	1,383	5.4	353	25.5	404	83	543	7,387	702	9.5	5,293	216	1,138
Jul-Sep 2008	1,390	5.4	360	25.9	402	88	540	7,373	715	9.7	5,280	207	1,130
Aug-Oct 2008	1,370	5.4	351	25.6	407	83	530	7,378	732	9.9	5,280	197	1,127
Sep-Nov 2008	1,403	5.5	364	26.0	399	84	555	7,446	753	10.1	5,312	199	1,138
Oct-Dec 2008	1,411	5.5	380	26.9	392	86	554	7,426	770	10.4	5,280	198	1,133
Nov-Jan 2009	1,425	5.6	397	27.8	390	91	546	7,441	815	11.0	5,256	191	1,133
Dec-Feb 2009	1,427	5.6	420	29.5	386	84	537	7,457	850	11.4	5,258	183	1,123
Jan-Mar 2009	1,428	5.6	426	29.8	386	81	536	7,466	875	11.7	5,257	184	1,111
Feb-Apr 2009	1,417	5.6	419	29.6	381	87	530	7,423	902	12.1	5,199	190	1,090
Mar-May 2009	1,404	5.6	417	29.7	384	92	512	7,419	936	12.6	5,163	191	1,087
Apr-Jun 2009	1,430	5.7	431	30.2	386	89	524	7,464	963	12.9	5,166	189	1,094
May-Jul 2009	1,429	5.7	443	31.0	371	84	531	7,465	972	13.0	5,176	181	1,086
Jun-Aug 2009	1,435	5.7	446	31.1	376	89	524	7,492	981	13.1	5,177	184	1,099
Jul-Sep 2009	1,450	5.8	464	32.0	377	85	525	7,547	1,002	13.3	5,196	189	1,115
Aug-Oct 2009	1,438	5.7	468	32.5	369	86	516	7,599	1,018	13.4	5,200	190	1,148
Sep-Nov 2009	1,437	5.7	490	34.1	365	76	506	7,608	1,038	13.6	5,198	183	1,144
Oct-Dec 2009	1,445	5.8	497	34.4	362	78	508	7,598	1,037	13.7	5,194	187	1,138
Nov-Jan 2010	1,451	5.8	499	34.4	370	77	505	7,611	1,045	13.7	5,197	185	1,141
Dec-Feb 2010	1,481	5.9	513	34.6	366	83	519	7,578	1,051	13.9	5,160	179	1,148
Jan-Mar 2010	1,482	6.0	513	34.6	366	79	524	7,612	1,071	14.1	5,187	168	1,140
Feb-Apr 2010	1,501	6.0	539	35.9	361	82	519	7,660	1,090	14.2	5,221	172	1,134
Mar-May 2010	1,541	6.2	554	36.0	375	80	532	7,710	1,073	13.9	5,280	167	1,148
Apr-Jun 2010	1,578	6.3	573	36.3	380	82	543	7,725	1,077	13.9	5,303	172	1,134
May-Jul 2010	1,577	6.3	571	36.2	383	80	543	7,814	1,115	14.3	5,313	171	1,175
Jun-Aug 2010	1,578	6.3	591	37.5	369	86	532	7,846	1,139	14.5	5,302	170	1,188
Jul-Sep 2010	1,588	6.3	600	37.8	370	87	531	7,868	1,153	14.7	5,311	165	1,190
Aug-Oct 2010	1,598	6.4	592	37.0	374	92	540	7,844	1,174	15.0	5,311	164	1,142
Sep-Nov 2010	1,575	6.3	589	37.4	354	94	538	7,828	1,178	15.0	5,341	172	1,085

4.2 Full-time, part-time and temporary workers

United Kingdom (thousands) seasonally adjusted

		Temporary employees (reasons for temporary working)							Part-time workers (reasons for working part-time)[3]					
	Total	Total as % of all employees	Could not find permanent job	% that could not find permanent job	Did not want permanent job	Had a contract with period of training	Some other reason		Total[4]	Could not find full-time job	% that could not find full-time job	Did not want full-time job	Ill or disabled	Student or at school
People (16+)	YCBZ	YCCC	YCCF	YCCI	YCCL	YCCO	YCCR		YCCU	YCCX	YCDA	YCDD	YCDG	YCDJ
Oct-Dec 2010	1,546	6.2	577	37.3	340	95	534		7,829	1,192	15.2	5,318	164	1,102
Nov-Jan 2011	1,567	6.2	579	37.0	341	93	553		7,828	1,180	15.1	5,349	164	1,080
Dec-Feb 2011	1,577	6.3	573	36.3	352	95	557		7,830	1,180	15.1	5,355	172	1,065
Jan-Mar 2011	1,595	6.3	579	36.3	357	100	558		7,828	1,188	15.2	5,338	182	1,063
Feb-Apr 2011	1,601	6.3	583	36.4	356	94	568		7,860	1,230	15.6	5,322	185	1,069
Mar-May 2011	1,605	6.4	582	36.3	363	92	568		7,862	1,259	16.0	5,312	180	1,056
Apr-Jun 2011	1,616	6.4	609	37.7	361	88	558		7,823	1,270	16.2	5,268	180	1,047
May-Jul 2011	1,568	6.2	578	36.9	354	85	551		7,749	1,288	16.6	5,188	182	1,033
Jun-Aug 2011	1,533	6.1	584	38.1	317	81	551		7,714	1,279	16.6	5,176	181	1,026
Jul-Sep 2011	1,525	6.1	582	38.2	330	85	528		7,726	1,275	16.5	5,177	189	1,033
Aug-Oct 2011	1,538	6.2	605	39.3	331	84	517		7,755	1,286	16.6	5,199	184	1,040
Sep-Nov 2011	1,553	6.2	594	38.2	354	89	516		7,799	1,331	17.1	5,191	184	1,049
Oct-Dec 2011	1,545	6.2	602	39.0	346	91	506		7,821	1,361	17.4	5,186	189	1,043
Nov-Jan 2012	1,559	6.2	610	39.1	342	98	509		7,822	1,397	17.9	5,164	189	1,028
Dec-Feb 2012	1,587	6.3	630	39.7	350	96	512		7,877	1,406	17.9	5,194	181	1,050
Jan-Mar 2012	1,570	6.3	618	39.4	337	90	524		7,921	1,414	17.9	5,217	191	1,048
Feb-Apr 2012	1,558	6.2	609	39.1	329	96	524		7,909	1,412	17.9	5,211	191	1,043
Mar-May 2012	1,578	6.3	638	40.4	319	95	526		7,899	1,396	17.7	5,216	191	1,044
Apr-Jun 2012	1,613	6.4	644	39.9	327	103	539		7,965	1,427	17.9	5,237	183	1,068
May-Jul 2012	1,655	6.6	661	40.0	347	100	546		8,032	1,431	17.8	5,306	181	1,066
Jun-Aug 2012	1,641	6.5	651	39.7	342	99	548		8,038	1,420	17.7	5,313	182	1,074
Jul-Sep 2012	1,628	6.4	656	40.3	336	92	542		8,016	1,414	17.6	5,317	181	1,053
Aug-Oct 2012	1,631	6.5	655	40.2	332	92	552		8,005	1,406	17.6	5,323	184	1,037
Sep-Nov 2012	1,649	6.5	655	39.7	344	90	560		8,004	1,404	17.5	5,334	182	1,024
Oct-Dec 2012	1,655	6.5	659	39.8	341	96	559		7,986	1,390	17.4	5,333	185	1,014
Nov-Jan 2013	1,640	6.5	655	40.0	334	96	555		7,972	1,407	17.7	5,323	186	996
Dec-Feb 2013	1,602	6.3	644	40.2	332	100	526		7,966	1,422	17.9	5,304	184	999
Jan-Mar 2013	1,615	6.4	651	40.3	331	104	528		7,947	1,419	17.9	5,278	178	1,016
Feb-Apr 2013	1,595	6.3	631	39.6	337	100	526		7,974	1,441	18.1	5,261	181	1,034
Mar-May 2013	1,589	6.3	625	39.3	328	103	534		7,936	1,463	18.4	5,212	180	1,017
Apr-Jun 2013	1,568	6.2	605	38.6	324	107	531		7,955	1,453	18.3	5,245	187	1,007
May-Jul 2013	1,571	6.2	607	38.7	314	112	537		7,951	1,464	18.4	5,228	187	1,009
Jun-Aug 2013	1,582	6.2	609	38.5	300	123	550		7,951	1,464	18.4	5,260	192	973
Jul-Sep 2013	1,606	6.3	603	37.5	319	126	559		7,973	1,464	18.4	5,257	193	993
Aug-Oct 2013	1,594	6.2	593	37.2	327	124	550		8,029	1,467	18.3	5,307	194	1,001
Sep-Nov 2013	1,602	6.2	583	36.4	329	130	559		8,010	1,444	18.0	5,298	191	1,026
Oct-Dec 2013	1,621	6.3	600	37.0	337	117	567		7,983	1,428	17.9	5,280	191	1,033
Nov-Jan 2014	1,621	6.3	593	36.6	347	116	566		8,002	1,437	18.0	5,282	194	1,038
Dec-Feb 2014	1,630	6.3	587	36.0	358	113	573		8,090	1,419	17.5	5,393	194	1,038
Jan-Mar 2014	1,655	6.4	593	35.9	357	117	589		8,092	1,419	17.5	5,415	191	1,024
Feb-Apr 2014	1,683	6.5	601	35.7	369	118	594		8,088	1,399	17.3	5,425	185	1,038
Mar-May 2014	1,684	6.5	602	35.7	370	121	591		8,114	1,361	16.8	5,490	192	1,032
Apr-Jun 2014	1,651	6.4	604	36.6	370	117	560		8,109	1,342	16.6	5,522	192	1,010
May-Jul 2014	1,676	6.5	613	36.6	373	121	568		8,135	1,340	16.5	5,560	182	1,011
Jun-Aug 2014	1,696	6.5	617	36.4	388	119	571		8,105	1,351	16.7	5,516	172	1,022
Jul-Sep 2014	1,701	6.5	597	35.1	420	122	563		8,095	1,340	16.5	5,522	174	1,017
Aug-Oct 2014	1,688	6.5	575	34.0	428	120	566		8,088	1,319	16.3	5,556	173	995
Sep-Nov 2014	1,679	6.4	578	34.4	416	121	564		8,127	1,319	16.2	5,570	186	1,010
Oct-Dec 2014	1,704	6.5	581	34.1	412	114	598		8,148	1,312	16.1	5,565	189	1,033
Nov-Jan 2015	1,678	6.4	573	34.1	391	123	592		8,146	1,322	16.2	5,569	193	1,016
Dec-Feb 2015	1,686	6.4	591	35.0	379	117	600		8,203	1,348	16.4	5,600	194	1,016
Jan-Mar 2015	1,688	6.4	589	34.9	369	123	608		8,207	1,319	16.1	5,616	208	1,015
Feb-Apr 2015	1,681	6.4	583	34.7	367	124	607		8,169	1,297	15.9	5,600	206	1,014
Mar-May 2015	1,672	6.4	552	33.0	389	127	604		8,138	1,275	15.7	5,591	211	1,007
Apr-Jun 2015	1,644	6.2	565	34.4	376	134	569		8,145	1,287	15.8	5,584	216	1,007
May-Jul 2015	1,679	6.4	562	33.5	402	129	586		8,219	1,275	15.5	5,638	228	1,028
Jun-Aug 2015	1,660	6.3	582	35.1	407	127	544		8,221	1,266	15.4	5,638	222	1,046
Jul-Sep 2015	1,661	6.3	565	34.0	410	127	559		8,290	1,257	15.2	5,698	220	1,069
Aug-Oct 2015	1,649	6.2	577	35.0	405	117	550		8,304	1,287	15.5	5,660	219	1,093
Sep-Nov 2015	1,641	6.2	578	35.2	391	134	537		8,306	1,245	15.0	5,707	226	1,081
Oct-Dec 2015	1,616	6.1	552	34.2	393	135	536		8,296	1,237	14.9	5,682	233	1,084

Source: Labour Force Survey
Inquiries: Email: labour.market@ons.gsi.gov.uk
Tel: 01633 455400

Note: When comparing quarterly changes ONS recommends comparing with the previous non-overlapping 3-month average time period (eg, compare Apr-Jun with Jan-Mar, not with Mar-May).

1. The split between full-time and part-time employment is based on respondents' self-classification.

2. This series does not include all people on these programmes; it only includes those engaging in any form of work, work experience or work-related training.

3. These series cover Employees and Self-employed only. These series include some temporary employees.

4. The total includes those who did not give a reason for working part-time and it therefore does not equal the sum of the other columns in this section of the table.

4.2 Full-time, part-time and temporary workers

United Kingdom (thousands) seasonally adjusted

	All in employment					Full-time and part-time workers[1]						
	Total	Employees	Self employed	Unpaid family workers	Government supported training & employment programmes[2]	Total people working full-time	Total people working part-time	Employees working full-time	Employees working part-time	Self-employed people working full-time	Self-employed people working part-time	Total workers with second jobs
Men (16+)	MGSA	MGRO	MGRR	MGRU	MGRX	YCBF	YCBI	YCBL	YCBO	YCBR	YCBU	YCBX
Nov-Jan 2005	15,504	12,740	2,652	40	72	13,865	1,639	11,501	1,239	2,316	336	455
Dec-Feb 2005	15,515	12,751	2,650	42	71	13,877	1,638	11,518	1,234	2,313	338	449
Jan-Mar 2005	15,530	12,769	2,650	42	69	13,887	1,643	11,529	1,240	2,310	340	454
Feb-Apr 2005	15,517	12,749	2,658	42	69	13,870	1,647	11,502	1,247	2,319	339	456
Mar-May 2005	15,508	12,726	2,675	39	68	13,868	1,640	11,478	1,248	2,339	336	467
Apr-Jun 2005	15,527	12,762	2,658	37	70	13,894	1,633	11,509	1,253	2,332	326	463
May-Jul 2005	15,539	12,776	2,659	35	69	13,909	1,630	11,527	1,249	2,331	327	464
Jun-Aug 2005	15,553	12,798	2,658	33	64	13,929	1,624	11,570	1,227	2,313	346	464
Jul-Sep 2005	15,571	12,799	2,678	31	62	13,945	1,626	11,570	1,229	2,330	348	459
Aug-Oct 2005	15,571	12,809	2,672	32	58	13,942	1,629	11,582	1,227	2,320	352	451
Sep-Nov 2005	15,570	12,788	2,694	30	58	13,932	1,638	11,552	1,236	2,338	356	434
Oct-Dec 2005	15,573	12,777	2,706	29	60	13,927	1,646	11,542	1,235	2,343	363	445
Nov-Jan 2006	15,604	12,797	2,717	31	58	13,961	1,642	11,564	1,233	2,354	363	455
Dec-Feb 2006	15,614	12,809	2,717	29	59	13,960	1,654	11,566	1,244	2,351	365	457
Jan-Mar 2006	15,609	12,820	2,700	31	58	13,966	1,642	11,579	1,241	2,345	355	440
Feb-Apr 2006	15,656	12,859	2,710	30	57	14,015	1,641	11,612	1,247	2,362	348	442
Mar-May 2006	15,639	12,853	2,696	33	56	13,991	1,648	11,597	1,256	2,356	340	434
Apr-Jun 2006	15,652	12,864	2,697	36	54	13,993	1,659	11,601	1,263	2,355	343	449
May-Jul 2006	15,683	12,894	2,698	38	53	14,013	1,670	11,626	1,268	2,346	352	452
Jun-Aug 2006	15,722	12,922	2,711	42	48	14,057	1,665	11,657	1,265	2,360	351	449
Jul-Sep 2006	15,740	12,909	2,731	42	58	14,040	1,700	11,629	1,280	2,366	365	455
Aug-Oct 2006	15,738	12,894	2,743	42	59	14,007	1,731	11,591	1,303	2,372	371	456
Sep-Nov 2006	15,744	12,880	2,756	40	68	14,035	1,709	11,602	1,279	2,389	367	450
Oct-Dec 2006	15,751	12,902	2,747	41	60	14,048	1,703	11,621	1,281	2,386	362	462
Nov-Jan 2007	15,760	12,886	2,773	39	63	14,064	1,696	11,606	1,280	2,416	356	447
Dec-Feb 2007	15,752	12,885	2,768	40	58	14,052	1,700	11,609	1,276	2,403	366	461
Jan-Mar 2007	15,758	12,885	2,775	43	56	14,034	1,724	11,597	1,288	2,399	376	463
Feb-Apr 2007	15,782	12,913	2,772	40	57	14,064	1,718	11,635	1,278	2,392	380	461
Mar-May 2007	15,846	12,979	2,771	38	59	14,134	1,712	11,703	1,275	2,393	377	457
Apr-Jun 2007	15,839	12,965	2,775	36	62	14,126	1,713	11,696	1,269	2,393	382	456
May-Jul 2007	15,846	12,969	2,771	37	68	14,120	1,726	11,705	1,264	2,378	393	460
Jun-Aug 2007	15,861	12,991	2,771	38	61	14,137	1,724	11,714	1,278	2,388	383	456
Jul-Sep 2007	15,884	13,027	2,760	37	60	14,141	1,742	11,733	1,294	2,374	386	450
Aug-Oct 2007	15,903	13,036	2,774	37	56	14,176	1,726	11,754	1,282	2,390	384	458
Sep-Nov 2007	15,942	13,061	2,783	37	61	14,181	1,762	11,755	1,306	2,385	398	454
Oct-Dec 2007	15,947	13,057	2,787	39	63	14,182	1,766	11,741	1,317	2,395	392	450
Nov-Jan 2008	15,968	13,074	2,789	39	66	14,180	1,788	11,733	1,341	2,398	391	453
Dec-Feb 2008	15,993	13,054	2,825	40	74	14,197	1,796	11,714	1,340	2,435	390	461
Jan-Mar 2008	16,005	13,070	2,822	40	73	14,209	1,796	11,739	1,331	2,427	395	451
Feb-Apr 2008	16,024	13,106	2,805	42	70	14,229	1,795	11,769	1,337	2,415	391	458
Mar-May 2008	16,019	13,101	2,809	40	68	14,254	1,764	11,792	1,309	2,419	390	458
Apr-Jun 2008	16,011	13,097	2,810	40	64	14,221	1,790	11,758	1,340	2,423	387	461
May-Jul 2008	15,987	13,089	2,798	36	64	14,178	1,809	11,726	1,363	2,415	383	451
Jun-Aug 2008	15,927	13,059	2,775	30	64	14,105	1,822	11,685	1,374	2,389	386	451
Jul-Sep 2008	15,910	13,049	2,769	28	64	14,081	1,829	11,664	1,385	2,387	382	456
Aug-Oct 2008	15,864	13,029	2,736	33	67	14,024	1,840	11,639	1,390	2,355	381	452
Sep-Nov 2008	15,885	13,017	2,766	37	65	14,045	1,840	11,634	1,383	2,381	385	471
Oct-Dec 2008	15,870	12,991	2,774	41	64	14,012	1,858	11,598	1,393	2,386	388	473
Nov-Jan 2009	15,859	12,977	2,784	38	61	13,995	1,865	11,572	1,405	2,399	385	479
Dec-Feb 2009	15,786	12,921	2,771	33	61	13,935	1,851	11,504	1,417	2,399	372	483
Jan-Mar 2009	15,739	12,876	2,773	32	58	13,900	1,839	11,475	1,402	2,394	379	492
Feb-Apr 2009	15,678	12,807	2,779	33	59	13,841	1,836	11,417	1,391	2,391	388	500
Mar-May 2009	15,577	12,711	2,774	36	56	13,718	1,859	11,318	1,393	2,369	405	489
Apr-Jun 2009	15,513	12,658	2,756	40	59	13,646	1,866	11,268	1,390	2,341	415	480
May-Jul 2009	15,465	12,607	2,761	36	61	13,618	1,847	11,229	1,379	2,356	405	480
Jun-Aug 2009	15,471	12,608	2,770	33	61	13,616	1,856	11,206	1,402	2,375	395	491
Jul-Sep 2009	15,447	12,608	2,749	29	61	13,606	1,841	11,215	1,392	2,359	390	489
Aug-Oct 2009	15,448	12,588	2,769	33	58	13,591	1,857	11,189	1,400	2,373	396	494
Sep-Nov 2009	15,438	12,593	2,757	32	56	13,568	1,870	11,188	1,405	2,354	403	483
Oct-Dec 2009	15,436	12,570	2,770	37	60	13,558	1,879	11,168	1,402	2,363	407	485
Nov-Jan 2010	15,407	12,538	2,773	36	60	13,514	1,893	11,127	1,411	2,360	413	467
Dec-Feb 2010	15,404	12,539	2,763	41	63	13,511	1,893	11,129	1,409	2,354	408	457
Jan-Mar 2010	15,397	12,516	2,775	41	66	13,486	1,911	11,096	1,420	2,363	411	434
Feb-Apr 2010	15,417	12,527	2,780	42	69	13,501	1,917	11,103	1,425	2,368	412	452
Mar-May 2010	15,499	12,593	2,787	42	77	13,551	1,948	11,152	1,441	2,365	422	476
Apr-Jun 2010	15,539	12,633	2,788	41	77	13,567	1,972	11,165	1,468	2,368	420	472
May-Jul 2010	15,634	12,684	2,820	43	87	13,622	2,012	11,206	1,478	2,379	441	467
Jun-Aug 2010	15,654	12,690	2,839	42	83	13,617	2,036	11,182	1,508	2,396	442	458
Jul-Sep 2010	15,696	12,706	2,864	43	83	13,635	2,061	11,183	1,523	2,414	450	465
Aug-Oct 2010	15,658	12,726	2,808	43	81	13,590	2,068	11,202	1,524	2,357	451	459
Sep-Nov 2010	15,644	12,704	2,825	33	82	13,587	2,057	11,189	1,514	2,367	458	462
Oct-Dec 2010	15,679	12,736	2,834	34	75	13,623	2,057	11,217	1,519	2,375	459	469

4.2 Full-time, part-time and temporary workers

United Kingdom (thousands) seasonally adjusted

Men (16+)	All in employment					Full-time and part-time workers[1]						
	Total	Employees	Self employed	Unpaid family workers	Government supported training & employment programmes[2]	Total people working full-time	Total people working part-time	Employees working full-time	Employees working part-time	Self-employed people working full-time	Self-employed people working part-time	Total workers with second jobs
	MGSA	MGRO	MGRR	MGRU	MGRX	YCBF	YCBI	YCBL	YCBO	YCBR	YCBU	YCBX
Nov-Jan 2011	15,711	12,774	2,823	35	80	13,672	2,039	11,281	1,493	2,363	460	488
Dec-Feb 2011	15,717	12,786	2,820	33	77	13,695	2,022	11,322	1,464	2,350	470	509
Jan-Mar 2011	15,692	12,791	2,795	31	76	13,670	2,022	11,326	1,465	2,323	472	496
Feb-Apr 2011	15,742	12,817	2,827	28	70	13,689	2,053	11,323	1,494	2,345	481	488
Mar-May 2011	15,739	12,816	2,832	31	60	13,690	2,049	11,335	1,480	2,336	495	490
Apr-Jun 2011	15,728	12,795	2,838	38	56	13,687	2,041	11,316	1,479	2,350	488	488
May-Jul 2011	15,655	12,731	2,836	38	49	13,628	2,027	11,257	1,474	2,353	483	498
Jun-Aug 2011	15,620	12,685	2,849	40	46	13,647	1,973	11,253	1,432	2,373	476	476
Jul-Sep 2011	15,588	12,608	2,897	42	42	13,617	1,971	11,196	1,412	2,401	496	487
Aug-Oct 2011	15,607	12,604	2,919	41	43	13,616	1,991	11,155	1,449	2,434	485	492
Sep-Nov 2011	15,620	12,610	2,916	43	51	13,593	2,027	11,137	1,472	2,423	493	491
Oct-Dec 2011	15,632	12,652	2,886	41	53	13,597	2,035	11,164	1,488	2,403	483	479
Nov-Jan 2012	15,638	12,647	2,890	42	58	13,601	2,037	11,166	1,481	2,406	484	463
Dec-Feb 2012	15,690	12,684	2,902	38	66	13,592	2,098	11,153	1,531	2,404	497	488
Jan-Mar 2012	15,725	12,693	2,915	44	73	13,601	2,124	11,158	1,535	2,404	511	488
Feb-Apr 2012	15,757	12,704	2,929	45	79	13,624	2,133	11,161	1,543	2,423	506	489
Mar-May 2012	15,800	12,710	2,947	46	97	13,664	2,136	11,163	1,547	2,449	497	487
Apr-Jun 2012	15,862	12,754	2,973	42	92	13,706	2,156	11,186	1,568	2,468	505	487
May-Jul 2012	15,872	12,748	2,981	43	99	13,722	2,151	11,182	1,566	2,475	507	477
Jun-Aug 2012	15,900	12,779	2,973	46	103	13,741	2,159	11,222	1,557	2,454	519	470
Jul-Sep 2012	15,892	12,761	2,973	49	109	13,749	2,144	11,223	1,538	2,454	519	462
Aug-Oct 2012	15,904	12,769	2,972	47	115	13,774	2,130	11,244	1,525	2,457	516	460
Sep-Nov 2012	15,933	12,834	2,942	46	110	13,808	2,124	11,300	1,534	2,441	501	452
Oct-Dec 2012	15,950	12,847	2,948	45	110	13,833	2,117	11,323	1,524	2,444	504	453
Nov-Jan 2013	15,932	12,859	2,917	43	112	13,814	2,118	11,334	1,526	2,414	504	442
Dec-Feb 2013	15,882	12,805	2,932	39	107	13,783	2,100	11,306	1,498	2,410	522	438
Jan-Mar 2013	15,884	12,820	2,918	38	108	13,797	2,087	11,317	1,502	2,414	504	434
Feb-Apr 2013	15,902	12,823	2,933	37	109	13,761	2,142	11,294	1,529	2,413	520	449
Mar-May 2013	15,889	12,831	2,921	31	106	13,768	2,121	11,316	1,515	2,409	512	455
Apr-Jun 2013	15,932	12,855	2,927	43	107	13,797	2,135	11,345	1,510	2,405	522	459
May-Jul 2013	15,969	12,894	2,932	39	102	13,838	2,131	11,379	1,515	2,417	515	470
Jun-Aug 2013	15,995	12,897	2,951	45	102	13,850	2,145	11,371	1,526	2,435	516	488
Jul-Sep 2013	16,052	12,963	2,945	40	103	13,881	2,170	11,408	1,555	2,430	515	491
Aug-Oct 2013	16,095	12,969	2,977	43	106	13,911	2,184	11,414	1,555	2,452	525	490
Sep-Nov 2013	16,149	12,978	3,033	44	94	13,966	2,183	11,430	1,548	2,490	543	500
Oct-Dec 2013	16,138	12,966	3,039	45	88	13,962	2,176	11,415	1,550	2,498	541	508
Nov-Jan 2014	16,177	12,951	3,103	46	78	14,003	2,174	11,400	1,551	2,555	548	514
Dec-Feb 2014	16,257	13,008	3,122	46	82	14,075	2,182	11,441	1,567	2,578	544	516
Jan-Mar 2014	16,279	13,008	3,139	58	74	14,090	2,189	11,438	1,570	2,596	543	517
Feb-Apr 2014	16,324	13,060	3,128	63	73	14,167	2,156	11,512	1,547	2,593	535	510
Mar-May 2014	16,353	13,086	3,140	59	68	14,200	2,153	11,544	1,542	2,598	542	508
Apr-Jun 2014	16,326	13,053	3,143	56	74	14,206	2,119	11,556	1,497	2,591	552	510
May-Jul 2014	16,318	13,057	3,123	55	83	14,171	2,146	11,538	1,518	2,572	552	493
Jun-Aug 2014	16,362	13,119	3,114	54	75	14,211	2,151	11,573	1,546	2,580	533	517
Jul-Sep 2014	16,388	13,153	3,113	53	70	14,240	2,149	11,605	1,548	2,586	526	508
Aug-Oct 2014	16,384	13,168	3,099	52	65	14,240	2,144	11,623	1,545	2,576	523	512
Sep-Nov 2014	16,375	13,189	3,070	49	66	14,208	2,167	11,627	1,562	2,539	531	496
Oct-Dec 2014	16,427	13,262	3,051	48	66	14,273	2,154	11,713	1,550	2,525	526	489
Nov-Jan 2015	16,458	13,278	3,068	50	61	14,305	2,154	11,723	1,555	2,545	523	490
Dec-Feb 2015	16,544	13,342	3,085	53	63	14,357	2,187	11,774	1,568	2,549	536	517
Jan-Mar 2015	16,570	13,389	3,067	54	60	14,383	2,187	11,811	1,578	2,535	533	521
Feb-Apr 2015	16,524	13,356	3,054	52	62	14,357	2,167	11,790	1,567	2,523	531	532
Mar-May 2015	16,459	13,308	3,042	45	64	14,341	2,117	11,774	1,534	2,514	528	531
Apr-Jun 2015	16,499	13,307	3,086	45	61	14,360	2,140	11,778	1,529	2,531	555	540
May-Jul 2015	16,542	13,353	3,082	43	64	14,365	2,177	11,816	1,538	2,509	573	524
Jun-Aug 2015	16,572	13,409	3,062	38	63	14,374	2,198	11,848	1,560	2,484	578	489
Jul-Sep 2015	16,607	13,404	3,102	41	60	14,376	2,231	11,806	1,598	2,526	576	489
Aug-Oct 2015	16,697	13,472	3,129	41	55	14,453	2,243	11,855	1,618	2,556	573	490
Sep-Nov 2015	16,731	13,507	3,130	49	45	14,495	2,236	11,907	1,600	2,552	578	505
Oct-Dec 2015	16,770	13,514	3,152	49	56	14,520	2,250	11,894	1,620	2,587	564	499

Source: Labour Force Survey
Inquiries: Email: labour.market@ons.gsi.gov.uk
Tel: 01633 455400

Note: When comparing quarterly changes ONS recommends comparing with the previous non-overlapping 3-month average time period (eg, compare Apr-Jun with Jan-Mar, not with Mar-May).

1. The split between full-time and part-time employment is based on respondents' self-classification.
2. This series does not include all people on these programmes; it only includes those engaging in any form of work, work experience or work-related training.
3. These series cover Employees and Self-employed only. These series include some temporary employees.
4. The total includes those who did not give a reason for working part-time and it therefore does not equal the sum of the other columns in this section of the table.

4.2 Full-time, part-time and temporary workers

United Kingdom (thousands) seasonally adjusted

		Temporary employees (reasons for temporary working)						Part-time workers (reasons for working part-time)[3]					
	Total	Total as % of all employees	Could not find permanent job	% that could not find permanent job	Did not want permanent job	Had a contract with period of training	Some other reason	Total[4]	Could not find full-time job	% that could not find full-time job	Did not want full-time job	Ill or disabled	Student or at school
Men (16+)	YCCA	YCCD	YCCG	YCCJ	YCCM	YCCP	YCCS	YCCV	YCCY	YCDB	YCDE	YCDH	YCDK
Nov-Jan 2005	706	5.5	203	28.7	185	54	264	1,575	228	14.5	755	66	517
Dec-Feb 2005	703	5.5	202	28.7	175	52	274	1,571	225	14.3	769	66	500
Jan-Mar 2005	693	5.4	202	29.1	173	51	267	1,580	231	14.6	769	69	498
Feb-Apr 2005	689	5.4	205	29.7	168	52	264	1,586	229	14.4	773	76	494
Mar-May 2005	687	5.4	210	30.6	159	57	262	1,584	235	14.8	766	72	497
Apr-Jun 2005	692	5.4	210	30.3	166	56	259	1,579	235	14.9	755	72	499
May-Jul 2005	691	5.4	207	30.0	172	60	252	1,576	241	15.3	748	73	500
Jun-Aug 2005	678	5.3	212	31.2	173	57	236	1,573	227	14.5	758	75	499
Jul-Sep 2005	680	5.3	212	31.2	167	59	242	1,577	228	14.4	771	76	494
Aug-Oct 2005	668	5.2	206	30.9	169	55	237	1,579	233	14.8	774	77	484
Sep-Nov 2005	660	5.2	202	30.6	166	51	242	1,592	248	15.6	779	76	478
Oct-Dec 2005	651	5.1	195	30.0	165	43	248	1,598	246	15.4	786	77	477
Nov-Jan 2006	652	5.1	195	30.0	163	50	244	1,596	245	15.3	786	76	476
Dec-Feb 2006	660	5.2	191	28.9	168	55	247	1,609	250	15.5	786	76	484
Jan-Mar 2006	666	5.2	192	28.8	168	60	247	1,596	247	15.4	778	76	482
Feb-Apr 2006	669	5.2	194	29.0	175	55	245	1,595	247	15.5	775	72	489
Mar-May 2006	666	5.2	187	28.1	173	55	251	1,596	248	15.5	774	73	490
Apr-Jun 2006	654	5.1	187	28.7	173	53	241	1,606	252	15.7	770	70	504
May-Jul 2006	643	5.0	179	27.9	168	48	248	1,620	256	15.8	772	75	509
Jun-Aug 2006	663	5.1	186	28.1	172	47	258	1,616	263	16.3	760	77	507
Jul-Sep 2006	667	5.2	193	28.9	173	47	254	1,645	270	16.4	769	74	519
Aug-Oct 2006	687	5.3	206	30.0	176	46	259	1,674	279	16.7	789	75	518
Sep-Nov 2006	700	5.4	211	30.1	182	49	258	1,646	280	17.0	780	76	498
Oct-Dec 2006	707	5.5	214	30.2	185	48	259	1,643	278	16.9	785	78	492
Nov-Jan 2007	712	5.5	209	29.3	187	56	260	1,636	281	17.2	770	83	491
Dec-Feb 2007	703	5.5	212	30.2	185	51	255	1,642	267	16.2	787	82	495
Jan-Mar 2007	713	5.5	215	30.1	183	53	261	1,664	274	16.5	798	81	500
Feb-Apr 2007	696	5.4	211	30.3	177	48	260	1,658	273	16.5	799	80	497
Mar-May 2007	696	5.4	219	31.4	174	43	261	1,653	277	16.8	804	76	487
Apr-Jun 2007	693	5.3	223	32.2	172	40	258	1,652	275	16.7	821	75	469
May-Jul 2007	689	5.3	219	31.8	177	39	255	1,658	281	17.0	832	79	453
Jun-Aug 2007	694	5.3	218	31.4	185	38	252	1,661	290	17.5	828	70	460
Jul-Sep 2007	682	5.2	206	30.2	189	37	249	1,680	293	17.4	831	72	471
Aug-Oct 2007	668	5.1	202	30.3	187	38	241	1,666	292	17.5	817	71	474
Sep-Nov 2007	684	5.2	203	29.6	192	42	247	1,704	288	16.9	834	72	498
Oct-Dec 2007	696	5.3	200	28.8	193	45	258	1,709	291	17.0	836	71	498
Nov-Jan 2008	685	5.2	188	27.4	189	43	265	1,731	292	16.9	857	69	500
Dec-Feb 2008	663	5.1	181	27.4	181	43	258	1,730	292	16.9	857	69	498
Jan-Mar 2008	657	5.0	185	28.1	182	39	251	1,726	289	16.7	860	69	494
Feb-Apr 2008	656	5.0	179	27.3	183	42	252	1,727	287	16.6	860	73	492
Mar-May 2008	648	4.9	178	27.5	165	45	259	1,699	268	15.8	859	76	479
Apr-Jun 2008	628	4.8	176	28.1	159	46	247	1,727	271	15.7	864	78	499
May-Jul 2008	611	4.7	182	29.7	143	47	239	1,747	290	16.6	858	82	503
Jun-Aug 2008	615	4.7	180	29.2	154	44	238	1,760	303	17.2	858	83	504
Jul-Sep 2008	633	4.8	184	29.1	158	46	244	1,766	315	17.8	860	81	497
Aug-Oct 2008	627	4.8	177	28.2	170	42	239	1,772	322	18.2	857	80	498
Sep-Nov 2008	635	4.9	186	29.4	155	42	251	1,767	333	18.8	847	79	492
Oct-Dec 2008	639	4.9	195	30.5	152	42	250	1,780	353	19.9	840	80	490
Nov-Jan 2009	659	5.1	215	32.6	153	47	243	1,789	379	21.2	832	77	485
Dec-Feb 2009	662	5.1	225	34.1	158	38	240	1,789	385	21.5	830	78	481
Jan-Mar 2009	664	5.2	232	35.0	155	37	239	1,781	394	22.1	821	77	474
Feb-Apr 2009	662	5.2	228	34.4	155	40	238	1,779	405	22.8	812	79	464
Mar-May 2009	649	5.1	219	33.7	153	48	229	1,798	425	23.6	806	80	467
Apr-Jun 2009	676	5.3	231	34.1	156	47	243	1,805	438	24.3	793	79	472
May-Jul 2009	680	5.4	231	34.0	151	45	253	1,784	438	24.6	789	73	466
Jun-Aug 2009	679	5.4	235	34.7	151	47	246	1,797	432	24.0	802	70	472
Jul-Sep 2009	671	5.3	240	35.8	146	44	241	1,783	433	24.3	785	79	468
Aug-Oct 2009	672	5.3	245	36.5	140	49	237	1,796	435	24.2	778	79	486
Sep-Nov 2009	685	5.4	262	38.2	145	43	235	1,807	449	24.8	787	76	478
Oct-Dec 2009	690	5.5	268	38.8	146	42	235	1,809	447	24.7	799	77	471
Nov-Jan 2010	683	5.4	259	37.9	147	41	236	1,823	449	24.6	811	75	470
Dec-Feb 2010	709	5.7	273	38.5	149	46	241	1,817	457	25.2	800	72	474
Jan-Mar 2010	707	5.6	268	37.9	151	43	245	1,832	463	25.3	808	69	479
Feb-Apr 2010	715	5.7	283	39.6	151	42	239	1,836	463	25.2	807	68	487
Mar-May 2010	733	5.8	291	39.7	158	41	244	1,863	459	24.6	834	63	497
Apr-Jun 2010	760	6.0	304	40.0	163	40	253	1,889	468	24.8	847	70	492
May-Jul 2010	753	5.9	300	39.8	160	40	253	1,920	480	25.0	848	70	509
Jun-Aug 2010	760	6.0	314	41.3	157	43	246	1,950	492	25.2	851	77	515
Jul-Sep 2010	756	5.9	319	42.2	150	44	243	1,973	501	25.4	859	72	525
Aug-Oct 2010	761	6.0	314	41.3	156	48	242	1,975	522	26.4	867	72	500
Sep-Nov 2010	744	5.9	303	40.7	151	52	238	1,972	520	26.4	878	78	482
Oct-Dec 2010	718	5.6	289	40.3	147	53	228	1,978	519	26.3	882	73	488

4.2 Full-time, part-time and temporary workers

United Kingdom (thousands) seasonally adjusted

	Temporary employees (reasons for temporary working)							Part-time workers (reasons for working part-time)[3]					
	Total	Total as % of all employees	Could not find permanent job	% that could not find permanent job	Did not want permanent job	Had a contract with period of training	Some other reason	Total[4]	Could not find full-time job	% that could not find full-time job	Did not want full-time job	Ill or disabled	Student or at school
Men (16+)	YCCA	YCCD	YCCG	YCCJ	YCCM	YCCP	YCCS	YCCV	YCCY	YCDB	YCDE	YCDH	YCDK
Nov-Jan 2011	738	5.8	299	40.5	145	51	244	1,952	511	26.2	880	73	471
Dec-Feb 2011	741	5.8	296	40.0	145	51	249	1,935	513	26.5	872	76	454
Jan-Mar 2011	752	5.9	300	40.0	146	56	250	1,937	523	27.0	869	81	441
Feb-Apr 2011	769	6.0	314	40.8	145	51	259	1,975	540	27.3	880	83	452
Mar-May 2011	771	6.0	311	40.4	149	49	262	1,976	554	28.0	889	74	438
Apr-Jun 2011	792	6.2	329	41.6	151	46	265	1,967	564	28.7	877	71	437
May-Jul 2011	760	6.0	304	40.0	154	45	257	1,959	579	29.5	865	71	423
Jun-Aug 2011	747	5.9	309	41.4	134	42	261	1,907	569	29.8	841	66	415
Jul-Sep 2011	735	5.8	302	41.1	141	43	249	1,908	555	29.1	850	66	419
Aug-Oct 2011	736	5.8	311	42.3	138	41	246	1,934	563	29.1	852	68	432
Sep-Nov 2011	733	5.8	302	41.2	152	41	238	1,964	579	29.5	857	69	441
Oct-Dec 2011	727	5.7	308	42.4	142	41	235	1,971	593	30.1	854	70	438
Nov-Jan 2012	732	5.8	313	42.7	140	45	234	1,965	604	30.7	846	73	430
Dec-Feb 2012	739	5.8	327	44.2	135	45	232	2,029	625	30.8	862	73	455
Jan-Mar 2012	742	5.8	319	43.0	139	44	240	2,046	635	31.0	868	74	457
Feb-Apr 2012	740	5.8	311	42.0	137	47	246	2,049	639	31.2	867	75	452
Mar-May 2012	738	5.8	323	43.8	134	46	235	2,045	633	31.0	866	76	453
Apr-Jun 2012	751	5.9	326	43.4	134	50	241	2,073	650	31.4	871	73	459
May-Jul 2012	761	6.0	335	44.0	135	50	241	2,074	644	31.0	881	71	458
Jun-Aug 2012	757	5.9	327	43.2	134	49	247	2,076	633	30.5	888	74	458
Jul-Sep 2012	760	6.0	335	44.0	129	45	251	2,057	632	30.7	886	70	447
Aug-Oct 2012	766	6.0	340	44.3	127	46	254	2,041	632	31.0	892	69	425
Sep-Nov 2012	778	6.1	347	44.5	135	40	256	2,034	635	31.2	896	62	413
Oct-Dec 2012	785	6.1	357	45.5	136	42	250	2,028	639	31.5	889	66	404
Nov-Jan 2013	777	6.0	350	45.1	137	42	248	2,029	640	31.6	897	64	399
Dec-Feb 2013	769	6.0	343	44.6	140	45	241	2,021	641	31.7	895	63	400
Jan-Mar 2013	755	5.9	338	44.8	138	42	236	2,006	639	31.8	878	61	406
Feb-Apr 2013	749	5.8	330	44.1	145	36	238	2,049	661	32.2	878	63	421
Mar-May 2013	753	5.9	324	43.1	140	43	246	2,027	665	32.8	863	64	408
Apr-Jun 2013	736	5.7	315	42.8	139	40	242	2,032	657	32.3	877	67	407
May-Jul 2013	743	5.8	315	42.4	133	49	246	2,032	660	32.5	878	65	407
Jun-Aug 2013	741	5.7	310	41.9	131	60	240	2,042	665	32.6	892	66	398
Jul-Sep 2013	756	5.8	306	40.5	137	67	246	2,071	668	32.3	902	72	404
Aug-Oct 2013	742	5.7	300	40.4	139	62	241	2,080	664	31.9	909	74	411
Sep-Nov 2013	756	5.8	297	39.3	136	63	259	2,089	658	31.5	909	76	430
Oct-Dec 2013	769	5.9	299	38.9	143	62	265	2,091	639	30.5	917	77	439
Nov-Jan 2014	770	5.9	299	38.9	146	59	265	2,098	652	31.1	908	79	440
Dec-Feb 2014	771	5.9	297	38.5	152	56	267	2,111	639	30.3	935	79	437
Jan-Mar 2014	783	6.0	303	38.7	144	59	278	2,114	642	30.4	947	80	425
Feb-Apr 2014	782	6.0	307	39.2	144	61	270	2,082	604	29.0	952	80	428
Mar-May 2014	777	5.9	309	39.8	143	62	264	2,085	599	28.7	959	88	419
Apr-Jun 2014	766	5.9	316	41.2	137	58	255	2,050	585	28.5	956	83	407
May-Jul 2014	778	6.0	322	41.4	140	63	253	2,071	588	28.4	973	86	405
Jun-Aug 2014	805	6.1	329	40.9	154	57	264	2,080	593	28.5	971	78	417
Jul-Sep 2014	801	6.1	308	38.5	177	62	253	2,074	586	28.3	975	79	415
Aug-Oct 2014	806	6.1	293	36.4	190	64	259	2,067	574	27.8	987	76	411
Sep-Nov 2014	793	6.0	301	37.9	179	64	249	2,092	576	27.5	992	84	423
Oct-Dec 2014	812	6.1	308	37.9	171	59	274	2,076	565	27.2	994	84	414
Nov-Jan 2015	804	6.1	309	38.4	160	63	272	2,079	576	27.7	990	86	411
Dec-Feb 2015	816	6.1	317	38.9	155	64	280	2,105	587	27.9	1,018	85	403
Jan-Mar 2015	816	6.1	313	38.4	156	67	280	2,110	576	27.3	1,019	87	415
Feb-Apr 2015	808	6.0	313	38.8	156	65	274	2,097	553	26.4	1,023	85	420
Mar-May 2015	793	6.0	292	36.8	170	60	271	2,061	546	26.5	1,000	86	414
Apr-Jun 2015	769	5.8	298	38.8	160	63	247	2,084	555	26.6	1,016	90	409
May-Jul 2015	783	5.9	288	36.8	171	59	265	2,112	553	26.2	1,028	94	421
Jun-Aug 2015	774	5.8	301	38.9	175	58	240	2,139	555	25.9	1,050	87	428
Jul-Sep 2015	791	5.9	297	37.5	182	57	255	2,174	557	25.6	1,070	84	448
Aug-Oct 2015	786	5.8	308	39.2	181	46	251	2,191	567	25.9	1,055	88	467
Sep-Nov 2015	768	5.7	301	39.2	175	59	233	2,179	543	24.9	1,075	90	455
Oct-Dec 2015	751	5.6	283	37.6	177	60	232	2,184	547	25.1	1,064	96	457

Source: Labour Force Survey
Inquiries: Email: labour.market@ons.gsi.gov.uk
Tel: 01633 455400

Note: When comparing quarterly changes ONS recommends comparing with the previous non-overlapping 3-month average time period (eg, compare Apr-Jun with Jan-Mar, not with Mar-May).

1. The split between full-time and part-time employment is based on respondents' self-classification.
2. This series does not include all people on these programmes; it only includes those engaging in any form of work, work experience or work-related training.
3. These series cover Employees and Self-employed only. These series include some temporary employees.
4. The total includes those who did not give a reason for working part-time and it therefore does not equal the sum of the other columns in this section of the table.

4.2 Full-time, part-time and temporary workers

United Kingdom (thousands) seasonally adjusted

	All in employment					Full-time and part-time workers[1]						
	Total	Employees	Self employed	Unpaid family workers	Government supported training & employment programmes[2]	Total people working full-time	Total people working part-time	Employees working full-time	Employees working part-time	Self-employed people working full-time	Self-employed people working part-time	Total workers with second jobs
Women (16+)	MGSB	MGRP	MGRS	MGRV	MGRY	YCBG	YCBJ	YCBM	YCBP	YCBS	YCBV	YCBY
Nov-Jan 2005	13,222	12,163	951	58	51	7,565	5,657	7,070	5,093	467	484	611
Dec-Feb 2005	13,279	12,193	969	63	55	7,633	5,646	7,115	5,078	486	483	617
Jan-Mar 2005	13,258	12,180	958	62	57	7,622	5,636	7,101	5,079	488	470	608
Feb-Apr 2005	13,242	12,177	952	61	52	7,602	5,640	7,093	5,084	478	473	611
Mar-May 2005	13,272	12,200	963	63	46	7,585	5,687	7,073	5,127	482	481	617
Apr-Jun 2005	13,276	12,212	958	63	43	7,575	5,700	7,072	5,140	474	484	615
May-Jul 2005	13,316	12,247	968	60	42	7,611	5,705	7,097	5,149	486	481	607
Jun-Aug 2005	13,353	12,280	979	52	42	7,666	5,687	7,145	5,134	497	482	602
Jul-Sep 2005	13,357	12,267	988	58	44	7,680	5,677	7,151	5,116	501	487	612
Aug-Oct 2005	13,342	12,264	974	60	43	7,683	5,659	7,160	5,104	493	481	611
Sep-Nov 2005	13,311	12,219	986	62	44	7,672	5,639	7,149	5,069	492	493	602
Oct-Dec 2005	13,307	12,221	977	61	48	7,696	5,611	7,177	5,044	490	487	587
Nov-Jan 2006	13,330	12,249	975	60	46	7,699	5,632	7,182	5,067	488	488	583
Dec-Feb 2006	13,374	12,282	998	58	35	7,718	5,656	7,195	5,087	500	498	589
Jan-Mar 2006	13,439	12,322	1,024	58	35	7,738	5,701	7,195	5,128	520	504	589
Feb-Apr 2006	13,429	12,311	1,029	55	35	7,742	5,686	7,206	5,105	512	517	592
Mar-May 2006	13,424	12,326	1,006	53	39	7,754	5,671	7,236	5,090	496	510	591
Apr-Jun 2006	13,454	12,346	1,013	55	39	7,753	5,701	7,230	5,116	499	515	599
May-Jul 2006	13,457	12,331	1,029	60	37	7,757	5,701	7,221	5,110	512	517	601
Jun-Aug 2006	13,502	12,361	1,038	64	39	7,764	5,738	7,219	5,143	520	518	611
Jul-Sep 2006	13,443	12,301	1,040	62	39	7,722	5,721	7,188	5,114	511	529	613
Aug-Oct 2006	13,451	12,302	1,052	56	42	7,702	5,749	7,164	5,137	516	536	612
Sep-Nov 2006	13,459	12,319	1,032	60	47	7,710	5,749	7,177	5,142	507	525	609
Oct-Dec 2006	13,463	12,315	1,042	60	46	7,701	5,763	7,166	5,149	511	531	619
Nov-Jan 2007	13,441	12,299	1,036	62	44	7,689	5,752	7,155	5,144	507	529	625
Dec-Feb 2007	13,423	12,269	1,048	59	47	7,696	5,727	7,151	5,118	520	528	616
Jan-Mar 2007	13,436	12,284	1,047	61	44	7,721	5,715	7,186	5,099	509	538	611
Feb-Apr 2007	13,450	12,298	1,048	61	43	7,734	5,717	7,194	5,104	513	535	634
Mar-May 2007	13,468	12,331	1,030	61	45	7,762	5,706	7,223	5,109	513	517	643
Apr-Jun 2007	13,483	12,344	1,027	62	49	7,776	5,706	7,239	5,106	514	514	651
May-Jul 2007	13,506	12,350	1,040	66	50	7,801	5,705	7,260	5,090	519	521	658
Jun-Aug 2007	13,514	12,339	1,060	64	52	7,810	5,704	7,269	5,070	516	544	661
Jul-Sep 2007	13,536	12,353	1,072	59	52	7,847	5,689	7,293	5,061	529	543	653
Aug-Oct 2007	13,568	12,386	1,066	60	56	7,861	5,706	7,313	5,073	520	546	657
Sep-Nov 2007	13,584	12,410	1,060	66	49	7,874	5,711	7,331	5,079	516	543	661
Oct-Dec 2007	13,628	12,464	1,047	67	51	7,893	5,735	7,364	5,100	503	544	676
Nov-Jan 2008	13,646	12,472	1,058	70	45	7,903	5,743	7,375	5,097	503	556	659
Dec-Feb 2008	13,683	12,503	1,067	70	43	7,932	5,751	7,386	5,117	520	547	665
Jan-Mar 2008	13,678	12,511	1,056	69	42	7,925	5,753	7,384	5,128	519	537	652
Feb-Apr 2008	13,682	12,517	1,045	73	47	7,931	5,751	7,381	5,136	524	521	663
Mar-May 2008	13,730	12,556	1,047	76	51	7,972	5,758	7,424	5,132	523	524	658
Apr-Jun 2008	13,710	12,544	1,048	72	47	7,968	5,742	7,418	5,125	524	524	669
May-Jul 2008	13,709	12,540	1,056	65	48	7,993	5,716	7,441	5,100	527	529	680
Jun-Aug 2008	13,684	12,532	1,052	60	41	7,976	5,709	7,433	5,099	525	527	670
Jul-Sep 2008	13,670	12,518	1,049	61	43	7,980	5,690	7,434	5,084	528	521	670
Aug-Oct 2008	13,671	12,515	1,058	58	38	7,986	5,685	7,437	5,079	532	527	675
Sep-Nov 2008	13,672	12,516	1,064	54	37	7,914	5,758	7,382	5,134	519	545	673
Oct-Dec 2008	13,659	12,515	1,054	53	36	7,939	5,720	7,409	5,106	511	542	670
Nov-Jan 2009	13,680	12,530	1,061	50	39	7,957	5,722	7,421	5,109	519	542	673
Dec-Feb 2009	13,643	12,495	1,055	52	41	7,908	5,735	7,363	5,133	520	535	671
Jan-Mar 2009	13,627	12,458	1,071	55	43	7,868	5,759	7,320	5,139	524	547	669
Feb-Apr 2009	13,594	12,413	1,081	56	45	7,874	5,721	7,330	5,083	520	561	656
Mar-May 2009	13,578	12,386	1,082	64	46	7,867	5,711	7,324	5,062	523	559	655
Apr-Jun 2009	13,575	12,385	1,087	58	46	7,832	5,742	7,285	5,100	527	559	646
May-Jul 2009	13,553	12,355	1,097	55	46	7,793	5,759	7,234	5,121	539	559	641
Jun-Aug 2009	13,604	12,379	1,124	51	50	7,830	5,774	7,260	5,119	548	576	648
Jul-Sep 2009	13,622	12,394	1,132	48	48	7,782	5,840	7,218	5,176	544	588	654
Aug-Oct 2009	13,636	12,430	1,111	50	44	7,759	5,877	7,203	5,227	536	575	652
Sep-Nov 2009	13,654	12,420	1,139	43	52	7,777	5,877	7,213	5,207	544	595	647
Oct-Dec 2009	13,665	12,418	1,142	50	55	7,791	5,874	7,214	5,204	555	588	644
Nov-Jan 2010	13,650	12,409	1,133	50	59	7,777	5,873	7,207	5,201	546	587	627
Dec-Feb 2010	13,620	12,364	1,146	51	59	7,770	5,850	7,190	5,174	559	587	624
Jan-Mar 2010	13,616	12,329	1,180	50	58	7,749	5,867	7,151	5,177	577	603	633
Feb-Apr 2010	13,630	12,329	1,194	50	58	7,720	5,910	7,119	5,211	581	613	645
Mar-May 2010	13,645	12,367	1,172	51	54	7,715	5,930	7,125	5,242	567	605	658
Apr-Jun 2010	13,653	12,387	1,161	49	56	7,734	5,919	7,151	5,236	560	601	664
May-Jul 2010	13,691	12,410	1,169	60	52	7,712	5,979	7,117	5,293	570	599	667
Jun-Aug 2010	13,686	12,415	1,154	67	49	7,697	5,989	7,109	5,306	566	589	662
Jul-Sep 2010	13,689	12,400	1,181	62	46	7,706	5,983	7,111	5,289	576	606	656
Aug-Oct 2010	13,650	12,375	1,172	57	46	7,699	5,950	7,104	5,271	575	597	655
Sep-Nov 2010	13,640	12,352	1,177	61	49	7,695	5,945	7,095	5,257	577	600	652

4.2 Full-time, part-time and temporary workers

United Kingdom (thousands) seasonally adjusted

	All in employment					Full-time and part-time workers[1]						
	Total	Employees	Self employed	Unpaid family workers	Government supported training & employment programmes[2]	Total people working full-time	Total people working part-time	Employees working full-time	Employees working part-time	Self-employed people working full-time	Self-employed people working part-time	Total workers with second jobs
Women (16+)	MGSB	MGRP	MGRS	MGRV	MGRY	YCBG	YCBJ	YCBM	YCBP	YCBS	YCBV	YCBY
Oct-Dec 2010	13,645	12,362	1,174	59	50	7,703	5,942	7,120	5,242	562	612	653
Nov-Jan 2011	13,680	12,364	1,202	65	49	7,715	5,965	7,126	5,238	565	636	663
Dec-Feb 2011	13,725	12,406	1,205	65	49	7,739	5,987	7,150	5,256	566	639	666
Jan-Mar 2011	13,749	12,444	1,189	66	50	7,767	5,982	7,181	5,263	561	628	670
Feb-Apr 2011	13,694	12,400	1,182	65	46	7,726	5,968	7,151	5,249	548	634	665
Mar-May 2011	13,728	12,434	1,191	60	43	7,761	5,967	7,183	5,251	555	636	661
Apr-Jun 2011	13,719	12,452	1,171	58	39	7,789	5,930	7,211	5,241	556	615	648
May-Jul 2011	13,690	12,431	1,164	56	39	7,824	5,866	7,245	5,186	562	603	644
Jun-Aug 2011	13,679	12,381	1,202	60	35	7,794	5,884	7,198	5,184	579	623	647
Jul-Sep 2011	13,689	12,359	1,225	63	42	7,789	5,900	7,188	5,172	579	646	656
Aug-Oct 2011	13,690	12,340	1,236	69	44	7,781	5,909	7,167	5,173	588	648	649
Sep-Nov 2011	13,704	12,357	1,232	69	46	7,783	5,920	7,171	5,187	583	649	654
Oct-Dec 2011	13,707	12,367	1,228	69	44	7,766	5,941	7,156	5,210	586	642	648
Nov-Jan 2012	13,713	12,362	1,235	69	47	7,764	5,948	7,155	5,208	586	649	655
Dec-Feb 2012	13,696	12,330	1,250	62	54	7,754	5,942	7,150	5,181	582	668	658
Jan-Mar 2012	13,735	12,356	1,270	53	55	7,774	5,961	7,164	5,192	588	682	664
Feb-Apr 2012	13,738	12,364	1,265	54	55	7,792	5,946	7,182	5,182	587	678	659
Mar-May 2012	13,759	12,403	1,240	65	52	7,812	5,947	7,217	5,186	572	668	654
Apr-Jun 2012	13,801	12,426	1,251	70	55	7,815	5,987	7,218	5,207	567	684	637
May-Jul 2012	13,874	12,469	1,274	76	55	7,815	6,059	7,223	5,246	564	710	649
Jun-Aug 2012	13,880	12,498	1,262	66	53	7,824	6,056	7,238	5,260	560	702	647
Jul-Sep 2012	13,861	12,487	1,260	61	53	7,813	6,048	7,225	5,262	563	697	648
Aug-Oct 2012	13,836	12,471	1,253	61	51	7,780	6,056	7,191	5,280	568	685	661
Sep-Nov 2012	13,914	12,507	1,289	65	53	7,851	6,063	7,237	5,271	588	701	670
Oct-Dec 2012	13,959	12,533	1,303	68	56	7,905	6,054	7,278	5,255	598	705	694
Nov-Jan 2013	13,963	12,565	1,285	63	51	7,941	6,022	7,318	5,248	590	695	700
Dec-Feb 2013	13,945	12,551	1,283	64	46	7,920	6,024	7,293	5,258	596	687	684
Jan-Mar 2013	13,967	12,591	1,264	66	45	7,943	6,024	7,313	5,279	602	662	675
Feb-Apr 2013	13,987	12,585	1,281	69	52	7,973	6,013	7,329	5,256	613	668	649
Mar-May 2013	13,967	12,572	1,266	72	57	7,962	6,006	7,323	5,249	606	660	666
Apr-Jun 2013	14,004	12,599	1,274	72	58	7,989	6,014	7,337	5,262	615	660	665
May-Jul 2013	14,030	12,622	1,274	71	63	8,027	6,003	7,361	5,261	618	656	662
Jun-Aug 2013	14,033	12,605	1,293	72	63	8,041	5,993	7,356	5,249	633	660	669
Jul-Sep 2013	14,047	12,609	1,296	73	69	8,052	5,995	7,369	5,240	633	662	671
Aug-Oct 2013	14,113	12,660	1,318	74	61	8,071	6,042	7,388	5,272	641	677	675
Sep-Nov 2013	14,139	12,655	1,364	68	52	8,131	6,009	7,423	5,232	675	689	683
Oct-Dec 2013	14,150	12,661	1,373	62	53	8,175	5,974	7,457	5,204	684	689	669
Nov-Jan 2014	14,145	12,638	1,390	64	53	8,156	5,988	7,440	5,198	685	706	666
Dec-Feb 2014	14,234	12,711	1,402	70	51	8,164	6,070	7,452	5,258	681	721	640
Jan-Mar 2014	14,255	12,707	1,433	67	47	8,191	6,064	7,489	5,218	673	760	659
Feb-Apr 2014	14,305	12,757	1,435	64	48	8,215	6,090	7,517	5,240	670	765	669
Mar-May 2014	14,365	12,793	1,459	60	53	8,246	6,118	7,549	5,244	673	786	680
Apr-Jun 2014	14,355	12,778	1,465	59	52	8,206	6,149	7,506	5,272	678	787	699
May-Jul 2014	14,364	12,808	1,441	65	50	8,205	6,159	7,510	5,298	676	765	708
Jun-Aug 2014	14,401	12,866	1,410	72	53	8,271	6,130	7,576	5,291	674	735	706
Jul-Sep 2014	14,404	12,874	1,408	70	53	8,283	6,121	7,598	5,276	663	744	700
Aug-Oct 2014	14,412	12,861	1,437	63	51	8,302	6,110	7,599	5,262	678	759	691
Sep-Nov 2014	14,426	12,877	1,450	53	46	8,316	6,110	7,612	5,265	680	770	702
Oct-Dec 2014	14,469	12,918	1,450	54	47	8,325	6,145	7,625	5,294	672	778	708
Nov-Jan 2015	14,481	12,915	1,458	63	45	8,336	6,145	7,639	5,275	667	791	710
Dec-Feb 2015	14,505	12,959	1,438	61	47	8,331	6,174	7,655	5,304	643	795	698
Jan-Mar 2015	14,527	12,981	1,437	65	44	8,352	6,175	7,661	5,320	659	778	693
Feb-Apr 2015	14,528	13,005	1,419	60	45	8,387	6,142	7,692	5,313	659	760	681
Mar-May 2015	14,523	12,999	1,427	62	36	8,377	6,147	7,700	5,299	647	780	665
Apr-Jun 2015	14,535	13,009	1,426	58	43	8,404	6,131	7,706	5,303	667	759	655
May-Jul 2015	14,553	13,016	1,431	60	46	8,372	6,181	7,675	5,341	664	767	664
Jun-Aug 2015	14,550	13,018	1,435	54	42	8,399	6,151	7,696	5,322	675	760	672
Jul-Sep 2015	14,605	13,057	1,449	54	44	8,420	6,185	7,710	5,347	681	768	680
Aug-Oct 2015	14,605	13,043	1,478	44	40	8,427	6,178	7,717	5,327	692	786	672
Sep-Nov 2015	14,658	13,079	1,488	47	44	8,465	6,193	7,748	5,331	691	796	659
Oct-Dec 2015	14,647	13,047	1,503	50	46	8,464	6,183	7,742	5,305	697	807	643

Source: Labour Force Survey
Inquiries: Email: labour.market@ons.gsi.gov.uk
Tel: 01633 455400

Note: When comparing quarterly changes ONS recommends comparing with the previous non-overlapping 3-month average time period (eg, compare Apr-Jun with Jan-Mar, not with Mar-May).

1. The split between full-time and part-time employment is based on respondents' self-classification.
2. This series does not include all people on these programmes; it only includes those engaging in any form of work, work experience or work-related training.
3. These series cover Employees and Self-employed only. These series include some temporary employees.
4. The total includes those who did not give a reason for working part-time and it therefore does not equal the sum of the other columns in this section of the table.

4.2 Full-time, part-time and temporary workers

United Kingdom (thousands) seasonally adjusted

	Temporary employees (reasons for temporary working)							Part-time workers (reasons for working part-time)[3]					
	Total	Total as % of all employees	Could not find permanent job	% that could not find permanent job	Did not want permanent job	Had a contract with period of training	Some other reason	Total[4]	Could not find full-time job	% that could not find full-time job	Did not want full-time job	Ill or disabled	Student or at school
Women (16+)	YCCB	YCCE	YCCH	YCCK	YCCN	YCCQ	YCCT	YCCW	YCCZ	YCDC	YCDF	YCDI	YCDL
Nov-Jan 2005	794	6.5	155	19.5	240	59	340	5,577	311	5.6	4,493	101	653
Dec-Feb 2005	799	6.6	156	19.5	242	62	340	5,561	324	5.8	4,469	100	648
Jan-Mar 2005	773	6.3	156	20.2	230	51	336	5,549	337	6.1	4,452	97	642
Feb-Apr 2005	755	6.2	152	20.1	215	52	337	5,557	335	6.0	4,463	100	640
Mar-May 2005	758	6.2	147	19.4	221	49	341	5,608	351	6.3	4,505	96	641
Apr-Jun 2005	759	6.2	147	19.3	219	43	350	5,623	353	6.3	4,500	92	661
May-Jul 2005	781	6.4	148	19.0	229	47	357	5,631	351	6.2	4,498	88	673
Jun-Aug 2005	793	6.5	166	21.0	223	43	361	5,616	362	6.4	4,490	91	650
Jul-Sep 2005	801	6.5	181	22.6	226	45	348	5,604	370	6.6	4,477	93	645
Aug-Oct 2005	766	6.2	181	23.6	218	45	322	5,586	361	6.5	4,467	93	645
Sep-Nov 2005	760	6.2	169	22.2	213	51	328	5,563	366	6.6	4,448	92	635
Oct-Dec 2005	739	6.1	152	20.6	213	51	324	5,531	359	6.5	4,435	92	623
Nov-Jan 2006	780	6.4	169	21.7	225	55	331	5,555	368	6.6	4,440	93	631
Dec-Feb 2006	791	6.4	173	21.9	233	48	337	5,585	370	6.6	4,447	101	642
Jan-Mar 2006	820	6.7	182	22.2	242	54	341	5,631	373	6.6	4,478	98	651
Feb-Apr 2006	816	6.6	175	21.5	242	60	339	5,621	371	6.6	4,470	100	653
Mar-May 2006	812	6.6	181	22.4	239	60	331	5,601	363	6.5	4,454	97	657
Apr-Jun 2006	808	6.5	182	22.6	245	57	324	5,631	370	6.6	4,473	101	659
May-Jul 2006	795	6.5	179	22.5	247	51	318	5,627	376	6.7	4,461	102	661
Jun-Aug 2006	806	6.5	177	22.0	260	49	319	5,660	381	6.7	4,476	109	676
Jul-Sep 2006	799	6.5	174	21.7	260	47	318	5,644	376	6.7	4,459	112	677
Aug-Oct 2006	792	6.4	180	22.7	252	42	317	5,675	381	6.7	4,470	113	685
Sep-Nov 2006	795	6.5	181	22.7	255	45	315	5,667	382	6.7	4,459	114	679
Oct-Dec 2006	805	6.5	178	22.1	265	43	319	5,679	386	6.8	4,458	116	688
Nov-Jan 2007	817	6.6	190	23.2	256	49	322	5,673	388	6.8	4,465	115	675
Dec-Feb 2007	818	6.7	185	22.6	254	55	324	5,646	380	6.7	4,468	110	663
Jan-Mar 2007	821	6.7	190	23.1	251	58	321	5,636	386	6.9	4,459	107	662
Feb-Apr 2007	817	6.6	192	23.5	249	56	320	5,639	399	7.1	4,465	98	655
Mar-May 2007	817	6.6	189	23.1	248	58	323	5,626	408	7.3	4,443	101	653
Apr-Jun 2007	814	6.6	194	23.9	237	57	326	5,619	406	7.2	4,429	99	662
May-Jul 2007	812	6.6	192	23.6	235	54	331	5,612	415	7.4	4,397	102	678
Jun-Aug 2007	798	6.5	188	23.5	232	49	329	5,613	407	7.3	4,420	95	668
Jul-Sep 2007	803	6.5	186	23.2	232	47	337	5,605	401	7.2	4,428	97	656
Aug-Oct 2007	794	6.4	182	23.0	235	46	330	5,620	409	7.3	4,440	97	650
Sep-Nov 2007	794	6.4	177	22.3	240	41	336	5,622	409	7.3	4,453	102	638
Oct-Dec 2007	799	6.4	179	22.4	256	36	327	5,642	438	7.8	4,424	99	654
Nov-Jan 2008	788	6.3	179	22.7	250	35	324	5,653	447	7.9	4,416	105	660
Dec-Feb 2008	782	6.3	181	23.2	247	40	314	5,664	437	7.7	4,419	108	671
Jan-Mar 2008	773	6.2	178	23.1	244	44	307	5,665	416	7.3	4,431	115	674
Feb-Apr 2008	783	6.3	179	22.8	248	44	312	5,657	409	7.2	4,415	114	691
Mar-May 2008	772	6.1	179	23.1	239	39	316	5,657	402	7.1	4,422	117	686
Apr-Jun 2008	767	6.1	171	22.3	245	38	313	5,649	408	7.2	4,419	126	669
May-Jul 2008	774	6.2	169	21.9	248	40	316	5,629	399	7.1	4,410	134	659
Jun-Aug 2008	768	6.1	173	22.6	251	39	305	5,627	399	7.1	4,435	133	634
Jul-Sep 2008	757	6.0	176	23.2	244	42	295	5,606	399	7.1	4,420	126	633
Aug-Oct 2008	743	5.9	174	23.4	237	41	291	5,606	409	7.3	4,423	117	629
Sep-Nov 2008	768	6.1	178	23.1	244	42	304	5,678	420	7.4	4,465	120	646
Oct-Dec 2008	772	6.2	185	24.0	240	44	303	5,646	417	7.4	4,439	118	643
Nov-Jan 2009	766	6.1	182	23.7	237	44	303	5,651	437	7.7	4,424	114	648
Dec-Feb 2009	765	6.1	195	25.5	227	46	297	5,668	465	8.2	4,428	105	643
Jan-Mar 2009	764	6.1	193	25.3	230	44	297	5,685	481	8.5	4,436	107	638
Feb-Apr 2009	755	6.1	191	25.3	226	47	292	5,644	497	8.8	4,387	112	626
Mar-May 2009	755	6.1	198	26.2	231	44	282	5,621	511	9.1	4,357	111	620
Apr-Jun 2009	754	6.1	200	26.6	230	42	282	5,660	525	9.3	4,373	110	622
May-Jul 2009	750	6.1	212	28.3	220	39	279	5,681	534	9.4	4,387	108	620
Jun-Aug 2009	756	6.1	211	27.9	225	42	279	5,695	549	9.6	4,375	114	627
Jul-Sep 2009	779	6.3	223	28.7	230	41	284	5,765	569	9.9	4,411	110	648
Aug-Oct 2009	767	6.2	223	29.0	228	36	279	5,803	583	10.0	4,422	112	662
Sep-Nov 2009	752	6.1	228	30.3	220	34	271	5,801	589	10.2	4,411	107	666
Oct-Dec 2009	755	6.1	229	30.4	216	36	273	5,789	591	10.2	4,395	110	666
Nov-Jan 2010	768	6.2	240	31.2	223	36	269	5,789	596	10.3	4,386	109	671
Dec-Feb 2010	772	6.2	240	31.1	217	37	278	5,761	594	10.3	4,360	107	674
Jan-Mar 2010	775	6.3	245	31.6	215	37	278	5,780	608	10.5	4,379	99	661
Feb-Apr 2010	786	6.4	256	32.6	210	40	280	5,824	627	10.8	4,413	104	647
Mar-May 2010	808	6.5	263	32.6	217	39	289	5,847	613	10.5	4,446	104	651
Apr-Jun 2010	818	6.6	269	32.9	217	42	290	5,837	608	10.4	4,456	102	642
May-Jul 2010	824	6.6	272	33.0	222	40	289	5,894	635	10.8	4,465	101	666
Jun-Aug 2010	818	6.6	277	33.9	211	43	286	5,896	646	11.0	4,451	93	673
Jul-Sep 2010	832	6.7	281	33.8	220	42	288	5,895	652	11.1	4,452	93	665
Aug-Oct 2010	836	6.8	277	33.2	217	44	297	5,868	652	11.1	4,444	92	642
Sep-Nov 2010	831	6.7	286	34.4	203	42	300	5,857	657	11.2	4,464	94	603

4.2 Full-time, part-time and temporary workers

United Kingdom (thousands) seasonally adjusted

Women (16+)	Temporary employees (reasons for temporary working)							Part-time workers (reasons for working part-time)[3]					
	Total	Total as % of all employees	Could not find permanent job	% that could not find permanent job	Did not want permanent job	Had a contract with period of training	Some other reason	Total[4]	Could not find full-time job	% that could not find full-time job	Did not want full-time job	Ill or disabled	Student or at school
	YCCB	YCCE	YCCH	YCCK	YCCN	YCCQ	YCCT	YCCW	YCCZ	YCDC	YCDF	YCDI	YCDL
Oct-Dec 2010	828	6.7	287	34.7	193	42	306	5,851	672	11.5	4,437	91	614
Nov-Jan 2011	829	6.7	281	33.9	196	43	309	5,875	669	11.4	4,469	91	609
Dec-Feb 2011	836	6.7	277	33.1	208	44	308	5,895	668	11.3	4,483	96	611
Jan-Mar 2011	843	6.8	279	33.1	211	45	308	5,891	665	11.3	4,468	100	622
Feb-Apr 2011	831	6.7	269	32.4	210	43	309	5,885	689	11.7	4,441	102	617
Mar-May 2011	834	6.7	271	32.5	214	43	306	5,886	705	12.0	4,423	106	617
Apr-Jun 2011	824	6.6	280	34.0	210	41	293	5,856	707	12.1	4,391	109	611
May-Jul 2011	807	6.5	274	34.0	200	40	293	5,790	709	12.2	4,322	111	610
Jun-Aug 2011	786	6.3	275	35.0	182	39	290	5,807	711	12.2	4,336	115	611
Jul-Sep 2011	790	6.4	280	35.4	189	42	279	5,818	720	12.4	4,326	123	614
Aug-Oct 2011	802	6.5	294	36.6	194	43	272	5,821	723	12.4	4,346	116	608
Sep-Nov 2011	820	6.6	292	35.6	202	48	278	5,835	753	12.9	4,334	115	608
Oct-Dec 2011	818	6.6	294	35.9	204	50	271	5,850	768	13.1	4,332	119	605
Nov-Jan 2012	827	6.7	297	35.9	203	52	275	5,857	794	13.6	4,319	116	599
Dec-Feb 2012	848	6.9	303	35.7	215	51	280	5,849	781	13.4	4,332	108	594
Jan-Mar 2012	828	6.7	300	36.2	198	46	284	5,875	779	13.3	4,349	117	590
Feb-Apr 2012	818	6.6	298	36.4	193	49	278	5,860	773	13.2	4,344	116	591
Mar-May 2012	840	6.8	315	37.5	185	50	291	5,854	763	13.0	4,350	116	591
Apr-Jun 2012	862	6.9	318	36.9	194	53	297	5,892	777	13.2	4,366	110	609
May-Jul 2012	893	7.2	327	36.6	211	51	305	5,958	787	13.2	4,425	110	608
Jun-Aug 2012	884	7.1	324	36.7	209	50	301	5,962	787	13.2	4,425	108	615
Jul-Sep 2012	867	6.9	322	37.1	207	47	291	5,959	782	13.1	4,431	111	607
Aug-Oct 2012	865	6.9	316	36.5	204	46	299	5,965	774	13.0	4,430	116	612
Sep-Nov 2012	871	7.0	309	35.4	209	49	304	5,970	769	12.9	4,438	120	610
Oct-Dec 2012	870	6.9	302	34.7	205	54	310	5,959	752	12.6	4,444	118	610
Nov-Jan 2013	864	6.9	306	35.4	196	54	307	5,943	767	12.9	4,425	122	597
Dec-Feb 2013	833	6.6	301	36.1	192	55	285	5,945	781	13.1	4,410	121	599
Jan-Mar 2013	859	6.8	313	36.4	193	62	292	5,940	781	13.1	4,399	117	610
Feb-Apr 2013	846	6.7	301	35.6	192	65	288	5,925	780	13.2	4,383	118	613
Mar-May 2013	837	6.7	301	36.0	188	60	288	5,908	798	13.5	4,349	116	609
Apr-Jun 2013	831	6.6	290	34.9	185	67	289	5,922	796	13.4	4,368	120	600
May-Jul 2013	827	6.6	292	35.3	181	63	292	5,919	804	13.6	4,350	122	602
Jun-Aug 2013	840	6.7	298	35.5	169	63	310	5,909	799	13.5	4,369	126	575
Jul-Sep 2013	850	6.7	296	34.9	182	59	313	5,903	796	13.5	4,355	122	590
Aug-Oct 2013	852	6.7	293	34.4	188	62	309	5,949	803	13.5	4,399	120	590
Sep-Nov 2013	846	6.7	286	33.8	193	67	301	5,921	786	13.3	4,389	116	596
Oct-Dec 2013	852	6.7	301	35.4	194	56	301	5,892	790	13.4	4,363	114	594
Nov-Jan 2014	852	6.7	293	34.4	201	57	300	5,903	785	13.3	4,374	115	599
Dec-Feb 2014	859	6.8	290	33.8	206	57	306	5,979	780	13.0	4,457	115	602
Jan-Mar 2014	872	6.9	291	33.3	213	58	311	5,979	776	13.0	4,468	111	599
Feb-Apr 2014	901	7.1	295	32.7	225	57	324	6,006	794	13.2	4,473	105	610
Mar-May 2014	907	7.1	293	32.3	228	59	327	6,029	762	12.6	4,531	104	613
Apr-Jun 2014	885	6.9	288	32.6	233	59	305	6,059	758	12.5	4,566	109	603
May-Jul 2014	897	7.0	291	32.4	233	58	315	6,064	752	12.4	4,587	96	606
Jun-Aug 2014	892	6.9	288	32.3	235	62	308	6,026	758	12.6	4,544	95	606
Jul-Sep 2014	901	7.0	289	32.1	243	60	310	6,020	753	12.5	4,547	95	602
Aug-Oct 2014	882	6.9	281	31.9	238	56	307	6,021	745	12.4	4,569	97	583
Sep-Nov 2014	886	6.9	278	31.3	237	57	315	6,035	743	12.3	4,578	102	587
Oct-Dec 2014	892	6.9	273	30.7	240	54	324	6,072	746	12.3	4,571	105	619
Nov-Jan 2015	874	6.8	264	30.2	231	59	320	6,067	746	12.3	4,580	108	605
Dec-Feb 2015	871	6.7	274	31.4	224	52	320	6,098	761	12.5	4,582	109	612
Jan-Mar 2015	872	6.7	276	31.6	212	56	328	6,097	744	12.2	4,597	121	600
Feb-Apr 2015	873	6.7	269	30.9	212	59	333	6,072	743	12.2	4,577	121	594
Mar-May 2015	879	6.8	260	29.6	220	66	333	6,077	729	12.0	4,591	125	593
Apr-Jun 2015	876	6.7	267	30.5	216	70	322	6,061	733	12.1	4,568	127	598
May-Jul 2015	896	6.9	274	30.6	231	70	321	6,107	722	11.8	4,610	134	607
Jun-Aug 2015	886	6.8	281	31.7	232	69	304	6,082	712	11.7	4,588	134	618
Jul-Sep 2015	870	6.7	268	30.8	229	69	304	6,116	700	11.4	4,628	136	621
Aug-Oct 2015	863	6.6	269	31.1	224	71	300	6,113	720	11.8	4,605	132	625
Sep-Nov 2015	872	6.7	277	31.8	216	75	304	6,128	702	11.5	4,632	136	626
Oct-Dec 2015	864	6.6	270	31.2	216	75	304	6,112	689	11.3	4,618	138	627

Source: Labour Force Survey Force Survey
Inquiries: Email: labour.market@ons.gsi.gov.uk ns.gsi.gov.uk
Tel: 01633 455400/1633 455400

Note: When comparing quarterly changes ONS recommends comparing with the previous non-overlapping 3-month average time period (eg, compare Apr-Jun with Jan-Mar, not with Mar-May).

1. The split between full-time and part-time employment is based on respondents' self-classification.
2. This series does not include all people on these programmes; it only includes those engaging in any form of work, work experience or work-related training.
3. These series cover Employees and Self-employed only. These series include some temporary employees.
4. The total includes those who did not give a reason for working part-time and it therefore does not equal the sum of the other columns in this section of the table.

4.3 Employment: by sex and age: United Kingdom

United Kingdom (thousands) seasonally adjusted

Aged 16 and over / Aged 16-64

		Employment Level	Employment Rate	Unemployment Level	Unemployment Rate	Inactivity Level	Inactivity Rate	Employment Level	Employment Rate	Unemployment Level	Unemployment Rate	Inactivity Level	Inactivity Rate
People		MGRZ	MGSR	MGSC	MGSX	MGSI	YBTC	LF2G	LF24	LF2I	LF2Q	LF2M	LF2S
	Oct-Dec 2012	29,910	58.5	2,529	7.8	18,662	36.5	28,927	71.4	2,507	8.0	9,082	22.4
	Oct-Dec 2013	30,288	58.9	2,348	7.2	18,800	36.6	29,213	72.0	2,318	7.4	9,047	22.3
	Oct-Dec 2014	30,896	59.7	1,862	5.7	19,016	36.7	29,769	73.2	1,844	5.8	9,052	22.3
	Jan-Mar 2015	31,098	60.0	1,827	5.5	18,933	36.5	29,902	73.5	1,805	5.7	8,983	22.1
	Apr-Jun 2015	31,035	59.8	1,852	5.6	19,053	36.7	29,894	73.4	1,829	5.8	8,990	22.1
	Jul-Sep 2015	31,211	60.0	1,749	5.3	19,061	36.6	30,043	73.7	1,729	5.4	8,968	22.0
	Oct-Dec 2015	**31,417**	**60.3**	**1,690**	**5.1**	**18,996**	**36.5**	**30,215**	**74.1**	**1,671**	**5.2**	**8,880**	**21.8**
	Change on quarter	206	0.3	-59	-0.2	-65	-0.1	172	0.4	-58	-0.2	-88	-0.2
	Change %	0.7		-3.4		-0.3		0.6		-3.4		-1.0	
	Change on year	521	0.6	-172	-0.6	-20	-0.2	446	0.9	-173	-0.6	-172	-0.5
	Change %	1.7		-9.2		-0.1		1.5		-9.4		-1.9	
Men		MGSA	MGSS	MGSD	MGSY	MGSJ	YBTD	YBSF	MGSV	YBSI	YBTJ	YBSO	YBTM
	Oct-Dec 2012	15,950	64.1	1,419	8.2	7,512	30.2	15,347	76.4	1,400	8.4	3,340	16.6
	Oct-Dec 2013	16,138	64.4	1,321	7.6	7,612	30.4	15,490	76.9	1,303	7.8	3,338	16.6
	Oct-Dec 2014	16,427	65.0	1,039	6.0	7,793	30.9	15,745	78.0	1,025	6.1	3,418	16.9
	Jan-Mar 2015	16,570	65.5	1,006	5.7	7,729	30.5	15,845	78.4	990	5.9	3,368	16.7
	Apr-Jun 2015	16,499	65.1	1,014	5.8	7,838	30.9	15,808	78.2	1,001	6.0	3,410	16.9
	Jul-Sep 2015	16,607	65.4	957	5.4	7,834	30.8	15,894	78.5	943	5.6	3,398	16.8
	Oct-Dec 2015	**16,770**	**65.9**	**924**	**5.2**	**7,750**	**30.5**	**16,033**	**79.2**	**913**	**5.4**	**3,306**	**16.3**
	Change on quarter	163	0.5	-33	-0.2	-84	-0.3	139	0.7	-30	-0.2	-92	-0.5
	Change %	1.0		-3.4		-1.1		0.9		-3.2		-2.7	
	Change on year	343	0.9	-115	-0.8	-43	-0.4	288	1.2	-112	-0.7	-112	-0.6
	Change %	2.1		-11.1		-0.6		1.8		-10.9		-3.3	
Women		MGSB	MGST	MGSE	MGSZ	MGSK	YBTE	LF2H	LF25	LF2J	LF2R	LF2N	LF2T
	Oct-Dec 2012	13,959	53.2	1,110	7.4	11,150	42.5	13,580	66.5	1,106	7.5	5,742	28.1
	Oct-Dec 2013	14,150	53.7	1,027	6.8	11,188	42.4	13,723	67.1	1,015	6.9	5,709	27.9
	Oct-Dec 2014	14,469	54.6	822	5.4	11,223	42.3	14,024	68.5	819	5.5	5,635	27.5
	Jan-Mar 2015	14,527	54.7	821	5.3	11,203	42.2	14,056	68.6	815	5.5	5,615	27.4
	Apr-Jun 2015	14,535	54.7	838	5.5	11,215	42.2	14,086	68.7	828	5.6	5,580	27.2
	Jul-Sep 2015	14,605	54.9	793	5.1	11,227	42.2	14,149	69.0	785	5.3	5,570	27.2
	Oct-Dec 2015	**14,647**	**54.9**	**766**	**5.0**	**11,247**	**42.2**	**14,182**	**69.1**	**758**	**5.1**	**5,574**	**27.2**
	Change on quarter	42	0.0	-27	-0.1	20	0.0	33	0.1	-27	-0.2	4	0.0
	Change %	0.3		-3.4		0.2		0.2		-3.4		0.1	
	Change on year	178	0.3	-56	-0.4	24	-0.1	158	0.6	-61	-0.4	-61	-0.3
	Change %	1.2		-6.8		0.2		1.1		-7.4		-1.1	

Aged 16-17 / Aged 18-24

		Employment Level	Employment Rate	Unemployment Level	Unemployment Rate	Inactivity Level	Inactivity Rate	Employment Level	Employment Rate	Unemployment Level	Unemployment Rate	Inactivity Level	Inactivity Rate
People		YBTO	YBUA	YBVH	YBVK	YCAS	LWEX	YBTR	YBUD	YBVN	YBVQ	YCAV	LWFA
	Oct-Dec 2012	334	22.1	201	37.6	976	64.6	3,402	58.2	787	18.8	1,652	28.6
	Oct-Dec 2013	328	21.7	188	36.4	993	65.8	3,402	58.4	740	17.9	1,680	28.9
	Oct-Dec 2014	346	23.2	157	31.2	986	66.3	3,494	60.2	583	14.3	1,722	29.7
	Jan-Mar 2015	353	23.8	148	29.5	981	66.2	3,535	61.0	588	14.3	1,669	28.8
	Apr-Jun 2015	354	24.0	148	29.5	973	66.0	3,526	61.0	591	14.3	1,667	28.8
	Jul-Sep 2015	369	25.1	135	26.8	963	65.7	3,577	62.0	518	12.7	1,674	29.0
	Oct-Dec 2015	**359**	**24.6**	**131**	**26.8**	**969**	**66.4**	**3,601**	**62.6**	**491**	**12.0**	**1,661**	**28.9**
	Change on quarter	-10	-0.5	-4	0.0	6	0.7	24	0.6	-27	-0.7	-13	-0.1
	Change %	-2.7		-3.0		0.6		0.7		-5.2		-0.8	
	Change on year	13	1.4	-26	-4.4	-17	0.1	107	2.4	-92	-2.3	-61	-0.8
	Change %	3.8		-16.6		-1.7		3.1		-15.8		-3.5	
Men		YBTP	YBUB	YBVI	YBVL	YCAT	LWEY	YBTS	YBUE	YBVO	YBVR	YCAW	LWFB
	Oct-Dec 2012	145	18.7	110	43.2	521	67.2	1,742	59.1	463	21.0	742	25.2
	Oct-Dec 2013	148	19.1	98	39.9	528	68.2	1,743	59.1	444	20.3	761	25.8
	Oct-Dec 2014	150	19.7	82	35.4	529	69.5	1,811	61.6	340	15.8	791	26.9
	Jan-Mar 2015	147	19.4	88	37.4	524	69.1	1,839	62.6	341	15.6	757	25.8
	Apr-Jun 2015	150	19.9	82	35.4	522	69.2	1,810	61.7	344	16.0	780	26.6
	Jul-Sep 2015	157	21.0	77	33.0	516	68.7	1,860	63.5	292	13.6	775	26.5
	Oct-Dec 2015	**170**	**22.8**	**71**	**29.3**	**506**	**67.8**	**1,865**	**63.9**	**283**	**13.2**	**772**	**26.4**
	Change on quarter	13	1.8	-6	-3.7	-10	-0.9	5	0.4	-9	-0.4	-3	-0.1
	Change %	8.3		-7.8		-1.9		0.3		-3.1		-0.4	
	Change on year	20	3.1	-11	-6.1	-23	-1.7	54	2.3	-57	-2.6	-19	-0.5
	Change %	13.3		-13.4		-4.3		3.0		-16.8		-2.4	
Women		YBTQ	YBUC	YBVJ	YBVM	YCAU	LWEZ	YBTT	YBUF	YBVP	YBVS	YCAX	LWFC
	Oct-Dec 2012	189	25.7	91	32.5	455	61.9	1,660	57.4	324	16.3	910	31.4
	Oct-Dec 2013	180	24.5	90	33.3	466	63.3	1,659	57.7	296	15.2	919	32.0
	Oct-Dec 2014	195	26.9	75	27.6	457	62.9	1,683	58.9	244	12.6	932	32.6
	Jan-Mar 2015	206	28.5	60	22.6	457	63.2	1,696	59.4	246	12.7	912	31.9
	Apr-Jun 2015	204	28.3	65	24.3	451	62.6	1,717	60.2	246	12.6	887	31.1
	May-Jul 2014	211	29.5	58	21.4	447	62.5	1,717	60.4	226	11.6	899	31.6
	Oct-Dec 2015	**189**	**26.5**	**61**	**24.3**	**463**	**65.0**	**1,736**	**61.3**	**208**	**10.7**	**889**	**31.4**
	Change on quarter	-22	-3.0	3	2.9	16	2.5	19	0.9	-18	-0.9	-10	-0.2
	Change %	-10.4		5.2		3.6		1.1		-8.0		-1.1	
	Change on year	-6	-0.4	-14	-3.3	6	2.1	53	2.4	-36	-1.9	-43	-1.2
	Change %	-3.1		-18.7		1.3		3.1		-14.8		-4.6	

Source: Labour Force Survey

Labour market statistics enquiries: labour.market@ons.gsi.gov.uk

Note: When comparing quarterly changes ONS recommends comparing with the previous non-overlapping 3-month average time period (eg, compare Apr-Jun with Jan-Mar, not with Mar-May).

4.3 Employment: by sex and age: United Kingdom

United Kingdom (thousands) seasonally adjusted

	Aged 25-34						Aged 35-49					
	Employment		Unemployment		Inactivity		Employment		Unemployment		Inactivity	
	Level	Rate	Level	Rate	Level	Rate	Level	Rate	Level	Rate	Level	Rate
People	YBTU	YBUG	YCGM	YCGP	YCAY	LWFD	YBTX	YBUJ	YCGS	YCGV	YCBB	LWFG
Oct-Dec 2012	6,723	78.8	531	7.3	1,274	14.9	10,771	82.0	607	5.3	1,755	13.4
Oct-Dec 2013	6,884	79.7	492	6.7	1,260	14.6	10,663	82.1	529	4.7	1,803	13.9
Oct-Dec 2014	7,006	80.5	390	5.3	1,308	15.0	10,794	83.7	414	3.7	1,685	13.1
Jan-Mar 2015	7,045	80.8	363	4.9	1,311	15.0	10,780	83.7	420	3.8	1,672	13.0
Apr-Jun 2015	7,047	80.7	382	5.1	1,304	14.9	10,728	83.5	416	3.7	1,707	13.3
Jul-Sep 2015	7,114	81.3	369	4.9	1,269	14.5	10,672	83.2	399	3.6	1,761	13.7
Oct-Dec 2015	**7,166**	**81.7**	**387**	**5.1**	**1,220**	**13.9**	**10,701**	**83.5**	**362**	**3.3**	**1,751**	**13.7**
Change on quarter	*52*	*0.4*	*18*	*0.2*	*-49*	*-0.6*	*29*	*0.3*	*-37*	*-0.3*	*-10*	*0.0*
Change %	*0.7*		*4.9*		*-3.9*		*0.3*		*-9.3*		*-0.6*	
Change on year	*160*	*1.2*	*-3*	*-0.2*	*-88*	*-1.1*	*-93*	*-0.2*	*-52*	*-0.4*	*66*	*0.6*
Change %	*2.3*		*-0.8*		*-6.7*		*-0.9*		*-12.6*		*3.9*	
Men	YBTV	YBUH	YCGN	YCGQ	YCAZ	LWFE	YBTY	YBUK	YCGT	YCGW	YCBC	LWFH
Oct-Dec 2012	3,655	86.5	281	7.1	290	6.9	5,698	88.0	296	4.9	484	7.5
Oct-Dec 2013	3,726	86.9	280	7.0	280	6.5	5,636	87.9	264	4.5	510	8.0
Oct-Dec 2014	3,785	87.3	207	5.2	341	7.9	5,685	89.4	214	3.6	462	7.3
Jan-Mar 2015	3,817	87.9	196	4.9	331	7.6	5,702	89.8	200	3.4	449	7.1
Apr-Jun 2015	3,797	87.2	215	5.4	343	7.9	5,672	89.4	191	3.3	478	7.5
Jul-Sep 2015	3,844	88.0	195	4.8	330	7.5	5,635	89.0	196	3.4	500	7.9
Oct-Dec 2015	**3,891**	**88.8**	**202**	**4.9**	**291**	**6.6**	**5,658**	**89.5**	**174**	**3.0**	**491**	**7.8**
Change on quarter	*47*	*0.8*	*7*	*0.1*	*-39*	*-0.9*	*23*	*0.5*	*-22*	*-0.4*	*-9*	*-0.1*
Change %	*1.2*		*3.6*		*-11.8*		*0.4*		*-11.2*		*-1.8*	
Change on year	*106*	*1.5*	*-5*	*-0.3*	*-50*	*-1.3*	*-27*	*0.1*	*-40*	*-0.6*	*29*	*0.5*
Change %	*2.8*		*-2.4*		*-14.7*		*-0.5*		*-18.7*		*6.3*	
Women	YBTW	YBUI	YCGO	YCGR	YCBA	LWFF	YBTZ	YBUL	YCGU	YCGX	YCBD	LWFI
Oct-Dec 2012	3,069	71.3	250	7.5	984	22.9	5,073	76.2	311	5.8	1,272	19.1
Oct-Dec 2013	3,158	72.6	211	6.3	980	22.5	5,027	76.3	266	5.0	1,292	19.6
Oct-Dec 2014	3,222	73.7	183	5.4	968	22.1	5,109	78.2	200	3.8	1,223	18.7
Jan-Mar 2015	3,228	73.8	167	4.9	980	22.4	5,078	77.9	220	4.2	1,223	18.8
Apr-Jun 2015	3,250	74.2	166	4.9	961	22.0	5,056	77.7	224	4.3	1,229	18.9
Jul-Sep 2015	3,270	74.6	174	5.0	940	21.4	5,036	77.5	203	3.9	1,261	19.4
Oct-Dec 2015	**3,274**	**74.6**	**186**	**5.4**	**929**	**21.2**	**5,043**	**77.7**	**188**	**3.6**	**1,260**	**19.4**
Change on quarter	*4*	*0.0*	*12*	*0.4*	*-11*	*-0.2*	*7*	*0.2*	*-15*	*-0.3*	*-1*	*0.0*
Change %	*0.1*		*6.9*		*-1.2*		*0.1*		*-7.4*		*-0.1*	
Change on year	*52*	*0.9*	*3*	*0.0*	*-39*	*-0.9*	*-66*	*-0.5*	*-12*	*-0.2*	*37*	*0.7*
Change %	*1.6*		*1.6*		*-4.0*		*-1.3*		*-6.0*		*3.0*	

	Aged 50-64						Age 65+					
	Employment		Unemployment		Inactivity		Employment		Unemployment		Inactivity	
	Level	Rate	Level	Rate	Level	Rate	Level	Rate	Level	Rate	Level	Rate
People	LF26	LF2U	LF28	LF2E	LF2A	LF2W	LFK4	LFK6	K5HU	K5HW	LFL4	LFL6
Oct-Dec 2012	7,697	66.9	381	4.7	3,425	29.8	983	9.3	22	2.2	9,580	90.5
Oct-Dec 2013	7,937	68.3	369	4.4	3,310	28.5	1,075	9.9	30	2.7	9,753	89.8
Oct-Dec 2014	8,129	69.0	301	3.6	3,350	28.4	1,127	10.1	18	1.5	9,963	89.7
Jan-Mar 2015	8,189	69.2	286	3.4	3,350	28.3	1,196	10.7	22	1.8	9,950	89.1
Apr-Jun 2015	8,239	69.4	293	3.4	3,339	28.1	1,140	10.2	23	2.0	10,063	89.6
Jul-Sep 2015	8,312	69.7	307	3.6	3,300	27.7	1,168	10.4	21	1.8	10,093	89.5
Oct-Dec 2015	**8,389**	**70.1**	**299**	**3.4**	**3,278**	**27.4**	**1,201**	**10.6**	**18**	**1.5**	**10,116**	**89.2**
Change on quarter	*77*	*0.4*	*-8*	*-0.2*	*-22*	*-0.3*	*33*	*0.2*	*-3*	*-0.3*	*23*	*-0.3*
Change %	*0.9*		*-2.6*		*-0.7*		*2.8*		*-14.3*		*0.2*	
Change on year	*260*	*1.1*	*-2*	*-0.2*	*-72*	*-1.0*	*74*	*0.5*	*0*	*0.0*	*153*	*-0.5*
Change %	*3.2*		*-0.7*		*-2.1*		*6.6*		*0.0*		*1.5*	
Men	MGUX	YBUN	MGVM	MGXF	MGWB	LWFK	MGVA	YBUQ	MGVP	MGXI	MGWE	LWFN
Oct-Dec 2012	4,108	72.6	250	5.7	1,303	23.0	603	12.6	19	3.0	4,171	87.0
Oct-Dec 2013	4,238	74.2	217	4.9	1,259	22.0	648	13.1	17	2.6	4,274	86.5
Oct-Dec 2014	4,313	74.5	183	4.1	1,295	22.4	682	13.4	14	2.0	4,375	86.3
Jan-Mar 2015	4,340	74.7	165	3.7	1,308	22.5	725	14.5	16	2.2	4,361	85.5
Apr-Jun 2015	4,380	75.1	168	3.7	1,287	22.1	691	13.5	14	1.9	4,428	86.3
Jul-Sep 2015	4,397	75.1	182	4.0	1,277	21.8	713	13.8	13	1.9	4,436	85.9
Oct-Dec 2015	**4,449**	**75.7**	**185**	**4.0**	**1,246**	**21.2**	**737**	**14.2**	**11**	**1.4**	**4,444**	**85.6**
Change on quarter	*52*	*0.6*	*3*	*0.0*	*-31*	*-0.6*	*24*	*0.4*	*-2*	*-0.5*	*8*	*-0.3*
Change %	*1.2*		*1.6*		*-2.4*		*3.4*		*-15.4*		*0.2*	
Change on year	*136*	*1.2*	*2*	*-0.1*	*-49*	*-1.2*	*55*	*0.8*	*-3*	*-0.6*	*69*	*-0.7*
Change %	*3.2*		*1.1*		*-3.8*		*8.1*		*-21.4*		*1.6*	
Women	LF27	LF2V	LF29	LF2F	LF2B	LF2X	LFK5	LFK7	K5HV	K5HX	LFL5	LFL7
Oct-Dec 2012	3,589	61.4	131	3.5	2,121	36.3	380	6.6	*	*	5,408	93.4
Oct-Dec 2013	3,699	62.7	152	3.9	2,051	34.8	427	7.2	13	2.9	5,479	92.6
Oct-Dec 2014	3,815	63.7	118	3.0	2,056	34.3	445	7.4	*	*	5,588	92.6
Jan-Mar 2015	3,849	64.0	121	3.1	2,043	34.0	471	7.8	6	1.2	5,589	92.1
Apr-Jun 2015	3,860	63.9	125	3.1	2,052	34.0	449	7.4	10	2.1	5,634	92.5
Jul-Sep 2015	3,915	64.6	125	3.1	2,023	33.4	456	7.5	7	1.6	5,656	92.4
Oct-Dec 2015	**3,940**	**64.7**	**115**	**2.8**	**2,032**	**33.4**	**465**	**7.6**	**8**	**1.6**	**5,672**	**92.3**
Change on quarter	*25*	*0.1*	*-10*	*-0.3*	*9*	*0.0*	*9*	*0.1*	*1*	*0.0*	*16*	*-0.1*
Change %	*0.6*		*-8.0*		*0.4*		*2.0*		*14.3*		*0.3*	
Change on year	*125*	*1.0*	*-3*	*-0.2*	*-24*	*-0.9*	*20*	*0.2*	*0*	*0.0*	*84*	*-0.3*
Change %	*3.3*		*-2.5*		*-1.2*		*4.5*		*0.0*		*1.5*	

Source: Labour Force Survey

* grossed up total less than 9,500.

Labour market statistics enquiries: labour.market@ons.gsi.gov.uk

Note: When comparing quarterly changes ONS recommends comparing with the previous non-overlapping 3-month average time period (eg, compare Apr-Jun with Jan-Mar, not with Mar-May).

4.4: All in employment by industry Sector

United Kingdom (thousands) not seasonally adjusted

Standard Industrial Classification (SIC) 2007

People	All in employment¹	Public sector	Private sector	Agriculture, forestry & fishing A	Mining, energy and water supply B, D, E	Manufacturing C	Construction F	Wholesale, retail & repair of motor vehicles G	Transport & storage H	Accommodation & food services I	Information & communication J	Financial & insurance activities K	Real estate activities L	Professional, scientific & technical activities M	Administrative & support services N	Public admin & defence; social security O	Education P	Human health & social work activities Q	Other services R, S, T
Jan-Mar 2006	28,966	7,130	21,735	273	404	3,242	2,431	4,163	1,564	1,286	1,014	1,270	252	1,835	1,276	2,020	2,836	3,576	1,426
Apr-Jun 2006	29,032	7,096	21,824	268	414	3,285	2,460	4,117	1,555	1,340	1,024	1,259	263	1,806	1,280	1,990	2,849	3,579	1,446
Jul-Sep 2006	29,289	7,018	22,165	293	424	3,280	2,510	4,154	1,574	1,382	1,045	1,252	248	1,824	1,323	1,970	2,758	3,630	1,528
Oct-Dec 2006	29,276	6,940	22,216	302	436	3,234	2,542	4,198	1,585	1,329	1,057	1,270	248	1,825	1,328	1,962	2,813	3,522	1,508
Jan-Mar 2007	29,108	6,954	22,040	288	450	3,216	2,527	4,120	1,566	1,324	1,056	1,263	257	1,874	1,304	1,980	2,798	3,500	1,473
Apr-Jun 2007	29,242	6,987	22,131	294	464	3,281	2,544	4,034	1,559	1,371	1,051	1,272	245	1,883	1,347	1,985	2,823	3,461	1,513
Jul-Sep 2007	29,525	6,919	22,466	297	469	3,269	2,558	4,090	1,556	1,406	1,062	1,304	266	1,912	1,432	1,990	2,782	3,505	1,512
Oct-Dec 2007	29,640	7,018	22,479	307	461	3,216	2,537	4,187	1,576	1,395	1,019	1,312	279	1,952	1,399	1,996	2,840	3,531	1,517
Jan-Mar 2008	29,596	7,047	22,404	334	452	3,148	2,535	4,184	1,605	1,382	1,024	1,288	263	1,939	1,398	2,011	2,847	3,566	1,509
Apr-Jun 2008	29,637	7,101	22,383	321	446	3,087	2,512	4,195	1,590	1,355	1,033	1,287	253	1,969	1,417	2,035	2,861	3,642	1,519
Jul-Sep 2008	29,685	7,039	22,508	313	463	3,068	2,583	4,248	1,606	1,355	1,063	1,272	259	1,919	1,404	2,033	2,805	3,648	1,533
Oct-Dec 2008	29,593	7,167	22,289	306	507	2,981	2,564	4,221	1,626	1,335	1,036	1,244	252	1,849	1,347	2,037	2,848	3,748	1,584
Jan-Mar 2009	29,277	7,224	21,913	322	489	2,857	2,482	4,107	1,571	1,324	1,035	1,227	273	1,842	1,309	2,009	2,919	3,772	1,579
Apr-Jun 2009	29,003	7,238	21,624	311	483	2,777	2,385	3,989	1,510	1,360	1,015	1,235	268	1,882	1,301	1,967	2,929	3,739	1,583
Jul-Sep 2009	29,170	7,278	21,745	329	491	2,813	2,311	4,031	1,463	1,428	1,020	1,246	265	1,890	1,301	1,977	2,960	3,778	1,599
Oct-Dec 2009	29,167	7,324	21,691	323	482	2,799	2,311	4,017	1,455	1,406	1,014	1,223	254	1,886	1,328	1,944	3,045	3,846	1,579
Jan-Mar 2010	28,924	7,255	21,488	336	472	2,815	2,208	3,943	1,462	1,388	1,011	1,210	263	1,882	1,319	1,930	3,062	3,824	1,549
Apr-Jun 2010	29,110	7,325	21,586	341	463	2,875	2,207	4,004	1,443	1,461	979	1,175	262	1,893	1,326	1,925	3,129	3,848	1,532
Jul-Sep 2010	29,484	7,298	21,973	369	474	2,888	2,234	4,112	1,483	1,503	1,045	1,165	301	1,852	1,341	1,925	3,120	3,821	1,594
Oct-Dec 2010	29,390	7,315	21,929	366	489	2,902	2,238	4,082	1,436	1,427	1,030	1,171	300	1,882	1,379	1,867	3,120	3,884	1,555
Jan-Mar 2011	29,350	7,315	21,842	357	497	2,860	2,212	4,034	1,451	1,417	1,059	1,179	299	1,857	1,299	1,875	3,121	3,967	1,544
Apr-Jun 2011	29,367	7,183	22,021	342	521	2,868	2,198	4,051	1,445	1,458	1,073	1,173	308	1,851	1,321	1,844	3,129	3,931	1,587
Jul-Sep 2011	29,376	7,009	22,216	370	519	2,842	2,237	4,019	1,428	1,498	1,061	1,192	300	1,888	1,339	1,852	2,986	3,981	1,639
Oct-Dec 2011	29,405	6,970	22,276	356	527	2,884	2,172	4,078	1,432	1,499	1,083	1,215	293	1,898	1,353	1,864	3,021	3,927	1,583
Jan-Mar 2012	29,365	6,952	22,208	374	534	2,850	2,148	4,018	1,430	1,438	1,124	1,199	333	1,903	1,369	1,847	3,088	3,865	1,554
Apr-Jun 2012	29,587	6,847	22,517	353	532	2,920	2,171	4,103	1,416	1,496	1,098	1,229	328	1,945	1,357	1,803	3,078	3,871	1,574
Jul-Sep 2012	29,851	6,884	22,721	356	547	2,934	2,175	4,129	1,457	1,527	1,113	1,216	329	1,983	1,372	1,827	3,021	3,948	1,607
Oct-Dec 2012	29,974	6,985	22,751	316	518	2,910	2,149	4,105	1,482	1,523	1,146	1,169	346	1,967	1,376	1,824	3,141	3,992	1,592
Jan-Mar 2013	29,750	6,990	22,503	304	537	2,921	2,101	4,031	1,487	1,504	1,161	1,150	344	2,000	1,354	1,852	3,115	3,986	1,587
Apr-Jun 2013	29,860	6,965	22,637	308	526	2,868	2,155	4,021	1,456	1,505	1,162	1,144	344	2,023	1,423	1,864	3,104	4,029	1,592
Jul-Sep 2013	30,195	7,013	22,932	324	510	2,954	2,188	4,000	1,520	1,566	1,177	1,177	326	2,073	1,450	1,880	3,082	4,036	1,642
Oct-Dec 2013	30,362	6,905	23,225	322	511	2,957	2,200	4,098	1,543	1,555	1,198	1,171	340	2,095	1,437	1,817	3,095	4,068	1,639
Jan-Mar 2014	30,446	6,935	23,310	379	508	2,945	2,228	4,063	1,490	1,579	1,150	1,171	369	2,168	1,388	1,851	3,108	4,076	1,663
Apr-Jun 2014	30,627	6,937	23,495	395	511	2,997	2,216	3,994	1,466	1,633	1,174	1,157	358	2,141	1,441	1,806	3,219	4,105	1,693
Jul-Sep 2014	30,920	6,915	23,808	386	543	3,020	2,242	3,976	1,470	1,666	1,237	1,207	340	2,139	1,487	1,853	3,198	4,062	1,781
Oct-Dec 2014	31,022	6,903	23,916	375	537	3,078	2,268	4,125	1,479	1,595	1,250	1,182	339	2,136	1,452	1,798	3,234	4,142	1,753
Jan-Mar 2015	31,082	6,982	23,922	348	567	3,007	2,266	4,068	1,512	1,618	1,276	1,184	334	2,189	1,415	1,845	3,286	4,170	1,766
Apr-Jun 2015	31,047	6,932	23,923	340	552	3,018	2,198	4,001	1,537	1,665	1,243	1,222	339	2,147	1,500	1,831	3,265	4,156	1,758
Jul-Sep 2015	31,426	6,852	24,386	349	553	2,969	2,225	4,097	1,576	1,700	1,276	1,254	348	2,174	1,540	1,840	3,267	4,162	1,813
Oct-Dec 2015	31,617	6,900	24,531	383	546	2,991	2,265	4,209	1,610	1,639	1,260	1,279	347	2,205	1,564	1,878	3,329	4,130	1,756
Change on year	595	-3	615	8	10	-86	-3	84	131	45	11	97	8	69	111	80	95	-12	3
Change %	1.9	0.0	2.6	2.1	1.8	-2.8	-0.1	2.0	8.8	2.8	0.8	8.2	2.3	3.3	7.7	4.4	2.9	-0.3	0.2

Source: Labour Force Survey

4.4: All in employment by industry Sector

United Kingdom (thousands) not seasonally adjusted

Standard Industrial Classification (SIC) 2007

Men	All in employment[1]	Public sector	Private sector	Agriculture, forestry & fishing A	Mining, energy and water supply B, D, E	Manufacturing C	Construction F	Wholesale, retail & repair of motor vehicles G	Transport & storage H	Accommodation & food services I	Information & communication J	Financial & insurance activities K	Real estate activities L	Professional, scientific & technical activities M	Administrative & support services N	Public admin & defence, social security O	Education P	Human health & social work activities Q	Other services R, S, T
Jan-Mar 2006	15,541	2,563	12,912	199	322	2,491	2,105	2,077	1,261	584	723	637	134	1,023	714	1,015	809	754	629
Apr-Jun 2006	15,603	2,531	13,007	201	322	2,507	2,127	2,082	1,264	603	727	639	144	998	706	994	817	750	663
Jul-Sep 2006	15,821	2,513	13,244	218	328	2,493	2,183	2,142	1,266	629	742	628	124	1,028	712	996	785	777	711
Oct-Dec 2006	15,790	2,449	13,276	221	338	2,463	2,212	2,157	1,262	580	751	646	131	1,024	733	989	795	731	688
Jan-Mar 2007	15,691	2,436	13,197	204	346	2,452	2,210	2,135	1,242	587	758	662	125	1,024	735	1,001	770	717	661
Apr-Jun 2007	15,789	2,459	13,259	208	359	2,506	2,216	2,084	1,244	618	749	658	116	1,024	771	991	788	709	684
Jul-Sep 2007	15,964	2,423	13,465	214	363	2,464	2,244	2,103	1,245	647	754	681	126	1,052	827	1,005	784	703	686
Oct-Dec 2007	15,987	2,444	13,467	210	358	2,429	2,225	2,131	1,268	648	713	703	133	1,064	823	1,021	799	720	678
Jan-Mar 2008	15,938	2,483	13,374	223	352	2,379	2,204	2,132	1,293	631	722	692	130	1,060	804	1,039	786	756	664
Apr-Jun 2008	15,961	2,509	13,371	222	349	2,354	2,181	2,144	1,274	633	730	675	131	1,082	823	1,053	780	800	659
Jul-Sep 2008	15,990	2,488	13,422	218	370	2,316	2,249	2,177	1,275	620	752	648	143	1,066	802	1,037	741	805	704
Oct-Dec 2008	15,909	2,538	13,293	219	409	2,252	2,233	2,161	1,292	616	744	629	137	1,022	774	1,028	777	830	717
Jan-Mar 2009	15,670	2,572	13,020	247	390	2,144	2,213	2,103	1,255	604	722	624	132	1,069	715	1,003	803	828	722
Apr-Jun 2009	15,464	2,558	12,828	240	383	2,102	2,127	2,056	1,208	620	717	635	124	1,105	710	985	791	812	710
Jul-Sep 2009	15,526	2,572	12,867	252	389	2,128	2,065	2,089	1,171	645	725	642	122	1,094	695	996	831	805	726
Oct-Dec 2009	15,477	2,581	12,814	246	384	2,122	2,070	2,069	1,173	633	722	637	115	1,064	706	995	868	820	719
Jan-Mar 2010	15,326	2,533	12,694	252	380	2,154	1,971	2,037	1,181	643	710	628	118	1,089	707	984	857	792	693
Apr-Jun 2010	15,493	2,576	12,807	264	373	2,207	1,961	2,094	1,160	681	692	622	113	1,092	725	1,003	864	810	697
Jul-Sep 2010	15,773	2,601	13,047	284	381	2,213	1,992	2,159	1,173	684	748	624	132	1,070	760	994	872	804	735
Oct-Dec 2010	15,720	2,582	13,035	283	394	2,214	1,991	2,147	1,133	668	748	640	130	1,097	788	949	843	852	702
Jan-Mar 2011	15,620	2,582	12,930	270	413	2,179	1,955	2,115	1,167	643	756	647	133	1,091	724	963	848	855	697
Apr-Jun 2011	15,685	2,547	13,050	262	428	2,170	1,940	2,112	1,172	651	766	644	144	1,100	752	913	887	863	725
Jul-Sep 2011	15,666	2,453	13,136	271	422	2,167	2,005	2,082	1,149	678	752	650	154	1,105	741	904	842	851	758
Oct-Dec 2011	15,672	2,436	13,158	261	424	2,196	1,939	2,124	1,154	710	788	654	151	1,104	732	922	838	843	714
Jan-Mar 2012	15,649	2,426	13,113	270	434	2,152	1,910	2,093	1,158	678	812	635	177	1,116	741	912	867	823	696
Apr-Jun 2012	15,821	2,359	13,329	257	436	2,203	1,928	2,155	1,140	674	802	660	162	1,146	745	889	867	836	735
Jul-Sep 2012	15,968	2,385	13,423	256	440	2,219	1,942	2,159	1,173	681	803	671	156	1,151	754	922	850	841	746
Oct-Dec 2012	15,985	2,404	13,430	235	404	2,198	1,916	2,161	1,190	677	814	642	164	1,138	765	952	897	853	724
Jan-Mar 2013	15,800	2,378	13,261	220	418	2,226	1,858	2,082	1,202	696	827	637	169	1,177	743	955	866	828	706
Apr-Jun 2013	15,888	2,359	13,372	234	419	2,197	1,894	2,092	1,175	701	848	634	163	1,183	782	953	836	849	715
Jul-Sep 2013	16,122	2,403	13,573	236	409	2,241	1,912	2,109	1,227	750	849	650	149	1,211	804	956	857	841	739
Oct-Dec 2013	16,173	2,322	13,724	233	409	2,225	1,936	2,126	1,251	733	842	653	144	1,242	805	918	847	860	763
Jan-Mar 2014	16,198	2,344	13,743	271	414	2,199	1,947	2,130	1,207	756	819	666	161	1,270	769	927	842	872	767
Apr-Jun 2014	16,289	2,356	13,822	286	414	2,240	1,946	2,064	1,171	764	850	657	152	1,262	816	922	885	889	780
Jul-Sep 2014	16,474	2,373	13,981	291	437	2,256	1,968	2,067	1,152	788	891	677	162	1,255	818	947	902	873	823
Oct-Dec 2014	16,484	2,384	13,982	279	422	2,308	2,004	2,139	1,141	729	892	657	168	1,253	792	924	929	889	794
Jan-Mar 2015	16,531	2,410	14,024	267	444	2,264	1,999	2,141	1,159	755	901	638	173	1,261	776	945	949	918	814
Apr-Jun 2015	16,496	2,360	14,025	259	439	2,276	1,933	2,106	1,195	779	894	670	169	1,232	813	934	940	906	802
Jul-Sep 2015	16,745	2,352	14,293	252	442	2,224	1,969	2,165	1,231	811	930	686	173	1,227	820	915	972	931	846
Oct-Dec 2015	16,876	2,365	14,407	267	432	2,269	2,005	2,225	1,277	790	925	707	173	1,241	834	925	977	912	790
Change on year	392	-19	426	-12	10	-39	1	86	136	62	32	50	5	-13	42	2	48	23	-4
Change %	2.4	-0.8	3.0	-4.3	2.4	-1.7	0.1	4.0	11.9	8.4	3.6	7.6	3.2	-1.0	5.3	0.2	5.2	2.6	-0.6

Source: Labour Force Survey

4.4: All in employment by industry Sector

United Kingdom (thousands) not seasonally adjusted

Standard Industrial Classification (SIC) 2007

Women	All in employment[1]	Public sector	Private sector	Agriculture, forestry & fishing A	Mining, energy and water supply B,D,E	Manufacturing C	Construction F	Wholesale, retail & repair of motor vehicles G	Transport & storage H	Accommodation & food services I	Information & communication J	Financial & insurance activities K	Real estate activities L	Professional, scientific & technical activities M	Administrative & support services N	Public admin & defence; social security O	Education P	Human health & social work activities Q	Other services R, S, T
Jan-Mar 2006	13,424	4,566	8,823	75	82	752	326	2,086	303	703	291	632	119	812	562	1,006	2,026	2,822	797
Apr-Jun 2006	13,428	4,565	8,817	67	92	778	333	2,035	292	737	296	620	119	808	573	996	2,032	2,829	783
Jul-Sep 2006	13,468	4,505	8,922	75	96	787	327	2,012	308	753	303	624	123	796	611	975	1,973	2,853	817
Oct-Dec 2006	13,486	4,491	8,939	81	99	771	331	2,040	322	749	306	624	117	801	596	973	2,018	2,790	820
Jan-Mar 2007	13,417	4,519	8,842	85	104	764	328	1,985	315	737	298	601	131	851	569	979	2,029	2,783	812
Apr-Jun 2007	13,453	4,528	8,872	87	105	775	314	1,950	311	753	301	614	129	858	576	993	2,035	2,752	830
Jul-Sep 2007	13,561	4,496	9,001	83	105	805	312	1,986	308	759	308	623	139	860	604	986	1,998	2,802	826
Oct-Dec 2007	13,653	4,574	9,012	98	103	787	331	2,056	311	747	306	609	145	888	576	975	2,041	2,811	839
Jan-Mar 2008	13,658	4,563	9,030	112	100	769	331	2,052	316	751	302	595	133	879	594	972	2,061	2,810	845
Apr-Jun 2008	13,677	4,593	9,011	99	97	733	334	2,051	332	722	302	612	122	887	594	982	2,081	2,842	860
Jul-Sep 2008	13,695	4,551	9,086	95	93	753	331	2,071	334	734	310	624	117	853	602	996	2,065	2,843	828
Oct-Dec 2008	13,683	4,629	8,996	88	98	728	270	2,060	316	719	292	614	115	827	574	1,009	2,071	2,917	866
Jan-Mar 2009	13,606	4,652	8,894	75	99	713	258	2,004	302	719	313	603	142	773	594	1,006	2,116	2,944	857
Apr-Jun 2009	13,539	4,680	8,796	71	100	674	246	1,933	291	740	298	600	145	778	591	982	2,138	2,927	872
Jul-Sep 2009	13,644	4,705	8,878	77	102	686	241	1,942	282	783	295	605	143	796	606	981	2,130	2,973	873
Oct-Dec 2009	13,690	4,743	8,877	77	98	677	237	1,948	281	773	292	586	139	822	622	950	2,177	3,026	860
Jan-Mar 2010	13,597	4,721	8,794	84	92	661	246	1,906	283	745	301	583	144	793	613	946	2,206	3,032	856
Apr-Jun 2010	13,616	4,748	8,780	78	89	668	241	1,910	309	780	287	553	149	801	601	923	2,266	3,039	835
Jul-Sep 2010	13,710	4,697	8,926	86	93	676	247	1,953	303	819	297	542	169	782	581	931	2,247	3,017	859
Oct-Dec 2010	13,670	4,696	8,894	84	95	688	257	1,935	285	759	281	531	171	785	592	918	2,277	3,032	853
Jan-Mar 2011	13,730	4,732	8,912	87	85	681	258	1,919	273	774	303	532	167	766	575	913	2,273	3,112	847
Apr-Jun 2011	13,682	4,636	8,972	80	93	698	232	1,939	279	807	307	529	164	751	569	932	2,242	3,068	862
Jul-Sep 2011	13,710	4,556	9,080	98	96	675	234	1,937	278	820	308	542	147	783	598	948	2,144	3,130	881
Oct-Dec 2011	13,733	4,534	9,118	95	103	688	237	1,954	272	789	295	561	143	794	621	942	2,183	3,084	869
Jan-Mar 2012	13,716	4,526	9,095	104	100	698	243	1,924	275	760	312	564	156	787	628	935	2,221	3,042	858
Apr-Jun 2012	13,766	4,488	9,188	96	97	718	233	1,948	284	823	297	569	166	799	611	914	2,211	3,035	839
Jul-Sep 2012	13,883	4,498	9,298	100	107	715	233	1,970	291	846	310	545	173	832	619	905	2,172	3,107	861
Oct-Dec 2012	13,989	4,581	9,321	80	114	712	244	1,945	285	846	332	527	182	830	611	872	2,244	3,139	867
Jan-Mar 2013	13,950	4,611	9,242	84	119	695	262	1,949	281	809	333	512	175	823	611	897	2,250	3,157	880
Apr-Jun 2013	13,973	4,606	9,266	74	107	670	276	1,929	292	803	314	509	180	840	641	911	2,268	3,181	877
Jul-Sep 2013	14,073	4,610	9,359	88	110	713	264	1,890	292	817	328	527	177	862	646	924	2,225	3,176	903
Oct-Dec 2013	14,189	4,583	9,501	88	102	732	274	1,972	283	822	356	518	196	898	632	899	2,248	3,209	876
Jan-Mar 2014	14,248	4,591	9,567	108	94	746	281	1,933	296	824	331	506	208	878	619	924	2,266	3,203	896
Apr-Jun 2014	14,338	4,581	9,673	109	96	757	270	1,930	318	869	324	500	207	884	626	884	2,334	3,215	913
Jul-Sep 2014	14,446	4,541	9,827	95	106	764	274	1,909	339	878	345	530	178	882	669	906	2,297	3,190	958
Oct-Dec 2014	14,538	4,519	9,935	96	115	769	265	1,985	353	866	358	525	171	928	660	874	2,305	3,253	959
Jan-Mar 2015	14,551	4,572	9,898	81	124	743	267	1,927	342	863	375	547	161	915	639	900	2,337	3,253	952
Apr-Jun 2015	14,552	4,571	9,899	81	113	742	265	1,895	345	886	349	552	170	946	687	898	2,325	3,250	955
Jul-Sep 2015	14,681	4,500	10,092	98	111	745	256	1,932	345	889	346	568	175	946	720	925	2,295	3,231	966
Oct-Dec 2015	14,741	4,534	10,124	116	114	722	260	1,983	333	849	336	571	173	964	730	952	2,352	3,218	967
Change on year	204	16	190	20	-1	-47	-4	-2	-5	-17	-22	47	2	82	70	78	47	-35	7
Change %	1.4	0.3	1.9	20.7	-0.5	-6.1	-1.6	-0.1	-1.6	-2.0	-6.1	8.9	1.3	9.3	10.6	8.9	2.0	-1.1	0.8

Source: Labour Force Survey

[1] The breakdown by industry sector for Q1 2009 onwards is not entirely consistent with those of previous quarters. This is because:
(a) LFS data on industrial activity were coded directly to SIC 1992 for all quarters up to and including Q4 2008 and then mapped to the new industrial classification, SIC 2007, according to the assumed relationship between the two classifications;
(b) data for Q1 2009 onwards have been coded directly to SIC 2007; and
(c) a new, automatic coding tool was introduced in January 2009.

The effect of these changes on the time series was significant for some of the industry sectors shown. Consequently some adjustments have been made to the pre-2009 estimates to account for the estimated combined effects of the new classification and the new coding tool. This also means that the pre-2009 estimates in this table are not the same as those obtained from LFS microdata.
More information and analysis of these effects are available in the Labour Force Survey User Guide (Volume 1) and from Labour Force Assessment Branch (tel 01633 455839 or email labour.market.assessment@ons.gov.uk).
[2] Includes people with workplace outside UK and those who did not state their industry.
[3] In the LFS the distinction between public and private sector is based on respondents' views about the organisation for which they work. The public sector estimates provided here do not correspond to the official Public Sector Employment estimates which are based on National Accounts definitions.
Totals may not sum due to rounding

4.5a International Comparisons of Employment and Unemployment

		Latest period	Employment rate (%)[1][2]	Change on year %				Latest Period	Unemployment rate (%)[3]	Change on month %	Change on year %
Employment rates as published by EUROSTAT: (not seasonally adjusted)						**Unemployment rates as published by EUROSTAT on 2 February 2016 (seasonally adjusted)**					
European Union (EU)						**European Union (EU)**					
Austria	YXSN	Jul-Sep 15	72.1	0.2		Austria	ZXDS	Dec 15	5.8	0.0	0.2
Belgium	YXSO	Jul-Sep 15	62.1	0.1		Belgium	ZXDI	Dec 15	7.9	0.0	-0.7
Bulgaria	A495	Jul-Sep 15	64.5	1.7		Bulgaria	A492	Dec 15	8.8	0.0	-1.4
Croatia	GUMI	Jul-Sep 15	57.5	0.6		Croatia	GUMJ	Dec 15	16.5	-0.1	-1.2
Cyprus	A4AC	Jul-Sep 15	62.2	-0.4		Cyprus	A4AN	Dec 15	15.7	0.0	-0.8
Czech Republic	A4AD	Jul-Sep 15	70.5	1.2		Czech Republic	A4AO	Dec 15	4.5	0.0	-1.3
Denmark	YXSP	Jul-Sep 15	73.7	0.0		Denmark	ZXDJ	Dec 15	6.0	0.0	-0.2
Estonia	A4AE	Jul-Sep 15	74.0	3.7		Estonia	A4AP	Nov 15	6.5	0.2	0.0
Finland	YXSQ	Jul-Sep 15	69.9	0.1		Finland	ZXDU	Dec 15	9.5	0.0	0.5
France	YXSR	Jul-Sep 15	64.1	0.0		France	ZXDN	Dec 15	10.2	0.0	-0.3
Germany	YXSS	Jul-Sep 15	74.2	0.0		Germany	ZXDK	Dec 15	4.5	0.0	-0.4
Greece	YXST	Jul-Sep 15	51.7	1.5		Greece	ZXDL	Oct 15	24.5	-0.1	-1.5
Hungary	A4AF	Jul-Sep 15	64.8	2.2		Hungary	A4AQ	Nov 15	6.3	-0.1	-1.0
Ireland	YXSU	Jul-Sep 15	63.8	1.6		Ireland	ZXDO	Jan 16	8.6	-0.2	-1.5
Italy	YXSV	Jul-Sep 15	56.7	0.7		Italy	ZXDP	Dec 15	11.4	0.0	-1.0
Latvia	A4AG	Jul-Sep 15	68.6	2.3		Latvia	A4AR	Dec 15	10.2	0.2	0.1
Lithuania	A4AH	Jul-Sep 15	68.0	0.8		Lithuania	A4AS	Dec 15	8.5	0.1	-1.5
Luxembourg	YXSW	Jul-Sep 15	65.5	-0.5		Luxembourg	ZXDQ	Dec 15	6.1	0.0	-0.2
Malta	A4AI	Jul-Sep 15	65.2	1.7		Malta	A4AT	Dec 15	5.1	0.0	-0.8
Netherlands	YXSX	Jul-Sep 15	74.5	1.0		Netherlands	ZXDR	Dec 15	6.6	-0.1	-0.6
Poland	A4AJ	Jul-Sep 15	63.5	1.0		Poland	A4AU	Dec 15	7.1	-0.1	-1.1
Portugal	YXSY	Jul-Sep 15	64.4	1.0		Portugal	ZXDT	Dec 15	11.8	-0.4	-1.8
Romania	A494	Jul-Sep 15	63.2	0.6		Romania	A48Z	Dec 15	6.7	0.0	0.1
Slovak Republic	A4AK	Jul-Sep 15	63.0	1.7		Slovak Republic	A4AV	Dec 15	10.6	-0.2	-1.8
Slovenia	A4AL	Jul-Sep 15	66.7	2.1		Slovenia	A4AW	Dec 15	8.8	0.1	-0.5
Spain	YXSZ	Jul-Sep 15	58.4	1.9		Spain	ZXDM	Dec 15	20.8	-0.2	-2.8
Sweden	YXTA	Jul-Sep 15	76.9	0.4		Sweden[5]	ZXDV	Dec 15	7.2	0.3	-0.4
United Kingdom (*)	ANZ6	Jul-Sep 15	72.9	0.7		United Kingdom (*)	ZXDW	Oct 15	5.1	-0.1	-0.7
Total EU [4]	**A496**	**Jul-Sep 15**	**66.1**	**0.8**		**Total EU [4]**	**A493**	**Dec 15**	**9.0**	**0.0**	**-0.9**
Eurozone [4]	YXTC	Jul-Sep 15	64.9	0.7		Eurozone [4]	ZXDH	Dec 15	10.4	-0.1	-1.0
Employment rates published by the OECD (seasonally adjusted)						**Unemployment rates as published by national statistical offices (seasonally adjusted)**					
Canada	A48O	Oct-Dec 15	72.4	-0.1		Canada	ZXDZ	Jan 16	7.2	0.1	0.6
Japan	A48P	Oct-Dec 15	73.6	0.7		Japan	ZXDY	Dec 15	3.3	0.0	-0.1
United States	A48Q	Oct-Dec 15	68.9	0.4		United States	ZXDX	Jan 16	4.9	-0.1	-0.8

Sources: EUROSTAT, OECD, national statistical offices. Labour market statistics enquiries: labour.market@ons.gsi.gov.uk

(*) Note: The UK rates shown in this table are as published by EUROSTAT (the EUs statistical office). See Table 1 for the latest rates for the UK as published by ONS.

1. All employment rates shown in this table are for those aged from 15 to 64 except for the rate for the United States published by OECD which are for those aged from 16 to 64.
2. The employment rates for the EU are published by EUROSTAT and are not seasonally adjusted. EUROSTAT do not publish seasonally adjusted (SA) employment rates but SA rates for some EU countries are published by OECD. These OECD employment rates are available at data table A10.
3. Unemployment rates published by EUROSTAT for most EU countries (but not for the UK), are calculated by extrapolating from the most recent LFS data using monthly registered unemployment data. A standard population basis (15-74) is used by EUROSTAT except for Spain, Italy and the UK (16-74). The unemployment rate for the US is based on those aged 16 and over, but the rates for Canada and Japan are for those aged 15 and over. All unemployment rates shown in this table are seasonally adjusted.
4. The "Total EU" series consist of all 28 EU countries. The Eurozone figures consist of the following EU countries: Austria, Belgium, Cyprus, Estonia, Finland, France, Germany, Greece, Ireland, Italy, Latvia, Lithuania, Luxembourg, Malta, Netherlands, Portugal, Slovak Republic, Slovenia and Spain.
5. The EU unemployment rates are as published on the EUROSTAT database. For Sweden the rates on the database differ from those shown in the EUROSTAT News Release published on 2 February 2016. This is because the figures for Sweden on the database are seasonally adjusted estimates but the figures for Sweden shown in the News Release are the trend component.

4.5b: Labour Disputes

United Kingdom, not seasonally adjusted

	Working days lost (thousands)	Working days lost in the Public Sector (thousands)	Working days lost in the Private Sector (thousands)	Number of stoppages	Number of stoppages in the Public Sector	Number of stoppages in the Private Sector	Workers involved (thousands)
	1	2	3	4	5	6	7
	BBFW	F8XZ	F8Y2	BLUU	F8Y3	F8Y4	BLUT
2013 Dec	38	6	32	8	4	4	55
2014 Dec	13	11	3	15	8	7	11
2015 Jan	22	5	17	18	11	7	21
2015 Feb	24	10	14	11	5	6	23
2015 Mar	23	19	3	17	12	5	17
2015 Apr	7	4	3	19	10	9	2
2015 May	12	10	2	17	9	8	2
2015 Jun	8	5	3	20	9	11	3
2015 Jul	18	12	5	14	10	4	12
2015 Aug	22	12	10	12	7	5	11
2015 Sep	8	6	2	17	9	8	4
2015 Oct	3	2	1	11	6	5	2
2015 Nov	13	2	11	11	6	5	15
2015 Dec	9	1	8	10	4	6	11
Cumulative totals 12 months to:							
Dec 14	786	716	74	211	90	121	817
Dec 15	169	88	79	177	98	79	123

Relationship between columns 1=4+5; 2=6+7

Source: ONS Labour Disputes Survey. Labour Disputes Statistics Helpline 01633 456724

1. Due to rounding the working days lost for the public and private sector may not add up to the working days lost.

4.6: Civil Service employment; regional distribution by government department[12]

All employees   Headcount

Tuesday, 31 March 2015

	North West	North East	Yorkshire and The Humber	West Midlands	East Midlands	East	London	South East	South West	Scotland	Wales	Northern Ireland	Overseas	Not reported
Attorney General's Departments														
Attorney General's Office	0	0	0	0	0	0	40	0	0	0	0	0	0	0
Crown Prosecution Service	910	320	830	560	360	440	1,540	700	250	0	340	0	20	0
Crown Prosecution Service Inspectorate	0	0	10	0	0	0	30	0	0	0	0	0	0	0
Serious Fraud Office	0	0	0	0	0	0	410	0	0	0	0	0	0	0
Treasury Solicitor	..	0	10	0	0	0	1,630	0	20	0	0	0	0	0
Business, Innovation and Skills														
Business, Innovation and Skills (excl. agencies)	50	30	260	50	30	30	2,560	10	20	20	50	0	0	0
Advisory Conciliation and Arbitration Service	120	70	60	60	60	50	220	50	50	80	60	0	0	0
Companies House	0	0	0	0	0	0	10	0	0	20	820	20	0	0
Competition and Markets Authority	0	0	0	0	0	0	570	0	0	..	..	..	0	0
Insolvency Service	190	50	80	400	40	90	410	110	90	40	50	0	0	0
Land Registry	600	430	240	420	620	240	260	0	1,140	0	420	0	0	0
Met Office	30	0	30	20	40	40	40	90	1,600	120	20	10	30	0
National Measurement Office	0	0	0	0	0	0	80	0	0	0	0	0	0	0
Ordnance Survey [3]	30	10	30	30	20	30	20	990	30	30	20	0	0	0
Skills Funding Agency	70	50	80	420	20	30	120	70	40	0	0	0	0	0
UK Intellectual Property Office	0	0	0	0	0	0	40	0	0	0	1,040	0	0	0
UK Space Agency	0	0	0	0	0	0	10	0	60	0	0	0	0	0
Cabinet Office														
Cabinet Office (excl. agencies)	..	..	30	0	..	30	2,050	30	..	0	0	0	0	0
Other Cabinet Office agencies														
Crown Commercial Service	300	0	30	..	..	180	160	..	..	..	120	0	0	0
Government in Parliament	0	0	0	0	0	0	100	0	0	0	0	0	0	0
Chancellor's other departments														
Government Actuary's Department	0	0	0	0	0	0	160	0	0	0	0	0	0	0
National Savings and Investments	10	10	0	0	0	0	150	0	0	10	0	0	0	0
Charity Commission														
Charity Commission	150	0	0	0	0	0	80	0	80	0	10	0	0	0
Communities and Local Government														
Department for Communities and Local Government (excl. agencies)	70	40	50	70	30	80	1,230	20	70	0	0	0	0	0
Planning Inspectorate	0	0	0	0	0	0	0	0	720	0	40	0	0	0
Queen Elizabeth II Centre	0	0	0	0	0	0	40	0	0	0	0	0	0	0
Culture, Media and Sport														
Department for Culture Media and Sport	0	0	0	0	0	0	480	0	0	0	0	0	0	0
Royal Parks	0	0	0	0	0	0	120	0	0	0	0	0	0	0
Defence														
Ministry of Defence	1,750	290	2,700	2,880	1,570	3,860	3,570	8,900	14,310	3,920	850	1,290	1,510	240
Defence Science and Technology Laboratory	0	0	0	..	10	10	0	2,010	1,790	0	0	0	0	0
Defence Support Group [4]	0	0	90	960	..	90	10	80	730	90	380	10	0	0
Royal Fleet Auxiliary	0	0	0	0	0	0	0	0	0	0	0	0	0	1,890
UK Hydrographic Office	0	0	0	0	0	0	0	0	970	0	0	0	..	0
Education														
Department for Education	180	320	370	80	40	10	1,220	0	10	0	0	0	0	0
Education Funding Agency	80	100	100	180	30	..	340	0	30	0	0	0	0	0
Standards and Testing Agency	..	..	..	60	..	0	30	0	0	0	0	0	0	0
The National College for Teaching and Leadership	100	..	10	50	120	0	30	0	0	0	0	0	0	0
Energy and Climate Change														
Department of Energy and Climate Change	0	0	0	0	0	0	1,440	0	0	110	0	0	0	0
Environment, Food and Rural Affairs														
Department for Environment Food and Rural Affairs (excl. agencies)	30	30	240	90	10	30	1,490	50	120	..	0	0	0	0
Animal and Plant Health Agency [5]	180	50	160	340	100	150	80	640	320	120	230	0	0	0
Centre for Environment Fisheries and Aquaculture Science	..	0	..	0	0	390	..	0	140	0	0	0	0	0
Food and Environment Research Agency [6]	0	0	580	0	0	0	0	0	0	0	0	0	0	0
Office of Water Services	..	0	0	120	0	..	30	..	0	0	0	0	0	0
Rural Payments Agency	740	310	230	50	30	50	10	430	330	..	..	..	0	0
Veterinary Medicines Directorate	0	0	0	0	0	0	0	160	0	0	0	0	0	0
ESTYN														
ESTYN	0	0	0	0	0	0	0	0	0	0	110	0	0	0
Food Standards Agency														
Food Standards Agency	90	20	200	90	80	130	210	80	90	150	80	40	0	0
Foreign and Commonwealth Office														
Foreign and Commonwealth Office (excl. agencies)	0	0	0	0	0	0	2,450	300	0	0	0	0	1,730	0
FCO Services	0	0	0	0	0	0	180	700	0	0	0	0	110	0
Wilton Park Executive Agency	0	0	0	0	0	0	0	80	0	0	0	0	0	0
Health														
Department of Health (excl. agencies)	50	0	670	0	0	0	1,290	20	0	0	0	0	0	..
Medicines and Healthcare Products Regulatory Agency	0	0	20	0	0	340	850	0	0	0	0	0	0	0
Public Health England	450	150	310	400	110	400	2,140	600	1,240	20	..	0	0	0
HM Revenue and Customs														
HM Revenue and Customs	11,370	10,800	4,250	3,810	3,390	3,110	8,180	3,960	2,180	8,330	3,290	1,640	0	10
Valuation Office	430	240	460	300	230	250	710	450	400	60	270	0	0	0
HM Treasury														
HM Treasury	0	0	0	0	0	30	1,100	0	0	..	0	0	0	0
Debt Management Office	0	0	0	0	0	0	110	0	0	0	0	0	0	0

4.6: Civil Service employment; regional distribution by government department[12]

All employees   *Headcount*

	North West	North East	Yorkshire and The Humber	West Midlands	East Midlands	East	London	South East	South West	Scotland	Wales	Northern Ireland	Overseas	Not reported
Tuesday, 31 March 2015														
Office for Budget Responsibility	0	0	0	0	0	0	20	0	0	0	0	0	0	0
Home Office														
Home Office[78]	4,360	1,370	2,730	830	220	1,990	12,450	3,130	340	820	520	470	600	10
International Development														
Department for International Development	0	0	0	0	0	0	840	0	0	610	0	0	570	0
Justice														
Ministry of Justice (excl. agencies)	120	30	80	140	70	30	2,440	40	40	20	110	..	0	0
Criminal Injuries Compensation Authority	0	0	0	0	0	0	0	0	0	300	0	0	0	0
Her Majesty's Courts and Tribunals Service	2,430	860	1,650	1,740	1,590	1,220	4,280	1,690	1,110	220	970	0	0	0
Legal Aid Agency	300	270	50	110	210	10	410	30	90	0	60	0	0	0
National Archives	0	0	0	0	0	0	..	650	0	0	0	0	0	0
National Offender Management Service	6,210	2,930	5,670	4,520	4,510	4,790	5,840	7,020	3,470	0	1,470	0	0	0
Office of the Public Guardian	0	0	0	690	160	0	30	0	0	0	0	0	0	0
National Crime Agency														
National Crime Agency	710	60	170	340	130	190	1,420	550	220	40	50	70	150	80
Northern Ireland Office														
Northern Ireland Office	0	0	0	0	0	0	50	0	0	0	0	60	0	0
Office for Standards in Education														
Office for Standards in Education, Children's Services and Skills	440	0	100	90	130	70	360	0	190	0	0	0	0	0
Office of Gas and Electricity Markets														
Office of Gas and Electricity Markets	0	0	0	0	0	0	780	0	0	110	..	0	0	0
Office of Qualifications and Examinations Regulation														
Ofqual	0	0	0	180	0	0	0	0	0	0	0	..	0	0
Scotland Office														
Scotland Office (incl. Office of the Advocate General for Scotland)	0	0	0	0	0	0	30	0	0	80	0	0	0	0
Scottish Government														
Scottish Government (excl. agencies)	0	0	0	0	0	0	0	0	0	5,370	0	0	10	0
Crown Office and Procurator Fiscal Service	0	0	0	0	0	0	0	0	0	1,710	0	0	0	0
Disclosure Scotland	0	0	0	0	0	0	0	0	0	280	0	0	0	0
Education Scotland	0	0	0	0	0	0	0	0	0	290	0	0	0	0
Historic Scotland	0	0	0	0	0	0	0	0	0	1,050	0	0	0	0
National Records of Scotland	0	0	0	0	0	0	0	0	0	400	0	0	0	0
Office of Accountant in Bankruptcy	0	0	0	0	0	0	0	0	0	150	0	0	0	0
Office of the Scottish Charity Regulator	0	0	0	0	0	0	0	0	0	50	0	0	0	0
Registers of Scotland	0	0	0	0	0	0	0	0	0	980	0	0	0	0
Revenue Scotland	0	0	0	0	0	0	0	0	0	50	0	0	0	0
Scottish Court Service	0	0	0	0	0	0	0	0	0	1,540	0	0	0	0
Scottish Housing Regulator	0	0	0	0	0	0	0	0	0	50	0	0	0	0
Scottish Prison Service	0	0	0	0	0	0	0	0	0	4,600	0	0	0	0
Scottish Public Pensions Agency	0	0	0	0	0	0	0	0	0	300	0	0	0	0
Student Awards Agency	0	0	0	0	0	0	0	0	0	250	0	0	0	0
Transport Scotland	0	0	0	0	0	0	0	0	0	410	0	0	0	0
	0													
Transport														
Department for Transport (excl. agencies)	0	10	0	..	30	0	1,590	200	10	0	..	0	..	0
Driver and Vehicle Licensing Agency	..	..	..	..	..	10	10	..	..	10	5,750	0	0	0
Driver and Vehicle Standards Agency[9]	420	340	410	370	480	380	410	450	520	310	420	0	0	0
Highways Agency[10]	520	20	490	1,040	140	480	40	650	390	0	0	0	0	0
Maritime and Coastguard Agency	20	20	60	0	..	20	20	490	100	160	130	40	0	0
Office of Rail Regulation	20	..	10	10	..	..	200	10	10	20	..	0	0	0
Vehicle Certification Agency	0	0	0	0	50	..	0	..	100	0	0	0	10	0
United Kingdom Statistics Authority														
United Kingdom Statistics Authority	0	0	0	0	0	0	40	1,780	..	0	1,880	0	0	0
UK Export Finance														
UK Export Finance	..	..	..	..	..	10	230	..	..	..	..	..	0	0
UK Supreme Court														
UK Supreme Court	0	0	0	0	0	0	50	0	0	0	0	0	0	0
Wales Office														
Wales Office	0	0	0	0	0	0	30	0	0	0	20	0	0	0
Welsh Government														
Welsh Government	0	0	0	0	0	0	10	0	0	0	5,700	0	10	0
Work and Pensions														
Department for Work and Pensions	17,710	9,560	9,390	8,290	4,960	4,420	8,660	5,970	5,250	10,120	5,430	0	0	270
The Health and Safety Executive	940	70	330	120	480	130	160	110	90	240	100	0	0	0
All employees	52,150	28,880	33,260	29,890	20,080	23,830	79,020	42,620	38,730	43,620	30,800	3,660	4,750	2,500

Source: Annual Civil Service Employment Survey

1 Numbers are rounded to the nearest ten, and cells containing between one and five employees are represented by "..".
2 Workplace postcode data are used to derive geographical information.
3 As of 1 April 2015, Ordnance Survey will no longer operate as Trading Fund and will convert to a Government Owned Company (GovCo). This means that from this date employees will no longer be civil servants.
4 Defence Support Group moved to the private sector on 1 April 2015 and all employees ceased to be civil servants.
5 Animal Health and Veterinary Laboratories Agency was renamed Animal and Plant Health Agency on 1 October 2014.
6 As of 1 April 2015, FERA became part of the private sector, owned by Capita PLC and will no longer be civil servants.
7 Home Office estimates for 31 March 2015 include staff paid via the Foreign and Commonwealth Office employee records system (PRISM).
8 Home Office no longer has any Executive Agencies. United Kingdom Border Agency ceased Agency status on 1st April 2013 with 12,268 (FTE) staff moved in to core Home Office. 3,578 HM Passport Office staff moved in to core Home Office on 1st October 2014.
9 Driver and Vehicle Standards Agency was formally launched on 1 April 2014, taking over the responsibilities of the Driving Standards Agency and Vehicle and Operators Services Agency.
10 Highways Agency became Highways England as of 1 April 2015 and all employees ceased to be civil servants.

4.7: Unemployment by age and duration

United Kingdom (thousands) seasonally adjusted

	All aged 16 & over							All aged 16 - 64						
	All	Rate (%)[1]	Up to 6 months	Over 6 and up to 12 months	All over 12 months	% over 12 months	All over 24 months	All	Rate (%)[1]	Up to 6 months	Over 6 and up to 12 months	All over 12 months	% over 12 months	All over 24 months
	1	2	3	4	5	6	7	8	9	10	11	12	13	14
People	MGSC	MGSX	YBWF	YBWG	YBWH	YBWI	YBWL	LF2I	LF2Q	LF2Y	LF32	LF34	LF36	LF38
Nov-Jan 2007	1,703	5.5	1,026	276	400	23.5	185	1,691	5.6	1,019	275	398	23.5	183
Dec-Feb 2007	1,708	5.5	1,041	269	398	23.3	180	1,696	5.6	1,033	266	397	23.4	178
Jan-Mar 2007	1,704	5.5	1,033	277	393	23.1	179	1,689	5.6	1,026	275	388	23.0	175
Feb-Apr 2007	1,692	5.5	1,012	278	402	23.7	177	1,677	5.5	1,006	277	393	23.5	173
Mar-May 2007	1,670	5.4	999	271	399	23.9	181	1,655	5.5	993	270	392	23.7	177
Apr-Jun 2007	1,658	5.4	999	263	396	23.9	175	1,640	5.4	988	261	391	23.9	172
May-Jul 2007	1,645	5.3	988	262	394	24.0	179	1,629	5.4	981	261	388	23.8	176
Jun-Aug 2007	1,645	5.3	986	267	392	23.8	175	1,631	5.4	980	265	386	23.7	172
Jul-Sep 2007	1,650	5.3	991	268	391	23.7	176	1,638	5.4	985	267	386	23.6	173
Aug-Oct 2007	1,629	5.2	985	261	384	23.6	177	1,617	5.3	978	261	379	23.4	174
Sep-Nov 2007	1,633	5.2	984	257	391	24.0	176	1,621	5.3	979	257	385	23.8	173
Oct-Dec 2007	1,608	5.2	969	256	384	23.9	170	1,600	5.2	964	254	382	23.9	167
Nov-Jan 2008	1,617	5.2	974	262	381	23.6	180	1,606	5.3	967	259	381	23.7	177
Dec-Feb 2008	1,622	5.2	960	273	389	24.0	190	1,609	5.3	953	269	387	24.1	187
Jan-Mar 2008	1,622	5.2	958	267	398	24.5	198	1,610	5.3	952	264	394	24.5	196
Feb-Apr 2008	1,667	5.3	989	268	410	24.6	197	1,651	5.4	982	264	404	24.5	195
Mar-May 2008	1,625	5.2	954	265	406	25.0	191	1,610	5.2	947	262	401	24.9	190
Apr-Jun 2008	1,680	5.4	989	275	416	24.8	192	1,666	5.4	980	271	415	24.9	190
May-Jul 2008	1,724	5.5	1,011	278	435	25.2	206	1,711	5.6	1,005	274	432	25.2	203
Jun-Aug 2008	1,793	5.7	1,075	277	442	24.6	207	1,777	5.8	1,067	272	438	24.6	205
Jul-Sep 2008	1,840	5.9	1,112	284	444	24.1	204	1,822	5.9	1,104	279	438	24.0	203
Aug-Oct 2008	1,875	6.0	1,146	289	440	23.5	202	1,855	6.0	1,134	287	433	23.4	200
Sep-Nov 2008	1,941	6.2	1,189	313	440	22.7	199	1,922	6.2	1,177	310	434	22.6	197
Oct-Dec 2008	2,003	6.4	1,225	324	454	22.7	211	1,987	6.4	1,214	320	453	22.8	209
Nov-Jan 2009	2,057	6.5	1,250	347	460	22.4	209	2,042	6.6	1,240	342	459	22.5	206
Dec-Feb 2009	2,128	6.7	1,290	355	483	22.7	224	2,110	6.8	1,280	351	479	22.7	220
Jan-Mar 2009	2,235	7.1	1,345	381	508	22.8	232	2,215	7.2	1,335	378	502	22.7	229
Feb-Apr 2009	2,296	7.3	1,365	408	523	22.8	236	2,278	7.4	1,356	405	517	22.7	233
Mar-May 2009	2,395	7.6	1,417	442	536	22.4	237	2,376	7.7	1,407	439	531	22.3	234
Apr-Jun 2009	2,448	7.8	1,413	483	552	22.6	240	2,427	7.9	1,400	479	549	22.6	236
May-Jul 2009	2,478	7.9	1,403	495	581	23.4	246	2,455	8.0	1,390	491	574	23.4	241
Jun-Aug 2009	2,484	7.9	1,357	516	611	24.6	252	2,464	8.0	1,349	515	600	24.4	246
Jul-Sep 2009	2,475	7.8	1,306	539	631	25.5	236	2,451	8.0	1,298	534	619	25.3	229
Aug-Oct 2009	2,484	7.9	1,293	567	624	25.1	237	2,457	8.0	1,283	562	612	24.9	231
Sep-Nov 2009	2,455	7.8	1,250	568	637	25.9	236	2,428	7.9	1,239	560	629	25.9	232
Oct-Dec 2009	2,453	7.8	1,251	539	663	27.0	247	2,430	7.9	1,239	532	659	27.1	242
Nov-Jan 2010	2,434	7.7	1,199	550	685	28.1	246	2,409	7.8	1,187	542	680	28.2	242
Dec-Feb 2010	2,496	7.9	1,209	556	731	29.3	272	2,472	8.0	1,199	550	723	29.3	265
Jan-Mar 2010	2,526	8.0	1,213	546	768	30.4	283	2,501	8.1	1,203	541	756	30.2	277
Feb-Apr 2010	2,510	8.0	1,191	531	788	31.4	294	2,487	8.1	1,184	526	776	31.2	287
Mar-May 2010	2,508	7.9	1,185	521	801	32.0	303	2,486	8.1	1,178	518	790	31.8	297
Apr-Jun 2010	2,488	7.9	1,173	512	803	32.3	314	2,468	8.0	1,164	507	797	32.3	308
May-Jul 2010	2,488	7.8	1,198	486	803	32.3	322	2,469	8.0	1,189	483	797	32.3	315
Jun-Aug 2010	2,476	7.8	1,181	472	823	33.2	334	2,456	7.9	1,174	469	812	33.1	328
Jul-Sep 2010	2,470	7.8	1,197	450	823	33.3	330	2,451	7.9	1,193	447	811	33.1	325
Aug-Oct 2010	2,513	7.9	1,204	468	842	33.5	335	2,495	8.1	1,201	465	828	33.2	330
Sep-Nov 2010	2,502	7.9	1,214	452	837	33.4	337	2,481	8.0	1,206	448	827	33.3	330
Oct-Dec 2010	2,503	7.9	1,209	456	838	33.5	342	2,482	8.0	1,199	452	831	33.5	335
Nov-Jan 2011	2,524	7.9	1,220	452	852	33.8	349	2,503	8.1	1,212	449	843	33.7	342
Dec-Feb 2011	2,492	7.8	1,194	444	853	34.2	372	2,474	8.0	1,188	442	845	34.1	366
Jan-Mar 2011	2,483	7.8	1,182	443	859	34.6	389	2,466	8.0	1,177	441	848	34.4	384
Feb-Apr 2011	2,462	7.7	1,185	436	840	34.1	389	2,444	7.9	1,178	434	832	34.1	384
Mar-May 2011	2,500	7.8	1,234	447	820	32.8	388	2,482	8.0	1,228	447	807	32.5	382
Apr-Jun 2011	2,540	7.9	1,259	434	846	33.3	411	2,522	8.1	1,250	433	839	33.3	407
May-Jul 2011	2,556	8.0	1,254	442	860	33.6	420	2,535	8.2	1,243	440	851	33.6	415
Jun-Aug 2011	2,612	8.2	1,261	475	876	33.6	426	2,589	8.3	1,254	470	864	33.4	421
Jul-Sep 2011	2,664	8.3	1,283	503	878	33.0	425	2,637	8.5	1,273	498	866	32.9	420
Aug-Oct 2011	2,680	8.4	1,297	505	878	32.7	434	2,648	8.5	1,285	501	862	32.6	428
Sep-Nov 2011	2,708	8.5	1,316	527	865	31.9	427	2,680	8.6	1,299	522	859	32.0	423
Oct-Dec 2011	2,684	8.4	1,301	516	867	32.3	427	2,657	8.5	1,285	510	862	32.4	422
Nov-Jan 2012	2,670	8.3	1,298	512	859	32.2	409	2,646	8.5	1,285	506	855	32.3	403
Dec-Feb 2012	2,653	8.3	1,255	510	887	33.5	424	2,628	8.4	1,242	507	879	33.4	417
Jan-Mar 2012	2,633	8.2	1,225	521	887	33.7	429	2,604	8.4	1,212	517	874	33.6	422
Feb-Apr 2012	2,624	8.2	1,203	530	890	33.9	436	2,597	8.3	1,190	525	882	34.0	431
Mar-May 2012	2,605	8.1	1,199	515	890	34.2	444	2,581	8.3	1,188	509	884	34.2	440
Apr-Jun 2012	2,582	8.0	1,192	502	888	34.4	424	2,562	8.2	1,183	496	883	34.5	419
May-Jul 2012	2,600	8.0	1,196	495	908	34.9	444	2,577	8.2	1,188	489	899	34.9	436
Jun-Aug 2012	2,550	7.9	1,183	464	903	35.4	442	2,530	8.1	1,181	461	888	35.1	435

4.7: Unemployment by age and duration

United Kingdom (thousands) seasonally adjusted

	All aged 16 & over							All aged 16 - 64						
	All	Rate (%)[1]	Up to 6 months	Over 6 and up to 12 months	All over 12 months	% over 12 months	All over 24 months	All	Rate (%)[1]	Up to 6 months	Over 6 and up to 12 months	All over 12 months	% over 12 months	All over 24 months
	1	2	3	4	5	6	7	8	9	10	11	12	13	14
	MGSC	MGSX	YBWF	YBWG	YBWH	YBWI	YBWL	LF2I	LF2Q	LF2Y	LF32	LF34	LF36	LF38
People														
Jul-Sep 2012	2,538	7.9	1,191	445	903	35.6	440	2,518	8.0	1,188	443	888	35.2	433
Aug-Oct 2012	2,534	7.9	1,183	440	912	36.0	449	2,513	8.0	1,180	437	896	35.7	445
Sep-Nov 2012	2,530	7.8	1,197	435	897	35.5	437	2,506	8.0	1,186	432	888	35.4	431
Oct-Dec 2012	2,535	7.8	1,205	445	885	34.9	443	2,513	8.0	1,195	441	877	34.9	437
Nov-Jan 2013	2,537	7.8	1,195	453	890	35.1	452	2,520	8.0	1,186	450	884	35.1	447
Dec-Feb 2013	2,587	8.0	1,214	467	906	35.0	464	2,571	8.2	1,209	465	896	34.9	459
Jan-Mar 2013	2,541	7.8	1,196	437	908	35.7	467	2,523	8.0	1,190	435	898	35.6	461
Feb-Apr 2013	2,530	7.8	1,208	418	903	35.7	460	2,508	8.0	1,197	415	896	35.7	453
Mar-May 2013	2,511	7.8	1,173	418	919	36.6	475	2,490	7.9	1,160	418	911	36.6	469
Apr-Jun 2013	2,515	7.7	1,173	428	914	36.3	476	2,489	7.9	1,158	426	906	36.4	468
May-Jul 2013	2,492	7.7	1,146	445	901	36.2	471	2,467	7.8	1,130	443	895	36.3	464
Jun-Aug 2013	2,502	7.7	1,154	444	904	36.1	469	2,477	7.9	1,142	442	892	36.0	463
Jul-Sep 2013	2,481	7.6	1,163	425	894	36.0	460	2,460	7.8	1,153	422	884	35.9	457
Aug-Oct 2013	2,403	7.4	1,131	399	873	36.3	446	2,378	7.5	1,123	396	859	36.1	444
Sep-Nov 2013	2,338	7.2	1,101	397	841	36.0	450	2,314	7.3	1,085	394	835	36.1	447
Oct-Dec 2013	2,358	7.2	1,111	400	847	35.9	453	2,327	7.4	1,093	396	838	36.0	449
Nov-Jan 2014	2,341	7.2	1,118	394	829	35.4	452	2,310	7.3	1,102	390	818	35.4	448
Dec-Feb 2014	2,260	6.9	1,076	374	811	35.9	432	2,229	7.0	1,062	369	797	35.8	429
Jan-Mar 2014	2,213	6.8	1,044	353	816	36.9	447	2,187	6.9	1,032	349	806	36.9	442
Feb-Apr 2014	2,167	6.6	1,031	342	795	36.7	433	2,138	6.8	1,014	337	787	36.8	428
Mar-May 2014	2,110	6.4	1,012	346	753	35.7	419	2,082	6.6	998	344	740	35.6	412
Apr-Jun 2014	2,061	6.3	990	331	740	35.9	408	2,035	6.4	977	327	731	35.9	403
May-Jul 2014	2,009	6.1	968	317	724	36.0	400	1,989	6.3	957	315	717	36.1	394
Jun-Aug 2014	1,968	6.0	944	312	712	36.2	389	1,949	6.2	938	311	700	35.9	383
Jul-Sep 2014	1,957	6.0	950	317	690	35.3	377	1,936	6.1	943	316	677	35.0	371
Aug-Oct 2014	1,952	6.0	936	331	685	35.1	377	1,932	6.1	933	330	670	34.7	371
Sep-Nov 2014	1,922	5.9	948	317	657	34.2	355	1,902	6.0	939	315	648	34.1	350
Oct-Dec 2014	1,872	5.7	931	304	637	34.0	340	1,854	5.9	926	300	628	33.9	333
Nov-Jan 2015	1,861	5.7	947	287	627	33.7	339	1,840	5.8	938	283	620	33.7	333
Dec-Feb 2015	1,845	5.6	938	284	623	33.8	352	1,825	5.7	932	282	611	33.5	343
Jan-Mar 2015	1,830	5.5	958	283	589	32.2	342	1,808	5.7	950	279	579	32.0	333
Feb-Apr 2015	1,822	5.5	955	291	576	31.6	327	1,802	5.7	947	287	568	31.6	318
Mar-May 2015	1,847	5.6	974	304	569	30.8	318	1,829	5.8	969	300	561	30.7	311
Apr-Jun 2015	1,848	5.6	967	304	577	31.3	325	1,825	5.7	958	299	568	31.1	318
May-Jul 2015	1,820	5.5	979	294	547	30.1	309	1,796	5.6	968	289	539	30.0	303
Jun-Aug 2015	1,772	5.4	957	287	528	29.8	302	1,747	5.5	947	282	518	29.7	298
Jul-Sep 2015	1,752	5.3	958	278	516	29.4	290	1,731	5.4	950	273	508	29.3	287
Aug-Oct 2015	1,713	5.2	937	264	512	29.9	288	1,693	5.3	933	261	499	29.5	283
Sep-Nov 2015	1,684	5.1	935	258	491	29.2	269	1,665	5.2	926	256	483	29.0	263
Oct-Dec 2015	1,692	5.1	949	254	489	28.9	261	1,673	5.2	941	251	482	28.8	256
Change on qtr	*-60*	*-0.2*	*-9*	*-24*	*-27*	*-0.5*	*-29*	*-58*	*-0.2*	*-10*	*-23*	*-26*	*-0.5*	*-30*
Change %	*-3.5*		*-1.0*	*-8.8*	*-5.2*		*-10.0*	*-3.4*		*-1.0*	*-8.2*	*-5.1*		*-10.6*
Change on year	*-180*	*-0.6*	*18*	*-50*	*-148*	*-5.1*	*-78*	*-181*	*-0.6*	*15*	*-49*	*-147*	*-5.1*	*-77*
Change %	*-9.6*		*1.9*	*-16.5*	*-23.3*		*-23.0*	*-9.8*		*1.6*	*-16.4*	*-23.3*		*-23.1*
Men	MGSD	MGSY	MGYK	MGYM	MGYO	YBWJ	YBWM	YBSI	YBTJ	YBWP	YBWS	YBVV	YBWY	YBXB
Nov-Jan 2007	967	5.8	530	162	274	28.4	129	958	5.9	527	161	270	28.2	128
Dec-Feb 2007	974	5.8	541	155	278	28.6	128	966	5.9	537	153	276	28.5	126
Jan-Mar 2007	970	5.8	535	163	272	28.1	127	960	5.9	531	161	268	27.9	124
Feb-Apr 2007	968	5.8	528	163	277	28.6	126	956	5.9	524	161	271	28.4	123
Mar-May 2007	953	5.7	518	161	274	28.7	131	942	5.7	513	160	269	28.5	128
Apr-Jun 2007	941	5.6	518	152	271	28.8	124	928	5.7	512	151	264	28.5	121
May-Jul 2007	935	5.6	516	152	267	28.5	126	924	5.6	512	151	261	28.3	123
Jun-Aug 2007	933	5.6	514	153	267	28.6	123	923	5.6	509	152	262	28.4	120
Jul-Sep 2007	935	5.6	516	155	263	28.2	125	927	5.7	511	155	261	28.1	124
Aug-Oct 2007	918	5.5	505	154	259	28.2	130	909	5.5	499	154	255	28.1	127
Sep-Nov 2007	923	5.5	506	151	266	28.8	129	914	5.6	502	150	262	28.7	127
Oct-Dec 2007	909	5.4	499	151	259	28.5	122	903	5.5	497	149	256	28.4	120
Nov-Jan 2008	926	5.5	513	152	261	28.2	130	918	5.6	511	150	258	28.1	128
Dec-Feb 2008	933	5.5	506	162	265	28.4	140	924	5.6	503	159	263	28.4	138
Jan-Mar 2008	935	5.5	507	155	272	29.1	146	925	5.6	503	154	269	29.0	144
Feb-Apr 2008	945	5.6	513	155	277	29.3	142	933	5.7	507	153	273	29.3	141
Mar-May 2008	936	5.5	508	152	276	29.5	139	925	5.6	502	149	273	29.5	137
Apr-Jun 2008	978	5.8	529	159	290	29.7	142	968	5.9	524	157	287	29.7	140
May-Jul 2008	1,008	5.9	541	163	304	30.1	150	998	6.0	537	160	301	30.1	149
Jun-Aug 2008	1,048	6.2	575	162	311	29.7	150	1,036	6.3	568	158	309	29.8	149

4.7: Unemployment by age and duration

United Kingdom (thousands) seasonally adjusted

	All aged 16 & over							All aged 16 - 64						
	All	Rate (%)[1]	Up to 6 months	Over 6 and up to 12 months	All over 12 months	% over 12 months	All over 24 months	All	Rate (%)[1]	Up to 6 months	Over 6 and up to 12 months	All over 12 months	% over 12 months	All over 24 months
	1	2	3	4	5	6	7	8	9	10	11	12	13	14
	MGSD	MGSY	MGYK	MGYM	MGYO	YBWJ	YBWM	YBSI	YBTJ	YBWP	YBWS	YBWV	YBWY	YBXB
Men														
Jul-Sep 2008	1,075	6.3	605	162	308	28.6	147	1,061	6.4	597	158	305	28.8	146
Aug-Oct 2008	1,100	6.5	638	161	300	27.3	144	1,084	6.6	628	159	297	27.4	143
Sep-Nov 2008	1,147	6.7	670	180	297	25.9	140	1,132	6.8	660	178	294	25.9	138
Oct-Dec 2008	1,191	7.0	693	190	309	25.9	151	1,180	7.1	686	187	307	26.1	150
Nov-Jan 2009	1,225	7.2	708	204	313	25.6	149	1,214	7.3	703	201	309	25.5	147
Dec-Feb 2009	1,272	7.5	739	208	325	25.6	158	1,260	7.6	733	205	321	25.5	156
Jan-Mar 2009	1,338	7.8	776	224	338	25.2	161	1,323	8.0	769	220	334	25.2	160
Feb-Apr 2009	1,383	8.1	795	247	341	24.6	164	1,370	8.2	789	244	338	24.7	162
Mar-May 2009	1,450	8.5	834	272	345	23.8	166	1,439	8.7	827	269	343	23.8	164
Apr-Jun 2009	1,490	8.8	829	305	355	23.8	164	1,475	8.9	822	303	351	23.8	161
May-Jul 2009	1,521	9.0	821	318	382	25.1	172	1,504	9.1	812	315	377	25.1	169
Jun-Aug 2009	1,531	9.0	782	341	407	26.6	179	1,515	9.2	775	340	400	26.4	175
Jul-Sep 2009	1,522	9.0	740	362	419	27.5	167	1,504	9.1	733	358	412	27.4	162
Aug-Oct 2009	1,523	9.0	728	381	414	27.2	166	1,503	9.1	719	377	407	27.1	161
Sep-Nov 2009	1,496	8.8	711	370	415	27.7	162	1,475	9.0	703	364	409	27.7	158
Oct-Dec 2009	1,485	8.8	703	344	438	29.5	169	1,469	8.9	696	340	433	29.5	167
Nov-Jan 2010	1,490	8.8	681	351	458	30.7	172	1,473	9.0	675	346	452	30.7	170
Dec-Feb 2010	1,518	9.0	669	353	496	32.7	191	1,501	9.1	663	348	489	32.6	187
Jan-Mar 2010	1,542	9.1	671	350	522	33.8	203	1,523	9.3	663	345	515	33.8	199
Feb-Apr 2010	1,524	9.0	650	336	537	35.3	211	1,507	9.2	645	332	530	35.2	207
Mar-May 2010	1,500	8.8	635	321	543	36.2	216	1,483	9.0	629	317	536	36.1	211
Apr-Jun 2010	1,476	8.7	618	309	548	37.1	223	1,461	8.8	614	306	542	37.1	218
May-Jul 2010	1,454	8.5	624	283	547	37.7	226	1,441	8.7	618	280	542	37.6	221
Jun-Aug 2010	1,439	8.4	613	269	557	38.7	234	1,425	8.6	607	266	551	38.7	230
Jul-Sep 2010	1,432	8.4	627	252	553	38.6	236	1,417	8.5	623	248	547	38.6	232
Aug-Oct 2010	1,455	8.5	637	258	560	38.5	239	1,440	8.7	632	255	554	38.4	236
Sep-Nov 2010	1,470	8.6	650	255	564	38.4	236	1,453	8.8	646	251	557	38.3	230
Oct-Dec 2010	1,457	8.5	638	258	561	38.5	237	1,442	8.7	634	255	553	38.4	232
Nov-Jan 2011	1,468	8.5	640	260	568	38.7	241	1,453	8.7	638	258	557	38.3	236
Dec-Feb 2011	1,445	8.4	626	252	568	39.3	263	1,433	8.6	623	249	560	39.1	258
Jan-Mar 2011	1,436	8.4	614	251	571	39.8	273	1,424	8.6	610	250	564	39.6	269
Feb-Apr 2011	1,428	8.3	622	247	559	39.1	279	1,415	8.5	618	245	552	39.0	275
Mar-May 2011	1,443	8.4	638	261	544	37.7	281	1,429	8.6	634	261	534	37.3	277
Apr-Jun 2011	1,461	8.5	658	245	558	38.2	290	1,450	8.7	655	244	551	38.0	288
May-Jul 2011	1,465	8.6	655	253	557	38.0	297	1,451	8.8	650	252	549	37.9	295
Jun-Aug 2011	1,508	8.8	672	270	566	37.5	302	1,495	9.0	669	266	560	37.5	299
Jul-Sep 2011	1,545	9.0	694	286	565	36.6	303	1,530	9.2	689	282	559	36.5	300
Aug-Oct 2011	1,546	9.0	699	283	564	36.5	307	1,529	9.2	692	280	556	36.4	302
Sep-Nov 2011	1,560	9.1	707	295	558	35.8	296	1,543	9.3	699	292	552	35.8	292
Oct-Dec 2011	1,543	9.0	696	290	557	36.1	292	1,526	9.2	689	287	550	36.0	288
Nov-Jan 2012	1,527	8.9	700	283	544	35.6	271	1,512	9.1	696	279	537	35.5	266
Dec-Feb 2012	1,508	8.8	669	285	554	36.7	286	1,492	9.0	662	283	546	36.6	280
Jan-Mar 2012	1,500	8.7	652	295	553	36.9	292	1,480	8.9	643	292	545	36.8	287
Feb-Apr 2012	1,492	8.6	632	300	559	37.5	299	1,474	8.8	624	297	552	37.5	295
Mar-May 2012	1,482	8.6	642	285	555	37.5	298	1,468	8.8	635	281	551	37.5	295
Apr-Jun 2012	1,465	8.5	628	278	558	38.1	286	1,453	8.7	625	275	553	38.0	282
May-Jul 2012	1,478	8.5	627	283	568	38.4	300	1,463	8.7	624	279	560	38.3	294
Jun-Aug 2012	1,446	8.3	621	264	560	38.7	300	1,431	8.5	618	261	552	38.6	294
Jul-Sep 2012	1,430	8.3	616	264	551	38.5	297	1,416	8.5	611	261	544	38.4	293
Aug-Oct 2012	1,431	8.3	611	258	562	39.3	310	1,414	8.5	604	254	555	39.3	306
Sep-Nov 2012	1,418	8.2	609	250	559	39.4	302	1,398	8.4	602	247	550	39.3	298
Oct-Dec 2012	1,420	8.2	619	244	557	39.2	304	1,401	8.4	613	241	547	39.0	298
Nov-Jan 2013	1,435	8.3	622	250	563	39.2	307	1,422	8.5	618	248	556	39.1	303
Dec-Feb 2013	1,449	8.4	635	254	560	38.6	305	1,437	8.6	632	252	554	38.5	301
Jan-Mar 2013	1,437	8.3	639	233	565	39.3	305	1,424	8.5	634	232	558	39.2	302
Feb-Apr 2013	1,425	8.2	646	218	562	39.4	301	1,408	8.4	639	216	554	39.3	297
Mar-May 2013	1,429	8.3	627	229	573	40.1	312	1,412	8.5	618	228	566	40.1	307
Apr-Jun 2013	1,437	8.3	630	238	569	39.6	313	1,416	8.5	618	237	561	39.6	307
May-Jul 2013	1,420	8.2	609	249	563	39.6	312	1,402	8.4	598	248	556	39.7	306
Jun-Aug 2013	1,417	8.1	611	249	557	39.3	310	1,398	8.3	599	248	550	39.4	305
Jul-Sep 2013	1,387	8.0	599	234	554	39.9	306	1,371	8.2	591	232	549	40.0	304
Aug-Oct 2013	1,347	7.7	597	217	533	39.6	292	1,330	7.9	587	214	528	39.7	290
Sep-Nov 2013	1,310	7.5	576	218	516	39.4	299	1,295	7.7	567	217	512	39.5	298
Oct-Dec 2013	1,321	7.6	575	226	520	39.3	306	1,304	7.8	564	225	515	39.5	304
Nov-Jan 2014	1,290	7.4	551	228	512	39.7	303	1,271	7.6	539	227	505	39.7	300
Dec-Feb 2014	1,264	7.2	540	215	509	40.3	289	1,245	7.4	529	213	503	40.4	286
Jan-Mar 2014	1,232	7.0	519	197	515	41.8	299	1,213	7.2	511	196	506	41.7	294
Feb-Apr 2014	1,207	6.9	517	185	506	41.9	290	1,187	7.1	507	182	497	41.9	286

4.7: Unemployment by age and duration

	All aged 16 & over							All aged 16 - 64						
	All	Rate (%)[1]	Up to 6 months	Over 6 and up to 12 months	All over 12 months	% over 12 months	All over 24 months	All	Rate (%)[1]	Up to 6 months	Over 6 and up to 12 months	All over 12 months	% over 12 months	All over 24 months
	1	2	3	4	5	6	7	8	9	10	11	12	13	14
Men	MGSD	MGSY	MGYK	MGYM	MGYO	YBWJ	YBWM	YBSI	YBTJ	YBWP	YBWS	YBWV	YBWY	YBXB
Mar-May 2014	1,160	6.6	495	183	482	41.5	283	1,138	6.8	486	180	472	41.5	278
Apr-Jun 2014	1,140	6.5	493	180	467	41.0	267	1,122	6.7	485	177	460	41.0	263
May-Jul 2014	1,116	6.4	489	168	459	41.2	267	1,101	6.6	482	165	453	41.2	262
Jun-Aug 2014	1,094	6.3	482	164	447	40.9	251	1,080	6.4	478	163	440	40.7	247
Jul-Sep 2014	1,086	6.2	489	171	426	39.3	233	1,070	6.4	482	169	419	39.2	228
Aug-Oct 2014	1,086	6.2	485	178	422	38.9	233	1,071	6.4	481	175	415	38.8	228
Sep-Nov 2014	1,068	6.1	488	173	407	38.1	225	1,053	6.3	482	170	400	38.0	221
Oct-Dec 2014	1,042	6.0	477	164	401	38.5	220	1,027	6.1	474	161	392	38.2	216
Nov-Jan 2015	1,026	5.9	481	152	392	38.3	223	1,010	6.0	477	150	384	38.0	218
Dec-Feb 2015	1,017	5.8	476	153	388	38.2	234	1,003	6.0	472	151	381	37.9	227
Jan-Mar 2015	1,007	5.7	483	154	371	36.8	232	991	5.9	478	151	363	36.6	226
Feb-Apr 2015	1,010	5.8	487	160	363	35.9	217	995	5.9	483	157	355	35.6	211
Mar-May 2015	1,010	5.8	495	161	353	35.0	208	995	5.9	491	158	346	34.7	203
Apr-Jun 2015	1,015	5.8	499	159	357	35.1	211	1,002	5.9	494	158	350	34.9	207
May-Jul 2015	985	5.6	502	150	333	33.8	194	971	5.8	496	148	327	33.7	190
Jun-Aug 2015	970	5.5	497	151	323	33.3	190	955	5.7	491	147	317	33.2	188
Jul-Sep 2015	958	5.4	500	143	315	32.9	184	945	5.6	494	140	311	32.9	181
Aug-Oct 2015	936	5.3	485	144	307	32.8	186	924	5.4	481	141	302	32.7	182
Sep-Nov 2015	921	5.2	490	141	290	31.5	172	911	5.4	486	140	286	31.3	169
Oct-Dec 2015	923	5.2	490	142	290	31.5	172	912	5.4	486	140	286	31.4	169
Change on qtr	*-36*	*-0.2*	*-9*	*-2*	*-25*	*-1.4*	*-13*	*-33*	*-0.2*	*-8*	*0*	*-24*	*-1.5*	*-13*
Change %	*-3.7*		*-1.9*	*-1.1*	*-7.9*		*-7.0*	*-3.5*		*-1.7*	*-0.2*	*-7.9*		*-7.0*
Change on year	*-119*	*-0.8*	*14*	*-22*	*-110*	*-7.0*	*-49*	*-116*	*-0.8*	*12*	*-21*	*-106*	*-6.8*	*-47*
Change %	*-11.4*		*2.8*	*-13.6*	*-27.6*		*-22.2*	*-11.2*		*2.5*	*-13.2*	*-27.0*		*-21.7*
Women	MGSE	MGSZ	MGYL	MGYN	MGYP	YBWK	YBWN	LF2J	LF2R	LF2Z	LF33	LF35	LF37	LF39
Nov-Jan 2007	736	5.2	496	114	126	17.1	56	733	5.3	492	113	128	17.5	55
Dec-Feb 2007	734	5.2	500	114	120	16.3	52	731	5.2	496	113	121	16.6	52
Jan-Mar 2007	733	5.2	498	114	121	16.5	52	729	5.2	495	114	120	16.5	51
Feb-Apr 2007	725	5.1	484	115	125	17.2	51	721	5.2	483	116	122	16.9	51
Mar-May 2007	717	5.1	482	110	126	17.5	50	712	5.1	480	110	123	17.3	49
Apr-Jun 2007	717	5.0	481	111	125	17.4	51	713	5.1	476	109	127	17.8	51
May-Jul 2007	710	5.0	472	110	128	18.0	53	705	5.0	469	109	127	18.0	52
Jun-Aug 2007	712	5.0	472	114	126	17.7	52	708	5.1	471	113	124	17.5	51
Jul-Sep 2007	715	5.0	474	113	128	17.9	50	712	5.1	474	113	125	17.6	50
Aug-Oct 2007	712	5.0	480	107	125	17.6	47	709	5.0	479	107	123	17.4	47
Sep-Nov 2007	710	5.0	478	106	126	17.7	47	707	5.0	477	106	123	17.4	47
Oct-Dec 2007	699	4.9	470	105	125	17.9	47	696	4.9	467	105	125	18.0	47
Nov-Jan 2008	691	4.8	461	110	120	17.4	49	689	4.9	456	109	123	17.9	49
Dec-Feb 2008	689	4.8	454	111	124	17.9	50	685	4.9	450	110	125	18.2	49
Jan-Mar 2008	688	4.8	451	111	126	18.3	53	684	4.8	450	110	125	18.3	52
Feb-Apr 2008	722	5.0	476	113	133	18.5	55	718	5.1	475	112	131	18.2	55
Mar-May 2008	689	4.8	446	113	130	18.8	52	685	4.8	445	112	128	18.7	52
Apr-Jun 2008	702	4.9	461	116	126	17.9	50	698	4.9	456	114	128	18.3	50
May-Jul 2008	716	5.0	470	115	131	18.4	55	713	5.0	468	114	131	18.4	54
Jun-Aug 2008	745	5.2	500	114	131	17.6	57	741	5.2	499	113	129	17.4	56
Jul-Sep 2008	765	5.3	507	122	136	17.8	57	761	5.4	507	121	133	17.4	56
Aug-Oct 2008	775	5.4	508	128	140	18.0	58	770	5.4	507	128	136	17.6	57
Sep-Nov 2008	794	5.5	519	132	143	18.0	59	789	5.6	517	132	140	17.8	59
Oct-Dec 2008	812	5.6	532	134	145	17.9	60	807	5.7	528	133	146	18.1	59
Nov-Jan 2009	833	5.7	543	143	147	17.7	60	828	5.8	537	141	150	18.1	59
Dec-Feb 2009	856	5.9	551	147	158	18.5	66	851	6.0	546	146	158	18.6	63
Jan-Mar 2009	897	6.2	569	158	171	19.1	72	892	6.3	566	158	168	18.8	70
Feb-Apr 2009	914	6.3	570	161	182	20.0	72	909	6.4	567	162	180	19.8	71
Mar-May 2009	944	6.5	583	170	191	20.2	71	938	6.6	580	170	188	20.0	70
Apr-Jun 2009	958	6.6	584	177	197	20.6	76	952	6.7	578	176	198	20.8	75
May-Jul 2009	957	6.6	582	177	198	20.7	74	951	6.7	578	176	197	20.7	72
Jun-Aug 2009	953	6.5	574	175	204	21.4	73	949	6.7	574	175	200	21.1	71
Jul-Sep 2009	954	6.5	566	176	211	22.2	69	947	6.6	565	175	207	21.8	68
Aug-Oct 2009	961	6.6	565	186	210	21.8	71	955	6.7	564	186	205	21.5	70
Sep-Nov 2009	959	6.6	540	198	222	23.1	75	953	6.7	536	196	221	23.1	74
Oct-Dec 2009	968	6.6	548	195	225	23.3	77	961	6.7	543	192	226	23.5	75
Nov-Jan 2010	944	6.5	518	199	226	24.0	74	936	6.6	512	196	228	24.4	72
Dec-Feb 2010	978	6.7	540	203	235	24.0	80	971	6.8	536	202	234	24.0	78
Jan-Mar 2010	984	6.7	542	196	246	25.0	81	977	6.8	541	196	241	24.6	78

4.7: Unemployment by age and duration

United Kingdom (thousands) seasonally adjusted

	All aged 16 & over							All aged 16 - 64						
	All	Rate (%)[1]	Up to 6 months	Over 6 and up to 12 months	All over 12 months	% over 12 months	All over 24 months	All	Rate (%)[1]	Up to 6 months	Over 6 and up to 12 months	All over 12 months	% over 12 months	All over 24 months
	1	2	3	4	5	6	7	8	9	10	11	12	13	14
Women	MGSE	MGSZ	MGYL	MGYN	MGYP	YBWK	YBWN	LF2J	LF2R	LF2Z	LF33	LF35	LF37	LF39
Feb-Apr 2010	986	6.7	541	194	250	25.4	83	980	6.9	540	194	246	25.1	81
Mar-May 2010	1,008	6.9	549	201	258	25.6	87	1,003	7.0	549	200	254	25.3	85
Apr-Jun 2010	1,012	6.9	554	203	255	25.2	92	1,007	7.0	550	201	255	25.3	90
May-Jul 2010	1,034	7.0	575	203	256	24.7	96	1,028	7.2	571	203	255	24.8	94
Jun-Aug 2010	1,037	7.0	569	203	266	25.6	100	1,032	7.2	568	203	261	25.3	98
Jul-Sep 2010	1,038	7.1	570	199	270	26.0	94	1,034	7.2	571	199	264	25.6	92
Aug-Oct 2010	1,058	7.2	567	210	281	26.6	96	1,054	7.3	569	211	275	26.0	94
Sep-Nov 2010	1,032	7.0	563	197	272	26.4	101	1,028	7.2	560	197	271	26.3	100
Oct-Dec 2010	1,046	7.1	571	198	277	26.4	104	1,040	7.3	565	198	277	26.7	103
Nov-Jan 2011	1,056	7.2	580	192	284	26.9	108	1,050	7.3	574	191	285	27.2	106
Dec-Feb 2011	1,046	7.1	569	192	286	27.3	110	1,041	7.2	565	192	284	27.3	108
Jan-Mar 2011	1,047	7.1	568	191	288	27.5	116	1,042	7.2	567	192	284	27.2	115
Feb-Apr 2011	1,034	7.0	563	189	281	27.2	110	1,029	7.2	560	189	280	27.2	109
Mar-May 2011	1,058	7.2	596	186	276	26.1	107	1,053	7.3	594	186	273	25.9	105
Apr-Jun 2011	1,078	7.3	601	190	288	26.7	120	1,072	7.4	596	188	288	26.8	119
May-Jul 2011	1,091	7.4	599	189	303	27.8	122	1,084	7.5	593	188	302	27.9	121
Jun-Aug 2011	1,104	7.5	589	205	310	28.1	125	1,094	7.6	586	205	304	27.8	123
Jul-Sep 2011	1,119	7.6	589	217	313	28.0	122	1,107	7.7	584	216	307	27.8	120
Aug-Oct 2011	1,134	7.6	598	222	314	27.7	127	1,119	7.7	592	221	306	27.3	125
Sep-Nov 2011	1,149	7.7	609	232	307	26.7	131	1,137	7.8	600	230	307	27.0	131
Oct-Dec 2011	1,141	7.7	605	226	310	27.2	135	1,131	7.8	596	223	312	27.6	135
Nov-Jan 2012	1,143	7.7	598	229	315	27.6	138	1,134	7.8	589	227	318	28.0	138
Dec-Feb 2012	1,144	7.7	587	224	333	29.1	138	1,136	7.9	580	224	333	29.3	137
Jan-Mar 2012	1,133	7.6	573	226	334	29.5	137	1,123	7.7	569	225	329	29.3	135
Feb-Apr 2012	1,132	7.6	571	230	332	29.3	137	1,123	7.7	566	228	329	29.3	136
Mar-May 2012	1,123	7.5	557	230	335	29.9	146	1,113	7.7	553	228	333	29.9	145
Apr-Jun 2012	1,118	7.5	564	224	330	29.5	138	1,110	7.6	558	222	330	29.8	138
May-Jul 2012	1,121	7.5	569	212	340	30.3	144	1,114	7.6	565	210	339	30.4	142
Jun-Aug 2012	1,105	7.4	562	199	343	31.1	142	1,099	7.5	563	199	336	30.6	141
Jul-Sep 2012	1,108	7.4	575	181	352	31.7	143	1,102	7.6	577	181	343	31.2	140
Aug-Oct 2012	1,103	7.4	572	181	350	31.7	139	1,099	7.5	575	183	341	31.0	138
Sep-Nov 2012	1,112	7.4	589	185	338	30.4	134	1,107	7.6	584	185	338	30.5	133
Oct-Dec 2012	1,115	7.4	586	201	328	29.5	139	1,112	7.6	582	200	330	29.7	139
Nov-Jan 2013	1,103	7.3	573	203	327	29.7	145	1,099	7.5	569	202	328	29.8	144
Dec-Feb 2013	1,138	7.5	578	213	346	30.4	160	1,134	7.7	578	214	343	30.2	158
Jan-Mar 2013	1,104	7.3	557	204	343	31.0	161	1,100	7.5	556	203	340	30.9	159
Feb-Apr 2013	1,105	7.3	563	201	342	30.9	158	1,100	7.5	558	199	343	31.2	157
Mar-May 2013	1,081	7.2	546	189	346	32.0	163	1,077	7.4	543	190	345	32.0	161
Apr-Jun 2013	1,078	7.1	543	190	345	32.0	163	1,074	7.3	540	189	345	32.1	161
May-Jul 2013	1,071	7.1	537	196	338	31.6	159	1,065	7.2	532	195	338	31.8	158
Jun-Aug 2013	1,085	7.2	544	194	347	32.0	158	1,079	7.3	543	194	342	31.7	158
Jul-Sep 2013	1,095	7.2	564	191	340	31.1	153	1,088	7.4	563	191	335	30.8	153
Aug-Oct 2013	1,056	7.0	534	182	340	32.2	154	1,049	7.1	536	182	331	31.5	154
Sep-Nov 2013	1,028	6.8	525	178	324	31.6	150	1,019	6.9	519	177	323	31.7	149
Oct-Dec 2013	1,036	6.8	535	173	327	31.6	147	1,023	6.9	529	171	323	31.6	145
Nov-Jan 2014	1,051	6.9	567	167	317	30.2	149	1,039	7.0	562	163	314	30.2	148
Dec-Feb 2014	996	6.5	536	159	301	30.3	144	984	6.6	533	156	295	30.0	143
Jan-Mar 2014	982	6.4	524	156	302	30.7	148	974	6.6	521	153	300	30.8	148
Feb-Apr 2014	960	6.3	514	157	289	30.1	143	951	6.4	507	155	289	30.4	142
Mar-May 2014	951	6.2	516	163	271	28.5	135	944	6.4	511	164	269	28.5	134
Apr-Jun 2014	921	6.0	497	151	273	29.6	142	913	6.2	492	150	272	29.8	140
May-Jul 2014	893	5.8	479	150	265	29.6	133	888	6.0	474	149	264	29.8	132
Jun-Aug 2014	874	5.7	461	148	265	30.3	138	868	5.9	460	148	260	30.0	137
Jul-Sep 2014	871	5.7	461	146	264	30.3	144	865	5.8	461	147	258	29.8	143
Aug-Oct 2014	866	5.7	450	153	263	30.4	144	861	5.8	452	155	254	29.5	143
Sep-Nov 2014	854	5.6	461	144	249	29.2	130	849	5.7	457	144	248	29.2	129
Oct-Dec 2014	830	5.4	454	140	236	28.5	119	826	5.6	452	138	236	28.6	118
Nov-Jan 2015	835	5.4	465	135	235	28.1	116	830	5.6	461	133	236	28.4	115
Dec-Feb 2015	828	5.4	462	131	234	28.3	118	822	5.5	460	131	231	28.1	115
Jan-Mar 2015	823	5.3	476	130	218	26.4	110	817	5.5	472	129	216	26.4	107
Feb-Apr 2015	812	5.3	468	131	213	26.3	110	807	5.4	463	129	214	26.5	107
Mar-May 2015	838	5.4	479	142	216	25.8	110	834	5.6	477	142	215	25.8	108
Apr-Jun 2015	832	5.4	468	144	221	26.5	114	823	5.5	464	142	218	26.5	111
May-Jul 2015	835	5.4	477	144	214	25.7	115	825	5.5	472	141	212	25.7	112
Jun-Aug 2015	802	5.2	460	136	205	25.6	112	792	5.3	456	135	201	25.4	110
Jul-Sep 2015	794	5.1	458	135	201	25.3	106	786	5.2	456	133	197	25.1	106
Aug-Oct 2015	777	5.0	452	120	205	26.3	102	769	5.1	453	120	197	25.5	101
Sep-Nov 2015	763	4.9	445	117	201	26.4	96	754	5.0	440	116	198	26.2	94

4.7: Unemployment by age and duration

United Kingdom (thousands) seasonally adjusted

	All aged 16 & over							All aged 16 - 64						
	All	Rate (%)[1]	Up to 6 months	Over 6 and up to 12 months	All over 12 months	% over 12 months	All over 24 months	All	Rate (%)[1]	Up to 6 months	Over 6 and up to 12 months	All over 12 months	% over 12 months	All over 24 months
	MGSE	MGSZ	MGYL	MGYN	MGYP	YBWK	YBWN	LF2J	LF2R	LF2Z	LF33	LF35	LF37	LF39
	1	2	3	4	5	6	7	8	9	10	11	12	13	14
Women														
Oct-Dec 2015	769	5.0	459	112	199	25.8	90	761	5.1	455	111	195	25.7	88
Change on qtr	*-25*	*-0.2*	*0*	*-23*	*-2*	*0.5*	*-16*	*-25*	*-0.2*	*-1*	*-22*	*-2*	*0.6*	*-18*
Change %	*-3.1*		*0.1*	*-16.9*	*-1.1*		*-15.2*	*-3.2*		*-0.3*	*-16.8*	*-0.8*		*-16.9*
Change on year	*-61*	*-0.4*	*4*	*-28*	*-38*	*-2.7*	*-29*	*-65*	*-0.5*	*3*	*-28*	*-41*	*-2.9*	*-30*
Change %	*-7.4*		*1.0*	*-19.8*	*-16.0*		*-24.6*	*-7.9*		*0.7*	*-20.1*	*-17.2*		*-25.5*

	16-17							18-24						
	All	Rate (%)[1]	Up to 6 months	Over 6 and up to 12 months	All over 12 months	% over 12 months	All over 24 months	All	Rate (%)[1]	Up to 6 months	Over 6 and up to 12 months	All over 12 months	% over 12 months	All over 24 months
	YBVH	YBVK	YBXD	YBXG	YBXJ	YBXM	YBXP	YBVN	YBVQ	YBXS	YBXV	YBXY	YBYB	YBYE
	15	16	17	18	19	20	21	22	23	24	25	26	27	28
People														
Nov-Jan 2007	185	25.3	144	27	14	7.6	*	505	12.3	357	72	76	15.1	29
Dec-Feb 2007	189	26.2	146	28	15	7.7	*	512	12.5	356	69	87	16.9	31
Jan-Mar 2007	188	26.3	147	27	14	7.4	*	514	12.5	349	78	88	17.1	31
Feb-Apr 2007	187	26.2	145	27	15	8.1	*	519	12.6	342	86	91	17.5	28
Mar-May 2007	188	26.5	147	26	15	8.1	*	523	12.7	347	87	88	16.9	29
Apr-Jun 2007	193	27.5	150	28	14	7.4	*	515	12.5	339	85	91	17.7	30
May-Jul 2007	206	28.4	156	30	20	9.7	*	496	12.1	330	79	87	17.6	31
Jun-Aug 2007	205	28.3	151	35	19	9.1	*	500	12.2	333	73	93	18.7	35
Jul-Sep 2007	212	29.1	154	37	21	9.8	*	488	11.9	328	71	89	18.3	33
Aug-Oct 2007	201	27.6	147	40	14	7.0	*	485	11.8	325	67	93	19.1	35
Sep-Nov 2007	192	26.1	141	36	15	7.6	*	490	11.9	325	70	94	19.2	32
Oct-Dec 2007	185	25.0	136	33	16	8.5	*	488	11.9	322	70	96	19.7	36
Nov-Jan 2008	176	24.1	131	31	14	7.7	*	497	12.0	332	70	95	19.2	40
Dec-Feb 2008	174	24.2	129	33	13	7.3	*	496	12.0	332	73	91	18.4	39
Jan-Mar 2008	172	24.2	127	33	12	7.0	*	505	12.2	338	72	96	19.0	42
Feb-Apr 2008	184	25.3	136	35	14	7.3	*	510	12.4	340	65	105	20.7	40
Mar-May 2008	182	25.3	134	36	13	7.1	*	497	12.0	325	66	105	21.2	39
Apr-Jun 2008	186	26.1	143	32	11	5.9	*	519	12.6	341	74	104	20.0	36
May-Jul 2008	186	26.0	142	32	12	6.6	*	530	12.8	349	78	102	19.3	38
Jun-Aug 2008	192	26.9	153	28	11	5.9	*	545	13.3	355	81	109	20.1	39
Jul-Sep 2008	187	26.5	147	29	12	6.1	*	566	13.7	377	81	108	19.0	39
Aug-Oct 2008	190	27.2	153	24	12	6.5	*	577	14.0	390	91	96	16.7	35
Sep-Nov 2008	193	27.8	147	29	16	8.3	*	597	14.4	398	99	99	16.7	36
Oct-Dec 2008	191	28.2	144	32	16	8.2	*	606	14.6	401	103	103	17.0	37
Nov-Jan 2009	198	28.5	143	38	16	8.1	*	614	14.8	402	110	102	16.6	38
Dec-Feb 2009	187	27.6	135	35	17	9.0	*	624	15.2	408	110	106	17.0	40
Jan-Mar 2009	196	29.2	143	32	22	11.0	*	668	16.3	429	123	116	17.4	45
Feb-Apr 2009	192	29.7	136	34	22	11.6	*	692	16.9	432	130	131	18.9	51
Mar-May 2009	200	31.0	144	35	21	10.5	*	722	17.6	454	135	134	18.5	49
Apr-Jun 2009	206	32.3	144	40	22	10.7	*	710	17.4	427	143	140	19.7	50
May-Jul 2009	221	35.1	156	44	21	9.5	*	711	17.5	412	148	151	21.2	54
Jun-Aug 2009	214	34.5	144	47	24	11.1	*	719	17.6	409	154	156	21.7	55
Jul-Sep 2009	206	33.7	137	42	26	12.7	*	728	18.0	407	153	168	23.1	54
Aug-Oct 2009	198	32.6	130	40	28	14.3	*	734	18.3	424	150	159	21.7	50
Sep-Nov 2009	200	32.9	128	42	29	14.5	*	704	17.6	405	145	154	21.8	50
Oct-Dec 2009	196	33.0	130	38	29	14.6	*	704	17.5	409	140	156	22.1	51
Nov-Jan 2010	199	33.7	134	38	27	13.5	*	700	17.5	390	145	165	23.6	49
Dec-Feb 2010	199	34.1	134	35	30	15.1	*	715	17.8	388	156	171	23.9	57
Jan-Mar 2010	205	34.8	136	43	26	12.4	*	732	18.1	385	161	187	25.5	64
Feb-Apr 2010	217	36.5	143	49	25	11.6	*	721	17.8	376	154	191	26.5	71
Mar-May 2010	220	36.1	143	54	23	10.7	*	719	17.7	378	149	192	26.8	70
Apr-Jun 2010	199	33.7	132	45	22	11.2	*	728	17.9	403	141	184	25.3	72
May-Jul 2010	194	33.2	131	40	23	11.7	*	726	17.7	409	128	190	26.1	70
Jun-Aug 2010	189	32.7	128	36	25	13.3	*	741	18.0	410	126	205	27.7	70
Jul-Sep 2010	196	34.0	130	37	28	14.4	*	711	17.3	402	120	190	26.7	65
Aug-Oct 2010	213	36.2	143	41	30	14.0	*	735	17.9	405	132	198	26.9	68
Sep-Nov 2010	208	36.9	147	36	25	12.1	*	738	18.2	400	135	203	27.5	71
Oct-Dec 2010	215	37.5	154	35	26	12.0	*	745	18.2	395	141	209	28.1	76
Nov-Jan 2011	217	37.2	152	36	29	13.4	*	751	18.3	409	142	200	26.6	69
Dec-Feb 2011	220	37.4	153	39	27	12.3	*	740	18.0	406	136	198	26.8	75

4.7: Unemployment by age and duration

United Kingdom (thousands) seasonally adjusted

	16-17							18-24						
	All	Rate (%)[1]	Up to 6 months	Over 6 and up to 12 months	All over 12 months	% over 12 months	All over 24 months	All	Rate (%)[1]	Up to 6 months	Over 6 and up to 12 months	All over 12 months	% over 12 months	All over 24 months
	15	16	17	18	19	20	21	22	23	24	25	26	27	28
People	YBVH	YBVK	YBXD	YBXG	YBXJ	YBXM	YBXP	YBVN	YBVQ	YBXS	YBXV	YBXY	YBYB	YBYE
Jan-Mar 2011	215	37.2	150	38	26	12.1	*	728	17.9	393	137	199	27.3	82
Feb-Apr 2011	210	36.5	144	41	26	12.2	*	702	17.3	391	124	187	26.6	84
Mar-May 2011	207	36.4	138	43	25	12.3	*	728	17.8	413	133	182	25.0	79
Apr-Jun 2011	211	37.0	145	40	26	12.2	*	756	18.4	423	129	204	27.0	94
May-Jul 2011	211	37.5	141	41	29	13.9	*	782	19.0	428	136	219	28.0	91
Jun-Aug 2011	220	38.8	143	44	33	14.9	*	803	19.5	427	147	229	28.5	96
Jul-Sep 2011	226	40.1	142	47	37	16.4	*	809	19.8	427	159	224	27.6	88
Aug-Oct 2011	217	39.5	139	46	32	14.9	*	830	20.2	441	162	228	27.4	98
Sep-Nov 2011	218	38.5	135	46	37	16.9	*	834	20.3	456	166	211	25.3	92
Oct-Dec 2011	213	37.5	134	46	33	15.6	*	826	20.1	445	168	212	25.7	94
Nov-Jan 2012	221	38.9	138	45	38	17.3	*	818	20.0	435	166	216	26.4	88
Dec-Feb 2012	219	38.0	138	46	34	15.5	*	813	19.8	415	171	227	27.9	96
Jan-Mar 2012	210	37.2	133	45	33	15.7	*	818	19.9	415	172	231	28.2	99
Feb-Apr 2012	209	37.1	137	42	30	14.2	*	814	19.9	407	184	224	27.5	99
Mar-May 2012	203	36.3	135	40	29	14.4	*	828	20.0	404	183	241	29.1	111
Apr-Jun 2012	205	36.4	137	40	29	14.2	*	819	19.6	403	177	239	29.1	99
May-Jul 2012	204	36.6	134	41	29	14.2	*	825	19.6	407	167	251	30.5	103
Jun-Aug 2012	200	36.1	131	38	32	15.9	*	781	18.8	395	140	245	31.4	104
Jul-Sep 2012	199	35.3	127	35	36	18.1	*	786	19.0	408	141	237	30.1	102
Aug-Oct 2012	204	36.9	133	34	37	18.3	*	757	18.3	391	133	233	30.8	101
Sep-Nov 2012	203	37.2	136	34	33	16.4	*	777	18.6	408	133	236	30.3	91
Oct-Dec 2012	203	37.9	138	34	30	15.0	*	788	18.8	405	133	250	31.7	102
Nov-Jan 2013	197	37.4	133	37	27	13.6	*	807	19.4	419	128	259	32.1	107
Dec-Feb 2013	199	38.5	136	37	26	13.1	*	790	19.1	403	133	254	32.1	108
Jan-Mar 2013	194	37.5	132	34	28	14.3	*	773	18.7	401	126	247	31.9	101
Feb-Apr 2013	187	36.1	128	30	28	15.1	*	769	18.6	405	127	237	30.8	96
Mar-May 2013	196	37.4	130	36	30	15.1	*	771	18.8	399	120	252	32.7	108
Apr-Jun 2013	198	37.5	136	38	24	12.0	*	787	19.3	403	129	254	32.3	113
May-Jul 2013	200	37.9	138	40	22	11.1	*	779	19.1	387	131	260	33.4	117
Jun-Aug 2013	192	36.5	133	33	26	13.5	*	789	19.3	391	148	251	31.8	115
Jul-Sep 2013	191	36.6	135	30	27	14.3	*	793	19.2	397	139	258	32.5	113
Aug-Oct 2013	192	36.2	130	32	30	15.3	*	765	18.6	388	137	240	31.4	105
Sep-Nov 2013	196	36.4	137	35	24	12.4	*	741	18.0	375	134	233	31.4	106
Oct-Dec 2013	190	36.9	129	36	25	13.1	*	741	18.0	376	131	234	31.6	113
Nov-Jan 2014	191	37.0	140	31	20	10.7	*	731	17.7	377	130	225	30.7	103
Dec-Feb 2014	182	36.6	128	32	22	12.3	*	706	17.1	361	121	223	31.6	103
Jan-Mar 2014	182	36.0	129	30	24	13.0	*	686	16.8	347	115	224	32.7	104
Feb-Apr 2014	176	34.9	119	31	26	14.6	*	672	16.3	349	108	215	32.0	103
Mar-May 2014	169	34.1	118	26	25	14.6	*	647	15.7	349	106	192	29.7	92
Apr-Jun 2014	163	33.5	114	23	25	15.7	*	602	14.7	319	102	180	29.9	86
May-Jul 2014	160	33.5	111	25	24	15.2	*	588	14.5	310	99	179	30.5	84
Jun-Aug 2014	160	33.2	109	30	21	13.2	*	571	14.0	290	92	189	33.1	89
Jul-Sep 2014	160	32.9	113	30	16	10.1	*	585	14.4	304	89	192	32.8	87
Aug-Oct 2014	158	32.6	109	32	17	10.5	*	599	14.7	309	88	203	33.8	95
Sep-Nov 2014	157	32.2	109	29	18	11.7	*	614	15.2	333	94	187	30.4	84
Oct-Dec 2014	160	31.7	113	28	19	11.6	*	592	14.5	326	83	183	31.0	83
Nov-Jan 2015	157	31.2	112	25	20	12.5	*	590	14.4	332	78	180	30.5	82
Dec-Feb 2015	157	31.1	115	23	19	11.9	*	585	14.3	327	79	180	30.7	91
Jan-Mar 2015	148	29.7	110	21	17	11.4	*	584	14.2	343	85	156	26.7	81
Feb-Apr 2015	151	30.2	111	22	18	12.0	*	583	14.2	350	87	146	25.1	71
Mar-May 2015	145	28.7	110	20	16	10.7	*	576	14.1	344	92	139	24.2	66
Apr-Jun 2015	144	28.7	111	18	16	11.0	*	583	14.2	343	94	145	24.9	66
May-Jul 2015	143	27.7	111	19	12	8.7	*	569	13.9	342	91	136	23.9	62
Jun-Aug 2015	139	27.4	106	21	12	8.6	*	535	13.1	326	83	126	23.5	54
Jul-Sep 2015	137	26.6	102	21	13	9.6	*	514	12.5	319	75	119	23.2	51
Aug-Oct 2015	124	24.5	95	18	10	8.4	*	501	12.2	313	71	116	23.2	52
Sep-Nov 2015	128	25.7	96	18	15	11.5	*	504	12.3	317	72	114	22.6	47
Oct-Dec 2015	134	27.1	102	18	14	10.8	*	494	12.0	309	73	112	22.6	44
Change on qtr	-3	0.5	0	-4	1	1.1	*	-20	-0.5	-9	-2	-8	-0.7	-7
Change %	-2.3		-0.5	-17.8	9.2		*	-3.8		-3.0	-3.1	-6.6		-14.1
Change on year	-26	-4.6	-11	-11	-4	-0.8	*	-98	-2.5	-17	-9	-72	-8.4	-39
Change %	-16.4		-10.1	-37.4	-22.4		*	-16.5		-5.1	-11.4	-39.1		-47.4

4.7: Unemployment by age and duration

United Kingdom (thousands) seasonally adjusted

	16-17							18-24						
	All	Rate (%)[1]	Up to 6 months	Over 6 and up to 12 months	All over 12 months	% over 12 months	All over 24 months	All	Rate (%)[1]	Up to 6 months	Over 6 and up to 12 months	All over 12 months	% over 12 months	All over 24 months
	15	16	17	18	19	20	21	22	23	24	25	26	27	28
Men	YBVI	YBVL	YBXE	YBXH	YBXK	YBXN	YBXQ	YBVO	YBVR	YBXT	YBXW	YBXZ	YBYC	YBYF
Nov-Jan 2007	105	29.6	79	17	9	8.8	*	297	13.6	195	46	57	19.2	22
Dec-Feb 2007	105	29.5	77	17	10	9.8	*	301	13.8	195	43	63	20.9	23
Jan-Mar 2007	104	29.1	78	17	9	9.0	*	300	13.7	190	49	61	20.4	23
Feb-Apr 2007	101	28.4	76	14	10	10.0	*	308	14.0	187	56	65	21.0	21
Mar-May 2007	105	29.6	79	15	11	10.1	*	307	14.0	188	56	63	20.5	23
Apr-Jun 2007	106	31.0	81	15	10	9.7	*	306	14.0	186	53	67	21.8	23
May-Jul 2007	114	32.2	85	18	12	10.5	*	290	13.5	180	48	61	21.2	25
Jun-Aug 2007	114	31.5	82	21	11	9.6	*	296	13.7	182	47	67	22.7	28
Jul-Sep 2007	114	31.4	78	22	13	11.3	*	292	13.5	185	44	64	21.7	26
Aug-Oct 2007	113	30.7	80	25	8	6.9	*	287	13.3	181	40	66	22.8	28
Sep-Nov 2007	108	28.7	77	21	10	9.2	*	289	13.3	181	43	65	22.6	27
Oct-Dec 2007	108	28.7	78	20	11	10.1	*	288	13.3	176	44	67	23.4	31
Nov-Jan 2008	101	27.0	71	19	11	11.0	*	296	13.6	182	45	69	23.3	35
Dec-Feb 2008	100	27.3	69	22	9	8.8	*	303	13.9	189	45	69	22.8	35
Jan-Mar 2008	97	26.7	68	21	8	8.3	*	310	14.2	194	44	72	23.3	38
Feb-Apr 2008	103	28.7	74	20	9	9.0	*	307	14.1	192	40	74	24.2	34
Mar-May 2008	100	28.4	74	17	9	9.1	*	299	13.7	183	42	73	24.4	31
Apr-Jun 2008	99	28.1	75	16	8	8.4	*	320	14.7	197	48	75	23.3	28
May-Jul 2008	100	28.1	76	17	8	7.6	*	333	15.3	209	51	74	22.2	29
Jun-Aug 2008	101	28.3	80	15	6	6.1	*	342	15.6	212	51	78	22.9	29
Jul-Sep 2008	101	28.0	83	12	5	5.4	*	350	15.9	220	52	78	22.2	28
Aug-Oct 2008	100	28.3	85	9	5	5.5	*	354	16.2	223	60	71	20.1	25
Sep-Nov 2008	104	29.6	80	16	8	7.8	*	365	16.7	228	64	73	20.0	25
Oct-Dec 2008	102	29.6	75	19	8	7.9	*	373	16.9	231	66	75	20.2	26
Nov-Jan 2009	104	30.2	74	21	9	9.0	*	380	17.3	233	72	76	19.9	28
Dec-Feb 2009	102	30.0	73	17	11	11.3	*	386	17.8	239	74	73	19.0	29
Jan-Mar 2009	106	31.9	78	14	14	13.4	*	406	18.8	247	80	79	19.4	33
Feb-Apr 2009	103	32.2	71	19	13	12.9	*	418	19.4	251	84	84	20.0	37
Mar-May 2009	108	34.1	75	20	14	12.5	*	437	20.2	264	88	85	19.5	37
Apr-Jun 2009	116	36.8	76	24	15	12.9	*	436	20.2	251	94	91	20.9	37
May-Jul 2009	122	39.4	79	27	15	12.7	*	450	20.8	245	99	106	23.5	42
Jun-Aug 2009	120	39.5	78	27	15	12.6	*	448	20.8	229	107	112	25.0	43
Jul-Sep 2009	109	37.7	69	26	14	12.6	*	449	21.1	224	107	118	26.3	40
Aug-Oct 2009	106	37.1	67	24	15	14.3	*	449	21.2	233	108	109	24.3	35
Sep-Nov 2009	108	39.1	69	26	14	12.6	*	426	20.3	223	95	108	25.4	39
Oct-Dec 2009	107	38.9	69	23	14	13.3	*	424	20.2	220	90	114	27.0	38
Nov-Jan 2010	108	39.8	72	23	13	12.1	*	422	20.2	208	89	125	29.6	40
Dec-Feb 2010	109	40.0	72	21	16	14.3	*	429	20.4	206	98	125	29.1	44
Jan-Mar 2010	115	41.6	74	28	13	11.4	*	444	21.0	207	102	136	30.6	50
Feb-Apr 2010	122	42.6	77	32	12	10.3	*	438	20.5	201	97	139	31.7	54
Mar-May 2010	123	41.7	76	34	13	10.8	*	429	20.1	197	91	141	32.9	55
Apr-Jun 2010	107	37.3	67	26	14	12.8	*	429	20.1	207	88	135	31.4	55
May-Jul 2010	105	37.0	69	22	14	13.4	*	424	19.6	208	79	136	32.2	53
Jun-Aug 2010	101	36.0	67	18	15	15.2	*	431	19.9	216	71	144	33.4	53
Jul-Sep 2010	105	37.4	68	21	17	15.8	*	407	18.6	214	65	128	31.5	47
Aug-Oct 2010	107	38.6	70	22	16	14.6	*	424	19.4	220	72	132	31.1	48
Sep-Nov 2010	109	39.5	74	20	15	13.4	*	432	19.9	217	79	137	31.6	46
Oct-Dec 2010	112	40.5	79	19	14	12.7	*	435	19.9	214	80	141	32.4	47
Nov-Jan 2011	118	40.7	79	21	19	16.0	*	431	19.8	216	84	131	30.4	43
Dec-Feb 2011	115	41.4	79	21	14	12.6	*	429	19.7	218	82	129	30.0	47
Jan-Mar 2011	110	40.5	77	19	14	13.0	*	431	19.9	212	87	132	30.7	53
Feb-Apr 2011	110	40.6	74	21	16	14.1	*	429	19.7	220	80	129	30.0	59
Mar-May 2011	109	40.3	68	25	16	14.6	*	436	20.0	228	86	122	28.0	56
Apr-Jun 2011	113	41.6	71	24	18	15.7	*	446	20.4	235	78	133	29.9	64
May-Jul 2011	112	42.5	68	24	20	18.0	*	459	21.2	232	85	142	31.0	65
Jun-Aug 2011	119	43.7	72	25	22	18.8	*	479	22.0	238	89	153	31.9	70
Jul-Sep 2011	125	45.5	77	26	23	18.3	*	488	22.6	244	97	147	30.0	66
Aug-Oct 2011	118	44.0	73	25	20	16.9	*	504	23.3	254	98	151	30.0	73
Sep-Nov 2011	113	41.3	65	24	24	21.5	*	509	23.5	269	101	138	27.2	66
Oct-Dec 2011	108	39.5	65	22	21	19.0	*	513	23.6	261	106	146	28.4	70
Nov-Jan 2012	118	43.2	72	23	24	20.0	*	514	23.6	262	103	148	28.9	63
Dec-Feb 2012	114	40.7	72	22	20	17.3	*	511	23.4	247	110	154	30.1	72
Jan-Mar 2012	108	39.1	68	22	18	16.6	*	508	23.2	242	110	156	30.7	73
Feb-Apr 2012	105	38.2	70	20	16	14.8	*	507	23.2	234	118	154	30.5	73
Mar-May 2012	107	38.7	75	17	15	13.9	*	512	23.2	228	117	167	32.6	79
Apr-Jun 2012	105	38.8	74	16	15	14.0	*	505	22.7	229	113	164	32.4	70
May-Jul 2012	100	37.7	69	19	11	11.0	*	506	22.7	227	110	169	33.4	73

4.7: Unemployment by age and duration

United Kingdom (thousands) seasonally adjusted

	16-17							18-24						
	All	Rate (%)[1]	Up to 6 months	Over 6 and up to 12 months	All over 12 months	% over 12 months	All over 24 months	All	Rate (%)[1]	Up to 6 months	Over 6 and up to 12 months	All over 12 months	% over 12 months	All over 24 months
	15	16	17	18	19	20	21	22	23	24	25	26	27	28
Men	YBVI	YBVL	YBXE	YBXH	YBXK	YBXN	YBXQ	YBVO	YBVR	YBXT	YBXW	YBXZ	YBYC	YBYF
Jun-Aug 2012	101	38.5	66	20	15	14.8	*	474	21.5	221	89	164	34.6	71
Jul-Sep 2012	100	37.7	63	21	16	15.7	*	473	21.5	225	88	160	33.8	70
Aug-Oct 2012	107	40.4	68	19	19	18.0	*	457	20.7	216	83	158	34.6	70
Sep-Nov 2012	108	42.0	72	19	17	15.5	*	463	21.0	215	83	165	35.6	66
Oct-Dec 2012	111	43.6	73	20	18	16.7	*	464	21.1	213	80	171	36.9	71
Nov-Jan 2013	105	41.6	68	22	15	14.3	*	478	21.8	226	80	173	36.1	72
Dec-Feb 2013	100	41.1	67	18	14	13.8	*	458	21.1	219	75	164	35.8	72
Jan-Mar 2013	101	41.1	68	19	14	14.1	*	450	20.8	219	66	165	36.7	68
Feb-Apr 2013	98	40.4	64	18	16	16.1	*	446	20.6	218	64	163	36.6	67
Mar-May 2013	104	42.0	66	24	15	14.3	*	452	21.0	219	66	167	37.1	71
Apr-Jun 2013	106	41.6	71	25	10	9.6	*	466	21.7	227	72	167	35.9	75
May-Jul 2013	112	43.2	75	26	11	9.6	*	459	21.2	217	74	168	36.6	81
Jun-Aug 2013	104	40.2	72	21	11	10.2	*	468	21.7	214	90	165	35.3	82
Jul-Sep 2013	101	39.9	71	18	12	12.0	*	467	21.4	217	84	167	35.7	80
Aug-Oct 2013	103	40.4	70	19	14	13.5	*	460	21.2	221	84	155	33.7	73
Sep-Nov 2013	108	41.9	76	20	12	11.3	*	439	20.2	206	81	151	34.5	77
Oct-Dec 2013	99	40.6	67	20	12	12.3	*	445	20.4	204	83	157	35.4	84
Nov-Jan 2014	96	39.1	69	17	10	10.2	*	432	19.9	198	84	150	34.7	75
Dec-Feb 2014	91	39.3	60	18	13	14.3	*	427	19.6	199	80	148	34.7	75
Jan-Mar 2014	91	38.8	58	18	15	16.4	*	415	19.2	190	74	151	36.3	77
Feb-Apr 2014	93	40.3	59	18	17	17.9	*	410	18.7	194	66	150	36.5	77
Mar-May 2014	85	37.4	55	14	17	19.8	*	393	18.0	191	62	139	35.5	69
Apr-Jun 2014	78	35.6	49	12	17	22.1	*	368	17.1	180	64	123	33.5	63
May-Jul 2014	76	35.7	50	11	15	19.7	*	361	16.9	178	63	119	33.1	59
Jun-Aug 2014	77	35.3	51	12	13	17.1	*	351	16.4	167	58	126	35.8	62
Jul-Sep 2014	78	35.8	56	11	11	13.7	*	355	16.6	166	60	129	36.4	59
Aug-Oct 2014	77	35.4	52	14	10	13.3	*	357	16.6	165	57	134	37.6	63
Sep-Nov 2014	80	36.2	55	16	9	11.6	*	352	16.4	172	56	123	35.1	55
Oct-Dec 2014	85	36.8	61	15	9	10.5	*	343	16.0	175	43	125	36.3	57
Nov-Jan 2015	85	37.2	63	12	11	12.3	*	345	16.0	177	42	127	36.7	64
Dec-Feb 2015	93	39.1	69	12	12	12.5	*	339	15.7	171	42	127	37.4	69
Jan-Mar 2015	87	37.5	66	11	10	10.9	*	342	15.8	183	48	111	32.4	61
Feb-Apr 2015	89	37.6	67	12	10	10.9	*	344	15.9	187	53	104	30.3	53
Mar-May 2015	82	34.8	64	10	8	9.5	*	340	15.9	189	53	98	28.8	49
Apr-Jun 2015	81	34.4	62	11	8	10.3	*	339	15.8	188	51	100	29.5	47
May-Jul 2015	80	33.1	61	11	8	10.0	*	332	15.4	191	47	94	28.4	42
Jun-Aug 2015	76	32.2	56	12	8	10.3	*	315	14.6	185	44	85	27.1	36
Jul-Sep 2015	78	32.0	55	13	9	11.8	*	291	13.5	177	36	77	26.5	34
Aug-Oct 2015	73	29.7	52	13	7	9.7	*	279	13.0	171	34	75	26.7	35
Sep-Nov 2015	74	30.4	50	12	12	16.3	*	288	13.4	180	38	70	24.4	32
Oct-Dec 2015	72	29.5	50	11	11	14.8	*	283	13.1	174	40	68	24.2	27
Change on qtr	*-6*	*-2.4*	*-5*	*-2*	*1*	*3.0*	*	*-8*	*-0.3*	*-3*	*3*	*-9*	*-2.3*	*-6*
Change %	*-7.5*		*-9.2*	*-16.7*	*16.1*		*	*-2.7*		*-1.6*	*9.5*	*-11.0*		*-18.6*
Change on year	*-14*	*-7.3*	*-11*	*-4*	*2*	*4.3*	*	*-60*	*-2.9*	*-1*	*-3*	*-56*	*-12.1*	*-30*
Change %	*-15.9*		*-18.4*	*-26.1*	*18.6*		*	*-17.6*		*-0.4*	*-8.1*	*-45.0*		*-52.0*
Women	YBVJ	YBVM	YBXF	YBXI	YBXL	YBXO	YBXR	YBVP	YBVS	YBXU	YBXX	YBYA	YBYD	YBYG
Nov-Jan 2007	80	21.3	65	10	5	6.1	*	208	10.8	162	27	19	9.2	7
Dec-Feb 2007	84	23.0	69	11	*	5.2	*	211	11.0	161	26	24	11.2	8
Jan-Mar 2007	84	23.4	70	10	5	5.5	*	214	11.1	159	28	27	12.4	9
Feb-Apr 2007	86	24.0	68	12	5	6.0	*	211	11.0	156	30	26	12.3	7
Mar-May 2007	83	23.5	68	11	5	5.5	*	215	11.2	159	31	25	11.8	7
Apr-Jun 2007	86	24.1	70	13	*	4.7	*	209	10.8	153	31	24	11.7	7
May-Jul 2007	92	24.8	72	13	8	8.6	*	206	10.6	150	30	26	12.5	7
Jun-Aug 2007	92	25.0	69	15	8	8.5	*	204	10.5	151	26	26	12.9	8
Jul-Sep 2007	98	27.0	76	14	8	8.1	*	195	10.1	143	27	26	13.1	7
Aug-Oct 2007	88	24.4	67	15	6	7.0	*	198	10.1	144	27	27	13.7	7
Sep-Nov 2007	84	23.4	64	15	5	5.6	*	200	10.3	144	28	29	14.3	5
Oct-Dec 2007	77	21.2	59	13	5	6.2	*	200	10.3	145	26	28	14.2	5
Nov-Jan 2008	74	21.1	60	12	*	3.3	*	201	10.3	150	25	26	13.1	6
Dec-Feb 2008	75	21.1	59	11	*	5.3	*	193	9.9	143	27	22	11.6	4
Jan-Mar 2008	75	21.6	60	11	*	5.3	*	194	10.0	144	27	24	12.2	5
Feb-Apr 2008	81	22.0	62	15	*	5.3	*	204	10.5	148	25	31	15.3	6
Mar-May 2008	82	22.4	60	18	*	4.7	*	198	10.1	142	24	32	16.3	8
Apr-Jun 2008	88	24.1	69	16	*	3.1	*	198	10.2	144	25	29	14.6	8
May-Jul 2008	86	24.0	66	15	5	5.4	*	197	10.1	141	27	29	14.6	9

4.7: Unemployment by age and duration

United Kingdom (thousands) seasonally adjusted

	16-17							18-24						
	All	Rate (%)[1]	Up to 6 months	Over 6 and up to 12 months	All over 12 months	% over 12 months	All over 24 months	All	Rate (%)[1]	Up to 6 months	Over 6 and up to 12 months	All over 12 months	% over 12 months	All over 24 months
	YBVJ	YBVM	YBXF	YBXI	YBXL	YBXO	YBXR	YBVP	YBVS	YBXU	YBXX	YBYA	YBYD	YBYG
	15	16	17	18	19	20	21	22	23	24	25	26	27	28
Women														
Jun-Aug 2008	91	25.4	73	13	5	5.7	*	204	10.6	143	30	31	15.3	10
Jul-Sep 2008	86	24.9	64	17	6	7.0	*	216	11.1	157	29	30	13.9	11
Aug-Oct 2008	90	26.0	68	15	7	7.5	*	223	11.5	167	31	25	11.3	10
Sep-Nov 2008	89	25.9	67	14	8	9.0	*	231	11.8	170	35	26	11.4	11
Oct-Dec 2008	89	26.7	69	13	8	8.5	*	234	12.0	170	37	27	11.7	11
Nov-Jan 2009	94	26.9	69	18	7	7.2	*	234	12.0	169	38	26	11.3	10
Dec-Feb 2009	85	25.2	62	18	5	6.3	*	238	12.3	170	36	33	13.7	11
Jan-Mar 2009	90	26.5	65	18	7	8.2	*	262	13.5	182	43	37	14.2	12
Feb-Apr 2009	89	27.3	65	14	9	10.1	*	274	14.1	181	46	47	17.2	14
Mar-May 2009	92	28.1	69	15	7	8.1	*	285	14.7	190	48	48	16.9	13
Apr-Jun 2009	90	27.9	68	16	7	7.8	*	274	14.2	176	49	49	17.9	13
May-Jul 2009	99	30.9	76	17	6	5.7	*	261	13.8	168	48	45	17.3	12
Jun-Aug 2009	94	29.7	66	19	9	9.3	*	271	14.1	180	47	44	16.3	12
Jul-Sep 2009	97	30.0	68	16	12	12.8	*	279	14.5	183	46	50	17.9	14
Aug-Oct 2009	92	28.7	63	16	13	14.2	*	284	14.9	192	43	50	17.6	15
Sep-Nov 2009	92	27.7	60	16	15	16.8	*	278	14.6	183	50	46	16.4	12
Oct-Dec 2009	90	27.9	61	15	14	16.0	*	280	14.6	189	50	41	14.8	13
Nov-Jan 2010	91	28.6	62	15	14	15.1	*	278	14.5	181	57	40	14.5	9
Dec-Feb 2010	90	29.0	62	14	15	16.1	*	286	14.9	182	58	46	16.0	13
Jan-Mar 2010	90	28.8	62	15	12	13.8	*	288	15.0	178	59	51	17.7	14
Feb-Apr 2010	96	30.8	66	17	13	13.3	*	284	14.7	175	56	52	18.5	17
Mar-May 2010	97	30.9	67	20	10	10.4	*	289	15.0	181	58	51	17.6	15
Apr-Jun 2010	92	30.3	65	19	9	9.4	*	299	15.4	196	53	50	16.6	16
May-Jul 2010	89	29.5	62	18	9	9.7	*	303	15.5	201	49	53	17.6	17
Jun-Aug 2010	88	29.5	61	17	10	11.0	*	310	15.9	194	55	61	19.8	17
Jul-Sep 2010	91	30.8	63	16	12	12.9	*	304	15.7	188	55	61	20.2	17
Aug-Oct 2010	106	34.0	73	18	14	13.4	*	312	16.2	185	60	66	21.2	20
Sep-Nov 2010	100	34.4	73	16	11	10.6	*	306	16.3	183	56	66	21.7	25
Oct-Dec 2010	102	34.7	75	16	11	11.2	*	310	16.3	181	61	68	22.0	29
Nov-Jan 2011	100	33.8	73	16	10	10.3	*	320	16.6	194	58	69	21.6	27
Dec-Feb 2011	105	33.9	74	18	13	12.0	*	310	16.2	188	54	69	22.3	28
Jan-Mar 2011	105	34.3	74	19	12	11.2	*	297	15.5	181	50	66	22.3	28
Feb-Apr 2011	100	32.9	70	20	10	10.1	*	273	14.5	171	43	58	21.3	26
Mar-May 2011	98	32.9	70	18	10	9.8	*	292	15.2	185	47	60	20.4	23
Apr-Jun 2011	98	32.9	74	16	8	8.1	*	310	16.0	188	51	71	22.8	31
May-Jul 2011	99	33.1	73	17	9	9.2	*	323	16.7	196	50	76	23.7	27
Jun-Aug 2011	100	34.2	71	20	10	10.2	*	324	16.8	189	59	76	23.5	26
Jul-Sep 2011	100	34.8	65	21	14	13.9	*	322	16.7	182	62	77	23.9	22
Aug-Oct 2011	99	35.2	66	20	12	12.5	*	327	16.8	186	64	76	23.4	24
Sep-Nov 2011	105	35.8	70	22	12	11.9	*	325	16.7	187	65	72	22.2	26
Oct-Dec 2011	105	35.6	69	23	13	12.2	*	313	16.2	184	62	67	21.3	24
Nov-Jan 2012	103	35.0	66	22	15	14.2	*	304	15.9	173	63	68	22.4	25
Dec-Feb 2012	105	35.5	66	24	14	13.5	*	303	15.8	168	61	73	24.3	24
Jan-Mar 2012	102	35.3	64	23	15	14.6	*	310	16.1	173	61	75	24.2	26
Feb-Apr 2012	104	36.1	67	22	14	13.6	*	308	16.0	172	66	69	22.6	26
Mar-May 2012	96	33.9	59	23	14	15.0	*	317	16.4	176	66	74	23.4	32
Apr-Jun 2012	100	34.3	62	23	15	14.5	*	314	16.1	174	65	75	23.8	28
May-Jul 2012	104	35.6	64	22	18	17.2	*	318	16.2	179	57	82	25.9	30
Jun-Aug 2012	100	34.0	65	18	17	16.9	*	306	15.7	174	51	81	26.4	33
Jul-Sep 2012	99	33.1	64	15	20	20.6	*	313	16.2	183	53	77	24.6	33
Aug-Oct 2012	98	33.8	65	15	18	18.6	*	300	15.6	175	50	75	24.9	31
Sep-Nov 2012	96	33.0	64	15	17	17.5	*	314	16.0	193	50	71	22.5	25
Oct-Dec 2012	92	32.7	65	15	12	12.9	*	324	16.3	191	54	78	24.2	31
Nov-Jan 2013	92	33.5	65	15	12	12.8	*	329	16.6	194	49	87	26.4	35
Dec-Feb 2013	99	36.2	69	18	12	12.4	*	332	16.9	184	58	90	27.1	36
Jan-Mar 2013	93	34.1	64	15	13	14.5	*	324	16.4	182	60	82	25.2	33
Feb-Apr 2013	89	32.3	64	12	12	14.0	*	323	16.4	187	63	74	22.8	29
Mar-May 2013	92	33.3	64	13	15	16.0	*	320	16.5	181	55	84	26.4	37
Apr-Jun 2013	92	33.7	65	14	14	14.7	*	321	16.7	177	57	87	27.1	38
May-Jul 2013	88	32.9	63	14	11	13.0	*	319	16.7	170	57	92	28.8	36
Jun-Aug 2013	89	32.9	61	12	15	17.3	*	321	16.7	177	58	86	26.7	33
Jul-Sep 2013	90	33.4	63	12	15	16.9	*	327	16.7	181	55	91	27.9	32
Aug-Oct 2013	90	32.3	60	14	16	17.5	*	305	15.7	167	53	86	28.0	32
Sep-Nov 2013	88	31.4	62	14	12	13.8	*	303	15.6	168	53	82	27.0	29
Oct-Dec 2013	91	33.6	62	16	13	13.9	*	296	15.2	171	48	76	25.8	29
Nov-Jan 2014	96	35.2	71	14	11	11.1	*	299	15.3	178	46	74	24.9	29
Dec-Feb 2014	91	34.2	68	14	9	10.2	*	278	14.3	162	41	74	26.8	29
Jan-Mar 2014	91	33.6	70	12	9	9.7	*	271	14.1	156	41	74	27.1	28

4.7: Unemployment by age and duration

United Kingdom (thousands) seasonally adjusted

	16-17							18-24						
	All	Rate (%)[1]	Up to 6 months	Over 6 and up to 12 months	All over 12 months	% over 12 months	All over 24 months	All	Rate (%)[1]	Up to 6 months	Over 6 and up to 12 months	All over 12 months	% over 12 months	All over 24 months
	15	16	17	18	19	20	21	22	23	24	25	26	27	28
Women	YBVJ	YBVM	YBXF	YBXI	YBXL	YBXO	YBXR	YBVP	YBVS	YBXU	YBXX	YBYA	YBYD	YBYG
Feb-Apr 2014	82	30.2	61	12	9	10.8	*	262	13.5	155	42	66	25.1	26
Mar-May 2014	83	31.3	64	12	8	9.2	*	254	13.1	158	43	53	20.7	22
Apr-Jun 2014	84	31.8	66	10	8	9.7	*	234	12.1	139	38	57	24.3	24
May-Jul 2014	84	31.7	61	13	9	11.1	*	228	11.8	132	36	60	26.3	25
Jun-Aug 2014	84	31.5	57	18	8	9.7	*	220	11.4	123	34	63	28.8	27
Jul-Sep 2014	82	30.6	58	19	5	6.6	*	229	11.9	137	29	63	27.4	28
Aug-Oct 2014	81	30.4	57	18	6	7.9	*	243	12.6	144	31	68	28.1	32
Sep-Nov 2014	76	28.9	54	13	9	11.7	*	262	13.7	160	38	63	24.2	28
Oct-Dec 2014	75	27.3	52	13	10	12.8	*	249	12.9	151	39	59	23.6	26
Nov-Jan 2015	71	26.2	50	13	9	12.8	*	245	12.7	156	36	53	21.7	19
Dec-Feb 2015	64	24.1	46	11	7	11.1	*	246	12.7	156	37	53	21.4	22
Jan-Mar 2015	61	22.9	44	10	7	12.0	*	243	12.5	160	37	45	18.5	20
Feb-Apr 2015	63	23.6	44	10	9	13.6	*	239	12.3	163	34	42	17.7	18
Mar-May 2015	63	23.3	46	9	8	12.3	*	237	12.2	155	40	42	17.6	17
Apr-Jun 2015	64	23.7	49	7	8	12.0	*	243	12.4	155	43	45	18.6	18
May-Jul 2015	63	22.9	50	8	*	7.1	*	237	12.1	151	44	42	17.6	20
Jun-Aug 2015	63	23.3	51	8	*	6.6	*	220	11.4	141	39	40	18.4	19
Jul-Sep 2015	59	21.8	47	8	*	6.8	*	223	11.5	142	39	42	19.0	17
Aug-Oct 2015	51	19.5	43	5	*	6.5	*	221	11.4	143	37	41	18.7	16
Sep-Nov 2015	54	21.2	46	6	*	4.9	*	216	11.1	137	35	44	20.3	15
Oct-Dec 2015	62	24.7	52	6	*	6.1	*	211	10.8	135	33	43	20.4	16
Change on qtr	3	2.9	5	-2	*	-0.7	*	-12	-0.6	-7	-6	1	1.4	-1
Change %	4.5		9.6	-19.6	*		*	-5.3		-4.7	-14.9	1.6		-5.1
Change on year	-13	-2.6	0	-7	*	-6.8	*	-37	-2.1	-16	-6	-16	-3.2	-10
Change %	-16.9		-0.3	-50.6	*		*	-15.0		-10.5	-15.1	-26.5		-37.2

	25-49							50 and over						
	All	Rate (%)[1]	Up to 6 months	Over 6 and up to 12 months	All over 12 months	% over 12 months	All over 24 months	All	Rate (%)[1]	Up to 6 months	Over 6 and up to 12 months	All over 12 months	% over 12 months	All over 24 months
	29	30	31	32	33	34	35	36	37	38	39	40	41	42
People	MGVI	MGXB	YBYH	YBYK	YBYN	YBYQ	YBYT	YBVT	YBVW	YBYW	YBYZ	YBZC	YBZF	YBZI
Nov-Jan 2007	774	4.3	410	142	221	28.6	103	239	3.0	115	35	89	37.2	54
Dec-Feb 2007	765	4.2	414	132	218	28.6	102	241	3.1	124	39	78	32.5	47
Jan-Mar 2007	755	4.2	416	129	211	27.9	101	246	3.1	122	44	81	32.7	46
Feb-Apr 2007	735	4.0	399	124	212	28.8	100	252	3.2	126	42	84	33.4	48
Mar-May 2007	710	3.9	389	118	203	28.6	102	249	3.1	116	41	93	37.3	49
Apr-Jun 2007	700	3.8	393	108	199	28.4	96	251	3.1	117	42	92	36.6	48
May-Jul 2007	694	3.8	389	110	196	28.2	97	248	3.1	114	44	91	36.7	49
Jun-Aug 2007	697	3.8	386	119	192	27.5	90	243	3.0	116	39	88	36.3	48
Jul-Sep 2007	705	3.9	391	125	188	26.7	89	246	3.1	117	36	93	37.9	51
Aug-Oct 2007	703	3.9	398	118	187	26.7	92	241	3.0	115	36	90	37.4	50
Sep-Nov 2007	710	3.9	401	116	193	27.1	92	241	3.0	116	35	90	37.4	52
Oct-Dec 2007	701	3.8	397	114	190	27.0	91	234	2.9	113	38	82	35.3	43
Nov-Jan 2008	714	3.9	399	124	190	26.6	97	230	2.8	111	37	82	35.8	43
Dec-Feb 2008	716	3.9	391	128	198	27.6	103	235	2.9	108	40	87	37.0	48
Jan-Mar 2008	714	3.9	387	126	202	28.3	103	231	2.8	106	37	88	38.1	53
Feb-Apr 2008	733	4.0	404	127	203	27.6	102	240	2.9	109	42	89	37.1	52
Mar-May 2008	715	3.9	388	124	203	28.4	100	230	2.8	107	39	85	36.8	51
Apr-Jun 2008	735	4.0	394	130	210	28.6	103	240	2.9	110	39	91	38.0	53
May-Jul 2008	760	4.1	409	128	223	29.3	109	248	3.0	111	39	97	39.3	58
Jun-Aug 2008	793	4.3	446	122	225	28.3	111	263	3.2	120	46	96	36.7	56
Jul-Sep 2008	813	4.4	456	126	231	28.4	113	273	3.3	131	48	94	34.4	53
Aug-Oct 2008	824	4.5	459	129	236	28.7	112	283	3.4	144	45	95	33.5	55
Sep-Nov 2008	855	4.7	487	141	227	26.5	110	297	3.6	156	43	97	32.8	53
Oct-Dec 2008	894	4.9	518	142	233	26.1	114	311	3.8	162	47	102	32.8	60
Nov-Jan 2009	932	5.0	542	147	243	26.1	116	314	3.8	163	51	99	31.6	56
Dec-Feb 2009	982	5.3	576	152	255	25.9	120	335	4.0	171	59	106	31.5	65
Jan-Mar 2009	1,024	5.5	595	166	263	25.7	124	347	4.2	178	61	108	31.1	62
Feb-Apr 2009	1,052	5.7	615	183	254	24.1	118	360	4.3	182	62	116	32.2	65
Mar-May 2009	1,110	6.0	635	203	272	24.5	127	362	4.3	184	68	109	30.2	59
Apr-Jun 2009	1,158	6.3	655	227	277	23.9	130	374	4.5	188	73	113	30.3	59
May-Jul 2009	1,170	6.3	643	230	297	25.4	135	376	4.5	191	73	112	29.6	56

4.7: Unemployment by age and duration

United Kingdom (thousands) seasonally adjusted

	25-49							50 and over						
	All	Rate (%)[1]	Up to 6 months	Over 6 and up to 12 months	All over 12 months	% over 12 months	All over 24 months	All	Rate (%)[1]	Up to 6 months	Over 6 and up to 12 months	All over 12 months	% over 12 months	All over 24 months
	29	30	31	32	33	34	35	36	37	38	39	40	41	42
People	MGVI	MGXB	YBYH	YBYK	YBYN	YBYQ	YBYT	YBVT	YBVW	YBYW	YBYZ	YBZC	YBZF	YBZI
Jun-Aug 2009	1,172	6.4	621	237	314	26.8	139	378	4.5	183	79	116	30.8	57
Jul-Sep 2009	1,165	6.3	593	255	317	27.2	126	377	4.5	169	88	120	31.8	57
Aug-Oct 2009	1,166	6.3	577	274	316	27.1	127	386	4.6	162	103	120	31.2	59
Sep-Nov 2009	1,158	6.3	552	277	329	28.4	123	393	4.7	164	103	125	31.9	62
Oct-Dec 2009	1,155	6.2	542	267	346	30.0	131	397	4.7	171	94	132	33.4	65
Nov-Jan 2010	1,142	6.2	516	270	355	31.1	132	393	4.7	159	96	137	34.9	67
Dec-Feb 2010	1,191	6.5	530	272	389	32.6	152	391	4.6	157	93	141	36.1	63
Jan-Mar 2010	1,200	6.5	542	251	408	34.0	155	388	4.6	150	91	147	37.9	64
Feb-Apr 2010	1,196	6.5	534	248	414	34.6	156	375	4.4	138	80	157	41.9	67
Mar-May 2010	1,179	6.4	520	243	415	35.2	158	390	4.6	144	76	170	43.7	74
Apr-Jun 2010	1,166	6.3	492	249	424	36.4	169	394	4.6	145	77	172	43.6	72
May-Jul 2010	1,170	6.3	504	245	421	36.0	172	398	4.6	154	74	170	42.7	77
Jun-Aug 2010	1,153	6.2	488	238	427	37.0	178	393	4.6	155	72	166	42.2	84
Jul-Sep 2010	1,164	6.3	507	227	430	37.0	185	399	4.6	158	66	175	43.8	80
Aug-Oct 2010	1,166	6.3	502	225	439	37.6	188	399	4.6	154	69	175	43.9	77
Sep-Nov 2010	1,166	6.3	514	211	441	37.8	187	390	4.5	153	69	168	43.0	76
Oct-Dec 2010	1,152	6.2	509	206	438	38.0	186	391	4.5	150	75	165	42.2	78
Nov-Jan 2011	1,165	6.3	511	201	453	38.9	198	391	4.5	148	72	171	43.6	79
Dec-Feb 2011	1,143	6.2	496	197	450	39.4	212	389	4.5	139	72	178	45.7	83
Jan-Mar 2011	1,142	6.2	490	202	451	39.5	212	398	4.6	149	66	183	46.0	92
Feb-Apr 2011	1,152	6.2	498	204	450	39.0	206	397	4.6	151	67	178	44.9	96
Mar-May 2011	1,169	6.3	524	204	441	37.7	207	397	4.5	159	67	171	43.1	99
Apr-Jun 2011	1,184	6.4	530	200	453	38.3	212	389	4.5	161	65	163	42.0	99
May-Jul 2011	1,176	6.3	524	200	453	38.5	221	386	4.5	162	66	159	41.1	102
Jun-Aug 2011	1,199	6.5	532	210	457	38.1	224	390	4.5	159	73	158	40.5	101
Jul-Sep 2011	1,208	6.5	541	221	446	36.9	229	421	4.8	174	76	172	40.8	106
Aug-Oct 2011	1,212	6.5	546	223	443	36.5	233	420	4.8	171	74	175	41.7	100
Sep-Nov 2011	1,215	6.6	549	234	432	35.6	224	442	5.0	176	81	185	41.9	107
Oct-Dec 2011	1,208	6.5	554	228	426	35.3	218	437	5.0	168	75	195	44.5	113
Nov-Jan 2012	1,198	6.5	553	227	418	34.9	206	433	4.9	172	73	187	43.1	113
Dec-Feb 2012	1,187	6.4	528	227	432	36.4	208	434	4.9	174	65	194	44.8	120
Jan-Mar 2012	1,180	6.4	516	233	430	36.4	209	425	4.8	161	71	193	45.5	120
Feb-Apr 2012	1,175	6.3	504	230	442	37.6	214	426	4.8	156	75	195	45.8	123
Mar-May 2012	1,161	6.2	498	220	443	38.1	221	412	4.6	162	72	178	43.1	110
Apr-Jun 2012	1,155	6.2	496	219	439	38.1	218	403	4.5	156	67	181	44.9	105
May-Jul 2012	1,158	6.2	507	214	437	37.7	222	413	4.6	149	73	191	46.3	115
Jun-Aug 2012	1,158	6.2	512	214	432	37.3	219	411	4.6	146	71	195	47.3	116
Jul-Sep 2012	1,152	6.2	516	199	437	37.9	220	401	4.5	139	69	193	48.0	116
Aug-Oct 2012	1,166	6.3	515	207	444	38.1	232	407	4.5	143	67	197	48.5	113
Sep-Nov 2012	1,142	6.1	506	199	436	38.2	231	408	4.5	147	69	192	47.1	110
Oct-Dec 2012	1,140	6.1	510	209	422	37.0	232	405	4.5	153	68	183	45.3	106
Nov-Jan 2013	1,134	6.1	487	222	425	37.5	235	400	4.4	155	65	179	44.8	107
Dec-Feb 2013	1,188	6.4	525	223	440	37.0	238	411	4.5	149	75	186	45.3	116
Jan-Mar 2013	1,159	6.2	505	209	445	38.4	249	415	4.5	159	68	188	45.3	115
Feb-Apr 2013	1,146	6.2	512	193	441	38.5	244	428	4.7	163	68	197	46.0	117
Mar-May 2013	1,120	6.0	483	195	441	39.4	249	424	4.6	161	67	196	46.3	116
Apr-Jun 2013	1,104	5.9	473	195	437	39.6	242	426	4.6	161	67	199	46.6	118
May-Jul 2013	1,095	5.9	463	208	424	38.7	234	418	4.5	157	66	194	46.5	116
Jun-Aug 2013	1,105	5.9	470	201	434	39.3	238	415	4.5	160	62	193	46.5	112
Jul-Sep 2013	1,084	5.8	469	198	417	38.5	234	412	4.4	162	59	191	46.4	109
Aug-Oct 2013	1,036	5.6	454	170	412	39.7	230	410	4.4	159	59	192	46.8	107
Sep-Nov 2013	1,008	5.4	436	169	403	40.0	234	392	4.2	153	59	180	45.9	107
Oct-Dec 2013	1,024	5.5	446	170	408	39.8	232	403	4.3	160	62	181	44.8	106
Nov-Jan 2014	1,015	5.5	438	172	405	39.9	241	403	4.3	163	62	178	44.3	104
Dec-Feb 2014	974	5.2	423	161	389	40.0	226	398	4.2	163	60	176	44.2	101
Jan-Mar 2014	961	5.1	416	153	392	40.8	233	385	4.1	152	56	176	45.9	108
Feb-Apr 2014	940	5.0	414	154	373	39.7	222	380	4.0	149	49	181	47.6	108
Mar-May 2014	915	4.9	399	163	353	38.6	212	379	4.0	145	52	183	48.2	115
Apr-Jun 2014	922	4.9	404	161	357	38.7	207	375	3.9	152	45	178	47.5	113
May-Jul 2014	904	4.8	402	154	347	38.4	198	357	3.8	145	39	173	48.4	113
Jun-Aug 2014	888	4.8	400	150	339	38.1	190	348	3.6	145	40	163	46.8	107
Jul-Sep 2014	870	4.7	384	155	330	38.0	183	342	3.6	148	43	152	44.3	103
Aug-Oct 2014	860	4.6	377	165	317	36.9	174	335	3.5	140	46	149	44.4	104
Sep-Nov 2014	826	4.4	374	147	304	36.9	167	325	3.4	132	46	147	45.1	100
Oct-Dec 2014	801	4.3	371	145	285	35.6	155	320	3.3	122	48	151	47.1	101
Nov-Jan 2015	806	4.3	376	137	293	36.4	160	308	3.2	126	47	135	43.7	93
Dec-Feb 2015	797	4.3	367	135	295	37.0	164	306	3.2	129	47	129	42.3	94
Jan-Mar 2015	789	4.2	378	131	280	35.5	164	309	3.2	127	46	136	43.9	95

4.7: Unemployment by age and duration

United Kingdom (thousands) seasonally adjusted

	25-49							50 and over						
	All	Rate (%)[1]	Up to 6 months	Over 6 and up to 12 months	All over 12 months	% over 12 months	All over 24 months	All	Rate (%)[1]	Up to 6 months	Over 6 and up to 12 months	All over 12 months	% over 12 months	All over 24 months
	29	30	31	32	33	34	35	36	37	38	39	40	41	42
People	MGVI	MGXB	YBYH	YBYK	YBYN	YBYQ	YBYT	YBVT	YBVW	YBYW	YBYZ	YBZC	YBZF	YBZI
Feb-Apr 2015	787	4.2	367	135	284	36.2	167	301	3.1	126	47	127	42.2	89
Mar-May 2015	811	4.3	385	137	289	35.7	169	315	3.3	135	55	125	39.8	84
Apr-Jun 2015	802	4.3	375	133	294	36.7	176	319	3.3	138	59	122	38.2	83
May-Jul 2015	779	4.2	380	121	278	35.7	162	329	3.4	146	63	120	36.6	84
Jun-Aug 2015	766	4.1	384	122	260	33.9	156	332	3.4	141	61	131	39.3	90
Jul-Sep 2015	772	4.1	398	122	252	32.6	146	330	3.4	140	59	132	39.9	92
Aug-Oct 2015	758	4.1	393	119	245	32.3	141	331	3.4	136	55	140	42.4	93
Sep-Nov 2015	723	3.9	381	118	225	31.1	132	329	3.3	141	50	138	41.9	88
Oct-Dec 2015	746	4.0	399	118	229	30.7	134	318	3.2	139	45	134	42.2	81
Change on qtr	*-26*	*-0.2*	*2*	*-4*	*-23*	*-1.9*	*-11*	*-12*	*-0.2*	*-1*	*-14*	*3*	*2.3*	*-11*
Change %	*-3.3*		*0.4*	*-3.6*	*-9.1*		*-7.9*	*-3.6*		*-0.5*	*-23.5*	*2.0*		*-11.6*
Change on year	*-55*	*-0.3*	*29*	*-27*	*-56*	*-4.9*	*-21*	*-2*	*-0.1*	*17*	*-3*	*-16*	*-4.9*	*-20*
Change %	*-6.9*		*7.7*	*-18.9*	*-19.7*		*-13.3*	*-0.6*		*14.1*	*-5.5*	*-10.9*		*-19.6*
Men	MGVJ	MGXC	YBYI	YBYL	YBYO	YBYR	YBYU	YBVU	YBVX	YBYX	YBZA	YBZD	YBZG	YBZJ
Nov-Jan 2007	414	4.2	196	77	141	34.1	66	150	3.4	61	22	67	44.5	41
Dec-Feb 2007	416	4.3	198	71	147	35.3	70	152	3.4	70	24	58	38.1	35
Jan-Mar 2007	408	4.2	197	69	142	34.9	68	159	3.6	71	28	59	37.4	36
Feb-Apr 2007	395	4.0	188	66	141	35.8	68	165	3.7	77	27	61	37.2	36
Mar-May 2007	381	3.9	182	67	133	34.8	71	159	3.6	69	23	67	42.3	37
Apr-Jun 2007	366	3.7	180	59	126	34.5	65	163	3.6	71	25	68	41.5	36
May-Jul 2007	371	3.8	185	59	127	34.4	65	160	3.6	67	27	66	41.1	36
Jun-Aug 2007	368	3.8	181	60	127	34.5	60	155	3.5	69	25	62	39.7	34
Jul-Sep 2007	370	3.8	185	64	121	32.8	61	158	3.5	67	26	66	41.3	37
Aug-Oct 2007	365	3.7	182	63	121	33.1	65	152	3.4	62	25	65	42.5	36
Sep-Nov 2007	369	3.8	185	61	123	33.2	62	157	3.5	64	26	68	43.1	39
Oct-Dec 2007	363	3.7	185	59	119	32.8	59	150	3.3	61	28	61	40.8	32
Nov-Jan 2008	375	3.8	196	61	119	31.6	63	153	3.4	63	27	62	40.8	32
Dec-Feb 2008	376	3.8	185	66	124	33.1	67	154	3.4	62	29	63	40.9	37
Jan-Mar 2008	378	3.8	184	65	129	34.1	67	149	3.3	62	25	63	42.1	41
Feb-Apr 2008	384	3.9	186	68	130	33.8	66	151	3.3	60	27	64	42.3	41
Mar-May 2008	384	3.9	189	65	130	33.7	67	153	3.3	62	26	65	42.2	40
Apr-Jun 2008	400	4.1	196	69	134	33.6	72	159	3.5	60	26	73	45.8	42
May-Jul 2008	408	4.1	195	71	142	34.8	73	166	3.6	62	24	80	48.2	48
Jun-Aug 2008	433	4.4	216	67	151	34.8	75	171	3.7	66	30	75	44.0	46
Jul-Sep 2008	447	4.5	226	68	153	34.2	77	178	3.9	76	30	72	40.5	42
Aug-Oct 2008	459	4.7	242	65	152	33.0	77	186	4.0	87	27	72	38.6	42
Sep-Nov 2008	479	4.9	259	76	144	30.0	76	199	4.3	102	25	72	36.2	38
Oct-Dec 2008	503	5.1	279	74	150	29.9	80	214	4.6	108	30	75	35.1	45
Nov-Jan 2009	528	5.3	295	76	157	29.7	80	212	4.6	106	35	71	33.5	41
Dec-Feb 2009	556	5.6	316	75	164	29.5	81	228	4.9	111	41	76	33.5	48
Jan-Mar 2009	584	5.9	334	86	164	28.1	81	242	5.2	117	44	80	33.2	46
Feb-Apr 2009	607	6.1	349	100	158	26.1	78	254	5.4	125	44	85	33.6	49
Mar-May 2009	646	6.5	369	114	164	25.4	84	258	5.5	126	51	82	31.6	45
Apr-Jun 2009	672	6.8	375	134	163	24.3	82	267	5.7	127	53	86	32.3	45
May-Jul 2009	683	6.9	370	136	177	25.8	86	266	5.7	126	56	85	31.7	44
Jun-Aug 2009	690	7.0	350	151	189	27.4	89	273	5.8	126	56	91	33.3	47
Jul-Sep 2009	694	7.0	334	163	197	28.3	83	270	5.8	113	66	91	33.6	44
Aug-Oct 2009	689	7.0	317	174	198	28.7	85	278	5.9	111	75	91	32.9	46
Sep-Nov 2009	684	6.9	309	173	201	29.5	78	278	5.9	110	76	92	33.0	45
Oct-Dec 2009	677	6.9	300	164	212	31.4	84	277	5.9	113	67	97	34.8	47
Nov-Jan 2010	681	6.9	292	170	219	32.1	85	279	5.9	108	70	101	36.3	48
Dec-Feb 2010	704	7.2	286	167	251	35.6	100	276	5.9	105	66	104	37.9	48
Jan-Mar 2010	707	7.2	288	156	263	37.2	103	275	5.8	102	64	109	39.8	49
Feb-Apr 2010	698	7.1	278	150	270	38.6	105	266	5.7	94	57	116	43.6	51
Mar-May 2010	676	6.9	265	142	269	39.8	107	271	5.8	97	54	120	44.2	54
Apr-Jun 2010	667	6.8	249	140	278	41.6	114	272	5.8	95	55	122	45.0	52
May-Jul 2010	652	6.6	245	132	275	42.2	116	273	5.7	101	51	122	44.6	56
Jun-Aug 2010	645	6.5	234	133	278	43.1	119	262	5.5	95	46	120	45.9	61
Jul-Sep 2010	649	6.6	247	123	279	43.0	128	271	5.7	99	42	130	47.8	60
Aug-Oct 2010	655	6.6	252	118	285	43.6	134	269	5.7	95	46	128	47.5	56
Sep-Nov 2010	660	6.7	262	111	287	43.5	130	269	5.6	97	46	126	47.0	58
Oct-Dec 2010	646	6.5	253	108	285	44.2	130	264	5.5	92	51	121	45.9	59
Nov-Jan 2011	653	6.6	253	107	293	44.9	138	266	5.5	93	48	125	47.0	59
Dec-Feb 2011	635	6.4	240	100	295	46.4	153	266	5.5	89	48	129	48.7	61
Jan-Mar 2011	623	6.3	231	101	291	46.8	151	272	5.7	95	44	133	48.9	67

4.7: Unemployment by age and duration

United Kingdom (thousands) seasonally adjusted

			25-49								50 and over				
	All	Rate (%)[1]	Up to 6 months	Over 6 and up to 12 months	All over 12 months	% over 12 months	All over 24 months	All	Rate (%)[1]	Up to 6 months	Over 6 and up to 12 months	All over 12 months	% over 12 months	All over 24 months
	29	30	31	32	33	34	35	36	37	38	39	40	41	42
Men	MGVJ	MGXC	YBYI	YBYL	YBYO	YBYR	YBYU	YBVU	YBVX	YBYX	YBZA	YBZD	YBZG	YBZJ
Feb-Apr 2011	620	6.2	235	100	285	46.0	147	269	5.6	94	46	129	48.1	71
Mar-May 2011	628	6.3	248	104	277	44.1	148	269	5.6	95	45	129	47.9	75
Apr-Jun 2011	640	6.5	254	99	287	44.8	149	262	5.4	99	43	120	45.9	74
May-Jul 2011	635	6.4	255	101	279	43.9	153	259	5.4	100	43	115	44.5	76
Jun-Aug 2011	653	6.6	264	108	281	43.0	155	257	5.4	98	48	110	43.0	73
Jul-Sep 2011	654	6.6	270	111	273	41.7	158	278	5.8	103	52	123	44.1	77
Aug-Oct 2011	651	6.6	271	112	268	41.2	159	273	5.7	101	48	124	45.4	72
Sep-Nov 2011	652	6.6	270	119	263	40.4	150	286	5.9	103	51	132	46.2	77
Oct-Dec 2011	645	6.5	276	116	253	39.2	139	278	5.8	94	46	137	49.5	80
Nov-Jan 2012	623	6.3	266	113	244	39.2	128	272	5.7	100	44	128	47.1	77
Dec-Feb 2012	611	6.2	252	114	245	40.0	128	272	5.7	97	39	136	49.8	87
Jan-Mar 2012	608	6.1	247	117	244	40.2	131	275	5.7	95	46	135	49.0	88
Feb-Apr 2012	609	6.1	240	114	254	41.8	134	271	5.6	88	49	134	49.6	91
Mar-May 2012	603	6.1	244	104	256	42.3	141	260	5.3	95	47	118	45.5	76
Apr-Jun 2012	599	6.0	236	107	255	42.6	140	255	5.2	88	42	125	48.9	75
May-Jul 2012	607	6.1	244	106	257	42.3	144	265	5.4	86	48	131	49.5	83
Jun-Aug 2012	600	6.0	247	106	247	41.2	142	271	5.5	88	49	134	49.4	87
Jul-Sep 2012	592	6.0	245	104	243	41.1	140	266	5.4	82	51	132	49.7	88
Aug-Oct 2012	597	6.0	242	107	247	41.4	151	271	5.5	84	49	138	50.9	88
Sep-Nov 2012	576	5.8	236	100	240	41.6	151	271	5.5	85	48	138	50.8	83
Oct-Dec 2012	578	5.8	243	96	239	41.3	155	267	5.4	90	49	128	48.0	75
Nov-Jan 2013	585	5.9	235	102	247	42.3	156	267	5.4	93	46	128	48.0	78
Dec-Feb 2013	633	6.4	261	110	262	41.4	156	259	5.2	89	50	120	46.3	76
Jan-Mar 2013	627	6.3	256	104	267	42.5	162	259	5.2	96	44	119	46.0	74
Feb-Apr 2013	616	6.2	265	93	258	41.9	154	265	5.3	98	43	125	47.0	77
Mar-May 2013	605	6.1	242	98	265	43.8	160	269	5.4	101	42	126	46.7	78
Apr-Jun 2013	596	6.0	233	100	263	44.1	154	269	5.3	99	42	128	47.7	82
May-Jul 2013	593	6.0	228	108	257	43.3	147	256	5.1	89	41	127	49.5	82
Jun-Aug 2013	589	5.9	234	101	255	43.2	146	256	5.0	91	38	127	49.6	80
Jul-Sep 2013	574	5.8	227	97	251	43.7	149	245	4.8	85	36	124	50.6	74
Aug-Oct 2013	544	5.5	218	80	246	45.2	147	241	4.7	88	34	119	49.4	70
Sep-Nov 2013	535	5.4	210	83	242	45.2	151	228	4.5	84	34	111	48.6	69
Oct-Dec 2013	544	5.5	213	90	241	44.3	151	234	4.6	91	34	109	46.6	69
Nov-Jan 2014	526	5.3	196	90	240	45.6	160	236	4.6	87	37	112	47.5	66
Dec-Feb 2014	510	5.1	194	84	232	45.5	147	236	4.6	87	33	116	49.1	67
Jan-Mar 2014	498	5.0	190	75	233	46.7	148	227	4.4	81	31	116	51.1	73
Feb-Apr 2014	483	4.9	187	73	223	46.1	141	221	4.3	77	27	117	52.7	71
Mar-May 2014	458	4.6	174	76	208	45.3	134	224	4.3	75	31	118	52.7	77
Apr-Jun 2014	470	4.7	186	74	210	44.6	125	224	4.4	77	30	117	52.2	77
May-Jul 2014	458	4.6	181	69	208	45.5	126	221	4.3	80	24	116	52.6	80
Jun-Aug 2014	454	4.6	182	71	201	44.4	117	212	4.1	81	24	106	50.2	71
Jul-Sep 2014	443	4.5	177	76	190	42.8	107	209	4.0	89	23	97	46.2	65
Aug-Oct 2014	445	4.5	183	83	180	40.4	98	207	4.0	85	24	98	47.3	69
Sep-Nov 2014	428	4.3	178	75	175	40.9	98	207	4.0	82	26	99	47.9	69
Oct-Dec 2014	418	4.2	172	77	169	40.3	96	196	3.8	69	28	99	50.4	66
Nov-Jan 2015	412	4.2	171	72	169	41.0	98	183	3.5	71	26	86	47.1	59
Dec-Feb 2015	408	4.1	167	72	169	41.3	103	177	3.4	69	27	81	45.8	61
Jan-Mar 2015	398	4.0	165	68	166	41.7	106	180	3.4	68	27	85	47.0	63
Feb-Apr 2015	402	4.1	164	68	170	42.3	107	175	3.3	69	27	79	45.0	55
Mar-May 2015	405	4.1	165	69	171	42.3	106	183	3.5	77	29	77	41.7	51
Apr-Jun 2015	412	4.2	172	66	174	42.3	112	184	3.5	77	33	74	40.4	51
May-Jul 2015	389	3.9	170	58	161	41.4	102	183	3.5	80	34	69	37.6	50
Jun-Aug 2015	388	3.9	179	58	151	38.9	98	192	3.6	77	36	79	41.2	56
Jul-Sep 2015	392	4.0	186	59	147	37.6	92	198	3.7	82	35	82	41.2	57
Aug-Oct 2015	385	3.9	185	60	140	36.3	89	199	3.7	77	36	86	43.1	60
Sep-Nov 2015	362	3.6	177	59	125	34.7	84	197	3.7	83	32	82	41.7	56
Oct-Dec 2015	373	3.7	186	59	127	34.1	86	195	3.6	80	31	84	43.1	56
Change on qtr	*-20*	*-0.2*	*0*	*0*	*-20*	*-3.5*	*-6*	*-3*	*-0.1*	*-2*	*-3*	*3*	*1.9*	*-1*
Change %	*-5.0*		*0.2*	*0.7*	*-13.8*		*-6.9*	*-1.3*		*-2.3*	*-9.3*	*3.2*		*-1.8*
Change on year	*-45*	*-0.5*	*14*	*-18*	*-42*	*-6.3*	*-10*	*-1*	*-0.1*	*11*	*3*	*-14*	*-7.3*	*-10*
Change %	*-10.8*		*8.3*	*-23.2*	*-24.6*		*-10.6*	*-0.2*		*16.1*	*10.9*	*-14.7*		*-15.0*

4.7: Unemployment by age and duration

United Kingdom (thousands) seasonally adjusted

				25-49							50 and over			
	All	Rate (%)[1]	Up to 6 months	Over 6 and up to 12 months	All over 12 months	% over 12 months	All over 24 months	All	Rate (%)[1]	Up to 6 months	Over 6 and up to 12 months	All over 12 months	% over 12 months	All over 24 months
	29	30	31	32	33	34	35	36	37	38	39	40	41	42
Women	MGVK	MGXD	YBYJ	YBYM	YBYP	YBYS	YBYV	YBVV	YBVY	YBYY	YBZB	YBZE	YBZH	YBZK
Nov-Jan 2007	359	4.3	214	65	80	22.3	37	89	2.5	54	13	22	24.9	13
Dec-Feb 2007	348	4.2	216	61	71	20.5	32	90	2.6	54	15	21	22.9	12
Jan-Mar 2007	348	4.2	219	60	69	19.7	33	87	2.5	50	16	21	24.2	11
Feb-Apr 2007	340	4.1	211	59	70	20.7	32	87	2.5	49	15	23	26.3	11
Mar-May 2007	329	3.9	208	51	70	21.4	31	90	2.6	47	17	25	28.3	12
Apr-Jun 2007	334	4.0	213	49	72	21.7	31	88	2.5	46	17	24	27.6	12
May-Jul 2007	323	3.9	204	51	68	21.1	32	89	2.5	47	16	26	28.9	13
Jun-Aug 2007	329	3.9	205	59	65	19.8	30	87	2.5	47	14	26	30.3	14
Jul-Sep 2007	334	4.0	206	61	67	20.0	28	87	2.5	50	10	28	31.6	15
Aug-Oct 2007	338	4.0	216	55	67	19.7	27	88	2.5	53	10	25	28.5	14
Sep-Nov 2007	341	4.0	217	55	70	20.5	30	84	2.4	53	9	23	26.8	13
Oct-Dec 2007	338	4.0	213	55	70	20.8	32	84	2.4	53	10	21	25.5	11
Nov-Jan 2008	338	4.0	204	63	71	21.1	34	77	2.2	47	10	20	25.9	11
Dec-Feb 2008	340	4.0	205	61	73	21.6	36	81	2.3	46	11	24	29.4	11
Jan-Mar 2008	336	4.0	203	61	73	21.7	36	82	2.3	45	12	25	30.7	12
Feb-Apr 2008	349	4.1	218	59	73	20.9	36	88	2.5	49	14	25	28.2	11
Mar-May 2008	331	3.9	199	59	73	22.2	33	77	2.2	45	12	20	25.9	11
Apr-Jun 2008	335	3.9	198	61	76	22.6	31	81	2.3	50	13	18	22.5	10
May-Jul 2008	352	4.1	214	57	81	23.0	36	82	2.3	49	15	17	21.1	10
Jun-Aug 2008	360	4.2	231	55	74	20.6	36	91	2.5	54	16	21	22.8	11
Jul-Sep 2008	366	4.3	230	58	78	21.3	36	96	2.6	56	18	22	23.2	11
Aug-Oct 2008	365	4.3	217	64	85	23.2	35	97	2.7	56	18	23	23.6	13
Sep-Nov 2008	376	4.4	228	65	83	22.1	34	98	2.7	54	19	25	25.8	15
Oct-Dec 2008	391	4.6	240	68	83	21.3	34	98	2.7	54	17	27	27.8	16
Nov-Jan 2009	404	4.7	247	71	86	21.3	36	101	2.8	58	16	28	27.7	16
Dec-Feb 2009	427	5.0	260	76	91	21.3	39	107	2.9	60	18	29	27.2	16
Jan-Mar 2009	440	5.1	261	80	99	22.5	42	105	2.9	61	17	27	26.0	16
Feb-Apr 2009	445	5.2	266	83	96	21.5	40	106	2.9	58	18	31	28.9	16
Mar-May 2009	463	5.4	266	90	108	23.2	43	103	2.8	58	18	28	26.6	14
Apr-Jun 2009	487	5.7	280	93	114	23.4	48	107	2.9	61	19	27	25.2	13
May-Jul 2009	486	5.7	273	93	120	24.7	49	110	3.0	65	18	27	24.5	12
Jun-Aug 2009	482	5.6	271	86	126	26.1	49	105	2.8	57	23	25	24.1	10
Jul-Sep 2009	471	5.5	259	92	120	25.5	43	107	2.9	56	22	29	27.3	13
Aug-Oct 2009	477	5.5	260	99	118	24.7	42	108	2.9	51	28	29	26.8	14
Sep-Nov 2009	475	5.5	243	104	127	26.8	45	114	3.1	54	27	33	29.2	16
Oct-Dec 2009	478	5.5	241	103	134	28.0	47	120	3.2	57	27	36	29.9	18
Nov-Jan 2010	461	5.3	224	100	137	29.7	47	114	3.0	52	26	36	31.5	19
Dec-Feb 2010	487	5.7	244	105	138	28.3	52	115	3.1	52	26	37	31.8	16
Jan-Mar 2010	493	5.7	253	95	145	29.4	52	113	3.0	49	27	38	33.4	15
Feb-Apr 2010	498	5.8	255	98	144	29.0	51	109	2.9	45	23	41	37.7	15
Mar-May 2010	503	5.8	256	101	146	29.1	51	119	3.1	47	22	51	42.5	21
Apr-Jun 2010	499	5.8	243	109	147	29.5	54	122	3.2	51	22	50	40.6	20
May-Jul 2010	517	6.0	259	113	145	28.1	56	125	3.3	53	23	48	38.6	21
Jun-Aug 2010	508	5.9	254	105	149	29.4	60	131	3.4	60	26	46	34.8	22
Jul-Sep 2010	516	6.0	260	103	152	29.4	57	128	3.3	59	24	45	35.2	20
Aug-Oct 2010	511	5.9	250	108	154	30.0	54	130	3.4	59	23	48	36.6	21
Sep-Nov 2010	506	5.8	252	100	154	30.4	57	121	3.1	56	24	41	34.3	18
Oct-Dec 2010	507	5.9	256	98	153	30.2	55	127	3.3	58	24	44	34.7	19
Nov-Jan 2011	512	5.9	258	94	160	31.2	60	125	3.2	55	24	45	36.4	20
Dec-Feb 2011	508	5.9	256	97	155	30.6	59	123	3.2	50	24	48	39.3	22
Jan-Mar 2011	519	6.0	259	101	159	30.7	61	127	3.2	55	22	50	39.9	25
Feb-Apr 2011	533	6.2	264	105	164	30.8	59	128	3.3	58	21	49	38.2	25
Mar-May 2011	540	6.2	277	100	164	30.4	60	128	3.3	63	22	42	33.1	23
Apr-Jun 2011	543	6.3	277	101	166	30.5	63	127	3.3	62	22	43	34.0	25
May-Jul 2011	541	6.3	269	99	174	32.1	68	128	3.3	61	23	44	34.2	26
Jun-Aug 2011	546	6.3	268	102	176	32.3	69	133	3.4	61	25	48	35.6	28
Jul-Sep 2011	555	6.4	271	110	173	31.3	71	143	3.6	70	23	49	34.3	30
Aug-Oct 2011	562	6.5	276	112	174	31.0	74	147	3.7	70	25	51	34.8	29
Sep-Nov 2011	563	6.5	279	115	169	30.0	74	156	3.9	73	30	53	34.2	30
Oct-Dec 2011	563	6.5	278	112	173	30.8	78	160	4.0	74	29	57	35.9	34
Nov-Jan 2012	575	6.6	287	115	174	30.3	77	160	4.0	72	30	58	36.4	35
Dec-Feb 2012	576	6.7	275	113	187	32.5	81	162	4.1	77	26	59	36.3	33
Jan-Mar 2012	571	6.6	269	116	186	32.5	78	150	3.7	66	25	59	39.1	32
Feb-Apr 2012	567	6.5	263	116	188	33.1	80	154	3.8	68	26	60	39.1	32
Mar-May 2012	557	6.4	254	116	187	33.6	80	152	3.8	67	26	59	39.0	33
Apr-Jun 2012	556	6.4	260	112	184	33.2	78	148	3.7	68	24	56	38.0	29
May-Jul 2012	551	6.4	263	108	180	32.6	78	148	3.6	63	25	60	40.7	32

4.7: Unemployment by age and duration

United Kingdom (thousands) seasonally adjusted

	25-49							50 and over						
	All	Rate (%)[1]	Up to 6 months	Over 6 and up to 12 months	All over 12 months	% over 12 months	All over 24 months	All	Rate (%)[1]	Up to 6 months	Over 6 and up to 12 months	All over 12 months	% over 12 months	All over 24 months
	29	30	31	32	33	34	35	36	37	38	39	40	41	42
Women	MGVK	MGXD	YBYJ	YBYM	YBYP	YBYS	YBYV	YBVV	YBVY	YBYY	YBZB	YBZE	YBZH	YBZK
Jun-Aug 2012	558	6.4	265	108	185	33.1	77	141	3.5	58	22	61	43.2	29
Jul-Sep 2012	561	6.5	271	96	194	34.6	80	135	3.3	57	18	60	44.6	28
Aug-Oct 2012	569	6.6	273	99	197	34.6	81	136	3.4	58	18	60	43.9	26
Sep-Nov 2012	566	6.5	270	99	197	34.7	79	137	3.4	62	20	54	39.8	28
Oct-Dec 2012	563	6.5	267	113	183	32.5	76	137	3.3	63	19	55	40.1	31
Nov-Jan 2013	549	6.3	252	120	178	32.4	79	133	3.2	63	19	51	38.2	29
Dec-Feb 2013	555	6.4	264	113	178	32.0	82	152	3.7	61	25	66	43.7	40
Jan-Mar 2013	532	6.1	248	105	179	33.6	87	156	3.8	64	23	69	44.2	41
Feb-Apr 2013	530	6.1	247	100	183	34.5	90	163	3.9	66	25	72	44.4	40
Mar-May 2013	515	5.9	242	97	177	34.3	89	155	3.7	60	25	70	45.5	38
Apr-Jun 2013	508	5.8	240	94	174	34.2	88	157	3.7	62	25	70	44.8	36
May-Jul 2013	503	5.8	235	100	167	33.3	87	161	3.8	69	25	67	41.8	34
Jun-Aug 2013	516	5.9	237	100	179	34.8	92	160	3.8	69	24	66	41.6	32
Jul-Sep 2013	510	5.9	242	101	166	32.6	86	168	4.0	78	23	68	40.3	35
Aug-Oct 2013	492	5.7	236	90	166	33.7	84	169	4.0	71	25	73	43.0	37
Sep-Nov 2013	474	5.5	226	86	162	34.2	83	164	3.8	69	26	69	42.1	38
Oct-Dec 2013	480	5.5	233	80	166	34.7	81	169	3.9	69	29	72	42.3	37
Nov-Jan 2014	489	5.6	242	81	166	33.9	81	167	3.9	76	25	66	39.8	38
Dec-Feb 2014	463	5.3	230	77	157	34.0	79	163	3.7	76	27	60	37.1	34
Jan-Mar 2014	463	5.3	226	77	159	34.4	85	157	3.6	72	25	60	38.3	35
Feb-Apr 2014	457	5.2	227	80	150	32.8	81	159	3.7	72	22	64	40.4	37
Mar-May 2014	457	5.2	225	87	146	31.8	78	156	3.6	70	21	65	41.7	37
Apr-Jun 2014	452	5.2	218	87	147	32.5	82	151	3.5	74	16	61	40.4	36
May-Jul 2014	446	5.1	221	86	139	31.2	72	136	3.1	65	15	57	41.6	34
Jun-Aug 2014	434	5.0	218	79	137	31.6	72	136	3.1	63	17	56	41.4	36
Jul-Sep 2014	427	4.9	207	79	141	33.0	76	133	3.0	59	19	55	41.2	38
Aug-Oct 2014	415	4.7	194	83	138	33.2	76	128	2.9	55	22	51	39.8	35
Sep-Nov 2014	397	4.5	195	73	129	32.5	69	118	2.7	50	20	48	40.3	31
Oct-Dec 2014	383	4.4	199	68	116	30.4	59	124	2.8	53	19	52	41.9	34
Nov-Jan 2015	394	4.5	205	65	124	31.5	62	125	2.8	56	21	48	38.8	34
Dec-Feb 2015	389	4.4	200	63	126	32.5	62	128	2.9	59	21	48	37.6	34
Jan-Mar 2015	391	4.5	213	63	114	29.3	59	128	2.9	59	19	51	39.5	32
Feb-Apr 2015	385	4.4	203	67	114	29.7	60	126	2.8	57	20	48	38.3	33
Mar-May 2015	406	4.6	220	68	118	29.1	63	132	3.0	57	25	49	37.2	32
Apr-Jun 2015	390	4.5	202	68	120	30.8	64	135	3.0	61	26	48	35.3	31
May-Jul 2015	390	4.5	210	63	117	30.0	60	145	3.2	66	28	51	35.2	34
Jun-Aug 2015	378	4.3	205	64	109	28.9	58	140	3.1	64	25	51	36.7	33
Jul-Sep 2015	379	4.3	212	63	104	27.5	53	132	2.9	58	24	50	37.9	34
Aug-Oct 2015	373	4.3	209	59	105	28.3	52	132	2.9	58	19	54	41.2	33
Sep-Nov 2015	361	4.1	203	59	99	27.5	48	132	2.9	58	18	56	42.2	32
Oct-Dec 2015	373	4.3	213	59	102	27.2	48	123	2.7	59	14	50	40.8	25
Change on qtr	*-6*	*-0.1*	*1*	*-5*	*-3*	*-0.2*	*-5*	*-10*	*-0.2*	*1*	*-11*	*0*	*2.9*	*-10*
Change %	*-1.6*		*0.6*	*-7.6*	*-2.4*		*-9.6*	*-7.2*		*2.0*	*-43.9*	*0.0*		*-28.1*
Change on year	*-10*	*-0.1*	*14*	*-9*	*-15*	*-3.1*	*-10*	*-1*	*-0.1*	*6*	*-6*	*-2*	*-1.0*	*-10*
Change %	*-2.6*		*7.2*	*-13.9*	*-12.6*		*-17.7*	*-1.2*		*11.5*	*-29.4*	*-3.6*		*-28.4*

[1] Denominator = economically active for that age group.

* Sample size too small for reliable estimate.

Totals may not sum due to rounding

Note: When comparing quarterly changes ONS recommends comparing with the previous non-overlapping 3-month average time period (eg, compare Apr-Jun with Jan-Mar, not with Mar-May). For the change on quarter for this table, comparisons were made between Jul-Sep 2015 and Oct-Dec 2015

Source: Labour Force Survey

Labour market statistics enquiries: labour.market@ons.gsi.gov.uk

4.8: Regional labour market summary (employment, unemployment, economic activity, inactivity)

Thousands, seasonally adjusted

Headline estimates for November 2015 to January 2016

	Economically active		Employment		Unemployment		Economically inactive	
	Aged 16+	Aged 16-64	Aged 16+	Aged 16-64	Aged 16+	Aged 16+	Aged 16-64	Aged 16-64
	Level	Rate (%)[2]	Level	Rate (%)[2]	Level	Rate (%)[3]	Level	Rate (%)[2]
	1	2	3	4	5	6	7	8
North East	1,313	76.6	1,211	70.6	102	7.8	389	23.4
North West	3,573	77.0	3,396	73.2	177	4.9	1,037	23.0
Yorkshire and The Humber	2,692	76.7	2,529	71.9	163	6.1	789	23.3
East Midlands	2,353	78.0	2,250	74.5	104	4.4	637	22.0
West Midlands	2,766	75.3	2,616	71.1	150	5.4	875	24.7
East of England	3,142	81.0	3,030	78.0	112	3.6	705	19.0
London	4,622	77.6	4,332	72.7	290	6.3	1,295	22.4
South East	4,640	81.1	4,463	77.9	177	3.8	1,039	18.9
South West	2,792	80.3	2,686	77.1	106	3.8	649	19.7
England	**27,893**	**78.4**	**26,512**	**74.4**	**1,381**	**5.0**	**7,415**	**21.6**
Wales	1,520	75.6	1,440	71.5	79	5.2	466	24.4
Scotland	2,803	79.5	2,631	74.5	171	6.1	701	20.5
Great Britain	**32,216**	**78.3**	**30,584**	**74.3**	**1,632**	**5.1**	**8,582**	**21.7**
Northern Ireland	887	73.6	834	69.0	53	6.0	308	26.4
United Kingdom	**33,102**	**78.2**	**31,418**	**74.1**	**1,685**	**5.1**	**8,890**	**21.8**

Change on quarter (change since August to October 2015)[4]

	Economically active		Employment		Unemployment		Economically inactive	
	Aged 16+	Aged 16-64	Aged 16+	Aged 16-64	Aged 16+	Aged 16+	Aged 16-64	Aged 16-64
	Level	Rate (%)[2]	Level	Rate (%)[2]	Level	Rate (%)[3]	Level	Rate (%)[2]
North East	22	1.3	33	2.0	-11	-1.0	-22	-1.3
North West	17	0.6	24	0.7	-7	-0.2	-25	-0.6
Yorkshire and The Humber	17	0.2	19	0.2	-2	-0.1	-5	-0.2
East Midlands	20	0.4	17	0.3	3	0.1	-11	-0.4
West Midlands	-4	-0.3	-1	-0.3	-3	-0.1	12	0.3
East of England	5	-0.2	20	0.2	-15	-0.5	9	0.2
London	-22	-0.3	-18	-0.3	-4	-0.1	20	0.3
South East	3	0.3	-4	0.2	8	0.2	-14	-0.3
South West	-37	-1.1	-33	-0.9	-4	-0.1	36	1.1
England	**21**	**0.0**	**56**	**0.1**	**-35**	**-0.1**	**0**	**0.0**
Wales	25	0.7	33	1.1	-8	-0.7	-13	-0.7
Scotland	32	0.6	17	0.1	16	0.5	-21	-0.6
Great Britain	**78**	**0.1**	**106**	**0.2**	**-28**	**-0.1**	**-33**	**-0.1**
Northern Ireland	10	0.6	10	0.6	0	-0.1	-7	-0.6
United Kingdom	**87**	**0.1**	**116**	**0.2**	**-28**	**-0.1**	**-40**	**-0.1**

Change on year (change since November 2014 to January 2015)

	Economically active		Employment		Unemployment		Economically inactive	
	Aged 16+	Aged 16-64	Aged 16+	Aged 16-64	Aged 16+	Aged 16+	Aged 16-64	Aged 16-64
	Level	Rate (%)[2]	Level	Rate (%)[2]	Level	Rate (%)[3]	Level	Rate (%)[2]
North East	26	0.4	23	0.3	3	0.1	-5	-0.4
North West	38	1.1	80	2.0	-42	-1.2	-43	-1.1
Yorkshire and The Humber	21	-0.4	19	-0.5	2	0.0	18	0.4
East Midlands	5	-0.1	19	0.4	-14	-0.6	5	0.1
West Midlands	-22	-1.0	10	-0.1	-32	-1.1	38	1.0
East of England	38	0.2	83	1.4	-45	-1.5	-7	-0.2
London	23	0.6	16	0.4	7	0.1	-31	-0.6
South East	36	0.7	67	1.4	-31	-0.7	-38	-0.7
South West	55	0.3	71	0.9	-16	-0.7	-9	-0.3
England	**219**	**0.3**	**388**	**0.8**	**-169**	**-0.6**	**-72**	**-0.3**
Wales	38	1.2	51	1.8	-13	-1.0	-24	-1.2
Scotland	30	0.7	21	0.4	9	0.3	-25	-0.7
Great Britain	**287**	**0.4**	**460**	**0.8**	**-172**	**-0.6**	**-120**	**-0.4**
Northern Ireland	20	1.4	19	1.3	1	0.0	-16	-1.4
United Kingdom	**307**	**0.4**	**478**	**0.8**	**-171**	**-0.6**	**-136**	**-0.4**

Relationship between columns: 1=3+5

1. Labour Force Survey is tabulated by region of residence.

2. Denominator = all persons aged 16 to 64.

3. Denominator = Total economically active.

4. Quarter on quarter changes at regional level are particularly subject to sampling variability and should be interpreted in the context of changes over several quarters rather than in isolation.

Source: Labour Force Survey
Labour market statistics enquiries: labour.market@ons.gsi.gov.uk

4.9 claimant count rates: by region

ONS Crown Copyright Reserved [from Nomis on 18 August 2017]

Sex: Total
Rate: Workplace-based estimates

Area		January 2004 - December 2004 (inclusive)		January 2005 - December 2005 (inclusive)		January 2006 - December 2006 (inclusive)		January 2007 - December 2007 (inclusive)	
		number	rate	number	rate	number	rate	number	rate
England	E92000001	690,317	2.6	706,092	2.6	785,550	2.8	723,100	2.6
United Kingdom	K02000001	853,342	2.7	861,775	2.7	944,967	2.9	864,467	2.6
North East	E12000001	46,275	3.9	45,942	3.8	50,233	4.0	49,275	3.9
North West	E12000002	99,200	2.8	101,242	2.9	115,550	3.3	110,092	3.1
Yorkshire and The Humber	E12000003	73,400	2.8	76,017	2.9	87,358	3.3	81,158	3.0
East Midlands	E12000004	52,483	2.5	54,083	2.5	61,975	2.8	58,483	2.6
West Midlands	E12000005	88,258	3.2	93,958	3.4	108,325	3.8	102,525	3.6
East	E12000006	55,408	1.9	58,100	2.1	65,583	2.2	61,225	2.1
London	E12000007	162,750	3.4	162,950	3.4	166,833	3.4	145,450	2.9
South East	E12000008	70,675	1.6	71,625	1.6	81,675	1.8	71,950	1.6
South West	E12000009	41,867	1.6	42,175	1.6	48,017	1.8	42,942	1.6
Wales	W92000004	40,208	2.9	41,200	2.9	44,217	3.0	40,692	2.8
Scotland	S92000003	92,000	3.4	85,892	3.1	87,258	3.1	76,300	2.7
Northern Ireland	N92000002	30,817	3.6	28,592	3.3	27,875	3.2	24,375	2.8

Area		January 2008 - December 2008 (inclusive)		January 2009 - December 2009 (inclusive)		January 2010 - December 2010 (inclusive)		January 2011 - December 2011 (inclusive)	
		number	rate	number	rate	number	rate	number	rate
England	E92000001	754,108	2.7	1,275,583	4.5	1,230,708	4.4	1,258,225	4.5
United Kingdom	K02000001	906,083	2.7	1,527,683	4.6	1,496,358	4.5	1,534,408	4.6
North East	E12000001	53,717	4.3	83,775	6.6	81,417	6.5	85,367	6.9
North West	E12000002	119,708	3.4	191,708	5.3	184,017	5.1	190,200	5.3
Yorkshire and The Humber	E12000003	88,033	3.3	149,817	5.6	148,008	5.5	153,267	5.7
East Midlands	E12000004	61,408	2.7	108,300	4.8	101,492	4.5	103,142	4.5
West Midlands	E12000005	106,167	3.7	173,775	6.2	163,667	5.9	164,025	5.9
East	E12000006	63,625	2.2	115,992	3.9	111,067	3.8	111,800	3.8
London	E12000007	137,658	2.7	211,150	4.1	217,283	4.3	228,000	4.5
South East	E12000008	76,942	1.7	149,225	3.3	139,858	3.1	137,242	3.0
South West	E12000009	46,850	1.7	91,842	3.3	83,900	3.0	85,183	3.1
Wales	W92000004	45,517	3.1	77,133	5.2	73,192	5.1	74,850	5.2
Scotland	S92000003	78,633	2.7	125,958	4.5	135,733	5.0	141,508	5.1
Northern Ireland	N92000002	27,825	3.1	49,008	5.5	56,725	6.2	59,825	6.6

Area		January 2012 - December 2012 (inclusive)		January 2013 - December 2013 (inclusive)		January 2014 - December 2014 (inclusive)		January 2015 - December 2015 (inclusive)	
		number	rate	number	rate	number	rate	number	rate
England	E92000001	1,301,583	4.6	1,157,878	4.1	828,727	2.8	631,305	2.1
United Kingdom	K02000001	1,585,575	4.7	1,421,326	4.2	1,036,164	3.0	798,052	2.3
North East	E12000001	93,425	7.6	84,494	6.8	61,859	5.0	47,601	3.8
North West	E12000002	200,275	5.6	179,102	5.0	128,486	3.5	106,336	2.9
Yorkshire and The Humber	E12000003	164,075	6.1	149,861	5.6	110,507	4.1	83,010	3.0
East Midlands	E12000004	108,842	4.7	95,520	4.2	67,771	2.9	49,372	2.1
West Midlands	E12000005	164,983	5.8	149,178	5.3	109,447	3.8	81,161	2.8
East	E12000006	115,075	3.8	101,690	3.4	68,625	2.2	49,623	1.6
London	E12000007	226,708	4.2	202,011	3.7	148,079	2.6	114,937	2.0
South East	E12000008	139,333	3.0	119,459	2.6	81,414	1.7	60,401	1.3
South West	E12000009	88,867	3.2	76,563	2.7	52,540	1.8	38,865	1.3
Wales	W92000004	79,600	5.5	72,896	5.0	56,856	3.8	45,378	3.0
Scotland	S92000003	141,433	5.1	127,998	4.6	96,566	3.4	78,405	2.8
Northern Ireland	N92000002	62,958	7.1	62,555	7.0	54,016	5.9	54,016	5.9

Seasonally adjusted

Source: Office for National Statistics

From May 2013 onwards these figures are not designated as National Statistics.
From May 2013 onwards these figures are considered Experimental Statistics.
Under Universal Credit a broader span of claimants are required to look for work than under Jobseeker's Allowance. As Universal Credit Full Service is rolled out in particular areas, the number of people recorded as being on the Claimant Count is therefore likely to rise.
Rate figures for dates from 2015 onwards are calculated using mid-2015 workforce estimates.

4.10 Claimant count by sex and Unitary and Local Authority
from Nomis 24 August 2017
Age 16+

| | Claimant Count December 2015 | | | | | | Change on Year | | | | | |
| | Levels | | | Percentage of Pop | | | Levels | | | Percentage of Pop | | |
	Total	Male	Female	Total	Male	Female	Total	Male	Female	Total	Male	Female
United Kingdom	733,945	472,740	261,205	1.8	2.3	1.3	-105,260	-67,240	-38,020	-0.3	-0.3	-0.2
Great Britain	695,695	445,855	249,840	1.7	2.2	1.2	-94,440	-59,570	-34,870	-0.2	-0.3	-0.2
England and Wales	624,525	396,520	228,010	1.7	2.2	1.2	-85,530	-53,690	-31,835	-0.2	-0.3	-0.2
England	582,515	369,615	212,900	1.7	2.1	1.2	-80,235	-49,510	-30,725	-0.2	-0.3	-0.2
North East	46,740	32,010	14,730	2.8	3.9	1.8	-4,075	-2,185	-1,885	-0.2	-0.3	-0.2
Darlington	1,860	1,265	595	2.9	4.0	1.8	-110	-45	-65	-0.2	-0.1	-0.2
County Durham	6,945	4,530	2,415	2.1	2.8	1.5	-730	-545	-180	-0.2	-0.3	-0.1
Hartlepool	2,595	1,825	765	4.5	6.5	2.6	60	130	-70	0.1	0.5	-0.2
Middlesbrough	4,060	2,930	1,130	4.6	6.6	2.5	-80	5	-85	-0.1	0.0	-0.2
Northumberland	4,275	2,810	1,465	2.2	3.0	1.5	-565	-400	-165	-0.3	-0.4	-0.2
Redcar and Cleveland	3,445	2,630	815	4.2	6.6	1.9	95	370	-275	0.1	0.9	-0.6
Stockton-on-Tees	3,760	2,680	1,075	3.1	4.4	1.7	-425	-220	-205	-0.3	-0.3	-0.3
Tyne and Wear (Met County)	19,800	13,335	6,465	2.7	3.7	1.8	-2,315	-1,480	-840	-0.3	-0.4	-0.2
Gateshead	3,025	2,035	985	2.4	3.2	1.5	-720	-480	-235	-0.6	-0.8	-0.4
Newcastle upon Tyne	4,915	3,330	1,585	2.5	3.2	1.6	-525	-285	-240	-0.3	-0.3	-0.3
North Tyneside	2,890	2,020	870	2.3	3.2	1.3	-385	-250	-135	-0.3	-0.4	-0.2
South Tyneside	3,945	2,685	1,260	4.2	5.8	2.6	-200	-85	-115	-0.2	-0.2	-0.2
Sunderland	5,025	3,265	1,760	2.8	3.7	2.0	-490	-380	-110	-0.3	-0.4	-0.1
North West	101,090	65,815	35,275	2.2	2.9	1.6	-1,145	-615	-530	0.0	0.0	0.0
Blackburn with Darwen	2,440	1,595	845	2.7	3.4	1.9	105	60	45	0.1	0.1	0.1
Blackpool	3,395	2,335	1,055	4.0	5.4	2.5	-195	-80	-115	-0.2	-0.1	-0.2
Cheshire East	2,450	1,620	830	1.1	1.4	0.7	-165	-80	-80	-0.1	-0.1	-0.1
Cheshire West and Chester	2,690	1,725	960	1.3	1.7	0.9	-55	-40	-15	0.0	0.0	0.0
Halton	2,125	1,300	825	2.7	3.3	2.0	0	-15	10	0.0	0.0	0.0
Warrington	2,200	1,425	775	1.7	2.2	1.2	-260	-160	-100	-0.2	-0.2	-0.2
Cumbria	4,545	3,065	1,480	1.5	2.0	1.0	-290	-100	-190	-0.1	-0.1	-0.1
Allerdale	1,060	710	350	1.8	2.5	1.2	-120	-40	-80	-0.2	-0.1	-0.3
Barrow-in-Furness	1,170	825	345	2.8	4.0	1.7	-70	-15	-50	-0.1	-0.1	-0.2
Carlisle	865	550	315	1.3	1.7	0.9	-20	0	-20	0.0	0.0	-0.1
Copeland	885	600	290	2.1	2.7	1.4	-35	-25	-5	-0.1	-0.1	0.0
Eden	200	135	65	0.6	0.9	0.4	-15	-5	-10	0.0	0.0	-0.1
South Lakeland	365	250	115	0.6	0.8	0.4	-35	-10	-25	-0.1	0.0	-0.1
Greater Manchester (Met County)	43,200	27,980	15,220	2.4	3.2	1.7	990	655	340	0.0	0.1	0.0
Bolton	4,910	3,165	1,745	2.8	3.6	2.0	-150	-125	-25	-0.1	-0.1	0.0
Bury	2,685	1,720	965	2.3	3.0	1.6	180	105	75	0.2	0.2	0.1
Manchester	10,010	6,485	3,525	2.7	3.4	1.9	-220	-110	-110	-0.1	-0.1	-0.1
Oldham	3,870	2,380	1,490	2.7	3.4	2.1	195	120	80	0.1	0.1	0.1
Rochdale	3,415	2,110	1,305	2.5	3.2	1.9	440	295	145	0.3	0.4	0.2
Salford	4,170	2,760	1,405	2.6	3.3	1.8	195	140	60	0.1	0.1	0.1
Stockport	3,390	2,285	1,105	1.9	2.6	1.2	120	100	25	0.1	0.1	0.0
Tameside	3,605	2,330	1,275	2.6	3.4	1.8	120	50	75	0.1	0.1	0.1
Trafford	2,250	1,505	745	1.5	2.1	1.0	20	10	10	0.0	0.0	0.0
Wigan	4,895	3,235	1,660	2.4	3.2	1.6	85	80	10	0.0	0.1	0.0
Lancashire	12,500	8,170	4,330	1.7	2.2	1.2	430	275	155	0.1	0.1	0.0
Burnley	1,395	905	490	2.6	3.4	1.8	-25	15	-40	0.0	0.1	-0.1
Chorley	920	580	340	1.3	1.6	1.0	75	25	50	0.1	0.1	0.1
Fylde	565	345	220	1.3	1.5	1.0	-30	-30	-5	-0.1	-0.1	0.0
Hyndburn	1,065	705	360	2.2	2.9	1.5	130	100	30	0.3	0.4	0.1
Lancaster	1,625	1,095	530	1.8	2.4	1.2	-35	-30	-5	-0.1	-0.1	0.0
Pendle	1,100	715	385	2.0	2.6	1.4	120	90	30	0.2	0.3	0.1
Preston	1,800	1,195	605	1.9	2.5	1.3	-90	-55	-35	-0.1	-0.1	-0.1
Ribble Valley	250	165	85	0.7	0.9	0.5	20	15	0	0.1	0.1	0.0
Rossendale	850	540	310	2.0	2.5	1.4	35	35	0	0.1	0.2	0.0
South Ribble	755	465	290	1.1	1.4	0.9	10	-10	20	0.0	0.0	0.1
West Lancashire	1,280	865	415	1.8	2.6	1.2	295	185	110	0.4	0.5	0.3
Wyre	895	595	300	1.4	1.9	0.9	-75	-70	-5	-0.1	-0.2	0.0
Merseyside (Met County)	25,550	16,600	8,950	2.9	3.8	2.0	-1,700	-1,125	-575	-0.2	-0.3	-0.1
Knowsley	3,045	1,870	1,175	3.2	4.2	2.4	-125	-60	-65	-0.1	-0.1	-0.1
Liverpool	10,825	7,070	3,755	3.3	4.3	2.3	-800	-505	-295	-0.3	-0.4	-0.2
Sefton	4,330	2,835	1,500	2.6	3.5	1.8	-190	-160	-30	-0.1	-0.2	0.0
St. Helens	3,200	2,075	1,125	2.9	3.8	2.0	-100	-35	-65	-0.1	-0.1	-0.1
Wirral	4,150	2,755	1,395	2.1	2.9	1.4	-485	-365	-120	-0.2	-0.4	-0.1
Yorkshire and The Humber	73,005	47,870	25,140	2.1	2.8	1.5	-17,330	-11,255	-6,075	-0.5	-0.7	-0.4
East Riding of Yorkshire	3,030	2,000	1,030	1.5	2.0	1.0	-595	-380	-215	-0.3	-0.4	-0.2

4.10 Claimant count by sex and Unitary and Local Authority
from Nomis 24 August 2017
Age 16+

| | Claimant Count December 2015 | | | | | | Change on Year | | | | | |
| | Levels | | | Percentage of Pop | | | Levels | | | Percentage of Pop | | |
	Total	Male	Female	Total	Male	Female	Total	Male	Female	Total	Male	Female
Kingston upon Hull, City of	6,845	4,635	2,205	4.0	5.3	2.6	-1,450	-885	-570	-0.9	-1.0	-0.7
North East Lincolnshire	3,465	2,305	1,160	3.5	4.7	2.4	-415	-290	-125	-0.4	-0.6	-0.2
North Lincolnshire	2,405	1,600	805	2.3	3.1	1.5	-230	-100	-130	-0.2	-0.2	-0.2
York	905	625	285	0.7	0.9	0.4	-265	-165	-100	-0.2	-0.3	-0.2
North Yorkshire	3,540	2,275	1,265	1.0	1.3	0.7	-670	-505	-165	-0.2	-0.3	-0.1
Craven	235	150	80	0.7	0.9	0.5	-90	-55	-35	-0.3	-0.4	-0.2
Hambleton	405	280	120	0.8	1.1	0.5	-35	10	-50	-0.1	0.0	-0.2
Harrogate	525	340	185	0.6	0.7	0.4	-115	-90	-25	-0.1	-0.2	0.0
Richmondshire	200	125	75	0.6	0.7	0.5	25	10	15	0.1	0.1	0.1
Ryedale	270	160	105	0.9	1.1	0.7	-55	-60	0	-0.2	-0.4	0.0
Scarborough	1,245	790	455	2.0	2.6	1.4	-305	-265	-40	-0.5	-0.8	-0.1
Selby	665	425	240	1.2	1.6	0.9	-95	-60	-35	-0.2	-0.2	-0.1
South Yorkshire (Met County)	21,510	14,150	7,360	2.5	3.2	1.7	-3,425	-2,200	-1,225	-0.4	-0.5	-0.3
Barnsley	3,355	2,125	1,230	2.2	2.8	1.6	-400	-260	-140	-0.3	-0.4	-0.2
Doncaster	4,990	3,135	1,855	2.6	3.3	2.0	-860	-550	-310	-0.4	-0.6	-0.3
Rotherham	4,120	2,760	1,365	2.6	3.4	1.7	-940	-605	-335	-0.6	-0.8	-0.4
Sheffield	9,045	6,130	2,915	2.4	3.2	1.6	-1,225	-790	-435	-0.4	-0.5	-0.3
West Yorkshire (Met County)	31,310	20,280	11,035	2.2	2.8	1.5	-10,275	-6,730	-3,550	-0.7	-0.9	-0.5
Bradford	8,775	5,535	3,240	2.7	3.4	2.0	-3,445	-2,185	-1,260	-1.1	-1.3	-0.8
Calderdale	2,490	1,675	815	1.9	2.6	1.2	-785	-520	-265	-0.6	-0.8	-0.4
Kirklees	5,455	3,530	1,925	2.0	2.6	1.4	-1,430	-935	-490	-0.5	-0.7	-0.4
Leeds	10,975	7,280	3,695	2.2	2.9	1.4	-3,560	-2,370	-1,190	-0.7	-1.0	-0.5
Wakefield	3,615	2,260	1,355	1.7	2.2	1.3	-1,055	-715	-340	-0.5	-0.7	-0.3
East Midlands	42,985	27,535	15,450	1.5	1.9	1.0	-9,660	-5,815	-3,840	-0.3	-0.4	-0.3
Derby	2,195	1,330	865	1.4	1.6	1.1	-870	-555	-315	-0.6	-0.7	-0.4
Leicester	4,430	2,715	1,715	1.9	2.4	1.5	-1,805	-1,020	-785	-0.8	-0.9	-0.7
Nottingham	6,845	4,630	2,215	3.1	4.1	2.0	-1,545	-835	-710	-0.8	-0.8	-0.7
Rutland	125	80	40	0.5	0.7	0.4	-30	-25	-5	-0.1	-0.2	-0.1
Derbyshire	5,440	3,510	1,930	1.1	1.5	0.8	-1,480	-885	-595	-0.3	-0.4	-0.2
Amber Valley	855	520	335	1.1	1.4	0.9	-125	-85	-40	-0.2	-0.2	-0.1
Bolsover	595	375	220	1.2	1.5	0.9	-170	-100	-70	-0.4	-0.4	-0.3
Chesterfield	1,070	755	315	1.6	2.3	1.0	-315	-175	-140	-0.5	-0.5	-0.4
Derbyshire Dales	215	135	80	0.5	0.6	0.4	-50	-35	-15	-0.1	-0.1	-0.1
Erewash	1,105	725	380	1.5	2.1	1.0	-220	-125	-95	-0.3	-0.4	-0.3
High Peak	640	420	220	1.1	1.5	0.8	-150	-95	-55	-0.3	-0.3	-0.2
North East Derbyshire	670	430	240	1.1	1.4	0.8	-240	-130	-110	-0.4	-0.4	-0.4
South Derbyshire	295	160	135	0.5	0.5	0.4	-205	-140	-65	-0.3	-0.5	-0.2
Leicestershire	3,345	2,095	1,250	0.8	1.0	0.6	-590	-380	-210	-0.1	-0.2	-0.1
Blaby	420	260	160	0.7	0.9	0.5	-110	-70	-45	-0.2	-0.2	-0.1
Charnwood	850	535	315	0.7	0.9	0.6	-150	-100	-50	-0.1	-0.2	-0.1
Harborough	260	165	100	0.5	0.6	0.4	-25	-25	0	-0.1	-0.1	0.0
Hinckley and Bosworth	680	430	250	1.0	1.3	0.7	25	10	10	0.0	0.0	0.0
Melton	295	200	95	1.0	1.3	0.6	15	35	-25	0.0	0.2	-0.1
North West Leicestershire	520	330	185	0.9	1.1	0.6	-200	-130	-70	-0.3	-0.4	-0.2
Oadby and Wigston	320	175	145	0.9	1.0	0.8	-140	-105	-35	-0.4	-0.6	-0.2
Lincolnshire	7,235	4,740	2,495	1.6	2.2	1.1	-1,310	-875	-435	-0.3	-0.4	-0.2
Boston	615	395	220	1.5	1.9	1.1	-125	-85	-40	-0.3	-0.4	-0.2
East Lindsey	1,730	1,130	600	2.2	3.0	1.5	-435	-280	-155	-0.5	-0.7	-0.4
Lincoln	1,530	1,070	460	2.3	3.3	1.4	-280	-170	-110	-0.4	-0.5	-0.3
North Kesteven	585	385	200	0.9	1.2	0.6	-80	-70	-15	-0.1	-0.2	0.0
South Holland	580	330	245	1.1	1.2	0.9	-140	-110	-30	-0.3	-0.4	-0.1
South Kesteven	1,005	635	370	1.2	1.6	0.9	-50	-45	-5	-0.1	-0.1	0.0
West Lindsey	1,195	790	400	2.2	3.0	1.4	-195	-110	-80	-0.4	-0.4	-0.3
Northamptonshire	6,195	3,855	2,340	1.4	1.7	1.0	-535	-215	-320	-0.1	-0.1	-0.1
Corby	755	520	235	1.8	2.4	1.1	40	90	-50	0.1	0.4	-0.2
Daventry	440	275	165	0.9	1.1	0.7	35	40	-5	0.1	0.1	0.0
East Northamptonshire	530	320	205	1.0	1.2	0.7	-35	-5	-30	-0.1	0.0	-0.1
Kettering	1,005	620	385	1.7	2.1	1.3	0	-25	25	0.0	-0.1	0.1
Northampton	2,390	1,460	930	1.7	2.0	1.3	-435	-240	-195	-0.3	-0.4	-0.3
South Northamptonshire	260	160	100	0.5	0.6	0.4	-30	-15	-15	-0.1	-0.1	-0.1
Wellingborough	815	500	315	1.7	2.2	1.3	-110	-60	-50	-0.2	-0.3	-0.2
Nottinghamshire	7,180	4,575	2,605	1.4	1.8	1.0	-1,490	-1,025	-460	-0.3	-0.4	-0.2
Ashfield	1,435	895	545	1.9	2.3	1.4	-270	-175	-95	-0.4	-0.5	-0.3
Bassetlaw	1,125	705	420	1.6	2.0	1.2	-205	-160	-45	-0.3	-0.5	-0.1
Broxtowe	875	550	325	1.2	1.6	0.9	-125	-80	-40	-0.2	-0.2	-0.1
Gedling	975	635	340	1.4	1.8	0.9	-300	-210	-90	-0.4	-0.6	-0.2
Mansfield	1,345	880	465	2.0	2.6	1.4	-300	-195	-100	-0.5	-0.6	-0.3
Newark and Sherwood	865	520	345	1.2	1.4	1.0	-160	-130	-30	-0.2	-0.4	-0.1
Rushcliffe	560	395	165	0.8	1.1	0.5	-130	-75	-55	-0.2	-0.2	-0.2

4.10 Claimant count by sex and Unitary and Local Authority

from Nomis 24 August 2017

Age 16+

| | Claimant Count December 2015 | | | | | | Change on Year | | | | | |
| | Levels | | | Percentage of Pop | | | Levels | | | Percentage of Pop | | |
	Total	Male	Female	Total	Male	Female	Total	Male	Female	Total	Male	Female
West Midlands	**74,145**	**47,335**	**26,810**	**2.1**	**2.6**	**1.5**	**-11,010**	**-6,475**	**-4,535**	**-0.3**	**-0.4**	**-0.3**
Herefordshire, County of	895	570	325	0.8	1.0	0.6	-120	-85	-35	-0.1	-0.2	-0.1
Shropshire	1,835	1,200	630	1.0	1.3	0.7	-575	-355	-220	-0.3	-0.4	-0.2
Stoke-on-Trent	2,905	1,820	1,085	1.8	2.3	1.4	-640	-450	-190	-0.4	-0.5	-0.2
Telford and Wrekin	1,470	905	565	1.4	1.7	1.0	-450	-310	-140	-0.4	-0.6	-0.3
Staffordshire	4,470	2,760	1,710	0.8	1.0	0.6	-610	-395	-215	-0.1	-0.1	-0.1
Cannock Chase	695	405	290	1.1	1.3	0.9	-75	-80	0	-0.1	-0.2	0.0
East Staffordshire	520	315	205	0.7	0.9	0.6	-235	-125	-110	-0.3	-0.3	-0.3
Lichfield	365	225	140	0.6	0.7	0.5	-35	-40	0	-0.1	-0.1	0.0
Newcastle-under-Lyme	860	545	315	1.1	1.3	0.8	-40	-25	-20	-0.1	-0.1	-0.1
South Staffordshire	685	440	245	1.0	1.3	0.7	-140	-65	-75	-0.2	-0.2	-0.2
Stafford	545	335	210	0.7	0.8	0.5	-120	-85	-30	-0.1	-0.2	-0.1
Staffordshire Moorlands	425	270	155	0.7	0.9	0.5	-45	-25	-20	-0.1	-0.1	-0.1
Tamworth	370	225	150	0.8	0.9	0.6	85	50	35	0.2	0.2	0.1
Warwickshire	3,055	1,885	1,170	0.9	1.1	0.7	-585	-385	-205	-0.2	-0.2	-0.1
North Warwickshire	340	215	125	0.9	1.1	0.6	-25	-10	-15	-0.1	-0.1	-0.1
Nuneaton and Bedworth	1,325	780	545	1.7	2.0	1.4	-255	-195	-65	-0.3	-0.5	-0.2
Rugby	600	360	235	0.9	1.1	0.7	-120	-70	-55	-0.2	-0.2	-0.2
Stratford-on-Avon	265	170	95	0.4	0.5	0.3	-90	-55	-35	-0.1	-0.2	-0.1
Warwick	530	360	170	0.6	0.8	0.4	-95	-55	-35	-0.1	-0.1	-0.1
West Midlands (Met County)	**55,620**	**35,635**	**19,985**	**3.1**	**4.0**	**2.2**	**-7,180**	**-3,970**	**-3,210**	**-0.4**	**-0.5**	**-0.4**
Birmingham	28,100	18,240	9,860	3.9	5.2	2.7	-2,545	-1,445	-1,100	-0.4	-0.5	-0.3
Coventry	3,915	2,485	1,430	1.7	2.1	1.3	-785	-465	-320	-0.4	-0.5	-0.3
Dudley	5,205	3,395	1,810	2.7	3.5	1.9	-600	-290	-310	-0.3	-0.3	-0.3
Sandwell	6,305	4,000	2,305	3.2	4.0	2.3	-1,135	-575	-560	-0.6	-0.6	-0.6
Solihull	1,920	1,215	705	1.5	2.0	1.1	-265	-170	-95	-0.2	-0.3	-0.1
Walsall	4,285	2,610	1,675	2.5	3.1	2.0	-680	-360	-320	-0.4	-0.5	-0.4
Wolverhampton	5,890	3,690	2,200	3.7	4.6	2.8	-1,175	-665	-505	-0.7	-0.8	-0.6
Worcestershire	3,900	2,555	1,340	1.1	1.5	0.8	-845	-525	-320	-0.2	-0.3	-0.2
Bromsgrove	530	340	190	0.9	1.2	0.7	-75	-40	-35	-0.1	-0.1	-0.1
Malvern Hills	375	270	105	0.9	1.3	0.5	-110	-40	-70	-0.2	-0.2	-0.3
Redditch	785	500	285	1.5	1.9	1.1	-25	-35	10	0.0	-0.1	0.0
Worcester	865	580	285	1.3	1.8	0.9	-315	-210	-100	-0.5	-0.6	-0.3
Wychavon	615	405	210	0.9	1.1	0.6	-125	-60	-60	-0.2	-0.2	-0.2
Wyre Forest	725	460	265	1.2	1.6	0.9	-200	-135	-65	-0.3	-0.5	-0.2
East of England	**44,780**	**27,965**	**16,810**	**1.2**	**1.5**	**0.9**	**-7,625**	**-4,585**	**-3,040**	**-0.2**	**-0.3**	**-0.2**
Bedford	**2,040**	**1,255**	**785**	**2.0**	**2.4**	**1.5**	**-145**	**-100**	**-45**	**-0.2**	**-0.2**	**-0.1**
Central Bedfordshire	**1,360**	**850**	**510**	**0.8**	**1.0**	**0.6**	**-160**	**-65**	**-95**	**-0.1**	**-0.1**	**-0.1**
Luton	**2,445**	**1,450**	**995**	**1.8**	**2.1**	**1.5**	**-345**	**-165**	**-180**	**-0.3**	**-0.3**	**-0.3**
Peterborough	**1,530**	**910**	**620**	**1.2**	**1.5**	**1.0**	**-710**	**-380**	**-330**	**-0.6**	**-0.6**	**-0.6**
Southend-on-Sea	**2,125**	**1,395**	**730**	**1.9**	**2.5**	**1.3**	**-350**	**-170**	**-180**	**-0.3**	**-0.3**	**-0.3**
Thurrock	**1,905**	**1,130**	**770**	**1.8**	**2.2**	**1.5**	**-265**	**-115**	**-150**	**-0.3**	**-0.2**	**-0.3**
Cambridgeshire	2,720	1,675	1,040	0.7	0.8	0.5	-420	-300	-125	-0.1	-0.2	-0.1
Cambridge	695	460	235	0.7	0.9	0.5	-5	-15	10	0.0	0.0	0.0
East Cambridgeshire	340	210	130	0.6	0.8	0.5	-70	-35	-35	-0.1	-0.1	-0.1
Fenland	610	345	265	1.0	1.1	0.9	-120	-90	-30	-0.2	-0.3	-0.1
Huntingdonshire	610	385	225	0.6	0.7	0.4	-195	-130	-70	-0.2	-0.2	-0.1
South Cambridgeshire	460	275	185	0.5	0.6	0.4	-30	-35	0	0.0	-0.1	0.0
Essex	11,580	7,125	4,455	1.3	1.6	1.0	-1,400	-780	-620	-0.2	-0.2	-0.1
Basildon	1,985	1,180	805	1.7	2.1	1.4	-215	-120	-95	-0.2	-0.2	-0.2
Braintree	1,030	615	415	1.1	1.3	0.9	-175	-100	-75	-0.2	-0.2	-0.2
Brentwood	315	180	135	0.7	0.8	0.6	-100	-80	-25	-0.2	-0.3	-0.1
Castle Point	670	400	270	1.3	1.5	1.0	-55	-55	0	-0.1	-0.2	0.0
Chelmsford	1,095	665	430	1.0	1.2	0.8	-275	-165	-110	-0.3	-0.3	-0.2
Colchester	1,415	895	520	1.2	1.5	0.9	5	0	0	0.0	0.0	0.0
Epping Forest	920	500	420	1.1	1.3	1.0	-135	-80	-55	-0.2	-0.2	-0.1
Harlow	955	585	370	1.8	2.2	1.4	-235	-110	-120	-0.4	-0.5	-0.4
Maldon	340	215	125	0.9	1.1	0.7	-55	-25	-30	-0.1	-0.1	-0.2
Rochford	445	295	150	0.9	1.2	0.6	-65	-15	-50	-0.1	-0.1	-0.2
Tendring	2,175	1,435	740	2.8	3.9	1.9	5	15	-10	0.0	0.0	0.0
Uttlesford	235	150	85	0.5	0.6	0.3	-100	-50	-50	-0.2	-0.2	-0.2
Hertfordshire	7,485	4,475	3,010	1.0	1.2	0.8	-1,310	-900	-405	-0.2	-0.3	-0.1
Broxbourne	695	370	330	1.2	1.3	1.1	-175	-115	-60	-0.3	-0.4	-0.2
Dacorum	1,005	595	410	1.0	1.2	0.9	-200	-140	-60	-0.2	-0.3	-0.1
East Hertfordshire	605	365	235	0.7	0.8	0.5	-160	-120	-40	-0.2	-0.3	-0.1
Hertsmere	740	460	280	1.2	1.5	0.9	-75	-10	-65	-0.1	0.0	-0.2
North Hertfordshire	905	545	360	1.1	1.3	0.9	-95	-65	-30	-0.1	-0.2	-0.1
St Albans	575	350	225	0.6	0.8	0.5	-130	-90	-35	-0.1	-0.2	-0.1

4.10 Claimant count by sex and Unitary and Local Authority
from Nomis 24 August 2017
Age 16+

| | Claimant Count December 2015 | | | | | | Change on Year | | | | | |
| | Levels | | | Percentage of Pop | | | Levels | | | Percentage of Pop | | |
	Total	Male	Female	Total	Male	Female	Total	Male	Female	Total	Male	Female
Stevenage	830	500	330	1.5	1.8	1.2	-295	-205	-90	-0.5	-0.7	-0.3
Three Rivers	455	275	180	0.8	1.0	0.6	-60	-50	-15	-0.1	-0.2	-0.1
Watford	790	495	295	1.2	1.6	0.9	-115	-75	-45	-0.2	-0.2	-0.1
Welwyn Hatfield	885	530	355	1.1	1.3	0.9	0	-30	30	0.0	-0.1	0.0
Norfolk	**6,460**	**4,355**	**2,105**	**1.2**	**1.7**	**0.8**	**-1,720**	**-1,030**	**-690**	**-0.3**	**-0.4**	**-0.3**
Breckland	790	520	265	1.0	1.3	0.7	-180	-75	-100	-0.2	-0.2	-0.3
Broadland	445	290	150	0.6	0.8	0.4	-130	-55	-70	-0.2	-0.2	-0.2
Great Yarmouth	1,795	1,245	550	3.1	4.3	1.9	-255	-150	-105	-0.4	-0.5	-0.3
King`s Lynn and West Norfolk	830	535	295	1.0	1.2	0.7	-360	-225	-135	-0.4	-0.5	-0.3
North Norfolk	520	340	180	0.9	1.2	0.6	-135	-85	-50	-0.2	-0.3	-0.2
Norwich	1,545	1,085	460	1.6	2.3	1.0	-485	-305	-180	-0.5	-0.7	-0.4
South Norfolk	535	340	200	0.7	0.9	0.5	-180	-125	-50	-0.2	-0.4	-0.1
Suffolk	**5,130**	**3,345**	**1,785**	**1.2**	**1.5**	**0.8**	**-800**	**-580**	**-220**	**-0.2**	**-0.3**	**-0.1**
Babergh	390	230	160	0.8	0.9	0.6	-85	-75	-10	-0.2	-0.3	0.0
Forest Heath	285	175	110	0.7	0.9	0.6	-50	-25	-25	-0.1	-0.1	-0.1
Ipswich	1,620	1,085	535	1.9	2.5	1.2	-410	-300	-105	-0.5	-0.7	-0.2
Mid Suffolk	420	240	180	0.7	0.8	0.6	-105	-75	-30	-0.2	-0.3	-0.1
St Edmundsbury	635	430	210	0.9	1.2	0.6	-95	-40	-55	-0.1	-0.1	-0.2
Suffolk Coastal	420	275	145	0.6	0.8	0.4	-95	-80	-15	-0.1	-0.2	0.0
Waveney	1,360	915	445	2.1	2.9	1.3	40	20	20	0.1	0.1	0.1
London	**106,430**	**61,655**	**44,775**	**1.8**	**2.1**	**1.5**	**-16,450**	**-10,350**	**-6,100**	**-0.3**	**-0.4**	**-0.2**
Inner London	**50,215**	**29,440**	**20,775**	**2.0**	**2.3**	**1.7**	**-9,270**	**-5,835**	**-3,435**	**-0.4**	**-0.5**	**-0.3**
Camden	2,595	1,535	1,060	1.5	1.8	1.3	-270	-175	-95	-0.2	-0.3	-0.1
City of London	50	35	15	0.8	1.0	0.5	-20	-10	-10	-0.4	-0.4	-0.4
Hackney	4,605	2,720	1,885	2.4	2.8	1.9	-1,135	-770	-365	-0.6	-0.9	-0.4
Hammersmith and Fulham	2,955	1,800	1,155	2.3	2.8	1.8	-195	-80	-115	-0.2	-0.2	-0.2
Haringey	4,475	2,730	1,745	2.3	2.8	1.8	-1,150	-650	-505	-0.7	-0.7	-0.6
Islington	3,290	1,955	1,330	1.9	2.3	1.6	-670	-435	-235	-0.5	-0.6	-0.3
Kensington and Chelsea	1,595	910	680	1.5	1.7	1.2	-225	-135	-90	-0.2	-0.3	-0.2
Lambeth	5,765	3,410	2,355	2.4	2.8	2.0	-940	-635	-305	-0.4	-0.6	-0.3
Lewisham	4,975	2,915	2,060	2.4	2.8	2.0	-815	-485	-330	-0.4	-0.5	-0.4
Newham	4,315	2,500	1,810	1.8	2.0	1.7	-1,490	-810	-680	-0.7	-0.7	-0.7
Southwark	4,965	2,870	2,095	2.2	2.5	1.8	-1,180	-765	-415	-0.6	-0.7	-0.4
Tower Hamlets	4,955	2,825	2,130	2.3	2.5	2.1	-525	-455	-75	-0.3	-0.5	-0.1
Wandsworth	3,210	1,855	1,355	1.4	1.7	1.1	-400	-230	-165	-0.2	-0.2	-0.1
Westminster	2,470	1,370	1,100	1.4	1.5	1.3	-255	-200	-55	-0.2	-0.3	-0.1
Outer London	**56,215**	**32,215**	**24,005**	**1.7**	**1.9**	**1.4**	**-7,185**	**-4,515**	**-2,670**	**-0.2**	**-0.3**	**-0.2**
Barking and Dagenham	3,100	1,685	1,415	2.4	2.7	2.2	-495	-315	-175	-0.4	-0.6	-0.3
Barnet	3,600	2,060	1,540	1.5	1.7	1.2	-260	-185	-75	-0.1	-0.2	-0.1
Bexley	1,810	995	815	1.2	1.3	1.0	-400	-190	-210	-0.3	-0.3	-0.3
Brent	5,540	3,320	2,225	2.5	2.9	2.1	-340	-280	-60	-0.2	-0.3	-0.1
Bromley	2,120	1,245	875	1.0	1.3	0.8	-495	-275	-220	-0.3	-0.3	-0.2
Croydon	4,780	2,815	1,965	1.9	2.4	1.6	-35	-30	-5	0.0	0.0	0.0
Ealing	4,895	2,965	1,930	2.1	2.6	1.7	-260	-110	-150	-0.1	-0.1	-0.1
Enfield	4,365	2,370	1,995	2.1	2.3	1.8	-970	-545	-425	-0.5	-0.6	-0.4
Greenwich	3,830	2,190	1,645	2.1	2.3	1.8	-450	-280	-170	-0.3	-0.4	-0.2
Harrow	1,825	1,010	815	1.1	1.3	1.0	-385	-250	-135	-0.2	-0.3	-0.2
Havering	2,325	1,300	1,020	1.5	1.7	1.3	-315	-235	-80	-0.2	-0.3	-0.1
Hillingdon	2,510	1,415	1,095	1.3	1.4	1.1	-190	-150	-40	-0.1	-0.2	-0.1
Hounslow	2,825	1,685	1,145	1.6	1.8	1.3	-305	-165	-140	-0.2	-0.2	-0.2
Kingston upon Thames	1,085	615	470	0.9	1.1	0.8	-115	-65	-50	-0.1	-0.1	-0.1
Merton	1,975	1,130	845	1.4	1.7	1.2	-335	-215	-120	-0.2	-0.3	-0.2
Redbridge	2,690	1,480	1,210	1.4	1.5	1.3	-610	-390	-215	-0.3	-0.4	-0.2
Richmond upon Thames	1,200	705	495	1.0	1.1	0.8	-110	-45	-65	-0.1	-0.1	-0.1
Sutton	1,645	880	765	1.3	1.4	1.2	-60	-105	45	-0.1	-0.2	0.1
Waltham Forest	4,090	2,345	1,745	2.2	2.5	1.9	-1,060	-680	-380	-0.6	-0.8	-0.4
South East	**56,125**	**35,285**	**20,840**	**1.0**	**1.3**	**0.7**	**-8,975**	**-5,755**	**-3,220**	**-0.2**	**-0.2**	**-0.1**
Bracknell Forest	**570**	**345**	**225**	**0.7**	**0.9**	**0.6**	**-95**	**-60**	**-35**	**-0.1**	**-0.2**	**-0.1**
Brighton and Hove	**2,885**	**1,830**	**1,060**	**1.4**	**1.8**	**1.1**	**-565**	**-380**	**-185**	**-0.3**	**-0.4**	**-0.2**
Isle of Wight	**1,700**	**1,095**	**605**	**2.1**	**2.8**	**1.5**	**-270**	**-200**	**-65**	**-0.3**	**-0.5**	**-0.2**
Medway	**3,465**	**2,170**	**1,295**	**1.9**	**2.4**	**1.5**	**-315**	**-180**	**-135**	**-0.2**	**-0.2**	**-0.2**
Milton Keynes	**2,050**	**1,240**	**810**	**1.2**	**1.5**	**1.0**	**-480**	**-300**	**-175**	**-0.3**	**-0.4**	**-0.2**
Portsmouth	**1,995**	**1,315**	**680**	**1.4**	**1.8**	**1.0**	**-670**	**-420**	**-250**	**-0.5**	**-0.6**	**-0.4**
Reading	**1,410**	**890**	**520**	**1.3**	**1.6**	**1.0**	**-130**	**-90**	**-40**	**-0.1**	**-0.2**	**-0.1**
Slough	**1,260**	**745**	**520**	**1.3**	**1.5**	**1.1**	**-300**	**-180**	**-125**	**-0.3**	**-0.4**	**-0.3**
Southampton	**2,320**	**1,555**	**760**	**1.3**	**1.7**	**0.9**	**-180**	**-70**	**-105**	**-0.1**	**-0.1**	**-0.1**
West Berkshire	**480**	**295**	**190**	**0.5**	**0.6**	**0.4**	**-160**	**-110**	**-50**	**-0.2**	**-0.2**	**-0.1**
Windsor and Maidenhead	**650**	**405**	**245**	**0.7**	**0.9**	**0.5**	**-90**	**-40**	**-50**	**-0.1**	**-0.1**	**-0.1**

4.10 Claimant count by sex and Unitary and Local Authority
from Nomis 24 August 2017
Age 16+

| | Claimant Count December 2015 | | | | | | Change on Year | | | | | |
| | Levels | | | Percentage of Pop | | | Levels | | | Percentage of Pop | | |
	Total	Male	Female	Total	Male	Female	Total	Male	Female	Total	Male	Female
Wokingham	505	300	205	0.5	0.6	0.4	-40	-35	-5	0.0	-0.1	0.0
Buckinghamshire	2,325	1,410	910	0.7	0.9	0.6	-460	-325	-140	-0.1	-0.2	-0.1
Aylesbury Vale	690	405	285	0.6	0.7	0.5	-155	-125	-30	-0.1	-0.2	-0.1
Chiltern	265	165	105	0.5	0.6	0.4	-110	-70	-40	-0.2	-0.3	-0.2
South Bucks	255	145	110	0.6	0.7	0.5	-15	-15	0	0.0	-0.1	0.0
Wycombe	1,115	700	415	1.0	1.3	0.8	-180	-115	-65	-0.2	-0.2	-0.1
East Sussex	4,410	2,830	1,580	1.4	1.8	1.0	-840	-560	-280	-0.3	-0.4	-0.2
Eastbourne	1,095	695	400	1.8	2.3	1.3	-200	-150	-45	-0.3	-0.5	-0.2
Hastings	1,470	970	500	2.6	3.5	1.7	-290	-180	-110	-0.5	-0.6	-0.4
Lewes	645	435	210	1.1	1.5	0.7	-170	-90	-80	-0.3	-0.3	-0.3
Rother	605	380	225	1.2	1.6	0.9	-140	-100	-45	-0.3	-0.4	-0.2
Wealden	595	350	245	0.7	0.8	0.5	-45	-45	0	-0.1	-0.1	0.0
Hampshire	6,045	3,765	2,280	0.7	0.9	0.5	-825	-595	-230	-0.1	-0.1	-0.1
Basingstoke and Deane	750	455	295	0.7	0.8	0.5	-70	-50	-20	-0.1	-0.1	0.0
East Hampshire	430	255	175	0.6	0.7	0.5	-15	-20	5	0.0	-0.1	0.0
Eastleigh	515	340	175	0.6	0.9	0.4	-90	-70	-20	-0.1	-0.2	0.0
Fareham	435	290	140	0.6	0.8	0.4	-55	-35	-20	-0.1	-0.1	-0.1
Gosport	580	365	215	1.1	1.4	0.8	-155	-90	-65	-0.3	-0.3	-0.3
Hart	235	150	85	0.4	0.5	0.3	-45	-30	-15	-0.1	-0.1	-0.1
Havant	1,120	710	410	1.5	2.0	1.1	-155	-100	-55	-0.2	-0.3	-0.2
New Forest	660	395	265	0.7	0.8	0.5	-155	-135	-20	-0.2	-0.3	0.0
Rushmoor	560	325	230	0.9	1.0	0.7	-15	-25	15	0.0	-0.1	0.0
Test Valley	410	260	150	0.6	0.7	0.4	-50	-5	-45	-0.1	0.0	-0.1
Winchester	355	215	135	0.5	0.6	0.4	-25	-35	10	0.0	-0.1	0.0
Kent	13,340	8,450	4,890	1.4	1.8	1.0	-1,495	-860	-635	-0.2	-0.2	-0.1
Ashford	1,000	630	370	1.3	1.7	1.0	20	25	-5	0.0	0.1	0.0
Canterbury	1,070	695	370	1.0	1.4	0.7	-25	-30	5	0.0	-0.1	0.0
Dartford	670	360	310	1.0	1.1	0.9	-125	-45	-85	-0.2	-0.1	-0.3
Dover	1,240	830	415	1.8	2.5	1.2	-265	-185	-85	-0.4	-0.5	-0.2
Gravesham	1,235	780	455	1.9	2.4	1.4	-75	-35	-40	-0.1	-0.1	-0.1
Maidstone	1,070	650	420	1.0	1.3	0.8	-95	-35	-60	-0.1	-0.1	-0.1
Sevenoaks	515	315	195	0.7	0.9	0.5	-85	-55	-30	-0.1	-0.2	-0.1
Shepway	1,285	845	440	2.0	2.6	1.3	-265	-160	-100	-0.4	-0.5	-0.3
Swale	1,770	1,090	680	2.0	2.5	1.5	5	-25	25	0.0	-0.1	0.0
Thanet	2,345	1,550	800	2.9	3.9	1.9	-520	-310	-210	-0.7	-0.8	-0.5
Tonbridge and Malling	680	420	260	0.9	1.1	0.7	-50	-15	-35	-0.1	0.0	-0.1
Tunbridge Wells	465	290	175	0.7	0.8	0.5	-15	5	-20	0.0	0.0	-0.1
Oxfordshire	2,495	1,560	935	0.6	0.7	0.4	-375	-250	-125	-0.1	-0.1	-0.1
Cherwell	440	255	185	0.5	0.6	0.4	-130	-95	-35	-0.1	-0.2	-0.1
Oxford	920	620	300	0.8	1.1	0.5	-55	-50	0	-0.1	-0.1	0.0
South Oxfordshire	365	210	155	0.4	0.5	0.4	-85	-45	-35	-0.1	-0.1	-0.1
Vale of White Horse	400	245	155	0.5	0.6	0.4	-35	-25	-10	-0.1	-0.1	0.0
West Oxfordshire	370	225	145	0.6	0.7	0.4	-70	-30	-40	-0.1	-0.1	-0.1
Surrey	3,925	2,400	1,525	0.5	0.7	0.4	-955	-565	-390	-0.1	-0.2	-0.1
Elmbridge	345	225	120	0.4	0.6	0.3	-75	-35	-40	-0.1	-0.1	-0.1
Epsom and Ewell	255	165	90	0.5	0.7	0.4	-55	-30	-25	-0.1	-0.1	-0.1
Guildford	495	320	175	0.5	0.7	0.4	-150	-70	-80	-0.2	-0.2	-0.2
Mole Valley	250	155	95	0.5	0.6	0.4	-60	-45	-10	-0.1	-0.2	0.0
Reigate and Banstead	625	375	250	0.7	0.8	0.6	-100	-45	-55	-0.1	-0.1	-0.1
Runnymede	300	175	125	0.5	0.6	0.4	-10	-5	-10	0.0	0.0	0.0
Spelthorne	450	240	210	0.7	0.8	0.7	-85	-75	-10	-0.1	-0.2	0.0
Surrey Heath	205	130	75	0.4	0.5	0.3	-115	-75	-40	-0.2	-0.3	-0.2
Tandridge	330	190	140	0.6	0.7	0.5	-95	-45	-50	-0.2	-0.2	-0.2
Waverley	335	210	125	0.5	0.6	0.3	-95	-65	-30	-0.1	-0.2	-0.1
Woking	340	215	130	0.6	0.7	0.4	-115	-75	-35	-0.2	-0.2	-0.1
West Sussex	4,295	2,680	1,615	0.9	1.1	0.6	-730	-530	-200	-0.2	-0.2	-0.1
Adur	430	260	165	1.1	1.4	0.9	-25	-25	0	-0.1	-0.1	0.0
Arun	895	570	330	1.0	1.3	0.7	-230	-145	-85	-0.3	-0.4	-0.2
Chichester	565	345	220	0.8	1.1	0.6	-145	-115	-30	-0.2	-0.4	-0.1
Crawley	880	530	350	1.2	1.5	1.0	-40	-5	-35	-0.1	0.0	-0.1
Horsham	455	300	155	0.6	0.8	0.4	-110	-80	-30	-0.1	-0.2	-0.1
Mid Sussex	380	225	160	0.4	0.5	0.4	-55	-50	-5	-0.1	-0.1	0.0
Worthing	685	445	240	1.1	1.4	0.7	-125	-100	-20	-0.2	-0.3	-0.1
South West	37,210	24,145	13,065	1.1	1.4	0.8	-3,970	-2,475	-1,495	-0.1	-0.2	-0.1
Bath and North East Somerset	1,010	665	345	0.8	1.1	0.6	-190	-125	-65	-0.2	-0.2	-0.1
Bournemouth	1,760	1,165	595	1.4	1.8	1.0	-240	-175	-65	-0.2	-0.3	-0.1
Bristol, City of	4,790	3,155	1,630	1.6	2.0	1.1	-1,145	-720	-425	-0.4	-0.5	-0.3
Cornwall	4,420	2,885	1,535	1.4	1.8	0.9	-235	-125	-105	-0.1	-0.1	-0.1
Isles of Scilly	5	5	0	0.5	0.7	#	0	0	-5	-0.2	0.1	-0.4

4.10 Claimant count by sex and Unitary and Local Authority
from Nomis 24 August 2017
Age 16+

| | Claimant Count December 2015 | | | | | | Change on Year | | | | | |
| | Levels | | | Percentage of Pop | | | Levels | | | Percentage of Pop | | |
	Total	Male	Female	Total	Male	Female	Total	Male	Female	Total	Male	Female
North Somerset	1,195	785	410	1.0	1.3	0.7	-230	-130	-100	-0.2	-0.2	-0.2
Plymouth	3,155	2,135	1,020	1.9	2.5	1.2	100	60	40	0.1	0.1	0.0
Poole	865	535	335	1.0	1.2	0.7	-120	-100	-25	-0.1	-0.2	0.0
South Gloucestershire	1,450	900	550	0.8	1.0	0.6	-195	-80	-115	-0.1	-0.1	-0.1
Swindon	1,765	1,065	700	1.3	1.5	1.0	-105	-25	-80	-0.1	0.0	-0.1
Torbay	1,520	1,025	490	2.0	2.7	1.3	-200	-125	-75	-0.2	-0.3	-0.2
Wiltshire	2,320	1,455	865	0.8	1.0	0.6	-235	-160	-75	-0.1	-0.1	-0.1
Devon	3,865	2,455	1,410	0.8	1.1	0.6	-135	-90	-45	0.0	0.0	0.0
East Devon	600	360	240	0.8	1.0	0.6	25	5	20	0.0	0.0	0.0
Exeter	705	465	240	0.8	1.0	0.6	-45	-40	-10	-0.1	-0.1	0.0
Mid Devon	345	210	135	0.7	0.9	0.6	-40	-25	-15	-0.1	-0.1	-0.1
North Devon	540	350	190	1.0	1.3	0.7	-15	-5	-5	0.0	0.0	0.0
South Hams	320	205	115	0.7	0.9	0.5	25	35	-10	0.1	0.1	0.0
Teignbridge	620	385	235	0.8	1.1	0.6	-25	-5	-20	0.0	0.0	-0.1
Torridge	525	355	170	1.4	1.9	0.9	-60	-35	-25	-0.2	-0.2	-0.1
West Devon	205	120	85	0.6	0.8	0.5	0	-20	20	0.0	-0.1	0.1
Dorset	1,895	1,230	665	0.8	1.1	0.6	-225	-140	-85	-0.1	-0.1	-0.1
Christchurch	220	140	80	0.8	1.1	0.6	-35	-40	0	-0.1	-0.3	0.0
East Dorset	275	175	100	0.6	0.8	0.4	-20	0	-20	0.0	0.0	-0.1
North Dorset	225	155	70	0.5	0.7	0.4	-10	5	-15	0.0	0.0	-0.1
Purbeck	175	120	55	0.7	0.9	0.4	-60	-35	-25	-0.2	-0.3	-0.2
West Dorset	350	215	140	0.6	0.8	0.5	0	-5	5	0.0	0.0	0.0
Weymouth and Portland	645	430	215	1.7	2.2	1.1	-100	-70	-30	-0.2	-0.3	-0.2
Gloucestershire	3,865	2,580	1,290	1.0	1.4	0.7	-750	-455	-295	-0.2	-0.2	-0.2
Cheltenham	720	490	230	1.0	1.3	0.6	-210	-135	-75	-0.3	-0.3	-0.2
Cotswold	305	200	105	0.6	0.8	0.4	-10	-15	0	0.0	-0.1	0.0
Forest of Dean	640	420	220	1.3	1.7	0.9	40	30	10	0.1	0.1	0.0
Gloucester	1,215	815	400	1.5	2.0	1.0	-425	-280	-145	-0.5	-0.7	-0.4
Stroud	510	340	170	0.7	1.0	0.5	-80	-35	-45	-0.1	-0.1	-0.1
Tewkesbury	480	315	165	0.9	1.2	0.6	-70	-25	-45	-0.1	-0.1	-0.2
Somerset	3,330	2,105	1,225	1.0	1.3	0.8	-65	-85	20	0.0	-0.1	0.0
Mendip	570	360	210	0.9	1.1	0.6	-40	-40	5	-0.1	-0.1	0.0
Sedgemoor	1,065	645	420	1.5	1.8	1.2	-90	-80	-10	-0.1	-0.2	0.0
South Somerset	775	490	285	0.8	1.0	0.6	100	80	20	0.1	0.2	0.0
Taunton Deane	750	495	250	1.1	1.5	0.7	-20	-35	15	0.0	-0.1	0.0
West Somerset	165	110	55	0.9	1.2	0.6	-15	-10	-5	-0.1	-0.1	0.0
Wales	42,015	26,905	15,110	2.2	2.8	1.6	-5,290	-4,180	-1,115	-0.3	-0.4	-0.1
Anglesey	1,255	845	410	3.1	4.1	2.0	5	-5	10	0.0	0.0	0.1
Gwynedd	1,495	1,000	495	2.0	2.7	1.3	-160	-100	-65	-0.2	-0.3	-0.2
Conwy	1,515	1,010	505	2.3	3.1	1.5	-150	-115	-35	-0.2	-0.3	-0.1
Denbighshire	1,305	860	445	2.4	3.1	1.6	-120	-105	-20	-0.2	-0.3	-0.1
Flintshire	1,510	940	570	1.6	2.0	1.2	-255	-190	-65	-0.3	-0.4	-0.1
Wrexham	1,685	1,070	615	2.0	2.5	1.5	-370	-260	-110	-0.4	-0.6	-0.3
Powys	815	540	275	1.1	1.4	0.7	-140	-85	-55	-0.2	-0.2	-0.1
Ceredigion	550	355	195	1.2	1.5	0.9	-20	-35	15	0.0	-0.1	0.1
Pembrokeshire	1,730	1,180	550	2.4	3.3	1.5	-110	-110	0	-0.1	-0.3	0.0
Carmarthenshire	1,910	1,195	715	1.7	2.2	1.3	-80	-115	35	-0.1	-0.2	0.1
Swansea	3,170	2,065	1,105	2.1	2.6	1.5	-95	-175	85	-0.1	-0.2	0.1
Neath Port Talbot	1,980	1,225	755	2.3	2.8	1.7	35	-20	55	0.0	0.0	0.1
Bridgend	1,800	1,130	670	2.0	2.5	1.5	-70	-50	-20	-0.1	-0.1	0.0
The Vale of Glamorgan	1,430	930	500	1.8	2.4	1.3	-140	-135	-5	-0.2	-0.3	0.0
Cardiff	5,410	3,550	1,860	2.2	3.0	1.5	-1,290	-965	-325	-0.6	-0.8	-0.3
Rhondda, Cynon, Taff	3,505	2,195	1,310	2.4	3.0	1.7	-445	-300	-140	-0.3	-0.4	-0.2
Merthyr Tydfil	1,000	630	370	2.7	3.4	1.9	-135	-95	-40	-0.4	-0.5	-0.2
Caerphilly	3,545	2,160	1,385	3.1	3.9	2.4	-275	-230	-40	-0.2	-0.4	-0.1
Blaenau Gwent	1,630	1,000	635	3.7	4.6	2.9	-250	-195	-55	-0.5	-0.9	-0.2
Torfaen	1,450	930	520	2.5	3.3	1.8	-215	-185	-30	-0.4	-0.6	-0.1
Monmouthshire	620	380	245	1.1	1.4	0.9	-120	-90	-30	-0.2	-0.3	-0.1
Newport	2,710	1,720	990	2.9	3.8	2.1	-900	-615	-285	-1.0	-1.4	-0.6
Scotland	71,170	49,335	21,835	2.0	2.9	1.2	-8,910	-5,880	-3,035	-0.3	-0.4	-0.2
Aberdeen City	2,525	1,860	665	1.6	2.3	0.8	1,005	790	215	0.6	0.9	0.3
Aberdeenshire	1,760	1,255	505	1.1	1.5	0.6	800	605	195	0.5	0.7	0.2
Angus	1,230	850	380	1.7	2.4	1.0	-60	-20	-45	-0.1	0.0	-0.1
Argyll and Bute	875	615	260	1.7	2.3	1.0	-110	-90	-15	-0.2	-0.3	-0.1
Clackmannanshire	780	545	235	2.4	3.4	1.4	-250	-130	-120	-0.8	-0.8	-0.7
Dumfries and Galloway	1,530	1,035	495	1.7	2.4	1.1	-160	-105	-55	-0.2	-0.2	-0.1
Dundee City	2,890	2,110	780	2.9	4.4	1.5	-505	-320	-185	-0.5	-0.7	-0.4
East Ayrshire	2,540	1,785	755	3.3	4.7	1.9	-250	-155	-95	-0.3	-0.4	-0.2

4.10 Claimant count by sex and Unitary and Local Authority
from Nomis 24 August 2017
Age 16+

	Claimant Count December 2015						Change on Year					
	Levels			Percentage of Pop			Levels			Percentage of Pop		
	Total	Male	Female	Total	Male	Female	Total	Male	Female	Total	Male	Female
East Dunbartonshire	670	470	200	1.0	1.5	0.6	-180	-125	-55	-0.3	-0.4	-0.2
East Lothian	1,000	640	360	1.6	2.1	1.1	-175	-145	-30	-0.3	-0.5	-0.1
East Renfrewshire	560	380	180	1.0	1.4	0.6	-135	-110	-30	-0.2	-0.4	-0.1
Edinburgh, City of	5,065	3,450	1,615	1.5	2.0	0.9	-1,005	-705	-300	-0.3	-0.4	-0.2
Eilean Siar	330	250	80	2.1	3.1	1.0	-20	-15	0	-0.1	-0.2	0.0
Falkirk	2,065	1,420	650	2.0	2.8	1.3	-465	-265	-205	-0.5	-0.5	-0.4
Fife	4,935	3,430	1,505	2.1	3.0	1.3	-950	-585	-360	-0.4	-0.5	-0.3
Glasgow City	12,670	8,835	3,835	3.0	4.2	1.8	-2,400	-1,615	-785	-0.6	-0.9	-0.4
Highland	2,230	1,580	650	1.5	2.2	0.9	-180	-85	-90	-0.1	-0.1	-0.1
Inverclyde	1,290	905	385	2.5	3.7	1.5	-140	-140	0	-0.3	-0.5	0.0
Midlothian	895	620	275	1.6	2.3	1.0	-80	-60	-20	-0.2	-0.2	-0.1
Moray	750	535	215	1.3	1.8	0.7	-10	30	-40	0.0	0.1	-0.1
North Ayrshire	3,380	2,265	1,115	4.0	5.6	2.5	-90	-120	30	-0.1	-0.3	0.1
North Lanarkshire	5,770	3,895	1,875	2.6	3.6	1.7	-940	-660	-280	-0.4	-0.6	-0.2
Orkney Islands	85	65	25	0.6	0.9	0.3	-25	-20	-5	-0.2	-0.3	-0.1
Perth and Kinross	960	660	295	1.0	1.4	0.6	-165	-115	-50	-0.2	-0.3	-0.1
Renfrewshire	2,705	1,910	795	2.4	3.5	1.4	-320	-240	-80	-0.3	-0.4	-0.1
Scottish Borders	1,070	715	355	1.6	2.1	1.0	-70	-65	-5	-0.1	-0.2	0.0
Shetland Islands	125	90	35	0.9	1.2	0.5	50	35	15	0.4	0.5	0.2
South Ayrshire	1,685	1,160	520	2.5	3.6	1.5	-305	-190	-115	-0.4	-0.6	-0.3
South Lanarkshire	4,075	2,775	1,300	2.0	2.8	1.2	-1,175	-815	-360	-0.6	-0.8	-0.3
Stirling	845	555	295	1.4	1.9	0.9	-160	-110	-55	-0.3	-0.4	-0.2
West Dunbartonshire	2,125	1,520	605	3.7	5.5	2.0	-180	-145	-35	-0.3	-0.5	-0.1
West Lothian	1,755	1,155	600	1.5	2.0	1.0	-260	-185	-75	-0.2	-0.3	-0.1
Northern Ireland	**38,245**	**26,885**	**11,365**	**3.3**	**4.6**	**1.9**	**-10,820**	**-7,670**	**-3,145**	**-0.9**	**-1.3**	**-0.5**
Antrim	780	550	230	2.3	3.3	1.3	-145	-85	-60	-0.4	-0.5	-0.3
Ards	1,505	1,075	435	3.1	4.5	1.7	-260	-170	-95	-0.5	-0.7	-0.4
Armagh	860	570	290	2.3	3.0	1.5	-400	-295	-105	-1.1	-1.5	-0.6
Ballymena	975	670	305	2.4	3.3	1.5	-370	-220	-150	-0.9	-1.1	-0.7
Ballymoney	615	440	175	3.0	4.3	1.7	-80	-45	-35	-0.4	-0.4	-0.3
Banbridge	630	440	185	2.0	2.8	1.2	-195	-160	-35	-0.6	-1.0	-0.2
Belfast	8,105	5,990	2,115	4.3	6.5	2.2	-2,840	-2,085	-755	-1.5	-2.3	-0.8
Carrickfergus	700	505	195	2.8	4.2	1.5	-120	-70	-50	-0.5	-0.6	-0.4
Castlereagh	895	675	220	2.1	3.2	1.0	-175	-110	-65	-0.4	-0.5	-0.3
Coleraine	1,275	870	405	3.4	4.7	2.2	-220	-190	-30	-0.6	-1.1	-0.2
Cookstown	490	300	190	2.0	2.5	1.6	-225	-155	-70	-0.9	-1.3	-0.6
Craigavon	1,855	1,265	590	3.0	4.1	1.9	-605	-385	-220	-1.0	-1.3	-0.7
Derry	4,560	3,220	1,340	6.5	9.4	3.7	-940	-625	-310	-1.3	-1.8	-0.8
Down	1,475	1,040	430	3.4	4.8	1.9	-440	-340	-100	-1.0	-1.5	-0.4
Dungannon	800	510	290	2.1	2.6	1.5	-255	-160	-95	-0.7	-0.9	-0.5
Fermanagh	1,315	900	415	3.4	4.5	2.2	-350	-270	-80	-0.9	-1.3	-0.4
Larne	560	400	160	2.8	4.0	1.6	-85	-60	-25	-0.4	-0.6	-0.2
Limavady	930	655	280	4.2	5.8	2.6	-230	-180	-55	-1.0	-1.6	-0.5
Lisburn	2,195	1,480	715	2.8	3.8	1.8	-510	-395	-115	-0.7	-1.1	-0.3
Magherafelt	610	410	200	2.1	2.7	1.4	-270	-160	-110	-0.9	-1.1	-0.8
Moyle	445	290	155	4.2	5.4	2.9	-80	-85	5	-0.8	-1.6	0.1
Newry and Mourne	1,820	1,260	560	2.8	3.9	1.7	-785	-580	-205	-1.2	-1.8	-0.6
Newtownabbey	1,335	980	355	2.5	3.7	1.3	-265	-180	-85	-0.5	-0.7	-0.3
North Down	1,165	845	320	2.4	3.6	1.3	-365	-245	-120	-0.8	-1.1	-0.5
Omagh	875	580	290	2.6	3.5	1.8	-345	-215	-130	-1.0	-1.3	-0.8
Strabane	1,475	960	515	5.8	7.5	4.1	-260	-205	-55	-1.0	-1.6	-0.4

Source: ONS Labour Market Statistics; Nomisweb

Under Universal Credit a broader span of claimants are required to look for work than under Jobseeker's Allowance. As Universal Credit Full Service is rolled out in particular areas, the number of people recorded as being on the Claimant Count is therefore likely to rise.

All data are rounded to the nearest 5 and may not precisely add to the sum of the number of people claiming JSA, published on Nomis, and the number of people claiming Universal Credit required to seek work, published by DWP, due to independent rounding.

4.11a   Weekly pay - Gross (£) - For all employee jobs[a]: United Kingdom, 2015

Description	Code	Number of jobs[b] (thousand)	Median	Annual percentage change	Mean	Annual percentage change	Percentiles 10	20	25	30	40	60	70	75	80	90
ALL EMPLOYEES		25,997	425.1	1.7	507.2	1.1	130.2	217.4	259.1	292.5	357.2	500.6	594.4	652.4	717.8	922.4
All Industries and Services		25,988	425.2	1.7	507.3	1.1	130.3	217.5	259.1	292.6	357.3	500.7	594.4	652.5	717.8	922.5
All Index of Production Industries		2,839	532.5	1.1	607.8	1.4	280.2	348.5	377.9	405.5	468.5	606.4	689.8	742.8	804.3	1,006.2
All Manufacturing		2,475	519.5	0.8	590.8	1.0	276.3	341.9	369.2	397.6	458.6	589.5	672.1	724.5	783.9	970.4
All Service Industries		22,114	403.5	1.8	491.7	1.2	118.8	198.8	238.4	273.9	338.2	480.0	574.9	632.4	699.5	907.9
AGRICULTURE, FORESTRY AND FISHING	A	136	357.7	-0.1	390.7	2.5	124.4	202.4	235.9	271.5	314.2	399.0	463.2	498.8	533.7	658.2
Crop and animal production, hunting and related service activities	1	121	349.5	-0.1	377.4	1.8	123.5	200.0	232.8	265.9	310.6	390.2	450.1	482.9	518.3	640.5
Forestry and logging	2	11	439.8	-4.7	506.7	2.9	x	230.0	299.0	321.0	368.7	490.7	x	x	x	x
Fishing and aquaculture	3	x	x		x		x	x	x	x	x	x	x	x	x	x
MINING AND QUARRYING	B	49	720.1	3.2	877.4	2.7	400.2	503.0	539.7	574.9	638.9	791.3	910.7	1,038.4	1,134.5	x
Mining of coal and lignite	5	x	x		x		x	x	x	x	x	x	x	x	x	x
Extraction of crude petroleum and natural gas	6	7	1,128.2	10.3	1,433.1	18.2	x	721.9	748.4	767.5	956.3	x	x	x	x	x
Mining of metal ores	7	..														
Other mining and quarrying	8	22	622.2	9.7	671.2	6.0	379.9	460.8	482.2	510.6	556.9	671.5	737.8	781.7	804.1	x
Mining support service activities	9	17	789.7	5.7	917.1	3.4	433.2	520.5	581.8	597.3	663.2	882.6	1,043.6	x	x	x
MANUFACTURING	C	2,475	519.5	0.8	590.8	1.0	276.3	341.9	369.2	397.6	458.6	589.5	672.1	724.5	783.9	970.4
Manufacture of food products	10	378	402.9	0.7	489.0	2.4	228.7	278.6	295.7	318.4	358.3	460.9	535.5	582.5	643.4	810.3
Manufacture of beverages	11	47	612.8	-2.7	705.1	1.1	345.0	414.2	453.1	483.2	528.9	690.9	777.4	848.3	892.7	x
Manufacture of tobacco products	12	x	910.7	16.4	928.5	21.3	x	x	x	x	873.6	x	x	x	x	x
Manufacture of textiles	13	44	377.8	2.3	462.1	1.5	207.3	266.3	279.5	295.4	334.7	425.4	505.0	547.0	579.7	x
Manufacture of wearing apparel	14	22	270.8	-8.3	360.5	4.3	126.0	164.4	187.5	195.6	242.9	331.0	380.6	x	x	x
Manufacture of leather and related products	15	9	356.7	4.2	368.3	0.7	x	x	271.3	287.8	332.5	409.6	442.5	452.5	x	x
Manufacture of wood and of products of wood and cork, except furniture; manufacture of articles of straw and plaiting materials	16	55	429.5	3.8	466.8	-1.2	259.9	308.9	329.9	348.4	386.8	471.7	525.0	557.7	583.5	x
Manufacture of paper and paper products	17	59	520.5	2.9	566.8	0.7	285.8	354.8	383.9	408.2	465.8	571.2	626.4	670.0	715.1	x
Printing and reproduction of recorded media	18	97	465.2	2.9	540.5	4.5	239.1	324.9	345.8	375.6	420.2	526.6	609.1	650.8	705.9	x
Manufacture of coke and refined petroleum products	19	9	928.1	0.4	989.0	0.9	x	539.3	672.8	701.2	797.4	1,008.3	1,131.2	x	x	x
Manufacture of chemicals and chemical products	20	91	592.7	3.0	659.3	1.1	306.6	388.2	419.4	451.6	506.6	668.8	739.2	792.6	860.5	1,089.2
Manufacture of basic pharmaceutical products and pharmaceutical preparations	21	43	628.3	-7.3	750.7	-4.4	344.0	411.2	438.7	475.6	545.3	700.2	785.9	857.6	952.0	x
Manufacture of rubber and plastic products	22	152	448.2	0.8	537.5	1.7	270.0	321.5	344.6	364.2	400.0	504.8	572.3	608.5	650.4	854.3
Manufacture of other non-metallic mineral products	23	84	517.3	0.8	563.1	0.5	285.7	347.6	370.7	399.0	459.1	584.2	643.9	679.6	722.7	867.1
Manufacture of basic metals	24	84	652.1	3.7	668.3	1.3	359.8	443.0	483.6	522.8	592.0	711.4	777.6	830.8	873.8	966.0
Manufacture of fabricated metal products, except machinery and equipment	25	289	499.5	2.5	545.4	1.8	269.6	344.9	367.7	393.6	445.5	561.3	619.9	661.2	711.6	843.4
Manufacture of computer, electronic and optical products	26	129	592.4	0.0	669.7	3.6	314.2	376.7	408.1	442.8	511.5	666.0	759.1	814.6	906.6	1,064.7
Manufacture of electrical equipment	27	94	508.7	3.7	577.4	0.8	286.4	340.9	360.1	385.8	440.8	564.0	636.6	676.3	754.7	966.5
Manufacture of machinery and equipment n.e.c.	28	212	565.4	0.6	632.0	0.4	339.8	401.6	429.7	462.1	508.3	634.4	704.2	750.8	803.1	983.0
Manufacture of motor vehicles, trailers and semi-trailers	29	173	628.4	3.3	697.7	3.5	344.9	415.0	452.5	488.9	558.1	698.3	797.8	858.5	939.5	1,131.6
Manufacture of other transport equipment	30	176	705.2	0.2	753.5	-0.8	431.2	516.4	546.2	578.0	642.9	762.5	836.7	876.9	928.2	1,099.7
Manufacture of furniture	31	65	397.7	2.2	445.6	-2.3	258.5	297.0	319.6	337.4	364.3	427.2	486.6	521.5	577.9	x
Other manufacturing	32	68	452.6	3.2	505.5	4.4	242.5	299.0	325.6	350.1	407.0	493.6	579.0	620.5	668.5	x
Repair and installation of machinery and equipment	33	91	618.2	4.0	686.1	0.2	284.9	400.3	456.8	482.4	548.2	708.4	805.1	857.9	926.3	1,149.9
ELECTRICITY, GAS, STEAM AND AIR CONDITIONING SUPPLY	D	169	691.4	4.2	775.1	3.7	361.3	445.3	487.3	535.9	621.2	786.0	905.6	966.8	1,061.0	1,286.4
Electricity, gas, steam and air conditioning supply	35	169	691.4	4.2	775.1	3.7	361.3	445.3	487.3	535.9	621.2	786.0	905.6	966.8	1,061.0	1,286.4
WATER SUPPLY; SEWERAGE, WASTE MANAGEMENT AND REMEDIATION ACTIVITIES	E	147	532.5	0.8	613.1	3.9	285.2	358.1	386.1	426.3	478.8	599.3	670.7	726.0	788.4	1,009.8
Water collection, treatment and supply	36	44	608.1	3.8	674.8	5.1	372.2	437.8	456.5	484.8	538.7	666.7	738.0	771.0	814.3	x
Sewerage	37	12	562.6	-4.6	626.0	-1.2	x	417.8	488.0	492.5	512.1	612.9	680.2	768.1	x	x
Waste collection, treatment and disposal activities; materials recovery	38	89	497.8	1.7	582.4	3.5	265.9	330.5	353.1	376.9	439.5	558.9	634.8	675.9	750.5	x
Remediation activities and other waste management services	39	x	x		556.5		x	x	x	x	x	x	x	x	x	x
CONSTRUCTION	F	899	529.0	1.1	592.2	0.1	218.5	350.0	383.7	417.6	475.0	592.8	674.4	728.3	785.8	990.3
Construction of buildings	41	262	534.9	2.2	630.9	0.3	214.2	348.5	383.3	418.7	476.4	607.2	725.3	779.8	872.8	1,133.4
Civil engineering	42	179	585.5	-0.6	653.0	-0.9	292.7	388.5	423.0	456.9	521.9	662.1	764.4	821.0	876.4	1,091.0
Specialised construction activities	43	458	507.2	1.4	546.3	1.0	203.9	339.7	373.0	401.0	459.5	565.2	632.4	670.8	719.2	862.8

4.11a Weekly pay - Gross (£) - For all employee jobs[a]: United Kingdom, 2015

Description	Code	Number of jobs[b] (thousand)	Median	Annual percentage change	Mean	Annual percentage change	Percentiles 10	20	25	30	40	60	70	75	80	90
WHOLESALE AND RETAIL TRADE; REPAIR OF MOTOR VEHICLES AND MOTORCYCLES	G	3,769	320.3	2.9	395.4	1.5	103.6	152.1	178.9	209.3	271.4	373.7	450.0	494.2	550.4	738.0
Wholesale and retail trade and repair of motor vehicles and motorcycles	45	449	414.4	2.2	465.4	1.2	183.0	280.0	302.1	322.0	367.5	467.6	523.6	556.7	591.9	728.9
Wholesale trade, except of motor vehicles and motorcycles	46	1,031	460.0	1.8	555.5	-0.5	230.0	306.6	330.8	351.9	400.0	521.6	602.0	661.2	728.3	979.1
Retail trade, except of motor vehicles and motorcycles	47	2,289	245.0	3.0	309.7	2.9	82.5	119.3	136.6	154.7	196.8	289.3	341.5	373.7	420.2	589.9
TRANSPORTATION AND STORAGE	H	1,105	520.4	3.8	596.3	5.4	275.5	359.1	391.5	418.6	467.3	580.7	654.8	704.9	766.6	968.9
Land transport and transport via pipelines	49	489	530.2	4.9	569.0	5.2	260.0	370.0	398.6	425.2	477.4	582.8	645.8	694.0	751.4	925.8
Water transport	50	10	527.4	4.2	590.8	2.2	x	361.1	401.9	430.1	481.6	590.8	650.5	x	x	x
Air transport	51	77	625.3	-3.5	827.1	7.6	287.9	373.4	411.1	448.6	529.8	728.8	845.3	963.9	1,106.9	x
Warehousing and support activities for transportation	52	323	542.0	3.2	636.6	3.9	294.4	356.6	386.2	414.0	475.9	618.4	705.0	766.6	850.1	1,107.1
Postal and courier activities	53	206	470.3	4.2	512.3	5.2	259.7	341.2	376.3	406.0	436.4	512.5	563.5	594.4	638.7	755.5
ACCOMMODATION AND FOOD SERVICE ACTIVITIES	I	1,417	213.6	1.7	252.3	1.4	56.9	97.5	111.2	130.2	168.0	261.0	306.6	334.3	366.3	461.8
Accommodation	55	313	268.5	0.1	302.3	0.7	75.0	126.3	155.5	178.8	229.8	303.9	346.5	374.7	405.8	536.6
Food and beverage service activities	56	1,103	195.2	2.6	238.0	1.8	53.1	91.0	104.0	120.3	155.6	245.1	292.3	322.1	354.3	451.9
INFORMATION AND COMMUNICATION	J	1,002	648.9	3.7	744.6	2.5	287.5	395.7	443.7	479.1	557.4	737.9	858.8	923.1	1,020.2	1,314.7
Publishing activities	58	146	542.0	4.8	638.5	-2.4	243.7	355.7	383.3	413.9	479.5	623.2	701.7	766.6	843.4	1,085.0
Motion picture, video and television programme production, sound recording and music publishing activities	59	54	480.6	-1.0	572.7	2.7	111.3	177.7	247.5	316.6	414.5	555.5	689.7	765.4	862.4	x
Programming and broadcasting activities	60	47	733.7	1.9	839.2	5.3	402.5	503.5	549.6	594.7	664.0	809.3	898.1	961.0	1,059.5	x
Telecommunications	61	213	660.0	6.5	746.1	4.5	337.7	440.8	479.1	525.5	574.9	738.7	835.4	905.1	1,004.8	1,245.7
Computer programming, consultancy and related activities	62	487	672.8	1.0	779.5	1.9	287.5	404.9	460.0	498.3	575.0	779.5	900.9	967.8	1,072.6	1,380.0
Information service activities	63	55	699.6	3.7	801.0	5.7	308.3	422.1	459.5	496.6	606.9	821.4	971.7	1,033.9	1,138.0	x
FINANCIAL AND INSURANCE ACTIVITIES	K	961	628.9	0.7	870.1	-2.5	295.8	368.2	402.8	444.5	530.8	766.6	949.1	1,070.6	1,217.8	1,724.9
Financial service activities, except insurance and pension funding	64	490	673.1	3.5	923.4	-1.4	305.2	378.0	413.9	454.3	547.1	814.5	1,024.3	1,150.0	1,312.8	1,820.7
Insurance, reinsurance and pension funding, except compulsory social security	65	115	606.0	1.7	767.0	-0.4	313.2	372.7	411.6	446.3	528.1	718.5	855.5	905.4	1,028.9	1,428.2
Activities auxiliary to financial services and insurance activities	66	357	592.8	-3.3	830.1	-3.8	270.7	349.2	386.1	425.3	504.3	718.7	874.6	997.0	1,139.4	1,679.7
REAL ESTATE ACTIVITIES	L	358	450.7	1.9	518.1	1.3	157.2	271.1	310.9	340.8	388.6	507.9	575.2	623.8	689.9	893.2
Real estate activities	68	358	450.7	1.9	518.1	1.3	157.2	271.1	310.9	340.8	388.6	507.9	575.2	623.8	689.9	893.2
PROFESSIONAL, SCIENTIFIC AND TECHNICAL ACTIVITIES	M	1,676	553.2	0.5	667.2	1.0	195.1	308.4	350.9	392.7	477.8	651.4	766.6	833.5	919.9	1,245.7
Legal and accounting activities	69	511	507.9	1.2	639.0	0.3	201.4	292.9	326.0	360.1	425.7	610.6	728.3	799.9	876.7	1,245.7
Activities of head offices; management consultancy activities	70	328	517.3	-2.0	692.1	2.1	154.5	241.9	296.3	345.0	421.6	621.8	766.6	862.4	987.2	1,389.5
Architectural and engineering activities; technical testing and analysis	71	414	613.3	0.1	700.6	-1.2	272.9	383.3	431.2	469.4	536.6	699.0	798.4	862.4	938.3	1,219.0
Scientific research and development	72	131	726.9	5.7	831.1	5.0	388.8	506.5	540.5	578.5	656.6	810.5	931.2	992.0	1,135.0	1,386.9
Advertising and market research	73	129	547.6	2.3	638.9	1.6	191.7	345.0	383.3	422.3	479.1	614.3	728.3	783.5	864.1	1,149.9
Other professional, scientific and technical activities	74	115	481.0	9.8	546.7	6.5	144.8	230.0	277.9	319.0	411.4	537.0	644.6	699.5	768.0	1,054.1
Veterinary activities	75	49	358.9	-1.1	432.0	-4.0	135.0	188.3	218.7	246.9	306.5	437.1	531.1	576.4	648.5	x
ADMINISTRATIVE AND SUPPORT SERVICE ACTIVITIES	N	1,806	338.6	4.7	402.7	3.4	95.5	162.2	202.6	242.0	287.7	393.5	470.9	514.6	572.6	743.3
Rental and leasing activities	77	140	467.7	2.7	521.8	1.8	217.7	322.3	345.0	367.1	415.4	515.0	574.9	613.6	670.8	877.5
Employment activities	78	665	311.5	2.3	370.2	1.5	113.3	188.5	218.9	243.8	276.3	359.0	421.6	460.0	503.1	652.0
Travel agency, tour operator and other reservation service and related activities	79	79	411.9	-2.3	528.4	3.0	191.4	263.7	288.0	313.2	362.4	496.4	574.9	613.3	685.0	x
Security and investigation activities	80	105	402.1	4.3	401.3	-0.5	129.7	249.5	276.3	309.0	359.5	443.2	480.3	510.4	540.1	619.4
Services to buildings and landscape activities	81	459	238.0	21.1	305.8	8.9	65.0	91.0	104.0	120.0	164.9	301.4	370.6	410.7	468.0	641.8
Office administrative, office support and other business support activities	82	359	414.9	8.2	513.3	4.4	149.5	249.6	275.4	300.0	353.3	494.8	596.4	651.6	713.8	967.1
PUBLIC ADMINISTRATION AND DEFENCE; COMPULSORY SOCIAL SECURITY	O	1,278	557.6	1.4	583.7	1.5	264.7	360.6	389.5	424.8	487.2	618.9	698.5	736.3	780.0	916.1
Public administration and defence; compulsory social security	84	1,278	557.6	1.4	583.7	1.5	264.7	360.6	389.5	424.8	487.2	618.9	698.5	736.3	780.0	916.1
EDUCATION	P	3,778	427.8	2.4	475.1	2.3	110.9	199.8	238.2	276.4	353.6	516.4	616.9	668.6	718.6	871.8
Education	85	3,778	427.8	2.4	475.1	2.3	110.9	199.8	238.2	276.4	353.6	516.4	616.9	668.6	718.6	871.8
HUMAN HEALTH AND SOCIAL WORK ACTIVITIES	Q	3,950	380.2	2.1	464.2	1.1	145.9	214.5	244.7	272.9	325.2	446.3	534.8	582.8	643.9	811.7
Human health activities	86	2,516	451.0	1.3	541.5	0.8	184.4	270.0	302.4	335.3	388.6	531.1	614.0	663.8	717.6	911.5
Residential care activities	87	724	284.1	4.8	331.2	4.1	125.6	175.7	196.4	214.3	249.9	320.3	373.0	404.5	451.3	578.9
Social work activities without accommodation	88	710	282.8	2.7	325.6	2.1	91.3	145.7	170.5	196.5	244.8	328.2	389.5	424.6	469.0	607.1
ARTS, ENTERTAINMENT AND RECREATION	R	498	293.3	4.6	371.4	4.8	38.4	94.2	125.6	156.8	229.0	350.8	422.3	468.4	515.7	680.2

4.11a   Weekly pay - Gross (£) - For all employee jobs[a]: United Kingdom, 2015

Description	Code	Number of jobs[b] (thousand)	Median	Annual percentage change	Mean	Annual percentage change	Percentiles									
							10	20	25	30	40	60	70	75	80	90
Creative, arts and entertainment activities	90	50	453.6	1.4	540.6	5.7	x	156.4	217.8	285.8	366.1	529.2	617.6	664.1	710.0	x
Libraries, archives, museums and other cultural activities	91	56	416.7	1.9	435.5	3.5	110.2	191.1	246.5	285.1	352.9	473.7	545.4	581.2	622.7	x
Gambling and betting activities	92	103	305.5	1.4	342.7	0.0	121.8	179.3	202.6	226.7	269.5	345.0	384.6	416.2	450.7	552.2
Sports activities and amusement and recreation activities	93	290	236.1	10.9	340.3	5.2	26.0	55.4	75.5	100.1	161.0	303.1	373.6	416.0	472.8	662.2
OTHER SERVICE ACTIVITIES	S	444	335.4	-0.5	405.4	0.8	100.7	149.5	178.0	207.2	272.6	406.2	474.2	517.5	580.8	778.1
Activities of membership organisations	94	197	410.5	2.9	455.2	4.1	74.4	154.6	197.2	242.4	336.6	464.4	548.6	605.9	675.2	879.8
Repair of computers and personal and household goods	95	36	479.1	-5.3	565.6	-6.9	231.8	300.7	338.7	354.1	420.4	537.1	624.2	669.2	750.8	x
Other personal service activities	96	210	268.2	5.3	330.9	3.1	104.0	135.0	153.0	172.5	228.3	311.4	375.9	415.4	450.1	606.1
ACTIVITIES OF HOUSEHOLDS AS EMPLOYERS; UNDIFFERENTIATED GOODS-AND SERVICES-PRODUCING ACTIVITIES OF HOUSEHOLDS FOR OWN USE	T	73	128.7	-0.9	192.7	4.2	31.5	50.0	62.3	73.8	100.5	177.6	226.0	256.6	295.1	x
Activities of households as employers of domestic personnel	97	73	128.7	-0.9	192.7	4.2	31.5	50.0	62.3	73.8	100.5	177.6	226.0	256.6	295.1	x
Undifferentiated goods- and services-producing activities of private households for own use	98	:														
ACTIVITIES OF EXTRATERRITORIAL ORGANISATIONS AND BODIES	U	x	x		493.2		x	x	x	x	x	x	x	x	x	x
Activities of extraterritorial organisations and bodies	99	x	x		493.2		x	x	x	x	x	x	x	x	x	x
NOT CLASSIFIED		9	x		300.3	12.9	x	92.0	103.8	x	x	x	x	x	x	x

a Employees on adult rates whose pay for the survey pay-period was not affected by absence.

b Figures for Number of Jobs are for indicative purposes only and should not be considered an accurate estimate of employee job counts.

KEY - The colour coding indicates the quality of each estimate; jobs, median, mean and percentiles but not the annual percentage change.

The quality of an estimate is measured by its coefficient of variation (CV), which is the ratio of the standard error of an estimate to the estimate.

Source: Annual Survey of Hours and Earnings, Office for National Statistics.

Key	Statistical robustness
CV <= 5%	Estimates are considered precise
CV > 5% and <= 10%	Estimates are considered reasonably precise
CV > 10% and <= 20%	Estimates are considered acceptable
x = CV > 20%	Estimates are considered unreliable for practical purposes
.. = disclosive	
: = not applicable	
- = nil or negligible	

4.11b - Hourly pay - Gross (£) - For all employee jobs[a]: United Kingdom, 2015

Description	Code	Number of jobs[b] (thousand)	Median	Annual percentage change	Mean	Annual percentage change	Percentiles 10	20	25	30	40	60	70	75	80	90
ALL EMPLOYEES		25,997	11.78	1.4	15.26	0.9	6.88	7.81	8.33	8.92	10.17	13.80	16.32	17.88	19.73	25.63
All Industries and Services		25,988	11.78	1.4	15.26	0.9	6.88	7.81	8.33	8.92	10.18	13.80	16.32	17.88	19.73	25.63
All Index of Production Industries		2,839	13.13	1.5	15.50	1.7	7.61	8.95	9.57	10.21	11.59	14.96	17.31	18.71	20.45	25.93
All Manufacturing		2,475	12.83	1.4	15.07	1.4	7.50	8.75	9.38	10.00	11.33	14.52	16.77	18.14	19.81	24.92
All Service Industries		22,114	11.51	1.4	15.26	0.8	6.80	7.66	8.14	8.70	9.97	13.61	16.23	17.84	19.70	25.70
AGRICULTURE, FORESTRY AND FISHING	A	136	8.94	0.8	10.56	3.5	6.57	7.04	7.35	7.62	8.19	9.90	10.89	11.58	12.50	16.30
Crop and animal production, hunting and related service activities	1	121	8.71	0.6	10.11	1.8	6.53	7.00	7.26	7.50	8.00	9.62	10.48	11.20	11.79	14.45
Forestry and logging	2	11	12.27	2.9	14.69	10.4	x	8.57	8.87	9.19	10.72	13.01	15.18	x	x	x
Fishing and aquaculture	3	x	x		14.28	19.5	x	x	x	8.78	9.27	x	x	x	x	x
MINING AND QUARRYING	B	49	17.57	3.3	21.28	2.0	9.71	11.64	12.41	13.23	15.26	20.06	23.12	25.88	27.60	x
Mining of coal and lignite	5	x	x		x		x	x	x	x	x	16.92	x	x	x	x
Extraction of crude petroleum and natural gas	6	7	x		39.09	18.1	x	19.97	21.38	22.43	25.50	34.36	x	x	x	x
Mining of metal ores	7	..														
Other mining and quarrying	8	22	13.24	3.4	15.39	4.5	9.20	9.97	10.25	11.19	12.41	14.82	18.06	19.10	20.59	x
Mining support service activities	9	17	20.33	4.6	23.29	2.8	11.08	14.37	15.24	15.54	17.33	22.58	26.45	x	x	x
MANUFACTURING	C	2,475	12.83	1.4	15.07	1.4	7.50	8.75	9.38	10.00	11.33	14.52	16.77	18.14	19.81	24.92
Manufacture of food products	10	378	9.56	-0.2	12.33	3.0	6.79	7.31	7.61	7.94	8.62	10.88	12.61	13.75	15.39	19.81
Manufacture of beverages	11	47	15.93	3.2	18.68	1.1	9.32	11.08	11.98	12.45	13.95	17.92	19.91	21.84	24.18	x
Manufacture of tobacco products	12	x	22.74	6.3	23.94	13.9	x	x	x	x	x	24.99	x	x	x	x
Manufacture of textiles	13	44	9.46	2.9	12.01	3.2	6.70	7.11	7.28	7.55	8.70	10.62	12.03	13.01	14.06	x
Manufacture of wearing apparel	14	22	7.91	-9.5	11.07	5.4	x	6.50	6.52	6.73	7.39	9.01	10.66	x	x	x
Manufacture of leather and related products	15	9	9.18	3.3	10.40	3.5	7.00	7.65	7.87	8.08	8.83	10.29	11.40	12.01	x	x
Manufacture of wood and of products of wood and cork, except furniture; manufacture of articles of straw and plaiting materials	16	55	10.09	0.4	11.52	-1.9	7.40	8.03	8.38	8.70	9.50	11.14	11.97	12.49	13.14	x
Manufacture of paper and paper products	17	59	12.87	1.3	14.58	1.0	7.85	9.22	9.81	10.35	11.70	14.06	15.85	17.15	18.48	x
Printing and reproduction of recorded media	18	97	11.83	0.6	14.22	3.4	7.47	8.71	9.24	9.70	10.66	13.22	15.16	16.23	17.54	x
Manufacture of coke and refined petroleum products	19	9	24.50	-0.3	25.27	-2.1	x	x	16.59	20.44	22.31	25.85	26.95	28.61	x	x
Manufacture of chemicals and chemical products	20	91	15.23	2.8	17.31	1.6	8.35	10.00	10.92	11.54	13.22	17.05	19.58	20.78	22.81	x
Manufacture of basic pharmaceutical products and pharmaceutical preparations	21	43	16.49	-8.7	19.94	-4.5	9.43	10.80	11.71	12.70	14.40	18.62	20.81	22.13	25.49	x
Manufacture of rubber and plastic products	22	152	10.94	2.5	13.56	2.0	7.23	8.30	8.67	9.10	9.98	12.26	13.99	15.00	16.15	21.54
Manufacture of other non-metallic mineral products	23	84	12.03	0.4	14.02	-0.1	7.65	8.91	9.50	9.98	10.99	13.62	15.63	16.97	17.86	x
Manufacture of basic metals	24	84	16.01	4.0	16.57	0.3	9.18	11.20	12.01	12.80	14.41	17.45	19.06	20.44	22.19	24.63
Manufacture of fabricated metal products, except machinery and equipment	25	289	12.03	2.3	13.58	3.3	7.70	8.90	9.40	9.88	11.00	13.42	14.79	15.59	16.64	21.15
Manufacture of computer, electronic and optical products	26	129	15.39	0.0	17.60	3.5	8.30	9.78	10.76	11.34	13.40	17.64	20.35	21.68	23.45	28.80
Manufacture of electrical equipment	27	94	12.65	1.9	14.81	-1.2	7.79	8.99	9.54	10.17	11.38	13.85	16.15	17.42	18.83	24.07
Manufacture of machinery and equipment n.e.c.	28	212	14.10	2.2	16.14	1.9	8.96	10.31	10.94	11.76	12.94	15.62	17.78	19.03	20.58	25.94
Manufacture of motor vehicles, trailers and semi-trailers	29	173	15.69	2.9	17.42	4.8	8.78	10.44	11.26	12.23	13.82	17.77	20.10	21.49	22.78	27.80
Manufacture of other transport equipment	30	176	18.15	1.8	19.38	0.6	11.14	13.17	14.07	14.72	16.43	19.56	21.56	22.67	23.89	28.74
Manufacture of furniture	31	65	9.87	3.5	11.22	-1.2	6.93	7.73	8.01	8.42	9.08	10.70	11.79	12.61	13.48	x
Other manufacturing	32	68	11.95	4.3	13.80	3.4	7.41	8.36	8.94	9.50	10.70	13.29	15.33	16.41	17.76	x
Repair and installation of machinery and equipment	33	91	14.94	3.7	17.11	1.8	8.41	10.48	11.44	12.15	13.42	17.06	19.12	20.60	22.69	28.30
ELECTRICITY, GAS, STEAM AND AIR CONDITIONING SUPPLY	D	169	18.51	4.2	20.80	2.9	10.31	12.24	13.22	14.44	16.69	20.74	23.66	25.81	28.17	33.67
Electricity, gas, steam and air conditioning supply	35	169	18.51	4.2	20.80	2.9	10.31	12.24	13.22	14.44	16.69	20.74	23.66	25.81	28.17	33.67
WATER SUPPLY; SEWERAGE, WASTE MANAGEMENT AND REMEDIATION ACTIVITIES	E	147	12.59	0.4	15.11	3.9	7.65	9.06	9.70	10.26	11.35	14.03	16.21	17.72	19.78	25.44
Water collection, treatment and supply	36	44	15.38	3.3	17.65	4.5	9.95	11.69	12.18	12.70	13.95	16.96	18.59	19.97	20.82	x
Sewerage	37	12	14.17	4.6	16.13	2.1	8.31	10.65	10.79	11.63	12.53	15.13	17.66	x	x	x
Waste collection, treatment and disposal activities; materials recovery	38	89	11.11	4.3	13.87	3.4	7.13	8.05	8.65	9.13	10.22	12.25	14.02	15.19	16.87	x
Remediation activities and other waste management services	39	x	11.48	21.0	13.99		x	x	x	x	10.95	x	x	x	x	x
CONSTRUCTION	F	899	12.94	0.8	15.10	0.8	8.06	9.50	10.00	10.52	11.75	14.35	16.10	17.31	18.86	24.02
Construction of buildings	41	262	13.31	1.2	16.62	1.4	8.15	9.62	10.19	10.76	12.01	15.23	17.88	19.56	21.80	28.35
Civil engineering	42	179	13.34	-1.1	15.62	-0.1	8.23	9.77	10.23	10.94	12.04	14.98	17.04	18.74	20.23	25.57

4.11b - Hourly pay - Gross (£) - For all employee jobs[a]: United Kingdom, 2015

Description	Code	Number of jobs[b] (thousand)	Median	Annual percentage change	Mean	Annual percentage change	Percentiles 10	20	25	30	40	60	70	75	80	90
Specialised construction activities	43	458	12.60	1.6	14.03	1.0	8.00	9.29	10.00	10.30	11.50	13.79	15.16	16.07	17.09	20.39
WHOLESALE AND RETAIL TRADE; REPAIR OF MOTOR VEHICLES AND MOTORCYCLES	G	3,769	8.82	2.3	12.24	1.4	6.52	6.99	7.15	7.39	8.00	9.92	11.49	12.57	13.99	19.25
Wholesale and retail trade and repair of motor vehicles and motorcycles	45	449	10.07	1.9	11.99	1.2	6.71	7.46	7.81	8.30	9.18	11.20	12.49	13.14	14.12	17.91
Wholesale trade, except of motor vehicles and motorcycles	46	1,031	11.54	1.4	14.80	-0.3	7.17	8.16	8.64	9.12	10.22	13.22	15.49	17.02	18.89	26.07
Retail trade, except of motor vehicles and motorcycles	47	2,289	7.86	2.7	10.80	2.7	6.50	6.73	6.91	7.08	7.39	8.55	9.53	10.20	11.25	15.52
TRANSPORTATION AND STORAGE	H	1,105	12.19	3.3	14.92	5.0	8.00	9.23	9.78	10.30	11.18	13.61	15.59	16.72	18.77	25.99
Land transport and transport via pipelines	49	489	11.50	2.8	13.59	4.2	7.90	8.89	9.35	9.80	10.60	12.78	14.51	15.72	17.20	24.52
Water transport	50	10	13.78	-0.2	15.64	-3.1	x	9.91	10.74	11.58	12.67	14.25	15.76	x	x	x
Air transport	51	77	18.14	-3.8	24.64	8.7	9.34	11.74	12.82	13.49	15.53	21.85	26.95	29.99	34.26	x
Warehousing and support activities for transportation	52	323	12.92	1.4	15.98	3.6	8.00	9.08	9.67	10.17	11.44	14.85	17.26	18.71	20.88	28.69
Postal and courier activities	53	206	11.85	5.7	13.40	6.0	8.44	10.25	10.97	11.01	11.30	12.76	13.66	14.30	15.25	17.66
ACCOMMODATION AND FOOD SERVICE ACTIVITIES	I	1,417	7.00	2.9	8.76	1.9	5.77	x	x	6.50	6.70	7.47	8.00	8.50	9.16	11.51
Accommodation	55	313	7.35	1.5	9.54	3.1	6.49	x	6.50	6.62	7.00	8.00	8.91	9.60	10.18	13.36
Food and beverage service activities	56	1,103	6.96	4.3	8.51	1.6	5.54	x	x	6.50	6.65	7.28	7.90	8.23	8.82	11.06
INFORMATION AND COMMUNICATION	J	1,002	17.44	2.7	20.75	1.6	9.25	11.29	12.27	13.29	15.31	19.91	22.99	24.64	27.11	35.07
Publishing activities	58	146	15.49	3.0	19.10	-7.4	8.60	10.26	11.20	12.23	13.51	17.42	19.64	21.89	23.65	30.61
Motion picture, video and television programme production, sound recording and music publishing activities	59	54	13.11	-1.3	17.32	3.4	6.55	7.71	8.52	9.57	11.43	15.49	18.81	20.38	22.77	x
Programming and broadcasting activities	60	47	20.45	5.1	22.99	3.8	11.29	14.17	15.26	16.06	18.29	22.70	24.25	26.80	28.71	x
Telecommunications	61	213	16.66	5.4	19.74	4.8	9.58	11.75	12.54	13.85	15.08	19.28	21.48	22.94	25.37	31.88
Computer programming, consultancy and related activities	62	487	18.39	1.3	21.67	1.7	9.66	11.72	12.77	13.80	16.03	21.09	24.27	26.06	28.75	37.02
Information service activities	63	55	18.74	2.9	21.97	5.1	9.61	11.47	12.67	13.88	16.31	22.01	26.23	28.02	30.13	x
FINANCIAL AND INSURANCE ACTIVITIES	K	961	17.93	0.2	25.32	-2.6	9.36	11.00	11.86	12.85	15.18	21.76	26.64	30.31	34.46	48.18
Financial service activities, except insurance and pension funding	64	490	19.17	2.7	27.15	-1.4	9.73	11.35	12.31	13.32	15.90	23.29	29.04	32.83	37.08	51.12
Insurance, reinsurance and pension funding, except compulsory social security	65	115	17.26	3.0	21.99	-0.7	9.17	10.79	11.86	12.72	14.87	20.10	23.84	25.90	29.51	39.41
Activities auxiliary to financial services and insurance activities	66	357	16.90	-3.6	23.94	-3.7	8.97	10.46	11.26	12.21	14.31	20.13	24.76	27.94	31.92	46.51
REAL ESTATE ACTIVITIES	L	358	12.70	3.0	15.50	2.6	7.75	8.84	9.40	10.00	11.31	14.24	16.03	17.44	19.16	24.86
Real estate activities	68	358	12.70	3.0	15.50	2.6	7.75	8.84	9.40	10.00	11.31	14.24	16.03	17.44	19.16	24.86
PROFESSIONAL, SCIENTIFIC AND TECHNICAL ACTIVITIES	M	1,676	15.56	0.7	19.53	0.5	8.15	9.89	10.73	11.65	13.42	18.06	21.04	23.00	25.40	34.19
Legal and accounting activities	69	511	15.11	0.4	19.46	0.0	8.16	9.70	10.36	11.12	12.82	17.88	20.93	22.92	25.26	35.25
Activities of head offices; management consultancy activities	70	328	14.80	-1.3	20.74	2.3	7.46	9.15	9.84	10.54	12.54	17.73	21.72	24.02	27.05	37.40
Architectural and engineering activities; technical testing and analysis	71	414	16.31	0.6	19.16	-1.6	8.93	10.98	11.78	12.65	14.37	18.44	21.18	23.13	25.05	32.10
Scientific research and development	72	131	19.67	5.7	23.12	4.2	11.57	13.91	14.85	15.87	17.97	21.97	25.21	27.21	31.01	37.97
Advertising and market research	73	129	15.02	0.5	18.69	-1.6	8.50	10.17	11.02	11.98	13.29	16.75	19.91	21.73	23.46	31.36
Other professional, scientific and technical activities	74	115	13.57	5.3	16.74	5.3	7.50	9.06	9.99	10.51	11.98	15.33	17.88	19.41	21.57	28.65
Veterinary activities	75	49	10.64	3.0	13.75	-1.8	6.98	7.67	8.29	8.65	9.65	12.61	15.42	16.83	18.27	x
ADMINISTRATIVE AND SUPPORT SERVICE ACTIVITIES	N	1,806	9.25	4.5	12.15	3.0	6.50	6.99	7.24	7.53	8.29	10.49	12.33	13.59	15.11	19.85
Rental and leasing activities	77	140	11.05	0.3	13.05	1.6	7.03	8.00	8.53	8.97	9.92	12.25	13.69	14.84	16.17	21.08
Employment activities	78	665	9.00	4.7	11.14	1.8	6.50	6.80	7.07	7.41	8.12	10.13	11.96	13.00	14.35	18.57
Travel agency, tour operator and other reservation service and related activities	79	79	11.24	-2.7	15.14	2.0	7.21	8.12	8.51	8.94	10.12	13.27	15.36	16.63	18.28	x
Security and investigation activities	80	105	8.73	0.1	9.79	-0.6	6.85	7.28	7.58	7.83	8.18	9.30	10.00	10.72	11.25	13.97
Services to buildings and landscape activities	81	459	7.79	6.2	10.85	4.3	6.50	6.51	6.65	6.83	7.23	8.53	9.88	10.62	11.83	16.00
Office administrative, office support and other business support activities	82	359	11.76	8.4	15.14	4.0	7.03	7.89	8.41	8.97	10.13	13.83	16.32	17.49	19.69	26.07

4.11b - Hourly pay - Gross (£) - For all employee jobs[a]: United Kingdom, 2015

Description	Code	Number of jobs[b] (thousand)	Median	Annual percentage change	Mean	Annual percentage change	Percentiles									
							10	20	25	30	40	60	70	75	80	90
PUBLIC ADMINISTRATION AND DEFENCE; COMPULSORY SOCIAL SECURITY	O	1,278	14.91	1.4	16.35	1.1	9.49	10.63	11.41	12.19	13.55	16.42	18.23	19.06	20.17	23.59
Public administration and defence; compulsory social security	84	1,278	14.91	1.4	16.35	1.1	9.49	10.63	11.41	12.19	13.55	16.42	18.23	19.06	20.17	23.59
EDUCATION	P	3,778	14.05	1.7	16.62	1.6	7.66	8.64	9.18	9.98	11.73	16.74	19.46	21.18	22.76	27.49
Education	85	3,778	14.05	1.7	16.62	1.6	7.66	8.64	9.18	9.98	11.73	16.74	19.46	21.18	22.76	27.49
HUMAN HEALTH AND SOCIAL WORK ACTIVITIES	Q	3,950	11.77	0.5	14.63	0.5	7.09	8.00	8.51	9.09	10.21	13.85	15.89	17.25	18.43	22.79
Human health activities	86	2,516	14.39	0.8	16.85	0.3	8.46	9.63	10.13	10.98	12.42	16.05	17.90	19.12	20.78	25.09
Residential care activities	87	724	8.11	2.7	10.08	2.8	6.56	6.84	7.00	7.15	7.58	8.88	10.14	11.14	12.51	15.15
Social work activities without accommodation	88	710	9.01	1.2	11.19	2.3	6.69	7.15	7.38	7.64	8.23	10.16	11.64	12.61	13.86	17.69
ARTS, ENTERTAINMENT AND RECREATION	R	498	9.10	3.0	13.21	2.9	6.50	6.85	7.14	7.50	8.28	10.28	11.94	13.29	14.90	19.79
Creative, arts and entertainment activities	90	50	13.29	4.0	17.86	12.2	7.20	8.71	9.37	10.22	11.20	15.40	17.56	18.65	20.33	x
Libraries, archives, museums and other cultural activities	91	56	11.50	-0.1	13.67	-1.7	7.00	7.97	8.42	8.89	10.37	13.13	15.00	15.92	17.28	x
Gambling and betting activities	92	103	8.32	2.7	10.23	0.3	6.57	6.79	7.00	7.28	7.99	8.85	9.64	10.20	11.05	x
Sports activities and amusement and recreation activities	93	290	8.69	2.2	13.55	2.2	6.50	6.67	6.99	7.20	7.87	9.82	11.37	12.48	14.17	19.43
OTHER SERVICE ACTIVITIES	S	444	10.24	0.6	13.41	0.0	6.50	7.18	7.53	8.00	8.99	11.62	13.47	14.82	16.48	22.13
Activities of membership organisations	94	197	12.39	5.2	15.90	4.1	7.29	8.30	9.00	9.73	11.01	13.89	16.29	17.71	19.98	24.89
Repair of computers and personal and household goods	95	36	12.70	-3.0	15.29	-4.8	7.17	8.63	9.08	9.96	10.93	14.69	16.81	18.08	20.06	x
Other personal service activities	96	210	8.29	1.7	10.83	0.6	6.50	6.55	6.86	7.00	7.61	9.20	10.50	11.23	12.26	16.03
ACTIVITIES OF HOUSEHOLDS AS EMPLOYERS; UNDIFFERENTIATED GOODS-AND SERVICES-PRODUCING ACTIVITIES OF HOUSEHOLDS FOR OWN USE	T	73	9.00	0.0	10.30	5.5	7.13	7.79	8.00	8.10	8.60	9.81	10.00	10.50	11.00	x
Activities of households as employers of domestic personnel	97	73	9.00	0.0	10.30	5.5	7.13	7.79	8.00	8.10	8.60	9.81	10.00	10.50	11.00	x
Undifferentiated goods- and services-producing activities of private households for own use	98	:														
ACTIVITIES OF EXTRATERRITORIAL ORGANISATIONS AND BODIES	U	x	x		14.50	-5.0	x	x	x	x	x	x	x	x	x	x
Activities of extraterritorial organisations and bodies	99	x	x		14.50	-5.0	x	x	x	x	x	x	x	x	x	x
NOT CLASSIFIED		9	8.34	5.9	11.12	18.6	6.50	6.61	7.00	7.39	7.69	9.53	x	x	x	x

a Employees on adult rates whose pay for the survey pay-period was not affected by absence.

b Figures for Number of Jobs are for indicative purposes only and should not be considered an accurate estimate of employee job counts.

KEY - The colour coding indicates the quality of each estimate; jobs, median, mean and percentiles but not the annual percentage change.

The quality of an estimate is measured by its coefficient of variation (CV), which is the ratio of the standard error of an estimate to the estimate.

Source: Annual Survey of Hours and Earnings, Office for National Statistics.

Key	Statistical robustness
CV <= 5%	Estimates are considered precise
CV > 5% and <= 10%	Estimates are considered reasonably precise
CV > 10% and <= 20%	Estimates are considered acceptable
x = CV > 20%	Estimates are considered unreliable for practical purposes
.. = disclosive	
: = not applicable	
- = nil or negligible	

4.12a - Weekly pay - Gross (£) - For all employee jobs[a]: United Kingdom, 2015

Description	Number of jobs[b] (thousand)	Median	Annual % change	Mean	Annual % change	Percentiles									
						10	20	25	30	40	60	70	75	80	90
ALL EMPLOYEES	25,997	425.1	1.7	507.2	1.1	130.2	217.4	259.1	292.5	357.2	500.6	594.4	652.4	717.8	922.4
Male	13,072	517.5	2.0	612.6	1.1	203.1	310.5	345.0	379.1	445.9	595.1	691.9	752.7	826.5	1,079.9
Female	12,926	337.1	2.0	400.6	1.4	102.9	161.3	192.3	221.9	280.0	401.1	480.0	531.3	592.4	761.7
Full-Time	18,637	527.1	1.7	627.0	1.0	296.1	351.3	378.4	404.8	462.4	599.9	687.6	741.6	805.0	1,034.9
Part-Time	7,360	166.5	3.4	203.9	0.2	52.0	88.2	103.6	115.9	143.7	193.7	225.7	247.6	277.5	387.8
Male Full-Time	11,231	567.2	1.5	680.3	0.9	316.6	378.4	406.8	438.5	498.4	643.5	737.8	796.4	872.0	1,140.3
Male Part-Time	1,841	155.5	2.7	199.9	-0.3	44.8	78.0	93.3	105.4	135.0	181.5	207.7	230.0	254.8	374.6
Female Full-Time	7,407	470.2	1.9	546.2	1.3	276.6	323.0	345.0	366.9	416.0	535.1	615.1	665.9	716.7	878.0
Female Part-Time	5,519	171.2	3.1	205.3	0.4	54.5	91.9	105.3	119.4	146.3	197.5	230.4	253.6	284.0	391.3

a Employees on adult rates whose pay for the survey pay-period was not affected by absence.   Source: Annual Survey of Hours and Earnings, Office for National Statistics.

b Figures for Number of Jobs are for indicative purposes only and should not be considered an accurate estimate of employee job counts.

The quality of an estimate is measured by its coefficient of variation (CV), which is the ratio of the standard error of an estimate to the estimate.

4.12b - Hourly pay - Excluding overtime (£) - For all employee jobs[a]: United Kingdom, 2015

Description	Code	Number of jobs[b] (thousand)	Median	Annual % change	Mean	Annual % change	10	20	25	30	40	60	70	75	80	90
ALL EMPLOYEES		25,997	11.72	1.6	15.29	0.8	6.86	7.77	8.28	8.87	10.11	13.73	16.27	17.84	19.68	25.59
All Industries and Services		25,988	11.73	1.6	15.29	0.8	6.86	7.77	8.28	8.87	10.11	13.74	16.27	17.84	19.68	25.59
All Index of Production Industries		2,839	12.93	1.4	15.45	1.6	7.50	8.79	9.41	10.03	11.43	14.74	17.10	18.55	20.33	25.87
All Manufacturing		2,475	12.63	1.6	15.01	1.3	7.43	8.60	9.20	9.84	11.16	14.32	16.58	17.96	19.65	24.87
All Service Industries		22,114	11.50	1.8	15.31	0.7	6.78	7.64	8.10	8.66	9.94	13.58	16.18	17.83	19.67	25.68
AGRICULTURE, FORESTRY AND FISHING	A	136	8.75	2.3	10.47	3.8	6.50	7.00	7.25	7.50	8.04	9.58	10.57	11.50	12.39	16.36
Crop and animal production, hunting and related service activities	1	121	8.57	1.7	9.99	2.2	6.50	7.00	7.14	7.48	8.00	9.25	10.06	10.91	11.70	14.43
Forestry and logging	2	11	12.27	2.9	14.65	10.3	x	8.55	8.87	9.19	10.71	12.93	14.72	x	x	x
Fishing and aquaculture	3	x	x		13.89	16.3	x	x	x	8.41	x	x	x	x	x	x
MINING AND QUARRYING	B	49	17.37	3.1	21.38	1.9	9.36	11.10	11.99	13.08	15.17	20.09	23.31	24.95	27.50	x
Mining of coal and lignite	5	x	x		x		x	x	x	x	x	14.60	x	x	x	x
Extraction of crude petroleum and natural gas	6	7	x		39.17	18.2	x	19.97	21.38	22.43	24.43	34.36	x	x	x	x
Mining of metal ores	7	..														
Other mining and quarrying	8	22	13.20	3.1	15.25	4.4	8.79	9.68	10.01	10.34	11.99	14.62	17.49	18.98	20.24	x
Mining support service activities	9	17	20.50	5.4	23.24	2.1	11.08	13.81	14.80	15.63	17.14	22.68	25.40	x	x	x
MANUFACTURING	C	2,475	12.63	1.6	15.01	1.3	7.43	8.60	9.20	9.84	11.16	14.32	16.58	17.96	19.65	24.87
Manufacture of food products	10	378	9.39	-0.4	12.32	3.1	6.73	7.20	7.44	7.79	8.47	10.73	12.56	13.61	15.33	19.78
Manufacture of beverages	11	47	15.94	5.6	18.70	1.3	9.24	11.08	11.83	12.30	13.86	17.83	19.78	21.84	24.18	x
Manufacture of tobacco products	12	x	22.75	7.2	22.52	10.0	x	x	x	x	x	23.79	x	x	x	x
Manufacture of textiles	13	44	9.45	3.6	11.98	3.4	6.63	7.00	7.25	7.48	8.60	10.61	11.89	12.77	13.87	x
Manufacture of wearing apparel	14	22	7.91	-10.4	11.01	5.3	x	x	6.50	6.73	7.36	9.25	10.11	x	x	x
Manufacture of leather and related products	15	9	9.02	1.7	10.34	3.7	7.00	7.53	7.78	8.08	8.69	10.29	11.40	12.05	x	x
Manufacture of wood and of products of wood and cork, except furniture; manufacture of articles of straw and plaiting materials	16	55	9.97	2.5	11.40	-2.5	7.31	7.89	8.09	8.50	9.18	10.86	11.63	12.16	12.97	x
Manufacture of paper and paper products	17	59	12.61	1.0	14.53	0.9	7.79	8.99	9.51	10.17	11.33	13.96	15.78	17.10	18.17	x
Printing and reproduction of recorded media	18	97	11.75	0.4	14.19	3.4	7.40	8.62	9.08	9.48	10.46	13.11	14.76	16.00	17.28	x
Manufacture of coke and refined petroleum products	19	9	23.66	-1.6	24.83	-4.0	x	x	16.59	20.44	22.28	25.32	26.52	x	x	x
Manufacture of chemicals and chemical products	20	91	14.95	2.1	17.27	1.8	8.21	10.00	10.78	11.50	13.09	16.98	19.26	20.56	22.45	x
Manufacture of basic pharmaceutical products and pharmaceutical preparations	21	43	16.40	-8.6	19.92	-4.5	9.18	10.76	11.61	12.56	14.30	18.54	20.66	22.04	25.49	x
Manufacture of rubber and plastic products	22	152	10.71	1.0	13.57	2.1	7.13	8.20	8.58	8.96	9.90	12.17	13.85	14.93	16.12	21.54
Manufacture of other non-metallic mineral products	23	84	12.00	0.9	14.01	-0.6	7.53	8.81	9.24	9.78	10.78	13.58	15.47	16.94	17.84	x
Manufacture of basic metals	24	84	15.76	4.0	16.57	0.3	8.96	10.79	11.80	12.61	14.09	17.33	19.04	20.31	22.21	24.66
Manufacture of fabricated metal products, except machinery and equipment	25	289	11.75	2.5	13.42	2.9	7.55	8.68	9.11	9.75	10.75	12.94	14.46	15.33	16.51	21.09
Manufacture of computer, electronic and optical products	26	129	15.19	-0.2	17.61	3.7	8.16	9.63	10.59	11.29	13.15	17.59	20.17	21.54	23.45	28.80
Manufacture of electrical equipment	27	94	12.38	1.5	14.74	-1.4	7.74	8.86	9.44	10.02	11.19	13.82	15.88	17.20	18.69	x
Manufacture of machinery and equipment n.e.c.	28	212	13.82	2.4	16.06	2.0	8.77	10.17	10.81	11.48	12.75	15.28	17.63	19.01	20.51	25.90
Manufacture of motor vehicles, trailers and semi-trailers	29	173	15.46	2.1	17.26	4.6	8.61	10.28	11.05	12.08	13.60	17.64	19.80	21.41	22.51	28.07
Manufacture of other transport equipment	30	176	17.83	1.0	19.35	0.0	11.01	12.93	13.92	14.68	16.15	19.52	21.45	22.61	23.88	28.84
Manufacture of furniture	31	65	9.76	3.7	11.08	-1.5	6.83	7.65	7.96	8.25	9.00	10.55	11.50	12.29	13.08	x
Other manufacturing	32	68	11.93	5.4	13.74	3.1	7.34	8.31	8.82	9.43	10.61	13.15	15.27	16.07	17.62	x
Repair and installation of machinery and equipment	33	91	14.74	5.3	16.95	2.3	8.41	10.32	11.25	12.03	13.21	16.49	18.80	20.35	22.38	28.30
ELECTRICITY, GAS, STEAM AND AIR CONDITIONING SUPPLY	D	169	18.25	3.9	20.63	2.8	10.27	12.19	13.10	14.37	16.51	20.49	23.53	25.60	27.96	33.43
Electricity, gas, steam and air conditioning supply	35	169	18.25	3.9	20.63	2.8	10.27	12.19	13.10	14.37	16.51	20.49	23.53	25.60	27.96	33.43
WATER SUPPLY; SEWERAGE, WASTE MANAGEMENT AND REMEDIATION ACTIVITIES	E	147	12.41	0.9	15.08	4.2	7.50	8.97	9.46	10.00	11.14	13.88	15.87	17.27	19.72	25.43
Water collection, treatment and supply	36	44	14.97	1.0	17.61	4.5	9.90	11.65	12.12	12.54	13.74	16.69	18.48	19.85	20.82	x
Sewerage	37	12	13.92	2.7	16.11	0.8	8.31	10.00	10.66	11.48	12.51	14.81	17.66	x	x	x
Waste collection, treatment and disposal activities; materials recovery	38	89	10.91	4.2	13.80	4.1	7.01	8.00	8.50	9.00	9.97	12.13	13.66	14.97	16.72	x
Remediation activities and other waste management services	39	x	11.47	21.0	14.02		x	x	x	x	10.78	x	x	x	x	x

4.12b - Hourly pay - Excluding overtime (£) - For all employee jobs[a]: United Kingdom, 2015

Description	Code	Number of jobs[b] (thousand)	Median	Annual % change	Mean	Annual % change	10	20	25	30	40	60	70	75	80	90
CONSTRUCTION	F	899	12.81	1.3	15.04	0.8	8.00	9.38	10.00	10.50	11.60	14.12	15.95	17.18	18.71	24.02
Construction of buildings	41	262	13.18	0.5	16.67	1.6	8.13	9.58	10.19	10.74	11.91	15.08	17.86	19.51	21.60	28.35
Civil engineering	42	179	13.16	-1.3	15.60	-0.1	8.09	9.50	10.05	10.59	11.84	14.75	16.97	18.57	20.22	25.59
Specialised construction activities	43	458	12.50	2.1	13.88	0.9	8.00	9.20	9.93	10.25	11.42	13.59	15.00	15.82	16.96	20.30
WHOLESALE AND RETAIL TRADE; REPAIR OF MOTOR VEHICLES AND MOTORCYCLES	G	3,769	8.71	2.0	12.30	1.2	6.51	6.96	7.12	7.34	7.92	9.78	11.36	12.50	13.92	19.23
Wholesale and retail trade and repair of motor vehicles and motorcycles	45	449	10.01	1.8	11.97	1.2	6.66	7.38	7.74	8.23	9.12	11.06	12.41	13.00	13.99	17.92
Wholesale trade, except of motor vehicles and motorcycles	46	1,031	11.50	1.7	14.84	-0.4	7.11	8.11	8.62	9.07	10.12	13.11	15.38	16.94	18.81	26.07
Retail trade, except of motor vehicles and motorcycles	47	2,289	7.78	2.3	10.86	2.6	6.50	6.73	6.90	7.05	7.34	8.45	9.36	10.04	11.08	15.50
TRANSPORTATION AND STORAGE	H	1,105	12.15	3.4	15.02	5.2	8.00	9.10	9.69	10.23	11.14	13.58	15.53	16.71	18.77	25.94
Land transport and transport via pipelines	49	489	11.45	3.1	13.61	4.5	7.76	8.75	9.25	9.70	10.52	12.72	14.39	15.64	17.10	24.51
Water transport	50	10	13.74	-0.4	15.63	-2.9	x	9.89	10.42	11.23	12.46	14.17	15.76	x	x	x
Air transport	51	77	18.26	-2.6	24.86	9.3	9.39	11.74	12.89	13.42	15.34	21.81	26.95	29.99	34.26	x
Warehousing and support activities for transportation	52	323	12.82	0.8	16.05	3.6	7.90	9.00	9.55	10.06	11.37	14.75	17.24	18.70	21.11	28.73
Postal and courier activities	53	206	11.91	6.8	13.54	6.3	8.38	10.23	11.01	11.01	11.30	12.81	13.81	14.47	15.44	17.87
ACCOMMODATION AND FOOD SERVICE ACTIVITIES	I	1,417	7.00	2.9	8.76	1.7	5.77	x	x	6.50	6.69	7.46	8.00	8.50	9.15	11.50
Accommodation	55	313	7.35	1.6	9.54	3.0	6.49	x	6.50	6.61	6.99	7.99	8.88	9.60	10.16	13.36
Food and beverage service activities	56	1,103	6.95	4.2	8.50	1.4	5.52	x	x	6.50	6.65	7.28	7.88	8.22	8.82	11.06
INFORMATION AND COMMUNICATION	J	1,002	17.38	2.5	20.75	1.4	9.24	11.26	12.26	13.29	15.07	19.85	22.94	24.58	27.06	35.07
Publishing activities	58	146	15.48	3.3	19.10	-7.5	8.58	10.26	11.20	12.17	13.47	17.50	19.80	21.89	23.55	30.61
Motion picture, video and television programme production, sound recording and music publishing activities	59	54	13.15	0.3	17.35	3.5	6.52	7.69	8.51	9.54	11.40	15.58	18.81	20.34	22.77	x
Programming and broadcasting activities	60	47	20.36	3.3	22.95	3.6	11.25	13.95	15.13	16.05	18.29	22.68	24.21	26.65	28.71	x
Telecommunications	61	213	16.28	3.7	19.66	4.4	9.60	11.54	12.42	13.68	14.89	19.21	21.36	22.69	24.85	31.78
Computer programming, consultancy and related activities	62	487	18.39	1.8	21.68	1.6	9.58	11.60	12.77	13.80	15.99	21.06	24.24	26.00	28.70	37.05
Information service activities	63	55	18.74	3.8	22.01	5.3	9.56	11.47	12.67	13.83	16.31	22.07	26.23	28.02	30.13	x
FINANCIAL AND INSURANCE ACTIVITIES	K	961	17.89	0.3	25.39	-2.6	9.32	10.96	11.82	12.79	15.17	21.75	26.60	30.30	34.39	48.29
Financial service activities, except insurance and pension funding	64	490	19.16	3.0	27.23	-1.4	9.72	11.32	12.26	13.28	15.89	23.27	29.04	32.83	37.11	51.12
Insurance, reinsurance and pension funding, except compulsory social security	65	115	17.04	1.8	21.97	-0.8	9.11	10.72	11.82	12.68	14.80	20.10	23.82	25.82	29.51	39.41
Activities auxiliary to financial services and insurance activities	66	357	16.83	-3.9	24.00	-3.8	8.94	10.44	11.21	12.14	14.26	20.11	24.70	27.91	31.87	46.51
REAL ESTATE ACTIVITIES	L	358	12.70	3.1	15.54	2.5	7.74	8.83	9.38	9.97	11.30	14.24	16.04	17.40	19.13	24.83
Real estate activities	68	358	12.70	3.1	15.54	2.5	7.74	8.83	9.38	9.97	11.30	14.24	16.04	17.40	19.13	24.83
PROFESSIONAL, SCIENTIFIC AND TECHNICAL ACTIVITIES	M	1,676	15.51	0.9	19.56	0.5	8.14	9.86	10.70	11.60	13.40	17.99	21.00	23.00	25.37	34.20
Legal and accounting activities	69	511	15.08	0.2	19.47	0.0	8.15	9.67	10.36	11.11	12.80	17.87	20.93	22.92	25.23	35.23
Activities of head offices; management consultancy activities	70	328	14.78	-0.7	20.79	2.3	7.45	9.14	9.82	10.54	12.52	17.71	21.67	24.02	26.98	37.40
Architectural and engineering activities; technical testing and analysis	71	414	16.23	0.3	19.17	-1.5	8.89	10.89	11.72	12.62	14.31	18.38	21.16	23.00	25.00	32.11
Scientific research and development	72	131	19.62	5.5	23.16	4.4	11.52	13.88	14.74	15.63	17.97	21.72	25.21	27.34	30.99	37.97
Advertising and market research	73	129	15.04	0.7	18.70	-1.6	8.50	10.13	11.02	11.98	13.29	16.68	19.91	21.73	23.46	31.36
Other professional, scientific and technical activities	74	115	13.59	5.5	16.75	5.0	7.47	9.00	9.99	10.50	11.98	15.33	17.88	19.20	21.57	28.65
Veterinary activities	75	49	10.59	3.1	13.76	-2.0	6.98	7.67	8.20	8.62	9.64	12.58	15.12	16.83	18.27	x
ADMINISTRATIVE AND SUPPORT SERVICE ACTIVITIES	N	1,806	9.21	4.7	12.17	3.2	6.50	6.95	7.20	7.50	8.24	10.41	12.27	13.53	15.01	19.85
Rental and leasing activities	77	140	10.89	0.6	13.03	1.6	7.00	8.00	8.50	8.92	9.80	12.04	13.53	14.70	16.14	21.12
Employment activities	78	665	9.00	5.7	11.14	2.1	6.50	6.75	7.00	7.34	8.07	10.04	11.89	12.96	14.30	18.57
Travel agency, tour operator and other reservation service and related activities	79	79	11.20	-2.5	15.17	2.0	7.21	8.09	8.50	8.89	10.07	13.27	15.47	16.65	18.28	x
Security and investigation activities	80	105	8.73	0.0	9.76	-0.5	6.83	7.28	7.55	7.83	8.14	9.30	10.00	10.74	11.23	13.92
Services to buildings and landscape activities	81	459	7.75	6.1	10.83	4.7	6.50	6.51	6.62	6.83	7.21	8.50	9.86	10.57	11.65	15.77

4.12b - Hourly pay - Excluding overtime (£) - For all employee jobs[a]: United Kingdom, 2015

Description	Code	Number of jobs[b] (thousand)	Median	Annual % change	Mean	Annual % change	Percentiles 10	20	25	30	40	60	70	75	80	90
Office administrative, office support and other business support activities	82	359	11.73	8.2	15.17	4.1	7.00	7.85	8.34	8.92	10.07	13.79	16.22	17.46	19.69	26.07
PUBLIC ADMINISTRATION AND DEFENCE; COMPULSORY SOCIAL SECURITY	O	1,278	14.90	1.3	16.31	1.0	9.47	10.52	11.39	12.17	13.54	16.38	18.13	18.98	20.00	23.52
Public administration and defence; compulsory social security	84	1,278	14.90	1.3	16.31	1.0	9.47	10.52	11.39	12.17	13.54	16.38	18.13	18.98	20.00	23.52
EDUCATION	P	3,778	14.04	2.0	16.68	1.6	7.65	8.63	9.18	9.96	11.70	16.73	19.45	21.16	22.75	27.49
Education	85	3,778	14.04	2.0	16.68	1.6	7.65	8.63	9.18	9.96	11.70	16.73	19.45	21.16	22.75	27.49
HUMAN HEALTH AND SOCIAL WORK ACTIVITIES	Q	3,950	11.78	0.6	14.64	0.3	7.09	8.00	8.51	9.09	10.22	13.85	15.89	17.25	18.39	22.75
Human health activities	86	2,516	14.39	0.8	16.81	0.0	8.46	9.63	10.12	11.02	12.43	16.02	17.87	19.06	20.73	25.01
Residential care activities	87	724	8.11	2.7	10.13	2.5	6.55	6.83	6.99	7.14	7.58	8.89	10.15	11.15	12.54	15.08
Social work activities without accommodation	88	710	9.02	1.2	11.25	2.3	6.69	7.14	7.38	7.64	8.23	10.21	11.67	12.62	13.86	17.73
ARTS, ENTERTAINMENT AND RECREATION	R	498	9.11	3.5	13.34	2.9	6.50	6.83	7.12	7.50	8.29	10.23	11.93	13.29	14.86	19.72
Creative, arts and entertainment activities	90	50	13.26	3.8	17.95	12.7	7.20	8.75	9.37	10.22	11.22	15.38	17.56	18.65	20.33	x
Libraries, archives, museums and other cultural activities	91	56	11.50	-0.1	13.71	-1.8	6.93	7.93	8.41	8.88	10.47	13.13	15.00	15.92	17.28	x
Gambling and betting activities	92	103	8.31	2.6	10.38	0.1	6.57	6.79	6.94	7.26	8.00	8.84	9.66	10.21	11.09	x
Sports activities and amusement and recreation activities	93	290	8.70	2.4	13.61	2.2	6.50	6.67	6.98	7.20	7.87	9.77	11.32	12.47	14.17	19.39
OTHER SERVICE ACTIVITIES	S	444	10.22	0.9	13.41	0.0	6.50	7.15	7.50	8.00	8.95	11.62	13.48	14.77	16.42	22.17
Activities of membership organisations	94	197	12.40	5.5	15.90	4.0	7.29	8.28	9.00	9.71	11.02	13.90	16.23	17.71	19.98	24.89
Repair of computers and personal and household goods	95	36	12.68	-2.3	15.27	-3.8	7.17	8.57	9.06	9.96	10.89	14.60	16.80	17.86	20.02	x
Other personal service activities	96	210	8.27	1.4	10.80	0.4	6.50	6.55	6.85	7.00	7.59	9.18	10.47	11.19	12.25	16.00
ACTIVITIES OF HOUSEHOLDS AS EMPLOYERS; UNDIFFERENTIATED GOODS-AND SERVICES-PRODUCING ACTIVITIES OF HOUSEHOLDS FOR OWN USE	T	73	9.00	0.4	10.28	5.5	7.13	7.76	8.00	8.10	8.60	9.81	10.00	10.50	11.00	x
Activities of households as employers of domestic personnel	97	73	9.00	0.4	10.28	5.5	7.13	7.76	8.00	8.10	8.60	9.81	10.00	10.50	11.00	x
Undifferentiated goods- and services-producing activities of private households for own use	98	:														
ACTIVITIES OF EXTRATERRITORIAL ORGANISATIONS AND BODIES	U	x	x		14.52	-4.9	x	x	x	x	x	x	x	x	x	x
Activities of extraterritorial organisations and bodies	99	x	x		14.52	-4.9	x	x	x	x	x	x	x	x	x	x
NOT CLASSIFIED		9	8.34	5.7	11.11	18.3	6.50	6.61	7.00	7.39	7.69	9.53	x	x	x	x

a Employees on adult rates whose pay for the survey pay-period was not affected by absence.

b Figures for Number of Jobs are for indicative purposes only and should not be considered an accurate estimate of employee job counts.

KEY - The colour coding indicates the quality of each estimate; jobs, median, mean and percentiles but not the annual percentage change.
The quality of an estimate is measured by its coefficient of variation (CV), which is the ratio of the standard error of an estimate to the estimate.

Source: Annual Survey of Hours and Earnings, Office for National Statistics.

Key	Statistical robustness
CV <= 5%	Estimates are considered precise
CV > 5% and <= 10%	Estimates are considered reasonably precise
CV > 10% and <= 20%	Estimates are considered acceptable
x = CV > 20%	Estimates are considered unreliable for practical purposes
.. = disclosive	
: = not applicable	
- = nil or negligible	

4.13 Average weekly earnings: main industrial sectors Great Britain
Great Britain
Standard Industrial Classification 2007

	Whole economy		Manufacturing		Construction		Services		Distribution Hotels and Restuarants	
	Actual	Seasonally adjusted	Actual	Seasonally adjusted	Actual	Seasonally adjusted	Actual	Seasonally adjusted	Actual	Seasonally adjusted
	KA46	KAB9	K55I	K5CA	K55L	K5CD	K55O	K5BZ	K55R	K5CG
2000	313	313	363	364	370	370	298	297	212	212
2001	329	330	377	377	399	398	315	314	221	220
2002	340	340	390	391	409	409	326	324	229	229
2003	350	351	405	405	427	427	336	335	234	234
2004	366	366	425	424	439	439	352	351	242	242
2005	382	383	440	440	452	452	369	369	251	252
2006	400	401	457	457	480	480	387	386	260	260
2007	420	420	476	475	512	512	406	405	276	276
2008	436	435	490	490	520	521	422	421	283	283
2009	435	435	495	496	525	525	420	420	286	286
2010	445	444	516	515	525	525	430	430	293	293
2011	455	455	524	522	534	534	442	441	296	296
2012	461	461	533	532	538	538	447	447	304	304
2013	466	466	545	544	536	535	452	452	312	311
2014	472	471	555	554	542	542	457	456	316	316
2015	484	483	564	564	557	556	469	469	331	330

	Finance and Business Industries		Private Sector		Public Sector		Private Sector Excl Financial Services	
	Actual	Seasonally adjusted	Actual	Seasonally adjusted	Actual	Seasonally adjusted	Actual	Seasonally adjusted
	K55U	K5C4	KA4O	KAC4	KA4R	KAC7	KA4U	KAD8
2000	380	382	312	312	314	314	314	314
2001	408	408	328	328	331	330	331	330
2002	414	414	338	338	344	343	344	342
2003	424	424	347	348	360	360	360	359
2004	447	448	363	363	376	375	375	374
2005	474	475	378	379	396	395	395	394
2006	507	507	397	398	410	409	410	408
2007	534	532	419	419	424	422	424	421
2008	560	557	434	434	439	437	438	436
2009	540	541	429	429	452	452	450	448
2010	566	566	438	437	467	467	459	459
2011	597	596	448	448	479	479	468	467
2012	597	596	454	454	487	487	476	476
2013	598	598	460	460	490	489	480	479
2014	599	598	467	466	493	492	487	486
2015	615	615	480	480	497	497	492	492

Source: Office for National Statistics: 01633 456780

4.14a Average Weekly Earnings by Industry (Not Seasonally Adjusted)

All figures are in pounds (£)

	Agriculture, Forestry and Fishing (A)			Mining and Quarrying (B)			Manufacturing - Food Products, Beverages and Tobacco (C1)			Manufacturing - Textiles, Leather and Clothing (C2)		
	Average Weekly Earnings	of which		Average Weekly Earnings	Of which		Average Weekly Earnings	Of which		Average Weekly Earnings	Of which	
		Bonuses	Arrears		Bonuses	Arrears		Bonuses	Arrears		Bonuses	Arrears
CDID	K57A	K57B	K57C	K57D	K57E	K57F	K57G	K57H	K57I	K57J	K57K	K57L
2011 Jan	329	5	0	1049	110	0	465	6	3	364	13	0
2011 Feb	322	4	0	1091	173	1	463	11	0	360	15	0
2011 Mar	358	15	0	1583	659	1	549	86	0	385	38	1
2011 Apr	334	2	0	1062	133	0	501	30	0	360	12	0
2011 May	317	2	0	1023	66	1	464	6	0	361	8	0
2011 Jun	307	1	0	1011	56	0	471	14	0	365	10	0
2011 Jul	335	24	0	1057	97	1	457	5	0	362	8	0
2011 Aug	328	11	0	994	36	0	462	5	0	358	6	0
2011 Sep	312	2	0	1007	48	0	498	34	1	364	9	0
2011 Oct	331	10	0	1004	34	0	462	5	0	366	8	0
2011 Nov	325	6	0	1021	40	1	470	4	0	369	10	0
2011 Dec	371	38	0	1067	97	1	509	32	0	378	22	0
2012 Jan	323	3	0	1250	261	6	462	8	0	355	8	0
2012 Feb	327	6	0	1141	161	0	465	10	0	369	18	0
2012 Mar	339	17	0	1538	551	2	513	47	0	367	20	0
2012 Apr	313	3	0	1135	137	0	475	15	1	359	10	0
2012 May	313	5	0	1071	60	0	472	12	1	367	10	0
2012 Jun	323	3	0	1034	54	0	479	12	0	370	16	0
2012 Jul	343	14	0	1038	57	0	468	8	0	381	14	0
2012 Aug	337	8	0	1023	36	0	468	4	0	375	9	0
2012 Sep	335	6	0	1027	36	1	492	23	0	382	11	0
2012 Oct	328	4	1	1040	42	3	474	11	0	380	10	0
2012 Nov	334	5	0	1071	59	5	467	4	0	389	17	0
2012 Dec	359	28	2	1075	83	4	504	27	0	396	29	0
2013 Jan	340	6	0	1210	227	0	473	7	8	377	10	0
2013 Feb	345	5	0	1200	199	3	489	16	0	381	12	0
2013 Mar	342	3	0	1538	541	3	540	46	2	397	26	0
2013 Apr	352	4	0	1269	272	1	497	14	0	387	14	0
2013 May	347	3	0	1186	166	0	490	5	1	383	10	0
2013 Jun	335	3	0	1091	57	2	496	9	1	386	10	0
2013 Jul	337	2	0	1087	40	0	485	7	1	385	8	0
2013 Aug	335	3	0	1102	45	6	481	5	0	385	13	0
2013 Sep	342	3	0	1132	51	1	500	18	0	397	15	0
2013 Oct	346	2	0	1139	52	3	491	10	0	388	10	1
2013 Nov	335	3	0	1118	49	1	492	4	0	394	10	0
2013 Dec	390	53	0	1150	85	0	535	44	0	401	34	0
2014 Jan	339	3	0	1189	115	2	498	6	0	379	8	0
2014 Feb	350	5	0	1209	143	8	510	20	1	378	9	0
2014 Mar	352	2	1	1629	580	3	524	53	0	383	15	0
2014 Apr	345	3	0	1308	237	0	490	9	0	376	11	0
2014 May	334	3	0	1277	178	1	485	5	1	369	6	0
2014 Jun	336	5	0	1148	78	0	493	16	0	374	7	0
2014 Jul	347	13	0	1130	60	1	484	8	0	372	8	0
2014 Aug	331	2	0	1119	45	3	481	4	0	368	6	0
2014 Sep	337	5	0	1133	54	0	498	19	0	375	8	0
2014 Oct	345	3	0	1142	63	0	480	6	0	378	10	0
2014 Nov	342	3	0	1111	46	0	498	23	0	384	8	0
2014 Dec	394	43	1	1152	93	1	521	43	0	399	23	0
2015 Jan	352	13	0	1139	105	0	485	10	0	385	12	0
2015 Feb	353	4	0	1178	130	0	495	18	0	385	10	0
2015 Mar	370	7	0	1534	488	0	521	52	0	401	26	0
2015 Apr	374	4	0	1235	173	1	487	14	0	389	20	1
2015 May	362	5	0	1153	93	0	481	10	1	378	11	0
2015 Jun	357	8	0	1147	73	0	476	9	0	381	7	0
2015 Jul	374	18	0	1101	37	1	474	7	0	387	12	0
2015 Aug	374	10	0	1113	39	0	470	2	1	382	5	0
2015 Sep	372	7	0	1132	60	0	492	18	0	388	10	0
2015 Oct	370	7	0	1122	50	1	485	9	0	389	10	0
2015 Nov	388	3	0	1119	63	0	488	10	1	390	11	0
2015 Dec	396	17	0	1135	72	0	525	37	3	410	32	0
2016 Jan	396	20	0	1199	134	0	488	10	1	389	9	0
2016 Feb	393	5	0	1365	312	2	499	18	1	378	8	0
2016 Mar	408	6	0	1656	600	2	565	79	1	387	22	0
2016 Apr	410	12	0	1252	181	2	505	16	0	391	14	0
2016 May	391	6	0	1114	52	2	503	11	0	383	10	0
2016 Jun	381	3	0	1131	72	1	492	8	0	379	7	0
2016 Jul	393	15	0	1118	54	0	491	7	0	380	6	0
2016 Aug	381	3	0	1102	44	1	489	3	1	375	4	0
2016 Sep	402	2	0	1088	53	3	515	26	0	381	7	0
2016 Oct	410	6	0	1095	42	1	498	6	0	383	8	0
2016 Nov	396	2	0	1116	63	1	497	5	0	392	11	0
2016 Dec	434	39	0	1134	75	1	524	27	0	408	28	0
2017 Jan	398	4	0	1184	127	0	494	7	0	394	7	0
2017 Feb (r)	408	6	0	1462	409	1	506	19	0	387	10	0
2017 Mar (p)	409	1	0	1424	365	1	563	76	0	412	30	0

p = Provisional
r = Revised

Source: Monthly wages and salaries survey
Inquiries: Email: earnings@ons.gsi.gov.uk   Tel: 01633 456120

4.14a Average Weekly Earnings by Industry (Not Seasonally Adjusted)

	Manufacturing - Chemicals and Man-made Fibres (C3)			Manufacturing - Basic Metals and Metal Products (C4)			Manufacturing - Engineering and Allied Industries (C5)			Other Manufacturing (C6)		
	Average Weekly Earnings	Of which Bonuses	Arrears	Average Weekly Earnings	Of which Bonuses	Arrears	Average Weekly Earnings	Of which Bonuses	Arrears	Average Weekly Earnings	Of which Bonuses	Arrears
CDID	K57M	K57N	K57O	K57P	K57Q	K57R	K57S	K57T	K57U	K57V	K57W	K57X
2011 Jan	661	28	0	524	21	2	593	28	0	467	11	0
2011 Feb	660	27	0	516	15	1	590	31	1	478	21	0
2011 Mar	958	324	1	564	54	0	638	70	3	502	42	1
2011 Apr	698	67	1	527	22	0	595	30	1	471	15	0
2011 May	664	16	1	534	23	0	580	17	2	468	9	1
2011 Jun	663	18	1	532	14	0	591	24	1	472	14	0
2011 Jul	678	29	1	544	24	1	581	15	1	476	15	1
2011 Aug	660	11	1	520	7	1	571	9	1	470	9	0
2011 Sep	665	22	2	523	7	0	576	10	1	472	8	0
2011 Oct	655	14	1	534	16	1	582	9	5	474	12	0
2011 Nov	661	12	3	527	13	1	593	13	4	480	15	0
2011 Dec	687	36	4	529	29	1	595	24	2	491	26	0
2012 Jan	676	25	10	533	20	0	593	19	1	474	14	0
2012 Feb	666	25	2	528	16	0	612	42	1	479	17	0
2012 Mar	906	266	0	557	39	0	643	66	1	516	46	1
2012 Apr	734	85	1	558	37	1	608	27	2	489	20	0
2012 May	674	19	1	545	24	1	600	18	1	483	13	0
2012 Jun	682	24	1	534	21	0	613	28	1	483	13	1
2012 Jul	681	21	4	541	21	0	602	17	0	480	12	0
2012 Aug	676	19	1	518	8	0	596	13	1	481	10	0
2012 Sep	666	13	1	520	9	0	591	7	4	483	10	0
2012 Oct	671	17	0	523	12	0	596	8	1	484	13	0
2012 Nov	687	17	2	530	14	2	599	15	1	490	15	0
2012 Dec	720	36	1	538	24	4	610	27	0	497	23	0
2013 Jan	701	21	6	532	13	6	605	20	0	484	12	0
2013 Feb	705	31	0	527	17	4	616	28	0	491	16	0
2013 Mar	952	271	0	556	42	1	668	78	1	524	46	0
2013 Apr	818	150	1	542	25	0	634	36	1	504	26	1
2013 May	695	22	2	534	21	0	615	16	1	491	13	0
2013 Jun	698	15	0	533	21	0	644	42	1	489	11	0
2013 Jul	694	12	0	527	17	0	626	22	2	490	13	0
2013 Aug	700	17	0	511	6	0	613	15	1	488	9	1
2013 Sep	690	21	1	526	11	0	602	6	0	490	11	1
2013 Oct	689	16	1	536	12	0	611	11	1	493	10	1
2013 Nov	691	16	0	543	17	0	621	14	1	498	16	2
2013 Dec	709	28	1	561	33	9	627	23	1	512	26	0
2014 Jan	675	21	0	537	15	0	642	30	3	498	14	1
2014 Feb	687	23	0	543	20	0	642	25	2	501	18	1
2014 Mar	1024	352	1	560	34	0	693	76	1	538	53	1
2014 Apr	785	115	0	542	18	0	653	32	1	517	28	1
2014 May	696	14	1	545	17	1	637	20	1	507	15	1
2014 Jun	694	15	1	552	22	0	668	46	3	506	13	0
2014 Jul	709	34	1	549	18	0	639	23	0	500	13	1
2014 Aug	704	28	0	528	6	2	621	8	1	500	12	0
2014 Sep	700	24	1	547	12	4	622	9	0	503	13	1
2014 Oct	691	16	1	553	14	0	627	9	0	502	11	0
2014 Nov	673	13	0	555	16	0	631	10	1	504	13	0
2014 Dec	689	31	0	572	39	1	663	41	2	518	31	0
2015 Jan	682	25	0	550	17	0	642	16	2	502	19	0
2015 Feb	716	38	1	543	13	6	645	18	1	503	17	0
2015 Mar	1033	347	1	580	45	6	714	82	2	555	70	0
2015 Apr	797	118	1	562	22	0	670	30	2	522	32	0
2015 May	708	13	0	549	12	1	652	17	1	505	14	0
2015 Jun	710	17	0	563	19	0	693	56	1	514	19	0
2015 Jul	734	44	2	567	17	3	647	17	1	519	22	1
2015 Aug	710	15	1	548	6	1	631	9	1	515	17	0
2015 Sep	722	19	4	561	11	1	630	7	0	506	11	0
2015 Oct	721	25	1	564	13	1	634	9	0	509	13	1
2015 Nov	706	15	0	566	16	0	638	10	0	517	14	0
2015 Dec	738	42	1	583	37	0	656	25	0	536	35	0
2016 Jan	705	14	2	558	10	0	654	18	1	517	18	0
2016 Feb	714	22	0	566	19	1	651	18	1	517	20	0
2016 Mar	1129	431	1	586	40	0	707	72	1	553	50	1
2016 Apr	800	89	0	576	25	0	681	35	1	535	28	0
2016 May	740	23	0	582	30	1	665	17	0	522	16	0
2016 Jun	742	16	1	581	24	0	700	51	0	525	20	0
2016 Jul	756	26	0	565	10	0	676	22	1	524	18	1
2016 Aug	713	16	0	559	9	0	663	13	1	518	13	0
2016 Sep	719	19	0	569	10	1	654	8	1	520	13	1
2016 Oct	717	28	0	563	8	1	659	11	0	518	11	0
2016 Nov	715	27	0	567	17	0	660	10	1	528	20	0
2016 Dec	743	47	0	583	40	0	684	32	5	540	33	1
2017 Jan	711	30	0	567	15	2	680	16	1	528	17	0
2017 Feb (r)	731	32	6	574	23	0	685	26	1	530	22	1
2017 Mar (p)	976	282	1	598	44	0	759	94	1	556	44	0

p = Provisional
r = Revised

Source: Monthly wages and salaries survey
Inquiries: Email: earnings@ons.gsi.gov.uk   Tel: 01633 456120

4.14a Average Weekly Earnings by Industry (Not Seasonally Adjusted)

	Electricity, Gas and Water Supply (D , E)			Construction (F)			Wholesale Trade (G46)			Retail Trade and Repairs (G45 & G47)		
	Average Weekly Earnings	Of which		Average Weekly Earnings	Of which		Average Weekly Earnings	Of which		Average Weekly Earnings	Of which	
		Bonuses	Arrears		Bonuses	Arrears		Bonuses	Arrears		Bonuses	Arrears
CDID	K57Y	K57Z	K582	K583	K584	K585	K586	K587	K588	K589	K58A	K58B
2011 Jan	607	27	1	540	14	0	510	43	0	263	12	0
2011 Feb	604	24	3	547	21	1	504	45	0	265	19	0
2011 Mar	644	81	1	585	56	0	566	99	0	285	38	0
2011 Apr	615	42	1	532	14	0	503	37	0	272	18	0
2011 May	582	17	5	532	11	0	501	30	1	270	16	0
2011 Jun	653	89	3	546	18	0	522	53	1	272	20	0
2011 Jul	637	69	0	537	12	0	519	48	1	267	16	0
2011 Aug	592	31	1	530	9	0	507	38	0	262	10	0
2011 Sep	592	19	2	545	20	0	501	30	0	260	9	0
2011 Oct	597	18	1	537	12	0	511	34	0	264	13	0
2011 Nov	607	21	6	548	21	0	504	27	1	261	11	0
2011 Dec	611	25	3	548	27	0	540	61	0	258	10	0
2012 Jan	602	24	0	542	13	0	538	56	0	266	12	0
2012 Feb	603	31	1	543	15	0	533	54	0	270	18	0
2012 Mar	659	86	1	592	51	3	584	103	1	289	34	0
2012 Apr	618	36	0	547	16	0	527	42	0	275	18	1
2012 May	595	17	2	551	13	0	526	39	1	275	16	0
2012 Jun	660	80	1	557	22	0	542	54	0	277	16	0
2012 Jul	640	59	2	547	16	0	533	43	1	273	15	0
2012 Aug	593	15	1	528	8	0	532	43	0	271	15	0
2012 Sep	598	17	2	540	18	0	523	34	0	268	11	0
2012 Oct	611	19	5	538	15	0	535	38	1	272	15	0
2012 Nov	618	24	2	543	17	0	528	31	1	268	14	0
2012 Dec	613	22	1	541	25	0	542	49	1	266	14	0
2013 Jan	601	20	0	528	12	1	557	58	0	270	13	0
2013 Feb	612	26	4	539	13	1	559	63	0	271	19	0
2013 Mar	655	72	0	559	29	1	585	82	2	292	35	0
2013 Apr	640	47	1	567	29	1	593	83	0	280	21	1
2013 May	611	23	0	547	14	1	550	42	1	283	23	0
2013 Jun	667	70	1	551	20	1	564	53	0	280	16	0
2013 Jul	642	54	0	544	16	1	571	60	1	283	18	0
2013 Aug	615	23	1	538	11	1	559	50	0	285	21	0
2013 Sep	601	11	2	554	24	1	547	39	0	276	11	0
2013 Oct	612	18	2	537	13	1	554	38	0	282	18	0
2013 Nov	617	14	7	546	17	1	544	43	0	276	13	0
2013 Dec	620	20	3	552	25	1	574	65	0	275	13	0
2014 Jan	623	19	1	559	16	1	592	60	1	282	14	0
2014 Feb	624	18	1	546	15	0	551	49	0	279	14	0
2014 Mar	694	81	5	568	40	0	613	110	1	305	38	0
2014 Apr	666	48	12	544	19	0	564	62	1	296	25	0
2014 May	629	23	2	539	13	0	534	31	0	298	25	0
2014 Jun	676	72	1	555	22	0	555	54	0	288	14	0
2014 Jul	663	56	3	566	28	0	547	49	1	288	16	0
2014 Aug	638	26	2	545	14	1	534	42	1	288	14	0
2014 Sep	622	17	1	566	29	1	540	38	0	289	11	0
2014 Oct	622	13	2	551	14	0	541	39	0	294	18	0
2014 Nov	637	18	8	562	22	0	536	39	0	290	16	0
2014 Dec	624	13	1	571	34	1	565	66	1	288	13	0
2015 Jan	626	21	1	548	16	0	564	60	0	304	18	0
2015 Feb	645	36	6	553	13	0	563	65	0	300	15	0
2015 Mar	695	87	1	600	46	0	677	172	1	328	40	0
2015 Apr	669	56	4	562	21	0	559	57	0	319	26	0
2015 May	641	23	2	572	30	0	549	39	0	318	26	0
2015 Jun	692	70	2	567	20	0	559	52	0	309	18	0
2015 Jul	661	51	1	605	31	0	567	58	0	310	20	0
2015 Aug	642	30	1	582	14	0	552	40	0	305	17	0
2015 Sep	621	15	3	595	28	0	536	36	0	304	15	0
2015 Oct	619	11	1	590	17	1	536	36	0	307	19	0
2015 Nov	626	17	2	598	21	1	542	41	1	303	16	0
2015 Dec	627	13	3	603	35	0	583	72	1	303	16	0
2016 Jan	622	16	1	602	22	1	563	51	0	308	18	0
2016 Feb	653	32	4	602	20	0	594	72	0	307	17	0
2016 Mar	705	88	1	637	51	1	650	122	1	327	35	0
2016 Apr	700	75	1	615	29	0	584	50	0	329	30	1
2016 May	655	18	5	623	40	0	567	32	1	327	29	1
2016 Jun	714	66	12	609	23	0	578	44	1	317	15	1
2016 Jul	700	62	2	628	37	1	575	44	0	323	24	1
2016 Aug	664	26	2	605	15	1	566	36	0	317	16	1
2016 Sep	651	14	1	627	34	0	566	35	1	316	15	1
2016 Oct	651	12	2	642	46	0	578	46	0	321	21	1
2016 Nov	663	20	2	631	28	1	575	44	0	320	18	0
2016 Dec	658	18	5	634	42	1	589	60	0	317	18	0
2017 Jan	655	19	1	611	16	1	595	45	1	320	20	0
2017 Feb (r)	666	27	2	617	24	0	618	80	1	314	16	0
2017 Mar (p)	726	82	1	640	48	1	670	122	1	334	34	1

p = Provisional
r = Revised

Source: Monthly wages and salaries survey
Inquiries: Email: earnings@ons.gsi.gov.uk   Tel: 01633 456120

4.14a Average Weekly Earnings by Industry (Not Seasonally Adjusted)

	Transport and Storage (H)			Accommodation and Food Service Activities (I)			Information and Communication (J)			Financial & Insurance Activities (K)		
	Average Weekly Earnings	Of which Bonuses	Arrears	Average Weekly Earnings	Of which Bonuses	Arrears	Average Weekly Earnings	Of which Bonuses	Arrears	Average Weekly Earnings	Of which Bonuses	Arrears
CDID	K58F	K58G	K58H	K58C	K58D	K58E	K5E9	K5EA	K5EB	K58I	K58J	K58K
2011 Jan	505	7	0	218	5	0	753	72	2	1235	473	0
2011 Feb	504	7	0	225	9	0	765	83	1	1662	901	1
2011 Mar	524	31	1	224	8	0	858	178	1	1541	783	2
2011 Apr	514	14	1	222	5	0	736	55	1	850	86	0
2011 May	512	10	1	225	8	0	747	61	1	892	121	1
2011 Jun	515	14	3	223	3	1	808	128	1	1064	296	1
2011 Jul	520	18	2	224	6	1	744	62	1	878	114	1
2011 Aug	509	6	1	222	3	0	782	96	1	814	50	2
2011 Sep	509	5	2	221	4	0	738	51	1	871	105	1
2011 Oct	508	5	1	222	5	1	745	65	1	830	51	1
2011 Nov	519	6	7	226	9	1	745	57	0	825	47	0
2011 Dec	523	10	2	228	8	0	746	64	1	903	121	0
2012 Jan	514	7	0	230	6	0	761	82	1	1091	323	0
2012 Feb	525	17	0	234	11	0	781	97	1	1486	712	2
2012 Mar	535	26	0	227	7	0	857	168	2	1504	728	3
2012 Apr	534	17	1	227	5	1	756	70	1	896	117	0
2012 May	529	9	1	231	8	0	768	80	2	874	95	1
2012 Jun	549	26	2	229	4	0	816	136	2	999	225	3
2012 Jul	530	6	1	231	5	0	769	80	1	860	88	0
2012 Aug	544	18	1	232	4	0	779	81	1	841	67	1
2012 Sep	534	12	0	229	3	0	768	71	3	855	85	1
2012 Oct	534	13	1	226	5	0	747	51	1	819	47	1
2012 Nov	529	7	2	230	6	0	766	65	1	819	41	1
2012 Dec	551	23	2	234	8	1	757	56	1	898	114	0
2013 Jan	526	7	0	222	5	1	779	78	2	1130	351	1
2013 Feb	529	15	0	226	8	0	809	104	2	1532	746	1
2013 Mar	546	26	1	227	7	0	837	138	1	1551	763	0
2013 Apr	549	21	5	230	8	0	811	100	2	1063	267	1
2013 May	541	9	1	234	9	0	776	62	2	968	170	0
2013 Jun	565	34	1	228	4	0	830	111	5	1049	258	0
2013 Jul	538	10	1	231	5	0	778	64	2	865	75	1
2013 Aug	539	13	1	231	4	0	789	70	2	852	64	0
2013 Sep	533	4	1	230	4	0	780	66	1	875	87	0
2013 Oct	537	7	2	229	3	0	770	54	2	839	51	1
2013 Nov	542	7	5	232	6	0	762	49	1	841	53	1
2013 Dec	573	35	1	237	8	1	773	54	1	939	142	0
2014 Jan	534	7	1	232	7	1	793	76	3	1138	351	0
2014 Feb	634	38	68	234	8	0	817	98	2	1659	856	3
2014 Mar	556	29	1	232	7	0	851	141	2	1643	826	3
2014 Apr	556	20	1	232	7	0	825	107	2	941	131	1
2014 May	551	13	1	238	11	0	783	70	1	961	155	1
2014 Jun	568	33	2	232	8	0	838	114	2	991	187	1
2014 Jul	559	23	0	232	6	0	773	49	3	865	60	2
2014 Aug	540	5	0	232	4	0	799	75	2	903	66	2
2014 Sep	539	5	1	228	5	1	761	39	2	933	91	1
2014 Oct	548	13	1	231	4	1	786	58	1	897	53	3
2014 Nov	548	7	1	234	8	1	786	59	2	898	54	0
2014 Dec	579	31	0	242	12	1	815	64	2	1056	202	2
2015 Jan	547	9	3	237	5	1	825	85	4	1190	339	1
2015 Feb	553	18	0	242	10	1	856	107	3	1592	732	5
2015 Mar	554	19	1	243	10	1	921	170	1	1816	958	1
2015 Apr	562	20	4	240	8	1	830	80	1	1062	189	2
2015 May	555	13	0	248	11	1	828	80	2	1025	155	1
2015 Jun	577	38	1	240	5	1	857	107	1	1002	126	7
2015 Jul	549	10	1	244	5	1	834	82	0	967	94	3
2015 Aug	555	10	2	242	4	0	843	99	1	963	91	1
2015 Sep	552	8	1	240	5	0	793	51	2	963	91	1
2015 Oct	550	6	0	244	5	0	822	79	1	936	63	1
2015 Nov	552	10	1	246	8	0	804	61	2	927	49	1
2015 Dec	578	32	0	251	12	0	824	76	3	1097	208	2
2016 Jan	555	8	2	243	6	0	845	99	1	1267	382	0
2016 Feb	561	19	1	246	9	0	830	94	1	1460	567	5
2016 Mar	576	34	0	249	12	0	889	150	1	1955	1067	5
2016 Apr	566	23	0	245	7	0	828	79	2	1072	171	4
2016 May	552	10	1	250	11	0	828	81	1	1081	182	1
2016 Jun	580	29	6	245	6	0	842	91	2	1084	186	1
2016 Jul	557	11	2	248	5	1	836	84	1	1030	125	2
2016 Aug	564	16	1	249	4	0	836	86	1	964	72	2
2016 Sep	558	9	1	249	6	0	808	52	1	970	76	2
2016 Oct	553	7	1	248	4	0	822	66	1	967	72	1
2016 Nov	564	12	2	249	8	0	823	64	1	955	58	0
2016 Dec	588	35	1	255	10	0	835	72	1	1116	219	1
2017 Jan	557	10	1	246	5	1	867	101	1	1267	377	0
2017 Feb (r)	570	20	4	250	11	0	860	100	1	1539	637	2
2017 Mar (p)	580	30	1	253	11	0	914	150	2	2163	1261	3

p = Provisional
r = Revised

Source: Monthly wages and salaries survey
Inquiries: Email: earnings@ons.gsi.gov.uk   Tel: 01633 456120

4.14a Average Weekly Earnings by Industry (Not Seasonally Adjusted)

	Real Estate Activities			Professional, Scientific & Technical Activities			Administrative and Support Service Activities			Public Administration		
	(L)			(M)			(N)			(O)		
	Average Weekly Earnings	Of which		Average Weekly Earnings	Of which		Average Weekly Earnings	Of which		Average Weekly Earnings	Of which	
		Bonuses	Arrears		Bonuses	Arrears		Bonuses	Arrears		Bonuses	Arrears
CDID	K58L	K58M	K58N	K5EC	K5ED	K5EE	K5EF	K5EG	K5EH	K58O	K58P	K58Q
2011 Jan	489	33	1	660	29	0	338	13	0	536	1	0
2011 Feb	480	26	1	673	35	1	329	12	0	534	2	0
2011 Mar	529	69	1	780	144	1	351	33	0	537	4	0
2011 Apr	495	34	0	670	28	0	326	13	0	537	2	0
2011 May	484	27	0	674	32	0	330	8	0	537	2	0
2011 Jun	506	48	0	672	33	0	340	14	0	542	6	0
2011 Jul	501	41	1	699	56	0	344	16	0	539	5	0
2011 Aug	486	35	0	660	21	1	340	13	0	545	11	0
2011 Sep	479	27	0	663	18	0	332	9	0	545	1	0
2011 Oct	488	35	0	679	29	0	338	11	0	538	1	0
2011 Nov	501	43	3	684	36	1	335	9	0	537	2	0
2011 Dec	511	48	1	711	59	0	355	24	0	540	6	0
2012 Jan	487	30	0	684	38	1	351	12	0	535	1	0
2012 Feb	498	38	0	698	50	1	353	13	0	538	1	0
2012 Mar	605	140	0	789	136	1	381	38	0	541	2	0
2012 Apr	499	33	0	694	41	0	351	13	0	545	0	0
2012 May	488	32	0	683	31	0	350	10	0	543	1	0
2012 Jun	511	51	0	687	29	0	347	10	0	550	5	0
2012 Jul	513	55	0	711	61	1	351	12	0	551	5	0
2012 Aug	481	29	0	677	27	1	352	9	0	547	3	0
2012 Sep	494	37	1	669	24	1	346	9	0	554	7	1
2012 Oct	497	41	0	664	24	1	348	10	0	547	2	1
2012 Nov	493	37	0	671	29	1	346	8	0	544	2	0
2012 Dec	506	53	0	711	72	1	358	21	0	543	2	2
2013 Jan	498	49	2	658	23	0	348	11	0	546	1	1
2013 Feb	477	33	1	682	36	1	350	13	0	535	0	0
2013 Mar	533	85	1	740	89	2	371	36	0	536	3	0
2013 Apr	533	83	0	706	56	2	357	20	0	537	1	0
2013 May	501	47	0	672	33	1	357	15	0	537	0	0
2013 Jun	504	48	0	676	39	1	345	9	0	540	3	0
2013 Jul	522	68	0	691	48	2	355	15	0	543	6	0
2013 Aug	501	46	1	661	24	0	351	9	0	540	1	4
2013 Sep	493	46	0	669	29	1	344	9	0	547	7	0
2013 Oct	500	51	0	669	24	1	344	10	0	537	1	0
2013 Nov	485	43	0	666	22	1	343	8	0	537	1	0
2013 Dec	512	52	0	713	67	0	364	26	0	540	2	1
2014 Jan	488	41	0	666	22	1	359	19	1	545	1	1
2014 Feb	480	34	0	674	34	0	349	16	0	541	1	1
2014 Mar	562	106	1	749	103	1	370	34	0	548	2	4
2014 Apr	525	68	2	693	46	1	352	17	0	553	7	3
2014 May	509	53	0	683	43	1	355	12	0	547	1	1
2014 Jun	516	52	2	697	57	1	356	13	0	549	3	0
2014 Jul	538	80	1	689	47	1	362	13	0	549	4	3
2014 Aug	496	40	0	669	27	1	365	10	0	547	3	1
2014 Sep	496	31	1	670	27	1	367	10	0	555	7	0
2014 Oct	508	42	1	679	26	1	375	13	0	552	1	1
2014 Nov	499	36	0	674	25	1	364	10	0	549	1	1
2014 Dec	540	70	1	736	85	1	378	27	0	554	1	1
2015 Jan	505	36	0	671	21	1	370	14	0	551	0	1
2015 Feb	502	40	1	708	54	0	381	23	1	551	2	1
2015 Mar	625	162	1	783	124	1	398	35	0	548	2	0
2015 Apr	504	41	1	698	46	1	388	18	0	552	1	1
2015 May	522	64	0	684	36	1	392	14	1	552	1	0
2015 Jun	530	64	3	696	46	1	389	13	1	551	2	0
2015 Jul	569	97	1	693	50	1	383	13	0	554	4	0
2015 Aug	506	35	1	674	34	2	383	11	0	552	2	1
2015 Sep	506	32	0	662	20	0	377	11	0	561	8	1
2015 Oct	510	38	1	669	29	1	384	12	0	556	2	1
2015 Nov	499	29	0	667	23	1	381	11	0	553	1	1
2015 Dec	520	45	0	731	78	1	394	22	0	550	1	0
2016 Jan	509	33	0	678	25	1	395	17	1	556	0	1
2016 Feb	517	38	0	703	56	1	405	22	0	555	1	0
2016 Mar	693	210	1	779	126	3	418	37	0	553	2	1
2016 Apr	550	67	0	725	67	1	409	19	0	566	6	0
2016 May	546	69	0	675	32	0	405	21	0	557	1	0
2016 Jun	542	58	1	686	43	1	406	18	0	561	1	1
2016 Jul	571	94	0	699	63	1	406	18	0	556	1	0
2016 Aug	507	29	2	672	33	2	399	10	0	570	8	1
2016 Sep	507	37	0	662	23	1	401	11	0	562	2	0
2016 Oct	508	34	0	662	29	1	405	15	0	566	2	1
2016 Nov	501	27	0	665	28	1	403	10	0	564	1	1
2016 Dec	521	43	1	690	51	0	420	24	1	562	0	0
2017 Jan	517	37	0	684	29	1	411	15	0	563	0	0
2017 Feb (r)	517	38	1	692	41	1	424	27	0	562	0	0
2017 Mar (p)	661	180	1	753	100	0	459	59	0	562	1	0

p = Provisional
r = Revised

Source: Monthly wages and salaries survey
Inquiries: Email: earnings@ons.gsi.gov.uk   Tel: 01633 456120

4.14a Average Weekly Earnings by Industry (Not Seasonally Adjusted)

	Education			Health and Social Work			Arts, Entertainment and Recreation			Other Service Activities		
	(P)			(Q)			(R)			(S)		
	Average Weekly Earnings	Of which		Average Weekly Earnings	Of which		Average Weekly Earnings	Of which		Average Weekly Earnings	Of which	
		Bonuses	Arrears		Bonuses	Arrears		Bonuses	Arrears		Bonuses	Arrears
CDID	K58R	K58S	K58T	K58U	K58V	K58W	K5EI	K5EJ	K5EK	K58X	K58Y	K58Z
2011 Jan	397	0	0	398	0	0	329	13	0	350	14	1
2011 Feb	398	0	1	398	1	1	319	15	1	361	17	1
2011 Mar	401	2	0	398	1	0	331	23	0	400	50	1
2011 Apr	403	1	0	400	1	0	314	9	0	363	12	0
2011 May	400	1	0	401	0	0	311	10	2	355	10	1
2011 Jun	401	1	0	401	0	0	312	9	0	358	8	1
2011 Jul	402	1	0	399	1	0	320	13	0	362	11	1
2011 Aug	407	1	0	397	0	0	327	17	0	357	8	1
2011 Sep	409	1	0	400	1	0	323	12	0	355	8	0
2011 Oct	404	1	0	399	1	0	313	5	0	357	7	0
2011 Nov	401	1	0	401	0	0	323	9	0	364	13	1
2011 Dec	401	2	0	402	1	0	339	14	0	365	14	0
2012 Jan	395	0	0	402	0	0	342	16	0	352	14	1
2012 Feb	396	1	0	403	1	0	331	7	0	350	19	0
2012 Mar	398	1	0	403	2	0	340	26	0	348	22	0
2012 Apr	400	1	0	404	0	0	331	10	1	343	12	0
2012 May	399	1	0	407	0	0	334	11	0	341	12	0
2012 Jun	402	1	0	404	0	0	361	24	0	346	15	0
2012 Jul	402	1	0	405	1	0	346	11	1	342	13	0
2012 Aug	409	1	0	404	1	0	358	10	0	344	12	0
2012 Sep	411	1	0	403	1	0	361	13	0	332	7	0
2012 Oct	407	0	0	404	1	0	349	6	0	329	8	0
2012 Nov	406	0	0	406	0	0	355	13	0	337	13	0
2012 Dec	407	1	1	407	1	0	371	14	0	341	14	0
2013 Jan	402	1	1	409	0	0	363	16	0	342	11	0
2013 Feb	399	0	0	402	1	0	354	5	0	338	11	0
2013 Mar	400	2	0	404	2	0	356	19	0	344	20	0
2013 Apr	403	0	0	410	1	0	361	18	0	346	13	0
2013 May	404	1	0	408	1	0	364	19	0	346	9	0
2013 Jun	404	1	0	406	1	0	372	18	0	349	7	0
2013 Jul	406	1	0	406	1	0	362	10	0	347	10	0
2013 Aug	411	1	1	401	0	0	365	12	0	348	9	0
2013 Sep	414	0	0	404	1	0	364	19	0	341	6	0
2013 Oct	413	1	1	403	1	0	348	4	0	353	6	5
2013 Nov	411	1	1	404	1	0	350	13	0	356	9	1
2013 Dec	415	1	1	406	1	0	346	14	0	360	10	0
2014 Jan	408	0	0	408	1	0	364	12	1	362	13	1
2014 Feb	409	0	0	404	1	0	335	6	0	437	79	0
2014 Mar	410	3	0	403	1	0	330	13	0	390	30	2
2014 Apr	412	1	1	407	1	0	353	14	0	369	15	0
2014 May	413	1	2	408	1	0	346	13	0	368	11	1
2014 Jun	412	1	0	408	1	0	357	15	0	364	8	0
2014 Jul	414	1	0	405	0	0	353	7	0	369	12	0
2014 Aug	421	1	0	402	1	0	342	6	1	373	12	0
2014 Sep	424	1	0	408	1	0	348	16	0	373	7	1
2014 Oct	421	1	0	406	0	0	338	9	1	372	9	0
2014 Nov	418	1	0	408	1	0	341	8	1	356	10	0
2014 Dec	425	2	2	408	1	0	347	19	1	364	15	0
2015 Jan	419	1	0	410	1	0	357	15	1	360	16	0
2015 Feb	417	0	0	407	0	0	337	11	0	362	17	0
2015 Mar	419	3	0	408	1	0	348	22	0	381	34	0
2015 Apr	419	1	0	412	1	0	355	25	0	369	19	0
2015 May	418	0	0	414	1	0	343	11	0	366	13	0
2015 Jun	421	2	0	414	0	0	375	19	0	369	12	0
2015 Jul	422	1	0	411	0	0	381	17	1	370	16	0
2015 Aug	427	2	0	407	0	0	374	20	0	367	15	0
2015 Sep	430	1	0	412	2	0	390	30	0	358	10	0
2015 Oct	426	1	0	408	0	0	356	11	0	359	10	0
2015 Nov	426	1	2	410	1	0	354	7	0	361	10	0
2015 Dec	428	1	1	411	1	0	367	15	3	367	17	0
2016 Jan	424	2	1	412	1	0	375	10	0	386	24	1
2016 Feb	423	1	0	412	0	1	366	11	0	383	21	0
2016 Mar	423	1	0	411	1	1	371	15	0	397	32	0
2016 Apr	424	1	0	416	0	0	393	37	0	407	28	1
2016 May	422	2	0	416	1	0	373	17	0	394	14	0
2016 Jun	426	1	1	418	0	1	386	20	0	399	19	0
2016 Jul	425	1	1	415	0	0	410	16	0	399	15	0
2016 Aug	432	1	0	415	0	0	408	36	0	399	17	0
2016 Sep	436	1	0	416	1	0	404	25	0	396	13	0
2016 Oct	432	1	1	416	0	0	387	13	0	400	12	0
2016 Nov	431	1	1	419	2	1	393	10	1	404	18	1
2016 Dec	433	1	1	418	1	0	390	17	0	414	21	0
2017 Jan	429	1	0	418	1	0	396	21	0	393	17	0
2017 Feb (r)	429	0	0	419	1	0	461	92	0	396	18	0
2017 Mar (p)	430	1	0	417	1	0	387	23	0	402	22	0

p = Provisional

r = Revised

Source: Monthly wages and salaries survey

Inquiries: Email: earnings@ons.gsi.gov.uk   Tel: 01633 456120

4.14b Average Weekly Earnings - Regular Pay

Great Britain, seasonally adjusted

Standard Industrial Classification (2007)

	Whole Economy				Private sector [3][4][5]				Public sector [3][4][5]		
	Weekly Earnings (£)	% changes year on year		Weekly Earnings (£)	% changes year on year		Weekly Earnings (£)	% changes year on year	
		Single month	3 month average [2]		Single month	3 month average [2]		Single month	3 month average [2]
	KAI7	KAI8	KAI9	KAJ2	KAJ3	KAJ4	KAJ5	KAJ6	KAJ7
Jan 03	334	3.4	3.1	330	3.2	2.8	348	4.1	4.2
Feb 03	335	2.9	3.1	331	2.5	2.7	350	4.4	4.3
Mar 03	335	2.9	3.1	331	2.4	2.7	351	4.3	4.3
Apr 03	336	3.0	3.0	332	2.6	2.5	352	4.5	4.4
May 03	337	3.3	3.1	333	3.0	2.7	353	4.3	4.4
Jun 03	338	2.9	3.1	334	2.3	2.6	355	4.4	4.4
Jul 03	339	2.9	3.0	334	2.4	2.6	359	4.8	4.5
Aug 03	340	3.6	3.1	334	2.7	2.5	362	6.3	5.2
Sep 03	341	3.6	3.4	336	3.0	2.7	361	5.6	5.6
Oct 03	342	3.7	3.6	337	3.2	3.0	361	4.9	5.6
Nov 03	344	3.8	3.7	338	3.4	3.2	363	4.9	5.2
Dec 03	345	4.3	3.9	340	4.1	3.6	363	4.6	4.8
Jan 04	345	3.4	3.8	340	3.1	3.5	364	4.5	4.7
Feb 04	346	3.3	3.7	340	2.8	3.3	365	4.1	4.4
Mar 04	347	3.4	3.4	341	3.1	3.0	366	4.3	4.3
Apr 04	348	3.5	3.4	343	3.2	3.0	369	4.7	4.4
May 04	350	3.6	3.5	344	3.2	3.2	370	4.9	4.6
Jun 04	351	3.7	3.6	345	3.4	3.3	371	4.5	4.7
Jul 04	352	3.8	3.7	346	3.7	3.4	373	4.0	4.5
Aug 04	353	3.9	3.8	348	4.0	3.7	375	3.5	4.0
Sep 04	354	3.7	3.8	348	3.5	3.7	376	4.2	3.9
Oct 04	356	3.9	3.8	350	3.7	3.7	378	4.7	4.1
Nov 04	356	3.7	3.8	350	3.5	3.6	379	4.3	4.4
Dec 04	359	4.1	3.9	354	4.1	3.8	378	4.1	4.4
Jan 05	360	4.2	4.0	353	3.9	3.8	382	4.9	4.4
Feb 05	360	4.2	4.1	354	4.2	4.0	383	4.9	4.7
Mar 05	362	4.4	4.3	356	4.2	4.1	386	5.4	5.1
Apr 05	363	4.3	4.3	357	4.0	4.1	389	5.4	5.3
May 05	364	4.2	4.3	357	3.7	4.0	391	5.5	5.4
Jun 05	365	4.2	4.2	358	3.9	3.9	391	5.3	5.4
Jul 05	367	4.4	4.3	361	4.2	3.9	392	5.1	5.3
Aug 05	369	4.4	4.3	362	4.1	4.1	394	5.0	5.1
Sep 05	370	4.6	4.5	363	4.4	4.2	396	5.2	5.1
Oct 05	371	4.2	4.4	363	4.0	4.2	397	5.1	5.1
Nov 05	371	4.2	4.3	364	4.0	4.1	398	5.2	5.2
Dec 05	372	3.7	4.0	365	3.3	3.8	400	5.7	5.3
Jan 06	374	4.1	4.0	367	4.0	3.8	400	4.8	5.2
Feb 06	375	4.2	4.0	369	4.0	3.7	403	5.2	5.2
Mar 06	376	3.8	4.1	370	4.0	4.0	400	3.6	4.5
Apr 06	377	3.7	3.9	371	4.0	4.0	401	3.1	3.9
May 06	379	4.0	3.8	373	4.5	4.1	401	2.6	3.1
Jun 06	381	4.2	4.0	374	4.5	4.3	405	3.4	3.0
Jul 06	381	3.6	3.9	374	3.7	4.2	405	3.3	3.1
Aug 06	381	3.4	3.7	375	3.6	3.9	405	3.0	3.3
Sep 06	383	3.5	3.5	377	3.9	3.7	406	2.6	3.0
Oct 06	386	4.0	3.7	379	4.4	4.0	409	2.9	2.9
Nov 06	386	4.0	3.8	380	4.4	4.2	409	2.7	2.8
Dec 06	388	4.1	4.0	382	4.5	4.4	412	3.0	2.9
Jan 07	388	3.7	3.9	381	3.8	4.2	414	3.4	3.0
Feb 07	390	3.8	3.9	384	4.2	4.1	413	2.7	3.0
Mar 07	392	4.2	3.9	386	4.3	4.1	415	3.6	3.3
Apr 07	392	4.0	4.0	386	4.2	4.2	414	3.3	3.2

4.14b Average Weekly Earnings - Regular Pay

Great Britain, seasonally adjusted

Standard Industrial Classification (2007)

	Whole Economy			Private sector [3][4][5]			Public sector [3][4][5]		
	Weekly Earnings (£)	% changes year on year		Weekly Earnings (£)	% changes year on year		Weekly Earnings (£)	% changes year on year	
		Single month	3 month average [2]		Single month	3 month average [2]		Single month	3 month average [2]
	KAI7	KAI8	KAI9	KAJ2	KAJ3	KAJ4	KAJ5	KAJ6	KAJ7
May 07	395	4.2	4.1	389	4.4	4.3	416	3.7	3.6
Jun 07	397	4.2	4.1	391	4.5	4.3	417	3.1	3.4
Jul 07	398	4.6	4.3	393	5.1	4.7	417	3.0	3.3
Aug 07	400	4.9	4.6	395	5.2	4.9	419	3.4	3.2
Sep 07	400	4.5	4.7	395	4.8	5.1	420	3.4	3.3
Oct 07	401	3.9	4.4	395	4.1	4.7	421	2.9	3.2
Nov 07	403	4.2	4.2	397	4.5	4.5	423	3.3	3.2
Dec 07	403	4.0	4.0	397	4.1	4.3	425	3.2	3.1
Jan 08	404	4.1	4.1	398	4.5	4.4	426	3.0	3.1
Feb 08	406	4.2	4.1	401	4.4	4.3	429	3.7	3.3
Mar 08	408	4.1	4.1	402	4.1	4.3	430	3.8	3.5
Apr 08	411	4.8	4.4	405	4.8	4.4	433	4.4	4.0
May 08	409	3.8	4.2	404	3.7	4.2	431	3.6	4.0
Jun 08	411	3.5	4.0	405	3.7	4.1	430	3.0	3.7
Jul 08	412	3.4	3.6	406	3.2	3.5	433	3.9	3.5
Aug 08	413	3.3	3.4	407	3.1	3.3	435	3.7	3.5
Sep 08	414	3.3	3.3	408	3.1	3.2	436	3.8	3.8
Oct 08	415	3.6	3.4	409	3.6	3.3	436	3.6	3.7
Nov 08	416	3.2	3.4	410	3.1	3.3	437	3.5	3.6
Dec 08	416	3.1	3.3	410	3.1	3.2	438	3.1	3.4
Jan 09	416	2.8	3.1	410	2.8	3.0	439	3.0	3.2
Feb 09	417	2.6	2.9	410	2.4	2.8	442	3.0	3.0
Mar 09	417	2.1	2.5	410	2.2	2.5	440	2.3	2.7
Apr 09	418	1.8	2.2	411	1.5	2.0	444	2.6	2.6
May 09	419	2.2	2.1	411	1.9	1.9	446	3.5	2.8
Jun 09	419	2.0	2.0	411	1.4	1.6	448	4.3	3.5
Jul 09	418	1.4	1.9	408	0.6	1.3	450	3.7	3.9
Aug 09	418	1.3	1.6	409	0.4	0.8	451	3.7	3.9
Sep 09	419	1.4	1.4	410	0.5	0.5	452	3.8	3.7
Oct 09	419	1.0	1.2	410	0.1	0.3	452	3.7	3.7
Nov 09	420	1.0	1.1	410	0.0	0.2	455	3.9	3.8
Dec 09	421	1.3	1.1	411	0.4	0.2	455	4.0	3.9
Jan 10	423	1.8	1.4	414	1.0	0.5	457	4.2	4.0
Feb 10	423	1.5	1.6	413	0.6	0.7	459	3.8	4.0
Mar 10	425	2.1	1.8	416	1.3	1.0	457	3.8	4.0
Apr 10	424	1.4	1.7	414	0.6	0.9	460	3.6	3.7
May 10	424	1.2	1.6	413	0.4	0.8	461	3.2	3.5
Jun 10	425	1.4	1.3	414	0.8	0.6	460	2.6	3.1
Jul 10	427	2.2	1.6	416	1.9	1.0	462	2.7	2.8
Aug 10	428	2.3	2.0	417	2.2	1.6	463	2.5	2.6
Sep 10	428	2.2	2.2	417	1.8	2.0	464	2.7	2.6
Oct 10	429	2.2	2.2	418	2.0	2.0	466	3.1	2.8
Nov 10	430	2.4	2.3	418	2.2	2.0	467	2.8	2.8
Dec 10	429	1.9	2.2	418	1.5	1.9	468	2.8	2.9
Jan 11	433	2.2	2.2	422	1.9	1.9	470	2.7	2.8
Feb 11	432	2.1	2.1	420	1.9	1.8	471	2.6	2.7
Mar 11	432	1.7	2.0	420	1.1	1.6	472	3.2	2.9
Apr 11	433	2.1	1.9	421	1.8	1.6	471	2.6	2.8
May 11	433	2.3	2.0	422	2.3	1.8	472	2.4	2.7
Jun 11	433	2.0	2.1	422	1.9	2.0	471	2.5	2.5
Jul 11	434	1.6	2.0	423	1.7	2.0	471	2.1	2.3
Aug 11	434	1.5	1.7	423	1.4	1.7	472	2.1	2.2
Sep 11	436	1.7	1.6	425	1.7	1.6	474	2.1	2.1
Oct 11	437	1.8	1.7	426	1.9	1.7	475	1.9	2.0
Nov 11	438	1.8	1.8	427	2.0	1.9	476	1.8	1.9

4.14b Average Weekly Earnings - Regular Pay

Great Britain, seasonally adjusted

Standard Industrial Classification (2007)

	Whole Economy			Private sector [3][4][5]			Public sector [3][4][5]		
	Weekly Earnings (£)	% changes year on year		Weekly Earnings (£)	% changes year on year		Weekly Earnings (£)	% changes year on year	
		Single month	3 month average [2]		Single month	3 month average [2]		Single month	3 month average [2]
	KAI7	KAI8	KAI9	KAJ2	KAJ3	KAJ4	KAJ5	KAJ6	KAJ7
Dec 11	438	1.9	1.9	427	2.2	2.0	475	1.3	1.7
Jan 12	437	1.0	1.6	427	1.2	1.8	474	1.0	1.4
Feb 12	439	1.7	1.5	429	2.0	1.8	476	1.2	1.2
Mar 12	441	1.9	1.5	430	2.2	1.8	477	1.2	1.1
Apr 12	440	1.7	1.8	429	2.0	2.1	478	1.4	1.3
May 12	441	1.7	1.8	430	1.9	2.0	479	1.4	1.3
Jun 12	442	2.0	1.8	431	2.2	2.0	482	2.3	1.7
Jul 12	442	1.9	1.9	431	1.9	2.0	484	2.7	2.2
Aug 12	444	2.1	2.0	432	2.1	2.0	487	3.1	2.7
Sep 12	442	1.5	1.9	431	1.6	1.8	484	2.2	2.7
Oct 12	442	1.3	1.6	431	1.3	1.7	484	1.9	2.4
Nov 12	444	1.4	1.4	433	1.5	1.5	484	1.8	2.0
Dec 12	443	1.2	1.3	432	1.3	1.4	483	1.8	1.8
Jan 13	442	1.1	1.2	431	1.0	1.2	483	1.9	1.8
Feb 13	443	0.7	1.0	432	0.8	1.0	482	1.1	1.6
Mar 13	443	0.6	0.8	432	0.6	0.8	483	1.3	1.4
Apr 13	446	1.4	0.9	436	1.5	1.0	485	1.4	1.3
May 13	446	1.1	1.0	435	1.1	1.0	485	1.4	1.4
Jun 13	446	0.9	1.1	436	1.1	1.2	485	0.5	1.1
Jul 13	446	1.0	1.0	436	1.3	1.1	485	0.2	0.7
Aug 13	446	0.6	0.8	436	1.0	1.1	483	-0.7	0.0
Sep 13	446	0.8	0.8	436	1.0	1.1	485	0.1	-0.1
Oct 13	447	1.0	0.8	437	1.3	1.1	487	0.6	0.0
Nov 13	447	0.7	0.8	437	1.0	1.1	486	0.3	0.4
Dec 13	449	1.3	1.0	439	1.6	1.3	488	1.0	0.6
Jan 14	450	1.7	1.2	440	2.2	1.6	488	0.9	0.7
Feb 14	448	1.2	1.4	438	1.4	1.7	487	1.2	1.0
Mar 14	447	1.0	1.3	437	1.1	1.6	489	1.2	1.1
Apr 14	448	0.5	0.9	439	0.7	1.1	487	0.5	0.9
May 14	449	0.7	0.7	440	1.1	1.0	487	0.3	0.7
Jun 14	449	0.8	0.7	440	1.1	1.0	488	0.7	0.5
Jul 14	450	0.8	0.8	441	1.0	1.1	488	0.8	0.6
Aug 14	451	1.1	0.9	443	1.4	1.2	489	1.3	0.9
Sep 14	454	1.8	1.2	446	2.3	1.6	489	0.9	1.0
Oct 14	456	2.0	1.7	448	2.5	2.1	490	0.5	0.9
Nov 14	455	1.8	1.9	447	2.1	2.3	489	0.8	0.7
Dec 14	456	1.7	1.8	448	2.0	2.2	491	0.6	0.6
Jan 15	457	1.6	1.7	449	2.0	2.0	491	0.8	0.7
Feb 15	458	2.3	1.9	450	2.7	2.2	493	1.1	0.8
Mar 15	460	2.8	2.3	453	3.6	2.8	493	0.7	0.9
Apr 15	461	2.8	2.7	453	3.2	3.2	493	1.2	1.0
May 15	461	2.8	2.8	454	3.3	3.4	494	1.4	1.1
Jun 15	462	2.8	2.8	455	3.3	3.3	494	1.3	1.3
Jul 15	463	2.9	2.9	456	3.4	3.3	494	1.2	1.3
Aug 15	463	2.6	2.8	456	2.9	3.2	495	1.1	1.2
Sep 15	463	1.9	2.4	455	2.0	2.8	496	1.4	1.2
Oct 15	463	1.6	2.0	456	1.8	2.3	496	1.3	1.3
Nov 15	465	2.2	1.9	457	2.4	2.1	498	1.6	1.5
Dec 15	465	2.1	2.0	459	2.4	2.2	497	1.2	1.4
Jan 16	467	2.3	2.2	460	2.5	2.4	499	1.7	1.5

Source: Monthly wages and salaries survey

Inquiries: Email: labour.market@ons.gsi.gov.uk

Earnings enquiries: 01633 456773

1. Estimates of regular pay exclude bonuses and arrears of pay.

2. The three month average figures are the changes in the average seasonally adjusted values for the three months ending with the relevant month compared with the same period a year earlier.

3. From July 2009 Royal Bank of Scotland Group plc is classified to the public sector; for earlier time periods it is classified to the private sector. Between July 2009 and March 2014 Lloyds Banking Group plc is classified to the public sector; it is classified to the private sector for earlier and later time periods.

4. Between June 2010 and May 2012 English Further Education Corporations and Sixth Form College Corporations are classified to the public sector. Before June 2010 and after May 2012 they are classified to the private sector.

5. From October 2013 Royal Mail plc is classified to the private sector; previously it is in the public sector.

4.14b Average Weekly Earnings - Regular Pay
Great Britain, seasonally adjusted

Standard Industrial Classification (2007)

	Services, SIC 2007 sections G-S			Finance and business services, SIC 2007 sections K-N			Public sector excluding financial services [4][5]		
	Weekly Earnings (£)	% changes year on year		Weekly Earnings (£)	% changes year on year		Weekly Earnings (£)	% changes year on year	
		Single month	3 month average [2]		Single month	3 month average [2]		Single month	3 month average [2]
	K5DL	K5DM	K5DN	K5DO	K5DP	K5DQ	KAK6	KAK7	KAK8
Jan 03	319	3.7	3.3	390	3.4	2.4	348	4.2	4.3
Feb 03	320	3.1	3.3	392	2.9	2.5	350	4.3	4.3
Mar 03	321	2.9	3.3	392	2.9	3.1	351	4.3	4.3
Apr 03	322	3.3	3.1	393	3.0	2.9	352	4.6	4.4
May 03	323	3.5	3.3	395	3.9	3.3	352	4.1	4.3
Jun 03	324	2.9	3.2	393	2.7	3.2	355	4.6	4.4
Jul 03	324	3.2	3.2	393	2.7	3.1	359	4.7	4.4
Aug 03	326	4.0	3.4	393	2.8	2.7	362	6.4	5.2
Sep 03	327	3.9	3.7	395	2.8	2.8	361	5.6	5.6
Oct 03	328	4.0	4.0	398	3.3	3.0	361	5.0	5.7
Nov 03	329	4.0	4.0	398	3.0	3.0	362	4.8	5.2
Dec 03	330	4.6	4.2	399	4.4	3.6	364	4.7	4.9
Jan 04	331	3.5	4.0	399	2.5	3.3	363	4.3	4.6
Feb 04	331	3.3	3.8	398	1.7	2.8	366	4.7	4.6
Mar 04	331	3.3	3.4	400	2.1	2.1	367	4.5	4.5
Apr 04	333	3.6	3.4	402	2.1	2.0	369	4.6	4.6
May 04	334	3.7	3.5	405	2.6	2.3	370	5.0	4.7
Jun 04	336	3.8	3.7	404	2.6	2.5	371	4.5	4.7
Jul 04	337	3.9	3.8	405	3.0	2.8	372	3.9	4.4
Aug 04	338	3.9	3.8	407	3.6	3.1	375	3.6	4.0
Sep 04	339	3.8	3.9	409	3.4	3.3	376	4.1	3.9
Oct 04	341	4.2	4.0	410	3.1	3.4	378	4.6	4.1
Nov 04	341	3.9	4.0	411	3.2	3.2	379	4.5	4.4
Dec 04	345	4.5	4.2	415	4.1	3.5	379	4.0	4.4
Jan 05	345	4.4	4.2	416	4.2	3.8	382	5.0	4.5
Feb 05	346	4.7	4.5	420	5.5	4.6	382	4.3	4.5
Mar 05	348	5.1	4.7	422	5.4	5.0	386	5.3	4.9
Apr 05	349	4.8	4.8	423	5.2	5.4	388	5.4	5.0
May 05	350	4.7	4.8	423	4.5	5.0	391	5.7	5.4
Jun 05	351	4.7	4.7	423	4.7	4.8	390	5.2	5.4
Jul 05	354	5.0	4.8	429	5.9	5.0	392	5.2	5.4
Aug 05	355	4.8	4.8	429	5.3	5.3	394	5.1	5.1
Sep 05	356	5.0	4.9	430	5.3	5.5	396	5.2	5.1
Oct 05	356	4.4	4.7	430	4.9	5.1	397	5.1	5.1
Nov 05	357	4.5	4.6	431	4.7	5.0	398	5.2	5.2
Dec 05	358	3.8	4.2	430	3.6	4.4	399	5.5	5.3
Jan 06	360	4.4	4.2	435	4.5	4.3	400	4.7	5.1
Feb 06	360	4.1	4.1	433	3.1	3.7	402	5.4	5.2
Mar 06	361	3.8	4.1	439	4.0	3.8	400	3.6	4.5
Apr 06	362	3.6	3.9	439	3.9	3.7	400	3.1	4.0
May 06	363	3.7	3.7	440	4.0	4.0	401	2.6	3.1
Jun 06	366	4.1	3.8	443	4.9	4.3	404	3.4	3.0
Jul 06	366	3.4	3.7	443	3.3	4.0	405	3.5	3.2
Aug 06	366	3.3	3.6	445	3.8	4.0	405	2.9	3.3
Sep 06	368	3.4	3.3	446	3.6	3.6	406	2.7	3.0
Oct 06	370	4.0	3.5	447	4.0	3.8	408	2.8	2.8
Nov 06	371	4.0	3.8	448	3.9	3.8	409	2.8	2.8
Dec 06	373	4.2	4.1	452	5.0	4.3	411	3.0	2.9
Jan 07	372	3.5	3.9	444	2.2	3.7	414	3.7	3.1
Feb 07	375	4.1	3.9	450	4.0	3.7	413	2.7	3.1
Mar 07	376	4.1	3.9	452	3.1	3.1	414	3.7	3.4
Apr 07	377	4.2	4.1	455	3.7	3.6	413	3.3	3.2

4.14b Average Weekly Earnings - Regular Pay

Great Britain, seasonally adjusted

Standard Industrial Classification (2007)

	Services, SIC 2007 sections G-S			Finance and business services, SIC 2007 sections K-N			Public sector excluding financial services [4] [5]		
	Weekly Earnings (£)	% changes year on year		Weekly Earnings (£)	% changes year on year		Weekly Earnings (£)	% changes year on year	
		Single month	3 month average [2]		Single month	3 month average [2]		Single month	3 month average [2]
	K5DL	K5DM	K5DN	K5DO	K5DP	K5DQ	KAK6	KAK7	KAK8
May 07	380	4.6	4.3	459	4.2	3.6	415	3.6	3.5
Jun 07	381	4.3	4.4	461	4.0	3.9	416	3.1	3.3
Jul 07	382	4.5	4.5	463	4.5	4.2	417	2.8	3.1
Aug 07	384	4.8	4.6	464	4.1	4.2	419	3.5	3.1
Sep 07	385	4.6	4.6	467	4.8	4.5	420	3.3	3.2
Oct 07	385	3.9	4.4	468	4.6	4.5	421	3.1	3.3
Nov 07	387	4.3	4.3	471	5.3	4.9	422	3.1	3.2
Dec 07	388	4.0	4.1	473	4.7	4.8	425	3.4	3.2
Jan 08	389	4.3	4.2	470	5.8	5.2	426	2.8	3.1
Feb 08	390	4.1	4.1	475	5.5	5.3	428	3.6	3.3
Mar 08	393	4.3	4.2	476	5.2	5.5	430	3.8	3.4
Apr 08	395	4.9	4.4	479	5.2	5.3	431	4.4	3.9
May 08	394	3.7	4.3	477	4.0	4.8	431	3.7	4.0
Jun 08	395	3.5	4.0	483	4.7	4.6	428	2.9	3.7
Jul 08	396	3.7	3.6	486	5.1	4.6	433	4.0	3.6
Aug 08	398	3.6	3.6	489	5.4	5.1	434	3.6	3.5
Sep 08	399	3.6	3.7	489	4.7	5.1	435	3.8	3.8
Oct 08	400	3.9	3.7	490	4.7	4.9	436	3.5	3.6
Nov 08	400	3.3	3.6	490	4.0	4.5	437	3.6	3.6
Dec 08	400	3.3	3.5	488	3.3	4.0	438	3.0	3.4
Jan 09	400	3.0	3.2	490	4.4	3.9	439	3.0	3.2
Feb 09	402	3.1	3.1	491	3.4	3.7	441	3.1	3.1
Mar 09	402	2.3	2.8	493	3.6	3.8	439	2.0	2.7
Apr 09	403	2.0	2.5	494	3.1	3.4	443	2.8	2.7
May 09	404	2.6	2.3	494	3.6	3.4	445	3.3	2.7
Jun 09	404	2.4	2.3	494	2.5	3.1	447	4.3	3.5
Jul 09	404	1.8	2.3	494	1.6	2.5	446	2.8	3.5
Aug 09	403	1.4	1.9	495	1.2	1.7	448	3.1	3.4
Sep 09	404	1.5	1.6	495	1.2	1.3	448	2.8	2.9
Oct 09	404	1.1	1.3	495	1.0	1.1	448	2.9	2.9
Nov 09	404	1.1	1.2	498	1.6	1.3	450	2.8	2.8
Dec 09	405	1.2	1.1	498	2.0	1.5	451	2.8	2.8
Jan 10	408	1.8	1.4	502	2.3	1.9	452	2.9	2.9
Feb 10	407	1.2	1.4	498	1.3	1.8	453	2.7	2.8
Mar 10	409	1.8	1.6	506	2.7	2.1	452	3.1	2.9
Apr 10	408	1.2	1.4	503	1.9	2.0	455	2.5	2.8
May 10	408	1.1	1.4	504	2.0	2.2	456	2.4	2.6
Jun 10	409	1.2	1.2	504	1.9	1.9	453	1.5	2.1
Jul 10	412	2.1	1.5	511	3.5	2.4	457	2.5	2.1
Aug 10	413	2.3	1.9	513	3.7	3.0	457	2.0	2.0
Sep 10	414	2.3	2.2	515	4.2	3.8	459	2.7	2.4
Oct 10	414	2.3	2.3	518	4.6	4.2	460	2.6	2.4
Nov 10	415	2.6	2.4	519	4.3	4.4	462	2.7	2.7
Dec 10	415	2.4	2.5	523	5.0	4.6	463	2.8	2.7
Jan 11	418	2.6	2.5	530	5.6	5.0	464	2.8	2.8
Feb 11	418	2.5	2.5	526	5.6	5.4	465	2.5	2.7
Mar 11	418	2.0	2.4	525	3.8	5.0	466	3.1	2.8
Apr 11	418	2.5	2.4	527	4.8	4.7	465	2.3	2.6
May 11	419	2.7	2.4	531	5.4	4.7	465	2.0	2.5
Jun 11	419	2.3	2.5	531	5.4	5.2	465	2.5	2.3
Jul 11	419	1.8	2.3	531	3.9	4.9	464	1.6	2.1
Aug 11	419	1.6	1.9	529	3.1	4.1	466	2.1	2.1
Sep 11	421	1.7	1.7	533	3.4	3.4	467	1.6	1.8
Oct 11	422	2.1	1.8	537	3.8	3.4	467	1.5	1.8
Nov 11	423	1.9	1.9	537	3.4	3.5	467	1.1	1.4

4.14b Average Weekly Earnings - Regular Pay

Great Britain, seasonally adjusted

Standard Industrial Classification (2007)

	Services, SIC 2007 sections G-S			Finance and business services, SIC 2007 sections K-N			Public sector excluding financial services [4][5]		
	Weekly Earnings (£)	% changes year on year		Weekly Earnings (£)	% changes year on year		Weekly Earnings (£)	% changes year on year	
		Single month	3 month average [2]		Single month	3 month average [2]		Single month	3 month average [2]
	K5DL	K5DM	K5DN	K5DO	K5DP	K5DQ	KAK6	KAK7	KAK8
Dec 11	423	2.0	2.0	541	3.4	3.5	467	0.8	1.1
Jan 12	422	1.0	1.7	537	1.4	2.8	466	0.4	0.7
Feb 12	425	1.7	1.6	540	2.8	2.6	469	0.9	0.7
Mar 12	425	1.9	1.6	543	3.3	2.5	470	0.8	0.7
Apr 12	425	1.6	1.7	541	2.6	2.9	470	1.1	0.9
May 12	426	1.5	1.7	540	1.7	2.6	470	1.2	1.0
Jun 12	427	1.9	1.7	542	2.2	2.2	474	2.1	1.4
Jul 12	427	1.8	1.8	540	1.7	1.9	476	2.6	2.0
Aug 12	429	2.3	2.0	542	2.5	2.1	479	2.7	2.5
Sep 12	428	1.6	1.9	540	1.5	1.9	477	2.1	2.5
Oct 12	428	1.3	1.7	538	0.1	1.4	477	2.0	2.3
Nov 12	429	1.5	1.5	540	0.5	0.7	477	2.1	2.1
Dec 12	429	1.3	1.4	538	-0.5	0.1	475	1.9	2.0
Jan 13	427	1.2	1.3	537	0.0	0.0	476	2.0	2.0
Feb 13	427	0.6	1.0	539	-0.3	-0.3	474	1.0	1.7
Mar 13	428	0.5	0.7	538	-0.8	-0.4	475	1.1	1.4
Apr 13	430	1.2	0.7	540	-0.1	-0.4	477	1.5	1.2
May 13	430	1.0	0.9	539	-0.3	-0.4	478	1.6	1.4
Jun 13	430	0.8	1.0	536	-1.1	-0.5	477	0.6	1.2
Jul 13	431	1.0	0.9	538	-0.4	-0.6	478	0.4	0.8
Aug 13	431	0.4	0.8	536	-1.0	-0.9	477	-0.3	0.2
Sep 13	431	0.7	0.7	535	-1.1	-0.8	478	0.4	0.2
Oct 13	432	0.9	0.7	534	-0.7	-0.9	481	0.9	0.3
Nov 13	431	0.5	0.7	534	-1.0	-0.9	480	0.8	0.7
Dec 13	434	1.1	0.8	539	0.2	-0.5	481	1.2	0.9
Jan 14	433	1.3	1.0	536	-0.2	-0.4	482	1.4	1.1
Feb 14	431	1.0	1.1	533	-1.2	-0.4	482	1.8	1.5
Mar 14	432	1.0	1.1	538	-0.1	-0.5	482	1.4	1.5
Apr 14	432	0.5	0.8	535	-1.0	-0.8	482	1.2	1.4
May 14	433	0.6	0.7	535	-0.7	-0.6	483	1.2	1.2
Jun 14	434	0.8	0.6	536	0.1	-0.5	484	1.4	1.2
Jul 14	434	0.6	0.7	538	0.0	-0.2	484	1.2	1.3
Aug 14	436	1.1	0.8	543	1.3	0.5	484	1.4	1.3
Sep 14	439	1.9	1.2	548	2.5	1.3	485	1.4	1.4
Oct 14	440	2.0	1.7	552	3.4	2.4	486	1.0	1.3
Nov 14	439	1.8	1.9	548	2.6	2.8	486	1.1	1.2
Dec 14	441	1.7	1.9	548	1.6	2.5	488	1.5	1.2
Jan 15	442	2.1	1.9	550	2.6	2.3	488	1.1	1.2
Feb 15	443	2.7	2.2	552	3.6	2.6	489	1.4	1.3
Mar 15	445	3.0	2.6	555	3.2	3.1	489	1.5	1.3
Apr 15	445	3.0	2.9	557	4.2	3.7	489	1.4	1.4
May 15	446	3.0	3.0	558	4.3	3.9	489	1.2	1.4
Jun 15	447	3.0	3.0	559	4.2	4.2	491	1.4	1.3
Jul 15	447	2.9	3.0	556	3.3	3.9	490	1.3	1.3
Aug 15	446	2.4	2.8	556	2.3	3.3	491	1.5	1.4
Sep 15	446	1.7	2.3	556	1.5	2.4	493	1.5	1.4
Oct 15	447	1.4	1.8	558	1.0	1.6	493	1.4	1.5
Nov 15	448	2.0	1.7	561	2.3	1.6	494	1.8	1.6
Dec 15	449	1.8	1.7	564	3.0	2.1	494	1.1	1.4
Jan 16	451	1.9	1.9	567	3.0	2.8	496	1.6	1.5

Source: Monthly wages and salaries survey

Inquiries Email: labour.market@ons.gsi.gov.uk

Earnings enquiries: 01633 456773

1. Estimates of regular pay exclude bonuses and arrears of pay.

2. The three month average figures are the changes in the average seasonally adjusted values for the three months ending with the relevant month compared with the same period a year earlier.

3. From July 2009 Royal Bank of Scotland Group plc is classified to the public sector; for earlier time periods it is classified to the private sector. Between July 2009 and March 2014 Lloyds Banking Group plc is classified to the public sector; it is classified to the private sector for earlier and later time periods.

4. Between June 2010 and May 2012 English Further Education Corporations and Sixth Form College Corporations are classified to the public sector. Before June 2010 and after May 2012 they are classified to the private sector.

5. From October 2013 Royal Mail plc is classified to the private sector; previously it is in the public sector.

4.14b Average Weekly Earnings - Regular Pay
Great Britain, seasonally adjusted

Standard Industrial Classification (2007)

	Manufacturing, SIC 2007 section C			Construction, SIC 2007 section F			Wholesaling, retailing, hotels & restaurants, SIC 2007 sections G & I		
	Weekly Earnings (£)	% changes year on year		Weekly Earnings (£)	% changes year on year		Weekly Earnings (£)	% changes year on year	
		Single month	3 month average [2]		Single month	3 month average [2]		Single month	3 month average [2]
	K5DU	K5DV	K5DW	K5DX	K5DY	K5DZ	K5E2	K5E3	K5E4
Jan 03	389	3.1	3.2	407	4.5	2.9	223	5.4	4.5
Feb 03	390	2.9	3.2	411	3.1	3.1	221	4.1	4.5
Mar 03	389	2.9	3.0	412	3.7	3.8	221	3.2	4.2
Apr 03	392	2.9	2.9	414	5.0	3.9	222	3.4	3.6
May 03	394	2.8	2.9	412	3.3	4.0	223	3.5	3.4
Jun 03	396	3.0	2.9	418	5.0	4.4	223	1.6	2.8
Jul 03	397	2.9	2.9	414	3.6	4.0	222	1.5	2.2
Aug 03	398	3.2	3.1	415	4.1	4.2	223	1.6	1.6
Sep 03	401	4.0	3.4	420	4.8	4.2	224	2.1	1.8
Oct 03	401	3.6	3.6	421	5.3	4.7	223	1.8	1.9
Nov 03	402	4.3	4.0	421	3.9	4.7	224	2.1	2.0
Dec 03	405	4.1	4.0	427	5.9	5.0	226	3.2	2.4
Jan 04	406	4.4	4.2	426	4.6	4.8	226	1.7	2.3
Feb 04	407	4.5	4.3	427	3.9	4.8	227	2.6	2.5
Mar 04	410	5.2	4.7	431	4.8	4.4	227	2.8	2.4
Apr 04	409	4.4	4.7	432	4.3	4.3	229	3.3	2.9
May 04	412	4.6	4.8	431	4.6	4.6	230	3.1	3.1
Jun 04	414	4.6	4.5	426	1.9	3.6	231	3.7	3.4
Jul 04	416	4.9	4.7	427	3.2	3.2	232	4.2	3.7
Aug 04	417	4.7	4.7	433	4.4	3.2	232	4.1	4.0
Sep 04	418	4.4	4.7	426	1.5	3.0	232	3.8	4.0
Oct 04	421	5.0	4.7	424	0.6	2.2	234	4.7	4.2
Nov 04	422	4.8	4.7	426	1.2	1.1	234	4.2	4.2
Dec 04	421	4.0	4.6	428	0.4	0.7	236	4.5	4.5
Jan 05	422	4.0	4.2	439	3.0	1.5	237	4.5	4.4
Feb 05	423	3.9	3.9	425	-0.4	1.0	237	4.5	4.5
Mar 05	426	3.9	3.9	430	-0.4	0.7	238	4.6	4.5
Apr 05	427	4.5	4.1	429	-0.8	-0.5	239	4.1	4.4
May 05	427	3.7	4.0	432	0.3	-0.3	237	2.9	3.9
Jun 05	428	3.6	3.9	433	1.6	0.4	239	3.3	3.5
Jul 05	430	3.4	3.5	435	1.7	1.2	240	3.6	3.3
Aug 05	432	3.7	3.6	443	2.3	1.9	242	4.6	3.8
Sep 05	434	3.7	3.6	443	4.0	2.7	241	4.0	4.1
Oct 05	434	3.2	3.5	447	5.4	3.9	244	4.3	4.3
Nov 05	435	3.1	3.3	449	5.5	5.0	244	4.6	4.3
Dec 05	437	3.7	3.3	446	4.1	5.0	244	3.4	4.1
Jan 06	436	3.3	3.4	452	3.0	4.2	245	3.7	3.9
Feb 06	442	4.5	3.8	456	7.3	4.8	246	3.5	3.5
Mar 06	441	3.5	3.8	454	5.7	5.3	245	3.1	3.4
Apr 06	443	3.7	3.9	460	7.3	6.8	245	2.6	3.1
May 06	446	4.3	3.8	466	7.9	7.0	248	4.5	3.4
Jun 06	444	3.6	3.9	467	8.0	7.7	248	3.8	3.7
Jul 06	442	2.7	3.5	472	8.6	8.2	248	3.5	3.9
Aug 06	446	3.2	3.2	468	5.6	7.4	248	2.3	3.2
Sep 06	448	3.4	3.1	472	6.5	6.9	250	3.7	3.2
Oct 06	450	3.7	3.4	474	6.2	6.1	253	3.6	3.2
Nov 06	451	3.7	3.6	474	5.4	6.0	255	4.3	3.9
Dec 06	450	3.0	3.5	476	6.8	6.1	256	4.8	4.2
Jan 07	456	4.6	3.8	476	5.3	5.8	254	3.5	4.2
Feb 07	457	3.4	3.7	471	3.4	5.1	257	4.7	4.3
Mar 07	460	4.5	4.2	480	5.6	4.7	258	5.2	4.5
Apr 07	457	3.3	3.7	479	4.1	4.4	260	5.9	5.3

4.14b Average Weekly Earnings - Regular Pay

Great Britain, seasonally adjusted

Standard Industrial Classification (2007)

	Manufacturing, SIC 2007 section C			Construction, SIC 2007 section F			Wholesaling, retailing, hotels & restaurants, SIC 2007 sections G & I		
	Weekly Earnings (£)	% changes year on year		Weekly Earnings (£)	% changes year on year		Weekly Earnings (£)	% changes year on year	
		Single month	3 month average [2]		Single month	3 month average [2]		Single month	3 month average [2]
	K5DU	K5DV	K5DW	K5DX	K5DY	K5DZ	K5E2	K5E3	K5E4
May 07	459	2.9	3.6	480	3.1	4.3	260	4.8	5.3
Jun 07	461	3.7	3.3	485	3.8	3.7	261	5.3	5.3
Jul 07	462	4.7	3.8	505	7.0	4.7	262	5.6	5.2
Aug 07	462	3.6	4.0	507	8.5	6.5	263	6.2	5.7
Sep 07	463	3.2	3.8	509	7.8	7.8	263	5.0	5.6
Oct 07	464	3.2	3.3	501	5.7	7.3	264	4.4	5.2
Nov 07	464	3.0	3.1	504	6.5	6.6	264	3.6	4.3
Dec 07	465	3.3	3.2	504	5.8	6.0	263	2.8	3.6
Jan 08	469	2.8	3.0	493	3.7	5.3	265	4.4	3.6
Feb 08	472	3.3	3.1	502	6.5	5.3	265	3.0	3.4
Mar 08	472	2.5	2.8	500	4.3	4.8	268	3.7	3.7
Apr 08	474	3.6	3.1	504	5.2	5.3	271	4.2	3.6
May 08	474	3.3	3.2	506	5.4	4.9	269	3.5	3.8
Jun 08	475	3.1	3.3	509	4.9	5.2	268	2.9	3.6
Jul 08	476	3.0	3.2	509	0.8	3.7	267	2.0	2.8
Aug 08	476	2.9	3.0	503	-0.9	1.6	269	2.1	2.3
Sep 08	476	2.9	2.9	511	0.3	0.1	270	2.9	2.3
Oct 08	477	2.8	2.9	515	2.6	0.7	269	2.2	2.4
Nov 08	481	3.5	3.1	514	1.8	1.6	268	1.5	2.2
Dec 08	480	3.2	3.2	513	1.9	2.1	271	2.9	2.2
Jan 09	479	2.1	2.9	516	4.6	2.8	271	2.2	2.2
Feb 09	478	1.2	2.2	514	2.3	2.9	274	3.5	2.8
Mar 09	478	1.2	1.5	515	2.9	3.3	272	1.7	2.5
Apr 09	480	1.3	1.2	516	2.5	2.6	271	0.1	1.7
May 09	481	1.6	1.4	514	1.6	2.3	272	1.1	1.0
Jun 09	484	2.0	1.6	506	-0.7	1.1	272	1.3	0.8
Jul 09	480	0.8	1.4	513	0.7	0.6	273	2.0	1.4
Aug 09	484	1.7	1.5	517	2.9	1.0	272	1.3	1.5
Sep 09	486	2.1	1.5	516	1.1	1.6	274	1.2	1.5
Oct 09	488	2.2	2.0	521	1.2	1.7	274	1.8	1.4
Nov 09	489	1.7	2.0	521	1.3	1.2	274	2.2	1.8
Dec 09	499	4.0	2.6	524	2.0	1.5	276	1.9	2.0
Jan 10	499	4.2	3.3	522	1.3	1.6	275	1.7	1.9
Feb 10	500	4.8	4.3	523	1.8	1.7	277	1.2	1.6
Mar 10	504	5.4	4.8	520	1.1	1.4	279	2.4	1.7
Apr 10	501	4.5	4.9	522	1.1	1.3	277	2.1	1.9
May 10	501	4.1	4.7	516	0.4	0.9	276	1.4	2.0
Jun 10	502	3.7	4.1	514	1.7	1.1	278	2.2	1.9
Jul 10	501	4.4	4.1	512	-0.2	0.6	278	2.0	1.9
Aug 10	504	4.3	4.1	512	-1.1	0.1	279	2.6	2.3
Sep 10	504	3.7	4.1	514	-0.4	-0.6	279	2.0	2.2
Oct 10	504	3.3	3.7	518	-0.6	-0.7	278	1.2	2.0
Nov 10	504	3.2	3.4	516	-0.8	-0.6	278	1.5	1.6
Dec 10	505	1.2	2.5	512	-2.3	-1.2	277	0.4	1.0
Jan 11	506	1.5	2.0	523	0.2	-1.0	279	1.3	1.0
Feb 11	505	0.9	1.2	526	0.5	-0.5	278	0.4	0.7
Mar 11	506	0.6	1.0	523	0.6	0.4	278	-0.2	0.5
Apr 11	506	0.9	0.8	518	-0.9	0.1	281	1.5	0.5
May 11	507	1.1	0.9	521	1.0	0.2	281	2.1	1.1
Jun 11	508	1.1	1.0	524	1.9	0.7	280	0.9	1.5
Jul 11	510	1.6	1.3	524	2.4	1.8	280	0.7	1.2
Aug 11	511	1.3	1.3	527	2.9	2.4	281	0.6	0.7
Sep 11	513	1.8	1.6	526	2.3	2.6	281	0.5	0.6
Oct 11	512	1.5	1.5	525	1.4	2.2	282	1.6	0.9
Nov 11	514	1.9	1.7	526	2.0	1.9	284	2.2	1.4

4.14b Average Weekly Earnings - Regular Pay
Great Britain, seasonally adjusted

Standard Industrial Classification (2007)

	Manufacturing, SIC 2007 section C			Construction, SIC 2007 section F			Wholesaling, retailing, hotels & restaurants, SIC 2007 sections G & I		
	Weekly Earnings (£)	% changes year on year		Weekly Earnings (£)	% changes year on year		Weekly Earnings (£)	% changes year on year	
		Single month	3 month average [2]		Single month	3 month average [2]		Single month	3 month average [2]
	K5DU	K5DV	K5DW	K5DX	K5DY	K5DZ	K5E2	K5E3	K5E4
Dec 11	513	1.6	1.7	525	2.6	2.0	284	2.5	2.1
Jan 12	513	1.2	1.6	526	0.5	1.7	285	2.2	2.3
Feb 12	514	1.7	1.5	528	0.4	1.2	286	3.0	2.5
Mar 12	516	1.8	1.6	532	1.7	0.9	286	2.7	2.6
Apr 12	517	2.2	1.9	531	2.6	1.6	286	1.9	2.5
May 12	519	2.4	2.2	538	3.3	2.5	287	2.0	2.2
Jun 12	519	2.2	2.3	532	1.5	2.5	289	3.2	2.4
Jul 12	521	2.2	2.3	531	1.2	2.0	289	3.0	2.7
Aug 12	522	2.3	2.2	524	-0.5	0.8	288	2.7	3.0
Sep 12	522	1.8	2.1	523	-0.6	0.0	288	2.7	2.8
Oct 12	522	2.1	2.1	524	-0.2	-0.4	289	2.3	2.5
Nov 12	522	1.5	1.8	525	-0.2	-0.3	291	2.4	2.5
Dec 12	525	2.2	1.9	520	-0.8	-0.4	290	2.0	2.2
Jan 13	523	2.0	1.9	513	-2.5	-1.2	287	0.7	1.7
Feb 13	527	2.6	2.3	525	-0.6	-1.3	287	0.3	1.0
Mar 13	529	2.6	2.4	528	-0.9	-1.3	290	1.3	0.7
Apr 13	530	2.5	2.6	534	0.6	-0.3	291	1.9	1.1
May 13	530	2.2	2.4	534	-0.9	-0.4	291	1.5	1.6
Jun 13	531	2.4	2.4	528	-0.8	-0.4	294	1.8	1.7
Jul 13	532	2.1	2.2	526	-0.9	-0.9	296	2.7	2.0
Aug 13	532	1.8	2.1	530	1.2	-0.2	296	2.8	2.4
Sep 13	532	1.9	1.9	530	1.3	0.5	296	2.8	2.8
Oct 13	534	2.2	2.0	525	0.2	0.9	298	3.1	2.9
Nov 13	537	2.9	2.3	527	0.4	0.6	297	2.1	2.6
Dec 13	538	2.4	2.5	531	2.0	0.9	298	2.9	2.7
Jan 14	540	3.2	2.9	541	5.4	2.6	301	4.8	3.3
Feb 14	543	3.0	2.9	531	1.1	2.8	297	3.4	3.7
Mar 14	537	1.6	2.6	521	-1.3	1.7	296	2.3	3.5
Apr 14	540	1.8	2.1	527	-1.4	-0.5	297	1.9	2.5
May 14	540	1.9	1.8	528	-1.1	-1.2	298	2.3	2.2
Jun 14	541	1.8	1.8	531	0.6	-0.6	297	0.9	1.7
Jul 14	540	1.5	1.7	535	1.8	0.4	297	0.0	1.1
Aug 14	541	1.7	1.7	533	0.5	1.0	298	0.5	0.5
Sep 14	542	2.0	1.7	536	1.3	1.2	301	1.5	0.7
Oct 14	543	1.8	1.8	538	2.5	1.4	302	1.3	1.1
Nov 14	542	1.0	1.6	538	2.0	1.9	302	1.7	1.5
Dec 14	542	0.8	1.2	541	2.0	2.2	303	1.7	1.6
Jan 15	542	0.5	0.8	531	-1.8	0.7	306	1.9	1.8
Feb 15	546	0.6	0.6	540	1.6	0.6	308	3.5	2.4
Mar 15	543	1.0	0.7	548	5.2	1.6	309	4.3	3.2
Apr 15	547	1.4	1.0	543	3.1	3.3	309	4.1	4.0
May 15	547	1.2	1.2	543	3.0	3.7	310	4.0	4.1
Jun 15	548	1.2	1.3	545	2.7	2.9	309	4.1	4.1
Jul 15	549	1.7	1.4	571	6.7	4.1	311	4.8	4.3
Aug 15	549	1.6	1.5	570	7.0	5.5	311	4.3	4.4
Sep 15	550	1.5	1.6	567	5.7	6.5	308	2.5	3.9
Oct 15	550	1.3	1.5	573	6.5	6.4	310	3.0	3.2
Nov 15	552	1.8	1.5	575	6.8	6.3	312	3.4	2.9
Dec 15	554	2.2	1.8	572	5.7	6.3	314	3.4	3.3
Jan 16	555	2.3	2.1	578	8.8	7.1	312	1.8	2.9

Source: Monthly wages and salaries survey
Inquiries: Email: labour.market@ons.gsi.gov.uk
Earnings enquiries: 01633 456773

1. Estimates of regular pay exclude bonuses and arrears of pay.

2. The three month average figures are the changes in the average seasonally adjusted values for the three months ending with the relevant month compared with the same period a year earlier.

3. From July 2009 Royal Bank of Scotland Group plc is classified to the public sector; for earlier time periods it is classified to the private sector. Between July 2009 and March 2014 Lloyds Banking Group plc is classified to the public sector; it is classified to the private sector for earlier and later time periods.

4. Between June 2010 and May 2012 English Further Education Corporations and Sixth Form College Corporations are classified to the public sector. Before June 2010 and after May 2012 they are classified to the private sector.

5. From October 2013 Royal Mail plc is classified to the private sector; previously it is in the public sector.

4.14c Average Weekly Earnings - Bonus Pay

Great Britain, seasonally adjusted

Standard Industrial Classification (2007)

	Whole Economy			Private sector [234]			Public sector [234]		
	Weekly Earnings (£)	% changes year on year		Weekly Earnings (£)	% changes year on year		Weekly Earnings (£)	% changes year on year	
		Single month	3 month average [1]		Single month	3 month average [1]		Single month	3 month average [1]
	KAF4	KAF5	KAF6	KAF7	KAF8	KAF9	KAG2	KAG3	KAG4
Jan 03	16	-13.7	-6.9	16	-18.2	-7.0	3	-12.5	35.1
Feb 03	17	-3.3	-7.0	19	-3.2	-7.9	3	-20.9	10.0
Mar 03	20	18.7	0.1	24	20.8	-0.4	3	-11.0	-15.0
Apr 03	16	-10.9	1.2	20	-5.6	3.7	3	-19.8	-17.4
May 03	17	-9.1	-0.8	19	-6.2	2.6	3	-28.5	-20.1
Jun 03	17	-3.7	-7.9	20	-4.3	-5.4	4	38.3	-5.8
Jul 03	18	-2.3	-5.1	22	2.0	-2.8	3	-9.6	-2.2
Aug 03	17	-7.2	-4.4	20	-6.0	-2.8	3	27.7	17.1
Sep 03	18	0.7	-3.0	22	3.6	-0.2	3	-8.6	0.5
Oct 03	20	15.2	2.7	24	18.1	5.0	3	-8.5	1.0
Nov 03	18	0.8	5.5	22	6.5	9.3	2	-28.7	-15.2
Dec 03	18	-0.7	5.0	21	4.7	9.7	3	3.4	-11.6
Jan 04	20	27.1	8.5	30	83.2	27.5	3	16.5	-4.0
Feb 04	17	-1.9	7.7	21	7.4	28.4	3	3.1	7.5
Mar 04	21	3.1	8.7	25	5.4	27.5	3	14.8	11.5
Apr 04	21	33.2	10.5	24	21.7	11.1	3	6.8	8.3
May 04	20	21.0	17.9	26	31.9	18.7	3	11.0	10.9
Jun 04	20	13.9	22.5	24	20.8	24.7	3	-20.8	-4.0
Jul 04	20	10.8	15.1	23	5.7	18.9	3	-4.4	-7.2
Aug 04	20	21.0	15.1	23	15.1	13.6	3	9.1	-7.2
Sep 04	22	21.3	17.7	26	17.9	12.8	3	-2.4	0.7
Oct 04	24	18.6	20.2	27	11.6	14.7	3	2.8	3.2
Nov 04	22	25.2	21.6	26	15.1	14.7	3	38.7	10.9
Dec 04	22	24.1	22.4	24	12.7	13.1	3	10.1	15.4
Jan 05	23	11.1	19.7	31	3.7	9.8	3	-2.4	13.0
Feb 05	21	23.0	18.9	25	20.2	11.1	3	7.4	4.9
Mar 05	21	2.5	11.5	25	2.3	7.8	3	-9.1	-1.8
Apr 05	22	4.6	9.1	26	8.1	9.7	4	18.8	5.1
May 05	22	11.2	6.0	26	1.0	3.8	4	21.6	9.5
Jun 05	21	9.0	8.2	26	8.3	5.7	4	10.2	16.6
Jul 05	22	13.2	11.1	26	14.0	7.5	4	38.0	22.6
Aug 05	26	26.1	16.2	30	26.8	16.3	4	32.5	26.4
Sep 05	24	8.9	16.0	28	9.2	16.4	5	55.3	41.6
Oct 05	24	-0.4	10.9	28	2.6	12.3	5	53.5	46.7
Nov 05	25	13.0	7.0	30	16.0	9.2	4	23.2	43.5
Dec 05	25	15.0	8.9	29	18.7	12.2	5	34.1	36.6
Jan 06	23	1.6	9.8	30	-4.9	8.8	6	69.9	42.2
Feb 06	25	21.0	12.3	30	18.7	9.6	5	54.3	52.3
Mar 06	27	25.7	15.8	32	24.6	11.5	5	51.8	58.8
Apr 06	26	17.2	21.3	31	18.4	20.6	5	36.7	47.1
May 06	26	17.7	20.1	30	17.0	20.0	5	37.4	41.5
Jun 06	29	34.0	22.8	34	32.4	22.6	5	28.0	34.0
Jul 06	29	28.4	26.6	34	29.2	26.2	5	19.4	27.9
Aug 06	28	8.6	22.8	32	9.7	23.1	5	7.9	17.9
Sep 06	25	5.7	13.8	29	5.3	14.3	4	-18.5	2.1
Oct 06	27	11.6	8.6	32	15.3	10.1	6	21.1	3.6
Nov 06	28	8.7	8.7	33	11.6	10.7	3	-20.3	-5.0
Dec 06	32	26.8	15.7	38	32.2	19.6	5	7.5	4.0
Jan 07	31	35.7	23.3	39	32.6	25.3	4	-22.8	-12.1
Feb 07	33	30.1	30.7	38	29.0	31.3	4	-29.3	-15.6
Mar 07	30	10.4	24.8	34	8.0	22.9	5	9.6	-14.8
Apr 07	29	11.2	17.0	34	12.1	16.1	5	4.2	-5.3

4.14c Average Weekly Earnings - Bonus Pay

Great Britain, seasonally adjusted

Standard Industrial Classification (2007)

	Whole Economy				Private sector [2][3][4]				Public sector [2][3][4]		
	Weekly Earnings (£)	Single month	3 month average [1]	Weekly Earnings (£)	Single month	3 month average [1]		Weekly Earnings (£)	Single month	3 month average [1]	
	KAF4	KAF5	KAF6	KAF7	KAF8	KAF9		KAG2	KAG3	KAG4	
May 07	29	10.4	10.7	35	14.5	11.5		5	8.6	7.4	
Jun 07	30	4.9	8.7	35	4.7	10.2		6	23.5	11.9	
Jul 07	31	6.7	7.2	36	8.0	8.8		5	3.7	11.8	
Aug 07	31	10.4	7.3	37	13.0	8.5		5	3.9	10.3	
Sep 07	34	34.8	16.6	40	35.3	18.1		5	27.3	10.4	
Oct 07	30	14.0	19.3	37	16.2	21.1		3	-49.4	-11.4	
Nov 07	32	16.5	21.5	40	18.2	22.8		5	55.5	-0.2	
Dec 07	29	-8.6	6.5	36	-6.3	8.6		5	-6.9	-10.1	
Jan 08	31	0.2	2.1	40	2.3	4.1		4	-7.1	9.0	
Feb 08	35	6.4	-0.6	40	4.9	0.3		5	42.7	6.7	
Mar 08	32	10.0	5.5	36	6.2	4.4		4	-30.1	-3.0	
Apr 08	31	8.1	8.1	38	10.5	7.1		4	-24.1	-9.6	
May 08	33	12.6	10.2	41	17.9	11.6		5	-7.8	-20.5	
Jun 08	30	0.6	7.0	37	3.5	10.6		5	-10.6	-14.0	
Jul 08	30	-0.6	4.1	37	0.4	7.1		6	21.1	0.0	
Aug 08	29	-4.5	-1.5	36	-1.8	0.6		6	19.7	8.8	
Sep 08	29	-13.1	-6.3	34	-13.5	-5.2		6	16.0	19.0	
Oct 08	30	-0.2	-6.2	37	-0.5	-5.5		5	78.8	31.9	
Nov 08	26	-18.1	-10.7	32	-18.1	-10.9		6	22.6	33.0	
Dec 08	27	-7.0	-8.6	34	-4.6	-8.0		6	20.9	34.9	
Jan 09	27	-12.5	-12.7	25	-37.2	-20.6		5	35.3	25.7	
Feb 09	18	-48.5	-24.0	21	-47.3	-30.7		5	0.7	17.6	
Mar 09	19	-42.2	-35.0	26	-27.4	-37.6		6	68.9	31.4	
Apr 09	30	-5.4	-32.7	37	-1.8	-25.8		6	39.7	32.7	
May 09	26	-21.5	-23.2	30	-25.9	-18.4		4	-10.5	28.3	
Jun 09	21	-29.6	-18.7	32	-11.6	-13.4		4	-22.2	-0.9	
Jul 09	25	-19.0	-23.3	30	-17.6	-18.6		4	-37.9	-24.5	
Aug 09	25	-14.1	-21.0	31	-14.1	-14.4		4	-38.7	-33.4	
Sep 09	24	-17.2	-16.8	31	-11.1	-14.3		6	6.3	-24.1	
Oct 09	25	-17.7	-16.4	31	-15.6	-13.6		5	-5.0	-13.1	
Nov 09	27	1.1	-11.8	33	2.6	-8.4		5	-21.6	-7.3	
Dec 09	28	3.5	-4.9	34	-0.2	-4.8		4	-31.4	-19.8	
Jan 10	23	-17.5	-4.4	23	-7.7	-1.3		6	5.0	-16.5	
Feb 10	27	53.7	8.0	33	56.7	12.4		5	5.6	-7.6	
Mar 10	27	42.2	19.9	36	34.8	26.4		4	-29.6	-7.7	
Apr 10	23	-21.8	16.6	30	-20.1	16.1		5	-4.6	-10.8	
May 10	26	-0.2	1.9	34	13.6	6.1		5	21.0	-7.1	
Jun 10	24	12.9	-4.9	28	-13.1	-7.7		5	23.9	11.8	
Jul 10	22	-9.2	0.6	28	-6.9	-2.4		5	30.1	24.8	
Aug 10	23	-7.8	-2.1	28	-8.4	-9.6		5	40.6	31.2	
Sep 10	25	4.5	-4.2	32	3.7	-3.9		5	-23.1	9.2	
Oct 10	25	2.2	-0.4	31	1.3	-1.1		6	19.9	7.4	
Nov 10	26	-3.6	0.9	32	-4.7	0.0		6	22.6	4.4	
Dec 10	26	-7.6	-3.2	32	-6.1	-3.3		5	28.2	23.2	
Jan 11	30	35.0	6.3	35	49.3	8.7		5	-18.7	7.9	
Feb 11	27	0.2	7.5	33	0.6	10.6		6	10.3	4.0	
Mar 11	28	5.0	12.1	36	0.6	12.9		6	44.5	9.4	
Apr 11	25	5.8	3.6	32	6.4	2.4		5	0.0	16.6	
May 11	26	0.9	3.9	34	-1.1	1.7		5	-6.2	10.6	
Jun 11	30	23.4	9.9	36	26.4	9.7		6	20.2	4.4	
Jul 11	31	37.6	19.8	36	26.6	16.0		20	305.7	101.9	
Aug 11	28	18.1	26.1	34	18.5	23.8		6	9.7	109.8	
Sep 11	26	3.4	19.0	32	0.5	14.6		5	18.3	112.4	
Oct 11	27	7.8	9.5	34	7.0	8.3		4	-29.7	-2.8	
Nov 11	27	6.9	6.0	33	5.6	4.3		5	-7.2	-8.2	

4.14c Average Weekly Earnings - Bonus Pay

Great Britain, seasonally adjusted

Standard Industrial Classification (2007)

	Whole Economy				Private sector [2][3][4]				Public sector [2][3][4]		
	Weekly Earnings (£)	% changes year on year		Weekly Earnings (£)		% changes year on year		Weekly Earnings (£)		% changes year on year	
		Single month	3 month average [1]			Single month	3 month average [1]			Single month	3 month average [1]
	KAF4	KAF5	KAF6	KAF7	KAF8	KAF9		KAG2	KAG3	KAG4	
Dec 11	27	2.9	5.9	32	1.5	4.7		5	-4.4	-14.3	
Jan 12	27	-12.4	-1.6	32	-9.1	-0.9		6	35.6	6.4	
Feb 12	26	-5.1	-5.3	32	-4.7	-4.3		4	-30.5	-2.5	
Mar 12	27	-4.9	-7.6	33	-7.2	-7.0		5	-22.6	-9.5	
Apr 12	27	8.2	-1.0	34	7.0	-1.9		4	-18.4	-24.0	
May 12	26	0.4	0.9	33	-3.1	-1.4		5	7.6	-12.1	
Jun 12	28	-6.9	0.1	34	-5.8	-0.9		6	-9.0	-6.9	
Jul 12	29	-6.1	-4.4	35	-0.9	-3.2		5	-72.5	-46.9	
Aug 12	29	5.7	-2.7	34	0.6	-2.1		10	77.4	-33.8	
Sep 12	28	6.9	1.8	33	4.6	1.4		6	10.0	-31.1	
Oct 12	27	-0.2	4.1	32	-3.6	0.5		9	118.1	64.6	
Nov 12	28	1.2	2.6	33	-0.6	0.0		6	16.8	42.5	
Dec 12	27	0.7	0.6	32	-1.8	-2.0		7	44.3	55.2	
Jan 13	27	2.3	1.4	33	4.3	0.6		5	-16.8	12.1	
Feb 13	27	3.2	2.1	33	3.1	1.8		3	-31.1	-1.4	
Mar 13	25	-7.3	-0.6	30	-9.9	-1.0		5	-6.5	-17.4	
Apr 13	41	53.1	16.4	52	51.7	15.5		4	-3.7	-13.2	
May 13	31	18.4	21.4	39	17.5	20.1		5	-14.5	-8.7	
Jun 13	29	4.0	24.9	35	5.2	25.0		6	-0.8	-6.5	
Jul 13	28	-3.4	5.9	34	-3.8	6.1		4	-32.2	-15.8	
Aug 13	29	-0.4	0.0	35	4.1	1.8		5	-52.5	-33.4	
Sep 13	29	4.7	0.3	35	5.4	1.8		5	-19.6	-38.1	
Oct 13	28	2.2	2.1	33	2.9	4.1		3	-63.7	-48.7	
Nov 13	27	-1.0	2.0	33	-0.7	2.6		4	-42.6	-45.2	
Dec 13	29	7.7	2.9	34	7.9	3.3		2	-70.1	-59.6	
Jan 14	28	3.4	3.3	34	3.8	3.6		4	-16.1	-45.4	
Feb 14	29	7.7	6.2	35	8.3	6.6		4	48.4	-28.8	
Mar 14	27	9.4	6.7	32	6.2	6.1		5	2.5	5.2	
Apr 14	30	-26.5	-6.9	36	-29.7	-9.4		5	23.7	21.3	
May 14	30	-3.8	-10.0	36	-6.3	-13.2		3	-45.3	-7.6	
Jun 14	28	-1.7	-12.4	39	9.5	-11.5		3	-53.9	-28.6	
Jul 14	27	-2.9	-2.8	31	-9.1	-2.0		5	39.1	-26.1	
Aug 14	27	-7.7	-4.1	32	-8.3	-2.6		2	-53.7	-28.9	
Sep 14	28	-5.2	-5.3	33	-5.9	-7.8		3	-45.5	-24.5	
Oct 14	29	4.7	-2.8	34	3.0	-3.9		3	-16.5	-41.0	
Nov 14	30	9.1	2.7	36	8.6	1.7		3	-29.7	-32.4	
Dec 14	32	10.3	8.0	38	11.5	7.7		4	101.3	5.1	
Jan 15	27	-4.4	5.0	32	-5.3	4.9		1	-72.1	-21.1	
Feb 15	28	-2.7	1.1	34	-2.6	1.2		2	-41.5	-26.3	
Mar 15	31	14.2	2.1	37	15.2	2.1		2	-59.0	-57.8	
Apr 15	31	2.2	4.3	37	1.2	4.2		2	-58.0	-53.4	
May 15	31	3.8	6.5	37	1.5	5.6		3	2.2	-45.9	
Jun 15	26	-8.0	-0.5	36	-7.6	-1.8		2	-18.4	-33.1	
Jul 15	32	19.4	4.8	38	21.8	4.1		3	-42.3	-25.3	
Aug 15	33	22.1	10.9	39	19.5	9.9		3	25.7	-21.3	
Sep 15	30	8.9	16.7	36	8.4	16.4		4	51.2	-3.0	
Oct 15	32	10.0	13.5	38	9.2	12.3		2	-10.3	21.3	
Nov 15	30	0.4	6.4	36	1.0	6.1		2	-3.9	12.0	
Dec 15	31	-3.7	2.1	36	-4.7	1.6		2	-56.5	-28.8	
Jan 16	29	9.1	1.6	36	9.8	1.7		3	138.1	-9.7	

Source: Monthly wages and salaries survey

Inquiries: Email: labour.market@ons.gsi.gov.uk

Earnings enquiries: 01633 456773

1. Estimates of regular pay exclude bonuses and arrears of pay.

2. The three month average figures are the changes in the average seasonally adjusted values for the three months ending with the relevant month compared with the same period a year earlier.

3. From July 2009 Royal Bank of Scotland Group plc is classified to the public sector; for earlier time periods it is classified to the private sector. Between July 2009 and March 2014 Lloyds Banking Group plc is classified to the public sector; it is classified to the private sector for earlier and later time periods.

4. Between June 2010 and May 2012 English Further Education Corporations and Sixth Form College Corporations are classified to the public sector. Before June 2010 and after May 2012 they are classified to the private sector.

5. From October 2013 Royal Mail plc is classified to the private sector; previously it is in the public sector.

4.14c Average Weekly Earnings - Bonus Pay

Great Britain, seasonally adjusted

	Services, SIC 2007 sections G-S			Finance and business services, SIC 2007 sections K-N			Public sector excluding financial services [3][4]		
	Weekly Earnings (£)	% changes year on year		Weekly Earnings (£)	% changes year on year		Weekly Earnings (£)	% changes year on year	
		Single month	3 month average [1]		Single month	3 month average [1]		Single month	3 month average [1]
	K5CS	K5CT	K5CU	K5CV	K5CW	K5CX	KAH3	KAH4	KAH5
Jan 03	16	-18.0	-8.5	31	-24.8	-12.2	2	-14.5	33.3
Feb 03	17	-6.5	-10.0	41	-2.4	-12.2	2	-9.1	15.6
Mar 03	18	15.2	-4.2	42	14.5	-5.1	2	-13.8	-12.5
Apr 03	17	-11.3	-1.7	38	-3.7	2.4	2	-24.4	-16.1
May 03	17	-9.7	-2.9	39	-3.1	2.2	2	-29.4	-22.9
Jun 03	18	-5.1	-8.7	37	-9.0	-5.3	3	36.6	-8.3
Jul 03	18	-4.1	-6.3	40	-10.1	-7.5	2	-12.5	-4.0
Aug 03	17	-10.6	-6.6	38	-7.7	-9.0	2	24.3	14.4
Sep 03	18	-4.1	-6.3	38	-12.5	-10.1	2	-10.3	-2.1
Oct 03	20	12.7	-0.9	47	14.3	-2.2	2	-9.8	-0.9
Nov 03	18	-2.6	1.9	42	2.6	1.1	2	-30.8	-16.9
Dec 03	18	-2.0	2.6	31	-18.9	-0.3	2	1.2	-13.5
Jan 04	21	29.4	7.3	49	56.9	10.5	2	14.6	-6.3
Feb 04	17	-1.6	7.9	38	-7.0	6.9	2	-0.5	4.9
Mar 04	21	10.9	12.4	50	20.9	20.7	2	11.1	8.3
Apr 04	23	36.9	15.0	54	44.1	18.6	2	6.5	5.7
May 04	20	16.2	21.0	54	39.6	34.5	2	9.5	9.1
Jun 04	20	14.1	22.2	47	27.6	37.2	2	-21.7	-5.0
Jul 04	20	9.9	13.4	50	26.0	31.1	2	-5.3	-8.3
Aug 04	21	19.8	14.5	38	0.4	18.1	2	7.6	-8.3
Sep 04	22	23.4	17.6	47	22.0	16.3	2	-4.9	-0.9
Oct 04	24	20.7	21.3	65	38.9	21.8	2	-0.2	0.8
Nov 04	23	25.9	23.2	51	22.8	28.5	2	34.4	7.6
Dec 04	23	26.9	24.3	53	70.4	41.5	2	8.3	12.4
Jan 05	23	11.3	20.9	55	11.0	30.2	2	-3.6	10.8
Feb 05	21	22.3	19.7	51	32.9	33.7	2	4.2	2.9
Mar 05	21	3.3	11.7	52	4.4	14.7	2	-5.1	-1.7
Apr 05	23	0.1	7.4	54	0.0	10.4	2	12.0	3.4
May 05	23	13.6	5.4	51	-6.6	-0.9	2	14.8	6.9
Jun 05	22	9.3	7.3	60	27.4	6.0	2	4.4	10.2
Jul 05	23	12.6	11.8	54	7.7	8.7	3	32.9	16.7
Aug 05	26	28.4	16.8	67	76.8	33.9	3	27.4	21.0
Sep 05	24	9.6	16.7	64	37.4	37.4	3	50.8	36.7
Oct 05	24	-1.9	11.1	60	-8.1	27.6	3	53.0	43.2
Nov 05	26	14.6	7.2	67	31.7	17.5	3	19.3	40.7
Dec 05	26	15.9	9.2	62	16.6	11.7	3	30.3	33.9
Jan 06	23	1.5	10.6	57	4.5	17.3	4	71.9	40.1
Feb 06	25	21.2	12.6	65	28.0	16.1	4	74.4	57.9
Mar 06	28	30.0	17.1	71	35.8	22.5	3	50.4	65.6
Apr 06	27	16.0	22.2	70	28.7	30.8	3	36.2	53.2
May 06	27	19.8	21.7	71	38.9	34.4	3	35.4	40.4
Jun 06	30	35.8	23.7	96	60.4	43.4	3	25.7	32.3
Jul 06	30	32.4	29.3	82	51.5	50.9	3	17.4	25.8
Aug 06	29	8.6	24.6	77	15.5	41.2	3	6.7	16.0
Sep 06	25	4.0	14.4	61	-4.4	19.1	2	-21.5	0.0
Oct 06	27	10.6	7.8	73	23.0	11.2	4	17.8	1.2
Nov 06	29	11.3	8.7	81	20.3	12.9	2	-21.5	-7.2
Dec 06	37	40.1	20.9	107	72.8	38.4	3	4.5	1.8
Jan 07	32	38.4	29.6	81	42.8	44.6	3	-25.4	-14.5
Feb 07	33	29.9	36.1	84	28.1	47.7	3	-24.6	-16.4
Mar 07	30	8.6	24.8	75	4.7	23.8	3	-0.8	-17.7
Apr 07	30	12.3	16.7	77	10.4	14.0	3	-3.2	-10.4

4.14c Average Weekly Earnings - Bonus Pay

Great Britain, seasonally adjusted

Standard Industrial Classification (2007)

	Services, SIC 2007 sections G-S			Finance and business services, SIC 2007 sections K-N			Public sector excluding financial services [3 4]		
	Weekly Earnings (£)	% changes year on year		Weekly Earnings (£)	% changes year on year		Weekly Earnings (£)	% changes year on year	
		Single month	3 month average [1]		Single month	3 month average [1]		Single month	3 month average [1]
	K5CS	K5CT	K5CU	K5CV	K5CW	K5CX	KAH3	KAH4	KAH5
May 07	30	9.9	10.3	75	5.5	6.9	3	5.8	0.6
Jun 07	30	1.8	7.8	75	-22.0	-4.2	4	19.6	7.3
Jul 07	31	4.6	5.3	77	-5.2	-8.6	3	0.6	8.6
Aug 07	32	10.4	5.6	80	4.0	-8.7	3	1.4	7.1
Sep 07	35	39.4	17.1	92	49.3	13.2	3	24.3	7.5
Oct 07	31	18.6	22.2	74	1.2	16.2	2	-50.8	-14.0
Nov 07	33	14.8	23.7	80	-1.0	14.0	3	54.1	-3.1
Dec 07	31	-14.9	4.1	75	-29.8	-12.2	3	-9.7	-12.7
Jan 08	32	0.4	-1.0	80	-1.4	-12.6	2	-8.6	6.8
Feb 08	35	6.7	-3.1	87	4.5	-10.7	2	-13.9	-10.7
Mar 08	33	9.6	5.5	83	11.5	4.7	2	-40.4	-21.9
Apr 08	33	8.7	8.3	79	1.8	5.9	3	2.9	-17.6
May 08	33	11.0	9.8	91	22.6	11.9	3	-9.5	-15.8
Jun 08	31	2.8	7.5	92	22.8	15.6	3	-14.8	-7.7
Jul 08	31	-0.6	4.3	79	2.0	15.6	4	19.8	-2.4
Aug 08	31	-3.0	-0.3	73	-8.6	5.1	4	18.6	6.7
Sep 08	30	-13.8	-6.1	82	-10.0	-5.8	3	15.6	18.0
Oct 08	32	1.8	-5.3	88	18.7	-0.9	3	79.5	31.7
Nov 08	28	-16.1	-9.7	65	-19.4	-4.4	4	27.7	35.3
Dec 08	30	-2.1	-5.7	81	7.2	1.6	3	16.0	35.6
Jan 09	29	-8.7	-9.1	77	-3.6	-5.5	2	-6.0	13.8
Feb 09	18	-50.2	-21.5	44	-49.3	-16.7	4	60.5	22.7
Mar 09	18	-43.8	-34.8	47	-43.1	-32.6	4	96.2	45.9
Apr 09	31	-4.9	-33.5	85	8.5	-29.0	5	55.2	67.3
May 09	26	-20.5	-23.1	53	-42.4	-26.8	3	-12.6	39.1
Jun 09	22	-30.6	-18.5	55	-40.8	-26.6	2	-26.3	5.6
Jul 09	26	-17.3	-22.8	63	-20.9	-35.4	2	-46.4	-29.7
Aug 09	26	-14.9	-21.0	68	-7.7	-24.5	2	-55.0	-43.5
Sep 09	26	-15.7	-16.0	60	-27.2	-19.0	3	-10.9	-38.1
Oct 09	25	-20.5	-17.1	64	-27.5	-21.5	2	-39.8	-35.7
Nov 09	27	-2.3	-13.2	69	6.7	-18.0	2	-53.3	-35.5
Dec 09	30	0.1	-7.9	84	4.3	-7.0	2	-43.4	-46.0
Jan 10	24	-18.1	-6.8	63	-19.3	-3.2	2	-6.6	-38.5
Feb 10	27	55.4	5.7	75	70.2	9.7	2	-54.4	-38.8
Mar 10	26	42.0	18.5	66	38.8	20.4	4	18.0	-16.1
Apr 10	24	-22.3	15.8	63	-26.8	15.0	1	-69.9	-38.9
May 10	26	-1.5	0.6	77	46.7	10.8	2	-26.0	-30.5
Jun 10	25	16.2	-4.8	68	23.9	7.7	2	-14.5	-45.0
Jul 10	24	-7.9	1.5	57	-8.2	19.2	2	-22.9	-21.3
Aug 10	24	-8.9	-1.2	66	-2.8	3.3	2	1.7	-12.8
Sep 10	26	1.7	-5.1	73	22.1	3.3	2	-49.4	-28.8
Oct 10	26	0.5	-2.3	72	12.8	10.2	2	-0.5	-22.2
Nov 10	26	-3.2	-0.4	73	5.3	13.0	2	-3.6	-23.0
Dec 10	27	-12.8	-5.6	69	-18.0	-1.5	2	-10.0	-4.6
Jan 11	33	36.9	5.0	99	57.8	11.5	1	-36.6	-17.9
Feb 11	27	0.2	6.2	76	0.2	9.5	2	15.8	-12.2
Mar 11	29	9.4	14.7	78	18.4	23.7	2	-57.0	-36.2
Apr 11	25	3.0	4.2	68	8.0	8.5	2	48.4	-19.8
May 11	26	0.2	4.2	72	-7.2	5.6	2	-18.9	-27.7
Jun 11	31	23.1	8.8	87	28.9	9.2	1	-42.2	-9.1
Jul 11	33	39.9	20.5	86	50.4	21.2	4	128.7	14.7
Aug 11	28	19.2	27.3	71	7.3	27.9	2	10.2	25.9
Sep 11	26	1.8	19.7	72	-2.3	16.3	2	4.3	46.7
Oct 11	28	10.3	10.2	73	1.4	1.9	1	-26.8	-5.6

4.14c Average Weekly Earnings - Bonus Pay
Great Britain, seasonally adjusted

Standard Industrial Classification (2007)

	Services, SIC 2007 sections G-S			Finance and business services, SIC 2007 sections K-N			Public sector excluding financial services [3][4]		
	Weekly Earnings (£)	% changes year on year		Weekly Earnings (£)	% changes year on year		Weekly Earnings (£)	% changes year on year	
		Single month	3 month average [1]		Single month	3 month average [1]		Single month	3 month average [1]
	K5CS	K5CT	K5CU	K5CV	K5CW	K5CX	KAH3	KAH4	KAH5
Nov 11	28	4.8	5.6	76	5.0	1.3	2	4.4	-7.3
Dec 11	27	1.7	5.5	71	2.8	3.1	2	-6.6	-10.4
Jan 12	28	-15.9	-4.1	73	-26.3	-8.5	2	49.7	13.5
Feb 12	26	-4.9	-7.1	67	-11.6	-13.5	2	-25.2	1.3
Mar 12	28	-1.9	-8.0	74	-4.4	-15.2	2	-14.5	-1.8
Apr 12	28	11.4	1.2	75	11.4	-2.0	1	-31.7	-24.2
May 12	26	-1.4	2.4	59	-18.3	-4.1	2	7.8	-14.8
Jun 12	28	-9.3	-0.5	67	-22.8	-11.2	2	57.2	1.7
Jul 12	30	-8.3	-6.7	78	-10.3	-17.1	2	-50.7	-16.4
Aug 12	30	5.8	-4.3	76	7.6	-9.6	2	24.8	-10.6
Sep 12	29	10.1	1.7	69	-4.0	-2.8	2	33.7	-11.3
Oct 12	28	-2.1	4.5	67	-7.4	-1.4	4	188.3	76.0
Nov 12	28	1.4	3.0	68	-11.4	-7.7	2	18.4	73.7
Dec 12	27	1.0	0.1	71	0.1	-6.4	3	73.9	86.9
Jan 13	28	0.7	1.0	74	1.5	-3.5	2	-18.7	20.4
Feb 13	27	4.1	1.9	69	4.0	1.8	1	-35.4	4.7
Mar 13	26	-6.0	-0.5	68	-8.2	-1.1	2	11.5	-14.3
Apr 13	44	57.8	18.8	128	69.8	22.7	2	33.3	2.9
May 13	31	20.8	24.1	82	39.3	33.4	2	11.0	18.0
Jun 13	29	4.1	27.6	76	12.3	41.7	2	27.1	23.3
Jul 13	29	-4.5	6.1	70	-10.2	11.5	2	-7.4	10.3
Aug 13	29	-1.9	-0.9	71	-6.1	-1.9	2	-33.6	-7.4
Sep 13	30	4.1	-0.9	74	8.1	-3.1	2	-23.8	-22.9
Oct 13	28	2.7	1.6	71	5.9	2.3	1	-74.5	-50.9
Nov 13	28	0.6	2.5	70	3.4	5.8	1	-55.8	-56.9
Dec 13	29	7.0	3.4	74	4.3	4.5	1	-70.4	-68.8
Jan 14	28	1.5	3.0	72	-1.8	1.9	1	-27.0	-54.5
Feb 14	30	10.0	6.1	75	8.4	3.5	1	-6.5	-45.3
Mar 14	28	7.5	6.3	70	3.2	3.2	1	-28.2	-22.9
Apr 14	32	-27.7	-7.6	72	-43.9	-18.1	5	159.3	54.2
May 14	30	-3.5	-11.0	76	-7.2	-21.5	1	-34.8	34.7
Jun 14	28	-2.5	-13.4	69	-8.1	-23.9	1	-44.5	24.0
Jul 14	26	-9.0	-5.0	65	-6.8	-7.4	3	65.6	-10.5
Aug 14	27	-8.6	-6.7	71	-0.1	-5.1	1	-52.9	-14.0
Sep 14	28	-9.0	-8.8	71	-4.0	-3.6	1	-18.1	-1.1
Oct 14	30	4.9	-4.4	72	0.5	-1.3	1	36.5	-17.0
Nov 14	30	7.6	0.9	74	5.3	0.5	1	41.8	13.6
Dec 14	32	10.4	7.6	80	8.0	4.6	2	99.7	56.4
Jan 15	28	-2.8	5.1	64	-12.3	0.3	1	-53.0	18.7
Feb 15	29	-1.7	2.0	69	-8.7	-4.3	3	205.7	69.0
Mar 15	32	13.9	3.1	77	9.1	-4.1	1	-1.0	35.7
Apr 15	32	0.9	4.2	80	12.1	3.9	1	-76.8	-27.9
May 15	31	2.3	5.5	73	-3.1	5.9	1	4.3	-50.8
Jun 15	26	-8.7	-1.7	54	-23.0	-4.4	1	-26.1	-55.2
Jul 15	33	23.1	5.0	79	21.6	-2.0	1	-50.5	-31.4
Aug 15	33	23.4	12.1	89	24.5	7.5	1	52.9	-27.8
Sep 15	31	13.2	19.8	69	-3.7	13.9	2	45.3	-7.6
Oct 15	33	9.8	15.2	77	7.4	9.4	1	-13.4	22.5
Nov 15	31	2.4	8.3	69	-5.8	-0.7	1	3.1	10.9
Dec 15	31	-2.6	3.0	73	-8.6	-2.6	1	-56.0	-23.9
Jan 16	30	10.1	3.0	71	11.6	-1.7	2	167.4	2.8

Source: Monthly wages and salaries survey

Inquiries: Email: labour.market@ons.gsi.gov.uk

Earnings enquiries: 01633 456773

1. Estimates of regular pay exclude bonuses and arrears of pay.

2. The three month average figures are the changes in the average seasonally adjusted values for the three months ending with the relevant month compared with the same period a year earlier.

3. From July 2009 Royal Bank of Scotland Group plc is classified to the public sector; for earlier time periods it is classified to the private sector. Between July 2009 and March 2014 Lloyds Banking Group plc is classified to the public sector; it is classified to the private sector for earlier and later time periods.

4. Between June 2010 and May 2012 English Further Education Corporations and Sixth Form College Corporations are classified to the public sector. Before June 2010 and after May 2012 they are classified to the private sector.

5. From October 2013 Royal Mail plc is classified to the private sector; previously it is in the public sector.

4.14c Average Weekly Earnings - Bonus Pay
Great Britain, seasonally adjusted

Standard Industrial Classification (2007)

	Manufacturing, SIC 2007 section C			Construction, SIC 2007 section F			Wholesaling, retailing, hotels & restaurants, SIC 2007 sections G & I		
	Weekly Earnings (£)	% changes year on year		Weekly Earnings (£)	% changes year on year		Weekly Earnings (£)	% changes year on year	
		Single month	3 month average [1]		Single month	3 month average [1]		Single month	3 month average [1]
	K5D3	K5D4	K5D5	K5D6	K5D7	K5D8	K5D9	K5DA	K5DB
Jan 03	16	16.9	8.0	22	36.2	-1.0	16	-0.4	-1.4
Feb 03	17	25.9	15.6	20	2.4	10.9	15	2.9	-0.1
Mar 03	16	5.6	15.8	24	18.6	17.9	14	-5.0	-0.9
Apr 03	13	-11.3	6.4	20	-27.3	-4.9	12	-20.2	-7.7
May 03	16	14.8	2.9	17	-11.0	-8.8	13	-19.7	-15.1
Jun 03	13	-16.8	-5.1	18	-10.9	-17.7	14	-16.6	-18.8
Jul 03	17	16.5	4.0	19	-9.2	-10.4	14	2.9	-11.7
Aug 03	17	24.9	7.1	20	-13.4	-11.3	13	-15.1	-10.1
Sep 03	16	11.0	17.4	22	9.2	-4.9	14	-9.2	-7.5
Oct 03	16	11.3	15.7	24	40.2	9.3	15	-5.8	-10.0
Nov 03	19	31.0	18.0	22	29.8	25.3	13	-16.7	-10.6
Dec 03	15	-3.7	12.7	21	8.8	25.6	18	20.7	-1.1
Jan 04	17	8.5	11.7	21	-3.5	10.3	14	-12.2	-3.2
Feb 04	14	-18.1	-5.0	20	1.9	2.1	15	0.4	2.7
Mar 04	16	-0.3	-3.8	23	-2.5	-1.5	13	-4.4	-5.5
Apr 04	16	23.8	-0.3	21	4.9	1.2	15	24.3	5.8
May 04	19	19.8	13.7	25	52.0	15.0	14	9.2	9.0
Jun 04	16	24.6	22.5	20	7.0	19.8	14	6.3	12.9
Jul 04	17	3.1	15.1	22	12.6	22.8	15	1.3	5.4
Aug 04	18	6.8	10.5	18	-10.7	2.7	15	14.5	7.1
Sep 04	20	27.7	12.2	15	-33.3	-11.6	16	17.6	10.9
Oct 04	19	16.3	16.6	18	-23.5	-22.9	14	-1.5	9.9
Nov 04	17	-12.0	9.0	26	21.4	-12.4	15	11.1	8.8
Dec 04	22	45.1	13.8	20	-1.7	-2.1	15	-14.0	-2.8
Jan 05	18	7.7	11.1	24	14.6	11.6	16	13.5	1.8
Feb 05	17	19.9	23.6	23	14.2	9.0	16	4.5	0.0
Mar 05	17	5.7	10.7	26	10.7	13.1	13	-4.8	4.5
Apr 05	18	16.1	13.6	24	14.3	13.0	15	-1.0	-0.3
May 05	17	-11.6	2.5	26	4.3	9.4	15	8.1	0.8
Jun 05	16	-0.5	0.5	23	16.6	11.1	14	-2.3	1.5
Jul 05	18	6.8	-2.1	24	9.4	9.6	14	-4.0	0.5
Aug 05	19	1.5	2.6	20	10.9	12.3	14	-5.3	-3.9
Sep 05	17	-16.7	-3.4	21	41.3	18.6	15	-9.4	-6.3
Oct 05	18	-4.5	-6.8	25	34.6	28.3	15	2.4	-4.4
Nov 05	19	13.6	-3.3	26	-0.8	20.7	15	-0.2	-2.7
Dec 05	19	-11.3	-1.6	25	21.5	16.2	16	4.7	2.3
Jan 06	19	6.8	2.0	26	7.6	8.5	15	-5.8	-0.4
Feb 06	21	22.6	4.7	27	17.7	15.3	13	-15.6	-5.6
Mar 06	19	13.0	14.0	23	-8.0	5.3	15	13.7	-3.6
Apr 06	20	10.8	15.4	24	0.7	3.1	14	-3.8	-2.9
May 06	19	14.5	12.7	25	-6.2	-4.6	14	-7.1	0.3
Jun 06	20	20.1	14.9	27	15.9	3.0	15	5.3	-2.0
Jul 06	19	2.8	12.1	27	15.3	7.7	17	19.1	5.5
Aug 06	18	-1.9	6.4	27	38.0	22.3	15	4.2	9.5
Sep 06	21	24.9	8.0	21	-1.3	16.9	15	-1.3	7.2
Oct 06	24	36.6	19.4	25	2.7	12.1	15	0.5	1.1
Nov 06	20	1.0	20.1	23	-11.8	-3.7	15	1.2	0.1
Dec 06	20	2.7	12.8	25	1.4	-2.7	15	-4.6	-1.0
Jan 07	21	9.7	4.5	25	-1.9	-4.2	16	9.1	1.7
Feb 07	22	4.5	5.6	46	68.5	24.0	17	26.6	9.3
Mar 07	21	8.0	7.3	26	10.1	27.0	19	28.2	21.1
Apr 07	21	1.4	4.5	29	20.0	34.7	18	25.1	26.6

4.14c Average Weekly Earnings - Bonus Pay

Great Britain, seasonally adjusted

Standard Industrial Classification (2007)

	Manufacturing, SIC 2007 section C			Construction, SIC 2007 section F			Wholesaling, retailing, hotels & restaurants, SIC 2007 sections G & I		
	Weekly Earnings (£)	% changes year on year		Weekly Earnings (£)	% changes year on year		Weekly Earnings (£)	% changes year on year	
		Single month	3 month average [1]		Single month	3 month average [1]		Single month	3 month average [1]
	K5D3	K5D4	K5D5	K5D6	K5D7	K5D8	K5D9	K5DA	K5DB
May 07	22	17.6	8.8	31	24.8	18.4	19	37.5	30.2
Jun 07	24	21.3	13.2	35	32.8	26.1	20	37.6	33.4
Jul 07	23	24.7	21.2	28	4.3	20.4	20	20.9	31.4
Aug 07	23	23.3	23.0	27	0.4	12.3	18	21.0	26.3
Sep 07	23	10.9	19.3	32	55.8	17.0	21	40.8	27.2
Oct 07	23	-5.5	8.2	29	15.0	21.0	21	42.5	34.8
Nov 07	24	24.1	8.8	33	45.3	37.3	19	30.0	37.8
Dec 07	24	23.2	12.5	35	37.9	32.3	19	22.0	31.4
Jan 08	22	2.9	16.4	32	28.7	37.0	17	7.4	19.5
Feb 08	23	3.7	9.5	32	-31.3	2.4	18	8.9	12.6
Mar 08	19	-6.1	0.2	28	8.7	-5.1	20	5.7	7.3
Apr 08	24	13.9	3.8	26	-11.0	-15.2	19	8.6	7.7
May 08	35	54.0	21.5	27	-11.6	-5.3	20	5.1	6.4
Jun 08	24	1.9	23.1	23	-35.4	-20.3	18	-9.9	0.8
Jul 08	27	16.3	23.6	23	-18.9	-22.7	19	-8.3	-4.6
Aug 08	22	-3.5	5.0	26	-6.6	-21.6	17	-2.1	-7.0
Sep 08	22	-5.2	2.7	28	-14.6	-13.5	16	-21.4	-11.0
Oct 08	24	5.4	-1.1	22	-23.2	-14.9	16	-26.4	-17.4
Nov 08	19	-20.3	-7.0	22	-33.5	-23.9	18	-6.7	-18.5
Dec 08	21	-11.9	-9.3	21	-39.8	-32.7	16	-13.5	-15.9
Jan 09	21	-3.8	-12.3	18	-42.8	-38.7	18	5.8	-5.1
Feb 09	19	-18.5	-11.5	21	-33.8	-38.9	18	-2.4	-3.7
Mar 09	22	10.4	-4.7	24	-13.8	-30.9	16	-19.6	-6.1
Apr 09	25	5.0	-1.5	24	-4.9	-18.6	17	-13.5	-12.1
May 09	20	-40.9	-14.1	18	-34.4	-17.9	18	-12.6	-15.2
Jun 09	19	-22.2	-22.2	19	-15.7	-18.7	17	-8.8	-11.7
Jul 09	18	-33.9	-33.4	19	-19.2	-23.8	16	-11.5	-11.0
Aug 09	19	-13.5	-23.9	19	-24.5	-20.0	18	4.5	-5.5
Sep 09	20	-9.7	-20.1	18	-36.3	-27.2	17	4.9	-1.1
Oct 09	18	-25.7	-16.6	20	-9.2	-24.3	17	9.7	6.3
Nov 09	21	7.1	-10.6	22	0.1	-16.7	17	-5.5	2.6
Dec 09	21	-3.7	-8.6	21	-1.2	-3.5	16	-1.0	0.7
Jan 10	20	-3.2	-0.1	22	18.9	5.3	18	-0.7	-2.4
Feb 10	22	18.1	3.1	21	0.2	5.4	19	7.6	2.0
Mar 10	22	4.2	5.9	24	-0.2	5.5	24	53.0	18.7
Apr 10	19	-22.9	-2.2	16	-35.1	-12.3	17	2.6	20.3
May 10	20	-0.7	-7.4	18	0.8	-12.7	16	-10.3	14.0
Jun 10	15	-19.3	-14.8	15	-24.8	-21.4	16	-4.0	-4.0
Jul 10	22	22.9	0.6	17	-7.3	-10.8	16	0.2	-4.8
Aug 10	22	18.6	7.2	17	-10.3	-14.2	16	-14.9	-6.5
Sep 10	22	11.6	17.5	17	-4.3	-7.4	17	-1.2	-5.6
Oct 10	26	43.0	23.9	14	-30.3	-15.6	17	-1.4	-6.0
Nov 10	20	-2.5	16.2	16	-29.1	-22.3	19	9.9	2.4
Dec 10	23	10.0	15.5	18	-13.0	-24.2	20	24.4	10.7
Jan 11	24	16.6	7.9	19	-12.3	-18.2	17	-5.1	9.1
Feb 11	21	-2.9	7.6	25	18.6	-2.3	18	-4.0	4.2
Mar 11	22	0.2	4.3	21	-13.5	-3.0	19	-20.4	-10.8
Apr 11	22	15.0	3.6	18	10.9	3.9	16	-10.1	-12.3
May 11	21	2.2	5.4	17	-6.8	-4.8	17	8.8	-9.3
Jun 11	20	30.5	14.5	19	33.7	11.1	23	40.7	12.6
Jul 11	22	0.3	8.9	15	-13.6	2.7	20	23.5	24.4
Aug 11	20	-12.5	3.2	17	-2.6	4.3	18	14.2	26.3
Sep 11	24	11.3	-0.4	17	3.9	-4.1	19	10.4	16.0
Oct 11	21	-18.8	-7.3	21	47.5	14.4	19	11.5	12.0

119

4.14c Average Weekly Earnings - Bonus Pay
Great Britain, seasonally adjusted

Standard Industrial Classification (2007)

	Manufacturing, SIC 2007 section C			Construction, SIC 2007 section F			Wholesaling, retailing, hotels & restaurants, SIC 2007 sections G & I		
	Weekly Earnings (£)	% changes year on year		Weekly Earnings (£)	% changes year on year		Weekly Earnings (£)	% changes year on year	
		Single month	3 month average [1]		Single month	3 month average [1]		Single month	3 month average [1]
	K5D3	K5D4	K5D5	K5D6	K5D7	K5D8	K5D9	K5DA	K5DB
Nov 11	22	6.0	-1.6	22	39.5	29.1	18	-4.3	5.5
Dec 11	21	-5.2	-7.0	19	7.2	29.7	19	-2.9	1.0
Jan 12	22	-8.8	-3.1	18	-5.6	12.1	20	14.4	2.0
Feb 12	24	13.7	-0.5	18	-27.3	-10.6	19	6.9	5.7
Mar 12	19	-14.7	-3.7	20	-5.1	-13.8	18	-4.9	5.1
Apr 12	23	2.7	0.3	20	13.3	-8.7	16	2.5	1.3
May 12	25	21.2	2.6	19	14.6	6.7	19	9.2	2.0
Jun 12	21	8.6	10.7	23	19.5	16.0	20	-10.5	-0.7
Jul 12	21	-4.3	8.2	18	21.4	18.5	18	-10.9	-5.0
Aug 12	25	27.8	10.0	16	-3.6	12.4	23	28.5	0.8
Sep 12	21	-14.9	1.2	16	-9.0	2.1	21	11.4	8.8
Oct 12	22	6.7	4.9	24	16.5	2.3	21	10.2	16.5
Nov 12	23	7.1	-1.1	17	-20.3	-4.3	20	11.3	11.0
Dec 12	20	-5.0	2.9	18	-9.0	-4.4	19	0.2	7.1
Jan 13	19	-11.4	-3.1	17	-7.3	-12.7	20	2.7	4.6
Feb 13	21	-11.4	-9.3	17	-4.6	-7.0	21	6.9	3.3
Mar 13	21	7.7	-5.8	12	-41.4	-18.5	17	-8.0	0.7
Apr 13	28	22.2	5.7	34	73.3	9.5	25	54.9	16.0
May 13	23	-10.2	5.9	19	1.2	11.2	23	22.9	21.8
Jun 13	23	8.4	6.2	21	-8.4	20.7	20	0.4	23.9
Jul 13	22	1.8	-0.6	17	-4.4	-4.1	23	29.7	17.0
Aug 13	25	-0.2	3.2	21	30.1	3.8	28	23.5	17.7
Sep 13	21	1.1	0.8	21	32.1	18.3	23	9.6	20.7
Oct 13	23	2.8	1.2	21	-15.8	10.8	22	6.8	13.6
Nov 13	23	-1.4	0.8	17	-2.1	1.5	22	10.5	9.0
Dec 13	23	12.8	4.4	18	0.6	-6.9	22	11.3	9.5
Jan 14	25	29.5	12.7	21	26.8	8.2	21	6.4	9.4
Feb 14	22	2.3	14.4	20	13.3	13.4	17	-19.8	-1.0
Mar 14	23	10.5	13.6	17	46.6	26.7	20	17.9	0.4
Apr 14	23	-16.3	-2.6	22	-36.2	-7.5	22	-9.1	-5.3
May 14	23	4.1	-2.0	17	-10.8	-14.0	22	-6.2	-1.0
Jun 14	25	8.4	-2.2	23	7.2	-17.4	21	3.3	-4.4
Jul 14	24	11.8	8.1	29	66.7	18.9	20	-13.9	-6.0
Aug 14	22	-10.0	2.9	27	26.7	31.3	21	-26.2	-13.9
Sep 14	25	19.4	6.2	26	24.0	37.4	22	-3.1	-15.3
Oct 14	21	-6.4	0.2	22	8.5	19.8	22	1.0	-10.8
Nov 14	25	8.0	6.7	24	39.2	23.0	23	4.8	0.8
Dec 14	28	20.2	7.3	24	36.3	26.8	22	3.0	2.9
Jan 15	23	-5.8	7.1	21	-3.9	21.8	23	8.0	5.3
Feb 15	20	-9.5	1.6	17	-11.7	5.6	21	24.6	10.8
Mar 15	25	10.5	-1.6	20	17.7	-0.2	26	28.3	19.8
Apr 15	25	6.1	2.5	24	8.8	4.5	22	0.2	16.6
May 15	22	-8.0	2.8	40	132.2	49.4	24	10.4	12.4
Jun 15	28	10.7	3.1	20	-11.4	35.9	22	2.6	4.4
Jul 15	25	3.4	2.3	31	6.0	32.0	24	18.3	10.3
Aug 15	24	5.1	6.5	26	-4.4	-2.6	22	6.9	9.1
Sep 15	22	-13.3	-1.9	24	-6.7	-1.5	24	11.8	12.2
Oct 15	24	13.6	1.0	27	19.8	2.0	23	1.9	6.8
Nov 15	22	-10.7	-4.3	23	-4.7	2.1	24	3.1	5.5
Dec 15	24	-12.2	-4.2	25	4.3	6.2	25	11.2	5.4
Jan 16	22	-7.7	-10.3	29	40.0	11.9	22	-5.1	2.9

Source: Monthly wages and salaries survey

Inquiries: Email: labour.market@ons.gsi.gov.uk

Earnings enquiries: 01633 456773

1. Estimates of regular pay exclude bonuses and arrears of pay.

2. The three month average figures are the changes in the average seasonally adjusted values for the three months ending with the relevant month compared with the same period a year earlier.

3. From July 2009 Royal Bank of Scotland Group plc is classified to the public sector; for earlier time periods it is classified to the private sector. Between July 2009 and March 2014 Lloyds Banking Group plc is classified to the public sector; it is classified to the private sector for earlier and later time periods.

4. Between June 2010 and May 2012 English Further Education Corporations and Sixth Form College Corporations are classified to the public sector. Before June 2010 and after May 2012 they are classified to the private sector.

5. From October 2013 Royal Mail plc is classified to the private sector; previously it is in the public sector.

4.14d Average Weekly Earnings in the public sector for selected activities (Not Seasonally Adjusted)

	Public Administration (Public Sector) (O)			Education (Public Sector) (P)			Health and Social Work (Public Sector) (Q)			Arts, Entertainment and Recreation (Public Sector) (R)		
	Average Weekly Earnings	Of which		Average Weekly Earnings	Of which		Average Weekly Earnings	Of which		Average Weekly Earnings	Of which	
		Bonuses	Arrears		Bonuses	Arrears		Bonuses	Arrears		Bonuses	Arrears
CDID	K5BE	K5BF	K5BG	K5BH	K5BI	K5BJ	K5BK	K5BL	K5BM	K5BN	K5BO	K5BP
2011 Jan	537	1	0	377	0	0	527	0	0	427	2	0
2011 Feb	535	2	0	378	0	0	527	0	0	423	0	0
2011 Mar	534	1	0	381	0	0	527	0	0	430	0	0
2011 Apr	537	1	0	384	0	1	530	0	1	433	5	0
2011 May	538	1	0	378	0	0	532	0	0	458	29	1
2011 Jun	542	6	0	379	0	0	534	0	0	428	3	0
2011 Jul	539	5	0	380	1	0	528	0	0	421	0	0
2011 Aug	545	11	0	383	0	0	524	0	0	424	4	0
2011 Sep	545	1	0	384	0	0	528	0	0	418	0	0
2011 Oct	538	1	0	381	1	0	529	0	0	419	0	0
2011 Nov	537	2	0	380	0	1	533	0	0	423	1	1
2011 Dec	540	6	0	379	0	0	533	0	0	427	0	0
2012 Jan	535	1	0	375	0	0	534	0	0	435	1	0
2012 Feb	538	1	0	377	0	0	537	0	0	463	0	0
2012 Mar	541	2	0	377	0	0	536	0	0	462	0	0
2012 Apr	545	0	0	381	0	0	540	0	0	463	1	1
2012 May	543	1	0	379	0	0	543	0	0	501	44	0
2012 Jun	550	5	0	381	0	0	541	0	0	463	5	0
2012 Jul	551	5	0	382	1	0	542	0	0	461	0	2
2012 Aug	547	3	0	387	0	0	536	0	0	455	0	0
2012 Sep	554	7	1	388	0	0	537	0	0	437	3	1
2012 Oct	547	2	1	385	0	0	536	0	0	462	41	0
2012 Nov	544	2	0	385	0	0	538	0	0	442	1	2
2012 Dec	543	2	2	385	0	0	537	0	0	444	5	0
2013 Jan	546	1	1	381	0	0	540	0	0	442	0	2
2013 Feb	535	0	0	380	0	0	538	0	0	441	0	0
2013 Mar	536	3	0	379	0	0	538	0	0	451	0	0
2013 Apr	537	1	0	384	0	0	547	0	0	450	3	0
2013 May	537	0	0	383	0	0	546	0	0	447	5	0
2013 Jun	540	3	0	382	0	0	545	0	0	449	4	1
2013 Jul	543	6	0	384	1	0	546	0	0	449	4	3
2013 Aug	540	1	4	386	0	1	536	0	0	442	1	1
2013 Sep	547	7	0	390	0	1	541	0	0	439	1	0
2013 Oct	537	1	0	390	0	1	543	0	0	441	1	1
2013 Nov	537	1	0	387	0	1	543	0	0	450	1	0
2013 Dec	540	2	1	391	0	1	543	0	0	444	0	0
2014 Jan	545	1	1	386	0	0	545	0	0	447	0	3
2014 Feb	541	1	1	388	0	0	544	0	1	450	0	0
2014 Mar	548	2	4	387	0	0	539	0	0	448	0	0
2014 Apr	553	7	3	392	0	2	547	0	0	454	1	0
2014 May	547	1	1	392	0	3	550	0	1	454	2	0
2014 Jun	549	3	0	390	0	0	549	0	0	453	5	0
2014 Jul	549	4	3	391	0	0	547	0	0	451	5	1
2014 Aug	547	3	1	393	1	0	538	0	0	448	6	0
2014 Sep	555	7	0	397	0	0	545	0	0	451	0	0
2014 Oct	552	1	1	395	0	0	540	0	0	448	1	3
2014 Nov	549	1	1	394	0	1	542	0	0	448	2	0
2014 DEC	554	1	1	405	2	3	543	0	0	456	3	1
2015 JAN	551	0	1	394	0	0	545	0	0	452	0	0
2015 FEB	551	2	1	395	0	0	545	0	0	447	0	0
2015 MAR	548	2	0	395	0	0	543	0	0	459	2	5
2015 APR	552	1	1	398	0	1	550	0	0	455	2	0
2015 MAY	552	1	0	395	0	0	551	0	0	454	0	0
2015 JUN	552	2	0	394	0	0	555	0	0	451	4	0
2015 JUL	554	4	1	396	0	0	547	0	0	456	7	1
2015 AUG	553	2	1	398	0	0	540	0	0	443	4	0
2015 SEP	561	8	1	403	0	0	548	0	0	447	1	1
2015 OCT	556	2	1	400	0	1	544	0	0	443	1	1
2015 NOV	553	1	1	401	0	2	549	0	0	447	1	0
2015 DEC	550	1	0	403	0	1	550	0	1	455	5	5

Source: Labour Force Survey, Office for National Statistics

All figures are in pounds (£)

4.15a Weekly pay - Gross (£) - For all employee jobs[a]: United Kingdom, 2015

Description	Code	Number of jobs[b] (thousand)	Median	Annual % change	Mean	Annual % change	10	20	25	30	40	60	70	75	80	90
All employees		25,997	425.1	1.7	507.2	1.1	130.2	217.4	259.1	292.5	357.2	500.6	594.4	652.4	717.8	922.4
18-21		1,306	199.3	3.0	209.6	2.6	44.8	77.1	92.1	108.3	148.2	243.9	280.5	298.4	320.1	380.7
22-29		4,481	383.2	3.2	409.9	1.8	145.5	239.5	268.7	293.0	337.4	433.0	489.8	521.5	558.1	670.8
30-39		5,950	489.1	1.0	553.3	0.5	171.6	274.5	314.2	349.4	418.2	567.3	656.1	704.3	766.4	958.0
40-49		6,555	491.9	2.3	588.7	1.2	160.3	255.5	297.1	337.3	412.0	583.8	688.3	749.7	820.4	1,075.1
50-59		5,490	458.0	2.5	558.2	1.3	154.3	238.1	279.1	316.2	383.3	543.8	650.2	709.6	781.9	1,016.3
60+		1,976	338.9	2.0	425.9	1.9	87.5	144.9	172.5	204.0	270.6	409.1	492.7	549.6	614.6	829.0
18-21 ALL OCCUPATIONS		1,306	199.3	3.0	209.6	2.6	44.8	77.1	92.1	108.3	148.2	243.9	280.5	298.4	320.1	380.7
18-21 Managers, directors and senior officials	1	24	327.2	-12.5	351.1	-9.7	x	x	x	308.0	x	339.3	x	383.1	440.0	x
18-21 Corporate managers and directors	11	17	324.5	-0.4	326.6	-13.0	x	x	x	x	307.9	326.3	x	x	x	x
18-21 Other managers and proprietors	12	x	352.1	-11.2	413.8	-2.5	x	x	x	x	x	x	x	x	x	x
18-21 Professional occupations	2	35	337.9	-3.0	357.6	4.0	x	249.1	277.7	291.9	315.8	362.6	415.7	426.4	452.8	x
18-21 Science, research, engineering and technology professionals	21	13	334.2	-8.2	386.1	1.0	x	x	288.9	292.7	315.9	350.6	x	x	x	x
18-21 Health professionals	22	11	328.2	-17.5	316.5	-5.9	x	x	x	x	304.8	373.8	416.0	x	x	x
18-21 Teaching and educational professionals	23	x	x		230.7	-7.1	x	x	x	x	x	x	x	x	x	x
18-21 Business, media and public service professionals	24	x	360.8	12.6	416.5	11.9	x	x	x	x	347.5	x	x	x	x	x
18-21 Associate professional and technical occupations	3	99	308.5	1.7	296.1	0.5	x	96.1	125.3	190.5	274.7	342.1	377.8	401.1	426.2	514.4
18-21 Science, engineering and technology associate professionals	31	26	314.7	-3.6	322.7	-8.2	x	243.4	261.1	274.6	293.5	333.0	359.4	386.3	407.0	x
18-21 Health and social care associate professionals	32	x	x		x		x	x	x	x	x	x	x	x	x	x
18-21 Protective service occupations	33	x	501.5	20.9	493.2	33.4	x	x	x	x	x	x	x	x	x	x
18-21 Culture, media and sports occupations	34	17	x		225.1	-3.0	x	x	x	x	x	x	x	x	x	x
18-21 Business and public service associate professionals	35	47	330.1	4.8	304.1	1.1	x	x	x	230.0	297.0	350.6	383.5	402.5	430.7	x
18-21 Administrative and secretarial occupations	4	130	265.8	5.3	248.7	1.7	67.6	127.2	159.2	191.7	234.4	287.5	315.1	328.6	345.0	390.6
18-21 Administrative occupations	41	109	270.5	4.6	255.3	2.6	73.2	135.9	172.0	201.5	244.2	294.4	320.3	335.4	347.5	392.1
18-21 Secretarial and related occupations	42	21	225.2	-2.4	214.2	-3.6	x	96.4	122.0	136.3	179.4	251.4	280.0	287.3	307.5	x
18-21 Skilled trades occupations	5	87	305.1	2.2	320.1	2.6	152.5	205.2	234.7	260.0	275.0	339.7	375.5	393.2	421.5	493.0
18-21 Skilled agricultural and related trades	51	6	290.6	3.0	286.8	7.4	x	x	x	272.0	277.7	298.2	x	x	x	x
18-21 Skilled metal, electrical and electronic trades	52	40	343.4	7.7	365.9	6.1	207.1	261.3	270.6	279.8	308.7	379.9	410.6	439.5	468.8	x
18-21 Skilled construction and building trades	53	13	289.3	-8.4	331.6	-5.5	x	199.5	205.2	218.2	262.1	347.5	414.1	431.6	x	x
18-21 Textiles, printing and other skilled trades	54	28	264.6	-0.7	256.4	3.4	x	149.3	170.0	191.2	234.1	288.0	324.3	344.8	357.0	x
18-21 Caring, leisure and other service occupations	6	190	217.1	4.7	202.3	1.4	40.3	88.2	103.6	126.7	180.1	242.7	270.4	280.7	293.2	334.5
18-21 Caring personal service occupations	61	145	228.1	4.0	212.8	2.0	51.9	103.7	126.0	151.0	203.2	250.0	276.2	284.1	298.0	335.4
18-21 Leisure, travel and related personal service occupations	62	45	147.6	-11.3	168.8	-1.9	24.2	45.8	60.9	80.9	102.0	201.6	241.4	260.0	273.4	x
18-21 Sales and customer service occupations	7	312	125.6	1.9	154.9	2.8	44.2	64.4	75.6	85.0	104.1	155.7	200.3	221.4	249.1	299.0
18-21 Sales occupations	71	271	119.2	4.7	145.0	1.6	41.7	60.8	70.2	80.3	98.7	144.5	181.1	205.1	227.5	284.0
18-21 Customer service occupations	72	40	220.1	26.6	221.9	14.1	79.1	101.3	114.3	124.1	167.6	270.1	287.7	300.4	317.3	x
18-21 Process, plant and machine operatives	8	39	295.7	3.3	305.6	3.6	142.9	210.6	240.3	257.5	279.0	320.0	341.4	352.3	383.0	450.2
18-21 Process, plant and machine operatives	81	31	299.4	2.7	307.7	0.1	155.4	223.9	243.8	263.3	287.2	320.3	344.1	355.3	383.1	450.2
18-21 Transport and mobile machine drivers and operatives	82	8	278.8	13.5	297.4	20.1	x	x	193.8	228.3	255.0	308.7	332.3	x	x	x
18-21 Elementary occupations	9	392	141.3	1.1	166.1	1.7	36.0	59.8	69.7	82.1	106.2	178.5	225.6	249.1	269.0	325.0
18-21 Elementary trades and related occupations	91	31	276.1	1.6	280.8	4.1	90.8	159.5	183.0	226.5	256.6	300.0	343.0	370.9	383.3	x
18-21 Elementary administration and service occupations	92	361	130.4	-1.0	156.2	0.8	33.6	56.6	66.4	77.5	100.5	166.8	210.0	231.6	258.2	307.7
22-29 ALL OCCUPATIONS		4,481	383.2	3.2	409.9	1.8	145.5	239.5	268.7	293.0	337.4	433.0	489.8	521.5	558.1	670.8
22-29 Managers, directors and senior officials	1	213	479.1	0.0	560.0	-2.8	296.8	350.2	370.4	385.3	436.0	527.1	595.0	659.5	714.1	966.5
22-29 Corporate managers and directors	11	160	501.6	-1.6	598.6	-2.4	312.6	364.6	383.3	403.9	453.5	569.2	660.1	709.1	786.1	1,054.1
22-29 Other managers and proprietors	12	54	423.5	2.9	445.1	-0.8	263.3	313.1	325.8	345.0	383.3	461.3	499.6	518.4	553.9	x
22-29 Professional occupations	2	889	537.2	0.1	569.7	0.7	345.0	422.1	444.9	465.3	502.9	578.7	632.1	663.5	702.1	831.2
22-29 Science, research, engineering and technology professionals	21	203	555.8	-0.3	593.0	1.1	375.1	440.8	463.6	479.1	518.0	595.7	655.3	689.9	731.9	857.4
22-29 Health professionals	22	236	535.8	-2.0	561.7	-1.7	320.4	429.9	446.2	469.0	504.0	572.3	617.5	652.4	700.3	854.2
22-29 Teaching and educational professionals	23	220	505.0	3.7	499.8	3.9	273.6	419.1	422.1	440.7	475.7	532.6	579.5	605.7	621.3	696.2
22-29 Business, media and public service professionals	24	229	574.9	0.8	624.7	1.9	354.3	421.6	460.0	480.0	527.9	622.9	684.9	724.4	766.6	953.6
22-29 Associate professional and technical occupations	3	675	479.1	1.5	508.0	0.7	300.0	359.4	383.3	401.1	441.1	519.8	571.0	594.1	632.4	745.5

4.15a Weekly pay - Gross (£) - For all employee jobs[a]: United Kingdom, 2015

Description	Code	Number of jobs[b] (thousand)	Median	Annual % change	Mean	Annual % change	Percentiles									
							10	20	25	30	40	60	70	75	80	90
22-29 Science, engineering and technology associate professionals	31	130	460.3	3.3	478.8	2.2	306.4	354.5	378.8	392.4	427.3	498.3	538.4	565.2	591.0	676.7
22-29 Health and social care associate professionals	32	46	401.6	1.3	399.7	5.5	x	302.1	326.6	345.0	377.7	435.3	466.5	482.0	499.6	x
22-29 Protective service occupations	33	44	568.5	-2.0	559.3	0.5	418.3	455.2	476.1	497.9	536.3	589.2	608.1	626.3	664.2	x
22-29 Culture, media and sports occupations	34	60	397.2	4.3	435.4		x	230.2	279.3	316.1	365.1	431.9	474.3	496.9	517.5	x
22-29 Business and public service associate professionals	35	395	498.3	2.0	535.4	2.3	321.6	374.2	392.9	421.6	460.0	542.0	594.1	626.9	670.8	789.6
22-29 Administrative and secretarial occupations	4	537	348.7	1.1	358.2	1.6	154.6	249.2	275.3	293.2	323.9	382.9	417.8	438.6	460.3	535.2
22-29 Administrative occupations	41	450	358.5	2.2	369.4	1.9	170.7	268.3	288.5	306.6	333.2	386.2	423.0	444.2	469.5	541.3
22-29 Secretarial and related occupations	42	87	295.1	1.1	300.3	-1.0	117.6	169.5	193.2	223.3	268.3	329.8	361.7	383.3	416.4	488.5
22-29 Skilled trades occupations	5	388	427.4	1.9	451.6	0.9	260.0	317.2	340.0	352.9	385.0	465.2	509.8	540.2	575.0	677.2
22-29 Skilled agricultural and related trades	51	21	346.0	6.4	345.0	6.5	x	276.8	285.8	299.3	319.9	364.1	390.9	400.0	430.7	x
22-29 Skilled metal, electrical and electronic trades	52	193	500.0	1.8	525.1	0.5	321.4	369.1	392.9	416.1	460.4	536.6	589.2	616.6	649.0	754.9
22-29 Skilled construction and building trades	53	61	450.0	0.7	479.0	-0.2	318.3	360.0	377.2	400.0	423.7	488.1	524.1	555.8	581.0	x
22-29 Textiles, printing and other skilled trades	54	113	341.9	4.3	330.3	0.3	156.0	237.5	264.0	286.0	315.0	359.8	384.4	402.5	422.8	461.8
22-29 Caring, leisure and other service occupations	6	475	269.6	4.9	266.3	3.7	104.0	152.8	177.4	201.2	242.3	293.9	320.2	339.0	359.9	421.8
22-29 Caring personal service occupations	61	388	269.1	4.6	263.4	3.0	103.5	156.0	178.9	201.2	240.3	292.8	318.8	336.4	354.4	412.6
22-29 Leisure, travel and related personal service occupations	62	87	270.1	6.4	279.5	6.9	105.7	141.0	162.5	200.0	245.6	297.9	331.4	358.3	395.9	454.0
22-29 Sales and customer service occupations	7	517	271.2	5.5	269.6	6.0	100.8	142.4	161.0	183.3	233.5	301.2	331.8	346.9	367.4	435.1
22-29 Sales occupations	71	387	246.5	7.2	247.8	5.7	90.9	127.3	144.4	160.9	201.3	277.5	309.5	325.8	345.0	405.0
22-29 Customer service occupations	72	130	330.6	7.9	334.6	8.9	160.5	242.9	267.2	282.7	306.5	352.0	385.0	402.4	422.3	496.3
22-29 Process, plant and machine operatives	8	199	383.5	6.0	411.8	4.8	246.7	283.3	300.3	316.9	349.2	425.9	471.7	501.1	534.4	625.0
22-29 Process, plant and machine operatives	81	127	379.9	5.6	411.0	4.5	255.1	286.1	300.7	318.0	345.8	419.3	467.6	498.3	523.2	624.4
22-29 Transport and mobile machine drivers and operatives	82	71	387.7	4.7	413.1	5.3	208.4	280.2	297.3	316.4	352.4	433.3	481.9	511.7	549.2	624.5
22-29 Elementary occupations	9	588	260.0	3.0	260.2	3.3	84.2	129.5	152.9	175.8	225.1	289.1	322.4	340.8	362.2	429.4
22-29 Elementary trades and related occupations	91	85	329.6	-0.5	334.4	-2.9	176.0	249.1	264.6	277.3	302.4	352.5	377.0	400.0	415.6	472.5
22-29 Elementary administration and service occupations	92	503	246.6	4.2	247.7	4.5	78.0	117.7	139.6	160.9	205.6	276.3	307.5	326.4	348.2	415.7
30-39 ALL OCCUPATIONS		5,950	489.1	1.0	553.3	0.5	171.6	274.5	314.2	349.4	418.2	567.3	656.1	704.3	766.4	958.0
30-39 Managers, directors and senior officials	1	589	716.8	-0.7	867.1	-0.8	324.5	432.4	479.1	528.8	621.1	836.8	983.9	1,093.7	1,237.6	1,573.0
30-39 Corporate managers and directors	11	493	774.9	-0.8	926.5	-0.4	340.4	460.0	517.3	574.7	670.8	910.3	1,078.2	1,186.7	1,303.3	1,642.3
30-39 Other managers and proprietors	12	96	522.8	-0.5	562.1	-2.9	276.6	362.0	383.3	403.8	464.6	576.1	644.0	672.4	721.5	862.4
30-39 Professional occupations	2	1,548	677.2	0.9	716.3	0.2	359.3	477.9	519.2	554.5	619.4	739.0	811.8	858.7	910.3	1,092.6
30-39 Science, research, engineering and technology professionals	21	381	750.1	1.3	790.1	-0.3	479.1	566.3	600.7	632.4	691.1	806.5	884.0	932.8	982.4	1,137.4
30-39 Health professionals	22	372	595.5	-0.8	648.9	-2.8	284.7	397.5	438.2	475.6	538.0	647.5	718.8	766.9	829.3	1,096.0
30-39 Teaching and educational professionals	23	386	668.3	1.0	639.0	2.0	294.9	422.1	466.6	520.6	611.3	716.9	770.3	801.2	833.3	923.2
30-39 Business, media and public service professionals	24	409	709.1	3.1	781.9	2.1	423.8	523.7	557.2	593.7	651.5	781.9	862.4	919.9	984.7	1,216.9
30-39 Associate professional and technical occupations	3	1,019	584.5	0.7	650.4	2.2	332.9	421.6	450.9	479.1	535.1	644.3	714.2	755.0	804.9	979.4
30-39 Science, engineering and technology associate professionals	31	170	538.4	0.2	568.4	-1.7	335.6	404.3	435.8	460.0	503.7	582.6	637.3	668.6	700.9	819.3
30-39 Health and social care associate professionals	32	91	436.9	-0.1	436.2	0.9	192.9	272.7	313.5	350.1	395.1	476.4	523.9	539.5	566.3	672.4
30-39 Protective service occupations	33	132	681.8	2.8	685.4	2.1	483.1	566.4	582.9	604.0	642.8	719.8	757.8	778.3	813.0	892.7
30-39 Culture, media and sports occupations	34	60	494.6	3.1	612.0	23.9	175.9	307.3	375.8	402.1	451.5	536.6	594.0	613.6	649.6	x
30-39 Business and public service associate professionals	35	566	616.5	1.5	705.2	1.7	357.0	437.2	471.0	498.3	560.2	682.3	766.6	823.1	897.6	1,149.9
30-39 Administrative and secretarial occupations	4	622	370.5	1.2	391.4	1.3	154.1	210.0	247.3	283.5	332.4	413.4	462.6	493.1	530.8	637.2
30-39 Administrative occupations	41	516	382.5	2.7	404.4	2.2	162.0	235.9	272.2	301.2	345.0	424.2	473.2	499.9	537.2	645.2
30-39 Secretarial and related occupations	42	106	296.6	-3.3	328.0	-2.3	119.6	159.4	182.1	197.8	241.1	347.7	404.7	431.8	468.7	586.8
30-39 Skilled trades occupations	5	452	478.3	2.2	502.2	1.6	268.4	345.0	364.9	388.2	435.9	521.0	574.9	604.7	646.5	749.6
30-39 Skilled agricultural and related trades	51	19	369.3	4.4	396.3	7.1	267.7	305.7	330.0	344.6	359.5	401.6	447.2	456.0	x	x
30-39 Skilled metal, electrical and electronic trades	52	229	550.0	1.6	582.7	0.9	360.1	421.6	452.8	474.1	514.3	598.9	657.6	685.5	719.0	845.8
30-39 Skilled construction and building trades	53	73	498.3	2.3	513.7	1.7	340.0	390.0	417.5	431.4	468.2	523.5	562.5	583.7	605.1	x
30-39 Textiles, printing and other skilled trades	54	131	360.5	1.8	370.5	1.0	160.4	236.1	271.0	297.1	326.7	389.5	425.2	447.1	467.6	550.8

4.15a Weekly pay - Gross (£) - For all employee jobs[a]: United Kingdom, 2015

Description	Code	Number of jobs[b] (thousand)	Median	Annual % change	Mean	Annual % change	Percentiles 10	20	25	30	40	60	70	75	80	90
30-39 Caring, leisure and other service occupations	6	492	257.0	1.8	271.4	1.6	104.0	149.5	166.5	185.6	220.9	293.5	333.1	357.8	381.2	452.1
30-39 Caring personal service occupations	61	415	254.0	2.1	264.2	2.2	101.0	147.2	165.6	184.4	217.8	287.5	325.6	346.9	372.5	438.1
30-39 Leisure, travel and related personal service occupations	62	78	291.6	0.8	309.7	-0.9	111.4	155.6	172.2	194.3	245.5	335.3	374.5	403.5	441.2	558.7
30-39 Sales and customer service occupations	7	365	279.5	1.7	299.9	2.5	108.6	143.8	161.1	185.9	235.3	322.9	365.2	391.0	425.4	522.5
30-39 Sales occupations	71	249	244.7	3.6	264.5	1.9	103.6	129.3	142.1	156.0	196.5	283.6	325.9	346.7	381.2	466.9
30-39 Customer service occupations	72	117	354.2	2.8	375.3	4.6	155.8	220.3	250.4	276.4	318.2	392.8	447.0	479.1	518.1	592.7
30-39 Process, plant and machine operatives	8	302	426.4	0.1	456.8	-1.3	253.7	302.0	326.5	346.0	387.9	478.0	523.1	560.2	598.0	699.3
30-39 Process, plant and machine operatives	81	162	403.2	-1.3	434.8	-4.2	252.5	287.9	311.8	329.3	362.5	445.9	500.3	529.1	565.7	668.4
30-39 Transport and mobile machine drivers and operatives	82	139	455.9	2.5	482.3	1.8	258.1	326.0	351.0	373.5	413.4	500.9	551.9	594.6	625.8	731.7
30-39 Elementary occupations	9	561	276.1	4.4	283.0	3.7	75.2	119.2	141.4	166.4	229.0	316.5	358.8	384.4	412.4	500.0
30-39 Elementary trades and related occupations	91	74	348.7	5.0	358.4	3.0	207.0	266.2	280.5	295.3	324.4	373.4	401.7	418.5	443.0	519.9
30-39 Elementary administration and service occupations	92	487	259.5	3.4	271.5	3.5	69.1	110.5	130.0	152.4	200.2	300.0	346.4	376.0	404.5	496.5
40-49 ALL OCCUPATIONS		6,555	491.9	2.3	588.7	1.2	160.3	255.5	297.1	337.3	412.0	583.8	688.3	749.7	820.4	1,075.1
40-49 Managers, directors and senior officials	1	822	826.6	1.8	1,001.1	-1.3	328.9	480.9	543.4	592.6	711.2	964.2	1,152.2	1,256.6	1,382.6	1,824.9
40-49 Corporate managers and directors	11	713	872.3	0.4	1,050.3	-1.6	336.5	512.3	574.9	635.6	752.1	1,027.5	1,217.9	1,315.7	1,451.7	1,889.8
40-49 Other managers and proprietors	12	109	579.9	-2.6	679.4	-1.7	306.1	383.3	423.8	463.8	525.2	670.6	771.8	843.0	893.0	1,132.0
40-49 Professional occupations	2	1,500	714.9	1.7	771.5	0.8	334.3	464.5	519.2	567.8	647.3	785.1	871.8	919.9	996.5	1,227.9
40-49 Science, research, engineering and technology professionals	21	338	825.6	1.0	873.1	0.5	488.4	611.0	651.6	686.8	758.7	890.4	978.2	1,039.6	1,102.0	1,290.5
40-49 Health professionals	22	430	619.6	0.9	715.1	0.1	280.2	397.7	436.4	480.0	552.7	671.6	758.0	792.9	869.0	1,315.7
40-49 Teaching and educational professionals	23	396	709.3	2.4	688.0	2.3	267.3	421.9	474.3	529.9	634.2	760.6	834.2	880.2	915.9	1,082.5
40-49 Business, media and public service professionals	24	337	752.6	3.9	839.6	1.4	387.6	512.8	562.5	602.0	675.2	831.4	920.5	992.0	1,072.6	1,351.6
40-49 Associate professional and technical occupations	3	973	620.3	1.1	689.9	-0.3	316.5	418.7	457.5	487.8	556.7	691.0	766.6	811.1	874.0	1,096.1
40-49 Science, engineering and technology associate professionals	31	154	575.2	0.7	602.4	0.9	331.3	400.6	445.2	471.9	522.2	630.0	676.8	710.0	741.3	887.7
40-49 Health and social care associate professionals	32	94	430.6	-3.1	441.6	-2.3	179.6	248.7	283.2	334.0	384.4	478.9	524.6	556.7	601.9	720.0
40-49 Protective service occupations	33	139	744.0	1.5	759.8	2.0	535.7	597.3	633.8	672.4	719.7	786.1	826.5	851.9	885.6	991.6
40-49 Culture, media and sports occupations	34	48	473.9	1.6	485.9	1.2	x	171.0	220.9	289.2	395.9	544.2	610.8	654.7	700.7	x
40-49 Business and public service associate professionals	35	539	642.4	0.9	758.3	-1.0	345.5	442.8	474.0	504.8	574.9	722.1	818.5	886.6	973.0	1,293.5
40-49 Administrative and secretarial occupations	4	760	359.8	2.0	387.6	1.8	151.8	202.6	230.0	261.6	313.8	402.5	457.6	489.1	530.0	654.0
40-49 Administrative occupations	41	602	372.9	2.1	401.4	2.1	154.3	216.1	250.0	281.5	330.6	417.6	471.3	500.9	540.7	668.4
40-49 Secretarial and related occupations	42	159	298.5	0.1	335.4	0.2	135.2	175.8	192.8	210.0	251.8	344.1	401.2	426.2	461.5	609.7
40-49 Skilled trades occupations	5	488	498.3	1.9	528.8	0.9	249.9	342.6	378.6	402.5	447.9	549.0	604.6	642.1	686.9	822.6
40-49 Skilled agricultural and related trades	51	27	381.7	0.6	396.5	-2.9	236.3	298.9	311.6	337.5	359.2	392.4	422.9	442.6	473.8	x
40-49 Skilled metal, electrical and electronic trades	52	259	574.9	1.0	619.3	1.0	380.0	439.3	466.3	487.4	533.3	624.3	686.5	721.1	767.6	913.6
40-49 Skilled construction and building trades	53	81	516.9	2.0	559.9	2.6	349.6	418.3	429.8	442.7	482.4	553.5	604.9	640.0	673.6	x
40-49 Textiles, printing and other skilled trades	54	122	324.9	1.5	344.7	0.3	151.9	191.8	219.0	250.0	293.6	374.5	419.2	437.3	466.3	546.0
40-49 Caring, leisure and other service occupations	6	637	262.8	1.9	282.3	0.9	109.4	160.9	181.8	200.0	232.4	298.4	337.7	361.1	386.8	460.5
40-49 Caring personal service occupations	61	554	260.0	2.8	272.7	1.5	109.2	160.8	182.5	200.1	230.3	293.9	329.2	353.6	377.7	446.4
40-49 Leisure, travel and related personal service occupations	62	83	301.4	0.8	346.8	1.1	110.5	160.6	179.3	199.0	245.1	341.9	402.2	432.1	480.8	632.3
40-49 Sales and customer service occupations	7	332	260.0	5.3	295.5	4.4	105.7	143.6	159.0	174.7	214.6	301.9	350.4	380.4	415.7	528.9
40-49 Sales occupations	71	242	222.6	3.3	256.0	4.1	103.1	131.4	144.4	156.8	187.8	261.5	302.1	325.8	352.2	456.6
40-49 Customer service occupations	72	90	368.1	7.2	401.5	8.0	158.9	227.3	259.3	284.8	337.2	406.6	467.9	503.5	546.5	664.6
40-49 Process, plant and machine operatives	8	416	467.0	2.6	495.6	1.9	260.0	324.9	347.1	369.0	414.5	518.3	577.7	610.3	649.9	772.6
40-49 Process, plant and machine operatives	81	189	429.4	0.8	472.6	0.1	252.0	299.1	325.9	344.5	381.6	481.4	540.0	580.7	629.4	759.7
40-49 Transport and mobile machine drivers and operatives	82	227	498.1	4.8	514.8	3.2	275.4	345.3	374.0	394.1	449.8	546.0	598.8	626.6	659.9	782.7
40-49 Elementary occupations	9	626	254.0	3.0	272.1	1.7	63.3	104.0	123.4	143.6	196.1	303.1	356.0	381.3	416.8	510.5
40-49 Elementary trades and related occupations	91	80	353.7	-2.0	370.4	-3.8	186.9	252.7	273.0	287.6	320.6	384.6	425.2	449.1	474.4	585.7
40-49 Elementary administration and service occupations	92	547	230.0	3.7	257.7	2.2	57.5	95.7	111.4	130.2	174.7	282.7	337.9	368.3	402.5	498.9
50-59 ALL OCCUPATIONS		5,490	458.0	2.5	558.2	1.3	154.3	238.1	279.1	316.2	383.3	543.8	650.2	709.6	781.9	1,016.3
50-59 Managers, directors and senior officials	1	647	788.5	1.7	976.0	-0.1	288.5	452.3	511.1	571.5	680.3	933.8	1,113.2	1,226.6	1,372.3	1,799.1
50-59 Corporate managers and directors	11	546	852.8	2.8	1,034.5	0.3	295.1	479.1	548.7	607.0	723.0	1,003.8	1,193.3	1,313.2	1,469.7	1,874.0

4.15a Weekly pay - Gross (£) - For all employee jobs[a]: United Kingdom, 2015

Description	Code	Number of jobs[b] (thousand)	Median	Annual % change	Mean	Annual % change	10	20	25	30	40	60	70	75	80	90
50-59 Other managers and proprietors	12	101	580.6	-2.0	659.4	-4.6	272.7	369.0	408.5	442.8	522.9	673.0	752.7	817.7	900.4	1,087.7
50-59 Professional occupations	2	1,141	703.6	1.2	766.5	2.0	299.7	436.4	497.5	545.9	637.1	781.2	862.4	911.5	981.2	1,219.6
50-59 Science, research, engineering and technology professionals	21	231	809.7	1.7	868.5	0.7	504.3	612.3	650.0	684.4	747.2	886.3	971.5	1,031.7	1,086.1	1,282.8
50-59 Health professionals	22	350	600.9	-0.2	717.7	1.3	235.5	358.2	397.5	439.1	526.7	670.3	766.3	792.9	859.8	1,188.9
50-59 Teaching and educational professionals	23	313	718.6	1.0	722.4	2.1	246.2	422.1	477.9	540.6	661.5	789.4	861.1	902.5	943.5	1,114.9
50-59 Business, media and public service professionals	24	247	709.1	2.8	796.2	3.5	357.7	479.0	525.8	574.9	642.8	785.1	888.7	958.2	1,028.9	1,260.6
50-59 Associate professional and technical occupations	3	698	588.8	1.4	658.8	-0.6	294.6	393.2	431.5	465.0	530.0	665.9	741.5	788.3	856.5	1,068.3
50-59 Science, engineering and technology associate professionals	31	135	573.7	1.5	597.2	0.4	316.5	388.6	426.1	459.6	520.5	623.2	687.4	717.0	759.9	896.8
50-59 Health and social care associate professionals	32	92	447.8	1.2	445.2	0.1	175.8	262.3	317.0	349.8	396.4	487.3	535.2	554.3	587.5	672.5
50-59 Protective service occupations	33	61	722.9	0.6	725.3	1.2	425.4	536.8	565.3	589.3	675.4	765.1	825.9	855.7	881.8	x
50-59 Culture, media and sports occupations	34	26	431.2	3.9	483.4	-3.7	x	x	x	x	368.6	505.3	595.5	669.8	x	x
50-59 Business and public service associate professionals	35	384	638.1	1.4	732.8	-0.7	340.9	430.3	469.0	493.6	567.6	714.8	806.5	864.5	947.1	1,244.9
50-59 Administrative and secretarial occupations	4	766	351.2	1.8	373.1	0.6	150.0	199.9	225.7	253.0	309.5	388.1	437.4	469.0	505.5	619.9
50-59 Administrative occupations	41	578	369.3	1.9	390.5	0.7	155.0	217.1	248.3	280.9	329.8	404.2	454.2	486.7	524.4	637.4
50-59 Secretarial and related occupations	42	188	291.6	-1.4	319.4	0.0	126.5	164.6	188.0	203.1	241.9	334.2	380.9	406.8	434.3	545.1
50-59 Skilled trades occupations	5	438	505.4	1.1	526.4	0.0	252.3	340.4	375.0	404.2	454.2	555.3	611.6	649.9	694.3	812.4
50-59 Skilled agricultural and related trades	51	24	351.7	1.0	363.9	-1.6	203.0	287.4	300.0	313.0	331.8	374.9	402.6	417.8	430.5	x
50-59 Skilled metal, electrical and electronic trades	52	249	577.0	0.4	613.2	0.3	388.3	447.3	474.8	498.0	534.6	623.8	685.3	716.8	749.8	858.9
50-59 Skilled construction and building trades	53	64	516.9	1.8	550.6	-0.4	358.8	419.8	434.9	448.4	481.2	556.1	600.9	632.7	683.8	x
50-59 Textiles, printing and other skilled trades	54	102	316.7	3.0	337.1	-1.0	138.1	184.6	214.1	243.3	281.2	352.1	395.2	418.4	445.4	526.1
50-59 Caring, leisure and other service occupations	6	537	278.7	3.3	296.9	2.9	114.1	168.5	189.0	207.6	241.9	317.9	358.2	380.0	406.6	482.3
50-59 Caring personal service occupations	61	452	273.1	2.2	284.7	1.1	110.6	168.4	186.8	204.2	238.6	309.2	346.0	370.8	391.8	462.4
50-59 Leisure, travel and related personal service occupations	62	85	323.5	12.0	361.3	10.8	122.6	170.0	202.4	223.7	271.5	374.3	423.8	455.8	500.3	628.5
50-59 Sales and customer service occupations	7	325	230.4	0.2	269.9	0.6	104.9	136.0	151.2	164.3	197.9	271.0	318.0	342.4	369.8	470.8
50-59 Sales occupations	71	246	206.2	0.8	233.6	-0.6	100.9	127.2	138.1	151.4	176.5	238.1	275.5	294.5	320.8	388.8
50-59 Customer service occupations	72	79	351.6	7.6	383.5	7.3	153.2	211.1	237.5	265.7	313.0	383.4	438.5	469.2	508.1	615.6
50-59 Process, plant and machine operatives	8	379	452.5	3.6	481.5	3.1	245.2	308.4	333.9	359.0	402.7	504.9	563.9	595.2	632.4	750.4
50-59 Process, plant and machine operatives	81	163	419.6	0.7	456.9	0.3	243.9	293.0	311.8	331.5	375.2	474.0	529.5	571.6	623.0	728.7
50-59 Transport and mobile machine drivers and operatives	82	216	477.8	6.7	500.0	4.8	250.3	328.2	353.1	380.2	429.5	527.1	582.0	608.9	642.6	772.5
50-59 Elementary occupations	9	560	257.6	-0.9	274.2	0.8	68.3	106.2	127.7	148.0	198.4	303.1	351.4	378.6	420.0	505.3
50-59 Elementary trades and related occupations	91	68	351.2	-1.6	372.9	0.7	180.5	266.5	280.9	298.8	326.8	380.3	425.6	445.7	474.0	567.5
50-59 Elementary administration and service occupations	92	492	233.0	-3.3	260.5	0.8	65.0	99.1	115.5	134.8	179.1	281.8	334.4	365.6	403.8	497.0
60+ ALL OCCUPATIONS		1,976	338.9	2.0	425.9	1.9	87.5	144.9	172.5	204.0	270.6	409.1	492.7	549.6	614.6	829.0
60+ Managers, directors and senior officials	1	212	596.2	0.4	786.2	2.9	176.5	276.7	324.2	373.4	479.1	722.7	898.2	1,007.4	1,149.9	1,530.6
60+ Corporate managers and directors	11	176	647.7	2.4	832.1	3.2	179.4	276.0	334.2	388.3	519.7	766.7	958.2	1,083.0	1,185.4	1,609.9
60+ Other managers and proprietors	12	36	459.2	-5.8	559.1	-1.1	155.6	283.5	301.2	324.0	395.2	534.5	608.4	684.1	732.1	x
60+ Professional occupations	2	330	555.2	2.8	624.4	0.9	146.0	258.3	310.8	357.2	453.0	661.0	764.0	821.0	888.3	1,133.9
60+ Science, research, engineering and technology professionals	21	62	757.0	1.5	774.2	2.6	347.2	491.8	549.2	579.6	667.2	824.0	917.9	999.5	1,043.0	x
60+ Health professionals	22	83	455.5	-0.7	610.2	0.9	185.5	252.2	285.8	323.6	392.4	538.5	622.3	673.6	785.1	x
60+ Teaching and educational professionals	23	104	461.0	2.4	549.4	0.6	90.5	159.1	217.9	264.7	354.7	611.9	717.5	781.8	870.8	1,082.7
60+ Business, media and public service professionals	24	82	583.9	1.6	620.2	-1.7	153.4	278.4	334.4	388.8	485.6	667.5	749.9	811.8	872.3	1,125.0
60+ Associate professional and technical occupations	3	182	483.6	4.1	524.1	2.7	169.7	266.3	325.1	360.7	426.7	545.5	613.3	660.5	708.3	899.3
60+ Science, engineering and technology associate professionals	31	38	519.8	5.2	545.3	3.3	285.6	359.9	383.4	405.2	463.4	550.8	617.4	668.1	707.6	x
60+ Health and social care associate professionals	32	23	348.8	2.6	365.7	10.6	x	169.4	208.7	228.8	283.8	418.1	491.9	506.1	541.7	x
60+ Protective service occupations	33	9	526.5	12.5	576.6	20.0	x	371.9	415.2	455.6	479.0	570.0	595.3	x	x	x
60+ Culture, media and sports occupations	34	10	x		315.7	3.1	x	x	x	x	x	x	x	x	x	x
60+ Business and public service associate professionals	35	103	504.6	2.0	566.8	-0.3	183.4	284.3	339.8	383.4	451.3	576.8	666.0	706.4	785.7	996.8
60+ Administrative and secretarial occupations	4	315	259.1	-1.0	291.9	-0.4	72.8	125.2	148.1	166.7	210.2	315.7	370.4	400.6	433.6	538.8
60+ Administrative occupations	41	228	278.8	-0.8	300.6	-0.6	66.6	127.4	150.8	172.2	221.6	338.7	382.3	413.5	447.9	551.8

4.15a Weekly pay - Gross (£) - For all employee jobs[a]: United Kingdom, 2015

Description	Code	Number of jobs[b] (thousand)	Median	Annual % change	Mean	Annual % change	10	20	25	30	40	60	70	75	80	90
60+ Secretarial and related occupations	42	88	227.3	-2.1	269.3	-0.2	80.0	122.2	140.4	156.5	193.2	266.7	321.3	354.9	392.8	500.1
60+ Skilled trades occupations	5	164	446.7	-1.3	465.2	0.0	189.4	287.5	319.4	347.9	400.6	504.3	562.7	590.5	626.4	736.3
60+ Skilled agricultural and related trades	51	16	307.4	4.2	295.6	0.8	x	x	x	215.2	269.9	330.4	366.5	377.6	x	x
60+ Skilled metal, electrical and electronic trades	52	86	540.6	3.3	553.2	1.7	305.9	383.0	410.6	435.6	492.6	579.9	631.9	656.8	698.2	804.8
60+ Skilled construction and building trades	53	25	470.3	-0.7	496.3	-2.2	252.9	393.5	408.7	424.1	440.0	514.8	550.0	584.1	610.2	x
60+ Textiles, printing and other skilled trades	54	38	313.0	5.1	312.5	4.0	109.2	153.1	188.4	207.9	265.0	346.9	383.2	410.1	431.5	x
60+ Caring, leisure and other service occupations	6	189	234.6	9.2	245.8	5.4	64.9	108.5	131.5	150.7	190.3	273.1	315.0	340.2	367.8	434.2
60+ Caring personal service occupations	61	147	234.0	8.5	244.0	4.7	64.6	112.2	135.2	153.8	193.5	269.0	312.4	336.0	364.7	426.4
60+ Leisure, travel and related personal service occupations	62	41	243.8	18.2	252.3	7.8	64.9	99.4	120.4	139.3	180.8	291.3	324.0	351.9	379.4	x
60+ Sales and customer service occupations	7	139	170.8	9.1	204.1	5.7	74.4	97.5	107.7	117.8	141.8	199.6	241.3	266.5	292.6	382.4
60+ Sales occupations	71	117	159.2	7.7	188.6	4.9	71.4	94.6	104.0	113.5	134.0	182.6	217.6	243.0	266.5	343.0
60+ Customer service occupations	72	22	269.9	18.2	287.7	13.1	82.1	131.0	159.3	184.9	227.8	305.7	362.4	389.1	405.8	x
60+ Process, plant and machine operatives	8	181	370.7	4.3	394.2	5.2	122.0	179.7	215.9	254.3	308.5	425.7	479.0	504.8	548.9	662.1
60+ Process, plant and machine operatives	81	64	365.6	1.0	391.7	-0.2	159.2	233.8	260.7	275.5	313.3	409.6	461.4	485.7	534.2	664.9
60+ Transport and mobile machine drivers and operatives	82	117	372.1	5.3	395.5	8.2	107.9	157.5	184.5	226.9	300.8	430.4	487.5	515.5	555.3	658.5
60+ Elementary occupations	9	264	175.0	-1.2	223.2	0.2	50.0	73.6	85.0	100.8	131.9	243.8	298.0	330.1	364.8	451.2
60+ Elementary trades and related occupations	91	29	323.6	-0.1	331.6	-2.3	125.7	187.4	234.8	265.7	291.8	360.4	396.9	414.8	435.3	x
60+ Elementary administration and service occupations	92	235	155.1	-1.5	209.8	0.8	48.1	69.8	80.3	91.6	120.0	210.6	273.8	307.2	345.6	438.3
Not Classified		:														

a Employees on adult rates whose pay for the survey pay-period was not affected by absence.

b Figures for Number of Jobs are for indicative purposes only and should not be considered an accurate estimate of employee job counts.

KEY - The colour coding indicates the quality of each estimate; jobs, median, mean and percentiles but not the annual percentage change.

The quality of an estimate is measured by its coefficient of variation (CV), which is the ratio of the standard error of an estimate to the estimate.

Source: Annual Survey of Hours and Earnings, Office for National Statistics.

Key	Statistical robustness
CV <= 5%	Estimates are considered precise
CV > 5% and <= 10%	Estimates are considered reasonably precise
CV > 10% and <= 20%	Estimates are considered acceptable
x = CV > 20%	Estimates are considered unreliable for practical purposes
.. = disclosive	
: = not applicable	
- = nil or negligible	

4.15b Hourly pay - Gross (£) - For all employee jobs[a]: United Kingdom, 2015

Description	Code	Number of jobs[b] (thousand)	Median	Annual % change	Mean	Annual % change	Percentiles									
							10	20	25	30	40	60	70	75	80	90
All employees		25,997	11.78	1.4	15.26	0.9	6.88	7.81	8.33	8.92	10.17	13.80	16.32	17.88	19.73	25.63
18-21		1,306	7.10	2.6	7.91	3.0	5.34	6.49	6.50	6.52	6.80	7.50	8.06	8.45	8.87	10.26
22-29		4,481	10.09	1.9	11.80	1.2	6.73	7.41	7.78	8.17	9.05	11.47	13.02	13.97	15.00	18.22
30-39		5,950	13.36	0.5	15.99	0.2	7.26	8.54	9.20	9.95	11.51	15.38	17.86	19.21	21.01	26.47
40-49		6,555	13.55	2.0	17.28	0.9	7.31	8.57	9.23	9.97	11.53	15.98	18.86	20.56	22.49	29.52
50-59		5,490	12.75	1.9	16.62	1.3	7.24	8.38	9.00	9.65	11.03	14.88	17.81	19.41	21.36	28.17
60+		1,976	10.92	1.6	14.71	1.4	6.98	7.73	8.14	8.63	9.72	12.50	14.81	16.46	18.40	25.12
18-21 ALL OCCUPATIONS		1,306	7.10	2.6	7.91	3.0	5.34	6.49	6.50	6.52	6.80	7.50	8.06	8.45	8.87	10.26
18-21 Managers, directors and senior officials	1	24	8.59	7.3	8.85	-3.4	x	x	7.13	7.63	8.16	8.67	9.21	x	10.03	x
18-21 Corporate managers and directors	11	17	7.92	-1.0	8.52	-7.2	x	x	x	x	7.63	x	x	x	x	x
18-21 Other managers and proprietors	12	x	9.16	8.1	9.60	5.5	x	x	x	x	x	x	x	x	x	x
18-21 Professional occupations	2	35	9.36	-9.4	10.45	-4.1	7.01	7.62	7.77	8.03	8.58	10.35	11.62	12.01	12.41	15.40
18-21 Science, research, engineering and technology professionals	21	13	8.58	-13.6	10.41	-6.4	x	x	7.78	8.01	8.49	9.40	x	x	x	x
18-21 Health professionals	22	11	10.51	-4.0	10.24	0.7	x	7.40	7.50	7.76	8.52	11.09	11.91	x	x	x
18-21 Teaching and educational professionals	23	x	11.14	-18.5	9.90	-29.1	x	x	x	x	x	x	x	x	x	x
18-21 Business, media and public service professionals	24	x	9.28	10.4	10.88	7.1	x	x	x	x	9.01	x	x	x	x	x
18-21 Associate professional and technical occupations	3	99	9.11	3.7	10.00	3.2	6.87	7.36	7.68	8.04	8.56	9.70	10.51	10.94	11.54	13.95
18-21 Science, engineering and technology associate professionals	31	26	8.75	-0.1	9.25	-3.0	6.74	7.12	7.29	7.62	8.32	9.35	10.03	10.49	10.83	x
18-21 Health and social care associate professionals	32	x	9.31	7.4	9.71	13.5	x	x	x	x	8.54	9.40	x	x	x	x
18-21 Protective service occupations	33	x	11.68	12.9	12.31	20.1	x	x	x	x	x	12.74	x	x	x	x
18-21 Culture, media and sports occupations	34	17	9.41	-3.0	11.78	-3.3	x	7.35	7.69	7.96	8.64	10.19	x	x	x	x
18-21 Business and public service associate professionals	35	47	8.88	4.1	9.86	6.2	6.77	7.36	7.63	7.97	8.40	9.55	10.25	10.82	11.41	x
18-21 Administrative and secretarial occupations	4	130	7.84	2.0	8.31	2.2	6.00	6.58	6.79	7.00	7.47	8.42	9.05	9.37	9.82	11.25
18-21 Administrative occupations	41	109	7.94	1.2	8.38	2.4	5.98	6.63	6.84	7.02	7.51	8.57	9.20	9.47	9.94	11.57
18-21 Secretarial and related occupations	42	21	7.47	4.4	7.91	0.8	6.11	6.50	6.60	6.75	7.00	7.73	8.27	8.53	8.96	x
18-21 Skilled trades occupations	5	87	7.65	5.1	8.29	2.8	5.41	x	6.50	6.71	7.03	8.23	9.00	9.49	9.99	11.14
18-21 Skilled agricultural and related trades	51	6	7.74	9.0	7.85	5.7	x	x	x	7.14	7.49	7.92	x	x	x	x
18-21 Skilled metal, electrical and electronic trades	52	40	8.45	8.3	8.91	4.6	5.73	6.52	6.78	7.20	7.68	9.03	9.97	10.20	10.71	x
18-21 Skilled construction and building trades	53	13	8.00	4.4	8.57	0.3	x	5.55	6.03	6.49	7.00	9.14	10.04	10.24	x	x
18-21 Textiles, printing and other skilled trades	54	28	6.92	1.6	7.23	2.0	5.29	6.30	x	6.50	6.70	7.07	7.75	8.02	8.21	x
18-21 Caring, leisure and other service occupations	6	190	7.15	2.2	7.44	3.7	5.80	x	6.50	6.62	6.87	7.50	7.96	8.24	8.53	9.40
18-21 Caring personal service occupations	61	145	7.24	2.7	7.46	3.5	6.10	6.50	6.59	6.68	6.95	7.55	8.02	8.30	8.59	9.47
18-21 Leisure, travel and related personal service occupations	62	45	6.96	5.3	7.34	4.4	5.14	6.00	6.33	6.50	6.60	7.25	7.70	8.00	8.25	x
18-21 Sales and customer service occupations	7	312	6.96	2.3	7.38	2.9	5.25	6.29	6.50	6.50	6.70	7.17	7.53	7.75	8.05	9.16
18-21 Sales occupations	71	271	6.89	2.1	7.24	1.6	5.18	6.05	6.50	6.50	6.63	7.11	7.44	7.66	7.92	8.95
18-21 Customer service occupations	72	40	7.33	5.2	8.08	9.7	6.39	6.63	6.73	6.91	7.08	7.64	8.08	8.47	8.99	x
18-21 Process, plant and machine operatives	8	39	7.50	4.4	8.05	0.0	6.08	6.50	6.65	6.77	7.13	7.96	8.50	8.86	9.06	10.41
18-21 Process, plant and machine operatives	81	31	7.56	5.3	8.04	-1.2	6.11	6.50	6.67	6.84	7.18	7.97	8.60	8.89	9.18	10.49
18-21 Transport and mobile machine drivers and operatives	82	8	7.40	3.8	8.06	5.6	6.00	x	x	6.56	6.77	7.84	8.18	8.68	x	x
18-21 Elementary occupations	9	392	6.61	3.3	7.11	4.0	5.15	5.76	6.13	x	6.50	6.88	7.19	7.37	7.69	8.69
18-21 Elementary trades and related occupations	91	31	7.08	1.2	7.79	6.1	6.00	x	6.50	6.57	6.90	7.50	8.00	8.19	8.79	x
18-21 Elementary administration and service occupations	92	361	6.57	3.0	7.02	3.6	5.15	5.70	6.00	6.48	6.50	6.82	7.09	7.30	7.56	8.50
22-29 ALL OCCUPATIONS		4,481	10.09	1.9	11.80	1.2	6.73	7.41	7.78	8.17	9.05	11.47	13.02	13.97	15.00	18.22
22-29 Managers, directors and senior officials	1	213	12.04	-1.6	14.45	-4.1	7.91	8.83	9.19	9.72	10.85	13.29	15.51	16.84	18.36	26.00
22-29 Corporate managers and directors	11	160	12.80	-1.8	15.55	-3.6	8.11	9.18	9.73	10.26	11.55	14.59	16.91	18.21	20.37	28.16
22-29 Other managers and proprietors	12	54	10.22	1.2	11.26	-2.6	7.31	8.00	8.34	8.63	9.20	11.07	12.41	12.81	13.23	x
22-29 Professional occupations	2	889	15.32	0.2	16.24	0.9	10.43	12.16	12.81	13.31	14.31	16.49	17.98	19.06	20.16	23.28
22-29 Science, research, engineering and technology professionals	21	203	14.65	-0.3	15.57	0.5	9.88	11.57	12.14	12.65	13.80	15.84	17.25	18.05	19.19	22.11
22-29 Health professionals	22	236	14.43	-1.3	15.52	-0.3	11.09	12.18	12.68	13.04	13.79	15.37	16.49	17.29	18.84	21.63
22-29 Teaching and educational professionals	23	220	16.57	0.7	16.80	1.1	11.78	13.36	14.03	14.67	15.60	17.70	19.10	19.96	20.65	23.52

4.15b Hourly pay - Gross (£) - For all employee jobs[a]: United Kingdom, 2015

Description	Code	Number of jobs[b] (thousand)	Median	Annual % change	Mean	Annual % change	Percentiles									
							10	20	25	30	40	60	70	75	80	90
22-29 Business, media and public service professionals	24	229	15.54	0.5	17.15	2.5	9.75	11.50	12.33	13.05	14.36	17.05	18.77	19.70	21.20	26.64
22-29 Associate professional and technical occupations	3	675	12.82	1.8	13.86	-0.3	8.67	9.87	10.34	10.91	11.88	13.94	15.00	15.73	16.62	19.70
22-29 Science, engineering and technology associate professionals	31	130	11.97	3.0	12.48	1.2	8.30	9.30	9.79	10.22	11.15	12.93	13.94	14.40	15.21	17.20
22-29 Health and social care associate professionals	32	46	11.42	1.4	12.12	1.5	8.55	9.49	9.87	10.16	10.80	12.16	13.07	13.49	14.36	x
22-29 Protective service occupations	33	44	14.12	-2.0	14.15	-0.3	10.97	11.89	12.48	12.83	13.65	14.67	15.19	15.61	16.17	x
22-29 Culture, media and sports occupations	34	60	11.46	-2.8	13.62		7.68	9.14	9.50	9.97	10.73	12.46	13.43	14.31	15.07	x
22-29 Business and public service associate professionals	35	395	13.35	2.1	14.51	1.9	8.76	10.10	10.65	11.23	12.28	14.51	15.84	16.69	17.89	21.70
22-29 Administrative and secretarial occupations	4	537	9.71	2.2	10.58	2.5	7.16	7.84	8.15	8.48	9.08	10.38	11.33	11.86	12.57	14.60
22-29 Administrative occupations	41	450	9.92	2.9	10.77	2.8	7.29	8.02	8.35	8.67	9.28	10.62	11.51	12.05	12.74	14.91
22-29 Secretarial and related occupations	42	87	8.51	0.1	9.50	0.1	6.72	7.20	7.39	7.58	8.05	9.19	9.96	10.37	11.03	13.26
22-29 Skilled trades occupations	5	388	10.04	0.4	11.08	1.8	7.00	7.84	8.13	8.50	9.29	11.07	12.34	12.95	13.69	15.77
22-29 Skilled agricultural and related trades	51	21	8.57	7.1	9.03	6.2	6.87	7.50	7.67	7.78	7.97	9.02	9.80	10.17	10.55	x
22-29 Skilled metal, electrical and electronic trades	52	193	11.98	1.3	12.53	0.9	8.00	9.01	9.54	10.00	10.88	12.97	13.93	14.61	15.34	17.79
22-29 Skilled construction and building trades	53	61	11.11	1.0	11.61	0.2	7.94	9.00	9.41	9.80	10.40	11.83	12.50	13.05	13.79	x
22-29 Textiles, printing and other skilled trades	54	113	8.01	4.1	8.48	2.6	6.50	7.00	7.07	7.40	7.69	8.38	8.97	9.34	9.62	10.56
22-29 Caring, leisure and other service occupations	6	475	8.02	2.0	8.66	2.9	6.54	6.88	7.03	7.23	7.61	8.52	9.22	9.66	10.17	11.66
22-29 Caring personal service occupations	61	388	8.05	2.3	8.59	2.9	6.58	6.94	7.09	7.26	7.64	8.55	9.23	9.62	10.14	11.58
22-29 Leisure, travel and related personal service occupations	62	87	7.91	1.5	8.95	2.9	6.50	6.69	6.92	7.04	7.48	8.34	9.09	9.85	10.37	12.28
22-29 Sales and customer service occupations	7	517	7.80	3.3	8.79	3.8	6.50	6.71	6.90	7.06	7.36	8.38	9.00	9.45	9.99	11.68
22-29 Sales occupations	71	387	7.50	2.7	8.43	3.4	6.50	6.63	6.74	6.90	7.15	7.96	8.53	8.90	9.35	10.79
22-29 Customer service occupations	72	130	8.97	5.7	9.69	5.4	6.83	7.35	7.61	7.90	8.48	9.60	10.40	10.80	11.45	12.93
22-29 Process, plant and machine operatives	8	199	9.06	3.1	9.95	2.6	6.68	7.22	7.50	7.77	8.42	9.75	10.74	11.32	11.93	13.96
22-29 Process, plant and machine operatives	81	127	9.11	3.6	10.11	3.7	6.74	7.28	7.50	7.95	8.52	9.88	11.04	11.63	12.38	14.78
22-29 Transport and mobile machine drivers and operatives	82	71	8.89	1.5	9.69	1.0	6.62	7.18	7.35	7.60	8.14	9.51	10.34	10.90	11.29	x
22-29 Elementary occupations	9	588	7.30	2.9	8.15	2.5	x	6.50	6.60	6.71	7.00	7.76	8.28	8.63	9.05	10.40
22-29 Elementary trades and related occupations	91	85	7.81	0.1	8.46	0.4	6.50	6.61	6.81	7.00	7.45	8.31	8.86	9.16	9.63	10.83
22-29 Elementary administration and service occupations	92	503	7.25	3.6	8.09	3.0	x	6.50	6.56	6.68	6.98	7.67	8.15	8.50	8.95	10.29
30-39 ALL OCCUPATIONS		5,950	13.36	0.5	15.99	0.2	7.26	8.54	9.20	9.95	11.51	15.38	17.86	19.21	21.01	26.47
30-39 Managers, directors and senior officials	1	589	18.89	-1.5	23.21	-1.0	9.23	11.50	12.60	13.78	16.36	22.22	26.51	29.20	33.31	43.14
30-39 Corporate managers and directors	11	493	20.92	0.1	24.90	-1.0	9.59	12.41	13.70	14.95	17.74	24.28	28.79	32.19	35.49	44.66
30-39 Other managers and proprietors	12	96	13.24	1.0	14.75	-1.1	8.21	9.51	10.00	10.42	11.72	14.86	16.72	17.59	18.70	22.16
30-39 Professional occupations	2	1,548	19.79	0.5	21.19	-0.2	12.99	15.07	15.94	16.79	18.25	21.48	23.53	24.68	26.17	31.00
30-39 Science, research, engineering and technology professionals	21	381	19.92	0.5	21.06	-0.4	12.94	15.19	16.09	16.86	18.38	21.56	23.51	24.60	25.96	29.98
30-39 Health professionals	22	372	17.77	-0.6	19.75	-2.5	12.51	14.34	14.77	15.36	16.56	18.98	20.75	21.82	23.60	29.88
30-39 Teaching and educational professionals	23	386	21.94	0.5	21.99	0.4	14.04	17.25	18.27	19.10	20.56	23.20	24.97	25.94	27.19	30.50
30-39 Business, media and public service professionals	24	409	19.55	2.1	21.90	1.5	12.74	14.92	15.81	16.62	18.00	21.48	23.77	25.07	26.85	33.22
30-39 Associate professional and technical occupations	3	1,019	15.62	0.8	17.76	1.3	10.22	11.76	12.48	13.14	14.36	17.01	18.67	19.66	21.04	26.07
30-39 Science, engineering and technology associate professionals	31	170	14.11	-0.6	15.09	-1.6	9.61	10.93	11.54	11.99	13.01	15.27	16.57	17.35	18.24	20.78
30-39 Health and social care associate professionals	32	91	12.68	-0.6	13.53	-0.1	9.21	10.15	10.58	11.10	11.92	13.66	14.63	15.30	16.02	18.26
30-39 Protective service occupations	33	132	16.74	1.4	16.82	0.5	13.09	14.08	14.70	15.19	15.98	17.85	18.48	18.81	19.35	20.99
30-39 Culture, media and sports occupations	34	60	13.98	0.1	18.32	18.7	9.48	10.95	11.27	11.76	12.69	15.01	16.05	16.92	17.67	x
30-39 Business and public service associate professionals	35	566	16.72	1.3	19.38	0.8	10.54	12.30	12.95	13.69	15.14	18.40	20.82	22.17	23.92	30.93
30-39 Administrative and secretarial occupations	4	622	10.80	1.4	12.17	1.3	7.61	8.55	8.95	9.28	9.97	11.76	12.95	13.73	14.69	17.32
30-39 Administrative occupations	41	516	10.99	2.1	12.33	1.7	7.76	8.73	9.10	9.48	10.06	11.98	13.19	14.03	14.90	17.51
30-39 Secretarial and related occupations	42	106	9.92	0.2	11.34	-0.7	7.10	7.82	8.15	8.49	9.19	10.86	11.77	12.53	13.23	16.29

4.15b Hourly pay - Gross (£) - For all employee jobs[a]: United Kingdom, 2015

Description	Code	Number of jobs[b] (thousand)	Median	Annual % change	Mean	Annual % change	Percentiles 10	20	25	30	40	60	70	75	80	90
30-39 Skilled trades occupations	5	452	11.51	2.9	12.35	1.8	7.44	8.46	9.00	9.50	10.50	12.53	13.75	14.49	15.27	17.58
30-39 Skilled agricultural and related trades	51	19	9.34	2.8	9.89	5.2	7.45	8.22	8.32	8.63	9.01	9.74	10.29	11.32	11.55	x
30-39 Skilled metal, electrical and electronic trades	52	229	13.36	3.4	13.95	1.4	9.00	10.31	10.89	11.41	12.40	14.34	15.45	16.15	16.85	19.48
30-39 Skilled construction and building trades	53	73	12.01	3.7	12.33	2.2	8.52	9.50	10.00	10.25	11.08	12.72	13.44	14.03	14.48	x
30-39 Textiles, printing and other skilled trades	54	131	8.57	-1.0	9.67	0.9	6.60	7.16	7.50	7.61	8.00	9.31	10.05	10.62	11.27	13.06
30-39 Caring, leisure and other service occupations	6	492	8.59	1.7	9.41	1.2	6.76	7.19	7.46	7.66	8.12	9.21	9.99	10.42	11.00	12.77
30-39 Caring personal service occupations	61	415	8.57	2.0	9.27	1.8	6.80	7.20	7.48	7.66	8.10	9.19	9.95	10.33	10.88	12.49
30-39 Leisure, travel and related personal service occupations	62	78	8.66	-1.6	10.11	-1.7	6.56	7.04	7.36	7.63	8.23	9.42	10.46	11.00	11.82	14.75
30-39 Sales and customer service occupations	7	365	8.39	2.4	9.82	1.8	6.51	6.90	7.07	7.25	7.74	9.13	10.20	10.77	11.52	13.87
30-39 Sales occupations	71	249	7.70	1.6	9.02	0.8	6.50	6.69	6.83	7.00	7.30	8.22	9.06	9.57	10.24	12.21
30-39 Customer service occupations	72	117	10.22	2.9	11.34	4.1	7.10	8.06	8.43	8.76	9.43	11.26	12.27	13.03	13.76	15.80
30-39 Process, plant and machine operatives	8	302	9.92	0.2	10.83	-0.5	6.94	7.66	8.03	8.42	9.09	10.75	11.67	12.38	13.14	15.37
30-39 Process, plant and machine operatives	81	162	9.59	-2.1	10.69	-2.2	6.80	7.49	7.83	8.11	8.79	10.60	11.57	12.35	13.32	15.68
30-39 Transport and mobile machine drivers and operatives	82	139	10.07	0.7	10.98	1.5	7.09	8.00	8.38	8.72	9.45	10.86	11.76	12.39	12.91	15.00
30-39 Elementary occupations	9	561	7.85	3.5	8.95	1.9	6.50	6.64	6.80	7.00	7.33	8.38	9.12	9.56	10.19	12.00
30-39 Elementary trades and related occupations	91	74	8.37	4.3	9.02	2.0	6.50	6.94	7.15	7.31	7.86	8.98	9.53	10.06	10.62	12.14
30-39 Elementary administration and service occupations	92	487	7.77	3.3	8.94	1.9	6.50	6.60	6.75	6.96	7.27	8.28	9.03	9.51	10.09	11.98
40-49 ALL OCCUPATIONS		6,555	13.55	2.0	17.28	0.9	7.31	8.57	9.23	9.97	11.53	15.98	18.86	20.56	22.49	29.52
40-49 Managers, directors and senior officials	1	822	21.92	2.2	27.11	-1.2	10.00	13.26	14.62	16.07	18.92	25.64	30.87	33.54	37.06	49.24
40-49 Corporate managers and directors	11	713	23.26	0.4	28.47	-1.7	10.39	14.11	15.63	16.94	20.05	27.40	32.45	35.17	39.00	50.91
40-49 Other managers and proprietors	12	109	15.32	-1.5	18.30	-1.0	8.81	10.37	11.13	11.97	13.61	17.70	20.46	21.87	23.75	x
40-49 Professional occupations	2	1,500	21.04	1.4	23.31	0.7	13.44	15.88	16.82	17.79	19.22	22.93	25.16	26.78	28.81	34.95
40-49 Science, research, engineering and technology professionals	21	338	22.12	1.6	23.69	1.2	14.21	16.84	17.81	18.68	20.44	24.02	26.25	27.68	29.57	34.12
40-49 Health professionals	22	430	18.40	0.6	22.01	-0.5	13.07	14.60	15.35	16.08	17.49	20.03	21.54	22.85	24.58	36.03
40-49 Teaching and educational professionals	23	396	23.32	2.5	23.94	1.4	14.44	18.01	18.98	19.91	21.85	24.71	26.81	28.15	29.59	33.96
40-49 Business, media and public service professionals	24	337	20.83	2.6	23.87	1.1	12.49	15.37	16.41	17.35	18.98	22.91	25.55	27.30	29.40	36.05
40-49 Associate professional and technical occupations	3	973	16.51	0.6	19.03	-0.5	10.28	12.10	12.89	13.58	15.04	18.20	19.95	21.05	22.59	28.45
40-49 Science, engineering and technology associate professionals	31	154	14.94	1.4	16.00	0.8	9.48	11.01	11.91	12.61	13.75	16.21	17.63	18.32	19.37	22.77
40-49 Health and social care associate professionals	32	94	12.75	-1.4	14.01	-0.5	9.33	10.33	10.84	11.22	11.91	13.69	14.84	15.78	17.00	18.87
40-49 Protective service occupations	33	139	18.46	0.8	18.43	0.4	13.60	14.95	15.73	16.29	17.84	19.26	20.06	20.59	21.19	22.57
40-49 Culture, media and sports occupations	34	48	15.00	0.7	16.45	-1.7	9.20	10.94	11.67	12.14	13.33	16.45	18.56	19.92	21.07	x
40-49 Business and public service associate professionals	35	539	17.45	1.4	21.07	-1.2	10.61	12.59	13.29	14.14	15.74	19.35	22.00	24.02	26.28	35.12
40-49 Administrative and secretarial occupations	4	760	10.83	1.3	12.46	1.5	7.76	8.61	9.01	9.33	10.00	11.77	13.08	13.88	14.99	18.18
40-49 Administrative occupations	41	602	11.06	1.6	12.68	1.9	7.92	8.82	9.18	9.58	10.21	12.06	13.34	14.23	15.21	18.48
40-49 Secretarial and related occupations	42	159	9.95	0.8	11.56	-0.2	7.35	8.03	8.36	8.69	9.21	10.91	11.69	12.50	13.50	17.07
40-49 Skilled trades occupations	5	488	12.00	0.3	13.22	1.2	7.55	8.89	9.46	10.00	11.00	13.10	14.31	15.07	16.01	19.15
40-49 Skilled agricultural and related trades	51	27	9.78	-0.4	10.57	-0.7	7.00	8.00	8.59	8.80	9.27	10.32	10.75	11.15	11.71	x
40-49 Skilled metal, electrical and electronic trades	52	259	13.60	1.3	14.69	1.4	9.42	10.76	11.25	11.75	12.76	14.67	15.98	16.79	17.85	20.94
40-49 Skilled construction and building trades	53	81	12.74	3.0	13.53	2.0	8.83	10.02	10.49	11.00	11.84	13.50	14.22	14.76	15.68	x
40-49 Textiles, printing and other skilled trades	54	122	8.67	1.8	9.86	0.5	6.63	7.04	7.43	7.60	8.07	9.55	10.44	10.80	11.36	13.13
40-49 Caring, leisure and other service occupations	6	637	8.79	1.7	9.65	0.1	6.83	7.32	7.58	7.79	8.25	9.38	10.11	10.57	11.18	12.89
40-49 Caring personal service occupations	61	554	8.75	1.8	9.34	0.6	6.86	7.34	7.58	7.78	8.21	9.28	10.00	10.44	11.00	12.50
40-49 Leisure, travel and related personal service occupations	62	83	9.01	0.4	11.67	0.3	6.63	7.24	7.58	7.99	8.50	10.03	11.19	12.05	13.00	x
40-49 Sales and customer service occupations	7	332	8.10	2.8	9.95	2.9	6.50	6.84	7.02	7.17	7.54	8.99	10.00	10.52	11.37	14.34
40-49 Sales occupations	71	242	7.59	2.9	9.01	3.2	6.50	6.70	6.85	7.02	7.26	8.10	8.89	9.34	9.86	11.98
40-49 Customer service occupations	72	90	10.64	6.8	12.11	4.2	6.98	7.78	8.28	8.90	9.93	11.60	12.78	13.67	14.65	17.28
40-49 Process, plant and machine operatives	8	416	10.47	2.6	11.60	2.2	7.13	8.02	8.52	8.92	9.62	11.37	12.56	13.18	14.07	16.81

4.15b Hourly pay - Gross (£) - For all employee jobs[a]: United Kingdom, 2015

Description	Code	Number of jobs[b] (thousand)	Median	Annual % change	Mean	Annual % change	Percentiles									
							10	20	25	30	40	60	70	75	80	90
40-49 Process, plant and machine operatives	81	189	10.34	1.2	11.66	0.4	6.87	7.72	8.10	8.62	9.48	11.45	12.71	13.50	14.60	17.92
40-49 Transport and mobile machine drivers and operatives	82	227	10.50	3.1	11.55	3.6	7.50	8.41	8.75	9.14	9.75	11.31	12.40	12.94	13.76	16.02
40-49 Elementary occupations	9	626	7.85	2.2	9.16	1.1	6.50	6.69	6.87	7.00	7.39	8.41	9.21	9.75	10.49	12.39
40-49 Elementary trades and related occupations	91	80	8.43	-2.8	9.38	-2.7	6.50	6.88	7.00	7.25	7.82	9.14	10.01	10.43	11.12	12.93
40-49 Elementary administration and service occupations	92	547	7.79	1.9	9.12	1.9	6.50	6.67	6.83	7.00	7.34	8.31	9.10	9.59	10.33	12.26
50-59 ALL OCCUPATIONS		5,490	12.75	1.9	16.62	1.3	7.24	8.38	9.00	9.65	11.03	14.88	17.81	19.41	21.36	28.17
50-59 Managers, directors and senior officials	1	647	21.17	1.2	26.66	-0.3	9.51	12.71	14.08	15.33	18.17	24.96	29.61	32.87	36.52	48.19
50-59 Corporate managers and directors	11	546	22.70	1.7	28.21	-0.2	9.80	13.34	14.82	16.40	19.34	26.67	31.60	35.00	38.97	50.53
50-59 Other managers and proprietors	12	101	15.79	0.2	18.16	-3.1	8.38	10.43	11.41	12.43	14.22	17.79	20.12	21.70	23.92	29.45
50-59 Professional occupations	2	1,141	20.93	1.0	23.50	1.8	13.10	15.45	16.57	17.59	19.09	22.76	25.12	26.63	28.83	35.40
50-59 Science, research, engineering and technology professionals	21	231	21.68	2.0	23.38	1.0	14.21	16.51	17.57	18.42	20.06	23.79	26.14	27.62	29.19	34.49
50-59 Health professionals	22	350	18.35	0.4	22.94	2.2	12.84	14.46	15.15	15.98	17.65	20.19	21.26	22.81	24.42	35.70
50-59 Teaching and educational professionals	23	313	23.80	0.3	24.96	0.2	14.57	18.46	19.11	19.99	22.12	25.62	27.54	29.14	30.46	35.92
50-59 Business, media and public service professionals	24	247	19.89	2.4	22.82	3.8	11.84	14.38	15.54	16.54	18.08	22.01	24.26	25.91	28.25	34.95
50-59 Associate professional and technical occupations	3	698	15.92	0.7	18.52	-0.3	10.08	11.74	12.51	13.01	14.49	17.75	19.58	20.87	22.36	28.42
50-59 Science, engineering and technology associate professionals	31	135	15.19	2.2	16.06	1.5	9.45	10.87	11.57	12.29	13.83	16.34	17.84	18.60	19.58	23.27
50-59 Health and social care associate professionals	32	92	13.00	0.2	14.01	1.4	9.18	10.26	10.78	11.28	12.17	13.92	14.76	15.67	16.43	18.71
50-59 Protective service occupations	33	61	17.99	-0.8	17.99	-0.9	11.43	13.93	14.65	15.02	16.54	19.03	20.08	20.84	21.37	x
50-59 Culture, media and sports occupations	34	26	14.63	2.3	17.91	-5.9	9.25	11.03	11.51	12.14	13.15	16.13	17.90	20.13	21.24	x
50-59 Business and public service associate professionals	35	384	17.28	1.7	20.50	-0.4	10.72	12.66	12.96	13.89	15.44	19.19	21.72	23.44	25.56	33.74
50-59 Administrative and secretarial occupations	4	766	10.53	1.1	12.09	0.6	7.72	8.60	9.00	9.25	9.95	11.40	12.51	13.29	14.25	17.25
50-59 Administrative occupations	41	578	10.88	2.5	12.36	0.8	7.86	8.87	9.14	9.52	10.12	11.73	12.93	13.66	14.64	17.65
50-59 Secretarial and related occupations	42	188	9.89	1.4	11.19	-0.2	7.42	8.06	8.36	8.60	9.22	10.47	11.37	11.97	12.83	15.33
50-59 Skilled trades occupations	5	438	12.39	1.2	13.37	0.4	7.72	8.97	9.60	10.19	11.35	13.49	14.80	15.52	16.39	19.29
50-59 Skilled agricultural and related trades	51	24	9.42	2.1	9.90	-0.1	7.10	7.67	8.00	8.26	8.83	9.92	10.46	10.86	11.58	x
50-59 Skilled metal, electrical and electronic trades	52	249	14.09	1.4	14.82	0.2	9.69	11.06	11.59	12.16	13.10	15.07	16.28	16.94	18.01	20.55
50-59 Skilled construction and building trades	53	64	12.49	-0.8	13.42	0.8	9.60	10.52	11.00	11.43	11.94	13.31	14.27	14.86	15.59	17.89
50-59 Textiles, printing and other skilled trades	54	102	8.72	2.7	9.92	-0.5	6.70	7.19	7.43	7.66	8.13	9.22	9.99	10.48	11.26	13.38
50-59 Caring, leisure and other service occupations	6	537	9.06	1.9	9.99	2.8	6.93	7.48	7.75	7.98	8.50	9.78	10.55	11.09	11.61	13.38
50-59 Caring personal service occupations	61	452	9.01	1.3	9.67	1.4	6.95	7.47	7.73	7.96	8.47	9.69	10.38	10.91	11.40	12.96
50-59 Leisure, travel and related personal service occupations	62	85	9.57	8.4	11.64	8.8	6.83	7.54	7.84	8.05	8.67	10.45	11.55	12.26	13.41	16.97
50-59 Sales and customer service occupations	7	325	7.83	2.4	9.47	2.2	6.50	6.79	6.98	7.08	7.36	8.50	9.30	9.80	10.48	12.93
50-59 Sales occupations	71	246	7.40	1.9	8.53	1.4	6.50	6.69	6.81	6.96	7.14	7.83	8.45	8.83	9.25	10.80
50-59 Customer service occupations	72	79	10.26	6.0	12.00	6.3	7.07	7.86	8.38	8.75	9.47	11.25	12.32	13.03	14.13	17.17
50-59 Process, plant and machine operatives	8	379	10.34	1.9	11.43	2.1	7.03	7.91	8.35	8.67	9.52	11.16	12.26	12.99	13.94	16.72
50-59 Process, plant and machine operatives	81	163	10.20	-0.7	11.46	0.4	6.95	7.60	8.04	8.46	9.31	11.34	12.66	13.59	14.58	17.23
50-59 Transport and mobile machine drivers and operatives	82	216	10.40	3.2	11.41	3.5	7.18	8.11	8.54	8.90	9.71	11.06	11.99	12.63	13.36	16.15
50-59 Elementary occupations	9	560	7.87	1.3	9.23	2.3	6.50	6.71	6.92	7.04	7.49	8.46	9.23	9.85	10.71	12.35
50-59 Elementary trades and related occupations	91	68	8.62	-0.1	9.51	0.8	6.50	6.94	7.17	7.53	8.01	9.30	10.11	10.75	11.29	12.94
50-59 Elementary administration and service occupations	92	492	7.84	2.1	9.17	2.6	6.50	6.69	6.88	7.00	7.41	8.31	9.10	9.69	10.52	12.24
60+ ALL OCCUPATIONS		1,976	10.92	1.6	14.71	1.4	6.98	7.73	8.14	8.63	9.72	12.50	14.81	16.46	18.40	25.12
60+ Managers, directors and senior officials	1	212	17.75	2.2	23.68	1.6	8.38	10.19	11.30	12.55	15.16	20.76	25.67	28.46	31.28	42.90
60+ Corporate managers and directors	11	176	18.96	1.4	25.05	1.0	8.42	10.78	12.00	13.45	16.38	22.44	27.15	30.00	33.08	45.59
60+ Other managers and proprietors	12	36	13.27	-4.7	16.85	1.5	7.95	9.14	9.87	10.50	12.20	15.51	17.92	19.42	20.44	x
60+ Professional occupations	2	330	20.32	0.2	22.66	-1.1	12.23	14.44	15.62	16.69	18.46	22.37	25.15	26.88	28.72	34.54
60+ Science, research, engineering and technology professionals	21	62	20.94	2.8	22.25	2.0	12.91	15.43	16.49	17.28	19.11	23.49	25.62	27.29	28.36	x
60+ Health professionals	22	83	17.82	0.8	22.58	-3.0	12.50	13.80	14.38	14.58	16.17	19.47	21.18	22.65	24.81	x

4.15b Hourly pay - Gross (£) - For all employee jobs[a]: United Kingdom, 2015

Description	Code	Number of jobs[b] (thousand)	Median	Annual % change	Mean	Annual % change	Percentiles									
							10	20	25	30	40	60	70	75	80	90
60+ Teaching and educational professionals	23	104	23.77	0.2	24.82	-2.3	13.66	17.65	18.64	19.23	21.60	25.56	28.35	29.59	31.05	36.22
60+ Business, media and public service professionals	24	82	18.87	5.5	21.05	-0.4	10.70	13.01	14.30	15.54	17.13	20.63	22.54	24.30	25.99	x
60+ Associate professional and technical occupations	3	182	14.24	1.9	16.34	-0.5	9.08	10.51	11.26	11.66	12.82	15.60	17.43	18.57	20.11	25.25
60+ Science, engineering and technology associate professionals	31	38	14.01	4.9	14.85	-0.5	9.01	10.56	11.25	11.44	12.46	15.11	15.90	17.04	17.95	x
60+ Health and social care associate professionals	32	23	12.69	4.3	13.79	5.7	8.73	9.85	10.25	10.85	11.51	13.61	14.58	15.35	16.23	x
60+ Protective service occupations	33	9	14.27	-1.3	15.84	4.6	x	11.56	12.01	12.39	13.60	14.73	x	x	x	x
60+ Culture, media and sports occupations	34	10	14.13	7.3	15.21	-2.6	x	9.65	9.97	10.80	12.51	15.14	16.55	x	x	x
60+ Business and public service associate professionals	35	103	14.80	-0.2	17.55	-1.8	9.11	10.90	11.44	12.16	13.18	16.54	19.01	20.47	22.57	28.12
60+ Administrative and secretarial occupations	4	315	10.05	0.5	11.54	0.4	7.51	8.25	8.62	9.00	9.58	10.95	11.97	12.61	13.42	16.56
60+ Administrative occupations	41	228	10.33	1.5	11.69	0.7	7.58	8.40	8.83	9.14	9.84	11.21	12.20	12.84	13.74	16.81
60+ Secretarial and related occupations	42	88	9.71	-0.5	11.10	-0.5	7.50	8.00	8.33	8.58	9.08	10.25	11.33	11.81	12.54	15.33
60+ Skilled trades occupations	5	164	11.56	0.5	12.72	1.8	7.48	8.50	9.12	9.71	10.69	12.80	13.93	14.64	15.31	18.11
60+ Skilled agricultural and related trades	51	16	9.02	10.0	9.73	3.3	6.64	7.18	7.30	7.59	8.39	9.73	10.10	10.48	x	x
60+ Skilled metal, electrical and electronic trades	52	86	13.51	3.5	14.10	2.8	8.80	10.52	10.97	11.53	12.47	14.33	15.25	16.01	16.70	19.59
60+ Skilled construction and building trades	53	25	11.74	-0.3	12.76	0.2	9.01	10.11	10.37	10.77	11.12	12.70	13.50	13.86	14.97	x
60+ Textiles, printing and other skilled trades	54	38	8.76	2.3	9.92	4.2	6.62	7.25	7.54	7.83	8.27	9.31	10.28	10.72	11.24	x
60+ Caring, leisure and other service occupations	6	189	8.89	1.5	9.61	3.0	6.91	7.43	7.66	7.86	8.38	9.39	10.08	10.64	11.19	12.79
60+ Caring personal service occupations	61	147	8.91	0.5	9.54	2.5	6.93	7.42	7.67	7.87	8.44	9.44	10.07	10.63	11.21	12.69
60+ Leisure, travel and related personal service occupations	62	41	8.66	4.8	9.86	4.7	6.86	7.43	7.57	7.84	8.22	9.21	10.16	10.63	11.07	x
60+ Sales and customer service occupations	7	139	7.45	2.3	8.74	4.7	6.50	6.71	6.83	6.95	7.19	7.85	8.53	8.98	9.51	11.28
60+ Sales occupations	71	117	7.31	2.9	8.32	4.0	6.50	6.63	6.77	6.90	7.08	7.59	8.06	8.48	8.93	10.31
60+ Customer service occupations	72	22	9.26	10.6	10.60	9.5	6.84	7.31	7.62	7.87	8.69	10.19	10.80	11.35	12.11	x
60+ Process, plant and machine operatives	8	181	9.50	4.3	10.86	5.3	6.67	7.25	7.59	7.96	8.72	10.28	11.12	11.61	12.22	14.20
60+ Process, plant and machine operatives	81	64	9.82	4.6	10.89	0.3	6.87	7.41	7.70	8.03	9.16	10.79	11.78	12.42	13.00	15.24
60+ Transport and mobile machine drivers and operatives	82	117	9.34	3.8	10.84	8.0	6.58	7.19	7.50	7.90	8.55	10.05	10.80	11.26	11.79	13.78
60+ Elementary occupations	9	264	7.68	2.3	8.91	2.7	6.50	6.66	6.80	7.00	7.28	8.05	8.74	9.23	9.82	11.50
60+ Elementary trades and related occupations	91	29	8.50	1.7	9.41	2.0	6.54	7.04	7.20	7.41	7.99	9.22	9.86	10.38	10.78	x
60+ Elementary administration and service occupations	92	235	7.60	2.2	8.82	2.9	6.50	6.63	6.76	6.96	7.23	7.94	8.58	9.03	9.63	11.29
Not Classified		:														

a Employees on adult rates whose pay for the survey pay-period was not affected by absence.

b Figures for Number of Jobs are for indicative purposes only and should not be considered an accurate estimate of employee job counts.

KEY - The colour coding indicates the quality of each estimate; jobs, median, mean and percentiles but not the annual percentage change.

The quality of an estimate is measured by its coefficient of variation (CV), which is the ratio of the standard error of an estimate to the estimate.

Source: Annual Survey of Hours and Earnings, Office for National Statistics.

Key	Statistical robustness
CV <= 5%	Estimates are considered precise
CV > 5% and <= 10%	Estimates are considered reasonably precise
CV > 10% and <= 20%	Estimates are considered acceptable
x = CV > 20%	Estimates are considered unreliable for practical purposes
.. = disclosive	
: = not applicable	
- = nil or negligible	

4.16 Median[1] weekly and hourly earnings of full-time employees[2] by age group: United Kingdom April 2006 to 2015

	18-21	22-29	30-39	40-49	50-59	60+
Median gross weekly earnings						
All	JRG9	JRH2	JRH3	JRH4	JEH5	JRH6
2006	250.6	376.5	496.1	502.5	465.4	400.0
2007	265.5	387.8	509.0	517.3	479.1	418.7
2008	271.6	400.0	532.7	539.9	504.1	437.5
2009	277.5	407.1	541.8	550.5	514.0	446.3
2010	277.4	411.2	547.8	559.6	528.2	457.3
2011	277.8	406.6	553.7	564.7	531.8	466.1
2012	279.7	412.0	557.7	573.1	535.9	476.1
2013	287.5	420.6	562.9	579.9	551.0	490.4
2014	290.0	424.8	566.0	588.2	556.1	491.3
2015	199.3	383.2	489.1	491.9	458.0	338.9
Men	JRH8	JRH9	JRI2	JRI3	JRI4	JRI5
2006	261.5	390.6	525.0	558.7	516.0	421.6
2007	275.9	402.5	539.0	574.9	534.4	440.9
2008	280.0	416.7	566.3	599.1	563.6	462.6
2009	285.7	421.6	571.1	605.2	569.7	469.0
2010	285.9	421.2	573.7	613.7	582.7	483.0
2011	288.2	413.7	574.9	618.9	586.7	496.3
2012	295.4	420.6	574.9	622.9	598.2	508.3
2013	299.0	430.6	579.6	637.8	613.3	527.5
2014	301.7	435.6	578.6	641.3	621.1	528.0
2015	233.0	411.6	556.5	618.8	593.9	443.1
Women	JRI7	JRI8	JRI9	JRJ2	JRJ3	JRJ4
2006	240.4	362.7	444.0	410.2	385.0	343.7
2007	254.3	374.1	460.6	420.3	395.6	356.1
2008	258.8	384.7	480.9	437.3	419.7	376.4
2009	268.3	392.9	497.9	457.7	432.8	382.1
2010	268.3	401.3	507.9	472.2	440.9	389.0
2011	264.7	398.5	519.4	477.1	449.1	399.6
2012	266.3	402.5	527.0	484.4	446.0	407.4
2013	276.2	405.7	533.8	494.1	463.5	416.1
2014	279.2	414.0	537.3	507.3	465.4	412.0
2015	166.6	347.5	401.0	365.2	342.8	235.7

4.16 Median[1] weekly and hourly earnings of full-time employees[2] by age group: United Kingdom April 2006 to 2015

	18-21	22-29	30-39	40-49	50-59	60+
Median hourly earnings (excluding overtime)						
All	**JRJ6**	**JRJ7**	**JRJ8**	**JRJ9**	**JRK2**	**JRK3**
2006	6.31	9.50	12.43	12.49	11.50	9.72
2007	6.60	9.80	12.77	12.77	11.87	10.09
2008	6.75	10.12	13.34	13.31	12.53	10.57
2009	7.00	10.43	13.82	13.83	12.95	10.97
2010	7.00	10.34	13.91	14.01	13.19	11.18
2011	6.97	10.23	14.07	14.16	13.34	11.46
2012	7.00	10.34	14.23	14.37	13.55	11.83
2013	7.20	10.60	14.37	14.63	13.89	12.13
2014	7.25	10.76	14.37	14.82	14.00	12.22
2015	7.08	10.03	13.31	13.49	12.68	10.88
Men	**JRK5**	**JRK6**	**JRK7**	**JRK8**	**JRK9**	**JRL2**
2006	6.37	9.51	12.78	13.46	12.28	9.96
2007	6.65	9.80	13.10	13.77	12.79	10.31
2008	6.85	10.13	13.70	14.37	13.52	10.89
2009	7.09	10.45	14.15	14.95	13.91	11.25
2010	7.05	10.26	14.07	14.95	14.25	11.50
2011	7.07	10.08	14.14	15.14	14.31	11.84
2012	7.24	10.22	14.28	15.27	14.68	12.15
2013	7.27	10.57	14.43	15.62	15.00	12.61
2014	7.42	10.73	14.35	15.69	15.13	12.78
2015	7.25	10.26	14.05	15.41	14.97	12.26
Women	**JRL4**	**JRL5**	**JRL6**	**JRL7**	**JRL8**	**JRL9**
2006	6.24	9.48	11.87	10.95	10.24	9.17
2007	6.55	9.79	12.28	11.14	10.54	9.48
2008	6.64	10.12	12.78	11.57	11.10	9.82
2009	6.93	10.40	13.29	12.21	11.52	10.23
2010	6.90	10.48	13.66	12.54	11.84	10.40
2011	6.76	10.45	13.99	12.77	12.02	10.64
2012	6.82	10.53	14.18	12.93	11.99	10.99
2013	7.15	10.64	14.28	13.18	12.38	11.10
2014	7.06	10.81	14.37	13.53	12.41	10.99
2015	7.00	9.83	12.41	11.55	10.84	9.60

1. Median values are less affected by extremes of earnings at either ends of the scale with half the employees earning above the stated amount and half below.
2. Data relate to full-time employees on adult rates whose pay for the survey pay-period was not affected by absence.

Source: Annual Survey of Hours and Earnings, Office for National Statistics

4.17: Trade Unions 2015-16

Trade unions: distribution by size

Number of Members	Number of Unions	Membership	Number of Unions		Membership of all Unions	
			Per cent	Cumulative Per cent	Per cent	Cumulative Per cent
Under 100	29	788	18.1	18.1	0.0	0.0
100-499	26	6,994	16.3	34.4	0.1	0.1
500-999	14	9,992	8.8	43.1	0.1	0.3
1,000-2,499	27	43,339	16.9	60.0	0.6	0.9
2,500-4,999	12	48,274	7.5	67.5	0.7	1.6
5,000-9,999	9	70,124	5.6	73.1	1.0	2.6
10,000-14,999	3	35,651	1.9	75.0	0.5	3.1
15,000-24,999	12	245,064	7.5	82.5	3.5	6.6
25,000-49,999	11	371,463	6.9	89.4	5.4	12.0
50,000-99,999	4	251,006	2.5	91.9	3.6	15.6
100,000-249,999	6	993,572	3.8	95.6	14.3	29.9
250,000 and over	7	4,872,458	4.4	100.0	70.1	100.0
Total	160	6,948,725	100.0	100.0	100.0	100.0

The trade union membership of 6,948,725 recorded in this annual report compares to 7,010,527 reported in the previous annual report. This indicates a decrease of 61,802 members or 0.88%. The total recorded membership of around 7 million compares with a peak of 13.2 million in 1979, a fall of about 47%.

The following table shows the trade unions whose membership has increased or decreased by 5,000 members or more since the previous reporting period.

4.17: Trade Unions 2015-16

Trade Union: Changes in Membership over 5,000 members

	Total Membership		
	2014-2015	*2013-2014*	*% changes*
Increases			
GMB	625,643	617,064	+1.4
Royal College of Nursing	429,414	421,558	+1.9
Decreases			
Union of Construction, Allied Trades and Technicians	61,229	86,983	-29.6
Public and Commercial Service Union	231,323	247,345	-6.48
Association of Teachers and Lecturers	189,479	198,102	-4.4
National Union of Teachers	376,208	387,610	-2.94
UNISON: The Public Service Union	1,270,248	1,282,560	-0.96

The annual returns submitted by unions to the Certification Officer require each union to provide figures for both total membership and members who pay contributions. There can be significant differences between these figures. This is usually the result of total membership figures including retired and unemployed members, members on long term sick and maternity/child care leave and those on career breaks. The returns submitted by unions during this reporting period show that the total number of contributing members was around 91.7% of the total number of members. This compared to 92.1% in the preceding year.

Source: Certification Office Annual Report 2015/16

this page is intentionally blank

Social protection

Chapter 5

Social Protection

(Tables 5.2 to 5.11, 5.13 and 5.15 to 5.19)

Tables 5.2 to 5.6, 5.9 to 5.11 and 5.13 to 5.19 give details of contributors and beneficiaries under the National Insurance and Industrial Injury Acts, supplementary benefits and war pensions.

There are five classes of National Insurance Contributions (NICs):

Class 1 Earnings-related contributions paid on earnings from employment. Employees pay primary Class 1 contributions and employers pay secondary Class 1 contributions. Payment of Class 1 contributions builds up entitlement to contributory benefits which include Basic State Pension; Additional State Pension (State Earnings Related Pension Scheme SERPS and from April 2002, State Second Pension, S2P); Contribution Based Jobseeker's Allowance; Bereavement Benefits and Employment and Support Allowance.

Class 1A or 1B Employers pay these directly on their employee's expenses or benefits

Primary class 1 contributions stop at State Pension age, but not Class 1 secondary contributions paid by employers. There are reduced contribution rates where the employee contracts out of S2P (previously SERPS). They still receive a Basic State Pension but an Occupational or Personal Pension instead of the Additional State Second Pension.

Class 2 Flat rate contributions paid by the self-employed whose profits are above the small earnings exception. Payment of Class 2 contributions builds up entitlement to the contributory benefits which include Basic State Pension; Bereavement Benefits; Maternity Allowance and the Employment and Support Allowance, but not Additional State Second Pension or Contribution Based Jobseeker's Allowance (JSA).

Class 2 contributions stop at State Pension age.

Class 3 Flat rate voluntary contributions, which can be paid by someone whose contribution record is insufficient. Payment of Class 3 contributions builds up entitlement to contributory benefits which include Basic State Pension and Bereavement Benefits. (Tables 5.2 to 5.11, 5.13 and 5.15 to 5.19) Tables 5.2 to 5.6, 5.9 to 5.11 and 5.13 to 5.19 give details of contributors and beneficiaries under the National Insurance and Industrial Injury Acts, supplementary benefits and war pensions.

Class 4 Profit-related contributions paid by the self employed in addition to Class 2 contributions. Class 4 contributions paid by self-employed people with a profit over £8,164 don't usually count towards state benefits.

Home Responsibilities Protection

Home Responsibilities Protection (HRP) was introduced to help to protect the basic State Pension of those precluded from regular employment because they are caring for children or a sick or disabled person at home. To be entitled to HRP, a person must have been precluded from regular employment for a full tax year. HRP reduces the amount of qualifying years a person would otherwise need for a Basic State Pension. **The scheme ceased on the 6th April 2010** and has been replaced by National Insurance credits which can be claimed if qualifying criteria are met.

National Insurance Credits

In addition to paying, or being treated as having paid contributions, a person can be credited with National Insurance contributions (NIC) credits. Contribution credits help to protect people's rights to State Retirement Pension and other Social Security Benefits.

A person is likely to be entitled to contributions credits if they are: a student in full time education or training, in receipt of Jobseeker's Allowance, unable to work due to sickness or disability, entitled to Statutory Maternity Pay or Statutory Adoption Pay, or they have received Carer's Allowance.

National Insurance Credits eligibility can be checked at: https://www.gov.uk/national-insurance-credits/eligibility

Jobseeker's Allowance (Table 5.6)

Jobseeker's Allowance (JSA) replaced Unemployment Benefit and Income Support for unemployed claimants on 7 October 1996. It is a unified benefit with two routes of entry: contribution-based, which depends mainly upon National Insurance contributions, and income-based, which depends mainly upon a means test. Some claimants can qualify by either route. In practice they receive income-based JSA but have an underlying entitlement to the contribution based element.

Employment and Support Allowance, and Incapacity Benefit (Table 5.7)

Incapacity Benefit replaced Sickness Benefit and Invalidity Benefit from 13 April 1995. The first condition for entitlement to these contributory benefits is that the claimants are incapable of work because of illness or disablement. The second is that they satisfy the contribution conditions, which depend on contributions paid as an employed (Class 1) or self-employed person (Class 2). Under Sickness and Invalidity Benefits the contribution conditions were automatically treated as satisfied if a person was incapable of work because of an industrial accident or prescribed disease. Under Incapacity Benefit those who do not satisfy the contribution conditions do not have them treated as satisfied. Class 1A contributions paid by employers are in respect of the benefit of cars provided for the private use of employees, and the free fuel provided for private use. These contributions do not provide any type of benefit cover.

Since 6 April 1983, most people working for an employer and paying National Insurance contributions as employed persons receive Statutory Sick Pay (SSP) from their employer when they are off work sick. Until 5 April 1986 SSP was payable for a maximum of eight weeks, since this date SSP has been payable for 28 weeks. People who do not work for an employer, and employees who are excluded from the SSP scheme, or those who have run out of SSP before reaching the maximum of 28 weeks and are still sick, can claim benefit. Any period of SSP is excluded from the tables.

Spells of incapacity of three days or less do not count as periods of interruption of employment and are excluded from the tables. Exceptions are where people are receiving regular weekly treatment by dialysis or treatment by radiotherapy, chemotherapy or plasmapheresis where two days in any six consecutive days make up a period of interruption of employment, and those whose incapacity for work ends within three days of the end of SSP entitlement.

At the beginning of a period of incapacity, benefit is subject to three waiting days, except where there was an earlier spell of incapacity of more than three days in the previous eight weeks. Employees entitled to SSP for less than 28 weeks and who are still sick can get Sickness Benefit or Incapacity Benefit Short Term (Low) until they reach a total of 28 weeks provided they satisfy the conditions.

After 28 weeks of SSP and/or Sickness Benefit (SB), Invalidity Benefit (IVB) was payable up to pension age for as long as the incapacity lasted. From pension age, IVB was paid at the person's State Pension rate, until entitlement ceased when SP was paid, or until deemed pension age (70 for a man, 65 for a woman). People who were on Sickness or Invalidity Benefit on 12 April 1995 were automatically transferred to Incapacity Benefit, payable on the same basis as before.

For people on Incapacity Benefit under State Pension age there are two short-term rates: the lower rate is paid for the first 28 weeks of sickness and the higher rate for weeks 29 to 52. From week 53 the Long Term rate Incapacity Benefit is payable. The Short Term rate Incapacity Benefit is based on State Pension entitlement for people over State Pension age and is paid for up to a year if incapacity began before pension age.

The long-term rate of Incapacity Benefit applies to people under State Pension age who have been sick for more than a year. People with a terminal illness, or who are receiving the higher rate care component of Disability Living Allowance, will get the Long Term rate. The Long Term rate is not paid for people over pension age.

Under Incapacity Benefit, for the first 28 weeks of incapacity, people previously in work will be assessed on the 'own occupation' test – the claimant's ability to do their own job. Otherwise, incapacity will be based on a personal capability assessment, which will assess ability to carry out a range of work-related activities. The test will apply after 28 weeks of incapacity or from the start of the claim for people who did not previously have a job. Certain people will be exempted from this test.

The tables exclude all men aged over 65 and women aged over 60 who are in receipt of State Pension, and all people over deemed pension age (70 for a man and 65 for a woman), members of the armed forces, mariners while at sea, and married women and certain widows who have chosen not to be insured for sickness benefit. The tables include a number of individuals who were unemployed prior to incapacity.

The Short Term (Higher) and Long Term rates of Incapacity Benefit are treated as taxable income. There were transitional provisions for people who were on Sickness or Invalidity Benefit on 12 April 1995. They were automatically transferred to Incapacity Benefit, payable on the same basis as before. Former IVB recipients continue to get Additional Pension entitlement, but frozen at 1994 levels. Also their IVB is not subject to tax. If they were over State Pension age on 12 April 1995 they may get Incapacity Benefit for up to five years beyond pension age.

Employment and Support Allowance (ESA) replaced Incapacity Benefit and Income Support paid on the grounds of incapacity for new claims from 27 October 2008. ESA consists of two phases. The first, the assessment phase rate, is paid for the first 13 weeks of the claim whilst a decision is made on the claimants capability through the 'Work Capability Asessment'. The second, or main phase begins after 14 weeks, but only if the 'Work Capability Assesment' has deemed the claimants illness or disability as a limitation on their ability to work.

Within the main phase there are two groups, 'The Work Related Activity Group' and 'The Support Group'. If a claimant is placed in the first, they are expected to take part in work focused interviews with a personal advisor. They will be given support to help them prepare for work and on gaining work will receive a work related activity component in addition to their basic rate. If the claimant is placed in the second group due to their illness or disability having a severe effect upon their ability to work, the claimant will not be expected to work at all, but can do so on a voluntary basis. These claimants will receive a support component in addition to their basic rate.

Child Benefits (Table 5.9a and 5.9b)

You get child benefit if you are responsible for a child under 16 (or under 20 if they stay in approved education or training.
Approved education
Education must be full-time (more than an average of 12 hours a week supervised study or course-related work experience) and can include:
A levels or similar - eg Pre-U, International Baccalaureate
Scottish Highers
NVQs and other vocational qualifications up to level 3
home education - if started before your child turned 16
traineeships in England
Courses are not approved if paid for by an employer or 'advanced', eg a university degree or BTEC Higher National Certificate.

Approved training
Approved training should be unpaid and can include:
Access to Apprenticeships in England
Foundation Apprenticeships or Traineeships in Wales
Employability Fund programmes or Get Ready for Work (if started before 1 April 2013) in Scotland
Training for Success, Pathways to Success or Collaboration and Innovation Programme in Northern Ireland
Courses that are part of a job contract are not approved.

Guardian's Allowance is an additional allowance for people bringing up a child because one or both of their parents has died. They must be getting Child Benefit (CB) for the child. The table shows the number of families in the UK in receipt of CB. The numbers shown in the table are estimates based on a random 5 per cent sample of awards current at 31 August, and are therefore subject to sampling error. The figures take no account of new claims, or revisions to claims that were received or processed after 31 August, even if they are backdated to start before 31 August.

Child and Working Tax Credits (New Tax Credits) (Table 5.10 and 5.11)

Child and Working Tax Credits (CTC and WTC) replaced Working Families' Tax Credit (WFTC) from 6th April 2003. CTC and WTC are claimed by individuals, or jointly by couples, whether or not they have children.

CTC provides support to families for the children (up to the 31 August after their 16th birthday) and the 'qualifying' young people (in full-time non-advanced education until their 20th birthday) for which they are responsible. It is paid in addition to CB.

WTC tops up the earnings of families on low or moderate incomes. People working for at least 16 hours a week can claim it if they: (a) are responsible for at least one child or qualifying young person, (b) have a disability which puts them at a disadvantage in getting a job or, (c) in the first year of work, having returned to work aged at least 50 after a period of at least six months receiving out-of-work benefits. Other adults also qualify if they are aged at least 25 and work for at least 30 hours a week.

Bereavement Benefits (Table 5.12 and 5.13)

If your husband, wife or civil partner died before 6 April 2017, you may be able to get one or more of the following:

Bereavement Payment (a one-off payment)
Bereavement Allowance (monthly payments)
Widowed Parent's Allowance (if you're bringing up children)

Bereavement Payment is a one-off, tax-free, lump-sum payment. The other two benefits are payable monthly. Widowed Parents' Allowance is payable if you are bringing up children. Eligibility requirements must be met. A full list of requirements can be viewed on gov.uk at: https://www.gov.uk/bereavement-allowance

You don't have to apply more than once - you'll be considered for all bereavement benefits when you apply for one.

5.1 National Insurance Fund (Great Britain)

For the year ended 31 March

£ 000

	2011	2012	2013	2014	2015
Receipts					
Opening balance	48,786,585 [3]	43,163,939	38,593,953	29,082,990	23,195,862
National Insurance Contributions	74,181,834	78,423,776	79,119,934	82,236,514	84,112,562
Treasury Grant	-	-	-	-	4,600,000
Compensation for statutory pay recoveries	2,100,796	3,008,707	2,559,760	2,319,000	2,465,000
Income from Investment Account	204,124	188,825	161,550	125,749	89,443
State Scheme Premiums[2]	47,299	36,733	30,861	56,408	32,622
Other receipts	46,657	46,401	36,164	29,586	23,292
Redundancy receipts	49,281	49,274	38,320	39,995	36,932
Total Receipts	**76,629,991**	**81,753,716**	**81,946,589**	**84,807,252**	**91,359,851**
Less					
Payments					
Benefit payments	77,799,137	82,357,733	87,464,810	88,933,118	91,759,523
of which					
State Pension	*69,346,701*	*74,110,982*	*80,008,745*	*82,522,101*	*85,893,497*
Incapacity Benefit	*5,598,835*	*4,981,255*	*3,355,345*	*1,213,380*	*233,704*
Employment and Support Alllowance	*958,990*	*1,410,890*	*2,312,374*	*3,554,301*	*4,130,282*
Jobseeker's Allowance (Contributory)	*811,621*	*757,582*	*669,184*	*533,630*	*375,940*
Bereavement Benefits	*615,455*	*605,011*	*598,431*	*587,821*	*579,061*
Maternity Allowance	*343,412*	*366,968*	*395,522*	*397,608*	*420,518*
Christmas Bonus	*122,215*	*123,203*	*123,308*	*122,356*	*124,521*
Guardian's Allowance and Child's Special Allowance	*1,908*	*1,842*	*1,901*	*1,921*	*2,000*
Personal Pensions[1]	2,313,669	2,139,042	2,124,560	15,913	*1,448*
Administrative costs	1,419,801	1,125,019	916,875	903,502	*806,386*
Redundancy payments	445,623	406,631	453,577	356,069	*276,708*
Transfers to Northern Ireland NIF	125,000	145,000	334,000	315,000	*609,000*
Other payments	149,407	150,277	163,730	170,778	*167,370*
Total Payments	**82,252,637**	**86,323,702**	**91,457,552**	**90,694,380**	**93,620,435**
Excess of payments over receipts	(5,622,646)	(4,569,986)	(9,510,963)	(5,887,128)	(2,260,584)
Opening balance	48,786,585	43,163,939	38,593,953	29,082,990	23,195,862
Less excess of payments over receipts	(5,622,646)	(4,569,986)	(9,510,963)	(5,887,128)	(2,260,584)
Closing balance	**43,163,939**	**38,593,953**	**29,082,990**	**23,195,862**	**20,935,278**

Source: HM Revenue and Customs, Department for Work and Pensions

1. On 5 April 2012 the abolition of contracting-out on a defined contribution basis took place resulting in these contributions no longer being received. As the payments were made a year in arrears, from April 2013, the number of transactions has greatly reduced as only late payments and recoveries are being dealt with.

2. State Scheme Premiums are payable to the Fund in respect of employed persons' who cease to be covered, in certain specified circumstances, by a contracted-out pension scheme.

3. Opening balance has been restated based on analysis of prior year data as better management information has become available.

5.2 National Insurance Contributions

For the year ended 31 March	Notes	2012	2013	2014	2015	2016
Class 1 (employed earner)	i	75,528,875	75,873,021	79,067,796	80,814,248	83,138,168
Class 1A and 1B	ii	987,226	1,047,965	1,118,263	1,078,274	1,119,605
Class 2 (Self-employed flat rate)	iii	229,516	341,361	327,180	353,608	191,127
Class 3 (Voluntary contributions)	iv	48,876	40,274	31,627	23,129	29,897
Class 3A (Voluntary contributions)	v	-	-	-	-	58,277
Class 4 (Self-employed earnings related)	vi	1,629,283	1,817,313	1,689,648	1,842,303	1,924,552
		78,423,776	79,119,934	82,236,514	84,112,562	86,461,626

Source: HMRC National Insurance Fund Account Great Britain

Notes

i. Class 1 contributions comprise two parts: primary contributions payable by employees and secondary contributions payable by employers.

ii. Class 1A contributions are paid by employers on most benefits provided to employees.
Class 1B contributions are payable by employers where they have entered into a PAYE settlement agreement for tax enabling them to settle their National Insurance and income tax liability in a lump sum after the end of the tax year. The figures for Class 1A and Class 1B have been combined.

iii. Class 2 self-employed persons pay flat rate weekly contributions.

iv. Class 3 voluntary flat rate contributions are paid to maintain contributors' National Insurance record for certain benefit and/or pension purposes.

v. Class 3A allows pensioners who have reached state pension age before 6 April 2016 to boost their retirement incomes by making voluntary payments of NICs. The scheme is available for 18 months from October 2015.

vi. Class 4 self employed persons pay earnings related contributions.

5.3 Main Features of National Insurance Contributions (NCIS) 1999-2000 to 2016-17

	Rate in 1999-2000	Rate in 2000-2001	Rate in 2001-2002	Rate in 2002-2003	Rate in 2003-2004	Rate in 2004-2005	Rate in 2005-2006	Rate in 2006-2007	Rate in 2007-2008	Rate in 2008-2009
Class 1										
Lower earnings limit (LEL) – a week	£66	£67	£72	£75	£77	£79	£82	£84	£87	£90
Primary threshold (PT) – a week	-	£76	£87	£89	£89	£91	£94	£97	£100	£105
Secondary threshold (ST) – a week	£83	£84	£87	£89	£89	£91	£94	£97	£100	£105
Upper accruals Point (UAP) – a week (1)	-	-	-	-	-	-	-	-	-	-
Upper earnings limit (UEL) – a week (2)	£500	£535	£575	£585	£595	£610	£630	£645	£670	£770
Primary contributions (employee)										
Main contribution rate (PT to UEL) (3)	10.0%	10.0%	10.0%	10.0%	11.0%	11.0%	11.0%	11.0%	11.0%	11.0%
Additional contribution rate (above UEL)	-	-	-	-	1.0%	1.0%	1.0%	1.0%	1.0%	1.0%
Contracted out rebate (LEL to UAP/UEL) (4) (5)	1.6%	1.6%	1.6%	1.6%	1.6%	1.6%	1.6%	1.6%	1.6%	1.6%
Reduced rate for married women and widow optants (6)	3.85%	3.85%	3.85%	3.85%	4.85%	4.85%	4.85%	4.85%	4.85%	4.85%
Secondary contributions (employer)										
Contribution rate (above ST)	12.2%	12.2%	11.9%	11.8%	12.8%	12.8%	12.8%	12.8%	12.8%	12.8%
Contracted out rebate (LEL to UAP/UEL) (5)										
- COSRS	3.0%	3.0%	3.0%	3.5%	3.5%	3.5%	3.5%	3.5%	3.7%	3.7%
- COMPS (7)	0.6%	0.6%	0.6%	1.0%	1.0%	1.0%	1.0%	1.0%	1.4%	1.4%
Class 1A and 1B										
Contribution rate (8)	12.2%	12.2%	11.9%	11.8%	12.8%	12.8%	12.8%	12.8%	12.8%	12.8%
Class 2										
Flat-rate contribution – a week	£6.55	£2.00	£2.00	£2.00	£2.00	£2.05	£2.10	£2.10	£2.20	£2.30
Small earnings exception / Small Profits Threshold – a year (11)	£3,770	£3,825	£3,955	£4,025	£4,095	£4,215	£4,345	£4,465	£4,635	£4,825
Class 3										
Flat-rate contribution – a week (9)	£6.45	£6.55	£6.75	£6.85	£6.95	£7.15	£7.35	£7.55	£7.80	£8.10
Class 4										
Lower profits limit (LPL) – a year	£7,530	£4,385	£4,535	£4,615	£4,615	£4,745	£4,895	£5,035	£5,225	£5,435
Upper profits limit (UPL) – a year (2)	£26,000	£27,820	£29,900	£30,420	£30,940	£31,720	£32,760	£33,540	£34,840	£40,040
Main contribution rate (LPL to UPL)	6%	7%	7%	7%	8%	8%	8%	8%	8%	8%
Additional contribution rate (above UPL)	-	-	-	-	1%	1%	1%	1%	1%	1%

Source: HM Revenue & Customs

5.3 Main Features of National Insurance Contributions (NCIS) 1999-2000 to 2016-17

	Rate in 2009-2010	Rate in 2010-11	Rate in 2011-12	Rate in 2012-13 (10)	Rate in 2013-14 (10)	Rate in 2014-15 (10)	Rate in 2015-16 (10)	Rate in 2016-17 (10)
Class 1								
Lower earnings limit (LEL) – a week	£95	£97	£102	£107	£109	£111	£112	£112
Primary threshold (PT) – a week	£110	£110	£139	£146	£149	£153	£155	£155
Secondary threshold (ST) – a week	£110	£110	£136	£144	£148	£153	£156	£156
Upper accruals Point (UAP) – a week (1)	£770	£770	£770	£770	£770	£770	£770	-
Upper earnings limit (UEL) – a week (2)	£844	£844	£817	£817	£797	£805	£815	£827
Primary contributions (employee)								
Main contribution rate (PT to UEL) (3)	11.0%	11.0%	12.0%	12.0%	12.0%	12.0%	12.0%	12.0%
Additional contribution rate (above UEL)	1.0%	1.0%	2.0%	2.0%	2.0%	2.0%	2.0%	2.0%
Contracted out rebate (LEL to UAP/UEL) (4) (5)	1.6%	1.6%	1.6%	1.4%	1.4%	1.4%	1.4%	-
Reduced rate for married women and widow optants (6)	4.85%	4.85%	5.85%	5.85%	5.85%	5.85%	5.85%	5.85%
Secondary contributions (employer)								
Contribution rate (above ST)	12.8%	12.8%	13.8%	13.8%	13.8%	13.8%	13.8%	13.8%
Contracted out rebate (LEL to UAP/UEL) (5)								
- COSRS	3.7%	3.7%	3.7%	3.4%	3.4%	3.4%	3.4%	-
- COMPS (7)	1.4%	1.4%	1.4%	-	-	-	-	-
Class 1A and 1B								
Contribution rate (8)	12.8%	12.8%	13.8%	13.8%	13.8%	13.8%	13.8%	13.8%
Class 2								
Flat-rate contribution – a week	£2.40	£2.40	£2.50	£2.65	£2.70	£2.75	£2.80	£2.80
Small earnings exception / Small Profits Threshold – a year (11)	£5,075	£5,075	£5,315	£5,595	£5,725	£5,885	£5,965	£5,965
Class 3								
Flat-rate contribution – a week (9)	£12.05	£12.05	£12.60	£13.25	£13.55	£13.90	£14.10	£14.10
Class 4								
Lower profits limit (LPL) – a year	£5,715	£5,715	£7,225	£7,605	£7,755	£7,956	£8,060	£8,060
Upper profits limit (UPL) – a year (2)	£43,875	£43,875	£42,475	£42,475	£41,450	£41,865	£42,385	£43,000
Main contribution rate (LPL to UPL)	8%	8%	9%	9%	9%	9%	9%	9%
Additional contribution rate (above UPL)	1%	1%	2%	2%	2%	2%	2%	2%

Source: HM Revenue & Customs

5.3 Main Features of National Insurance Contributions (NCIS) 1999-2000 to 2016-17

(1) The upper accruals point was introduced in April 2009 until April 2015-16. It is no longer needed after the contracting out rebates are abolished from 2016-17 onwards.

(2) From April 2009 the upper earnings limit and upper profits limit were aligned to the income tax higher rate threshold.

(3) Between LEL and UEL for 1999-2000.

(4) For Appropriate Personal Pension Schemes (APPS) both employer and employee pay NICs at the full contracted-out rate and in the following tax year on submission of the end-of-year returns HMRC pay an age related rebate direct to the schemes. The employee's share of this rebate is 1.6%.

(5) Up to and including 2008-09, the rebate applies between the LEL and the UEL. From 2009-10 onwards the rebate applies between the LEL and UAP. The rebates are abolished from 2016-17 onwards.

(6) Married women opting to pay contributions at the reduced rate earn no entitlement to contributory National Insurance benefits as a result of these contributions. No women have been allowed to exercise this option since 1977.

(7) For employers operating a COMPS, in addition to the reduction shown in secondary Class 1 contributions, in the following tax year on submission of end-of-year returns, HMRC pay an additional "top-up" rebate direct to the scheme. As with APPS, this rebate is age related. COMPs are abolished from 2012-13 onwards.

(8) From April 2000 the Class 1A liability for employers was extended from company cars and fuel to include other taxable benefits not already attracting a Class 1 liability. Class 1A and Class 1B contributions are paid in the year following accrual.

(9) Class 3 contribution rules changed in 2009-10 to allow those reaching state pension age before April 2015 with 20 qualifying years to purchase up to 6 additional years.

(10)   From 2012-13 the default indexation assumption for NICs is CPI (excluding the secondary threshold up until 2016-17).

(11)   The Small Profits Threshold replaced the Small Earnings Exception on 6 April 2015.

Notes:

Class 1 National Insurance Contributions (NICs)

Class 1 NICs are earnings related contributions paid by employed earners who are below State Pension age and their employers. The contributions are paid at either the contracted-out rate or the not contracted-out rate. The contracted-out rate is payable only where the employee is a member of a contracted-out occupational scheme in place of State Second Pension (formerly SERPS). Class 1 NICs are collected by HMRC along with income tax under the Pay As You Earn (PAYE) scheme.

Class 1A National Insurance Contributions (NICs)

Class 1A NICs are paid only by employers on the value of most taxable benefits-in-kind provided to employees, such as private use of company cars and fuel, private medical insurance, accommodation and loan benefits. They do not give any benefit rights.

Class 1B National Insurance Contributions (NICs)

Class 1B NICs were introduced on 6 April 1999. Like Class 1A they are also paid only by employers and cover PAYE Settlement Agreements (PSA) under which employers agree to meet the income tax liability arising on a restricted range of benefits. Class 1B is payable on the value of the items included in the PSA that would otherwise attract a Class 1 or Class 1A liability and the value of the income tax met by the employer. They do not give any benefit rights.

Class 2 National Insurance Contributions (NICs)

Class 2 contributions are a flat rate weekly liability payable by all self-employed people over 16 (up to State Pension age) with profits above the Small Profits Threshold. Self-employed people with profits below the Small Profits Threshold may pay Class 2 contributions voluntary. Voluntary payments of Class 2 NICs are typically collected through self-assessment but can usually be paid up to six years after the tax year. Class 4 NICs may also have to be paid by the self-employed if their profits for the year are over the lower profits limit (see below).

Class 3 National Insurance Contributions (NICs)

Class 3 NICs may be paid voluntarily by people aged 16 and over (but below State Pension age) to help them qualify for State Pension and Bereavement Benefits if their contribution record would not otherwise be sufficient. Contributions are flat rate and can be paid up to six years after the year in which they are due.

Class 4 National Insurance Contributions (NICs)

Class 4 NICS are paid by the self-employed whose profits are above the lower profits limit. They are profit related and do not count for any benefits themselves.

5.4 Proposed benefit and pension rates 2015 to 2016

Proposed benefit and pension rates 2015 to 2016 (Weekly rates unless otherwise shown)	RATES 2014	RATES 2015
ATTENDANCE ALLOWANCE		
higher rate	81.30	82.30
lower rate	54.45	55.10
BEREAVEMENT BENEFIT		
Bereavement payment (lump sum)	2000.00	2000.00
Widowed parent's allowance	111.20	112.55
Bereavement Allowance		
standard rate	111.20	112.55
age-related		
age 54	103.42	104.67
53	95.63	96.79
52	87.85	88.91
51	80.06	81.04
50	72.28	73.16
49	64.50	65.28
48	56.71	57.40
47	48.93	49.52
46	41.14	41.64
45	33.36	33.77
BENEFIT CAP		
In Housing Benefit (weekly rate)		
Couples and lone parents	500.00	500.00
Single persons without children	350.00	350.00
In Universal Credit (monthly rate)		
Joint claimants and single claimants with children	2167.00	2167.00
Single claimants, no dependent children	1517.00	1517.00

CAPITAL LIMITS - rules common to Income Support, income based Jobseeker's Allowance, income-related Employment and Support Allowance, Pension Credit, and Housing Benefit, and Universal Credit unless otherwise stated

	RATES 2014	RATES 2015
upper limit	16000.00	16000.00
upper limit - Pension Credit and those getting Housing Benefit and Pension Credit Guarantee Credit	No limit	No limit
Amount disregarded - all benefits except Pension Credit and Housing Benefit for those above the qualifying age for Guarantee Credit	6000.00	6000.00
Amount disregarded - Pension Credit and Housing Benefit for those above the qualifying age for Pension Credit	10000.00	10000.00

5.4 Proposed benefit and pension rates 2015 to 2016

Proposed benefit and pension rates 2015 to 2016 (Weekly rates unless otherwise shown)	RATES 2014	RATES 2015
child disregard (not Pension Credit, Employment and Support Allowance nor Housing Benefit)	3000.00	3000.00
amt disregarded (living in RC/NH)	10000.00	10000.00

Tariff income
£1 for every £250, or part thereof, between the amount of
capital disregarded and the capital upper limit

Tariff income - Pension Credit and Housing Benefit where clmt/ptner is over Guarantee Credit qualifying age
£1 for every £500, or part thereof, above or between the amount of
capital disregarded and any capital upper limit applicable

CARER'S ALLOWANCE	61.35	62.10

DEDUCTIONS - rules common to Income Support, Jobseeker's Allowance, Employment and Support Allowance, Pension Credit and Housing Benefit unless stated otherwise

Non-dependant deductions from housing benefit and from IS, JSA(IR), ESA(IR) and Pension Credit

aged 25 and over in receipt of IS and JSA(IR), or any age in receipt of main phase ESA(IR), aged 18 or over, not in remunerative work	14.15	14.55
aged 18 or over and in remunerative work		
- gross income: less than £129	14.15	14.55
- gross income: £129 to £188.99	32.45	33.40
- gross income: £189 to £245.99	44.55	45.85
- gross income: £246 to £327.99	72.95	75.05
- gross income: £328 to £407.99	83.05	85.45
- gross income: £408 and above	91.15	93.80
Deductions from housing benefit		
Service charges for fuel		
heating	27.55	28.80
hot water	3.20	3.35
lighting	2.20	2.30
cooking	3.20	3.35
Amount ineligible for meals		
three or more meals a day		
single claimant	26.55	26.85
each person in family aged 16 or over	26.55	26.85
each child under 16	13.45	13.60
less than three meals a day		
single claimant	17.65	17.85
each person in family aged 16 or over	17.65	17.85
each child under 16	8.90	9.00
breakfast only - claimant and each member of the family	3.25	3.30
Amount for personal expenses (not HB)	23.75	24.00

5.4 Proposed benefit and pension rates 2015 to 2016

Proposed benefit and pension rates 2015 to 2016 (Weekly rates unless otherwise shown)	RATES 2014	RATES 2015
Third party deductions from IS, JSA(IR), ESA(IR) and Pension Credit for;		
arrears of housing, fuel and water costs	3.65	3.70
council tax etc. and deductions for ELDS and ILS.		
child support, contribution towards maintenance (CTM)		
standard deduction	7.30	7.40
lower deduction	3.65	3.70
arrears of Community Charge		
court order against claimant	3.65	3.70
court order against couple	5.70	5.75
fine or compensation order		
standard rate	5.00	5.00
lower rate	3.65	3.70
Maximum deduction rates for recovery of overpayments (not JSA(C)/ESA(C))		
ordinary overpayments	10.95	11.10
Fraud Overpayments	18.25	18.50
Deductions from JSA(C) and ESA (C)		
Arrears of Comm. Charge & overpayment recovery		
Age 16 - 24	19.11	19.30
Age 25 +	24.13	24.36
Arrears of Council Tax & Fines		
Age 16 - 24	22.94	23.16
Age 25 +	28.96	29.24
Max. dedn for arrears of Child Maintenance		
Age 16 - 24	19.11	19.30
Age 25 +	24.13	24.36

DEPENDENCY INCREASES

Adult dependency increases for spouse or person looking after children - payable with;

	RATES 2014	RATES 2015
State Pension on own insurance (Cat A or B)	64.90	65.70
long term Incapacity Benefit	60.45	61.20
Severe Disablement Allowance	36.30	36.75
Carers Allowance	36.10	36.55
short-term Incapacity Benefit (over state pension age)	58.20	58.90
short-term Incapacity Benefit (under State Pension age)	47.10	47.65
Child Dependency Increases - payable with; State Pension; Widowed Mothers/Parents Allowance; short-term Incapacity benefit - higher rate or over state pension age;	11.35	11.35

5.4 Proposed benefit and pension rates 2015 to 2016

Proposed benefit and pension rates 2015 to 2016 (Weekly rates unless otherwise shown)	RATES 2014	RATES 2015
long-term Incapacity Benefit; Carer's Allowance; Severe Disablement Unemployability Supplement.		
NB - The rate of child dependency increase is adjusted where it is payable for the eldest child for whom child benefit is also paid. The weekly rate in such cases is reduced by the difference (less £3.65) between the ChB rates for the eldest and subsequent children.	8.05	8.00

DISABILITY LIVING ALLOWANCE
Care Component

Highest	81.30	82.30
Middle	54.45	55.10
Lowest	21.55	21.80

Mobility Component

Higher	56.75	57.45
Lower	21.55	21.80

DISREGARDS

Housing Benefit
Earnings disregards

standard (single claimant)	5.00	5.00
couple	10.00	10.00
higher (special occupations/circumstances)	20.00	20.00
lone parent	25.00	25.00
childcare charges	175.00	175.00
childcare charges (2 or more children)	300.00	300.00
permitted work higher	101.00	104.00
permitted work lower	20.00	20.00

Other Income disregards

adult maintenance disregard	15.00	15.00
war disablement pension and war widows pension	10.00	10.00
widowed mothers/parents allowance	15.00	15.00
Armed Forces Compensation Scheme	10.00	10.00
student loan	10.00	10.00
student's covenanted income	5.00	5.00
income from boarders (plus 50% of the balance)	20.00	20.00
additional earnings disregard	17.10	17.10
income from subtenants (£20 fixed from April 08)	20.00	20.00

Income Support, income-based Jobseeker's Allowance, Income-related Employment and Support Allowance (ESA(IR)) and Pension Credit
Earnings disregards

standard (single claimant) (not ESA(IR))	5.00	5.00
couple (not ESA(IR))	10.00	10.00
higher (special occupations/circumstances)	20.00	20.00
partner of claimant (ESA(IR))	20.00 (maximum)	20.00 (maximum)

Other Income disregards

war disablement pension and war widows pension	10.00	10.00
widowed mothers/parents allowance	10.00	10.00

5.4 Proposed benefit and pension rates 2015 to 2016

Proposed benefit and pension rates 2015 to 2016 (Weekly rates unless otherwise shown)	RATES 2014	RATES 2015
Armed Forces Compensation Scheme	10.00	10.00
student loan (not Pension Credit)	10.00	10.00
student's covenanted income (not Pension Credit)	5.00	5.00
income from boarders (plus 50% of the balance)	20.00	20.00
income from subtenants (£20 fixed from April 08)	20.00	20.00

EARNINGS RULES

	RATES 2014	RATES 2015
Carers Allowance	102.00	110.00
Limit of earnings from councillor's allowance	101.00	104.00
Permitted work earnings limit - higher	101.00	104.00
- lower	20.00	20.00
Industrial injuries unemployability supplement permitted earnings level (annual amount)	5252.00	5408.00
Earnings level at which adult dependency (ADI) increases are affected with:		
short-term incap.benefit where claimant is		
(a) under state pension age	47.10	47.65
(b) over state pension age	58.20	58.90
state pension, long term incapacity benefit, severe disablement allowance, unemployability supplement - payable when dependant		
(a) is living with claimant	72.40	73.10
(b) still qualifies for the tapered earnings rule	45.09	45.09
Earnings level at which ADI is affected when dependant is not living with claimant;		
state pension,	64.90	65.70
long-term incapacity benefit,	60.45	61.20
unemployability supplement,	61.35	62.10
severe disablement allowance	36.30	36.75
Carers allowance	36.10	36.55
Earnings level at which child dependency increases are affected		
for first child	225.00	230.00
additional amount for each subsequent child	30.00	30.00
Pension income threshold for incapacity benefit	85.00	85.00
Pension income threshold for contributory Employment Support Allowance	85.00	85.00

5.4 Proposed benefit and pension rates 2015 to 2016

Proposed benefit and pension rates 2015 to 2016 (Weekly rates unless otherwise shown)	RATES 2014	RATES 2015
EMPLOYMENT AND SUPPORT ALLOWANCE		
Personal Allowances		
Single		
under 25	57.35	57.90
25 or over	72.40	73.10
lone parent		
under 18	57.35	57.90
18 or over	72.40	73.10
couple		
both under 18	57.35	57.90
both under 18 with child	86.65	87.50
both under 18 (main phase)	72.40	73.10
both under 18 with child (main phase)	113.70	114.85
one 18 or over, one under 18 (certain conditions apply)	113.70	114.85
both over 18	113.70	114.85
claimant under 25, partner under 18	57.35	57.90
claimant 25 or over, partner under 18	72.40	73.10
claimant (main phase), partner under 18	72.40	73.10
Premiums		
enhanced disability		
single	15.55	15.75
couple	22.35	22.60
severe disability		
single	61.10	61.85
couple (lower rate)	61.10	61.85
couple (higher rate)	122.20	123.70
carer	34.20	34.60
pensioner		
single with WRAC	47.20	49.05
single with support component	40.20	41.90
single with no component	75.95	78.10
couple with WRAC	84.05	86.95
couple with support component	77.05	79.80
couple with no component	112.80	116.00
Components		
Work-related Activity	28.75	29.05
Support	35.75	36.20
HOUSING BENEFIT		
Personal allowances		
single		
under 25	57.35	57.90
25 or over	72.40	73.10

5.4 Proposed benefit and pension rates 2015 to 2016

Proposed benefit and pension rates 2015 to 2016 (Weekly rates unless otherwise shown)	RATES 2014	RATES 2015
entitled to main phase ESA	72.40	73.10
lone parent		
under 18	57.35	57.90
18 or over	72.40	73.10
entitled to main phase ESA	72.40	73.10
couple		
both under 18	86.65	87.50
one or both 18 or over	113.70	114.85
claimant entitled to main phase ESA	113.70	114.85
dependent children	66.33	66.90
pensioner		
single/lone parent has attained the qualifying age for Pension Credit but under 65.	148.35	151.20
couple – one or both has attained the qualifying age for Pension Credit but both under 65	226.50	230.85
single / lone parent - 65 and over	165.15	166.05
couple - one or both 65 and over	247.20	248.30
Premiums		
family	17.45	17.45
family (lone parent rate)	22.20	22.20
disability		
single	31.85	32.25
couple	45.40	45.95
enhanced disability		
single	15.55	15.75
disabled child	24.08	24.43
couple	22.35	22.60
severe disability		
single	61.10	61.85
couple (lower rate)	61.10	61.85
couple (higher rate)	122.20	123.70
disabled child	59.50	60.06
carer	34.20	34.60
ESA components		
work-related activity	28.75	29.05
support	35.75	36.20
INCAPACITY BENEFIT		
Long-term Incapacity Benefit	104.10	105.35

5.4 Proposed benefit and pension rates 2015 to 2016

Proposed benefit and pension rates 2015 to 2016 (Weekly rates unless otherwise shown)	RATES 2014	RATES 2015
Short-term Incapacity Benefit (under state pension age)		
lower rate	78.50	79.45
higher rate	92.95	94.05
Short-term Incapacity Benefit (over state pension age)		
lower rate	99.90	101.10
higher rate	104.10	105.35
Increase of Long-term Incapacity Benefit for age		
higher rate	11.00	11.15
lower rate	6.15	6.20
Invalidity Allowance (Transitional)		
higher rate	11.00	11.15
middle rate	6.15	6.20
lower rate	6.15	6.20
INCOME SUPPORT		
Personal Allowances		
single		
under 25	57.35	57.90
25 or over	72.40	73.10
lone parent		
under 18	57.35	57.90
18 or over	72.40	73.10
couple		
both under 18	57.35	57.90
both under 18 - higher rate	86.65	87.50
one under 18, one under 25	57.35	57.90
one under 18, one 25 and over	72.40	73.10
both 18 or over	113.70	114.85
dependent children	66.33	66.90
Premiums		
family / lone parent	17.45	17.45
pensioner (applies to couples only)	112.80	116.00
disability		
single	31.85	32.25
couple	45.40	45.95
enhanced disability		
single	15.55	15.75
disabled child	24.08	24.43
couple	22.35	22.60

5.4 Proposed benefit and pension rates 2015 to 2016

Proposed benefit and pension rates 2015 to 2016 (Weekly rates unless otherwise shown)	RATES 2014	RATES 2015
severe disability		
single	61.10	61.85
couple (lower rate)	61.10	61.85
couple (higher rate)	122.20	123.70
disabled child	59.50	60.06
carer	34.20	34.60
Relevant sum for strikers	40.00	40.50
INDUSTRIAL DEATH BENEFIT		
Widow's pension		
higher rate	113.10	115.95
lower rate	33.93	34.79
Widower's pension	113.10	115.95
INDUSTRIAL INJURIES DISABLEMENT BENEFIT		
Standard rate		
100%	166.00	168.00
90%	149.40	151.20
80%	132.80	134.40
70%	116.20	117.60
60%	99.60	100.80
50%	83.00	84.00
40%	66.40	67.20
30%	49.80	50.40
20%	33.20	33.60
Maximum life gratuity (lump sum)	11020.00	11150.00
Unemployability Supplement	102.60	103.85
increase for early incapacity		
higher rate	21.25	21.50
middle rate	13.70	13.90
lower rate	6.85	6.95
Maximum reduced earnings allowance	66.40	67.20
Maximum retirement allowance	16.60	16.80
Constant attendance allowance		
exceptional rate	132.80	134.40
intermediate rate	99.60	100.80
normal maximum rate	66.40	67.20
part-time rate	33.20	33.60
Exceptionally severe disablement allowance	66.40	67.20

5.4 Proposed benefit and pension rates 2015 to 2016

Proposed benefit and pension rates 2015 to 2016 (Weekly rates unless otherwise shown)	RATES 2014	RATES 2015
JOBSEEKER'S ALLOWANCE		
Contribution based JSA - Personal rates		
under 25	57.35	57.90
25 or over	72.40	73.10
Income-based JSA - personal allowances		
under 25	57.35	57.90
25 or over	72.40	73.10
lone parent		
under 18	57.35	57.90
18 or over	72.40	73.10
couple		
both under 18	57.35	57.90
both under 18 - higher rate	86.65	87.50
one under 18, one under 25	57.35	57.90
one under 18, one 25 and over	72.40	73.10
both 18 or over	113.70	114.85
dependent children	66.33	66.90
Premiums		
family / lone parent	17.45	17.45
pensioner		
single	75.95	78.10
couple	112.80	116.00
disability		
single	31.85	32.25
couple	45.40	45.95
enhanced disability		
single	15.55	15.75
disabled child	24.08	24.43
couple	22.35	22.60
severe disability		
single	61.10	61.85
couple (lower rate)	61.10	61.85
couple (higher rate)	122.20	123.70
disabled child	59.50	60.06
carer	34.20	34.60
Prescribed sum for strikers	40.00	40.50

5.4 Proposed benefit and pension rates 2015 to 2016

Proposed benefit and pension rates 2015 to 2016 (Weekly rates unless otherwise shown)	RATES 2014	RATES 2015
MATERNITY ALLOWANCE		
Standard rate	138.18	139.58
MA threshold	30.00	30.00
PENSION CREDIT		
Standard minimum guarantee		
single	148.35	151.20
couple	226.50	230.85
Additional amount for severe disability		
single	61.10	61.85
couple (one qualifies)	61.10	61.85
couple (both qualify)	122.20	123.70
Additional amount for carers	34.20	34.60
Savings credit		
threshold - single	120.35	126.50
threshold - couple	192.00	201.80
maximum - single	16.80	14.82
maximum - couple	20.70	17.43
Amount for claimant and first spouse in polygamous marriage	226.50	230.85
Additional amount for additional spouse	78.15	79.65
Non-State Pensions (for Pension Credit purposes)		
Statutory minimum increase to non-state pensions	2.70%	1.20%
PERSONAL INDEPENDENCE PAYMENT		
Daily living component		
Enhanced	81.30	82.30
Standard	54.45	55.10
Mobility component		
Enhanced	56.75	57.45
Standard	21.55	21.80
SEVERE DISABLEMENT ALLOWANCE		
Basic rate	73.75	74.65
Age-related addition (from Dec 90)		
Higher rate	11.00	11.15
Middle rate	6.15	6.20
Lower rate	6.15	6.20
STATE PENSION		
Category A or B	113.10	115.95

5.4 Proposed benefit and pension rates 2015 to 2016

Proposed benefit and pension rates 2015 to 2016 (Weekly rates unless otherwise shown)	RATES 2014	RATES 2015
Category B(lower) - spouse or civil partner's insurance	67.80	69.50
Category C or D - non-contributory	67.80	69.50
Additional pension	2.70%	1.20%
Increments to:-		
Basic pension	2.70%	1.20%
Additional pension	2.70%	1.20%
Graduated Retirement Benefit (GRB)	2.70%	1.20%
Inheritable lump sum	2.70%	1.20%
Contracted-out Deduction from AP in respect of pre-April 1988 contracted-out earnings	Nil	Nil
Contracted-out Deduction from AP in respect of contracted-out earnings from April 1988 to 1997	2.70%	1.20%
Graduated Retirement Benefit (unit)	0.1314	0.1330
Increase of long term incapacity for age	2.70%	1.20%
Addition at age 80	0.25	0.25
Increase of Long-term incapacity for age		
higher rate	21.25	21.50
lower rate	10.65	10.80
Invalidity Allowance (Transitional) for State Pension recipients		
higher rate	21.25	21.50
middle rate	13.70	13.90
lower rate	6.85	6.95
STATUTORY ADOPTION PAY		
Earnings threshold	111.00	112.00
Standard Rate	138.18	139.58
STATUTORY MATERNITY PAY		
Earnings threshold	111.00	112.00
Standard rate	138.18	139.58
STATUTORY PATERNITY PAY		
Earnings threshold	111.00	112.00
Standard Rate	138.18	139.58
Additional statutory paternity pay	138.18	139.58
STATUTORY SHARED PARENTAL PAY		
Earnings threshold	111.00	112.00

5.4 Proposed benefit and pension rates 2015 to 2016

Proposed benefit and pension rates 2015 to 2016 (Weekly rates unless otherwise shown)	RATES 2014	RATES 2015
Standard rate	138.18	139.58
STATUTORY SICK PAY		
Earnings threshold	111.00	112.00
Standard rate	87.55	88.45
UNIVERSAL CREDIT (monthly rates)		
Universal Credit Minimum Amount	0.01	0.01
Universal Credit Amounts		
Standard allowance		
Single		
Single under 25	249.28	251.77
Single 25 or over	314.67	317.82
Couple		
Joint claimants both under 25	391.29	395.20
Joint claimants, one or both 25 or over	493.95	498.89
Child element		
First child	274.58	277.08
Second/ subsequent child	229.17	231.67
Disabled child additions		
Lower rate addition	124.86	126.11
Higher rate addition	362.92	367.92
Limited Capabilty for Work element	124.86	126.11
Limited Capabilty for Work and Work-Related Activity element	311.86	315.60
Carer element	148.61	150.39
Childcare costs element		
Maximum for one child	532.29	532.29
Maximum for two or more children	912.50	912.50
Non-dependants' housing cost contributions	68.68	69.37
Work allowances		
Higher work allowance (no housing element)		
Single		
Single claimant, no dependent children	111.00	111.00
Single claimant, one or more children	734.00	734.00
Single claimant, limited capability for work	647.00	647.00
Joint claimants		
Joint claimant, no dependent children	111.00	111.00
Joint claimant, one or more children	536.00	536.00
Joint claimant, limited capability for work	647.00	647.00
Lower work allowance		
Single		
Single claimant, no dependent children	111.00	111.00
Single claimant, one or more children	263.00	263.00
Single claimant, limited capability for work	192.00	192.00
Joint claimants		
Joint claimant, no dependent children	111.00	111.00
Joint claimant, one or more children	222.00	222.00

5.4 Proposed benefit and pension rates 2015 to 2016

Proposed benefit and pension rates 2015 to 2016 (Weekly rates unless otherwise shown)	RATES 2014	RATES 2015
Joint claimant, limited capability for work	192.00	192.00
Assumed income from capital for every £250 or part thereof, between capital disregard and upper capital limit	4.35	4.35
Third Party Deductions at 5% of UC Standard Allowance (excludes deductions for rent and service charges included in rent)		
Single		
Single under 25	12.46	12.59
Single 25 or over	15.73	15.89
Couple		
Joint claimants both under 25	19.56	19.76
Joint claimants, one or both 25 or over	24.70	24.94
Maximum deductions for Fines	108.35	108.35
Minimum deductions for rent and service charges included in rent at 10% of UC Standard Allowance (10% minimum introduced from Nov 2014)		
Single		
Single under 25	24.93	25.18
Single 25 or over	31.47	31.78
Couple		
Joint claimants both under 25	39.13	39.52
Joint claimants, one or both 25 or over	49.40	49.89
Maximum deductions for rent and service charges included in rent at 20% of UC Standard Allowance (20% maximum introduced from Nov 2014)		
Single		
Single under 25	49.86	50.35
Single 25 or over	62.93	63.56
Couple		
Joint claimants both under 25	78.26	79.04
Joint claimants, one or both 25 or over	98.79	99.78
Overall Maximum deduction Rate at 40% of UC Standard Allowance:		
Single		
Single under 25	99.71	100.71
Single 25 or over	125.87	127.13
Couple		
Joint claimants both under 25	156.52	158.08
Joint claimants, one or both 25 or over	197.58	199.56
Fraud Overpayments, Recoverable Hardship Payments and Administrative Penalties at 40% of UC Standard Allowance		
Single		
Single under 25	99.71	100.71
Single 25 or over	125.87	127.13
Couple		
Joint claimants both under 25	156.52	158.08

5.4 Proposed benefit and pension rates 2015 to 2016

Proposed benefit and pension rates 2015 to 2016 (Weekly rates unless otherwise shown)	RATES 2014	RATES 2015
Joint claimants, one or both 25 or over	197.58	199.56
Ordinary Overpayments and Civil Penalties at 15% of UC Standard Allowance		
Single		
Single under 25	37.39	37.77
Single 25 or over	47.20	47.67
Couple		
Joint claimants both under 25	58.69	59.28
Joint claimants, one or both 25 or over	74.09	74.83
Ordinary Overpayments and Civil Penalties at 25% of UC Standard Allowance if claimant's and/or partner's earnings are over the Work Allowance		
Single		
Single under 25	62.32	62.94
Single 25 or over	78.67	79.46
Couple		
Joint claimants both under 25	97.82	98.80
Joint claimants, one or both 25 or over	123.49	124.72
WIDOW'S BENEFIT		
Widowed mother's allowance	111.20	112.55
Widow's pension		
standard rate	111.20	112.55
age-related		
age 54 (49)	103.42	104.67
53 (48)	95.63	96.79
52 (47)	87.85	88.91
51 (46)	80.06	81.04
50 (45)	72.28	73.16
49 (44)	64.50	65.28
48 (43)	56.71	57.40
47 (42)	48.93	49.52
46 (41)	41.14	41.64
45 (40)	33.36	33.77

Note: For deaths occurring before 11 April 1988
refer to age-points shown in brackets.

Source: Department for Work and Pensions

5.5 Number of Persons claiming benefits: Caseloads by age group, thousands

	2004/05 Outturn	2005/06 Outturn	2006/07 Outturn	2007/08 Outturn	2008/09 Outturn	2009/10 Outturn	2010/11 Outturn	2011/12 Outturn	2012/13 Outturn	2013/14 Outturn	2014/15 Outturn
Benefits directed at Children											
Attendance Allowance (in payment)	-	-	-	-	-	-	-	-	-	-	-
Child Benefit & One Parent Benefit	-	-	-	-	-	-	-	-	-	-	-
number of children covered	-	-	-	-	-	-	-	-	-	-	-
Disability Living Allowance	279	286	292	300	310	322	331	339	350	362	381
of which in payment	279	286	292	300	310	322	331	339	350	362	381
of which entitlement without payment	-	-	-	-	-	-	-	-	-	-	-
Mobility Allowance	-	-	-	-	-	-	-	-	-	-	-
Benefits Directed at People of Working Age											
Armed Forces Independence Payment										1	1
Attendance Allowance (in payment)	-	-	-	-	-	-	-	-	-	-	-
Bereavement Benefits	180	163	147	129	117	108	101	95	91	95	90
Carer's Allowance	467	475	485	496	519	550	584	615	650	685	731
of which in payment	407	422	432	442	462	491	523	558	595	633	678
of which entitlement without payment	60	53	52	54	57	59	61	57	55	51	53
Christmas Bonus - non-contributory	1,921	1,912	1,920	2,003	3,164	3,246	3,227	3,212	3,240	3,215	3,329
Council Tax Benefit	2,473	2,603	2,570	2,533	2,566	2,940	3,172	3,254	3,368		
Disability Living Allowance	1,596	1,627	1,657	1,692	1,733	1,780	1,819	1,847	1,877	1,866	1,761
of which in payment	1,582	1,612	1,641	1,676	1,715	1,761	1,800	1,828	1,858	1,846	1,742
of which entitlement without payment	14	15	16	16	17	19	19	20	20	20	19
Disability Working Allowance	-	-	-	-	-	-	-	-	-	-	-
Employment and Support Allowance	-	-	-	-	136	391	579	811	1,365	1,921	2,242
of which contributory	-	-	-	-	59	145	199	262	364	493	507
of which contributory and income-based	-	-	-	-	6	22	38	59	103	180	248
of which income-based	-	-	-	-	56	168	275	424	784	1,117	1,341
of which credits only	-	-	-	-	16	56	67	65	114	131	147
Family Credit	-	-	-				-	-	-	-	-
Housing Benefit	2,387	2,495	2,518	2,527	2,625	2,981	3,224	3,356	3,502	3,520	3,457
Incapacity Benefit, Invalidity Benefit & Sickness Benefit	2,510	2,475	2,443	2,415	2,332	2,031	1,827	1,577	965	366	133
of which in payment	1,543	1,500	1,456	1,413	1,346	1,177	1,054	909	566	192	38
of which credits only	967	975	987	1,002	986	854	773	668	399	174	95
Income Support	2,187	2,142	2,135	2,117	2,087	1,935	1,803	1,619	1,254	939	799
Industrial Injuries benefits	187	182	176	170	164	157	152	146	137	137	131
Jobseeker's Allowance	819	870	927	818	1,025	1,538	1,415	1,515	1,507	1,273	898
of which contributory	158	165	157	142	244	321	234	212	178	145	109
of which contributory and income-based	14	15	15	13	21	30	22	19	18	15	11
of which income-based	588	632	691	609	695	1,072	1,069	1,208	1,242	1,045	726
of which credits only	59	58	64	54	66	114	91	77	69	68	52
Maternity Allowance	26	29	27	44	54	56	54	57	60	58	60
Mobility Allowance	-	-	-	-	-	-	-	-	-	-	-
Personal Independence Payment	-	-	-	-	-	-	-	-	-	12	184
of which in payment	-	-	-	-	-	-	-	-	-	12	182
of which entitlement without payment	-	-	-	-	-	-	-	-	-	-	2
Severe Disablement Allowance	260	246	234	221	210	200	191	184	177	167	134
Statutory Maternity Pay	137	154	154	197	248	253	274	273	276	272	272
Unemployment Benefit	-	-	-	-	-	-	-	-	-	-	-
Benefits Directed at Pensioners											
Attendance Allowance	1,589	1,629	1,666	1,700	1,737	1,776	1,782	1,756	1,710	1,641	1,617
of which in payment	1,400	1,445	1,489	1,528	1,568	1,607	1,619	1,597	1,553	1,490	1,462
of which entitlement without payment	189	184	177	172	169	169	163	160	158	151	155
Bereavement Benefits	26	23	21	19	14	11	10	11	11	3	3
Carer's Allowance	235	279	319	356	388	411	420	417	405	387	375
of which in payment	22	24	26	28	30	31	30	26	22	20	18
of which entitlement without payment	213	255	292	327	357	381	390	391	383	367	357
Christmas Bonus - contributory	12,302	12,387	12,586	12,728	11,754	12,123	12,239	12,335	12,346	12,253	12,459
Council Tax Benefit	2,442	2,426	2,510	2,535	2,592	2,631	2,633	2,620	2,544	-	-
Disability Living Allowance	826	864	903	949	991	1,031	1,055	1,066	1,079	1,079	1,072
of which in payment	821	859	897	942	984	1,023	1,046	1,057	1,070	1,069	1,062
of which entitlement without payment	5	5	6	6	7	8	9	9	9	10	10
Housing Benefit	1,554	1,491	1,503	1,509	1,541	1,566	1,574	1,576	1,551	1,505	1,464
Incapacity Benefit, Invalidity Benefit & Sickness Benefit	-	-	-	-	-	-	-	-	-	-	-
of which in payment	-	-	-	-	-	-	-	-	-	-	-
of which credits only	-	-	-	-	-	-	-	-	-	-	-
Industrial Injuries benefits	153	156	159	171	172	176	182	185	187	189	189
Income Support	-	-	-	-	-	-	-	-	-	-	-
Mobility Allowance	-	-	-	-	-	-	-	-	-	-	-
Over-75 TV Licence	3,892	3,965	3,982	3,993	4,079	4,206	4,236	4,277	4,316	4,414	4,493
Pension Credit	2,594	2,700	2,729	2,732	2,724	2,736	2,718	2,649	2,505	2,380	2,228
Personal Independence Payment	-	-	-	-	-	-	-	-	-	1	17
of which in payment	-	-	-	-	-	-	-	-	-	1	16
of which entitlement without payment	-	-	-	-	-	-	-	-	-	-	-

5.5 Number of Persons claiming benefits: Caseloads by age group, thousands

	2004/05 Outturn	2005/06 Outturn	2006/07 Outturn	2007/08 Outturn	2008/09 Outturn	2009/10 Outturn	2010/11 Outturn	2011/12 Outturn	2012/13 Outturn	2013/14 Outturn	2014/15 Outturn
State Pension	11,477	11,585	11,715	11,938	12,160	12,410	12,566	12,667	12,810	12,888	12,958
of which contributory	11,454	11,562	11,692	11,913	12,134	12,382	12,537	12,634	12,775	12,846	12,912
of which basic element	11,384	11,492	11,617	11,837	12,053	12,285	12,460	12,556	12,737	12,814	12,887
of which earnings-related element ("Additional Pension", "SERPS" or "S2P")	7,425	7,700	7,963	8,324	8,673	9,052	9,320	9,549	9,848	10,021	10,207
of which Graduated Retirement Benefit	9,296	9,439	9,594	9,842	10,087	10,358	10,563	10,702	10,874	10,984	11,096
of which lump sums (covering all contributory elements)	-	-	8	24	46	58	66	59	56	56	50
of which new State Pension (excluding protected payments)											
of which new State Pension Protected Payments (including inherited elements)											
of which non-contributory ("Category D")	23	23	23	25	26	28	29	33	35	42	46
Severe Disablement Allowance	42	42	42	42	41	40	39	36	34	31	29
Winter Fuel Payments	11,430	11,555	11,750	12,123	12,421	12,681	12,783	12,686	12,683	12,585	12,467

Source: Department for Work and Pensions (DWP)

5.6 Jobseeker's Allowance[1,2,3] claimants: by benefit entitlement Great Britain

As at May   Thousands

		2005	2006	2007	2008	2009	2010	2011	2012	2013 *	2014 *	2015 *
All Persons												
All with benefit - total	KXDX	728.3	812	730.8	718	1316.4	1237.3	1298.3	1377	1433	1035.3	719.1
Contribution-based JSA only	KXDY	139.5	134.6	113.6	127.8	341.8	205.3	182.7	159.5	142.4	97.3	72.7
Contribution based JSA & income-based JSA	KXDZ	13.5	13	11.9	12.8	34.6	21.1	19.9	16.8	14.9	10.9	7.1
Income-based JSA only payment	KXEA	575.3	664.5	605.3	577.4	940	1010.9	1096	1201	1156	842.4	583.2
No benefit in payment	KXEB	72.4	83.9	76.4	69.9	126.6	117.3	105.8	107.2	119.4	84.7	56.1
Males												
All with benefit - total	KXED	545.3	606.8	537.8	529.9	978.9	890.9	879.8	930	938.4	665.7	460.9
Contribution-based JSA only	KXEE	99.5	95.8	79.6	90.6	248.7	143.4	118.9	103.5	94.1	62	45.8
Contribution based JSA & income-based JSA	KXEF	12.6	12	10.7	11.7	31.2	18.1	16.9	13.7	12.6	8.9	5.9
Income-based JSA only payment	KXEG	433.2	498.9	447.5	427.6	698.9	729.5	744	812.8	753	539.1	374.1
No benefit in payment	KXEH	49.8	56.6	51.7	46.7	88.8	82.2	69.3	71.6	78.7	55.8	35.1
Females												
All with benefit - total	KXEJ	182.9	205.3	193	188.1	337.6	346.4	418.4	447	494.3	369.5	258.2
Contribution-based JSA only	KXEK	40	38.7	34	37.2	93.1	61.9	63.7	56	48.3	35.3	26.9
Contribution based JSA & income-based JSA	KXEL	0.8	1	1.2	1.2	3.4	3.0	3	3.1	2.3	2	1.3
Income-based JSA only payment	KXEM	142.1	165.5	157.8	149.8	241.1	281.4	351.7	387.9	403	303.3	209.1
No benefit in payment	KXEN	22.6	27.2	24.8	23.2	37.7	35.1	36.5	35.5	40.7	28.9	21

Sources: Department for Work and Pensions

1. Jobseeker's Allowance (JSA) has two routes of entry: contrbution-based which depends mainly upon national insurance contributions and income-based which depends mainly on a means test. Some claimants can qualify by either route. In practice they receive income-based JSA but have an under lying entitlement to the contribution-based element.

2 Figures are given at May each year and have been derived by applying 5% proportions to 100% totals taken from the DWP 100% Work and Pensions Longitudinal Study (WPLS).

3 Figures are rounded to the nearest hundred and quoted in thousands. They may not sum due to rounding.

* 5% sample data - DWP recommends that, where the detail is only available on the 5% sample data, the proportions derived should be applied to the overall 100% total for the benefit.

5.7 Employment and Support Allowance and Incapacity Benefit[1,2,3] claimants: by sex, age and duration of spell
Great Britain and Overseas (excluding Northern Ireland).

end of May
Thousands

		2003	2004	2005	2006	2007	2008[4]	2009	2010	2011	2012	2013	2014	2015
Males														
All durations: All ages	KJJA	1525.02	1517.62	1492.38	1455.52	1428.65	1399.58	1419.43	1409.10	1358.24	1,312.25	1,252.36	1,250.99	1290.55
Under 20	KJJB	21.81	22.04	21.45	19.95	18.66	17.25	18.09	17.33	15.6	15.66	15.90	21.33	17.86
20-29	KJJC	138.54	142.68	143.24	141.8	146.07	149.47	159.1	160.91	156.22	156.71	159.44	180.29	189.19
30-39	KJJD	254.3	253.32	245.61	233.7	224.29	215.51	215.95	213.57	201.58	195.39	189.43	208.79	212.98
40-49	KJJE	311.85	318.04	320.77	319.77	320.24	319.22	330.96	335.93	328.57	319.31	304.49	309.69	306.33
50-59	KJJF	472.03	463.37	451.93	439.54	418.26	404.76	405.59	403.61	391.96	384.28	369.52	376.74	379.13
60-64	KJJG	326.45	318.12	309.36	300.73	301.1	293.33	289.57	277.30	263.8	240.26	212.72	153.15	184.12
65 and over	KJJH	0.05	0.05	0.04	0.02	0.03	0.04	0.17	0.46	0.48	0.60	0.82	0.98	0.93
Unknown										0.04	0.03	0.03	0.02	0.01
Over six months: All ages	KJJI	1359.53	1359.08	1347.43	1323.2	1291.32	1266.8	1253.91	1251.24	1213.77	1,050.73	950.15	1021.05	1101.36
Under 20	KJJJ	13.4	13.78	13.51	12.85	11.7	10.9	10.42	10.50	9.29	9.46	9.50	14.30	10.92
20-29	KJJK	105.72	110.85	114.57	115.21	117.83	121.9	124.5	128.76	125.36	115.47	114.37	137.80	150.76
30-39	KJJL	217.05	217.81	213.91	205.36	195.22	188.25	182.41	180.52	170.92	145.09	139.67	165.79	173.64
40-49	KJJM	278.53	285.9	290.72	291.36	289.94	289.72	293.13	298.29	294.15	249.83	230.62	256.27	262.66
50-59	KJJN	434.04	427.06	418.6	409.46	387.76	374.75	368.48	367.26	360.03	311.58	278.75	317.56	334.50
60-64	KJJO	310.75	303.64	296.1	288.93	288.85	281.25	274.93	265.52	253.54	218.74	176.44	128.44	167.98
65 and over	KJJP	0.03	0.04	0.02	0.02	0.03	0.03	0.05	0.39	0.43	0.53	0.76	0.86	0.89
Unknown										0.04	0.03	0.03	0.02	0.01
Females														
All durations: All ages	KJJQ	969.44	990.84	998.2	994.33	988.93	982.33	998.74	1007.13	1026.38	1,037.34	1,033.19	1067.92	1137.30
Under 20	KJJR	21.49	21.48	20.51	18.92	17.86	16.79	15.68	14.54	13.05	13.01	13.26	18.74	15.85
20-29	KJJS	100.78	105.02	108.61	109.73	114.42	117.91	121.5	122.82	121.54	121.56	123.93	140.27	145.75
30-39	KJJT	177.7	177.91	173.45	167.36	162.39	156.95	156.85	157.74	157.34	155.59	156.43	173.84	177.98
40-49	KJJU	262.2	270.9	276.62	279.32	283.45	285.84	296.87	305.06	305.31	299.72	287.89	301.47	291.46
50-59	KJJV	407.24	415.52	418.99	418.99	410.8	404.82	407.82	406.97	401.12	397.31	381.70	355.49	395.87
60 and over	KJJW	0.03	0.02	0.02	0.02	0.02	0.02	0.02	0.01	27.98	50.13	69.96	78.09	110.37
Unknown										0.03	0.02	0.02	0.02	0.01
Over six months: All ages	KJJX	858.03	880.52	894.57	896.33	885.69	881.41	882.94	888.73	905.11	817.68	787.01	881.84	975.54
Under 20	KJJY	12.35	12.4	12.1	11.13	10.2	9.55	8.75	8.15	7.16	7.31	7.46	12.15	9.00
20-29	KJJZ	79.63	84.02	88.98	90.99	93.6	97.24	99.15	100.81	99.22	90.34	89.68	107.74	116.32
30-39	KJKA	154.19	154.95	152.48	148	142.28	137.59	134.9	134.29	131.11	116.57	116.53	140.24	146.24
40-49	KJKB	234.71	243.52	250.11	253.5	255.99	258.74	263.7	269.48	269.38	234.09	222.46	253.55	251.44
50-59	KJKC	377.12	385.61	390.88	392.69	383.6	378.27	376.43	375.99	371.76	322.89	293.82	301.40	352.44
60 and over	KJKD	0.03	0.02	0.02	0.02	0.02	0.02	0.02	0.02	26.45	46.46	57.03	66.75	100.08
Unknown										0.03	0.02	0.02	0.01	0.01
Unknown Gender														
All durations	EW44	0.44	0.31	0.26	0.15	0.13	0.11	0.23	3.86	-	-	-	-	-
Over 6 months	EW45	0.21	0.16	0.13	0.1	0.09	0.09	0.1	3.67	-	-	-	-	-

Source: Department for Work and Pensions Work and Pensions Longitudinal Study 100% data

Definitions and conventions. Caseload figures are rounded to the nearest ten and displayed in thousands. Totals may not sum due to rounding.
Figures are given at May each year.
Table includes Employment and Support Allowance and Incapacity Benefit ONLY claimants and not those claiming Severe Disablement Allowance (SDA).
From 27th October 2008, new claims to Incapacity Benefit can also be allocated, on incapacity grounds, to the newly introduced Employment and Support Allowance (ESA).
Due to rounding errors several figures have been revised for May 2008.
2011 figures provided by IGS in relation to FOI 2013-2248 therefore 'Unknown' categories are different to previous years but match IGS published information on IB and ESA

5.8 Attendance allowance - cases in payment: Age and gender of claimant Great Britain

At May each year   Thousands

		2006	2007	2008	2009	2010	2011	2012	2013	2014	2015
Males: All ages	JT9Z	459.5	478.4	497.2	516.5	531.5	530.00	526.1	504.92	493.89	499.84
Unknown age	JTA2	–	–	–	–	–	0.02	0.02	0.02	0.02	0.02
65 - 69	JTA3	22.3	22.8	23.5	24.4	24.8	23.8	23.3	21.2	20.66	24.35
70 - 74	JTA4	64.2	66.8	70.2	73.7	74.9	71.9	68.8	63.6	59.93	60.94
75 - 79	JTA5	104.8	106.3	109.1	112.4	114.9	113.7	112.3	107.3	104.10	104.18
80 - 84	JTA6	130.4	133.1	135.4	137.8	139.9	137.6	135.3	130.0	125.69	125.81
85 - 89	JTA7	89.4	98.5	107.7	116	118.1	118.00	117.0	112.7	111.21	111.02
90 and over	JTA8	48.4	50.8	51.2	52.2	58.9	65.00	69.4	70.1	72.29	73.52
Females: All ages	JTA9	1006.2	1029.1	1049.5	1069.3	1082.8	1069.1	1047.5	997.9	963.27	951.99
Unknown age	JTB2	–	–	–	–	–	0.03	0.03	0.03	0.03	0.04
65 - 69	JTB3	28.3	28.4	29.1	30	30.3	28.7	27.2	23.8	22.52	26.63
70 - 74	JTB4	93.6	96.4	99.6	103.5	104.5	99.7	93.9	85.3	78.52	78.33
75 - 79	JTB5	186.8	185.8	186.7	188.4	188.4	182.2	176.5	166.3	158.57	156.09
80 - 84	JTB6	279.4	278.3	277.7	277.7	277.0	269.2	259.8	244.9	231.85	226.25
85 - 89	JTB7	241.6	259.3	276.7	290.9	286.6	279.8	271.7	258.8	250.12	244.97
90 and over	JTB8	176.4	180.9	179.6	178.8	196.0	209.6	218.5	218.7	221.66	219.68

Sources: Department for Work and Pensions (DWP);
Work and Pensions Longitudinal Study (WPLS)

Statistical disclosure control has been applied to this table to avoid the release of confidential data. Totals may not sum due to the disclosure control applied

The move to publishing benefit data via the Stat-Xplore instead of the DWP Tabulation Tool has involved adopting a new disclosure control methodology, in line with other benefits published via this new tool. Although the data still comes from the same source there may be small differences in the outputs displayed using this new tool, when compared to the Tabulation Tool.

".." denotes a nil or negligible number of claimants or award amount based on a nil or negligible number of claimants.

5.9a: Families and children receiving Child Benefit, in each country and English Region, 2003 to 2015

Time Series	United Kingdom[1]	Great Britain	England and Wales	England													Foreign and not known
					North East	North West	Yorkshire and the Humber	East Midlands	West Midlands	East	London	South East	South West	Wales	Scotland	Northern Ireland	
Area Codes[2]	K02000001	K03000001	K04000001	E92000001	E12000001	E12000002	E12000003	E12000004	E12000005	E12000006	E12000007	E12000008	E12000009	W92000004	S92000003	N92000002	n/a
Number of families																	
August 2003	7,246,335	7,000,770	6,394,870	6,037,500	318,470	861,775	619,630	517,590	663,400	653,695	876,120	956,080	570,735	357,370	605,900	225,885	19,675
August 2004	7,296,495	7,055,160	6,448,355	6,087,500	317,515	863,070	622,065	520,870	667,175	660,390	894,090	965,480	576,845	360,855	606,805	226,850	14,485
August 2005	7,315,165	7,074,665	6,470,575	6,110,190	315,855	860,660	622,475	522,195	667,565	664,155	909,045	970,225	578,015	360,385	604,085	226,800	13,705
August 2006	7,413,475	7,129,720	6,528,205	6,168,010	316,665	864,650	626,740	527,105	672,220	671,850	926,055	981,015	581,705	360,195	601,515	230,140	53,615
August 2007	7,475,035	7,212,565	6,605,270	6,241,895	318,020	869,475	631,995	535,775	678,300	683,780	937,480	995,990	591,085	363,375	607,290	230,825	31,650
August 2008	7,582,990	7,320,990	6,708,080	6,341,345	319,815	876,795	640,670	543,350	686,910	696,485	964,180	1,013,595	599,550	366,735	612,910	233,830	28,165
August 2009	7,769,880	7,485,730	6,864,935	6,492,290	324,525	892,240	653,645	554,925	701,070	713,455	1,002,815	1,038,010	611,600	372,650	620,795	238,605	45,545
August 2010	7,841,675	7,557,305	6,935,695	6,562,705	324,265	894,940	657,700	559,645	705,640	723,030	1,028,265	1,051,885	617,340	372,985	621,615	240,985	43,385
August 2011	7,884,760	7,600,115	6,979,465	6,606,285	323,155	895,670	659,240	561,885	708,325	730,180	1,044,355	1,061,870	621,605	373,180	620,650	242,310	42,335
August 2012	7,920,495	7,641,575	7,022,780	6,650,070	321,310	895,845	661,370	564,385	711,110	737,485	1,061,620	1,071,795	625,145	372,705	618,795	243,185	35,735
August 2013	7,550,265	7,279,100	6,691,985	6,328,460	311,725	868,775	643,560	545,720	692,110	690,410	996,490	979,075	600,590	363,525	587,115	239,125	32,040
August 2014	7,461,675	7,195,865	6,619,190	6,259,275	307,860	862,015	640,080	542,575	688,340	681,035	982,060	959,600	595,710	359,910	576,675	237,865	27,945
August 2015	7,416,800	7,153,935	6,584,675	6,227,865	305,000	857,415	636,600	541,540	687,010	678,260	977,940	951,060	593,040	356,810	569,260	236,890	25,970
Number of children																	
August 2003	13,138,075	12,670,975	11,625,050	10,983,290	552,970	1,549,900	1,116,630	934,450	1,219,985	1,200,175	1,613,235	1,754,585	1,041,360	641,755	1,045,925	439,870	27,230
August 2004	13,096,760	12,635,505	11,600,380	10,960,280	544,840	1,534,595	1,109,155	930,920	1,214,695	1,200,175	1,632,425	1,752,995	1,040,475	640,100	1,035,125	435,690	25,565
August 2005	13,111,665	12,654,135	11,626,490	10,988,765	540,940	1,528,255	1,109,150	932,310	1,215,315	1,204,750	1,658,755	1,758,520	1,040,780	637,725	1,027,640	431,995	25,535
August 2006	13,233,320	12,706,365	11,685,995	11,050,975	540,980	1,529,585	1,113,190	936,980	1,219,915	1,212,530	1,686,375	1,768,965	1,042,445	635,020	1,020,370	435,485	91,475
August 2007	13,267,355	12,778,460	11,754,415	11,117,770	540,610	1,529,060	1,117,760	946,090	1,225,025	1,225,485	1,699,215	1,782,530	1,052,000	636,645	1,024,045	433,370	55,525
August 2008	13,340,565	12,857,555	11,831,255	11,194,420	539,840	1,528,890	1,124,420	951,000	1,231,190	1,235,400	1,732,120	1,795,225	1,056,340	636,835	1,026,300	434,390	48,625
August 2009	13,604,375	13,088,240	12,054,140	11,409,950	546,125	1,549,625	1,143,245	967,010	1,251,900	1,258,520	1,794,220	1,827,530	1,071,775	644,190	1,034,095	440,570	75,565
August 2010	13,685,250	13,170,155	12,138,365	11,495,395	544,775	1,551,080	1,147,440	971,690	1,257,180	1,269,870	1,831,965	1,843,465	1,077,930	642,965	1,031,795	443,110	71,985
August 2011	13,721,160	13,207,465	12,179,715	11,537,505	542,680	1,549,475	1,148,450	973,310	1,259,770	1,276,525	1,853,670	1,852,950	1,080,680	642,210	1,027,750	444,285	69,410
August 2012	13,771,635	13,267,355	12,243,960	11,602,370	540,060	1,550,880	1,153,480	976,870	1,265,765	1,284,980	1,880,560	1,865,335	1,084,435	641,590	1,023,390	445,220	59,055
August 2013	13,107,460	12,618,675	11,651,810	11,026,465	525,215	1,505,780	1,124,295	943,980	1,233,780	1,198,215	1,763,895	1,693,670	1,037,630	625,345	966,865	437,440	51,345
August 2014	12,962,175	12,482,260	11,532,980	10,913,100	520,170	1,497,345	1,121,595	938,835	1,229,210	1,181,620	1,738,575	1,656,975	1,028,775	619,885	949,280	435,055	44,860
August 2015	12,895,530	12,420,785	11,482,570	10,867,625	517,125	1,494,870	1,118,980	938,125	1,229,805	1,176,055	1,729,510	1,639,590	1,023,565	614,945	938,215	433,940	40,805

Source: HM Revenue and Customs

Footnotes
1 Includes Foreign and not known
2 Area codes implemented from 1 January 2011; in line with the new GSS Coding and Naming policy.

5.9b: Families receiving Child Benefit nationally, in each country and English Region, August 2015

Area names	Area Codes [1]	Number of families, by size						Number of children in these families, by age				
		Total	One child	Two children	Three children	Four children	Five or more children	Total	Under 5	5-10	11-15	16 and over
United Kingdom [2]	K02000001	**7,416,800**	**3,551,205**	**2,702,915**	**840,540**	**234,325**	**87,810**	**12,895,530**	**3,537,900**	**4,283,230**	**3,238,795**	**1,835,605**
Great Britain	K03000001	**7,153,935**	**3,433,215**	**2,607,710**	**803,975**	**224,270**	**84,765**	**12,420,785**	**3,409,485**	**4,129,445**	**3,122,340**	**1,759,510**
England and Wales	K04000001	**6,584,675**	**3,139,635**	**2,403,930**	**748,370**	**211,650**	**81,095**	**11,482,570**	**3,154,555**	**3,811,620**	**2,875,540**	**1,640,855**
England	E92000001	6,227,865	2,967,350	2,273,615	708,260	201,230	77,415	10,867,625	2,990,000	3,610,440	2,719,595	1,547,590
North East	E12000001	305,000	152,865	108,460	31,965	8,525	3,190	517,125	140,590	170,695	129,795	76,040
North West	E12000002	857,415	414,720	304,790	97,850	28,635	11,420	1,494,870	409,900	494,855	373,365	216,750
Yorkshire and the Humber	E12000003	636,600	302,005	230,260	73,210	22,430	8,700	1,118,980	310,070	372,455	278,620	157,835
East Midlands	E12000004	541,540	258,735	200,655	59,455	16,440	6,250	938,125	258,275	309,985	235,585	134,285
West Midlands	E12000005	687,010	320,640	244,950	83,360	26,530	11,530	1,229,805	339,105	406,420	308,940	175,340
East	E12000006	678,260	318,150	257,485	76,495	19,755	6,380	1,176,055	323,600	389,120	295,945	167,395
London	E12000007	977,940	473,795	334,200	118,005	35,940	16,000	1,729,510	478,860	588,515	426,535	235,600
South East	E12000008	951,060	448,105	364,200	103,685	26,640	8,430	1,639,590	448,895	544,130	412,805	233,760
South West	E12000009	593,040	278,335	228,620	64,235	16,340	5,510	1,023,565	280,705	334,270	258,005	150,585
Wales	W92000004	356,810	172,285	130,310	40,110	10,420	3,685	614,945	164,555	201,180	155,945	93,270
Scotland	S92000003	569,260	293,585	203,780	55,610	12,620	3,670	938,215	254,930	317,825	246,800	118,655
Northern Ireland	N92000002	236,890	103,300	86,605	34,460	9,615	2,915	433,940	117,115	140,230	106,735	69,865
Foreign and not known	N/A	25,970	14,695	8,600	2,105	440	130	40,805	11,300	13,555	9,720	6,230

Source: HM Revenue and Customs

Footnotes
1 Area codes implemented from 1 January 2011; in line with the new GSS Coding and Naming policy.
2 Includes Foreign and not known.

5.10: Child Tax Credit and Working Tax Credit elements and thresholds

Annual rate (£), except where specified

	2003-04	2004-05	2005-06	2006-07	2007-08	2008-09	2009-10	2010-11	2011-12	2012-13	2013-14	2014-15	2015-16
Child Tax Credit													
Family element	545	545	545	545	545	545	545	545	545	545	545	545	545
Family element, baby addition[1]	545	545	545	545	545	545	545	545	-	-	-	-	-
Child element [2]	1,445	1,625	1,690	1,765	1,845	2,085	2,235	2,300	2,555	2,690	2,720	2,750	2,780
Disabled child additional element[3]	2,155	2,215	2,285	2,350	2,440	2,540	2,670	2,715	2,800	2,950	3,015	3,100	3,140
Severely disabled child additional element[4]	865	890	920	945	980	1,020	1,075	1,095	1,130	1,190	1,220	1,220	1,275
Working Tax Credit													
Basic element	1,525	1,570	1,620	1,665	1,730	1,800	1,890	1,920	1,920	1,920	1,920	1,940	1,960
Couples and lone parent element	1,500	1,545	1,595	1,640	1,700	1,770	1,860	1,890	1,950	1,950	1,970	1,990	2,010
30 hour element [5]	620	640	660	680	705	735	775	790	790	790	790	800	810
Disabled worker element	2,040	2,100	2,165	2,225	2,310	2,405	2,530	2,570	2,650	2,790	2,855	2,935	2,970
Severely disabled adult element	865	890	920	945	980	1,020	1,075	1,095	1,130	1,190	1,220	1,255	1,275
50+ return to work payment [6]													
16 but less than 30 hours per week	1,045	1,075	1,110	1,140	1,185	1,235	1,300	1,320	1,365	-	-	-	-
at least 30 hours per week	1,565	1,610	1,660	1,705	1,770	1,840	1,935	1,965	2,030	-	-	-	-
Childcare element													
Maximum eligible costs allowed (£ per week)													
Eligible costs incurred for 1 child	135	135	175	175	175	175	175	175	175	175	175	175	175
Eligible costs incurred for 2+ children	200	200	300	300	300	300	300	300	300	300	300	300	300
Percentage of eligible costs covered	*70%*	*70%*	*70%*	*80%*	*80%*	*80%*	*80%*	*80%*	*70%*	*70%*	*70%*	*70%*	*70%*
Common features													
First income threshold [7]	5,060	5,060	5,220	5,220	5,220	6,420	6,420	6,420	6,420	6,420	6,420	6,420	6,420
First withdrawal rate	*37%*	*37%*	*37%*	*37%*	*37%*	*39%*	*39%*	*39%*	*41%*	*41%*	*41%*	*41%*	*41%*
Second income threshold [8]	50,000	50,000	50,000	50,000	50,000	50,000	50,000	50,000	40,000	-	-	-	-
Second withdrawal rate	*1 in 15*	*1 in 15*	*1 in 15*	*1 in 15*	*1 in 15*	*1 in 15*	*1 in 15*	*1 in 15*	*41%*	-	-	-	-
First income threshold for those entitled to Child Tax Credit only[9]	13,230	13,480	13,910	14,155	14,495	15,575	16,040	16,190	15,860	15,860	15,910	16,010	16,105
Income increase disregard	2,500	2,500	2,500	25,000	25,000	25,000	25,000	25,000	10,000	10,000	5,000	5,000	5,000
Income fall disregard[10]										2,500	2,500	2,500	2,500
Minimum award payable	26	26	26	26	26	26	26	26	26	26	26	26	26

Source: HM Revenue and Customs

1 Payable to families for any period during which they have one or more children aged under 1. Abolished 6 April 2011.

2 Payable for each child up to 31 August after their 16th birthday, and for each young person for any period in which they are aged under 20 (under 19 to 2005-06) and in full-time non-advanced education, or under 19 and in their first 20 weeks of registration with the Careers service or Connexions.

3 Payable in addition to the child element for each disabled child.

4 Payable in addition to the disabled child element for each severely disabled child.

5 Payable for any period during which normal hours worked (for a couple, summed over the two partners) is at least 30 per week.

6 Payable for each qualifying adult for the first 12 months following a return to work.Abolished 6 April 2012.

7 Income is net of pension contributions, and excludes Child Benefit, Housing benefit, Council tax benefit, maintenance and the first £300 of family income other than from work or benefits. The award is reduced by the excess of income over the first threshold, multiplied by the first withdrawal rate.

8 For those entitled to the Child Tax Credit, the award is reduced only down to the family element, plus the baby addition where relevant, less the excess of income over the second threshold multiplied by the second withdrawal rate. Abolished 6 April 2012.

9 Those also receiving Income Support, income-based Jobseeker's Allowance or Pension Credit are passported to maximum CTC with no tapering.

10 Introduced from 6 April 2012, this drop in income is disregarded in the calculation of Tax Credit awards.

5.11: Number of families and children with Child Tax Credit or Working Tax Credit, by level of award, 2015-16

Thousands

	New Area Codes[1]	In-work families					Total in receipt (out-of-work and in-work families)	Number of children in recipient families		
		Total out-of-work families	With children		Of which, lone parents	With no children		Total out-of-work families	In-work families	
			Receiving WTC and CTC	Receiving CTC only		Receiving WTC only			Receiving WTC and CTC	Receiving CTC only
United Kingdom[2]	K02000001	1,240	1,759	805	1,151	480	4,284	2,386	3,247	1,665
Great Britain	K03000001	1,188	1,698	775	1,110	459	4,120	2,287	3,138	1,599
England and Wales	K04000001	1,092	1,573	716	1,013	414	3,794	2,116	2,931	1,481
England	E92000001	1,023	1,488	673	956	386	3,570	1,987	2,779	1,395
North East	E12000001	62	76	32	52	28	198	116	133	63
North West	E12000002	149	226	92	147	70	537	289	421	187
Yorkshire and the Humber	E12000003	112	168	74	100	50	404	220	319	152
East Midlands	E12000004	82	130	67	83	38	317	162	237	139
West Midlands	E12000005	126	174	80	103	44	425	254	339	167
East	E12000006	96	141	75	95	32	344	185	256	159
London	E12000007	192	262	80	162	45	578	366	516	163
South East	E12000008	125	183	96	129	41	446	241	332	204
South West	E12000009	80	127	76	85	39	322	152	227	159
Wales	W92000004	68	85	42	57	28	224	129	152	86
Scotland	S92000003	96	125	59	97	45	326	171	207	118
Northern Ireland	N92000002	50	58	29	39	20	156	95	104	63
Foreign and not known	n/a	2	3	2	2	2	8	4	5	3

Source: HM Revenue and Customs

Child and Working Tax Credits Finalised Awards 2015-16: Geographical Analysis

Footnotes

1 Area codes implemented from 1 January 2011 in line with the new GSS Coding and Naming policy.

2 Includes Foreign and not known

3 All figures are rounded to the nearest integer therefore not all totals may exactly equal the sums of their respective components.

4 "Foreign and not known" consists of a small proportion of recipient families and children who do not live within England, Scotland, Northern Island or Wales. They may for instance be a Crown servant posted overseas, or living in a British Crown Dependency. Due to the small size of this population we combine them into one group which also consists of those whom, at the time of publication, either have a UK postcode that does not match to a geographical office region code, or do not have a postcode in the available data.

5.12 Widows' Benefit (excluding bereavement payment[1,2,3]): by type of benefit Great Britain

Number in receipt of widows benefit as at May each year

Thousands

		2007	2008	2009	2010	2011	2012	2013	2014	2015
All Widows' Benefit (excluding bereavement allowance)										
All ages	KJGA	96.89	77.9	62.14	50.75	44	38	33	28.52	24.83
Unknown Age	EW4O	0.02	–	–	–	–	–	–	–	–
18 - 24	EW4P	–	–	–	–	–	–	–	–	–
25 - 29	EW4Q	0.04	0.02	0.01	–	–	–	–	–	–
30 - 34	EW4R	0.32	0.2	0.13	0.08	0.05	0.02	0.01	–	–
35 - 39	EW4S	1.53	1.08	0.74	0.50	0.34	0.22	0.14	0.09	0.05
40 - 44	EW4T	3.93	3.04	2.31	1.72	1.22	0.84	0.59	0.38	0.22
45 - 49	EW4U	7.58	6.26	5.14	4.20	3.38	2.71	2.07	1.52	1.09
50 - 54	EW4V	17.69	14.42	11.72	9.76	8.09	6.77	5.60	4.63	3.76
55 - 59	EW4W	45.78	36.86	30.37	24.62	20.00	16.31	13.26	10.80	9.02
60 - 64	EW4X	20.01	16.01	11.71	9.86	10.93	11.13	11.24	11.10	10.68
Widowed parents' allowance - with dependant children										
All ages	KJGG	15.6	12.6	9.98	7.91	6.11	4.61	3.35	2.34	1.56
Unknown Age	EW4Y	–	–	–	–	–	–	–	–	–
18 - 24	EW4Z	–	–	–	–	–	–	–	–	–
25 - 29	EW52	0.03	0.02	0.01	–	–	–	–	–	–
30 - 34	EW53	0.31	0.19	0.12	0.07	0.04	0.02	0.01	–	–
35 - 39	EW54	1.49	1.05	0.72	0.49	0.32	0.21	0.13	0.08	0.05
40 - 44	EW55	3.75	2.92	2.23	1.65	1.18	0.80	0.57	0.36	0.21
45 - 49	EW56	4.71	3.87	3.13	2.61	2.04	1.56	1.12	0.78	0.51
50 - 54	EW57	3.58	3.1	2.53	2.08	1.68	1.32	1.00	0.72	0.50
55 - 59	EW58	1.57	1.33	1.13	0.92	0.75	0.62	0.45	0.34	0.25
60 - 64	EW59	0.17	0.13	0.1	0.09	0.09	0.08	0.07	0.06	0.05
Widowed parents' allowance - without dependant children										
All ages	KJGM	0.69	0.54	0.46	0.39	0.28	0.22	0.17	0.12	0.07
Unknown Age	EW5A	–	–	–	–	–	–	–	–	–
18 - 24	EW5B	–	–	–	–	–	–	–	–	–
25 - 29	EW5C	–	–	–	–	–	–	–	–	–
30 - 34	EW5D	0.01	0.01	0.01	0.01	–	–	–	–	–
35 - 39	EW5E	0.04	0.03	0.02	0.02	0.01	0.01	0.01	0.01	–
40 - 44	EW5F	0.13	0.09	0.07	0.06	0.04	0.03	0.02	0.01	0.01
45 - 49	EW5G	0.21	0.17	0.15	0.12	0.09	0.07	0.05	0.03	0.02
50 - 54	EW5H	0.17	0.13	0.13	0.12	0.08	0.06	0.05	0.04	0.03
55 - 59	EW5I	0.11	0.1	0.07	0.06	0.04	0.04	0.02	0.02	0.01
60 - 64	EW5J	0.02	0.01	0.01	0.01	0.01	0.01	0.01	0.01	0.01
Age-related bereavement allowance										
All ages	KJGS	70.13	57.37	46.58	38.55	34.2	30.16	26.7	23.73	21.20
Unknown Age	EW5K	0.01	–	–	–	–	–	–	–	–
18 - 24	EW5L	–	–	–	–	–	–	–	–	–
25 - 29	EW5M	–	–	–	–	–	–	–	–	–
30 - 34	EW5N	–	–	–	–	–	–	–	–	–
35 - 39	EW5O	–	–	–	–	–	–	–	–	–
40 - 44	EW5P	0.06	0.03	0.01	–	–	–	–	–	–
45 - 49	EW5Q	2.66	2.23	1.86	1.47	1.24	1.08	0.90	0.72	0.57
50 - 54	EW5R	13.75	11.08	9.01	7.55	6.32	5.39	4.55	3.87	3.24
55 - 59	EW5S	40.57	32.61	26.83	21.74	17.71	14.44	11.80	9.68	8.16
60 - 64	EW5T	13.08	11.42	8.87	7.78	6.92	9.25	9.47	9.46	9.23
Bereavement allowance (Not age related)										
All ages	KJGW	10.47	7.39	5.12	3.90	3.41	3.02	2.67	2.33	2.00
Unknown Age	EW5U	–	–	–	–	–	–	–	–	–
18 - 24	EW5V	–	–	–	–	–	–	–	–	–
25 - 29	EW5W	–	–	–	–	–	–	–	–	–
30 - 34	EW5X	–	–	–	–	–	–	–	–	–
35 - 39	EW5Y	–	–	–	–	–	–	–	–	–
40 - 44	EW5Z	–	–	–	–	–	–	–	–	–
45 - 49	EW62	–	–	–	–	–	–	–	–	–
50 - 54	EW63	0.2	0.11	0.05	0.01	0.01	–	–	–	–
55 - 59	EW64	3.53	2.82	2.33	1.90	1.5	1.22	0.99	0.76	0.61
60 - 64	EW65	6.74	4.45	2.74	1.98	1.91	1.79	1.69	1.57	1.39

Source: DWP Work and Pensions Longitudinal Study 100% data.

1 "-" Nil or Negligible; "." Not applicable; Caseload figures are rounded to the nearest ten; Some additional disclosure control has also been applied. Average amounts are shown as pounds per week and rounded to the nearest penny. Totals may not sum due to rounding.
2 Caseload (Thousands) All Claimants of Widows Benefit are female. No new claims for WA have been accepted since April 2001 when it was replaced by Bereavement Allowance
3 Figures include overseas cases.
4. Please note that the figures supplied are derived from unpublished information and have not been quality assured to National Statistics or Official Statistics publication standard. They should therefore be treated with caution.

5.13 Bereavement Benefit[1,2] (excluding bereavement payment): by sex, type of benefit and age of widow/er Great Britain.

Thousands

		Males						Females				
		2011	2012	2013	2014	2015		2011	2012	2013	2014	2015
All Bereavement Benefit (excluding bereavement allowance)												
All ages	WLSX	18.59	18.78	18.76	18.56	18.48	WLTC	46.18	47.40	48.79	49.66	50.85
18 - 24	EVW9	–	.	.	.	.	EVY2	0.05	0.05	0.04	0.03	0.03
25 - 29	EVX2	0.06	0.05	0.04	0.05	0.06	EVY3	0.48	0.47	0.48	0.40	0.39
30 - 34	EVX3	0.24	0.25	0.26	0.26	0.26	EVY4	1.67	1.69	1.78	1.76	1.70
35 - 39	EVX4	0.88	0.84	0.79	0.75	0.74	EVY5	4.01	3.86	3.82	3.75	3.73
40 - 44	EVX5	2.13	2.15	2.10	1.94	1.84	EVY6	7.77	7.76	7.67	7.44	7.30
45 - 49	EVX6	4.00	3.92	3.81	3.75	3.58	EVY7	11.09	11.30	11.17	11.30	11.01
50 - 54	EVX7	3.82	3.97	4.10	4.16	4.21	EVY8	10.58	10.76	10.94	11.14	11.36
55 - 59	EVX8	3.41	3.53	3.57	3.59	3.65	EVY9	9.38	9.51	9.79	9.65	10.10
60 - 64	EVX9	4.05	4.08	4.08	4.05	4.14	EVZ2	1.15	1.99	3.11	4.18	5.24
Widowed parents' allowance - with dependant children												
All ages	WLUD	11.58	11.68	11.64	11.46	11.17	WLUH	33.27	33.90	34.30	34.46	34.42
18 - 24	EVZ3	–	.	.	.	.	EW24	0.05	0.05	0.04	0.03	0.03
25 - 29	EVZ4	0.06	0.05	0.04	0.05	0.06	EW25	0.48	0.46	0.47	0.40	0.39
30 - 34	EVZ5	0.24	0.25	0.26	0.26	0.25	EW26	1.66	1.68	1.76	1.76	1.69
35 - 39	EVZ6	0.88	0.84	0.79	0.75	0.74	EW27	3.98	3.85	3.81	3.74	3.72
40 - 44	EVZ7	2.12	2.15	2.09	1.94	1.84	EW28	0.73	7.73	7.64	7.41	7.27
45 - 49	EVZ8	3.51	3.41	3.33	3.25	3.08	EW29	9.56	9.81	9.81	9.93	9.68
50 - 54	EVZ9	2.7	2.86	2.97	3.03	3.00	EW2A	6.97	7.12	7.31	7.56	7.76
55 - 59	EW22	1.45	1.46	1.49	1.55	1.55	EW2B	2.69	2.93	3.09	3.16	3.37
60 - 64	EW23	0.63	0.66	0.65	0.63	0.65	EW2C	0.14	0.25	0.37	0.45	0.51
Widowed parents' allowance - without dependant children												
All ages	WLVK	0.03	0.03	0.02	0.02	0.01	WMMR	0.21	0.18	0.16	0.13	0.12
18 - 24	EW2D	–	.	.	.	.	EW2M	–	.	.	.	.
25 - 29	EW2E	–	.	.	.	.	EW2N	–	.	.	.	.
30 - 34	EW2F	–	.	.	.	.	EW2O	0.01	0.01	0.01	.	0.01
35 - 39	EW2G	–	.	.	.	.	EW2P	0.02	0.01	0.01	0.01	0.01
40 - 44	EW2H	0.01	0.01	0.01	.	.	EW2Q	0.04	0.04	0.03	0.02	0.02
45 - 49	EW2I	0.01	0.01	0.01	0.01	0.01	EW2R	0.06	0.06	0.05	0.04	0.03
50 - 54	EW2J	0.01	.	.	0.01	.	EW2S	0.05	0.04	0.04	0.04	0.03
55 - 59	EW2K	0.01	.	.	.	.	EW2T	0.02	0.01	0.01	0.01	0.01
60 - 64	EW2L	–	.	.	.	.	EW2U	–	.	.	.	.
Age-related bereavement allowance												
All ages	WMOB	1.75	1.75	1.75	1.78	1.89	WMOC	5.51	5.53	5.38	5.37	5.39
18 - 24	EW2V	–	.	.	.	.	EW36	–	.	.	.	.
25 - 29	EW2W	–	.	.	.	.	EW37	–	.	.	.	.
30 - 34	EW2X	–	.	.	.	.	EW38	–	.	.	.	.
35 - 39	EW2Y	–	.	.	.	.	EW39	–	.	.	.	.
40 - 44	EW2Z	–	.	.	.	.	EW3A	–	.	.	.	.
45 - 49	EW32	0.49	0.49	0.47	0.49	0.50	EW3B	1.46	1.43	1.32	1.34	1.31
50 - 54	EW33	1.11	0.11	0.12	1.13	1.20	EW3C	3.56	3.60	3.59	3.53	3.57
55 - 59	EW34	0.15	0.15	0.15	0.16	0.19	EW3D	0.49	0.51	0.48	0.50	0.51
60 - 64	EW35	–	.	.	.	.	EW3E	–	.	.	.	.
Bereavement allowance (not age related)												
All ages	WMOX	5.22	5.33	5.35	5.30	5.40	WMOY	7.19	7.80	8.94	9.69	10.92
18 - 24	EW3F	–	.	.	.	.	EW3O	–	.	.	.	.
25 - 29	EW3G	–	.	.	.	.	EW3P	–	.	.	.	.
30 - 34	EW3H	–	.	.	.	.	EW3Q	–	.	.	.	.
35 - 39	EW3I	–	.	.	.	.	EW3R	–	.	.	.	.
40 - 44	EW3J	–	.	.	.	.	EW3S	–	.	.	.	.
45 - 49	EW3K	–	.	.	.	.	EW3T	–	.	.	.	.
50 - 54	EW3L	–	.	.	.	.	EW3U	–	.	.	.	.
55 - 59	EW3M	1.8	1.91	1.91	1.88	1.91	EW3V	6.18	6.06	6.21	5.97	6.20
60 - 64	EW3N	3.42	3.42	3.43	3.42	3.48	EW3W	1.00	1.73	2.74	3.72	4.72

Source: DWP Work and Pensions Longitudinal Study 100% data

1 Figures are for Great Britain and Overseas and do not include figures for Northern Ireland

2 Figures are given at May each year and are taken from the DWP 100% Work and Pensions Longitudinal Study (WPLS).

"-" Nil or Negligible; "." Not applicable; Caseload figures are rounded to the nearest ten; Some additional disclosure control has also been applied. Average amounts are shown as pounds per week and rounded to the nearest penny. Totals may not sum due to rounding.

3 Please note that the figures supplied are derived from unpublished information and have not been quality assured to National Statistics or Official Statistics publication standard. They should therefore be treated with caution.

Notes:

Type of BA The category 'WPA with dependants' will include clients getting paid at the personal rate only due to the introduction of of Child Tax Credits in April 2003. To obtain figures for those who still receive Child Dependancy Increases, under the transitional protection arrangements, use the 'type of dependant' option.

5.14 Contributory and non-contributory retirement pensions:[1,2] by sex and age of claimant Great Britain and Overseas.

At May each year.   Thousands and percentages

		2006	2007	2008	2009	2010	2011	2012	2013	2014	2015
Men:											
Age-groups:											
65-69	KJSB	1341.5	1332.77	1350.61	1389.85	1,441.17	1,498.78	1,629.37	1705.34	1740.27	1751.69
Percentage	KJSC	30.6	30.03	29.84	29.99	30.28	30.77	32.14	32.59	32.35	31.95
70-74	KJSD	1160.1	1177.96	1205.7	1232.97	1,252.63	1249.42	1,256.65	1286.51	1330.41	1373.65
Percentage	KJSE	26.5	26.54	26.63	26.61	26.32	25.65	24.79	24.58	24.73	25.05
75-79	KJSF	903	918.47	932.17	942.03	958.54	975.17	996.90	1025.20	1054.99	1072.69
Percentage	KJSG	20.6	20.7	20.59	20.33	20.14	20.02	19.67	19.59	19.61	19.56
80-84	KJSH	596.9	604.74	614.77	627.28	644.94	663.35	680.67	695.95	710.47	724.92
Percentage	KJSI	13.6	13.63	13.58	13.54	13.55	13.62	13.43	13.30	13.21	13.22
85-89	KJSJ	273.1	296.36	317.9	335.49	340.87	348.51	357.78	365.24	378.93	389.92
Percentage	KJSK	6.2	6.68	7.02	7.24	7.16	7.16	7.06	6.98	7.04	7.11
90 and over	KJSL	103.6	106.13	105.33	105.62	120.82	135.62	147.15	154.43	164.14	169.77
Percentage	KJSM	2.4	2.39	2.33	2.28	2.54	2.79	2.90	2.95	3.05	3.10
Unknown age	EW3Y	1.2	1.45	0.19	0.24	0.23	0.27	0.27	0.29	0.29	0.32
Percentage	EW3Z	–	–	–	–	–	–	–	–	–	0.01
Total all ages	KJSA	4379.5	4437.99	4526.79	4633.62	4,759.36	4871.26	5068.96	5233.15	5379.68	5483.12
Women:											
Age-groups:											
65-69	KJSQ	1453.1	1456.08	1484.8	1527.47	1,576.10	1632.12	1768.96	1847.19	1883.33	1903.40
Percentage	KJSR	20	19.65	19.67	19.91	20.25	21.1	22.98	24.22	24.87	25.46
70-74	KJSS	1312.7	1322.14	1343.22	1366.91	1,382.42	1377.54	1385.36	1415.89	1459.75	1503.58
Percentage	KJST	18.1	17.85	17.8	17.82	17.77	17.79	18.00	18.56	19.28	20.12
75-79	KJSU	1165.5	1168.86	1170.01	1166.2	1,168.83	1172.33	1185.64	1207.02	1232.19	1246.03
Percentage	KJSV	16	15.78	15.5	15.2	15.02	15.14	15.40	15.82	16.27	16.67
80-84	KJSW	933.3	923.7	919.11	921.01	931.08	942.31	950.53	955.31	957.64	959.94
Percentage	KJSX	12.9	12.47	12.18	12.01	11.97	12.17	12.35	12.52	12.65	12.84
85-89	KJSY	552.7	587.91	621.15	643.5	634.29	628.71	626.68	625.48	634.32	640.44
Percentage	KJSZ	7.6	7.94	8.23	8.39	8.15	8.12	8.14	8.20	8.38	8.57
90 and over	KJTA	319.4	319.9	313.66	310.07	341.10	370.18	389.38	398.29	413.80	415.13
Percentage	KJTB	4.4	4.32	4.16	4.04	4.38	4.78	5.06	5.22	5.47	5.55
Unknown age	EW42	1.5	1.67	0.37	0.38	0.35	0.35	0.35	0.43	0.44	0.45
Percentage	EW43	–	–	–	–	–	–	–	–	–	0.01
Total all ages	KJSN	7262.3	7408.44	7548.2	7670.44	7,781.39	7744.98	7698.12	7627.94	7571.82	7474.83

Source: Department for Work and Pensions (DWP); Work and Pensions Longitudinal Study (WPLS)

1 See chapter text.

2 Caseloads include both contributory and non-contributory state pensioners.

"-" Nil or Negligible; "." Not applicable; Caseload figures are rounded to the nearest ten; Some additional disclosure control has also been applied. Average amounts are shown as pounds per week and rounded to the nearest penny. Totals may not sum due to rounding.

There may be a discrepancy between any sub-national November 2015 data reproduced in this table and the equivalent statistics produced by the DWP tabulation tool. The differences are small, at most 3% at regional level.

5.15a War pensions: estimated number of pensioners[1] Great Britain

At 31 March each year   Thousands

		2004	2005	2006[2]	2007	2008	2009	2010	2011	2012	2013	2014	2015
Disablement	KADH	201.55	191.75	182.8	173.85	165.17	157.13	148.95	141.72	134.43	127.60	121.90	116.05
Widows and dependants	KADI	46.04	43.55	41.05	38.69	36.1	33.62	31.45	29.20	27.11	25.10	23.11	21.17
Total	KADG	247.59	235.3	223.85	212.54	201.27	190.75	180.40	170.92	161.54	152.70	145.01	137.22

Source: War Pensions Computer System

1 See chapter text. From 1914 war, 1939 war and later service.

2 The discontinuity between 2005 and 2006 is due to improvements in data processing.

An additional validation check was introduced in 2014/15 on the 'not known' disablement pensioners to put them in the correct payment category.

The sum of the sub-totals may not sum to the totals due to rounding.

5.15b: War Pensions in payment by type of pension, gender and financial year end, 31 March 2011 to 31 March 2015, numbers[1]

	Awards in payment at:				
	31-Mar-11	31-Mar-12	31-Mar-13	31-Mar-14	31-Mar-15
ALL IN PAYMENT	**170,910**	**161,535**	**152,695**	**145,005**	**137,215**
Men	**135,740**	**128,720**	**122,105**	**116,610**	**110,935**
Women	**35,175**	**32,820**	**30,590**	**28,395**	**26,280**
Disablement Pensioners	**141,715**	**134,430**	**127,590**	**121,900**	**116,050**
Men	135,120	128,130	121,530	116,055	110,410
Women	6,595	6,305	6,060	5,845	5,640
War Widow(er)s	**28,425**	**26,375**	**24,415**	**22,445**	**20,535**
Men	75	80	85	80	70
Women	28,350	26,295	24,330	22,365	20,460
Other Pensioners	**770**	**730**	**690**	**660**	**635**
Men	540	510	490	470	455
Women	230	220	200	185	180

Source: War Pensions Computer System

1 The sum of the sub-totals may not sum to the totals due to rounding.

5.16 Income support[1],[2] by statistical group[3]: number of claimants receiving weekly payment

Great Britain

Thousands[4]

		2007	2008	2009	2010	2011	2012	2013	2014	2015
All income support claimants (including MIG from 2003)[5]	F8YY	2128.4	2102.3	1990.0	1852.3	1703.2	1417.1	1021.9	840.8	734.75
Incapacity Benefits	F8YZ	1193.5	1191.4	1097.0	996.6	924.9	654.13	328.09	167.64	92.12
Lone Parent	F8Z2	765.6	738.6	720.5	679.2	595.4	577.08	499.73	474.73	441.61
Carer	F8Z3	84.3	87.3	93.8	103.9	115.7	129.75	145.84	156.50	165.32
Others on Income Related Benefits	F8Z4	84.9	85.0	78.9	72.7	67.2	56.1	48.2	41.9	35.7

Sources: Department for Work and Pensions (DWP); Work and Pensions Longitudinal Study (WPLS)

1 Figures are given at May each year and are taken from the DWP 100% Work and Pensions Longitudinal Study (WPLS).

2 From 27th October 2008, new claims to Income Support can also be allocated, on incapacity grounds, to the newly introduced Employment and Support Allowance (ESA).

3 Statistical Group is a hierarchical variable. A person who fits into more than one category will only appear in the top-most one for which they are eligible. These statistical groups differ from the groups shown in the 5% sample tables. Lone Parents are defined as claimants on Income Support with child under 16 and no partner. Lone Parent Obligations were introduced from 24th November 2008 affecting the eligibility criteria based on the age of the youngest child.

4 Figures are rounded to the nearest hundred and quoted in thousands.

5 Totals may not sum due to rounding.

"-" Nil or Negligible; "." Not applicable; Caseload figures are rounded to the nearest ten; Some additional disclosure control has also been applied.

Time Series Universal Credit: Universal Credit (UC) is a new benefit that was introduced in April 2013 and will replace six existing benefits and tax credits with a single monthly payment. UC will eventually replace: Income-based Jobseeker's Allowance, Income-related Employment and Support Allowance, Income Support, Working Tax Credit, Child Tax Credit and Housing Benefit. After August 2003 there was a sharp decline in the number of claimants aged 60 or over. This is due to the migration of most existing Minimum Income Guarantee claimants (1.8 million) to Pension Credit, which was introduced in October 2003. Some residual cases remain.

There may be a discrepancy between any sub-national November 2015 data reproduced in this table and the equivalent statistics produced by the DWP tabulation tool. The differences are small, at most 3% at regional level.

5.17 Pension Credit[1]: number of claimants

Great Britain
End of May

Thousands[2]

		2007	2008	2009	2010	2011	2012	2013	2014	2015
All Pension Credit	F8Z5	2733.5	2719.1	2730.6	2733.9	2674.4	2541.3	2413.7	2270.1	2096.6
Guarantee Credit Only	F8Z6	805.7	882.1	925.7	954.2	936.8	1015.8	968.3	950.1	931.2
Guarantee Credit and Savings Credit	F8Z7	1330.1	1246.2	1205.2	1202.4	1148.0	964.2	906.6	824.3	739.7
Savings Credit	F8Z8	597.7	590.8	599.6	577.3	589.6	561.3	538.8	495.8	425.7

Source: Department for Work and Pensions (DWP); Work and Pensions Longitudinal Study (WPLS)

1 Source: DWP 100% Work and Pensions Longitudinal study (WPLS).
Caseload figures are rounded to the nearest ten. Totals may not sum due to rounding.

Caseload - number of claimants (Thousands) - Pension Credit was introduced on 6 October 2003 and replaced Minimum Income Guarantee (Income Support for people aged 60 or over). The vast majority of people who were previously in receipt of the Minimum Income Guarantee transferred to Pension Credit in October 2003. These Pension Credit statistics are produced on a different basis to the Early Estimates. The latter are more timely but operational processing times mean that a number of claim commencements and terminations are not reflected in them. Cases receiving a zero payment amount are recorded in the unknown payment category.

Type of Pension Credit - Certain aspects of the April 2012 uprating for Pension Credit were applied to the administrative computer system in advance, before the February 2012 statistics were extracted. Hence, the statistics in February 2012 show the Pension Credit type based on 2012/13 rates. However, the amounts in payment had not been adjusted and claimants were still being paid the correct rate of benefit, based on 2011/12 rates.

There may be a discrepancy between any sub-national November 2015 data reproduced in this table and the equivalent statistics produced by the DWP tabulation tool. The differences are small, at most 3% at regional level.

5.18 Income support: average weekly amounts of benefit[1,2,3]

Great Britain
As at May

£ per week

		2006	2007	2008	2009	2010	2011	2012	2013	2014	2015
All income support claimants	F8ZF	83.54	82.45	82.55	85.17	85.01	84.88	83.93	76.42	71.69	71.28
Incapacity benefits[4]	F8ZG	78.35	80.04	81.85	89.22	91.81	93.66	93.69	82.12	67.46	63.68
Lone Parent[4]	F8ZH	94.88	89.70	87.37	82.79	79.02	75.94	76.54	74.09	72.75	71.97
Carer[4]	F8ZI	71.13	70.82	70.21	71.85	70.90	69.94	72.23	72.32	72.16	72.82
Others on income related benefits[4]	F8ZJ	62.78	62.47	63.02	66.35	67.87	68.82	73.19	74.11	74.88	75.25

1 Figures are given at May each year and are taken from the DWP 100% (WPLS) Work and Pensions Longitudinal Study (WPLS).

Source: Department for Work and Pensions (DWP); Work and Pensions Longitudinal Study

2 The amount of Income Support is affected by the introduction in April 2003 of Child Tax Credit. From that date there were no new child dependency increases awarded to IS claimants, although existing CDIs were transitionally protected.

3 Average amounts are shown as pounds per week and rounded to the nearest penny.

4 Statistical Group is a hierarchical variable. A person who fits into more than one category will only appear in the top-most one for which they are eligible. These statistical groups differ from the groups shown in the 5% sample tables. Lone Parents are defined as claimants on Income Support with child under 16 and no partner. Lone Parent Obligations were introduced from 24th November 2008 affecting the eligibility criteria based on the age of the youngest child.

There may be a discrepancy between any sub-national November 2015 data reproduced in this table and the equivalent statistics produced by the DWP tabulation tool. The differences are small, at most 3% at regional level.

5.19 Pension Credit: average weekly amounts of benefit[1]

Great Britain

As at May

£ per week[2]

		2007	2008	2009	2010	2011	2012	2013	2014	2015
All Pension Credit	F8ZA	50.04	52.69	55.56	57.39	57.74	57.60	57.12	56.31	56.23
Guarantee Credit Only	F8ZB	83.74	85.07	88.86	90.73	92.51	90.12	90.06	88.33	86.84
Guarantee Credit and Savings Credit	F8ZC	46.11	48.29	50.81	51.75	52.04	52.26	49.41	47.38	45.17
Savings Credit only	F8ZD	13.36	13.62	13.71	14.01	13.57	11.36	10.87	9.80	8.47

Department for Work and Pensions (DWP); Work and Pensions Longitudinal Study (WPLS)

1 Figures are given in each May and are taken from the DWP 100% Work and Pensions Longitudinal Study (WPLS).
2 Average amounts are shown as pounds per week and rounded to the nearest penny.

There may be a discrepancy between any sub-national November 2015 data reproduced in this table and the equivalent statistics produced by the DWP tabulation tool. The differences are small, at most 3% at regional level.

this page is intentionally blank

External trade and investment

Chapter 6

External trade and investment

External trade (Table 6.1 and 6.3 to 6.6)

The statistics in this section are on the basis of Balance of Payments (BoP). They are compiled from information provided to HM Revenue and Customs (HMRC) by importers and exporters on the basis of Overseas Trade Statistics (OTS) which values exports 'f.o.b.' (free on board) and imports 'c.i.f.' (including insurance and freight). In addition to deducting these freight costs and insurance premiums from the OTS figures, coverage adjustments are made to convert the OTS data to a BoP basis. Adjustments are also made to the level of all exports and European Union (EU) imports to take account of estimated under-recording. The adjustments are set out and described in the annual United Kingdom *Balance of Payments Pink Book* (Office for National Statistics (ONS)). These adjustments are made to conform to the definitions in the 5th edition of the IMF Balance of Payments Manual.

Aggregate estimates of trade in goods, seasonally adjusted and on a BoP basis, are published monthly in the ONS statistical bulletin UK Trade. More detailed figures are available from time series data on the ONS website (www.ons.gov.uk) and are also published in the *Monthly Review of External Trade Statistics*. Detailed figures for EU and non-EU trade on an OTS basis are published in *Overseas trade statistics: United Kingdom trade with the European Community and the world* (HMRC).

Overseas Trade Statistics

HMRC provide accurate and up to date information via the website:
www.uktradeinfo.com
They also produce publications entitled 'Overseas Trade Statistics'.

Import penetration and export sales ratios (Table 6.2)

The ratios were first introduced in the August 1977 edition of *Economic Trends* in an article entitled 'The Home and Export Performance of United Kingdom Industries'. The article described the conceptual and methodological problems involved in measuring such variables as import penetration.

The industries are grouped according to the 2007 Standard Industrial Classification at 2-digit level.

Table 6.3 to 6.6

The series are now available as datasets in the UK Trade release, which is updated monthly

International trade in services (Tables 6.7 and 6.8)

These data relate to overseas trade in services and cover both production and non-production industries (excluding the public sector). In terms of the types of services traded these include royalties, various forms of consultancy, computing and telecommunications services, advertising and market research and other business services. A separate inquiry covers the film and television industries. The surveys cover receipts from the provision of services to residents of other countries (exports) and payments to residents of other countries for services rendered (imports).

Sources of data

The International Trade in Services (ITIS) surveys (which consist of a quarterly component addressed to the largest businesses and an annual component for the remainder) are based on a sample of companies derived from the Inter-departmental Business Register in addition to a reference list and from 2007 onwards a sample of approximately 5000 contributors from the Annual Business Inquiry (ABI). The companies are asked to show the amounts for their imports and exports against the geographical area to which they were paid or from which they were received, irrespective of where they were first earned.

The purpose of the ITIS survey is to record international transactions which impact on the UK's BoP. Exports and imports of goods are generally excluded, as they will have been counted in the estimate for trade in goods. However earnings from third country trade – that is, from arranging the sale of goods between two countries other than the UK and where the goods never physically enter the UK (known as merchanting) – are included. Earnings from commodity trading are also included. Together, these two comprise trade related services.

Royalties are a large part of the total trade in services collected in the ITIS survey. These cover transactions for items such as printed matter, sound recordings, performing rights, patents, licences, trademarks, designs, copyrights, manufacturing rights, the use of technical know-how and technical assistance.

Balance of Payments (Tables 6.9 to 6.12)

Tables 6.9 to 6.12 are derived from *United Kingdom Balance of Payments: The Pink Book.* The following general notes to the tables provide brief definitions and explanations of the figures and terms used. Further notes are included in the Pink Book.

Summary of Balance of Payments

The BoP consists of the current account, the capital account, the financial account and the International Investment Position (IIP). The current account consists of trade in goods and services, income, and current transfers. Income consists of investment income and compensation of employees. The capital account mainly consists of capital transfers and the financial account covers financial transactions. The IIP covers balance sheet levels of UK external assets and liabilities. Every credit entry in the balance of payments accounts should, in theory, be matched by a corresponding debit entry so that total current, capital and financial account credits should be equal to, and therefore offset by, total debits. In practice there is a discrepancy termed net errors and omissions.

Current account

Trade in goods

The goods account covers exports and imports of goods. Imports of motor cars from Japan, for example, are recorded as debits in the trade in goods account, whereas exports of vehicles manufactured in the UK are recorded as credits. Trade in goods forms a component of the expenditure measure of gross domestic product (GDP).

Trade in services

The services account covers exports and imports of services, for example civil aviation. Passenger tickets for travel on UK aircraft sold abroad, for example, are recorded as credits in the services account, whereas the purchases of airline tickets from foreign airlines by UK passengers are recorded as debits. Trade in services, along with trade in goods, forms a component of the expenditure measure of GDP.

Income

The income account consists of compensation of employees and investment income and is dominated by the latter. Compensation of employees covers employment income from cross-border and seasonal workers which is less significant in the UK than in other countries. Investment income covers earnings (for example, profits, dividends and interest payments and receipts) arising from cross-border investment in financial assets and liabilities. For example, earnings on foreign bonds and shares held by financial institutions based in the UK are recorded as credits in the investment income account, whereas earnings on UK company securities held abroad are recorded as investment income debits. Investment income forms a component of gross national income (GNI) but not GDP.

Current transfers

Current transfers are composed of central government transfers (for example, taxes and payments to and receipts from, the EU) and other transfers (for example gifts in cash or kind received by private individuals from abroad or receipts from the EU where the UK government acts as an agent for the ultimate beneficiary of the transfer). Current transfers do not form a component either of GDP or of GNI. For example, payments to the UK farming industry under the EU Agricultural Guarantee Fund are recorded as credits in the current transfers account, while payments of EU agricultural levies by the UK farming industry are recorded as debits in the current transfers account.

Capital account

Capital account transactions involve transfers of ownership of fixed assets, transfers of funds associated with acquisition or disposal of fixed assets and cancellation of liabilities by creditors without any counterparts being received in return. The main components are migrants transfers, EU transfers relating to fixed capital formation (regional development fund and agricultural guidance fund) and debt forgiveness. Funds brought into the UK by new immigrants would, for example, be recorded as credits in the capital account, while funds sent abroad by UK residents emigrating to other countries would be recorded as debits in the capital account. The size of capital account transactions are quite minor compared with the current and financial accounts.

Financial account

While investment income covers earnings arising from cross-border investments in financial assets and liabilities, the financial account of the balance of payments covers the flows of such investments. Earnings on foreign bonds and shares held by financial institutions based in the UK are, for example, recorded as credits in the investment income account, but the acquisition of such foreign securities by UK-based financial institutions are recorded as net debits in the financial account or portfolio investment abroad. Similarly, the acquisitions of UK company securities held by foreign residents are recorded in the financial account as net credits or portfolio investment in the UK.

International Investment Position

While the financial account covers the flows of foreign investments and financial assets and liabilities, the IIP records the levels of external assets and liabilities. While the acquisition of foreign securities by UK-based financial institutions are recorded in the financial account as net debits, the total holdings of foreign securities by UK-based financial institutions are recorded as levels of UK external assets. Similarly, the holdings of UK company securities held by foreign residents are recorded as levels of UK liabilities.

Foreign direct investment (Tables 6.13 to 6.18)

Direct investment refers to investment that adds to, deducts from, or acquires a lasting interest in an enterprise operating in an economy other than that of the investor – the investor's purpose being to have an effective voice in the management of the enterprise. (For the purposes of the statistical inquiry, an effective voice is taken as equivalent to a holding of 10 per cent or more in the foreign enterprise.) Other investments in which the investor does not have an effective voice in the management of the enterprise are mainly portfolio investments and these are not covered here.

Direct investment is a financial concept and is not the same as capital expenditure on fixed assets. It covers only the money invested in a related concern by the parent company and the concern will then decide how to use the money. A related concern may also raise money locally without reference to the parent company.

The investment figures are published on a net basis; that is they consist of investments net of disinvestments by a company into its foreign subsidiaries, associate companies and branches.

Definitional changes from 1997

The new European System of Accounts (ESA(95)) definitions were introduced from the 1997 estimates. The changes were as follows:

i.   Previously, for the measurement of direct investment, an effective voice in the management of an enterprise was taken as the equivalent of a 20 per cent shareholding. This is now 10 per cent

ii.   The Channel Islands and the Isle of Man have been excluded from the definition of the economic territory of the UK. Prior to 1987 these islands were considered to be part of the UK

iii.   Interest received or paid was replaced by interest accrued in the figures on earnings from direct investment. There is deemed to be little or no impact arising from this definitional change on the estimates

A further change caused by the move to ESA(95) is that withholding taxes payable on direct investment earnings are now measured. Earnings were shown gross of these taxes in the Balance of Payments 2005 Pink Book. However, for the purposes of this business monitor earnings are calculated net of tax, as before.

New register sources available from 1998 have led to revisions of the figures from that year onwards. These sources gave an improved estimate of the population satisfying the criteria for foreign direct investment.

From the 2005 surveys new data sources have allowed the inclusion of data for the previously excluded Private Property (outward & inward surveys) and Public Corporations (outward surveys) sectors. From the 2006 surveys the tax data previously excluded from the FDI surveys are now also included in the final earnings figures for both the outward & inward surveys. This now means that there are no coherence issues between the FDI annual surveys and the quarterly Balance of Payments figures as published in the latest Balance of Payments Pink Book.

Definitional changes have been introduced from 1997 and the register changes from 1998. Data prior to these years have not been reworked in Tables 6.13 to 6.18. For clarity, the Offshore Islands are identified separately on the tables. Breaks in the series for the other definitional changes are not quantified but are relatively small. More detailed information on the effect of these changes appears in the business monitor MA4 – Foreign Direct Investment 2002, which was published in February 2003 and is available from the ONS website.

Sources of data

The figures in Tables 6.13 to 6.18 are based on annual inquiries into foreign direct investment for 2015. These were sample surveys which involved sending approximately 1530 forms to UK businesses investing abroad, and 2370 forms to UK businesses in which foreign parents and associates had invested. The tables also contain some revisions as a result of new information coming to light in the course of the latest surveys. Further details from the latest annual surveys, including analyses by industry and by components of direct investment, are available in business monitor MA4.

Country allocation

The analysis of inward investment is based on the country of ownership of the immediate parent company. Thus, inward investment in a UK company may be attributed to the country of the intervening overseas subsidiary, rather than the country of the ultimate parent. Similarly, the country analysis of outward investment is based on the country of ownership of the immediate subsidiary; for example, to the extent that overseas investment in the UK is channelled through holding companies in the Netherlands, the underlying flow of investment from this country is overstated and the inflow from originating countries is understated.

Further information

More detailed statistics on foreign direct investment are available on request from Michael Hardie, Office for National Statistics, Telephone: +44 (0)1633 455923, email fdi@ons.gsi.gov.uk

6.1 Trade in goods[1]
United Kingdom
Balance of payments basis

£million and Indices 2013=100

		2003	2004	2005	2006	2007	2008	2009	2010	2011	2012	2013	2014	2015
Value (£ million)														
Exports of goods	BOKG	188546	191608	212053	243957	222964	254577	229107	270196	308171	301621	303147	292894	287584
Imports of goods	BOKH	239505	253549	282213	322920	313504	349603	315731	367580	403126	412528	423811	415469	407304
Balance on trade in goods	BOKI	-50959	-61941	-70160	-78963	-90540	-95026	-86624	-97384	-94955	-110907	-120664	-122575	-119720
Price index numbers														
Exports of goods	BQKR	69.7	70.3	72.8	74.0	73.6	83.7	84.5	90.3	97.4	97.3	100.0	94.2	87.0
Imports of goods	BQKS	73.0	72.5	75.7	78.1	78.2	89.2	90.2	94.5	102.5	102.7	100.0	98.6	94.3
Terms of trade[2]	BQKT	99.6	101.0	100.3	98.8	98.2	97.9	97.7	99.6	99.1	98.9	100.0	99.6	98.0
Volume index numbers														
Exports of goods	BQKU	83.2	84.5	91.3	103.6	95.3	96.7	86.4	96.2	102.7	101.0	100.0	101.6	108.7
Imports of goods	BQKV	76.7	82.1	88.1	98.1	95.2	93.7	84.4	94.1	95.6	98.0	100.0	103.3	108.1

Source: Office for National Statistics: 01633 456294

1 See chapter text. Statistics of trade in goods on a balance of payments basis are obtained by making certain adjustments in respect of valuation and coverage to the statistics recorded in the Overseas Trade Statistics. These adjustments are described in detail in The Pink Book.
2 Export price index as a percentage of the import price index.

Table 6.1 may show revisions to data going back over time. This is mainly to reflect revised data from HMRC and other data suppliers, later survey data and a re-assessment of seasonal factors.

6.2: Sales of products manufactured in the United Kingdom by Industry Division

Division	SIC(07) Division	£ Thousands			
		2011	2012	2013	2014
Other mining and quarrying	8	2,255,125	S	2,299,263	S
Manufacture of food products	10	60,663,124	62,897,838	66,030,444	67,053,056
Manufacture of beverages	11	12,875,926	12,375,786	12,386,202	12,968,981
Manufacture of tobacco products	12	1,672,839	1,793,420	1,723,231	S
Manufacture of textiles	13	4,047,168	4,134,488	S	S
Manufacture of wearing apparel	14	1,490,960	1,634,262	1,634,497	1,830,034
Manufacture of leather and related products	15	618,239	646,669	726,732	681,340
Manufacture of wood and of products of wood and cork, except furniture; manufacture of articles of straw and plaiting materials	16	5,577,606	5,739,940	6,096,793	S
Manufacture of paper and paper products	17	S	10,018,458	S	10,364,467
Printing and reproduction of recorded media	18	8,927,210	8,672,310	8,054,509	S
Manufacture of coke and refined petroleum products	19	S	S	S	S
Manufacture of chemicals and chemical products	20	S	S	S	21,430,541
Manufacture of basic pharmaceutical products and pharmaceutical preparations	21	13,901,544	12,288,627	12,047,139	10,914,046
Manufacture of rubber and plastic products	22	S	S	S	S
Manufacture of other non-metallic mineral products	23	10,249,359	10,167,511	10,358,525	11,467,693
Manufacture of basic metals	24	8,500,016	7,422,006	6,825,251	6,583,235
Manufacture of fabricated metal products, except machinery and equipment	25	S	S	24,266,120	25,551,331
Manufacture of computer, electronic and optical products	26	12,857,258	S	12,558,623	12,144,913
Manufacture of electrical equipment	27	11,864,709	S	S	S
Manufacture of machinery and equipment n.e.c.	28	S	26,920,747	S	27,581,071
Manufacture of motor vehicles, trailers and semi-trailers	29	38,446,099	39,296,813	S	47,381,993
Manufacture of other transport equipment	30	21,392,793	23,839,850	26,471,305	27,192,259
Manufacture of furniture	31	S	6,098,141	6,305,793	6,557,385
Other manufacturing	32	S	S	S	4,771,102
Repair and installation of machinery and equipment	33	12,589,466	S	13,987,075	14,085,966
Total		341,030,726	341,984,772	354,721,188	362,545,191

Source: Office for National Statistics (ONS)
Email: prodcompublications@ons.gsi.gov.uk
Tel: (01633) 456720

Note: Information in this table relates to products corresponding to a division irrespective of which division the business making the product is classified to.
S - A volume or unit value suppressed as disclosive

6.3 United Kingdom exports: by commodity[1,2]

Seasonally adjusted

£ million

		2005	2006	2007	2008	2009	2010	2011	2012	2013	2014	2015
0. Food and live animals	BOGG	6948	6878	7795	9099	9505	11715	14315	12014	12170	11781	11567
01. Meat and meat preparations	BOGS	705	712	783	1077	1158	1298	1566	1397	1146	1664	1460
02. Dairy products and eggs	BQMS	730	718	808	887	836	1051	1273	1164	1367	1499	1286
04 & 08. Cereals and animal feeding stuffs	BQMT	1560	1591	1801	2313	2394	2619	2808	2758	2807	2835	3036
05. Vegetables and fruit	BQMU	516	588	608	695	761	826	900	854	784	476	795
1. Beverages and tobacco	BQMZ	4130	4196	4405	5054	5383	6003	7050	6910	7224	6868	6605
11. Beverages	BQNB	3514	3731	4104	4606	4981	5677	6904	6836	6961	6607	6349
12. Tobacco	BQOW	616	465	301	448	402	326	146	74	263	261	256
2. Crude materials	BQOX	3627	4618	5192	6274	4824	6966	8658	7954	7125	6502	5666
of which:												
24. Wood, lumber and cork	BQOY	131	145	143	125	83	111	113	107	154	162	160
25. Pulp and waste paper	BQOZ	282	338	415	478	354	542	625	544	503	483	506
26. Textile fibres	BQPA	499	545	497	540	573	681	794	821	764	691	574
28. Metal ores	BQPB	1654	2418	2902	3683	2533	4139	5132	4495	4038	3659	3140
3. Fuels	BOPN	21468	24747	24426	35540	27024	35474	43445	43598	42768	36117	24150
33. Petroleum and petroleum products	ELBL	19821	22658	22516	32019	24700	31638	38667	39417	39184	32902	21048
32, 34 & 35. Coal, gas and electricity	BOQI	1647	2089	1910	3521	2324	3836	4778	4181	3584	3215	3102
4. Animal and vegetable oils and fats	BQPI	235	273	326	360	375	428	449	479	494	458	420
5. Chemicals	ENDG	33248	37230	38994	44000	47158	51314	53854	52787	48583	46771	51932
of which:												
51. Organic chemicals	BQPJ	6704	8019	7607	8416	9120	8921	9300	8977	7676	5825	8793
52. Inorganic chemicals	BQPK	1569	2146	2830	2993	2845	3513	3062	2880	2554	1756	1675
53. Colouring materials	CSCE	1612	1601	1670	1846	1693	1971	2196	1992	2027	2043	1879
54. Medicinal products	BQPL	12250	13821	14616	17378	20559	22526	23146	23389	20217	20976	24450
55. Toilet preparations	CSCF	3222	3447	3692	3958	4147	4339	4917	4831	5287	5133	4854
57 & 58. Plastics	BQQA	4236	4453	4619	4877	4411	5370	5960	5609	5529	5613	5403
6. Manufactures classified chiefly by material	BQQB	26588	27690	29376	32414	24554	29403	35240	32142	31450	28831	27068
of which:												
63. Wood and cork manufactures	BQQC	249	276	273	243	220	224	254	265	247	257	233
64. Paper and paperboard manufactures	BQQD	2068	2017	2126	2353	2289	2364	2416	2285	2269	2197	1964
65. Textile manufactures	BQQE	2644	2689	2597	2608	2382	2624	2833	2731	2776	2817	2695
67. Iron and steel	BQQF	5173	5151	6031	6878	4603	5080	6135	5726	6066	6049	4723
68. Non-ferrous metals	BQQG	3899	4842	5791	6871	3985	5878	8680	6805	7120	6752	6871
69. Metal manufactures	BQQH	4045	4493	4631	4989	4199	4466	4802	4767	4547	5321	5121
7. Machinery and transport equipment[3]	BQQI	89269	110404	82553	89066	79489	93133	104335	103843	108725	107938	108249
71-716, 72, 73 & 74. Mechanical machinery	BQQK	25703	28200	28972	32298	29391	33011	38897	39243	41466	39768	38424
716, 75, 76 & 77. Electrical machinery	BQQL	37234	55310	24010	25042	23990	25780	26296	23846	23485	24389	24027
78. Road vehicles	BQQM	19232	19385	21135	22535	17086	23531	27721	28865	31341	32054	32085
79. Other transport equipment	BQQN	7100	7509	8436	9191	9022	10811	11421	11889	12433	11727	13713
8. Miscellaneous manufactures[3]	BQQO	25138	25966	26723	28510	27775	31479	33906	35514	36937	38457	41670
of which:												
84. Clothing	CSCN	2704	2866	3101	3322	3451	3707	4292	4428	5117	5504	5795
85. Footwear	CSCP	476	523	543	622	723	864	950	1033	1282	1278	1449
87 & 88. Scientific and photographic	BQQQ	7245	7352	7059	8062	8308	9341	10286	10343	11103	11101	11308
9. Other commodities and transactions	BOQL	1402	1955	3174	4260	3020	4281	6919	6380	7671	9171	10257
Total United Kingdom exports	BOKG	212053	243957	222964	254577	229107	270196	308171	301621	303147	292894	287584

Source: Office for National Statistics: 01633 456294

1 See chapter text. The numbers on the left hand side of the table refer to the code numbers of the Standard International Trade Classification, Revision 3, which was introduced in January 1988.

2 Balance of payments consistent basis.

3 Sections 7 and 8 are shown by broad economic category in table G2 of the Monthly Review of External Trade Statistics.

6.4 United Kingdom imports: by commodity [1,2]

Seasonally adjusted

		2005	2006	2007	2008	2009	2010	2011	2012	2013	2014	2015
0. Food and live animals	BQQR	18626	19767	21303	25293	26332	27152	29387	29972	31237	31020	31118
of which:												
01. Meat and meat preparations	BQQS	3659	3788	3982	4612	4913	5004	5607	5596	5743	6138	5762
02. Dairy products and eggs	BQQT	1722	1805	1832	2285	2318	2427	2535	2604	2897	2835	2597
04 & 08. Cereals and animal feeding stuffs	BQQU	2384	2484	2912	3811	3926	3974	4137	4595	5540	5154	4978
05. Vegetables and fruit	BQQV	5358	5774	6207	7055	7048	7448	7890	7958	7271	7058	7541
1. Beverages and tobacco	BQQW	5384	5547	5760	6289	6499	6796	7025	6981	7496	7463	7390
11. Beverages	EGAT	3939	4158	4412	4811	5082	5313	5589	5693	5945	5875	5823
12. Tobacco	EMAI	1445	1389	1348	1478	1417	1483	1436	1288	1551	1588	1567
2. Crude materials	ENVB	6150	7087	8632	9587	6541	9119	10391	9211	11037	10519	9601
of which:												
24. Wood, lumber and cork	ENVC	1376	1451	1800	1408	1166	1463	1426	1456	2327	2631	2782
25. Pulp and waste paper	EQAH	474	533	516	612	452	596	629	517	519	524	555
26. Textile fibres	EQAP	303	299	322	338	290	355	455	379	403	416	385
28. Metalores	EHAA	2006	2646	3760	4647	2254	3891	4741	3925	4750	4106	3210
3. Fuels	BQAT	26352	31326	32204	48896	35416	44807	63043	67563	64533	52971	37906
33. Petroleum and petroleum products	ENXO	22398	26450	27126	38396	28033	36013	49395	53713	49109	42862	28961
32, 34 & 35. Coal, gas and electricity	BPBI	3954	4876	5078	10500	7383	8794	13648	13850	15424	10109	8945
4. Animal and vegetable oils and fats	EHAB	648	778	897	1398	1052	1128	1493	1413	1385	1200	1082
5. Chemicals	ENGA	31202	33219	36744	40419	41665	47174	50899	53066	51112	51866	52620
of which:												
51. Organic chemicals	EHAC	7324	7700	8645	8453	8274	9389	10078	10063	8119	6849	6628
52. Inorganic chemicals	EHAE	1533	2129	2690	2760	2742	2949	3606	3185	2545	2273	2280
53. Colouring materials	CSCR	1077	1082	1157	1228	1143	1253	1325	1360	1382	1390	1384
54. Medicinal products	EHAF	10231	10728	12050	13535	15888	17683	18442	21476	21152	23254	25411
55. Toilet preparations	CSCS	3070	3325	3441	3922	4162	4414	4653	4729	5049	5158	5490
57 & 58. Plastics	EHAG	5075	5354	5688	6225	5558	6843	7720	7484	7936	7987	7424
6. Manufactures classified chiefly by material	EHAH	33284	37636	39722	41899	35890	43547	49048	49656	46432	43535	42045
of which:												
63. Wood and cork manufactures	EHAI	1531	1579	1738	1730	1477	1664	1690	1660	1800	1976	2126
64. Paper and paperboard manufactures	EHAJ	4843	5025	5238	5486	5504	5896	6017	5680	5843	5937	5626
65. Textile manufactures	EHAK	3662	4000	4077	4076	3817	4282	4591	4498	4728	4885	4944
67. Iron and steel	EHAL	4350	5069	5930	6559	3853	5158	6476	6152	5344	5793	4991
68. Non-ferrous metals	EHAM	3938	6177	6235	6432	6351	8671	10120	12515	9559	7944	7259
69. Metal manufactures	EHAN	5355	5840	6546	6974	5968	6872	7532	7573	8016	8262	8297
7. Machinery and transport equipment [3]	EHAO	117189	139442	117428	120764	107206	129105	128558	130669	139384	146489	151828
71 - 716, 72, 73 & 74. Mechanical machinery	EHAQ	21900	22312	25506	29069	24404	28751	32735	34206	35797	36713	35834
716, 75, 76 & 77. Electrical machinery	EHAR	55443	75098	46009	47203	44529	50954	51090	50451	52244	51637	53469
78. Road vehicles	EHAS	31483	32561	36533	33881	26151	33644	36651	36455	40838	45587	49966
79. Other transport equipment	EHAT	8363	9471	9380	10611	12122	15756	8082	9557	10505	12552	12559
8. Miscellaneous manufactures [3]	EHAU	41102	44806	47938	51036	50072	54708	58544	59390	60653	63109	66773
of which:												
84. Clothing	CSDR	10207	11955	12365	13200	13850	14831	16129	15777	16484	17380	18091
85. Footwear	CSDS	2606	2712	2679	2843	3096	3601	3684	3838	4014	4317	4748
87 & 88. Scientific and photographic	EHAW	7482	7615	7529	8440	8497	9107	9558	10049	10725	10858	11493
9. Other commodities and transactions	BQAW	2276	3312	2876	4022	5058	4044	4738	4607	10542	7297	6941
Total United Kingdom imports	BOKH	282213	322920	313504	349603	315731	367580	403126	412528	423811	415469	407304

Source: Office for National Statistics: 01633 456294

1 See chapter text. The numbers on the left hand side of the table refer to the code numbers of the Standard International Trade Classification, Revision 3, which was introduced in January 1988.

2 Balance of payments consistent basis.

3 Sections 7 and 8 are shown by broad economic category in table G2 of the Monthly Review of External Trade Statistics.

6.5: Trade in goods - Exports

£ million

		2006	2007	2008	2009	2010	2011	2012	2013	2014	2015
Exports (Credits)											
Europe											
European Union (EU)											
Austria	QBRY	1674	1376	1480	1294	1485	1733	1553	1675	1669	1567
Belgium	QDOH	13009	11823	13417	10870	13478	16248	14212	13828	11856	11556
Bulgaria	QAMF	226	202	258	201	257	335	311	394	453	348
Croatia	QAMM	144	159	217	212	175	152	145	108	150	141
Cyprus	QDNZ	1042	414	539	625	569	708	443	452	493	374
Czech Republic	QDLF	1569	1400	1556	1446	1843	1967	1827	1929	2007	1978
Denmark	QBSE	3835	2181	2603	2484	2783	3077	2687	2878	2954	2334
Estonia	QAMN	469	228	224	140	197	288	288	331	283	221
Finland	QBSH	1810	1959	1916	1330	1516	1694	1548	1559	1635	1295
France	QDJA	28904	18137	18151	17255	19441	22475	20886	20977	19046	17920
Germany	QDJD	27135	25045	28308	24562	28788	34870	32544	29796	30664	30480
Greece	QDJG	1463	1354	1665	1630	1398	1234	909	943	1041	932
Hungary	QDLI	836	863	1012	855	1100	1216	1092	1234	1327	1282
Ireland	QDJJ	17131	17800	19176	15959	17085	18223	17234	18592	18104	16764
Italy	QDJM	9434	9206	9442	8385	8957	10248	8046	8513	8794	8485
Latvia	QAMO	585	145	172	109	172	246	257	380	336	218
Lithuania	QAMP	236	311	285	176	234	280	376	326	297	283
Luxembourg	QDOK	1622	272	210	198	254	283	227	239	223	198
Malta	QDOC	318	362	449	402	399	460	393	446	365	379
Netherlands	QDJP	16576	15193	20071	18299	22174	24992	25033	25424	22299	16870
Poland	QDLL	2774	2375	3024	2803	3840	4411	3417	3841	3885	3637
Portugal	QDJT	2325	1484	1648	1545	1857	1794	1371	1358	1350	1269
Romania	QAMQ	605	664	758	687	793	978	940	930	935	991
Slovak Republic	QAMR	275	380	455	378	472	567	528	471	447	449
Slovenia	QAMS	194	204	230	179	227	252	219	209	242	203
Spain	QDJW	12484	10062	10309	9249	10051	9952	8478	8663	9276	8910
Sweden	QDJZ	5151	4908	5236	4228	5628	6402	5721	5760	5341	4440
European Central Bank	QARP	-	-	-	-	-	-	-	-	-	-
EU Institutions	EOAY	-	-	-	-	-	-	-	-	-	-
Total EU28	L87R	151826	128507	142811	125501	145173	165085	150685	151256	145472	133524
European Free Trade Association (EFTA)											
Iceland	QDKW	190	202	188	128	132	148	190	172	138	231
Liechtenstein	EPOW	22	3	9	5	25	13	9	4	14	10
Norway	QDKZ	2168	2723	2832	2725	3105	3379	3564	3463	3758	3279
Switzerland	QDLC	4315	3942	4816	3993	5499	6307	7067	6140	10285	8143
Total EFTA	EPOT	6695	6870	7845	6851	8761	9847	10830	9779	14195	11663
Other Europe											
Albania	QAMC	17	19	16	18	21	19	22	21	22	17
Belarus	QAME	64	69	90	81	121	132	129	99	90	69
Russia	QDLO	2069	2851	4334	2457	3679	5217	5668	5278	4149	2831
Turkey	QDLR	2489	2348	2605	2368	3256	3937	3695	4085	3598	3575
Ukraine	QAMT	341	443	613	588	473	567	600	599	442	294
Serbia and Montenegro	QAMW	89	107	130	103	98	121	132	149	118	143
of which: Serbia	KN2P	89	99	120	99	94	113	122	134	114	134
Montenegro	KN2M	-	8	10	4	4	8	10	15	4	9
Other	BOQE	340	294	563	505	809	973	1053	1127	829	1138
Total Europe	EPLM	163930	141508	159007	138472	162391	185898	172814	172393	168915	153254
Americas											
Argentina	QAOM	217	225	319	255	358	414	388	376	234	306
Brazil	QDLU	920	1070	1691	1793	2224	2470	2667	2716	1923	2230
Canada	QATH	3884	3276	3245	3334	4134	4754	4164	4002	3228	4007
Chile	QAMG	188	183	267	514	632	799	682	1155	1028	469
Colombia	QAML	135	139	161	172	230	314	330	368	366	383
Mexico	QDLX	743	763	905	752	954	1007	1135	1175	896	1346
United States of America	J8V9	32179	32113	35278	34048	38139	40120	41261	39611	37116	47229
Uruguay	QAMU	42	36	65	60	79	122	115	174	108	228
Venezuela	QAMV	235	250	282	300	273	327	410	313	141	218
Other Central American											
Countries	BOQQ	759	767	943	704	849	899	951	886	805	973
Other	BOQT	173	183	248	234	394	477	657	607	430	540
Total Americas	EPLO	39475	39005	43404	42166	48266	51703	52760	51383	46275	57929
Asia											
China	QDMA	3495	4494	5798	5564	8131	10274	11338	13466	15520	12721
Hong Kong	QDMD	2875	2651	3665	3741	4468	5385	5394	5640	6344	5699
India	QDMG	2942	3770	4957	3088	4519	6660	5445	6426	6343	4250
Indonesia	QDMJ	319	294	394	365	462	672	655	704	499	480
Iran	QAON	434	399	442	406	307	190	109	84	87	98
Israel	QDMM	1318	1238	1339	1148	1391	1654	1548	1421	1133	1150
Japan	QAMJ	4135	3861	3916	3572	4348	4730	4932	4813	4264	4552
Malaysia	QDMP	887	953	1134	1052	1276	1486	1540	1649	1477	1409
Pakistan	QDMS	496	428	479	477	462	534	563	490	620	538
Philippines	QDMV	240	249	243	268	284	293	331	382	301	416
Saudi Arabia	QDMY	1698	1919	2284	2375	2533	2774	3156	3468	3840	4679
Singapore	QDNB	2329	2440	2814	2933	3416	3743	4403	4228	3412	3922
South Korea	QDNE	1754	1861	2560	2172	2350	2689	4943	5189	5605	4949

6.5: Trade in goods - Exports

£ million

		2006	2007	2008	2009	2010	2011	2012	2013	2014	2015
Taiwan	QDNH	915	935	887	797	1118	1388	1155	1239	1289	1217
Thailand	QDNK	572	599	758	916	1139	1418	2003	1965	1463	1289
Residual Gulf Arabian Countries	BOQW	5200	4514	6040	5783	6607	7479	8542	9546	9298	10058
Other Near & Middle Eastern Countries	QARJ	978	745	1031	1099	1319	1370	1346	1277	1332	1482
Other	BORB	673	1587	843	982	1216	1362	1333	1473	1341	1452
Total Asia	EPLP	31260	32937	39584	36738	45346	54101	58736	63460	64168	60361
Australasia & Oceania											
Australia	QDNN	2498	2582	3103	2962	3368	4396	4749	4311	3676	3970
New Zealand	QDNQ	377	359	388	350	414	543	619	650	591	597
Other	EGIZ	75	66	102	92	82	68	86	61	56	70
Total Australasia & Oceania	EPLQ	2950	3007	3593	3404	3864	5007	5454	5022	4323	4637
Africa											
Egypt	QDNT	588	689	945	1009	1200	1104	963	974	998	1061
Morocco	QAOO	306	313	517	311	567	567	649	476	529	516
South Africa	QDNW	2190	2155	2648	2257	2895	3466	3219	2572	2177	2314
Other North Africa	BORU	501	507	811	959	909	639	740	939	862	629
Other	BOQH	2757	2843	4068	3791	4758	5686	6286	5928	4647	4154
Total Africa	EPLN	6342	6507	8989	8327	10329	11462	11857	10889	9213	8674
International Organisations	EPLR	-	-	-	-	-	-	-	-	-	-
World total	LQAD	243957	222964	254577	229107	270196	308171	301621	303147	292894	284855

Source: Office for National Statistics

6.6: Trade in goods - Imports

£ million

		2006	2007	2008	2009	2010	2011	2012	2013	2014	2015
Imports (Debits)											
Europe											
European Union (EU)											
Austria	QBRZ	2789	2525	2388	2319	2670	2979	2633	2885	2973	3057
Belgium	QDOI	15391	15225	16705	15292	17348	19340	18501	20449	20982	20936
Bulgaria	QAMZ	198	241	215	183	233	289	285	418	365	381
Croatia	QANC	67	74	88	78	98	106	78	127	57	95
Cyprus	QDOA	1718	196	156	123	106	142	168	135	125	160
Czech Republic	QDLG	2961	3027	3658	3398	4050	4290	4544	4698	4739	4951
Denmark	QBSF	6539	3492	3998	3910	4180	6151	5929	5871	4628	3512
Estonia	QAND	2110	240	151	129	167	225	238	193	154	191
Finland	QBTG	3086	2655	2834	2147	2183	2464	2187	2515	2552	2084
France	QDJB	26854	22256	23657	20829	21913	23305	22865	24425	25165	24412
Germany	QDJE	42242	45268	45623	40936	47160	51071	53408	56808	60561	61789
Greece	QDJH	815	657	676	570	716	676	695	762	724	732
Hungary	QDLJ	2370	2408	2578	2585	3299	3120	2677	2665	2525	2574
Ireland	QDJK	10799	11494	12477	12659	13067	13200	13044	12537	11855	12803
Italy	QDJN	12973	13512	14427	12583	14162	14242	14491	15285	16508	16006
Latvia	QANE	806	638	423	341	443	448	412	600	435	518
Lithuania	QANF	282	313	361	377	562	613	842	907	1056	792
Luxembourg	QDOL	2727	707	846	628	956	937	685	368	436	475
Malta	QDOD	164	183	138	106	171	169	128	105	119	184
Netherlands	QDJQ	22601	23520	26387	22367	26865	28875	31750	35227	33017	31690
Poland	QDLM	3686	3749	4396	4759	6206	7157	7522	7956	7774	8251
Portugal	QDJU	3192	1534	1781	1455	1780	1826	1769	1980	2268	2407
Romania	QANG	835	960	822	803	1265	1302	1294	1507	1522	1569
Slovak Republic	QANH	850	1296	1665	1636	1648	1534	1607	1864	2010	2040
Slovenia	QANI	749	320	325	258	363	366	348	328	296	332
Spain	QDJX	12078	10643	10982	9756	10545	11931	11728	12436	13754	14079
Sweden	QDKA	6223	5381	6994	5835	6916	7797	9211	7613	8134	6972
European Central Bank	QARQ	-	-	-	-	-	-	-	-	-	-
EU Institutions	EOBS	-	-	-	-	-	-	-	-	-	-
Total EU28	L87T	185105	172514	184751	166062	189072	204555	209039	220664	224734	222992
European Free Trade Association (EFTA)											
Iceland	QDKX	406	414	467	489	433	418	393	379	429	466
Liechtenstein	EPOX	39	38	34	21	10	7	2	3	4	7
Norway	QDLA	14777	14563	21945	16200	21022	26493	24764	20437	18527	13263
Switzerland	QDLD	4421	4817	5363	5393	7460	7622	9047	8182	7790	8470
Total EFTA	EPOU	19643	19832	27809	22103	28925	34540	34206	29001	26750	22206
Other Europe											
Albania	QAMX	-	-	-	-	-	1	-	8	7	-
Belarus	QAMY	730	594	105	20	37	48	90	76	56	25
Russia	QDLP	5808	5428	6971	4638	5243	7440	8443	7116	6252	4403
Turkey	QDLS	3983	4679	4951	4659	5341	5549	5750	6178	6404	7047
Ukraine	QANJ	120	118	147	145	282	355	296	394	442	249
Serbia and Montenegro	QANM	65	74	90	74	93	97	83	114	83	145
of which: Serbia	KN2Q	65	74	88	74	92	96	80	113	83	145
Montenegro	KN2N	-	-	2	-	1	1	3	1	-	-
Other	BOQF	183	194	212	255	242	286	345	340	369	252
Total Europe	EPMM	215637	203433	225036	197956	229235	252871	258252	263891	265097	257319
Americas											
Argentina	QAOP	348	417	569	668	664	618	642	656	647	610
Brazil	QDLV	1940	2060	2654	2564	3109	2721	2446	2553	2634	2052
Canada	QATI	4933	5783	5716	4461	5762	6131	5532	5728	7181	6814
Chile	QANA	527	495	587	600	582	619	593	646	601	595
Colombia	QANB	304	367	699	582	675	921	938	827	655	648
Mexico	QDLY	429	553	780	756	1033	1083	719	757	786	1026
United States of America	J8VA	25504	25560	25508	24198	26946	28694	29837	27560	28099	34715
Uruguay	QANK	66	71	116	113	101	116	119	97	89	73
Venezuela	QANL	607	487	615	426	421	407	472	258	184	203
Other Central American											
Countries	BOQR	1387	1150	1368	1247	1141	1048	833	1091	1099	955
Other	BOQU	301	251	367	352	363	460	501	497	557	455
Total Americas	EPMO	36346	37194	38979	35967	40797	42818	42632	40670	42532	48146
Asia											
China	QDMB	16059	19038	23744	25255	30898	31847	31694	35921	36885	37968
Hong Kong	QDME	7473	6976	8161	7752	8164	7613	7389	7363	7421	6695
India	QDMH	3705	3971	4920	5408	6190	6594	6521	9673	7737	7185
Indonesia	QDMK	1034	1003	1217	1239	1391	1347	1275	1251	1052	1124
Iran	QAOQ	60	55	69	211	206	376	121	35	21	25
Israel	QDMN	961	1043	1172	1098	1562	2264	2410	1906	945	1072
Japan	QAMK	7860	7893	8534	6664	8093	8852	8523	7604	7242	6915
Malaysia	QDMQ	1923	1704	1893	1666	1835	1776	1716	1680	1739	1897
Pakistan	QDMT	508	494	635	701	808	886	842	956	940	1100
Philippines	QDMW	749	720	635	396	525	479	454	403	331	421
Saudi Arabia	QDMZ	1334	909	720	672	792	1098	1719	2837	2718	1907
Singapore	QDNC	3800	4077	4040	3586	4136	3872	3729	2704	3080	1947
South Korea	QDNF	3069	2984	3508	2859	2561	2612	3241	3394	3186	4458

6.6: Trade in goods - Imports

£ million

		2006	2007	2008	2009	2010	2011	2012	2013	2014	2015
Taiwan	QDNI	2388	2415	2628	2265	3110	3483	3963	3621	3511	3246
Thailand	QDNL	1966	2016	2448	2320	2680	2588	2617	2724	2434	2636
Residual Gulf Arabian Countries	BOQX	2245	2132	2395	2817	5381	8836	7218	7378	5329	5826
Other Near & Middle Eastern Countries	QARK	753	376	435	343	298	445	825	348	449	222
Other	BORD	2469	2638	3152	3622	3901	4959	6482	7152	5929	8136
Total Asia	EPMP	58356	60444	70306	68874	82531	89927	90739	96950	90949	92780
Australasia & Oceania											
Australia	QDNO	2087	2186	2379	2222	2306	2433	2419	2221	1735	1930
New Zealand	QDNR	603	657	751	819	842	871	893	890	716	922
Other	HFKF	130	117	169	168	107	197	164	185	155	156
Total Australasia & Oceania	EPMQ	2820	2960	3299	3209	3255	3501	3476	3296	2606	3008
Africa											
Egypt	QDNU	665	534	648	687	656	827	648	809	710	682
Morocco	QAOR	365	422	439	335	343	416	476	530	566	593
South Africa	QDNX	3965	3138	4780	3851	4417	2948	3303	2135	2678	2490
Other North Africa	BORW	1733	1703	2368	1843	2849	2245	4244	5248	3771	2067
Other	BOQJ	3033	3676	3748	3009	3497	7573	8758	10282	6560	4101
Total Africa	EPMN	9761	9473	11983	9725	11762	14009	17429	19004	14285	9933
International Organisations	EPMR	-	-	-	-	-	-	-	-	-	-
World total	LQBL	322920	313504	349603	315731	367580	403126	412528	423811	415469	411186

Source: Office for National Statistics

6.7 Total International Trade in Services all industries (excluding travel, transport and banking) analysed by product 2014-2015

£ million

	Exports		Imports		Balance	
	2014	2015	2014	2015	2014	2015
Agricultural and Mining Services						
Agricultural, forestry and fishing	55	15	116	10	-61	4
Mining and oil and gas extraction services	1,459	1,679	70	168	1,390	1,510
Total Agricultural and Mining services	**1,515**	**1,693**	**186**	**179**	**1,329**	**1,515**
Manufacturing, Maintenance and On-site Processing Services						
Waste treatment and depolution services	128	121	150	130	-21	-9
Manufacturing services on goods owned by others	2,103	2,350	581	627	1,521	1,723
Maintenance and repair services	2,012	2,089	440	890	1,572	1,199
Total Manufacturing, Maintenance and On-site Processing services	**4,243**	**4,560**	**1,171**	**1,647**	**3,072**	**2,913**
Business and Professional Services						
Accountancy, auditing, bookkeeping and tax consulting services	1,898	2,058	818	893	1,080	1,165
Advertising, market research and public opinion polling services	4,971	5,258	2,692	3,166	2,279	2,092
Business management and management consulting services	7,279	7,249	2,938	3,060	4,342	4,189
Public relations services	392	338	125	123	267	215
Recruitment services	1,359	1,365	428	519	931	846
Legal services	4,577	4,966	934	741	3,643	4,225
Operating leasing services	452	342	1,416	624	-964	-282
Procurement services	76	188	254	289	-178	-101
Property management services	583	409	167	145	415	265
Other business and professional services	3,867	3,724	2,197	2,093	1,670	1,631
Services between related enterprises	11,407	11,970	8,622	9,676	2,785	2,294
Total Business and Professional Services	**36,861**	**37,867**	**20,590**	**21,329**	**16,271**	**16,538**
Research and Development Services						
Provision of R&D services	5,086	5,224	3,750	4,559	1,336	665
Provision of product development and testing activities	975	1,141	307	422	668	719
Total Research and Development Services	**6,061**	**6,364**	**4,057**	**4,980**	**2,004**	**1,384**
Intellectual Property						
Trade marks, franchises, brands or design rights						
Outright sales and purchases	287	371	744	720	-457	-349
Charges or payments for the use of	5,453	5,468	3,150	3,435	2,303	2,034
Copyrighted literary works, sound recordings, films, television programmes and databases						
Outright sales and purchases	300	248	142	109	158	139
Charges or payments for the use of	4,734	5,223	3,247	4,236	1,487	987
Patents and other intellectual property that are the end result of research and development						
Outright sales and purchases	65	90	31	133	34	-43
Charges or payments for the use of	1,561	1,737	586	686	975	1,051
Total intellectual property	**12,400**	**13,137**	**7,901**	**9,319**	**4,499**	**3,819**
Telecommunication, Computer and Information Services						
Postal and courier	1,112	1,574	622	1,015	490	559
Telecommunications	7,256	6,783	4,640	4,444	2,616	2,339
Computer Services	7,739	7,673	4,635	4,729	3,104	2,944
Publishing Services	1,014	693	189	118	825	575
News agency Services	463	605	68	56	394	549
Information Services	1,700	2,080	559	903	1,141	1,177
Total Telecommunication, Computer and Information Services	**19,285**	**19,409**	**10,714**	**11,266**	**8,572**	**8,143**
Construction Services						
Construction in the UK	209	177	1,011	701	-802	-524
Construction outside the UK	2,522	1,416	947	503	1,575	913
Total Construction Services	**2,732**	**1,594**	**1,958**	**1,205**	**773**	**389**

6.7 Total International Trade in Services all industries (excluding travel, transport and banking) analysed by product 2014-2015

£ million

	Exports		Imports		Balance	
	2014	2015	2014	2015	2014	2015
Financial Services						
Financial	13,585	14,896	2,356	3,283	11,229	11,612
Insurance and Pension Services						
Insurance and Pension Services Claims	3,084	2,322			3,084	2,322
Insurance and Pension Services Premiums			596	403	-596	-403
Merchanting and Other Trade related Services						
Merchanting	1,395	2,241	1,099	372	296	1,870
Other trade - related services	1,788	2,208	634	817	1,154	1,390
Total Merchanting and Other Trade related Services	**3,183**	**4,449**	**1,733**	**1,189**	**1,451**	**3,260**
Personal, Cultural and Recreational Services						
Audio- Visual and related services	1,319	1,546	537	682	782	864
Medical Services	34	26	14	8	20	18
Training and educational services	317	296	47	79	269	217
Heritage and recreational services	208	354	42	137	165	218
Social, domestic and other personal services	70	74	36	41	34	33
Total Personal, Cultural and Recreational Services	**1,947**	**2,296**	**676**	**946**	**1,272**	**1,350**
Technical and Scientific Services						
Architectural services	451	468	120	31	330	437
Engineering Services	7,031	7,348	1,116	1,249	5,915	6,099
Scientific and other techinical services inc surveying	1,672	1,379	416	598	1,256	781
Total Technical Services	**9,153**	**9,194**	**1,652**	**1,878**	**7,501**	**7,316**
Other Trade in Services						
Other trade in services	5,654	5,449	866	886	4,789	4,563
Total International Trade in Services	**119,703**	**123,231**	**54,455**	**58,509**	**65,248**	**64,722**

Source: Office for National Statistics

- Denotes nil or less than £500,000

.. Denotes disclosive data

The sum of constituent items may not always agree exactly with the totals shown due to rounding

Data from 2013 has been collected in accordance with BPM6 regulations

6.8 Total International Trade in Services (excluding travel, transport and banking) analysed by continents and countries 2013 - 2015

£ million

	Export			Import			Balance		
	2013	2014	2015	2013	2014	2015	2013	2014	2015
Europe									
European Union (EU)									
Austria	365	373	388	245	380	345	120	-6	43
Belgium	2,064	1,730	2,078	1,199	1,010	1,264	865	720	814
Bulgaria	93	96	159	87	57	89	6	39	70
Croatia	45	55	53	25	16	21	20	40	33
Cyprus	456	230	287	285	141	181	171	89	106
Czech Republic	351	332	351	243	178	257	108	155	94
Denmark	1,539	1,514	1,427	563	713	553	976	801	874
Estonia	30	46	30	29	25	31	1	22	-1
Finland	624	791	604	229	216	181	395	574	423
France	4,798	4,650	5,346	3,274	3,586	3,568	1,524	1,064	1,778
Germany	7,490	7,171	7,276	4,736	5,287	4,910	2,754	1,883	2,366
Greece	438	398	342	152	111	119	286	287	223
Hungary	248	280	260	196	178	140	52	102	120
Irish Republic	6,697	6,598	7,188	4,084	3,335	3,791	2,613	3,263	3,398
Italy	2,411	2,292	3,035	1,324	1,542	1,401	1,087	750	1,634
Latvia	46	35	45	25	15	17	21	20	29
Lithuania	61	49	47	24	26	31	37	23	16
Luxembourg	2,090	2,255	2,189	1,404	1,693	1,905	686	562	284
Malta	265	207	240	65	55	73	200	152	168
Netherlands	5,584	7,580	6,854	2,727	2,393	2,720	2,857	5,187	4,134
Poland	679	818	805	521	506	619	158	312	186
Portugal	474	455	409	195	277	244	279	178	165
Romania	242	223	230	125	153	142	117	69	87
Slovakia	205	133	127	83	82	85	122	51	42
Slovenia	..	..	..	..	..	..	30	50	..
Spain	1,863	2,070	2,138	1,305	1,392	1,333	558	679	805
Sweden	1,930	2,009	2,123	1,183	1,167	1,824	747	841	299
EU Institutions	..	..	..	..	..	..	16	18	..
Total European Union (EU)	**41,148**	**42,475**	**44,098**	**24,342**	**24,554**	**25,866**	**16,806**	**17,921**	**18,232**
European Free Trade Association (EFTA)									
Iceland	74	96	118	9	24	16	65	72	102
Liechtenstein	32	36	65	3	2	23	29	34	42
Norway	2,194	2,212	1,624	459	466	400	1,735	1,746	1,224
Switzerland	7,712	7,204	6,863	2,179	1,791	2,603	5,533	5,413	4,261
Total EFTA	**10,012**	**9,548**	**8,670**	**2,650**	**2,283**	**3,041**	**7,362**	**7,265**	**5,629**
Other Europe									
Russia	944	1,133	1,080	390	288	294	554	845	786
Channel Islands	1,843	1,550	1,813	232	291	264	1,611	1,259	1,549
Isle of Man	93	435	197	13	14	9	80	421	188
Turkey	564	582	808	188	127	370	376	454	438
Rest of Europe	622	800	726	241	201	146	381	599	580
Europe Unallocated	1,924	2,188	2,126	1,303	1,326	1,494	621	862	632
Total Europe	**57,150**	**58,711**	**59,518**	**29,359**	**29,085**	**31,483**	**27,791**	**29,626**	**28,035**
America									
Brazil	819	797	781	140	149	184	679	648	597
Canada	1,815	1,414	1,476	760	791	563	1,055	623	913
Mexico	224	261	383	43	40	45	181	222	338
USA	26,504	27,821	27,991	11,642	12,945	13,880	14,862	14,875	14,110
Rest of America	3,182	2,806	3,094	697	861	683	2,485	1,945	2,412
America Unallocated	371	425	328	54	76	57	317	349	271
Total America	**32,915**	**33,523**	**34,053**	**13,336**	**14,863**	**15,413**	**19,579**	**18,661**	**18,641**
Asia									
China	1,180	1,058	1,647	591	521	861	589	537	785
Hong Kong	895	1,006	1,241	638	666	760	257	341	481
India	863	975	1,189	1,355	1,519	1,759	-492	-544	-570
Indonesia	167	171	180	43	55	72	124	115	108
Israel	329	351	452	363	241	375	-34	109	77
Japan	2,140	2,456	2,370	1,238	1,410	1,702	902	1,046	668

6.8 Total International Trade in Services (excluding travel, transport and banking) analysed by continents and countries 2013 - 2015

£ million

	Export			Import			Balance		
	2013	2014	2015	2013	2014	2015	2013	2014	2015
Malaysia	498	438	406	60	191	147	438	247	259
Pakistan	104	181	150	106	93	35	-2	88	115
Philippines	92	90	103	121	127	319	-29	-37	-216
Saudi Arabia	5,315	4,289	4,613	113	71	84	5,202	4,218	4,530
Singapore	1,411	2,077	2,311	1,192	1,507	1,196	219	570	1,115
South Korea	700	800	768	203	205	207	497	595	561
Taiwan	366	317	298	87	100	86	279	217	212
Thailand	294	286	317	57	172	64	237	114	253
Rest of Asia	4,580	4,494	4,634	1,452	946	1,188	3,128	3,548	3,446
Asia Unallocated	726	714	771	418	424	209	308	290	562
Total Asia	**19,660**	**19,703**	**21,452**	**8,037**	**8,248**	**9,065**	**11,623**	**11,454**	**12,386**
Australasia and Oceania									
Australia	..	1,863	1,787	..	873	1,096	1,101	990	691
New Zealand	219	220	175	75	39	70	144	181	106
Rest of Australia and Oceania	..	..	..	..	..	..	152	74	54
Oceania Unallocated	-	..	..	-	..	..	-	1	1
Total Australasia and Oceania	**2,365**	**2,175**	**2,023**	**968**	**929**	**1,172**	**1,397**	**1,246**	**851**
Africa									
Nigeria	562	493	867	297	75	97	265	418	770
South Africa	968	1,167	1,037	332	325	408	636	842	629
Rest of Africa	2,793	3,160	3,216	637	574	520	2,156	2,585	2,696
Africa Unallocated	233	261	216	239	186	114	-6	75	102
Total Africa	**4,556**	**5,081**	**5,335**	**1,505**	**1,160**	**1,138**	**3,051**	**3,921**	**4,196**
Total Unallocated	547	..	850	182	..	237	365	340	613
International Organisations	-	..	-	-	..	-	-	1	-
TOTAL INTERNATIONAL TRADE IN SERVICES	**117,193**	**119,703**	**123,231**	**53,387**	**54,455**	**58,508**	**63,806**	**65,248**	**64,722**

Source: Office for National Statistics

- Denotes nil or less than £500,000
.. Denotes disclosive data

The sum of constituent items may not always agree exactly with the totals shown due to rounding

Data from 2013 has been collected in accordance with BPM6 regulation

Excludes the activities of banking and travel industries

Estimates for Croatia have been published for the first time in 2013. Previously this was included in the Rest of Europe.

6.9 Summary of balance of payments in 2014

£ million

	Credits	Debits
1. Current account		
A. Goods and services	515 191	549 723
1. Goods	295 432	419 104
2. Services	219 759	130 619
2.1. Manufacturing physical inputs owned by others	1 965	709
2.2. Maintenance and repair	2 444	359
2.3. Transport	26 706	19 369
2.4. Travel	28 341	38 428
2.5. Construction	1 965	2 185
2.6. Insurance and pension services	20 110	1 374
2.7. Financial	49 223	10 004
2.8. Intellectual property	10 941	5 924
2.9. Telecommunications, computer and information services	16 332	9 413
2.10. Other business	57 135	35 508
2.11. Personal, cultural and recreational services	2 126	3 143
2.12. Government	2 471	4 203
B. Primary income	144 450	177 558
1. Compensation of employees	1 074	1 517
2. Investment income	141 067	173 081
2.1. Direct investment	72 642	70 642
2.2. Portfolio investment	44 705	67 652
2.3. Other investment	23 074	34 787
2.4. Reserve assets	646	
3. Other primary income	2 309	2 960
C. Secondary income	19 177	44 426
1. General government	5 032	25 933
2. Other sectors	14 145	18 493
Total current account	**678 818**	**771 707**
2. Capital account		
1. Capital transfers	1 478	1 727
2. Acquisition/disposal of non-produced, non-financial assets	546	1 059
Total capital account	**2 024**	**2 786**

	Net acquisition of financial assets	Net incurrence of liabilities
3. Financial account		
1. Direct investment	−19 021	23 429
Abroad	−19 021	
1.1. Equity capital other than reinvestment of earnings	−6 911	
1.2. Reinvestment of earnings	1 421	
1.3. Debt instruments[1]	−13 531	
In United Kingdom		23 429
1.1. Equity capital other than reinvestment of earnings		23 446
1.2. Reinvestment of earnings		11 094
1.3. Debt instruments[2]		−11 111
2. Portfolio investment	−5 719	45 006
Assets	−5 719	
2.1. Equity and investment fund shares	−22 783	
2.2. Debt securities	17 064	
Liabilities		45 006
2.1. Equity and investment fund shares		30 218
2.2. Debt securities		14 788
3. Financial derivatives and employee stock options (net)	13 947	
4. Other investment	−208 691	−213 819
Assets	−208 691	
4.1. Other equity	1 473	
4.2. Currency and deposits	−193 604	
4.3. Loans	−16 661	
4.4. Trade credit and advances	378	
4.5. Other accounts receivable	277	
Liabilities		−213 819
4.1. Currency and deposits		−278 145
4.2. Loans		63 598
4.3. Insurance, pensions and standardised guarantee schemes		−444
4.4. Trade credit and advances		−
4.5. Other accounts payable		1 172
4.6. Special drawing rights		−
5. Reserve assets	4 961	
5.1. Monetary gold	−	
5.2. Special drawing rights	43	
5.3. Reserve position in the IMF	−84	
5.4. Other reserve assets	5 002	
Total financial account	**−214 523**	**−145 384**

1 Debt instrument transactions on direct investment abroad represents claims on affiliated enterprises plus claims on direct investors.
2 Debt instrument transactions on direct investment in the United Kingdom represents liabilities to direct investors plus liabilities to affiliated enterprises

Source: Office for National Statistics

6.10 Summary of Balance of Payments: Balances (net credits less net debits)

£ million

			Current account										
	Trade in goods	Trade in services	**Total goods and services**	Compensat- ion of employees	Investment income	Other primary income	**Total primary income**	**Secondary income**	**Current balance**	Current balance as % of GDP[1]	Capital account	Financial account	Net errors & omissions
	LQCT	KTMS	KTMY	KTMP	HMBM	MT5W	HMBP	KTNF	HBOG	AA6H	FKMJ	-HBNT	HHDH
1946	−101	−274	−375	−20	76	−	56	166	−153	..	−21	−181	−7
1947	−358	−197	−555	−19	140	−	121	123	−311	..	−21	−552	−220
1948	−152	−64	−216	−20	223	−	203	96	83	0.7	−17	58	−8
1949	−138	−43	−181	−20	206	−	186	29	34	0.3	−12	103	81
1950	−55	−4	−59	−21	378	−	357	39	337	2.6	−10	447	120
1951	−693	32	−661	−21	322	−	301	29	−331	−2.3	−15	−426	−80
1952	−274	123	−151	−22	231	−	209	169	227	1.5	−15	229	17
1953	−246	122	−124	−25	207	−	182	143	201	1.2	−13	177	−11
1954	−213	114	−99	−27	227	−	200	55	156	0.9	−13	174	31
1955	−318	41	−277	−27	149	−	122	43	−112	−0.6	−15	−34	93
1956	44	25	69	−30	203	−	173	2	244	1.2	−13	250	19
1957	−39	120	81	−32	223	−	191	−5	267	1.2	−13	313	59
1958	22	117	139	−34	261	−	227	4	370	1.6	−10	411	51
1959	−129	116	−13	−37	233	−	196	−	183	0.7	−5	68	−110
1960	−418	36	−382	−35	201	−	166	−6	−222	−0.8	−6	7	235
1961	−160	48	−112	−35	223	−	188	−9	67	0.2	−12	−23	−78
1962	−122	47	−75	−37	301	−	264	−14	175	0.6	−12	195	32
1963	−142	1	−141	−38	364	−	326	−37	148	0.5	−16	30	−102
1964	−573	−37	−610	−33	365	−	332	−74	−352	−1.0	−17	−392	−23
1965	−288	−70	−358	−34	405	−	371	−75	−62	−0.2	−18	−49	31
1966	−144	39	−105	−39	358	−	319	−91	123	0.3	−19	−22	−126
1967	−646	151	−495	−39	354	−	315	−118	−298	−0.7	−25	−179	144
1968	−770	333	−437	−48	303	−	255	−119	−301	−0.7	−26	−688	−361
1969	−283	382	99	−47	468	−	421	−109	411	0.8	−23	794	406
1970	−94	443	349	−56	527	−	471	−89	731	1.3	−22	818	109
1971	120	602	722	−63	454	−	391	−90	1 023	1.6	−23	1 330	330
1972	−829	703	−126	−52	350	−	298	−142	30	−	−35	−477	−472
1973	−2 676	883	−1 793	−68	970	−	902	−336	−1 227	−1.5	−39	−1 031	235
1974	−5 357	1 258	−4 099	−92	1 010	−	918	−302	−3 483	−3.8	−34	−3 185	332
1975	−3 378	1 663	−1 715	−102	257	−	155	−313	−1 873	−1.6	−36	−1 569	340
1976	−4 079	2 815	−1 264	−140	760	−	620	−534	−1 178	−0.9	−12	−507	683
1977	−2 439	3 636	1 197	−152	−678	−	−830	−889	−522	−0.3	11	3 286	3 797
1978	−1 710	4 132	2 422	−140	−300	−	−440	−1 420	562	0.3	−79	2 655	2 172
1979	−3 514	4 469	955	−130	−342	−	−472	−1 777	−1 294	−0.6	−103	−864	533
1980	1 123	4 284	5 407	−82	−2 268	−	−2 350	−1 653	1 404	0.5	−4	2 157	757
1981	2 986	4 616	7 602	−66	−1 883	−	−1 949	−1 219	4 434	1.5	−79	5 312	957
1982	1 614	4 075	5 689	−95	−2 336	−	−2 431	−1 476	1 782	0.6	6	1 233	−555
1983	−1 892	5 191	3 299	−89	−1 050	−	−1 139	−1 391	769	0.2	75	3 287	2 443
1984	−5 736	5 867	131	−94	−326	−	−420	−1 566	−1 855	−0.5	107	7 130	8 878
1985	−3 755	8 243	4 488	−120	−2 609	−	−2 729	−2 924	−1 165	−0.3	185	1 657	2 637
1986	−9 968	7 878	−2 090	−156	71	−	−85	−2 094	−4 269	−1.0	135	122	4 256
1987	−12 093	8 610	−3 483	−174	−785	−	−959	−3 437	−7 879	−1.6	159	−9 690	−1 970
1988	−22 028	6 934	−15 094	−64	−1 234	−	−1 298	−3 293	−19 685	−3.6	−39	−15 271	4 453
1989	−25 214	6 891	−18 323	−138	−2 367	−	−2 505	−4 228	−25 056	−4.1	−56	−9 988	15 124
1990	−19 280	8 163	−11 117	−110	−4 644	−	−4 754	−4 802	−20 673	−3.1	222	−23 090	−2 639
1991	−10 919	8 369	−2 550	−63	−5 691	−	−5 754	−999	−9 303	−1.3	−55	−5 711	3 647
1992	−13 788	8 941	−4 847	−49	−990	−	−1 039	−5 228	−11 114	−1.5	35	−17 720	−6 641
1993	−13 881	11 223	−2 658	35	−2 488	−	−2 453	−5 056	−10 167	−1.3	32	−23 696	−13 561
1994	−11 972	11 787	−185	−170	1 625	−	1 455	−5 187	−3 917	−0.5	−252	3 259	7 428
1995	−12 985	15 379	2 394	−296	−435	−	−731	−7 363	−5 700	−0.7	97	−1 297	4 306
1996	−14 736	16 340	1 604	93	−2 351	−	−2 258	−4 539	−5 193	−0.6	806	−2 030	2 357
1997	−12 892	16 720	3 828	83	−299	686	470	−6 097	−1 799	−0.2	509	6 544	7 834
1998	−22 343	14 433	−7 910	−10	11 792	819	12 601	−8 878	−4 187	−0.4	−261	563	5 011
1999	−29 418	13 249	−16 169	201	−1 530	711	−618	−7 864	−24 651	−2.4	−258	−21 270	3 639
2000	−33 472	13 033	−20 439	150	6 673	441	7 264	−10 053	−23 228	−2.1	393	−13 653	9 182
2001	−41 913	15 805	−26 108	66	10 615	579	11 260	−6 893	−21 741	−1.9	73	−30 063	−8 395
2002	−48 953	16 008	−32 945	67	17 861	968	18 896	−9 382	−23 431	−2.0	−675	−22 443	1 663
2003	−50 959	20 573	−30 386	59	19 324	1 272	20 655	−10 822	−20 553	−1.7	−65	−14 150	−6 468
2004	−61 941	26 544	−35 397	−494	22 696	1 279	23 481	−11 090	−23 006	−1.8	90	−13 517	9 399
2005	−70 160	33 658	−36 502	−610	32 094	1 140	32 624	−12 865	−16 743	−1.2	−843	−12 304	−5 282
2006	−78 963	42 850	−36 113	−958	16 594	816	16 452	−12 702	−32 363	−2.2	−1 527	−28 587	5 303
2007	−90 540	50 598	−39 942	−734	16 626	537	16 429	−13 977	−37 490	−2.4	−169	−26 554	11 105
2008	−95 026	48 837	−46 189	−715	5 634	362	5 281	−14 094	−55 002	−3.5	220	−39 261	15 521
2009	−86 624	52 269	−34 355	−259	4 863	756	5 360	−15 836	−44 831	−3.0	404	−29 017	15 410
2010	−97 384	54 791	−42 593	−389	20 468	114	20 193	−20 662	−43 062	−2.7	3	−30 276	12 783
2011	−94 955	67 895	−27 060	−173	19 589	229	19 645	−21 673	−29 088	−1.8	−380	−23 455	6 013
2012	−110 907	73 573	−37 334	−148	−1 765	−273	−2 186	−21 913	−61 433	−3.7	−167	−52 786	−8 814
2013	−120 664	81 426	−39 238	−326	−9 544	−471	−10 341	−26 863	−76 442	−4.4	−472	−78 558	−1 644
2014	−122 575	86 352	−36 223	−470	−22 642	−654	−23 766	−25 009	−84 998	−4.7	−415	−78 589	6 824

1 Using series YBHA: GDP at current market prices.

Source: Office for National Statistics

6.11 Balance of payments: current account

£ million

		1994	1995	1996	1997	1998	1999	2000	2001	2002	2003	2004
Credits												
Exports of goods and services												
Exports of goods	LQAD	135 143	153 577	167 196	172 110	163 997	166 539	188 130	189 624	186 776	188 546	191 608
Exports of services	KTMQ	53 089	59 202	65 085	67 377	70 375	75 960	81 739	88 444	93 255	104 635	114 711
Total exports of goods and services	KTMW	188 232	212 779	232 281	239 487	234 372	242 499	269 869	278 068	280 031	293 181	306 319
Primary income												
Compensation of employees	KTMN	681	887	911	1 007	840	960	1 032	1 087	1 121	1 116	931
Investment income	HMBN	72 883	85 797	90 122	96 180	105 941	103 423	134 480	139 884	124 178	124 908	140 914
Other primary income	MT5S	–	–	–	3 068	2 937	2 781	2 571	2 679	2 912	3 227	3 449
Total primary income	HMBQ	73 564	86 684	91 033	100 255	109 718	107 164	138 083	143 650	128 211	129 251	145 294
Secondary income												
General government	FJUM	2 138	1 730	2 828	2 393	1 767	3 542	2 465	4 991	3 663	3 968	4 299
Other sectors	FJUN	8 918	10 213	11 372	8 503	8 439	6 215	6 280	6 020	7 695	8 148	8 563
Total secondary income	KTND	11 056	11 943	14 200	10 896	10 206	9 757	8 745	11 011	11 358	12 116	12 862
Total	HBOE	**272 852**	**311 406**	**337 514**	**350 638**	**354 296**	**359 420**	**416 697**	**432 729**	**419 600**	**434 548**	**464 475**
Debits												
Imports of goods and services												
Imports of goods	LQBL	147 115	166 562	181 932	185 002	186 340	195 957	221 602	231 537	235 729	239 505	253 549
Imports of services	KTMR	41 302	43 823	48 745	50 657	55 942	62 711	68 706	72 639	77 247	84 062	88 167
Total imports of goods and services	KTMX	188 417	210 385	230 677	235 659	242 282	258 668	290 308	304 176	312 976	323 567	341 716
Primary income												
Compensation of employees	KTMO	851	1 183	818	924	850	759	882	1 021	1 054	1 057	1 425
Investment income	HMBO	71 258	86 232	92 473	96 479	94 149	104 953	127 807	129 269	106 317	105 584	118 218
Other primary income	MT5U	–	–	–	2 382	2 118	2 070	2 130	2 100	1 944	1 955	2 170
Total primary income	HMBR	72 109	87 415	93 291	99 785	97 117	107 782	130 819	132 390	109 315	108 596	121 813
Secondary income												
General government	FJUO	4 795	4 811	5 081	8 370	10 701	10 913	11 819	11 056	11 968	13 648	13 803
Other sectors	FJUP	11 448	14 495	13 658	8 623	8 383	6 708	6 979	6 848	8 772	9 290	10 149
Total secondary income	KTNE	16 243	19 306	18 739	16 993	19 084	17 621	18 798	17 904	20 740	22 938	23 952
Total	HBOF	**276 769**	**317 106**	**342 707**	**352 437**	**358 483**	**384 071**	**439 925**	**454 470**	**443 031**	**455 101**	**487 481**
Balances												
Trade in goods and services												
Trade in goods	LQCT	−11 972	−12 985	−14 736	−12 892	−22 343	−29 418	−33 472	−41 913	−48 953	−50 959	−61 941
Trade in services	KTMS	11 787	15 379	16 340	16 720	14 433	13 249	13 033	15 805	16 008	20 573	26 544
Total trade in goods and services	KTMY	−185	2 394	1 604	3 828	−7 910	−16 169	−20 439	−26 108	−32 945	−30 386	−35 397
Primary income												
Compensation of employees	KTMP	−170	−296	93	83	−10	201	150	66	67	59	−494
Investment income	HMBM	1 625	−435	−2 351	−299	11 792	−1 530	6 673	10 615	17 861	19 324	22 696
Other primary income	MT5W	–	–	–	686	819	711	441	579	968	1 272	1 279
Total primary income	HMBP	1 455	−731	−2 258	470	12 601	−618	7 264	11 260	18 896	20 655	23 481
Secondary income												
General government	FJUQ	−2 657	−3 081	−2 253	−5 977	−8 934	−7 371	−9 354	−6 065	−8 305	−9 680	−9 504
Other sectors	FJUR	−2 530	−4 282	−2 286	−120	56	−493	−699	−828	−1 077	−1 142	−1 586
Total secondary income	KTNF	−5 187	−7 363	−4 539	−6 097	−8 878	−7 864	−10 053	−6 893	−9 382	−10 822	−11 090
Total (Current balance)	HBOG	**−3 917**	**−5 700**	**−5 193**	**−1 799**	**−4 187**	**−24 651**	**−23 228**	**−21 741**	**−23 431**	**−20 553**	**−23 006**

6.11 Balance of payments: current account

continued

£ million

		2005	2006	2007	2008	2009	2010	2011	2012	2013	2014
Credits											
Exports of goods and services											
Exports of goods	LQAD	212 053	243 957	222 964	254 577	229 107	270 196	308 171	301 621	303 147	292 894
Exports of services	KTMQ	129 285	145 836	157 679	166 223	169 473	174 121	188 816	197 520	214 495	218 760
Total exports of goods and services	KTMW	341 338	389 793	380 643	420 800	398 580	444 317	496 987	499 141	517 642	511 654
Primary income											
Compensation of employees	KTMN	974	938	984	1 046	1 176	1 097	1 121	1 124	1 094	1 080
Investment income	HMBN	193 049	249 298	307 890	287 868	175 117	174 003	199 995	170 279	157 261	139 005
Other primary income	MT5S	3 408	3 221	2 952	3 051	3 411	3 059	3 166	2 625	2 455	2 306
Total primary income	HMBQ	197 431	253 457	311 826	291 965	179 704	178 159	204 282	174 028	160 810	142 391
Secondary income											
General government	FJUM	4 385	4 471	4 408	5 720	6 271	3 843	3 536	3 719	4 302	5 086
Other sectors	FJUN	10 665	15 806	9 416	14 568	10 602	11 699	10 699	12 737	15 324	14 161
Total secondary income	KTND	15 050	20 277	13 824	20 288	16 873	15 542	14 235	16 456	19 626	19 247
Total	HBOE	**553 819**	**663 527**	**706 293**	**733 053**	**595 157**	**638 018**	**715 504**	**689 625**	**698 078**	**673 292**
Debits											
Imports of goods and services											
Imports of goods	LQBL	282 213	322 920	313 504	349 603	315 731	367 580	403 126	412 528	423 811	415 469
Imports of services	KTMR	95 627	102 986	107 081	117 386	117 204	119 330	120 921	123 947	133 069	132 408
Total imports of goods and services	KTMX	377 840	425 906	420 585	466 989	432 935	486 910	524 047	536 475	556 880	547 877
Primary income											
Compensation of employees	KTMO	1 584	1 896	1 718	1 761	1 435	1 486	1 294	1 272	1 420	1 550
Investment income	HMBO	160 955	232 704	291 264	282 234	170 254	153 535	180 406	172 044	166 805	161 647
Other primary income	MT5U	2 268	2 405	2 415	2 689	2 655	2 945	2 937	2 898	2 926	2 960
Total primary income	HMBR	164 807	237 005	295 397	286 684	174 344	157 966	184 637	176 214	171 151	166 157
Secondary income											
General government	FJUO	15 596	16 063	16 382	16 966	19 268	20 900	21 716	21 989	27 015	25 930
Other sectors	FJUP	12 319	16 916	11 419	17 416	13 441	15 304	14 192	16 380	19 474	18 326
Total secondary income	KTNE	27 915	32 979	27 801	34 382	32 709	36 204	35 908	38 369	46 489	44 256
Total	HBOF	**570 562**	**695 890**	**743 783**	**788 055**	**639 988**	**681 080**	**744 592**	**751 058**	**774 520**	**758 290**
Balances											
Trade in goods and services											
Trade in goods	LQCT	−70 160	−78 963	−90 540	−95 026	−86 624	−97 384	−94 955	−110 907	−120 664	−122 575
Trade in services	KTMS	33 658	42 850	50 598	48 837	52 269	54 791	67 895	73 573	81 426	86 352
Total trade in goods and services	KTMY	−36 502	−36 113	−39 942	−46 189	−34 355	−42 593	−27 060	−37 334	−39 238	−36 223
Primary income											
Compensation of employees	KTMP	−610	−958	−734	−715	−259	−389	−173	−148	−326	−470
Investment income	HMBM	32 094	16 594	16 626	5 634	4 863	20 468	19 589	−1 765	−9 544	−22 642
Other primary income	MT5W	1 140	816	537	362	756	114	229	−273	−471	−654
Total primary income	HMBP	32 624	16 452	16 429	5 281	5 360	20 193	19 645	−2 186	−10 341	−23 766
Secondary income											
General government	FJUQ	−11 211	−11 592	−11 974	−11 246	−12 997	−17 057	−18 180	−18 270	−22 713	−20 844
Other sectors	FJUR	−1 654	−1 110	−2 003	−2 848	−2 839	−3 605	−3 493	−3 643	−4 150	−4 165
Total secondary income	KTNF	−12 865	−12 702	−13 977	−14 094	−15 836	−20 662	−21 673	−21 913	−26 863	−25 009
Total (Current balance)	HBOG	**−16 743**	**−32 363**	**−37 490**	**−55 002**	**−44 831**	**−43 062**	**−29 088**	**−61 433**	**−76 442**	**−84 998**

Source: Office for National Statistics

6.12 Balance of payments: Summary of international investment position, financial account and investment income

£ billion

		2005	2006	2007	2008	2009	2010	2011	2012	2013	2014
Investment abroad											
International investment position											
Direct investment	N2V3	954.0	992.3	1 148.6	1 438.6	1 261.9	1 343.0	1 363.5	1 411.5	1 437.4	1 383.9
Portfolio investment	HHZZ	1 383.1	1 556.2	1 722.8	1 696.8	1 923.3	2 144.2	2 130.5	2 347.5	2 439.1	2 546.9
Financial derivatives	JX96	820.1	853.7	1 378.2	4 040.2	2 176.4	2 962.9	3 617.8	3 060.1	2 424.4	2 828.6
Other investment	HLXV	2 730.8	2 929.7	3 697.6	4 160.5	3 467.8	3 753.1	4 039.8	3 711.2	3 488.0	3 547.3
Reserve assets	LTEB	24.7	22.9	26.7	36.3	40.1	49.7	56.8	61.7	61.4	67.7
Total	HBQA	**5 912.8**	**6 354.8**	**7 973.9**	**11 372.4**	**8 869.6**	**10 252.8**	**11 208.3**	**10 591.9**	**9 850.4**	**10 374.4**
Financial account transactions[1]											
Direct investment	-N2SV	87.8	77.0	184.1	200.1	−32.8	35.8	50.0	7.7	28.6	−73.1
Portfolio investment	-HHZC	160.5	144.8	100.5	−113.0	179.8	100.8	12.5	131.9	−10.3	7.2
Financial derivatives (net)	-ZPNN	−5.8	−20.6	27.0	121.7	−29.1	−25.5	3.0	−36.9	11.6	−0.6
Other investment	-XBMM	498.3	394.8	660.5	−652.0	−350.1	238.5	103.2	−233.7	−209.2	110.8
Reserve assets	-LTCV	0.7	−0.4	1.2	−1.3	5.8	6.1	4.9	7.6	5.0	7.1
Total	-HBNR	**741.5**	**595.6**	**973.2**	**−444.6**	**−226.4**	**355.7**	**173.6**	**−123.5**	**−174.3**	**51.5**
Investment income											
Direct investment	N2QP	83.5	91.7	101.1	86.6	74.3	92.9	104.6	87.2	84.0	71.2
Portfolio investment	HLYX	46.9	57.0	68.8	69.7	56.1	50.0	53.9	50.8	47.0	44.3
Other investment	AIOP	61.9	99.9	137.5	130.8	43.9	30.3	40.7	31.6	25.6	22.9
Reserve assets	HHCB	0.7	0.6	0.6	0.8	0.8	0.7	0.8	0.7	0.6	0.6
Total	HMBN	**193.0**	**249.3**	**307.9**	**287.9**	**175.1**	**174.0**	**200.0**	**170.3**	**157.3**	**139.0**
Investment in the UK											
International investment position											
Direct investment	N2UG	692.0	774.4	788.1	944.3	881.2	948.2	994.1	1 250.9	1 265.3	1 349.7
Portfolio investment	HLXW	1 499.1	1 744.2	2 023.7	2 040.0	2 437.6	2 565.9	2 549.3	2 606.2	2 585.7	2 715.7
Financial derivatives	JX97	831.1	890.5	1 392.2	3 915.3	2 096.8	2 895.0	3 554.9	3 032.2	2 376.7	2 806.5
Other investment	HLYD	2 975.5	3 110.3	3 906.3	4 331.9	3 614.5	3 906.3	4 206.6	4 077.0	3 904.5	3 823.9
Total	HBQB	**5 997.8**	**6 519.4**	**8 110.4**	**11 231.6**	**9 030.1**	**10 315.4**	**11 305.0**	**10 966.4**	**10 132.2**	**10 695.8**
Financial account transactions											
Direct investment	N2SA	139.7	113.0	104.6	142.4	6.2	42.3	16.6	29.7	35.8	44.3
Portfolio investment	HHZF	206.6	199.3	206.9	132.4	210.8	87.0	5.4	−81.5	45.2	131.3
Other investment	XBMN	407.5	311.9	688.3	−680.2	−414.4	256.6	175.0	−18.9	−176.8	−45.5
Total	HBNS	**753.8**	**624.2**	**999.8**	**−405.3**	**−197.4**	**386.0**	**197.1**	**−70.7**	**−95.8**	**130.0**
Investment income											
Direct investment	N2Q4	32.1	51.9	61.7	60.5	50.6	45.1	51.1	52.3	56.2	57.9
Portfolio investment	HLZC	49.5	62.8	71.8	77.5	61.5	63.9	73.3	72.4	72.6	69.9
Other investment	HLZN	79.3	118.0	157.8	144.3	58.2	44.5	55.9	47.3	38.0	33.9
Total	HMBO	**161.0**	**232.7**	**291.3**	**282.2**	**170.3**	**153.5**	**180.4**	**172.0**	**166.8**	**161.6**
Net investment											
International investment position											
Direct investment	MU7O	262.0	217.9	360.5	494.2	380.7	394.8	369.4	160.6	172.2	34.2
Portfolio investment	CGNH	−116.0	−188.0	−300.9	−343.2	−514.3	−421.6	−418.9	−258.7	−146.6	−168.7
Financial derivatives	JX98	−11.0	−36.8	−14.1	124.9	79.6	67.8	62.9	27.9	47.7	22.1
Other investment	CGNG	−244.7	−180.6	−208.7	−171.3	−146.7	−153.2	−166.8	−365.9	−416.5	−276.6
Reserve assets	LTEB	24.7	22.9	26.7	36.3	40.1	49.7	56.8	61.7	61.4	67.7
Net investment position	HBQC	**−85.0**	**−164.6**	**−136.5**	**140.9**	**−160.5**	**−62.5**	**−96.7**	**−374.5**	**−281.8**	**−321.3**
Financial account transactions[1]											
Direct investment	-MU7M	−51.9	−36.0	79.5	57.7	−39.0	−6.5	33.3	−22.0	−7.2	−117.4
Portfolio investment	-HHZD	−46.1	−54.4	−106.4	−245.4	−31.0	13.8	7.1	213.4	−55.5	−124.1
Financial derivatives	-ZPNN	−5.8	−20.6	27.0	121.7	−29.1	−25.5	3.0	−36.9	11.6	−0.6
Other investment	-HHYR	90.8	82.9	−27.9	28.1	64.3	−18.1	−71.8	−214.9	−32.4	156.3
Reserve assets	-LTCV	0.7	−0.4	1.2	−1.3	5.8	6.1	4.9	7.6	5.0	7.1
Net transactions	-HBNT	**−12.3**	**−28.6**	**−26.6**	**−39.3**	**−29.0**	**−30.3**	**−23.5**	**−52.8**	**−78.6**	**−78.6**
Investment income											
Direct investment	MU7E	51.4	39.7	39.4	26.1	23.8	47.8	53.5	34.9	27.8	13.3
Portfolio investment	HLZX	−2.6	−5.7	−3.0	−7.8	−5.4	−13.9	−19.4	−21.6	−25.6	−25.6
Other investment	CGNA	−17.4	−18.1	−20.4	−13.4	−14.2	−14.2	−15.2	−15.8	−12.4	−10.9
Reserve assets	HHCB	0.7	0.6	0.6	0.8	0.8	0.7	0.8	0.7	0.6	0.6
Net earnings	HMBM	**32.1**	**16.6**	**16.6**	**5.6**	**4.9**	**20.5**	**19.6**	**−1.8**	**−9.5**	**−22.6**

1 **When downloading data from the Pink Book dataset users should reverse the sign of series that have an identifier that is prefixed with a minus sign.**

Source: Office for National Statistics

6.13 Net foreign direct investment flows abroad analysed by area and main country, 2006 to 2015 (Directional)

£ million

	2006	2007	2008	2009	2010	2011	2012	2013	2014	2015
EUROPE	**16,899**	**91,174**	**64,811**	**16,642**	**24,436**	**37,212**	**-3,964**	**-20,241**	**-107,766**	**-10,845**
EU	4,038	65,695	54,853	-13,416	20,191	25,441	-5,459	-11,656	-83,140	-9,764
AUSTRIA	-94	109	-73	-42	472	-49	-287	14	-131	229
BELGIUM	-4,356	2,246	1,784	-1,833	7,284	16,053	1,472	-4,054	373	1,355
BULGARIA	-5	-1	48	16	-101	-10	-43	4	13	29
CROATIA	..	-6	54	-2	-9	-3	-12	11	11	25
CYPRUS	98	371	470	60	-308	-340	296	36	-83	31
CZECH REPUBLIC	-160	63	387	-189	-175	-42	974	268	26	18
DENMARK	1,529	2,463	3,178	-2,177	479	-1,018	536	-124	-5	-790
ESTONIA	3	-4	-21	24	6	-10	-29	15	8	81
FINLAND	106	258	80	-88	-19	-615	-198	3	-107	111
FRANCE	1,175	8,256	8,507	845	5,180	-4,215	-6,925	-9,700	-2,631	1,574
GERMANY	3,186	2,798	1,000	3,027	-2,793	3,513	2,593	732	4,222	-2,721
GREECE	..	291	465	-349	106	-982	-46	35	-33	212
HUNGARY	39	60	186	89	116	-7	161	40	-115	175
IRISH REPUBLIC	5,161	3,367	223	3,619	-560	6,372	-4,185	-2,223	-192	178
ITALY	-397	7,266	508	-3,530	527	657	116	-341	1,883	-914
LATVIA	4	..	144	-60	..	-36	20	50	-10	-10
LITHUANIA	1	-1	..	..	4	4	-22	23	-5	4
LUXEMBOURG	-14,131	29,335	6,854	-2,760	6,945	11,717	3,267	-6,291	-76,928	-8,109
MALTA	891	-2,891	..	-422	-509	-266	350	278	505	198
NETHERLANDS	1,350	1,122	12,118	-15,664	949	-4,777	-4,549	8,966	-7,488	-3,365
POLAND	397	-575	-19	923	155	213	832	879	237	1,063
PORTUGAL	314	431	384	721	604	-252	82	173	-67	-322
ROMANIA	40	126	241	..	96	-28	133	187	15	78
SLOVAKIA	18	87	112	-34	-20	95	16	-26	-12	-46
SLOVENIA	14	..	12	9	..	127	-34	6	-3	-24
SPAIN	2,177	6,518	16,191	2,961	2,182	-371	9	-1,100	-1,526	565
SWEDEN	6,669	3,738	735	1,116	-486	-290	11	997	-1,098	609
EFTA	6,926	3,966	2,321	4,613	2,052	1,156	-2,594	3,284	2,045	605
of which										
NORWAY	3	1,280	1,630	1,884	-311	2,536	-833	-704	134	235
SWITZERLAND	6,948	2,796	742	2,885	2,354	-1,379	-1,744	3,554	1,900	372
OTHER EUROPEAN COUNTRIES	5,935	21,513	7,637	25,445	2,194	10,614	4,089	-11,869	-26,670	-1,687
of which										
RUSSIA	-13	860	3,747	-34	-2,497	373	3,382	..	4,144	816
UK OFFSHORE ISLANDS	5,023	19,134	2,961	24,591	3,222	10,775	493	-2,509	-27,050	-2,283
THE AMERICAS	**19,100**	**59,514**	**20,391**	**-3,872**	**-19,648**	**45,305**	**11,258**	**40,992**	**8,396**	**-20,175**
of which										
BERMUDA	908	2,122	4,254	-2,014	-65	-879	-334	1,785	1,269	-930
BRAZIL	354	846	932	390	1,687	2,283	321	-115	1,646	876
CANADA	8,130	15,453	-153	-2,698	-11,664	9,042	-3,638	655	333	-12,267
CHILE	25	99	-290	-	211	805	160	111	200	-541
COLOMBIA	315	109	169	188	..	-694	-486	115	-15	-119
MEXICO	334	302	498	29	501	965	654	279	601	670
PANAMA	7	-12	-2	59	29	58	10	59	-33	51
USA	-1,803	35,410	11,486	7,805	-13,691	34,813	12,478	37,199	2,474	-9,893
ASIA	**7,992**	**11,315**	**12,738**	**7,835**	**11,466**	**-22,989**	**1,253**	**-6,498**	**8,666**	**-11,838**
NEAR & MIDDLE EAST COUNTRIES	1,219	1,859	3,309	1,637	-5,736	-1,123	9,675	-9,139	1,788	-14,889
of which										
GULF ARABIAN COUNTRIES	329	706	928	1,559	-734	907	2,469	915	-1,450	-8,502
OTHER ASIAN COUNTRIES	6,773	9,456	9,429	6,197	17,202	-21,866	-8,422	2,641	6,878	3,051
of which										
CHINA	374	1,114	1,116	179	569	1,135	1,702	352	-251	-830
HONG KONG	1,674	2,267	1,115	-1,201	1,786	3,545	6,832	277	1,454	2,729
INDIA	104	4,893	784	547	2,567	8,977	-165	611	314	653
INDONESIA	196	-91	40	662	3,184	3,933	277	426	92	-163
JAPAN	440	893	980	1,031	-559	1,760	-729	516	-102	209
MALAYSIA	241	218	312	280	629	800	550	164	1,541	-1,062
SINGAPORE	2,621	-2,155	2,417	1,572	4,882	-43,882	-18,893	-1,533	1,662	2,034
SOUTH KOREA	679	436	672	498	937	370	1,725	196	350	-1,831
THAILAND	536	-15	275	300	141	164	272	137	204	484

6.13 Net foreign direct investment flows abroad analysed by area and main country, 2006 to 2015 (Directional)

£ million

	2006	2007	2008	2009	2010	2011	2012	2013	2014	2015
AUSTRALASIA & OCEANIA	**3,132**	**1,894**	**9,548**	**-3,399**	**8,530**	**6,655**	**2,902**	**8,406**	**-2,570**	**-9,899**
of which										
AUSTRALIA	2,743	1,790	8,450	-4,517	8,240	6,012	2,585	8,234	-2,840	-9,849
NEW ZEALAND	405	105	127	1,140	237	555	257	142	126	-131
AFRICA	**-235**	**3,969**	**318**	**1,388**	**6,339**	**-6,522**	**1,655**	**3,243**	**2,523**	**-190**
of which										
KENYA	62	77	56	43	93	-51	-69	39	94	79
NIGERIA	44	31	242	873	220	888	1,545	-940	-213	3,182
SOUTH AFRICA	1,466	1,406	1,394	-1,961	2,038	799	1,610	1,536	883	812
ZIMBABWE	8	2	-6	1	10	25	17	3	-10	..
WORLD TOTAL	**46,887**	**167,866**	**107,806**	**18,593**	**31,124**	**59,660**	**13,105**	**25,902**	**-90,751**	**-52,946**
OECD	21,276	127,963	78,285	-4,300	8,088	81,558	4,832	35,927	-80,685	-43,063
CENTRAL & EASTERN EUROPE	76	4	8	36	13	22	-16	66	41	-65

Source: Office for National Statistics

The sum of constituent items may not always agree exactly with the totals shown due to rounding.

A negative sign before values indicates a net disinvestment abroad.

For countries listed within regions see Geography tab.

  .. Indicates data are disclosive

  - Indicates nil data or less than £500,000

6.14 FDI International investment positions abroad analysed by area and main country, 2006 to 2015 (Directional)

£ million

	2006	2007	2008	2009	2010	2011	2012	2013	2014	2015
EUROPE	402,593	547,294	670,112	586,151	645,252	643,536	586,061	551,832	525,230	527,225
EU	314,481	429,073	538,044	504,202	564,615	557,436	504,848	454,904	445,048	449,144
AUSTRIA	2,402	2,711	3,069	3,932	1,119	1,036	347	862	993	996
BELGIUM	4,380	8,274	12,769	15,807	43,284	40,991	16,699	12,537	11,032	14,700
BULGARIA	46	48	141	116	..	95	74	137	160	104
CROATIA	..	..	282	282	246	244	185	248	224	230
CYPRUS	561	745	626	556	623	739	1,224	702	526	461
CZECH REPUBLIC	523	670	1,036	531	554	472	1,346	1,749	1,733	1,927
DENMARK	7,782	6,569	11,554	7,321	8,324	7,245	24,489	7,465	7,032	5,988
ESTONIA	-1	10	28	41	70	97	63	109	113	162
FINLAND	1,287	2,437	610	417	1,265	1,659	193	721	1,054	1,048
FRANCE	36,327	44,624	56,017	49,796	63,767	58,951	70,853	25,477	57,030	60,512
GERMANY	17,602	20,576	25,711	28,029	23,625	22,222	15,526	20,217	20,698	18,336
GREECE	562	911	1,186	960	2,125	1,510	1,301	1,612	1,442	623
HUNGARY	1,795	2,135	2,328	728	673	825	1,038	673	969	808
IRISH REPUBLIC	26,432	24,854	24,777	35,008	41,200	45,737	44,223	27,660	31,896	38,600
ITALY	7,924	15,310	12,454	12,735	12,903	12,308	10,836	10,200	11,165	11,157
LATVIA	27	..	106	10	-17	66	71	143	101	74
LITHUANIA	6	11	..	28	43	45	45	49	60	57
LUXEMBOURG	62,355	103,818	134,048	133,212	149,180	151,827	121,881	104,572	108,192	92,781
MALTA	2,399	3,741	1,961	1,884	1,152	487	1,765	243	1,858	1,908
NETHERLANDS	92,783	126,843	136,218	131,505	132,179	132,464	128,725	111,882	121,884	126,352
POLAND	2,519	2,086	3,232	4,676	3,874	4,075	4,053	4,585	4,974	5,999
PORTUGAL	3,167	3,948	4,741	4,177	4,432	3,397	3,097	1,056	3,202	3,041
ROMANIA	247	422	721	578	565	567	591	820	847	882
SLOVAKIA	..	200	..	262	275	295	203	267	307	957
SLOVENIA	53	64	55	55	..	343	262	101	77	96
SPAIN	25,233	39,479	76,835	47,132	48,454	44,751	36,194	4,781	40,532	44,997
SWEDEN	17,935	18,372	27,345	24,428	24,163	24,988	19,562	20,257	16,947	16,347
EFTA	12,637	15,985	21,392	25,463	26,055	23,789	26,254	28,581	17,025	22,133
of which										
NORWAY	2,116	2,433	4,402	5,417	5,837	4,976	4,820	3,754	2,384	2,792
SWITZERLAND	10,239	13,270	16,723	19,564	20,189	18,787	21,415	19,676	14,608	19,338
OTHER EUROPEAN COUNTRIES	75,475	102,236	110,675	56,485	54,582	62,310	54,958	68,347	63,157	55,948
of which										
RUSSIA	6,054	7,219	11,328	9,973	9,698	8,108	5,705	13,668	13,798	8,335
UK OFFSHORE ISLANDS	65,814	86,586	88,937	36,220	34,530	42,255	38,440	42,019	39,889	37,878
THE AMERICAS	256,423	285,615	337,475	296,105	263,684	288,127	293,686	326,729	367,527	342,806
of which										
BERMUDA	13,889	14,784	25,552	16,943	17,333	17,017	15,391	15,923	26,435	14,873
BRAZIL	2,824	3,132	6,144	4,105	6,121	14,331	14,582	9,241	14,639	15,455
CANADA	19,188	30,902	31,764	29,607	36,461	31,760	30,925	28,074	28,517	16,822
CHILE	563	506	369	275	574	838	718	877	1,327	1,175
COLOMBIA	985	1,188	1,785	2,101	2,661	465	-117	673	602	524
MEXICO	2,337	1,619	1,439	607	980	2,544	5,093	898	6,581	7,250
PANAMA	..	..	..	196	196	318	..	..	..	..
USA	180,629	193,958	236,081	222,237	181,511	203,918	198,001	169,146	254,153	237,260
ASIA	54,377	50,970	71,948	76,317	100,563	111,614	107,822	125,021	121,398	123,702
NEAR & MIDDLE EAST COUNTRIES	6,874	8,771	13,745	17,524	22,733	25,977	13,428	28,705	13,415	16,176
of which										
GULF ARABIAN COUNTRIES	4,756	5,238	7,881	11,915	14,980	18,412	10,529	23,899	6,943	8,943
OTHER ASIAN COUNTRIES	47,503	42,199	58,203	58,794	77,829	85,637	94,394	96,316	107,983	107,526
of which										
CHINA	2,228	2,942	4,504	4,614	6,001	6,598	6,501	4,588	9,165	9,667
HONG KONG	22,256	14,689	19,029	16,750	19,434	20,572	42,640	15,197	52,142	42,637
INDIA	1,977	4,984	4,827	10,629	12,345	13,632	5,088	3,547	3,148	12,088
INDONESIA	982	853	1,093	1,897	2,712	5,976	4,089	3,331	4,303	4,493
JAPAN	2,485	666	1,552	2,936	2,697	6,003	6,308	3,776	4,106	4,798
MALAYSIA	1,174	1,035	1,380	879	1,433	1,874	1,910	3,984	3,266	2,113
SINGAPORE	6,684	7,684	14,639	8,850	9,791	10,658	9,060	10,939	16,409	17,779
SOUTH KOREA	3,763	3,302	3,376	3,175	3,857	4,192	4,468	2,528	4,652	3,343
THAILAND	1,407	1,351	1,653	1,174	1,308	1,395	1,496	1,151	2,545	2,115
AUSTRALASIA & OCEANIA	12,665	17,334	19,891	19,218	34,036	39,716	43,490	50,632	21,814	19,464
of which										
AUSTRALIA	11,571	16,401	17,654	16,191	33,267	38,532	42,388	48,495	20,369	17,904
NEW ZEALAND	923	777	780	1,624	601	758	664	677	834	1,055

6.14 FDI International investment positions abroad analysed by area and main country, 2006 to 2015 (Directional)

£ million

	2006	2007	2008	2009	2010	2011	2012	2013	2014	2015
AFRICA	**15,105**	**20,618**	**19,827**	**36,608**	**33,604**	**35,036**	**42,403**	**36,424**	**42,723**	**38,884**
of which										
KENYA	313	345	405	393	466	590	483	348	530	503
NIGERIA	1,011	853	1,233	2,096	1,854	2,148	1,743	1,169	1,483	4,094
SOUTH AFRICA	8,255	11,544	8,395	21,124	13,672	13,782	13,013	8,189	12,949	11,460
ZIMBABWE	58	36	39	20	5	12	32	14	83	..
WORLD TOTAL	**741,163**	**921,831**	**1,119,252**	**1,014,399**	**1,077,139**	**1,118,030**	**1,073,462**	**1,090,639**	**1,078,692**	**1,052,081**
OECD	547,303	692,313	855,854	809,588	854,859	876,229	822,719	815,767	785,585	764,203
CENTRAL & EASTERN EUROPE	515	16	7	46	7	25	-8	122	204	384

Source: Office for National Statistics

The sum of constituent items may not always agree exactly with the totals shown due to rounding.

A negative sign before values indicates a net disinvestment abroad.

For countries listed within regions see Geography tab.

.. Indicates data are disclosive

- Indicates nil data or less than £500,000

6.15 Earnings from foreign direct investment abroad analysed by area and main country, 2006 to 2015 (Directional)

£ million

	2006	2007	2008	2009	2010	2011	2012	2013	2014	2015
EUROPE	**38,957**	**43,186**	**42,693**	**35,740**	**39,666**	**46,306**	**28,508**	**30,844**	**22,360**	**23,988**
EU	28,337	33,559	36,782	30,652	30,668	36,523	23,003	24,002	17,248	19,614
AUSTRIA	186	247	174	253	137	-14	-150	2	-8	15
BELGIUM	875	1,282	1,548	1,454	1,165	1,853	1,355	533	474	326
BULGARIA	3	-10	-4	5	-	8	-	21	24	17
CROATIA	..	-17	28	26	..	-13	-3	..	27	32
CYPRUS	171	367	331	56	-11	-86	133	30	-20	5
CZECH REPUBLIC	-64	72	-123	-122	-75	2	210	173	191	138
DENMARK	411	580	543	219	627	541	477	404	360	253
ESTONIA	11	5	6	27	17	22	14	6	16	9
FINLAND	69	281	131	120	184	218	62	67	152	128
FRANCE	3,344	3,012	1,956	1,406	3,222	3,566	2,859	795	554	2,479
GERMANY	2,189	2,748	2,783	2,743	1,474	1,392	207	1,126	-9	2,301
GREECE	151	218	114	204	-45	23	31	40	71	1
HUNGARY	83	91	72	34	21	89	114	71	1	91
IRISH REPUBLIC	2,525	2,940	1,892	-800	-2,857	730	1,318	2,429	1,211	1,067
ITALY	696	810	524	214	687	181	355	436	677	741
LATVIA	5	4	-18	-27	-20	-24	33	28	-6	-8
LITHUANIA	-	2	-1	-	3	4	4	2	5	13
LUXEMBOURG	7,626	7,982	13,309	11,422	10,353	12,092	7,368	3,769	3,553	1,310
MALTA	-185	-67	42	324	-5	-51	69	..	526	198
NETHERLANDS	7,251	9,441	10,363	7,915	11,820	11,796	4,739	8,462	5,985	7,008
POLAND	373	255	421	708	382	497	542	586	619	367
PORTUGAL	234	256	289	173	324	59	208	50	146	53
ROMANIA	43	79	108	93	12	61	76	126	103	131
SLOVAKIA	24	103	21	23	42	42	32	37	53	45
SLOVENIA	..	11	14	5	..	-32	-37	15	10	15
SPAIN	918	983	1,229	1,000	602	876	-366	518	988	937
SWEDEN	1,395	1,884	1,029	3,177	2,462	2,689	3,355	2,336	1,544	1,943
EFTA	3,759	4,591	4,392	2,739	5,251	5,090	3,410	4,219	1,755	1,339
of which										
NORWAY	345	297	602	580	538	472	-415	303	578	146
SWITZERLAND	3,411	4,294	3,786	2,174	4,714	4,617	3,832	3,421	1,175	1,193
OTHER EUROPEAN COUNTRIES	6,861	5,037	1,520	2,348	3,746	4,693	2,094	2,623	3,358	3,035
of which										
RUSSIA	1,715	1,158	1,835	1,509	1,652	2,961	313	1,802	1,326	1,210
UK OFFSHORE ISLANDS	4,580	3,543	-86	165	1,620	1,120	1,257	477	1,670	1,519
THE AMERICAS	**26,461**	**28,104**	**13,573**	**15,510**	**21,212**	**26,439**	**23,625**	**24,233**	**22,785**	**15,326**
of which										
BERMUDA	..	1,563	1,549	1,183	2,339	1,455	2,159	2,612	2,447	697
BRAZIL	577	706	728	1,212	1,045	1,270	1,052	43	1,246	915
CANADA	1,769	1,644	-2,248	-485	471	-325	417	359	263	-708
CHILE	771	775	601	531	125	322	89	91	95	81
COLOMBIA	274	189	321	137	280	657	-441	36	13	-21
MEXICO	531	555	293	255	544	1,362	760	169	724	686
PANAMA	23	43	..	66	54	84	61	76	72	177
USA	17,112	18,763	9,470	10,927	14,424	20,344	17,314	12,976	15,940	10,617
ASIA	**11,621**	**11,389**	**10,271**	**10,967**	**14,636**	**18,208**	**16,888**	**14,851**	**16,525**	**13,970**
NEAR & MIDDLE EAST COUNTRIES	1,430	2,580	3,661	1,830	2,023	2,645	782	3,172	2,531	1,561
of which										
GULF ARABIAN COUNTRIES	717	1,000	1,719	961	762	928	653	1,929	1,216	1,234
OTHER ASIAN COUNTRIES	10,191	8,809	6,611	9,137	12,613	15,563	16,107	11,680	13,994	12,408
of which										
CHINA	445	502	293	539	778	773	1,291	360	1,223	1,188
HONG KONG	3,786	4,062	1,410	797	2,736	4,179	5,023	1,056	4,845	4,757
INDIA	715	914	790	1,015	1,512	1,696	1,259	895	1,365	1,557
INDONESIA	336	170	178	400	560	1,065	1,047	661	772	412
JAPAN	388	144	431	364	299	391	242	517	385	310
MALAYSIA	494	587	526	674	734	536	562	435	988	998
SINGAPORE	2,285	469	959	2,423	2,278	3,158	3,039	-635	1,675	1,307
SOUTH KOREA	532	488	608	381	676	564	764	320	572	205
THAILAND	-121	11	-122	164	173	201	244	194	287	190
AUSTRALASIA & OCEANIA	**3,065**	**3,506**	**4,213**	**4,602**	**6,555**	**1,953**	**3,979**	**3,642**	**3,001**	**2,554**
of which										
AUSTRALIA	2,665	3,207	3,947	4,181	6,133	1,671	3,682	3,378	2,712	2,246
NEW ZEALAND	388	256	194	343	331	176	236	208	162	195

6.15 Earnings from foreign direct investment abroad analysed by area and main country, 2006 to 2015 (Directional)

£ million

	2006	2007	2008	2009	2010	2011	2012	2013	2014	2015
AFRICA	**3,488**	**4,449**	**3,792**	**2,885**	**5,581**	**6,060**	**7,506**	**5,113**	**3,801**	**1,109**
of which										
KENYA	88	82	93	68	87	114	5	25	83	117
NIGERIA	133	74	212	64	652	1,031	1,261	311	687	1,227
SOUTH AFRICA	1,620	2,190	1,173	1,025	2,358	2,494	3,180	1,803	1,590	1,665
ZIMBABWE	10	5	-5	-6	3	22	23	..	12	25
WORLD TOTAL	**83,591**	**90,634**	**74,542**	**69,704**	**87,649**	**98,966**	**80,507**	**78,682**	**68,473**	**56,946**
OECD	55,675	63,926	54,204	49,921	59,032	66,564	49,880	52,156	39,401	34,293
CENTRAL & EASTERN EUROPE	62	5	-	2	-1	6	-3	3	-6	78

Source: Office for National Statistics

The sum of constituent items may not always agree exactly with the totals shown due to rounding.
A negative sign before values indicates a net disinvestment abroad.
For countries listed within regions see Geography tab.

.. Indicates data are disclosive
- Indicates nil data or less than £500,000

6.16 Net foreign direct investment flows into the United Kingdom analysed by area and main country, 2006 to 2015 (Directional)

£ million

	2006	2007	2008	2009	2010	2011	2012	2013	2014	2015
EUROPE	**53,837**	**38,565**	**22,115**	**22,584**	**8,957**	**-28,258**	**22,830**	**9,456**	**-8**	**-12,088**
EU	47,698	32,508	21,267	15,181	-922	-23,682	15,381	-466	2,911	-14,330
AUSTRIA	..	223	75	89	170	876	-74	21	-87	47
BELGIUM	670	159	-533	86	416	5,416	2,048	724	-1,947	-443
BULGARIA	..	..	..	..	..	..	-2	-	-1	0
CROATIA	..	..	..	..	..	..	..	..	..	..
CYPRUS	18	84	73	27	..	-1,639	-192	265	61	340
CZECH REPUBLIC	..	1	1	-	1	-4	..	..	1	..
DENMARK	13	775	303	-432	-601	-822	506	-1,291	281	458
ESTONIA	-	..	..	-	..	..	..	..	..	..
FINLAND	44	75	41	170	62	42	44	139	46	60
FRANCE	..	925	-4,291	12,121	-9,065	2,127	6,499	-5,115	4,290	-2,781
GERMANY	5,566	12,545	6,421	4,056	11,221	561	1,358	2,790	976	5,544
GREECE	17	119	5	30	-193	-387	178	-10	3	15
HUNGARY	3	1	1	-	-34	5	..	-20	..	3
IRISH REPUBLIC	..	1,422	2,384	-629	3,408	216	634	98	35	458
ITALY	282	885	-209	166	467	-1,372	1,082	775	226	319
LATVIA	..	..	..	-	-	-	..	..	..	0
LITHUANIA	-	..	-	-	-	-	..	..	..	..
LUXEMBOURG	..	2,455	1,785	-6,548	-4,246	3,693	4,870	-1,040	1,107	92
MALTA	2	6	20	14	-16	346	-49	19	5	904
NETHERLANDS	13,715	2,356	9,866	-729	-3,274	-35,732	-1,594	1,251	-2,714	-22,554
POLAND	50	-10	9	-1	1	23	-	11	12	13
PORTUGAL	..	149	3	149	94	-81	63	-18	21	33
ROMANIA	..	..	1	-	-	-	..	-	0	0
SLOVAKIA	..	..	..	..	..	-1	-	..	..	..
SLOVENIA	..	..	1	1	-1	..	-	..	-1	0
SPAIN	..	10,396	4,530	6,389	2,226	2,578	-84	978	630	2,297
SWEDEN	508	-66	785	222	115	469	329	-25	211	847
EFTA of which	5,321	3,894	-4,930	3,209	5,194	-2,221	5,765	8,278	1,955	1,430
NORWAY	..	673	289	269	147	253	-384	483	477	613
SWITZERLAND	..	2,521	-5,258	2,985	4,176	-2,476	6,126	7,960	1,507	514
OTHER EUROPEAN COUNTRIES of which	817	2,163	5,778	4,194	4,686	-2,355	1,685	1,644	-4,875	813
RUSSIA	..	469	1,765	6	..	205	-40	-19	..	-96
UK OFFSHORE ISLANDS	733	1,690	4,115	4,003	4,322	-2,563	-691	1,662	-4,759	882
THE AMERICAS of which	**17,242**	**25,150**	**24,634**	**39,448**	**25,971**	**40,866**	**6,552**	**17,842**	**7,874**	**27,154**
BRAZIL	..	7	1	-	75	8	5	-4	-3	-5
CANADA	3,509	998	327	3	3,782	83	1,833	1,277	956	3,661
USA	12,313	20,309	24,073	37,575	17,131	40,118	4,237	16,528	9,159	20,141
ASIA	**11,806**	**23,046**	**3,530**	**-2,845**	**4,729**	**9,721**	**4,922**	**4,606**	**6,692**	**4,917**
NEAR & MIDDLE EAST COUNTRIES	5,034	-1,104	-880	333	1,049	5,070	498	542	..	785
OTHER ASIAN COUNTRIES of which	6,772	24,149	4,410	-3,178	3,680	4,651	4,423	4,065	..	4,132
CHINA	12	22	-23	100	12	..	845	..	604	491
HONG KONG	92	..	902	-323	1,030	878	623	1,009	276	1,004
INDIA	265	151	2,428	108	-8	1,470	94	-124	85	1,293
JAPAN	..	3,048	1,001	-2,433	1,608	1,106	1,666	2,240	1,552	2,001
SINGAPORE	..	..	250	47	-164	1,137	103	-28	2,118	-581
SOUTH KOREA	-85	50	214	38	..	-92	146	-18	112	-148
AUSTRALASIA & OCEANIA of which	**..**	**366**	**-1,137**	**-1,696**	**-2,083**	**3,175**	**810**	**934**	**36**	**1,185**
AUSTRALIA	..	373	-1,102	-1,676	-2,047	3,333	804	..	247	1,174
NEW ZEALAND	54	-8	-19	-16	-34	-20	-5	..	26	17

6.16 Net foreign direct investment flows into the United Kingdom analysed by area and main country, 2006 to 2015 (Directional)

£ million

	2006	2007	2008	2009	2010	2011	2012	2013	2014	2015
AFRICA	..	**1,252**	**990**	**95**	**92**	**835**	**-15**	**216**	**399**	**431**
of which										
SOUTH AFRICA	101	1,225	1,034	125	29	734	-60	216	370	334
WORLD TOTAL	**84,885**	**88,379**	**50,131**	**57,586**	**37,666**	**26,339**	**35,099**	**33,054**	**14,993**	**21,599**
OECD	73,961	61,034	40,745	51,967	28,179	20,016	30,093	28,461	16,904	12,479
CENTRAL & EASTERN EUROPE	..	..	..	..	..	..	..	..	..	..

Source: Office for National Statistics

The sum of constituent items may not always agree exactly with the totals shown due to rounding.

A negative sign before values indicates a net disinvestment in the UK.

For countries listed within regions see Geography tab.

.. Indicates data are disclosive

- Indicates nil data or less than £500,000

6.17 FDI International investment positions in the United Kingdom analysed by area and main country, 2006 to 2015 (Directional)

£ million

	2006	2007	2008	2009	2010	2011	2012	2013	2014	2015
EUROPE	**332,077**	**327,421**	**363,898**	**387,753**	**398,821**	**431,298**	**540,839**	**557,987**	**600,935**	**535,317**
EU	299,906	290,801	317,375	344,344	347,469	366,400	452,276	462,342	490,245	431,174
AUSTRIA	848	1,025	1,105	931	1,076	2,419	5,235	2,565	2,165	1,776
BELGIUM	5,609	4,475	4,278	3,577	7,133	15,971	10,480	24,841	26,162	20,406
BULGARIA	..	..	..	..	..	..	..	7	7	6
CROATIA	..	..	..	..	..	..	..	..	..	..
CYPRUS	162	430	501	311	1,827	2,577	4,090	3,605	3,942	4,070
CZECH REPUBLIC	..	8	19	1	6	23	11	26	11	..
DENMARK	4,344	5,008	8,626	4,944	3,079	3,538	5,959	8,861	5,910	6,340
ESTONIA	-	..	..	-	..	..	..	..	..	..
FINLAND	817	692	727	752	741	838	2,178	1,474	1,401	1,053
FRANCE	59,998	50,142	45,752	69,101	61,212	54,725	73,521	66,776	75,797	66,384
GERMANY	54,382	58,341	68,928	61,992	46,752	45,312	62,123	49,290	51,033	50,524
GREECE	121	151	221	414	661	757	325	511	179	364
HUNGARY	12	12	20	5	..	115	55	..	-8	136
IRISH REPUBLIC	8,186	7,192	8,613	9,248	7,565	10,619	9,008	11,911	13,825	12,350
ITALY	4,482	4,973	4,218	5,068	938	2,175	8,932	13,481	4,226	7,696
LATVIA	..	..	..	-	-	-	..	..	..	..
LITHUANIA	-	-	-	-	-	-	..	..	..	..
LUXEMBOURG	16,021	19,287	26,006	47,050	60,817	52,006	56,610	71,455	71,782	74,752
MALTA	12	62	143	48	606	271	913	969	514	582
NETHERLANDS	119,843	106,645	132,646	106,999	117,577	129,166	148,494	147,586	180,188	139,823
POLAND	96	75	78	18	24	88	76	209	105	251
PORTUGAL	122	217	301	558	761	308	479	515	486	569
ROMANIA	..	..	..	..	..	10	14	9	10	9
SLOVAKIA	-	..	..	..	..	-2	..	6	4	..
SLOVENIA	..	9	14	..	6	-1	..	7	9	1
SPAIN	20,658	27,681	10,731	26,825	32,997	39,895	56,116	49,470	43,062	37,217
SWEDEN	4,113	4,285	4,320	6,382	3,489	5,578	7,593	8,479	9,402	6,534
EFTA	22,358	23,913	22,773	20,078	25,167	31,056	35,368	45,986	46,916	45,236
of which										
NORWAY	969	1,503	1,425	1,764	1,600	2,229	4,852	3,861	4,954	4,573
SWITZERLAND	19,033	20,087	19,882	17,354	22,665	25,931	29,630	39,289	39,136	37,823
OTHER EUROPEAN COUNTRIES	9,813	12,707	23,750	23,331	26,186	33,841	53,195	49,659	63,774	58,906
of which										
RUSSIA	..	..	..	..	817	979	881	1,647	..	..
UK OFFSHORE ISLANDS	9,111	11,555	21,748	22,579	25,037	32,206	44,824	46,562	61,435	57,219
THE AMERICAS	**200,709**	**177,002**	**209,659**	**197,481**	**227,155**	**247,993**	**299,735**	**279,612**	**323,596**	**327,460**
of which										
BRAZIL	134	21	10	-	249	-5	-10	121	15	..
CANADA	19,369	19,843	18,625	18,833	18,201	17,012	14,606	19,656	20,872	16,726
USA	170,880	143,297	170,369	159,900	185,458	205,925	255,169	217,950	242,070	252,144
ASIA	**39,436**	**47,014**	**42,448**	**35,958**	**46,551**	**56,722**	**62,689**	**74,581**	**73,987**	**73,583**
NEAR & MIDDLE EAST COUNTRIES	10,160	5,278	3,397	2,991	3,646	4,445	3,710	4,900	5,983	6,337
OTHER ASIAN COUNTRIES	29,275	41,736	39,051	32,967	42,905	52,277	58,979	69,681	68,004	67,246
of which										
CHINA	99	196	199	607	367	767	1,118	..	1,100	1,844
HONG KONG	..	..	6,979	5,884	7,527	16,972	10,253	11,622	12,799	11,090
INDIA	798	1,323	3,284	1,875	2,749	2,774	2,072	1,676	1,942	8,893
JAPAN	14,766	20,321	24,801	19,263	22,501	26,071	36,036	36,194	39,756	40,518
SINGAPORE	4,046	12,202	1,518	3,454	5,739	3,635	4,064	3,655	8,482	1,576
SOUTH KOREA	798	768	884	696	2,752	889	2,516	2,389	2,076	1,841
AUSTRALASIA & OCEANIA	**7,623**	**8,601**	**7,026**	**11,468**	**8,399**	**10,879**	**8,230**	**3,953**	**11,858**	**11,490**
of which										
AUSTRALIA	7,093	8,165	6,750	11,229	8,171	10,022	7,633	..	11,192	10,820
NEW ZEALAND	428	429	275	239	224	271	579	..	338	498

6.17 FDI International investment positions in the United Kingdom analysed by area and main country, 2006 to 2015 (Directional)

£ million

	2006	2007	2008	2009	2010	2011	2012	2013	2014	2015
AFRICA	**469**	**1,332**	**1,994**	**1,009**	**1,403**	**1,769**	**1,368**	**2,345**	**2,887**	**2,466**
of which										
SOUTH AFRICA	130	898	1,558	490	553	819	353	1,274	2,060	1,603
WORLD TOTAL	**580,313**	**561,370**	**625,025**	**633,669**	**682,330**	**748,661**	**912,861**	**918,478**	**1,013,263**	**950,315**
OECD	535,218	507,478	561,816	574,328	607,930	653,463	799,380	781,800	847,247	792,332
CENTRAL & EASTERN EUROPE	..	..	..	..	..	..	..	..	..	..

The sum of constituent items may not always agree exactly with the totals shown due to rounding.
A negative sign before values indicates a net disinvestment in the UK.
For countries listed within regions see Geography tab.

Source: Office for National Statistics

.. Indicates data are disclosive
- Indicates nil data or less than £500,000

6.18 Earnings from foreign direct investment in the United Kingdom analysed by area and main country, 2006 to 2015 (Directional)

£ million

	2006	2007	2008	2009	2010	2011	2012	2013	2014	2015
EUROPE	**27,447**	**30,028**	**14,778**	**25,216**	**23,706**	**20,112**	**22,752**	**27,190**	**26,346**	**22,580**
EU	22,919	25,525	17,640	20,488	18,038	16,747	21,071	24,951	23,931	18,847
AUSTRIA	207	275	130	98	104	168	207	141	119	36
BELGIUM	646	622	697	-169	427	911	961	1,964	1,469	1,512
BULGARIA	-	..	..	..	..	..	-	1	-	-1
CROATIA	..	..	..	..	..	..	..	..	..	..
CYPRUS	44	82	75	33	104	86	197	235	246	305
CZECH REPUBLIC	..	1	1	-	-	30	..	6	1	..
DENMARK	204	-69	-8	-256	89	-71	156	421	326	641
ESTONIA	-	..	..	-	..	..	..	..	..	..
FINLAND	93	189	92	94	93	77	198	146	149	82
FRANCE	5,329	3,586	3,812	10,506	4,135	4,437	2,170	2,326	2,960	2,833
GERMANY	4,541	6,386	5,905	2,045	4,373	3,582	5,601	6,441	5,615	4,425
GREECE	70	126	304	190	328	71	122	122	68	58
HUNGARY	3	2	-	..	1	2	1	15	2	9
IRISH REPUBLIC	1,012	1,473	2,004	264	-1,089	382	486	493	506	919
ITALY	477	620	596	513	264	151	1,145	1,223	575	302
LATVIA	..	..	-	-	-	..	-	..	..
LITHUANIA	1	-	-	-	-	-	..	..	..	..
LUXEMBOURG	79	301	496	882	1,528	754	2,077	1,853	1,146	1,686
MALTA	3	9	11	1	31	18	91	71	35	11
NETHERLANDS	7,283	8,528	-1,334	652	2,872	3,679	4,337	6,062	6,634	3,107
POLAND	8	7	4	1	2	4	3	6	8	14
PORTUGAL	48	70	101	71	58	-66	67	38	152	121
ROMANIA	..	..	..	..	..	1	-1	1	1	1
SLOVAKIA	5	..	..	..	..	..	-	..	..	..
SLOVENIA	..	3	..	..	-	1	-1	1	-	-
SPAIN	2,536	2,892	4,272	5,281	4,245	2,009	2,677	2,689	3,182	2,069
SWEDEN	316	413	478	284	471	519	573	698	736	698
EFTA	3,366	2,940	-4,587	2,823	1,780	1,380	-410	353	983	2,016
of which										
NORWAY	169	202	265	12	18	194	398	686	255	200
SWITZERLAND	2,933	2,376	-4,901	2,771	1,004	804	-795	-499	422	1,477
OTHER EUROPEAN COUNTRIES	1,162	1,563	1,726	1,905	3,889	1,984	2,091	1,886	1,432	1,716
of which										
RUSSIA	..	8	31	3	59	125	-2	129	-44	-77
UK OFFSHORE ISLANDS	1,107	1,531	1,769	1,852	3,809	1,855	1,875	1,661	1,438	1,784
THE AMERICAS	**20,154**	**19,481**	**32,264**	**21,404**	**16,914**	**20,972**	**19,829**	**20,844**	**16,947**	**20,223**
of which										
BRAZIL	-4	9	-	-	28	16	12	17	5	6
CANADA	1,458	675	1,427	1,012	886	420	779	1,965	1,258	329
USA	16,828	16,566	29,498	19,135	14,648	18,894	17,889	17,608	12,659	17,546
ASIA	**2,710**	**289**	**471**	**-2,704**	**-742**	**4,051**	**3,198**	**2,486**	**4,781**	**5,340**
NEAR & MIDDLE EAST COUNTRIES	564	222	329	149	181	837	440	649	342	875
OTHER ASIAN COUNTRIES	2,145	67	142	-2,854	-923	3,213	2,758	1,836	4,439	4,465
of which										
CHINA	-35	21	-20	38	21	34	106	202	207	36
HONG KONG	-597	..	-358	-141	488	-4	589	1,179	949	1,604
INDIA	132	136	280	111	167	1,251	117	94	167	1,438
JAPAN	1,956	-257	-375	-3,126	-2,141	-147	1,441	640	1,733	1,882
SINGAPORE	259	597	161	-215	-101	1,508	230	-218	1,406	-604
SOUTH KOREA	104	126	117	54	111	60	99	136	-96	35

6.18 Earnings from foreign direct investment in the United Kingdom analysed by area and main country, 2006 to 2015 (Directional)

£ million

	2006	2007	2008	2009	2010	2011	2012	2013	2014	2015
AUSTRALASIA & OCEANIA	**1,259**	**1,254**	**683**	**1,913**	**-134**	**145**	**-99**	**272**	**-14**	**-309**
of which										
AUSTRALIA	876	1,225	697	1,922	-151	159	-128	228	266	-332
NEW ZEALAND	46	28	-11	-5	17	5	20	181	33	23
AFRICA	**80**	**159**	**226**	**121**	**73**	**199**	**-37**	**87**	**-49**	**39**
of which										
SOUTH AFRICA	31	103	171	119	20	110	-73	20	-108	2
WORLD TOTAL	**51,650**	**51,211**	**48,423**	**45,949**	**39,817**	**45,478**	**45,644**	**50,878**	**48,011**	**47,872**
OECD	47,476	46,754	44,372	42,328	33,089	37,143	40,498	45,693	40,280	39,748
CENTRAL & EASTERN EUROPE	..	..	..	..	..	..	..	..	..	..

Source: Office for National Statistics

The sum of constituent items may not always agree exactly with the totals shown due to rounding.
A negative sign before values indicates a net disinvestment in the UK.
For countries listed within regions see Geography tab.

.. Indicates data are disclosive
- Indicates nil data or less than £500,000

this page is intentionally blank

Research and development

Chapter 7

Research and development

(Tables 7.1 to 7.5)

Research and experimental development (R&D) is defined for statistical purposes as 'creative work undertaken on a systematic basis in order to increase the stock of knowledge, including knowledge of man, culture and society, and the use of this stock of knowledge to devise new applications'.

R&D is financed and carried out mainly by businesses, the Government, and institutions of higher education. A small amount is performed by non-profit-making bodies. Gross Expenditure on R&D (GERD) is an indicator of the total amount of R&D performed within the UK: it has been approximately 2 per cent of GDP in recent years. Detailed figures are reported each year in a statistical bulletin published in March. Table 7.1 shows the main components of GERD.

ONS conducts an annual survey of expenditure and employment on R&D performed by government, and of government funding of R&D. The survey collects data for the reference period along with future estimates. Until 1993 the detailed results were reported in the *Annual Review of Government Funded R&D*. From 1997 the results have appeared in the Science, Engineering and Technology (SET) Statistics published by the Department for Business, Innovation and Skills (BIS). Table 7.2 gives some broad totals for gross expenditure by government (expenditure before deducting funds received by government for R&D). Table 7.3 gives a breakdown of net expenditure (receipts are deducted).

The ONS conducts an annual survey of R&D in business. Tables 7.4 and 7.5 give a summary of the main trends up to 2014.

Statistics on expenditure and employment on R&D in higher education institutions (HEIs) are based on information collected by Higher Education Funding Councils and the Higher Education Statistics Agency (HESA). In 1994 a new methodology was introduced to estimate expenditure on R&D in HEIs. This is based on the allocation of various Funding Council Grants. Full details of the new methodology are contained in science, engineering and technology (SET) Statistics available on the BIS website at: https://www.gov.uk/government/collections/science-engineering-and-technology-statistics

The most comprehensive international comparisons of resources devoted to R&D appear in Main Science and Technology Indicators published by the Organisation for Economic Co-operation and Development (OECD). The Statistical Office of the European Union and the United Nations also compile R&D statistics based on figures supplied by member states.

To make international comparisons more reliable the OECD have published a series of manuals giving guidance on how to measure various components of R&D inputs and outputs. The most important of these is the Frascati Manual, which defines R&D and recommends how resources for R&D should be measured. The UK follows the Frascati Manual as far as possible.

For information on available aggregated data on Research and Development please call Office for National Statistics on 01633 456728.

7.1a Expenditure on R&D in the UK by Performing and Funding Sectors, 2014

Current prices			Sector performing the R&D				£ million
	Government	Research Councils	Higher Education	Business Enterprise	Private Non-Profit[1]	**Total**	Overseas
Sector providing the funds							
Government	944	83	436	1,856	75	**3,394**	617
Research Councils	62	599	2,143	2	138	**2,944**	208
Higher Education Funding Councils	-	-	2,341	-	-	**2,341**	-
Higher Education	4	12	307	-	56	**379**	-
Business Enterprise	237	29	336	14,083	17	**14,701**	5,632
Private Non-Profit	10	39	1,097	136	190	**1,473**	-
Overseas	144	58	1,228	3,859	78	**5,367**	-
TOTAL	**1,401**	**821**	**7,889**	**19,935**	**554**	**30,600**	**-**
of which:							
Civil	1,244	821	7,849	18,381	552	**28,846**	-
Defence	158	-	40	1,554	2	**1,754**	-

Source: Office for National Statistics

1. Private Non-Profit totals have been estimated using the 2013 data, as no survey data available for 2014.

 - denotes nil, figures unavailable or too small to display.

Please note:
Differences may occur between totals and the sum of their independently rounded components.

7.1b Expenditure on Research and Development in the UK by sector of performance: 2006 to 2014

£ million

Sector performing the R&D		2006	2007	2008	2009	2010	2011	2012	2013	2014
Current prices										
TOTAL	**GLBA**	**22,993**	**24,696**	**25,345**	**25,632**	**26,173**	**27,452**	**27,257** [†]	**29,269**	**30,600**
Government	**GLBK**	1,252	1,320	1,348	1,406	1,372	1,321	1,391 [†]	1,513	1,401
Research Councils	**DMRS**	1,061	1,034	1,041	1,097	1,141	1,035	804	814 [†]	821
Business Enterprise	**GLBL**	14,144	15,676	15,814	15,532	16,045	17,452	17,409 [†]	18,799	19,935
Higher Education	**GLBM**	6,022	6,119	6,545	6,931	6,963	7,117	7,133 [†]	7,625	7,889
Private Non-Profit [2]	**GLBN**	513	546	595	666	652	526	520 [†]	518	554
As % of GDP		1.61	1.65	1.69	1.70	1.66	1.69	1.62	1.67	1.67
Sector performing the R&D		2006	2007	2008	2009	2010	2011	2012	2013	2014
Constant prices (2014) [1]										
TOTAL	**GLBD**	**27,430**	**28,645**	**28,639**	**28,295**	**28,050**	**28,971**	**28,247**	**29,712**	**30,600**
Government	**GLBW**	1,494	1,531	1,523	1,552	1,470	1,394	1,442	1,536	1,401
Research Councils	**DMSU**	1,266	1,199	1,176	1,211	1,223	1,092	833	826	821
Business Enterprise	**GLBX**	16,874	18,183	17,870	17,146	17,196	18,418	18,042	19,083	19,935
Higher Education	**GLBY**	7,184	7,098	7,396	7,651	7,462	7,511	7,392	7,740	7,889
Private Non-Profit [2]	**GLBZ**	612	633	672	735	699	555	539	526	554

Source: Office for National Statistics

1. Please note that the latest deflators have been applied to the business research and development estimates in this bulletin which has resulted in small differences being observed between the BERD and GERD publications.

2. Private Non-Profit totals have been estimated using the 2013 data, as no survey data available for 2014.

† crosses denote earliest data revision.

Please Note:
Differences may occur between totals and the sum of their independently rounded components.

7.2 Expenditure on R&D in the UK by Performing and Funding Sectors, 2015

Current prices	Sector performing the R&D						£ million
	Government[1]	Research Councils	Higher Education	Business Enterprise	Private Non-Profit	Total[1]	Overseas
Sector funding the R&D							
Government	1,124	120	478	1,817	85	**3,624**	681
Research Councils	45	512	2,176	1	174	**2,908**	223
Higher Education Funding Councils	-	-	2,218	-	-	**2,218**	-
Higher Education	3	15	304	-	112	**433**	-
Business Enterprise[1]	19	28	349	15,069	19	**15,484**	7,423
Private Non-Profit	13	48	1,206	130	157	**1,553**	-
Overseas	121	50	1,279	3,868	87	**5,406**	-
TOTAL	**1,324**	**773**	**8,009**	**20,885**	**634**	**31,626**	-
of which:							
Civil	1,156	773	7,969	19,394	627	**29,919**	-
Defence	168	-	40	1,491	8	**1,707**	-

Source: Office for National Statistics

1. Estimates of launch investment loan repayments received by government from business have been removed following a review of how these payments should be reported. These loan repayments are in relation to loans given out in previous years and therefore should not be included in current totals of R&D expenditure. The total of loan repayments removed was £112 million, this value has also been removed from the total funding by business and the total performed by government.

- denotes nil, figures unavailable or too small to display.

Please note:
Differences may occur between totals and the sum of their independently rounded components.

7.3 UK Government net expenditure on R&D by socio-economic objective, percentage share: 2007 to 2015

Current prices

£ million

	2007	2008	2009	2010	2011	2012	2013	2014	2015
TOTAL	8,979 †	9,235	9,590	9,452	9,174	9,202	10,048	10,253	10,185

	2007	2008	2009	2010	2011	2012	2013	2014	2015
Per cent									
TOTAL	**100**	**100**	**100**	**100**	**100**	**100**	**100**	**100**	**100**
Health	16 †	18	19	20	21	21	22	22	23
General advancement of knowledge: R&D financed from General University Funds	25	24	25 †	24	25	24	23	22	22
Defence	24	22	18 †	18	14	16	15	17	16
General advancement of knowledge: R&D financed from other sources	17 †	18	16	18	13	13	13	12	12
Exploration and exploitation of the earth	3	3	3	3	3	3	3	4	4
Transport, telecommunication, other infrastructure	1	1	1	1	3	3	3	4	4
Industrial production and technology	2 †	2	4	3	4	3	4	4	4
Agriculture	3	3	4	3	4	4	4	3	3
Exploration and exploitation of space	2	2	2	2	3	3	4	3	3
Political and social systems, structures and processes	1	2	2	2	1	3	3	3	3
Energy	1	1	1	1	2	2	2	2	2
Environment	2	3	3	3	3	3	3	2	2
Culture, recreation, religion and mass media	2	2	2	2	2	1	1	1	1
Education	1	1	1	1	-	-	-	-	-

Source: Office for National Statistics

- denotes nil, figures unavailable or too small to display.

† denotes earliest data revision.

7.4 Expenditure on Civil and Defence R&D performed in UK businesses: broad product groups, 2012 - 2015

£ million

		Civil					Defence			
		2012	2013	2014	2015		2012	2013	2014	2015
CURRENT PRICES										
TOTAL	**DLBV**	**15,808**	**16,966** †	**18,272**	**19,394**	**DLBW**	**1,601**	**1,651** †	**1,547**	**1,491**
Manufacturing: Total	**DLEP**	**10,868**	**11,668** †	**12,270**	**13,228**	**DLEX**	**1,515**	**1,491**	**1,372** †	**1,322**
Chemicals	DLEQ	..	.. †	..	..	DLEY	..	..	..	..
Mechanical engineering	DLER	575	635 †	679	744	DLEZ	526	522	442 †	417
Electrical machinery	DLES	1,069	1,336 †	1,460	1,681	DLFA	270	199	189	100
Transport	DLET	..	.. †	..	..	DLFB	..	..	.. †	..
Aerospace	DLEU	1,162	1,229	1,309 †	1,315	DLFC	349	410	358 †	386
Other manufacturing	DLEV	1,388	1,522 †	1,754	1,713	DLFD	130	116	106 †	95
Services	**DLEW**	..	**4,738** †	..	..	**DLFE**	..	**161** †	..	..
Other: Total	**LDIL**	..	**561** †	..	..	**LDJJ**	..	-	..	..
Agriculture, hunting & forestry; Fishing	LDIN	132	121	135 †	139	LDJL	-	-	-	-
Extractive industries	LDIS	172	209 †	230	206	LDKF	-	-	-	-
Electricity, gas & water supply; Waste management	LDJB	..	140	167 †	184	LDKG	..	-	-	-
Construction	LDJG	..	91	.. †	..	LDKS	..	-	..	..

		Civil					Defence			
										£ million
		2012	2013	2014	2015		2012	2013	2014	2015
CONSTANT PRICES (2015)										
TOTAL	**DLBA**	**16,380**	**17,295**	**18,353**	**19,394**	**DLBB**	**1,659**	**1,683**	**1,554**	**1,491**
Manufacturing: Total	**DLBD**	**11,261**	**11,894**	**12,324**	**13,228**	**DLBL**	**1,570**	**1,520**	**1,378**	**1,322**
Chemicals	DLBE	..	..	..	..	DLBM	..	..	..	..
Mechanical engineering	DLBF	596	647	682	744	DLBN	545	532	444	417
Electrical machinery	DLBG	1,108	1,362	1,466	1,681	DLBO	280	203	190	100
Transport	DLBH	..	..	..	..	DLBP	..	..	..	..
Aerospace	DLBI	1,204	1,253	1,315	1,315	DLBQ	362	418	360	386
Other manufacturing	DLBJ	1,438	1,551	1,762	1,713	DLBR	135	118	106	95
Services	**DLBK**	..	**4,830**	..	..	**DLBS**	..	**164**	..	..
Other: Total	**C3ZE**	..	**572**	..	..	**C3ZJ**	..	-	..	..
Agriculture, hunting & forestry; Fishing	C3ZF	137	123	136	139	C3ZK	-	-	-	-
Extractive industries	C3ZG	178	213	231	206	C3ZL	-	-	-	-
Electricity, gas & water supply; Waste management	C3ZH	..	143	168	184	C3ZM	..	-	-	-
Construction	C3ZI	..	93	..	..	C3ZN	..	-	..	..

Source: Office for National Statistics

	2012	2013	2014	2015		2012	2013	2014	2015
GDP deflator used to convert current prices to constant prices	96.508	98.099	99.561	100		96.508	98.099	99.561	100

1. - denotes nil, figures unavailable or too small to display.
2. .. denotes disclosive figures.
3. † denotes earliest data revision.
4. Differences may occur between totals and the sum of their independently rounded components.

7.5a Sources of funds for R&D performed in UK businesses: 2012 to 2015

CURRENT PRICES

£ million		2012	2013	2014	2015
TOTAL	**DLBX**	**17,409**	**18,617** [†]	**19,819**	**20,885**
UK Government	DLDO	1,430	1,848 [†]	1,895	1,818
Overseas total of which:	DLHK	3,850	3,891 [†]	3,991	3,790
European Commission grants	DLDQ	55	65 [†]	65	67
Other Overseas	DLDS	3,796	3,826 [†]	3,926	3,723
Other UK Business	DLDU	344	364 [†]	393	413
Own funds	DLDW	11,696	12,407 [†]	13,409	14,657
Other	DLDY	88	107 [†]	130	209

Per cent		2012	2013	2014	2015
TOTAL		**100**	**100**	**100**	**100**
UK Government		8	10	10 [†]	9
Overseas total of which:		22	21 [†]	20	18
European Commission grants		-	-	-	-
Other Overseas		22	21 [†]	20	18
Other UK Business		2	2	2	2
Own funds		67	67 [†]	68	70
Other		1	1	1	1

Source: Office for National Statistics

1. - denotes nil, figures unavailable or too small to display.
2. [†] denotes earliest data revision.
3. Differences may occur between totals and the sum of their independently rounded components.
4. The sum of percentages may be more or less than 100 due to rounding.
5. 'Other' includes funds from UK Private Non-Profit organisations and Higher Education establishments, and from 2011, international organisations.

7.5b Sources of funds for R&D performed in UK businesses: Civil and Defence, 2012 to 2015

CURRENT PRICES   £ million

		Civil					Defence			
		2012	2013	2014	2015		2012	2013	2014	2015
UK Government	DLFG	366	767 †	848	821	DLFN	1,064	1,081 †	1,047	997
Overseas total of which:	DLHS	3,691	3,732 †	3,844	3,639	DLIF	159	160	147 †	151
European Commission grants	DLFH	52	64 †	64	65	DLFO	2	1	1	1
Other Overseas	DLFI	3,639	3,668 †	3,780	3,574	DLFP	157	158	146 †	149
Other UK Business	DLFJ	277	.. †	341	357	DLFQ	68	.. †	52	55
Own	DLFK	11,392	12,096 †	13,119	14,376	DLFR	304	312	290 †	280
Other	DLFL	82	.. †	119	201	DLFS	6	..	11	8
TOTAL	**DLBV**	**15,808**	**16,966** †	**18,272**	**19,394**	**DLBW**	**1,601**	**1,651** †	**1,547**	**1,491**

Source: Office for National Statistics

1. - denotes nil, figures unavailable or too small to display.
2. .. denotes disclosive figures.
3. † denotes earliest data revision.
4. Differences may occur between totals and the sum of their independently rounded components.
5. 'Other' includes funds from UK Private Non-Profit organisations and Higher Education establishments, and from 2011, international organisations.

this page is intentionally blank

Income and wealth

Chapter 8

Personal income, expenditure and wealth

Distribution of total incomes (Table 8.1)

The information shown in Table 8.1 comes from the Survey of Personal Income. This is an annual survey covering approximately 600,000 individuals across the whole of the UK. It is based on administrative data held by HM Revenue & Customs (HMRC) on individuals who could be liable for tax.

The table relates only to those individuals who are taxpayers. The distributions only cover incomes as computed for tax purposes, and above a level which for each year corresponds approximately to the single person's allowance. Incomes below these levels are not shown because the information about them is incomplete.

Some components of investment income (for example interest and dividends), from which tax has been deducted at source, are not always held on HMRC business systems. Estimates of missing bank and building society interest and dividends from UK companies are included in these tables. The missing investment income is distributed to cases, so that the population as a whole has amounts consistent with evidence from other sources. For example, amounts of tax accounted for by deposit takers and the tendency to hold interest-bearing accounts as indicated by household surveys.

Superannuation contributions are estimated and included in total income. They have been distributed among earners in the Survey of Personal Incomes sample, by a method consistent with information about the number of employees who are contracted in or out of the State Earnings Related Pension Scheme (SERPS) and the proportion of their earnings contributed.

When comparing results of these surveys across years, it should be noted that the Survey of Personal Incomes is not a longitudinal survey. However, sample sizes have increased in recent years to increase precision.

Effects of taxes and benefits, by household type (Table 8.2)

Original income is the total income in cash of all the members of the household before receipt of state benefits or the deduction of taxes. It includes income from employment, self-employment, investment income and occupational pensions. Gross income is original income plus cash benefits received from government (retirement pensions, child benefit, and so on). Disposal income is the income available for consumption; it is equal to gross income less direct taxes (which include income tax, national insurance contributions, and council tax). By further allowing for taxes paid on goods and services purchased, such as VAT, an estimate of post-tax income is derived. These income figures are derived from estimates made by the Office for National Statistics (ONS) based largely on information from the Living Costs and Food Survey (LFC) and published each year on the ONS website.

In Table 8.2, a retired household is defined as one where the combined income of retired members amounts to at least half the total gross income of the household; where a retired person is defined as anyone who describes themselves as retired, or anyone over the minimum National Insurance (NI) pension age describing themselves as 'unoccupied' or 'sick or injured but not intending to seek work.

Children are defined as persons aged under 16 or between 16 and 18, unmarried and receiving full-time non-advanced further education.

Living Costs and Food Survey (Tables 8.3–8.5)

The Living Costs and Food Survey (LCF) is a sample survey of private households in the UK. The LCF sample is representative of all regions of the UK and of different types of households. The survey is continuous, with interviews spread evenly over the year to ensure that estimates are not biased by seasonal variation. The survey results show how households spend their money; how much goes on food, clothing and so on, how spending patterns vary depending upon income, household composition, and regional location of households. In previous releases, Family Spending has reported on a calendar year basis. However, data used in these tables and subsequent Family Spending releases will report on a financial year basis (April to March). This change has been made to reduce disparities in estimates. The methodology in sampling and collecting Living Costs and Food Survey data has remained consistent to ensure that data in this release remain comparable with that of previous Family Spending releases.

One of the main purposes of the LCF is to define the 'basket of goods' for the Retail Prices Index (RPI) and the Consumer Prices Index (CPI). The RPI has a vital role in the up rating of state pensions and welfare benefits, while the CPI is a key instrument of the Government's monetary policy. Information from the survey is also a major source for estimates of household expenditure in the UK National Accounts. In addition, many other government departments use LCF data as a basis for policy making, for example in the areas of housing and transport. The Department for Environment, Food and Rural Affairs (Defra) uses LCF data to report on trends in food consumption and nutrient intake within the UK. Users of the LCF outside government include independent research institutes, academic researchers and business and market researchers. Like all surveys based on a sample of the population, its results are subject to sampling variability and potentially to some bias due to non-response. The results of the survey are published in an annual report called Family spending in the UK. The report includes a list of definitions used in the survey, items on which information is collected, and a brief account of the fieldwork procedure.

8.1 Distribution of total income before and after tax by gender, 2013-14

Taxpayers only

Numbers: thousands; Amounts: £ million

Total

Range of total income (lower limit) £	Before tax, by range of total income before tax				After tax, by range of total income after tax			
	No. of taxpayers	Total income before tax	Total tax	Total income after tax	No. of taxpayers	Total income before tax	Total tax	Total income after tax
9,440 [a]	610	5,800	41	5,760	727	6,990	61	6,930
10,000	2,760	30,500	656	29,800	3,410	38,800	1,020	37,700
12,000	4,240	57,100	2,950	54,200	5,070	72,600	4,420	68,200
15,000	5,850	102,000	8,550	93,200	6,530	125,000	11,800	113,000
20,000	7,500	184,000	21,200	162,000	7,450	207,000	25,800	181,000
30,000	6,330	240,000	34,000	206,000	5,390	241,000	38,900	202,000
50,000	1,590	92,500	18,800	73,700	1,010	77,600	18,900	58,700
70,000	791	65,400	16,500	49,000	478	55,100	16,400	38,600
100,000	405	48,500	14,700	33,800	201	36,000	12,100	23,900
150,000	143	24,500	8,190	16,300	60	16,000	5,820	10,200
200,000	95	22,800	8,240	14,600	45	17,600	6,700	10,900
300,000	56	21,300	8,140	13,100	26	16,100	6,310	9,740
500,000	31	20,800	8,170	12,600	15	16,100	6,390	9,760
1,000,000	15	36,600	14,500	22,100	6	25,400	9,930	15,500
All ranges	30,400	951,000	165,000	787,000	30,400	951,000	165,000	787,000

Male

Range of total income (lower limit) £	Before tax, by range of total income before tax				After tax, by range of total income after tax			
	No. of taxpayers	Total income before tax	Total tax	Total income after tax	No. of taxpayers	Total income before tax	Total tax	Total income after tax
9,440 [a]	272	2,570	21	2,550	323	3,080	32	3,050
10,000	1,170	12,900	284	12,700	1,470	16,700	449	16,300
12,000	1,960	26,500	1,370	25,100	2,420	34,800	2,130	32,600
15,000	3,090	53,800	4,490	49,300	3,580	68,800	6,480	62,300
20,000	4,450	109,000	12,700	96,800	4,560	127,000	16,000	111,000
30,000	4,100	157,000	22,400	134,000	3,620	163,000	26,800	137,000
50,000	1,150	66,700	13,700	53,000	749	57,600	14,200	43,500
70,000	592	49,000	12,400	36,600	370	42,900	12,900	30,000
100,000	317	38,000	11,600	26,400	162	29,200	9,810	19,400
150,000	116	19,900	6,660	13,200	50	13,500	4,890	8,560
200,000	79	19,000	6,850	12,100	39	15,200	5,770	9,380
300,000	48	18,200	6,980	11,300	23	14,200	5,600	8,610
500,000	27	18,400	7,260	11,200	13	14,600	5,790	8,810
1,000,000	14	33,600	13,400	20,200	6	23,500	9,210	14,200
All ranges	17,400	624,000	120,000	504,000	17,400	624,000	120,000	504,000

8.1 Distribution of total income before and after tax by gender, 2013-14

Taxpayers only

Numbers: thousands; Amounts: £ million

Range of total income (lower limit) £	Female							
	Before tax, by range of total income before tax				After tax, by range of total income after tax			
	No. of taxpayers	Total income before tax	Total tax	Total income after tax	No. of taxpayers	Total income before tax	Total tax	Total income after tax
9,440 [a]	338	3,230	20	3,210	405	3,910	29	3,880
10,000	1,590	17,500	373	17,200	1,940	22,100	575	21,500
12,000	2,280	30,600	1,580	29,000	2,650	37,800	2,290	35,500
15,000	2,770	48,000	4,060	44,000	2,950	56,300	5,310	51,000
20,000	3,050	74,200	8,480	65,700	2,890	79,900	9,820	70,100
30,000	2,230	83,800	11,700	72,100	1,770	77,500	12,100	65,400
50,000	447	25,900	5,140	20,700	263	20,000	4,760	15,200
70,000	199	16,500	4,070	12,400	108	12,200	3,530	8,680
100,000	88	10,500	3,120	7,390	39	6,860	2,270	4,590
150,000	27	4,610	1,530	3,080	10	2,570	929	1,640
200,000	16	3,850	1,380	2,460	6	2,480	931	1,550
300,000	8	3,040	1,160	1,880	3	1,850	716	1,130
500,000	3	2,320	908	1,420	1	1,550	601	948
1,000,000	1	2,990	1,120	1,880	1	1,990	719	1,280
All ranges	13,000	327,000	44,600	282,000	13,000	327,000	44,600	282,000

Source: Survey of Personal Incomes 2013-14

Footnote

(a) Can include some taxpayers who are not entitled to a Personal Allowance whose total income can be less than the Personal Allowance of £9,440 for 2013-14 (see Annex B for details).

Notes on the Table

Distribution of total income before and after tax by gender, 2013-14

1. This table only covers individuals with some liability to tax.

2. It should be noted that individuals may not necessarily fall into the same total income range for before and after tax breakdowns. Total income before tax is used to assign people to an income range for columns 2 to 5, whereas total income after the deduction of tax is used to assign individuals to an income band for columns 6 to 9.

3. For more information about the SPI and symbols used in this table, please refer to Personal Income Statistics release: https://www.gov.uk/government/collections/personal-incomes-statistics

8.2 Summary of the effects of taxes and benefits, by household type,[1] 2014/15

	All households	Retired households			
		1 adult Men	1 adult Women	All 1 adult	2 or more adults
Average per household (£ per year)					
Original income	34 718	9 802	6 433	7 536	18 006
plus Cash benefits	6 309	8 821	9 764	9 455	13 115
Gross income	41 027	18 623	16 197	16 991	31 121
less Direct taxes and employees' NIC	7 701	2 157	1 574	1 765	3 829
Disposable income	33 326	16 467	14 623	15 227	27 292
Equivalised[3] disposable income	30 895	24 700	21 935	22 840	26 448
less Indirect taxes	6 167	3 035	2 300	2 541	6 236
Post-tax income	27 159	13 432	12 323	12 686	21 056
plus Benefits in kind	6 991	4 399	5 227	4 955	7 680
Final income	34 150	17 830	17 550	17 641	28 736

	Non-Retired households								
	1 adult Men[2]	1 adult Women[2]	All 1 adult[2]	2 adults[2]	3 or more adults[2]	1 adult with children[3]	2 adults with 1 child	2 adults with 2 children	2 adults with 3 or more children	3 or more adults with children
Average per household (£ per year)									
Original income	21 774	23 101	22 323	48 216	56 325	13 433	47 290	51 648	51 701	57 303
plus Cash benefits	3 120	2 997	3 069	2 726	4 085	11 322	4 103	4 758	11 243	7 003
Gross income	24 894	26 098	25 393	50 941	60 409	24 755	51 393	56 406	62 944	64 306
less Direct taxes and employees' NIC	4 957	5 171	5 046	10 799	10 674	2 840	11 003	12 484	13 476	10 771
Disposable income	19 937	20 927	20 347	40 142	49 735	21 915	40 390	43 922	49 468	53 535
Equivalised[4] disposable income	29 905	31 390	30 520	40 142	34 070	20 610	32 836	30 501	28 079	29 253
less Indirect taxes	3 879	3 929	3 900	7 342	9 305	4 056	6 825	7 727	9 329	8 856
Post-tax income	16 058	16 998	16 447	32 800	40 430	17 860	33 565	36 195	40 139	44 679
plus Benefits in kind	1 480	1 713	1 577	3 322	5 982	12 968	7 929	14 123	21 257	16 256
Final income	17 538	18 711	18 024	36 122	46 412	30 828	41 494	50 318	61 396	60 935

Source: Office for National Statistics

Notes:
1 See chapter text
2 Without children.
3 Using the modified-OECD scale.
4 Children are defined as people aged under 16 or aged between 16 and 19, not married nor in a Civil Partnership, nor living with a partner; and living with parent(s)/guardian(s); and and receiving non-advanced further education or in unwaged-government training.

8.3 Income and source of income for all UK households, 1977 to 2015/16

(2015/16 prices[1])

| | Number of households in the population | Average annual household income | | Sources of income[2] | | | | | | |
		Disposable	Gross	Wages and salaries	Imputed income from benefits in kind	Self-employment income	Private pensions, annuities	Investment income	Other income	Total cash benefits
Year[3,4,5]	000s	£	£	Percentage of gross household income						
1977	7 199	16 502	21 404	73	-	7	3	3	1	13
1978	7 001	17 845	22 738	-	-	-	3	3	1	13
1979	6 777	18 507	23 263	74	-	6	3	3	1	14
1980	6 944	19 316	24 401	73	-	7	3	3	1	13
1981	7 525	18 992	24 286	70	-	7	3	4	1	14
1982	7 428	18 284	23 436	69	-	7	3	4	1	16
1983	6 973	18 472	23 726	67	-	8	4	4	1	17
1984	7 081	18 724	23 960	67	-	7	4	4	1	17
1985	7 012	19 723	25 159	66	-	8	5	4	1	16
1986	7 178	20 572	26 151	65	-	9	5	4	1	16
1987	7 396	21 880	27 835	65	-	10	5	5	1	15
1988	7 265	23 539	29 717	64	-	12	5	5	1	13
1989	7 410	23 753	29 767	65	-	11	5	5	1	13
1990	7 046	24 950	31 298	64	1	11	5	6	1	13
1991	7 056	24 796	30 806	63	1	9	5	7	1	13
1992	7 418	24 110	29 898	62	1	9	6	6	1	15
1993	6 979	23 920	29 727	62	1	8	6	5	1	16
1994/95	6 853	23 920	30 074	62	1	10	6	4	1	16
1995/96	6 796	23 814	29 998	62	1	9	7	5	1	16
1996/97	24 253	25 011	31 185	63	1	10	6	5	1	15
1997/98	24 556	25 980	32 450	65	1	8	7	4	1	14
1998/99	24 664	26 703	33 674	66	1	8	7	4	1	14
1999/00	25 334	27 715	34 837	64	1	10	7	5	1	14
2000/01	25 030	28 785	36 220	65	1	10	7	4	1	13
2001/02	24 888	30 573	38 529	67	1	8	7	4	1	13
2002/03	24 346	30 922	38 488	66	1	8	7	3	1	14
2003/04	24 670	31 324	39 520	66	1	9	7	3	1	14
2004/05	24 431	32 526	41 087	66	1	8	7	3	1	14
2005/06	24 799	32 681	41 310	65	1	8	7	3	1	14
2006/07	24 836	33 495	42 594	66	1	9	7	3	1	14
2007/08	25 289	33 217	42 245	66	1	9	7	3	1	14
2008/09	25 874	32 833	41 299	65	1	9	7	3	1	15
2009/10	26 053	33 166	41 547	65	1	8	8	3	1	16
2010/11	26 265	33 554	41 943	63	1	9	8	2	1	16
2011/12	26 436	31 911	39 958	65	1	7	9	2	1	16
2012/13	26 823	31 929	39 652	62	1	9	9	3	1	16
2013/14	26 675	32 282	39 929	63	1	8	9	3	1	16
2014/15	26 856	33 466	41 199	63	1	8	9	3	1	15
2015/16	27 204	33 778	41 545	63	1	8	10	3	1	15

Source: Office for National Statistics

Notes:

1 Income figures have been deflated to 2015/16 prices using the consumer price index including owner-occupiers' housing costs

2 See the ONS website for information relating to the composition of different sources of income.

3 For 1978 it is not possible to provide a breakdown of income from employment into employee wages and salaries and self-employment income.

4 Prior to 1990 imputed income from benefits in kind was not included in gross household income.

5 Prior to 1996/97 income figures are unweighted. From 1996/97 onwards income figures are based on weighted data.

This year and in the future, income data will be produced by the Household, Income and analysis area of ONS. Due to this change, table 8.3 will differ slightly to the one published in previous editions of Annual Abstract of Statistics.

8.4 Household expenditure at 2014-15 prices[1]

UK, financial year ending 2002 to financial year ending 2015

	2001-02	2002-03	2003-04	2004-05	2005-06	2006[2]	2006[3]	2007	2008	2009	2010	2011	2012	2013[4]	2014	2014-15
Weighted number of households (thousands)	24,450	24,350	24,670	24,430	24,800	24,790	25,440	25,350	25,690	25,980	26,320	26,110	26,410	26,840	26,600	26,760
Total number of households in sample	7,470	6,930	7,050	6,800	6,790	6,650	6,650	6,140	5,850	5,830	5,260	5,690	5,600	5,140	5,130	5,170
Total number of persons in sample	18,120	16,590	16,970	16,260	16,090	15,850	15,850	14,650	13,830	13,740	12,180	13,430	13,180	12,120	12,120	12,160
Total number of adults in sample	13,450	12,450	12,620	12,260	12,170	12,000	12,000	11,220	10,640	10,650	9,430	10,330	10,200	9,350	9,440	9,510
Weighted average number of persons per household	2.4	2.4	2.4	2.4	2.4	2.4	2.3	2.4	2.4	2.3	2.3	2.4	2.3	2.4	2.4	2.4

Commodity or service						Average weekly household expenditure (£)										
1 Food and non-alcoholic drinks	61.50	63.00	63.00	64.60	64.50	65.20	64.40	64.00	61.80	60.30	59.50	58.10	58.30	58.20	58.30	58.30
2 Alcoholic drinks, tobacco and narcotics	19.20	18.90	19.10	18.10	16.90	17.00	17.00	16.60	15.40	15.20	15.20	14.20	14.10	12.70	12.40	12.00
3 Clothing and footwear	15.50	16.20	17.10	19.00	19.00	20.00	19.80	19.70	20.70	21.70	24.50	22.30	23.80	22.80	23.80	23.70
4 Housing (net)[5], fuel and power	63.70	63.90	66.30	65.80	67.50	67.60	67.50	70.10	66.10	68.50	71.90	71.40	73.00	76.80	72.90	72.80
5 Household goods and services	36.30	36.10	37.50	37.90	36.10	36.60	36.20	36.50	35.10	31.50	34.40	28.50	29.00	33.40	35.40	36.70
6 Health	6.50	6.70	6.90	6.60	7.10	7.40	7.40	7.00	6.10	6.10	5.70	7.20	6.70	6.40	7.10	7.00
7 Transport	87.70	88.30	88.00	83.40	82.90	81.80	80.20	79.00	76.90	70.30	72.00	67.70	64.60	70.20	74.40	73.30
8 Communication	11.50	11.70	12.30	13.00	13.40	13.20	13.10	13.90	14.30	13.80	14.70	14.40	14.40	14.70	15.50	15.50
9 Recreation and culture	54.20	55.70	57.50	59.80	59.10	60.60	59.70	60.00	63.20	60.10	59.30	65.20	62.60	64.40	68.70	69.30
10 Education	16.00	14.10	13.30	15.80	15.10	15.70	15.20	13.00	10.60	11.10	15.10	10.10	8.90	9.90	10.00	9.00
11 Restaurants and hotels	50.00	51.30	49.00	49.30	48.40	48.80	48.40	46.40	45.30	45.00	44.70	43.20	42.80	41.60	42.70	42.50
12 Miscellaneous goods and services	41.50	43.70	43.20	43.30	41.30	41.70	41.30	40.00	39.40	38.00	38.00	39.80	38.80	39.10	39.90	40.40
1-12 All expenditure groups	463.60	469.60	473.10	476.60	471.30	475.70	470.10	466.10	454.80	441.70	455.00	442.20	437.10	450.20	461.10	460.50
13 Other expenditure items[6]	78.90	76.50	77.50	77.80	80.80	79.00	77.00	72.50	76.00	79.00	72.60	73.20	70.30	73.70	70.20	66.90
Total expenditure	**542.50**	**546.20**	**550.60**	**554.40**	**552.10**	**554.70**	**547.00**	**538.60**	**530.90**	**520.70**	**527.60**	**515.40**	**507.40**	**523.90**	**531.30**	**527.30**
Average weekly expenditure per person (£)																
Total expenditure	**228.30**	**229.30**	**233.60**	**232.30**	**234.20**	**234.60**	**234.00**	**228.60**	**225.20**	**222.50**	**226.30**	**218.90**	**216.60**	**222.20**	**221.80**	**221.20**

Note: The commodity and service categories are not comparable to those in publications before 2001-02.

Source: Family Spending in the UK; Office for National Statistics

1 Figures have been deflated to 2014-15 prices using deflators specific to the COICOP category.
2 From 2001-02 to this version of 2006, figures shown are based on weighted data using non-response weights based on the 1991 Census and population figures from the 1991 and 2001 Censuses.
3 From this version of 2006 until 2012, figures shown are based on weighted data using non-response weights and population figures based on the 2001 Census.
4 From 2013, figures are based on weighted data using non-response weights based on the 2001 Census and population estimates based on the 2011 Census.
5 Excluding mortgage interest payments, council tax and Northern Ireland rates.
6 An improvement to the imputation of mortgage interest payments has been implemented for 2006 data onwards. This means there is a slight discontinuity between 2006 and earlier years.

8.5 Percentage of households with durable goods
UK, 1998-99 to financial year ending 2015

	Car/ van	Central heating[1]	Washing machine	Tumble dryer	Dish- washer	Micro- wave	Tele- phone	Mobile phone	DVD Player	Home computer	Internet connection
1998-99 [2]	72	89	92	51	23	79	95	27	--	33	10
1999-2000	71	90	91	52	23	80	95	44	--	38	19
2000-01	72	91	93	53	25	84	93	47	--	44	32
2001-02 [3]	74	92	93	54	27	86	94	64	--	49	39
2002-03	74	93	94	56	29	87	94	70	31	55	45
2003-04	75	94	94	57	31	89	92	76	50	58	49
2004-05	75	95	95	58	33	90	93	78	67	62	53
2005-06	74	94	95	58	35	91	92	79	79	65	55
2006 [4]	76	95	96	59	38	91	91	80	83	67	59
2006 [5]	74	95	96	59	37	91	91	79	83	67	58
2007	75	95	96	57	37	91	89	78	86	70	61
2008	74	95	96	59	37	92	90	79	88	72	66
2009	76	95	96	58	39	93	88	81	90	75	71
2010	75	96	96	57	40	92	87	80	88	77	73
2011	75	96	97	56	41	92	88	87	88	79	77
2012	75	96	97	56	42	93	88	87	87	81	79
2013	76	96	97	56	42	92	89	92	85	83	82
2014	76	96	97	56	44	92	88	94	83	85	84
2014-15	76	96	97	56	44	92	88	94	83	85	84

Source: Family Spending in the UK; Office for National Statistics

-- Data not available.
1 Full or partial.
2 From this version of 1998-99, figures shown are based on weighted data and including children's expenditure.
3 From 2001-02 onwards, weighting is based on the population figures from the 2001 census.
4 From 1998-99 to this version of 2006, figures shown are based on weighted data using non-response weights based on the 1991 Census and population figures from the 1991 and 2001 Census.
5 From this version of 2006, figures shown are based on weighted data using updated weights, with non-response weights and population figures based on the 2001 Census.

this page is intentionally blank

232

Lifestyles

Chapter 9

Lifestyles

Expenditure by the Department for Culture, Media and Sport (Table 9.1)
The figures in this table are taken from the department's Annual Report and are outturn figures for each of the headings shown (later figures are the estimated outturn). The department's planned expenditure for future years is also shown.

International tourism and holidays abroad (Tables 9.8 and 9.9)
The figures in these tables are compiled using data from the International Passenger Survey (IPS). A holiday abroad is a visit made for holiday purposes. Business trips and visits to friends and relatives are excluded.

Domestic tourism (Table 9.10)
The figures in this table are compiled using data from the Visit England. Data includes total number of trips taken as well as number of bednights and expenditure, as well as average trip totals.

Gambling (Table 9.12)
The National Lottery figures in this table are the latest figures released by The National Lottery Commission at the time of going to press. They represent ticket sales (money staked1) for each of the games which comprise the lottery. The figures have been adjusted to real terms using the Retail Prices Index (RPI).
The National Lottery started on the 19 November 1994 with the first instant ticket being sold in March 1995. The sum of the individual games may not agree exactly with the figures for total sales which also include the Easy Play games which started in 1998 but were dropped in 1999. The other gambling figures in this table are obtained from the Gambling Commission (formerly the Gaming Board) and HM Revenue & Customs (HMRC). The figures have been adjusted to real terms using the Retail Prices Index (RPI).

9.1 Expenditure by the Department for Culture, Media and Sport

£'000

	2012-13 OUTTURN	2013-14 OUTTURN	2014-15 OUTTURN	2015-16 OUTTURN	2016-17 PLANS	2017-18 PLANS	2018-19 PLANS	2019-20 PLANS
Resource DEL								
Support for the Museums and Galleries sector	12,664	16,267	16,003	20,314	21,667	28,667	27,667	27,667
Museums and Galleries sponsored ALBs (net)	355,854	351,059	326,032	339,528	380,191	389,035	400,071	405,600
Libraries sponsored ALBs (net)	110,753	101,374	98,369	113,571	121,645	122,684	124,209	126,201
Museums, libraries and archives council (net)	8,632	-	-		-	-	-	-
Support for the Arts sector[1]	-53,218	-67,219	-58,465	-79,113	-73,967	1,133	533	533
Arts and culture ALBs (net)	452,545	448,788	433,475	439,548	442,189	356,753	369,009	369,436
Support for the Sports sector	6,847	21,147	18,075	11,159	7,124	7,124	7,124	7,124
Sport sponsored ALBs (net)	142,742	112,767	111,006	106,112	121,514	122,079	127,836	125,027
Ceremonial and support for the Heritage sector[2]	22,161	16,690	29,456	53,141	30,375	28,582	23,249	20,666
Heritage sponsored ALBs (net)[3]	90,277	105,685	115,478	84,350	104,647	79,196	77,365	75,741
The Royal Parks	16,955	13,637	14,600	12,320	13,596	13,128	12,702	12,306
Support for the Tourism sector	70	10	-200		6,500	6,500	6,500	6,500
Tourism sponsored ALBs (net)	47,824	48,200	46,502	66,374	34,772	39,492	49,732	27,232
Support for the Broadcasting and Media sector	15,607	15,862	42,315	19,498	30,283	23,606	13,010	10,157
Broadcasting and Media sponsored ALBs (net)[4]	188,279	101,810	88,099	95,600	104,635	41,566	41,585	41,211
Administration and Research	55,140	36,554	39,788	54,081	53,308	52,653	50,595	48,923
Support for Horseracing and the Gambling sector	-1,560	-1,603	-843	-2,858	-2,670	-	-	-
Gambling Commission(net)	1,959	3,097	1,449	365	3,162	368	343	310
Olympics - legacy programmes[5]	501,628	-18,083	-33,823	-55,210	7,432	4,492	-	-
London 2012(net)[5]	1,575,240	-29,477	55,715		-	-	-	-
Spectrum Management Receipts[6]	-60,142	-54,535	-52,594	-52,139	-61,800	-	-	-
Total Resource DEL	**3,490,257**	**1,222,030**	**1,290,437**	**1,226,641**	**1,344,603**	**1,317,058**	**1,331,530**	**1,304,634**
Of which:								
Staff costs	586,370	629,323	548,737	535,372	215,556	212,802	210,288	207,524
Purchase of goods and services	829,796	1,098,279	908,804	577,820	545,119	459,244	454,257	422,456
Income from sales of goods and services	-289,055	-490,412	-105,758	-55,262	-	-	-	-
Current grants to local government (net)	10,603	-7,008	27,686	45,826	-	-	-	-
Current grants to persons and non-profit bodies (net)	790,503	507,543	545,060	476,828	538,035	449,317	456,992	452,100
Current grants abroad (net)		-1,528	13,269	-1,819	-	-	-	-
Subsidies to private sector companies		157			-	-	-	-
Subsidies to public corporations	522,976	9,663	51,410	58,428	-	-	-	-
Rentals	3,432	32,444	25,203	22,996	-	-	-	-
Depreciation[7]	1,444,755	158,177	105,683	127,571	161,663	171,995	186,293	198,854
Change in pension scheme liabilities[8]		-44			-	-	-	-
Unwinding of the discount rate on pension scheme liabilities[8]				1,393				
Other resource	-409,123	-714,564	-829,657	-562,512	-115,770	23,700	23,700	23,700
Resource AME								
British Broadcasting Corporation(net)	3,204,478	3,046,611	3,363,162	3,138,249	3,411,359	3,792,043	3,661,584	3,604,113
Provisions, Impairments and other AME spend	21,202	18,414	-27,099	31,270	43,429	-	-	-
Lottery Grants[9]	1,450,239	1,352,673	1,594,409	1,070,465	1,189,222	1,189,222	1,189,222	1,189,222
London 2012(net)	-30,996	102,138	-	-	-	-	-	-
Levy bodies[10]	-10,268	-2,721	4,021	8,139	-	-	-	-
Total Resource AME	**4,634,655**	**4,517,115**	**4,934,493**	**4,248,123**	**4,644,010**	**4,981,265**	**4,850,806**	**4,793,335**
Of which:								
Staff costs	921,649	929,732	1,018,560	1,082,412	1,527,720	1,553,955	1,502,554	1,479,910
Purchase of goods and services	2,792,331	2,469,733	2,695,639	2,548,864	2,524,895	2,568,523	2,483,047	2,445,393
Income from sales of goods and services	-328,808	-	-		-187,784	-191,060	-184,642	-181,815
Current grants to local government (net)	20,812	34,896	32,218	24,145	35,623	35,623	35,623	35,623
Current grants to persons and non-profit bodies (net)	557,133	1,245,777	1,470,874	949,267	1,000,901	1,000,901	1,000,901	1,000,901
Current grants abroad (net)				37				
Subsidies to public corporations	-	24	4,823	7,245	-	-	-	-
Rentals	80,775	104,496	106,848	51,535	-	-	-	-
Depreciation[11]	237,372	274,590	211,087	212,835	187,814	-	-	-
Take up of provisions	592,197	29,932	21,917	46,670	863	-	-	-
Release of provision	-38,851	-10,526	-15,769	-3,412	-	-	-	-
Change in pension scheme liabilities[12]	162,422	178,831	192,115	165,013	-	-	-	-
Unwinding of the discount rate on pension scheme liabilities[12]	730,035	82,412	70,393	43,555	12,597	-	-	-
Release of provisions covering payments of pension benefits	-234	-14,336	-11,769	-10,237	-	-	-	-
Other resource	-1,092,178	-808,446	-862,443	-869,806	-458,619	13,323	13,323	13,323
Total Resource Budget[13]	**8,124,912**	**5,739,145**	**6,224,930**	**5,474,764**	**5,988,613**	**6,298,323**	**6,182,336**	**6,097,969**
Of which:								
Depreciation[10]	1,682,127	432,767	316,770	340,406	349,477	171,995	186,293	198,854
Capital DEL								
Support for the Museums and Galleries sector	2,100	100	1,981	1,170	1,934	1,934	-	-
Museums and Galleries sponsored ALBs (net)[14]	80,184	19,887	42,177	30,031	57,771	27,865	27,115	26,273

9.1 Expenditure by the Department for Culture, Media and Sport

£'000

	2012-13 OUTTURN	2013-14 OUTTURN	2014-15 OUTTURN	2015-16 OUTTURN	2016-17 PLANS	2017-18 PLANS	2018-19 PLANS	2019-20 PLANS
Libraries sponsored ALBs (net)	17,167	7,173	12,561	3,408	3,289	3,221	3,221	3,221
Support for the Arts sector	-	3,932	-	723	115	115	-	-
Arts and culture ALBs (net)[15]	18,222	18,679	14,432	21,413	35,484	59,314	38,334	17,634
Support for the Sports sector	-	250	-	154	-	-	-	-
Sport sponsored ALBs (net)	33,898	30,120	29,019	38,916	36,490	35,765	35,765	35,765
Ceremonial and support for the Heritage sector	7,581	6,882	2,182	5,491	4,321	4,123	-	-
Heritage sponsored ALBs (net)[16]	36,369	24,095	106,864	17,421	23,150	23,795	21,959	20,359
The Royal Parks	1,583	2,620	2,570	3,577	7,371	2,403	865	865
Tourism sponsored ALBs (net)	189	357	325	253	500	186	186	186
Support for the Broadcasting and Media sector[17]	9,136	55,198	229,066	213,138	133,633	128,177	83,338	41,480
Broadcasting and Media sponsored ALBs (net)[18]	41,638	23,525	4,290	4,720	74,272	105,242	163,857	154,857
Administration and Research	2,554	2,215	4,401	1,800	5,370	1,860	1,860	1,860
Support for Horseracing and the Gambling sector[19]	9,000	9,000	49,896		-40	-	-	-
Gambling Commission(net)	737	302	335	633	40	-	-	-
Olympics - legacy programmes[19]	42,053	-				-	-	-
London 2012(net)[20]	54,056	-184,059	-256,703		-	-	-	-
Total Capital DEL	**356,467**	**20,276**	**243,396**	**342,848**	**383,700**	**394,000**	**376,500**	**302,500**
Of which:								
Staff costs	10,214	11,332	11,450	10,660	11,350	11,650	11,650	11,650
Purchase of goods and services	3,900	3,900	3,900	3,900	4,000	4,000	4,000	4,000
Release of provision	-	3,815			-	-	-	-
Capital support for local government (net)	1,245,270	50,452	220,067	202,987	-	-	-	-
Capital grants to persons & non-profit bodies (net)	49,103	-103,067	-97,788	-81,098	279,759	329,547	325,452	250,336
Capital grants to private sector companies (net)	25,976	-13,457	18,443	36,438	12,000	-	-	-
Capital grants abroad (net)	-216	-202			-	-	-	-
Capital support for public corporations	46,818	-	80,050		-	-	-	-
Purchase of assets	374,707	531,860	262,826	191,713	76,631	48,803	35,398	36,514
Income from sales of assets	-1,242,875	-384,775	-260,065	-42,176	-	-	-	-
Net lending to the private sector and abroad	-26,761	-11,437	23,387	30,912	-	-	-	-
Other capital	-129,669	-68,145	-18,874	-10,488	-40	-	-	-
Capital AME								
British Broadcasting Corporation(net)[21]	-60,056	127,393	139,462	45,226	116,743	126,000	197,000	170,000
Lottery Grants[22]	536,954	523,705	601,444	453,717	447,593	447,593	447,593	447,593
London 2012(net)	-	-3,815	-		-	-	-	-
Levy bodies	-8,411	-1,763	1,991	-2,079	-	-	-	-
Total Capital AME	**468,487**	**645,520**	**742,897**	**496,864**	**564,336**	**573,593**	**644,593**	**617,593**
Of which:								
Staff costs	20,324	20,324	23,078	23,078	20,324	-	-	-
Release of provision	-7,400	-3,815	-		-	-	-	-
Capital support for local government (net)	99,230	132,060	188,770	21,803	-	-	-	-
Capital grants to persons & non-profit bodies (net)	355,026	311,789	329,681	30,932	407,454	407,454	407,454	407,454
Capital support for public corporations	-	18	417	-	-	-	-	-
Purchase of assets	135,451	129,856	124,090	120,203	136,558	166,139	237,139	210,139
Income from sales of assets	-208,487	-14,264	-6,342	-96,311	-	-	-	-
Net lending to the private sector and abroad	8,455	21,360	17,612	20,554	-	-	-	-
Other capital	65,888	48,192	65,591	376,605	-	-	-	-
Total Capital Budget[23]	**824,954**	**665,796**	**986,293**	**839,712**	**948,036**	**967,593**	**1,021,093**	**920,093**
Total departmental spending[24]	**7,267,739**	**5,972,174**	**6,894,453**	**5,974,070**	**6,587,172**	**7,093,921**	**7,017,136**	**6,819,208**
Of which:								
Total DEL[25]	2,401,969	1,084,129	1,428,150	1,441,918	1,566,640	1,539,063	1,521,737	1,408,280
Total AME[26]	4,865,770	4,888,045	5,466,303	4,532,152	5,020,532	5,554,858	5,495,399	5,410,928

Source: Department for Culture, Media and Sport

1 Support for the Art Sector. The income stream relates to contributions from Department for Education towards the cost of Music Hubs and other programmes managed by the Arts Council England. The funding profile is agreed on a year by year basis.

2 Ceremonial and Support for the Heritage sector included funding for World War One commemorations in 2013-14 through to 2015-16 including the Battle of Jutland and the Somme with funding for 2016-17 and 2017-18 allocated via the Supplementary Estimate.

3 The Heritage Sponsored Bodies line illustrates an initial reduction in 2012-13 as a result of the 2010 Spending Review cuts. In addition it includes funding for Church Roof repairs, announced in the 2014 Autumn Statement, via the National Heritage Memorial fund.

4 Broadcasting and Media includes the clearance and auction of the 800MHz band. The reduction in expenditure between 2016-17 and 2017-18 is due to Ofcom becoming self-funding from 2017-18 and so will not need the funding it currently receives from the Exchequer.

5 Olympics legacy and London 2012 relate to the staging of the Olympic and Paralympic games 2012. This includes income from the sale of the Olympic Village, residual costs and final settlements with the Greater London Authority (GLA) and Olympic Lottery Distribution Fund (OLDF).

6 Spectrum Management receipts which partially offset Administration expenditure cease after 2016-17 following the Spending Review 2015.

7 Depreciation includes impairment.

8 Pension schemes report under IAS 19 Employee Benefits accounting requirements. These figures, therefore, include cash payments made and contributions received, as well as certain non-cash items.

9.1 Expenditure by the Department for Culture, Media and Sport

£'000

	2012-13 OUTTURN	2013-14 OUTTURN	2014-15 OUTTURN	2015-16 OUTTURN	2016-17 PLANS	2017-18 PLANS	2018-19 PLANS	2019-20 PLANS

9 Lottery Grants: The Group Accounts exclude the Devolved Administrations and records expenditure on an accruals basis since 2014-15.

10 Levy Bodies: Levy Expenditure is only recorded at year end via the Annual Accounts, hence no forward plans data.

11 Depreciation includes impairment.

12 Pension schemes report under IAS 19 Employee Benefits accounting requirements. These figures, therefore, include cash payments made and contributions received, as well as certain non-cash items.

13 Total Resource Budget is the sum of the Resource DEL budget and the Resource AME budget, including depreciation.

14 Museums and Galleries Sponsored ALBs illustrate the efficiency Savings made by the Museums & Galleries following spending reviews of 2010 & 2013. Additional Capital funding was allocated for 2016-17 in the Spending review 2015.

15 Arts and culture ALBs includes funding in 2017-18 for the Factory Manchester as part of the Northern Powerhouse.

16 Heritage Sponsored ALBs saw an additional £80M allocated in 2014-15 to Historic England (formerly English Heritage) on implementation of the New Model whereby the management of historic bodies was transferred to a charity, the English Heritage Trust.

17 Support for Broadcasting and Media sector relates to the Broadband Delivery UK (BDUK) project delivered and completed over the years 2011 to 2017.

18 Broadcasting and Media sponsored ALBs sees an increase for 2016-17 onwards as it includes funding for the clearance and auction of the 700MHz band.

19 Support for Horseracing and Gambling sector - following the sale of the Tote in 2011-12 it was agreed that the proceeds would be return to the racing industry over a period of years. Initially at £9m a year and then with the industry it was agreed that the balance of £49.9m be repaid in 2014-15.

20 Olympics legacy and London 2012 relate to the staging of the Olympic and Paralympic games 2012. This includes income from the sale of the Olympic Village, residual costs and final settlements with the GLA and OLDF.

21 BBC Capital expenditure is net of property disposals in essence the sale of Television Centre in White City in 2015-16.

22 Lottery Grants: The Group Accounts exclude the Devolved Administrations and records expenditure on an accruals basis since 2014-15.

23 Total Capital Budget is the sum of the Capital DEL budget and the Capital AME budget.

24 Total departmental spending is the sum of the resource budget and the capital budget less depreciation.

25 Total DEL is the sum of the resource budget DEL and capital budget DEL less depreciation in DEL.

26 Total AME is the sum of the resource budget AME and the capital budget AME less depreciation in AME.

9.2 Estimates of Average Issue Readership of National Daily Newspapers

rolling 12 months' periods ending

000's

		2012 Mar	2012 Jun	2012 Sep	2012 Dec	2013 Mar	2013 Jun	2013 Sep	2013 Dec	2014 Mar	2014 Jun	2014 Sep	2014 Dec	2015 Mar	2015 Jun	2015 Sep	2015 Dec	2016 Mar
The Sun	WSDV	7,331	7,244	7,084	7,007	6,707	6,435	6,123	5,841	5,685	5,508	5,421	5,347	5,178	4878	4664	4490	4,392
Daily Mail	WSEI	4,426	4,385	4,320	4,258	4,245	4,298	4,269	4,215	4,074	3,866	3,833	3,745	3,704	3657	3605	3546	3,444
Daily Mirror/Daily Record	WSEH	4,046	3,995	3,849	3,773	3,614	3,512	3,357	3,167	2,975	2,893	2,908	2,881	2,796	2554	2433	2337	2,287
Daily Mirror	WSEM	3,196	3,178	3,062	2,995	2,856	2,775	2,639	2,456	2,309	2,230	2,251	2,281	2,211	2029	1953	1848	1,813
The Daily Telegraph	WSEN	1,468	1,387	1,394	1,346	1,352	1,348	1,312	1,318	1,313	1,261	1,237	1,192	1,119	1154	1150	1165	1,190
The Times	WSES	1,359	1,302	1,310	1,311	1,300	1,261	1,240	1,147	1,155	1,110	1,047	1,062	995	985	1014	1036	1,054
Daily Express	WSEP	1,329	1,304	1,265	1,192	1,157	1,123	1,114	1,095	1,114	1,097	1,079	1,079	993	948	845	777	758
Daily Star	WSEQ	1,409	1,439	1,421	1,358	1,279	1,211	1,158	1,113	1,090	1,039	978	1,010	943	878	838	808	791
The Guardian	WSET	1,058	1,081	1,062	1,050	1,027	935	890	843	793	748	744	748	761	793	793	814	809
i		-	564	561	612	579	545	568	559	563	584	573	579	549	561	533	536	569
The Independent	WSEU	533	537	506	490	443	397	393	348	309	261	264	262	272	284	270	270	285
Financial Times[1]	WSEY	301	300	285	319	312	305	296	235	-	-	-	-	-				-
Any national morning	WSEZ	18,679	18,466	18,069	17,825	17,403	20,852	20,181	19,347	19,092	18,384	18,106	17,929	17,331	16,716	16,161	15,794	15,591

Source: National Readership Surveys Ltd.

1. NRS ceased to publish estimates for Financial Times as of 2014 data, so data cannot be provided for March 2014 onwards.

9.3 Creative Industries group jobs by gender, 2014[1]

	Male	Female	% Female
Advertising and marketing	97,000	70,000	41.9%
Architecture	74,000	27,000	26.6%
Design: product, graphic and fashion design	77,000	59,000	43.5%
Film, TV, video, radio and photography	148,000	80,000	35.1%
IT, software and computer services	487,000	120,000	19.7%
Museums, galleries and libraries	33,000	52,000	61.3%
Music, performing and visual arts	139,000	146,000	51.2%
Publishing	88,000	105,000	54.5%
Creative Economy Total	1,145,000	663,000	36.7%

Source: Department for Culture, Media and Sport

1 Change for Crafts has not been shown due to small sample size.

9.4 Proportion of adults who participate in selected activities in their free time, 2015/16

	16-24	25-44	45-64	65-74	75+	All aged 16+
	%	%	%	%	%	%
Watching TV	88.1	88.1	90.4	93.6	93.1	89.9
Spending time with friends/family	91.1	91.4	87.7	89.6	85.4	89.4
Listening to music	91.1	80.1	78.6	74.5	69.3	79.4
Shopping	75.5	77.1	75.4	81.4	74.8	76.6
Eating out at restaurants	76.2	77.5	75.3	78.3	68.3	75.8
Internet/emailing	85.3	82.8	71.0	59.4	30.4	71.5
Reading	55.1	66.3	70.5	78.3	73.2	68.1
Days out or visits to places	66.9	72.8	69.8	73.9	55.2	69.4
Sport/exercise	66.0	63.4	57.5	50.7	37.5	57.9
Going to the cinema	72.3	62.2	50.1	39.8	26.2	53.7
Going to pubs/bars/clubs	57.6	52.9	51.7	47.0	26.7	49.9
Gardening	11.1	43.1	61.9	69.7	59.1	49.2
Theatre/music concerts	38.5	41.9	50.5	52.2	34.7	44.6
DIY	20.5	44.3	49.6	45.4	26.2	40.9
Visiting historic sites	23.6	39.9	49.0	53.5	33.5	41.4
Visiting museums/galleries	27.5	40.9	44.5	47.2	28.5	39.6
Playing computer games	59.5	37.7	20.4	17.3	7.8	30.0
Arts and crafts	17.6	24.4	23.1	28.0	23.3	23.3
Playing a musical instrument	13.3	10.8	9.7	8.2	6.1	10.0

Source: Taking Part Survey, Department for Digital, Culture, Media and Sport

9.5 Films

United Kingdom

	Production of UK films[1,4]		Expenditure on feature films			Numbers and £ million
	Films produced in the UK (numbers)	Production costs (current prices)	UK box office	Video[2] rental	Video[2] retail[3]	Video on Demand
	KWGD	KWGE	KWHU	KWHV	KWHW	
1998	83	389	547	437	453	33
1999	92	507	563	451	451	40
2000	80	578	583	601	601	50
2001	74	379	645	494	821	65
2002	119	551	755	494	1175	63
2003	214	1127	742	462	1392	68
2004	198	879	770	476	1557	73
2005	223	608	770	399	1399	74
2006	207	827	762	340	1302	67
2007	241	849	821	295	1440	75
2008	297	723	850	284	1454	101
2009	336	1256	944	285	1311	119
2010	374	1154	988	278	1267	129
2011	364	1328	1040	262	1165	149
2012	375	1010	1099	221	968	234
2013	361	1163	1083	146	940	337
2014	339	1514	1058	87	861	445

Source: BFI Statistical Yearbooks 2014-2016

1 Includes films with a production budget of £500,000 or more.

2 Video includes only rental and retail of physical discs, and does not include downloads.

3 In 2005 the British Video Association changed its methodology for producing market value which has necessitated a change to historical figures quoted.

4. Prior to 2010, the Research and Statistics Unit tracked all features shooting in the UK with a minimum budget of £500,000. However, evidence from a variety of sources (data on British film certification and the 2008 UK Film Council report Low and Micro-Budget Film Production in the UK) revealed a substantial number of films produced below this budget level. In order to broaden the evidence base, production tracking was extended to include feature films with budgets under £500,000 and data was collected from 2008 onwards.

Figures not adjusted for inflation

9.6 Box office top 20 films released in the UK and Republic of Ireland, 2014

	Title	Country of origin	Box office gross (£ million)	Number of opening weekend cinemas	Opening weekend gross (£ million)	Distributor
1	The Hobbit: The Battle of the Five Armies*	USA/NZ	41.2	598	9.8	Warner Bros
2	Paddington*	UK/Fra	36.9	520	5.2	StudioCanal
3	The Lego Movie	Aus/USA/Den	34.3	547	8	Warner Bros
4	The Inbetweeners 2	UK	33.4	509	12.5	Entertainment
5	Dawn of the Planet of the Apes	USA	32.7	563	8.7	20th Century Fox
6	The Hunger Games: Mockingjay - Part 1*	USA	31.1	565	12.6	Lionsgate
7	Gardians of the Galaxy*	UK/USA	28.5	557	6.4	Walt Disney
8	X-Men: Days of Future Past	USA	27.1	539	9.1	20th Century Fox
9	How to Train your Dragon 2	USA	25.1	135	0.6	20th Century Fox
10	The Amazing Spider-Man 2	USA	24.1	545	9	Sony Pictures
11	The Wolf of Wall Street	USA	22.7	501	4.6	Universal
12	Gone Girl*	USA	22.4	552	4.1	20th Century Fox
13	Interstellar*	USA	20.6	576	5.4	Warner Bros
14	12 Years a Slave	USA	20	207	2.5	eOne Films
15	Transformers: Age of Extinction	USA/China	19.5	533	11.7	Paramount
16	Maleficent	UK/USA	19.5	486	6.6	Walt Disney
17	Captain America: The Winter Soldier	USA	19.3	535	6	Walt Disney
18	22 Jump Street	USA	18.6	456	4.8	Sony Pictures
19	Godzilla	USA/Jap	17.2	551	6.4	Warner Bros
20	The Imitation Game*	UK/USA*	16.2	461	2.8	StudioCanal

Source: Rentrak, BFI RSU analysis

Notes:

Box office gross = cumulative total up to 22 February 2015.

* Film still on release on 22 February 2015.

9.7 Full year accommodation usage figures by visitors from overseas for 2004-2015 (Excluding 2013)

Data	Accommodation	Year										
		2004	2005	2006	2007	2008	2009	2010	2011	2012	2014	2015
Total Visits (000s)	All staying visits	25,677	28,038	30,654	30,871	30,142	28,208	28,300	29,197	29,282	32,613	34,436
	Bed & Breakfast	1,177	1,221	1,242	1,174	1,118	1,065	1,083	996	1,003	1,043	1,349
	Free guest with relatives or friends	10,174	11,144	12,081	11,944	12,056	11,165	10,570	10,646	10,811	11,120	11,881
	Holiday village/Centre	37	60	44	67	59	77	41	49	59	170	60
	Hostel/university/school	949	1,096	1,167	1,203	1,138	1,218	1,102	1,180	1,174	1,144	1,267
	Hotel/guest house	11,451	12,465	13,939	14,156	13,472	13,001	13,841	14,446	14,406	16,383	16,796
	Other	1,815	1,855	2,143	2,073	1,930	1,470	1,518	1,360	1,439	1,971	2,317
	Own home	413	412	466	446	418	385	358	392	364	382	401
	Paying guest family or friends house	610	616	595	567	650	461	465	577	537	583	736
	Camping/caravan	295	381	425	394	298	333	312	302	284	335	300
	Rented house/flat	740	806	832	836	868	934	882	958	1,002	1,361	1,421
Total Nights (000s)	All staying visits	227,406	249,181	273,417	251,522	245,775	229,391	227,960	234,363	230,149	264,366	272,941
	Bed & Breakfast	8,576	7,840	7,411	7,078	6,500	5,804	6,341	5,639	5,307	5,809	8,041
	Free guest with relatives or friends	113,736	121,487	133,209	121,272	122,898	111,947	107,642	108,703	107,575	111,173	120,308
	Holiday village/Centre	222	346	336	576	329	448	321	321	393	1,522	362
	Hostel/university/school	16,757	17,863	21,103	15,680	15,443	16,775	16,305	18,670	18,236	18,543	18,796
	Hotel/guest house	45,291	51,069	57,540	57,174	55,133	54,246	58,741	60,365	60,081	72,640	73,414
	Other	5,546	7,078	6,930	6,452	6,597	4,397	4,982	4,990	4,635	10,428	10,007
	Own home	4,638	5,507	7,895	5,169	5,110	4,524	5,068	5,625	4,895	5,412	6,413
	Paying guest family or friends house	8,807	8,716	9,692	8,240	7,961	5,423	5,148	6,574	7,433	7,060	8,614
	Camping/caravan	3,015	4,705	4,350	4,182	2,988	3,296	2,904	3,229	2,757	3,047	2,763
	Rented house/flat	20,818	24,570	24,950	25,695	22,817	22,362	20,482	20,237	18,838	28,731	24,223
Total Spend (£m)	All staying visits	12,798	14,011	15,759	15,699	16,058	16,354	16,649	17,666	18,245	21,578	21,787
	Bed & Breakfast	481	511	512	488	470	459	522	470	457	562	732
	Free guest with relatives or friends	3,822	3,972	4,498	4,207	4,501	4,425	4,254	4,371	4,515	4,593	4,878
	Holiday village/Centre	9	12	17	27	22	27	23	27	27	84	21
	Hostel/university/school	739	848	937	829	813	1,055	1,004	1,122	1,083	1,350	1,253
	Hotel/guest house	5,826	6,547	7,580	7,916	7,914	7,773	8,577	9,138	9,626	11,254	11,594
	Other	263	308	245	328	337	328	272	307	265	529	466
	Own home	354	357	412	402	429	531	354	377	505	515	532
	Paying guest family or friends house	345	393	439	385	379	364	340	426	475	445	501
	Camping/caravan	97	112	142	146	111	144	144	129	128	134	143
	Rented house/flat	861	951	977	971	1,084	1,245	1,172	1,305	1,181	2,111	1,666
Sample	All staying visits	37,321	39,977	40,410	36,432	31,854	41,952	41,948	38,144	37,666	37,359	37,058
	Bed & Breakfast	1,570	1,617	1,471	1,266	1,137	1,469	1,518	1,252	1,224	1,129	1,417
	Free guest with relatives or friends	15,167	16,363	16,256	14,386	12,831	16,976	16,003	14,233	14,207	13,133	13,090
	Holiday village/Centre	45	64	53	59	46	99	49	55	82	177	60
	Hostel/university/school	1,232	1,372	1,348	1,261	1,153	1,616	1,510	1,382	1,381	1,158	1,230
	Hotel/guest house	18,716	19,971	20,585	18,560	15,641	20,885	21,998	19,765	19,458	19,842	19,110
	Other	965	893	910	864	873	1,008	1,033	1,136	1,174	1,314	1,649
	Own home	730	744	740	645	522	656	637	545	594	528	516
	Paying guest family or friends house	562	599	527	487	507	529	538	637	548	558	666
	Camping/caravan	250	322	339	320	298	363	378	379	325	360	383
	Rented house/flat	1,101	1,161	1,164	1,034	973	1,457	1,397	1,291	1,334	1,607	1,525

Source: International Passenger Survey, Office for National Statistics

Please note: For 2013 the accommodation categories were reduced therefore we have included the analysis separately on the next page. ONS reverted back to the full accommodation options for 2014 data onwards, therefore 2014 and 2015 data is shown this this table.

9.7 Full year accommodation usage figures by visitors from overseas 2013

		Year
Data	Accommodation	**2013**
Total Visits (000s)	All staying visits	31,064
	Own Home	366
	Hotels or similar	16,852
	Camp/caravan sites	480
	Other Short Term Rented	2,100
	Friends or Relatives	10,569
	Other (Non Rented or Long Term Rented)	2,299
Total Nights (000s)	All staying visits	245,412
	Own Home	5,453
	Hotels or similar	77,553
	Camp/caravan sites	3,980
	Other Short Term Rented	34,680
	Friends or Relatives	105,763
	Other (Non Rented or Long Term Rented)	17,983
Total Spend (£m)	All staying visits	20,938
	Own Home	531
	Hotels or similar	11,956
	Camp/caravan sites	225
	Other Short Term Rented	2,514
	Friends or Relatives	4,656
	Other (Non Rented or Long Term Rented)	1,056
Sample	All staying visits	39,416
	Own Home	566
	Hotels or similar	22,514
	Camp/caravan sites	602
	Other Short Term Rented	2,561
	Friends or Relatives	13,609
	Other (Non Rented or Long Term Rented)	1,910

Source: International Passenger Survey, Office for National Statistics

Please note: For 2013 the accommodation categories were reduced therefore the analysis has been shown separately in this table. ONS reverted back to the full accommodation options for 2014. Therefore, 2014 and 2015 data is shown in the previous table.

9.8 International tourism[1]

Thousands and £ million

	Visits to the UK by overseas residents (thousands)	Spending in the UK by overseas residents		Visits overseas by UK residents (thousands)	Spending overseas by UK residents	
		Current prices	Constant 1995 prices		Current prices	Constant 1995 prices
2000	25,209	12,805	11,102	56,837	24,251	27,281
2001	22,835	11,306	9,528	58,281	25,332	27,710
2002	24,180	11,737	9,641	59,377	26,962	29,311
2003	24,715	11,855	9,451	61,424	28,550	28,677
2004	27,755	13,047	10,146	64,194	30,285	30,444
2005	29,970	14,248	10,714	66,441	32,154	30,954
2006	32,713	16,002	11,641	69,536	34,411	30,904
2007	32,778	15,960	11,389	69,450	35,013	32,477
2008	31,888	16,323	11,276	69,011	36,838	28,657
2009	29,889	16,592	11,032	58,614	31,694	22,673
2010	29,803	16,899	10,644	55,562	31,820	22,116
2011	30,798	17,998	10,870	56,836	31,701	20,569
2012	31,084	18,640	10,842	56,538	32,450	22,024
2013	32,692	21,258	11,740	57,792	34,510	23,613
2014	34,377	21,849	11,874	60,082	35,537	23,800
2015	36,115	22,072	11,730	65,720	39,028	24,381

1 See chapter text

Sources: International Passenger Survey
Office for National Statistics;
01633 456032

9.9 Holidays abroad:[1] by destination

Percentages

		2003	2004	2005	2006	2007	2008	2009	2010	2011	2012	2013	2014	2015
Spain	JTKC	29.8	28.4	27.2	27.8	26.5	26.6	26.5	25.9	25.8	27.0	27.5	28.2	27.1
France	JTKD	18.1	17.3	16.6	15.9	16.7	16.7	18.6	18.3	17.4	17.2	16.4	15.5	14.6
Greece	JTKF	6.6	5.7	5.1	5.0	5.0	4.2	4.4	4.8	4.8	4.5	4.4	4.5	4.9
USA	JTKE	5.5	6.1	6.0	5.1	5.2	5.4	5.4	4.9	5.2	5.2	5.0	5.4	5.4
Italy	JTKG	5	5	5.4	5.4	5.6	5.2	4.7	4.6	4.5	5.0	5.3	5.3	5.8
Irish Republic	JTKI	3.7	3.8	3.8	4.0	3.3	3.2	3.2	2.5	2.9	2.3	2.2	2.6	2.6
Portugal	JTKH	4	3.5	3.6	3.7	4.1	4.8	4.1	4.4	4.5	4.5	4.8	4.7	5.0
Cyprus	JTKL	2.7	2.6	2.8	2.4	2.4	2.4	2.1	2.1	2.2	2.0	1.5	1.3	1.3
Netherlands	JTKK	2.6	2.6	2.5	2.7	2.4	2.1	2.2	2.2	2.6	2.6	2.7	3.1	3.6
Turkey	JTKJ	2.3	2.3	2.7	2.7	2.8	3.7	3.5	4.7	3.7	3.3	2.8	2.9	2.8
Belgium	JTKM	2.2	1.8	1.9	2.0	2.2	2.0	1.9	1.7	2	2.5	2.3	2.5	2.2
Germany	JTKN	1.2	1.6	1.7	1.7	2.0	1.9	1.7	1.7	2.2	2.0	2.3	2.1	2.4
Austria	JTKP	1.1	1.4	1.3	1.2	1.2	1.4	1.4	1.5	1	1.1	1.2	1.0	1.0
Malta	JTKO	1	1	1.1	1.0	0.9	0.9	0.8	1.0	1	1.0	1.2	1.1	1.0
Other countries	JTKQ	14.2	16.8	18.4	20	19.6	19.5	19.5	19.6	20.2	13.3	13.4	13.3	12.5

1 See chapter text.

Sources: International Passenger Survey, Office for National Statistics;
01633 456032

9.10 All Tourism

	2009	2010	2011	2012	2013	2014	2015
TRIPS (millions)	122.537	115.711	126.635	126.019	122.905	114.242	124.426
BEDNIGHTS (millions)	387.448	361.398	387.329	388.24	373.607	349.546	377.101
EXPENDITURE (£ millions)	£20,971	£19,797	£22,666	£23,976	£23,294	£22,692	£24,825
Av. Trip Length	3.16	3.12	3.06	3.08	3.04	3.06	3.03
Av. £ / Night	£54	£55	£59	£62	£62	£65	£66
Av. £ / Trip	£171	£171	£179	£190	£190	£199	£200

Source: Visit England

Please note that the latest 2015 results are provisional and subject to minor changes in subsequent months due to the inclusion of trip-takers returning from late trips.

All expenditure figures are in historic prices

Due to a data processing issue, Visit England will not release the 2016 dataset until the end of 2017. Therefore this table will not be updated until the next edition of Annual Abstract

9.11 All tourism in Great Britain

	Trips				Nights				Spend			
	GB	England	Scotland	Wales	GB	England	Scotland	Wales	GB	England	Scotland	Wales
	Millions				Millions				£millions			
All tourism – 2014	114.24	92.61	12.52	10.00	349.5	272.9	41.6	35.1	£22,692	£18,085	£2,871	£1,735
All tourism – 2015	124.43	102.73	11.99	10.45	377.1	299.6	41.3	36.2	£24,825	£19,571	£3,279	£1,975
Purpose												
Leisure	102.51	84.28	9.83	9.04	326.0	258.2	35.2	32.6	£19,817	£15,380	£2,688	£1,749
Total holiday	85.18	68.92	8.66	8.19	283.1	220.9	32.1	30.1	£17,903	£13,790	£2,474	£1,640
Holiday	55.96	43.72	6.36	6.25	194.6	146.5	24.3	23.8	£14,171	£10,725	£2,068	£1,378
VFR-holiday	29.23	25.20	2.30	1.94	88.5	74.5	7.7	6.3	£3,732	£3,065	£405	£262
VFR-other	17.33	15.36	1.17	0.86	42.9	37.2	3.1	2.5	£1,914	£1,591	£214	£109
VFR	46.55	40.55	3.46	2.79	131.3	111.7	10.8	8.8	£5,646	£4,655	£619	£371
Total business	16.49	13.87	1.73	0.97	37.6	30.1	4.9	2.6	£4,013	£3,339	£503	£171
To attend a conference	1.29	1.13	0.12	0.04	3.0	2.6	0.3	0.1	£312	£261	£43	£8
To attend an exhibition/ trade show	0.71	0.56	0.12	0.04	1.3	1.0	0.3	0.1	£166	£132	£24	£10
Travel/transport is my work	0.57	0.50	0.08	0.02	1.0	0.8	0.2	*	£103	£92	£11	£1
To do paid work/ on business	14.50	12.18	1.49	0.90	33.3	26.6	4.3	2.5	£3,535	£2,946	£436	£153
School trip	0.56	0.44	0.02	0.11	1.4	1.1	*	0.2	£98	£86	£2	£9
Other reason	4.02	3.41	0.34	0.29	10.5	8.8	1.0	0.7	£749	£633	£74	£42

Source: The GB Tourist 2015

British residents made an estimated 124 million overnight trips in Great Britain in 2015, representing 377 million bed nights and £25 billion in spending.

Total holidays (including visiting friends and relatives) are the main purpose of trips taken, accounting for two thirds (68%) of trips taken and are even more important in terms of nights (75%) and spending (72%). Visits to friends and relatives (VFR) for mainly holiday purposes account for one in four trips and nights away (23%) but are less significant in terms of spending (15%). Business and work is the main purpose for around one in eight trips (13%), accounting for one in nine nights (10%). These are higher spending trips, accounting for 16% of all tourism spending.

Friends' and relatives' homes (including owned second homes) are a widely used type of accommodation accounting for almost four in ten of all trips (37%). This reflects not only visits to friends and relatives as such, but also holidays spent staying with friends and relatives. With no real accommodation costs, trips staying at friends' and relatives' homes account for only 19% of spending on all tourism trips.

Commercial accommodation is used on just over half of trips (58%), but these trips represent a much higher share of spending (75%). Commercial accommodation is mainly serviced (40% of trips) where trips tend to be shorter in duration (28% of nights) but higher spending (51%). Hotels and motels account for 34% of trips and 44% of spend; guest houses and B&Bs account for 6% of trips and 7% of spend. Self-catering rented accommodation is used on a lower volume of trips (19%), but these trips are longer (27% of nights) and therefore slightly above average in terms of spending (24%).

The car is the dominant form of transport with three quarters (74%) of trips using a private car for the longest part of the journey from home to the destination

Firm bookings are made before more than half of all trips (57%), but it would be higher were it not for the high level of staying at friends and relatives' homes and using personal transport, where advance booking is less relevant

Large cities/large towns (41%) are the major destinations of tourism trips, with small towns, the seaside and countryside/villages representing the remainder with a share of 20% each.

9.12 Gambling

United Kingdom

£ million[1] and numbers

		2002 /03	2003 /04	2004 /05	2005 /06	2006 /07	2007 /08	2008 /09	2009 /10	2010 /11	2011 /12	2012 /13	2013 /14	2014 /15
Money staked on gambling														
National Lottery -Total	C229	4,670	4,614	4,757	5,000	4,911	4,966	5,149	5,477	5,825	6,503	6,977	6,736	7,275
Lotto including on-line	C3PU	3,479	3,225	3,225	3,021	2,858	2,752	2,698	2,661	2,667	2,475	2,345	2,475	2,573
Lotto Plus 5[6]		-	-	-	-	-	-	-	-	-	101.7	78.7	36.4	-
Instants[2] (Scratchcards)	C3PV	592	641	729	804	943	1,109	1,221	1,340	1,436	1,726	2,062	2,141	2,629
Thunderball	C3PW	287	351	343	355	329	309	297	286	356	331	341	295	299
Lottery Extra[3]	C3PX	90	78	77	57	12	0	-	-	-	-	-	-	-
HotPicks	C3PY	222	244	219	228	222	210	211	210	206	200	193	179	178
Euromillions	C3Q2	..	15	104	427	464	476	618	881	1,056	1,666	1,984	1,609	1,597
Daily Play	C3Q3	..	45	59	54	49	50	50	49	46	4.3	-	-	-
Dream number[4]		..	..	..	..	59	59	54	50	39	-	-	-	-
Number operating in GB:														
Casinos	JE55	126	131	138	140	138	144	145	141	149	146	144	147	148
betting shops[5]	JE5B	..	..	..	..	..	8,800	8,872	8,822	9,067	9,128	9,100	8,983	8,867

Sources: National Lottery Commission;
Gambling Commission: 0121 230 6666;

1 Adjusted to real terms using the Retail Prices Index.
2 From 2003/04 includes Inter-active Instant Win Games
3 Discontinued games
4 Started July 2006 and discontinued February 2011. Replaced by Lotto Plus 5
5 The Gambling Commission started regulating the betting industry from 1 September 2007, the number of betting shops is an ABB estimate.
6 launched in February 2011 and discontinued September 2013

9.12 Gambling - Remote (Licensing and Advertising) Act Data

GB only remote data (£m)

Turnover

Turnover	Nov 2014 Mar 2015 Total	Apr 2015 Mar 2016 Proprietary	Revenue Share	Total
Betting	5,322.77	15,923.44	-00	15,923.44
Bingo	330.51	771.13	-00	771.13
Casino	6,757.05	22,292.77	-00	22,292.77
Pool Betting	29.54	58.80	-00	58.80
Total	12,439.87	39,046.15	-00	39,046.15

GGY

GGY	Nov 2014 Mar 2015 Total	Apr 2015 Mar 2016 Proprietary	Revenue Share	Total
Betting	456.41	1,053.19	513.63	1,566.83
Betting Exchange	52.44	151.86	-00	151.86
Bingo	66.98	52.05	100.62	152.66
Casino	899.63	1,009.82	1,561.60	2,571.42
Pool Betting	9.82	25.86	-00	25.86
Total	1,485.29	2,292.79	2,175.85	4,468.64

Betting Turnover

Betting Turnover	Nov 2014 Mar 2015 Total	Apr 2015 Mar 2016 Proprietary	Revenue Share	Total
Cricket	238.11	498.32	-00	498.32
Dogs	86.48	285.85	-00	285.85
Financials	56.50	231.62	-00	231.62
Football	2,119.33	5,878.80	-00	5,878.80
Golf	34.93	189.55	-00	189.55
Horses	1,630.94	5,293.74	-00	5,293.74
Other	741.97	2,133.17	-00	2,133.17
Tennis	444.05	1,471.20	-00	1,471.20
Total	5,352.31	15,982.24	-00	15,982.24

Betting GGY

Betting GGY	Nov 2014 Mar 2015 Total	Apr 2015 Mar 2016 Proprietary	Revenue Share	Total
Cricket	4.22	21.00	-00	21.00
Dogs	9.02	28.38	-00	28.38
Financials	3.10	12.35	-00	12.35
Football	160.71	580.56	-00	580.56
Golf	2.62	14.62	-00	14.62
Horses	115.47	345.78	-00	345.78
Other	41.17	155.80	-00	155.80
Tennis	23.06	72.42	-00	72.42
Unallocated rev share	159.32	-00	513.63	513.63
Total	518.67	1,230.92	513.63	1,744.55

Casino Turnover

Casino Turnover	Nov 2014 Mar 2015 Total	Apr 2015 Mar 2016 Proprietary	Revenue Share	Total
Card Game	492.81	1,872.52	-00	1,872.52
Other	223.16	781.84	-00	781.84
Slots	5,167.66	16,436.38	-00	16,436.38
Table Game	873.42	3,202.04	-00	3,202.04
Total	6,757.05	22,292.77	-00	22,292.77

Casino GGY

Casino GGY	Nov 2014 Mar 2015 Total	Apr 2015 Mar 2016 Proprietary	Revenue Share	Total
Card Game	66.45	32.88	155.94	188.83
Other	59.15	23.41	108.15	131.56
Peer to Peer	44.00	71.38	27.33	98.70
Slots	594.18	803.57	947.98	1,751.55
Table Game	135.87	78.58	322.20	400.79
Total	899.63	1,009.82	1,561.60	2,571.42

Total remote data (£m)

Turnover

Turnover	Nov 2014 Mar 2015 Total	Apr 2015 Mar 2016 Proprietary	Revenue Share	Total
Betting	5,476.00	16,338.17	-00	16,338.17
Bingo	331.21	772.73	-00	772.73
Casino	7,478.69	24,261.55	-00	24,261.55
Pool Betting	92.78	245.14	-00	245.14
Total	13,378.68	41,617.60	-00	41,617.60

GGY

GGY	Nov 2014 Mar 2015 Total	Apr 2015 Mar 2016 Proprietary	Revenue Share	Total
Betting	480.34	1,087.81	522.87	1,610.68
Betting Exchange	56.88	171.78	-00	171.78
Bingo	67.59	51.77	101.78	153.55
Casino	1,042.73	1,102.02	1,718.68	2,820.70
Pool Betting	37.29	86.44	-00	86.44
Total	1,684.82	2,499.83	2,343.32	4,843.15

Betting Turnover

Betting Turnover	Nov 2014 Mar 2015 Total	Apr 2015 Mar 2016 Proprietary	Revenue Share	Total
Cricket	240.18	504.39	-00	504.39
Dogs	95.75	293.99	-00	293.99
Financials	61.72	252.03	-00	252.03
Football	2,193.39	6,061.17	-00	6,061.17
Golf	36.24	193.82	-00	193.82
Horses	1,681.66	5,410.83	-00	5,410.83
Other	807.95	2,362.54	-00	2,362.54
Tennis	451.90	1,504.54	-00	1,504.54
Total	5,568.78	16,583.32	-00	16,583.32

Betting GGY

Betting GGY	Nov 2014 Mar 2015 Total	Apr 2015 Mar 2016 Proprietary	Revenue Share	Total
Cricket	4.31	21.81	-00	21.81
Dogs	10.97	30.07	-00	30.07
Financials	3.42	13.58	-00	13.58
Football	173.52	598.01	-00	598.01
Golf	2.73	14.89	-00	14.89
Horses	123.17	351.59	-00	351.59
Other	71.00	240.66	-00	240.66
Tennis	23.80	75.43	-00	75.43
Unallocated rev share	161.59	-00	522.87	522.87
Total	574.50	1,346.04	522.87	1,868.91

Casino Turnover

Casino Turnover	Nov 2014 Mar 2015 Total	Apr 2015 Mar 2016 Proprietary	Revenue Share	Total
Card Game	546.92	1,979.73	-00	1,979.73
Other	243.93	887.23	-00	887.23
Slots	5,725.33	18,028.28	-00	18,028.28
Table Game	962.51	3,366.32	-00	3,366.32
Total	7,478.69	24,261.55	-00	24,261.55

Casino GGY

Casino GGY	Nov 2014 Mar 2015 Total	Apr 2015 Mar 2016 Proprietary	Revenue Share	Total
Card Game	71.70	35.80	163.59	199.39
Other	139.19	27.72	182.77	210.49
Peer to Peer	49.44	74.96	33.60	108.56
Slots	641.75	880.81	1,010.53	1,891.35
Table Game	140.65	82.72	328.19	410.91
Total	1,042.73	1,102.02	1,718.68	2,820.70

Social responsibility data

Social responsibility data	Nov 2014 Mar 2015	Apr 2015 Mar 2016
Self Exclusions	180,166	611,531
Known breaches of self-exclusion	12,575	36,958
Number of individuals who cancelled their self-exclusion after minimum period	16,370	45,604
Challenged having gambled but unable to prove age	15,487	57,369

Accounts (£m)	Nov 2014 Mar 2015	Apr 2015 Mar 2016
Funds held in customer accounts	473.62	607.04
New account registrations	8.95	24.65
Active number accounts GC Licensed Facilities	17.53	22.87

Headcount	Nov 2014 Mar 2015	Apr 2015 Mar 2016
GB workforce	7,423	6,275

Accounts (Millions)	Nov 2014 Mar 2015	Apr 2015 Mar 2016
Funds held in customer accounts	495.51	638.87
Active number accounts GC Licensed Facilities	18.73	24.40

Source: Gambling Commission Industry Statistics

Turnover – the amount accrued through the sale of their product (bingo book/betting slip/lottery ticket/software etc) before winnings and overheads/expenses are deducted.
GGY can be higher than turnover as the GGY may not be accrued in the same reporting period.
Gross gambling yield (GGY) – the amount retained by operators after the payment of winnings but before the deduction of the costs of the operation.

9.13 Most Popular Boy and Girl Baby Names in England and Wales, 2014

Rank	Boys Name	Rank	Boys Name	Rank	Girls Name	Rank	Girls Name
1	OLIVER	51	REUBEN	1	AMELIA	51	WILLOW
2	JACK	52	MICHAEL	2	OLIVIA	52	BELLA
3	HARRY	53	ELIJAH	3	ISLA	53	ANNABELLE
4	JACOB	54	KIAN	4	EMILY	54	IVY
5	CHARLIE	55	TOMMY	5	POPPY	55	AMBER
6	THOMAS	56	MOHAMMAD	6	AVA	56	EMILIA
7	GEORGE	57	BLAKE	7	ISABELLA	57	EMMA
8	OSCAR	58	LUCA	8	JESSICA	58	SUMMER
9	JAMES	59	THEODORE	9	LILY	59	HANNAH
10	WILLIAM	60	STANLEY	10	SOPHIE	59	ELEANOR
11	NOAH	61	JENSON	11	GRACE	61	HARRIET
12	ALFIE	62	NATHAN	12	SOPHIA	62	ROSE
13	JOSHUA	63	CHARLES	13	MIA	63	AMELIE
14	MUHAMMAD	64	FRANKIE	14	EVIE	64	LEXI
15	HENRY	65	JUDE	15	RUBY	65	MEGAN
16	LEO	66	TEDDY	16	ELLA	66	GRACIE
17	ARCHIE	67	LOUIE	17	SCARLETT	67	ZARA
18	ETHAN	68	LOUIS	18	ISABELLE	68	LACEY
19	JOSEPH	69	RYAN	19	CHLOE	69	MARTHA
19	FREDDIE	70	HUGO	20	SIENNA	70	ANNA
21	SAMUEL	71	BOBBY	21	FREYA	71	VIOLET
22	ALEXANDER	72	ELLIOTT	22	PHOEBE	72	DARCEY
23	LOGAN	73	DEXTER	23	CHARLOTTE	73	MARIA
24	DANIEL	74	OLLIE	24	DAISY	74	MARYAM
25	ISAAC	74	ALEX	25	ALICE	75	BROOKE
26	MAX	76	LIAM	26	FLORENCE	76	AISHA
27	MOHAMMED	77	KAI	27	EVA	77	KATIE
28	BENJAMIN	78	GABRIEL	28	SOFIA	78	LEAH
29	MASON	79	CONNOR	29	MILLIE	79	THEA
30	LUCAS	80	AARON	30	LUCY	80	DARCIE
31	EDWARD	81	FREDERICK	31	EVELYN	81	HOLLIE
32	HARRISON	82	CALLUM	32	ELSIE	82	AMY
33	JAKE	83	ELLIOT	33	ROSIE	83	MOLLIE
34	DYLAN	84	ALBERT	34	IMOGEN	84	HEIDI
35	RILEY	85	LEON	35	LOLA	85	LOTTIE
36	FINLEY	86	RONNIE	36	MATILDA	86	BETHANY
37	THEO	87	RORY	37	ELIZABETH	87	FRANCESCA
38	SEBASTIAN	88	JAMIE	38	LAYLA	88	FAITH
39	ADAM	89	AUSTIN	39	HOLLY	89	HARPER
40	ZACHARY	90	SETH	40	LILLY	90	NANCY
41	ARTHUR	91	IBRAHIM	41	MOLLY	91	BEATRICE
42	TOBY	92	OWEN	42	ERIN	92	ISABEL
43	JAYDEN	93	CALEB	43	ELLIE	93	DARCY
44	LUKE	94	ELLIS	44	MAISIE	93	LYDIA
45	HARLEY	95	SONNY	45	MAYA	95	SARAH
46	LEWIS	96	ROBERT	46	ABIGAIL	96	SARA
47	TYLER	97	JOEY	47	ELIZA	97	JULIA
48	HARVEY	98	FELIX	48	GEORGIA	98	VICTORIA
49	MATTHEW	99	FINLAY	49	JASMINE	99	ZOE
50	DAVID	100	JACKSON	50	ESME	100=	ROBYN
						100=	SARA *

Source: Office for National Statistics (ONS)

Notes:

These rankings have been produced using the exact spelling of the name given at birth registration. Similar names with different spellings have been counted separately. Births where the name was not stated have been excluded from these figures. Of the 338,461 baby girls in the 2014 dataset, 9 were excluded for this reason.

* denotes new entry to top 100

9.14a Libraries overview
Great Britain

Percentages

	2006/07	2007/08	2008/09	2009/10	2010/11	2011/12	2012/13	2013/14	2014/15
	%	%	%	%	% (1)	% (1)	% (1)	% (1)	% (1)
Has visited a public library in the last year (2)	**46.1**	**45.0**	**41.1**	**39.4**	**39.7**	**38.8**	37.0	35.4	34.5
Frequency of attendance (2)									
1-2 times a year	10.3	10.5	**8.9**	**7.9**	**8.9**	**8.4**	8.7	8.5	7.9
3-4 times a year	12.9	13.0	**11.4**	**10.9**	**11.6**	**12.2**	10.8	9.9	10.9
At least once a month	15.7	**14.9**	**13.3**	**12.8**	**13.4**	**12.4**	12.4	12.2	10.8
At least once a week	**7.2**	**6.7**	**5.9**	**5.4**	**5.8**	**5.7**	5.0	4.9	4.9
Has not visited	**53.9**	**55.0**	**60.5**	**63.0**	**60.3**	**61.2**	63.0	64.6	65.5

Notes

(1) Figures in bold indicate a significant change from 2005/06.

(2) Figures exclude people who have visited a library for the purposes of paid work or academic study

Source: Department for Culture, Media and Sport Taking Part Survey 2014/15 Q4

https://www.gov.uk/government/publications/taking-part-201415-quarter-4-statistical-release

9.14b Proportion who have visited a public library in the last year - area-level breakdown

Percentages

	2005/06	2006/07	2007/08	2008/09	2009/10	2010/11	2011/12	2012/13	2013/14	2014/15
	%	%	%	%	%	% (1)	% (1)	% (1)	% (1)	% (1)
Index of deprivation										
1- Most deprived	N/A	N/A	N/A	N/A	37.6	39.8	37.3	40.1	40.4	37.6
2	N/A	N/A	N/A	N/A	32.8	38.2	37.0	35.7	35.3	34.8
3	N/A	N/A	N/A	N/A	38.3	39.2	39.2	33.5	33.4	33.5
4	N/A	N/A	N/A	N/A	36.1	41.2	39.1	35.0	33.3	37.8
5	N/A	N/A	N/A	N/A	42.1	38.4	40.6	35.3	35.7	33.9
6	N/A	N/A	N/A	N/A	38.7	36.4	38.3	37.5	36.1	32.2
7	N/A	N/A	N/A	N/A	39.9	40.7	40.4	34.8	33.3	31.8
8	N/A	N/A	N/A	N/A	34.6	40.1	33.8	37.1	32.7	34.5
9	N/A	N/A	N/A	N/A	45.4	**38.7**	42.2	41.8	37.1	35.7
10- Least deprived	N/A	N/A	N/A	N/A	46.3	43.5	39.8	38.4	36.8	33.8
Region										
North East	44.9	43.9	**40.1**	**37.1**	42.9	**38.8**	**36.3**	38.2	34.1	34.6
North West	46.9	46.2	45.0	**42.1**	41.4	**43.0**	**37.5**	37.8	35.4	34.0
Yorkshire and Humberside	42.1	40.5	**36.6**	**33.7**	**30.0**	**33.6**	**33.4**	34.9	33.1	31.0
East Midlands	44.7	42.9	44.3	**38.8**	42.7	**35.8**	**37.7**	34.9	32.3	30.9
West Midlands	47.6	47.1	**43.5**	**39.3**	**38.0**	**36.6**	**40.1**	35.5	34.8	35.0
East of England	50.5	47.5	**45.5**	**42.9**	**39.5**	**42.4**	**41.2**	37.5	37.0	32.2
London	52.6	**49.2**	**49.5**	**43.6**	**38.1**	**43.1**	**43.1**	41.9	40.9	40.2
South East	51.0	48.3	48.5	**44.5**	**43.5**	**40.5**	**37.4**	34.6	34.0	34.9
South West	47.9	45.1	45.5	**41.8**	**38.8**	**38.8**	**40.0**	36.3	33.6	34.4
Urban	48.5	**46.5**	**45.6**	**41.6**	**40.1**	**40.0**	**39.2**	37.8	36.4	35.4
Rural	47.1	44.7	**42.8**	**38.9**	**36.5**	**38.2**	**36.9**	33.7	31.4	30.9
ACORN										
Wealthy Achievers	50.9	48.9	**47.4**	**42.1**	**39.9**	**40.7**	**40.6**	38.4	33.8	32.9
Urban Prosperity	57.3	**51.0**	**52.0**	**41.8**	**42.6**	**43.9**	**41.9**	39.2	38.3	38.8
Comfortably Off	48.5	**46.4**	**44.2**	**41.9**	**41.9**	**38.2**	**37.9**	35.4	35.0	34.0
Moderate Means	45.3	45.0	**42.4**	**41.5**	**37.7**	**41.3**	**38.9**	36.9	35.7	35.1
Hard-pressed	40.9	39.8	41.0	**37.5**	**33.9**	**36.9**	**35.8**	36.4	35.9	34.5
Unclassified	61.7	50.0	**62.7**	**46.9**	*	*	*	*	40.3	*
All	48.2	**46.1**	**45.0**	**41.1**	**39.4**	**39.7**	**38.8**	37.0	35.4	34.5

Notes

(1) Figures in bold indicate a significant change from 2005/06.

(2) Index of deprivation data not available pre-2009/10. For Index of Deprivation data, figures in bold indicate a significant change from 2009/10.

(3) *= N too small to report

Source: Department for Culture, Media and Sport 2014/15 Q4

https://www.gov.uk/government/publications/taking-part-201415-quarter-4-statistical-release

9.14c Proportion who have visited a public library in the last year - demographic breakdown

Percentages

	2005/06	2006/07	2007/08	2008/09	2009/10	2010/11	2011/12	2012/13	2013/14	2014/15
						%	%	%	%	%
	%	%	%	%	%	(1)	(1)	(1)	(1)	(1)
Age										
16-24	51.0	**47.1**	**45.4**	**42.8**	**40.0**	**34.4**	**34.5**	32.3	33.4	28.5
25-44	51.2	50.2	49.5	**43.7**	**40.9**	**44.6**	**44.0**	42.2	40.4	41.3
45-64	45.7	44.3	**42.1**	**38.8**	**39.5**	**36.0**	**36.1**	33.1	30.9	30.6
65-74	46.7	44.4	44.7	**42.0**	**39.3**	44.3	**35.8**	38.6	37.1	35.2
75+	42.3	**37.1**	**37.6**	**35.0**	**32.9**	**37.1**	38.9	36.5	33.3	31.6
Sex										
Male	43.8	**42.1**	**40.2**	**35.3**	**35.5**	**34.3**	**33.6**	31.4	29.7	29.8
Female	52.3	**49.9**	**49.6**	**46.5**	**43.2**	**44.8**	**43.8**	42.3	40.8	39.0
NS-SEC										
Upper socio-economic group	52.1	**50.2**	**48.0**	**43.3**	**43.1**	**43.9**	**42.3**	39.7	36.7	35.9
Lower socio-economic group	40.1	**38.1**	38.7	**35.1**	**32.3**	**33.6**	**33.5**	33.0	32.4	31.2
Employment status										
Not working	49.7	**46.7**	**46.6**	**44.0**	**42.4**	**42.9**	**41.7**	41.0	38.3	37.8
Working	47.2	**45.7**	**44.0**	**39.0**	**37.4**	**37.5**	**36.8**	34.3	33.4	32.3
Tenure										
Owners	48.7	**46.4**	**44.8**	**41.1**	**39.8**	**40.1**	**39.2**	37.0	34.9	33.8
Social rented sector	41.9	40.5	42.2	39.0	**36.8**	**37.0**	**37.2**	38.6	38.1	39.1
Private rented sector	53.3	51.0	**49.2**	**43.0**	**39.8**	**40.2**	**38.7**	35.8	35.0	33.4
Ethnicity										
White	47.2	**44.9**	**43.6**	**40.1**	**37.9**	**38.3**	**37.8**	35.9	33.8	32.9
Black or ethnic minority	57.5	56.7	57.9	**50.2**	**50.6**	**50.0**	**46.5**	45.1	47.8	47.5
Religion										
No religion	46.8	45.5	45.3	40.1	**35.2**	**37.8**	**36.8**	33.2	34.4	33.2
Christian	47.3	**44.8**	**43.7**	**40.3**	**39.7**	**39.2**	**38.8**	37.7	34.3	33.4
Other religion	58.2	58.9	57.1	52.7	53.0	**48.2**	**44.4**	46.9	48.3	49.7
Long-standing illness or disability										
No	50.0	**48.0**	**46.0**	**42.1**	**40.4**	**40.1**	**39.2**	36.9	36.0	35.7
Yes	43.8	**41.5**	42.4	**38.4**	**36.8**	**38.5**	**37.9**	37.3	34.2	31.6
All	48.2	**46.1**	**45.0**	**41.1**	**39.4**	**39.7**	**38.8**	37.0	35.4	34.5

Notes

(1) Figures in bold indicate a significant change from 2005/06.

Source: Department for Culture, Media and Sport 2014/15 Q4
https://www.gov.uk/government/publications/taking-part-201415-quarter-4-statistical-release

9.15 Museums and Galleries overview (adults)

	2006/07	2007/08	2008/09	2009/10	2010/11	2011/12	2012/13	2013/14	2014/15
					%	%	%	%	%
	%	%	%	%	(1)	(1)	(1)	(1)	(1)
Has visited a museum or gallery in the last year[2]	41.5	**43.5**	43.4	**46.0**	**46.3**	**48.9**	52.8	53.1	52.0
Frequency of attendance [2]									
1-2 times a year	25.3	26.3	26.1	**27.9**	**27.4**	**29.6**	31.3	32.4	30.7
3-4 times a year	12.9	13.8	13.9	14.1	**14.7**	**15.3**	17.2	17.2	17.7
At least once a month	2.8	3.2	2.9	3.6	**3.6**	3.4	3.5	3.1	3.1
At least once a week	**0.4**	0.3	0.4	0.4	**0.5**	**0.5**	0.6	0.4	0.5
Has not visited	58.5	**56.5**	56.7	**54.0**	**53.7**	**51.1**	47.2	46.9	48.0

Notes

(1) Figures in bold indicate a significant change from 2005/06. For purpose of visit data, figures in bold indicate a significant change from 2008/09.
(2) Figures exclude people who have visited a library for the purposes of paid work or academic study
(3) * N to small to report

Source: Department for Culture, Media and Sport Taking Part Survey 2014/15 Q4
https://www.gov.uk/government/publications/taking-part-201415-quarter-4-statistical-release

9.16 Participation in voluntary activities, 2005 to 2015/16
England

Percentages

	2005	2007/08	2008/09	2009/10	2010/11	2012/13	2013/14	2014/15	2015/16
				At least once a month					
Informal volunteering[1]	37	35	35	29	29	36	35	34	34
Formal volunteering[2]	29	27	26	25	25	29	27	27	27
Any volunteering[3]	**50**	**48**	**47**	**42**	**41**	**49**	48	47	47
				At least once in last year					
Informal volunteering	68	64	62	54	55	62	64	59	60
Formal volunteering	44	43	41	40	39	44	41	42	41
Any volunteering	**76**	**73**	**71**	**66**	**65**	**72**	72	69	70

Source: Community Life Survey 2015/16

1 Informal volunteering: Giving unpaid help as an individual to people who are not relatives.

2 Formal volunteering: Giving unpaid help through groups, clubs or organisations to benefit other people or the

3 Participated in either formal or informal volunteering.

9.17 UK residents' visits to friends and relatives[1] abroad: by destination

United Kingdom

Percentages[2]

	2006	2009	2011	2012	2013	2014	2015
Irish Republic	15	14	13	10	10	11	10
France	11	11	10	10	10	11	9
Poland	6	9	9	9	9	9	10
Spain	9	8	7	8	8	8	7
Germany	6	5	5	5	5	5	5
USA	6	5	5	4	4	4	4
India	3	4	4	4	4	4	4
Italy	4	4	3	4	4	4	5
Netherlands	3	3	3	3	3	3	3
Pakistan	3	3	3	3	3	3	2
Other countries	35	36	39	39	39	37	35
All destinations (=100%) (millions)	12.0	11.6	11.6	11.8	12.3	13.3	14.7

Source: International Passenger Survey,
Office for National Statistics

1 As a proportion of all visits to friends and relatives taken abroad by residents of the UK. Excludes business trips and other miscellaneous visits.

2 Percentages may not add up to 100 per cent due to rounding.

9.18 The Internet

Internet activities, by age group, sex, 2015

Within the last 3 months   %

| | Age group | | | | | | Sex | | |
---	16-24	25-34	35-44	45-54	55-64	65+	Men	Women	All
Sending/receiving emails	82	88	88	78	72	50	79	74	76
Finding information about goods and services	69	77	82	76	73	45	73	67	69
Reading online news, newspapers or magazines	73	77	74	63	53	32	65	59	62
Social networking (eg Facebook or Twitter)	92	85	72	56	44	15	60	62	61
Internet banking	60	76	69	59	46	26	59	54	56
Consulting wikis to obtain knowledge or information	61	60	59	53	45	26	55	47	50
Looking for health-related information	46	62	63	52	47	27	43	53	49
Using services related to travel or travel related accommodation	45	53	53	53	48	27	47	44	46
Uploading content created by you to a website to be shared	55	56	54	42	32	16	42	42	42
Telephoning or making video calls over the internet via a webcam	48	53	46	30	27	15	39	36	37
Looking for information about education, training or courses	59	47	48	36	24	8	39	36	37
Downloading software (other than games software)	41	36	31	22	21	10	38	19	27
Looking for a job or sending a job application	50	35	28	24	9	1	30	22	25
Selling goods or services over the internet	23	28	32	20	15	6	23	18	20
Professional networking	15	22	24	16	9	2	21	10	15
Posting opinions on civic or political issues	19	19	17	15	10	4	16	13	14
Taking part in online consultations or voting on civic or political issues	9	9	12	9	8	4	8	8	8

Base: Adults (aged 16+) in Great Britain.   Source: Office for National Statistics

Purchases made over the internet, by age group and sex, 2015

Within the last 12 months   %

| | Age group | | | | | | Sex | | |
---	16-24	25-34	35-44	45-54	55-64	65+	Men	Women	All
Clothes or sports goods	74	69	70	57	42	19	53	56	55
Household goods (eg furniture, toys etc)	36	59	65	49	40	22	44	45	44
Travel arrangements (eg transport tickets, car hire)	34	44	46	44	37	19	40	34	37
Holiday accommodation	26	47	50	45	40	21	37	37	37
Tickets for events	39	39	48	43	34	12	36	34	35
Films, music (including downloads)	44	41	43	33	21	7	37	28	31
Books, magazines, newspapers (including e-books and downloads)	29	31	41	34	30	18	29	31	30
Food or groceries	20	31	40	27	16	7	20	26	23
Electronic equipment (including cameras)	26	27	33	24	14	9	31	16	22
Video games software, other computer software and upgrades (including downloads)	30	27	37	18	11	5	28	16	21
Share purchases, insurance policies etc	12	29	30	24	21	10	24	18	20
Telecommunication services	14	20	26	22	14	7	21	14	17
Computer hardware	18	12	16	11	10	4	19	7	12
Medicine	9	8	11	12	11	7	10	10	10
E-learning material	9	9	9	6	3	1	6	6	6

Base: Adults (aged 16+) in Great Britain.   Source: Office for National Statistics

Households with internet access, 2005 to 2015

Year	%	Year	%
GB 2005	55	2010	73
2006	57	2011	77
2007	61	2012	80
2008	65	2013	83
2009	70	2014	84
		2015	86

2015 estimates relate to January, February and April. Previous estimates relate to January to March, except 1998 which relates to April to June and 2005 which relates to May. During 2005, estimates were published at irregular intervals as Topic Based Summaries. These are no longer available on the ONS website.

9.19 Radio Listening

	Adult (15+) Population '000	Weekly Reach '000	Weekly Reach %	Average Hours per head	Average Hours per listener	Total Hours ('000's)	Share of Listening %
Quarterly Summary of Radio Listening - Survey period ending June 2016							
All Radio	54,029	48,687	90	19.3	21.5	1,044,635	100.0
All BBC Radio	54,029	35,066	65	10.1	15.6	545,585	52.2
BBC Local Radio	54,029	8,382	16	1.4	8.8	73,418	7.0
All Commercial Radio	54,029	35,570	66	8.7	13.3	472,093	45.2
All National Commercial	54,029	19,388	36	3.1	8.5	165,201	15.8
All Local Commercial (National TSA)	54,029	27,608	51	5.7	11.1	306,893	29.4
All BBC Network Radio	54,029	32,347	60	8.7	14.6	472,167	45.2
BBC Radio 1	54,029	9,455	17	1.1	6.2	59,066	5.7
BBC Radio 2	54,029	15,298	28	3.3	11.7	179,311	17.2
BBC Radio 3	54,029	2,201	4	0.2	5.9	12,964	1.2
BBC Radio 4	54,029	11,507	21	2.3	10.8	124,359	11.9
BBC Radio 4 (including 4 Extra)	54,029	11,887	22	2.5	11.6	137,412	13.2
BBC Radio 4 Extra	54,029	1,950	4	0.2	6.7	13,052	1.2
BBC Radio 5 live	54,029	5,858	11	0.8	7.0	40,968	3.9
BBC Radio 5 live (inc. sports extra)	54,029	6,181	11	0.8	7.2	44,494	4.3
BBC Radio 5 live sports extra	54,029	1,310	2	0.1	2.7	3,525	0.3
BBC 6 Music	54,029	2,266	4	0.4	9.7	21,916	2.1
1Xtra from the BBC	54,029	1,079	2	0.1	4.5	4,868	0.5
BBC Asian Network UK	54,029	676	1	0.1	5.8	3,911	0.4
BBC World Service	54,029	1,454	3	0.1	5.4	7,808	0.7

STATION SUMMARY ANALYSIS - RAJAR REPORTING PERIOD 2016 Q1
(Report 1690) All Radio, Adults Only
Quarterly Weighted Data

		Age Group of Respondent					
	Total	15-24	25-34	35-44	45-54	55-64	65+
Unw. Sample	26,112	2,859	2,979	3,699	4,802	4,691	7,082
Est. Pop'n	53,575	8,109	8,845	8,376	9,198	7,452	11,596
ALL RADIO							
Weekly Reach 000s	47,823	6,798	7,530	7,671	8,651	6,931	10,242
Weekly Reach %	89.3	83.8	85.1	91.6	94.1	93.0	88.3
Total Hours	1,006,462	95,015	129,916	152,542	200,305	166,013	262,670
Average Hours Per Head	18.8	11.7	14.7	18.2	21.8	22.3	22.7
Average Hours Per Listener	21	14.0	17.3	19.9	23.2	24.0	25.6

Source: RAJAR

this page is intentionally blank

Environment

Chapter 10

Environment

Air emissions (Table 10.2 to 10.8)

Emissions of air pollutants arise from a wide variety of sources. The National Atmospheric Emissions Inventory (NAEI) is prepared annually for the Government and the devolved administrations by AEA Energy and Environment, with the work being co-ordinated by the Department of Energy and Climate Change (DECC). Information is available for a range of point sources including the most significant polluters. However, a different approach has to be taken for diffuse sources such as transport and domestic emissions, where this type of information is not available. Estimates for these are derived from statistical information and from research on emission factors for stationary and mobile sources. Although for any given year considerable uncertainties surround the emission estimates for each pollutant, trends over time are likely to be more reliable.

UK national emission estimates are updated annually and any developments in methodology are applied retrospectively to earlier years. Adjustments in the methodology are made to accommodate new technical information and to improve international comparability.

Three different classification systems are used in the tables presented here; a National Accounts basis (Table 10.2), the format required by the Inter-governmental Panel on Climate Change (IPCC) (Table 10.3) and the National Communications (NC) categories (Tables 10.5-10.7).

The NC source categories are detailed below together with details of the main sources of these emissions:

Energy supply total: Power stations, refineries, manufacture of solid fuels and other energy industries, solid fuel transformation, exploration, production and transport of oils, offshore oil and gas – venting and flaring, power stations - FGD, coal mining and handling, and exploration, production and transport of gas.

Business total: Iron and steel – combustion, other industrial combustion, miscellaneous industrial and commercial combustion, energy recovery from waste fuels, refrigeration and air conditioning, foams, fire fighting, solvents, one components foams, and electronics, electrical insulation and sporting goods.

Transport total: Civil aviation (domestic, landing and take off, and cruise), passenger cars, light duty vehicles, buses, HGVs, mopeds & motorcycles, LPG emissions (all vehicles), other road vehicle engines, railways, railways – stationary combustion, national navigation, fishing vessels, military aircraft and shipping, and aircraft – support vehicles.

Residential total: Residential combustion, use of non aerosol consumer products, accidental vehicle fires, and aerosols and metered dose inhalers.

Agriculture total: Stationary and mobile combustion, breakdown of pesticides, enteric fermentation (cattle, sheep, goats, horses, pigs, and deer), wastes (cattle, sheep, goats, horses, pigs, poultry, and deer), manure liquid systems, manure solid storage and dry lot, other manure management, direct soil emission, and field burning of agricultural wastes.

Industrial process total: Sinter production, cement production, lime production, limestone and dolomite use, soda ash production and use, fletton bricks, ammonia production, iron and steel, nitric acid production, adipic acid production, other – chemical industry, halocarbon production, and magnesiun cover gas.

Land-use change: Forest land remaining forest land, forest land biomass burning, land converted to forest land, direct N2O emissions from N fertilisation of forest land, cropland liming, cropland remaining cropland, cropland biomass burning, land converted to cropland, N2O emissions from disturbance associated with land-use conversion to cropland, grassland biomass burning, grassland liming, grassland remaining grassland, land converted to grassland, wetlands remaining wetland, Non-CO2 emissions from drainage of soils and wetlands, settlements biomass burning, land converted to settlements, and harvested wood.

Waste management total: Landfill, waste-water handling, and waste incineration.

Atmospheric emissions on a National Accounts basis (Table 10.1)

The air and energy accounts are produced for ONS by AEA Technology plc based on data compiled for the National Atmospheric Emissions Inventory (NAEI)7 and UK Greenhouse Gas Inventory (GHGI)8. Every year a programme of development work is undertaken to optimise the methodologies employed in compiling the accounts. Assessments in previous years have indicated that a number of splits used to apportion road transport source data to more than one industry should be reviewed. The results of this review have been implemented in the 2011 UK Environmental Accounts for reference period 2009 and years back to 1990.

The industry breakdown used in the accounts has moved to using the Standard Industrial Classification 2007 (SIC 2007). Historically, the accounts were based on Environmental Accounts codes (EAcodes) based on SIC 2003. This change will allow the accounts which are broken down by industry to be more readily compared with other economic statistics. A methodology article that outlines this change in more detail was published on the ONS website in May 2011: http//www.statistics.gov.uk/cci/article.asp?id=2694. As a result while names given to the breakdown maybe similar they are not necessarily the same.

The National Accounts figures in Table 10.2 differ from those on an IPCC basis, in that they include estimated emissions from fuels purchased by UK resident households and companies either at home or abroad (including emissions from UK international shipping and aircraft operators), and exclude emissions in the UK resulting from the activities of non-residents. This allows for a more consistent comparison with key National Accounts indicators such as Gross Domestic Product (GDP).

Greenhouse gases include carbon dioxide, methane, nitrous oxide, hydro-fluorocarbons, perfluorocarbons and sulphur hexafluoride which are expressed in thousand tonnes of carbon dioxide equivalent.

Acid rain precursors include sulphur dioxide, nitrogen oxides and ammonia which are expressed as thousand tonnes of sulphur dioxide equivalent.

Road Transport Emissions (Table 10.2)

Various pollutants are emitted from road transport into the atmosphere. Table 10.2 shows emissions by pollutant generated from combustion by road vehicles.

Greenhouse gas emissions related to road transport generally increased from the early 1990s until 2007. However, since 2008 emissions have declined, which in part reflects both the economic downturn and the continuation of the trend toward more energy efficient vehicles.

Estimated total emissions of greenhouse gases on an IPCC basis (Table 10.3)

The IPCC classification is used to report greenhouse gas emissions under the UN Framework Convention on Climate Change (UNFCCC) and includes Land Use Change and all emissions from Domestic aviation and shipping, but excludes International aviation and shipping bunkers. Estimates of the relative contribution to global warming of the main greenhouse gases, or classes of gases, are presented weighted by their global warming potential.

Greenhouse gas emissions bridging table (Table 10.4)
National Accounts measure to UNFCCC measure
The air and energy accounts are produced for ONS by AEA Technology plc based on data compiled for the National Atmospheric Emissions Inventory (NAEI)7 and UK Greenhouse Gas Inventory (GHGI)8. Every year a programme of development work is undertaken to optimise the methodologies employed in compiling the accounts. Assessments in previous years have indicated that a number of splits used to apportion road transport source data to more than one industry should be reviewed. The results of this review have been implemented in the 2011 UK Environmental Accounts for reference period 2009 and years back to 1990. There are a number of formats for the reporting and recording of atmospheric emissions data, including those used by the Department of Energy and Climate Change (DECC) for reporting greenhouse gases under UNFCCC and the Kyoto Protocol, and for reporting air pollutant emissions to the UN Economic Commission for Europe (UNECE), which differ from the National Accounts consistent measure published by the Office for National Statistics (ONS).
Differences between the National Accounts measure and those for reporting under UNFCCC and the Kyoto Protocol, following the guidance of the IPCC, are shown in Table 10.4.

Emissions of carbon dioxide (Table 10.5)
Carbon dioxide is the main man-made contributor to global warming, with the highest source of emissions being energy supply.

Emissions of methane (Table 10.6)
The overall amount of methane emissions has fallen year on year since 2002, The highest source of emissions of methane for the 4th year running is Agriculture.

Emissions of nitrous oxide (Table 10.7)
Agriculture continues to be the highest source of nitrous oxide emissions for 2014.

Material Flow Account (Table 10.8)
Economy-wide material flow accounts estimate the physical flow of materials through our economy. As well as providing an aggregate overview of the annual extraction of raw materials, they also measure the physical amounts of imports and exports. This information is important in attempting to understand resource productivity. For example, they shed light on the depletion of natural resources and seek to promote a sustainable and more resource-efficient economy.

Annual rainfall (Table 10.9)

Regional rainfall is derived by the Met Office's National Climate Information Centre for the National Hydrological Monitoring Programme at the Centre for Ecology and Hydrology. These monthly area rainfalls are based initially on a subset of rain gauges (circa 350) but are updated after four to five months with figures using the majority of the UK's rain gauge network.

The regions of England shown in this table correspond to the original nine English regions of the National Rivers Authority (NRA). The NRA became part of the Environment Agency on its creation in April 1996. The figures in this table relate to the country of Wales, not the Environment Agency Welsh Region.

UK weather summary (Table 10.10)

Table 10.10 represents an initial assessment of the weather that was experienced across the UK and how it compares with the 1961 to 1990 average.

Final averages use quality controlled data from the UK climate network of observing stations. They show the Met Office's best assessment of the weather that was experienced across the UK during the years and how it compares with the 1961 to 1990 average. The columns headed 'Anom' (anomaly) show the difference from, or percentage of, the 1961 to 1990 long-term average.

Biological and chemical quality of rivers and canals (Table 10.11)

Table 10.11 shows a Summary of River Basin District Ecological and Chemical Status from 2009-2015. It looks at each river basin district in terms of Percent of surface water bodies that are at good chemical status or better and also Percent of surface water bodies are at good ecological status/potential or better. Improvements are measured in terms of the number of water bodies meeting good status

Status of Rivers and Canals in Scotland (Table 10.12)

Looks at the overall status of rivers & canals in Scotland, including water quality.

Reservoir stocks in England and Wales (Table 10.13)

Data are collected for a network of major reservoirs (or reservoir groups) in England and Wales for the National Hydrological Monitoring Programme at the Centre for Ecology and Hydrology. Figures of usable capacity are supplied by the Water PLCs and the Environment Agency at the start of each month and are aggregated to provide an index of the total reservoir stocks for England and Wales.

Water industry expenditure (Table 10.14)

So that water companies can benchmark themselves against each other, they collate and share historic information about their operations, investment and performance. Table 10.14 shows industry facts and figures for 20 water and sewerage companies.

Water pollution incidents (Table 10.15)

The Environment Agency responds to complaints and reported incidents of pollution in England and Wales. Each incident is then logged and categorised according to its severity. The category describes the impact of each incident on water, land and air. The impact of an incident on each medium is considered and reported separately. If no impact has occurred for a particular medium, the incident is reported as a category 4. Before 1999, the reporting system was used only for water pollution incidents; thus the total number of substantiated incidents was lower, as it did not include incidents not relating to the water environment.

Bathing waters (Table 10.16)

Table 10.16 shows statistics on UK bathing waters for 2015. These results summarise the compliance of coastal and inland bathing waters to the Bathing Water Directive (2006/7/EC) for the whole of the United Kingdom in 2015.

Surface and groundwater abstractions (Table 10.17)

Significant changes in the way data is collected and/or reported were made in 1991 (due to the Water Resources Act 1991) and 1999 (commission of National Abstraction Licensing Database). Figures are therefore not strictly comparable with those in previous/intervening years. From 1999, data have been stored and retrieved from one system nationally and are therefore more accurate and reliable. Some regions report licensed and actual abstracts for financial rather than calendar years. As figures represent an average for the whole year expressed as daily amounts, differences between amounts reported for financial and calendar years are small.

 Under the Water Act 2003, abstraction of less than 20 m3/day became exempt from the requirement to hold a licence as of 1 April 2005. As a result over 22,000 licences were deregulated, mainly for agricultural or private water supply purposes. However, due to the small volumes involved, this has had a minimal affect on the estimated licensed and actual abstraction totals.   The following changes have occurred in the classification of individual sources:

• Spray irrigation: this category includes small amounts of non-agricultural spray irrigation
• Mineral washing: from 1999 this was not reported as a separate category; licences for 'Mineral washing' are now contained in 'Other industry'
• Private water supply: this was shown as separate category from 1992 and includes private abstractions for domestic use and individual households
• Fish farming, cress growing, amenity ponds: includes amenity ponds, but excludes miscellaneous from 1991

Estimates of remaining recoverable oil and gas reserves (Table 10.18)

Only a small proportion of the estimated remaining recoverable reserves of oil and gas are known with any degree of certainty. The latest oil and gas data for 2014 shows that the upper range of total UK oil reserves was estimated to be around 2.4 billion tonnes, while UK gas reserves were around 1594 billion cubic metres. Of these, proven reserves of oil were 0.3 billion tonnes and proven reserves of gas were 205 billion cubic metres.

Local authority collected (Table 10.19)

Local authority collected includes household and non-household waste that is collected and disposed of by local authorities. It includes regular household collections, specific recycling collections, and special collections of bulky items, waste received at civic amenity sites, and waste collected from non-household sources that come under the control of local authorities.

Waste arisings from households (Table 10.20)

The 'waste from households' calculation was first published by Defra in May 2014. It was introduced for statistical purposes to provide a harmonised UK indicator with a comparable calculation in each of the four UK countries and to provide a consistent approach to report recycling rates at UK level on a calendar year basis under the Waste Framework Directive (2008/98/EC). The waste from household measure is a narrower measure than the 'household waste' measure which was previously used and excludes waste not considered to have come directly from households, such as recycling from street bins, parks and grounds.

Chartered Institute of Environmental Health Survey of Local Authority Noise Enforcement Activity (Table 10.21)

Every year the CIEH collects data on noise complaints made to local authorities and on the enforcement actions consequently taken by them. The data helps to inform policy and practice in environmental protection and public health and, in particular, the survey results provide the source of data for the Public Health England Outcome Indicator on noise. This, part of the Public Health Outcomes Framework, provides recognition of noise as one of the wider determinants of health.

Government revenue from environmental taxes (Table 10.22)

Environmental taxes data are based on the definition outlined in Regulation (EU) No 691/2011 on European environmental economic accounts. The European Statistical Office (Eurostat) define an environmental tax as a tax whose base is a physical unit (for example, a litre of petrol or a passenger flight) that has a proven negative impact on the environment. These taxes are designed to promote environmentally positive behaviour, reduce damaging effects on the environment and generate revenue that can potentially be used to promote further environmental protection.

In 2015, revenue from environmentally related taxes stood at £46 billion. This corresponded to 2.5% of the UK's gross domestic product (GDP). Looking over the time series as a whole, environmental taxes as a share of GDP has remained at a broadly consistent level of between 2% and 3%

10.1 Atmospheric emissions[1]
2014

	Total greenhouse gas emissions	Carbon Dioxide (CO2)	Methane (CH4)	Nitrous Oxide (N2O)	Hydrofluoro-carbons (HFCs)	Perfluoro-carbons (PFCs)	Sulphur hexafluoride (SF6)
Thousand tonnes CO2 equivalent							
Agriculture, forestry and fishing	51 462	7 690	27 407	16 319	46	–	–
Mining and quarrying	19 928	16 565	3 035	319	9	–	–
Manufacturing	91 214	87 966	261	648	1 903	278	157
Electricity, gas, steam and air conditioning supply; water supply, sewerage, waste management activities and remediation services	163 403	140 084	21 297	1 612	224	–	184
Construction	12 488	11 730	21	437	300	–	–
Wholesale and retail trade; repair of motor vehicles and motorcycles	17 797	12 345	22	157	5 273	–	–
Transport and storage; information and communication	86 588	83 913	166	885	1 624	–	–
Accommodation and food services	3 739	3 021	8	20	691	–	–
Financial and insurance activities	246	116	–	12	118	–	–
Real estate activities; professional scientific and technical activities; administration and support service activities	6 072	5 178	7	35	845	–	7
Public administration and defence; compulsory social security	5 438	5 066	6	51	197	–	118
Education	3 462	3 141	7	12	302	–	–
Human health and social work activities	5 326	4 257	9	594	465	–	1
Arts, entertainment and recreation; other service activities	2 832	2 595	5	15	217	–	–
Activities of households as employers; undifferentiated goods and services-producing activities of households for own use	236	234	1	1	–	–	–
Consumer expenditure	138 365	132 477	1 208	608	4 073	–	–
Total	608 595	516 378	53 458	21 726	16 285	278	468
Of which: emissions from road transport[2]	113 959	112 867	110	981	..	..	..

	Total acid rain precursors	Sulphur Dioxide (SO2)	Nitrogen Oxides (NOx)	Ammonia (NH3)
Thousand tonnes SO2 equivalent				
Agriculture, forestry and fishing	474	–	20	453
Mining and quarrying	53	9	45	–
Manufacturing	251	137	106	8
Electricity, gas, steam and air conditioning supply; water supply, sewerage, waste management activities and remediation services	309	122	165	23
Construction	34	–	34	–
Wholesale and retail trade; repair of motor vehicles and motorcycles	27	–	26	–
Transport and storage; information and communication	522	136	386	1
Accommodation and food services	4	–	4	–
Financial and insurance activities	1	–	1	–
Real estate activities; professional scientific and technical activities; administrative and support service activities	10	–	9	1
Public administration and defence; compulsory social security	26	4	16	5
Education	6	3	4	–
Human health and social work activities	5	–	5	–
Arts, entertainment and recreation; other service activities	12	–	4	7
Activities of households as employers; undifferentiated goods and services-producing activities of households for own use	–	–	–	–
Consumer expenditure	185	27	120	38
Total (excluding natural world)	1 918	438	944	537
Of which: emissions from road transport[2]	222	–	211	11

	Thousand tonnes						Tonnes		
	PM10[3]	PM2.5[3]	CO	NMVOC	Benzene	Butadiene	Lead	Cadmium	Mercury
Agriculture, forestry and fishing	26.72	13.18	90.40	180.02	0.12	0.04	0.42	0.04	0.02
Mining and quarrying	7.98	1.91	29.98	91.72	0.32	–	0.36	0.04	0.02
Manufacturing	28.82	20.55	711.93	258.14	1.76	0.22	53.45	1.51	2.60
Electricity, gas, steam and air conditioning supply; water supply, sewerage, waste management activities and remediation services	7.37	4.52	80.04	33.22	1.25	–	3.00	0.19	1.74
Construction	8.75	3.66	187.38	49.38	0.52	0.14	0.41	0.05	0.03
Wholesale and retail trade; repair of motor vehicles and motorcycles	2.49	1.74	22.35	37.54	0.08	0.03	1.57	0.03	0.02
Transport and storage; information and communication	38.15	35.12	106.46	29.93	2.40	0.20	3.33	1.45	0.13
Accommodation and food services	0.20	0.18	2.86	0.57	0.02	–	0.02	–	–
Financial and insurance activities	0.07	0.06	0.50	0.15	–	–	0.01	–	–
Real estate activities; professional scientific and technical activities; administration and support service activities	0.71	0.54	18.96	1.14	0.04	0.01	0.05	0.01	0.01
Public administration and defence: compulsory social security	0.84	0.74	19.74	1.94	0.12	0.02	0.12	0.02	0.01
Education	0.56	0.52	5.60	0.24	0.01	–	0.74	0.01	0.07
Human health and social work activities	0.17	0.15	3.22	0.99	0.02	–	0.01	–	–
Arts, entertainment and recreation; other service activities	0.32	0.26	5.46	1.94	0.02	–	0.09	0.01	0.56
Activities of households as employers; undifferentiated goods and services-producing activities of households for own use	–	–	49.92	1.18	0.08	0.02	–	–	–
Consumer expenditure	56.64	51.65	796.53	214.46	5.76	1.11	5.14	1.07	0.32
Total (excluding natural world)	179.78	134.79	2 131.32	902.55	12.51	1.80	68.72	4.43	5.52
Of which: emissions from road transport[2]	20.92	14.33	440.02	28.13	1.00	0.27	1.63	0.35	0.22

Source: Ricardo Energy & Environment, ONS

1 Components may not sum to totals due to rounding.
2 Includes emissions from fuel sources which are used by road vehicles (eg HGVs, LGVs, cars and motorcycles) across all industries.
3 PM10 and PM2.5 is particulate matter arising from various sources including fuel combustion, quarrying and construction, and formation of 'secondary' particles in the atmosphere from reactions involving other pollutants - sulphur dioxide, nitrogen oxides, ammonia and NMVOCs.

10.2 Road transport[1] emissions by pollutant, 2001 to 2014

UK resident basis

Weights in thousand tonnes

Pollutant	2001	2002	2003	2004	2005	2006	2007	2008	2009	2010	2011	2012	2013	2014
Greenhouse gases of which:	**118,235**	**120,545**	**120,067**	**120,808**	**121,536**	**121,849**	**123,516**	**119,488**	**115,747**	**114,939**	**113,228**	**112,512**	**112,078**	**113,959**
Carbon dioxide	116,286	118,714	118,388	119,239	120,054	120,461	122,195	118,372	114,745	113,944	112,224	111,489	111,030	112,867
Methane	535	482	425	381	349	315	281	251	188	166	149	134	119	110
Nitrous oxide	1,413	1,349	1,254	1,189	1,133	1,072	1,040	865	814	830	855	889	929	981
Acid rain precursors of which:	**535**	**504**	**474**	**452**	**429**	**412**	**393**	**366**	**304**	**286**	**266**	**248**	**233**	**222**
Sulphur dioxide	3	3	3	3	2	2	2	1	1	1	1	1	0	0
Nitrogen Oxides as NO_2	490	463	436	417	396	382	365	342	281	266	249	234	221	211
Ammonia	41	39	35	33	30	28	26	23	22	19	17	14	12	11
PM_{10}	34	33	32	32	31	30	29	28	26	26	24	23	22	21
$PM_{2.5}$	27	26	25	25	24	23	22	21	20	19	17	16	15	14
Carbon monoxide	2,637	2,372	2,142	1,934	1,710	1,512	1,303	1,165	893	764	633	563	483	440
Non Methane VOC	363	307	256	214	178	152	125	108	72	60	48	40	34	28
Benzene	10	9	8	7	7	6	5	5	3	2	2	2	1	1
1,3-Butadiene	3	3	2	2	2	1	1	1	1	1	1	0	0	0
Cadmium	0	0	0	0	0	0	0	0	0	0	0	0	0	0
Lead	2	2	2	2	2	2	2	2	2	2	2	2	2	2
Mercury	0	0	0	0	0	0	0	0	0	0	0	0	0	0

Source: Ricardo Energy and Environment, Office for National Statistics

Notes

[1] Emissions from fuel sources which are used by road vehicles across industry groups.

Greenhouse gases are made up of carbon dioxide, methane and nitrous oxide. Weight in carbon dioxide equivalent

Acid rain precursors are made of sulphur dioxide, nitrogen oxides and ammonia. Weight in sulphur dioxide equivalent

All figures are reported to 1 decimal place. Total figures are based on raw data and therefore may not sum due to rounding.

Enquiries about these data can be sent by email to: **environment.accounts@ons.gsi.gov.uk**

10.3 UK Greenhouse Gas Emissions headline results
UK 2000-2014, MtCO$_2$e

Mt CO$_2$e

	2000	2001	2002	2003	2004	2005	2006	2007	2008	2009	2010	2011	2012	2013	2014
Net CO$_2$ emissions (emissions minus removals)	554.3	563.4	546.2	557.3	557.5	554.1	551.7	542.5	528.5	477.5	495.8	452.6	472.1	463.3	422.0
Methane (CH$_4$)	114.4	109.5	107.3	102.2	97.4	92.1	88.1	84.1	78.1	71.7	66.2	63.3	60.6	55.8	53.5
Nitrous oxide (N$_2$O)	29.6	28.0	26.2	26.0	26.6	25.6	24.7	24.4	23.9	22.2	22.5	21.4	21.3	21.4	21.9
Hydrofluorocarbons (HFC)	9.8	10.8	11.3	12.8	11.9	13.1	14.0	14.5	14.9	15.7	16.6	15.1	15.7	16.0	16.3
Perfluorocarbons (PFC)	0.6	0.5	0.4	0.4	0.4	0.4	0.4	0.3	0.3	0.2	0.3	0.4	0.3	0.3	0.3
Sulphur hexafluoride (SF$_6$)	1.8	1.5	1.5	1.3	1.1	1.1	0.9	0.8	0.7	0.6	0.7	0.6	0.6	0.5	0.5
Nitrogen trifluoride (NF$_3$)	0.0	0.0	0.0	0.0	0.0	0.0	0.0	0.0	0.0	0.0	0.0	0.0	0.0	0.0	0.0
Total greenhouse gas emissions	710.6	713.7	692.9	699.9	694.9	686.3	679.7	666.6	646.3	587.8	602.1	553.4	570.5	557.3	514.4

Notes:

1. The entire time series is revised each year to take account of methodological improvements.

Uncertainty in estimates of UK Greenhouse Gas emissions

UK, Crown Dependencies and Overseas Territories 1990/2014

This table shows uncertainty estimates for the 2014 greenhouse gas inventory.

Pollutant		GWP[1]	1990 emissions[2]	2014 emissions[2]	Uncertainty[3] in 2014 emissions	Range of uncertainty in 2014 emissions		Percentage change between 2014 and 1990[2]	Range of likely % change between 2014 and 1990[3]	
			(thousand tonnes CO$_2$ equivalent)			2.5 percentile	97.5 percentile		2.5 percentile	97.5 percentile
Carbon dioxide[5]	CO$_2$	1	595,588	425,081	2%	414,648	435,444	-29%	-31%	-26%
Methane	CH$_4$	25	137,404	53,889	16%	46,467	63,265	-60%	-71%	-48%
Nitrous oxide	N$_2$O	298	49,752	22,331	29%	17,889	30,961	-54%	-69%	-34%
Hydrofluorocarbons	HFC	12 - 14,800	14,396	16,423	9%	14,914	17,945	15%	-4%	37%
Perfluorocarbons	PFC	7,390 - 17,340	1,652	278	24%	217	352	-83%	-87%	-79%
Sulphur hexafluoride	SF$_6$	22,800	1,279	468	13%	407	529	-63%	-69%	-57%
Nitrogen trifluoride	NF$_3$	17,200	0.4	0.4	47%	0.2	0.6	-4%	-51%	91%
All greenhouse gases weighted by GWP			800,070	518,472	3%	504,297	534,485	-35%	-39%	-32%

Source: Department of Energy and Climate Change (DECC)

Notes:

1. The GWP (Global Warming Potential) of a greenhouse gas measures its effectiveness in global warming over 100 years relative to carbon dioxide.

2. 1990 and 2014 estimates, and the percentage change, are presented as the central estimate from the model. These differ from the actual emissions estimates.

3. Expressed as a percentage relative to the mean value 2014 emissions. Calculated as 0.5*R/E where R is the difference between 2.5 and 97.5 percentiles and E is the mean.

4. Equivalent to a 95 per cent probability that the percentage change between 1990 and 2014 is between the two values shown. Values include uncertainties for overseas territories data.

5. CO$_2$ emissions are net emissions. Total emissions minus removals.

6. Figures include emissions for the UK, Crown Dependencies and the Overseas Territories. Uncertainties are not calculated for different geographical coverages but would be expected to be similar.

10.4 Summary Greenhouse Gas Emissions Bridging Table showing relationship of Environmental Accounts measure to UNFCCC[1] measure

United Kingdom [5][6]

Thousand tonnes CO$_2$ equivalent

	1990	1995	2000	2005	2010	2013	2014
Greenhouse gases[2] - CO$_2$, CH$_4$, N$_2$O, HFCs, PFCs SF$_6$ and NF$_3$							
Environmental Account	832,113	791,251	768,803	769,171	687,421	642,569	607,287
less							
Bunker emissions[3]	24,286	28,322	36,988	42,913	40,915	41,364	41,805
CO2 biomass[4]	2,973	5,709	6,639	11,860	20,576	26,673	30,933
Cross-boundary[5]	11,548	11,806	15,948	25,385	14,189	9,648	11,988
plus							
Land-Use, Land-Use Change and Forestry (LULUCF)[7]	5,718	3,058	511	-3,223	-5,828	-6,550	-7,430
BEIS reported (Excluding Crown Dependencies & Overseas Territories)[8]	799,023	748,472	709,739	685,791	605,912	558,334	515,131
plus							
Crown Dependencies[6] (including net emissions from LULUCF)	1,724	1,879	1,991	1,816	1,798	1,798	1,726
Overseas Territories (including net emissions from LULUCF)	1,013	995	1,115	1,280	1,282	1,369	1,368
UNFCCC reported in the UK Greenhouse Gas Inventory[8]	801,761	751,346	712,845	688,887	608,992	561,502	518,225

Source: Ricardo Energy and Environment, Department for Business, Energy & Industrial Strategy, Office for National Statistics

Notes

1 United Nations Framework Convention on Climate Change http://unfccc.int/2860.php

2 Carbon dioxide, methane, nitrous oxide, hydrofluorocarbons, perfluorocarbons, sulphur hexafluoride and nitrogen trifluoride expressed as thousand tonnes of carbon dioxide equivalent

3 Bunker emissions include IPCC memo items International Aviation and International Shipping

4 Emissions arising from wood, straw, biogases and poultry litter combustion for energy production

5 Emissions generated by UK households and business transport and travel abroad, net of emissions generated by non-residents travel and transport in the UK

6 Emissions of Crown dependencies; Guernsey, Jersey, Isle of Man.

7 Emissions from deforestation, soils and changes in forest and other woody biomass.

8 https://www.gov.uk/government/statistics/final-uk-greenhouse-gas-emissions-national-statistics-1990-2015

All figures are reported to 2 decimal places. Total figures are based on raw data and therefore may not sum due to rounding.

10.5 Estimated emissions of carbon dioxide by source, 1999 - 2014

UK 1999-2014, MtCO$_2$e

Mt CO$_2$e

Sector	1999	2000	2001	2002	2003	2004	2005	2006	2007	2008	2009	2010	2011	2012	2013	2014
(a) By source																
Energy Supply	192.6	203.3	213.9	211.9	219.4	217.4	218.6	224.2	219.1	212.8	189.8	196.7	182.3	193.2	180.8	155.6
Business	110.2	109.4	107.2	96.3	98.9	98.0	97.0	94.1	92.1	89.2	75.8	78.4	72.7	72.8	75.0	72.4
Transport	125.5	124.5	124.5	127.1	126.7	127.9	128.8	129.4	130.8	125.3	120.5	119.0	117.2	116.6	115.4	116.6
Public	12.8	12.0	12.2	10.3	10.3	11.2	11.1	10.1	9.4	10.7	9.2	9.7	9.3	9.2	9.4	8.1
Residential	85.4	85.6	87.9	84.5	85.3	86.8	82.5	79.9	76.4	78.2	74.9	84.5	64.5	74.0	74.1	61.1
Agriculture	6.2	5.7	5.8	5.8	5.9	5.7	5.6	5.4	5.3	4.9	5.2	5.2	5.4	5.2	5.3	5.3
Industrial Process	17.6	17.1	15.7	14.8	15.7	16.1	16.4	15.5	16.8	15.1	10.0	10.6	10.1	9.9	12.2	12.3
Land Use Change	-3.6	-4.0	-4.4	-5.1	-5.3	-6.0	-6.4	-7.1	-7.7	-8.1	-8.2	-8.6	-9.1	-9.2	-9.4	-9.7
Waste Management	0.5	0.5	0.5	0.5	0.5	0.5	0.4	0.3	0.3	0.3	0.3	0.3	0.3	0.3	0.3	0.3
Grand Total	547.1	554.3	563.4	546.2	557.3	557.5	554.1	551.7	542.5	528.5	477.5	495.8	452.6	472.1	463.3	422.0

Source: Department of Energy and Climate Change

Notes:

1. The entire time series is revised each year to take account of methodological improvements.

10.6 Estimated emissions of methane (CH_4) by source, 2002 - 2014
UK 2002-2014, $MtCO_2e$

Mt CO_2e

Sector	2002	2003	2004	2005	2006	2007	2008	2009	2010	2011	2012	2013	2014
(a) By source													
Energy Supply	14.6	13.1	12.8	11.1	10.3	9.8	9.4	9.3	9.0	8.8	8.7	7.6	7.3
Business	0.1	0.1	0.1	0.1	0.1	0.1	0.1	0.1	0.1	0.1	0.1	0.1	0.1
Transport	0.5	0.4	0.4	0.4	0.3	0.3	0.3	0.2	0.2	0.2	0.1	0.1	0.1
Public	0.0	0.0	0.0	0.0	0.0	0.0	0.0	0.0	0.0	0.0	0.0	0.0	0.0
Residential	0.8	0.7	0.7	0.6	0.6	0.6	0.7	0.7	0.8	0.7	0.8	0.9	0.8
Agriculture	28.6	28.8	29.1	28.7	28.5	28.1	27.5	27.1	27.2	27.1	27.0	27.0	27.4
Industrial Process	0.1	0.2	0.1	0.1	0.1	0.1	0.1	0.1	0.1	0.1	0.1	0.1	0.1
Land Use Change	0.0	0.1	0.0	0.0	0.0	0.0	0.0	0.0	0.0	0.0	0.1	0.0	0.0
Waste Management	62.5	58.8	54.2	51.0	48.1	44.9	40.0	34.1	28.7	26.2	23.6	19.9	17.6
Grand Total	107.3	102.2	97.4	92.1	88.1	84.1	78.1	71.7	66.2	63.3	60.6	55.8	53.5

Source: Department of Energy and Climate Change

Notes:
1. The entire time series is revised each year to take account of methodological improvements.

The geographical coverage for these statistics is UK only. This is a change from the 2013 statistics, where the main geographical coverage was the UK ad its Crown Dependencies. The publication of emissions of Methane in thousands of tonnes of gas has also ceased. it is now shown in Mt CO2e.

10.7 Estimated emissions of nitrous oxide (N_2O) by source, 2000 - 2014
UK 2000-2014, $MtCO_2e$

Mt CO_2e

Sector	2001	2002	2003	2004	2005	2006	2007	2008	2009	2010	2011	2012	2013	2014
(a) By source														
Energy Supply	1.2	1.3	1.2	1.2	1.2	1.2	1.1	1.1	1.0	1.0	1.0	1.2	1.1	1.0
Business	1.6	1.6	1.6	1.6	1.6	1.6	1.6	1.6	1.4	1.4	1.3	1.4	1.4	1.5
Transport	1.5	1.5	1.4	1.3	1.3	1.2	1.2	1.0	0.9	1.0	1.0	1.0	1.0	1.1
Public	0.0	0.0	0.0	0.0	0.0	0.0	0.0	0.0	0.0	0.0	0.0	0.0	0.0	0.0
Residential	0.2	0.2	0.2	0.1	0.1	0.1	0.1	0.1	0.1	0.2	0.1	0.2	0.2	0.2
Agriculture	17.2	17.4	17.2	16.9	16.6	16.3	15.8	15.7	15.7	15.9	15.8	15.6	15.8	16.3
Industrial Process	4.7	2.7	2.9	3.8	3.1	2.5	3.0	2.8	1.4	1.5	0.6	0.3	0.3	0.3
Land Use Change	1.0	1.0	1.0	0.9	0.9	0.8	0.8	0.8	0.8	0.8	0.8	0.8	0.7	0.7
Waste Management	0.7	0.7	0.6	0.7	0.7	0.8	0.8	0.8	0.8	0.9	0.9	0.9	0.9	0.9
Grand Total	28.0	26.2	26.0	26.6	25.6	24.7	24.4	23.9	22.2	22.5	21.4	21.3	21.4	21.9

Source: Department of Energy and Climate Change

Notes:
1. The entire time series is revised each year to take account of methodological improvements.

10.8 Material flows account for the United Kingdom 2002 to 2014

1,000 Metric tonnes

Domestic extraction	2002	2003	2004	2005	2006	2007	2008	2009	2010	2011	2012	2013	2014
Biomass	**140,774**	**138,305**	**139,314**	**138,422**	**134,642**	**129,458**	**138,403**	**134,338**	**131,214**	**136,158**	**128,581**	**132,368**	**135,593**
Crops	44,746	42,341	42,747	41,649	39,698	37,156	43,710	42,359	39,777	42,745	37,350	40,163	45,917
Crop residues (used), fodder crops and grazed biomass	90,682	90,546	90,997	91,064	89,357	86,371	89,139	86,296	85,095	86,906	84,636	85,202	89,676
Wood	4,617	4,775	4,915	5,039	4,963	5,311	4,958	5,092	5,730	5,907	5,963	6,371	:
Wild fish catch and aquatic plants/animals	729	644	655	670	625	620	596	591	613	601	632	632	:
Metal ores (gross ores)	**6**	**6**	**5**	**3**	**3**	**3**	**3**	**4**	**4**	**4**	**1**	**1**	**1**
Iron	0	1	1	0	0	0	0	0	0	0	0	0	0
Non-ferrous metal	6	6	4	3	3	3	3	4	4	4	1	1	1
Non-metallic minerals	**293,164**	**287,885**	**300,018**	**290,601**	**291,300**	**295,217**	**261,116**	**210,290**	**204,761**	**207,706**	**192,183**	**196,181**	**211,206**
Limestone and gypsum	82,388	80,635	83,334	79,296	81,928	85,191	75,345	61,311	58,185	59,300	56,000	58,100	67,500
Clays and kaolin	13,925	14,224	14,504	14,221	13,437	13,135	11,014	7,226	8,084	8,536	7,491	8,419	8,758
Sand and gravel	167,856	164,899	174,227	170,603	169,275	173,861	155,996	126,935	122,202	123,756	112,228	113,938	121,275
Other	28,995	28,127	27,953	26,481	26,660	23,030	18,762	14,818	16,290	16,114	16,464	15,724	13,673
Fossil energy materials/carriers	**248,955**	**237,442**	**216,568**	**193,416**	**175,259**	**165,428**	**159,059**	**145,689**	**138,520**	**115,841**	**100,362**	**90,402**	**88,260**
Coal and other solid energy materials/carriers	30,722	29,791	26,046	21,631	19,717	17,673	18,626	18,542	19,112	19,173	17,395	13,712	12,246
Crude oil, condensate and natural gas liquids	115,944	106,073	95,374	84,721	76,579	76,575	71,665	68,198	62,962	51,972	44,560	40,646	39,928
Natural gas	102,289	101,578	95,148	87,063	78,964	71,179	68,767	58,950	56,446	44,696	38,407	36,044	36,086
Total domestic extraction	**682,899**	**663,638**	**655,905**	**622,442**	**601,205**	**590,106**	**558,582**	**490,321**	**474,499**	**459,708**	**421,127**	**418,952**	**435,060**

Sources: Department for Environment, Food and Rural Affairs; Food and Agriculture Organization of the United Nations; Eurostat; Kentish Cobnuts Association; British Geological Survey

Notes

: denotes unavailable data.

All figures are reported to 1 decimal place. Total figures are based on raw data and therefore may not sum due to rounding.

Enquiries about these data can be sent by email to: **environment.accounts@ons.gsi.gov.uk**

1,000 Metric tonnes

Imports	2002	2003	2004	2005	2006	2007	2008	2009	2010	2011	2012	2013	2014
Biomass and biomass products	50,184	52,631	53,671	53,935	53,710	53,867	52,312	49,423	51,425	50,468	52,387	58,477	59,603
Metal ores and concentrates, raw and processed	41,035	42,348	45,964	43,623	45,291	47,862	42,605	26,955	32,936	33,476	33,856	37,972	40,595
Non-metallic minerals, raw and processed	17,013	16,240	16,989	16,752	16,454	17,160	16,337	12,684	15,078	15,904	13,904	14,505	18,308
Fossil energy materials/carriers, raw and processed	105,309	113,301	138,367	148,165	159,123	159,103	152,461	148,598	148,014	165,442	180,033	175,383	161,576
Other products	15,170	15,793	18,258	16,915	17,167	17,038	16,469	14,858	16,541	15,611	15,102	15,939	16,631
Waste imported for final treatment and disposal	4	2	1	1	15	10	13	19	22	5	5	30	17
Total imports	**228,715**	**240,314**	**273,252**	**279,392**	**291,759**	**295,039**	**280,197**	**252,537**	**264,016**	**280,906**	**295,287**	**302,306**	**296,729**

1,000 Metric tonnes

Exports	2002	2003	2004	2005	2006	2007	2008	2009	2010	2011	2012	2013	2014
Biomass and biomass products	15,686	20,289	19,118	20,005	20,704	21,374	21,543	20,159	22,413	21,950	22,103	21,239	21,978
Metal ores and concentrates, raw and processed	22,155	24,952	26,677	26,355	27,216	27,335	27,171	20,704	23,502	24,502	24,005	25,316	25,712
Non-metallic minerals, raw and processed	20,445	20,312	21,928	22,634	23,591	22,840	21,170	17,094	16,681	17,034	14,444	15,119	14,436
Fossil energy materials/carriers, raw and processed	129,791	114,128	108,739	98,716	93,760	90,402	89,444	87,836	95,693	92,063	88,728	84,759	82,491
Other products	8,596	8,934	8,685	9,423	8,504	9,539	8,754	7,721	7,716	7,739	7,705	7,693	7,855
Waste exported for final treatment and disposal	5	2	4	2	3	0	1	3	3	4	5	124	509
Total exports	**196,678**	**188,616**	**185,150**	**177,134**	**173,778**	**171,491**	**168,083**	**153,518**	**166,008**	**163,291**	**156,990**	**154,250**	**152,980**

Source: HM Revenue & Customs

Notes

All figures are reported to 1 decimal place. Total figures are based on raw data and therefore may not sum due to rounding.

Enquiries about these data can be sent by email to: **environment.accounts@ons.gsi.gov.uk**

10.8 Material flows account for the United Kingdom 2002 to 2014

1,000 Metric tonnes

Indicators	2002	2003	2004	2005	2006	2007	2008	2009	2010	2011	2012	2013	2014
Domestic material consumption (domestic extraction plus imports minus exports)[1]	722,082	723,006	751,956	732,639	724,007	718,850	675,064	592,945	577,039	582,227	563,288	569,997	563,030
Biomass	176,882	172,282	176,108	174,133	169,681	163,660	171,131	165,599	162,721	166,932	160,979	172,066	172,531
Metal ores	19,060	17,569	19,541	17,450	18,298	20,747	15,616	6,331	9,585	9,100	9,983	12,840	15,106
Non-metallic minerals	292,394	286,530	298,884	287,661	287,608	292,593	259,250	208,393	206,320	209,409	193,880	198,085	205,426
Fossil fuels	233,746	246,624	257,423	253,396	248,420	241,850	229,066	212,622	198,414	196,786	198,445	187,005	169,967
Physical trade balance (imports minus exports)	32,037	51,698	88,101	102,258	117,981	123,548	112,114	99,019	98,009	117,615	138,297	148,056	143,750
Direct material input (domestic extraction plus imports)	911,613	903,952	929,157	901,834	892,964	885,145	838,778	742,858	738,515	740,614	716,414	721,258	731,789

Sources: Office for National Statistics

Notes

1. 'Other' and 'waste for final treatment and disposal' imports and exports have been allocated to categories within Domestic Material Consumption using the same method that is used by Eurostat: http://ec.europa.eu/eurostat/statistics-explained/images/7/75/Raw_material_equivalents_2015.xlsx.

Latest estimates (2013) for raw material consumption are reported in another publication: 'How much material is the UK consuming?'
http://www.ons.gov.uk/economy/environmentalaccounts/articles/ukenvironmentalaccountshowmuchmaterialistheukconsuming/ukenvironmentalaccountshowmuchmaterialistheukconsuming

All figures are reported to 1 decimal place. Total figures are based on raw data and therefore may not sum due to rounding.

Metric tonnes

Per capita (person)	2002	2003	2004	2005	2006	2007	2008	2009	2010	2011	2012	2013	2014
Mid-year population estimates (persons)	59,365,677	59,636,662	59,950,364	60,413,276	60,827,067	61,319,075	61,823,772	62,260,486	62,759,456	63,285,145	63,705,030	64,105,654	64,596,752
Domestic extraction	11.5	11.1	10.9	10.3	9.9	9.6	9.0	7.9	7.6	7.3	6.6	6.5	6.7
Total imports	3.9	4.0	4.6	4.6	4.8	4.8	4.5	4.1	4.2	4.4	4.6	4.7	4.6
Total exports	3.3	3.2	3.1	2.9	2.9	2.8	2.7	2.5	2.6	2.6	2.5	2.4	2.4
Domestic material consumption (DMC)	12.2	12.1	12.5	12.1	11.9	11.7	10.9	9.5	9.2	9.2	8.8	8.9	8.7
Direct material input (DMI)	15.4	15.2	15.5	14.9	14.7	14.4	13.6	11.9	11.8	11.7	11.2	11.3	11.3

Sources: Office for National Statistics

Notes
Mid-year population estimates available here:
: denotes unavailable data.
All figures are reported to 1 decimal place. Total figures are based on raw data and therefore may not sum due to rounding.

10.9 Annual rainfall: by region

United Kingdom

Millimetres and percentages

Region		1971 - 2000[2] rainfall average (= 100%) millimetres	2001	2002	2003	2004	2005	2006	2007	2008	2009	2010	2011	2012	2013	2014	2015
United Kingdom	**JSJB**	1084	97	118	83	112	100	109	111	120	112	88	108	123	101	120	117
North West	**JSJC**	1177	94	121	85	116	96	114	110	126	113	84	116	136	97	111	128
Northumbria	**JSJD**	831	106	124	80	120	111	101	105	135	116	105	104	144	106	110	124
Severn Trent[1]	**JSJE**	759	104	119	81	110	92	103	123	121	103	84	74	139	100	121	99
Yorkshire	**JSJF**	814	100	126	82	114	96	110	115	130	105	91	89	143	91	114	115
Anglian	**JSJG**	603	124	118	86	115	89	102	118	116	99	97	73	138	93	122	95
Thames	**JSLK**	700	116	128	81	103	79	106	118	115	104	87	79	134	101	130	93
Southern	**JSLL**	782	114	129	85	97	79	101	106	108	109	94	81	130	107	137	100
Wessex	**JSLM**	866	100	132	83	98	89	100	113	116	107	80	84	140	101	128	95
South West	**JSLN**	1208	92	121	78	99	90	92	110	112	110	83	86	133	103	115	104
England	**JSLO**	819	105	123	83	109	91	103	114	120	107	89	87	137	99	120	106
Wales	**JSLP**	1373	98	119	83	108	95	107	108	121	109	82	94	124	98	113	114
Scotland	**JSLQ**	1440	91	112	84	117	110	114	109	120	117	87	131	112	102	122	129
Northern Ireland	**JSLR**	1111	81	127	84	98	96	104	99	114	114	94	115	107	103	117	119

Sources: Met Office; National Hydrological Monitoring Programme, Centre for Ecology and Hydrology

[1] The regions of England shown in this table correspond to the original nine English regions of the National Rivers Authority (NRA); the NRA became part of the Environment Agency upon its creation in April 1996. The exception to this is the Severn Trent region, part of which (the upper Severn) lies in Wales.

[2] 1971-2000 averages have been derived using arithmetic averages of Met Office areal rainfall.

10.10 UK Annual Weather Summary

	Max Temp		Min Temp		Mean Temp		Sunshine		Rainfall	
	Actual (degrees celsius)	Anomaly (degrees celsius)	Actual (degrees celsius)	Anomaly (degrees celsius)	Actual (degrees celsius)	Anomaly (degrees celsius)	Actual (hours/ day)	Anomaly (%)	Actual (mm)	Anomaly (%)
	WLRL	WLRM	WLRO	WLRP	WLRR	WLRS	WLRX	WLRY	WLSH	WLSI
1990	13.1	1.2	5.8	0.9	9.4	1.1	1490.7	111.4	1172.8	106.7
1991	12.1	0.3	5.1	0.2	8.6	0.3	1302.0	97.3	998.2	90.8
1992	12.3	0.4	5.2	0.4	8.7	0.4	1290.8	96.5	1186.8	107.9
1993	11.8	-0.1	5.0	0.1	8.4	0.0	1218.6	91.1	1121.1	102.0
1994	12.4	0.5	5.5	0.6	8.9	0.6	1366.9	102.2	1184.7	107.7
1995	13.0	1.1	5.4	0.6	9.2	0.9	1588.5	118.7	1023.7	93.1
1996	11.7	-0.1	4.7	-0.1	8.2	-0.2	1403.5	104.9	916.6	83.4
1997	13.1	1.3	5.8	1.0	9.4	1.1	1430.3	106.9	1024.0	93.1
1998	12.6	0.8	5.8	1.0	9.1	0.8	1268.4	94.8	1265.1	115.1
1999	13.0	1.1	5.9	1.0	9.4	1.1	1419.4	106.1	1239.1	112.5
2000	12.7	0.8	5.6	0.8	9.1	0.8	1367.5	102.2	1337.3	121.5
2001	12.4	0.6	5.3	0.5	8.8	0.5	1411.9	105.5	1052.8	95.5
2002	13.0	1.1	6.0	1.2	9.5	1.2	1304.0	97.5	1283.7	116.5
2003	13.5	1.6	5.6	0.7	9.5	1.2	1587.4	118.7	904.2	82.0
2004	13.0	1.2	6.0	1.2	9.5	1.2	1361.4	101.8	1210.1	110.1
2005	13.1	1.2	5.9	1.1	9.5	1.1	1399.2	104.6	1083.0	98.4
2006	13.4	1.5	6.1	1.3	9.7	1.4	1495.9	111.8	1175.9	106.8
2007	13.3	1.4	6.0	1.1	9.6	1.3	1450.7	108.4	1197.1	108.8
2008	12.7	0.8	5.5	0.6	9.1	0.7	1388.8	103.8	1295.0	117.7
2009	12.8	1.0	5.6	0.7	9.2	0.9	1467.4	109.7	1213.3	110.2
2010	11.7	-0.1	4.2	-0.6	8.0	-0.4	1456.0	108.8	950.5	86.4
2011	13.5	1.5	6.0	1.2	9.6	1.3	1406.2	105.0	1172.5	107
2012	12.4	0.5	5.2	0.4	8.8	0.4	1340.5	100	1334.8	121
2013	12.4	0.5	5.2	0.4	8.8	0.5	1421.1	106	1091	99
2014	13.5	1.7	6.3	1.5	9.9	1.6	1426.6	107	1300.5	118
2015	12.9	1.1	5.5	0.7	9.2	0.9	1456.7	109	1272.4	116

Source: Met Office

10.11 Summary of River Basin District Ecological and Chemical Status 2009-2015

River Basin District	Percent of surface water bodies are at good chemical status or better						
	2009	2010	2011	2012	2013	2014	2015
Solway Tweed	50	89	89	88	91	91	95
Northumbria	50	68	72	68	70	75	66
Humber	77	79	83	77	76	77	76
Anglian	85	89	92	87	84	83	84
Thames	75	76	79	74	72	70	70
South East	88	91	93	88	88	87	80
South West	77	80	83	84	79	79	83
Severn	78	83	88	82	82	83	83
Dee	75	92	92	87	82	67	100
North West	70	75	72	71	74	76	79

River Basin District	Percent of surface water bodies are at good ecological status/potential or better						
	2009	2010	2011	2012	2013	2014	2015
Solway Tweed	44	43	45	48	41	41	42
Northumbria	43	41	43	40	42	38	41
Humber	18	16	17	18	17	16	16
Anglian	18	19	18	18	17	13	13
Thames	23	22	22	18	19	14	14
South East	19	15	16	15	15	13	14
South West	33	31	34	32	31	27	25
Severn	29	30	30	30	29	26	27
Dee	28	26	30	30	25	15	15
North West	30	31	30	29	30	28	28

Source: Environment Agency

% of English water bodies only

Improvements measured in terms of the number of water bodies meeting good status

10.12 Overall status of rivers & canals in Scotland, 2014

	High	Max EP	Good	Good EP	Moderate	Moderate EP	Poor	Poor Ep	Bad	Bad EP
No. of river water bodies	166	0	999	133	465	116	321	79	76	52
Length of river water bodies (km)	1434	0	9832	1308	5647	1214	3472	862	891	454
% of length of river water bodies	5.7%	0.0%	39.2%	5.2%	22.5%	4.8%	13.8%	3.4%	3.5%	1.8%

Water Quality 2014

	High	Good	Moderate	Poor	bad
No. of river water bodies	827	1123	396	49	12
Length of river water bodies (km)	8331.6	11781.6	4370.7	505.7	122.8
% of length of river water bodies	33.2%	46.9%	17.4%	2.0%	0.5%

Source: Scottish Environment Protection Agency

10.13 Monthly reservoir stocks for England & Wales[1]

Percentages

		2003	2004	2005	2006	2007	2008	2009	2010	2011	2012	2013	2014	2015
January	JTAS	95.0	93.8	92.3	88.7	93.7	95.7	95.3	92.4	89.8	90.4	96.7	98.2	94.8
February	JTAT	92.1	92.1	92.1	91.2	96.7	95.6	93.4	91.8	93.7	92.0	93.8	98.1	95.5
March	JTAU	92.3	94.4	93.6	96.2	95.2	97.3	94.5	94.1	92.2	89.2	92.0	96.4	95.6
April	JTAV	88.6	94.7	95.0	93.4	91.9	95.1	92.0	91.9	88.9	94.0	94.5	95.4	93.1
May	JTAW	93.1	90.5	93.0	94.4	91.1	92.6	93.3	86.2	87.4	93.6	94.5	96.1	93.9
June	JTAX	87.0	84.8	85.6	88.4	94.4	90.6	88.6	79.0	86.7	97.8	90.8	91.3	88.7
July	JTAY	81.1	78.5	77.9	77.2	93.5	92.0	91.1	77.3	84.7	96.8	83.7	82.9	84.1
August	JTAZ	69.9	82.4	71.5	70.7	88.3	92.5	89.7	75.5	79.9	96.0	82.2	81.5	82.8
September	JTBA	60.4	84.2	67.4	67.8	86.1	90.9	84.0	81.1	81.0	95.3	77.7	73.6	79.7
October	JTBB	53.0	87.5	77.2	80.0	81.2	93.8	82.3	82.0	80.0	94.3	87.6	79.8	74.6
November	JTBC	60.9	86.2	83.8	89.8	82.4	93.1	93.0	86.9	79.7	95.8	88.3	83.6	89.4
December	JTBD	79.9	91.2	85.9	92.2	89.8	92.4	90.6	84.3	88.6	97.6	95.4	92.0	95.3

1 Reservoir stocks are the percentage of useable capacity based on a representative
 selection of reservoirs; the percentages relate to the end of each month.

Sources: Water PLCs;

Environment Agency;

National Hydrological Monitoring Programme, Centre for Ecology and Hydrology: 01491 838800

10.14a Current cost profit and loss account for the 12 months ended 31 March 2015 (appointed business only)

Description		Anglian	Welsh	Northumbrian	Severn Trent (WaSC)	Southern	South West	Thames	United Utilities	Wessex	Yorkshire	Affinity (WoC)	Bournemouth	Bristol	Dee Valley	Portsmouth	South East	South Staffs / Cambridge	Sutton and East Surrey	Northern Ireland (Total only)	Scottish
Water																					
Turnover																					
Unmeasured	- household	113.854	163.100	220.500	350.900	30.800	58.300	508.900	373.300	69.500	208.200	127.900	11.025	59.600	8.634	21.018	69.650	58.700	29.643		
	- non-household	0.538	2.500	2.600	2.800	1.200	1.400	7.600	4.400	2.500	1.200	2.592	0.454	1.200	0.111	0.304	1.605	1.393	0.252		
Measured	- household	250.634	63.800	126.000	208.500	119.200	114.000	218.300	186.500	68.100	133.700	102.336	18.229	38.700	8.106	6.331	93.328	35.030	19.607		
	- non-household	86.271	71.600	66.900	137.500	30.900	48.600	178.700	137.400	43.000	84.000	56.552	9.426	23.500	7.518	8.820	40.462	25.468	8.898		
Trade effluent		0.000	0.000	0.000	0.000	0.000	0.000	0.000	0.000	0.000	0.000	0.000	0.000	0.000	0.000	0.000	0.000	0.000	0.000		
Bulk supplies/inter company payments		6.499	9.800	0.800	5.300	2.600	8.100	3.400	0.700	0.400	0.400	3.040	0.010	0.600	0.004	0.226	0.003	0.461	0.038		
Other third party services (incl non-potable water)		12.562	21.800	9.300	37.300	6.600	5.200	2.700	6.200	0.100	0.200	1.104	0.197	1.200	0.096	1.407	0.000	0.808	1.123		
Other sources		36.608	8.400	28.400	1.700	7.400	0.000	42.900	59.800	15.100	36.700	0.000	5.507	6.200	0.000	0.095	4.918	0.513	1.240		
Total turnover		506.966	341.100	454.500	744.000	198.700	235.600	962.500	768.300	198.700	464.400	293.524	44.848	131.000	24.469	38.201	209.966	122.373	60.801		
Current cost operating costs - wholesale		-329.232	-233.100	-276.000	-486.700	-147.600	-127.900	-610.900	-448.500	-124.100	-287.800	-184.015	-29.021	-95.000	-16.430	-28.096	-127.929	-76.853	-40.321		
Current cost operating costs - retail		-37.948	-31.700	-43.500	-65.200	-30.400	-17.800	-111.800	-84.000	-15.700	-29.300	-36.295	-4.698	-11.300	-4.069	-5.255	-18.224	-18.308	-6.635		
Operating income		-0.154	0.000	-0.200	1.700	-2.400	0.500	8.000	-1.200	-0.200	1.100	-0.979	0.000	-0.200	0.000	0.003	-0.001	0.224	13.845		
Working capital adjustment		-0.299	0.000	-0.200	-0.200	0.100	-0.100	1.200	0.000	-0.100	0.400	0.192	-0.032	0.100	0.015	0.046	0.076	0.114	0.056		
Current cost operating profit		139.333	76.300	134.600	193.600	18.400	90.300	249.000	234.600	58.600	148.800	72.427	11.097	24.600	3.985	4.899	63.888	27.551	13.901		
Other income		0.000	0.000	0.000	0.000	0.000	0.000	0.900	0.000	0.000	0.000	0.000	0.115	0.300	0.054	0.000	0.658	0.000	0.892		
Net Interest		0.000	-75.900	0.000	0.000	0.000	0.000	0.000	0.000	0.000	0.000	-35.664	-4.970	-11.600	-2.557	-2.809	-47.997	-11.498	-9.873		
Financing adjustment		0.000	6.200	0.000	0.000	0.000	0.000	0.000	0.000	0.000	0.000	7.714	0.781	1.900	-0.029	0.021	6.759	0.097	0.265		
Current cost profit before taxation		139.333	6.600	134.600	193.600	18.400	90.300	249.900	234.600	58.600	148.800	44.477	7.023	15.200	1.453	2.111	23.308	16.150	5.185		
Net revenue movement out of tariff basket		0.698	0.200	0.000	-0.200	0.000	-0.400	1.200	0.500	0.100	0.100	-0.160	0.028	-0.100	0.000	-0.002	0.147	0.412	0.002		
Back-billing amount identified		0.000	0.000	0.000	0.000	0.000	0.000	4.100	0.000	0.000	0.200	3.540	0.000	0.000	0.000	0.000	0.000	0.127	0.000		
Sewerage																					
Turnover																					
Unmeasured	- household	185.523	226.000	161.700	375.900	174.400	70.400	523.900	408.000	136.600	249.300	0.000	0.000	0.000	0.000	0.000	0.000	0.000	0.000		
	- non-household	1.279	3.200	4.100	8.200	5.600	2.200	8.100	6.300	3.200	2.300	0.000	0.000	0.000	0.000	0.000	0.000	0.000	0.000		
Measured	- household	405.678	99.100	59.700	195.700	332.200	147.700	295.800	217.000	122.600	164.800	0.000	0.000	0.000	0.000	0.000	0.000	0.000	0.000		
	- non-household	82.924	60.700	61.000	181.500	81.000	44.700	150.300	252.800	52.300	78.100	0.000	0.000	0.000	0.000	0.000	0.000	0.000	0.000		
Trade effluent		8.184	9.700	3.000	13.200	7.700	4.400	8.200	22.400	4.300	11.900	0.000	0.000	0.000	0.000	0.000	0.000	0.000	0.000		
Bulk supplies/inter company payments		1.817	10.000	0.000	0.000	0.000	9.600	0.100	0.100	0.100	0.400	0.000	0.000	0.000	0.000	0.000	0.000	0.000	0.000		
Other third party services (incl non-potable water)		0.000	1.100	0.200	37.700	3.300	3.200	2.000	0.000	1.300	0.900	0.000	0.000	0.000	0.000	0.000	0.000	0.000	0.000		
Other sources		34.475	0.000	17.300	4.700	19.000	0.000	47.800	50.700	13.800	33.100	0.000	0.000	0.000	0.000	0.000	0.000	0.000	0.000		
Total turnover		719.880	409.800	307.000	816.900	623.200	282.200	1,036.100	957.300	334.200	540.000	0.000	0.000	0.000	0.000	0.000	0.000	0.000	0.000		
Current cost operating costs - wholesale		-475.520	-224.500	-183.200	-480.100	-365.600	-174.400	-652.900	-535.400	-175.300	-365.000	0.000	0.000	0.000	0.000	0.000	0.000	0.000	0.000		
Current cost operating costs - retail		-46.042	38.100	-17.100	-64.400	-54.200	-18.000	-84.100	-93.900	-16.300	-34.100	0.000	0.000	0.000	0.000	0.000	0.000	0.000	0.000		
Operating income		-0.126	0.000	0.700	1.700	-4.200	0.800	8.600	-4.800	-0.700	0.700	0.000	0.000	0.000	0.000	0.000	0.000	0.000	0.000		
Working capital adjustment		-0.299	0.100	-0.100	-0.200	0.500	-0.100	1.300	0.000	-0.400	0.500	0.000	0.000	0.000	0.000	0.000	0.000	0.000	0.000		
Current cost operating profit		197.893	147.300	107.300	273.900	199.700	90.500	309.000	323.200	141.500	142.500	0.000	0.000	0.000	0.000	0.000	0.000	0.000	0.000		
Other income		0.000	0.000	0.000	0.000	0.000	0.000	1.200	0.000	0.000	0.000	0.000	0.000	0.000	0.000	0.000	0.000	0.000	0.000		
Net Interest		0.000	-75.300	0.000	0.000	0.000	0.000	0.000	0.000	0.000	0.000	0.000	0.000	0.000	0.000	0.000	0.000	0.000	0.000		
Financing adjustment		0.000	6.200	0.000	0.000	0.000	0.000	0.000	0.000	0.000	0.000	0.000	0.000	0.000	0.000	0.000	0.000	0.000	0.000		
Current cost profit before taxation		197.893	78.200	107.300	273.900	199.700	90.500	310.200	323.200	141.500	142.500	0.000	0.000	0.000	0.000	0.000	0.000	0.000	0.000		
Net revenue movement out of tariff basket		0.743	0.000	0.200	-0.300	-1.000	-0.200	2.300	-0.300	0.000	-0.600	0.000	0.000	0.000	0.000	0.000	0.000	0.000	0.000		
Back-billing amount identified		0.000	0.000	0.000	0.000	0.000	0.000	2.900	0.000	0.000	0.200	0.000	0.000	0.000	0.000	0.000	0.000	0.000	0.000		
Total																					
Turnover																					
Unmeasured	- household	299.377	389.100	382.200	726.800	205.200	128.700	1,032.800	781.300	206.100	457.500	127.900	11.025	59.600	8.634	21.018	69.650	58.700	29.643		
	- non-household	1.817	5.700	6.700	11.000	6.800	3.600	15.700	10.700	5.700	3.500	2.592	0.454	1.200	0.111	0.304	1.605	1.393	0.252		
Measured	- household	656.312	162.900	185.700	404.200	451.400	261.700	514.100	403.500	190.700	298.500	102.336	18.229	38.700	8.106	6.331	93.328	35.030	19.607		
	- non-household	169.195	132.300	127.900	319.000	111.900	93.300	329.000	390.200	95.300	162.100	56.552	9.426	23.500	7.518	8.820	40.462	25.468	8.898		
Trade effluent		8.184	9.700	3.000	13.200	7.700	4.400	8.200	22.400	4.300	11.900	0.000	0.000	0.000	0.000	0.000	0.000	0.000	0.000		
Bulk supplies/inter company payments		8.316	19.800	0.800	5.300	2.600	17.700	3.500	0.800	0.500	0.800	3.040	0.010	0.600	0.004	0.226	0.003	0.461	0.038		
Other third party services (incl non-potable water)		12.562	22.900	9.500	75.000	9.900	8.400	4.700	6.200	1.400	1.100	1.104	0.197	1.200	0.096	1.407	0.000	0.808	1.123		
Other sources		71.083	8.400	45.700	6.400	26.400	0.000	90.700	110.500	28.900	69.800	0.000	5.507	6.200	0.000	0.095	4.918	0.513	1.240		

10.14a Current cost profit and loss account for the 12 months ended 31 March 2015 (appointed business only)

Description	WaSC										WoC								Northern Ireland (Total only)	Scottish (Total only)
	Anglian	Welsh	Northumbrian	Severn Trent	Southern	South West	Thames	United Utilities	Wessex	Yorkshire	Affinity	Bournemouth	Bristol	Dee Valley	Portsmouth	South East	South Staffs / Cambridge	Sutton and East Surrey		
Total turnover	1,226.846	750.900	761.500	1,560.900	821.900	517.800	1,998.600	1,725.600	532.900	1,004.800	293.524	44.848	131.000	24.469	38.201	209.966	122.373	60.801	364.407	
Current cost operating costs - wholesale	-804.752	-457.600	-459.200	-966.800	-513.200	-302.300	-1,263.800	-983.900	-299.400	-652.800	-184.015	-29.021	-95.000	-16.430	-28.096	-127.929	-76.853	-40.321	0.000	
Current cost operating costs - retail	-83.991	-69.800	-60.600	-129.600	-84.600	-35.800	-195.900	-177.900	-32.000	-63.400	-36.295	-4.698	-11.300	-4.069	-5.255	-18.224	-18.308	-6.635	0.000	
Current cost operating costs - total																			-306.136	
Operating income	-0.280	0.000	0.500	3.400	-6.600	1.300	16.600	-6.000	-0.900	1.800	-0.979	0.000	-0.200	0.000	0.003	-0.001	0.224	13.845	0.000	
Working capital adjustment	-0.598	0.100	-0.300	-0.400	0.600	-0.200	2.500	0.000	-0.500	0.900	0.192	-0.032	0.100	0.015	0.046	0.076	0.114	0.056	0.840	
Current cost operating profit	337.226	223.600	241.900	467.500	218.100	180.800	558.600	557.800	200.100	291.300	72.427	11.097	24.600	3.985	4.899	63.888	27.551	13.901	59.111	
Exceptional item						11.800														
Other income	0.000	0.000	0.100	1.200	2.600	0.400	2.100	1.000	0.400	2.000	0.000	0.115	0.300	0.054	0.000	0.658	0.000	0.892	0.000	
Net Interest	-101.561	-151.200	-123.300	-366.100	-125.700	-53.200	-365.300	-350.400	-79.000	-214.400	-35.664	-4.970	-11.600	-2.557	-2.809	-47.997	-11.498	-9.873	-51.957	
Financing adjustment	7.225	12.400	17.100	31.400	28.800	15.700	18.500	29.200	10.400	6.800	7.714	0.781	1.900	-0.029	0.021	6.759	0.097	0.265	9.183	
Current cost profit before taxation	242.890	84.800	135.800	134.000	123.800	155.500	213.300	237.600	131.900	85.700	44.477	7.023	15.200	1.453	2.111	23.308	16.150	5.185	16.337	
Net revenue movement out of tariff basket	1.441	0.200	0.200	-0.500	-1.000	-0.600	3.500	0.200	0.100	-0.500	-0.160	0.028	-0.100	0.000	-0.002	0.147	0.412	0.002	0.000	
Back-billing amount identified	0.000	0.000	0.000	0.000	0.000	0.000	7.000	0.000	0.000	0.400	3.540	0.000	0.000	0.000	0.000	0.000	0.127	0.000	0.000	

Source: OFWAT

Please note, this table has not been updated since the last edition of Annual Abstract of Statistics. This table was published by Water UK for the water industry using data collected from all water companies. They have confirmed they do not hold a later version of this table at this time.

10.14b Water Industry Regulatory Capital Values

RCV roll forward for indexation (£ million)	
RCV at 31 March 2017 as published in April 2016[1]	66,921
Indexation	2,102
RCV at 31 March 2017 in March 2017 prices	69,022

Wholesale water RCV (£ million)	2015-16	2016-17	2017-18	2018-19	2019-20
Opening RCV	28,305	28,762	29,377	29,905	30,239
RCV additions (from totex)	1,655	1,827	1,732	1,562	1,340
Less RCV run-off and depreciation	-1,197	-1,210	-1,202	-1,226	-1,251
Other adjustments[3]	0	-2	-2	-2	-2
Closing RCV	28,762	29,377	29,905	30,239	30,327
Average RCV (year average)	28,046	28,574	29,136	29,560	29,767

Wholesale water RCV breakdown (£ million)	2015-16	2016-17	2017-18	2018-19	2019-20
2015 RCV	27,141	26,035	25,012	24,033	23,091
Totex RCV	1,621	3,342	4,893	6,206	7,236
Total	28,762	29,377	29,905	30,239	30,327

Wholesale wastewater RCV (£ million)	2015-16	2016-17	2017-18	2018-19	2019-20
Opening RCV	38,439	38,996	39,645	40,302	40,831
RCV additions (from totex)	2,255	2,352	2,363	2,245	1,861
Less RCV run-off and depreciation	-1,697	-1,703	-1,706	-1,717	-1,709
Other adjustments[3]	0	0	0	0	0
Closing RCV	38,996	39,645	40,302	40,831	40,982
Average RCV (year average)	38,098	38,692	39,334	39,918	40,252

Wholesale wastewater RCV breakdown (£ million)	2015-16	2016-17	2017-18	2018-19	2019-20
2015 RCV	36,781	35,201	33,704	32,283	30,947
Totex RCV	2,215	4,445	6,598	8,547	10,035
Total	38,996	39,645	40,302	40,831	40,982

Notes

Source: OFWAT

1 Presented in March 2016 prices

2 Does not include the impact of the Competition and Markets Authority's (CMA) final determination for Bristol Water

3 Impact of the reduction in allowed totex and the associated RCV run-off as included in the CMA's final determination for Bristol Water

10.15 Summary of pollution incidents by area and incident category, England 2015

	Water						Land						Air					
	Cat 1	Cat 2	Cat 3	Cat 4	Total	Cat 1 and 2 Total	Cat 1	Cat 2	Cat 3	Cat 4	Total	Cat 1 and 2 Total	Cat 1	Cat 2	Cat 3	Cat 4	Total	Cat 1 and 2 Total
North and East																		
Northumberland, Durham and Tees	6	12	4	5	27	18	0	5	6	16	27	5	1	3	5	18	27	4
Cumbria and Lancashire	5	33	3	9	50	38	0	12	2	36	50	12	0	5	4	41	50	5
Yorkshire	5	28	6	20	59	33	1	11	6	41	59	12	2	16	5	36	59	18
Derbyshire, Nottinghamshire and Leicestershire	2	10	1	11	24	12	1	5	5	13	24	6	1	7	1	15	24	8
Lincolnshire and Northamptonshire	1	23	2	4	30	24	0	4	5	21	30	4	1	2	1	26	30	3
West																		
Greater Manchester, Merseyside and Cheshire	1	16	0	3	20	17	0	1	3	16	20	1	0	2	0	18	20	2
Staffordshire, Warwickshire and West Midlands	3	8	5	10	26	11	1	6	3	16	26	7	1	7	3	15	26	8
Shropshire, Herefordshire, Worcestershire and Gloucestershire	2	13	8	17	40	15	0	20	1	19	40	20	0	6	7	27	40	6
Wessex	6	20	0	10	36	26	0	4	8	24	36	4	1	8	3	24	36	9
Devon and Cornwall	3	29	3	12	47	32	1	9	8	29	47	10	1	8	8	30	47	9
South East																		
Cambridgeshire and Bedfordshire	2	11	3	7	23	13	0	5	5	13	23	5	0	6	2	15	23	6
Essex, Norfolk and Suffolk	6	15	0	16	37	21	2	9	2	24	37	11	1	8	1	27	37	9
Hertfordshire and North London	3	24	1	4	32	27	0	3	5	24	32	3	0	4	8	20	32	4
West Thames	3	7	0	0	10	10	0	0	1	9	10	0	0	0	1	9	10	0
Solent and South Downs	1	7	1	3	12	8	0	2	3	7	12	2	0	3	2	7	12	3
Kent and South London	2	18	2	4	26	20	0	5	2	19	26	5	0	3	0	23	26	3
Total	51	274	39	135	499	325	6	101	65	327	499	107	9	88	51	351	499	97

Source: Environment Agency

Data does not include incidents relating to:

Fisheries incidents – for incidents involving illegal fishing and illegal fish movements, fish disease, fishery management activities and fish kills from non-pollution causes, including low flows and low dissolved oxygen.

Water Resources incidents – for incidents involving the quantity of a water resource.

Waterways incidents – for incidents on a waterway where the Environment Agency are the competent authority for navigation.
Flood and Coastal Risk Management incidents – for incidents which involve actual or potential flooding and land drainage works on main river or where regional bylaws apply.

Only incidents where investigations and response have been completed are included. Some incidents may take an extended period of months, or exceptionally years, to be completed.

The dataset only includes substantiated incidents and their environmental impact. These are where the Environment Agency have confirmation that the incident took place either by a visit, or it is corroborated by other information.

10.16 Bathing Water Compliance Results 2015

(produced 29/10/15)

EA Area / County	Closed	Excellent	Good	Sufficient	Poor	Total (ex Closed)	Excellent %	Good %	Sufficient %	Poor %
Cambridgeshire and Bedfordshire	0	0	2	0	0	2	0.0	100.0	0.0	0.0
Cumbria and Lancashire	0	9	9	6	3	27	33.3	33.3	22.2	11.1
Derbyshire Nottinghamshire and Leicestershire	0	1	0	0	0	1	100.0	0.0	0.0	0.0
Devon and Cornwall	1	102	28	10	3	143	71.3	19.6	7.0	2.1
Essex Norfolk and Suffolk	0	22	5	1	1	29	75.9	17.2	3.4	3.4
Greater Manchester Merseyside and Cheshire	0	3	1	0	0	4	75.0	25.0	0.0	0.0
Hertfordshire and North London	0	2	1	1	0	4	50.0	25.0	25.0	0.0
Kent and South London	0	24	11	3	1	39	61.5	28.2	7.7	2.6
Lincolnshire and Northamptonshire	0	8	1	0	0	9	88.9	11.1	0.0	0.0
Northumberland Durham and Tees	0	19	11	3	1	34	55.9	32.4	8.8	2.9
Solent and South Downs	1	33	16	3	0	52	63.5	30.8	5.8	0.0
Wessex	1	30	16	1	2	49	61.2	32.7	2.0	4.1
West Thames	0	1	1	0	0	2	50.0	50.0	0.0	0.0
Yorkshire	0	10	8	1	1	20	50.0	40.0	5.0	5.0
England	3	264	110	29	12	415	63.6	26.5	7.0	2.9
Wales	0	82	16	4	0	102	80.4	15.7	3.9	0.0
Scotland	0	17	38	12	17	84	20.2	45.2	14.3	20.2
Northern Ireland	0	14	7	2	0	23	60.9	30.4	8.7	0.0
UK** Total	3	377	171	47	29	624	60.4	27.4	7.5	4.6

Source: Environment Agency

** Excluding Gibraltar

2014 was the final year of reporting under the original Bathing Water Directive (76/160/EEC). A new format is now being used to issue the classifications under the revised Directive (2006/7/EC). As such, this table is different to the one published in previous editions of Annual Abstract of Statistics. (Bathing and Shellfish Waters | Water and Flood Risk Management | Department for Environment, Food and Rural Affairs).

10.17 Estimated abstractions from all surface and groundwater sources: by purpose[1]

England and Wales

million cubic metres

		2003	2004	2005	2006	2007	2008	2009	2010	2011	2012	2013	2014	2015 [b]
Public water supply	JZLA	6,176	6,299	6,340	6,206	5,979	5,944	5,767	5,976	5,830	5,843	5,879	5,777	5,109
Spray irrigation [2]	JZLB	115	82	83	101	59	57	85	104	118	50	100	90	94
Agriculture (excl spray irrigation)	JZLC	48	45	22	17	26	14	16	25	26	26	26	27	25
Electricity supply industry[3]	JZLD	11,453	11,188	10,958	11,738	11,857	12,130	10,978	10,867	10,716	13,310	13,343	6,669	6,876
Other industry	JZLE	2,418	2,410	2,314	2,379	1,886	1,813	2,065	1,816	1,737	2,011	1,728	2,838	1,744
Fish farming, cress growing, amenity ponds	JYXG	1,123	1,489	1,334	1,322	1,245	1,043	953	1,058	847	974	947	962	841
Private water supply	JZLG	22	11	10	13	11	9	10	9	9	9	9	10	10
Other	JZLH	31	28	22	32	41	27	27	20	23	28	33	28	29
Total	JZLI	21,386	21,552	21,081	21,810	21,104	21,037	19,900	19,875	19,305	22,251	22,065	19,828	14,728

1 See chapter text.

Source: Environment Agency

2 Includes small amounts of non-agricultural spray irrigation

3 The Electricity Supply Industry category includes hydropower licences.

b - Indicates a break in the series where information concerning abstractions in the country of England and the Dee/Wye regional charge areas (formerly the Wales regional charge area) has been amalgamated into the North West and Midlands regional charge areas respectively

10.18 Estimates of remaining recoverable oil and gas reserves and resources, 2003-2014

	2003	2004	2005	2006	2007	2008	2009	2010	2011	2012	2013	2014
Oil *(million tonnes)*												
Annual production	106	95	85	77	77	72	68	63	52	45	41	40
Discovered reserves												
Proven	571	533	516	479	452	408	378	374	413	405	404	374
Probable	286	283	300	298	328	361	390	377	374	405	342	342
Proven + Probable	857	816	816	776	780	770	769	751	788	811	746	716
Possible reserves	410	512	451	478	399	360	343	342	319	253	338	344
Maximum reserves	1,267	1,328	1,267	1,254	1,179	1,130	1,112	1,093	1,106	1,064	1,084	1,060
Range of undiscovered resources												
Lower	323	396	346	438	379	454	397	475	422	455	453	444
Upper	1,826	1,830	1,581	1,637	1,577	1,561	1,477	1,374	1,321	1344	1331	1344
Range of total reserves and resources												
Lower[1]	1,590	1,724	1,613	1,692	1,558	1,584	1,509	1,568	1,528	1,519	1,537	1,504
Upper[2]	3,093	3,158	2,848	2,891	2,756	2,691	2,589	2,467	2,427	2,408	2,415	2,404
Expected level of reserves[3]												
Opening stocks	920	857	816	816	776	780	770	769	751	788	811	746
Extraction[4]	-106	-95	-85	-77	-77	-72	-68	-63	-52	-45	-41	-40
Other volume changes	43	54	85	37	81	62	67	45	89	68	106	70
Closing stocks	857	816	816	776	780	770	769	751	788	811	746	716
Gas (billion cubic metres)												
Annual production	102	95	86	78	70	68	57	55	43	37	34	35
Discovered reserves												
Proven	590	531	481	412	343	292	256	253	246	244	241	205
Probable	315	296	247	272	304	309	308	267	246	217	211	201
Proven plus Probable	905	826	728	684	647	601	564	520	493	461	452	407
Possible reserves	336	343	278	283	293	306	276	261	216	238	198	187
Maximum reserves	1,241	1,169	1,006	967	940	907	840	781	709	699	650	594
Range of undiscovered resources												
Lower	279	293	226	301	280	319	300	363	353	370	357	365
Upper	1,259	1,245	1,035	1,049	1,039	1,043	949	1,021	977	1011	997	1000
Range of total reserves and resources												
Lower[1]	1,520	1,462	1,232	1,268	1,220	1,226	1,140	1,144	1,062	1,069	1,007	959
Upper[2]	2,500	2,414	2,041	2,016	1,979	1,950	1,789	1,802	1,686	1,710	1,647	1,594
Expected Level of Reserves[3]												
Opening stocks	1,000	905	826	728	684	647	601	564	520	493	461	452
Extraction[4]	-102	-95	-86	-78	-70	-68	-57	-55	-43	-37	-34	-35
Other volume changes	7	16	-12	34	33	22	20	10	16	5	25	80
Closing stocks	905	826	728	684	647	601	564	520	493	461	452	407

Sources: Office for National Statistics, Department of Energy and Climate Change

All data refer to end of year.

Components may not sum to totals due to rounding.

1. The lower end of the range of total reserves and resources has been calculated as the sum of proven, probable and possible reserves and the lower end of the range of undiscovered resources.

2. The upper end of the range of total reserves and resources is the sum of proven, probable and possible reserves and the upper end of the range of undiscovered resources.

3. Expected reserves are the sum of proven and probable reserves.

4. The negative of extraction is shown here for the purposes of the calculation only. Of itself, extraction should be considered as a positive value.

10.19a Local Authority Collected Waste Generation from 2002/03 to 2014/15

England   *Thousand tonnes*

Household waste from:	2002/03	2003/04	2004/05	2005/06	2006/07r	2007/08	2008/09r	2009/10	2010/11	2011/12	2012/13	2013/14	2014/15
Regular household collection	16,528	16,066	15,470	14,616	14,050	13,046	12,076	11,432	11,048	10,586	10,317	10,308	10,392
Other household sources	1,351	1,244	1,205	1,314	1,173	1,073	1,026	1,070	1,047	997	1,027	1,099	1,058
Civic amenity sites	4,213	3,616	3,198	2,726	2,576	2,434	2,086	1,765	1,635	1,470	1,477	1,568	1,597
Household recycling	3,740	4,521	5,785	6,796	7,976	8,735	9,146	9,398	9,724	9,846	9,759	9,980	10,117
Total household	**25,832**	**25,448**	**25,658**	**25,454**	**25,775**	**25,287**	**24,334**	**23,666**	**23,454**	**22,899**	**22,580**	**22,967**	23,169
Non household sources (excl. recycling)	2,730	2,650	2,795	2,289	2,408	2,250	2,063	1,999	1,882	1,654	1,558	1,600	1,617
Non household recycling	832	1,016	1,167	1,003	961	969	936	877	864	866	817	950	950
Total LA collected waste	**29,394**	**29,114**	**29,619**	**28,745**	**29,144**	**28,506**	**27,334**	**26,541**	**26,200**	**25,419**	**24,955**	**25,518**	25,737

Source: Department for Environment, Food & Rural Affairs

There has been a revision to 2008/09 to include asbestos in "Other household sources" instead of "Non household sources".

10.19b Waste managed (tonnes) by management method and year 2012-13 onwards

	2012-13	2013-14	2014-15	2015-16
Total Municipal Waste Collected/Generated	1553511.53	1557229	1543357.32	1592177.68
Total Waste Reused/Recycled/Composted (Statutory Target) (1)	**811865.985**	**846091**	**868079.46**	**958258.84**
Household Waste Reused/Recycled (2)	499946.478	429863	430264.88	482303.1
Household Waste Composted (3)	265133.147	274265	281762.43	285800.99
Non-Household Waste Reused/Recycled (4)	28622.1164	128310	141705.77	176763.1
Non-Household Waste Composted (5)	18164.2443	13653	14346.36	13391.66
Waste sent for other recovery (6)	1801.856	4532	4923.87	3937.44
Other recovery: Recycling (7)	.	.	1488.15	781.57
Other recovery: Composting (8)	.	.	3435.72	3155.87
Waste Incinerated with Energy Recovery	71887.638	89907	182961.26	301905.74
Waste Incinerated without Energy Recovery	363.827	341	245.08	655.93
Waste Landfilled	640904.458	587390	453497.37	288820.05
Percentage of Waste Reused/Recycled/Composted (Statutory Target) (9)	**52.2600552**	**54.3331079**	**56.2461751**	**60.1854209**
Percentage of Household Waste Reused/Recycled (10)	32.1817036	27.604254	27.8785006	30.2920399
Percentage of Household Waste Composted (11)	17.0666996	17.6124159	18.2564612	17.9503201
Percentage of Non-Household Waste Reused/Recycled (12)	1.84241416	8.23962534	9.18165665	11.1019707
Percentage of Non-Household Waste Composted (13)	1.16923781	0.87687697	0.92955532	0.8410908

Source: WasteDataFlow, Natural Resources Wales

1. Total waste reused/recycled/composted as defined by the Statutory Local Authority Recovery Target (LART)
2. Household waste sent to be reused/recycled as defined by the Statutory Local Authority Recovery Target (LART)
3. Household waste sent to be composted as defined by the Statutory Local Authority Recovery Target (LART)
4. Non-Household waste sent to be reused/recycled as defined by the Statutory Local Authority Recovery Target (LART)
5. Non-Household waste sent to be composted as defined by the Statutory Local Authority Recovery Target (LART)
6. Other waste sent for recycling and/or composting that is not included in the statutory target definition
7. Other waste sent for recycling that is not included in the statutory target definition
8. Other waste sent for composting that is not included in the statutory target definition
9. Total waste reused/recycled/composted (as defined by the Statutory Local Authority Recovery Target, LART), as a percentage of total municipal waste collected/generated
10. Household waste sent to be reused/recycled (as defined by the Statutory Local Authority Recovery Target, LART), as a percentage of total municipal waste collected/generated
11. Household waste sent to be composted (as defined by the Statutory Local Authority Recovery Target, LART), as a percentage of total municipal waste collected/generated
12. Non-Household waste sent to be reused/recycled (as defined by the Statutory Local Authority Recovery Target, LART), as a percentage of total municipal waste collected/generated
13. Non-Household waste sent to be composted (as defined by the Statutory Local Authority Recovery Target, LART), as a percentage of total municipal waste collected/generated
. The data item is not applicable.

10.19c Household waste - Summary data 2015, Scotland

Local Authority	Generated (tonnes)	Recycled (tonnes)	Percentage Recycled (%)	Other diversion from landfill (tonnes)	Percentage Other diversion from Landfill (%)	Landfilled (tonnes)	Percentage Landfilled (%)
Aberdeen City	95,241	36,679	38.5	407	0.4	58,155	61.1
Aberdeenshire	130,249	56,902	43.7	172	0.1	73,175	56.2
Angus	57,609	34,102	59.2	10,810	18.8	12,697	22.0
Argyll & Bute	51,847	17,514	33.8	9,040	17.4	25,293	48.8
Clackmannanshire	26,621	12,792	48.1	2,433	9.1	11,397	42.8
Dumfries & Galloway	74,092	20,091	27.1	32,235	43.5	21,767	29.4
Dundee City	67,182	22,373	33.3	40,187	59.8	4,622	6.9
East Ayrshire	56,374	29,866	53.0	7,182	12.7	19,343	34.3
East Dunbartonshire	54,191	27,454	50.7	4,436	8.2	22,301	41.2
East Lothian	50,906	26,163	51.4	2,217	4.4	22,526	44.2
East Renfrewshire	46,880	26,449	56.4	290	0.6	20,141	43.0
Edinburgh, City of	189,574	80,130	42.3	13,631	7.2	95,813	50.5
Eilean Siar	14,013	2,973	21.2	1,948	13.9	9,092	64.9
Falkirk	72,329	39,011	53.9	4,592	6.3	28,727	39.7
Fife	191,153	99,965	52.3	9,088	4.8	82,100	42.9
Glasgow City	221,902	57,624	26.0	2,360	1.1	161,918	73.0
Highland	130,780	58,147	44.5	1,183	0.9	71,449	54.6
Inverclyde	28,493	15,592	54.7	141	0.5	12,760	44.8
Midlothian	42,076	20,136	47.9	7,714	18.3	14,227	33.8
Moray	50,116	28,778	57.4	0	0.0	21,338	42.6
North Ayrshire	64,194	35,949	56.0	1,587	2.5	26,658	41.5
North Lanarkshire	155,933	62,335	40.0	16,624	10.7	76,974	49.4
Orkney Islands	9,371	1,802	19.2	4,806	51.3	2,244	23.9
Perth & Kinross	76,187	41,328	54.2	8,011	10.5	26,849	35.2
Renfrewshire	83,068	36,427	43.9	19,821	23.9	26,819	32.3
Scottish Borders	49,848	18,600	37.3	892	1.8	30,355	60.9
Shetland Islands	10,250	939	9.2	7,052	68.8	2,258	22.0
South Ayrshire	55,653	28,653	51.5	7,500	13.5	19,499	35.0
South Lanarkshire	151,656	74,241	49.0	0	0.0	77,416	51.0
Stirling	41,924	22,582	53.9	1,563	3.7	18,029	43.0
West Dunbartonshire	45,088	20,915	46.4	4,138	9.2	20,036	44.4
West Lothian	74,000	35,092	47.4	4,331	5.9	34,559	46.7
Total Scotland	**2,468,800**	**1,091,602**	**44.2**	**226,390**	**9.2**	**1,150,537**	**46.6**

Source: Scottish Environment Protection Agency

10.19d Local authority collected (LAC) municipal waste sent for preparing for reuse, dry recycling, composting, energy recovery and landfill

Northern Ireland, 2014/15

Units: Tonnes
KPI (j)

Authority	LAC municipal waste preparing for reuse	LAC municipal waste dry recycling	LAC municipal waste composting	LAC municipal waste dry recycling and composting	LAC municipal waste preparing for reuse, dry recycling and composting	LAC municipal waste energy recovery (mixed residual LACMW)	LAC municipal waste energy recovery (specific streams e.g. wood)	LAC municipal waste energy recovery total	LAC municipal waste landfilled	LAC municipal waste unclassified	LAC municipal waste arisings
arc21											
Antrim	52	9,953	9,505	19,458	19,510	1,870	3,010	4,880	11,980	277	36,647
Ards	14	6,517	8,732	15,249	15,263	207	1,701	1,907	26,372	0	43,542
Ballymena	6	6,586	8,081	14,666	14,672	1,761	696	2,457	14,889	0	32,018
Belfast	107	38,191	19,515	57,706	57,814	32,803	891	33,694	56,744	1,539	149,791
Carrickfergus	0	4,506	3,845	8,351	8,351	471	408	879	11,411	0	20,641
Castlereagh	32	5,897	7,094	12,991	13,024	91	466	557	17,587	250	31,418
Down	0	5,694	4,696	10,390	10,390	1,734	812	2,546	19,361	-3	32,293
Larne	2	5,755	4,234	9,988	9,991	357	718	1,075	9,483	58	20,607
Lisburn	31	11,518	12,798	24,316	24,348	2,169	1,377	3,546	30,452	224	58,570
Newtownabbey	24	9,641	10,607	20,248	20,272	1,371	1,068	2,440	22,828	379	45,918
North Down	123	13,057	10,586	23,643	23,767	223	2,684	2,907	25,978	0	52,651
All arc21	392	117,315	99,693	217,008	217,400	43,056	13,832	56,888	247,085	2,724	524,097
NWRVMG											
Ballymoney	0	2,722	2,439	5,161	5,161	1,134	327	1,461	8,714	0	15,337
Coleraine	0	7,458	5,527	12,985	12,985	3,610	1,234	4,844	17,115	20	34,964
Derry	106	16,183	3,452	19,635	19,741	19,979	1,872	21,851	14,337	3	55,932
Limavady	101	5,796	2,195	7,991	8,092	3,378	570	3,948	6,256	0	18,296
Magherafelt	0	5,788	6,458	12,247	12,247	7,120	610	7,730	4,131	-1	24,107
Moyle	0	2,361	1,651	4,011	4,011	2,679	238	2,917	2,443	3	9,375
Strabane	0	4,086	1,062	5,148	5,148	1,892	553	2,446	10,430	39	18,062
All NWRVMG	207	44,395	22,784	67,179	67,386	39,793	5,405	45,198	63,426	64	176,074
SWaMP2008											
Armagh	84	6,399	5,553	11,952	12,037	8,676	155	8,831	6,636	87	27,591
Banbridge	0	6,369	8,953	15,323	15,323	7,713	408	8,121	1,813	21	25,278
Cookstown	0	4,939	4,802	9,741	9,741	1,911	183	2,095	9,493	21	21,349
Craigavon	0	12,331	9,400	21,731	21,731	15,614	311	15,925	10,497	154	48,308
Dungannon	0	6,222	6,194	12,416	12,416	237	546	783	17,854	-21	31,033
Fermanagh	79	8,504	2,657	11,160	11,239	159	212	371	15,594	44	27,248
Newry & Mourne	11	9,033	6,396	15,429	15,440	1,984	942	2,926	27,333	0	45,698
Omagh	5	6,576	4,446	11,022	11,027	0	698	698	13,025	-3	24,747
All SWaMP2008	179	60,373	48,402	108,775	108,954	36,294	3,455	39,749	102,244	304	251,252
Northern Ireland	778	222,084	170,878	392,962	393,740	119,144	22,692	141,835	412,755	3,093	951,423

Source: NIEA

Notes: The tonnage of waste sent for recycling includes recycling from both clean/source segregated collection sources (as shown in Table 8) and recycling from residual waste processes.
Unclassified waste is calculated as a residual amount of municipal waste after municipal waste sent for preparing for reuse, for dry recycling, composting, energy recovery and to landfill have been accounted for.
It is not extracted directly from the WasteDataFlow system. The majority of the total unclassified tonnage can be attributed to moisture and/or gaseous losses.
Small negative tonnages can arise in the unclassified column if more waste is sent for treatment in the year than was actually collected as is more likely at councils operating transfer stations.

10.19d Percentage of local authority collected (LAC) municipal waste sent for preparing for reuse, dry recycling, composting, energy recovery and landfill

Northern Ireland, 2014/15

Units: Percentages

Authority	KPI (e)				KPI (e2)				KPI(f)	
	LAC municipal waste preparing for reuse rate	LAC municipal waste dry recycling rate	LAC municipal waste composting rate	LAC municipal waste dry recycling and composting rate	LAC municipal waste preparing for reuse, dry recycling and composting rate	LAC municipal waste energy recovery rate (mixed residual LACMW)	LAC municipal waste energy recovery rate (specific streams e.g. wood)	LAC municipal waste recovery rate	LAC municipal waste landfill rate	LAC municipal waste unclassified
arc21										
Antrim	0.1	27.2	25.9	53.1	53.2	5.1	8.2	13.3	32.7	0.8
Ards	0.0	15.0	20.1	35.0	35.1	0.5	3.9	4.4	60.6	0.0
Ballymena	0.0	20.6	25.2	45.8	45.8	5.5	2.2	7.7	46.5	0.0
Belfast	0.1	25.5	13.0	38.5	38.6	21.9	0.6	22.5	37.9	1.0
Carrickfergus	0.0	21.8	18.6	40.5	40.5	2.3	2.0	4.3	55.3	0.0
Castlereagh	0.1	18.8	22.6	41.4	41.5	0.3	1.5	1.8	56.0	0.8
Down	0.0	17.6	14.5	32.2	32.2	5.4	2.5	7.9	60.0	0.0
Larne	0.0	27.9	20.5	48.5	48.5	1.7	3.5	5.2	46.0	0.3
Lisburn	0.1	19.7	21.9	41.5	41.6	3.7	2.4	6.1	52.0	0.4
Newtownabbey	0.1	21.0	23.1	44.1	44.1	3.0	2.3	5.3	49.7	0.8
North Down	0.2	24.8	20.1	44.9	45.1	0.4	5.1	5.5	49.3	0.0
All arc21	0.1	22.4	19.0	41.4	41.5	8.2	2.6	10.9	47.1	0.5
NWRWMG										
Ballymoney	0.0	17.8	15.9	33.7	33.7	7.4	2.1	9.5	56.8	0.0
Coleraine	0.0	21.3	15.8	37.1	37.1	10.3	3.5	13.9	49.0	0.1
Derry	0.2	28.9	6.2	35.1	35.3	35.7	3.3	39.1	25.6	0.0
Limavady	0.6	31.7	12.0	43.7	44.2	18.5	3.1	21.6	34.2	0.0
Magherafelt	0.0	24.0	26.8	50.8	50.8	29.5	2.5	32.1	17.1	0.0
Moyle	0.0	25.2	17.6	42.8	42.8	28.6	2.5	31.1	26.1	0.0
Strabane	0.0	22.6	5.9	28.5	28.5	10.5	3.1	13.5	57.7	0.2
All NWRWMG	0.1	25.2	12.9	38.2	38.3	22.6	3.1	25.7	36.0	0.0
SWaMP2008										
Armagh	0.3	23.2	20.1	43.3	43.6	31.4	0.6	32.0	24.0	0.3
Banbridge	0.0	25.2	35.4	60.6	60.6	30.5	1.6	32.1	7.2	0.1
Cookstown	0.0	23.1	22.5	45.6	45.6	9.0	0.9	9.8	44.5	0.1
Craigavon	0.0	25.5	19.5	45.0	45.0	32.3	0.6	33.0	21.7	0.3
Dungannon	0.0	20.0	20.0	40.0	40.0	0.8	1.8	2.5	57.5	-0.1
Fermanagh	0.3	31.2	9.7	41.0	41.2	0.6	0.8	1.4	57.2	0.2
Newry & Mourne	0.0	19.8	14.0	33.8	33.8	4.3	2.1	6.4	59.8	0.0
Omagh	0.0	26.6	18.0	44.5	44.6	0.0	2.8	2.8	52.6	0.0
All SWaMP2008	0.1	24.0	19.3	43.3	43.4	14.4	1.4	15.8	40.7	0.1
Northern Ireland	0.1	23.3	18.0	41.3	41.4	12.5	2.4	14.9	43.4	0.3

Source: NIEA

Notes: Rates calculated by dividing total tonnage of LAC municipal waste sent in each category by total LAC municipal waste arisings.

Unclassified waste is calculated as a residual amount of municipal waste after municipal waste sent for preparing for reuse, for dry recycling, composting, energy recovery and to landfill have been accounted for.

It is not extracted directly from the WasteDataFlow system. The majority of the total unclassified tonnage can be attributed to moisture and/or gaseous losses.

Small negative tonnages can arise in the unclassified column if more waste is sent for treatment in the year than was actually collected as is more likely at councils operating transfer stations.

10.19d Household waste sent for preparing for reuse, dry recycling, composting and landfill
Northern Ireland, 2014/15

Units: Tonnes

Authority	Household waste preparing for reuse	Household waste dry recycling	Household waste composting	Household waste dry recycling and composting	Household waste preparing for reuse, dry recycling and composting	Household waste landfilled	Household waste arisings
arc21							
Antrim	52	6,079	9,505	15,583	15,635	10,431	30,903
Ards	14	6,282	8,732	15,014	15,028	23,325	40,181
Ballymena	6	5,181	8,081	13,261	13,267	13,830	29,418
Belfast	107	35,061	18,978	54,039	54,146	42,504	123,368
Carrickfergus	0	3,213	3,845	7,058	7,058	10,010	17,810
Castlereagh	32	4,741	7,093	11,834	11,866	16,345	28,994
Down	0	5,599	4,656	10,256	10,256	17,528	30,162
Larne	2	3,530	4,234	7,764	7,766	8,297	17,083
Lisburn	31	8,791	12,798	21,589	21,620	27,657	52,825
Newtownabbey	24	7,328	10,409	17,737	17,762	20,619	40,756
North Down	123	7,496	10,394	17,890	18,013	21,175	42,025
All arc21	392	93,301	98,724	192,025	192,418	211,720	453,523
NWRWMG							
Ballymoney	0	2,425	2,439	4,864	4,864	7,677	13,900
Coleraine	0	6,642	5,527	12,168	12,168	14,598	30,840
Derry	106	13,450	2,978	16,428	16,534	13,360	50,401
Limavady	101	4,085	2,195	6,280	6,382	6,094	16,330
Magherafelt	0	4,552	6,458	11,010	11,010	3,444	21,044
Moyle	0	2,325	1,651	3,976	3,976	2,279	9,122
Strabane	0	3,965	1,062	5,027	5,027	9,362	16,730
All NWRWMG	207	37,443	22,310	59,753	59,960	56,813	158,367
SWaMP2008							
Armagh	84	5,280	5,363	10,642	10,727	6,209	25,282
Banbridge	0	5,352	8,492	13,845	13,845	1,751	23,448
Cookstown	0	4,141	4,802	8,943	8,943	7,611	18,215
Craigavon	0	10,238	9,343	19,581	19,581	9,454	43,570
Dungannon	0	6,075	6,194	12,270	12,270	16,150	29,146
Fermanagh	79	6,843	2,657	9,500	9,578	15,013	24,965
Newry & Mourne	11	8,903	6,396	15,299	15,310	22,088	40,097
Omagh	5	5,785	4,446	10,231	10,236	12,026	22,956
All SWaMP2008	179	52,616	47,693	100,310	100,489	90,302	227,680
Northern Ireland	778	183,361	168,728	352,088	352,867	358,836	839,569

Source: NIEA

Note: The tonnages of waste sent for preparing for reuse, for dry recycling, composting and landfill may not always equal the waste arisings because the recycling measures were defined to capture outputs from recycling processes which exclude energy recovery.

10.19d Percentage of household waste sent for preparing for reuse, dry recycling, composting and landfill

Northern Ireland, 2014/15

Units: Percentages

Authority	Household waste preparing for reuse rate	Household waste dry recycling rate	Household waste composting rate	KPI (a) Household waste dry recycling and composting rate	KPI (a2) Household waste preparing for reuse, dry recycling and composting rate	KPI (b) Household waste landfill rate
arc21						
Antrim	0.2	19.7	30.8	50.4	50.6	33.8
Ards	0.0	15.6	21.7	37.4	37.4	58.0
Ballymena	0.0	17.6	27.5	45.1	45.1	47.0
Belfast	0.1	28.4	15.4	43.8	43.9	34.5
Carrickfergus	0.0	18.0	21.6	39.6	39.6	56.2
Castlereagh	0.1	16.4	24.5	40.8	40.9	56.4
Down	0.0	18.6	15.4	34.0	34.0	58.1
Larne	0.0	20.7	24.8	45.4	45.5	48.6
Lisburn	0.1	16.6	24.2	40.9	40.9	52.4
Newtownabbey	0.1	18.0	25.5	43.5	43.6	50.6
North Down	0.3	17.8	24.7	42.6	42.9	50.4
All arc21	0.1	20.6	21.8	42.3	42.4	46.7
NWRWMG						
Ballymoney	0.0	17.4	17.5	35.0	35.0	55.2
Coleraine	0.0	21.5	17.9	39.5	39.5	47.3
Derry	0.2	26.7	5.9	32.6	32.8	26.5
Limavady	0.6	25.0	13.4	38.5	39.1	37.3
Magherafelt	0.0	21.6	30.7	52.3	52.3	16.4
Moyle	0.0	25.5	18.1	43.6	43.6	25.0
Strabane	0.0	23.7	6.3	30.0	30.0	56.0
All NWRWMG	0.1	23.6	14.1	37.7	37.9	35.9
SWaMP2008						
Armagh	0.3	20.9	21.2	42.1	42.4	24.6
Banbridge	0.0	22.8	36.2	59.0	59.0	7.5
Cookstown	0.0	22.7	26.4	49.1	49.1	41.8
Craigavon	0.0	23.5	21.4	44.9	44.9	21.7
Dungannon	0.0	20.8	21.3	42.1	42.1	55.4
Fermanagh	0.3	27.4	10.6	38.1	38.4	60.1
Newry & Mourne	0.0	22.2	16.0	38.2	38.2	55.1
Omagh	0.0	25.2	19.4	44.6	44.6	52.4
All SWaMP2008	0.1	23.1	20.9	44.1	44.1	39.7
Northern Ireland	0.1	21.8	20.1	41.9	42.0	42.7

Source: NIEA

Notes: Rates calculated by dividing total tonnage of household waste sent in each category by total household waste arisings.

The percentages of waste sent for preparing for reuse, for dry recycling, composting and landfill may not equal 100% because the recycling measures were defined to capture outputs from recycling processes which exclude energy recovery.

10.19d Household waste per capita and per household
Northern Ireland, 2014/15

Units: Kilogrammes per capita and tonnes per household

Authority	Household waste arisings	Population (2014)	KPI (p) Household waste arisings (kg per capita)	Housing stock (at Apr 2015)	KPI (h) Household waste arisings (tonnes per household)
arc21					
Antrim	30,903	54,111	571	20,178	1.532
Ards	40,181	78,924	509	32,424	1.239
Ballymena	29,418	65,221	451	25,568	1.151
Belfast	123,368	283,166	436	123,945	0.995
Carrickfergus	17,810	39,114	455	16,489	1.080
Castlereagh	28,994	68,388	424	28,409	1.021
Down	30,162	70,467	428	26,758	1.127
Larne	17,083	32,307	529	13,542	1.261
Lisburn	52,825	123,579	427	47,505	1.112
Newtownabbey	40,756	85,855	475	34,956	1.166
North Down	42,025	79,331	530	33,495	1.255
All arc21	453,523	980,463	463	403,269	1.125
NWRWMG					
Ballymoney	13,900	31,922	435	11,719	1.186
Coleraine	30,840	59,217	521	24,642	1.252
Derry	50,401	109,150	462	42,185	1.195
Limavady	16,330	34,011	480	12,527	1.304
Magherafelt	21,044	46,280	455	15,655	1.344
Moyle	9,122	17,153	532	6,932	1.316
Strabane	16,730	40,048	418	15,304	1.093
All NWRWMG	158,367	337,781	469	128,964	1.228
SWaMP2008					
Armagh	25,282	60,820	416	21,837	1.158
Banbridge	23,448	49,160	477	18,783	1.248
Cookstown	18,215	37,871	481	13,290	1.371
Craigavon	43,570	96,808	450	37,004	1.177
Dungannon	29,146	60,084	485	21,171	1.377
Fermanagh	24,965	62,985	396	24,824	1.006
Newry & Mourne	40,097	102,519	391	36,332	1.104
Omagh	22,956	52,007	441	19,423	1.182
All SWaMP2008	227,680	522,254	436	192,664	1.182
Northern Ireland	839,569	1,840,498	456	724,897	1.158

Source: NIEA, NISRA, LPS

Notes: The population figures are NISRA mid-year population estimates for 2014.
The number of occupied households is estimated from the total housing stock adjusted for vacant properties using the 2011 Census.

10.20a Waste arisings from households (Million tonnes) and household expenditure (2014 prices) UK, 2010 – 2015.

Waste from Households arisings (million tonnes)	2010	2011	2012	2013	2014	2015
UK	27.0	26.8	26.4	25.9	26.8	26.7
England	22.1	22.2	22.0	21.6	22.4	22.2
Scotland	2.6	2.5	2.4	2.3	2.3	2.4
Wales	1.3	1.3	1.3	1.3	1.3	1.3
Northern Ireland	0.8	0.8	0.8	0.8	0.8	0.8
UK total household annual expenditure £th (2014 prices)	27.4	26.8	26.4	27.2	27.6	N/a

10.20b Waste from households, England, 2011 – 2015 *(Waste Prevention Metric).*

	2011	2012	2013	2014	2015
Total waste generated from households (Million tonnes)	22.2	22.0	21.6	22.4	22.2
Waste generated (kg per person)	421	412	402	413	407

Notes: Waste from households' includes waste from: Regular household collection, Civic amenity sites, 'Bulky waste' 'Other household waste'. It does not include street cleaning/sweeping, gully emptying, separately collected healthcare waste, asbestos waste. 'Waste from households' is a narrower measure than 'municipal waste' and 'council collected waste'.

- The 'waste from households' calculation was first published by Defra in May 2014. It was introduced for statistical purposes to provide a harmonised UK indicator to be reported against the Waste Framework Directive (2008/98/EC). It is calculated on a calendar year basis by each of the four UK countries using almost identical methodologies.
- The waste from household measure is a narrower measure than the 'household waste' measure which was previously used in England. Waste from households excludes waste not considered to have come directly from households, such as recycling from street bins, parks and grounds.
- Waste arising from households in the UK decreased by 0.4 per cent between 2014 and 2015. The 2015 tonnage represents a decrease of 1.0 per cent since 2010.

Source: Department for Environment, Food & Rural Affairs; Office for National Statistics

10.20c Waste from Households, UK and country split, 2010-15

thousand tonnes and % recycled

Year	Measure	UK	England	NI	Scotland	Wales
2010	Arisings ('000 tonnes)	26,954	22,131	829	2,649	1,344
	Recycled ('000 tonnes)	10,878	9,112	314	861	591
	Recycling rate	40.4%	41.2%	37.8%	32.5%	44.0%
2011	Arisings ('000 tonnes)	26,792	22,170	810	2,482	1,329
	Recycled ('000 tonnes)	11,492	9,596	324	921	651
	Recycling rate	42.9%	43.3%	40.0%	37.1%	49.0%
2012	Arisings ('000 tonnes)	26,428	21,956	783	2,383	1,306
	Recycled ('000 tonnes)	11,594	9,684	319	911	681
	Recycling rate	43.9%	44.1%	40.7%	38.2%	52.1%
2013	Arisings ('000 tonnes)	25,929	21,564	781	2,311	1,274
	Recycled ('000 tonnes)	11,434	9,523	324	916	671
	Recycling rate	44.1%	44.2%	41.5%	39.6%	52.6%
2014	Arisings ('000 tonnes)	26,797	22,355	808	2,349	1,285
	Recycled ('000 tonnes)	12,036	10,025	344	962	705
	Recycling rate	44.9%	44.8%	42.5%	41.0%	54.8%
2015	Arisings ('000 tonnes)	26,677	22,225	821	2,354	1,278
	Recycled ('000 tonnes)	11,805	9,758	344	989	713
	Recycling rate	44.3%	43.9%	42.0%	42.0%	55.8%

Recycling rate = Recycled ('000 tonnes) as a percentage of Arisings ('000 tonnes)

Source: Waste Data Flow

Notes for users:

1) UK estimates for 'Waste from households' have been calculated in accordance with the Waste Framework Directive.

2) 'Waste from households' includes waste from:Regular household collection, Civic amenity sites, 'Bulky waste', 'Other household waste'

3) 'Waste from households' excludes waste from: Street cleaning/sweeping, Gully emptying, Separately collected healthcare waste, Soil, Rubble, Plasterboard & Asbestos wastes

4) Whilst the general approach is consistent across UK countries, aggregation method and the wording of some questions completed by Local Authorities varies.

5) Users should be aware that individual UK countries other than England publish household recycling estimates using alternative measures and as such may differ from the estimates published here.

6) Local Authorities in England may also use an alternative measure to 'Waste from Households'.

7) The NI waste from households data previously reported in Dec 2015 used the England WfH calculation for the years 2013 and 2014.

A new WfH calculation specific to NI has been used for 2015 which now correctly excludes certain Construction & Demolition wastes from the Recycled tonnage.

In order to provide a uniform comparison ALL previous years for NI have been recalculated as shown above

10.20d Packaging waste and recycling / recovery, split by material, UK

	Packaging waste arising (thousand tonnes)		Total recovered / recycled (thousand tonnes)		Achieved recovery / recycling rate (%)		EU target recovery / recycling rate (%)	
	2013	2014	2013	2014	2013	2014	2013	2014
Metal	806	736	462	428	57.4%	58.2%	50.0%	50.0%
of which: Aluminium	164	177	71	73	43.4%	41.0%	n/a	n/a
of which: Steel	642	559	391	356	60.9%	63.7%	n/a	n/a
Paper and cardboard	3,868	4,749	3,459	3,470	89.4%	73.1%	60.0%	60.0%
Glass	2,399	2,399	1,639	1,613	68.3%	67.2%	60.0%	60.0%
Plastic	2,260	2,220	714	842	31.6%	37.9%	22.5%	22.5%
Wood	1,029	1,310	436	412	42.3%	31.4%	15.0%	15.0%
Other materials	23	23	0	0	0.0%	0.0%	n/a	n/a
Total (for recycling)	10,384	11,436	6,710	6,765	64.6%	59.2%	55.0%	55.0%
Energy from Waste	10,384		838	566	8.1%	4.9%	n/a	n/a
Total (for recycling and recovery)	10,384	11,436	7,548	7,331	72.7%	64.1%	60.0%	60.0%

Source: Defra Statistics

1) Theses statistics have been calculated to fulfil a reporting requirement to Eurostat at UK level in relation to the EC Packaging and Packaging Waste Directive (94/62/EC). The 2014 figures were submitted to Eurostat in June 2016. The 2013 figures were submitted to Eurostat in June 2015.

2) Figures are compiled from the National Packaging Waste Database (NPWD) and industry reports.

3) Only includes obligated packaging producers (handle 50 tonnes of packaging materials or packaging and have a turnover more than £2 million a year)

4) "Recovery' in these tables refer specifically to waste used for energy recovery.

5) The recovery figure includes waste sent to facilities that did not meet the R1 recovery energy efficiency thresholds, but were considered eligible based on the Packaging Directive, which states "'energy recovery' shall mean the use of combustible packaging waste as a means to generate energy through direct incineration with or without other waste but with recovery of the heat".

10.21 CIEH Survey of Local Authority Noise Enforcement Activity 2014-15

England and Wales - Data represents 130 (37%) of 348 local authorities

	INDUSTRY		COMMERCE / LEISURE			RESIDENTIAL			CONSTRUCTION ETC	VME's	TOTAL'S	
	Agricultural Premises	Industrial / Warehousing / Distribution Premises	"On"-licensed Premises e.g. Pubs, Clubs, Restaurants	Commercial Premises e.g. Offices, Shops, Public transport	Leisure Premises e.g. Sports Facilities, Funfairs	Single Family House / Bungalow	Flats / Maisonettes	Other Residential e.g. Hostels, HMOs, Boarding Schools	Construction / Demolition Sites	Vehicles, Machinery and Equipment in Streets	SUM OF COLUMNS [4]	TOTAL OF ALL COMPLAINTS [5]
COMPLAINTS												
Number of Noise Complaints Received in Year	635	2,081	7,292	6,353	2,242	60,723	17,895	1,965	4,956	3,114	107,256	115,315
Number of Noise Complaints Resolved in Year	600	1,668	6,045	5,335	1,852	51,994	14,693	1,490	4,085	2,764	90,526	94,974
Number of Noise Incidents Complained-of	565	1,602	5,483	5,057	1,728	49,656	12,247	1,369	3,926	2,547	84,180	87,954
Number of Noise Incidents Per Million Population	45	91	312	287	100	2,817	717	92	225	152	4,838	4,881
Incidents Confirmed as Potentially Actionable [1,2]	139	459	1,640	1,625	461	15,494	3,056	358	1,322	652	25,230	
STATUTORY NUISANCES REMEDIED WITHOUT A NOTICE [3,6]												
Nuisance Ceased and Not Likely to Recur	21	69	261	241	55	3,228	583	51	119	89	4,717	
Referred to Other Services		32	52	52	40	498	106	12	19	40	851	
Resolved Informally	60	167	573	705	144	5,232	932	154	644	181	8,792	
No Action Possible	20	56	213	178	92	2,241	471	56	114	97	3,538	
NOTICES SERVED [6]												
S.80 EPA 1990 Abatement Notice	4	14	152	92	28	776	263	27	14	37	1,407	1,515
S.60 & S.61 CoPA 1974 Control of Construction Noise									185	1	186	201
Noise Act 1996 Warning Notice			1			22	2	1			26	65
Noise Act 1996 Fixed Penalty							1				1	1
S.80(4A) EPA 1990 Fixed Penalty (Lond)			4	1		2	2				9	9
APPEALS AGAINST NOTICES [6]												
Number of Appeals Allowed in Whole or in Part			3	1	2		1				7	
PROSECUTIONS BEGUN [6]												
Breach of Abatement Notice	1		18	3	1	91	43	3	3	6	169	171
Breach of Restriction on, or Prior Consent for, Construction Noise									2		2	5
Noise Act 1996							1					2
Convictions Gained	1		3	1	1	44	11		3	2	66	
OTHER REMEDIES [6]												
Nuisance Remedied by the LA in Default			4	5		48	5	1	1	6	70	71
Number of Seizures			3	1		50	29				83	

[1] Incidents Confirmed as Potentially Actionable includes all those 'triggers' giving rise to formal enforcement power (described previously as "incidents confirmed as statutory nuisances etc")

[2] The sum of actions taken to resolve nuisances may exceed the Incidents Confirmed as Potentially Actionable figure because not all local authorities could provide data on incidents and more than one formal action may be taken to resolve a nuisance

[3] "Nuisances" here means statutory nuisances

[4] The sum of columns value is calculated, information provided by local authorities providing sub-total data only is not included here

[5] The Total of all Complaints column includes noise activity unaccounted for in previous columns

[6] Figures reported from 2005-06 may seem lower than previous years as they have not been subject to a 'grossing' calculation. Before 2005-06, where responding authorities were not able to provide data on the questions concerning outcome of noise incidents, estimates were made by pro-rating on number of noise incidents complained of

Source: Chartered Institute of Environmental Health.
Website: http://www.cieh.org

10.22 Government revenue from environmental taxes in the UK, 2004 to 2015

£ million

Environmental tax	2004	2005	2006	2007	2008	2009	2010	2011	2012	2013	2014	2015
Energy taxes	**24,685**	**24,666**	**24,859**	**26,035**	**26,503**	**27,731**	**29,114**	**29,336**	**29,795**	**31,132**	**32,518**	**34,011**
Tax on Hydrocarbon oils[1,2]	23,412	23,346	23,448	24,512	24,790	25,894	27,013	26,923	26,703	26,697	27,094	27,415
Climate Change Levy[3]	756	747	711	690	717	693	666	675	624	1,098	1,506	1,752
Fossil Fuel Levy	0	0	0	0	0	0	0	0	0	0	0	0
Gas Levy	0	0	0	0	0	0	0	0	0	0	0	0
Hydro-Benefit	40	10	0	0	0	0	0	0	0	0	0	0
Renewable Energy Obligations	477	563	700	833	996	1,099	1,243	1,423	1,842	2,391	2,931	3,691
Emmision Trading Scheme (EU-ETS)	0	0	0	0	0	45	192	315	278	339	418	493
Carbon Reduction Commitment	0	0	0	0	0	0	0	0	348	607	569	660
Transport taxes	**5,824**	**5,756**	**6,096**	**7,526**	**7,704**	**7,944**	**8,742**	**9,434**	**9,930**	**10,352**	**10,646**	**10,645**
Air Passenger Duty	856	896	961	1,883	1,876	1,800	2,094	2,605	2,766	2,960	3,154	3,119
Rail Franchise Premia	205	98	125	244	285	496	792	993	1,275	1,275	1,501	1,611
Northern Ireland Driver Vehicle Agency	0	0	0	15	19	18	16	16	16	16	16	16
Motor vehicle duties paid by businesses	808	809	865	878	885	908	937	931	940	977	1,075	1,112
Motor vehicle duty paid by households	3,955	3,953	4,145	4,506	4,639	4,722	4,903	4,889	4,933	5,124	4,900	4,787
Boat Licenses	0	0	0	0	0	0	0	0	0	0	0	0
Pollution/Resources taxes	**1,019**	**1,080**	**1,145**	**1,236**	**1,308**	**1,137**	**1,375**	**1,403**	**1,379**	**1,494**	**1,506**	**1,403**
Landfill Tax	672	733	804	877	954	842	1,065	1,090	1,094	1,191	1,143	1,028
Fishing Licenses	19	20	20	20	20	20	20	23	21	21	21	21
Aggregates levy	328	327	321	339	334	275	290	290	264	282	342	354
Total environmental taxes	**31,528**	**31,502**	**32,100**	**34,797**	**35,515**	**36,812**	**39,231**	**40,173**	**41,104**	**42,978**	**44,670**	**46,059**
Total taxes and social contributions	427,480	456,460	492,500	514,272	527,082	490,551	526,595	555,343	558,691	577,095	596,449	622,097
As a percentage of total taxes and social contributions (%)	**7.4**	**6.9**	**6.5**	**6.8**	**6.7**	**7.5**	**7.5**	**7.2**	**7.4**	**7.5**	**7.5**	**7.4**
Gross Domestic Product (GDP)	1,304,874	1,379,457	1,455,644	1,530,890	1,564,252	1,519,459	1,572,439	1,628,274	1,675,044	1,739,563	1,822,480	1,872,714
As a percentage of GDP (%)	**2.4**	**2.3**	**2.2**	**2.3**	**2.3**	**2.4**	**2.5**	**2.5**	**2.5**	**2.5**	**2.5**	**2.5**

Source: Office for National Statistics

Notes

All data are presented in current prices i.e. not adjusted for inflation.

1 Includes unleaded petrol (including super unleaded), leaded petrol, lead replacement petrol, ultra low suplhur petrol, diesel and ultra low sulphur diesel.

2 Duty incentives have concentrated production on ultra low sulphur varieties.

3 Includes Carbon Price Floor from 2013.

Where figures have been rounded they are reported to 2 decimal places.

this page is intentionally blank

Housing

Chapter 11

Housing

Permanent dwellings (Table 11.1, 11.3)

Local housing authorities include: the Commission for the New Towns and New Towns Development Corporations; Communities Scotland; and the Northern Ireland Housing Executive. The figures shown for housing associations include dwellings provided by housing associations other than the Communities Scotland and the Northern Ireland Housing Executive and include those provided or authorised by government departments for the families of police, prison staff, the Armed Forces and certain other services.

Mortgage possession actions by region (Table 11.6)

The table shows mortgage possession actions in the county courts of England and Wales and excludes a small number of mortgage actions in the High Court.

A claimant begins an action for an order for possession of a property by issuing a claim in the county court, either by using the Possession Claim Online system or locally through a county court. In mortgage possession cases, the usual procedure is for the claim being issued to be given a hearing date before a district judge. The court, following a judicial hearing, may grant an order for possession immediately. This entitles the claimants to apply for a warrant to have the defendant evicted. However, even where a warrant for possession is issued, the parties can still negotiate a compromise to prevent eviction.

Frequently the court grants the claimant possession but suspends the operation of the order. Provided the defendant complies with the terms of suspension, which usually require the defendant to pay the current mortgage instalments plus some of the accrued arrears, the possession order cannot be enforced.

The mortgage possession figures do not indicate how many houses have actually been repossessed through the courts. Repossessions can occur without a court order being made while not all court orders result in repossession.

A new mortgage pre-action protocol (MPAP), approved by the Master of the Rolls, was introduced for possession claims in the County Courts with effect from 19 November 2008. The MPAP gives clear guidance on what the courts expect lenders and borrowers to have done prior to a claim being issued.

Evidence from administrative records from Qtr4 2008 suggests that this date coincided with a fall of around 50% in the daily and weekly numbers of new mortgage repossession claims being issued in the courts.

It therefore seems highly likely that the launch of the MPAP has led to a fall in the number of new claims being issued since introduction of MPAP (19th November to 31st December 2008). Mortgage possession orders are typically made (where necessary) around 8 weeks after the corresponding claims are issued.

Households in Temporary Accommodation under homelessness provisions (Tables 11.7, 11.8, 11.9)

Comprises households in accommodation arranged by local authorities pending enquiries or after being accepted as owed a main homeless duty under the 1996 Act (includes residual cases awaiting re-housing under the 1985 Act). Excludes "homeless at home" cases. The data shown for Wales includes "homeless at home" cases.

11.1a Dwelling stock: by tenure[1], England[2][3]

Thousands of dwellings

	Owner Occupied	Rented Privately or with a job or business	Rented from Private Registered Providers	Rented from Local Authorities	Other public sector dwellings	All Dwellings
2000	14,600	2,089	1,273	3,012	101	**21,075**
2001	14,735	2,133	1,424	2,812	103	**21,207**
2002	14,846	2,197	1,492	2,706	112	**21,354**
2003 [4]	14,752	2,549	1,651	2,457	104	**21,513**
2004 [4]	14,986	2,578	1,702	2,335	83	**21,684**
2005 [4]	15,100	2,720	1,802	2,166	82	**21,870**
2006 [4]	15,052	2,987	1,865	2,087	82	**22,073**
2007 [4]	15,093	3,182	1,951	1,987	75	**22,288**
2008 [4]	15,067	3,443	2,056	1,870	74	**22,511**
2009 [4]	14,968	3,705	2,128	1,820	74	**22,694**
2010 [4]	14,895	3,912	2,180	1,786	66	**22,839**
2011 [4]	14,827	4,105	2,255	1,726	63	**22,976**
2012 [4] P	14,754	4,286	2,304	1,693	75	**23,111**
2013 [4] P	14,685	4,465	2,331	1,682	73	**23,236**
2014 [4] P	14,674	4,623	2,343	1,669	64	**23,372**
2015 [4] PR	14,684	4,773	2,387	1,643	55	**23,543**

Source: Department for Communities and Local Government
Contact: 0303 44 41864
E-Mail: housing.statistics@communities.gsi.gov.uk

1. For detailed definitions of all tenures, see Definitions of housing terms in Housing Statistics home page.
2. Figures for census years are based on census output.
3. Series from 1992 to 2001 for England has been adjusted so that the 2001 total dwelling estimate matches the 2001 Census.
   Series from 2002 to 2011 for England has been adjusted so that the 2011 total dwelling estimate matches the 2011 Census.
   Estimates from 2002 are based on local authority and Private Registered Provider (housing association) dwelling counts,
   the Labour Force Survey and, from 2003, the English Housing Survey. Estimates may not be strictly comparable between periods.
4. From 2003 the figures for owner-occupied and the private rental sector for England have been produced using a new
   improved methodology as detailed in the dwelling stock release. Previous to this vacancy was not accounted for.

R- Revised from previous publication
P - Provisional

Data for earlier years are less reliable and definitions may not be consistent throughout the series Stock estimates are expressed to the nearest thousand but should not be regarded as accurate to the last digit Components may not sum to totals due to rounding

11.1b Dwelling stock: by tenure[1,2], Wales

Thousands of dwellings

	Owner Occupied	Rented Privately or with a job or business	Rented from Housing Associations	Rented from Local Authorities	All Dwellings
2000 [5]	914	106	54	193	1,267
2001 [5]	941	90	55	188	1,275
2002 [5]	957	89	57	183	1,285
2003 [5]	966	97	57	176	1,296
2004 [5]	979	104	64	160	1,307
2005 [5]	989	109	65	156	1,319
2006 [5]	997	113	66	154	1,331
2007 [5]	1,002	122	67	153	1,343
2008 [5]	1,001	135	89	130	1,355
2009 [5]	989	157	107	113	1,366
2010 [5]	984	170	110	111	1,375
2011 [5]	981	180	134	89	1,384
2012 [5]	977	189	135	88	1,389
2013 [5]	983	188	135	88	1,394
2014 [5]	981	196	135	88	1,400
2015 [5]	974	208	136	88	1,406

Source: Welsh Assembly Government
Contact: 0303 44 41864
E-Mail: housing.statistics@communities.gsi.gov.uk

1. For detailed definitions of all tenures, see Definitions of housing terms in Housing Statistics home page.
2. Owner-occupied tenure includes owner-occupied, intermediate and other.
3. April data for census years are based on census output.
4. Data for years 1969 to 1990 sourced from Department of Environment publications:
   Housing and Construction Statistics, 1967-1979, 1977-1987,1980-1990 and 1990-1997.
5. The tenure split between owner-occupied and privately rented dwellings has been calculated from 1997 onwards using
   information from the Labour Force Survey. These figures were revised in January 2011 following a re-weighting of the
   Labour Force Survey data.
R - Revised
P - Provisional

 These data are produced and published separately by the Welsh Assembly Government, and although the figures in this table are correct at the time of its latest update they may be superseded before the next update.

Data for earlier years are less reliable and definitions may not be consistent throughout the series.
Stock estimates are expressed to the nearest thousand but should not be regarded as accurate to the last digit.
Components may not sum to totals due to rounding.

11.1c Dwelling stock: by tenure[1,2,3,4,5], Scotland

Thousands of dwellings

	Owner Occupied	Rented Privately or with a job or business	Rented from Housing Associations	Rented from Local Authorities	All Dwellings
31 December[4]					
1999	1,435	155	131	583	**2,303**
2000	1,472	155	137	557	**2,322**
31 March[4]					
2001	1,439	181	139	553	**2,312**
2002	1,477	179	143	531	**2,329**
2003	1,505	188	238	416	**2,347**
2004	1,513	213	251	389	**2,367**
2005	1,536	225	251	374	**2,387**
2006	1,559	234	251	362	**2,406**
2007	1,562	259	261	346	**2,428**
2008	1,592	259	269	330	**2,451**
2009	1,590	285	268	326	**2,469**
2010	1,584	303	272	323	**2,482**
2011	1,580	320	275	320	**2,495**
2012	1,545	366	277	319	**2,508**
2013	1,537	389	277	318	**2,521**
2014	1,545	394	277	318	**2,534**
2015	1,552	402	278	317	**2,549**

Source: Scottish Government
Contact: 0303 44 41864
E-Mail: housing.statistics@communities.gsi.gov.uk

1. For detailed definitions of all tenures, see Definitions of housing terms in Housing Statistics home page
2. April data for census years are based on census output
3. Data for years 1969 to 1989 sourced from Department of Environment publications:
   Housing and Construction Statistics, 1967-1979, 1977-1987,1980-1990 and 1990-1997.
4. Estimates from 1990 onwards are based on the Census (1991, 2001, 2011), council tax records and exemptions,
   social sector stock counts, and private tenure splits from the Scottish Household Survey and are not strictly comparable
   with earlier figures. These are not all collected for the same timescales and may not be exact counts, even rounded to the nearest thousand
5. In order to include vacant private sector dwellings in table 107, estimates for vacant private sector stock in the Scottish
   statistics have been apportioned according to the % of occupied dwellings for the private sector tenures.

R- Revised from previous publication
P- Provisional

These data are produced and published separately by the Scottish Government, and although the figures in this table are correct at the time of its latest update they may be superseded before the next update.

Data for earlier years are less reliable and definitions may not be consistent throughout the series.
Stock estimates are expressed to the nearest thousand but should not be regarded as accurate to the last digit.
Components may not sum to totals due to rounding.

11.1d Household Tenure 2008-09 to 2015-16[1,2,3,4,5] Northern Ireland

All households   *Percentages*

Tenure	2008-09	2009-10	2010-11	2011-12	2012-13	2013-14	2014-15	2015-16
Owned outright	36	36	35	35	36	38	37	37
Owned with mortgage[2]	33	34	33	31	30	29	31	28
Rented- NIHE[3]	14	13	12	14	12	12	11	13
Rented other[4]	16	16	19	19	20	19	20	21
rented from housing association	..	..	..	..	*4*	*3*	*4*	*4*
rented privately	..	..	..	..	*16*	*16*	*16*	*17*
Rent free[5]	1	2	1	1	1	1	1	1
Bases=100%	**2,474**	**2,761**	**2,718**	**2,778**	**2,710**	**2,736**	**2,521**	**2,494**

Source: Continuous Household Survey

1. See Appendix 1: Data Sources - Supply: https://www.communities-ni.gov.uk/sites/default/files/publications/communities/ni-housing-stats-15-16-full-copy.pdf

2. Includes properties being purchased through the co-ownership scheme.

3. NIHE - Northern Ireland Housing Executive

4. Includes properties which are rented from a housing association, rented privately.

5. Includes squatting and rent free

11.2 Dwelling stock: by tenure[1], Great Britain

Thousands of dwellings

	Owner Occupied	Rented Privately or with a job or business	Rented from Housing Associations	Rented from Local Authorities	Other public sector dwellings	All Dwellings
1 April [2]						
1981	12,020	2,354	454	6,127	..	20,954
31 December [3]						
1981	11,936	2,288	468	6,388	..	21,077
1982	12,357	2,201	480	6,196	..	21,233
1983	12,740	2,121	497	6,060	..	21,419
1984	13,099	2,040	516	5,959	..	21,615
1985	13,440	1,963	537	5,863	..	21,803
1986	13,790	1,885	551	5,776	..	22,002
1987	13,968	2,139	586	5,599	..	22,293
1988	14,424	2,077	614	5,412	..	22,527
1989	14,832	2,069	652	5,190	..	22,743
1990	15,099	2,123	702	5,015	..	22,940
31 March [3,4]						
1991	15,155	1,990	701	4,966	167	22,979
1992	15,367	2,058	733	4,879	151	23,190
1993	15,523	2,120	811	4,759	153	23,366
1994	15,695	2,184	884	4,634	150	23,546
1995	15,869	2,255	976	4,496	145	23,739
1996	16,013	2,332	1,078	4,369	141	23,931
1997	16,215	2,361	1,132	4,273	132	24,113
1998	16,461	2,367	1,205	4,140	121	24,296
1999	16,734	2,324	1,319	3,983	110	24,469
2000	16,949	2,350	1,458	3,788	101	24,645
2001	17,115	2,404	1,618	3,553	103	24,794
2002	17,280	2,465	1,692	3,420	112	24,968
2003 [5]	17,223	2,834	1,946	3,049	104	25,156
2004 [5]	17,478	2,895	2,017	2,884	83	25,358
2005 [5]	17,625	3,054	2,118	2,696	82	25,576
2006 [5]	17,608	3,334	2,182	2,603	82	25,810
2007 [5]	17,657	3,563	2,279	2,486	75	26,059
2008 [5]	17,660	3,837	2,414	2,330	74	26,317
2009 [5]	17,547	4,147	2,503	2,259	74	26,529
2010 [5]	17,463	4,385	2,562	2,220	66	26,696
2011 [5]	17,388	4,605	2,664	2,135	63	26,855
2012 [5]	17,276	4,841	2,716	2,100	75	27,008
2013 [5]	17,205	5,042	2,743	2,088	73	27,151
2014 [5] R	17,200	5,213	2,755	2,075	64	27,306

1. For detailed definitions of all tenures, see Definitions of housing terms in Housing Statistics home page. 'Other public sector dwellings' figures
are currently only available for England.

2. Figures for census years are based on census output

3. Data for years 1969 to 1990 sourced from Department of Environment publications:
   Housing and Construction Statistics, 1967-1979, 1977-1987,1980-1990 and 1990-1997.
   Great Britain totals from 2002 are derived by summing country totals at 31st March.
   For 1991 to 2001 Scotland stock levels from the year before is added into the UK total.

4. Series from 1992 to 2011 for England has been adjusted so that the 2001 and 2011 total dwelling estimate matches the 2001 and 2011 Census.
   Estimates from 2002 are based on local authority and housing association dwelling counts,
   the Labour Force Survey and, from 2003, the English Housing Survey. Estimates may not be strictly comparable between periods.

5. From 2003 the figures for owner-occupied and the private rental sector for England have been produced using a new improved
   methodology as detailed in the dwelling stock release. Previous to this vacancy was not accounted for.

R- Revised from previous publication
P- Provisional

Data for earlier years are less reliable and definitions may not be consistent throughout the series.
Stock estimates are expressed to the nearest thousand but should not be regarded as accurate to the last digit.
Components may not sum to totals due to rounding

Source: Department for Communities and Local Government;
Welsh Assembly Government;
Scottish Government;
Department for Social Development (Northern Ireland)

Contact: 0303 44 41864
E-Mail: housing.statistics@Communities.gsi.gov.uk

11.3 House building: permanent dwellings completed, by tenure[1] and country[2, 3]

Number of dwellings

	Financial Year	United Kingdom	England	Wales	Scotland	Northern Ireland
All Dwellings	1993-94	186,850	147,710	9,870	22,110	7,160
	1994-95	195,580	157,970	9,070	21,810	6,730
	1995-96	197,710	154,600	9,170	24,690	9,250
	1996-97	185,940	146,250	10,090	20,700	8,910
	1997-98	190,760	149,560	8,430	22,590	10,180
	1998-99	178,290	140,260	7,740	20,660	9,640
	1999-00	184,010	141,800	8,710	23,110	10,400
	2000-01	175,370	133,260	8,330	22,110	11,670
	2001-02	174,200	129,870	8,270	22,570	13,490
	2002-03	183,210	137,740	8,310	22,750	14,420
	2003-04	190,590	143,960	8,300	23,820	14,510
	2004-05	205,390	155,890	8,490	26,470	14,540
	2005-06 [2]	210,310	163,400	8,250	24,950	13,710
	2006-07 [2]	215,210	167,680	9,330	24,270	13,930
	2007-08	215,860	170,610	8,660	25,790	10,800
	2008-09	178,550	140,990	7,120	21,010	9,430
	2009-10	151,220	119,910	6,170	17,120	8,020
	2010-11	136,020	107,870	5,510	16,420	6,210
	2011-12	145,780	118,510	5,580	15,980	5,720
	2012-13	133,000	107,980	5,450	14,050	5,530
	2013-14	138,350	112,330	5,840	14,870	5,320
	2014-15	152,520	124,640	6,170	16,210	5,500
Private Enterprise	1993-94	146,750	116,050	6,650	18,310	5,730
	1994-95	155,290	125,740	6,300	17,890	5,350
	1995-96	156,540	123,620	6,880	19,200	6,850
	1996-97	153,450	121,170	7,520	17,490	7,270
	1997-98	160,680	127,840	6,490	17,980	8,370
	1998-99	154,560	121,190	6,440	18,780	8,140
	1999-00	160,520	124,470	7,860	19,070	9,120
	2000-01	152,740	116,640	7,390	18,200	10,510
	2001-02	153,580	115,700	7,490	18,310	12,070
	2002-03	164,300	124,460	7,520	18,940	13,390
	2003-04	172,360	130,100	7,860	20,450	13,950
	2004-05	183,710	139,130	7,990	22,440	14,150
	2005-06 [2]	185,830	144,940	7,880	20,260	12,760
	2006-07 [2]	188,560	145,680	8,990	21,040	12,850
	2007-08	187,280	147,170	8,320	21,660	10,140
	2008-09	145,290	113,800	6,430	16,100	8,960
	2009-10	116,410	93,030	5,290	11,130	6,960
	2010-11	103,870	83,180	4,510	10,700	5,480
	2011-12	108,780	89,120	4,750	10,090	4,830
	2012-13	103,180	84,550	4,710	9,840	4,070
	2013-14	109,820	89,630	5,160	10,820	4,200
	2014-15	118,120	96,270	5,330	11,990	4,540
Housing Associations	1993-94	36,580	30,210	3,010	2,820	550
	1994-95	37,240	31,380	2,570	2,790	500
	1995-96	38,170	30,230	2,130	4,780	1,040
	1996-97	30,950	24,630	2,550	2,960	810
	1997-98	28,550	21,400	1,940	4,490	730
	1998-99	22,870	18,890	1,270	1,750	960
	1999-00	23,170	17,270	850	3,960	1,090
	2000-01	22,250	16,430	900	3,800	1,110
	2001-02	20,400	14,100	710	4,200	1,390
	2002-03	18,610	13,080	780	3,720	1,030
	2003-04	18,020	13,670	420	3,370	560
	2004-05	21,550	16,660	480	4,020	390
	2005-06 [2]	24,160	18,160	350	4,700	950

11.3 House building: permanent dwellings completed, by tenure[1] and country[2, 3]

Number of dwellings

	Financial Year	United Kingdom	England	Wales	Scotland	Northern Ireland
	2006-07 [2]	26,400	21,750	350	3,230	1,080
	2007-08	28,330	23,220	340	4,100	660
	2008-09	32,430	26,690	690	4,580	470
	2009-10	34,030	26,520	880	5,580	1,060
	2010-11	30,380	23,550	990	5,110	740
	2011-12	33,950	27,460	830	4,780	890
	2012-13	27,500	22,060	740	3,240	1,450
	2013-14	26,480	21,790	670	2,910	1,110
	2014-15	31,880	27,020	840	3,060	960
Local	1993-94	3,530	1,450	210	980	890
Authorities	1994-95	3,060	850	200	1,130	880
	1995-96	3,010	760	160	720	1,360
	1996-97	1,540	450	20	240	820
	1997-98	1,520	320	-	110	1,080
	1998-99	870	180	30	120	540
	1999-00	320	60	-	70	190
	2000-01	380	180	50	110	50
	2001-02	230	60	70	70	30
	2002-03	300	200	10	90	-
	2003-04	210	190	20	-	-
	2004-05	130	100	30	-	-
	2005-06 [2]	320	300	20	-	-
	2006-07 [2]	260	250	-	10	-
	2007-08	250	220	10	30	-
	2008-09	830	490	-	340	-
	2009-10	780	370	-	410	-
	2010-11	1,760	1,140	-	610	-
	2011-12	3,080	1,960	-	1,110	-
	2012-13	2,330	1,360	-	960	-
	2013-14	2,060	910	10	1,140	-
	2014-15	2,520	1,360	-	1,160	-

1. For detailed definitions of all tenures see definitions of housing terms on Housing Statistics home page

2. Northern Ireland data prior to 2005 is sourced from the Department of Communities, which use different definitions and adjust their data. Further information can be viewed at:
https://www.communities-ni.gov.uk/publications/review-new-dwelling-starts-and-completions

3. These figures are for new build dwellings only. The Department also publishes an annual release entitled 'Housing Supply: net additional dwellings, England' which is the primary and most comprehensive measure of housing supply in England.

4. Figures from October 2005 to March 2007 in England are missing a small number of starts and completions that were inspected by independent approved inspectors. These data are included from 'June 2007

Totals may not equal the sum of component parts due to rounding to the nearest 10

- Less than 5 dwellings

P Figure provisional and subject to revision

R Revised from previous release

.. Not available

Contact:
Telephone: 0303 444 1291
Email: housing.statistics@communities.gsi.gov.uk

Source:
P2 returns from local authorities
National House-Building Council (NHBC)
Approved inspector data returns
Welsh Assembly Government
Scottish Government
Department of Finance and Personnel (DFPNI)
District Council Building Control (NI)

11.4a Housebuilding: permanent dwellings completed, by house and flat, number of bedroom and tenure[1], ENGLAND

Percentage of all dwellings

Financial Year		2002 /03[2]	2003 /04[2]	2004 /05[2]	2005 /06[2]	2006 /07[2]	2007 /08[2]	2008 /09[2]	2009 /10[2]	2010 /11[2]	2011 /12[2]	2012 /13[2]	2013 /14[2]	2014 /15[2]
Private Enterprise														
Houses	1 bedroom	-	-	-	-		-	0	1	1	1	1	1	0
	2 bedrooms	9	8	7	6	6	7	8	8	9	10	10	9	9
	3 bedrooms	29	28	28	26	27	26	25	28	33	32	33	33	35
	4 or more bedrooms	36	31	25	22	22	21	21	24	27	26	28	31	33
	All	74	67	60	55	56	55	54	60	70	69	71	74	78
Flats	1 bedroom	5	7	9	9	9	9	12	11	6	8	7	7	6
	2 bedrooms	19	24	30	35	34	35	33	28	23	22	20	19	15
	3 bedrooms	1	1	1	1	1	1	1	1	1	1	1	1	1
	4 or more bedrooms	-	-	-	-	-	-	0	-	0	0	0	0	0
	All	26	33	40	45	44	45	46	40	30	31	29	26	22
Houses and flats	1 bedroom	6	8	9	9	9	10	12	11	7	8	8	7	6
	2 bedrooms	28	32	37	41	40	41	41	35	33	32	30	28	25
	3 bedrooms	30	29	29	28	28	27	26	29	34	33	34	34	36
	4 or more bedrooms	36	32	25	22	22	22	21	25	27	27	28	31	33
	All	100	100	100	100	100	100	100	100	100	100	100	100	100
Housing Associations														
Houses	1 bedroom	2	1	1	1	-	-	0	1	1	0	1	1	1
	2 bedrooms	24	23	19	18	15	15	17	16	19	21	22	26	27
	3 bedrooms	27	24	22	19	16	15	17	19	23	24	25	28	27
	4 or more bedrooms	8	6	5	4	3	3	3	5	6	5	5	5	4
	All	62	54	47	42	34	34	37	40	50	51	53	60	60
Flats	1 bedroom	14	13	17	18	23	18	17	17	13	11	12	10	12
	2 bedrooms	22	31	34	38	41	45	44	38	34	33	31	27	25
	3 bedrooms	2	1	2	2	1	2	2	3	3	4	4	3	3
	4 or more bedrooms	1	1	-	-	-	1	0	1	1	1	1	0	0
	All	39	46	53	58	66	66	63	60	50	49	47	40	40
Houses and flats	1 bedroom	17	14	18	19	24	18	17	18	14	12	13	11	13
	2 bedrooms	45	54	52	56	56	60	61	54	54	54	53	53	53
	3 bedrooms	29	25	24	21	17	18	18	22	26	28	29	30	30
	4 or more bedrooms	9	7	5	4	3	4	4	6	7	6	6	6	5
	All	100	100	100	100	100	100	100	100	100	100	100	100	100
All tenures														
Houses	1 bedroom	1	-	-	-		-	0	1	1	1	1	1	0
	2 bedrooms	10	9	8	8	8	8	10	10	12	13	12	13	13
	3 bedrooms	29	28	27	26	25	25	23	25	30	30	31	32	33
	4 or more bedrooms	34	30	23	20	20	19	16	19	22	21	23	26	27
	All	73	66	59	54	53	52	50	55	65	64	67	71	74
Flats	1 bedroom	6	8	10	10	11	11	13	12	8	9	8	7	7
	2 bedrooms	19	24	30	35	35	36	36	31	26	25	22	20	18
	3 bedrooms	1	1	1	1	1	1	1	1	1	2	2	1	1
	4 or more bedrooms	-	-	-	-	-	-	0	-	0	0	0	0	0
	All	27	34	41	46	47	48	50	45	35	36	33	29	26
Houses and flats	1 bedroom	6	8	10	10	11	11	13	13	8	9	9	8	8
	2 bedrooms	29	33	38	42	42	44	46	40	38	38	35	33	31
	3 bedrooms	30	29	28	27	27	26	24	27	32	32	33	33	35
	4 or more bedrooms	34	30	23	21	20	19	17	20	22	21	23	26	27
	All	100	100	100	100	100	100	100	100	100	100	100	100	100

Source: Department for Communities and Local Government
Telephone: 0303 444 1291
E-Mail: housing.statistics@communities.gsi.gov.uk

1. For detailed definitions of all tenures, see Definitions of housing terms in Housing Statistics home page
2. Figures for 2001/02 onwards are based on NHBC data only, so there is some degree of variability owing to partial coverage.
3. The England worksheet and charts have been corrected following initial publication.
4. Financial Year relates to April - April

11.4b Housebuilding completions: by number of bedrooms , Wales

Percentages

		2001 /02	2002 /03	2003 /04	2004 /05	2005 /06	2006 /07	2007 /08	2008 /09	2009 /10	2010 /11	2011 /12	2012 /13	2013 /14	2014 /15
Wales[1]															
1 bedroom	**JUWO**	4	6	6	7	9	11	10	16	11	10	11	7	11	9
2 bedrooms	**JUWP**	19	18	20	21	27	28	30	33	33	29	28	24	24	23
3 bedrooms	**JUWQ**	39	35	37	35	35	33	33	30	36	39	36	39	37	38
4 or more bedrooms	**JUWR**	38	41	37	37	30	28	27	22	20	22	25	29	28	30
All houses and flats	**JUWS**	100	100	100	100	100	100	100	100	100	100	100	100	100	100

Sources: Welsh Government

1 The information presented here is collected via quarterly returns from Local Authorities and the National Housing-Building Council (NHBC).

11.5 Mortgage possession workload in the county courts of England and Wales, 2003 - 2015

Year	Quarter	Claims Issued	Orders			Warrants[1]	Repossessions by county court bailiffs	Properties taken into possession[2] in UK
			Outright	Suspended	Total			
2003		65,373	16,495	24,547	41,042	31,481	6,692	8,500
2004		76,993	20,048	26,639	46,687	33,042	7,074	8,200
2005		114,733	32,757	38,211	70,968	48,513	12,794	14,500
2006		131,248	46,288	44,895	91,183	66,060	20,960	21,000
2007		137,725	58,250	49,259	107,509	73,890	23,831	25,900
2008		142,741	70,804	61,994	132,798	89,748	35,792	40,000
2009		93,533	44,856	38,039	82,895	77,461	32,457	48,300
2010		75,431	32,940	29,235	62,175	63,532	23,612	38,100
2011		73,181	30,190	29,697	59,887	65,371	25,463	37,100
2012		59,877	24,129	23,935	48,064	59,040	19,728	34,000
2013		53,659	20,718	19,585	40,303	52,305	15,692	28,900
2014		41,151	16,120	13,519	29,639	41,900	11,976	20,900
2015 (p)		19,853	7,987	6,035	14,022	23,218	5,594	
2011	Q1	19,608	8,122	7,732	15,854	17,330	6,538	9,600
	Q2	18,339	7,388	7,336	14,724	16,403	6,170	9,300
	Q3	18,763	7,790	7,762	15,552	16,409	7,274	9,500
	Q4	16,471	6,890	6,867	13,757	15,229	5,481	8,700
2012	Q1	16,963	6,763	7,116	13,879	16,136	6,072	9,600
	Q2	14,615	6,032	6,152	12,184	14,373	4,825	8,500
	Q3	14,168	5,556	5,437	10,993	14,557	4,676	8,200
	Q4	14,131	5,778	5,230	11,008	13,974	4,155	7,700
2013	Q1	14,375	5,674	5,260	10,934	13,580	4,474	8,000
	Q2	12,881	5,187	5,059	10,246	13,529	4,087	7,600
	Q3	14,256	4,974	4,723	9,697	13,039	3,733	7,200
	Q4	12,147	4,883	4,543	9,426	12,157	3,398	6,100
2014	Q1	12,706	4,648	4,277	8,925	12,391	3,709	6,400
	Q2	10,773	4,400	3,539	7,939	11,121	3,028	5,400
	Q3	9,731	3,940	3,201	7,141	10,067	2,805	5,000
	Q4	7,941	3,132	2,502	5,634	8,321	2,434	4,100
2015	Q1	5,643	2,298	1,926	4,224	6,343	1,658	3,000
	Q2	4,849	1,951	1,475	3,426	5,646	1,363	2,500
	Q3 (r)	5,012	2,055	1,385	3,440	6,255	1,423	2,500
	Q4 (p)	4,349	1,683	1,249	2,932	4,974	1,150	

Source: HM Courts and Tribunals Service CaseMan, Possession Claim On-Line (PCOL) and Council of Mortgage Lenders (CML)

Notes:

[1] Multiple warrants may be issued per claim

[2] Council of Mortgage Lenders (CML) statistics for the latest quarter are unavailable prior to this bulletin being published as the MOJ does not have pre-release access to them. Please also note this figure relates to repossessions made in the United Kingdom whereas all other statistics in this bulletin relate to England and Wales. It should also be noted that these figures are rounded by the CML to the nearest hundred. Please see the CML website http://www.cml.org.uk/ for more information about these statistics.

[3] Data relating to 1999 onwards are sourced from county court administrative systems and exclude duplicate observations. Data prior to 1999 are sourced from manual counts made by court staff.

.. = data not available

(p) = provisional

(r)= revised

11.6 Mortgage arrears and repossessions

Year	2003	2004	2005	2006	2007	2008	2009	2010	2011	2012	2013	2014	2015
Number of mortgages													
at year end (000s)	11,452	11,515	11,608	11,746	11,852	11,667	11,504	11,478	11,384	11,284	11,186	11,147	11,129
of which homeowners	11,035	10,989	10,909	10,910	10,827	10,498	10,257	10,169	9,996	9,835	9,658	9,491	9,342
Repossessions during year	8,500	8,200	14,500	21,000	25,900	40,000	48,900	38,500	37,300	33,900	28,900	20,900	10,200
of which homeowners	–	–	–	19,900	23,900	37,000	44,100	33,900	31,200	27,000	23,300	15,900	7,200
Cases in mortgage arrears													
12+ months arrears	12,600	11,000	15,000	15,700	15,300	29,500	69,500	63,700	54,400	48,500	41,100	30,700	30,600
+ 6 - 12 months arrears	31,000	29,900	38,600	34,900	40,500	72,000	93,900	80,500	72,200	69,900	60,700	45,100	38,700
+ 3 - 6 months arrears	55,800	60,500	69,400	64,900	71,700	117,400	112,400	103,300	99,000	97,200	86,600	68,800	55,100
= All 3+ months arrears	99,400	101,400	122,900	115,600	127,500	219,000	275,800	247,500	225,600	215,700	188,300	144,600	124,300
of which homeowners	98,000	98,600	118,400	110,800	120,000	192,000	250,700	225,600	206,600	199,200	174,200	133,200	114,000

Sources: Compendium of Housing Finance Statistics, Housing Finance and CML website, Council of Mortgage Lenders.

Notes: Properties taken into possession include those voluntarily surrendered. The CML arrears figures are for the end of the year. Changes in the mortgage rate have the effect of changing monthly mortgage repayments and hence the number of months in arrears which a given amount represents.

11.7 Households in temporary accommodation[1] by type of accommodation, at the end of each quarter, England, 2001 - 2015

		Total in TA[1] (Temporary Accommodation)				Bed and breakfast hotels (including shared annexes)[2]							Hostels (including women's refuges)		
		Total	% change on same quarter in previous year	of which: with children[4,7]	Total number of children[5,7]	Total	% of Total TA	of which: with children[4,7]	with children and resident more than 6 weeks	of which: pending review /appeal	of which: headed by a 16/17 year old	of which: resident more than 6 weeks	Total	% of Total TA	of which: with children[4]
Number and percentage of total households in TA (%)															
2001	Q1	75,200	15%	..	..	10,860	14%	..	..	..	..	..	10,610	14%	..
	Q2	75,920	12%	..	..	11,390	15%	..	..	..	..	..	10,320	14%	..
	Q3	77,800	8%	..	..	12,220	16%	..	..	..	..	..	11,270	14%	..
	Q4	77,510	6%	..	..	11,860	15%	..	..	..	..	..	10,680	14%	..
2002	Q1	80,200	7%	54,660	..	12,710	16%	6,960	..	..	..	..	9,570	12%	5,540
	Q2	81,660	8%	58,870	..	12,720	16%	6,830	..	..	..	..	9,770	12%	6,030
	Q3	85,010	9%	61,740	..	13,950	16%	6,970	..	..	..	..	9,720	11%	6,280
	Q4	85,140	10%	60,310	..	13,240	16%	5,870	3,050	..	..	..	9,650	11%	5,770
2003	Q1	89,040	11%	61,510	..	12,440	14%	5,230	2,910	..	..	..	10,050	11%	6,040
	Q2	91,870	13%	65,040	..	11,380	12%	3,940	2,120	..	..	..	10,420	11%	6,360
	Q3	94,440	11%	67,260	..	10,310	11%	3,200	1,590	..	..	..	10,800	11%	6,450
	Q4	94,610	11%	67,540	..	8,420	9%	1,730	940	..	..	..	10,370	11%	6,060
2004	Q1	97,680	10%	70,580	..	7,090	7%	820	30	..	..	..	10,790	11%	6,280
	Q2	99,530	8%	71,640	121,590	7,240	7%	1,100	60	..	..	..	10,570	11%	6,090
	Q3	101,300	7%	72,510	122,530	7,450	7%	1,420	180	..	..	..	10,380	10%	5,960
	Q4	101,030	7%	72,800	124,630	6,450	6%	820	100	..	..	..	10,070	10%	5,650
2005	Q1	101,070	3%	72,670	125,860	6,780	7%	1,180	110	..	..	..	10,280	10%	5,830
	Q2	100,970	1%	72,810	124,900	6,290	6%	1,300	130	50	..	..	9,870	10%	5,440
	Q3	101,020	0%	74,180	127,990	6,100	6%	1,470	150	40	..	..	10,020	10%	5,410
	Q4	98,730	-2%	72,920	127,620	4,950	5%	820	140	30	..	..	9,230	9%	4,990
2006	Q1	96,370	-5%	71,560	127,650	5,150	5%	1,020	110	30	..	..	9,010	9%	4,960
	Q2	93,910	-7%	69,790	130,470	4,890	5%	1,050	100	50	..	..	8,940	10%	4,820
	Q3	93,090	-8%	69,500	129,340	4,900	5%	1,100	120	40	..	..	8,460	9%	4,460
	Q4	89,510	-9%	65,770	122,080	4,210	5%	650	110	40	..	..	7,850	9%	3,950
2007	Q1	87,120	-10%	65,210	125,430	4,310	5%	980	80	30	..	..	7,640	9%	4,030
	Q2	84,900	-10%	64,020	117,340	4,070	5%	940	100	30	670	300	7,230	9%	3,890
	Q3	82,750	-11%	62,830	117,090	4,090	5%	900	130	30	690	300	7,180	9%	3,850
	Q4	79,500	-11%	59,990	112,260	3,530	4%	700	120	20	550	270	6,620	8%	3,490
2008	Q1	77,510	-11%	59,230	110,360	3,840	5%	1,030	160	30	560	250	6,450	8%	3,580
	Q2	74,690	-12%	57,210	107,050	3,440	5%	1,030	180	30	420	160	6,020	8%	3,350
	Q3	72,130	-13%	55,850	104,640	3,230	4%	940	160	30	400	150	5,800	8%	3,190
	Q4	67,480	-15%	52,290	98,880	2,560	4%	520	100	20	330	150	5,250	8%	2,830
2009	Q1	64,000	-17%	49,030	92,590	2,450	4%	470	70	10	340	120	5,170	8%	2,740
	Q2	60,230	-19%	45,940	87,030	2,150	4%	510	80	20	310	130	4,710	8%	2,430
	Q3	56,920	-21%	43,400	82,780	2,050	4%	510	130	20	230	100	4,480	8%	2,330
	Q4	53,370	-21%	40,560	77,990	1,880	4%	400	120	10	170	70	4,150	8%	2,150
2010	Q1	51,310	-20%	39,200	74,610	2,050	4%	630	100	10	180	60	4,240	8%	2,270
	Q2	50,400	-16%	37,940	72,590	2,410	5%	740	160	10	190	70	4,320	9%	2,380
	Q3	49,680	-13%	37,620	71,460	2,660	5%	930	140	10	210	80	4,360	9%	2,440
	Q4	48,010	-10%	36,230	69,050	2,310	5%	660	150	10	140	50	4,160	9%	2,270
2011	Q1	48,240	-6%	36,640	69,660	2,750	6%	1,030	200	10	160	50	4,250	9%	2,330
	Q2	48,330	-4%	35,950	68,770	3,120	6%	1,210	240	20	150	40	4,370	9%	2,340
	Q3	49,100	-1%	36,680	69,850	3,370	7%	1,340	310	40	140	50	4,380	9%	2,370
	Q4	48,920	2%	36,600	69,460	3,170	6%	1,310	450	60	100	30	4,310	9%	2,380
2012	Q1	50,430	5%	37,190	70,090	3,960	8%	1,660	480	60	150	50	4,360	9%	2,350
	Q2	51,630	7%	39,470	73,890	4,230	8%	1,900	680	70	140	50	4,350	8%	2,610
	Q3	52,960	8%	40,090	75,460	4,120	8%	1,920	870	100	120	50	4,390	8%	2,690
	Q4	53,140	9%	40,830	76,740	3,820	7%	1,600	770	100	80	50	4,280	8%	2,610
2013	Q1	55,320	10%	40,450	76,040	4,510	8%	1,970	760	50	100	40	4,480	8%	2,710
	Q2	55,840	8%	42,800	79,030	4,350	8%	2,090	740	70	80	20	4,590	8%	2,890
	Q3	57,410	8%	42,210	78,770	4,610	8%	2,110	800	80	70	20	4,700	8%	2,960
	Q4	56,940	7%	43,750	80,970	3,920	7%	1,560	500	60	70	20	4,710	8%	2,950
2014	Q1	58,410	6%	44,770	83,370	4,370	7%	1,900	440	40	60	20	4,880	8%	3,010
	Q2	59,570	7%	45,940	87,890	4,590	8%	2,130	610	50	70	20	4,980	8%	3,100
	Q3	60,900	6%	47,460	91,090	4,680	8%	2,140	470	60	70	20	5,010	8%	3,110
	Q4	61,930	9%	48,460	93,980	4,540	7%	2,040	780	60	40	20	5,090	8%	3,360
2015	Q1	64,710	11%	51,210	98,620	5,270	8%	2,560	920	50	50	10	5,040	8%	3,360
	Q2	66,980	12%	52,550	102,090	5,630	8%	2,660	880	40	40	10	5,180	8%	3,510
	Q3	68,560	13%	53,480	103,440	5,910	9%	3,000	1,050	100	30	10	5,310	8%	3,510
	Q4	69,140	12%	54,240	106,240	5,120	7%	2,270	910	100	40	20	5,360	8%	3,670

Source: Department for Communities and Local Government; P1E Homelessness returns (quarterly)

Notes

1. Households in accommodation arranged by local authorities pending enquiries or after being accepted as homeless under the 1996 Act (includes residual cases awaiting re-housing under the 1985 Act).

2. Other private sector accommodation includes accommodation that has been leased directly by the household from a private landlord where this arrangement is temporary, supported lodgings, and mobile homes such as caravans. The Homelessness (Suitability of Accommodation) (England) Order 2003 came into force on 1 April 2004. This prohibits the use of B&B accommodation for families except in an emergency and even then for no longer than six weeks.

3. "Duty owed, but no accommodation has been secured" are households accepted as owed a main duty but able to remain in their existing accommodation for the immediate future. Cases in the final two columns include those households awaiting a decision on their application. Since Q2 2005, this can only apply once an appeal has been accepted as owed a main duty.

4. Includes expectant mothers with no other dependent children.

5. Includes expected children.

6. Housing Association (HA) - this was previously known as "Registered Social Landlord".

.. - Data not collected.

R - Revised data

Totals may not equal the sum of components because of rounding.
Totals include estimated data to account for non-response.

11.7 Households in temporary accommodation[1] by type of accommodation, at the end of each quarter, England, 2001 - 2015

		Nightly paid, self contained accommodation			Local Authority or Housing Association (LA/HA) stock[6]			Leased from the Private Sector by an LA or HA[6]			Other accommodation[2,8] (including private landlord)		
		Total	% of Total TA	of which: with children[4]	Total	% of Total TA	of which: with children[4,7]	Total	% of Total TA	of which: with children[4,7]	Total	% of Total TA	of which: with children[4,7]
Number and percentage of total households in TA (%)													
2001	Q1	..	..	..	25,480	34%	..	21,900	29%	..	6,350	8%	..
	Q2	..	..	..	25,450	34%	..	21,970	29%	..	6,790	9%	..
	Q3	..	..	..	25,930	33%	..	20,050	26%	..	8,320	11%	..
	Q4	..	..	..	26,580	34%	..	20,600	27%	..	7,800	10%	..
2002	Q1	3,590	4%	2,550	27,760	35%	19,160	20,660	26%	17,070	5,920	7%	3,380
	Q2	3,690	5%	2,840	28,470	35%	21,360	22,610	28%	18,570	4,400	5%	3,250
	Q3	4,130	5%	3,170	28,870	34%	21,130	23,850	28%	20,600	4,490	5%	3,590
	Q4	4,060	5%	3,020	27,580	32%	20,380	25,940	30%	21,630	4,680	5%	3,640
2003	Q1	4,110	5%	3,070	28,250	32%	19,690	28,370	32%	23,240	5,810	7%	4,240
	Q2	5,020	5%	3,770	27,590	30%	19,900	31,460	34%	26,630	5,990	7%	4,450
	Q3	4,690	5%	3,460	27,560	29%	19,650	35,140	37%	29,950	5,950	6%	4,560
	Q4	3,250	3%	2,350	27,480	29%	19,450	38,730	41%	33,340	6,370	7%	4,600
2004	Q1	3,260	3%	2,350	27,890	29%	20,120	42,390	43%	36,390	6,270	6%	4,620
	Q2	4,140	4%	2,970	27,960	28%	20,070	42,630	43%	35,900	6,990	7%	5,510
	Q3	4,270	4%	2,920	28,220	28%	20,070	43,720	43%	36,650	7,260	7%	5,500
	Q4	4,180	4%	2,760	27,730	27%	19,730	46,140	46%	38,750	6,460	6%	5,080
2005	Q1	4,190	4%	2,850	26,630	26%	18,610	46,530	46%	39,170	6,670	7%	5,030
	Q2	4,520	4%	2,970	27,430	27%	19,070	46,990	47%	39,600	5,870	6%	4,420
	Q3	4,520	4%	3,140	25,030	25%	17,620	48,860	48%	41,500	6,500	6%	5,060
	Q4	4,450	5%	2,950	24,220	25%	17,110	49,910	51%	42,310	5,970	6%	4,750
2006	Q1	4,500	5%	2,990	22,350	23%	16,080	49,660	52%	41,960	5,700	6%	4,560
	Q2	4,570	5%	3,020	20,790	22%	14,880	49,320	53%	41,740	5,400	6%	4,270
	Q3	4,870	5%	3,190	20,180	22%	14,830	49,700	53%	41,980	4,980	5%	3,950
	Q4	4,900	5%	3,310	18,840	21%	13,930	48,850	55%	40,130	4,870	5%	3,810
2007	Q1	5,140	6%	3,470	18,040	21%	13,510	45,600	52%	38,600	6,400	7%	4,620
	Q2	5,410	6%	3,760	17,240	20%	12,970	44,610	53%	37,920	6,350	7%	4,540
	Q3	5,650	7%	3,990	16,490	20%	12,410	43,430	52%	37,100	5,920	7%	4,590
	Q4	5,780	7%	4,080	15,910	20%	11,780	41,730	52%	35,380	5,930	7%	4,560
2008	Q1	6,210	8%	4,450	14,740	19%	11,080	40,480	52%	34,610	5,790	7%	4,480
	Q2	5,980	8%	4,220	14,030	19%	10,660	41,130	55%	34,900	4,090	5%	3,050
	Q3	5,680	8%	4,120	13,420	19%	10,240	39,990	55%	34,390	4,020	6%	2,970
	Q4	5,230	8%	3,720	11,930	18%	8,990	38,790	57%	33,560	3,720	6%	2,680
2009	Q1	4,980	8%	3,470	10,480	16%	7,800	37,450	59%	32,050	3,480	5%	2,500
	Q2	4,570	8%	3,120	9,520	16%	6,970	35,920	60%	30,620	3,360	6%	2,290
	Q3	4,180	7%	2,870	8,780	15%	6,390	34,130	60%	29,090	3,310	6%	2,210
	Q4	3,620	7%	2,450	8,180	15%	5,950	32,430	61%	27,540	3,100	6%	2,070
2010	Q1	3,380	7%	2,320	7,790	15%	5,790	30,920	60%	26,310	2,940	6%	1,900
	Q2	3,340	7%	2,220	7,650	15%	5,570	29,820	59%	25,210	2,860	6%	1,830
	Q3	3,520	7%	2,380	7,610	15%	5,480	28,740	58%	24,570	2,800	6%	1,810
	Q4	3,590	7%	2,430	7,430	15%	5,440	27,730	58%	23,620	2,790	6%	1,810
2011	Q1	3,920	8%	2,730	7,490	16%	5,500	26,960	56%	23,170	2,870	6%	1,890
	Q2	4,200	9%	2,920	7,570	16%	5,460	26,240	54%	22,170	2,850	6%	1,860
	Q3	4,350	9%	3,100	7,890	16%	5,810	26,380	54%	22,250	2,740	6%	1,810
	Q4	4,460	9%	3,330	7,990	16%	5,840	26,080	53%	21,800	2,910	6%	1,950
2012	Q1	4,860	10%	3,670	8,270	16%	6,000	26,040	52%	21,490	2,940	6%	2,030
	Q2	5,370	10%	4,100	8,600	17%	6,470	25,960	50%	22,240	3,130	6%	2,160
	Q3	5,880	11%	4,580	8,930	17%	6,730	26,290	50%	21,880	3,360	6%	2,280
	Q4	6,190	12%	4,900	9,090	17%	6,830	26,310	50%	22,490	3,440	6%	2,400
2013	Q1	7,000	13%	5,450	9,270	17%	7,020	26,260	47%	21,020	3,800	7%	2,290
	Q2	7,630	14%	6,060	10,060	18%	7,860	24,780	44%	21,210	4,440	8%	2,690
	Q3	8,400	15%	6,420	9,810	17%	7,290	25,660	45%	21,460	4,230	7%	1,970
	Q4	8,660	15%	7,330	9,560	17%	7,280	25,460	45%	21,450	4,620	8%	3,190
2014	Q1	9,340	16%	7,960	9,880	17%	7,530	25,270	43%	21,150	4,680	8%	3,220
	Q2	10,100	17%	8,630	10,120	17%	7,870	24,800	42%	20,730	4,990	8%	3,490
	Q3	11,750	19%	10,100	10,070	17%	7,790	23,290	38%	19,550	6,110	10%	4,780
	Q4	12,540	20%	10,770	10,530	17%	8,110	23,460	38%	19,790	5,780	9%	4,400
2015	Q1	13,620	21%	11,770	10,920	17%	8,540	23,990	37%	20,410	5,860	9%	4,570
	Q2	14,870	22%	12,840	11,500	17%	8,750	23,820	36%	20,410	5,980	9%	4,390
	Q3	15,760	23%	13,280	12,210	18%	9,600	23,520	34%	19,800	5,860	9%	4,290
	Q4	16,210	23%	13,990	12,480	18%	9,790	25,580	37%	21,130	4,400	6%	3,400

Source: Department for Communities and Local Government; P1E Homelessness returns (quarterly)

Notes

1. Households in accommodation arranged by local authorities pending enquiries or after being accepted as homeless under the 1996 Act (includes residual cases awaiting re-housing under the 1985 Act).

2. Other private sector accommodation includes accommodation that has been leased directly by the household from a private landlord where this arrangement is temporary, supported lodgings, and mobile homes such as caravans. The Homelessness (Suitability of Accommodation) (England) Order 2003 came into force on 1 April 2004. This prohibits the use of B&B accommodation for families except in an emergency and even then for no longer than six weeks.

3. "Duty owed, but no accommodation has been secured" are households accepted as owed a main duty but able to remain in their existing accommodation for the immediate future. Cases in the final two columns include those households awaiting a decision on their application. Since Q2 2005, this can only apply once an appeal has been accepted as owed a main duty.

4. Includes expectant mothers with no other dependent children.

5. Includes expected children.

6. Housing Association (HA) - this was previously known as "Registered Social Landlord".

.. - Data not collected

R - Revised data

Totals may not equal the sum of components because of rounding.

Totals include estimated data to account for non-response.

11.7 Households in temporary accommodation[1] by type of accommodation, at the end of each quarter, England, 2001 - 2015

		Of which: in TA in another local authority district	a main duty accepted	% change from previous quarter	of which: with children[4]	All including decision pending	% change from previous quarter	Total with children[4], including decision pending
					Duty owed, no accommodation secured[3]			

Number and percentage of total households in TA (%)

Year	Qtr	Of which: in TA in another local authority district	a main duty accepted	% change from previous quarter	of which: with children[4]	All including decision pending	% change from previous quarter	Total with children[4], including decision pending
2001	Q1	6,150	8,420	11%	..	12,730	4%	..
	Q2	7,440	8,870	5%	..	13,240	4%	..
	Q3	8,240	8,090	-9%	..	11,820	-11%	..
	Q4	8,460	8,600	6%	..	12,000	2%	..
2002	Q1	9,670	8,620	0%	..	11,990	0%	3,320
	Q2	8,190	8,890	3%	..	12,440	4%	4,450
	Q3	11,550	10,390	17%	..	14,440	16%	6,760
	Q4	12,310	9,760	-6%	..	14,800	3%	5,830
2003	Q1	11,470	10,580	8%	..	16,280	10%	7,550
	Q2	10,880	13,310	26%	..	19,380	19%	9,410
	Q3	9,880	15,370	15%	..	23,060	19%	10,140
	Q4	10,440	17,500	14%	..	23,070	0%	10,990
2004	Q1	9,850	15,870	-9%	..	21,940	-5%	11,610
	Q2	9,480	17,030	7%	..	23,000	5%	13,230
	Q3	10,030	17,100	0%	..	23,200	1%	13,400
	Q4	8,610	16,100	-6%	..	20,930	-10%	11,880
2005	Q1	11,660	15,290	-5%	..	20,910	0%	12,850
	Q2	11,790	16,020	5%	10,470	..	..	..
	Q3	13,430	15,140	-6%	10,270	..	..	..
	Q4	10,700	11,570	-24%	7,840	..	..	..
2006	Q1	11,080	11,010	-5%	7,210	..	..	..
	Q2	11,590	10,210	-7%	6,920	..	..	..
	Q3	11,620	9,720	-5%	6,550	..	..	..
	Q4	9,950	8,470	-13%	5,740	..	..	..
2007	Q1	10,130	8,780	4%	5,910	..	..	..
	Q2	10,490	9,150	4%	6,280	..	..	..
	Q3	11,130	9,540	4%	6,300	..	..	..
	Q4	10,820	8,080	-15%	5,510	..	..	..
2008	Q1	10,200	7,470	-8%	5,180	..	..	..
	Q2	8,720	7,890	6%	5,630	..	..	..
	Q3	7,620	6,740	-15%	4,520	..	..	..
	Q4	7,360	6,070	-10%	4,030	..	..	..
2009	Q1	7,960	5,560	-9%	3,740	..	..	..
	Q2	7,880	4,560	-18%	2,940	..	..	..
	Q3	6,550	4,350	-5%	2,770	..	..	..
	Q4	5,780	4,150	-5%	2,540	..	..	..
2010	Q1	5,430	3,710	-11%	2,320	..	..	..
	Q2	5,630	3,780	2%	2,510	..	..	..
	Q3	5,880	4,100	8%	2,700	..	..	..
	Q4	5,810	4,410	8%	2,970	..	..	..
2011	Q1	6,300	4,770	8%	3,270	..	..	..
	Q2	6,290	4,770	0%	3,420	..	..	..
	Q3	6,850	5,110	7%	3,590	..	..	..
	Q4	7,350	5,490	8%	3,550	..	..	..
2012	Q1	7,870	5,400	-2%	3,860	..	..	..
	Q2	8,170	5,500	2%	3,830	..	..	..
	Q3	8,520	5,560	1%	4,080	..	..	..
	Q4	9,270	5,690	2%	3,950	..	..	..
2013	Q1	9,130	5,930	4%	4,270	..	..	..
	Q2	11,280	5,510	-7%	3,870	..	..	..
	Q3	11,860	5,010	-9%	3,520	..	..	..
	Q4	12,190	4,930	-2%	3,460	..	..	..
2014	Q1	12,910	5,620	14%	3,960	..	..	..
	Q2	14,130	5,310	-6%	3,880	..	..	..
	Q3	15,460	6,120	15%	4,420	..	..	..
	Q4	15,990	5,820	-5%	4,290	..	..	..
2015	Q1	16,810	6,900	19%	5,060	..	..	..
	Q2	17,640	6,370	-8%	4,640	..	..	..
	Q3	18,600	6,610	4%	4,830	..	..	..
	Q4	18,670	7,490	13%	4,800	..	..	..

Source: Department for Communities and Local Government; P1E Homelessness returns (quarterly)

Notes

1. Households in accommodation arranged by local authorities pending enquiries or after being accepted as homeless under the 1996 Act (includes residual cases awaiting re-housing under the 1985 Act).

2. Other private sector accommodation includes accommodation that has been leased directly by the household from a private landlord where this arrangement is temporary, supported lodgings, and mobile homes such as caravans. The Homelessness (Suitability of Accommodation) (England) Order 2003 came into force on 1 April 2004. This prohibits the use of B&B accommodation for families except in an emergency and even then for no longer than six weeks.

3. "Duty owed, but no accommodation has been secured" are households accepted as owed a main duty but able to remain in their existing accommodation for the immediate future. Cases in the final two columns include those households awaiting a decision on their application. Since Q2 2005, this can only apply once an appeal has been accepted as owed a main duty.

4. Includes expectant mothers with no other dependent children.

5. Includes expected children.

6. Housing Association (HA) - this was previously known as "Registered Social Landlord".

.. - Data not collected.

R - Revised data

Totals may not equal the sum of components because of rounding.

Totals include estimated data to account for non-response.

11.8 Homeless Households in temporary accomodation at the end of the period - as at 31 March each year, Wales

		2004-05 Annual	2005-06 Annual	2006-07 Annual	2007-08 Annual	2008-09 Annual	2009-10 Annual	2010-11 Annual	2011-12 Annual	2012-13 Annual	2013-14 Annual	2014-15 Annual
Total accommodated at the end of quarter		3350	3440	3150	2880	2815	2490	2640	2770	2525	2295	2050
Total accommodated at the end of quarter	Private sector accommodation (1)	415	505	710	900	1070	1050	1080	1065	1010	910	855
	Public sector accommodation (2)	460	615	575	445	415	390	435	380	380	440	440
	Hostels and women's refuges	310	450	405	475	510	400	415	485	505	510	475
	Bed and breakfast	760	595	380	280	255	235	240	310	300	185	195
	Other	170	300	230	190	105	*	*	5	10	*	*
	Homeless at home	1230	980	855	585	465	415	470	525	320	245	85
	Accommodation type unknown	.	.	.	.	.	.	.	.	.	.	.

Source: Welsh Government, Homelessness data collection

Contact: stats.housing@wales.gsi.gov.uk

1. Private sector accommodation includes private sector accommodation leased by the local authority, RSLs and directly with a private sector landlord

2. Public sector accommodation includes within local authority stock and RSL stock on assured shorthold tenancies

. The data item is not applicable.

* The data item is disclosive or not sufficiently robust for publication

11.9 Households in temporary accommodation by accommodation type, Scotland

Households in temporary accommodation by accommodation type											
All households		Social sector accommodation[1]		Hostel		Bed & Breakfast		Other[2]		Total	
		Number	%	Number	%	Number	%	Number	%	Number	%
2004	as at 31 March	3,537	55	1,586	25	1,190	18	132	2	6,445	100
	as at 30 June	3,754	56	1,514	23	1,273	19	105	2	6,646	100
	as at 30 September	3,894	56	1,590	23	1,331	19	110	2	6,925	100
	as at 31 December	4,071	59	1,521	22	1,243	18	117	2	6,952	100
2005	as at 31 March	4,136	57	1,490	20	1,516	21	159	2	7,301	100
	as at 30 June	4,324	59	1,340	18	1,413	19	264	4	7,341	100
	as at 30 September	4,606	60	1,320	17	1,424	19	333	4	7,683	100
	as at 31 December	4,525	60	1,295	17	1,323	18	356	5	7,499	100
2006	as at 31 March	4,747	59	1,328	17	1,494	19	416	5	7,985	100
	as at 30 June	4,732	60	1,342	17	1,362	17	452	6	7,888	100
	as at 30 September	4,880	60	1,301	16	1,491	18	439	5	8,111	100
	as at 31 December	4,981	62	1,235	15	1,391	17	482	6	8,089	100
2007	as at 31 March	5,164	60	1,242	14	1,528	18	643	7	8,577	100
	as at 30 June	5,075	60	1,170	14	1,588	19	690	8	8,523	100
	as at 30 September	5,104	61	1,134	13	1,492	18	671	8	8,401	100
	as at 31 December	5,460	63	1,104	13	1,348	16	721	8	8,633	100
2008	as at 31 March[3]	6,134	64	1,079	11	1,609	17	713	7	9,535	100
	as at 30 June	6,079	62	1,064	11	1,791	18	815	8	9,749	100
	as at 30 September	6,131	62	1,058	11	1,780	18	848	9	9,817	100
	as at 31 December	5,931	62	1,019	11	1,662	17	924	10	9,536	100
2009	as at 31 March	6,355	63	994	10	1,748	17	956	10	10,053	100
	as at 30 June	6,294	62	1,186	12	1,654	16	1,072	11	10,206	100
	as at 30 September	6,438	62	1,221	12	1,584	15	1,100	11	10,343	100
	as at 31 December	6,378	62	1,234	12	1,515	15	1,151	11	10,278	100
2010	as at 31 March	6,775	63	1,217	11	1,765	16	972	9	10,729	100
	as at 30 June	6,938	62	1,267	11	1,940	17	958	9	11,103	100
	as at 30 September	7,124	63	1,369	12	1,673	15	1,098	10	11,264	100
	as at 31 December	7,272	66	1,339	12	1,418	13	1,066	10	11,095	100
2011	as at 31 March	7,215	64	1,371	12	1,544	14	1,124	10	11,254	100
	as at 30 June	7,443	67	1,349	12	1,414	13	953	9	11,159	100
	as at 30 September	7,382	67	1,329	12	1,433	13	916	8	11,060	100
	as at 31 December	7,102	66	1,310	12	1,232	12	1,041	10	10,685	100
2012	as at 31 March	7,093	66	1,333	12	1,281	12	1,043	10	10,750	100
	as at 30 June	7,106	68	1,190	11	1,205	12	965	9	10,466	100
	as at 30 September	7,146	68	1,333	13	1,090	10	977	9	10,546	100
	as at 31 December	6,920	67	1,292	13	1,063	10	977	10	10,252	100
2013	as at 31 March	7,061	67	1,290	12	1,170	11	950	9	10,471	100
	as at 30 June	6,965	66	1,451	14	1,104	11	972	9	10,492	100
	as at 30 September	6,877	67	1,503	15	1,001	10	887	9	10,268	100
	as at 31 December	6,687	67	1,496	15	932	9	848	9	9,963	100
2014	as at 31 March	6,405	62	1,813	18	1,125	11	938	9	10,281	100
	as at 30 June	6,310	62	1,830	18	1,073	11	981	10	10,194	100
	as at 30 September	6,509	63	1,714	17	1,070	10	1,035	10	10,328	100
	as at 31 December	6,365	62	1,766	17	1,030	10	1,057	10	10,218	100
2015	as at 30 March	6,562	62	1,741	16	1,085	10	1,194	11	10,582	100
	as at 30 June	6,600	63	1,743	17	1,059	10	1,061	10	10,463	100
	as at 30 September	6,547	62	1,749	17	1,156	11	1,046	10	10,498	100
	as at 31 December	6,616	63	1,733	17	1,025	10	1,093	10	10,467	100

Source: Scottish Government

1. Includes Glasgow Housing Association stock from 2003, and all other housing associations from June 2005 onward.
2. The category 'other' includes mainly private landlords. Prior to June 1999 the figures may also include an unknown number of local authority-owned chalets or mobile homes.
3. From 31 March 2008 there is a break in comparability in numbers in temporary accommodation in Glasgow-see notes page.

Background to discontinuity in Glasgow data from 31 March 2008

From 31 March 2008 there is a break in comparability in the information on numbers of homeless applicants in temporary accommodation
in Glasgow. The number of homeless households in temporary accommodation in Glasgow includes asylum applications given indefinite
leave to remain in the United Kingdom and who are in temporary accommodation. From 31 March 2008 there was an significant increase in such households
as a consequence of the 'legacy' case reviews undertaken by the Home Office. This introduces a discontinuity in the statistics for both Glasgow and for
Scotland in the totals for all households and households with children. To bridge the discontinuity Glasgow have provided figures on the numbers
of such households included at the end of each quarter from 31 March 2008. The additional numbers included are:-

Banking, insurance

Chapter 12

Banking, insurance

Industrial analysis of monetary financial institutions deposits and lending (Tables 12.4 and 12.5)

These data collate information from UK MFIs on deposits from and lending to UK residents other than MFIs and are separated into 18 broad industrial categories, based upon the SIC classification system. Until Q3 2007, the analysis of lending covered loans, advances (including under reverse repos), finance leasing, acceptances and facilities (all in sterling and other currencies) provided by reporting MFIs to their UK resident non-MFI customers, as well as MFI holdings of sterling and euro commercial paper issued by these resident customers. Following a review of statistical data collected, acceptances and holdings of sterling and euro commercial paper are no longer collected at the industry level detail with effect from Q4 2007 data. Total lending therefore reflects loans and advances (including under reverse repos) only, from Q4 2007 data.

Consumer credit (Excluding Student Loans) (Table 12.12)

Following an ONS review in August 1997, data for 'other specialist lenders' were improved and revised back to January 1995. Total outstanding consumer credit was revised upwards by £2.6bn. Flows were break adjusted. Monthly data are available for lending by retailers from January 1997 but are not available for lending by insurance companies. The missing monthly data have been interpolated from quarterly data.

Within total consumer credit (excluding student loans) outstanding, credit card lending had been underestimated and 'other' consumer credit overestimated prior to January 1999 as a result of a longstanding inconsistency. The credit card element had previously covered sterling credit card lending to the UK household sector by only UK banks and building societies. Credit card lending by other specialist lenders and retailers (where they finance lending themselves) could not be separately identified and so was included within the 'other' consumer credit component.

From January 1999 onwards this inconsistency has been corrected, as credit card lending by other specialist lenders can be separately identified. As a result, data from January 1999 onwards for credit card lending and for 'other' consumer credit are not directly comparable with those for earlier periods. The change affects all three measures of credit card lending (gross, net and amounts outstanding), with an equal offsetting change to 'other' consumer credit. In non-seasonally adjusted terms, gross credit card lending was on average around £800 million per month higher since January 1999, whilst the amount outstanding of credit card debt was boosted by £4.8 billion in January 1999. The changes to net credit card lending are much smaller in absolute terms, with no discernible change to trend.

From November 2006, the Bank of England ceased to update the separate data on consumer credit provided by other specialist lenders, retailers, and insurance companies, previously contained in Table A5.6 of Monetary and Financial Statistics. The final month for which separate data are available on the Bank's Statistical Interactive Database is November 2006. The three categories have been merged into "other consumer credit lenders".

Prior to January 2008, building societies' lending was unsecured lending to individuals including sterling bridging loans (prior to October 1998 this was class 3 lending to individuals). Building societies gross lending through overdrafts is no longer included from January 2008.

http://www.bankofengland.co.uk/boeapps/iadb/newintermed.asp

12.1 The Bank of England's Annual Balance Sheet 1958-2015

This sheet gives consistent annual series for the Bank's liabilities and assets from 1958 to 1966, which were first published in the June 1967 Quarterly Bulletin and extended to 2006 using subsequent Quarterly Bulletins.   An extension to 2014 is made using the new reporting method introduced in 2006. The dates in each year to which the figures relate are: last Saturday in February; 1958-1966 - Published Bank Returns; last Wednesday in February: 1966-2006 - Published Bank Returns: third Wednesday in February (the dates on which the London Clearing Banks compiled their monthly figures); 2006-2014 - Published Bank Returns: third Wednesday in February. See links at the bottom of the table for more information on the data.

Assets, £

	Total	Government debt	Other Government securities	Other securities	Coin and bullion	Notes in the Bank
1958	2,327,196,165	11,015,100	2,222,675,614	49,533,147	5,727,986	38,244,318
1959	2,396,154,287	11,015,100	2,309,195,369	27,721,013	3,926,655	44,296,150
1960	2,509,611,487	11,015,100	2,412,801,707	44,040,161	3,309,613	38,444,906
1961	2,766,327,702	11,015,100	2,655,953,220	52,627,117	2,331,877	44,400,388
1962	2,920,525,859	11,015,100	2,819,589,302	65,236,067	1,468,171	23,217,219
1963	2,714,385,221	11,015,100	2,585,258,886	75,731,629	1,467,915	40,911,691
1964	2,831,080,950	11,015,100	2,738,352,963	58,944,838	1,451,304	21,316,745
1965	3,042,943,845	11,015,100	2,879,556,182	101,959,343	1,469,009	48,944,211
1966	3,302,225,248	11,015,100	3,165,623,387	102,383,926	1,460,584	21,742,251

3rd Wednesday in February

	Total	Government debt	Other Government securities	Other securities	Coin and bullion	Notes in the Bank
1966	3,294,800,000	11,015,100	3,165,884,900	100,500,000	17,400,000	
1967	3,532,700,000	11,015,100	3,326,484,900	153,800,000	41,400,000	
1968	3,742,400,000	11,015,100	3,513,084,900	179,700,000	38,600,000	
1969	3,870,700,000	11,015,100	3,724,084,900	116,900,000	18,700,000	
1970	3,887,000,000	11,015,100	3,655,984,900	198,000,000	22,000,000	
1971	4,668,000,000	11,015,100	4,166,984,900	446,000,000	44,000,000	
1972	4,242,000,000	11,015,100	3,598,984,900	594,000,000	38,000,000	
1973	5,484,000,000	11,015,100	4,572,984,900	866,000,000	34,000,000	
1974	6,564,000,000	11,015,100	5,208,984,900	1,320,000,000	24,000,000	
1975	6,945,000,000	11,015,100	6,037,984,900	877,000,000	19,000,000	
1976	7,677,000,000	11,015,100	6,508,984,900	1,138,000,000	19,000,000	
1977	8,156,000,000	11,015,100	6,600,984,900	1,537,000,000	7,000,000	
1978	10,004,000,000	11,015,100	8,541,984,900	1,428,000,000	23,000,000	
1979	10,193,000,000	11,015,100	8,491,984,900	1,683,000,000	7,000,000	
1980	11,065,000,000	11,015,100	8,760,984,900	2,269,000,000	24,000,000	
1981	12,112,000,000	11,015,100	7,336,984,900	4,749,000,000	15,000,000	
1982	12,701,000,000	11,015,100	4,765,984,900	7,919,000,000	5,000,000	
1983	15,961,000,000	11,015,100	4,369,984,900	11,565,000,000	15,000,000	
1984	14,315,000,000	11,015,100	2,109,984,900	12,184,000,000	10,000,000	
1985	19,603,000,000	11,015,100	2,893,984,900	16,693,000,000	5,000,000	
1986	19,219,000,000	11,015,100	3,227,984,900	15,972,000,000	8,000,000	
1987	17,256,000,000	11,015,100	2,150,984,900	15,087,000,000	7,000,000	
1988	16,889,000,000	11,015,100	2,713,984,900	14,157,000,000	7,000,000	
1989	17,350,000,000	11,015,100	6,114,984,900	11,214,000,000	10,000,000	
1990	18,679,000,000	11,015,100	11,681,984,900	6,976,000,000	10,000,000	
1991	19,694,000,000	11,015,100	9,952,984,900	9,726,000,000	4,000,000	
1992	20,280,000,000	11,015,100	8,448,984,900	11,808,000,000	12,000,000	
1993	24,569,000,000	11,015,100	7,976,984,900	16,574,000,000	7,000,000	
1994	26,351,000,000	11,015,100	6,954,984,900	19,381,000,000	4,000,000	
1995	24,195,000,000	0	14,311,000,000	9,876,000,000	8,000,000	
1996	25,181,000,000	0	13,552,000,000	11,624,000,000	5,000,000	
1997	26,917,000,000	0	10,309,000,000	16,596,000,000	12,000,000	
1998	32,681,000,000	0	6,174,000,000	26,503,000,000	4,000,000	
1999	101,956,000,000	0	6,936,000,000	95,008,000,000	12,000,000	
2000	80,756,000,000	0	7,255,000,000	73,489,000,000	12,000,000	
2001	37,850,000,000	0	15,061,000,000	22,782,000,000	7,000,000	
2002	41,352,000,000	0	15,298,000,000	26,050,000,000	4,000,000	
2003	46,712,000,000	0	15,735,000,000	30,970,000,000	7,000,000	
2004	48,565,000,000	0	16,426,000,000	32,132,000,000	7,000,000	
2005	55,714,000,000	0	15,193,000,000	40,512,000,000	9,000,000	
2006	61,799,000,000	0	15,538,000,000	46,254,000,000	7,000,000	

3rd Wednesday in February	Total	£ Short-term repo operations with BoE	£ long-term operations with BoE	Central Bank bonds and other securities acquired via market transactions	£ Ways and means advances to HM government	Other assets including loan to the Asset Purchase facility
2007	76,991,000,000	30,110,000,000	15,000,000,000	6,727,000,000	13,370,000,000	11,784,000,000
2008	97,616,000,000	6,609,000,000	31,999,000,000	7,618,000,000	7,370,000,000	44,020,000,000
2009	168,404,000,000	0	126,261,000,000	11,873,000,000	9,392,000,000	20,878,000,000
2010	247,280,000,000	0	20,607,000,000	12,691,000,000	370,000,000	213,612,000,000
2011	241,642,000,000	0	14,102,000,000	13,273,000,000	370,000,000	213,896,000,000
2012	311,459,000,000	0	5,545,000,000	13,892,000,000	370,000,000	291,653,000,000
2013	404,228,000,000	0	2,085,000,000	13,248,000,000	370,000,000	388,525,000,000
2014	403,089,000,000	0	1,165,000,000	16,312,000,000	370,000,000	385,242,000,000
2015*	406,582,000,000					

For more information on the data please use the following links: Source: Bank of England

Original 1967 Quarterly Bulletin article: http://www.bankofengland.co.uk/archive/Documents/historicpubs/qb/1967/qb67q2159163.pdf

Bank of England Statistical Abstracts: http://www.bankofengland.co.uk/archive/Pages/digitalcontent/historicpubs/statisticalabst.aspx

The implications of money market reform for data published in Monetary and Financial Statistics' in the June 2006 issue of Bank of England: Monetary and Financial Statistics.:

http://www.bankofengland.co.uk/statistics/Documents/ms/articles/artjun06.pdf

Changes to the Bank's weekly reporting regime - Quarterly Bulletin article, 2014Q3: http://www.bankofengland.co.uk/publications/Documents/quarterlybulletin/2014/qb300614.pdf

Other data

Weekly data on the Bank of England's balance sheet 1844-2006: http://www.bankofengland.co.uk/research/Documents/onebank/balanceweekly_final.xlsx

Three centuries of macroeconomic data: http://www.bankofengland.co.uk/research/Pages/onebank/threecenturies.aspx

* The total balance sheet is now published quarterly with a 5 quarter lag

Following changes to legislation in the 2009 Banking Act and the recommendations of the Plenderleith Review the Bank of England has decided to replace the Bank Return with a new Weekly Report. The information provided in the Weekly Report will be augmented on a quarterly basis, at a lag of five quarters, with data for those assets and liabilities which had not previously been disclosed to complete the balance sheet.

12.1 The Bank of England's Annual Balance Sheet 1958-2015

This sheet gives consistent annual series for the Bank's liabilities and assets from 1958 to 1966, which were first published in the June 1967 Quarterly Bulletin and extended to 2006 using subsequent Quarterly Bulletins. An extension to 2014 is made using the new reporting method introduced in 2006. The dates in each year to which the figures relate are: last Saturday in February; 1958-1966 - Published Bank Returns, last Wednesday in February: 1966-2006 - Published Bank Returns: third Wednesday in February (the dates on which the London Clearing Banks compiled their monthly figures); 2006-2014 - Published Bank Returns: third Wednesday in February. See links at the bottom of the table for more information on the data.

Liabilities, £

	Notes In circulation	Notes in the Bank	Capital	Rest	Deposits	o/w Public deposits	o/w Special deposits	o/w Bankers deposits	Other accounts	7 day and other Bills	Total
1958	1,962,114,543	38,244,318	14,553,000	3,900,136	308,384,168						2,327,196,165
1959	2,006,062,831	44,296,150	14,553,000	3,900,441	327,341,865						2,396,154,287
1960	2,111,915,274	38,444,906	14,553,000	3,898,192	340,800,115						2,509,611,487
1961	2,205,960,632	44,400,388	14,553,000	3,880,391	497,533,291		155,100,000				2,766,327,702
1962	2,302,141,403	23,217,219	14,553,000	3,917,764	576,696,473		241,400,000				2,920,525,859
1963	2,309,448,249	40,911,691	14,553,000	3,894,802	345,577,479						2,714,385,221
1964	2,429,044,275	21,316,745	14,553,000	3,896,193	362,270,737						2,831,080,950
1965	2,601,417,528	48,944,211	14,553,000	3,881,812	374,147,294						3,042,943,845
1966	2,778,619,008	21,742,251	14,553,000	3,882,025	483,428,964						3,302,225,248

3rd Wednesday in February

	Notes In circulation	Notes in the Bank	Capital	Rest	Deposits	o/w Public deposits	o/w Special deposits	o/w Bankers deposits	Other accounts	7 day and other Bills	Total
1966	2,783,800,000	16,600,000	14,553,000	3,747,000	476,100,000	12,600,000	97,500,000	274,800,000	91,200,000		3,294,800,000
1967	2,859,800,000	40,600,000	14,553,000	3,747,000	614,000,000	16,100,000	201,400,000	282,400,000	114,100,000		3,532,700,000
1968	3,012,500,000	38,000,000	14,553,000	3,747,000	673,600,000	14,400,000	218,200,000	308,400,000	132,600,000		3,742,400,000
1969	3,132,500,000	18,000,000	14,553,000	3,747,000	702,000,000	18,500,000	231,000,000	308,200,000	144,300,000		3,870,800,000
1970	3,231,000,000	20,000,000	14,553,000	0	621,447,000	15,000,000	220,000,000	248,000,000	138,000,000		3,887,000,000
1971	3,658,000,000	42,000,000	14,553,000	0	953,447,000	15,000,000	398,000,000	314,000,000	226,000,000		4,668,000,000
1972	3,663,000,000	37,000,000	14,553,000	0	527,447,000	15,000,000	0	178,000,000	334,000,000		4,242,000,000
1973	4,166,000,000	34,000,000	14,553,000	0	1,269,447,000	22,000,000	714,000,000	230,000,000	303,000,000		5,484,000,000
1974	4,552,000,000	23,000,000	14,553,000	0	1,974,447,000	28,000,000	1,368,000,000	266,000,000	312,000,000		6,564,000,000
1975	5,306,000,000	19,000,000	14,553,000	0	1,604,447,000	21,000,000	935,000,000	275,000,000	373,000,000		6,944,000,000
1976	5,981,000,000	19,000,000	14,553,000	0	1,662,447,000	20,000,000	980,000,000	269,000,000	394,000,000		7,677,000,000
1977	6,694,000,000	6,000,000	14,553,000	0	1,441,447,000	18,000,000	711,000,000	273,000,000	439,000,000		8,156,000,000
1978	7,652,000,000	23,000,000	14,553,000	0	2,315,447,000	25,000,000	1,229,000,000	386,000,000	675,000,000		10,005,000,000
1979	8,843,000,000	7,000,000	14,553,000	0	1,328,447,000	25,000,000	255,000,000	404,000,000	644,000,000		10,193,000,000
1980	9,651,000,000	24,000,000	14,553,000	0	1,376,447,000	26,000,000	104,000,000	579,000,000	667,000,000		11,066,000,000
1981	10,160,000,000	15,000,000	14,553,000	0	1,921,447,000	32,000,000	0	602,000,000	1,288,000,000		12,111,000,000
1982	10,570,000,000	5,000,000	14,553,000	0	2,111,447,000	39,000,000	0	518,000,000	1,554,000,000		12,701,000,000
1983	10,910,000,000	15,000,000	14,553,000	0	5,021,447,000	2,286,000,000	0	537,000,000	2,199,000,000		15,961,000,000
1984	11,400,000,000	10,000,000	14,553,000	0	2,890,447,000	742,000,000	0	778,000,000	1,371,000,000		14,315,000,000
1985	11,976,000,000	4,000,000	14,553,000	0	7,608,447,000	5,267,000,000	0	672,000,000	1,670,000,000		19,603,000,000
1986	11,962,000,000	8,000,000	14,553,000	0	7,234,447,000	4,885,000,000	0	823,000,000	1,527,000,000		19,219,000,000
1987	12,503,000,000	7,000,000	14,553,000	0	4,731,447,000	2,158,000,000	0	953,000,000	1,621,000,000		17,256,000,000
1988	13,253,000,000	7,000,000	14,553,000	0	3,614,447,000	104,000,000	0	1,057,000,000	2,452,000,000		16,889,000,000
1989	14,140,000,000	10,000,000	14,553,000	0	3,185,447,000	112,000,000	0	1,319,000,000	1,755,000,000		17,350,000,000
1990	14,951,000,000	9,000,000	14,553,000	0	3,704,447,000	54,000,000	0	1,736,000,000	1,915,000,000		18,679,000,000
1991	15,266,000,000	4,000,000	14,553,000	0	4,410,447,000	44,000,000	0	1,729,000,000	2,637,000,000		19,695,000,000
1992	15,436,000,000	12,000,000	14,553,000	0	4,815,447,000	119,000,000	0	1,417,000,000	3,278,000,000		20,278,000,000
1993	16,163,000,000	7,000,000	14,553,000	0	8,384,447,000	2,948,000,000	0	1,535,000,000	3,902,000,000		24,569,000,000
1994	17,096,000,000	4,000,000	14,553,000	0	9,236,447,000	1,129,000,000	0	1,628,000,000	6,479,000,000		26,351,000,000
1995	18,062,000,000	8,000,000	14,553,000	0	6,110,447,000	1,202,000,000	0	1,812,000,000	3,096,000,000		24,195,000,000
1996	19,405,000,000	5,000,000	14,553,000	0	5,756,447,000	873,000,000	0	1,842,000,000	3,042,000,000		25,181,000,000
1997	20,578,000,000	12,000,000	14,553,000	0	6,312,447,000	969,000,000	0	1,934,000,000	3,409,000,000		26,917,000,000
1998	22,026,000,000	4,000,000	14,553,000	0	10,636,447,000	1,103,000,000	0	2,716,000,000	6,817,000,000		32,681,000,000
1999	23,098,000,000	11,000,000	14,553,000	0	78,831,447,000	153,000,000	0	1,339,000,000	77,339,000,000		101,955,000,000
2000	24,918,000,000	12,000,000	14,553,000	0	55,811,447,000	217,000,000	0	1,360,000,000	54,235,000,000		80,756,000,000
2001	26,983,000,000	7,000,000	14,553,000	0	10,846,447,000	409,000,000	0	1,402,000,000	9,036,000,000		37,851,000,000
2002	29,046,000,000	4,000,000	14,553,000	0	12,288,447,000	372,000,000	0	1,656,000,000	10,261,000,000		41,353,000,000
2003	31,033,000,000	7,000,000	14,553,000	0	15,656,447,000	469,000,000	0	1,756,000,000	13,431,000,000		46,711,000,000
2004	33,013,000,000	7,000,000	14,553,000	0	15,530,447,000	650,000,000	0	1,929,000,000	12,951,000,000		48,565,000,000
2005	35,021,000,000	9,000,000	14,553,000	0	20,670,447,000	561,000,000	0	2,008,000,000	18,102,000,000		55,715,000,000
2006	36,793,000,000	7,000,000	14,553,000	0	24,983,447,000	803,000,000	0	2,857,000,000	21,324,000,000		61,798,000,000

3rd Wednesday in February

	Notes In circulation	£ Short-term repo operations with BoE	FC public securities issued	Cash ratio deposits	£ reserve balances	Other liabilities	Total
2007	38,214,000,000	0	3,314,000,000	2,568,000,000	17,716,000,000	15,180,000,000	76,992,000,000
2008	40,933,000,000	0	3,327,000,000	2,936,000,000	23,824,000,000	26,595,000,000	97,615,000,000
2009	44,494,000,000	43,940,000,000	2,893,000,000	2,427,000,000	33,700,000,000	40,951,000,000	168,405,000,000
2010	49,486,000,000	0	3,881,000,000	2,574,000,000	155,165,000,000	36,174,000,000	247,280,000,000
2011	51,542,000,000	0	3,783,000,000	2,444,000,000	138,015,000,000	45,857,000,000	241,641,000,000
2012	54,568,000,000	0	3,870,000,000	2,386,000,000	188,975,000,000	61,660,000,000	311,459,000,000
2013	57,242,000,000	0	3,943,000,000	2,479,000,000	279,727,000,000	60,836,000,000	404,227,000,000
2014	59,391,000,000	0	3,597,000,000	4,078,000,000	305,951,000,000	30,072,000,000	403,089,000,000
2015*							406,582,000,000

For more information on the data please use the following links:

Source: Bank of England

Original 1967 Quarterly Bulletin article: http://www.bankofengland.co.uk/archive/Documents/historicpubs/qb/1967/qb67q2159163.pdf

Bank of England Statistical Abstracts: http://www.bankofengland.co.uk/archive/Pages/digitalcontent/historicpubs/statisticalabst.aspx

The implications of money market reform for data published in Monetary and Financial Statistics' in the June 2006 issue of Bank of England: Monetary and Financial Statistics.:

http://www.bankofengland.co.uk/statistics/Documents/ms/articles/artjun06.pdf

Changes to the Bank's weekly reporting regime - Quarterly Bulletin article, 2014Q3: http://www.bankofengland.co.uk/publications/Documents/quarterlybulletin/2014/qb300614.pdf

Other data

Weekly data on the Bank of England's balance sheet 1844-2006: http://www.bankofengland.co.uk/research/Documents/onebank/balanceweekly_final.xlsx

Three centuries of macroeconomic data: http://www.bankofengland.co.uk/research/Pages/onebank/threecenturies.aspx

* The total balance sheet is now published quarterly with a 5 quarter lag

Following changes to legislation in the 2009 Banking Act and the recommendations of the Plenderleith Review the Bank of England has decided to replace the Bank Return with a new Weekly Report. The information provided in the Weekly Report will be augmented on a quarterly basis, at a lag of five quarters, with data for those assets and liabilities which had not previously been disclosed to complete the balance sheet.

12.2a Annual clearing volumes and values

Clearing volumes thousands

	Annual volumes			
	2015	2016	Change 2016 on 2015	%
Bacs				
Direct Credits	2,171,697	2,146,835	-24,862	-1%
Direct Debits	3,908,346	4,071,911	163,566	4%
Total BACS	**6,080,043**	**6,218,746**	138,704	**2%**
CHAPS Clearing Company				
Retail and Commercial (MT 103)	29,336	30,322	986	3%
Wholesale Financial (MT202)	8,212	8,641	429	5%
Total CHAPS	**37,548**	**38,964**	1,415	**4%**
Faster Payments				
Standing Order Payments	343,642	357,411	13,769	4%
Single Immediate Payments	730,675	882,226	151,551	21%
Forward Dated Payments	170,339	183,675	13,336	8%
Return Payments	2,378	2,780	402	17%
Total Faster Payments	**1,247,035**	**1,462,093**	179,058	**14%**
Cheque and Credit Clearing Company				
Cheques	404,134	344,621	-59,513	-15%
Credits	28,049	21,857	-6,193	-22%
Euro debits	89	80	-9	-10%
Total Cheque & Credit	**432,273**	**366,558**	-65,715	**-15%**
Currency Clearing: US Dollar	17.1	13.9	-3	-19%
Total all Clearing Companies	**7,809,333**	**8,061,631**	252,298	**3%**

Clearing values £ millions

	Annual values			
	2015	2016	Change 2016 on 2015	%
Bacs				
Direct Credits	3,374,815	3,514,313	139,498	4%
Direct Debits	1,215,396	1,262,235	46,839	4%
Total BACS	**4,590,211**	**4,776,549**	186,338	**4%**
CHAPS Clearing Company				
Retail and Commercial (MT 103)	16,730,137	18,879,635	2,149,498	13%
Wholesale Financial (MT202)	51,681,041	56,693,993	5,012,951	10%
Total CHAPS	**68,411,178**	**75,573,628**	7,162,450	**10%**
Faster Payments				
Standing Order Payments	107,202	113,558	6,355	6%
Single Immediate Payments	619,301	728,642	109,341	18%
Forward Dated Payments	313,099	313,099	345,630	10%
Return Payments	1,114	1,178	64	6%
Total Faster Payments	**1,040,717**	**1,189,008**	148,290	**14%**
Cheque and Credit Clearing Company				
Cheques	454,838	400,158	-54,679	-12%
Credits	17,216	15,022	-2,194	-13%
Euro debits	1,208	1,274	66	5%
Total	473,261	416,455	-58,806	4%
Currency Clearing: US Dollar	**273**	**285**	11	**4%**
Total all Clearing Companies	**74,536,146**	**81,975,063**	7,438,917	**10%**

Source: UK Payments Administration Ltd

(a) Totals, averages and percentages are calculated using unrounded data. The values of all euro and US Dollar clearings are shown as £ sterling equivalent.

(b) 253 clearing days were used to calculate the average daily statistics for both 2015 and 2016. In terms of Faster Payments, 253 clearing days were used for Standing Orders and 365 days for other payment types.

(c) A description of the United Kingdom payment clearings together with more comprehensive statistics over a longer period is available from the Information Management team. These data are published annually in UK Payment Statistics

12.2b Bacs volumes and values

Annual volumes thousands

	Bacs Direct Credits		Bacs Euro Credits		Direct Debits		Total volumes	
	Number	% Change	Number	% Change	Number	% Change	Number	% Change
2003	1,341,945	14.4	54	45.0	2,429,915	6.2	4,060,357	8.7
2004	1,710,673	27.5	84	55.5	2,589,934	6.6	4,602,570	13.4
2005	2,093,859	22.4	12	48.6	2,722,245	5.1	5,134,250	11.6
2006	2,171,586	3.7	157	25.9	2,857,761	5.0	5,361,749	4.4
2007	2,233,106	2.8	181	15.8	2,296,474	3.7	5,544,109	3.4
2008	2,254,875	1.0	176	-3.2	3,076,857	3.8	5,655,751	2.0
2009	2,289,813	1.5	193	10.0	3,149,153	2.3	5,638,919	-0.3
2010	2,292,942	0.1	143	26.0	3,229,338	2.5	5,672,730	0.6
2011	2,270,987	-1.0			3,322,360	2.9	5,716,999	0.8
2012	2,182,667	-3.9			3,416,651	2.8	5,616,392	-1.8
2013	2,151,718	-1.0			3,524,905	3.0	5,695,028	1.0
2014	2,150,557	-			3,671,997	4.0	5,841,232	3.0
2015	2,171,697	-			3,908,346	6.0	6,080,043	4.0
2016	2,146,835	-1.0 #			4,071,911	4.0	6,218,746	2.0

Average values £ millions

	Bacs Direct Credits [a]		Bacs Euro Credits		Direct Debits		Total volumes	
	Number	% Change	Number	% Change	Number	% Change	Number	% Change
2003	1,910,251	8.3	1,924	53.9	662,192	7.3	2,574,367	8.1
2004	2,131,031	11.6	2,040	6.0	750,381	13.3	2,883,452	12.0
2005	2,350,644	10.3	2,524	23.7	797,039	6.2	3,150,207	9.3
2006	2,581,682	9.8	2,819	11.7	844,832	6.0	3,429,333	8.9
2007	2,808,349	8.8	3,965	40.6	883,592	4.6	3,695,906	7.8
2008	3,006,159	7.0	4,806	21.2	935,356	5.9	3,946,321	6.8
2009	2,969,711	-1.2	5,255	9.3	885,708	-5.3	3,860,674	-2.2
2010	3,111,218	4.8	3,033	-42.3	948,137	7.0	4,062,388	5.2
2011	3,318,536	6.7			1,044,677	10.2	4,363,214	7.4
2012	3,036,714	-8.5			1,075,507	3.0	4,112,222	-5.8
2013	3,103,579	2.0			1,115,065	4.0	4,218,644	3.0
2014	3,253,279	5.0			1,167,266	5.0	4,420,546	5.0
2015	3,374,815	4.0			1,215,396	4.0	4,590,211	4.0
2016	3,541,313	4.0			1,262,235	4.0	4,776,549	4.0

Source: UK Payments Administration Ltd

(a) Values represent standing orders and Bacs Direct Credits combined

Bacs has 16 members and is responsible for the processing of bulk payments through its two principle payment schemes; Direct Debit and Bacs Direct Credit.

The Euro Debit Credit Service ceased operation on 29 October 2010

12.2c CHAPS volumes and values

Annual volumes thousands

	CHAPS Sterling [a]		CHAPS Euro						Total volumes [a]	
			Domestic (a)		Target					
					Transmitted to		Received from			
	Number	% Change	Number	% Change	Number	% Change	Number	% Change	Number	% Change
2003	27,215	6.5	1,399	13.1	2,904	19.2	1,685	4.7	33,202	7.6
2004	28,322	4.1	1,378	-1.5	3,314	14.1	1,849	9.7	34,862	5.0
2005	29,686	4.8	1,484	7.7	3,597	8.6	1,988	7.5	36,756	5.4
2006	33,030	11.3	1,461	-1.6	4,115	14.4	2,080	4.6	40,686	10.7
2007	35,588	7.7	1,455	-0.3	4,263	3.6	2,229	7.1	43,535	7.0
2008	34,606	-2.8	220	-84.9	379	-91.1	593	-73.4	35,797	-17.8
2009	31,926	-7.7							31,926	-10.8
2010	32,169	0.8							32,169	0.8
2011	34,024	5.8							34,024	5.8
2012	33,936	-0.3							33,936	-0.3
2013	34,976	3.0							34,976	3.0
2014	36,521	4.0							36,521	4.0
2015	37,548	3.0							37,548	3.0
2016	38,964	4.0							38,964	4.0

Annual Values £ millions

	CHAPS Sterling [a]		CHAPS Euro (sterling equivalent)						Total values [a]	
			Domestic (a)		Target					
					Transmitted to		Received from			
	Number	% Change	Number	% Change	Number	% Change	Number	% Change	Number	% Change
2003	51,613,456	-0.5	5,114,198	22.7	15,924,879	21.5	15,923,974	21.5	88,576,506	7.7
2004	52,347,525	1.4	4,509,924	-11.8	17,238,602	8.2	17,238,737	8.3	91,334,788	3.1
2005	52,671,592	0.6	6,069,146	34.6	19,180,194	11.3	19,179,273	11.3	97,100,206	6.3
2006	59,437,370	12.8	7,365,558	21.4	21,415,027	11.7	21,419,195	11.7	109,637,149	12.9
2007	69,352,322	16.7	6,781,942	-7.9	25,266,729	18.0	25,268,856	18.0	126,669,848	15.5
2008	73,625,908	6.2	574,610	-91.5	4,413,570	-82.5	4,403,022	-82.6	83,017,110	-34.5
2009	64,616,956	-12.2							64,616,956	-22.2
2010	61,587,609	-4.7							61,587,609	-4.7
2011	63,876,772	3.7							63,876,772	3.7
2012	71,716,857	12.3							71,716,857	12.3
2013	70,138,927	-2.0							70,138,927	-2.0
2014	67,959,491	-3.0							67,959,491	-3.0
2015	68,411,178	1.0							68,411,178	1.0
2016	75,573,628	10.0							75,573,628	10.0

Source: UK Payments Administration Ltd

(a) NewCHAPS was launched on 27 August 2001 and since this date CHAPS Sterling and CHAPS Euro Domestic figures include all CHAPS traffic

The CHAPS Scheme enables same-day bank-to-bank payments in sterling and has 23 direct participants

12.2d Faster Payments volumes and values

Annual volumes thousands

	Standing Order Payments		Single Immediate Payments		Forward Dated Payments		Return Payments		Total Volumes (a)	
	Number	% change	Number	% change	Number	% change	Number	% change	Number	% change
2003										
2004										
2005										
2006										
2007										
2008	37,574	*	36,325	*	8,708	*	182	*	82,789	*
2009	156,865	*	109,337	*	27,912	*	673	*	294,787	*
2010	203,055	29.4	181,195	65.7	40,632	45.6	880	30.6	425,761	44.4
2011	235,654	16.1	237,718	31.2	50,861	25.2	1,092	24.2	525,325	23.4
2012	299,630	27.1	379,844	59.8	129,829	155.3	1,788	63.6	811,090	54.4
2013	312,995	4	502,025	32	150,381	16.0	2,228	25.0	967,629	19.0
2014	329,858	5	609,879	21	159153	6.0	2,040	-8.0	1,100,930	14.0
2015	343,642	4	730,675	20	170339	7.0	2,378	17.0	1,247,035	13.0
2016	357,411	4.0	882226	21	183675	8.0	2,780	17.0	1,426,093	14

Annual values £ millions

	Standing Order Payments		Single Immediate Payments		Forward Dated Payments		Return Payments		Total Volumes (a)	
	Number	% change	Number	% change	Number	% change	Number	% change	Number	% change
2003										
2004										
2005										
2006										
2007										
2008	3,341	*	22,015	*	7,473	*	42	*	32,871	*
2009	26,527	*	59,015	*	20,544	*	136	*	106,223	*
2010	38,963	46.9	92,847	57.3	32,193	56.7	208	52.9	164,211	54.6
2011	50,206	28.9	135,101	45.5	49,492	53.5	308	47.9	235,044	43.1
2012	80,009	59.4	328,685	143.3	208,252	321.3	965	213	617,911	162.9
2013	88,885	11.0	423,571	29.0	257,794	24.0	1,111	15.0	771,361	25.0
2014	97,121	9.0	517,641	22.0	288,034	12.0	999	-10.0	903,794	17.0
2015	107,202	10.0	619,303	20.0	313,099	9.0	1,114	12.0	1,040,717	15.0
2016	113,558	6.0	728,642	18.0	345,630	10.0	1,178	6.0	1,189,008	14.0

Source: UK Payments Administration Ltd

(a) The UK Faster Payments Service was launched on 27 May 2008

The Faster Payment Service, operated by Faster Payments Scheme Ltd, enables internet, mobile and telephone banking payments as well as standing order payments to move from account to account, normally within seconds, 24 hours a day, 365 days a year. As at the end of 2016 there are 12 direct settling participants, with a number more intending to join in 2017. Given its scale and reach, it is considered one of the most advanced real-time payment services in the world.

12.2e Inter-bank cheque volumes and values

Annual volumes thousands

	Exchanged in Great Britain					
	Cheques		Euro Debits		Total Volumes	
	Number	% change	Number	% change	Number	% change
2003	1,519,117	-6.3	759	3.6	1,519,876	-6.3
2004	1,423,742	-6.3	724	-4.6	1,424,465	-6.3
2005	1,325,762	-6.9	637	-12.0	1,326,399	-6.9
2006	1,237,401	-6.7	586	-7.9	1,237,987	-6.7
2007	1,124,869	-9.1	531	-9.5	1,125,400	-9.1
2008	1,007,379	-23.5	445	-16.1	1,007,824	-10.4
2009	875,533	-11.4	351	-21.2	875,884	-13.1
2010	775,643	-12.1	279	-20.5	775,922	-11.4
2011	682,082	-12.1	223	-20.1	6,822,305	-12.1
2012	597,076	-12.5	165	-25.7	597,241	-12.5
2013	525,295	-12.0	131	-21.0	525,426	-12.0
2014	464,191	-12.0	108	-17.0	464,299	-12.0
2015	404,134	-13.0	89	-18.0	432,273	-13.0
2016	344,621	15.0	80	-10.0	366,558	-15.0

Annual values £ millions

	Exchanged in Great Britain					
	Cheques		Euro Debits		Total Volumes	
	Number	% change	Number	% change	Number	% change
2003	1,240,685	-3.2	3,898	13.8	1,244,583	-3.1
2004	1,210,057	-2.5	3,456	-11.4	1,213,513	-2.5
2005	1,152,256	-4.8	3,206	-7.2	1,155,642	-4.8
2006	1,171,062	1.6	3,111	-3.0	1,174,174	1.6
2007	1,156,684	-1.2	2,970	-4.6	1,159,653	-1.2
2008	1,075,694	-7.0	2,980	0.4	1,078,674	-7.0
2009	870,591	-19.1	2,993	0.4	873,584	-19.0
2010	761,081	-12.6	1,767	-41	762,848	-12.7
2011	675,706	-11.2	1,559	-11.8	667,226	-11.2
2012	601,256	-11	1,188	-23.9	602,444	-11.0
2013	535,513	-11.0	1,166	-2.0	536,679	-11.0
2014	498,729	-7.0	1,289	11.0	500,018	-7.0
2015	454,838	-9.0	1,208	-6.0	473,261	-8.8
2016	400,158	-12.0	1,274	5.0	416,455	-12.0

Source: UK Payments Administration Ltd

The Cheque and Credit Clearing Company has managed the cheque clearing system in England and Wales since 1985 and in Scotland since 1996. As well as clearing cheques, the system processes bankers' drafts, postal orders, warrants, government payable orders and travellers' cheques. The company also managed the systems for the clearing of paper bank giro credits, euro cheques (drawn on GB banks) and US dollar cheques (drawn on GB banks). There are 11 participants in the cheque cleaing system and the credit clearing system, 10 in the eurp debit clearing system and 5 participants in the curency clearing system.

12.2f Inter-bank credit volumes and values

Annual volumes thousands

	Exchanged in Great Britain			
	Number	% change	Number	% change
2003	140,792	-6.4	140,792	-6.4
2004	132,899	-5.6	132,899	-5.6
2005	123,280	-7.2	123,280	-7.2
2006	108,309	-12.1	108,309	-12.1
2007	96,90	-11.1	96,90	-11.1
2008	86,442	-10.2	86,442	-10.2
2009	73,686	-14.8	73,686	-14.8
2010	61,662	-16.3	61,662	-16.3
2011	53,934	-12.5	53,934	-12.5
2012	46,927	-12.9	46,927	-12.9
2013	40,569	-14.0	40,569	-14.0
2014	34,962	-14.0	34,962	-14.0
2015	28,049	-20.0	28,049	-20.0
2016	21,857	22.0	21,857	22.0

Annual values £ millions

	Exchanged in Great Britain			
	Number	% change	Number	% change
2003	74,366	-7.6	74,366	-7.6
2004	68,261	-8.2	68,261	-8.2
2005	61,844	-9.4	61,844	-9.4
2006	59,309	-4.1	59,309	-4.1
2007	57,347	-3.3	57,347	-3.3
2008	51,641	-9.9	51,641	-9.9
2009	41,624	-19.4	41,624	-19.4
2010	32,312	-22.4	32,312	-22.4
2011	27,990	-13.4	27,990	-13.4
2012	23,802	-15	23,802	-15
2013	21,109	-11.0	21,109	-11.0
2014	19,659	-7.0	19,659	-7.0
2015	17,216	-12.0	17,216	-12.0
2016	15,022	-13.0	15,022	-13.0

Source: UK Payments Administration Ltd

The Cheque and Credit Clearing Company has managed the cheque clearing system in England and Wales since 1985 and in Scotland since 1996. As well as clearing cheques, the system processes bankers' drafts, postal orders, warrants, government payable orders and travellers' cheques. The company also managed the systems for the clearing of paper bank giro credits, euro cheques (drawn on GB banks) and US dollar cheques (drawn on GB banks). There are 11 participants in the cheque cleaing system and the credit clearing system, 10 in the eurp debit clearing system and 5 participants in the curency clearing system.

12.3a Monetary financial institutions' (excluding central bank) balance sheet

£ millions

Amounts outstanding of sterling liabilities

Not seasonally adjusted

	Notes	Sight deposits					Time deposits						
	outstanding and cash loaded cards	UK MFIs	of which intragroup banks	UK public sector	Other UK residents	Non-residents	UK MFIs	of which intragroup banks	UK public sector	Other UK residents	of which SAYE	of which cash ISAs	Non-residents
RPM	B3LM	B3GL	B8ZC	B3MM	B3NM	B3OM	B3HL	B8ZE	B3PM	B3QM	B3RM	B3SM	B3TM
2015 Aug	6,920	114,575	96,536	15,292	1,180,716	150,071	137,550	132,179	19,624	694,980	1,187	260,670	191,724
Sep	7,003	114,839	97,975	15,160	1,198,656	158,909	131,347	126,145	19,546	683,894	1,169	261,334	202,359
Oct	7,018	118,714	102,816	15,570	1,204,978	143,841	141,442	135,968	19,566	686,144	1,192	261,875	193,505
Nov	7,108	122,413	105,979	15,351	1,215,760	150,548	143,778	137,477	19,339	682,340	1,166	262,321	193,282
Dec	7,232	120,345	106,354	15,880	1,219,920	150,148	146,287	140,366	18,741	682,826	1,120	262,591	208,259
2016 Jan	6,997	116,615	101,441	16,617	1,218,570	158,484	138,517	132,667	18,463	674,235	1,119	262,923	200,850
Feb	6,966	116,650	100,824	16,012	1,237,202	158,086	138,712	132,503	17,581	670,527	972	263,504	176,619
Mar	7,065	106,174	89,056	15,189	1,264,267	166,282	142,403	136,776	15,435	654,894 (a)	975	265,493	178,697
Apr	7,065	101,243	85,379	16,398	1,249,182	161,550	143,038	135,012	16,559	662,888	1,000	270,998	185,514
May	7,145	101,341	85,893	15,747	1,266,291	152,548	138,641	131,217	16,828	660,096	1,012	271,719	177,644
Jun	7,118	95,237	79,259	15,764	1,294,533	166,716	162,142	154,324	17,087	661,180	1,046	271,941	183,339
Jul	7,122	102,532	83,544	16,423	1,299,441	176,575	158,302	151,103	17,941	661,500	962	272,368	185,186
Aug	7,238	97,833	79,415	16,266	1,305,093	177,915	154,919	148,019	17,991	663,883	932	271,966	182,842
Sep	7,321	104,476	87,166	15,155	1,323,496	170,492	158,982	151,736	17,763	657,004	887	271,617	183,587
Oct	7,355	106,085	86,216	15,701	1,322,805	171,335	150,903	142,332	17,845	657,516	901	270,962	183,697
Nov	7,426	99,860	82,335	14,917	1,324,085	169,995	156,550	144,352	17,626	651,071	894	270,176	182,511
Dec	7,852	104,913	89,263	15,030	1,333,224	172,218	191,696	165,240	16,955	652,271	899	269,783	184,000
2017 Jan	7,696	111,503	94,478	15,241	1,316,897	174,390	199,656	159,778	16,586	642,895	911	268,988	179,714
Feb	7,704	120,382	104,905	14,312	1,319,172	172,824	220,016	171,176	15,772	639,394	904	268,217	179,606
Mar	7,718	138,906	123,951	13,916	1,353,802	177,016	247,893	186,401	14,051	634,702	926	268,855	173,634
Apr	7,804	140,045	123,758	15,609	1,345,004	173,275	249,930	185,931	14,052	645,780	931	272,693	176,180

Source: Bank of England

Source: Bank of England

Source: Bank of England

Source: Bank of England

Source: Bank of England

Source: Bank of England

12.3a Monetary financial institutions' (excluding central bank) balance sheet

£ millions

Amounts outstanding of sterling liabilities

	Sale and repurchase agreements					Acceptances	CDs and other paper Issued				Total	Sterling	Net	Accrued	Sterling	Total
	UK MFIs	of which intragroup banks	UK public sector	Other UK residents	Non-residents	granted	CDs and Commercial paper	Bonds with maturity of up to and incl. 5 years	Bonds with maturity of greater than 5 years	Total	sterling deposits	items in suspense and transmission	derivatives	amounts payable	capital and other internal funds	sterling liabilities
RPM	B3IL	B8ZA	B3UM	B3VM	B3WM	B3XM	B2TL	B6OI	B2TM	B3YM	B3ZM	B3GN	B3HN	B3IN	B3JN	B3KN
2015 Aug	76,837	43,273	9,014	100,388	62,624	207	98,382	24,606	37,515	160,502	2,914,104	40,934	-32,257	22,037	443,887	3,395,625
Sep	76,057	44,758	100	76,264	62,230	206	94,308	26,069	37,478	157,854	2,897,419	33,900	-49,440	20,775	470,328	3,379,984
Oct	54,981	24,988	1,779	80,450	64,883	203	94,050	25,411	37,324	156,785	2,882,841	40,003	-39,511	20,288	441,532	3,352,172
Nov	48,202	21,953	1,998	85,158	67,449	193	93,462	24,799	36,056	154,317	2,900,129	39,850	-40,962	21,010	439,618	3,366,752
Dec	48,670	21,220	1,852	73,380	61,785	192	97,325	25,743	35,743	158,811	2,915,095	20,822	-54,546	21,136	446,084	3,355,823
2016 Jan	46,043	18,401	1,774	75,871	68,286	185	96,077	26,313	35,670	158,060	2,892,570	54,025	-28,529	22,582	434,102	3,381,747
Feb	48,599	19,209	1,609	78,575	58,133	169	97,325	27,341	35,693	160,359	2,878,833	40,442	1,782	23,742	409,127	3,360,891
Mar	54,471	18,309	310	70,684	68,543	157	101,297	26,186	35,841	163,325	2,900,830 (a)	36,852	-56,499	21,771	411,758	3,321,777 (a)
Apr	58,104	18,055	5,857	73,912	69,809	163	102,166	27,012	36,191	165,368	2,909,588	41,766	-61,178	20,810	401,950 (b)	3,320,001 (b)
May	55,967	15,678	6,107	78,066	73,496	161	106,273	26,088	35,886	168,247	2,911,180	44,957	-68,283	22,189	411,919	3,329,107
Jun	61,906	16,733	6,290	76,670	75,146	198	106,257	25,970	36,581	168,808	2,985,018	45,506	11,460	22,337	392,682	3,464,121
Jul	52,310	11,110	4,286	90,674	63,811	204	115,539	25,914	36,276	177,729	3,006,915	52,385	4,332	22,022	379,922	3,472,699
Aug	52,894	11,710	5,199	99,551	67,808	207	117,437	26,009	36,379	179,826	3,022,228	37,638	-2,697	21,597	386,255	3,472,259
Sep	51,065	11,418	2,011	83,126	70,165	173	121,666	25,863	36,346	183,875	3,021,369	44,922	14,223	22,233	361,127	3,471,195
Oct	48,409	13,522	3,485	102,510	78,151	189	120,983	25,822	36,052	182,857	3,041,488	37,203	80,682	22,767	331,138	3,520,634
Nov	46,054	12,981	3,775	116,898	83,119	208	118,027	26,007	35,185	179,219	3,045,889	46,521	3,667	22,620	380,019	3,506,142
Dec	40,851	12,828	2,176	96,054	83,951	181	120,150	24,948	35,177	180,275	3,073,797	20,592	11,417	21,423	388,720	3,523,800
2017 Jan	43,286	17,314	1,765	122,405	84,315	186	119,299	24,223	34,520	178,042	3,086,880	42,929	-12,810	21,392	415,255	3,561,342
Feb	41,658	16,843	3,815	123,232	85,681	187	124,491	24,053	34,543	183,087	3,119,136	44,997	21,903	21,907	426,770	3,642,417
Mar	41,275	14,102	2,613	123,066	95,220	252	134,753	23,161	34,305	192,219	3,208,566	48,528	-3,748	19,133	407,664	3,687,861
Apr	40,387	14,752	2,108	138,104	87,075	258	137,516	20,958	34,136	192,610	3,220,418	48,361	-38,604	18,570	409,362	3,665,911

Source: Bank of England

Notes to table

Movements in amounts outstanding can reflect breaks in data series as well as underlying flows. For changes data, users are recommended to refer directly to the appropriate series or data tables. Further explanation can be found at: www.bankofengland.co.uk/statistics/Pages/iadb/notesiadb/Changes flows growth rates.aspx.

(a) Due to changes in reporting at one institution, the amounts outstanding decreased by £5bn. This effect has been adjusted out of the flows for March 2016.

(b) Due to a loan transfer by one reporting institution, the amounts outstanding increased by £7bn. This effect has been adjusted out of the flows for April 2016.

(c) Due to improvements in reporting at one institution, the amounts outstanding increased by £17bn. This effect has been adjusted out of the flows for June 2017.

(d) Due to improvements in reporting at one institution, the amounts outstanding decreased by £5bn. This effect has been adjusted out of the flows for June 2017.

(e) Due to improvements in reporting at one institution, the amounts outstanding increased by £10bn. This effect has been adjusted out of the flows for June 2017.

Explanatory notes can be found here: http://www.bankofengland.co.uk/statistics/Pages/iadb/notesiadb/MFIs_extICB.aspx

Copyright guidance and the related UK Open Government Licence can be viewed here: www.bankofengland.co.uk/Pages/disclaimer.aspx.

12.3b Monetary financial institutions' (excluding central bank) balance sheet

£ millions   Not seasonally adjusted

Not seasonally adjusted

Amounts outstanding of foreign currency liabilities (including euro)

	Sight and time deposits					Acceptances granted	Sale and repurchase agreements				
	UK MFIs	of which intragroup banks	UK public sector	Other UK residents	Non-residents		UK MFIs	of which intragroup banks	UK public sector	Other UK residents	Non-residents
RPM	B3JL	B8ZM	B2UP	B2UV	B3NN	B3KQ	B3KL	B8ZK	B3PN	B3QN	B3RN
2015 Aug	214,788	143,310	2,210	257,472	1,645,700	2,591	92,212	55,587	883	103,610	482,597
Sep	213,562	145,493	2,197	257,835	1,634,396	2,661	89,565	55,966	466	106,396	476,000
Oct	207,649	143,258	2,259	255,116	1,590,307	2,672	86,375	52,933	634	101,705	480,363
Nov	205,433	144,698	2,288	255,561	1,616,872 (f)	2,498	90,517	56,718	522	104,582	489,453
Dec	207,571	148,067	2,194	255,042	1,631,182	2,767	84,360	51,732	1,531	104,574	457,350
2016 Jan	208,903	145,866	2,353	274,162	1,692,801	2,405	79,019	49,908	1,414	112,701	510,595
Feb	220,714	153,042	2,575	280,680	1,734,659	2,085	78,876	48,844	1,268	116,940	500,825
Mar	209,638	147,854	2,341	282,593	1,696,245	2,380	72,791	43,819	112	116,514	485,146
Apr	218,926	157,901	2,484	279,813	1,649,995	2,508	75,762	44,160	1,293	118,184	494,252
May	198,818	138,756	2,474	283,405	1,639,167	2,554	74,490	40,150	695	114,914	508,905
Jun	214,995	143,433	3,048	316,335	1,836,238	3,331	79,468	42,394	341	121,389	557,941
Jul	215,741	149,522	3,027	322,784	1,849,173	3,010	80,325	43,607	1,414	126,677	559,416
Aug	224,844	158,074	3,229	332,357	1,854,568	2,962	81,244	43,715	1,134	125,868	563,987
Sep	214,530	146,290	2,437	331,529	1,855,029 (g)	3,618	76,859	37,621	250	138,404	580,709
Oct	219,974	152,278	2,531	345,850	1,885,003	3,558	78,399	36,074	626	140,847	621,158
Nov	215,864	152,245	2,667	341,390	1,820,717	3,691	72,668	34,845	1,588	145,662	606,381
Dec	217,773	149,050	2,518	324,792	1,836,539	4,015	75,148	33,036	530	139,651	609,476
2017 Jan	217,530	153,305	2,689	336,977	1,817,696	3,288	78,312	35,890	1,317	151,236	628,041
Feb	206,752	144,109	2,633	336,848	1,842,486	3,789	76,870	35,761	339	181,024	653,853
Mar	197,174	136,947	2,383	328,699	1,813,204	4,008	82,344	39,816	70	172,708	648,760
Apr	192,379	133,353	2,674	329,056	1,783,247	3,580	77,778	38,108	1,340	171,046	632,021

Source: Bank of England

Notes to table

Movements in amounts outstanding can reflect breaks in data series as well as underlying flows. For changes data, users are recommended to refer directly to the appropriate series or data tables. Further explanation can be found at: www.bankofengland.co.uk/statistics/Pages/iadb/notesiadb/Changes_flows_growth_rates.aspx.

(f) Due to changes in reporting at one institution, the amounts outstanding decreased by £18bn. This effect has been adjusted out of the flows for November 2015.
(g) Due to a change in treatment at one institution, the amounts outstanding decreased by £14bn. This effect has been adjusted out of the flows for September 2016.
(h) Due to a transfer of business by one institution, amounts outstanding increased by £29 billion. This amount has been adjusted out of the flows for July 2017.
(i) Due to changes in reporting at one institution, the amounts outstanding decreased by £5bn. This effect has been adjusted out of the flows for March 2016.
(j) Due to a loan transfer by one reporting institution, the amounts outstanding increased by £7bn. This effect has been adjusted out of the flows for April 2016.

Explanatory notes can be found here: http://www.bankofengland.co.uk/statistics/Pages/iadb/notesiadb/MFIs_exICB.aspx

Copyright guidance and the related UK Open Government Licence can be viewed here: www.bankofengland.co.uk/Pages/disclaimer.aspx.

322

12.3b Monetary financial institutions' (excluding central bank) balance sheet

£ millions   Not seasonally adjusted

Amounts outstanding of foreign currency liabilities (including euro)

RPM	CDs and Commercial paper	CDs and other paper Issued		Total	Total foreign currency deposits	Items in suspense and transmission	Net derivatives	Accrued amounts payable	Capital and other internal funds	Total foreign currency liabilities	Total liabilities
		Bonds with maturity of up to and incl. 5 years	Bonds with maturity of greater than 5 years								
	B2TP	B6OK	B2TQ	B3SN	B3TN	B3UN	B3VN	B3WN	B3XN	B3YN	B3ZN
2015 Aug	120,184	177,053	210,055	507,292	3,309,353	131,345	14,041	14,519	131,383	3,600,641	6,996,265
Sep	109,758	172,859	215,890	498,507	3,281,585	142,124	15,285	14,440	112,295	3,565,730	6,945,714
Oct	105,051	170,570	216,084	491,704	3,218,784	176,321	7,407	13,786	124,784	3,541,082	6,893,254
Nov	101,608	171,133	214,350	487,091	3,254,818 (f)	165,454	8,540	14,782	138,760	3,582,354 (f)	6,949,106 (f)
Dec	98,101	172,035	218,066	488,202	3,234,772	84,019	21,951	14,273	151,705	3,506,720	6,862,543
2016 Jan	104,410	174,158	223,095	501,663	3,386,015	187,523	-13,622	12,320	166,672	3,738,908	7,120,654
Feb	110,507	178,379	230,433	519,319	3,457,942	186,073	-38,983	12,265	190,236	3,807,533	7,168,425
Mar	108,703	172,030	229,819	510,552	3,378,313	175,831	16,255	12,075	179,606	3,762,080	7,083,857 (i)
Apr	108,985	174,550	231,396	514,930	3,358,148	205,202	20,055	12,088	192,957	3,788,451	7,108,452 (j)
May	110,243	170,178	226,793	507,214	3,332,634	195,730	23,939	12,924	174,757	3,739,984	7,069,091
Jun	117,122	184,737	249,064	550,923	3,684,009	209,928	-55,571	13,368	206,776	4,058,510	7,522,631
Jul	112,175	185,495	253,075	550,746	3,712,312	207,744	-49,869	13,397	218,433	4,102,018	7,574,717
Aug	109,377	187,228	253,232	549,838	3,740,030	199,952	-45,574	13,355	215,958	4,123,721	7,595,980
Sep	109,113	211,662	252,924	573,699	3,777,065 (g)	228,135	-54,715	14,051	229,804	4,194,340 (g)	7,665,535 (g)
Oct	118,695	217,314	263,901	599,910	3,897,855	230,663	-134,521	15,506	267,587	4,277,090	7,797,724
Nov	117,042	206,511	244,788	568,340	3,778,969	257,720	-53,599	15,710	219,775	4,218,575	7,724,717
Dec	112,712	208,052	247,044	567,808	3,778,250	107,579	-59,185	13,881	232,269	4,072,795	7,596,595
2017 Jan	113,498	207,223	247,708	568,429	3,805,515	231,738	-31,677	14,500	205,652	4,225,728	7,787,070
Feb	124,665	214,881	256,400	595,945	3,900,539	242,484	-67,864	16,901	224,225	4,316,285	7,958,702
Mar	125,439	208,200	252,862	586,502	3,835,852	205,851	-41,321	16,370	207,097	4,223,848	7,911,709
Apr	121,172	215,507	251,092	587,771	3,780,891	237,729	-3,794	17,993	190,410	4,223,229	7,889,139

Source: Bank of England

Notes to table

Movements in amounts outstanding can reflect breaks in data series as well as underlying flows. For changes data, users are recommended to refer directly to the appropriate series or data tables. Further explanation can be found at: www.bankofengland.co.uk/statistics/Pages/iadb/notesiadb/Changes_flows_growth_rates.aspx.

(f) Due to changes in reporting at one institution, the amounts outstanding decreased by £18bn. This effect has been adjusted out of the flows for November 2015.
(g) Due to a change in treatment at one institution, the amounts outstanding decreased by £14bn. This effect has been adjusted out of the flows for September 2016.
(h) Due to a transfer of business by one institution, amounts outstanding increased by £29 billion. This amount has been adjusted out of the flows for July 2017.
(i) Due to changes in reporting at one institution, the amounts outstanding decreased by £5bn. This effect has been adjusted out of the flows for March 2016.
(j) Due to a loan transfer by one reporting institution, the amounts outstanding increased by £7bn. This effect has been adjusted out of the flows for April 2016.

Explanatory notes can be found here: http://www.bankofengland.co.uk/statistics/Pages/iadb/notesiadb/MFIs_exICB.aspx

12.3c Monetary financial institutions' (excluding central bank) balance sheet

£ millions   Not seasonally adjusted

Amounts outstanding of sterling assets

	Notes	With UK central bank		Loans					Acceptances granted			
	coin	Cash ratio deposits	Other	UK MFIs	of which intragroup banks	UK MFIs CDs	UK MFIs commercial paper	Non-residents	UK MFIs	UK public sector	Other UK residents	Non-residents
RPM	B3UO	B3VO	B3WO	B3NL	B8ZI	B3OL	B3PL	B3XO	B3QL	B3YO	B3ZO	B3GP
2015 Aug	9,335	4,075	312,599	249,423	229,078	3,977	246	111,015	15	-	156	36
Sep	9,530	4,075	294,725	244,999	224,354	3,703	123	123,614	15	-	157	34
Oct	9,559	4,075	304,625	257,960	238,638	3,912	143	112,837	15	-	156	33
Nov	9,373	4,079	305,635	264,325	243,833	3,850	171	110,479	-	-	159	34
Dec	10,943	4,136	302,471	263,449	246,696	3,478	164	117,292	-	-	157	35
2016 Jan	9,460	4,136	304,721	251,630	234,082	3,875	183	116,236	-	-	152	33
Feb	9,309	4,136	305,759	253,020	233,981	3,798	85	111,677	-	-	136	33
Mar	10,730	4,136	301,075	247,946	225,945	3,638	44	120,187	-	-	126	31
Apr	9,907	4,137	310,603	242,961	220,690	3,484	44	122,328	-	-	127	36
May	10,187	4,155	305,681	239,632	217,320	3,475	43	121,830	-	-	126	35
Jun	10,717	4,215	302,755	256,043	234,542	3,300	43	122,793	-	-	163	35
Jul	10,116	4,215	306,966	258,489	235,689	3,845	71	132,507	-	-	171	33
Aug	10,825	4,215	318,346	251,400	228,514	3,795	50	132,255	-	-	175	32
Sep	10,247	4,216	314,556	262,442	240,715	3,638	43	136,040	-	-	141	31
Oct	9,769	4,217	326,529	251,643	227,915	3,602	33	136,124	-	-	155	33
Nov	10,346	4,242	342,425	246,527	223,861	3,502	25	134,727	-	-	175	33
Dec	11,867	4,424	356,687	275,269	253,758	3,278	25	127,565	-	-	141	39
2017 Jan	10,365	4,424	375,664	273,300	250,356	3,478	27	136,718	1	-	146	40
Feb	10,186	4,424	393,306	295,742	273,393	3,219	21	127,280	-	-	145	41
Mar	10,263	4,424	409,678	329,741	310,074	3,139	21	127,998	1	-	142	110
Apr	10,246	4,426	415,469	329,257	308,686	2,837	21	134,524	1	-	147	110

Source: Bank of England

Notes to table

Movements in amounts outstanding can reflect breaks in data series as well as underlying flows. For changes data, users are recommended to refer directly to the appropriate series or data tables. Further explanation can be found at:
www.bankofengland.co.uk/statistics/Pages/iadb/notesiadb/Changes_flows_growth_rates.aspx

(o) In order to bring reporting in line with the National Accounts, English housing associations were reclassified from PNFCs to public corporations with effect from July 2017 data. The amounts outstanding increased by £34bn. This effect has been adjusted out of the flows for July 2017.

(p) Due to a loan transfer by one reporting institution, the amounts outstanding increased by £7bn. This effect has been adjusted out of the flows for April 2016.

(q) In order to bring reporting in line with the National Accounts, English housing associations were reclassified from PNFCs to public corporations with effect from July 2017 data. The amounts outstanding decreased by £34bn. This effect has been adjusted out of the flows for July 2017.

(r) Due to improvements in reporting at one institution, the amounts outstanding increased by £15bn. This effect has been adjusted out of the flows for June 2017.

(s) Due to improvements in reporting at one institution, the amounts outstanding decreased by £5bn. This effect has been adjusted out of the flows for June 2017.

(t) Due to improvements in reporting at one institution, the amounts outstanding increased by £10bn. This effect has been adjusted out of the flows for June 2017.

Explanatory notes can be found here: http://www.bankofengland.co.uk/statistics/Pages/iadb/notesiadb/MFIs_exICB.aspx

12.3c Monetary financial institutions' (excluding central bank) balance

£ millions

Amounts outstanding of sterling assets

Not seasonally adjusted

RPM	Bills				Sales and repurchase agreements					Advances		
	Treasury bills	UK MFIs bills	Other UK residents	Non-residents	UK MFIs	of which intragroup banks	UK public sector	Other UK residents	Non-residents	UK public sector	Other UK residents	Non-residents
	B3HP	B3RL	B3IP	B3JP	B3SL	B8ZG	B3KP	B3LP	B3MP	B2UK	B3OP	B3PP
2015 Aug	9,797	77	113	850	60,692	43,733	849	136,738	47,191	8,695	1,826,000	91,434
Sep	9,317	82	160	834	60,889	45,190	2	131,829	51,411	8,536	1,830,196	89,657
Oct	9,605	86	110	826	41,334	25,599	-	123,011	49,596	8,333	1,834,682	89,228
Nov	9,027	85	104	822	35,069	22,762	31	129,523	52,029	8,694	1,833,644	89,243
Dec	8,393	162	111	825	33,023	21,350	9	126,685	49,812	8,483	1,839,562	89,712
2016 Jan	9,489	231	152	749	30,696	18,831	75	123,963	52,458	8,577	1,849,610	90,255
Feb	9,359	213	19	663	33,874	19,491	102	129,285	46,728	8,607	1,861,142	88,432
Mar	7,582	210	78	670	35,338	18,457	35	131,574	48,390	8,565	1,866,642	88,688
Apr	6,994	241	76	779	38,433	18,203	29	130,010	52,215	8,618	1,860,447 (p)	90,280
May	6,201	248	41	579	37,923	16,009	11	146,215	53,538	8,830	1,861,454	95,840
Jun	8,821	273	104	402	38,128	16,865	11	157,700	55,618	8,316	1,871,114	99,973
Jul	14,084	270	147	586	27,958	11,223	11	155,061	57,090	8,495	1,879,028	96,632
Aug	12,725	270	76	595	29,009	11,804	224	154,650	59,769	8,417	1,887,402	100,322
Sep	11,779	274	84	388	30,692	11,493	497	159,840	61,495	8,235	1,890,474	98,555
Oct	10,589	297	93	473	30,458	13,597	1,491	165,219	58,909	8,643	1,889,663	99,873
Nov	8,997	298	152	417	29,190	13,056	428	182,007	61,076	8,667	1,881,345	95,257
Dec	7,630	311	153	364	30,026	12,903	-	175,957	67,530	8,515	1,886,203	104,938
2017 Jan	5,357	269	126	619	34,699	17,364	2,388	182,328	61,003	8,460	1,891,296	102,614
Feb	4,131	265	188	426	32,510	17,098	530	180,222	65,973	8,344	1,893,382	106,713
Mar	3,751	265	138	595	29,889	14,177	1,372	194,529	73,256	8,312	1,899,967	106,385
Apr	2,167	294	183	666	27,148	14,827	422	194,147	71,776	8,359	1,907,448	109,180

Source: Bank of England

Notes to table

Movements in amounts outstanding can reflect breaks in data series as well as underlying flows. For changes data, users are recommended to refer directly to the appropriate series or data tables. Further explanation can be found at: www.bankofengland.co.uk/statistics/Pages/iadb/notesiadb/Changes flows growth rates.aspx.

(o) In order to bring reporting in line with the National Accounts, English housing associations were reclassified from PNFCs to public corporations with effect from July 2017 data. The amounts outstanding increased by £34bn. This effect has been adjusted out of the flows for July 2017.

(p) Due to a loan transfer by one reporting institution, the amounts outstanding increased by £7bn. This effect has been adjusted out of the flows for April 2016.

(q) In order to bring reporting in line with the National Accounts, English housing associations were reclassified from PNFCs to public corporations with effect from July 2017 data. The amounts outstanding decreased by £34bn. This effect has been adjusted out of the flows for July 2017.

(r) Due to improvements in reporting at one institution, the amounts outstanding increased by £15bn. This effect has been adjusted out of the flows for June 2017.

(s) Due to improvements in reporting at one institution, the amounts outstanding decreased by £5bn. This effect has been adjusted out of the flows for June 2017.

(t) Due to improvements in reporting at one institution, the amounts outstanding increased by £10bn. This effect has been adjusted out of the flows for June 2017.

Explanatory notes can be found here: http://www.bankofengland.co.uk/statistics/Pages/iadb/notesiadb/MFIs_exICB.aspx

12.3c Monetary financial institutions' (excluding central bank) balance sheet

£ millions

Amounts outstanding of sterling assets   Not seasonally adjusted

	UK government bonds	Other UK public sector	Investments UK MFIs	Other UK residents	Non-residents	Items in suspense and collection	Accrued amounts receivable	Other assets	Total sterling assets
RPM	B3QP	B3RP	B3TL	B3SP	B3TP	B3UP	B3VP	B3WP	B3XP
2015 Aug	144,085	201	49,466	196,262	50,932	38,926	14,932	28,043	3,396,160
Sep	139,145	214	48,573	195,280	49,538	32,249	14,121	28,529	3,371,536
Oct	139,788	192	48,896	198,504	49,279	35,990	14,593	28,809	3,366,177
Nov	144,760	182	49,788	201,057	48,211	38,742	14,992	28,933	3,383,039
Dec	136,527	178	53,257	203,648	46,118	18,684	14,377	28,537	3,360,227
2016 Jan	138,282	235	52,931	197,906	47,819	52,625	14,729	28,597	3,389,805
Feb	141,394	260	50,889	193,750	50,205	39,343	15,445	28,808	3,386,472
Mar	141,039	236	50,165	195,393	50,315	36,483	14,641	29,469	3,393,425
Apr	143,385	233	50,336	195,431	47,414	43,176	14,444	29,463	3,405,634 (p)
May	141,552	244	50,197	194,426	49,141	42,399	15,609	29,513	3,419,126
Jun	144,619	582	50,082	195,532	49,148	43,775	15,121	29,582	3,468,966
Jul	143,879	598	49,955	196,977	52,165	54,099	15,437	29,815	3,498,700
Aug	152,551	664	50,017	197,912	54,176	38,360	15,637	29,927	3,513,797
Sep	151,526	647	50,406	195,925	54,460	43,470	14,070	30,379	3,534,547
Oct	151,472	604	50,985	190,374	56,783	35,727	13,909	30,644	3,528,309
Nov	150,012	581	50,189	191,266	55,710	44,096	14,162	30,689	3,546,544
Dec	150,107	574	51,387	193,520	55,106	17,728	13,807	30,867	3,574,017
2017 Jan	144,060	548	29,133	223,121	57,269	39,719	13,789	30,795	3,631,756
Feb	143,570	590	27,934	220,789	56,822	46,371	13,960	30,451	3,667,534
Mar	145,809	484	28,183	219,078	54,960	52,979	13,014	30,552	3,749,034
Apr	147,043	435	27,899	223,042	55,334	48,866	13,308	30,484	3,765,239

Source: Bank of England

Notes to table

Movements in amounts outstanding can reflect breaks in data series as well as underlying flows. For changes data, users are recommended to refer directly to the appropriate series or data tables. Further explanation can be found at: www.bankofengland.co.uk/statistics/Pages/iadb/notesiadb/Changes_flows_growth_rates.aspx.

(o) In order to bring reporting in line with the National Accounts, English housing associations were reclassified from PNFCs to public corporations with effect from July 2017 data. This effect has been adjusted out of the flows for July 2017.

(p) Due to a loan transfer by one reporting institution, the amounts outstanding increased by £7bn. This effect has been adjusted out of the flows for April 2016.

(q) In order to bring reporting in line with the National Accounts, English housing associations were reclassified from PNFCs to public corporations with effect from July 2017 data. The amounts outstanding decreased by £34bn. This effect has been adjusted out of the flows for July 2017.

(r) Due to improvements in reporting at one institution, the amounts outstanding increased by £15bn. This effect has been adjusted out of the flows for June 2017.

(s) Due to improvements in reporting at one institution, the amounts outstanding decreased by £5bn. This effect has been adjusted out of the flows for June 2017.

(t) Due to improvements in reporting at one institution, the amounts outstanding increased by £10bn. This effect has been adjusted out of the flows for June 2017.

Explanatory notes can be found here: http://www.bankofengland.co.uk/statistics/Pages/iadb/notesiadb/MFIs_exICB.aspx

12.3d Monetary financial institutions' (excluding central bank) balance she

£ millions

Not seasonally adjusted

Amounts outstanding of foreign currency assets (including euro)

	Loans and advances						Sale and repurchase agreements					Acceptances granted	Total bills
	UK MFIs	of which intragroup banks	UK MFIs' CDs etc.	UK public sector	Other UK residents	Non-residents	UK MFIs	of which intragroup banks	UK public sector	Other UK residents	Non-residents		
RPM	B3UL	B8ZQ	B3VL	B2UN	B3ZP	B2UH	B3WL	B8ZO	B3HQ	B3IQ	B3JQ	B3KQ	B3LQ
2015 Aug	209,801	144,212	2,362	493	224,429	1,677,387	88,542	55,763	614	111,866	527,482	2,591	36,064
Sep	200,903	145,590	2,191	528	227,153	1,650,999	86,526	55,905	1,209	112,038	541,150	2,661	38,204
Oct	196,990	143,371	1,815	483	227,366	1,604,135	81,502	52,913	1,542	105,680	514,778	2,672	37,991
Nov	197,812	145,797	1,465	446	223,831	1,636,970	85,340	56,703	872	105,282	517,221	2,498	41,643
Dec	197,651	148,459	1,110	494	220,646	1,691,114	77,282	51,805	1,417	100,525	516,203	2,767	44,279
2016 Jan	195,957	146,249	1,052	568	232,201	1,766,536	76,412	49,968	1,600	111,056	543,274	2,405	42,382
Feb	207,542	153,751	1,218	656	246,339	1,772,048	76,697	49,377	1,163	122,409	561,171	2,085	45,599
Mar	199,514	148,544	1,310	624	233,809	1,731,340	69,105	44,479	275	114,579	564,808	2,380	45,031
Apr	209,821	158,534	1,314	579	236,631	1,683,644	71,991	44,765	1,326	120,361	566,334	2,508	42,023
May	189,081	139,117	1,295	509	233,587	1,696,042	70,777	40,171	1,473	121,308	563,487	2,554	41,010
Jun	204,057	143,873	1,489	641	258,388	1,923,479	76,452	42,394	922	132,391	631,881	3,331	40,564
Jul	206,542	149,625	1,576	711	260,296	1,930,097	76,466	43,610	1,316	131,352	630,828	3,010	38,970
Aug	214,079	158,988	1,571	680	262,614	1,947,698	77,153	43,719	1,014	130,628	620,260	2,962	38,339
Sep	203,684	147,291	1,412	11	241,896	1,992,264 (u)	72,088	37,621	1,628	136,365	668,115	3,618	36,123
Oct	211,952	152,778	1,810	9	248,968	2,053,109	73,408	36,061	426	138,097	686,863	3,558	38,843
Nov	207,664	152,537	1,193	3	250,122	1,997,339	69,252	34,846	1,527	141,062	668,495	3,691	36,273
Dec	203,308	149,424	1,153	12	241,795	2,021,172	70,567	33,036	1,813	122,640	671,554	4,015	36,204
2017 Jan	206,911	154,446	1,201	7	248,512	1,978,013	74,364	35,740	1,989	137,091	687,479	3,288	39,168
Feb	199,983	144,529	1,112	35	254,679	2,028,597	75,379	35,565	1,072	159,167	698,801	3,789	37,152
Mar	194,249	137,113	1,037	11	245,880	1,970,277	81,217	39,816	197	154,816	705,335	4,008	36,559
Apr	187,594	133,417	896	24	247,590	1,936,008	75,737	38,118	3,253	158,797	678,921	3,580	32,843

Source: Bank of England

Notes to table

Movements in amounts outstanding can reflect breaks in data series as well as underlying flows. For changes data, users are recommended to refer directly to the appropriate series or data tables. Further explanation can be found at: www.bankofengland.co.uk/statistics/Pages/iadb/notesiadb/Changes_flows_growth_rates.aspx.

(u) Due to a change in treatment at one institution, the amounts outstanding decreased by £14bn. This effect has been adjusted out of the flows for September 2016.

(v) Due to transfer of business by one institution, amounts outstanding increased by £34 billion. This amount has been adjusted out of the flows for July 2017.

Explanatory notes can be found here: http://www.bankofengland.co.uk/statistics/Pages/iadb/notesiadb/MFIs_exICB.aspx

12.3d Monetary financial institutions' (excluding central bank) balance sheet

£ millions

Not seasonally adjusted

Amounts outstanding of foreign currency assets (including euro)

RPM	UK government bonds	Other UK public sector	Investments UK MFIs	Other UK residents	Non-residents	Items in suspense and collection	Accrued amounts receivable	Other assets	Total foreign currency assets	Total assets	Holdings of own sterling acceptances	Holdings of own foreign currency acceptances
	B3MQ	B3NQ	B3XL	B3OQ	B3PQ	B3QQ	B3RQ	B3SQ	B3TQ	B3UQ	B3IM	B3JM
2015 Aug	463	-	13,310	22,406	479,567	147,106	11,788	43,831	3,600,105	6,996,265	126	1,276
Sep	428	-	12,482	22,558	468,933	150,192	11,326	44,698	3,574,178	6,945,714	184	1,252
Oct	420	-	12,382	20,605	482,378	182,474	11,025	42,841	3,527,078	6,893,254	194	1,248
Nov	422	-	14,847	19,681	491,695	173,396	11,385	41,261	3,566,067	6,949,106	187	1,264
Dec	471	-	14,218	19,525	475,134	89,329	10,761	39,389	3,502,316	6,862,543	189	1,173
2016 Jan	473	-	14,898	19,107	475,717	197,818	11,153	38,239	3,730,849	7,120,654	176	1,123
Feb	504	1	14,918	19,378	459,136	197,071	10,893	43,124	3,781,952	7,168,425	156	1,028
Mar	569	2	14,124	19,651	446,141	192,914	11,202	43,053	3,690,431	7,083,857	118	1,017
Apr	661	1	15,609	17,793	457,143	222,009	10,053	43,019	3,702,819	7,108,452	128	884
May	711	3	14,996	17,267	442,661	204,291	10,454	38,461	3,649,966	7,069,091	139	932
Jun	778	4	14,814	16,779	466,404	225,679	11,088	44,525	4,053,665	7,522,631	151	1,094
Jul	691	3	14,589	14,941	492,137	215,369	10,356	46,767	4,076,017	7,574,717	154	1,198
Aug	703	2	14,534	15,155	486,311	206,322	10,688	51,469	4,082,182	7,595,979	187	1,111
Sep	692	-	13,889	13,730	462,304	227,515	10,583	45,071	4,130,988 (u)	7,665,535 (u)	184	1,011
Oct	582	-	14,477	14,097	490,431	235,684	11,673	45,429	4,269,415	7,797,724	198	897
Nov	499	-	13,605	14,862	450,162	266,521	11,892	44,011	4,178,173	7,724,717	201	936
Dec	464	-	13,855	13,104	457,809	108,868	9,392	44,851	4,022,578	7,596,595	189	1,011
2017 Jan	426	-	13,113	12,548	459,369	239,807	9,653	42,375	4,155,313	7,787,070	193	920
Feb	401	-	15,007	13,465	484,150	264,093	12,637	41,647	4,291,167	7,958,702	184	1,113
Mar	473	-	13,240	12,917	461,730	228,757	11,733	40,240	4,162,675	7,911,709	158	1,436
Apr	438	-	12,953	11,541	451,983	268,152	13,022	40,569	4,123,901	7,889,139	160	1,096

Source: Bank of England

Notes to table

Movements in amounts outstanding can reflect breaks in data series as well as underlying flows. For changes data, users are recommended to refer directly to the appropriate series or data tables. Further explanation can be found at: www.bankofengland.co.uk/statistics/Pages/iadb/notesiadb/Changes_flows_growth_rates.aspx.

(u) Due to a change in treatment at one institution, the amounts outstanding decreased by £14bn. This effect has been adjusted out of the flows for September 2016.
(v) Due to transfer of business by one institution, amounts outstanding increased by £34 billion. This amount has been adjusted out of the flows for July 2017.

Explanatory notes can be found here: http://www.bankofengland.co.uk/statistics/Pages/iadb/notesiadb/MFIs_extICB.aspx

Copyright guidance and the related UK Open Government Licence can be viewed here:www.bankofengland.co.uk/Pages/disclaimer.aspx.

12.3e Monetary financial institutions' (excluding central bank) balance sheet

£ millions

Not seasonally adjusted

Changes in sterling liabilities

RPM	Notes outstanding & cash loaded cards	UK MFIs	of which intragroup banks	Sight deposits UK public sector	Sight deposits Other UK residents	Sight deposits Non-residents	UK MFIs	of which intragroup banks	Time deposits UK public sector	Time deposits Other UK residents	of which SAYE	of which cash ISAs	Non-residents
	B4IJ	B4GA	B8ZD	B4CF	B4BH	B4DD	B4HA	B8ZF	B4DF	B4CH	B4FH	B4DH	B4ED
2015 Aug	138	-8,087	-9,329	-244	-8,522	5,453	4,089	4,049	-19	-6,617	44	885	-8
Sep	83	263	1,438	-132	17,255	7,510	-6,203	-6,034	-78	-11,151	-18	664	12,099
Oct	16	3,875	4,841	410	6,322	-15,068	1,085	813	20	2,754	24	541	-9,167
Nov	89	4,066	3,164	-219	10,855	6,717	2,336	1,509	-227	-3,054	-26	446	-223
Dec	125	-2,068	374	528	4,170	7,175	2,510	2,889	-598	-275	-47	270	14,976
2016 Jan	-236	-3,677	-4,910	737	-1,586	264	-7,735	-7,698	-278	-8,443	-1	267	-7,442
Feb	-31	35	-617	-612	18,511	-432	195	-165	-892	-3,516	16	581	-24,251
Mar	99	-10,476	-11,768	-809	27,036	8,195	3,699	4,281	-2,146	-10,425	3	1,989	2,078
Apr	1	-4,752	-3,677	1,232	-16,073	-4,469	443	-1,764	1,103	7,179	24	5,505	6,487
May	80	98	514	-652	17,109	-9,002	-4,397	-3,796	269	-2,518	12	722	-7,870
Jun	-26	-6,104	-6,634	18	28,593	12,322	23,501	23,107	259	1,084	34	222	3,142
Jul	4	7,295	4,285	659	5,368	9,859	-3,840	-3,221	854	-140	-84	426	1,847
Aug	116	-4,699	-4,129	-157	5,752	1,240	-3,383	-3,083	50	2,383	-29	-402	-2,344
Sep	82	6,644	7,751	-1,110	18,058	-7,423	4,063	3,717	-229	-6,485	-45	-349	996
Oct	34	1,609	-950	736	-246	1,443	-8,079	-9,404	-108	-535	13	-656	109
Nov	71	-6,282	-3,881	-784	2,491	-1,040	5,647	2,020	-219	-6,261	-6	-620	-1,186
Dec	426	5,084	6,929	114	9,113	2,225	34,946	20,603	-648	2,618	5	-393	1,522
2017 Jan	-156	6,589	5,214	211	-16,328	2,172	7,960	-5,462	-370	-9,377	12	-795	-4,286
Feb	8	9,369	10,427	-907	1,763	-1,565	20,360	11,398	-814	-6,711	-7	-771	-108
Mar	14	18,524	19,046	-388	30,254	3,243	27,877	15,225	-1,721	-4,309	21	638	-5,971
Apr	86	1,139	-194	1,693	-9,026	-1,488	2,037	-470	1	11,247	5	3,838	4,143

Source: Bank of England

Notes to table

Explanatory notes can be found here: http://www.bankofengland.co.uk/statistics/Pages/iadb/notesiadb/MFIs_exICB.aspx

Copyright guidance and the related UK Open Government Licence can be viewed here: www.bankofengland.co.uk/Pages/disclaimer.aspx.

12.3e Monetary financial institutions' (excluding central bank) balance sheet

£ millions

Changes in sterling liabilities

RPM	UK MFIs	Liabilities under sale and repurchase agreements				Acceptances granted	CDs and other paper issued				Total sterling deposits	Sterling items in suspense and transmission	Net derivatives	Accrued amounts payable	Sterling capital and other internal funds	Total sterling liabilities
		of which intragroup banks	UK public sector	Other UK residents	Non-residents		CDs and Commercial paper	Bonds with maturity of up to and incl. 5 years	Bonds with maturity of greater than 5 years	Total						
	B4IA	B8ZB	B4EF	B4EH	B4FD	B4BK	B2SU	B6OH	B2TK	B4EJ	B4FJ	B4AK	B4GJ	B4CJ	B4DJ	B4JJ
2015 Aug	4,831	2,260	1,496	2,433	-8,648	6	3,698	-209	-256	3,233	-10,603	-4,111	1,318	-135	30,242	16,849
Sep	-780	1,485	-8,914	-24,124	-395	-1	-4,074	1,463	-37	-2,648	-17,298	-7,034	-15,616	-1,266	25,364	-15,767
Oct	-21,076	-19,770	1,679	4,186	2,653	-3	-258	-658	-153	-1,069	-23,398	6,103	9,929	-485	-27,704	-35,539
Nov	-6,779	-3,035	220	4,708	2,566	-10	-588	-612	-1,268	-2,468	18,488	-153	-1,451	722	-7,657	10,038
Dec	218	-982	-147	-12,053	-5,140	-1	3,863	944	-314	4,494	13,790	-19,028	-12,298	99	2,825	-14,488
2016 Jan	-2,627	-2,819	-78	2,491	6,501	-7	-1,249	570	-72	-752	-22,631	33,204	26,017	1,450	-14,222	23,583
Feb	2,556	809	-165	2,704	-10,152	-16	1,249	1,028	22	2,299	-13,737	-13,422	30,311	625	-24,086	-20,340
Mar	5,872	-900	-1,298	-7,892	10,409	-12	3,972	-1,155	148	2,966	27,199	-3,590	-58,281	-1,970	-3,467	-40,010
Apr	3,633	-255	5,547	3,297	1,267	6	869	748	12	1,628	6,527	5,155	-5,248	-1,020	-13,865	-8,450
May	-2,137	-2,377	250	4,155	3,687	-2	4,108	-924	-305	2,878	1,867	2,536	-7,105	1,379	10,130	8,886
Jun	5,939	1,055	183	-1,396	1,650	37	-16	-118	695	562	69,791	1,205	79,742	148	-32,889	117,970
Jul	-9,596	-5,623	-2,005	14,004	-11,335	6	9,281	-55	-305	8,920	21,897	6,879	-7,127	-315	-22,436	-1,099
Aug	584	600	913	8,877	3,997	3	1,899	95	103	2,097	15,313	-14,747	-7,030	-425	-1,793	-8,566
Sep	-1,829	-292	-3,188	-16,919	2,357	-34	4,228	-231	-33	3,964	-1,136	7,284	16,923	722	-18,203	5,672
Oct	-2,656	2,104	1,474	19,384	7,986	16	-682	-42	-293	-1,017	20,116	-7,718	66,459	533	-23,379	56,045
Nov	-2,355	-540	290	14,388	4,968	19	-2,956	185	-867	-3,638	6,038	9,318	-77,015	-147	56,387	-5,347
Dec	-5,288	-153	-1,599	-20,844	833	-27	2,122	-1,058	-8	1,056	29,104	-25,930	7,750	-835	1,431	11,946
2017 Jan	2,436	4,486	-411	26,351	364	5	-851	-725	-657	-2,233	13,083	22,337	-24,227	-31	30,126	41,132
Feb	-1,629	-471	2,049	-1,031	1,366	1	5,192	-170	23	5,045	27,188	2,118	35,703	1,193	1,644	67,855
Mar	-383	-2,740	-1,202	-166	9,538	66	10,262	-892	-238	9,133	84,494	3,531	-25,650	-2,775	-15,569	44,045
Apr	-1,532	649	-505	15,039	-7,500	5	2,763	-2,203	-170	391	15,644	-167	-34,857	-565	1,312	-18,546

Source: Bank of England

Notes to table

12.3f Monetary financial institutions' (excluding central bank) balance sheet

£ millions

Not seasonally adjusted

Changes in foreign currency liabilities (including euro)

RPM	Sight and time deposits					Acceptances granted	Sale and repurchase agreements				
	UK MFIs	of which intragroup banks	UK public sector	Other UK residents	Non-residents		UK MFIs	of which intragroup banks	UK public sector	Other UK residents	Non-residents
	B4GB	B8ZN	B2VP	B2VV	B2VJ	B4HM	B4HB	B8ZL	B4GG	B4GI	B4HE
2015 Aug	8,097	3,562	133	9,975	17,491	474	-3,204	-3,371	-793	442	5,101
Sep	-3,214	720	-34	-3,244	-30,236	50	-3,505	-207	-421	1,569	-12,568
Oct	-1,102	1,317	109	2,912	-8,475	55	-926	-1,639	184	-2,006	15,177
Nov	-1,082	1,632	16	-1,972	37,026	-197	4,275	3,890	-101	2,990	4,192
Dec	-3,072	-1,355	-151	-5,363	-28,787	216	-8,386	-7,011	975	-2,520	-39,373
2016 Jan	-5,606	-7,719	81	9,258	-1,288	-444	-8,501	-3,767	-173	3,989	34,433
Feb	7,619	3,999	176	829	5,211	-358	-1,777	-2,047	-174	1,249	-20,970
Mar	-9,991	-4,290	-286	6,191	-19,595	328	-6,044	-5,074	-1,155	-237	-7,846
Apr	11,021	12,400	179	3,189	-15,012	162	3,571	989	1,198	3,464	16,184
May	-18,299	-17,836	6	5,126	85	48	-395	-3,486	-584	-1,586	16,798
Jun	916	-6,127	369	9,548	64,505	583	-1,111	-901	-385	-3,577	5,520
Jul	-2,111	4,055	-63	2,226	-11,744	-355	-380	543	1,067	3,380	-6,002
Aug	7,613	7,169	171	5,634	-12,516	-73	126	-304	-294	-1,985	-1,440
Sep	-12,950	-13,684	-817	-4,560	-7,969	622	-5,481	-6,659	-890	8,788	10,010
Oct	-3,501	-615	-30	-2,564	-55,398	-230	-1,909	-3,042	367	-3,519	9,954
Nov	3,955	5,979	207	6,970	2,332	226	-2,434	446	993	11,889	7,047
Dec	-3,854	-4,940	-181	-17,014	-60	279	1,560	-2,177	-1,063	-7,458	-4,475
2017 Jan	4,959	5,615	213	8,957	987	-675	3,849	2,982	796	12,516	26,574
Feb	-12,411	-9,523	-74	-943	16,425	472	-1,554	-41	-975	25,197	22,265
Mar	-10,131	-6,995	-245	-7,369	-24,977	233	5,631	4,095	-272	-8,694	-3,197
Apr	-615	-404	358	9,071	13,871	-335	-2,760	-993	1,279	1,956	-1

Source: Bank of England

Notes to table

Explanatory notes can be found here: http://www.bankofengland.co.uk/statistics/Pages/iadb/notesiadb/MFIs_exICB.aspx

Copyright guidance and the related UK Open Government Licence can be viewed here: www.bankofengland.co.uk/Pages/disclaimer.aspx

12.3f Monetary financial institutions' (excluding central bank) balance sheet

£ millions

Changes in foreign currency liabilities (including euro)

Not seasonally adjusted

RPM	CDs and Commercial paper	CDs and other paper Issued		Total	Total foreign currency deposits	Items in suspense and transmission	Net derivatives	Accrued amounts payable	Capital and other internal funds	Total foreign currency liabilities	Total liabilities
		Bonds with maturity of up to and incl. 5 years	Bonds with maturity of greater than 5 years								
	B2TN	B6OJ	B2TO	B4CM	B4DM	B4GM	B4EM	B4AM	B4BM	B4FM	B4JM
2015 Aug	4,943	-616	-2,528	1,799	39,514	-25,204	-3,925	1,237	-10,582	1,039	17,888
Sep	-11,646	-6,106	2,755	-14,996	-66,601	10,197	482	-132	-14,829	-70,883	-86,650
Oct	-2,055	1,767	5,702	5,413	11,343	36,709	-7,667	-480	11,726	51,631	16,092
Nov	-3,739	-199	-2,471	-6,409	38,738	-9,495	1,740	1,111	8,769	40,863	50,901
Dec	-6,584	-3,740	-3,710	-14,034	-100,494	-84,569	7,656	143	16,625	-160,640	-175,128
2016 Jan	2,358	-4,401	-3,155	-5,198	26,550	101,753	-36,162	-2,113	10,281	100,309	123,891
Feb	3,798	-113	2,141	5,826	-2,370	-3,510	-26,192	190	9,836	-22,046	-42,385
Mar	-854	-4,838	-414	-6,106	-44,741	-11,346	55,926	-270	-11,548	-11,979	-51,989
Apr	2,026	835	8,137	10,998	34,954	30,918	4,079	-168	12,304	82,087	73,636
May	2,047	-2,813	-1,616	-2,383	-1,183	-7,532	4,730	943	-20,412	-23,455	-14,569
Jun	-1,941	593	3,968	2,620	78,988	7,081	-83,278	35	8,337	11,163	129,133
Jul	-6,757	-1,875	209	-8,423	-22,405	-3,796	4,912	-69	214	-21,144	-22,243
Aug	-3,950	-13	-2,173	-6,136	-8,900	-8,588	4,097	-93	-3,590	-17,073	-25,640
Sep	-1,669	20,468	-3,996	14,803	1,556	26,599	-11,644	626	17,073	34,211	39,883
Oct	4,412	-4,348	16	80	-56,750	-873	-79,577	1,252	36,517	-99,431	-43,386
Nov	2,931	-2,184	-7,803	-7,056	24,129	32,908	84,112	538	-29,123	112,564	107,217
Dec	-5,738	-855	-1,475	-8,067	-40,333	-150,332	-4,737	-1,606	6,497	-190,511	-178,565
2017 Jan	1,966	1,404	2,218	5,589	63,764	124,391	27,279	620	-23,761	192,292	233,424
Feb	10,850	6,608	8,403	25,860	74,263	11,241	-34,557	5,186	-1,030	55,103	122,958
Mar	990	-6,285	-3,403	-8,698	-57,718	-37,128	26,530	-551	-12,149	-81,015	-36,971
Apr	-1,318	12,947	3,732	15,361	38,184	33,661	37,838	1,739	-13,010	98,412	79,866

Source: Bank of England

Notes to table

Explanatory notes can be found here: http://www.bankofengland.co.uk/statistics/Pages/iadb/notesiadb/MFIs_exICB.aspx

Copyright guidance and the related UK Open Government Licence can be viewed here: www.bankofengland.co.uk/Pages/disclaimer.aspx.

12.3g Monetary financial institutions' (excluding central bank) balance sheet

£ millions

Not seasonally adjusted

Changes in sterling assets

| | Notes and coin | With UK central bank | | Loans | | | | | Acceptances granted | | | |
| | | Cash ratio deposits | Other | UK MFIs | of which intragroup banks | UK MFIs' CDs etc | UK MFIs commercial paper | Non-residents | UK MFIs | UK public sector | Other UK residents | Non-residents |
RPM	B4II	B3YR	B3ZR	B4DC	B8ZJ	B4JB	B4BC	B4BD	B4EC	B4FF	B3TR	B4GD
2015 Aug	-254	-	-2,641	-4,721	-5,063	97	82	-52	-	-	4	1
Sep	195	-	-17,874	-4,438	-4,724	-238	-14	12,502	-	-	2	-3
Oct	29	-	9,900	3,965	5,274	209	20	-10,777	-	-	-2	-1
Nov	-186	4	1,035	6,366	5,195	-63	28	-2,358	-14	-	3	1
Dec	1,558	57	-3,164	753	2,863	-371	-7	6,813	-	-	-2	1
2016 Jan	-1,483	-	2,250	-11,778	-12,612	397	19	-1,056	-	-	-5	-2
Feb	-151	-	1,038	1,390	-101	-77	-98	-4,559	-	-	-17	-
Mar	1,420	-	-4,684	-5,013	-7,976	-160	-41	8,482	-	-	-10	-2
Apr	-822	1	9,514	-4,979	-5,254	-154	1	2,152	-	-	1	5
May	279	18	-4,938	-3,329	-3,370	-10	-1	-498	-	-	-1	-1
Jun	230	60	-2,941	16,407	17,222	-175	-	-4,032	-	-	37	-
Jul	-601	-	4,211	2,446	1,146	546	27	9,715	-	-	8	-2
Aug	709	-	11,380	-7,089	-7,175	-50	-21	-252	-	-	4	-1
Sep	-578	-	-3,777	11,032	12,202	-158	-7	4,035	-	-	-34	-1
Oct	-478	1	11,973	-10,793	-12,800	-35	-10	83	-	-	14	2
Nov	577	26	15,896	-5,599	-4,054	-100	-7	-1,397	-	-	19	-
Dec	1,553	182	14,262	28,569	29,612	-224	-	-7,161	-	-	-33	6
2017 Jan	-1,502	-	18,977	-1,969	-3,402	200	2	9,152	-	-	5	1
Feb	-179	-	17,641	22,441	23,037	-259	-6	-9,438	-	-	-1	1
Mar	77	-	16,359	35,248	36,682	-80	-	948	-	-	-3	69
Apr	-17	2	5,792	-483	-1,388	-302	-	10,274	-	-	5	-

Source: Bank of England

Notes to table

Explanatory notes can be found here: http://www.bankofengland.co.uk/statistics/Pages/iadb/notesiadb/MFIs_exICB.aspx

Copyright guidance and the related UK Open Government Licence can be viewed here: www.bankofengland.co.uk/Pages/disclaimer.aspx

12.3g Monetary financial institutions' (excluding central bank) balance sheet

£ millions

Not seasonally adjusted

Changes in sterling assets

	Bills				Claims under sale and repurchase agreements					Advances		
	Treasury bills	UK MFIs bills	Other UK	Non-residents	UK MFIs	of which intragroup banks	UK public sector	Other UK residents	Non-residents	UK public sector	Other UK residents	Non-residents
RPM	B4BA	B4IB	B4HG	B4IC	B4FA	B8ZH	B4BF	B4AH	B4CD	B2VK	B2VQ	B4HC
2015 Aug	1,826	25	-6	-7	4,057	2,410	823	6,712	-654	390	-143	711
Sep	-494	5	47	-17	196	1,457	-847	-4,909	4,220	-159	4,913	-1,106
Oct	288	3	-50	-8	-19,554	-19,591	-2	-8,817	-1,815	-203	5,039	-409
Nov	-626	-	-6	-4	-6,266	-2,837	31	6,512	2,433	361	-528	38
Dec	-634	77	7	3	-2,046	-1,412	-22	-2,838	-2,217	-211	2,416	489
2016 Jan	821	68	40	-76	-2,327	-2,519	66	-2,722	2,647	93	9,586	566
Feb	-660	-17	-133	-86	3,178	661	26	5,321	-5,730	30	12,404	-2,539
Mar	-1,777	-3	59	7	1,464	-1,035	-67	2,289	1,662	-42	5,862	272
Apr	-588	31	-2	108	3,287	-253	-6	-1,756	3,825	66	-12,975	707
May	-793	7	-35	-200	-510	-2,195	-19	15,064	2,464	227	1,374	6,157
Jun	2,620	25	63	-176	205	857	-	11,484	2,080	-214	10,048	4,993
Jul	5,262	-4	43	184	-10,170	-5,642	-	-2,639	1,472	179	8,671	-3,466
Aug	-1,359	1	-71	9	1,051	581	213	-411	2,679	-56	8,716	3,661
Sep	-951	4	7	-208	1,683	-311	273	4,696	1,727	-183	3,841	-1,729
Oct	-1,190	23	10	85	-234	2,104	994	5,379	-2,586	408	-639	1,336
Nov	-1,592	1	59	-56	-1,268	-540	-1,063	16,789	2,167	24	-6,045	-4,599
Dec	-1,346	12	-	-53	836	-153	-428	-6,051	6,453	-152	6,731	9,702
2017 Jan	-2,273	-41	-27	255	4,673	4,461	2,388	6,372	-6,527	-54	5,020	-2,379
Feb	-1,227	-4	62	-193	-1,428	-266	-2,095	-3,805	4,288	-117	2,275	4,134
Mar	-379	-	-50	169	-2,621	-2,921	842	14,306	7,283	-32	4,863	-1,241
Apr	-1,584	29	46	70	-2,741	649	-950	-381	-1,480	48	7,292	1,193

Source: Bank of England

Notes to table

Explanatory notes can be found here: http://www.bankofengland.co.uk/statistics/Pages/iadb/notesiadb/MFIs_exICB.aspx

Copyright guidance and the related UK Open Government Licence can be viewed here: www.bankofengland.co.uk/Pages/disclaimer.aspx.

12.3g Monetary financial institutions' (excluding central bank) balance sheet

£ millions   Not seasonally adjusted

Changes in sterling assets

RPM	UK government bonds	Other UK public sector	Investments UK MFIs	Other UK residents	Non-residents	Items in suspense and collection	Accrued amounts receivable	Other assets	Total sterling assets
	B4CA	B4IE	B4CC	B4IG	B4JC	B4BJ	B4HI	B4JI	B4AJ
2015 Aug	7,155	14	334	-9,045	-1,703	-2,800	1,691	-181	1,716
Sep	-6,710	13	-802	-296	-2,020	-6,677	-972	470	-25,013
Oct	2,297	-21	346	1,418	376	3,741	472	280	-13,276
Nov	4,507	-10	777	-958	-2,032	2,752	399	124	12,320
Dec	-6,764	-4	1,755	2,130	-2,888	-20,058	-805	-398	-26,370
2016 Jan	-2,527	57	-107	-1,468	-454	33,993	380	61	27,038
Feb	2,730	25	-1,759	-39	-742	-13,282	891	36	-2,817
Mar	592	-24	-920	-485	474	-2,859	-804	366	6,057
Apr	3,298	-3	-26	-565	-2,284	6,692	-185	-8	5,338
May	-3,520	10	-243	-244	1,573	-776	1,165	49	13,273
Jun	-4,896	53	-86	849	-4,794	1,375	-488	67	32,795
Jul	-3,295	16	-554	-4,573	1,708	10,324	316	233	20,057
Aug	5,820	66	-143	-3,839	1,382	-15,739	200	112	6,971
Sep	2,597	-17	501	477	21	5,111	-1,443	487	27,408
Oct	5,855	-43	312	-2,741	283	-7,743	-161	265	368
Nov	1,244	-23	-731	2,503	1,886	8,369	254	46	27,381
Dec	-2,608	-6	993	-1,480	-1,453	-26,368	-349	171	21,758
2017 Jan	-3,029	-27	-22,212	29,208	3,215	21,991	-18	-71	61,330
Feb	-3,887	43	-1,415	-4,787	-1,879	2,574	161	-344	22,557
Mar	1,754	-106	291	-1,943	-1,409	6,607	-946	97	80,100
Apr	885	-49	-230	5,472	597	-4,112	294	-61	19,608

Source: Bank of England

Notes to table

Explanatory notes can be found here: http://www.bankofengland.co.uk/statistics/Pages/iadb/notesiadb/MFIs_exICB.aspx

Copyright guidance and the related UK Open Government Licence can be viewed here: www.bankofengland.co.uk/Pages/disclaimer.aspx

12.3h Monetary financial institutions' (excluding central bank) balance sheet

£ millions

Not seasonally adjusted

Changes in foreign currency assets (including euro)

	Loans and advances						Claims under sale and repurchase agreements					Acceptances granted	Total Bills
	UK MFIs	of which intragroup banks	UK MFIs' CDs etc.	UK public sector	Other UK residents	Non-residents	UK MFIs	of which intragroup banks	UK public sector	Other UK residents	Non-residents		
RPM	B4EB	B8ZR	B4AF	B2VN	B2VT	B2VH	B4FB	B8ZP	B4EG	B4EI	B4FE	B4HM	B4GL
2015 Aug	10,481	4,999	12	-9	1,484	18,270	-1,571	-3,381	-1,306	-133	3,404	474	770
Sep	-10,223	-52	-37	30	-86	-41,653	-2,910	-414	586	-1,066	6,855	50	1,641
Oct	526	1,277	-325	-31	5,334	-9,905	-2,916	-1,640	354	-3,645	-14,655	55	678
Nov	1,814	2,684	-330	-29	-3,941	43,141	3,983	3,944	-680	-212	-3,604	-197	3,390
Dec	-5,076	-1,651	-408	28	-8,924	9,129	-10,693	-6,829	524	-8,080	-6,826	216	1,395
2016 Jan	-8,136	-7,722	-96	56	3,210	10,029	-3,780	-3,778	131	6,624	5,939	-444	-3,606
Feb	7,196	4,306	142	75	9,278	-32,502	-1,247	-1,582	-467	8,394	4,895	-358	843
Mar	-7,077	-4,472	82	-41	-8,909	-23,453	-7,491	-4,943	-880	-7,366	13,870	328	84
Apr	13,306	12,322	19	-38	6,314	-18,251	4,423	946	1,067	7,038	8,683	162	-2,623
May	-19,066	-18,097	-	-60	-1,523	25,526	-460	-4,067	162	2,508	-709	48	-660
Jun	424	-6,054	102	87	5,309	86,110	-54	-967	-599	446	18,324	583	-3,892
Jul	-214	3,706	66	59	-1,548	-19,997	-1,158	539	384	-3,034	-9,591	-355	-2,178
Aug	5,746	7,987	-16	-37	-915	-115	-79	-307	-314	-1,902	-17,294	-73	-1,012
Sep	-12,229	-13,622	-177	-672	-23,535	32,476	-6,075	-6,680	595	2,086	39,948	622	-2,745
Oct	-258	-1,181	349	-2	-4,613	-30,536	-1,883	-3,099	-1,281	-3,829	-15,827	-230	1,091
Nov	3,506	5,810	-562	-7	10,178	21,958	-1,093	493	1,129	9,943	6,471	226	-767
Dec	-6,556	-4,864	-48	10	-8,027	1,348	455	-2,187	265	-19,524	-4,937	279	-381
2017 Jan	5,246	6,372	54	-6	9,613	-23,703	4,417	2,846	199	15,213	24,494	-675	3,224
Feb	-7,356	-10,232	-90	28	4,837	41,081	924	-94	-922	17,464	6,937	472	-2,244
Mar	-5,454	-7,270	-74	-24	-7,618	-55,084	5,981	4,291	-882	-4,336	8,385	233	-531
Apr	-2,586	-550	-124	13	8,127	12,916	-3,703	-966	3,086	7,245	-8,239	-335	-2,807

Source: Bank of England

Notes to table

Explanatory notes can be found ere: http://www.bankofengland.co.uk/statistics/Pages/iadb/notesiadb/MFIs_exICB.aspx

Copyright guidance and the related UK Open Government Licence can be viewed here: www.bankofengland.co.uk/Pages/disclaimer.aspx.

12.3h Monetary financial institutions' (excluding central bank) balance sheet

£ millions

Not seasonally adjusted

Changes in foreign currency assets (including euro)

RPM	UK government bonds	Other UK public sector	Investments UK MFIs	Other UK residents	Non-residents	Items in suspense and collection	Accrued amounts receivable	Other assets	Total foreign currency assets	Total assets	Holdings of own sterling acceptances	Holdings of own foreign currency acceptances
	B4EA	B4CG	B4AG	B4CI	B4DE	B4JL	B4FL	B4HL	B4IL	B4IM	B3VR	B3XR
2015 Aug	33	-	529	-1,395	4,392	-21,284	361	1,675	16,185	17,902	22	102
Sep	-40	-	-940	184	-14,684	1,549	-588	-300	-61,631	-86,644	58	-39
Oct	-	-	180	-1,491	19,932	36,233	-59	-1,104	29,162	15,885	11	19
Nov	-3	-	869	-1,297	6,715	-9,107	269	-2,192	38,589	50,909	-7	-12
Dec	1	-	-1,078	-974	-27,027	-88,388	10	-2,609	-148,779	-175,149	2	-109
2016 Jan	-15	-	220	-569	-14,737	104,504	6	-2,526	96,810	123,849	-13	-96
Feb	22	1	-278	113	-33,659	-4,884	-484	3,312	-39,608	-42,425	-20	-114
Mar	77	1	-826	250	-15,097	-2,972	430	940	-58,050	-51,993	-38	20
Apr	119	-1	584	-1,324	17,092	31,840	-675	573	68,308	73,646	10	-119
May	48	2	-412	-32	-13,181	-15,787	464	-4,719	-27,851	-14,578	11	44
Jun	15	1	366	-1,586	-18,226	5,624	-181	3,424	96,278	129,072	12	84
Jul	-95	-1	-416	-2,040	10,185	-13,346	-877	1,820	-42,338	-22,281	3	93
Aug	5	-1	-167	-253	-9,670	-10,977	234	4,224	-32,617	-25,645	32	-101
Sep	-16	-2	-812	-1,740	-26,839	18,448	-195	-6,665	12,472	39,879	-3	-108
Oct	-143	-	79	-574	16,366	-1,318	587	-1,793	-43,815	-43,447	14	-171
Nov	-71	-	-360	556	-11,880	40,480	658	-464	79,901	107,282	3	60
Dec	-40	-	152	-3,072	30	-158,118	-2,597	409	-200,352	-178,594	-12	62
2017 Jan	-30	-	-697	-752	8,164	129,083	356	-2,080	172,122	233,452	4	-73
Feb	-29	-	1,879	217	16,374	18,922	2,936	-1,070	100,362	122,919	-9	183
Mar	74	-	-1,750	125	-19,524	-34,487	-893	-1,203	-117,061	-36,961	-26	333
Apr	-21	-	-48	-830	-118	44,768	1,580	1,377	60,301	79,909	3	-303

Source: Bank of England

Notes to table

Explanatory notes can be found ere: http://www.bankofengland.co.uk/statistics/Pages/iadb/notesiadb/MFIs_extICB.aspx

Copyright guidance and the related UK Open Government Licence can be viewed here: www.bankofengland.co.uk/Pages/disclaimer.aspx

12.4a Industrial analysis of monetary financial institutions' lending to UK residents

£ millions

Not seasonally adjusted

Amounts outstanding of lending in sterling

RPM	Agriculture, hunting and forestry	Fishing	Mining and quarrying	Manufacturing									Electricity, gas and water supply			
				Food, beverages and tobacco	Textiles, wearing apparel and leather	Pulp, paper, and printing	Chemicals, pharmaceuticals, rubber and plastics	Non-metallic mineral products and metals	Machinery, equipment and transport equipment	Electrical, medical and optical equipment	Other manufacturing	Total	Electricity, gas steam and air conditioning	Water collection and sewerage	Waste management related services and remediation activities	Total
	TBUC	TBUD	TBUE	TBUG	TBUH	TBUI	TBUJ	TBUK	TBUL	TBUM	TBUN	TBUF	TBUO	TBUP	B3F9	B3FN
2015 Aug	17,020	243	1,982	4,499	735	2,020	3,039	3,318	5,652	1,965	2,717	23,946	8,002	2,617	2,031	12,650
Sep	17,291	242	1,966	4,502	772	2,023	3,064	3,219	5,743	2,067	2,740	24,130	8,047	2,566	1,988	12,601
Oct	17,519	244	1,921	4,339	766	1,816	3,045	3,335	5,919	2,254	2,834	24,308	8,464	2,504	2,042	13,010
Nov	17,623	239	1,794	4,382	744	1,887	3,230	3,291	5,756	2,261	2,798	24,349	8,369	2,639	2,071	13,080
Dec	17,539	228	1,761	4,429	747	1,816	3,114	3,054	5,600	2,002	2,766	23,529	8,584	2,869	2,051	13,504
2016 Jan	17,435	234	1,840	4,419	729	1,883	3,355	3,062	5,773	1,855	2,640	23,715	8,572	2,969	2,086	13,627
Feb	17,370	229	1,820	4,344	690	1,847	3,242	3,100	5,946	1,872	2,632	23,672	8,930	2,958	2,144	14,032
Mar	17,456	229	1,770	4,382	700	1,844	3,491	3,024	5,807	1,739	2,605	23,592	8,988	3,211	2,093	14,292
Apr	17,458	226	1,712	4,738	700	1,823	3,459	3,085	5,366	1,838	2,591	23,600	9,206	3,361	2,127	14,694
May	17,578	225	1,771	4,864	696	1,823	3,657	3,345	5,428	2,055	2,599	24,467	9,056	3,364	2,130	14,550
Jun	17,760	269	2,040	4,741	727	1,816	3,350	3,409	5,358	1,672	2,623	23,696	8,934	3,457	1,927	14,317
Jul	17,909	269	1,956	4,686	734	1,809	3,547	3,423	5,402	1,761	2,639	23,999	9,067	3,615	2,024	14,705
Aug	17,947	268	1,851	4,623	748	1,824	3,659	3,213	5,456	1,784	2,632	23,937	9,385	3,575	2,114	15,074
Sep	17,946	262	1,888	4,351	759	1,801	3,612	3,269	5,599	1,759	2,587	23,737	9,373	3,481	2,019	14,874
Oct	17,954	275	1,934	4,499	748	1,821	3,656	3,276	5,536	1,727	2,485	23,746	9,090	3,501	2,173	14,763
Nov	17,994	278	1,932	4,531	748	1,824	3,671	3,145	5,659	1,574	2,485	23,637	8,976	3,609	2,177	14,762
Dec	17,591	289	1,824	4,672	756	1,842	3,702	3,144	5,495	1,518	2,479	23,609	8,998	3,436	2,231	14,666
2017 Jan	17,698	286	1,812	4,542	721	1,862	4,055	3,218	5,443	1,420	2,487	23,750	9,005	3,442	2,299	14,746
Feb	17,814	285	1,895	4,453	723	1,839	3,570	3,201	5,681	1,541	2,505	23,513	9,207	3,175	2,350	14,733
Mar	17,934	285	1,833	4,297	744	1,865	3,352	3,336	5,814	1,737	2,486	23,631	10,936	2,972	2,230	16,138
Apr	18,048	282	1,849	4,630	733	1,787	3,292	3,340	5,874	1,627	2,615	23,899	11,054	2,982	2,245	16,281

Source: Bank of England

12.4a Industrial analysis of monetary financial institutions' lending to UK residents

£ millions

Not seasonally adjusted

Amounts outstanding of lending in sterling

| | | Construction | | | | | Wholesale and retail trade | | | | | Transport, storage and communication | | |
	Development of buildings	Construction of commercial buildings	Construction of domestic buildings	Civil Engineering	Other construction activities	Total	Wholesale and retail trade and repair of motor vehicles and motorcycles	Wholesale trade, excluding motor vehicles and motor cycles	Retail trade excluding motor vehicles and motor cycles	Total	Accommodation and food service activities	Transportation and storage	Information and communication	Total
RPM	B7EB	B3I6	B3LX	B4PK	B4PX	TBUQ	TBUS	TBUT	TBUU	TBUR	TBUV	B5PK	B5PR	TBUW
2015 Aug	16,938	4,568	4,387	2,757	5,859	34,509	11,575	10,547	14,509	36,631	22,362	11,946	9,186	21,133
Sep	16,639	4,595	4,468	2,860	5,800	34,363	11,222	10,422	15,011	36,655	21,875	11,701	9,659	21,360
Oct	16,300	4,890	4,412	2,949	5,562	34,113	11,426	10,601	15,322	37,350	21,890	11,895	9,980	21,875
Nov	16,146	5,063	4,677	2,971	5,560	34,417	11,591	10,604	15,256	37,451	22,032	12,028	9,655	21,684
Dec	15,970	4,555	3,935	2,350	5,457	32,269	11,572	10,146	15,021	36,739	22,142	12,142	9,781	21,924
2016 Jan	15,971	4,757	4,221	2,887	5,645	33,481	12,205	10,939	15,176	38,319	22,453	12,351	12,472	24,823
Feb	16,742 (a)	4,454	4,573	3,280	5,555	34,603 (a)	13,360	10,857	15,754	39,971	22,479	12,612	11,339	23,952
Mar	14,967 (b)	4,282	4,655	3,175	5,477	32,556 (b)	12,637	10,518	16,191	39,345	22,600	11,928	8,968	20,896
Apr	14,865	4,325	4,560	3,195	5,506	32,451	12,166	10,578	16,284	39,028	22,818	12,009	8,376	20,386
May	14,834	4,277	4,949	3,198	5,607	32,865	11,804	10,619	16,075	38,498	22,912	11,905	8,647	20,553
Jun	14,828	3,971	4,813	2,876	5,573	32,061	12,218	10,361	16,439	39,019	22,829	11,713	8,516	20,229
Jul	14,894	4,195	4,777	2,956	5,645	32,467	12,526	10,217	16,629	39,372	22,963	12,096	8,776	20,872
Aug	14,806	4,230	4,899	3,087	5,647	32,670	12,598	10,319	16,198	39,114	23,192	11,924	8,777	20,700
Sep	15,203	4,224	4,833	3,242	5,694	33,196	11,316	10,431	16,377	38,124	22,998	12,098	8,521	20,620
Oct	15,198	4,258	5,012	3,391	5,748	33,607	11,116	10,439	16,742	38,297	23,053	11,909	8,707	20,616
Nov	15,215	4,255	5,189	3,458	5,831	33,948	11,103	10,589	16,699	38,390	23,004	11,221	8,555	19,776
Dec	14,838	3,992	4,646	3,139	5,612	32,227	11,269	10,666	16,430	38,365	23,238	10,801	8,600	19,402
2017 Jan	15,159	4,260	4,974	3,209	5,703	33,304	11,620	10,641	17,019	39,280	23,786	11,044	8,108	19,152
Feb	15,237	4,302	5,285	3,303	5,755	33,881	12,873	10,679	16,738	40,289	24,236	11,241	7,760	19,001
Mar	15,323	4,248	5,475	3,681	5,674	34,400	12,086	10,957	17,049	40,092	24,163	11,526	7,435	18,961
Apr	15,375	4,224	5,552	3,326	5,701	34,178	11,827	10,533	17,010	39,371	24,287	11,477	7,651	19,128

Source: Bank of England

12.4a Industrial analysis of monetary financial institutions' lending to UK residents

£ millions

Not seasonally adjusted

Amounts outstanding of lending in sterling

RPM	Real estate, professional services and support activities				Public administration and defence	Education	Human health and social work	Recreational, personal and community service activities			Financial intermediation (excluding insurance and pension funds)				
	Buying, selling and renting of real estate	Professional, scientific and technical activities	Administrative and support services	Total				Recreational, cultural and sporting activities	Personal and community service activities	Total	Financial leasing corporations	Non-bank credit grantors excluding credit unions and SPVs	Credit unions	Factoring corporations	Mortgage and housing credit corporations excluding SPVs
	TBUY	B6PD	B6PO	TBUX	TBVD	TBVE	TBVF	TBVH	TBVG	B6PT	TBVJ	TBVK	TBVL	TBVM	TBVN
2015 Aug	134,616	15,695	19,474	169,784	8,818	11,156	20,187	4,924	3,306	8,230	24,587	18,696	1	5,425	49,734
Sep	134,284	15,742	19,381	169,408	7,903	10,838	19,981	4,932	3,267	8,199	24,777	19,591	1	5,061	48,669
Oct	133,757	15,696	19,910	169,362	7,917	10,863	19,783	5,165	3,287	8,452	24,861	19,312	1	4,759	49,285
Nov	133,011	15,558	20,364	168,933	7,982	10,785	20,097	5,171	3,323	8,494	24,801	19,245	1	4,882	49,074
Dec	133,825	14,971	20,448	169,244	8,107	10,756	19,851	5,069	3,240	8,309	24,528	19,347	1	4,624	52,488 (k)
2016 Jan	133,281	15,977	20,032	169,289	7,946	10,671	20,211	5,034	3,233	8,267	23,603	18,341 (i)	1	4,559	53,410
Feb	132,844 (c)	16,013	20,651	169,508 (c)	7,973	10,722	20,237	4,982	3,308	8,290	23,477	18,678	1	4,534	53,822
Mar	136,349 (d)	15,789	21,018	173,156 (d)	7,769	10,730	20,229	5,126	3,286	8,412	23,953	19,066	2	5,288	54,677
Apr	135,509	15,510	21,470	172,488	8,073	10,668	19,986	5,002	3,344	8,345	24,150	19,628	1	5,378	49,019
May	135,563	15,330	21,407	172,299	7,968	10,629	20,179	4,921	3,338	8,259	24,068	19,329	1	5,365	48,925
Jun	136,467	15,624	22,214	174,305	7,573	10,655	20,316	4,662	3,313	7,975	23,888	19,461	1	5,692	49,670
Jul	136,397	15,952	22,686	175,035	7,670	10,826	20,389	4,659	3,316	7,976	24,005	19,864	1	5,342	49,908
Aug	136,002	16,286	23,154	175,442	7,808	10,846	20,185	4,489	3,312	7,801	24,014	19,882	-	5,190	49,316
Sep	135,591 (e)	16,288	23,241	175,119 (e)	8,115	10,587	19,961	4,578	3,310	7,888	23,964	22,861 (j)	-	5,647	49,895
Oct	135,125	16,048	23,926	175,099	9,172	10,538	20,147	4,690	3,345	8,035	24,236	23,351	-	5,542	50,555
Nov	134,689	15,966	23,992	174,648	8,103	10,465	20,109	5,017	3,311	8,328	24,963	23,729	-	5,566	48,506
Dec	135,351	15,248	24,185	174,784	7,779	10,445	19,631	5,278	3,326	8,604	25,327	23,656	1	5,833	48,373
2017 Jan	134,203	16,154	24,081	174,439	10,078	10,351	19,976	5,311	3,297	8,609	24,880	23,495	1	5,257	48,768
Feb	134,408	16,014	24,270	174,691	8,122	10,321	20,005	5,265	3,206	8,470	24,752	19,841	1	5,579	43,605
Mar	134,749	15,821	24,320 (g)	174,890 (g)	8,988	10,330	20,183	5,517	3,358	8,874	24,700	20,329	1	5,825	47,639
Apr	135,473 (f)	15,706	25,383 (h)	176,562 (f)(h)	8,284	10,364	19,867	5,617	3,431	9,049	24,322	20,090	1	5,879	47,634

Source: Bank of England

12.4a Industrial analysis of monetary financial institutions' lending to UK residents

£ millions

Not seasonally adjusted

Amounts outstanding of lending in sterling

RPM	Investment and unit trusts excluding money market mutual funds	Money market mutual funds	Financial intermediation (excluding insurance and pension funds)							Insurance companies & pension funds		
			Bank holding companies	Securities dealers	SPVs related to securitisation	Other financial intermediaries	of which intragroup activity	Total		Insurance companies	Pension funds	Total
	TBVO	TBVP	TBVQ	TBVR	B6PY	TBVS	B3U8	TBVI		B3V6	B3W4	TBVT
2015 Aug	5,326	26	18,536	25,606	16,616	63,916	55,150	228,467		9,003	9,374	18,378
Sep	6,138	28	18,527	28,584	18,410	61,027	52,346	230,813		6,541	9,960	16,501
Oct	6,000	26	19,953 (m)	24,207	18,971	59,410 (q)	50,955	226,786 (m)(q)		5,172	10,952	16,123
Nov	6,401	38	19,901	24,213	17,874	53,157	44,805	219,587		6,987	11,002	17,989
Dec	7,152	46	19,360	25,202	19,220 (n)	50,907	43,000	222,874 (k)(n)		5,672	10,463	16,135
2016 Jan	8,510	49	19,531	25,197	19,787 (o)	46,637	39,732	219,627 (i)(o)		6,054	11,108	17,162
Feb	8,678	53	20,071	26,491	19,708	47,131	40,218	222,644		6,971	13,158	20,129
Mar	9,683	97	19,984	27,885	19,702	43,234	36,330	223,571		7,553	13,120	20,673
Apr	9,802	78	20,192	30,386	16,072	40,662	34,179	215,369		6,540	11,323	17,863
May	11,152	86	18,954	26,160	15,593	42,487	33,916	212,119		7,356	11,572	18,928
Jun	11,173	72	11,767	29,303	16,259	41,614	33,164	208,900		8,592	14,763	23,355
Jul	10,812	77	13,382	29,332	16,036	41,573	32,388	210,332		7,980	15,719	23,699
Aug	10,364	112	13,241	26,726	13,893	42,696	33,397	205,436		9,933	15,947	25,881
Sep	10,814	100	13,258	25,592	13,409	41,882	32,424	207,422 (j)		10,013	16,318	26,331
Oct	11,040	158	13,546	23,923	11,340	40,457	31,902	204,150		8,632	14,270	22,902
Nov	11,563	146	13,543	25,773	10,266	35,981	28,557	200,037		8,622	15,906	24,529
Dec	10,719	119	16,068	22,659	9,876	37,598	29,906	200,229		8,592	18,920	27,512
2017 Jan	9,703	119	18,859	21,908	9,771	37,996	29,801	200,758		8,460	15,742	24,202
Feb	11,085	101	18,296	22,155	9,503	38,103	29,814	193,022		8,162	16,744	24,906
Mar	9,597 (l)	119	13,376	20,107	9,291	38,267 (r)	31,501	189,250 (l)(r)		8,713	25,179 (s)	33,892 (s)
Apr	9,735	92	13,509	21,308	10,417	38,386	31,906	191,372		9,898	27,311	37,209

Source: Bank of England

12.4a Industrial analysis of monetary financial institutions' lending to UK residents

£ millions

Not seasonally adjusted

Amounts outstanding of lending in sterling

RPM	Fund management activities	Activities auxiliary to financial intermediation				Total financial and non-financial businesses	Individuals and individual trusts			Total UK residents
		Other			Total		Lending secured on dwellings inc. bridging finance	Other loans and advances	Total	
		Central clearing counterparties	Other auxiliary activities	Total						
	TBVU	B7FX	B8FD	TBVV	B8FJ	Z949	TBVX	TBVY	TBVW	TBUA
2015 Aug	68,094	59,759	2,685	62,444	130,538	766,034	1,086,800	119,447	1,206,247	1,972,281
Sep	72,955	50,434	2,598	53,032	125,987	760,113	1,090,374	120,075	1,210,449	1,970,562
Oct	70,853 (t)	46,081 (z)	2,810	48,891 (z)	119,744 (t)(z)	751,259 (m)(q)(t)(z)	1,094,581	120,186	1,214,767	1,966,026 (m)(q)(t)(z)
Nov	72,481	50,259	2,670	52,929	125,409	751,945	1,098,575	121,372	1,219,947	1,971,892
Dec	74,221	45,326	2,645	47,971	122,191	747,102 (k)(n)	1,105,445 (ad)	122,193	1,227,638 (ad)	1,974,740 (k)(n)(ad)
2016 Jan	80,338 (u)	39,274 (aa)	2,814	42,088 (aa)	122,426 (u)(aa)	751,525 (i)(o)(u)(aa)	1,108,163	122,216	1,230,379	1,981,904 (i)(o)(u)(aa)
Feb	89,728	36,301	2,920	39,221	128,948	766,580 (a)(c)	1,109,821	122,735	1,232,556	1,999,136 (a)(c)
Mar	92,832	33,196	2,871	36,067	128,899	766,178	1,116,891	123,746	1,240,637	2,006,815
Apr	90,058	33,328 (ab)	3,227	36,555 (ab)	126,613 (ab)	751,778 (ab)	1,123,534 (ae)	123,792	1,247,326 (ae)	1,999,104 (ab)(ae)
May	98,386 (v)	40,599	3,305	43,904	142,290 (v)	766,089 (v)	1,125,346	125,075	1,250,421	2,016,510 (v)
Jun	107,126	44,789	3,511	48,301	155,426	780,726	1,130,284	126,131	1,256,415	2,037,141
Jul	106,520	41,753	3,693	45,446	151,965	782,406	1,133,579	126,611	1,260,189	2,042,595
Aug	107,048	46,868	3,098	49,966	157,015	785,166	1,137,641	127,885	1,265,526	2,050,693
Sep	112,388	44,451	3,074	47,525	159,913	788,980 (e)(j)	1,141,851	128,209	1,270,060	2,059,039 (e)(j)
Oct	113,124	50,543	3,115	53,659	166,783	791,071	1,145,235	128,709	1,273,944	2,065,016
Nov	113,975	57,907	3,144	61,052	175,027	794,968	1,147,616 (af)	129,864	1,277,480 (af)	2,072,447 (af)
Dec	115,853	51,003	3,384	54,387	170,239	790,436	1,150,155	130,084	1,280,238	2,070,674
2017 Jan	113,025	63,583	3,017	66,600	179,624	801,852	1,152,375	130,246	1,282,620	2,084,472
Feb	113,115	65,067 (ac)	4,066	69,133 (ac)	182,248 (ac)	797,433 (ac)	1,154,709	130,336	1,285,045	2,082,478 (ac)
Mar	116,626 (w)(x)(y)	70,283	3,434	73,718	190,344 (w)(x)(y)	814,189 (g)	1,159,064	130,926	1,289,991	2,104,180 (g)
Apr	111,909	73,265	3,301	76,566	188,475	818,504 (f)(h)	1,160,471	131,401	1,291,872	2,110,376 (f)(h)

Source: Bank of England

12.4a Industrial analysis of monetary financial institutions' lending to UK residents

Notes to table

Movements in amounts outstanding can reflect breaks in data series as well as underlying flows. For changes data, users are recommended to refer directly to the appropriate series or data tables.
www.bankofengland.co.uk/statistics/Pages/iadb/notesiadb/Changes_flows_growth_rates.aspx.

(a) Due to improvements in reporting at one institution, the amounts outstanding increased by £1bn. This effect has been adjusted out of the flows for February 2016.

(b) Due to improvements in reporting at one institution, the amounts outstanding decreased by £1bn. This effect has been adjusted out of the flows for March 2016.

(c) Due to improvements in reporting at one institution, the amounts outstanding decreased by £1bn. This effect has been adjusted out of the flows for February 2016.

(d) Due to improvements in reporting at one institution, the amounts outstanding increased by £1bn. This effect has been adjusted out of the flows for March 2016.

(e) Due to a change in the reporting population, the amounts outstanding decreased by £1bn. This effect has been adjusted out of the flows for September 2016.

(f) Due to reporting improvements at one institution, amounts outstanding increased by £1 billion. This has been adjusted out of the flows for April 2017.

(g) Due to loan transfers by one institution, amounts outstanding decreased by £1 billion. This amount has been adjusted out of the flows for March 2017.

(h) Due to loan transfers by one institution, amounts outstanding increased by £1 billion. This amount has been adjusted out of the flows for April 2017.

(i) Due to improvements in reporting at one institution, the amounts outstanding decreased by £1bn. This effect has been adjusted out of the flows for January 2016.

(j) Due to a change in the reporting population, the amounts outstanding increased by £2bn. This effect has been adjusted out of the flows for September 2016.

(k) Due to a restructuring at one reporting institution, the amounts outstanding decreased by £4bn. This effect has been adjusted out of the flows for December 2015.

(l) Due to reporting improvements at one institution, amounts outstanding decreased by £2bn. This has been adjusted out of flows for March 2017.

(m) Due to improvements in reporting at one institution, the amounts outstanding increased by £1bn. This effect has been adjusted out of the flows for October 2015.

(n) Due to a restructuring at one reporting institution, the amounts outstanding decreased by £4bn. This effect has been adjusted out of the flows for December 2015.

(o) Due to improvements in reporting at one institution, the amounts outstanding increased by £1bn. This effect has been adjusted out of the flows for January 2016.

(p) Due to a change in accounting treatment at one reporting institution, the amounts outstanding decreased by £2bn. This effect has been adjusted out of the flows for June 2017.

(q) Due to improvements in reporting at one institution, the amounts outstanding decreased by £1bn. This effect has been adjusted out of the flows for October 2015.

(r) Due to reporting improvements at one institution, amounts outstanding decreased by £2bn. This has been adjusted out of flows for March 2017.

(s) Due to reporting improvements at one institution, amounts outstanding increased by £5bn. This has been adjusted out of flows for March 2017.

(t) Due to a change in the reporting population, the amounts outstanding decreased by £2bn. This effect has been adjusted out of the flows for October 2015.

(u) Due to a change in the reporting population, the amounts outstanding increased by £3bn. This effect has been adjusted out of the flows for January 2016.

(v) Due to improvements in reporting at one institution, the amounts outstanding increased by £1bn. This effect has been adjusted out of the flows for May 2016.

(w) Due to reporting improvements at one institution, amounts outstanding decreased by £5bn. This has been adjusted out of flows for March 2017.

(x) Due to reporting improvements at one institution, amounts outstanding increased by £2bn. This has been adjusted out of flows for March 2017.

(y) Due to reporting improvements at one institution, amounts outstanding increased by £2bn. This has been adjusted out of flows for March 2017.

(z) Due to a change in the reporting population, the amounts outstanding decreased by £3bn. This effect has been adjusted out of the flows for October 2015.

(aa) Due to a change in the reporting population, the amounts outstanding decreased by £4bn. This effect has been adjusted out of the flows for January 2016.

(ab) Due to improvements in reporting at one institution, the amounts outstanding increased by £1bn. This effect has been adjusted out of the flows for April 2016.

(ac) Due to improvements in reporting at one institution, the amounts outstanding increased by £2bn. This effect has been adjusted out of the flows for February 2017.

(ad) Due to a loan transfer by one reporting institution, the amounts outstanding increased by £3bn. This effect has been adjusted out of the flows for December 2015.

(ae) Due to a loan transfer by one reporting institution, the amounts outstanding increased by £7bn. This effect has been adjusted out of the flows for April 2016.

(af) Due to improvements in reporting at one institution, the amounts outstanding decreased by £2bn. This effect has been adjusted out of the flows for November 2016.

Explanatory notes can be found here: http://www.bankofengland.co.uk/statistics/Pages/iadb/notesiadb/industrial.aspx

Copyright guidance and the related UK Open Government Licence can be viewed here: www.bankofengland.co.uk/Pages/disclaimer.aspx.

12.4b Industrial analysis of monetary financial institutions' lending to UK residents

£ millions

Not seasonally adjusted

Amounts outstanding of lending in all currencies

RPM	Agriculture, hunting and forestry	Fishing	Mining and quarrying	Food, beverages and tobacco	Textiles, wearing apparel and leather	Pulp, paper, and printing	Chemicals, pharmaceuticals, rubber and plastics	Manufacturing Non-metallic mineral products and metals	Machinery, equipment and transport equipment	Electrical, medical and optical equipment	Other manufacturing	Total
	TBSC	TBSD	TBSE	TBSG	TBSH	TBSI	TBSJ	TBSK	TBSL	TBSM	TBSN	TBSF
2015 Aug	17,227	246	6,579	6,173	1,163	2,859	6,222	5,165	8,621	2,974	3,675	36,853
Sep	17,486	246	6,982	6,249	1,214	2,549	5,855	5,067	8,926	3,115	3,525	36,499
Oct	17,709	248	6,859	5,650	1,204	2,197	5,803	5,127	9,089	3,356	3,678	36,104
Nov	17,812	243	6,362	5,790	1,154	2,331	6,021	4,940	9,270	3,469	3,633	36,607
Dec	17,752	232	6,416	5,974	1,140	2,321	5,783	4,714	8,715	3,053	3,489	35,189
2016 Jan	17,653	259	6,229	5,941	1,167	2,421	5,874	4,746	8,849	2,881	3,635	35,513
Feb	17,558	253	6,512	5,973	1,105	2,421	6,242	4,937	8,778	2,972	3,746	36,174
Mar	17,657	254	6,465	5,877	1,152	2,388	6,539	4,878	8,563	2,731	3,966	36,095
Apr	17,659	248	6,221	6,494	1,114	2,276	6,600	4,870	7,993	2,898	4,031	36,277
May	17,761	248	6,469	7,427	1,109	2,330	7,005	5,148	7,519	3,133	4,005	37,676
Jun	17,969	296	7,695	7,239	1,206	2,424	7,088	5,336	7,363	3,043	3,595	37,294
Jul	18,130	294	7,098	7,152	1,235	2,310	6,382	4,967	7,294	2,953	3,667	35,960
Aug	18,184	293	7,005	6,794	1,221	2,380	6,831	4,717	7,218	3,031	3,401	35,593
Sep	18,186	284	8,471	7,375	1,232	2,326	6,719	4,779	7,940	3,177	3,298	36,847
Oct	18,209	299	9,417	7,512	1,253	2,245	6,787	4,780	8,189	3,242	3,251	37,258
Nov	18,207	301	9,577	7,104	1,235	2,521	6,675	4,591	8,107	3,099	3,267	36,599
Dec	17,811	312	9,639	7,914	1,203	2,486	6,871	4,541	8,026	2,975	3,198	37,214
2017 Jan	17,924	309	10,251	6,655	1,179	2,463	7,193	4,685	8,018	2,850	3,233	36,276
Feb	18,030	309	9,886	6,990	1,114	2,502	6,791	4,730	8,257	2,805	3,256	36,446
Mar	18,159	308	9,613	6,448	1,134	2,483	7,198	5,206	8,042	2,868	3,416	36,796
Apr	18,295	304	7,212 (av)	6,852	1,130	2,393	7,133	4,787	8,380	2,835	3,382	36,892

Source: Bank of England

343

12.4b Industrial analysis of monetary financial institutions' lending to UK residents

£ millions

Not seasonally adjusted

Amounts outstanding of lending in all currencies

| | Electricity, gas steam and air conditioning | Electricity, gas and water supply | | | Construction | | | | | | Wholesale and retail trade | | | Total |
| | | Water collection and sewerage | Waste management related services and remediation activities | Total | Development of buildings | Construction of commercial buildings | Construction of domestic buildings | Civil Engineering | Other construction activities | Total | Wholesale and retail trade and repair of motor vehicles and motorcycles | Wholesale trade, excluding motor vehicles and motor cycles | Retail trade excluding motor vehicles and motor cycles | |
RPM	TBSO	TBSP	B3FA	B3FO	B7EC	B3I7	B3LY	B4PL	B4PY	TBSQ	TBSS	TBST	TBSU	TBSR
2015 Aug	8,525	2,617	2,074	13,216	17,088	4,635	4,434	3,093	5,946	35,196	12,187	14,553	15,896	42,636
Sep	8,539	2,567	2,021	13,127	16,811	4,662	4,476	3,326	5,910	35,184	11,899	14,312	16,422	42,633
Oct	9,019	2,504	2,093	13,615	16,453	4,956	4,415	3,272	5,677	34,774	12,009	14,771	16,614	43,394
Nov	9,020	2,639	2,146	13,805	16,321	5,130	4,681	3,296	5,677	35,105	12,172	14,589	16,584	43,344
Dec	9,213	2,869	2,125	14,207	16,154	4,629	3,939	2,683	5,570	32,974	12,138	14,515	16,381	43,034
2016 Jan	9,499	2,969	2,192	14,660	16,164	4,838	4,225	3,230	5,764	34,222	12,828	15,019	16,666	44,513
Feb	9,922	2,960	2,247	15,129	16,909 (ax)	4,549	4,578	3,627	5,681	35,344 (ax)	13,996	15,146	17,537	46,679
Mar	9,898	3,211	2,326	15,436	15,097 (ay)	4,382	4,660	3,537	5,600	33,276 (ay)	13,288	14,741	18,145	46,173
Apr	9,741	3,361	2,320	15,422	14,995	4,429	4,564	3,570	5,629	33,188	12,919	14,634	18,482	46,035
May	9,542	3,365	2,225	15,132	14,962	4,382	4,953	3,587	5,760	33,643	12,495	15,191	18,336	46,022
Jun	9,403	3,458	2,091	14,952	14,971	4,084	4,818	3,301	5,718	32,891	12,947	15,436	18,686	47,068
Jul	9,559	3,624	2,259	15,442	15,042	4,316	4,782	3,392	5,798	33,329	13,174	15,274	18,804	47,252
Aug	9,980	3,576	2,308	15,864	14,954	4,354	4,904	3,529	5,789	33,530	13,255	15,732	18,515	47,502
Sep	10,054	3,482	2,150	15,687	15,352	4,350	4,833	3,619	5,769	33,923	11,970	15,541	18,881	46,392
Oct	9,764	3,502	2,398	15,664	15,354	4,387	5,016	3,738	5,871	34,367	11,816	16,161	19,161	47,139
Nov	9,526	3,610	2,311	15,446	15,359	4,376	5,193	3,803	5,908	34,639	11,771	16,233	18,933	46,937
Dec	9,588	3,438	2,323	15,349	14,986	4,139	4,657	3,489	5,683	32,955	12,058	16,056	18,810	46,924
2017 Jan	9,580	3,443	2,462	15,486	15,317	4,402	4,974	3,571	5,774	34,039	12,385	16,202	19,294	47,882
Feb	9,748	3,177	2,365	15,289	15,402	4,449	5,286	3,663	5,829	34,628	13,600	16,373	19,120	49,094
Mar	11,516	2,973	2,323	16,813	15,488	4,403	5,475	4,047	5,746	35,160	12,842	16,843 (az)	19,477	49,162 (az)
Apr	11,644	2,983	2,349	16,975	15,534	4,368	5,552	3,675	5,785	34,915	12,650	17,947 (ba)	19,122	49,720 (ba)

Source: Bank of England

12.4b Industrial analysis of monetary financial institutions' lending to UK res

£ millions

Not seasonally adjusted

Amounts outstanding of lending in all currencies

| | Accommodation and food service activities | Transport, storage and communication | | | Real estate, professional services and support activities | | | | Public administration and defence | Education | Human health and social work | Recreational, personal and community service activities | | |
		Transportation and storage	Information and communication	Total	Buying, selling and renting of real estate	Professional, scientific and technical activities	Administrative and support services	Total				Recreational, cultural and sporting activities	Personal and community service activities	Total
RPM	TBSV	B5PL	B5PS	TBSW	TBSY	B6PE	B6PP	TBSX	TBTD	TBTE	TBTF	TBTH	TBTG	B6H5
2015 Aug	22,784	14,731	13,821	28,552	135,766	19,009	22,744	177,518	9,900	11,194	20,398	5,255	3,408	8,664
Sep	22,316	14,327	13,898	28,225	135,552	19,184	23,071	177,807	9,633	10,867	20,196	5,368	3,346	8,714
Oct	22,331	14,512	14,293	28,805	135,765	19,151	23,378	178,294	9,934	10,880	19,975	5,614	3,365	8,979
Nov	22,487	14,416	13,709	28,125	134,877	18,914	23,970	177,761	9,299	10,802	20,265	5,657	3,395	9,052
Dec	22,539	14,903	14,142	29,044	135,684	18,446	23,821	177,951	9,986	10,773	19,960	5,612	3,314	8,926
2016 Jan	22,798	15,412	17,197	32,610	135,168	19,565	23,494	178,226	10,125	10,689	20,330	5,598	3,309	8,907
Feb	22,832	16,400	15,813	32,213	134,300 (bb)	19,426	24,521	178,247 (bb)	9,781	10,742	20,363	5,577	3,391	8,969
Mar	22,986	15,414	13,418	28,832	137,417 (bc)	19,353	25,134	181,905 (bc)	8,657	10,754	20,391	5,695	3,382	9,077
Apr	23,163	15,470	12,114	27,584	136,322	19,035	25,714	181,071	9,927	10,706	20,140	5,498	3,429	8,926
May	23,509	15,364	12,269	27,632	136,384	19,097	25,380	180,862	9,938	10,662	20,314	5,413	3,453	8,866
Jun	23,451	15,405	12,570	27,975	137,193	19,798	26,904	183,895	9,131	10,691	20,473	5,205	3,437	8,642
Jul	23,511	16,309	12,989	29,299	137,262	20,157	27,541	184,961	9,703	10,864	20,561	5,227	3,438	8,664
Aug	23,561	15,627	12,911	28,538	136,893	20,663	28,157	185,713	9,520	10,890	20,355	5,059	3,433	8,493
Sep	23,765	16,192	12,722	28,914	136,346 (bd)	21,368	28,107	185,821 (bd)	9,757	10,630	20,306	5,351	3,427	8,778
Oct	23,832	16,292	13,869	30,161	135,761	21,146	29,208	186,115	9,633	10,563	20,509	5,514	3,473	8,987
Nov	23,817	15,140	14,591	29,731	135,301	20,839	28,800	184,941	9,648	10,521	20,405	5,820	3,428	9,248
Dec	24,138	14,585	14,066	28,652	135,990	19,863	30,159	186,011	9,605	10,504	19,866	6,065	3,442	9,506
2017 Jan	24,346	15,139	13,526	28,665	134,831	20,771	29,994	185,596	12,073	10,403	20,179	6,095	3,411	9,506
Feb	24,912	15,364	13,095	28,458	135,104	20,639	29,909	185,652	9,222	10,375	20,209	6,077	3,324	9,401
Mar	24,884	15,667	12,552	28,220	135,514	20,248	29,252 (bf)	185,015 (bf)	9,196	10,379	20,405	6,284	3,476	9,760
Apr	24,968	15,468	12,698	28,166	136,035 (be)	20,085	29,712 (bg)(bh)	185,832 (be)(bg)(bh)	11,595	10,410	20,059	6,368	3,600	9,968

Source: Bank of England

12.4b Industrial analysis of monetary financial institutions' lending to UK

£ millions

Amounts outstanding of lending in all currencies

Not seasonally adjusted

RPM	Financial leasing corporations	Non-bank credit grantors excluding credit unions and SPVs	Credit unions	Factoring corporations	Mortgage and housing credit corporations excluding SPVs	Financial intermediation (excluding insurance and pension funds)						of which intragroup activity	Total
						Investment and unit trusts excluding money market mutual funds	Money market mutual funds	Bank holding companies	Securities dealers	SPVs related to securitisation	Other financial intermediaries		
	TBTJ	TBTK	TBTL	TBTM	TBTN	TBTO	TBTP	TBTQ	TBTR	B6PZ	TBTS	B3U9	TBTI
2015 Aug	28,390	19,026	1	5,850	50,537	9,527	26	27,010	122,309	17,806	97,621	82,050	**378,104**
Sep	28,519	19,910	1	5,557	49,448	10,166	29	26,778	132,118	19,687	96,227	79,333	**388,440**
Oct	29,340	19,619	1	5,214	50,029	9,811	28	28,399 (bm)	118,976	20,124	93,884 (br)	78,081	**375,425 (bm)(br)**
Nov	29,368	19,536	1	5,330	49,862	10,326	38	28,831	115,982	19,028	87,677	72,354	**365,979**
Dec	29,233	19,556	1	5,063	53,415 (bk)	11,602	70	29,608	112,357	21,295 (bo)	85,901	70,198	**368,101 (bk)(bo)**
2016 Jan	28,376	18,651 (bi)	1	5,020	54,374	13,530	76	30,252	117,325	20,453 (bp)	83,373	67,685	**371,432 (bi)(bp)**
Feb	28,563	18,999	1	4,956	54,865	13,320	77	31,706	124,430	20,443	85,484	69,861	**382,845**
Mar	28,875	19,347	4	5,784	55,731	14,226	163	31,074	117,994	20,470	78,936	63,819	**372,604**
Apr	29,003	19,926	1	5,854	50,002	14,327	130	30,865	129,828	16,854	82,784 (bs)(bt)	67,798 (bs)(bt)	**379,574 (bs)(bt)**
May	28,807	19,625	1	5,832	49,790	16,121	155	29,310	121,890	16,168	85,141	68,463	**372,841**
Jun	29,046	19,759	1	6,662	50,659	16,648	154	20,354	135,599	16,871	88,370	70,305	**384,122**
Jul	29,835	20,161	1	6,322	50,926	15,957	146	21,858	135,968	16,607	88,034	69,321	**385,816**
Aug	29,614	20,223	1	5,850	50,343	15,295	208	22,278	128,888	14,472	89,414	71,023	**376,588**
Sep	29,918	23,183 (bj)	1	6,240	50,940	15,433	172	21,834	135,687 (bn)	13,985	88,691	69,363	**386,084 (bj)(bn)**
Oct	31,165	23,752	1	6,143	51,653	15,858	226	21,789	137,565	12,263	90,258	71,583	**390,673**
Nov	31,211	24,131	1	6,269	48,991	16,295	203	21,487	147,781	11,002	84,948	67,968	**392,317**
Dec	31,580	24,071	1	7,164	48,863	15,323	197	23,615	132,197	12,074	82,800 (bu)	66,739	**377,886 (bu)**
2017 Jan	31,054	23,942	1	6,265	49,258	14,204	180	26,225	136,033	12,015	83,163	67,279	**382,340**
Feb	30,586	20,243	1	6,462	44,089	15,477	162	25,702	136,382	11,669	95,627	72,332	**386,399**
Mar	30,473	20,764	1	6,763	48,131	13,974 (bl)	191	20,854	137,486	11,425	89,378 (bv)	74,340	**379,440 (bl)(bv)**
Apr	29,649	20,501	2	6,684	48,084	13,651	188	20,756	142,980	12,463	88,948	73,995	**383,906**

Source: Bank of England

12.4b Industrial analysis of monetary financial institutions' lending to UK residents

£ millions

Not seasonally adjusted

Amounts outstanding of lending in all currencies

	Insurance companies & pension funds			Activities auxiliary to financial intermediation					Total financial and non-financial businesses
	Insurance companies	Pension funds	Total	Fund management activities	Other auxiliary to financial intermediation			Total	
					Central clearing counterparties	Other auxiliary activities	Total		
RPM	B3V7	B3W5	TBTT	TBTU	B3X2	B8FE	TBTV	B5H8	Z92T
2015 Aug	14,672	10,184	24,857	140,596	113,627	13,774	127,401	267,997	1,101,921
Sep	12,880	10,808	23,688	143,201	101,707	12,556	114,263	257,465	1,099,510
Oct	11,084	12,621	23,705	146,772 (bx)	94,626 (cd)	12,406	107,032 (cd)	253,804 (bx)(cd)	1,084,837 (bm)(br)(bx)(cd)
Nov	12,704	12,399	25,103	143,672	99,859 (ce)	15,195 (ck)	115,054	258,726	1,080,877
Dec	10,973	11,734	22,706	138,054	95,503	15,511	111,014	249,068	1,068,859 (bk)(bo)
2016 Jan	11,857	12,158	24,015	152,697 (by)	94,171 (cf)	16,875	111,046 (cf)	263,743 (by)(cf)	1,095,922 (bi)(bp)(by)(cf)
Feb	14,299	14,388	28,686	167,131	99,323	17,398	116,721	283,852	1,136,178 (ax)(bb)
Mar	14,930	14,144	29,074	167,690	90,045	17,072	107,117	274,806	1,114,440
Apr	13,594	12,149	25,743	165,282	90,802 (cg)	11,692 (cl)(cm)	102,494 (cg)(cl)(cm)	267,776 (cg)(cl)(cm)	1,109,661 (cg)
May	14,850	12,795	27,645	174,228 (bz)	96,380	12,154	108,534	282,762 (bz)	1,121,981 (bz)
Jun	16,912	16,136	33,048	188,209	111,499	12,679	124,177	312,386	1,171,980
Jul	16,676	17,192	33,868	189,902	107,530	12,756	120,286	310,188	1,174,942
Aug	18,767	17,536	36,303	193,809	114,201	13,004	127,206	321,015	1,178,945
Sep	16,515	17,929	34,444	177,567	109,304	12,521	121,825	299,392	1,167,679 (bd)(bj)(bn)
Oct	14,431	15,590	30,020	174,835	118,451	11,217	129,668	304,503	1,177,350
Nov	13,912	17,110	31,022	172,659	129,379	11,071	140,450	313,108	1,186,465
Dec	13,823	20,263	34,087	176,823	107,185	11,042	118,227	295,050	1,155,509 (bu)
2017 Jan	13,499	16,980	30,478	175,239	136,194	11,056	147,250	322,489	1,188,241
Feb	13,394	17,927	31,321	183,337	146,347 (ch)(ci)	11,844	158,191 (ch)(ci)	341,529 (ch)(ci)	1,211,160 (ch)(ci)
Mar	13,785	26,393 (bw)	40,178 (bw)	187,607 (ca)(cb)(cc)	140,926	11,702	152,628	340,235 (ca)(cb)(cc)	1,213,720 (az)(bf)
Apr	15,502	28,661	44,163	185,279	146,561	11,642	158,203	343,482	1,226,862 (be)(bg)(bh)

Source: Bank of England

12.4b Industrial analysis of monetary financial institutions' lending to UK residents

£ millions

Not seasonally adjusted

Amounts outstanding of lending in all currencies

RPM	Individuals and individual trusts			Total UK residents
	Lending secured on dwellings inc. bridging finance	Other loans and advances	Total	
	TBTX	TBTY	TBTW	TBSA
2015 Aug	1,086,972	120,792	1,207,764	2,309,685
Sep	1,090,549	121,431	1,211,980	2,311,489
Oct	1,094,753	121,507	1,216,260	2,301,097 (bm)(br)(bx)(cd)
Nov	1,098,747	122,698	1,221,445	2,302,322
Dec	1,105,593 (cn)	123,616	1,229,210 (cn)	2,298,068 (bk)(bo)(cn)
2016 Jan	1,108,314	122,974	1,231,288	2,327,210 (bi)(bp)(by)(cf)
Feb	1,109,972	123,552	1,233,524	2,369,702 (ax)(bb)
Mar	1,117,040	124,621	1,241,662	2,356,102
Apr	1,123,678 (co)	124,662	1,248,339 (co)	2,358,000 (cg)(co)
May	1,125,483	125,922	1,251,406	2,373,387 (bz)
Jun	1,130,427	127,075	1,257,502	2,429,482
Jul	1,133,722	127,606	1,261,328	2,436,270
Aug	1,137,784	128,900	1,266,684	2,445,629
Sep	1,141,990	129,256	1,271,246	2,438,925 (bd)(bj)(bn)
Oct	1,145,380	129,785	1,275,166	2,452,516
Nov	1,147,753 (cp)	130,943	1,278,696 (cp)	2,465,162 (cp)
Dec	1,150,306	131,121	1,281,426	2,436,935 (bu)
2017 Jan	1,152,531	131,298	1,283,829	2,472,070
Feb	1,154,866	131,405	1,286,271	2,497,432 (ch)(ci)
Mar	1,159,213	132,150	1,291,363	2,505,083 (az)(bf)
Apr	1,160,600	132,578	1,293,177	2,520,040 (be)(bg)(bh)

Source: Bank of England

Notes to table

Movements in amounts outstanding can reflect breaks in data series as well as underlying flows. For changes data, users are recommended to refer directly to the appropriate series or data tables. Further explanation can be found at: www.bankofengland.co.uk/statistics/Pages/iadb/notesiadb/Changes_flows_growth_rates.aspx.

(av) Due to reporting improvements at one institution, amounts outstanding decreased by £2 billion. This has been adjusted out of the flows for April 2017.

(aw) Due to loan transfers by one institution, amounts outstanding increased by £1 billion. This amount has been adjusted out of the flows for July 2017.

(ax) Due to improvements in reporting at one institution, the amounts outstanding increased by £1bn. This effect has been adjusted out of the flows for February 2016.

(ay) Due to improvements in reporting at one institution, the amounts outstanding decreased by £1bn. This effect has been adjusted out of the flows for March 2016.

(az) Due to changes in the reporting population, amounts outstanding increased by £1bn. This has been adjusted out of flows for March 2017.

(ba) Due to reporting improvements at one institution, amounts outstanding increased by £2 billion. This has been adjusted out of the flows for April 2017.

(bb) Due to improvements in reporting at one institution, the amounts outstanding decreased by £1bn. This effect has been adjusted out of the flows for February 2016.

(bc) Due to improvements in reporting at one institution, the amounts outstanding increased by £1bn. This effect has been adjusted out of the flows for March 2016.

(bd) Due to a change in the reporting population, the amounts outstanding decreased by £1bn. This effect has been adjusted out of the flows for September 2016.

(be) Due to reporting improvements at one institution, amounts outstanding increased by £1 billion. This has been adjusted out of the flows for April 2017.

(bf) Due to loan transfers by one institution, amounts outstanding decreased by £1 billion. This amount has been adjusted out of the flows for March 2017.

(bg) Due to reporting improvements at one institution, amounts outstanding decreased by £1 billion. This has been adjusted out of the flows for April 2017.

(bh) Due to loan transfers by one institution, amounts outstanding increased by £1 billion. This amount has been adjusted out of the flows for April 2017.

(bi) Due to improvements in reporting at one institution, the amounts outstanding decreased by £1bn. This effect has been adjusted out of the flows for January 2016.

(bj) Due to a change in the reporting population, the amounts outstanding increased by £2bn. This effect has been adjusted out of the flows for September 2016.

(bk) Due to a restructuring at one reporting institution, the amounts outstanding decreased by £4bn. This effect has been adjusted out of the flows for December 2015.

(bl) Due to improvements in reporting at one institution, the amounts outstanding decreased by £2bn. This has been adjusted out of flows for March 2017.

(bm) Due to improvements in reporting at one institution, the amounts outstanding increased by £1bn. This effect has been adjusted out of the flows for October 2015.

(bn) Due to a change in treatment at one institution, the amounts outstanding increased by £2bn. This effect has been adjusted out of the flows for September 2016.

(bo) Due to a restructuring at one reporting institution, the amounts outstanding decreased by £4bn. This effect has been adjusted out of the flows for December 2015.

(bp) Due to improvements in reporting at one institution, the amounts outstanding increased by £1bn. This effect has been adjusted out of the flows for January 2016.

(bq) Due to a change in accounting treatment at one reporting institution, the amounts outstanding decreased by £2bn. This effect has been adjusted out of the flows for June 2017.

(br) Due to improvements in reporting at one institution, the amounts outstanding decreased by £1bn. This effect has been adjusted out of the flows for October 2015.

(bs) Due to improvements in reporting at one institution, the amounts outstanding increased by £1bn. This effect has been adjusted out of the flows for April 2016.

(bt) Due to improvements in reporting at one institution, the amounts outstanding increased by £4bn. This effect has been adjusted out of the flows for April 2016.

(bu) Due to improvements in reporting at one institution, the amounts outstanding decreased by £2bn. This effect has been adjusted out of the flows for December 2016.

(bv) Due to improvements in reporting at one institution, amounts outstanding decreased by £2bn. This has been adjusted out of flows for March 2017.

(bw) Due to reporting improvements at one institution, amounts outstanding increased by £5bn. This has been adjusted out of the flows for March 2017.

(bx) Due to a change in the reporting population, the amounts outstanding decreased by £2bn. This effect has been adjusted out of the flows for October 2015.

(by) Due to a change in the reporting population, the amounts outstanding increased by £3bn. This effect has been adjusted out of the flows for January 2016.

(bz) Due to improvements in reporting at one institution, the amounts outstanding increased by £1bn. This effect has been adjusted out of the flows for May 2016.

(ca) Due to reporting improvements at one institution, amounts outstanding decreased by £5bn. This has been adjusted out of flows for March 2017.

(cb) Due to reporting improvements at one institution, amounts outstanding increased by £2bn. This has been adjusted out of flows for March 2017.

(cc) Due to reporting improvements at one institution, amounts outstanding increased by £2bn. This has been adjusted out of flows for March 2017.

(cd) Due to a transfer of business by one reporting institution, the amounts outstanding increased by £2bn. This effect has been adjusted out of the flows for July 2017.

(ce) Due to changes in reporting at one institution, the amounts outstanding increased by £3bn. This effect has been adjusted out of the flows for October 2015.

(cf) Due to a change in the reporting population, the amounts outstanding decreased by £2bn. This effect has been adjusted out of the flows for November 2015.

(cg) Due to a change in the reporting population, the amounts outstanding decreased by £4bn. This effect has been adjusted out of the flows for January 2016.

(ch) Due to improvements in reporting at one institution, the amounts outstanding increased by £1bn. This effect has been adjusted out of the flows for April 2016.

(ci) Due to improvements in reporting at one institution, the amounts outstanding increased by £2bn. This effect has been adjusted out of the flows for February 2017.

(cj) Due to improvements in reporting at one institution, the amounts outstanding increased by £4bn. This effect has been adjusted out of the flows for February 2017.

(ck) Due to improvements in reporting at one institution, the amounts outstanding increased by £2bn. This effect has been adjusted out of the flows for November 2015.

(cl) Due to improvements in reporting at one institution, the amounts outstanding decreased by £1bn. This effect has been adjusted out of the flows for April 2016.

(cm) Due to improvements in reporting at one institution, the amounts outstanding decreased by £4bn. This effect has been adjusted out of the flows for April 2016.

(cn) Due to a loan transfer by one reporting institution, the amounts outstanding increased by £3bn. This effect has been adjusted out of the flows for December 2015.

(co) Due to a loan transfer by one reporting institution, the amounts outstanding increased by £7bn. This effect has been adjusted out of the flows for April 2016.

(cp) Due to improvements in reporting at one institution, the amounts outstanding decreased by £2bn. This effect has been adjusted out of the flows for November 2016.

Explanatory notes can be found here: http://www.bankofengland.co.uk/statistics/Pages/iadb/notesiadb/industrial.aspx
Copyright guidance and the related UK Open Government Licence can be viewed here: www.bankofengland.co.uk/Pages/disclaimer.aspx.

12.4c Industrial analysis of monetary financial institutions' lending to UK residents

£ millions

Not seasonally adjusted

Amounts outstanding of facilities granted in sterling

RPM	Agriculture, hunting and forestry	Fishing	Mining and quarrying	Manufacturing								Total
				Food, beverages and tobacco	Textiles, wearing apparel and leather	Pulp, paper, and printing	Chemicals, pharmaceuticals, rubber and plastics	Non-metallic mineral products and metals	Machinery, equipment and transport equipment	Electrical, medical and optical equipment	Other manufacturing	
	TCCC	TCCD	TCCE	TCCG	TCCH	TCCI	TCCJ	TCCK	TCCL	TCCM	TCCN	TCCF
2015 Aug	23,535	310	7,195	8,693	1,085	2,721	7,093	5,422	10,922	3,160	4,076	43,173
Sep	23,839	296	7,387	8,893	1,141	2,853	7,140	5,398	11,097	3,316	4,205	44,044
Oct	24,029	291	7,464	8,664	1,156	2,706	6,840	5,468	11,115	3,391	4,369	43,708
Nov	24,080	288	7,273	8,584	1,131	2,740	7,196	5,390	10,870	3,384	4,319	43,614
Dec	24,136	277	7,237	8,796	1,147	2,585	7,143	5,246	11,120	3,102	4,343	43,483
2016 Jan	24,105	282	7,454	8,717	1,130	2,612	7,428	5,191	11,193	3,040	4,168	43,477
Feb	24,070	281	2,939	8,573	1,101	2,612	7,554	5,187	11,398	3,058	4,147	43,629
Mar	24,202	282	2,856	8,790	1,100	2,613	7,471	5,149	11,306	3,048	4,111	43,589
Apr	24,171	276	2,869	9,242	1,090	2,725	7,599	5,185	11,032	3,054	4,076	44,003
May	24,234	277	2,899	9,319	1,108	2,671	7,696	5,294	11,128	3,394	4,132	44,742
Jun	24,389	320	3,019	9,325	1,173	2,626	7,480	5,293	11,138	2,994	4,093	44,122
Jul	24,487	331	3,022	9,351	1,151	2,587	7,710	5,371	10,846	2,965	4,001	43,981
Aug	24,584	328	3,442	9,297	1,153	2,569	7,743	5,263	10,887	3,295	3,914	44,121
Sep	24,675	326	3,376	8,979	1,164	2,636	7,982	5,257	11,252	3,312	3,782	44,364
Oct	24,700	330	3,400	9,119	1,146	2,687	8,093	5,264	10,973	3,102	3,705	44,089
Nov	24,687	330	3,388	9,140	1,160	2,582	8,049	5,214	11,151	3,159	3,759	44,216
Dec	24,684	342	3,356	9,253	1,177	2,672	7,970	5,186	11,112	3,215	3,752	44,336
2017 Jan	24,722	339	3,197	9,640	1,151	2,666	7,999	5,458	11,195	3,139	3,729	44,978
Feb	24,772	339	3,240	9,623	1,135	2,687	7,972	5,426	11,399	3,156	3,740	45,137
Mar	24,883	343	3,192	9,512	1,186	2,747	8,032	5,497	11,518	3,467	3,836	45,795
Apr	24,917	333	3,120	10,434	1,180	2,731	7,971	5,471	11,705	3,164	3,843	46,498

Source: Bank of England

12.4c Industrial analysis of monetary financial institutions' lending to UK residents

£ millions

Not seasonally adjusted

Amounts outstanding of facilities granted in sterling

	Electricity, gas and water supply				Construction						Wholesale and retail trade			Total
	Electricity, gas steam and air conditioning	Water collection and sewerage	Waste management related services and remediation activities	Total	Development of buildings	Construction of commercial buildings	Construction of domestic buildings	Civil Engineering	Other construction activities	Total	Wholesale and retail trade and repair of motor vehicles and motorcycles	Wholesale trade, excluding motor vehicles and motor cycles	Retail trade excluding motor vehicles and motor cycles	
RPM	TCCO	TCCP	B3FE	B3FS	B7EG	B3ID	B4PC	B4PP	B5QH	TCCQ	TCCS	TCCT	TCCU	TCCR
2015 Aug	13,328	6,334	2,858	22,520	21,082	6,174	7,945	4,960	7,936	48,097	14,307	18,032	25,993	58,332
Sep	14,232	6,390	2,829	23,451	20,599	6,216	7,947	4,948	8,058	47,768	14,049	19,258	26,388	59,696
Oct	14,899	6,361	2,955	24,215	20,302	6,479	7,991	5,045	7,817	47,633	14,164	18,947	26,480	59,591
Nov	14,761	6,669	2,976	24,406	20,292	6,636	8,169	5,085	7,773	47,955	14,324	19,130	26,613	60,067
Dec	15,496	7,130	2,951	25,577	20,045	6,274	7,891	4,784	7,718	46,712	14,372	18,588	26,704	59,664
2016 Jan	15,563	7,212	2,893	25,669	19,971	6,347	8,066	5,032	7,836	47,252	14,888	19,597	27,007	61,493
Feb	16,184	7,208	2,956	26,347	21,587 (cq)	5,405 (cs)	9,065	5,316	7,694	49,067 (cq)(cs)	16,285	20,068	27,332	63,685
Mar	15,978	7,313	2,889	26,180	19,015 (cr)	5,188	9,252	5,175	7,625	46,255 (cr)	15,719	19,948	27,445	63,112
Apr	16,445	7,341	2,891	26,677	19,165	5,287	9,224	5,179	7,718	46,572	16,473 (ct)	19,414	27,705	63,592 (ct)
May	17,636	7,602	2,869	28,107	19,092	5,191	9,508	5,212	7,870	46,874	16,227	19,619	27,460	63,307
Jun	18,321	7,712	2,647	28,680	19,298	4,908	9,683	5,152	7,872	46,913	16,702	19,243	27,525	63,471
Jul	17,984	7,872	2,734	28,590	19,568	5,166	9,625	5,056	7,888	47,303	16,725	18,937	27,706	63,368
Aug	18,056	8,110	2,834	29,001	19,508	5,234	9,774	5,104	7,897	47,518	16,489	19,334	27,133	62,955
Sep	17,416	8,080	2,863	28,359	20,305	5,165	9,851	5,123	8,028	48,472	15,697	18,987	27,216	61,901
Oct	17,428	7,959	2,969	28,355	20,290	5,190	10,047	5,353	8,064	48,944	15,268	19,419	27,555	62,242
Nov	17,544	7,912	2,907	28,362	20,143	5,230	10,028	5,388	8,166	48,955	15,593	19,348	27,930	62,871
Dec	17,853	7,773	3,033	28,659	19,801	4,952	9,990	5,232	8,053	48,028	15,642	19,194	28,081	62,917
2017 Jan	18,468	7,766	2,998	29,233	20,060	5,194	10,237	5,235	8,113	48,840	16,217	19,606	28,130	63,953
Feb	18,334	7,428	3,054	28,816	20,344	5,211	10,330	5,339	8,111	49,335	17,079	19,993	28,053	65,124
Mar	20,307	7,320	2,945	30,572	20,299	5,148	10,461	5,897	8,042	49,847	17,007	19,697	27,994	64,698
Apr	20,273	7,320	2,885	30,478	20,396	5,095	10,498	5,497	8,058	49,544	16,644	18,809	28,443	63,896

Source: Bank of England

12.4c Industrial analysis of monetary financial institutions' lending to UK residents

£ millions

Not seasonally adjusted

Amounts outstanding of facilities granted in sterling

| RPM | Accommodation and food service activities | Transport, storage and communication | | | Real estate, professional services and support activities | | | | Public administration and defence | Education | Human health and social work | Recreational, personal and community service activities | | Total |
| | | Transportation and storage | Information and communication | Total | Buying, selling and renting of real estate | Professional, scientific and technical activities | Administrative and support services | Total | | | | Recreational, cultural and sporting activities | Personal and community service activities | |
	TCCV	B5PP	B5PW	TCCW	TCCY	B6PH	B3S2	TCCX	TCDD	TCDE	TCDF	TCDH	TCDG	B3SR
2015 Aug	26,835	20,313	18,108	38,421	162,211	22,521	26,826	211,558	11,030	13,944	23,526	6,717	4,242	10,959
Sep	27,031	20,429	19,048	39,478	161,568	22,851	27,374	211,793	10,114	13,719	23,301	6,669	4,225	10,894
Oct	27,032	20,465	20,008	40,473	160,923	23,049	28,099	212,070	10,047	13,744	23,095	7,125	4,247	11,373
Nov	26,978	20,510	19,925	40,435	160,937	23,212	28,345	212,495	10,052	13,599	23,333	7,295	4,325	11,620
Dec	26,900	20,722	20,154	40,876	161,978 (cu)	22,614	28,912	213,504 (cu)	10,331	13,310	23,098	7,038	4,161	11,198
2016 Jan	27,305	20,760	20,405	41,164	161,868	23,371	28,560	213,799	9,956	13,224	23,447	7,083	4,161	11,244
Feb	27,204	20,835	19,216	40,051	161,364 (cv)(cw)	23,014	28,891	213,269 (cv)(cw)	10,157	13,328	23,470	7,249	4,248	11,497
Mar	27,478	20,218	17,654	37,871	165,885 (cx)	23,190	29,167	218,242 (cx)	10,043	13,294	23,389	7,378	4,230	11,608
Apr	27,636	20,377	16,301	36,678	165,937	23,020	29,664	218,621	10,247	13,213	23,295	7,356	4,302	11,659
May	27,756	20,332	14,329	34,661	166,400	23,185	29,731	219,316	10,235	13,268	23,357	7,318	4,279	11,596
Jun	27,766	20,519	14,396	34,915	167,282	23,365	30,470	221,118	9,975	13,220	23,408	7,040	4,302	11,343
Jul	27,852	20,757	14,453	35,209	167,276	23,483	31,010	221,769	9,895	13,268	23,401	7,065	4,328	11,393
Aug	28,314	20,560	14,644	35,205	167,629	23,393	31,280	222,301	10,406	13,229	23,206	6,994	4,348	11,342
Sep	28,419	20,630	13,981	34,611	166,956 (cy)	23,516	31,405	221,876 (cy)	10,682	13,042	22,980	7,124	4,358	11,482
Oct	28,476	20,534	14,677	35,211	166,666	23,276	32,555	222,497	11,517	13,013	23,097	7,411	4,368	11,779
Nov	28,303	19,754	14,595	34,349	167,329	23,237	32,743	223,309	10,398	12,906	23,197	7,265	4,328	11,593
Dec	28,631	19,198	14,241	33,440	168,592	22,806	33,283	224,681	10,025	12,913	22,713	7,609	4,344	11,953
2017 Jan	29,128	18,967	14,156	33,123	167,262	23,591	33,285	224,138	12,404	12,865	23,336	7,678	4,295	11,973
Feb	29,522	19,722	14,007	33,729	166,919	23,180	32,756	222,855	10,639	12,866	23,021	7,709	4,129	11,838
Mar	29,632	19,739	14,415	34,153	166,799	23,360	33,133 (da)	223,292 (da)	11,918	12,904	23,237	7,714	4,328	12,042
Apr	30,192	19,676	14,400	34,076	167,428 (cz)	23,537	33,921 (db)	224,885 (cz)(db)	11,208	12,926	23,048	7,847	4,425	12,272

Source: Bank of England

12.4c Industrial analysis of monetary financial institutions' lending to UK residents

£ millions

Not seasonally adjusted

Amounts outstanding of facilities granted in sterling

RPM	Financial leasing corporations	Non-bank credit grantors excluding credit unions and SPVs	Credit unions	Factoring corporations	Financial intermediation (excluding insurance and pension funds)									Total
					Mortgage and housing credit corporations excluding SPVs	Investment and unit trusts excluding money market mutual funds	Money market mutual funds	Bank holding companies	Securities dealers	SPVs related to securitisation	Other financial intermediaries	of which intragroup activity		
	TCDJ	TCDK	TCDL	TCDM	TCDN	TCDO	TCDP	TCDQ	TCDR	B8EX	TCDS	B7FF		TCDI
2015 Aug	29,086	25,039	2	5,969	50,741	6,652	30	18,772	26,305	19,315	67,827	55,442		**249,739**
Sep	29,321	25,160	2	5,696	49,572	7,944	33	18,878	29,254	21,563	64,615	52,410		**252,038**
Oct	29,364	24,988	2	4,978	50,082	8,019	32	20,229 (dg)	24,948	21,528	63,226 (dk)	51,021		**247,395 (dg)(dk)**
Nov	29,265	24,780	2	5,106	49,999	8,555	43	20,197	24,924	22,378	57,289	44,898		**242,537**
Dec	28,950	24,862	2	4,847	53,335 (de)	9,178	51	19,660	25,867	21,810 (dh)	54,578	43,066		**243,139 (de)(dh)**
2016 Jan	27,974	23,879 (dc)	2	4,812	54,251	10,438	54	19,862	26,007	23,708 (di)	50,008	39,746		**240,997 (dc)(di)**
Feb	27,853	24,117	2	4,725	54,663	10,626	58	20,396	27,313	23,237	50,378	40,882		**243,368**
Mar	28,282	20,249	3	5,404	54,975	11,458	104	20,308	28,872	23,485	46,862	36,995		**240,001**
Apr	28,215	20,874	1	5,580	49,310	11,982	87	20,600	31,229	19,981	44,615	34,844		**232,474**
May	28,135	20,770	1	5,569	49,215	13,376	93	19,322	26,903	19,425	46,324	34,580		**229,133**
Jun	27,893	20,581	1	5,808	49,949	13,417	118	12,150	31,030	20,844	45,764	33,789		**227,556**
Jul	28,035	20,923	1	5,469	50,163	13,397	123	13,535	30,015	20,554	45,496	33,023		**227,711**
Aug	28,034	21,001	1	5,283	49,597	12,983	154	13,395	27,389	18,970	46,474	34,188		**223,282**
Sep	28,011	23,878 (dd)	1	5,706	50,171	13,404	159	13,547	26,299	18,637	45,743	33,213		**225,556 (dd)**
Oct	28,012	24,502	1	5,657	51,061	14,409	214	13,919	24,535	16,251	44,507	32,679		**223,071**
Nov	28,791	24,906	1	5,679	48,970	14,277	206	13,748	26,587	15,222	39,898	29,091		**218,285**
Dec	27,807	24,816	1	5,985	48,760	13,653	160	16,327	23,355	14,764	41,351	30,379		**216,977**
2017 Jan	27,443	25,028	3	5,369	49,147	12,830	164	19,114	22,851	14,397	41,794	30,276		**218,141**
Feb	27,290	21,293	3	5,730	44,004	13,854	169	18,536	23,022	14,108	41,731	30,311		**209,740**
Mar	26,406	21,844	3	5,949	47,998	12,177 (df)	168	13,632	21,018	14,052	41,590 (dl)	31,987		**204,836 (df)(dl)**
Apr	25,879	21,519	3	5,984	47,980	12,394	120	13,774	22,208	15,107	41,813	32,394		**206,781**

Source: Bank of England

12.4c Industrial analysis of monetary financial institutions' lending to UK residents

£ millions

Not seasonally adjusted

Amounts outstanding of facilities granted in sterling

RPM	Insurance companies & pension funds			Fund management activities	Activities auxiliary to financial intermediation			Total	Total financial and non-financial businesses
	Insurance companies	Pension funds	Total		Other		Total		
					Central clearing counterparties	Other auxiliary activities			
	B7FK	B3W9	TCDT	TCDU	B3X6	B3Y4	TCDV	B8FO	Z94D
2015 Aug	13,846	10,025	23,870	69,574	59,779	3,797	63,576	133,151	945,196
Sep	11,586	10,614	22,201	74,461	50,443	4,016	54,459	128,920	945,970
Oct	10,188	11,611	21,799	72,242 (dn)	46,122 (dt)	4,151	50,273 (dt)	122,516 (dn)(dt)	936,476 (dg)(dk)(dn)(dt)
Nov	11,962	11,617	23,579	73,904	50,360	4,123	54,482	128,386	940,699
Dec	10,526	11,079	21,605	76,208	45,522	3,925	49,446	125,654	936,701 (cu)(de)(dh)
2016 Jan	11,263	11,721	22,984	81,983 (do)	39,532 (du)	4,078	43,611 (du)	125,594 (do)(du)	939,446 (dc)(di)(do)(du)
Feb	11,920	13,836	25,756	91,390	36,539	3,930	40,468	131,859	949,978 (cq)(cs)(cv)(cw)
Mar	12,486	13,783	26,269	94,585	33,517	3,890	37,407	131,992	946,665
Apr	11,382	11,988	23,370	91,875	33,503 (dv)	4,234	37,737 (dv)	129,612 (dv)	934,967 (ct)(dv)
May	12,152	12,276	24,428	99,856 (dp)	40,764	4,352	45,117	144,972 (dp)	949,162 (dp)
Jun	13,342	15,464	28,805	108,813	45,084	5,084	50,169	158,982	968,002
Jul	12,986	16,425	29,411	107,998	42,082	5,117	47,199	155,197	966,187
Aug	14,573	16,654	31,227	108,377	47,141	4,482	51,623	160,000	970,460
Sep	14,668	17,018	31,686	113,893	44,664	4,530	49,194	163,087	974,892 (cy)(dd)
Oct	13,371	14,970	28,342	114,693	50,751	4,591	55,341	170,034	979,096
Nov	12,915	16,648	29,563	115,626	58,167	4,575	62,743	178,369	983,082
Dec	13,373	19,678	33,051	117,544	51,256	4,888	56,144	173,689	980,396
2017 Jan	13,440	16,552	29,992	114,829	63,796	4,377	68,174	183,003	993,365
Feb	12,949	17,505	30,454	115,191	65,273 (dw)	5,688	70,961 (dw)	186,152 (dw)	987,578 (dw)
Mar	13,861	25,911 (dm)	39,772 (dm)	118,714 (dq)(dr)(ds)	70,475	5,108	75,583	194,297 (dq)(dr)(ds)	1,005,414 (da)
Apr	15,067	28,080	43,147	114,149	73,433	4,880	78,314	192,463	1,009,783 (cz)(db)

Source: Bank of England

12.4c Industrial analysis of monetary financial institutions' lending to UK residents

£ millions

Not seasonally adjusted

RPM		Individuals and individual trusts			Total UK residents
	Lending secured on dwellings inc. bridging finance	Other loans and advances	Total		
	TCDX	TCDY	TCDW		TCCA
2015 Aug	1,136,217	198,003	1,334,220		2,280,415
Sep	1,140,079	199,088	1,339,166		2,285,136
Oct	1,144,725	199,885	1,344,610		2,281,086 (dg)(dk)(dn)(dt)
Nov	1,149,226	200,713	1,349,939		2,290,638
Dec	1,159,523 (dx)(dy)	198,236 (eb)	1,357,759 (dx)(dy)(eb)		2,294,461 (cu)(de)(dh)(dx)(dy)(eb)
2016 Jan	1,160,485	199,024	1,359,508		2,298,954 (dc)(di)(do)(du)
Feb	1,163,166	200,123	1,363,289		2,313,266 (cq)(cs)(cv)(cw)
Mar	1,169,891	201,195	1,371,086		2,317,751
Apr	1,178,808 (dz)	201,962	1,380,771 (dz)		2,315,738 (ct)(dv)(dz)
May	1,182,762	202,771	1,385,533		2,334,695 (dp)
Jun	1,189,355	203,780	1,393,134		2,361,136
Jul	1,192,336	204,633	1,396,969		2,363,156
Aug	1,194,588	205,871	1,400,459		2,370,919
Sep	1,198,478	204,981	1,403,458		2,378,350 (cy)(dd)
Oct	1,201,672	205,496	1,407,168		2,386,264
Nov	1,206,523	206,461	1,412,984		2,396,066
Dec	1,207,758	206,822	1,414,580		2,394,976
2017 Jan	1,209,427	207,224	1,416,650		2,410,015
Feb	1,212,619	207,735	1,420,354		2,407,932 (dw)
Mar	1,219,164	208,675	1,427,839		2,433,253 (da)
Apr	1,220,500	209,396	1,429,896		2,439,679 (cz)(db)

Source: Bank of England

12.4c Industrial analysis of monetary financial institutions' lending to UK residents

Notes to table

Movements in amounts outstanding can reflect breaks in data series as well as underlying flows. For changes data, users are recommended to refer directly to the appropriate series or data tables. Further explanation can be found at: www.bankofengland.co.uk/statistics/Pages/iadb/notesiadb/Changes_flows_growth_rates.aspx.

(cq) Due to improvements in reporting at one institution, the amounts outstanding increased by £1bn. This effect has been adjusted out of the flows for February 2016.

(cr) Due to improvements in reporting at one institution, the amounts outstanding decreased by £2bn. This effect has been adjusted out of the flows for March 2016.

(cs) Due to improvements in reporting at one institution, the amounts outstanding decreased by £1bn. This effect has been adjusted out of the flows for February 2016.

(ct) Due to improvements in reporting at one institution, the amounts outstanding increased by £1bn. This effect has been adjusted out of the flows for April 2016.

(cu) Due to a change in the reporting population, the amounts outstanding increased by £1bn. This effect has been adjusted out of the flows for December 2015.

(cv) Due to improvements in reporting at one institution the amounts outstanding decreased by £1bn. This effect has been adjusted out of the flows for February 2016.

(cw) Due to improvements in reporting at one institution, the amounts outstanding decreased by £1bn. This effect has been adjusted out of the flows for February 2016.

(cx) Due to improvements in reporting at one institution, the amounts outstanding increased by £2bn. This effect has been adjusted out of the flows for March 2016.

(cy) Due to a change in the reporting population, the amounts outstanding decreased by £1bn. This effect has been adjusted out of the flows for September 2016.

(cz) Due to reporting improvements at one institution, amounts outstanding increased by £1 billion. This has been adjusted out of the flows for April 2017.

(da) Due to loan transfers by one institution, the amounts outstanding decreased by £1 billion. This amount has been adjusted out of the flows for March 2017.

(db) Due to loan transfers by one institution, amounts outstanding increased by £1 billion. This amount has been adjusted out of the flows for April 2017.

(dc) Due to improvements in reporting at one institution, the amounts outstanding decreased by £1bn. This effect has been adjusted out of the flows for January 2016.

(dd) Due to a change in the reporting population, the amounts outstanding increased by £2bn. This effect has been adjusted out of the flows for September 2016.

(de) Due to a restructuring at one reporting institution, the amounts outstanding increased by £4bn. This effect has been adjusted out of the flows for December 2015.

(df) Due to reporting improvements at one institution, amounts outstanding decreased by £2bn. This has been adjusted out of flows for March 2017.

(dg) Due to improvements in reporting at one institution, the amounts outstanding increased by £1bn. This effect has been adjusted out of the flows for October 2015.

(dh) Due to a restructuring at one reporting institution, the amounts outstanding decreased by £4bn. This effect has been adjusted out of the flows for December 2015.

(di) Due to improvements in reporting at one institution, the amounts outstanding increased by £1bn. This effect has been adjusted out of the flows for January 2016.

(dj) Due to a change in accounting treatment at one reporting institution, the amounts outstanding decreased by £2bn. This effect has been adjusted out of the flows for June 2017.

(dk) Due to improvements in reporting at one institution, the amounts outstanding decreased by £1bn. This effect has been adjusted out of the flows for October 2015.

(dl) Due to reporting improvements at one institution, amounts outstanding decreased by £2bn. This has been adjusted out of flows for March 2017.

(dm) Due to reporting improvements at one institution, amounts outstanding increased by £5bn. This has been adjusted out of flows for March 2017.

(dn) Due to improvements in reporting at one institution, the amounts outstanding decreased by £2bn. This effect has been adjusted out of the flows for October 2015.

(do) Due to a change in the reporting population, the amounts outstanding increased by £3bn. This effect has been adjusted out of the flows for January 2016.

(dp) Due to improvements in reporting at one institution, the amounts outstanding increased by £1bn. This effect has been adjusted out of the flows for May 2016.

(dq) Due to reporting improvements at one institution, amounts outstanding decreased by £5bn. This has been adjusted out of flows for March 2017.

(dr) Due to reporting improvements at one institution, amounts outstanding increased by £2bn. This has been adjusted out of flows for March 2017.

(ds) Due to reporting improvements at one institution, amounts outstanding increased by £2bn. This has been adjusted out of flows for March 2017.

(dt) Due to a change in the reporting population, the amounts outstanding decreased by £3bn. This effect has been adjusted out of the flows for October 2015.

(du) Due to a change in the reporting population, the amounts outstanding decreased by £4bn. This effect has been adjusted out of the flows for January 2016.

(dv) Due to improvements in reporting at one institution, the amounts outstanding increased by £1bn. This effect has been adjusted out of the flows for April 2016.

(dw) Due to improvements in reporting at one institution, the amounts outstanding increased by £2bn. This effect has been adjusted out of the flows for February 2017.

(dx) Due to a loan transfer by one reporting institution, the amounts outstanding increased by £3bn. This effect has been adjusted out of the flows for December 2015.

(dy) Due to improvements in reporting at one institution, the amounts outstanding increased by £5bn. This effect has been adjusted out of the flows for December 2015.

(dz) Due to a loan transfer by one reporting institution, the amounts outstanding increased by £7bn. This effect has been adjusted out of the flows for April 2016.

(ea) Due to improvements in reporting at one institution, the amounts outstanding decreased by £4bn. This effect has been adjusted out of the flows for July 2017.

(eb) Due to improvements in reporting at one institution, the amounts outstanding decreased by £3bn. This effect has been adjusted out of the flows for December 2015.

(ec) Due to improvements in reporting at one institution, the amounts outstanding decreased by £6bn. This effect has been adjusted out of the flows for July 2017.

Explanatory notes can be found here: http://www.bankofengland.co.uk/statistics/Pages/iadb/notesiadb/industrial.aspx

Copyright guidance and the related UK Open Government Licence can be viewed here: www.bankofengland.co.uk/Pages/disclaimer.aspx.

12.4d Industrial analysis of monetary financial institutions' lending to UK residents

£ millions

Not seasonally adjusted

Amounts outstanding of facilities granted in all currencies

RPM	Agriculture, hunting and forestry	Fishing	Mining and quarrying	Manufacturing								Total
				Food, beverages and tobacco	Textiles, wearing apparel and leather	Pulp, paper, and printing	Chemicals, pharmaceuticals, rubber and plastics	Non-metallic mineral products and metals	Machinery, equipment and transport equipment	Electrical, medical and optical equipment	Other manufacturing	
	TCAC	TCAD	TCAE	TCAG	TCAH	TCAI	TCAJ	TCAK	TCAL	TCAM	TCAN	TCAF
2015 Aug	23,837	314	33,606	19,513	1,761	4,158	16,205	8,965	17,497	5,099	5,807	79,006
Sep	24,123	319	31,810	19,036	1,799	3,965	16,083	8,972	17,641	5,313	5,760	78,570
Oct	24,311	295	31,355	18,021	1,832	3,710	15,630	9,121	17,644	5,367	5,950	77,276
Nov	24,365	293	31,575	17,830	1,786	3,805	16,490	8,851	17,838	5,510	5,944	78,055
Dec	24,446	286	32,380 (ed)	17,783	1,791	3,702	16,636	8,871	18,321	5,219	5,858	78,181
2016 Jan	24,431	312	32,661	17,856	1,814	3,745	16,689	8,723	18,416	5,090	5,867	78,200
Feb	24,380	311	28,697	18,202	1,746	3,726	17,901	8,880	18,507	5,178	5,973	80,113
Mar	24,508	315	28,223	18,150	1,778	3,708	17,690	8,833	18,330	5,161	6,241	79,893
Apr	24,479	307	25,933	19,147	1,716	3,826	17,206	8,792	18,069	5,157	6,324	80,237
May	24,525	308	25,898	20,863	1,716	3,793	17,546	8,849	17,318	5,449	6,453	81,986
Jun	24,706	356	28,309	21,523	1,841	3,782	18,252	8,758	17,826	5,485	6,064	83,531
Jul	24,797	365	27,614	21,300	1,849	3,687	17,613	8,716	17,607	5,467	6,125	82,363
Aug	24,911	361	27,953	21,236	1,826	3,789	18,158	8,596	17,403	5,631	5,818	82,457
Sep	25,002	356	29,533	22,713	1,871	3,915	18,491	8,570	18,176	6,131	5,631	85,499
Oct	25,048	368	31,828	23,342	1,892	4,100	18,911	8,706	18,346	5,964	5,724	86,985
Nov	24,983	359	30,871	24,662	1,921	4,268	18,727	8,550	18,207	6,292	5,693	88,320
Dec	24,987	371	32,056	23,385	1,884	4,263	19,333	8,512	18,442	6,285	5,741	87,845
2017 Jan	25,031	370	30,930	32,304	1,851	4,669	19,292	8,731	18,583	6,147	5,678	97,255
Feb	25,066	370	30,720	33,695	1,785	4,813	32,120	8,750	18,988	6,024	5,692	111,867
Mar	25,183	373	30,176	33,313	1,831	4,840	27,766	9,258	18,818	6,139	6,051	108,016
Apr	25,258	362	27,259 (ee)	36,031	1,826	4,801	28,194	8,728	19,050	6,037	5,701	110,366

Source: Bank of England

12.4d Industrial analysis of monetary financial institutions' lending to UK residents

£ millions

Not seasonally adjusted

Amounts outstanding of facilities granted in all currencies

	Electricity, gas and water supply				Construction						Wholesale and retail trade			
	Electricity, gas steam and air conditioning	Water collection and sewerage	Waste management related services and remediation activities	Total	Development of buildings	Construction of commercial buildings	Construction of domestic buildings	Civil Engineering	Other construction activities	Total	Wholesale and retail trade and repair of motor vehicles and motorcycles	Wholesale trade, excluding motor vehicles and motor cycles	Retail trade excluding motor vehicles and motor cycles	Total
RPM	TCAO	TCAP	B3FF	B3FT	B7EH	B3IE	B4PD	B3KK	B5PC	TCAQ	TCAS	TCAT	TCAU	TCAR
2015 Aug	21,904	7,022	3,166	32,091	21,558	6,727	8,120	5,886	8,118	50,409	15,572	26,403	32,652	74,628
Sep	22,492	7,077	3,072	32,642	21,081	6,722	8,086	5,818	8,254	49,960	15,381	27,183	32,658	75,222
Oct	22,449	7,048	3,176	32,674	20,740	6,993	8,141	5,772	8,009	49,655	15,413	26,878	32,666	74,957
Nov	22,557	7,381	3,225	33,162	20,787	7,122	8,330	5,984	7,968	50,191	15,460	26,781	32,964	75,205
Dec	23,611	7,842	3,206	34,659	20,550	6,974	8,089	5,618	7,940	49,171	15,563	26,802	33,151	75,516
2016 Jan	23,900	7,891	3,244	35,035	20,494	6,926	8,260	5,800	8,048	49,528	16,077	27,660	33,424	77,161
Feb	24,155	7,899	3,207	35,261	22,155 (eg)	5,876 (ei)	9,317	6,013	7,909	51,269 (eg)(ei)	17,479	28,771	33,951	80,201
Mar	23,830	7,938	3,290	35,058	19,550 (eh)	5,703	9,494	6,031	7,830	48,607 (eh)	16,954	28,603	34,151	79,708
Apr	22,571	7,944	3,239	33,754	19,694	5,766	9,489	5,974	7,918	48,840	17,941 (ei)	28,008	34,568	80,517 (ej)
May	24,062	8,229	3,096	35,386	19,613	5,682	9,756	5,959	8,135	49,146	17,608	28,400	34,613	80,622
Jun	25,101	8,377	2,951	36,428	19,835	5,627	9,946	6,046	8,143	49,597	18,244	29,266	34,713	82,223
Jul	24,813	8,435	3,095	36,343	20,120	5,655	9,864	5,944	8,147	49,731	18,188	28,570	34,733	81,491
Aug	25,129	8,716	3,133	36,979	20,057	5,694	9,994	6,012	8,179	49,936	18,082	29,287	33,997	81,366
Sep	25,140	8,666	3,120	36,926	20,837	5,576	10,079	5,916	8,265	50,673	17,345	28,800	34,594	80,739
Oct	26,117	8,554	3,339	38,011	20,832	5,626	10,278	6,167	8,375	51,277	16,779	30,481	34,463	81,722
Nov	25,635	8,481	3,189	37,305	20,517	5,650	10,244	6,201	8,369	50,982	16,978	30,030	34,795	81,803
Dec	26,097	8,349	3,279	37,724	20,178	5,558	10,222	6,156	8,300	50,414	16,973	29,146	35,555	81,674
2017 Jan	26,783	8,477	3,315	38,575	20,481	5,701	10,506	6,267	8,347	51,302	17,660	29,520	35,513	82,693
Feb	26,697	8,167	3,222	38,087	20,763	5,709	10,604	6,362	8,347	51,785	18,414	29,928	35,403	83,746
Mar	28,612	8,063	3,223	39,898	20,724	5,654	10,734	6,806	8,278	52,196	18,365	30,109 (ek)	35,260	83,734 (ek)
Apr	28,049	8,173	3,113	39,335	20,780	5,583	10,774	6,308	8,298	51,744	17,969	30,899 (el)	35,274	84,143 (el)

Source: Bank of England

12.4d Industrial analysis of monetary financial institutions' lending to UK residents

£ millions

Amounts outstanding of facilities granted in all currencies

RPM	Accommodation and food service activities	Transport, storage and communication			Real estate, professional services and support activities				Public administration and defence	Education	Human health and social work
		Transportation and storage	Information and communication	Total	Buying, selling and renting of real estate	Professional, scientific and technical activities	Administrative and support services	Total			
	TCAV	B3NF	B5PX	TCAW	TCAY	B3QF	B3S3	TCAX	TCBD	TCBE	TCBF
2015 Aug	28,656	26,551	31,077	57,628	165,427	29,484	33,735	228,647	12,153	14,003	23,972
Sep	28,927	26,991	32,469	59,460	165,307	30,108	34,597	230,012	11,869	13,769	23,744
Oct	28,950	26,713	33,203	59,916	165,386	30,058	34,803	230,246	12,094	13,781	23,482
Nov	28,930	26,605	33,831	60,436	165,117	30,490	35,332	230,939	11,391	13,643	23,735
Dec	28,780	27,537	35,472	63,009	166,285 (ed)	30,149	35,789 (ed)	232,223 (ed)	12,239	13,353	23,411
2016 Jan	29,171	27,803	36,467	64,270	166,283	30,937	35,302	232,521	12,154	13,271	23,761
Feb	29,078	28,267	35,475	63,742	165,259 (em)(en)	30,621	36,444	232,324 (em)(en)	11,977	13,375	23,823
Mar	29,417	27,530	33,719	61,249	169,336 (eo)	30,361	36,850	236,547 (eo)	10,942	13,333	23,782
Apr	29,504	27,698	31,620	59,319	169,111	30,101	37,523	236,735	12,113	13,264	23,620
May	29,624	27,699	29,481	57,180	169,367	30,461	37,388	237,217	12,216	13,314	23,675
Jun	29,708	28,321	30,778	59,099	170,175	31,113	38,795	240,083	11,545	13,282	23,886
Jul	29,797	28,967	30,669	59,636	170,282	31,204	39,330	240,816	11,940	13,325	23,897
Aug	30,258	28,228	31,395	59,623	170,588	31,212	40,069	241,869	12,257	13,306	23,744
Sep	31,165	29,011	31,136	60,147	170,069 (ep)	32,310	40,219	242,597 (ep)	12,467	13,120	23,644
Oct	31,435	29,307	33,746	63,053	169,472	31,993	42,064	243,529	12,126	13,105	23,768
Nov	31,244	28,111	31,955	60,066	170,247	31,176	41,558	242,981	11,956	13,018	23,834
Dec	31,999	27,522	31,474	58,996	171,590	31,102	43,805	246,497	11,863	13,026	23,153
2017 Jan	32,050	27,505	31,449	58,954	170,347	31,621	43,648	245,616	14,412	12,969	23,746
Feb	32,426	28,439	31,490	59,928	170,011	31,128	42,984	244,122	11,751	12,966	23,420
Mar	32,679	28,163	31,991	60,154	169,639	31,391	42,640 (er)	243,670 (er)	12,142	13,001	23,643
Apr	33,344	27,934	31,470	59,404	170,163 (eq)	31,417	42,392 (es)(et)	243,972 (eq)(es)(et)	14,650	13,020	23,442

Source: Bank of England

12.4d Industrial analysis of monetary financial institutions' lending to UK residents

£ millions

Amounts outstanding of facilities granted in all currencies

RPM	Recreational, personal and community service activities				Non-bank credit grantors excluding credit unions and SPVs	Credit unions	Factoring corporations	Financial intermediation (excluding insurance and pension funds)							
	Recreational, cultural and sporting activities	Personal and community service activities	Total	Financial leasing corporations				Mortgage and housing credit corporations excluding SPVs	Investment and unit trusts excluding money market mutual funds	Money market mutual funds	Bank holding companies	Securities dealers	SPVs related to securitisation	Other financial intermediaries
	TCBH	TCBG	B3T2	TCBJ	TCBK	TCBL	TCBM	TCBN	TCBO	TCBP	TCBQ	TCBR	B7FB	TCBS
2015 Aug	7,916	4,719	12,635	32,988	25,980	3	6,460	51,724	13,922	31	27,475	124,397	20,891	112,390
Sep	7,898	4,591	12,489	33,471	26,103	2	6,262	50,530	15,301	34	27,152	134,202	23,232	110,544
Oct	8,483	4,622	13,105	33,870	25,900	2	5,484	51,014	15,805	34	28,721 (ez)	121,427 (ez)	23,041	108,576 (ff)
Nov	8,597	4,690	13,287	33,860	25,558	2	5,609	50,964	16,742	44	29,173	118,394	23,997	103,125
Dec	8,398	4,530	12,928	33,663	25,619	3	5,347	54,440 (ew)	16,775	125	29,953	114,898	24,325 (fc)	101,502
2016 Jan	8,431	4,543	12,974	32,754	24,803 (eu)	3	5,311	55,390	18,638	135	30,632	119,914	24,811 (fd)	98,803
Feb	8,608	4,625	13,233	32,947	25,158	2	5,183	55,881	18,795	122	32,150	127,023	24,531	100,749
Mar	8,727	4,662	13,389	33,216	25,265	5	5,932	56,203	19,481	193	31,501	120,520	24,747	95,167
Apr	8,622	4,629	13,251	33,083	21,867	2	6,104	50,466	20,009	164	31,385	137,673 (fa)	21,376	99,024 (fg)(fh)
May	8,598	4,614	13,212	32,923	21,796	2	6,086	50,253	21,662	176	29,780	129,941	20,540	100,867
Jun	8,441	4,735	13,177	33,095	21,470	2	6,833	51,112	22,063	202	20,815	145,185	22,006	104,521
Jul	8,505	4,765	13,270	33,892	21,806	2	6,591	51,348	21,380	205	22,074	146,215	21,670	103,884
Aug	8,435	4,779	13,214	33,664	21,839	2	6,004	50,795	21,244	298	22,470	139,229	20,151	100,139 (fi)
Sep	8,823	4,771	13,593	34,673	24,682 (ev)	2	6,447	51,386	21,290	322	22,138	146,705 (fb)	19,775	99,899
Oct	9,249	4,803	14,052	35,037	25,427	2	6,406	52,338	22,785	407	22,189	148,947	18,053	101,433
Nov	8,884	4,736	13,620	35,258	25,869	2	6,523	49,623	22,017	350	21,719	157,109	16,706	94,705
Dec	9,216	4,745	13,961	34,173	25,743	2	7,448	49,415	21,617	350	23,901	141,134	17,437	92,045 (fj)
2017 Jan	9,309	4,713	14,022	33,744	26,251	3	6,542	49,802	20,757	342	26,508	144,833	17,262	92,318
Feb	9,429	4,487	13,916	33,252	22,421	3	6,747	44,654	22,020	342	25,970	145,280	16,767	104,803
Mar	9,247	4,710	13,957	32,330	23,046	3	7,068	48,654	20,100 (ex)	346	21,137	145,852	16,823	97,733 (fk)
Apr	9,424	4,825	14,249	31,337	22,678	3	6,969	49,035	20,073	320	21,048	151,075	17,760	97,519

Source: Bank of England

12.4d Industrial analysis of monetary financial institutions' lending to UK residents

£ millions

Not seasonally adjusted

Amounts outstanding of facilities granted in all currencies

RPM	Financial intermediation (excluding insurance and pension funds)		Insurance companies & pension funds			Fund management activities	Activities auxiliary to financial intermediation			Total
	of which intragroup activity	Total	Insurance companies	Pension funds	Total		Central clearing counterparties	Other auxiliary activities	Total	
	B7FG	TCBI	B7FL	B7FQ	TCBT	TCBU	B3X7	B3Y5	TCBV	B3Z2
2015 Aug	84,863	416,262	22,994	10,837	33,831	143,270	113,740	15,640	129,380	272,650
Sep	81,924	426,834	21,553	11,464	33,017	146,117	101,803	14,748	116,551	262,667
Oct	80,646	413,875 (ey)(ez)(ff)	19,728	13,282	33,009	149,530 (fm)	94,755 (fs)	14,593	109,349 (fs)	258,879 (fm)(fs)
Nov	74,984	407,468	21,077	13,016	34,092	146,842	100,031 (ft)	17,655 (fz)	117,686	264,528
Dec	72,770	406,650 (ew)(fc)	19,314	12,352	31,666	141,519	95,700	17,692	113,392	254,911
2016 Jan	70,293	411,194 (eu)(fd)	20,723	12,773	33,495	155,912 (fn)	94,430 (fu)	19,004	113,434 (fu)	269,346 (fn)(fu)
Feb	72,519	422,541	22,963	15,067	38,030	170,699	99,561	19,284	118,845	289,544
Mar	68,437	408,232	23,498	14,808	38,307	171,096	90,367	18,932	109,299	280,395
Apr	71,971 (fg)(fh)	421,150 (fa)(fg)(fh)	21,922	12,816	34,737	168,896	90,977 (fv)	13,533 (ga)(gb)	104,510 (fv)(ga)(gb)	273,406 (fv)(ga)(gb)
May	72,837	414,027	23,178	13,502	36,680	178,038 (fo)	96,545	14,009	110,554	288,592 (fo)
Jun	74,880	427,303	25,432	16,839	42,272	192,754	111,794	15,231	127,025	319,779
Jul	73,818	429,066	25,385	17,901	43,286	194,220	107,859	15,478	123,337	317,557
Aug	75,395	415,835 (fi)	27,301	18,246	45,547	197,932	114,475	15,617	130,092	328,024
Sep	74,161	427,318 (ev)(fb)	25,171	18,632	43,803	181,779	109,639	15,461	125,099	306,878
Oct	76,396	433,024	23,282	16,293	39,574	179,067	118,813	14,025	132,837	311,904
Nov	71,219	429,880	22,309	17,855	40,163	177,142	129,755	13,793	143,548	320,690
Dec	69,484	413,265 (fj)	22,620	21,580	44,200	181,132	107,555	13,751	121,306	302,437
2017 Jan	70,107	418,361	22,604	17,909	40,512	180,013	136,409	13,668	150,076	330,089
Feb	75,245	422,260	22,317	18,690	41,006	188,212	146,574 (fw)(fx)	14,578	161,152 (fw)(fx)	349,364 (fw)(fx)
Mar	77,207	413,093 (ex)(fk)	22,953	27,127 (fl)	50,080 (fl)	192,443 (fp)(fq)(fr)	141,123	14,514	155,637	348,080 (fp)(fq)(fr)
Apr	76,765	417,816	24,560	29,431	53,991	189,333	146,738	14,507	161,245	350,578

Source: Bank of England

12.4d Industrial analysis of monetary financial institutions' lending to UK residents

Amounts outstanding of facilities granted in all currencies

Not seasonally adjusted

	Total financial and non-financial businesses	Individuals and individual trusts			Total UK residents
		Lending secured on dwellings inc. bridging finance	Other loans and advances	Total	
RPM	Z94H	TCBX	TCBY	TCBW	TCAA
2015 Aug	1,394,327	1,136,392	199,398	1,335,790	2,730,117
Sep	1,395,435	1,140,256	200,581	1,340,837	2,736,272
Oct	1,377,861 (ey)(ez)(ff)(fm)(fs)	1,144,899	201,346	1,346,245	2,724,106 (ey)(ez)(ff)(fm)(fs)
Nov	1,381,296	1,149,399	202,269	1,351,668	2,732,963 (gi)
Dec	1,373,810 (ed)(ew)(fc)	1,159,673 (gc)(gd)	199,775 (gg)	1,359,448 (gc)(gd)(gg)	2,733,259 (ed)(ew)(fc)(gc)(gd)(gg)
2016 Jan	1,399,484 (eu)(fd)(fn)(fu)	1,160,637	199,838	1,360,475	2,759,959 (eu)(fd)(fn)(fu)
Feb	1,437,898 (eg)(ei)(em)(en)	1,163,318	200,997	1,364,315	2,802,213 (eg)(ei)(em)(en)
Mar	1,411,904	1,170,040	202,130	1,372,171	2,784,075
Apr	1,411,166 (ej)(fa)(fv)	1,178,952 (ge)	202,890	1,381,841 (ge)	2,793,008 (ej)(fa)(fv)(ge)
May	1,423,607 (fo)	1,182,900	203,688	1,386,588	2,810,195 (fo)
Jun	1,485,284	1,189,498	204,788	1,394,287	2,879,570
Jul	1,485,295	1,192,480	205,693	1,398,172	2,883,467
Aug	1,487,641 (fi)	1,194,731	206,951	1,401,682	2,889,323 (fi)
Sep	1,483,464 (ep)(ev)(fb)	1,198,617	206,097	1,404,714	2,888,178 (ep)(ev)(fb)
Oct	1,500,810	1,201,820	206,681	1,408,501	2,909,311
Nov	1,502,076	1,206,662	207,641	1,414,303	2,916,379
Dec	1,474,467 (fj)	1,207,911	207,965	1,415,876	2,890,343 (fj)
2017 Jan	1,516,889	1,209,585	208,372	1,417,957	2,934,845
Feb	1,552,801 (fw)(fx)	1,212,778	208,883	1,421,661	2,974,462 (fw)(fx)
Mar	1,550,074 (ek)(er)	1,219,315	209,987	1,429,302	2,979,376 (ek)(er)
Apr	1,562,935 (eq)(es)(et)	1,220,632	210,664	1,431,296	2,994,231 (eq)(es)(et)

Source: Bank of England

Notes to table

Movements in amounts outstanding can reflect breaks in data series as well as underlying flows. For changes data, users are recommended to refer directly to the appropriate series or data tables. Further explanation can be found at: www.bankofengland.co.uk/statistics/Pages/iadb/notesiadb/Changes_flows_growth_rates.aspx.

(ed)   Due to a change in the reporting population, the amounts outstanding increased by £1bn. This effect has been adjusted out of the flows for December 2015.
(ee)   Due to reporting improvements at one institution, amounts outstanding decreased by £2 billion. This has been adjusted out of the flows for April 2017.
(ef)   Due to loan transfers by one institution, amounts outstanding increased by £1 billion. This amount has been adjusted out of the flows for July 2017.
(eg)   Due to improvements in reporting at one institution, the amounts outstanding increased by £1bn. This effect has been adjusted out of the flows for February 2016.
(eh)   Due to improvements in reporting at one institution, the amounts outstanding decreased by £2bn. This effect has been adjusted out of the flows for March 2016.
(ei)   Due to improvements in reporting at one institution, the amounts outstanding decreased by £1bn. This effect has been adjusted out of the flows for February 2016.
(ej)   Due to improvements in reporting at one institution, the amounts outstanding increased by £1bn. This effect has been adjusted out of the flows for April 2016.
(ek)   Due to changes in the reporting population, amounts outstanding increased by £1bn. This has been adjusted out of flows for March 2017.
(el)   Due to reporting improvements at one institution, amounts outstanding increased by £2 billion. This has been adjusted out of the flows for April 2017.

12.4d Industrial analysis of monetary financial institutions' lending to UK residents

(em) Due to improvements in reporting at one institution the amounts outstanding decreased by £1bn. This effect has been adjusted out of the flows for February 2016.

(en) Due to improvements in reporting at one institution, the amounts outstanding decreased by £1bn. This effect has been adjusted out of the flows for February 2016.

(eo) Due to improvements in reporting at one institution, the amounts outstanding increased by £2bn. This effect has been adjusted out of the flows for March 2016.

(ep) Due to a change in the reporting population, the amounts outstanding decreased by £1bn. This effect has been adjusted out of the flows for September 2016.

(eq) Due to reporting improvements at one institution, amounts outstanding increased by £1 billion. This has been adjusted out of the flows for April 2017.

(er) Due to loan transfers by one institution, amounts outstanding decreased by £1 billion. This amount has been adjusted out of the flows for March 2017.

(es) Due to reporting improvements at one institution, amounts outstanding decreased by £1 billion. This has been adjusted out of the flows for April 2017.

(et) Due to loan transfers by one institution, amounts outstanding increased by £1 billion. This amount has been adjusted out of the flows for April 2017.

(eu) Due to improvements in reporting at one institution, the amounts outstanding decreased by £1bn. This effect has been adjusted out of the flows for January 2016.

(ev) Due to a change in the reporting population, the amounts outstanding increased by £2bn. This effect has been adjusted out of the flows for September 2016.

(ew) Due to a restructuring at one reporting institution, the amounts outstanding increased by £4bn. This effect has been adjusted out of the flows for December 2015.

(ex) Due to reporting improvements at one institution, amounts outstanding decreased by £2bn. This effect has been adjusted out of flows for March 2017.

(ey) Due to improvements in reporting at one institution, the amounts outstanding increased by £1bn. This effect has been adjusted out of the flows for October 2015.

(ez) Due to a change in the reporting population, the amounts outstanding decreased by £1bn. This effect has been adjusted out of the flows for October 2015.

(fa) Due to improvements in reporting at one institution, the amounts outstanding increased by £5bn. This effect has been adjusted out of the flows for April 2016.

(fb) Due to a change in treatment at one institution, the amounts outstanding increased by £2bn. This effect has been adjusted out of the flows for September 2016.

(fc) Due to a restructuring at one reporting institution, the amounts outstanding decreased by £4bn. This effect has been adjusted out of the flows for December 2015.

(fd) Due to improvements in reporting at one institution, the amounts outstanding increased by £1bn. This effect has been adjusted out of the flows for January 2016.

(fe) Due to a change in accounting treatment at one reporting institution, the amounts outstanding decreased by £2bn. This effect has been adjusted out of the flows for June 2017.

(ff) Due to improvements in reporting at one institution, the amounts outstanding decreased by £1bn. This effect has been adjusted out of the flows for October 2015.

(fg) Due to improvements in reporting at one institution, the amounts outstanding increased by £1bn. This effect has been adjusted out of the flows for April 2016.

(fh) Due to improvements in reporting at one institution, the amounts outstanding increased by £4bn. This effect has been adjusted out of the flows for April 2016.

(fi) Due to improvements in reporting at one institution, the amounts outstanding decreased by £4bn. This effect has been adjusted out of the flows for August 2016.

(fj) Due to improvements in reporting at one institution, the amounts outstanding decreased by £2bn. This effect has been adjusted out of the flows for December 2016.

(fk) Due to reporting improvements at one institution, amounts outstanding decreased by £1bn. This effect has been adjusted out of the flows for January 2016.

(fl) Due to reporting improvements at one institution, amounts outstanding decreased by £1bn. This has been adjusted out of flows for March 2017.

(fm) Due to reporting improvements at one institution, amounts outstanding increased by £5bn. This has been adjusted out of flows for March 2017.

(fn) Due to a change in the reporting population, the amounts outstanding decreased by £2bn. This effect has been adjusted out of the flows for October 2015.

(fo) Due to a change in the reporting population, the amounts outstanding increased by £3bn. This effect has been adjusted out of the flows for January 2016.

(fp) Due to improvements in reporting at one institution, the amounts outstanding increased by £1bn. This effect has been adjusted out of the flows for May 2016.

(fq) Due to reporting improvements at one institution, amounts outstanding decreased by £5bn. This has been adjusted out of flows for March 2017.

(fr) Due to reporting improvements at one institution, amounts outstanding increased by £2bn. This has been adjusted out of flows for March 2017.

(fs) Due to reporting improvements at one institution, amounts outstanding increased by £2bn. This has been adjusted out of flows for March 2017.

(ft) Due to a change in the reporting population, the amounts outstanding increased by £3bn. This effect has been adjusted out of the flows for October 2015.

(fu) Due to changes in reporting at one institution, the amounts outstanding decreased by £2bn. This effect has been adjusted out of the flows for November 2015.

(fv) Due to a change in the reporting population, the amounts outstanding decreased by £4bn. This effect has been adjusted out of the flows for January 2016.

(fw) Due to improvements in reporting at one institution, the amounts outstanding increased by £1bn. This effect has been adjusted out of the flows for April 2016.

(fx) Due to improvements in reporting at one institution, the amounts outstanding increased by £2bn. This effect has been adjusted out of the flows for February 2017.

(fy) Due to a transfer of business by one reporting institution, the amounts outstanding increased by £4bn. This effect has been adjusted out of the flows for February 2017.

(fz) Due to changes in reporting at one institution, the amounts outstanding increased by £2bn. This effect has been adjusted out of the flows for July 2017.

(ga) Due to improvements in reporting at one institution, the amounts outstanding increased by £2bn. This effect has been adjusted out of the flows for November 2015.

(gb) Due to improvements in reporting at one institution, the amounts outstanding decreased by £1bn. This effect has been adjusted out of the flows for April 2016.

(gc) Due to a loan transfer by one reporting institution, the amounts outstanding decreased by £4bn. This effect has been adjusted out of the flows for April 2016.

(gd) Due to improvements in reporting at one institution, the amounts outstanding increased by £3bn. This effect has been adjusted out of the flows for December 2015.

(ge) Due to a loan transfer by one reporting institution, the amounts outstanding increased by £5bn. This effect has been adjusted out of the flows for December 2015.

(gf) Due to improvements in reporting at one institution, the amounts outstanding increased by £7bn. This effect has been adjusted out of the flows for November 2015.

(gg) Due to improvements in reporting at one institution, the amounts outstanding decreased by £4bn. This effect has been adjusted out of the flows for April 2016.

(gh) Due to improvements in reporting at one institution, the amounts outstanding decreased by £3bn. This effect has been adjusted out of the flows for July 2017.

(gi) Due to improvements in reporting at one institution, the amounts outstanding decreased by £6bn. This effect has been adjusted out of the flows for December 2015.

(gi) Due to changes in reporting at one institution, the amounts outstanding increased by £7bn. This effect has been adjusted out of the flows for November 2015.

Explanatory notes can be found here: http://www.bankofengland.co.uk/statistics/Pages/iadb/notesiadb/industrial.aspx
Copyright guidance and the related UK Open Government Licence can be viewed here: www.bankofengland.co.uk/Pages/disclaimer.aspx

12.5a Industrial analysis of monetary financial institutions' deposits from UK residents

£ millions

Amounts outstanding of deposit liabilities (including under repo) in sterling

RPM	Agriculture, hunting and forestry	Fishing	Mining and quarrying	Food, beverages and tobacco	Textiles, wearing apparel and leather	Pulp, paper, and printing	Chemicals, pharmaceuticals, rubber and plastics	Manufacturing Non-metallic mineral products and metals	Machinery, equipment and transport equipment	Electrical, medical and optical equipment	Other manufacturing	Total
	TDCB	TDCC	TDCD	TDCF	TDCG	TDCH	TDCI	TDCJ	TDCK	TDCL	TDCM	TDCE
2015 Aug	5,815	236	6,872 (a)	3,740	1,131	1,343	5,120	5,543	8,642	4,595	4,135	34,250
Sep	5,862	243	8,991	3,954	1,265	1,332	5,520	5,805	8,652	4,656	4,386	35,569
Oct	5,795	234	9,642	4,275	1,264	1,369	5,242	5,822	9,203	4,783	4,337	36,296
Nov	5,840	245	11,127	4,428	1,296	1,466	5,424	5,970	8,694	4,764	4,476	36,518
Dec	6,083	250	9,573	4,154	1,360	1,551	5,399	6,214	10,708	4,738	4,631	38,756
2016 Jan	6,225	239	10,389	4,081	1,355	1,667	5,370	5,826	9,906	4,721	4,466	37,392
Feb	6,201	260	3,508	3,688	1,353	1,640	5,466	5,731	9,960	4,724	4,505	37,068
Mar	6,160	267	3,208	3,828	1,335	1,668	5,361	5,801	10,056	4,523	4,718	37,290
Apr	6,162	259	2,919	3,788	1,316	1,651	4,915	5,815	9,531	4,572	4,670	36,257
May	6,182	263	2,805	3,886	1,349	1,583	5,027	5,944	9,547	4,658	4,682	36,676
Jun	6,236	258	2,887	4,165	1,347	1,648	5,102	6,151	9,978	4,751	4,847	37,989
Jul	6,225	260	3,006	3,788	1,354	1,646	4,832	5,997	9,752	4,636	4,602	36,608
Aug	6,183	293	4,167	3,984	1,351	1,628	5,079	5,979	10,055	4,686	4,772	37,535
Sep	6,227	300	6,303	4,077	1,374	1,681	4,972	6,246	9,832	4,653	4,785	37,621
Oct	6,297	307	5,029	3,930	1,421	1,748	5,272	6,455	9,440	4,815	4,880	37,960
Nov	6,436	335	5,050	4,060	1,432	1,707	5,161	6,401	9,654	4,622	4,974	38,011
Dec	7,216	355	5,090	4,011	1,339	1,778	4,763	6,495	10,166	4,667	5,208	38,426
2017 Jan	7,066	354	4,325	3,904	1,254	1,685	4,642	6,392	9,791	4,666	4,860	37,193
Feb	6,924	368	4,930	3,571	1,183	1,675	4,527	6,127	9,318	4,561	4,732	35,694
Mar	6,873	370	5,291	3,502	1,173	1,736	5,053	6,316	9,972	4,573	5,116	37,442
Apr	6,801	348	4,772	3,567	1,138	1,678	4,867	6,009	9,367	4,807	4,949	36,381

Source: Bank of England

12.5a Industrial analysis of monetary financial institutions' deposits from UK residents

£ millions

Not seasonally adjusted

Amounts outstanding of deposit liabilities (including under repo) in sterling

| | Electricity, gas steam and air conditioning | Electricity, gas and water supply | | | Construction | | | | | | Wholesale and retail trade | | | | Total |
| | | Water collection and sewerage | Waste management related services and remediation activities | Total | Development of buildings | Construction of commercial buildings | Construction of domestic buildings | Civil Engineering | Other construction activities | Total | Wholesale and retail trade and repair of motor vehicles and motorcycles | Wholesale trade, excluding motor vehicles and motor cycles | Retail trade excluding motor vehicles and motor cycles | |
RPM	TDCN	TDCO	BE2M	B3FI	B3FW	B7EK	B3LS	B3JO	B4PS	TDCP	TDCR	TDCS	TDCT	TDCQ
2015 Aug	5,721	2,589	1,532	9,842	7,464	3,790	3,682	5,145	10,768	30,850	5,191	14,274	14,855	34,321
Sep	5,749	2,407	1,625	9,781	7,585	3,772	3,408	5,137	10,888	30,789	5,363	14,590	14,975	34,928
Oct	5,251	2,358	1,550	9,159	7,576	3,733	3,619	5,257	11,305	31,490	5,067	14,849	16,992	36,908
Nov	5,708	2,373	1,560	9,641	7,637	3,820	3,751	5,464	11,487	32,159	5,111	15,218	16,908	37,237
Dec	6,335	2,294	1,578	10,207	7,941	4,049	4,184	5,762	11,735	33,671	5,040	15,554	19,592	40,186
2016 Jan	5,122	2,205	1,509	8,836	7,781	3,795	3,607	5,192	11,214	31,590	5,086	15,314	15,493	35,892
Feb	5,638	2,310	1,502	9,450	7,774	3,860	3,650	5,260	11,037	31,580	5,529	15,277	16,483	37,288
Mar	6,436	2,286	1,733	10,455	8,118	4,046	3,647	5,714	11,181	32,705	5,427	15,344	16,015	36,786
Apr	6,140	2,151	1,522	9,812	7,954	4,045	3,610	5,438	11,386	32,433	5,545	14,665	16,166	36,376
May	6,650	2,344	1,489	10,483	7,885	4,136	3,641	5,403	11,462	32,526	5,648	15,031	17,553	38,232
Jun	6,356	2,472	1,653	10,481	8,216	4,503	4,647	5,655	11,935	34,956	6,207	15,199	16,754	38,159
Jul	6,380	2,076	1,688	10,145	8,144	4,364	4,213	5,539	12,003	34,263	5,851	15,076	16,688	37,615
Aug	5,839	2,021	1,777	9,637	8,138	4,438	4,083	5,783	12,257	34,699	6,215	15,203	17,700	39,118
Sep	5,821	2,284	1,736	9,842	8,273	4,662	4,351	5,580	12,539	35,405	5,904	16,360	16,113	38,377
Oct	6,471	2,397	1,807	10,675	8,291	4,815	4,296	5,754	12,835	35,991	6,131	16,186	15,404	37,721
Nov	6,290	2,427	1,679	10,396	8,150	4,545	4,517	5,905	13,073	36,190	6,101	16,134	17,887	40,122
Dec	6,104	2,643	1,633	10,381	8,616	4,954	5,091	6,303	13,238	38,202	5,921	17,113	20,273	43,307
2017 Jan	6,548	2,738	1,752	11,038	8,842	4,508	4,401	6,205	12,729	36,685	5,732	15,569	17,825	39,126
Feb	6,169	2,434	1,768	10,370	8,412	4,498	4,630	5,990	12,402	35,932	5,915	15,701	17,734	39,350
Mar	7,771	2,105	1,779	11,655	8,947	5,037	4,803	6,560	12,813	38,161	6,442	16,715	16,701	39,858
Apr	7,788	2,130	1,699	11,617	8,899	4,834	4,838	6,665	12,846	38,082	6,232	16,345	15,913	38,490

Source: Bank of England

12.5a Industrial analysis of monetary financial institutions' deposits from UK residents

£ millions

Amounts outstanding of deposit liabilities (including under repo) in sterling

Not seasonally adjusted

| | Accommodation and food service activities | Transport, storage and communication | | | Real estate, professional services and support activities | | | | Public administration and defence | Education | Human health and social work | Recreational, personal and community service activities | | |
		Transportation and storage	Information and communication	Total	Buying, selling and renting of real estate	Professional, scientific and technical activities	Administrative and support services	Total				Recreational, cultural and sporting activities	Personal and community service activities	Total
RPM	TDCU	B5PF	B3NI	TDCV	TDCX	B3ON	B6PK	TDCW	TDDB	TDDC	TDDD	TDDF	TDDE	B3S6
2015 Aug	7,968	12,742	21,892	34,633	39,295	71,390	23,247	133,932	38,481	18,835	19,008	11,272	17,673	28,945
Sep	8,431	13,257	21,954	35,211	42,641	72,227	23,404	138,272	29,504	19,677	18,981	10,998	17,886	28,884
Oct	8,408	14,413	22,180	36,594	41,652	72,358	22,753	136,763	30,092	20,533	19,270	10,793	17,931	28,723
Nov	8,409	13,586	23,195	36,782	41,106	76,425	22,851	140,383	31,109	19,388	19,521	10,604	17,874	28,478
Dec	8,416	12,538	23,719	36,257	42,913	72,009	22,705	137,628	31,112	18,507	19,538	10,635	17,858	28,493
2016 Jan	7,881	13,720	22,843	36,563	41,705	72,505	22,315	136,526	30,361	19,768	19,216	11,138	18,041	29,179
Feb	7,945	13,848	25,630	39,478	40,940	73,319	23,015	137,273	28,983	20,180	19,466	11,181	18,246	29,426
Mar	8,325	14,049	25,820	39,868	44,000	79,880	24,136	148,016	25,512	18,926	19,470	11,104	18,142	29,246
Apr	7,916	13,435	24,415	37,850	42,164	71,673	23,895	137,732	33,459	20,083	19,630	10,996	18,251	29,247
May	8,402	13,882	24,123	38,006	41,576	72,993	24,529	139,098	32,918	22,012	19,884	11,046	18,163	29,209
Jun	8,523	13,801	23,088	36,889	44,837	75,350	25,954	146,142	33,403	21,209	20,177	11,300	18,046	29,347
Jul	8,551	13,239	23,404	36,643	42,963	74,594	26,102	143,660	32,988	20,240	20,377	11,956	18,035	29,991
Aug	9,092	13,180	23,390	36,570	42,503	74,012	26,526	143,040	33,617	19,874	20,392	12,148	17,999	30,147
Sep	8,917	13,513	23,057	36,570	45,181	74,601	26,700	146,481	29,529	20,859	20,363	11,961	17,916	29,877
Oct	9,189	13,178	23,119	36,297	43,097	75,034	26,704	144,835	31,752	22,102	20,410	11,774	18,206	29,980
Nov	9,432	14,287	23,123	37,411	42,741	75,742	26,378	144,862	30,474	20,797	20,928	11,885	18,304	30,189
Dec	8,903	13,378	23,100	36,479	46,050	73,461	26,158	145,669	29,121	19,477	21,246	12,406	18,024	30,430
2017 Jan	8,378	13,192	23,506	36,698	43,820	73,203	26,282	143,305	28,169	20,610	20,855	12,869	18,223	31,092
Feb	8,489	13,874	23,920	37,794	43,619	73,357	26,636	143,612	28,169	20,836	21,123	12,930	18,190	31,120
Mar	8,771	13,763	24,455	38,218	46,472	76,023	27,889	150,384	25,524	19,378	21,162	12,702	18,573	31,275
Apr	9,032	13,887	24,332	38,219	45,350	74,500	27,667	147,517	26,379	20,807	20,965	12,214	18,534	30,748

Source: Bank of England

12.5a Industrial analysis of monetary financial institutions' deposits from UK residents

£ millions | Not seasonally adjusted

Amounts outstanding of deposit liabilities (including under repo) in sterling

	Financial leasing corporations	Non-bank credit grantors excluding credit unions and SPVs	Credit unions	Factoring corporations	Mortgage and housing credit corporations excluding SPVs	Financial intermediation (excluding insurance and pension funds)		Bank holding companies	Securities dealers	SPVs related to securitisation	Other financial intermediaries	of which intragroup activity	Total
						Investment and unit trusts excluding money market mutual funds	Money market mutual funds						
RPM	TDDH	TDDI	TDDJ	TDDK	TDDL	TDDM	TDDN	TDDO	TDDP	B3T5	TDDQ	B3U3	TDDG
2015 Aug	10,715	3,196	1,046	1,130	9,646	17,365	710	17,167	30,473	108,882	66,060 (e)	44,688	266,390 (e)
Sep	10,838	3,460	1,058	873	9,428	17,668	756	10,288	29,099	110,781	66,275	43,927	260,523
Oct	11,062	3,484	1,102	899	9,440	18,151	592	9,345	27,574	110,153	65,644	43,513	257,447
Nov	10,456	3,770	1,041	949	9,569	17,938	770	9,928	28,535	107,148	64,673	43,024	254,777
Dec	9,825	3,749	1,049	948	9,309	18,725	547	10,105	26,853	107,854	67,101	44,576	256,066
2016 Jan	8,967	3,323	1,059	960	9,336	18,644	1,022	10,293	28,556	99,845	65,344	42,707	247,348
Feb	9,026	3,562	1,089	861	9,285	19,842	910	11,512	28,374	100,449 (b)	63,546	41,805	248,455 (b)
Mar	8,987	3,581	1,103	981	8,823	19,704	939	10,565	28,342	98,834	63,699 (f)	42,579	245,557 (f)
Apr	9,067	3,761	1,104	1,052	8,954	17,994	606	10,135	27,202	97,692 (c)	61,397	41,087	238,965 (c)
May	9,110	3,540	1,100	1,033	8,831	18,126	923	9,834	26,129	100,684	60,915	40,703	240,226
Jun	8,560	3,925	1,079	951	8,944	20,220	940	14,472	27,346	100,744	60,509	40,171	247,691
Jul	8,414	3,642	1,068	912	8,796	19,843	1,256	15,243	30,539	95,505	60,737	38,881	245,956
Aug	8,371	3,799	1,078	925	8,037	18,968	553	17,329	28,489	92,642	63,071	40,016	243,263
Sep	8,119	3,837	1,098	1,129	8,618	21,894	502	18,329	30,237	90,901	60,922	38,572	245,587
Oct	8,357	3,987	1,113	942	8,652	19,634	622	17,993	32,421	88,444	60,702	38,817	242,869
Nov	8,153	4,019	1,073	895	8,611	20,200	677	17,084	31,134	89,450	58,613	37,253	239,910
Dec	8,247	3,931	1,049	1,026	7,360	20,324	1,483	18,422	31,874	88,612	58,592	37,173	240,921
2017 Jan	7,900	3,985	1,062	894	7,457	19,541	868	17,141	31,628	82,137	57,942	36,785	230,556
Feb	7,869	3,620	1,063	886	3,559	18,941	1,047	17,122	32,537	77,728 (d)	59,012	37,176	223,384 (d)
Mar	7,866	3,749	1,063	765	7,621	20,435	398	14,602	35,114	78,135	60,350	37,442	230,099
Apr	7,700	3,779	1,084	758	7,232	22,208	648	15,235	32,588	76,705	59,350	37,769	227,287

Source: Bank of England

12.5a Industrial analysis of monetary financial institutions' deposits from UK residents

£ millions

Not seasonally adjusted

Amounts outstanding of deposit liabilities (including under repo) in sterling

	Insurance companies & pension funds			Activities auxiliary to financial intermediation					Total financial and non-financial businesses	Individuals and individual trusts	Total UK residents
	Insurance companies	Pension funds	Total	Fund management activities	Other			Total			
					Central clearing counterparties	Other auxiliary activities	Total				
RPM	B7FI	B3VH	TDDR	TDDS	B7FT	B7FY	TDDT	B3Y8	Z945	TDDU	TDCA
2015 Aug	23,269	23,413	46,681	72,622 (h)	85,089	15,205	100,294	172,917 (h)	889,976 (a)	1,130,038	2,020,013 (a)
Sep	22,838	24,103	46,942	76,067	58,326	15,603	73,929	149,997	862,584	1,131,035	1,993,619
Oct	22,324	23,177	45,501	75,889	64,657	15,199	79,856	155,745	868,599	1,139,888	2,008,487
Nov	22,742	22,971	45,714	74,900	69,361	15,899	85,260	160,159	877,488	1,142,458	2,019,946
Dec	21,628	23,332	44,960	66,949	58,570	15,945	74,514	141,464	861,167	1,151,799	2,012,966
2016 Jan	21,519	25,317	46,835	72,871	60,589	16,514	77,103	149,974	854,213	1,151,007	2,005,221
Feb	21,478	25,279	46,757	77,978	65,712	17,512	83,224	161,202	864,521 (b)	1,156,985 (n)	2,021,506
Mar	23,321	20,627 (g)	43,948 (g)	76,955 (i)	51,431	18,302	69,732	146,687 (i)	852,426 (g)	1,168,353	2,020,779 (g)
Apr	20,973	21,685	42,657	76,988	54,906	17,666	72,572	149,560	841,318 (c)	1,183,479	2,024,797 (c)
May	21,114	21,162	42,277	83,049	59,551	18,264	77,815	160,864	860,064	1,183,071	2,043,135
Jun	23,654	22,278	45,932	85,468	58,251	18,364	76,615	162,083	882,361	1,189,164	2,071,525
Jul	24,314	22,774	47,088	94,051	66,946	18,040	84,986	179,038	892,652	1,197,613	2,090,265
Aug	23,732	20,813	44,544	94,202	84,253	18,929	103,182	197,384	909,555	1,198,428	2,107,983
Sep	27,328	23,785	51,113	88,844	58,209	19,483	77,693	166,537	889,908	1,208,647 (o)	2,098,555 (o)
Oct	24,696	24,766	49,462	92,763 (j)	75,363 (k)	20,469	95,832 (k)	188,594	909,470	1,210,392	2,119,862
Nov	26,320	23,924	50,244	86,709	89,479	20,346	109,825	196,535	917,322	1,211,050 (p)	2,128,372 (p)
Dec	26,297	24,412	50,709	81,879	67,747	20,785	88,532	170,410	896,340	1,219,371	2,115,712
2017 Jan	25,204	26,248	51,452	86,344	94,528	20,264	114,792	201,135	908,036	1,207,752	2,115,788
Feb	24,529	26,638	51,167	88,091	95,776 (l)	18,856	114,633 (l)	202,724 (l)	901,986 (d)(l)	1,213,710	2,115,696 (d)(l)
Mar	26,749	28,541	55,289	86,962	90,887 (m)	20,856	111,743 (m)	198,706 (m)	918,456 (m)	1,223,694	2,142,150 (m)
Apr	23,591	27,929	51,521	90,778	112,001	19,666	131,668	222,446	931,411	1,229,246	2,160,657

Source: Bank of England

12.5a Industrial analysis of monetary financial institutions' deposits from UK residents

Notes to table

Movements in amounts outstanding can reflect breaks in data series as well as underlying flows. For changes data, users are recommended to refer directly to the appropriate series or data tables. www.bankofengland.co.uk/statistics/Pages/iadb/notesiadb/Changes_flows_growth_rates.aspx.

(a) Due to improvements in reporting at one institution, the amounts outstanding decreased by £1bn. This effect has been adjusted out of the flows for August 2015.

(b) Due to improvements in reporting at one institution, the amounts outstanding decreased by £1bn. This effect has been adjusted out of the flows for February 2016.

(c) Due to a loan transfer by one reporting institution, the amounts outstanding increased by £1bn. This effect has been adjusted out of the flows for April 2016.

(d) Due to improvements in reporting at one institution, the amounts outstanding increased by £3bn. This effect has been adjusted out of the flows for February 2017.

(e) Due to improvements in reporting at one institution, the amounts outstanding decreased by £4bn. This effect has been adjusted out of the flows for August 2015.

(f) Due to improvements in reporting at one institution, the amounts outstanding decreased by £2bn. This effect has been adjusted out of the flows for March 2016.

(g) Due to changes in reporting at one institution, the amounts outstanding decreased by £5bn. This effect has been adjusted out of the flows for March 2016.

(h) Due to improvements in reporting at one institution, the amounts outstanding increased by £5bn. This effect has been adjusted out of the flows for August 2015.

(i) Due to improvements in reporting at one institution, the amounts outstanding increased by £2bn. This effect has been adjusted out of the flows for March 2016.

(j) Due to a revision by one reporting institution, this series has been revised downwards by £4bn for October 2016.

(k) Due to a revision by one reporting institution, this series has been revised upwards by £4bn for October 2016.

(l) Due to improvements in reporting at one institution, the amounts outstanding increased by £2bn. This effect has been adjusted out of the flows for February 2017.

(m) Due to reporting improvements at one institution, amounts outstanding increased by £1bn. This has been adjusted out of flows for March 2017.

(n) Due to improvements in reporting at one institution, the amounts outstanding increased by £1bn. This effect has been adjusted out of the flows for February 2016.

(o) Due to a change in the reporting population, the amounts outstanding increased by £1bn. This effect has been adjusted out of the flows for September 2016.

(p) Due to improvements in reporting at one institution, the amounts outstanding decreased by £2bn. This effect has been adjusted out of the flows for November 2016.

Explanatory notes can be found here: http://www.bankofengland.co.uk/statistics/Pages/iadb/notesiadb/industrial.aspx

Copyright guidance and the related UK Open Government Licence can be viewed here: www.bankofengland.co.uk/Pages/disclaimer.aspx.

12.5b Industrial analysis of monetary financial institutions' deposits from UK residents

£ millions

Amounts outstanding of deposit liabilities (including under repo) in all currencies

RPM	Agriculture, hunting and forestry	Fishing	Mining and quarrying	Food, beverages and tobacco	Textiles, wearing apparel and leather	Pulp, paper, and printing	Chemicals, pharmaceuticals, rubber and plastics	Manufacturing Non-metallic mineral products and metals	Machinery, equipment and transport equipment	Electrical, medical and optical equipment	Other manufacturing	Total
	TDAB	TDAC	TDAD	TDAF	TDAG	TDAH	TDAI	TDAJ	TDAK	TDAL	TDAM	TDAE
2015 Aug	5,951	263	21,726	5,142	1,507	1,922	11,104	6,700	11,454	6,788	4,971	49,588
Sep	5,991	266	21,526	6,177	1,637	1,775	11,085	6,840	11,633	6,815	5,180	51,141
Oct	5,926	258	21,062	5,338	1,619	1,820	10,621	6,938	12,123	6,975	5,097	50,531
Nov	5,985	279	24,371	5,321	1,648	1,909	11,086	7,104	11,546	6,904	5,207	50,726
Dec	6,235	265	22,570	4,790	1,704	2,052	10,875	7,391	14,795	7,041	5,382	54,031
2016 Jan	6,384	256	21,783	5,110	1,686	2,153	10,716	7,107	13,086	7,421	5,473	52,751
Feb	6,368	284	11,922	4,645	1,602	2,163	11,163	7,113	13,769	7,193	5,769	53,417
Mar	6,320	289	12,480	4,812	1,602	2,064	10,990	6,990	14,004	6,979	5,916	53,356
Apr	6,345	285	11,713	4,770	1,578	2,112	10,426	6,970	13,209	6,695	6,062	51,822
May	6,352	289	14,406	5,051	1,645	2,168	11,236	7,145	12,610	6,885	5,988	52,727
Jun	6,392	282	14,716	5,378	1,774	2,368	12,007	9,719	14,140	7,068	6,067	58,520
Jul	6,373	286	14,540	4,954	1,756	2,114	10,635	7,398	13,033	6,980	6,284	53,154
Aug	6,323	318	15,370	5,447	1,756	2,084	11,068	7,428	13,344	7,084	5,797	54,007
Sep	6,352	315	21,457	5,484	1,643	1,983	11,024	7,475	13,455	7,235	5,833	54,132
Oct	6,437	323	19,552	4,704	1,725	2,048	11,573	7,728	13,752	7,677	6,031	55,238
Nov	6,609	365	21,657	5,105	1,874	2,115	11,254	7,676	13,818	7,595	5,949	55,386
Dec	7,427	384	22,565	5,106	2,005	2,137	11,609	7,775	15,545	7,863	6,398	58,438
2017 Jan	7,234	380	21,176	4,979	1,720	2,046	11,444	7,699	14,188	7,685	5,974	55,735
Feb	7,089	416	22,134	4,866	1,535	2,028	10,574	7,544	14,630	7,272	5,879	54,329
Mar	7,142	421	21,866	4,798	1,652	2,139	10,872	7,472	15,210	7,457	6,287	55,887
Apr	7,074	400	18,858 (ad)	4,740	1,622	2,073	10,931	7,228	14,529	7,503	5,958	54,585

Source: Bank of England

12.5b Industrial analysis of monetary financial institutions' deposits from UK residents

£ millions

Not seasonally adjusted

Amounts outstanding of deposit liabilities (including under repo) in all currencies

| | | Electricity, gas and water supply | | | Construction | | | | | | Wholesale and retail trade | | | |
	Electricity, gas steam and air conditioning	Water collection and sewerage	Waste management related services and remediation activities	Total	Development of buildings	Construction of commercial buildings	Construction of domestic buildings	Civil Engineering	Other construction activities	Total	Wholesale and retail trade and repair of motor vehicles and motorcycles	Wholesale trade, excluding motor vehicles and motor cycles	Retail trade excluding motor vehicles and motor cycles	Total
RPM	TDAN	TDAO	BE2N	B3FJ	B3FX	B7EL	B3LT	B4PG	B4PT	TDAP	TDAR	TDAS	TDAT	TDAQ
2015 Aug	7,030	2,611	1,703	11,344	7,503	3,833	3,697	5,446	10,941	31,419	5,556	19,578	16,306	41,440
Sep	6,883	2,427	1,771	11,082	7,621	3,801	3,419	5,499	11,044	31,385	5,724	19,764	16,487	41,975
Oct	6,412	2,384	1,679	10,475	7,621	3,763	3,631	5,640	11,469	32,125	5,388	20,283	18,524	44,195
Nov	6,954	2,394	1,692	11,040	7,685	3,856	3,763	5,876	11,662	32,841	5,541	20,849	18,426	44,816
Dec	7,509	2,320	1,685	11,515	7,992	4,105	4,198	6,178	11,915	34,389	5,325	20,498	21,306	47,129
2016 Jan	6,057	2,231	1,627	9,915	7,834	3,846	3,617	5,688	11,403	32,388	5,444	20,135	17,257	42,836
Feb	6,695	2,334	1,656	10,685	7,833	3,916	3,661	5,822	11,238	32,471	5,961	20,605	18,297	44,864
Mar	7,363	2,304	1,909	11,576	8,179	4,121	3,659	6,215	11,388	33,562	5,845	20,514	17,861	44,220
Apr	7,103	2,170	1,691	10,964	8,013	4,085	3,620	5,834	11,549	33,101	5,895	19,905	17,987	43,788
May	7,636	2,362	1,673	11,671	7,939	4,177	3,650	5,807	11,635	33,209	6,158	19,883	19,281	45,322
Jun	7,591	2,496	1,828	11,916	8,277	4,566	4,668	6,082	12,127	35,719	6,748	20,330	18,473	45,552
Jul	7,671	2,094	1,861	11,627	8,198	4,419	4,219	5,963	12,175	34,974	6,337	20,625	18,487	45,449
Aug	7,079	2,047	2,021	11,147	8,190	4,475	4,092	6,266	12,448	35,471	6,636	21,166	19,693	47,495
Sep	7,066	2,303	1,977	11,346	8,330	4,702	4,359	5,980	12,744	36,115	6,346	23,044	17,998	47,388
Oct	7,986	2,419	2,022	12,427	8,356	4,857	4,305	6,269	13,054	36,839	6,789	23,770	17,500	48,059
Nov	7,929	2,446	1,919	12,293	8,219	4,592	4,527	6,474	13,375	37,188	6,736	22,711	20,265	49,711
Dec	7,725	2,662	1,955	12,342	8,690	5,003	5,107	6,752	13,652	39,204	6,479	24,935	22,475	53,889
2017 Jan	7,747	2,758	1,985	12,490	8,905	4,576	4,418	6,656	12,941	37,495	6,249	22,925	20,038	49,212
Feb	7,483	2,454	2,076	12,013	8,475	4,557	4,641	6,424	12,628	36,724	6,444	22,875	19,950	49,270
Mar	9,067	2,129	2,066	13,262	9,005	5,102	4,811	7,066	13,044	39,029	7,104	24,385	18,679	50,168
Apr	8,958	2,147	1,942	13,048	8,954	4,893	4,846	7,099	13,077	38,869	6,808	25,252 (ae)	17,926	49,986 (ae)

Source: Bank of England

12.5b Industrial analysis of monetary financial institutions' deposits from UK residents

£ millions

Not seasonally adjusted

Amounts outstanding of deposit liabilities (including under repo) in all currencies

	Accommodation and food service activities	Transport, storage and communication			Real estate, professional services and support activities				Public administration and defence	Education	Human health and social work	Recreational, personal and community service activities		Total
		Transportation and storage	Information and communication	Total	Buying, selling and renting of real estate	Professional, scientific and technical activities	Administrative and support services	Total				Recreational, cultural and sporting activities	Personal and community service activities	
	RPM	B5PG	B3NJ	TDAV	TDAX	B3TK	B6PL	TDAW	TDBB	TDBC	TDBD	TDBF	TDBE	B3S7
	TDAU													
2015 Aug	8,523	15,951	26,537	42,489	40,073	78,416	27,936	146,425	41,418	19,583	19,786	12,690	18,532	31,222
Sep	8,973	16,310	26,754	43,064	43,570	79,328	28,317	151,214	32,012	20,474	19,782	12,491	18,667	31,158
Oct	8,946	17,210	26,442	43,652	42,486	78,834	27,371	148,691	32,867	21,339	20,076	12,262	18,672	30,934
Nov	8,951	16,722	27,589	44,310	41,955	83,050	26,929	151,934	33,819	20,149	20,326	12,138	18,606	30,744
Dec	8,876	15,679	28,705	44,384	43,804	79,167	26,788	149,758	34,745	19,327	20,371	12,110	18,781	30,891
2016 Jan	8,364	17,166	27,846	45,012	42,621	79,936	26,592	149,148	34,061	20,554	20,053	12,618	18,917	31,536
Feb	8,454	17,254	31,332	48,586	41,771	80,519	27,701	149,992	32,719	20,964	20,250	12,724	19,240	31,964
Mar	8,797	17,120	32,020	49,140	44,780	87,206	29,485	161,471	27,841	19,742	20,279	12,888	19,049	31,937
Apr	8,395	16,280	29,775	46,055	43,007	78,612	29,110	150,728	37,132	20,844	20,445	12,744	19,194	31,938
May	8,822	16,629	29,706	46,335	42,553	79,946	30,173	152,671	35,995	22,788	20,720	12,855	19,091	31,945
Jun	8,970	17,037	30,017	47,054	45,611	82,683	32,442	160,736	36,638	21,976	21,102	13,430	19,001	32,431
Jul	9,266	16,397	30,838	47,235	43,958	82,118	32,185	158,261	37,301	21,059	21,267	13,932	19,005	32,937
Aug	9,882	16,361	29,936	46,297	43,360	81,653	33,103	158,117	37,839	20,743	21,326	13,593	19,004	32,596
Sep	9,755	16,926	29,652	46,578	46,089	82,201	33,195	161,486	32,081	21,842	21,343	13,824	18,918	32,742
Oct	10,150	16,938	31,448	48,386	44,073	83,038	33,119	160,229	34,460	23,149	21,337	13,684	19,231	32,916
Nov	10,398	18,490	30,419	48,909	43,633	83,839	32,075	159,547	33,634	21,746	21,855	13,744	19,248	32,991
Dec	9,630	16,485	30,647	47,132	46,947	82,667	32,112	161,726	32,087	20,592	22,195	14,258	19,052	33,311
2017 Jan	9,013	16,596	31,199	47,794	44,721	82,465	32,054	159,240	31,663	21,637	21,854	14,612	19,222	33,834
Feb	9,160	16,887	31,891	48,779	44,497	82,290	32,192	158,979	31,018	21,835	22,189	14,608	19,202	33,810
Mar	9,388	17,204	32,445	49,649	47,351	84,952	33,848	166,151	27,917	20,375	22,247	14,663	19,646	34,309
Apr	9,718	17,134	31,565	48,699	46,207	83,711	33,482	163,400	30,330	21,769	22,029	14,116	19,565	33,681

Source: Bank of England

12.5b Industrial analysis of monetary financial institutions' deposits from UK residents

£ millions

Amounts outstanding of deposit liabilities (including under repo) in all currencies

RPM	Financial leasing corporations	Non-bank credit grantors excluding credit unions and SPVs	Credit unions	Factoring corporations	Mortgage and housing credit corporations excluding SPVs	Investment and unit trusts excluding money market mutual funds	Money market mutual funds	Bank holding companies	Securities dealers	SPVs related to securitisation	Other financial intermediaries	of which intragroup activity	Total
	TDBH	TDBI	TDBJ	TDBK	TDBL	TDBM	TDBN	TDBO	TDBP	B3T6	TDBQ	B3U4	TDBG
2015 Aug	11,092	3,750	1,047	1,211	9,721	23,966	879	46,268	95,240	110,307	100,251 (an)	71,616	403,730 (an)
Sep	11,239	3,964	1,058	935	9,523	23,849	923	37,965	92,822	112,134	101,810	71,141	396,221
Oct	11,556	3,992	1,102	965	9,522	24,510	861	36,234	89,530	112,272	99,835	70,368	390,381
Nov	11,257	4,261	1,042	1,029	9,631	25,051	1,007	37,209	89,715	109,480	100,124	70,437	389,805
Dec	10,530	4,010	1,049	1,083	9,400	25,261	727	42,879	83,844	109,943	102,697	72,446	391,424
2016 Jan	9,585	3,616	1,060	1,031	9,458	25,802	1,184	49,779	93,021	102,005	102,266	71,114	398,806
Feb	9,753	3,872	1,090	942	9,437	27,185	972	51,441	93,430	102,719 (ak)	101,482	71,948	402,325 (ak)
Mar	9,678	3,886	1,104	1,055	8,969	26,194	1,069	61,005	90,293	100,951	99,342 (ao)	70,926	403,546 (ao)
Apr	9,756	4,260	1,105	1,144	9,097	25,571	773	54,987	93,058 (ah)	99,800 (al)	95,885	67,932 (aq)	395,437 (ah)(al)(aq)
May	9,705	3,861	1,101	1,122	8,950	25,175	1,038	58,304	86,144	102,703	95,377	67,638	393,479
Jun	9,169	4,301	1,080	1,021	9,109	28,315	1,115	63,499	91,842	102,752	99,164	70,343	411,367
Jul	9,160	4,167	1,069	986	8,950	27,530	1,614	73,286	97,258	98,229	98,459	68,484	420,710
Aug	9,060	4,215	1,079	1,025	8,251	26,710	760	84,961	90,317	95,023	102,584	71,512	423,984
Sep	8,823	4,206	1,099	1,178	8,907	29,577	550	87,782	100,571 (ai)	93,776	100,037	69,595	436,506 (ai)
Oct	9,447	4,376	1,114	993	8,969	27,992	678	90,970	102,289	98,355	97,767	66,386	442,949
Nov	8,980	4,411	1,074	951	8,874	27,840	748	87,726	109,995	98,498	95,162	64,232	444,259
Dec	8,926	4,359	1,054	1,137	7,556	28,388	1,639	87,846	92,642 (aj)	97,430	91,925	61,253	422,900 (aj)
2017 Jan	8,520	4,413	1,062	944	7,648	27,286	898	97,072 (ag)	99,934	90,715	90,697	60,955	429,190 (ag)
Feb	8,278	4,075	1,063	942	4,048	26,805	1,066	98,909	92,825	86,365 (am)	94,261 (ap)	62,919 (ap)	418,637 (am)(ap)
Mar	8,254	4,135	1,063	870	8,122	29,035	418	89,221	96,233	87,356	94,401	63,427	419,110
Apr	8,025	4,120	1,084	943	7,681	30,613	684	87,521	96,984	85,593	96,443	66,999	419,691

Financial intermediation (excluding insurance and pension funds)

Source: Bank of England

12.5b Industrial analysis of monetary financial institutions' deposits from UK residents

£ millions Not seasonally adjusted

Amounts outstanding of deposit liabilities (including under repo) in all currencies

RPM	Insurance companies & pension funds			Activities auxiliary to financial intermediation					Total financial and non-financial businesses	Individuals and individuals trusts	Total UK residents
	Insurance companies	Pension funds	Total	Fund management activities	Other			Total			
					Central clearing counterparties	Other auxiliary activities	Total				
	B3V2	B7FO	TDBR	TDBS	B7FU	B7FZ	TDBT	B5H5	Z8ZX	TDBU	TDAA
2015 Aug	29,685	27,954	57,640	147,689 (as)	144,440	23,257	167,698	315,387 (as)	1,247,936	1,136,252	2,384,187
Sep	29,109	28,205	57,314	156,076	119,320	24,325	143,646	299,722	1,223,300	1,137,214	2,360,514
Oct	28,829	27,484	56,313	161,118	119,659	23,705	143,365	304,483	1,222,255	1,145,947	2,368,201
Nov	30,006	27,007	57,013	154,119	127,764	25,204	152,968	307,087	1,234,196	1,148,704	2,382,900
Dec	28,902	27,445	56,347	139,452	121,444	25,003	146,448	285,900	1,218,155	1,158,155	2,376,310
2016 Jan	29,208	29,451	58,659	153,437	127,205	26,213	153,418	306,855	1,239,361	1,157,062	2,396,423
Feb	28,925	30,066	58,991	162,933	135,008	27,851	162,860	325,792	1,260,047 (ak)	1,162,923 (bb)	2,422,970
Mar	30,218	24,482 (ar)	54,700 (ar)	159,546 (at)	120,337	28,874	149,210	308,756 (at)	1,248,013 (ar)	1,174,327	2,422,340 (ar)
Apr	28,038	26,564	54,602	162,821	122,689	27,853	150,542	313,363	1,236,957 (ah)(al)(aq)	1,189,615	2,426,572 (ah)(al)(aq)
May	28,843	25,247	54,089	168,929	126,645	28,854	155,499	324,428	1,255,249	1,189,373	2,444,623
Jun	31,190	26,905	58,095	178,535	136,880	29,963	166,844	345,378	1,316,844	1,195,795	2,512,638
Jul	32,452	27,163	59,614	188,679	147,501	29,597	177,098	365,777	1,339,830	1,204,337	2,544,167
Aug	31,902	25,347	57,249	191,104	165,566	30,536	196,102	387,206	1,365,371	1,205,199	2,570,570
Sep	35,305	29,124	64,429	186,301	133,809	31,573	165,382	351,683	1,355,549 (ai)	1,215,627 (bc)	2,571,176 (ai)(bc)
Oct	34,268	30,806	65,074	190,781 (au)	152,317 (aw)	31,449	183,765 (aw)	374,546	1,392,071	1,217,645	2,609,715
Nov	34,639	29,283	63,923	181,348	167,885	31,685	199,570	380,917	1,401,388	1,218,291 (bd)	2,619,679 (bd)
Dec	34,272	29,893	64,164	178,128	138,410	31,682	170,091	348,220	1,356,208 (aj)	1,226,995	2,583,203 (aj)
2017 Jan	33,530	31,106	64,637	183,825	174,364	31,736	206,100	389,926	1,392,510 (ag)	1,215,497	2,608,007 (ag)
Feb	32,788	31,453	64,241	200,346	192,734 (ax)(ay)	31,129	223,862 (ax)(ay)	424,208 (ax)(ay)	1,414,830 (am)(ap)(ax)(ay)	1,221,710	2,636,540 (am)(ap)(ax)(ay)
Mar	34,838	33,673	68,511	203,155	172,233 (az)	33,262	205,495 (az)	408,650 (az)	1,414,081 (az)	1,231,928	2,646,009 (az)
Apr	32,206	33,362	65,568	204,287	192,878	32,382	225,260	429,547	1,427,251	1,237,522	2,664,773

Source: Bank of England

12.5b Industrial analysis of monetary financial institutions' deposits from UK residents

Notes to table

Movements in amounts outstanding can reflect breaks in data series as well as underlying flows. For changes data, users are recommended to refer directly to the appropriate series or data tables. www.bankofengland.co.uk/statistics/Pages/iadb/notesiadb/Changes_flows_growth_rates.aspx.

(ad) Due to reporting improvements at one institution, amounts outstanding decreased by £2 billion. This has been adjusted out of the flows for April 2017.

(ae) Due to reporting improvements at one institution, amounts outstanding increased by £2 billion. This has been adjusted out of the flows for April 2017.

(af) Due to a transfer of business by one reporting institution, the amounts outstanding increased by £1bn. This effect has been adjusted out of the flows for July 2017.

(ag) Due to improvements in reporting at one institution, the amounts outstanding increased by £8bn. This effect has been adjusted out of the flows for January 2017.

(ah) Due to improvements in reporting at one institution, the amounts outstanding decreased by £1bn. This effect has been adjusted out of the flows for April 2016.

(ai) Due to a change in treatment at one institution, the amounts outstanding increased by £2bn. This effect has been adjusted out of the flows for September 2016.

(aj) Due to improvements in reporting at one institution, the amounts outstanding decreased by £3bn. This effect has been adjusted out of the flows for December 2016.

(ak) Due to improvements in reporting at one institution, the amounts outstanding decreased by £1bn. This effect has been adjusted out of the flows for February 2016.

(al) Due to a loan transfer by one reporting institution, the amounts outstanding increased by £1bn. This effect has been adjusted out of the flows for April 2016.

(am) Due to improvements in reporting at one institution, the amounts outstanding increased by £3bn. This effect has been adjusted out of the flows for February 2017.

(an) Due to improvements in reporting at one institution, the amounts outstanding decreased by £4bn. This effect has been adjusted out of the flows for August 2015.

(ao) Due to improvements in reporting at one institution, the amounts outstanding decreased by £2bn. This effect has been adjusted out of the flows for March 2016.

(ap) Due to improvements in reporting at one institution, the amounts outstanding decreased by £1bn. This effect has been adjusted out of the flows for February 2017.

(aq) Due to improvements in reporting at one institution, the amounts outstanding decreased by £2bn. This effect has been adjusted out of the flows for April 2016.

(ar) Due to changes in reporting at one institution, the amounts outstanding decreased by £5bn. This effect has been adjusted out of the flows for March 2016.

(as) Due to improvements in reporting at one institution, the amounts outstanding increased by £5bn. This effect has been adjusted out of the flows for August 2015.

(at) Due to improvements in reporting at one institution, the amounts outstanding increased by £2bn. This effect has been adjusted out of the flows for March 2016.

(au) Due to a revision by one reporting institution, this series has been revised downwards by £4bn for October 2016.

(av) Due to a transfer of business by one reporting institution, the amounts outstanding increased by £1bn. This effect has been adjusted out of the flows for July 2017.

(aw) Due to a revision by one reporting institution, this series has been revised upwards by £4bn for October 2016.

(ax) Due to improvements in reporting at one institution, the amounts outstanding increased by £2bn. This effect has been adjusted out of the flows for February 2017.

(ay) Due to improvements in reporting at one institution, the amounts outstanding increased by £4bn. This effect has been adjusted out of the flows for February 2017.

(az) Due to reporting improvements at one institution, amounts outstanding increased by £1bn. This has been adjusted out of flows for March 2017.

(ba) Due to a transfer of business by one reporting institution, the amounts outstanding increased by £6bn. This effect has been adjusted out of the flows for July 2017.

(bb) Due to improvements in reporting at one institution, the amounts outstanding increased by £1bn. This effect has been adjusted out of the flows for February 2016.

(bc) Due to a change in the reporting population, the amounts outstanding increased by £1bn. This effect has been adjusted out of the flows for September 2016.

(bd) Due to improvements in reporting at one institution, the amounts outstanding decreased by £2bn. This effect has been adjusted out of the flows for November 2016.

Explanatory notes can be found here: http://www.bankofengland.co.uk/statistics/Pages/iadb/notesiadb/industrial.aspx

Copyright guidance and the related UK Open Government Licence can be viewed here: www.bankofengland.co.uk/Pages/disclaimer.aspx.

12.6a Components of M4

£ millions   Seasonally adjusted

Amounts outstanding

		Retail deposits and cash in M4			Wholesale deposits in M4		M4	M3
		Deposits	Notes and coin	Total	Deposits	of which repos		(estimate of EMU aggregate for the UK)
LPM		**B3SF**	**VQJO**	**VQWK (a)**	**VRGP**	**VZZQ**	**AUYN**	**VWYZ**
2015 Aug		1,482,180	65,295	**1,547,475**	559,707	92,098	**2,117,400**	**2,378,414**
Sep		1,489,207	65,716	**1,554,923**	539,540	82,655	**2,094,548**	**2,373,366**
Oct		1,500,458	65,791	**1,566,248**	540,170	77,081	**2,107,864**	**2,382,152**
Nov		1,505,731	66,232	**1,571,964**	538,317	79,261	**2,121,853**	**2,377,554**
Dec		1,514,730	66,817	**1,581,547**	535,318	79,444	**2,117,127**	**2,401,885**
2016 Jan		1,522,351	67,031	**1,589,382**	531,487	74,829	**2,121,424**	**2,421,548**
Feb		1,532,748	67,705	**1,600,453**	540,034	75,778	**2,141,414**	**2,443,245**
Mar		1,487,564 (b)	68,024	**1,555,588 (b)**	579,329 (d)(e)	74,845	**2,127,222 (e)**	**2,450,329**
Apr		1,496,666	68,782	**1,565,448**	567,359	73,341	**2,124,480**	**2,440,989**
May		1,503,493	69,502	**1,572,995**	581,197	77,600	**2,151,488**	**2,454,405**
Jun		1,514,422	69,705	**1,584,126**	603,229 (f)	80,582	**2,181,264 (f)**	**2,536,219 (h)**
Jul		1,528,075	69,865	**1,597,940**	611,415	87,859	**2,210,442**	**2,563,011**
Aug		1,534,555	71,034	**1,605,590**	616,095	93,634	**2,235,463**	**2,588,747**
Sep		1,544,929	71,202	**1,616,132**	611,401	87,796	**2,225,093**	**2,605,501**
Oct		1,549,974	71,982	**1,621,955**	623,376	99,289	**2,250,976**	**2,640,027**
Nov		1,552,151	72,346	**1,624,497**	625,648	112,821	**2,260,972**	**2,636,981**
Dec		1,557,469	72,143	**1,629,611**	620,596	103,685	**2,248,868**	**2,641,111**
2017 Jan		1,558,669	73,523	**1,632,192**	636,058	122,457	**2,270,907**	**2,661,279**
Feb		1,557,563	73,484	**1,631,046**	637,534 (g)	121,606	**2,268,889 (g)**	**2,688,298 (g)(i)**
Mar		1,568,879	73,608	**1,642,487**	651,794	129,926	**2,280,317**	**2,706,990**
Apr		1,574,217	73,505	**1,647,721**	670,366	139,364	**2,309,233**	**2,722,997**

Notes to table

Source: Bank of England

Movements in amounts outstanding can reflect breaks in data series as well as underlying flows. For changes and growth rates data, users are recommended to refer directly to the appropriate series or data tables. Further details can be found at www.bankofengland.co.uk/statistics/Pages/iadb/notesiadb/Changes_flows_growth_rates.aspx

(a) A minor change was made to the definition of Retail M4 in October 2007. From October data onwards, non-interest-bearing bank deposits are only included in Retail M4 when reporters identify them explicitly as being taken from retail sources. There was also a change to the reporting population in October 2007. Together these led to a break in the amount outstanding of Retail M4 in October 2007. The effect of this has been removed from the flows data.

(b) Due to improvements in reporting at one institution, the amounts outstanding decreased by £52bn. This effect has been adjusted out of the flows for March 2016.

(c) In order to bring reporting in line with the National Accounts, English housing associations were reclassified from PNFCs to public corporations with effect from July 2017 data. The amounts outstanding decreased by £3bn. This effect has been adjusted out of the flows for July 2017.

(d) Due to improvements in reporting at one institution, the amounts outstanding increased by £52bn. This effect has been adjusted out of the flows for March 2016.

(e) Due to changes in reporting at one institution, the amounts outstanding decreased by £5bn. This effect has been adjusted out of the flows for March 2016.

(f) Due to improvements in reporting at one institution, the amounts outstanding increased by £6bn. This effect has been adjusted out of the flows for June 2016.

(g) Due to improvements in reporting at one institution, the amounts outstanding increased by £3bn. This effect has been adjusted out of the flows for February 2017.

(h) Due to improvements in reporting at one institution, the amounts outstanding increased by £9bn. This effect has been adjusted out of the flows for June 2016.

(i) Due to improvements in reporting at one institution, the amounts outstanding increased by £4bn. This effect has been adjusted out of the flows for February 2017.

(j) Due to a transfer of business by one reporting institution, the amounts outstanding increased by £6bn. This effect has been adjusted out of the flows for July 2017.

Explanatory notes can be found here: http://www.bankofengland.co.uk/statistics/Pages/iadb/notesiadb/m4.aspx

Copyright guidance and the related UK Open Government Licence can be viewed here: www.bankofengland.co.uk/Pages/disclaimer.aspx.

12.6b Components of M4

£ millions Not seasonally adjusted

Changes

LPM	Retail deposits and cash in M4					Wholesale deposits in M4		M4	M3
	Deposits			Notes and	Total	Deposits	of which		(estimate of
	Total	of which:		coin			repos		EMU aggregate
		Private non-financial corporations	Household sector						for the UK)
	VRLW	Z599	Z59A	VQLU	VQZA	VRLR	VWDN	AUZI	VWXK
2015 Aug	2,813	-1,746	4,783	649	3,462	-14,614	2,433	-11,151	-778
Sep	11,979	6,492	1,726	-836	11,143	-31,171	-24,124	-20,027	-19,738
Oct	8,748	677	9,125	1,232	9,980	5,717	4,186	15,697	16,073
Nov	6,782	3,797	1,978	873	7,656	3,375	4,708	11,030	14,871
Dec	14,750	4,095	8,768	754	15,504	-19,438	-12,053	-3,934	-15,451
2016 Jan	-10,121	-7,372	-1,399	-889	-11,009	236	2,491	-10,773	4,406
Feb	11,877	528	4,168	276	12,153	7,726	2,704	19,880	20,985
Mar	22,444	7,658	11,061	605	23,049	-12,840	-7,892	10,209	14,010
Apr	4,036	-8,035	15,465	1,188	5,224	-10,169	3,297	-4,945	2,692
May	6,085	3,429	27	-13	6,071	17,305	4,155	23,377	26,568
Jun	15,544	8,271	5,914	374	15,918	16,882	-1,396	32,800	38,732
Jul	6,313	-2,295	6,774	1,663	7,976	14,014	14,004	21,990	27,233
Aug	5,022	3,055	-56	-428	4,594	12,460	8,877	17,054	18,014
Sep	15,678	5,210	9,581	1,075	16,752	-17,240	-16,919	-488	-445
Oct	2,693	90	1,909	921	3,614	17,662	19,384	21,276	15,257
Nov	4,901	1,504	940	292	5,193	6,063	14,388	11,256	28,990
Dec	11,475	3,197	8,135	1,621	13,096	-20,902	-20,844	-7,806	-28,151
2017 Jan	-18,116	-5,853	-10,767	-2,054	-20,170	21,120	26,351	950	18,526
Feb	3,228	-622	5,316	187	3,415	-4,406	-1,031	-991	26,260
Mar	22,311	8,180	8,157	890	23,201	6,871	-166	30,072	17,855
Apr	3,399	-1,447	7,788	939	4,338	21,506	15,039	25,843	33,567

Notes to table   Source: Bank of England

Explanatory notes can be found here: http://www.bankofengland.co.uk/statistics/Pages/iadb/notesiadb/m4.aspx

Copyright guidance and the related UK Open Government Licence can be viewed here: www.bankofengland.co.uk/Pages/disclaimer.aspx.

12.7 Counterparts to changes in M4: alternative presentation

£ millions

Changes

	Public sector net cash requirement (PSNCR)		M4 private sector net purchases (-) of Central Government debt						M4 private sector net purchases of other public sector debt			
		Gilts	Sterling treasury bills	Tax instruments	National Savings	Other	Total	Local government debt (-)	Public corporatio debt (-)	Other public sector purchases of M4 private sector debt (+)	Total
LPM	ABEN (f)	AVBY	VQLK	VQLG	VQLJ	VQLI	RCMD	VQLL	VQLO	VQLQ	AVBV
2015 Aug	1,344	-3,137	-938	-20	-728	6,008	1,185	-74	-	105	31
Sep	20,561	5,742	-2,838	36	-662	-23,766	-21,489	39	-	99	138
Oct	-2,378	6,118	3,646	-20	-940	12,304	21,107	162	-	331	493
Nov	9,518	11,101	-4,593	-5	-655	-591	5,257	-20	-	-213	-233
Dec	21,186	-13,552	-6,959	-61	-710	-4,945	-26,227	122	-	-776	-654
2016 Jan	-21,121	7,316	2,722	-17	107	-2,415	7,714	59	-	455	514
Feb	1,821	-6,781	2,880	241	-690	3,134	-1,216	311	-	-634	-323
Mar	23,519	346	-3,901	19	-571	-5,583	-9,691	503	-	-1,662	-1,159
Apr	-1,435	-11,782	5,328	-47	-1,004	1,564	-5,941	-443	-	1,884	1,441
May	8,268	-13,912	84	-65	957	3,162	-9,774	-31	-	-1	-32
Jun	18,150	-3,062	-6,804	-67	319	-3,740	-13,354	-177	-	1,207	1,030
Jul	2,253	-11,033	473	-85	-322	6,721	-4,246	-165	-	752	587
Aug	4,807	13,033	-12,305	44	-719	8,017	8,069	119	-	-311	-192
Sep	22,165	36,134	-5,454	-81	-977	-21,092	8,530	-11	-	217	206
Oct	-4,689	16,896	1,626	-67	-1,745	8,041	24,752	182	-	321	503
Nov	10,245	14,582	1,261	-181	-2,257	1,026	14,431	-192	-	-441	-633
Dec	21,608	-7,787	-4,737	-62	-2,063	-5,816	-20,464	9	-	-371	-362
2017 Jan	-27,125	2,893	6,913	-18	-1,688	9,668	17,767	-105	-	353	248
Feb	-3,204	-9,636	5,500	179	-1,551	4,608	-899	369	-	-1,200	-831
Mar	22,477	-5,603	6,902	72	-599	-11,268	-10,496	576	-	-1,946	-1,370
Apr	-17,578	-6,961	12,343	-74	-884	10,135	14,559	-444	-	1,532	1,088

£ millions

Changes

	Purchases of public sector net debt (-)	External and foreign currency finance of public sector				Public sector contribution	M4 lending			
		Non-residents' purchases of gilts (-)	Non-residents' purchases of £TBs (-)	Other	Total		Loans	of which reverse repos	Investments	Total
LPM	VQLN	VQCZ	VRME	VQOC	VQDC	VWZL (g)	Z5MB	VWDP	VYAP (h)	BF37 (i)(j)
2015 Aug	1,216	4,136	-612	1,081	4,605	7,165	6,649	6,712	-9,045	-2,396
Sep	-21,351	3,169	43	-3,947	-735	-1,525	374	-4,909	-296	79
Oct	21,600	-18,252	-396	2,488	-16,161	3,061	-5,001	-8,817	1,418	-3,583
Nov	5,024	-12,986	-1,702	2,301	-12,387	2,156	7,221	6,512	-958	6,263
Dec	-26,881	1,688	-318	-1,479	-109	-5,804	-1,437	-2,838	2,130	693
2016 Jan	8,228	6,273	-750	1,348	6,871	-6,022	8,092	-2,722	-1,468	6,624
Feb	-1,539	3,029	1,320	3,426	7,776	8,058	17,447	5,321	-39	17,408
Mar	-10,850	-7,811	189	-2,032	-9,654	3,014	8,566	2,289	-485	8,081
Apr	-4,500	-249	-75	-989	-1,313	-7,248	-14,454	-1,756	-565	-15,018
May	-9,806	-3,748	-32	1,993	-1,787	-3,326	14,988	15,064	-244	14,745
Jun	-12,323	-8,140	-842	1,081	-7,901	-2,075	21,105	11,484	849	21,954
Jul	-3,659	4,403	-870	1,201	4,734	3,327	7,536	-2,639	-4,573	2,964
Aug	7,877	-1,793	-117	3,864	1,955	14,638	8,521	-411	-3,839	4,682
Sep	8,736	-13,272	-1,996	-5,011	-20,279	10,623	6,893	4,696	639	7,532
Oct	25,254	-10,515	3,272	3,437	-3,805	16,760	4,432	5,379	-1,722 (k)	2,710
Nov	13,797	-15,577	479	1,582	-13,516	10,526	10,251	16,789	3,488	13,739
Dec	-20,827	2,970	2,470	-7	5,432	6,214	1,001	-6,051	-942	59
2017 Jan	18,015	7,574	815	-2,887	5,502	-3,608	11,269	6,372	29,824	41,093
Feb	-1,730	-758	2,142	3,774	5,159	225	-1,022	-3,805	-3,716	-4,738
Mar	-11,867	-218	1,522	-15	1,288	11,899	19,902	14,306	-1,009	18,893
Apr	15,648	-1,949	547	630	-772	-2,703	5,714	-381	6,068	11,782

Source: Bank of England

12.7 Counterparts to changes in M4: alternative presentation

£ millions   Not seasonally adjusted

Changes

	External and foreign currency flows			Total	Net	M4
	Net sterling deposits from non-residents (-)	Net foreign currency liabilities (-)	Total	external counterparts	non-deposit £ liabilities (-)	
LPM	B69P	B72P	AVBW	VQLP	VWZV	AUZI
2015 Aug	-2,480	15,368	12,889	17,493	-28,809	-11,151
Sep	-16,796	9,218	-7,579	-8,313	-11,003	-20,027
Oct	16,704	-22,518	-5,814	-21,974	22,033	15,697
Nov	-6,147	-2,276	-8,423	-20,810	11,035	11,030
Dec	-18,214	12,049	-6,165	-6,274	7,343	-3,934
2016 Jan	3,175	-3,236	-61	6,810	-11,314	-10,773
Feb	19,776	-17,344	2,431	10,207	-8,018	19,880
Mar	-13,563	-45,943	-59,506	-69,160	58,619	10,209
Apr	7,571	-13,716	-6,145	-7,458	23,466	-4,945
May	19,451	-4,610	14,841	13,054	-2,883	23,377
Jun	-21,420	84,966	63,546	55,645	-50,625	32,800
Jul	6,266	-21,976	-15,710	-10,976	31,409	21,990
Aug	4,393	-16,223	-11,830	-9,876	9,563	17,054
Sep	6,604	-22,610	-16,005	-36,284	-2,637	-488
Oct	-13,510	55,417	41,907	38,102	-40,101	21,276
Nov	-1,093	-33,134	-34,227	-47,743	21,217	11,256
Dec	9,024	-10,030	-1,005	4,427	-13,074	-7,806
2017 Jan	5,397	-20,642	-15,245	-9,743	-21,290	950
Feb	-2,226	45,416	43,190	48,348	-39,667	-991
Mar	-4,929	-35,790	-40,718	-39,430	39,999	30,072
Apr	15,735	-37,920	-22,185	-22,958	38,949	25,843

Source: Bank of England

Notes to table

(f) This estimate of the Public Sector Net Cash Requirement may differ from the headline measure published by the Office for National Statistics (ONS). The Bank of England's measure is maintained to ensure ensure the "Alternative Count Counterparts" analysis continues to balance. More details on this can can be found in article www.bankofengland.co.uk/statistics/Documents/ms/articles/art2may09.pdf.

(g) Net sterling lending to the public sector includes holdings of coin. Coin is a liability of Central Government and therefore outside of the MFIs' consolidated balance sheet. Holdings of coin are a component of M4 and are therefore included here in order to reconcile the counterparts.

(h) This series includes purchases of bonds made as part of the Bank of England's Corporate Bond Purchase Scheme. Data on Central Bank holdings of securities can be found in Bankstats Table B2.2. For further information on the Bank's treatment of securities transactions in credit statistics, see: www.bankofengland.co.uk/statistics/Documents/articles/2015/2may.pdf.

(i) Please note that the compilation and descriptions of some credit series have changed from publication of April 2015 data, as described in Bankstats, April 2015, 'Changes to the treatment of loan transfers and lending to housing associations', available at www.bankofengland.co.uk/statistics/Documents/ms/articles/art1apr15.pdf.

(j) This series includes purchases of bonds made as part of the Bank of England's Corporate Bond Purchase Scheme. Data on Central Bank holdings of securities can be found in Bankstats Table B2.2. For further information on the Bank's treatment of securities transactions in credit statistics, see: www.bankofengland.co.uk/statistics/Documents/articles/2015/2may.pdf.

(k) The data for PNFCs M4 lending in October 2016 take account of a redemption of MFIs UK equity holdings of £4bn, following a merger of a UK corporate with a non-UK entity.

Explanatory notes can be found here: http://www.bankofengland.co.uk/statistics/Pages/iadb/notesiadb/M4_counterparts.aspx

Copyright guidance and the related UK Open Government License can be viewed here:www.bankofengland.co.uk/Pages/disclaimer.aspx.

12.8 Selected retail banks' base rate

Daily average of 4 UK Banks' base rates

Date of change	New rate	Date of change	New rate	Date of change	New rate
09-Jan-86	12.5	17-Sep-92	10.5	05-Jul-07	5.75
19-Mar-86	11.5	18-Sep-92	10	06-Dec-07	5.5
08-Apr-86	11.13	22-Sep-92	9	07-Feb-08	5.25
09-Apr-86	11	16-Oct-92	8.25	10-Apr-08	5
21-Apr-86	10.5	19-Oct-92	8	08-Oct-08	4.5
23-May-86	10.25	13-Nov-92	7	06-Nov-08	3
27-May-86	10	26-Jan-93	6	04-Dec-08	2
14-Oct-86	10.5	23-Nov-93	5.5	08-Jan-09	1.5
15-Oct-86	11	08-Feb-94	5.25	05-Feb-09	1
10-Mar-87	10.5	12-Sep-94	5.75	05-Mar-09	0.5
18-Mar-87	10.25	07-Dec-94	6.25	04-Jan-10	0.5
19-Mar-87	10	02-Feb-95	6.63	31-Dec-10	0.5
28-Apr-87	9.88	03-Feb-95	6.75	04-Jan-11	0.5
29-Apr-87	9.5	13-Dec-95	6.5	30-Dec-11	0.5
11-May-87	9	18-Jan-96	6.25	03-Jan-12	0.5
06-Aug-87	9.25	08-Mar-96	6	31-Dec-12	0.5
07-Aug-87	10	06-Jun-96	5.75	02-Jan-13	0.5
23-Oct-87	9.88	30-Oct-96	5.94	31-Dec-13	0.5
26-Oct-87	9.5	31-Oct-96	6	02-Jan-13	0.5
04-Nov-87	9.38	06-May-97	6.25	31-Dec-13	0.5
05-Nov-87	9	06-Jun-97	6.44	31-Jan-14	0.5
04-Dec-87	8.5	09-Jun-97	6.5	31-Dec-15	0.5
02-Feb-88	9	10-Jul-97	6.75	31-Jan-15	0.5
17-Mar-88	8.63	07-Aug-97	7	31-Dec-15	0.5
18-Mar-88	8.5	06-Nov-97	7.25		
11-Apr-88	8	04-Jun-98	7.5		
17-May-88	7.88	08-Oct-98	7.25		
18-May-88	7.5	06-Nov-98	6.75		
02-Jun-88	7.75	10-Dec-98	6.25		
03-Jun-88	8	07-Jan-99	6		
06-Jun-88	8.25	04-Feb-99	5.5		
07-Jun-88	8.5	08-Apr-99	5.25		
22-Jun-88	8.88	10-Jun-99	5		
23-Jun-88	9	08-Sep-99	5.19		
28-Jun-88	9.25	10-Sep-99	5.25		
29-Jun-88	9.5	04-Nov-99	5.5		
04-Jul-88	9.88	14-Jan-00	5.75		
05-Jul-88	10	10-Feb-00	6		
18-Jul-88	10.38	08-Feb-01	5.75		
19-Jul-88	10.5	05-Apr-01	5.5		
08-Aug-88	10.88	10-May-01	5.25		
09-Aug-88	11	02-Aug-01	5		
25-Aug-88	11.75	18-Sep-01	4.75		
26-Aug-88	12	04-Oct-01	4.5		
25-Nov-88	13	08-Nov-01	4		
24-May-89	14	07-Feb-03	3.75		
05-Oct-89	15	11-Jul-03	3.5		
08-Oct-90	14	06-Nov-03	3.75		
13-Feb-91	13.5	05-Feb-04	4		
27-Feb-91	13	07-May-04	4.25		
22-Mar-91	12.5	10-Jun-04	4.5		
12-Apr-91	12	05-Aug-04	4.75		
24-May-91	11.5	04-Aug-05	4.5		
12-Jul-91	11	03-Aug-06	4.75		
04-Sep-91	10.5	09-Nov-06	5		
05-May-92	10	11-Jan-07	5.25		
16-Sep-92	12	10-May-07	5.5		

Source: Bank of England: 020 7601 3644

1 Data obtained from Barclays Bank, Lloyds/TSB Bank, HSBC Bank and National Westminster Bank whose rates are used to compile this series.

2 Where all the rates did not change on the same day a spread is shown.

12.9 Average three month sterling money market rates

Monthly average rate of discount, 3 month Treasury bills, Sterling IUMAAJNB		Monthly average of Eligible bills discount rate, 3 month (a) IUMAAJND		Monthly average Sterling 3 month mean interbank lending rate IUMAAMIJ		Monthly average of Sterling certificates of deposit interest rate, 3 months, mean offer/bid IUMAVCDA	
31-Jan-00	5.7218	31-Jan-00	5.9	31-Jan-00	6.0578	31-Jan-00	6.0152
29-Feb-00	5.8346	29-Feb-00	6.01	29-Feb-00	6.1492	29-Feb-00	6.0991
31-Mar-00	5.8582	31-Mar-00	5.98	31-Mar-00	6.1458	31-Mar-00	6.0878
30-Apr-00	5.9178	30-Apr-00	6.05	30-Apr-00	6.2129	30-Apr-00	6.1728
31-May-00	5.9501	31-May-00	6.09	31-May-00	6.2289	31-May-00	6.187
30-Jun-00	5.8535	30-Jun-00	6.03	30-Jun-00	6.1423	30-Jun-00	6.0958
31-Jul-00	5.8333	31-Jul-00	5.97	31-Jul-00	6.1146	31-Jul-00	6.0826
31-Aug-00	5.8103	31-Aug-00	5.97	31-Aug-00	6.1365	31-Aug-00	6.0913
30-Sep-00	5.7798	30-Sep-00	5.95	30-Sep-00	6.1191	30-Sep-00	6.0811
31-Oct-00	5.7482	31-Oct-00	5.92	31-Oct-00	6.081	31-Oct-00	6.0485
30-Nov-00	5.6833	30-Nov-00	5.88	30-Nov-00	6.0007	30-Nov-00	5.9794
31-Dec-00	5.6229	31-Dec-00	5.78	31-Dec-00	5.8882	31-Dec-00	5.8512
31-Jan-01	5.4852	31-Jan-01	5.64	31-Jan-01	5.7642	31-Jan-01	5.7338
28-Feb-01	5.4582	28-Feb-01	5.56	28-Feb-01	5.6854	28-Feb-01	5.661
31-Mar-01	5.2286	31-Mar-01	5.37	31-Mar-01	5.473	31-Mar-01	5.4443
30-Apr-01	5.1158	30-Apr-01	5.21	30-Apr-01	5.3323	30-Apr-01	5.3037
31-May-01	4.9765	31-May-01	5.06	31-May-01	5.1727	31-May-01	5.1479
30-Jun-01	4.991	30-Jun-01	5.08	30-Jun-01	5.189	30-Jun-01	5.1621
31-Jul-01	5.0052	31-Jul-01	5.07	31-Jul-01	5.1917	31-Jul-01	5.1673
31-Aug-01	4.7198	31-Aug-01	4.82	31-Aug-01	4.9269	31-Aug-01	4.8991
30-Sep-01	4.4297	30-Sep-01	4.57	30-Sep-01	4.6485	30-Sep-01	4.6223
31-Oct-01	4.1567	31-Oct-01	4.26	31-Oct-01	4.3594	31-Oct-01	4.3304
30-Nov-01	3.7799	30-Nov-01	3.85	30-Nov-01	3.9326	30-Nov-01	3.9084
31-Dec-01	3.8296	31-Dec-01	3.88	31-Dec-01	3.9852	31-Dec-01	3.9568
31-Jan-02	3.8321	31-Jan-02	3.91	31-Jan-02	3.978	31-Jan-02	3.957
28-Feb-02	3.868	28-Feb-02	3.92	28-Feb-02	3.9805	28-Feb-02	3.9618
31-Mar-02	3.9672	31-Mar-02	3.99	31-Mar-02	4.0609	31-Mar-02	4.0413
30-Apr-02	3.9693	30-Apr-02	4.04	30-Apr-02	4.1086	30-Apr-02	4.0802
31-May-02	3.9525	31-May-02	4.01	31-May-02	4.0795	31-May-02	4.0627
30-Jun-02	3.9767	30-Jun-02	4.04	30-Jun-02	4.112	30-Jun-02	4.0889
31-Jul-02	3.8408	31-Jul-02	3.94	31-Jul-02	3.9925	31-Jul-02	3.9704
31-Aug-02	3.7663	31-Aug-02	3.86	31-Aug-02	3.9174	31-Aug-02	3.9005
30-Sep-02	3.7861	30-Sep-02	3.86	30-Sep-02	3.9315	30-Sep-02	3.9057
31-Oct-02	3.7509	31-Oct-02	3.82	31-Oct-02	3.9015	31-Oct-02	3.8802
30-Nov-02	3.8033	30-Nov-02	3.84	30-Nov-02	3.9091	30-Nov-02	3.8876
31-Dec-02	3.8418	31-Dec-02	3.71	31-Dec-02	3.9488	31-Dec-02	3.929
31-Jan-03	3.7993	31-Jan-03	3.87	31-Jan-03	3.9132	31-Jan-03	3.9036
28-Feb-03	3.4993	28-Feb-03	3.65	28-Feb-03	3.6888	28-Feb-03	3.675
31-Mar-03	3.4721	31-Mar-03	3.54	31-Mar-03	3.5838	31-Mar-03	3.5729
30-Apr-03	3.4537	30-Apr-03	3.52	30-Apr-03	3.576	30-Apr-03	3.567
31-May-03	3.4366	31-May-03	3.52	31-May-03	3.5665	31-May-03	3.556
30-Jun-03	3.4724	30-Jun-03	3.45	30-Jun-03	3.5702	30-Jun-03	3.5602
31-Jul-03	3.3119	31-Jul-03	3.39	31-Jul-03	3.42	31-Jul-03	3.4089
31-Aug-03	3.3998	31-Aug-03	3.42	31-Aug-03	3.4518	31-Aug-03	3.4413
30-Sep-03	3.5239	30-Sep-03	3.59	30-Sep-03	3.6311	30-Sep-03	3.6216
31-Oct-03	3.6514	31-Oct-03	3.69	31-Oct-03	3.727	31-Oct-03	3.7204
30-Nov-03	3.808	30-Nov-03	3.88	30-Nov-03	3.9085	30-Nov-03	3.9038
31-Dec-03	3.8298	31-Dec-03	3.9	31-Dec-03	3.949	31-Dec-03	3.9419
31-Jan-04	3.8983	31-Jan-04	3.94	31-Jan-04	3.986	31-Jan-04	3.9771
29-Feb-04	3.9788	29-Feb-04	4.06	29-Feb-04	4.101	29-Feb-04	4.0908
31-Mar-04	4.1025	31-Mar-04	4.19	31-Mar-04	4.2328	31-Mar-04	4.2235
30-Apr-04	4.1862	30-Apr-04	4.28	30-Apr-04	4.3288	30-Apr-04	4.321
31-May-04	4.34	31-May-04	4.42	31-May-04	4.4555	31-May-04	4.4505
30-Jun-04	4.5793	30-Jun-04	4.68	30-Jun-04	4.7305	30-Jun-04	4.7211

12.9 Average three month sterling money market rates

Monthly average rate of discount, 3 month Treasury bills, Sterling IUMAAJNB		Monthly average of Eligible bills discount rate, 3 month (a) IUMAAJND		Monthly average Sterling 3 month mean interbank lending rate IUMAAMIJ		Monthly average of Sterling certificates of deposit interest rate, 3 months, mean offer/bid IUMAVCDA	
31-Jul-04	4.6424	31-Jul-04	4.75	31-Jul-04	4.7859	31-Jul-04	4.7859
31-Aug-04	4.7218	31-Aug-04	4.85	31-Aug-04	4.8938	31-Aug-04	4.8864
30-Sep-04	4.6937	30-Sep-04	4.83	30-Sep-04	4.8743	30-Sep-04	4.868
31-Oct-04	4.679	31-Oct-04	4.79	31-Oct-04	4.8336	31-Oct-04	4.8319
30-Nov-04	4.6578	30-Nov-04	4.78	30-Nov-04	4.8159	30-Nov-04	4.8098
31-Dec-04	4.677	31-Dec-04	4.77	31-Dec-04	4.8057	31-Dec-04	4.7967
31-Jan-05	4.6568	31-Jan-05	4.75	31-Jan-05	4.8045	31-Jan-05	4.801
28-Feb-05	4.6858	28-Feb-05	4.78	28-Feb-05	4.822	28-Feb-05	4.8183
31-Mar-05	4.7691	31-Mar-05	4.88	31-Mar-05	4.9186	31-Mar-05	4.9069
30-Apr-05	4.7047	30-Apr-05	4.84	30-Apr-05	4.8756	30-Apr-05	4.8645
31-May-05	4.6618	31-May-05	4.8	31-May-05	4.8253	31-May-05	4.821
30-Jun-05	4.6175	30-Jun-05	4.76	30-Jun-05	4.7777	30-Jun-05	4.782
31-Jul-05	4.4609	31-Jul-05	4.57	31-Jul-05	4.5948	31-Jul-05	4.5967
31-Aug-05	4.4057	31-Aug-05	4.51	31-Aug-05	4.533	31-Aug-05	4.5336
30-Sep-05	4.4037	30-Sep-05	-	30-Sep-05	4.5359	30-Sep-05	4.5377
31-Oct-05	4.402	31-Oct-05	-	31-Oct-05	4.525	31-Oct-05	4.5202
30-Nov-05	4.4169	30-Nov-05	-	30-Nov-05	4.5614	30-Nov-05	4.5627
31-Dec-05	4.4287	31-Dec-05	-	31-Dec-05	4.587	31-Dec-05	4.5845
31-Jan-06	4.3906	31-Jan-06	-	31-Jan-06	4.5369	31-Jan-06	4.5398
28-Feb-06	4.3839	28-Feb-06	-	28-Feb-06	4.5203	28-Feb-06	4.519
31-Mar-06	4.3956	31-Mar-06	-	31-Mar-06	4.5263	31-Mar-06	4.5257
30-Apr-06	4.4196	30-Apr-06	-	30-Apr-06	4.5725	30-Apr-06	4.5719
31-May-06	4.5012	31-May-06	-	31-May-06	4.6519	31-May-06	4.6467
30-Jun-06	4.5414	30-Jun-06	-	30-Jun-06	4.6927	30-Jun-06	4.692
31-Jul-06	4.534	31-Jul-06	-	31-Jul-06	4.6838	31-Jul-06	4.681
31-Aug-06	4.7544	31-Aug-06	-	31-Aug-06	4.8968	31-Aug-06	4.8945
30-Sep-06	4.8359	30-Sep-06	-	30-Sep-06	4.9819	30-Sep-06	4.9807
31-Oct-06	4.9357	31-Oct-06	-	31-Oct-06	5.0909	31-Oct-06	5.0886
30-Nov-06	5.0095	30-Nov-06	-	30-Nov-06	5.1791	30-Nov-06	5.1782
31-Dec-06	5.0759	31-Dec-06	-	31-Dec-06	5.2453	31-Dec-06	5.2429
31-Jan-07	5.304	31-Jan-07	-	31-Jan-07	5.4545	31-Jan-07	5.4491
28-Feb-07	5.3393	28-Feb-07	-	28-Feb-07	5.5248	28-Feb-07	5.5143
31-Mar-07	5.3274	31-Mar-07	-	31-Mar-07	5.5041	31-Mar-07	5.5177
30-Apr-07	5.4329	30-Apr-07	-	30-Apr-07	5.6058	30-Apr-07	5.6939
31-May-07	5.5516	31-May-07	-	31-May-07	5.7221	31-May-07	5.835
30-Jun-07	5.6702	30-Jun-07	-	30-Jun-07	5.8348	30-Jun-07	5.9379
31-Jul-07	5.7742	31-Jul-07	-	31-Jul-07	5.9789	31-Jul-07	6.1118
31-Aug-07	5.7943	31-Aug-07	-	31-Aug-07	6.3389	31-Aug-07	6.3464
30-Sep-07	5.6896	30-Sep-07	-	30-Sep-07	6.5813	30-Sep-07	6.537
31-Oct-07	5.6058	31-Oct-07	-	31-Oct-07	6.2122	31-Oct-07	6.2052
30-Nov-07	5.4986	30-Nov-07	-	30-Nov-07	6.3564	30-Nov-07	6.3445
31-Dec-07	5.3034	31-Dec-07	-	31-Dec-07	6.3542	31-Dec-07	6.3489
31-Jan-08	5.1215	31-Jan-08	-	31-Jan-08	5.6071	31-Jan-08	5.6059
29-Feb-08	5.0178	29-Feb-08	-	29-Feb-08	5.6083	29-Feb-08	5.6
31-Mar-08	4.8835	31-Mar-08	-	31-Mar-08	5.8555	31-Mar-08	5.8482
30-Apr-08	4.8258	30-Apr-08	-	30-Apr-08	5.8961	30-Apr-08	5.8882
31-May-08	4.9496	31-May-08	-	31-May-08	5.7933	31-May-08	5.787
30-Jun-08	5.1138	30-Jun-08	-	30-Jun-08	5.9002	30-Jun-08	5.8924
31-Jul-08	5.0843	31-Jul-08	-	31-Jul-08	5.803	31-Jul-08	5.7996
31-Aug-08	4.9539	31-Aug-08	-	31-Aug-08	5.7588	31-Aug-08	5.7535
30-Sep-08	4.7425	30-Sep-08	-	30-Sep-08	5.8698	30-Sep-08	5.8573
31-Oct-08	3.6788	31-Oct-08	-	31-Oct-08	6.1772	31-Oct-08	6.1598
30-Nov-08	1.9948	30-Nov-08	-	30-Nov-08	4.3955	30-Nov-08	4.4
31-Dec-08	1.2875	31-Dec-08	-	31-Dec-08	3.2143	31-Dec-08	3.2107

12.9 Average three month sterling money market rates

Monthly average rate of discount, 3 month Treasury bills, Sterling IUMAAJNB		Monthly average of Eligible bills discount rate, 3 month (a) IUMAAJND		Monthly average Sterling 3 month mean interbank lending rate IUMAAMIJ		Monthly average of Sterling certificates of deposit interest rate, 3 months, mean offer/bid IUMAVCDA	
31-Jan-09	0.8945	31-Jan-09	-	31-Jan-09	2.28	31-Jan-09	2.2869
28-Feb-09	0.7177	28-Feb-09	-	28-Feb-09	2.0758	28-Feb-09	2.0625
31-Mar-09	0.6035	31-Mar-09	-	31-Mar-09	1.8273	31-Mar-09	1.7864
30-Apr-09	0.625	30-Apr-09	-	30-Apr-09	1.4838	30-Apr-09	1.425
31-May-09	0.5271	31-May-09	-	31-May-09	1.3026	31-May-09	1.2697
30-Jun-09	0.5037	30-Jun-09	-	30-Jun-09	1.2057	30-Jun-09	1.1386
31-Jul-09	0.4397	31-Jul-09	-	31-Jul-09	1.0293	31-Jul-09	0.9185
31-Aug-09	0.3946	31-Aug-09	-	31-Aug-09	0.7963	31-Aug-09	0.69
30-Sep-09	0.3761	30-Sep-09	-	30-Sep-09	0.617	30-Sep-09	0.5136
31-Oct-09	0.4315	31-Oct-09	-	31-Oct-09	0.5636	31-Oct-09	0.5023
30-Nov-09	0.4459	30-Nov-09	-	30-Nov-09	0.5976	30-Nov-09	0.575
31-Dec-09	0.3587	31-Dec-09	-	31-Dec-09	0.6071	31-Dec-09	0.575
31-Jan-10	0.4874	31-Jan-10	-	31-Jan-10	0.6013	31-Jan-10	0.575
28-Feb-10	0.4878	28-Feb-10	-	28-Feb-10	0.5995	28-Feb-10	0.575
31-Mar-10	0.5109	31-Mar-10	-	31-Mar-10	0.6002	31-Mar-10	0.6011
30-Apr-10	0.5083	30-Apr-10	-	30-Apr-10	0.6	30-Apr-10	0.625
31-May-10	0.4976	31-May-10	-	31-May-10	0.6645	31-May-10	0.6776
30-Jun-10	0.4839	30-Jun-10	-	30-Jun-10	0.7045	30-Jun-10	0.7682
31-Jul-10	0.498	31-Jul-10	-	31-Jul-10	0.75	31-Jul-10	0.775
31-Aug-10	0.4945	31-Aug-10	-	31-Aug-10	0.75	31-Aug-10	0.7655
30-Sep-10	0.4966	30-Sep-10	-	30-Sep-10	0.7545	30-Sep-10	0.725
31-Oct-10	0.5061	31-Oct-10	-	31-Oct-10	0.75	31-Oct-10	0.725
30-Nov-10	0.4935	30-Nov-10	-	30-Nov-10	0.75	30-Nov-10	0.725
31-Dec-10	0.4913	31-Dec-10	-	31-Dec-10	0.755	31-Dec-10	0.7655
31-Jan-11	0.5055	31-Jan-11	-	31-Jan-11	0.7785	31-Jan-11	0.825
28-Feb-11	0.5363	28-Feb-11	-	28-Feb-11	0.775	28-Feb-11	0.825
31-Mar-11	0.5603	31-Mar-11	-	31-Mar-11	0.7811	31-Mar-11	0.8315
30-Apr-11	0.5676	30-Apr-11	-	30-Apr-11	0.8	30-Apr-11	0.875
31-May-11	0.5265	31-May-11	-	31-May-11	0.8	31-May-11	0.875
30-Jun-11	0.5174	30-Jun-11	-	30-Jun-11	0.8464	30-Jun-11	0.875
31-Jul-11	0.4996	31-Jul-11	-	31-Jul-11	0.86	31-Jul-11	0.875
31-Aug-11	0.4531	31-Aug-11	-	31-Aug-11	0.8873	31-Aug-11	0.9114
30-Sep-11	0.4649	30-Sep-11	-	30-Sep-11	0.9664	30-Sep-11	1.0077
31-Oct-11	0.4608	31-Oct-11	-	31-Oct-11	1.0179	31-Oct-11	1.0593
30-Nov-11	0.4387	30-Nov-11	-	30-Nov-11	1.0511	30-Nov-11	1.0968
31-Dec-11	0.2996	31-Dec-11	-	31-Dec-11	1.0878	31-Dec-11	1.15
31-Jan-12	0.3239	31-Jan-12	-	31-Jan-12	1.1086	31-Jan-12	1.175
29-Feb-12	0.3912	29-Feb-12	-	29-Feb-12	1.0971	29-Feb-12	1.156
31-Mar-12	0.4248	31-Mar-12	-	31-Mar-12	1.0752	31-Mar-12	1.1164
30-Apr-12	0.4236	30-Apr-12	-	30-Apr-12	1.0558	30-Apr-12	1.0992
31-May-12	0.3561	31-May-12	-	31-May-12	1.0143	31-May-12	1.0891
30-Jun-12	0.3422	30-Jun-12	-	30-Jun-12	0.9658	30-Jun-12	1.0376
31-Jul-12	0.2943	31-Jul-12	-	31-Jul-12	0.8627	31-Jul-12	0.8691
31-Aug-12	0.2398	31-Aug-12	-	31-Aug-12	0.7048	31-Aug-12	0.7405
30-Sep-12	0.2478	30-Sep-12	-	30-Sep-12	0.6418	30-Sep-12	0.6825
31-Oct-12	0.2368	31-Oct-12	-	31-Oct-12	0.535	31-Oct-12	0.575
30-Nov-12	0.2243	30-Nov-12	-	30-Nov-12	0.5034	30-Nov-12	0.575
31-Dec-12	0.249	31-Dec-12	-	31-Dec-12	0.5	31-Dec-12	0.575
31-Jan-13	0.2677	31-Jan-13	-	31-Jan-13	0.4927	31-Jan-13	0.575
28-Feb-13	0.3147	28-Feb-13	-	28-Feb-13	0.49	28-Feb-13	0.575
31-Mar-13	0.3391	31-Mar-13	-	31-Mar-13	0.4865	31-Mar-13	0.5655
30-Apr-13	0.3447	30-Apr-13	-	30-Apr-13	0.485	30-Apr-13	0.5731
31-May-13	0.3065	31-May-13	-	31-May-13	0.485	31-May-13	0.5512
30-Jun-13	0.3066	30-Jun-13	-	30-Jun-13	0.485	30-Jun-13	0.525

12.9 Average three month sterling money market rates

Monthly average rate of discount, 3 month Treasury bills, Sterling IUMAAJNB		Monthly average of Eligible bills discount rate, 3 month (a) IUMAAJND		Monthly average Sterling 3 month mean interbank lending rate IUMAAMIJ		Monthly average of Sterling certificates of deposit interest rate, 3 months, mean offer/bid IUMAVCDA	
31-Jul-13	0.3124	31-Jul-13	-	31-Jul-13	0.4839	31-Jul-13	0.525
31-Aug-13	0.2812	31-Aug-13	-	31-Aug-13	0.485	31-Aug-13	0.525
30-Sep-13	0.289	30-Sep-13	-	30-Sep-13	0.4931	30-Sep-13	0.525
31-Oct-13	0.3141	31-Oct-13	-	31-Oct-13	0.495	31-Oct-13	0.525
30-Nov-13	0.2865	30-Nov-13	-	30-Nov-13	0.5017	30-Nov-13	0.5512
31-Dec-13	0.2555	31-Dec-13	-	31-Dec-13	0.5335	31-Dec-13	0.575
31-Jan-14	0.3211	31-Jan-14	-	31-Jan-14	0.5318	31-Jan-14	0.575
28-Feb-14	0.3624	28-Feb-14	-	28-Feb-14	0.5288	28-Feb-14	0.575
31-Mar-14	0.3882	31-Mar-14	-	31-Mar-14	0.53	31-Mar-14	0.575
30-Apr-14	0.3688	30-Apr-14	-	30-Apr-14	0.532	30-Apr-14	0.575
31-May-14	0.284	31-May-14	-	31-May-14	0.55	31-May-14	0.575
30-Jun-14	0.3586	30-Jun-14	-	30-Jun-14	0.55	30-Jun-14	0.575
31-Jul-14	0.4271	31-Jul-14	-	31-Jul-14	0.5487	31-Jul-14	0.575
31-Aug-14	0.3978	31-Aug-14	-	31-Aug-14	0.545	31-Aug-14	0.575
30-Sep-14	0.4351	30-Sep-14	-	30-Sep-14	0.5505	30-Sep-14	0.567
31-Oct-14	0.3964	31-Oct-14	-	31-Oct-14	0.5426	31-Oct-14	0.5511
30-Nov-14	0.4114	30-Nov-14	-	30-Nov-14	0.53	30-Nov-14	0.5538
31-Dec-14	0.4101	31-Dec-14	-	31-Dec-14	0.53	31-Dec-14	0.5524
31-Jan-15	0.377	31-Jan-15	-	31-Jan-15	0.53	31-Jan-15	0.5512
28-Feb-15	0.338	28-Feb-15	-	28-Feb-15	0.53	28-Feb-15	0.55
31-Mar-15	0.4295	31-Mar-15	-	31-Mar-15	0.53	31-Mar-15	0.5511
30-Apr-15	0.4322	30-Apr-15	-	30-Apr-15	0.533	30-Apr-15	0.55
31-May-15	0.4511	31-May-15	-	31-May-15	0.54	31-May-15	0.5532
30-Jun-15	0.467	30-Jun-15	-	30-Jun-15	0.5505	30-Jun-15	0.55
31-Jul-15	0.4895	31-Jul-15	-	31-Jul-15	0.567	31-Jul-15	0.55
31-Aug-15	0.4643	31-Aug-15	-	31-Aug-15	0.57	31-Aug-15	0.55
30-Sep-15	0.4532	30-Sep-15	-	30-Sep-15	0.57	30-Sep-15	0.55
31-Oct-15	0.48	31-Oct-15	-	31-Oct-15	0.57	31-Oct-15	0.55
30-Nov-15	0.4806	30-Nov-15	-	30-Nov-15	0.57	30-Nov-15	0.55
31-Dec-15	0.4551	31-Dec-15	-	31-Dec-15	0.57	31-Dec-15	0.5786
31-Jan-16	0.4823	31-Jan-16	-	31-Jan-16	0.566	31-Jan-16	0.6475
28-Feb-16	0.4711	28-Feb-16	-	28-Feb-16	0.565	28-Feb-16	0.65
31-Mar-16	0.4505	31-Mar-16	-	31-Mar-16	0.565	31-Mar-16	0.6476
30-Apr-16	0.4489	30-Apr-16	-	30-Apr-16	0.565	30-Apr-16	0.65
31-May-16	0.4362	31-May-16	-	31-May-16	0.565	31-May-16	0.65
30-Jun-16	0.4046	30-Jun-16	-	30-Jun-16	0.563	30-Jun-16	0.6386
31-Jul-16	0.3689	31-Jul-16	-	31-Jul-16	0.5414	31-Jul-16	0.4869
31-Aug-16	0.2281	31-Aug-16	-	31-Aug-16	0.468	31-Aug-16	0.367
30-Sep-16	0.2104	30-Sep-16	-	30-Sep-16	0.3627	30-Sep-16	0.3509
31-Oct-16	0.1711	31-Oct-16	-	31-Oct-16	0.3748	31-Oct-16	0.3524
30-Nov-16	0.1385	30-Nov-16	-	30-Nov-16	0.38	30-Nov-16	0.3523
31-Dec-16	0.0518	31-Dec-16	-	31-Dec-16	0.3775	31-Dec-16	0.35

Source: Bank of England

Notes:

[a] These data have been discontinued with effect from 20th July 2017.

[b] Data provided is for general reference purposes. Every effort is made to ensure that it is up to date and accurate. The Bank of England does not warrant, or accept responsibility/liability for, the accuracy/completeness of content, or loss/damage, whether direct, indirect or consequential, which may arise from reliance on said data. We reserve the right to change information published, including timing and methods used. We give no assurance that data currently published will be in the future.

12.10 Average Foreign Exchange rates

Monthly average Old IMF-based Effective exchange rate index, Sterling (a) (1990 average = 100) XUMAGBG		Monthly average Effective exchange rate index, Sterling (Jan 2005 = 100) XUMABK67		Monthly average Spot exchange rate, US$ into Sterling XUMAUSS		Monthly average Spot exchange rate, Euro into Sterling XUMAERS	
31-Jan-00	108.55	31-Jan-00	102.5163	31-Jan-00	1.6402	31-Jan-00	1.6201
29-Feb-00	108.44	29-Feb-00	102.1478	29-Feb-00	1.5998	29-Feb-00	1.6266
31-Mar-00	108.41	31-Mar-00	101.9463	31-Mar-00	1.5802	31-Mar-00	1.6377
30-Apr-00	110.06	30-Apr-00	103.3007	30-Apr-00	1.5837	30-Apr-00	1.673
31-May-00	108.52	31-May-00	101.3378	31-May-00	1.5075	31-May-00	1.6655
30-Jun-00	104.64	30-Jun-00	98.3084	30-Jun-00	1.5089	30-Jun-00	1.5882
31-Jul-00	105.63	31-Jul-00	99.0767	31-Jul-00	1.5088	31-Jul-00	1.6052
31-Aug-00	107.38	31-Aug-00	100.188	31-Aug-00	1.491	31-Aug-00	1.6478
30-Sep-00	106.21	30-Sep-00	98.7465	30-Sep-00	1.4355	30-Sep-00	1.6471
31-Oct-00	109.19	31-Oct-00	101.3391	31-Oct-00	1.4511	31-Oct-00	1.6994
30-Nov-00	107.27	30-Nov-00	99.6623	30-Nov-00	1.4256	30-Nov-00	1.6664
31-Dec-00	106.39	31-Dec-00	99.4118	31-Dec-00	1.4625	31-Dec-00	1.6302
31-Jan-01	104.43	31-Jan-01	98.2362	31-Jan-01	1.4769	31-Jan-01	1.5753
28-Feb-01	104.14	28-Feb-01	97.7179	28-Feb-01	1.4529	28-Feb-01	1.5786
31-Mar-01	105.02	31-Mar-01	98.4528	31-Mar-01	1.4454	31-Mar-01	1.5901
30-Apr-01	105.85	30-Apr-01	99.0733	30-Apr-01	1.435	30-Apr-01	1.6084
31-May-01	106.56	31-May-01	99.3906	31-May-01	1.4259	31-May-01	1.6304
30-Jun-01	106.77	30-Jun-01	99.2172	30-Jun-01	1.4014	30-Jun-01	1.6434
31-Jul-01	107.18	31-Jul-01	99.7551	31-Jul-01	1.4139	31-Jul-01	1.6433
31-Aug-01	105.09	31-Aug-01	98.4283	31-Aug-01	1.4365	31-Aug-01	1.5955
30-Sep-01	106.08	30-Sep-01	99.5949	30-Sep-01	1.4635	30-Sep-01	1.606
31-Oct-01	105.78	31-Oct-01	99.3536	31-Oct-01	1.4517	31-Oct-01	1.6024
30-Nov-01	106.14	30-Nov-01	99.4505	30-Nov-01	1.4358	30-Nov-01	1.6166
31-Dec-01	106.49	31-Dec-01	100.0899	31-Dec-01	1.4409	31-Dec-01	1.6151
31-Jan-02	106.9	31-Jan-02	100.26	31-Jan-02	1.4323	31-Jan-02	1.6222
28-Feb-02	107.36	28-Feb-02	100.4838	28-Feb-02	1.4231	28-Feb-02	1.6348
31-Mar-02	106.48	31-Mar-02	99.7945	31-Mar-02	1.4225	31-Mar-02	1.6224
30-Apr-02	107.13	30-Apr-02	100.5217	30-Apr-02	1.4434	30-Apr-02	1.6282
31-May-02	105.32	31-May-02	99.1553	31-May-02	1.4593	31-May-02	1.5914
30-Jun-02	103.58	30-Jun-02	98.0057	30-Jun-02	1.4863	30-Jun-02	1.5515
31-Jul-02	105.29	31-Jul-02	100.1562	31-Jul-02	1.5546	31-Jul-02	1.5665
31-Aug-02	105.38	31-Aug-02	100.0907	31-Aug-02	1.5377	31-Aug-02	1.5723
30-Sep-02	106.46	30-Sep-02	101.2329	30-Sep-02	1.5561	30-Sep-02	1.5861
31-Oct-02	106.67	31-Oct-02	101.4447	31-Oct-02	1.5574	31-Oct-02	1.5868
30-Nov-02	105.87	30-Nov-02	100.8857	30-Nov-02	1.5723	30-Nov-02	1.5694
31-Dec-02	105.48	31-Dec-02	100.6652	31-Dec-02	1.5863	31-Dec-02	1.5566
31-Jan-03	104.04	31-Jan-03	99.8966	31-Jan-03	1.6169	31-Jan-03	1.5222
28-Feb-03	102.42	28-Feb-03	98.4726	28-Feb-03	1.6085	28-Feb-03	1.4924
31-Mar-03	100.6	31-Mar-03	96.8021	31-Mar-03	1.5836	31-Mar-03	1.4649
30-Apr-03	99.8	30-Apr-03	95.9557	30-Apr-03	1.5747	30-Apr-03	1.4505
31-May-03	97.9	31-May-03	94.8862	31-May-03	1.623	31-May-03	1.403
30-Jun-03	99.64	30-Jun-03	96.6136	30-Jun-03	1.6606	30-Jun-03	1.4234
31-Jul-03	99.4	31-Jul-03	95.9155	31-Jul-03	1.6242	31-Jul-03	1.4277
31-Aug-03	99.01	31-Aug-03	95.2462	31-Aug-03	1.595	31-Aug-03	1.4286
30-Sep-03	99.24	30-Sep-03	95.5651	30-Sep-03	1.6131	30-Sep-03	1.4338
31-Oct-03	99.82	31-Oct-03	96.7185	31-Oct-03	1.6787	31-Oct-03	1.4334
30-Nov-03	100.42	30-Nov-03	97.317	30-Nov-03	1.6901	30-Nov-03	1.4426
31-Dec-03	100.29	31-Dec-03	97.8697	31-Dec-03	1.7507	31-Dec-03	1.4246
31-Jan-04	102.38	31-Jan-04	100.1608	31-Jan-04	1.8234	31-Jan-04	1.4447
29-Feb-04	104.84	29-Feb-04	102.5025	29-Feb-04	1.8673	29-Feb-04	1.4774
31-Mar-04	104.99	31-Mar-04	102.1884	31-Mar-04	1.8267	31-Mar-04	1.489
30-Apr-04	105.18	30-Apr-04	102.137	30-Apr-04	1.8005	30-Apr-04	1.5022
31-May-04	104.63	31-May-04	101.7871	31-May-04	1.7876	31-May-04	1.4894
30-Jun-04	105.8	30-Jun-04	103.059	30-Jun-04	1.8275	30-Jun-04	1.505
31-Jul-04	105.89	31-Jul-04	103.1662	31-Jul-04	1.8429	31-Jul-04	1.5023

12.10 Average Foreign Exchange rates

Monthly average Old IMF-based Effective exchange rate index, Sterling (a) (1990 average = 100) XUMAGBG		Monthly average Effective exchange rate index, Sterling (Jan 2005 = 100) XUMABK67		Monthly average Spot exchange rate, US$ into Sterling XUMAUSS		Monthly average Spot exchange rate, Euro into Sterling XUMAERS	
31-Aug-04	105.16	31-Aug-04	102.4289	31-Aug-04	1.8216	31-Aug-04	1.4933
30-Sep-04	103.32	30-Sep-04	100.7156	30-Sep-04	1.7922	30-Sep-04	1.4676
31-Oct-04	102.17	31-Oct-04	99.8303	31-Oct-04	1.8065	31-Oct-04	1.4455
30-Nov-04	101.73	30-Nov-04	99.7587	30-Nov-04	1.8603	30-Nov-04	1.4311
31-Dec-04	103.15	31-Dec-04	101.2974	31-Dec-04	1.9275	31-Dec-04	1.4401
31-Jan-05	102.1	31-Jan-05	100	31-Jan-05	1.8764	31-Jan-05	1.4331
28-Feb-05	103.29	28-Feb-05	100.9792	28-Feb-05	1.8871	28-Feb-05	1.4499
31-Mar-05	103.21	31-Mar-05	101.0494	31-Mar-05	1.9078	31-Mar-05	1.444
30-Apr-05	104.38	30-Apr-05	102.0108	30-Apr-05	1.896	30-Apr-05	1.4652
31-May-05	103.55	31-May-05	100.9896	31-May-05	1.8538	31-May-05	1.4611
30-Jun-05	104.92	30-Jun-05	101.7515	30-Jun-05	1.8179	30-Jun-05	1.4952
31-Jul-05	102.14	31-Jul-05	98.8169	31-Jul-05	1.7509	31-Jul-05	1.4547
31-Aug-05	102.85	31-Aug-05	99.7011	31-Aug-05	1.7943	31-Aug-05	1.4592
30-Sep-05	103.91	30-Sep-05	100.6456	30-Sep-05	1.8081	30-Sep-05	1.4761
31-Oct-05	103.09	31-Oct-05	99.6486	31-Oct-05	1.764	31-Oct-05	1.4674
30-Nov-05	103.16	30-Nov-05	99.4195	30-Nov-05	1.7341	30-Nov-05	1.4719
31-Dec-05	103.32	31-Dec-05	99.5011	31-Dec-05	1.7462	31-Dec-05	1.4725
31-Jan-06	102.67	31-Jan-06	99.0364	31-Jan-06	1.7678	31-Jan-06	1.4582
28-Feb-06	102.83	28-Feb-06	98.9167	28-Feb-06	1.747	28-Feb-06	1.4637
31-Mar-06	102.09	31-Mar-06	98.3582	31-Mar-06	1.7435	31-Mar-06	1.45
30-Apr-06	101.87	30-Apr-06	98.3685	30-Apr-06	1.7685	30-Apr-06	1.4402
31-May-06	104.14	31-May-06	101.2652	31-May-06	1.8702	31-May-06	1.4637
30-Jun-06	-	30-Jun-06	100.9564	30-Jun-06	1.8428	30-Jun-06	1.456
31-Jul-06	-	31-Jul-06	100.9424	31-Jul-06	1.8447	31-Jul-06	1.454
31-Aug-06	-	31-Aug-06	102.9584	31-Aug-06	1.8944	31-Aug-06	1.4785
30-Sep-06	-	30-Sep-06	103.0141	30-Sep-06	1.8847	30-Sep-06	1.4811
31-Oct-06	-	31-Oct-06	103.1453	31-Oct-06	1.8755	31-Oct-06	1.4869
30-Nov-06	-	30-Nov-06	103.4686	30-Nov-06	1.9119	30-Nov-06	1.4834
31-Dec-06	-	31-Dec-06	104.5334	31-Dec-06	1.9633	31-Dec-06	1.486
31-Jan-07	-	31-Jan-07	105.5735	31-Jan-07	1.9587	31-Jan-07	1.5079
28-Feb-07	-	28-Feb-07	105.0313	28-Feb-07	1.9581	28-Feb-07	1.4969
31-Mar-07	-	31-Mar-07	103.5671	31-Mar-07	1.9471	31-Mar-07	1.4703
30-Apr-07	-	30-Apr-07	104.2682	30-Apr-07	1.9909	30-Apr-07	1.4713
31-May-07	-	31-May-07	103.9117	31-May-07	1.9836	31-May-07	1.4677
30-Jun-07	-	30-Jun-07	104.5063	30-Jun-07	1.9864	30-Jun-07	1.4805
31-Jul-07	-	31-Jul-07	105.2357	31-Jul-07	2.0338	31-Jul-07	1.4821
31-Aug-07	-	31-Aug-07	104.5357	31-Aug-07	2.0111	31-Aug-07	1.4762
30-Sep-07	-	30-Sep-07	103.3042	30-Sep-07	2.0185	30-Sep-07	1.4515
31-Oct-07	-	31-Oct-07	102.8113	31-Oct-07	2.0446	31-Oct-07	1.437
30-Nov-07	-	30-Nov-07	101.8978	30-Nov-07	2.0701	30-Nov-07	1.4106
31-Dec-07	-	31-Dec-07	99.9273	31-Dec-07	2.0185	31-Dec-07	1.3863
31-Jan-08	-	31-Jan-08	96.6594	31-Jan-08	1.9698	31-Jan-08	1.3383
29-Feb-08	-	29-Feb-08	96.1702	29-Feb-08	1.9638	29-Feb-08	1.3316
31-Mar-08	-	31-Mar-08	94.7859	31-Mar-08	2.0032	31-Mar-08	1.2897
30-Apr-08	-	30-Apr-08	93.0097	30-Apr-08	1.9817	30-Apr-08	1.258
31-May-08	-	31-May-08	93.0105	31-May-08	1.9641	31-May-08	1.2633
30-Jun-08	-	30-Jun-08	93.1297	30-Jun-08	1.9658	30-Jun-08	1.2636
31-Jul-08	-	31-Jul-08	93.2514	31-Jul-08	1.988	31-Jul-08	1.2615
31-Aug-08	-	31-Aug-08	91.6752	31-Aug-08	1.8889	31-Aug-08	1.2614
30-Sep-08	-	30-Sep-08	90.0272	30-Sep-08	1.7986	30-Sep-08	1.2531
31-Oct-08	-	31-Oct-08	89.6321	31-Oct-08	1.69	31-Oct-08	1.2718
30-Nov-08	-	30-Nov-08	83.8159	30-Nov-08	1.5338	30-Nov-08	1.2041
31-Dec-08	-	31-Dec-08	78.4569	31-Dec-08	1.4859	31-Dec-08	1.1043
31-Jan-09	-	31-Jan-09	77.2822	31-Jan-09	1.4452	31-Jan-09	1.0919
28-Feb-09	-	28-Feb-09	79.1632	28-Feb-09	1.4411	28-Feb-09	1.1264

12.10 Average Foreign Exchange rates

Monthly average Old IMF-based Effective exchange rate index, Sterling (a) (1990 average = 100) XUMAGBG		Monthly average Effective exchange rate index, Sterling (Jan 2005 = 100) XUMABK67		Monthly average Spot exchange rate, US$ into Sterling XUMAUSS		Monthly average Spot exchange rate, Euro into Sterling XUMAERS	
31-Mar-09	-	31-Mar-09	77.2402	31-Mar-09	1.4174	31-Mar-09	1.0867
30-Apr-09	-	30-Apr-09	79.1169	30-Apr-09	1.4715	30-Apr-09	1.1157
31-May-09	-	31-May-09	80.65	31-May-09	1.5429	31-May-09	1.1295
30-Jun-09	-	30-Jun-09	84.1934	30-Jun-09	1.6366	30-Jun-09	1.1682
31-Jul-09	-	31-Jul-09	83.777	31-Jul-09	1.6366	31-Jul-09	1.1622
31-Aug-09	-	31-Aug-09	83.66	31-Aug-09	1.6539	31-Aug-09	1.1597
30-Sep-09	-	30-Sep-09	81.3425	30-Sep-09	1.6328	30-Sep-09	1.1212
31-Oct-09	-	31-Oct-09	79.5602	31-Oct-09	1.6199	31-Oct-09	1.0928
30-Nov-09	-	30-Nov-09	81.1213	30-Nov-09	1.6597	30-Nov-09	1.1126
31-Dec-09	-	31-Dec-09	80.4832	31-Dec-09	1.6239	31-Dec-09	1.1127
31-Jan-10	-	31-Jan-10	81.0259	31-Jan-10	1.6162	31-Jan-10	1.1327
28-Feb-10	-	28-Feb-10	80.305	28-Feb-10	1.5615	28-Feb-10	1.1415
31-Mar-10	-	31-Mar-10	77.526	31-Mar-10	1.5053	31-Mar-10	1.1092
30-Apr-10	-	30-Apr-10	79.3964	30-Apr-10	1.534	30-Apr-10	1.1436
31-May-10	-	31-May-10	79.2556	31-May-10	1.4627	31-May-10	1.1685
30-Jun-10	-	30-Jun-10	81.0387	30-Jun-10	1.4761	30-Jun-10	1.2082
31-Jul-10	-	31-Jul-10	81.4282	31-Jul-10	1.5299	31-Jul-10	1.1959
31-Aug-10	-	31-Aug-10	82.643	31-Aug-10	1.566	31-Aug-10	1.2132
30-Sep-10	-	30-Sep-10	81.219	30-Sep-10	1.5578	30-Sep-10	1.1901
31-Oct-10	-	31-Oct-10	79.5102	31-Oct-10	1.5862	31-Oct-10	1.1412
30-Nov-10	-	30-Nov-10	80.9631	30-Nov-10	1.5961	30-Nov-10	1.1701
31-Dec-10	-	31-Dec-10	80.4151	31-Dec-10	1.5603	31-Dec-10	1.1802
31-Jan-11	-	31-Jan-11	80.7146	31-Jan-11	1.5795	31-Jan-11	1.1817
28-Feb-11	-	28-Feb-11	81.4914	28-Feb-11	1.613	28-Feb-11	1.1815
31-Mar-11	-	31-Mar-11	80.2504	31-Mar-11	1.6159	31-Mar-11	1.1527
30-Apr-11	-	30-Apr-11	79.6662	30-Apr-11	1.6345	30-Apr-11	1.1331
31-May-11	-	31-May-11	79.7728	31-May-11	1.6312	31-May-11	1.1403
30-Jun-11	-	30-Jun-11	78.875	30-Jun-11	1.6214	30-Jun-11	1.1261
31-Jul-11	-	31-Jul-11	78.7586	31-Jul-11	1.6145	31-Jul-11	1.1308
31-Aug-11	-	31-Aug-11	79.633	31-Aug-11	1.6348	31-Aug-11	1.1422
30-Sep-11	-	30-Sep-11	79.259	30-Sep-11	1.5783	30-Sep-11	1.147
31-Oct-11	-	31-Oct-11	79.5315	31-Oct-11	1.576	31-Oct-11	1.1487
30-Nov-11	-	30-Nov-11	80.472	30-Nov-11	1.5804	30-Nov-11	1.1659
31-Dec-11	-	31-Dec-11	80.9061	31-Dec-11	1.5585	31-Dec-11	1.1843
31-Jan-12	-	31-Jan-12	81.1135	31-Jan-12	1.551	31-Jan-12	1.2034
29-Feb-12	-	29-Feb-12	80.9907	29-Feb-12	1.5802	29-Feb-12	1.1941
31-Mar-12	-	31-Mar-12	81.4144	31-Mar-12	1.5823	31-Mar-12	1.1981
30-Apr-12	-	30-Apr-12	82.5592	30-Apr-12	1.6014	30-Apr-12	1.2161
31-May-12	-	31-May-12	83.8064	31-May-12	1.5905	31-May-12	1.244
30-Jun-12	-	30-Jun-12	83.09	30-Jun-12	1.5571	30-Jun-12	1.2416
31-Jul-12	-	31-Jul-12	84.0002	31-Jul-12	1.5589	31-Jul-12	1.2688
31-Aug-12	-	31-Aug-12	84.0151	31-Aug-12	1.5719	31-Aug-12	1.2676
30-Sep-12	-	30-Sep-12	84.2259	30-Sep-12	1.6116	30-Sep-12	1.2524
31-Oct-12	-	31-Oct-12	83.6192	31-Oct-12	1.6079	31-Oct-12	1.2393
30-Nov-12	-	30-Nov-12	83.6804	30-Nov-12	1.5961	30-Nov-12	1.244
31-Dec-12	-	31-Dec-12	83.5787	31-Dec-12	1.6144	31-Dec-12	1.231
31-Jan-13	-	31-Jan-13	82.1836	31-Jan-13	1.5957	31-Jan-13	1.2
28-Feb-13	-	28-Feb-13	79.7009	28-Feb-13	1.5478	28-Feb-13	1.1594
31-Mar-13	-	31-Mar-13	79.1385	31-Mar-13	1.5076	31-Mar-13	1.1634
30-Apr-13	-	30-Apr-13	80.1286	30-Apr-13	1.5316	30-Apr-13	1.175
31-May-13	-	31-May-13	80.4282	31-May-13	1.5285	31-May-13	1.1777
30-Jun-13	-	30-Jun-13	80.9963	30-Jun-13	1.5478	30-Jun-13	1.174
31-Jul-13	-	31-Jul-13	79.9695	31-Jul-13	1.5172	31-Jul-13	1.16
31-Aug-13	-	31-Aug-13	80.989	31-Aug-13	1.5507	31-Aug-13	1.1649
30-Sep-13	-	30-Sep-13	82.7389	30-Sep-13	1.5865	30-Sep-13	1.1883

12.10 Average Foreign Exchange rates

Monthly average Old IMF-based Effective exchange rate index, Sterling (a) (1990 average = 100) XUMAGBG		Monthly average Effective exchange rate index, Sterling (Jan 2005 = 100) XUMABK67		Monthly average Spot exchange rate, US$ into Sterling XUMAUSS		Monthly average Spot exchange rate, Euro into Sterling XUMAERS	
31-Oct-13	-	31-Oct-13	82.6672	31-Oct-13	1.6094	31-Oct-13	1.1797
30-Nov-13	-	30-Nov-13	83.5614	30-Nov-13	1.6104	30-Nov-13	1.1938
31-Dec-13	-	31-Dec-13	84.4199	31-Dec-13	1.6375	31-Dec-13	1.1947
31-Jan-14	-	31-Jan-14	85.4256	31-Jan-14	1.647	31-Jan-14	1.2097
28-Feb-14	-	28-Feb-14	85.7374	28-Feb-14	1.6567	28-Feb-14	1.2122
31-Mar-14	-	31-Mar-14	85.5266	31-Mar-14	1.6622	31-Mar-14	1.2021
30-Apr-14	-	30-Apr-14	86.1739	30-Apr-14	1.6743	30-Apr-14	1.2125
31-May-14	-	31-May-14	86.8392	31-May-14	1.6844	31-May-14	1.2267
30-Jun-14	-	30-Jun-14	87.6791	30-Jun-14	1.6906	30-Jun-14	1.2436
31-Jul-14	-	31-Jul-14	88.7384	31-Jul-14	1.7069	31-Jul-14	1.2611
31-Aug-14	-	31-Aug-14	87.7641	31-Aug-14	1.6709	31-Aug-14	1.2542
30-Sep-14	-	30-Sep-14	87.5035	30-Sep-14	1.6305	30-Sep-14	1.2639
31-Oct-14	-	31-Oct-14	87.353	31-Oct-14	1.6068	31-Oct-14	1.2678
30-Nov-14	-	30-Nov-14	86.9779	30-Nov-14	1.578	30-Nov-14	1.2646
31-Dec-14	-	31-Dec-14	87.5043	31-Dec-14	1.564	31-Dec-14	1.2686
31-Jan-15	-	31-Jan-15	87.7721	31-Jan-15	1.5143	31-Jan-15	1.3045
28-Feb-15	-	28-Feb-15	90.0828	28-Feb-15	1.5334	28-Feb-15	1.3503
31-Mar-15	-	31-Mar-15	90.4409	31-Mar-15	1.4957	31-Mar-15	1.3825
30-Apr-15	-	30-Apr-15	90.1919	30-Apr-15	1.4967	30-Apr-15	1.3856
31-May-15	-	31-May-15	91.3478	31-May-15	1.547	31-May-15	1.3852
30-Jun-15	-	30-Jun-15	92.1334	30-Jun-15	1.5568	30-Jun-15	1.3879
31-Jul-15	-	31-Jul-15	93.3352	31-Jul-15	1.556	31-Jul-15	1.4139
31-Aug-15	-	31-Aug-15	93.482	31-Aug-15	1.5583	31-Aug-15	1.4004
30-Sep-15	-	30-Sep-15	91.8347	30-Sep-15	1.5326	30-Sep-15	1.3665
31-Oct-15	-	31-Oct-15	91.5953	31-Oct-15	1.5339	31-Oct-15	1.3657
30-Nov-15	-	30-Nov-15	93.4031	30-Nov-15	1.519	30-Nov-15	1.4168
31-Dec-15	-	31-Dec-15	91.551	31-Dec-15	1.4983	31-Dec-15	1.3769
31-Jan-16	-	31-Jan-16	88.4994	31-Jan-16	1.4379	31-Jan-16	1.3257
28-Feb-16	-	28-Feb-16	86.6959	28-Feb-16	1.4296	28-Feb-16	1.289
31-Mar-16	-	31-Mar-16	85.7815	31-Mar-16	1.425	31-Mar-16	1.2809
30-Apr-16	-	30-Apr-16	84.9485	30-Apr-16	1.4312	30-Apr-16	1.2622
31-May-16	-	31-May-16	86.6711	31-May-16	1.4518	31-May-16	1.2846
30-Jun-16	-	30-Jun-16	84.9386	30-Jun-16	1.4209	30-Jun-16	1.2646
31-Jul-16	-	31-Jul-16	79.3988	31-Jul-16	1.3141	31-Jul-16	1.1884
31-Aug-16	-	31-Aug-16	78.3767	31-Aug-16	1.31	31-Aug-16	1.1687
30-Sep-16	-	30-Sep-16	78.6967	30-Sep-16	1.3142	30-Sep-16	1.1722
31-Oct-16	-	31-Oct-16	74.7185	31-Oct-16	1.2329	31-Oct-16	1.119
30-Nov-16	-	30-Nov-16	76.7199	30-Nov-16	1.2431	30-Nov-16	1.1533
31-Dec-16	-	31-Dec-16	78.3192	31-Dec-16	1.2488	31-Dec-16	1.1838

(a) This series was discontinued in May 2006

Source: Bank of England

12.11 Average zero coupon yields

End month level of yield from British Government Securities, 5 year Nominal Zero Coupon IUMSNZC [a] [b]		End month level of yield from British Government Securities, 10 year Nominal Zero Coupon IUMMNZC [a] [b]		End month level of yield from British Government Securities, 20 year Nominal Zero Coupon IUMLNZC [a] [b]		Monthly average yield from British Government Securities, 10 year Real Zero Coupon IUMAMRZC [c]		Monthly average yield from British Government Securities, 20 year Real Zero Coupon IUMALRZC [c]	
31-Jan-01	4.3694	31-Jan-01	4.6718	31-Jan-01	4.978	31-Jan-01	4.6718	31-Jan-01	4.978
28-Feb-01	4.378	28-Feb-01	4.7079	28-Feb-01	4.9824	28-Feb-01	4.7079	28-Feb-01	4.9824
31-Mar-01	4.5984	31-Mar-01	4.7218	31-Mar-01	4.8425	31-Mar-01	4.7218	31-Mar-01	4.8425
30-Apr-01	4.8872	30-Apr-01	5.065	30-Apr-01	5.126	30-Apr-01	5.065	30-Apr-01	5.126
31-May-01	5.0197	31-May-01	5.1627	31-May-01	5.2777	31-May-01	5.1627	31-May-01	5.2777
30-Jun-01	5.0078	30-Jun-01	5.2329	30-Jun-01	5.4376	30-Jun-01	5.2329	30-Jun-01	5.4376
31-Jul-01	4.7653	31-Jul-01	5.0002	31-Jul-01	5.1702	31-Jul-01	5.0002	31-Jul-01	5.1702
31-Aug-01	4.682	31-Aug-01	4.8652	31-Aug-01	4.9746	31-Aug-01	4.8652	31-Aug-01	4.9746
30-Sep-01	4.8559	30-Sep-01	4.9172	30-Sep-01	4.8735	30-Sep-01	4.9172	30-Sep-01	4.8735
31-Oct-01	4.4576	31-Oct-01	4.5368	31-Oct-01	4.5126	31-Oct-01	4.5368	31-Oct-01	4.5126
30-Nov-01	4.5089	30-Nov-01	4.6479	30-Nov-01	4.6523	30-Nov-01	4.6479	30-Nov-01	4.6523
31-Dec-01	4.782	31-Dec-01	5.0326	31-Dec-01	5.0788	31-Dec-01	5.0326	31-Dec-01	5.0788
31-Jan-02	4.6689	31-Jan-02	4.8138	31-Jan-02	4.9044	31-Jan-02	4.8138	31-Jan-02	4.9044
28-Feb-02	4.7928	28-Feb-02	4.923	28-Feb-02	4.9428	28-Feb-02	4.923	28-Feb-02	4.9428
31-Mar-02	5.0823	31-Mar-02	5.2456	31-Mar-02	5.3046	31-Mar-02	5.2456	31-Mar-02	5.3046
30-Apr-02	5.0257	30-Apr-02	5.1553	30-Apr-02	5.1522	30-Apr-02	5.1553	30-Apr-02	5.1522
31-May-02	5.1364	31-May-02	5.2282	31-May-02	5.2156	31-May-02	5.2282	31-May-02	5.2156
30-Jun-02	4.8164	30-Jun-02	4.9715	30-Jun-02	5.0148	30-Jun-02	4.9715	30-Jun-02	5.0148
31-Jul-02	4.8015	31-Jul-02	4.9201	31-Jul-02	4.7231	31-Jul-02	4.9201	31-Jul-02	4.7231
31-Aug-02	4.4857	31-Aug-02	4.6394	31-Aug-02	4.4976	31-Aug-02	4.6394	31-Aug-02	4.4976
30-Sep-02	4.3797	30-Sep-02	4.412	30-Sep-02	4.1825	30-Sep-02	4.412	30-Sep-02	4.1825
31-Oct-02	4.5466	31-Oct-02	4.5992	31-Oct-02	4.3315	31-Oct-02	4.5992	31-Oct-02	4.3315
30-Nov-02	4.6549	30-Nov-02	4.6898	30-Nov-02	4.5062	30-Nov-02	4.6898	30-Nov-02	4.5062
31-Dec-02	4.4607	31-Dec-02	4.3967	31-Dec-02	4.1583	31-Dec-02	4.3967	31-Dec-02	4.1583
31-Jan-03	4.374	31-Jan-03	4.2807	31-Jan-03	4.0136	31-Jan-03	4.2807	31-Jan-03	4.0136
28-Feb-03	4.4687	28-Feb-03	4.227	28-Feb-03	3.7987	28-Feb-03	4.227	28-Feb-03	3.7987
31-Mar-03	4.5931	31-Mar-03	4.3549	31-Mar-03	3.9584	31-Mar-03	4.3549	31-Mar-03	3.9584
30-Apr-03	4.6491	30-Apr-03	4.4202	30-Apr-03	4.0086	30-Apr-03	4.4202	30-Apr-03	4.0086
31-May-03	4.4323	31-May-03	4.1579	31-May-03	3.7737	31-May-03	4.1579	31-May-03	3.7737
30-Jun-03	4.6015	30-Jun-03	4.2698	30-Jun-03	3.8401	30-Jun-03	4.2698	30-Jun-03	3.8401
31-Jul-03	4.8344	31-Jul-03	4.6075	31-Jul-03	4.2291	31-Jul-03	4.6075	31-Jul-03	4.2291
31-Aug-03	4.6988	31-Aug-03	4.6562	31-Aug-03	4.4574	31-Aug-03	4.6562	31-Aug-03	4.4574
30-Sep-03	4.6736	30-Sep-03	4.5844	30-Sep-03	4.3404	30-Sep-03	4.5844	30-Sep-03	4.3404
31-Oct-03	4.859	31-Oct-03	5.0093	31-Oct-03	4.9274	31-Oct-03	5.0093	31-Oct-03	4.9274
30-Nov-03	4.8909	30-Nov-03	5.0473	30-Nov-03	4.911	30-Nov-03	5.0473	30-Nov-03	4.911
31-Dec-03	4.7034	31-Dec-03	4.7733	31-Dec-03	4.612	31-Dec-03	4.7733	31-Dec-03	4.612
31-Jan-04	4.7485	31-Jan-04	4.8572	31-Jan-04	4.7324	31-Jan-04	4.8572	31-Jan-04	4.7324
29-Feb-04	4.7232	29-Feb-04	4.735	29-Feb-04	4.5996	29-Feb-04	4.735	29-Feb-04	4.5996
31-Mar-04	4.6453	31-Mar-04	4.7184	31-Mar-04	4.6154	31-Mar-04	4.7184	31-Mar-04	4.6154
30-Apr-04	4.839	30-Apr-04	4.9564	30-Apr-04	4.8491	30-Apr-04	4.9564	30-Apr-04	4.8491
31-May-04	4.8917	31-May-04	5.1062	31-May-04	5.1163	31-May-04	5.1062	31-May-04	5.1163
30-Jun-04	4.84	30-Jun-04	5.0587	30-Jun-04	5.039	30-Jun-04	5.0587	30-Jun-04	5.039
31-Jul-04	4.7933	31-Jul-04	5.0518	31-Jul-04	5.0958	31-Jul-04	5.0518	31-Jul-04	5.0958
31-Aug-04	4.6547	31-Aug-04	4.881	31-Aug-04	4.8585	31-Aug-04	4.881	31-Aug-04	4.8585
30-Sep-04	4.6312	30-Sep-04	4.7878	30-Sep-04	4.7433	30-Sep-04	4.7878	30-Sep-04	4.7433
31-Oct-04	4.5693	31-Oct-04	4.7002	31-Oct-04	4.6267	31-Oct-04	4.7002	31-Oct-04	4.6267
30-Nov-04	4.4453	30-Nov-04	4.5606	30-Nov-04	4.473	30-Nov-04	4.5606	30-Nov-04	4.473
31-Dec-04	4.4097	31-Dec-04	4.4872	31-Dec-04	4.4287	31-Dec-04	4.4872	31-Dec-04	4.4287
31-Jan-05	4.4811	31-Jan-05	4.5419	31-Jan-05	4.4769	31-Jan-05	4.5419	31-Jan-05	4.4769
28-Feb-05	4.5249	28-Feb-05	4.6514	28-Feb-05	4.6761	28-Feb-05	4.6514	28-Feb-05	4.6761
31-Mar-05	4.5618	31-Mar-05	4.6357	31-Mar-05	4.6106	31-Mar-05	4.6357	31-Mar-05	4.6106
30-Apr-05	4.4264	30-Apr-05	4.4735	30-Apr-05	4.444	30-Apr-05	4.4735	30-Apr-05	4.444
31-May-05	4.3326	31-May-05	4.2823	31-May-05	4.2051	31-May-05	4.2823	31-May-05	4.2051
30-Jun-05	4.2073	30-Jun-05	4.1519	30-Jun-05	4.0387	30-Jun-05	4.1519	30-Jun-05	4.0387
31-Jul-05	4.3179	31-Jul-05	4.2892	31-Jul-05	4.2154	31-Jul-05	4.2892	31-Jul-05	4.2154
31-Aug-05	4.1705	31-Aug-05	4.1248	31-Aug-05	4.0641	31-Aug-05	4.1248	31-Aug-05	4.0641
30-Sep-05	4.2336	30-Sep-05	4.2489	30-Sep-05	4.1884	30-Sep-05	4.2489	30-Sep-05	4.1884
31-Oct-05	4.238	31-Oct-05	4.2833	31-Oct-05	4.2874	31-Oct-05	4.2833	31-Oct-05	4.2874
30-Nov-05	4.0854	30-Nov-05	4.1685	30-Nov-05	4.2061	30-Nov-05	4.1685	30-Nov-05	4.2061
31-Dec-05	3.9626	31-Dec-05	4.0505	31-Dec-05	4.1019	31-Dec-05	4.0505	31-Dec-05	4.1019
31-Jan-06	3.8631	31-Jan-06	4.0817	31-Jan-06	4.172	31-Jan-06	4.0817	31-Jan-06	4.172
28-Feb-06	3.9088	28-Feb-06	4.1211	28-Feb-06	4.2134	28-Feb-06	4.1211	28-Feb-06	4.2134
31-Mar-06	4.1388	31-Mar-06	4.3444	31-Mar-06	4.3946	31-Mar-06	4.3444	31-Mar-06	4.3946
30-Apr-06	4.3286	30-Apr-06	4.5855	30-Apr-06	4.6102	30-Apr-06	4.5855	30-Apr-06	4.6102
31-May-06	4.2978	31-May-06	4.5395	31-May-06	4.6302	31-May-06	4.5395	31-May-06	4.6302

12.11 Average zero coupon yields

End month level of yield from British Government Securities, 5 year Nominal Zero Coupon IUMSNZC [a] [b]		End month level of yield from British Government Securities, 10 year Nominal Zero Coupon IUMMNZC [a] [b]		End month level of yield from British Government Securities, 20 year Nominal Zero Coupon IUMLNZC [a] [b]		Monthly average yield from British Government Securities, 10 year Real Zero Coupon IUMAMRZC [c]		Monthly average yield from British Government Securities, 20 year Real Zero Coupon IUMALRZC [c]	
30-Jun-06	4.4151	30-Jun-06	4.6536	30-Jun-06	4.7356	30-Jun-06	4.6536	30-Jun-06	4.7356
31-Jul-06	4.2984	31-Jul-06	4.5482	31-Jul-06	4.6631	31-Jul-06	4.5482	31-Jul-06	4.6631
31-Aug-06	4.163	31-Aug-06	4.4391	31-Aug-06	4.6343	31-Aug-06	4.4391	31-Aug-06	4.6343
30-Sep-06	4.1548	30-Sep-06	4.4471	30-Sep-06	4.6412	30-Sep-06	4.4471	30-Sep-06	4.6412
31-Oct-06	4.0629	31-Oct-06	4.4201	31-Oct-06	4.6979	31-Oct-06	4.4201	31-Oct-06	4.6979
30-Nov-06	4.0858	30-Nov-06	4.4113	30-Nov-06	4.6926	30-Nov-06	4.4113	30-Nov-06	4.6926
31-Dec-06	4.2526	31-Dec-06	4.6318	31-Dec-06	4.9131	31-Dec-06	4.6318	31-Dec-06	4.9131
31-Jan-07	4.4219	31-Jan-07	4.855	31-Jan-07	5.1482	31-Jan-07	4.855	31-Jan-07	5.1482
28-Feb-07	4.3078	28-Feb-07	4.6791	28-Feb-07	4.9735	28-Feb-07	4.6791	28-Feb-07	4.9735
31-Mar-07	4.4697	31-Mar-07	4.8548	31-Mar-07	5.1338	31-Mar-07	4.8548	31-Mar-07	5.1338
30-Apr-07	4.5536	30-Apr-07	4.9284	30-Apr-07	5.194	30-Apr-07	4.9284	30-Apr-07	5.194
31-May-07	4.6951	31-May-07	5.1283	31-May-07	5.448	31-May-07	5.1283	31-May-07	5.448
30-Jun-07	4.8891	30-Jun-07	5.3604	30-Jun-07	5.6348	30-Jun-07	5.3604	30-Jun-07	5.6348
31-Jul-07	4.6572	31-Jul-07	5.1173	31-Jul-07	5.3529	31-Jul-07	5.1173	31-Jul-07	5.3529
31-Aug-07	4.5484	31-Aug-07	4.9347	31-Aug-07	5.1209	31-Aug-07	4.9347	31-Aug-07	5.1209
30-Sep-07	4.6447	30-Sep-07	4.9495	30-Sep-07	4.9798	30-Sep-07	4.9495	30-Sep-07	4.9798
31-Oct-07	4.5916	31-Oct-07	4.8667	31-Oct-07	4.9395	31-Oct-07	4.8667	31-Oct-07	4.9395
30-Nov-07	4.5157	30-Nov-07	4.6361	30-Nov-07	4.5718	30-Nov-07	4.6361	30-Nov-07	4.5718
31-Dec-07	4.3859	31-Dec-07	4.5151	31-Dec-07	4.4137	31-Dec-07	4.5151	31-Dec-07	4.4137
31-Jan-08	4.4193	31-Jan-08	4.4877	31-Jan-08	4.2964	31-Jan-08	4.4877	31-Jan-08	4.2964
29-Feb-08	4.503	29-Feb-08	4.5274	29-Feb-08	4.1991	29-Feb-08	4.5274	29-Feb-08	4.1991
31-Mar-08	4.6048	31-Mar-08	4.424	31-Mar-08	3.9541	31-Mar-08	4.424	31-Mar-08	3.9541
30-Apr-08	4.7139	30-Apr-08	4.733	30-Apr-08	4.4429	30-Apr-08	4.733	30-Apr-08	4.4429
31-May-08	4.8293	31-May-08	4.9984	31-May-08	4.94	31-May-08	4.9984	31-May-08	4.94
30-Jun-08	4.8995	30-Jun-08	5.1663	30-Jun-08	5.1659	30-Jun-08	5.1663	30-Jun-08	5.1659
31-Jul-08	4.7434	31-Jul-08	4.8448	31-Jul-08	4.7675	31-Jul-08	4.8448	31-Jul-08	4.7675
31-Aug-08	4.5953	31-Aug-08	4.5222	31-Aug-08	4.4108	31-Aug-08	4.5222	31-Aug-08	4.4108
30-Sep-08	4.6924	30-Sep-08	4.5137	30-Sep-08	4.208	30-Sep-08	4.5137	30-Sep-08	4.208
31-Oct-08	4.9258	31-Oct-08	4.713	31-Oct-08	3.9697	31-Oct-08	4.713	31-Oct-08	3.9697
30-Nov-08	4.5731	30-Nov-08	4.0317	30-Nov-08	3.3664	30-Nov-08	4.0317	30-Nov-08	3.3664
31-Dec-08	4.066	31-Dec-08	3.4126	31-Dec-08	2.708	31-Dec-08	3.4126	31-Dec-08	2.708
31-Jan-09	4.7012	31-Jan-09	4.0861	31-Jan-09	2.8834	31-Jan-09	4.0861	31-Jan-09	2.8834
28-Feb-09	4.7151	28-Feb-09	3.8159	28-Feb-09	2.6227	28-Feb-09	3.8159	28-Feb-09	2.6227
31-Mar-09	4.2558	31-Mar-09	3.311	31-Mar-09	2.4459	31-Mar-09	3.311	31-Mar-09	2.4459
30-Apr-09	4.5822	30-Apr-09	3.6361	30-Apr-09	2.594	30-Apr-09	3.6361	30-Apr-09	2.594
31-May-09	4.7127	31-May-09	3.8141	31-May-09	2.7154	31-May-09	3.8141	31-May-09	2.7154
30-Jun-09	4.5708	30-Jun-09	3.703	30-Jun-09	2.9717	30-Jun-09	3.703	30-Jun-09	2.9717
31-Jul-09	4.7431	31-Jul-09	3.9125	31-Jul-09	3.083	31-Jul-09	3.9125	31-Jul-09	3.083
31-Aug-09	4.1118	31-Aug-09	3.6313	31-Aug-09	2.6877	31-Aug-09	3.6313	31-Aug-09	2.6877
30-Sep-09	4.1499	30-Sep-09	3.7123	30-Sep-09	2.6807	30-Sep-09	3.7123	30-Sep-09	2.6807
31-Oct-09	4.2789	31-Oct-09	3.7684	31-Oct-09	2.7662	31-Oct-09	3.7684	31-Oct-09	2.7662
30-Nov-09	4.2359	30-Nov-09	3.6987	30-Nov-09	2.6607	30-Nov-09	3.6987	30-Nov-09	2.6607
31-Dec-09	4.5939	31-Dec-09	4.203	31-Dec-09	2.9821	31-Dec-09	4.203	31-Dec-09	2.9821
31-Jan-10	4.5279	31-Jan-10	4.1135	31-Jan-10	2.9411	31-Jan-10	4.1135	31-Jan-10	2.9411
28-Feb-10	4.7692	28-Feb-10	4.2373	28-Feb-10	2.7834	28-Feb-10	4.2373	28-Feb-10	2.7834
31-Mar-10	4.6577	31-Mar-10	4.1764	31-Mar-10	2.7852	31-Mar-10	4.1764	31-Mar-10	2.7852
30-Apr-10	4.6279	30-Apr-10	4.1034	30-Apr-10	2.7534	30-Apr-10	4.1034	30-Apr-10	2.7534
31-May-10	4.4818	31-May-10	3.7919	31-May-10	2.4101	31-May-10	3.7919	31-May-10	2.4101
30-Jun-10	4.3767	30-Jun-10	3.5853	30-Jun-10	2.2133	30-Jun-10	3.5853	30-Jun-10	2.2133
31-Jul-10	4.4956	31-Jul-10	3.5691	31-Jul-10	2.2281	31-Jul-10	3.5691	31-Jul-10	2.2281
31-Aug-10	3.9415	31-Aug-10	3.0217	31-Aug-10	1.7575	31-Aug-10	3.0217	31-Aug-10	1.7575
30-Sep-10	4.0071	30-Sep-10	3.1512	30-Sep-10	1.813	30-Sep-10	3.1512	30-Sep-10	1.813
31-Oct-10	4.3031	31-Oct-10	3.3042	31-Oct-10	1.878	31-Oct-10	3.3042	31-Oct-10	1.878
30-Nov-10	4.4002	30-Nov-10	3.4591	30-Nov-10	2.0313	30-Nov-10	3.4591	30-Nov-10	2.0313
31-Dec-10	4.3314	31-Dec-10	3.6174	31-Dec-10	2.314	31-Dec-10	3.6174	31-Dec-10	2.314
31-Jan-11	4.5822	31-Jan-11	3.8827	31-Jan-11	2.5858	31-Jan-11	3.8827	31-Jan-11	2.5858
28-Feb-11	4.5184	28-Feb-11	3.8872	28-Feb-11	2.6508	28-Feb-11	3.8872	28-Feb-11	2.6508
31-Mar-11	4.5078	31-Mar-11	3.8974	31-Mar-11	2.6575	31-Mar-11	3.8974	31-Mar-11	2.6575
30-Apr-11	4.3435	30-Apr-11	3.7116	30-Apr-11	2.4534	30-Apr-11	3.7116	30-Apr-11	2.4534
31-May-11	4.3125	31-May-11	3.5655	31-May-11	2.2507	31-May-11	3.5655	31-May-11	2.2507
30-Jun-11	4.4964	30-Jun-11	3.6665	30-Jun-11	2.2036	30-Jun-11	3.6665	30-Jun-11	2.2036
31-Jul-11	4.2227	31-Jul-11	3.1755	31-Jul-11	1.7512	31-Jul-11	3.1755	31-Jul-11	1.7512
31-Aug-11	4.0173	31-Aug-11	2.9038	31-Aug-11	1.6065	31-Aug-11	2.9038	31-Aug-11	1.6065
30-Sep-11	3.5397	30-Sep-11	2.5096	30-Sep-11	1.4048	30-Sep-11	2.5096	30-Sep-11	1.4048
31-Oct-11	3.4276	31-Oct-11	2.5642	31-Oct-11	1.3719	31-Oct-11	2.5642	31-Oct-11	1.3719

12.11 Average zero coupon yields

End month level of yield from British Government Securities, 5 year Nominal Zero Coupon IUMSNZC [a] [b]		End month level of yield from British Government Securities, 10 year Nominal Zero Coupon IUMMNZC [a] [b]		End month level of yield from British Government Securities, 20 year Nominal Zero Coupon IUMLNZC [a] [b]		Monthly average yield from British Government Securities, 10 year Real Zero Coupon IUMAMRZC [c]		Monthly average yield from British Government Securities, 20 year Real Zero Coupon IUMALRZC [c]	
30-Nov-11	3.1294	30-Nov-11	2.4275	30-Nov-11	1.2752	30-Nov-11	2.4275	30-Nov-11	1.2752
31-Dec-11	3.0454	31-Dec-11	2.105	31-Dec-11	1.001	31-Dec-11	2.105	31-Dec-11	1.001
31-Jan-12	3.0189	31-Jan-12	2.0983	31-Jan-12	0.9544	31-Jan-12	2.0983	31-Jan-12	0.9544
29-Feb-12	3.2967	29-Feb-12	2.2582	29-Feb-12	1.001	29-Feb-12	2.2582	29-Feb-12	1.001
31-Mar-12	3.447	31-Mar-12	2.3289	31-Mar-12	1.0698	31-Mar-12	2.3289	31-Mar-12	1.0698
30-Apr-12	3.3938	30-Apr-12	2.2516	30-Apr-12	1.1164	30-Apr-12	2.2516	30-Apr-12	1.1164
31-May-12	2.8994	31-May-12	1.673	31-May-12	0.6748	31-May-12	1.673	31-May-12	0.6748
30-Jun-12	2.9815	30-Jun-12	1.8661	30-Jun-12	0.8284	30-Jun-12	1.8661	30-Jun-12	0.8284
31-Jul-12	2.7932	31-Jul-12	1.6099	31-Jul-12	0.566	31-Jul-12	1.6099	31-Jul-12	0.566
31-Aug-12	2.8217	31-Aug-12	1.6346	31-Aug-12	0.5849	31-Aug-12	1.6346	31-Aug-12	0.5849
30-Sep-12	2.9454	30-Sep-12	1.6958	30-Sep-12	0.6798	30-Sep-12	1.6958	30-Sep-12	0.6798
31-Oct-12	3.0256	31-Oct-12	1.879	31-Oct-12	0.8255	31-Oct-12	1.879	31-Oct-12	0.8255
30-Nov-12	2.9544	30-Nov-12	1.794	30-Nov-12	0.8264	30-Nov-12	1.794	30-Nov-12	0.8264
31-Dec-12	3.023	31-Dec-12	1.8782	31-Dec-12	0.8853	31-Dec-12	1.8782	31-Dec-12	0.8853
31-Jan-13	3.3222	31-Jan-13	2.2055	31-Jan-13	1.098	31-Jan-13	2.2055	31-Jan-13	1.098
28-Feb-13	3.2498	28-Feb-13	2.1054	28-Feb-13	0.9145	28-Feb-13	2.1054	28-Feb-13	0.9145
31-Mar-13	3.0961	31-Mar-13	1.8933	31-Mar-13	0.7439	31-Mar-13	1.8933	31-Mar-13	0.7439
30-Apr-13	2.9541	30-Apr-13	1.7929	30-Apr-13	0.73	30-Apr-13	1.7929	30-Apr-13	0.73
31-May-13	3.2631	31-May-13	2.1641	31-May-13	1.02	31-May-13	2.1641	31-May-13	1.02
30-Jun-13	3.5337	30-Jun-13	2.618	30-Jun-13	1.3933	30-Jun-13	2.618	30-Jun-13	1.3933
31-Jul-13	3.5392	31-Jul-13	2.5513	31-Jul-13	1.2511	31-Jul-13	2.5513	31-Jul-13	1.2511
31-Aug-13	3.6373	31-Aug-13	2.8265	31-Aug-13	1.5644	31-Aug-13	2.8265	31-Aug-13	1.5644
30-Sep-13	3.5437	30-Sep-13	2.7601	30-Sep-13	1.5498	30-Sep-13	2.7601	30-Sep-13	1.5498
31-Oct-13	3.4942	31-Oct-13	2.7053	31-Oct-13	1.5122	31-Oct-13	2.7053	31-Oct-13	1.5122
30-Nov-13	3.6515	30-Nov-13	2.8783	30-Nov-13	1.6323	30-Nov-13	2.8783	30-Nov-13	1.6323
31-Dec-13	3.7316	31-Dec-13	3.1577	31-Dec-13	1.9931	31-Dec-13	3.1577	31-Dec-13	1.9931
31-Jan-14	3.5521	31-Jan-14	2.8386	31-Jan-14	1.7819	31-Jan-14	2.8386	31-Jan-14	1.7819
28-Feb-14	3.5484	28-Feb-14	2.8582	28-Feb-14	1.798	28-Feb-14	2.8582	28-Feb-14	1.798
31-Mar-14	3.5515	31-Mar-14	2.8707	31-Mar-14	1.8714	31-Mar-14	2.8707	31-Mar-14	1.8714
30-Apr-14	3.4992	30-Apr-14	2.8105	30-Apr-14	1.857	30-Apr-14	2.8105	30-Apr-14	1.857
31-May-14	3.412	31-May-14	2.7043	31-May-14	1.7997	31-May-14	2.7043	31-May-14	1.7997
30-Jun-14	3.4523	30-Jun-14	2.8146	30-Jun-14	1.9945	30-Jun-14	2.8146	30-Jun-14	1.9945
31-Jul-14	3.3233	31-Jul-14	2.7619	31-Jul-14	1.9847	31-Jul-14	2.7619	31-Jul-14	1.9847
31-Aug-14	2.9663	31-Aug-14	2.3948	31-Aug-14	1.6987	31-Aug-14	2.3948	31-Aug-14	1.6987
30-Sep-14	3.0612	30-Sep-14	2.4682	30-Sep-14	1.781	30-Sep-14	2.4682	30-Sep-14	1.781
31-Oct-14	2.9766	31-Oct-14	2.3054	31-Oct-14	1.5647	31-Oct-14	2.3054	31-Oct-14	1.5647
30-Nov-14	2.6605	30-Nov-14	1.9853	30-Nov-14	1.3003	30-Nov-14	1.9853	30-Nov-14	1.3003
31-Dec-14	2.4808	31-Dec-14	1.8196	31-Dec-14	1.1987	31-Dec-14	1.8196	31-Dec-14	1.1987
31-Jan-15	2.0083	31-Jan-15	1.3867	31-Jan-15	0.9086	31-Jan-15	1.3867	31-Jan-15	0.9086
28-Feb-15	2.4648	28-Feb-15	1.8567	28-Feb-15	1.2811	28-Feb-15	1.8567	28-Feb-15	1.2811
31-Mar-15	2.2909	31-Mar-15	1.6605	31-Mar-15	1.0851	31-Mar-15	1.6605	31-Mar-15	1.0851
30-Apr-15	2.5347	30-Apr-15	1.9447	30-Apr-15	1.3017	30-Apr-15	1.9447	30-Apr-15	1.3017
31-May-15	2.5294	31-May-15	1.9178	31-May-15	1.263	31-May-15	1.9178	31-May-15	1.263
30-Jun-15	2.7485	30-Jun-15	2.1552	30-Jun-15	1.4567	30-Jun-15	2.1552	30-Jun-15	1.4567
31-Jul-15	2.5863	31-Jul-15	2.0074	31-Jul-15	1.3892	31-Jul-15	2.0074	31-Jul-15	1.3892
31-Aug-15	2.5998	31-Aug-15	1.9669	31-Aug-15	1.3454	31-Aug-15	1.9669	31-Aug-15	1.3454
30-Sep-15	2.5118	30-Sep-15	1.7919	30-Sep-15	1.184	30-Sep-15	1.7919	30-Sep-15	1.184
31-Oct-15	2.6502	31-Oct-15	1.9457	31-Oct-15	1.2853	31-Oct-15	1.9457	31-Oct-15	1.2853
30-Nov-15	2.5946	30-Nov-15	1.8741	30-Nov-15	1.2399	30-Nov-15	1.8741	30-Nov-15	1.2399
31-Dec-15	2.7092	31-Dec-15	2.0097	31-Dec-15	1.3752	31-Dec-15	2.0097	31-Dec-15	1.3752
31-Jan-16	2.3858	31-Jan-16	1.6355	31-Jan-16	0.9573	31-Jan-16	1.6355	31-Jan-16	0.9573
28-Feb-16	2.3061	28-Feb-16	1.4096	28-Feb-16	0.6909	28-Feb-16	1.4096	28-Feb-16	0.6909
31-Mar-16	2.3188	31-Mar-16	1.5041	31-Mar-16	0.8064	31-Mar-16	1.5041	31-Mar-16	0.8064
30-Apr-16	2.4476	30-Apr-16	1.6947	30-Apr-16	0.9684	30-Apr-16	1.6947	30-Apr-16	0.9684
31-May-16	2.2818	31-May-16	1.5474	31-May-16	0.9044	31-May-16	1.5474	31-May-16	0.9044
30-Jun-16	1.7905	30-Jun-16	1.0263	30-Jun-16	0.3959	30-Jun-16	-	30-Jun-16	-
31-Jul-16	1.567	31-Jul-16	0.7998	31-Jul-16	0.2752	31-Jul-16	-	31-Jul-16	-
31-Aug-16	1.2793	31-Aug-16	0.6615	31-Aug-16	0.2182	31-Aug-16	-	31-Aug-16	-
30-Sep-16	1.5211	30-Sep-16	0.7968	30-Sep-16	0.2591	30-Sep-16	-	30-Sep-16	-
31-Oct-16	1.9205	31-Oct-16	1.2877	31-Oct-16	0.6341	31-Oct-16	-	31-Oct-16	-
30-Nov-16	2.1026	30-Nov-16	1.4765	30-Nov-16	0.6747	30-Nov-16	-	30-Nov-16	-
31-Dec-16	1.9308	31-Dec-16	1.2955	31-Dec-16	0.5495	31-Dec-16	-	31-Dec-16	-

Source: Bank of England

Notes:

[a] Calculated by the Bank of England using the Variable Roughness Penalty (VRP) model

[b] There have been small revisions to the UK government VRP curves (nominal, real and inflation) going back to the beginning of January 01 (31 Jan 01)

[c] The Bank of England have suspended publication of real yields and the inflation compensation term structure temporarily.

12.12 Consumer credit excluding student loans

£ millions   Not seasonally adjusted

Net lending - monthly changes

	Monthly changes of					
	MFIs sterling net unsecured lending for individuals	of which: mutuals	Other consumer credit lenders (excluding Student Loans Company) sterling net unsecured lending for individuals	Total (excluding Student Loans Company) sterling net unsecured lending for individuals	of which:	
					credit card lending to individuals	other consumer credit lending to individuals
	LPMVVXP [a] [b]	LPMB3VC [a] [c]	LPMB4TH [a]	LPMB3PT	LPMVZQS	LPMB4TV
31-Jan-12	-881	10	-203	-1084	-969	-116
29-Feb-12	-973	5	-245	-1219	-518	-701
31-Mar-12	-192	23	755	563	-22	585
30-Apr-12	-19	55	41	22	192	-169
31-May-12	-178	48	180	2	-19	21
30-Jun-12	193	10	407	600	568	33
31-Jul-12	-25	74	70	45	-218	263
31-Aug-12	-337	46	-66	-404	227	-630
30-Sep-12	635	27	830	1465	424	1040
31-Oct-12	-442	24	136	-306	-354	48
30-Nov-12	-1	27	352	352	680	-328
31-Dec-12	1688	61	432	2121	1158	963
31-Jan-13	-534	-6	-277	-811	-1052	241
28-Feb-13	244	75	-447	-202	-22	-180
31-Mar-13	-46	38	901	855	-40	895
30-Apr-13	729	45	93	822	374	448
31-May-13	250	7	171	421	268	153
30-Jun-13	314	13	289	603	522	81
31-Jul-13	718	14	123	841	-43	884
31-Aug-13	584	-1	53	637	544	93
30-Sep-13	941	-9	961	1902	276	1627
31-Oct-13	-327	-27	316	-11	-151	140
30-Nov-13	269	-35	511	780	999	-219
31-Dec-13	1259	-	582	1840	917	924
31-Jan-14	-762	-	-17	-780	-825	46
28-Feb-14	4	-	-160	-155	-90	-66
31-Mar-14	787	-	1012	1799	-276	2075
30-Apr-14	528	-	-18	510	602	-92
31-May-14	501	-	230	731	210	521
30-Jun-14	840	-	143	983	352	630
31-Jul-14	751	-	346	1097	166	931
31-Aug-14	480	-	216	696	542	154
30-Sep-14	1021	-	1125	2146	143	2003
31-Oct-14	59	-	316	375	92	283
30-Nov-14	862	-	522	1384	851	533
31-Dec-14	1115	-	496	1611	1150	461
31-Jan-15	-732	-	41	-691	-920	229
28-Feb-15	47	-	-138	-91	-118	27
31-Mar-15	1397	-	1140	2537	-203	2740
30-Apr-15	590	-	400	990	823	167
31-May-15	303	-	418	721	94	627
30-Jun-15	1327	-	418	1745	552	1193
31-Jul-15	833	-	510	1343	345	997
31-Aug-15	916	-	172	1088	580	508
30-Sep-15	1013	-	1455	2468	234	2234
31-Oct-15	75	-	456	532	14	518
30-Nov-15	1579	-	755	2334	1267	1067
31-Dec-15	860	-	771	1630	1130	501

Source: Bank of England

Notes:

[a] These series may be affected by securitisations and loan transfers.

[b] Please note that the compilation and descriptions of some credit series have changed from publication of April 2015 data, as described in Bankstats, April 2015, 'Changes to the treatment of loan transfers and lending to housing associations', available at www.bankofengland.co.uk/statistics/Documents/ms/articles/art1apr15.pdf.

[c] This series will be discontinued with effect from December 2013 data. Further information can be found in Bankstats, December 2013, `Changes to publication of data for mutually owned monetary financial institutions', available at www.bankofengland.co.uk/statistics/Documents/ms/articles/art1dec13.pdf.

12.13a INVESTMENT TRUSTS' ASSETS AND LIABILITIES AT MARKET VALUES

£ million at end of year

		2004	2005	2006	2007	2008	2009	2010	2011	2012	2013	2014
ASSETS												
UK government securities denominated in sterling	RLLT	466	768	533	715	628	585	466	681	857	487	302
Index-linked	AFIS	0	0	0	0	0	0	8	95	c	45	47
Other[1]	K5HJ	466	768	533	715	628	585	458	586	c	442	255
UK government securities denominated in foreign currency	CBPP	0	0	0	0	0	0	0	0	0	0	0
UK local authority investments[2]	AHBR	0	0	0	0	0	0	0	0	0	0	0
Other UK public sector investments[3]	AHBS	0	0	0	0	0	0	0	0	0	0	0
UK ordinary shares												
Quoted[4]	AHBM	22,598	24,021	21,843	21,848	13,428	16,297	17,547	17,329	18,655	18,907	19,384
Unquoted	AHBQ	1,343	1,016	1,027	1,186	938	1,349	1,336	1,437	1,363	1,323	1,616
Overseas ordinary shares	AHCC	18,967	23,065	21,659	25,795	18,385	23,865	29,341	29,083	30,758	31,859	31,491
Other corporate securities[5]												
UK	CBGZ	1,270	673	1,071	1,259	813	665	560	529	470	498	350
Overseas	CBHA	682	937	741	1,038	623	939	1,304	1,344	1,129	1,217	775
UK authorised unit trust units	AHBT	149	140	24	0	28	33	42	76	53	86	119
Overseas government, provincial and municipal securities	AHBY	33	168	4	151	410	256	410	254	251	118	107
UK existing buildings, property, land and new construction work	CBHB	39	117	252	154	142	141	197	1,522	1,538	158	202
Other longer-term assets not elsewhere classified[6]	AMSE	1,665	2,359	2,898	3,462	3,684	3,824	4,618	5,439	5,744	6,240	8,168
LONGER-TERM ASSETS	**AHBD**	**47,212**	**53,264**	**50,052**	**55,608**	**39,079**	**47,954**	**55,821**	**57,694**	**60,818**	**60,893**	**62,514**
Short-term assets	CBGX	3,100	3,032	2,138	3,303	3,397	2,522	2,174	2,893	3,015	2,848	3,377
TOTAL ASSETS	**CBGW**	**50,312**	**56,296**	**52,190**	**58,911**	**42,476**	**50,476**	**57,995**	**60,587**	**63,833**	**63,741**	**65,891**
LIABILITIES												
Borrowing from UK and overseas banks[7]	CBHD	2,797	2,771	2,900	2,708	2,553	2,216	2,359	2,897	2,845	3,652	3,373
Other UK borrowing[8]	CBHG	843	670	952	988	1,012	1,062	1,123	914	865	989	1,099
Other overseas borrowing[9]	CBHI	0	0	2	0	225	185	186	126	117	11	c
Issued share and loan capital[10]	CBHK	8,210	7,155	5,492	5,659	3,834	3,627	3,361	4,395	4,345	3,741	3,237
TOTAL LIABILITIES	**CBHO**	**11,850**	**10,596**	**9,346**	**9,355**	**7,624**	**7,090**	**7,029**	**8,332**	**8,172**	**8,393**	**7,810**
NET ASSETS	**CBHM**	**38,462**	**45,700**	**42,844**	**49,556**	**34,852**	**43,386**	**50,966**	**52,255**	**55,661**	**55,348**	**58,081**

c Suppressed to avoid the disclosure of confidential data. *Source: Office for National Statistics*

1 Includes securities of: 0 up to 15 years maturity; over 15 years maturity and undated maturity. Excludes treasury bills and index-linked securities.
2 Includes local authority securities; negotiable bonds; loans and mortgages.
3 Includes public corporation loans and mortgages and other public sector investments not elsewhere classified.
4 Includes investment trust securities.
5 Includes corporate bonds and preference shares.
6 Includes UK unauthorised unit trust units; UK open-ended investment companies; overseas mutual fund investments; other UK fixed assets; overseas fixed assets; overseas direct investment and other UK and overseas assets not elsewhere classified.
7 Sterling and foreign currency. Includes foreign currency liabilities on back-to-back loans and overdrafts.

8 Includes sterling and foreign currency borrowing from building societies; issue of securities (other than ordinary shares); issue of sterling commercial paper and other borrowing not elsewhere classified (such as borrowing from parent, subsidiary and associate companies and other related concerns).
9 Includes borrowing from related companies and other borrowing not elsewhere classified.
10 Quoted and unquoted. Includes ordinary shares; preference shares; deferred stocks; bonds; debentures and loan stocks.

12.13b UNIT TRUSTS AND PROPERTY UNIT TRUSTS' BALANCE SHEET ASSETS AND LIABILITIES AT MARKET VALUES

£ million at end of year

		2004	2005	2006	2007	2008	2009	2010	2011	2012	2013	2014
ASSETS												
UK government securities denominated in sterling[1]	CBHT	9,768	25,181	31,603	32,120	33,466	29,331	33,306	37,116	36,033	37,275	44,970
Ordinary shares[2]												
UK	RLIB	130,230	157,149	185,637	195,009	143,550	167,401	204,616	179,940	201,822	234,866	241,783
Overseas	RLIC	81,034	105,443	127,409	142,211	113,667	150,863	200,028	187,714	215,705	265,209	288,079
Other corporate securities[3]												
UK	CBHU	22,467	29,293	29,876	30,626	30,174	36,646	52,786	52,735	63,546	60,803	66,686
Overseas	CBHV	13,142	16,057	25,617	30,029	30,442	43,301	49,098	48,388	62,870	67,946	78,566
Overseas government, provincial and municipal securities	CBHW	2,347	3,412	3,532	3,880	5,754	5,810	9,251	14,797	19,604	19,698	23,184
UK existing buildings, property, land and new construction work	RLIE	5,909	9,623	12,781	12,480	8,518	7,248	9,484	13,220	13,498	13,576	15,706
Other longer-term assets not elsewhere classified[4]	CBHX	14,261	22,327	29,765	38,707	42,670	49,417	60,029	66,640	81,849	105,015	110,193
Short-term assets	CBHS	11,497	16,417	20,653	27,969	35,224	37,263	48,382	45,001	53,734	62,021	56,686
of which:												
Derivative contracts with UK and overseas counterparties which have a positive (asset) value[5]	KUU5	2,099	4,745	4,552	7,271	13,151	17,132	25,944	18,168	25,644	27,923	13,320
TOTAL ASSETS	**CBHR**	**290,655**	**384,902**	**466,873**	**513,031**	**443,465**	**527,280**	**666,980**	**645,551**	**748,661**	**866,409**	**925,853**
LIABILITIES												
Borrowing from UK and overseas	RLLF	413	1,456	2,544	2,603	3,486	1,541	991	1,992	3,430	3,154	2,834
Other UK borrowing[7]	RLLH	27	130	16	36	80	26	74	350	83	34	109
Other overseas borrowing[8]	RLLI	1	1	0	0	0	54	0	0	0	0	0
Derivative contracts with UK and counterparties which have a negative (liability) value[5]	KUU6	1,611	2,814	3,701	6,382	11,890	15,294	23,676	17,464	22,832	26,255	12,122
Other creditors, provisions and liabilities not elsewhere classified	KUU7	1,835	2,425	3,370	2,562	3,442	5,524	7,228	14,087	5,460	1,740	4,424
Liability attributable to unit and share holders	RLLG	286,768	378,076	457,242	501,448	424,567	504,841	635,011	611,658	716,856	835,226	906,364
TOTAL LIABILITIES	**RLLE**	**290,655**	**384,902**	**466,873**	**513,031**	**443,465**	**527,280**	**666,980**	**645,551**	**748,661**	**866,409**	**925,853**

c Suppressed to avoid the disclosure of confidential data.

Source: Office for National Statistics

1 Includes securities of: 0 up to 15 years maturity; over 15 years maturity;
2 UK and overseas. Quoted and unquoted. Includes investment trust securities.
3 Includes corporate bonds and preference shares.
4 UK and overseas. Includes UK government securities denominated in foreign currency; local authority and public corporation securities; mutual fund investments; other UK fixed assets; overseas fixed assets; direct investment and other assets not elsewhere classified.
5 Includes credit default products; employee stock options; other options; other swaps; futures; forwards and other derivative contracts not elsewhere classified.
6 Sterling and foreign currency. Includes foreign currency liabilities on back-to-back loans and overdrafts.

7 Includes sterling and foreign currency borrowing from building societies; issue of securities (other than ordinary shares); issue of sterling commercial paper and other borrowing not elsewhere classified (such as borrowing from parent, subsidiary and associate companies and other related concerns).
8 Includes borrowing from related companies and other borrowing not elsewhere classified.

12.14 SELF-ADMINISTERED PENSION FUNDS'[1] BALANCE SHEET ASSETS AND LIABILITIES AT MARKET VALUES

£ million at end of year

		2004	2005	2006	2007	2008	2009	2010	2011	2012	2013	2014
ASSETS												
UK government securities denominated in sterling	AHVK	87,579	94,325	104,910	113,617	98,577	108,871	122,007	167,372	199,400	227,528	260,553
Index-linked	AHWC	46,333	48,821	53,858	64,797	58,564	70,317	83,016	110,808	142,565	159,843	178,465
Other[2]	J8Y5	41,246	45,504	51,052	48,820	40,013	38,554	38,991	56,564	56,835	67,685	82,088
UK government securities denominated in foreign currency	RYEX	44	45	27	42	4	126	89	1,287	5,695	275	351
UK local authority investments[3]	AHVO	4	4	2	5	0	2	274	113	263	291	284
Other UK public sector investments[4]	JE5J	656	846	1,118	1,351	1,259	2,347	2,911	1,703	1,611	3,862	582
UK PUBLIC SECTOR SECURITIES	**RYHC**	**88,283**	**95,220**	**106,057**	**115,015**	**99,840**	**111,346**	**125,281**	**170,475**	**206,969**	**231,956**	**261,770**
UK corporate bonds[5]	JX62	42,871	47,912	54,626	57,306	55,741	64,351	59,469	61,586	64,508	64,581	76,987
Sterling	GQFT	42,151	47,061	53,190	55,550	53,765	62,073	57,086	59,322	61,896	61,938	73,601
Foreign currency	GQFU	720	851	1,436	1,756	1,976	2,278	2,383	2,264	2,612	2,643	3,386
UK ordinary shares[6]	AHVP	180,561	199,199	208,473	152,048	110,571	116,710	121,882	108,631	111,913	109,777	95,981
UK preference shares[6]	J8YF	156	153	276	235	775	833	16	11	29	51	77
Overseas corporate securities	JRS8	156,278	203,562	224,514	215,068	175,747	214,230	222,751	211,562	226,274	232,277	259,644
Bonds	RLPF	15,794	19,891	30,867	44,387	47,612	57,920	60,826	61,129	60,424	61,655	70,977
Ordinary shares	AHVR	140,282	183,060	192,978	169,598	127,525	155,577	161,043	149,638	165,141	170,007	187,923
Preference shares	RLPC	202	611	669	1,083	610	733	882	795	709	615	744
Mutual fund investments	JRS9	144,265	192,033	215,218	254,936	211,724	286,493	369,955	385,337	448,583	476,623	449,664
UK	J8Y7	115,622	150,316	168,635	194,833	148,798	203,523	266,058	264,652	293,071	302,024	283,997
Unit trust units[7]	JX63	86,005	105,429	115,872	147,536	110,558	148,642	178,027	172,120	208,155	212,566	191,218
Other[8]	JX64	29,617	44,887	52,763	47,297	38,240	54,881	88,031	92,532	84,916	89,458	92,779
Overseas	JE4P	28,643	41,717	46,583	60,103	62,926	82,970	103,897	120,685	155,512	174,599	165,667
CORPORATE SECURITIES	**RYHN**	**524,131**	**642,859**	**703,107**	**679,593**	**554,558**	**682,617**	**774,073**	**767,127**	**851,307**	**883,309**	**882,353**
Overseas government, provincial and municipal securities	AHVT	15,075	19,037	21,776	22,434	21,527	16,900	17,335	21,424	23,768	23,462	22,643
Loans	JRT4	44	9	42	417	518	1,768	2,343	1,656	1,313	324	94
UK[9]	JE5E	44	6	6	12	0	116	81	77	170	c	c
Overseas[10]	AHVZ	0	3	36	405	518	1,652	2,262	1,579	1,143	c	c
Fixed assets[11]	JRT5	30,676	31,742	34,608	30,466	22,892	24,957	30,159	32,991	30,705	33,695	37,734
UK	JE5F	30,554	31,616	34,435	30,306	22,818	24,718	28,991	32,178	30,372	33,064	36,937
Overseas	GOLB	122	126	173	160	74	239	1,168	813	333	631	797
Investment in insurance managed funds, insurance policies and annuities	RYHS	67,936	86,336	92,387	103,610	86,541	70,318	80,613	93,823	99,896	110,723	122,194
Other longer-term assets not elsewhere classified[12]	J8YA	17,071	21,423	31,234	41,455	45,301	51,100	69,419	81,562	90,893	109,368	84,875
OTHER LONGER-TERM ASSETS	**RYHW**	**130,802**	**158,547**	**180,047**	**198,382**	**176,779**	**165,043**	**199,869**	**231,456**	**246,575**	**277,572**	**267,540**
LONGER-TERM ASSETS	**RYHX**	**743,216**	**896,626**	**989,211**	**992,990**	**831,177**	**959,006**	**1,099,223**	**1,169,058**	**1,304,851**	**1,392,837**	**1,411,663**

c Suppressed to avoid the disclosure of confidential data.   *Source: Office for National Statistics*

1 Combined public and private sector. Data from the pension funds surveys are of lower quality than equivalent data from other institutional groups because of the difficulties in constructing a suitable sampling frame of pension funds.

2 Includes securities of: 0 up to 15 years maturity; over 15 years maturity and undated maturity. Excludes treasury bills and index-linked securities.

3 Includes local authority securities; negotiable bonds; loans and mortgages.

4 Includes public corporation loans and mortgages and other public sector investments not elsewhere classified.

5 Issued by: banks; building societies and other corporates.

6 Quoted and unquoted.

7 Authorised and unauthorised.

8 Includes property unit trusts; investment trust securities; open-ended investment companies; hedge funds and other mutual fund investments not elsewhere classified.

9 Includes sterling asset backed loans; loans to individuals secured on dwellings; other loans to individuals (including policy loans); loans to businesses and other loans not elsewhere classified. Excludes loans to UK associate companies; bank term deposits and building society investments.

10 Includes loans to parent companies; subsidiaries; associates and other loans not elsewhere classified. Excludes loans categorised as direct investment; loans covered by Export Credit Guarantee Department (ECGD), specific bank guarantees or ECGD buyer credit guarantees.

11 UK and overseas. Includes existing buildings; property; land; new construction work; vehicles; machinery and equipment; valuables and intangibles. Includes the capital value of assets bought on hire purchase or acquired (as lessee) under a finance leasing arrangement and assets acquired for hiring, renting and operating leasing purposes. Excludes the capital value of assets acquired but leased out to others under finance leasing arrangements.

12 UK and overseas. Includes certificates of tax deposit; insurance policies; annuities and loans covered by Export Credit Guarantee Department (ECGD), specific bank guarantees or ECGD buyer credit guarantees. Excludes pre-payments and debtors.

12.14 SELF-ADMINISTERED PENSION FUNDS'[1] BALANCE SHEET ASSETS AND LIABILITIES AT MARKET VALUES

continued   £ million at end of year

		2004	2005	2006	2007	2008	2009	2010	2011	2012	2013	2014
ASSETS												
Cash	GNOR	0	0	0	0	0	0	0	0	0	0	0
Balances with banks and building societies in the UK	JX5Q	16,216	17,789	22,823	25,974	20,133	23,054	23,736	23,854	22,929	22,701	25,881
Sterling	JX5S	14,064	15,510	20,211	22,615	16,802	19,099	20,043	20,159	18,901	18,193	21,841
Foreign currency	JX5U	2,152	2,279	2,612	3,359	3,331	3,955	3,693	3,695	4,028	4,508	4,040
Balances with overseas banks	GNOW	287	361	525	807	351	134	197	72	157	349	c
Other liquid deposits [13]	GNOX	1,782	3,010	3,891	5,392	4,300	12,431	9,631	11,956	15,265	20,505	15,084
Certificates of deposit issued by banks and building societies in the UK [14]	IX8H	1,678	2,649	4,932	8,156	6,480	2,269	2,472	6,498	2,069	1,288	455
Money market instruments issued by HM Treasury [15]	IX9J	69	89	22	304	548	1,709	1,109	1,734	4,116	1,167	1,698
UK local authority debt	AHVF	337	270	221	205	323	210	116	157	232	130	c
Commercial paper issued by UK companies [16]	GQFR	175	476	401	857	367	664	1,135	993	1,254	334	286
Other UK money market instruments [17]	GOZR	1,428	883	1,174	1,893	1,959	2,822	3,416	3,936	2,716	4,655	3,928
Money market instruments issued by non-resident businesses	GOZS	413	384	449	1,279	911	963	2,067	3,709	2,752	2,752	6,099
Other short-term assets not elsewhere classified [18]	JX5W	1,365	1,854	1,898	1,304	3,474	3,113	3,644	2,311	1,904	1,788	2,592
Balances outstanding from stockbrokers and securities dealers [19]	RYIL	8,939	18,879	24,812	28,297	30,536	11,281	7,145	8,241	6,213	5,989	5,379
Income accrued on investments and rents	RYIM	1,921	1,970	2,303	2,744	2,576	2,714	2,761	2,930	2,872	3,169	2,651
Amounts outstanding from HM Revenue and Customs [19]	RYIN	28	29	16	15	23	32	37	53	67	54	65
Other debtors and assets not elsewhere classified	RYIO	22,838	25,006	35,224	22,454	24,565	21,464	13,159	8,902	11,387	7,543	5,933
Derivative contracts with UK counterparties which have a positive (asset) value [20]	JRO3	10,235	22,157	24,357	29,789	35,194	61,862	99,420	170,170	186,184	191,511	222,296
Derivative contracts with overseas counterparties which have a positive (asset) value [20]	GOJU	2,962	2,668	5,995	8,652	5,835	20,534	19,803	29,445	38,324	49,910	79,679
TOTAL ASSETS	RYIR	813,889	995,100	1,118,254	1,131,112	968,752	1,124,262	1,289,071	1,444,019	1,603,292	1,706,682	1,784,104
LIABILITIES												
Borrowing [23]	GQED	8,133	11,678	14,661	16,180	4,461	3,859	2,830	3,361	10,603	16,050	27,135
Balances owed to stockbrokers and securities dealers [24]	RYIS	9,248	18,722	25,954	33,965	37,912	13,707	7,312	9,688	7,816	8,267	9,869
Pensions due but not paid [24]	RYIT	138	86	285	220	167	280	271	300	5,152	2,672	3,693
Derivative contracts with UK counterparties which have a negative (liability) value [20]	JRP9	7,873	16,818	17,231	26,187	27,533	37,689	78,322	147,217	149,493	161,962	181,946
Derivative contracts with overseas counterparties which have a negative (liability) value [20]	GKGR	3,082	2,785	7,036	11,275	6,335	41,110	37,345	42,712	60,725	73,848	109,217
Other creditors, provisions and liabilities not elsewhere classified	RYIU	22,107	24,834	36,208	18,327	20,577	21,603	18,889	9,905	9,011	13,236	3,006
Market value of pension funds [25]	AHVA	763,308	920,177	1,016,879	1,024,958	871,767	1,006,014	1,144,102	1,230,836	1,360,492	1,430,647	1,449,238
TOTAL LIABILITIES	RYIR	813,889	995,100	1,118,254	1,131,112	968,752	1,124,262	1,289,071	1,444,019	1,603,292	1,706,682	1,784,104

c Suppressed to avoid the disclosure of confidential data.   *Source: Office for National Statistics*

1 Combined public and private sector. Data from the pension funds surveys are of lower quality than equivalent data from other institutional groups because of the difficulties in constructing a suitable sampling frame of pension funds.

13 Includes money market funds; liquidity funds and cash liquidity funds.

14 Sterling and foreign currency.

15 Includes treasury bills. Excludes UK government securities.

16 Sterling and foreign currency commercial paper issued by: banks; building societies; other financial institutions and other issuing companies.

17 Includes floating rate notes maturing within one year of issue.

18 UK and overseas. Excludes derivative contracts.

19 Gross value.

20 Includes credit default products; employee stock options; other options; other swaps; futures; forwards and other derivative contracts not elsewhere classified.

22 Gross value.

23 UK and overseas. Includes from a UK perspective: sterling and foreign currency borrowing from UK banks

24 Excludes any estimated future liabilities.

25 Net value as found in statement of net assets.

2.15a INSURANCE COMPANIES' BALANCE SHEET: LONG-TERM BUSINESS ASSETS AND LIABILITIES AT MARKET VALUES

£ million at end of year

		2004	2005	2006	2007	2008	2009	2010	2011	2012	2013	2014
ASSETS												
UK government securities denominated in sterling	AHNJ	157,019	161,906	161,641	158,694	166,879	167,247	182,506	205,223	187,145	170,950	179,602
Index-linked	AHQI	28,673	33,722	41,104	45,902	54,387	57,157	66,115	78,354	72,499	71,234	81,181
Other[1]	J5HZ	128,346	128,184	120,537	112,792	112,492	110,090	116,391	126,869	114,646	99,716	98,421
UK government securities denominated in foreign currency	RGBV	0	206	12	0	0	0	0	0	0	0	0
UK local authority investments[2]	AHNN	2,044	1,840	1,614	998	776	655	768	813	770	3,168	8,390
Other UK public sector investments[3]	RGCS	254	801	651	634	872	1,461	2,189	2,207	2,197	3,684	2,496
UK PUBLIC SECTOR SECURITIES	**RYEK**	**159,317**	**164,753**	**163,918**	**160,326**	**168,527**	**169,363**	**185,463**	**208,243**	**190,112**	**177,802**	**190,488**
UK corporate bonds[4]	IFLF	150,884	165,918	159,073	159,273	159,789	160,532	158,987	163,348	178,627	167,021	177,937
Sterling	IFLG	144,280	158,995	150,907	153,694	154,525	155,184	156,477	160,842	174,682	165,453	176,486
Foreign currency	IFLH	6,604	6,923	8,166	5,579	5,264	5,348	2,510	2,506	3,945	1,568	1,451
UK ordinary shares[5]	IFLI	237,610	273,679	299,717	293,655	188,430	209,992	207,971	177,480	162,949	170,841	160,294
UK preference shares[5]	RLOL	1,198	1,228	1,231	983	724	624	648	536	375	340	271
Overseas corporate securities	IFLJ	130,098	165,452	194,997	234,388	219,957	266,280	278,930	262,823	303,565	315,453	331,122
Bonds	RLOP	40,281	45,970	57,774	69,696	85,077	111,866	112,338	115,744	127,629	119,631	122,217
Ordinary shares	AHNQ	89,654	119,207	136,652	163,249	134,211	153,500	165,216	145,932	173,982	194,250	207,643
Preference shares	RLOM	163	275	571	1,443	669	914	1,376	1,147	1,954	1,572	1,262
Mutual fund investments[6]	IFLK	108,019	168,896	192,516	222,081	186,950	230,247	259,457	265,750	328,657	360,502	390,694
CORPORATE SECURITIES	**RYEO**	**627,809**	**775,173**	**847,534**	**910,380**	**755,850**	**867,675**	**905,993**	**869,937**	**974,173**	**1,014,157**	**1,060,318**
Overseas government, provincial and municipal securities	AHNS	20,161	16,065	21,078	25,787	29,053	24,601	25,363	23,727	26,928	30,013	34,234
Other longer-term assets not elsewhere classified[7]	JX8D	89,063	83,665	92,326	99,316	76,139	67,531	74,900	81,916	81,039	74,737	80,064
OTHER LONGER-TERM ASSETS	**RYER**	**109,224**	**99,730**	**113,404**	**125,103**	**105,192**	**92,132**	**100,263**	**105,643**	**107,967**	**104,750**	**114,298**
LONGER-TERM ASSETS	**RYES**	**896,350**	**1,039,656**	**1,124,856**	**1,195,809**	**1,029,569**	**1,129,170**	**1,191,719**	**1,183,823**	**1,272,252**	**1,296,709**	**1,365,104**

Suppressed to avoid the disclosure of confidential data.

Source: Office for National Statistics

Includes securities of: 0 up to 15 years maturity; over 15 years maturity and undated maturity. Excludes treasury bills and index-linked securities.
Includes local authority securities; negotiable bonds; loans and mortgages.
Includes public corporation loans and mortgages and other public sector investments not elsewhere classified.
Issued by: banks; building societies and other corporates.
Quoted and unquoted.
UK and overseas. Includes authorised and unauthorised unit trust units; investment trust securities; open-ended investment companies; hedge funds and other mutual fund investments not elsewhere classified.
UK and overseas. Includes loans; fixed assets and other longer-term assets not elsewhere classified.

12.15a INSURANCE COMPANIES' BALANCE SHEET: LONG-TERM BUSINESS ASSETS AND LIABILITIES AT MARKET VALUES

continued

£ million at end of

		2004	2005	2006	2007	2008	2009	2010	2011	2012	2013	2
ASSETS												
Cash	HLGW	15	29	0	0	0	0	0	0	0	0	
Balances with banks and building societies in the UK	JX2C	28,018	31,606	34,454	48,619	51,139	44,483	34,026	34,998	35,424	26,785	26
Sterling	JX3R	26,116	30,221	32,653	45,948	47,456	42,097	32,387	32,698	33,805	24,616	23,
Foreign currency	JX3T	1,902	1,385	1,801	2,671	3,683	2,386	1,639	2,300	1,619	2,169	2
Balances with overseas banks	HLHB	1,086	1,454	1,022	1,484	2,816	3,758	2,766	1,726	1,381	3,143	3
Other liquid deposits[8]	HLHC	1,522	1,215	333	678	1,638	12,385	14,076	15,891	17,257	38,843	39,
Certificates of deposit issued by banks and building societies in the UK[9]	AHND	18,733	14,200	17,256	15,177	11,401	8,177	8,622	6,158	5,769	5,318	6,
Money market instruments issued by HM Treasury[10]	RGBM	534	537	685	785	179	1,344	509	1,392	1,081	2,688	1
UK local authority debt	AHNF	0	0	0	0	0	0	0	0	0	1	
Commercial paper issued by UK companies[11]	JF77	2,884	5,130	2,714	2,723	2,268	1,806	646	891	496	648	
Other UK money market instruments[12]	HLHL	1,997	2,670	3,538	3,071	3,159	2,959	3,208	5,501	3,540	2,055	2,
Money market instruments issued by non-resident businesses	HLHM	952	1,681	405	859	689	1,755	2,956	1,530	2,068	907	1,
Other short-term assets not elsewhere classified[13]	JX2E	2,615	10,432	10,749	20,965	19,555	10,076	5,232	6,159	6,008	5,582	
Balances due from stockbrokers and securities dealers[14]	RGBU	-228	-1,052	-345	140	-399	-1,159	-834	-1,245	-1,145	-1,228	-1
SHORT-TERM ASSETS (excluding derivatives)	**RYEW**	**58,128**	**67,902**	**70,811**	**94,501**	**92,445**	**85,584**	**71,207**	**73,001**	**71,879**	**84,742**	**82**
Derivative contracts with UK and overseas counterparties which have a positive (asset) value[15]	IFKX	3,743	5,739	5,937	5,205	17,892	10,317	12,399	24,060	20,805	18,144	39,
Agents' balances and outstanding premiums in respect of direct insurance and facultative reinsurance contracts[16]												
UK	RYPA	269	500	669	738	535	467	515	554	620	769	
Overseas	RYPB	106	-103	-136	-177	0	1	3	3	0	0	
Reinsurance, coinsurance and treaty balances[17]												
UK	RYPC	2,965	2,607	3,462	-413	-1,000	3,817	-838	-1,147	-1,778	2,109	7,
Overseas	RYPD	415	929	1,105	836	-7,355	-8,232	-6,020	-6,035	-6,425	-5,590	-5,
Outstanding interest, dividends and rents[18]	RYPH	7,476	7,897	7,330	8,690	9,256	9,158	8,591	8,511	8,716	7,762	7,
Other debtors and assets not elsewhere classified[19]	RYPF	23,028	19,694	44,923	51,373	37,342	33,162	30,366	28,806	27,717	28,595	21,
Direct investment for non-insurance subsidiary and associate companies in the UK[20]	RYET	3,971	8,390	13,016	9,186	11,484	10,129	5,097	7,249	8,880	8,125	5,
Direct investment for UK insurance subsidiary, associate and holding companies[20]	RYEU	3,473	2,528	6,114	7,578	7,890	7,234	6,720	7,152	4,275	3,865	6,
Direct investment for overseas subsidiaries, associates, branches and agencies[20]	RYEV	2,181	4,455	3,341	3,832	5,011	4,141	4,131	3,340	3,470	4,296	3,
TOTAL ASSETS	**RKBI**	**1,002,105**	**1,160,194**	**1,281,428**	**1,377,158**	**1,203,069**	**1,284,948**	**1,323,890**	**1,329,317**	**1,410,411**	**1,449,526**	**1,535,**

c Suppressed to avoid the disclosure of confidential data.

Source: Office for National Statis

8 Includes money market funds; liquidity funds and cash liquidity funds.
9 Sterling and foreign currency.
10 Includes treasury bills. Excludes UK government securities.
11 Sterling and foreign currency commercial paper issued by: banks; building societies; other financial institutions and other issuing companies.
12 Includes floating rate notes maturing within one year of issue.
13 UK and overseas. Excludes derivative contracts.
14 Net of balances owed. Includes amounts due on securities bought and sold for future settlement.
15 Includes credit default products; employee stock options; other options; other swaps; futures; forwards and other derivative contracts not elsewhere classified.
16 Net of insurance liabilities.
17 Net of reinsurance bought and sold.
18 Net value.
19 Includes deferred acquisition costs.
20 Net asset value of attributable companies.

12.15a INSURANCE COMPANIES' BALANCE SHEET: LONG-TERM BUSINESS ASSETS AND LIABILITIES AT MARKET VALUES

continued

£ million at end of year

		2004	2005	2006	2007	2008	2009	2010	2011	2012	2013	2014
LIABILITIES												
Borrowing	AHNI	14,536	15,224	14,369	12,426	12,467	10,866	12,542	12,084	10,660	10,112	9,578
Banks and building societies in the UK[9]	JX2G	5,362	5,043	2,867	3,801	5,089	3,305	2,099	1,980	961	1,011	461
Other UK[21]	ICXU	8,381	9,030	9,537	6,699	4,832	5,460	8,112	8,730	9,075	8,368	8,340
Overseas[22]	RGDD	793	1,151	1,965	1,926	2,546	2,101	2,331	1,374	624	733	777
Long-term business insurance and investment contract liabilities[23]	RKDC	873,071	1,037,658	1,125,221	1,205,183	1,069,993	1,153,944	1,178,823	1,171,844	1,241,671	1,277,415	1,346,456
Claims admitted but not paid[23]	RKBM	3,579	3,481	3,513	3,848	3,426	4,637	2,946	3,072	3,387	3,608	3,649
Provisions for taxation and dividends payable[24]	KVE9	4,961	8,245	8,120	7,489	60	1,781	2,973	1,993	2,400	2,919	4,041
Other creditors, provisions and liabilities not elsewhere classified[25]	RYPL	16,738	16,907	33,192	39,527	52,849	47,803	53,826	66,466	69,971	68,289	89,296
Excess of total assets over liabilities in respect of: long-term business; minority interests in UK subsidiary companies; shareholders' capital and reserves and any other reserves[26]	A4YP	89,220	78,679	97,013	108,685	64,274	65,917	72,780	73,858	82,322	87,183	82,527
TOTAL LIABILITIES	RKBI	1,002,105	1,160,194	1,281,428	1,377,158	1,203,069	1,284,948	1,323,890	1,329,317	1,410,411	1,449,526	1,535,547

c Suppressed to avoid the disclosure of confidential data.

Source: Office for National Statistics

9 Sterling and foreign currency.
21 Includes issue of securities (other than ordinary shares); issue of sterling commercial paper and other borrowing not elsewhere classified.
22 Includes borrowing from banks; related companies and other borrowing not elsewhere classified.
23 Net of reinsurers share.
24 UK and overseas. Includes deferred tax net of amounts receivable.
25 UK and overseas. Includes derivative contracts which have a negative (liability) value.
26 Includes unallocated divisible surplus and the 'net worth' of UK branches of overseas companies, including profit and loss account balances.

12.15b INSURANCE COMPANIES' BALANCE SHEET: GENERAL BUSINESS ASSETS AND LIABILITIES AT MARKET VALUES

£ million at end of year

		2004	2005	2006	2007	2008	2009	2010	2011	2012	2013	2014
ASSETS												
UK government securities denominated in sterling	AHMJ	19,662	19,818	19,296	16,026	18,441	16,969	13,631	13,384	11,774	12,855	14,712
Index-linked	AHMZ	345	538	603	297	1,622	1,991	1,731	1,724	2,150	2,355	3,009
Other[1]	J8EX	19,317	19,280	18,693	15,729	16,819	14,978	11,900	11,660	9,624	10,500	11,703
UK government securities denominated in foreign currency	RYMQ	35	12	72	69	3	0	0	c	13	18	0
UK local authority investments[2]	AHMN	49	44	0	3	0	0	0	c	0	0	0
Other UK public sector investments[3]	RYMU	54	6	0	10	0	65	249	c	252	209	446
UK PUBLIC SECTOR SECURITIES	**RYMV**	**19,800**	**19,880**	**19,368**	**16,108**	**18,444**	**17,034**	**13,880**	**13,907**	**12,039**	**13,082**	**15,158**
UK corporate bonds[4]	IFVV	9,826	10,815	11,797	13,397	12,060	13,550	10,487	10,817	12,127	12,355	12,462
Sterling	IFVW	9,637	9,932	11,057	12,647	11,009	12,288	9,544	10,217	11,264	11,610	11,716
Foreign currency	IFVX	189	883	740	750	1,051	1,262	943	600	863	745	746
UK ordinary shares[5]	IFVY	8,724	9,864	10,138	9,006	10,501	9,963	9,525	8,435	8,732	7,846	3,500
UK preference shares[5]	RLOT	54	40	9	44	29	26	26	25	21	21	25
Overseas corporate securities	IFVZ	11,520	12,645	18,636	14,773	20,258	23,002	17,594	18,636	24,380	24,638	27,748
Bonds	RLOX	9,762	10,866	16,128	12,872	18,081	21,017	15,847	16,939	21,872	21,834	24,276
Ordinary shares	AHMQ	1,758	1,779	2,507	1,901	2,175	1,976	1,741	1,692	2,501	c	3,462
Preference shares	RLOU	0	0	1	0	2	9	6	5	7	c	10
Mutual fund investments[6]	IFWA	2,470	1,270	1,256	1,780	1,911	3,498	4,878	5,802	4,236	4,686	4,951
CORPORATE SECURITIES	**RYNF**	**32,594**	**34,634**	**41,836**	**39,000**	**44,759**	**50,039**	**42,510**	**43,715**	**49,496**	**49,546**	**48,686**
Overseas government, provincial and municipal securities	AHMS	6,662	7,341	8,035	4,869	8,505	7,204	5,126	5,524	9,355	9,584	8,373
Other longer-term assets not elsewhere classified[7]	JX8E	4,451	6,362	6,746	7,059	8,269	7,338	9,158	9,938	10,148	9,606	10,518
OTHER LONGER-TERM ASSETS	**RYNO**	**11,113**	**13,703**	**14,781**	**11,928**	**16,774**	**14,542**	**14,284**	**15,462**	**19,503**	**19,190**	**18,891**
LONGER-TERM ASSETS	**RYNP**	**63,507**	**68,217**	**75,985**	**67,036**	**79,977**	**81,615**	**70,674**	**73,084**	**81,038**	**81,818**	**82,735**

c Suppressed to avoid the disclosure of confidential data.

Source: Office for National Statistics

1 Includes securities of: 0 up to 15 years maturity; over 15 years maturity and undated maturity. Excludes treasury bills and index-linked securities.
2 Includes local authority securities; negotiable bonds; loans and mortgages.
3 Includes public corporation loans and mortgages and other public sector investments not elsewhere classified.
4 Issued by: banks; building societies and other corporates.
5 Quoted and unquoted.
6 UK and overseas. Includes authorised and unauthorised unit trust units; investment trust securities; open-ended investment companies; hedge funds and other mutual fund investments not elsewhere classified.
7 UK and overseas. Includes loans; fixed assets and other longer-term assets not elsewhere classified.

12.15b INSURANCE COMPANIES' BALANCE SHEET: GENERAL BUSINESS ASSETS AND LIABILITIES AT MARKET VALUES

continued

£ million at end of year

		2004	2005	2006	2007	2008	2009	2010	2011	2012	2013	2014
ASSETS												
Cash	HLMN	23	63	0	0	0	0	0	0	0	0	0
Balances with banks and building societies in the UK	JX3H	18,051	9,116	9,327	8,949	9,871	10,227	7,961	7,619	7,032	6,970	5,161
Sterling	JX43	16,485	7,952	6,501	6,907	8,170	8,763	6,730	6,532	5,988	5,583	3,974
Foreign currency	JX45	1,566	1,164	2,826	2,042	1,701	1,464	1,231	1,087	1,044	1,387	1,187
Balances with overseas banks	HLMS	1,523	1,116	1,031	1,015	1,250	1,138	981	1,150	1,841	1,369	617
Other liquid deposits[8]	HLMT	204	70	396	375	869	2,476	3,326	2,916	3,753	3,021	3,390
Certificates of deposit issued by banks and building societies in the UK[9]	IX8K	6,808	8,402	7,708	8,264	7,775	2,002	558	843	1,223	1,403	2,557
Money market instruments issued by HM Treasury[10]	ICWI	444	1,670	379	342	708	979	327	237	1,675	1,214	1,659
UK local authority debt	AHMF	0	0	0	0	0	0	0	0	0	0	0
Commercial paper issued by UK companies[11]	JF75	441	610	732	2,682	1,640	1,630	275	281	509	461	498
Other UK money market instruments[12]	HLNC	160	139	68	90	278	346	359	360	253	340	324
Money market instruments issued by non-resident businesses	HLND	1,619	2,429	3,516	3,261	2,277	2,321	545	745	449	1,120	570
Other short-term assets not elsewhere classified[13]	JX2I	138	2,992	1,733	612	1,576	718	725	933	1,064	781	1,413
Balances due from stockbrokers and securities dealers[14]	RYMA	-61	3	-66	25	891	52	90	26	-1	37	-48
SHORT-TERM ASSETS (excluding derivatives)	**RYME**	**29,350**	**26,610**	**24,824**	**25,615**	**27,135**	**21,889**	**15,147**	**15,110**	**17,798**	**16,716**	**16,141**
Derivative contracts with UK and overseas counterparties which have a positive (asset) value[15]	IFVJ	122	44	45	208	685	455	906	629	3,032	4,099	3,608
Agents' balances and outstanding premiums in respect of direct insurance and facultative reinsurance contracts[16]												
UK	RYMF	8,450	7,991	9,060	8,216	9,022	8,171	8,470	8,222	9,584	9,089	8,829
Overseas	RYMG	1,385	572	480	575	55	73	-15	-200	711	868	702
Reinsurance, coinsurance and treaty balances[17]												
UK	RYMH	942	934	1,290	1,164	1,092	1,730	-165	-258	-182	-233	-921
Overseas	RYMI	-919	-1,501	-48	-23	537	491	375	921	-4	217	244
Outstanding interest, dividends and rents[18]	RYPN	1,156	905	1,067	1,255	1,108	958	765	726	724	881	581
Other debtors and assets not elsewhere classified[19]	RKAC	11,462	12,405	15,814	19,096	17,189	10,785	11,064	10,683	14,281	12,905	11,407
Direct investment for non-insurance subsidiary and associate companies in the UK[20]	RYNR	19,028	20,530	20,111	21,954	21,259	21,181	18,206	18,627	19,876	20,510	7,674
Direct investment for UK insurance subsidiary, associate and holding companies[20]	RYNS	2,280	6,071	4,745	6,936	7,669	7,159	6,252	6,795	6,365	6,886	c
Direct investment for overseas subsidiaries, associates, branches and agencies[20]	RYNT	5,507	6,446	9,657	9,445	10,815	12,124	9,868	9,073	8,004	7,147	c
TOTAL ASSETS	**RKBY**	**142,270**	**149,224**	**163,030**	**161,477**	**176,543**	**166,631**	**141,547**	**143,412**	**161,227**	**160,903**	**142,025**

c Suppressed to avoid the disclosure of confidential data.

Source: Office for National Statistics

8 Includes money market funds; liquidity funds and cash liquidity funds.
9 Sterling and foreign currency.
10 Includes treasury bills. Excludes UK government securities.
11 Sterling and foreign currency commercial paper issued by: banks; building societies; other financial institutions and other issuing companies.
12 Includes floating rate notes maturing within one year of issue.
13 UK and overseas. Excludes derivative contracts.
14 Net of balances owed. Includes amounts due on securities bought and sold for future settlement.
15 Includes credit default products; employee stock options; other options; other swaps; futures; forwards and other derivative contracts not elsewhere classified.
16 Net of insurance liabilities.
17 Net of reinsurance bought and sold.
18 Net value.
19 Includes deferred acquisition costs.
20 Net asset value of attributable companies.

12.15b INSURANCE COMPANIES' BALANCE SHEET: GENERAL BUSINESS ASSETS AND LIABILITIES AT MARKET VALUES

continued   £ million at end of year

		2004	2005	2006	2007	2008	2009	2010	2011	2012	2013	2014
LIABILITIES												
Borrowing	AHMI	17,256	14,790	19,052	18,597	20,214	15,602	14,431	14,281	12,460	12,133	7,081
Banks and building societies in the UK[9]	JX3J	4,519	893	3,148	675	343	744	621	606	819	794	734
Other UK[21]	IFHX	10,261	11,080	10,445	10,885	13,179	9,965	9,835	8,991	8,401	8,792	5,200
Overseas[22]	RYMD	2,476	2,817	5,459	7,037	6,692	4,893	3,975	4,684	3,240	2,547	1,147
General business technical reserves[23]	RKCT	67,241	71,710	77,221	71,146	76,980	70,947	58,484	57,539	61,771	59,738	59,744
Provisions for taxation and dividends payable[24]	KVF2	2,429	1,806	2,656	2,486	858	345	40	7	240	424	595
Other creditors, provisions and liabilities not elsewhere classified[25]	RYPR	10,817	10,718	16,226	22,069	21,149	19,976	18,367	19,362	25,757	24,989	16,985
Excess of total assets over liabilities in respect of minority interests in UK subsidiary companies, shareholders' capital and reserves and any other reserves[26]	A8SI	44,527	50,200	47,875	47,179	57,342	59,761	50,225	52,223	60,999	63,619	57,620
TOTAL LIABILITIES	**RKBY**	**142,270**	**149,224**	**163,030**	**161,477**	**176,543**	**166,631**	**141,547**	**143,412**	**161,227**	**160,903**	**142,025**

c Suppressed to avoid the disclosure of confidential data.

Source: Office for National Statistics

9 Sterling and foreign currency.
21 Includes issue of securities (other than ordinary shares); issue of sterling commercial paper and other borrowing not elsewhere classified.
22 Includes borrowing from banks; related companies and other borrowing not elsewhere classified.
23 Net of reinsurers share.
24 UK and overseas. Includes deferred tax net of amounts receivable.
25 UK and overseas. Includes derivative contracts which have a negative (liability) value.
26 Includes the 'net worth' of UK branches of overseas companies, including profit and loss account balances.

12.16a Individual insolvencies

England and Wales, not seasonally adjusted

	Total individual insolvencies	Bankruptcies[1]	Debt relief orders[2]	Individual voluntary arrangements[3]
2007	106,645	64,480	z	42,165
2008	106,544	67,428	z	39,116
2009	134,142	74,670	11,831	47,641
2010	135,045	59,173	25,179	50,693
2011	119,943	41,876	29,009	49,058
2012	109,640	31,787	31,179	46,674
2013	100,998	24,571	27,546	48,881
2014	99,223	20,345	26,688	52,190
2015	80,404	15,845	24,175	40,384

Source: The Insolvency Service.

[1] Figures from 2011 Q2 onwards based on the date the bankruptcy order was granted by the court or the Adjudicator. From 6 April 2016, the process for people making themselves bankrupt moved online and out of the courts.

[2] Debt Relief Orders (DROs) came into effect on 6 April 2009 as an alternative route into individual insolvency. In April 2011 a change was introduced to the legislation to allow those who have built up value in a pension scheme to apply for debt relief under these provisions.

[3] Includes Deeds of Arrangement.

12.16b Individual insolvencies

Scotland, not seasonally adjusted

	Total individual insolvencies	Sequestrations (of which LILA/MAP)[1,2]		Protected trust deeds
2007	13,924	6,331	z	7,593
2008	19,991	12,449	(7,133)	7,542
2009	23,541	14,415	(8,774)	9,126
2010	20,344	11,906	(6,801)	8,438
2011	19,650	11,128	(4,812)	8,522
2012	18,402	9,630	(3,886)	8,772
2013	14,250	7,189	(2,728)	7,061
2014	11,622	6,747	(2,533)	4,875
2015	8,785	4,477	(1,509)	4,308

Source: Accountant in Bankruptcy.

[1] On 1 April 2008, Part 1 of the Bankruptcy and Diligence etc. (Scotland) Act 2007 came into force making significant changes to some aspects of sequestration (bankruptcy), debt relief and debt enforcement in Scotland. This included the introduction of the new route into bankruptcy for people with low income and low assets (LILA). Of the number or sequestrations, individuals who meet LILA criteria are shown in brackets.

[2] On 1 April 2015, part of the Bankruptcy and Debt Advice (Scotland) Act came into force making significant changes to some aspects of sequestration (bankruptcy). This included the introduction of the Minimal Asset Process (MAP), which replaced the LILA route into sequestration; mandatory debt advice for people seeking statutory debt relief; a new online process for applying for sequestration; and an additional year for people to make contributions to repaying their debts (increasing from three years to four, in line with protected trust deeds).

12.16c Individual insolvencies

Northern Ireland, not seasonally adjusted

	Total individual insolvencies	Bankruptcies	Debt relief orders[1]	Individual voluntary arrangements
2007	1,338	898	z	440
2008	1,638	1,079	z	559
2009	1,958	1,236	z	722
2010	2,323	1,321	z	1,002
2011	2,839	1,615	112	1,112
2012	3,189	1,452	506	1,231
2013	3,373	1,347	593	1,433
2014	3,395	1,367	536	1,492
2015	2,690	1,071	472	1,147

Source: Department for Enterprise, Trade and Investment, Northern Ireland.

1 Debt relief orders came into effect on 30 June 2011.

12.17a Company insolvencies[1,2]

England and Wales, not seasonally adjusted

	Total new company insolvencies[2,3]	Compulsory liquidations[3,4]	New creditors' voluntary liquidations[3]	Administrations[5,6,7]	Company voluntary arrangements[8]	Receivership appointments[9]
2007	15,866	5,165	7,625	2,531	417	128
2008	21,072	5,494	9,995	4,808	586	189
2009	24,011	5,643	13,509	4,019	723	117
2010	19,795	4,792	11,506	2,682	766	49
2011	20,285	5,003	11,947	2,539	748	48
2012	19,349	4,261	11,906	2,334	816	32
2013	17,682	3,632	11,453	2,009	571	17
2014	16,317 r	3,755	10,399 r	1,587	554	22
2015	14,660 r	2,889	9,995 r	1,402	363	11

Sources: Insolvency Service (compulsory liquidations only); Companies House (all other insolvency types).

1 Data from 2000Q1 are not consistent with earlier data because of a change to the methodology. This does not affect compulsory liquidations.

2 Excludes creditors' voluntary liquidations following administration

3 Includes partnership winding-up orders.

4 Figures from 2011 Q2 onwards based on the date the winding-up order was granted by the court.

5 Releases prior to 2012 Q4 showed administrations separately as "Administrator Appointments" and "In Administration - Enterprise Act".

6 The figure for Q4 2006 includes 844 separate, limited companies created and managed by "Safe Solutions Accountancy Limited" for which Grant Thornton was appointed administrator.

7 The figure for Q3 2008 includes 728 separate managed service companies.

8 The figure for Q2 2012 includes 104 new CVAs recorded under "Health and Social Work" in June reflecting the fact that on 20 June 2012 156 companies in the Southern Cross Healthcare Group had CVAs approved.

9 Data before 2000 Q1 include Law of Property Act and fixed charge receiverships, which are not insolvencies but which cannot be identified separately to insolvent receiverships under the previous methodology.

12.17b Company insolvencies[2]

Scotland, not seasonally adjusted

	Total new company insolvencies[2]	Compulsory liquidations[3]	New creditors' voluntary liquidations[2]	Administrations	Company voluntary arrangements	Receivership appointments
2007	640	400	122	64	7	47
2008	893	561	104	190	4	34
2009	1,027	556	171	259	8	33
2010	1,302	780	252	212	7	51
2011	1,453	923	269	211	13	37
2012	1,377 r	920 r	233	169	24	31
2013	897	484	258	122	16	17
2014	963	650	207	87	14	5
2015	948	576	253	109	4	6

Source: Companies House.

[1] Data from 2000 Q1 are not consistent with earlier data because of a change to the methodology.

[2] Data before 2000 Q1 includes creditors' voluntary liquidations following administration as under the previous methodology it is not possible to separate these CVLs out.

[3] Includes provisional liquidations.

12.17c Company insolvencies[1,2]

Northern Ireland, not seasonally adjusted

	Total new company insolvencies[4]	Compulsory liquidations[3]	New creditors' voluntary liquidations[4,5]	Administrations[4]	Company voluntary arrangements[4]	Administrative receiverships[4]
2007	:	122	42	:	:	:
2008	:	158	51	:	:	:
2009	:	164	86	:	:	:
2010	494	250	116	78	42	8
2011	437	208	116	68	26	19
2012	526	252	136	83	41	14
2013	357	178	98	47	33	1
2014	380	221	90	29	37	3
2015	378	225	76	35	39	3

Source: Department for Enterprise, Trade and Investment, Northern Ireland; Companies House

[1] Includes partnerships.

[2] Data from 2009 Q4 are not consistent with earlier data because of a change to the methodology. This does not affect compulsory liquidations. Data for Northern Ireland prior to 2010 are not available under the new methodology.

[3] Source: Department for Enterprise, Trade and Investment, Northern Ireland.

[4] Source: Companies House.

[5] Data before 2009 Q4 includes creditors' voluntary liquidations following administration as under the previous methodology it is not possible to separate these CVLs out.

12.18a Monetary financial institutions' consolidated balance sheet

£ millions   Not seasonally adjusted

Amounts outstanding of liabilities

LPM	Currency, deposits and money market instruments						Financial derivatives (net)		Other securities issued		Other liabilities		Total liabilities/assets
	Private sector		Public sector		Non-residents								
	Sterling	Foreign currency	Sterling	Foreign currency	Sterling	Foreign currency	Sterling	Foreign currency	Sterling	Foreign currency	Sterling	Foreign currency	
	VYAX	VYAY	VYAZ	VYBA	VYBB	VYBC	VWKM	VWKN	VWKO	VWKP	VWKQ	VWKR	VYBF
2015 Aug	2,110,711	421,133	50,819	3,337	456,937	2,363,068	-7,316	13,914	37,515	210,055	469,229	145,922	6,275,324
Sep	2,091,524	426,143	42,073	2,929	487,315	2,337,970	-19,802	15,023	37,478	215,890	494,349	126,742	6,257,633
Oct	2,106,712	418,220	42,930	3,134	458,170	2,294,801	-16,499	6,889	37,324	216,084	465,060	138,585	6,171,410
Nov	2,116,647	420,328	45,234	3,187	462,345	2,325,241 (aa)	-14,733	7,684	36,056	214,350	463,862	153,565	6,233,766 (aa)
Dec	2,114,369	421,919	43,063	4,027	482,528	2,307,176	-32,442	21,615	35,743	218,066	470,386	165,995	6,252,446
2016 Jan	2,103,709	448,793	43,256	4,165	481,514	2,426,142	5,172	-13,794	35,670	223,095	460,059	179,012	6,396,792
Feb	2,123,558	460,909	41,638	4,372	448,076	2,466,958	41,133	-39,043	35,693	230,433	436,441	203,328	6,453,495
Mar	2,128,434 (v)	458,653	37,235	2,787	472,627	2,404,210	-18,147	16,777	35,841	229,819	437,545	191,690	6,397,472 (v)
Apr	2,125,195	458,240	47,402	4,105	469,387	2,370,539	-31,444	20,394	36,191	231,396	426,774 (ad)	205,058	6,363,237 (ad)
May	2,148,693	459,325	46,498	3,585	459,282	2,376,140	-32,261	23,825	35,886	226,793	438,191	187,700	6,373,656
Jun	2,186,240 (w)	502,635	45,800	3,797	481,787	2,636,668	67,183	-55,297	36,581	249,064	419,353	220,168	6,793,978 (w)
Jul	2,207,952	515,132	44,587	4,865	485,403	2,650,594	68,127	-49,553	36,276	253,075	406,487	231,860	6,854,804
Aug	2,224,788	525,091	46,421	4,783	488,900	2,662,013	70,967	-45,365	36,379	253,232	412,451	229,348	6,909,008
Sep	2,224,869	545,796	40,018	2,820	485,923	2,701,375 (ab)	78,794	-54,554	36,346	252,924	387,780	243,870	6,945,961 (ab)
Oct	2,246,503	563,526	43,686	3,273	498,638	2,780,936	125,231	-134,589	36,052	263,901	358,295	283,112	7,068,564
Nov	2,256,203	559,766	44,200	4,630	498,083	2,691,192	42,454	-53,667	35,185	244,788	406,917	235,508	6,965,259
Dec	2,246,902	540,650	40,362	3,322	497,082	2,712,601	57,778	-59,585	35,177	247,044	414,410	246,180	6,981,922
2017 Jan	2,247,924	561,878 (y)	39,543	4,246	495,978	2,707,400	23,929	-31,287	34,520	247,708	441,077	220,183	6,993,100
Feb	2,249,735 (x)	590,128 (z)	41,731	3,278	496,189	2,769,490	72,207	-68,084	34,543	256,400	453,116	241,162	7,139,895
Mar	2,284,128	569,426	35,921	2,673	508,322	2,727,870	47,413	-41,079	34,305	252,862	431,358	223,483	7,076,683
Apr	2,310,347	569,418	37,002	4,276	499,020	2,679,143	9,723	-3,761	34,136	251,092	432,532	208,425	7,031,353
May	2,304,147	579,697	41,812	4,599	508,864	2,715,335	32,377	-21,323	33,460	257,713	455,403	178,343	7,090,429

Source: Bank of England

Notes to table

Movements in amounts outstanding can reflect breaks in data series as well as underlying flows. For changes data, users are recommended to refer directly to the appropriate series or data tables. Further explanation can be found at: www.bankofengland.co.uk/statistics/Pages/iadb/notesiadb/Changes_flows_growth_rates.aspx.

(v) Due to changes in reporting at one institution, the amounts outstanding decreased by £5bn. This effect has been adjusted out of the flows for March 2016.
(w) Due to improvements in reporting at one institution, the amounts outstanding increased by £8bn. This effect has been adjusted out of the flows for June 2016.
(x) Due to improvements in reporting at one institution, the amounts outstanding increased by £3bn. This effect has been adjusted out of the flows for February 2017.
(y) Due to improvements in reporting at one institution, the amounts outstanding increased by £8bn. This effect has been adjusted out of the flows for January 2017.
(z) Due to improvements in reporting at one institution, the amounts outstanding increased by £4bn. This effect has been adjusted out of the flows for February 2017.
(aa) Due to changes in reporting at one institution, the amounts outstanding decreased by £18bn. This effect has been adjusted out of the flows for November 2015.
(ab) Due to a change in treatment at one institution, the amounts outstanding decreased by £14bn. This effect has been adjusted out of the flows for September 2016.
(ac) Due to a transfer of business by one institution, amounts outstanding increased by £29 billion. This amount has been adjusted out of the flows for July 2017.
(ad) Due to a loan transfer by one reporting institution, the amounts outstanding increased by £7bn. This effect has been adjusted out of the flows for April 2016.

Explanatory notes can be found here: http://www.bankofengland.co.uk/mfsd/iadb/notesiadb/mfi_bs.htm

Copyright guidance and the related UK Open Government Licence can be viewed here: www.bankofengland.co.uk/Pages/disclaimer.aspx.

12.18b Monetary financial institutions' consolidated balance shee

£ millions

Not seasonally adjusted

Amounts outstanding of assets

	Loans						Securities (other than financial derivatives)						Other assets	
	Private sector		Public sector		Non-residents		Private sector		Public sector		Non-residents			
	Sterling	Foreign currency	Sterling	Foreign currency	Sterling	Foreign currency	Sterling	Foreign currency	Sterling	Foreign currency	Sterling	Foreign currency	Sterling	Foreign currency
LPM	VYBG	VYBH	VYBI	VYBJ	VYBK	VYBL	VYBM (ah)	VYBN	VYBO	VYBP	VYBQ	VYBR	VYBS	VYBT
2015 Aug	1,960,495	339,399	19,680	1,107	249,574	2,277,746	196,262	22,406	551,938	463	51,180	483,669	83,562	37,841
Sep	1,960,156	338,891	18,222	1,737	264,683	2,264,604	195,280	22,558	548,147	428	49,786	473,485	82,500	37,154
Oct	1,954,598	332,938	18,297	2,024	251,523	2,190,161	198,504	20,605	546,048	420	49,526	486,960	83,563	36,243
Nov	1,961,428	330,069	18,102	1,317	251,696	2,227,058	201,057	19,681	554,544	422	48,457	496,268	84,758	38,908
Dec	1,962,835	321,152	17,258	1,911	256,181	2,280,659	203,648	19,525	540,558	471	46,245	479,855	85,489	36,658
2016 Jan	1,971,390	343,714	18,534	2,169	258,686	2,383,122	197,906	19,107	551,779	473	47,946	481,025	85,260	35,681
Feb	1,988,011	369,669	18,429	1,819	246,392	2,414,046	193,750	19,378	564,855	505	50,332	465,036	84,264	37,008
Mar	1,996,196	350,676	16,532	899	256,817	2,378,322	195,392	19,651	560,108	572	50,567	452,454	83,232	36,054
Apr	1,988,741 (ai)	359,437	16,008	1,905	264,290	2,330,742	195,431	17,793	557,763	662	47,539	464,077	82,944	35,905
May	2,004,319	356,063	15,382	1,981	270,344	2,331,529	194,426	17,267	562,445	713	49,266	449,618	83,931	36,370
Jun	2,028,408 (ai)	393,287	17,516	1,563	278,705	2,632,461	195,532	16,779	583,134	782	49,272	474,023	83,289	39,227
Jul	2,035,188	392,944	22,946	2,027	287,077	2,635,179	196,976	14,941	591,342	694	52,289	499,600	83,912	39,689
Aug	2,043,367	393,778	21,758	1,694	293,539	2,646,503	197,911	15,155	621,774	705	54,299	493,898	84,392	40,233
Sep	2,049,984	378,685	20,877	1,639	296,913	2,725,452 (ak)	196,086	13,730	611,511	692	54,742	469,613	83,446	42,592
Oct	2,054,241	388,360	21,072	435	295,660	2,813,453	191,548	14,097	608,802	583	57,892	497,465	83,659	41,297
Nov	2,062,369	392,925	18,478	1,530	291,779	2,737,328	193,402	14,862	613,938	499	57,505	456,801	83,145	40,699
Dec	2,061,468	363,774	16,542	1,826	300,851	2,759,544	196,238	13,104	625,768	464	57,350	464,714	81,114	39,165
2017 Jan	2,072,809	385,805	16,586	1,995	301,412	2,737,797	226,409	12,548	610,527	426	60,028	465,869	63,446	37,442

Source: Bank of England

Notes to table

Movements in amounts outstanding can reflect breaks in data series as well as underlying flows. For changes data, users are recommended to refer directly to the appropriate series or data tables. Further explanation can be found at: www.bankofengland.co.uk/statistics/Pages/iadb/notesiadb/Changes_flows_growth_rates.aspx.

(ah) This series includes purchases of bonds made as part of the Bank of England's Corporate Bond Purchase Scheme. Data on Central Bank holdings of securities can be found in Bankstats Table B2.2. For further information on the Bank's treatment of securities transactions in credit statistics, see: www.bankofengland.co.uk/statistics/Documents/articles/2015/2may.pdf.

(ai) Due to a loan transfer by one reporting institution, the amounts outstanding increased by £7bn. This effect has been adjusted out of the flows for April 2016.

(ai) Due to improvements in reporting at one institution, the amounts outstanding increased by £3bn. This effect has been adjusted out of the flows for June 2016.

(ak) Due to a change in treatment at one institution, the amounts outstanding decreased by £14bn. This effect has been adjusted out of the flows for September 2016.

Explanatory notes can be found here : http://www.bankofengland.co.uk/statistics/Pages/iadb/notesiadb/mfi_bs.aspx

Copyright guidance and the related UK Open Government Licence can be viewed here: www.bankofengland.co.uk/Pages/disclaimer.aspx.

12.18c Monetary financial institutions' consolidated balance sheet

£ millions

Not seasonally adjusted

Changes in liabilities

	Currency, deposits and money market instruments						Financial derivatives (net)		Other securities issued		Other liabilities		Total liabilities/ assets
	Private sector		Public sector		Non-residents								
	Sterling	Foreign currency	Sterling	Foreign currency	Sterling	Foreign currency	Sterling	Foreign currency	Sterling	Foreign currency	Sterling	Foreign currency	
LPM	VYAA	VYAB	VYAC	VYAD	VYAE	VYAF	VWKG	VWKH	VWKI	VWKJ	VWKK	VWKL	VYAI
2015 Aug	-11,175	8,584	3,100	-633	533	24,027	2,318	-3,494	-256	-2,528	28,203	-9,491	39,188
Sep	-20,034	-494	-8,746	-437	30,454	-52,415	-10,919	333	-37	2,755	20,790	-14,956	-53,707
Oct	15,671	1,415	857	276	-29,465	8,352	3,303	-7,876	-153	5,702	-24,117	11,416	-14,619
Nov	10,953	-142	2,303	56	4,256	35,689	1,766	1,434	-1,268	-2,471	-10,357	10,324	52,542
Dec	-3,994	-7,289	-2,170	734	19,990	-74,178	-16,422	8,097	-314	-3,710	8,163	16,409	-54,685
2016 Jan	-10,772	10,846	193	-8	-1,114	29,558	37,614	-36,119	-72	-3,155	-26,217	8,065	8,818
Feb	19,880	2,386	-1,619	124	-33,531	-11,472	35,961	-26,157	22	2,141	-28,871	10,669	-30,466
Mar	10,197	2,406	-4,388	-1,570	24,583	-34,776	-59,280	56,534	148	-414	-813	-13,124	-20,496
Apr	-4,951	6,133	10,167	1,376	-3,350	4,382	-13,866	3,930	12	8,137	-10,075	12,197	14,090
May	23,368	4,868	-904	-481	-10,089	20,446	-817	4,313	-305	-1,616	4,958	-19,207	24,533
Jun	32,785	6,339	-698	-57	19,474	69,211	99,444	-83,104	695	3,968	-50,113	7,946	105,890
Jul	21,985	5,651	-1,213	1,013	3,684	-21,272	943	4,902	-305	209	-31,511	-161	-16,074
Aug	17,027	4,532	1,834	-131	3,420	-14,357	2,841	3,959	103	-2,173	-12,119	-3,682	1,253
Sep	-502	11,894	-6,403	-1,997	-2,761	20,339	7,829	-11,737	-33	-3,996	-5,920	17,602	24,314
Oct	21,271	-7,582	3,669	314	13,374	-46,425	46,437	-79,940	-293	16	-5,796	38,015	-16,939
Nov	11,192	17,103	514	1,470	-204	7,806	-82,777	84,258	-867	-7,803	61,913	-28,161	64,444
Dec	-7,859	-22,844	-3,816	-1,347	-950	-5,819	15,324	-5,105	-8	-1,475	-4,340	4,893	-33,347
2017 Jan	966	21,178	-818	974	-1,118	27,151	-33,848	28,087	-657	2,218	38,100	-23,247	58,985

Source: Bank of England

Notes to table

Explanatory notes can be found here: http://www.bankofengland.co.uk/statistics/Pages/iadb/notesiadb/mfi_bs.aspx

Copyright guidance and the related UK Open Government Licence can be viewed here: www.bankofengland.co.uk/Pages/disclaimer.aspx.

12.18d Monetary financial institutions' consolidated balance sheet

£ millions

Changes in assets

Not seasonally adjusted

	Loans						Securities (other than financial derivatives)						Other assets	
	Private sector		Public sector		Non-residents		Private sector		Public sector		Non-residents			
	Sterling	Foreign currency	Sterling	Foreign currency	Sterling	Foreign currency	Sterling	Foreign currency	Sterling	Foreign currency	Sterling	Foreign currency	Sterling	Foreign currency
LPM	VYAJ	VYAK	VYAL	VYAM	VYAN	VYAO	VYAP (aq)	VYAQ	VYAR	VYAS	VYAT	VYAU	VYAV	VYAW
2015 Aug	6,649	3,143	3,022	-1,315	-242	26,023	-9,045	-1,395	7,220	33	-1,705	4,454	1,456	892
Sep	374	-4,489	-1,471	616	15,682	-36,905	-296	184	-8,806	-40	-2,024	-14,271	-1,168	-1,092
Oct	-5,001	1,990	74	323	-13,138	-23,916	1,418	-1,491	3,818	-	378	20,028	1,066	-166
Nov	7,221	-3,284	-243	-709	147	40,269	-958	-1,297	4,624	-3	-2,038	6,693	1,175	944
Dec	-1,437	-18,822	-843	552	4,787	593	2,130	-974	-7,190	1	-3,011	-26,988	-1,231	-2,251
2016 Jan	8,092	10,120	1,001	187	2,520	12,714	-1,468	-475	-6,828	-15	-460	-14,322	11	-2,259
Feb	17,447	17,783	-640	-392	-13,009	-23,931	-39	113	7,081	23	-746	-33,275	-905	26
Mar	8,566	-14,667	-1,898	-921	10,420	-6,415	-485	250	512	78	600	-14,715	-1,325	-496
Apr	-14,454	14,370	-511	1,030	6,629	-9,296	-565	-1,324	3,423	118	-2,408	17,800	-463	-259
May	14,988	-320	-611	102	7,790	16,384	-244	-32	-3,628	50	1,572	-13,118	952	646
Jun	21,105	6,044	2,434	-511	2,861	101,777	849	-1,586	-5,222	16	-4,808	-18,228	-597	1,756
Jul	7,536	-5,971	5,430	443	8,246	-33,747	-4,573	-2,040	-3,321	-97	1,704	9,772	537	7
Aug	8,521	-3,833	-1,166	-352	6,433	-14,212	-3,839	-253	17,611	4	1,380	-9,601	388	170
Sep	6,893	-21,507	-887	-76	3,663	58,027	639	-1,740	5,092	-18	181	-27,171	-762	1,981
Oct	4,432	-8,319	195	-1,283	-1,235	-42,559	-1,722 (ar)	-574	20,228	-143	1,099	15,912	247	-3,217
Nov	10,251	21,055	-2,594	1,122	-3,928	30,066	3,488	556	13,570	-72	2,631	-11,873	-514	684
Dec	1,001	-28,951	-1,916	275	9,107	-8,191	-942	-3,072	4,260	-40	-1,032	184	-2,098	-1,931
2017 Jan	11,269	24,384	44	193	505	5,416	29,824	-752	-4,454	-30	3,774	7,857	-17,696	-1,351

Source: Bank of England

Notes to table

(aq) This series includes purchases of bonds made as part of the Bank of England's Corporate Bond Purchase Scheme. Data on Central Bank holdings of securities can be found in Bankstats Table B2.2. For further information on the Bank's treatment of securities transactions in credit statistics, see: www.bankofengland.co.uk/statistics/Documents/articles/2015/2may.pdf.

(ar) The data for PNFCs M4 lending in October 2016 take account of a redemption of MFIs UK equity holdings of £4bn, following a merger of a UK corporate with a non-UK entity.

Explanatory notes can be found here: http://www.bankofengland.co.uk/statistics/Pages/iadb/notesiadb/mfi_bs.aspx

Copyright guidance and the related UK Open Government Licence can be viewed here: www.bankofengland.co.uk/Pages/disclaimer.aspx

12.19 Selected interest rates, exchange rates and security prices

Monthly average of 4 UK Banks' base rates		Monthly average rate of discount, 3 month Treasury bills, Sterling		Monthly average yield from British Government Securities, 20 year Nominal Par Yield		Monthly average Spot exchange rate, US$ into Sterling	
IUMAAMIH [a] [b]		IUMAAJNB		IUMALNPY [c] [d]		XUMAUSS	
31-Jan-08	5.5	31-Jan-08	5.1215	31-Jan-08	4.4578	31-Jan-08	1.9698
29-Feb-08	5.2976	29-Feb-08	5.0178	29-Feb-08	4.6173	29-Feb-08	1.9638
31-Mar-08	5.25	31-Mar-08	4.8835	31-Mar-08	4.5401	31-Mar-08	2.0032
30-Apr-08	5.0795	30-Apr-08	4.8258	30-Apr-08	4.7315	30-Apr-08	1.9817
31-May-08	5	31-May-08	4.9496	31-May-08	4.8539	31-May-08	1.9641
30-Jun-08	5	30-Jun-08	5.1138	30-Jun-08	5.0261	30-Jun-08	1.9658
31-Jul-08	5	31-Jul-08	5.0843	31-Jul-08	4.9391	31-Jul-08	1.988
31-Aug-08	5	31-Aug-08	4.9539	31-Aug-08	4.7438	31-Aug-08	1.8889
30-Sep-08	5	30-Sep-08	4.7425	30-Sep-08	4.6619	30-Sep-08	1.7986
31-Oct-08	4.6087	31-Oct-08	3.6788	31-Oct-08	4.7579	31-Oct-08	1.69
30-Nov-08	3.225	30-Nov-08	1.9948	30-Nov-08	4.6898	30-Nov-08	1.5338
31-Dec-08	2.1429	31-Dec-08	1.2875	31-Dec-08	4.1461	31-Dec-08	1.4859
31-Jan-09	1.5952	31-Jan-09	0.8945	31-Jan-09	4.2758	31-Jan-09	1.4452
28-Feb-09	1.075	28-Feb-09	0.7177	28-Feb-09	4.3394	28-Feb-09	1.4411
31-Mar-09	0.5682	31-Mar-09	0.6035	31-Mar-09	4.007	31-Mar-09	1.4174
30-Apr-09	0.5	30-Apr-09	0.625	30-Apr-09	4.2419	30-Apr-09	1.4715
31-May-09	0.5	31-May-09	0.5271	31-May-09	4.3752	31-May-09	1.5429
30-Jun-09	0.5	30-Jun-09	0.5037	30-Jun-09	4.471	30-Jun-09	1.6366
31-Jul-09	0.5	31-Jul-09	0.4397	31-Jul-09	4.4588	31-Jul-09	1.6366
31-Aug-09	0.5	31-Aug-09	0.3946	31-Aug-09	4.2164	31-Aug-09	1.6539
30-Sep-09	0.5	30-Sep-09	0.3761	30-Sep-09	4.0688	30-Sep-09	1.6328
31-Oct-09	0.5	31-Oct-09	0.4315	31-Oct-09	4.05	31-Oct-09	1.6199
30-Nov-09	0.5	30-Nov-09	0.4459	30-Nov-09	4.2177	30-Nov-09	1.6597
31-Dec-09	0.5	31-Dec-09	0.3587	31-Dec-09	4.3306	31-Dec-09	1.6239
31-Jan-10	0.5	31-Jan-10	0.4874	31-Jan-10	4.4161	31-Jan-10	1.6162
28-Feb-10	0.5	28-Feb-10	0.4878	28-Feb-10	4.5158	28-Feb-10	1.5615
31-Mar-10	0.5	31-Mar-10	0.5109	31-Mar-10	4.5698	31-Mar-10	1.5053
30-Apr-10	0.5	30-Apr-10	0.5083	30-Apr-10	4.558	30-Apr-10	1.534
31-May-10	0.5	31-May-10	0.4976	31-May-10	4.3143	31-May-10	1.4627
30-Jun-10	0.5	30-Jun-10	0.4839	30-Jun-10	4.2079	30-Jun-10	1.4761
31-Jul-10	0.5	31-Jul-10	0.498	31-Jul-10	4.1754	31-Jul-10	1.5299
31-Aug-10	0.5	31-Aug-10	0.4945	31-Aug-10	3.9824	31-Aug-10	1.566
30-Sep-10	0.5	30-Sep-10	0.4966	30-Sep-10	3.8954	30-Sep-10	1.5578
31-Oct-10	0.5	31-Oct-10	0.5061	31-Oct-10	3.8876	31-Oct-10	1.5862
30-Nov-10	0.5	30-Nov-10	0.4935	30-Nov-10	4.1149	30-Nov-10	1.5961
31-Dec-10	0.5	31-Dec-10	0.4913	31-Dec-10	4.2568	31-Dec-10	1.5603
31-Jan-11	0.5	31-Jan-11	0.5055	31-Jan-11	4.3204	31-Jan-11	1.5795
28-Feb-11	0.5	28-Feb-11	0.5363	28-Feb-11	4.405	28-Feb-11	1.613
31-Mar-11	0.5	31-Mar-11	0.5603	31-Mar-11	4.298	31-Mar-11	1.6159
30-Apr-11	0.5	30-Apr-11	0.5676	30-Apr-11	4.2933	30-Apr-11	1.6345
31-May-11	0.5	31-May-11	0.5265	31-May-11	4.1371	31-May-11	1.6312
30-Jun-11	0.5	30-Jun-11	0.5174	30-Jun-11	4.1277	30-Jun-11	1.6214
31-Jul-11	0.5	31-Jul-11	0.4996	31-Jul-11	4.0974	31-Jul-11	1.6145
31-Aug-11	0.5	31-Aug-11	0.4531	31-Aug-11	3.7132	31-Aug-11	1.6348
30-Sep-11	0.5	30-Sep-11	0.4649	30-Sep-11	3.4205	30-Sep-11	1.5783
31-Oct-11	0.5	31-Oct-11	0.4608	31-Oct-11	3.2581	31-Oct-11	1.576
30-Nov-11	0.5	30-Nov-11	0.4387	30-Nov-11	3.0313	30-Nov-11	1.5804
31-Dec-11	0.5	31-Dec-11	0.2996	31-Dec-11	2.9803	31-Dec-11	1.5585
31-Jan-12	0.5	31-Jan-12	0.3239	31-Jan-12	2.906	31-Jan-12	1.551
29-Feb-12	0.5	29-Feb-12	0.3912	29-Feb-12	3.089	29-Feb-12	1.5802
31-Mar-12	0.5	31-Mar-12	0.4248	31-Mar-12	3.1744	31-Mar-12	1.5823
30-Apr-12	0.5	30-Apr-12	0.4236	30-Apr-12	3.1259	30-Apr-12	1.6014
31-May-12	0.5	31-May-12	0.3561	31-May-12	2.9073	31-May-12	1.5905
30-Jun-12	0.5	30-Jun-12	0.3422	30-Jun-12	2.725	30-Jun-12	1.5571
31-Jul-12	0.5	31-Jul-12	0.2943	31-Jul-12	2.6453	31-Jul-12	1.5589
31-Aug-12	0.5	31-Aug-12	0.2398	31-Aug-12	2.65	31-Aug-12	1.5719

12.19 Selected interest rates, exchange rates and security prices

Monthly average of 4 UK Banks' base rates		Monthly average rate of discount, 3 month Treasury bills, Sterling		Monthly average yield from British Government Securities, 20 year Nominal Par Yield		Monthly average Spot exchange rate, US$ into Sterling	
IUMAAMIH [a] [b]		IUMAAJNB		IUMALNPY [c] [d]		XUMAUSS	
30-Sep-12	0.5	30-Sep-12	0.2478	30-Sep-12	2.7497	30-Sep-12	1.6116
31-Oct-12	0.5	31-Oct-12	0.2368	31-Oct-12	2.7969	31-Oct-12	1.6079
30-Nov-12	0.5	30-Nov-12	0.2243	30-Nov-12	2.7846	30-Nov-12	1.5961
31-Dec-12	0.5	31-Dec-12	0.249	31-Dec-12	2.8391	31-Dec-12	1.6144
31-Jan-13	0.5	31-Jan-13	0.2677	31-Jan-13	3.0069	31-Jan-13	1.5957
28-Feb-13	0.5	28-Feb-13	0.3147	28-Feb-13	3.1035	28-Feb-13	1.5478
31-Mar-13	0.5	31-Mar-13	0.3391	31-Mar-13	2.9654	31-Mar-13	1.5076
30-Apr-13	0.5	30-Apr-13	0.3447	30-Apr-13	2.776	30-Apr-13	1.5316
31-May-13	0.5	31-May-13	0.3065	31-May-13	2.9096	31-May-13	1.5285
30-Jun-13	0.5	30-Jun-13	0.3066	30-Jun-13	3.1584	30-Jun-13	1.5478
31-Jul-13	0.5	31-Jul-13	0.3124	31-Jul-13	3.2719	31-Jul-13	1.5172
31-Aug-13	0.5	31-Aug-13	0.2812	31-Aug-13	3.4083	31-Aug-13	1.5507
30-Sep-13	0.5	30-Sep-13	0.289	30-Sep-13	3.4662	30-Sep-13	1.5865
31-Oct-13	0.5	31-Oct-13	0.3141	31-Oct-13	3.3198	31-Oct-13	1.6094
30-Nov-13	0.5	30-Nov-13	0.2865	30-Nov-13	3.3978	30-Nov-13	1.6104
31-Dec-13	0.5	31-Dec-13	0.2555	31-Dec-13	3.497	31-Dec-13	1.6375
31-Jan-14	0.5	31-Jan-14	0.3211	31-Jan-14	3.4287	31-Jan-14	1.647
28-Feb-14	0.5	28-Feb-14	0.3624	28-Feb-14	3.3668	28-Feb-14	1.6567
31-Mar-14	0.5	31-Mar-14	0.3882	31-Mar-14	3.3469	31-Mar-14	1.6622
30-Apr-14	0.5	30-Apr-14	0.3688	30-Apr-14	3.3127	30-Apr-14	1.6743
31-May-14	0.5	31-May-14	0.284	31-May-14	3.2387	31-May-14	1.6844
30-Jun-14	0.5	30-Jun-14	0.3586	30-Jun-14	3.3055	30-Jun-14	1.6906
31-Jul-14	0.5	31-Jul-14	0.4271	31-Jul-14	3.228	31-Jul-14	1.7069
31-Aug-14	0.5	31-Aug-14	0.3978	31-Aug-14	2.9986	31-Aug-14	1.6709
30-Sep-14	0.5	30-Sep-14	0.4351	30-Sep-14	2.978	30-Sep-14	1.6305
31-Oct-14	0.5	31-Oct-14	0.3964	31-Oct-14	2.7955	31-Oct-14	1.6068
30-Nov-14	0.5	30-Nov-14	0.4114	30-Nov-14	2.7235	30-Nov-14	1.578
31-Dec-14	0.5	31-Dec-14	0.4101	31-Dec-14	2.4744	31-Dec-14	1.564
31-Jan-15	0.5	31-Jan-15	0.377	31-Jan-15	2.1112	31-Jan-15	1.5143
28-Feb-15	0.5	28-Feb-15	0.338	28-Feb-15	2.2503	28-Feb-15	1.5334
31-Mar-15	0.5	31-Mar-15	0.4295	31-Mar-15	2.2853	31-Mar-15	1.4957
30-Apr-15	0.5	30-Apr-15	0.4322	30-Apr-15	2.2061	30-Apr-15	1.4967
31-May-15	0.5	31-May-15	0.4511	31-May-15	2.4791	31-May-15	1.547
30-Jun-15	0.5	30-Jun-15	0.467	30-Jun-15	2.6379	30-Jun-15	1.5568
31-Jul-15	0.5	31-Jul-15	0.4895	31-Jul-15	2.5968	31-Jul-15	1.556
31-Aug-15	-	31-Aug-15	0.4643	31-Aug-15	2.4307	31-Aug-15	1.5583
30-Sep-15	-	30-Sep-15	0.4532	30-Sep-15	2.4175	30-Sep-15	1.5326
31-Oct-15	-	31-Oct-15	0.48	31-Oct-15	2.4421	31-Oct-15	1.5339
30-Nov-15	-	30-Nov-15	0.4806	30-Nov-15	2.5375	30-Nov-15	1.519
31-Dec-15	-	31-Dec-15	0.4551	31-Dec-15	2.4749	31-Dec-15	1.4983

Source: Bank of England

[a] Data obtained from Barclays Bank, Lloyds Bank, HSBC, and National Westminster Bank whose rates are used to compile this series. Where all the rates did not change on the same day a spread is shown.
[b] This series will end on 31-July-2015
[c] Calculated using the Variable Roughness Penalty (VRP) model.
[d] The monthly average figure is calculated using the available daily observations within each month.

12.20 Mergers and Acquisitions in the UK by other UK Companies: Category of Expenditure

£ million

| | Expenditure | | | | | Percentage of Expenditure | | |
| | | Cash | | | | | | |
	Total	Independent Companies	Subsidiaries	Issues of Ordinary Shares[2]	Issues of Fixed Interest Securities[2]	Cash	Issues of Ordinary Shares	Issues of Fixed Interest Securities
	DUCM	DWVW	DWVX	AIHD	AIHE	DWVY	DWVZ	DWWA
Annual								
2004	31,408	12,080	7,822	10,338	1,168	63	33	4
2005	25,134	13,425	8,510	2,768	431	87	11	2
2006	28,511	..	8,131	..	335	..	..	2
2007	26,778	13,671	6,507	4,909	1,691	76	18	6
2008	36,469	31,333	2,851	1,910	375	94	5	1
2009	12,195	2,937	709	8,435	114	30	69	1
2010[1]	12,605	6,175	4,520	1,560	350	85	12	3
2011	8,089	4,432	2,667	719	271	87	10	4
2012	3,413	1,937	789	419	268	82	10	8
2013	7,665	3,690	3,475	353	147	92	6	2
2014	8,032	3,249	1,947	2,782	51	65	35	–
2015	6,920 †	3,365 †	1,871 †	1,418 †	265 †	74	22	4
Quarterly								
2009 Q2	729	130	150	437	12	38	60	2
2009 Q3	1,886	1,409	214	254	9	87	13	–
2009 Q4	1,374	1,066	217	45	46	94	3	3
2010 Q1[1]	1,361	765	525	58	13	95	4	1
2010 Q2	2,032	986	714	275	57	83	14	3
2010 Q3	2,949	1,165	814	839	131	68	28	4
2010 Q4	6,263	3,259	2,467	388	149	92	6	2
2011 Q1	1,500	552	651	240	57	80	16	4
2011 Q2	3,346	2,355	704	204	83	92	6	2
2011 Q3	1,452	828	462	75	87	89	5	6
2011 Q4	1,791	697	850	200	44	87	11	2
2012 Q1	1,070	518	199	323	30	67	30	3
2012 Q2	1,041	575	269	54	143	81	5	14
2012 Q3	610	409	100	8	93	84	1	15
2012 Q4	692	435	221	34	2	95	5	–
2013 Q1	2,825	567	2,216	26	16	98	1	1
2013 Q2	2,438	1,992	316	80	50	95	3	2
2013 Q3	1,166	587	332	230	17	79	20	1
2013 Q4	1,236	544	611	17	64	94	1	5
2014 Q1	1,613	896	103	612	2	62	38	–
2014 Q2	1,625	478	1,051	50	45 †	94	3	3
2014 Q3	3,152	476	656	2,019	–	36	64	–
2014 Q4	1,642	1,399	137	101	4	94	6	–
2015 Q1	1,755 †	1,075 †	314 †	281	84	79	16	5
2015 Q2	2,739	854	789	1,019	77	60	37	3
2015 Q3	1,195	666	464	64 †	2	95 †	5 †	–
2015 Q4	1,231	770	304	54	102 †	88	4	8 †
2016 Q1	11,609	408	3,585	7,598	18	34	66	–

Source: Mergers and Acquisitions Surveys, Office for National Statistics

† indicates earliest revision, if any

– indicates data is zero or less than £0.5m

Disclosive data indicated by ..

1 The deal identification threshold has been increased from Q1 2010 from £0.1m to £1.0m and as a consequence there may be a discontinuity in the number and value of transactions reported.

2 Issued to the vendor company as payment.

Service industry

Chapter 13

Service industry

Annual Business Inquiry (Tables 13.1, 13.3 and 13.4)

The Annual Business Inquiry (ABI) estimates cover all UK businesses registered for Value Added Tax (VAT) and/or Pay As You Earn (PAYE). The businesses are classified to the 2007 Standard Industrial Classification (SIC(2007)) headings listed in the tables. The ABI obtains details on these businesses from the Office for National Statistics (ONS) Inter-Departmental Business Register (IDBR).

As with all its statistical inquiries, ONS is concerned to minimise the form-filling burden of individual contributors and as such the ABI is a sample inquiry. The sample was designed as a stratified random sample of about 66,600 businesses; the inquiry population is stratified by SIC(2007) and employment using the information from the register.

The inquiry results are grossed up to the total population so that they relate to all active UK businesses on the IDBR for the sectors covered.

The results meet a wide range of needs for government, economic analysts and the business community at large. In official statistics the inquiry is an important source for the national accounts and input-output tables, and also provides weights for the indices of production and producer prices. Additionally, inquiry results enable the UK to meet statistical requirements of the European Union.

Data from 1995 and 1996 were calculated on a different basis from those for 1997 and later years. In order to provide a link between the two data series, the 1995 and 1996 data were subsequently reworked to provide estimates on a consistent basis.

Revised ABI results down to SIC(2007) 4 digit class level for 1995–2007, giving both analysis and tabular detail, are available from the ONS website at: www.statistics.gov.uk, with further extracts and bespoke analyses available on request. This service replaces existing publications.

Retail trade: index numbers of value and volume (Table 13.2)

The main purpose of the Retail Sales Inquiry (RSI) is to provide up-to-date information on short period movements in the level of retail sales. In principle, the RSI covers the retail activity of every business classified in the retail sector (Division 52 of the 2007 Standard Industrial Classification (SIC(2007)) in Great Britain. A business will be classified to the retail sector if its main activity is one of the individual 4 digit SIC categories within Division 52. The retail activity of a business is then defined by its retail turnover, that is the sale of all retail goods (note that petrol, for example, is not a retail good).

The RSI is compiled from the information returned to the statutory inquiries into the distribution and services sector. The inquiry is addressed to a stratified sample of 5,000 businesses classified to the retail sector, the stratification being by 'type of store' (the individual 4 digit SIC categories within Division 52) and by size. The sample structure is designed to ensure that the inquiry estimates are as accurate as possible. In terms of the selection, this means that:

• each of the individual 4 digit SIC categories are represented – their coverage depending upon the relative size of the category and the variability of the data

• within each 4 digit SIC category the larger retailers tend to be fully enumerated with decreasing proportions of medium and smaller retailers

The structure of the inquiry is updated periodically by reference to the more comprehensive results of the Annual Business Inquiry (ABI). The monthly inquiry also incorporates a rotation element for the smallest retailers. This helps to spread the burden more fairly, as well as improving the representativeness between successive benchmarks.

13.1a Retail Trade, except of motor vehicles and motorcycles

Standard Industrial Classification (Revised 2007) Division Group Class	Description	Year	Number of enterprises	Total turnover	Approximate gross value added at basic prices (aGVA)	Total purchases of goods, materials and services	Total employment - point in time [1]	Total employment - average during the year [1]
			Number	£ million	£ million	£ million	Thousand	Thousand
47	Retail trade, except of motor vehicles and motorcycles	2008	194,677	311,745	65,123	246,237	3,054	3,106
		2009	187,890	319,318	69,924	249,058	3,073	3,139
		2010	187,230	332,131	71,500	261,676	3,016	3,040
		2011	189,119	342,147	70,871	271,203	3,032	3,060
		2012	187,616	349,327	73,876	275,052	3,029	3,062
		2013	189,828	359,088	81,368	278,326	3,052	3,084
		2014	186,737	371,522	83,728	288,613	3,130	3,154

Standard Industrial Classification (Revised 2007) Division Group Class	Description	Year	Total employment costs	Total net capital expenditure (Inc NYIP) [2]	Total capital expenditure-acquisitions (Inc NYIP) [2]	Total capital expenditure - disposals (Inc NYIP) [2]	Total stocks and work in progress - value at end of year	Total stocks and work in progress - value at beginning of year	Total stocks and work in progress - increase during year
			£ million	£ million	£ million	£ million	£ million	£ million	£ million
47	Retail trade, except of motor vehicles and motorcycles	2008	38,466	9,069	10,495	1,426	26,110	25,519	591
		2009	38,914	7,784	9,113	1,330	26,539	25,759	781
		2010	39,816	6,149	9,258	3,108	28,743	26,425	2,317
		2011	41,592	9,051	10,879	1,828	30,356	28,964	1,392
		2012	42,184	9,477	10,789	1,312	30,021	28,720	1,301
		2013	43,441	9,510	10,627	1,117	31,791	29,863	1,929
		2014	44,996	11,228	12,543	1,314	33,571	32,461	1,110

Source: Annual Business Survey (ABS)

The sum of constituent items in tables may not always agree exactly with the totals shown due to rounding.

1. Total employment - point in time and Total employment - average during the year are from the Business Register and Employment Survey (BRES). Caution should be taken when combining financial data from the ABS with employment data from BRES due to differences in methodology.

2. From 2008 to 2014 the Total net capital expenditure, Total capital expenditure - acquisitions, and Total capital expenditure - disposals published values included a small element of Not yet in production (NYIP). From 2015 onwards NYIP is not estimated for and is no longer included in the published values.

More information can be found in the ABS Technical Report.:
http://www.ons.gov.uk/file?uri=/businessindustryandtrade/business/businessservices/methodologies/annualbusinesssurveyabs/abstechnicalreport2014tcm77368873.pdf

13.1b Retail trade, except of motor vehicles and motor-cycles

£ million (Inclusive of VAT)

	2010	2011	2012	2013	2014
TOTAL TURNOVER	**367,446**	**385,692**	**393,423**	**404,534**	**418,185**
RETAIL TURNOVER	**347,144**	**363,280**	**368,176**	**378,917**	**387,983**
Fruit (including fresh, chilled, dried, frozen, canned and processed)	6,821	7,662	6,846	7,132	7,351
Vegetables (including fresh, chilled, dried, frozen canned and processed)	10,533	10,677	12,380	13,219	13,273
Meat (including fresh, chilled, smoked, frozen, canned and processed)	17,909	19,541	20,254	21,230	21,794
Fish, crustaceans and molluscs (including fresh, chilled, smoked, frozen, canned and processed)	2,978	3,295	3,453	3,458	3,486
Bakery products and cereals (including rice and pasta products)	17,875	18,818	20,078	20,352	20,372
Sugar, jam, honey, chocolate and confectionery (including ice-cream)	8,844	8,688	9,162	9,829	10,233
Alcoholic drink	16,618	17,445	18,184	19,219	19,605
Non-alcoholic beverages (including tea, coffee, fruit drinks and vegetable drinks)	8,018	9,176	9,161	9,652	9,860
Tobacco (excluding smokers requisites e.g. pipes, lighters etc)	11,369	11,838	11,885	11,405	11,607
Milk, cheese and eggs (including yoghurts and cream)	10,918	11,219	11,441	11,579	11,767
Oils and fats (including butter and margarine)	1,444	1,613	1,611	1,695	1,826
Food products not elsewhere classified (including sauces, herbs spices, soups)	4,427	4,528	3,890	3,858	3,971
Pharmaceutical products	3,946	4,390	4,725	4,916	5,359
National Health Receipts	12,067	11,405	11,680	11,100	12,262
Other medical products and therapeutic appliances and equipment	4,210	3,638	4,067	3,913	3,712
Other appliances, articles and products for personal care	14,109	15,107	15,702	16,776	17,172
Other articles of clothing, accessories for making clothing	3,395	3,781	4,051	4,317	4,321
Garments	36,706	37,976	38,730	41,466	43,253
Footwear (excluding sports shoes)	7,458	7,720	8,720	8,765	9,213
Travel goods and other personal effects not elsewhere classified	2,352	2,518	2,506	3,183	3,081
Household textiles (including furnishing fabrics, curtains etc)	4,862	4,188	4,158	4,731	4,786
Household and personal appliances whether electric or not	6,917	7,278	7,367	6,768	8,351
Glassware, tableware and household utensils (including non-electric)	2,754	3,369	3,668	3,899	3,622
Furniture and furnishings	12,313	13,475	12,395	13,606	14,492
Audio and visual equipment (including radios, televisions and video recorders)	6,245	5,353	5,821	4,916	4,124
Recording material for pictures and sound (including audio and video tapes, blank and pre recorded records etc)	2,787	2,547	2,668	2,560	2,034
Information processing equipment (including printers, software, calculators and typewriters)	4,530	5,425	4,862	5,475	5,058
Decorating and DIY supplies	7,319	7,528	5,580	6,500	6,952
Tools and equipment for house and garden	3,088	3,566	3,887	4,235	3,916
Books	2,648	2,579	3,084	2,623	2,636
Newspapers and periodicals	3,947	3,675	3,410	2,906	3,022
Stationery and drawing materials and miscellaneous printed matter	4,025	4,432	4,397	4,620	4,304
Carpets and other floor coverings (excluding bathroom mats, rush and door mats)	2,824	3,159	3,144	2,806	3,114
Photographic and cinematographic equipment and optical instruments	1,625	1,643	1,298	736	809
Telephone and telefax equipment (including mobile phones)	3,143	3,665	4,437	4,481	3,277
Jewellery, silverware and plate; watches and clocks	6,045	6,235	6,626	6,340	7,449
Works of art and antiques (including furniture, floor coverings and jewellery)	1,756	1,493	1,254	1,807	2,374
Equipment and accessories for sport, camping, recreation and musical instruments	4,864	5,118	4,944	4,355	5,350
Spare parts and accessories for all types of vehicle and sales of bicycles	1,148	983	950	1,244	1,520
Games, toys, hobbies (including video game software, video game computers that plug into the tv, video-games cassettes and CD-ROM'S)	7,514	7,492	7,154	7,018	7,855
Other goods not elsewhere classified (including sale of new postage stamps and sales of liquid and solid fuels)	5,896	5,929	5,788	6,689	7,570
Non-durable household goods (including household cleaning, maintenance products) & paper products and other non-durable household goods	4,727	4,923	4,936	5,596	6,199
Natural or artificial plants and flowers	3,609	4,023	3,501	3,772	3,523
Pets and related products (including pet food)	3,896	4,166	4,154	4,664	4,697
Petrol, diesel, lubricating oil and other petroleum products	36,664	40,001	40,171	39,507	37,432

Source: Annual Business Survey (ABS)

The following symbols and abbreviations are used throughout the ABS releases;

*   Information suppressed to avoid disclosure

..   not available

-     nil or less than half the level of rounding

The sum of constituent items in tables may not always agree exactly with the totals shown due to rounding.

13.2 Retail trade: index numbers of value and volume of sales[1]

Great Britain
Non-seasonally adjusted

			2005	2006	2007	2008	2009	2010	2011	2012	2013	2014	2015
		Sales in 2015 £ thousand									Weekly average (2013=100)		
Value													
All retailing	J5AH	374,817,448	78.2	81.1	84.3	87.5	88.2	90.6	95.3	97.5	100	103	104.1
Large	J5AI	297,903,888	73.4	76.8	80.5	84.4	85.8	89.9	94.6	97.2	100	102.5	104.3
Small	J5AJ	76,913,548	96.5	97.7	98.9	99.6	97.4	93.4	97.9	98.7	100	104.9	103.4
All retailing excluding automotive fuel	J43S	339,445,505	79.6	81.6	84.5	87.1	88.9	91.1	94.3	96.8	100	103.8	105.7
Predominantly food stores	EAFS	151,742,468	74	76.7	79.9	84.5	89.1	90.5	94.4	97.1	100	101.1	101.2
Predominantly non-food stores	EAFT	159,233,953	90	91.3	94.1	94.5	93	95.3	96.7	98.3	100	105.4	107.9
Non specialised predominantly non-food stores	EAGE	32,459,816	76.7	78.9	81.9	79.7	81.1	86.8	90.2	95.7	100	105.4	109.7
Textile, clothing, footwear and leather	EAFU	46,726,281	81.1	84.8	87.2	86.9	87.9	92.7	96.2	97.7	100	103.6	106.8
Household goods stores	EAFV	32,359,744	114.6	115.4	119.4	116.8	111	106.6	104.2	103.2	100	105.6	111.2
Other specialised non-food stores	EAFW	47,688,112	91.4	90.3	92.5	97.1	94	96.1	96.8	97.3	100	107	105.6
Non-store retailing	J596	28,469,084	50.8	51.9	54	57.7	61.5	68	78.1	85.6	100	111.4	121.6
Automotive fuel	J43H	35,371,943	66	77.1	82.6	90.7	82.9	86.8	103.4	103.2	100	96.3	90.6
Volume													
All retailing	J5DD	374,817,448	93.1	95.9	98.6	98.6	99	98	98.2	98.7	100	103.7	108.2
All retailing excluding automotive fuel	J448	339,445,505	92	94.1	96.5	97	97.6	97.7	97.4	98.3	100	104	108.2
Predominantly food stores	EAGW	151,742,468	101.2	102.6	103.4	102.4	103.5	101.7	100.5	100.3	100	100.8	103.1
Predominantly non-food stores	EAGX	159,233,953	90	92.7	96.5	97.7	97.2	98.2	97.4	98.2	100	106.1	110.7
Non specialised predominantly non-food stores	EAHI	32,459,816	83.1	85.6	88.4	85.3	86	90	91.1	95.8	100	106.1	112.8
Textile, clothing, footwear and leather	EAGY	46,726,281	75.1	80.4	84.2	86.8	92.6	97.5	98.4	98.9	100	103.5	107.1
Household goods stores	EAGZ	32,359,744	115.9	119.4	124.7	122.4	115.7	108.5	103.8	102.2	100	106.7	115.7
Other specialised non-food stores	EAHA	47,688,112	93	92.5	95.9	100.5	97.1	97.6	96.3	96.6	100	108.4	109.4
Non-store retailing	J5CL	28,469,084	53.3	54.6	56.9	60	64.5	70	78.7	85.9	100	111.8	125.3
Automotive fuel	J43V	35,371,943	102.2	113.4	117.8	113.2	111.5	100.5	104.8	102.4	100	101.1	108.8

1 See chapter text.

Please note that the indices have been re-referenced so the value of 100 is in 2013

Source: Office for National Statistics

13.3 Wholesale and retail trade and repair of motor vehicles and motorcycles

Standard Industrial Classification (Revised 2007) Division Group Class	Description	Year	Number of enterprises	Total turnover	Approximate gross value added at basic prices (aGVA)	Total purchases of goods, materials and services	Total employment - point in time [1]	Total employment - average during the year [1]	Total employment costs
			Number	£ million	£ million	£ million	Thousand	Thousand	£ million
45	Wholesale and retail trade and repair of motor vehicles and motorcycles	2008	67,683	135,669	20,957	115,372	532	535	10,925
		2009	66,372	125,764	18,348	105,457	500	539	10,445
		2010	66,239	132,077	22,150	111,243	511	510	10,439
		2011	67,298	137,364	23,419	115,292	523	535	10,658
		2012	67,274	142,461	22,347	120,649	510	522	10,615
		2013	67,754	152,510	24,236	129,877	525	537	11,570
		2014	68,108	168,247	26,857	143,563	547	521	11,895

Standard Industrial Classification (Revised 2007) Division Group Class	Description	Year	Total net capital expenditure (Inc NYIP) [2]	Total capital expenditure- acquisitions (Inc NYIP) [2]	Total capital expenditure - disposals (Inc NYIP) [2]	Total stocks and work in progress - value at end of year	Total stocks and work in progress - value at beginning of year	Total stocks and work in progress - increase during year
			£ million	£ million	£ million	£ million	£ million	£ million
45	Wholesale and retail trade and repair of motor vehicles and motorcycles	2008	1,044	2,110	1,066	16,136	15,402	735
		2009	885	1,669	784	13,624	15,545	-1,921
		2010	1,035	1,747	711	15,008	13,640	1,368
		2011	1,292	2,067	775	16,451	15,107	1,344
		2012	1,174	1,927	753	17,067	16,490	577
		2013	1,530	2,296	766	18,139	16,525	1,613
		2014	2,155	2,873	718	20,692	18,606	2,086

Source: Annual Business Survey (ABS)

The following symbols and abbreviations are used throughout the ABS releases;
* Information suppressed to avoid disclosure
.. not available
- nil or less than half the level of rounding

The sum of constituent items in tables may not always agree exactly with the totals shown due to rounding.

Notes:

1. Total employment - point in time and Total employment - average during the year are from the Business Register and Employment Survey (BRES). Caution should be taken when combining financial data from the ABS with employment data from BRES due to differences in methodology. More information can be found in the ABS Technical Report.

2. From 2008 to 2014 the Total net capital expenditure, Total capital expenditure - acquisitions, and Total capital expenditure - disposals published values included a small element of Not yet in production (NYIP). From 2015 onwards NYIP is not estimated for and is no longer included in the published values.

13.4 Accommodation and food service activities

Standard Industrial Classification (Revised 2007) Section, Division, Group, Class,	Description	Year	Number of enterprises	Total turnover	Approximate gross value added at basic prices (aGVA)	Total purchases of goods, materials and services	Total employment - point in time [1]	Total employment - average during the year [1]	Total employment costs
			Number	£ million	£ million	£ million	Thousand	Thousand	£ million
I	Accommodation and food service activities	2009	129,112	66,195	29,375	36,745	1,919	1,812	19,012
		2010	127,844	68,346	31,435	36,883	1,869	1,855	19,074
		2011	130,336	72,322	34,826	37,563	1,937	1,869	19,987
		2012	128,831	74,355	37,764	37,272	1,970	1,910	21,132
		2013	131,322	77,033	38,357	38,625	2,029	1,970	21,611
		2014	131,982	82,194	43,046	39,595	2,108	2,043	22,697
55	Accommodation	2009	15,157	17,235	9,231	7,973	393	360	4,724
		2010	15,075	17,650	9,087	8,603	388	377	5,075
		2011	15,159	18,566	9,838	8,775	429	407	5,331
		2012	15,205	19,822	11,149	8,677	426	409	5,752
		2013	15,365	20,222	11,353	8,860	433	416	5,646
		2014	15,513	22,918	14,035	9,063	440	418	5,812
55.1	Hotels and similar accommodation	2009	9,687	13,624	7,439	6,171	325	297	3,942
		2010	9,559	13,493	7,102	6,399	321	316	4,173
		2011	9,575	14,150	7,619	6,532	358	342	4,424
		2012	9,449	15,186	8,572	6,609	351	339	4,823
		2013	9,364	15,764	8,925	6,852	356	344	4,703
		2014	9,300	17,762	10,794	7,075	357	347	4,716
55.2	Holiday and other short stay accommodation	2009	3,351	1,219	661	554	30	29	289
		2010	3,318	1,603	846	776	29	26	339
		2011	3,296	1,476	726	774	33	30	351
		2012	3,247	1,497	913	590	33	31	344
		2013	3,411	1,562	969	601	32	30	343
		2014	3,581	1,855	1,263	602	36	31	412
55.3	Camping grounds, recreational vehicle parks and trailer parks	2009	1,711	2,230	1,033	1,184	34	31	448
		2010	1,735	2,325	1,031	1,307	*	*	495
		2011	1,775	2,739	1,385	1,378	34	31	507
		2012	1,796	2,771	1,415	1,360	37	34	516
		2013	1,818	2,630	1,292	1,310	39	37	524
		2014	1,855	2,955	1,706	1,273	*	*	583
55.9	Other accommodation	2009	408	162	98	64	3	3	46
		2010	463	229	108	121	*	*	69
		2011	513	200	108	92	4	4	49
		2012	713	368	250	118	5	4	70
		2013	772	265	168	98	6	5	76
		2014	777	346	272	113	*	*	101
56	Food and beverage service activities	2009	113,955	48,960	20,144	28,772	1,526	1,452	14,288
		2010	112,769	50,696	22,348	28,281	1,481	1,478	13,998
		2011	115,177	53,756	24,988	28,787	1,507	1,462	14,656
		2012	113,626	54,533	26,615	28,594	1,544	1,501	15,380
		2013	115,957	56,811	27,003	29,765	1,596	1,553	15,964
		2014	116,469	59,277	29,012	30,532	1,668	1,625	16,884
56.1	Restaurants and mobile food service activities	2009	61,192	22,658	9,910	12,765	737	644	6,460
		2010	61,387	23,017	10,407	12,623	705	684	6,306
		2011	63,712	25,690	12,301	13,447	767	765	6,886
		2012	64,460	25,934	13,367	13,332	782	783	7,187
		2013	67,144	28,740	14,328	14,454	859	860	8,067
		2014	68,879	29,534	15,002	14,724	885	833	8,524
56.2	Event catering and other food service activities	2009	7,049	6,811	2,786	4,029	210	235	2,952
		2010	7,031	7,971	4,003	3,970	227	253	3,149
		2011	7,967	8,553	4,418	4,138	231	212	3,204
		2012	7,651	8,925	4,430	4,521	262	249	3,688
		2013	8,003	8,269	3,928	4,343	233	222	3,381
		2014	8,221	9,139	4,667	4,473	255	261	3,685
56.21	Event catering activities	2009	6,070	6,139	2,505	3,636	197	222	2,782
		2010	5,767	7,289	3,710	3,581	211	236	2,957
		2011	6,267	7,837	4,119	3,715	213	196	2,993
		2012	5,514	7,844	3,879	3,968	241	228	3,411
		2013	5,885	3,196	1,394	1,809	86	82	967
		2014	6,149	3,458	1,529	1,936	96	98	1,009
56.29	Other food service activities	2009	979	672	281	393	12	12	170
		2010	1,264	682	293	389	16	17	192
		2011	1,700	716	299	422	18	17	211
		2012	2,137	1,081	551	552	21	20	278
		2013	2,118	5,073	2,534	2,534	147	140	2,414
		2014	2,072	5,681	3,138	2,537	159	163	2,676
56.3	Beverage serving activities	2009	45,714	19,491	7,448	11,979	579	574	4,876
		2010	44,351	19,709	7,938	11,688	549	540	4,543
		2011	43,498	19,513	8,269	11,203	509	484	4,566
		2012	41,515	19,675	8,817	10,742	501	469	4,504
		2013	40,810	19,802	8,748	10,968	503	471	4,516
		2014	39,369	20,604	9,342	11,335	528	531	4,675

The following symbols and abbreviations are used throughout the ABS releases;

Source: Annual Business Survey (ABS)

* Information suppressed to avoid disclosure   .. not available   - nil or less than half the level of rounding

The sum of constituent items in tables may not always agree exactly with the totals shown due to rounding.

1. Total employment - point in time and Total employment - average during the year are from the Business Register and Employment Survey (BRES). Caution should be taken when combining financial data from the ABS with employment data from BRES due to differences in methodology. More information can be found in the ABS Technical Report.

13.4 Accommodation and food service activities

Standard Industrial Classification (Revised 2007) Section, Division, Group, Class,	Description	Year	Total net capital expenditure	Total capital expenditure -acquisitions	Total capital expenditure - disposals	Total stocks and work in progress - value at end of year	Total stocks and work in progress - value at beginning of year	Total stocks and work in progress - increase during year
			£ million	£ million	£ million	£ million	£ million	£ million
I	Accommodation and food service activities	2009	3,443	3,803	360	1,318	1,303	15
		2010	2,807	3,804	997	1,481	1,403	79
		2011	3,311	4,339	1,028	1,484	1,368	117
		2012	3,930	4,704	774	1,716	1,713	3
		2013	3,946	4,837	891	1,544	1,523	21
		2014	5,626	6,888	1,261	1,580	1,501	78
55	Accommodation	2009	1,628	1,728	100	359	391	-32
		2010	1,301	1,489	188	488	445	43
		2011	1,416	1,641	225	506	443	63
		2012	1,898	2,050	152	469	452	17
		2013	1,836	2,045	209	397	413	-16
		2014	1,657	2,277	620	470	442	27
55.1	Hotels and similar accommodation	2009	1,390	1,433	43	181	197	-15
		2010	936	1,072	136	250	231	20
		2011	946	1,137	191	201	176	25
		2012	1,282	1,397	115	185	172	13
		2013	1,173	1,335	162	207	189	18
		2014	1,158	1,727	569	198	194	4
55.2	Holiday and other short stay accommodation	2009	50	67	17	24	29	-5
		2010	186	214	28	75	66	9
		2011	169	184	15	59	45	15
		2012	254	269	16	64	58	6
		2013	195	216	21	37	34	3
		2014	224	235	11	52	47	5
55.3	Camping grounds, recreational vehicle parks and trailer parks	2009	138	*	*	153	164	-11
		2010	160	181	21	159	145	14
		2011	238	257	18	245	222	23
		2012	258	279	21	217	219	-3
		2013	254	278	24	152	190	-38
		2014	238	270	32	217	199	18
55.9	Other accommodation	2009	50	*	*	1	1	-
		2010	19	22	4	3	3	-
		2011	62	63	1	1	1	-
		2012	104	105	1	3	3	-
		2013	214	216	2	1	-	-
		2014	36	44	8	3	2	-
56	Food and beverage service activities	2009	1,815	2,075	260	959	912	47
		2010	1,507	2,316	809	993	958	35
		2011	1,895	2,698	803	978	925	54
		2012	2,032	2,654	622	1,247	1,261	-13
		2013	2,110	2,792	682	1,147	1,110	37
		2014	3,970	4,611	641	1,110	1,059	51
56.1	Restaurants and mobile food service activities	2009	1,104	1,250	146	437	408	29
		2010	998	1,185	187	429	402	27
		2011	1,203	1,327	123	412	379	33
		2012	1,380	1,512	132	562	532	30
		2013	1,449	1,645	196	480	454	26
		2014	2,428	2,601	173	454	421	32
56.2	Event catering and other food service activities	2009	44	49	5	103	98	5
		2010	135	176	41	126	122	4
		2011	175	188	14	145	140	5
		2012	127	135	8	158	154	4
		2013	110	117	7	176	167	9
		2014	125	158	32	180	180	-
56.21	Event catering activities	2009	33	37	4	87	84	3
		2010	117	155	38	111	107	4
		2011	116	129	13	123	124	-1
		2012	113	120	7	133	131	2
		2013	48	52	5	77	68	9
		2014	73	95	22	75	72	3
56.29	Other food service activities	2009	11	12	1	16	14	2
		2010	18	21	2	15	15	-
		2011	59	60	1	22	16	6
		2012	14	15	1	24	23	1
		2013	62	65	3	100	99	1
		2014	52	63	11	105	107	-3
56.3	Beverage serving activities	2009	667	776	109	419	406	13
		2010	374	955	581	438	434	5
		2011	517	1,183	666	421	405	16
		2012	524	1,007	483	527	575	-47
		2013	551	1,030	479	491	488	2
		2014	1,416	1,852	435	477	458	19

The following symbols and abbreviations are used throughout the ABS releases;
Source: Annual Business Survey (ABS)
* Information suppressed to avoid disclosure   .. not available   - nil or less than half the level of rounding
The sum of constituent items in tables may not always agree exactly with the totals shown due to rounding.
1. Total employment - point in time and Total employment - average during the year are from the Business Register and Employment Survey (BRES). Caution should be taken when combining financial data from the ABS with employment data from BRES due to differences in methodology. More information can be found in the ABS Technical Report.

Defence

Chapter 14

Defence

This section includes figures on Defence expenditure, on the size and role of the Armed Forces and on related support activities. Much of the material used in this section can be found in UK Defence Statistics

Table 14.1 United Kingdom Defence Expenditure by Commodity Block

This table shows a breakdown of Resource & Capital DEL and AME by Commodity Block. Under Clear Line of Sight (CLoS), the main MOD expenditure categories are now presented as Commodity Blocks. This provides a more meaningful description of the Department's planned and actual spend, and enables a clearer understanding of the MOD's plans and expenditure over the Spending Review period.

Please refer to the Resource Accounting & Budgeting section of UK Defence Statistics to view important information relating to the introduction of the International Financial Reporting Standard (IFRS), the implementation of the Clear Line of Sight (CLoS) Alignment project and accounting changes from 2011/12, which have led to presentational changes to the reporting of MOD accounts.

Prior to 2011/12, when Commodity Block reporting was first introduced, information contained in this table was reported in Table 1.3a of UK Defence Statistics 2012.

The data are derived directly from the MOD Departmental Resource Accounts.

Further information about the quality of data and methods used in the production of these statistics, along with details of their intended use can be found in the Background Quality Report - Departmental Resources Statistics.

Table 14.2 Intake to UK Regular Forces by gender
Women accounted for 9.8 per cent of the intake to UK Regular Forces in September 2015, which represents an overall increase since 2012.

Table 14.3 provides information on the formation of the United Kingdom's Armed Forces

Table 14.3a shows the number of submarines and ships in the Royal Navy and Royal Fleet Auxiliary, Royal Marine Commando units, squadrons of helicopters and fixed-wing aircraft in the Fleet Air Arm, and Reserve Units.

Table 14.3b shows the numbers of Regiments and Infantry battalions in the Regular Army and Army Reserves; and Corps, Divisional and Brigade headquarters.

Table 14.3c shows the number of squadrons in the Royal Air Force (RAF) and the Royal Auxiliary Air Force (RAuxAF).

There was a delay between the last edition of Formations, Vessels and Aircraft (published in February 2015) and the first edition of the UK Armed Forces Equipment and Formations (published September 2016). Initially this delay was caused by investigations into data errors and concerns over the accuracy of the statistics in the 2014 edition. The publication was then further delayed due to an internal review of equipment statistics and a subsequent public consultation which was held for a period of six weeks. As a result, no 2015 data for tables 14.3 a, b and c was produced.

Table 14.4 Outflow from UK Regular Forces, trained and untrained
Figures show outflow from UK Regular Forces, both trained and untrained, including personnel leaving the Services, deaths and recalled reservists on release. They do not include promotion from Ranks to Officers or flows between Services.
UK Regular Forces comprises trained and untrained Full-time personnel but does not include Gurkhas, FTRS personnel and reservists.

Table 14.5 United Kingdom Armed Forces Full-time trained strength and requirement, at 1 April each year
The Full-Time Trained Strength of the UK Armed Forces is defined as comprising of trained UK Regular Forces, trained Gurkhas and elements of the FTRS (Full Time Reserve Service) personnel. It does not include mobilised reservists.
The full-time trained strength of the UK Armed Forces was 144,120 at 1 April 2015, down 6770 since 1 April 2014 and down 46,150 since 1 April 2000.
The requirement for the UK's full-time trained Armed Forces decreased from 198,160 in 2000 to 174,840 in 2012 and 150,700 in 2015. The rate of decrease has been greatest in the RAF, followed by the Naval Service and least in the Army.
The deficit between strength and requirement of full-time trained Armed Forces has decreased from 7,880 at 1 April 2000 to 4,830 at 1 April 2012 to 6,580 in April 2015. The largest deficit as a percentage of requirement is in the Royal Air Force (6.0% deficit).

Table 14.6 Trends in Service and civilian personnel strengths, at 1 April each year
The Ministry of Defence civilian population (Level 0) has continued to decrease, falling from 71,008 at 1 April 2012 to 56,243 at 1 April 2016, a reduction of 14,765.
Between 1 April 2012 and 1 April 2016 the overall strength in Level 1 MOD personnel fell from 54,509 to 37,656, a reduction of 16,853 personnel over the period.

Table 14.7a Land holdings by parent Service area and whether owned, leased or with legal rights, at 1 April each year
At 1st April 2015, the MOD owned 222,600 hectares of land and foreshore (either freehold or leasehold), and held rights over a further 217,000 hectares.

Table 14.7b Service Family Accommodation in the United Kingdom, at 31 March each year
At 31 March 2015 there were 49,600 Service Family Accommodation (SFA) properties in the UK, which is broadly unchanged over the past year.

10,400 properties are currently vacant (21% of the total), a further increase from the recent low of 6,000 properties (12%) in 2011. The increase in the vacancy rate since 2011 can be partly explained by the Armed Forces Redundancy Program, the Army Basing Strategy and development of the new MOD Footprint Strategy, which have resulted in some SFA, previously earmarked for disposal, being retained.

Table 14.8a Location of Service and civilian personnel in the United Kingdom, at 1 April each year
The strength of UK-based civilian personnel has reduced from 51,610 in 2014 to 49,520 in 2015. The total strength of MOD personnel based in Northern Ireland has continued to reduce, falling from 3,790 in 2014 to 3,470 in 2015. Since 2000, the number of Service personnel stationed in Northern Ireland has been reduced from 8,390 to 2,190, whilst the civilian strength has fallen during the same period from 3,250 to 1,280. The South East Region has the largest population of UK Service personnel, with 39,080, although the South West has the largest population of civilians, with 16,610.

Table 14.8b Global locations of Service and civilian personnel, at 1 April each year
At 1 April 2015, 88% of UK Regular Armed Forces and 90% of MOD civilians excluding LEC personnel were stationed in the UK.

The strength of UK Regular Forces stationed in the UK fell by 3,060 between 1 April 2014 and 1 April 2015 from 141,180 to 138,120. Over the same period, the number of UK civilian personnel decreased by 2,09 from 51,610 to 49,520.

The strength of UK Regular Forces stationed overseas decreased from 18,070 to 15,300 between 1 April 2014 and 1 April 2015. Over the same period, the number of MOD civilian personnel based overseas decreased from 8,580 to 6,410.

The number of UK Regular Armed Forces personnel stationed in Germany continued to decrease from 12,960 to 10,020 between 1 April 2014 and 1 April 2015 in line with the announcement made during the Strategic Defence & Security Review (SDSR). Despite this decrease, Germany still has the second largest population of MOD personnel after the UK

Table 14.9a UK regular Armed Forces deaths by Service, Year of occurrence 2005-2014, numbers, age and gender standardised rates
In 2015, there were 60 deaths in the regular Armed Forces. Of these, 11 deaths were in the Naval Service, 39 in the Army and 10 in the RAF. In 2015 the mortality rate for the UK Armed Forces was 39 per 100,000. This was a decrease from the previous year

Table 14.10a UK Military Search and Rescue - UK & Overseas Callouts, Incidents and Persons Moved, 2006 to 2015
Table 14.10a shows the number of incidents, callouts and persons moved each year between 2006 and 2015. Between 2006 and 2009 the number of callouts increased year-on-year. Callout numbers peaked in 2009, and since then the number of callouts fell year-on-year.

14.10b Search and Rescue Helicopters - UK & Overseas Callouts and Persons Moved by Unit
This data focuses on SAR helicopter callouts, excluding Mountain Rescue Teams.
Table 14.10b presents the number of callouts by unit and number of Persons moved by Unit between 2006 and 2015. The unit with the highest number of callouts during 2015 was HMS Gannet, with 317, closely followed by RNAS Culdrose with 282.
RAF Leconfield moved the lowest number of persons of the UK units during 2015, with 25.

14.10c Search and Rescue Helicopters: UK & Overseas Callouts by Assistance Type, 2006 to 2015
14.10c presents callout numbers by assistance type between 2006 and 2015. The assistance type with the largest number of callouts during 2015 was Medrescue with 546 helicopter callouts. Most of the other callout types have very low numbers. The second half of the table shows the number of persons moved by assistance type between 2006 and 2015. In 2015, most number of persons moved were for Medrescue, with a similar proportion to recent years.

14.10d Strength of United Kingdom Medical Staff
The figures shown in 14.10d are for regular personnel only and therefore do not represent the strength of either Reserve or veterinarian personnel.

14.11 Number of vessels boarded by the Royal Navy Fishery Protection Squadron within British fishing limits and convictions arising from these boardings each financial year
This table shows the activities of the Royal Navy Fishery Protection Squadron operating within British fishery limits under contract to the Marine Maritime Organisation (MMO. Boardings carried out by vessels of the Scottish Executive Environment Directorate and the Department of Agriculture and Rural Development for Northern Ireland are not included. The data in this Table are outside the scope of National Statistics since they have not been put forward for assessment by the UK Statistics Authority.

Convictions arising from Royal Navy boardings are convictions of infringements detected by the Royal Navy Fishery Protection vessels in that year operating under contract to DEFRA. Figures may change retrospectively as some cases may not be heard in court until a year or more after the initial Royal Navy boarding.
in financial year 08/09, the Marine and Fisheries Agency introduced the Fisheries Administration Penalty (FAP. This has streamlined the penalty process, and has removed the necessity for most of the crews of vessels that would previously have been sent to Court from actually having to attend Court, where they would probably have been convicted. Convictions from 2008/09 onwards are based on the number of offences addressed by the Courts that resulted in a Court conviction, not the number of fishing vessel crews that attended Court. That is, the same fishing vessel crew could be required to attend Court for one or more offences to be heard and each offence would count separately.

From April 2013, an agreement that FPS ships would no longer be exclusively tasked with Marine Enforcement came into effect, meaning there would be less less time available for boardings.

In 2014/15 567 vessels were boarded by the Royal Navy Fisheries Protection Squadron, the lowest figure in the last six years. This had resulted in 8 court convictions by the time the information was available.

14.1 Defence Expenditure by Commodity Block

	Outturn 2011/12	Outturn 2012/13	Outturn 2013/14	Outturn 2014/15
Defence Spending	**37 169**	**34 260**	**34 559**	**34 365** [1]
Departmental Expenditure Limits (DEL)	**46 994**	**43 718**	**44 020**	**42 891**
Cash Resource DEL	**37 980**	**35 874**	**36 448**	**35 105**
Personnel Costs	12 846	11 921	11 473	10 903
of which: Service Personnel Costs[2]	10 101	9 598	9 156	8 588
Civilian Personnel Costs[3]	2 745	2 323	2 318	2 315
Infrastructure Costs[4]	4 580	4 594	4 707	4 664
Inventory Consumption[5]	2 535	2 312	2 161	1 822
Equipment Support Costs[6]	6 256	5 588	6 411	6 528
Other Costs & Services[7]	1 850	1 923	2 027	2 395
Receipts & Other Income[8]	-1 327	-1 277	-1 196	-1 133
Depreciation & Impairment[9]	9 825	9 458	9 462	8 510
Cash Release of Provisions[10]	348	239	178	219
Research & Development Costs[11]	833	944	988	1 012
Conflict Pool	46	44	50	56
Arm's Length Bodies[1,12]	187	127	187	130
Capital DEL[13]	**9 014**	**7 843**	**7 572**	**7 786**
Single Use Military Equipment[14]	5 284	4 768	4 528	4 889
Other (Fiscal)[15]	3 883	3 141	3 091	3 202
Asset/Estate Disposal Costs	- 150	- 64	- 44	- 251
New Loans and Loan Repayments	- 5	- 6	- 6	- 57
Arm's Length Bodies	2	3	3	2
Annually Managed Expenditure (AME)	**957**	**1 831**	**835**	**1 915**
Resource AME	**967**	**1 867**	**963**	**1 864**
Depreciation & Impairment	510	1 062	- 208	461
Provisions	- 460	318	148	742
Cash Release of Provisions	- 345	- 239	- 203	- 219
Movement on Fair Value of Financial Instruments	347	- 183	368	43
War Pensions Benefits	916	908	859	838
Capital AME	**- 10**	**- 35**	**- 129**	**51**
Provision Costs (Release)	- 10	- 35	- 129	51

Source: Defence Economics (Defence Expenditure Analysis) and Defence Resources

1. From 2014/15 a small amount of Depreciation (£16m), from the Arm's Length Bodies Resource DEL total, has been included in the calculation of Defence Spending.
2. Military officers and other ranks pay and other allowances; SCAPE; Employer's National Insurance Contributions (ERNIC).
3. Civilian pay and other allowances; pension contributions; Employer's National Insurance Contributions (ERNIC).
4. Property management; service charges; IT & communications costs; utilities costs.
5. Munitions; stores; fuel (marine & aviation); clothing; other materials consumed e.g. stationary, sundries, general stores etc.
6. Equipment support costs, including leases & hire charges for plant, machinery and transport.
7. Travel & subsistence; professional services & fees; training.
8. Receipts from various sources; costs recoveries; dividends; interest.
9. Depreciation & impairments on Non-Current Assets (Property, SUME, dual purpose).
10. Nuclear and non nuclear provisions e.g. staff redundancies, legal costs, environmental, etc.
11. Research and Development expenditure is incurred mainly for the future benefit of the Department. Such expenditure is primarily incurred on the development of new Single Use Military Equipment (SUME) and on the improvement of the effectiveness and capability of existing SUME.Council of Reserve Forces and Cadet Associations; Royal Hospital Chelsea; National Army Museum; RAF Museum; National Museum of the Royal Navy; Commonwealth War Graves Commission; From 2014/15 includes the Single Source Regulations Office.

12. Expenditure on the acquisition of Non-Current Assets.
13. Single Use Military Equipment (SUME) are assets which only have a military use, such as tanks and fighter aircraft. Dual use items i.e. those that also have a civilian use are recorded under the other category.
14. Expenditure on Property, Plant and dual use military equipment that could be used by civilian organisations for the production of goods and services.

14.2 Intake to UK Regular Forces by Gender

12 Months Ending:

	2012 31 Mar		2012 30 Sep		2013 31 Mar		2013 30 Sep		2014 31 Mar		2014 30 Sep		2015 31 Mar		2015 30 Sep		1 Apr 2015 to 30 Sep 2015	
	Number	%	Number	%	Number	%	Number	%	Number	%	Number	%	Number	%	Number	%	Number	%
All Services	**14 800**		**14 530**		**14 370**		**13 390**		**11 880**		**12 040**		**12 980**		**13 580**		**7 180**	
of which female	1 290	8.7	1 200	8.3	1 200	8.4	1 200	9.0	1 140	9.6	1 220	10.1	1 400	10.8	1 330	9.8	650	9.1
of which male	13 510	91.3	13 320	91.7	13 170	91.6	12 190	91.0	10 740	90.4	10 830	89.9	11 580	89.2	12 250	90.2	6 530	90.9
Officers	**1 070**	**100.0**	**960**	**100.0**	**1 060**	**100.0**	**1 050**	**100.0**	**1 070**	**100.0**	**1 110**	**100.0**	**1 130**	**100.0**	**1 220**	**100.0**	**740**	**100.0**
of which female	180	16.8	170	17.9	170	16.4	170	15.9	160	15.2	170	15.1	180	15.5	170	14.0	90	12.4
of which male	890	83.2	790	82.1	880	83.6	880	84.1	900	84.8	940	84.9	960	84.5	1 050	86.0	650	87.6
Other Ranks	**13 730**	**100.0**	**13 570**	**100.0**	**13 310**	**100.0**	**12 340**	**100.0**	**10 820**	**100.0**	**10 940**	**100.0**	**11 850**	**100.0**	**12 360**	**100.0**	**6 440**	**100.0**
of which female	1 110	8.1	1 030	7.6	1 030	7.7	1 040	8.4	980	9.1	1 050	9.6	1 220	10.3	1 160	9.4	560	8.7
of which male	12 620	91.9	12 540	92.4	12 280	92.3	11 310	91.6	9 840	90.9	9 890	90.4	10 630	89.7	11 210	90.6	5 880	91.3
Royal Navy/Royal Marines	**2 220**		**2 570**		**2 770**		**2 910**		**3 170**		**2 990**		**2 930**		**2 980**		**1 400**	
of which female	180	8.3	200	7.6	200	7.3	210	7.3	250	8.0	270	9.1	310	10.6	310	10.4	140	10.0
of which male	2 030	91.7	2 380	92.4	2 570	92.7	2 700	92.7	2 920	92.0	2 720	90.9	2 620	89.4	2 670	89.6	1 260	90.0
Officers	**280**	**100.0**	**230**	**100.0**	**280**	**100.0**	**280**	**100.0**	**290**	**100.0**	**310**	**100.0**	**360**	**100.0**	**400**	**100.0**	**240**	**100.0**
of which female	40	13.5	30	12.3	40	12.5	40	12.9	40	12.2	30	10.6	50	13.6	50	13.3	30	10.9
of which male	240	86.5	200	87.7	240	87.5	240	87.1	250	87.8	280	89.4	310	86.4	350	86.7	210	89.1
Other Ranks	**1 940**	**100.0**	**2 350**	**100.0**	**2 490**	**100.0**	**2 630**	**100.0**	**2 890**	**100.0**	**2 680**	**100.0**	**2 570**	**100.0**	**2 580**	**100.0**	**1 160**	**100.0**
of which female	150	7.5	170	7.2	170	6.7	180	6.7	220	7.5	240	8.9	260	10.1	260	9.9	110	9.8
of which male	1 790	92.5	2 180	92.8	2 320	93.3	2 460	93.3	2 670	92.5	2 440	91.1	2 310	89.9	2 320	90.1	1 050	90.2
Army	**11 190**		**10 740**		**10 300**		**9 020**		**7 020**		**7 230**		**8 160**		**8 580**		**4 710**	
of which female	920	8.3	860	8.0	830	8.1	790	8.8	660	9.3	660	9.2	800	9.8	720	8.4	340	7.3
of which male	10 260	91.7	9 880	92.0	9 460	91.9	8 230	91.2	6 370	90.7	6 560	90.8	7 360	90.2	7 850	91.6	4 370	92.7
Officers	**710**	**100.0**	**640**	**100.0**	**640**	**100.0**	**610**	**100.0**	**580**	**100.0**	**550**	**100.0**	**520**	**100.0**	**560**	**100.0**	**390**	**100.0**
of which female	110	16.0	110	18.0	100	15.3	90	15.0	80	13.9	80	14.7	80	15.5	70	12.7	40	11.0
of which male	600	84.0	520	82.0	540	84.7	520	85.0	500	86.1	470	85.3	440	84.5	490	87.3	350	89.0
Other Ranks	**10 480**	**100.0**	**10 100**	**100.0**	**9 660**	**100.0**	**8 420**	**100.0**	**6 440**	**100.0**	**6 680**	**100.0**	**7 650**	**100.0**	**8 010**	**100.0**	**4 320**	**100.0**
of which female	810	7.7	750	7.4	740	7.6	700	8.3	580	8.9	580	8.7	720	9.4	650	8.1	300	6.9
of which male	9 670	92.3	9 360	92.6	8 920	92.4	7 720	91.7	5 860	91.1	6 090	91.3	6 930	90.6	7 360	91.9	4 020	93.1
Royal Air Force	**1 390**		**1 220**		**1 310**		**1 460**		**1 690**		**1 830**		**1 880**		**2 020**		**1 070**	
of which female	180	13.1	150	12.2	170	12.9	200	13.7	230	13.8	280	15.4	290	15.2	300	14.6	170	15.9
of which male	1 210	86.9	1 070	87.8	1 140	87.1	1 260	86.3	1 460	86.2	1 550	84.6	1 600	84.8	1 730	85.4	900	84.1
Officers	**80**	**100.0**	**100**	**100.0**	**140**	**100.0**	**160**	**100.0**	**200**	**100.0**	**240**	**100.0**	**250**	**100.0**	**250**	**100.0**	**120**	**100.0**
of which female	30	36.3	30	31.3	40	29.7	40	24.4	50	23.4	50	21.6	50	18.2	40	18.1	20	20.0
of which male	50	63.8	70	68.8	100	70.3	120	75.6	150	76.6	190	78.4	210	81.8	200	81.9	90	80.0
Other Ranks	**1 310**	**100.0**	**1 120**	**100.0**	**1 170**	**100.0**	**1 290**	**100.0**	**1 490**	**100.0**	**1 590**	**100.0**	**1 630**	**100.0**	**1 780**	**100.0**	**960**	**100.0**
of which female	150	11.7	120	10.5	130	10.9	160	12.3	190	12.5	230	14.4	240	14.7	250	14.1	150	15.4
of which male	1 160	88.3	1 000	89.5	1 040	89.1	1 130	87.7	1 300	87.5	1 360	85.6	1 390	85.3	1 530	85.9	810	84.6

Source: Defence Statistics (Tri Service)

14.3a Number of vessels in the Royal Navy and Royal Fleet Auxiliary, and squadrons in the Fleet Air Arm, at 1 April each year

These figures show overall unit numbers only; they do not reflect the level of readiness at which each unit is held, which changes throughout the year. Readiness refers to the length of time it would take for a vessel to be ready for deployment.

This table is a National Statistic.

		2000	2008	2009	2010	2011	2012	2013	2014
Royal Navy submarines	**Total**	**16**	**13**	**12**	**11**	**11**	**11**	**11**	**11**
Of which:									
Trident / Polaris	Vessels	4	4	4	4	4	4	4	4
Fleet	Vessels	12	9	8 [2]	7 [3]	7	7	7 [4,5]	7
Royal Navy ships	**Total**	**89**	**74**	**73**	**71**	**67**	**65**	**66**	**65**
Of which:									
Aircraft Carriers	Vessels	3	2	2	2	- [6,7]	-	-	-
Landing Platform Docks / Helicopter	Vessels	3	3	3	3	4 [7]	4	4	4
Destroyers	Vessels	11	8	7 [8]	6 [9]	6 [10]	5 [11]	6	6
Frigates	Vessels	21	17	17	17	15 [12]	13 [13]	13	13
Mine countermeasures vessels	Vessels	21	16	16	16	15 [14]	15	15	15
Patrol ships and craft	Vessels	23	22 [15]	22	22	22	22	22	22
Survey ships	Vessels	6	5	5	4 [16]	4	4	4	4
Ice patrol ships	Vessels	1	1	1	1 [17]	1 [17]	2 [18]	2 [18]	1 #
Royal Fleet Auxiliary Service	**Total**	**22**	**18**	**16**	**16**	**14**	**13**	**13**	**13**
Of which:									
Tankers	Vessels	9 [r]	6 [r, 19]	6	6	6 [r, 22]	5	5	5
Fleet Replenishment Ships	Vessels	- [r]	2	2 [r, 20]	2 [r, 21]	1 [r]	1 [r]	1 [r]	1
Solid Support Ships	Vessels	4	4	2 [20]	2	2	2	2	2
Primary Casualty Receiving Ship[23]	Vessels	1	1	1	1	1	1	1	1
Landing Ships	Vessels	5	4 [24,25]	4	4	3 [26]	3	3	3
Forward Repair Ships	Vessels	1	1	1	1	1	1	1	1
Roll-on Roll-off vessels[27]	Vessels	2	- [r]	- [r]	- [r]	- [r]	- [r]	- [r]	-
Royal Marines									
RM Commando	Commando	3	3	3	3	3	3	3	3
Command Support Group	Commando	1	1	1	1	1	1	1	1
Infantry Battalion	Battalion	-	1 [28]	1	1	1	1	1	- #
Logistic unit	Regiments	1	1	1	1	1	1	1	1
Artillery unit	Regiments	1	1	1	1	1	1	1	1
Engineer unit	Squadrons	1	1	1	1	1	1	1	1
Nuclear Guarding and Fleet Security	Squadrons	1	3	3	4 [29]	4	4	4	3 #
Assault (landing craft)	Squadrons	3	4	4	4	4	4	3 [30]	3
Naval Aircraft									
Fixed Wing Aircraft[32]	Squadrons	1	- [r]	- [r]	- [r]	-	-	-	1
Helicopters[33, 34]	Squadrons	10 [r]	8 [r]	8 [r]	8 [r]	8 [r]	8 [r]	8 [r]	8
Reserve Units									
Royal Navy Reserve Units	Units	..	14	14	14	14	14	14	14
Royal Marine Reserve Units	Units	..	5	5	5	5	5	5	5

Source: MOD Finance & Military Capability

Footnotes located on the next page.

14.3a Number of vessels in the Royal Navy and Royal Fleet Auxiliary, as at 1 April each year.

This table is a National Statistic.

Number

	2016	
	In Service[1]	Total
Royal Navy Submarine Service	**11**	**11**
Ballistic Nuclear Submarine	4	4
Nuclear Submarine	7	7
Royal Navy Surface Fleet	**64**	**64**
Aircraft Carriers	-	-
Landing Platform Docks/Helicopters	3	3
Destroyers	6	6
Frigates	13	13
Mine Countermeasures Vessels (MCMV)	15	15
Inshore Patrol Vessels	18	18
Offshore Patrol Vessels	4	4
Survey Ships	4	4
Ice Patrol Ship	1	1
Royal Fleet Auxiliary	**12**	**12**
Fleet Tanker	2	2
Small Fleet Tanker	2	2
Fleet Replenishment Ship[2]	3	3
Landing Ship Dock	3	3
Primary Casualty Receiving Ship[3]	1	1
Forward Repair Ship	1	1

Source: Navy Command

1. In service here is defined as any element held at a state of "Readiness". Readiness time is the period required for an element to be ready to deploy form their home base (or current location) to undertake specific tasks, with appropriate Manpower, Equipment, Training and Sustainability (METS) criteria, to conduct the allocated task.

2. Consists of the Auxiliary Oiler Replenishment vessel RFA Fort Victoria, and the Auxiliary Fleet Support Helicopter carrying vesseels RFA Fort Austin and RFA Rosalie.

3. Primary Casualty Receiving Ship has a secondary role of Aviation Training Ship.

There was a delay between the last edition of Formations, Vessels and Aircraft (published in February 2015) and the first edition of the UK Armed Forces Equipment and Formations (published September 2016). Initially this delay was caused by investigations into data errors and concerns over the accuracy of the statistics in the 2014 edition. The publication was then further delayed due to an internal review of equipment statistics and a subsequent public consultation which was held for a period of six weeks. As a result, no 2015 data for table 14.3a was produced.

14.3b Number of Regiments, Infantry Battalions and Major Headquarters in the Regular Army and Army Reserves[1], at 1 April each year

This table is a National Statistic.

		2000	2008	2009	2010	2011	2012	2013	2014
Combat arms									
Armour									
Regular Army	Regiments	10	10	10	10	10	10	10	10
Army Reserves	Regiments	4	4	4	4	4	4	4	4
Infantry									
Regular Army [2]	Battalions	40	36	36	36	36	36	36	33 [3]
Army Reserves	Battalions	15	14	14	14	14	14	14	14
Home Service Forces	Battalions	7	-	-	-	-	-	-	-
Combat support									
Artillery									
Regular Army [4]	Regiments	15	14	14	14	14	14	13	13
Army Reserves [5]	Regiments	7	7	7	7	7	7	7	7
Engineers									
Regular Army	Regiments	11	11	11	12 [6]	12	14	13 [7]	13
Army Reserves	Regiments	6	6	6	5	5	5	5	5
Signals									
Regular Army	Regiments	11	12	12	12	12	11	11	11
Army Reserves	Regiments	11	11	5 [8]	5	5	5	5	5
Combat service support									
Equipment support									
Regular Army	Battalions	7	7	7	7	7	7	6 [9]	6
Army Reserves	Battalions	4	2 #	2	2	2	2	2	2
Logistics									
Regular Army	Regiments	22	17	17	17	17	17	16 #	14 [12]
Army Reserves	Regiments	17	17	17	17	17	17	17	17 [13]
Medical Regiments / Field Hospitals									
Regular Army	Number	8	8	8	9	9	9	9	9
Army Reserves	Number	15	15	15	15	15	15	15	15
Corps, Division & Brigade HQ									
NATO Corps HQ		1	1	1	1	1	1	1	1
Division / District HQ									
Deployable		2	2	2	2	2	2	2	2
Non-deployable		4	5	5	5	5	5	4 #	4
Brigade HQ [15]									
Deployable		7	7	7	7	7	7	6 #	6
Non-deployable		15	9	9	10	10	10	10	10

Source: Army HQ Plans Directorate

1. Previously known as the Territorial Army.
2. Excludes Special Forces Support Group.
3. 1 R WELSH and 2 R WELSH merged Mar 14; 2 YORKS and 3 YORKS merged 2013; 5 SCOTS regiment reduced to a Public Duties Independent Company Mar 14.
4. Excludes 14th Regiment Royal Artillery. Also excludes 40th Regiment Royal Artillery which was disbanded due to Planning Round 2011.
5. Includes the Honourable Artillery Company.
6. 101 Engr Regt (EOD) was 'regularised' under Op ENTIRETY, in order to support ongoing operations in Afghanistan.
7. 38 Engineer Regiment were disbanded in Planning Round 2011.
8. Restructuring of Royal Electrical and Mechanical Engineers was announced in 2008.
9. 19 Combat Service Support Batallion REME disbanded in January 2013 in Planning Round 2011. 01 Bn & 104 Bn REME form a single Regular Force Support Battalion.
10. As a result of Planning Round 2009, six R Signals Regiments (V) were removed from the force structure.
11. 8 Regiment Royal Logistics Corps disbanded in Planning Round 2011.
12. 24 Regiment and 12 Logistic Support Regiment removed from ORBAT as at Mar 14.
13. 168 Pioneer Regiment Royal Logistics Corp disbanded Feb 2014, with effect post 1 Apr 2014.
14. HQ 2 DIV, HQ 4 DIV and HQ 5 DIV all disbanded in 12/13; HQ Sp Comd was established in 12/13.
15. Brigade HQ figures do not include Logistics or Specialist Brigades.
16. HQ 19 Lt Brigade were disbanded in Planning Round 2011.

14.3b Land Formations of the UK Armed Forces

The number of formations, which are all or primarily land-based, in the Army.
Note: Hybrid (Regular and Reserve) units are counted as Regular Army units.

This table is a National Statistic.

		Number
		2016
Combat Forces		
Infantry		
Regular Army	Battalions	31
Army Reserves	Battalions	14
Royal Armoured Corps		
Regular Army	Regiments	9
Army Reserves	Regiments	4
Combat Support Forces		
Royal Artillery		
Regular Army	Regiments	13
Army Reserves	Regiments	5
Royal Engineers		
Regular Army	Regiments	13
Army Reserves	Regiments	4
Royal Signals		
Regular Army	Regiments	11
Army Reserves	Regiments	4
Intelligence Corps		
Regular Army	Regiments	5
Army Reserves	Regiments	5
Combat Service Support		
Royal Electrical and Mechanical Engineers		
Regular Army	Battalions	7
Army Reserves	Battalions	6
Royal Logistic Corps		
Regular Army[1]	Regiments	12
Army Reserves	Regiments	12
Royal Army Medical Corps		
Regular Army	Regiments	9
Army Reserves	Regiments	15
Royal Military Police		
Regular Army	Regiments	6
Army Reserves	Regiments	-
Corps, Division & Brigade HQ		
NATO Corps HQ	HQs	1
Division / District HQ		
Deployable	HQs	2
Non-deployable	HQs	4
Brigade HQ[2]		
Deployable	HQs	7
Non-deployable	HQs	4

1. Includes Commando Logistic Regimentt (Navy).

2. Brigade HQ figures do not include Logistics or Specialist Brigades.

Source: Army Org Branch

There was a delay between the last edition of Formations, Vessels and Aircraft (published in February 2015) and the first edition of the UK Armed Forces Equipment and Formations (published September 2016). Initially this delay was caused by investigations into data errors and concerns over the accuracy of the statistics in the 2014 edition. The publication was then further delayed due to an internal review of equipment statistics and a subsequent public consultation which was held for a period of six weeks. As a result, no 2015 data for table 14.3b was produced.

14.3c Number of Squadrons in the Royal Air Force and the Royal Auxiliary Air Force, at 1 April each year

This table excludes Operational Conversion Units, which train qualified aircrew for different aircraft types.
This table is a National Statistic.

		2000	2008	2009	2010	2011	2012	2013	2014
Regular Air Force									
Multi-roled Fast Jet Squadrons [1,2]	Squadrons	17	11	11	10 [3]	10 [4]	8 [5]	9 [6]	7 [20]
Maritime patrol	Squadrons	3	2	2	2	2	- [7]	-	-
ISTAR (inc Airborne Early Warning)	Squadrons	2	4	4	4	4	5 [8]	6 [9]	6
Air transport / Air Refuelling	Squadrons	8	8	8	8	7 [10]	7	7	6 [21]
Search and Rescue	Squadrons	2	2	2	2	2	2	2	2
RAF FP Wg	HQs	..	7	7	8	8	8	8	8
RAF Ground based air defence [11]	Squadrons	*	-	-	-	-	-	-	-
RAF Regiment Field [11]	Squadrons	*	7	7	8	8	8	8	8
RAF Regt (Jt CBRN) [12]	Squadrons	-	1	1	1	1	-	-	-
Defence CBRN Wing [12,25]	HQs	-	-	-	-	-	1	1	1
	Squadrons	-	-	-	-	-	2	2	2
RAF Police Force [13]	HQs	*	*	*	*	*	* ||[13]	3	3
	Squadrons	*	*	*	*	*	* ||	9	9
Tactical Provost Wg	HQs	-	1	1	1	1	1 ||	*	*
	Squadrons	-	1	1	1	1	1 ||	*	*
Specialist Policing Wg	HQs	-	1	1	1	1	1 ||	*	*
	Squadrons	-	3	3	3	3	3 ||	*	*
General Policing Wg	HQs	-	1	1	1	1	1 ||	*	*
	Squadrons	-	4	4	4	4	4 ||	*	*
Tactical Communications Wg [14]	Squadrons	*	4	4	4	4	4	4	4
Auxiliary Air Force [25]									
Air Movements	Squadrons	1	1	1	1	1	1	1	1
Aeromedical	Squadrons	2	2	2	2	2	2	2	2
Flight Operations	Squadrons	-	-	-	-	-	1	1	1
General Support	Squadrons	-	-	-	-	-	-	2 [15]	3
HQ Augmentation	Squadrons	1	1	1	1	1	1	1 [r]	1
Intelligence	Squadrons	2	2	2	2	2	2	2	2
Photographic Interpretation	Squadrons	1	1	1	1	1	1	1	1
Public Relations	Squadrons	1	1	1	1	1	1	1	1
RAuxAF Regt Field	Squadrons	4	3	3	3	3	3	4 [16]	5 [22]
FP Operations Support	Squadrons	4	4	4	4	4	4	1 [17]	- [22]
RAF Police	Squadrons	-	1	1	1	1	1	2 [18]	2
RAuxAF Regt CBRN [24]	Squadrons	-	1	1	1	1	1	1	1
A4 - Logs	Squadrons	-	-	-	-	-	-	2 [19]	2
Reserve Aircrew - Air Mobility	Squadrons	-	-	- -	-	-	-	1	1
RAF Reserve - Sponsored Reserves									
Meteorological [23]	Units	1	1	1	1	1	1	1	1

Source: MOD Finance & Military Capability

Footnotes continued on the next page.

1. Excludes Joint Force Harrier squadrons. See Table 4.01.07 - Joint units.

2. From 2006, four Air Defence squadrons amalgamated with Strike/Attack, Offensive support and Reconnaissance squadrons to form multi-roled fast jet squadrons. One Reconnaissance squadron was re-roled ISTAR. One squadron was disbanded.

3. 43 Sqn was stood down on 1 July 2009.

4. 6 Sqn (Typhoon) stood up 6 Sep 2010. 111 Sqn (Tornado F3) stood down 22 Mar 2011.

5. 13 Sqn and 14 Sqn (both Tornado GR4) were disbanded on 1 Jun 2011. (See further footnote below on 14 Sqn)

6. 1 Sqn (Typhoon) reformed 15 Sep 2012.

7. 201 Sqn and 120 Sqn were disbanded on 26 May 2011.

8. 14 Sqn was subsequently stood up on 14 October 2011. This unit replaced the flight within 5 Sqn operating the R1 Shadow aircraft.

9. 13 Sqn (MQ9) reformed 26 Oct 2012.

10. 70 Sqn disbanded 10 Sep 2010.

11. Delivery of Ground based air defence has been vested with the Army since 2008. The remaining 2 squadrons were combined on 1 Apr 2008 to provide a 7th Field Sqn (15 Sqn RAF Regt).

12. Defence CBRN Wing was established on 14 Dec 2011 on the disbandment of the Joint CBRN Regiment.

13. RAF Police re-brigaded on 1 Apr 2012 following a Planning Round 2011 option that directed a 15% reduction in manning numbers. The previous definitions of Tactical Provost, Specialist and General Wings are no longer appropriate.

14. TCW has existed as a formed unit since 1969 and is currently subordinate to 90 Signals Unit at RAF Leeming. 90 Signals Unit comprises one HQ and 8 Sqns; 4 x TCW and 4 x Force Generation Wg (FGW); it has existed since 2006. All but 2 Sqns have some form of deployable function.

15. 611 Sqn stood up Oct 2012, 502 Sqn stood up Jan 2013

16. 501 Sqn RAuxAF Ops Spt - Regt staff regenerated into newly created 2624 RAuxAF Regt Sqn at BZN.

17. 501 and 504 RAuxAF Ops Spt Sqns transfer to A4. 603 RAuxAF Sqn transfered to RAFP.

18. Reflects the transfer of 603 Sqn to RAF Police.

19. 501 and 504 RAuxAF Logs Sqns.

20. 12 Sqn and 617 Sqn stood down on 31 March 2014.

21. Number 216 Sqn disbanded March 2014.

22. 609 Sqn now Regt Field previously reported as Operations Support.

23. Previously reported as an Royal Auxillary Air Force squadron.

24. CBRN is also known as: Chemical, Biological, Radiological and Nuclear.

25. Note that this is not a comprehensive list of Auxiliary Air Force squadrons, as for example some units that form part of the Air Combat Service Support Units are not included.

r The 2013 edition of this publication incorrectly stated that there were three HQ Augmentation Squadrons in 2013. The reason for this error is that 2 General Support Squadrons were incorrectly declared as HQ Augmentation Squadrons.

14.3c Numbers of formations in the Royal Air Force and Royal Auxiliary Air Force, and in the air components of the Royal Navy and the Army, as at 1 April each year.

This table is a National Statistic.

		Number
		2016
Royal Navy Fleet Air Arm		
Battlefield Helicopter	Squadrons	1
Flying Training	Squadrons	4
Maritime Helicopter	Squadrons	6
Remotely Piloted Air Systems	Squadrons	1
Support	Squadrons	2
Support Helicopter	Squadrons	2
Commando Helicopter Force	HQ	1
Fixed Wing Force	HQ	1
Lynx Wildcat Maritime Force	HQ	1
Merlin Helicopter Force	HQ	1
Sea King Force	HQ	1
Army Air Corps		
Regular Army[1]	Regiments	4
Army Reserves	Regiments	1
Royal Air Force		
Flying Support		
Air Transport & Air-to-Air Refuelling	Squadrons	8
Airborne Command and Control	Squadrons	1
Combat Air	Squadrons	8
Flying Training & Operational Training Support	Squadrons	12
Intelligence, Surveillance and Reconnaissance	Squadrons	3
Operational Conversion and Evaluation Units	Squadrons	9
Remotely Piloted Aircraft Systems	Squadrons	2
Search and Rescue	Squadrons	1
Support Helicopter	Squadrons	5
Combat Support - Force Protection		
RAF Force Protection Wing	HQs	6
RAF Regiment Field	Squadrons	6
RAF Police Wing	HQs	3
RAF Police	Squadrons	5
Defence CBRN Wing	HQ	1
Defence CBRN Wing	Squadrons	2
Combat Support - Communications		
Operational Information Services Wing	Squadrons	3
Tactical Communications Wing	Squadrons	3
Technical Information Assurance	Squadrons	1
Combat Support - Engineering and Logistics		
Air Mobility Wing	Squadrons	2
Engineering Support Wing	Squadrons	4
Expeditionary Logistics Wing	Squadrons	5
Royal Auxiliary Air Force		
Aeromedical Evacuation & Medical Support	Squadrons	2
Air Operations & Aerospace Battle Management	Squadrons	1
Air Transport & Air-to-Air Refuelling	Squadrons	1
Expeditionary Logistics Wing	Squadrons	5
Force Protection	Squadrons	7
General Operations Support	Squadrons	5
Intelligence and Imagery Analyst Support	Squadrons	3
Musical & Ceremonial Support	HQ	1
Provost Wing	Wing	1
Public Relations	Squadrons	1
Support Helicopter	Squadrons	1
RAF Reserve - Sponsored Reserves	**Units/Squadrons**	**3**

1. Includes two training regiments.   Sources: Navy Command; Army Org Branch; Air Command

There was a delay between the last edition of Formations, Vessels and Aircraft (published in February 2015) and the first edition of the UK Armed Forces Equipment and Formations (published September 2016). Initially this delay was caused by investigations into data errors and concerns over the accuracy of the statistics in the 2014 edition. The publication was then further delayed due to an internal review of equipment statistics and a subsequent public consultation which was held for a period of six weeks. As a result, no 2015 data for table 14.3c was produced.

14.3d Number of Regiments and Squadrons in selected Joint Units, at 1 April each year

This table excludes Operational Conversion Units, which train qualified aircrew for different aircraft types.

This table is a National Statistic.

		2008	2009	2010	2011	2012	2013	2014
Joint Units								
Joint Nuclear Biological Chemical	Regiments	1	1	1	1	-[3]	-	-
Special Forces								
Special Air Service	Regiments	1	1	1	1	1	1	1
Special Air Service - Army Reserves	Regiments	2	2	2	2	2	2	2
Special Boat Service	Units[1]	1	1	1	1	1	1	1
Special Forces Support Group Battalion [2]	Battalions	1	1	1	1	1	1	1
Joint Helicopter Command								
Royal Navy Helicopter	Squadrons[4]	4	4	4	4	4	4	4 [14]
Army Aviation [5]	Regiments	5	5	5	5	5	5	5
Army Aviation - Army Reserves	Regiments	2	1 [7]	1	1	1	1	1
Royal Air Force Helicopter	Squadrons[4]	6 [8]	6	6	6	6	6 [r]	6 [15]
Royal Auxiliary Air Force [9]	Squadrons[4]	1	1	1	1	1	1	1
Joint Special Forces Air Wing	Units	1	1	1	1	1	1	1
Joint Force Harrier								
Royal Navy	Squadrons[4]	2	2	1 [#]	- [#]	-	-	-
Royal Air Force	Squadrons[4]	2	2	1 [#]	- [#]	-	-	-

Source: MOD Finance & Military Capability

1. The units for the Special Boat Service have been changed from Squadrons to Units so that the same level of formation is given for all Special Forces.

2. The Special Forces Support Group was formed as a result of the Ministerial Announcement on 16 Dec 2004 as part of The Future Army Structure. It is a Tri-Service Unit based on 1 PARA, to provide specialist support to Special Forces.

3. The JNBC regiment disbanded on the formation of the Defence CBRN Wing on 14 December 2011.

4. The term "squadron" has different meanings among the three Services: see the Glossary for details.

5. These figures exclude the School of Army Aviation, 667 (D&T) Sqn and 657 Sqn and three independent Army Air Corps flights (7, 25 and 29 Flts).

6. 6 Regt AAC(V) formed on 1 April 2007.

7. 7 Regt AAC(V) was disbanded 31 March 2009.

8. Reflects the standing up of 78 Sqn RAF to accommodate the endorsed increase in Merlin Mk3 crews and aircraft.

9. No 606 (Chiltern) Squadron provides a pool of trained personnel to provide combat service support to the Support Helicopter Force in training and on operations in times of crisis and war.

10. On the reduction in the Joint Force Harrier force from 1 April 2010, the Fleet Air Arm Strike Wing was counted as 1 Sqn.

11. 800 RNAS was disbanded on 28 January 2011.

12. 20 Sqn was disbanded 31 March 2010.

13. 1 Sqn was disbanded on 28 January 2011.

14. Although Commando Helicopter Force have 4x Sqns, currently the Merlin Sqn are going through transition to Merlin based out of RAF Benson under Command of the RAF until they move to Yeovilton under RN in March 15 and March 16.

15. Merlin Sqns (2x RAF Sqn) currently going through transition to RN.

r The 2013 edition of this publication incorrectly stated that there were 7 RAF Helicopter squadrons in 2013.

Please note that this table has now ceased to be published and has therefore not been updated by the Ministry of Defence since the last edition of Annual Abstract of Statistics.

14.4 Outflow from UK Regular Forces, trained or untrained

	12 Months Ending:												1 Apr 2015 'to
	2015 31 Jan	2015 28 Feb	2015 31 Mar	2015 30 Apr	2015 31 May	2015 30 Jun	2015 31 Jul	2015 31 Aug	2015 30 Sep	2015 31 Oct	2015 30 Nov	2015 31 Dec	30 Nov 2015
All Services Outflow	**18 705**	**18 683**	**18 912**	**18 879**	**18 737**	**18 323**	**18 107**	**18 075**	**18 081**	**18 076**	**18 093**	**17 232**	**11 635**
Trained[1][2]	16 191	16 185	16 324	16 214	16 062	15 547	15 301	15 233	15 209	15 163	15 129	14 274	9 624 ‖
Untrained[1][2]	2 514	2 498	2 588	2 665	2 675	2 776	2 806	2 842	2 872	2 913	2 964	2 958	2 011 ‖
Officers	**2 222**	**2 227**	**2 216**	**2 242**	**2 234**	**2 237**	**2 236**	**2 266**	**2 273**	**2 310**	**2 278**	**2 239**	**1 583**
Trained[1][2]	2 102	2 109	2 105	2 132	2 126	2 130	2 128	2 162	2 169	2 207	2 180	2 145	1 517 ‖
Untrained[1][2]	120	118	111	110	108	107	108	104	104	103	98	94	66 ‖
Other Ranks	**16 483**	**16 456**	**16 696**	**16 637**	**16 503**	**16 086**	**15 871**	**15 809**	**15 808**	**15 766**	**15 815**	**14 993**	**10 052**
Trained[1][2]	14 089	14 076	14 219	14 082	13 936	13 417	13 173	13 071	13 040	12 956	12 949	12 129	8 107 ‖
Untrained[1][2]	2 394	2 380	2 477	2 555	2 567	2 669	2 698	2 738	2 768	2 810	2 866	2 864	1 945 ‖
Royal Navy/Royal Marines	**3 485**	**3 486**	**3 519**	**3 500**	**3 433**	**3 449**	**3 412**	**3 384**	**3 398**	**3 431**	**3 411**	**3 372**	**2 253**
Trained	2 815	2 833	2 870	2 840	2 796	2 799	2 758	2 718	2 704	2 691	2 652	2 635	1 735
Untrained	670	653	649	660	637	650	654	666	694	740	759	737	518
Officers	**459**	**472**	**477**	**490**	**499**	**508**	**498**	**498**	**506**	**514**	**507**	**514**	**344**
Trained	408	421	428	440	447	457	446	446	454	459	454	460	306
Untrained	51	51	49	50	52	51	52	52	52	55	53	54	38
Other Ranks	**3 026**	**3 014**	**3 042**	**3 010**	**2 934**	**2 941**	**2 914**	**2 886**	**2 892**	**2 917**	**2 904**	**2 858**	**1 909**
Trained	2 407	2 412	2 442	2 400	2 349	2 342	2 312	2 272	2 250	2 232	2 198	2 175	1 429
Untrained	619	602	600	610	585	599	602	614	642	685	706	683	480
Army	**12 015**	**12 005**	**12 209**	**12 223**	**12 179**	**11 782**	**11 705**	**11 723**	**11 717**	**11 751**	**11 813**	**11 043**	**7 493**
Trained[1][2]	10 352	10 337	10 448	10 401	10 327	9 835	9 716	9 713	9 688	9 709	9 744	8 956	6 091 ‖
Untrained[1][2]	1 663	1 668	1 761	1 822	1 852	1 947	1 989	2 010	2 029	2 042	2 069	2 087	1 402 ‖
Officers	**1 166**	**1 152**	**1 144**	**1 157**	**1 150**	**1 127**	**1 147**	**1 152**	**1 146**	**1 174**	**1 162**	**1 133**	**818**
Trained[1][2]	1 119	1 106	1 102	1 116	1 112	1 088	1 107	1 116	1 110	1 138	1 126	1 103	796 ‖
Untrained[1][2]	47	46	42	41	38	39	40	36	36	36	36	30	22 ‖
Other Ranks	**10 849**	**10 853**	**11 065**	**11 066**	**11 029**	**10 655**	**10 558**	**10 571**	**10 571**	**10 577**	**10 651**	**9 910**	**6 675**
Trained[1][2]	9 233	9 231	9 346	9 285	9 215	8 747	8 609	8 597	8 578	8 571	8 618	7 853	5 295 ‖
Untrained[1][2]	1 616	1 622	1 719	1 781	1 814	1 908	1 949	1 974	1 993	2 006	2 033	2 057	1 380 ‖
Royal Air Force	**3 205**	**3 192**	**3 184**	**3 156**	**3 125**	**3 092**	**2 990**	**2 968**	**2 966**	**2 894**	**2 869**	**2 817**	**1 889**
Trained	3 024	3 015	3 006	2 973	2 939	2 913	2 827	2 802	2 817	2 763	2 733	2 683	1 798
Untrained	181	177	178	183	186	179	163	166	149	131	136	134	91
Officers	**597**	**603**	**595**	**595**	**585**	**602**	**591**	**616**	**621**	**622**	**609**	**592**	**421**
Trained	575	582	575	576	567	585	575	600	605	610	600	582	415
Untrained	22	21	20	19	18	17	16	16	16	12	9	10	6
Other Ranks	**2 608**	**2 589**	**2 589**	**2 561**	**2 540**	**2 490**	**2 399**	**2 352**	**2 345**	**2 272**	**2 260**	**2 225**	**1 468**
Trained	2 449	2 433	2 431	2 397	2 372	2 328	2 252	2 202	2 212	2 153	2 133	2 101	1 383
Untrained	159	156	158	164	168	162	147	150	133	119	127	124	85

Source: Defence Statistics (Tri-Service)

Notes
1. Due to the change in definition of trained strength for Army in 1 October 2016, intake and outflow by trained and untrained will not be available until October 2017 when 12 months of data under the new definition is available.
2. As the definition has changed part-way through the year we will not be able to priovde the figures for the 1 Apr 2016 to 30 Sep 2016 totals.
3. Figures show outflow from UK Regular Forces, both trained and untrained, including personnel leaving the Services, deaths and recalled reservists on release. They do not include promotion from Ranks to Officers or flows between Services.
4. Figures are not comparable with gains to trained strength figures which include promotion from Ranks to Officers.

14.5 Full-Time Trained Strength[1] and Requirement, at 1 April each year

This table is a National Statistic.

								Number of personnel (unless stated otherwise)	
	2000	**2008**	**2009**	**2010**	**2011**	**2012**	**2013**	**2014**	**2015**
All Services									
Requirement	198 160	179 270	178 860	178 750	179 250	174 840	162 940	159 640	150 700
Strength[2]	190 270	173 530	174 170	177 890	176 860	170 010	160 710	150 890	144 120
Surplus/Deficit	-7 880	-5 740	-4 690	- 860	-2 390	-4 830	-2 230	-8 750	-6 580
Surplus/Deficit as % of requirement	*-4.0*	*-3.2*	*-2.6*	*-0.5*	*-1.3*	*-2.8*	*-1.4*	*-5.5*	*-4.4*
By Service:									
RN/RM									
Requirement	39 860	36 260	35 760	35 790	35 700	34 800	30 530	30 340	30 280
Strength[2]	38 880	35 050	35 020	35 500	35 420	33 290	31 420	30 510	30 060
Surplus/Deficit	- 990	-1 210	- 740	- 290	- 280	-1 510	890	170	- 230
Surplus/Deficit as % of requirement	*-2.5*	*-3.3*	*-2.1*	*-0.8*	*-0.8*	*-4.3*	*2.9*	*0.6*	*-0.7*
Army									
Requirement	106 400	101 800	101 790	102 160	102 210	101 210	96 790	94 100	86 540
Strength[2]	100 190	98 070	99 510	102 260	101 340	98 600	93 940	87 180	82 230
Surplus/Deficit	-6 210	-3 730	-2 280	100	- 870	-2 610	-2 850	-6 930	-4 300
Surplus/Deficit as % of requirement	*-5.8*	*-3.7*	*-2.2*	*0.1*	*-0.8*	*-2.6*	*-2.9*	*-7.4*	*-5.0*
Royal Air Force									
Requirement	51 900	41 210	41 310	40 800	41 340	38 830	35 620	35 200	33 880
Strength[2]	51 210	40 400	39 640	40 130	40 090	38 120	35 350	33 210	31 830
Surplus/Deficit	- 690	- 800	-1 670	- 670	-1 250	- 700	- 270	-1 990	- 2 050
Surplus/Deficit as % of requirement	*-1.3*	*-1.9*	*-4.1*	*-1.7*	*-3.0*	*-1.8*	*-0.8*	*-5.7*	*-6.0*

Source: Defence Statistics (Tri-Service)

1. The Full-Time Trained Strength of the UK Armed Forces is defined as comprising of trained UK Regular Forces, trained Gurkhas and elements of the FTRS (Full Time Reserve Service) personnel. It does not include mobilised reservists.
2. From 1 April 2010 some elements of the FTRS are excluded.

14.6a Trends in Service and civilian personnel strengths, at 1 April each year

Full Time Equivalent (FTE)

	2012 1 Apr	2013 1 Apr	2014 1 Apr	2015 1 Apr	2016 1 Apr
MOD Personnel	**256 908**	**242 261**	**228 576**	**218 726**	**214 854**
Service	**185 900**	**176 861**	**166 075**	**160 565**	**158 610**
UK Regulars	179 804	170 712	159 627	153 724	150 996
FTRS	2 064	2 438	3 184	3 750	4 559
Gurkhas	3 824	3 510	3 047	2 866	2 855
Locally Engaged Personnel	208	201	217	225	200
Civilian (Level 0)	**71 008**	**65 400**	**62 501**	**58 161**	**56 243**
Civilian (Level 1)	54 509	49 977	48 400	48 648 ‖	37 656
DE&S Trading Entity	*	*	*	* ‖	9 836
Trading Funds	7 113	7 171	7 110	4 495	4 405
Locally engaged civilians	9 387 e	8 252	6 991	5 018	4 347

Notes   Source: Defence Statistics (Tri-Service)

1. April 2012 Locally engaged civilians figures are estimates due to partial non-availability of d
2. Civilian Level 1 includes: Top Level Budgetary Areas (TLBs) and Royal Fleet Auxiliary (RFA).
3. From July 2015 Defence Equipment & Support (DE&S) has been reported in a separate row as 'DE&S Trading Entity' outside of Level 1.
4. Full Time Equivalent (FTE) is a measure of the size of the workforce that takes account of the fact that some Civilian personnel work part-time.
5. Service personnel in this table includes trained and untrained Full-time UK Regular Forces, FTRS, Gurkhas and Locally Engaged Personnel.
6. Civilian Personnel data have been provided on a Full Time Equivalent (FTE) basis as it enables a fair comparison with Service figures. These data have been provided to the nearest whole number, therefore adding individual components together may not match the sub-total.

14.6b Civilian personnel by Top Level Budgetary Area (Full Time Equivalent)

	2015	2016	FTE 2016
	1 Jul	1 Jul	1 Oct
Top Level Budgetary areas (TLBs)	**36,126**	**35,604**	**35,549**
Navy Command	2,511	2,562	2,550
Army TLB	10,649	10,207	10,141
HQ Air Command	4,981	4,726	4,676
Head Office & Corporate Services	7,803	7,828	7,885
Joint Forces Command	6,026	6,038	6,035
Defence Infrastructure Organisation	4,154	4,235	4,260
DG Nuclear	*	*	*
Unallocated	2	8	3
Royal Fleet Auxiliary (RFA)	**1,912**	**1,955**	**1,949**
Apprentices	14	99	119
Cadets	90	79	87
Civilians	181	169	161
Sponsored Reserves	1,627	1,608	1,582
Civilian Level 1 Total	**38,038**	**37,559**	**37,498**
DE&S Trading Entity	**10,531**	**9,815**	**10,116**
Trading Funds & Executive Agency Total	**4,560**	**4,383**	**4,426**
Defence Science & Technology Laboratory	3,652	3,537	3,585
Hydrographic Office	908	847	841
Locally engaged civilians (LEC)	**5,073**	**4,388**	**4,382**
Civilian Level 0 Total	**58,203**	**56,145**	**56,422**

Source: Defence Statistics (Civilian)

14.6c Civilian personnel by grade equivalence[1] (Full Time Equivalent)

	2015	2016	FTE 2016
	1 Jul	1 Jul	1 Oct
Civilian Level 0 Total	**58,203**	**56,145**	**56,422**
Non Industrial Total	**30,455**	**30,363**	**30,392**
SCS & Equivalent[2]	186	200	203
Band B1 & Equivalent	408	435	447
Band B2 & Equivalent	1,207	1,299	1,316
Band C1 & Equivalent	3,277	3,356	3,343
Band C2 & Equivalent	6,444	6,345	6,301
Band D & Equivalent	6,302	6,253	6,225
Band E1 & Equivalent	9,141	9,182	9,179
Band E2 & Equivalent	3,426	3,218	3,232
Other[3]	62	75	147
Industrial Total	**5,672**	**5,241**	**5,157**
Firefighter	798	739	736
Skill Zone 4	405	378	382
Skill Zone 3	1,634	1,478	1,452
Skill Zone 2	1,748	1,670	1,638
Skill Zone 1	1,082	974	947
Apprentice	5	2	1
Royal Fleet Auxiliary[4]	**1,912**	**1,955**	**1,949**
DE&S Trading Entity	**10,531**	**9,815**	**10,116**
Trading Funds & Executive Agency Total[4]	**4,560**	**4,383**	**4,426**
Locally engaged civilians[4]	**5,073**	**4,388**	**4,382**

Source: Defence Statistics (Civilian)

1. Grade equivalence is shown in terms of the broader banding structure and is based on paid grade.

2. Includes personnel outside the Senior Civil Service but of equivalent grade, primarily Senior Medical Specialists.

3. 'Other' represents core civilian personnel for whom no grade information is available.

4. Data by grade are not available for Royal Fleet Auxiliary, Trading Funds, Executive Agency and Locally engaged civilians.

14.7a Land holdings by parent Service area and whether owned, leased or with legal rights, at 1 April each year

These holdings include land declared as surplus to defence requirements.
A thousand hectares is 3.86 square miles.
This table is a National Statistic.

Thousand hectares

	2000	2009[1]	2010[1]	2011[2,3]	2012	2013	2014[4]	2015[5]
Total land & foreshore holdings and Rights held[5]	**363.3**	**372.0**	**371.0** ‖	**435.3**	**434.1**	**432.9** ‖	**449.3**	**439.6**
Land and foreshore holdings	238.5	239.0	238.0 ‖	230.4	229.1	228.0	227.3 ‖	222.6
Freehold	219.9	219.0	218.0 ‖	209.8	208.8	207.7	207.0	207.1
Leasehold	18.6	20.0	20.0 ‖	20.6	20.3	20.3	20.3 ‖	15.5
Rights held[6]	124.8	133.0	133.0 ‖	204.9	204.9	204.9 ‖	222.0 ‖	217.0
Of which:								
Naval Service	**39.3**	**44.0**	**44.0** ‖	**2.3**	**2.3**	**2.3**	**2.3**	**3.8**
Land and foreshore holdings	13.1	18.0	18.0 ‖	2.2	2.3	2.3	2.2	3.7
Freehold	10.7	15.0	15.0 ‖	2.1	2.1	2.1	2.0	3.5
Leasehold	2.4	3.0	3.0 ‖	0.1	0.2	0.2	0.2	0.2
Rights held[6]	26.2	26.0	26.0 ‖	0.1	0.1	0.1	0.1	0.1
Army	**243.9**	**245.0**	**245.0** ‖	**15.1**	**15.1**	**14.7**	**14.6**	**13.6**
Land and foreshore holdings	155.9	157.0	157.0 ‖	14.7	14.6	14.3	14.2	13.2
Freehold	152.1	151.0	151.0 ‖	14.2	14.1	13.8	13.7	12.7
Leasehold	3.8	6.0	6.0 ‖	0.5	0.5	0.5	0.5	0.5
Rights held[6]	88.0	88.0	88.0 ‖	0.5	0.5	0.4	0.4	0.4
Royal Air Force	**48.6**	**46.0**	**45.0** ‖	**21.7**	**21.7**	**21.7**	**21.4**	**20.7**
Land and foreshore holdings	39.3	37.0	36.0 ‖	21.7	21.6	21.6	21.4	20.7
Freehold	30.9	28.0	28.0 ‖	17.8	17.7	17.7	17.5	17.0
Leasehold	8.4	8.0	8.0 ‖	3.9	3.9	3.9	3.9	3.7
Rights held[6]	9.3	9.0	9.0 ‖	-	-	-	-	-
The Centre[7]	**27.4**	**34.0**	**34.0** ‖	**392.8**	**391.8**	**391.1** ‖	**406.6**	**396.6**
Land and foreshore holdings	26.1	25.0	25.0 ‖	188.6	187.4	186.8	185.2 ‖	180.1
Freehold	25.1	24.0	24.0 ‖	172.7	171.9	171.2	169.7	169.2
Leasehold	1.0	1.0	1.0 ‖	15.9	15.5	15.6	15.5 ‖	10.9
Rights held[6]	1.3	10.0	10.0 ‖	204.3	204.4	204.4 ‖	221.4 ‖	216.5
Other[8]	**4.1**	**4.0**	**4.0** ‖	**3.3**	**3.2**	**3.1**	**4.3**	**4.9**
Land and foreshore holdings	4.1	4.0	4.0 ‖	3.3	3.1	3.1	4.3	4.8
Freehold	1.0	1.0	1.0 ‖	3.2	3.0	3.0	4.1	4.7
Leasehold	3.1	3.0	3.0 ‖	0.1	0.1	0.1	0.2	0.1
Rights held[6]	-	-	- ‖	-	-	-	-	-

Source: MOD Defence Infrastructure Organisation (DIO)

1. The figures presented for years 2009 and 2010 were rounded to the nearest thousand hectares.
2. Data from 2011 has been compiled using a new spatial dataset which allows for greater accuracy in the measurement of the estate. Because of this new dataset, comparable figures for earlier years are not available. Figures have been rounded to the nearest hundred hectares.
3. The large changes in the allocations to parent service areas between 2010 and 2011 reflect the outcome of the Defence Estate Training Review, with the Training Estate now transferred to the Defence Infrastructure Organisation, part of the Centre.
4. Part of the Kinlochleven Training Area in Scotland, over which MOD holds rights, is included from 2014 onwards, having been omitted from figures previously reported. It was highlighted by data quality improvement work as a result of the introduction of the DIO's Infrastructure Management System.
5. Balduff Training Area (2,000 hectares), which was shown as leasehold in 2014, has been updated to rights held in 2015.
6. Rights held are land and foreshore that are not owned by, or leased to MOD, but over which the Department has limited rights under grants and rights.
7. The Centre includes Defence Equipment & Support, Defence Infrastructure Organisation (including former Defence Training Estate (hence marked increase in values from 2011) and Service family quarters leased from Annington Property Ltd.) and Centre TLBs.
8. Includes Permanent Joint Headquarters and Trading Funds.

14.7b Service Family Accommodation in the United Kingdom at 31 March each year

This table is a National Statistic.

Numbers of dwellings are rounded to the nearest thousand

Thousands of dwellings

	2000	2009	2010	2011	2012	2013	2014	2015
Permanent holdings	**64.8**	**49.9**	**49.1**	**49.2**	**49.0**	**49.4**	**49.4**	**49.6**
By country:								
England & Wales	55.9	44.9	44.1	44.2	44.0	44.5	44.5	44.7
Scotland	5.7	3.2	3.2	3.2	3.3	3.3	3.3	3.3
Northern Ireland	3.2	1.8	1.8	1.7	1.7	1.6	1.6	1.6
Vacant properties	**14.7**	**8.4**	**7.3**	**6.0**	**6.5**	**7.7**	**9.3**	**10.4**
By country:								
England & Wales	12.6	7.3	6.1	5.0	5.0	6.1	7.5	8.4
Scotland	1.7	0.6	0.6	0.5	0.7	0.7	0.8	1.0
Northern Ireland	0.4	0.5	0.6	0.5	0.8	0.9	1.0	1.0
Vacant properties as a percentage of all dwellings	*23*	*17*	*15*	*12*	*13*	*16*	*19*	*21*
By country:								
England & Wales	*23*	*16*	*14*	*11*	*11*	*14*	*17*	*19*
Scotland	*30*	*19*	*18*	*16*	*21*	*21*	*23*	*30*
Northern Ireland	*13*	*28*	*34*	*29*	*47*	*56*	*63*	*62*

Source: MOD Defence Infrastructure Organisation

14.8a Location of Service and civilian personnel[1,2] in the United Kingdom, at 1 April each year

FTE

	2000 [3]	2009	2010	2011	2012	2013	2014	2015
United Kingdom	**267 700**	**233 290**	**236 710**	**229 400**	**214 190**	**203 360**	**192 800**	**187 650**
Service	170 300	162 670	166 100	161 790	156 970	150 310	141 180	138 120
Civilian	97 410	70 620	70 610	67 610	57 220	53 050	51 610	49 520
England	**222 560**	**204 400**	**207 890**	**201 320**	**188 810**	**180 080**	**170 680**	**167 400**
Service	143 040	143 540	146 950	142 860	139 260	133 810	125 640	124 070
Civilian	79 520	60 860	60 940	58 450	49 560	46 270	45 040	43 330
Wales	**8 260**	**4 730**	**4 900**	**4 580**	**4 150**	**3 910**	**3 810**	**3 550**
Service	3 220	2 720	2 930	2 820	2 780	2 650	2 600	2 400
Civilian	5 040	2 010	1 970	1 760	1 370	1 260	1 210	1 160
Scotland	**24 680**	**17 880**	**17 840**	**17 630**	**15 880**	**15 340**	**14 510**	**13 230**
Service	15 080	12 020	12 080	12 090	11 190	11 310	10 600	9 460
Civilian	9 600	5 860	5 760	5 540	4 690	4 020	3 910	3 760
Northern Ireland	**11 640**	**6 280**	**6 080**	**5 870**	**5 350**	**4 030**	**3 790**	**3 470**
Service	8 390	4 390	4 140	4 010	3 740	2 530	2 340	2 190
Civilian	3 250	1 890	1 930	1 850	1 610	1 500	1 450	1 280

Source: Defence Statistics (Tri-Service)

Service and Civilian personnel[1,2] by Region

FTE

	Service				Civilian		
	2014	2015	% change		2014	2015	% change
United Kingdom	**141 180**	**138 120**	**-2.2**		**51 610**	**49 520**	*-4.0*
England	**125 640**	**124 070**	*-1.2*		**45 040**	**43 330**	*-3.8*
East of England	14 540	14 140	*-2.6*		3 890	3 740	*-3.9*
East Midlands	8 890	8 660	*-2.6*		1 580	1 530	*-3.2*
London	4 670	4 100	*-12.2*		3 490	3 520	*0.9*
North East	1 220	1 030	*-15.6*		290	280	*-3.4*
North West	1 560	2 130	*36.5*		1 640	1 670	*1.8*
South East	39 300	39 080	*-0.6*		10 520	10 470	*-0.5*
South West	36 520	36 510	*-0.02*		17 040	16 610	*- 2.5*
West Midlands	6 300	6 610	*4.9*		3 770	3 870	*2.7*
Yorkshire and The Humber	12 640	11 800	*-6.6*		2 810	2 650	*-5.7*
Wales	**2 600**	**2 400**	*-7.7*		**1 210**	**1 160**	*-4.1*
Scotland	**10 600**	**9 460**	*-10.7*		**3 910**	**3 760**	*-3.8*
Northern Ireland	**2 340**	**2 190**	*-6.4*		**1 450**	**1 280**	*-11.7*

Source: Defence Statistics (Tri-Service)

1. UK Regular Forces - Figures are for UK Regular Forces (including both Trained and Untrained personnel), and therefore exclude Gurkhas, Full Time Reserve Service personnel and mobilised reservists. Royal Navy / Royal Marines personnel on sea service are included against the local authority containing the home port of their ship. RAF Other Ranks serving in the South Atlantic are shown against the location containing their home base.

2. MOD Civilian Personnel - Civilian figures are reported as Full Time Equivalent (FTE). FTE is a measure of the size of the workforce taking into account that some people work part-time. Part-time staff are counted according to the number of hours they work per week as a proportion of normal hours for their grade and location.

3. 2000 figures are as at 1 July.

14.8b Global locations of Service[1] and civilian personnel [2,3], at 1 April each year

Number: FTE

		2000 [4]	2009	2010	2011	2012	2013	2014	2015
Global Total		**333 960**	**275 220**	**277 560**	**269 420**	**250 810**	**236 110**	**222 130**	**211 880**
	Service	213 220	188 600	191 710	186 360	179 800	170 710	159 630	153 720
	Civilian Level 0	120 740	86 620	85 850	83 060	71 010	65 400	62 500	58 160
United Kingdom Total		**267 700**	**233 290**	**236 710**	**229 390**	**214 190**	**203 360**	**192 800**	**187 650**
	Service	170 300	162 670	166 100	161 790	156 970	150 310	141 180	138 120
	Civilian	97 410	70 620	70 610	67 610	57 220	53 050	51 610	49 520
Overseas Total		**54 000**	**38 240**	**37 650**	**36 910**	**33 710**	**30 050**	**26 660**	**21 710**
	Service	37 200	25 350	25 260	24 230	22 440	20 060	18 070	15 300
	Civilian	16 800	12 890	12 400	12 680	11 270	10 000	8 580	6 410
EUROPE (exc. UK)		..	**33 670**	**33 000**	**31 300**	**29 050**	**25 610**	**22 570**	**18 190**
of which:									
Germany	Service	..	19 100	19 100	18 240	16 990	14 840	12 960	10 020
	Civilian	..	7 420	7 020	6 470	5 800	5 300	4 250	2 850
Cyprus	Service	3 510	2 910	2 880	2 830	2 590	2 400	2 340	2 400
	Civilian	..	1 640	1 610	1 570	1 670	1 380	1 330	1 180
Belgium	Service	..	410	410	340	330	330	320	310
	Civilian	..	..	140	100	100	40	60	70
Gibraltar	Service	550	260	270	260	230	200	180	160
	Civilian	..	730	730	750	650	530	550	600
Italy	Service	..	260	250	210	170	140	140	180
	Civilian	..	..	60	50	50	20	30	20
ASIA (EXC. MIDDLE EAST)		..	**1 600**	**1 920**	**2 080**	**2 110**	**2 020**	**1 710**	**1 070**
	Service	970	260	260	280	260	260	260	260
	Civilian	..	1 340	1 660	1 800	1 860	1 760	1 450	810
NORTH AFRICA / MIDDLE EAST		..	**730**	**460**	**500**	**430**	**420**	**440**	**460**
	Service	1 300	370	380	420	340	330	350	370
	Civilian	..	360	80	80	90	90	90	100
SUB SAHARAN AFRICA		..	**680**	**690**	**1 540**	**890**	**730**	**670**	**670**
of which:									
Kenya[6]	Service	-	80	90	140	180	180	200	200
	Civilian	..	320	360	1 190	640	480	420	400
Sierra Leone	Service	-	60	30	30	20	20	10	10
	Civilian	..	150	150	130	-	-	-	-

Continued on the next page

14.8b Global locations of Service[1] and civilian personnel [2,3], at 1 April each year

		2000 [4]	2009	2010	2011	2012	2013	2014	2015
NORTH AMERICA		..	**920**	**990**	**980**	**990**	**1 000**	**1 010**	**1 070**
of which:									
United States	Service	910	470	520	550	560	560	570	610
	Civilian	..	160	160	150	150	150	160	160
Canada	Service	1 610	270	270	270	270	280	270	280
	Civilian	..	10	50	10	10	10	10	10
CENTRAL AMERICA / CARIBBEAN		..	**250**	**240**	**240**	**70**	**70**	**70**	**70**
	Service	-	70	70	70	10	10	10	10
	Civilian	..	180	170	160	60	60	60	60
SOUTH AMERICA		..	**20**	**20**	**20**	**20**	**20**	**20**	**20**
	Service	-	10	10	10	10	10	10	10
	Civilian	..	10	10	10	10	10	10	10
SOUTH ATLANTIC		..	**310**	**270**	**180**	**80**	**110**	**100**	**100**
of which:									
Falkland Islands	Service	780	250	220	120	50	70	70	70
	Civilian	..	50	40	40	30	30	30	30
OCEANIA		..	**60**	**60**	**70**	**70**	**70**	**70**	**60**
	Service	20	50	50	50	60	60	60	50
	Civilian	..	20	10	20	10	10	10	10
Unallocated		-	**1 390**	**860**	**760**	**910**	**800**	**860**	**630**
	Service	5 720	580	350	340	390	350	370	300
	Civilian	4 080	800	520	420	520	450	490	330

Source: Defence Statistics (Tri-Service)

1.UK Regular Forces - Figures are for UK Regular Forces (including both Trained and Untrained personnel), and therefore exclude Gurkhas, Full Time Reserve Service personnel and mobilised reservists. Royal Navy / Royal Marines personnel on sea service are included against the local authority containing the home port of their ship. RAF Other Ranks serving in the South Atlantic are shown against the location containing their home base.

2.MOD Civilian Personnel - Civilian figures are reported as Full Time Equivalent (FTE). FTE is a measure of the size of the workforce taking into account that some people work part-time. Part-time staff are counted according to the number of hours they work per week as a proportion of normal hours for their grade and location.

3. UK civilian totals include Trading Fund personnel but exclude RFA and LEC personnel and those with an unknown location. Overseas civilian includes LEC personnel.

4. Detailed break down of LEC data for 2000 are not available. The "Overseas Total" for year 2000 subsumes the total LEC figure. 2000 figures as at 1 July.

5. The increase in civilian numbers in 2011 reflects the additional requirements for locally engaged civilian to support military exercises.

14.9a UK Regular Armed Forces deaths by Service,by year of registration, numbers, age and gender standardised rates[1]. 2007 - 2015

Year	All		Naval Service[2]		Army		RAF	
	number	rate	number	rate	number	rate	number	rate
2007	204	106	27	73	145	127	32	75
2008	137	74	40	108	79	75	18	37
2009	205	105	23	58	158	131	24	55
2010	187	96	30	76	136	115	21	50
2011	132	69	19	51	98	88	15	33
2012	130	72	20	63	95	90	15	42
2013	86	50	13	42	63	65	10	22
2014	68	42	12	35	40	42	16	40
2015	60	39	11	32	39	45	10	27

Source: Defence Statistics (Health)

[1] Rates have been age and gender standardised to the 2016 Regular Armed Forces population, expressed per 100,000 personnel at risk.

[2] Naval Service includes Royal Navy and Royal Marines.

14.9b UK Regular Armed Forces deaths by Service, 2005-2015, numbers, Standardised Mortality Ratios (SMR) (95% confidence intervals (CI)).

Year	All			Naval Service			Army			RAF		
	Number	SMR	(95% CI)	Number	SMR	(95% CI)	Number	SMR	(95% CI)	Number	SMR	(95% CI)
2005	160	75	(64-88)	27	62	(41-91)	93	87.61153956	(71-107)	40	62.48911	(46-85)
2006	191	87	(76-101)	33	73	(52-103)	111	99.70681409	(83-120)	47	75.41417	(57-100)
2007	204	96	(84-110)	27	61	(40-89)	145	132.0440764	(112-155)	32	55.0789	(39-78)
2008	137	65	(55-76)	40	89	(65-122)	79	71.88921705	(58-90)	18	31.54793	(19-50)
2009	205	99	(86-113)	23	53	(33-79)	158	145.5606818	(125-170)	24	43.24544	(28-64)
2010	187	94	(81-108)	30	71	(50-102)	136	130.9681753	(111-155)	21	39.37523	(24-60)
2011	132	71	(60-84)	19	48	(29-76)	98	100.2919584	(82-122)	15	30.44807	(17-50)
2012	130	76	(64-90)	20	56	(34-86)	95	104.7418751	(86-128)	15	33.68819	(19-56)
2013	86	52	(42-65)	13	37	(20-63)	63	72.5911087	(57-93)	10	23.72698	(11-44)
2014	68	44	(35-56)	12	35	(18-61)	40	49.84235416	(37-68)	16	39.60561	(23-64)
2015	60	40	(31-51)	11	32	(16-57)	39	50.32644230	(37-69)	10	25.70606	(12-47)

Source: Defence Statistics (Health)

1. Rates have been age and gender standardised to the 2015 Regular Armed Forces population, expressed per 100,000 personnel at risk.
   Individual rates may not add up to totals due to rounding.
2. Standardised mortality ratios have been age and gender standardised.
3. Naval Service includes Royal Navy and Royal Marines.

14.10a UK Military Search and Rescue - UK & Overseas Callouts, Incidents and Persons Moved, 2006 to 2015

	Incidents			Callouts			Persons Moved		
	All	UK	Overseas	All	UK	Overseas	All	UK	Overseas
2006	1,767	1,703	64	1,948	1,875	73	1,538	1,463	75
2007	1,877	1,803	74	2,065	1,973	92	1,817	1,767	50
2008	2,025	1,941	84	2,179	2,083	96	1,763	1,607	156
2009	2,262	2,191	71	2,418	2,337	81	1,873	1,810	63
2010	1,960	1,901	59	2,050	1,983	67	1,647	1,605	42
2011	1,864	1,801	63	1,921	1,856	65	1,560	1,501	59
2012	1,774	1,733	41	1,879	1,837	42	1,550	1,522	28
2013	1,817	1,777	40	1,918	1,874	44	1,696	1,660	36
2014	1,811	1,767	44	1,906	1,862	44	1,580	1,530	50
2015	1,298	1,245	53	1,341	1,286	55	1,056	974	82

Source: UK Defence Statistics, Ministry of Defence

14.10b UK & Overseas Callouts and Persons Moved by Unit, 2006 to 2015

UK & Overseas Callouts by Unit, 2006 to 2015

	RAF Boulmer	RAF Lossiemouth	RAF Leconfield	RAF Valley	RAF Chivenor	RAF Wattisham	RAF UK Total	RNAS Culdrose	HMS Gannet	RN Total	UK Other	UK Total	Cyprus	Falklands	Overseas Total
2006	206	217	147	225	293	163	1,251	228	269	497	8	1,756	35	38	73
2007	170	188	222	234	256	183	1,253	231	359	590	7	1,850	53	39	92
2008	211	275	232	222	262	174	1,376	204	382	586	1	1,963	30	66	96
2009	214	236	204	322	340	162	1,478	311	447	758	1	2,237	36	45	81
2010	193	175	174	268	339	133	1,282	260	379	639	0	1,921	29	38	67
2011	181	207	168	276	267	157	1,256	244	298	542	1	1,799	24	41	65
2012	141	216	129	300	266	160	1,212	251	298	549	0	1,761	20	22	42
2013	157	231	134	335	238	121	1,216	257	329	586	0	1,802	12	32	44
2014	160	212	135	329	285	127	1,248	252	299	551	0	1,799	6	38	44
2015	115	53	25	126	221	69	609	282	317	599	0	1,208	14	41	55

Table 6 UK & Overseas Persons Moved by Unit, 2006 to 2015

	RAF Boulmer	RAF Lossiemouth	RAF Leconfield	RAF Valley	RAF Chivenor	RAF Wattisham	RAF UK Total	RNAS Culdrose	HMS Gannet	RN Total	UK Other	UK Total	Cyprus	Falklands	Overseas Total
2006	132	180	125	202	213	110	962	176	303	479	6	1,447	5	70	75
2007	136	160	315	236	224	122	1,193	220	286	506	27	1,726	11	39	50
2008	185	199	163	217	211	87	1,062	169	347	516	0	1,578	5	151	156
2009	149	171	132	296	304	82	1,134	278	378	656	1	1,791	9	54	63
2010	169	156	120	263	256	83	1,047	215	324	539	0	1,586	5	37	42
2011	121	239	125	246	203	96	1,030	219	240	459	0	1,489	15	44	59
2012	129	205	97	284	187	80	982	235	285	520	0	1,502	3	25	28
2013	145	219	94	352	191	83	1,084	212	327	539	0	1,623	2	34	36
2014	115	213	86	299	225	84	1,022	221	255	476	0	1,498	2	48	50
2015	86	39	17	100	148	43	433	250	260	510	0	943	10	72	82

Source: UK Defence Statistics, ARCC Database

14.10c Search and Rescue Helicopters: UK & Overseas callouts and Persons Moved by Assistance Type, 2006 to 2015

UK & Overseas Callouts by Assistance Type, 2006 to 2015

	2006	2007	2008	2009	2010	2011	2012	2013	2014	2015
Rescue	100	106	99	97	105	87	81	77	88	57
Search-Rescue	0	30	33	75	40	30	39	56	50	12
Medrescue	751	703	744	914	839	843	808	873	823	546
Search-Medrescue	0	38	55	59	61	53	46	54	57	36
Medtransfer	191	209	229	224	210	182	169	201	193	175
Recovery	33	15	29	19	13	14	21	13	16	12
Search-Recovery	0	2	8	16	7	7	8	15	8	9
Transfer	24	18	16	15	12	10	9	11	5	2
Civil Aid	23	41	26	17	20	10	5	2	0	3
Search	289	284	291	297	189	202	178	137	185	132
Top Cover	28	35	15	28	22	24	19	19	8	5
Assist	33	25	27	34	31	20	35	21	36	16
Search-Assist	0	37	53	49	19	27	36	28	28	29
Recall	222	212	277	280	243	224	221	209	209	142
Not Required	83	113	80	104	88	94	97	85	82	44
False Alarm	9	25	31	36	29	10	9	12	21	18
Hoax	10	12	14	11	15	7	3	5	5	5
Precaution	8	5	1	2	9	6	5	2	4	0
Aborted	25	27	23	34	33	9	9	22	19	7
Search-Aborted	0	5	8	7	3	5	5	4	6	13
Total Callouts	**1,829**	**1,942**	**2,059**	**2,318**	**1,988**	**1,864**	**1,803**	**1,846**	**1,843**	**1,263**

UK & Overseas Persons Moved by Assistance Type, 2006 to 2015

	2006	2007	2008	2009	2010	2011	2012	2013	2014	2015
Rescue	407	575	383	289	290	301	287	238	272	171
Search-Rescue	0	56	70	155	82	55	100	112	90	15
Medrescue	852	839	821	1,026	917	910	860	949	869	579
Search-Medrescue	0	56	65	70	68	59	48	62	68	40
Medtransfer	192	212	243	238	227	190	185	220	215	188
Recovery	39	16	28	22	15	14	27	24	20	15
Search-Recovery	0	2	9	20	8	7	10	16	9	9
Transfer	32	20	115	34	21	12	13	38	5	8
Total Persons Moved	**1,522**	**1,776**	**1,734**	**1,854**	**1,628**	**1,548**	**1,530**	**1,659**	**1,548**	**1,025**

Source: UK Defence Statistics, ARCC Database

14.10d Strength of Uniformed United Kingdom Medical Staff, 2011-2015

	2011	2012	2013	2014	2015
Qualified Doctors	588	575	578	604	616
Qualified Dentists	245	244	226	207	183
Nursing Services	1329	1461	1286	1298	1262
Support Staff	4038	4000	4127	4125	3838
Total	**6200**	**6280**	**6217**	**6234**	**5899**

Source: Headquarters of the Surgeon General

14.11 Number of vessels boarded by the Royal Navy Fishery Protection Squadron within British fishery limits each financial year

The data in this table are not National Statistics, and they have not been put forward to the UK Statistics Authority for assessment.

								Number of vessels boarded
	2000/01	2008/09	2009/10	2010/11	2011/12	2012/13	2013/14 [1]	2014/15
Vessels boarded	**1 603**	**1 102**	**1 201**	**1 399**	**1 408**	**898 ‖**	**575**	**567**
By sea areas [2] :								
North Sea	627	306	338	411	417	169 ‖	172	78
Bristol Channel, Celtic Sea, English Channel, Irish Sea, and Western Approaches	976	796	863	988	991	729 ‖	403	489

Source: Marine Management Organisation

1. From April 2013, an agreement that FPS ships would no longer be exclusively tasked with Marine Enforcement came into effect, meaning there would be less less time available for boardings.

2. The Faroes, Rockall and West of Scotland are not covered by the Royal Navy Fishery Protection Squadron.

Convictions and Financial Administration Penalties arising from the boarding of vessels by the Royal Navy Fishery Protection Squadron within British fishery limits each financial year

The data in this Table are not National Statistics, and they have not been put forward to the UK Statistics Authority for assessment.

								Number of convictions and Financial Administration Penalties
	2000/01		2008/09 [1]	2009/10	2010/11	2011/12	2012/13	2013/14	2014/15
Convictions and FAPs arising from boardings	**48**	**‖**	**30**	**10**	**29**	**17**	**13**	**17** [r]	**8** [p]
By nationality:									
Belgium	4	‖	5	3	1	2	2	1	-
Denmark	3	‖	-	-	-	-	-	-	-
Eire	4	‖	-	1	3	3	1	2	4
Faroes	3	‖	-	-	-	-	-	-	-
France	8	‖	12	1	14	6	6	4 [r]	1
Germany	-	‖	-	-	2	-	-	-	2
Netherlands	6	‖	2	-	3	2	2	1 [r]	1
Spain	-	‖	3	1	1	2	-	-	-
United Kingdom	20	‖	8	4	5	2	2	9 [r]	-

Source: Marine Management Organisation

1. From 2008/09, these figures include Financial Administration Penalties.

[p] The number of convictions and FAPs is provisional and may increase due to some cases being concluded a year or more after the initial boarding.

[r] Since the publication of the 2013/14 bulletin in June 2014, the total number of convictions arising from boardings in the 2013/14 financial year has increased from 8 to 17. The number of UK convictions has increased from 2 to 9, Netherlands convictions have increased from 0 to 1, and France convictions have increased from 3 to 4.

Population and vital statistics

Chapter 15

Population and Vital Statistics

This section begins with a summary of population figures for the United Kingdom and constituent countries for 1851 to 2046 and for Great Britain from 1801 (Table 15.1). Table 15.2 analyses the components of population change. Table 15.3 gives details of the national sex and age structures for years up to the present date, with projected figures up to the year 2114. Legal marital condition of the population is shown in Table 15.4. The distribution of population at regional and local levels is summarised in Table 15.5.

In the main, historical series relate to census information, while mid-year estimates, which make allowance for under-enumeration in the census, are given for the recent past and the present (from 1961 onwards).

Population
(Tables 15.1 - 15.3)

Figures shown in these tables relate to the population enumerated at successive censuses, (up to 1961), mid-year estimates (from 1973 to 2015) and population projections (up to 2046). Further information can be found on the National Statistics website www.ons.gov.uk.

Definition of resident population

The estimated resident population of an area includes all people who usually live there, whatever their nationality. Members of HM and US Armed Forces in England and Wales are included on a residential basis wherever possible. HM Forces stationed outside England and Wales are not included. Students are taken to be resident at their term time address.

The projections of the resident population of the United Kingdom and constituent countries were prepared by the National Statistics Centre for Demography within ONS, in consultation with the Registrars General, as a common framework for use in national planning in a number of different fields. New projections are made every second year on assumptions regarding future fertility, mortality and migration which seem most appropriate on the basis of the statistical evidence available at the time. The population projections in Tables 15.1 -15.3 are based on the estimates of the population of the United Kingdom at mid-2014 made by the Registrars General.

Marital condition (de jure): estimated population
(Table 15.4)

This table shows population estimates by marital status

Geographical distribution of the population
(Table 15.5)

The mid-year population estimates are provided for standard regions of the United Kingdom, for metropolitan areas, for broad groupings of local authority districts by type within England and Wales, and for some of the larger cities. Projections of future sub-national population levels are prepared from time to time by the Registrar General, but are not shown in this publication.

Migration into and out of the United Kingdom
(Tables 15.7 - 15.8)

A long-term international migrant is defined as a person who changes his or her country of usual residence for a period of at least a year,so that the country of destination effectively becomes the country of usual residence.

The main source of long-term international migration data is the International Passenger Survey (IPS). This is a continuous voluntary sample survey that provides information on passengers entering and leaving the UK by the principal air, sea and tunnel routes. Being a sample survey, the IPS is subject to some uncertainty; therefore it should be noted that long-term international migration estimates, in particular the difference between inflow and outflow, may be subject to large sampling errors. The IPS excludes routes between the Channel Islands and Isle of Man and the rest of the world.

The IPS data are supplemented with four types of additional information in order to provide a full picture of total long-term international migration, known as Long-Term International Migration or LTIM:

1. The IPS is based on intentions to migrate and intentions are liable to change. Adjustments are made for visitor switchers (those who intend to stay in the UK or abroad for less than one year but subsequently stay for longer and become migrants) and for migrant switchers (those who intend to stay in the UK or abroad for one year or more but then return earlier so are no longer migrants). These adjustments are primarily based on IPS data but for years prior to 2001, Home Office data on short-term visitors who were subsequently granted an extension of stay for a year or longer for other reasons have been incorporated.

2. Home Office data on applications for asylum and dependants of asylum seekers entering the UK are used to estimate inflows of asylum seekers and dependants not already captured by the I PS. In addition, Home Office data on removals and refusals are used to estimate outflows of failed asylum seekers not identified by the IPS.

3. Migration flows between the UK and the Irish Republic were added to the data to 2007 as the IPS did not cover this route until recently. These flows were obtained mainly from the Quarterly National Household Survey and were agreed between the Irish Central Statistics Office and ONS. From 2008 onwards, estimates of migration between the UK and Irish Republic come from the IPS.

4. Migration flows to and from Northern Ireland are added to the IPS data for Great Britain from 2008 onwards. These flows are obtained from the Irish Quarterly National Household Survey (from CSO Ireland) and health card registration data (from Northern Ireland Statistics Research Agency (NISRA)). These data are now deemed a better source for Northern Irish flows than IPS data. Prior to 2008, estimates of migration to and from Northern Ireland came from the IPS.

Grants for settlement in the United Kingdom
(Table 15.9)

This table presents in geographic regions, the statistics of individual countries of nationality, arranged alphabetically within each region. The figures are on a different basis from those derived from IPS (Tables 15.9 and 15.10) and relate only to people subject to immigration control. Persons granted settlement are allowed to stay indefinitely in the United Kingdom. They exclude temporary migrants such as students and generally relate only to non-EEA nationals. Settlement can occur several years after entry to the country.

Applications received for asylum in the United Kingdom, excluding dependants
(Table 15.10)

This table shows statistics of applications for asylum in the United Kingdom. Figures are shown for the main applicant nationalities by geographic region. The basis of assessing asylum applications, and hence of deciding whether to grant asylum in the United Kingdom, is the 1951 United Nations Convention on Refugees.

Marriages
(Table 15.11)
This table shows the number of marriages by type of ceremony and denomination.

Births
(Tables 15.14 –15.16)

For Scotland and Northern Ireland the number of births relate to those registered during the year. For England and Wales the figures up to and including 1930-32 are for those registered, while later figures relate to births occurring in each year.

All data for England and Wales and for Scotland include births occurring in those countries to mothers not usually resident in them. Data for Northern Ireland, and hence UK, prior to 1981 include births occurring in Northern Ireland to non-resident mothers; from 1981, such births are excluded.

Deaths
(Tables 15.17 - 15.18)

The figures relate to the number of deaths registered during each calendar year.

Infant and maternal mortality
(Table 15.18)

On 1 October 1992 the legal definition of a stillbirth was altered from a baby born dead after 28 completed weeks gestation or more, to one born after 24 completed weeks of gestation or more. The 258 stillbirths of 24 to 27 weeks gestation that which occurred between 1 October and 31 December 1992 are excluded from this table.

Life tables
(Table 15.19)

The current set of interim life tables are constructed from the estimated populations in 2013-2015
and corresponding data on births, infant deaths and deaths by individual age registered
in those years.

Adoptions
(Table 15.20)

The figures shown within these tables relate to the date the adoption was entered in the Adopted
Children Register. Figures based on the date of court order are available for England and Wales in
the volumes Adoptions in England and Wales, Marriages in England and Wales and Divorces in
England and Wales available on the National Statistics website www.statistics.gov.uk.

15.1 Population summary: by country and sex

Thousands

	United Kingdom			England and Wales			Wales	Scotland			Northern Ireland		
	Persons	Males	Females	Persons	Males	Females	Persons	Persons	Males	Females	Persons	Males	Females
Enumerated population: census figures													
1801	..	..	..	8,893	4,255	4,638	587	1,608	739	869	..	..	..
1851	22,259	10,855	11,404	17,928	8,781	9,146	1,163	2,889	1,376	1,513	1,442	698	745
1901	38,237	18,492	19,745	32,528	15,729	16,799	2,013	4,472	2,174	2,298	1,237	590	647
1911	42,082	20,357	21,725	36,070	17,446	18,625	2,421	4,761	2,309	2,452	1,251	603	648
1921 [1]	44,027	21,033	22,994	37,887	18,075	19,811	2,656	4,882	2,348	2,535	1,258	610	648
1931 [1]	46,038	22,060	23,978	39,952	19,133	20,819	2,593	4,843	2,326	2,517	1,243	601	642
1951	50,225	24,118	26,107	43,758	21,016	22,742	2,599	5,096	2,434	2,662	1,371	668	703
1961	52,709	25,481	27,228	46,105	22,304	23,801	2,644	5,179	2,483	2,697	1,425	694	731
Resident population: mid-year estimates													
	DYAY	BBAB	BBAC	BBAD	BBAE	BBAF	KGJM	BBAG	BBAH	BBAI	BBAJ	BBAK	BBAL
1973	56,223	27,332	28,891	49,459	24,061	25,399	2,773	5,234	2,515	2,719	1,530	756	774
1974	56,236	27,349	28,887	49,468	24,075	25,393	2,785	5,241	2,519	2,722	1,527	755	772
1975	56,226	27,361	28,865	49,470	24,091	25,378	2,795	5,232	2,516	2,716	1,524	753	770
1976	56,216	27,360	28,856	49,459	24,089	25,370	2,799	5,233	2,517	2,716	1,524	754	769
1977	56,190	27,345	28,845	49,440	24,076	25,364	2,801	5,226	2,515	2,711	1,523	754	769
1978	56,178	27,330	28,848	49,443	24,067	25,375	2,804	5,212	2,509	2,704	1,523	754	770
1979	56,240	27,373	28,867	49,508	24,113	25,395	2,810	5,204	2,505	2,699	1,528	755	773
1980	56,330	27,411	28,919	49,603	24,156	25,448	2,816	5,194	2,501	2,693	1,533	755	778
1981	56,357	27,412	28,946	49,634	24,160	25,474	2,813	5,180	2,495	2,685	1,543	757	786
1982	56,291	27,364	28,927	49,582	24,119	25,462	2,804	5,165	2,487	2,677	1,545	757	788
1983	56,316	27,371	28,944	49,617	24,133	25,484	2,803	5,148	2,479	2,669	1,551	759	792
1984	56,409	27,421	28,989	49,713	24,185	25,528	2,801	5,139	2,475	2,664	1,557	761	796
1985	56,554	27,489	29,065	49,861	24,254	25,606	2,803	5,128	2,470	2,658	1,565	765	800
1986	56,684	27,542	29,142	49,999	24,311	25,687	2,811	5,112	2,462	2,649	1,574	768	805
1987	56,804	27,599	29,205	50,123	24,371	25,752	2,823	5,099	2,455	2,644	1,582	773	809
1988	56,916	27,652	29,265	50,254	24,434	25,820	2,841	5,077	2,444	2,633	1,585	774	812
1989	57,076	27,729	29,348	50,408	24,510	25,898	2,855	5,078	2,443	2,635	1,590	776	814
1990	57,237	27,819	29,419	50,561	24,597	25,964	2,862	5,081	2,444	2,637	1,596	778	818
1991	57,439	27,909	29,530	50,748	24,681	26,067	2,873	5,083	2,445	2,639	1,607	783	824
1992	57,585	27,977	29,608	50,876	24,739	26,136	2,878	5,086	2,445	2,640	1,623	792	831
1993	57,714	28,039	29,675	50,986	24,793	26,193	2,884	5,092	2,448	2,644	1,636	798	837
1994	57,862	28,108	29,754	51,116	24,853	26,263	2,887	5,102	2,453	2,649	1,644	802	842
1995	58,025	28,204	29,821	51,272	24,946	26,326	2,889	5,104	2,453	2,650	1,649	804	845
1996	58,164	28,287	29,877	51,410	25,030	26,381	2,891	5,092	2,447	2,645	1,662	810	851
1997	58,314	28,371	29,943	51,560	25,113	26,446	2,895	5,083	2,442	2,641	1,671	816	856
1998	58,475	28,458	30,017	51,720	25,201	26,519	2,900	5,077	2,439	2,638	1,678	819	859
1999	58,684	28,578	30,106	51,933	25,323	26,610	2,901	5,072	2,437	2,635	1,679	818	861
2000	58,886	28,690	30,196	52,140	25,438	26,702	2,907	5,063	2,432	2,631	1,683	820	862
2001	59,113	28,832	30,281	52,360	25,574	26,786	2,910	5,064	2,434	2,630	1,689	824	865
2002	59,366	28,973	30,393	52,602	25,708	26,894	2,923	5,066	2,436	2,630	1,697	829	868
2003	59,637	29,125	30,511	52,863	25,854	27,009	2,938	5,069	2,438	2,630	1,705	833	872
2004	59,950	29,297	30,653	53,152	26,012	27,140	2,957	5,084	2,447	2,638	1,714	838	876
2005	60,413	29,541	30,872	53,575	26,234	27,341	2,969	5,110	2,461	2,649	1,728	845	882
2006	60,827	29,762	31,065	53,951	26,433	27,518	2,986	5,133	2,475	2,658	1,743	853	890
2007	61,319	30,028	31,291	54,387	26,669	27,718	3,006	5,170	2,497	2,673	1,762	862	899
2009	62,260	30,532	31,728	55,235	27,122	28,114	3,039	5,232	2,532	2,700	1,793	879	915
2010	62,759	30,805	31,954	55,692	27,373	28,320	3,050	5,262	2,548	2,714	1,805	885	920
2011	63,285	31,097	32,188	56,171	27,638	28,533	3,064	5,300	2,570	2,730	1,814	889	925
2012	63,705	31,315	32,390	56,568	27,843	28,724	3,074	5,314	2,577	2,736	1,824	895	929
2013	64,106	31,533	32,571	56,948	28,049	28,899	3,082	5,328	2,587	2,741	1,830	897	933
2014	64,597	31,794	32,803	57,409	28,295	29,114	3,092	5,347	2,597	2,751	1,840	903	938
2015	65,110	32,074	33,035	57,885	28,554	29,330	3,099	5,373	2,610	2,762	1,851	909	942
Resident population: projections (mid-year) [2]													
	C59J	C59K	C59L	C59M	C59N	C59O	C59P	C59Q	C59R	C59S	C59T	C59U	C59V
2021	67,781	33,531	34,251	60,406	30,136	30,481	3,158	5,462	2,663	2,799	1,913	943	970
2026	69,844	34,632	35,212	62,341	31,149	31,387	3,206	5,548	2,712	2,837	1,954	965	989
2031	71,707	35,622	36,086	64,098	32,059	32,213	3,245	5,624	2,754	2,870	1,986	983	1,003
2036	73,361	36,504	36,857	65,674	32,882	32,952	3,270	5,678	2,786	2,892	2,009	996	1,013
2041	74,884	37,326	37,558	67,140	33,510	33,630	3,286	5,715	2,808	2,907	2,029	1,008	1,021
2046	76,342	38,277	38,221	68,557	34,279	34,278	3,300	5,741	2,826	2,915	2,044	1,017	1,027

1 Figures for Northern Ireland are estimated. The population at the Census of 1926 was
  1,257 thousand (608 thousand males and 648 thousand females).
2 These projections are 2014-based.

Sources: Office for National Statistics: 01329 444661;
National Records of Scotland
Northern Ireland Statistics and Research Agency;

Figures may not add exactly due to rounding

15.2a Population projections by the Office for National Statistics
United Kingdom, PERSONS, thousands

2014-based
Principal projection

Components of change (mid-year to mid-year), total fertility rate and expectation of life at birth based on the mortality rates for the year

	2014-2015	2015-2016	2016-2017	2017-2018	2018-2019	2019-2020	2020-2021	2021-2022	2022-2023	2023-2024	2024-2025	2025-2026	2026-2027	2027-2028	2028-2029	2029-2030	2030-2031	2031-2032	2032-2033	2033-2034
Population at start	64,597	65,097	65,572	66,030	66,487	66,928	67,360	67,781	68,203	68,622	69,036	69,444	69,844	70,234	70,616	70,989	71,353	71,707	72,053	72,391
Births	776	784	791	797	802	805	808	810	812	811	809	807	804	803	801	800	799	800	800	802
Deaths	605	565	565	566	567	569	571	574	578	582	587	592	599	606	613	621	630	639	648	657
Natural change	171	219	226	231	234	236	237	236	234	229	223	214	206	197	188	179	170	161	153	145
International migration inflows	653	582	559	555	537	528	518	518	518	518	518	518	518	518	518	518	518	518	518	518
Crossborder migration inflows	-	-	-	-	-	-	-	-	-	-	-	-	-	-	-	-	-	-	-	-
International migration outflows	324	326	327	329	330	332	333	333	333	333	333	333	333	333	333	333	333	333	333	333
Crossborder migration outflows	-	-	-	-	-	-	-	-	-	-	-	-	-	-	-	-	-	-	-	-
Net international migration	329	256	232	226	206	196	185	185	185	185	185	185	185	185	185	185	185	185	185	185
Net crossborder migration	-	-	-	-	-	-	-	-	-	-	-	-	-	-	-	-	-	-	-	-
Net migration	329	256	232	226	206	196	185	185	185	185	185	185	185	185	185	185	185	185	185	185
Total change	500	475	458	457	441	432	422	421	419	414	408	399	391	382	373	364	355	346	338	330
Population at end	65,097	65,572	66,030	66,487	66,928	67,360	67,781	68,203	68,622	69,036	69,444	69,844	70,234	70,616	70,989	71,353	71,707	72,053	72,391	72,721
Annual growth rate	0.77%	0.73%	0.70%	0.69%	0.66%	0.65%	0.63%	0.62%	0.61%	0.60%	0.59%	0.58%	0.56%	0.54%	0.53%	0.51%	0.50%	0.48%	0.47%	0.46%
Total fertility rate (TFR)	1.81	1.81	1.82	1.83	1.84	1.84	1.85	1.86	1.87	1.87	1.87	1.87	1.88	1.88	1.88	1.88	1.88	1.88	1.89	1.89
EOLB Males	78.9	79.8	80.0	80.3	80.5	80.8	81.0	81.2	81.4	81.7	81.9	82.1	82.2	82.4	82.6	82.8	82.9	83.1	83.3	83.4
Females	82.5	83.4	83.5	83.7	83.9	84.1	84.3	84.5	84.6	84.8	85.0	85.1	85.3	85.5	85.6	85.8	85.9	86.0	86.2	86.3

	2034-2035	2035-2036	2036-2037	2037-2038	2038-2039	2039-2040	2040-2041	2041-2042	2042-2043	2043-2044	2044-2045	2045-2046	2046-2047	2047-2048	2048-2049	2049-2050	2050-2051	2051-2052	2052-2053	2053-2054
Population at start	72,721	73,044	73,361	73,673	73,980	74,284	74,585	74,884	75,180	75,474	75,766	76,055	76,342	76,626	76,907	77,184	77,457	77,726	77,991	78,252
Births	805	808	812	817	823	828	834	839	844	848	852	855	858	859	861	862	863	864	865	865
Deaths	667	676	685	695	704	712	720	728	735	741	747	753	759	764	769	774	779	784	788	792
Natural change	138	132	127	123	119	116	113	111	109	107	105	102	99	96	92	88	84	80	76	73
International migration inflows	518	518	518	518	518	518	518	518	518	518	518	518	518	518	518	518	518	518	518	518
Crossborder migration inflows	-	-	-	-	-	-	-	-	-	-	-	-	-	-	-	-	-	-	-	-
International migration outflows	333	333	333	333	333	333	333	333	333	333	333	333	333	333	333	333	333	333	333	333
Crossborder migration outflows	-	-	-	-	-	-	-	-	-	-	-	-	-	-	-	-	-	-	-	-
Net international migration	185	185	185	185	185	185	185	185	185	185	185	185	185	185	185	185	185	185	185	185
Net crossborder migration	-	-	-	-	-	-	-	-	-	-	-	-	-	-	-	-	-	-	-	-
Net migration	185	185	185	185	185	185	185	185	185	185	185	185	185	185	185	185	185	185	185	185
Total change	323	317	312	308	304	301	298	296	294	292	290	287	284	281	277	273	269	265	261	258
Population at end	73,044	73,361	73,673	73,980	74,284	74,585	74,884	75,180	75,474	75,766	76,055	76,342	76,626	76,907	77,184	77,457	77,726	77,991	78,252	78,510
Annual growth rate	0.44%	0.43%	0.43%	0.42%	0.41%	0.41%	0.40%	0.40%	0.39%	0.39%	0.38%	0.38%	0.37%	0.37%	0.36%	0.35%	0.35%	0.34%	0.34%	0.33%
Total fertility rate (TFR)	1.89	1.89	1.89	1.89	1.89	1.89	1.89	1.89	1.89	1.89	1.89	1.89	1.89	1.89	1.89	1.89	1.89	1.89	1.89	1.89
EOLB Males	83.5	83.7	83.8	83.9	84.1	84.2	84.3	84.4	84.6	84.7	84.8	84.9	85.1	85.2	85.3	85.4	85.6	85.7	85.8	85.9
Females	86.4	86.6	86.7	86.8	86.9	87.0	87.1	87.2	87.4	87.5	87.6	87.7	87.8	87.9	88.0	88.2	88.3	88.4	88.5	88.6

15.2a Population projections by the Office for National Statistics
United Kingdom, PERSONS, thousands

2014-based
Principal projection

Components of change (mid-year to mid-year), total fertility rate
and expectation of life at birth based on the mortality rates for the year

	2054 -2055	2055 -2056	2056 -2057	2057 -2058	2058 -2059	2059 -2060	2060 -2061	2061 -2062	2062 -2063	2063 -2064	2064 -2065	2065 -2066	2066 -2067	2067 -2068	2068 -2069	2069 -2070	2070 -2071	2071 -2072	2072 -2073	2073 -2074
Population at start	78,510	78,765	79,016	79,266	79,513	79,759	80,004	80,249	80,495	80,743	80,992	81,244	81,499	81,758	82,020	82,287	82,557	82,830	83,107	83,387
Births	866	866	867	868	868	869	870	871	872	874	876	878	880	883	885	888	891	895	898	901
Deaths	796	800	803	805	807	809	810	810	810	809	808	807	806	805	804	803	803	803	803	803
Natural change	70	67	64	62	61	60	60	61	62	64	67	70	74	77	81	85	89	92	95	98
International migration inflows	518	518	518	518	518	518	518	518	518	518	518	518	518	518	518	518	518	518	518	518
Crossborder migration inflows	-	-	-	-	-	-	-	-	-	-	-	-	-	-	-	-	-	-	-	-
International migration outflows	333	333	333	333	333	333	333	333	333	333	333	333	333	333	333	333	333	333	333	333
Crossborder migration outflows	-	-	-	-	-	-	-	-	-	-	-	-	-	-	-	-	-	-	-	-
Net international migration	185	185	185	185	185	185	185	185	185	185	185	185	185	185	185	185	185	185	185	185
Net crossborder migration	-	-	-	-	-	-	-	-	-	-	-	-	-	-	-	-	-	-	-	-
Net migration	185	185	185	185	185	185	185	185	185	185	185	185	185	185	185	185	185	185	185	185
Total change	255	252	249	247	246	245	245	246	247	249	252	255	259	262	266	270	274	277	280	283
Population at end	78,765	79,016	79,266	79,513	79,759	80,004	80,249	80,495	80,743	80,992	81,244	81,499	81,758	82,020	82,287	82,557	82,830	83,107	83,387	83,670
Annual growth rate	0.32%	0.32%	0.32%	0.31%	0.31%	0.31%	0.31%	0.31%	0.31%	0.31%	0.31%	0.32%	0.32%	0.32%	0.32%	0.33%	0.33%	0.33%	0.34%	0.34%
Total fertility rate (TFR)	1.89	1.89	1.89	1.89	1.89	1.89	1.89	1.89	1.89	1.89	1.89	1.89	1.89	1.89	1.89	1.89	1.89	1.89	1.89	1.89
EOLB Males	86.1	86.2	86.3	86.4	86.5	86.7	86.8	86.9	87.0	87.1	87.3	87.4	87.5	87.6	87.8	87.9	88.0	88.1	88.2	88.4
Females	88.7	88.8	89.0	89.1	89.2	89.3	89.4	89.5	89.6	89.7	89.9	90.0	90.1	90.2	90.3	90.4	90.5	90.6	90.8	90.9

	2074 -2075	2075 -2076	2076 -2077	2077 -2078	2078 -2079	2079 -2080	2080 -2081	2081 -2082	2082 -2083	2083 -2084	2084 -2085	2085 -2086	2086 -2087	2087 -2088	2088 -2089	2089 -2090	2090 -2091	2091 -2092	2092 -2093	2093 -2094
Population at start	83,670	83,955	84,241	84,529	84,817	85,105	85,394	85,683	85,971	86,259	86,546	86,833	87,121	87,408	87,696	87,984	88,273	88,563	88,854	89,146
Births	904	907	909	912	914	916	918	920	921	923	924	925	926	927	928	930	931	932	933	935
Deaths	804	805	807	809	811	813	815	817	818	820	822	823	824	825	825	826	826	826	826	826
Natural change	100	101	102	103	104	104	104	103	103	102	102	102	102	103	103	104	105	106	107	109
International migration inflows	518	518	518	518	518	518	518	518	518	518	518	518	518	518	518	518	518	518	518	518
Crossborder migration inflows	-	-	-	-	-	-	-	-	-	-	-	-	-	-	-	-	-	-	-	-
International migration outflows	333	333	333	333	333	333	333	333	333	333	333	333	333	333	333	333	333	333	333	333
Crossborder migration outflows	-	-	-	-	-	-	-	-	-	-	-	-	-	-	-	-	-	-	-	-
Net international migration	185	185	185	185	185	185	185	185	185	185	185	185	185	185	185	185	185	185	185	185
Net crossborder migration	-	-	-	-	-	-	-	-	-	-	-	-	-	-	-	-	-	-	-	-
Net migration	185	185	185	185	185	185	185	185	185	185	185	185	185	185	185	185	185	185	185	185
Total change	285	286	287	288	289	289	289	288	288	287	287	287	287	288	288	289	290	291	292	294
Population at end	83,955	84,241	84,529	84,817	85,105	85,394	85,683	85,971	86,259	86,546	86,833	87,121	87,408	87,696	87,984	88,273	88,563	88,854	89,146	89,440
Annual growth rate	0.34%	0.34%	0.34%	0.34%	0.34%	0.34%	0.34%	0.34%	0.33%	0.33%	0.33%	0.33%	0.33%	0.33%	0.33%	0.33%	0.33%	0.33%	0.33%	0.33%
Total fertility rate (TFR)	1.89	1.89	1.89	1.89	1.89	1.89	1.89	1.89	1.89	1.89	1.89	1.89	1.89	1.89	1.89	1.89	1.89	1.89	1.89	1.89
EOLB Males	88.5	88.6	88.7	88.8	89.0	89.1	89.2	89.3	89.4	89.6	89.7	89.8	89.9	90.0	90.2	90.3	90.4	90.5	90.7	90.8
Females	91.0	91.1	91.2	91.3	91.4	91.5	91.7	91.8	91.9	92.0	92.1	92.2	92.3	92.4	92.6	92.7	92.8	92.9	93.0	93.1

15.2a Population projections by the Office for National Statistics
United Kingdom, PERSONS, thousands

2014-based
Principal projection

Components of change (mid-year to mid-year), total fertility rate
and expectation of life at birth based on the mortality rates for the year

	2094 -2095	2095 -2096	2096 -2097	2097 -2098	2098 -2099	2099 -2100	2100 -2101	2101 -2102	2102 -2103	2103 -2104	2104 -2105	2105 -2106	2106 -2107	2107 -2108	2108 -2109	2109 -2110	2110 -2111	2111 -2112	2112 -2113	2113 -2114
Population at start	89,440	89,735	90,031	90,329	90,628	90,927	91,228	91,528	91,830	92,131	92,432	92,733	93,033	93,332	93,631	93,929	94,226	94,523	94,818	95,113
Births	937	938	940	942	944	947	949	951	953	956	958	960	963	965	967	969	971	973	975	976
Deaths	827	827	828	829	830	831	833	835	837	840	842	845	848	851	854	857	860	862	865	867
Natural change	110	111	113	114	115	115	116	116	116	116	116	115	115	114	113	112	111	111	110	109
International migration inflows	518	518	518	518	518	518	518	518	518	518	518	518	518	518	518	518	518	518	518	518
Crossborder migration inflows	-	-	-	-	-	-	-	-	-	-	-	-	-	-	-	-	-	-	-	-
International migration outflows	333	333	333	333	333	333	333	333	333	333	333	333	333	333	333	333	333	333	333	333
Crossborder migration outflows	-	-	-	-	-	-	-	-	-	-	-	-	-	-	-	-	-	-	-	-
Net international migration	185	185	185	185	185	185	185	185	185	185	185	185	185	185	185	185	185	185	185	185
Net crossborder migration	-	-	-	-	-	-	-	-	-	-	-	-	-	-	-	-	-	-	-	-
Net migration	185	185	185	185	185	185	185	185	185	185	185	185	185	185	185	185	185	185	185	185
Total change	295	296	298	299	300	300	301	301	301	301	301	300	300	299	298	297	296	296	295	294
Population at end	89,735	90,031	90,329	90,628	90,927	91,228	91,528	91,830	92,131	92,432	92,733	93,033	93,332	93,631	93,929	94,226	94,523	94,818	95,113	95,408
Annual growth rate	0.33%	0.33%	0.33%	0.33%	0.33%	0.33%	0.33%	0.33%	0.33%	0.33%	0.33%	0.32%	0.32%	0.32%	0.32%	0.32%	0.31%	0.31%	0.31%	0.31%
Total fertility rate (TFR)	1.89	1.89	1.89	1.89	1.89	1.89	1.89	1.89	1.89	1.89	1.89	1.89	1.89	1.89	1.89	1.89	1.89	1.89	1.89	1.89
EOLB Males	90.9	91.0	91.1	91.3	91.4	91.5	91.6	91.7	91.9	92.0	92.1	92.2	92.3	92.5	92.6	92.7	92.8	92.9	93.1	93.2
Females	93.2	93.3	93.5	93.6	93.7	93.8	93.9	94.0	94.1	94.3	94.4	94.5	94.6	94.7	94.8	94.9	95.0	95.2	95.3	95.4

Source: Office for National Statistics

Note: Figures may not add exactly due to rounding.
* Children under 16. Working age and pensionable age populations based on state pension age (SPA) for given year.
Between 2012 and 2018, SPA will change from 65 years for men and 61 years for women, to 65 years for both sexes.
Then between 2019 and 2020, SPA will change from 65 years to 66 years for both men and women.
Between 2026 and 2027 SPA will increase to 67 years and between 2044 and 2046 to 68 years for both sexes. This is based on SPA under the 2014 Pensions Act.
** This is consistent with the age-group definitions used in ONS Labour Market Statistics.

National Population Projections are currently produced every two years. The 2016-based projections are not due to be published until November/December 2017. Therefore, this table series will be updated in the next edition

15.2b Population projections by the Office for National Statistics
England and Wales, PERSONS, thousands

2014-based
Principal projection

Components of change (mid-year to mid-year), total fertility rate
and expectation of life at birth based on the mortality rates for the year

	2014 -2015	2015 -2016	2016 -2017	2017 -2018	2018 -2019	2019 -2020	2020 -2021	2021 -2022	2022 -2023	2023 -2024	2024 -2025	2025 -2026	2026 -2027	2027 -2028	2028 -2029	2029 -2030	2030 -2031	2031 -2032	2032 -2033	2033 -2034
Population at start	57,409	57,881	58,330	58,761	59,191	59,606	60,011	60,406	60,801	61,194	61,583	61,966	62,341	62,708	63,067	63,419	63,763	64,098	64,426	64,747
Births	696	704	711	717	722	725	727	730	731	730	729	726	724	723	721	721	720	721	722	724
Deaths	531	496	496	497	498	500	502	504	507	511	516	521	527	533	540	547	554	562	571	579
Natural change	165	208	215	220	223	225	225	225	223	219	213	206	198	190	182	174	166	158	151	145
International migration inflows	602	536	513	508	490	481	472	472	472	472	472	472	472	472	472	472	472	472	472	472
Crossborder migration inflows	48	48	49	49	49	48	48	48	48	48	48	48	48	48	48	48	48	48	48	48
International migration outflows	289	291	292	293	295	296	297	297	297	297	297	297	297	297	297	297	297	297	297	297
Crossborder migration outflows	53	53	53	53	53	53	53	53	53	53	53	53	53	53	53	53	53	53	53	53
Net international migration	312	245	221	215	196	185	175	175	175	175	175	175	175	175	175	175	175	175	175	175
Net crossborder migration	-5	-5	-5	-5	-5	-5	-5	-5	-5	-5	-5	-5	-5	-5	-5	-5	-5	-5	-5	-5
Net migration	308	240	217	211	191	180	170	170	170	170	170	170	170	170	170	170	170	170	170	170
Total change	472	448	431	431	414	405	395	393	389	383	375	367	359	352	344	336	328	321	314	
Population at end	57,881	58,330	58,761	59,191	59,606	60,011	60,406	60,801	61,194	61,583	61,966	62,341	62,708	63,067	63,419	63,763	64,098	64,426	64,747	65,062
Annual growth rate	0.82%	0.77%	0.74%	0.73%	0.70%	0.68%	0.66%	0.65%	0.65%	0.64%	0.62%	0.61%	0.59%	0.57%	0.56%	0.54%	0.53%	0.51%	0.50%	0.49%
Total fertility rate (TFR)	1.82	1.83	1.84	1.85	1.85	1.86	1.87	1.88	1.88	1.89	1.89	1.89	1.89	1.89	1.89	1.90	1.90	1.90	1.90	1.90
EOLB Males	79.2	80.0	80.3	80.5	80.8	81.0	81.2	81.4	81.7	81.9	82.1	82.3	82.5	82.6	82.8	83.0	83.1	83.3	83.5	83.6
Females	82.7	83.6	83.8	83.9	84.1	84.3	84.5	84.7	84.9	85.0	85.2	85.4	85.5	85.7	85.8	86.0	86.1	86.2	86.4	86.5

	2034 -2035	2035 -2036	2036 -2037	2037 -2038	2038 -2039	2039 -2040	2040 -2041	2041 -2042	2042 -2043	2043 -2044	2044 -2045	2045 -2046	2046 -2047	2047 -2048	2048 -2049	2049 -2050	2050 -2051	2051 -2052	2052 -2053	2053 -2054
Population at start	65,062	65,370	65,674	65,973	66,269	66,562	66,852	67,140	67,427	67,712	67,995	68,277	68,557	68,834	69,109	69,380	69,648	69,913	70,175	70,432
Births	726	730	734	739	744	749	754	759	764	768	772	775	778	780	781	783	784	785	785	786
Deaths	588	596	605	613	621	629	636	643	649	655	660	665	670	675	680	684	689	693	697	701
Natural change	139	134	129	126	123	120	119	117	115	114	112	110	108	105	102	99	95	92	88	85
International migration inflows	472	472	472	472	472	472	472	472	472	472	472	472	472	472	472	472	472	472	472	472
Crossborder migration inflows	48	48	48	48	48	48	48	48	48	48	48	48	48	48	48	48	48	48	48	48
International migration outflows	297	297	297	297	297	297	297	297	297	297	297	297	297	297	297	297	297	297	297	297
Crossborder migration outflows	53	53	53	53	53	53	53	53	53	53	53	53	53	53	53	53	53	53	53	53
Net international migration	175	175	175	175	175	175	175	175	175	175	175	175	175	175	175	175	175	175	175	175
Net crossborder migration	-5	-5	-5	-5	-5	-5	-5	-5	-5	-5	-5	-5	-5	-5	-5	-5	-5	-5	-5	-5
Net migration	170	170	170	170	170	170	170	170	170	170	170	170	170	170	170	170	170	170	170	170
Total change	309	304	299	296	293	290	288	287	285	284	282	280	277	275	271	268	265	261	258	255
Population at end	65,370	65,674	65,973	66,269	66,562	66,852	67,140	67,427	67,712	67,995	68,277	68,557	68,834	69,109	69,380	69,648	69,913	70,175	70,432	70,687
Annual growth rate	0.47%	0.46%	0.46%	0.45%	0.44%	0.44%	0.43%	0.43%	0.42%	0.42%	0.41%	0.41%	0.40%	0.40%	0.39%	0.39%	0.38%	0.37%	0.37%	0.36%
Total fertility rate (TFR)	1.90	1.90	1.90	1.90	1.90	1.90	1.90	1.90	1.90	1.90	1.90	1.90	1.90	1.90	1.90	1.90	1.90	1.90	1.90	1.90
EOLB Males	83.7	83.9	84.0	84.1	84.3	84.4	84.5	84.6	84.8	84.9	85.0	85.1	85.2	85.4	85.5	85.6	85.7	85.9	86.0	86.1
Females	86.6	86.8	86.9	87.0	87.1	87.2	87.3	87.5	87.6	87.7	87.8	87.9	88.0	88.1	88.2	88.4	88.5	88.6	88.7	88.8

2014-based Principal projection

15.2b Population projections by the Office for National Statistics
England and Wales, PERSONS, thousands

Components of change (mid-year to mid-year), total fertility rate and expectation of life at birth based on the mortality rates for the year

	2054 -2055	2055 -2056	2056 -2057	2057 -2058	2058 -2059	2059 -2060	2060 -2061	2061 -2062	2062 -2063	2063 -2064	2064 -2065	2065 -2066	2066 -2067	2067 -2068	2068 -2069	2069 -2070	2070 -2071	2071 -2072	2072 -2073	2073 -2074
Population at start	70,687	70,939	71,187	71,434	71,679	71,922	72,164	72,407	72,649	72,893	73,139	73,387	73,638	73,891	74,149	74,409	74,673	74,941	75,211	75,485
Births	787	788	788	789	790	791	791	793	794	796	797	800	802	804	807	810	813	816	820	823
Deaths	705	708	711	714	716	718	719	720	720	720	719	719	718	717	716	716	716	716	716	717
Natural change	82	79	77	75	74	73	73	74	76	78	81	84	87	91	94	98	101	104	106	
International migration inflows	472	472	472	472	472	472	472	472	472	472	472	472	472	472	472	472	472	472	472	472
Crossborder migration inflows	48	48	48	48	48	48	48	48	48	48	48	48	48	48	48	48	48	48	48	48
International migration outflows	297	297	297	297	297	297	297	297	297	297	297	297	297	297	297	297	297	297	297	297
Crossborder migration outflows	53	53	53	53	53	53	53	53	53	53	53	53	53	53	53	53	53	53	53	53
Net international migration	175	175	175	175	175	175	175	175	175	175	175	175	175	175	175	175	175	175	175	175
Net crossborder migration	-5	-5	-5	-5	-5	-5	-5	-5	-5	-5	-5	-5	-5	-5	-5	-5	-5	-5	-5	-5
Net migration	170	170	170	170	170	170	170	170	170	170	170	170	170	170	170	170	170	170	170	170
Total change	252	249	247	245	243	242	242	243	244	246	248	251	254	257	261	264	267	271	273	276
Population at end	70,939	71,187	71,434	71,679	71,922	72,164	72,407	72,649	72,893	73,139	73,387	73,638	73,891	74,149	74,409	74,673	74,941	75,211	75,485	75,761
Annual growth rate	0.36%	0.35%	0.35%	0.34%	0.34%	0.34%	0.34%	0.34%	0.34%	0.34%	0.34%	0.34%	0.35%	0.35%	0.35%	0.35%	0.36%	0.36%	0.36%	0.37%
Total fertility rate (TFR)	1.90	1.90	1.90	1.90	1.90	1.90	1.90	1.90	1.90	1.90	1.90	1.90	1.90	1.90	1.90	1.90	1.90	1.90	1.90	1.90
EOLB Males	86.2	86.3	86.5	86.6	86.7	86.8	86.9	87.1	87.2	87.3	87.4	87.5	87.7	87.8	87.9	88.0	88.1	88.3	88.4	88.5
Females	88.9	89.0	89.1	89.3	89.4	89.5	89.6	89.7	89.8	89.9	90.0	90.1	90.3	90.4	90.5	90.6	90.7	90.8	90.9	91.0

	2074 -2075	2075 -2076	2076 -2077	2077 -2078	2078 -2079	2079 -2080	2080 -2081	2081 -2082	2082 -2083	2083 -2084	2084 -2085	2085 -2086	2086 -2087	2087 -2088	2088 -2089	2089 -2090	2090 -2091	2091 -2092	2092 -2093	2093 -2094
Population at start	75,761	76,038	76,317	76,598	76,879	77,161	77,442	77,724	78,005	78,286	78,567	78,847	79,128	79,408	79,689	79,970	80,252	80,535	80,818	81,103
Births	826	828	831	834	836	838	840	842	843	844	846	847	848	849	851	852	853	854	856	857
Deaths	718	719	720	722	724	726	728	730	732	733	735	736	737	738	739	740	740	740	741	741
Natural change	108	110	111	112	112	112	112	112	111	111	111	111	111	111	112	112	113	114	115	116
International migration inflows	472	472	472	472	472	472	472	472	472	472	472	472	472	472	472	472	472	472	472	472
Crossborder migration inflows	48	48	48	48	48	48	48	48	48	48	48	48	48	48	48	48	48	48	48	48
International migration outflows	297	297	297	297	297	297	297	297	297	297	297	297	297	297	297	297	297	297	297	297
Crossborder migration outflows	53	53	53	53	53	53	53	53	53	53	53	53	53	53	53	53	53	53	53	53
Net international migration	175	175	175	175	175	175	175	175	175	175	175	175	175	175	175	175	175	175	175	175
Net crossborder migration	-5	-5	-5	-5	-5	-5	-5	-5	-5	-5	-5	-5	-5	-5	-5	-5	-5	-5	-5	-5
Net migration	170	170	170	170	170	170	170	170	170	170	170	170	170	170	170	170	170	170	170	170
Total change	278	279	280	281	282	282	282	281	281	281	281	280	280	281	281	282	283	284	285	286
Population at end	76,038	76,317	76,598	76,879	77,161	77,442	77,724	78,005	78,286	78,567	78,847	79,128	79,408	79,689	79,970	80,252	80,535	80,818	81,103	81,389
Annual growth rate	0.37%	0.37%	0.37%	0.37%	0.37%	0.37%	0.36%	0.36%	0.36%	0.36%	0.36%	0.35%	0.35%	0.35%	0.35%	0.35%	0.35%	0.35%	0.35%	0.35%
Total fertility rate (TFR)	1.90	1.90	1.90	1.90	1.90	1.90	1.90	1.90	1.90	1.90	1.90	1.90	1.90	1.90	1.90	1.90	1.90	1.90	1.90	1.90
EOLB Males	88.6	88.7	88.9	89.0	89.1	89.2	89.3	89.5	89.6	89.7	89.8	89.9	90.1	90.2	90.3	90.4	90.5	90.7	90.8	90.9
Females	91.2	91.3	91.4	91.5	91.6	91.7	91.8	91.9	92.0	92.2	92.3	92.4	92.5	92.6	92.7	92.8	92.9	93.0	93.2	93.3

15.2b Population projections by the Office for National Statistics
England and Wales, PERSONS, thousands

2014-based
Principal projection

Components of change (mid-year to mid-year), total fertility rate
and expectation of life at birth based on the mortality rates for the year

	2094 -2095	2095 -2096	2096 -2097	2097 -2098	2098 -2099	2099 -2100	2100 -2101	2101 -2102	2102 -2103	2103 -2104	2104 -2105	2105 -2106	2106 -2107	2107 -2108	2108 -2109	2109 -2110	2110 -2111	2111 -2112	2112 -2113	2113 -2114
Population at start	81,389	81,676	81,964	82,253	82,543	82,834	83,125	83,417	83,709	84,001	84,293	84,584	84,875	85,166	85,455	85,744	86,032	86,320	86,606	86,892
Births	859	861	863	865	867	869	871	874	876	878	881	883	885	887	889	892	893	895	897	899
Deaths	742	742	743	744	746	747	749	751	753	756	759	761	764	767	770	773	776	778	781	783
Natural change	117	118	119	120	121	122	122	122	122	122	122	121	121	120	119	119	118	117	116	116
International migration inflows	472	472	472	472	472	472	472	472	472	472	472	472	472	472	472	472	472	472	472	472
Crossborder migration inflows	48	48	49	49	49	49	49	49	49	49	49	49	49	49	49	49	49	49	49	49
International migration outflows	297	297	297	297	297	297	297	297	297	297	297	297	297	297	297	297	297	297	297	297
Crossborder migration outflows	53	53	53	53	53	53	53	54	54	54	54	54	54	54	54	54	54	54	54	54
Net international migration	175	175	175	175	175	175	175	175	175	175	175	175	175	175	175	175	175	175	175	175
Net crossborder migration	-5	-5	-5	-5	-5	-5	-5	-5	-5	-5	-5	-5	-5	-5	-5	-5	-5	-5	-5	-5
Net migration	170	170	170	170	170	170	170	170	170	170	170	170	170	170	170	170	170	170	170	170
Total change	287	288	289	290	291	291	292	292	292	292	292	291	290	290	289	288	287	287	286	285
Population at end	81,676	81,964	82,253	82,543	82,834	83,125	83,417	83,709	84,001	84,293	84,584	84,875	85,166	85,455	85,744	86,032	86,320	86,606	86,892	87,178
Annual growth rate	0.35%	0.35%	0.35%	0.35%	0.35%	0.35%	0.35%	0.35%	0.35%	0.35%	0.35%	0.34%	0.34%	0.34%	0.34%	0.34%	0.33%	0.33%	0.33%	0.33%
Total fertility rate (TFR)	1.90	1.90	1.90	1.90	1.90	1.90	1.90	1.90	1.90	1.90	1.90	1.90	1.90	1.90	1.90	1.90	1.90	1.90	1.90	1.90
EOLB Males	91.0	91.1	91.3	91.4	91.5	91.6	91.7	91.9	92.0	92.1	92.2	92.3	92.4	92.6	92.7	92.8	92.9	93.0	93.2	93.3
Females	93.4	93.5	93.6	93.7	93.8	93.9	94.1	94.2	94.3	94.4	94.5	94.6	94.7	94.8	95.0	95.1	95.2	95.3	95.4	95.5

Source: Office for National Statistics

Note: Figures may not add exactly due to rounding.
* Children under 16. Working age and pensionable age populations based on state pension age (SPA) for given year.
Between 2012 and 2018, SPA will change from 65 years for men and 61 years for women, to 65 years for both sexes.
Then between 2019 and 2020, SPA will change from 65 years to 66 years for both men and women.
Between 2026 and 2027 SPA will increase to 67 years and between 2044 and 2046 to 68 years for both sexes. This is based on SPA under the 2014 Pensions Act.
** This is consistent with the age-group definitions used in ONS Labour Market Statistics.

National Population Projections are currently produced every two years. The 2016-based projections are not due to be published until November/December 2017. Therefore, this table series will be updated in the next edition

458

15.2c Population projections by the Office for National Statistics
Scotland, PERSONS, thousands

2014-based
Principal projection

Components of change (mid-year to mid-year), total fertility rate
and expectation of life at birth based on the mortality rates for the year

	2014-2015	2015-2016	2016-2017	2017-2018	2018-2019	2019-2020	2020-2021	2021-2022	2022-2023	2023-2024	2024-2025	2025-2026	2026-2027	2027-2028	2028-2029	2029-2030	2030-2031	2031-2032	2032-2033	2033-2034
Population at start	5,348	5,365	5,380	5,396	5,412	5,428	5,445	5,462	5,480	5,497	5,514	5,532	5,548	5,565	5,581	5,596	5,610	5,624	5,636	5,648
Births	56	56	55	56	56	57	57	57	57	57	58	58	57	57	57	57	56	56	56	56
Deaths	58	54	54	54	54	54	54	55	55	55	55	56	56	57	57	58	58	59	60	60
Natural change	-2	2	1	2	2	2	3	3	3	2	2	2	1	1	0	-1	-2	-3	-3	-4
International migration inflows	39	33	33	33	33	33	33	33	33	33	33	33	33	33	33	33	33	33	33	33
Crossborder migration inflows	47	47	47	47	47	47	47	47	47	47	46	46	47	47	47	47	47	47	47	47
International migration outflows	25	25	25	25	24	24	24	24	24	24	24	24	24	24	24	24	24	24	24	24
Crossborder migration outflows	41	41	42	42	42	42	41	41	41	41	41	41	41	41	41	41	41	41	41	41
Net international migration	14	8	9	9	9	9	9	9	9	9	9	9	9	9	9	9	9	9	9	9
Net crossborder migration	6	5	5	5	5	5	5	5	5	5	6	6	6	6	6	6	6	6	6	6
Net migration	19	14	14	14	14	15	15	15	15	15	15	15	15	15	15	15	15	15	15	15
Total change	17	16	15	16	16	17	17	17	17	17	17	17	16	16	15	14	13	13	12	11
Population at end	5,365	5,380	5,396	5,412	5,428	5,445	5,462	5,480	5,497	5,514	5,532	5,548	5,565	5,581	5,596	5,610	5,624	5,636	5,648	5,659
Annual growth rate	0.32%	0.29%	0.29%	0.29%	0.30%	0.31%	0.32%	0.32%	0.32%	0.32%	0.31%	0.30%	0.30%	0.28%	0.27%	0.26%	0.24%	0.22%	0.21%	0.19%
Total fertility rate (TFR)	1.59	1.58	1.56	1.57	1.58	1.59	1.60	1.61	1.62	1.63	1.65	1.66	1.66	1.67	1.68	1.68	1.69	1.69	1.70	1.70
EOLB Males	76.6	77.7	77.9	78.2	78.5	78.7	78.9	79.2	79.4	79.6	79.9	80.1	80.3	80.5	80.7	80.9	81.0	81.2	81.4	81.5
Females	80.7	81.5	81.7	81.9	82.0	82.2	82.4	82.5	82.7	82.9	83.0	83.2	83.3	83.5	83.6	83.8	83.9	84.1	84.2	84.3

	2034-2035	2035-2036	2036-2037	2037-2038	2038-2039	2039-2040	2040-2041	2041-2042	2042-2043	2043-2044	2044-2045	2045-2046	2046-2047	2047-2048	2048-2049	2049-2050	2050-2051	2051-2052	2052-2053	2053-2054
Population at start	5,659	5,669	5,678	5,686	5,694	5,701	5,708	5,715	5,721	5,726	5,732	5,737	5,741	5,745	5,749	5,753	5,756	5,759	5,761	5,764
Births	56	56	56	56	56	56	56	56	56	56	56	56	56	56	56	56	56	56	56	56
Deaths	61	61	62	63	63	64	65	65	66	66	67	67	67	68	68	68	68	69	69	69
Natural change	-5	-6	-6	-7	-8	-8	-9	-9	-9	-10	-10	-11	-11	-11	-12	-12	-12	-12	-12	-12
International migration inflows	33	33	33	33	33	33	33	33	33	33	33	33	33	33	33	33	33	33	33	33
Crossborder migration inflows	46	46	46	46	46	46	46	46	46	47	47	47	47	47	47	47	47	47	47	47
International migration outflows	24	24	24	24	24	24	24	24	24	24	24	24	24	24	24	24	24	24	24	24
Crossborder migration outflows	41	41	41	41	41	41	41	41	41	41	41	41	41	41	41	41	41	41	41	41
Net international migration	9	9	9	9	9	9	9	9	9	9	9	9	9	9	9	9	9	9	9	9
Net crossborder migration	6	5	5	5	6	6	6	6	5	5	6	6	6	6	6	6	6	6	6	6
Net migration	15	15	15	15	15	15	15	15	15	15	15	15	15	15	15	15	15	15	15	15
Total change	10	9	8	8	7	7	6	6	6	5	5	5	4	4	3	3	3	3	3	3
Population at end	5,669	5,678	5,686	5,694	5,701	5,708	5,715	5,721	5,726	5,732	5,737	5,741	5,745	5,749	5,753	5,756	5,759	5,761	5,764	5,767
Annual growth rate	0.18%	0.16%	0.15%	0.14%	0.13%	0.12%	0.11%	0.11%	0.10%	0.09%	0.09%	0.08%	0.07%	0.07%	0.06%	0.06%	0.05%	0.05%	0.05%	0.04%
Total fertility rate (TFR)	1.70	1.70	1.70	1.70	1.70	1.70	1.70	1.70	1.70	1.70	1.70	1.70	1.70	1.70	1.70	1.70	1.70	1.70	1.70	1.70
EOLB Males	81.7	81.8	82.0	82.1	82.3	82.4	82.5	82.7	82.8	82.9	83.0	83.2	83.3	83.4	83.6	83.7	83.8	84.0	84.1	84.2
Females	84.5	84.6	84.7	84.8	85.0	85.1	85.2	85.3	85.4	85.5	85.7	85.8	85.9	86.0	86.1	86.3	86.4	86.5	86.6	86.7

15.2c Population projections by the Office for National Statistics
Scotland, PERSONS, thousands

2014-based
Principal projection

Components of change (mid-year to mid-year), total fertility rate
and expectation of life at birth based on the mortality rates for the year

	2054 -2055	2055 -2056	2056 -2057	2057 -2058	2058 -2059	2059 -2060	2060 -2061	2061 -2062	2062 -2063	2063 -2064	2064 -2065	2065 -2066	2066 -2067	2067 -2068	2068 -2069	2069 -2070	2070 -2071	2071 -2072	2072 -2073	2073 -2074
Population at start	5,767	5,769	5,772	5,774	5,777	5,780	5,783	5,786	5,790	5,794	5,798	5,802	5,807	5,812	5,817	5,823	5,828	5,834	5,840	5,846
Births	56	56	56	56	56	56	56	56	56	56	56	56	56	56	56	56	56	56	56	56
Deaths	69	69	69	69	68	68	68	68	67	67	67	66	66	66	65	65	65	65	65	65
Natural change	-13	-12	-12	-12	-12	-12	-12	-11	-11	-11	-11	-10	-10	-10	-10	-9	-9	-9	-9	-9
International migration inflows	33	33	33	33	33	33	33	33	33	33	33	33	33	33	33	33	33	33	33	33
Crossborder migration inflows	47	47	47	47	47	46	46	46	46	46	46	46	47	47	47	47	47	47	47	47
International migration outflows	24	24	24	24	24	24	24	24	24	24	24	24	24	24	24	24	24	24	24	24
Crossborder migration outflows	41	41	41	41	41	41	41	41	41	41	41	41	41	41	41	41	41	41	41	41
Net international migration	9	9	9	9	9	9	9	9	9	9	9	9	9	9	9	9	9	9	9	9
Net crossborder migration	6	6	6	6	6	6	6	6	6	6	6	6	6	6	6	6	6	6	6	6
Net migration	15	15	15	15	15	15	15	15	15	15	15	15	15	15	15	15	15	15	15	15
Total change	3	3	3	3	3	3	3	4	4	4	4	5	5	5	5	6	6	6	6	6
Population at end	5,769	5,772	5,774	5,777	5,780	5,783	5,786	5,790	5,794	5,798	5,802	5,807	5,812	5,817	5,823	5,828	5,834	5,840	5,846	5,853
Annual growth rate	0.04%	0.04%	0.05%	0.05%	0.05%	0.05%	0.06%	0.06%	0.07%	0.07%	0.08%	0.08%	0.09%	0.09%	0.09%	0.10%	0.10%	0.10%	0.11%	0.11%
Total fertility rate (TFR)	1.70	1.70	1.70	1.70	1.70	1.70	1.70	1.70	1.70	1.70	1.70	1.70	1.70	1.70	1.70	1.70	1.70	1.70	1.70	1.70
EOLB Males	84.4	84.5	84.6	84.7	84.9	85.0	85.1	85.3	85.4	85.5	85.6	85.8	85.9	86.0	86.2	86.3	86.4	86.5	86.7	86.8
Females	86.9	87.0	87.1	87.2	87.3	87.4	87.6	87.7	87.8	87.9	88.0	88.2	88.3	88.4	88.5	88.6	88.7	88.9	89.0	89.1

	2074 -2075	2075 -2076	2076 -2077	2077 -2078	2078 -2079	2079 -2080	2080 -2081	2081 -2082	2082 -2083	2083 -2084	2084 -2085	2085 -2086	2086 -2087	2087 -2088	2088 -2089	2089 -2090	2090 -2091	2091 -2092	2092 -2093	2093 -2094
Population at start	5,853	5,859	5,865	5,871	5,877	5,884	5,890	5,896	5,902	5,908	5,913	5,919	5,925	5,931	5,937	5,943	5,950	5,956	5,963	5,970
Births	56	56	56	56	56	56	56	56	56	56	56	56	56	56	56	56	56	56	56	56
Deaths	65	65	65	65	65	65	65	65	65	65	65	65	65	65	65	65	65	64	64	64
Natural change	-9	-9	-9	-9	-9	-9	-9	-9	-9	-9	-9	-9	-9	-9	-9	-9	-9	-8	-8	-8
International migration inflows	33	33	33	33	33	33	33	33	33	33	33	33	33	33	33	33	33	33	33	33
Crossborder migration inflows	47	47	47	47	47	47	47	47	47	47	47	47	47	47	47	47	47	47	47	47
International migration outflows	24	24	24	24	24	24	24	24	24	24	24	24	24	24	24	24	24	24	24	24
Crossborder migration outflows	41	41	41	41	41	41	41	41	41	41	41	41	41	41	41	41	41	41	41	41
Net international migration	9	9	9	9	9	9	9	9	9	9	9	9	9	9	9	9	9	9	9	9
Net crossborder migration	6	6	6	6	6	6	6	6	6	6	6	6	6	6	6	6	6	6	6	6
Net migration	15	15	15	15	15	15	15	15	15	15	15	15	15	15	15	15	15	15	15	15
Total change	6	6	6	6	6	6	6	6	6	6	6	6	6	6	6	6	6	7	7	7
Population at end	5,859	5,865	5,871	5,877	5,884	5,890	5,896	5,902	5,908	5,913	5,919	5,925	5,931	5,937	5,943	5,950	5,956	5,963	5,970	5,977
Annual growth rate	0.11%	0.11%	0.11%	0.11%	0.10%	0.10%	0.10%	0.10%	0.10%	0.10%	0.10%	0.10%	0.10%	0.10%	0.10%	0.11%	0.11%	0.11%	0.11%	0.12%
Total fertility rate (TFR)	1.70	1.70	1.70	1.70	1.70	1.70	1.70	1.70	1.70	1.70	1.70	1.70	1.70	1.70	1.70	1.70	1.70	1.70	1.70	1.70
EOLB Males	86.9	87.1	87.2	87.3	87.4	87.6	87.7	87.8	87.9	88.1	88.2	88.3	88.5	88.6	88.7	88.8	89.0	89.1	89.2	89.3
Females	89.2	89.3	89.5	89.6	89.7	89.8	89.9	90.0	90.2	90.3	90.4	90.5	90.6	90.8	90.9	91.0	91.1	91.2	91.3	91.5

15.2c Population projections by the Office for National Statistics
Scotland, PERSONS, thousands

2014-based
Principal projection

Components of change (mid-year to mid-year), total fertility rate
and expectation of life at birth based on the mortality rates for the year

	2094 -2095	2095 -2096	2096 -2097	2097 -2098	2098 -2099	2099 -2100	2100 -2101	2101 -2102	2102 -2103	2103 -2104	2104 -2105	2105 -2106	2106 -2107	2107 -2108	2108 -2109	2109 -2110	2110 -2111	2111 -2112	2112 -2113	2113 -2114
Population at start	5,977	5,984	5,991	5,999	6,006	6,014	6,022	6,030	6,038	6,046	6,054	6,062	6,070	6,079	6,087	6,095	6,103	6,111	6,119	6,127
Births	56	56	56	56	56	56	56	56	56	56	56	56	56	56	56	56	56	56	56	56
Deaths	64	64	63	63	63	63	63	63	63	63	63	63	63	63	63	63	63	63	63	63
Natural change	-8	-8	-8	-7	-7	-7	-7	-7	-7	-7	-7	-7	-7	-7	-7	-7	-7	-7	-7	-7
International migration inflows	33	33	33	33	33	33	33	33	33	33	33	33	33	33	33	33	33	33	33	33
Crossborder migration inflows	47	47	47	47	47	47	47	47	47	47	47	47	47	47	47	47	47	47	47	47
International migration outflows	24	24	24	24	24	24	24	24	24	24	24	24	24	24	24	24	24	24	24	24
Crossborder migration outflows	41	41	41	41	41	41	41	41	41	41	41	41	41	41	41	41	41	41	42	42
Net international migration	9	9	9	9	9	9	9	9	9	9	9	9	9	9	9	9	9	9	9	9
Net crossborder migration	6	6	6	6	6	6	6	6	6	6	6	6	6	6	6	6	6	6	6	6
Net migration	15	15	15	15	15	15	15	15	15	15	15	15	15	15	15	15	15	15	15	15
Total change	7	7	7	8	8	8	8	8	8	8	8	8	8	8	8	8	8	8	8	8
Population at end	5,984	5,991	5,999	6,006	6,014	6,022	6,030	6,038	6,046	6,054	6,062	6,070	6,079	6,087	6,095	6,103	6,111	6,119	6,127	6,135
Annual growth rate	0.12%	0.12%	0.12%	0.13%	0.13%	0.13%	0.13%	0.13%	0.13%	0.13%	0.13%	0.13%	0.13%	0.13%	0.13%	0.13%	0.13%	0.13%	0.13%	0.13%
Total fertility rate (TFR)	1.70	1.70	1.70	1.70	1.70	1.70	1.70	1.70	1.70	1.70	1.70	1.70	1.70	1.70	1.70	1.70	1.70	1.70	1.70	1.70
EOLB Males	89.5	89.6	89.7	89.9	90.0	90.1	90.2	90.4	90.5	90.6	90.7	90.9	91.0	91.1	91.3	91.4	91.5	91.6	91.8	91.9
Females	91.6	91.7	91.8	91.9	92.1	92.2	92.3	92.4	92.5	92.6	92.8	92.9	93.0	93.1	93.2	93.4	93.5	93.6	93.7	93.8

Source: Office for National Statistics

Note: Figures may not add exactly due to rounding.
* Children under 16. Working age and pensionable age populations based on state pension age (SPA) for given year.
Between 2012 and 2018, SPA will change from 65 years for men and 61 years for women, to 65 years for both sexes.
Then between 2019 and 2020, SPA will change from 65 years to 66 years for both men and women.
Between 2026 and 2027 SPA will increase to 67 years and between 2044 and 2046 to 68 years for both sexes. This is based on SPA under the 2014 Pensions Act.
** This is consistent with the age-group definitions used in ONS Labour Market Statistics.

National Population Projections are currently produced every two years. The 2016-based projections are not due to be published until November/December 2017. Therefore, this table series will be updated in the next edition

15.2d Population projections by the Office for National Statistics
Northern Ireland, PERSONS, thousands

2014-based
Principal projection

**Components of change (mid-year to mid-year), total fertility rate
and expectation of life at birth based on the mortality rates for the year**

	2014 -2015	2015 -2016	2016 -2017	2017 -2018	2018 -2019	2019 -2020	2020 -2021	2021 -2022	2022 -2023	2023 -2024	2024 -2025	2025 -2026	2026 -2027	2027 -2028	2028 -2029	2029 -2030	2030 -2031	2031 -2032	2032 -2033	2033 -2034
Population at start	1,840	1,851	1,863	1,874	1,884	1,894	1,904	1,913	1,922	1,930	1,939	1,947	1,954	1,961	1,968	1,974	1,980	1,986	1,991	1,996
Births	24	24	24	24	24	24	24	24	24	23	23	23	23	23	23	23	22	22	22	22
Deaths	16	15	15	15	15	15	15	15	15	16	16	16	16	16	17	17	17	17	18	18
Natural change	9	10	9	9	9	9	9	9	8	8	8	7	7	7	6	6	5	5	5	5
International migration inflows	13	13	13	13	13	13	13	13	13	13	13	13	13	13	13	13	13	13	13	13
Crossborder migration inflows	11	11	11	11	11	11	10	10	10	10	10	10	10	10	10	10	10	10	10	10
International migration outflows	10	10	11	11	11	12	12	12	12	12	12	12	12	12	12	12	12	12	12	12
Crossborder migration outflows	11	11	11	11	11	11	11	11	11	11	11	11	11	11	11	11	11	11	11	11
Net international migration	3	3	2	2	2	1	1	1	1	1	1	1	1	1	1	1	1	1	1	1
Net crossborder migration	-1	-1	-1	-1	-1	-1	-1	-1	-1	-1	-1	-1	-1	-1	-1	-1	-1	-1	-1	-1
Net migration	2	2	1	1	1	1	0	0	0	0	0	0	0	0	0	0	0	0	0	0
Total change	11	11	11	10	10	10	9	9	9	8	8	8	7	7	6	6	6	5	5	5
Population at end	1,851	1,863	1,874	1,884	1,894	1,904	1,913	1,922	1,930	1,939	1,947	1,954	1,961	1,968	1,974	1,980	1,986	1,991	1,996	2,000
Annual growth rate	0.58%	0.62%	0.58%	0.56%	0.54%	0.51%	0.48%	0.47%	0.45%	0.43%	0.41%	0.39%	0.36%	0.34%	0.32%	0.30%	0.28%	0.26%	0.25%	0.24%
Total fertility rate (TFR)	1.95	1.97	1.97	1.97	1.98	1.98	1.99	1.99	2.00	2.00	2.00	2.00	2.00	2.00	2.00	2.00	2.00	2.00	2.00	2.00
EOLB Males	78.2	78.9	79.1	79.4	79.7	79.9	80.2	80.4	80.6	80.8	81.0	81.2	81.4	81.6	81.8	82.0	82.2	82.3	82.5	82.6
Females	82.1	82.9	83.1	83.3	83.5	83.7	83.9	84.1	84.2	84.4	84.6	84.7	84.9	85.0	85.2	85.3	85.5	85.6	85.8	85.9

	2034 -2035	2035 -2036	2036 -2037	2037 -2038	2038 -2039	2039 -2040	2040 -2041	2041 -2042	2042 -2043	2043 -2044	2044 -2045	2045 -2046	2046 -2047	2047 -2048	2048 -2049	2049 -2050	2050 -2051	2051 -2052	2052 -2053	2053 -2054
Population at start	2,000	2,005	2,009	2,013	2,017	2,021	2,025	2,029	2,032	2,035	2,039	2,042	2,044	2,047	2,049	2,051	2,053	2,054	2,055	2,056
Births	22	23	23	23	23	23	23	23	23	23	23	23	23	23	23	23	23	23	23	23
Deaths	18	18	19	19	19	20	20	20	20	21	21	21	21	21	22	22	22	22	22	22
Natural change	4	4	4	4	4	4	3	3	3	3	3	2	2	2	2	1	1	1	1	0
International migration inflows	13	13	13	13	13	13	13	13	13	13	13	13	13	13	13	13	13	13	13	13
Crossborder migration inflows	10	10	10	10	10	10	10	10	10	10	10	10	10	10	10	10	10	10	10	10
International migration outflows	12	12	12	12	12	12	12	12	12	12	12	12	12	12	12	12	12	12	12	12
Crossborder migration outflows	11	11	11	11	11	11	11	11	11	11	11	11	11	11	11	11	11	11	11	11
Net international migration	1	1	1	1	1	1	1	1	1	1	1	1	1	1	1	1	1	1	1	1
Net crossborder migration	-1	-1	-1	-1	-1	-1	-1	-1	-1	-1	-1	-1	-1	-1	-1	-1	-1	-1	-1	-1
Net migration	0	0	0	0	0	0	0	0	0	0	0	0	0	0	0	0	0	0	0	0
Total change	5	4	4	4	4	4	4	3	3	3	3	3	2	2	2	2	1	1	1	1
Population at end	2,005	2,009	2,013	2,017	2,021	2,025	2,029	2,032	2,035	2,039	2,042	2,044	2,047	2,049	2,051	2,053	2,054	2,055	2,056	2,057
Annual growth rate	0.23%	0.21%	0.21%	0.20%	0.19%	0.19%	0.18%	0.17%	0.16%	0.15%	0.14%	0.13%	0.12%	0.11%	0.10%	0.08%	0.07%	0.06%	0.04%	0.03%
Total fertility rate (TFR)	2.00	2.00	2.00	2.00	2.00	2.00	2.00	2.00	2.00	2.00	2.00	2.00	2.00	2.00	2.00	2.00	2.00	2.00	2.00	2.00
EOLB Males	82.8	82.9	83.1	83.2	83.3	83.4	83.6	83.7	83.8	83.9	84.1	84.2	84.3	84.5	84.6	84.7	84.8	85.0	85.1	85.2
Females	86.0	86.1	86.3	86.4	86.5	86.6	86.7	86.8	86.9	87.1	87.2	87.3	87.4	87.5	87.6	87.7	87.9	88.0	88.1	88.2

15.2d Population projections by the Office for National Statistics
Northern Ireland, PERSONS, thousands

2014-based
Principal projection

Components of change (mid-year to mid-year), total fertility rate
and expectation of life at birth based on the mortality rates for the year

	2054 -2055	2055 -2056	2056 -2057	2057 -2058	2058 -2059	2059 -2060	2060 -2061	2061 -2062	2062 -2063	2063 -2064	2064 -2065	2065 -2066	2066 -2067	2067 -2068	2068 -2069	2069 -2070	2070 -2071	2071 -2072	2072 -2073	2073 -2074
Population at start	2,057	2,057	2,057	2,057	2,057	2,057	2,057	2,056	2,056	2,056	2,055	2,055	2,055	2,054	2,055	2,055	2,055	2,055	2,056	2,056
Births	23	23	22	22	22	22	22	22	22	22	22	22	22	22	22	22	22	22	22	22
Deaths	23	23	23	23	23	23	23	23	23	23	23	23	23	22	22	22	22	22	22	22
Natural change	0	0	-1	-1	-1	-1	-1	-1	-1	-1	-1	-1	-1	0	0	0	0	0	0	0
International migration inflows	13	13	13	13	13	13	13	13	13	13	13	13	13	13	13	13	13	13	13	13
Crossborder migration inflows	10	10	10	10	10	10	10	10	10	10	10	10	10	10	10	10	10	10	10	10
International migration outflows	12	12	12	12	12	12	12	12	12	12	12	12	12	12	12	12	12	12	12	12
Crossborder migration outflows	11	11	11	11	11	11	11	11	11	11	11	11	11	11	11	11	11	11	11	11
Net international migration	1	1	1	1	1	1	1	1	1	1	1	1	1	1	1	1	1	1	1	1
Net crossborder migration	-1	-1	-1	-1	-1	-1	-1	-1	-1	-1	-1	-1	-1	-1	-1	-1	-1	-1	-1	-1
Net migration	0	0	0	0	0	0	0	0	0	0	0	0	0	0	0	0	0	0	0	0
Total change	0	0	0	0	0	0	0	0	0	0	0	0	0	0	0	0	0	0	1	1
Population at end	2,057	2,057	2,057	2,057	2,057	2,056	2,056	2,056	2,055	2,055	2,055	2,054	2,055	2,055	2,055	2,055	2,056	2,056	2,056	2,057
Annual growth rate	0.02%	0.01%	0.00%	-0.01%	-0.01%	-0.02%	-0.02%	-0.02%	-0.02%	-0.02%	-0.01%	-0.01%	-0.01%	0.00%	0.01%	0.01%	0.02%	0.02%	0.03%	0.03%
Total fertility rate (TFR)	2.00	2.00	2.00	2.00	2.00	2.00	2.00	2.00	2.00	2.00	2.00	2.00	2.00	2.00	2.00	2.00	2.00	2.00	2.00	2.00
EOLB Males	85.3	85.5	85.6	85.7	85.8	86.0	86.1	86.2	86.3	86.5	86.6	86.7	86.8	87.0	87.1	87.2	87.3	87.5	87.6	87.7
Females	88.3	88.4	88.5	88.6	88.8	88.9	89.0	89.1	89.2	89.3	89.4	89.5	89.7	89.8	89.9	90.0	90.1	90.2	90.3	90.5

	2074 -2075	2075 -2076	2076 -2077	2077 -2078	2078 -2079	2079 -2080	2080 -2081	2081 -2082	2082 -2083	2083 -2084	2084 -2085	2085 -2086	2086 -2087	2087 -2088	2088 -2089	2089 -2090	2090 -2091	2091 -2092	2092 -2093	2093 -2094
Population at start	2,057	2,058	2,059	2,059	2,060	2,061	2,062	2,063	2,064	2,065	2,066	2,067	2,067	2,068	2,069	2,070	2,071	2,072	2,073	2,074
Births	22	22	22	22	22	22	22	22	22	22	22	22	22	22	22	22	22	22	22	22
Deaths	22	22	22	22	22	22	22	22	22	22	22	22	21	21	21	21	21	21	21	21
Natural change	0	1	1	1	1	1	1	1	1	1	1	1	1	1	1	1	1	1	1	1
International migration inflows	13	13	13	13	13	13	13	13	13	13	13	13	13	13	13	13	13	13	13	13
Crossborder migration inflows	10	10	10	10	10	10	10	10	10	10	10	10	10	10	10	10	10	10	10	10
International migration outflows	12	12	12	12	12	12	12	12	12	12	12	12	12	12	12	12	12	12	12	12
Crossborder migration outflows	11	11	11	11	11	11	11	11	11	11	11	11	11	11	11	11	11	11	11	11
Net international migration	1	1	1	1	1	1	1	1	1	1	1	1	1	1	1	1	1	1	1	1
Net crossborder migration	-1	-1	-1	-1	-1	-1	-1	-1	-1	-1	-1	-1	-1	-1	-1	-1	-1	-1	-1	-1
Net migration	0	0	0	0	0	0	0	0	0	0	0	0	0	0	0	0	0	0	0	0
Total change	1	1	0	1	1	1	1	1	1	1	1	0	1	1	1	1	1	1	1	0
Population at end	2,058	2,059	2,059	2,060	2,061	2,062	2,063	2,064	2,065	2,066	2,067	2,067	2,068	2,069	2,070	2,071	2,072	2,073	2,074	2,074
Annual growth rate	0.04%	0.04%	0.04%	0.04%	0.04%	0.04%	0.04%	0.04%	0.04%	0.04%	0.04%	0.04%	0.04%	0.04%	0.04%	0.04%	0.04%	0.04%	0.04%	0.05%
Total fertility rate (TFR)	2.00	2.00	2.00	2.00	2.00	2.00	2.00	2.00	2.00	2.00	2.00	2.00	2.00	2.00	2.00	2.00	2.00	2.00	2.00	2.00
EOLB Males	87.8	88.0	88.1	88.2	88.3	88.5	88.6	88.7	88.8	88.9	89.1	89.2	89.3	89.4	89.6	89.7	89.8	89.9	90.1	90.2
Females	90.6	90.7	90.8	90.9	91.0	91.1	91.2	91.4	91.5	91.6	91.7	91.8	91.9	92.0	92.1	92.3	92.4	92.5	92.6	92.7

15.2d Population projections by the Office for National Statistics
Northern Ireland, PERSONS, thousands

2014-based
Principal projection

Components of change (mid-year to mid-year), total fertility rate
and expectation of life at birth based on the mortality rates for the year

	2094 -2095	2095 -2096	2096 -2097	2097 -2098	2098 -2099	2099 -2100	2100 -2101	2101 -2102	2102 -2103	2103 -2104	2104 -2105	2105 -2106	2106 -2107	2107 -2108	2108 -2109	2109 -2110	2110 -2111	2111 -2112	2112 -2113	2113 -2114
Population at start	2,074	2,075	2,076	2,078	2,079	2,080	2,081	2,082	2,083	2,084	2,085	2,086	2,087	2,088	2,089	2,090	2,091	2,092	2,093	2,094
Births	22	22	22	22	22	22	22	22	22	22	22	22	22	22	22	22	22	22	22	22
Deaths	21	21	21	21	21	21	21	21	21	21	21	21	21	21	21	21	21	21	21	21
Natural change	1	1	1	1	1	1	1	1	1	1	1	1	1	1	1	1	1	1	1	1
International migration inflows	13	13	13	13	13	13	13	13	13	13	13	13	13	13	13	13	13	13	13	13
Crossborder migration inflows	10	10	10	10	10	10	10	10	10	10	10	10	10	10	10	10	10	10	10	10
International migration outflows	12	12	12	12	12	12	12	12	12	12	12	12	12	12	12	12	12	12	12	12
Crossborder migration outflows	11	11	11	11	11	11	11	11	11	11	11	11	11	11	11	11	11	11	11	10
Net international migration	1	1	1	1	1	1	1	1	1	1	1	1	1	1	1	1	1	1	1	1
Net crossborder migration	-1	-1	-1	-1	-1	-1	-1	-1	-1	-1	-1	-1	-1	-1	-1	-1	-1	-1	-1	-1
Net migration	0	0	0	0	0	0	0	0	0	0	0	0	0	0	0	0	0	0	0	0
Total change	1	1	1	1	1	1	1	1	1	1	1	1	1	1	1	1	1	1	1	1
Population at end	2,075	2,076	2,078	2,079	2,080	2,081	2,082	2,083	2,084	2,085	2,086	2,087	2,088	2,089	2,090	2,091	2,092	2,093	2,094	2,095
Annual growth rate	0.05%	0.05%	0.05%	0.05%	0.05%	0.05%	0.05%	0.05%	0.05%	0.05%	0.05%	0.05%	0.05%	0.05%	0.05%	0.05%	0.04%	0.04%	0.04%	0.04%
Total fertility rate (TFR)	2.00	2.00	2.00	2.00	2.00	2.00	2.00	2.00	2.00	2.00	2.00	2.00	2.00	2.00	2.00	2.00	2.00	2.00	2.00	2.00
EOLB Males	90.3	90.4	90.6	90.7	90.8	90.9	91.0	91.2	91.3	91.4	91.5	91.7	91.8	91.9	92.0	92.2	92.3	92.4	92.5	92.6
Females	92.8	92.9	93.0	93.2	93.3	93.4	93.5	93.6	93.7	93.8	94.0	94.1	94.2	94.3	94.4	94.5	94.6	94.7	94.9	95.0

Source: Office for National Statistics

Note: Figures may not add exactly due to rounding.
* Children under 16. Working age and pensionable age populations based on state pension age (SPA) for given year.
Between 2012 and 2018, SPA will change from 65 years for men and 61 years for women, to 65 years for both sexes.
Then between 2019 and 2020, SPA will change from 65 years to 66 years for both men and women.
Between 2026 and 2027 SPA will increase to 67 years and between 2044 and 2046 to 68 years for both sexes. This is based on SPA under the 2014 Pensions Act.
** This is consistent with the age-group definitions used in ONS Labour Market Statistics.

National Population Projections are currently produced every two years. The 2016-based projections are not due to be published until November/December 2017. Therefore, this table series will be updated in the next edition

15.3a Mid-2015 Population estimates for United Kingdom by sex and single year of age

Ages	Persons	Males	females	Ages	Persons	Males	Females
ALL AGES	65,110,034	32,074,445	33,035,589	45	902,356	444,995	457,361
0	776,769	398,539	378,230	46	925,304	455,570	469,734
1	786,125	403,020	383,105	47	926,005	456,082	469,923
2	806,704	413,548	393,156	48	938,658	464,148	474,510
3	834,076	427,117	406,959	49	938,422	461,581	476,841
4	823,418	421,505	401,913	50	946,132	465,548	480,584
5	808,040	413,235	394,805	51	936,939	461,048	475,891
6	799,539	408,987	390,552	52	917,310	452,399	464,911
7	805,819	412,479	393,340	53	897,508	443,862	453,646
8	778,761	399,245	379,516	54	867,448	429,088	438,360
9	762,287	389,988	372,299	55	832,633	411,759	420,874
10	732,631	375,072	357,559	56	814,617	402,345	412,272
11	720,030	368,574	351,456	57	796,445	393,423	403,022
12	699,694	358,439	341,255	58	767,256	378,415	388,841
13	689,008	352,759	336,249	59	739,711	364,674	375,037
14	707,888	361,698	346,190	60	712,293	350,167	362,126
15	727,076	373,264	353,812	61	713,366	349,645	363,721
16	750,567	385,048	365,519	62	704,081	345,319	358,762
17	762,441	391,202	371,239	63	683,633	333,812	349,821
18	787,378	403,985	383,393	64	688,346	335,678	352,668
19	796,411	410,770	385,641	65	700,832	340,422	360,410
20	807,063	414,063	393,000	66	716,743	348,975	367,768
21	840,560	431,038	409,522	67	753,906	366,002	387,904
22	852,056	433,886	418,170	68	814,536	395,680	418,856
23	885,913	446,514	439,399	69	628,572	303,869	324,703
24	909,091	462,222	446,869	70	607,549	292,273	315,276
25	894,540	455,341	439,199	71	604,201	290,461	313,740
26	887,394	446,764	440,630	72	561,866	267,272	294,594
27	897,168	448,965	448,203	73	501,307	236,273	265,034
28	876,658	434,633	442,025	74	450,240	210,093	240,147
29	885,474	443,500	441,974	75	463,055	215,612	247,443
30	887,089	443,494	443,595	76	455,990	210,995	244,995
31	866,565	431,902	434,663	77	439,548	202,447	237,101
32	874,105	434,309	439,796	78	413,693	188,015	225,678
33	873,336	432,286	441,050	79	389,763	174,775	214,988
34	880,428	437,099	443,329	80	365,463	162,277	203,186
35	880,371	437,332	443,039	81	333,965	145,722	188,243
36	844,460	420,414	424,046	82	312,353	133,787	178,566
37	787,673	392,107	395,566	83	296,904	124,667	172,237
38	775,965	387,285	388,680	84	274,824	112,442	162,382
39	790,469	392,441	398,028	85	249,042	98,571	150,471
40	805,939	399,874	406,065	86	218,287	84,424	133,863
41	819,263	405,771	413,492	87	189,763	71,190	118,573
42	856,619	425,003	431,616	88	167,274	61,372	105,902
43	893,968	443,067	450,901	89	145,225	51,143	94,082
44	923,575	454,825	468,750	90	556,266	163,519	392,747

Source: Office for National Statistics

1. These unrounded estimates are published to enable and encourage further calculations and analysis. However, the estimates should not be taken to be accurate to the level of detail provided

2. The estimates are produced using a variety of data sources and statistical models, including some statistical disclosure control methods, and small estimates should not be taken to refer to particular individuals.

3. The estimated resident population of an area includes all those people who usually live there, regardless of nationality. Arriving international migrants are included in the usually resident population if they remain in the UK for at least a year. Emigrants are excluded if they remain outside the UK for at least a year. This is consistent with the United Nations definition of a long-term migrant. Armed forces stationed outside of the UK are excluded. Students are taken to be usually resident at their term time address.

4. Some of the administrative data used in estimating international migration at LA level was not available at the time of production of the mid-2015 population estimates.

5. Note that age 90 comprises data for ages 90 and above.

15.3b Population projections by the Office for National Statistics
United Kingdom, PERSONS, thousands

2014-based
Principal projection

Projected populations at mid-years by age last birthday

Ages	2014	2015	2016	2017	2018	2019	2020	2021	2022	2023	2024	2025	2026	2027	2028	2029	2030	2031	2032	2033
Thousands																				
0-14	11,408	11,509	11,629	11,768	11,901	12,012	12,111	12,180	12,232	12,258	12,286	12,303	12,299	12,278	12,280	12,299	12,321	12,336	12,345	12,349
15-29	12,556	12,595	12,570	12,518	12,449	12,396	12,334	12,272	12,239	12,258	12,271	12,319	12,386	12,468	12,546	12,615	12,701	12,812	12,946	13,073
30-44	12,741	12,751	12,731	12,734	12,801	12,898	13,025	13,191	13,361	13,497	13,580	13,603	13,624	13,651	13,656	13,658	13,615	13,553	13,476	13,387
45-59	12,973	13,135	13,290	13,389	13,425	13,408	13,360	13,266	13,129	12,988	12,886	12,814	12,751	12,683	12,631	12,573	12,563	12,535	12,534	12,596
60-74	9,707	9,834	10,013	10,175	10,314	10,438	10,582	10,746	10,777	10,889	11,057	11,252	11,453	11,660	11,840	12,013	12,166	12,317	12,417	12,457
75 & over	5,211	5,274	5,340	5,445	5,596	5,776	5,947	6,128	6,463	6,731	6,955	7,154	7,331	7,493	7,663	7,831	7,986	8,154	8,335	8,528
All ages	64,597	65,097	65,572	66,030	66,487	66,928	67,360	67,781	68,203	68,622	69,036	69,444	69,844	70,234	70,616	70,989	71,353	71,707	72,053	72,391
Percentages																				
0-14	17.7	17.7	17.7	17.8	17.9	17.9	18.0	18.0	17.9	17.9	17.8	17.7	17.6	17.5	17.4	17.3	17.3	17.2	17.1	17.1
15-29	19.4	19.3	19.2	19.0	18.7	18.5	18.3	18.1	17.9	17.9	17.8	17.7	17.7	17.8	17.8	17.8	17.8	17.9	18.0	18.1
30-44	19.7	19.6	19.4	19.3	19.3	19.3	19.3	19.5	19.6	19.7	19.7	19.6	19.5	19.4	19.3	19.2	19.1	18.9	18.7	18.5
45-59	20.1	20.2	20.3	20.3	20.2	20.0	19.8	19.6	19.3	18.9	18.7	18.5	18.3	18.1	17.9	17.7	17.6	17.5	17.4	17.4
60-74	15.0	15.1	15.3	15.4	15.5	15.6	15.7	15.9	15.8	15.9	16.0	16.2	16.4	16.6	16.8	16.9	17.1	17.2	17.2	17.2
75 & over	8.1	8.1	8.1	8.2	8.4	8.6	8.8	9.0	9.5	9.8	10.1	10.3	10.5	10.7	10.9	11.0	11.2	11.4	11.6	11.8
All ages	100.0	100.0	100.0	100.0	100.0	100.0	100.0	100.0	100.0	100.0	100.0	100.0	100.0	100.0	100.0	100.0	100.0	100.0	100.0	100.0
Mean age	40.3	40.4	40.5	40.6	40.8	40.9	41.0	41.2	41.3	41.4	41.6	41.7	41.9	42.0	42.1	42.3	42.4	42.6	42.7	42.8
Median age	40.0	40.0	40.0	40.0	40.1	40.2	40.3	40.5	40.6	40.7	40.9	41.0	41.1	41.3	41.4	41.6	41.7	41.9	42.0	42.2

Ages	2034	2035	2036	2037	2038	2039	2040	2041	2042	2043	2044	2045	2046	2047	2048	2049	2050	2051	2052	2053
Thousands																				
0-14	12,350	12,350	12,350	12,353	12,359	12,371	12,391	12,418	12,453	12,494	12,542	12,594	12,650	12,708	12,767	12,826	12,884	12,940	12,991	13,039
15-29	13,182	13,280	13,349	13,403	13,428	13,457	13,474	13,470	13,450	13,452	13,472	13,494	13,509	13,518	13,522	13,524	13,524	13,525	13,528	13,534
30-44	13,324	13,258	13,198	13,168	13,188	13,203	13,252	13,320	13,403	13,483	13,552	13,639	13,750	13,884	14,011	14,120	14,219	14,288	14,342	14,368
45-59	12,691	12,816	12,983	13,152	13,288	13,372	13,398	13,422	13,451	13,458	13,463	13,423	13,364	13,291	13,206	13,146	13,085	13,030	13,004	13,028
60-74	12,448	12,411	12,332	12,216	12,096	12,015	11,964	11,921	11,873	11,839	11,800	11,805	11,795	11,809	11,880	11,979	12,106	12,271	12,437	12,571
75 & over	8,726	8,928	9,148	9,382	9,621	9,866	10,108	10,333	10,550	10,748	10,937	11,101	11,274	11,416	11,520	11,588	11,639	11,672	11,689	11,712
All ages	72,721	73,044	73,361	73,673	73,980	74,284	74,585	74,884	75,180	75,474	75,766	76,055	76,342	76,626	76,907	77,184	77,457	77,726	77,991	78,252
Percentages																				
0-14	17.0	16.9	16.8	16.8	16.7	16.7	16.6	16.6	16.6	16.6	16.6	16.6	16.6	16.6	16.6	16.6	16.6	16.6	16.7	16.7
15-29	18.1	18.2	18.2	18.2	18.2	18.1	18.1	18.0	17.9	17.8	17.8	17.7	17.7	17.6	17.6	17.5	17.5	17.4	17.3	17.3
30-44	18.3	18.2	18.0	17.9	17.8	17.8	17.8	17.8	17.8	17.9	17.9	17.9	18.0	18.1	18.2	18.3	18.4	18.4	18.4	18.4
45-59	17.5	17.5	17.7	17.9	18.0	18.0	18.0	17.9	17.9	17.8	17.8	17.6	17.5	17.3	17.2	17.0	16.9	16.8	16.7	16.6
60-74	17.1	17.0	16.8	16.6	16.3	16.2	16.0	15.9	15.8	15.7	15.6	15.5	15.4	15.4	15.4	15.5	15.6	15.8	15.9	16.1
75 & over	12.0	12.2	12.5	12.7	13.0	13.3	13.6	13.8	14.0	14.2	14.4	14.6	14.8	14.9	15.0	15.0	15.0	15.0	15.0	15.0
All ages	100.0	100.0	100.0	100.0	100.0	100.0	100.0	100.0	100.0	100.0	100.0	100.0	100.0	100.0	100.0	100.0	100.0	100.0	100.0	100.0
Mean age	42.9	43.1	43.2	43.3	43.4	43.5	43.5	43.6	43.7	43.8	43.8	43.9	43.9	44.0	44.0	44.1	44.1	44.2	44.2	44.3
Median age	42.3	42.5	42.6	42.7	42.8	42.9	43.0	43.0	43.0	43.0	43.0	42.9	42.9	42.9	42.8	42.9	42.9	43.0	43.0	43.1

15.3b Population projections by the Office for National Statistics
United Kingdom, PERSONS, thousands

2014-based
Principal projection

Projected populations at mid-years by age last birthday

Ages	2054	2055	2056	2057	2058	2059	2060	2061	2062	2063	2064	2065	2066	2067	2068	2069	2070	2071	2072	2073
Thousands																				
0-14	13,082	13,120	13,153	13,182	13,206	13,227	13,244	13,259	13,273	13,286	13,299	13,313	13,327	13,344	13,362	13,382	13,405	13,431	13,458	13,489
15-29	13,547	13,566	13,594	13,629	13,670	13,718	13,770	13,826	13,885	13,944	14,004	14,061	14,117	14,169	14,217	14,260	14,298	14,331	14,360	14,384
30-44	14,398	14,416	14,413	14,394	14,397	14,417	14,441	14,456	14,466	14,471	14,473	14,474	14,476	14,480	14,487	14,500	14,520	14,549	14,584	14,627
45-59	13,046	13,098	13,169	13,254	13,336	13,407	13,495	13,607	13,740	13,867	13,977	14,076	14,147	14,202	14,230	14,262	14,282	14,282	14,266	14,272
60-74	12,658	12,690	12,721	12,756	12,769	12,779	12,747	12,698	12,634	12,560	12,511	12,462	12,420	12,407	12,441	12,470	12,530	12,608	12,700	12,788
75 & over	11,780	11,875	11,967	12,052	12,135	12,211	12,307	12,403	12,497	12,614	12,728	12,858	13,012	13,157	13,283	13,412	13,521	13,629	13,738	13,828
All ages	78,510	78,765	79,016	79,266	79,513	79,759	80,004	80,249	80,495	80,743	80,992	81,244	81,499	81,758	82,020	82,287	82,557	82,830	83,107	83,387
Percentages																				
0-14	16.7	16.7	16.6	16.6	16.6	16.6	16.6	16.5	16.5	16.5	16.4	16.4	16.4	16.3	16.3	16.3	16.2	16.2	16.2	16.2
15-29	17.3	17.2	17.2	17.2	17.2	17.2	17.2	17.2	17.2	17.3	17.3	17.3	17.3	17.3	17.3	17.3	17.3	17.3	17.3	17.3
30-44	18.3	18.3	18.2	18.2	18.1	18.1	18.0	18.0	18.0	17.9	17.9	17.8	17.8	17.7	17.7	17.6	17.6	17.6	17.5	17.5
45-59	16.6	16.6	16.7	16.7	16.8	16.8	16.9	17.0	17.1	17.2	17.3	17.3	17.4	17.4	17.3	17.3	17.3	17.2	17.2	17.1
60-74	16.1	16.1	16.1	16.1	16.1	16.0	15.9	15.8	15.7	15.6	15.4	15.3	15.2	15.2	15.2	15.2	15.2	15.2	15.3	15.3
75 & over	15.0	15.1	15.1	15.2	15.3	15.3	15.4	15.5	15.5	15.6	15.7	15.8	16.0	16.1	16.2	16.3	16.4	16.5	16.5	16.6
All ages	100.0	100.0	100.0	100.0	100.0	100.0	100.0	100.0	100.0	100.0	100.0	100.0	100.0	100.0	100.0	100.0	100.0	100.0	100.0	100.0
Mean age	44.3	44.4	44.4	44.4	44.5	44.5	44.5	44.6	44.6	44.7	44.7	44.7	44.8	44.8	44.9	44.9	45.0	45.0	45.1	45.1
Median age	43.1	43.2	43.3	43.3	43.4	43.4	43.5	43.5	43.6	43.6	43.7	43.7	43.8	43.8	43.9	44.0	44.0	44.1	44.1	44.2

Ages	2074	2075	2076	2077	2078	2079	2080	2081	2082	2083	2084	2085	2086	2087	2088	2089	2090	2091	2092	2093
Thousands																				
0-14	13,522	13,557	13,594	13,633	13,673	13,714	13,755	13,795	13,836	13,875	13,912	13,948	13,982	14,014	14,043	14,071	14,097	14,121	14,144	14,166
15-29	14,405	14,423	14,438	14,452	14,465	14,479	14,492	14,507	14,524	14,542	14,563	14,586	14,611	14,639	14,670	14,703	14,738	14,775	14,814	14,854
30-44	14,675	14,728	14,785	14,844	14,903	14,963	15,022	15,078	15,130	15,178	15,222	15,261	15,295	15,324	15,349	15,370	15,388	15,404	15,419	15,433
45-59	14,294	14,319	14,337	14,349	14,356	14,360	14,363	14,367	14,373	14,383	14,398	14,421	14,451	14,488	14,532	14,582	14,639	14,695	14,755	14,816
60-74	12,864	12,955	13,068	13,201	13,327	13,437	13,537	13,611	13,670	13,705	13,742	13,768	13,776	13,769	13,781	13,809	13,839	13,862	13,880	13,893
75 & over	13,910	13,973	14,019	14,051	14,092	14,153	14,225	14,324	14,438	14,576	14,709	14,850	15,006	15,174	15,320	15,449	15,573	15,705	15,841	15,984
All ages	83,670	83,955	84,241	84,529	84,817	85,105	85,394	85,683	85,971	86,259	86,546	86,833	87,121	87,408	87,696	87,984	88,273	88,563	88,854	89,146
Percentages																				
0-14	16.2	16.1	16.1	16.1	16.1	16.1	16.1	16.1	16.1	16.1	16.1	16.1	16.0	16.0	16.0	16.0	16.0	15.9	15.9	15.9
15-29	17.2	17.2	17.1	17.1	17.1	17.0	17.0	16.9	16.9	16.9	16.8	16.8	16.8	16.7	16.7	16.7	16.7	16.7	16.7	16.7
30-44	17.5	17.5	17.6	17.6	17.6	17.6	17.6	17.6	17.6	17.6	17.6	17.6	17.6	17.5	17.5	17.5	17.4	17.4	17.4	17.3
45-59	17.1	17.1	17.0	17.0	16.9	16.9	16.8	16.8	16.7	16.7	16.6	16.6	16.6	16.6	16.6	16.6	16.6	16.6	16.6	16.6
60-74	15.4	15.4	15.5	15.6	15.7	15.8	15.9	15.9	15.9	15.9	15.9	15.9	15.8	15.7	15.7	15.7	15.7	15.7	15.6	15.6
75 & over	16.6	16.6	16.6	16.6	16.6	16.6	16.7	16.7	16.8	16.9	17.0	17.1	17.2	17.4	17.5	17.6	17.6	17.7	17.8	17.9
All ages	100.0	100.0	100.0	100.0	100.0	100.0	100.0	100.0	100.0	100.0	100.0	100.0	100.0	100.0	100.0	100.0	100.0	100.0	100.0	100.0
Mean age	45.2	45.2	45.3	45.3	45.3	45.4	45.4	45.5	45.5	45.6	45.6	45.7	45.7	45.8	45.8	45.9	45.9	46.0	46.1	46.1
Median age	44.2	44.2	44.3	44.3	44.3	44.4	44.4	44.4	44.5	44.5	44.6	44.6	44.7	44.7	44.8	44.8	44.9	45.0	45.0	45.1

15.3b Population projections by the Office for National Statistics
United Kingdom, PERSONS, thousands

2014-based
Principal projection

Projected populations at mid-years by age last birthday

Ages	2094	2095	2096	2097	2098	2099	2100	2101	2102	2103	2104	2105	2106	2107	2108	2109	2110	2111	2112	2113	2114
Thousands																					
0-14	14,187	14,207	14,228	14,249	14,270	14,292	14,315	14,339	14,364	14,390	14,418	14,447	14,477	14,508	14,539	14,571	14,604	14,637	14,669	14,702	14,734
15-29	14,895	14,937	14,978	15,018	15,057	15,095	15,131	15,165	15,196	15,226	15,254	15,280	15,305	15,328	15,349	15,371	15,391	15,412	15,433	15,454	15,476
30-44	15,447	15,461	15,476	15,493	15,512	15,534	15,557	15,583	15,612	15,643	15,676	15,712	15,750	15,789	15,830	15,871	15,913	15,954	15,995	16,034	16,072
45-59	14,877	14,937	14,994	15,048	15,098	15,143	15,183	15,218	15,249	15,275	15,298	15,318	15,335	15,352	15,367	15,382	15,398	15,415	15,434	15,454	15,477
60-74	13,903	13,913	13,923	13,936	13,952	13,973	14,001	14,037	14,080	14,129	14,183	14,242	14,304	14,369	14,434	14,498	14,562	14,622	14,680	14,733	14,782
75 & over	16,130	16,280	16,432	16,585	16,739	16,891	17,041	17,187	17,329	17,467	17,602	17,734	17,862	17,988	18,112	18,236	18,359	18,483	18,608	18,736	18,867
All ages	89,440	89,735	90,031	90,329	90,628	90,927	91,228	91,528	91,830	92,131	92,432	92,733	93,033	93,332	93,631	93,929	94,226	94,523	94,818	95,113	95,408
Percentages																					
0-14	15.9	15.8	15.8	15.8	15.7	15.7	15.7	15.7	15.6	15.6	15.6	15.6	15.6	15.5	15.5	15.5	15.5	15.5	15.5	15.5	15.4
15-29	16.7	16.6	16.6	16.6	16.6	16.6	16.6	16.6	16.5	16.5	16.5	16.5	16.5	16.4	16.4	16.4	16.3	16.3	16.3	16.2	16.2
30-44	17.3	17.2	17.2	17.2	17.1	17.1	17.1	17.0	17.0	17.0	17.0	16.9	16.9	16.9	16.9	16.9	16.9	16.9	16.9	16.9	16.8
45-59	16.6	16.6	16.7	16.7	16.7	16.7	16.6	16.6	16.6	16.6	16.6	16.5	16.5	16.4	16.4	16.4	16.3	16.3	16.3	16.2	16.2
60-74	15.5	15.5	15.5	15.4	15.4	15.4	15.3	15.3	15.3	15.3	15.3	15.4	15.4	15.4	15.4	15.4	15.5	15.5	15.5	15.5	15.5
75 & over	18.0	18.1	18.3	18.4	18.5	18.6	18.7	18.8	18.9	19.0	19.0	19.1	19.2	19.3	19.3	19.4	19.5	19.6	19.6	19.7	19.8
All ages	100.0	100.0	100.0	100.0	100.0	100.0	100.0	100.0	100.0	100.0	100.0	100.0	100.0	100.0	100.0	100.0	100.0	100.0	100.0	100.0	100.0
Mean age	46.2	46.2	46.3	46.3	46.4	46.5	46.5	46.6	46.7	46.7	46.8	46.8	46.9	46.9	47.0	47.1	47.1	47.2	47.2	47.3	47.3
Median age	45.2	45.3	45.3	45.4	45.5	45.5	45.6	45.7	45.7	45.8	45.8	45.9	46.0	46.0	46.1	46.1	46.2	46.2	46.3	46.3	46.4

Source: Office for National Statistics

Note: Figures may not add exactly due to rounding.
* Children under 16. Working age and pensionable age populations based on state pension age (SPA) for given year.
Between 2012 and 2018, SPA will change from 65 years for men and 61 years for women, to 65 years for both sexes.
Then between 2019 and 2020, SPA will change from 65 years to 66 years for both men and women.
Between 2026 and 2027 SPA will increase to 67 years and between 2044 and 2046 to 68 years for both sexes. This is based on SPA under the 2014 Pensions Act.
** This is consistent with the age-group definitions used in ONS Labour Market Statistics.

National Population Projections are currently produced every two years. The 2016-based projections are not due to be published until November/December 2017. Therefore, this table series will be updated in the next edition

15.3b Population projections by the Office for National Statistics
United Kingdom, MALES, thousands

2014-based
Principal projection

Projected populations at mid-years by age last birthday

Ages	2014	2015	2016	2017	2018	2019	2020	2021	2022	2023	2024	2025	2026	2027	2028	2029	2030	2031	2032	2033
Thousands																				
0-14	5,841	5,893	5,956	6,028	6,097	6,155	6,206	6,242	6,270	6,284	6,299	6,309	6,307	6,297	6,297	6,307	6,318	6,326	6,330	6,332
15-29	6,369	6,405	6,406	6,398	6,376	6,359	6,332	6,304	6,296	6,308	6,314	6,339	6,372	6,414	6,456	6,492	6,536	6,595	6,664	6,730
30-44	6,323	6,332	6,328	6,328	6,364	6,419	6,494	6,588	6,679	6,759	6,815	6,842	6,871	6,902	6,921	6,938	6,931	6,911	6,889	6,856
45-59	6,403	6,478	6,549	6,595	6,610	6,597	6,571	6,521	6,454	6,384	6,336	6,301	6,271	6,234	6,208	6,181	6,178	6,169	6,168	6,201
60-74	4,700	4,762	4,851	4,931	5,000	5,060	5,131	5,210	5,227	5,281	5,361	5,454	5,549	5,650	5,735	5,817	5,888	5,958	6,005	6,024
75 & over	2,159	2,202	2,244	2,303	2,385	2,481	2,571	2,665	2,832	2,965	3,077	3,175	3,262	3,342	3,425	3,506	3,581	3,663	3,750	3,843
All ages	31,794	32,073	32,334	32,584	32,832	33,071	33,304	33,531	33,757	33,981	34,202	34,419	34,632	34,839	35,042	35,240	35,433	35,622	35,806	35,985
Percentages																				
0-14	18.4	18.4	18.4	18.5	18.6	18.6	18.6	18.6	18.6	18.5	18.4	18.3	18.2	18.1	18.0	17.9	17.8	17.8	17.7	17.6
15-29	20.0	20.0	19.8	19.6	19.4	19.2	19.0	18.8	18.6	18.6	18.5	18.4	18.4	18.4	18.4	18.4	18.4	18.5	18.6	18.7
30-44	19.9	19.7	19.6	19.4	19.4	19.4	19.5	19.6	19.8	19.9	19.9	19.9	19.8	19.8	19.8	19.7	19.6	19.4	19.2	19.1
45-59	20.1	20.2	20.3	20.2	20.1	19.9	19.7	19.4	19.1	18.8	18.5	18.3	18.1	17.9	17.7	17.5	17.4	17.3	17.2	17.2
60-74	14.8	14.8	15.0	15.1	15.2	15.3	15.4	15.5	15.5	15.5	15.7	15.8	16.0	16.2	16.4	16.5	16.6	16.7	16.8	16.7
75 & over	6.8	6.9	6.9	7.1	7.3	7.5	7.7	7.9	8.4	8.7	9.0	9.2	9.4	9.6	9.8	9.9	10.1	10.3	10.5	10.7
All ages	100.0	100.0	100.0	100.0	100.0	100.0	100.0	100.0	100.0	100.0	100.0	100.0	100.0	100.0	100.0	100.0	100.0	100.0	100.0	100.0
Mean age	39.3	39.4	39.5	39.6	39.8	39.9	40.1	40.2	40.3	40.5	40.6	40.8	40.9	41.0	41.2	41.3	41.5	41.6	41.7	41.8
Median age	38.8	38.8	38.8	38.8	38.9	39.0	39.2	39.3	39.4	39.5	39.6	39.7	39.9	40.0	40.1	40.3	40.4	40.6	40.8	40.9

Ages	2034	2035	2036	2037	2038	2039	2040	2041	2042	2043	2044	2045	2046	2047	2048	2049	2050	2051	2052	2053
Thousands																				
0-14	6,333	6,333	6,333	6,335	6,338	6,344	6,354	6,368	6,386	6,407	6,431	6,458	6,487	6,517	6,547	6,577	6,607	6,635	6,662	6,686
15-29	6,787	6,838	6,874	6,902	6,916	6,932	6,941	6,940	6,930	6,931	6,940	6,952	6,960	6,964	6,966	6,967	6,967	6,968	6,969	6,973
30-44	6,833	6,804	6,778	6,771	6,784	6,792	6,817	6,851	6,894	6,936	6,973	7,018	7,077	7,146	7,212	7,269	7,320	7,357	7,385	7,399
45-59	6,255	6,328	6,422	6,513	6,592	6,649	6,677	6,708	6,740	6,760	6,778	6,772	6,755	6,734	6,704	6,683	6,657	6,633	6,629	6,644
60-74	6,017	5,997	5,957	5,901	5,845	5,808	5,786	5,766	5,742	5,727	5,710	5,716	5,717	5,723	5,762	5,818	5,892	5,985	6,073	6,150
75 & over	3,938	4,034	4,139	4,250	4,362	4,476	4,589	4,693	4,795	4,886	4,973	5,048	5,127	5,193	5,241	5,271	5,293	5,307	5,315	5,326
All ages	36,161	36,334	36,504	36,672	36,837	37,001	37,164	37,326	37,487	37,647	37,806	37,964	38,122	38,277	38,432	38,585	38,736	38,885	39,033	39,179
Percentages																				
0-14	17.5	17.4	17.3	17.3	17.2	17.1	17.1	17.1	17.0	17.0	17.0	17.0	17.0	17.0	17.0	17.0	17.1	17.1	17.1	17.1
15-29	18.8	18.8	18.8	18.8	18.8	18.7	18.7	18.6	18.5	18.4	18.4	18.3	18.3	18.2	18.1	18.1	18.0	17.9	17.9	17.8
30-44	18.9	18.7	18.6	18.5	18.4	18.4	18.3	18.4	18.4	18.4	18.4	18.5	18.6	18.7	18.8	18.8	18.9	18.9	18.9	18.9
45-59	17.3	17.4	17.6	17.8	17.9	18.0	18.0	18.0	18.0	18.0	17.9	17.8	17.7	17.6	17.4	17.3	17.2	17.1	17.0	17.0
60-74	16.6	16.5	16.3	16.1	15.9	15.7	15.6	15.4	15.3	15.2	15.1	15.1	15.0	15.0	15.0	15.1	15.2	15.4	15.6	15.7
75 & over	10.9	11.1	11.3	11.6	11.8	12.1	12.3	12.6	12.8	13.0	13.2	13.3	13.4	13.6	13.6	13.7	13.7	13.6	13.6	13.6
All ages	100.0	100.0	100.0	100.0	100.0	100.0	100.0	100.0	100.0	100.0	100.0	100.0	100.0	100.0	100.0	100.0	100.0	100.0	100.0	100.0
Mean age	42.0	42.1	42.2	42.3	42.4	42.5	42.6	42.6	42.7	42.8	42.8	42.9	43.0	43.0	43.1	43.1	43.2	43.2	43.3	43.3
Median age	41.1	41.2	41.3	41.4	41.5	41.6	41.6	41.7	41.7	41.6	41.6	41.6	41.6	41.6	41.6	41.7	41.8	41.8	41.9	42.0

15.3b Population projections by the Office for National Statistics
United Kingdom, MALES, thousands

2014-based
Principal projection

Projected populations at mid-years by age last birthday

Ages	2054	2055	2056	2057	2058	2059	2060	2061	2062	2063	2064	2065	2066	2067	2068	2069	2070	2071	2072	2073
Thousands																				
0-14	6,708	6,728	6,745	6,759	6,772	6,782	6,791	6,799	6,806	6,813	6,820	6,827	6,834	6,843	6,852	6,862	6,874	6,887	6,901	6,917
15-29	6,979	6,989	7,003	7,021	7,043	7,067	7,094	7,123	7,153	7,183	7,214	7,243	7,272	7,298	7,323	7,345	7,365	7,382	7,397	7,409
30-44	7,416	7,426	7,425	7,416	7,417	7,427	7,439	7,448	7,453	7,455	7,457	7,457	7,459	7,461	7,465	7,472	7,482	7,497	7,515	7,537
45-59	6,654	6,681	6,716	6,761	6,804	6,842	6,888	6,947	7,016	7,082	7,139	7,191	7,228	7,257	7,273	7,291	7,302	7,303	7,296	7,299
60-74	6,208	6,240	6,273	6,308	6,330	6,351	6,349	6,335	6,319	6,294	6,279	6,260	6,244	6,246	6,267	6,283	6,315	6,355	6,403	6,450
75 & over	5,358	5,403	5,446	5,485	5,524	5,561	5,609	5,659	5,704	5,765	5,827	5,901	5,987	6,065	6,139	6,215	6,282	6,349	6,415	6,471
All ages	39,324	39,467	39,609	39,750	39,891	40,031	40,171	40,311	40,451	40,593	40,735	40,879	41,024	41,170	41,319	41,468	41,620	41,773	41,927	42,083
Percentages																				
0-14	17.1	17.0	17.0	17.0	17.0	16.9	16.9	16.9	16.8	16.8	16.7	16.7	16.7	16.6	16.6	16.5	16.5	16.5	16.5	16.4
15-29	17.7	17.7	17.7	17.7	17.7	17.7	17.7	17.7	17.7	17.7	17.7	17.7	17.7	17.7	17.7	17.7	17.7	17.7	17.6	17.6
30-44	18.9	18.8	18.7	18.7	18.6	18.6	18.5	18.5	18.4	18.4	18.3	18.2	18.2	18.1	18.1	18.0	18.0	17.9	17.9	17.9
45-59	16.9	16.9	17.0	17.0	17.1	17.1	17.1	17.2	17.3	17.4	17.5	17.6	17.6	17.6	17.6	17.6	17.5	17.5	17.4	17.3
60-74	15.8	15.8	15.8	15.9	15.9	15.9	15.8	15.7	15.6	15.5	15.4	15.3	15.2	15.2	15.2	15.2	15.2	15.2	15.3	15.3
75 & over	13.6	13.7	13.7	13.8	13.8	13.9	14.0	14.0	14.1	14.2	14.3	14.4	14.6	14.7	14.9	15.0	15.1	15.2	15.3	15.4
All ages	100.0	100.0	100.0	100.0	100.0	100.0	100.0	100.0	100.0	100.0	100.0	100.0	100.0	100.0	100.0	100.0	100.0	100.0	100.0	100.0
Mean age	43.4	43.4	43.4	43.5	43.5	43.6	43.6	43.7	43.7	43.8	43.8	43.9	43.9	44.0	44.1	44.1	44.2	44.2	44.3	44.4
Median age	42.1	42.2	42.2	42.3	42.3	42.4	42.4	42.5	42.6	42.7	42.7	42.8	42.9	43.0	43.0	43.1	43.2	43.2	43.3	43.3

Ages	2074	2075	2076	2077	2078	2079	2080	2081	2082	2083	2084	2085	2086	2087	2088	2089	2090	2091	2092	2093
Thousands																				
0-14	6,934	6,952	6,971	6,991	7,011	7,032	7,053	7,074	7,095	7,115	7,134	7,152	7,170	7,186	7,201	7,215	7,229	7,241	7,253	7,264
15-29	7,420	7,429	7,437	7,444	7,451	7,458	7,465	7,472	7,481	7,490	7,501	7,513	7,526	7,540	7,556	7,573	7,591	7,610	7,630	7,650
30-44	7,562	7,589	7,618	7,648	7,679	7,710	7,740	7,769	7,796	7,820	7,843	7,863	7,880	7,895	7,908	7,919	7,929	7,937	7,945	7,952
45-59	7,310	7,323	7,333	7,339	7,343	7,346	7,348	7,350	7,354	7,359	7,368	7,379	7,395	7,415	7,438	7,463	7,492	7,522	7,553	7,584
60-74	6,491	6,538	6,598	6,666	6,732	6,789	6,841	6,880	6,912	6,931	6,952	6,967	6,973	6,970	6,977	6,992	7,008	7,021	7,031	7,038
75 & over	6,523	6,565	6,597	6,623	6,653	6,692	6,736	6,794	6,859	6,935	7,009	7,086	7,171	7,261	7,340	7,411	7,478	7,549	7,622	7,697
All ages	42,239	42,396	42,554	42,711	42,869	43,026	43,183	43,340	43,496	43,651	43,806	43,960	44,114	44,267	44,421	44,574	44,726	44,879	45,033	45,186
Percentages																				
0-14	16.4	16.4	16.4	16.4	16.4	16.3	16.3	16.3	16.3	16.3	16.3	16.3	16.3	16.2	16.2	16.2	16.2	16.1	16.1	16.1
15-29	17.6	17.5	17.5	17.4	17.4	17.3	17.3	17.2	17.2	17.2	17.1	17.1	17.1	17.0	17.0	17.0	17.0	17.0	16.9	16.9
30-44	17.9	17.9	17.9	17.9	17.9	17.9	17.9	17.9	17.9	17.9	17.9	17.9	17.9	17.8	17.8	17.8	17.7	17.7	17.6	17.6
45-59	17.3	17.3	17.2	17.2	17.1	17.1	17.0	17.0	16.9	16.9	16.8	16.8	16.8	16.7	16.7	16.7	16.7	16.8	16.8	16.8
60-74	15.4	15.4	15.5	15.6	15.7	15.8	15.8	15.9	15.9	15.9	15.9	15.8	15.8	15.7	15.7	15.7	15.7	15.6	15.6	15.6
75 & over	15.4	15.5	15.5	15.5	15.5	15.6	15.6	15.7	15.8	15.9	16.0	16.1	16.3	16.4	16.5	16.6	16.7	16.8	16.9	17.0
All ages	100.0	100.0	100.0	100.0	100.0	100.0	100.0	100.0	100.0	100.0	100.0	100.0	100.0	100.0	100.0	100.0	100.0	100.0	100.0	100.0
Mean age	44.4	44.5	44.5	44.6	44.7	44.7	44.8	44.8	44.9	44.9	45.0	45.1	45.1	45.2	45.2	45.3	45.4	45.4	45.5	45.5
Median age	43.4	43.4	43.5	43.5	43.6	43.6	43.7	43.7	43.8	43.8	43.9	43.9	44.0	44.1	44.1	44.2	44.3	44.3	44.4	44.5

15.3b Population projections by the Office for National Statistics
United Kingdom, MALES, thousands

2014-based
Principal projection

Projected populations at mid-years by age last birthday

Ages	2094	2095	2096	2097	2098	2099	2100	2101	2102	2103	2104	2105	2106	2107	2108	2109	2110	2111	2112	2113	2114
Thousands																					
0-14	7,275	7,285	7,296	7,307	7,317	7,329	7,340	7,353	7,366	7,379	7,393	7,408	7,423	7,439	7,455	7,472	7,489	7,505	7,522	7,539	7,555
15-29	7,671	7,693	7,714	7,734	7,754	7,774	7,792	7,810	7,826	7,841	7,856	7,869	7,881	7,893	7,904	7,915	7,926	7,937	7,947	7,958	7,970
30-44	7,959	7,967	7,975	7,984	7,993	8,004	8,016	8,030	8,045	8,061	8,078	8,096	8,116	8,136	8,157	8,178	8,199	8,221	8,242	8,262	8,282
45-59	7,616	7,647	7,676	7,704	7,730	7,753	7,774	7,792	7,808	7,822	7,834	7,844	7,854	7,862	7,871	7,879	7,887	7,896	7,906	7,917	7,929
60-74	7,044	7,050	7,057	7,064	7,073	7,085	7,100	7,119	7,142	7,168	7,196	7,227	7,259	7,293	7,327	7,360	7,393	7,425	7,455	7,482	7,508
75 & over	7,774	7,852	7,931	8,010	8,090	8,168	8,245	8,320	8,393	8,463	8,532	8,599	8,665	8,729	8,792	8,855	8,917	8,980	9,044	9,110	9,176
All ages	45,340	45,494	45,648	45,803	45,957	46,113	46,268	46,423	46,579	46,734	46,889	47,044	47,198	47,352	47,506	47,659	47,812	47,964	48,116	48,268	48,419
Percentages																					
0-14	16.0	16.0	16.0	16.0	15.9	15.9	15.9	15.8	15.8	15.8	15.8	15.7	15.7	15.7	15.7	15.7	15.7	15.6	15.6	15.6	15.6
15-29	16.9	16.9	16.9	16.9	16.9	16.9	16.8	16.8	16.8	16.8	16.8	16.7	16.7	16.7	16.6	16.6	16.6	16.5	16.5	16.5	16.5
30-44	17.6	17.5	17.5	17.4	17.4	17.4	17.3	17.3	17.3	17.2	17.2	17.2	17.2	17.2	17.2	17.2	17.1	17.1	17.1	17.1	17.1
45-59	16.8	16.8	16.8	16.8	16.8	16.8	16.8	16.8	16.8	16.7	16.7	16.7	16.6	16.6	16.6	16.5	16.5	16.5	16.4	16.4	16.4
60-74	15.5	15.5	15.5	15.4	15.4	15.4	15.3	15.3	15.3	15.3	15.3	15.4	15.4	15.4	15.4	15.4	15.5	15.5	15.5	15.5	15.5
75 & over	17.1	17.3	17.4	17.5	17.6	17.7	17.8	17.9	18.0	18.1	18.2	18.3	18.4	18.4	18.5	18.6	18.7	18.7	18.8	18.9	19.0
All ages	100.0	100.0	100.0	100.0	100.0	100.0	100.0	100.0	100.0	100.0	100.0	100.0	100.0	100.0	100.0	100.0	100.0	100.0	100.0	100.0	100.0
Mean age	45.6	45.7	45.7	45.8	45.9	45.9	46.0	46.0	46.1	46.2	46.2	46.3	46.4	46.4	46.5	46.5	46.6	46.6	46.7	46.8	46.8
Median age	44.6	44.6	44.7	44.8	44.8	44.9	45.0	45.0	45.1	45.2	45.2	45.3	45.3	45.4	45.4	45.5	45.5	45.6	45.6	45.7	45.8

Source: Office for National Statistics

Note: Figures may not add exactly due to rounding.
* Children under 16. Working age and pensionable age populations based on state pension age (SPA) for given year.
Between 2012 and 2018, SPA will change from 65 years for men and 61 years for women, to 65 years for both sexes.
Then between 2019 and 2020, SPA will change from 65 years to 66 years for both men and women.
Between 2026 and 2027 SPA will increase to 67 years and between 2044 and 2046 to 68 years for both sexes. This is based on SPA under the 2014 Pensions Act.
** This is consistent with the age-group definitions used in ONS Labour Market Statistics.

National Population Projections are currently produced every two years. The 2016-based projections are not due to be published until November/December 2017. Therefore, this table series will be updated in the next edition

471

15.3b Population projections by the Office for National Statistics
United Kingdom, FEMALES, thousands

2014-based
Principal projection

Projected populations at mid-years by age last birthday

Ages	2014	2015	2016	2017	2018	2019	2020	2021	2022	2023	2024	2025	2026	2027	2028	2029	2030	2031	2032	2033
Thousands																				
0-14	5,567	5,616	5,673	5,740	5,804	5,857	5,905	5,937	5,963	5,974	5,987	5,994	5,991	5,981	5,983	5,992	6,003	6,010	6,015	6,016
15-29	6,188	6,190	6,164	6,121	6,073	6,037	6,002	5,968	5,944	5,950	5,957	5,980	6,014	6,054	6,091	6,123	6,165	6,217	6,282	6,343
30-44	6,418	6,419	6,403	6,406	6,437	6,479	6,531	6,603	6,682	6,739	6,766	6,762	6,753	6,749	6,735	6,720	6,685	6,642	6,588	6,531
45-59	6,571	6,657	6,741	6,794	6,816	6,810	6,790	6,744	6,676	6,604	6,551	6,513	6,480	6,449	6,422	6,392	6,384	6,365	6,367	6,395
60-74	5,007	5,072	5,162	5,244	5,314	5,378	5,452	5,536	5,551	5,608	5,696	5,798	5,904	6,010	6,105	6,196	6,278	6,359	6,412	6,434
75 & over	3,053	3,072	3,096	3,141	3,211	3,295	3,376	3,463	3,631	3,766	3,878	3,979	4,069	4,152	4,238	4,325	4,405	4,491	4,585	4,685
All ages	32,803	33,024	33,239	33,446	33,654	33,857	34,056	34,251	34,446	34,641	34,834	35,025	35,212	35,395	35,574	35,749	35,920	36,086	36,248	36,405
Percentages																				
0-14	17.0	17.0	17.1	17.2	17.2	17.3	17.3	17.3	17.3	17.2	17.2	17.1	17.0	16.9	16.8	16.8	16.7	16.7	16.6	16.5
15-29	18.9	18.7	18.5	18.3	18.0	17.8	17.6	17.4	17.3	17.2	17.1	17.1	17.1	17.1	17.1	17.1	17.2	17.2	17.3	17.4
30-44	19.6	19.4	19.3	19.2	19.1	19.1	19.2	19.3	19.4	19.5	19.4	19.3	19.2	19.1	18.9	18.8	18.6	18.4	18.2	17.9
45-59	20.0	20.2	20.3	20.3	20.3	20.1	19.9	19.7	19.4	19.1	18.8	18.6	18.4	18.2	18.1	17.9	17.8	17.6	17.6	17.6
60-74	15.3	15.4	15.5	15.7	15.8	15.9	16.0	16.2	16.1	16.2	16.4	16.6	16.8	17.0	17.2	17.3	17.5	17.6	17.7	17.7
75 & over	9.3	9.3	9.3	9.4	9.5	9.7	9.9	10.1	10.5	10.9	11.1	11.4	11.6	11.7	11.9	12.1	12.3	12.4	12.6	12.9
All ages	100.0	100.0	100.0	100.0	100.0	100.0	100.0	100.0	100.0	100.0	100.0	100.0	100.0	100.0	100.0	100.0	100.0	100.0	100.0	100.0
Mean age	41.3	41.3	41.5	41.6	41.7	41.8	42.0	42.1	42.2	42.4	42.5	42.7	42.8	42.9	43.1	43.2	43.4	43.5	43.6	43.8
Median age	41.1	41.1	41.2	41.3	41.3	41.4	41.5	41.6	41.8	41.9	42.1	42.2	42.4	42.5	42.7	42.9	43.0	43.2	43.3	43.5

Ages	2034	2035	2036	2037	2038	2039	2040	2041	2042	2043	2044	2045	2046	2047	2048	2049	2050	2051	2052	2053
Thousands																				
0-14	6,017	6,017	6,017	6,018	6,021	6,027	6,037	6,050	6,067	6,087	6,110	6,136	6,163	6,191	6,220	6,249	6,277	6,304	6,330	6,353
15-29	6,396	6,443	6,475	6,501	6,512	6,525	6,532	6,530	6,520	6,522	6,531	6,542	6,550	6,554	6,556	6,556	6,556	6,557	6,558	6,561
30-44	6,490	6,454	6,420	6,397	6,404	6,411	6,434	6,469	6,509	6,546	6,579	6,621	6,673	6,738	6,799	6,852	6,899	6,931	6,957	6,969
45-59	6,436	6,488	6,561	6,639	6,696	6,724	6,721	6,714	6,711	6,698	6,684	6,650	6,610	6,557	6,502	6,463	6,428	6,396	6,375	6,384
60-74	6,431	6,414	6,375	6,314	6,251	6,207	6,178	6,154	6,131	6,112	6,090	6,089	6,078	6,086	6,118	6,161	6,215	6,287	6,364	6,420
75 & over	4,789	4,894	5,009	5,132	5,259	5,389	5,519	5,640	5,755	5,862	5,964	6,052	6,147	6,223	6,279	6,317	6,346	6,365	6,374	6,387
All ages	36,559	36,710	36,857	37,001	37,143	37,283	37,421	37,558	37,693	37,827	37,960	38,091	38,221	38,349	38,475	38,599	38,721	38,841	38,958	39,074
Percentages																				
0-14	16.5	16.4	16.3	16.3	16.2	16.2	16.1	16.1	16.1	16.1	16.1	16.1	16.1	16.1	16.2	16.2	16.2	16.2	16.2	16.3
15-29	17.5	17.6	17.6	17.6	17.5	17.5	17.5	17.4	17.3	17.2	17.2	17.2	17.1	17.1	17.0	17.0	16.9	16.9	16.8	16.8
30-44	17.8	17.6	17.4	17.3	17.2	17.2	17.2	17.2	17.3	17.3	17.3	17.4	17.5	17.6	17.7	17.8	17.8	17.8	17.9	17.8
45-59	17.6	17.7	17.8	17.9	18.0	18.0	18.0	17.9	17.8	17.7	17.6	17.5	17.3	17.1	16.9	16.7	16.6	16.5	16.4	16.3
60-74	17.6	17.5	17.3	17.1	16.8	16.6	16.5	16.4	16.3	16.2	16.0	16.0	15.9	15.9	15.9	16.0	16.0	16.2	16.3	16.4
75 & over	13.1	13.3	13.6	13.9	14.2	14.5	14.7	15.0	15.3	15.5	15.7	15.9	16.1	16.2	16.3	16.4	16.4	16.4	16.4	16.3
All ages	100.0	100.0	100.0	100.0	100.0	100.0	100.0	100.0	100.0	100.0	100.0	100.0	100.0	100.0	100.0	100.0	100.0	100.0	100.0	100.0
Mean age	43.9	44.0	44.1	44.2	44.3	44.4	44.5	44.6	44.7	44.7	44.8	44.9	44.9	45.0	45.0	45.1	45.1	45.2	45.2	45.2
Median age	43.6	43.8	44.0	44.1	44.2	44.3	44.3	44.4	44.4	44.4	44.4	44.4	44.3	44.2	44.2	44.2	44.1	44.2	44.2	44.2

15.3b Population projections by the Office for National Statistics
United Kingdom, FEMALES, thousands

2014-based
Principal projection

Projected populations at mid-years by age last birthday

Ages	2054	2055	2056	2057	2058	2059	2060	2061	2062	2063	2064	2065	2066	2067	2068	2069	2070	2071	2072	2073
Thousands																				
0-14	6,374	6,392	6,408	6,422	6,434	6,444	6,453	6,460	6,467	6,473	6,479	6,486	6,493	6,501	6,510	6,520	6,531	6,543	6,557	6,572
15-29	6,567	6,577	6,590	6,607	6,628	6,651	6,676	6,704	6,732	6,761	6,790	6,818	6,845	6,870	6,894	6,915	6,933	6,950	6,964	6,975
30-44	6,982	6,990	6,988	6,978	6,980	6,990	7,001	7,009	7,013	7,016	7,016	7,017	7,017	7,019	7,022	7,029	7,038	7,052	7,069	7,090
45-59	6,392	6,417	6,452	6,493	6,531	6,565	6,607	6,660	6,724	6,785	6,838	6,885	6,918	6,945	6,957	6,971	6,980	6,979	6,970	6,973
60-74	6,450	6,450	6,447	6,448	6,438	6,428	6,399	6,362	6,315	6,266	6,232	6,202	6,176	6,161	6,174	6,186	6,215	6,254	6,297	6,338
75 & over	6,422	6,472	6,521	6,567	6,611	6,651	6,698	6,744	6,793	6,849	6,902	6,958	7,025	7,091	7,144	7,197	7,239	7,280	7,323	7,357
All ages	39,187	39,298	39,408	39,516	39,622	39,728	39,833	39,939	40,044	40,150	40,257	40,365	40,475	40,588	40,702	40,818	40,937	41,057	41,180	41,305
Percentages																				
0-14	16.3	16.3	16.3	16.3	16.2	16.2	16.2	16.2	16.1	16.1	16.1	16.1	16.0	16.0	16.0	16.0	16.0	15.9	15.9	15.9
15-29	16.8	16.7	16.7	16.7	16.7	16.7	16.8	16.8	16.8	16.8	16.9	16.9	16.9	16.9	16.9	16.9	16.9	16.9	16.9	16.9
30-44	17.8	17.8	17.7	17.7	17.6	17.6	17.6	17.5	17.5	17.5	17.4	17.4	17.3	17.3	17.3	17.2	17.2	17.2	17.2	17.2
45-59	16.3	16.3	16.4	16.4	16.5	16.5	16.6	16.7	16.8	16.9	17.0	17.1	17.1	17.1	17.1	17.1	17.1	17.0	16.9	16.9
60-74	16.5	16.4	16.4	16.3	16.2	16.2	16.1	15.9	15.8	15.6	15.5	15.4	15.3	15.2	15.2	15.2	15.2	15.2	15.3	15.3
75 & over	16.4	16.5	16.5	16.6	16.7	16.7	16.8	16.9	17.0	17.1	17.1	17.2	17.4	17.5	17.6	17.6	17.7	17.7	17.8	17.8
All ages	100.0	100.0	100.0	100.0	100.0	100.0	100.0	100.0	100.0	100.0	100.0	100.0	100.0	100.0	100.0	100.0	100.0	100.0	100.0	100.0
Mean age	45.3	45.3	45.3	45.4	45.4	45.4	45.5	45.5	45.5	45.5	45.6	45.6	45.6	45.7	45.7	45.7	45.8	45.8	45.8	45.9
Median age	44.3	44.3	44.4	44.5	44.5	44.5	44.5	44.6	44.6	44.6	44.7	44.7	44.7	44.8	44.8	44.9	44.9	45.0	45.0	45.0

Ages	2074	2075	2076	2077	2078	2079	2080	2081	2082	2083	2084	2085	2086	2087	2088	2089	2090	2091	2092	2093
Thousands																				
0-14	6,588	6,605	6,623	6,642	6,661	6,681	6,701	6,721	6,741	6,760	6,778	6,796	6,812	6,828	6,842	6,856	6,868	6,880	6,891	6,902
15-29	6,985	6,994	7,002	7,008	7,015	7,021	7,028	7,035	7,043	7,052	7,062	7,073	7,086	7,099	7,114	7,130	7,147	7,165	7,184	7,204
30-44	7,113	7,139	7,166	7,195	7,224	7,253	7,282	7,309	7,334	7,358	7,379	7,398	7,414	7,428	7,441	7,451	7,460	7,467	7,474	7,481
45-59	6,984	6,996	7,004	7,009	7,012	7,014	7,015	7,017	7,019	7,024	7,031	7,041	7,055	7,073	7,095	7,119	7,145	7,173	7,202	7,232
60-74	6,373	6,417	6,470	6,534	6,595	6,648	6,696	6,730	6,758	6,774	6,790	6,801	6,803	6,798	6,804	6,817	6,831	6,842	6,849	6,855
75 & over	7,387	7,408	7,422	7,428	7,440	7,461	7,489	7,530	7,579	7,641	7,700	7,764	7,836	7,913	7,980	8,038	8,095	8,156	8,220	8,287
All ages	41,431	41,559	41,687	41,817	41,948	42,079	42,211	42,343	42,475	42,608	42,740	42,873	43,007	43,141	43,275	43,410	43,546	43,683	43,821	43,960
Percentages																				
0-14	15.9	15.9	15.9	15.9	15.9	15.9	15.9	15.9	15.9	15.9	15.9	15.9	15.8	15.8	15.8	15.8	15.8	15.7	15.7	15.7
15-29	16.9	16.8	16.8	16.8	16.7	16.7	16.6	16.6	16.6	16.6	16.5	16.5	16.5	16.5	16.4	16.4	16.4	16.4	16.4	16.4
30-44	17.2	17.2	17.2	17.2	17.2	17.2	17.3	17.3	17.3	17.3	17.3	17.3	17.2	17.2	17.2	17.2	17.1	17.1	17.1	17.0
45-59	16.9	16.8	16.8	16.8	16.7	16.7	16.6	16.6	16.5	16.5	16.4	16.4	16.4	16.4	16.4	16.4	16.4	16.4	16.4	16.5
60-74	15.4	15.4	15.5	15.6	15.7	15.8	15.9	15.9	15.9	15.9	15.9	15.9	15.8	15.7	15.7	15.7	15.7	15.7	15.6	15.6
75 & over	17.8	17.8	17.8	17.8	17.7	17.7	17.7	17.8	17.8	17.9	18.0	18.1	18.2	18.3	18.4	18.5	18.6	18.7	18.8	18.9
All ages	100.0	100.0	100.0	100.0	100.0	100.0	100.0	100.0	100.0	100.0	100.0	100.0	100.0	100.0	100.0	100.0	100.0	100.0	100.0	100.0
Mean age	45.9	45.9	46.0	46.0	46.1	46.1	46.1	46.2	46.2	46.2	46.3	46.3	46.4	46.4	46.5	46.5	46.5	46.6	46.6	46.7
Median age	45.1	45.1	45.1	45.1	45.2	45.2	45.2	45.2	45.3	45.3	45.3	45.4	45.4	45.4	45.5	45.5	45.6	45.7	45.7	45.8

15.3b Population projections by the Office for National Statistics
United Kingdom, FEMALES, thousands

2014-based
Principal projection

Projected populations at mid-years by age last birthday

Ages	2094	2095	2096	2097	2098	2099	2100	2101	2102	2103	2104	2105	2106	2107	2108	2109	2110	2111	2112	2113	2114
Thousands																					
0-14	6,912	6,922	6,932	6,942	6,953	6,963	6,974	6,986	6,998	7,011	7,025	7,039	7,053	7,068	7,084	7,099	7,115	7,131	7,147	7,163	7,179
15-29	7,224	7,244	7,264	7,284	7,303	7,321	7,338	7,355	7,371	7,385	7,399	7,411	7,423	7,434	7,445	7,455	7,465	7,475	7,486	7,496	7,507
30-44	7,487	7,494	7,502	7,510	7,519	7,529	7,541	7,553	7,567	7,582	7,598	7,616	7,634	7,653	7,673	7,693	7,713	7,733	7,753	7,772	7,791
45-59	7,261	7,290	7,318	7,344	7,368	7,390	7,409	7,426	7,441	7,453	7,464	7,473	7,482	7,489	7,496	7,504	7,511	7,519	7,528	7,538	7,548
60-74	6,859	6,863	6,867	6,872	6,879	6,888	6,901	6,918	6,938	6,961	6,987	7,015	7,045	7,076	7,107	7,138	7,168	7,198	7,225	7,250	7,274
75 & over	8,356	8,428	8,501	8,575	8,649	8,723	8,796	8,867	8,936	9,004	9,070	9,134	9,197	9,259	9,320	9,381	9,441	9,502	9,564	9,626	9,690
All ages	44,100	44,241	44,383	44,526	44,670	44,815	44,960	45,105	45,251	45,397	45,543	45,689	45,835	45,980	46,125	46,270	46,415	46,559	46,702	46,845	46,988
Percentages																					
0-14	15.7	15.6	15.6	15.6	15.6	15.5	15.5	15.5	15.5	15.4	15.4	15.4	15.4	15.4	15.4	15.3	15.3	15.3	15.3	15.3	15.3
15-29	16.4	16.4	16.4	16.4	16.3	16.3	16.3	16.3	16.3	16.3	16.2	16.2	16.2	16.2	16.1	16.1	16.1	16.1	16.0	16.0	16.0
30-44	17.0	16.9	16.9	16.9	16.8	16.8	16.8	16.7	16.7	16.7	16.7	16.7	16.7	16.6	16.6	16.6	16.6	16.6	16.6	16.6	16.6
45-59	16.5	16.5	16.5	16.5	16.5	16.5	16.5	16.5	16.4	16.4	16.4	16.4	16.3	16.3	16.3	16.2	16.2	16.1	16.1	16.1	16.1
60-74	15.6	15.5	15.5	15.4	15.4	15.4	15.4	15.3	15.3	15.3	15.3	15.4	15.4	15.4	15.4	15.4	15.4	15.5	15.5	15.5	15.5
75 & over	18.9	19.0	19.2	19.3	19.4	19.5	19.6	19.7	19.7	19.8	19.9	20.0	20.1	20.1	20.2	20.3	20.3	20.4	20.5	20.5	20.6
All ages	100.0	100.0	100.0	100.0	100.0	100.0	100.0	100.0	100.0	100.0	100.0	100.0	100.0	100.0	100.0	100.0	100.0	100.0	100.0	100.0	100.0
Mean age	46.7	46.8	46.9	46.9	47.0	47.0	47.1	47.2	47.2	47.3	47.3	47.4	47.4	47.5	47.6	47.6	47.7	47.7	47.8	47.8	47.9
Median age	45.9	45.9	46.0	46.1	46.1	46.2	46.3	46.3	46.4	46.4	46.5	46.6	46.6	46.7	46.7	46.8	46.8	46.9	46.9	47.0	47.0

Source: Office for National Statistics

Note: Figures may not add exactly due to rounding.
* Children under 16. Working age and pensionable age populations based on state pension age (SPA) for given year.
Between 2012 and 2018, SPA will change from 65 years for men and 61 years for women, to 65 years for both sexes.
Then between 2019 and 2020, SPA will change from 65 years to 66 years for both men and women.
Between 2026 and 2027 SPA will increase to 67 years and between 2044 and 2046 to 68 years for both sexes. This is based on SPA under the 2014 Pensions Act.
** This is consistent with the age-group definitions used in ONS Labour Market Statistics.

National Population Projections are currently produced every two years. The 2016-based projections are not due to be published until November/December 2017. Therefore, this table series will be updated in the next edition

15.3c Mid-2015 Population estimates: England and Wales by sex and single year of age

Ages	Persons	Males	females	Ages	Persons	Males	Females
ALL AGES	57,885,413	28,554,847	29,330,566	45	800,846	395,897	404,949
0	696,519	357,381	339,138	46	820,510	404,902	415,608
1	704,962	361,337	343,625	47	819,192	404,319	414,873
2	723,873	371,298	352,575	48	831,345	411,737	419,608
3	748,880	383,366	365,514	49	831,566	409,599	421,967
4	736,368	377,084	359,284	50	835,965	411,852	424,113
5	724,129	370,477	353,652	51	828,296	408,357	419,939
6	713,780	365,251	348,529	52	809,624	399,787	409,837
7	720,162	368,849	351,313	53	792,333	392,314	400,019
8	696,654	357,193	339,461	54	764,439	378,702	385,737
9	682,541	349,291	333,250	55	733,327	363,081	370,246
10	653,896	334,541	319,355	56	716,577	354,517	362,060
11	642,623	328,736	313,887	57	700,839	346,705	354,134
12	624,447	320,067	304,380	58	674,586	333,033	341,553
13	613,943	314,445	299,498	59	650,168	320,716	329,452
14	630,339	322,203	308,136	60	626,693	308,234	318,459
15	647,287	332,069	315,218	61	629,074	308,188	320,886
16	667,536	342,463	325,073	62	621,467	304,930	316,537
17	677,805	347,818	329,987	63	604,132	294,950	309,182
18	699,829	359,255	340,574	64	608,277	296,646	311,631
19	706,823	364,756	342,067	65	620,767	301,356	319,411
20	715,172	367,210	347,962	66	635,505	309,482	326,023
21	745,367	383,113	362,254	67	670,917	325,837	345,080
22	755,077	385,653	369,424	68	726,423	353,348	373,075
23	783,791	395,818	387,973	69	559,209	270,523	288,686
24	807,064	411,283	395,781	70	541,670	261,077	280,593
25	795,805	405,948	389,857	71	537,683	258,815	278,868
26	789,261	397,787	391,474	72	498,350	237,729	260,621
27	798,384	399,930	398,454	73	443,736	209,777	233,959
28	780,238	387,025	393,213	74	397,592	186,225	211,367
29	789,335	396,008	393,327	75	410,486	191,900	218,586
30	791,532	396,594	394,938	76	404,720	187,969	216,751
31	773,589	386,313	387,276	77	390,576	180,530	210,046
32	780,403	388,578	391,825	78	367,618	168,014	199,604
33	778,754	386,367	392,387	79	346,269	156,098	190,171
34	785,715	390,743	394,972	80	324,938	145,013	179,925
35	787,094	391,686	395,408	81	296,883	130,225	166,658
36	754,489	376,282	378,207	82	278,088	119,702	158,386
37	703,432	351,122	352,310	83	264,593	111,789	152,804
38	692,830	346,302	346,528	84	245,732	101,110	144,622
39	703,748	349,937	353,811	85	223,300	88,973	134,327
40	718,167	357,070	361,097	86	195,581	76,067	119,514
41	729,956	361,981	367,975	87	170,607	64,428	106,179
42	762,316	378,828	383,488	88	150,400	55,604	94,796
43	794,854	394,896	399,958	89	130,672	46,368	84,304
44	821,043	405,438	415,605	90	504,030	148,630	355,400

Source: Office for National Statistics

1. These unrounded estimates are published to enable and encourage further calculations and analysis. However, the estimates should not be taken to be accurate to the level of detail provided

2. The estimates are produced using a variety of data sources and statistical models, including some statistical disclosure control methods, and small estimates should not be taken to refer to particular individuals.

3. The estimated resident population of an area includes all those people who usually live there, regardless of nationality. Arriving international migrants are included in the usually resident population if they remain in the UK for at least a year. Emigrants are excluded if they remain outside the UK for at least a year. This is consistent with the United Nations definition of a long-term migrant. Armed forces stationed outside of the UK are excluded. Students are taken to be usually resident at their term time address.

4. Some of the administrative data used in estimating international migration at LA level was not available at the time of production of the mid-2015 population estimates.

5. Note that age 90 comprises data for ages 90 and above.

15.3d Population projections by the Office for National Statistics
England, PERSONS, thousands

2014-based
Principal projection

Projected populations at mid-years by age last birthday

Ages	2014	2015	2016	2017	2018	2019	2020	2021	2022	2023	2024	2025	2026	2027	2028	2029	2030	2031	2032	2033
Thousands																				
0-14	9,676	9,773	9,887	10,016	10,138	10,241	10,333	10,397	10,448	10,477	10,508	10,526	10,528	10,512	10,516	10,535	10,557	10,572	10,581	10,586
15-29	10,556	10,598	10,585	10,550	10,501	10,465	10,420	10,378	10,362	10,387	10,406	10,458	10,523	10,605	10,683	10,751	10,833	10,937	11,061	11,178
30-44	10,811	10,830	10,822	10,831	10,893	10,979	11,089	11,231	11,373	11,488	11,557	11,575	11,594	11,617	11,622	11,625	11,590	11,541	11,481	11,411
45-59	10,822	10,968	11,109	11,205	11,248	11,246	11,219	11,152	11,051	10,945	10,873	10,820	10,783	10,736	10,703	10,665	10,664	10,648	10,653	10,709
60-74	8,077	8,183	8,334	8,470	8,586	8,686	8,804	8,938	8,961	9,053	9,195	9,360	9,534	9,712	9,867	10,019	10,155	10,291	10,385	10,430
75 & over	4,375	4,428	4,481	4,568	4,696	4,849	4,997	5,152	5,439	5,668	5,857	6,025	6,174	6,311	6,454	6,594	6,724	6,864	7,014	7,176
All ages	54,317	54,780	55,219	55,640	56,061	56,466	56,862	57,248	57,634	58,017	58,396	58,769	59,135	59,493	59,844	60,188	60,524	60,853	61,175	61,491
Percentages																				
0-14	17.8	17.8	17.9	18.0	18.1	18.1	18.2	18.2	18.1	18.1	18.0	17.9	17.8	17.7	17.6	17.5	17.4	17.4	17.3	17.2
15-29	19.4	19.3	19.2	19.0	18.7	18.5	18.3	18.1	18.0	17.9	17.8	17.8	17.8	17.8	17.9	17.9	17.9	18.0	18.1	18.2
30-44	19.9	19.8	19.6	19.5	19.4	19.4	19.5	19.6	19.7	19.8	19.8	19.7	19.6	19.5	19.4	19.3	19.1	19.0	18.8	18.6
45-59	19.9	20.0	20.1	20.1	20.1	19.9	19.7	19.5	19.2	18.9	18.6	18.4	18.2	18.0	17.9	17.7	17.6	17.5	17.4	17.4
60-74	14.9	14.9	15.1	15.2	15.3	15.4	15.5	15.6	15.5	15.6	15.7	15.9	16.1	16.3	16.5	16.6	16.8	16.9	17.0	17.0
75 & over	8.1	8.1	8.1	8.2	8.4	8.6	8.8	9.0	9.4	9.8	10.0	10.3	10.4	10.6	10.8	11.0	11.1	11.3	11.5	11.7
All ages	100.0	100.0	100.0	100.0	100.0	100.0	100.0	100.0	100.0	100.0	100.0	100.0	100.0	100.0	100.0	100.0	100.0	100.0	100.0	100.0
Mean age	40.2	40.2	40.4	40.5	40.6	40.7	40.9	41.0	41.1	41.3	41.4	41.5	41.7	41.8	42.0	42.1	42.2	42.4	42.5	42.6
Median age	39.7	39.7	39.8	39.8	39.8	39.9	40.1	40.2	40.3	40.5	40.6	40.7	40.9	41.0	41.1	41.3	41.4	41.6	41.8	41.9

Ages	2034	2035	2036	2037	2038	2039	2040	2041	2042	2043	2044	2045	2046	2047	2048	2049	2050	2051	2052	2053
Thousands																				
0-14	10,589	10,592	10,596	10,602	10,612	10,628	10,650	10,679	10,716	10,758	10,805	10,857	10,911	10,968	11,025	11,083	11,139	11,192	11,242	11,288
15-29	11,280	11,372	11,437	11,489	11,517	11,549	11,567	11,569	11,553	11,557	11,576	11,598	11,613	11,622	11,627	11,631	11,634	11,638	11,645	11,655
30-44	11,364	11,314	11,273	11,259	11,284	11,305	11,358	11,424	11,508	11,587	11,657	11,740	11,844	11,968	12,085	12,186	12,278	12,343	12,395	12,424
45-59	10,792	10,901	11,042	11,183	11,297	11,367	11,387	11,408	11,433	11,439	11,444	11,412	11,365	11,308	11,242	11,198	11,152	11,116	11,105	11,134
60-74	10,434	10,415	10,361	10,275	10,186	10,132	10,101	10,074	10,043	10,025	10,001	10,013	10,011	10,027	10,090	10,176	10,285	10,425	10,563	10,674
75 & over	7,341	7,510	7,695	7,892	8,094	8,301	8,506	8,700	8,886	9,055	9,219	9,362	9,514	9,640	9,736	9,802	9,854	9,891	9,915	9,945
All ages	61,800	62,104	62,404	62,700	62,992	63,282	63,569	63,854	64,138	64,421	64,702	64,981	65,259	65,534	65,806	66,076	66,342	66,605	66,864	67,120
Percentages																				
0-14	17.1	17.1	17.0	16.9	16.8	16.8	16.8	16.7	16.7	16.7	16.7	16.7	16.7	16.7	16.8	16.8	16.8	16.8	16.8	16.8
15-29	18.3	18.3	18.3	18.3	18.3	18.2	18.2	18.1	18.0	17.9	17.9	17.8	17.8	17.7	17.7	17.6	17.5	17.5	17.4	17.4
30-44	18.4	18.2	18.1	18.0	17.9	17.9	17.9	17.9	17.9	18.0	18.0	18.1	18.1	18.3	18.4	18.4	18.5	18.5	18.5	18.5
45-59	17.5	17.6	17.7	17.8	17.9	18.0	17.9	17.9	17.8	17.8	17.7	17.6	17.4	17.3	17.1	16.9	16.8	16.7	16.6	16.6
60-74	16.9	16.8	16.6	16.4	16.2	16.0	15.9	15.8	15.7	15.6	15.5	15.4	15.3	15.3	15.3	15.4	15.5	15.7	15.8	15.9
75 & over	11.9	12.1	12.3	12.6	12.8	13.1	13.4	13.6	13.9	14.1	14.2	14.4	14.6	14.7	14.8	14.8	14.9	14.8	14.8	14.8
All ages	100.0	100.0	100.0	100.0	100.0	100.0	100.0	100.0	100.0	100.0	100.0	100.0	100.0	100.0	100.0	100.0	100.0	100.0	100.0	100.0
Mean age	42.8	42.9	43.0	43.1	43.2	43.3	43.4	43.4	43.5	43.6	43.6	43.7	43.7	43.8	43.9	43.9	43.9	44.0	44.0	44.1
Median age	42.1	42.2	42.3	42.4	42.5	42.6	42.6	42.7	42.7	42.7	42.6	42.6	42.5	42.5	42.5	42.6	42.6	42.7	42.7	42.8

15.3d Population projections by the Office for National Statistics
England, PERSONS, thousands

2014-based
Principal projection

Projected populations at mid-years by age last birthday

Ages	2054	2055	2056	2057	2058	2059	2060	2061	2062	2063	2064	2065	2066	2067	2068	2069	2070	2071	2072	2073
Thousands																				
0-14	11,330	11,368	11,401	11,430	11,455	11,476	11,495	11,512	11,527	11,541	11,556	11,571	11,588	11,605	11,625	11,646	11,670	11,697	11,725	11,756
15-29	11,671	11,693	11,722	11,759	11,801	11,849	11,900	11,955	12,012	12,069	12,127	12,183	12,236	12,287	12,333	12,375	12,413	12,446	12,475	12,500
30-44	12,456	12,475	12,478	12,463	12,468	12,488	12,510	12,526	12,536	12,541	12,545	12,549	12,554	12,561	12,572	12,588	12,611	12,641	12,678	12,721
45-59	11,157	11,212	11,281	11,366	11,447	11,518	11,602	11,706	11,829	11,946	12,047	12,139	12,205	12,257	12,288	12,322	12,343	12,348	12,336	12,342
60-74	10,746	10,771	10,798	10,827	10,839	10,848	10,824	10,784	10,735	10,679	10,643	10,608	10,583	10,582	10,619	10,651	10,712	10,786	10,876	10,961
75 & over	10,012	10,102	10,189	10,268	10,346	10,418	10,506	10,594	10,678	10,782	10,882	10,996	11,129	11,252	11,361	11,472	11,565	11,659	11,753	11,832
All ages	67,373	67,622	67,869	68,113	68,356	68,597	68,837	69,077	69,317	69,558	69,801	70,046	70,293	70,544	70,797	71,054	71,314	71,577	71,843	72,112
Percentages																				
0-14	16.8	16.8	16.8	16.8	16.8	16.7	16.7	16.7	16.6	16.6	16.6	16.5	16.5	16.5	16.4	16.4	16.4	16.3	16.3	16.3
15-29	17.3	17.3	17.3	17.3	17.3	17.3	17.3	17.3	17.3	17.4	17.4	17.4	17.4	17.4	17.4	17.4	17.4	17.4	17.4	17.3
30-44	18.5	18.4	18.4	18.3	18.2	18.2	18.2	18.1	18.1	18.0	18.0	17.9	17.9	17.8	17.8	17.7	17.7	17.7	17.6	17.6
45-59	16.6	16.6	16.6	16.7	16.7	16.8	16.9	16.9	17.1	17.2	17.3	17.3	17.4	17.4	17.4	17.3	17.3	17.3	17.2	17.1
60-74	16.0	15.9	15.9	15.9	15.9	15.8	15.7	15.6	15.5	15.4	15.2	15.1	15.1	15.0	15.0	15.0	15.0	15.1	15.1	15.2
75 & over	14.9	14.9	15.0	15.1	15.1	15.2	15.3	15.3	15.4	15.5	15.6	15.7	15.8	15.9	16.0	16.1	16.2	16.3	16.4	16.4
All ages	100.0	100.0	100.0	100.0	100.0	100.0	100.0	100.0	100.0	100.0	100.0	100.0	100.0	100.0	100.0	100.0	100.0	100.0	100.0	100.0
Mean age	44.1	44.2	44.2	44.2	44.3	44.3	44.4	44.4	44.4	44.5	44.5	44.6	44.6	44.6	44.7	44.7	44.8	44.8	44.9	44.9
Median age	42.9	42.9	43.0	43.1	43.1	43.1	43.2	43.2	43.3	43.3	43.4	43.5	43.5	43.6	43.6	43.7	43.8	43.8	43.8	43.9

Ages	2074	2075	2076	2077	2078	2079	2080	2081	2082	2083	2084	2085	2086	2087	2088	2089	2090	2091	2092	2093
Thousands																				
0-14	11,789	11,824	11,861	11,900	11,940	11,980	12,020	12,060	12,100	12,138	12,176	12,211	12,245	12,276	12,306	12,334	12,361	12,385	12,409	12,431
15-29	12,521	12,540	12,557	12,572	12,587	12,602	12,617	12,633	12,651	12,671	12,693	12,717	12,743	12,772	12,803	12,836	12,871	12,908	12,947	12,987
30-44	12,769	12,821	12,876	12,933	12,992	13,049	13,106	13,160	13,210	13,257	13,300	13,338	13,371	13,401	13,426	13,448	13,467	13,484	13,500	13,515
45-59	12,364	12,388	12,405	12,416	12,424	12,429	12,435	12,441	12,451	12,463	12,481	12,506	12,538	12,576	12,620	12,669	12,723	12,779	12,837	12,897
60-74	11,036	11,121	11,226	11,348	11,463	11,564	11,656	11,724	11,780	11,815	11,853	11,879	11,891	11,886	11,898	11,924	11,952	11,974	11,990	12,002
75 & over	11,904	11,961	12,005	12,036	12,077	12,134	12,201	12,293	12,397	12,520	12,639	12,767	12,906	13,058	13,192	13,310	13,425	13,546	13,672	13,803
All ages	72,383	72,656	72,930	73,206	73,482	73,759	74,035	74,312	74,589	74,865	75,141	75,417	75,693	75,969	76,245	76,522	76,799	77,077	77,356	77,636
Percentages																				
0-14	16.3	16.3	16.3	16.3	16.2	16.2	16.2	16.2	16.2	16.2	16.2	16.2	16.2	16.2	16.1	16.1	16.1	16.1	16.0	16.0
15-29	17.3	17.3	17.2	17.2	17.1	17.1	17.0	17.0	17.0	16.9	16.9	16.9	16.8	16.8	16.8	16.8	16.8	16.7	16.7	16.7
30-44	17.6	17.6	17.7	17.7	17.7	17.7	17.7	17.7	17.7	17.7	17.7	17.7	17.7	17.6	17.6	17.6	17.5	17.5	17.5	17.4
45-59	17.1	17.0	17.0	17.0	16.9	16.9	16.8	16.7	16.7	16.6	16.6	16.6	16.6	16.6	16.6	16.6	16.6	16.6	16.6	16.6
60-74	15.2	15.3	15.4	15.5	15.6	15.7	15.7	15.8	15.8	15.8	15.8	15.8	15.7	15.6	15.6	15.6	15.6	15.5	15.5	15.5
75 & over	16.4	16.5	16.5	16.4	16.4	16.5	16.5	16.5	16.6	16.7	16.8	16.9	17.1	17.2	17.3	17.4	17.5	17.6	17.7	17.8
All ages	100.0	100.0	100.0	100.0	100.0	100.0	100.0	100.0	100.0	100.0	100.0	100.0	100.0	100.0	100.0	100.0	100.0	100.0	100.0	100.0
Mean age	45.0	45.0	45.1	45.1	45.2	45.2	45.3	45.3	45.4	45.4	45.5	45.5	45.6	45.6	45.7	45.7	45.8	45.8	45.9	45.9
Median age	43.9	44.0	44.0	44.0	44.1	44.1	44.1	44.2	44.2	44.3	44.3	44.4	44.4	44.5	44.5	44.6	44.7	44.7	44.8	44.9

15.3d Population projections by the Office for National Statistics
England, PERSONS, thousands

2014-based
Principal projection

Projected populations at mid-years by age last birthday

Ages	2094	2095	2096	2097	2098	2099	2100	2101	2102	2103	2104	2105	2106	2107	2108	2109	2110	2111	2112	2113	2114
Thousands																					
0-14	12,453	12,475	12,496	12,518	12,540	12,562	12,586	12,610	12,636	12,663	12,691	12,720	12,750	12,781	12,812	12,844	12,877	12,909	12,942	12,974	13,006
15-29	13,027	13,068	13,108	13,148	13,186	13,223	13,259	13,293	13,324	13,354	13,382	13,409	13,434	13,457	13,480	13,502	13,523	13,545	13,566	13,588	13,611
30-44	13,531	13,546	13,563	13,581	13,602	13,624	13,648	13,675	13,704	13,735	13,769	13,805	13,842	13,881	13,921	13,962	14,003	14,044	14,084	14,123	14,160
45-59	12,955	13,013	13,067	13,119	13,167	13,210	13,249	13,284	13,315	13,341	13,365	13,385	13,404	13,421	13,437	13,454	13,471	13,489	13,508	13,530	13,553
60-74	12,013	12,024	12,036	12,051	12,069	12,092	12,121	12,157	12,200	12,248	12,301	12,358	12,417	12,479	12,541	12,602	12,662	12,720	12,774	12,825	12,871
75 & over	13,937	14,074	14,211	14,350	14,489	14,626	14,760	14,891	15,018	15,142	15,262	15,380	15,495	15,609	15,720	15,831	15,942	16,054	16,167	16,283	16,401
All ages	77,917	78,199	78,482	78,766	79,051	79,337	79,623	79,910	80,197	80,484	80,770	81,056	81,342	81,627	81,912	82,195	82,478	82,760	83,041	83,322	83,602
Percentages																					
0-14	16.0	16.0	15.9	15.9	15.9	15.8	15.8	15.8	15.8	15.7	15.7	15.7	15.7	15.7	15.6	15.6	15.6	15.6	15.6	15.6	15.6
15-29	16.7	16.7	16.7	16.7	16.7	16.7	16.7	16.6	16.6	16.6	16.6	16.5	16.5	16.5	16.5	16.4	16.4	16.4	16.3	16.3	16.3
30-44	17.4	17.3	17.3	17.2	17.2	17.2	17.1	17.1	17.1	17.1	17.0	17.0	17.0	17.0	17.0	17.0	17.0	17.0	17.0	16.9	16.9
45-59	16.6	16.6	16.7	16.7	16.7	16.7	16.6	16.6	16.6	16.6	16.5	16.5	16.5	16.4	16.4	16.4	16.3	16.3	16.3	16.2	16.2
60-74	15.4	15.4	15.3	15.3	15.3	15.2	15.2	15.2	15.2	15.2	15.2	15.2	15.3	15.3	15.3	15.3	15.4	15.4	15.4	15.4	15.4
75 & over	17.9	18.0	18.1	18.2	18.3	18.4	18.5	18.6	18.7	18.8	18.9	19.0	19.0	19.1	19.2	19.3	19.3	19.4	19.5	19.5	19.6
All ages	100.0	100.0	100.0	100.0	100.0	100.0	100.0	100.0	100.0	100.0	100.0	100.0	100.0	100.0	100.0	100.0	100.0	100.0	100.0	100.0	100.0
Mean age	46.0	46.1	46.1	46.2	46.2	46.3	46.4	46.4	46.5	46.6	46.6	46.7	46.7	46.8	46.9	46.9	47.0	47.0	47.1	47.1	47.2
Median age	44.9	45.0	45.1	45.2	45.2	45.3	45.4	45.4	45.5	45.5	45.6	45.7	45.7	45.8	45.8	45.9	45.9	46.0	46.0	46.1	46.1

Source: Office for National Statistics

Note: Figures may not add exactly due to rounding.
* Children under 16. Working age and pensionable age populations based on state pension age (SPA) for given year.
Between 2012 and 2018, SPA will change from 65 years for men and 61 years for women, to 65 years for both sexes.
Then between 2019 and 2020, SPA will change from 65 years to 66 years for both men and women.
Between 2026 and 2027 SPA will increase to 67 years and between 2044 and 2046 to 68 years for both sexes. This is based on SPA under the 2014 Pensions Act.
** This is consistent with the age-group definitions used in ONS Labour Market Statistics.

National Population Projections are currently produced every two years. The 2016-based projections are not due to be published until November/December 2017. Therefore, this table series will be updated in the next edition

15.3d Population projections by the Office for National Statistics
England, MALES, thousands

Projected populations at mid-years by age last birthday

Ages	2014	2015	2016	2017	2018	2019	2020	2021	2022	2023	2024	2025	2026	2027	2028	2029	2030	2031	2032	2033
Thousands																				
0-14	4,954	5,005	5,065	5,131	5,195	5,249	5,297	5,331	5,357	5,373	5,390	5,400	5,401	5,393	5,394	5,404	5,415	5,423	5,428	5,430
15-29	5,357	5,393	5,398	5,396	5,383	5,373	5,354	5,335	5,333	5,348	5,359	5,385	5,418	5,460	5,502	5,538	5,580	5,635	5,700	5,760
30-44	5,378	5,391	5,391	5,393	5,426	5,474	5,539	5,619	5,696	5,763	5,810	5,832	5,857	5,883	5,899	5,914	5,908	5,893	5,877	5,853
45-59	5,351	5,421	5,486	5,532	5,550	5,546	5,530	5,495	5,444	5,393	5,359	5,336	5,315	5,290	5,273	5,255	5,256	5,252	5,252	5,281
60-74	3,913	3,965	4,040	4,107	4,164	4,213	4,271	4,336	4,348	4,393	4,461	4,541	4,624	4,711	4,785	4,857	4,922	4,985	5,030	5,051
75 & over	1,820	1,856	1,890	1,939	2,008	2,089	2,167	2,247	2,389	2,502	2,596	2,678	2,751	2,817	2,887	2,954	3,017	3,084	3,156	3,234
All ages	26,773	27,030	27,270	27,499	27,727	27,944	28,157	28,363	28,569	28,773	28,974	29,172	29,365	29,555	29,740	29,921	30,099	30,273	30,443	30,610
Percentages																				
0-14	18.5	18.5	18.6	18.7	18.7	18.8	18.8	18.8	18.8	18.7	18.6	18.5	18.4	18.2	18.1	18.1	18.0	17.9	17.8	17.7
15-29	20.0	20.0	19.8	19.6	19.4	19.2	19.0	18.8	18.7	18.6	18.5	18.5	18.4	18.5	18.5	18.5	18.5	18.6	18.7	18.8
30-44	20.1	19.9	19.8	19.6	19.6	19.6	19.7	19.8	19.9	20.0	20.1	20.0	19.9	19.9	19.8	19.8	19.6	19.5	19.3	19.1
45-59	20.0	20.1	20.1	20.1	20.0	19.8	19.6	19.4	19.1	18.7	18.5	18.3	18.1	17.9	17.7	17.6	17.5	17.3	17.3	17.3
60-74	14.6	14.7	14.8	14.9	15.0	15.1	15.2	15.3	15.2	15.3	15.4	15.6	15.7	15.9	16.1	16.2	16.4	16.5	16.5	16.5
75 & over	6.8	6.9	6.9	7.1	7.2	7.5	7.7	7.9	8.4	8.7	9.0	9.2	9.4	9.5	9.7	9.9	10.0	10.2	10.4	10.6
All ages	100.0	100.0	100.0	100.0	100.0	100.0	100.0	100.0	100.0	100.0	100.0	100.0	100.0	100.0	100.0	100.0	100.0	100.0	100.0	100.0
Mean age	39.2	39.3	39.4	39.5	39.6	39.8	39.9	40.0	40.2	40.3	40.5	40.6	40.7	40.9	41.0	41.1	41.3	41.4	41.5	41.7
Median age	38.6	38.6	38.6	38.6	38.7	38.8	38.9	39.1	39.2	39.3	39.4	39.5	39.6	39.8	39.9	40.0	40.2	40.4	40.5	40.7

Ages	2034	2035	2036	2037	2038	2039	2040	2041	2042	2043	2044	2045	2046	2047	2048	2049	2050	2051	2052	2053
Thousands																				
0-14	5,432	5,433	5,435	5,439	5,444	5,452	5,463	5,478	5,497	5,518	5,543	5,569	5,597	5,626	5,656	5,685	5,714	5,741	5,767	5,790
15-29	5,813	5,862	5,896	5,923	5,938	5,955	5,965	5,967	5,959	5,960	5,970	5,981	5,989	5,994	5,996	5,998	6,000	6,002	6,006	6,011
30-44	5,837	5,815	5,797	5,797	5,812	5,823	5,851	5,884	5,927	5,970	6,006	6,049	6,105	6,169	6,229	6,282	6,331	6,365	6,392	6,407
45-59	5,328	5,391	5,472	5,548	5,614	5,661	5,684	5,710	5,737	5,754	5,770	5,765	5,751	5,737	5,714	5,700	5,681	5,665	5,667	5,684
60-74	5,051	5,040	5,012	4,971	4,930	4,906	4,893	4,881	4,865	4,857	4,847	4,855	4,858	4,865	4,899	4,946	5,010	5,089	5,163	5,227
75 & over	3,313	3,394	3,482	3,575	3,670	3,767	3,861	3,951	4,038	4,117	4,193	4,259	4,329	4,388	4,432	4,461	4,484	4,500	4,511	4,525
All ages	30,774	30,935	31,094	31,252	31,408	31,563	31,717	31,871	32,023	32,176	32,328	32,479	32,629	32,778	32,926	33,073	33,218	33,362	33,504	33,645
Percentages																				
0-14	17.7	17.6	17.5	17.4	17.3	17.3	17.2	17.2	17.2	17.2	17.1	17.1	17.2	17.2	17.2	17.2	17.2	17.2	17.2	17.2
15-29	18.9	18.9	19.0	19.0	18.9	18.9	18.8	18.7	18.6	18.5	18.5	18.4	18.4	18.3	18.2	18.1	18.1	18.0	17.9	17.9
30-44	19.0	18.8	18.6	18.5	18.5	18.4	18.4	18.5	18.5	18.6	18.6	18.6	18.7	18.8	18.9	19.0	19.1	19.1	19.1	19.0
45-59	17.3	17.4	17.6	17.8	17.9	17.9	17.9	17.9	17.9	17.9	17.8	17.8	17.6	17.5	17.4	17.2	17.1	17.0	16.9	16.9
60-74	16.4	16.3	16.1	15.9	15.7	15.5	15.4	15.3	15.2	15.1	15.0	14.9	14.9	14.8	14.9	15.0	15.1	15.3	15.4	15.5
75 & over	10.8	11.0	11.2	11.4	11.7	11.9	12.2	12.4	12.6	12.8	13.0	13.1	13.3	13.4	13.5	13.5	13.5	13.5	13.5	13.5
All ages	100.0	100.0	100.0	100.0	100.0	100.0	100.0	100.0	100.0	100.0	100.0	100.0	100.0	100.0	100.0	100.0	100.0	100.0	100.0	100.0
Mean age	41.8	41.9	42.0	42.1	42.2	42.3	42.4	42.4	42.5	42.6	42.6	42.7	42.8	42.8	42.9	42.9	43.0	43.0	43.1	43.1
Median age	40.8	40.9	41.0	41.1	41.2	41.3	41.3	41.4	41.4	41.3	41.3	41.3	41.3	41.3	41.3	41.4	41.5	41.5	41.6	41.7

15.3d Population projections by the Office for National Statistics
England, MALES, thousands

2014-based
Principal projection

Projected populations at mid-years by age last birthday

Ages	2054	2055	2056	2057	2058	2059	2060	2061	2062	2063	2064	2065	2066	2067	2068	2069	2070	2071	2072	2073
Thousands																				
0-14	5,812	5,831	5,848	5,863	5,876	5,887	5,896	5,905	5,913	5,920	5,928	5,935	5,944	5,953	5,963	5,974	5,986	6,000	6,014	6,030
15-29	6,019	6,030	6,046	6,064	6,086	6,110	6,137	6,165	6,194	6,223	6,253	6,282	6,309	6,335	6,359	6,380	6,399	6,416	6,431	6,444
30-44	6,425	6,436	6,438	6,431	6,432	6,442	6,454	6,462	6,467	6,470	6,473	6,475	6,477	6,481	6,487	6,495	6,507	6,523	6,542	6,564
45-59	5,697	5,726	5,760	5,804	5,848	5,885	5,929	5,984	6,048	6,108	6,161	6,209	6,244	6,272	6,288	6,307	6,319	6,322	6,317	6,320
60-74	5,275	5,300	5,328	5,357	5,377	5,394	5,393	5,383	5,372	5,354	5,344	5,330	5,322	5,328	5,350	5,368	5,400	5,438	5,486	5,531
75 & over	4,557	4,600	4,640	4,676	4,713	4,747	4,791	4,836	4,876	4,929	4,983	5,047	5,121	5,188	5,251	5,316	5,372	5,430	5,487	5,535
All ages	33,785	33,923	34,060	34,196	34,331	34,466	34,600	34,735	34,870	35,005	35,141	35,278	35,417	35,557	35,698	35,840	35,984	36,130	36,276	36,424
Percentages																				
0-14	17.2	17.2	17.2	17.1	17.1	17.1	17.0	17.0	17.0	16.9	16.9	16.8	16.8	16.7	16.7	16.7	16.6	16.6	16.6	16.6
15-29	17.8	17.8	17.7	17.7	17.7	17.7	17.7	17.7	17.8	17.8	17.8	17.8	17.8	17.8	17.8	17.8	17.8	17.8	17.7	17.7
30-44	19.0	19.0	18.9	18.8	18.7	18.7	18.7	18.6	18.5	18.5	18.4	18.4	18.3	18.2	18.2	18.1	18.1	18.1	18.0	18.0
45-59	16.9	16.9	16.9	17.0	17.0	17.1	17.1	17.2	17.3	17.4	17.5	17.6	17.6	17.6	17.6	17.6	17.6	17.5	17.4	17.4
60-74	15.6	15.6	15.6	15.7	15.7	15.7	15.6	15.5	15.4	15.3	15.2	15.1	15.0	15.0	15.0	15.0	15.0	15.1	15.1	15.2
75 & over	13.5	13.6	13.6	13.7	13.7	13.8	13.8	13.9	14.0	14.1	14.2	14.3	14.5	14.6	14.7	14.8	14.9	15.0	15.1	15.2
All ages	100.0	100.0	100.0	100.0	100.0	100.0	100.0	100.0	100.0	100.0	100.0	100.0	100.0	100.0	100.0	100.0	100.0	100.0	100.0	100.0
Mean age	43.2	43.2	43.3	43.3	43.4	43.4	43.5	43.5	43.6	43.6	43.7	43.7	43.8	43.8	43.9	43.9	44.0	44.1	44.1	44.2
Median age	41.8	41.9	41.9	42.0	42.1	42.1	42.2	42.3	42.3	42.4	42.5	42.6	42.6	42.7	42.8	42.8	42.9	43.0	43.0	43.1

Ages	2074	2075	2076	2077	2078	2079	2080	2081	2082	2083	2084	2085	2086	2087	2088	2089	2090	2091	2092	2093
Thousands																				
0-14	6,047	6,065	6,084	6,104	6,124	6,145	6,166	6,186	6,206	6,226	6,245	6,263	6,281	6,297	6,312	6,327	6,340	6,353	6,365	6,376
15-29	6,455	6,465	6,473	6,481	6,489	6,497	6,504	6,513	6,522	6,532	6,543	6,555	6,569	6,584	6,600	6,617	6,635	6,654	6,674	6,694
30-44	6,588	6,615	6,644	6,673	6,703	6,732	6,761	6,789	6,815	6,839	6,861	6,881	6,898	6,913	6,926	6,937	6,947	6,956	6,964	6,972
45-59	6,331	6,343	6,352	6,358	6,363	6,366	6,369	6,373	6,378	6,385	6,394	6,407	6,424	6,444	6,466	6,492	6,519	6,549	6,579	6,609
60-74	5,571	5,615	5,671	5,734	5,793	5,846	5,894	5,930	5,960	5,979	6,000	6,015	6,022	6,020	6,027	6,041	6,056	6,067	6,076	6,083
75 & over	5,580	5,617	5,646	5,670	5,698	5,734	5,775	5,827	5,886	5,954	6,019	6,088	6,164	6,245	6,318	6,382	6,444	6,509	6,576	6,645
All ages	36,572	36,721	36,871	37,020	37,170	37,320	37,469	37,618	37,767	37,915	38,062	38,210	38,356	38,503	38,649	38,795	38,941	39,087	39,233	39,380
Percentages																				
0-14	16.5	16.5	16.5	16.5	16.5	16.5	16.5	16.4	16.4	16.4	16.4	16.4	16.4	16.4	16.3	16.3	16.3	16.3	16.2	16.2
15-29	17.7	17.6	17.6	17.5	17.5	17.4	17.4	17.3	17.3	17.2	17.2	17.2	17.1	17.1	17.1	17.1	17.0	17.0	17.0	17.0
30-44	18.0	18.0	18.0	18.0	18.0	18.0	18.0	18.0	18.0	18.0	18.0	18.0	18.0	18.0	17.9	17.9	17.8	17.8	17.8	17.7
45-59	17.3	17.3	17.2	17.2	17.1	17.1	17.0	16.9	16.9	16.8	16.8	16.8	16.7	16.7	16.7	16.7	16.7	16.8	16.8	16.8
60-74	15.2	15.3	15.4	15.5	15.6	15.7	15.7	15.8	15.8	15.8	15.8	15.7	15.7	15.6	15.6	15.6	15.6	15.5	15.5	15.4
75 & over	15.3	15.3	15.3	15.3	15.3	15.4	15.4	15.5	15.6	15.7	15.8	15.9	16.1	16.2	16.3	16.5	16.5	16.7	16.8	16.9
All ages	100.0	100.0	100.0	100.0	100.0	100.0	100.0	100.0	100.0	100.0	100.0	100.0	100.0	100.0	100.0	100.0	100.0	100.0	100.0	100.0
Mean age	44.2	44.3	44.4	44.4	44.5	44.5	44.6	44.7	44.7	44.8	44.8	44.9	44.9	45.0	45.1	45.1	45.2	45.2	45.3	45.4
Median age	43.1	43.2	43.2	43.3	43.3	43.3	43.4	43.4	43.5	43.5	43.6	43.7	43.7	43.8	43.9	43.9	44.0	44.1	44.2	44.2

15.3d Population projections by the Office for National Statistics
England, MALES, thousands

2014-based
Principal projection

Projected populations at mid-years by age last birthday

Ages	2094	2095	2096	2097	2098	2099	2100	2101	2102	2103	2104	2105	2106	2107	2108	2109	2110	2111	2112	2113	2114
Thousands																					
0-14	6,388	6,399	6,409	6,420	6,432	6,443	6,456	6,468	6,481	6,495	6,509	6,524	6,540	6,555	6,571	6,588	6,604	6,621	6,638	6,654	6,671
15-29	6,715	6,735	6,756	6,776	6,796	6,815	6,834	6,851	6,867	6,883	6,897	6,910	6,923	6,935	6,947	6,958	6,969	6,980	6,991	7,003	7,014
30-44	6,980	6,988	6,997	7,006	7,017	7,028	7,041	7,055	7,070	7,086	7,103	7,121	7,141	7,161	7,181	7,202	7,223	7,244	7,265	7,285	7,304
45-59	6,639	6,669	6,697	6,724	6,748	6,771	6,791	6,809	6,825	6,839	6,851	6,862	6,871	6,880	6,889	6,898	6,907	6,916	6,926	6,937	6,950
60-74	6,090	6,096	6,103	6,111	6,121	6,134	6,149	6,169	6,191	6,216	6,244	6,274	6,305	6,336	6,368	6,400	6,432	6,461	6,490	6,516	6,540
75 & over	6,715	6,786	6,857	6,929	7,000	7,071	7,139	7,206	7,271	7,334	7,396	7,456	7,514	7,572	7,628	7,685	7,741	7,798	7,855	7,914	7,974
All ages	39,526	39,673	39,820	39,967	40,114	40,262	40,410	40,557	40,705	40,853	41,000	41,147	41,293	41,440	41,586	41,731	41,876	42,021	42,165	42,309	42,453
Percentages																					
0-14	16.2	16.1	16.1	16.1	16.0	16.0	16.0	15.9	15.9	15.9	15.9	15.9	15.8	15.8	15.8	15.8	15.8	15.8	15.7	15.7	15.7
15-29	17.0	17.0	17.0	17.0	16.9	16.9	16.9	16.9	16.9	16.8	16.8	16.8	16.8	16.7	16.7	16.7	16.6	16.6	16.6	16.6	16.5
30-44	17.7	17.6	17.6	17.5	17.5	17.5	17.4	17.4	17.4	17.3	17.3	17.3	17.3	17.3	17.3	17.3	17.2	17.2	17.2	17.2	17.2
45-59	16.8	16.8	16.8	16.8	16.8	16.8	16.8	16.8	16.8	16.7	16.7	16.7	16.6	16.6	16.6	16.5	16.5	16.5	16.4	16.4	16.4
60-74	15.4	15.4	15.3	15.3	15.3	15.2	15.2	15.2	15.2	15.2	15.2	15.2	15.3	15.3	15.3	15.3	15.4	15.4	15.4	15.4	15.4
75 & over	17.0	17.1	17.2	17.3	17.5	17.6	17.7	17.8	17.9	18.0	18.0	18.1	18.2	18.3	18.3	18.4	18.5	18.6	18.6	18.7	18.8
All ages	100.0	100.0	100.0	100.0	100.0	100.0	100.0	100.0	100.0	100.0	100.0	100.0	100.0	100.0	100.0	100.0	100.0	100.0	100.0	100.0	100.0
Mean age	45.4	45.5	45.6	45.6	45.7	45.8	45.8	45.9	45.9	46.0	46.1	46.1	46.2	46.3	46.3	46.4	46.4	46.5	46.5	46.6	46.6
Median age	44.3	44.4	44.5	44.5	44.6	44.7	44.7	44.8	44.9	44.9	45.0	45.0	45.1	45.1	45.2	45.3	45.3	45.4	45.4	45.5	45.5

Source: Office for National Statistics

Note: Figures may not add exactly due to rounding.
* Children under 16. Working age and pensionable age populations based on state pension age (SPA) for given year.
Between 2012 and 2018, SPA will change from 65 years for men and 61 years for women, to 65 years for both sexes.
Then between 2019 and 2020, SPA will change from 65 years to 66 years for both men and women.
Between 2026 and 2027 SPA will increase to 67 years and between 2044 and 2046 to 68 years for both sexes. This is based on SPA under the 2014 Pensions Act.
** This is consistent with the age-group definitions used in ONS Labour Market Statistics.

National Population Projections are currently produced every two years. The 2016-based projections are not due to be published until November/December 2017. Therefore, this table series will be updated in the next edition

15.3d Population projections by the Office for National Statistics
England, FEMALES, thousands

2014-based
Principal projection

Projected populations at mid-years by age last birthday

Ages	2014	2015	2016	2017	2018	2019	2020	2021	2022	2023	2024	2025	2026	2027	2028	2029	2030	2031	2032	2033
Thousands																				
0-14	4,722	4,768	4,822	4,884	4,943	4,992	5,036	5,066	5,091	5,104	5,118	5,126	5,127	5,119	5,122	5,131	5,142	5,149	5,153	5,156
15-29	5,198	5,205	5,187	5,154	5,118	5,092	5,066	5,043	5,029	5,039	5,048	5,072	5,105	5,144	5,181	5,213	5,253	5,302	5,362	5,418
30-44	5,433	5,439	5,432	5,438	5,467	5,505	5,550	5,612	5,677	5,725	5,747	5,743	5,737	5,734	5,722	5,710	5,682	5,647	5,603	5,558
45-59	5,471	5,547	5,623	5,674	5,697	5,700	5,689	5,657	5,606	5,552	5,515	5,490	5,467	5,446	5,430	5,410	5,408	5,397	5,401	5,428
60-74	4,164	4,218	4,294	4,364	4,422	4,473	4,533	4,602	4,613	4,660	4,734	4,819	4,910	5,001	5,083	5,162	5,233	5,306	5,355	5,379
75 & over	2,555	2,572	2,591	2,629	2,688	2,760	2,831	2,905	3,050	3,165	3,261	3,347	3,423	3,494	3,567	3,640	3,707	3,780	3,858	3,942
All ages	27,543	27,750	27,949	28,142	28,335	28,522	28,705	28,885	29,065	29,245	29,423	29,598	29,770	29,939	30,104	30,267	30,425	30,581	30,732	30,881
Percentages																				
0-14	17.1	17.2	17.3	17.4	17.4	17.5	17.5	17.5	17.5	17.5	17.4	17.3	17.2	17.1	17.0	17.0	16.9	16.8	16.8	16.7
15-29	18.9	18.8	18.6	18.3	18.1	17.9	17.6	17.5	17.3	17.2	17.2	17.1	17.1	17.2	17.2	17.2	17.3	17.3	17.4	17.5
30-44	19.7	19.6	19.4	19.3	19.3	19.3	19.3	19.4	19.5	19.6	19.5	19.4	19.3	19.2	19.0	18.9	18.7	18.5	18.2	18.0
45-59	19.9	20.0	20.1	20.2	20.1	20.0	19.8	19.6	19.3	19.0	18.7	18.5	18.4	18.2	18.0	17.9	17.8	17.6	17.6	17.6
60-74	15.1	15.2	15.4	15.5	15.6	15.7	15.8	15.9	15.9	15.9	16.1	16.3	16.5	16.7	16.9	17.1	17.2	17.4	17.4	17.4
75 & over	9.3	9.3	9.3	9.3	9.5	9.7	9.9	10.1	10.5	10.8	11.1	11.3	11.5	11.7	11.8	12.0	12.2	12.4	12.6	12.8
All ages	100.0	100.0	100.0	100.0	100.0	100.0	100.0	100.0	100.0	100.0	100.0	100.0	100.0	100.0	100.0	100.0	100.0	100.0	100.0	100.0
Mean age	41.1	41.2	41.3	41.4	41.5	41.7	41.8	41.9	42.1	42.2	42.3	42.5	42.6	42.8	42.9	43.0	43.2	43.3	43.5	43.6
Median age	40.8	40.9	40.9	41.0	41.0	41.1	41.2	41.3	41.5	41.7	41.8	42.0	42.1	42.3	42.4	42.6	42.7	42.9	43.1	43.2

Ages	2034	2035	2036	2037	2038	2039	2040	2041	2042	2043	2044	2045	2046	2047	2048	2049	2050	2051	2052	2053
Thousands																				
0-14	5,157	5,158	5,160	5,164	5,168	5,176	5,187	5,201	5,219	5,239	5,262	5,287	5,314	5,342	5,370	5,398	5,425	5,451	5,475	5,498
15-29	5,467	5,511	5,541	5,566	5,579	5,593	5,602	5,602	5,594	5,597	5,606	5,617	5,624	5,629	5,631	5,633	5,634	5,636	5,639	5,644
30-44	5,527	5,499	5,476	5,462	5,472	5,482	5,507	5,541	5,580	5,618	5,650	5,690	5,739	5,799	5,856	5,904	5,948	5,978	6,003	6,016
45-59	5,464	5,509	5,571	5,636	5,683	5,706	5,703	5,698	5,696	5,685	5,674	5,647	5,614	5,572	5,528	5,498	5,472	5,450	5,438	5,450
60-74	5,384	5,375	5,348	5,304	5,256	5,226	5,208	5,193	5,178	5,168	5,155	5,158	5,153	5,162	5,192	5,229	5,275	5,336	5,400	5,447
75 & over	4,028	4,117	4,213	4,317	4,424	4,535	4,645	4,749	4,847	4,938	5,026	5,103	5,186	5,253	5,304	5,341	5,370	5,391	5,404	5,419
All ages	31,026	31,169	31,310	31,448	31,584	31,718	31,852	31,984	32,115	32,245	32,374	32,503	32,630	32,756	32,880	33,003	33,124	33,243	33,360	33,475
Percentages																				
0-14	16.6	16.5	16.5	16.4	16.4	16.3	16.3	16.3	16.3	16.2	16.3	16.3	16.3	16.3	16.3	16.4	16.4	16.4	16.4	16.4
15-29	17.6	17.7	17.7	17.7	17.7	17.6	17.6	17.5	17.4	17.4	17.3	17.3	17.2	17.2	17.1	17.1	17.0	17.0	16.9	16.9
30-44	17.8	17.6	17.5	17.4	17.3	17.3	17.3	17.3	17.4	17.4	17.5	17.5	17.6	17.7	17.8	17.9	18.0	18.0	18.0	18.0
45-59	17.6	17.7	17.8	17.9	18.0	18.0	17.9	17.8	17.7	17.6	17.5	17.4	17.2	17.0	16.8	16.7	16.5	16.4	16.3	16.3
60-74	17.4	17.2	17.1	16.9	16.6	16.5	16.4	16.2	16.1	16.0	15.9	15.9	15.8	15.8	15.8	15.8	15.9	16.1	16.2	16.3
75 & over	13.0	13.2	13.5	13.7	14.0	14.3	14.6	14.8	15.1	15.3	15.5	15.7	15.9	16.0	16.1	16.2	16.2	16.2	16.2	16.2
All ages	100.0	100.0	100.0	100.0	100.0	100.0	100.0	100.0	100.0	100.0	100.0	100.0	100.0	100.0	100.0	100.0	100.0	100.0	100.0	100.0
Mean age	43.7	43.8	43.9	44.1	44.2	44.2	44.3	44.4	44.5	44.6	44.6	44.7	44.7	44.8	44.8	44.9	44.9	45.0	45.0	45.0
Median age	43.4	43.5	43.7	43.8	43.9	43.9	44.0	44.1	44.1	44.1	44.1	44.0	43.9	43.9	43.8	43.8	43.8	43.8	43.9	43.9

15.3d Population projections by the Office for National Statistics
England, FEMALES, thousands

2014-based
Principal projection

Projected populations at mid-years by age last birthday

Ages	2054	2055	2056	2057	2058	2059	2060	2061	2062	2063	2064	2065	2066	2067	2068	2069	2070	2071	2072	2073
Thousands																				
0-14	5,518	5,537	5,553	5,567	5,579	5,590	5,599	5,607	5,614	5,621	5,628	5,636	5,644	5,652	5,662	5,672	5,684	5,697	5,711	5,726
15-29	5,652	5,663	5,677	5,695	5,715	5,738	5,764	5,790	5,818	5,846	5,874	5,901	5,927	5,952	5,974	5,995	6,013	6,030	6,044	6,056
30-44	6,031	6,039	6,040	6,033	6,036	6,045	6,056	6,064	6,068	6,071	6,072	6,074	6,076	6,080	6,085	6,093	6,104	6,118	6,136	6,157
45-59	5,461	5,487	5,521	5,562	5,599	5,633	5,673	5,722	5,781	5,838	5,886	5,930	5,960	5,985	6,000	6,015	6,024	6,026	6,019	6,023
60-74	5,471	5,471	5,469	5,470	5,462	5,454	5,431	5,402	5,364	5,325	5,299	5,277	5,261	5,254	5,269	5,283	5,312	5,348	5,391	5,430
75 & over	5,455	5,503	5,549	5,592	5,633	5,671	5,715	5,758	5,802	5,853	5,900	5,949	6,008	6,064	6,110	6,156	6,193	6,229	6,267	6,297
All ages	33,588	33,699	33,809	33,918	34,025	34,131	34,237	34,342	34,448	34,553	34,660	34,768	34,877	34,987	35,099	35,214	35,330	35,447	35,567	35,688
Percentages																				
0-14	16.4	16.4	16.4	16.4	16.4	16.4	16.4	16.3	16.3	16.3	16.2	16.2	16.2	16.2	16.1	16.1	16.1	16.1	16.1	16.0
15-29	16.8	16.8	16.8	16.8	16.8	16.8	16.8	16.9	16.9	16.9	16.9	17.0	17.0	17.0	17.0	17.0	17.0	17.0	17.0	17.0
30-44	18.0	17.9	17.9	17.8	17.7	17.7	17.7	17.7	17.6	17.6	17.5	17.5	17.4	17.4	17.3	17.3	17.3	17.3	17.3	17.3
45-59	16.3	16.3	16.3	16.4	16.5	16.5	16.6	16.7	16.8	16.9	17.0	17.1	17.1	17.1	17.1	17.1	17.1	17.0	16.9	16.9
60-74	16.3	16.2	16.2	16.1	16.1	16.0	15.9	15.7	15.6	15.4	15.3	15.2	15.1	15.0	15.0	15.0	15.0	15.1	15.2	15.2
75 & over	16.2	16.3	16.4	16.5	16.6	16.6	16.7	16.8	16.8	16.9	17.0	17.1	17.2	17.3	17.4	17.5	17.5	17.6	17.6	17.6
All ages	100.0	100.0	100.0	100.0	100.0	100.0	100.0	100.0	100.0	100.0	100.0	100.0	100.0	100.0	100.0	100.0	100.0	100.0	100.0	100.0
Mean age	45.1	45.1	45.1	45.2	45.2	45.2	45.3	45.3	45.3	45.4	45.4	45.4	45.5	45.5	45.5	45.6	45.6	45.6	45.7	45.7
Median age	44.0	44.0	44.1	44.2	44.2	44.2	44.2	44.3	44.3	44.4	44.4	44.4	44.5	44.5	44.6	44.6	44.7	44.7	44.7	44.8

Ages	2074	2075	2076	2077	2078	2079	2080	2081	2082	2083	2084	2085	2086	2087	2088	2089	2090	2091	2092	2093
Thousands																				
0-14	5,742	5,759	5,777	5,796	5,815	5,835	5,855	5,874	5,894	5,912	5,930	5,948	5,964	5,980	5,994	6,008	6,021	6,033	6,044	6,055
15-29	6,066	6,075	6,084	6,091	6,098	6,105	6,113	6,121	6,129	6,139	6,150	6,161	6,174	6,188	6,203	6,219	6,236	6,255	6,273	6,293
30-44	6,180	6,206	6,233	6,260	6,289	6,317	6,344	6,371	6,395	6,418	6,439	6,457	6,473	6,488	6,500	6,511	6,520	6,528	6,536	6,543
45-59	6,033	6,044	6,052	6,058	6,061	6,063	6,066	6,069	6,073	6,079	6,087	6,099	6,114	6,132	6,154	6,178	6,203	6,231	6,259	6,288
60-74	5,465	5,506	5,555	5,614	5,670	5,718	5,762	5,794	5,820	5,836	5,853	5,865	5,869	5,866	5,871	5,883	5,896	5,906	5,914	5,919
75 & over	6,324	6,344	6,358	6,366	6,379	6,400	6,427	6,466	6,511	6,566	6,620	6,678	6,742	6,813	6,874	6,928	6,981	7,037	7,097	7,159
All ages	35,811	35,935	36,060	36,185	36,312	36,439	36,566	36,694	36,822	36,951	37,079	37,208	37,337	37,466	37,596	37,727	37,858	37,990	38,123	38,256
Percentages																				
0-14	16.0	16.0	16.0	16.0	16.0	16.0	16.0	16.0	16.0	16.0	16.0	16.0	16.0	16.0	15.9	15.9	15.9	15.9	15.9	15.8
15-29	16.9	16.9	16.9	16.8	16.8	16.8	16.7	16.7	16.6	16.6	16.6	16.6	16.5	16.5	16.5	16.5	16.5	16.5	16.5	16.4
30-44	17.3	17.3	17.3	17.3	17.3	17.3	17.4	17.4	17.4	17.4	17.4	17.4	17.3	17.3	17.3	17.3	17.2	17.2	17.1	17.1
45-59	16.8	16.8	16.8	16.7	16.7	16.6	16.6	16.5	16.5	16.5	16.4	16.4	16.4	16.4	16.4	16.4	16.4	16.4	16.4	16.4
60-74	15.3	15.3	15.4	15.5	15.6	15.7	15.8	15.8	15.8	15.8	15.8	15.8	15.7	15.7	15.6	15.6	15.6	15.5	15.5	15.5
75 & over	17.7	17.7	17.6	17.6	17.6	17.6	17.6	17.6	17.7	17.8	17.9	17.9	18.1	18.2	18.3	18.4	18.4	18.5	18.6	18.7
All ages	100.0	100.0	100.0	100.0	100.0	100.0	100.0	100.0	100.0	100.0	100.0	100.0	100.0	100.0	100.0	100.0	100.0	100.0	100.0	100.0
Mean age	45.7	45.8	45.8	45.8	45.9	45.9	46.0	46.0	46.0	46.1	46.1	46.2	46.2	46.2	46.3	46.3	46.4	46.4	46.5	46.5
Median age	44.8	44.8	44.8	44.9	44.9	44.9	44.9	45.0	45.0	45.0	45.1	45.1	45.1	45.2	45.2	45.3	45.4	45.4	45.5	45.5

15.3d Population projections by the Office for National Statistics
England, FEMALES, thousands

2014-based
Principal projection

Projected populations at mid-years by age last birthday

Ages	2094	2095	2096	2097	2098	2099	2100	2101	2102	2103	2104	2105	2106	2107	2108	2109	2110	2111	2112	2113	2114
Thousands																					
0-14	6,066	6,076	6,087	6,097	6,108	6,119	6,130	6,142	6,155	6,168	6,181	6,196	6,210	6,225	6,241	6,256	6,272	6,288	6,304	6,319	6,335
15-29	6,312	6,332	6,352	6,371	6,390	6,408	6,425	6,442	6,457	6,472	6,486	6,498	6,511	6,522	6,533	6,544	6,554	6,565	6,575	6,586	6,597
30-44	6,550	6,558	6,566	6,575	6,585	6,595	6,607	6,620	6,634	6,650	6,666	6,683	6,702	6,721	6,740	6,760	6,780	6,799	6,819	6,838	6,856
45-59	6,316	6,344	6,370	6,395	6,418	6,440	6,458	6,475	6,490	6,503	6,514	6,524	6,532	6,540	6,548	6,556	6,564	6,573	6,582	6,592	6,603
60-74	5,923	5,928	5,933	5,939	5,947	5,958	5,972	5,989	6,009	6,032	6,057	6,084	6,113	6,142	6,172	6,202	6,231	6,258	6,285	6,309	6,331
75 & over	7,223	7,288	7,354	7,421	7,488	7,555	7,621	7,684	7,747	7,807	7,867	7,924	7,981	8,037	8,092	8,147	8,201	8,256	8,312	8,369	8,427
All ages	38,391	38,526	38,662	38,799	38,937	39,075	39,214	39,353	39,492	39,631	39,770	39,910	40,049	40,187	40,326	40,464	40,602	40,739	40,876	41,013	41,149
Percentages																					
0-14	15.8	15.8	15.7	15.7	15.7	15.7	15.6	15.6	15.6	15.6	15.5	15.5	15.5	15.5	15.5	15.5	15.4	15.4	15.4	15.4	15.4
15-29	16.4	16.4	16.4	16.4	16.4	16.4	16.4	16.4	16.4	16.3	16.3	16.3	16.3	16.2	16.2	16.2	16.1	16.1	16.1	16.1	16.0
30-44	17.1	17.0	17.0	16.9	16.9	16.9	16.8	16.8	16.8	16.8	16.8	16.7	16.7	16.7	16.7	16.7	16.7	16.7	16.7	16.7	16.7
45-59	16.5	16.5	16.5	16.5	16.5	16.5	16.5	16.5	16.4	16.4	16.4	16.3	16.3	16.3	16.2	16.2	16.2	16.1	16.1	16.1	16.0
60-74	15.4	15.4	15.3	15.3	15.3	15.2	15.2	15.2	15.2	15.2	15.2	15.2	15.3	15.3	15.3	15.3	15.3	15.4	15.4	15.4	15.4
75 & over	18.8	18.9	19.0	19.1	19.2	19.3	19.4	19.5	19.6	19.7	19.8	19.9	19.9	20.0	20.1	20.1	20.2	20.3	20.3	20.4	20.5
All ages	100.0	100.0	100.0	100.0	100.0	100.0	100.0	100.0	100.0	100.0	100.0	100.0	100.0	100.0	100.0	100.0	100.0	100.0	100.0	100.0	100.0
Mean age	46.6	46.6	46.7	46.8	46.8	46.9	46.9	47.0	47.1	47.1	47.2	47.2	47.3	47.4	47.4	47.5	47.5	47.6	47.6	47.7	47.7
Median age	45.6	45.7	45.8	45.8	45.9	46.0	46.0	46.1	46.1	46.2	46.3	46.3	46.4	46.4	46.5	46.5	46.6	46.6	46.7	46.7	46.8

Source: Office for National Statistics

Note: Figures may not add exactly due to rounding.
* Children under 16. Working age and pensionable age populations based on state pension age (SPA) for given year.
Between 2012 and 2018, SPA will change from 65 years for men and 61 years for women, to 65 years for both sexes.
Then between 2019 and 2020, SPA will change from 65 years to 66 years for both men and women.
Between 2026 and 2027 SPA will increase to 67 years and between 2044 and 2046 to 68 years for both sexes. This is based on SPA under the 2014 Pensions Act.
** This is consistent with the age-group definitions used in ONS Labour Market Statistics.

National Population Projections are currently produced every two years. The 2016-based projections are not due to be published until November/December 2017. Therefore, this table series will be updated in the next edition

15.3d Population projections by the Office for National Statistics
Wales, PERSONS, thousands

2014-based
Principal projection

Projected populations at mid-years by age last birthday

Ages	2014	2015	2016	2017	2018	2019	2020	2021	2022	2023	2024	2025	2026	2027	2028	2029	2030	2031	2032	2033
Thousands																				
0-14	519	520	522	525	528	531	533	534	535	535	535	535	533	533	533	534	535	535	536	536
15-29	598	599	597	594	590	585	580	574	570	568	565	564	565	565	565	565	565	567	570	573
30-44	546	542	537	534	534	538	543	551	559	567	572	574	576	579	580	582	581	579	575	571
45-59	626	630	635	636	634	629	622	612	601	590	580	572	565	557	551	543	539	533	530	531
60-74	526	531	537	542	547	551	555	561	560	561	567	573	579	585	590	596	600	605	607	605
75 & over	276	279	283	289	297	307	316	324	342	356	368	378	387	395	404	412	418	425	433	441
All ages	3,092	3,101	3,111	3,120	3,130	3,139	3,149	3,158	3,168	3,177	3,187	3,196	3,206	3,215	3,223	3,231	3,238	3,245	3,251	3,257
Percentages																				
0-14	16.8	16.8	16.8	16.8	16.9	16.9	16.9	16.9	16.9	16.8	16.8	16.7	16.6	16.6	16.5	16.5	16.5	16.5	16.5	16.5
15-29	19.3	19.3	19.2	19.0	18.8	18.6	18.4	18.2	18.0	17.9	17.7	17.7	17.6	17.6	17.5	17.5	17.5	17.5	17.5	17.6
30-44	17.7	17.5	17.3	17.1	17.1	17.1	17.3	17.5	17.6	17.8	18.0	18.0	18.0	18.0	18.0	18.0	17.9	17.8	17.7	17.5
45-59	20.3	20.3	20.4	20.4	20.3	20.0	19.7	19.4	19.0	18.6	18.2	17.9	17.6	17.3	17.1	16.8	16.6	16.4	16.3	16.3
60-74	17.0	17.1	17.3	17.4	17.5	17.5	17.6	17.8	17.7	17.7	17.8	17.9	18.1	18.2	18.3	18.4	18.5	18.7	18.7	18.6
75 & over	8.9	9.0	9.1	9.3	9.5	9.8	10.0	10.3	10.8	11.2	11.5	11.8	12.1	12.3	12.5	12.7	12.9	13.1	13.3	13.5
All ages	100.0	100.0	100.0	100.0	100.0	100.0	100.0	100.0	100.0	100.0	100.0	100.0	100.0	100.0	100.0	100.0	100.0	100.0	100.0	100.0
Mean age	41.6	41.7	41.9	42.0	42.2	42.3	42.5	42.6	42.8	42.9	43.0	43.2	43.3	43.4	43.6	43.7	43.8	43.9	44.0	44.2
Median age	42.1	42.2	42.4	42.4	42.5	42.5	42.5	42.5	42.6	42.7	42.8	42.9	43.0	43.1	43.1	43.2	43.3	43.4	43.5	43.7

Ages	2034	2035	2036	2037	2038	2039	2040	2041	2042	2043	2044	2045	2046	2047	2048	2049	2050	2051	2052	2053
Thousands																				
0-14	536	535	534	533	532	530	529	529	528	528	528	528	528	529	529	530	531	531	532	533
15-29	576	578	579	580	579	580	579	578	578	578	579	580	581	581	581	581	580	579	578	576
30-44	566	562	557	553	551	549	548	548	548	547	547	547	549	552	555	558	560	561	562	562
45-59	534	540	548	556	564	570	572	573	577	579	580	579	577	574	570	565	561	556	553	551
60-74	601	594	586	576	565	556	550	544	537	531	525	521	517	515	516	520	526	534	542	550
75 & over	449	457	466	476	485	496	505	514	522	528	535	540	546	550	552	551	549	547	543	540
All ages	3,262	3,266	3,270	3,273	3,277	3,280	3,283	3,286	3,289	3,291	3,294	3,296	3,298	3,300	3,302	3,305	3,307	3,308	3,310	3,312
Percentages																				
0-14	16.4	16.4	16.3	16.3	16.2	16.2	16.1	16.1	16.1	16.0	16.0	16.0	16.0	16.0	16.0	16.0	16.1	16.1	16.1	16.1
15-29	17.7	17.7	17.7	17.7	17.7	17.7	17.7	17.6	17.6	17.6	17.6	17.6	17.6	17.6	17.6	17.6	17.5	17.5	17.4	17.4
30-44	17.4	17.2	17.0	16.9	16.8	16.7	16.7	16.7	16.7	16.6	16.6	16.6	16.6	16.7	16.8	16.9	16.9	17.0	17.0	17.0
45-59	16.4	16.5	16.8	17.0	17.2	17.4	17.4	17.5	17.5	17.6	17.6	17.6	17.5	17.4	17.2	17.1	17.0	16.8	16.7	16.6
60-74	18.4	18.2	17.9	17.6	17.2	17.0	16.7	16.5	16.3	16.1	15.9	15.8	15.7	15.6	15.6	15.7	15.9	16.1	16.4	16.6
75 & over	13.8	14.0	14.3	14.5	14.8	15.1	15.4	15.6	15.9	16.1	16.3	16.4	16.6	16.7	16.7	16.7	16.6	16.5	16.4	16.3
All ages	100.0	100.0	100.0	100.0	100.0	100.0	100.0	100.0	100.0	100.0	100.0	100.0	100.0	100.0	100.0	100.0	100.0	100.0	100.0	100.0
Mean age	44.3	44.4	44.5	44.5	44.6	44.7	44.8	44.8	44.9	44.9	45.0	45.0	45.1	45.1	45.1	45.2	45.2	45.2	45.3	45.3
Median age	43.8	44.0	44.1	44.3	44.4	44.5	44.6	44.7	44.8	44.8	44.8	44.8	44.7	44.7	44.6	44.5	44.5	44.5	44.6	44.6

15.3d Population projections by the Office for National Statistics
Wales, PERSONS, thousands

2014-based
Principal projection

Projected populations at mid-years by age last birthday

Ages	2054	2055	2056	2057	2058	2059	2060	2061	2062	2063	2064	2065	2066	2067	2068	2069	2070	2071	2072	2073
Thousands																				
0-14	533	534	534	534	535	535	535	535	535	535	534	534	534	534	533	533	533	533	532	532
15-29	575	574	573	573	573	573	573	574	574	575	575	576	577	578	578	579	579	580	580	580
30-44	562	562	560	560	560	561	562	563	563	563	563	562	561	560	559	558	557	557	556	556
45-59	548	548	548	548	548	547	548	550	553	556	559	561	563	564	564	564	564	563	562	562
60-74	556	559	561	565	567	568	568	566	563	559	555	551	547	544	543	541	541	542	542	542
75 & over	539	540	541	541	541	541	542	543	545	548	551	556	562	568	574	581	586	590	596	600
All ages	3,314	3,316	3,318	3,321	3,323	3,325	3,327	3,330	3,332	3,335	3,338	3,341	3,344	3,348	3,351	3,355	3,360	3,364	3,368	3,373
Percentages																				
0-14	16.1	16.1	16.1	16.1	16.1	16.1	16.1	16.1	16.0	16.0	16.0	16.0	16.0	15.9	15.9	15.9	15.9	15.8	15.8	15.8
15-29	17.4	17.3	17.3	17.3	17.2	17.2	17.2	17.2	17.2	17.2	17.2	17.2	17.3	17.3	17.3	17.3	17.2	17.2	17.2	17.2
30-44	17.0	16.9	16.9	16.9	16.9	16.9	16.9	16.9	16.9	16.9	16.9	16.8	16.8	16.7	16.7	16.6	16.6	16.5	16.5	16.5
45-59	16.5	16.5	16.5	16.5	16.5	16.5	16.5	16.5	16.6	16.7	16.7	16.8	16.8	16.8	16.8	16.8	16.8	16.7	16.7	16.7
60-74	16.8	16.9	16.9	17.0	17.1	17.1	17.1	17.0	16.9	16.8	16.6	16.5	16.4	16.3	16.2	16.1	16.1	16.1	16.1	16.1
75 & over	16.3	16.3	16.3	16.3	16.3	16.3	16.3	16.3	16.3	16.4	16.5	16.6	16.8	17.0	17.1	17.3	17.4	17.5	17.7	17.8
All ages	100.0	100.0	100.0	100.0	100.0	100.0	100.0	100.0	100.0	100.0	100.0	100.0	100.0	100.0	100.0	100.0	100.0	100.0	100.0	100.0
Mean age	45.3	45.3	45.3	45.4	45.4	45.4	45.4	45.5	45.5	45.5	45.5	45.6	45.6	45.6	45.7	45.7	45.8	45.8	45.9	45.9
Median age	44.6	44.7	44.8	44.8	44.8	44.8	44.8	44.8	44.8	44.9	44.9	44.9	45.0	45.1	45.1	45.2	45.3	45.3	45.4	45.5

Ages	2074	2075	2076	2077	2078	2079	2080	2081	2082	2083	2084	2085	2086	2087	2088	2089	2090	2091	2092	2093
Thousands																				
0-14	532	532	532	533	533	533	533	534	534	534	535	535	535	536	536	536	536	536	536	536
15-29	580	580	580	580	580	580	580	579	579	579	579	578	578	578	578	578	578	578	578	579
30-44	556	556	557	557	558	558	559	560	561	561	562	562	563	563	563	563	563	563	563	563
45-59	563	565	565	566	566	566	566	565	564	563	562	561	560	560	560	560	560	561	561	562
60-74	542	543	545	549	552	555	558	560	561	561	562	562	561	561	562	563	565	566	566	567
75 & over	603	605	607	607	608	609	611	614	618	623	627	631	637	642	645	648	651	653	656	660
All ages	3,378	3,382	3,387	3,392	3,397	3,402	3,407	3,412	3,416	3,421	3,426	3,430	3,435	3,439	3,444	3,449	3,453	3,458	3,462	3,467
Percentages																				
0-14	15.8	15.7	15.7	15.7	15.7	15.7	15.7	15.6	15.6	15.6	15.6	15.6	15.6	15.6	15.6	15.5	15.5	15.5	15.5	15.5
15-29	17.2	17.2	17.1	17.1	17.1	17.0	17.0	17.0	17.0	16.9	16.9	16.9	16.8	16.8	16.8	16.8	16.7	16.7	16.7	16.7
30-44	16.5	16.4	16.4	16.4	16.4	16.4	16.4	16.4	16.4	16.4	16.4	16.4	16.4	16.4	16.4	16.3	16.3	16.3	16.3	16.2
45-59	16.7	16.7	16.7	16.7	16.7	16.6	16.6	16.6	16.5	16.5	16.4	16.4	16.3	16.3	16.3	16.2	16.2	16.2	16.2	16.2
60-74	16.1	16.1	16.1	16.2	16.3	16.3	16.4	16.4	16.5	16.4	16.4	16.4	16.3	16.3	16.3	16.2	16.4	16.4	16.4	16.4
75 & over	17.9	17.9	17.9	17.9	17.9	17.9	17.9	18.0	18.1	18.2	18.3	18.4	18.5	18.7	18.7	18.8	18.8	18.9	19.0	19.0
All ages	100.0	100.0	100.0	100.0	100.0	100.0	100.0	100.0	100.0	100.0	100.0	100.0	100.0	100.0	100.0	100.0	100.0	100.0	100.0	100.0
Mean age	46.0	46.1	46.1	46.2	46.2	46.3	46.3	46.4	46.4	46.5	46.5	46.6	46.6	46.7	46.7	46.8	46.8	46.9	46.9	47.0
Median age	45.5	45.6	45.7	45.7	45.8	45.8	45.8	45.9	45.9	46.0	46.0	46.1	46.1	46.2	46.2	46.3	46.3	46.4	46.4	46.5

15.3d Population projections by the Office for National Statistics
Wales, PERSONS, thousands

2014-based
Principal projection

Projected populations at mid-years by age last birthday

Ages	2094	2095	2096	2097	2098	2099	2100	2101	2102	2103	2104	2105	2106	2107	2108	2109	2110	2111	2112	2113	2114
Thousands																					
0-14	536	536	536	536	536	536	536	536	536	536	536	536	536	536	536	536	537	537	537	537	537
15-29	579	579	580	580	580	581	581	581	582	582	582	582	582	582	582	582	582	582	582	582	582
30-44	563	563	563	562	562	562	562	562	561	561	561	562	562	562	562	562	563	563	563	564	564
45-59	563	564	565	565	566	567	567	568	568	569	569	569	569	569	569	569	569	569	568	568	568
60-74	567	567	566	566	565	564	564	563	563	563	564	564	565	566	567	568	569	570	571	572	573
75 & over	664	668	672	677	682	687	692	697	702	706	711	715	719	723	727	731	735	739	742	746	750
All ages	3,472	3,477	3,481	3,486	3,491	3,496	3,502	3,507	3,512	3,517	3,523	3,528	3,533	3,538	3,544	3,549	3,554	3,560	3,565	3,570	3,575
Percentages																					
0-14	15.4	15.4	15.4	15.4	15.4	15.3	15.3	15.3	15.3	15.2	15.2	15.2	15.2	15.2	15.1	15.1	15.1	15.1	15.1	15.0	15.0
15-29	16.7	16.7	16.7	16.6	16.6	16.6	16.6	16.6	16.6	16.5	16.5	16.5	16.5	16.5	16.4	16.4	16.4	16.4	16.3	16.3	16.3
30-44	16.2	16.2	16.2	16.1	16.1	16.1	16.0	16.0	16.0	16.0	15.9	15.9	15.9	15.9	15.9	15.8	15.8	15.8	15.8	15.8	15.8
45-59	16.2	16.2	16.2	16.2	16.2	16.2	16.2	16.2	16.2	16.2	16.1	16.1	16.1	16.1	16.1	16.0	16.0	16.0	15.9	15.9	15.9
60-74	16.3	16.3	16.3	16.2	16.2	16.1	16.1	16.1	16.0	16.0	16.0	16.0	16.1	16.0	16.0	16.0	16.0	16.0	16.0	16.0	16.0
75 & over	19.1	19.2	19.3	19.4	19.5	19.6	19.8	19.9	20.0	20.1	20.2	20.3	20.3	20.4	20.5	20.6	20.7	20.8	20.8	20.9	21.0
All ages	100.0	100.0	100.0	100.0	100.0	100.0	100.0	100.0	100.0	100.0	100.0	100.0	100.0	100.0	100.0	100.0	100.0	100.0	100.0	100.0	100.0
Mean age	47.0	47.1	47.1	47.2	47.2	47.3	47.4	47.4	47.5	47.5	47.6	47.7	47.7	47.8	47.8	47.9	48.0	48.0	48.1	48.1	48.2
Median age	46.5	46.6	46.7	46.7	46.8	46.9	46.9	47.0	47.1	47.1	47.2	47.2	47.3	47.4	47.4	47.5	47.6	47.6	47.7	47.7	47.8

Source: Office for National Statistics

Note: Figures may not add exactly due to rounding.
* Children under 16. Working age and pensionable age populations based on state pension age (SPA) for given year.
Between 2012 and 2018, SPA will change from 65 years for men and 61 years for women, to 65 years for both sexes.
Then between 2019 and 2020, SPA will change from 65 years to 66 years for both men and women.
Between 2026 and 2027 SPA will increase to 67 years and between 2044 and 2046 to 68 years for both sexes. This is based on SPA under the 2014 Pensions Act.
*** This is consistent with the age-group definitions used in ONS Labour Market Statistics.

National Population Projections are currently produced every two years. The 2016-based projections are not due to be published until November/December 2017. Therefore, this table series will be updated in the next edition

15.3d Population projections by the Office for National Statistics
Wales, MALES, thousands

2014-based
Principal projection

Projected populations at mid-years by age last birthday

Ages	2014	2015	2016	2017	2018	2019	2020	2021	2022	2023	2024	2025	2026	2027	2028	2029	2030	2031	2032	2033
Thousands																				
0-14	266	267	267	269	270	272	273	274	274	274	274	274	273	273	273	273	274	274	274	274
15-29	307	308	308	307	306	304	301	299	297	296	294	294	294	294	294	294	294	295	297	298
30-44	270	269	267	265	266	268	271	276	280	285	288	290	292	294	296	297	297	297	296	294
45-59	307	309	311	311	310	307	304	299	294	288	283	280	276	272	269	266	264	262	260	261
60-74	256	258	261	264	266	267	269	272	272	272	274	277	280	283	285	288	290	292	293	292
75 & over	115	117	120	123	128	133	138	142	151	158	164	169	174	178	182	185	189	192	195	199
All ages	1,521	1,528	1,534	1,539	1,545	1,551	1,557	1,562	1,568	1,573	1,579	1,584	1,589	1,594	1,599	1,604	1,608	1,612	1,616	1,619
Percentages																				
0-14	17.5	17.5	17.4	17.5	17.5	17.5	17.6	17.5	17.5	17.4	17.4	17.3	17.2	17.1	17.1	17.0	17.0	17.0	17.0	17.0
15-29	20.2	20.2	20.1	20.0	19.8	19.6	19.4	19.1	19.0	18.8	18.7	18.6	18.5	18.4	18.4	18.3	18.3	18.3	18.4	18.4
30-44	17.8	17.6	17.4	17.2	17.2	17.3	17.4	17.7	17.9	18.1	18.3	18.3	18.4	18.5	18.5	18.5	18.5	18.4	18.3	18.2
45-59	20.2	20.2	20.3	20.2	20.0	19.8	19.5	19.1	18.7	18.3	17.9	17.7	17.4	17.1	16.9	16.6	16.4	16.2	16.1	16.1
60-74	16.8	16.9	17.0	17.1	17.2	17.2	17.3	17.4	17.3	17.3	17.4	17.5	17.6	17.8	17.8	18.0	18.0	18.1	18.1	18.0
75 & over	7.6	7.7	7.8	8.0	8.3	8.6	8.9	9.1	9.6	10.1	10.4	10.7	10.9	11.1	11.4	11.6	11.7	11.9	12.1	12.3
All ages	100.0	100.0	100.0	100.0	100.0	100.0	100.0	100.0	100.0	100.0	100.0	100.0	100.0	100.0	100.0	100.0	100.0	100.0	100.0	100.0
Mean age	40.5	40.6	40.8	41.0	41.1	41.3	41.4	41.6	41.7	41.8	42.0	42.1	42.2	42.4	42.5	42.6	42.7	42.9	43.0	43.1
Median age	40.8	40.8	40.8	40.8	40.8	40.8	40.9	41.0	41.1	41.2	41.2	41.3	41.3	41.4	41.5	41.6	41.7	41.8	42.0	42.1

Ages	2034	2035	2036	2037	2038	2039	2040	2041	2042	2043	2044	2045	2046	2047	2048	2049	2050	2051	2052	2053
Thousands																				
0-14	274	274	274	273	272	272	271	271	271	270	270	271	271	271	271	272	272	272	273	273
15-29	300	301	301	302	301	302	301	301	301	301	301	302	302	302	302	302	302	301	301	300
30-44	292	290	288	287	286	285	284	284	284	284	284	284	285	286	288	289	290	291	291	291
45-59	264	267	272	276	280	284	286	288	291	292	293	294	294	293	291	289	287	285	284	284
60-74	290	287	283	278	273	269	266	263	260	257	254	253	251	250	252	254	258	263	267	271
75 & over	203	206	211	215	220	224	229	233	236	239	243	245	248	249	250	250	249	247	246	244
All ages	1,622	1,625	1,628	1,630	1,633	1,635	1,637	1,639	1,642	1,644	1,646	1,648	1,650	1,652	1,654	1,656	1,658	1,660	1,661	1,663
Percentages																				
0-14	16.9	16.9	16.8	16.7	16.7	16.6	16.6	16.5	16.5	16.5	16.4	16.4	16.4	16.4	16.4	16.4	16.4	16.4	16.4	16.4
15-29	18.5	18.5	18.5	18.5	18.5	18.4	18.4	18.3	18.3	18.3	18.3	18.3	18.3	18.3	18.3	18.2	18.2	18.1	18.1	18.0
30-44	18.0	17.9	17.7	17.6	17.5	17.4	17.4	17.3	17.3	17.3	17.2	17.2	17.3	17.3	17.4	17.5	17.5	17.5	17.5	17.5
45-59	16.2	16.4	16.7	16.9	17.2	17.4	17.5	17.6	17.7	17.8	17.8	17.8	17.8	17.7	17.6	17.5	17.3	17.2	17.1	17.1
60-74	17.9	17.6	17.4	17.0	16.7	16.4	16.2	16.0	15.8	15.6	15.5	15.3	15.2	15.2	15.2	15.4	15.5	15.8	16.0	16.3
75 & over	12.5	12.7	12.9	13.2	13.5	13.7	14.0	14.2	14.4	14.6	14.7	14.9	15.0	15.1	15.1	15.1	15.0	14.9	14.8	14.7
All ages	100.0	100.0	100.0	100.0	100.0	100.0	100.0	100.0	100.0	100.0	100.0	100.0	100.0	100.0	100.0	100.0	100.0	100.0	100.0	100.0
Mean age	43.2	43.3	43.4	43.4	43.5	43.6	43.7	43.7	43.8	43.8	43.9	43.9	44.0	44.0	44.0	44.1	44.1	44.2	44.2	44.2
Median age	42.3	42.4	42.6	42.8	42.9	43.0	43.1	43.2	43.2	43.2	43.2	43.2	43.1	43.1	43.1	43.1	43.1	43.2	43.3	43.3

15.3d Population projections by the Office for National Statistics
Wales, MALES, thousands

2014-based
Principal projection

Projected populations at mid-years by age last birthday

Ages	2054	2055	2056	2057	2058	2059	2060	2061	2062	2063	2064	2065	2066	2067	2068	2069	2070	2071	2072	2073
Thousands																				
0-14	273	273	274	274	274	274	274	274	274	274	274	274	273	273	273	273	273	273	273	273
15-29	299	299	298	298	298	298	298	298	299	299	299	300	300	301	301	301	301	302	302	302
30-44	291	291	291	290	290	291	291	292	292	292	292	292	291	291	290	289	289	289	288	288
45-59	282	282	282	282	282	282	282	283	284	286	287	289	289	290	290	290	290	290	289	289
60-74	275	277	280	282	284	286	286	286	285	284	282	280	279	278	278	277	276	277	277	277
75 & over	244	245	245	245	246	246	247	248	249	251	253	256	260	263	267	271	274	277	281	284
All ages	1,665	1,667	1,669	1,671	1,674	1,676	1,678	1,680	1,683	1,685	1,687	1,690	1,693	1,695	1,698	1,701	1,704	1,707	1,710	1,713
Percentages																				
0-14	16.4	16.4	16.4	16.4	16.4	16.3	16.3	16.3	16.3	16.3	16.2	16.2	16.2	16.1	16.1	16.1	16.0	16.0	16.0	15.9
15-29	18.0	17.9	17.9	17.8	17.8	17.8	17.8	17.8	17.8	17.7	17.7	17.7	17.7	17.7	17.7	17.7	17.7	17.7	17.6	17.6
30-44	17.5	17.5	17.4	17.4	17.4	17.4	17.4	17.4	17.3	17.3	17.3	17.2	17.2	17.1	17.1	17.0	17.0	16.9	16.9	16.8
45-59	16.9	16.9	16.9	16.8	16.8	16.8	16.8	16.8	16.9	17.0	17.0	17.1	17.1	17.1	17.1	17.1	17.0	16.9	16.9	16.9
60-74	16.5	16.6	16.7	16.9	17.0	17.0	17.0	17.0	17.0	16.8	16.7	16.6	16.5	16.4	16.3	16.3	16.2	16.2	16.2	16.2
75 & over	14.7	14.7	14.7	14.7	14.7	14.7	14.7	14.7	14.8	14.9	15.0	15.2	15.4	15.5	15.7	15.9	16.1	16.3	16.4	16.5
All ages	100.0	100.0	100.0	100.0	100.0	100.0	100.0	100.0	100.0	100.0	100.0	100.0	100.0	100.0	100.0	100.0	100.0	100.0	100.0	100.0
Mean age	44.3	44.3	44.3	44.4	44.4	44.4	44.5	44.5	44.6	44.6	44.7	44.7	44.8	44.8	44.9	45.0	45.0	45.1	45.2	45.2
Median age	43.4	43.5	43.6	43.6	43.6	43.7	43.7	43.7	43.8	43.8	43.9	44.0	44.1	44.1	44.2	44.3	44.4	44.5	44.6	44.7

Ages	2074	2075	2076	2077	2078	2079	2080	2081	2082	2083	2084	2085	2086	2087	2088	2089	2090	2091	2092	2093
Thousands																				
0-14	273	273	273	273	273	273	273	273	274	274	274	274	274	274	275	275	275	275	275	275
15-29	302	302	302	302	302	302	302	301	301	301	301	301	301	301	301	301	301	301	301	301
30-44	288	288	289	289	289	290	290	290	291	291	291	292	292	292	292	292	292	292	292	292
45-59	290	291	291	291	291	291	291	291	290	290	289	289	289	288	288	289	289	289	290	290
60-74	278	278	279	281	282	284	285	286	287	287	288	288	288	288	288	289	289	290	290	291
75 & over	286	288	289	290	291	292	293	295	297	300	303	305	308	311	313	315	317	318	320	322
All ages	1,716	1,719	1,722	1,726	1,729	1,732	1,735	1,738	1,741	1,743	1,746	1,749	1,752	1,754	1,757	1,760	1,762	1,765	1,768	1,770
Percentages																				
0-14	15.9	15.9	15.8	15.8	15.8	15.8	15.8	15.7	15.7	15.7	15.7	15.7	15.7	15.6	15.6	15.6	15.6	15.6	15.5	15.5
15-29	17.6	17.6	17.5	17.5	17.5	17.4	17.4	17.3	17.3	17.3	17.2	17.2	17.2	17.1	17.1	17.1	17.1	17.1	17.0	17.0
30-44	16.8	16.8	16.8	16.7	16.7	16.7	16.7	16.7	16.7	16.7	16.7	16.7	16.7	16.6	16.6	16.6	16.6	16.6	16.5	16.5
45-59	16.9	16.9	16.9	16.9	16.9	16.8	16.8	16.5	16.5	16.5	16.5	16.5	16.5	16.4	16.4	16.4	16.4	16.4	16.4	16.4
60-74	16.2	16.2	16.2	16.3	16.3	16.4	16.5	16.5	16.5	16.5	16.5	16.5	16.4	16.4	16.4	16.4	16.4	16.4	16.4	16.4
75 & over	16.7	16.7	16.8	16.8	16.8	16.9	16.9	17.0	17.1	17.2	17.3	17.5	17.6	17.7	17.8	17.9	18.0	18.0	18.1	18.2
All ages	100.0	100.0	100.0	100.0	100.0	100.0	100.0	100.0	100.0	100.0	100.0	100.0	100.0	100.0	100.0	100.0	100.0	100.0	100.0	100.0
Mean age	45.3	45.4	45.5	45.5	45.6	45.7	45.7	45.8	45.8	45.9	46.0	46.0	46.1	46.1	46.2	46.3	46.3	46.4	46.4	46.5
Median age	44.7	44.8	44.9	45.0	45.0	45.1	45.1	45.2	45.2	45.3	45.3	45.4	45.5	45.5	45.6	45.6	45.7	45.8	45.8	45.9

15.3d Population projections by the Office for National Statistics
Wales, MALES, thousands

2014-based
Principal projection

Projected populations at mid-years by age last birthday

Ages	2094	2095	2096	2097	2098	2099	2100	2101	2102	2103	2104	2105	2106	2107	2108	2109	2110	2111	2112	2113	2114
Thousands																					
0-14	275	275	275	275	275	275	275	275	275	275	275	275	275	275	275	275	275	275	275	275	275
15-29	301	301	302	302	302	302	302	303	303	303	303	303	303	303	303	303	303	303	303	303	303
30-44	292	292	292	292	292	292	291	291	291	291	291	291	291	292	292	292	292	292	292	293	293
45-59	290	290	291	291	292	292	292	293	293	293	293	293	293	293	293	293	293	293	293	293	293
60-74	291	291	291	290	290	289	289	289	289	289	290	290	290	291	291	292	293	293	294	294	295
75 & over	324	326	329	331	334	336	339	342	344	347	349	351	353	355	358	360	362	364	366	368	370
All ages	1,773	1,776	1,778	1,781	1,784	1,786	1,789	1,792	1,795	1,798	1,800	1,803	1,806	1,809	1,812	1,815	1,817	1,820	1,823	1,826	1,829
Percentages																					
0-14	15.5	15.5	15.4	15.4	15.4	15.4	15.3	15.3	15.3	15.3	15.2	15.2	15.2	15.2	15.2	15.1	15.1	15.1	15.1	15.1	15.1
15-29	17.0	17.0	17.0	16.9	16.9	16.9	16.9	16.9	16.9	16.8	16.8	16.8	16.8	16.8	16.7	16.7	16.7	16.6	16.6	16.6	16.6
30-44	16.5	16.4	16.4	16.4	16.4	16.3	16.3	16.3	16.2	16.2	16.2	16.2	16.1	16.1	16.1	16.1	16.1	16.1	16.0	16.0	16.0
45-59	16.4	16.4	16.4	16.3	16.4	16.4	16.3	16.3	16.3	16.3	16.3	16.3	16.2	16.2	16.2	16.2	16.1	16.1	16.1	16.1	16.1
60-74	16.4	16.4	16.4	16.3	16.2	16.2	16.2	16.1	16.1	16.1	16.1	16.1	16.1	16.1	16.1	16.1	16.1	16.1	16.1	16.1	16.1
75 & over	18.3	18.4	18.5	18.6	18.7	18.8	19.0	19.1	19.2	19.3	19.4	19.5	19.6	19.7	19.7	19.8	19.9	20.0	20.1	20.1	20.2
All ages	100.0	100.0	100.0	100.0	100.0	100.0	100.0	100.0	100.0	100.0	100.0	100.0	100.0	100.0	100.0	100.0	100.0	100.0	100.0	100.0	100.0
Mean age	46.5	46.6	46.6	46.7	46.8	46.8	46.9	46.9	47.0	47.1	47.1	47.2	47.3	47.3	47.4	47.4	47.5	47.6	47.6	47.7	47.7
Median age	45.9	46.0	46.1	46.1	46.2	46.3	46.4	46.4	46.5	46.6	46.6	46.7	46.8	46.8	46.9	46.9	47.0	47.1	47.1	47.2	47.2

Source: Office for National Statistics

Note: Figures may not add exactly due to rounding.
* Children under 16. Working age and pensionable age populations based on state pension age (SPA) for given year.
Between 2012 and 2018, SPA will change from 65 years for men and 61 years for women, to 65 years for both sexes.
Then between 2019 and 2020, SPA will change from 65 years to 66 years for both men and women.
Between 2026 and 2027 SPA will increase to 67 years and between 2044 and 2046 to 68 years for both sexes. This is based on SPA under the 2014 Pensions Act.
** This is consistent with the age-group definitions used in ONS Labour Market Statistics.

National Population Projections are currently produced every two years. The 2016-based projections are not due to be published until November/December 2017. Therefore, this table series will be updated in the next edition

15.3d Population projections by the Office for National Statistics
Wales, FEMALES, thousands

2014-based
Principal projection

Projected populations at mid-years by age last birthday

Ages	2014	2015	2016	2017	2018	2019	2020	2021	2022	2023	2024	2025	2026	2027	2028	2029	2030	2031	2032	2033
Thousands																				
0-14	253	253	254	256	258	259	260	261	261	261	261	261	260	260	260	260	261	261	261	261
15-29	291	291	289	287	284	281	279	276	273	272	270	270	271	271	271	271	271	272	274	275
30-44	276	274	270	269	268	270	272	275	279	282	284	284	284	285	285	285	283	282	279	276
45-59	319	322	324	325	324	322	318	313	308	302	297	293	289	285	281	277	275	271	270	269
60-74	270	273	276	279	281	283	286	289	289	289	292	296	299	302	305	308	310	313	314	313
75 & over	161	162	163	166	169	174	178	182	191	198	204	209	214	218	222	226	230	234	238	242
All ages	1,571	1,574	1,577	1,581	1,585	1,588	1,592	1,596	1,600	1,604	1,608	1,612	1,616	1,620	1,624	1,627	1,630	1,633	1,635	1,637
Percentages																				
0-14	16.1	16.1	16.1	16.2	16.3	16.3	16.3	16.3	16.3	16.3	16.2	16.2	16.1	16.0	16.0	16.0	16.0	16.0	16.0	16.0
15-29	18.6	18.5	18.3	18.1	17.9	17.7	17.5	17.3	17.1	16.9	16.8	16.8	16.8	16.7	16.7	16.6	16.6	16.7	16.7	16.8
30-44	17.6	17.4	17.1	17.0	16.9	17.0	17.1	17.2	17.4	17.6	17.7	17.6	17.6	17.6	17.5	17.5	17.4	17.2	17.1	16.9
45-59	20.3	20.4	20.6	20.6	20.5	20.2	20.0	19.6	19.2	18.8	18.5	18.2	17.9	17.6	17.3	17.0	16.9	16.6	16.5	16.5
60-74	17.2	17.3	17.5	17.6	17.7	17.8	18.0	18.1	18.0	18.0	18.2	18.3	18.5	18.7	18.8	18.9	19.0	19.2	19.2	19.1
75 & over	10.3	10.3	10.4	10.5	10.7	10.9	11.2	11.4	11.9	12.3	12.7	13.0	13.2	13.4	13.7	13.9	14.1	14.3	14.5	14.8
All ages	100.0	100.0	100.0	100.0	100.0	100.0	100.0	100.0	100.0	100.0	100.0	100.0	100.0	100.0	100.0	100.0	100.0	100.0	100.0	100.0
Mean age	42.7	42.8	42.9	43.0	43.2	43.3	43.5	43.6	43.8	43.9	44.1	44.2	44.3	44.5	44.6	44.7	44.9	45.0	45.1	45.2
Median age	43.4	43.5	43.7	43.9	44.0	44.1	44.2	44.2	44.2	44.3	44.4	44.5	44.6	44.7	44.8	44.9	45.0	45.1	45.2	45.3

Ages	2034	2035	2036	2037	2038	2039	2040	2041	2042	2043	2044	2045	2046	2047	2048	2049	2050	2051	2052	2053
Thousands																				
0-14	261	261	260	260	259	259	258	258	258	257	257	257	258	258	258	258	259	259	259	260
15-29	276	277	278	278	278	278	278	277	277	277	278	278	279	279	279	279	278	278	277	277
30-44	274	271	269	266	265	264	264	264	264	264	263	263	264	266	267	269	270	270	271	271
45-59	271	273	276	280	284	286	286	286	286	287	287	285	284	281	278	276	273	271	268	267
60-74	311	308	303	298	293	288	284	281	277	274	270	268	265	264	264	266	268	272	276	279
75 & over	246	251	256	261	266	271	276	281	285	289	293	295	299	301	302	302	301	299	297	296
All ages	1,639	1,641	1,642	1,643	1,644	1,645	1,646	1,646	1,647	1,647	1,648	1,648	1,648	1,649	1,649	1,649	1,649	1,649	1,649	1,649
Percentages																				
0-14	15.9	15.9	15.9	15.8	15.8	15.7	15.7	15.7	15.6	15.6	15.6	15.6	15.6	15.6	15.7	15.7	15.7	15.7	15.7	15.8
15-29	16.9	16.9	16.9	16.9	16.9	16.9	16.9	16.9	16.8	16.8	16.9	16.9	16.9	16.9	16.9	16.9	16.9	16.8	16.8	16.8
30-44	16.7	16.5	16.4	16.2	16.1	16.0	16.0	16.0	16.0	16.0	16.0	16.0	16.0	16.1	16.2	16.3	16.4	16.4	16.4	16.4
45-59	16.5	16.6	16.8	17.1	17.2	17.4	17.4	17.3	17.4	17.4	17.4	17.3	17.2	17.1	16.9	16.7	16.6	16.5	16.3	16.2
60-74	19.0	18.8	18.5	18.1	17.8	17.5	17.3	17.0	16.8	16.6	16.4	16.3	16.1	16.0	16.0	16.1	16.3	16.5	16.7	16.9
75 & over	15.0	15.3	15.6	15.9	16.2	16.5	16.8	17.1	17.3	17.5	17.8	17.9	18.1	18.2	18.3	18.3	18.2	18.1	18.0	17.9
All ages	100.0	100.0	100.0	100.0	100.0	100.0	100.0	100.0	100.0	100.0	100.0	100.0	100.0	100.0	100.0	100.0	100.0	100.0	100.0	100.0
Mean age	45.3	45.4	45.5	45.6	45.7	45.8	45.9	45.9	46.0	46.0	46.1	46.1	46.2	46.2	46.2	46.2	46.3	46.3	46.3	46.3
Median age	45.4	45.6	45.7	45.9	46.0	46.1	46.2	46.3	46.3	46.4	46.4	46.4	46.4	46.3	46.2	46.1	46.0	46.0	46.0	45.9

15.3d Population projections by the Office for National Statistics
Wales, FEMALES, thousands

2014-based
Principal projection

Projected populations at mid-years by age last birthday

Ages	2054	2055	2056	2057	2058	2059	2060	2061	2062	2063	2064	2065	2066	2067	2068	2069	2070	2071	2072	2073
Thousands																				
0-14	260	260	260	261	261	261	261	261	261	261	261	260	260	260	260	260	260	260	260	260
15-29	276	275	275	275	275	275	275	275	275	276	276	276	277	277	277	278	278	278	278	278
30-44	271	271	270	269	270	270	271	271	271	271	271	271	270	270	269	269	268	268	268	268
45-59	266	266	266	266	266	266	266	267	269	270	272	273	273	274	274	274	274	273	273	273
60-74	281	282	282	283	283	283	282	280	278	275	273	270	268	266	265	264	264	265	265	265
75 & over	295	295	295	295	295	295	295	295	296	297	298	300	303	305	308	310	311	313	315	316
All ages	1,649	1,649	1,649	1,649	1,649	1,649	1,649	1,649	1,650	1,650	1,650	1,651	1,652	1,652	1,653	1,654	1,655	1,657	1,658	1,660
Percentages																				
0-14	15.8	15.8	15.8	15.8	15.8	15.8	15.8	15.8	15.8	15.8	15.8	15.8	15.8	15.7	15.7	15.7	15.7	15.7	15.7	15.6
15-29	16.7	16.7	16.7	16.7	16.7	16.7	16.7	16.7	16.7	16.7	16.7	16.7	16.8	16.8	16.8	16.8	16.8	16.8	16.8	16.8
30-44	16.4	16.4	16.4	16.3	16.3	16.4	16.4	16.4	16.4	16.4	16.4	16.4	16.4	16.3	16.3	16.2	16.2	16.2	16.1	16.1
45-59	16.1	16.1	16.2	16.1	16.1	16.1	16.1	16.2	16.3	16.4	16.5	16.5	16.6	16.6	16.6	16.6	16.5	16.5	16.4	16.4
60-74	17.0	17.1	17.1	17.1	17.1	17.2	17.1	17.0	16.8	16.7	16.5	16.4	16.2	16.1	16.0	16.0	16.0	16.0	16.0	16.0
75 & over	17.9	17.9	17.9	17.9	17.9	17.9	17.9	17.9	17.9	18.0	18.1	18.2	18.3	18.5	18.6	18.7	18.8	18.9	19.0	19.0
All ages	100.0	100.0	100.0	100.0	100.0	100.0	100.0	100.0	100.0	100.0	100.0	100.0	100.0	100.0	100.0	100.0	100.0	100.0	100.0	100.0
Mean age	46.3	46.3	46.4	46.4	46.4	46.4	46.4	46.4	46.4	46.4	46.4	46.4	46.5	46.5	46.5	46.5	46.6	46.6	46.6	46.7
Median age	46.0	46.0	46.0	46.0	46.1	46.1	46.0	46.0	46.0	46.0	46.0	46.0	46.0	46.0	46.1	46.1	46.2	46.2	46.3	46.3

Ages	2074	2075	2076	2077	2078	2079	2080	2081	2082	2083	2084	2085	2086	2087	2088	2089	2090	2091	2092	2093
Thousands																				
0-14	260	260	260	260	260	260	260	260	260	261	261	261	261	261	261	261	261	261	261	261
15-29	278	278	278	278	278	278	278	278	278	278	278	277	277	277	277	277	277	277	277	278
30-44	268	268	268	268	268	269	269	269	270	270	270	271	271	271	271	271	271	271	271	271
45-59	274	274	274	275	275	275	274	274	274	273	272	272	272	272	272	272	272	272	272	273
60-74	265	265	266	268	270	271	272	273	274	274	274	274	274	274	274	275	275	276	276	276
75 & over	317	318	318	317	317	317	318	319	320	322	324	326	328	330	332	333	334	335	337	338
All ages	1,661	1,663	1,665	1,667	1,668	1,670	1,672	1,674	1,676	1,678	1,680	1,681	1,683	1,685	1,687	1,689	1,691	1,693	1,695	1,697
Percentages																				
0-14	15.6	15.6	15.6	15.6	15.6	15.6	15.6	15.5	15.5	15.5	15.5	15.5	15.5	15.5	15.5	15.5	15.5	15.4	15.4	15.4
15-29	16.8	16.7	16.7	16.7	16.7	16.7	16.6	16.6	16.6	16.6	16.5	16.5	16.5	16.5	16.4	16.4	16.4	16.4	16.4	16.4
30-44	16.1	16.1	16.1	16.1	16.1	16.1	16.1	16.1	16.1	16.1	16.1	16.1	16.1	16.1	16.1	16.1	16.0	16.0	16.0	16.0
45-59	16.5	16.5	16.5	16.5	16.5	16.4	16.4	16.4	16.3	16.3	16.2	16.2	16.1	16.1	16.1	16.1	16.1	16.1	16.1	16.1
60-74	15.9	16.0	16.0	16.1	16.2	16.2	16.3	16.3	16.3	16.3	16.3	16.3	16.3	16.2	16.2	16.3	16.3	16.3	16.3	16.3
75 & over	19.1	19.1	19.1	19.0	19.0	19.0	19.0	19.1	19.1	19.2	19.3	19.4	19.5	19.6	19.7	19.7	19.8	19.8	19.9	19.9
All ages	100.0	100.0	100.0	100.0	100.0	100.0	100.0	100.0	100.0	100.0	100.0	100.0	100.0	100.0	100.0	100.0	100.0	100.0	100.0	100.0
Mean age	46.7	46.7	46.8	46.8	46.9	46.9	47.0	47.0	47.0	47.1	47.1	47.2	47.2	47.3	47.3	47.3	47.4	47.4	47.5	47.5
Median age	46.4	46.4	46.5	46.5	46.5	46.6	46.6	46.6	46.7	46.7	46.7	46.8	46.8	46.8	46.9	46.9	47.0	47.0	47.1	47.1

15.3d Population projections by the Office for National Statistics
Wales, FEMALES, thousands

2014-based
Principal projection

Projected populations at mid-years by age last birthday

Ages	2094	2095	2096	2097	2098	2099	2100	2101	2102	2103	2104	2105	2106	2107	2108	2109	2110	2111	2112	2113	2114
Thousands																					
0-14	261	261	261	261	261	261	261	261	261	261	261	261	261	261	262	262	262	262	262	262	262
15-29	278	278	278	278	278	279	279	279	279	279	279	279	279	279	279	279	279	279	279	279	279
30-44	271	271	271	271	270	270	270	270	270	270	270	270	270	270	270	271	271	271	271	271	271
45-59	273	273	274	274	274	275	275	275	275	275	276	276	276	276	276	276	275	275	275	275	275
60-74	276	276	276	275	275	275	274	274	274	274	274	275	275	275	276	276	277	277	278	278	279
75 & over	340	342	344	346	348	351	353	355	357	360	362	364	366	368	369	371	373	375	377	379	381
All ages	1,699	1,701	1,703	1,706	1,708	1,710	1,712	1,715	1,717	1,720	1,722	1,725	1,727	1,729	1,732	1,734	1,737	1,739	1,742	1,744	1,747
Percentages																					
0-14	15.4	15.4	15.3	15.3	15.3	15.3	15.3	15.2	15.2	15.2	15.2	15.2	15.1	15.1	15.1	15.1	15.1	15.1	15.0	15.0	15.0
15-29	16.3	16.3	16.3	16.3	16.3	16.3	16.3	16.3	16.2	16.2	16.2	16.2	16.2	16.1	16.1	16.1	16.1	16.1	16.0	16.0	16.0
30-44	15.9	15.9	15.9	15.9	15.8	15.8	15.8	15.8	15.7	15.7	15.7	15.7	15.6	15.6	15.6	15.6	15.6	15.6	15.6	15.5	15.5
45-59	16.1	16.1	16.1	16.1	16.1	16.1	16.1	16.0	16.0	16.0	16.0	16.0	16.0	15.9	15.9	15.9	15.9	15.8	15.8	15.8	15.7
60-74	16.3	16.2	16.2	16.1	16.1	16.1	16.0	16.0	16.0	15.9	15.9	15.9	15.9	15.9	15.9	15.9	15.9	15.9	15.9	15.9	15.9
75 & over	20.0	20.1	20.2	20.3	20.4	20.5	20.6	20.7	20.8	20.9	21.0	21.1	21.2	21.3	21.3	21.4	21.5	21.6	21.6	21.7	21.8
All ages	100.0	100.0	100.0	100.0	100.0	100.0	100.0	100.0	100.0	100.0	100.0	100.0	100.0	100.0	100.0	100.0	100.0	100.0	100.0	100.0	100.0
Mean age	47.5	47.6	47.6	47.7	47.7	47.8	47.9	47.9	48.0	48.0	48.1	48.1	48.2	48.3	48.3	48.4	48.4	48.5	48.5	48.6	48.7
Median age	47.2	47.2	47.3	47.3	47.4	47.5	47.5	47.6	47.7	47.7	47.8	47.8	47.9	48.0	48.0	48.1	48.1	48.2	48.3	48.3	48.4

Source: Office for National Statistics

Note: Figures may not add exactly due to rounding.
* Children under 16. Working age and pensionable age populations based on state pension age (SPA) for given year.
Between 2012 and 2018, SPA will change from 65 years for men and 61 years for women, to 65 years for both sexes.
Then between 2019 and 2020, SPA will change from 65 years to 66 years for both men and women.
Between 2026 and 2027 SPA will increase to 67 years and between 2044 and 2046 to 68 years for both sexes. This is based on SPA under the 2014 Pensions Act.
** This is consistent with the age-group definitions used in ONS Labour Market Statistics.

National Population Projections are currently produced every two years. The 2016-based projections are not due to be published until November/December 2017. Therefore, this table series will be updated in the next edition

15.3e Mid-2015 Population estimates: Scotland by sex and single year of age

Ages	Persons	Males	females	Ages	Persons	Males	Females
ALL AGES	5,373,000	2,610,469	2,762,531	45	75,732	36,546	39,186
0	56,001	28,765	27,236	46	78,720	37,963	40,757
1	56,678	29,135	27,543	47	80,228	38,692	41,536
2	57,813	29,527	28,286	48	80,816	39,457	41,359
3	59,341	30,503	28,838	49	80,322	38,907	41,415
4	61,341	31,354	29,987	50	83,200	40,490	42,710
5	58,497	29,801	28,696	51	82,142	39,635	42,507
6	60,030	30,513	29,517	52	81,807	39,711	42,096
7	59,905	30,453	29,452	53	79,957	39,209	40,748
8	57,571	29,438	28,133	54	78,187	38,177	40,010
9	56,353	28,689	27,664	55	75,506	37,015	38,491
10	55,960	28,779	27,181	56	74,932	36,388	38,544
11	54,864	28,216	26,648	57	72,849	35,448	37,401
12	53,191	27,119	26,072	58	70,878	34,653	36,225
13	52,935	26,995	25,940	59	68,655	33,567	35,088
14	55,192	28,050	27,142	60	65,720	31,963	33,757
15	56,590	29,133	27,457	61	64,782	31,625	33,157
16	58,760	30,163	28,597	62	63,577	30,952	32,625
17	60,074	30,796	29,278	63	61,183	29,767	31,416
18	62,576	32,041	30,535	64	61,736	29,940	31,796
19	65,983	33,634	32,349	65	61,768	30,116	31,652
20	68,431	34,514	33,917	66	63,190	30,668	32,522
21	71,367	35,638	35,729	67	65,005	31,496	33,509
22	73,141	36,142	36,999	68	70,181	33,786	36,395
23	77,485	38,305	39,180	69	52,811	25,421	27,390
24	77,246	38,562	38,684	70	49,594	23,449	26,145
25	74,147	37,083	37,064	71	50,402	23,965	26,437
26	73,527	36,676	36,851	72	48,067	22,259	25,808
27	73,839	36,683	37,156	73	43,865	20,048	23,817
28	71,408	35,205	36,203	74	40,398	18,201	22,197
29	70,965	35,146	35,819	75	40,800	18,333	22,467
30	70,533	34,548	35,985	76	39,510	17,682	21,828
31	68,276	33,488	34,788	77	37,998	16,944	21,054
32	69,258	33,813	35,445	78	35,493	15,270	20,223
33	70,132	34,009	36,123	79	33,768	14,474	19,294
34	69,701	34,142	35,559	80	31,477	13,378	18,099
35	68,314	33,487	34,827	81	28,857	11,995	16,862
36	66,079	32,708	33,371	82	26,397	10,877	15,520
37	61,363	29,894	31,469	83	25,116	10,003	15,113
38	60,428	29,942	30,486	84	22,494	8,767	13,727
39	63,953	31,434	32,519	85	19,821	7,412	12,409
40	64,459	31,390	33,069	86	17,425	6,435	10,990
41	65,347	32,144	33,203	87	14,672	5,175	9,497
42	69,421	33,994	35,427	88	12,855	4,389	8,466
43	73,863	35,763	38,100	89	11,239	3,715	7,524
44	76,735	36,869	39,866	90	39,795	11,423	28,372

Source: Office for National Statistics

1. These unrounded estimates are published to enable and encourage further calculations and analysis. However, the estimates should not be taken to be accurate to the level of detail provided

2. The estimates are produced using a variety of data sources and statistical models, including some statistical disclosure control methods, and small estimates should not be taken to refer to particular individuals.

3. The estimated resident population of an area includes all those people who usually live there, regardless of nationality. Arriving international migrants are included in the usually resident population if they remain in the UK for at least a year. Emigrants are excluded if they remain outside the UK for at least a year. This is consistent with the United Nations definition of a long-term migrant. Armed forces stationed outside of the UK are excluded. Students are taken to be usually resident at their term time address.

4. Some of the administrative data used in estimating international migration at LA level was not available at the time of production of the mid-2015 population estimates.

5. Note that age 90 comprises data for ages 90 and above.

15.3f Population projections by the Office for National Statistics
Scotland, PERSONS, thousands

2014-based
Principal projection

Projected populations at mid-years by age last birthday

Ages	2014	2015	2016	2017	2018	2019	2020	2021	2022	2023	2024	2025	2026	2027	2028	2029	2030	2031	2032	2033
Thousands																				
0-14	853	854	856	860	865	867	870	872	873	872	871	871	868	867	867	868	869	870	871	872
15-29	1,035	1,032	1,025	1,014	1,002	993	983	970	959	954	949	945	944	943	943	942	944	946	951	955
30-44	1,019	1,015	1,009	1,007	1,012	1,020	1,030	1,045	1,063	1,076	1,085	1,090	1,093	1,094	1,093	1,093	1,088	1,081	1,072	1,060
45-59	1,157	1,163	1,168	1,168	1,163	1,151	1,139	1,123	1,103	1,082	1,065	1,050	1,039	1,029	1,019	1,009	1,004	999	998	1,003
60-74	851	862	878	894	908	923	940	957	961	973	987	1,004	1,018	1,034	1,047	1,058	1,065	1,071	1,073	1,069
75 & over	433	438	444	452	462	474	484	495	521	540	557	572	586	599	612	626	640	656	672	689
All ages	5,348	5,365	5,380	5,396	5,412	5,428	5,445	5,462	5,480	5,497	5,514	5,532	5,548	5,565	5,581	5,596	5,610	5,624	5,636	5,648
Percentages																				
0-14	15.9	15.9	15.9	15.9	16.0	16.0	16.0	16.0	15.9	15.9	15.8	15.7	15.6	15.6	15.5	15.5	15.5	15.5	15.5	15.4
15-29	19.3	19.2	19.0	18.8	18.5	18.3	18.1	17.8	17.5	17.4	17.2	17.1	17.0	16.9	16.9	16.8	16.8	16.8	16.9	16.9
30-44	19.1	18.9	18.8	18.7	18.7	18.8	18.9	19.1	19.4	19.6	19.7	19.7	19.7	19.7	19.6	19.5	19.4	19.2	19.0	18.8
45-59	21.6	21.7	21.7	21.7	21.5	21.2	20.9	20.6	20.1	19.7	19.3	19.0	18.7	18.5	18.3	18.0	17.9	17.8	17.7	17.8
60-74	15.9	16.1	16.3	16.6	16.8	17.0	17.3	17.5	17.5	17.7	17.9	18.1	18.4	18.6	18.8	18.9	19.0	19.0	19.0	18.9
75 & over	8.1	8.2	8.3	8.4	8.5	8.7	8.9	9.1	9.5	9.8	10.1	10.3	10.6	10.8	11.0	11.2	11.4	11.7	11.9	12.2
All ages	100.0	100.0	100.0	100.0	100.0	100.0	100.0	100.0	100.0	100.0	100.0	100.0	100.0	100.0	100.0	100.0	100.0	100.0	100.0	100.0
Mean age	41.3	41.5	41.7	41.8	42.0	42.2	42.3	42.5	42.7	42.8	43.0	43.1	43.3	43.4	43.5	43.7	43.8	44.0	44.1	44.2
Median age	41.9	42.0	42.1	42.2	42.3	42.4	42.4	42.5	42.6	42.7	42.9	43.0	43.1	43.2	43.4	43.5	43.7	43.8	44.0	44.1

Ages	2034	2035	2036	2037	2038	2039	2040	2041	2042	2043	2044	2045	2046	2047	2048	2049	2050	2051	2052	2053
Thousands																				
0-14	871	871	870	868	866	865	863	862	860	859	859	858	858	858	859	859	860	860	861	862
15-29	958	960	962	963	962	961	961	958	957	958	958	959	961	962	962	962	962	960	959	957
30-44	1,051	1,042	1,030	1,019	1,015	1,010	1,006	1,006	1,005	1,004	1,004	1,005	1,007	1,012	1,016	1,019	1,022	1,024	1,025	1,024
45-59	1,012	1,022	1,037	1,056	1,069	1,078	1,084	1,086	1,088	1,088	1,088	1,083	1,077	1,067	1,056	1,048	1,039	1,027	1,016	1,012
60-74	1,059	1,048	1,035	1,017	998	984	972	963	955	947	940	937	934	935	941	950	961	976	995	1,008
75 & over	707	725	744	763	784	803	823	839	856	871	884	894	904	911	914	914	913	911	905	901
All ages	5,659	5,669	5,678	5,686	5,694	5,701	5,708	5,715	5,721	5,726	5,732	5,737	5,741	5,745	5,749	5,753	5,756	5,759	5,761	5,764
Percentages																				
0-14	15.4	15.4	15.3	15.3	15.2	15.2	15.1	15.1	15.0	15.0	15.0	15.0	14.9	14.9	14.9	14.9	14.9	14.9	14.9	14.9
15-29	16.9	16.9	16.9	16.9	16.9	16.9	16.8	16.8	16.7	16.7	16.7	16.7	16.7	16.7	16.7	16.7	16.7	16.7	16.6	16.6
30-44	18.6	18.4	18.1	17.9	17.8	17.7	17.6	17.6	17.6	17.5	17.5	17.5	17.5	17.6	17.7	17.7	17.8	17.8	17.8	17.8
45-59	17.9	18.0	18.3	18.6	18.8	18.9	19.0	19.0	19.0	19.0	19.0	18.9	18.8	18.6	18.4	18.2	18.1	17.8	17.6	17.6
60-74	18.7	18.5	18.2	17.9	17.5	17.3	17.0	16.9	16.7	16.5	16.4	16.3	16.3	16.3	16.4	16.5	16.7	17.0	17.3	17.5
75 & over	12.5	12.8	13.1	13.4	13.8	14.1	14.4	14.7	15.0	15.2	15.4	15.6	15.7	15.9	15.9	15.9	15.9	15.8	15.7	15.6
All ages	100.0	100.0	100.0	100.0	100.0	100.0	100.0	100.0	100.0	100.0	100.0	100.0	100.0	100.0	100.0	100.0	100.0	100.0	100.0	100.0
Mean age	44.4	44.5	44.6	44.7	44.8	44.9	45.0	45.1	45.2	45.3	45.3	45.4	45.5	45.5	45.6	45.6	45.7	45.7	45.7	45.8
Median age	44.3	44.5	44.7	44.9	45.1	45.2	45.3	45.4	45.5	45.6	45.7	45.7	45.7	45.7	45.6	45.6	45.5	45.5	45.5	45.6

15.3f Population projections by the Office for National Statistics
Scotland, PERSONS, thousands

2014-based
Principal projection

Projected populations at mid-years by age last birthday

Ages	2054	2055	2056	2057	2058	2059	2060	2061	2062	2063	2064	2065	2066	2067	2068	2069	2070	2071	2072	2073
Thousands																				
0-14	862	863	863	863	864	864	863	863	863	863	863	862	862	861	861	861	860	860	859	859
15-29	955	954	952	951	950	949	949	949	949	949	950	950	951	952	952	953	954	954	954	954
30-44	1,023	1,024	1,021	1,020	1,020	1,021	1,022	1,023	1,025	1,025	1,025	1,025	1,024	1,022	1,021	1,019	1,018	1,016	1,015	1,014
45-59	1,009	1,004	1,004	1,004	1,004	1,004	1,005	1,008	1,013	1,017	1,021	1,023	1,026	1,027	1,027	1,026	1,027	1,024	1,023	1,024
60-74	1,017	1,023	1,026	1,028	1,029	1,029	1,025	1,019	1,011	1,001	993	986	975	966	963	961	958	959	960	960
75 & over	900	902	905	908	911	914	918	924	930	938	947	956	969	983	993	1,003	1,013	1,021	1,029	1,035
All ages	5,767	5,769	5,772	5,774	5,777	5,780	5,783	5,786	5,790	5,794	5,798	5,802	5,807	5,812	5,817	5,823	5,828	5,834	5,840	5,846
Percentages																				
0-14	15.0	15.0	15.0	15.0	14.9	14.9	14.9	14.9	14.9	14.9	14.9	14.9	14.8	14.8	14.8	14.8	14.8	14.7	14.7	14.7
15-29	16.6	16.5	16.5	16.5	16.4	16.4	16.4	16.4	16.4	16.4	16.4	16.4	16.4	16.4	16.4	16.4	16.4	16.4	16.3	16.3
30-44	17.7	17.7	17.7	17.7	17.7	17.7	17.7	17.7	17.7	17.7	17.7	17.7	17.6	17.7	17.5	17.5	17.5	17.4	17.4	17.3
45-59	17.5	17.4	17.4	17.4	17.4	17.4	17.4	17.4	17.5	17.6	17.6	17.6	17.7	17.7	17.7	17.6	17.6	17.6	17.5	17.5
60-74	17.6	17.7	17.8	17.8	17.8	17.8	17.7	17.6	17.5	17.3	17.1	17.0	16.8	16.6	16.6	16.5	16.4	16.4	16.4	16.4
75 & over	15.6	15.6	15.7	15.7	15.8	15.8	15.9	16.0	16.1	16.2	16.3	16.5	16.7	16.9	17.1	17.2	17.4	17.5	17.6	17.7
All ages	100.0	100.0	100.0	100.0	100.0	100.0	100.0	100.0	100.0	100.0	100.0	100.0	100.0	100.0	100.0	100.0	100.0	100.0	100.0	100.0
Mean age	45.8	45.8	45.9	45.9	45.9	46.0	46.0	46.1	46.1	46.1	46.1	46.2	46.2	46.3	46.3	46.4	46.4	46.5	46.5	46.6
Median age	45.6	45.6	45.7	45.8	45.8	45.8	45.8	45.9	45.9	45.9	45.9	45.9	46.0	46.0	46.1	46.1	46.2	46.3	46.3	46.4

Ages	2074	2075	2076	2077	2078	2079	2080	2081	2082	2083	2084	2085	2086	2087	2088	2089	2090	2091	2092	2093
Thousands																				
0-14	858	858	858	857	857	857	857	858	858	858	858	858	859	859	859	859	859	859	859	859
15-29	954	954	954	954	954	954	953	953	952	952	952	951	951	950	950	949	949	949	948	948
30-44	1,013	1,013	1,013	1,013	1,014	1,014	1,015	1,016	1,017	1,017	1,018	1,019	1,019	1,019	1,020	1,020	1,020	1,020	1,020	1,019
45-59	1,025	1,026	1,028	1,029	1,030	1,030	1,030	1,029	1,028	1,027	1,025	1,024	1,023	1,022	1,021	1,021	1,021	1,021	1,021	1,022
60-74	961	964	967	971	976	980	983	986	988	988	988	989	988	988	989	991	993	995	997	998
75 & over	1,040	1,043	1,046	1,046	1,046	1,048	1,051	1,054	1,059	1,065	1,072	1,078	1,086	1,093	1,099	1,104	1,109	1,113	1,118	1,123
All ages	5,853	5,859	5,865	5,871	5,877	5,884	5,890	5,896	5,902	5,908	5,913	5,919	5,925	5,931	5,937	5,943	5,950	5,956	5,963	5,970
Percentages																				
0-14	14.7	14.6	14.6	14.6	14.6	14.6	14.6	14.5	14.5	14.5	14.5	14.5	14.5	14.5	14.5	14.5	14.4	14.4	14.4	14.4
15-29	16.3	16.3	16.3	16.2	16.2	16.2	16.2	16.2	16.1	16.1	16.1	16.1	16.0	16.0	16.0	16.0	15.9	15.9	15.9	15.9
30-44	17.3	17.3	17.3	17.3	17.2	17.2	17.2	17.2	17.2	17.2	17.2	17.2	17.2	17.2	17.2	17.2	17.1	17.1	17.1	17.1
45-59	17.5	17.5	17.5	17.5	17.5	17.5	17.5	17.5	17.4	17.4	17.3	17.3	17.3	17.2	17.2	17.2	17.2	17.1	17.1	17.1
60-74	16.4	16.4	16.5	16.5	16.6	16.7	16.7	16.7	16.7	16.7	16.7	16.7	16.7	16.7	16.7	16.7	16.7	16.7	16.7	16.7
75 & over	17.8	17.8	17.8	17.8	17.8	17.8	17.8	17.9	17.9	18.0	18.1	18.2	18.3	18.4	18.5	18.6	18.6	18.7	18.7	18.8
All ages	100.0	100.0	100.0	100.0	100.0	100.0	100.0	100.0	100.0	100.0	100.0	100.0	100.0	100.0	100.0	100.0	100.0	100.0	100.0	100.0
Mean age	46.6	46.7	46.7	46.8	46.8	46.9	46.9	47.0	47.0	47.1	47.1	47.2	47.2	47.3	47.3	47.3	47.4	47.4	47.5	47.5
Median age	46.5	46.5	46.6	46.6	46.7	46.7	46.8	46.8	46.8	46.9	46.9	46.9	47.0	47.0	47.1	47.1	47.1	47.2	47.3	47.3

15.3f Population projections by the Office for National Statistics
Scotland, PERSONS, thousands

2014-based
Principal projection

Projected populations at mid-years by age last birthday

Ages	2094	2095	2096	2097	2098	2099	2100	2101	2102	2103	2104	2105	2106	2107	2108	2109	2110	2111	2112	2113	2114
Thousands																					
0-14	859	859	859	858	858	858	858	858	857	857	857	857	857	857	857	856	856	856	856	856	857
15-29	948	948	948	949	949	949	949	950	950	950	950	950	950	950	950	950	950	950	950	949	949
30-44	1,019	1,019	1,019	1,018	1,018	1,018	1,017	1,017	1,016	1,016	1,016	1,015	1,015	1,015	1,015	1,015	1,015	1,015	1,016	1,016	1,016
45-59	1,023	1,023	1,024	1,025	1,026	1,027	1,028	1,029	1,029	1,030	1,030	1,030	1,030	1,030	1,030	1,030	1,030	1,030	1,030	1,030	1,029
60-74	999	999	999	998	997	996	995	995	994	994	994	995	996	997	998	999	1,000	1,002	1,003	1,004	1,006
75 & over	1,129	1,135	1,142	1,150	1,158	1,166	1,174	1,182	1,191	1,199	1,207	1,215	1,223	1,230	1,237	1,244	1,251	1,258	1,265	1,272	1,279
All ages	5,977	5,984	5,991	5,999	6,006	6,014	6,022	6,030	6,038	6,046	6,054	6,062	6,070	6,079	6,087	6,095	6,103	6,111	6,119	6,127	6,135
Percentages																					
0-14	14.4	14.4	14.3	14.3	14.3	14.3	14.2	14.2	14.2	14.2	14.2	14.1	14.1	14.1	14.1	14.1	14.0	14.0	14.0	14.0	14.0
15-29	15.9	15.8	15.8	15.8	15.8	15.8	15.8	15.7	15.7	15.7	15.7	15.7	15.7	15.6	15.6	15.6	15.6	15.5	15.5	15.5	15.5
30-44	17.1	17.0	17.0	17.0	16.9	16.9	16.9	16.9	16.8	16.8	16.8	16.7	16.7	16.7	16.7	16.7	16.6	16.6	16.6	16.6	16.6
45-59	17.1	17.1	17.1	17.1	17.1	17.1	17.1	17.1	17.0	17.0	17.0	17.0	17.0	16.9	16.9	16.9	16.9	16.9	16.9	16.8	16.8
60-74	16.7	16.7	16.7	16.6	16.6	16.6	16.5	16.5	16.5	16.4	16.4	16.4	16.4	16.4	16.4	16.4	16.4	16.4	16.4	16.4	16.4
75 & over	18.9	19.0	19.1	19.2	19.3	19.4	19.5	19.6	19.7	19.8	19.9	20.0	20.1	20.2	20.3	20.4	20.5	20.6	20.7	20.8	20.8
All ages	100.0	100.0	100.0	100.0	100.0	100.0	100.0	100.0	100.0	100.0	100.0	100.0	100.0	100.0	100.0	100.0	100.0	100.0	100.0	100.0	100.0
Mean age	47.6	47.6	47.7	47.7	47.8	47.9	47.9	48.0	48.0	48.1	48.2	48.2	48.3	48.3	48.4	48.5	48.5	48.6	48.6	48.7	48.8
Median age	47.4	47.4	47.5	47.5	47.6	47.7	47.7	47.8	47.8	47.9	48.0	48.0	48.1	48.2	48.2	48.3	48.4	48.4	48.5	48.5	48.6

Source: Office for National Statistics

Note: Figures may not add exactly due to rounding.
* Children under 16. Working age and pensionable age populations based on state pension age (SPA) for given year.
Between 2012 and 2018, SPA will change from 65 years for men and 61 years for women, to 65 years for both sexes.
Then between 2019 and 2020, SPA will change from 65 years to 66 years for both men and women.
Between 2026 and 2027 SPA will increase to 67 years and between 2044 and 2046 to 68 years for both sexes. This is based on SPA under the 2014 Pensions Act.
** This is consistent with the age-group definitions used in ONS Labour Market Statistics.

National Population Projections are currently produced every two years. The 2016-based projections are not due to be published until November/December 2017. Therefore, this table series will be updated in the next edition

15.3f Population projections by the Office for National Statistics
Scotland, MALES, thousands

2014-based
Principal projection

Projected populations at mid-years by age last birthday

Ages	2014	2015	2016	2017	2018	2019	2020	2021	2022	2023	2024	2025	2026	2027	2028	2029	2030	2031	2032	2033
Thousands																				
0-14	436	436	438	440	442	443	444	445	446	446	445	445	444	443	444	444	444	445	446	446
15-29	519	519	515	511	505	501	497	491	486	484	481	479	478	478	477	477	478	479	481	484
30-44	498	496	494	493	496	500	506	514	523	530	535	538	541	543	544	545	543	541	537	532
45-59	563	566	567	566	563	558	551	543	533	523	515	508	503	497	492	488	486	484	484	487
60-74	408	414	422	430	437	444	453	461	463	468	475	482	489	496	502	507	510	512	512	510
75 & over	173	176	180	184	190	197	202	209	222	232	242	250	257	264	271	278	285	293	301	309
All ages	2,596	2,606	2,616	2,625	2,634	2,643	2,653	2,663	2,673	2,683	2,693	2,702	2,712	2,721	2,730	2,738	2,746	2,754	2,761	2,768
Percentages																				
0-14	16.8	16.7	16.7	16.8	16.8	16.8	16.7	16.7	16.7	16.6	16.5	16.5	16.4	16.3	16.2	16.2	16.2	16.2	16.1	16.1
15-29	20.0	19.9	19.7	19.5	19.2	19.0	18.7	18.4	18.2	18.0	17.9	17.7	17.6	17.6	17.5	17.4	17.4	17.4	17.4	17.5
30-44	19.2	19.0	18.9	18.8	18.8	18.9	19.1	19.3	19.6	19.7	19.9	19.9	19.9	19.9	19.9	19.9	19.8	19.6	19.4	19.2
45-59	21.7	21.7	21.7	21.6	21.4	21.1	20.8	20.4	20.0	19.5	19.1	18.8	18.5	18.3	18.0	17.8	17.7	17.6	17.5	17.6
60-74	15.7	15.9	16.1	16.4	16.6	16.8	17.1	17.3	17.3	17.5	17.6	17.8	18.0	18.2	18.4	18.5	18.6	18.6	18.5	18.4
75 & over	6.7	6.8	6.9	7.0	7.2	7.4	7.6	7.9	8.3	8.7	9.0	9.2	9.5	9.7	9.9	10.1	10.4	10.6	10.9	11.2
All ages	100.0	100.0	100.0	100.0	100.0	100.0	100.0	100.0	100.0	100.0	100.0	100.0	100.0	100.0	100.0	100.0	100.0	100.0	100.0	100.0
Mean age	40.2	40.4	40.6	40.8	40.9	41.1	41.3	41.5	41.6	41.8	42.0	42.1	42.3	42.4	42.6	42.7	42.9	43.0	43.1	43.3
Median age	40.7	40.7	40.8	40.9	40.9	41.0	41.1	41.2	41.3	41.5	41.6	41.7	41.8	41.9	42.1	42.2	42.4	42.6	42.7	42.9

Ages	2034	2035	2036	2037	2038	2039	2040	2041	2042	2043	2044	2045	2046	2047	2048	2049	2050	2051	2052	2053
Thousands																				
0-14	446	445	445	444	443	442	442	441	440	440	439	439	439	439	439	439	440	440	440	441
15-29	485	486	487	488	487	487	487	486	485	485	486	486	487	488	488	488	488	487	486	485
30-44	528	524	518	513	511	509	507	506	506	506	505	506	507	510	512	513	515	516	517	516
45-59	492	498	505	515	522	527	531	533	535	537	538	537	534	531	526	522	518	513	508	506
60-74	506	500	494	485	476	470	464	461	456	453	450	449	448	449	452	457	463	471	480	487
75 & over	318	327	336	346	355	364	374	381	389	396	402	406	410	413	415	415	414	413	411	409
All ages	2,774	2,780	2,786	2,791	2,795	2,800	2,804	2,808	2,812	2,816	2,819	2,823	2,826	2,829	2,832	2,834	2,837	2,840	2,842	2,845
Percentages																				
0-14	16.1	16.0	16.0	15.9	15.9	15.8	15.7	15.7	15.6	15.6	15.6	15.6	15.5	15.5	15.5	15.5	15.5	15.5	15.5	15.5
15-29	17.5	17.5	17.5	17.5	17.4	17.4	17.4	17.3	17.3	17.2	17.2	17.2	17.2	17.2	17.2	17.2	17.2	17.1	17.1	17.1
30-44	19.0	18.8	18.6	18.4	18.3	18.2	18.1	18.0	18.0	18.0	17.9	17.9	18.0	18.0	18.1	18.1	18.1	18.2	18.2	18.1
45-59	17.7	17.9	18.1	18.4	18.7	18.8	18.9	19.0	19.0	19.1	19.1	19.0	18.9	18.8	18.6	18.4	18.3	18.0	17.9	17.8
60-74	18.2	18.0	17.7	17.4	17.0	16.8	16.6	16.4	16.2	16.1	15.9	15.9	15.9	15.9	16.0	16.1	16.3	16.6	16.9	17.1
75 & over	11.5	11.8	12.1	12.4	12.7	13.0	13.3	13.6	13.8	14.1	14.2	14.4	14.5	14.6	14.7	14.6	14.6	14.5	14.5	14.4
All ages	100.0	100.0	100.0	100.0	100.0	100.0	100.0	100.0	100.0	100.0	100.0	100.0	100.0	100.0	100.0	100.0	100.0	100.0	100.0	100.0
Mean age	43.4	43.5	43.6	43.7	43.9	44.0	44.1	44.1	44.2	44.3	44.4	44.4	44.5	44.6	44.6	44.7	44.7	44.8	44.8	44.8
Median age	43.1	43.3	43.5	43.7	43.8	44.0	44.1	44.2	44.3	44.3	44.4	44.4	44.3	44.3	44.3	44.3	44.3	44.3	44.4	44.4

15.3f Population projections by the Office for National Statistics
Scotland, MALES, thousands

2014-based
Principal projection

Projected populations at mid-years by age last birthday

Ages	2054	2055	2056	2057	2058	2059	2060	2061	2062	2063	2064	2065	2066	2067	2068	2069	2070	2071	2072	2073
Thousands																				
0-14	441	441	442	442	442	442	442	442	442	441	441	441	441	441	441	440	440	440	440	439
15-29	484	484	483	482	482	481	481	481	481	481	481	482	482	483	483	483	484	484	484	484
30-44	516	516	515	514	515	515	516	516	517	517	517	517	516	516	514	514	513	513	512	512
45-59	504	502	502	502	502	502	503	504	507	509	511	512	513	514	514	514	514	513	513	513
60-74	493	497	499	502	503	505	504	502	498	494	491	488	483	479	478	477	475	476	476	477
75 & over	409	410	411	413	414	415	418	421	424	429	434	439	446	453	459	464	470	475	480	484
All ages	2,847	2,850	2,852	2,855	2,857	2,860	2,863	2,866	2,869	2,872	2,875	2,878	2,882	2,885	2,889	2,893	2,897	2,901	2,905	2,909
Percentages																				
0-14	15.5	15.5	15.5	15.5	15.5	15.4	15.4	15.4	15.4	15.4	15.3	15.3	15.3	15.3	15.2	15.2	15.2	15.2	15.1	15.1
15-29	17.0	17.0	16.9	16.9	16.9	16.8	16.8	16.8	16.8	16.8	16.7	16.7	16.7	16.7	16.7	16.7	16.7	16.7	16.7	16.6
30-44	18.1	18.1	18.1	18.0	18.0	18.0	18.0	18.0	18.0	18.0	18.0	18.0	17.9	17.9	17.8	17.8	17.7	17.7	17.6	17.6
45-59	17.7	17.6	17.6	17.6	17.6	17.5	17.6	17.5	17.7	17.7	17.8	17.8	17.8	17.8	17.8	17.8	17.8	17.7	17.7	17.6
60-74	17.3	17.4	17.5	17.6	17.6	17.6	17.6	17.5	17.4	17.2	17.1	16.9	16.8	16.6	16.5	16.5	16.4	16.4	16.4	16.4
75 & over	14.4	14.4	14.4	14.5	14.5	14.5	14.6	14.7	14.8	14.9	15.1	15.2	15.5	15.7	15.9	16.1	16.2	16.4	16.5	16.6
All ages	100.0	100.0	100.0	100.0	100.0	100.0	100.0	100.0	100.0	100.0	100.0	100.0	100.0	100.0	100.0	100.0	100.0	100.0	100.0	100.0
Mean age	44.9	44.9	45.0	45.0	45.0	45.1	45.1	45.2	45.2	45.3	45.3	45.4	45.4	45.5	45.5	45.6	45.7	45.7	45.8	45.8
Median age	44.5	44.5	44.6	44.7	44.7	44.8	44.8	44.8	44.8	44.9	44.9	45.0	45.0	45.1	45.2	45.3	45.3	45.4	45.5	45.6

Ages	2074	2075	2076	2077	2078	2079	2080	2081	2082	2083	2084	2085	2086	2087	2088	2089	2090	2091	2092	2093
Thousands																				
0-14	439	439	439	439	439	439	439	439	439	439	439	439	439	439	439	439	440	440	440	440
15-29	484	484	484	484	484	484	483	483	483	483	483	482	482	482	482	481	481	481	481	481
30-44	511	511	511	516	512	512	512	513	513	514	514	514	515	515	515	515	515	515	515	515
45-59	514	515	515	516	517	517	517	516	516	515	514	514	513	513	513	512	512	512	513	513
60-74	477	478	480	483	485	487	489	490	492	492	492	493	492	492	493	494	495	496	497	498
75 & over	487	489	491	492	492	494	496	498	501	505	508	512	516	520	523	526	529	532	534	537
All ages	2,913	2,917	2,921	2,925	2,928	2,932	2,936	2,940	2,943	2,947	2,951	2,954	2,958	2,961	2,965	2,968	2,972	2,976	2,980	2,983
Percentages																				
0-14	15.1	15.0	15.0	15.0	15.0	15.0	14.9	14.9	14.9	14.9	14.9	14.9	14.8	14.8	14.8	14.8	14.8	14.8	14.8	14.7
15-29	16.6	16.6	16.6	16.5	16.5	16.5	16.5	16.4	16.4	16.4	16.4	16.3	16.3	16.3	16.2	16.2	16.2	16.2	16.1	16.1
30-44	17.6	17.5	17.5	17.5	17.5	17.5	17.5	17.4	17.4	17.5	17.4	17.4	17.4	17.4	17.4	17.3	17.3	17.3	17.2	17.3
45-59	17.6	17.6	17.6	17.7	17.6	17.6	17.6	17.6	17.5	17.5	17.4	17.4	17.3	17.3	17.3	17.3	17.2	17.2	17.2	17.2
60-74	16.4	16.4	16.4	16.5	16.6	16.6	16.6	16.7	16.7	16.7	16.7	16.7	16.7	16.6	16.6	16.6	16.7	16.7	16.7	16.7
75 & over	16.7	16.8	16.8	16.8	16.8	16.8	16.9	16.9	17.0	17.1	17.2	17.3	17.5	17.6	17.7	17.7	17.8	17.9	17.9	18.0
All ages	100.0	100.0	100.0	100.0	100.0	100.0	100.0	100.0	100.0	100.0	100.0	100.0	100.0	100.0	100.0	100.0	100.0	100.0	100.0	100.0
Mean age	45.9	46.0	46.0	46.1	46.2	46.2	46.3	46.3	46.4	46.4	46.5	46.5	46.6	46.6	46.7	46.7	46.8	46.9	46.9	47.0
Median age	45.6	45.7	45.8	45.8	45.9	45.9	46.0	46.0	46.1	46.1	46.2	46.2	46.3	46.3	46.4	46.4	46.5	46.5	46.6	46.6

15.3f Population projections by the Office for National Statistics
Scotland, MALES, thousands

2014-based
Principal projection

Projected populations at mid-years by age last birthday

Ages	2094	2095	2096	2097	2098	2099	2100	2101	2102	2103	2104	2105	2106	2107	2108	2109	2110	2111	2112	2113	2114
Thousands																					
0-14	439	439	439	439	439	439	439	439	439	439	438	438	438	438	438	438	438	438	438	438	438
15-29	481	481	481	481	481	481	481	482	482	482	482	482	482	482	482	482	482	482	482	482	481
30-44	515	515	514	514	514	514	514	514	513	513	513	513	513	513	513	513	513	513	513	513	513
45-59	514	514	515	515	516	516	517	517	517	517	518	518	518	518	518	518	518	518	518	518	518
60-74	498	499	499	498	498	498	497	497	497	497	497	497	498	498	499	500	500	501	502	503	503
75 & over	540	544	547	551	555	560	564	568	573	577	581	585	589	593	597	600	604	607	611	614	618
All ages	2,987	2,991	2,995	2,999	3,003	3,008	3,012	3,016	3,020	3,025	3,029	3,033	3,038	3,042	3,046	3,051	3,055	3,059	3,063	3,068	3,072
Percentages																					
0-14	14.7	14.7	14.7	14.6	14.6	14.6	14.6	14.5	14.5	14.5	14.5	14.5	14.4	14.4	14.4	14.4	14.3	14.3	14.3	14.3	14.3
15-29	16.1	16.1	16.1	16.0	16.0	16.0	16.0	16.0	15.9	15.9	15.9	15.9	15.9	15.8	15.8	15.8	15.8	15.7	15.7	15.7	15.7
30-44	17.2	17.2	17.2	17.1	17.1	17.1	17.1	17.0	17.0	17.0	16.9	16.9	16.9	16.9	16.8	16.8	16.8	16.8	16.7	16.7	16.7
45-59	17.2	17.2	17.2	17.2	17.2	17.2	17.2	17.1	17.1	17.1	17.1	17.1	17.0	17.0	17.0	17.0	17.0	16.9	16.9	16.9	16.8
60-74	16.7	16.7	16.6	16.6	16.6	16.5	16.5	16.5	16.5	16.4	16.4	16.4	16.4	16.4	16.4	16.4	16.4	16.4	16.4	16.4	16.4
75 & over	18.1	18.2	18.3	18.4	18.5	18.6	18.7	18.8	19.0	19.1	19.2	19.3	19.4	19.5	19.6	19.7	19.8	19.9	19.9	20.0	20.1
All ages	100.0	100.0	100.0	100.0	100.0	100.0	100.0	100.0	100.0	100.0	100.0	100.0	100.0	100.0	100.0	100.0	100.0	100.0	100.0	100.0	100.0
Mean age	47.0	47.1	47.1	47.2	47.2	47.3	47.4	47.4	47.5	47.6	47.6	47.7	47.7	47.8	47.9	47.9	48.0	48.1	48.1	48.2	48.2
Median age	46.7	46.8	46.8	46.9	47.0	47.0	47.1	47.1	47.2	47.3	47.4	47.4	47.5	47.6	47.6	47.7	47.7	47.8	47.9	47.9	48.0

Source: Office for National Statistics

Note: Figures may not add exactly due to rounding.
* Children under 16. Working age and pensionable age populations based on state pension age (SPA) for given year.
Between 2012 and 2018, SPA will change from 65 years for men and 61 years for women, to 65 years for both sexes.
Then between 2019 and 2020, SPA will change from 65 years to 66 years for both men and women.
Between 2026 and 2027 SPA will increase to 67 years and between 2044 and 2046 to 68 years for both sexes. This is based on SPA under the 2014 Pensions Act.
** This is consistent with the age-group definitions used in ONS Labour Market Statistics.

National Population Projections are currently produced every two years. The 2016-based projections are not due to be published until November/December 2017. Therefore, this table series will be updated in the next edition

15.3f Population projections by the Office for National Statistics
Scotland, FEMALES, thousands

2014-based
Principal projection

Projected populations at mid-years by age last birthday

Ages	2014	2015	2016	2017	2018	2019	2020	2021	2022	2023	2024	2025	2026	2027	2028	2029	2030	2031	2032	2033
Thousands																				
0-14	417	418	419	421	422	424	425	426	427	426	425	425	424	423	423	424	424	425	425	426
15-29	516	514	509	503	497	491	486	480	473	470	468	466	466	465	465	465	466	467	469	471
30-44	522	519	515	514	516	520	524	531	541	547	550	552	552	551	550	548	544	541	535	529
45-59	594	598	601	602	599	594	588	580	570	559	550	542	537	532	526	521	518	515	514	516
60-74	443	448	456	464	471	479	487	496	498	505	513	522	529	538	545	551	555	559	561	558
75 & over	260	262	264	267	272	277	281	286	298	308	316	323	329	335	342	348	355	363	371	380
All ages	2,751	2,758	2,765	2,771	2,778	2,785	2,792	2,799	2,807	2,814	2,822	2,829	2,837	2,844	2,851	2,858	2,864	2,870	2,875	2,880
Percentages																				
0-14	15.2	15.1	15.1	15.2	15.2	15.2	15.2	15.2	15.2	15.1	15.1	15.0	14.9	14.9	14.9	14.8	14.8	14.8	14.8	14.8
15-29	18.8	18.6	18.4	18.2	17.9	17.6	17.4	17.1	16.9	16.7	16.6	16.5	16.4	16.4	16.3	16.3	16.3	16.3	16.3	16.4
30-44	19.0	18.8	18.6	18.5	18.6	18.7	18.8	19.0	19.3	19.4	19.5	19.5	19.5	19.4	19.3	19.2	19.0	18.8	18.6	18.4
45-59	21.6	21.7	21.7	21.7	21.6	21.3	21.1	20.7	20.3	19.9	19.5	19.2	18.9	18.7	18.5	18.2	18.1	17.9	17.9	17.9
60-74	16.1	16.3	16.5	16.7	16.9	17.2	17.4	17.7	17.8	17.9	18.2	18.4	18.7	18.9	19.1	19.3	19.4	19.5	19.5	19.4
75 & over	9.5	9.5	9.6	9.6	9.8	9.9	10.1	10.2	10.6	10.9	11.2	11.4	11.6	11.8	12.0	12.2	12.4	12.6	12.9	13.2
All ages	100.0	100.0	100.0	100.0	100.0	100.0	100.0	100.0	100.0	100.0	100.0	100.0	100.0	100.0	100.0	100.0	100.0	100.0	100.0	100.0
Mean age	42.4	42.5	42.7	42.8	43.0	43.2	43.3	43.5	43.6	43.8	43.9	44.1	44.2	44.3	44.5	44.6	44.8	44.9	45.0	45.2
Median age	43.0	43.2	43.4	43.5	43.6	43.7	43.8	43.8	43.8	43.9	44.1	44.2	44.4	44.5	44.6	44.8	44.9	45.1	45.2	45.4

Ages	2034	2035	2036	2037	2038	2039	2040	2041	2042	2043	2044	2045	2046	2047	2048	2049	2050	2051	2052	2053
Thousands																				
0-14	426	425	425	424	423	422	422	421	420	420	419	419	419	419	419	420	420	420	421	421
15-29	473	474	475	475	475	474	474	472	472	472	473	473	474	474	474	474	474	473	473	472
30-44	524	519	512	506	503	501	499	499	499	498	498	499	500	502	504	506	507	508	509	508
45-59	520	525	532	541	547	551	553	553	552	551	550	546	542	537	531	526	521	515	509	506
60-74	553	548	541	531	522	514	507	503	499	495	490	489	486	486	489	493	498	505	509	520
75 & over	389	398	407	417	428	439	449	458	467	475	482	488	494	498	500	499	499	497	494	492
All ages	2,885	2,889	2,892	2,896	2,899	2,902	2,904	2,907	2,909	2,911	2,912	2,914	2,915	2,916	2,917	2,918	2,919	2,919	2,919	2,919
Percentages																				
0-14	14.8	14.7	14.7	14.6	14.6	14.6	14.5	14.5	14.4	14.4	14.4	14.4	14.4	14.4	14.4	14.4	14.4	14.4	14.4	14.4
15-29	16.4	16.4	16.4	16.4	16.4	16.3	16.3	16.3	16.2	16.2	16.2	16.2	16.2	16.3	16.3	16.3	16.2	16.2	16.2	16.2
30-44	18.2	18.0	17.7	17.5	17.4	17.3	17.2	17.2	17.1	17.1	17.1	17.1	17.2	17.2	17.3	17.3	17.4	17.4	17.4	17.4
45-59	18.0	18.2	18.4	18.7	18.9	19.0	19.0	19.0	19.0	18.9	18.9	18.7	18.6	18.4	18.2	18.0	17.8	17.6	17.4	17.3
60-74	19.2	19.0	18.7	18.4	18.0	17.7	17.5	17.3	17.2	17.0	16.8	16.8	16.7	16.7	16.8	16.9	17.1	17.3	17.6	17.8
75 & over	13.5	13.8	14.1	14.4	14.8	15.1	15.5	15.8	16.0	16.3	16.6	16.7	16.9	17.1	17.1	17.1	17.1	17.0	16.9	16.9
All ages	100.0	100.0	100.0	100.0	100.0	100.0	100.0	100.0	100.0	100.0	100.0	100.0	100.0	100.0	100.0	100.0	100.0	100.0	100.0	100.0
Mean age	45.3	45.4	45.5	45.6	45.7	45.8	45.9	46.0	46.1	46.2	46.3	46.3	46.4	46.4	46.5	46.5	46.6	46.6	46.7	46.7
Median age	45.5	45.7	45.9	46.1	46.3	46.4	46.6	46.7	46.8	46.9	46.9	47.0	47.0	47.0	46.9	46.9	46.8	46.8	46.7	46.7

15.3f Population projections by the Office for National Statistics
Scotland, FEMALES, thousands

2014-based
Principal projection

Projected populations at mid-years by age last birthday

Ages	2054	2055	2056	2057	2058	2059	2060	2061	2062	2063	2064	2065	2066	2067	2068	2069	2070	2071	2072	2073
Thousands																				
0-14	421	421	422	422	422	422	422	422	422	421	421	421	421	421	421	420	420	420	420	419
15-29	471	470	469	469	468	468	468	468	468	468	468	468	469	469	470	470	470	470	470	470
30-44	507	507	506	506	506	506	507	507	508	508	508	508	507	506	506	505	504	503	503	502
45-59	504	502	502	502	502	502	503	504	506	508	510	511	512	513	513	512	512	511	510	511
60-74	524	526	527	526	525	524	521	518	513	507	502	498	493	487	485	484	482	483	483	484
75 & over	491	492	494	496	497	498	501	503	506	510	513	517	523	530	534	539	543	546	549	551
All ages	2,920	2,920	2,920	2,920	2,920	2,920	2,920	2,921	2,921	2,922	2,923	2,924	2,925	2,926	2,928	2,930	2,932	2,933	2,936	2,938
Percentages																				
0-14	14.4	14.4	14.4	14.4	14.4	14.4	14.4	14.4	14.4	14.4	14.4	14.4	14.4	14.4	14.4	14.3	14.3	14.3	14.3	14.3
15-29	16.1	16.1	16.1	16.1	16.0	16.0	16.0	16.0	16.0	16.0	16.0	16.0	16.0	16.0	16.0	16.0	16.0	16.0	16.0	16.0
30-44	17.4	17.4	17.3	17.3	17.3	17.3	17.3	17.4	17.4	17.4	17.4	17.4	17.3	17.3	17.3	17.2	17.2	17.2	17.1	17.1
45-59	17.3	17.2	17.2	17.2	17.2	17.2	17.2	17.3	17.5	17.4	17.4	17.5	17.5	17.5	17.5	17.5	17.5	17.4	17.4	17.4
60-74	18.0	18.0	18.0	18.0	18.0	18.0	17.8	17.7	17.5	17.4	17.2	17.0	16.8	16.6	16.6	16.5	16.5	16.5	16.5	16.5
75 & over	16.8	16.9	16.9	17.0	17.0	17.1	17.1	17.2	17.3	17.4	17.6	17.7	17.9	18.1	18.2	18.4	18.5	18.6	18.7	18.8
All ages	100.0	100.0	100.0	100.0	100.0	100.0	100.0	100.0	100.0	100.0	100.0	100.0	100.0	100.0	100.0	100.0	100.0	100.0	100.0	100.0
Mean age	46.7	46.8	46.8	46.8	46.8	46.8	46.9	46.9	46.9	46.9	47.0	47.0	47.0	47.1	47.1	47.1	47.2	47.2	47.3	47.3
Median age	46.7	46.7	46.8	46.8	46.9	46.9	46.9	46.9	46.9	46.9	46.9	46.9	46.9	47.0	47.0	47.0	47.1	47.1	47.2	47.2

Ages	2074	2075	2076	2077	2078	2079	2080	2081	2082	2083	2084	2085	2086	2087	2088	2089	2090	2091	2092	2093
Thousands																				
0-14	419	419	419	419	419	419	419	419	419	419	419	419	419	419	419	420	420	420	420	420
15-29	470	470	470	470	470	470	470	470	469	469	469	469	469	468	468	468	468	468	467	467
30-44	502	502	502	502	502	502	503	503	503	504	504	504	505	505	505	505	505	505	505	505
45-59	511	512	512	513	513	514	513	513	512	512	511	510	509	509	508	508	508	508	508	509
60-74	484	485	486	489	491	493	494	496	497	496	496	496	496	496	496	497	498	498	499	500
75 & over	553	554	555	554	554	554	555	556	558	561	564	566	570	573	576	578	580	582	584	586
All ages	2,940	2,942	2,945	2,947	2,949	2,951	2,954	2,956	2,958	2,961	2,963	2,965	2,968	2,970	2,972	2,975	2,978	2,980	2,983	2,986
Percentages																				
0-14	14.3	14.2	14.2	14.2	14.2	14.2	14.2	14.2	14.2	14.2	14.1	14.1	14.1	14.1	14.1	14.1	14.1	14.1	14.1	14.0
15-29	16.0	16.0	16.0	16.0	15.9	15.9	15.9	15.9	15.9	15.8	15.8	15.8	15.8	15.8	15.7	15.7	15.7	15.7	15.7	15.7
30-44	17.1	17.1	17.0	17.0	17.0	17.0	17.0	17.0	17.0	17.0	17.0	17.0	17.0	17.0	17.0	17.0	17.0	16.9	16.9	16.9
45-59	17.4	17.4	17.4	17.4	17.4	17.4	17.4	17.3	17.3	17.3	17.2	17.2	17.2	17.1	17.1	17.1	17.1	17.1	17.0	17.0
60-74	16.5	16.5	16.5	16.6	16.6	16.7	16.7	16.8	16.8	16.8	16.7	16.7	16.7	16.7	16.7	16.7	16.7	16.7	16.7	16.7
75 & over	18.8	18.8	18.8	18.8	18.8	18.8	18.8	18.8	18.9	18.9	19.0	19.1	19.2	19.3	19.4	19.4	19.5	19.5	19.6	19.6
All ages	100.0	100.0	100.0	100.0	100.0	100.0	100.0	100.0	100.0	100.0	100.0	100.0	100.0	100.0	100.0	100.0	100.0	100.0	100.0	100.0
Mean age	47.3	47.4	47.4	47.5	47.5	47.6	47.6	47.6	47.7	47.7	47.8	47.8	47.8	47.9	47.9	47.9	48.0	48.0	48.1	48.1
Median age	47.3	47.3	47.4	47.4	47.5	47.5	47.5	47.6	47.6	47.6	47.6	47.7	47.7	47.7	47.8	47.8	47.8	47.9	47.9	48.0

15.3f Population projections by the Office for National Statistics
Scotland, FEMALES, thousands

2014-based
Principal projection

Projected populations at mid-years by age last birthday

Ages	2094	2095	2096	2097	2098	2099	2100	2101	2102	2103	2104	2105	2106	2107	2108	2109	2110	2111	2112	2113	2114
Thousands																					
0-14	420	419	419	419	419	419	419	419	419	419	419	418	418	418	418	418	418	418	418	418	418
15-29	467	467	468	468	468	468	468	468	468	468	468	468	468	468	468	468	468	468	468	468	468
30-44	505	504	504	504	504	504	503	503	503	503	503	502	502	502	502	502	502	502	502	503	503
45-59	509	509	510	510	511	511	512	512	512	512	512	512	512	512	512	512	512	512	512	512	512
60-74	500	500	500	500	499	499	498	498	498	497	497	498	498	498	499	499	500	500	501	502	502
75 & over	589	592	595	599	602	606	610	614	618	622	626	630	633	637	641	644	647	651	654	657	661
All ages	2,989	2,993	2,996	2,999	3,003	3,006	3,010	3,014	3,017	3,021	3,025	3,029	3,033	3,037	3,040	3,044	3,048	3,052	3,056	3,060	3,063
Percentages																					
0-14	14.0	14.0	14.0	14.0	14.0	13.9	13.9	13.9	13.9	13.9	13.8	13.8	13.8	13.8	13.8	13.7	13.7	13.7	13.7	13.7	13.7
15-29	15.6	15.6	15.6	15.6	15.6	15.6	15.5	15.5	15.5	15.5	15.5	15.5	15.4	15.4	15.4	15.4	15.4	15.3	15.3	15.3	15.3
30-44	16.9	16.9	16.8	16.8	16.8	16.8	16.7	16.7	16.7	16.6	16.6	16.6	16.6	16.5	16.5	16.5	16.5	16.5	16.4	16.4	16.4
45-59	17.0	17.0	17.0	17.0	17.0	17.0	17.0	17.0	17.0	17.0	16.9	16.9	16.9	16.9	16.9	16.8	16.8	16.8	16.8	16.7	16.7
60-74	16.7	16.7	16.7	16.7	16.6	16.6	16.6	16.5	16.5	16.5	16.4	16.4	16.4	16.4	16.4	16.4	16.4	16.4	16.4	16.4	16.4
75 & over	19.7	19.8	19.9	20.0	20.1	20.2	20.3	20.4	20.5	20.6	20.7	20.8	20.9	21.0	21.1	21.2	21.2	21.3	21.4	21.5	21.6
All ages	100.0	100.0	100.0	100.0	100.0	100.0	100.0	100.0	100.0	100.0	100.0	100.0	100.0	100.0	100.0	100.0	100.0	100.0	100.0	100.0	100.0
Mean age	48.2	48.2	48.3	48.3	48.4	48.4	48.5	48.5	48.6	48.6	48.7	48.8	48.8	48.9	48.9	49.0	49.1	49.1	49.2	49.2	49.3
Median age	48.0	48.1	48.1	48.2	48.3	48.3	48.4	48.4	48.5	48.6	48.6	48.7	48.7	48.8	48.9	48.9	49.0	49.0	49.1	49.2	49.2

Source: Office for National Statistics

Note: Figures may not add exactly due to rounding.
* Children under 16. Working age and pensionable age populations based on state pension age (SPA) for given year.
Between 2012 and 2018, SPA will change from 65 years for men and 61 years for women, to 65 years for both sexes.
Then between 2019 and 2020, SPA will change from 65 years to 66 years for both men and women.
Between 2026 and 2027 SPA will increase to 67 years and between 2044 and 2046 to 68 years for both sexes. This is based on SPA under the 2014 Pensions Act.
** This is consistent with the age-group definitions used in ONS Labour Market Statistics.

National Population Projections are currently produced every two years. The 2016-based projections are not due to be published until November/December 2017. Therefore, this table series will be updated in the next edition

15.3g Mid-2015 Population estimates: Northern Ireland by sex and single year of age

Ages	Persons	Males	females	Ages	Persons	Males	Females
ALL AGES	1,851,621	909,129	942,492	45	25,778	12,552	13,226
0	24,249	12,393	11,856	46	26,074	12,705	13,369
1	24,485	12,548	11,937	47	26,585	13,071	13,514
2	25,018	12,723	12,295	48	26,497	12,954	13,543
3	25,855	13,248	12,607	49	26,534	13,075	13,459
4	25,709	13,067	12,642	50	26,967	13,206	13,761
5	25,414	12,957	12,457	51	26,501	13,056	13,445
6	25,729	13,223	12,506	52	25,879	12,901	12,978
7	25,752	13,177	12,575	53	25,218	12,339	12,879
8	24,536	12,614	11,922	54	24,822	12,209	12,613
9	23,393	12,008	11,385	55	23,800	11,663	12,137
10	22,775	11,752	11,023	56	23,108	11,440	11,668
11	22,543	11,622	10,921	57	22,757	11,270	11,487
12	22,056	11,253	10,803	58	21,792	10,729	11,063
13	22,130	11,319	10,811	59	20,888	10,391	10,497
14	22,357	11,445	10,912	60	19,880	9,970	9,910
15	23,199	12,062	11,137	61	19,510	9,832	9,678
16	24,271	12,422	11,849	62	19,037	9,437	9,600
17	24,562	12,588	11,974	63	18,318	9,095	9,223
18	24,973	12,689	12,284	64	18,333	9,092	9,241
19	23,605	12,380	11,225	65	18,297	8,950	9,347
20	23,460	12,339	11,121	66	18,048	8,825	9,223
21	23,826	12,287	11,539	67	17,984	8,669	9,315
22	23,838	12,091	11,747	68	17,932	8,546	9,386
23	24,637	12,391	12,246	69	16,552	7,925	8,627
24	24,781	12,377	12,404	70	16,285	7,747	8,538
25	24,588	12,310	12,278	71	16,116	7,681	8,435
26	24,606	12,301	12,305	72	15,449	7,284	8,165
27	24,945	12,352	12,593	73	13,706	6,448	7,258
28	25,012	12,403	12,609	74	12,250	5,667	6,583
29	25,174	12,346	12,828	75	11,769	5,379	6,390
30	25,024	12,352	12,672	76	11,760	5,344	6,416
31	24,700	12,101	12,599	77	10,974	4,973	6,001
32	24,444	11,918	12,526	78	10,582	4,731	5,851
33	24,450	11,910	12,540	79	9,726	4,203	5,523
34	25,012	12,214	12,798	80	9,048	3,886	5,162
35	24,963	12,159	12,804	81	8,225	3,502	4,723
36	23,892	11,424	12,468	82	7,868	3,208	4,660
37	22,878	11,091	11,787	83	7,195	2,875	4,320
38	22,707	11,041	11,666	84	6,598	2,565	4,033
39	22,768	11,070	11,698	85	5,921	2,186	3,735
40	23,313	11,414	11,899	86	5,281	1,922	3,359
41	23,960	11,646	12,314	87	4,484	1,587	2,897
42	24,882	12,181	12,701	88	4,019	1,379	2,640
43	25,251	12,408	12,843	89	3,314	1,060	2,254
44	25,797	12,518	13,279	90	12,441	3,466	8,975

Source: Office for National Statistics

1. These unrounded estimates are published to enable and encourage further calculations and analysis. However, the estimates should not be taken to be accurate to the level of detail provided

2. The estimates are produced using a variety of data sources and statistical models, including some statistical disclosure control methods, and small estimates should not be taken to refer to particular individuals.

3. The estimated resident population of an area includes all those people who usually live there, regardless of nationality. Arriving international migrants are included in the usually resident population if they remain in the UK for at least a year. Emigrants are excluded if they remain outside the UK for at least a year. This is consistent with the United Nations definition of a long-term migrant. Armed forces stationed outside of the UK are excluded. Students are taken to be usually resident at their term time address.

4. Some of the administrative data used in estimating international migration at LA level was not available at the time of production of the mid-2015 population estimates.

5. At a subnational level, the population estimates reflect boundaries in place as of the reference year; for Northern Ireland the 11 New Local Government Districts (LGD2014) introduced

6. Note that age 90 comprises data for ages 90 and above.

15.3h Population projections by the Office for National Statistics
Northern Ireland, PERSONS, thousands

2014-based
Principal projection

Projected populations at mid-years by age last birthday

Ages	2014	2015	2016	2017	2018	2019	2020	2021	2022	2023	2024	2025	2026	2027	2028	2029	2030	2031	2032	2033
Thousands																				
0-14	360	362	365	368	371	373	375	376	376	374	373	371	369	366	364	363	361	359	357	356
15-29	368	366	363	360	356	354	351	349	348	349	350	352	354	355	356	357	359	361	364	366
30-44	365	363	362	362	361	362	363	364	366	366	366	364	363	362	361	359	356	353	349	345
45-59	368	373	377	380	381	381	380	378	375	371	368	366	364	361	358	356	355	354	353	353
60-74	253	258	264	269	274	278	284	290	295	302	308	316	322	329	335	341	345	349	352	354
75 & over	127	129	132	135	140	146	151	156	162	168	173	178	183	188	193	198	204	209	215	222
All ages	1,840	1,851	1,863	1,874	1,884	1,894	1,904	1,913	1,922	1,930	1,939	1,947	1,954	1,961	1,968	1,974	1,980	1,986	1,991	1,996
Percentages																				
0-14	19.5	19.5	19.6	19.6	19.7	19.7	19.7	19.7	19.6	19.4	19.2	19.1	18.9	18.7	18.5	18.4	18.2	18.1	18.0	17.8
15-29	20.0	19.8	19.5	19.2	18.9	18.7	18.5	18.3	18.1	18.1	18.1	18.1	18.1	18.1	18.1	18.1	18.1	18.2	18.3	18.4
30-44	19.8	19.6	19.5	19.3	19.2	19.1	19.0	19.0	19.0	19.0	18.9	18.7	18.6	18.4	18.3	18.2	18.0	17.8	17.5	17.3
45-59	20.0	20.2	20.2	20.3	20.2	20.1	20.0	19.7	19.5	19.2	19.0	18.8	18.6	18.4	18.2	18.1	17.9	17.8	17.7	17.7
60-74	13.8	13.9	14.2	14.4	14.5	14.7	14.9	15.2	15.4	15.6	15.9	16.2	16.5	16.8	17.0	17.3	17.4	17.6	17.7	17.7
75 & over	6.9	7.0	7.1	7.2	7.5	7.7	7.9	8.2	8.4	8.7	8.9	9.2	9.4	9.6	9.8	10.0	10.3	10.5	10.8	11.1
All ages	100.0	100.0	100.0	100.0	100.0	100.0	100.0	100.0	100.0	100.0	100.0	100.0	100.0	100.0	100.0	100.0	100.0	100.0	100.0	100.0
Mean age	38.7	38.8	39.0	39.2	39.4	39.6	39.8	40.0	40.2	40.4	40.6	40.8	41.0	41.2	41.4	41.6	41.8	42.0	42.2	42.4
Median age	38.0	38.1	38.3	38.5	38.7	38.9	39.2	39.4	39.6	39.8	40.1	40.3	40.5	40.8	41.0	41.2	41.5	41.7	41.9	42.1

Ages	2034	2035	2036	2037	2038	2039	2040	2041	2042	2043	2044	2045	2046	2047	2048	2049	2050	2051	2052	2053
Thousands																				
0-14	354	352	351	350	349	349	348	349	349	349	350	351	352	353	354	355	355	356	356	356
15-29	369	370	371	371	370	368	366	364	362	360	359	357	355	353	352	350	349	347	346	346
30-44	343	340	338	337	338	339	340	342	343	344	345	347	349	352	355	357	359	360	360	358
45-59	353	354	355	357	358	358	356	354	353	352	351	348	345	341	338	335	333	331	330	331
60-74	354	353	351	349	346	343	341	340	338	336	334	334	333	332	332	333	334	336	337	338
75 & over	229	235	243	250	258	265	273	280	287	294	300	305	310	314	318	321	323	324	326	327
All ages	2,000	2,005	2,009	2,013	2,017	2,021	2,025	2,029	2,032	2,035	2,039	2,042	2,044	2,047	2,049	2,051	2,053	2,054	2,055	2,056
Percentages																				
0-14	17.7	17.6	17.5	17.4	17.3	17.2	17.2	17.2	17.2	17.2	17.2	17.2	17.2	17.3	17.3	17.3	17.3	17.3	17.3	17.3
15-29	18.4	18.5	18.5	18.4	18.3	18.2	18.1	18.0	17.8	17.7	17.6	17.5	17.4	17.3	17.2	17.1	17.0	16.9	16.9	16.8
30-44	17.1	17.0	16.8	16.7	16.7	16.8	16.8	16.8	16.9	16.9	16.9	17.0	17.1	17.2	17.3	17.4	17.5	17.5	17.5	17.4
45-59	17.6	17.6	17.7	17.7	17.7	17.7	17.6	17.5	17.4	17.3	17.2	17.1	16.9	16.7	16.5	16.3	16.2	16.1	16.0	16.1
60-74	17.7	17.6	17.5	17.3	17.1	17.0	16.9	16.8	16.6	16.5	16.4	16.3	16.3	16.2	16.2	16.2	16.3	16.3	16.4	16.5
75 & over	11.4	11.7	12.1	12.4	12.8	13.1	13.5	13.8	14.1	14.4	14.7	14.9	15.2	15.4	15.5	15.7	15.7	15.8	15.8	15.9
All ages	100.0	100.0	100.0	100.0	100.0	100.0	100.0	100.0	100.0	100.0	100.0	100.0	100.0	100.0	100.0	100.0	100.0	100.0	100.0	100.0
Mean age	42.6	42.7	42.9	43.1	43.2	43.3	43.5	43.6	43.7	43.8	43.9	44.0	44.1	44.2	44.2	44.3	44.4	44.5	44.5	44.6
Median age	42.3	42.5	42.7	42.8	42.9	43.0	43.2	43.3	43.3	43.4	43.4	43.4	43.3	43.3	43.3	43.4	43.4	43.5	43.6	43.7

15.3h Population projections by the Office for National Statistics
Northern Ireland, PERSONS, thousands

2014-based
Principal projection

Projected populations at mid-years by age last birthday

Ages	2054	2055	2056	2057	2058	2059	2060	2061	2062	2063	2064	2065	2066	2067	2068	2069	2070	2071	2072	2073
Thousands																				
0-14	356	356	355	354	353	352	351	350	348	347	346	345	344	343	343	342	342	342	342	342
15-29	345	345	346	346	347	347	348	349	350	351	352	352	353	353	353	353	352	352	351	350
30-44	357	355	353	351	349	348	346	345	343	341	340	338	337	336	335	335	335	335	336	336
45-59	332	333	335	336	337	338	340	343	346	348	350	352	353	353	352	350	349	347	345	343
60-74	339	337	336	335	334	333	331	328	325	322	319	317	315	315	316	317	319	321	323	324
75 & over	328	331	333	335	337	338	340	342	344	346	348	350	352	354	355	357	357	359	360	361
All ages	2,057	2,057	2,057	2,057	2,057	2,057	2,057	2,056	2,056	2,056	2,055	2,055	2,055	2,054	2,055	2,055	2,055	2,055	2,056	2,056
Percentages																				
0-14	17.3	17.3	17.3	17.2	17.2	17.1	17.1	17.0	16.9	16.9	16.8	16.8	16.8	16.7	16.7	16.7	16.6	16.6	16.6	16.6
15-29	16.8	16.8	16.8	16.8	16.8	16.9	16.9	17.0	17.0	17.1	17.1	17.1	17.2	17.2	17.2	17.2	17.1	17.1	17.1	17.0
30-44	17.3	17.3	17.2	17.1	17.0	16.9	16.8	16.8	16.7	16.6	16.5	16.5	16.4	16.4	16.3	16.3	16.3	16.3	16.3	16.3
45-59	16.1	16.2	16.3	16.3	16.4	16.4	16.5	16.7	16.8	16.9	17.1	17.1	17.2	17.2	17.1	17.1	17.0	16.9	16.8	16.7
60-74	16.5	16.4	16.3	16.3	16.3	16.2	16.1	15.9	15.8	15.6	15.5	15.4	15.4	15.3	15.4	15.4	15.5	15.6	15.7	15.8
75 & over	16.0	16.1	16.2	16.3	16.4	16.5	16.6	16.7	16.8	16.8	16.9	17.0	17.1	17.2	17.3	17.4	17.4	17.4	17.5	17.6
All ages	100.0	100.0	100.0	100.0	100.0	100.0	100.0	100.0	100.0	100.0	100.0	100.0	100.0	100.0	100.0	100.0	100.0	100.0	100.0	100.0
Mean age	44.6	44.7	44.8	44.8	44.9	44.9	45.0	45.0	45.1	45.1	45.2	45.2	45.2	45.3	45.3	45.4	45.4	45.5	45.5	45.6
Median age	43.8	43.9	44.0	44.1	44.1	44.2	44.3	44.4	44.4	44.5	44.6	44.6	44.7	44.8	44.8	44.9	44.9	45.0	45.0	45.0

Ages	2074	2075	2076	2077	2078	2079	2080	2081	2082	2083	2084	2085	2086	2087	2088	2089	2090	2091	2092	2093
Thousands																				
0-14	342	342	342	343	343	343	344	344	344	344	344	344	343	343	342	342	341	341	340	339
15-29	349	348	347	345	344	343	342	342	341	340	340	340	339	339	339	340	340	340	340	341
30-44	337	338	339	340	340	341	342	342	343	343	343	342	342	341	340	339	338	337	336	335
45-59	342	340	339	337	336	334	333	332	331	330	330	330	330	331	331	332	333	334	335	336
60-74	325	327	330	333	335	338	339	341	341	340	338	337	335	334	332	331	330	328	327	326
75 & over	362	363	362	362	361	361	362	363	365	368	371	374	377	381	384	387	389	392	395	398
All ages	2,057	2,058	2,059	2,059	2,060	2,061	2,062	2,063	2,064	2,065	2,066	2,067	2,067	2,068	2,069	2,070	2,071	2,072	2,073	2,074
Percentages																				
0-14	16.6	16.6	16.6	16.6	16.6	16.7	16.7	16.7	16.7	16.7	16.6	16.6	16.6	16.6	16.5	16.5	16.5	16.4	16.4	16.4
15-29	17.0	16.9	16.8	16.8	16.7	16.7	16.6	16.6	16.5	16.5	16.5	16.4	16.4	16.4	16.4	16.4	16.4	16.4	16.4	16.4
30-44	16.4	16.4	16.5	16.5	16.5	16.6	16.6	16.6	16.6	16.6	16.6	16.6	16.5	16.5	16.4	16.4	16.3	16.3	16.2	16.1
45-59	16.6	16.5	16.5	16.4	16.3	16.2	16.1	16.1	16.0	16.0	16.0	16.0	16.0	16.0	16.0	16.0	16.1	16.1	16.2	16.2
60-74	15.8	15.9	16.0	16.1	16.3	16.4	16.5	16.5	16.5	16.5	16.4	16.3	16.2	16.1	16.1	16.0	15.9	15.9	15.8	15.7
75 & over	17.6	17.6	17.6	17.6	17.5	17.5	17.5	17.6	17.7	17.8	18.0	18.1	18.3	18.4	18.6	18.7	18.8	18.9	19.0	19.2
All ages	100.0	100.0	100.0	100.0	100.0	100.0	100.0	100.0	100.0	100.0	100.0	100.0	100.0	100.0	100.0	100.0	100.0	100.0	100.0	100.0
Mean age	45.6	45.6	45.7	45.7	45.8	45.8	45.9	45.9	46.0	46.0	46.1	46.1	46.2	46.2	46.3	46.3	46.4	46.4	46.5	46.6
Median age	45.0	45.1	45.1	45.1	45.1	45.1	45.1	45.2	45.2	45.2	45.3	45.3	45.4	45.5	45.6	45.6	45.7	45.8	45.9	46.0

15.3h Population projections by the Office for National Statistics
Northern Ireland, PERSONS, thousands

2014-based
Principal projection

Projected populations at mid-years by age last birthday

Ages	2094	2095	2096	2097	2098	2099	2100	2101	2102	2103	2104	2105	2106	2107	2108	2109	2110	2111	2112	2113	2114
Thousands																					
0-14	339	338	337	337	336	336	335	335	335	335	334	334	334	334	334	334	334	334	334	334	334
15-29	341	341	341	341	342	341	341	341	341	340	340	339	338	338	337	336	336	335	335	334	334
30-44	334	333	332	331	331	330	330	330	330	330	330	330	331	331	331	331	332	332	332	332	332
45-59	337	337	338	338	338	338	338	337	337	336	335	334	333	332	331	330	330	328	327	327	326
60-74	324	323	322	322	321	321	321	322	322	323	324	325	326	327	328	329	330	331	331	331	331
75 & over	400	403	406	408	411	413	415	417	419	421	422	424	425	427	428	429	430	432	433	435	437
All ages	2,074	2,075	2,076	2,078	2,079	2,080	2,081	2,082	2,083	2,084	2,085	2,086	2,087	2,088	2,089	2,090	2,091	2,092	2,093	2,094	2,095
Percentages																					
0-14	16.3	16.3	16.2	16.2	16.2	16.1	16.1	16.1	16.1	16.1	16.0	16.0	16.0	16.0	16.0	16.0	16.0	16.0	16.0	16.0	16.0
15-29	16.4	16.4	16.4	16.4	16.4	16.4	16.4	16.4	16.4	16.3	16.3	16.3	16.2	16.2	16.1	16.1	16.1	16.0	16.0	16.0	15.9
30-44	16.1	16.0	16.0	15.9	15.9	15.9	15.9	15.8	15.8	15.8	15.8	15.8	15.8	15.8	15.8	15.9	15.9	15.9	15.9	15.9	15.8
45-59	16.2	16.3	16.3	16.3	16.3	16.3	16.2	16.2	16.2	16.1	16.1	16.0	15.9	15.9	15.8	15.7	15.7	15.7	15.6	15.6	15.6
60-74	15.6	15.6	15.5	15.5	15.5	15.4	15.4	15.4	15.5	15.5	15.5	15.6	15.6	15.7	15.7	15.7	15.8	15.8	15.8	15.8	15.6
75 & over	19.3	19.4	19.5	19.7	19.8	19.9	20.0	20.0	20.1	20.2	20.3	20.3	20.4	20.4	20.5	20.5	20.6	20.6	20.7	20.8	20.9
All ages	100.0	100.0	100.0	100.0	100.0	100.0	100.0	100.0	100.0	100.0	100.0	100.0	100.0	100.0	100.0	100.0	100.0	100.0	100.0	100.0	100.0
Mean age	46.6	46.7	46.8	46.8	46.9	47.0	47.0	47.1	47.1	47.2	47.3	47.3	47.4	47.4	47.5	47.5	47.6	47.6	47.7	47.7	47.8
Median age	46.1	46.1	46.2	46.3	46.4	46.5	46.5	46.6	46.7	46.7	46.8	46.8	46.9	46.9	46.9	47.0	47.0	47.1	47.1	47.1	47.2

Source: Office for National Statistics

Note: Figures may not add exactly due to rounding.
* Children under 16. Working age and pensionable age populations based on state pension age (SPA) for given year.
Between 2012 and 2018, SPA will change from 65 years for men and 61 years for women, to 65 years for both sexes.
Then between 2019 and 2020, SPA will change from 65 years to 66 years for both men and women.
Between 2026 and 2027 SPA will increase to 67 years and between 2044 and 2046 to 68 years for both sexes. This is based on SPA under the 2014 Pensions Act.
** This is consistent with the age-group definitions used in ONS Labour Market Statistics.

National Population Projections are currently produced every two years. The 2016-based projections are not due to be published until November/December 2017. Therefore, this table series will be updated in the next edition

15.3h Population projections by the Office for National Statistics
Northern Ireland, MALES, thousands

2014-based
Principal projection

Projected populations at mid-years by age last birthday

Ages	2014	2015	2016	2017	2018	2019	2020	2021	2022	2023	2024	2025	2026	2027	2028	2029	2030	2031	2032	2033
Thousands																				
0-14	184	185	187	188	190	191	192	192	192	191	190	190	189	187	186	185	185	184	183	182
15-29	186	186	185	183	182	181	180	179	179	180	180	181	181	182	183	183	184	185	186	188
30-44	177	177	177	177	177	177	178	179	180	181	182	182	182	182	182	182	181	180	179	177
45-59	182	183	185	186	187	186	186	184	183	180	179	177	176	175	173	172	172	171	171	171
60-74	123	125	128	131	133	136	138	141	144	147	151	154	157	160	163	165	167	169	170	170
75 & over	51	52	54	56	59	61	64	67	70	72	75	78	81	83	86	89	91	94	97	100
All ages	903	909	915	921	927	932	938	943	948	952	957	961	965	969	973	977	980	983	986	989
Percentages																				
0-14	20.4	20.4	20.4	20.4	20.5	20.5	20.5	20.4	20.3	20.1	19.9	19.7	19.5	19.3	19.1	19.0	18.8	18.7	18.5	18.4
15-29	20.6	20.4	20.2	19.9	19.6	19.4	19.2	19.0	18.9	18.9	18.8	18.8	18.8	18.8	18.8	18.7	18.7	18.8	18.9	19.0
30-44	19.7	19.5	19.3	19.2	19.0	19.0	19.0	19.0	19.0	19.0	19.0	18.9	18.8	18.8	18.7	18.6	18.5	18.3	18.1	17.9
45-59	20.1	20.2	20.2	20.2	20.1	20.0	19.8	19.5	19.3	19.0	18.7	18.4	18.2	18.0	17.8	17.6	17.5	17.4	17.4	17.3
60-74	13.6	13.8	14.0	14.2	14.4	14.6	14.7	15.0	15.2	15.5	15.7	16.0	16.3	16.5	16.7	16.9	17.0	17.1	17.2	17.2
75 & over	5.6	5.7	5.9	6.1	6.3	6.6	6.8	7.1	7.3	7.6	7.9	8.1	8.4	8.6	8.8	9.1	9.3	9.6	9.9	10.2
All ages	100.0	100.0	100.0	100.0	100.0	100.0	100.0	100.0	100.0	100.0	100.0	100.0	100.0	100.0	100.0	100.0	100.0	100.0	100.0	100.0
Mean age	37.7	37.8	38.0	38.2	38.4	38.6	38.8	39.0	39.2	39.4	39.6	39.8	40.0	40.2	40.5	40.7	40.9	41.0	41.2	41.4
Median age	36.9	37.0	37.1	37.3	37.5	37.7	37.9	38.1	38.3	38.5	38.7	39.0	39.2	39.4	39.6	39.8	40.0	40.3	40.5	40.7

Ages	2034	2035	2036	2037	2038	2039	2040	2041	2042	2043	2044	2045	2046	2047	2048	2049	2050	2051	2052	2053
Thousands																				
0-14	181	180	179	179	178	178	178	178	178	179	179	180	180	181	181	181	182	182	182	182
15-29	189	189	190	190	189	188	187	186	185	184	183	183	182	181	180	179	178	178	177	177
30-44	176	175	175	174	175	175	176	176	177	177	178	179	180	181	183	184	185	185	185	184
45-59	172	172	174	175	176	177	177	177	177	177	177	177	175	174	173	172	171	170	170	170
60-74	170	170	169	167	166	164	163	162	161	160	159	159	159	159	159	160	161	162	163	164
75 & over	104	107	110	114	117	121	124	128	131	134	136	139	141	143	144	146	146	147	147	147
All ages	991	994	996	999	1,001	1,003	1,005	1,008	1,010	1,012	1,014	1,015	1,017	1,019	1,020	1,021	1,023	1,024	1,025	1,026
Percentages																				
0-14	18.3	18.1	18.0	17.9	17.8	17.8	17.7	17.7	17.7	17.7	17.7	17.7	17.7	17.7	17.7	17.8	17.8	17.8	17.8	17.8
15-29	19.0	19.1	19.1	19.0	18.9	18.7	18.6	18.5	18.3	18.2	18.1	18.0	17.9	17.8	17.6	17.5	17.4	17.4	17.3	17.2
30-44	17.8	17.6	17.5	17.5	17.5	17.5	17.5	17.5	17.5	17.5	17.6	17.6	17.7	17.8	17.9	18.0	18.1	18.1	18.1	18.0
45-59	17.3	17.3	17.4	17.5	17.6	17.6	17.6	17.6	17.5	17.5	17.5	17.4	17.2	17.1	16.9	16.8	16.7	16.6	16.6	16.6
60-74	17.2	17.1	16.9	16.7	16.5	16.3	16.2	16.1	16.0	15.8	15.7	15.7	15.6	15.6	15.6	15.6	15.7	15.8	15.9	16.0
75 & over	10.4	10.7	11.1	11.4	11.7	12.0	12.4	12.7	13.0	13.2	13.5	13.7	13.8	14.0	14.2	14.2	14.3	14.3	14.3	14.4
All ages	100.0	100.0	100.0	100.0	100.0	100.0	100.0	100.0	100.0	100.0	100.0	100.0	100.0	100.0	100.0	100.0	100.0	100.0	100.0	100.0
Mean age	41.6	41.8	41.9	42.1	42.2	42.4	42.5	42.6	42.7	42.8	42.9	43.0	43.1	43.2	43.2	43.3	43.4	43.4	43.5	43.6
Median age	40.9	41.0	41.2	41.4	41.5	41.6	41.7	41.8	41.9	41.9	41.9	41.9	41.9	41.9	42.0	42.1	42.2	42.3	42.4	42.5

15.3h Population projections by the Office for National Statistics
Northern Ireland, MALES, thousands

2014-based
Principal projection

Projected populations at mid-years by age last birthday

Ages	2054	2055	2056	2057	2058	2059	2060	2061	2062	2063	2064	2065	2066	2067	2068	2069	2070	2071	2072	2073
Thousands																				
0-14	182	182	182	181	181	180	179	179	178	178	177	177	176	176	175	175	175	175	175	175
15-29	177	177	177	177	177	178	178	179	179	180	180	180	181	181	181	181	180	180	180	179
30-44	183	183	182	181	180	179	178	177	177	176	175	174	174	173	173	173	173	173	173	173
45-59	171	171	172	173	173	174	175	176	177	179	180	181	181	181	181	180	179	178	177	176
60-74	165	166	166	166	166	166	166	165	164	163	162	161	161	161	161	162	163	163	164	165
75 & over	148	149	150	151	151	152	153	154	155	156	158	159	160	162	163	164	165	166	168	169
All ages	1,026	1,027	1,028	1,028	1,029	1,029	1,030	1,030	1,031	1,031	1,031	1,032	1,032	1,033	1,033	1,034	1,035	1,036	1,036	1,037
Percentages																				
0-14	17.7	17.7	17.7	17.6	17.6	17.5	17.4	17.4	17.3	17.2	17.2	17.1	17.1	17.0	17.0	16.9	16.9	16.9	16.9	16.9
15-29	17.2	17.2	17.2	17.2	17.2	17.3	17.3	17.3	17.4	17.4	17.5	17.5	17.5	17.5	17.5	17.5	17.4	17.4	17.3	17.3
30-44	17.9	17.8	17.7	17.6	17.5	17.4	17.3	17.2	17.1	17.1	17.0	16.9	16.8	16.8	16.7	16.7	16.7	16.7	16.7	16.7
45-59	16.7	16.7	16.7	16.8	16.8	16.9	17.0	17.1	17.2	17.4	17.4	17.5	17.6	17.5	17.5	17.4	17.3	17.2	17.1	17.0
60-74	16.1	16.1	16.1	16.2	16.2	16.2	16.1	16.0	15.9	15.8	15.7	15.6	15.6	15.5	15.6	15.7	15.7	15.8	15.9	15.9
75 & over	14.4	14.5	14.6	14.6	14.7	14.8	14.9	15.0	15.1	15.2	15.3	15.4	15.5	15.6	15.7	15.9	16.0	16.1	16.2	16.3
All ages	100.0	100.0	100.0	100.0	100.0	100.0	100.0	100.0	100.0	100.0	100.0	100.0	100.0	100.0	100.0	100.0	100.0	100.0	100.0	100.0
Mean age	43.6	43.7	43.8	43.8	43.9	44.0	44.0	44.1	44.1	44.2	44.3	44.3	44.4	44.5	44.5	44.6	44.7	44.7	44.8	44.8
Median age	42.7	42.8	42.9	43.0	43.1	43.2	43.3	43.4	43.4	43.5	43.6	43.7	43.8	43.9	44.0	44.0	44.1	44.1	44.2	44.2

Ages	2074	2075	2076	2077	2078	2079	2080	2081	2082	2083	2084	2085	2086	2087	2088	2089	2090	2091	2092	2093
Thousands																				
0-14	175	175	175	175	175	176	176	176	176	176	176	176	176	175	175	175	175	174	174	174
15-29	179	178	177	177	176	176	175	175	175	174	174	174	174	174	174	174	174	174	174	174
30-44	174	174	175	175	176	176	176	177	177	177	177	176	176	176	175	175	174	174	173	173
45-59	176	175	174	173	172	172	171	171	170	170	170	172	170	170	170	171	171	172	172	173
60-74	166	166	168	169	171	172	173	173	173	173	172	172	171	170	169	169	168	167	167	166
75 & over	170	171	171	171	171	172	173	173	175	177	179	180	182	184	186	187	189	190	192	193
All ages	1,038	1,039	1,040	1,041	1,042	1,043	1,044	1,044	1,045	1,046	1,047	1,048	1,048	1,049	1,050	1,050	1,051	1,052	1,052	1,053
Percentages																				
0-14	16.8	16.8	16.8	16.8	16.8	16.8	16.8	16.8	16.8	16.8	16.8	16.8	16.8	16.7	16.7	16.6	16.6	16.6	16.5	16.5
15-29	17.2	17.1	17.1	17.0	16.9	16.9	16.8	16.7	16.7	16.7	16.6	16.6	16.6	16.6	16.6	16.6	16.6	16.6	16.6	16.6
30-44	16.7	16.8	16.8	16.8	16.8	16.9	16.9	16.9	16.9	16.9	16.9	16.8	16.8	16.8	16.7	16.6	16.6	16.5	16.5	16.4
45-59	16.9	16.8	16.7	16.6	16.6	16.5	16.4	16.3	16.3	16.2	16.2	16.2	16.2	16.2	16.2	16.3	16.3	16.4	16.4	16.4
60-74	16.0	16.0	16.1	16.3	16.4	16.5	16.5	16.6	16.6	16.5	16.4	16.4	16.3	16.2	16.1	16.1	16.0	15.9	15.8	15.8
75 & over	16.4	16.4	16.4	16.4	16.4	16.5	16.5	16.6	16.7	16.9	17.1	17.2	17.4	17.6	17.7	17.8	18.0	18.1	18.2	18.4
All ages	100.0	100.0	100.0	100.0	100.0	100.0	100.0	100.0	100.0	100.0	100.0	100.0	100.0	100.0	100.0	100.0	100.0	100.0	100.0	100.0
Mean age	44.9	45.0	45.0	45.1	45.1	45.2	45.3	45.3	45.4	45.5	45.5	45.6	45.6	45.7	45.8	45.8	45.9	46.0	46.0	46.1
Median age	44.3	44.3	44.4	44.4	44.4	44.5	44.5	44.6	44.6	44.7	44.7	44.8	44.9	45.0	45.0	45.1	45.2	45.3	45.4	45.5

15.3h Population projections by the Office for National Statistics
Northern Ireland, MALES, thousands

2014-based
Principal projection

Projected populations at mid-years by age last birthday

Ages	2094	2095	2096	2097	2098	2099	2100	2101	2102	2103	2104	2105	2106	2107	2108	2109	2110	2111	2112	2113	2114
Thousands																					
0-14	173	173	172	172	172	172	171	171	171	171	171	171	171	171	171	171	171	171	171	171	171
15-29	175	175	175	175	175	175	175	175	174	174	174	174	173	173	173	172	172	172	171	171	171
30-44	172	172	171	171	171	171	170	170	170	170	170	171	171	171	171	171	171	171	171	171	171
45-59	173	173	174	174	174	174	174	174	173	173	172	172	171	171	170	170	169	169	169	168	168
60-74	165	165	164	164	164	164	164	164	165	165	165	166	167	167	168	168	169	169	169	169	169
75 & over	195	196	198	199	200	202	203	204	205	206	206	207	208	209	209	210	211	212	212	213	214
All ages	1,053	1,054	1,055	1,055	1,056	1,057	1,057	1,058	1,058	1,059	1,060	1,060	1,061	1,062	1,062	1,063	1,063	1,064	1,064	1,065	1,065
Percentages																					
0-14	16.4	16.4	16.4	16.3	16.3	16.2	16.2	16.2	16.2	16.2	16.1	16.1	16.1	16.1	16.1	16.1	16.1	16.1	16.1	16.1	16.0
15-29	16.6	16.6	16.6	16.6	16.6	16.5	16.5	16.5	16.5	16.4	16.4	16.4	16.3	16.3	16.3	16.2	16.2	16.1	16.1	16.1	16.0
30-44	16.3	16.3	16.2	16.2	16.2	16.1	16.1	16.1	16.1	16.1	16.1	16.1	16.1	16.1	16.1	16.1	16.1	16.1	16.1	16.1	16.1
45-59	16.4	16.5	16.5	16.5	16.5	16.5	16.4	16.4	16.4	16.3	16.3	16.2	16.2	16.1	16.0	16.0	15.9	15.9	15.9	15.8	15.8
60-74	15.7	15.6	15.6	15.6	15.5	15.5	15.5	15.5	15.5	15.6	15.6	15.7	15.7	15.7	15.8	15.8	15.9	15.9	15.9	15.9	15.9
75 & over	18.5	18.6	18.8	18.9	19.0	19.1	19.2	19.3	19.3	19.4	19.5	19.5	19.6	19.7	19.7	19.8	19.8	19.9	20.0	20.0	20.1
All ages	100.0	100.0	100.0	100.0	100.0	100.0	100.0	100.0	100.0	100.0	100.0	100.0	100.0	100.0	100.0	100.0	100.0	100.0	100.0	100.0	100.0
Mean age	46.2	46.3	46.3	46.4	46.5	46.5	46.6	46.7	46.7	46.8	46.8	46.9	47.0	47.0	47.1	47.1	47.2	47.2	47.3	47.3	47.4
Median age	45.6	45.7	45.7	45.8	45.9	46.0	46.0	46.1	46.2	46.2	46.3	46.3	46.4	46.4	46.5	46.5	46.6	46.6	46.6	46.7	46.7

Source: Office for National Statistics

Note: Figures may not add exactly due to rounding.
* Children under 16. Working age and pensionable age populations based on state pension age (SPA) for given year.
Between 2012 and 2018, SPA will change from 65 years for men and 61 years for women, to 65 years for both sexes.
Then between 2019 and 2020, SPA will change from 65 years to 66 years for both men and women.
Between 2026 and 2027 SPA will increase to 67 years and between 2044 and 2046 to 68 years for both sexes. This is based on SPA under the 2014 Pensions Act.
** This is consistent with the age-group definitions used in ONS Labour Market Statistics.

National Population Projections are currently produced every two years. The 2016-based projections are not due to be published until November/December 2017. Therefore, this table series will be updated in the next edition

15.3h Population projections by the Office for National Statistics
Northern Ireland, FEMALES, thousands

2014-based
Principal projection

Projected populations at mid-years by age last birthday

Ages	2014	2015	2016	2017	2018	2019	2020	2021	2022	2023	2024	2025	2026	2027	2028	2029	2030	2031	2032	2033
Thousands																				
0-14	175	176	178	179	181	182	183	184	184	183	182	181	180	179	178	177	176	176	175	174
15-29	182	180	178	177	174	173	171	170	169	170	170	171	172	173	174	174	175	176	177	179
30-44	187	186	186	185	185	185	185	185	186	185	184	182	181	180	178	177	175	173	170	168
45-59	187	190	192	194	195	195	195	193	192	191	190	188	188	186	185	184	183	182	182	181
60-74	131	133	135	138	140	143	145	149	151	154	158	162	165	169	172	176	178	181	182	183
75 & over	76	77	78	80	82	84	87	89	92	95	98	100	103	105	107	110	112	115	118	122
All ages	938	942	948	952	957	962	966	970	974	978	982	985	989	992	995	998	1,000	1,003	1,005	1,007
Percentages																				
0-14	18.7	18.7	18.8	18.8	18.9	18.9	19.0	18.9	18.9	18.7	18.6	18.4	18.2	18.0	17.9	17.8	17.6	17.5	17.4	17.3
15-29	19.4	19.1	18.8	18.5	18.2	18.0	17.7	17.5	17.4	17.3	17.3	17.4	17.4	17.4	17.4	17.4	17.5	17.6	17.7	17.7
30-44	20.0	19.8	19.6	19.5	19.3	19.2	19.1	19.1	19.0	18.9	18.8	18.5	18.3	18.1	17.9	17.7	17.5	17.2	17.0	16.7
45-59	19.9	20.1	20.3	20.3	20.3	20.3	20.1	19.9	19.7	19.5	19.3	19.1	19.0	18.8	18.6	18.5	18.3	18.2	18.1	18.0
60-74	13.9	14.1	14.3	14.5	14.7	14.8	15.1	15.3	15.5	15.8	16.1	16.4	16.7	17.0	17.3	17.6	17.8	18.0	18.1	18.2
75 & over	8.1	8.1	8.2	8.4	8.6	8.8	9.0	9.2	9.5	9.7	10.0	10.2	10.4	10.6	10.8	11.0	11.2	11.5	11.8	12.1
All ages	100.0	100.0	100.0	100.0	100.0	100.0	100.0	100.0	100.0	100.0	100.0	100.0	100.0	100.0	100.0	100.0	100.0	100.0	100.0	100.0
Mean age	39.7	39.8	40.0	40.1	40.3	40.5	40.7	40.9	41.1	41.3	41.5	41.7	41.9	42.1	42.3	42.5	42.7	42.9	43.1	43.3
Median age	39.1	39.2	39.4	39.6	39.8	40.0	40.3	40.6	40.8	41.1	41.3	41.6	41.9	42.1	42.4	42.6	42.9	43.1	43.3	43.6

Ages	2034	2035	2036	2037	2038	2039	2040	2041	2042	2043	2044	2045	2046	2047	2048	2049	2050	2051	2052	2053
Thousands																				
0-14	173	172	171	171	171	170	170	170	170	171	171	172	172	172	173	173	174	174	174	174
15-29	180	181	181	181	181	180	179	178	177	176	175	174	173	173	172	171	170	170	169	169
30-44	166	165	163	163	163	164	165	165	166	167	167	168	169	171	172	173	174	175	175	174
45-59	181	181	182	182	182	181	179	177	176	175	174	172	169	167	165	163	162	161	160	160
60-74	184	183	183	181	180	179	178	178	177	176	175	174	174	173	173	173	173	174	174	174
75 & over	125	129	133	136	140	144	149	153	156	160	163	166	169	172	174	176	177	178	179	179
All ages	1,009	1,011	1,013	1,015	1,016	1,018	1,020	1,021	1,023	1,024	1,025	1,026	1,027	1,028	1,029	1,029	1,030	1,030	1,030	1,030
Percentages																				
0-14	17.1	17.0	16.9	16.8	16.8	16.7	16.7	16.7	16.7	16.7	16.7	16.7	16.7	16.8	16.8	16.8	16.9	16.9	16.9	16.9
15-29	17.8	17.9	17.9	17.9	17.8	17.7	17.6	17.4	17.3	17.2	17.1	17.0	16.9	16.8	16.7	16.6	16.5	16.5	16.4	16.4
30-44	16.5	16.3	16.1	16.0	16.0	16.1	16.1	16.2	16.2	16.3	16.3	16.4	16.5	16.6	16.7	16.8	16.9	17.0	17.0	16.9
45-59	17.9	17.9	17.9	17.9	17.9	17.8	17.5	17.4	17.3	17.1	16.9	16.7	16.5	16.3	16.1	15.9	15.7	15.6	15.5	15.5
60-74	18.2	18.1	18.0	17.9	17.7	17.6	17.5	17.4	17.3	17.2	17.1	17.0	16.9	16.9	16.8	16.8	16.8	16.9	16.9	16.9
75 & over	12.4	12.7	13.1	13.4	13.8	14.2	14.6	14.9	15.3	15.6	15.9	16.2	16.5	16.7	16.9	17.1	17.2	17.3	17.3	17.4
All ages	100.0	100.0	100.0	100.0	100.0	100.0	100.0	100.0	100.0	100.0	100.0	100.0	100.0	100.0	100.0	100.0	100.0	100.0	100.0	100.0
Mean age	43.5	43.7	43.9	44.0	44.2	44.3	44.4	44.6	44.7	44.8	44.9	45.0	45.1	45.2	45.3	45.3	45.4	45.5	45.5	45.6
Median age	43.8	44.0	44.2	44.3	44.5	44.6	44.6	44.7	44.8	44.9	44.9	44.9	44.9	44.8	44.8	44.7	44.7	44.7	44.8	44.9

15.3h Population projections by the Office for National Statistics
Northern Ireland, FEMALES, thousands

2014-based
Principal projection

Projected populations at mid-years by age last birthday

Ages	2054	2055	2056	2057	2058	2059	2060	2061	2062	2063	2064	2065	2066	2067	2068	2069	2070	2071	2072	2073
Thousands																				
0-14	174	174	173	173	173	172	171	171	170	170	169	169	168	168	168	167	167	167	167	167
15-29	169	169	169	169	169	170	170	170	171	171	172	172	172	172	172	172	172	172	171	171
30-44	173	172	171	170	169	169	168	167	166	165	165	164	163	163	163	162	162	162	163	163
45-59	161	162	163	163	164	164	165	167	168	169	171	172	172	172	171	171	170	169	168	167
60-74	173	171	170	169	168	167	165	163	161	159	157	156	155	154	155	155	157	157	158	159
75 & over	181	182	183	184	185	186	187	188	189	190	190	191	192	192	192	193	192	192	192	192
All ages	1,030	1,030	1,030	1,029	1,028	1,028	1,027	1,026	1,025	1,025	1,024	1,023	1,022	1,022	1,021	1,020	1,020	1,020	1,019	1,019
Percentages																				
0-14	16.9	16.9	16.8	16.8	16.8	16.7	16.7	16.6	16.6	16.6	16.5	16.5	16.5	16.4	16.4	16.4	16.4	16.4	16.4	16.4
15-29	16.4	16.4	16.4	16.4	16.5	16.5	16.6	16.6	16.7	16.7	16.8	16.8	16.8	16.9	16.9	16.9	16.9	16.8	16.8	16.8
30-44	16.8	16.7	16.6	16.5	16.5	16.4	16.3	16.3	16.2	16.1	16.1	16.0	16.0	15.9	15.9	15.9	15.9	15.9	16.0	16.0
45-59	15.6	15.7	15.8	15.9	15.9	16.0	16.1	16.3	16.4	16.5	16.7	16.8	16.8	16.9	16.8	16.7	16.7	16.6	16.5	16.4
60-74	16.8	16.6	16.5	16.4	16.3	16.2	16.1	15.9	15.7	15.5	15.4	15.2	15.1	15.1	15.2	15.2	15.3	15.4	15.5	15.6
75 & over	17.5	17.7	17.8	17.9	18.0	18.1	18.2	18.3	18.4	18.5	18.6	18.7	18.7	18.8	18.8	18.9	18.8	18.8	18.9	18.9
All ages	100.0	100.0	100.0	100.0	100.0	100.0	100.0	100.0	100.0	100.0	100.0	100.0	100.0	100.0	100.0	100.0	100.0	100.0	100.0	100.0
Mean age	45.7	45.7	45.8	45.8	45.8	45.9	45.9	46.0	46.0	46.0	46.1	46.1	46.1	46.1	46.2	46.2	46.2	46.2	46.3	46.3
Median age	44.9	45.0	45.1	45.2	45.3	45.3	45.4	45.4	45.5	45.5	45.6	45.6	45.7	45.7	45.7	45.8	45.8	45.8	45.8	45.8

Ages	2074	2075	2076	2077	2078	2079	2080	2081	2082	2083	2084	2085	2086	2087	2088	2089	2090	2091	2092	2093
Thousands																				
0-14	167	167	167	167	168	168	168	168	168	168	168	168	168	167	167	167	167	166	166	166
15-29	170	170	169	169	168	168	167	167	166	166	166	166	166	166	166	166	166	166	166	166
30-44	163	164	164	165	165	165	166	166	166	166	166	166	165	165	165	164	164	163	163	163
45-59	166	166	165	164	163	162	162	161	161	160	160	160	160	161	161	161	162	162	163	163
60-74	159	161	162	163	165	166	167	167	167	167	166	166	165	164	163	162	162	161	160	160
75 & over	193	192	191	191	190	190	189	189	190	191	193	194	195	197	198	199	200	202	203	204
All ages	1,019	1,019	1,019	1,019	1,019	1,019	1,019	1,019	1,019	1,019	1,019	1,019	1,019	1,019	1,019	1,020	1,020	1,020	1,020	1,021
Percentages																				
0-14	16.4	16.4	16.4	16.4	16.5	16.5	16.5	16.5	16.5	16.5	16.5	16.5	16.5	16.4	16.4	16.4	16.3	16.3	16.3	16.2
15-29	16.7	16.7	16.6	16.6	16.5	16.5	16.4	16.4	16.3	16.3	16.3	16.3	16.3	16.2	16.2	16.3	16.3	16.3	16.3	16.3
30-44	16.0	16.1	16.1	16.2	16.2	16.2	16.3	16.3	16.3	16.3	16.3	16.3	16.2	16.2	16.2	16.1	16.0	16.0	15.9	15.9
45-59	16.3	16.3	16.2	16.1	16.0	16.0	15.9	15.8	15.8	15.8	15.7	15.7	15.7	15.8	15.8	15.8	15.9	15.9	15.9	15.9
60-74	15.7	15.8	15.9	16.0	16.2	16.3	16.4	16.4	16.4	16.4	16.3	16.2	16.2	16.1	16.0	15.9	15.9	15.8	15.7	15.6
75 & over	18.9	18.8	18.8	18.7	18.7	18.6	18.6	18.6	18.7	18.8	18.9	19.0	19.2	19.3	19.4	19.5	19.6	19.8	19.9	20.0
All ages	100.0	100.0	100.0	100.0	100.0	100.0	100.0	100.0	100.0	100.0	100.0	100.0	100.0	100.0	100.0	100.0	100.0	100.0	100.0	100.0
Mean age	46.3	46.3	46.4	46.4	46.4	46.4	46.5	46.5	46.5	46.6	46.6	46.6	46.7	46.7	46.8	46.8	46.9	46.9	47.0	47.0
Median age	45.8	45.8	45.8	45.8	45.8	45.8	45.8	45.8	45.8	45.9	45.9	45.9	46.0	46.0	46.1	46.2	46.2	46.3	46.4	46.5

15.3h Population projections by the Office for National Statistics
Northern Ireland, FEMALES, thousands

2014-based
Principal projection

Projected populations at mid-years by age last birthday

Ages	2094	2095	2096	2097	2098	2099	2100	2101	2102	2103	2104	2105	2106	2107	2108	2109	2110	2111	2112	2113	2114
Thousands																					
0-14	165	165	165	164	164	164	164	164	164	163	163	163	163	163	163	163	163	163	163	163	163
15-29	166	166	167	167	167	167	166	166	166	166	166	165	165	165	164	164	164	164	163	163	163
30-44	162	161	161	160	160	160	160	160	160	160	160	160	160	160	160	160	160	160	161	161	161
45-59	163	164	164	164	164	164	164	164	163	163	162	162	161	161	160	160	159	159	159	158	158
60-74	159	158	158	157	157	157	157	157	158	158	158	159	159	160	160	161	161	162	162	162	162
75 & over	205	207	208	209	210	211	212	213	214	215	216	217	217	218	218	219	220	220	221	222	223
All ages	1,021	1,021	1,022	1,022	1,023	1,023	1,024	1,024	1,024	1,025	1,025	1,026	1,026	1,027	1,027	1,027	1,028	1,028	1,029	1,029	1,029
Percentages																					
0-14	16.2	16.2	16.1	16.1	16.1	16.0	16.0	16.0	16.0	15.9	15.9	15.9	15.9	15.9	15.9	15.9	15.9	15.9	15.9	15.9	15.9
15-29	16.3	16.3	16.3	16.3	16.3	16.3	16.3	16.2	16.2	16.2	16.2	16.1	16.1	16.1	16.0	16.0	15.9	15.9	15.9	15.9	15.9
30-44	15.8	15.8	15.7	15.7	15.6	15.6	15.6	15.6	15.6	15.6	15.6	15.6	15.6	15.6	15.6	15.6	15.6	15.6	15.6	15.6	15.6
45-59	16.0	16.0	16.1	16.1	16.1	16.0	16.0	16.0	15.9	15.9	15.8	15.8	15.7	15.7	15.6	15.7	15.7	15.7	15.7	15.7	15.7
60-74	15.6	15.5	15.4	15.4	15.4	15.4	15.4	15.4	15.4	15.4	15.4	15.5	15.5	15.6	15.6	15.6	15.7	15.7	15.7	15.7	15.7
75 & over	20.1	20.2	20.4	20.5	20.6	20.7	20.8	20.8	20.9	21.0	21.0	21.1	21.2	21.2	21.3	21.3	21.4	21.4	21.5	21.6	21.6
All ages	100.0	100.0	100.0	100.0	100.0	100.0	100.0	100.0	100.0	100.0	100.0	100.0	100.0	100.0	100.0	100.0	100.0	100.0	100.0	100.0	100.0
Mean age	47.1	47.2	47.2	47.3	47.3	47.4	47.5	47.5	47.6	47.7	47.7	47.8	47.8	47.9	47.9	48.0	48.0	48.1	48.1	48.2	48.2
Median age	46.6	46.7	46.7	46.8	46.9	47.0	47.0	47.1	47.2	47.2	47.3	47.3	47.4	47.4	47.4	47.5	47.5	47.5	47.6	47.6	47.7

Source: Office for National Statistics

Note: Figures may not add exactly due to rounding.
* Children under 16. Working age and pensionable age populations based on state pension age (SPA) for given year.
Between 2012 and 2018, SPA will change from 65 years for men and 61 years for women, to 65 years for both sexes.
Then between 2019 and 2020, SPA will change from 65 years to 66 years for both men and women.
Between 2026 and 2027 SPA will increase to 67 years and between 2044 and 2046 to 68 years for both sexes. This is based on SPA under the 2014 Pensions Act.
** This is consistent with the age-group definitions used in ONS Labour Market Statistics.

National Population Projections are currently produced every two years. The 2016-based projections are not due to be published until November/December 2017. Therefore, this table series will be updated in the next edition

15.4 Families by family type and presence of children
United Kingdom, 1999-2015

thousands

Number of families	1999 Estimate	1999 CI+/-	2000 Estimate	2000 CI+/-	2001 Estimate	2001 CI+/-	2002 Estimate	2002 CI+/-	2003 Estimate	2003 CI+/-	2004 Estimate	2004 CI+/-	2005 Estimate	2005 CI+/-	2006 Estimate	2006 CI+/-	2007 Estimate	2007 CI+/-	2008 Estimate	2008 CI+/-	2009 Estimate	2009 CI+/-	2010 Estimate	2010 CI+/-	2011 Estimate	2011 CI+/-	2012 Estimate	2012 CI+/-	2013 Estimate	2013 CI+/-	2014 Estimate	2014 CI+/-	2015 Estimate	2015 CI+/-
Married couple family	12,417	69	12,443	69	12,280	71	12,252	72	12,219	74	12,210	77	12,278	78	12,237	80	12,246	82	12,216	83	12,267	85	12,287	88	12,208	102	12,303	102	12,376	106	12,476	104	12,465	110
No children	5,880	65	5,977	66	5,892	67	5,958	67	5,976	69	5,922	71	6,006	71	6,046	72	5,997	74	6,042	75	5,961	76	6,039	79	5,983	92	5,987	91	5,942	95	6,083	94	6,075	99
Dependent children	4,936	52	4,918	53	4,833	54	4,777	54	4,746	54	4,689	57	4,732	58	4,682	59	4,689	60	4,642	61	4,709	63	4,701	65	4,641	67	4,697	67	4,748	69	4,751	67	4,704	69
Non-dependent children only	1,601	46	1,548	43	1,555	44	1,517	44	1,497	45	1,599	47	1,539	47	1,509	47	1,560	48	1,532	49	1,597	50	1,548	51	1,584	52	1,619	53	1,686	55	1,642	54	1,685	57
Civil partner couple family	N/A	N/A	N/A	N/A	N/A	N/A	N/A	N/A	N/A	N/A	N/A	N/A	N/A	N/A	13	5	33	9	40	9	41	9	45	10	60	12	67	12	64	13	61	12	48	11
No children or non-dependent children only	N/A	N/A	N/A	N/A	N/A	N/A	N/A	N/A	N/A	N/A	N/A	N/A	N/A	N/A	13	5	29	8	37	9	37	9	43	10	54	12	61	12	55	13	49	11	44	11
Dependent children	N/A	N/A	N/A	N/A	N/A	N/A	N/A	N/A	N/A	N/A	N/A	N/A	N/A	N/A			4	3	3	2	4	3	2	2	5	3	6	3	9	4	12	5	4	3
Opposite sex cohabiting couple family	1,855	53	1,984	52	2,129	55	2,156	55	2,242	58	2,298	60	2,392	62	2,457	63	2,549	65	2,653	67	2,689	69	2,749	71	2,863	76	2,880	75	2,826	78	2,975	78	3,087	82
No children	1,083	41	1,184	42	1,260	44	1,267	44	1,354	47	1,331	48	1,409	49	1,419	50	1,480	52	1,522	53	1,564	55	1,556	56	1,632	60	1,619	60	1,524	60	1,666	63	1,689	65
Dependent children	718	32	739	32	808	34	809	34	819	36	885	38	899	38	954	40	974	40	1,040	42	1,025	43	1,077	45	1,107	47	1,130	47	1,170	49	1,163	48	1,251	51
Non-dependent children only	54	9	61	10	61	10	79	12	68	11	81	12	85	13	85	13	96	14	92	14	101	15	116	16	123	17	130	18	133	18	146	19	147	20
Same sex cohabiting couple family	31	7	38	8	45	9	46	9	53	10	61	11	57	11	68	12	52	11	61	11	54	11	51	11	63	13	70	13	89	16	84	15	90	18
No children or non-dependent children only	30	7	37	8	44	9	45	9	52	10	60	11	54	11	65	12	48	10	58	11	51	11	48	11	61	13	64	13	84	16	75	14	88	18
Dependent children	1	1											3	2	3	2	4	3	3	2	3	2	3	2	3	2	6	3	5	3	9	4	3	2
Lone parent family	2,490	55	2,428	55	2,512	58	2,548	57	2,597	60	2,685	62	2,697	63	2,695	63	2,692	64	2,759	66	2,889	68	2,943	70	2,909	71	3,043	74	3,004	77	3,005	75	3,022	79
Dependent children	1,742	43	1,698	44	1,745	45	1,809	45	1,804	47	1,869	49	1,883	49	1,870	50	1,880	50	1,905	52	1,989	54	2,002	54	1,991	56	2,056	57	1,974	58	1,981	57	1,963	59
Non-dependent children only	748	34	731	34	767	35	740	35	793	37	817	38	814	39	825	39	812	39	854	41	901	43	942	44	918	45	986	47	1,030	50	1,024	49	1,059	51
Lone mother family	2,162	50	2,108	50	2,159	51	2,207	51	2,250	53	2,320	55	2,352	56	2,347	57	2,339	57	2,414	59	2,512	61	2,562	63	2,565	65	2,637	66	2,597	69	2,611	68	2,586	70
Dependent children	1,579	40	1,550	41	1,575	42	1,636	42	1,626	43	1,686	45	1,708	46	1,701	46	1,713	47	1,736	48	1,803	50	1,813	51	1,826	53	1,878	54	1,806	55	1,810	54	1,762	55
Non-dependent children only	583	29	558	29	584	30	571	30	625	32	634	33	644	34	646	34	627	33	678	35	709	37	749	39	739	39	759	40	791	43	801	43	824	45
Lone father family	328	22	320	22	353	24	342	24	347	24	366	26	345	25	347	26	353	26	345	26	377	28	381	28	344	28	405	30	408	31	395	30	437	33
Dependent children	163	16	147	15	170	16	172	17	178	17	183	19	175	18	169	18	167	18	169	18	185	19	188	20	165	19	178	20	168	20	171	20	201	22
Non-dependent children only	165	16	173	17	184	18	169	17	168	17	183	19	170	18	178	19	186	20	176	19	192	20	193	21	179	20	227	24	240	25	223	24	235	25
All families	16,793	71	16,893	59	16,966	61	17,002	62	17,110	65	17,254	67	17,424	67	17,470	69	17,571	71	17,729	72	17,940	73	18,075	75	18,102	90	18,362	89	18,359	94	18,601	93	18,712	97
No children	6,993	73	7,198	73	7,196	75	7,270	75	7,383	78	7,314	80	7,469	81	7,542	82	7,553	84	7,657	85	7,612	87	7,686	90	7,730	103	7,727	101	7,602	102	7,871	106	7,894	110
Dependent children	7,398	44	7,355	44	7,386	44	7,396	44	7,370	46	7,444	47	7,517	48	7,509	48	7,550	50	7,592	50	7,729	52	7,784	53	7,747	55	7,896	55	7,905	57	7,916	55	7,926	57
Non-dependent children only	2,403	56	2,339	52	2,383	53	2,336	53	2,358	54	2,497	57	2,438	57	2,420	58	2,469	59	2,480	60	2,599	62	2,605	64	2,625	65	2,739	66	2,851	69	2,813	68	2,893	71

Source: Labour Force Survey (LFS), Office for National Statistics
Produced by Demographic Analysis Unit, Office for National Statistics
families@ons.gsi.gov.uk

1. Totals may not sum due to rounding.
2. In the table .. indicates that the data are not sufficiently reliable to be published.
3. The robustness of an estimate is presented in two ways:
The coefficient of variation (CV) indicates the robustness of each estimate. It is defined a standard error.

The coloured shading on the table indicates the precision of each estimate as follows:

Statistical Robustness

CV ≤ 5	Estimates are considered precise
CV > 5 and ≤ 10	Estimates are considered reasonably precise
CV > 10 and ≤ 20	Estimates are considered acceptable
CV > 20	Estimates are considered unreliable for practical purposes

$$\frac{\text{standard error}}{\text{estimate}} \times 100 \text{, where standard error is an estimate of the margin of error associated with a sample survey.}$$

Confidence intervals are also presented. CI+/- is the upper(+) and lower(-) 95% confidence interval. It is defined as 1.96 x standard error. The confidence interval provides an estimated range of values in which an actual data value is likely to fall 95% of the time.

For example, there were 12,280,000 married couple families in 2001. This estimate has a confidence interval of 71,000, meaning that there is 95 per cent confidence that the true value is 12,280,000 ± 71,000 or between 12,209,000 and 12,351,000.

4. Civil partnerships were introduced in the UK in December 2005.
5. Marriages of same sex couples were introduced in England and Wales in March 2014 and in Scotland in December 2014. Estimates relating to same sex married couples are presented along with opposite sex married couples within the 'Married couple family' category.
6. Families with no children and non-dependent children only have been added together for civil partner couple families and same sex cohabiting couple families to improve the robustness of the estimates.
7. A family is a married, civil partnered or cohabiting couple with or without children, or a lone parent with at least one child. Children may be dependent or non-dependent.
8. Dependent children are those living with their parent(s) and either (a) aged under 16, or (b) aged 16 to 18 in full-time education, excluding children aged 16 to 18 who have a spouse, partner or child living in the household.
9. Non-dependent children are those living with their parent(s), and either (a) aged 19 or over, or (b) aged 16 to 18 who are not in full-time education or who have a spouse, partner or child living in the household. Non-dependent children are sometimes called adult children.
10. Families with no children are families where there are no children currently living in the household. This does not necessarily indicate that the adult(s) in the household have never had children.

15.5 Geographical distribution of the population
ALL PERSONS

Name	Code	Mid-year population estimate	
		2014	2015
UNITED KINGDOM	**K02000001**	**64,596,752**	**65,110,034**
GREAT BRITAIN	**K03000001**	**62,756,254**	**63,258,413**
ENGLAND AND WALES	K04000001	57,408,654	57,885,413
ENGLAND	E92000001	54,316,618	54,786,327
WALES	W92000004	3,092,036	3,099,086
SCOTLAND	S92000003	5,347,600	5,373,000
NORTHERN IRELAND	N92000002	1,840,498	1,851,621
NORTH EAST	**E12000001**	**2,618,710**	**2,624,621**
County Durham	E06000047	517,773	519,695
Darlington	E06000005	105,367	105,389
Hartlepool	E06000001	92,590	92,493
Middlesbrough	E06000002	139,119	139,509
Northumberland	E06000057	315,987	315,263
Redcar and Cleveland	E06000003	135,042	135,275
Stockton-on-Tees	E06000004	194,119	194,803
Tyne and Wear (Met County)	E11000007	1,118,713	1,122,194
Gateshead	E08000037	200,505	200,996
Newcastle upon Tyne	E08000021	289,835	292,883
North Tyneside	E08000022	202,744	202,494
South Tyneside	E08000023	148,740	148,671
Sunderland	E08000024	276,889	277,150
NORTH WEST	**E12000002**	**7,132,991**	**7,173,835**
Blackburn with Darwen	E06000008	146,743	146,846
Blackpool	E06000009	140,501	139,578
Cheshire East	E06000049	374,179	375,392
Cheshire West and Chester	E06000050	332,210	333,917
Halton	E06000006	126,354	126,528
Warrington	E06000007	206,428	207,695
Cumbria	E10000006	497,874	497,996
Allerdale	E07000026	96,471	96,660
Barrow-in-Furness	E07000027	67,648	67,515
Carlisle	E07000028	108,022	108,155
Copeland	E07000029	69,832	69,647
Eden	E07000030	52,630	52,565
South Lakeland	E07000031	103,271	103,454
Greater Manchester (Met County)	E11000001	2,732,854	2,756,162
Bolton	E08000001	280,439	281,619
Bury	E08000002	187,474	187,884
Manchester	E08000003	520,215	530,292
Oldham	E08000004	228,765	230,823
Rochdale	E08000005	212,962	214,195
Salford	E08000006	242,040	245,614
Stockport	E08000007	286,755	288,733
Tameside	E08000008	220,771	221,692
Trafford	E08000009	232,458	233,288
Wigan	E08000010	320,975	322,022
Lancashire	E10000017	1,184,735	1,191,691
Burnley	E07000117	87,291	87,371
Chorley	E07000118	111,607	112,969
Fylde	E07000119	77,042	77,322
Hyndburn	E07000120	80,208	80,228
Lancaster	E07000121	141,277	142,283
Pendle	E07000122	89,840	90,111
Preston	E07000123	140,452	141,302
Ribble Valley	E07000124	58,091	58,480
Rossendale	E07000125	69,168	69,487
South Ribble	E07000126	109,077	109,651
West Lancashire	E07000127	111,940	112,742
Wyre	E07000128	108,742	109,745

15.5 Geographical distribution of the population
ALL PERSONS

Name	Code	Mid-year population estimate	
		2014	2015
Merseyside (Met County)	E11000002	1,391,113	1,398,030
Knowsley	E08000011	146,407	147,231
Liverpool	E08000012	473,073	478,580
Sefton	E08000014	273,531	273,707
St. Helens	E08000013	177,188	177,612
Wirral	E08000015	320,914	320,900
YORKSHIRE AND THE HUMBER	**E12000003**	**5,360,027**	**5,390,576**
East Riding of Yorkshire	E06000011	337,115	336,685
Kingston upon Hull, City of	E06000010	257,710	258,995
North East Lincolnshire	E06000012	159,804	159,570
North Lincolnshire	E06000013	169,247	169,820
York	E06000014	204,439	206,856
North Yorkshire	E10000023	601,536	602,277
Craven	E07000163	55,696	55,801
Hambleton	E07000164	89,828	90,035
Harrogate	E07000165	157,267	157,016
Richmondshire	E07000166	52,729	52,510
Ryedale	E07000167	52,655	53,052
Scarborough	E07000168	108,006	107,902
Selby	E07000169	85,355	85,961
South Yorkshire (Met County)	E11000003	1,365,847	1,374,655
Barnsley	E08000016	237,843	239,319
Doncaster	E08000017	304,185	304,813
Rotherham	E08000018	260,070	260,786
Sheffield	E08000019	563,749	569,737
West Yorkshire (Met County)	E11000006	2,264,329	2,281,718
Bradford	E08000032	528,155	531,176
Calderdale	E08000033	207,376	208,402
Kirklees	E08000034	431,020	434,321
Leeds	E08000035	766,399	774,060
Wakefield	E08000036	331,379	333,759
EAST MIDLANDS	**E12000004**	**4,637,413**	**4,677,038**
Derby	E06000015	252,463	254,251
Leicester	E06000016	337,653	342,627
Nottingham	E06000018	314,268	318,901
Rutland	E06000017	38,022	38,046
Derbyshire	E10000007	779,804	782,365
Amber Valley	E07000032	123,942	124,069
Bolsover	E07000033	77,155	77,780
Chesterfield	E07000034	104,288	104,407
Derbyshire Dales	E07000035	71,281	71,145
Erewash	E07000036	114,048	114,510
High Peak	E07000037	91,364	91,496
North East Derbyshire	E07000038	99,352	99,639
South Derbyshire	E07000039	98,374	99,319
Leicestershire	E10000018	667,905	675,309
Blaby	E07000129	95,851	96,544
Charnwood	E07000130	173,545	176,720
Harborough	E07000131	88,008	89,284
Hinckley and Bosworth	E07000132	107,722	108,769
Melton	E07000133	50,969	50,912
North West Leicestershire	E07000134	95,882	97,247
Oadby and Wigston	E07000135	55,928	55,833
Lincolnshire	E10000019	731,516	736,665
Boston	E07000136	66,458	66,902
East Lindsey	E07000137	137,623	137,887
Lincoln	E07000138	96,202	97,065
North Kesteven	E07000139	111,046	111,876
South Holland	E07000140	90,419	91,214
South Kesteven	E07000141	137,981	138,909

15.5 Geographical distribution of the population
ALL PERSONS

Name	Code	Mid-year population estimate	
		2014	2015
West Lindsey	E07000142	91,787	92,812
Northamptonshire	E10000021	714,392	723,026
Corby	E07000150	65,434	66,854
Daventry	E07000151	79,036	80,014
East Northamptonshire	E07000152	88,872	89,746
Kettering	E07000153	96,945	97,650
Northampton	E07000154	219,495	222,462
South Northamptonshire	E07000155	88,164	89,116
Wellingborough	E07000156	76,446	77,184
Nottinghamshire	E10000024	801,390	805,848
Ashfield	E07000170	122,508	123,574
Bassetlaw	E07000171	114,143	114,533
Broxtowe	E07000172	111,780	112,253
Gedling	E07000173	115,638	115,889
Mansfield	E07000174	105,893	106,556
Newark and Sherwood	E07000175	117,758	118,569
Rushcliffe	E07000176	113,670	114,474
WEST MIDLANDS	**E12000005**	**5,713,284**	**5,751,000**
Herefordshire, County of	E06000019	187,160	188,099
Shropshire	E06000051	310,121	311,380
Stoke-on-Trent	E06000021	251,027	251,648
Telford and Wrekin	E06000020	169,440	171,159
Staffordshire	E10000028	860,165	862,562
Cannock Chase	E07000192	98,549	98,535
East Staffordshire	E07000193	115,663	116,040
Lichfield	E07000194	102,093	102,706
Newcastle-under-Lyme	E07000195	126,052	127,045
South Staffordshire	E07000196	110,692	110,726
Stafford	E07000197	132,241	132,488
Staffordshire Moorlands	E07000198	97,763	97,881
Tamworth	E07000199	77,112	77,141
Warwickshire	E10000031	551,594	554,002
North Warwickshire	E07000218	62,468	62,787
Nuneaton and Bedworth	E07000219	126,174	126,319
Rugby	E07000220	102,500	103,443
Stratford-on-Avon	E07000221	121,056	121,522
Warwick	E07000222	139,396	139,931
West Midlands (Met County)	E11000005	2,808,356	2,833,557
Birmingham	E08000025	1,101,360	1,111,307
Coventry	E08000026	337,428	345,385
Dudley	E08000027	315,799	316,464
Sandwell	E08000028	316,719	319,455
Solihull	E08000029	209,890	210,445
Walsall	E08000030	274,173	276,095
Wolverhampton	E08000031	252,987	254,406
Worcestershire	E10000034	575,421	578,593
Bromsgrove	E07000234	95,485	95,768
Malvern Hills	E07000235	75,911	75,731
Redditch	E07000236	84,471	84,743
Worcester	E07000237	100,842	101,328
Wychavon	E07000238	119,752	121,520
Wyre Forest	E07000239	98,960	99,503
EAST	**E12000006**	**6,018,383**	**6,076,451**
Bedford	E06000055	163,924	166,252
Central Bedfordshire	E06000056	269,076	274,022
Luton	E06000032	210,962	214,710
Peterborough	E06000031	190,461	193,980
Southend-on-Sea	E06000033	177,931	178,702
Thurrock	E06000034	163,270	165,184
Cambridgeshire	E10000003	639,818	647,238

15.5 Geographical distribution of the population
ALL PERSONS

Name	Code	Mid-year population estimate	
		2014	2015
Cambridge	E07000008	128,515	130,907
East Cambridgeshire	E07000009	86,685	87,306
Fenland	E07000010	97,732	99,171
Huntingdonshire	E07000011	173,605	174,966
South Cambridgeshire	E07000012	153,281	154,888
Essex	E10000012	1,431,953	1,443,151
Basildon	E07000066	180,521	181,721
Braintree	E07000067	149,985	150,360
Brentwood	E07000068	75,645	76,057
Castle Point	E07000069	88,907	89,173
Chelmsford	E07000070	171,633	172,638
Colchester	E07000071	180,420	183,939
Epping Forest	E07000072	128,777	129,677
Harlow	E07000073	84,564	85,397
Maldon	E07000074	62,767	62,743
Rochford	E07000075	84,776	85,144
Tendring	E07000076	139,916	141,183
Uttlesford	E07000077	84,042	85,119
Hertfordshire	E10000015	1,154,766	1,166,339
Broxbourne	E07000095	95,748	96,217
Dacorum	E07000096	149,741	151,350
East Hertfordshire	E07000242	143,021	144,719
Hertsmere	E07000098	102,427	102,998
North Hertfordshire	E07000099	131,046	131,696
St Albans	E07000240	144,834	145,797
Stevenage	E07000243	85,997	86,469
Three Rivers	E07000102	90,423	91,674
Watford	E07000103	95,505	96,403
Welwyn Hatfield	E07000241	116,024	119,016
Norfolk	E10000020	877,710	884,978
Breckland	E07000143	133,986	135,480
Broadland	E07000144	125,961	126,628
Great Yarmouth	E07000145	98,172	98,667
King's Lynn and West Norfolk	E07000146	150,026	151,013
North Norfolk	E07000147	102,867	103,308
Norwich	E07000148	137,472	138,872
South Norfolk	E07000149	129,226	131,010
Suffolk	E10000029	738,512	741,895
Babergh	E07000200	88,845	89,215
Forest Heath	E07000201	62,812	63,691
Ipswich	E07000202	134,966	135,600
Mid Suffolk	E07000203	99,121	99,632
St Edmundsbury	E07000204	112,073	112,523
Suffolk Coastal	E07000205	124,776	125,052
Waveney	E07000206	115,919	116,182
LONDON	**E12000007**	**8,538,689**	**8,673,713**
Camden	E09000007	234,846	241,059
City of London	E09000001	8,072	8,760
Hackney	E09000012	263,150	269,009
Hammersmith and Fulham	E09000013	178,365	179,410
Haringey	E09000014	267,541	272,864
Islington	E09000019	221,030	227,692
Kensington and Chelsea	E09000020	156,190	157,711
Lambeth	E09000022	318,216	324,431
Lewisham	E09000023	291,933	297,325
Newham	E09000025	324,322	332,817
Southwark	E09000028	302,538	308,901
Tower Hamlets	E09000030	284,015	295,236
Wandsworth	E09000032	312,145	314,544
Westminster	E09000033	233,292	242,299

15.5 Geographical distribution of the population
ALL PERSONS

Name	Code	Mid-year population estimate	
		2014	2015
Barking and Dagenham	E09000002	198,294	201,979
Barnet	E09000003	374,915	379,691
Bexley	E09000004	239,865	242,142
Brent	E09000005	320,762	324,012
Bromley	E09000006	321,278	324,857
Croydon	E09000008	376,040	379,031
Ealing	E09000009	342,118	343,059
Enfield	E09000010	324,574	328,433
Greenwich	E09000011	268,678	274,803
Harrow	E09000015	246,011	247,130
Havering	E09000016	245,974	249,085
Hillingdon	E09000017	292,690	297,735
Hounslow	E09000018	265,568	268,770
Kingston upon Thames	E09000021	169,958	173,525
Merton	E09000024	203,515	204,565
Redbridge	E09000026	293,055	296,793
Richmond upon Thames	E09000027	193,585	194,730
Sutton	E09000029	198,134	200,145
Waltham Forest	E09000031	268,020	271,170
SOUTH EAST	**E12000008**	**8,873,818**	**8,947,913**
Bracknell Forest	E06000036	118,025	118,982
Brighton and Hove	E06000043	281,076	285,276
Isle of Wight	E06000046	139,105	139,395
Medway	E06000035	274,015	276,492
Milton Keynes	E06000042	259,245	261,762
Portsmouth	E06000044	209,085	211,758
Reading	E06000038	160,825	161,739
Slough	E06000039	144,575	145,734
Southampton	E06000045	245,290	249,537
West Berkshire	E06000037	155,732	156,020
Windsor and Maidenhead	E06000040	147,400	147,708
Wokingham	E06000041	159,097	160,409
Buckinghamshire	E10000002	521,922	528,400
Aylesbury Vale	E07000004	184,560	188,707
Chiltern	E07000005	93,972	94,545
South Bucks	E07000006	68,512	69,120
Wycombe	E07000007	174,878	176,028
East Sussex	E10000011	539,766	544,064
Eastbourne	E07000061	101,547	102,465
Hastings	E07000062	91,093	91,497
Lewes	E07000063	100,229	100,693
Rother	E07000064	92,130	92,908
Wealden	E07000065	154,767	156,501
Hampshire	E10000014	1,346,136	1,353,043
Basingstoke and Deane	E07000084	172,870	173,856
East Hampshire	E07000085	117,483	118,077
Eastleigh	E07000086	128,877	129,027
Fareham	E07000087	114,331	114,799
Gosport	E07000088	84,287	84,672
Hart	E07000089	93,325	93,912
Havant	E07000090	122,210	122,927
New Forest	E07000091	178,907	179,023
Rushmoor	E07000092	95,296	95,342
Test Valley	E07000093	119,332	120,712
Winchester	E07000094	119,218	120,696
Kent	E10000016	1,510,354	1,524,719
Ashford	E07000105	123,285	124,250
Canterbury	E07000106	157,649	159,965
Dartford	E07000107	102,234	103,892
Dover	E07000108	113,066	113,228

15.5 Geographical distribution of the population
ALL PERSONS

Name	Code	Mid-year population estimate	
		2014	2015
Gravesham	E07000109	105,261	106,299
Maidstone	E07000110	161,819	164,499
Sevenoaks	E07000111	117,811	118,409
Shepway	E07000112	109,452	110,034
Swale	E07000113	140,836	142,417
Thanet	E07000114	138,410	139,772
Tonbridge and Malling	E07000115	124,426	125,713
Tunbridge Wells	E07000116	116,105	116,241
Oxfordshire	E10000025	672,516	677,810
Cherwell	E07000177	144,494	145,550
Oxford	E07000178	157,997	159,574
South Oxfordshire	E07000179	137,015	137,412
Vale of White Horse	E07000180	124,852	126,663
West Oxfordshire	E07000181	108,158	108,611
Surrey	E10000030	1,161,256	1,168,809
Elmbridge	E07000207	132,769	132,670
Epsom and Ewell	E07000208	78,318	78,950
Guildford	E07000209	142,958	146,080
Mole Valley	E07000210	86,234	86,104
Reigate and Banstead	E07000211	143,094	144,100
Runnymede	E07000212	84,584	85,594
Spelthorne	E07000213	98,106	98,469
Surrey Heath	E07000214	87,533	88,067
Tandridge	E07000215	85,374	86,025
Waverley	E07000216	122,860	123,315
Woking	E07000217	99,426	99,435
West Sussex	E10000032	828,398	836,256
Adur	E07000223	63,176	63,429
Arun	E07000224	154,414	155,732
Chichester	E07000225	115,527	116,976
Crawley	E07000226	109,883	110,864
Horsham	E07000227	134,158	135,868
Mid Sussex	E07000228	144,377	145,651
Worthing	E07000229	106,863	107,736
SOUTH WEST	**E12000009**	**5,423,303**	**5,471,180**
Bath and North East Somerset	E06000022	182,021	184,874
Bournemouth	E06000028	191,390	194,516
Bristol, City of	E06000023	442,474	449,328
Cornwall	E06000052	545,335	549,404
Isles of Scilly	E06000053	2,280	2,324
North Somerset	E06000024	208,154	209,944
Plymouth	E06000026	261,546	262,712
Poole	E06000029	150,109	150,577
South Gloucestershire	E06000025	271,556	274,661
Swindon	E06000030	215,799	217,160
Torbay	E06000027	132,984	133,373
Wiltshire	E06000054	483,143	486,093
Devon	E10000008	765,302	773,077
East Devon	E07000040	136,374	138,141
Exeter	E07000041	124,328	127,308
Mid Devon	E07000042	79,198	79,510
North Devon	E07000043	94,059	94,172
South Hams	E07000044	84,108	84,470
Teignbridge	E07000045	127,357	128,826
Torridge	E07000046	65,618	66,265
West Devon	E07000047	54,260	54,385
Dorset	E10000009	418,269	420,585
Christchurch	E07000048	48,895	49,057
East Dorset	E07000049	88,186	88,690
North Dorset	E07000050	70,043	70,713

15.5 Geographical distribution of the population
ALL PERSONS

Name	Code	Mid-year population estimate	
		2014	2015
Purbeck	E07000051	45,679	46,212
West Dorset	E07000052	100,474	100,747
Weymouth and Portland	E07000053	64,992	65,166
Gloucestershire	E10000013	611,332	617,162
Cheltenham	E07000078	116,495	116,781
Cotswold	E07000079	84,637	85,162
Forest of Dean	E07000080	83,674	84,544
Gloucester	E07000081	125,649	127,158
Stroud	E07000082	115,093	116,627
Tewkesbury	E07000083	85,784	86,890
Somerset	E10000027	541,609	545,390
Mendip	E07000187	110,844	111,724
Sedgemoor	E07000188	119,057	120,260
South Somerset	E07000189	164,569	164,982
Taunton Deane	E07000190	112,817	114,021
West Somerset	E07000191	34,322	34,403
WALES	**W92000004**	**3,092,036**	**3,099,086**
Isle of Anglesey	W06000001	70,169	69,979
Gwynedd	W06000002	122,273	122,864
Conwy	W06000003	116,287	116,218
Denbighshire	W06000004	94,791	94,691
Flintshire	W06000005	153,804	154,074
Wrexham	W06000006	136,714	136,647
Ceredigion	W06000008	75,425	74,642
Pembrokeshire	W06000009	123,666	123,464
Carmarthenshire	W06000010	184,898	185,123
Swansea	W06000011	241,297	242,382
Neath Port Talbot	W06000012	140,490	140,992
Bridgend	W06000013	141,214	142,092
Vale of Glamorgan	W06000014	127,685	127,592
Cardiff	W06000015	354,294	357,160
Rhondda Cynon Taf	W06000016	236,888	237,411
Caerphilly	W06000018	179,941	180,164
Blaenau Gwent	W06000019	69,674	69,544
Torfaen	W06000020	91,609	91,836
Monmouthshire	W06000021	92,336	92,476
Newport	W06000022	146,841	147,769
Powys	W06000023	132,675	132,642
Merthyr Tydfil	W06000024	59,065	59,324
SCOTLAND	**S92000003**	**5,347,600**	**5,373,000**
Aberdeen City	S12000033	228,920	230,350
Aberdeenshire	S12000034	260,530	261,960
Angus	S12000041	116,740	116,900
Argyll and Bute	S12000035	87,650	86,890
City of Edinburgh	S12000036	492,610	498,810
Clackmannanshire	S12000005	51,190	51,360
Dumfries and Galloway	S12000006	149,960	149,670
Dundee City	S12000042	148,130	148,210
East Ayrshire	S12000008	122,130	122,060
East Dunbartonshire	S12000045	106,710	106,960
East Lothian	S12000010	102,090	103,050
East Renfrewshire	S12000011	92,410	92,940
Falkirk	S12000014	157,690	158,460
Fife	S12000015	367,250	368,080
Glasgow City	S12000046	599,640	606,340
Highland	S12000017	233,080	234,110
Inverclyde	S12000018	79,890	79,500
Midlothian	S12000019	86,220	87,390

15.5 Geographical distribution of the population
ALL PERSONS

Name	Code	Mid-year population estimate	
		2014	2015
Moray	S12000020	94,770	95,510
Na h-Eileanan Siar	S12000013	27,250	27,070
North Ayrshire	S12000021	136,480	136,130
North Lanarkshire	S12000044	338,000	338,260
Orkney Islands	S12000023	21,580	21,670
Perth and Kinross	S12000024	148,930	149,930
Renfrewshire	S12000038	174,230	174,560
Scottish Borders	S12000026	114,040	114,030
Shetland Islands	S12000027	23,220	23,200
South Ayrshire	S12000028	112,530	112,400
South Lanarkshire	S12000029	315,300	316,230
Stirling	S12000030	91,520	92,830
West Dunbartonshire	S12000039	89,710	89,590
West Lothian	S12000040	177,200	178,550
NORTHERN IRELAND	**N92000002**	**1,840,498**	**1,851,621**
Antrim and Newtownabbey	N09000001	139,966	140,467
Ards and North Down	N09000011	157,931	158,797
Armagh City, Banbridge and Craigavon	N09000002	205,711	207,797
Belfast	N09000003	336,830	338,907
Causeway Coast and Glens	N09000004	142,303	143,148
Derry City and Strabane	N09000005	149,198	149,473
Fermanagh and Omagh	N09000006	114,992	115,311
Lisburn and Castlereagh	N09000007	138,627	140,205
Mid and East Antrim	N09000008	136,642	137,145
Mid Ulster	N09000009	142,895	144,002
Newry, Mourne and Down	N09000010	175,403	176,369

Source: Office for National Statistics

15.6 Overseas-born population in the United Kingdom, excluding some residents in communal establishments, by sex, by country of birth[1,2,3] January 2014 to December 2014

United Kingdom
thousands

60 most common countries of birth

	Country	Total		Male		Female	
		estimate	CI[4,5] +/-	estimate	CI +/-	estimate	CI +/-
1	India	793	40	407	28	386	28
2	Poland	790	39	373	27	417	29
3	Pakistan	523	32	282	24	241	22
4	Republic of Ireland	383	27	168	18	215	21
5	Germany	301	24	135	16	166	18
6	Bangladesh	212	20	112	15	100	14
7	South Africa	201	20	93	14	108	15
8	China	196	20	84	13	112	15
9	United States of America	187	19	89	13	97	14
10	Nigeria	178	19	88	13	89	13
11	Romania	170	18	89	13	81	13
12	Italy	150	17	77	12	73	12
13	France	147	17	67	11	80	13
14	Sri Lanka	139	17	74	12	65	11
15	Lithuania	137	16	62	11	75	12
16	Jamaica	136	16	54	10	83	13
17	Kenya	129	16	61	11	69	12
18	Philippines	128	16	49	10	79	12
19	Portugal	127	16	57	11	70	12
20	Australia	126	16	64	11	62	11
21	Zimbabwe	120	15	56	10	65	11
22	Spain	119	15	53	10	66	11
23	Somalia	114	15	48	10	66	11
24	Latvia	102	14	48	10	54	10
25	Ghana	92	13	39	9	53	10
26	Canada	86	13	35	8	51	10
27	Turkey	82	13	45	9	37	9
28	Afghanistan	81	13	47	10	34	8
29	Iran	80	13	46	10	34	8
30	Hungary	79	12	42	9	37	9
31	Iraq	79	12	47	10	32	8
32	Slovakia	75	12	33	8	41	9
33	Nepal	70	12	34	8	36	8
34	Netherlands	66	11	33	8	33	8
35	Bulgaria	65	11	31	8	34	8
36	Malaysia	64	11	28	7	36	8
37	New Zealand	63	11	32	8	31	8
38	Cyprus (European Union)	60	11	27	7	33	8
39	Greece	52	10	27	7	25	7
40	Uganda	51	10	25	7	26	7
41	Brazil	47	10	22	7	25	7
42	Singapore	46	10	21	6	25	7
43	Czech Republic	42	9	16	6	26	7
44	Mauritius	41	9	21	6	20	6
45	Russia	40	9	13	5	27	7
46	Thailand	40	9	9	4	31	8
47	Taiwan	38	9	14	5	24	7
48	Egypt	35	8	20	6	15	5
49	Saudi Arabia	34	8	20	6	14	5
50	Tanzania	34	8	16	6	18	6
51	Zambia	31	8	16	6	14	5
52	Japan	30	8	9	4	20	6
53	Vietnam	28	7	13	5	15	5
54	Malta	27	7	14	5	13	5
55	Sweden	26	7	9	4	18	6
56	Denmark	25	7	10	4	15	5
57	Congo (Democratic Republic)	24	7	11	5	13	5
58	Libya	24	7	15	5	9	4
59	Colombia	24	7	10	4	13	5
60	Sierra Leone	24	7	10	4	13	5

Totals may not sum due to rounding   Source: Annual Population Survey (APS), ONS

. = no contact   : = not available

c = not available due to disclosure control   0~ = rounded to zero

1. Estimates are based on the Annual Population Survey (APS) which is made up of wave 1 and wave 5 of the Labour Force Survey (LFS) plus annual sample boosts which are included primarily to enhance the geographical coverage. As some residents of communal establishments are excluded from the coverage of this survey the estimates in this table are different from the standard ONS mid-year population estimates, which cover all usual residents. For a more comprehensive estimate of the UK population, please refer to: http://www.ons.gov.uk/ons/rel/pop-estimate/population-estimates-for-uk--england-and-wales--scotland-and-northern-ireland/index.html

2. It should be noted that the LFS :-

* excludes students in halls who do not have a UK resident parent

* excludes people in most other types of communal establishments (eg hotels, boarding houses, hostels, mobile home sites, etc)

* is grossed to population estimates of those living in private households. An adjustment is made for those who live in some NHS accommodation and halls of residence whose parents live in the UK. For this reason the sum of those born in the UK and outside the UK may not agree with the published population estimate.

3. The LFS weighting does not adjust for non-response bias by the country of birth variable.

4. CI+/- is the upper(+) and lower(-) 95% confidence limits. It is defined as:

   1.96 x standard error

5. If the confidence interval is higher than the estimate, it is not considered reliable for practical purposes.

15.7 Long-Term International Migration 1991 to 2015
United Kingdom, England and Wales
Citizenship (old country groupings)   *thousands*

Year	All citizenships 2011 Census Revisions[1] Estimate	+/-CI	British Estimate	+/-CI	Non-British Estimate	+/-CI	European Union[2] Estimate	+/-CI	European Union EU15 Estimate	+/-CI	European Union EU8 Estimate	+/-CI	Non-EU All Estimate	+/-CI	Commonwealth[4] All[4] Estimate	+/-CI	Old Estimate	+/-CI	New[4] Estimate	+/-CI	Other Foreign[5] Estimate	+/-CI	All citizenships Original Estimates[1] Estimate	+/-CI
United Kingdom																							
Inflow																							
1991	**329**	23	110	17	219	16	53	11	53	11	z	z	167	12	85	9	26	7	59	5	82	9		
1992	**268**	20	93	16	175	13	44	9	44	9	z	z	131	9	65	6	18	4	46	5	67	7		
1993	**266**	19	86	13	179	13	44	7	44	7	z	z	135	11	70	8	23	6	47	4	65	8		
1994	**315**	23	109	17	206	15	50	9	50	9	z	z	156	12	80	7	21	4	59	5	76	10		
1995	**312**	22	84	14	228	17	61	11	61	11	z	z	167	13	85	8	27	6	58	5	82	10		
1996	**318**	25	94	17	224	18	72	13	72	13	z	z	152	12	78	9	29	7	49	5	74	9		
1997	**327**	27	90	15	237	23	71	18	71	18	z	z	166	13	90	11	31	6	59	9	76	8		
1998	**391**	27	104	16	287	22	82	15	82	15	z	z	206	16	105	13	54	8	51	10	101	8		
1999	**454**	31	115	18	338	25	66	16	66	16	z	z	272	19	123	14	55	9	68	11	150	13		
2000	**479**	31	99	17	379	26	63	14	63	14	z	z	316	22	147	18	56	15	91	9	169	13		
2001	**481**	30	110	18	370	25	58	16	58	16	z	z	313	19	149	14	65	10	84	10	164	12		
2002	**516**	32	98	19	418	26	61	16	61	16	z	z	357	20	155	13	63	8	92	10	201	16		
2003	**511**	33	100	18	411	27	66	18	66	18	z	z	344	20	167	14	62	8	105	11	177	15		
2004	**589**	40	89	14	500	38	130	22	77	15	53	16	370	30	215	20	73	12	141	16	155	23		
2005	**567**	37	98	18	469	33	152	23	73	14	76	18	317	24	180	16	62	10	117	13	137	17		
2006	**596**	39	83	17	513	35	170	26	74	13	92	22	343	24	201	19	62	10	139	16	143	16		
2007	**574**	40	74	14	500	37	195	29	77	17	112	24	305	23	174	17	45	7	129	15	131	16		
2008	**590**	39	85	16	505	36	198	28	90	19	89	19	307	22	165	16	44	9	121	13	142	15		
2009	**567**	30	96	14	471	26	167	19	82	13	68	13	303	18	171	13	30	6	141	12	132	12		
2010	**591**	31	93	15	498	27	176	21	76	13	86	16	322	17	187	12	31	6	156	11	135	12		
2011	**566**	28	78	12	488	25	174	18	83	12	77	12	314	18	179	13	29	6	151	12	135	12		
2012	**498**	27	80	12	418	25	158	18	85	12	60	13	260	17	129	12	31	7	98	10	131	12		
2013	**526**	29	76	12	450	27	201	20	104	13	70	12	248	18	101	10	23	5	78	8	147	15		
2014	**632**	36	81	14	551	34	264	25	129	17	80	15	287	22	127	14	37	7	90	13	160	17		
2015	**631**	33	84	12	548	30	269	24	130	15	73	12	279	19	116	12	33	7	83	10	163	14		
Outflow																							
1991	285	23	154	18	130	15	53	10	53	10	z	z	77	10	35	6	18	4	17	5	43	8		
1992	281	21	155	17	126	13	38	5	38	5	z	z	88	12	31	5	18	4	13	3	57	11		
1993	266	20	149	16	118	11	40	7	40	7	z	z	77	9	34	6	17	4	17	4	43	7		
1994	238	20	125	15	113	13	42	8	42	8	z	z	71	10	31	6	14	4	17	4	40	9		
1995	236	19	135	15	101	11	38	7	38	7	z	z	63	9	29	6	18	5	12	3	34	6		
1996	264	28	156	25	108	11	44	7	44	7	z	z	64	9	32	6	17	4	14	4	32	7		
1997	279	24	149	19	131	15	53	10	53	10	z	z	77	10	40	7	20	6	20	4	37	7		
1998	251	22	126	18	126	12	49	8	49	8	z	z	77	9	33	6	20	4	13	4	44	8		
1999	291	24	139	16	152	18	59	13	59	13	z	z	93	13	41	8	29	7	12	4	52	10		
2000	321	27	161	19	160	19	57	13	57	13	z	z	103	14	47	8	32	6	15	4	55	12		
2001	309	25	159	19	150	17	51	12	51	12	z	z	99	12	51	8	32	6	19	5	49	9		
2002	363	29	186	23	177	19	54	13	54	13	z	z	122	14	58	9	42	8	16	4	64	11		
2003	363	32	191	23	172	22	51	17	51	17	z	z	121	15	59	9	42	8	17	4	62	11		
2004	344	28	196	23	148	16	43	10	39	9	3	3	104	13	53	8	33	6	19	5	52	10		
2005	361	31	186	22	175	21	56	13	40	11	15	8	119	17	60	9	37	7	23	6	59	14		
2006	398	34	207	26	192	22	66	16	44	11	22	11	126	15	66	11	42	8	24	6	60	11		
2007	341	27	171	20	169	18	69	15	41	11	25	10	101	10	58	7	31	4	26	6	43	7		
2008	427	41	173	22	255	34	134	32	54	15	69	21	120	12	66	9	35	6	31	7	55	8		
2009	368	22	140	11	228	18	109	16	53	11	52	12	119	9	66	6	32	5	34	4	53	6		
2010	339	20	136	11	203	16	99	14	58	12	37	8	104	8	52	5	22	4	30	4	52	6		
2011	351	22	149	13	202	17	92	14	49	10	37	9	110	10	60	6	21	4	39	5	50	8		
2012	321	20	143	14	179	14	75	11	41	8	30	8	103	8	53	6	17	3	36	5	51	6		
2013	317	19	134	12	183	15	78	12	47	10	26	7	105	9	53	5	18	3	36	4	52	7		
2014	319	22	137	13	182	18	89	15	51	12	32	9	93	10	42	5	14	3	28	4	51	9		
2015	299	20	124	13	175	16	86	13	50	10	27	7	90	9	42	6	13	3	29	5	48	6		
Balance																							
1991	**+ 44**	33	- 44	24	+ 89	22	- 1	15	- 1	15	z	z	+ 89	16	+ 50	11	+ 8	8	+ 42	7	+ 39	12		
1992	**- 13**	29	- 62	23	+ 49	18	+ 5	10	+ 5	10	z	z	+ 44	15	+ 34	8	0~	5	+ 33	6	+ 10	13		
1993	**- 1**	27	- 62	21	+ 62	17	+ 4	10	+ 4	10	z	z	+ 58	14	+ 36	10	+ 6	8	+ 30	6	+ 22	11		
1994	**+ 77**	30	- 16	23	+ 94	20	+ 9	12	+ 9	12	z	z	+ 85	16	+ 49	9	+ 7	6	+ 42	7	+ 36	14		
1995	**+ 76**	29	- 51	21	+ 127	20	+ 23	13	+ 23	13	z	z	+ 104	16	+ 56	10	+ 9	8	+ 46	6	+ 48	12		
1996	**+ 55**	37	- 62	30	+ 116	21	+ 28	15	+ 28	15	z	z	+ 88	15	+ 47	10	+ 12	8	+ 35	7	+ 41	11		
1997	**+ 48**	36	- 59	24	+ 107	27	+ 18	21	+ 18	21	z	z	+ 88	17	+ 50	13	+ 11	9	+ 39	10	+ 38	11		
1998	**+ 140**	35	- 22	24	+ 162	25	+ 33	17	+ 33	17	z	z	+ 129	18	+ 72	14	+ 34	9	+ 38	11	+ 57	11		
1999	**+ 163**	39	- 24	24	+ 187	31	+ 8	20	+ 8	20	z	z	+ 179	23	+ 82	16	+ 26	11	+ 56	12	+ 98	17		
2000	**+ 158**	41	- 62	25	+ 220	32	+ 6	19	+ 6	19	z	z	+ 214	26	+ 100	19	+ 24	16	+ 76	10	+ 114	18		
2001	**+ 179**	:	- 48	26	+ 220	30	+ 7	20	+ 7	20	z	z	+ 213	22	+ 98	16	+ 33	12	+ 65	11	+ 115	15	**+ 171**	40
2002	**+ 172**	:	- 88	29	+ 241	32	+ 7	21	+ 7	21	z	z	+ 234	24	+ 97	15	+ 21	11	+ 77	10	+ 137	19	**+ 153**	43
2003	**+ 185**	:	- 91	29	+ 239	35	+ 15	25	+ 15	25	z	z	+ 224	25	+ 109	17	+ 20	12	+ 88	12	+ 115	19	**+ 148**	46
2004	**+ 268**	:	- 107	27	+ 352	41	+ 87	24	+ 38	18	+ 49	17	+ 266	33	+ 162	22	+ 40	14	+ 122	17	+ 104	25	**+ 245**	49
2005	**+ 267**	:	- 88	29	+ 294	39	+ 96	27	+ 33	17	+ 61	20	+ 198	29	+ 120	19	+ 25	12	+ 94	14	+ 78	22	**+ 206**	49
2006	**+ 265**	:	- 124	31	+ 322	41	+ 104	30	+ 30	17	+ 71	24	+ 218	29	+ 135	21	+ 20	13	+ 115	17	+ 83	19	**+ 198**	52
2007	**+ 273**	:	- 97	24	+ 330	41	+ 127	33	+ 36	20	+ 87	26	+ 204	25	+ 116	18	+ 13	8	+ 103	16	+ 88	17	**+ 233**	48
2008	**+ 229**	:	- 87	28	+ 251	50	+ 63	43	+ 37	24	+ 20	28	+ 187	25	+ 100	18	+ 9	10	+ 91	15	+ 87	17	**+ 163**	57
2009	**+ 229**	:	- 44	18	+ 242	32	+ 58	25	+ 29	17	+ 16	18	+ 184	20	+ 105	15	- 2	8	+ 107	12	+ 79	13	**+ 198**	37
2010	**+ 256**	:	- 43	18	+ 294	32	+ 77	25	+ 18	17	+ 49	18	+ 217	19	+ 135	13	+ 9	7	+ 126	12	+ 83	13	**+ 252**	37

15.7 Long-Term International Migration 1991 to 2015
United Kingdom, England and Wales
Citizenship (old country groupings)

thousands

Year	All citizenships 2011 Census Revisions[1] Estimate	+/-CI	British Estimate	+/-CI	Non-British Estimate	+/-CI	European Union[2] Estimate	+/-CI	European Union EU15 Estimate	+/-CI	European Union EU8 Estimate	+/-CI	Non-European Union[3] All Estimate	+/-CI	Commonwealth[4] All[4] Estimate	+/-CI	Old Estimate	+/-CI	New[4] Estimate	+/-CI	Other Foreign[5] Estimate	+/-CI	All citizenships Original Estimates[1] Estimate	+/-CI
2011	+ 205	:	- 70	18	+ 286	31	+ 82	23	+ 34	16	+ 40	15	+ 204	20	+ 119	15	+ 8	7	+ 111	13	+ 85	14	+ 215	35
2012	+ 177	34	- 63	19	+ 239	28	+ 82	21	+ 44	14	+ 30	15	+ 157	19	+ 76	13	+ 15	7	+ 61	11	+ 81	14		
2013	+ 209	35	- 57	16	+ 267	31	+ 123	24	+ 58	16	+ 44	14	+ 143	19	+ 48	11	+ 6	6	+ 42	9	+ 95	16		
2014	+ 313	43	- 55	19	+ 368	38	+ 174	29	+ 79	21	+ 48	18	+ 194	25	+ 85	15	+ 23	8	+ 62	13	+ 109	19		
2015	+ 332	38	- 40	18	+ 372	34	+ 184	27	+ 80	18	+ 46	14	+ 189	20	+ 74	14	+ 19	7	+ 54	11	+ 115	15		

England and Wales

Inflow

Year	Estimate	+/-CI	British Estimate	+/-CI	Non-British Estimate	+/-CI	EU Estimate	+/-CI	EU15 Estimate	+/-CI	EU8 Estimate	+/-CI	Non-EU All Estimate	+/-CI	Commonwealth All Estimate	+/-CI	Old Estimate	+/-CI	New Estimate	+/-CI	Other Foreign Estimate	+/-CI
1991	304	22	98	15	207	16	50	11	50	11	z	z	157	12	81	9	25	7	57	5	76	8
1992	251	20	87	16	164	12	42	9	42	9	z	z	123	8	60	6	18	4	42	4	63	6
1993	249	18	80	12	170	13	40	6	40	6	z	z	130	11	67	7	22	6	45	4	62	8
1994	292	21	94	15	199	15	47	9	47	9	z	z	151	12	78	6	21	4	58	5	73	10
1995	299	22	79	14	220	17	59	11	59	11	z	z	162	13	83	8	25	6	58	5	79	10
1996	300	23	86	15	214	17	67	13	67	13	z	z	147	12	77	9	29	7	48	5	70	8
1997	310	26	85	15	226	22	69	18	69	18	z	z	157	12	86	10	29	5	57	8	71	7
1998	370	26	96	15	274	21	76	15	76	15	z	z	198	15	101	13	53	8	48	10	97	8
1999	424	29	101	16	323	24	63	16	63	16	z	z	260	18	117	13	51	8	65	11	143	13
2000	446	28	95	16	351	23	53	12	53	12	z	z	298	20	140	17	51	14	89	9	158	11
2001	449	29	99	17	350	24	56	16	56	16	z	z	295	18	139	13	59	9	79	10	156	12
2002	485	31	92	18	394	25	57	16	57	16	z	z	337	19	149	12	61	8	89	9	188	14
2003	480	31	93	17	387	26	61	18	61	18	z	z	326	19	159	13	58	8	101	11	167	14
2004	549	38	82	13	467	36	122	21	72	14	50	16	345	29	199	19	70	12	129	15	146	22
2005	523	36	87	17	436	32	143	22	66	13	74	18	293	22	167	15	56	9	111	13	126	16
2006	549	36	78	16	471	33	149	23	67	12	78	19	322	23	186	18	55	9	131	15	136	15
2007	524	38	65	13	460	35	175	28	68	16	101	23	285	21	163	15	43	7	120	14	122	15
2008	528	36	67	13	461	34	178	27	75	17	84	19	283	21	157	15	40	8	117	13	126	15
2009	507	28	83	13	424	25	142	18	69	12	58	13	282	17	160	12	25	5	135	11	122	11
2010	532	29	80	14	451	26	151	20	68	12	72	15	300	16	175	12	28	5	147	11	124	11
2011	515	26	71	12	445	24	153	17	74	12	67	12	291	17	169	12	27	5	142	11	122	12
2012	451	26	72	11	380	23	138	16	74	11	52	11	241	16	121	11	30	7	92	9	120	12
2013	484	28	70	11	413	26	183	19	94	12	63	12	230	17	95	9	22	5	72	8	135	14
2014	583	34	76	14	507	31	240	25	116	16	74	15	267	19	120	12	35	7	84	10	147	14
2015	581	31	73	11	508	29	248	23	122	15	63	11	260	17	110	11	31	7	79	9	150	14

Outflow

Year	Estimate	+/-CI	British Estimate	+/-CI	Non-British Estimate	+/-CI	EU Estimate	+/-CI	EU15 Estimate	+/-CI	EU8 Estimate	+/-CI	Non-EU All Estimate	+/-CI	Commonwealth All Estimate	+/-CI	Old Estimate	+/-CI	New Estimate	+/-CI	Other Foreign Estimate	+/-CI
1991	253	21	138	17	115	13	45	9	45	9	z	z	71	9	32	6	17	4	14	4	39	7
1992	248	19	135	15	113	12	34	5	34	5	z	z	79	11	29	5	17	4	12	3	49	9
1993	244	19	137	16	107	11	37	7	37	7	z	z	70	8	31	5	15	4	16	4	39	7
1994	216	19	113	14	103	12	36	7	36	7	z	z	67	10	29	6	13	4	16	4	38	8
1995	216	18	124	15	92	11	33	7	33	7	z	z	59	8	28	6	17	5	11	3	31	6
1996	238	27	141	24	97	11	39	6	39	6	z	z	58	8	28	5	16	4	12	4	30	7
1997	244	21	125	16	120	14	48	10	48	10	z	z	72	10	37	7	19	6	18	4	35	7
1998	223	20	107	16	116	12	44	8	44	8	z	z	72	9	31	5	19	4	12	3	41	7
1999	273	24	129	16	144	18	56	12	56	12	z	z	88	12	39	8	28	7	11	4	49	10
2000	291	26	141	18	151	19	55	13	55	13	z	z	96	14	44	7	30	6	14	4	52	12
2001	282	24	143	18	138	16	46	12	46	12	z	z	93	11	48	8	30	6	18	5	44	8
2002	328	28	168	21	159	18	47	12	47	12	z	z	112	13	52	8	38	7	14	4	60	10
2003	333	31	174	22	159	22	47	16	47	16	z	z	112	14	54	9	38	8	16	4	59	11
2004	311	27	175	22	135	15	41	10	37	9	3	3	94	12	48	7	31	6	17	4	46	9
2005	328	29	171	22	157	19	50	13	35	10	15	8	106	15	55	9	34	7	21	6	51	12
2006	369	33	192	25	177	21	60	15	38	10	22	11	117	15	62	10	39	8	22	6	55	10
2007	307	25	152	19	155	17	60	14	38	11	20	9	94	9	53	6	29	4	23	5	42	7
2008	393	40	157	21	235	34	126	32	49	15	65	20	110	11	59	8	32	5	27	6	50	8
2009	328	20	123	10	205	18	98	16	49	11	46	11	107	8	61	6	31	5	31	4	46	5
2010	308	19	123	10	184	16	89	14	54	11	32	8	95	7	48	5	21	4	27	4	47	5
2011	312	20	134	12	178	16	78	13	42	9	31	9	100	9	55	6	18	3	37	5	45	7
2012	286	19	126	13	160	14	66	11	38	8	24	7	94	8	49	6	16	3	34	5	45	6
2013	280	18	118	11	163	14	68	12	42	9	22	7	95	8	48	5	16	3	32	4	46	6
2014	285	21	124	12	161	17	76	14	44	11	27	8	85	10	39	5	13	3	26	4	45	9
2015	272	20	114	12	158	15	75	13	47	10	21	7	83	8	40	6	12	3	27	5	43	6

Balance

Year	Estimate	+/-CI	British Estimate	+/-CI	Non-British Estimate	+/-CI	EU Estimate	+/-CI	EU15 Estimate	+/-CI	EU8 Estimate	+/-CI	Non-EU All Estimate	+/-CI	Commonwealth All Estimate	+/-CI	Old Estimate	+/-CI	New Estimate	+/-CI	Other Foreign Estimate	+/-CI
1991	+ 51	31	- 40	23	+ 91	20	+ 5	14	+ 5	14	z	z	+ 86	15	+ 50	10	+ 7	8	+ 42	7	+ 37	10
1992	+ 4	27	- 48	21	+ 51	17	+ 7	10	+ 7	10	z	z	+ 44	14	+ 30	7	+ 1	5	+ 29	5	+ 14	11
1993	+ 5	26	- 57	20	+ 62	16	+ 3	9	+ 3	9	z	z	+ 59	14	+ 36	9	+ 7	7	+ 30	6	+ 23	10
1994	+ 77	28	- 19	20	+ 96	19	+ 12	11	+ 12	11	z	z	+ 84	16	+ 49	9	+ 8	6	+ 42	7	+ 35	13
1995	+ 83	28	- 45	20	+ 129	20	+ 25	13	+ 25	13	z	z	+ 103	15	+ 55	10	+ 8	8	+ 47	6	+ 48	11
1996	+ 62	35	- 55	29	+ 117	20	+ 27	14	+ 27	14	z	z	+ 90	15	+ 49	10	+ 12	8	+ 37	6	+ 41	11
1997	+ 66	34	- 40	22	+ 106	26	+ 21	21	+ 21	21	z	z	+ 85	15	+ 49	12	+ 10	8	+ 39	9	+ 36	10
1998	+ 147	33	- 10	22	+ 157	24	+ 31	17	+ 31	17	z	z	+ 126	18	+ 70	14	+ 34	9	+ 36	10	+ 56	11
1999	+ 151	38	- 28	23	+ 179	30	+ 7	20	+ 7	20	z	z	+ 171	22	+ 77	15	+ 23	10	+ 54	11	+ 94	16
2000	+ 154	38	- 46	24	+ 200	30	- 2	17	- 2	17	z	z	+ 202	24	+ 96	18	+ 22	15	+ 74	10	+ 105	16
2001	+ 167	38	- 45	24	+ 212	29	+ 10	20	+ 10	20	z	z	+ 202	21	+ 90	16	+ 29	11	+ 61	11	+ 112	14
2002	+ 158	41	- 77	28	+ 234	30	+ 9	20	+ 9	20	z	z	+ 225	23	+ 97	15	+ 22	11	+ 75	10	+ 128	18
2003	+ 147	44	- 81	28	+ 228	34	+ 14	24	+ 14	24	z	z	+ 214	24	+ 105	16	+ 21	11	+ 84	12	+ 108	18
2004	+ 238	47	- 94	26	+ 332	39	+ 81	23	+ 35	17	+ 46	16	+ 251	31	+ 151	20	+ 38	13	+ 112	15	+ 100	24
2005	+ 195	46	- 84	27	+ 279	37	+ 92	26	+ 31	16	+ 59	20	+ 186	27	+ 112	18	+ 22	11	+ 90	14	+ 75	20
2006	+ 180	49	- 114	30	+ 294	39	+ 89	27	+ 29	16	+ 56	22	+ 205	28	+ 124	20	+ 16	12	+ 109	16	+ 81	19

15.7 Long-Term International Migration 1991 to 2015
United Kingdom, England and Wales
Citizenship (old country groupings)   *thousands*

Year	All citizenships 2011 Census Revisions[1] Estimate	+/-CI	British Estimate	+/-CI	Non-British Estimate	+/-CI	European Union[2] Estimate	+/-CI	European Union EU15 Estimate	+/-CI	European Union EU8 Estimate	+/-CI	Non-European Union[3] All Estimate	+/-CI	Commonwealth[4] All[4] Estimate	+/-CI	Old Estimate	+/-CI	New[4] Estimate	+/-CI	Other Foreign[5] Estimate	+/-CI	All citizenships Original Estimates[1] Estimate	+/-CI
2007	+ 217	45	- 88	23	+ 305	39	+ 115	32	+ 30	19	+ 81	25	+ 190	23	+ 110	17	+ 14	8	+ 97	15	+ 80	16		
2008	+ 135	54	- 90	25	+ 225	48	+ 52	42	+ 26	22	+ 19	28	+ 173	24	+ 97	17	+ 8	10	+ 89	14	+ 76	16		
2009	+ 179	35	- 40	17	+ 219	30	+ 44	24	+ 20	16	+ 12	17	+ 174	18	+ 99	14	- 5	7	+ 104	12	+ 76	12		
2010	+ 224	35	- 43	17	+ 267	30	+ 62	24	+ 14	17	+ 39	17	+ 205	18	+ 127	13	+ 7	6	+ 120	11	+ 78	12		
2011	+ 203	33	- 64	17	+ 267	29	+ 75	21	+ 32	15	+ 37	15	+ 192	19	+ 114	13	+ 8	6	+ 106	12	+ 77	14		
2012	+ 165	32	- 54	18	+ 219	27	+ 73	19	+ 37	13	+ 28	13	+ 147	18	+ 72	13	+ 14	7	+ 58	10	+ 75	13		
2013	+ 203	33	- 47	15	+ 250	29	+ 115	23	+ 52	15	+ 40	13	+ 136	19	+ 47	10	+ 7	6	+ 40	9	+ 89	16		
2014	+ 298	40	- 49	18	+ 347	36	+ 165	28	+ 72	20	+ 47	17	+ 182	21	+ 81	13	+ 22	7	+ 59	10	+ 102	17		
2015	+ 309	37	- 42	17	+ 351	33	+ 173	26	+ 75	18	+ 43	13	+ 177	19	+ 70	13	+ 19	7	+ 52	10	+ 107	15		

Source: Office for National Statistics (ONS), Home Office, Central Statistics Office (CSO) Ireland, Northern Ireland Statistics and Research Agency (NISRA).

Totals may not sum due to rounding.

"z" - Not applicable, ":" - Not available, "0~" - Rounds to zero. Please see the Notes worksheet for more information.

1 Net migration ("Balance") figures for the United Kingdom for 2001 to 2011 have been revised in light of the results of the 2011 Census. The original published estimates are shown to the right of the table. The revisions are not reflected in the remainder of the table. The sums of the disaggregated estimates will not therefore match the revised balances. Users should continue to use the estimates in the table to analyse detailed breakdowns of inflows and outflows of long-term international migrants but, in doing so, should bear in mind that the headline net migration estimates have been revised.

2 European Union estimates are for the EU15 (Austria, Belgium, Denmark, Finland, France, Germany, Greece, Republic of Ireland, Italy, Luxembourg, Netherlands, Portugal, Spain and Sweden) up to 2003, the EU25 (the EU15 and the EU8 groupings plus Malta and Cyprus) from 2004 to 2006, the EU27 (the EU25 plus Bulgaria and Romania) from 2007 and the EU28 (the EU27 plus Croatia) from July 2013. Estimates are also shown separately for the EU15, the EU8 (Czech Republic, Estonia, Hungary, Latvia, Lithuania, Poland, Slovakia and Slovenia) and the EU2 (Bulgaria and Romania). British citizens are excluded from all citizenship groupings and are shown separately.

3 Excludes British and other European Union citizens as defined in footnote 2.

4 From 2004 onwards, All and New Commonwealth exclude Malta and Cyprus.

5 From 2004 onwards, Other Foreign excludes the eight central and eastern European member states that joined the EU in May 2004 (the EU8). From 2007 onwards, Other Foreign excludes Bulgaria and Romania which joined the EU in January 2007. From July 2013 onwards, Other Foreign excludes Croatia which joined the EU in July 2013.

Statistically Significant Increase   Statistically Significant Decrease

The latest estimates (2015) have been compared with the corresponding estimates for the period one year earlier (2014)."," Where changes have been found to be statistically significant, the relevant pair of estimates have been highlighted by setting their background colour.E202

Highlights significant changes over the last year

15.8 Long-Term International Migration 1991 to 2015
United Kingdom, England and Wales
Country of Last or Next Residence (old country groupings)

thousands

Year	All countries (2011 Census Revisions[1]) Estimate	+/-CI	European Union² Estimate	+/-CI	European Union EU15 Estimate	+/-CI	European Union EU8 Estimate	+/-CI	Non-European Union³ All Estimate	+/-CI	Commonwealth⁴ All⁴ Estimate	+/-CI	Old Commonwealth All Estimate	+/-CI	Australia Estimate	+/-CI	Canada Estimate	+/-CI	New Zealand Estimate	+/-CI	South Africa Estimate	+/-CI
United Kingdom																						
Inflow																						
1991	329	23	95	17	95	17	z	z	234	16	130	12	51	9	28	6	6	2	10	4	7	4
1992	268	20	89	17	89	17	z	z	179	12	96	8	38	6	20	4	4	2	8	3	6	3
1993	266	19	75	13	75	13	z	z	191	14	103	10	42	8	22	6	5	2	6	2	9	3
1994	315	23	95	17	95	17	z	z	220	16	112	9	42	6	19	4	6	2	8	3	9	3
1995	312	22	89	15	89	15	z	z	223	16	111	10	41	7	19	4	8	4	9	4	5	2
1996	318	25	98	18	98	18	z	z	220	17	112	11	48	8	22	5	7	3	9	4	11	4
1997	327	27	100	22	100	22	z	z	226	16	121	12	53	8	22	5	9	4	10	3	13	4
1998	391	27	109	18	109	18	z	z	282	20	148	16	84	11	38	7	9	5	16	4	20	6
1999	454	31	96	20	96	20	z	z	358	23	174	17	92	12	40	7	6	3	16	5	29	7
2000	479	31	89	19	89	19	z	z	389	25	189	20	85	17	35	7	10	5	18	6	22	13
2001	481	30	84	19	84	19	z	z	397	23	199	17	99	13	52	10	7	3	17	7	23	5
2002	516	32	90	22	90	22	z	z	426	24	188	14	86	10	38	6	8	3	13	4	28	6
2003	511	33	101	23	101	23	z	z	410	23	204	16	92	11	40	7	12	4	12	4	28	6
2004	589	40	153	24	98	18	54	16	436	32	249	21	96	12	39	7	7	4	13	4	37	9
2005	567	37	186	27	107	19	76	18	381	26	219	19	90	12	39	7	7	3	15	6	29	7
2006	596	39	210	30	110	20	93	22	386	25	219	19	80	11	40	8	7	2	12	4	21	6
2007	574	40	220	31	100	19	113	24	354	25	200	18	65	9	31	6	6	3	10	3	17	5
2008	590	39	224	30	114	22	89	19	366	25	196	18	68	11	29	7	10	6	9	2	20	7
2009	567	30	198	21	114	15	67	13	368	21	204	15	56	9	29	6	8	4	8	3	11	4
2010	591	31	208	24	110	17	81	15	383	19	219	14	57	8	30	5	9	3	11	5	7	3
2011	566	28	203	20	107	15	77	12	363	19	204	14	51	8	26	5	9	5	8	3	8	3
2012	498	27	182	20	112	14	57	13	316	19	153	13	51	8	28	6	9	3	9	3	5	3
2013	526	29	220	22	125	17	70	12	306	19	133	11	46	7	29	6	7	3	5	2	5	2
2014	632	36	287	27	155	20	79	15	345	24	154	16	59	9	31	6	14	5	8	3	6	2
2015	631	33	295	25	160	17	70	11	336	21	141	14	53	9	28	7	8	3	9	3	8	3
Outflow																						
1991	285	23	95	16	95	16	z	z	189	16	101	12	68	9	38	6	15	5	9	3	7	3
1992	281	21	86	13	86	13	z	z	195	16	87	8	57	7	35	5	7	2	10	3	5	3
1993	266	20	88	14	88	14	z	z	178	14	92	10	61	8	38	6	9	4	10	3	4	2
1994	238	20	76	14	76	14	z	z	162	15	81	10	51	8	28	5	7	3	12	5	4	2
1995	236	19	76	13	76	13	z	z	161	13	81	9	58	7	33	5	7	3	12	3	6	3
1996	264	28	94	23	94	23	z	z	170	15	94	11	63	8	36	5	9	4	13	3	5	2
1997	279	24	92	18	92	18	z	z	187	17	100	11	65	9	35	6	9	4	13	4	8	4
1998	251	22	85	17	85	17	z	z	167	14	83	10	59	8	36	6	7	4	11	3	6	2
1999	291	24	103	17	103	17	z	z	188	17	101	11	80	10	53	8	8	3	12	3	7	3
2000	321	27	103	17	103	17	z	z	217	20	111	12	86	11	54	9	8	3	17	4	7	3
2001	309	25	95	19	95	19	z	z	214	17	114	12	88	11	54	7	10	5	16	4	8	3
2002	363	29	128	23	128	23	z	z	234	19	123	12	94	11	53	7	13	5	18	4	10	4
2003	363	32	123	24	123	24	z	z	240	21	131	14	104	12	62	10	7	4	21	5	14	5
2004	344	28	125	21	111	19	6	4	219	19	125	14	95	12	54	9	12	5	20	5	9	4
2005	361	31	138	23	118	21	17	9	223	21	128	14	99	12	51	8	12	5	22	5	13	4
2006	398	34	145	26	118	23	24	11	253	21	148	16	114	14	68	11	11	5	21	5	14	5
2007	341	27	131	22	98	19	25	10	210	15	127	11	94	9	58	7	8	3	17	4	11	3
2008	427	41	202	38	123	26	66	20	225	15	119	10	86	8	55	6	11	4	13	2	7	3
2009	368	22	144	18	88	14	50	11	224	12	127	9	88	7	57	6	11	3	14	3	6	2
2010	339	20	136	16	92	14	38	8	204	11	102	7	64	6	40	4	9	2	9	2	7	2
2011	351	22	124	16	80	13	36	9	226	15	124	10	74	8	48	5	8	2	14	5	3	1
2012	321	20	114	16	79	13	26	6	207	12	114	8	69	6	48	5	9	3	8	2	4	2
2013	317	19	114	15	79	13	26	7	203	12	109	8	68	7	44	6	11	3	10	3	3	1
2014	319	22	127	18	87	15	33	8	192	14	95	8	61	7	38	5	10	3	10	2	3	2
2015	299	20	124	16	89	13	25	7	175	12	83	8	50	6	33	5	8	3	6	2	3	2
Balance																						
1991	+ 44	33	0~	24	0~	24	z	z	+ 44	23	+ 29	16	- 17	12	- 10	8	- 10	6	+ 2	5	+ 1	6
1992	- 13	29	+ 3	21	+ 3	21	z	z	- 16	20	+ 9	12	- 19	9	- 15	6	- 3	3	- 2	4	+ 1	4
1993	- 1	27	- 14	19	- 14	19	z	z	+ 13	19	+ 10	14	- 18	11	- 15	9	- 5	4	- 3	4	+ 5	4
1994	+ 77	30	+ 19	22	+ 19	22	z	z	+ 58	21	+ 31	13	- 9	10	- 9	6	- 2	4	- 4	6	+ 5	4
1995	+ 76	29	+ 13	20	+ 13	20	z	z	+ 63	21	+ 30	13	- 17	10	- 13	6	0~	5	- 3	5	- 1	3
1996	+ 55	37	+ 5	30	+ 5	30	z	z	+ 50	22	+ 17	16	- 15	12	- 14	8	- 2	6	- 4	5	+ 5	5
1997	+ 48	36	+ 9	28	+ 9	28	z	z	+ 39	23	+ 21	16	- 12	12	- 13	8	0~	6	- 4	4	+ 5	6
1998	+ 140	35	+ 24	25	+ 24	25	z	z	+ 116	24	+ 65	19	+ 25	14	+ 3	9	+ 2	6	+ 5	6	+ 15	6
1999	+ 163	39	- 7	27	- 7	27	z	z	+ 170	29	+ 73	20	+ 12	15	- 13	11	- 2	5	+ 5	6	+ 22	8
2000	+ 158	41	- 14	25	- 14	25	z	z	+ 172	32	+ 78	23	- 1	20	- 18	12	+ 2	6	+ 1	7	+ 15	13
2001	+ 179	:	- 11	27	- 11	27	z	z	+ 183	29	+ 85	21	+ 11	17	- 1	12	- 3	6	+ 1	8	+ 14	6
2002	+ 172	:	- 38	31	- 38	31	z	z	+ 191	30	+ 65	19	- 8	14	- 15	10	- 5	6	- 6	6	+ 17	7
2003	+ 185	:	- 23	34	- 23	34	z	z	+ 170	31	+ 74	21	- 12	17	- 23	12	+ 5	6	- 8	6	+ 14	8
2004	+ 268	:	+ 28	32	- 14	28	+ 47	17	+ 217	37	+ 123	26	+ 2	17	- 16	11	- 4	6	- 7	7	+ 28	9
2005	+ 267	:	+ 48	35	- 11	29	+ 59	20	+ 158	34	+ 91	24	- 9	16	- 12	11	- 5	6	- 8	8	+ 15	8
2006	+ 265	:	+ 65	40	- 8	31	+ 69	25	+ 133	33	+ 72	25	- 34	18	- 28	13	- 4	5	- 9	7	+ 7	8
2007	+ 273	:	+ 88	38	+ 2	27	+ 88	26	+ 145	29	+ 73	21	- 29	13	- 27	10	- 2	4	- 7	5	+ 6	6
2008	+ 229	:	+ 21	49	- 9	34	+ 23	28	+ 142	29	+ 76	20	- 18	14	- 26	9	- 1	7	- 4	3	+ 14	7
2009	+ 229	:	+ 54	28	+ 26	21	+ 18	17	+ 144	24	+ 77	17	- 32	12	- 27	9	- 3	4	- 6	4	+ 4	5
2010	+ 256	:	+ 73	29	+ 18	22	+ 43	17	+ 179	23	+ 117	16	- 7	10	- 10	7	0~	4	+ 2	5	+ 1	4
2011	+ 205	:	+ 79	26	+ 27	19	+ 41	15	+ 137	24	+ 80	17	- 23	12	- 22	8	+ 1	6	- 6	6	+ 5	3
2012	+ 177	34	+ 67	26	+ 33	19	+ 31	14	+ 109	22	+ 39	15	- 19	10	- 20	8	+ 1	4	+ 1	4	+ 1	3
2013	+ 209	35	+ 106	26	+ 46	21	+ 44	14	+ 104	23	+ 24	14	- 21	10	- 15	8	- 3	5	- 5	3	+ 2	3
2014	+ 313	43	+ 160	33	+ 67	25	+ 47	17	+ 153	28	+ 59	17	- 2	11	- 7	8	+ 4	6	- 1	4	+ 3	3
2015	+ 332	38	+ 171	30	+ 71	22	+ 45	13	+ 161	24	+ 58	16	+ 3	10	- 5	8	0~	4	+ 3	4	+ 5	4

15.8 Long-Term International Migration 1991 to 2015
United Kingdom, England and Wales
Country of Last or Next Residence (old country groupings)

thousands

Year	All countries 2011 Census Revisions[1] Estimate	+/-CI	European Union[2] Estimate	+/-CI	European Union EU15 Estimate	+/-CI	European Union EU8 Estimate	+/-CI	Non-European Union[3] All Estimate	+/-CI	Commonwealth[4] All[4] Estimate	+/-CI	Old Commonwealth All Estimate	+/-CI	Australia Estimate	+/-CI	Canada Estimate	+/-CI	New Zealand Estimate	+/-CI	South Africa Estimate	+/-CI

England and Wales

Inflow

1991	304	22	89	17	89	17	z	z	215	14	120	11	44	8	25	5	5	2	10	4	4	2
1992	251	20	85	17	85	17	z	z	166	11	87	8	35	5	19	4	4	2	7	3	5	2
1993	249	18	67	11	67	11	z	z	183	14	98	10	40	8	22	6	5	2	6	2	8	3
1994	292	21	86	15	86	15	z	z	207	15	108	9	40	6	18	4	6	2	8	3	8	3
1995	299	22	85	15	85	15	z	z	214	15	107	9	37	7	18	4	6	2	9	4	4	2
1996	300	23	89	17	89	17	z	z	210	16	108	11	45	8	21	5	6	3	9	4	9	3
1997	310	26	99	22	99	22	z	z	212	15	116	11	50	7	21	5	7	3	9	2	13	4
1998	370	26	101	18	101	18	z	z	269	19	139	15	79	11	36	7	8	4	16	4	20	6
1999	424	29	92	20	92	20	z	z	332	21	162	16	83	10	37	7	6	3	13	3	27	6
2000	446	28	77	16	77	16	z	z	369	23	182	19	80	16	33	7	6	3	18	6	22	13
2001	449	29	80	19	80	19	z	z	369	22	183	16	89	12	45	8	5	2	17	7	22	4
2002	485	31	84	21	84	21	z	z	401	22	179	14	82	9	36	6	7	2	12	4	27	6
2003	480	31	93	22	93	22	z	z	387	22	192	15	83	10	37	7	9	3	11	3	27	6
2004	549	38	144	24	92	17	51	16	404	30	231	20	91	12	37	7	7	4	12	4	35	8
2005	523	36	175	26	98	19	74	18	348	24	202	18	80	10	35	6	6	2	12	4	28	7
2006	549	36	190	28	104	19	79	19	359	24	203	18	71	10	34	6	7	2	11	4	19	6
2007	524	38	195	30	86	18	102	23	330	23	187	17	60	9	29	6	6	3	10	3	15	5
2008	528	36	199	28	95	19	84	19	329	23	183	16	61	10	27	6	6	3	8	2	19	7
2009	507	28	168	20	95	14	58	13	339	20	188	14	46	7	25	5	7	3	6	2	7	3
2010	532	29	178	23	94	16	69	15	353	18	205	14	53	8	28	5	7	3	10	5	7	3
2011	515	26	179	19	95	14	68	12	336	18	191	13	46	7	24	5	8	3	7	2	7	3
2012	451	26	160	18	98	13	50	11	291	18	142	12	46	8	25	6	9	3	8	3	5	3
2013	484	28	199	21	112	16	63	12	285	19	126	11	44	7	28	6	7	3	5	2	5	2
2014	583	34	261	27	138	20	73	15	322	21	145	13	56	8	29	6	13	5	8	3	6	2
2015	581	31	270	24	148	17	61	11	311	19	132	12	49	8	25	6	7	3	9	3	8	3

Outflow

1991	253	21	87	16	87	16	z	z	166	14	89	10	58	7	34	5	11	4	8	3	5	2
1992	248	19	78	13	78	13	z	z	170	14	79	8	53	6	32	5	7	2	9	3	4	2
1993	244	19	82	14	82	14	z	z	162	13	85	9	56	7	36	6	8	3	9	3	3	2
1994	216	19	67	13	67	13	z	z	149	14	72	9	44	7	24	4	7	3	9	3	4	2
1995	216	18	69	13	69	13	z	z	147	12	74	8	54	7	30	5	7	3	11	3	6	3
1996	238	27	85	23	85	23	z	z	152	14	83	10	55	7	31	5	6	3	13	3	5	2
1997	244	21	78	15	78	15	z	z	166	15	90	10	58	8	32	5	6	2	12	3	8	4
1998	223	20	74	16	74	16	z	z	148	13	70	8	49	7	30	5	4	2	9	3	6	2
1999	273	24	96	17	96	17	z	z	177	16	95	11	75	10	49	8	7	3	11	3	7	3
2000	291	26	95	17	95	17	z	z	196	19	102	12	78	10	49	9	7	3	15	4	7	3
2001	282	24	89	18	89	18	z	z	193	16	104	11	79	10	48	7	8	4	15	4	8	3
2002	328	28	113	21	113	21	z	z	214	18	110	11	85	10	49	7	11	5	16	4	10	3
2003	333	31	115	24	115	24	z	z	218	20	117	13	92	12	56	9	5	2	18	5	13	5
2004	311	27	116	20	104	19	6	4	195	18	113	13	86	11	49	8	10	5	18	5	9	4
2005	328	29	126	22	106	20	17	9	202	19	116	13	90	11	47	8	10	4	20	5	13	4
2006	369	33	137	26	111	23	24	11	232	20	137	15	105	13	62	10	10	5	19	5	14	5
2007	307	25	119	21	90	19	20	9	188	14	112	10	83	8	50	6	7	3	15	3	11	3
2008	393	40	186	37	111	25	62	20	207	14	111	9	80	7	53	6	9	3	13	2	6	2
2009	328	20	128	17	78	13	43	11	201	11	115	8	79	7	50	6	10	3	13	3	6	2
2010	308	19	122	16	84	13	33	8	186	10	94	7	59	5	36	4	8	2	9	2	6	2
2011	312	20	108	15	71	12	30	8	204	14	112	9	66	8	43	5	8	2	13	5	3	1
2012	286	19	101	16	71	12	20	5	186	11	104	8	63	6	43	5	8	2	7	2	4	2
2013	280	18	101	14	72	12	22	6	180	11	94	8	57	6	37	5	9	3	8	2	3	1
2014	285	21	111	17	77	14	28	8	173	13	87	8	55	6	34	5	9	3	9	2	3	2
2015	272	20	111	16	83	13	19	6	161	12	76	8	44	6	29	5	7	3	5	2	3	2

Balance

1991	+ 51	31	+ 2	23	+ 2	23	z	z	+ 49	20	+ 32	15	- 14	11	- 9	8	- 6	4	+ 2	5	- 1	3
1992	+ 4	27	+ 8	21	+ 8	21	z	z	- 4	18	+ 8	11	- 18	8	- 13	6	- 3	3	- 2	4	+ 1	3
1993	+ 5	26	- 16	18	- 16	18	z	z	+ 21	18	+ 14	13	- 15	11	- 14	9	- 3	4	- 3	3	+ 5	4
1994	+ 77	28	+ 18	20	+ 18	20	z	z	+ 58	20	+ 36	12	- 4	9	- 6	6	- 1	4	- 2	5	+ 5	4
1995	+ 83	28	+ 16	20	+ 16	20	z	z	+ 67	20	+ 33	12	- 17	9	- 11	6	- 1	4	- 2	5	- 2	3
1996	+ 62	35	+ 4	29	+ 4	29	z	z	+ 58	21	+ 26	15	- 10	10	- 10	7	0~	4	- 4	5	+ 4	4
1997	+ 66	34	+ 21	26	+ 21	26	z	z	+ 45	21	+ 26	15	- 8	11	- 10	7	+ 1	4	- 3	4	+ 5	5
1998	+ 147	33	+ 26	24	+ 26	24	z	z	+ 120	23	+ 69	17	+ 30	13	+ 5	9	+ 3	5	+ 7	5	+ 14	6
1999	+ 151	38	- 4	26	- 4	26	z	z	+ 155	27	+ 68	19	+ 8	14	- 12	10	- 1	5	+ 2	5	+ 20	7
2000	+ 154	38	- 18	24	- 18	24	z	z	+ 172	30	+ 80	23	+ 2	19	- 16	11	0~	4	+ 3	7	+ 15	13
2001	+ 167	38	- 9	27	- 9	27	z	z	+ 176	27	+ 79	19	+ 10	15	- 3	11	- 3	5	+ 1	8	+ 14	5
2002	+ 158	41	- 29	30	- 29	30	z	z	+ 187	29	+ 69	18	- 4	14	- 13	9	- 4	5	- 4	5	+ 18	7
2003	+ 147	44	- 23	33	- 23	33	z	z	+ 169	29	+ 75	20	- 9	15	- 19	11	+ 4	4	- 8	5	+ 13	8
2004	+ 238	47	+ 28	31	- 12	26	+ 45	16	+ 210	35	+ 118	24	+ 5	16	- 12	11	- 3	6	- 6	6	+ 26	9
2005	+ 195	46	+ 49	34	- 8	27	+ 57	20	+ 146	31	+ 85	22	- 10	15	- 12	10	- 4	5	- 8	7	+ 15	8
2006	+ 180	49	+ 52	38	- 7	30	+ 55	22	+ 127	31	+ 66	24	- 34	17	- 28	12	- 4	5	- 8	6	+ 6	8
2007	+ 217	45	+ 76	37	- 4	26	+ 82	25	+ 141	27	+ 75	19	- 23	12	- 21	8	- 1	4	- 5	5	+ 5	5
2008	+ 135	54	+ 12	47	- 16	31	+ 22	27	+ 123	27	+ 71	19	- 20	12	- 25	8	- 3	4	- 4	3	+ 13	7
2009	+ 179	35	+ 41	26	+ 18	19	+ 14	17	+ 138	22	+ 73	16	- 34	10	- 25	8	- 3	4	- 7	3	+ 1	3
2010	+ 224	35	+ 57	27	+ 10	21	+ 36	17	+ 167	21	+ 111	15	- 6	10	- 8	7	- 1	3	+ 2	5	+ 1	4
2011	+ 203	33	+ 71	24	+ 24	18	+ 38	15	+ 132	23	+ 79	16	- 20	11	- 18	7	0~	4	- 6	6	+ 5	3
2012	+ 165	32	+ 59	24	+ 27	18	+ 30	12	+ 106	21	+ 38	15	- 17	10	- 18	8	0~	4	+ 1	3	0~	3
2013	+ 203	33	+ 98	25	+ 41	20	+ 41	13	+ 105	22	+ 31	13	- 13	13	- 9	7	- 3	4	- 3	3	+ 2	3
2014	+ 298	40	+ 149	32	+ 61	24	+ 45	17	+ 149	25	+ 58	15	+ 1	11	- 5	7	+ 4	6	- 1	4	+ 3	3
2015	+ 309	37	+ 159	29	+ 65	21	+ 42	13	+ 150	23	+ 57	15	+ 5	10	- 4	8	0~	4	+ 4	3	+ 5	4

Source: Office for National Statistics (ONS), Home Office, Central Statistics Office (CSO) Ireland, Northern Ireland Statistics and Research Agency (NISRA).

15.8 Long-Term International Migration 1991 to 2015
United Kingdom, England and Wales
Country of Last or Next Residence (old country groupings)

thousands

Year	Commonwealth[4] All[4] Estimate	+/-CI	New Commonwealth Other African Estimate	+/-CI	Indian Subcontinent Estimate	+/-CI	Other[4] Estimate	+/-CI	Non-European Union[3] Other Foreign[5] All[5] Estimate	+/-CI	Remainder of Europe[5] Estimate	+/-CI	United States of America Estimate	+/-CI	Rest of America Estimate	+/-CI	Middle East Estimate	+/-CI	Other Estimate	+/-CI	All countries Original Estimates[1] Estimate	+/-CI
United Kingdom																						
Inflow																						
1991	79	8	27	5	33	4	19	4	104	10	23	5	24	5	4	1	11	2	42	7		
1992	57	6	17	2	23	3	17	4	84	8	21	5	18	4	5	1	8	2	32	5		
1993	60	6	18	2	27	5	15	3	88	10	23	7	23	5	4	1	10	2	29	4		
1994	71	6	23	3	27	3	20	4	108	13	26	8	29	7	5	2	12	4	36	6		
1995	71	7	23	2	28	4	21	5	112	12	23	6	27	6	4	1	13	4	45	8		
1996	64	7	19	4	27	4	18	4	109	12	20	5	32	8	4	1	14	4	39	7		
1997	67	9	13	4	31	6	23	5	106	11	23	5	23	6	5	2	15	4	39	6		
1998	64	11	20	9	27	4	17	4	134	12	32	4	37	8	4	2	13	4	48	6		
1999	83	12	24	8	40	7	19	5	183	16	57	11	31	7	7	3	15	3	74	9		
2000	104	11	30	7	50	6	24	5	200	14	50	7	24	5	12	5	30	5	85	9		
2001	101	12	30	7	51	8	19	5	197	15	37	6	25	5	6	2	31	8	99	10		
2002	102	10	41	7	46	6	15	4	237	19	47	9	29	9	7	2	33	4	122	12		
2003	113	12	40	8	58	8	15	4	206	16	35	9	30	6	8	3	26	5	107	11		
2004	152	17	45	9	90	14	17	5	187	24	18	6	27	8	9	5	29	11	104	18		
2005	130	15	32	7	86	13	11	4	162	18	20	7	25	6	7	2	19	5	90	14		
2006	139	16	23	5	102	14	14	5	167	16	21	7	23	5	8	4	21	5	93	12		
2007	135	15	24	5	95	13	16	6	154	17	17	8	23	5	10	4	23	5	82	12		
2008	128	14	31	8	80	10	17	6	171	18	14	5	28	7	12	6	30	9	87	11		
2009	148	12	31	6	101	10	16	4	164	15	13	7	31	8	9	3	26	5	84	9		
2010	162	11	23	4	121	9	19	5	163	13	14	4	22	5	10	4	24	5	94	10		
2011	153	12	19	4	122	10	12	4	159	13	12	4	23	5	6	2	26	5	91	10		
2012	102	10	19	4	69	8	14	4	163	14	16	5	27	6	7	3	24	5	89	10		
2013	87	9	17	3	55	7	15	5	173	16	18	5	21	4	8	3	25	4	102	13		
2014	95	13	15	4	66	12	14	4	191	19	15	6	28	7	20	8	34	7	95	12		
2015	88	11	19	5	51	8	17	5	195	16	18	5	27	6	10	6	38	6	102	11		
Outflow																						
1991	33	7	9	5	10	3	14	5	88	12	12	5	35	8	5	2	14	4	23	5		
1992	29	5	8	3	8	2	14	4	108	14	20	8	40	8	5	3	15	4	28	6		
1993	31	5	8	3	9	3	14	4	86	10	12	4	36	7	5	3	11	3	22	4		
1994	30	6	7	3	7	2	16	4	81	11	18	7	27	5	6	3	13	4	18	3		
1995	23	5	5	2	6	2	12	4	80	10	12	4	30	6	3	2	10	3	25	5		
1996	31	8	9	5	6	3	15	5	76	10	16	7	26	5	3	1	8	3	23	5		
1997	35	6	7	3	9	3	18	4	88	13	21	9	28	7	2	1	13	3	22	5		
1998	24	5	5	3	7	2	11	3	84	11	17	6	27	5	4	2	9	3	27	5		
1999	21	5	3	2	5	2	14	5	87	13	16	7	33	8	4	2	10	4	24	6		
2000	26	6	7	4	8	2	10	4	106	16	22	11	33	8	6	3	15	5	30	7		
2001	26	5	5	2	11	3	10	3	100	13	24	7	28	6	4	2	9	3	34	8		
2002	29	6	5	2	11	3	13	5	112	14	28	8	37	8	3	2	12	4	31	7		
2003	27	6	6	3	11	4	10	4	109	15	35	10	27	7	6	3	7	4	34	8		
2004	31	8	6	3	9	4	15	6	93	13	13	5	25	7	7	4	11	4	37	8		
2005	29	7	6	3	16	5	7	4	95	16	17	6	24	9	8	5	11	3	34	10		
2006	33	8	7	3	17	5	10	5	106	15	17	7	29	7	6	3	16	6	38	8		
2007	33	6	5	1	18	5	9	3	83	10	15	6	18	4	7	3	11	2	31	6		
2008	34	6	8	2	17	4	9	3	105	11	15	6	23	5	10	3	21	5	36	5		
2009	39	4	8	2	23	3	8	2	97	8	11	3	27	5	5	2	15	3	39	5		
2010	38	4	8	2	21	3	8	2	102	9	15	4	25	4	5	2	15	3	43	5		
2011	50	6	7	3	29	4	13	3	103	11	17	8	24	4	4	2	17	3	41	5		
2012	45	5	8	3	26	4	10	3	93	8	9	3	20	3	5	2	14	3	45	6		
2013	41	5	7	2	24	3	11	3	94	8	12	4	24	5	4	1	14	3	41	5		
2014	34	4	6	2	20	3	9	2	97	11	13	4	17	3	4	2	19	4	44	9		
2015	33	5	7	2	19	4	8	3	92	10	11	5	22	4	7	2	14	3	39	6		
Balance																						
1991	+ 46	11	+ 18	7	+ 23	5	+ 5	7	+ 16	16	+ 11	7	- 10	9	- 1	2	- 3	4	+ 19	9		
1992	+ 28	8	+ 9	4	+ 15	4	+ 3	6	- 25	16	0~	10	- 22	9	0~	3	- 7	4	+ 4	8		
1993	+ 29	8	+ 10	4	+ 19	5	+ 1	5	+ 3	14	+ 12	8	- 13	8	- 1	3	- 1	4	+ 7	6		
1994	+ 41	8	+ 16	4	+ 20	4	+ 4	6	+ 27	17	+ 9	11	+ 2	9	- 1	3	- 1	6	+ 18	7		
1995	+ 47	8	+ 17	3	+ 22	4	+ 8	6	+ 32	16	+ 12	7	- 3	9	+ 1	2	+ 3	5	+ 20	9		
1996	+ 33	11	+ 10	6	+ 20	5	+ 2	7	+ 33	16	+ 4	8	+ 7	9	+ 1	2	+ 5	5	+ 16	9		
1997	+ 32	11	+ 6	5	+ 22	7	+ 5	7	+ 18	17	+ 2	10	- 5	9	+ 3	2	+ 2	5	+ 16	8		
1998	+ 40	12	+ 14	10	+ 20	5	+ 6	6	+ 50	16	+ 15	7	+ 10	10	0~	3	+ 4	5	+ 21	8		
1999	+ 62	13	+ 22	8	+ 35	8	+ 5	7	+ 97	21	+ 41	13	- 2	11	+ 3	4	+ 5	5	+ 50	10		
2000	+ 79	12	+ 23	8	+ 42	7	+ 14	7	+ 94	22	+ 28	13	- 10	9	+ 6	6	+ 15	7	+ 55	12		
2001	+ 74	13	+ 25	7	+ 40	8	+ 10	6	+ 98	20	+ 13	10	- 3	8	+ 2	3	+ 21	8	+ 65	13	+ 171	40
2002	+ 73	12	+ 36	7	+ 36	7	+ 2	6	+ 126	24	+ 19	12	- 9	12	+ 4	3	+ 21	6	+ 91	14	+ 153	43
2003	+ 86	14	+ 34	8	+ 47	9	+ 5	6	+ 97	22	0~	13	+ 3	9	+ 2	4	+ 19	6	+ 73	14	+ 148	46
2004	+ 122	19	+ 39	10	+ 81	14	+ 2	8	+ 94	27	+ 5	8	+ 2	10	+ 2	6	+ 18	12	+ 68	20	+ 245	49
2005	+ 101	17	+ 26	8	+ 70	14	+ 4	6	+ 67	24	+ 3	9	+ 1	11	- 1	5	+ 8	6	+ 56	17	+ 206	49
2006	+ 106	17	+ 16	6	+ 85	15	+ 4	7	+ 61	22	+ 4	10	- 6	9	+ 3	5	+ 6	8	+ 55	14	+ 198	52
2007	+ 103	17	+ 19	6	+ 77	14	+ 7	7	+ 72	20	+ 2	10	+ 4	7	+ 2	5	+ 12	6	+ 51	13	+ 233	48
2008	+ 94	15	+ 23	8	+ 63	11	+ 8	6	+ 65	21	- 2	8	+ 5	8	+ 2	7	+ 9	11	+ 51	13	+ 163	57
2009	+ 109	13	+ 23	6	+ 78	10	+ 8	5	+ 67	17	+ 2	7	+ 4	9	+ 4	4	+ 11	6	+ 46	10	+ 198	37
2010	+ 124	12	+ 15	5	+ 99	10	+ 11	6	+ 62	16	- 1	6	- 3	6	+ 5	4	+ 10	6	+ 52	12	+ 252	37
2011	+ 103	13	+ 12	5	+ 93	11	- 1	5	+ 56	17	- 5	8	- 1	6	+ 2	3	+ 9	6	+ 50	11	+ 215	35
2012	+ 58	11	+ 10	5	+ 43	9	+ 4	5	+ 70	16	+ 7	5	+ 7	7	+ 2	3	+ 10	6	+ 44	12		
2013	+ 46	10	+ 10	4	+ 31	7	+ 4	5	+ 79	18	+ 6	6	- 3	6	+ 4	3	+ 11	5	+ 61	14		
2014	+ 60	14	+ 10	5	+ 45	12	+ 5	4	+ 95	22	+ 2	8	+ 11	8	+ 16	8	+ 14	8	+ 50	15		
2015	+ 54	12	+ 13	5	+ 33	9	+ 9	6	+ 103	18	+ 7	7	+ 6	7	+ 3	6	+ 24	7	+ 63	13		

15.8 Long-Term International Migration 1991 to 2015
United Kingdom, England and Wales
Country of Last or Next Residence (old country groupings)

thousands

Year	\[Commonwealth\] All[4] Estimate	+/-CI	Other African Estimate	+/-CI	Indian Subcontinent Estimate	+/-CI	Other[4] Estimate	+/-CI	\[Other Foreign\] All[5] Estimate	+/-CI	Remainder of Europe[5] Estimate	+/-CI	United States of America Estimate	+/-CI	Rest of America Estimate	+/-CI	Middle East Estimate	+/-CI	Other Estimate	+/-CI	Original Estimates[1] Estimate	+/-CI
England and Wales																						
Inflow																						
1991	76	8	26	5	32	4	18	4	95	9	20	4	21	4	4	1	10	2	39	6		
1992	52	5	17	2	22	3	13	3	79	8	20	5	17	4	4	1	8	2	30	4		
1993	58	6	17	2	27	4	14	3	84	10	22	7	21	4	3	1	10	2	28	4		
1994	68	6	23	3	27	3	18	4	99	12	25	8	22	5	5	2	11	4	35	6		
1995	70	7	22	2	27	4	20	5	107	12	23	6	23	6	4	1	13	4	44	8		
1996	63	7	19	4	26	4	18	4	102	11	18	4	29	7	4	1	12	4	38	7		
1997	66	9	13	4	30	6	23	5	96	9	22	5	20	5	5	2	14	3	35	5		
1998	60	10	17	8	27	4	16	4	129	11	31	4	35	8	4	2	12	4	47	6		
1999	79	12	23	8	38	7	18	5	170	14	56	10	25	5	7	3	14	3	68	7		
2000	102	11	30	7	49	6	24	5	187	13	49	7	22	4	9	4	29	5	78	8		
2001	94	11	28	7	48	7	17	4	187	15	35	6	22	4	6	2	29	8	95	10		
2002	98	10	39	7	45	6	14	4	222	17	45	9	26	8	7	2	30	4	114	11		
2003	108	12	39	8	55	7	15	4	196	16	32	8	29	6	7	3	25	5	102	11		
2004	139	16	40	8	85	13	15	4	174	23	17	5	25	7	8	4	27	11	96	17		
2005	121	15	30	6	81	12	10	4	147	17	18	7	21	5	7	2	17	5	83	14		
2006	132	15	22	5	96	13	14	5	157	15	20	7	22	5	7	3	20	5	88	12		
2007	126	14	23	5	88	12	16	6	143	16	15	8	21	5	9	4	21	5	77	11		
2008	122	13	29	7	78	10	16	6	147	15	12	5	24	7	10	5	23	5	78	11		
2009	143	12	30	6	97	9	16	4	150	14	12	7	26	7	9	3	24	5	79	9		
2010	152	11	21	4	114	9	17	5	148	12	12	4	19	4	9	3	22	4	87	10		
2011	145	11	18	4	116	10	11	3	145	13	12	4	20	4	6	2	24	5	84	10		
2012	96	9	17	4	67	8	12	4	149	14	14	4	25	6	6	3	22	5	82	10		
2013	82	8	16	3	51	6	14	4	159	15	15	5	19	4	7	3	23	4	96	13		
2014	89	10	15	4	62	8	13	4	177	16	13	4	26	7	19	8	31	6	87	10		
2015	83	9	19	5	49	6	16	5	178	15	16	5	23	5	8	5	35	6	96	10		
Outflow																						
1991	30	7	8	5	9	3	13	5	78	10	10	5	29	6	5	2	13	4	21	5		
1992	27	5	7	2	7	2	12	3	91	12	17	8	31	6	5	3	13	3	25	5		
1993	29	5	7	3	8	3	13	4	77	9	10	4	31	5	5	3	10	3	21	4		
1994	28	5	7	3	6	2	15	4	77	10	16	7	26	5	6	3	12	4	17	3		
1995	20	4	5	2	5	2	11	3	73	9	11	4	28	6	3	2	9	3	22	4		
1996	27	7	8	5	5	2	14	5	70	10	14	6	25	5	3	1	7	3	21	4		
1997	32	6	7	3	9	3	16	4	76	12	20	9	23	5	2	1	11	3	19	4		
1998	21	5	4	3	7	2	10	3	78	10	14	5	25	5	4	2	8	3	27	5		
1999	20	5	3	2	5	2	12	4	82	12	16	7	31	7	4	2	10	4	22	5		
2000	24	6	6	4	8	2	10	4	95	15	21	11	29	7	5	3	12	4	28	7		
2001	25	5	5	2	11	3	9	3	89	11	23	7	26	6	4	2	9	3	27	5		
2002	24	6	5	2	10	3	10	4	104	14	27	8	34	7	3	1	11	4	30	7		
2003	24	6	5	3	10	3	9	4	101	15	33	9	25	6	5	2	5	3	33	8		
2004	27	7	6	3	9	4	12	5	82	12	12	5	22	6	7	4	8	3	33	8		
2005	26	7	6	3	14	5	7	4	86	14	16	6	19	6	6	3	10	3	33	10		
2006	32	6	6	3	16	5	10	5	95	14	16	7	25	7	5	3	15	6	33	8		
2007	29	5	5	1	16	4	8	2	77	10	15	6	16	4	7	3	10	2	28	5		
2008	31	6	8	4	15	4	8	3	95	11	15	6	20	4	9	3	19	5	31	5		
2009	36	4	7	2	22	3	7	2	86	7	11	3	22	4	5	2	14	3	34	4		
2010	35	4	8	2	20	3	8	2	92	8	14	4	23	4	5	2	13	3	38	4		
2011	46	5	7	3	27	4	12	3	92	10	15	7	22	4	4	2	15	3	36	4		
2012	41	5	8	3	24	4	9	2	82	8	8	3	18	3	5	2	11	3	39	5		
2013	38	5	6	2	21	3	10	3	85	8	11	4	20	3	3	1	13	3	38	5		
2014	32	4	5	2	19	3	8	2	86	10	11	4	16	3	4	2	17	3	39	8		
2015	32	5	6	2	18	4	8	3	85	9	10	5	20	4	6	2	13	3	36	6		
Balance																						
1991	+ 45	11	+ 18	7	+ 23	5	+ 5	7	+ 17	13	+ 11	6	- 7	7	- 1	2	- 2	4	+ 17	8		
1992	+ 25	7	+ 9	3	+ 15	4	+ 1	5	- 12	14	+ 3	9	- 14	7	- 1	3	- 5	4	+ 5	7		
1993	+ 29	8	+ 10	4	+ 18	5	+ 1	5	+ 7	13	+ 12	8	- 10	7	- 1	3	0~	4	+ 7	6		
1994	+ 40	8	+ 17	4	+ 20	4	+ 3	6	+ 22	16	+ 9	10	- 3	7	- 1	3	- 1	5	+ 18	6		
1995	+ 49	8	+ 18	3	+ 22	4	+ 9	6	+ 34	15	+ 13	7	- 6	8	+ 1	2	+ 3	5	+ 23	9		
1996	+ 36	10	+ 11	6	+ 21	4	+ 3	7	+ 32	15	+ 4	8	+ 4	8	+ 1	2	+ 5	4	+ 18	9		
1997	+ 34	10	+ 6	5	+ 21	6	+ 7	6	+ 20	15	+ 2	10	- 3	7	+ 2	2	+ 3	5	+ 16	6		
1998	+ 39	12	+ 13	9	+ 20	5	+ 7	5	+ 51	15	+ 17	6	+ 10	9	0~	3	+ 4	5	+ 20	8		
1999	+ 59	13	+ 21	8	+ 33	7	+ 6	7	+ 88	19	+ 40	13	- 7	9	+ 3	4	+ 4	5	+ 47	9		
2000	+ 79	12	+ 24	8	+ 41	7	+ 14	7	+ 92	20	+ 28	13	- 7	8	+ 4	5	+ 17	6	+ 50	11		
2001	+ 69	12	+ 23	7	+ 38	8	+ 8	5	+ 98	19	+ 12	10	- 4	7	+ 2	3	+ 20	8	+ 68	11		
2002	+ 73	12	+ 34	7	+ 35	7	+ 4	6	+ 118	22	+ 19	12	- 8	11	+ 4	3	+ 19	6	+ 84	13		
2003	+ 84	13	+ 34	8	+ 44	8	+ 6	6	+ 94	22	- 1	13	+ 4	9	+ 3	4	+ 19	6	+ 70	13		
2004	+ 112	17	+ 34	8	+ 76	13	+ 3	7	+ 92	26	+ 5	7	+ 3	9	+ 1	6	+ 19	12	+ 64	19		
2005	+ 95	16	+ 24	7	+ 67	13	+ 3	6	+ 61	22	+ 1	9	+ 2	8	+ 1	4	+ 7	6	+ 50	17		
2006	+ 100	17	+ 16	6	+ 80	14	+ 5	7	+ 62	21	+ 4	10	- 3	8	+ 1	4	+ 4	7	+ 55	14		
2007	+ 97	15	+ 18	5	+ 72	13	+ 8	7	+ 66	19	0~	10	+ 5	6	+ 2	5	+ 11	5	+ 49	12		
2008	+ 91	14	+ 21	8	+ 62	10	+ 8	6	+ 52	19	- 3	8	+ 3	8	0~	6	+ 4	8	+ 47	12		
2009	+ 107	13	+ 22	6	+ 76	10	+ 9	5	+ 65	16	+ 2	7	+ 4	8	+ 4	4	+ 10	5	+ 45	10		
2010	+ 117	12	+ 14	5	+ 94	9	+ 9	5	+ 56	15	- 3	6	- 4	6	+ 4	4	+ 9	5	+ 49	10		
2011	+ 99	12	+ 11	5	+ 89	11	- 1	4	+ 53	16	- 3	8	- 2	6	+ 2	3	+ 9	6	+ 47	11		
2012	+ 55	11	+ 9	5	+ 42	8	+ 3	4	+ 68	15	+ 6	5	+ 7	7	+ 2	3	+ 10	6	+ 43	11		
2013	+ 44	9	+ 10	4	+ 30	7	+ 4	5	+ 74	17	+ 4	6	- 1	5	+ 4	3	+ 10	5	+ 58	14		
2014	+ 57	11	+ 10	5	+ 43	9	+ 5	4	+ 91	19	+ 2	6	+ 10	8	+ 15	8	+ 15	7	+ 48	13		
2015	+ 51	10	+ 13	5	+ 31	7	+ 8	6	+ 93	18	+ 6	7	+ 3	7	+ 2	6	+ 23	7	+ 60	12		

Source: Office for National Statistics (ONS), Home Office, Central Statistics Office (CSO) Ireland, Northern Ireland Statistics and Research Agency (NISRA).

15.8 Long-Term International Migration 1991 to 2015
United Kingdom, England and Wales
Country of Last or Next Residence (old country groupings)

thousands

Totals may not sum due to rounding.
"z" - Not applicable, ":" - Not available, "0~" - Rounds to zero.

1   Net migration ("Balance") figures for the United Kingdom for 2001 to 2011 have been revised in light of the results of the 2011 Census. The original published estimates are shown to the right of the table. The revisions are not reflected in the remainder of the table. The sums of the disaggregated estimates will not therefore match the revised balances. Users should continue to use the estimates in the table to analyse detailed breakdowns of inflows and outflows of long-term international migrants but, in doing so, should bear in mind that the headline net migration estimates have been revised.

2   European Union estimates are for the EU15 (Austria, Belgium, Denmark, Finland, France, Germany, Greece, Republic of Ireland, Italy, Luxembourg, Netherlands, Portugal, Spain and Sweden) up to 2003, the EU25 (the EU15 and the EU8 groupings plus Malta and Cyprus) from 2004 to 2006, the EU27 (the EU25 plus Bulgaria and Romania) from 2007 and the EU28 (the EU27 plus Croatia) from July 2013. Estimates are also shown separately for the EU15 and the EU8 (Czech Republic, Estonia, Hungary, Latvia, Lithuania, Poland, Slovakia and Slovenia).

3   Excludes migrants to and from European Union countries as defined in footnote 2.

4   From 2004 onwards, All, New and Other Commonwealth exclude Malta and Cyprus.

5   From 2004 onwards, Other Foreign and Remainder of Europe excludes the eight central and eastern European member states that joined the EU in May 2004 (the EU8). From 2007 onwards, Other Foreign and Remainder of Europe excludes Bulgaria and Romania which joined the EU in January 2007. From July 2013 onwards, Other Foreign and Remainder of Europe excludes Croatia which joined the EU in July 2013.

Statistically Significant Increase   Statistically Significant Decrease

The latest estimates (2015) have been compared with the corresponding estimates for the period one year earlier (2014). Where changes have been found to be statistically significant, the relevant pair of estimates have been highlighted by setting their background colour. Please see the Notes worksheet for more information.

```
Highlights significant changes over the last year
```

15.9 Grants of settlement by country of nationality and category and in-country refusals of settlement

Year	Geographical region	Country of nationality	Total grants of settlement
2015	*Total	*Total	90,839
2015	Africa North	*Total Africa North	2,576
2015	Africa Sub-Saharan	*Total Africa Sub-Saharan	20,927
2015	America North	*Total America North	3,265
2015	America Central and South	*Total America Central and South	2,315
2015	Asia Central	*Total Asia Central	2,031
2015	Asia East	*Total Asia East	4,846
2015	Asia South	*Total Asia South	37,107
2015	Asia South East	*Total Asia South East	5,035
2015	EU 14	*Total EU 14	z
2015	EU 2	*Total EU 2	z
2015	EU 8	*Total EU 8	z
2015	EU Other	*Total EU Other	z
2015	Europe Other	*Total Europe Other	4,823
2015	Middle East	*Total Middle East	5,004
2015	Oceania	*Total Oceania	2,367
2015	Other	*Total Other	543
2015	Asia Central	Afghanistan	1,741
2015	Europe Other	Albania	244
2015	Africa North	Algeria	218
2015	Oceania	American Samoa	0
2015	Europe Other	Andorra	0
2015	Africa Sub-Saharan	Angola	65
2015	Other	Anguilla (British)	0
2015	America Central and South	Antigua and Barbuda	9
2015	America Central and South	Argentina	41
2015	Europe Other	Armenia	54
2015	America Central and South	Aruba	0
2015	Oceania	Australia	1,444
2015	EU 14	Austria	z
2015	Europe Other	Azerbaijan	123
2015	America Central and South	Bahamas, The	5
2015	Middle East	Bahrain	18
2015	Asia South	Bangladesh	3,335
2015	America Central and South	Barbados	36
2015	Europe Other	Belarus	109
2015	EU 14	Belgium	z
2015	America Central and South	Belize	12
2015	Africa Sub-Saharan	Benin	4
2015	Other	Bermuda (British)	0
2015	Asia South	Bhutan	31
2015	America Central and South	Bolivia	61
2015	America Central and South	Bonaire, Sint Eustatius and Saba	0
2015	Europe Other	Bosnia and Herzegovina	32
2015	Africa Sub-Saharan	Botswana	45
2015	America Central and South	Brazil	338
2015	Other	British overseas citizens	2
2015	Asia South East	Brunei	4
2015	EU 2	Bulgaria	z
2015	Africa Sub-Saharan	Burkina	1
2015	Asia South East	Burma	402
2015	Africa Sub-Saharan	Burundi	31
2015	Asia South East	Cambodia	8
2015	Africa Sub-Saharan	Cameroon	305
2015	America North	Canada	809
2015	Africa Sub-Saharan	Cape Verde	1
2015	Other	Cayman Islands (British)	0
2015	Africa Sub-Saharan	Central African Republic	4
2015	Africa Sub-Saharan	Chad	17
2015	America Central and South	Chile	32
2015	Asia East	China	3,728
2015	Oceania	Christmas Island	0
2015	Oceania	Cocos (Keeling) Islands	0
2015	America Central and South	Colombia	190
2015	Africa Sub-Saharan	Comoros	0
2015	Africa Sub-Saharan	Congo	43
2015	Africa Sub-Saharan	Congo (Democratic Republic)	597
2015	Oceania	Cook Islands	0

15.9 Grants of settlement by country of nationality and category and in-country refusals of settlement

Year	Geographical region	Country of nationality	Total grants of settlement
2015	America Central and South	Costa Rica	11
2015	EU Other	Croatia	z
2015	America Central and South	Cuba	28
2015	America Central and South	Curacao	0
2015	EU Other	Cyprus	z
2015	Europe Other	Cyprus (Northern part of)	1
2015	EU 8	Czech Republic	z
2015	EU 14	Denmark	z
2015	Africa Sub-Saharan	Djibouti	4
2015	America Central and South	Dominica	14
2015	America Central and South	Dominican Republic	11
2015	Asia South East	East Timor	0
2015	America Central and South	Ecuador	30
2015	Africa North	Egypt	546
2015	America Central and South	El Salvador	5
2015	Africa Sub-Saharan	Equatorial Guinea	0
2015	Africa Sub-Saharan	Eritrea	1,486
2015	EU 8	Estonia	z
2015	Africa Sub-Saharan	Ethiopia	503
2015	Other	Falkland Islands (British)	0
2015	Europe Other	Faroe Islands	0
2015	Oceania	Fiji	201
2015	EU 14	Finland	z
2015	Europe Other	Former Yugoslavia	1
2015	EU 14	France	z
2015	America Central and South	French Guiana	0
2015	Oceania	French Polynesia	0
2015	Africa Sub-Saharan	Gabon	10
2015	Africa Sub-Saharan	Gambia, The	540
2015	Europe Other	Georgia	86
2015	EU 14	Germany	z
2015	Africa Sub-Saharan	Ghana	983
2015	Other	Gibraltar (British)	0
2015	EU 14	Greece	z
2015	Europe Other	Greenland	0
2015	America Central and South	Grenada	37
2015	America Central and South	Guadeloupe	0
2015	Oceania	Guam	0
2015	America Central and South	Guatemala	8
2015	Africa Sub-Saharan	Guinea	137
2015	Africa Sub-Saharan	Guinea-Bissau	1
2015	America Central and South	Guyana	56
2015	America Central and South	Haiti	4
2015	Oceania	Heard Island and McDonald Islands	0
2015	America Central and South	Honduras	5
2015	Asia East	Hong Kong	174
2015	EU 8	Hungary	z
2015	Europe Other	Iceland	z
2015	Asia South	India	18,741
2015	Asia South East	Indonesia	116
2015	Middle East	Iran	2,453
2015	Middle East	Iraq	1,087
2015	EU 14	Ireland	z
2015	Middle East	Israel	194
2015	EU 14	Italy	z
2015	Africa Sub-Saharan	Ivory Coast	114
2015	America Central and South	Jamaica	821
2015	Asia East	Japan	349
2015	Middle East	Jordan	142
2015	Asia Central	Kazakhstan	102
2015	Africa Sub-Saharan	Kenya	542
2015	Oceania	Kiribati	0
2015	Asia East	Korea (North)	22
2015	Asia East	Korea (South)	405
2015	Europe Other	Kosovo	108
2015	Middle East	Kuwait	40
2015	Asia Central	Kyrgyzstan	23
2015	Asia South East	Laos	2

15.9 Grants of settlement by country of nationality and category and in-country refusals of settlement

Year	Geographical region	Country of nationality	Total grants of settlement
2015	EU 8	Latvia	z
2015	Middle East	Lebanon	137
2015	Africa Sub-Saharan	Lesotho	5
2015	Africa Sub-Saharan	Liberia	26
2015	Africa North	Libya	187
2015	Europe Other	Liechtenstein	z
2015	EU 8	Lithuania	z
2015	EU 14	Luxembourg	z
2015	Asia East	Macau	0
2015	Europe Other	Macedonia	18
2015	Africa Sub-Saharan	Madagascar	4
2015	Africa Sub-Saharan	Malawi	189
2015	Asia South East	Malaysia	738
2015	Asia South	Maldives	22
2015	Africa Sub-Saharan	Mali	3
2015	EU Other	Malta	z
2015	Oceania	Marshall Islands	0
2015	America Central and South	Martinique	0
2015	Africa North	Mauritania	1
2015	Africa Sub-Saharan	Mauritius	847
2015	Africa Sub-Saharan	Mayotte	0
2015	America Central and South	Mexico	156
2015	Oceania	Micronesia	0
2015	Europe Other	Moldova	24
2015	Europe Other	Monaco	0
2015	Asia East	Mongolia	37
2015	Europe Other	Montenegro	6
2015	Other	Montserrat (British)	0
2015	Africa North	Morocco	209
2015	Africa Sub-Saharan	Mozambique	6
2015	Africa Sub-Saharan	Namibia	31
2015	Oceania	Nauru	0
2015	Asia South	Nepal	1,469
2015	EU 14	Netherlands	z
2015	America Central and South	Netherlands Antilles	z
2015	Oceania	New Caledonia	0
2015	Oceania	New Zealand	718
2015	America Central and South	Nicaragua	2
2015	Africa Sub-Saharan	Niger	4
2015	Africa Sub-Saharan	Nigeria	4,397
2015	Oceania	Niue	0
2015	Oceania	Norfolk Island	0
2015	Oceania	Northern Mariana Islands	0
2015	Europe Other	Norway	z
2015	Middle East	Occupied Palestinian Territories	92
2015	Middle East	Oman	6
2015	Other	Other and unknown	14
2015	Asia South	Pakistan	10,564
2015	Oceania	Palau	0
2015	America Central and South	Panama	7
2015	Oceania	Papua New Guinea	2
2015	America Central and South	Paraguay	3
2015	America Central and South	Peru	48
2015	Asia South East	Philippines	2,929
2015	Other	Pitcairn Islands (British)	0
2015	EU 8	Poland	z
2015	EU 14	Portugal	z
2015	America North	Puerto Rico	0
2015	Middle East	Qatar	2
2015	Other	Refugee	343
2015	Africa Sub-Saharan	Reunion	0
2015	EU 2	Romania	z
2015	Europe Other	Russia	1,182
2015	Africa Sub-Saharan	Rwanda	43
2015	Oceania	Samoa	0
2015	Europe Other	San Marino	0
2015	Africa Sub-Saharan	Sao Tome and Principe	0
2015	Middle East	Saudi Arabia	63

15.9 Grants of settlement by country of nationality and category and in-country refusals of settlement

Year	Geographical region	Country of nationality	Total grants of settlement
2015	Africa Sub-Saharan	Senegal	34
2015	Europe Other	Serbia	76
2015	Europe Other	Serbia and Montenegro	z
2015	Africa Sub-Saharan	Seychelles	21
2015	Africa Sub-Saharan	Sierra Leone	209
2015	Asia South East	Singapore	133
2015	EU 8	Slovakia	z
2015	EU 8	Slovenia	z
2015	Oceania	Solomon Islands	0
2015	Africa Sub-Saharan	Somalia	2,367
2015	Africa Sub-Saharan	South Africa	1,747
2015	Other	South Georgia and South Sandwich Islands	0
2015	EU 14	Spain	z
2015	Asia South	Sri Lanka	2,945
2015	Other	St. Helena (British)	0
2015	America Central and South	St. Kitts and Nevis	12
2015	America Central and South	St. Lucia	53
2015	America Central and South	St. Maarten (Dutch Part)	0
2015	America Central and South	St. Martin (French Part)	0
2015	America Central and South	St. Pierre and Miquelon	0
2015	America Central and South	St. Vincent and the Grenadines	38
2015	Other	Stateless	184
2015	Africa North	Sudan	1,326
2015	Africa Sub-Saharan	Sudan (South)	5
2015	America Central and South	Surinam	0
2015	Europe Other	Svalbard and Jan Mayen	0
2015	Africa Sub-Saharan	Swaziland	18
2015	EU 14	Sweden	z
2015	Europe Other	Switzerland	z
2015	Middle East	Syria	650
2015	Asia East	Taiwan	131
2015	Asia Central	Tajikistan	13
2015	Africa Sub-Saharan	Tanzania	155
2015	Asia South East	Thailand	455
2015	Africa Sub-Saharan	Togo	17
2015	Oceania	Tokelau	0
2015	Oceania	Tonga	2
2015	America Central and South	Trinidad and Tobago	148
2015	Africa North	Tunisia	87
2015	Europe Other	Turkey	2,354
2015	Asia Central	Turkmenistan	36
2015	Other	Turks and Caicos Islands (British)	0
2015	Oceania	Tuvalu	0
2015	Africa Sub-Saharan	Uganda	391
2015	Europe Other	Ukraine	405
2015	Middle East	United Arab Emirates	1
2015	America North	United States	2,456
2015	America Central and South	Uruguay	3
2015	Asia Central	Uzbekistan	116
2015	Oceania	Vanuatu	0
2015	Europe Other	Vatican City	0
2015	America Central and South	Venezuela	91
2015	Asia South East	Vietnam	248
2015	Other	Virgin Islands (British)	0
2015	America North	Virgin Islands (US)	0
2015	Oceania	Wallis and Futuna	0
2015	Africa North	Western Sahara	2
2015	Middle East	Yemen	119
2015	Africa Sub-Saharan	Zambia	128
2015	Africa Sub-Saharan	Zimbabwe	4,847

Source: Home Office Immigration Statistics

z = Not applicable.
: = Not available.

15.10 Asylum applications and initial decisions for main applicants, by country of nationality

Year	Geographical region	Country of nationality	Total applications
2015	***Total**	***Total**	**32,733**
2015	**Africa North**	***Total Africa North**	**3,883**
2015	**Africa Sub-Saharan**	***Total Africa Sub-Saharan**	**7,634**
2015	**America North**	***Total America North**	**42**
2015	**America Central and South**	***Total America Central and South**	**327**
2015	**Asia Central**	***Total Asia Central**	**2,293**
2015	**Asia East**	***Total Asia East**	**541**
2015	**Asia South**	***Total Asia South**	**5,642**
2015	**Asia South East**	***Total Asia South East**	**881**
2015	**EU 14**	***Total EU 14**	**23**
2015	**EU 2**	***Total EU 2**	**23**
2015	**EU 8**	***Total EU 8**	**194**
2015	**EU Other**	***Total EU Other**	**0**
2015	**Europe Other**	***Total Europe Other**	**2,118**
2015	**Middle East**	***Total Middle East**	**8,432**
2015	**Oceania**	***Total Oceania**	**7**
2015	**Other**	***Total Other**	**693**
2015	Asia Central	Afghanistan	2,261
2015	Europe Other	Albania	1,519
2015	Africa North	Algeria	136
2015	Oceania	American Samoa	0
2015	Europe Other	Andorra	0
2015	Africa Sub-Saharan	Angola	48
2015	Other	Anguilla (British)	0
2015	America Central and South	Antigua and Barbuda	1
2015	America Central and South	Argentina	0
2015	Europe Other	Armenia	18
2015	America Central and South	Aruba	0
2015	Oceania	Australia	4
2015	EU 14	Austria	0
2015	Europe Other	Azerbaijan	15
2015	America Central and South	Bahamas, The	0
2015	Middle East	Bahrain	7
2015	Asia South	Bangladesh	1,110
2015	America Central and South	Barbados	2
2015	Europe Other	Belarus	14
2015	EU 14	Belgium	2
2015	America Central and South	Belize	1
2015	Africa Sub-Saharan	Benin	1
2015	Other	Bermuda (British)	0
2015	Asia South	Bhutan	3
2015	America Central and South	Bolivia	11
2015	America Central and South	Bonaire, Sint Eustatius and Saba	0
2015	Europe Other	Bosnia and Herzegovina	2
2015	Africa Sub-Saharan	Botswana	12
2015	America Central and South	Brazil	17
2015	Other	British overseas citizens	9
2015	Asia South East	Brunei	0
2015	EU 2	Bulgaria	3
2015	Africa Sub-Saharan	Burkina	2
2015	Asia South East	Burma	161
2015	Africa Sub-Saharan	Burundi	14
2015	Asia South East	Cambodia	2
2015	Africa Sub-Saharan	Cameroon	132
2015	America North	Canada	8
2015	Africa Sub-Saharan	Cape Verde	1
2015	Other	Cayman Islands (British)	0
2015	Africa Sub-Saharan	Central African Republic	3
2015	Africa Sub-Saharan	Chad	24
2015	America Central and South	Chile	0
2015	Asia East	China	487
2015	Oceania	Christmas Island	0
2015	Oceania	Cocos (Keeling) Islands	0
2015	America Central and South	Colombia	12
2015	Africa Sub-Saharan	Comoros	1
2015	Africa Sub-Saharan	Congo	20
2015	Africa Sub-Saharan	Congo (Democratic Republic)	198
2015	Oceania	Cook Islands	0
2015	America Central and South	Costa Rica	0

15.10 Asylum applications and initial decisions for main applicants, by country of nationality

Year	Geographical region	Country of nationality	Total applications
2015	EU Other	Croatia	0
2015	America Central and South	Cuba	4
2015	America Central and South	Curacao	0
2015	EU Other	Cyprus	0
2015	Europe Other	Cyprus (Northern part of)	0
2015	EU 8	Czech Republic	3
2015	EU 14	Denmark	1
2015	Africa Sub-Saharan	Djibouti	1
2015	America Central and South	Dominica	4
2015	America Central and South	Dominican Republic	0
2015	Asia South East	East Timor	2
2015	America Central and South	Ecuador	2
2015	Africa North	Egypt	321
2015	America Central and South	El Salvador	11
2015	Africa Sub-Saharan	Equatorial Guinea	1
2015	Africa Sub-Saharan	Eritrea	3,695
2015	EU 8	Estonia	3
2015	Africa Sub-Saharan	Ethiopia	751
2015	Other	Falkland Islands (British)	0
2015	Europe Other	Faroe Islands	0
2015	Oceania	Fiji	1
2015	EU 14	Finland	1
2015	Europe Other	Former Yugoslavia	1
2015	EU 14	France	1
2015	America Central and South	French Guiana	0
2015	Oceania	French Polynesia	0
2015	Africa Sub-Saharan	Gabon	1
2015	Africa Sub-Saharan	Gambia, The	186
2015	Europe Other	Georgia	34
2015	EU 14	Germany	2
2015	Africa Sub-Saharan	Ghana	172
2015	Other	Gibraltar (British)	0
2015	EU 14	Greece	1
2015	Europe Other	Greenland	0
2015	America Central and South	Grenada	3
2015	America Central and South	Guadeloupe	0
2015	Oceania	Guam	0
2015	America Central and South	Guatemala	3
2015	Africa Sub-Saharan	Guinea	28
2015	Africa Sub-Saharan	Guinea-Bissau	3
2015	America Central and South	Guyana	7
2015	America Central and South	Haiti	0
2015	Oceania	Heard Island and McDonald Islands	0
2015	America Central and South	Honduras	7
2015	Asia East	Hong Kong	3
2015	EU 8	Hungary	5
2015	Europe Other	Iceland	0
2015	Asia South	India	1,014
2015	Asia South East	Indonesia	5
2015	Middle East	Iran	3,242
2015	Middle East	Iraq	2,216
2015	EU 14	Ireland	3
2015	Middle East	Israel	3
2015	EU 14	Italy	1
2015	Africa Sub-Saharan	Ivory Coast	42
2015	America Central and South	Jamaica	182
2015	Asia East	Japan	0
2015	Middle East	Jordan	20
2015	Asia Central	Kazakhstan	1
2015	Africa Sub-Saharan	Kenya	78
2015	Oceania	Kiribati	0
2015	Asia East	Korea (North)	29
2015	Asia East	Korea (South)	11
2015	Europe Other	Kosovo	23
2015	Middle East	Kuwait	88
2015	Asia Central	Kyrgyzstan	8
2015	Asia South East	Laos	3
2015	EU 8	Latvia	29
2015	Middle East	Lebanon	35

15.10 Asylum applications and initial decisions for main applicants, by country of nationality

Year	Geographical region	Country of nationality	Total applications
2015	Africa Sub-Saharan	Lesotho	0
2015	Africa Sub-Saharan	Liberia	3
2015	Africa North	Libya	410
2015	Europe Other	Liechtenstein	0
2015	EU 8	Lithuania	45
2015	EU 14	Luxembourg	0
2015	Asia East	Macau	0
2015	Europe Other	Macedonia	1
2015	Africa Sub-Saharan	Madagascar	0
2015	Africa Sub-Saharan	Malawi	68
2015	Asia South East	Malaysia	51
2015	Asia South	Maldives	15
2015	Africa Sub-Saharan	Mali	16
2015	EU Other	Malta	0
2015	Oceania	Marshall Islands	0
2015	America Central and South	Martinique	0
2015	Africa North	Mauritania	1
2015	Africa Sub-Saharan	Mauritius	40
2015	Africa Sub-Saharan	Mayotte	0
2015	America Central and South	Mexico	9
2015	Oceania	Micronesia	0
2015	Europe Other	Moldova	1
2015	Europe Other	Monaco	0
2015	Asia East	Mongolia	11
2015	Europe Other	Montenegro	0
2015	Other	Montserrat (British)	0
2015	Africa North	Morocco	69
2015	Africa Sub-Saharan	Mozambique	2
2015	Africa Sub-Saharan	Namibia	16
2015	Oceania	Nauru	0
2015	Asia South	Nepal	69
2015	EU 14	Netherlands	2
2015	America Central and South	Netherlands Antilles	z
2015	Oceania	New Caledonia	0
2015	Oceania	New Zealand	2
2015	America Central and South	Nicaragua	0
2015	Africa Sub-Saharan	Niger	1
2015	Africa Sub-Saharan	Nigeria	917
2015	Oceania	Niue	0
2015	Oceania	Norfolk Island	0
2015	Oceania	Northern Mariana Islands	0
2015	Europe Other	Norway	0
2015	Middle East	Occupied Palestinian Territories	129
2015	Middle East	Oman	2
2015	Other	Other and unknown	9
2015	Asia South	Pakistan	2,470
2015	Oceania	Palau	0
2015	America Central and South	Panama	0
2015	Oceania	Papua New Guinea	0
2015	America Central and South	Paraguay	0
2015	America Central and South	Peru	0
2015	Asia South East	Philippines	51
2015	Other	Pitcairn Islands (British)	0
2015	EU 8	Poland	100
2015	EU 14	Portugal	6
2015	America North	Puerto Rico	0
2015	Middle East	Qatar	2
2015	Other	Refugee	173
2015	Africa Sub-Saharan	Reunion	0
2015	EU 2	Romania	20
2015	Europe Other	Russia	70
2015	Africa Sub-Saharan	Rwanda	10
2015	Oceania	Samoa	0
2015	Europe Other	San Marino	0
2015	Africa Sub-Saharan	Sao Tome and Principe	0
2015	Middle East	Saudi Arabia	34
2015	Africa Sub-Saharan	Senegal	26
2015	Europe Other	Serbia	4
2015	Europe Other	Serbia and Montenegro	z

15.10 Asylum applications and initial decisions for main applicants, by country of nationality

Year	Geographical region	Country of nationality	Total applications
2015	Africa Sub-Saharan	Seychelles	2
2015	Africa Sub-Saharan	Sierra Leone	62
2015	Asia South East	Singapore	1
2015	EU 8	Slovakia	9
2015	EU 8	Slovenia	0
2015	Oceania	Solomon Islands	0
2015	Africa Sub-Saharan	Somalia	386
2015	Africa Sub-Saharan	South Africa	56
2015	Other	South Georgia and South Sandwich Islands	0
2015	EU 14	Spain	3
2015	Asia South	Sri Lanka	961
2015	Other	St. Helena (British)	0
2015	America Central and South	St. Kitts and Nevis	3
2015	America Central and South	St. Lucia	11
2015	America Central and South	St. Maarten (Dutch Part)	0
2015	America Central and South	St. Martin (French Part)	0
2015	America Central and South	St. Pierre and Miquelon	0
2015	America Central and South	St. Vincent and the Grenadines	6
2015	Other	Stateless	502
2015	Africa North	Sudan	2,912
2015	Africa Sub-Saharan	Sudan (South)	11
2015	America Central and South	Surinam	0
2015	Europe Other	Svalbard and Jan Mayen	0
2015	Africa Sub-Saharan	Swaziland	23
2015	EU 14	Sweden	0
2015	Europe Other	Switzerland	0
2015	Middle East	Syria	2,539
2015	Asia East	Taiwan	0
2015	Asia Central	Tajikistan	1
2015	Africa Sub-Saharan	Tanzania	34
2015	Asia South East	Thailand	23
2015	Africa Sub-Saharan	Togo	8
2015	Oceania	Tokelau	0
2015	Oceania	Tonga	0
2015	America Central and South	Trinidad and Tobago	24
2015	Africa North	Tunisia	32
2015	Europe Other	Turkey	233
2015	Asia Central	Turkmenistan	3
2015	Other	Turks and Caicos Islands (British)	0
2015	Oceania	Tuvalu	0
2015	Africa Sub-Saharan	Uganda	256
2015	Europe Other	Ukraine	183
2015	Middle East	United Arab Emirates	1
2015	America North	United States	34
2015	America Central and South	Uruguay	0
2015	Asia Central	Uzbekistan	19
2015	Oceania	Vanuatu	0
2015	Europe Other	Vatican City	0
2015	America Central and South	Venezuela	7
2015	Asia South East	Vietnam	582
2015	Other	Virgin Islands (British)	0
2015	America North	Virgin Islands (US)	0
2015	Oceania	Wallis and Futuna	0
2015	Africa North	Western Sahara	2
2015	Middle East	Yemen	114
2015	Africa Sub-Saharan	Zambia	17
2015	Africa Sub-Saharan	Zimbabwe	266

z = Not applicable.

: = Not available.

Source: Home Office Immigration Statistics

Data, after April 2000 for asylum applications and May 2000 for asylum decisions, have been taken from the Asylum Case Information Database. Prior to this date manual counts were taken.

The tables do not include grants of asylum or ELR (exceptional leave to remain) or refusals on non-compliance grounds under the backlog criteria in 1999 and 2000 which aimed to reduce the pre-1996 asylum application backlog.

Fresh claims' are when a human rights or asylum claim has been refused, withdrawn or treated as withdrawn under paragraph 333C of Immigration Rule 353 and any appeal relating to that claim is no longer pending, the decision maker will consider any further submissions and, if rejected, will then determine whether they amount to a fresh claim. The submissions will amount to a fresh claim if they are significantly different from the material that has previously been considered. The submissions will only be significantly different if the content: had not already been considered; and taken together with the previously considered material, created a realistic prospect of success, not withstanding its rejection.

'Pending' cases are those asylum applications, including fresh claims, lodged since 1 April 2006 which are still under consideration at the end of the reference period.

15.11 Number of marriages by type of ceremony and denomination, 1837 to 2014 [1]
England and Wales

Year (selected years only prior to 1962[2])	All marriages	All marriages to opposite sex couples	Civil ceremonies		Religious ceremonies				
			All	Approved Premises[3]	All	Church of England and Church in Wales	Roman Catholic	Other Christian denominations[4]	Other[5]
2014	252,222	247,372	179,344	158,057	68,028	49,717	7,598	7,895	2,818
2013	240,854	240,854	172,254	147,875	68,600	50,226	7,550	8,035	2,789
2012	263,640	263,640	184,167	156,548	79,473	58,797	8,664	9,027	2,985
2011	249,133	249,133	174,681	143,296	74,452	54,463	8,390	8,844	2,755
2010	243,808	243,808	165,680	125,612	78,128	57,607	8,622	9,032	2,867
2009	232,443	232,443	155,950	111,313	76,493	56,236	8,426	8,973	2,858
2008	235,794	235,794	157,296	106,298	78,498	57,057	8,909	9,745	2,787
2007	235,367	235,367	156,198	101,158	79,169	57,101	8,904	10,351	2,813
2006	239,454	239,454	158,350	95,763	81,104	57,963	9,263	11,249	2,629
2005	247,805	247,805	162,169	90,239	85,636	61,155	9,599	12,315	2,567
2004	273,069	273,069	184,913	85,154	88,156	62,006	9,850	13,578	2,722
2003	270,109	270,109	183,124	73,784	86,985	60,385	9,858	14,188	2,554
2002	255,596	255,596	169,210	61,749	86,386	58,980	10,044	14,844	2,518
2001	249,227	249,227	160,238	50,149	88,989	60,878	10,518	15,210	2,383
2000	267,961	267,961	170,800	45,792	97,161	65,536	11,312	17,751	2,562
1999	263,515	263,515	162,679	37,709	100,836	67,219	12,399	18,690	2,528
1998	267,303	267,303	163,072	28,879	104,231	69,494	12,615	19,746	2,376
1997	272,536	272,536	165,516	22,052	107,020	70,310	13,125	21,211	2,374
1996	278,975	278,975	164,158	15,210	114,817	75,147	13,989	23,605	2,076
1995 [3]	283,012	283,012	155,490	2,496	127,522	83,685	15,181	26,622	2,034
1994	291,069	291,069	152,113	z	138,956	90,703	16,429	29,807	2,017
1993	299,197	299,197	152,930	z	146,267	96,060	17,465	30,804	1,938
1992	311,564	311,564	156,967	z	154,597	101,883	18,795	32,006	1,913
1991	306,756	306,756	151,333	z	155,423	102,840	19,551	31,069	1,963
1990	331,150	331,150	156,875	z	174,275	115,328	22,455	34,599	1,893
1989	346,697	346,697	166,651	z	180,046	118,956	23,737	35,551	1,802
1988	348,492	348,492	168,897	z	179,595	118,423	24,372	34,975	1,825
1987	351,761	351,761	168,190	z	183,571	121,293	25,020	35,589	1,669
1986	347,924	347,924	168,255	z	179,669	117,804	24,578	35,507	1,780
1985	346,389	346,389	169,025	z	177,364	116,378	25,207	33,938	1,841
1984	349,186	349,186	170,506	z	178,680	117,506	25,609	33,866	1,699
1983	344,334	344,334	167,327	z	177,007	116,854	25,211	33,252	1,690
1982	342,166	342,166	165,089	z	177,077	116,978	24,834	33,835	1,430
1981	351,973	351,973	172,514	z	179,459	118,435	26,097	33,439	1,488
1980	370,022	370,022	183,395	z	186,627	123,400	28,553	33,164	1,510
1979	368,853	368,853	187,381	z	181,472	119,420	28,477	32,007	1,568
1978	368,258	368,258	186,239	z	182,019	119,970	28,654	31,882	1,513
1977	356,954	356,954	180,446	z	176,508	116,749	28,204	30,008	1,547
1976	358,567	358,567	179,330	z	179,237	119,569	28,714	29,462	1,492
1975	380,620	380,620	181,824	z	198,796	133,074	32,307	31,845	1,570
1974 [6]	384,389	384,389	178,710	z	205,679	137,767	33,702	34,210	
1973	400,435	400,435	184,724	z	215,711	143,853	36,267	35,591	
1972	426,241	426,241	194,134	z	232,107	155,538	39,694	36,875	
1971	404,737	404,737	167,101	z	237,636	160,165	41,399	36,072	
1970	415,487	415,487	164,119	z	251,368	170,146	43,658	37,564	
1969	396,746	396,746	143,115	z	253,631	172,067	43,441	38,123	
1968	407,822	407,822	144,572	z	263,250	178,700	44,931	39,619	
1967	386,052	386,052	131,576	z	254,476	173,278	43,305	37,893	
1966	384,497	384,497	127,502	z	256,995	175,254	43,814	37,927	
1965	371,127	371,127	118,034	z	253,093	171,848	43,192	38,053	
1964	359,307	359,307	111,053	z	248,254	167,742	42,525	37,987	
1963	351,329	351,329	107,384	z	243,945	163,837	42,272	37,836	
1962	347,732	347,732	103,102	z	244,630	164,707	42,788	37,135	
1957	346,903	346,903	97,084	z	249,819	172,010	39,960	37,849	
1952	349,308	349,308	106,777	z	242,531	173,282	33,050	36,199	
1934	342,307	342,307	97,120	z	245,187	183,123	22,323	39,741	
1929	313,316	313,316	80,475	z	232,841	176,113	18,711	38,017	
1924	296,416	296,416	70,604	z	225,812	171,480	16,286	38,046	
1919	369,411	369,411	85,330	z	284,081	220,557	19,078	44,446	
1914	294,401	294,401	70,880	z	223,521	171,700	13,729	38,092	
1913	286,583	286,583	62,328	z	224,255	172,640	13,349	38,266	
1912	283,834	283,834	58,367	z	225,467	174,357	12,715	38,395	
1911	274,943	274,943	57,435	z	217,508	167,925	12,002	37,581	
1910	267,721	267,721	54,678	z	213,043	164,945	11,312	36,786	
1909	260,544	260,544	53,505	z	207,039	159,991	10,962	36,086	

15.11 Number of marriages by type of ceremony and denomination, 1837 to 2014 [1]
England and Wales

Year (selected years only prior to 1962[2])	All marriages	All marriages to opposite sex couples	Civil ceremonies		Religious ceremonies				
			All	Approved Premises[3]	All	Church of England and Church in Wales	Roman Catholic	Other Christian denominations[4]	Other[5]
1908	264,940	264,940	54,048	z	210,892	163,086	10,940	36,866	
1907	276,421	276,421	54,026	z	222,395	172,497	11,700	38,198	
1906	270,038	270,038	50,682	z	219,356	170,579	11,455	37,322	
1905	260,742	260,742	47,768	z	212,974	165,747	10,812	36,415	
1904	257,856	257,856	46,247	z	211,609	165,519	10,450	35,640	
1903	261,103	261,103	44,520	z	216,583	170,044	10,621	35,918	
1902	261,750	261,750	42,761	z	218,989	173,011	10,606	35,372	
1901	259,400	259,400	41,067	z	218,333	172,679	10,624	35,030	
1900	257,480	257,480	39,471	z	218,009	173,060	10,267	34,682	
1899	262,334	262,334	39,403	z	222,931	177,896	10,686	34,349	
1898	255,379	255,379	37,938	z	217,441	174,826	10,164	32,451	
1897	249,145	249,145	36,626	z	212,519	170,806	10,095	31,618	
1896	242,764	242,764	35,439	z	207,325	166,871	10,042	30,412	
1895	228,204	228,204	33,749	z	194,455	156,469	9,405	28,581	
1894	226,449	226,449	33,550	z	192,899	155,352	9,453	28,094	
1893	218,689	218,689	31,379	z	187,310	151,309	9,019	26,982	
1892	227,135	227,135	31,416	z	195,719	158,632	9,133	27,954	
1891	226,526	226,526	30,809	z	195,717	158,439	9,517	27,761	
1890	223,028	223,028	30,376	z	192,652	156,371	9,596	26,685	
1889	213,865	213,865	29,779	z	184,086	149,356	8,988	25,742	
1888	203,821	203,821	27,809	z	176,012	142,863	8,632	24,517	
1887	200,518	200,518	27,335	z	173,183	140,607	8,611	23,965	
1886	196,071	196,071	25,590	z	170,481	138,571	8,220	23,690	
1885	197,745	197,745	25,851	z	171,894	139,913	8,162	23,819	
1884	204,301	204,301	26,786	z	177,515	144,344	8,783	24,388	
1883	206,384	206,384	26,547	z	179,837	147,000	8,980	23,857	
1882	204,405	204,405	25,717	z	178,688	146,102	9,235	23,351	
1881	197,290	197,290	25,055	z	172,235	140,995	8,784	22,456	
1880	191,965	191,965	24,180	z	167,785	137,661	8,210	21,914	
1879	182,082	182,082	21,769	z	160,313	131,689	7,437	21,187	
1878	190,054	190,054	22,056	z	167,998	137,969	7,980	22,049	
1877	194,352	194,352	21,269	z	173,083	142,396	8,277	22,410	
1876	201,874	201,874	21,709	z	180,165	148,910	8,577	22,678	
1875	201,212	201,212	21,002	z	180,210	149,685	8,411	22,114	
1874	202,010	202,010	21,256	z	180,754	150,819	8,179	21,756	
1873	205,615	205,615	21,178	z	184,437	154,581	8,222	21,634	
1872	201,267	201,267	19,995	z	181,272	152,364	8,427	20,481	
1871	190,112	190,112	18,378	z	171,734	144,663	7,647	19,424	
1870	181,655	181,655	17,848	z	163,807	137,986	7,391	18,430	
1869	176,970	176,970	16,745	z	160,225	135,082	7,231	17,912	
1868	176,962	176,962	15,878	z	161,084	136,038	7,517	17,529	
1867	179,154	179,154	15,058	z	164,096	138,930	7,918	17,248	
1866	187,776	187,776	15,246	z	172,530	146,040	8,911	17,579	
1865	185,474	185,474	14,792	z	170,682	145,104	8,742	16,836	
1864	180,387	180,387	14,611	z	165,776	141,083	8,659	16,034	
1863	173,510	173,510	13,589	z	159,921	136,743	8,095	15,083	
1862	164,030	164,030	12,723	z	151,307	129,733	7,345	14,229	
1861	163,706	163,706	11,725	z	151,981	130,697	7,782	13,502	
1860	170,156	170,156	11,257	z	158,899	137,370	7,800	13,729	
1859	167,723	167,723	10,844	z	156,879	136,210	7,756	12,913	
1858	156,070	156,070	9,952	z	146,118	128,082	6,643	11,393	
1857	159,097	159,097	9,642	z	149,455	131,031	7,360	11,064	
1856	159,337	159,337	8,097	z	151,240	133,619	7,527	10,094	
1855	152,113	152,113	7,441	z	144,672	127,751	7,344	9,577	
1854	159,727	159,727	7,593	z	152,134	134,109	7,813	10,212	
1853	164,520	164,520	7,598	z	156,922	138,042	8,375	10,505	
1852	158,782	158,782	7,100	z	151,682	133,882	7,479	10,321	
1851	154,206	154,206	6,813	z	147,393	130,958	6,570	9,865	
1850	152,744	152,744	6,207	z	146,537	130,959	5,623	9,955	
1849	141,883	141,883	5,558	z	136,325	123,182	4,199	8,944	
1848	138,230	138,230	4,790	z	133,440	121,469	3,658	8,313	
1847	135,845	135,845	4,258	z	131,587	120,876	2,961	7,750	
1846	145,664	145,664	4,167	z	141,497	130,509	3,027	7,961	
1845	143,743	143,743	3,977	z	139,766	129,515	2,816	7,435	
1844	132,249	132,249	3,446	z	128,803	120,009	2,280	6,514	
1843	123,818	123,818	2,817	z	121,001	113,637	7,213		151

15.11 Number of marriages by type of ceremony and denomination, 1837 to 2014 [1]
England and Wales

Year (selected years only prior to 1962[2])	All marriages	All marriages to opposite sex couples	Civil ceremonies		Religious ceremonies				
			All	Approved Premises[3]	All	Church of England and Church in Wales	Roman Catholic	Other Christian denominations[4]	Other[5]
1842	118,825	118,825	2,357	z	116,468	110,047		6,258	163
1841	122,496	122,496	2,064	z	120,432	114,371		5,948	113
1841 - Year ending 30 June	122,482	122,482	2,036	z	120,446	114,448		5,882	116
1840 - Year ending 30 June	124,329	124,329	1,938	z	122,391	117,018		5,221	152
1839 - Year ending 30 June	121,083	121,083	1,564	z	119,519	114,632		4,727	160
1838 - Year ending 30 June	111,481	111,481	1,093	z	110,388	107,201		3,052	135
1837 - 1 July 1937 to 31 December 1937	58,479	58,479	431	z	58,048	56,832		1,142	74

Year (selected years only prior to 1962[2])	All marriages	All marriages to same sex couples	Marriages of same sex couples		Civil ceremonies		Religious ceremonies
			Male	Female	All	Approved Premises[3]	
2014	252,222	4,850	2,129	2,721	4,827	4,200	23

(prior to 2014 - data not applicable)

Source: Office for National Statistics

1 The first marriages of same sex couples took place on 29 March 2014. Figures for 2014 therefore represent a part-year.

2 Data are not available for years not shown.

3 Approved premises are buildings such as hotels, historic buildings and stately homes licensed for civil marriages. Data on approved premises is from 1 April 1995.

4 'Other Christian denominations' include Methodist, Calvinistic Methodist, United Reform Church, Congregationalist, Baptist, Presbyterian, Society of Friends (Quakers), Salvation Army, Brethren, Mormon, Unitarian and Jehovah's Witnesses.

5 'Other' include Jews, Muslim and Sikh.

6 Prior to 1975 further information on denominations was not published.

15.12 Duration of marriage at divorce by age of wife at marriage, 1983-2013

England and Wales Numbers

Year of divorce	Age of wife at marriage	All durations	Duration of marriage (completed years)								
			0-2 years	0 years	1 year	2 years	3 years	4 years	5-9 years	5 years	6 years
2013	**All ages**	**114,720**	**6,271**	**79**	**2,055**	**4,137**	**5,647**	**6,272**	**30,996**	**6,449**	**6,410**
	Under 20	**8,115**	185	3	62	120	184	243	1,462	304	302
	20-24	**35,388**	1,428	19	447	962	1,370	1,561	7,540	1,538	1,568
	25-29	**33,404**	1,959	19	634	1,306	1,814	1,863	8,858	1,934	1,898
	30-44	**33,340**	2,196	29	720	1,447	1,897	2,204	11,422	2,251	2,288
	45 and over	**4,473**	503	9	192	302	382	401	1,714	422	354
2012	**All ages**	**118,140**	**6,268**	**49**	**2,033**	**4,186**	**5,710**	**6,550**	**33,027**	**6,748**	**6,542**
	Under 20	**9,195**	193	3	47	143	248	326	1,790	349	316
	20-24	**37,445**	1,513	7	485	1,021	1,454	1,674	8,183	1,695	1,613
	25-29	**34,055**	1,937	19	632	1,286	1,738	1,958	9,374	2,038	1,895
	30-44	**33,018**	2,120	13	689	1,418	1,908	2,160	11,925	2,247	2,349
	45 and over	**4,427**	505	7	180	318	362	432	1,755	419	369
2011	**All ages**	**117,558**	**5,803**	**30**	**1,748**	**4,025**	**5,890**	**6,654**	**32,989**	**6,727**	**7,111**
	Under 20	**9,727**	238	1	59	178	309	329	1,915	344	400
	20-24	**38,327**	1,392	10	416	966	1,535	1,681	8,320	1,745	1,751
	25-29	**33,379**	1,783	11	544	1,228	1,734	1,986	9,406	1,949	2,001
	30-44	**31,999**	1,924	4	576	1,344	1,931	2,246	11,736	2,332	2,604
	45 and over	**4,126**	466	4	153	309	381	412	1,612	357	355
2010	**All ages**	**119,589**	**6,278**	**17**	**1,897**	**4,364**	**6,109**	**6,936**	**33,700**	**7,418**	**7,652**
	Under 20	**10,619**	255	0	85	170	332	351	2,085	450	489
	20-24	**39,963**	1,528	4	429	1,095	1,551	1,849	8,624	1,895	2,072
	25-29	**33,309**	1,874	3	583	1,288	1,795	1,947	9,609	2,072	2,123
	30-44	**31,660**	2,134	8	624	1,502	2,009	2,404	11,834	2,597	2,607
	45 and over	**4,038**	487	2	176	309	422	385	1,548	404	361
2009	**All ages**	**113,949**	**6,270**	**21**	**1,951**	**4,298**	**5,884**	**6,947**	**31,290**	**7,561**	**6,864**
	Under 20	**10,529**	267	1	60	206	293	371	1,943	478	439
	20-24	**39,231**	1,540	1	472	1,067	1,516	1,813	8,350	2,065	1,889
	25-29	**31,400**	1,808	8	572	1,228	1,715	1,986	8,994	2,106	1,898
	30-44	**29,021**	2,184	7	683	1,494	1,981	2,389	10,610	2,554	2,307
	45 and over	**3,768**	471	4	164	303	379	388	1,393	358	331
2008	**All ages**	**121,708**	**6,937**	**27**	**2,103**	**4,807**	**6,776**	**7,929**	**31,803**	**7,369**	**6,714**
	Under 20	**11,657**	319	1	78	240	365	500	1,948	478	407
	20-24	**42,578**	1,685	10	463	1,212	1,798	2,103	8,401	2,043	1,879
	25-29	**33,050**	2,044	7	621	1,416	1,875	2,148	9,287	1,985	1,863
	30-44	**30,642**	2,379	7	741	1,631	2,349	2,751	10,819	2,512	2,304
	45 and over	**3,781**	510	2	200	308	389	427	1,348	351	261
2007	**All ages**	**128,131**	**8,195**	**38**	**2,558**	**5,599**	**7,206**	**7,574**	**32,419**	**7,164**	**7,046**
	Under 20	**13,224**	411	1	120	290	417	487	2,053	430	470
	20-24	**45,806**	2,039	7	623	1,409	1,905	1,977	8,481	1,928	1,814
	25-29	**34,564**	2,234	13	668	1,553	1,990	2,115	9,987	2,099	2,106
	30-44	**30,808**	2,942	11	929	2,002	2,521	2,591	10,617	2,403	2,366
	45 and over	**3,729**	569	6	218	345	373	404	1,281	304	290
2006	**All ages**	**132,140**	**8,763**	**37**	**2,793**	**5,933**	**7,226**	**7,376**	**33,736**	**7,398**	**7,310**
	Under 20	**14,441**	503	2	157	344	376	447	2,232	474	506
	20-24	**48,396**	2,240	9	668	1,563	1,975	1,997	8,954	1,967	1,901
	25-29	**35,054**	2,381	13	796	1,572	2,052	2,172	10,416	2,182	2,181
	30-44	**30,613**	3,087	6	966	2,115	2,441	2,424	10,858	2,473	2,437
	45 and over	**3,636**	552	7	206	339	382	336	1,276	302	285
2005	**All ages**	**141,322**	**9,573**	**49**	**3,181**	**6,343**	**7,520**	**8,175**	**36,064**	**7,920**	**7,697**
	Under 20	**16,473**	537	2	148	387	515	579	2,389	576	544
	20-24	**52,884**	2,469	15	783	1,671	2,025	2,203	9,961	2,083	2,016
	25-29	**36,992**	2,545	9	845	1,691	2,081	2,507	11,296	2,367	2,431
	30-44	**31,213**	3,413	17	1,171	2,225	2,540	2,554	11,025	2,545	2,406
	45 and over	**3,760**	609	6	234	369	359	332	1,393	349	300
2004	**All ages**	**152,923**	**10,101**	**42**	**3,345**	**6,714**	**8,319**	**8,894**	**39,681**	**8,840**	**8,375**
	Under 20	**18,655**	626	3	201	422	557	662	2,626	667	581
	20-24	**59,356**	2,662	7	854	1,801	2,361	2,494	11,818	2,477	2,359
	25-29	**39,459**	2,871	8	947	1,916	2,480	2,642	12,426	2,674	2,593
	30-44	**31,631**	3,353	15	1,122	2,216	2,542	2,724	11,356	2,679	2,515
	45 and over	**3,822**	589	9	221	359	379	372	1,455	343	327

15.12 Duration of marriage at divorce by age of wife at marriage, 1983-2013

England and Wales   Numbers

Year of divorce	Age of wife at marriage	Duration of marriage (completed years)								Not stated	Median duration
		7 years	8 years	9 years	10-14 years	15-19 years	20-24 years	25-29 years	30 years and over		
2013	All ages	6,005	6,152	5,980	21,652	15,687	11,880	7,691	8,624	0	11.7
	Under 20	258	304	294	1,125	822	883	969	2,242	0	:
	20-24	1,460	1,515	1,459	5,130	4,742	5,039	4,074	4,504	0	:
	25-29	1,719	1,691	1,616	6,792	5,316	3,772	1,762	1,268	0	:
	30-44	2,266	2,318	2,299	7,743	4,408	2,049	839	582	0	:
	45 and over	302	324	312	862	399	137	47	28	0	:
2012	All ages	6,919	6,961	5,857	22,356	15,733	12,215	7,649	8,632	0	11.5
	Under 20	361	406	358	1,259	795	1,056	1,088	2,440	0	:
	20-24	1,700	1,746	1,429	5,523	5,142	5,498	4,024	4,434	0	:
	25-29	1,910	1,843	1,688	7,188	5,426	3,541	1,669	1,224	0	:
	30-44	2,576	2,634	2,119	7,551	4,048	1,984	816	506	0	:
	45 and over	372	332	263	835	322	136	52	28	0	:
2011	All ages	7,263	6,389	5,499	22,126	15,547	12,228	7,712	8,609	0	11.5
	Under 20	487	384	300	1,276	901	1,111	1,130	2,518	0	:
	20-24	1,902	1,619	1,303	5,749	5,361	5,834	4,052	4,403	0	:
	25-29	2,042	1,756	1,658	7,097	5,198	3,370	1,644	1,161	0	:
	30-44	2,488	2,323	1,989	7,267	3,754	1,804	831	506	0	:
	45 and over	344	307	249	737	333	109	55	21	0	:
2010	All ages	7,101	5,995	5,534	22,105	15,772	12,412	7,639	8,638	0	11.4
	Under 20	432	381	333	1,280	1,012	1,305	1,366	2,633	0	:
	20-24	1,825	1,481	1,351	5,967	5,920	5,929	4,117	4,478	0	:
	25-29	2,018	1,690	1,706	7,163	5,134	3,369	1,351	1,067	0	:
	30-44	2,527	2,189	1,914	6,961	3,419	1,693	770	436	0	:
	45 and over	299	254	230	734	287	116	35	24	0	:
2009	All ages	5,968	5,634	5,263	20,591	15,390	11,855	7,490	8,225	7	11.4
	Under 20	355	357	314	1,177	1,092	1,337	1,484	2,565	0	:
	20-24	1,629	1,466	1,301	5,909	5,944	5,964	3,956	4,235	4	:
	25-29	1,679	1,648	1,663	6,704	4,926	2,983	1,299	985	0	:
	30-44	2,068	1,919	1,762	6,090	3,128	1,494	713	429	3	:
	45 and over	237	244	223	711	300	77	38	11	0	:
2008	All ages	6,365	6,034	5,321	21,561	16,945	12,706	8,136	8,907	8	11.5
	Under 20	358	363	342	1,174	1,274	1,526	1,749	2,800	2	:
	20-24	1,619	1,528	1,332	6,315	6,881	6,511	4,247	4,632	5	:
	25-29	1,880	1,862	1,697	7,075	5,204	2,945	1,389	1,082	1	:
	30-44	2,228	2,032	1,743	6,324	3,295	1,620	722	383	0	:
	45 and over	280	249	207	673	291	104	29	10	0	:
2007	All ages	6,560	6,072	5,577	23,427	18,203	13,117	8,701	9,282	7	11.7
	Under 20	423	395	335	1,240	1,542	1,929	2,099	3,045	1	:
	20-24	1,650	1,607	1,482	7,397	7,930	6,757	4,498	4,820	2	:
	25-29	2,021	1,953	1,808	7,777	5,240	2,802	1,377	1,039	3	:
	30-44	2,203	1,890	1,755	6,343	3,219	1,526	686	362	1	:
	45 and over	263	227	197	670	272	103	41	16	0	:
2006	All ages	6,769	6,249	6,010	24,606	18,735	13,472	8,764	9,449	13	11.6
	Under 20	490	397	365	1,491	1,831	2,191	2,241	3,128	1	:
	20-24	1,751	1,681	1,654	8,443	8,470	6,949	4,415	4,947	6	:
	25-29	2,159	2,004	1,890	7,708	5,157	2,745	1,365	1,053	5	:
	30-44	2,107	1,939	1,902	6,263	3,034	1,483	717	305	1	:
	45 and over	262	228	199	701	243	104	26	16	0	:
2005	All ages	7,343	6,801	6,303	26,310	20,310	14,268	9,241	9,852	9	11.6
	Under 20	478	429	362	1,722	2,299	2,605	2,571	3,255	1	:
	20-24	2,007	1,920	1,935	9,570	9,450	7,368	4,636	5,200	2	:
	25-29	2,291	2,173	2,034	8,364	5,146	2,683	1,310	1,058	2	:
	30-44	2,266	2,040	1,768	5,965	3,161	1,526	699	326	4	:
	45 and over	301	239	204	689	254	86	25	13	0	:
2004	All ages	7,900	7,683	6,883	28,984	21,515	15,431	9,705	10,293	0	11.5
	Under 20	498	485	395	2,133	2,737	3,103	2,804	3,407	0	:
	20-24	2,324	2,389	2,269	11,471	10,355	7,893	4,792	5,510	0	:
	25-29	2,517	2,436	2,206	8,671	5,082	2,823	1,427	1,037	0	:
	30-44	2,274	2,111	1,777	6,064	3,093	1,539	639	321	0	:
	45 and over	287	262	236	645	248	73	43	18	0	:

15.12 Duration of marriage at divorce by age of wife at marriage, 1983-2013

England and Wales   Numbers

Year of divorce	Age of wife at marriage	All durations	Duration of marriage (completed years)								
			0-2 years	0 years	1 year	2 years	3 years	4 years	5-9 years	5 years	6 years
2003	All ages	153,065	10,286	42	3,283	6,961	8,276	8,882	40,497	8,968	8,639
	Under 20	20,008	694	0	198	496	591	662	2,644	614	562
	20-24	60,883	2,735	11	825	1,899	2,352	2,587	12,944	2,636	2,564
	25-29	38,628	2,954	9	903	2,042	2,554	2,715	12,663	2,778	2,716
	30-44	29,873	3,304	10	1,131	2,163	2,444	2,554	10,865	2,600	2,468
	45 and over	3,673	599	12	226	361	335	364	1,381	340	329
2002	All ages	147,735	10,239	31	3,326	6,882	8,325	8,780	39,730	8,823	8,370
	Under 20	19,828	684	3	184	497	623	597	2,589	591	541
	20-24	60,353	2,833	6	878	1,949	2,411	2,696	13,727	2,739	2,754
	25-29	36,387	2,903	8	906	1,989	2,581	2,778	12,269	2,795	2,602
	30-44	27,803	3,250	7	1,132	2,111	2,366	2,387	9,865	2,374	2,171
	45 and over	3,364	569	7	226	336	344	322	1,280	324	302
2001	All ages	143,818	10,190	36	3,413	6,741	8,206	8,591	39,079	8,632	8,329
	Under 20	20,218	738	3	225	510	634	560	2,676	574	498
	20-24	60,211	2,809	12	870	1,927	2,472	2,711	14,418	2,900	2,938
	25-29	34,759	3,041	10	973	2,058	2,571	2,737	11,728	2,648	2,600
	30-44	25,405	3,054	6	1,116	1,932	2,177	2,246	9,059	2,202	2,028
	45 and over	3,225	548	5	229	314	352	337	1,198	308	265
2000	All ages	141,135	10,438	52	3,494	6,892	8,296	8,740	38,206	8,506	8,148
	Under 20	20,930	846	2	284	560	598	575	2,937	571	594
	20-24	59,874	2,954	8	925	2,021	2,631	2,978	14,663	3,014	3,021
	25-29	33,282	3,095	17	1,038	2,040	2,567	2,675	11,443	2,625	2,510
	30-44	23,912	2,971	14	1,012	1,945	2,159	2,179	8,082	2,032	1,779
	45 and over	3,137	572	11	235	326	341	333	1,081	264	244
1999	All ages	144,556	11,350	49	3,813	7,488	8,833	9,124	39,676	8,958	8,521
	Under 20	22,486	868	5	268	595	658	625	3,367	604	691
	20-24	62,853	3,445	15	1,125	2,305	2,965	3,366	16,221	3,440	3,404
	25-29	32,867	3,182	6	1,074	2,102	2,710	2,745	11,170	2,670	2,432
	30-44	23,270	3,197	14	1,082	2,101	2,147	2,076	7,898	1,982	1,735
	45 and over	3,080	658	9	264	385	353	312	1,020	262	259
1998	All ages	145,214	12,247	68	4,191	7,988	9,270	9,619	40,239	9,180	8,497
	Under 20	24,276	976	7	327	642	704	785	3,858	753	762
	20-24	64,453	4,000	16	1,303	2,681	3,475	3,737	17,413	3,800	3,586
	25-29	31,533	3,510	21	1,144	2,345	2,697	2,787	10,518	2,569	2,289
	30-44	22,076	3,162	18	1,140	2,004	2,062	2,027	7,478	1,801	1,631
	45 and over	2,876	599	6	277	316	332	283	972	257	229
1997	All ages	146,689	12,596	61	4,369	8,166	9,410	9,761	41,260	9,326	8,580
	Under 20	25,579	1,024	7	359	658	757	809	4,424	857	851
	20-24	66,167	4,412	10	1,449	2,953	3,773	4,114	18,226	3,917	3,736
	25-29	31,022	3,576	13	1,213	2,350	2,706	2,712	10,417	2,591	2,263
	30-44	21,017	2,958	20	1,073	1,865	1,879	1,818	7,241	1,719	1,513
	45 and over	2,904	626	11	275	340	295	308	952	242	217
1996	All ages	157,107	14,021	76	5,010	8,935	10,467	10,436	44,609	10,042	9,850
	Under 20	29,927	1,178	4	383	791	970	1,022	5,543	1,128	1,165
	20-24	71,123	5,289	20	1,744	3,525	4,236	4,392	20,221	4,408	4,417
	25-29	31,396	3,872	23	1,384	2,465	2,901	2,778	10,373	2,557	2,359
	30-44	21,640	3,018	15	1,197	1,806	2,008	1,919	7,480	1,702	1,691
	45 and over	3,021	664	14	302	348	352	325	992	247	218
1995	All ages	155,499	14,015	95	4,944	8,976	10,209	10,283	44,304	10,447	9,812
	Under 20	31,322	1,374	8	418	948	1,090	1,158	5,894	1,224	1,180
	20-24	71,360	5,634	28	1,948	3,658	4,375	4,477	20,360	4,748	4,457
	25-29	29,441	3,568	17	1,257	2,294	2,591	2,576	9,892	2,523	2,255
	30-44	20,506	2,817	26	1,034	1,757	1,842	1,792	7,208	1,684	1,707
	45 and over	2,870	622	16	287	319	311	280	950	268	213
1994	All ages	158,175	13,841	81	4,895	8,865	10,400	11,454	44,769	10,836	9,896
	Under 20	34,069	1,582	6	518	1,058	1,297	1,468	6,805	1,404	1,418
	20-24	73,291	5,689	19	1,956	3,714	4,518	5,106	21,102	4,975	4,681
	25-29	28,360	3,408	24	1,208	2,176	2,520	2,698	9,187	2,414	2,077
	30-44	19,686	2,574	17	959	1,598	1,749	1,838	6,807	1,806	1,523
	45 and over	2,769	588	15	254	319	316	344	868	237	197

545

15.12 Duration of marriage at divorce by age of wife at marriage, 1983-2013

England and Wales

Numbers

Year of divorce	Age of wife at marriage	Duration of marriage (completed years)								Not stated	Median duration
		7 years	8 years	9 years	10-14 years	15-19 years	20-24 years	25-29 years	30 years and over		
2003	All ages	8,228	7,686	6,976	29,751	20,863	14,974	9,627	9,907	2	11.3
	Under 20	551	495	422	2,613	2,911	3,559	2,985	3,349	0	:
	20-24	2,569	2,622	2,553	12,281	10,413	7,534	4,708	5,327	2	:
	25-29	2,594	2,361	2,214	8,537	4,508	2,409	1,333	955	0	:
	30-44	2,232	1,965	1,600	5,679	2,811	1,391	564	261	0	:
	45 and over	282	243	187	641	220	81	37	15	0	:
2002	All ages	8,020	7,564	6,953	28,592	19,784	13,989	9,106	9,190	0	11.1
	Under 20	481	517	459	2,774	3,160	3,439	2,891	3,071	0	:
	20-24	2,795	2,770	2,669	12,516	9,810	6,845	4,480	5,035	0	:
	25-29	2,514	2,265	2,093	7,524	4,032	2,279	1,175	846	0	:
	30-44	1,985	1,796	1,539	5,249	2,577	1,355	523	231	0	:
	45 and over	245	216	193	529	205	71	37	7	0	:
2001	All ages	7,909	7,463	6,746	28,176	18,603	13,318	8,986	8,667	2	10.9
	Under 20	524	513	567	2,999	3,309	3,607	2,830	2,865	0	:
	20-24	2,925	2,943	2,712	12,875	9,251	6,432	4,505	4,736	2	:
	25-29	2,398	2,183	1,899	7,075	3,587	2,052	1,158	810	0	:
	30-44	1,810	1,612	1,407	4,721	2,270	1,157	475	246	0	:
	45 and over	252	212	161	506	186	70	18	10	0	:
2000	All ages	7,778	7,183	6,591	27,459	17,870	12,907	9,017	8,196	6	10.7
	Under 20	566	604	602	3,230	3,413	3,556	3,003	2,770	2	:
	20-24	2,959	2,909	2,760	12,720	8,839	6,142	4,479	4,465	3	:
	25-29	2,356	2,046	1,906	6,521	3,192	1,995	1,078	715	1	:
	30-44	1,665	1,429	1,177	4,461	2,250	1,145	433	232	0	:
	45 and over	232	195	146	527	176	69	24	14	0	:
1999	All ages	7,861	7,338	6,998	27,384	18,072	12,888	9,349	7,871	9	10.5
	Under 20	620	722	730	3,532	3,886	3,874	3,040	2,633	3	:
	20-24	3,217	3,111	3,049	12,984	8,729	5,960	4,871	4,308	4	:
	25-29	2,205	2,044	1,819	6,209	3,127	1,950	1,053	720	1	:
	30-44	1,622	1,312	1,247	4,191	2,156	1,037	362	205	1	:
	45 and over	197	149	153	468	174	67	23	5	0	:
1998	All ages	7,785	7,757	7,020	26,698	17,934	12,675	9,056	7,468	8	10.2
	Under 20	740	823	780	3,986	4,364	4,020	3,075	2,508	0	:
	20-24	3,435	3,413	3,179	12,757	8,469	5,833	4,738	4,028	3	:
	25-29	2,026	1,955	1,679	5,599	2,955	1,851	896	716	4	:
	30-44	1,398	1,419	1,229	3,907	1,993	911	325	210	1	:
	45 and over	186	147	153	449	153	60	22	6	0	:
1997	All ages	8,324	7,935	7,095	26,215	18,027	13,148	9,058	7,202	12	10.0
	Under 20	923	894	899	4,197	4,648	4,284	2,957	2,476	3	:
	20-24	3,750	3,540	3,283	12,447	8,298	6,082	4,971	3,837	7	:
	25-29	2,065	1,918	1,580	5,353	2,881	1,860	834	681	2	:
	30-44	1,409	1,400	1,200	3,776	2,006	869	274	196	0	:
	45 and over	177	183	133	442	194	53	22	12	0	:
1996	All ages	9,092	8,171	7,454	27,332	19,321	14,236	9,511	7,165	9	9.9
	Under 20	1,120	1,116	1,014	5,084	5,507	4,867	3,294	2,461	1	:
	20-24	4,029	3,776	3,591	12,921	8,558	6,549	5,112	3,841	4	:
	25-29	2,168	1,734	1,555	5,119	2,998	1,882	805	665	3	:
	30-44	1,549	1,375	1,163	3,765	2,087	887	285	190	1	:
	45 and over	226	170	131	443	171	51	15	8	0	:
1995	All ages	8,822	7,965	7,258	27,365	18,943	14,483	8,925	6,962	10	9.6
	Under 20	1,161	1,176	1,153	5,768	5,604	5,009	3,072	2,350	3	:
	20-24	4,051	3,668	3,436	12,640	8,476	6,815	4,860	3,718	5	:
	25-29	2,023	1,664	1,427	4,781	2,832	1,796	711	692	2	:
	30-44	1,426	1,275	1,116	3,727	1,868	795	268	189	0	:
	45 and over	161	182	126	449	163	68	14	13	0	:
1994	All ages	8,881	7,900	7,256	28,073	19,200	14,891	8,801	6,739	7	9.8
	Under 20	1,403	1,327	1,253	6,458	6,077	5,101	3,050	2,230	1	14.6
	20-24	4,222	3,727	3497	12,808	8,351	7,303	4,777	3,633	4	10.1
	25-29	1,774	1,559	1,363	4,733	2,804	1,663	675	670	2	7.6
	30-44	1,315	1,144	1,019	3,693	1,785	761	278	201	0	7.1
	45 and over	167	143	124	381	183	63	21	5	0	5.5

15.12 Duration of marriage at divorce by age of wife at marriage, 1983-2013

England and Wales

Numbers

Year of divorce	Age of wife at marriage	All durations	Duration of marriage (completed years)								
			0-2 years	0 years	1 year	2 years	3 years	4 years	5-9 years	5 years	6 years
1993	All ages	165,018	14,096	74	4,708	9,314	11,357	11,799	46,536	11,137	10,352
	Under 20	38,811	1,867	9	583	1,275	1,668	1,653	8,196	1,713	1,685
	20-24	76,853	6,163	12	2,045	4,106	5,066	5,470	21,731	5,194	4,901
	25-29	27,178	3,051	27	953	2,071	2,439	2,506	8,777	2,282	1,970
	30-44	19,357	2,419	18	878	1,523	1,832	1,827	6,920	1,722	1,562
	45 and over	2,819	596	8	249	339	352	343	912	226	234
1992	All ages	160,385	14,247	62	4,630	9,555	11,299	11,352	43,745	10,417	9,459
	Under 20	39,734	1,990	3	590	1,397	1,736	1,739	8,544	1,798	1,697
	20-24	74,701	6,208	19	1,949	4,240	5,159	5,510	20,464	4,952	4,469
	25-29	25,173	2,992	11	1,010	1,971	2,241	2,213	7,759	1,952	1,796
	30-44	18,011	2,430	16	832	1,582	1,822	1,631	6,054	1,476	1,275
	45 and over	2,766	627	13	249	365	341	259	924	239	222
1991	All ages	158,745	15,332	62	5,239	10,031	11,321	11,126	42,735	10,049	9,345
	Under 20	40,594	2,387	1	780	1,606	1,894	2,014	9,143	1,857	1,805
	20-24	74,050	6,863	17	2,271	4,575	5,308	5,292	19,926	4,808	4,493
	25-29	24,025	2,942	12	1,003	1,927	2,162	2,014	7,048	1,776	1,571
	30-44	17,359	2,486	16	892	1,578	1,640	1,556	5,765	1,390	1,269
	45 and over	2,717	654	16	293	345	317	250	853	218	207
1990	All ages	153,386	15,122	64	5,142	9,916	10,863	10,314	42,061	9,883	9,025
	Under 20	41,116	2,558	6	788	1,764	1,993	1,961	9,790	2,030	1,917
	20-24	71,489	6,919	20	2,312	4,587	5,115	4,981	19,248	4,702	4,265
	25-29	21,701	2,637	11	906	1,720	1,898	1,721	6,567	1,627	1,462
	30-44	16,387	2,378	16	866	1,496	1,533	1,386	5,608	1,297	1,214
	45 and over	2,693	630	11	270	349	324	265	848	227	167
1989	All ages	150,872	15,231	56	5,420	9,755	10,372	10,116	42,108	9,569	8,928
	Under 20	42,612	2,915	11	980	1,924	2,059	2,144	10,798	2,209	2,199
	20-24	69,424	6,956	18	2,424	4,514	4,886	4,783	18,725	4,377	4,042
	25-29	20,369	2,468	8	887	1,573	1,651	1,580	6,189	1,476	1,360
	30-44	15,774	2,272	12	853	1,407	1,487	1,338	5,535	1,286	1,118
	45 and over	2,693	620	7	276	337	289	271	861	221	209
1988	All ages	152,633	15,003	88	5,403	9,512	10,213	10,376	42,617	9,730	9,080
	Under 20	44,693	3,151	7	1,055	2,089	2,296	2,472	11,676	2,374	2,424
	20-24	69,489	6,676	31	2,339	4,306	4,751	4,777	18,310	4,378	3,936
	25-29	20,267	2,298	16	854	1,428	1,525	1,543	6,167	1,464	1,331
	30-44	15,472	2,207	17	852	1,338	1,328	1,368	5,584	1,302	1,182
	45 and over	2,712	671	17	303	351	313	216	880	212	207
1987	All ages	151,007	14,549	:	:	:	10,248	10,626	43,150	10,262	9,626
	Under 20	46,097	3,387	:	:	:	2,554	2,755	12,428	2,823	2,628
	20-24	68,345	6,393	:	:	:	4,643	4,751	18,180	4,461	4,190
	25-29	19,049	2,045	:	:	:	1,449	1,449	6,088	1,420	1,353
	30-44	14,802	2,085	:	:	:	1,293	1,405	5,549	1,327	1,242
	45 and over	2,714	639	:	:	:	309	266	905	231	213
1986	All ages	153,903	14,596	:	:	:	11,683	12,358	42,187	10,656	9,329
	Under 20	48,621	3,735	:	:	:	3,239	3,618	12,978	3,204	2,863
	20-24	68,387	6,216	:	:	:	5,020	5,257	17,059	4,446	3,713
	25-29	18,990	1,955	:	:	:	1,504	1,561	5,845	1,369	1,296
	30-44	15,064	2,068	:	:	:	1,553	1,583	5,369	1,387	1,248
	45 and over	2,841	622	:	:	:	367	339	936	250	209
1985	All ages	160,300	14,662	:	:	:	16,929	14,185	41,537	10,942	9,352
	Under 20	52,858	4,034	:	:	:	5,320	4,481	13,455	3,471	3,008
	20-24	69,663	5,927	:	:	:	6,983	5,735	16,294	4,374	3,607
	25-29	18,689	1,748	:	:	:	1,894	1,720	5,620	1,408	1,269
	30-44	15,765	2,160	:	:	:	2,187	1,827	5,181	1,403	1,249
	45 and over	3,325	793	:	:	:	545	422	987	286	219
1984	All ages	144,501	1,336	:	:	:	15,296	13,868	40,866	10,434	8,830
	Under 20	49,610	304	:	:	:	5,084	4,577	13,821	3,452	2,994
	20-24	62,642	427	:	:	:	6,107	5,443	15,716	4,020	3,371
	25-29	16,811	183	:	:	:	1,707	1,737	5,477	1,329	1,118
	30-44	12,944	289	:	:	:	1,921	1,739	4,895	1,362	1,126
	45 and over	2,494	133	:	:	:	477	372	957	271	221
1983	All ages	147,479	1,528	:	:	:	15,706	13,863	42,041	10,413	8,785
	Under 20	52,547	389	:	:	:	5,529	4,866	15,084	3,693	3,129
	20-24	63,382	477	:	:	:	6,054	5,228	15,887	3,942	3,294
	25-29	16,351	196	:	:	:	1,723	1,654	5,362	1,270	1,130
	30-44	12,675	326	:	:	:	1,904	1,725	4,726	1,253	1,027
	45 and over	2,524	140	:	:	:	496	390	982	255	205

Source: Office for National Statistics

15.12 Duration of marriage at divorce by age of wife at marriage, 1983-2013

England and Wales											Numbers
		Duration of marriage (completed years)									
Year of divorce	Age of wife at marriage	7 years	8 years	9 years	10-14 years	15-19 years	20-24 years	25-29 years	30 years and over	Not stated	Median duration
1993	All ages	9,029	8,475	7,543	30,156	20,233	15,503	8,426	6,907	5	9.8
	Under 20	1,593	1,621	1,584	7,812	6,830	5,452	3,065	2,267	1	13.9
	20-24	4,311	3,892	3,433	13,538	8,796	7,909	4,434	3,743	3	10.0
	25-29	1,624	1,627	1,274	4,753	2,808	1,497	671	675	1	7.8
	30-44	1,328	1,177	1,131	3,667	1,648	588	242	214	0	7.0
	45 and over	173	158	121	386	151	57	14	8	0	5.4
1992	All ages	8,708	7,914	7,247	29,285	20,160	15,488	8,098	6,704	7	9.9
	Under 20	1,708	1,670	1,671	8,192	6,920	5,395	3,090	2,125	3	13.5
	20-24	4,090	3,694	3,259	12,837	8,721	8,038	4,067	3,694	3	10.0
	25-29	1,513	1,340	1,158	4,401	2,791	1,448	633	694	1	7.9
	30-44	1,219	1,059	1,025	3,477	1,552	570	289	186	0	6.9
	45 and over	178	151	134	378	176	37	19	5	0	5.6
1991	All ages	8,423	7,797	7,121	28,791	20,127	14,957	7,845	6,492	19	9.8
	Under 20	1,808	1,883	1,790	8,295	6,988	5,112	2,825	1,930	6	12.7
	20-24	3,902	3,506	3,217	12,304	8,775	7,924	4,066	3,581	11	9.9
	25-29	1,438	1,228	1,035	4,417	2,686	1,318	685	751	2	8.1
	30-44	1,118	1,033	955	3,355	1,521	553	261	222	0	7.0
	45 and over	157	147	124	420	157	50	8	8	0	5.7
1990	All ages	8,289	7,634	7,230	27,310	19,819	14,186	7,479	6,216	16	9.8
	Under 20	1,950	1,933	1,960	8,313	7,122	4,974	2,648	1,755	2	12.4
	20-24	3,767	3,380	3,134	11,542	8,786	7,500	3,897	3,490	11	9.8
	25-29	1,316	1,144	1,018	3,893	2,416	1,156	639	772	2	8.2
	30-44	1,101	1,016	980	3,163	1,330	514	283	191	1	7.0
	45 and over	155	161	138	399	165	42	12	8	0	6.0
1989	All ages	8,392	7,887	7,332	26,281	19,418	13,575	7,333	6,419	19	9.7
	Under 20	2,233	2,037	2,120	8,289	6,951	4,963	2,632	1,854	7	11.9
	20-24	3,698	3,538	3,070	10,775	8,890	7,051	3,758	3,590	10	9.8
	25-29	1,210	1,113	1,030	3,900	2,201	1,026	640	713	1	8.4
	30-44	1,094	1,054	983	2,885	1,226	491	286	253	1	7.0
	45 and over	157	145	129	432	150	44	17	9	0	5.8
1988	All ages	8,784	7,906	7,117	26,545	20,132	13,723	7,476	6,548	0	9.7
	Under 20	2,410	2,352	2,116	8,648	7,126	4,896	2,571	1,857	0	11.5
	20-24	3,813	3,247	2,936	10,753	9,646	7,074	3,915	3,587	0	10.1
	25-29	1,256	1,083	1,033	3,962	2,046	1,180	698	848	0	8.7
	30-44	1,137	1,069	894	2,787	1,149	527	274	248	0	7.0
	45 and over	168	155	138	395	165	46	18	8	0	5.7
1987	All ages	8,781	7,827	6,654	26,194	19,576	12,970	7,314	6,380	0	9.5
	Under 20	2,592	2,324	2,061	8,925	7,019	4,820	2,472	1,737	0	11.0
	20-24	3,652	3,212	2,665	10,656	9,671	6,602	3,861	3,588	0	10.1
	25-29	1,196	1,127	992	3,723	1,791	1,021	694	789	0	8.5
	30-44	1,163	993	824	2,475	975	488	276	256	0	6.8
	45 and over	178	171	112	415	120	39	11	10	0	5.1
1986	All ages	8,457	7,465	6,280	26,718	19,547	12,909	7,357	6,539	9	9.4
	Under 20	2,616	2,313	1,982	9,208	6,946	4,810	2,317	1,766	4	10.4
	20-24	3,410	2,981	2509	10,953	9,857	6,376	3,986	3,661	2	10.3
	25-29	1,205	1,044	931	3,679	1,688	1,145	736	874	3	8.6
	30-44	1,034	969	731	2,477	940	541	301	232	0	6.4
	45 and over	192	158	127	401	116	37	17	6	0	5.4
1985	All ages	7,932	6,884	6,427	27,087	19,460	12,463	7,388	6,576	13	8.9
	Under 20	2,553	2,262	2,161	9,658	7,125	4,645	2,347	1,789	4	9.6
	20-24	3,114	2,705	2,494	11,276	9,665	6,122	4,016	3,638	7	10.0
	25-29	1,054	981	908	3,388	1,630	1,122	700	865	2	8.3
	30-44	1,015	781	733	2,348	935	538	315	274	0	6.0
	45 and over	196	155	131	417	105	36	10	10	0	4.8
1984	All ages	7,854	7,105	6,643	27,336	19,108	12,516	7,528	6,637	10	10.1
	Under 20	2,640	2,450	2,285	9,933	7,127	4,614	2,410	1,737	3	10.4
	20-24	3,060	2,687	2,578	11,723	9,412	6,154	3,942	3,711	7	11.5
	25-29	1,048	1,034	948	3,209	1,578	1,159	827	934	0	9.3
	30-44	911	793	703	2,093	884	545	328	250	0	6.8
	45 and over	195	141	129	378	107	44	21	5	0	6.0
1983	All ages	8,072	7,662	7,109	28,432	19,103	12,579	7,529	6,661	37	10.1
	Under 20	2,867	2,752	2,643	10,412	7,596	4,599	2,331	1,728	13	10.2
	20-24	3,111	2,916	2,624	12,764	8,987	6,227	4,045	3,699	14	11.6
	25-29	1,042	997	923	2,999	1,551	1,129	786	943	8	9.2
	30-44	846	825	775	1,899	865	587	355	286	2	7.1
	45 and over	206	172	144	358	104	37	12	5	0	5.9

Source: Office for National Statistics

This table will be updated in November/December 2017. The updated table will appear in the next edition of Annual Abstract

15.13 Duration of marriage at divorce by age of husband at marriage, 2003-2013

England and Wales   Numbers

Year of divorce	Age of husband at marriage	All durations	Duration of marriage (completed years)								
			0-2 years	0 years	1 year	2 years	3 years	4 years	5-9 years	5 years	6 years
2013	All ages	114,720	6,271	79	2,055	4,137	5,647	6,272	30,996	6,449	6,410
	Under 20	2,390	67	1	20	46	55	62	441	94	103
	20-24	25,080	852	9	273	570	830	932	4,599	946	964
	25-29	35,535	1,860	23	600	1,237	1,682	1,870	8,492	1,808	1,738
	30-44	44,049	2,725	35	887	1,803	2,497	2,762	14,505	2,946	2,967
	45 and over	7,666	767	11	275	481	583	646	2,959	655	638
2012	All ages	118,140	6,268	49	2,033	4,186	5,710	6,550	33,027	6,748	6,542
	Under 20	2,710	61	1	19	41	74	96	468	86	92
	20-24	26,783	907	4	257	646	857	1,032	5,132	1,050	985
	25-29	36,697	1,814	21	596	1,197	1,699	1,921	9,215	2,005	1,801
	30-44	44,375	2,706	16	884	1,806	2,483	2,824	15,263	2,949	3,070
	45 and over	7,575	780	7	277	496	597	677	2,949	658	594
2011	All ages	117,558	5,803	30	1,748	4,025	5,890	6,654	32,989	6,727	7,111
	Under 20	2,871	75	0	19	56	87	101	536	108	124
	20-24	27,934	813	4	213	596	910	1,034	5,343	1,092	1,135
	25-29	36,299	1,679	13	489	1,177	1,780	1,890	9,183	1,919	1,883
	30-44	43,304	2,547	6	793	1,748	2,493	2,965	15,209	3,022	3,345
	45 and over	7,150	689	7	234	448	620	664	2,718	586	624
2010	All ages	119,589	6,278	17	1,897	4,364	6,109	6,936	33,700	7,418	7,652
	Under 20	2,958	74	0	20	54	86	97	542	115	120
	20-24	29,661	909	2	251	656	951	1,145	5,437	1,240	1,247
	25-29	36,920	1,740	5	522	1,213	1,723	1,969	9,584	1,998	2,185
	30-44	43,027	2,763	8	829	1,926	2,697	3,070	15,439	3,380	3,468
	45 and over	7,023	792	2	275	515	652	655	2,698	685	632
2009	All ages	113,949	6,270	21	1,951	4,298	5,884	6,947	31,290	7,561	6,864
	Under 20	3,066	74	0	24	50	75	114	543	129	98
	20-24	29,150	883	1	246	636	894	1,193	5,281	1,305	1,221
	25-29	35,305	1,746	4	553	1,189	1,702	1,991	9,186	2,188	1,912
	30-44	39,984	2,810	9	856	1,945	2,623	3,032	13,948	3,370	3,104
	45 and over	6,444	757	7	272	478	590	617	2,332	569	529
2008	All ages	121,708	6,937	27	2,103	4,807	6,776	7,929	31,803	7,369	6,714
	Under 20	3,364	91	0	29	62	98	130	564	125	125
	20-24	32,151	1,006	4	236	766	1,090	1,319	5,161	1,281	1,132
	25-29	37,895	1,978	9	604	1,365	1,889	2,278	9,594	2,013	1,972
	30-44	41,529	3,051	9	941	2,101	3,040	3,544	14,089	3,345	2,979
	45 and over	6,769	811	5	293	513	659	658	2,395	605	506
2007	All ages	128,131	8,195	38	2,558	5,599	7,206	7,574	32,419	7,164	7,046
	Under 20	4,036	132	0	36	96	122	146	611	131	151
	20-24	35,408	1,238	4	364	870	1,214	1,275	5,430	1,198	1,153
	25-29	39,546	2,202	13	659	1,530	1,986	2,109	10,074	2,129	2,133
	30-44	42,408	3,736	12	1,171	2,553	3,279	3,351	13,960	3,163	3,085
	45 and over	6,733	887	9	328	550	605	693	2,344	543	524
2006	All ages	132,140	8,763	37	2,793	5,933	7,226	7,376	33,736	7,398	7,310
	Under 20	4,115	140	0	49	91	119	132	630	142	143
	20-24	38,096	1,400	4	411	985	1,192	1,239	5,727	1,211	1,204
	25-29	40,683	2,304	10	724	1,570	2,054	2,176	10,907	2,285	2,295
	30-44	42,417	4,002	14	1,287	2,701	3,234	3,238	14,093	3,209	3,146
	45 and over	6,829	917	9	322	586	627	591	2,379	551	522
2005	All ages	141,322	9573	49	3,181	6,343	7,520	8,175	36,064	7,920	7,697
	Under 20	4,685	175	0	53	122	159	139	634	166	134
	20-24	42,354	1,516	5	497	1,014	1,308	1,415	6,526	1,328	1,309
	25-29	43,807	2,625	18	836	1,771	2,175	2,529	11,853	2,547	2,481
	30-44	43,631	4,287	13	1,472	2,802	3,250	3,466	14,547	3,270	3,219
	45 and over	6,845	970	13	323	634	628	626	2,504	609	554
2004	All ages	152,923	10,101	42	3,345	6,714	8,319	8,894	39,681	8,840	8,375
	Under 20	5,392	178	0	52	126	146	187	680	186	136
	20-24	47,794	1,680	7	552	1,121	1,475	1,538	7,762	1,572	1,540
	25-29	48,067	2,863	7	881	1,975	2,568	2,974	13,672	2,982	2,812
	30-44	44,701	4,428	19	1,507	2,902	3,468	3,531	15,035	3,505	3,299
	45 and over	6,969	952	9	353	590	662	664	2,532	595	588
2003	All ages	153,065	10,286	42	3,283	6,961	8,276	8,882	40,497	8,968	8,639
	Under 20	5,764	191	0	58	133	157	169	690	176	148
	20-24	50,015	1,720	4	483	1,233	1,484	1,658	8,685	1,675	1,718
	25-29	47,353	3,021	5	927	2,089	2,702	2,960	13,881	3,000	2,901
	30-44	43,173	4,386	17	1,456	2,913	3,362	3,459	14,702	3,519	3,328
	45 and over	6,760	968	16	359	593	571	636	2,539	598	544

Source: Office for National Statistics

15.13 Duration of marriage at divorce by age of husband at marriage, 2003-2013

England and Wales
Numbers

Year of divorce	Age of husband at marriage	Duration of marriage (completed years)									Median duration
		7 years	8 years	9 years	10-14 years	15-19 years	20-24 years	25-29 years	30 years and over	Not stated	
2013	All ages	6,005	6,152	5,980	21,652	15,687	11,880	7,691	8,624	0	11.7
	Under 20	62	91	91	322	222	246	261	714	0	:
	20-24	902	916	871	3,203	2,999	3,707	3,214	4,744	0	
	25-29	1,661	1,649	1,636	6,582	5,829	4,464	2,628	2,128	0	
	30-44	2,818	2,924	2,850	9,981	5,925	3,173	1,489	992	0	
	45 and over	562	572	532	1,564	712	290	99	46	0	
2012	All ages	6,919	6,961	5,857	22,356	15,733	12,215	7,649	8,632	0	11.5
	Under 20	99	99	92	359	243	285	296	828	0	:
	20-24	1,095	1,056	946	3,388	3,318	4,039	3,334	4,776	0	
	25-29	1,810	1,953	1,646	7,133	5,902	4,518	2,447	2,048	0	
	30-44	3,241	3,277	2,726	10,022	5,629	3,056	1,461	931	0	
	45 and over	674	576	447	1,454	641	317	111	49	0	:
2011	All ages	7,263	6,389	5,499	22,126	15,547	12,228	7,712	8,609	0	11.5
	Under 20	116	115	73	365	226	309	358	814	0	:
	20-24	1,228	1,024	864	3,599	3,622	4,365	3,444	4,804	0	
	25-29	2,062	1,766	1,553	7,217	5,803	4,318	2,380	2,049	0	
	30-44	3,264	2,997	2,581	9,549	5,252	2,962	1,434	893	0	
	45 and over	593	487	428	1,396	644	274	96	49	0	:
2010	All ages	7,101	5,995	5,534	22,105	15,772	12,412	7,639	8,638	0	11.4
	Under 20	98	123	86	345	277	323	371	843	0	:
	20-24	1,167	904	879	3,769	4,147	4,715	3,596	4,992	0	
	25-29	2,022	1,726	1,653	7,523	5,757	4,398	2,234	1,992	0	
	30-44	3,269	2,801	2,521	9,150	5,021	2,738	1,373	776	0	
	45 and over	545	441	395	1,318	570	238	65	35	0	:
2009	All ages	5,968	5,634	5,263	20,591	15,390	11,855	7,490	8,225	7	11.4
	Under 20	106	108	102	316	296	343	429	876	0	:
	20-24	1,004	912	839	3,716	4,298	4,673	3,545	4,665	2	
	25-29	1,732	1,719	1,635	7,059	5,566	4,022	2,124	1,907	2	
	30-44	2,690	2,458	2,326	8,270	4,620	2,617	1,306	755	3	
	45 and over	436	437	361	1,230	610	200	86	22	0	:
2008	All ages	6,365	6,034	5,321	21,561	16,945	12,706	8,136	8,907	8	11.5
	Under 20	113	90	111	321	342	407	501	909	1	:
	20-24	987	922	839	4,134	4,924	5,257	3,993	5,265	2	
	25-29	1,910	1,908	1,791	7,677	6,168	4,089	2,233	1,984	5	
	30-44	2,860	2,697	2,208	8,147	4,911	2,701	1,317	729	0	
	45 and over	495	417	372	1,282	600	252	92	20	0	:
2007	All ages	6,560	6,072	5,577	23,427	18,203	13,117	8,701	9,282	7	11.7
	Under 20	139	108	82	353	425	516	661	1,070	0	:
	20-24	1,045	1,077	957	4,993	5,878	5,654	4,230	5,494	2	
	25-29	2,003	1,961	1,848	8,330	6,392	4,045	2,396	2,009	3	
	30-44	2,892	2,522	2,298	8,441	4,939	2,695	1,332	673	2	
	45 and over	481	404	392	1,310	569	207	82	36	0	:
2006	All ages	6,769	6,249	6,010	24,606	18,735	13,472	8,764	9,449	13	11.6
	Under 20	145	106	94	370	463	569	666	1,025	1	:
	20-24	1,130	1,099	1,083	5,866	6,495	5,991	4,431	5,752	3	
	25-29	2,199	2,085	2,043	8,483	6,388	4,053	2,268	2,044	6	
	30-44	2,783	2,571	2,384	8,503	4,814	2,615	1,317	598	3	
	45 and over	512	388	406	1,384	575	244	82	30	0	:
2005	All ages	7,343	6,801	6,303	26,310	20,310	14,268	9,241	9,852	9	11.6
	Under 20	116	125	93	445	575	734	761	1,062	1	:
	20-24	1,303	1,317	1,269	6,815	7,425	6,596	4,831	5,921	1	
	25-29	2,437	2,267	2,121	9,377	6,742	4,049	2,313	2,142	2	
	30-44	2,951	2,651	2,456	8,448	4,979	2,672	1,274	703	5	
	45 and over	536	441	364	1,225	589	217	62	24	0	:
2004	All ages	7,900	7,683	6,883	28,984	21,515	15,431	9,705	10,293	0	11.5
	Under 20	127	120	111	596	710	894	849	1,152	0	:
	20-24	1,543	1,585	1,522	8,361	8,403	7,232	5,081	6,262	0	
	25-29	2,699	2,699	2,480	10,158	6,893	4,251	2,510	2,178	0	
	30-44	3,016	2,851	2,364	8,605	4,924	2,838	1,200	672	0	
	45 and over	515	428	406	1,264	585	216	65	29	0	:
2003	All ages	8,228	7,686	6,976	29,751	20,863	14,974	9,627	9,907	2	11.3
	Under 20	127	122	117	705	798	1,064	902	1,087	1	:
	20-24	1,751	1,760	1,781	9,169	8,627	7,216	5,204	6,251	1	
	25-29	2,781	2,745	2,454	10,243	6,314	3,938	2,330	1,964	0	
	30-44	3,015	2,616	2,224	8,378	4,617	2,573	1,119	577	0	
	45 and over	554	443	400	1,256	507	183	72	28	0	:

Source: Office for National Statistics

This table will be updated in November/December 2017. The updated table will appear in the next edition of Annual Abstract

15.14 Live births by administrative area of usual residence, numbers, sex, General Fertility Rates and Total Fertility Rates, 2015

England and Wales: regions (within England), unitary authorities, counties, districts, London Boroughs, local health boards (within Wales)

Area of usual residence	Total Live Births	Male	Female	General Fertility Rate (GFR)[2]	Total Fertility Rate (TFR)[3]
UNITED KINGDOM	777,165	398,983	378,182	61.7	1.80
ENGLAND, WALES AND ELSEWHERE	697,852	358,136	339,716	62.3	1.82
ENGLAND	664,399	341,098	323,301	62.5	1.82
NORTH EAST	28,400	14,664	13,736	57.9	1.71
County Durham	5,355	2,806	2,549	56.6	1.70
Darlington	1,217	631	586	63.2	1.94
Hartlepool	1,080	526	554	63.3	1.87
Middlesbrough	1,925	1,001	924	69.5	2.01
Northumberland	2,832	1,446	1,386	56.6	1.75
Redcar and Cleveland	1,431	735	696	61.2	1.82
Stockton-on-Tees	2,274	1,159	1,115	62.1	1.82
Tyne and Wear (Met County)	12,286	6,360	5,926	55.4	1.63
Gateshead	2,214	1,150	1,064	58.2	1.70
Newcastle upon Tyne	3,329	1,707	1,622	49.7	1.55
North Tyneside	2,207	1,140	1,067	59.2	1.77
South Tyneside	1,647	882	765	61.2	1.81
Sunderland	2,889	1,481	1,408	55.0	1.62
NORTH WEST	85,838	44,254	41,584	62.9	1.86
Blackburn with Darwen	2,115	1,098	1,017	73.2	2.18
Blackpool	1,665	881	784	67.8	2.03
Cheshire East	3,848	2,001	1,847	61.6	1.94
Cheshire West and Chester	3,558	1,837	1,721	59.6	1.83
Halton	1,489	740	749	62.2	1.86
Warrington	2,395	1,247	1,148	62.7	1.88
Cumbria	4,789	2,479	2,310	59.7	1.86
Allerdale	893	456	437	58.5	1.84
Barrow-in-Furness	770	390	380	66.3	2.04
Carlisle	1,206	645	561	62.2	1.87
Copeland	718	346	372	62.9	1.92
Eden	395	216	179	51.1	1.64
South Lakeland	807	426	381	54.5	1.77
Greater Manchester (Met County)	36,644	18,799	17,845	65.3	1.88
Bolton	3,788	1,880	1,908	70.6	2.09
Bury	2,356	1,255	1,101	67.4	2.00
Manchester	8,051	4,146	3,905	58.9	1.69
Oldham	3,336	1,742	1,594	75.0	2.21
Rochdale	2,894	1,481	1,413	69.5	2.05
Salford	3,558	1,753	1,805	67.8	1.87
Stockport	3,378	1,693	1,685	64.9	1.93
Tameside	2,874	1,463	1,411	68.4	2.00
Trafford	2,828	1,476	1,352	64.7	1.92
Wigan	3,581	1,910	1,671	60.3	1.81
Lancashire	13,202	6,717	6,485	61.2	1.85
Burnley	1,197	580	617	73.6	2.14
Chorley	1,269	636	633	63.2	1.91
Fylde	633	328	305	57.4	1.80
Hyndburn	1,077	528	549	71.6	2.11
Lancaster	1,447	725	722	50.9	1.61
Pendle	1,261	636	625	75.5	2.18
Preston	1,879	987	892	63.0	1.87
Ribble Valley	426	217	209	46.9	1.57
Rossendale	763	382	381	60.0	1.84
South Ribble	1,208	627	581	62.2	1.90
West Lancashire	1,076	553	523	52.8	1.77
Wyre	966	518	448	58.1	1.81
Merseyside (Met County)	16,133	8,455	7,678	59.7	1.76
Knowsley	1,930	1,042	888	67.2	1.96
Liverpool	5,883	3,065	2,818	54.4	1.60
Sefton	2,777	1,456	1,321	60.9	1.86
St. Helens	1,980	1,077	903	61.4	1.83
Wirral	3,563	1,815	1,748	63.9	1.94
YORKSHIRE AND THE HUMBER	63,858	32,720	31,138	61.9	1.83
East Riding of Yorkshire	2,900	1,516	1,384	55.9	1.83
Kingston upon Hull, City of	3,579	1,817	1,762	66.1	1.83
North East Lincolnshire	1,918	980	938	67.0	1.96
North Lincolnshire	1,872	927	945	64.0	1.92
York	2,023	1,072	951	45.0	1.44

15.14 Live births by administrative area of usual residence, numbers, sex, General Fertility Rates and Total Fertility Rates, 2015

England and Wales: regions (within England), unitary authorities, counties, districts, London Boroughs, local health boards (within Wales)

Area of usual residence	Total Live Births	Male	Female	General Fertility Rate (GFR)[2]	Total Fertility Rate (TFR)[3]
North Yorkshire	**5,643**	**2,922**	**2,721**	**60.7**	**1.93**
Craven	464	248	216	57.2	1.90
Hambleton	764	376	388	57.4	1.85
Harrogate	1,494	791	703	60.6	1.95
Richmondshire	540	285	255	69.1	2.13
Ryedale	476	248	228	61.3	2.00
Scarborough	976	501	475	59.2	1.81
Selby	929	473	456	62.7	1.94
South Yorkshire (Met County)	**16,017**	**8,156**	**7,861**	**59.4**	**1.74**
Barnsley	2,811	1,412	1,399	64.3	1.92
Doncaster	3,562	1,820	1,742	64.8	1.91
Rotherham	3,062	1,549	1,513	64.6	1.94
Sheffield	6,582	3,375	3,207	53.3	1.62
West Yorkshire (Met County)	**29,906**	**15,330**	**14,576**	**64.9**	**1.91**
Bradford	7,931	4,026	3,905	74.8	2.20
Calderdale	2,433	1,267	1,166	64.0	1.95
Kirklees	5,375	2,755	2,620	64.2	1.92
Leeds	10,182	5,211	4,971	59.5	1.77
Wakefield	3,985	2,071	1,914	64.5	1.91
EAST MIDLANDS	**53,641**	**27,511**	**26,130**	**61.3**	**1.84**
Derby	**3,389**	**1,751**	**1,638**	**66.1**	**1.91**
Leicester	**5,156**	**2,607**	**2,549**	**64.8**	**1.87**
Nottingham	**4,308**	**2,249**	**2,059**	**54.8**	**1.72**
Rutland	**340**	**179**	**161**	**59.7**	**2.05**
Derbyshire	**7,861**	**3,998**	**3,863**	**58.0**	**1.79**
Amber Valley	1,172	609	563	54.5	1.69
Bolsover	903	459	444	64.7	1.96
Chesterfield	1,097	570	527	58.4	1.77
Derbyshire Dales	547	264	283	54.9	1.85
Erewash	1,300	676	624	61.9	1.85
High Peak	842	433	409	53.5	1.68
North East Derbyshire	883	448	435	54.8	1.73
South Derbyshire	1,117	539	578	60.6	1.87
Leicestershire	**6,962**	**3,570**	**3,392**	**57.3**	**1.76**
Blaby	1,057	553	504	61.6	1.85
Charnwood	1,875	961	914	53.2	1.65
Harborough	875	459	416	60.8	1.99
Hinckley and Bosworth	1,111	534	577	59.3	1.80
Melton	457	242	215	54.5	1.72
North West Leicestershire	1,026	540	486	59.2	1.83
Oadby and Wigston	561	281	280	55.0	1.79
Lincolnshire	**7,773**	**3,980**	**3,793**	**61.8**	**1.89**
Boston	816	444	372	68.6	2.01
East Lindsey	1,211	615	596	62.8	1.98
Lincoln	1,287	688	599	56.2	1.70
North Kesteven	1,124	542	582	61.3	1.94
South Holland	957	473	484	63.0	1.94
South Kesteven	1,477	764	713	63.1	1.99
West Lindsey	901	454	447	61.1	1.97
Northamptonshire	**9,054**	**4,629**	**4,425**	**67.1**	**2.03**
Corby	1,004	543	461	74.9	2.16
Daventry	763	387	376	58.9	1.91
East Northamptonshire	901	462	439	58.2	1.87
Kettering	1,272	655	617	70.8	2.18
Northampton	3,249	1,634	1,615	70.0	2.01
South Northamptonshire	886	463	423	59.9	1.93
Wellingborough	979	485	494	70.3	2.18
Nottinghamshire	**8,798**	**4,548**	**4,250**	**61.6**	**1.87**
Ashfield	1,488	773	715	64.9	1.94
Bassetlaw	1,231	647	584	64.2	2.03
Broxtowe	1,196	618	578	58.5	1.73
Gedling	1,305	675	630	62.7	1.90
Mansfield	1,284	641	643	65.6	1.91
Newark and Sherwood	1,225	631	594	61.5	1.92
Rushcliffe	1,069	563	506	53.5	1.65
WEST MIDLANDS	**69,806**	**36,014**	**33,792**	**63.9**	**1.90**
Herefordshire, County of	**1,733**	**918**	**815**	**57.7**	**1.76**
Shropshire	**2,795**	**1,486**	**1,309**	**56.9**	**1.80**
Stoke-on-Trent	**3,391**	**1,758**	**1,633**	**69.0**	**1.98**
Telford and Wrekin	**2,075**	**1,054**	**1,021**	**64.1**	**1.93**

15.14 Live births by administrative area of usual residence, numbers, sex, General Fertility Rates and Total Fertility Rates, 2015

England and Wales: regions (within England), unitary authorities, counties, districts, London Boroughs, local health boards (within Wales)

Area of usual residence	Total Live Births	Male	Female	General Fertility Rate (GFR)[2]	Total Fertility Rate (TFR)[3]
Staffordshire	**8,508**	**4,372**	**4,136**	**57.1**	**1.75**
Cannock Chase	1,056	548	508	57.6	1.73
East Staffordshire	1,449	767	682	70.8	2.14
Lichfield	910	458	452	54.4	1.71
Newcastle-under-Lyme	1,244	641	603	52.0	1.58
South Staffordshire	915	470	445	52.6	1.69
Stafford	1,228	625	603	55.8	1.72
Staffordshire Moorlands	798	408	390	52.2	1.69
Tamworth	908	455	453	61.2	1.83
Warwickshire	**6,086**	**3,137**	**2,949**	**61.8**	**1.88**
North Warwickshire	664	356	308	62.7	1.95
Nuneaton and Bedworth	1,589	855	734	68.0	2.02
Rugby	1,266	642	624	67.6	2.05
Stratford-on-Avon	1,103	576	527	59.5	1.92
Warwick	1,464	708	756	53.6	1.65
West Midlands (Met County)	**39,197**	**20,148**	**19,049**	**67.0**	**1.95**
Birmingham	16,828	8,677	8,151	68.1	1.99
Coventry	4,517	2,325	2,192	58.7	1.69
Dudley	3,672	1,876	1,796	64.1	1.92
Sandwell	4,786	2,449	2,337	74.5	2.15
Solihull	2,259	1,150	1,109	61.9	1.92
Walsall	3,752	1,939	1,813	71.3	2.09
Wolverhampton	3,383	1,732	1,651	67.5	1.96
Worcestershire	**6,021**	**3,141**	**2,880**	**60.6**	**1.86**
Bromsgrove	900	467	433	58.0	1.82
Malvern Hills	563	292	271	51.4	1.69
Redditch	1,080	580	500	66.7	1.96
Worcester	1,279	673	606	60.0	1.79
Wychavon	1,110	573	537	58.5	1.87
Wyre Forest	1,089	556	533	66.5	2.06
EAST	**72,505**	**37,128**	**35,377**	**64.7**	**1.92**
Bedford	**2,158**	**1,116**	**1,042**	**68.0**	**2.02**
Central Bedfordshire	**3,303**	**1,728**	**1,575**	**64.8**	**1.91**
Luton	**3,553**	**1,808**	**1,745**	**76.6**	**2.13**
Peterborough	**3,170**	**1,648**	**1,522**	**81.1**	**2.34**
Southend-on-Sea	**2,233**	**1,128**	**1,105**	**66.5**	**1.99**
Thurrock	**2,505**	**1,328**	**1,177**	**72.7**	**2.12**
Cambridgeshire	**7,469**	**3,813**	**3,656**	**60.3**	**1.80**
Cambridge	1,447	734	713	44.2	1.45
East Cambridgeshire	1,042	526	516	66.7	2.02
Fenland	1,175	641	534	69.4	2.09
Huntingdonshire	2,033	1,040	993	65.3	1.97
South Cambridgeshire	1,772	872	900	64.6	1.95
Essex	**16,335**	**8,440**	**7,895**	**63.1**	**1.91**
Basildon	2,457	1,263	1,194	69.6	2.06
Braintree	1,607	848	759	60.0	1.83
Brentwood	890	464	426	65.5	1.95
Castle Point	848	437	411	58.7	1.85
Chelmsford	1,876	989	887	58.5	1.72
Colchester	2,242	1,129	1,113	60.5	1.78
Epping Forest	1,627	823	804	68.1	2.00
Harlow	1,222	668	554	71.5	2.05
Maldon	575	298	277	59.7	1.97
Rochford	753	371	382	53.3	1.74
Tendring	1,340	688	652	66.0	2.09
Uttlesford	898	462	436	62.4	1.97
Hertfordshire	**14,699**	**7,411**	**7,288**	**64.5**	**1.89**
Broxbourne	1,249	635	614	67.2	1.96
Dacorum	1,945	1,023	922	67.6	1.98
East Hertfordshire	1,594	805	789	59.3	1.81
Hertsmere	1,347	666	681	68.6	2.01
North Hertfordshire	1,564	810	754	63.8	1.90
St Albans	1,851	909	942	66.8	1.90
Stevenage	1,168	545	623	67.2	1.91
Three Rivers	1,079	532	547	63.6	1.89
Watford	1,505	782	723	70.4	1.92
Welwyn Hatfield	1,397	704	693	53.7	1.64
Norfolk	**9,052**	**4,610**	**4,442**	**60.0**	**1.80**
Breckland	1,386	725	661	63.4	1.93
Broadland	1,141	579	562	57.3	1.84
Great Yarmouth	1,070	535	535	65.5	1.97

15.14 Live births by administrative area of usual residence, numbers, sex, General Fertility Rates and Total Fertility Rates, 2015

England and Wales: regions (within England), unitary authorities, counties, districts, London Boroughs, local health boards (within Wales)

Area of usual residence	Total Live Births	Male	Female	General Fertility Rate (GFR)[2]	Total Fertility Rate (TFR)[3]
King's Lynn and West Norfolk	1,641	826	815	68.4	2.08
North Norfolk	774	403	371	56.5	1.79
Norwich	1,711	887	824	51.0	1.46
South Norfolk	1,329	655	674	61.9	1.95
Suffolk	**8,028**	**4,098**	**3,930**	**65.0**	**1.98**
Babergh	819	429	390	61.0	1.98
Forest Heath	991	481	510	80.8	2.22
Ipswich	1,978	1,013	965	72.2	2.06
Mid Suffolk	879	459	420	56.2	1.80
St Edmundsbury	1,174	618	556	62.7	1.90
Suffolk Coastal	1,060	543	517	59.2	2.01
Waveney	1,127	555	572	61.9	1.89
LONDON	**129,615**	**66,407**	**63,208**	**63.9**	**1.73**
Inner London	**51,017**	**26,253**	**24,764**	**56.3**	**1.51**
Camden	2,699	1,408	1,291	43.8	1.22
City of London	69	30	39	38.4	1.00
Hackney	4,500	2,292	2,208	60.9	1.69
Hammersmith and Fulham	2,345	1,169	1,176	50.5	1.35
Haringey	4,108	2,089	2,019	61.9	1.69
Islington	2,939	1,507	1,432	45.6	1.29
Kensington and Chelsea	1,805	931	874	51.0	1.32
Lambeth	4,620	2,413	2,207	52.2	1.44
Lewisham	4,814	2,495	2,319	65.5	1.78
Newham	6,226	3,211	3,015	77.7	2.08
Southwark	4,587	2,381	2,206	55.5	1.51
Tower Hamlets	4,560	2,392	2,168	54.2	1.40
Wandsworth	5,038	2,527	2,511	55.8	1.44
Westminster	2,707	1,408	1,299	46.9	1.22
Outer London	**78,598**	**40,154**	**38,444**	**70.2**	**1.96**
Barking and Dagenham	3,850	1,948	1,902	84.8	2.42
Barnet	5,261	2,685	2,576	64.5	1.77
Bexley	3,162	1,603	1,559	65.4	1.91
Brent	5,204	2,634	2,570	72.4	1.99
Bromley	4,098	2,115	1,983	64.3	1.84
Croydon	5,833	2,975	2,858	72.7	2.08
Ealing	5,210	2,718	2,492	69.2	1.90
Enfield	5,027	2,545	2,482	70.9	2.01
Greenwich	4,644	2,353	2,291	72.7	2.00
Harrow	3,601	1,777	1,824	72.0	2.01
Havering	3,275	1,685	1,590	67.4	1.95
Hillingdon	4,394	2,281	2,113	68.1	1.91
Hounslow	4,455	2,263	2,192	73.9	1.99
Kingston upon Thames	2,350	1,212	1,138	59.0	1.66
Merton	3,412	1,734	1,678	73.2	1.93
Redbridge	4,798	2,449	2,349	73.4	2.02
Richmond upon Thames	2,609	1,323	1,286	65.2	1.74
Sutton	2,764	1,437	1,327	66.9	1.90
Waltham Forest	4,651	2,417	2,234	74.4	2.02
SOUTH EAST	**102,703**	**52,550**	**50,153**	**61.7**	**1.86**
Bracknell Forest	**1,488**	**795**	**693**	**61.8**	**1.81**
Brighton and Hove	**2,952**	**1,479**	**1,473**	**43.7**	**1.36**
Isle of Wight	**1,296**	**677**	**619**	**62.3**	**1.98**
Medway	**3,609**	**1,844**	**1,765**	**65.2**	**1.92**
Milton Keynes	**3,882**	**1,996**	**1,886**	**72.3**	**2.10**
Portsmouth	**2,686**	**1,394**	**1,292**	**57.9**	**1.70**
Reading	**2,521**	**1,328**	**1,193**	**66.8**	**1.86**
Slough	**2,590**	**1,347**	**1,243**	**79.6**	**2.23**
Southampton	**3,305**	**1,719**	**1,586**	**56.3**	**1.64**
West Berkshire	**1,721**	**863**	**858**	**62.3**	**1.97**
Windsor and Maidenhead	**1,617**	**851**	**766**	**60.4**	**1.76**
Wokingham	**1,787**	**916**	**871**	**61.4**	**1.86**
Buckinghamshire	**6,140**	**3,116**	**3,024**	**64.3**	**1.95**
Aylesbury Vale	2,330	1,178	1,152	66.2	1.98
Chiltern	872	419	453	57.7	1.89
South Bucks	744	381	363	63.9	1.92
Wycombe	2,194	1,138	1,056	65.5	1.97
East Sussex	**5,046**	**2,538**	**2,508**	**58.7**	**1.85**
Eastbourne	1,070	508	562	60.6	1.83
Hastings	1,099	552	547	66.1	1.98
Lewes	877	456	421	56.0	1.78
Rother	677	361	316	54.7	1.77
Wealden	1,323	661	662	56.1	1.84

15.14 Live births by administrative area of usual residence, numbers, sex, General Fertility Rates and Total Fertility Rates, 2015

England and Wales: regions (within England), unitary authorities, counties, districts, London Boroughs, local health boards (within Wales)

Area of usual residence	Total Live Births	Male	Female	General Fertility Rate (GFR)[2]	Total Fertility Rate (TFR)[3]
Hampshire	**14,357**	**7,247**	**7,110**	**60.9**	**1.89**
Basingstoke and Deane	2,166	1,083	1,083	65.7	1.96
East Hampshire	1,043	540	503	55.2	1.83
Eastleigh	1,468	719	749	61.4	1.83
Fareham	1,094	534	560	57.9	1.83
Gosport	977	503	474	64.2	1.94
Hart	1,000	516	484	62.5	1.98
Havant	1,309	668	641	63.7	1.96
New Forest	1,438	755	683	54.1	1.74
Rushmoor	1,334	657	677	66.6	1.93
Test Valley	1,333	687	646	65.4	2.06
Winchester	1,195	585	610	53.7	1.79
Kent	**17,297**	**8,869**	**8,428**	**62.4**	**1.91**
Ashford	1,523	767	756	67.6	2.09
Canterbury	1,375	718	657	41.1	1.47
Dartford	1,500	778	722	69.8	1.96
Dover	1,130	561	569	61.3	1.91
Gravesham	1,410	700	710	68.6	2.03
Maidstone	2,006	1,038	968	66.4	1.97
Sevenoaks	1,300	654	646	65.2	2.05
Shepway	1,056	540	516	59.3	1.82
Swale	1,707	878	829	66.7	2.04
Thanet	1,677	864	813	70.0	2.13
Tonbridge and Malling	1,358	668	690	59.7	1.90
Tunbridge Wells	1,255	703	552	61.2	1.93
Oxfordshire	**7,893**	**4,085**	**3,808**	**59.7**	**1.78**
Cherwell	1,848	956	892	67.9	2.02
Oxford	1,899	1,002	897	45.7	1.48
South Oxfordshire	1,544	798	746	67.2	2.08
Vale of White Horse	1,413	707	706	64.4	1.94
West Oxfordshire	1,189	622	567	64.1	1.96
Surrey	**13,542**	**6,933**	**6,609**	**63.0**	**1.91**
Elmbridge	1,755	849	906	76.5	2.31
Epsom and Ewell	958	481	477	63.0	1.95
Guildford	1,513	778	735	50.0	1.58
Mole Valley	802	423	379	58.6	1.91
Reigate and Banstead	1,743	892	851	65.2	1.90
Runnymede	964	488	476	52.1	1.68
Spelthorne	1,291	638	653	70.0	2.02
Surrey Heath	972	512	460	63.5	1.98
Tandridge	964	537	427	64.5	2.01
Waverley	1,282	669	613	63.1	2.05
Woking	1,298	666	632	69.3	2.04
West Sussex	**8,974**	**4,553**	**4,421**	**62.9**	**1.92**
Adur	724	376	348	67.2	2.05
Arun	1,517	753	764	63.4	1.95
Chichester	1,051	509	542	58.5	1.90
Crawley	1,642	873	769	69.7	1.95
Horsham	1,264	661	603	57.2	1.85
Mid Sussex	1,593	815	778	62.7	1.91
Worthing	1,183	566	617	62.2	1.89
SOUTH WEST	**58,033**	**29,850**	**28,183**	**60.0**	**1.82**
Bath and North East Somerset	**1,808**	**957**	**851**	**48.4**	**1.65**
Bournemouth	**2,264**	**1,124**	**1,140**	**55.1**	**1.61**
Bristol, City of	**6,263**	**3,174**	**3,089**	**58.6**	**1.69**
Cornwall and Isles of Scilly [5]	**5,412**	**2,767**	**2,645**	**60.2**	**1.91**
North Somerset	**2,234**	**1,154**	**1,080**	**64.7**	**1.99**
Plymouth	**3,160**	**1,625**	**1,535**	**59.6**	**1.76**
Poole	**1,568**	**794**	**774**	**60.1**	**1.80**
South Gloucestershire	**3,161**	**1,631**	**1,530**	**61.8**	**1.85**
Swindon	**2,847**	**1,502**	**1,345**	**66.6**	**1.97**
Torbay	**1,380**	**689**	**691**	**66.5**	**2.05**
Wiltshire	**5,050**	**2,596**	**2,454**	**62.0**	**1.98**
Devon	**7,095**	**3,675**	**3,420**	**56.5**	**1.76**
East Devon	1,180	595	585	61.6	1.99
Exeter	1,322	696	626	43.6	1.40
Mid Devon	803	421	382	62.6	1.98
North Devon	868	434	434	59.4	1.85
South Hams	677	362	315	58.2	1.88
Teignbridge	1,177	598	579	60.3	1.88
Torridge	614	332	282	62.8	1.99
West Devon	454	237	217	58.5	1.89
Dorset	**3,470**	**1,782**	**1,688**	**57.8**	**1.86**

15.14 Live births by administrative area of usual residence, numbers, sex, General Fertility Rates and Total Fertility Rates, 2015

England and Wales: regions (within England), unitary authorities, counties, districts, London Boroughs, local health boards (within Wales)

Area of usual residence	Total Live Births	Male	Female	General Fertility Rate (GFR)[2]	Total Fertility Rate (TFR)[3]
Christchurch	385	203	182	56.5	1.82
East Dorset	652	346	306	54.5	1.80
North Dorset	640	321	319	59.5	1.91
Purbeck	387	196	191	58.2	1.85
West Dorset	748	387	361	54.6	1.80
Weymouth and Portland	658	329	329	64.7	2.02
Gloucestershire	**6,697**	**3,454**	**3,243**	**61.8**	**1.89**
Cheltenham	1,247	641	606	52.4	1.55
Cotswold	732	380	352	56.7	1.88
Forest of Dean	786	400	386	58.8	1.94
Gloucester	1,796	919	877	71.8	2.07
Stroud	1,166	595	571	62.1	1.99
Tewkesbury	970	519	451	67.0	2.02
Somerset	**5,624**	**2,926**	**2,698**	**64.0**	**2.00**
Mendip	1,171	576	595	64.1	2.08
Sedgemoor	1,288	694	594	65.8	2.05
South Somerset	1,674	876	798	64.3	2.00
Taunton Deane	1,222	647	575	62.4	1.91
West Somerset	269	133	136	61.4	1.89
WALES	**33,279**	**16,943**	**16,336**	**59.1**	**1.77**
Isle of Anglesey	692	338	354	63.4	1.92
Gwynedd	1,156	582	574	53.1	1.70
Conwy	1,117	578	539	64.1	2.00
Denbighshire	1,045	520	525	69.0	2.16
Flintshire	1,577	809	768	58.7	1.79
Wrexham	1,499	779	720	61.1	1.81
Powys	1,123	581	542	57.8	1.86
Ceredigion	632	314	318	48.2	1.75
Pembrokeshire	1,180	608	572	61.0	1.90
Carmarthenshire	1,855	967	888	60.7	1.85
Swansea	2,524	1,290	1,234	54.8	1.65
Neath Port Talbot	1,488	743	745	59.4	1.79
Bridgend	1,503	775	728	59.9	1.82
The Vale of Glamorgan	1,333	687	646	60.5	1.91
Cardiff	4,540	2,279	2,261	54.6	1.64
Rhondda, Cynon, Taff	2,692	1,348	1,344	59.3	1.74
Merthyr Tydfil	749	392	357	66.1	1.90
Caerphilly	2,050	1,061	989	60.2	1.79
Blaenau Gwent	757	372	385	58.3	1.69
Torfaen	1,004	512	492	59.7	1.76
Monmouthshire	782	406	376	55.8	1.84
Newport	1,981	1,002	979	69.5	2.03
Betsi Cadwaladr University	7,086	3,606	3,480	60.7	1.85
Powys Teaching	1,123	581	542	57.8	1.86
Hywel Dda	3,667	1,889	1,778	58.2	1.81
Abertawe Bro Morgannwg University	5,515	2,808	2,707	57.3	1.71
Cwm Taf	3,441	1,740	1,701	60.7	1.77
Aneurin Bevan	6,574	3,353	3,221	61.8	1.84
Cardiff and Vale University	5,873	2,966	2,907	55.8	1.68
Usual residence outside England and Wales where birth occurred in England and Wales	**174**	**95**	**79**	:	:

Source: Office for National Statistics (ONS)

A birth to a mother whose usual residence is outside England and Wales is assigned to the country of residence. These births are included in total figures for "England, Wales and elsewhere " but are excluded from any sub-divisions of England and Wales.
The England and Wales and elsewhere figures correspond to figures published at the national level for England and Wales not based on area of usual residence.

The Human Fertilisation and Embryology Act (HFEA) 2008 contained provisions enabling two females in a same sex couple to register a birth from 1 September 2009 onwards. Due to the small numbers, births registered to a same sex couple in a marriage/civil partnership (881 in 2015) are included with marital births while births registered to a same sex couple outside a marriage/civil partnership (339 in 2015) are included with births outside marriage.

Births registered under HFEA are reported only for England and Wales and no sub division thereof.

1 Live births per 1,000 population (all persons and all ages). This has been calculated using the mid-2015 population estimates.
2 The General Fertility Rate (GFR) is the number of live births per 1,000 women aged 15 to 44. The GFRs have been calculated using the mid-2015 population estimates.
3 The Total Fertility Rate (TFR) is the average number of live children that a group of women would bear if they experienced the age-specific fertility rates of the calendar year in question throughout their childbearing lifespan.
 The national TFRs have been calculated using the number of live births by single year of age and the mid-2015 population estimates.
 The sub-national TFRs have been calculated using the number of live births by five year age groups and the mid-2015 population estimates.
4 Maternities per 1,000 women aged 15 to 44. A maternity is a pregnancy resulting in the birth of one or more children, including stillbirths.
5 To preserve confidentiality, counts for Isles of Scilly have been combined with Cornwall

: denotes not available

15.15 Live births by age of mother and registration type[1], 1982-2013

England and Wales

Year	Type of Registration		Age of mother at birth						
		All ages	Under 20	20-24	25-29	30-34	35-39	40-44	45 and over
		Numbers of births							
2013	All	698,512	29,136	119,719	196,693	212,306	111,500	27,148	2,010
	Within Marriage/Civil Partnership[1]	367,618	1,272	25,794	102,106	144,376	76,046	16,783	1,241
	Outside Marriage/Civil Partnership[1]	330,894	27,864	93,925	94,587	67,930	35,454	10,365	769
	Joint Registrations same address	218,049	11,220	56,805	66,103	49,922	26,234	7,282	483
	Joint Registrations different address	73,546	10,628	25,440	18,908	11,195	5,499	1,736	140
	Sole Registrations	39,299	6,016	11,680	9,576	6,813	3,721	1,347	146
2012	All	729,674	33,815	132,456	202,370	216,242	114,797	28,019	1,975
	Within Marriage/Civil Partnership[1]	383,189	1,295	29,627	106,555	148,403	78,689	17,380	1,240
	Outside Marriage/Civil Partnership[1]	346,485	32,520	102,829	95,815	67,839	36,108	10,639	735
	Joint Registrations same address	227,337	13,326	62,151	67,031	50,094	26,731	7,528	476
	Joint Registrations different address	77,269	12,327	27,867	18,759	10,872	5,529	1,809	106
	Sole Registrations	41,879	6,867	12,811	10,025	6,873	3,848	1,302	153
2011	All	723,913	36,435	134,946	200,587	207,151	115,444	27,518	1,832
	Within Marriage/Civil Partnership[1]	382,574	1,410	31,785	107,383	143,519	79,951	17,388	1,138
	Outside Marriage/Civil Partnership[1]	341,339	35,025	103,161	93,204	63,632	35,493	10,130	694
	Joint Registrations same address	226,057	14,600	63,287	66,102	47,706	26,688	7,213	461
	Joint Registrations different address	73,464	12,960	26,826	17,379	9,489	5,093	1,603	114
	Sole Registrations	41,818	7,465	13,048	9,723	6,437	3,712	1,314	119
2010	All	723,165	40,591	137,312	199,233	202,457	115,841	25,973	1,758
	Within Marriage/Civil Partnership[1]	384,375	1,684	33,955	108,465	141,873	80,846	16,404	1,148
	Outside Marriage/Civil Partnership[1]	338,790	38,907	103,357	90,768	60,584	34,995	9,569	610
	Joint Registrations same address	224,001	16,401	63,816	64,656	45,498	26,453	6,769	408
	Joint Registrations different address	72,297	14,352	26,184	16,393	8,838	4,903	1,525	102
	Sole Registrations	42,492	8,154	13,357	9,719	6,248	3,639	1,275	100
2009	All	706,248	43,243	136,012	194,129	191,600	114,288	25,357	1,619
	Within Marriage/Civil Partnership[1]	380,069	2,334	35,920	108,499	135,802	80,156	16,318	1,040
	Outside Marriage/Civil Partnership[1]	326,179	40,909	100,092	85,630	55,798	34,132	9,039	579
	Joint Registrations same address	214,189	17,200	61,813	60,876	41,831	25,637	6,444	388
	Joint Registrations different address	68,251	14,778	24,376	14,811	7,991	4,790	1,420	85
	Sole Registrations	43,739	8,931	13,903	9,943	5,976	3,705	1,175	106
2008	All	708,711	44,691	135,971	192,960	192,450	116,220	24,991	1,428
	Within Marriage	387,930	2,739	38,239	110,353	138,066	81,602	15,991	940
	Outside Marriage	320,781	41,952	97,732	82,607	54,384	34,618	9,000	488
	Joint Registrations same address	210,076	17,231	59,913	59,104	41,178	26,036	6,289	325
	Joint Registrations different address	65,241	15,161	23,102	13,543	7,257	4,662	1,441	75
	Sole Registrations	45,464	9,560	14,717	9,960	5,949	3,920	1,270	88
2007	All	690,013	44,805	130,784	182,570	191,124	115,380	24,041	1,309
	Within Marriage	384,463	3,087	38,859	106,603	138,157	81,399	15,484	874
	Outside Marriage	305,550	41,718	91,925	75,967	52,967	33,981	8,557	435
	Joint Registrations same address	198,470	17,036	55,904	54,040	39,783	25,383	6,050	274
	Joint Registrations different address	61,379	14,714	21,415	12,204	7,024	4,587	1,359	76
	Sole Registrations	45,701	9,968	14,606	9,723	6,160	4,011	1,148	85
2006	All	669,601	45,509	127,828	172,642	189,407	110,509	22,512	1,194
	Within Marriage	378,225	3,199	40,126	103,348	137,996	78,269	14,511	776
	Outside Marriage	291,376	42,310	87,702	69,294	51,411	32,240	8,001	418
	Joint Registrations same address	185,461	17,061	52,162	48,474	38,133	23,897	5,469	265
	Joint Registrations different address	60,460	14,870	20,755	11,651	7,159	4,578	1,375	72
	Sole Registrations	45,455	10,379	14,785	9,169	6,119	3,765	1,157	81

15.15 Live births by age of mother and registration type[1], 1982-2013

England and Wales

Year	Type of Registration		Age of mother at birth						
		All ages	Under 20	20-24	25-29	30-34	35-39	40-44	45 and over
		Numbers of births							
2005	All	645,835	44,830	122,145	164,348	188,153	104,113	21,155	1,091
	Within Marriage	369,330	3,654	40,010	99,957	137,401	73,810	13,760	738
	Outside Marriage	276,505	41,176	82,135	64,391	50,752	30,303	7,395	353
	Joint Registrations same address	175,555	16,316	48,755	45,165	37,764	22,265	5,057	233
	Joint Registrations different address	55,780	14,108	18,909	10,320	6,801	4,289	1,287	66
	Sole Registrations	45,170	10,752	14,471	8,906	6,187	3,749	1,051	54
2004	All	639,721	45,094	121,072	159,984	190,550	102,228	19,884	909
	Within Marriage	369,997	4,063	41,285	98,539	139,838	72,555	13,098	619
	Outside Marriage	269,724	41,031	79,787	61,445	50,712	29,673	6,786	290
	Joint Registrations same address	171,498	16,262	47,793	43,038	37,820	21,758	4,648	179
	Joint Registrations different address	52,854	13,608	17,628	9,620	6,713	4,133	1,096	56
	Sole Registrations	45,372	11,161	14,366	8,787	6,179	3,782	1,042	55
2003	All	621,469	44,236	116,622	156,931	187,214	97,386	18,205	875
	Within Marriage	364,244	4,338	40,887	98,694	138,002	69,595	12,113	615
	Outside Marriage	257,225	39,898	75,735	58,237	49,212	27,791	6,092	260
	Joint Registrations same address	163,374	16,000	45,225	40,867	36,630	20,335	4,151	166
	Joint Registrations different address	48,976	12,706	16,076	8,815	6,488	3,831	1,014	46
	Sole Registrations	44,875	11,192	14,434	8,555	6,094	3,625	927	48
2002	All	596,122	43,467	110,959	153,379	180,532	90,449	16,441	895
	Within Marriage	354,090	4,582	40,712	97,583	134,093	65,369	11,110	641
	Outside Marriage	242,032	38,885	70,247	55,796	46,439	25,080	5,331	254
	Joint Registrations same address	154,086	15,824	42,315	39,554	34,326	18,236	3,656	175
	Joint Registrations different address	44,817	11,832	14,333	8,109	6,164	3,471	866	42
	Sole Registrations	43,129	11,229	13,599	8,133	5,949	3,373	809	37
2001	All	594,634	44,189	108,844	159,926	178,920	86,495	15,499	761
	Within Marriage	356,548	4,640	40,736	103,131	133,710	63,202	10,582	547
	Outside Marriage	238,086	39,549	68,108	56,795	45,210	23,293	4,917	214
	Joint Registrations same address	150,421	16,215	40,843	39,797	33,306	16,790	3,341	129
	Joint Registrations different address	43,921	11,665	13,682	8,416	6,029	3,290	800	39
	Sole Registrations	43,744	11,669	13,583	8,582	5,875	3,213	776	46
2000	All	604,441	45,846	107,741	170,701	180,113	84,974	14,403	663
	Within Marriage	365,836	4,742	40,262	111,606	136,165	62,671	9,910	480
	Outside Marriage	238,605	41,104	67,479	59,095	43,948	22,303	4,493	183
	Joint Registrations same address	149,510	17,011	40,450	41,236	31,795	15,836	3,055	127
	Joint Registrations different address	43,322	11,634	13,110	8,646	6,037	3,158	706	31
	Sole Registrations	45,773	12,459	13,919	9,213	6,116	3,309	732	25
1999	All	621,872	48,375	110,722	181,931	185,311	81,281	13,617	635
	Within Marriage	379,983	5,333	43,190	120,716	140,330	60,470	9,466	478
	Outside Marriage	241,889	43,042	67,532	61,215	44,981	20,811	4,151	157
	Joint Registrations same address	149,584	17,833	40,190	42,126	32,152	14,455	2,725	103
	Joint Registrations different address	44,102	12,015	12,865	9,153	6,214	3,135	695	25
	Sole Registrations	48,203	13,194	14,477	9,936	6,615	3,221	731	29
1998	All	635,901	48,285	113,537	193,144	188,499	78,881	12,980	575
	Within Marriage	395,290	5,278	45,724	130,747	144,599	59,320	9,189	433
	Outside Marriage	240,611	43,007	67,813	62,397	43,900	19,561	3,791	142
	Joint Registrations same address	146,521	17,589	39,818	42,212	30,938	16,410	3,118	114
	Joint Registrations different address	44,130	11,588	13,157	9,513	6,194			
	Sole Registrations	49,960	13,830	14,838	10,672	6,768	3,151	673	28

.15 Live births by age of mother and registration type[1], 1982-2013

England and Wales

Year	Type of Registration		Age of mother at birth						
		All ages	Under 20	20-24	25-29	30-34	35-39	40-44	45 and over
		Numbers of births							
1997	All	643,095	46,372	118,589	202,792	187,528	74,900	12,332	582
	Within Marriage	404,873	5,233	49,068	139,383	145,293	56,671	8,797	428
	Outside Marriage	238,222	41,139	69,521	63,409	42,235	18,229	3,535	154
	Joint Registrations same address	141,740	16,551	39,784	42,020	28,715	15,179	2,860	122
	Joint Registrations different address	45,900	11,365	14,147	10,374	6,523			
	Sole Registrations	50,582	13,223	15,590	11,015	6,997	3,050	675	32
1996	All	649,485	44,667	125,732	211,103	186,377	69,503	11,516	587
	Within Marriage	416,822	5,365	54,651	148,770	145,898	53,265	8,421	452
	Outside Marriage	232,663	39,302	71,081	62,333	40,479	16,238	3,095	135
	Joint Registrations same address	135,282	15,410	39,978	40,384	26,875	13,347	2,517	107
	Joint Registrations different address	46,365	10,946	14,858	10,599	6,626			
	Sole Registrations	51,016	12,946	16,245	11,350	6,978	2,891	578	28
1995	All	648,138	41,938	130,744	217,418	181,202	65,517	10,779	540
	Within Marriage	428,189	5,623	61,029	157,855	144,200	51,129	7,944	409
	Outside Marriage	219,949	36,315	69,715	59,563	37,002	14,388	2,835	131
	Joint Registrations same address	127,789	14,424	39,274	38,376	24,376	11,859	2,335	99
	Joint Registrations different address	44,244	10,011	14,815	10,323	6,141			
	Sole Registrations	47,916	11,880	15,626	10,864	6,485	2,529	500	32
1994	All	664,726	42,026	140,240	229,102	179,568	63,061	10,241	488
	Within Marriage	449,190	6,099	69,227	170,605	145,563	49,668	7,662	366
	Outside Marriage	215,536	35,927	71,013	58,497	34,005	13,393	2,579	122
	Joint Registrations same address	123,874	14,168	39,827	37,168	22,288	10,892	2,084	97
	Joint Registrations different address	42,632	9,752	14,778	9,939	5,513			
	Sole Registrations	49,030	12,007	16,408	11,390	6,204	2,501	495	25
1993	All	673,467	45,121	151,975	235,961	171,061	58,824	9,986	539
	Within Marriage	456,919	6,875	76,950	178,456	139,671	46,919	7,621	427
	Outside Marriage	216,548	38,246	75,025	57,505	31,390	11,905	2,365	112
	Joint Registrations same address	118,758	14,134	40,168	35,307	20,084	9,569	1,882	85
	Joint Registrations different address	47,548	11,577	17,381	10,780	5,339			
	Sole Registrations	50,242	12,535	17,476	11,418	5,967	2,336	483	27
1992	All	689,656	47,861	163,311	244,798	166,839	56,650	9,696	501
	Within Marriage	474,431	7,787	86,220	188,928	137,904	45,733	7,456	403
	Outside Marriage	215,225	40,074	77,091	55,870	28,935	10,917	2,240	98
	Joint Registrations same address	119,239	15,236	42,063	34,756	18,673	8,784	1,811	78
	Joint Registrations different address	44,514	11,381	16,658	9,693	4,620			
	Sole Registrations	51,472	13,457	18,370	11,421	5,642	2,133	429	20
1991	All	699,217	52,396	173,356	248,727	161,259	53,644	9,316	519
	Within Marriage	487,923	8,948	95,605	196,281	135,542	43,810	7,294	443
	Outside Marriage	211,294	43,448	77,751	52,446	25,717	9,834	2,022	76
	Joint Registrations same address	115,298	16,351	42,245	32,532	16,468	7,861	1,594	60
	Joint Registrations different address	41,865	11,848	15,835	8,518	3,851			
	Sole Registrations	54,131	15,249	19,671	11,396	5,398	1,973	428	16
1990	All	706,140	55,541	180,136	252,577	156,264	51,905	9,220	497
	Within Marriage	506,141	10,958	106,188	204,701	133,384	43,179	7,302	429
	Outside Marriage	199,999	44,583	73,948	47,876	22,880	8,726	1,918	68
	Joint Registrations same address	106,001	16,311	39,062	29,181	14,585	6,793	1,505	55
	Joint Registrations different address	39,167	12,081	14,751	7,555	3,289			
	Sole Registrations	54,831	16,191	20,135	11,140	5,006	1,933	413	13

15.15 Live births by age of mother and registration type[1], 1982-2013

England and Wales

Year	Type of Registration	All ages	Under 20	20-24	25-29	30-34	35-39	40-44	45 and over
		Numbers of births							
1989	All	687,725	55,543	185,239	242,822	145,320	49,465	8,845	491
	Within Marriage	501,921	12,027	114,456	200,961	125,439	41,528	7,079	431
	Outside Marriage	185,804	43,516	70,783	41,861	19,881	7,937	1,766	60
	Joint Registrations same address	95,858	15,686	36,582	24,859	12,543	6,156	1,341	49
	Joint Registrations different address	36,409	11,688	14,022	6,603	2,738			
	Sole Registrations	53,537	16,142	20,179	10,399	4,600	1,781	425	11
1988	All	693,577	58,741	193,726	243,460	140,974	47,649	8,520	507
	Within Marriage	516,225	14,099	125,575	205,292	123,384	40,400	7,025	450
	Outside Marriage	177,352	44,642	68,151	38,168	17,590	7,249	1,495	57
	Joint Registrations same address	87,601	15,304	33,994	22,070	10,765	5,607	1,159	44
	Joint Registrations different address	35,807	12,240	13,807	5,913	2,505			
	Sole Registrations	53,944	17,098	20,350	10,185	4,320	1,642	336	13
1987	All	681,511	57,545	193,232	238,929	136,558	46,604	8,112	531
	Within Marriage	523,080	15,588	132,809	206,036	121,252	40,159	6,751	485
	Outside Marriage	158,431	41,957	60,423	32,893	15,306	6,445	1,361	46
	Joint Registrations same address	75,572	13,808	29,114	18,671	9,210	4,836	1,026	31
	Joint Registrations different address	32,385	11,362	12,365	5,313	2,221			
	Sole Registrations	50,474	16,787	18,944	8,909	3,875	1,609	335	15
1986	All	661,018	57,406	192,064	229,035	129,487	45,465	7,033	528
	Within Marriage	519,673	17,793	137,985	201,323	116,369	39,753	5,959	491
	Outside Marriage	141,345	39,613	54,079	27,712	13,118	5,712	1,074	37
	Joint Registrations same address	65,844	12,908	25,760	15,300	7,849	4,233	768	26
	Joint Registrations different address	27,679	10,326	10,397	4,166	1,790			
	Sole Registrations	47,822	16,379	17,922	8,246	3,479	1,479	306	11
1985	All	656,417	56,929	193,958	227,486	126,185	44,393	6,882	584
	Within Marriage	530,167	20,057	146,262	203,272	114,862	39,293	5,883	538
	Outside Marriage	126,250	36,872	47,696	24,214	11,323	5,100	999	46
	Joint Registrations	81,792	21,000	31,256	16,856	8,177	3,736	734	33
	Sole Registrations	44,458	15,872	16,440	7,358	3,146	1,364	265	13
1984	All	636,818	54,508	191,455	218,031	122,774	42,921	6,576	553
	Within Marriage	526,353	21,373	150,371	197,401	112,660	38,350	5,691	507
	Outside Marriage	110,465	33,135	41,084	20,630	10,114	4,571	885	46
	Joint Registrations	69,872	18,207	26,208	14,247	7,290	3,302	591	27
	Sole Registrations	40,593	14,928	14,876	6,383	2,824	1,269	294	19
1983	All	629,134	54,059	191,852	214,078	120,996	41,277	6,210	662
	Within Marriage	529,923	23,636	155,209	196,162	111,722	37,160	5,422	612
	Outside Marriage	99,211	30,423	36,643	17,916	9,274	4,117	788	50
	Joint Registrations	60,794	16,072	22,550	12,097	6,623	2,892	526	34
	Sole Registrations	38,417	14,351	14,093	5,819	2,651	1,225	262	16
1982	All	625,931	55,435	192,322	211,905	120,758	38,992	5,886	633
	Within Marriage	536,074	26,696	159,911	195,839	112,625	35,310	5,118	575
	Outside Marriage	89,857	28,739	32,411	16,066	8,133	3,682	768	58
	Joint Registrations	53,404	14,286	19,420	10,683	5,835	2,596	539	45
	Sole Registrations	36,453	14,453	12,991	5,383	2,298	1,086	229	13

1. . The Human Fertilisation and Embryology Act 2008 contained provisions enabling two females in a same-sex couple to register birth from 1 September 2009 onwards. Due to the small numbers, births registered to a same-sex couple in a civil partnership (655 in 2013) are included with marital births while births registered to a same-sex couple outside a civil partnership (259 in 2013) are included with births outside marriage.

2. . 1981 births for age-groups are based on a 10 per cent sample

Source: Office for National Statistics

This table will be updated in October/November 2017. The updated table will appear in the next edition of Annual Abstract

15.16 Legal abortions: countries of Great Britain by (i) age, (ii) gestation weeks, (iii) procedure, (iv) parity, (v) previous abortions, (vi) grounds and (vii) principal medical condition for abortions performed under ground E, 2015

Country of abortion

numbers and percentages

	England & Wales		Scotland		Great Britain	
All legal abortions	**191,014**	*100%*	**12,082**	*100%*	**203,096**	*100%*
(i) Age						
Under 16	1,895	*1*	136	*1*	2,031	*1*
16-17	8,084	*4*	595	*5*	8,679	*4*
18-19	16,640	*9*	1,212	*10*	17,852	*9*
20-24	52,746	*28*	3,600	*30*	56,346	*28*
25-29	46,466	*24*	2,810	*23*	49,276	*24*
30-34	34,412	*18*	1,980	*16*	36,392	*18*
35+	30,771	*16*	1,749	*14*	32,520	*16*
(ii) Gestation weeks						
3 - 9	152,469	*80*	9,742	*81*	162,211	*80*
10 - 12	22,008	*12*	1,481	*12*	23,489	*12*
13 - 19	13,306	*7*	792	*7*	14,098	*7*
20 and over	3,231	*2*	67	*1*	3,298	*2*
(iii) Procedure						
Surgical	87,906	*46*	2,287	*19*	90,193	*44*
Medical	103,108	*54*	9,795 [2]	*81*	112,903	*56*
(iv) Parity (number of previous pregnancies resulting in live or stillbirth)						
0	87,377	*46*	5,836	*48*	93,213	*46*
1+	103,637	*54*	6,246	*52*	109,883	*54*
(v) Number of previous pregnancies resulting in abortion under the Act						
0	119,684	*63*	8 295	*69*	127,979	*63*
1+	71,330	*37*	3 787	*31*	75,117	*37*
(vi) Grounds						
A (alone or with B, C or D) or F or G	92	*0*	*	.	*	.
B (alone or with C or D)	132	*0*	*	.	*	.
C (alone)	186,211	*97*	11,874	*98*	198,085	*98*
D (alone or with C)	1,160	*1*	6	*0*	1,166	*1*
E (alone or with A, B, C or D)	3,419	*2*	186	*2*	3,605	*2*
(vii) Principal medical condition for abortions performed under ground E						
Total Ground E	**3,298**	*100%*	**186**	*100%*	**3,484**	*100*
The nervous system (Q00 - Q07)	729	*22*	30	*16*	759	*22*
Other congenital malformations (Q10-Q89)	758	*23*	47	*25*	805	*23*
Chromosomal abnormalities (Q90 - Q99)	1,208	*37*	78	*42*	1,286	*37*
Other	603	*18*	31	*17*	634	*18*

Source: ISD Scotland, Department of Health

* Adhering to ISD Statistical Disclosure Control Protocol.

. Not available

[1] Some notifications record more than one Statutory Ground, therefore totals may not match with the numbers released by ISD Scotland.

[2] Ten cases where method of diagnosis was not known were included in total for 'medical'.

Note: percentages are rounded and may not add up to 100

15.17 Death[1] rates per 1,000 population: by age and sex, 2015
England and Wales

Age	Males	Females	Age	Males	Females	Age	Males	Females
All ages	9.01	9.29						
0-4	0.99	0.76	**35-39**	1.13	0.69	**70-74**	23.63	15.90
0	4.43	3.36	35	0.95	0.55	70	19.20	12.90
1	0.30	0.27	36	1.10	0.66	71	21.12	14.18
2	0.16	0.12	37	1.09	0.70	72	23.50	15.35
3	0.12	0.11	38	1.25	0.77	72	26.08	18.05
4	0.11	0.07	39	1.30	0.81	74	30.77	20.45
5-9	0.08	0.07	**40-44**	1.71	1.04	**75-79**	40.61	27.89
5	0.08	0.07	40	1.45	0.91	75	33.25	22.09
6	0.08	0.07	41	1.58	0.88	76	36.79	25.05
7	0.09	0.08	42	1.75	1.12	77	40.55	27.16
8	0.07	0.08	43	1.75	1.07	78	44.41	30.90
9	0.08	0.07	44	1.97	1.19	79	50.27	35.45
10-14	0.10	0.08	**45-49**	2.50	1.61	**80-84**	72.28	53.81
10	0.10	0.06	45	2.07	1.40	80	57.11	41.03
11	0.11	0.05	46	2.25	1.53	81	63.42	47.38
12	0.09	0.07	47	2.59	1.55	82	73.69	53.12
13	0.10	0.12	48	2.58	1.72	83	82.74	60.77
14	0.10	0.11	49	2.99	1.84	84	92.21	70.51
15-19	0.31	0.18	**50-54**	3.70	2.50	**85-89**	129.44	101.98
15	0.18	0.16	50	3.46	2.08	85	105.59	78.77
16	0.19	0.15	51	3.33	2.21	86	118.83	90.45
17	0.29	0.15	52	3.56	2.47	87	132.16	103.38
18	0.40	0.21	53	3.93	2.80	88	149.32	118.83
19	0.46	0.23	54	4.26	2.99	89	164.98	134.58
20-24	0.50	0.20	**55-59**	5.81	3.82	**90+**	244.41	219.30
20	0.45	0.21	55	4.89	3.20			
21	0.47	0.17	56	5.40	3.47			
22	0.50	0.19	57	5.93	3.72			
23	0.53	0.24	58	6.28	4.05			
24	0.54	0.20	59	6.69	4.77			
25-29	0.59	0.28	**60-64**	9.53	6.14			
25	0.63	0.23	60	8.00	5.32			
26	0.52	0.28	61	8.59	5.52			
27	0.58	0.24	62	9.19	6.09			
28	0.63	0.28	63	10.52	6.78			
29	0.60	0.37	64	11.47	7.01			
30-34	0.80	0.42	**65-69**	14.32	9.46			
30	0.63	0.37	65	12.08	7.72			
31	0.67	0.36	66	13.09	8.56			
32	0.92	0.44	67	14.35	9.37			
33	0.85	0.43	68	14.95	10.30			
34	0.93	0.48	69	17.36	11.42			

Source: Office for National Statistics

1. Death figures are based on deaths registered rather than deaths occurring in a calendar year.

15.18 Stillbirth[1,2] and infant death[3] rates: age at death, 1921 to 2015

England and Wales

Period Infant mortality per 1,000 live births[3] at various ages

Stillbirths[2] and infant deaths per 1,000 total births

Period	Under 1 year	Neonatal mortality					Postneonatal mortality				Still-births	Still-births plus deaths under 1 week	Still-births plus deaths under 4 weeks	Still-births plus deaths under 1 year
		Under 4 weeks	Early neonatal			Late neo-natal	4 weeks and under 1 year	4 weeks and under 3 months	3 months and under 6 months	6 months and under 1 year				
			Under 1 week	Under 1 day	1 day and under 1 week	1 week and under 4 weeks								
1921	82.8	35.3	22.4	10.8	11.6	12.9	47.5	14.8	14.0	18.6	:	:	:	:
1922	77.1	34.1	22.0	10.4	11.6	12.1	43.0	12.7	11.0	19.3	:	:	:	:
1923	69.4	31.9	21.1	10.2	10.9	10.8	37.5	11.3	10.0	16.1	:	:	:	:
1924	75.1	33.1	21.8	10.6	11.2	11.3	42.0	12.5	10.9	18.6	:	:	:	:
1925	75.0	32.3	21.2	10.1	11.1	11.1	42.7	12.6	11.3	18.8	:	:	:	:
1926	70.2	31.9	21.3	10.0	11.3	10.6	38.3	11.6	10.4	16.3	:	:	:	:
1927	69.7	32.3	22.2	10.6	11.6	10.1	37.4	10.7	9.7	16.9	38.8	59.6	69.3	105.3
1928	65.1	31.1	21.6	10.4	11.2	9.5	34.0	10.7	9.2	14.1	40.1	60.8	69.9	102.6
1929	74.4	32.8	22.3	10.4	11.9	10.6	41.5	11.6	10.7	19.3	40.0	61.4	71.6	111.4
1930	60.0	30.9	22.0	10.4	11.6	8.9	29.1	9.6	7.8	11.6	40.8	61.9	70.4	98.3
1931	65.7	31.5	22.1	10.4	11.7	9.5	34.2	10.8	9.2	14.2	40.9	62.1	71.2	104.5
1932	64.5	31.5	22.4	10.6	11.8	9.2	33.0	10.8	9.0	13.2	41.3	62.8	71.6	103.7
1933	62.7	32.1	22.9	11.0	11.8	9.3	30.6	9.8	8.6	12.2	41.4	63.4	72.3	102.5
1934	59.3	31.4	22.7	10.9	11.8	8.7	27.9	8.9	7.7	11.3	40.5	62.2	70.5	96.7
1935	57.0	30.4	22.0	10.7	11.3	8.4	26.6	9.1	7.7	9.8	40.7	61.9	69.9	95.4
1936	58.7	30.2	21.9	10.7	11.3	8.2	28.5	9.3	8.3	10.9	39.7	60.8	68.7	95.9
1937	57.7	29.7	22.0	10.8	11.2	7.8	28.0	9.4	8.3	10.3	39.0	60.2	67.6	94.4
1938	52.8	28.3	21.1	10.3	10.8	7.1	24.5	8.2	7.3	9.0	38.3	58.6	65.5	88.9
1939	50.6	28.3	21.2	10.3	10.9	7.1	22.2	7.9	7.0	7.3	38.1	58.5	65.3	86.9
1940	56.8	29.6	21.3	9.8	11.5	8.3	27.2	9.3	8.2	9.7	37.2	57.7	65.7	92.5
1941	60.0	29.0	20.7	10.1	10.6	8.3	31.1	11.3	9.7	10.1	34.8	54.7	62.7	92.4
1942	50.6	27.2	19.6	9.6	10.0	7.7	23.4	8.7	7.5	7.2	33.2	52.1	59.4	81.1
1943	49.1	25.2	18.3	9.1	9.2	6.9	23.9	8.8	7.8	7.3	30.1	47.9	54.6	77.5
1944	45.4	24.4	17.5	8.8	8.8	6.9	21.1	8.0	7.0	6.1	27.6	44.5	51.1	70.9
1945	46.0	24.8	18.0	9.0	9.0	6.8	21.3	8.2	7.0	6.1	27.6	45.2	51.8	73.4
1946	42.9	24.5	17.8	8.7	9.1	6.7	18.4	7.1	6.1	5.2	27.2	44.3	50.7	66.9
1947	41.4	22.7	16.5	7.8	8.7	6.2	18.6	6.9	6.0	5.7	24.1	40.3	46.4	65.0
1948	33.9	19.7	15.6	7.8	7.9	4.1	14.2	5.5	4.8	3.9	23.2	38.5	42.5	56.8
1949	32.4	19.3	15.6	7.6	8.0	3.7	13.0	4.8	4.4	3.8	22.7	38.0	41.5	54.6
1950	29.6	18.5	15.2	7.2	8.0	3.3	11.1	4.3	3.7	3.1	22.6	37.4	40.7	51.7
1951	29.7	18.8	15.5	7.5	8.0	3.3	10.9	4.1	3.6	3.2	23.0	38.2	41.5	52.2
1952	27.6	18.3	15.2	7.6	7.6	3.2	9.3	3.7	3.0	2.6	22.7	37.5	40.6	49.6
1953	26.8	17.7	14.8	7.4	7.4	2.9	9.1	3.4	3.0	2.7	22.4	36.9	39.7	48.6
1954	25.4	17.7	14.9	7.6	7.4	2.8	7.7	3.0	2.6	2.1	23.5	38.1	40.8	48.4
1955	24.9	17.3	14.6	7.6	7.0	2.6	7.6	2.9	2.6	2.1	23.2	37.4	40.0	47.5
1956	23.7	16.8	14.2	7.4	6.8	2.6	6.9	2.7	2.3	1.8	22.9	36.7	39.3	46.0
1957	23.1	16.5	14.1	7.6	6.5	2.4	6.7	2.6	2.1	1.9	22.5	36.2	38.5	45.1
1958	22.5	16.2	13.8	7.5	6.3	2.4	6.4	2.6	2.1	1.7	21.5	35.0	37.3	43.6
1959	22.2	15.9	13.6	7.6	6.0	2.3	6.3	2.4	2.1	1.8	20.8	34.1	36.3	42.6
1960	21.8	15.5	13.3	7.5	5.8	2.2	6.3	2.5	2.1	1.6	19.8	32.8	35.0	41.1
1961	21.4	15.3	13.3	7.6	5.7	2.1	6.1	2.4	2.0	1.7	19.0	32.0	34.1	40.0
1962	21.7	15.1	13.0	7.4	5.6	2.1	6.6	2.5	2.3	1.8	18.1	30.8	32.9	39.4
1963	21.1	14.3	12.3	7.2	5.1	2.0	6.9	2.7	2.4	1.8	17.2	29.3	31.3	38.0
1964	19.9	13.8	12.0	7.1	4.9	1.8	6.1	2.4	2.1	1.6	16.3	28.2	29.9	35.9
1965	19.0	13.0	11.3	6.6	4.7	1.7	6.0	2.4	2.1	1.6	15.8	26.9	28.6	34.5
1966	19.0	12.9	11.1	6.5	4.6	1.7	6.1	2.5	2.0	1.6	15.3	26.3	28.0	34.1
1967	18.3	12.5	10.7	6.3	4.4	1.8	5.8	2.4	2.0	1.4	14.8	25.4	27.2	32.9
1968	18.3	12.4	10.6	6.3	4.3	1.8	5.9	2.4	2.1	1.5	14.3	24.7	26.4	32.3
1969	18.0	12.0	10.3	6.0	4.3	1.7	6.0	2.5	2.1	1.5	13.2	23.4	25.1	31.0
1970	18.2	12.3	10.6	6.3	4.3	1.7	5.9	2.6	2.0	1.3	13.0	23.5	25.2	31.0
1971	17.5	11.6	9.9	6.0	3.9	1.7	5.9	2.6	2.0	1.3	12.5	22.3	24.0	29.8
1972	17.2	11.5	9.8	5.8	4.1	1.7	5.7	2.4	2.0	1.4	12.0	21.7	23.4	29.0
1973	16.9	11.1	9.5	5.5	4.0	1.6	5.7	2.5	1.9	1.3	11.6	21.0	22.6	28.3
1974	16.3	11.0	9.4	5.2	4.2	1.7	5.3	2.3	1.9	1.1	11.1	20.4	22.0	27.3
1975	15.7	10.7	9.1	5.0	4.1	1.7	5.0	2.2	1.7	1.1	10.3	19.3	20.9	25.9
1976	14.3	9.7	8.2	4.7	3.5	1.5	4.6	1.9	1.6	1.1	9.7	17.7	19.3	23.8
1977	13.8	9.3	7.6	4.2	3.5	1.6	4.5	1.9	1.6	1.1	9.4	17.0	18.6	23.0
1978	13.2	8.7	7.1	3.7	3.4	1.6	4.5	1.9	1.6	1.0	8.5	15.5	17.1	21.6
1979	12.8	8.2	6.8	3.7	3.0	1.5	4.6	1.9	1.7	1.0	8.0	14.7	16.1	20.7
1980	12.0	7.7	6.2	3.4	2.8	1.5	4.4	1.8	1.5	1.1	7.2	13.3	14.8	19.2
1981	11.1	6.7	5.3	2.9	2.3	1.4	4.4	1.8	1.6	1.0	6.6	11.8	13.2	17.6
1982	10.8	6.3	5.0	2.8	2.2	1.2	4.6	1.9	1.6	1.1	6.3	11.3	12.5	17.0
1983	10.1	5.9	4.7	2.6	2.1	1.2	4.3	1.9	1.5	0.9	5.7	10.4	11.6	15.8
1984	9.5	5.6	4.4	2.6	1.9	1.1	3.9	1.6	1.3	0.9	5.7	10.1	11.2	15.1
1985	9.4	5.4	4.3	2.5	1.9	1.0	4.0	1.7	1.4	0.9	5.5	9.8	10.9	14.8
1986	9.6	5.3	4.3	2.4	1.8	1.0	4.3	1.8	1.5	1.0	5.3	9.6	10.6	14.8
1987	9.2	5.1	3.9	2.3	1.6	1.1	4.1	1.8	1.5	0.9	5.0	8.9	10.0	14.2
1988	9.0	4.9	3.9	2.2	1.7	1.0	4.1	1.7	1.5	0.9	4.9	8.7	9.8	13.8
1989	8.4	4.8	3.7	2.1	1.6	1.1	3.7	1.6	1.3	0.8	4.7	8.3	9.4	13.1

15.18 Stillbirth[1,2] and infant death[3] rates: age at death, 1921 to 2015

England and Wales

Period   Infant mortality per 1,000 live births[3] at various ages

Stillbirths[2] and infant deaths per 1,000 total births

Period	Under 1 year	Neonatal mortality					Postneonatal mortality				Still-births	Still-births plus deaths under 1 week	Still-births plus deaths under 4 weeks	Still-births plus deaths under 1 year
		Under 4 weeks	Early neonatal			Late neo-natal	4 weeks and under 1 year	4 weeks and under 3 months	3 months and under 6 months	6 months and under 1 year				
			Under 1 week	Under 1 day	1 day and under 1 week	1 week and under 4 weeks								
1990	7.9	4.6	3.5	2.0	1.5	1.0	3.3	1.3	1.2	0.7	4.6	8.1	9.1	12.4
1991	7.4	4.4	3.4	2.0	1.4	0.9	3.0	1.2	1.0	0.7	4.6	8.0	9.0	12.0
1992	6.6	4.3	3.3	2.0	1.4	1.0	2.3	1.0	0.8	0.6	4.3	7.6	8.5	10.8
1993	6.3	4.2	3.2	1.9	1.3	0.9	2.1	0.9	0.7	0.6	5.7	8.9	9.8	12.0
1994	6.2	4.1	3.2	1.9	1.4	0.9	2.1	0.8	0.7	0.6	5.7	8.9	9.8	11.9
1995	6.1	4.2	3.2	1.8	1.5	0.9	2.0	0.9	0.6	0.5	5.5	8.7	9.7	11.6
1996	6.1	4.1	3.2	1.9	1.3	0.9	2.0	0.9	0.6	0.5	5.4	8.6	9.5	11.5
1997	5.9	3.9	3.0	1.8	1.2	0.9	2.0	0.9	0.6	0.5	5.3	8.3	9.2	11.2
1998	5.7	3.8	2.9	1.7	1.2	0.9	1.9	0.9	0.6	0.4	5.3	8.2	9.1	11.0
1999	5.8	3.9	2.9	1.7	1.2	1.0	1.9	0.9	0.6	0.5	5.3	8.2	9.2	11.1
2000	5.6	3.9	2.9	1.7	1.2	1.0	1.7	0.8	0.5	0.4	5.3	8.2	9.1	10.8
2001	5.4	3.6	2.7	1.7	1.0	0.9	1.9	0.8	0.5	0.5	5.3	8.0	8.9	10.7
2002	5.2	3.6	2.7	1.7	1.0	1.0	1.7	0.8	0.0	0.0	5.6	8.0	9.0	11.0
2003	5.3	3.6	2.8	1.8	1.0	0.8	1.7	0.8	0.4	0.4	5.8	8.6	9.4	11.1
2004	5.0	3.5	2.7	1.7	1.0	0.8	1.6	0.8	0.4	0.4	5.7	8.4	9.2	10.7
2005	5.0	3.4	2.6	1.7	1.0	0.8	1.6	0.8	0.5	0.4	5.4	8.0	8.8	10.4
2006	5.0	3.5	2.6	1.7	0.9	0.9	1.5	0.7	0.4	0.3	5.4	8.0	8.8	10.3
2007	4.7	3.3	2.5	1.6	0.9	0.7	1.5	0.7	0.4	0.4	5.2	7.7	8.4	9.9
2008	4.6	3.2	2.4	1.6	0.8	0.7	1.4	0.7	0.4	0.3	5.1	7.5	8.3	9.7
2009	4.5	3.1	2.4	1.5	0.9	0.7	1.4	0.7	0.4	0.3	5.2	7.6	8.3	9.7
2010	4.3	2.9	2.3	1.5	0.8	0.6	1.3	0.7	0.3	0.3	5.1	7.4	8.0	9.3
2011	4.2	2.9	2.3	1.5	0.7	0.7	1.2	0.6	0.3	0.3	5.2	7.5	8.2	9.4
2012	4.0	2.8	2.2	1.5	0.6	0.6	1.2	0.6	0.3	0.3	4.9	7.0	7.6	8.8
2013	3.8	2.7	2.0	1.4	0.6	0.6	1.2	0.6	0.3	0.3	4.7	6.7	7.3	8.5
2014	3.6	2.5	2.0	1.3	0.6	0.6	1.1	0.5	0.3	0.2	4.7	6.6	7.2	8.3
2015	3.7	2.6	2.1	1.5	0.6	0.6	1.1	0.5	0.3	0.3	4.5	6.5	7.1	8.2

Source: Office for National Statistics

1 Registration of stillbirths commenced on 1 July 1927. Annual figures for 1927 are estimated.
2 From 1927 to 30 September 1992 stillbirths relate to fetal deaths at or over 28 weeks gestation, and from 1 October 1992 at or over 24 weeks gestation.
3 Infant deaths are based on the live births occurring in the year, except in the years 1931-56 when they were based on related live births - that is, the combined live births of the associated and preceding years to which they relate.

15.19 Interim Life Tables
Period expectation of life based on data for the years 2013-2015

United Kingdom

Age	Males		Females	
x	l_x	e_x	l_x	e_x
0	100000.0	79.09	100000.0	82.82
5	99500.3	74.49	99593.7	78.16
10	99457.2	69.52	99557.6	73.18
15	99404.7	64.56	99517.1	68.21
20	99249.8	59.65	99431.8	63.27
25	99001.4	54.79	99325.9	58.33
30	98690.0	49.96	99181.3	53.41
35	98278.2	45.16	98959.4	48.53
40	97683.2	40.42	98615.2	43.69
45	96816.0	35.75	98086.4	38.91
50	95575.9	31.18	97291.2	34.21
55	93782.5	26.73	96053.5	29.61
60	90996.6	22.47	94155.1	25.16
65	86681.2	18.45	91247.2	20.87
70	80502.2	14.66	86926.7	16.78
75	71064.8	11.26	80022.6	12.99
80	57713.1	8.25	69305.2	9.59
85	39781.4	5.81	52805.7	6.76
90	20359.6	4.00	31499.9	4.60
95	6432.2	2.78	12204.4	3.15
100	1023.6	1.99	2521.5	2.22

England & Wales

Age	Males		Females	
x	l_x	e_x	l_x	e_x
0	100000.0	79.32	100000.0	83.01
5	99498.9	74.72	99592.3	78.35
10	99455.7	69.75	99554.9	73.38
15	99404.3	64.78	99513.9	68.41
20	99254.7	59.88	99431.5	63.46
25	99015.0	55.01	99327.5	58.53
30	98718.5	50.17	99186.3	53.61
35	98328.7	45.36	98973.4	48.72
40	97763.2	40.61	98639.7	43.87
45	96934.8	35.93	98125.8	39.09
50	95735.2	31.35	97354.8	34.38
55	93986.5	26.88	96152.3	29.77
60	91263.4	22.61	94305.1	25.30
65	87019.3	18.58	91459.0	21.01
70	80967.1	14.77	87242.9	16.90
75	71694.7	11.33	80484.9	13.09
80	58455.2	8.30	69969.4	9.65
85	40496.1	5.84	53554.7	6.80
90	20853.7	4.02	32136.3	4.63
95	6614.7	2.79	12533.1	3.16
100	1066.7	2.01	2602.6	2.23

Scotland

Age	Males		Females	
x	l_x	e_x	l_x	e_x
0	100000	77.09	100000	81.14
5	99576.8	72.42	99633.0	76.43
10	99535.1	67.45	99615.4	71.45
15	99475.7	62.49	99578.1	66.47
20	99288.6	57.60	99471.9	61.54
25	98996.0	52.76	99355.3	56.61
30	98567.1	47.98	99174.9	51.71
35	97947.2	43.27	98858.4	46.87
40	97049.2	38.64	98392.1	42.08
45	95763.1	34.13	97714.4	37.35
50	94138.0	29.67	96686.8	32.72
55	91931.6	25.32	95146.6	28.20
60	88542.4	21.19	92809.9	23.85
65	83603.8	17.28	89397.9	19.66
70	76259.7	13.69	84128.9	15.72
75	65288.5	10.54	75841.4	12.15
80	50988.4	7.77	63529.7	8.98
85	33428.3	5.49	46324.0	6.35
90	16002.7	3.86	26005.6	4.36
95	4817.9	2.61	9362.7	3.02
100	680.5	1.87	1816.5	2.07

Northern Ireland

Age	Males		Females	
x	l_x	e_x	l_x	e_x
0	100000.0	78.28	100000.0	82.27
5	99363.9	73.78	99544.0	77.65
10	99319.3	68.81	99498.9	72.68
15	99256.4	63.85	99465.7	67.71
20	99032.7	58.99	99351.0	62.78
25	98640.1	54.22	99220.9	57.86
30	98195.0	49.45	99073.5	52.94
35	97657.4	44.71	98835.9	48.07
40	96969.0	40.01	98505.1	43.22
45	96085.5	35.35	97954.0	38.45
50	94756.0	30.81	97129.6	33.75
55	92893.0	26.37	95773.5	29.19
60	90169.8	22.09	93750.7	24.76
65	85692.6	18.10	90533.3	20.54
70	79172.2	14.37	85850.0	16.52
75	69582.3	10.99	79011.4	12.72
80	55924.1	8.03	67553.8	9.43
85	37718.6	5.66	51020.7	6.63
90	18747.8	3.87	29947.7	4.50
95	5838.4	2.50	11306.9	3.08
100			2323.3	2.18

Data published to age 95 due to very low numbers of deaths and population.   Source: Office for National Statistics

l_x is the number of survivors to exact age x of 100,000 live births of the same sex who are assumed to be subject throughout their lives to the mortality rates experienced in the three year period to which the National Life Table relates.

e_x is the average period expectation of life at exact age x, that is the average number of years that those aged x exact will live thereafter based on the mortality rates experienced in the three year period to which the National Life Table relates.

15.20a Adoption Orders[1] granted by sex and age band, 2011-2015

England & Wales

Year	Total adoption orders: All Ages	adoption orders granted by Age of adopted child					
		< 1 year	1-4 yrs	5-9 yrs	10-14 yrs	15-17 yrs	Other[2]
Total							
2011	**4,709**	90	2,924	1,075	457	133	30
2012	**5,260**	121	3,286	1,238	439	158	18
2013	**6,078**	169	4,037	1,338	368	141	25
2014	**6,750**	235	4,628	1,358	345	146	38
2015	**6,195**	251	3,935	1,431	379	165	34
Males							
2011	2,330	53	530	1465	216	61	5
2012	2,648	58	621	1683	205	70	11
2013	2,985	80	679	1996	173	51	6
2014	3,435	111	2428	655	165	60	16
2015	3,187	140	2092	705	168	70	13
Females							
2011	2,365	37	545	1459	241	72	11
2012	2,611	63	617	1603	234	88	6
2013	3,090	89	659	2041	195	90	16
2014	3,305	124	2200	703	180	86	12
2015	3,008	112	1843	726	211	95	21
Gender Unknown							
2011	14	0	0	0	0	0	14
2012	1	0	0	0	0	0	1
2013	3	0	0	0	0	0	3
2014	10	0	0	0	0	0	10
2015	0	0	0	0	0	0	0

Source: Ministry of Justice, Family Court Statistics

Notes:

1) Figures are for adoption orders only. Figures for orders issued for related non-adoption orders are not included in this summary

2) 'Other' includes those who were aged 18 by the time the order was made, or where the age was not correctly recorded.

Note:

Prior to 2011, National Statistics on Adoptions in england and Wales were published by ONS: http://www.ons.gov.uk/ons/taxonomy/index.html?nscl=AdoptionsData in ONS publications are based on adoption data provided by the General Register Office, which maintains the Adopted Child Register using copies of adoption orders issued by courts. There are small differences between the number of adoptions as recorded by the two sets of statistics.

During the transition period over 2009/2010 when courts were starting to implement the new administrative data systems not all adoption orders made were recorded on the system, resulting in MoJ figures held for adoptions being around 15 per cent lower than those published by ONS. Since 2011 all courts dealing with family matters in England and Wales have been using the Familyman administrative system and hand-written notifications of adoptions to GRO have been phased out. This has resulted in figures for the ONS and MoJ being much closer.

Please see the joint statement produced by MoJ, ONS and GRO on the differences in these adoption statistics attached to the 2012 Q4 edition of Court Statistics Quarterly for further details.

15.20b Adoptions by age of child and relationship of the adopter(s), 2015

Age and sex of child		Total	Relationship of adopter(s)				
			Both parents	Step-parent	Grandparent(s)	Other relation(s)	No relation
All ages	**P**	**504**	**2**	**115**	**1**	**18**	**368**
	M	**259**	**-**	**57**	**-**	**8**	**194**
	F	**245**	**2**	**58**	**1**	**10**	**174**
Months							
less than 6	M	-	-	-	-	-	-
	F	-	-	-	-	-	-
6-8	M	9	-	6	-	-	3
	F	2	-	1	-	-	1
9-11	M	2	-	-	-	-	2
	F	5	1	-	-	-	4
12-17	M	14	-	1	-	1	12
	F	18	-	-	-	1	17
18-23	M	13	-	1	-	1	11
	F	13	-	-	-	1	12
Years							
2	M	50	-	2	-	1	47
	F	53	-	1	-	1	51
3-4	M	69	-	2	-	4	63
	F	46	1	4	-	4	37
5-9	M	69	-	17	-	-	52
	F	70	-	22	1	1	46
10-14	M	24	-	20	-	1	3
	F	24	-	19	-	2	3
15 and over	M	9	-	8	-	-	1
	F	14	-	11	-	-	3

Source: GRO-Scotland

15.20c Adoptions - Northern Ireland, 2009-2014

Persons	All ages		Under 1		1-4		5-9		10-14		15-17	
Year	Numbers	Percentage	Numbers	Percentage	Numbers	Percentage	Numbers	Percentage	Numbers	Percentage	Numbers	Percentage
2009	116	100%	1	1%	43	37%	46	40%	20	17%	6	5%
2010	116	100%	3	3%	46	40%	46	40%	17	15%	4	3%
2011	104	100%	3	3%	40	38%	40	38%	13	13%	8	8%
2012	127	100%	1	1%	66	52%	39	31%	13	10%	8	6%
2013	130	100%	0	0%	67	52%	51	39%	9	7%	3	2%
2014	104	100%	1	1%	63	61%	28	27%	9	9%	3	3%

Males	All ages		Under 1		1-4		5-9		10-14		15-17	
Year	Numbers	Percentage	Numbers	Percentage	Numbers	Percentage	Numbers	Percentage	Numbers	Percentage	Numbers	Percentage
2009	55	100%	0	0%	24	44%	20	36%	10	18%	1	2%
2010	56	100%	2	4%	26	46%	21	38%	6	11%	1	2%
2011	47	100%	0	0%	19	40%	18	38%	6	13%	4	9%
2012	68	100%	0	0%	33	49%	21	31%	10	15%	4	6%
2013	69	100%	0	0%	30	43%	32	46%	6	9%	1	1%
2014	50	100%	0	0%	27	54%	18	36%	3	6%	2	4%

Females	All ages		Under 1		1-4		5-9		10-14		15-17	
Year	Numbers	Percentage	Numbers	Percentage	Numbers	Percentage	Numbers	Percentage	Numbers	Percentage	Numbers	Percentage
2009	61	100%	1	2%	19	31%	26	43%	10	16%	5	8%
2010	60	100%	1	2%	20	33%	25	42%	11	18%	3	5%
2011	57	100%	3	5%	21	37%	22	39%	7	12%	4	7%
2012	59	100%	1	2%	33	56%	18	31%	3	5%	4	7%
2013	61	100%	0	0%	37	61%	19	31%	3	5%	2	3%
2014	54	100%	1	2%	36	67%	10	19%	6	11%	1	2%

Source: Northern Ireland Statistics and Research Agency (NISRA)

Health

Chapter 16

Health

Deaths: analysed by cause (Table 16.6)
All figures in this table for England and Wales represent
the number of deaths occurring in each calendar year.
All data for Scotland and Northern Ireland relate to the
number of deaths registered during each calendar
year. From 2001, all three constituent countries of the
UK are coding their causes of death using
the latest, tenth, revision of the International Statistical
Classification of Diseases and Related Health
Problems (ICD-10). All cause of death information from
2001 (also for 2000 for Scotland) presented in this table
is based on the revised classification.

To assist users in assessing any discontinuities arising
from the introduction of the revised classification, bridge-
coding exercises were carried out on all deaths
registered in 1999 in England and Wales and also in
Scotland. For further information about ICD-10 and the
bridge-coding carried out by The Office for National
Statistics (ONS), see the ONS Report: Results of the
ICD-10 bridge-coding study, England and Wales,
Statistics Quarterly 14 (2002), pages 75–83 or log on to
the Office for National Statistics (ONS) website at: www.ons.gov.uk.
For information on the Scottish bridge-coding exercise,
consult the Annual Report of the General Register
Office for Scotland or log on to their website at: www.gro-
scotland.gov.uk. No bridge-coding exercise was
conducted for Northern Ireland.

Neonatal deaths and homicide and assault
For England and Wales, neonatal deaths (those at age
under 28 days) are included in the number of total
deaths but excluded from the cause figures. This has
particular impact on the totals shown for the chapters
covered by the ranges P and Q, 'Conditions originating
in the perinatal period' and 'Congenital malformations,
deformations and chromosomal abnormalities'. These
are considerably lower than the actual number of deaths
because it is not possible to assign an underlying
cause of death from the neonatal death certificate used
in England and Wales.
Also, for England and Wales only, the total number
shown for Homicide and assault, X85–Y09, will not be
a true representation because the registration of these
deaths is often delayed by adjourned inquests.

Occupational ill health (Tables 16.8 and 16.9)

There are a number of sources of data on the extent of occupational or work-related ill health in Great Britain. For some potentially severe lung diseases caused by exposures which are highly unlikely to be found in a non-occupational setting, it is useful to count the number of death certificates issued each year. This is also true for mesothelioma, a cancer affecting the lining of the lungs and stomach, for which the number of cases with non-occupational causes is likely to be larger (although still a minority). Table 16.9 shows the number of deaths for mesothelioma and asbestosis (linked to exposure to asbestos), pneumoconiosis (linked to coal dust or silica), byssinosis (linked to cotton dust) and some forms of allergic alveolitis (including farmer's lung). For asbestos-related diseases the figures are derived from a special register maintained by HSE.

Most conditions which can be caused or made worse by work can also arise from other factors. The remaining sources of data on work-related ill health rely on attribution of individual cases of illness to work causes. In The Health and Occupation Reporting Network (THOR), this is done by specialist doctors – either occupational physicians or those working in particular disease specialisms (covering musculoskeletal, psychological, respiratory, skin, audio logical and infectious disease). Table 16.8 presents data from THOR for the last three years. It should be noted that not all cases of occupational disease will be seen by participating specialists; for example, the number of deaths due to mesothelioma (shown in Table 16.9) is known to be greater than the number of cases reported to THOR.

Injuries at work (Table 16.10)

The Reporting of Injuries, Diseases and Dangerous Occurrences Regulations 1995 (RIDDOR) places a legal duty on employers to report injuries arising from work activity to the relevant enforcing authority, namely HSE, local authorities and the Office of Rail Regulation (ORR). These include injuries to employees, self-employed people and members of the public. From 12 September 2011 the reporting of all RIDDOR incidents will move to a predominantly online system.

While the enforcing authorities are informed about almost all relevant fatal workplace injuries, it is known that non-fatal injuries are substantially under-reported. Currently, it is estimated that just over half of all such injuries to employees are actually reported, with the self-employed reporting a much smaller proportion. These results are achieved by comparing reported non-fatal injuries (major as well as over-3-day), with results from the Labour Force Survey (LFS).

16.1a NHS Hospital and Community Health Services (HCHS): Ambulance staff and Support to ambulance staff in NHS Trusts and CCGs in England

Headcount

Staff Group 1	Staff Group 2	Level	Sep-09	Sep-10	Sep-11	Sep-12	Sep-13	Sep-14	Sep-15
All Ambulance Staff			**31,796**	**32,707**	**32,414**	**31,608**	**32,289**	**33,041**	**34,808**
015_Ambulance staff			**17,666**	**18,169**	**18,393**	**18,379**	**18,419**	**18,374**	**18,862**
	015_Ambulance staff		**17,666**	**18,169**	**18,393**	**18,379**	**18,419**	**18,374**	**18,862**
		001_Manager	695	693	697	653	603	616	625
		002_Emergency Care Practitioner	763	773	764	731	687	661	654
		003_Ambulance Paramedic	9,946	10,522	11,172	11,785	12,362	12,538	12,646
		004_Ambulance Technician	6,264	6,185	5,764	5,212	4,775	4,563	4,942
027_Support to ambulance staff			**14,159**	**14,563**	**14,043**	**13,249**	**13,898**	**14,687**	**15,969**
	028_Ambulance personnel & trainees		**7,667**	**7,851**	**7,525**	**7,077**	**7,250**	**8,002**	**8,499**
		001_Ambulance Personnel	6,283	6,377	6,348	6,216	6,592	6,815	6,544
		003_Trainee Ambulance Technician	1,384	1,474	1,177	861	658	1,187	1,955
	029_Healthcare assistants & support workers		**2,233**	**2,207**	**2,092**	**1,662**	**1,593**	**1,082**	**1,370**
		004_Healthcare Assistant	925	956	955	973	912	354	643
		005_Support Worker	1,308	1,251	1,137	689	681	728	727
	030_Clerical & administrative		**4,080**	**4,290**	**4,203**	**4,281**	**4,843**	**5,430**	**5,918**
		006_Clerical & administrative	4,080	4,290	4,203	4,281	4,843	5,430	5,918
	031_Estates (maintenance & works)		**193**	**226**	**231**	**237**	**224**	**187**	**189**
		007_Estates (maintenance & works)	193	226	231	237	224	187	189

Source: NHS Digital
NHS Digital is the trading name of the Health and Social Care Information Centre.

Headcount totals are unlikely to equal the sum of components.
For more information regarding staff group categorisation, please refer to the lookup guide in the Occupation Code manual.
http://content.digital.nhs.uk/article/2268/NHS-Occupation-Codes

Following a public consultation in 2015, categorisation of Trusts and staff groups has changed from September 2009 onwards, therefore restricting comparability with previous publications. Because of these changes, these statistics are classed as experimental.
More details regarding these changes can be found in the outcomes of the consultation document available at the link below.
http://content.digital.nhs.uk/hchs

Data Quality:
NHS Digital seeks to minimise inaccuracies and the effect of missing and invalid data but responsibility for data accuracy lies with the organisations providing the data. Methods are continually being updated to improve data quality. Where changes impact on figures already published, this is assessed but unless it is significant at national level figures are not changed. Impact at detailed or local level is footnoted in relevant analyses.

16.1b NHS Labour Turnover and Stability Analysis
Welsh Ambulance Trust

As of 31 Dec 2015		Headcount	FTE
	Role		
	Urgent Care Assistant	184	182.53
	Paramedic Manager	29	28.80
	Paramedic	917	898.81
	Paramedic Specialist Practitioner	50	46.49
	Emergency Medical Technician	414	406.41
	Grand Total	1594	1563.04

Source: Welsh Ambulance Service NHS Trust

16.1c Ambulance Staff by type: Scotland
As of December 2015

Whole-time equivalent (WTE)

	Total	Under 20	20 - 24	25 - 29	30 - 34	35 - 39	40 - 44	45 - 49	50 - 54	55 - 59	60 - 64	65 +
Ambulance services	2,451.7	5.7	110.8	218.6	207.3	252.3	337.8	393.2	381.2	316.2	186.0	42.7
Ambulance care assistant	790.6	-	3.0	6.0	11.7	38.5	107.3	144.5	179.7	152.3	116.9	30.7
Auxiliary	1.0	-	-	-	-	-	-	-	1.0	-	-	-
Driver	46.6	-	-	1.0	1.0	0.8	1.3	8.2	8.7	7.9	12.1	5.5
EMDC / control	345.2	5.7	34.8	47.6	53.6	58.6	38.9	43.2	27.1	26.9	8.6	-
Paramedic[1]	x	x	x	x	x	x	x	x	x	x	x	x
Technician	1,183.2	-	73.0	164.0	138.0	144.3	175.2	180.3	148.7	111.0	42.3	6.5
Other	85.0	-	-	-	3.0	10.0	15.0	17.0	16.0	18.0	6.0	-
Not assimilated / not known	-	-	-	-	-	-	-	-	-	-	-	-

Source: Scottish Workforce Information Standard System (SWISS)

1. From 1st April 2013 paramedics have been reclassified from ambulance services staff to allied health professions.

Whole time equivalent (WTE) adjusts headcount staff figures to take account of part time staff.

- nil

x not applicable

16.1d Ambulance Staff by Type: Northern Ireland

											Headcount
		2006	2007	2008	2009	2010	2011	2012	2013	2014	2015
Northern Ireland											
Total Ambulance staff	JHQ9	989	1,007	1,025	1,036	1026	1045	1052	1086	1060	1092
Emergency Medical Technicians and Paramedics	JHR2	637	659	625	629	598	610	618	620	600	639
Other/Patient care services	JHR3	220	219	231	227	244	240	231	263	257	243
Control Assistants	JHR4	63	67	94	108	106	102	107	108	108	122
Ambulance Officers	JHR5	69	62	75	72	78	93	96	95	95	88

Source: Human Resource, Payroll, Travel & Subsistence System; Department of Health, Northern Ireland

16.2 Hospital and primary care services Scotland

			2001 /02	2002 /03	2003 /04	2004 /05	2005 /06	2006 /07	2007 /08
Hospital and community services In-patients:[1,2]									
Average available staffed beds	KDEA	Thousands	30.9	29.8	28.9	28.1	27.4	26.9	26.3
Average occupied beds:									
All departments	KDEB	"	25.1	24.2	23.2	22.5	22.1	21.7	21.0
Psychiatric and learning disability	KDEC	"	6.3	6.0	5.8	5.5	5.2	5.0	4.6
Discharges or deaths[3]	KDED	"	969	959	989	1,003	1,015	1,037	1,066
Outpatients:[2,4]									
New cases	KDEE	"	2,728	2,731	2,750	2,718	1,342	1,324	1,337
Total attendances	KDEF	"	6,254	6,193	6,147	5,981	4,447	4,377	4,371
Medical and dental staff:[5,6,22]	JYXO	Headcount	9,644	10,256	10,407	10,658	10,871	11,201	11,822
Whole-time	KDEG	"	7,530	8,115	8,349	8,612	8,796	9,201	9,828
Part-time	KDEH	"	1,681	1,697	1,636	1,630	1,670	1,607	2,028
Honorary	JYXN	"	468	468	437	431	418	411	418
Professional and technical staff:[6,7,22]									
Whole-time	KDEI	"	11,705	12,265	12,942	13,258	13,750	14,323	13,642
Part-time	KDEJ	"	5,852	6,273	6,708	6,968	7,440	7,990	7,953
Nursing and midwifery staff:[6,8,22]									
Whole-time	KDEK	"	33,334	34,294	34,939	35,338	36,093	37,104	37,071
Part-time	KDEL	"	29,004	29,015	29,354	29,484	29,688	29,995	29,544
Administrative and clerical staff:[6,9,22]									
Whole-time	KDEM	"	15,361	16,200	17,260	17,806	18,434	18,907	18,181
Part-time	KDEN	"	8,075	8,630	9,307	9,943	10,707	11,375	10,836
Domestic, transport, etc, staff:[6,10,22]									
Whole-time	KDEO		7,625	7,768	8,234	8,305	8,516	8,697	10,205
Part-time	KDEP		11 522	11 915	12 588	12 324	12 545	12 675	12,819
Primary care services									
Primary Medical services									
General medical practitioners (GPs):[11,23]	JX4B	Headcount	4,346	4,361	4,447	4,456	4,521	4,597	4,686
Performer[12,23]	KDET	"	3,761	3,770	3,805	3,782	3,763	3,770	3,785
Performer salaried[13,23]	KDEU	"	108	114	155	188	288	354	418
Performer registrar	JX4C	"	283	284	281	282	300	308	325
Performer retainee[14,23]	JX4D	"	196	194	209	208	176	169	164
Expenditure on Primary Medical Services[15,23]	KDEW	£million	430	468	519	628	701	700	705
Pharmaceutical services[16]									
Prescriptions dispensed	KDEX	Millions	66	70	72	75	77	80	82
Payments to pharmacists (gross)	KDEY	£million	808	887	963	984	1016	1045	1067
Average gross cost per prescription	KDEZ	£	12.2	12.8	13.3	12.6	12.5	12.1	11.7
Dental services									
Dentists on list[17]	KDFA	Headcount	1,844	1,869	1,882	1,900	1,936	2,009	2,099
Number of courses of treatment completed	KDFB	Thousands	3,359	3,420	3,359	3,375	3,348	3,387	3,401
Payments to dentists (gross)	KDFC	£million	165	172	170	174	179	188	199
Payments by patients	KDFD	"	52	55	53	54	54	46	47
Payments out of public funds	KDFE	"	113	118	117	120	125	143	152
Average gross cost per course	KDFF	£	38	40	40	40	41	42	43
General ophthalmic services Number of Eye Exams given[18,19,20,21]	KDFG	Thousands	-	-	-	-	-	1,578	1,630
Number of vouchers claimed to provide pairs of glasses/ contact lenses[19,22]	KDFH	"	-	-	-	-	-	465	468
Payments out of public funds forsight testing and dispensing[21]	KDFK	£ million	..	..	..	..	..	66	79

Source: ISD Scotland, Scottish Workforce Information Standard System (SWISS); NHS National Services Scotland

16.2 Hospital and primary care services Scotland

			2008 /09	2009 /10	2010 /11	2011 /12	2012 /13	2013 /14	2014 /15
Hospital and community services In-patients:[1,2]									
Average available staffed beds	KDEA	Thousands	26.6	25.8	24.8	24.1	23.5	23.2	23.0
Average occupied beds:									
All departments	KDEB	"	20.6	19.9	19.2	18.8	18.7	18.5	19.0
Psychiatric and learning disability	KDEC	"	4.3	4.2	4.0	3.8	3.7	3.6	3.6
Discharges or deaths[3]	KDED	"	1,156	1,156	1,149	1,170	1,184	1,205	1,221
Outpatients:[2,4]									
New cases	KDEE	"	1,437	1,442	1,447	1,448	1,460	1,480	1,475
Total attendances	KDEF	"	4,551	4,484	4,485	4,487	4,530	4,582	4,456
Medical and dental staff:[5,6,22]	JYXO	Headcount	12,534	12,619	12,757	13,336	13,317	13,569	14,086
Whole-time	KDEG	"	9,971	9,975	9,973	10,360	10,296	10,511	10,906
Part-time	KDEH	"	2,252	2,444	2,563	2,797	2,849	2,878	3,003
Honorary	JYXN	"	377	247	263	252	243	238	245
Professional and technical staff:[6,7,22]									
Whole-time	KDEI	"	14,567	15,403	15,590	15,021	14,866	16,403	16,651
Part-time	KDEJ	"	8,375	9,036	9,504	9,689	9,924	10,319	10,580
Nursing and midwifery staff:[6,8,22]									
Whole-time	KDEK	"	37,654	37,995	37,165	35,547	35,015	35,803	36,574
Part-time	KDEL	"	29,555	29,949	30,261	30,065	30,518	30,719	30,878
Administrative and clerical staff:[6,9,22]									
Whole-time	KDEM	"	18,158	19,007	18,686	17,639	17,147	17,370	17,649
Part-time	KDEN	"	11,231	11,679	11,703	11,345	11,140	11,242	11,322
Domestic, transport, etc, staff:[6,10,22]									
Whole-time	KDEO		10,623	11,037	10,927	10,522	10,469	9,251	9,338
Part-time	KDEP		12,874	13,138	12,576	12,042	12,051	12,001	12,007
Primary care services									
Primary Medical services									
General medical practitioners (GPs):[11,23]	JX4B	Headcount	4,890	4,906	4,905	4,889	4,865	4,881	4,921
Performer[12,23]	KDET	"	3,785	3,808	3,781	3,753	3,758	3,726	3,719
Performer salaried[13,23]	KDEU	"	458	482	479	519	522	542	596
Performer registrar/ST	JX4C	"	490	465	497	478	455	491	499
Performer retainee[14,23]	JX4D	"	163	158	155	144	138	132	115
Expenditure on Primary Medical Services[15,23]	KDEW	£million	701	729	741	747	756	763	771
Pharmaceutical services[16]									
Prescriptions dispensed	KDEX	Millions	86	89	91	95	97	99	101
Payments to pharmacists (gross)	KDEY	£million	1107	1139	1160	1177	1118	1145	1191
Average gross cost per prescription	KDEZ	£	11.4	11.1	11.0	10.7	9.9	9.9	10.0
Dental services									
Dentists on list[17]	KDFA	Headcount	2,204	2,313	2,354	2,486	2,520	2564	2663
Number of courses of treatment completed	KDFB	Thousands	3,548	3,686	3,830	4,100	4,289	4,418	4,490
Payments to dentists (gross)	KDFC	£million	227	246	254	267	271	274	280
Payments by patients	KDFD	"	50	52	55	59	62	N/A	N/A
Payments out of public funds	KDFE	"	170	180	188	196	198	N/A	N/A
Average gross cost per course	KDFF	£	39	43	44	46	47	47	48
General ophthalmic services Number of Eye Exams given[18,19,20,21]	KDFG	Thousands	1,728	1,775	1,804	1,913	1,932	2306	2021
Number of vouchers claimed to provide pairs of glasses/ contact lenses[19,22]	KDFH	"	483	493	489	504	487	494	453
Payments out of public funds forsight testing and dispensing[21]	KDFK	£ million	86	91	90	96	96	N/A	N/A

Source: ISD Scotland, Scottish Workforce Information Standard System (SWISS); NHS National Services Scotland

16.2 Hospital and primary care services Scotland

1 Excludes joint user and contractual hospitals.

2 In year to 31 March.

3 figures prior to 2008/09 were sourced from the ISD(S)1 dataset and may have included an element of estimation for any incomplete or outstanding data submissions. Discharges data from 2008/09 is sourced from the SMR01 dataset, where no such estimation is applied

4 Including all specialities but excluding A & E. Outpatients are based on ISD(S)1 data.

5 As at 30 September. Figures exclude officers holding honorary locum appointments. Part-time includes maximum part-time appointments. There is an element of double counting of "heads" in this table as doctors can hold more than one contract. For example, they may hold contracts of different type, eg part time and honorary. Doctors holding two or more contracts of the same type, eg part time, are not double counted. Doctors, whose sum of contracts amounts to whole time, are classed as such. Figures have been revised due to coding changes.

6 The change in both collection and presentation of workforce data due to changes to staff groupings under Agenda for Change has inevitably meant that the amount of historical trend analysis of data is limited, though still available for some high level groupings.

7 As at 30 September. Comprises Therapeutic, Healthcare science, Technical and Pharmacy staff.

8 As at 30 September.Figures post 2003 have been amended due to a coding error resulting in some staff previously in this group being moved to the admin and clerical group.

9 As at 30 September. Comprises Senior Management and Administrative and Clerical staff. Figures for 2003 onwards have been amended due to the inclusion of some staff previously in the nursing and midwifery staff group

10 As at 30 September.Comprises Ambulance, Works, Ancillary and Trades.

11 Please note that GPs may hold multiple posts simultaneously therefore the total number of GPs may not equal the sum of the different GP post types.

12 Performer (GP performers that are not salaried, retainees or registrars - i.e. generally the practice partners). Known prior to 2004/05 as Principal GPs.

13 Performer salaried (GPs who are employed by the practice or NHS Board on a salaried basis)

14 Performer retainee (A GP, typically part-time, who can be utilised by a practice as they are required). Data on the number of GP retainees not available prior to 2000.

15 Total expenditure on General Medical Services/Primary Medical Services Source: NHS Scotland Costs Book "R390" tables, www.isdscotland.org/costs

Note, the contractual arrangements for payments to many general practices changed with the introduction of the new GMS contract in April 2004.

16 For prescriptions dispensed in financial year by all community pharmacists (including stock orders), dispensing doctors and appliance suppliers. Gross total excludes patient charges.

17 Comprises of non-salaried GDS principal dentists only as at 31 March.

18 As a result of a number of data quality issues, eye examination data have been revised. It is therefore strongly advised that any previously held data are discarded and the revised data reported here are used.

19 Data on eye examinations and vouchers are sourced from OPTIX, the electronic system for recording ophtalmic payment information.

20 Figures represent the total number of fully funded NHS eye examinations.

21 Fully funded NHS eye examinations were extended to all on 1st April 2006.

22 General Ophthalmic Service GOS(S)3 forms are referred to as 'vouchers' and are used to provide eye glasses/contact lenses Headcount refers to the actual number of individuals (employees) working within the NHSS. This eliminates any double counting that may exist as a result of an employee holding more than one post. Please note due to revisions in the headcount measure, it is not possible to compare data prior to 2007.

23 Figures have been revised and differ from those previously published due to improvements in source data quality.

*** Figures not yet published.

Update to Secondary Care Notes

Average available staffed beds: The daily average number of beds which are staffed and are available for the reception of inpatients (borrowed and temporary beds are included).

Average occupied beds: The average of available staffed beds that were occupied by inpatients during the financial year.

Source: ISD Scotland, Scottish Workforce Information Standard System (SWISS); NHS National Services Scotland

16.3 Hospital and general health services
Northern Ireland

			2004	2005	2006	2007	2008	2009
Hospital services[1]								
In-patients:								
Beds available[2]	KDGA	Numbers	8,323	8,238	7,976	7,827	7,636	7,274
Average daily occupation of beds	KDGB	Percentages	84	84	83	83	82	82
Discharges or deaths[3]	KDGC	Thousands	337	296	295	306	311	300
Out-patients:[4]								
New cases	KDGD	"	1,027	1,040	1,081	1,115	1,149	1,150
Total attendances	KDGE	"	2,175	2,219	2,233	2,282	2,256	2,231
General health services								
Medical services[1]								
Doctors (principals) on the list[5,6]	KDGF	Numbers	1,078	1,084	1,100	1,127	1,148	1,156
Number of patients per doctor	KDGG	"	1,663	1,655	1,631	1,626	1,618	1,615
Gross Payments to doctors[7]	KDGH	£ thousand	..	..	..	..	..	..
Pharmaceutical services[8]								
Prescription forms dispensed	KDGI	Thousands	15,283	15,860	16,393	17,280	17,910	19,241
Number of prescriptions	KDGJ	"	27,401	28,417	29,599	30,864	32,107	34,263
Gross Cost[9]	KDGK	£ thousand	382,789	390,763	408,771	425,440	445,184	470,049
Charges[10]	KDGL	"	10,262	10,676	11,298	11,943	10,243	4,447
Net Cost[9]	KDGM	"	372,527	380,087	397,473	413,497	434,940	465,603
Average gross cost per prescription[9]	KDGN	£	14	14	14	14	14	14
Dental services[8,11]								
Dentists on the list[5]	KDGO	Numbers	720	722	751	763	795	816
Number of courses of paid treatment	KDGP	Thousands	1,086	1,084	1,064	1,002	1,034	1,051
Gross cost	KDGQ	£ thousand	67,294	69,480	65,172	68,775	71,401	73,741
Patients	KDGR	Thousands	907	910	900	859	868	885
Contributions (Net cost)	KDGS	£ thousand	50,498	52,308	50,068	53,301	55,801	57,897
Average gross cost per paid treatment	KDGT	£	62	64	61	69	69	70
Ophthalmic services[8]								
Number of sight tests given[12]	KDGU	Thousands	347	360	368	385	404	413
Number of optical appliances supplied[13]	KDGV	"	189	194	196	200	210	212
Cost of service (gross)[14]	KDGW	£ thousand	14,395	15,868	16,280	16,970	18,468	19,638
Health and social services[15]								
Medical and dental staff:								
Whole-time	KDGZ	Numbers	2,749	2,947	3,152	3,250	3,278	3,301
Part-time	KDHA	"	626	561	554	587	603	599
Nursing and midwifery staff:								
Whole-time	KDHB	"	11,116	11,395	11,454	11,623	11,512	11,716
Part-time	KDHC	"	8,850	9,015	9,072	9,310	9,251	9,277
Administrative and clerical staff:								
Whole-time	KDHD	"	8,676	8,878	8,938	8,683	8,255	8,197
Part-time	KDHE	"	3,828	4,160	4,221	4,226	4,196	4,286
Professional and technical staff:								
Whole-time	KDHF	"	4,518	4,685	4,758	4,936	4,619	4,704
Part-time	KDHG	"	1,724	1,822	2,021	2,076	2,347	2,423
Social services staff(excluding casual home helps):								
Whole-time	KDHH	"	3,709	3,773	3,889	4,014	4,441	4,619
Part-time	KDHI	"	1,197	1,289	1,417	2,041	2,808	2,863
Ancillary and other staff:								
Whole-time	KDHJ	"	3,469	3,722	3,833	3,857	3,831	3,816
Part-time	KDHK	"	5,580	5,486	5,892	5,667	4,794	4,904
Cost of services (gross)[14]	KDHL	£ thousand	..	..	..	..	..	..
Payments by recipients	KDHM	Thousands	..	..	..	..	..	..
Payments out of public funds	KDHN	£ thousand	..	..	..	..	..	..

16.3 Hospital and general health services
Northern Ireland

			2010	2011	2012	2013	2014	2015
Hospital services[1]								
In-patients:								
Beds available[2]	KDGA	Numbers	6,732	6,439	6,288	6,172	6,056	5,925
Average daily occupation of beds	KDGB	Percentages	83	84	84	83	83	83
Discharges or deaths[3]	KDGC	Thousands	295	295	301	304	308	306
Out-patients:[4]								
New cases	KDGD	"	1,148	1,123	1,124	1,144	1,146	1,186
Total attendances	KDGE	"	2,234	2,239	2,247	2,288	2,240	2,283
General health services								
Medical services[1]								
Doctors (principals) on the list[5,6]	KDGF	Numbers	1,160	1,163	1,170	1,171	1,211	1,274
Number of patients per doctor	KDGG	"	1,623	1,631	1,631	1,639	1,599	1,529
Gross Payments to doctors[7]	KDGH	£ thousand	..	..	..	..	..	..
Pharmaceutical services[8]								
Prescription forms dispensed	KDGI	Thousands	20,411	20,860	21,416	21,723	22,473	22,809
Number of prescriptions	KDGJ	"	36,298	36,916	38,614	40,019	40,377	40,712
Gross Cost[9]	KDGK	£ thousand	490,670	462,947	457,492	463,206	478,328	496,397
Charges[10]	KDGL	"	0	0	0	0	0	0
Net Cost[9]	KDGM	"	490,670	462,947	457,492	463,206	478,328	496,397
Average gross cost per prescription[9]	KDGN	£	14	13	12	12	12	12
Dental services[8,11]								
Dentists on the list[5]	KDGO	Numbers	889	1,010	1,044	1,049	1,125	1,055
Number of courses of paid treatment	KDGP	Thousands	1,172	1,231	1,283	1,335	1,336	1,355
Gross cost	KDGQ	£ thousand	81,621	84,659	90,759	92,984	94,681	96,690
Patients	KDGR	Thousands	1,001	1,119	1,147	1,166	1,175	1,195
Contributions (Net cost)	KDGS	£ thousand	64,280	66,533	69,960	73,520	74,640	74,127
Average gross cost per paid treatment	KDGT	£	70	69	71	70	71	71
Ophthalmic services[8]								
Number of sight tests given[12]	KDGU	Thousands	425	435	438	446	454	469
Number of optical appliances supplied[13]	KDGV	"	219	226	233	235	236	237
Cost of service (gross)[14]	KDGW	£ thousand	19,823	20,220	20,836	21,346	21,815	22,357
Health and social services[15]								
Medical and dental staff:								
Whole-time	KDGZ	Numbers	3,294	3,347	3,415	3,358	3,539	3,596
Part-time	KDHA	"	618	649	677	697	810	827
Nursing and midwifery staff:								
Whole-time	KDHB	"	11,292	11,171	11,426	11,722	11,970	12,342
Part-time	KDHC	"	9,470	9,356	9,422	9,453	9,436	9,312
Administrative and clerical staff:								
Whole-time	KDHD	"	7,880	7,795	8,106	8,201	8,237	8,093
Part-time	KDHE	"	4,280	4,304	4,447	4,498	4,512	4,619
Professional and technical staff:								
Whole-time	KDHF	"	4,748	4,807	5,069	5,233	5,340	5,416
Part-time	KDHG	"	2,533	2,639	2,725	2,859	3,005	3,123
Social services staff(excluding casual home helps):								
Whole-time	KDHH	"	4,632	4,581	4,622	4,689	4,778	4,843
Part-time	KDHI	"	2,877	2,896	2,919	2,930	2,844	2,913
Ancillary and other staff:								
Whole-time	KDHJ	"	3,855	3,814	3,740	3,726	3,731	3,710
Part-time	KDHK	"	4,805	4,582	4,598	4,636	4,338	4,290
Cost of services (gross)[14]	KDHL	£ thousand	..	..	..	..	..	..
Payments by recipients	KDHM	Thousands	..	..	..	..	..	..
Payments out of public funds	KDHN	£ thousand	..	..	..	..	..	..

Sources: Business Services Organisation (BSO) Northern Ireland: 028 9053 2975;
Dept of Health Northern Ireland: 028 9052 2509;
(Figures on Hospital Services: 028 9052 2800)

16.3 Hospital and general health services
Northern Ireland

1 Financial Year.

2 Average available beds in wards open overnight during the year.

3 Includes transfers to other hospitals. This figure also excludes day case admissions.

4 Includes consultant outpatient clinics and Accident and Emergency departments.

5 At beginning of period for Dentists. Doctors numbers at 2002 (Oct), 2003 (Nov), 2004, 2005 & 2006 (Oct).

6 From 2003 onwards (UPE's).

7 These costs refer to the majority of non-cash limited services: further expenditure under GMS is allocated through HSS Boards on a cash limited basis. Change between 2002 and 2003 is due to advance payments being made in relation to the new GMS contract introduced in April 2004.

8 From 1995 onwards figures are taken from financial year.

9 Gross cost is defined as net ingredient costs plus on-cost, fees and other payments.

10 Excludes amount paid by patients for pre-payment certificates.

11 Due to changes in the Dental Contract which came into force in October 1990 dentists are paid under a combination of headings relating to Capitation and Continuing Care patients. Prior to this, payment was simply on an item of service basis.

12 Excluding sight tests given in hospitals and under the school health service and in the home.

13 Relates to the number of vouchers supplied and excludes repair/replace spectacles.

14 Figures relate to the costs of the hospital, community health and personal social services,and have been estimated from financial year data.

15 Workforce figures are headcounts at 30th September and are taken from the Human Resources Management System system. All workforce figures have been revised and now exclude Home Helps, Bank staff, staff on career breaks, Chairperson / Members of Boards and staff with a whole-time equivalent equal to or less than 0.03. The Ancillary and Other staff category includes Ancillary & General/Support Services staff, Works & Maintenance/Estates staff and Ambulance staff for all years, and from 2008 also includes Generic staff who are multidisciplinary staff. Due to Agenda for Change, new grade codes were introduced (from 2007 onwards) which resulted in some staff moving between categories. Backward comparison of the workforce is therefore not advised due to variations in definitions. 2014 figures onwards will include Northern Ireland Medical & Dental Training Agency staff and GP trainees working in Trusts.

16.4 Workforce in General Practice and Hospital and Community Health Services in NHS Trusts and Clinical Commissioning Groups as at 30 September each year

Provisional Experimental statistics
England

Headcount & Percentages

	Sep-09	Sep-10	Sep-11	Sep-12	Sep-13	Sep-14	Sep-15	Change 2014-2015	% change 2014-2015	Change 2009-2015	Average Annual % change
HEADCOUNT											
Total (excluding GP Locums)	1,301,673	1,333,197	1,310,849	1,290,904	1,286,234	1,306,946	1,318,038	11,092	0.8%	16,365	0.2%
Professionally qualified clinical staff	651,927	662,621	663,956	656,787	664,288	671,218	677,524	6,306	0.9%	25,597	0.6%
Total Doctors (excluding GP Locums)	137,571	142,071	144,219	145,869	147,574	148,348	149,808	1,460	1.0%	12,237	1.4%
HCHS doctors	102,172	103,865	105,207	106,150	107,639	109,944	111,127	1,183	1.1%	8,955	1.4%
Consultant (including Directors of Public Health)	36,932	38,507	39,758	40,997	42,125	43,602	45,349	1,747	4.0%	8,417	3.5%
Associate Specialist	3,770	3,758	3,730	3,479	3,218	2,967	2,727	-240	-8.1%	-1,043	-5.3%
Specialty Doctor	3,974	5,053	5,866	6,301	6,578	6,985	7,156	171	2.4%	3,182	10.3%
Staff Grade	2,440	1,421	854	616	502	449	478	29	6.5%	-1,962	-23.8%
Specialty Registrar	30,128	29,763	29,857	29,981	30,581	31,237	30,569	-668	-2.1%	441	0.2%
Core Medical Training	5,861	6,949	7,315	7,648	7,731	7,939	8,173	234	2.9%	2,312	5.7%
Core Dental Training	1,658	1,336	1,241	1,145	1,066	934	874	-60	-6.4%	-784	-10.1%
Foundation Doctor Year 2	6,190	6,394	6,458	6,482	6,491	6,648	6,626	-22	-0.3%	436	1.1%
Foundation Doctor Year 1	6,121	6,180	6,193	6,180	6,413	6,310	6,391	81	1.3%	270	0.7%
Hospital Practitioner / Clinical Assistant	3,753	3,237	2,707	2,239	1,942	1,817	1,762	-55	-3.0%	-1,991	-11.8%
Other and Unknown HCHS Doctor Grades	1,981	1,850	1,743	1,523	1,428	1,447	1,407	-40	-2.8%	-574	-5.5%
GPs total	**40,269**	**39,409**	**40,008**	**40,463**	**40,236**	**41,105**	**41,877**	**..**	**..**	**..**	**..**
GPs (excluding Locums)	**36,388**	**35,532**	**35,775**	**35,844**	**35,842**	**36,078**	**40,697**	**-408**	**-1.0%**	**428**	**0.2%**
GPs (excluding Registrars & Locums)	35,917	35,120	35,415	35,527	35,561	35,819	35,734	-344	-1.0%	-654	-0.3%
GPs (excluding Registrars, Retainers and Locums)	:	:	:	:	:	:	35,586	-233	-0.7%	-331	-0.2%
GP Providers	27,613	27,036	27,218	26,886	26,635	26,183	22,390	:	:	:	:
Other GPs	8304	8,319	8,585	8,898	9,153	9,885	10,063	:	:	:	:
GP Registrars	3881	3,880	4,241	4,624	4,404	5,033	4,982	:	:	:	:
GP Retainers	471	419	365	321	284	262	148	:	:	:	:
GP Locums	:	:	:	:	:	:	1,321	:	:	:	:
GPs not stated	:	:	:	:	:	:	3,228	:	:	:	:
Nurses & health visitors	315,436	316,861	313,379	305,846	308,316	312,176	314,966	2,790	0.9%	-470	0.0%
Midwives	23,540	24,151	24,519	24,765	25,006	25,333	25,418	85	0.3%	1,878	1.3%
Ambulance staff	17,666	18,169	18,393	18,379	18,419	18,374	18,862	488	2.7%	1,196	1.1%
Scientific, therapeutic & technical staff	137,252	140,599	141,782	140,035	142,701	144,540	146,792	2,252	1.6%	9,540	1.1%
Nurses in GP Practices	21,935	23,846	23,584	23,458	23,833	23,832	23,066	:	:	:	:
Support to clinical staff	341,282	345,328	334,787	325,251	330,407	340,720	350,053	9,333	2.7%	8,771	0.4%
Support to doctors, nurses & midwives	268,874	270,747	261,922	255,021	259,002	265,590	272,588	6,998	2.6%	3,714	0.2%
Support to ambulance staff	14,159	14,563	14,043	13,249	13,898	14,687	15,969	1,282	8.7%	1,810	2.0%
Support to ST&T staff	58,784	60,568	59,399	57,500	58,031	60,934	61,982	1,048	1.7%	3,198	0.9%

16.4 Workforce in General Practice and Hospital and Community Health Services in NHS Trusts and Clinical Commissioning Groups as at 30 September each year

Provisional Experimental statistics
England

Headcount & Percentages

	Sep-09	Sep-10	Sep-11	Sep-12	Sep-13	Sep-14	Sep-15	Change 2014 -2015	% change 2014 -2015	Change 2009 -2015	Average Annual % change
NHS infrastructure support	215,502	214,414	201,939	195,223	177,311	178,704	181,961	3,257	1.8%	-33,541	-2.8%
Central functions	102,682	104,306	97,329	93,745	83,060	84,738	87,228	2,490	2.9%	-15,454	-2.7%
Hotel, property & estates	73,779	73,570	71,088	69,111	66,648	64,954	63,900	-1,054	-1.6%	-9,879	-2.4%
Senior managers	12,322	11,485	10,467	10,203	8,672	9,243	9,733	490	5.3%	-2,589	-3.9%
Managers	26,922	25,233	23,238	22,327	19,070	19,911	21,219	1,308	6.6%	-5,703	-3.9%
Other HCHS staff or those with unknown classification	4,906	4,307	4,228	4,002	3,896	4,240	4,291	51	1.2%	-615	-2.2%
GP Direct Patient Care and Admin Staff	92,333										
GP Direct Patient Care staff	..	14,297	13,620	15,631	16,339	16,800	14,469	..	..	..	..
GP Admin/Non-Clinical staff	..	98,688	96,973	98,201	97,884	98,720	93,301	..	..	..	..

Source: NHS Digital

Copyright: © 2016, Health and Social Care Information Centre. The Health and Social Care Information Centre is a non-departmental body created by statute, also known as NHS Digital.

HCHS Figures for September 2010, 2011 and 2014 that were published on 30 March 2016 have been updated in April 2016.
From 2015 GP figures are sourced from the workforce Minimum Dataset (wMDS).
GP data is classed as Experimental, Provisional
For lines where a GP headcount percentage change is given, the working assumption is that the 2014 and 2015 figures are broadly comparable, despite the change in data source. For Practice staff headcount the figures are not comparable.
As comparisons between the data sources are explored in even further depth, as part of the publication scheduled for September 2016, there may be some revisions to improve comparability.
Headcount totals are unlikely to equal the sum of components due to some staff working in more than one role.
2009 Practice Staff data include imputed data based on previous censuses for a number of PCTs who did not submit returns.
'..' denotes not applicable
Data as at 30 September each year

Please note that this table is different to previous versions. This is because the non-medical staff in post census no longer exists, the last one produced was for data as at September 2014. Following a public consultation in 2015, categorisation of Trusts and staff groups has changed from September 2009 onwards, therefore restricting comparability with previous publications. Because of these changes, these statistics are classed as experimental. More details regarding these changes can be found in the outcomes of the consultation document available at the link below.
http://content.digital.nhs.uk/hchs

16.5 Staffing summary

Wales

	Unit (a)	2011	2012	2013	2014	2015 (g)
Directly employed NHS staff:						
Medical and dental staff (b):						
Hospital medical staff	Fte	5,490	5,544	5,713	5,654	5,765
Of which consultants	Fte	2,128	2,180	2,230	2,221	2,255
Community/Public health medical staff	Fte	84	88	79	76	72
Hospital dental staff	Fte	161	161	168	164	165
Of which consultants	Fte	44	44	46	49	48
Community/Public health dental staff	Fte	109	115	114	117	119
Total	**Fte**	**5,844**	**5,909**	**6,073**	**6,011**	**6,120**
Nursing, midwifery and health visiting staff	Fte	27,980	28,068	28,254	28,300	28,684
of which qualified	Fte	21,748	21,823	22,005	22,053	22,192
Scientific, therapeutic and technical staff	Fte	11,472	11,549	11,616	11,671	11,971
Health care assistants and other support staff	Fte	9,718	9,793	9,699	9,650	9,753
Administration and estates staff	Fte	15,192	15,039	15,120	15,172	15,724
Ambulance staff	Fte	1,457	1,511	1,499	1,544	1,598
Other (c)	Fte	173	133	131	115	108
Total	**Fte**	**71,836**	**72,002**	**72,393**	**72,464**	**73,958**
Family Practitioners:						
General medical practitioners (d)	Number	2,009	1,997	2,026	2,006	1,997
General dental practitioners (e)	Number	1,349	1,360	1,392	1,438	1,439
Ophthalmic medical practitioners (f)	Number	12	14	8	7	7
Ophthalmic opticians (f)	Number	756	795	773	769	811

Source: Health Statistics and Analysis Unit, Welsh Government

(a) Fte = whole-time equivalent.

(b) Excludes locum staff.

© Professional advisors and staff on general payments, eg Macmillan and Marie Curie nurses.

(d) At 30 September. All practitioners excluding GP registrars, GP Retainers and locums

(e) Number of dental performers who have any NHS activity recorded against them via FP17 claim forms at any time in the year ending 31 March.

(f) At 31 December.

(g) NHS Wales Shared Services Partnership (NWSSP) became the lead employer for General Practice (Doctors in Training only) from 2015 onwards. Previously GPs in training who rotated into a GP surgery would be employed by the surgery and therefore leave the NHS Wales payroll. Now NWSSP keeps continuous employment and these figures are shown against Velindre NHS Trust, which hosts NWSSP. In addition to these, GP trainees who are on hospital rotations are recorded under the specialty of their current role against Velindre NHS trust from 2015 onwards. Previously these trainees were recorded against the Local Health Boards (LHBs) which hosted the trainee. As a result the numbers recorded against the LHBs in the relevant specialties have fallen.

16.6 Deaths[1]: underlying cause, sex and age-group, Summary

ICD-10 code	England and Wales		2013		2014		2015
	Underlying cause (excludes deaths under 28 days for individual causes)		Age-group		Age-group		Age-group
			All ages		All ages		All ages
A00-R99, U00-Y89	All causes, all ages	M	245,585	M	245,585	M	257,207
		F	261,205	F	261,205	F	272,448
	All causes, ages under 28 days	M	1,084	M	1,084	M	1,108
		F	813	F	813	F	795
A00-R99, U00-Y89	All causes, ages 28 days and over	M	244,501	M	244,501	M	256,099
		F	260,392	F	260,392	F	271,653
A00-B99	Certain infectious and parasitic diseases	M	2,403	M	2,403	M	2,660
		F	2,902	F	2,902	F	3,123
C00-D48	Neoplasms	M	76,962	M	76,962	M	78,735
		F	68,382	F	68,382	F	69,022
D50-D89	Diseases of the blood and blood-forming organs and certain disorders involving the immune mechanism	M	440	M	440	M	516
		F	516	F	516	F	614
E00-E90	Endocrine, nutritional and metabolic diseases	M	3,184	M	3,184	M	3,712
		F	3,594	F	3,594	F	3,957
F00-F99	Mental and behavioural disorders	M	12,655	M	12,655	M	16,398
		F	25,578	F	25,578	F	31,919
G00-G99	Diseases of the nervous system	M	10,173	M	10,173	M	12,367
		F	12,331	F	12,331	F	16,006
H00-H59	Diseases of the eye and adnexa	M	2	M	2	M	6
		F	10	F	10	F	10
H60-H95	Diseases of the ear and mastoid process	M	2	M	2	M	20
		F	10	F	10	F	14
I00-I99	Diseases of the circulatory system	M	70,336	M	70,336	M	70,357
		F	69,965	F	69,965	F	68,257
J00-J99	Diseases of the respiratory system	M	35,115	M	35,115	M	36,114
		F	39,114	F	39,114	F	39,420
K00-K93	Diseases of the digestive system	M	11,712	M	11,712	M	12,212
		F	12,646	F	12,646	F	12,889
L00-L99	Diseases of the skin and subcutaneous tissue	M	605	M	605	M	637
		F	1,115	F	1,115	F	1,264
M00-M99	Diseases of the musculoskeletal system and connective tissue	M	1,368	M	1,368	M	1,367
		F	2,853	F	2,853	F	2,696
N00-N99	Diseases of the genitourinary system	M	4,073	M	4,073	M	4,090
		F	5,558	F	5,558	F	5,269
O00-O99	Pregnancy, childbirth and the puerperium	F	47	F	47	F	29
P00-P96	Certain conditions originating in the perinatal period	M	111	M	111	M	115
		F	56	F	56	F	75
Q00-Q99	Congenital malformations, deformations and chromosomal abnormalities	M	576	M	576	M	679
		F	550	F	550	F	578
R00-R99	Symptoms, signs and abnormal clinical and laboratory findings, not elsewhere classified	M	2,851	M	2,851	M	3,173
		F	8,167	F	8,167	F	8,676
U509, V01-Y89	External causes of morbidity and mortality	M	11,923	M	11,923	M	12,941
		F	6,998	F	6,998	F	7,835

Source: Office for National Statistics

1 Death figures are based on deaths registered rather than deaths occurring in a calendar year. For more infomation on registration delays see www.ons.gov.uk/ons/guide-method/user-guidance/health-and-life-events/impact-of-registration-delays-on-mortality-statistics/index.html

16.7a Notifications of infectious diseases , 2006-2015

England and Wales

Disease	2006	2007	2008	2009	2010	2011	2012	2013	2014	2015
Acute encephalitis	19	18	24	16	16	13	9	15	11	9
Acute infectious hepatitis	.	.	.	.	475	408	253	253	865	559
Acute Meningitis	1494	1251	1181	1219	922	538	522	545	474	524
Acute poliomyelitis	.	.	.	1	.	1	.	.	1	.
Anthrax	1	.	1	.	5	.	2	1	.	.
Botulism	.	.	.	.	2	.	.	.	.	3
Brucellosis	.	.	.	.	.	3	3	1	4	3
Cholera	37	41	40	35	35	16	7	3	10	13
Diphtheria	10	9	6	11	9	2	4	9	14	9
Dysentery	1122	1217	1166	1218	267	.	.	.	.	.
Enteric fever (typhoid or paratyphoid fever)	.	.	.	.	272	224	137	127	157	128
Food poisoning	70603	72382	68962	74974	57041	24384	20680	15350	17402	15716
Haemolytic uraemic syndrome (HUS)	.	.	.	.	1	5	1	4	6	4
Infectious bloody diarrhoea	.	.	.	.	386	469	418	399	511	463
Invasive group A streptococcal disease	.	.	.	.	215	186	194	223	369	403
Legionnaires' Disease	.	.	.	.	102	73	80	82	151	139
Leprosy	.	.	.	.	1	1	8	4	8	4
Leptospirosis	24	37	44	29	5	.	.	.	.	.
Malaria	613	426	386	381	327	296	267	226	201	195
Measles	3705	3670	5088	5191	2235	2355	4211	6193	1851	1193
Meningococcal septicaemia	657	673	528	495	367	261	301	300	277	227
Mumps	12841	7196	7827	18629	10402	6888	7530	10095	8334	6114
Ophthalmia neonatorum	100	83	77	90	18	.	.	.	.	.
Other	.	.	.	.	1974	2780	4751	5017	4660	4424
Paratyphoid fever	185	126	170	130	33	.	.	.	.	.
Rabies	.	.	.	.	.	.	1	.	.	.
Rubella	1221	1082	1096	1130	631	476	756	553	425	398
SARS	.	.	.	.	.	.	.	.	.	1
Scarlet fever	2166	1948	2920	4176	2969	2719	4254	4643	15637	17696
Tetanus	.	4	7	6	6	2	7	2	4	3
Tuberculosis	7621	6989	7319	7241	8333	9227	9101	8137	7261	6599
Typhoid fever	201	208	240	210	68	.	.	.	.	.
Typhus fever	6	.	4	.	2	.	4	2	1	.
Viral haemorrhagic fever	5	1	3	5	3	3	7	6	11	10
Viral hepatitis	4007	3857	4756	4979	1043	.	.	.	.	.
Whooping cough	550	1089	1512	1155	405	911	6557	3273	2506	3083
Grand Total	107188	102307	103357	121321	88570	52241	60065	55463	61151	57920

Source: Public Health England

1. As from 6th April 2010 the following diseases are no longer notifiable but may still be reported under the Other disease category: Dysentery, Leptospirosis, Ophthalmia neonatorum, Viral hepatitis

2. As from 6th April 2010 the following diseases became notifiable: Botulism, Brucellosis, Haemolytic Uraemic Syndrome (HUS), Infectious bloody diarrhoea, Legionnaire's disease,

3. As from 6th April 2010 Typhoid and Paratyphoid fever have been grouped under Enteric fever.

4. As from week 35 of 2010 Food poisoning 'otherwise ascertained' cases are no longer collected.

5. As from 6th April 2010 the Other disease category may be used to notify any cases that may present a significant risk to human health.

6. A proportion of notified cases are shown subsequently not to be the implicated infection.

7. Any disease not mentioned on a table may be assumed Where a disease is not mentioned on a table it may be assumed that no notifications were received.

16.7b Notifications of infectious diseases, 2003 - 2014

Scotland

Notifiable Disease[1,2,3]	Confirmed notifications											
	2003	2004	2005	2006	2007	2008	2009	2010	2011	2012	2013	2014
Botulism	..	.. ..	..		..	..	..	0	3	0	..	1
Anthrax	0	0	0	1	0	0	4	39	0	4	1	2
Brucellosis	..	..	..	..	..	..	..	1	1	0	1	..
Cholera	1	1	6	3	8	3	5	3	3	1	1	5
Clinical Syndrome E.coli O 157 infection	..	..	..	..	..	..	..	33	4	17	3	10
Diphtheria	0	0	0	0	1	0	0	0	0	0	1	3
Haemolytic Uraemic Syndrome (HUS)	..	..	..	..	..	..	..	5	3	1	5	4
Haemophilus influenzae type b (Hib)	..	..	..	..	..	..	..	3	6	0	..	2
Measles	181	257	186	259	168	219	172	93	82	99	162	55
Meningococcal disease	117	147	139	140	150	120	122	93	103	89	83	68
Mumps	181	3 595	5 698	2 917	2 741	720	1129	727	607	920	503	335
Necrotizing fasciitis	..	..	..	..	..	..	..	2	12	4	7	9
Paratyphoid	0	0	0	0	1	4	2	2	1	0	..	10
Pertussis (Whooping cough)	60	87	51	67	98	134	104	45	85	2068	1 134	413
Poliomyelitis	0	0	0	0	0	0	0	0	0	0	..	..
Rabies	0	0	0	0	0	0	0	0	0	0	..	..
Rubella	130	222	141	153	146	106	93	39	21	43	22	24
Tetanus	1	1	1	0	0	0	0	0	0	0	..	1
Typhoid	2	2	1	3	3	3	1	6	3	2	8	6
Viral haemorrhagic fevers	0	0	0	0	0	0	0	0	0	1	..	..

Source: Health Protection Scotland (HPS SIDSS2)
Queries to: nss.hpsenquiries@nhs.net (tel 0141 300 1100)

.. Not available

1 Figures for all years are confirmed notifications

2 The following diseases were also notifiable but there were no cases in 2012: Plague, Severe Acute Respiratory Syndrome (SARS), Smallpox, Tularemia, West Nile fever, Yellow fever

3 From 2010 the following diseases are no longer notifiable - Bacillary dysentery, Chickenpox, Erysipelas, Food poisoning, Legionellosis, Leptospirosis, Lyme disease, Malaria, Puerperal fever, Scarlet fever, Toxoplasmosis, Typhus fever and Viral hepatitis

16.7c Notifications of Infectious diseases
Northern Ireland

Description	2011	2012	2013	2014	2015
Acute Encephalitis/Meningitis Bacterial	28	37	61	62	46
Acute Encephalitis/Meningitis Viral	13	10	7	16	5
Anthrax	0	0	2	0	0
Chickenpox	1566	2126	1574	1675	1439
Cholera	0	0	0	0	0
Diphtheria	0	0	0	0	0
Dysentery	7	11	6	24	48
Food Poisoning	1575	1777	1707	1820	1913
Gastroenteritis (< 2years)	661	799	571	447	309
Hepatitis A	0	4	4	3	7
Hepatitis B	129	130	114	126	93
Hepatitis Unspecified	0	0	0	0	5
Legionnaires' Disease	4	6	10	7	10
Leptospirosis	3	3	2	0	3
Malaria	1	5	5	6	7
Measles	27	43	57	17	16
Meningococcal Septicaemia	45	33	27	22	19
Mumps	123	298	694	126	352
Paratyphoid Fever	0	0	1	1	0
Plague	0	0	0	0	0
Poliomyelitis (Acute)	0	0	0	0	0
Poliomyelitis (Paralytic)	0	0	0	0	0
Rabies	0	0	0	0	0
Relapsing Fever	0	0	0	0	0
Rubella	18	13	17	10	5
Scarlet Fever	130	196	190	625	363
Smallpox	0	0	0	0	0
Tetanus	1	1	1	0	2
Tuberculosis (Non Pulmonary)	14	45	40	71	44
Tuberculosis (Pulmonary)	44	51	34	36	36
Typhoid	1	1	1	0	1
Typhus	0	0	0	0	0
Viral Haemorraghic Fever	0	2	1	0	0
Whooping Cough	18	394	76	41	118
Yellow Fever	0	0	0	0	0

Public Health Agency, Northern Ireland

Food poisoning notifications include those formally notified by clinicians and reports of Salmonella, Campylobacter, Cryptosporidium, Giardia, Listeria and E Coli O 157 informally ascertained from laboratories.

16.8a Work-related and occupational respiratory disease: estimated number of cases reported by chest physicians to SWORD 2007-2014 and by occupational physicians to OPRA 2006-2010 by sex and diagnostic category

Sex		Chest physicians (SWORD)								Occupational Physicians (OPRA) (c)				
All cases (b)	Diagnostic category	2007	2008	2009	2010	2011	2012	2013	2014r	2006	2007	2008	2009	2010
	Allergic alveolitis	19	87	39	29	25	56	53	14	-	-	-	13	-
	Asthma	251	307	181	205	159	189	189	132	145	104	55	47	65
	Bronchitis/emphysema	15	18	69	18	52	19	26	17	-	2	12	-	-
	Infectious diseases	28	24	25	2	60	25	14	36	2	36	-	24	12
	Inhalation accidents	5	38	50	3	14	3	1	1	4	16	1	-	50
	Lung cancer	104	91	86	71	133	16	100	96	2	-	-	-	-
	Malignant mesothelioma	884	611	559	522	472	577	658	369	16	1	14	-	-
	Benign pleural disease	1008	1114	893	790	831	708	708	581	12	-	-	12	1
	Pneumoconiosis	167	145	208	110	224	159	276	275	3	5	-	-	-
	Other	81	56	100	61	105	61	105	80	47	114	80	77	30
	Total diagnoses	**2562**	**2491**	**2210**	**1811**	**2075**	**1813**	**2130**	**1601**	**231**	**278**	**162**	**173**	**158**
	Total cases (a)	**2534**	**2442**	**2135**	**1760**	**2009**	**1747**	**2045**	**1552**	**230**	**278**	**161**	**172**	**157**

Source: Health and Safety Executive (HSE)

Notes:

(a) Individuals may have more than one diagnosis.

(b) May not equal males plus females because sex is not recorded for some cases.

(c) No OPRA data are available for the annual statistics after 2010.

(d) Some physicians report on a sample basis, for one month in each year. Estimated totals for these are calculated by multiplying the actual number of cases reported by 12.

"-" means zero.

p Provisional data.

r Revised

16.8b Work-related mental ill-health cases reported to THOR-GP by diagnosis 2013 to 2015

Mental ill-health diagnoses	*Number of cases reported to THOR-GP aggregate total 2013 to 2015	% of all diagnoses
Anxiety/depression	792	35
Post-traumatic stress disorder (PTSD)	12	1
Other stress	1332	59
Alcohol & drug abuse	60	3
Other diagnoses	36	2
Other stress symptoms	24	1
Total diagnoses	2256	100
Total cases	2172	

Source: Health and Safety Executive (HSE)

* This estimate has an adjustment applied for sample reporting, but not an adjustment for the response rate. This is because there is no evidence indicating that non-responding GPs would report, on average, the same number of cases as those who responded.

16.8c Work-related skin disease: estimated number of cases reported by dermatologists to EPIDERM 2008 - 2014 and by occupational physicians to OPRA 2006 - 2010, by diagnostic category

Sex	Diagnostic category	2008	2009	2010	2011	2012	2013	2014r	Occupational physicians (OPRA) (c)				
									2006	2007	2008	2009	2010
All cases(b)	Contact dermatitis	1325	1423	1281	1208	1151	964	1106	596	488	322	373	342
	Contact urticaria	43	44	55	38	31	11	33	26	15	13	14	13
	Folliculitis /acne	17	3	-	1	-	-	-	-	-	1	-	-
	Infective skin disease	2	13	14	1	-	1	-	-	14	36	2	12
	Mechanical skin disease	9	18	18	14	6	26	2	1	-	1	12	-
	Nail conditions	13	13	1	-	1	13	2	-	-	-	-	-
	Skin neoplasia	418	492	390	231	314	296	229	-	-	-	-	-
	Other dermatoses	30	72	30	72	3	28	12	68	40	36	40	37
	Total number of diagnoses	1857	2078	1789	1565	1506	1339	1384	691	557	409	441	404
	Total number of individuals[a]	1839	2015	1745	1550	1480	1310	1368	679	556	409	440	392

Source: Health and Safety Executive (HSE)

Notes:
(a) Individuals may have more than one diagnosis.
(b) May not equal males plus females because sex is not recorded for some cases.
(c) No OPRA data are available for the annual statistics after 2010.
(d) Some physicians report on a sample basis, for one month in each year. Estimated totals for these are calculated by multiplying the actual number of cases reported by 12.
"-" means zero.
p Provisional data.
r Revised

16.8d Work-related musculoskeletal cases reported to THOR-GP by anatomical site 2013 to 2015

Anatomical site	*Number of cases reported to THOR-GP aggregate total 2013 to 2015	% of all diagnoses
Hand/wrist/arm	780	23
Elbow	264	8
Shoulder	408	12
Neck/thoracic spine	240	7
Lumbar spine/trunk	972	29
Hip/knee	372	11
Ankle/foot	192	6
Other	144	4
Total diagnoses	3372	100
Total cases	3108	

Source: Health and Safety Executive (HSE)

* This estimate has an adjustment applied for sample reporting, but not an adjustment for the response rate. This is because there is no evidence indicating that non-responding GPs would report, on average, the same number of cases as those who responded.

16.9 Deaths due to occupationally related lung disease in Great Britain, 2001 to 2014

Numbers

	2001	2002	2003	2004	2005	2006	2007	2008	2009	2010	2011	2012	2013	2014r
Asbestosis (without Mesothelioma) [1,3]	233	234	236	268	303	327	320	367	412	414	429	464	482	431
Mesothelioma [2,4]	1860	1867	1887	1978	2049	2060	2176	2265	2336	2360	2312	2549	2560	2519
Pneumoconiosis due to dust containing silica(a)	19 (1)	28	13	13 (1)	10	14	7	10 (2)	18 (2)	13	16	11	18 (1)	10
Other non-asbestosis pneumoconiosis(b)	221 (1)	243 (8)	218 (1)	201 (1)	184 (1)	153	142 (1)	129 (1)	131	121	136	140	147	141
Byssinosis(c)	2 (1)	0	3 (2)	4 (3)	3 (1)	5 (3)	2 (1)	1	2 (1)	2 (2)	1 (1)	1 (1)	1 (1)	1
Farmer's lung and other occupational allergic alveolitis(d)	7 (1)	6 (2)	7 (2)	5	13	10	5 (2)	7 (2)	7 (1)	8	9 (2)	10	4	7 (2)
Total	**2342**	**2378**	**2364**	**2469**	**2562**	**2569**	**2652**	**2779**	**2906**	**2918**	**2903**	**3175**	**3212**	**3109**

Source: ONS, GRO(S), Health and Safety Executive

(a) ICD9 code 502; ICD10 code J62

(b) ICD9 codes 500, 503, 505; ICD10 codes J60, J63-J64

(c) ICD9 code 504; ICD10 code J66

(d) ICD9 codes 495.0, 495.3, 495.4, 495.5, 495.6, 495.8; ICD10 codes J670, J673-J676, J678

The figure is the number of deaths coded to the disease as underlying cause.

Figures in brackets show the number of females. Where no figure is given, all cases were male.

1. some death certificates mention asbestosis with lung cancer and/or mesothelioma. In some cases - particularly where mesothelioma is mentioned - the word "asbestosis" may have been used incorrectly to indicate the role of asbestos in causing mesothelioma and/or lung cancer

2. the Office for National Statistics (ONS) discontinued medical enquiries in 1993. Therefore, for deaths registered from 1993 onwards, there is often less information available to accurately code the specific site of the mesothelioma.

3. For inclusion into the Asbestosis register the cause of death on the death certificate must mention the word Asbestosis

4. Total for Great Britain may include a small number of persons with overseas addresses.

16.10a Fatal injuries to workers (employees and the self-employed) in Great Britain, by detailed industry 2014/15r

		Number of fatal injuries			Rate of fatal injury per 100,000 workers (or employees / self-employed)		
		Workers	Of which…		Workers	Of which…	
SIC 2007 code [1]	Industry		Employees	Self-employed		Employees	Self-employed
All (01-99)	All industry	142	97	45	0.46	0.37	0.93
A (01-03)	Agriculture, forestry and fishing	32	13	19	8.85	7.47	10.14
01	Crop and animal production, hunting and related service activities	30	13	17	9.31	8.59	9.95
02	Forestry and logging	2		2	7.62		18.59
03	Fishing and aquaculture (2)						
B (05-09)	Mining and quarrying	1	1		0.71	0.77	
05	Mining of coal and lignite						
06	Extraction of crude petroleum and natural gas	1	1		4.12	4.71	
07	Mining of metal ores						
08	Other mining and quarrying						
09	Mining support service activities						
C (10-33)	Manufacturing	18	15	3	0.62	0.56	1.42
10	Manufacture of food products	2	2		0.59	0.61	
11	Manufacture of beverages						
12	Manufacture of tobacco products						
13	Manufacture of textiles						
14	Manufacture of wearing apparel						
15	Manufacture of leather and related products						
16	Manufacture of wood and of products of wood and cork, except furniture; manufacture of articles of straw and plaiting materials	2	1	1	2.75	1.74	6.51
17	Manufacture of paper and paper products						
18	Printing and reproduction of recorded media	1	1		0.81	0.90	
19	Manufacture of coke and refined petroleum products						
20	Manufacture of chemicals and chemical products	1	1		1.05	1.08	
21	Manufacture of basic pharmaceutical products and pharmaceutical preparations						
22	Manufacture of rubber and plastic products	2	2		1.34	1.46	
23	Manufacture of other non-metallic mineral products	3	3		3.10	3.43	
24	Manufacture of basic metals						
25	Manufacture of fabricated metal products, except machinery and equipment	3	2	1	1.27	0.92	5.15
26	Manufacture of computer, electronic and optical products						
27	Manufacture of electrical equipment						
28	Manufacture of machinery and equipment n.e.c.	1	1		0.40	0.42	
29	Manufacture of motor vehicles, trailers and semi-trailers						
30	Manufacture of other transport equipment	1		1	0.54		*
31	Manufacture of furniture						
32	Other manufacturing						
33	Repair and installation of machinery and equipment	2	2		0.87	1.01	
D (35)	Electricity, gas, steam and air conditioning supply	1	1		0.55	0.58	
35	Electricity, gas, steam and air conditioning supply	1	1		0.55	0.58	
E (36-39)	Water supply; sewerage, waste management and remediation activities	5	4	1	2.45	2.05	*
36,37	Water collection, treatment and supply; Sewerage						
38	Waste collection, treatment and disposal activities; materials recovery	5	4	1	4.33	3.66	*
39	Remediation activities and other waste management services.						
F (41-43)	Construction	35	24	11	1.63	1.86	1.28
41,43	Construction of buildings; Specialised construction activities	32	21	11	1.73	2.04	1.35
42	Civil engineering	3	3		0.98	1.15	
G,I (45-47,55-56)	Wholesale and retail trade; repair of motor vehicles and motorcycles; accommodation and food service activities	11	8	3	0.19	0.16	0.51
G (45-47)	Wholesale and retail trade; repair of motor vehicles and motorcycles	10	7	3	0.25	0.19	0.70
45	Wholesale and retail trade and repair of motor vehicles and motorcycles	4	2	2	0.87	0.53	2.40
46	Wholesale trade, except of motor vehicles and motorcycles	3	2	1	0.42	0.31	1.27
47	Retail trade, except of motor vehicles and motorcycles	3	3		0.10	0.11	
I (55-56)	Accommodation and food service activities	1	1		0.06	0.07	
55	Accommodation	1	1		0.26	0.30	
56	Food and beverage service activities						
H (49-53)	Transportation and storage	16	10	6	1.09	0.83	2.25
49	Land transport and transport via pipelines	11	8	3	1.54	1.61	1.36
50	Water transport (3)						
51	Air transport						
52	Warehousing and support activities for transportation	4	2	2	1.16	0.59	*
53	Postal and courier activities	1		1	0.33		3.22
J-N (58-82)	Information and communication; financial and insurance activities; real estate activities; professional, scientific and technical activities; administrative and support service activities	11	11		0.17	0.22	
J (58-63)	Information and communication						
58	Publishing activities						
59	Motion picture, video and television programme production, sound recording and music publishing activities						
60	Programming and broadcasting activities						
61	Telecommunications						
62	Computer programming, consultancy and related activities						
63	Information service activities						

16.10a Fatal injuries to workers (employees and the self-employed) in Great Britain, by detailed industry 2014/15r

SIC 2007 code [1]	Industry	Number of fatal injuries			Rate of fatal injury per 100,000 workers (or employees / self-employed)		
		Workers	Of which...		Workers	Of which...	
			Employees	Self-employed		Employees	Self-employed
K (64-66)	*Financial and insurance activities*						
64	Financial service activities, except insurance and pension funding						
65	Insurance, reinsurance and pension funding, except compulsory social security						
66	Activities auxiliary to financial services and insurance activities						
L (68)	*Real estate activities*	2	2		0.56	0.74	
68	Real estate activities	2	2		0.56	0.74	
M (69-75)	*Professional, scientific and technical activities*	1	1		0.05	0.06	
69	Legal and accounting activities						
70	Activities of head offices; management consultancy activities	1	1		0.21	0.29	
71	Architectural and engineering activities; technical testing and analysis						
72	Scientific research and development						
73	Advertising and market research						
74	Other professional, scientific and technical activities						
75	Veterinary activities						
N (77-82)	*Administrative and support service activities*	8	8		0.55	0.72	
77	Rental and leasing activities	2	2		1.76	2.01	
78	Employment activities	1	1		0.49	0.55	
79	Travel agency, tour operator and other reservation service and related activities						
80	Security and investigation activities	1	1		0.53	0.58	
81	Services to buildings and landscape activities	2	2		0.30	0.49	
82	Office administrative, office support and other business support activities	2	2		1.09	1.27	
O-Q (84-88)	**Public administration and defence; compulsory social security; education; human health and social work activities**	8	7	1	0.09	0.08	0.14
O (84)	**Public administration and defence; compulsory social security**	3	3		0.16	0.17	
84	Public administration and defence; compulsory social security	3	3		0.16	0.17	
P (85)	**Education**	3	2	1	0.09	0.07	0.35
85	Education	3	2	1	0.09	0.07	0.35
Q (86-88)	**Human health and social work activities**	2	2		0.05	0.05	
86	Human health activities	2	2		0.09	0.10	
87	Residential care activities						
88	Social work activities without accommodation						
R-U (90-99)	**Arts, entertainment and recreation; other service activities; activities of households as employers; undifferentiated goods-and services-producing activities of households for own use; activities of extraterritorial organisations and bodies**	4	3	1	0.21	0.24	0.17
R (90-93)	**Arts, entertainment and recreation**	3	3		0.34	0.47	
90	Creative, arts and entertainment activities	1	1		0.45	1.57	
91	Libraries, archives, museums and other cultural activities	1	1		0.96	1.01	
92	Gambling and betting activities						
93	Sports activities and amusement and recreation activities	1	1		0.21	0.26	
S (94-96)	**Other service activities**	1		1	0.12		0.33
94	Activities of membership organisations	1		1	0.32		2.07
95	Repair of computers and personal and household goods						
96	Other personal service activities						
T (97-98)	**Activities of households as employers; undifferentiated goods-and services-producing activities of households for own use**						
97	Activities of households as employers of domestic personnel						
98	Undifferentiated goods- and services-producing activities of private households for own use						
U (99)	**Activities of extraterritorial organisations and bodies**						
99	Activities of extraterritorial organisations and bodies						

Source: Reporting of Injuries, Diseases and Dangerous Occurrences Regulations (RIDDOR)

r=revised

(1) Standard Industrial Classification (SIC): The current system used in UK official statistics for classifying businesses by type of activity they are engaged in.

(2) Excludes sea fishing.

(3) Injuries arising from shore-based services only. Excludes incidents reported under merchant shipping legislation.

Includes injuries that were classified as 'major' for the period April-September 2013 and as 'specified' thereafter (many injuries previously categorised as major continue to be categorised as specified, primarily most fractures and amputations)

* Employment numbers are too small to provide reliable rate estimates.

Table presents annual reportable fatal injury statistics to workers (employees and self employed). Because the numbers of fatalities for some groupings are relatively small they are susceptible to considerable year-on-year variation in both the number and rate.

16.10b Non-fatal injuries to employees and the self-employed in Great Britain, by broad industry group 2014/15

Employment Status	Year	Industry	Important notes — Regulations Injuries reported under[1]	Industry classification[2]	Source of employment data for rates[3]	Number of reported non-fatal injuries to employees / self employed — Total reported non-fatal injury[4]	Of which... Major/ Specified# injury[5]	Over-3-day injury[6]	Over 7-day injury[6]	Rate of reported non-fatal injury per 100,000 employees[7] — Total reported non-fatal injury[4]	Of which... Major/ Specified# injury[5]	Over-3-day injury[6]	Over 7-day injury[6]
Employee	2014/15r	All industries	(g)	(l)	(o)	77,270	18,328	-	58,942	297	71	-	227
Employee	2014/15r	Agriculture, forestry and fishing[8]	(g)	(l)	(o)	936	367	-	569	538	211	-	327
Employee	2014/15r	Mining and Quarrying	(g)	(l)	(o)	355	76	-	279	273	58	-	215
Employee	2014/15r	Gas, electricity and water supply; sewerage, waste and recycling	(g)	(l)	(o)	2,564	655	-	1,909	700	179	-	521
Employee	2014/15r	Manufacturing	(g)	(l)	(o)	13,223	2,881	-	10,342	492	107	-	384
Employee	2014/15r	Construction	(g)	(l)	(o)	5,449	1,842	-	3,607	422	143	-	279
Employee	2014/15r	Service industries	(g)	(l)	(o)	54,743	12,507	-	42,236	259	59	-	200
Self employed	2014/15r	All industries	(g)	(l)	-	2,033	1,040	-	993	-	-	-	-
Self employed	2014/15r	Agriculture, forestry and fishing[8]	(g)	(l)	-	104	68	-	36	-	-	-	-
Self employed	2014/15r	Mining and Quarrying	(g)	(l)	-	2	1	-	1	-	-	-	-
Self employed	2014/15r	Gas, electricity and water supply; sewerage, waste and recycling	(g)	(l)	-	38	20	-	18	-	-	-	-
Self employed	2014/15r	Manufacturing	(g)	(l)	-	139	75	-	64	-	-	-	-
Self employed	2014/15r	Construction	(g)	(l)	-	1,339	639	-	700	-	-	-	-
Self employed	2014/15r	Service industries	(g)	(l)	-	411	237	-	174	-	-	-	-

Source: Reporting of Injuries, Diseases and Dangerous Occurrences Regulations (RIDDOR) and earlier regulations

r=revised

Note: Great care needs to be taken when comparing estimates over time because this non-fatal injury series is not consistent over the entire time period.

1. Since 1974 (and earlier), there has been a requirement to report cases of workplace injury to the appropriate authority. The criteria for reporting has changed during this period as new and revised regulations have come into force. Figures in the table represent cases that have been reported. Because of changes in reporting requirements this has introduced discontinuities into the time series and care must be taken when making comparisons over time. The table below details the various regulations that reports have been made under, and the main impacts on the statistics

2. From 1981, reports have been classified by industry using the Standard Industrial Classification (SIC), an industry coding framework used in UK official statistics. (Prior to this they were classified according to the regulations they were reported under. The SIC coding classification is periodically updated to take account of changes in the industry composition of the labour market. Since 1980 there have been 3 revisions of the Classification in 1980, 1992 and 2007. The table below shows the classification system that applies in different time periods for which the statistics are presented in these tables. This change in classification system will also have introduced discontinuities in the data series. While mostly the discontinuities at the top level industry groupings presented in these tables are small, for extractive and utility supply, these industries were classified in separate SIC sections under SIC2007. Hence no estimates for this exact industry grouping are available post 2004/05. Instead estimates are presented separately for mining and quarrying and Gas, electricity and water supply; sewerage, waste and recycling industries.

3. The estimation of injury incidence rates requires the use of employment estimates. The rate of injury is calculated by dividing the number of injury cases (the numerator) by the employment estimate (the denominator), and then multiplying by a factor of 100,000. Rate estimates use a different source of employment data prior to 2004/05, as shown in the table below. The change in employment estimates from 2004/05 means that these rates are not directly comparable with earlier periods

4. Because of differences in reporting requirements between years then great care needs to be taken when comparing estimates of non-fatal injury over time.

5. # Includes injuries that were classified as 'major' for the period April-September 2013 and as 'specified' thereafter (many injuries previously categorised as major continue to be categorised as specified, primarily most fractures and amputations)

6. RIDDOR 2012, introduced in April 2012, changed the threshold for reporting non-fatal injuries from over 3-days absence to over 7-days absence

7. Rates of non-fatal injury in table 3 are presented for employees only. Injuries to the self-employed suffer from severe under-reporting meaning that rate estimates may be misleading

8. Excludes sea fishing.

9. Figures prior to 1996/97 also include injuries in the offshore oil and gas industry reported under offshore installations safety legislation.

-. Estimate not available

*. Employment numbers are too small to provide reliable rate estimates.

(g) 2014/15 onwards - Reporting of Injuries, Diseases and Dangerous Occurrence Regulations 2013 (RIDDOR 2013): The list of non-fatal 'major' injuries was revised and re-named as 'Specified' injuries (many injuries previously categorised as major continue to be categorised as specified, primarily most fractures and amputations). The introduction of RIDDOR 2013 also removed the requirement to report suicides on railway systems (introduced under RIDDOR 1995).

(l) 2004/05 onwards - Industry Classsification: SIC 2007

(o) 2004/05 onwards - Source of employment data for estimating rates: The Annual Population Survey (APS) is the source of employment data used as the denominator for rates of injury for estimates from 2004/05. For more information see: www.hse.gov.uk/statistics/sources.pdf

Prices

Chapter 17

Prices

Producer price index numbers
(Tables 17.1 and 17.2)

The producer price indices (PPIs) were published for the first time in August 1983, replacing the former wholesale price indices. Full details of the differences between the two indices were given in an article published in British Business, 15 April 1983. The producer price indices are calculated using the same general methodology as that used by the wholesale price indices.

The high level index numbers in Tables 17.1 and 17.2 are constructed on a net sector basis. That is to say, they are intended to measure only transactions between the sector concerned and other sectors. Within-sector transactions are excluded. Index numbers for the whole of manufacturing are thus not weighted averages of sector index numbers.

The index numbers for selected industries in Tables 17.1 and 17.2 are constructed on a gross sector basis, that is, all transactions are included in deriving the weighting patterns, including sales within the same industry.

Producer Prices has implemented the change to the Standard Industrial Classification 2007 (SIC 2007). The most significant change to PPI output prices involves the reclassification of 'recovered secondary raw materials' and 'publishing'. These are no longer classified in the manufacturing sector, but are classified under services. In addition to this, a new SIC division, 'repair, installation and maintenance of machinery and equipment' has been created.

Fundamental changes have been made to the classification of the PPI Trade surveys, Import Price indices (IPI) and Export Price Indices (EPI). As part of the reclassification project the classification of these trade surveys have become compliant with Eurostat's Short Term Statistics Regulation. The collection of IPI and EPI will now be on an SIC basis, a switch from the Standard International Trade Classification (SITC) and Combined Nomenclature (CN) previously used. PPI input prices are heavily dependant on IPI.

Further details are available from the Office for National Statistics website: www.ons.gov.uk.

Purchasing power of the pound
(Table 17.3)

Changes in the internal purchasing power of a currency may be defined as the 'inverse' of changes in the levels of prices; when prices go up, the amount which can be purchased with a given sum of money goes down. Movements in the internal purchasing power of the pound are based on the consumers' expenditure deflator (CED) prior to 1962 and on the general index of retail prices (RPI) from January 1962 onwards. The CED shows the movement in prices implied by the national accounts estimates of consumers' expenditure valued at current and at constant prices, while the RPI is constructed directly by weighting together monthly movements in prices according to a given pattern of household expenditure derived from the Expenditure and Food Survey. If the purchasing power of the pound is taken to be 100p in a particular month (quarter, year), the comparable purchasing power in a subsequent month (quarter, year) is:

$$100 \times \frac{\text{earlier period price index}}{\text{later period price index}}$$

where the price index used is the CED for years 1946–1961

Consumer prices index
(Table 17.4)

The CPI is the main UK domestic measure of consumer price inflation for macroeconomic purposes. It forms the basis for the Government's target for inflation that the Bank of England's Monetary Policy Committee (MPC) is required to achieve. From April 2011 the CPI is also being used for the indexation of benefits, tax credits and public service pensions. The uprating is based on the 12-month change in the September CPI.

Internationally, the CPI is known as the Harmonised Index of Consumer Prices (HICP). HICPs are calculated in each Member State of the European Union, according to rules specified in a series of European regulations developed by Eurostat in conjunction with the EU Member States. HICPs are used to compare inflation rates across the European Union. Since January 1999, the HICP has also been used by the European Central Bank (ECB) as the measure of price stability across the euro area.

The official CPI series starts in 1996 but estimates for earlier periods are available back to 1988. These estimates are broadly consistent with data from 1996 but should be treated with some caution.

A full description of how the CPI is compiled is given in the Consumer Price Indices Technical Manual at: www.ons.gov.uk/ons/guide-method/user-guidance/prices/cpi-and-rpi/index.html

Retail prices index
(Table 17.5)

The all items retail prices index (RPI) is the most long-standing general purpose measure of inflation in the UK. Historically the uses of the RPI include the indexation of various prices and incomes and the uprating of pensions, state benefits and index-linked gilts, as well as the revalorisation of excise duties. Please note, though, that from April 2011 the CPI is being used to uprate benefits, tax credits and public service pensions. RPI data are available back to 1947 but have been re-referenced on several occasions since then, generally accompanied by changes to the coverage and/or structure of the detailed sub-components.

A full description of how the RPI is compiled is given in the Consumer Price Indices Technical Manual at: www.ons.gov.uk/ons/guide-method/user-guidance/prices/cpi-and-rpi/index.html

Further details are available from the Office for National Statistics website: www.ons.gov.uk/ons/taxonomy/index.html?nscl=Price+Indices+and+Inflation

Tax and price index (TPI)
(Table 17.6)

The purpose and methodology of the TPI were described in an article in the August 1979 issue (No. 310) of Economic Trends. The TPI measures the change in gross taxable income needed for taxpayers to maintain their purchasing power, allowing for changes in retail prices. The TPI thus takes account of the changes to direct taxes (and employees' National Insurance (NI) contributions) faced by a representative cross-section of taxpayers as well as changes in the retail prices index (RPI).
When direct taxation or employees' NI contributions change, the TPI will rise by less than or more than the RPI according to the type of changes made. Between Budgets, the monthly increase in the TPI is normally slightly larger than that in the RPI, since all the extra income needed to offset any rise in retail prices is fully taxed.

Index numbers of agricultural prices
(Tables 17.7 and 17.8)
The indices of producer prices of agricultural products are designed to provide short-term and medium-term indications of movements in these prices. All annual series are baseweighted Laspeyres type, using value weights derived from the Economic Accounts for Agriculture prepared for the Statistical Office of the European Union. Prices are measured exclusive of VAT. For Table 17.7, it has generally been necessary to measure the prices of materials (inputs) ex-supplier. For Table 17.8, it has generally been necessary to measure the prices received by producers (outputs) at the first marketing stage. The construction of the indices enables them to be combined with similar indices for other member countries of the EU to provide an overall indication of trends within the Union which appears in the Union's Eurostat series of publications.

Index numbers at a more detailed level and for earlier based series are available from the Department for Environment, Food and Rural Affairs, Room 309, Foss House, Kingspool 1–2 Peasholme Green, York, YO1 7PX, tel 01904 456561

Room 309, Foss House, Kingspool 1–2 Peasholme Green, York, YO1 7PX, tel 01904 456561

17.1 Producer Price Index (2010=100, SIC2007)

2010=100, SIC2007

Net Sector Input Price Indices of Materials & Fuel purchased

	6207000050: NSI - All Manufacturing including CCL	6207000010: NSI - All Manufacturing, materials only	6207000060: NSI - Fuel Purchased by Manufacturing Industry including CCL	6207990050: NSI - Materials & Fuels Purchased other than FBTP Industries, NSA	6207998950: NSI - All Manufacturing excl FBTP (incl CCL) - SA	6207990010: NSI - Materials Purchased other than FBTP Industries, NSA
	K646 NSA	K644 NSA	K647 NSA	K655 NSA	K658 SA	K653 NSA
2009	92.6	90.9	107.4	95.6	95.6	93.6
2010	100	100	100	100	100	100
2011	114.5	115.1	109.7	109.1	109.1	109.1
2012	116	115.9	117.6	108.8	108.9	107.5
2013	117.4	116.6	125	109.3	109.3	106.8
2014	109.7	108.3	122.4	105.3	105	102.4
2015	95.7	93.2	117	99.8	99.7	96.9
2012 JAN	115.8	115.7	117.7	110.1	109.6	109
FEB	118.3	118.1	121.1	111	110	109.5
MAR	119.8	120.2	117.4	110.9	109.4	110.1
APR	118.3	118.5	117.4	110.1	109.3	109
MAY	115.5	115.6	115.3	108.9	108.6	107.9
JUN	113.4	113.3	114.4	108.4	108.8	107.5
JUL	113.1	113.1	113.3	107.3	108	106.4
AUG	115.1	115.5	112.3	107.1	108	106.3
SEP	115	115	116.1	107.2	108.2	105.8
OCT	115.6	115.3	119.5	108	108.6	106.2
NOV	116	115.3	122.8	108.6	108.9	106.3
DEC	116.3	115.4	124.5	108.7	108.9	106.2
2013 JAN	117.7	117.1	123.8	109.9	109.6	107.7
FEB	120.7	120.4	124	112.1	111.2	110.1
MAR	120.9	120	129.9	112.7	111.3	110
APR	118.6	117.6	127.3	111.1	110.4	108.6
MAY	117.1	116.6	121.9	109.3	109.2	107.2
JUN	116.8	116.4	120.4	108.4	108.9	106.4
JUL	118.4	117.9	123.5	109.5	110.1	107.2
AUG	117.2	116.6	122.7	108.6	109.5	106.4
SEP	116.1	115.5	121.5	107.6	108.5	105.3
OCT	115.6	114.4	126.5	107.8	108.2	104.8
NOV	114.9	113.5	127.9	107.5	107.7	104.2
DEC	115.3	113.5	130.8	107.2	107.2	103.4
2014 JAN	114.3	112.6	130.4	106.8	103.2	103.1
FEB	113.7	112.1	127.9	106.4	105.8	102.9
MAR	113.3	111.7	127.5	106.6	105.4	103.2
APR	112.3	111.1	122.4	105.5	105.1	102.6
MAY	112.5	111.6	120.3	105	105.1	102.4
JUN	111.4	110.7	117.2	104.6	105.1	102.4
JUL	109.5	108.8	114.7	103.8	104.8	102
AUG	108.4	107.6	115.1	104.3	105.1	102.4
SEP	107.5	106.4	117.7	104.7	105.5	102.5
OCT	106.2	104.3	122.3	105.2	105.3	102.4
NOV	105.4	103	127.3	105.7	105.4	102.2
DEC	101.9	99.1	126.1	104.7	104.5	101.2
2015 JAN	98.2	95.3	123	103.4	103.2	100.2
FEB	98.4	95.5	122.8	102.1	101.6	98.6
MAR	98.5	95.8	122	101.9	100.9	98.6
APR	99.8	97.7	117.2	101.5	101	98.8
MAY	99.1	97.1	116.4	100.8	100.8	98.2
JUN	96.9	94.7	115.4	99.9	100.2	97.3
JUL	95.5	93.1	115.7	98.9	99.8	96.1
AUG	92.6	90.3	111.5	97.9	98.4	95.5
SEP	93.1	90.8	113.2	98.7	99	96.2
OCT	93.1	90.7	113.9	98	97.7	95.2
NOV	91.6	89	114.3	96.7	96.2	93.7
DEC	91.3	88.2	118.4	97.8	97.3	94.3
2016 JAN	90.1	87.3	113.3	98	97.6	95.3
FEB	90.5	87.7	113	98.5	98.2	96
MAR	92	89.7	111.9	99	98.4	96.8
APR	92.7	90.9	107.3	99.3	99.2	97.8
MAY	94.8	93.5	105.1	98.9	99.5	97.7
JUN	96.4	95.2	105.3	99.6	100.2	98.5

17.1 Producer Price Index (2010=100, SIC2007)

2010=100, SIC2007

Gross Sector Price Indices of Materials & Fuel purchased

	6107113140: GSI Sub section - Inputs for Manuf of Textiles & Textile products	6107215000: GSI (excl. CCL) - Inputs for Manuf of Leather & Related products	6107216000: GSI (excl. CCL) - Inputs for Manuf of Wood & products of Wood/Cork	6107117180: GSI Sub section - Inputs for Manuf of Pulp, Paper & Paper products	6107219000: GSI (excl. CCL) - Inputs for Manuf of Coke & Refined Petroleum products	6107120000: GSI Sub section - Inputs for Manuf of Chemicals, Chemical products	6107222000: GSI (excl. CCL) - Inputs for Manufacture of Rubber/Plastic products
	MC36 NSA	MC3O NSA	MC3P NSA	MC39 NSA	MC3R NSA	MC3B NSA	MB4R NSA
2009	97.4	97.5	94.9	98.3	78.1	95.8	95.2
2010	100	100	100	100	100	100	100
2011	108.2	108.8	106.3	106.9	133.4	111.5	108.7
2012	110.4	110.7	108.5	107.4	136.9	111.8	108.9
2013	111.2	114	109.9	108.2	135.5	110.3	108.7
2014	110.5	113.2	111.9	107.6	118.3	106.3	105.9
2015	108.5	110.9	110.7	105.7	73.4	100	101.6
2012 JAN	110.2	109.6	107.7	108.6	136.2	111.1	107.9
FEB	110.4	109.7	108.1	108.1	144.1	112.1	109.1
MAR	110.7	109.9	108.5	107.8	151.8	113.4	110
APR	109.9	111.1	108.9	107.9	146.1	113.9	110.4
MAY	109.9	111.2	108.6	107.5	136.6	113.3	110.2
JUN	109.5	110.7	108.4	107.4	123.3	111.4	108.9
JUL	110	110.3	108.4	107	127.3	109.5	107.1
AUG	110.3	110.2	108.6	106.6	137.7	110.7	108
SEP	110.7	110.8	108.8	106.6	137.1	111.3	108.5
OCT	111.2	111.4	108.7	106.9	136.4	111.6	108.9
NOV	111.3	111.5	108.6	107.1	134.2	111.6	109
DEC	110.4	111.5	108.5	107.2	132.5	111.5	109.1
2013 JAN	110.7	112	108.8	107.5	136.5	111.5	109.3
FEB	111.3	112.5	109.4	108	144.1	112.1	109.7
MAR	111.9	113.5	109.9	108.8	141.2	113	110.6
APR	111.4	114.1	110	108.4	132.9	111.6	109.6
MAY	111.3	114.1	109.4	107.9	131.7	110.2	108.5
JUN	111.1	114.3	109.4	107.8	130	109.7	108.3
JUL	111.5	114.9	109.8	108.2	137.8	110	108.2
AUG	111.3	114.8	109.9	108.1	139	110.2	108.5
SEP	111	115	109.8	108	138	109.8	108.1
OCT	110.7	114.8	110.6	108.4	133	108.9	108
NOV	110.7	114.4	110.6	108.5	130.1	108	107.5
DEC	110.9	114.1	110.8	108.5	132.1	108	107.5
2014 JAN	111	114.3	111	108.7	129.2	107.8	107.3
FEB	110.9	113.9	111.2	108.6	128.7	108	107.3
MAR	111	114	111.3	108.7	126.6	108.1	107.3
APR	110.8	114.5	112	108.1	125.6	107.6	106.7
MAY	110.7	114.2	112	107.7	126.5	107.1	106.4
JUN	110.4	113.7	112	107.2	127.6	106.4	105.9
JUL	110.1	113.2	111.9	106.7	123.3	105.8	105.4
AUG	110	112.5	112.1	106.7	120.1	105.5	105.2
SEP	110.2	111.9	112.2	106.8	116.5	105.3	105
OCT	110.5	111.9	112.3	107.2	107.9	105.2	105.2
NOV	110.6	112.3	112.3	107.6	101.4	104.9	105
DEC	110.3	111.8	112	107.5	85.8	103.7	104.3
2015 JAN	109.7	111.5	111.5	107	72.2	101.9	102.8
FEB	109.4	111.6	111.5	106.7	76.7	101.3	102.2
MAR	109.2	112.1	111.5	106.4	80.2	101.2	102
APR	108.9	112.7	111.3	106	82	101.2	102
MAY	108.7	112	111.2	106	84.2	101.9	102.6
JUN	108.5	111.6	111.1	105.5	81.2	101.3	102.4
JUL	108.1	111.3	110.7	105.6	77.5	100.7	102
AUG	107.7	110.5	110.1	104.9	67.6	99.5	101.4
SEP	108	109.9	110.1	105.1	67.4	99.1	101.2
OCT	108.1	109.7	110	105.1	68.3	98.3	100.6
NOV	107.8	109	109.5	104.8	64.7	97.1	99.8
DEC	108	108.8	109.6	105.5	59.1	96.6	99.7
2016 JAN	108.2	109	108.9	105.4	53.2	96.7	99.9
FEB	108.7	109.3	108.6	105.5	52.4	96.7	100
MAR	108.8	110	109	105.5	59.9	96.4	99.9
APR	108.9	109.8	108.9	105.1	63.2	96.8	100.1
MAY	108.1	109.4	108.9	104.9	68.6	96.8	100.1
JUN	107.4	109.5	109.6	105.1	72.5	97.1	100.5

17.1 Producer Price Index (2010=100, SIC2007)

2010=100, SIC2007

Gross Sector Price Indices of Materials & Fuel purchased

	6107123000: GSI - Purchases of materials and fuels for Manufacture of Other Non-Metallic Mineral Products MC3E	6107124250: GSI Sub-section - Inputs of Manuf of Basic Metals & Fabricated products MC3F NSA	6107126270: GSI Sub-section - Inputs for Manuf of Computer, Elect & Opt products MC3G NSA	6107228000: GSI (excl. CCL) - Inputs for Manufacture of Machinery & Equipment MB4U NSA	6107129300: GSI Sub-section - Inputs for Manufacture of Motor Vehicles MC3I NSA	6107131330: GSI Sub-section - Inputs for Manuf of Other Manufactured Goods n.e.c MC3J NSA
2009	98	92.5	97	96.8	97.4	96.4
2010	100	100	100	100	100	100
2011	109.1	110.1	103.3	105.3	104.1	104.5
2012	111.7	108.4	103.1	105.3	104	105.4
2013	111.9	107	103.1	105.6	104.3	106.3
2014	110.4	103.6	103	104.4	103.1	106.4
2015	108.5	95.5	102.1	102.1	101.3	105.8
2012 JAN	111.9	109.4	103.3		104.2	105.3
FEB	112.7	111.2	103.7		104.8	105.8
MAR	113.1	111.6	103.9		104.9	106
APR	113.1	110.5	103.5		104.3	105.9
MAY	112.1	108.8	103.3		103.9	105.6
JUN	111.1	107.1	103		104.1	105.5
JUL	110.1	106.6	102.8		103.6	105.2
AUG	109.6	106.5	102.7		103.4	105
SEP	110.6	107.4	102.6		103.4	105
OCT	111.5	107.5	102.8		103.7	105.2
NOV	111.9	106.9	102.7		103.8	105.1
DEC	112.1	107.1	102.3		103.8	105
2013 JAN	112.3	108	102.7	105.5	104.6	105.8
FEB	113.1	109.9	103.6	106.7	105.4	106.8
MAR	114.1	110.2	104.2	107	105.3	107.2
APR	112.8	108.2	103.8	106.4	104.8	106.8
MAY	111.3	106.9	103.4	105.6	104.4	106.5
JUN	110.7	106	103.1	105.3	104.1	106.2
JUL	111.9	106.5	103.3	105.6	104.5	106.6
AUG	111.4	106.8	103.2	105.5	104.3	106.3
SEP	111.2	106	102.9	105	103.7	105.9
OCT	111.3	105.5	102.7	104.9	103.8	105.8
NOV	111.5	105.2	102.5	104.7	103.6	105.7
DEC	111.5	105	102.3	104.5	103.4	105.5
2014 JAN	112.1	104.8	102.8	104.6	103.3	106.3
FEB	111.9	104.6	102.7	104.4	103.3	106.4
MAR	111.9	104.7	102.8	104.7	103.5	106.5
APR	110.3	103.8	102.5	104.2	103.1	106.1
MAY	110.1	103.9	102.4	104.3	103.1	106.1
JUN	109.8	103.9	103	104.2	102.9	106.3
JUL	108.8	103.4	102.7	104	102.7	106
AUG	108.8	103.8	103.1	104.4	103	106.3
SEP	109.7	103.4	103.2	104.3	102.9	106.5
OCT	110.4	103	103.4	104.5	103.2	106.7
NOV	110.9	102.7	103.5	104.6	103.3	106.9
DEC	110.3	101.2	103.4	104.3	103	106.7
2015 JAN	110	99.2	103.3	103.7	102.5	106.5
FEB	109.7	98.5	102.8	103.3	102	106.6
MAR	109.9	98.3	102.8	103.1	101.8	106.7
APR	109	97.7	102.7	102.8	101.9	106.6
MAY	109.4	97.6	102.6	102.8	101.9	106.2
JUN	108.8	96.4	102.3	102.3	101.5	105.9
JUL	108.6	95.2	101.8	101.9	101	105.6
AUG	107.4	93.5	101.5	101.4	101	105.3
SEP	107.5	93.1	101.6	101.4	101.3	105.4
OCT	107.3	93	101.4	101.3	100.6	105
NOV	106.7	91.8	101.1	100.7	100	104.7
DEC	107.1	91.2	101.3	100.8	100.4	104.9
2016 JAN	107.1	90.6	101.7	101	101	105.8
FEB	107.1	90.8	102	101.4	101.3	106.1
MAR	107.2	92.6	102.2	102.1	101.5	106.5
APR	106.8	94.1	102.6	102.8	102	107
MAY	106.3	95.5	102.5	103.1	101.9	107
JUN	107	96.4	103.2	103.9	102.5	107.7

Source: Office for National Statistics (ONS)

Climate change Levy was introduced in April 2001

Rebasing the Producer Price Index, including trade prices (PPI) and the Services Producer Price Index (SPPI) onto 2010=100 occurred at the end of 2013.
Further information can be found at: http://www.ons.gov.uk/ons/rel/ppi2/producer-price-index/ppi-rebasing-2010---100/index.html

Abreviations
NSI - Net Sector Input
FBTP - Food, Beverages and Tobacco Products
NSA - Not Seasonally Adjusted
SA - Seasonally Adjusted
GSI - Gross Sector Input
CCL - Climate Change Levy

17.2 Producer Price Index of Output (2010=100, SIC2007)

	Net Sector Output Price Indices of Materials & Fuel purchased			Gross Sector Output Price Indices of Materials & Fuel purchased (All Manufacturing & Selected Industries)			
	7200700000: Net Sector Output - Output of Manufactured products	7200799000: Net Sector Output - All Manufacturing excl Food, Beverages Tobacco	7111101280: Gross Sector Output - Food Products, Beverages & Tobacco incl duty	7112130000: Textiles	7112140000: Wearing Apparel	7112150000: Leather & related products	7112160000: Wood, Products of Wood & Cork, except Furniture; Articles of Straw
	JVZ7 NSA	K3BI NSA	K65A NSA	K37R NSA	K37S NSA	K37T NSA	K37U NSA
2008	96.9	97.1	95.7	95.6	99.6	98.7	94.8
2009	97.4	98.5	98.9	98.2	99.7	93.7	96.2
2010	100	100	100	100	100	100	100
2011	104.8	102.8	106.6	107	102.8	116.5	105.2
2012	107	103.9	110.9	110.6	106.1	119	109
2013	108.4	104.8	114.8	111.4	106.9	123.9	110.4
2014	108.4	105.7	113.7	112.5	110.7	124.2	113.9
2015	106.6	105.9	111.3	112.3	112.3	121.8	114.9
2012 JAN	105.9	103.4	108.8	110.6	104.7	114.8	107.6
FEB	106.3	103.7	109	110.2	105.1	114.8	107.9
MAR	106.8	103.8	109.8	110.4	105.4	115.6	108.3
APR	107.2	104	110.4	108.8	105.7	119.4	108.9
MAY	107	104	110.8	109.1	106.5	119.6	108.9
JUN	106.6	103.9	110.9	109.2	105.9	120.1	109.1
JUL	106.8	104	111	111.2	106.7	119.6	109.4
AUG	107.2	104	111.3	111.4	106.6	118.9	109.4
SEP	107.5	104.1	111.7	111.9	106.7	119.7	109.6
OCT	107.6	104.1	111.8	112.1	106.7	121.2	109.5
NOV	107.4	104.1	112.5	112.3	106.4	122.2	109.4
DEC	107.2	103.9	112.7	110.5	106.5	122.3	109.6
2013 JAN	107.6	104.2	113.2	110.8	106.6	122.3	109.7
FEB	108.1	104.4	113.4	111.2	106.6	122.4	109.7
MAR	108.4	104.7	114	111.2	106.6	122.5	109.9
APR	108.3	104.8	114.7	111.1	106.6	123.6	110.1
MAY	108.3	104.8	115	111.8	107.3	124.4	109.7
JUN	108.4	104.8	115.3	111.8	107.3	124.5	109.9
JUL	108.7	104.9	115.5	111.8	107.3	124.3	110.1
AUG	108.8	104.9	115.4	111.7	106.7	124.4	110.5
SEP	108.8	104.9	115.5	111.7	106.7	124.7	110.7
OCT	108.5	104.9	115.2	111	106.7	124.7	111.1
NOV	108.3	104.8	115.3	111.3	107	124.7	111.4
DEC	108.3	104.9	114.9	111.6	107	124.7	111.5
2014 JAN	108.6	105.4	114.9	112	109.5	124.5	112
FEB	108.7	105.6	114.9	112.1	109.6	124.6	112.9
MAR	108.8	105.8	115.1	112.2	110	125	113
APR	108.9	105.8	115.2	112.6	110.2	125.8	113.2
MAY	108.8	105.8	114.7	112.7	110.2	124.7	113.6
JUN	108.7	105.8	114	112.7	111.3	124.3	114
JUL	108.6	105.7	113.9	112.7	111.3	124.5	114.4
AUG	108.5	105.8	113.2	112.3	111.4	124.1	114.8
SEP	108.3	105.7	112.8	112.7	111.4	122.9	115
OCT	107.7	105.5	112	112.7	111.4	123.8	114.8
NOV	107.6	105.7	111.7	112.7	111.1	124.4	114.7
DEC	107.1	105.7	111.8	112.7	111.1	122.2	114.9
2015 JAN	106.6	105.9	111.8	112.8	112.1	123.1	115.1
FEB	106.8	105.9	111.7	112.9	112.1	123.6	115.4
MAR	106.9	105.9	112.1	112.6	112.1	123.5	115.4
APR	107	105.9	112.1	112.5	112	123.6	115.3
MAY	107.1	105.9	111.8	112	112	122.2	115.1
JUN	107.1	105.9	111.9	111.9	112	122.3	115.1
JUL	106.9	105.9	111.8	111.7	112.3	122.2	115
AUG	106.4	105.8	111.2	111.6	112.9	121.7	114.8
SEP	106.3	105.9	110.7	111.8	112.9	120.7	114.5
OCT	106.1	105.8	110.3	112.4	112.9	119.4	114.5
NOV	105.9	105.6	110	112.5	112.2	119.4	114.5
DEC	105.6	105.8	109.8	112.5	112.3	119.5	114.3
2016 JAN	105.5	106	109.9	112.6	112.3	119.9	114.1
FEB	105.6	106.1	110.1	113.4	112.3	120.5	113.4
MAR	106.1	106.2	111	113.3	112.6	120.5	113.9
APR	106.5	106.4	111.2	113.6	113.3	119.8	113.7
MAY	106.6	106.5	110.3	112.4	113.4	120.4	113.6
JUN	106.9	106.6	110.1	110.3	113.4	120.7	114.2

17.2 Producer Price Index of Output (2010=100, SIC2007)

Gross Sector Output Price Indices of Materials & Fuel purchased (All Manufacturing & Selected Industries)

	7112170000: Paper & Paper products	7112180000: Printing & Recording Services	7112200000: Chemicals & Chemical products	7112220000: Rubber & Plastics products	7112230000: Other Non-Metallic Mineral products	7112240000: Basic Metals	7112260000: Computer, Electronic & Optical products
	K37V NSA	K37W NSA	K37Z NSA	K383 NSA	K384 NSA	K385 NSA	K387 NSA
2008	97.1	99.6	96.4	96.5	97.2	99.7	97.5
2009	97.4	100.6	98.8	97.8	99.5	90.8	98.3
2010	100	100	100	100	100	100	100
2011	107.7	100.4	107.8	105.4	102.7	108.8	98.2
2012	106.9	99.9	108.4	107	106.4	104.7	96.5
2013	106.6	99.3	106.5	108.5	107.7	102	96.9
2014	106.9	100	104.8	108.7	109.6	99.7	97.5
2015	106.3	100.2	101.6	107.9	111.7	91.4	97.9
2012 JAN	109.3	100.4	107.7	106.2	105	106.1	97.2
FEB	107.6	100.4	108.6	106.1	105.9	107.6	97.2
MAR	107.5	100.1	109.6	106.5	106.3	107.5	97.2
APR	107.6	100.2	109.9	106.8	106.6	106.8	96.6
MAY	107.4	100.4	109.7	107	106.4	105.8	96.5
JUN	107.5	100.2	108.3	106.9	106.3	104.8	96.3
JUL	107.3	100.2	106.9	106.9	106.3	103.9	96.8
AUG	106.4	99.4	107.7	107.1	106.5	102.3	96.6
SEP	105.7	99.5	108.1	107.4	106.6	103.4	96.5
OCT	105.7	99.4	108	107.5	106.9	103.2	96.3
NOV	105.6	99.3	107.9	107.3	106.8	102.4	95.9
DEC	105.5	99.3	108.1	107.7	106.7	102.6	94.7
2013 JAN	105.7	99.5	108	108.4	107.5	103.3	94.9
FEB	105.6	99.3	107.9	108.3	107.7	104.3	95.1
MAR	106.2	99.2	108.4	108.3	107.7	104.3	95.9
APR	106.3	99.1	107.7	108.4	107.7	102.9	96.9
MAY	106.4	99	106.8	108.5	107.2	102.3	97.2
JUN	106.4	99.1	106.2	108.7	107.3	101.3	97.1
JUL	106.4	99.1	105.9	108.4	107.5	100.9	97.2
AUG	106.7	99	106.2	108.7	107.6	101.5	97.3
SEP	107	99.4	106	108.6	107.8	101.1	97.8
OCT	107.2	99.6	105.3	108.7	107.9	100.8	97.8
NOV	107.6	99.4	104.6	108.6	108.2	100.8	97.6
DEC	107.2	99.6	104.6	108.5	108.1	100.4	97.5
2014 JAN	107.4	99.7	105.1	108.6	108.8	100.5	97.4
FEB	107.6	100.5	105.6	109.1	109.5	100.3	97.3
MAR	107.7	100.1	105.7	109.2	109.8	100.6	97.4
APR	107.6	100	105.7	108.7	109.9	99.1	97.4
MAY	107.2	100.4	105.6	108.6	109.5	99.4	97.4
JUN	107	100.3	105.1	108.6	109.7	100.1	97.2
JUL	106.5	100.4	104.8	108.6	109.6	99.8	97.2
AUG	106.4	100.5	104.5	108.7	109.6	100.4	97.6
SEP	106.3	99.7	104.2	108.6	109.4	99.2	97.5
OCT	106.4	99.6	104.1	108.5	109.5	99.3	97.6
NOV	106.4	99.6	104.1	108.4	109.7	99.2	97.6
DEC	106.6	99.7	103.7	108.5	109.6	98.5	97.8
2015 JAN	106.7	99.5	102.9	108.2	110.8	96.6	98.1
FEB	106.7	99.9	102.7	108	111.3	95.5	98
MAR	106	99.9	102.5	107.8	111.8	95	97.9
APR	106.5	100.2	102.6	107.5	111.9	93.9	98.1
MAY	106.5	100.3	102.7	107.3	111.9	93	97.9
JUN	106.3	100.3	102.5	107.4	112	92	97.9
JUL	106.8	100.2	102.1	108	111.7	91	97.8
AUG	106.1	100.2	101.3	108.1	111.7	89.8	97.9
SEP	106.1	100.3	101	108.3	111.7	88.6	98
OCT	105.9	100.2	100.3	108.4	111.8	88.4	98
NOV	105.8	100.5	99.6	108.1	111.7	87.1	97.9
DEC	106.4	100.9	99.2	108.2	111.9	86.3	97.9
2016 JAN	107.1	99.7	99.4	109.2	113	85.6	98.1
FEB	107.2	99.6	99.2	109.3	113	85.9	98.3
MAR	107.2	99.8	98.8	109.3	113.2	88.4	98.3
APR	107	99.7	98.8	109.5	113.3	91	98.3
MAY	107.3	99.8	98.7	109.5	113.6	93.8	98.2
JUN	107.4	100.1	98.5	109.5	113.4	95.3	98.5

17.2 Producer Price Index of Output (2010=100, SIC2007)

2010=100, SIC2007

Gross Sector Output Price Indices of Materials & Fuel purchased (All Manufacturing & Selected Industries)

	7112270000: Electrical Equipment	7112280000: Machinery & Equipment n.e.c.	7112290000: Motor Vehicles, Trailers & Semi-trailers	7112300000: Other Transport Equipment	7112310000: Furniture	7112320000: Other Manufactured Goods	Output in the Construction Industry All New Work *	Mix-adjusted house price index of new dwellings **
	K388 NSA	K389 NSA	K38A NSA	K38B NSA	K38C NSA	K38D NSA	(2013=100)	(2015=100)
2008	94.3	97.5	96.2	97.1	96.7	97.2	99.7	94.1
2009	96.9	98.8	99.4	99.1	98.3	98.9	97.5	84.7
2010	100	100	100	100	100	100	92.6	87.1
2011	102.9	103.3	100.9	101.3	102.7	102	93.6	88.4
2012	102.8	105.5	101.5	102.9	105.1	104	96.6	88.1
2013	103	108.2	102.5	105.1	105.8	105.3	100.0	90.7
2014	103.7	109.8	102	107.4	107.2	107.2	103.7	98.0
2015	104.2	111.1	100.5	108.7	108.7	108.2	106.2	102.9
2012 JAN	102.1	104.4	100.9	102	104.2	103.5	95.5	86.8
FEB	102.5	104.4	101.2	102	104.4	105.3	95.8	86.6
MAR	103	105.1	101.2	102.1	104.3	104.1	96.0	87.7
APR	102.9	105.4	101.6	102	105	104.1	96.2	88.2
MAY	102.8	105.5	101.4	102.5	105.3	104.1	96.4	88.2
JUN	102.6	105.7	101.5	102.9	105.3	104.1	96.6	88.4
JUL	102.8	105.5	101.3	103.9	105.4	104	96.9	86.8
AUG	102.9	105.4	101.3	103.8	105.4	103.8	97.1	87.4
SEP	102.8	105.8	101.8	102.9	105.6	103.6	97.2	88.0
OCT	103	105.9	101.9	103.5	105.6	103.6	97.2	89.1
NOV	103	106.1	101.7	103.7	105.5	103.8	97.4	89.7
DEC	103	106.2	101.9	103.7	105.4	104	97.6	89.9
2013 JAN	103.3	106.4	102.4	103.8	105.6	104.4	98.0	86.6
FEB	103.3	107.5	102.6	104.5	105.6	104.6	98.3	87.2
MAR	103.4	107.8	102.5	104.9	105.5	104.8	98.7	89.6
APR	103.4	108.2	102.2	105.1	105.6	104.9	99.0	90.1
MAY	103.3	108.2	102.2	105.2	105.7	104.9	99.4	89.8
JUN	103.3	108.3	102.3	105	105.6	105.5	99.6	90.2
JUL	103.1	108.8	102.8	105.2	105.8	105.5	100.0	90.4
AUG	102.6	108.6	102.7	105.6	105.8	105.7	100.4	90.9
SEP	102.6	108.4	102.5	105.5	106	105.8	100.8	92.6
OCT	102.6	108.6	102.6	105.5	106	105.8	101.4	92.4
NOV	102.8	108.7	102.3	105.5	106	105.6	101.9	92.9
DEC	102.7	108.5	102.3	105.4	106.2	105.5	102.5	95.1
2014 JAN	103.1	109.1	102.4	106.3	106.8	105.9	104.2	93.4
FEB	103.3	109.3	102.5	106.4	106.8	105.9	103.5	94.9
MAR	103.3	109.5	102.6	106.7	106.9	107.1	103.2	95.0
APR	103.2	109.6	102.2	107	107	107.1	102.9	97.1
MAY	103.5	109.6	102.3	107.4	107.3	107.2	102.8	98.8
JUN	103.7	109.5	102	107.5	107.3	107.2	103.6	98.5
JUL	103.7	109.6	101.6	107.8	107.3	107.3	104.1	98.9
AUG	103.8	109.9	101.8	107.8	107.3	107.3	103.5	99.3
SEP	104.1	110	101.6	107.9	107.4	107.4	104.0	99.4
OCT	104.1	110.2	101.5	107.8	107.5	107.9	104.1	100.0
NOV	104	110.3	101.5	107.9	107.6	108	104.3	99.0
DEC	104	110.4	101.5	107.9	107.5	107.9	104.1	101.1
2015 JAN	104.5	110.6	101.2	108.4	107.7	108	104.4	100.0
FEB	104.5	111.1	100.8	109.1	107.7	108	104.9	100.8
MAR	104.5	110.9	100.5	108.5	107.7	107.6	106.2	101.2
APR	104.6	110.8	100.4	108.5	108.4	107.8	105.1	101.3
MAY	104.5	110.9	100.5	108.4	108.6	107.9	105.2	101.7
JUN	104.5	111.1	100.4	108.4	108.8	107.8	105.5	100.7
JUL	103.9	111.2	100.1	108.6	108.9	109.5	107.5	103.5
AUG	104	111	100.2	108.6	109.1	108.2	106.9	103.5
SEP	103.9	111.3	100.6	108.7	109.1	108.3	106.8	103.9
OCT	103.8	111.6	100.7	108.7	109.1	108.4	107.2	105.0
NOV	103.9	111.5	100.2	108.9	109.4	108.6	107.6	105.3
DEC	104.2	111.7	100.5	109	109.5	108.4	106.8	108.3
2016 JAN	104	112.2	101	109.6	109.7	108.7	108.0	107.3
FEB	104.2	112.3	101.2	109.7	109.3	108.9	108.3	105.8
MAR	103.1	112.5	101.2	109.9	109.4	109.4	108.6	104.9
APR	103.3	112.6	101.5	110	109.4	110.7	108.8	112.0
MAY	103.4	112.4	101.3	110.6	109.8	110.9	108.6	115.0
JUN	104.1	112.6	101.5	111	110	110.8	108.8	112.4

Climate change Levy was introduced in April 2001

Rebasing the Producer Price Index, including trade prices (PPI) and the Services Producer Price Index (SPPI) onto 2010=100 occurred at the end of 2013. Further information can be found at:
http://www.ons.gov.uk/ons/rel/ppi2/producer-price-index/ppi-rebasing-2010---100/index.html
* All New Work uses the base of 2013=100
** House Price Index uses the base of 2015=100

Source: Office for National Statistics
Department for Communities and Local Government

Abreviations
NSI - Net Sector Input
FBTP - Food, Beverages and Tobacco Products
NSA - Not Seasonally Adjusted
SA - Seasonally Adjusted
GSI - Gross Sector Input
CCL - Climate Change Levy

17.3 Internal purchasing power of the pound (based on RPI) [1,2,3,4]: 1992 to 2015

pence	1992	1993	1994	1995	1996	1997	1998	1999	2000	2001	2002	2003	2004	2005	2006	2007	2008	2009	2010	2011	2012	2013	2014	2015
	CZVM	CBXX	DOFX	DOHR	DOLM	DTUL	CDQG	JKZZ	ZMHO	IKHI	FAUI	SEZH	C687	E9AO	GB4Y	HT4R	J5TL	JRT3	K9AD	KO2K	KVO5	MF5D	MZX3	DU4B
1991	104	105	108	112	114	118	122	124	128	130	132	136	140	144	148	155	161	160	167	176	182	187	193	194
1992	100	102	104	108	110	114	118	119	123	125	127	131	135	139	143	149	155	154	161	170	175	181	186	187
1993	98	100	102	106	109	112	116	118	121	123	125	129	133	136	141	147	153	152	159	167	173	178	183	184
1994	96	98	100	103	106	109	113	115	118	120	122	126	130	133	137	143	149	148	155	163	168	174	179	179
1995	93	94	97	100	102	106	109	111	114	116	118	122	125	129	133	139	144	143	150	158	163	168	173	173
1996	91	92	94	98	100	103	107	108	112	113	115	119	122	126	130	135	141	140	146	154	159	164	169	169
1997	88	89	92	95	97	100	103	105	108	110	112	115	119	122	126	131	136	136	142	149	154	159	163	164
1998	85	86	88	92	94	97	100	102	105	106	108	111	115	118	122	127	132	131	137	144	149	154	158	159
1999	84	85	87	90	92	95	98	100	103	105	107	110	113	116	120	125	130	129	135	142	147	151	156	156
2000	81	83	85	88	90	92	96	97	100	102	103	106	110	113	116	121	126	125	131	138	143	147	151	152
2001	80	81	83	86	88	91	94	95	98	100	102	105	108	111	114	119	124	123	129	136	140	144	149	149
2002	79	80	82	85	87	89	92	94	97	98	100	103	106	109	112	117	122	121	127	133	138	142	146	147
2003	76	78	79	82	84	87	90	91	94	96	97	100	103	106	109	114	118	118	123	130	134	138	142	143
2004	74	75	77	80	82	84	87	89	91	93	94	97	100	103	106	111	115	114	120	126	130	134	138	138
2005	72	73	75	78	80	82	85	86	89	90	92	94	97	100	103	108	112	111	116	123	126	130	134	135
2006	70	71	73	75	77	80	82	83	86	87	89	92	94	97	100	104	108	108	113	119	123	126	130	131
2007	67	68	70	72	74	76	79	80	82	84	85	88	90	93	96	100	104	103	108	114	117	121	125	125
2008	64	65	67	69	71	73	76	77	79	81	82	84	87	89	92	96	100	99	104	109	113	116	120	120
2009	65	66	67	70	71	74	76	77	80	81	82	85	87	90	93	97	101	100	105	110	114	117	120	121
2010	62	63	64	67	68	70	73	74	76	78	79	81	84	86	89	92	96	96	100	105	109	112	115	116
2011	59	60	61	63	65	67	69	70	72	74	75	77	79	82	84	88	91	91	95	100	103	106	109	110
2012	57	58	59	61	63	65	67	68	70	71	73	75	77	79	82	85	89	88	92	97	100	103	106	107
2013	55	56	58	60	61	63	65	66	68	69	70	72	75	77	79	83	86	85	89	94	97	100	103	103
2014	54	55	56	58	59	61	63	64	66	67	68	70	73	75	77	80	83	83	87	91	94	97	100	100
2015	54	54	56	59	61	63	64	66	67	68	70	72	74	77	80	83	83	86	91	94	97	100	100	100

1. To find the purchasing power of the pound in 2001, given that it was 100 pence in 1990, select the column headed 1990 and look at the 2001 row. The result is 73 pence.

2. Changes in the internal purchasing power of a currency may be defined as the 'inverse' of changes in the levels of prices; when prices go up, the amount which can be purchased with a given sum of money goes down. The monthly figures of the all items RPI can be used to obtain estimates of the changes in prices or in purchasing power between any 2 months. To find the purchasing power of the pound in one month, given that it was 100p in a previous month the calculation is: 100p multiplied by the earlier month RPI then divided by the later month RPI

3. Comparisons between any 2 years may be made in the same way using the annual averages of the RPI found in table 5.3. These figure are reproduced in the above table.

4. In accordance with the *Statistics and Registration Service Act 2007*, the Retail Prices Index and its derivatives have been assessed against the Code of Practice for Official Statistics and found not to meet the required standards for designation as National Statistics. A full report can be found at: http://www.statisticsauthority.gov.uk/

Source:
Office for National Statistics
Prices Division
2.001 Cardiff Road
Newport
South Wales
NP10 8XG
Tel: +44 (0) 1633 456900

17.4 CPI: Detailed figures by division [1,2]

	Food and non-alcoholic beverages	Alcoholic beverages and tobacco	Clothing and footwear	Housing, water, electricity, gas & other fuels	Furniture, household equipment & routine maintenance	Health[3]	Transport	Commun-ication	Recreation and culture	Education 3	Restaurants and hotels	Miscell-aneous goods and services[3]	CPI (overall index)
COICOP Division	1	2	3	4	5	6	7	8	9	10	11	12	
	CHZR	CHZS	CHZT	CHZU	CHZV	CHZW	CHZX	CHZY	CHZZ	CJUU	CJUV	CJUW	CHZQ
Weights 2016	103	42	71	120	59	28	153	32	148	25	123	96	1000

Monthly indices (2015=100)

	D7BU	D7BV	D7BW	D7BX	D7BY	D7BZ	D7C2	D7C3	D7C4	D7C5	D7C6	D7C7	D7BT
Jul 2014	102.2	97.7	95.1	99.8	99.0	98.5	104.4	98.5	100.7	89.8	98.7	99.2	99.9
Aug	102.0	98.7	97.6	99.8	100.0	99.0	105.2	98.4	100.6	89.8	98.5	99.4	100.2
Sep	101.8	99.3	101.5	99.9	100.6	98.7	102.7	98.5	100.5	91.5	98.7	99.7	100.3
Oct	101.9	100.0	102.1	100.0	99.5	98.4	101.5	98.6	101.0	98.7	99.0	99.6	100.4
Nov	101.7	98.8	102.8	100.0	99.6	98.1	100.3	98.3	100.7	98.7	99.0	99.5	100.1
Dec	102.0	98.5	101.7	100.0	101.2	98.3	100.1	98.9	100.5	98.7	99.0	99.4	100.1
Jan	101.3	99.9	98.0	99.9	98.7	99.0	98.1	98.9	99.6	98.7	98.9	99.3	99.3
Feb	101.0	99.5	99.3	99.8	100.1	99.1	98.5	99.7	99.5	98.7	99.1	99.6	99.5
Mar	100.9	99.3	99.2	99.5	100.5	99.5	99.2	99.9	100.0	98.7	99.3	99.8	99.7
Apr	100.5	99.8	99.9	99.9	99.3	100.2	100.3	99.9	100.1	98.7	99.6	99.8	99.9
May	100.4	100.5	100.5	99.9	99.8	100.5	100.9	99.7	100.0	98.7	99.8	99.6	100.1
Jun	100.2	100.7	100.1	99.9	100.2	99.9	101.1	99.5	99.9	98.7	100.2	99.8	100.2
Jul 2015	99.5	99.6	96.7	100.2	98.7	100.8	102.3	99.7	100.1	98.7	100.3	99.9	100.0
Aug	99.5	100.7	98.2	100.2	100.4	100.7	102.4	99.5	99.7	98.7	100.3	100.3	100.3
Sep	99.5	100.7	100.9	100.0	101.1	100.7	99.9	99.9	99.7	99.9	100.5	100.3	100.2
Oct	99.1	100.3	102.9	100.2	100.2	100.0	98.9	100.5	100.6	103.4	100.6	100.4	100.3
Nov	99.2	100.1	102.8	100.3	100.0	99.8	98.2	101.1	100.6	103.4	100.8	100.7	100.3
Dec	99.0	98.8	101.5	100.3	101.0	99.8	100.0	101.5	100.3	103.4	100.7	100.5	100.3
Jan	98.6	101.2	98.3	100.2	98.7	101.1	97.5	101.0	99.5	103.4	100.4	100.7	99.5
Feb	98.8	100.6	99.6	100.1	100.3	101.1	97.5	101.8	99.4	103.4	100.9	100.8	99.8
Mar	98.1	100.3	100.6	99.9	101.1	101.3	99.1	101.4	99.7	103.4	101.4	100.8	100.2
Apr	98.0	101.1	100.3	99.8	99.5	102.2	99.0	101.6	100.5	103.4	101.9	100.8	100.2
May	97.6	101.5	100.1	99.9	100.0	102.4	99.9	102.5	100.1	103.4	102.4	100.9	100.4
Jun	97.2	101.1	99.4	100.0	99.6	102.6	100.9	103.1	100.8	103.4	102.6	100.9	100.6
Jul 2016	96.9	101.4	96.0	100.1	98.0	102.6	102.6	103.4	100.7	103.4	103.0	100.8	100.6

Percentage change on a year earlier

	D7G8	D7G9	D7GA	D7GB	D7GC	D7GD	D7GE	D7GF	D7GG	D7GH	D7GI	D7GJ	D7G7
Jul 2014	-0.4	3.6	-0.2	3.2	1.1	2.6	1.3	0.7	1.5	10.3	2.8	-0.6	1.6
Aug	-1.1	4.6	0.4	3.2	0.4	2.9	1.2	0.8	1.4	10.3	2.6	-0.4	1.5
Sep	-1.4	4.9	0.2	3.1	0.8	2.5	0.1	0.9	0.7	10.3	2.3	-0.5	1.2
Oct	-1.4	5.2	-0.2	3.2	0.1	2.2	0.5	0.6	1.0	10.0	2.5	-0.3	1.3
Nov	-1.7	4.0	-0.2	3.3	0.3	2.0	-0.2	0.5	0.3	10.0	2.4	-0.8	1.0
Dec	-1.7	5.0	-0.3	1.0	0.2	2.1	-1.4	0.7	0.6	10.0	2.3	-0.6	0.5
Jan	-2.5	3.3	1.4	1.0	0.8	2.2	-2.8	0.2	0.1	10.0	2.4	-0.4	0.3
Feb	-3.3	3.8	1.7	0.9	-0.3	1.8	-2.7	0.9	-0.8	10.0	2.2	-0.4	-
Mar	-3.0	3.4	-0.2	0.7	-0.2	2.1	-1.9	0.9	-0.7	10.0	2.0	-0.5	-
Apr	-2.8	3.0	-0.4	0.5	-0.5	2.0	-2.8	1.0	-0.4	10.0	2.0	-0.1	-0.1
May	-1.8	2.2	0.2	0.4	-0.5	2.2	-1.5	1.2	-1.0	10.0	1.9	-0.1	0.1
Jun	-2.2	2.3	-0.8	0.4	-0.3	1.6	-1.8	1.1	-1.0	10.0	1.9	0.1	-
Jul 2015	-2.7	1.9	1.7	0.4	-0.3	2.3	-1.9	1.3	-0.6	10.0	1.6	0.7	0.1
Aug	-2.4	2.1	0.6	0.4	0.4	1.8	-2.6	1.1	-0.9	10.0	1.8	0.8	-
Sep	-2.3	1.4	-0.6	0.1	0.5	2.0	-2.7	1.4	-0.8	9.1	1.8	0.6	-0.1
Oct	-2.7	0.3	0.8	0.2	0.6	1.7	-2.6	2.0	-0.4	4.8	1.6	0.8	-0.1
Nov	-2.4	1.4	-	0.3	0.4	1.7	-2.1	2.9	-0.1	4.8	1.8	1.3	0.1
Dec	-2.9	0.3	-0.3	0.3	-0.2	1.5	-0.2	2.7	-0.3	4.8	1.7	1.1	0.2
Jan	-2.6	1.3	0.4	0.4	-0.1	2.1	-0.7	2.2	-0.1	4.8	1.6	1.4	0.3
Feb	-2.3	1.2	0.3	0.3	0.2	2.0	-1.1	2.1	-0.1	4.8	1.9	1.2	0.3
Mar	-2.7	1.0	1.4	0.4	0.6	1.8	-0.1	1.4	-0.2	4.8	2.1	1.0	0.5
Apr	-2.5	1.3	0.3	-0.1	0.3	2.0	-1.3	1.7	0.4	4.8	2.3	1.0	0.3
May	-2.8	1.0	-0.4	-	0.2	1.9	-1.0	2.8	0.1	4.8	2.6	1.3	0.3
Jun	-2.9	0.5	-0.7	0.1	-0.5	2.7	-0.2	3.7	0.8	4.8	2.3	1.1	0.5
Jul 2016	-2.6	1.8	-0.7	-0.1	-0.8	1.8	0.2	3.6	0.6	4.8	2.7	0.9	0.6

Source: Office for National Statistics

Key: - zero or negligible
1. For the release of January consumer price inflation data on 16 February 2016, CPI and CPIH indices have been re-referenced and published with 2015=100
Full historic series for each of the re-referenced indices are now available for users to view or download. Regular re-referencing of indices is methodological good practice as it avoids rounding issues that can arise from small index values.
Please note that re-referencing does not impact on published inflation rates, although when using the indices to calculate inflation rates, it is important to use indices that are calculated in the same reference year. Re-referencing does not impact on RPI and RPIJ. For more information, please contact cpi@ons.gsi.gov.uk.
2. More detailed CPI data are available at: http://www.ons.gov.uk
3. The coverage of these categories was extended in January 2000; further extensions to coverage came into effect in January 2001 for health and miscellaneous goods and services; the coverage of miscellaneous goods and services was further extended with effect from January 2002. (Details are given in a series of Economic Trends articles available on the National Statistics website)

17.5 Retail Prices Index[1] United Kingdom

Indices (13 January 1987=100)

| | All items (RPI) | All items excluding | | | | | | | | | | | All items excluding |
		mortgage interest payments (RPIX)	mortgage interest payments and depreci-ation	Housing	All items excluding Food	All items excluding Seasonal food[2]	Food and catering	Alcohol and tobacco	Housing and household expend-iture	Pesonal expend-iture	Travel and leisure	Consumer durables[4]	mortgage interest payments and indirect taxes (RPIY)[3]
Weights													
	CZGU	CZGY	DOGZ	CZGX	CZGV	CZGW	CBVV	CBVW	CBVX	CBVY	CBVZ	CBWA	
2001	1000	954	914	795	884	982	169	97	362	96	276	125	
2002	1000	964	924	801	886	980	166	99	363	94	278	126	
2003	1000	961	919	797	891	983	160	98	365	92	285	126	
2004	1000	961	914	791	889	981	160	97	367	93	283	121	
2005	1000	950	901	776	890	981	159	96	387	89	269	122	
2006	1000	950	906	778	895	983	155	96	392	90	267	117	
2007	1000	945	895	762	895	981	152	95	408	83	262	109	
2008	1000	940	885	746	889	980	158	86	417	83	256	104	
2009	1000	959	909	764	882	979	168	90	416	80	246	106	
2010	1000	966	911	763	888	981	159	91	403	81	266	105	
2011	1000	968	914	762	882	980	165	88	408	82	257	106	
2012	1000	971	915	763	886	981	161	85	412	84	258	100	
2013	1000	971	913	746	884	980	163	91	419	83	244	96	
2014	1000	970	912	747	886	981	161	87	424	85	243	98	
2015	1000	971	898	737	891	982	156	83	432	83	246	94	
2016	1000	972	892	734	898	982	149	82	436	83	250	98	
Annual averages													
	CHAW	CHMK	CHON	CHAZ	CHAY	CHAX	CHBS	CHBT	CHBU	CHBV	CHBW	CHBY	CBZW
2001	173.3	171.3	169.5	163.7	178.0	174.3	162.2	216.9	180.0	135.7	172.0	105.0	163.7
2002	176.2	175.1	172.5	166.0	181.1	177.2	164.8	222.3	184.6	133.2	174.2	101.9	167.5
2003	181.3	180.0	176.2	168.9	186.7	182.4	167.9	228.0	194.3	133.2	177.0	99.8	172.0
2004	186.7	184.0	179.1	170.9	192.8	187.9	170.0	233.6	207.4	131.5	178.1	97.7	175.5
2005	192.0	188.2	182.6	173.7	198.7	193.3	172.9	239.8	219.4	131.0	179.2	95.3	179.4
2006	198.1	193.7	187.8	178.3	205.2	199.5	176.9	247.1	231.8	131.7	181.1	94.0	184.8
2007	206.6	199.9	193.3	183.2	213.9	207.9	184.3	256.2	248.1	132.9	183.8	93.3	190.8
2008	214.8	208.5	201.9	191.3	221.2	216.0	198.5	266.7	258.6	132.4	189.0	91.6	199.2
2009	213.7	212.6	207.2	196.3	218.3	214.6	207.6	276.7	247.4	131.4	191.2	90.7	204.8
2010	223.6	222.7	217	206.5	228.8	224.5	214.1	289.9	253.8	138.2	207.6	94.4	211.9
2011	235.2	234.5	229.3	219.6	240.5	236.3	225.6	311.3	262.5	149.8	220.1	99.7	220.4
2012	242.7	242.0	237.0	227.4	248.2	243.9	232.9	327.1	270.9	158.2	224.1	104.1	227.7
2013	250.1	249.4	244.4	235.1	255.5	251.2	240.8	341.9	279.7	166.8	226.8	108.8	235.0
2014	256.0	255.5	249.5	240.2	262.4	257.3	242.5	354.9	288.2	175.0	228.7	113.5	241.2
2015	258.5	258.1	251.0	240.9	266.0	260.0	239.8	362.7	293.7	182.6	226.7	117.6	243.3
Monthly figures													
2015 Sep	259.6	259.3	251.8	241.7	267.4	261.2	239.3	364.4	295.3	185.0	227.3	119.5	244.6
Oct	259.5	259.2	251.6	241.3	267.4	261.1	238.7	363.8	295.5	186.4	226.5	119.8	244.5
Nov	259.8	259.4	251.8	241.4	267.6	261.3	239.0	364.1	296.1	186.6	226.2	119.7	244.5
Dec	260.6	260.3	252.5	242.2	268.6	262.1	239.1	362.3	297.2	185.0	228.6	119.5	245.5
2016 Jan	258.8	258.4	250.5	239.8	266.7	260.3	238.1	366.5	296.4	182.8	224.0	116.1	243.4
Feb	260.0	259.7	251.8	241.2	268.1	261.6	238.6	365.8	297.8	186.9	224.7	120.0	244.7
Mar	261.1	260.8	252.9	242.5	269.4	262.7	238.1	366.3	298.1	188.9	227.3	122.1	245.9
Apr	261.4	261.1	253.0	242.3	269.8	263.1	238.0	368.5	298.8	189.4	226.9	121.0	245.7
May	262.1	261.9	253.7	243.0	270.8	263.8	237.5	369.6	299.5	189.4	228.6	121.1	246.4
June	263.1	262.9	254.6	244.0	272.0	264.8	237.1	369.3	300.3	188.8	231.3	121.1	247.5
July	263.4	263.2	254.7	244.0	272.4	265.2	236.5	370.1	300.2	185.9	233.8	118.3	247.9
Aug	264.4	264.5	255.8	245.3	273.5	266.2	237.5	371.7	300.9	187.8	234.7	120.2	249.4

1 See chapter text.
2 Seasonal food is defined as items of food the prices of which show significant
seasonal variations. These are fresh fruit and vegetables, fresh fish, eggs and home-killed lamb.
3 There are no weights available for RPIY. The taxes excluded are council tax, VAT, duties, car purchase tax and vehicle excise duty, insurance premium tax and airport tax.
4 Consumer durables: Furniture, furnishings, electrical appliances and other household equipment, men's, women's and children's outerwear, footwear, audio-visual equipment, CDs and tapes, toys, photographic and sports goods.

Source: Office for National Statistics: 020 7533 5874

In accordance with the *Statistics and Registration Service Act 2007*, the Retail Prices Index and its derivatives have been assessed against the Code of Practice for Official Statistics and found not to meet the required standards for designation as National Statistics. A full report can be found at: http://www.statisticsauthority.gov.uk/

17.6 Tax and Price Index[1] United Kingdom

Indices and percentages

	Tax and Price Index: (January 1987=100)															
	DQAB															
	2001	2002	2003	2004	2005	2006	2007	2008	2009	2010	2011	2012	2013	2014	2015	2016
January	156.7	156.5	161.4	166.9	172.1	175.9	183.3	190.7	188.6	194.7	205.5	212.8	218.8	222.7	223.9	225.8
February	157.6	157.0	162.3	167.6	172.8	176.7	184.8	192.3	189.8	196.0	207.7	214.6	220.5	224.2	225.2	226.9
March	157.8	157.7	163.0	168.4	173.7	177.4	186.1	192.9	189.7	197.4	208.8	215.6	221.6	224.8	225.6	228.0
April	156.3	158.6	164.9	168.9	174.1	178.3	186.3	192.2	188.5	199.5	209.2	215.6	219.7	224.2	225.1	228.8
May	157.4	159.1	165.2	169.7	174.5	179.5	187.1	193.4	189.7	200.3	210.0	215.5	220.2	224.4	225.5	229.5
June	157.6	159.1	165.0	170.0	174.7	180.3	188.2	195.1	190.2	200.8	210.0	214.9	219.9	224.8	225.9	230.4
July	156.5	158.8	165.0	170.0	174.7	180.3	187.0	194.8	190.2	200.3	209.5	215.2	219.9	224.5	225.6	230.7
August	157.2	159.3	165.4	170.6	175.1	181.0	188.2	195.5	191.3	201.2	210.9	216.1	221.1	225.5	226.7	231.7
September	157.8	160.6	166.3	171.3	175.6	181.9	188.9	196.7	192.2	201.9	212.7	217.2	222.0	226.1	226.6	232.1
October	157.5	160.9	166.4	171.8	175.8	182.2	189.8	196.0	192.9	202.4	212.8	218.6	222.0	226.1	226.5	232.0
November	156.8	161.2	166.5	172.2	176.1	182.8	190.6	194.3	193.4	203.4	213.2	218.6	222.2	225.6	226.7	232.7
December	156.6	161.5	167.3	173.1	176.6	184.4	191.8	191.2	194.8	204.9	214.1	219.8	223.5	226.0	227.6	234.1

	Retail Prices Index: (January 1987=100)															
	CHAW															
	2001	2002	2003	2004	2005	2006	2007	2008	2009	2010	2011	2012	2013	2014	2015	2016
January	171.1	173.3	178.4	183.1	188.9	193.4	201.6	209.8	210.1	217.9	229.0	238.0	245.8	252.6	255.4	258.8
February	172.0	173.8	179.3	183.8	189.6	194.2	203.1	211.4	211.4	219.2	231.3	239.9	247.6	254.2	256.7	260.0
March	172.2	174.5	179.9	184.6	190.5	195.0	204.4	212.1	211.3	220.7	232.5	240.8	248.7	254.8	257.1	261.1
April	173.1	175.7	181.2	185.7	191.6	196.5	205.4	214.0	211.5	222.8	234.4	242.5	249.5	255.7	258.0	261.4
May	174.2	176.2	181.5	186.5	192.0	197.7	206.2	215.1	212.8	223.6	235.2	242.4	250.0	255.9	258.5	262.1
June	174.4	176.2	181.3	186.8	192.2	198.5	207.3	216.8	213.4	224.1	235.2	241.8	249.7	256.3	258.9	263.1
July	173.3	175.9	181.3	186.8	192.2	198.5	206.1	216.5	213.4	223.6	234.7	242.1	249.7	256.0	258.6	263.4
August	174.0	176.4	181.6	187.4	192.6	199.2	207.3	217.2	214.4	224.5	236.1	243.0	251.0	257.0	259.8	264.4
September	174.6	177.6	182.5	188.1	193.1	200.1	208.0	218.4	215.3	225.3	237.9	244.2	251.9	257.6	259.6	264.9
October	174.3	177.9	182.6	188.6	193.3	200.4	208.9	217.7	216.0	225.8	238.0	245.6	251.9	257.7	259.5	264.8
November	173.6	178.2	182.7	189.0	193.6	201.1	209.7	216.0	216.6	226.8	238.5	245.6	252.1	257.1	259.8	265.5
December	173.4	178.5	183.5	189.9	194.1	202.7	210.9	212.9	218.0	228.4	239.4	246.8	253.4	257.5	260.6	267.1

	Percentage changes on one year earlier[1] CZVL															
	2001	2002	2003	2004	2005	2006	2007	2008	2009	2010	2011	2012	2013	2014	2015	2016
Tax and Price Index[1]																
January	2.6	-0.1	3.1	3.4	3.1	2.2	4.2	4.0	-1.1	3.2	5.5	3.6	2.8	1.8	0.5	0.8
February	2.5	-0.4	3.4	3.3	3.1	2.3	4.6	4.1	-1.3	3.3	6.0	3.3	2.7	1.7	0.4	0.8
March	2.1	-0.1	3.4	3.3	3.1	2.1	4.9	3.7	-1.7	4.1	5.8	3.3	2.8	1.4	0.4	1.1
April	0.4	1.5	4.0	2.4	3.1	2.4	4.5	3.2	-1.9	5.8	4.9	3.1	1.9	2.0	0.4	1.6
May	0.7	1.1	3.8	2.7	2.8	2.9	4.2	3.4	-1.9	5.6	4.8	2.6	2.2	1.9	0.5	1.8
June	0.6	1.0	3.7	3.0	2.8	3.2	4.4	3.7	-2.5	5.6	4.6	2.3	2.3	2.2	0.5	2.0
July	0.3	1.5	3.9	3.0	2.8	3.2	3.7	4.2	-2.4	5.3	4.6	2.7	2.2	2.1	0.5	2.3
August	0.7	1.3	3.8	3.1	2.6	3.4	4.0	3.9	-2.1	5.2	4.8	2.5	2.3	2.0	0.5	2.2
September	0.3	1.8	3.5	3.0	2.5	3.6	3.8	4.1	-2.3	5.0	5.3	2.1	2.2	1.8	0.2	2.4
October	0.2	2.2	3.4	3.2	2.3	3.6	4.2	3.3	-1.6	4.9	5.1	2.7	1.6	1.8	0.2	2.4
November	-0.6	2.8	3.3	3.4	2.3	3.8	4.3	1.9	-0.5	5.2	4.8	2.5	1.6	1.5	0.5	2.6
December	-0.8	3.1	3.6	3.5	2.0	4.4	4.0	-0.3	1.9	5.2	4.5	2.7	1.7	1.1	0.7	2.9
Retail Prices Index - CZBH																
January	2.7	1.3	2.9	2.6	3.2	2.4	4.2	4.1	0.1	3.7	5.1	3.9	3.3	2.8	1.1	1.3
February	2.7	1.0	3.2	2.5	3.2	2.4	4.6	4.1	-	3.7	5.5	3.7	3.2	2.7	1.0	1.3
March	2.3	1.3	3.1	2.6	3.2	2.4	4.8	3.8	-0.4	4.4	5.3	3.6	3.3	2.5	0.9	1.6
April	1.8	1.5	3.1	2.5	3.2	2.6	4.5	4.2	-1.2	5.3	5.2	3.5	2.9	2.5	0.9	1.3
May	2.1	1.1	3.0	2.8	2.9	3.0	4.3	4.3	-1.1	5.1	5.2	3.1	3.1	2.4	1.0	1.4
June	1.9	1.0	2.9	3.0	2.9	3.3	4.4	4.6	-1.6	5.0	5.0	2.8	3.3	2.6	1.0	1.6
July	1.6	1.5	3.1	3.0	2.9	3.3	3.8	5.0	-1.4	4.8	5.0	3.2	3.1	2.5	1.0	1.9
August	2.1	1.4	2.9	3.2	2.8	3.4	4.1	4.8	-1.3	4.7	5.2	2.9	3.3	2.4	1.1	1.8
September	1.7	1.7	2.8	3.1	2.7	3.6	3.9	5.0	-1.4	4.6	5.6	2.6	3.2	2.3	0.8	2.0
October	1.6	2.1	2.6	3.3	2.5	3.7	4.2	4.2	-0.8	4.5	5.4	3.2	2.6	2.3	0.7	2.0
November	0.9	2.6	2.5	3.4	2.4	3.9	4.3	3.0	0.3	4.7	5.2	3.0	2.6	2.0	1.1	2.2
December	0.7	2.9	2.8	3.5	2.2	4.4	4.0	0.9	2.4	4.8	4.8	3.1	2.7	1.6	1.2	2.5

Source: Office for National Statistics: 020 7533 5874

Key: - zero or negligible .. not available

1. In accordance with the *Statistics and Registration Service Act 2007*, the Retail Prices Index and its derivatives have been assessed against the Code of Practice for Official Statistics and found not to meet the required standards for designation as National Statistics. A full report can be found at: http://www.statisticsauthority.gov.uk/

17.7 Index of Producer Prices of Agricultural Products, UK (2010=100)

Table 4 Inputs annual series		2006	2007	2008	2009	2010	2011	2012	2013	2014	2015
Total Inputs	a	78.1	84.8	103.2	95.9	100.0	112.3	114.2	117.0	112.1	106.8
All goods and services currently consumed in agriculture	a	76.2	83.6	105.0	95.7	100.0	114.0	116.6	119.7	112.8	106.2
Seeds	a	86.3	97.2	111.2	105.0	100.0	106.9	105.2	113.9	100.9	95.6
Energy and lubricants		75.8	78.2	107.0	88.3	100.0	118.1	122.3	123.3	119.0	101.2
Electricity		79.7	84.4	100.5	102.2	100.0	108.8	113.4	121.9	128.4	128.0
Fuels for heating		68.2	75.0	101.4	81.4	100.0	109.5	118.8	126.8	132.1	127.9
Motor fuels		75.5	76.7	109.6	85.0	100.0	122.0	125.4	123.3	114.6	89.9
Fertilisers and soil improvers		62.6	67.8	148.5	102.3	100.0	130.4	125.2	113.1	106.5	101.5
Straight fertilisers		66.0	69.8	152.9	93.7	100.0	140.7	128.2	115.2	111.2	103.6
Straight fertilisers - nitrogenous		68.8	71.6	151.8	89.1	100.0	144.5	130.7	118.0	114.9	106.2
Straight fertilisers - phosphatic		48.0	69.0	184.3	111.3	100.0	131.0	120.2	97.5	90.0	94.9
Straight fertilisers - potassic		44.8	51.3	148.2	134.6	100.0	105.2	105.5	94.7	82.2	80.1
Compound fertilisers		55.4	62.4	147.1	112.6	100.0	120.5	123.6	111.3	100.6	97.7
Other fertilisers and soil improvers		96.2	100.8	105.6	105.8	100.0	100.0	102.4	105.5	109.1	114.2
Plant protection products	a	97.3	98.8	100.9	102.8	100.0	100.7	102.0	97.7	102.6	102.5
Fungicides		98.3	99.6	101.9	103.5	100.0	110.6	109.3	99.9	103.5	102.5
Insecticides		85.7	89.6	91.4	102.2	100.0	89.5	67.3	61.0	67.5	67.4
Herbicides	a	98.4	99.8	101.9	102.3	100.0	95.1	89.1	91.6	96.7	95.7
Other plant protection products		96.5	97.8	99.5	102.7	100.0	98.6	151.3	137.3	145.2	151.4
Veterinary services	a	89.8	91.2	87.6	88.0	100.0	102.0	103.5	106.1	107.0	107.7
Animal feedingstuffs	q	66.0	80.1	103.7	95.4	100.0	120.7	128.5	139.4	120.7	108.1
Straight feedingstuffs		62.6	81.7	106.1	90.1	100.0	122.9	135.7	147.6	120.1	103.6
Cereal and milling by products		69.0	96.7	127.2	90.5	100.0	151.6	153.8	161.4	124.1	105.4
Feed wheat		65.5	91.2	123.8	91.3	100.0	143.8	144.6	157.0	124.3	102.8
Feed barley		73.5	105.1	132.5	90.0	100.0	159.9	163.7	165.8	124.4	109.2
Feed oats		74.3	90.8	111.7	80.3	100.0	184.8	198.4	180.7	111.1	102.8
Oilcakes		51.2	64.7	93.8	90.5	100.0	96.6	124.2	138.7	111.9	98.5
Soya bean meal		49.8	66.2	108.6	93.4	100.0	117.3	134.4	137.3	108.4	102.2
Sunflower seed meal		49.8	60.6	90.9	97.1	100.0	97.8	126.0	141.3	112.6	92.9
Rape seed meal		53.9	72.9	99.1	77.6	100.0	91.6	113.4	131.2	105.5	109.2
Products of animal origin (incl. white fish meal)		61.0	58.0	58.6	67.2	100.0	101.9	103.5	108.8	113.6	115.7
Other straights		68.8	84.9	96.6	90.0	100.0	120.8	128.4	142.8	125.4	107.4
Field peas		55.6	99.3	119.9	93.2	100.0	126.4	140.4	171.1	144.8	109.3
Field beans		54.8	97.7	114.9	88.8	100.0	125.3	141.1	177.4	142.3	109.7
Soya beans		60.1	59.3	67.8	81.1	100.0	103.9	110.6	122.0	122.8	121.3
Compound feedingstuffs	q	68.2	79.1	102.2	98.9	100.0	119.2	123.7	134.0	121.1	111.1
Compound feedingstuffs for cattle and calves	q	69.8	80.1	103.8	101.0	100.0	117.8	125.6	135.6	124.7	114.7
Compound feedingstuffs for pigs	q	68.1	79.3	98.6	95.3	100.0	118.7	123.5	128.6	117.4	109.5
Compound feedingstuffs for poultry	q	65.8	77.4	101.5	97.3	100.0	120.8	121.2	132.9	116.9	106.2
Compound feedingstuffs for sheep	q	72.7	81.9	103.8	103.3	100.0	119.8	127.3	142.2	130.7	119.7
Maintenance of Materials		83.5	86.6	91.6	95.8	100.0	104.9	106.5	108.3	110.3	110.8
Maintenance of Buildings		81.6	87.7	94.0	93.8	100.0	107.4	109.8	110.1	110.9	109.0
Other goods and services	a	83.6	88.3	93.0	93.3	100.0	106.0	106.7	109.1	109.9	109.2
Goods and services contributing to investment	a	87.9	90.9	94.3	96.9	100.0	103.6	101.7	102.9	108.7	110.0
Materials	a	90.0	91.8	94.3	97.3	100.0	103.0	99.1	100.4	108.5	110.5
Machinery and other equipment	a	88.5	92.1	97.4	99.7	100.0	103.8	94.3	96.8	115.9	121.4
Plant and machinery for cultivation		86.2	90.4	96.6	99.5	100.0	104.7	93.4	95.9	117.7	123.8
Farm machinery and installations	a	96.8	98.2	100.3	100.1	100.0	100.6	97.4	100.4	109.0	112.4
Transport Equipment		91.1	91.6	92.0	95.6	100.0	102.4	102.8	103.0	103.0	102.2
Tractors		87.8	89.1	91.4	95.9	100.0	103.7	104.6	105.3	105.1	104.5
Other vehicles		104.8	102.1	95.1	94.4	100.0	98.2	96.3	95.0	95.0	92.9
Buildings		83.7	89.3	95.0	95.2	100.0	105.8	107.4	107.7	108.4	107.2
Other (Engineering and soil improvement operations)		84.9	89.0	93.1	97.9	100.0	102.5	104.5	107.2	110.7	113.4

a:- Part or all of the series is made up of annual data
q:- Part or all of the series is made up of quarterly data

Source: Department for Environment, Food and Rural Affairs
Enquiries Defra prices team. Tel: ++44(0)20802 66280
email: prices@defra.gsi.gov.uk

17.8 Index of Producer Prices of Agricultural Products, UK (2010=100)

		2006	2007	2008	2009	2010	2011	2012	2013	2014	2015
Total Outputs (1)	a	72.3	82.2	98.9	95.0	100.0	113.5	118.8	125.8	114.6	105.0
Crop products (1)	a	73.2	88.0	103.6	89.1	100.0	119.0	124.2	128.7	109.2	102.7
Cereals	a	66.2	96.8	124.0	89.6	100.0	144.8	149.7	153.1	120.6	102.8
Wheat	a	64.2	93.2	121.5	90.5	100.0	141.7	144.3	151.9	121.3	101.3
Wheat - Feeding	a	65.1	92.1	120.0	89.5	100.0	141.0	143.7	152.8	120.8	101.2
Wheat - Breadmaking		60.2	95.5	124.0	95.7	100.0	138.3	141.7	141.9	122.4	102.0
Wheat - Other Milling		63.4	98.6	129.1	90.0	100.0	152.2	152.7	158.4	123.8	101.7
Barley	a	71.5	107.9	132.6	88.0	100.0	150.3	160.9	154.4	119.2	106.4
Barley - Feeding	a	71.4	103.8	126.0	86.3	100.0	155.5	159.9	158.6	120.2	106.3
Barley - Malting		71.6	117.1	147.1	91.7	100.0	138.9	163.2	145.2	117.2	106.6
Oats	a	73.6	91.9	113.1	82.7	100.0	177.8	190.1	173.7	112.6	108.3
Oats - Milling		71.6	91.1	110.0	82.6	100.0	170.4	183.2	155.8	108.4	107.3
Oats - Feeding	a	76.6	93.1	118.0	82.7	100.0	189.7	201.0	202.0	119.3	110.1
Potatoes		92.1	104.4	108.7	86.6	100.0	107.3	122.7	156.5	103.9	106.1
Potatoes - Earlies		79.3	61.7	89.4	61.4	100.0	65.9	125.2	122.6	65.0	100.6
Potatoes - Main Crop		93.6	108.6	110.9	88.5	100.0	111.1	122.2	160.7	107.3	106.3
Industrial Crops	a	64.7	73.6	112.4	93.5	100.0	132.0	130.0	121.5	101.8	98.6
Oilseed Rape (non set aside)		58.9	69.7	118.7	91.5	100.0	143.3	139.1	127.0	99.7	95.1
Sugar Beet	a	81.2	83.7	93.6	99.0	100.0	99.9	104.3	105.7	108.9	110.1
Forage plants		62.8	73.7	80.5	84.1	100.0	112.6	106.2	114.8	107.4	94.5
Hay and dried grass		54.8	69.0	65.0	69.5	100.0	136.9	100.4	86.3	84.7	71.7
Straw		51.4	63.1	70.9	80.1	100.0	113.5	100.6	104.3	99.4	85.5
Other forage plants		54.9	94.3	111.1	87.6	100.0	127.5	136.9	168.3	138.6	108.1
Fresh Vegetables (1)		85.3	93.3	91.9	87.8	100.0	92.8	108.6	110.2	103.1	105.9
Cauliflowers		77.9	91.5	93.4	89.4	100.0	96.3	118.4	102.0	105.3	99.4
Tomatoes		80.8	82.3	87.1	75.9	100.0	78.9	90.7	88.3	90.1	88.3
Cabbages		83.1	102.5	99.2	92.0	100.0	108.4	120.3	113.4	94.9	106.9
Lettuce		82.8	78.7	91.4	79.4	100.0	85.5	110.1	104.9	100.0	98.7
Carrots		91.9	106.4	110.7	114.7	100.0	108.0	124.2	124.4	89.8	113.0
Onions		56.1	77.1	56.1	57.1	100.0	94.1	68.3	96.9	94.9	93.2
Beans (Green)		87.9	106.2	94.8	84.4	100.0	89.8	132.6	124.1	103.5	107.3
Mushrooms		100.9	95.0	79.6	86.0	100.0	87.4	104.4	117.7	144.3	142.9
Fresh Fruit		77.3	84.0	96.6	95.6	100.0	98.7	103.7	104.8	97.6	101.2
Dessert Apples		76.1	86.7	92.1	96.6	100.0	107.0	118.0	117.1	104.0	104.7
Cooking Apples		87.0	97.5	122.5	99.6	100.0	104.0	132.0	158.1	109.1	104.2
Dessert Pears		82.2	80.3	106.2	113.3	100.0	101.2	116.9	129.4	102.8	99.8
Strawberries		70.5	73.1	83.8	90.9	100.0	91.8	87.4	84.0	91.4	95.1
Raspberries		83.9	96.6	97.7	99.0	100.0	102.2	96.5	96.2	88.7	104.9
Flowers and plants	a	73.6	77.5	83.6	86.6	100.0	107.3	109.3	110.9	109.5	107.2
Other crop products	a	93.1	83.7	79.1	103.7	100.0	97.7	102.9	102.9	102.9	102.9
Seeds	a	93.1	83.7	79.1	103.7	100.0	97.7	102.9	102.9	102.9	102.9
Animals and animal products	a	71.7	78.0	95.6	99.3	100.0	109.5	114.8	123.8	118.6	106.5
Animals (for slaughter & export)		71.0	73.9	90.2	100.8	100.0	109.6	114.8	121.0	113.5	109.6
Cattle and calves		73.8	75.0	98.4	104.9	100.0	116.4	129.3	137.7	123.2	126.0
Cattle (clean)		75.2	76.3	98.4	105.0	100.0	115.1	129.0	139.0	124.5	128.3
Cows and Bulls		65.7	67.5	98.2	103.9	100.0	123.8	131.2	131.1	116.5	113.2
Calves		80.1	84.7	102.5	128.6	100.0	112.7	126.7	118.4	110.3	140.8
Pigs		74.2	76.0	89.5	103.1	100.0	102.1	106.3	116.7	111.7	92.2
Pigs (clean)		74.0	76.3	89.2	102.9	100.0	102.2	106.2	116.9	112.2	93.0
Sows and Boars		76.5	60.8	97.3	114.1	100.0	96.1	114.1	107.2	91.7	56.7
Sheep and lambs		63.4	56.7	72.1	91.1	100.0	111.7	105.9	104.8	106.9	99.0
Sheep and lambs (clean)		65.4	58.0	74.5	92.0	100.0	111.1	105.6	107.4	107.4	97.5
Ewes and Rams		48.3	47.2	54.7	84.0	100.0	116.2	108.6	85.8	103.1	109.9
All Poultry	a	70.1	81.0	89.5	99.5	100.0	103.0	105.1	111.1	106.0	104.5
Chickens	a	70.5	82.1	87.4	99.3	100.0	102.1	103.7	109.6	103.3	101.2
Turkeys		63.7	74.2	101.4	101.6	100.0	106.8	112.4	118.5	118.4	119.8
Animal products	a	72.7	84.3	104.1	96.9	100.0	109.4	114.8	128.1	126.4	101.7
Milk		72.8	84.3	105.2	96.1	100.0	111.0	113.8	128.2	127.7	99.1
Eggs	q	76.9	87.8	103.2	105.7	100.0	99.9	124.0	130.8	122.2	118.6
Intensive eggs	q	71.4	80.6	98.1	103.5	100.0	101.6	135.7	139.6	127.4	120.5
Free range eggs	q	80.7	92.6	106.6	107.2	100.0	98.7	116.2	124.9	118.7	117.3
Wool clip	a	16.6	35.4	32.4	47.1	100.0	121.6	75.5	101.0	102.9	83.3

Source: Department for Environment, Food and Rural Affairs
Enquiries Defra prices team. Tel: ++44(0)20802 66280
email: prices@defra.gsi.gov.uk

a:- Part or all of the series is made up of annual data
q:- Part or all of the series is made up of quarterly data

17.9 Harmonised Indices of Consumer Prices (HICPs) - International Comparisons: EU Countries: 2010 to 2016 Percentage change over 12 months

per cent

	Austria	Belgium	Bulgaria	Cyprus	Czech Republic	Denmark	Estonia	Finland	France	Germany	Greece	Hungary	Ireland	Italy	Latvia
Annual average															
	D7SK	D7SL	GHY8	D7RO	D7RP	D7SM	D7RQ	D7SN	D7SO	D7SP	D7SQ	D7RR	D7SS	D7ST	D7RS
2010	1.7	2.3	3.0	2.6	1.2	2.2	2.7	1.7	1.7	1.1	4.7	4.7	-1.6	1.6	-1.2
2011	3.6	3.4	3.4	3.5	2.2	2.7	5.1	3.3	2.3	2.5	3.1	3.9	1.2	2.9	4.2
2012	2.6	2.6	2.4	3.1	3.5	2.4	4.2	3.2	2.2	2.1	1.0	5.7	1.9	3.3	2.3
2013	2.1	1.2	0.4	0.4	1.4	0.5	3.2	2.2	1.0	1.6	-0.9	1.7	0.5	1.2	-
2014	1.5	0.5	-1.6	-0.3	0.4	0.4	0.5	1.2	0.6	0.8	-1.4	-	0.3	0.2	0.7
2015	0.8	0.6	-1.1	-1.5	0.3	0.2	0.1	-0.2	0.1	0.1	-1.1	0.1	-	0.1	0.2
Monthly															
Jul 2015	1.1	0.9	-1.0	-2.4	0.5	0.5	0.1	-0.1	0.2	0.1	-1.3	0.5	0.2	0.4	-0.2
Aug	1.0	0.8	-0.8	-1.9	0.2	0.3	0.2	-0.2	0.1	0.1	-0.4	0.1	0.2	0.3	0.2
Sep	0.6	0.9	-1.0	-1.9	0.3	0.3	-0.3	-0.7	0.1	-0.1	-0.8	-0.1	-0.1	0.2	-0.4
Oct	0.7	1.2	-1.2	-1.8	0.1	0.1	-	-0.3	0.2	0.2	-0.1	0.2	-0.1	0.3	-0.1
Nov	0.5	1.4	-0.9	-1.5	-	0.1	0.5	-0.2	0.1	0.2	-0.1	0.6	-0.1	0.1	-
Dec	1.1	1.5	-0.9	-0.6	-0.1	0.3	-0.2	-0.2	0.3	0.2	0.4	1.0	0.2	0.1	0.4
Jan 2016	1.4	1.8	-0.4	-1.1	0.5	0.4	0.1	-	0.3	0.4	-0.1	1.0	-	0.4	-0.3
Feb	1.0	1.1	-1.0	-2.2	0.5	0.1	0.4	-0.1	-0.1	-0.2	0.1	0.3	-0.2	-0.2	-0.6
Mar	0.7[†]	1.6	-1.9	-2.2	0.3	-0.3	0.5	-	-0.1	0.1	-0.7	-0.2	-0.6	-0.2	-0.6
Apr	0.6	1.5	-2.5	-2.1	0.5	-0.3	-	0.3	-0.1	-0.3	-0.4	0.3	-0.2	-0.4	-0.7
May	0.6	1.6	-2.5	-1.9	-	-0.1	-	0.3	0.1	-	-0.2	-0.1	-0.2	-0.3	-0.8
Jun	..	..	..	..	..	..	..	..	..	..	..	..	..	..	..

per cent

	Lithuania	Luxem-bourg	Malta	Nether-lands	Poland	Portugal	Romania	Slovakia	Slovenia	Spain	Sweden	United Kingdom [1]	EICP [2] EU 25 average [3]	EICP [2] EU 28 average [3]	MUICP average [4]
Annual average															
	D7RT	D7SU	D7RU	D7SV	D7RV	D7SX	GHY7	D7RW	D7RX	D7SY	D7SZ	D7G7	D7RY	GJ2E	D7SR
2010	1.2	2.8	2.0	0.9	2.6	1.4	6.1	0.7	2.1	2.0	1.9	3.3	..	2.1	1.6
2011	4.1	3.7	2.5	2.5	3.9	3.6	5.8	4.1	2.1	3.0	1.4	4.5	..	3.1	2.7
2012	3.2	2.9	3.2	2.8	3.7	2.8	3.4	3.7	2.8	2.4	0.9	2.8	..	2.6	2.5
2013	1.2	1.7	1.0	2.6	0.8	0.4	3.2	1.5	1.9	1.5	0.4	2.6	..	1.5	1.4
2014	0.2	0.7	0.8	0.3	0.1	-0.2	1.4	-0.1	0.4	-0.2	0.2	1.5	..	0.5	0.4
2015	-0.7	0.1	1.2	0.2	-0.7	0.5	-0.4	-0.3	-0.8	-0.6	0.7	-	..	- *	-
Monthly															
Jul 2015	-0.2	0.2	1.2	0.8	-0.5	0.7	-1.4	-0.2	-0.7	-	0.8	0.1	..	0.2	0.2
Aug	-1.0	0.1	1.4	0.4	-0.4	0.7	-1.7	-0.2	-0.6	-0.5	0.6	-	..	-	0.1
Sep	-0.8	-0.2	1.6	0.3	-0.7	0.9	-1.5	-0.5	-1.0	-1.1	0.9	-0.1	..	-0.1	-0.1
Oct	-0.4	-0.1	1.6	0.4	-0.6	0.7	-1.4	-0.5	-1.2	-0.9	0.9	-0.1	..	-	0.1
Nov	-0.5	0.4	1.3	0.4	-0.5	0.6	-0.9	-0.4	-0.9	-0.4	0.8	0.1	..	0.1	0.1
Dec	-0.2	0.9	1.3	0.5	-0.4	0.3	-0.7	-0.5	-0.6	-0.1	0.7	0.2	..	0.2	0.2
Jan 2016	0.7	0.5	0.8	0.2	-0.3	0.7	-1.5	-0.6	-0.8	-0.4	1.3	0.3	..	0.3	0.3
Feb	0.5	-0.3	1.0	0.3	-0.2	0.2	-2.1	-0.3	-0.9	-1.0	0.8	0.3	..	-0.1	-0.2
Mar	0.8	-0.6	1.0	0.5	-0.4	0.5	-2.4	-0.5	-0.9	-1.0	1.2	0.5	..	-	-
Apr	0.8	-0.6	0.8	-0.2	-0.5	0.5	-2.6	-0.4	-0.7	-1.2	1.0	0.3	..	-0.2	-0.2
May	0.2	-0.6	1.0	-0.2	-0.4	0.4	-3.0	-0.7	-0.5	-1.1	0.8	0.3	..	-0.1	-0.1
Jun	..	..	..	..	..	..	..	..	..	..	..	0.5	..	..	0.1

Key: - zero or negligible   .. Not available   * Provisional

[†] Date of earliest revision   [ᵠ] Estimated

1. Published as the CPI in the UK.

2. The EICP (European Index of Consumer Prices) is the official EU aggregate. It covers 15 member states until April 2004, 25 member states from May 2004 to Dec 2006, and 27 member states from Jan 2007. The EU 25 annual average for 2004 is calculated from the EU 15 average from January to April and the EU 25 average from May to December.

3. The coverage of the European Union was extended to include Cyprus, Czech Republic, Estonia, Hungary, Latvia, Lithuania, Malta, Poland, Slovakia and Slovenia with effect from 1 May 2004, and Bulgaria and Romania from 1 Jan 2007. Data for the EU 25 average is available from May 2004 and for the EU 27 average from Jan 2007.

4. The coverage of the Monetary Union Indices of Consumer Prices (MUICP) was extended to include Greece with effect from Jan 2001 and Slovakia from Jan 2009.

Source:

Office for National Statistics
Prices Division
2.001 Cardiff Road
Newport
South Wales
NP10 8XG

http://www.ons.gov.uk

Eurostat
www.ec.europa.eu/eurostat

this page is intentionally blank

Production

Chapter 18

Production

Annual Business Survey
(Table 18.1)

The Annual Business Survey (ABS) estimates cover all UK businesses registered for Value Added Tax (VAT) and/or Pay As You Earn (PAYE) classified to the 2007 Standard Industrial Classification (SIC (2007)) headings listed in the tables. The ABS obtains details on these businesses from the Office for National Statistics (ONS) Inter-Departmental Business Register (IDBR).

As with all its statistical inquiries, ONS is concerned to minimise the form-filling burden of individual contributors and as such the ABS is a sample inquiry. The sample was designed as a stratified random sample of about 66,300 businesses; the inquiry population is stratified by SIC (2007) and employment using the information from the register.

The inquiry results are grossed up to the total population so that they relate to all active UK businesses on the IDBR for the sectors covered.

The results meet a wide range of needs for government, economic analysts and the business community at large. In official statistics the inquiry is an important source for the national accounts and input-output tables, and also provides weights for the indices of production and producer prices. Inquiry results also enable the UK to meet statistical requirements of the European Union.

UK Manufacturer's Sales by Industry
(Table 18.2)

Table 18.2 lists total UK manufacturers' sales by industry.

Number of local units in manufacturing industries
(Table 18.3)

The table shows the number of local units (sites) in manufacturing by employment size band. The classification breakdown is at division level (two digit) as classified to SIC(2007) held on the Inter-Departmental Business Register (IDBR).
UK Business: Activity, Size and Location provides further details and contains detailed information regarding enterprises in the UK including size, classification, and local units in the UK including size, classification and location.

Production of primary fuels
(Table 18.4)

This table shows indigenous production of primary fuels. It includes the extraction or capture of primary commodities and the generation or manufacture of secondary commodities. Production is always gross; that is, it includes the quantities used during the extraction or manufacturing process. Primary fuels are coal, natural gas (including colliery methane), oil, primary electricity (that is, electricity generated by hydro, nuclear wind and tide stations and also electricity imported from France through the interconnector) and renewables (includes solid renewables such as wood, straw and waste and gaseous renewables such as landfill gas and sewage gas). The figures are presented on a common basis expressed in million tonnes of oil equivalent. Estimates of the gross calorific values used for converting the statistics for the various fuels to these are given in the Digest of UK Energy Statistics available on the Department for Business, Energy & Industrial Strategy website.

Total inland energy consumption
(Table 18.5)

This table shows energy consumption by fuel and final energy consumption by fuel and class of consumer. Primary energy consumption covers consumption of all primary fuels (defined above) for energy purposes. This measure of energy consumption includes energy that is lost by converting primary fuels into secondary fuels (the energy lost burning coal to generate electricity or the energy used by refineries to separate crude oil into fractions) in addition to losses in distribution. The other common way of measuring energy consumption is to measure the energy content of the fuels supplied to consumers. This is called final energy consumption. It is net of fuel used by the energy industries, conversion, transmission and distribution losses. The figures are presented on a common basis, measured as energy supplied and expressed in million tonnes of oil equivalent. Estimates of the gross calorific values used for converting the statistics for the various fuels to these are given in the Digest of UK Energy Statistics available on the Department for Business, Energy & Industrial Strategy website.

So far as practicable the user categories have been grouped on the basis of the SIC(2007) although the methods used by each of the supply industries to identify end users are slightly different. Chapter 1 of the Digest of UK Energy Statistics gives more information on these figures.

Coal
(Table 18.6)

Since 1995, aggregate data on coal production have been obtained from the Coal Authority. In addition, main coal producers provide data in response to an annual Department for Business, Energy & Industrial Strategy inquiry which covers production (deep mined and opencast), trade, stocks and disposals. HM Revenue & Customs (HMRC) also provides trade data for solid fuels. Department for Business, Energy & Industrial Strategy collects information on the use of coal from the UK Iron and Steel Statistics Bureau and consumption of coal for electricity generation is covered by data provided by the electricity generators.

Gas
(Table 18.7)

Production figures, covering the production of gas from the UK Continental Shelf offshore and onshore gas fields and gas obtained during the production of oil, are obtained from returns made under the Department for Business, Energy & Industrial Strategy Petroleum Production Reporting System. Additional information is used on imports and exports of gas and details from the operators of gas terminals in the UK to complete the picture.

It is no longer possible to present information on fuels input into the gas industry and gas output and sales in the same format as in previous editions of this table. As such, users are directed to Chapter 4 of the Digest of UK Energy Statistics, where more detailed information on gas production and consumption in the UK is available.

The Department for Business, Energy & Industrial Strategy carry out an annual survey of gas suppliers to obtain details of gas sales to the various categories of consumer. Estimates are included for the suppliers with the smallest market share, since the inquiry covers only the largest suppliers (that is, those known to supply more than 1,750 GWh per year).

Electricity
(Tables 18.8–18.10)

Tables 18.8 to 18.10 cover all generators and suppliers of electricity in the UK. The relationship between generation, supply, availability and consumption is as follows:

Electricity generated

less electricity used on works

equals electricity supplied (gross)

less electricity used in pumping at pumped storage stations.

equals electricity supplied (net)

plus imports (net of exports) of electricity

equals electricity available

less losses and statistical differences

equals electricity consumed

In Table 18.8 'major power producers' are those generating companies corresponding to the old public sector supply system:
• AES Electric Ltd.
• Baglan Generation Ltd.
• Barking Power Ltd.
• British Energy plc
• Centrica Energy
• Coolkeeragh ESB Ltd.
• Corby Power Ltd.
• Coryton Energy Company Ltd.
• Derwent Cogeneration Ltd.
• Drax Power Ltd.
• EDF Energy plc
• E.ON UK plc
• Energy Power Resources Ltd.
• Gaz De France
• GDF Suez Teesside Power Ltd
• Immingham CHP
• International Power plc
• Magnox Electric Ltd.
• Premier Power Ltd.
• RGS Energy Ltd.
• Rocksavage Power Company Ltd.
• RWE Npower plc
• Scottish Power plc
• Scottish and Southern Energy plc
• Seabank Power Ltd.
• SELCHP Ltd.
• Spalding Energy Company Ltd.
• Uskmouth Power Company Ltd.
• Western Power Generation Ltd.

Additionally, from 2007, the following major wind farm companies are included as 'major power producers':

• Airtricity
• Cumbria Wind Farms
• Fred Olsen
• H G Capital
• Renewable Energy Systems
• Vattenfall Wind

In Table 18.10 all fuels are converted to the common unit of million tonnes of oil equivalent, that is, the amounts of oil which would be needed to produce the output of electricity generated from those fuels.

More detailed statistics on energy are given in the Digest of United Kingdom Energy Statistics. Readers may wish to note that the production and consumption of fuels are presented using commodity balances. A commodity balance shows the flows of an individual fuel through from production to final consumption, showing its use in transformation and energy industry own use.

Oil and oil products
(Tables 18.11–18.13)

Data on the production of crude oil, condensates and natural gases given in Table 18.11 are collected directly from the operators of production facilities and terminals situated on UK territory, either onshore or offshore, that is, on the UK Continental Shelf. Data are also collected from the companies on their trade in oil and oil products. These data are used in preference to the foreign trade as recorded by HMRC in Overseas Trade Statistics.

Data on the internal UK oil industry (that is, on the supply, refining and distribution of oil and oil products in the UK) are collected by the UK Petroleum Industry Association. These data, reported by individual refining companies and wholesalers and supplemented where necessary by data from other sources, provide the contents of Tables 18.12 and 18.13. The data are presented in terms of deliveries to the inland UK market. This is regarded as an acceptable proxy for actual consumption of products. The main shortcoming is that, while changes in stocks held by companies in central storage areas are taken into account, changes in the levels of stocks further down the retail ladder (such as stocks held on petrol station forecourts) are not. This is not thought to result in a significant degree of difference in the data.

Iron and steel
(Tables 18.14–18.16)
Iron and steel industry
The general definition of the UK iron and steel industry is based on groups 271 'ECSC iron and steel', 272 'Tubes', and 273 'Primary Transformation' of the UK SIC(92), except those parts of groups 272 and 273 which cover cast iron pipes, drawn wire, cold formed sections and Ferro alloys.

The definition excludes certain products which may be made by works within the industry, such as refined iron, finished steel castings, steel tyres, wheels, axles and rolled rings, open and closed die forgings, colliery arches and springs. Iron foundries and steel stockholders are also considered to be outside of the industry.

Statistics

The statistics for the UK iron and steel industry are compiled by the Iron and Steel Statistics Bureau (ISSB) Ltd from data collected from UK steel producing companies, with the exception of trade data which is based on HMRC data.

'Crude steel' is the total of usable ingots, usable continuously cast semi-finished products and liquid steel for castings.

'Production of finished products' is the total production at the mill of that product after deduction of any material which is immediately scrapped

'Deliveries' are based on invoiced tonnages and will include deliveries made to steel stockholders and service centres by the UK steel industry.

For more detailed information on definitions etc please contact ISSB Ltd. on 020 7343 3900.

Fertilisers
(Table 18.17)
Table 18.17 gives the quantity of the fertiliser nutrients nitrogen (N), phosphate (P2O5) and potash (K2O) used by UK farmers during the growing season, or fertiliser year, which is taken as the year ending in June.

Minerals
(Table 18.18)
Table 18.18 gives, separately for Great Britain and Northern Ireland, the production of minerals extracted from the ground. The figures for chemicals and metals are estimated from the quality of the ore which is extracted.

Building materials
(Table 18.19)
Table 18.19 gives the production and deliveries of a number of building materials, including bricks, concrete blocks, sand and gravel, slate, cement, concrete roofing tiles and ready mixed cement. This data comes from the Monthly Bulletin of Building Materials and Components.

Construction
(Tables 18.20–18.21)
The value of output represents the value of construction work done during the quarter in Great Britain and is derived from returns made by private contractors and public authorities with their own direct labour forces. The series (and the accompanying index of the volume of output) include estimates of the output of small firms and self-employed workers not recorded in the regular quarterly output inquiry.

The new orders statistics are collected from private contractors and analysed by the principal types of construction work involved. The series includes speculative work for eventual sale or lease undertaken on the initiative of the respondent where no formal contract or order is involved.

Engineering turnover and orders
(Tables 18.22–18.23)
The figures represent the output of UK-based manufacturers classified to Subsections DK and DL of the SIC(2007). They are derived from the monthly production inquiry (MPI) and include estimates for non-responders and for establishments which are not sampled.

Drink and tobacco
(Tables 18.24–18.25)

Data for these tables are derived by HMRC from the systems for collecting excise duties. Alcoholic drinks and tobacco products become liable for duty when released for consumption in the UK. Figures for releases include both home-produced products and commercial imports. Production figures are also available for potable spirits distilled and beer brewed in the UK.

Alcoholic drink
(Table 18.24)

The figures for imported ad other spirits released for home consumption include gin and other UK produced spirits for which a breakdown is not available.

Since June 1993 beer duty has been charged when the beer leaves the brewery or other registered premises. Previously duty was chargeable at an earlier stage (the worts stage) in the brewing process and an allowance was made for wastage. Figures for years prior to 1994 include adjustments to bring them into line with current data. The change in June 1993 also led to the availability of data on the strength; a series in hectolitres of pure alcohol is shown from 1994.

Made wine with alcoholic strength from 1.2 per cent to 5.5 per cent is termed 'coolers'. Included in 'coolers' are alcoholic lemonade and similar products of appropriate strength. From 28 April 2002 duty on spirit-based 'coolers' (ready to drink products) is charged at the same rate as spirits per litre of alcohol. Made wine coolers include only wine based 'coolers' from this period.

Tobacco products
(Table 18.25)

Releases of cigarettes and other tobacco products tend to be higher in the period before a Budget. Products may then be stocked, duty paid, before being sold.

The industries are now grouped according to the 2007 Standard Industrial Classification at 2-digit level.

18.1 Production and Construction Industries

Description	Year	Number of enterprises	Total turnover	Approximate gross value added at basic prices (aGVA)	Total purchases of goods, materials and services	Total employment - point in time [1]	Total employment - average during the year [1]
Standard Industrial Classification (Revised 2007)		Number	£ million	£ million	£ million	Thousand	Thousand
B-F	2012	391,516	893,690	288,924	587,760	4,156	4,161
	2013	401,360	909,589	295,200	599,281	4,125	4,129
	2014	408,057	921,897	300,407	610,407	4,243	4,188
B-E Production industries	2012	134,410	703,277	215,117	470,931	2,855	2,865
	2013	138,848	711,301	217,593	477,694	2,827	2,835
	2014	137,455	705,616	215,117	475,408	2,885	2,851
B Mining and quarrying	2012	1,263	51,173	24,581	27,945	76	75
	2013	1,308	49,409	22,055	28,886	66	65
	2014	1,255	41,555	16,258	27,007	68	67
05 Mining of coal and lignite	2012	*	*	*	*	7	8
	2013	20	*	*	506	5	5
	2014	*	*	*	*	*	*
06 Extraction of crude petroleum and natural gas	2012	151	37,430	19,720	19,167	16	15
	2013	157	34,884	17,060	19,486	15	14
	2014	143	27,155	11,597	17,308	*	*
07 Mining of metal ores	2012	*	*	*	*	*	*
	2013	7	*	*	2	*	*
	2014	*	*	*	*	*	*
08 Other mining and quarrying	2012	703	5,359	1,501	3,726	27	27
	2013	715	6,144	1,878	4,130	20	20
	2014	688	5,792	1,839	3,864	21	19
09 Mining support service activities	2012	378	7,083	2,961	4,189	*	*
	2013	409	7,566	2,807	4,761	*	*
	2014	403	7,911	2,495	5,449	27	27
C Manufacturing	2012	124,514	513,437	149,498	344,634	2,482	2,500
	2013	127,900	517,798	155,099	344,303	2,466	2,483
	2014	125,870	517,732	155,489	344,448	2,520	2,491
10 Manufacture of food products	2012	6,642	76,445	18,664	57,977	363	359
	2013	6,890	77,571	20,187	57,580	373	369
	2014	7,107	78,241	20,385	58,089	379	371
11 Manufacture of beverages	2012	1,127	18,396	*	*	43	43
	2013	1,340	*	*	*	44	44
	2014	1,489	*	*	10,062	*	*
12 Manufacture of tobacco products	2012	11	10,990	*	*	*	*
	2013	10	*	*	*	*	*
	2014	10	*	*	416	*	*
13 Manufacture of textiles	2012	3,778	5,313	2,262	3,053	55	54
	2013	3,842	5,285	2,110	3,147	56	56
	2014	3,878	5,336	1,913	3,463	60	63
14 Manufacture of wearing apparel	2012	3,384	2,653	744	1,895	29	29
	2013	3,392	2,749	911	1,848	33	34
	2014	3,413	2,916	897	2,070	34	34
15 Manufacture of leather and related products	2012	559	970	313	647	*	*
	2013	551	975	386	602	*	*
	2014	575	1,030	391	650	*	*
16 Manufacture of wood and of products of wood and cork, except furniture; manufacture of articles of straw and plaiting materials	2012	7,105	6,752	2,673	4,136	68	66
	2013	7,327	7,156	2,582	4,566	67	64
	2014	7,631	7,973	2,763	5,289	75	79

18.1 Production and Construction Industries

Description	Year	Number of enterprises	Total turnover	Approximate gross value added at basic prices (aGVA)	Total purchases of goods, materials and services	Total employment - point in time [1]	Total employment - average during the year [1]
Standard Industrial Classification (Revised 2007)							
		Number	£ million	£ million	£ million	Thousand	Thousand
17 Manufacture of paper and paper products	2012	1,576	10,827	3,859	6,910	56	58
	2013	1,550	10,906	3,693	7,295	53	54
	2014	1,514	10,991	3,796	7,200	55	58
18 Printing and reproduction of recorded media	2012	13,259	10,943	4,966	5,955	115	120
	2013	12,988	10,755	5,056	5,729	104	108
	2014	12,561	10,831	4,762	6,135	117	113
19 Manufacture of coke and refined petroleum products	2012	149	53,725	2,226	42,590	11	10
	2013	131	48,260	1,321	38,584	*	*
	2014	131	42,188	733	31,568	*	*
20 Manufacture of chemicals and chemical products	2012	2,468	31,201	8,500	22,758	109	111
	2013	2,549	31,388	8,534	22,900	104	106
	2014	2,617	31,653	8,951	22,829	103	99
21 Manufacture of basic pharmaceutical products and pharmaceutical preparations	2012	510	16,027	6,736	9,402	50	50
	2013	529	15,021	6,334	8,548	*	*
	2014	536	13,650	5,725	8,020	40	37
22 Manufacture of rubber and plastic products	2012	5,696	21,925	8,048	13,969	155	154
	2013	5,693	22,658	8,154	14,502	162	161
	2014	5,715	24,025	8,331	15,733	176	175
23 Manufacture of other non-metallic mineral products	2012	3,625	12,462	3,735	8,680	86	87
	2013	3,625	12,756	3,831	8,827	78	78
	2014	3,584	13,001	3,952	9,060	87	85
24 Manufacture basic metals	2012	1,400	17,548	3,628	13,653	71	71
	2013	1,485	18,284	4,065	14,148	70	71
	2014	1,595	17,844	4,328	13,509	72	71
25 Manufacture of fabricated metal products, except machinery and equipment	2012	24,050	33,093	14,483	18,711	292	296
	2013	24,364	33,221	14,259	19,088	297	300
	2014	24,870	34,354	15,598	19,178	299	304
26 Manufacture of computer, electronic and optical products	2012	5,874	18,358	8,025	10,403	123	128
	2013	6,009	19,642	7,808	11,683	132	138
	2014	5,959	19,338	7,789	11,531	128	126
27 Manufacture of electrical equipment	2012	2,971	14,446	4,869	9,567	87	86
	2013	3,017	13,561	4,551	9,051	86	85
	2014	3,053	13,421	4,620	8,895	82	82
28 Manufacture of machinery and equipment n.e.c.	2012	7,948	37,173	14,455	22,696	208	205
	2013	7,932	34,755	13,026	21,992	202	200
	2014	7,917	34,744	13,433	21,571	188	183
29 Manufacture of motor vehicles, trailers and semi-trailers	2012	2,614	55,353	10,856	44,758	137	135
	2013	2,672	60,654	14,592	46,142	145	143
	2014	2,751	63,569	17,603	46,591	150	150
30 Manufacture of other transport equipment	2012	1,876	29,197	9,680	19,839	134	131
	2013	1,943	31,595	11,562	20,202	134	131
	2014	2,032	31,343	7,906	23,494	138	137
31 Manufacture of furniture	2012	6,131	6,589	2,585	4,026	79	86
	2013	6,022	7,006	2,838	4,187	77	83
	2014	5,934	7,429	2,870	4,594	80	71
32 Other manufacturing	2012	9,988	8,949	3,812	5,194	91	100
	2013	9,759	9,241	3,644	5,715	74	81
	2014	9,449	8,932	3,386	5,593	78	81
33 Repair and installation of machinery and equipment	2012	11,773	14,104	6,564	7,686	107	109
	2013	14,280	15,604	7,761	8,025	106	108
	2014	11,549	16,144	7,422	8,907	109	106

18.1 Production and Construction Industries

Description		Year	Number of enterprises	Total turnover	Approximate gross value added at basic prices (aGVA)	Total purchases of goods, materials and services	Total employment - point in time [1]	Total employment - average during the year [1]
Standard Industrial Classification (Revised 2007)								
			Number	£ million	£ million	£ million	Thousand	Thousand
D	Electricity, gas, steam and air conditioning supply	2012	1,825	106,916	24,151	82,879	136	129
		2013	2,574	111,056	23,848	87,897	129	122
		2014	3,284	111,834	24,675	87,557	132	129
E	Water supply, sewerage, waste management and remediation activities	2012	6,808	31,751	16,887	15,473	162	161
		2013	7,066	33,038	16,591	16,608	165	164
		2014	7,046	34,495	18,696	16,396	165	164
36	Water collection, treatment and supply	2012	120	11,049	9,033	2,681	*	*
		2013	107	11,859	9,483	2,912	40	40
		2014	99	11,940	9,831	2,888	*	*
37	Sewerage	2012	899	2,586	1,921	818	15	15
		2013	920	2,741	1,648	1,090	18	18
		2014	920	3,091	1,938	1,153	15	14
38	Waste collection, treatment and disposal activities; materials recovery	2012	5,186	17,804	5,734	11,851	105	104
		2013	5,343	18,066	5,286	12,402	102	102
		2014	5,258	18,730	6,484	12,053	106	106
39	Remediation activities and other waste management services	2012	603	311	199	123	*	*
		2013	696	372	173	204	4	4
		2014	769	734	443	302	*	*
F	Construction	2012	257,106	190,413	73,807	116,829	1,300	1,296
		2013	262,512	198,288	77,607	121,587	1,299	1,295
		2014	270,602	216,281	85,289	134,999	1,358	1,337
41	Construction of buildings	2012	67,554	75,292	27,312	47,548	369	376
		2013	69,672	79,069	29,152	50,411	363	371
		2014	73,841	87,791	34,168	57,246	412	405
42	Civil engineering	2012	19,682	37,025	12,485	24,794	207	205
		2013	20,285	39,756	13,687	26,346	196	194
		2014	20,785	42,104	13,386	28,855	199	196
43	Specialised construction activities	2012	169,870	78,095	34,010	44,487	725	715
		2013	172,555	79,463	34,768	44,829	740	730
		2014	175,976	86,387	37,735	48,897	748	736

Source: Annual Business Survey (ABS)

The following symbols and abbreviations are used throughout the ABS releases;
* Information suppressed to avoid disclosure
.. not available
- nil or less than half the level of rounding

The sum of constituent items in tables may not always agree exactly with the totals shown due to rounding.

Notes:
1. Total employment - point in time and Total employment - average during the year are from the Business Register and Employment Survey (BRES). Caution should be taken when combining financial data from the ABS with employment data from BRES due to differences in methodology. More information can be found in the ABS Technical Report.

18.1 Production and Construction Industries

Description		Year	Total employment costs	Total net capital expenditure	Total capital expenditure- acquisitions	Total capital expenditure - disposals	Total stocks and work in progress - value at end of year	Total stocks and work in progress - value at beginning of year	Total stocks and work in progress - increase during year
Standard Industrial Classification (Revised 2007)									
			£ million	£ million	£ million	£ million	£ million	£ million	£ million
B-F		2012	127,164	42,749	54,088	11,339	95,111	93,980	1,132
		2013	130,688	46,383	56,725	10,344	96,944	93,511	3,433
		2014	135,812	59,483	69,604	10,122	102,054	96,792	5,261
B-E	Production industries	2012	92,982	40,694	44,742	4,048	59,641	58,850	791
		2013	96,158	41,672	46,231	4,560	62,099	59,804	2,295
		2014	98,808	49,093	52,803	3,709	63,280	61,894	1,386
B	Mining and quarrying	2012	5,263	9,402	10,887	1,484	2,019	1,906	113
		2013	5,745	12,092	13,459	1,368	2,173	2,039	134
		2014	5,953	14,884	15,610	726	2,107	1,940	167
05	Mining of coal and lignite	2012	*	*	*	*	*	*	*
		2013	254	*	*	*	52	55	-3
		2014	*	*	*	*	*	*	*
06	Extraction of crude petroleum and natural gas	2012	2,388	8,927	10,201	1,274	1,055	979	76
		2013	2,757	*	*	*	1,239	1,097	142
		2014	2,814	13,813	14,420	607	1,209	1,092	117
07	Mining of metal ores	2012	*	*	*	*	*	*	*
		2013	-	1	1	-	-	-	-
		2014	*	*	*	*	*	*	*
08	Other mining and quarrying	2012	854	160	238	78	417	418	-1
		2013	866	142	223	81	457	468	-11
		2014	932	300	338	38	427	396	31
09	Mining support service activities	2012	1,665	360	398	38	476	402	74
		2013	1,867	544	582	38	425	419	6
		2014	2,017	755	832	76	400	406	-5
C	Manufacturing	2012	76,955	12,589	14,614	2,026	53,081	52,507	575
		2013	79,182	11,723	14,245	2,522	54,954	53,269	1,684
		2014	81,138	16,546	18,746	2,200	55,747	54,733	1,014
10	Manufacture of food products	2012	9,609	1,822	1,989	167	5,013	4,801	212
		2013	9,739	2,128	2,250	122	5,280	5,097	183
		2014	10,014	2,235	2,413	178	5,362	5,187	175
11	Manufacture of beverages	2012	1,780	714	*	*	5,729	5,392	337
		2013	1,880	666	811	146	6,267	5,722	546
		2014	1,815	819	898	79	6,892	6,383	509
12	Manufacture of tobacco products	2012	135	84	*	*	177	173	4
		2013	154	47	49	1	170	179	-9
		2014	141	51	56	6	178	174	4
13	Manufacture of textiles	2012	1,086	131	143	12	710	703	7
		2013	1,094	95	106	11	740	744	-4
		2014	1,153	137	156	20	805	756	49
14	Manufacture of wearing apparel	2012	444	13	29	16	336	348	-13
		2013	522	33	39	6	310	301	9
		2014	543	34	35	2	379	330	48
15	Manufacture of leather and related products	2012	199	29	31	2	160	166	-6
		2013	187	21	22	2	160	144	16
		2014	198	29	30	-	155	137	18
16	Manufacture of wood and of products of wood and cork, except furniture; manufacture of articles of straw and plaiting materials	2012	1,403	122	171	49	659	621	38
		2013	1,419	202	233	31	662	665	-3
		2014	1,590	180	239	59	717	646	71
17	Manufacture of paper and paper products	2012	1,794	340	379	39	831	897	-66
		2013	1,842	307	368	61	886	813	72
		2014	1,868	353	383	29	873	876	-3
18	Printing and reproduction of recorded media	2012	2,811	288	458	170	428	437	-10
		2013	2,788	368	436	68	469	444	24
		2014	2,707	587	670	83	482	462	20

18.1 Production and Construction Industries

Description	Year	Total employment costs	Total net capital expenditure	Total capital expenditure- acquisitions	Total capital expenditure - disposals	Total stocks and work in progress - value at end of year	Total stocks and work in progress - value at beginning of year	Total stocks and work in progress - increase during year
Standard Industrial Classification (Revised 2007)								
		£ million	£ million	£ million	£ million	£ million	£ million	£ million
19 Manufacture of coke and refined petroleum products	2012	1,111	509	531	22	2,841	3,759	-919
	2013	781	506	563	57	3,045	2,893	152
	2014	808	201	411	210	1,876	3,104	-1,228
20 Manufacture of chemicals and chemical products	2012	4,293	1,174	1,266	92	3,473	3,426	46
	2013	4,350	981	1,177	196	3,495	3,415	80
	2014	4,319	1,280	1,934	653	3,500	3,429	71
21 Manufacture of basic pharmaceutical products and pharmaceutical preparations	2012	2,478	428	453	24	2,075	1,984	90
	2013	2,457	473	475	3	1,934	2,008	-75
	2014	2,431	431	445	14	2,027	1,914	113
22 Manufacture of rubber and plastic products	2012	4,222	610	725	115	1,986	1,900	85
	2013	4,352	582	693	111	2,014	2,012	2
	2014	4,562	648	777	129	2,062	2,016	46
23 Manufacture of other non-metallic mineral products	2012	2,527	353	522	168	1,380	1,339	41
	2013	2,541	456	581	125	1,293	1,319	-25
	2014	2,478	478	545	68	1,348	1,319	29
24 Manufacture basic metals	2012	2,766	454	495	42	2,474	2,746	-272
	2013	2,780	364	373	9	2,362	2,479	-117
	2014	2,908	382	418	37	2,293	2,323	-30
25 Manufacture of fabricated metal products, except machinery and equipment	2012	8,287	896	1,068	172	3,596	3,513	83
	2013	8,169	849	988	139	3,682	3,566	116
	2014	8,424	1,525	1,652	127	3,721	3,438	282
26 Manufacture of computer, electronic and optical products	2012	4,138	542	610	68	2,623	2,563	60
	2013	4,629	442	527	85	2,632	2,803	-172
	2014	4,579	601	667	66	2,999	3,075	-76
27 Manufacture of electrical equipment	2012	2,727	190	297	107	1,729	1,722	7
	2013	2,821	312	357	45	1,767	1,748	19
	2014	2,915	343	383	40	1,711	1,621	89
28 Manufacture of machinery and equipment n.e.c.	2012	6,674	853	962	109	4,054	4,082	-28
	2013	7,210	633	788	155	4,494	4,199	295
	2014	7,542	830	987	157	4,714	4,481	233
29 Manufacture of motor vehicles, trailers and semi-trailers	2012	5,889	1,650	1,945	295	4,092	3,755	337
	2013	6,060	*	1,525	*	4,192	4,065	128
	2014	6,538	3,309	3,369	60	4,427	4,051	377
30 Manufacture of other transport equipment	2012	5,544	802	920	118	5,463	5,149	314
	2013	5,870	*	1,012	*	5,721	5,567	154
	2014	5,958	1,019	1,050	31	5,737	5,740	-3
31 Manufacture of furniture	2012	1,613	124	137	13	680	656	24
	2013	1,664	142	160	18	587	570	17
	2014	1,918	248	281	33	596	563	34
32 Other manufacturing	2012	2,069	266	308	42	1,125	1,069	57
	2013	2,057	360	392	33	1,228	1,123	106
	2014	2,045	458	473	16	1,171	1,146	24
33 Repair and installation of machinery and equipment	2012	3,356	193	298	105	1,448	1,304	144
	2013	3,817	248	317	69	1,565	1,394	170
	2014	3,686	370	473	102	1,723	1,560	163
D Electricity, gas, steam and air conditioning supply	2012	6,028	11,961	12,357	396	3,557	3,446	111
	2013	6,215	11,189	11,634	446	4,055	3,458	598
	2014	6,149	10,948	11,588	641	4,364	4,103	261
E Water supply, sewerage, waste management and remediation activities	2012	4,736	6,742	6,884	142	983	991	-8
	2013	5,016	6,668	6,893	225	917	1,038	-121
	2014	5,568	6,715	6,858	143	1,062	1,118	-57
36 Water collection, treatment and supply	2012	1,534	4,330	4,356	26	180	175	5
	2013	1,656	4,315	4,348	33	193	183	10
	2014	1,841	4,091	4,129	37	173	193	-20
37 Sewerage	2012	395	*	*	24	18	18	-
	2013	404	*	*	22	18	21	-3
	2014	464	*	*	13	60	60	-

18.1 Production and Construction Industries

	Description	Year	Total employment costs	Total net capital expenditure	Total capital expenditure- acquisitions	Total capital expenditure - disposals	Total stocks and work in progress - value at end of year	Total stocks and work in progress - value at beginning of year	Total stocks and work in progress - increase during year
Standard Industrial Classification (Revised 2007)			£ million	£ million	£ million	£ million	£ million	£ million	£ million
38	Waste collection, treatment and disposal activities; materials recovery	2012	2,740	*	*	91	766	791	-24
		2013	2,893	*	*	169	691	824	-133
		2014	3,120	*	*	92	795	843	-48
39	Remediation activities and other waste management services	2012	67	11	13	2	18	7	11
		2013	63	7	8	1	14	9	5
		2014	144	54	56	2	33	22	11
F	Construction	2012	34,182	2,055	9,346	7,291	35,471	35,130	341
		2013	34,530	4,711	10,494	5,783	34,845	33,707	1,138
		2014	37,004	10,390	16,802	6,412	38,774	34,898	3,876
41	Construction of buildings	2012	9,636	165	6,675	6,510	28,637	29,005	-368
		2013	10,358	2,998	8,060	5,062	27,688	27,093	595
		2014	10,473	7,074	12,819	5,745	32,803	29,427	3,376
42	Civil engineering	2012	7,576	597	848	251	2,829	2,604	226
		2013	7,567	410	700	290	2,263	2,013	250
		2014	8,102	810	1,016	206	2,217	2,086	132
43	Specialised construction activities	2012	16,970	1,293	1,823	530	4,004	3,522	483
		2013	16,606	1,302	1,734	432	4,894	4,602	292
		2014	18,428	2,506	2,967	461	3,754	3,385	369

Source: Annual Business Survey (ABS)

The following symbols and abbreviations are used throughout the ABS releases;
* Information suppressed to avoid disclosure
.. not available
- nil or less than half the level of rounding

The sum of constituent items in tables may not always agree exactly with the totals shown due to rounding.

Notes:
1. Total employment - point in time and Total employment - average during the year are from the Business Register and Employment Survey (BRES).
Caution should be taken when combining financial data from the ABS with employment data from BRES due to differences in methodology.
More information can be found in the ABS Technical Report.

18.2 UK Manufacturer's Sales by Industry

Industry	SIC(07)	2009	2010	2011	2012	2013	2014	£ million 2015
Other mining and quarrying								
Quarrying of ornamental and building stone, limestone, gypsum, chalk and slate	08110	9	S	12	383	S	S	S
Operation of gravel and sand pits; mining of clays and kaolin	08120	68	74	54	1,330	S	S	S
Mining of chemical and fertiliser minerals	08910	S	S	S	S	S	S	S
Extraction of salt	08930	S	S	S	331	S	S	S
Other mining and quarrying n.e.c.	08990	S	S	S	33	S	S	S
Manufacture of food products								
Processing and preserving of meat	10110	4,473	4,637	5,035	5,835	6,189	6,596	6,699
Processing and preserving of poultry meat	10120	2,682	2,732	2,894	2,947	3,402	3,712	3,756
Production of meat and poultry meat products	10130	5,222	5,383	5,318	5,593	5,266	5,476	5,602
Processing and preserving of fish, crustaceans and molluscs	10200	1,620	1,887	2,106	2,220	2,108	2,224	2,189
Processing and preserving of potatoes	10310	S	S	S	S	S	1,212	1,177
Manufacture of fruit and vegetable juice	10320	491	495	549	574	611	650	598
Other processing and preserving of fruit and vegetables	10390	2,720	2,841	2,910	2,900	3,030	3,165	3,131
Manufacture of oils and fats	10410	981	930	1,198	1,150	1,130	1,066	1,093
Manufacture of margarine and similar edible fats	10420	S	S	S	484	466	S	454
Operation of dairies and cheese making	10510	6,445	6,829	7,075	6,792	7,068	7,929	7,539
Manufacture of ice cream	10520	562	600	566	591	634	681	733
Manufacture of grain mill products	10610	3,506	3,410	3,770	3,736	S	S	S
Manufacture of starches and starch products	10620	374	304	S	319	385	325	265
Manufacture of bread; manufacture of fresh pastry goods and cakes	10710	5,282	S	S	5,752	6,023	6,281	6,541
Manufacture of rusks and biscuits; manufacture of preserved pastry goods and cakes	10720	S	3,695	S	3,958	4,434	4,307	4,175
Manufacture of macaroni, noodles, couscous and similar farinaceous products	10730	S	35	S	S	S	S	S
Manufacture of sugar	10810	1,128	1,076	S	1,183	1,210	1,049	S
Manufacture of cocoa, chocolate and sugar confectionery	10820	3,528	3,781	2,707	2,613	2,620	2,648	2,701
Processing of tea and coffee	10830	S	S	S	S	S	S	S
Manufacture of condiments and seasonings	10840	1,416	1,482	1,636	1,812	1,936	1,959	2,079
Manufacture of prepared meals and dishes	10850	2,302	2,477	2,546	S	S	3,116	3,257
Manufacture of homogenised food preparations and dietetic food	10860	30	29	33	30	29	18	S
Manufacture of other food products n.e.c.	10890	2,991	3,019	3,295	3,588	3,759	3,648	3,664
Manufacture of prepared feeds for farm animals	10910	3,002	3,278	3,811	3,787	4,329	4,113	3,801
Manufacture of prepared pet foods	10920	1,508	1,536	1,541	1,537	1,666	1,662	1,730
Manufacture of beverages								
Distilling, rectifying and blending of spirits	11010	2,502	S	S	3,723	S	S	S
Manufacture of wine from grape	11020	S	S	S	S	S	S	S
Manufacture of cider and other fruit wines	11030	641	574	760	771	921	859	959
Manufacture of other non-distilled fermented beverages	11040	0	0	0	0	0	0	0
Manufacture of beer	11050	4,766	3,914	4,081	3,269	3,297	3,286	S
Manufacture of malt	11060	418	S	377	S	S	S	S
Manufacture of soft drinks; production of mineral waters and other bottled waters	11070	3,538	3,963	S	S	S	S	4,832
Manufacture of tobacco products								
Manufacture of tobacco products	12000	1,912	1,626	1,673	1,793	1,723	1,614	S
Manufacture of textiles								
Preparation and spinning of textile fibres	13100	315	367	384	385	396	387	405
Weaving of textiles	13200	469	542	591	608	619	627	616
Finishing of textiles	13300	414	490	517	492	500	534	466
Manufacture of knitted and crocheted fabrics	13910	134	S	S	S	S	S	120
Manufacture of made-up textile articles, except apparel	13920	1,042	1,094	1,064	1,169	1,094	1,146	1,302
Manufacture of carpets and rugs	13930	691	675	S	700	708	737	758
Manufacture of cordage, rope, twine and netting	13940	64	46	52	56	50	59	62
Manufacture of non-wovens and articles made from non-wovens, except apparel	13950	S	S	172	S	178	174	178
Manufacture of other technical and industrial textiles	13960	S	279	309	293	315	332	322
Manufacture of other textiles n.e.c.	13990	102	108	108	106	114	130	129
Manufacture of wearing apparel								
Manufacture of leather clothes	14110	6	S	S	4	4	5	8
Manufacture of workwear	14120	214	191	171	147	107	100	106
Manufacture of other outerwear	14130	551	538	474	595	620	697	725

18.2 UK Manufacturer's Sales by Industry

Industry	SIC(07)	2009	2010	2011	2012	2013	2014	£ million 2015
Manufacture of underwear	14140	397	S	388	415	388	393	495
Manufacture of other wearing apparel and accessories	14190	242	215	198	223	258	285	319
Manufacture of articles of fur	14200	0	S	S	1	1	S	S
Manufacture of knitted and crocheted hosiery	14310	S	108	95	86	84	89	81
Manufacture of other knitted and crocheted apparel	14390	113	124	159	162	172	191	176
Manufacture of leather and related products								
Tanning and dressing of leather; dressing and dyeing of fur	15110	150	228	263	248	310	249	225
Manufacture of luggage, handbags and the like, saddlery and harness	15120	111	134	119	147	133	205	214
Manufacture of footwear	15200	S	S	236	252	284	264	281
Manufacture of wood and of products of wood and cork; except furniture; manufacture of articles of straw and plaiting materials								
Sawmilling and planing of wood	16100	797	897	968	985	1,037	1,136	1,050
Manufacture of veneer sheets and wood-based panels	16210	801	836	856	928	909	1,011	998
Manufacture of assembled parquet floors	16220	S	S	2	3	5	4	S
Manufacture of other builders' carpentry and joinery	16230	2,803	3,212	3,014	2,983	3,317	3,719	3,405
Manufacture of wooden containers	16240	388	434	401	513	492	568	624
Manufacture of other products of wood; manufacture of articles of cork, straw and plaiting materials	16290	334	332	336	328	337	415	451
Manufacture of paper and paper products								
Manufacture of pulp	17110	S	S	S	S	S	S	S
Manufacture of paper and paperboard	17120	2,309	2,437	2,507	2,481	2,384	2,357	2,124
Manufacture of corrugated paper and paperboard and of containers of paper and paperboard	17210	3,097	3,399	3,815	3,921	3,967	3,974	4,179
Manufacture of household and sanitary goods and of toilet requisites	17220	2,201	S	2,302	S	2,067	S	S
Manufacture of paper stationery	17230	641	548	548	531	419	456	411
Manufacture of wallpaper	17240	113	136	132	134	141	122	121
Manufacture of other articles of paper and paperboard	17290	970	962	989	945	999	1,153	1,111
Printing and reproduction of recorded media								
Printing of newspapers	18110	217	218	219	S	159	S	S
Other printing	18120	7,478	7,659	7,965	7,722	7,162	7,468	7,656
Pre-press and pre-media services	18130	470	455	404	387	381	392	482
Binding and related services	18140	275	271	232	238	243	216	205
Reproduction of recorded media	18200	167	111	S	S	110	98	85
Manufacture of coke and refined petroleum products								
Manufacture of coke oven products	19100	S	S	S	S	S	S	S
Manufacture of chemicals and chemical products								
Manufacture of industrial gases	20110	528	594	623	631	692	667	S
Manufacture of dyes and pigments	20120	930	1,001	1,066	914	932	972	893
Manufacture of other inorganic basic chemicals	20130	1,100	1,187	1,209	949	955	775	704
Manufacture of other organic basic chemicals	20140	3,111	3,579	3,597	2,940	2,792	2,641	2,340
Manufacture of fertilisers and nitrogen compounds	20150	1,118	1,294	1,550	1,603	1,647	1,477	1,048
Manufacture of plastics in primary forms	20160	3,038	3,518	3,930	3,524	3,543	3,530	3,513
Manufacture of synthetic rubber in primary forms	20170	298	392	S	S	303	173	113
Manufacture of pesticides and other agrochemical products	20200	624	577	582	605	622	651	675
Manufacture of paints, varnishes and similar coatings, printing ink and mastics	20300	2,761	2,847	3,086	2,950	3,068	3,357	3,140
Manufacture of soap and detergents, cleaning and polishing preparations	20410	1,662	1,755	1,752	1,784	1,754	1,749	2,106
Manufacture of perfumes and toilet preparations	20420	2,243	2,380	2,356	2,392	2,602	2,655	2,728
Manufacture of explosives	20510	186	171	159	154	S	133	138
Manufacture of glues	20520	340	342	357	382	383	374	S
Manufacture of essential oils	20530	642	690	878	860	717	771	674
Manufacture of other chemical products n.e.c.	20590	2,645	2,612	2,606	2,456	2,630	2,548	2,479
Manufacture of man-made fibres	20600	211	208	256	300	200	167	166
Manufacture of basic pharmaceutical products and pharmaceutical preparations								
Manufacture of basic pharmaceutical products	21100	495	559	936	794	777	752	769
Manufacture of pharmaceutical preparations	21200	12,702	14,159	12,965	11,495	11,270	10,133	10,352

18.2 UK Manufacturer's Sales by Industry

Industry	SIC(07)	2009	2010	2011	2012	2013	2014	£ million 2015
Manufacture of rubber and plastic products								
Manufacture of rubber tyres and tubes; retreading and rebuilding of rubber tyres	22110	S	S	S	S	S	S	S
Manufacture of other rubber products	22190	1,276	1,399	1,607	1,602	1,571	1,607	1,536
Manufacture of plastic plates, sheets, tubes and profiles	22210	4,065	4,471	4,574	4,707	4,740	5,031	4,919
Manufacture of plastic packing goods	22220	2,651	2,852	3,295	3,441	3,255	3,426	3,295
Manufacture of buildersâ€™ ware of plastic	22230	3,634	3,795	3,478	3,368	4,108	4,333	4,148
Manufacture of other plastic products	22290	2,762	3,011	3,424	3,537	4,288	4,598	4,481
Manufacture of other non-metallic mineral products								
Manufacture of flat glass	23110	S	S	S	S	177	S	S
Shaping and processing of flat glass	23120	1,143	1,237	1,115	1,123	1,116	1,105	1,123
Manufacture of hollow glass	23130	635	654	694	724	726	750	S
Manufacture of glass fibres	23140	374	424	432	423	397	414	392
Manufacture and processing of other glass, including technical glassware	23190	119	125	172	174	S	137	172
Manufacture of refractory products	23200	237	234	276	259	246	238	225
Manufacture of ceramic tiles and flags	23310	88	76	74	78	90	95	92
Manufacture of bricks, tiles and construction products, in baked clay	23320	S	S	478	465	S	598	626
Manufacture of ceramic household and ornamental articles	23410	205	236	S	S	S	295	306
Manufacture of ceramic sanitary fixtures	23420	S	S	110	S	S	S	S
Manufacture of ceramic insulators and insulating fittings	23430	34	35	31	S	S	S	16
Manufacture of other technical ceramic products	23440	S	26	28	S	S	S	S
Manufacture of other ceramic products	23490	18	19	27	28	22	S	S
Manufacture of cement	23510	814	S	714	702	673	S	820
Manufacture of lime and plaster	23520	S	184	S	208	S	235	241
Manufacture of concrete products for construction purposes	23610	S	S	1,474	S	S	1,950	2,160
Manufacture of plaster products for construction purposes	23620	S	S	S	S	S	S	S
Manufacture of ready-mixed concrete	23630	1,208	1,095	1,127	1,088	1,180	1,299	1,543
Manufacture of mortars	23640	104	118	S	S	S	S	S
Manufacture of fibre cement	23650	S	S	S	76	70	81	67
Manufacture of other articles of concrete, plaster and cement	23690	134	S	146	167	S	S	S
Cutting, shaping and finishing of stone	23700	463	402	420	414	404	418	430
Production of abrasive products	23910	109	90	100	S	140	139	151
Manufacture of other non-metallic mineral products n.e.c.	23990	1,280	1,320	1,484	1,517	1,459	1,578	1,686
Manufacture of basic metals								
Manufacture of tubes, pipes, hollow profiles and related fittings, of steel	24200	S	1,266	1,544	1,557	1,317	1,197	1,025
Cold drawing of bars	24310	76	128	190	168	150	152	153
Cold rolling of narrow strip	24320	31	S	S	S	S	S	35
Cold forming or folding	24330	S	S	S	S	S	S	S
Cold drawing of wire	24340	S	S	S	157	153	140	S
Precious metals production	24410	443	643	875	481	371	260	229
Aluminium production	24420	1,211	1,478	1,646	1,259	1,124	1,177	1,355
Lead, zinc and tin production	24430	S	541	529	507	506	513	S
Copper production	24440	454	637	727	615	577	471	446
Other non-ferrous metal production	24450	923	1,046	1,011	1,017	970	933	873
Casting of iron	24510	256	316	421	415	411	413	385
Casting of steel	24520	299	287	388	333	351	297	277
Casting of light metals	24530	294	362	388	359	401	432	425
Casting of other non-ferrous metals	24540	157	184	224	224	188	184	214
Manufacture of fabricated metal products; except machinery and equipment								
Manufacture of metal structures and parts of structures	25110	5,801	5,418	5,682	5,463	5,407	6,015	5,585
Manufacture of doors and windows of metal	25120	1,278	1,235	1,217	1,286	1,375	1,516	1,655
Manufacture of central heating radiators and boilers	25210	S	787	798	803	870	900	1,001
Manufacture of other tanks, reservoirs and containers of metal	25290	379	324	395	430	429	415	399
Manufacture of steam generators, except central heating hot water boilers	25300	S	S	S	S	S	S	S
Manufacture of weapons and ammunition	25400	2,912	2,032	1,941	1,881	1,667	1,478	1,901
Forging, pressing, stamping and roll-forming of metal; powder metallurgy	25500	1,319	1,608	1,839	1,968	1,900	1,968	1,975
Treatment and coating of metals	25610	1,054	1,045	1,187	1,263	1,325	1,341	1,244
Machining	25620	3,383	3,629	4,243	4,559	4,825	5,068	5,393
Manufacture of cutlery	25710	21	20	23	25	22	24	20
Manufacture of locks and hinges	25720	491	537	561	514	498	534	525
Manufacture of tools	25730	730	796	799	825	867	959	877

18.2 UK Manufacturer's Sales by Industry

Industry	SIC(07)	2009	2010	2011	2012	2013	2014	£ million 2015
Manufacture of steel drums and similar containers	25910	96	107	112	106	S	S	85
Manufacture of light metal packaging	25920	S	1,533	1,499	1,395	S	S	S
Manufacture of wire products, chain and springs	25930	768	857	904	782	800	780	748
Manufacture of fasteners and screw machine products	25940	340	364	454	469	476	512	454
Manufacture of other fabricated metal products n.e.c.	25990	1,386	1,595	1,747	1,810	1,906	2,020	2,264
Manufacture of computer; electronic and optical products								
Manufacture of electronic components	26110	1,048	1,296	1,301	897	1,104	828	815
Manufacture of loaded electronic boards	26120	937	1,044	1,256	1,167	1,017	887	886
Manufacture of computers and peripheral equipment	26200	1,359	1,182	1,270	1,182	1,403	S	S
Manufacture of communication equipment	26300	1,754	1,736	1,691	1,460	1,362	1,269	1,247
Manufacture of consumer electronics	26400	S	S	404	383	355	405	419
Manufacture of instruments and appliances for measuring, testing and navigation	26510	4,817	5,112	5,544	5,658	5,668	5,895	5,887
Manufacture of watches and clocks	26520	S	34	30	31	24	22	21
Manufacture of irradiation, electromedical and electrotherapeutic equipment	26600	787	S	S	S	S	S	S
Manufacture of optical instruments and photographic equipment	26700	304	332	394	374	333	351	416
Manufacture of magnetic and optical media	26800	12	9	S	13	S	11	S
Manufacture of electrical equipment								
Manufacture of electric motors, generators and transformers	27110	2,187	2,602	3,153	3,060	2,763	2,581	2,675
Manufacture of electricity distribution and control apparatus	27120	1,465	1,891	2,086	2,173	2,288	2,352	2,286
Manufacture of batteries and accumulators	27200	224	247	S	259	S	274	260
Manufacture of fibre optic cables	27310	92	124	S	114	97	106	115
Manufacture of other electronic and electric wires and cables	27320	952	1,263	1,399	1,311	1,206	1,218	1,305
Manufacture of wiring devices	27330	423	576	601	S	590	560	552
Manufacture of electric lighting equipment	27400	1,020	1,142	1,293	1,334	1,352	1,542	1,577
Manufacture of electric domestic appliances	27510	1,272	1,277	1,268	1,156	1,186	900	887
Manufacture of non-electric domestic appliances	27520	406	427	463	346	359	S	S
Manufacture of other electrical equipment	27900	1,101	1,356	1,211	1,231	1,208	1,191	1,058
Manufacture of machinery and equipment n.e.c.								
Manufacture of engines and turbines, except aircraft, vehicle and cycle engines	28110	3,263	3,662	4,303	4,232	3,623	3,782	3,371
Manufacture of fluid power equipment	28120	606	791	977	1,037	979	1,054	870
Manufacture of other pumps and compressors	28130	1,984	2,175	2,447	2,215	2,167	2,014	1,754
Manufacture of other taps and valves	28140	1,063	1,103	1,303	1,400	1,729	2,435	2,200
Manufacture of bearings, gears, gearing and driving elements	28150	812	903	1,027	1,004	993	1,048	988
Manufacture of ovens, furnaces and furnace burners	28210	239	222	271	295	220	203	209
Manufacture of lifting and handling equipment	28220	1,965	1,842	2,132	2,326	2,365	2,549	2,475
Manufacture of office machinery and equipment (except computers and peripheral equipment)	28230	410	524	548	607	S	700**	S
Manufacture of power-driven hand tools	28240	70	100	S	151	166	174	S
Manufacture of non-domestic cooling and ventilation equipment	28250	S	2,502	2,371	2,260	2,286	2,558	S
Manufacture of other general-purpose machinery n.e.c.	28290	1,969	1,990	2,090	2,125	2,163	2,350	2,138
Manufacture of agricultural and forestry machinery	28300	1,177	1,275	1,483	1,767	1,618	1,592	1,450
Manufacture of metal forming machinery	28410	334	389	554	679	663	650	534
Manufacture of other machine tools	28490	247	280	329	351	303	324	304
Manufacture of machinery for metallurgy	28910	60	76	97	82	88	86	77
Manufacture of machinery for mining, quarrying and construction	28920	2,171	2,894	4,087	4,471	4,291	4,238	3,818
Manufacture of machinery for food, beverage and tobacco processing	28930	424	467	461	428	479	481	478
Manufacture of machinery for textile, apparel and leather production	28940	77	67	82	59	58	63	75
Manufacture of machinery for paper and paperboard production	28950	109	134	135	126	125	107	128
Manufacture of plastics and rubber machinery	28960	51	68	86	78	70	60	61
Manufacture of other special-purpose machinery n.e.c.	28990	972	1,181	1,252	1,227	1,051	1,197	1,331
Manufacture of motor vehicles; trailers and semi-trailers								
Manufacture of motor vehicles	29100	18,506	25,590	27,516	28,004	34,204	35,926	36,212
Manufacture of bodies (coachwork) for motor vehicles; manufacture of trailers and semi-trailers	29200	1,890	2,097	2,165	2,153	1,904	2,058	2,356
Manufacture of electrical and electronic equipment for motor vehicles	29310	515	S	544	346	S	258	263
Manufacture of other parts and accessories for motor vehicles	29320	6,345	8,301	8,222	8,794	8,618	9,100	9,608
Manufacture of other transport equipment								
Building of ships and floating structures	30110	2,456	2,756	2,903	S	3,775	S	4,320
Building of pleasure and sporting boats	30120	842	850	792	824	747	665	679

18.2 UK Manufacturer's Sales by Industry

Industry	SIC(07)	2009	2010	2011	2012	2013	2014	£ million 2015
Manufacture of railway locomotives and rolling stock	30200	S	S	1,366	S	S	1,083	894
Manufacture of air and spacecraft and related machinery	30300	15,815	15,378	15,853	17,265	20,316	20,692	22,055
Manufacturer of military fighting vehicles	30400	430	513	S	S	S	S	S
Manufacture of motorcycles	30910	S	S	S	S	S	S	S
Manufacture of bicycles and invalid carriages	30920	115	115	113	129	134	148	155
Manufacture of other transport equipment n.e.c.	30990	51	41	S	S	40	44	49
Manufacture of furniture								
Manufacture of office and shop furniture	31010	1,032	1,011	1,100	1,217	1,081	1,189	1,136
Manufacture of kitchen furniture	31020	1,016	1,036	1,055	1,094	1,356	1,349	1,378
Manufacture of mattresses	31030	544	587	S	579	612	694	783
Manufacture of other furniture	31090	2,783	2,988	3,084	3,208	3,257	3,356	3,182
Other manufacturing								
Striking of coins	32110	184	206	S	S	S	S	S
Manufacture of jewellery and related articles	32120	S	411	437	420	428	428	452
Manufacture of imitation jewellery and related articles	32130	44	48	45	37	36	41	46
Manufacture of musical instruments	32200	24	16	18	20	22	21	29
Manufacture of sports goods	32300	S	324	369	344	348	353	326
Manufacture of games and toys	32400	210	171	162	155	210	316	311
Manufacture of medical and dental instruments and supplies	32500	2,783	2,667	2,541	2,629	2,597	2,719	2,868
Manufacture of brooms and brushes	32910	105	105	91	85	79	100	102
Other manufacturing n.e.c.	32990	589	531	572	662	694	634	773
Repair and installation of machinery and equipment								
Repair of fabricated metal products	33110	455	800	977	1,017	1,236	1,119	1,093
Repair of machinery	33120	3,130	2,759	2,983	3,034	3,150	3,114	2,916
Repair of electronic and optical equipment	33130	654	618	631	598	S	772	805
Repair of electrical equipment	33140	522	439	476	528	537	492	605
Repair and maintenance of ships and boats	33150	327	338	331	404	456	459	464
Repair and maintenance of aircraft and spacecraft	33160	2,904	2,557	S	3,333	3,488	3,589	3,708
Repair and maintenance of other transport equipment	33170	S	S	S	855	1,119	S	1,285
Repair of other equipment	33190	S	S	S	S	S	S	5
Installation of industrial machinery and equipment	33200	2,914	S	3,379	3,273	3,214	3,348	3,552
Total		299,845	324,799	341,031	341,985	354,721	363,947	364,596

Source: Office for National Statistics

Note: Information in this table relate to products corresponding to an industry irrespective of which SIC the business making the product is classified.
**Note: This value has been unsuppressed and rounded to the nearest £100 million to allow it to be published
S   A volume or unit value suppressed as disclosive

S* A value suppressed as disclosive and aggregated within the UK Manufacturer Sales of "Other" products

Suppression of data
Statistical disclosure control methodology is applied to PRODCOM data. This ensures that information attributable to an individual or individual organisation is not identifiable in any published outputs. The Code of Practice for Official Statistics, and specifically the Principle on Confidentiality (P.C) set out practices for how ONS protects data from being disclosed. The P.C includes the statement that ONS outputs should "ensure that official statistics do not reveal the identity of an individual or organisation, or any private information relating to them, taking into account other relevant sources of information". More information can be found in National Statistician's Guidance: Confidentiality of Official Statistics, on the statistical disclosure control methodology page of the ONS website, and also in the PRODCOM technical report above.

Previous PRODCOM codes and the incorporation of additional back data
Following user feedback for a longer time series to aid statistical analysis of trends, 2008 and 2009 back data were included to these reference tables at provisional 2014 results, in addition to the 2010 to 2014 data. However, caution should be exercised when comparing certain values, due to the continuously evolving nature of the PRODCOM question list which is set by Eurostat, the European Union's Statistical Authority, in the face of new or changing products and industries. The changes can make backwards comparability difficult, as some codes may appear or disappear in future publications. In this publication, only products included in the most recent PRODCOM list have been included. This leads to difficulties with some aggregate figures in previous years, where the parts do not sum to the whole; this is caused by some of those parts being now-defunct product codes that are not included here, so the sum of the actual values in the table may not equal the aggregate total.

18.3 United Kingdom Business Entities - Number of Local Units by 2 Digit SIC and Employment Size Band, 2015

Local Units

	Total	\multicolumn{7}{c}{Employment Size Bands:}
		0-4	5-9	10-19	20-49	50-99	100-249	250+
SIC07 : Total	2,907,555	2,018,940	411,585	235,170	151,250	51,245	27,435	11,930
SIC07 : 01 : Crop and animal production; hunting and related service activities	142,020	124,980	12,480	3,060	1,100	240	125	35
SIC07 : 02 : Forestry and logging	4,125	3,455	410	170	65	15	10	0
SIC07 : 03 : Fishing and aquaculture	4,060	3,610	340	90	20	0	0	0
SIC07 : 05 : Mining of coal and lignite	30	0	0	5	10	10	0	5
SIC07 : 06 : Extraction of crude petroleum and natural gas	175	85	20	15	10	15	10	20
SIC07 : 07 : Mining of metal ores	0	0	0	0	0	0	0	0
SIC07 : 08 : Other mining and quarrying	1,465	710	315	240	155	30	15	0
SIC07 : 09 : Mining support service activities	425	270	40	30	25	30	15	15
SIC07 : 10 : Manufacture of food products	8,975	3,815	1,720	1,175	965	500	420	380
SIC07 : 11 : Manufacture of beverages	1,805	1,105	260	180	130	35	60	35
SIC07 : 12 : Manufacture of tobacco products	0	0	0	0	0	0	0	0
SIC07 : 13 : Manufacture of textiles	4,285	2,500	775	475	335	110	70	20
SIC07 : 14 : Manufacture of wearing apparel	3,950	2,570	670	405	225	65	10	5
SIC07 : 15 : Manufacture of leather and related products	625	390	105	50	50	20	10	0
SIC07 : 16 : Manufacture of wood and of products of wood and cork; except furniture; manufacture of articles of straw and plaiting materials	8,665	5,785	1,365	845	455	140	60	15
SIC07 : 17 : Manufacture of paper and paper products	1,720	705	225	245	240	140	135	30
SIC07 : 18 : Printing and reproduction of recorded media	13,165	8,875	2,080	1,160	685	225	110	30
SIC07 : 19 : Manufacture of coke and refined petroleum products	145	55	20	20	25	15	5	5
SIC07 : 20 : Manufacture of chemicals and chemical products	3,090	1,395	455	385	420	230	150	55
SIC07 : 21 : Manufacture of basic pharmaceutical products and pharmaceutical preparations	640	380	65	45	35	25	35	55
SIC07 : 22 : Manufacture of rubber and plastic products	6,360	2,545	1,155	1,050	820	435	265	90
SIC07 : 23 : Manufacture of other non-metallic mineral products	5,045	2,770	845	640	440	190	125	35
SIC07 : 24 : Manufacture of basic metals	1,770	825	240	215	255	110	80	45
SIC07 : 25 : Manufacture of fabricated metal products; except machinery and equipment	27,420	16,230	4,455	3,325	2,285	760	295	70
SIC07 : 26 : Manufacture of computer; electronic and optical products	6,640	3,950	925	665	595	280	160	65
SIC07 : 27 : Manufacture of electrical equipment	3,350	1,580	475	470	435	200	140	50
SIC07 : 28 : Manufacture of machinery and equipment n.e.c.	8,620	4,480	1,450	985	940	395	260	110
SIC07 : 29 : Manufacture of motor vehicles; trailers and semi-trailers	3,160	1,770	440	300	255	155	130	110
SIC07 : 30 : Manufacture of other transport equipment	2,440	1,635	250	150	125	95	95	90
SIC07 : 31 : Manufacture of furniture	6,325	3,740	1,115	700	470	175	95	30
SIC07 : 32 : Other manufacturing	9,970	6,845	1,725	775	390	125	80	30
SIC07 : 33 : Repair and installation of machinery and equipment	12,795	9,690	1,380	880	490	195	100	60
SIC07 : 35 : Electricity; gas; steam and air conditioning supply	4,505	3,020	555	345	210	135	125	115
SIC07 : 36 : Water collection; treatment and supply	915	365	190	125	120	45	35	35
SIC07 : 37 : Sewerage	1,415	770	250	175	150	50	20	0
SIC07 : 38 : Waste collection; treatment and disposal activities; materials recovery	7,825	3,995	1,455	975	840	355	170	35
SIC07 : 39 : Remediation activities and other waste management services	825	570	135	80	40	0	0	0
SIC07 : 41 : Construction of buildings	84,225	70,940	7,735	3,135	1,440	550	335	90

18.3 United Kingdom Business Entities - Number of Local Units by 2 Digit SIC and Employment Size Band, 2015

| | Local Units | | | | | | | |
| | | Employment Size Bands: | | | | | | |
	Total	0-4	5-9	10-19	20-49	50-99	100-249	250+
SIC07 : 42 : Civil engineering	22,895	17,155	2,720	1,370	950	370	230	100
SIC07 : 43 : Specialised construction activities	186,705	155,150	18,445	8,145	3,560	980	350	75
SIC07 : 45 : Wholesale and retail trade and repair of motor vehicles and motorcycles	81,955	54,725	15,600	6,170	4,085	1,075	275	25
SIC07 : 46 : Wholesale trade; except of motor vehicles and motorcycles	125,100	77,500	22,485	14,095	7,530	2,220	930	340
SIC07 : 47 : Retail trade; except of motor vehicles and motorcycles	290,320	163,965	67,060	34,760	16,905	3,875	2,420	1,335
SIC07 : 49 : Land transport and transport via pipelines	58,135	43,875	6,010	3,880	2,510	925	630	305
SIC07 : 50 : Water transport	1,545	1,075	195	145	85	25	15	5
SIC07 : 51 : Air transport	1,115	700	120	85	60	40	65	45
SIC07 : 52 : Warehousing and support activities for transportation	19,690	10,910	3,090	2,220	1,875	795	520	280
SIC07 : 53 : Postal and courier activities	19,145	14,040	1,970	910	1,050	700	345	130
SIC07 : 55 : Accommodation	20,880	8,345	3,660	3,395	3,415	1,295	660	110
SIC07 : 56 : Food and beverage service activities	165,415	70,565	45,650	28,800	17,060	2,565	645	130
SIC07 : 58 : Publishing activities	11,955	8,940	1,295	790	535	190	110	95
SIC07 : 59 : Motion picture; video and television programme production; sound recording and music publishing activities	23,470	20,760	1,115	680	560	230	100	25
SIC07 : 60 : Programming and broadcasting activities	2,190	1,725	175	115	95	25	40	15
SIC07 : 61 : Telecommunications	11,355	7,890	1,310	850	660	290	200	155
SIC07 : 62 : Computer programming; consultancy and related activities	143,885	129,280	6,650	3,970	2,495	860	440	190
SIC07 : 63 : Information service activities	8,210	6,560	810	435	220	90	60	35
SIC07 : 64 : Financial service activities; except insurance and pension funding	27,160	15,005	5,800	3,635	1,830	330	245	315
SIC07 : 65 : Insurance; reinsurance and pension funding; except compulsory social security	6,475	5,700	210	160	130	85	75	115
SIC07 : 66 : Activities auxiliary to financial services and insurance activities	34,835	25,335	4,590	2,305	1,335	585	420	265
SIC07 : 68 : Real estate activities	101,905	79,110	14,060	5,890	1,840	525	370	110
SIC07 : 69 : Legal and accounting activities	79,280	58,995	9,955	5,850	2,915	860	455	250
SIC07 : 70 : Activities of head offices; management consultancy activities	165,935	150,705	7,640	3,905	2,130	790	470	295
SIC07 : 71 : Architectural and engineering activities; technical testing and analysis	99,325	85,055	6,770	4,025	2,245	740	340	150
SIC07 : 72 : Scientific research and development	5,360	3,690	545	405	335	160	135	90
SIC07 : 73 : Advertising and market research	22,735	18,035	2,175	1,230	765	260	180	90
SIC07 : 74 : Other professional; scientific and technical activities	77,130	68,785	5,510	1,880	720	165	55	15
SIC07 : 75 : Veterinary activities	5,515	2,430	1,340	1,145	530	60	10	0
SIC07 : 77 : Rental and leasing activities	20,655	13,615	3,475	2,135	1,020	255	135	20
SIC07 : 78 : Employment activities	29,170	17,535	3,330	2,430	2,340	1,565	1,335	635
SIC07 : 79 : Travel agency; tour operator and other reservation service and related activities	11,100	6,730	2,655	970	430	190	90	35
SIC07 : 80 : Security and investigation activities	9,835	6,670	1,165	780	575	290	205	150
SIC07 : 81 : Services to buildings and landscape activities	60,450	42,305	9,330	4,640	2,450	855	505	365
SIC07 : 82 : Office administrative; office support and other business support activities	100,965	86,395	8,350	3,570	1,510	565	345	230
SIC07 : 84 : Public administration and defence; compulsory social security	25,025	10,270	3,100	3,270	3,590	1,905	1,645	1,245
SIC07 : 85 : Education	72,050	25,250	9,100	9,165	14,690	8,350	4,550	945
SIC07 : 86 : Human health activities	72,960	37,730	12,590	10,830	7,630	2,080	1,250	850
SIC07 : 87 : Residential care activities	30,830	8,340	4,575	5,960	7,740	3,415	715	85

18.3 United Kingdom Business Entities - Number of Local Units by 2 Digit SIC and Employment Size Band, 2015

| | Local Units | | | | | | | |
| | | Employment Size Bands: | | | | | | |
	Total	0-4	5-9	10-19	20-49	50-99	100-249	250+
SIC07 : 88 : Social work activities without accommodation	63,605	25,565	13,865	12,400	8,250	2,290	1,000	235
SIC07 : 90 : Creative; arts and entertainment activities	29,295	26,445	1,535	675	365	165	100	10
SIC07 : 91 : Libraries; archives; museums and other cultural activities	6,110	2,855	1,330	890	670	220	105	40
SIC07 : 92 : Gambling and betting activities	11,560	4,930	5,590	420	435	95	80	10
SIC07 : 93 : Sports activities and amusement and recreation activities	34,160	19,440	5,565	4,320	3,060	1,165	500	110
SIC07 : 94 : Activities of membership organisations	26,215	17,040	4,795	2,435	1,290	370	215	70
SIC07 : 95 : Repair of computers and personal and household goods	9,140	7,510	910	425	175	75	25	20
SIC07 : 96 : Other personal service activities	81,840	57,905	17,250	5,025	1,355	190	95	20
SIC07 : 97 : Activities of households as employers of domestic personnel	0	0	0	0	0	0	0	0
SIC07 : 98 : Undifferentiated goods- and services-producing activities of private households for own use	0	0	0	0	0	0	0	0
SIC07 : 99 : Activities of extraterritorial organisations and bodies	0	0	0	0	0	0	0	0

Source: Office for National Statistics

18.4 Production of primary fuels

United Kingdom

Million tonnes of oil equivalent

	2000	2001	2002	2003	2004	2005	2006	2007	2008	2009	2010	2011	2012	2013	2014	2015
Coal	19.6	20.0	18.8	17.6	15.6	12.7	11.4	10.7	11.3	11.0	11.4	11.5	10.6	8.0	7.3	5.4
Petroleum [1]	138.3	127.8	127.0	116.2	104.5	92.9	84.0	83.9	78.7	74.7	69.0	56.9	48.8	44.5	43.7	49.5
Natural Gas [2]	108.4	105.9	103.6	103.0	96.4	88.2	80.0	72.1	69.7	59.7	55.3r	44.0r	37.4r	35.3r	35.8r	38.8r
Primary electricity [3]	20.2	21.2	20.6	20.4	18.7	19.0	17.9	14.9	13.0r	16.5r	15.1r	17.5r	17.5r	18.5	17.5	20.1
Renewable energy [4]	2.3	2.5	2.8	3.0	3.1	3.7	4.0	4.3	18.0	21.9	76.5r	67.8r	61.9r	42.9r	44.0r	48.7r
Total Production	288.7	277.4	272.9	260.3	238.4	216.5	197.2	186.0	177.7	167.4	156.9r	136.2r	121.3r	113.9r	112.5r	123.7r

r - revised data

Source: Department for Business, Energy & Industrial Strategy

(1) Crude oil plus all condensates and petroleum gases extracted at gas separation plants.

(2) Includes colliery methane.

(3) Nuclear and natural flow hydro electricty excluding generation of pumped storage stations. From 1988 includes generation at wind stations.

(4) Includes solar and geothermal heat, solid renewable sources (wood, waste, etc), and gaseous renewable sources (landfill gas, sewage gas) from 1988.

Datasource
DUKES 1.1.2

18.5 Total inland energy consumption

United Kingdom

Million tonnes of oil equivalent

	2000	2001	2002	2003	2004	2005	2006	2007	2008	2009	2010	2011	2012	2013	2014	2015
Inland energy consumption of primary fuels and equivalents	234.8	236.9	229.6	231.9	233.6	236.3	233.1	227.5r	225.6r	211.6r	219.5r	203.7r	208.1r	206.8r	194.0r	195.5r
Coal	38.5	40.8	37.7	40.5	39.1	39.9	43.4	41.0	38.2	31.2	32.6	32.2	40.9	39.0r	31.5r	25.1r
Petroleum	76.7	75.9	73.5	73.0	75.1	78.2	77.4	76.3	74.4	70.9	70.2	67.8	67.0	65.8r	66.0r	67.3r
Primary electricity	21.4	22.1	21.3	20.6	19.4	19.8	18.5	15.4	13.9	16.7	15.4r	18.0r	18.5r	19.7r	19.2r	21.9r
Natural gas	95.9	95.6	94.3	94.6	96.6	94.3	89.4	90.2	93.1r	86.2r	93.5r	77.6r	73.3r	72.6r	66.1r	68.1r
Renewables and waste	2.3	2.5	2.8	3.1	3.5	4.2	4.4	5.0r	6.0r	6.6r	7.8r	8.1r	8.4r	9.7r	11.2r	13.1r
Total consumption by final users	159.4	160.9	156.5	158.1	159.9	159.7	157.0	154.3	154.2r	144.2r	150.5r	138.6r	142.3r	143.0r	135.6r	138.5
Final energy consumption by type of fuel																
Coal (direct use)	2.7	2.7	2.2	2.1	2.0	1.7	1.6	1.8	1.8	1.7	1.9	1.8	1.7	2.1r	2.1r	1.8
Coke and breeze	0.8	0.8	0.7	0.7	0.6	0.6	0.5	0.5	0.5	0.4	0.3	0.3	0.4	0.5r	0.5r	0.4
Other solid fuel	0.6	0.5	0.5	0.4	0.4	0.4	0.4	0.4	0.4	0.2	0.2	0.2	0.2	0.2	0.2	0.2
Coke oven gas	0.2	0.2	0.1	0.1	0.1	0.1	0.1	0.1	0.1	0.0	0.1	0.1	0.0	0.1	0.1	0.1
Natural gas (direct use)	57.1	57.8	55.2	56.7	57.1	55.4	52.6	50.0	51.5r	46.8r	51.6r	42.9r	46.9r	47.4r	40.4r	42.0
Electricity	28.3	28.6	28.7	28.9	29.1	30.0	29.7	29.4	29.4	27.7	28.3r	27.3r	27.4r	27.2r	26.0r	26.1
Petroleum (direct use)	66.3	67.1	66.1	66.8	68.6	69.5	69.8	69.5	66.5	63.4	63.2	61.5	61.1	60.2r	60.9r	62.2
Renewables [6]	0.9	0.9	0.9	0.6	0.7	0.7	1.1	1.3	2.5	2.8	3.6	3.3	3.4	4.1	4.2	4.6
Heat	2.5	2.3	2.1	1.8	1.3	1.3	1.2	1.3	1.5	1.2	1.3	1.2	1.2r	1.2r	1.2r	1.1
Final energy consumption by class of consumer																
Agriculture	1.2	1.3	1.2	0.9	0.9	1.0	0.9	0.9	0.9r	0.9r	1.0r	0.9r	1.0r	1.1r	1.3r	1.1r
Iron and steel industry	2.2	2.3	2.0	1.9	1.9	1.8	1.9	1.8	1.6r	1.2r	1.4r	1.3r	1.2r	1.3r	1.4r	1.3r
Other industries	33.3	33.2	31.8	32.1	31.0	30.5	29.6	28.8	28.6r	24.5r	25.6r	24.0r	23.7r	23.5r	22.9r	23.1r
Railways	1.4	1.4	1.4	1.4	1.0	1.0	1.0	1.0	1.0r	1.0r	1.0r	1.0r	1.1r	1.0r	1.1r	1.0r
Road transport	41.1	41.1	41.9	41.8	42.2	42.6	42.7	43.2	41.9r	40.7	40.4r	39.8r	39.5r	39.3r	40.0r	40.5r
Water transport	1.0	0.8	0.7	1.2	1.2	1.4	1.8	1.6	1.0r	1.0r	0.9r	0.9r	0.8r	0.7r	0.7r	0.7r
Air transport	12.0	11.8	11.7	11.9	12.9	13.9	14.0	13.9	13.4r	12.8r	12.3r	12.8r	12.4r	12.4r	12.4r	12.5r
Domestic	46.9	48.2	47.5	48.3	49.3	47.8	46.6	44.9	46.0r	44.7r	49.4r	40.9r	44.4r	44.9r	38.7r	40.0r
Public administration	8.1	8.0	7.0	6.7	7.2	7.1	6.6	6.3	6.5	6.0	6.2	5.5	6.0	6.1	5.5	5.7
Commercial and other services	12.2	12.8	11.3	11.8	12.2	12.7	12.0	11.8	13.1r	11.6r	12.2r	11.5r	12.3r	12.6r	11.7r	12.5r

Source: Department for Business, Energy & Industrial Strategy

r revisions to data for 2008 to 2015

18.6 Coal: supply and demand

United Kingdom   Million tonnes

	2000	2001	2002	2003	2004	2005	2006	2007	2008	2009	2010	2011	2012	2013	2014	2015
Supply																
Production of deep-mined coal	17.2	17.3	16.4	15.6	12.5	9.6	9.4	7.7	8.1	7.5	7.4	7.3	6.2	4.1	3.7	2.8
Surface mining (1)	13.4	14.2	13.1	12.1	12.0	10.4	8.6	8.9	9.5	9.9	10.4	10.6	10.1	8.6	8.0	5.8
Total	30.6	31.5	29.5	27.8	24.5	20.0	18.1	16.5	17.6	17.4	17.8	17.9	16.3	12.7	11.6	8.6
Recovered slurry, fines, etc (2)	0.6	0.4	0.4	0.5	0.6	0.5	0.4	0.5	0.4	0.5	0.5	0.7	0.7	0.1	0.0	0.0
Imports	23.4	35.5	28.7	31.9	36.2	44.0	50.5	43.4	43.9	38.2	26.5	32.5	44.8	50.6r	42.2	22.5
Total	54.6	67.5	58.7	60.2	61.2	64.5	69.0	60.4	61.9	56.0	44.9	51.1	61.8	63.4r	53.9	31.1
Change in stocks at collieries and opencast sites	3.5	0.1	-0.9	0.9	0.4	0.1	0.3	0.0	-0.1	-0.6	-0.1	0.6	-0.2	0.1r	0.0r	0.0
Total supply	58.2	67.5	57.8	61.0	61.7	64.6	69.4	60.4	61.8	55.4	44.8	51.7	61.6	63.5r	53.9	31.1
Home consumption																
Total home consumption	59.8	63.5	58.6	62.9	60.6	61.8	67.3	62.9	58.2	48.8	51.4	51.4	64.3	60.1r	48.3r	37.6
Overseas shipments and bunkers	0.7	0.5	0.5	0.5	0.6	0.5	0.4	0.5	0.6	0.6	0.7	0.5	0.5	0.6	0.4	0.4
Total consumption and shipments	60.5	64.1	59.2	63.4	61.2	62.3	67.8	63.4	58.8	49.4	52.1	51.9	64.3	60.1	48.3	37.6
Change in distributed stocks	2.3	-3.5	1.4	2.4	-0.5	-1.9	-1.9	3.0	-3.0	-6.2	7.3	0.3	3.0	-2.6	-5.1	6.9
Balance	0.0	0.0	0.0	0.0	0.0	0.3	-0.3	0.0	0.0	-0.2	0.0	0.0	0.2	-0.1	0.0	0.0
Stocks at end of year																
Distributed	12.4	15.9	14.5	12.1	12.6	14.5	16.4	13.4	16.4	22.6	15.4	15.1	11.9	15.1r	20.1r	13.5
At collieries and opencast sites	1.6	1.6	2.5	1.6	1.2	1.1	0.8	0.7	0.9	1.4	1.5	0.9	1.1	0.5	0.6	0.4
Total stocks	14.1	17.5	17.0	13.7	13.8	15.6	17.2	14.2	17.2	24.1	16.9	16.0	13.0	15.6	20.7	13.9

Source: Department for Business, Energy & Industrial Strategy

Datasource
DUKES 2.4
location
https://www.gov.uk/government/publications/solid-fuels-and-derived-gases-chapter-2-digest-of-united-kingdom-energy-statistics-dukes

(1) The term 'surface mining' has now replaced opencast production. Opencast production is a surface mining technique.
(2) Estimates of slurry etc. recovered from ponds, dumps, rivers, etc.

18.7 Fuel input and gas output: gas consumption

United Kingdom   Giga-watt hours

	2002	2003	2004	2005	2006	2007	2008	2009	2010	2011	2012	2013	2014	2015
Analysis of gas consumption														
Transformation sector	351,856	344,410	362,668	354,146	333,431	379,518	402,236	382,061	400,828r	332,012r	239,631r	230,170r	243,468r	238,025
Electricity generation	329,847	324,580	340,824	331,658	311,408	355,878	376,810	359,303	377,121	309,076	216,543	205,869	217,837r	212,632
Heat generation	22,009	19,830	21,844	22,488	22,023	23,640	25,426	22,758	23,707	22,936	23,089r	24,302	25,631	25,393
Energy industry use total	91,260	88,907	88,468	87,161	81,859	76,025	72,280	70,597	71,219r	62,905r	56,236r	53,219r	52,470r	58,645
Oil and gas extraction	79,364	76,837	77,753	73,372	69,252	64,230	61,292	61,110	61,124	53,163	48,461	46,000r	45,391	51,024
Petroleum refineries	3,350	2,773	3,076	5,163	5,161	5,206	4,971	1,601	1,785	1,757	1,522r	1,151r	1,201r	1,201
Coal extraction and coke manufacture	196	188	150	114	112	91	95	217	260	223	194	60r	100r	79
Blast furnaces	222	539	728	941	611	719	718	450	641	453	266	363	338	323
Other	8,128	8,570	6,761	7,572	6,723	5,779	5,204	7,218	7,409r	7,309r	5,793	5,645	5,440r	6,018
Final consumption total	653,151	669,457	673,860	652,024	620,035	591,274	599,018	550,142	611,526	503,762	550,672r	557,201r	475,601r	493,994
Iron and steel industry	8,791	10,327	9,715	8,453	8,391	7,323	6,920	5,346	6,124	5,829	5,091	5,338	5,454	5,374
Other industries	156,375	155,890	144,238	142,988	136,150	126,028	127,013	4,900	5,373	5,155	7,571r	7,171r	7,022r	6,745
Domestic	376,372	386,486	396,411	381,879	366,928	352,868	359,554	344,499	389,595	293,400	343,180r	344,501r	283,691r	297,582
Public administration	42,998	44,362	51,934	50,319	45,803	42,444	45,665	42,372	45,473	42,960	41,323r	42,251r	34,972r	36,545
Commercial	36,224	39,537	37,595	38,197	34,273	33,098	38,448	53,025	57,320	55,757	45,331r	47,276r	40,189r	44,097
Agriculture	2,346	2,324	2,355	2,261	2,013	1,998	2,161	1,468	1,619	1,351	1,162	1,096	1,073r	983
Miscellaneous	19,265	20,510	21,591	20,014	18,564	17,286	11,052	10,627	10,501	9,830	11,311r	11,465r	9,609r	10,310
Non energy use	10,780	10,021	10,021	7,913	7,913	10,228	8,206	6,887	8,089	5,949	5,771	5,598	5,430	5,267
Total gas consumption	1,096,267	1,102,774	1,124,996	1,093,331	1,035,325	1,046,817	1,073,535	1,013,943	1,096,368	908,605	854,430r	848,064r	778,395r	797,132r

Source: Department for Business, Energy & Industrial Strategy

18.8 Electricity: generation, supply and consumption

United Kingdom

Gigawatt-hours

	2003	2004	2005	2006	2007	2008	2009	2010	2011	2012	2013	2014	2015
Electricity generated													
Major power producers: total	362,600	358,313	362,212	361,232	361,317	355,209	342,374	347,846	332,461	328,291r	324,623r	300,822r	295,991
Conventional thermal and other	147,536	140,576	143,091	160,566	146,706	128,944	106,939	111,127	111,255	147,946	141,011r	114,534	95,606
Combined cycle gas turbine stations	121,076	131,182	130,748	117,669	140,011	160,109	151,454	160,518	131,886	85,647	82,533	88,259	87,732
Nuclear stations	88,686	79,999	81,618	75,451	63,028	52,486	69,098	62,140	68,980	70,405	70,607	63,748	70,345
Hydro-electric stations:													
Natural flow	2,568	3,908	3,826	3,693	4,144	4,224	4,294	2,703	4,594	4,170r	3,609	4,635	4,907
Pumped storage	2,734	2,649	2,930	3,853	3,859	4,089	3,685	3,150	2,906	2,966	2,904	2,883	2,739
Renewables other than hydro	1,154	1,471	2,744	2,928	5,910	7,966	9,574	11,893	17,358	23,270r	33,170r	39,460r	52,355
Other generators: total	35,609	35,616	36,148	36,050	35,513	33,663	34,378	33,926	34,960	35,582r	33,661r	37,274r	42,926
Conventional thermal and other	17,244	14,419	13,407	12,354	13,865	19,457	20,218	18,862	20,258	20,813r	15,162r	18,794r	21,519
Combined cycle gas turbine stations	10,879	11,852	11,792	11,561	11,516	11,522	10,790	12,113	10,560	9,582r	10,953r	7,974r	6,812
Hydro-electric stations (natural flow)	660	936	1,096	900	933	931	947	862	1,086	1,140r	1,092r	1,253r	1,392
Renewables other than hydro	6,825	8,408	9,853	11,235	8,702	8,680	10,428	10,325	11,491	12,669r	15,342r	19,175r	24,750
All generating companies: total	398,209	393,929	398,360	397,282	396,830	388,872	376,753	381,772	367,422r	363,874r	358,283r	338,096r	338,917
Conventional thermal and other	164,780	154,995	156,498	172,920	160,571	148,401	127,157	129,989	131,513	168,758r	156,173r	133,328r	117,125
Combined cycle gas turbine stations	131,955	143,034	142,540	129,230	151,527	171,631	162,244	172,631	142,447	95,229r	93,486r	96,233r	94,544
Nuclear stations	88,686	79,999	81,618	75,451	63,028	52,486	69,098	62,140	68,980	70,405	70,607	63,748	70,345
Hydro-electric stations:													
Natural flow	3,228	4,844	4,922	4,593	5,077	5,155	5,241	3,565	5,680	5,310r	4,701r	1,253r	6,298
Pumped storage	2,734	2,649	2,930	3,853	3,859	4,089	3,685	3,150	2,906	2,966	2,904	2,883	2,739
Renewables other than hydro	7,979	9,879	12,597	14,164	14,612	16,645	20,002	22,218	28,849	35,939r	48,512r	58,769	58,635
Electricity used on works: Total	18,136	17,032	17,873	18,503	17,694	16,340	16,571	16,112	16,430	17,983r	17,850r	16,480r	16,654
Major generating companies	16,747	15,582	16,265	17,031	16,090	14,662	14,750	14,403	14,479	15,860r	15,658r	13,958	16,654
Other generators	1,389	1,451	1,608	1,472	1,605	1,678	1,821	1,710	1,951	2,124r	2,191r	2,522r	2,836
Electricity supplied (gross)													
Major power producers: total	345,854	342,732	345,947	344,201	345,227	340,547	327,624	333,443	317,983	312,431r	308,964r	286,864r	282,173
Conventional thermal and other	140,196	133,607	135,999	151,866	138,793	121,816	101,100	105,142	105,345	139,994	133,238r	107,945	89,741
Combined cycle gas turbine stations	118,546	128,983	128,179	115,695	137,657	157,417	148,907	157,818	129,669	84,207	81,145	86,775	86,256
Nuclear stations	81,911	73,682	75,173	69,237	57,249	47,673	62,762	56,442	62,655	63,949	64,133	57,903	63,895
Hydro-electric stations:													
Natural flow	2,559	3,901	3,821	3,680	4,114	4,209	4,279	2,694	4,578	4,168	3,596	4,606	4,889
Pumped storage	2,641	2,559	2,776	3,722	3,846	4,075	3,672	3,139	2,895	2,956	2,894	2,873	2,730
Renewables other than hydro	1,059	1,367	2,486	2,643	5,675	7,704	9,306	11,523	16,904	22,656r	32,245r	38,185r	50,579
Other generators: total	34,220	34,165	34,539	34,578	33,908	31,985	32,558	32,216	33,009	33,459r	31,470r	34,752r	40,090
Conventional thermal and other	21,942	20,046	19,494	18,598	19,801	18,371	18,952	17,771	18,854	19,189r	13,539r	16,697r	19,056
Combined cycle gas turbine stations	10,336	11,260	11,204	10,859	11,471	10,947	10,251	11,509	10,033	9,104r	10,406r	7,576r	6,473
Hydro-electric stations (natural flow)	653	919	930	885	918	915	930	847	1,066	1,118r	1,071r	1,226r	1,358
Renewables other than hydro	6,519	8,000	9,380	10,702	8,147	8,000	9,584	9,584	10,502	11,486r	13,842r	17,362r	22,671
All generating companies: total	380,074	376,896	380,486	378,779	379,136	372,532	360,182	365,660	350,992	345,890r	340,434r	321,616r	322,263
Conventional thermal and other	162,138	153,653	155,493	170,464	158,594	140,186	120,052	122,914r	124,200r	159,183r	146,777r	124,642r	108,797
Combined cycle gas turbine stations	128,882	140,243	139,382	126,554	149,127	168,364	159,159	169,327	139,702	93,311r	91,552r	94,351r	92,729
Nuclear stations	81,911	73,682	75,173	69,237	57,249	47,673	62,762	56,442	62,655	63,949	64,133	57,903	63,895
Hydro-electric stations:													
Natural flow	3,212	4,821	4,750	4,566	5,032	5,124	5,209	3,541	5,643	5,286r	4,667r	5,831r	6,247
Pumped storage	2,641	2,559	2,776	3,722	3,846	4,075	3,672	3,139	2,895	2,956	2,894	2,873	2,730
Renewables other than hydro	7,578	9,367	11,867	13,345	13,822	15,704	18,889	21,107	27,406	34,142r	46,086r	55,547	73,250
Electricity used in pumping													
Major power producers	3,546	3,497	3,707	4,918	5,071	5,371	4,843	4,212	3,843	3,978	3,930	3,884	3,711
Electricity supplied (net): Total	376,528	373,399	376,780	373,861	374,064	367,161	355,339	361,448	347,149	341,912r	336,504r	317,732r	318,552
Major power producers	342,308	339,235	342,240	339,283	340,156	335,175	322,781	329,231	314,140	308,454r	305,034r	282,980r	278,462
Other generators	34,220	34,165	34,539	34,578	33,908	31,985	32,558	32,216	33,009	33,459r	31,470r	34,752r	40,090
Net imports	8,414	2,160	7,490	8,321	7,517	5,215	11,022	2,663	6,222	11,864r	14,431r	20,520	20,938
Electricity available	378,687	380,889	385,101	381,378	379,279	378,183	358,200	364,111	353,371	353,776r	350,935r	338,253r	339,491
Losses in transmission etc	29,862	30,728	27,674	27,410	28,223	27,852	28,043	27,037r	28,140r	28,917r	27,667r	28,514r	27,319
Electricity consumption: Total	346,126	347,246	356,685	353,367	350,970	349,648	329,555	337,203	325,620	318,272r	316,271r	302,786r	303,448
Fuel industries	9,908	8,299	8,010	8,137	9,313	7,825	7,807	8,377	7,793	4,187	4,058	3,698	3,846
Final users: total	336,218	338,948	348,675	345,229	341,656	341,822	321,748	328,825	317,827	318,757r	316,844r	303,347r	303,860
Industrial sector	109,278	111,467	116,024	114,896	112,799	114,151	99,738	104,538r	102,416r	98,456r	96,981r	93,005r	92,907
Domestic sector	123,001	124,200	125,711	124,704	123,076	119,800	118,541	118,832r	111,586r	114,663r	113,412r	108,076r	107,764
Other sectors	103,939	103,280	106,939	105,629	105,781	107,871	103,469	105,468	103,871	105,153	105,878	101,705	102,778

Source: Department for Business, Energy & Industrial Strategy

18.9 Electricity: plant capacity and demand

United Kingdom
At end of December

Megawatts

	2003	2004	2005	2006	2007	2008	2009	2010	2011	2012	2013	2014	2015
Major power producers													
Total declared net capability [1]	71,471	73,293	73,941	74,996	75,979	76,993	77,881	83,438	81,789	81,877	77,167	75,694	71,928
Conventional steam stations	31,867	31,982	32,292	33,608	34,134	32,823	32,831	32,839	31,763	28,523	23,141	21,282	18,714
Combined cycle gas turbine stations	21,452	23,178	23,678	24,274	24,269	26,203	26,785	31,724	30,183	33,113	32,967	31,994	30,080
Nuclear stations	11,852	11,852	11,852	10,969	10,979	10,979	10,858	10,865	10,663	9,946	9,906	9,937	9,487
Gas turbines and oil engines	1,582	1,540	1,541	1,629	1,630	1,641	1,779	1,779	1,706	1,651	1,639	1,643	1,386r
Hydro-electric stations:													
Natural flow [2]	1,273	1,276	1,273	1,294	1,293	1,392	1,395	1,397	1,397	1,398	1,399	1,400	1,400
Pumped storage	2,788	2,788	2,788	2,726	2,744	2,744	2,744	2,744	2,744	2,744	2,744	2,744	2,744
Renewables other than hydro, wind & solar [3]	117	117	117	96	134	213	213	223	1,092	1,226r	1,424r	2,166r	2,911
Other generators:													
Total capacity of own generating plant [4]	6,793	6,829	7,422	7,407	6,763	6,700	6,945	7,006r	7,315r	7,423r	7,430	8,718r	9,098r
Conventional steam stations [5]	3,480	3,275	3,269	3,059	2,924	2,749	2,408	2,360r	2,437r	2,373r	2,045r	2,108r	2,171r
Combined cycle gas turbine stations	1,927	1,968	2,182	2,106	2,076	1,988	2,267	2,302r	2,005r	2,037r	1,905	1,813	1,616r
Hydro-electric stations (natural flow) [2]	129	132	127	123	126	125	127	130r	153r	158r	163r	169r	186r
Renewables other than hydro, wind & solar [3]	945	1,061	1,194	1,296	1,391	1,353	1,519	1,683r	1,954r	1,949r	1,914r	2,594r	2,554r
All generating companies: Total capacity	78,264	80,122	81,363	82,403	82,742	83,693	84,826	90,444r	89,104r	89,301r	84,596r	84,412r	81,026r
Conventional steam stations [5]	35,347	35,257	35,561	36,667	37,058	35,572	35,239	35,199r	34,201r	30,897r	25,186r	23,390r	20,885r
Combined cycle gas turbine stations	23,379	25,146	25,860	26,380	26,345	28,191	29,051	34,026r	32,188r	35,150r	34,872	33,807r	31,696r
Nuclear stations	11,852	11,852	11,852	10,969	10,979	10,979	10,858	10,865	10,663	9,946	9,906	9,937	9,487
Gas turbines and oil engines	1,582	1,540	1,541	1,629	1,630	1,641	1,779	1,779	1,706	1,651	1,639	1,643	1,386r
Hydro-electric stations:													
Natural flow [2]	1,402	1,408	1,400	1,417	1,419	1,517	1,523	1,527r	1,550r	1,556r	1,561r	1,569r	1,586r
Pumped storage	2,788	2,788	2,788	2,726	2,744	2,744	2,744	2,744	2,744	2,744	2,744	2,744	2,744
Renewables other than hydro, wind & solar [3]	1,062	1,178	1,310	1,392	1,525	1,566	1,732	1,905r	3,046r	3,175r	3,338r	4,760r	5,465r
Major power producers:													
Simultaneous maximum load met [6, 7]	60,501	61,013	61,697	59,071	61,527	60,289	60,231	60,893	57,086	57,490	53,420	53,858	52,753
System load factor (percentages) [8]	67	67	66	69	66	68	64	65	67	66	71	67	68

Source: Department for Business, Energy & Industrial Strategy

(1) Data before 2006 are based on declared net capacity.

(2) Small-scale hydro, wind and solar photovoltaics capacity are shown on declared net capability basis, and are de-rated to account for intermittency, by factors of 0.365, 0.43 and 0.17 respectively. See paragraph 5.77

(3) For Major Power Producers, this includes bioenergy; for other generators, this includes bioenergy wave and tidal.

(4) "Other generators" capacities are given in declared net capacity terms, see paragraph 5.77

(5) For other generators, conventional steam stations include combined heat and power plants (electrical capacity only) but exclude combined cycle gas turbine plants, hydro-electric stations and plants using renewable sources.

(6) Load met by transmission network, net of demand met by embedded generation

(7) Data cover the 12 months ending March of the following year, e.g. 2015 data are for the year ending March 2016

(8) Average electricity available as percentage of maximum demand.

18.10 Electricity: fuel used in generation
United Kingdom
At end of December

Million tonnes of oil equivalent

	2003	2004	2005	2006	2007	2008	2009	2010	2011	2012	2013	2014	2015
Major power producers: total all fuels	77.5	76.8	78.2	78.7	76.0	74.2	70.2	70.9	68.4	69.7	68.1r	62.0	59.3
Coal	31.6	30.4	31.7	35.0	32.0	29.0	23.8	24.8	25.2	33.7	31.3	24.0	18.3
Oil [1]	0.7	0.6	0.9	1.0	0.7	1.1	1.0	0.6	0.3	0.4	0.2	0.2	0.2
Gas	24.5	26.2	25.4	23.9	27.5	29.6	28.2	29.7	23.9	15.9	15.1	16.3	16.0
Nuclear	20.0	18.2	18.4	17.1	14.0	11.9	15.2	13.9	15.6	15.2	15.4	13.9	15.5
Hydro (natural flow)	0.2	0.3	0.3	0.3	0.4	0.4	0.4	0.2	0.4	0.4	0.3	0.4	0.4
Wind	0.0	0.0	0.0	0.0	0.3	0.5	0.6	0.7	1.1	1.5	2.1	2.3	2.9
Other renewables	0.4	0.5	0.8	0.7	0.6	0.8	0.7	1.0	1.3	1.8	2.2	3.0	3.6
Net imports	0.2	0.6	0.7	0.6	0.4	0.9	0.2	0.2	0.5	1.0	1.2	1.8	1.8
Other generators: total all fuels	8.7	8.4	9.2	9.0	8.8	8.3	8.5	8.4	8.7	8.5	7.9	8.4	9.2
Transport under takings													
Gas [2]	0.008	0.002	0.003	0.002	0.002	0.002	0.001	0.002	0.001	0.001	0.001	0.001	0.001
Under takings in industrial sector													
Coal [3]	1.0	0.9	0.9	0.9	0.9	1.0	0.9	0.8	0.8	0.7	0.0	0.0	0.0
Oil [4]	0.5	0.5	0.4	0.5	0.5	0.5	0.5	0.5	0.4	0.3	0.3	0.4	0.4
Gas	3.4	3.1	3.1	2.9	3.1	2.8	2.7	2.7	2.7	2.8	2.6	2.4	2.3
Hydro (natural flow)	0.1	0.1	0.1	0.1	0.1	0.1	0.1	0.1	0.1	0.1	0.1	0.1	0.1
Wind, wave and solar photovoltaics	0.1	0.2	0.3	0.4	0.1	0.2	0.2	0.2	0.3	0.3	0.6	0.8	1.1
Other renewables	2.0	2.2	2.5	2.7	2.8	2.7	3.1	3.3	3.3	3.2	2.8	3.1	3.6
Other fuels [5]	1.5	1.4	1.9	1.6	1.3	1.1	1.0	0.8	1.0	1.1	1.4	1.6	1.7
All generating companies: total fuels	86.2	85.2	87.4	87.7	84.7	82.5	78.7	79.6	77.1	78.3	75.8	70.2	68.1
Coal [3]	32.5	31.3	32.6	35.9	32.9	30.0	24.7	25.6	26.0	34.3	31.3	24.0	18.3
Oil [4, 6]	1.2	1.1	1.3	1.4	1.2	1.6	1.5	1.2	0.8	0.7	0.6	0.6	0.6
Gas	27.9	29.3	28.5	26.8	30.6	32.4	30.9	32.4	26.6	18.6	17.7	18.7	18.3
Nuclear	20.0	18.2	18.4	17.1	14.0	11.9	15.2	13.9	15.6	15.2	15.4	13.9	15.5
Hydro (natural flow)	0.3	0.4	0.4	0.4	0.4	0.4	0.4	0.3	0.5	0.5	0.4	0.5	0.5
Wind, wave and solar photovoltaics	0.1	0.2	0.3	0.4	0.5	0.6	0.8	0.9	1.4	1.8	2.6	3.1	4.1
Other renewables	2.4	2.8	3.4	3.5	3.4	3.5	3.9	4.3	4.6	5.0	5.0	6.1	7.2
Other fuels [7]	1.5	1.4	1.9	1.6	1.3	1.1	1.0	0.8	1.0	1.1	1.4	1.6	1.7
Net imports	0.2	0.6	0.7	0.6	0.4	0.9	0.2	0.2	0.5	1.0	1.2	1.8	1.8

Source: Department for Business, Energy & Industrial Strategy

Data source
DUKES 5.3 - Fuel used in generation

(1) Includes orimulsion, oil used in gas turbine and diesel plant, and oil used for lighting up coal fired boilers.
(2) Includes colliery methane
(3) Includes coke oven coke.
(4) Includes refinery gas.
(5) Main fuels included are coke oven gas, blast furnace gas, and waste products from chemical processes.
(6) Includes orimulsion, oil used in gas turbine and diesel plant, and oil used for lighting up coal fired boilers.
(7) Includes gas turbines and oil engines and plants producing electricity from renewable sources other than hydro.

18.11 Indigenous petroleum production, refinery receipts, imports and exports of oil

Thousand tonnes

	2001	2002	2003	2004	2005	2006	2007	2008	2009	2010	2011	2012	2013	2014	2015
Total indigenous petroleum production	116,678	115,944	106,073	95,374	84,721	76,578	76,575	71,789	68,199	62,962	51,972	44,561	41,101r	40,328r	45,698r
Crude petroleum:															
Refinery receipts total	83,343	84,784	84,585	89,821	86,134	83,213	81,477	81,034	75,551	73,543	75,080	71,839	65,972r	61,063r	61,391r
Foreign trade															
Imports	53,551	56,968	54,177	62,517	58,885	59,443	57,357	60,335	55,002r	55,064	58,092	60,476	58,967r	53,638r	50,604
Exports	86,930	87,144	74,898	64,504	54,099	50,195	50,999	48,235	45,351	42 064	33,625	30,946	33,105	30,869r	33,709
Net imports	-33,378	-30,176	-20,720	-1,987	4,786	9,249	6,357	12,100	9,651	13,000	24,467	29,530	25,862r	22,769	16,895
Petroleum products															
Foreign trade															
Imports	17,234	14,900	16,472	18,545	22,481	26,836	25,110	23,741	22,172	23,665	22,656	26,207	28,418r	29,384r	32,133
Exports	19,088	23,444	23,323	30,495	29,722	28,945	29,983	28,803	25,491	26,065	27,800	29,904	26,910	22,748	22,926
Net imports	-1,854	-8,544	-6,851	-11,950	-7,241	-2,109	-4,874	-5,062	-3,319	-2,400	-5,145	-3,697	1,508	6,636	9,207
International marine bunkers	2,274	1,913	1,764	2,085	2,055	2,348	2,371	3,472	3,306	2,807	3,130	2,663	2,720	2,824	2,509

Source: Department for Business, Energy & Industrial Strategy

18.12 Throughput of crude and process oils and output of refined products from refineries

United Kingdom   Thousand tonnes

	2002	2003	2004	2005	2006	2007	2008	2009	2010	2011	2012	2013	2014	2015
Throughput of crude and process oils	84356	84814	89710	86069	83130	81509	81241	75754	73,543	75,080	71,839	65,972	61,063	61,391
less: Refinery fuel:	5677	5456	5417	5601	4879	4676	4706	4304	4,378	4,585	4,299	3,759	3,198	3,344r
Losses	788	56	-7	371	374	293	470	777	566	373	209	575	671	462r
Total output of refined products	77891	79302	84301	80097	77877	76541	76065	70674	68599	70122	67331	61638	57194	57585
Gases:														
Butane and propane	2149	2300	2170	2222	2142	2298	2250	2113	2247	2598	2512	2326	2127r	2207
Other petroleum	537	715	520	427	661	517	369	449	518	434	285	352r	348r	402
Naphtha and other feedstock	3153	3503	3168	3019	2734	2561	2660	2507	2440	2526	2328	2013	2290	2368
Aviation spirit	28	26	31	32	25	0	0	0	0	0	0	0	0	0
Motor spirit	22944	22627	24589	22604	21443	21313	19,521	19,184	19,074	18,823	18,650	17,691	15,709	16,894
Industrial and white spirit	121	104	100	136	107	70	55	61	66	65	72	106	165	151
Kerosene:														
Aviation turbine fuel	5365	5277	5615	5167	6261	6176	6549	6022	5781	6411	5775	4527	4635	4973
Burning oil	3506	3521	3613	3325	3374	2968	3092	2830	2570	2377	2268	2705	2093	2031
DERV				19056	15821	16138	16350	15908	15332	16801	15772	14831	13,726	13,483
Gas/diesel oil	28343	27380	28646	9430	10215	10165	10566	9487	9505	8683	8941	8193	8,049	7,204
Fuel oil	8507	9495	11308	10155	11280	10433	10483	8043	7004	7432	7158	6230	5269r	4818
Lubricating oil	509	576	1136	936	617	547	514	530	412	430	457	387	373	350
Bitumen	1918	1925	2196	1912	1749	1628	1485	1338	1276	1476	1222	777	1,006	990
Petroleum coke	441	612	633	660	606	676	781	847	817	654	640r	528	605r	610
Other products	818	1030	702	1103	964	1058	1182	1204	1557	1412	1252	1029r	798r	1104

Source: Department for Business, Energy & Industrial Energy

Data source
DUKES 3.5 - Supply and disposal of petroleum

DUKES 3.2-3.4 - Petroleum product

18.13 Deliveries of pertoleum products for inland consumption
United Kingdom

	2002	2003	2004	2005	2006	2007	2008	2009	2010	2011	2012	2013	2014	2015
Total (including refinery fuel)	76233	77154	79066	80736	79812	77424	75160	71252	70,673	68,829	67,347	66,156	66,051r	68,097
Total (excluding refinery fuel)	70557	71697	73649	75135	74933	72748	70455	66948	66,295	64,244	63,048	62,397	62,852	64,753
Butane and propane	2553	3017	3115	3310	3123	2823	3315	3223	3026	3065	2475	2290r	2358r	2,819
Other Petroleum Gases (includes Ethane)	1953	1885	1737	1838	1714	1563	1459	1344	1199	1003	899	884r	944r	1030
Naphtha	1592	2332	2029	1916	2278	1608	741r	988	1037	1061	1094	1012	986r	1195
Aviation spirit	50	46	49	52	46	33	30	22	21	21	17	16	18	11
Motor spirit														
Retail deliveries														
Lead Replacement Petrol/Super premium unleaded	1107	1044	884	851	737	787	757	745	647	560	446	-	-	-
Premium unleaded	19167	18291	17795	17221	16615	16322	15250	14300	13435	12870	12357	-	-	-
Total retail deliveries	20274	19335	18679	18071	17351	17109	16007	15045	14082	13430	12803	-	-	-
Commercial consumers														
Lead Replacement Petrol/Super premium unleaded (6)	36	41	40	22	21	16	12	12	11	11	2	-	-	-
Premium unleaded	499	542	765	759	719	624	523	555	509	454	426	-	-	-
Total commercial consumers	535	583	805	781	739	641	535	567	520	465	428	-	-	-
Total motor spirit	20808	19918	19484	18852	18091	17615	16542	15613	14602	13895	13231	12570	12326	12082
Industrial and white spirits	157	147	281	284	156	167	145	174	224	143	219	279	126	160
Kerosene														
Aviation turbine fuel	10519	10765	11637	12497	12641	12574	12142	11533	11116	11574	11221	11240	11220	11332
Burning oil	3578	3569	3950	3870	4017	3629	3681	3732	4012	3288	3329	3510	3187	3192
Gas/diesel oil														
DERV fuel														
Retail deliveries	8153	9057	9517	10532	11501	12685	12777	12669	13157	13549	13965	-	-	-
Commercial consumers	8774	8655	8997	8845	8660	8730	7724	7443	7583	7442	7573	-	-	-
Total DERV fuel	16926	17712	18514	19377	20161	21038	20501	20112	20740	20991	21538	21930	22675	23656
Other gas/diesel oil (includes MDF)	6099	6326	6023	6719	6525	6116	5632	5034	5059	4721	5148	4730	4837	5149
Fuel oil	3767	3562	3743	3780	3248	3228	2660	2113	1892	1415	1052	820	695	838
Lubricating oils	829	868	914	750	713	672	510	510	580	491	412	437	436	411
Bitumen	2002	1959	1991	1906	1610	1563	1741	1381	1370	1621	1,355	1,358	1,410	1,464
Petroleum coke	893	880	1146	1042	925	366	281	207	301	262	154	101	149	138
Miscellaneous products	647	506	526	556	437	338	590	573	671	592	542	358	526	505

Source: Department for Business, Energy & Industrial Strategy

- Data no longer available

Datasource
Supply and demand of petroleum (DUKES Table 3.5)
Additional information on inland deliveries of selected products (DUKES 3.6)
Additional information on inland deliveries for non-energy uses (DUKES 3.8)
Inland deliveries of petroleum (DUKES 3.1.2)
Commodity (DUKES 3.2-3.4)

18.14 Iron and steel:[1] summary of steel supplies, deliveries and stocks

United Kingdom

		2010	2011	2012	2013	2014	2015
Supply, disposal and consumption -(Finished product weight -Thousand tonnes)							
UK producers' home deliveries	**KLTA**	4685	4604	4256	4166	4194	4253
Imports excluding steelworks receipts	**KLTB**	5168	5613	5554	5420	6445	6199
Total deliveries to home market (a)	**KLTC**	9853	10217	9810	9586	10639	10452
Total exports (producers, consumers, merchants)	**KLTD**	5830	5779	6185	8162	8254	7012
Exports by UK producers	**KLTE**	4767	4614	4950	7041	7643	6189
Derived consumers' and merchants' exports (b)	**KLTF**	1063	1165	1235	1121	611	823
Net home disposals (a)-(b)	**KLTG**	8790	9052	8575	8465	10028	9629
Estimated home consumption	**KLTI**	8790	9052	8575	8465	10028	9629
Stocks -(Finished product weight - Thousand tonnes)							
Producers							
-ingots & semis	**KLTJ**	552	470	564	507	427	433
-finished steel	**KLTK**	704	632	632	705	653	641
Estimated home consumption -(Crude steel equivalent -Million tonnes)							
Crude steel production2	**KLTN**	9.71	9.48	9.58	11.86	12.03	10.91
Producers' stock change	**KLTO**	-0.18	-0.20	0.14	0.01	-0.13	-0.01
Re-usable material	**KLTP**	0.00	0.00	0.00	0.00	0.00	0.00
Total supply from home sources	**KLTQ**	9.89	9.68	9.44	11.85	12.16	10.92
Total imports3	**KLTR**	6.86	8.03	7.83	6.95	8.14	7.88
Total exports3	**KLTS**	6.67	6.66	7.02	9.11	9.27	7.94
Net home disposals	**KLTT**	10.08	11.05	10.25	9.69	11.03	10.86
Estimated home consumption	**KLTV**	10.08	11.05	10.25	9.69	11.03	10.86

The figures relate to periods of 52 weeks.　　　　Source: International Steel Statistics Bureau (ISSB)
2 Includes liquid steel for castings only up to 2003.

18.15 Iron and steel:[1] iron ore, manganese ore, pig iron and iron and steel scrap
United Kingdom

Thousand tonnes

		2010	2011	2012	2013	2014	2015
Iron ore consumption	**KLOF**	10572	9735	10511	14034	14353	12975
Manganese ore consumption	**KLOG**	0	0	0	3	0	0
Pig iron (and blast furnace ferro-alloys)							
Average number of furnaces in blast during period	**KLOH**	5	5	5	4	4	5
Production							
Steelmaking iron	**KLOI**	7233	6625	7183	9471	9705	8774
In blast furnaces: total	**KLOL**	7233	6625	7183	9471	9705	8774
In steel works	**KLOM**	7233	6625	7183	9471	9705	8774
Consumption of pig iron: total	**KLOO**	7233	6625	7183	9471	9705	8774
Iron and steel scrap							
Steelworks and steel foundries							
Circulating scrap	**KLOQ**	1256	1317	1413	1689	1756	1626
Purchased receipts	**KLOR**	2507	2517	2384	2456	2379	1997
Consumption	**KLOS**	3713	3890	3675	4085	4145	3700
Stocks (end of period)	**KLOT**	179	123	245	306	296	219

1 The figures relate to periods of 52 weeks.
2 Consumption.

Source: International Steel Statistics Bureau (ISSB)

18.16 Iron and steel:[1] furnaces and production of steel

United Kingdom   Number and thousand tonnes

		2010	2011	2012	2013	2014	2015
Steel furnaces (numbers[2])	**KLPA**						
Oxygen converters	**KLPC**						
Electric	**KLPD**						
Production of crude steel	**KLPF**	9708	9478	9579	11858	12034	10907
by process							
Oxygen converters	**KLPH**	7323	6946	7525	9915	10079	9051
Electric	**KLPI**	2385	2532	2054	1943	1955	1856
by cast method							
Cast to ingot	**KLPK**	153	205	189	158	171	151
Continuously cast	**KLPL**	9555	9273	9390	11699	11863	10756
Steel for castings	**KLPM**						
by quality							
Non alloy steel	**KLPN**	9201	8835	8992	11303	11418	10405
Stainless and other alloy steel	**KLPO**	508	643	587	555	616	502

Production of finished steel products (All qualities)[3]

		2010	2011	2012	2013	2014	2015
Rods and bars for reinforcement (in coil and lengths)	**KLPP**	792	637	606	578	553	674
Wire rods and other rods and bars in coil	**KLPQ**	874	787	728	738	726	701
Hot rolled bars in lengths	**KLPR**	887	1002	849	809	845	742
Bright steel bars[4]	**KLPS**	239	225	102	154	175	155
Light sections other than rails	**KLPT**	129	117	112	125	128	145
Heavy sections	**KGQZ**	1069	978	883	927	1006	1171
Hot rolled plates, sheets and strip in coil and lengths	**KLPW**	4733	4575	3962	4944	4975	4617
Cold rolled plates and sheets in coil and lengths	**KLPX**	2200	2215	1939	2419	2437	2282
Cold rolled strip[4]	**KLPZ**	81	73	39	45	39	33
Tinplate	**KLQW**	468	411	411	401	430	407
Other coated sheet	**KLQX**	1278	1262	1161	1373	1383	1380
Tubes and pipes[4]	**KLQY**	991	842	515	702	666	645
Forged bars[4]	**KLQZ**	0	0	0	0	16	11

1 The figures relate to periods of 52 weeks.   Source: International Steel Statistics Bureau (ISSB)
2 Includes steel furnaces at steel foundries, only up to 2003.

18.17 Fertilisers - UK consumption

Years ending 30 June   Thousand tonnes

		2002	2003	2004	2005	2006	2007	2008	2009	2010	2011	2012	2013	2014	2015
Nutrient Content															
Nitrogen (N):	**XXXX**	1197	1131	1125	1061	1003	1008	1001	948	1016	1022	1000	999	1060	1049
Straight	**KGRM**	751	664	662	691	631	656	744	733	771					
Compounds	**KGRN**	446	467	463	370	372	352	292	180	245					
Phosphate (P2O5)	**KGRO**	283	282	278	259	235	224	215	129	184	192	188	194	201	196
Potash (K2O)	**KGRP**	391	375	375	352	325	317	325	208	251	283	259	267	284	272
Compounds - total product	**KGRQ**	2,511	2,558	2,550	2,221	2,134	2,039	1,827	1,116	1,529					

Source: British Survey of Fertiliser Practice (Defra)

Table 18.17 gives the quantity of the fertiliser nutrients nitrogen (N), phosphate (P2O5) and potash (K2O)
used by UK farmers during the fertiliser year, which runs from 1st July to 30th June. The year shown in the
table is the year in which the harvest takes place, at the end of each fertiliser year.

18.18a United Kingdom production of minerals 2008–2014

Thousand tonnes

Mineral	2008	2009	2010	2011	2012	2013	2014
Coal:							
Deep-mined	8,096	7,520	7,390	7,312	6,153	4,089	3,685
Opencast	9,509	9,854	10,426	10,580	10,134	8,584	7,962
Other (a)	449	500	540	660	680	95	—
Natural gas and oil:							
Methane (oil equivalent)							
Colliery	63	62	71	58	52	52	48
Onshore	92	89	88	27	15	10	38
Offshore	69,525	59,581	57,036	45,204	38,850	36,460	36,479
Crude oil							
Onshore	1,248	1,181	941	678	870	1,003	1,014
Offshore	64,249	61,639	57,106	47,893	41,182	37,453	36,460
Condensates and other (c)							
Onshore	33	32	17	0	13	20	19
Offshore	6,135	5,346	4,898	3,401	2,495	2,170	2,435
Iron ore	0.1	—	—	—	—	—	—
Non-ferrous ores (metal content):							
Tin	—	—	—	—	—	—	—
Lead (h)	0.3	0.4	0.4	0.3	0.1	0.1	0.1
Gold (kg)	163	187	177	202	102	42	0
Silver (kg)	398	514	506	531	230	82	0
Chalk (e)	5,874	4,047	3,626	3,996	3,473	3,528	3,312
Clay and shale (e)	8,459	5,310	5,934	6,154	5,497	6,464	6,806
Igneous rock (j) (k)	53,490	44,618	44,876	(l) 44 400	(l) 40 200	(l) 40 500	(l) 43 700
Limestone (excluding dolomite)	74,145	60,111	56,985	(l) 58 100	(l) 54 800	(l) 56 900	(l) 66 300
Dolomite (excluding limestone)	5,509	3,164	4,540	4,490	4,896	3,432	3,730
Sand and gravel:							
Land	66,640	50,973	47,167	(l) 45 800	(l) 41 800	(l) 43 400	(l) 46 800
Marine (i)	18,833	15,253	14,533	17,287	14,840	14,577	14,327
Sandstone	12,255	12,335	11,556	(l) 12 300	(l) 11 500	(l) 11 500	(l) 12 500
Slate (g)	1,058	683	695	763	701	885	868
Ball clay (sales)	1,020	727	(h) 900	(h) 930	(h) 748	(h) 740	(h) 733
Barytes	43	36	34	31	30	30	44
Chert and flint	1	1	…	…	…	…	…
China clay (sales) (d)	1,355	1,060	(h) 1 140	(h) 1 290	(h) 1 150	(h) 1 110	(h) 1 090
China stone	0.5	—	—	—	—	—	—
Fireclay (e)	180	129	110	162	96	105	129
Fluorspar (h)	37	19	26	—	—	16	24
Gypsum (natural) (h)	1,200	1,200	1,200	1,200	1,200	1,200	1,200
Lignite	…	…	…	…	…	…	…
Peat (000 m^3)	760	887	1,004	825	568	1,254	795
Potash (b)	673	(h) 700	(h) 700	(h) 770	(h) 900	(h) 900	(h) 1 000
Salt	5,565	6,166	6,666	6,060	6,460	6,930	4,690
Silica sand	4,777	3,755	4,070	3,969	3,888	3,961	3,948
Talc	2	3	3	4	4	3	5

(a) Slurry etc. recovered from dumps, ponds, rivers etc.
(b) Marketable product (KCl).
(c) Including ethane, propane and butane, in addition to condensates.
(d) Dry weight.
(e) Excluding a small production in Northern Ireland.
(f) BGS estimates based on data from producing companies.
(g) Slate figures include waste used for constructional fill and powder and granules used in industry.
(h) BGS estimate.
(i) Including marine-dredged landings at foreign ports (exports).
(j) Excluding a small production of granite in Northern Ireland.

(k) In addition, the following amounts of igneous rock were produced in Guernsey (thousand tonnes):2007: 160; 2008: 139; 2009: 120; 2010: 116; 2011: 156; 2012: 169; 2014: 117 and Jersey: 2007: 295; 2008: 325; 2009: 249; 2010: 238; 2011: 220; 2012: 239 ; 2013: 176 2013: 149.
(l) Contains an estimate related to Northern Ireland production.

Sources: Office for National Statistics, Department of Business, Innovation and Skills, Dept. of Enterprise, Trade & Investment (Northern Ireland), Crown Estate Commissioners (marine sand and gravel produced for export), and company data.

18.18b Minerals produced in Northern Ireland, the Isle of Man, Guernsey and Jersey 2010-2014

Thousand tonnes

		2010	2011	2012	2013	2014
Northern Ireland						
Gold (kg)		177	202	102	42	0
Silver (kg)		506	531	230	82	0
Lead (tonnes)		251	280	61	36	0
Limestone		3,689	...	...	...	...
Sand and gravel		2,178	...	...	...	...
Basalt and igneous rock (a)		5,438	...	...	...	...
Sandstone		2,768	...	...	...	...
Granite		...	...	...	...	...
Clay and shale		...	...	...	...	...
Others (b)		2,087	...	...	...	...
	Total	16,160	...	...	...	...
Isle of Man						
Limestone		71	82	72	56	53
Sand and gravel		145	141	101	96	97
Igneous rock		109	96	94	110	98
Slate		28	29	23	17	26
	Total	353	347	290	279	274
Guernsey						
Igneous rock		116	156	169	149	117
Jersey						
Igneous rock (c)		238	220	239	176	...
Sand and gravel		57	74	46	44	48

(a) Excluding granite.
(b) Including rock salt, chalk, dolomite, fireclay and granite.
(c) BGS estimates.

Sources: Department of Enterprise, Trade & Investment (Northern Ireland), Department of Economic Development (Isle of Man), Company data (Guernsey and Jersey).

18.19a Building materials and components

Bricks - Production, Deliveries and Stocks

Great Britain

Millions of Bricks

Brick Type		Seasonally Adjusted Deliveries	All Types			Commons			Facings			Engineerings		
		All Types	Production	Deliveries (from)	Stocks*	Production	Deliveries (from)	Stocks*	Production	Deliveries (from)	Stocks*	Production	Deliveries (from)	Stocks*
2011		1,646	1554	1646	610	172	185	82	1230	1304	494	152	157	34
2012		1,551	1459	1551	515	137	166	52	1172	1239	425	150	146	38
2013		1,736	1555	1736	339	151	169	35	1244	1384	288	160	183	16
2014		1,812	1824	1812	349	169	173	29	1489	1470	306	167	169	15
2015		1,694 p	1804	1809	544	167	166	33	1466	1492	446	171	151	66
	Q4	461	442	419	349	40	37	29	363	343	306	38	39	15
2015	Q1	433	464	403	415	42	35	36	372	329	354	50	39	25
	Q2	439	511	475	452	41	45	33	419	383	391	51	47	28
	Q3	424	510	462	502	41	44	31	412	374	430	57	44	41
	Q4	399 p	430	364	561	38	36	33	347	300	477	45	35	51
2016	Q1	426 p	489	391	624	43	37	39	362	323	515	49	30	70
	Q2	444 p	496	492	628	44	45	38	404	404	516	47	43	74
	Q3	455 p	476	509	544	44	45	33	395	422	446	37	41	66
2014	November	147	161	138	343	15	12	28	132	113	301	13	13	14
	December	163	120	113	349	10	9	29	98	94	306	11	10	15
2015	January	145	140	117	373	16	10	35	107	96	317	18	11	21
	February	143	151	128	400	14	12	37	122	103	340	16	13	23
	March	144	173	158	415	12	13	36	144	130	354	17	15	25
	April	150	162	158	420	13	14	35	132	126	360	16	17	24
	May	143	175	149	446	12	15	33	146	120	386	17	14	27
	June	146	174	168	452	15	16	33	141	136	391	18	16	28
	July	145	176	169	461	16	17	33	141	135	398	19	17	30
	August	141	163	143	481	11	13	31	132	116	414	19	13	37
	September	138	171	151	502	14	14	31	139	123	430	19	14	41
	October	131	174	141	529	15	15	30	145	119	456	15	14	42
	November	134 p	151	131	549	14	13	32	122	107	471	15	12	45
	December	134 p	105	92	561	9	9	33	80	75	477	15	9	51
2016	January	140 p	130	109	582	14	10	36	100	91	487	16	8	59
	February	142 p	157	132	607	15	13	38	124	108	502	18	10	67
	March	144 p	167	150	624	15	14	39	137	124	515	15	12	70
	April	148 p	166	163	626	16	15	39	132	133	514	18	14	73
	May	148 p	167	158	635	13	14	38	138	131	521	16	13	76
	June	149 p	163	170	628	16	16	38	134	139	516	13	15	74
	July	147 p	146	159	615	15	15	38	117	130	504	13	14	74
	August	156 p	129	167	577	12	15	35	107	138	474	9	14	69
	September	152 p	154	164	568	14	14	34	129	136	466	12	13	68
	October	163 p	164	170	562	16	16	33	137	140	462	12	13	67
	November	172 p	157	175	544	14	15	33	129	146	446	13	14	66

* Refers to stocks at end of period

In the March 2015 edition of these tables, entries for clay, sand-lime and concrete bricks were removed. This is because data for these categories of bricks have been confidential since 2009. We will continue to monitor these material types and will reinstate them if they become publishable at a later date.

From March 2015, seasonally adjusted figures for deliveries of bricks have been included in this table. In the production of these figures, brick deliveries data back to January 1983 have been seasonally adjusted. This long run data series is available on request.

Source: Department for Business, Energy & Industrial Strategy

18.19b Building and components
Concrete Blocks - Production, Deliveries and Stocks

Great Britain | Thousand square metres

	All Types	All Types			Dense			Lightweight			Aerated		
	Seasonally Adjusted Deliveries	Production	Deliveries (from)	Stocks*	Production	Deliveries (from)	Stocks*	Production	Deliveries (from)	Stocks*	Production	Deliveries (from)	Stocks*
2005	89,551	89,997	89,551	9,680	36,188	36,473	3,465	25,561	25,673	2,173	28,248	27,405	4,042
2006	87,015	87,510	87,015	:	34,956	34,741	:	25,345	25,222	:	27,209	27,051	:
2007	88,746	89,951	88,746	:	36,686	35,396	:	25,965	25,667	:	27,300	27,682	:
2008	67,136	67,743	67,136	8,920	29,675	29,889	3,498	18,168	18,363	2,149	19,900	18,884	3,273
2009	50,639	50,394	50,639	8,320	22,607	22,748	3,291	13,421	13,989	1,522	14,367	13,903	3,507
2010	51,758	53,629	51,758	10,152	22,393	21,731	3,833	14,415	13,923	2,044	16,822	16,104	4,276
2011	52,901	54,583	52,901	10,810	22,940	22,101	4,486	15,153	14,821	1,728	16,490	15,978	4,596
2012	52,021	51,693	52,021	10,700	21,551	22,323	3,808	14,383	14,103	2,024	15,759	15,595	4,868
2013	57,995	56,031	57,995	4,171	23,599	24,340	1,894	17,055	17,508	1,208	15,377	16,147	1,069
2014	56,953	57,943	56,953	5,413	25,088	24,943	2,147	17,499	17,447	1,402	15,356	14,563	1,864
2015	64,585 p	64,718	64,920	6,282	25,828	25,474	2,393	19,036	18,727	1,712	19,853	20,719	2,177
2011 Q3	12,922	14,208	14,076	12,352	6,217	5,931	4,862	3,908	3,970	2,218	4,083	4,175	5,272
Q4	13,566	11,632	12,120	10,810	4,864	5,021	4,486	3,321	3,359	1,728	3,447	3,739	4,596
2012 Q1	12,999	13,323	12,642	11,493	5,374	5,426	4,456	3,559	3,314	1,964	4,389	3,903	5,074
Q2	12,523	13,268	13,235	11,595	5,535	5,824	4,209	3,487	3,437	2,006	4,245	3,973	5,380
Q3	12,863	12,584	13,795	10,471	5,360	5,773	3,773	3,756	3,887	1,904	3,467	4,135	4,794
Q4	13,635	12,519	12,349	10,700	5,281	5,300	3,808	3,580	3,465	2,024	3,658	3,584	4,868
2013 Q1	13,702	12,125	12,713	10,165	5,212	5,430	3,643	3,094	3,389	1,730	3,818	3,893	4,793
Q2	15,082	14,960	16,188	4,401	6,351	6,655	2,190	4,691	4,809	1,303	3,918	4,723	908
Q3	14,703	15,333	16,042	3,683	6,345	6,609	1,875	5,079	5,162	1,210	3,909	4,271	597
Q4	14,508	13,614	13,052	4,171	5,691	5,646	1,894	4,191	4,147	1,208	3,732	3,259	1,069
2014 Q1	13,533	14,021	12,907	5,311	5,918	5,595	2,236	4,164	4,058	1,320	3,939	3,254	1,755
Q2	14,365	14,867	15,095	5,228	6,257	6,627	1,867	4,503	4,710	1,256	4,107	3,758	2,104
Q3	14,554	15,399	16,038	4,610	7,012	7,112	1,784	4,854	4,794	1,322	3,533	4,133	1,504
Q4	14,500	13,656	12,913	5,413	5,902	5,610	2,147	3,977	3,885	1,402	3,777	3,418	1,864
2015 Q1	15,458	15,878	14,520	6,648	6,693	6,285	2,542	4,517	4,334	1,624	4,668	3,902	2,483
Q2	15,474	15,512	16,562	5,433	6,490	6,648	2,243	5,343	5,486	1,456	3,679	4,428	1,734
Q3	16,956	17,197	18,615	5,419	6,789	6,816	2,286	4,894	4,859	1,499	5,514	6,940	1,635
Q4	16,697 p	16,130	15,223	6,282	5,857	5,726	2,393	4,282	4,047	1,712	5,991	5,449	2,177
2016 Q1	16,847 p	15,124	15,545	5,974	5,734	5,782	2,409	4,434	4,332	1,864	4,956	5,431	1,702
Q2	17,626 p	18,648	19,273	5,280	6,864	7,126	2,146	5,164	5,594	1,364	6,620	6,552	1,770
Q3	17,098 p	18,750 r	18,713 r	5,330 r	7,461 r	7,463 r	2,151 r	5,539 r	5,569 r	1,341 r	5,749	5,681	1,838
2014 November	4,762	4,740	4,239	:	1,993	1,823	:	1,392	1,316	:	1,354	1,101	:
December	5,260	3,876	3,761	5,413	1,731	1,620	2,147	1,045	1,015	1,402	1,100	1,126	1,864
2015 January	5,153	4,841	4,213	7,099	1,721	1,592	2,217	1,296	1,190	1,519	1,824	1,431	3,363
February	4,993	5,221	4,571	6,566	2,370	2,151	2,504	1,500	1,382	1,638	1,351	1,038	2,423
March	5,312	5,816	5,737	6,648	2,602	2,541	2,542	1,721	1,762	1,624	1,493	1,434	2,483
April	5,162	4,987	5,552	6,401	2,200	2,267	2,469	1,780	1,945	1,783	1,007	1,340	2,149
May	5,149	5,095	5,284	6,190	2,049	2,074	2,427	1,887	1,794	1,871	1,158	1,415	1,892
June	5,163	5,430	5,726	5,433	2,240	2,307	2,243	1,676	1,747	1,456	1,514	1,672	1,734
July	5,560	5,896	6,474	6,204	2,349	2,364	2,240	1,918	1,782	1,603	1,628	2,328	2,361
August	5,826	5,112	5,945	5,350	2,130	2,225	2,148	1,432	1,463	1,549	1,551	2,257	1,654
September	5,571	6,189	6,196	5,419	2,310	2,227	2,286	1,544	1,614	1,499	2,335	2,355	1,635
October	5,818	6,393	6,252	5,473	2,403	2,358	2,261	1,653	1,627	1,508	2,337	2,268	1,704
November	5,524 p	5,876	5,106	6,300	2,166	2,007	2,476	1,464	1,448	1,525	2,247	1,651	2,299
December	5,355 p	3,860	3,864	6,282	1,288	1,361	2,393	1,164	973	1,712	1,408	1,530	2,177
2016 January	6,185 p	4,414	4,904	5,791	1,691	1,638	2,446	1,272	1,279	1,705	1,451	1,987	1,641
February	5,809 p	5,209	5,512	5,552	1,899	1,989	2,388	1,575	1,505	1,806	1,735	2,018	1,358
March	4,854 p	5,501	5,130	5,974	2,143	2,155	2,409	1,588	1,548	1,864	1,770	1,426	1,702
April	5,875 p	5,942	6,483	5,364	2,107	2,313	2,203	1,765	1,739	1,820	2,070	2,431	1,341
May	5,772 p	5,943	6,107	5,199	2,256	2,291	2,168	1,636	1,832	1,624	2,051	1,985	1,407
June	5,980 p	6,762	6,682	5,280	2,500	2,522	2,146	1,764	2,023	1,364	2,498	2,136	1,770
July	5,560 p	5,829	6,066	5,042	2,331	2,423	2,055	1,843	1,830	1,377	1,654	1,814	1,610
August	5,715 p	6,044	6,220	4,866	2,600	2,484	2,171	1,760	1,870	1,268	1,684	1,867	1,427
September	5,823 p	6,878	6,427	5,330	2,531	2,557	2,151	1,936	1,870	1,341	2,411	2,001	1,838
October	6,113 p	6,456 r	6,313 r	5,327 r	2,499 r	2,485 r	2,025 r	1,901 r	1,927 r	1,312 r	2,055 r	1,902 r	1,991 r
November	6,773 p	6,824	6,473	5,678	2,610	2,480	2,155	2,034	2,046	1,299	2,180	1,947	2,225

Source: Department for Business, Energy & Industrial Strategy

* Refers to stocks at end of period

From March 2015, seasonally adjusted figures for deliveries of concrete blocks have been included in this table. In the production of these figures, blocks deliveries data back to January 1983 have been seasonally adjusted. This long run data series is available on request.

Data from December 2011 to June 2012 has been revised following receipt of corrected data. The period August 2007 to November 2011 may also be affected, but non-availability of a back-series of corrected data means that this period cannot be revised, and should be treated with caution. Full details are available in the 'Summary of revision to monthly statistics of building materials and components publication' document on our website.

18.19c Building materials and components
Concrete Roofing Tiles and Ready-Mixed Concrete

		Great Britain			United Kingdom	United Kingdom
						Seasonally Adjusted
		Concrete Roofing Tiles (Th.sq.m. of roof area covered)			**Ready-Mixed Concrete #** (Th.cu.m.)	**Ready-Mixed Concrete** (Th.cu.m.)
		Production	Deliveries	Stocks *	Deliveries	Deliveries
2005		25,719	24,489	4,902	22,432	22,432
2006		23,730	24,118	4,426	23,029	23,029
2007		23,551	23,812	3,646	23,548	23,548
2008		20,084	19,926	3,899	20,051	20,051
2009		14,079	15,612	2,344	14,069	14,069
2010		17,817	17,146	3,023	14,038	14,038
2011		17,712	17,684	3,126	15,121	15,121
2012		17,476	17,578	3,061	13,758	13,758
2013		18,745	19,580	2,214	15,089	15,089
2014		24,086	23,058	3,275	15,348	15,348
2015		25,105	24,475	3,904	16,294	16,339 p
2007	Q3	5,129	6,541	3,929	6,205	5,942
	Q4	6,028	5,914	3,646	5,686	5,930
2008	Q1	5,708	5,421	3,922	5,193	5,711
	Q2	5,815	5,679	4,488	5,773	5,274
	Q3	4,657	4,977	3,840	4,902	4,697
	Q4	3,903	3,849	3,899	4,183	4,369
2009	Q1	3,664	3,281	4,273	3,583	3,716
	Q2	3,055	3,936	3,391	3,637	3,509
	Q3	3,580	4,447	2,522	3,628	3,476
	Q4	3,779	3,949	2,344	3,221	3,368
2010	Q1	4,129	3,505	2,967	3,328	3,444
	Q2	4,961	4,922	3,008	3,819	3,709
	Q3	4,783	4,824	2,967	3,831	3,678
	Q4	3,945	3,894	3,023	3,060	3,206
2011	Q1	4,820	4,079	3,858	3,827	3,947
	Q2	4,565	4,398	4,022	3,907	3,798
	Q3	4,210	4,901	3,316	3,908	3,739
	Q4	4,116	4,306	3,126	3,479	3,636
2012	Q1	4,673	3,928	3,872	3,463	3,554
	Q2	4,236	4,100	4,008	3,399	3,310
	Q3	4,095	5,004	3,136	3,556	3,396
	Q4	4,471	4,547	3,061	3,340	3,498
2013	Q1	4,514	4,055	3,520	3,325	3,602
	Q2	4,209	4,598	3,131	4,108	3,815
	Q3	4,550	5,468	2,214	3,972	3,802
	Q4	5,471	5,459	2,214	3,684	3,870
2014	Q1	6,151	5,414	2,932	3,475	3,570
	Q2	6,195	5,491	3,687	3,977	3,895
	Q3	5,815	6,238	3,261	4,183	3,993
	Q4	5,925	5,915	3,275	3,713	3,891
2015	Q1	6,547	5,400	4,422	4,035	4,136
	Q2	6,296	5,843	4,875	3,992	3,936
	Q3	5,697	6,420	4,152	4,225	4,036 p
	Q4	6,565	6,812	3,904	4,042	4,231 p
2016	Q1	6,323	5,837	4,391	4,159	4,341 p
	Q2	6,082	6,292	4,185	4,251	4,069 p
	Q3	5,857	6,912	3,129	4,390	4,194 p

Source: Department for Business, Energy and Industrial Strategy

* Refers to stocks at the end of the period.

In April 2012, the Mineral Products Association (who provide these figures), estimated that data understates UK deliveries by around 20-25%. Previously, they had estimated that figures understate UK deliveries by 14-18%.

Concrete roofing tiles data have included imputation for non-responders in each quarter since 2012Q1.

From March 2015, seasonally adjusted figures for deliveries of ready-mixed concrete have been included in this table. In the production of these figures, ready-mixed concrete deliveries data back to Q1 1983 have been seasonally adjusted. This long run data series is available on request.

18.19d Builfing materials and components
Slate - Production, Deliveries and Stocks

Great Britain   Tonnes

	Production			Deliveries			Stocks [1]			Deliveries
	Roofing [2]	Cladding, decorative & crude blocks	Powder & Granules	Roofing [2]	Cladding, decorative & crude blocks	Powder & Granules	Roofing [2]	Cladding, decorative & crude blocks	Powder & Granules	Fill & Other Uses
2004	c	c	c	c	c	c	c	c	c	c
2005	c	c	c	c	c	c	2,824	10,281	5,347	c
2006	c	61,612	22,967	c	64,037	22,719	c	6,454	4,274	860,395
2007	c	65,260	19,141	c	62,646	19,431	2,563	2,521	3,746	c
2008	c	59,644	16,915	c	58,129	18,402	c	2,749	2,253	c
2009	c	33,759	9,150	22,555	34,322	10,637	2,420	2,186	766	615,346
2010	c	28,001	c	c	27,355	c	c	3,063	c	582,111
2011	c	30,665	c	c	30,437	c	c	3,245	c	662,003
2012	c	29,634	c	c	28,083	c	c	1,351	c	607,127
2013	c	32,419	c	c	31,375	c	c	c	665	692,319
2014	19,358	30,900	15,467	18,596	31,268	15,393	2,925	1,076	0	620,887
2015	c	29,990	c	c	29,996	c	2,130	605	0	534,879
2008 Q3	c	13,811	3,843	c	13,841	5,511	3,851	2,749	1,816	c
Q4	c	11,760	4,052	c	11,760	3,615	c	2,749	2,253	c
2009 Q1	c	7,370	2,128	5,315	7,688	2,724	c	2,431	1,658	148,722
Q2	5,084	9,124	2,046	5,328	9,319	3,385	4,142	2,236	318	169,661
Q3	5,503	8,263	2,046	6,534	8,267	2,163	3,111	2,232	201	154,862
Q4	4,687	9,002	2,930	5,378	9,048	2,365	2,420	2,186	766	142,101
2010 Q1	c	6,772	c	c	6,662	c	c	2,296	c	88,805
Q2	c	7,517	c	c	7,388	c	2,049	3,284	683	175,098
Q3	c	7,335	c	c	7,184	c	1,326	3,332	281	159,574
Q4	4,907	6,377	c	4,909	6,121	c	c	3,063	c	158,634
2011 Q1	4,736	6,516	3,314	4,449	6,504	3,399	c	3,029	c	198,547
Q2	4,677	8,167	3,370	4,630	8,187	3,094	2,012	3,009	472	216,524
Q3	c	9,851	c	c	9,732	c	c	3,128	c	139,359
Q4	c	6,131	c	c	6,014	c	c	3,245	c	107,573
2012 Q1	c	9,247	c	c	8,829	c	c	2,646	c	131,311
Q2	c	8,216	c	c	9,677	c	c	1,154	c	177,748
Q3	c	6,219	c	c	6,167	c	c	1,206	c	146,152
Q4	c	5,952	c	c	3,410	c	c	1,351	c	151,916
2013 Q1	c	6,052	c	c	9,220	c	c	c	802	157,215
Q2	c	9,638	c	c	9,440	c	c	c	736	216,035
Q3	c	10,429	c	c	6,843	c	c	c	537	169,995
Q4	c	6,300	c	c	5,872	c	c	c	665	149,074
2014 Q1	4,670	5,639	4,036	4,337	5,637	4,209	2,721	1,134	492	159,818
Q2	4,693	7,413	3,946	4,299	7,428	3,657	3,085	1,049	781	179,396
Q3	5,141	8,533	3,837	4,996	8,145	4,054	3,034	988	564	152,155
Q4	4,854	9,315	3,648	4,964	10,058	3,473	2,925	1,076	0	129,518
2015 Q1	c	7,488	c	c	7,564	c	c	833	c	156,704
Q2	3,575	8,461	3,421	4,075	8,443	3,692	2,143	583	0	148,002
Q3	4,115	7,209	3,636	3,940	7,177	3,667	2,318	615	0	130,949
Q4	3,519	6,832	3,380	3,713	6,812	2,921	2,130	605	0	99,224
2016 Q1	4,276	6,533	3,341	4,046	6,541	3,618	2,360	587	0	111,123
Q2	3,538	7,062	3,419	3,865	7,120	3,419	2,033	529	0	168,008
Q3 p	3,655	7,996	3,465	3,786	7,836	3,870	1,902	689	0	167,602

Source: Department for Business, Energy & Industrial Strategy

Note : 1) We have improved our sampling panel to include some new sites and have removed some non-pure slate sites. In line with the
Code of Practice we have revised the data for Q2, Q3 and Q4 2010.
2) From Q1 1995, the coverage of 'powder & granules' has been extended to include non-quarry manufacture

[1]   Refers to stocks at the end of the period.

[2]   Consists of all slate tiles which could be used as roofing tiles.

c   Confidential

18.19e Building materials and components

Cement & Clinker - Production and Deliveries

Great Britain   Thousand tonnes

	Cement							Clinker
	Production		Deliveries	Imports *(into GB)*		Cementitious Material		Production
		of which . **Exports**	*(into GB from*	by	by			
		(from GB)	*GB production)*	'Manuf.	Others*	other	total	
2003	11,215	164	11,072	576	646	2,329	14,623	10,146
2004	11,405	141	11,074	609	825	2,443	14,951	10,402
2005	11,216	110	11,004	306	971	2,385	14,666	10,074
2006	11,469	127	11,221	124	1,089	2,648	15,082	10,069
2007	11,887	74	11,638	255	1,121	2,769	15,783	10,227
2008	10,071	61	9,937	283	1,084	2,432	13,660	8,700
2009	7,623	21	7,474	99	1,085	1,680	10,338	6,421
2010	7,883	0	7,767	61	1,153	1,535	10,515	6,598
2011	8,529	0	8,318	86	1,173	1,736	11,312	7,096
2012	7,952	0	7,728	61	1,122	1,605	10,515	6,555
2013	8,203	0	8,204	117	1,322	1,892	11,535	6,712
2014	8,958	3	8,751	227	1,590	1,864	12,433	7,197
2015	9,235	0	9,526	635	1,425	2,382	13,967	7,804

Source: Department for Business, Energy & Industrial Strategy

1. Arrangements for publication of the cementitious data have been revised following discussion and agreement by the Mineral Products Association (MPA) Cement members. Data are now provided on an annual basis. For quarterly and monthly data up to September 2013, please refer to earlier editions of this publication.

2. Where the coverage is for Great Britain, the figures for imports & exports are defined accordingly and have been estimated. Cementitious material covers cement itself, fly ash to EN 450 Part 1 where used as part of the cement in concrete (previously known as pulverised fuel ash (pfa) to BS 3892 Part 1) and ground granulated blast furnace slag (ggbs) to EN 15167 Part 1 (previously BS 6699)

* Estimated

18.19f Building materials and components
Sales of Sand and Gravel in Great Britain

Great Britain   Thousand tonnes

	Seasonally Adjusted Sand & Gravel Total	Sand for Building	Sand for Concreting	Gravel for Concreting & other uses	Sand & Gravel for Coating	Sand, Gravel & Hoggin for Fill	Sand & Gravel Total	of which Marine-Dredged
2006	77,896	9,499	29,893	31,963	2,346	4,195	77,896	13,974
2007	75,515	8,649	29,803	31,114	1,695	4,254	75,515	13,777
2008	74,651	8,864	28,922	28,297	c	c	74,651	12,582
2009	58,482	7,270	21,582	c	c	c	58,482	9,589
2010	54,530	6,074	19,887	c	c	c	54,530	9,341
2011	57,062	6,041	23,489	c	c	c	57,062	11,169
2012	57,972	6,499	21,994	23,077	c	c	57,972	10,320
2013	52,591	5,722	19,036	18,890	c	c	52,591	10,489
2014	52,430	5,803	19,217	20,356	1,416	5,640	52,430	11,713
2015	52,725	5,814	20,529	19,315	1,412	5,650	52,721	11,737
2016	57,160 p	6,309	22,363	21,442	1,813	5,235	57,160	11,772
2010 Q4	13,414	1,366	4,684	c	c	c	12,767	2,174
2011 Q1	14,547	1,572	5,665	c	c	c	14,150	2,746
Q2	14,454	1,579	6,127	5,291	c	c	14,831	2,923
Q3	13,981	1,533	6,085	5,160	c	c	14,684	2,937
Q4	14,080	1,357	5,612	4,719	c	c	13,397	2,563
2012 Q1	14,350	1,481	5,635	5,039	c	c	13,894	2,675
Q2	14,070	1,712	5,608	5,633	c	c	14,474	2,609
Q3	14,399	1,778	5,612	6,259	c	c	15,192	2,749
Q4	15,153	1,528	5,139	6,146	c	c	14,412	2,287
2013 Q1	13,482	1,380	4,854	5,107	c	c	12,957	2,260
Q2	13,239	1,570	4,665	4,908	c	c	13,662	2,681
Q3	13,149	1,545	5,007	4,760	322	2,264	13,898	2,914
Q4	12,721	1,227	4,510	4,115	c	c	12,074	2,634
2014 Q1	12,502	1,379	4,221	4,393	394	1,533	11,919	2,447
Q2	13,037	1,472	4,744	5,627	302	1,379	13,524	3,296
Q3	13,559	1,593	5,456	5,511	387	1,388	14,334	3,138
Q4	13,332	1,359	4,796	4,825	333	1,340	12,653	2,832
2015 Q1	13,257	1,352	4,722	4,643	283	1,598	12,599	2,905
Q2	13,757	1,626	5,539	5,170	413	1,617	14,364	3,150
Q3	12,554	1,465	5,140	4,841	386	1,464	13,297	3,003
Q4	13,156	1,371	5,128	4,661	330	971	12,461	2,679
2016 Q1	13,740 p	1,406	5,213	4,893	349	1,167	13,027	2,593
Q2	14,513 p	1,796	5,775	5,587	600	1,408	15,165	3,116
Q3	14,540 p	1,661	6,042	5,912	449	1,312	15,376	3,245
Q4	14,367 p	1,446	5,333	5,050	415	1,348	13,592	2,818

Note : The figures above are from a quarterly sample inquiry whereas those below are from the Annual Minerals Raised Inquiry, a census. The two inquiries differ because some respondents are only able to provide estimated information for the quarterly inquiry.

From March 2015, seasonally adjusted figures for sales of sand and gravel have been included in this table. In the production of these figures, data back to 1983Q1 have been seasonally adjusted. This long run data series is available on request.

		Sand for Building	Sand for Concreting	Gravel for Concreting & other uses	Sand & Gravel for Coating	Sand, Gravel & Hoggin for Fill	Sand & Gravel Total	of which Marine-Dredged
2000		11,758	31,167	31,797	2,461	12,051	89,234	14,356
2001		11,515	31,656	35,135	2,257	7,647	88,210	13,611
2002		11,190	31,224	32,434	2,031	5,842	82,721	12,832
2003		11,851	31,411	30,236	1,766	4,957	80,221	12,131
2004		10,688	32,529	32,346	2,437	8,058	86,057	12,996
2005		11,558	29,848	32,163	2,172	6,651	82,392	13,024
2006		9,907	29,815	31,002	2,648	6,869	80,242	13,974
2007		9,877	30,202	29,350	2,636	6,436	78,501	13,777
2008		8,527	26,885	23,388	2,222	11,106	72,127	12,621
2009		6,296	21,570	19,553	2,270	6,021	55,709	9,592
2010		6,110	20,947	18,540	2,112	6,621	54,330	9,341
2011		6,140	22,591	18,712	1,913	5,659	55,015	11,189
2012		5,474	19,697	18,072	1,817	4,985	50,044	10,291
2013		5,204	20,361	18,175	1,225	6,960	51,925	10,487
2014		5,790	22,335	19,601	1,351	7,052	56,129	11,332

Source: Department for Business, Energy & Industrial Strategy

c   confidential

p   Provisional

18.20 Volume of construction output in Great Britain. Seasonally adjusted index numbers by sector

2013=100

Period	New Housing			Other New Work				All New Work	Repair and Maintenance				All Repair and Maintenance	All Work
			Total Housing	Infrastruc-ture	Excluding Infrastructure				Housing			Non Housing R&M		
	Public	Private			Public	Private Industrial	Private Commercial		Public	Private	Total			
	MV36	MV37	MVL7	MV38	MV39	MV3A	MV3B	MV3C	MV3D	MV3E	MV3F	MV3G	MV3H	MV3I
2010 Q1	101.3	77.0	81.7	102.8	147.1	105.9	104.5	103.0	109.5	93.2	98.5	86.0	92.2	98.9
Q2	105.5	84.7	88.8	107.6	154.2	108.4	107.4	108.1	114.8	101.0	105.4	92.3	98.9	104.5
Q3	117.2	91.2	96.2	101.7	149.5	126.8	113.6	111.4	111.1	107.8	108.8	90.5	99.7	106.9
Q4	114.7	90.7	95.3	91.6	154.9	103.1	107.5	106.8	108.8	106.0	106.9	92.4	99.7	104.0
2011 Q1	119.6	92.5	97.8	104.2	156.6	99.3	106.2	109.7	103.5	102.4	102.7	95.0	98.9	105.5
Q2	114.3	93.3	97.4	114.6	143.3	102.7	110.7	111.4	104.2	101.6	102.4	94.8	98.6	106.5
Q3	109.5	95.5	98.2	109.2	133.7	99.8	112.6	109.8	99.9	101.3	100.9	97.4	99.1	105.7
Q4	104.9	93.3	95.6	109.5	126.4	100.4	114.0	108.5	100.6	106.0	104.3	98.3	101.3	105.7
2012 Q1	100.8	97.1	97.8	98.6	121.0	107.9	104.0	103.5	100.7	102.8	102.1	97.2	99.7	102.0
Q2	89.3	89.3	89.3	91.8	111.4	108.1	103.6	98.1	103.9	98.2	100.1	96.6	98.3	98.2
Q3	93.3	87.8	88.9	99.1	107.3	107.7	95.4	96.3	106.3	96.4	99.6	94.5	97.1	96.6
Q4	91.8	91.4	91.5	101.7	102.7	116.9	96.9	97.9	106.1	93.5	97.6	95.6	96.6	97.4
2013 Q1	91.1	90.9	90.9	99.0	99.5	108.5	97.9	96.7	102.4	96.6	98.4	96.6	97.5	97.0
Q2	95.6	98.8	98.1	98.6	101.1	98.6	97.5	98.5	99.8	98.8	99.1	99.1	99.1	98.7
Q3	101.3	102.2	102.0	98.8	102.8	97.6	103.6	101.8	98.0	101.9	100.6	101.4	101.0	101.5
Q4	112.1	108.2	108.9	103.6	96.6	95.3	101.0	103.1	99.8	102.7	101.8	103.0	102.4	102.8
2014 Q1	122.4	115.9	117.1	95.6	96.1	106.6	105.1	105.7	101.5	108.6	106.3	103.1	104.7	105.3
Q2	130.2	119.9	121.9	91.9	98.6	118.0	105.7	107.5	102.0	107.3	105.6	107.6	106.6	107.1
Q3	138.2	128.6	130.4	95.7	100.3	118.0	105.9	111.2	102.2	109.9	107.4	108.4	107.9	109.9
Q4	132.0	130.1	130.4	102.3	100.6	113.9	107.6	112.8	100.7	107.0	105.0	107.1	106.0	110.2
2015 Q1	123.7	131.8	130.2	122.8	96.2	124.9	106.7	116.6	103.0	106.0	105.1	105.8	105.4	112.3
Q2	115.7	135.4	131.6	126.7	98.8	123.9	108.3	118.6	103.3	111.3	108.7	101.4	105.0	113.4
Q3	97.6	131.1	124.6	127.5	98.9	133.2	106.4	116.5	102.9	112.2	109.2	101.1	105.1	112.1
Q4	97.2	136.9	129.2	125.2	97.8	122.7	108.6	117.4	100.3	111.5	107.9	103.4	105.7	112.9
2016 Q1	96.8	144.7	135.4	118.2	96.5	105.9	110.2	117.5	100.9	111.8	108.3	101.0	104.7	112.5

Source: Office for National Statistics (ONS)

18.21 Value of orders for new construction obtained by main contractors in Great Britain, by sector: Seasonally Adjusted

£million

		New Housing			Other New Work						Period on period growths (%)	Period on same period one year ago growths (%)
	Public	Private	All New Housing	Infra-structure	Excluding Infrastructure			All Other Work	All New Work		
					Public	Private Industrial	Private Commercial				
2010	3,093	8,600	11,694	8,720	12,485	2,150	13,441	36,796	48,490	0.3	
2011	2,434	8,963	11,397	7,239	8,440	2,069	12,897	30,645	42,042	-13.3	
2012	2,257	8,996	11,252	10,133	7,211	2,480	11,488	31,313	42,565	1.2	
2013	3,656	11,844	15,500	8,432	7,826	3,257	12,463	31,978	47,478	11.5	
2014	1,820	12,994	14,814	7,229	8,256	3,476	14,916	33,877	48,691	2.6	
2015	1,316	12,806	14,122	10,865	6,384	4,333	14,365	35,947	50,069	2.8	
2010 Q1	870	1,943	2,813	2,678	3,312	542	3,264	9,797	12,609	7.7	23.1
Q2	774	1,769	2,543	2,363	3,155	597	3,435	9,550	12,093	-4.1	-6.5
Q3	537	2,628	3,164	1,650	2,550	516	3,592	8,308	11,472	-5.1	-14.8
Q4	913	2,261	3,174	2,029	3,467	494	3,151	9,141	12,315	7.3	5.2
2011 Q1	837	2,365	3,202	1,708	2,701	571	3,267	8,247	11,449	-7.0	-9.2
Q2	605	2,142	2,747	1,380	1,974	522	3,156	7,033	9,780	-14.6	-19.1
Q3	543	2,281	2,825	1,722	2,134	489	3,823	8,169	10,993	12.4	-4.2
Q4	448	2,174	2,622	2,429	1,630	488	2,651	7,197	9,819	-10.7	-20.3
2012 Q1	514	2,056	2,570	2,656	1,514	768	3,424	8,361	10,931	11.3	-4.5
Q2	535	2,145	2,680	1,801	1,868	524	2,719	6,912	9,592	-12.2	-1.9
Q3	582	2,281	2,862	2,408	1,870	652	2,535	7,466	10,328	7.7	-6.1
Q4	627	2,513	3,140	3,269	1,959	536	2,810	8,574	11,714	13.4	19.3
2013 Q1	709	2,619	3,328	1,578	2,201	607	3,040	7,426	10,754	-8.2	-1.6
Q2	939	3,098	4,037	2,521	1,888	681	3,276	8,367	12,404	15.3	29.3
Q3	1,045	2,995	4,040	2,338	1,755	838	3,008	7,939	11,979	-3.4	16.0
Q4	963	3,132	4,095	1,995	1,983	1,130	3,138	8,246	12,341	3.0	5.3
2014 Q1	531	3,277	3,809	1,449	2,082	968	3,167	7,666	11,474	-7.0	6.7
Q2	582	3,084	3,666	1,700	2,295	936	3,655	8,586	12,252	6.8	-1.2
Q3	389	3,476	3,865	1,889	1,984	555	4,313	8,741	12,606	2.9	5.2
Q4	318	3,156	3,474	2,192	1,895	1,017	3,780	8,884	12,358	-2.0	0.1
2015 Q1	303	3,334	3,637	2,468	1,721	1,100	3,641	8,930	12,567	1.7	9.5
Q2	328	3,156	3,484	3,088	1,495	1,155	3,204	8,941	12,425	-1.1	1.4
Q3	272	3,023	3,295	3,066	1,643	1,125	3,383	9,217	12,512	0.7	-0.7
Q4	413	3,293	3,706	2,243	1,525	954	4,137	8,859	12,565	0.4	1.7
2016 Q1	438	2,726	3,164	2,857	1,323	1,014	4,054	9,248	12,413	-1.2	-1.2

Source: Office for National Statistics (ONS)

18.22 Total engineering[1]

Values at current prices

£ million

	Turnover			New Orders		
	Export	Home	Total	Export	Home	Total
	JWO5	JWO6	JWO7	JWO8	JWO9	JWP2
2009	29,994.1	56,556.9	86,550.6	26,189.2	44,661.1	70,850.7
2010	37,532.0	61,679.2	99,211.2	35,537.8	54,997.3	90,535.1
2011	40,021.3	63,718.0	103,739.3	38,364.0	53,445.6	91,809.6
2012	40,458.8	66,938.9	107,397.7	38,569.9	52,650.2	91,220.1
2013	41,248.8	61,547.6	102,796.4	-	-	-
2014	40,394.7	64,246.7	104,641.4	-	-	-
2015	36,561.2	61,585.5	98,146.7	-	-	-
2010 Q1	8,405.6	14,561.7	22,967.3	8,184.8	13,131.0	21,315.8
Q2	9,268.8	15,326.0	24,594.8	9,293.0	14,418.4	23,711.4
Q3	9,498.2	16,005.1	25,503.3	8,595.8	13,589.2	22,185.0
Q4	10,359.4	15,786.4	26,145.8	9,464.2	13,858.7	23,322.9
2011 Q1	10,003.1	15,286.3	25,289.4	10,198.5	12,874.7	23,073.2
Q2	10,216.5	15,953.7	26,170.2	10,357.6	13,311.0	23,668.6
Q3	9,737.5	16,471.0	26,208.5	8,777.4	13,159.5	21,936.9
Q4	10,064.2	16,007.0	26,071.2	9,030.5	14,100.4	23,130.9
2012 Q1	9784.2	16,486.3	26,270.5	10,167.2	13,636.5	23,803.7
Q2	10224.1	17,159.1	27,383.2	9,528.5	13,034.2	22,562.7
Q3	9862.7	16,861.3	26,724.0	8,794.5	12,945.7	21,740.2
Q4	10587.8	16,432.2	27,020.0	10,079.7	13,033.8	23,113.5
2013 Q1	10,034.20	14,750.6	24,784.8	-	-	-
Q2	10,682.30	15,189.0	25,871.3	-	-	-
Q3	10,154.90	15,767.1	25,922.0	-	-	-
Q4	10,377.40	15,840.9	26,218.3	-	-	-
2014 Q1	9,857.3	15,703.2	25,560.5	-	-	-
Q2	10,127.1	16,002.1	26,129.2	-	-	-
Q3	9,778.6	16,277.0	26,055.6	-	-	-
Q4	10,631.7	16,264.4	26,896.1	-	-	-
2015 Q1	9,128.9	15,403.7	24,532.6	-	-	-
Q2	9,437.4	15,423.6	24,861.0	-	-	-
Q3	9,028.4	15,450.3	24,478.7	-	-	-
Q4	8,966.5	15,307.9	24,274.4	-	-	-
2014 Jan	3,116.0	4,929.5	8,045.5	-	-	-
Feb	3,017.4	5,003.9	8,021.3	-	-	-
Mar	3,723.9	5,769.8	9,493.7	-	-	-
Apr	3,188.3	5,125.5	8,313.8	-	-	-
May	3,275.8	5,206.0	8,481.8	-	-	-
June	3,663.0	5,670.6	9,333.6	-	-	-
July	3,266.4	5,623.0	8,889.4	-	-	-
August	2,853.5	4,923.6	7,777.1	-	-	-
September	3,658.7	5,730.4	9,389.1	-	-	-
October	3,521.5	5,619.5	9,141.0	-	-	-
November	3,407.3	5,317.2	8,724.5	-	-	-
December	3,702.9	5,327.7	9,030.6	-	-	-
2015 Jan	2,696.7	4,672.8	7,369.5	-	-	-
Feb	2,849.7	4,876.0	7,725.7	-	-	-
Mar	3,582.5	5,854.9	9,437.4	-	-	-
Apr	3,149.4	4,974.9	8,124.3	-	-	-
May	2,773.2	4,869.1	7,642.3	-	-	-
June	3,514.8	5,579.6	9,094.4	-	-	-
July	2,981.5	5,242.3	8,223.8	-	-	-
August	2,665.1	4,783.6	7,448.7	-	-	-
September	3,381.8	5,424.4	8,806.2	-	-	-
October	2,997.3	5,263.5	8,260.8	-	-	-
November	2,908.0	5,208.0	8,116.0	-	-	-
December	3,061.2	4,836.4	7,897.6	-	-	-

Source: Office for National Statistics : 01633 646659

- As of January 2013, New Orders data is no longer being collected

1 The data for this table is based on SIC 2007 (the Industrial Classification for 2007). The change is a result of the SIC 2003 based MPI survey (which provided figures up to the April edition of the Monthly Digest) becoming part of the SIC 2007 based Monthly Business Survey (MBS). This is part of an ONS wide project to convert all data series to the latest SIC. This means that this table is now Total engineering (SIC 07 25-28) Please note this new table does not include Orders on Hand.

18.23 Manufacture of fabricated metal products and machinery and equipment n.e.c.[1]

Values at current prices

£ million

	Turnover			New Orders		
	Export	Home	Total	Export	Home	Total
	JWM9	JWN2	JWN3	JWN4	JWN5	JWN6
2009	16,407.4	37,694.8	54,102.1	14,092.0	26,752.2	40,844.4
2010	22,257.5	42,731.1	64,988.6	21,727.5	34,866.8	56,594.3
2011	24,209.6	46,149.6	70,359.2	24,884.9	35,766.8	60,651.7
2012	24,794.0	47,704.2	72,498.2	24,489.3	34,234.2	58,723.5
2013	23,644.6	43,936.4	67,581.0	-	-	-
2014	23,079.1	46,767.2	69,846.3	-	-	-
2015	21,651.8	44,430.1	66,081.9	-	-	-
2010 Q1	4,838.8	9,902.9	14,741.7	4,810.6	8,203.9	13,014.5
Q2	5,567.2	10,577.9	16,145.1	5,852.1	9,155.6	15,007.7
Q3	5,622.2	11,313.3	16,935.5	5,113.6	8,520.7	13,634.3
Q4	6,229.3	10,937.0	17,166.3	5,951.2	8,986.6	14,937.8
2011 Q1	6,033.3	10,736.0	16,769.3	6,554.6	8,407.0	14,961.6
Q2	6,110.9	11,745.8	17,856.7	6,830.3	9,006.5	15,836.8
Q3	5,978.8	12,137.6	18,116.4	5,756.8	8,804.5	14,561.3
Q4	6,086.6	11,530.2	17,616.8	5,743.2	9,548.8	15,292.0
2012 Q1	5,995.6	11,728.6	17,724.2	6,493.8	8,721.4	15,215.2
Q2	6,327.4	12,382.9	18,710.3	6,089.3	8,674.9	14,764.2
Q3	6,095.4	12,006.9	18,102.3	5,459.0	8,355.3	13,814.3
Q4	6,375.6	11,585.8	17,961.4	6,447.2	8,482.6	14,929.8
2013 Q1	10,034.2	14,750.6	24,784.8	-	-	-
Q2	10,682.3	15,189.0	25,871.3	-	-	-
Q3	10,154.9	15,767.1	25,922.0	-	-	-
Q4	10,377.4	15,840.9	26,218.3	-	-	-
2014 Q1	5,836.5	11,255.1	17,091.6	-	-	-
Q2	5,875.0	11,827.6	17,702.6	-	-	-
Q3	5,579.8	12,006.1	17,585.9	-	-	-
Q4	5,787.8	11,678.4	17,466.2	-	-	-
2015 Q1	5,484.4	11,130.8	16,615.2	-	-	-
Q2	5,667.9	11,227.1	16,895.0	-	-	-
Q3	5,361.8	11,176.8	16,538.6	-	-	-
Q4	5,137.7	10,895.4	16,033.1	-	-	-
2014 Jan	1,848.3	3,549.6	5,397.9	-	-	-
Feb	1,850.1	3,597.0	5,447.1	-	-	-
Mar	2,138.1	4,108.5	6,246.6	-	-	-
Apr	1,875.2	3,736.4	5,611.6	-	-	-
May	1,945.2	3,869.3	5,814.5	-	-	-
June	2,054.6	4,221.9	6,276.5	-	-	-
July	1,958.6	4,180.0	6,138.6	-	-	-
August	1,569.2	3,641.5	5,210.7	-	-	-
September	2,052.0	4,184.6	6,236.6	-	-	-
October	2,017.0	4,119.2	6,136.2	-	-	-
November	1,902.6	3,834.9	5,737.5	-	-	-
December	1,868.2	3,724.3	5,592.5	-	-	-
2015 Jan	1,596.1	3,386.6	4,982.7	-	-	-
Feb	1,753.7	3,541.9	5,295.6	-	-	-
Mar	2,134.6	4,202.3	6,336.9	-	-	-
Apr	1,881.7	3,642.3	5,524.0	-	-	-
May	1,667.5	3,543.8	5,211.3	-	-	-
June	2,118.7	4,041.0	6,159.7	-	-	-
July	1,782.2	3,833.9	5,616.1	-	-	-
August	1,572.0	3,462.6	5,034.6	-	-	-
September	2,007.6	3,880.3	5,887.9	-	-	-
October	1,724.0	3,828.8	5,552.8	-	-	-
November	1,687.0	3,698.8	5,385.8	-	-	-
December	1,726.7	3,367.8	5,094.5	-	-	-

Source: Office for National Statistics : 01633 646659

- As of Jan 2013, new orders data is no longer collected

1 The data for this table is based on SIC 2007 (the Industrial Classification for 2007). The change is a result of the SIC 2003 based MPI survey (which provided figures up to the April edition of the Monthly Digest) becoming part of the SIC 2007 based Monthly Business Survey (MBS). This is part of an ONS wide project to convert all data series to the latest SIC. Manufacture of fabricated metal products and machinery and equipment n.e.c. (SIC 07 25, 28). Please note this new table does not include Orders on Hand.

18.24 Alcoholic drink

| | Spirits | | | | | Beer | | | |
Calendar Year	Production (hl of pure alcohol)	Whisky (hl of pure alcohol)	RTD (hl of pure alcohol)	Imported and other (hl of pure alcohol)	Total (hl of pure alcohol)	Production (thousand hl)	Released for home consumption (thousand hl)	Production (thousand hl of pure alcohol)	Clearances (thousand hl of pure alcohol)
2002	4508	321	105	689	1115	56672	59384	2352	2473
2003	4553	318	124	744	1187	58014	60301	2414	2515
2004	4081	319	114	792	1226	57461	59194	2433	2499
2005	4365	301	84	822	1206	56255	57572	2338	2398
2006	4485	283	65	767	1114	53768	55751	2250	2335
2007	5498	286	52	832	1170	51341	53465	2160	2247
2008	6072	289	42	817	1148	49611	51498	2062	2145
2009	5757	258	32	802	1091	45141	46817	1891	1957
2010	5074	267	35	842	1144	44997	45872	1905	1932
2011	5697	257	30	828	1116	45694	42527	1934	1881
2012	6185	258	24	836	1117	42047	42962	1752	1790
2013	8434	245	22	821	1087	41956	42422	1735	1758
2014	8668	233	16	835	1085	41204	43752	1713	1819

| | Wine of Fresh Grapes | | | | Made Wine | | | | Cider and Perry |
Calendar Year	Fortified (hl)	Still table (hl)	Sparkling (hl)	Total (hl)	Still (hl)	Sparkling (hl)	Coolers (hl)	Total (hl)	Released for home consumption (thousand hl)
2002	325	10319	578	11222	366	2	1606	1974	5939
2003	296	10647	640	11584	338	1	423	762	5876
2004	298	11768	676	12742	351	1	508	859	6139
2005	306	12117	721	13143	334	0	597	931	6377
2006	302	11655	715	12672	316	1	528	844	7523
2007	305	12559	838	13702	343	5	720	1068	8046
2008	324	12402	757	13483	374	7	611	993	8412
2009	219	11729	731	12680	390	2	597	989	9404
2010	220	11870	810	12900	400	5	758	1162	9399
2011	217	11844	800	12860	440	7	828	1275	9280
2012	224	11705	872	12808	424	3	1000	1427	8737
2013	228	11586	925	12739	422	5	1395	1822	8640
2014	201	11244	1117	12562	465	7	1715	2187	7937

Source: Her Majesty's Revenue and Customs

Published in the HMRC Alcohol Bulletin

18.25 Tobacco products: recent receipts

| | Cigarettes | | | Other | | | Overall |
Calendar Year	Home Produced (million sticks)	Imported (million sticks)	Total (million sticks)	Cigars (thousand kg)	HRT (thousand kg)	Other (thousand kg)	Total (thousand kg)
2008	7005	579	7585	86	473	27	8171
2009	7473	578	8051	92	607	29	8779
2010	7590	662	8252	86	683	29	9051
2011	7899	657	8556	87	845	28	9517
2012	7954	637	8591	88	991	29	9699
2013	7723	625	8348	82	1073	27	9530
2014	7557	668	8225	83	1108	27	9442

Source: Her Majesty's Revenue and Customs

Published in the HMRC Tobacco Bulletin

National accounts

Chapter 19

National accounts

The tables are based on those in The Blue Book 2016 Edition. The Blue Book presents the full set of economic accounts for the United Kingdom. The accounts are based on the European System of Accounts 1995 (ESA 95), a system of national accounts that all European Union members have agreed to use. ESA 95 is fully compliant with the System of National Accounts 1993 (SNA93), which was unanimously approved by the Statistical Commission of the United Nations, and is used by statistical offices throughout the world.

The Blue Book contains an introduction which provides an overview of the accounts and an explanation of the underlying framework. A detailed description of the structure of the accounts and the methods used to derive the figures is provided in a separate Office for National Statistics (ONS) publication United Kingdom National Accounts: Concepts, Sources and Methods (TSO 1998). Further information on the financial accounts is given in the Financial Statistics Explanatory Handbook.

Brief definitions of some national accounting terms used in this chapter are included here. Current prices (or, more precisely, current price estimates) describe values during the period of the observation. Hence, in a time series, they will describe changes to price and to volume. Chain volume measures exclude the effects of price change. Basic prices do not include taxes and subsidies on products, whereas these are included in market prices.

Gross Domestic Product and Gross National Income
(Tables 19.1, 19.2, 19.3)

Table 19.1 shows three of the most important economic aggregates: Gross Domestic Product (GDP), Gross National Income (GNI) and Gross National Disposable Income (GNDI). In all three cases 'gross' denotes that depreciation (or consumption) of fixed capital is ignored. GDP is the total value of the UK's output. GNI is GDP plus primary incomes received from the rest of the world minus primary incomes paid to the rest of the world. Primary income comprises taxes on production and imports, property income and compensation of employees. These measures are given as current price estimates and chained volume measures. GNDI equals GNI plus net current transfers to the rest of the world. Transfers are unrequited payments such as taxes, social benefits and remittances.

There are three different approaches to measuring GDP: output, income and expenditure. Table 19.2 shows the various money flows which are used in these different approaches, and those that are used to measure GNI at current prices. The output approach to measuring GDP takes the gross value added for the entire economy (that is, the value of the UK's output minus the goods and services consumed in the productive process) to give gross value added at basic prices. This figure is then adjusted to include taxes and exclude subsidies on products. This gives gross value added at market prices for the UK, which is equivalent to GDP.

The expenditure approach to GDP shows consumption expenditure by households and government, gross capital formation and expenditure on UK exports. The sum of these items overstates the amount of income generated in the UK by the value of imported goods and services. This item is therefore subtracted to produce GDP at market prices.

The income approach to GDP shows gross operating surplus, mixed income and compensation of employees (previously known as income from employment). Production taxes less subsidies are added to produce the total of the income-based components at market prices.

Table 19.2 also shows the primary incomes received from the rest of the world, which are added to GDP, and primary incomes payable to non-resident units, which are deducted from GDP, to arrive at GNI. Primary income comprises compensation of employees, taxes less subsidies on production, and property and entrepreneurial income. The data in Table 19.2 are in current prices. This means that changes between years will be driven by a combination of price effects and changes in the volume of production. The second of these components is often referred to as 'real growth'.

Table 19.3 shows the expenditure approach to the chained volume measure of GDP, that is to say the effects of price change have been removed. In chained volume series, volume measures for each year are produced in prices of the previous year. These volume measures are then 'chain-linked' together to produce a continuous time series.

Industrial analysis
(Tables 19.4, 19.5)

The analysis of gross value added by industry at current prices shown in Table 19.4 reflects the estimates based on the 2007 Standard Industrial Classification (SIC2007). The table is based on current price data reconciled through the input–output process for 2005 to 2012.

Table 19.5 shows chained volume measures of gross value added by industry. These indices are based on basic price measures. Chained volume measures of gross value added provides a lead economic indicator. The analysis of gross value added is estimated in terms of change and expressed in index number form.

Sector analysis – Distribution of income accounts and capital account
(Tables 19.6 to 19.13)

The National Accounts accounting framework includes the sector accounts which provide, by institutional sector, a description of the different stages of the economic process, from the income generated by production and its distribution and re-distribution to different economic units, and finally, capital accumulation and financing. Tables 19.6 to 19.12 show the 'allocation of primary income account' and the 'secondary distribution of income account' for the non-financial corporations, financial corporations, government and households sectors. Additionally, Table 19.12 shows the 'use of income account' for the households sector and Table 19.13 provides a summary of the capital account. The full sequence of accounts is shown in The Blue Book.

The allocation of primary income account shows the resident units and institutional sectors as recipients rather than producers of primary income. The balancing item of this account is the gross balance of primary income (B.5g) for each sector and, if the gross balance is aggregated across all sectors of the economy, the result is Gross National Income.

The secondary distribution of income account describes how the balance of income for each sector is allocated by redistribution; through transfers such as taxes on income, social contributions and benefits, and other current transfers. The balancing item of this account is Gross Disposable Income (GDI). For the households sector, the chained volume measure of GDI is shown as real household disposable income.

Table 19.12 shows, for the household sector, the use of disposable income where the balancing item is saving (B.8g). For the non-financial corporations sector the balancing item of the secondary distribution of income account, gross disposable income (B.6g), is equal to saving (B.8g).

The summary capital account (Table 19.13) brings together the saving and investment of the sectors of the economy. It shows saving, capital transfers, gross capital formation and net acquisition of non-financial assets for each of these.

Households' and non-profit institutions serving households' consumption expenditure at current market prices and chained volume measures (Tables 19.14 to 19.17)

Households' and non-profit institutions serving households' (NPISH) final consumption expenditure is a major component of the expenditure measure of GDP. In Table 19.2 this expenditure is given at current market prices, broken down by the type of good or service purchased. Table 19.3 supplies the same breakdown in chain volume measures. Household final consumption expenditure includes the value of income-in-kind and imputed rent of owner-occupied dwellings. It includes expenditure on durable goods (for instance motor cars) which, from the point of view of the individual might more appropriately be treated as capital expenditure. The purchase of land and dwellings (including costs incurred in connection with the transfer of their ownership) and expenditure on major improvements by occupiers are treated as personal capital expenditure. Other goods and services purchased by the household sector (with the exception of goods and services that are to be used in self-employment) are treated as final consumption expenditure. The most detailed figures are published quarterly in Consumer Trends

Change in inventories (previously known as value of physical increase in stocks and work in progress)(Table 19.18)

This table gives a broad analysis by industry of the value of entries less withdrawals and losses of inventories (stocks), and analysis by asset for manufacturing industry.

Gross fixed capital formation (Table 19.19 to 19.22)

Gross fixed capital formation is the total value of the acquisition less disposal of fixed assets, and improvements to land.

19.1 UK national and domestic product
Main aggregates: Index numbers and values
Current prices and chained volume measures (reference year 2013)

			2008	2009	2010	2011	2012	2013	2014	2015
Indices (2013=100)										
Values at current prices										
Gross domestic product at market prices ("Money GDP")	YBEU	B.1*g	89.9	87.3	90.4	93.6	96.3	100.0	104.8	107.5
Gross value added at basic prices	YBEX	B.1g	91.1	89.1	91.2	93.6	96.4	100.0	104.7	107.4
Chained volume measures										
Gross domestic product at market prices	YBEZ	B.1*g	97.9	93.6	95.4	96.9	98.1	100.0	103.1	105.4
Gross national disposable income at market prices	YBFP	B.6*g	98.2	94.2	97.0	98.1	98.2	100.0	103.0	104.8
Gross value added at basic prices	CGCE	B.1g	98.7	94.3	96.3	97.6	98.6	100.0	103.4	105.8
Implied deflator										
Implied deflator of GDP at market prices	YBGB		91.9	93.3	94.7	96.6	98.1	100.0	101.6	102.0
Values at current prices (£million)										
Gross measures (before deduction of consumption of fixed capital) at current market prices										
Gross domestic product ("Money GDP")	YBHA	B.1*g	1 564 252	1 519 459	1 572 439	1 628 274	1 675 044	1 739 563	1 822 480	1 869 560
Employment, property and entrepreneurial income from rest of the world (receipts less payments)	YBGG	D.1+D.4	4 919	4 604	20 079	19 416	−1 913	−9 870	−23 112	−35 959
Subsidies (receipts) less taxes (payments) on products from/to rest of the world	QZOZ	-D.21+D.31	2 689	2 655	2 945	2 937	2 898	2 926	2 960	3 087
Other subsidies on production from/to rest of the world	IBJL	+D.29-D.39	−3 051	−3 411	−3 059	−3 166	−2 625	−2 455	−2 306	−2 030
Gross balance of primary incomes/ gross national income (GNI)	ABMX	B.5*g	1 569 536	1 524 820	1 592 635	1 647 922	1 672 858	1 729 222	1 798 714	1 832 544
Current transfers from rest of the world (receipts less payments)	YBGF	D.5,6,7	14 094	15 836	20 662	21 673	21 913	26 863	25 009	24 677
Gross national disposable income	NQCO	B.6*g	1 555 442	1 508 984	1 571 973	1 626 249	1 650 945	1 702 359	1 773 705	1 807 867
Adjustment to current basic prices										
Gross domestic product (at market prices)	YBHA	B.1*g	1 564 252	1 519 459	1 572 439	1 628 274	1 675 044	1 739 563	1 822 480	1 869 560
Adjustment to current basic prices (less taxes plus subsidies on products)	NQBU	D.21-D.31	150 145	137 230	157 804	176 199	179 468	188 010	198 204	203 218
Gross value added (at basic prices)	ABML	B.1g	1 414 107	1 382 229	1 414 635	1 452 075	1 495 576	1 551 553	1 624 276	1 666 342
Net measures (after deduction of consumption of fixed capital) at current market prices										
Consumption of fixed capital	NQAE	P.51c	202 586	204 323	206 080	212 636	219 710	228 826	238 657	245 144
Net domestic product	NHRK	B.1*n	1 361 666	1 315 136	1 366 359	1 415 638	1 455 334	1 510 737	1 583 823	1 624 416
Net national income	NSRX	B.5*n	1 366 950	1 320 497	1 386 555	1 435 286	1 453 148	1 500 396	1 560 057	1 587 400
Net national disposable income	NQCP	B.6*n	1 352 856	1 304 661	1 365 893	1 413 613	1 431 235	1 473 533	1 535 048	1 562 723
Chained volume measures (reference year 2013, £million)										
Gross measures (before deduction of consumption of fixed capital) at market prices										
Gross domestic product	ABMI	B.1*g	1 702 252	1 628 583	1 659 772	1 684 820	1 706 942	1 739 563	1 792 976	1 833 233
Terms of trade effect ("trading gain or loss")	YBGJ	TGL	−21 362	−13 300	−7 590	−12 524	−11 154	−	8 062	11 528
Real gross domestic income	YBGL	GDI	1 680 890	1 615 283	1 652 182	1 672 296	1 695 788	1 739 563	1 801 038	1 844 761
Real employment, property and entrepreneurial income from rest of the world (receipts less payments)	YBGI	D.1+D.4	5 290	4 899	21 096	19 939	−1 936	−9 870	−22 860	−35 568
Subsidies (receipts) less taxes (payments) on products from/to rest of the world	QZPB	-D.21+D.31	2 891	2 824	3 093	3 015	2 933	2 926	2 928	3 053
Other subsidies on production from/to rest of the world	IBJN	+D.29-D.39	−3 281	−3 629	−3 213	−3 251	−2 657	−2 455	−2 281	−2 008
Gross balance of primary incomes/ gross national income (GNI)	YBGM	B.5*g	1 686 590	1 621 006	1 673 403	1 692 475	1 693 578	1 729 222	1 777 531	1 808 148
Real current transfers from rest of the world (receipts less payments)	YBGP	D.5,6,7	15 155	16 847	21 705	22 252	22 180	26 863	24 737	24 408
Gross national disposable income	YBGO	B.6*g	1 671 432	1 604 157	1 651 699	1 670 224	1 671 399	1 702 359	1 752 794	1 783 740
Adjustment to basic prices										
Gross domestic product (at market prices)	ABMI	B.1*g	1 702 252	1 628 583	1 659 772	1 684 820	1 706 942	1 739 563	1 792 976	1 833 233
Adjustment to basic prices (less taxes plus subsidies on products)	NTAQ	-D.21+D.31	171 538	166 456	165 764	170 812	176 805	188 010	188 807	191 861
Gross value added (at basic prices)	ABMM	B.1g	1 531 690	1 463 182	1 494 588	1 514 583	1 530 435	1 551 553	1 604 169	1 641 372
Net measures (after deduction of consumption of fixed capital) at market prices										
Consumption of fixed capital	CIHA	P.51c	217 070	211 878	216 240	219 457	223 016	228 826	236 707	239 697
Net national income at market prices	YBET	B.5*n	1 469 099	1 408 710	1 456 913	1 472 761	1 470 399	1 500 396	1 540 824	1 568 451
Net national disposable income at market prices	YBEY	B.6*n	1 453 954	1 391 874	1 435 207	1 450 508	1 448 218	1 473 533	1 516 087	1 544 043

Source: Office for National Statistics, Blue Book 2016

19.2 UK gross domestic product and national income
Current prices

£ million

			2008	2009	2010	2011	2012	2013	2014	2015
Gross domestic product										
Gross domestic product: production										
Gross value added, at basic prices		B.1g								
Output of goods and services[1]	KN26	P.1	2 726 505	2 672 874	2 742 824	2 835 130	2 917 373	3 041 257	3 143 890	..
less intermediate consumption[1]	KN25	P.2	1 312 398	1 290 645	1 328 189	1 383 055	1 421 797	1 489 704	1 519 614	..
Total gross value added	ABML	**B.1g**	**1 414 107**	**1 382 229**	**1 414 635**	**1 452 075**	**1 495 576**	**1 551 553**	**1 624 276**	**1 666 342**
Value added taxes (VAT) on products	QYRC	D.211	92 002	79 900	95 865	111 437	113 859	118 234	124 211	128 816
Other taxes on products	NSUI	D.212,4	63 825	63 815	68 876	71 057	72 667	76 530	81 264	82 943
less subsidies on products	NZHC	D.31	5 682	6 485	6 937	6 295	7 058	6 754	7 271	8 541
Gross domestic product at market prices	YBHA	**B.1*g**	**1 564 252**	**1 519 459**	**1 572 439**	**1 628 274**	**1 675 044**	**1 739 563**	**1 822 480**	**1 869 560**
Gross domestic product: expenditure										
Final consumption expenditure		P.3								
Actual individual consumption		P.41								
Household final consumption expenditure	ABPB	P.3	975 508	948 481	974 938	1 004 276	1 042 914	1 084 011	1 126 230	1 157 989
Final consumption expenditure of NPISH[2]	ABNV	P.3	46 616	49 958	50 488	52 862	52 849	54 535	56 672	58 124
Individual govt. final consumption expenditure	NNAQ	P.31	193 138	205 878	210 631	212 551	217 319	221 336	228 239	231 816
Total	NQEO	P.41	1 215 262	1 204 317	1 236 057	1 269 689	1 313 082	1 359 882	1 411 141	1 447 929
Collective govt. final consumption expenditure	NQEP	P.32	123 804	125 622	127 757	127 423	129 806	128 279	130 290	129 012
Total final consumption expenditure		P.3								
Households and NPISH	NSSG	P.3	1 022 124	998 439	1 025 426	1 057 138	1 095 763	1 138 546	1 182 902	1 216 113
Central government	NMBJ	P.3	189 992	199 154	204 393	209 441	219 740	222 787	232 500	236 405
Local government	NMMT	P.3	126 950	132 346	133 995	130 533	127 385	126 828	126 029	124 423
Total	ABKW	P.3	1 339 066	1 329 939	1 363 814	1 397 112	1 442 888	1 488 161	1 541 431	1 576 941
Gross capital formation		P.5								
Gross fixed capital formation	NPQX	P.51g	271 152	236 583	245 687	255 231	266 761	280 224	302 495	316 806
Changes in inventories	ABMP	P.52	535	−14 441	5 458	2 686	1 900	5 074	13 073	5 000
Acquisitions less disposals of valuables	NPJO	P.53	−312	1 733	73	305	829	5 342	1 704	6 049
Total gross capital formation	NQFM	P.5	271 375	223 875	251 218	258 222	269 490	290 640	317 272	327 855
External balance of goods and services		B.11								
Exports of goods and services	KTMW	P.6	420 800	398 580	444 317	496 987	499 141	517 642	511 654	510 340
less imports of goods and services	KTMX	P.7	466 989	432 935	486 910	524 047	536 475	556 880	547 877	548 908
Total	KTMY	B.11	−46 189	−34 355	−42 593	−27 060	−37 334	−39 238	−36 223	−38 568
Statistical discrepancy between expenditure components and GDP	RVFD	de	–	–	–	–	–	–	–	3 332
Gross domestic product at market prices	YBHA	**B.1*g**	**1 564 252**	**1 519 459**	**1 572 439**	**1 628 274**	**1 675 044**	**1 739 563**	**1 822 480**	**1 869 560**
Gross domestic product: income										
Operating surplus, gross		B.2g								
Non-financial corporations										
Public non-financial corporations	NRJT		9 644	9 322	9 552	9 156	9 379	9 477	8 909	8 793
Private non-financial corporations	NRJK		279 852	251 396	268 903	282 923	285 798	304 034	331 709	336 390
Financial corporations	NQNV		46 671	61 453	45 424	49 480	50 325	51 469	53 671	50 004
General government	NMXV		21 624	22 694	23 892	25 321	26 549	27 441	28 304	29 234
Households and NPISH	QWLS		152 363	129 108	129 146	134 923	143 263	145 103	157 594	164 976
Total	ABNF	B.2g	510 154	473 973	476 917	501 803	515 314	537 524	580 187	589 397
Mixed income	QWLT	B.3g	94 984	95 088	95 324	98 255	107 181	111 380	120 736	123 870
Compensation of employees	HAEA	D.1	792 367	795 449	819 664	831 143	850 503	879 055	899 342	929 216
Taxes on production and imports	NZGX	D.2	178 809	167 914	192 758	208 227	213 722	223 142	234 476	241 443
less subsidies	AAXJ	D.3	12 062	12 965	12 224	11 154	11 676	11 538	12 261	13 844
Statistical discrepancy between income components and GDP	RVFC	di	–	–	–	–	–	–	–	−522
Gross domestic product at market prices	YBHA	**B.1*g**	**1 564 252**	**1 519 459**	**1 572 439**	**1 628 274**	**1 675 044**	**1 739 563**	**1 822 480**	**1 869 560**
Gross national income at market prices										
Gross domestic product at market prices	YBHA	**B.1*g**	**1 564 252**	**1 519 459**	**1 572 439**	**1 628 274**	**1 675 044**	**1 739 563**	**1 822 480**	**1 869 560**
Compensation of employees		D.1								
Receipts from rest of the world	KTMN		1 046	1 176	1 097	1 121	1 124	1 094	1 080	1 295
less payments to rest of the world	KTMO		1 761	1 435	1 486	1 294	1 272	1 420	1 550	1 498
Total	KTMP	D.1	−715	−259	−389	−173	−148	−326	−470	−203
Subsidies (receipts) less taxes (payments) on products from/to rest of the world	QZOZ	-D.21+D.31	2 689	2 655	2 945	2 937	2 898	2 926	2 960	3 087
Other subsidies on production from/ to rest of the world	IBJL	+D.29-D.39	−3 051	−3 411	−3 059	−3 166	−2 625	−2 455	−2 306	−2 030
Property and entrepreneurial income		D.4								
from rest of the world	HMBN		287 868	175 117	174 003	199 995	170 279	157 261	139 005	136 331
(receipts less payments)	HMBO		282 234	170 254	153 535	180 406	172 044	166 805	161 647	172 087
Total	HMBM	D.4	5 634	4 863	20 468	19 589	−1 765	−9 544	−22 642	−35 756
Gross balance of primary incomes/ gross national income (GNI)	ABMX	**B.5*g**	**1 569 536**	**1 524 820**	**1 592 635**	**1 647 922**	**1 672 858**	**1 729 222**	**1 798 714**	**1 832 544**

1 These series are not available for the latest year   2 Non-profit institutions serving households   Source: Office for National Statistics, Blue Book 2016

19.3 UK gross domestic product
Chained volume measures (reference year 2013)

£ million

			2008	2009	2010	2011	2012	2013	2014	2015
Gross domestic product										
Gross domestic product: expenditure approach										
Final consumption expenditure		P.3								
Actual individual consumption		P.41								
Household final consumption expenditure	ABPF	P.3	1 084 930	1 047 083	1 053 933	1 046 647	1 066 530	1 084 011	1 107 154	1 135 788
Final consumption expenditure of NPISH[1]	ABNU	P.3	52 652	53 920	53 421	55 642	54 539	54 535	55 982	56 848
Individual government final consumption expenditure	NSZK	P.31	201 695	207 159	209 916	212 315	216 908	221 336	228 251	234 308
Total	YBIO	P.41	1 338 163	1 307 689	1 316 900	1 314 521	1 337 948	1 359 882	1 391 387	1 426 944
Collective government final consumption expenditure	NSZL	P.32	136 462	134 678	132 391	130 598	131 726	128 279	129 339	128 123
Total	ABKX	P.3	1 474 737	1 442 476	1 449 362	1 445 150	1 469 695	1 488 161	1 520 726	1 555 067
Gross capital formation		P.5								
Gross fixed capital formation	NPQR	P.51g	292 575	248 099	260 396	265 327	271 534	280 224	298 872	308 866
Changes in inventories	ABMQ	P.52	−8 916	−18 195	5 596	−4 328	−361	5 074	16 630	12 201
Acquisitions less disposals of valuables	NPJP	P.53	−841	56	−659	−1 374	743	5 342	2 561	7 822
Total	NPQU	P.5	257 382	215 372	249 011	254 822	264 291	290 640	318 063	328 889
Gross domestic final expenditure	YBIK		1 732 253	1 653 100	1 697 056	1 699 051	1 733 256	1 778 801	1 838 789	1 883 956
Exports of goods and services	KTMZ	P.6	498 530	454 739	481 082	509 069	512 159	517 642	525 176	550 370
Gross final expenditure	ABME		2 230 516	2 109 120	2 178 696	2 208 051	2 245 333	2 296 443	2 363 965	2 434 326
less imports of goods and services	KTNB	P.7	528 606	480 099	519 251	523 536	538 482	556 880	570 989	604 362
Statistical discrepancy between expenditure components and GDP	GIXS	de	−	−	−	−	−	−	−	3 269
Gross domestic product at market prices	ABMI	B.1*g	**1 702 252**	**1 628 583**	**1 659 772**	**1 684 820**	**1 706 942**	**1 739 563**	**1 792 976**	**1 833 233**
Of which: external balance of goods and services	KTNC	B.11	−30 076	−25 360	−38 169	−14 467	−26 323	−39 238	−45 813	−53 992

1 Non-profit institutions serving households

Source: Office for National Statistics, Blue Book 2016

19.4 Output and capital formation: by industry[1,2]
Gross value added at current basic prices

£ million

			2008	2009	2010	2011	2012	2013	2014
Agriculture									
Output									
Compensation of employees	KLR2	D.1	4 002	4 151	4 234	4 298	4 452	4 736	4 650
Taxes less subsidies on production other than those on products	KLR3	D.29-D.39	−2 678	−3 515	−2 609	−2 559	−2 160	−2 245	−2 350
Operating surplus and mixed income, gross	KLR4	B.2g+B.3g	8 535	7 701	8 707	8 119	7 681	8 602	8 698
Gross value added at basic prices	KLR5	B.1g	9 859	8 337	10 332	9 858	9 973	11 093	10 998
Intermediate consumption at purchasers' prices	KLR6	P.2	13 671	15 665	14 872	15 948	16 196	17 066	17 743
Total output at basic prices	KLR7	P.1	23 530	24 002	25 204	25 806	26 169	28 159	28 741
Gross capital formation	KLR8	P.5	4 593	4 847	4 442	5 024	5 320	5 489	5 361
Production									
Output									
Compensation of employees	KLR9	D.1	119 530	115 564	118 580	121 921	124 027	128 883	130 533
Taxes less subsidies on production other than those on products	KLS4	D.29-D.39	3 958	3 895	3 808	3 760	3 950	4 212	4 311
Operating surplus and mixed income, gross	KLS3	B.2g+B.3g	85 925	79 056	81 390	84 014	86 900	94 198	95 677
Gross value added at basic prices	KLS5	B.1g	209 413	198 515	203 778	209 695	214 877	227 293	230 521
Intermediate consumption at purchasers' prices	KLS6	P.2	379 241	358 762	387 603	415 882	429 644	443 425	446 924
Total output at basic prices	KLS7	P.1	588 654	557 277	591 381	625 577	644 521	670 718	677 445
Gross capital formation	KLS8	P.5	44 072	34 550	37 815	47 869	50 794	54 393	58 696
Construction									
Output									
Compensation of employees	KLS9	D.1	46 277	44 801	45 126	46 521	47 611	49 339	51 350
Taxes less subsidies on production other than those on products	KLT3	D.29-D.39	918	965	1 002	903	1 124	984	916
Operating surplus and mixed income, gross	KLT2	B.2g+B.3g	42 391	31 331	34 614	37 749	37 701	40 487	44 490
Gross value added at basic prices	KLT4	B.1g	89 586	77 097	80 742	85 173	86 436	90 810	96 756
Intermediate consumption at purchasers' prices	KLT5	P.2	135 006	118 923	121 368	124 327	128 469	133 615	141 125
Total output at basic prices	KLT6	P.1	224 592	196 020	202 110	209 500	214 905	224 425	237 881
Gross capital formation	KLT7	P.5	19 289	13 073	18 293	18 086	20 837	19 129	23 465

1 The contribution of each industry to the gross domestic product before providing for consumption of fixed capital. The industrial composition in this table is consistent with the Supply-Use Table.

2 Components may not sum to totals due to rounding.

Source: Office for National Statistics, Blue Book 2016

19.4 Output and capital formation: by industry[1,2]
Gross value added at current basic prices

£ million

			2008	2009	2010	2011	2012	2013	2014
Distribution, transport, hotels and restaurants									
Output									
Compensation of employees	KLT8	D.1	166 840	165 134	169 403	172 940	176 127	184 002	193 109
Taxes less subsidies on production other than		D.29-D.39							
those on products	KLU2		10 300	11 422	11 567	12 123	12 623	13 078	13 374
Operating surplus and mixed income, gross	KLT9	B.2g+B.3g	75 168	67 240	73 666	73 784	74 800	81 608	91 998
Gross value added at basic prices	KLU3	B.1g	252 308	243 796	254 636	258 847	263 550	278 688	298 481
Intermediate consumption at purchasers' prices	KLU4	P.2	247 899	239 312	241 927	247 259	259 498	271 466	280 285
Total output at basic prices	KLU5	P.1	500 207	483 108	496 563	506 106	523 048	550 154	578 766
Gross capital formation	KLU6	P.5	36 546	26 735	40 220	34 143	36 907	40 146	46 754
Information and communication									
Output									
Compensation of employees	KLU7	D.1	52 795	50 141	51 353	54 086	56 748	58 937	58 900
Taxes less subsidies on production other than		D.29-D.39							
those on products	KLU9		910	742	785	804	704	799	824
Operating surplus and mixed income, gross	KLU8	B.2g+B.3g	33 911	34 548	33 982	36 346	35 582	37 266	41 705
Gross value added at basic prices	KLV2	B.1g	87 616	85 431	86 120	91 236	93 034	97 002	101 429
Intermediate consumption at purchasers' prices	KLV3	P.2	64 097	63 582	68 382	68 141	69 705	74 142	76 072
Total output at basic prices	KLV4	P.1	151 713	149 013	154 502	159 377	162 739	171 144	177 501
Gross capital formation	KLV5	P.5	19 466	17 670	17 569	17 475	17 541	18 978	18 652
Financial and insurance									
Output									
Compensation of employees	KLV6	D.1	58 434	61 289	63 500	61 022	58 830	62 187	63 655
Taxes less subsidies on production other than									
those on products	KLV8	D.29-D.39	1 783	1 762	5 457	2 445	2 533	2 609	2 792
Operating surplus and mixed income, gross	KLV7	B.2g+B.3g	48 185	62 873	46 716	50 661	51 507	53 251	55 457
Gross value added at basic prices	KLV9	B.1g	108 402	125 924	115 673	114 128	112 870	118 047	121 904
Intermediate consumption at purchasers' prices	KLW2	P.2	133 792	122 121	116 578	129 406	127 322	136 447	136 491
Total output at basic prices	KLW3	P.1	242 194	248 045	232 251	243 534	240 192	254 494	258 395
Gross capital formation	KLW4	P.5	8 174	6 511	8 363	8 074	9 833	8 103	8 855

1 The contribution of each industry to the gross domestic product before providing for consumption of fixed capital. The industrial composition in this table is consistent with the Supply-Use Table.

2 Components may not sum to totals due to rounding.

Source: Office for National Statistics, Blue Book 2016

19.4
Output and capital formation: by industry[1,2]
Gross value added at current basic prices

£ million

			2008	2009	2010	2011	2012	2013	2014
Real estate									
Output									
Compensation of employees	KLW5	D.1	10 482	9 450	9 868	10 074	11 439	11 714	12 078
Taxes less subsidies on production other than		D.29-D.39							
those on products	KLW7		−1 666	−1 005	−733	−281	−328	−247	−415
Operating surplus and mixed income, gross	KLW6	B.2g+B.3g	172 889	151 390	155 004	165 397	178 054	177 934	193 586
Gross value added at basic prices	KLW8	B.1g	181 705	159 835	164 139	175 190	189 165	189 401	205 249
Intermediate consumption at purchasers' prices	KLW9	P.2	35 999	62 619	66 217	63 307	60 757	68 558	63 048
Total output at basic prices	KLX2	P.1	217 704	222 454	230 356	238 497	249 922	257 959	268 297
Gross capital formation	KLX3	P.5	3 919	−1 002	−1 580	−1 843	−2 268	−2 476	−3 251
Professional and support									
Output									
Compensation of employees	KLX4	D.1	96 047	95 973	96 027	98 366	103 994	110 412	111 971
Taxes less subsidies on production other than		D.29-D.39							
those on products	KLX6		1 930	2 104	2 115	2 459	2 544	2 708	2 868
Operating surplus and mixed income, gross	KLX5	B.2g+B.3g	60 647	55 817	60 264	63 169	67 084	71 532	81 373
Gross value added at basic prices	KLX7	B.1g	158 624	153 894	158 406	163 994	173 622	184 652	196 212
Intermediate consumption at purchasers' prices	KLX8	P.2	120 543	115 741	119 380	123 186	128 575	132 958	140 825
Total output at basic prices	KLX9	P.1	279 167	269 635	277 786	287 180	302 197	317 610	337 037
Gross capital formation	KLY2	P.5	17 554	14 910	17 247	20 251	19 850	22 214	23 009
Government, health and education									
Output									
Compensation of employees	KLY3	D.1	210 483	220 923	228 569	228 825	233 192	233 717	237 497
Taxes less subsidies on production other		D.29-D.39							
than those on products	KLY5		401	368	475	457	575	628	707
Operating surplus and mixed income, gross	KLY4	B.2g+B.3g	53 266	55 318	55 015	57 781	58 290	58 429	60 644
Gross value added at basic prices	KLY6	B.1g	264 150	276 609	284 059	287 063	292 057	292 774	298 848
Intermediate consumption at purchasers' prices	KLY7	P.2	149 700	162 462	161 978	163 168	167 139	175 836	180 355
Total output at basic prices	KLY8	P.1	413 850	439 071	446 037	450 231	459 196	468 610	479 203
Gross capital formation	KLY9	P.5	35 125	37 736	38 068	35 717	34 938	35 638	37 502

1 The contribution of each industry to the gross domestic product before providing for consumption of fixed capital. The industrial composition in this table is consistent with the Supply-Use Table.

2 Components may not sum to totals due to rounding.

Source: Office for National Statistics, Blue Book 2016

19.4 Output and capital formation: by industry[1,2]
Gross value added at current basic prices

£ million

			2008	2009	2010	2011	2012	2013	2014
Other services									
Output									
Compensation of employees	KLZ2	D.1	27 477	28 023	33 004	33 090	34 083	35 128	35 599
Taxes less subsidies on production other		D.29-D.39							
than those on products	KLZ4		746	981	863	763	1 013	1 068	984
Operating surplus and mixed income, gross	KLZ3	B.2g+B.3g	24 221	23 787	22 883	23 038	24 896	25 597	27 295
Gross value added at basic prices	KLZ5	B.1g	52 444	52 791	56 750	56 891	59 992	61 793	63 878
Intermediate consumption at purchasers' prices	KLZ6	P.2	32 450	31 458	29 884	32 431	34 492	36 191	36 746
Total output at basic prices	KLZ7	P.1	84 894	84 249	86 634	89 322	94 484	97 984	100 624
Gross capital formation	KLZ8	P.5	5 380	5 405	5 536	5 493	5 781	5 801	5 767
Not allocated to industries									
Gross capital formation[3]	KN28	P.5	77 257	63 440	65 245	67 933	69 957	83 225	92 462
All industries									
Output									
Compensation of employees	HAEA	D.1	792 367	795 449	819 664	831 143	850 503	879 055	899 342
Taxes less subsidies on production other		D.29-D.39							
than those on products	KN22		16 602	17 719	22 730	20 874	22 578	23 594	24 011
Operating surplus, gross	ABNF	B.2g	510 154	473 973	476 917	501 803	515 314	537 524	580 187
Mixed income, gross	QWLT	B.3g	94 984	95 088	95 324	98 255	107 181	111 380	120 736
Statistical discrepancy between income and GDP	RVFC	di	–	–	–	–	–	–	–
Gross value added at basic prices	ABML	B.1g	1 414 107	1 382 229	1 414 635	1 452 075	1 495 576	1 551 553	1 624 276
Intermediate consumption at purchasers' prices	KN25	P.2	1 312 398	1 290 645	1 328 189	1 383 055	1 421 797	1 489 704	1 519 614
Total output at basic prices	KN26	P.1	2 726 505	2 672 874	2 742 824	2 835 130	2 917 373	3 041 257	3 143 890
Gross capital formation									
Gross fixed capital formation	NPQX	P.51g	271 152	236 583	245 687	255 231	266 761	280 224	302 495
Changes in inventories	ABMP	P.52	535	–14 441	5 458	2 686	1 900	5 074	13 073
Acquisitions less disposals of valuables	NPJO	P.53	–312	1 733	73	305	829	5 342	1 704
Total gross capital formation	NQFM	P.5	271 375	223 875	251 218	258 222	269 490	290 640	317 272

1 The contribution of each industry to the gross domestic product before providing for consumption of fixed capital. The industrial composition in this table is consistent with the Supply-Use Table.

2 Components may not sum to totals due to rounding.

3 Gross fixed capital formation of dwellings and costs associated with the transfer of non-produced assets and acquisitions less disposals of valuables

Source: Office for National Statistics, Blue Book 2016

19.5 Gross value added at basic prices: by industry[1,2,3]
Chained volume indices

Indices 2013=100

		Weight per 1000[1]		2008	2009	2010	2011	2012	2013	2014	2015
		2013									
Agriculture	A	7.1	L2KL	103.4	97.1	96.5	107.1	99.3	100.0	113.9	115.1
Production and construction	B-F										
Production	B-E										
Mining and quarrying	B	17.6	L2KR	152.5	138.9	134.5	115.3	102.8	100.0	100.6	109.4
Manufacturing	C										
Food products, beverages and tobacco	CA	16.7	KN3D	95.3	93.9	97.9	104.4	101.7	100.0	104.2	104.1
Textiles, wearing apparel and leather products	CB	3.7	KN3E	114.0	103.7	106.9	108.3	104.6	100.0	97.4	96.8
Wood, paper products and printing	CC	7.5	KN3F	117.0	108.6	109.4	103.3	97.8	100.0	101.1	101.7
Coke and refined petroleum product	CD	1.3	KN3G	120.6	113.7	111.9	113.4	102.0	100.0	91.1	93.7
Chemicals and chemical products	CE	5.8	KN3H	111.7	97.1	96.5	103.1	101.1	100.0	102.8	108.9
Basic pharmaceutical products and preparations	CF	8.6	KN3I	127.5	135.6	126.1	109.1	102.7	100.0	95.0	95.5
Rubber, plastic and other non-metallic mineral products	CG	8.1	KN3J	124.5	107.4	107.5	107.3	102.8	100.0	113.1	109.7
Basic metals and metal products	CH	12.2	KN3K	111.9	90.4	95.8	100.0	102.9	100.0	101.5	101.9
Computer, electronic and optical products	CI	5.3	KN3L	112.2	107.5	102.9	101.6	102.1	100.0	103.9	101.7
Electrical equipment	CJ	3.1	KN3M	113.6	88.2	98.3	94.6	104.9	100.0	96.8	97.6
Machinery and equipment n.e.c.	CK	7.4	KN3N	108.5	86.4	103.3	112.2	113.4	100.0	104.3	90.7
Transport equipment	CL	13.5	KN3O	75.2	65.8	80.8	89.0	92.9	100.0	103.5	110.2
Other manufacturing and repair	CM	9.4	KN3P	97.5	92.9	96.9	102.1	95.6	100.0	105.6	103.6
Total manufacturing	C	102.6	L2KX	105.8	95.9	100.3	102.5	101.0	100.0	102.9	102.7
Electricity, gas, steam and air conditioning supply	D	15.3	L2MW	105.9	103.4	107.6	101.0	100.2	100.0	94.0	94.8
Water supply, sewerage, waste mgmt and remediation	E	10.9	L2N2	96.4	89.0	90.8	96.0	95.9	100.0	100.7	103.9
Total production	B - E	146.5	L2KQ	110.5	100.9	104.2	103.5	100.7	100.0	101.5	102.8
Construction	F	58.5	L2N8	109.9	95.4	103.6	105.9	98.6	100.0	108.0	112.6
Total production and construction	B - F	205.0	L2KP	110.3	99.3	104.0	104.2	100.1	100.0	103.4	105.6

1 The weights shown are in proportion to total gross value added (GVA) in 2013 and are used to combine the industry output indices to calculate the totals. For 2012 and earlier, totals are calculated using the equivalent weights for the previous year (e.g. totals for 2009 use 2008 weights). Weights may not sum to totals due to rounding.

2 As GVA is expressed in index number form, it is inappropriate to show as a statistical adjustment any divergence from the other measures of GDP. Such an adjustment does, however, exist implicitly.

3 Because of differences in the annual and monthly production inquiries, estimates of current price output and gross value added by industry derived from the current price Input-Output Supply and Use Tables are not consistent with the equivalent measures of chained volume measures growth given in 2.3. These differences do not affect GDP totals.

Source: Office for National Statistics, Blue Book 2016

19.5 Gross value added at basic prices: by industry[1,2,3]
Chained volume indices

Indices 2013=100

			Weight per 1000[1]		2008	2009	2010	2011	2012	2013	2014	2015
			2013									
Services	G-T											
Distribution, transport, hotels and restaurants	G-I											
Wholesale, retail, repair of motor vehicles and m/cycles	G	107.3	L2NE	97.4	91.8	92.9	94.2	95.2	100.0	105.2	110.1
Transportation and storage	H	43.5	L2NI	107.1	95.4	96.6	99.1	98.6	100.0	105.6	106.9
Accommodation and food service activities	I	28.9	L2NQ	99.6	94.1	96.6	98.8	102.7	100.0	103.1	107.9
Total distribution, transport, hotels and restaurants	G - I	179.6	L2ND	99.9	93.1	94.4	96.1	97.1	100.0	105.0	109.0
Information and communication	J										
Publishing, audiovisual and broadcasting activities	JA	16.3	L2NU	92.5	86.0	88.0	91.5	95.3	100.0	96.4	106.0
Telecommunications	JB	18.0	L2NZ	95.3	98.3	103.1	105.1	104.7	100.0	95.5	98.5
IT and other information service activities	JC	28.2	L2O3	86.2	80.8	89.1	90.1	95.8	100.0	107.5	113.4
Total information and communication	J	62.5	L2NT	90.0	86.7	92.3	94.3	98.0	100.0	101.1	107.2
Financial and insurance	K	76.1	L2O6	113.5	113.0	104.3	102.8	103.4	100.0	98.2	100.0
Real estate	L	122.1	L2OC	91.2	92.2	94.8	95.7	98.1	100.0	103.6	105.2
Professional and support	M-N										
Professional, scientific and technical activitie	M										
Legal, accounting, management, architect, engineering etc	MA	53.0	L2OJ	91.9	85.0	85.7	89.4	92.9	100.0	106.8	112.0
Scientific research and d velopment	MB	5.4	L2OQ	90.5	86.9	97.2	91.5	94.9	100.0	105.3	112.5
Other professional, scientific and technical activitie	MC	14.3	L2OS	83.4	74.4	79.8	92.6	98.7	100.0	107.3	110.1
Total professional, scientific and technical activitie	M	72.7	L2OI	90.0	83.0	85.4	90.2	94.1	100.0	106.8	111.6
Administrative and support service activities	N	46.3	L2OX	84.2	73.4	82.0	87.9	95.1	100.0	109.7	115.3
Total professional and support	M - N	119.0	L2OH	87.6	79.0	84.1	89.3	94.5	100.0	107.9	113.1
Government, health and education	O-Q										
Public admin, defence, compulsory social security	O	52.0	L2P8	108.4	109.4	108.4	103.6	102.2	100.0	98.4	95.9
Education	P	63.2	L2PA	97.7	97.0	96.2	96.6	99.6	100.0	101.2	102.4
Human health and social work activities	Q										
Human health activities	QA	55.0	L2PD	84.6	88.6	91.1	93.2	97.0	100.0	102.4	104.5
Residential care and social work activities	QB	18.6	L2PF	87.9	88.5	96.3	96.8	99.3	100.0	101.0	99.0
Total human health and social work activities	Q	73.5	L2PC	85.2	88.4	92.3	94.1	97.5	100.0	102.0	103.1
Total government, health and education	O - Q	188.7	L2P7	95.3	96.6	97.8	97.4	99.5	100.0	100.8	100.9
Other services	R-T										
Arts, entertainment and recreation	R	14.3	L2PJ	106.9	96.2	94.8	97.8	103.6	100.0	102.2	101.3
Other service activities	S	21.3	L2PP	97.0	99.6	97.0	102.9	99.5	100.0	111.3	114.3
Activities of households as employers, undiff. Goods	T	4.1	L2PT	97.4	88.3	98.8	93.1	98.0	100.0	94.6	95.6
Total other services	R - T	39.8	L2PI	100.6	97.0	96.3	100.0	100.8	100.0	106.3	107.7
Total service industries	G - T	787.8	L2NC	95.9	93.1	94.5	96.0	98.3	100.0	103.3	106.0
All industries	B.1g	1 000.0	CGCE	98.7	94.3	96.3	97.6	98.6	100.0	103.4	105.8

1 The weights shown are in proportion to total gross value added (GVA) in 2013 and are used to combine the industry output indices to calculate the totals. For 2012 and earlier, totals are calculated using the equivalent weights for the previous year (e.g. totals for 2009 use 2008 weights). Weights may not sum to totals due to rounding.

2 As GVA is expressed in index number form, it is inappropriate to show as a statistical adjustment any divergence from the other measures of GDP. Such an adjustment does, however, exist implicitly.

3 Because of differences in the annual and monthly production inquiries, estimates of current price output and gross value added by industry derived from the current price Input-Output Supply and Use Tables are not consistent with the equivalent measures of chained volume measures growth given in 2.3. These differences do not affect GDP totals.

Source: Office for National Statistics, Blue Book 2016

19.6 Non-financial corporations
ESA 2010 sector S.11

£ million

			2008	2009	2010	2011	2012	2013	2014	2015
Allocation of primary income account		II.1.2								
Resources										
Operating surplus, gross	NQBE	B.2g	289 496	260 718	278 455	292 079	295 177	313 511	340 618	345 183
Property income, received		D.4								
Interest		D.41								
Interest before FISIM allocation[1]	J4WQ	D.41g	26 055	9 281	9 089	9 183	8 714	9 363	9 345	8 502
plus FISIM[1]	IV89	P.119	5 769	3 305	2 664	3 749	3 585	3 118	4 788	5 558
Total	EABC	D.41	31 824	12 586	11 753	12 932	12 299	12 481	14 133	14 060
Distributed income of corporations	EABD	D.42	47 124	62 614	57 887	68 098	62 539	64 344	84 852	70 342
Reinvested earnings on foreign direct investment	WEYD	D.43	37 714	12 455	26 240	27 262	11 717	6 982	−21 635	−14 292
Other investment income		D.44								
Attributable to insurance policy holders	L8GM	D.441	972	975	430	297	219	279	339	160
Attributable to collective investment fund shareholders		D.443								
Dividends	L8H9	D.4431	6	2	5	3	–	2	4	4
Retained earnings	L8HG	D.4432	8	4	8	4	4	4	4	4
Total	L8H2	D.443	14	6	13	7	4	6	8	8
Total other investment income	FAOF	D.44	986	981	443	304	223	285	347	168
Rent	FAOG	D.45	126	132	130	132	132	132	132	132
Total	FAKY	D.4	117 774	88 768	96 453	108 728	86 910	84 224	77 829	70 410
Total resources	FBXJ	TR	407 270	349 486	374 908	400 807	382 087	397 735	418 447	415 593
Uses										
Property income, paid		D.4								
Interest		D.41								
Interest before FISIM allocation[1]	J4WS	D.41g	74 556	50 386	38 609	36 678	38 035	35 702	36 414	35 385
less FISIM[1]	IV88	P.119	5 588	9 081	9 521	8 466	7 968	7 980	6 452	5 916
Total	EABG	D.41	68 968	41 305	29 088	28 212	30 067	27 722	29 962	29 469
Distributed income of corporations	NVCS	D.42	113 873	119 926	122 545	139 681	141 557	141 570	147 769	149 312
Of which: PNFCs dividends[2]	NETZ	D.421	88 073	84 637	82 534	103 728	106 074	103 570	109 673	110 013
Reinvested earnings on foreign direct investment	HDVB	D.43	3 656	−4 539	156	−5 971	−5 363	5 263	3 817	11 379
Rent	FBXO	D.45	1 259	1 285	1 281	1 287	1 303	1 429	1 423	1 406
Total	FBXK	D.4	187 756	157 977	153 070	163 209	167 564	175 984	182 971	191 566
Balance of primary incomes, gross	NQBG	B.5g	**219 514**	**191 509**	**221 838**	**237 598**	**214 523**	**221 751**	**235 476**	**224 027**
Total uses	FBXJ	TU	407 270	349 486	374 908	400 807	382 087	397 735	418 447	415 593
less consumption of fixed capital	DBGF	P.51c	108 424	111 803	110 567	113 891	116 317	119 176	121 866	125 281
Balance of primary incomes, net	FBXQ	B.5n	111 090	79 706	111 271	123 707	98 206	102 575	113 610	98 746

1 Financial intermediation services indirectly measured.
2 Private non-financial corporations.

Source: Office for National Statistics, Blue Book 2016

19.7 Non-financial corporations
ESA 2010 sector S.11

£ million

Secondary distribution of income account		II.2	2008	2009	2010	2011	2012	2013	2014	2015
Resources											
Balance of primary incomes, gross	NQBG	B.5g	219 514	191 509	221 838	237 598	214 523	221 751	235 476	224 027
Net social contributions		D.61								
Employers' imputed social contributions	L8RD	D.612	3 710	4 179	3 301	2 969	3 520	3 471	3 517	3 041
Total	L8TP	D.61	3 710	4 179	3 301	2 969	3 520	3 471	3 517	3 041
Current transfers other than taxes,		D.7								
social contributions and benefits										
Non-life insurance claims	FCBP	D.72	5 230	5 578	5 775	3 745	3 523	6 360	5 697	4 823
Miscellaneous current transfers	CY8C	D.75	–	–	–	–	724	136	–	–
Total	NRJB	D.7	5 230	5 578	5 775	3 745	4 247	6 496	5 697	4 823
Total resources	FCBR	TR	228 454	201 266	230 914	244 312	222 290	231 718	244 690	231 891
Uses											
Current taxes on income, wealth etc.		D.5								
Taxes on income	FCBS	D.51	40 973	33 992	35 667	35 731	32 821	32 406	30 680	31 901
Social benefits other than social transfers in kind		D.62								
Other social insurance benefits	L8S3	D.622	3 710	4 179	3 301	2 969	3 520	3 471	3 517	3 041
Total	L8TD	D.62	3 710	4 179	3 301	2 969	3 520	3 471	3 517	3 041
Current transfers other than taxes,		D.7								
social contributions and benefits										
Net non-life insurance premiums	FCBY	D.71	5 230	5 578	5 775	3 745	3 523	6 360	5 697	4 823
Miscellaneous current transfers	CY8B	D.75	488	488	488	488	488	488	488	488
Total	FCBX	D.7	5 718	6 066	6 263	4 233	4 011	6 848	6 185	5 311
Gross disposable income	NRJD	B.6g	**178 053**	**157 029**	**185 683**	**201 379**	**181 938**	**188 993**	**204 308**	**191 638**
Total uses	FCBR	TU	228 454	201 266	230 914	244 312	222 290	231 718	244 690	231 891
less consumption of fixed capital	DBGF	P.51c	108 424	111 803	110 567	113 891	116 317	119 176	121 866	125 281
Disposable income, net	FCCF	B.6n	69 629	45 226	75 116	87 488	65 621	69 817	82 442	66 357

Source: Office for National Statistics, Blue Book 2016

19.8 Private non-financial corporations
ESA 2010 sectors S.11002 and S.11003[1]

£ million

			2008	2009	2010	2011	2012	2013	2014	2015
Allocation of primary income account		II.1.2								
before deduction of fixed capital consumption										
Resources										
Operating surplus, gross	NRJK	B.2g	279 852	251 396	268 903	282 923	285 798	304 034	331 709	336 390
Property income, received		D.4								
Interest		D.41								
Interest before FISIM allocation[2]	I69R	D.41g	25 221	9 004	8 793	8 946	8 494	9 187	9 189	8 360
plus FISIM[2]	IV87	P.119	5 765	3 313	2 662	3 745	3 574	3 105	4 759	5 534
Total	DSZR	D.41	30 986	12 317	11 455	12 691	12 068	12 292	13 948	13 894
Distributed income of corporations	DSZS	D.42	46 389	62 589	57 803	68 012	62 456	64 263	84 751	70 267
Reinvested earnings on foreign direct investment	HDVR	D.43	37 890	12 337	26 179	27 201	11 656	6 911	−21 651	−14 356
Other investment income		D.44								
Attributable to insurance policy holders	KZI4	D.441	972	975	430	297	219	279	339	160
Attributable to collective investment fund shares		D.443								
Dividends	KZI6	D.4431	6	2	5	3	–	2	4	4
Retained earnings	KZI7	D.4432	8	4	8	4	4	4	4	4
Total	L5U6	D.443	14	6	13	7	4	6	8	8
Total	FCFP	D.44	986	981	443	304	223	285	347	168
Rent	FAOL	D.45	126	132	130	132	132	132	132	132
Total	FACV	D.4	116 377	88 356	96 010	108 340	86 535	83 883	77 527	70 105
Total resources	FCFQ	TR	396 229	339 752	364 913	391 263	372 333	387 917	409 236	406 495
Uses										
Property income, paid		D.4								
Interest		D.41								
Interest before FISIM allocation[2]	I6A2	D.41g	72 142	48 380	37 290	35 666	37 243	34 692	35 611	34 270
less FISIM[2]	IV86	P.119	5 518	9 023	9 483	8 424	7 944	7 967	6 444	5 909
Total	DSZV	D.41	66 624	39 357	27 807	27 242	29 299	26 725	29 167	28 361
Distributed income of corporations	NVDC	D.42	113 222	119 129	121 783	138 606	140 305	140 428	146 815	148 593
Of which: dividend payments	NETZ	D.421	88 073	84 637	82 534	103 728	106 074	103 570	109 673	110 013
Reinvested earnings on foreign direct investment	HDVB	D.43	3 656	−4 539	156	−5 971	−5 363	5 263	3 817	11 379
Rent	FCFU	D.45	1 259	1 285	1 281	1 287	1 303	1 429	1 423	1 406
Total	FCFR	D.4	184 761	155 232	151 027	161 164	165 544	173 845	181 222	189 739
Balance of primary incomes, gross	NRJM	B.5g	**211 468**	**184 520**	**213 886**	**230 099**	**206 789**	**214 072**	**228 014**	**216 756**
Total uses	FCFQ	TU	396 229	339 752	364 913	391 263	372 333	387 917	409 236	406 495
less consumption of fixed capital	NSRK	P.51c	100 480	103 680	102 609	105 886	108 308	110 857	113 410	116 735
Balance of primary incomes, net	FCFW	B.5n	110 988	80 840	111 277	124 213	98 481	103 215	114 604	100 021

1 S.11002 National controlled and S.11003 Foreign controlled
2 Financial intermediation services indirectly measured

Source: Office for National Statistics, Blue Book 2016

19.9 Private non-financial corporations
ESA 2010 sectors S.11002 and S.11003[1]

£ million

			2008	2009	2010	2011	2012	2013	2014	2015
Secondary distribution of income account		II.2								
Resources										
Balance of primary incomes, gross	NRJM	**B.5g**	**211 468**	**184 520**	**213 886**	**230 099**	**206 789**	**214 072**	**228 014**	**216 756**
Net social contributions		D.61								
Employers' imputed social contributions	L8RJ	D.612	3 559	4 019	3 181	2 859	3 407	3 370	3 432	2 961
Total	L8TV	D.61	3 559	4 019	3 181	2 859	3 407	3 370	3 432	2 961
Other current transfers		D.7								
Net non-life insurance claims	FDBA	D.72	5 230	5 578	5 775	3 745	3 523	6 360	5 697	4 823
Total resources	FDBC	TR	220 257	194 117	222 842	236 703	213 719	223 802	237 143	224 540
Uses										
Current taxes on income, wealth etc.		D.5								
Taxes on income	FCCP	D.51	40 719	33 741	35 518	35 622	32 715	32 333	30 645	31 852
Social security benefits other than social transfers in kind		D.62								
Other social insurance benefits	L8S9	D.622	3 559	4 019	3 181	2 859	3 407	3 370	3 432	2 961
Total	L8TH	D.62	3 559	4 019	3 181	2 859	3 407	3 370	3 432	2 961
Current transfers other than taxes, social contributions and benefits		D.7								
Net non-life insurance premiums	FDBH	D.71	5 230	5 578	5 775	3 745	3 523	6 360	5 697	4 823
Miscellaneous current transfers	CY88	D.75	488	488	488	488	488	488	488	488
Total	FCCN	D.7	5 718	6 066	6 263	4 233	4 011	6 848	6 185	5 311
Gross disposable income	NRJQ	**B.6g**	**170 261**	**150 291**	**177 880**	**193 989**	**173 586**	**181 251**	**196 881**	**184 416**
Total uses	FDBC	TU	220 257	194 117	222 842	236 703	213 719	223 802	237 143	224 540
less consumption of fixed capital	NSRK	P.51c	100 480	103 680	102 609	105 886	108 308	110 857	113 410	116 735
Disposable income, net	FDBK	B.6n	69 781	46 611	75 271	88 103	65 278	70 394	83 471	67 681

1 S.11002 National controlled and S.11003 Foreign controlled

Source: Office for National Statistics, Blue Book 2016

19.10 Households and non-profit institutions serving households
ESA 2010 sectors S.14 and S.15

£ million

			2008	2009	2010	2011	2012	2013	2014	2015
Allocation of primary income account before deduction of fixed capital consumption		II.1.2								
Resources										
Operating surplus, gross	QWLS	B.2g	152 363	129 108	129 146	134 923	143 263	145 103	157 594	164 976
Mixed income, gross	QWLT	B.3g	94 984	95 088	95 324	98 255	107 181	111 380	120 736	123 870
Compensation of employees		D.1								
Wages and salaries	QWLW	D.11	661 717	662 719	671 533	681 981	695 166	717 359	741 947	770 891
Employers' social contributions	QWLX	D.12	129 935	132 471	147 742	148 989	155 189	161 370	156 925	158 122
Total	QWLY	D.1	791 652	795 190	819 275	830 970	850 355	878 729	898 872	929 013
Property income, received		D.4								
Interest		D.41								
Interest before FISIM[1] allocation	J4WY	D.41g	43 529	20 831	20 411	22 299	23 532	21 366	17 567	16 096
plus FISIM	IV8W	P.119	23 517	3 015	−695	548	216	−607	8 086	10 619
Total	QWLZ	D.41	67 046	23 846	19 716	22 847	23 748	20 759	25 653	26 715
Distributed income of corporations	QWMA	D.42	46 411	54 392	58 179	56 690	51 201	53 294	53 624	54 729
Other investment income		D.44								
Attributable to insurance policy holders	L8GL	D.441	28 990	24 219	24 936	24 480	21 982	21 611	19 976	18 195
Payable on pension entitlements	L8GS	D.442	79 922	69 283	80 106	77 775	70 166	67 748	82 519	77 932
Attributable to collective investment fund shareholders		D.443								
Dividends	L8H8	D.4431	1 656	771	1 660	772	716	711	925	1 099
Retained earnings	L8HF	D.4432	2 588	1 203	2 596	1 207	1 125	1 114	1 444	1 720
Total	L8GZ	D.443	4 244	1 974	4 256	1 979	1 841	1 825	2 369	2 819
Total	QWMC	D.44	113 156	95 476	109 298	104 234	93 989	91 184	104 864	98 946
Rent	QWMD	D.45	115	115	118	123	127	128	128	128
Total	QWME	D.4	226 728	173 829	187 311	183 894	169 065	165 365	184 269	180 518
Total resources	QWMF	TR	1 265 727	1 193 215	1 231 056	1 248 042	1 269 864	1 300 577	1 361 471	1 398 377
Uses										
Property income, paid		D.4								
Interest		D.41								
Interest before FISIM allocation	J4WZ	D.41g	98 724	72 196	64 957	62 194	61 813	61 670	60 515	58 590
less FISIM	IV8X	P.119	9 958	44 708	44 908	38 619	36 458	39 821	33 151	31 590
Interest	QWMG	D.41	88 766	27 488	20 049	23 575	25 355	21 849	27 364	27 000
Rent	QWMH	D.45	233	239	239	243	247	248	248	248
Total	QWMI	D.4	88 999	27 727	20 288	23 818	25 602	22 097	27 612	27 248
Balance of primary incomes, gross	QWMJ	B.5g	**1 176 728**	**1 165 488**	**1 210 768**	**1 224 224**	**1 244 262**	**1 278 480**	**1 333 859**	**1 371 129**
Total uses	QWMF	TU	1 265 727	1 193 215	1 231 056	1 248 042	1 269 864	1 300 577	1 361 471	1 398 377
less consumption of fixed capital	QWLL	P.51c	66 324	63 059	64 773	66 251	69 265	74 462	80 242	81 845
Balance of primary incomes, net	QWMK	B.5n	1 110 404	1 102 429	1 145 995	1 157 973	1 174 997	1 204 018	1 253 617	1 289 284

1 Financial intermediation services indirectly measured

Source: Office for National Statistics, Blue Book 2016

19.11 Households and non-profit institutions serving households
ESA 2010 sectors S.14 and S.15

£ million

			2008	2009	2010	2011	2012	2013	2014	2015
Secondary distribution of income account		II.2								
Resources										
Balance of primary incomes, gross	QWMJ	B.5g	1 176 728	1 165 488	1 210 768	1 224 224	1 244 262	1 278 480	1 333 859	1 371 129
Employers' imputed social contributions	L8RF	D.612	657	764	607	546	571	561	593	566
Social benefits other than social transfers in kind		D.62								
Social security benefits in cash	L8QF	D.621	73 871	80 826	82 117	83 826	89 187	91 231	93 650	96 370
Other social insurance benefits	L8QT	D.622	93 461	100 129	105 933	108 158	117 483	120 635	119 959	129 941
Social assistance benefits in cash	MT3B	D.623R	94 147	105 596	112 739	116 117	119 418	120 142	121 109	122 076
Total	QWML	D.62	261 479	286 551	300 789	308 101	326 088	332 008	334 718	348 387
Other current transfers		D.7								
Non-life insurance claims	QWMM	D.72	21 674	21 975	30 811	32 085	30 112	31 335	27 986	27 551
Miscellaneous current transfers	QWMN	D.75	37 899	39 502	40 728	39 451	43 373	39 282	36 302	36 922
Total	QWMO	D.7	59 573	61 477	71 539	71 536	73 485	70 617	64 288	64 473
Total resources	QWMP	TR	1 498 437	1 514 280	1 583 703	1 604 407	1 644 406	1 681 666	1 733 458	1 784 555
Uses										
Current taxes on income, wealth, etc		D.5								
Taxes on income	QWMQ	D.51	159 860	151 348	152 424	157 598	153 734	158 990	162 612	171 782
Other current taxes	NVCO	D.59	32 909	33 752	34 578	34 924	35 390	36 554	37 448	38 070
Total	QWMS	D.5	192 769	185 100	187 002	192 522	189 124	195 544	200 060	209 852
Net social contributions		D.61								
Employers' actual social contributions	L8NJ	D.611	106 047	106 770	121 198	123 082	128 734	134 487	130 232	130 156
Employers' imputed social contributions	M9X2	D.612	23 887	25 699	26 544	25 907	26 455	26 883	26 693	27 966
Households' actual social contributions	L8PR	D.613	60 186	57 155	58 668	60 422	63 597	65 366	67 949	68 806
Households' social contribution supplements	L8Q7	D.614	79 922	69 283	80 106	77 775	70 166	67 748	82 519	77 932
Social insurance scheme service charge	L8LT	D.61SC	−12 777	−11 101	−12 568	−14 740	−17 046	−18 322	−18 809	−19 275
Total	QWMY	D.61	257 265	247 806	273 948	272 446	271 906	276 162	288 584	285 585
Social benefits other than social transfers in kind		D.62								
Other social insurance benefits	L8S5	D.622	657	764	607	546	571	561	593	566
Social assistance benefits in cash	MT3D	D.623U	496	494	486	496	496	496	496	496
Total	QWMZ	D.62	1 153	1 258	1 093	1 042	1 067	1 057	1 089	1 062
Other current transfers		D.7								
Net non-life insurance premiums	QWNA	D.71	21 674	21 975	30 811	32 085	30 112	31 335	27 986	27 551
Miscellaneous current transfers	QWNB	D.75	13 616	13 939	14 113	14 387	15 378	16 026	16 525	16 535
Total	QWNC	D.7	35 290	35 914	44 924	46 472	45 490	47 361	44 511	44 086
Gross disposable income	QWND	B.6g	1 011 960	1 044 202	1 076 736	1 091 925	1 136 819	1 161 542	1 199 214	1 243 970
Total uses	QWMP	TU	1 498 437	1 514 280	1 583 703	1 604 407	1 644 406	1 681 666	1 733 458	1 784 555
less consumption of fixed capital	QWLL	P.51c	66 324	63 059	64 773	66 251	69 265	74 462	80 242	81 845
Disposable income, net	QWNE	B.6n	945 636	981 143	1 011 963	1 025 674	1 067 554	1 087 080	1 118 972	1 162 125
Real households disposable income: (Chained volume measures)										
£ Million (reference year 2013)[1]	RVGK		1 126 252	1 151 402	1 162 678	1 138 534	1 163 065	1 161 542	1 179 175	1 219 955
Index (2013=100)	OSXR		97.0	99.1	100.1	98.0	100.1	100.0	101.5	105.0

1 Gross household disposable income deflated by the households and NPISH final consumption deflator

Source: Office for National Statistics, Blue Book 2016

19.12 Households and non-profit institutions serving households
ESA 2010 sectors S.14 and S.15

£ million

Redistribution of income in kind account		II.3	2008	2009	2010	2011	2012	2013	2014	2015
Resources										
Gross disposable income	QWND	B.6g	1 011 960	1 044 202	1 076 736	1 091 925	1 136 819	1 161 542	1 199 214	1 243 970
Social transfers in kind		D.63								
Non-market produced	QWNH	D.631	203 631	218 422	222 601	225 667	229 722	235 397	241 044	247 558
Purchased market production	NSSA	D.632	36 123	37 414	38 518	39 746	40 446	40 474	43 867	42 382
Total	NSSB	D.63	239 754	255 836	261 119	265 413	270 168	275 871	284 911	289 940
Total resources	NSSC	TR	1 251 714	1 300 038	1 337 855	1 357 338	1 406 987	1 437 413	1 484 125	1 533 910
Uses										
Social transfers in kind		D.63								
Non-market produced	DPSD	D.631	46 616	49 958	50 488	52 862	52 849	54 535	56 672	58 124
Total	HAEK	D.63	46 616	49 958	50 488	52 862	52 849	54 535	56 672	58 124
Adjusted disposable income, gross	NSSD	B.7g	1 205 098	1 250 080	1 287 367	1 304 476	1 354 138	1 382 878	1 427 453	1 475 786
Total uses	NSSC	TU	1 251 714	1 300 038	1 337 855	1 357 338	1 406 987	1 437 413	1 484 125	1 533 910

£ million

			2008	2009	2010	2011	2012	2013	2014	2015
Use of income account		II.4								
Use of disposable income account		II.4.1								
Resources										
Households' gross disposable income	QWND	B.6g	1 011 960	1 044 202	1 076 736	1 091 925	1 136 819	1 161 542	1 199 214	1 243 970
Adjustment for the change in pension entitlements	NSSE	D.8	68 265	56 907	75 076	68 888	58 408	58 157	69 963	51 786
Total resources	NSSF	TR	1 080 225	1 101 109	1 151 812	1 160 813	1 195 227	1 219 699	1 269 177	1 295 756
Uses										
Final consumption expenditure		P.3								
Individual consumption expenditure	NSSG	P.31	1 022 124	998 439	1 025 426	1 057 138	1 095 763	1 138 546	1 182 902	1 216 113
Gross saving	NSSH	B.8g	58 101	102 670	126 386	103 675	99 464	81 153	86 275	79 643
Total uses	NSSF	TU	1 080 225	1 101 109	1 151 812	1 160 813	1 195 227	1 219 699	1 269 177	1 295 756
less consumption of fixed capital	QWLL	P.51c	66 324	63 059	64 773	66 251	69 265	74 462	80 242	81 845
Saving, net	NSSI	B.8n	–8 223	39 611	61 613	37 424	30 199	6 691	6 033	–2 202
Use of adjusted disposable income account		II.4.2								
Resources										
Adjusted disposable income, gross	NSSD	B.7g	1 205 098	1 250 080	1 287 367	1 304 476	1 354 138	1 382 878	1 427 453	1 475 786
Adjustment for the change in pension entitlements	NSSE	D.8	68 265	56 907	75 076	68 888	58 408	58 157	69 963	51 786
Total resources	NSSJ	TR	1 273 363	1 306 987	1 362 443	1 373 364	1 412 546	1 441 035	1 497 416	1 527 572
Uses										
Actual final consumption		P.4								
Actual individual consumption	ABRE	P.41	1 215 262	1 204 317	1 236 057	1 269 689	1 313 082	1 359 882	1 411 141	1 447 929
Gross saving	NSSH	B.8g	58 101	102 670	126 386	103 675	99 464	81 153	86 275	79 643
Total uses	NSSJ	TU	1 273 363	1 306 987	1 362 443	1 373 364	1 412 546	1 441 035	1 497 416	1 527 572
Households saving ratio (per cent)	RVGL		5.4	9.3	11.0	8.9	8.3	6.7	6.8	6.1

Source: Office for National Statistics, Blue Book 2016

19.13 The sector accounts: Key economic indicators

£ million

			2008	2009	2010	2011	2012	2013	2014	2015
Net lending(+)/borrowing(-) by:										
Non-financial corporations	EABO	B.9	40 814	59 453	59 488	69 094	38 837	34 059	33 943	19 470
Financial corporations	NHCQ	B.9	−5 845	6 029	−23 194	−15 672	2 825	−15 067	−17 939	−25 488
General government	NNBK	B.9	−76 825	−160 520	−150 439	−124 569	−139 423	−99 473	−101 740	−80 623
Households and NPISH[1]	NSSZ	B.9	−12 923	50 612	71 089	41 682	36 161	3 567	323	−10 895
Rest of the world	NHRB	B.9	54 782	44 427	43 059	29 468	61 600	76 914	85 413	101 390
Private non-financial corporations										
Gross trading profits										
Continental shelf profits	CAGD		28 120	21 452	25 379	29 806	25 246	23 470	16 702	10 253
Others	CAED		243 235	212 042	229 039	237 954	237 494	256 906	287 608	294 138
Rental of buildings	DTWR		22 050	22 115	22 920	23 961	25 791	26 806	26 773	26 929
less holding gains of inventories	DLRA		13 553	4 213	8 435	8 798	2 733	3 148	−626	−5 070
Gross operating surplus	CAER	B.2g	279 852	251 396	268 903	282 923	285 798	304 034	331 709	336 390
Households and NPISH										
Disposable income, gross	QWND	B.6g	1 011 960	1 044 202	1 076 736	1 091 925	1 136 819	1 161 542	1 199 214	1 243 970
Implied deflator of households and NPISH Individual consumption expenditure Index (2013=100)[2]	YBFS		89.9	90.7	92.6	95.9	97.7	100.0	101.7	102.0
Real households disposable income:										
Chained volume measures (reference year 2013)	RVGK		1 126 252	1 151 402	1 162 678	1 138 534	1 163 065	1 161 542	1 179 175	1 219 955
Index (2013=100)[2]	OSXR		97.0	99.1	100.1	98.0	100.1	100.0	101.5	105.0
Gross saving	NSSH	B.8g	58 101	102 670	126 386	103 675	99 464	81 153	86 275	79 643
Households total resources	NSSF		1 080 225	1 101 109	1 151 812	1 160 813	1 195 227	1 219 699	1 269 177	1 295 756
Saving ratio (per cent)	RVGL		5.4	9.3	11.0	8.9	8.3	6.7	6.8	6.1

1 Non-profit institutions serving households
2 Rounded to one decimal place

Source: Office for National Statistics, Blue Book 2016

19.14 Household final consumption expenditure: classified by purpose
At current market prices

£ million

			2008	2009	2010	2011	2012	2013	2014	2015
Final consumption expenditure of households		P.31								
Durable goods										
Furnishings, household equipment and routine maintenance of the house	LLIJ	05	23 094	20 419	20 773	21 584	21 398	21 579	23 431	25 051
Health	LLIK	06	3 069	3 167	2 979	2 963	3 094	3 628	3 633	3 454
Transport	LLIL	07	35 493	35 067	35 410	35 908	38 684	41 481	45 295	49 255
Communication	LLIM	08	802	869	761	754	919	994	937	1 064
Recreation and culture	LLIN	09	24 372	23 230	23 719	22 547	21 813	22 897	23 690	24 260
Miscellaneous goods and services	LLIO	12	5 525	5 312	5 678	6 553	7 502	7 372	8 087	8 228
Total durable goods	UTIA	D	92 355	88 064	89 320	90 309	93 410	97 951	105 073	111 312
Semi-durable goods										
Clothing and footwear	LLJL	03	48 607	48 333	50 243	53 248	54 820	57 258	60 900	64 396
Furnishings, household equipment and routine maintenance of the house	LLJM	05	13 893	13 862	14 336	13 939	14 671	15 763	16 235	17 711
Transport	LLJN	07	4 102	4 121	3 929	3 831	4 281	4 674	4 683	4 514
Recreation and culture	LLJO	09	30 642	28 281	28 244	26 780	27 687	27 056	27 755	29 556
Miscellaneous goods and services	LLJP	12	3 275	3 556	5 505	5 765	5 818	7 091	6 181	6 151
Total semi-durable goods	UTIQ	SD	100 519	98 153	102 257	103 563	107 277	111 842	115 754	122 328
Non-durable goods										
Food and drink	ABZV	01	78 818	80 526	83 600	86 896	91 263	96 534	97 515	95 849
Alcoholic beverages, tobacco and narcotics	ADFL	02	36 408	38 363	39 104	41 948	43 052	43 765	44 936	44 710
Housing, water, electricity, gas and other fuels	LLIX	04	33 661	34 164	35 464	34 571	38 318	40 863	37 890	37 492
Furnishings, household equipment and routine maintenance of the house	LLIY	05	3 887	4 276	4 286	4 146	4 183	4 372	4 429	4 478
Health	LLIZ	06	4 894	4 627	4 802	5 017	6 441	6 943	7 119	7 243
Transport	LLJA	07	29 727	26 622	30 818	35 407	35 500	34 236	32 660	28 396
Recreation and culture	LLJB	09	16 094	15 292	15 213	15 173	15 261	15 958	16 053	16 680
Miscellaneous goods and services	LLJC	12	15 880	15 984	16 079	16 840	17 477	18 429	19 695	20 673
Total non-durable goods	UTII	ND	219 369	219 854	229 366	239 998	251 495	261 100	260 297	255 521
Total goods	UTIE		412 243	406 071	420 943	433 870	452 182	470 893	481 124	489 161
Services										
Clothing and footwear	LLJD	03	1 115	1 199	1 129	1 003	1 015	1 008	1 050	895
Housing, water, electricity, gas and other fuels	LLJE	04	208 761	212 404	220 062	226 396	233 772	241 002	250 377	256 594
Furnishings, household equipment and routine maintenance of the house	LLJF	05	6 465	5 962	6 757	6 589	6 743	7 133	7 272	7 485
Health	LLJG	06	6 418	7 070	7 983	8 389	8 319	8 627	8 470	9 311
Transport	LLJH	07	57 256	55 781	57 843	60 735	64 127	69 807	73 854	78 957
Communication	LLJI	08	18 015	17 613	18 626	18 840	18 939	20 143	20 255	21 444
Recreation and culture	LLJJ	09	34 185	33 339	34 277	35 912	37 741	38 262	39 166	41 763
Education	ADIE	10	13 494	14 659	14 878	14 822	15 783	16 923	17 795	18 330
Restaurants and hotels	ADIF	11	87 890	82 280	86 512	92 265	97 017	101 712	105 788	110 598
Miscellaneous goods and services	LLJK	12	112 614	98 661	93 564	94 884	97 292	99 747	112 108	112 724
Total services	UTIM	S	546 213	528 968	541 631	559 835	580 748	604 364	636 135	658 101
Final consumption expenditure in the UK by resident and non-resident households (domestic concept)	ABQI	0	958 456	935 039	962 574	993 705	1 032 930	1 075 257	1 117 259	1 147 262
Final consumption expenditure outside the UK by UK resident households	ABTA	P.33	37 112	33 273	33 852	32 997	33 725	35 583	37 459	41 444
Final consumption expenditure in the UK by households resident in rest of the world	CDFD	P.34	−20 060	−19 831	−21 488	−22 426	−23 741	−26 829	−28 488	−30 717
Final consumption expenditure by UK resident households in the UK and abroad (national concept)	ABPB	P.31	975 508	948 481	974 938	1 004 276	1 042 914	1 084 011	1 126 230	1 157 989

Source: Office for National Statistics, Blue Book 2016

19.15 Household final consumption expenditure: classified by purpose
Chained volume measures (reference year 2013)

£ million

			2008	2009	2010	2011	2012	2013	2014	2015
Final consumption expenditure of households		P.31								
Durable goods										
Furnishings, household equipment and routine maintenance of the house	LLME	05	26 234	22 416	22 113	22 260	21 534	21 579	23 372	25 083
Health	LLMF	06	3 126	3 211	2 990	2 958	3 072	3 628	3 559	3 346
Transport	LLMG	07	39 105	39 503	36 477	35 546	38 232	41 481	44 683	48 587
Communication	LLMH	08	931	1 002	838	800	943	994	928	1 036
Recreation and culture	LLMI	09	17 094	17 738	18 926	19 820	20 799	22 897	24 283	26 672
Miscellaneous goods and services	LLMJ	12	7 320	6 680	6 696	7 180	7 669	7 372	8 097	8 288
Total durable goods	UTIC	D	91 942	89 534	87 752	88 436	92 177	97 951	104 922	113 012
Semi-durable goods										
Clothing and footwear	LLNG	03	46 155	49 747	52 204	54 118	55 314	57 258	60 666	64 360
Furnishings, household equipment and routine maintenance of the house	LLNH	05	15 937	15 634	15 757	14 378	14 696	15 763	16 118	17 463
Transport	LLNI	07	4 674	4 547	4 158	3 903	4 319	4 674	4 630	4 506
Recreation and culture	LLNJ	09	29 328	27 534	27 603	26 918	27 935	27 056	27 665	29 826
Miscellaneous goods and services	LLNK	12	3 422	3 670	5 722	5 965	5 933	7 091	6 172	6 140
Total semi-durable goods	UTIS	SD	99 329	101 076	105 405	105 281	108 202	111 842	115 251	122 295
Non-durable goods										
Food and drink	ADIP	01	96 838	93 837	94 359	92 903	94 625	96 534	97 754	98 693
Alcoholic beverages, tobacco and narcotics	ADIS	02	49 078	47 101	47 469	45 223	45 647	43 765	43 514	42 650
Housing, water, electricity, gas and other fuels	LLMS	04	43 545	41 402	44 043	39 504	40 704	40 863	36 537	37 371
Furnishings, household equipment and routine maintenance of the house	LLMT	05	4 770	4 890	4 751	4 319	4 236	4 372	4 398	4 581
Health	LLMU	06	5 254	4 889	4 996	5 157	6 511	6 943	7 007	7 030
Transport	LLMV	07	36 825	35 754	34 481	35 365	35 147	34 236	34 369	34 328
Recreation and culture	LLMW	09	19 017	17 393	16 577	15 887	15 618	15 958	15 615	16 126
Miscellaneous goods and services	LLMX	12	17 261	16 917	16 606	16 942	17 436	18 429	19 888	21 175
Total non-durable goods	UTIK	ND	272 040	261 667	262 795	255 293	259 877	261 100	259 082	261 954
Total goods	UTIG		461 456	451 364	455 142	448 686	460 063	470 893	479 255	497 261
Services										
Clothing and footwear	LLMY	03	1 248	1 313	1 211	1 037	1 030	1 008	1 026	854
Housing, water, electricity, gas and other fuels	LLMZ	04	228 231	228 304	232 722	235 311	237 926	241 002	246 232	247 186
Furnishings, household equipment and routine maintenance of the house	LLNA	05	7 044	6 378	7 084	6 783	6 842	7 133	7 109	7 099
Health	LLNB	06	7 524	7 948	8 663	8 840	8 581	8 627	8 272	8 849
Transport	LLNC	07	69 536	65 745	66 374	66 030	67 436	69 807	72 945	76 042
Communication	LLND	08	21 196	20 510	20 679	20 144	19 489	20 143	20 022	20 911
Recreation and culture	LLNE	09	41 213	38 677	38 290	38 248	39 046	38 262	38 093	39 647
Education	ADMJ	10	20 494	20 667	19 914	18 867	18 515	16 923	16 163	15 322
Restaurants and hotels	ADMK	11	103 082	94 413	96 762	97 980	99 243	101 712	102 832	104 520
Miscellaneous goods and services	LLNF	12	102 321	97 965	95 582	95 433	97 773	99 747	103 779	101 425
Total services	UTIO	S	601 261	581 442	586 688	588 316	595 660	604 364	616 473	621 855
Final consumption expenditure in the UK by resident and non-resident households (domestic concept)	ABQJ	0	1 062 701	1 032 742	1 041 767	1 036 932	1 055 705	1 075 257	1 095 728	1 119 116
Final consumption expenditure outside the UK by UK resident households	ABTC	P.33	46 007	36 846	35 990	33 674	35 394	35 583	39 193	46 089
Final consumption expenditure in the UK by households resident in rest of the world	CCHX		−22 880	−22 447	−23 797	−23 901	−24 539	−26 829	−27 767	−29 417
Final consumption expenditure by UK resident households in the UK and abroad (national concept)	ABPF	P.3	1 084 930	1 047 083	1 053 933	1 046 647	1 066 530	1 084 011	1 107 154	1 135 788

Source: Office for National Statistics, Blue Book 2016

19.16 Individual consumption expenditure at current market prices by households, non-profit institutions serving households and general government
Classified by function (COICOP/COPNI/COFOG)[1]

£ million

			2008	2009	2010	2011	2012	2013	2014	2015
Final consumption expenditure of households		P.31								
Food and non-alcoholic beverages	ABZV	01	78 818	80 526	83 600	86 896	91 263	96 534	97 515	95 849
Food	ABZW	01.1	69 743	71 186	73 903	76 302	80 287	85 128	85 949	84 292
Non-alcoholic beverages	ADFK	01.2	9 075	9 340	9 697	10 594	10 976	11 406	11 566	11 557
Alcoholic beverages, tobacco and narcotics	ADFL	02	36 408	38 363	39 104	41 948	43 052	43 765	44 936	44 710
Alcoholic beverages	ADFM	02.1	14 133	14 578	15 383	16 178	16 975	17 495	18 085	18 486
Tobacco	ADFN	02.2	15 879	16 210	17 292	18 203	18 698	18 916	19 830	19 189
Narcotics	MNC2	02.3	6 396	7 575	6 429	7 567	7 379	7 354	7 021	7 035
Clothing and footwear	ADFP	03	49 722	49 532	51 372	54 251	55 835	58 266	61 950	65 291
Clothing	ADFQ	03.1	42 499	42 018	43 718	46 589	47 670	49 960	52 638	55 272
Footwear	ADFR	03.2	7 223	7 514	7 654	7 662	8 165	8 306	9 312	10 019
Housing, water, electricity, gas and other fuels	ADFS	04	242 422	246 568	255 526	260 967	272 090	281 865	288 267	294 086
Actual rentals for housing	ADFT	04.1	40 828	43 411	48 927	53 026	55 434	56 965	59 243	60 079
Imputed rentals for housing	ADFU	04.2	162 269	163 251	165 345	167 423	172 038	177 519	184 473	190 140
Maintenance and repair of the dwelling	ADFV	04.3	2 452	2 358	2 229	2 242	2 443	2 592	3 028	2 808
Water supply and miscellaneous dwelling services	ADFW	04.4	8 057	8 255	8 596	8 877	9 191	9 528	9 764	9 864
Electricity, gas and other fuels	ADFX	04.5	28 816	29 293	30 429	29 399	32 984	35 261	31 759	31 195
Furnishings, household equipment and routine		05								
maintenance of the house	ADFY		47 339	44 519	46 152	46 258	46 995	48 847	51 367	54 725
Furniture, furnishings, carpets and other floor coverings	ADFZ	05.1	17 595	15 699	15 740	16 775	16 380	16 736	18 244	19 772
Household textiles	ADGG	05.2	5 509	5 719	6 305	4 921	5 242	6 002	6 393	7 109
Household appliances	ADGL	05.3	6 082	5 695	6 076	6 215	6 323	6 135	6 592	6 896
Glassware, tableware and household utensils	ADGM	05.4	4 408	4 222	4 131	4 676	4 805	5 054	5 050	5 423
Tools and equipment for house and garden	ADGN	05.5	3 861	3 407	3 365	3 568	3 912	3 995	3 996	4 200
Goods and services for routine household maintenance	ADGO	05.6	9 884	9 777	10 535	10 103	10 333	10 925	11 092	11 325
Health	ADGP	06	14 381	14 864	15 764	16 369	17 854	19 198	19 222	20 008
Medical products, appliances and equipment	ADGQ	06.1	7 963	7 794	7 781	7 980	9 535	10 571	10 752	10 697
Out-patient services	ADGR	06.2	3 621	3 953	4 849	5 309	5 152	5 613	5 316	5 920
Hospital services	ADGS	06.3	2 797	3 117	3 134	3 080	3 167	3 014	3 154	3 391
Transport	ADGT	07	126 578	121 591	128 000	135 881	142 592	150 198	156 492	161 122
Purchase of vehicles	ADGU	07.1	35 493	35 067	35 410	35 908	38 684	41 481	45 295	49 255
Operation of personal transport equipment	ADGV	07.2	56 646	53 514	58 647	63 237	64 583	65 125	65 445	62 930
Transport services	ADGW	07.3	34 439	33 010	33 943	36 736	39 325	43 592	45 752	48 937
Communication	ADGX	08	18 817	18 482	19 387	19 594	19 858	21 137	21 192	22 508
Postal services	CDEF	08.1	1 024	1 055	908	752	585	781	721	717
Telephone and telefax equipment	ADWO	08.2	802	869	761	754	919	994	937	1 064
Telephone and telefax services	ADWP	08.3	16 991	16 558	17 718	18 088	18 354	19 362	19 534	20 727
Recreation and culture	ADGY	09	105 293	100 142	101 453	100 412	102 502	104 173	106 664	112 259
Audio-visual, photographic and information processing equipment	ADGZ	09.1	23 538	21 321	21 076	20 100	19 113	18 715	17 605	16 617
Other major durables for recreation and culture	ADHL	09.2	7 154	7 379	7 729	7 204	7 618	8 594	10 490	12 167
Other recreational items and equipment; flowers, garden and pets	ADHZ	09.3	30 500	29 170	30 026	28 640	29 622	30 058	31 789	34 232
Recreational and cultural services	ADIA	09.4	31 605	30 585	31 218	33 051	34 608	34 953	35 720	38 179
Newspapers, books and stationery	ADIC	09.5	12 496	11 687	11 404	11 417	11 541	11 853	11 060	11 064
Package holidays[2]	ADID	09.6	–	–	–	–	–	–	–	–
Education		10								
Education services	ADIE	10	13 494	14 659	14 878	14 822	15 783	16 923	17 795	18 330
Restaurants and hotels	ADIF	11	87 890	82 280	86 512	92 265	97 017	101 712	105 788	110 598
Catering services	ADIG	11.1	70 408	65 340	68 456	73 058	76 113	79 898	82 169	84 463
Accommodation services	ADIH	11.2	17 482	16 940	18 056	19 207	20 904	21 814	23 619	26 135
Miscellaneous goods and services	ADII	12	137 294	123 513	120 826	124 042	128 089	132 639	146 071	147 776
Personal care	ADIJ	12.1	22 363	22 771	23 560	24 162	24 807	26 003	27 578	28 774
Prostitution	MNC8	12.2	4 071	4 189	4 336	4 454	4 562	4 674	4 701	4 723
Personal effects n.e.c.	ADIK	12.3	7 825	7 700	9 824	10 933	11 980	13 036	12 854	13 092
Social protection	ADIL	12.4	13 517	13 141	13 259	13 042	13 488	15 170	16 112	16 605
Insurance	ADIM	12.5	19 237	21 449	20 243	21 295	23 737	23 430	26 571	22 610
Financial services n.e.c.	ADIN	12.6	61 041	45 093	41 440	41 502	39 629	40 034	48 178	51 759
Other services n.e.c.	ADIO	12.7	9 240	9 170	8 164	8 654	9 886	10 292	10 077	10 213
Final consumption expenditure in the UK by resident and non-resident households(domestic concept)	ABQI	0	958 456	935 039	962 574	993 705	1 032 930	1 075 257	1 117 259	1 147 262
Final consumption expenditure outside the UK by UK resident households	ABTA	P.33	37 112	33 273	33 852	32 997	33 725	35 583	37 459	41 444
Final consumption expenditure in the UK by households resident in rest of the world	CDFD	P.34	−20 060	−19 831	−21 488	−22 426	−23 741	−26 829	−28 488	−30 717
Final consumption expenditure by UK resident households in the UK and abroad (national concept)	ABPB	P.31	975 508	948 481	974 938	1 004 276	1 042 914	1 084 011	1 126 230	1 157 989

19.16 Individual consumption expenditure at current market prices by households, non-profit institutions serving households and general government

Classified by function (COICOP/COPNI/COFOG)[1]

£ million

			2008	2009	2010	2011	2012	2013	2014	2015
Consumption expenditure of UK resident households		P.31								
Final consumption expenditure of UK resident households in theUK and abroad	ABPB	P.31	975 508	948 481	974 938	1 004 276	1 042 914	1 084 011	1 126 230	1 157 989
Final individual consumption expenditure of NPISH		13								
Final individual consumption expenditure of NPISH	ABNV	P.31	46 616	49 958	50 488	52 862	52 849	54 535	56 672	58 124
Final individual consumption expenditure of general government		14								
Health	IWX5	14.1	100 888	109 096	111 872	115 251	117 284	120 294	126 086	130 318
Recreation and culture	IWX6	14.2	6 047	6 285	6 187	6 246	6 469	5 859	5 791	5 854
Education	IWX7	14.3	55 758	58 862	60 788	59 941	60 092	61 083	61 936	61 660
Social protection	IWX8	14.4	30 445	31 635	31 784	31 113	33 474	34 100	34 426	33 984
Final individual consumption expenditure of general government	NNAQ	P.31	193 138	205 878	210 631	212 551	217 319	221 336	228 239	231 816
Total, individual consumption expenditure/ actual individual consumption	ABRE	P.31 P.41	1 215 262	1 204 317	1 236 057	1 269 689	1 313 082	1 359 882	1 411 141	1 447 929

1 "Purpose" or "function" classifications are designed to indicate the "socio-economic objectives" that institutional units aim to achieve through various kinds of outlays. COICOP is the Classification of Individual Consumption by Purpose and applies to households. COPNI is the Classification of the Purposes of Non-profit Institutions Serving Households and COFOG is the Classification of the Functions of Government.
2 Package holidays data are dispersed between components (transport etc).

Source: Office for National Statistics, Blue Book 2016

19.17 Individual consumption expenditure by households, NPISH and general government. Chained volume measures (reference year 2013)

Classified by function (COICOP/COPNI/COFOG)[1]

£ million

			2008	2009	2010	2011	2012	2013	2014	2015
Final consumption expenditure of households		P.31								
Food and non-alcoholic beverages	ADIP	01	96 838	93 837	94 359	92 903	94 625	96 534	97 754	98 693
Food	ADIQ	01.1	85 292	82 472	83 224	81 720	83 493	85 128	86 197	86 989
Non-alcoholic beverages	ADIR	01.2	11 547	11 373	11 128	11 181	11 133	11 406	11 557	11 704
Alcoholic beverages, tobacco and narcotics	ADIS	02	49 078	47 101	47 469	45 223	45 647	43 765	43 514	42 650
Alcoholic beverages	ADIT	02.1	18 339	17 631	18 101	17 612	17 765	17 495	17 930	18 341
Tobacco	ADIU	02.2	22 614	22 163	22 050	20 950	19 997	18 916	18 364	17 157
Narcotics	MNC4	02.3	8 380	7 588	7 582	6 909	7 895	7 354	7 220	7 152
Clothing and footwear	ADIW	03	47 384	51 044	53 408	55 154	56 344	58 266	61 692	65 214
Clothing	ADIX	03.1	40 747	43 898	46 087	47 590	48 257	49 960	52 400	55 139
Footwear	ADIY	03.2	6 634	7 142	7 331	7 574	8 085	8 306	9 292	10 075
Housing, water, electricity, gas and other fuels	ADIZ	04	271 074	269 296	276 166	274 861	278 617	281 865	282 769	284 557
Actual rentals for housing	ADJA	04.1	51 875	52 802	53 108	56 150	56 817	56 965	57 897	57 076
Imputed rentals for housing	ADJB	04.2	169 671	169 131	173 087	172 704	174 549	177 519	181 855	183 955
Maintenance and repair of the dwelling	ADJC	04.3	2 723	2 547	2 332	2 260	2 430	2 592	3 032	2 841
Water supply and miscellaneous dwelling services	ADJD	04.4	9 797	9 548	9 829	9 814	9 632	9 528	9 492	9 581
Electricity, gas and other fuels	ADJE	04.5	37 622	35 742	38 398	33 903	35 221	35 261	30 493	31 104
Furnishings, household equipment and routine maintenance of the house	ADJF	05	53 974	49 256	49 667	47 737	47 306	48 847	50 997	54 226
Furniture, furnishings, carpets and other floor coverings	ADJG	05.1	19 923	17 297	16 869	17 395	16 482	16 736	18 157	19 716
Household textiles	ADJH	05.2	6 030	6 245	6 802	5 033	5 265	6 002	6 483	7 193
Household appliances	ADJI	05.3	6 899	6 107	6 259	6 257	6 343	6 135	6 645	6 938
Glassware, tableware and household utensils	ADJJ	05.4	5 044	4 711	4 434	4 786	4 842	5 054	4 952	5 329
Tools and equipment for house and garden	ADJK	05.5	4 850	4 189	4 006	3 786	3 869	3 995	3 872	4 020
Goods and services for routine household maintenance	ADJL	05.6	11 348	10 774	11 331	10 487	10 503	10 925	10 888	11 030
Health	ADJM	06	15 943	16 060	16 622	16 923	18 149	19 198	18 838	19 225
Medical products, appliances and equipment	ADJN	06.1	8 387	8 117	7 997	8 122	9 579	10 571	10 566	10 376
Out-patient services	ADJO	06.2	3 953	4 202	5 065	5 459	5 271	5 613	5 276	5 677
Hospital services	ADJP	06.3	3 677	3 853	3 635	3 386	3 317	3 014	2 996	3 172
Transport	ADJQ	07	150 078	145 646	141 511	140 787	145 135	150 198	156 627	163 463
Purchase of vehicles	ADJR	07.1	39 105	39 503	36 477	35 546	38 232	41 481	44 683	48 587
Operation of personal transport equipment	ADJS	07.2	67 707	65 743	64 473	64 071	64 724	65 125	66 522	67 672
Transport services	ADJT	07.3	43 296	40 208	40 535	41 269	42 211	43 592	45 422	47 204
Communication	ADJU	08	22 126	21 512	21 516	20 942	20 431	21 137	20 950	21 947
Postal services	CCGZ	08.1	1 699	1 609	1 306	993	652	781	693	678
Telephone and telefax equipment	ADQF	08.2	930	1 001	838	800	943	994	928	1 036
Telephone and telefax services	ADQG	08.3	19 714	19 100	19 497	19 206	18 829	19 362	19 329	20 233
Recreation and culture	ADJV	09	104 722	100 312	100 889	100 639	103 263	104 173	105 656	112 271
Audio-visual, photographic and information processing equipment	ADJW	09.1	14 672	15 141	16 014	17 280	18 059	18 715	18 487	19 652
Other major durables for recreation and culture	ADJX	09.2	8 418	8 394	8 397	7 526	7 702	8 594	10 281	11 716
Other recreational items and equipment; flowers, gardens and pets	ADJY	09.3	31 064	29 194	29 780	28 702	29 728	30 058	31 638	34 486
Recreational and cultural services	ADJZ	09.4	38 135	35 538	34 931	35 267	35 844	34 953	34 721	36 163
Newspapers, books and stationery	ADKM	09.5	14 563	13 191	12 380	12 023	12 001	11 853	10 529	10 254
Package holidays[2]	ADMI	09.6	–	–	–	–	–	–	–	–
Education		10								
Education services	ADMJ	10	20 494	20 667	19 914	18 867	18 515	16 923	16 163	15 322
Restaurants and hotels	ADMK	11	103 082	94 413	96 762	97 980	99 243	101 712	102 832	104 520
Catering services	ADML	11.1	84 163	75 884	77 335	77 901	77 945	79 898	79 804	80 055
Accommodation services	ADMM	11.2	19 096	18 588	19 462	20 096	21 297	21 814	23 028	24 465
Miscellaneous goods and services	ADMN	12	130 485	125 394	124 691	125 540	128 813	132 639	137 936	137 028
Personal care	ADMO	12.1	24 420	24 283	24 503	24 433	24 838	26 003	27 691	29 090
Prostitution	MND2	12.2	4 454	4 488	4 556	4 600	4 638	4 674	4 611	4 546
Personal effects n.e.c.	ADMP	12.3	9 388	8 894	11 025	11 755	12 265	13 036	12 842	13 116
Social protection	ADMQ	12.4	15 722	14 608	14 284	13 649	13 760	15 170	15 661	15 574
Insurance	ADMR	12.5	23 169	24 674	21 929	21 853	24 167	23 430	25 571	20 556
Financial services n.e.c.	ADMS	12.6	41 623	38 295	39 236	39 867	38 922	40 034	41 630	44 315
Other services n.e.c.	ADMT	12.7	10 719	10 417	9 011	9 220	10 228	10 292	9 930	9 831
Final consumption expenditure in the UK by resident and non-resident households (domestic concept)	ABQJ	0	1 062 701	1 032 742	1 041 767	1 036 932	1 055 705	1 075 257	1 095 728	1 119 116
Final consumption expenditure outside the UK by UK resident households	ABTC	P.33	46 007	36 846	35 990	33 674	35 394	35 583	39 193	46 089
Final consumption expenditure in the UK by households resident in rest of the world	CCHX	P.34	–22 880	–22 447	–23 797	–23 901	–24 539	–26 829	–27 767	–29 417
Final consumption expenditure by UK resident households in the UK and abroad (national concept)	ABPF	P.31	1 084 930	1 047 083	1 053 933	1 046 647	1 066 530	1 084 011	1 107 154	1 135 788

19.17 Individual consumption expenditure by households, NPISH and general government. Chained volume measures (reference year 2013)

Classified by function (COICOP/COPNI/COFOG)[1]

£ million

			2008	2009	2010	2011	2012	2013	2014	2015
Consumption expenditure of UK resident households		P.31								
Final consumption expenditure of UK resident households in the UK and abroad	ABPF	P.31	1 084 930	1 047 083	1 053 933	1 046 647	1 066 530	1 084 011	1 107 154	1 135 788
Final individual consumption expenditure of NPISH		13								
Final individual consumption expenditure of NPISH	ABNU	P.31	52 652	53 920	53 421	55 642	54 539	54 535	55 982	56 848
Final individual consumption expenditure of general government		14								
Health	K4CP	14.1	106 274	110 062	112 230	114 742	117 033	120 294	125 881	130 083
Recreation and culture	K4CQ	14.2	6 661	6 758	6 513	6 452	6 560	5 859	5 718	5 743
Education	K4CR	14.3	56 900	57 390	58 099	58 911	60 289	61 083	62 590	64 329
Social protection	K4CS	14.4	31 938	33 056	33 153	32 227	33 047	34 100	34 062	34 153
Final individual consumption expenditure of general government	NSZK	P.31	201 695	207 159	209 916	212 315	216 908	221 336	228 251	234 308
Total, individual consumption expenditure/ actual individual consumption	YBIO	P.31 P.41	1 338 163	1 307 689	1 316 900	1 314 521	1 337 948	1 359 882	1 391 387	1 426 944

1 "Purpose" or "function" classifications are designed to indicate the "socio-economic objectives" that institutional units aim to achieve through various kinds of outlays. COICOP is the Classification of Individual Consumption by Purpose and applies to households. COPNI is the Classification of the Purposes of Non-profit Institutions Serving Households and COFOG is the Classification of the Functions of Government

2 Package holidays data are dispersed between components (transport etc).

Source: Office for National Statistics, Blue Book 2016

19.18 Change in inventories at chained volume measures [1]

Reference year 2012, £ million

| | Manufacturing industries | | | | | | Distributive trades | | | |
	Mining and quarrying	Materials and fuel	Work in progress	Finished goods	Total	Electricity, gas and water supply	Wholesale [2]	Retail [2]	Other industries	Changes in inventories [3]
Level of inventories held at end-December 2013 [4]	536	20 395	17 219	18 995	56 600	36 408	37 064	5 487	67 630	204 229
	FAEA	FBNF	FBNG	FBNH	DHBM	FAEB	FAJX	FBYN	DLWX	CAFU
Seasonally adjusted										
2011	- 367	620	- 898	- 522	- 800	- 437	299	- 852	- 2 135	- 4 247
2012	210	- 1 140	635	707	202	- 138	1 626	625	- 992	1 533
2013	88	900	- 3	- 528	369	- 208	676	1 284	11 423	13 632
2014	2 127	1 741	1 957	3 903	7 601	2 921	- 2 849	2 868	3 994	16 662
2015	7 834	61	- 209	- 1 347	- 1 495	- 157	- 1 051	1 980	2 918	10 029
Seasonally adjusted										
2011 Q1	- 269	- 197	199	- 1 048	- 1 051	183	- 1 174	- 16	- 5 137	- 7 497
2011 Q2	- 35	432	- 1 165	- 993	- 1 722	- 96	509	- 584	56	- 1 867
2011 Q3	- 70	217	278	2 092	2 586	- 42	- 333	- 330	1 580	3 403
2011 Q4	7	168	- 210	- 573	- 613	- 482	1 297	78	1 366	1 714
2012 Q1	- 180	- 1 459	- 138	- 436	- 2 033	- 167	- 980	- 543	- 8 134	- 12 037
2012 Q2	480	- 215	68	1 053	906	- 128	1 152	644	- 903	2 151
2012 Q3	- 157	- 184	166	348	330	- 149	1 792	- 509	3 088	4 395
2012 Q4	67	718	539	- 258	999	306	- 338	1 033	4 957	7 024
2013 Q1	98	443	229	- 422	250	278	- 1 552	1 393	655	1 122
2013 Q2	220	107	270	- 72	305	- 80	2 560	1 046	- 935	3 116
2013 Q3	- 160	152	- 390	- 400	- 638	- 42	1 912	- 112	1 220	2 180
2013 Q4	- 70	198	- 112	366	452	- 364	- 2 244	- 1 043	10 483	7 214
2014 Q1	268	1 069	1 642	973	3 684	609	1 276	250	- 1 161	4 926
2014 Q2	20	81	167	1 016	1 264	693	- 1 967	421	1 501	1 932
2014 Q3	420	452	249	901	1 601	355	- 792	790	2 454	4 828
2014 Q4	1 419	139	- 101	1 013	1 052	1 264	- 1 366	1 407	1 200	4 976
2015 Q1	1 847	112	126	1 469	1 707	- 225	872	514	1 462	6 177
2015 Q2	165	900	- 322	- 1 113	- 535	- 57	- 1 508	1 213	- 713	- 1 435
2015 Q3	2 445	- 204	349	- 587	- 442	- 485	247	- 220	331	1 876
2015 Q4	3 377	- 747	- 362	- 1 116	- 2 225	610	- 662	473	1 838	3 411

1. Estimates are given to the nearest £ million but cannot be regarded as accurate to this degree.

2. Wholesaling and retailing estimates exclude the motor trades.

3. Quarterly alignment adjustment included in this series.

4. Estimates of level based on previously available data.

Source: Office for National Statistics (ONS)

19.19

Gross fixed capital formation at current purchasers' prices[1]
Analysis by broad sector and type of asset
Total economy

£ million

			2008	2009	2010	2011	2012	2013	2014	2015
Private sector										
New dwellings, excluding land	L5ZQ		51 780	42 044	44 638	48 125	48 121	52 904	60 736	63 839
Other buildings and structures	EQBU		37 473	30 392	29 419	34 301	41 272	42 915	45 062	49 752
Transport equipment	EQBV		10 408	9 330	12 770	8 001	9 165	9 035	10 469	15 667
ICT[2] equipment and other machinery and equipment and cultivated biological resources	EQBW		42 951	34 840	37 316	43 931	46 319	48 150	49 355	49 270
Intellectual property products	EQBX		52 085	48 437	50 170	52 632	54 635	57 571	59 662	60 699
Costs associated with the transfer of ownership of non-produced assets	L5ZR		21 424	11 903	12 633	12 244	13 462	16 400	19 760	19 756
Total	EQBZ	P.51g	216 121	176 946	186 947	199 233	212 975	226 975	245 043	258 984
Public non-financial corporations		S.11001								
New dwellings, excluding land	L5YQ		3 966	4 068	3 883	3 340	3 135	3 352	3 835	4 281
Other buildings and structures	DEES		1 736	1 836	1 890	1 645	1 400	1 297	1 441	1 487
Transport equipment	DEEP		274	340	196	156	510	455	393	404
ICT equipment and other machinery and equipment and cultivated biological resources	DEEQ		1 778	1 155	903	945	923	890	868	829
Intellectual property products	DLXJ		2 081	2 055	2 055	2 024	2 024	2 014	2 005	1 995
Costs associated with the transfer of ownership of non-produced assets	L5ZL		−1 654	−370	−406	−388	−427	−505	−621	−622
Total	FCCJ	P.51g	8 181	9 084	8 521	7 722	7 565	7 503	7 921	8 374
General government		S.13								
New dwellings, excluding land	L5ZU		15	1	−5	−8	115	130	190	208
Other buildings and structures	EQCH		31 383	31 758	28 760	27 413	26 667	25 326	27 080	26 988
Transport equipment	EQCI		512	605	702	602	460	438	460	478
ICT equipment, other machinery and equipment, Cultivated biological resources, weapons	EQCJ		9 211	10 254	11 175	11 046	9 369	9 429	9 812	10 161
Intellectual property products	EQCK		3 691	3 874	5 159	4 907	4 890	4 822	5 131	4 755
Costs associated with the transfer of ownership of non-produced assets	L5ZV		2 038	4 061	4 429	4 315	4 722	5 602	6 858	6 859
Total	NNBF	P.51g	46 850	50 553	50 220	48 275	46 223	45 747	49 531	49 449
Total gross fixed capital formation	NPQX	P.51g	271 152	236 583	245 687	255 231	266 761	280 224	302 495	316 806

1 Components may not sum to totals due to rounding
2 Information Communication Technology.

Source: Office for National Statistics, Blue Book 2016

19.20

Gross fixed capital formation at current purchasers' prices[1]
Analysis by type of asset
Total economy

£ million

			2008	2009	2010	2011	2012	2013	2014	2015
Tangible fixed assets										
New dwellings, excluding land	DFDK		55 761	46 113	48 516	51 457	51 371	56 386	64 761	68 328
Other buildings and structures	DLWS		70 592	63 986	60 069	63 359	69 339	69 538	73 583	78 227
Transport equipment	DLWZ		11 194	10 275	13 668	8 759	10 135	9 928	11 322	16 549
ICT[2] equipment, other machinery and equipment, cultivated biological resources, weapons[3]	DLXI		53 940	46 249	49 394	55 922	56 611	58 469	60 035	60 260
Total	EQCQ		191 487	166 623	171 647	179 497	187 456	194 321	209 701	223 364
Intellectual property products	DLXP		57 857	54 366	57 384	59 563	61 549	64 407	66 798	67 449
Costs associated with the transfer of ownership of non-produced assets	DFBH		21 808	15 594	16 656	16 171	17 757	21 497	25 997	25 993
Total gross fixed capital formation	NPQX	P.51g	271 152	236 583	245 687	255 231	266 761	280 224	302 495	316 806

1 Components may not sum to totals due to rounding
2 Information Communication Technology
3 Weapons data are central government only.

Source: Office for National Statistics, Blue Book 2016

19.21 Gross fixed capital formation[1,2]
Chained volume measures (reference year 2013)
Total economy: Analysis by broad sector and type of asset

£ million

			2008	2009	2010	2011	2012	2013	2014	2015
Private sector										
New dwellings, excluding land	L62K		59 187	46 044	48 784	51 540	49 588	52 904	58 967	61 131
Other buildings and structures	EQCU		37 950	31 097	31 729	36 899	42 783	42 914	43 297	47 179
Transport equipment	EQCV		10 722	9 503	13 038	7 883	9 111	9 035	11 124	16 486
ICT[3] equipment and other machinery and equipment and cultivated biological resources	EQCW		49 200	35 728	38 776	44 314	46 210	48 150	50 191	48 393
Intellectual property products	EQCX		54 778	51 209	52 173	53 351	55 185	57 571	59 317	60 363
Costs associated with the transfer of ownership of non-produced assets	L62L		24 004	12 671	13 215	12 493	13 512	16 400	19 638	19 689
Total	EQCZ	P.51g	234 978	186 348	197 917	206 390	216 350	226 974	242 534	253 240
Public non-financial corporations		S.11001								
New dwellings, excluding land	L62M		4 547	4 458	4 245	3 583	3 232	3 352	3 722	4 107
Other buildings and structures	DEEX		1 778	1 905	2 043	1 767	1 449	1 297	1 388	1 400
Transport equipment	DEEU		285	350	206	157	511	455	416	434
ICT equipment and other machinery and equipment and cultivated biological resources	DEEV		2 054	1 190	949	961	928	890	894	851
Intellectual property products	EQDE		2 480	2 349	2 295	2 183	2 108	2 014	2 001	1 967
Costs associated with the transfer of ownership of non-produced assets	L62N		−1 853	−394	−425	−396	−429	−505	−617	−620
Total	EQDG	P.51g	9 281	9 830	9 279	8 226	7 798	7 503	7 804	8 140
General government		S.13								
New dwellings, excluding land costs	L62O		17	5	−5	−7	120	130	185	200
Other buildings and structures	EQDI		31 683	32 361	30 859	29 522	27 692	25 326	26 011	25 164
Transport equipment	EQDJ		530	613	722	599	458	438	485	512
ICT equipment, other machinery and equipment, Cultivated biological resources, weapons	EQDK		10 377	10 638	11 775	11 331	9 491	9 429	9 986	10 171
Intellectual property services	EQDL		3 928	4 113	5 430	5 011	4 963	4 822	5 052	4 605
Costs associated with the transfer of ownership of non-produced assets	L62P		2 283	4 323	4 633	4 403	4 739	5 602	6 816	6 836
Total	EQDN	P.51g	48 982	52 103	53 391	50 843	47 418	45 747	48 535	47 487
Total gross fixed capital formation	NPQR	P.51g	292 575	248 099	260 396	265 327	271 534	280 224	298 872	308 866

1 For the years before the reference year (2013), totals differ from the sum of their components
2 Components may not sum to totals due to rounding
3 Information Communication Technology.

Source: Office for National Statistics, Blue Book 2016

19.22 Gross fixed capital formation[1,2]
Chained volume measures (reference year 2013)
Total economy: Analysis by type of asset

£ million

			2008	2009	2010	2011	2012	2013	2014	2015
Tangible fixed assets										
New dwellings, excluding land	DFDV		63 754	50 505	53 023	55 116	52 940	56 386	62 874	65 438
Other buildings and structures	EQDP		71 484	65 387	64 643	68 185	71 923	69 537	70 696	73 743
Transport equipment	DLWJ		11 542	10 470	13 971	8 641	10 079	9 928	12 025	17 432
ICT[3] equipment, other machinery and equipment, cultivated biological resources, weapons[4]	DLWM		61 524	47 521	51 461	56 581	56 624	58 469	61 071	59 414
Total	EQDS		208 304	173 881	183 098	188 522	191 566	194 320	206 666	216 027
Intellectual property products	EQDT		61 156	57 636	59 868	60 530	62 250	64 407	66 370	66 935
Costs associated with the transfer of ownership of non-produced assets	DFDW		24 434	16 601	17 423	16 502	17 822	21 497	25 836	25 904
Total gross fixed capital formation	NPQR	P.51g	292 575	248 099	260 396	265 327	271 534	280 224	298 872	308 866

1 For the years before the reference year (2013), totals differ from the sum of their components
2 Components may not sum to totals due to rounding
3 Information Communication Technology
4 Weapons data are central government only.

Source: Office for National Statistics, Blue Book 2016

Education

Chapter 20

Education

Educational establishments in the UK are administered and financed in several ways. Most schools are controlled by local authorities, which are part of the structure of local government, but some are 'assisted', receiving grants direct from central government sources and being controlled by governing bodies who have a substantial degree of autonomy. Completely outside the public sector are non.maintained schools run by individuals, companies or charitable institutions.

For the purposes of UK education statistics, schools fall under the following broad categories:

Mainstream state schools
(In Northern Ireland, grant-aided mainstream schools)

These schools work in partnership with other schools and local authorities and they receive funding from local authorities. Since 1 September 1999, the categories (typically in England) are:

Community – schools formerly known as 'county' plus some former grant-maintained (GM) schools

Foundation – most former GM schools

Voluntary Aided – schools formerly known as 'aided' and some former GM schools

Voluntary Controlled – schools formerly known as 'controlled'

Non-maintained mainstream schools

These consist of:

(a) Independent schools

Schools which charge fees and may also be financed by individuals, companies or charitable institutions. These include Direct Grant schools, where the governing bodies are assisted by departmental grants and a proportion of the pupils attending them do so free or under an arrangement by which local authorities meet tuition fees. City Technology Colleges (CTCs) and Academies (applicable in England only) are also included as independent schools.

(b) Non-maintained schools
Run by voluntary bodies who may receive some grant from central government for capital work and for equipment, but their current expenditure is met primarily from the fees charged to local authorities for pupils placed in schools.

Special schools

Special schools provide education for children with Special Educational Needs (SEN) (in Scotland, Record of Needs or a Coordinated Support Plan), who cannot be educated satisfactorily in an ordinary school. Maintained special schools are run by local authorities, while non-maintained special schools are financed as described at (b) above.

Pupil Referral Units

Pupil Referral Units (PRUs) operate in England and Wales and provide education outside of a mainstream or special school setting, to meet the needs of difficult or disruptive children.

Schools in Scotland are categorised as Education Authority, Grant-aided, Opted-out/Self-governing (these three being grouped together as 'Publicly funded' schools), Independent schools and Partnership schools.

The home government departments dealing with education statistics are:

Department for Education (DfE)
Welsh Government (WG)
Scottish Government (SG)
Northern Ireland Department of Education (DENI)
Northern Ireland Department for Employment and Learning (DELNI)

Each of the home education departments in Great Britain, along with the Northern Ireland Department of Education, have overall responsibility for funding the schools sectors in their own country.

Up to March 2001, further education (FE) courses in FE sector colleges in England and in Wales were largely funded through grants from the respective FE funding councils. In April 2001, however, the Learning and Skills Council (LSC) took over the responsibility for funding the FE sector in England, and the National Council for Education and Training for Wales (part of Education and Learning Wales – ELWa) did so for Wales. The Apprenticeships, Skills, Children and Learning Act 2009 received Royal Assent on 12 November 2009 for the dissolution of the Learning and Skills Council by 2010 and the transfer of its functions on 1 April 2010 to local authorities and two new agencies: the Young People's Learning Agency (YPLA) and the Skills Funding Agency. The YPLA champions young people's learning by providing financial support to young learners; by funding academies, general FE and sixth form colleges and other 16 to 19 providers; and supporting local authorities to secure sufficient education and training places for all 16 to 19 year olds in England. The Skills Funding Agency funds further education colleges and training providers in England to deliver adult skills and apprenticeships. In Wales, the National Council – ELWa, funds FE provision made by FE institutions via a third party or sponsored arrangements. The Scottish Further Education Funding Council (SFEFC) funds FE colleges in Scotland, while the Department for Employment and Learning funds FE colleges in Northern Ireland.

From 1 April 2012, funding for the education and training of 3 to 19 year olds in England will become the responsibility of the Education Funding Agency (EFA), which will be a new executive agency of the Department for Education. The EFA will directly fund academies, free schools, university technology colleges, studio schools and 16 to 19 providers. It will distribute funding to local authorities for them to pass on to their maintained schools and it will also be responsible for the distribution of capital funding.

Higher education (HE) courses in higher education establishments are largely publicly funded through block grants from the HE funding councils in England and Scotland, the Higher Education Council – ELWa in Wales, and the Department for Employment and Learning in Northern Ireland. In addition, some designated HE (mainly HND/HNC Diplomas and Certificates of HE) is also funded by these sources. The FE sources mentioned above fund the remainder.

Statistics for the separate systems obtained in England, Wales, Scotland and Northern Ireland are collected and processed separately in accordance with the particular needs of the responsible departments. Since 1994/95 the Higher Education Statistics Agency (HESA) has undertaken the data collection for all higher education institutions (HEIs) in the UK. This includes the former Universities Funding Council (UFC) funded UK universities previously collected by the Universities Statistical Record. There are some structural differences in the information collected for schools, FE and HE in each of the four home countries and in some tables the GB/UK data presented are amalgamations from sources that are not entirely comparable.

Stages of education

There are five stages of education: early years, primary, secondary, FE and HE, and education is compulsory for all children between the ages of 5 (4 in Northern Ireland) and 16. The non-compulsory fourth stage, FE, covers non-advanced education, which can be taken at further (including tertiary) education colleges, HE institutions (HEIs) and increasingly in secondary schools. The fifth stage, HE, is study beyond GCE A levels and their equivalent which, for most full-time students, takes place in universities and other HEIs.

Early years education

Children under 5 attend a variety of settings including state nursery schools, nursery classes within primary schools and, in England and Wales, reception classes within primary schools, as well as s ettings outside the state sector such as voluntary pre-schools or privately run nurseries. In recent years there has been a major expansion of early years education, and the Education Act 2002 extended the National Curriculum for England to include the foundation stage. The foundation stage was introduced in September 2000, and covered children's education from the age of 3 to the end of the reception year, when most are just 5 and some almost 6 years old. The Early Years Foundation Stage (EYFS), came into force in September 2008, and is a single regulatory and quality framework for the provision of learning, development and care for children in all registered early years settings between birth and the academic year in which they turn 5.

Children born in Scotland between March and December are eligible for early years education at the time the Pre-School Education and Day Care Census is carried out. In Scotland, early years education is called ante-pre-school education for those aged 3 to 4 years old, and pre-school education for those aged 4.

Primary education

The primary stage covers three age ranges: nursery (under 5), infant (5 to 7 or 8) and junior (up to 11 or 12) but in Scotland and Northern Ireland there is generally no distinction between infant and junior schools. Most public sector primary schools take both boys and girls in mixed classes. It is usual to transfer straight to secondary school at age 11 (in England, Wales and Northern Ireland) or 12 (in Scotland), but in England some children make the transition via middle schools catering for various age ranges between 8 and 14. Depending on their individual age ranges middle schools are classified as either primary or secondary.

Secondary education

Public provision of secondary education in an area may consist of a combination of different types of school, the pattern reflecting historical circumstance and the policy adopted by the local authority. Comprehensive schools largely admit pupils without reference to ability or aptitude and cater for all the children in a neighbourhood, but in some areas they co.exist with grammar, secondary modern or technical schools. In 2005/06, 88 per cent of secondary pupils in England attended comprehensive schools while all secondary schools in Wales are comprehensive schools.

The majority of education authority secondary schools in Scotland are comprehensive in character and offer six years of secondary education; however, in remote areas there are several two-year and four-year secondary schools.

In Northern Ireland, post-primary education is provided by grammar schools and non-selective secondary schools.

In England, the Specialist Schools Programme helps schools, in partnership with private sector sponsors and supported by additional government funding, to establish distinctive identities through their chosen specialisms and achieve their targets to raise standards. Specialist schools have a special focus on their chosen subject area but must meet the National Curriculum requirements and deliver a broad and balanced education to all pupils. Any maintained secondary school in England can apply to be designated as a specialist school in one of ten specialist areas: arts, business & enterprise, engineering, humanities, languages, mathematics & computing, music, science, sports and technology. Schools can also combine any two specialisms.

Academies, operating in England, are publicly funded independent local schools that provide free education. They are all-ability schools established by sponsors from business, faith or voluntary groups working with partners from the local community.

Academies benefit from greater freedoms to help innovate and raise standards. These include freedom from local authority control, ability to set pay and conditions for staff, freedom from following the National Curriculum and the ability to change the lengths of terms and school days.

The Academies Programme was first introduced in March 2000 with the objective of replacing poorly performing schools. Academies were established and driven by external sponsors, to achieve a transformation in education performance.

The Academies Programme was expanded through legislation in the Academies Act 2010. This enables all maintained primary, secondary and special schools to apply to become an Academy. The early focus is on schools rated outstanding by Ofsted and the first of these new academies opened in September 2010. These schools do not have a sponsor but instead are expected to work with underperforming schools to help raise standards.

Special schools

Special schools (day or boarding) provide education for children who require specialist support to complete their education, for example because they have physical or other difficulties. Many pupils with special educational needs are educated in mainstream schools. All children attending special schools are offered a curriculum designed to overcome their learning difficulties and to enable them to become self-reliant. Since December 2005, special schools have also been able to apply for the Special Educational Needs (SEN) specialism, under the Specialist Schools Programme. They can apply for a curriculum specialism, but not for both the SEN and a curriculum specialism.

Further education

The term further education may be used in a general sense to cover all non.advanced courses taken after the period of compulsory education, but more commonly it excludes those staying on at secondary school and those in higher education, that is, courses in universities and colleges leading to qualifications above GCE A Level, Scottish Certificate of Education (SCE) Higher Grade, GNVQ/NVQ level 3, and their equivalents. Since 1 April 1993, sixth form colleges in England and Wales have been included in the further education sector.

Higher education

Higher education is defined as courses that are of a standard that is higher than GCE A level, the Higher Grade of the SCE/National Qualification, GNVQ/NVQ level 3 or the Edexcel (formerly BTEC) or SQA National Certificate/Diploma. There are three main levels of HE course:

(i) Postgraduate courses leading to higher degrees, diplomas and certificates (including postgraduate certificates of education (PGCE) and professional qualifications) which usually require a first degree as entry qualification.

(ii) Undergraduate courses which include first degrees, first degrees with qualified teacher status, enhanced first degrees, first degrees obtained concurrently with a diploma, and intercalated first degrees (where first degree students, usually in medicine, dentistry or veterinary medicine, interrupt their studies to complete a one-year course of advanced studies in a related topic).

(iii) Other undergraduate courses which include all other higher education courses, for example HNDs and Diplomas in HE.

As a result of the Further and Higher Education Act 1992, former polytechnics and some other HEIs were designated as universities in 1992/93. Students normally attend HE courses at HEIs, but some attend at FE colleges. Some also attend institutions which do not receive public grant (such as the University of Buckingham) and these numbers are excluded from the tables. However, the University of Buckingham is included in Tables 20.6 and 20.7.

20.1: Number of schools by type of school - time series

United Kingdom   **Numbers**

	2000/01	2011/12	2012/13	2013/14	2014/15
UNITED KINGDOM					
Public sector mainstream					
Nursery	3,228	3,095	3,085	3,031	2,969
Primary	22,902	21,165	21,069	21,040	20,980
Middle(1)	.	.	4	4	6
Secondary(2)	4,352	4,072	4,077	4,116	4,158
of which Middle deemed secondary	316	196	189	176	154
Non-maintained mainstream	2,397	2,502	2,497	2,497	2,437
Special schools	1,498	1,281	1,269	1,264	1,263
of which state-funded	1,401	1,209	1,198	1,195	1,194
of which non-maintained	97	72	71	69	69
Pupil referral units	338	403	400	371	362
ALL SCHOOLS	34,715	32,518	32,401	32,323	32,175
ENGLAND					
Public sector mainstream					
Maintained nursery	506	423	417	414	411
State-funded primary(3)	18,069	16,818	16,784	16,788	16,766
State-funded secondary(2)	3,496	3,268	3,281	3,329	3,381
of which Middle deemed secondary	316	196	189	176	154
Non-maintained mainstream(4)	2,190	2,421	2,414	2,412	2,357
Special schools	1,175	1,039	1,032	1,033	1,040
of which state-funded(5)	1,113	967	961	964	971
of which non-maintained	62	72	71	69	69
Pupil referral units	308	403	400	371	362
ALL SCHOOLS	25,744	24,372	24,328	24,347	24,317
WALES					
Public sector mainstream					
Nursery	41	22	20	17	13
Primary	1,631	1,412	1,374	1,357	1,330
Middle(1)	.	.	4	4	6
Secondary	229	221	216	213	207
Non-maintained mainstream	54	66	68	70	66
Special (maintained)	45	43	42	42	39
Pupil referral units	30	..	..	..	..
ALL SCHOOLS	2,030	1,764	1,724	1,703	1,661
SCOTLAND					
Public sector mainstream					
Nursery(6)	2,586	2,553	2,551	2,504	2,449
Primary	2,278	2,081	2,064	2,056	2,048
Secondary	389	367	365	364	362
Non-maintained mainstream	127	..	..	..	..
Special schools	230	158	155	149	145
of which maintained	195	158	155	149	145
of which non-maintained	35	..	..	..	..
ALL SCHOOLS	5,610	5,159	5,135	5,073	5,004
NORTHERN IRELAND					
Grant aided mainstream					
Nursery(7)	95	97	97	96	96
Primary	924	854	847	839	836
Secondary	238	216	215	210	208
Non-maintained mainstream	26	15	15	15	14
Special (maintained)	48	41	40	40	39
ALL SCHOOLS	1,331	1,223	1,214	1,200	1,193

Source: Department for Education; Welsh Government; Scottish Government; Northern Ireland Department of Education

1 In Wales, the Middle School for pupils of both primary and secondary school age was introduced in 2012/13.

2 In England, includes secondary sponsor-led academies, secondary converter academies and secondary free schools.

3 In England, includes middle deemed primary schools as well as primary sponsor-led academies, primary convertor academies and primary free schools.

4 In England, includes direct grant nurseries.

5 In England, includes special academies and general hospital schools.

6 In Scotland, there was a change in the timing of the Pre-School Education Census in 2010/11, from January to September.
    September figures from 2010/11 may not be directly comparable with previously published January figures.

7 In Northern Ireland, excludes voluntary and private pre-school education centres.

20.2 Full-time and part-time pupils by gender(1)(2), age and school type, 2015/16

United Kingdom   Thousands

| | | Maintained schools(3) | | | | | | | | Non-maintained(4) | | | |
| | | Primary Schools(5)(6)(7) | | | | | | | | | | | |
Age at 31 August 2015(14)	Nursery Schools(8)	Nursery Classes	Other Classes(9)	Total	Middle Schools(10)	Secondary Schools(5)(11)	Special schools(12)	Pupil Referral Units(13)	All maintained schools	Special schools	Other Schools	All non-maintained schools	All schools
All													
2-4(15)	50.6	258.9	548.8	1,065.6	0.4	11.7	6.7	0.0	1,135.2	0.1	63.8	64.6	1,199.8
5(16)	-	-	596.1	754.8	0.2	7.1	5.6	0.0	767.7	0.1	28.4	28.8	796.5
6	-	-	594.0	749.0	0.2	6.0	6.2	0.1	761.5	0.1	29.5	29.9	791.4
7	-	-	590.1	751.8	0.2	5.8	6.9	0.2	764.9	0.1	32.9	33.4	798.3
8	-	-	569.7	724.4	0.2	5.1	7.1	0.2	737.0	0.1	34.8	35.3	772.3
9	-	-	540.2	687.2	0.2	17.4	7.4	0.3	712.5	0.2	36.1	36.8	749.2
10	-	-	526.6	669.7	0.2	19.5	8.0	0.3	697.7	0.2	37.1	37.8	735.5
11	-	-	53.8	54.0	0.7	613.2	10.7	0.3	678.9	0.3	43.6	44.6	723.5
12	-	-	4.8	5.0	0.7	643.0	11.0	1.0	660.7	0.3	43.6	44.6	705.4
13	-	-	-	-	0.6	625.8	11.2	1.8	639.4	0.4	44.1	45.2	684.6
14	-	-	-	-	0.6	629.4	11.6	3.1	644.8	0.4	46.5	47.8	692.5
15	-	-	-	-	0.7	634.5	12.1	7.2	654.5	0.4	49.2	50.5	705.1
16	-	-	-	-	0.3	299.0	7.0	0.3	306.5	0.4	42.6	43.9	350.4
17	-	-	-	-	0.2	250.0	5.9	0.1	256.3	0.4	40.6	41.9	298.1
18	-	-	-	-	-	26.8	4.3	-	31.2	0.3	7.9	8.6	39.8
19 and over	-	-	-	-	-	0.8	0.1	-	0.9	-	2.9	3.0	3.9
Total(17)	147.9	258.9	4,024.1	5,461.5	5.4	3,795.1	122.0	15.0	9,546.9	3.8	583.8	596.5	10,143.4
of which													
England	43.7	249.6	3,464.0	4,615.2	.	3,193.4	105.4	15.0	7,972.7	3.8	583.1	586.9	8,559.6
Wales	1.0	..	..	277.0	5.4	178.7	4.5	..	466.6	..	..	8.9	475.4
Scotland	97.3	.	391.1	391.1	.	281.9	6.9	.	777.3	..	..	..	777.3
Northern Ireland	5.9	9.3	168.9	178.2	.	141.1	5.2	.	330.4	.	0.7	0.7	331.1
Males													
2-4(15)	26.5	130.9	280.4	542.7	0.2	6.0	4.7	-	580.1	0.1	32.0	32.4	612.5
5(16)	-	-	304.1	385.2	0.1	3.5	4.1	-	393.0	0.0	14.4	14.6	407.5
6	-	-	303.0	382.0	0.1	3.0	4.6	0.1	389.7	0.1	15.0	15.2	404.9
7	-	-	300.7	383.1	0.1	2.9	5.1	0.2	391.4	0.1	16.8	17.1	408.5
8	-	-	290.3	369.2	0.1	2.6	5.3	0.2	377.4	0.1	18.0	18.3	395.7
9	-	-	274.8	349.9	0.1	8.8	5.5	0.3	364.5	0.1	18.5	18.9	383.4
10	-	-	267.8	340.6	0.1	10.0	5.8	0.3	356.9	0.2	19.4	19.7	376.6
11	-	-	27.7	27.9	0.3	311.6	7.7	0.2	347.7	0.2	22.4	23.0	370.6
12	-	-	3.0	3.1	0.4	326.2	8.0	0.8	338.5	0.3	22.5	23.1	361.5
13	-	-	-	-	0.3	317.6	8.1	1.3	327.4	0.3	22.6	23.3	350.6
14	-	-	-	-	0.3	318.8	8.3	2.2	329.6	0.3	23.9	24.6	354.3
15	-	-	-	-	0.3	321.2	8.6	4.8	334.9	0.3	25.3	26.1	361.0
16	-	-	-	-	0.1	143.5	4.6	0.1	148.3	0.3	21.8	22.5	170.9
17	-	-	-	-	0.1	116.5	3.9	-	120.5	0.3	20.9	21.6	142.1
18	-	-	-	-	-	14.1	2.8	-	17.0	0.2	4.3	4.7	21.6
19 and over	-	-	-	-	-	0.4	0.1	-	0.4	-	1.8	1.8	2.2
Total(17)	26.5	130.9	2,051.9	2,783.7	2.6	1,906.8	87.0	10.6	4,817.2	2.8	299.4	306.7	5,124.0
of which													
England	22.9	126.2	1,766.3	2,352.1	.	1,604.8	75.4	10.6	4,065.7	2.8	299.1	301.9	4,367.6
Wales	0.5	..	..	141.3	2.6	90.1	3.3	..	237.9	..	..	4.5	242.4
Scotland	..	.	199.6	199.6	.	141.8	4.8	.	346.3	..	..	..	346.3
Northern Ireland	3.1	4.7	85.9	90.7	.	70.1	3.6	.	167.4	.	0.3	0.3	167.7
Females													
2-4(15)	24.1	128.0	268.4	523.0	0.2	5.7	2.1	-	555.0	-	31.8	32.3	587.3
5(16)	-	-	291.9	369.6	0.1	3.5	1.5	-	374.7	-	14.0	14.2	389.0
6	-	-	291.0	367.0	0.1	3.0	1.7	-	371.8	-	14.5	14.7	386.5
7	-	-	289.4	368.7	0.1	2.9	1.8	-	373.5	-	16.1	16.3	389.9
8	-	-	279.4	355.1	0.1	2.5	1.9	-	359.7	-	16.8	17.0	376.7
9	-	-	265.4	337.2	0.1	8.7	1.9	-	348.0	0.1	17.6	17.9	365.8
10	-	-	258.8	329.1	0.1	9.5	2.1	-	340.9	-	17.8	18.0	358.9
11	-	-	26.1	26.2	0.4	301.6	3.0	-	331.2	0.1	21.2	21.6	352.8
12	-	-	1.8	1.9	0.4	316.8	3.1	0.2	322.3	0.1	21.2	21.6	343.8
13	-	-	-	-	0.3	308.2	3.1	0.4	312.0	0.1	21.5	21.9	334.0
14	-	-	-	-	0.3	310.5	3.3	0.9	315.1	0.1	22.7	23.1	338.3
15	-	-	-	-	0.3	313.3	3.5	2.5	319.6	0.1	23.9	24.4	344.1
16	-	-	-	-	0.2	155.4	2.4	0.1	158.1	0.1	20.8	21.4	179.5
17	-	-	-	-	0.1	133.5	2.1	0.1	135.8	0.1	19.7	20.3	156.0
18	-	-	-	-	-	12.7	1.5	-	14.3	0.1	3.7	3.9	18.1
19 and over	-	-	-	-	-	0.4	-	-	0.4	-	1.2	1.2	1.6

20.2 Full-time and part-time pupils by gender(1)(2), age and school type, 2015/16

United Kingdom   Thousands

| | | Maintained schools(3) | | | | | | | | Non-maintained(4) | | | |
| | | Primary Schools(5)(6)(7) | | | | | | | | | | | |
	Nursery Schools(8)	Nursery Classes	Other Classes(9)	Total	Middle Schools(10)	Secondary Schools(5)(11)	Special schools(12)	Pupil Referral Units(13)	All maintained schools	Special schools	Other Schools	All non-maintained schools	All schools
Age at 31 August 2015(14)													
Total(17)	24.1	128.0	1,972.2	2,677.8	2.8	1,888.4	35.0	4.4	4,632.4	1.0	284.3	289.7	4,922.2
of which													
England	20.8	123.4	1,697.7	2,263.1	.	1,588.7	30.0	4.4	3,907.0	1.0	284.0	285.1	4,192.0
Wales	0.5	..	..	135.6	2.8	88.5	1.3	..	228.7	..	..	4.4	233.1
Scotland	..	.	191.5	191.5	.	140.1	2.1	.	333.7	..	..	..	333.7
Northern Ireland	2.8	4.6	83.0	87.6	.	71.1	1.6	.	163.0	.	0.3	0.3	163.4

Sources: Department for Education; Welsh Government; Scottish Government; Northern Ireland Department of Education

1. In Scotland gender split is not collected by age but has been calculated according to figures collected in September each year. There are a small number of pupils for whom it has not been possible to assign an age; these pupils are included in the Scotland total but excluded from the age breakdowns.

2. In Northern Ireland a gender split is not available by age but is available by year group and so this is used as a proxy. For example pupils in Year 1 are counted as age 4, pupils in Year 2 are counted as age 5 etc.

3. Maintained school figures includes all state-funded schools (Grant-aided schools in Northern Ireland).

4. In Scotland figures for the Non-maintained sector have not been provided, the collection was discontinued in 2010. In Wales all non-maintained schools are counted as a single group.

5. In England includes middle schools as deemed.

6. In England includes primary converter academies, primary sponsor led academies and primary free schools.

7. A Primary school breakdown by class type is not available in Wales.

8. For centres providing early learning and childcare in Scotland (this includes nursery classes within schools); children are counted once for each centre they are registered with. Only the 'All' figures are provided for early learning and childcare registrations in Scotland, as these cannot be split by gender.

9. Includes reception pupils in primary classes and, in Northern Ireland, pupils in preparatory departments of grammar schools.

10. In Wales, the Middle School for pupils of both primary and secondary school age was introduced in 2012/13.

11. Includes City Technology Colleges (CTCs) and Academies in England. Also includes secondary free schools, university technical colleges and studio schools.

12. Includes general hospital schools. Also includes special converter academies, special sponsored academies and special free schools. Hospital schools not included in Northern Ireland figures.

13. Only England and Wales have pupil referral units. Data for England includes alternative provision academies and free schools, and sole and dual main registrations. Data are not available for Wales.

14. 1 July for Northern Ireland, 28 February for maintained primary and secondary school pupils in Scotland and age at census date in September for pupils in early learning and childcare provision in Scotland.

15. Includes the so-called rising five's (i.e. those pupils who became 5 during the autumn term). Also includes under twos for England and Scotland in 2015/16.

16. In Scotland, includes some 4-year-olds.

17. Some figures do not equal the sum of the component parts due to rounding.

20.3 Pupil: teacher ratios and pupil: adult ratios within schools by type of school - time series

United Kingdom

	Pupil: teacher ratio within schools(1)					Pupil: adult ratio within schools(2)				
	2000/01	2011/12	2012/13	2013/14	2014/15	2000/01	2011/12	2012/13	2013/14	2014/15
United Kingdom										
Public sector mainstream										
Nursery schools(3)	23.1	17.7	17.5	18.0	19.2	..	..	..	..	..
Primary schools(4)(5)	22.3	20.5	20.5	20.5	20.7	..	..	..	..	..
Middle(6)	.	.	16.2	15.8	14.9	..	..	..	..	..
Secondary schools(7)	16.5	15.3	15.2	15.4	15.4	..	..	..	..	..
Non-maintained mainstream schools	9.7	8.0	8.0	8.1	7.9	..	..	..	..	..
Special schools										
Maintained(8)	6.4	6.0	5.9	5.7	6.1	..	..	..	..	..
Non-maintained	..	..	..	..	..	..	..	..	..	..
All schools(9)	17.9	16.2	16.2	16.3	16.4	..	..	..	..	..
England(10)										
Public sector mainstream										
Nursery schools	17.7	16.7	16.5	17.1	18.4	6.8	4.9	4.9	4.8	4.9
State-funded primary schools(5)	22.9	21.0	20.9	21.0	21.0	15.7	11.9	11.5	11.3	11.1
State-funded secondary schools(7)	17.1	15.6	15.5	15.7	15.8	14.0	10.6	10.5	10.6	10.5
Non-maintained mainstream schools	9.7	8.0	8.0	8.1	7.9	..	..	..	..	..
Special schools										
State-funded(8)	6.7	6.3	6.2	5.9	6.4	..	..	..	..	..
Non-maintained	4.8	..	..	..	..	..	..	..	..	..
All schools	18.1	16.3	16.2	16.3	16.5	..	..	..	..	..
Wales										
Public sector mainstream										
Nursery schools	17.3	15.2	15.1	14.9	14.6	..	5.6	5.4	5.3	5.4
Primary schools	21.5	20.7	20.7	20.8	21.2	..	10.2	9.9	9.8	10.0
Middle(6)	.	.	16.2	15.8	14.9	..	.	10.6	10.2	9.2
Secondary schools	16.6	16.7	16.3	16.1	16.2	..	11.9	11.5	11.2	11.3
Non-maintained mainstream schools	9.6	8.1	7.9	7.9	8.2	..	..	..	..	5.8
Special schools (maintained)	6.8	6.6	6.7	6.5	6.6	..	..	..	..	1.7
All schools	18.4	17.9	17.8	17.7	18.0	..	..	..	..	9.8
Scotland										
Public sector mainstream										
Nursery schools(3)	28.5	..	..	..	..	..	..	..	..	..
Primary schools(11)	19.0	16.0	16.3	16.5	16.7	..	11.7	11.8	11.9	12.1
Secondary schools	13.0	12.3	12.2	12.2	12.1	..	9.9	10.3	10.3	10.2
Non-maintained mainstream schools	10.1	..	..	..	..	..	..	..	..	..
Special schools										
Maintained	4.2	3.5	3.4	3.5	3.5	..	..	..	..	..
Non-maintained	3.3	..	..	..	..	..	..	..	..	..
All schools	15.4	13.7	13.8	13.9	14.0	..	..	..	..	..
Northern Ireland(12)										
Grant-aided sector mainstream										
Nursery schools	24.4	26.1	25.6	25.5	25.4	..	..	..	..	..
Primary schools(4)	20.1	21.4	21.1	21.1	21.0	..	..	..	..	..
Secondary schools	14.5	15.2	15.3	15.4	15.2	..	..	..	..	..
Non-maintained mainstream schools	9.3	6.7	6.8	6.8	6.5	..	..	..	..	..
Special schools (maintained)	5.9	6.3	6.0	5.9	6.4	..	..	..	..	..
All schools	16.6	17.5	17.5	17.5	17.4	..	..	..	..	..

Source: Department for Education; Welsh Government; Scottish Government; Northern Ireland Department of Education

1. The Pupil: teacher ratio (PTR) within schools is calculated by dividing the total full-time equivalent (FTE) number of pupils on roll in schools by the total FTE number of qualified teachers. It excludes centrally employed teachers regularly employed in schools.

2. The Pupil: adult ratio (PAR) within schools is calculated by dividing the total FTE number of pupils on roll in schools by the total FTE number of all teachers and support staff employed in schools, excluding administrative and clerical staff.

3. Excludes pre-school education figures for Scotland as FTE pupil numbers are not available.

4. Includes figures for preparatory departments attached to grammar schools in Northern Ireland.

5. Figures for England include primary converter academies, primary sponsor-led academies and primary free schools.

6. In Wales, the Middle School for pupils of both primary and secondary school age was introduced in 2012/13.

7. Figures for England include secondary converter academies, secondary sponsor-led academies and secondary free schools.

8. Figures for England include special converter academies. Excludes general hospital schools.

9. The UK PTR excludes pupil referral units and non-maintained special schools.

10. Figures for England from 2010 are derived from the School Workforce Census and are not comparable with figures for earlier years.

11. In Scotland, 2010, 2011 and 2012 pre-school and primary school teacher FTEs and PTRs were revised to remove double counting across these two sectors.

12. Figures for Northern Ireland exclude temporary teachers i.e. teachers filling vacant posts, secondments or career breaks.

20.4 PUPILS WITH STATEMENTS OF SPECIAL EDUCATIONAL NEEDS (SEN) OR EDUCATION, HEALTH AND CARE (EHC) PLANS (1)(2)

As at January each year: 2007-2015
England

	2007	2008	2009	2010	2011	2012	2013	2014	2015
ALL SCHOOLS									
Pupils with statements or EHC plans	232,760	227,315	225,400	223,945	224,210	226,125	229,390	232,190	236,165
Pupils on roll	8,167,715	8,121,955	8,092,280	8,098,360	8,123,865	8,178,200	8,249,810	8,331,385	8,438,145
Incidence (%) (3)	2.8	2.8	2.8	2.8	2.8	2.8	2.8	2.8	2.8
STATE-FUNDED SCHOOLS									
Maintained nursery									
Pupils with statements or EHC plans	310	265	285	265	250	305	245	265	265
Pupils on roll	37,640	37,440	37,285	37,575	38,830	39,395	38,820	39,915	41,455
Incidence (%) (3)	0.8	0.7	0.8	0.7	0.6	0.8	0.6	0.7	0.6
Placement (%) (4)	0	0	0	0.1	0.1	0.1	0.1	0.1	0.1
State-funded primary (5)(6)									
Pupils with statements or EHC plans	61,800	59,695	58,505	57,850	57,855	58,535	59,710	60,830	61,970
Pupils on roll	4,110,750	4,090,400	4,077,350	4,096,580	4,137,755	4,217,000	4,309,580	4,416,710	4,510,310
Incidence (%) (3)	1.5	1.5	1.4	1.4	1.4	1.4	1.4	1.4	1.4
Placement (%) (4)	26.6	26.3	26.0	25.8	25.8	25.9	26.0	26.2	26.2
State-funded secondary (5)(7)									
Pupils with statements or EHC plans	71,190	67,875	65,890	64,605	63,720	62,630	61,615	59,700	58,100
Pupils on roll	3,325,625	3,294,575	3,278,130	3,278,485	3,262,635	3,234,875	3,210,120	3,181,360	3,184,730
Incidence (%) (3)	2.1	2.1	2.0	2.0	2.0	1.9	1.9	1.9	1.8
Placement (%) (4)	30.6	29.9	29.2	28.8	28.4	27.7	26.9	25.7	24.6
Maintained special (8)									
Pupils with statements or EHC plans	83,645	83,600	84,295	85,445	86,660	88,230	90,845	94,120	97,830
Pupils on roll	87,010	87,135	87,615	88,690	89,860	91,590	94,350	97,395	101,250
Incidence (%) (3)	96.1	95.9	96.2	96.3	96.4	96.3	96.3	96.6	96.6
Placement (%) (4)	35.9	36.8	37.4	38.2	38.7	39.0	39.6	40.5	41.4
Pupil Referral Units (9)									
Pupils with statements or EHC plans	3,425	3,260	3,230	1,910	1,695	1,610	1,630	1,545	1,565
Pupils on roll	24,165	25,290	24,760	15,550	14,050	13,495	12,950	12,895	13,585
Incidence (%) (3)	14.2	12.9	13.0	12.3	12.1	11.9	12.6	12.0	11.5
Placement (%) (4)	1.5	1.4	1.4	0.9	0.8	0.7	0.7	0.7	0.7
OTHER SCHOOLS									
Independent (10)									
Pupils with statements or EHC plans	7,760	8,055	8,690	9,470	9,750	10,630	11,265	11,790	12,565
Pupils on roll	577,785	582,425	582,490	576,940	576,325	577,515	579,740	579,035	582,865
Incidence (%) (3)	1.3	1.4	1.5	1.6	1.7	1.8	1.9	2.0	2.2
Placement (%) (4)	3.3	3.5	3.9	4.2	4.3	4.7	4.9	5.1	5.3
Non-maintained special									
Pupils with statements or EHC plans	4,630	4,565	4,500	4,400	4,280	4,185	4,085	3,945	3,870
Pupils on roll	4,740	4,695	4,655	4,540	4,415	4,325	4,245	4,080	3,955
Incidence (%) (3)	97.7	97.3	96.7	97.0	97.0	96.7	96.1	96.7	97.9
Placement (%) (4)	2.0	2.0	2.0	2.0	1.9	1.9	1.8	1.7	1.6

Source: School Census and School Level Annual School Census

(1) Includes pupils who are sole or dual main registrations.
(2) Education, Health and Care (EHC) plans were introduced from September 2014 as part of a range of SEND reforms.
(3) Incidence of pupils - the number of pupils with statements or EHC plans expressed as a proportion of the number of pupils on roll.
(4) Placement of pupils - the number of pupils with statements or EHC plans expressed as a proportion of the number of pupils with statements in all schools.
(5) Includes middle schools as deemed.
(6) Includes all primary academies, including free schools.
(7) Includes city technology colleges, university technology colleges, studio schools and all secondary academies, including free schools. Includes all-through schools
(8) Includes general hospital schools and special academies, including free schools.
(9) Includes pupils registered with other providers, in alternative provision academies, including free schools and in further education colleges.
Prior to 2010 includes dual subsidiary registered pupils.
(10) Includes direct grant nursery schools.

Totals may not appear to equal the sum of the component parts because numbers have been rounded to the nearest 5.

20.5: GCSE, A level, SCE/NQ[1] and vocational qualifications obtained by pupils and students - time series

United Kingdom   Percentages and thousands

	2000/01	2010/11	2011/12	2012/13	2013/14
All					
Pupils in their last year of compulsory education[2]					
England, Wales and Northern Ireland [3]					
Percentage achieving GCSE or equivalent					
5 or more grades A*-C[4]	51.0	78.7	81.2	81.5	..
5 or more grades A*-C incl English and Maths	..	58.5	59.0	58.9	..
Any Passes	..	99.1	99.4	99.6	..
Pupils/students in education[5,6]					
England, Wales and Northern Ireland[3]					
Percentage achieving A Levels and equivalent[7]					
2 or more passes	37.4	52.8	54.7	54.8	54.3
Population aged 17 (thousands)[8]	717.9	707.4	700.4	709.0	711.0
School leavers					
Scotland [9]					
Percentage of school leavers attaining					
1 or more qualifications at SCQF level 4 or better	..	..	95.8	96.3	96.3
1 or more qualifications at SCQF level 5 or better	..	..	81.6	82.7	84.4
1 or more qualifications at SCQF level 6 or better	..	..	55.8	55.8	58.8
Males					
Pupils in their last year of compulsory education[2]					
England, Wales and Northern Ireland [3]					
Percentage achieving GCSE or equivalent					
5 or more grades A*-C[4]	45.7	75.0	77.6	77.7	..
5 or more grades A*-C incl English and Maths	..	54.8	54.3	53.7	..
Any Passes	..	98.9	99.1	99.3	..
Pupils/students in education[5,6]					
England, Wales and Northern Ireland[3]					
Percentage achieving A levels and equivalent[7]					
2 or more passes	33.4	48.0	49.7	50.1	49.2
Population aged 17 (thousands)[8]	366.6	364.0	359.9	364.1	366.8
School leavers					
Scotland[9]					
Percentage of school leavers attaining					
1 or more qualifications at SCQF level 4 or better	..	..	95.1	95.8	95.7
1 or more qualifications at SCQF level 5 or better	..	..	79.8	81.0	82.3
1 or more qualifications at SCQF level 6 or better	..	..	50.6	50.6	53.6
Females					
Pupils in their last year of compulsory education[2]					
England, Wales and Northern Ireland[3]					
Percentage achieving GCSE or equivalent					
5 or more grades A*-C[4]	56.5	82.6	85.0	85.4	..
5 or more grades A*-C incl English and Maths	..	62.4	63.9	64.4	..
Any Passes	..	99.4	99.8	100.0	..
Pupils/students in education[5,6]					
England, Wales and Northern Ireland[3]					
Percentage achieving A levels and equivalent[7]					
2 or more passes	41.6	57.9	60.1	59.9	59.7
Population aged 17 (thousands)[8]	351.3	343.4	340.4	345.0	344.2
School leavers					
Scotland[9]					
Percentage of school leavers attaining					
1 or more qualifications at SCQF level 4 or better	..	..	96.5	96.8	96.9
1 or more qualifications at SCQF level 5 or better	..	..	83.4	84.5	86.6
1 or more qualifications at SCQF level 6 or better	..	..	61.1	61.1	64.1

Source: Department for Education; Welsh Government; Scottish Government; Northern Ireland Department of Education

20.5: GCSE, A level, SCE/NQ[1] and vocational qualifications obtained by pupils and students - time series

1   National Qualifications (NQ) include Standard Grades, Intermediate 1 & 2 and Higher Grades.

2   Pupils aged 15 at the start of the academic year in Wales; pupils in Year S4 in Scotland. From 2004/05, pupils at the end of Key Stage 4 in England.

3   Also includes Scotland for 2009/10 and earlier.

4   Standard Grades 1-3/Intermediate 2 A-C/Intermediate 1 A in England for 2009/10 and earlier.

5   The number of pupils in schools and students in further education colleges in England, Wales and Northern Ireland expressed as a percentage of the of the 17-year-old population. Pupils and students are generally aged 16-18 at the start of the academic year in England, and aged 17 at the start of the academic year in Wales. Figures from 2002/03 for Wales and Northern Ireland relate to schools only.

6   Figures, other than for Scotland, include Vocational Certificates of Education (VCE) and, previously, Advanced level GNVQ, which is equivalent to 2 A levels or AS equivalents. From 2006/07, figures included for England cover achievements in all Level 3 qualifications approved under Section 96 of the Learning and Skills Act (2000), therefore UK aggregates are not comparable with previous years.

7   2 AS levels or 2 Highers/1 Advanced Higher or 1 each in Scotland, count as 1 A level pass for 2009/10 and earlier.

8   For 2013/14, based on mid-2013 based population projections. These take into account the 2011 Census. The figures for UK excluding Scotland are derived by the summation of England, Wales and Northern Ireland.

9   Qualifications in Scotland are based on the Scottish Credit and Qualifications Framework (SCQF). There are 12 levels on the framework, SCQF levels 1 to 7 are covered by school education. The new National qualifications, along with Standard Grades and Intermediates make up SCQF levels 3 to 5. Since 2013/14, under Curriculum for Excellence, Standard Grades are being phased out and replaced with National 3, 4 and 5 qualifications, and Intermediates will cease to exist from 2015/16. For most young people in Scotland S4 is the last compulsory year of school, but the majority will choose to stay on and complete S5 and S6. Highers (SCQF level 6) are generally taken in S5/S6; Highers, sometimes along with Advanced Highers (SCQF level 7, usually taken in S6) are the qualifications required for entry to Higher Education. School leaver data looks at a pupil's attainment throughout their school education. The leaver cohort is made up of all pupils who leave during or at the end of that year, so it contains pupils who leave at various stages of their schooling. Although Standard Grades were not available in 2013/14, the 2013/14 school leaver data will include Standard Grade attainment of leavers who sat these qualifications in earlier years of their schooling.

20.6 HE qualifications obtained by sex, subject area** and level of qualification obtained 2011/12 to 2014/15

	2011/12 All levels	2012/13 All levels	2013/14 All levels	2014/15 Postgraduate research	Postgraduate taught	Total postgraduate	First degree	Foundation degree	Other undergraduate	Total undergraduate	All levels
Female											
Medicine & dentistry	10650	10755	10630	1440	3590	5025	5645	0	210	5855	10880
Subjects allied to medicine	68470	70440	67190	1060	14070	15135	34790	1420	13695	49905	65035
Biological sciences	34450	36685	38180	2250	7715	9965	24170	470	2505	27145	37105
Veterinary science	875	800	880	55	95	150	815	0	20	835	985
Agriculture & related subjects	3635	3920	3800	135	805	940	1755	485	515	2755	3695
Physical sciences	11110	11395	11505	1150	2380	3530	6810	120	550	7480	11010
Mathematical sciences	4720	5015	5005	200	850	1050	3410	0	230	3640	4695
Computer science	5750	5455	5085	205	1785	1990	2705	80	390	3180	5170
Engineering & technology	8595	8755	8705	795	3775	4570	3850	130	460	4440	9010
Architecture, building & planning	7340	7125	6720	205	3100	3305	2860	45	490	3390	6700
Total - Science subject areas	155590	160340	157695	7495	38165	45660	86810	2755	19065	108625	154285
Percentage - Science subject areas	35%	36%	35%	60%	28%	30%	39%	27%	46%	39%	36%
Social studies	46255	46720	46400	1205	13500	14705	23325	1445	3730	28500	43205
Law	19585	19590	19025	220	6455	6675	10960	65	1165	12190	18870
Business & administrative studies	69655	69835	68210	525	32185	32705	30365	1220	3955	35540	68245
Mass communications & documentation	11815	11645	12090	115	4305	4420	6175	90	490	6750	11170
Languages	25345	25555	25425	965	4415	5380	16090	5	2255	18350	23730
Historical & philosophical studies	15000	14780	14805	790	2850	3640	8670	140	1000	9805	13450
Creative arts & design	37680	38165	39090	425	7175	7605	24500	1275	2435	28205	35810
Education	61430	58815	57650	770	28150	28920	15800	3125	6230	25155	54075
Combined	4100	4025	3875	0	65	65	2390	10	915	3315	3380
Total - All subject areas	446450	449470	444270	12505	137270	149775	225080	10130	41235	276445	426220
Male											
Medicine & dentistry	7555	7670	7610	1085	2290	3375	4370	0	95	4470	7840
Subjects allied to medicine	17280	17640	17070	675	4305	4980	8160	485	2995	11635	16620
Biological sciences	20970	23460	24530	1455	3585	5040	15255	735	2155	18145	23185
Veterinary science	255	260	275	30	50	80	265	0	5	275	355
Agriculture & related subjects	2255	2380	2260	95	605	700	950	385	295	1630	2330
Physical sciences	15100	15770	16265	2080	2630	4710	9960	200	1085	11245	15950
Mathematical sciences	6765	7430	7175	500	1305	1805	4900	0	490	5395	7200
Computer science	24765	22880	21895	815	4990	5805	12880	500	2420	15800	21605
Engineering & technology	42085	41585	41475	2520	11515	14035	21580	1295	4490	27360	41395
Architecture, building & planning	14405	13600	12015	250	4000	4250	5335	185	1240	6760	11010
Total - Science subject areas	151440	152675	150575	9505	35280	44785	83655	3780	15275	102710	147495
Percentage - Science subject areas	44%	45%	45%	67%	36%	40%	49%	56%	51%	50%	46%
Social studies	27485	27850	28290	1160	8435	9595	14730	450	1490	16670	26265
Law	13480	13100	12850	270	4785	5050	6365	50	895	7315	12365
Business & administrative studies	70370	68650	66720	690	28225	28915	29355	1295	4520	35175	64090
Mass communications & documentation	8090	7870	7825	120	1850	1970	4410	105	490	5000	6970
Languages	11495	11400	11235	640	1760	2400	6385	0	1455	7840	10240
Historical & philosophical studies	13170	13440	13210	985	2425	3415	7615	115	780	8510	11920
Creative arts & design	23520	23000	22605	365	3595	3960	13940	690	1650	16275	20235
Education	18915	17965	17590	395	11270	11660	2380	250	2670	5300	16960
Combined	2705	2410	2295	0	35	35	1615	10	480	2105	2145
Total - All subject areas	340670	338355	333195	14130	97660	111790	170445	6745	29705	206900	318685
All sexes											
Medicine & dentistry	18200	18425	18245	2525	5875	8400	10015	0	305	10325	18725
Subjects allied to medicine	85750	88085	84265	1735	18380	20115	42950	1905	16690	61545	81660
Biological sciences	55420	60150	62715	3705	11300	15005	39425	1205	4660	45290	60295
Veterinary science	1135	1060	1155	80	150	230	1080	0	30	1110	1340
Agriculture & related subjects	5885	6300	6060	230	1410	1640	2700	870	815	4390	6030
Physical sciences	26210	27170	27775	3230	5010	8240	16770	315	1635	18725	26965
Mathematical sciences	11485	12445	12180	700	2155	2855	8310	0	725	9035	11895
Computer science	30520	28340	26980	1025	6775	7800	15595	580	2810	18985	26785
Engineering & technology	50680	50345	50185	3315	15295	18605	25435	1425	4945	31805	50410
Architecture, building & planning	21745	20730	18735	455	7100	7560	8195	225	1730	10150	17710
Total - Science subject areas	307025	313045	308295	17000	73450	90450	170480	6535	34345	211355	301805
Percentage - Science subject areas	39%	40%	40%	64%	31%	35%	43%	39%	48%	44%	41%
Social studies	73740	74585	74715	2365	21945	24310	38055	1895	5220	45175	69485
Law	33065	32695	31880	490	11245	11735	17330	115	2060	19505	31240
Business & administrative studies	140020	138490	134940	1210	60410	61625	59725	2515	8480	70720	132345
Mass communications & documentation	19905	19515	19920	235	6155	6390	10585	190	980	11755	18145
Languages	36845	36955	36660	1610	6170	7780	22475	10	3710	26195	33975
Historical & philosophical studies	28170	28220	28025	1775	5280	7060	16290	255	1780	18320	25380
Creative arts & design	61200	61175	61705	795	10780	11570	38450	1960	4085	44495	56065
Education	80340	76785	75250	1165	39420	40585	18180	3375	8900	30460	71045
Combined	6810	6435	6165	0	100	100	4005	25	1395	5420	5525
Total - All subject areas*	787120	787900	777555	26640	234960	261600	395580	16875	70950	483405	745005

Soure: Higher Education Statistics Agency Limited

In this table 0,1, 2 are rounded to 0. All other numbers are rounded up or down to the nearest multiple of 5.

Percentages are calculated on un-rounded data. Percentages are rounded to the nearest whole number. Percentages calculated on populations which contain fewer than 22.5 individuals are suppressed and represented as "..".

* Students with a sex of 'other' are included in total figures but not in separate breakdowns.

** Analyses of subject information show Full-person equivalent (FPE). These are derived by splitting student instances between the different subjects that make up their course aim.

20.7 HE qualifications obtained by sex, level of qualification obtained and mode of study 2011/12 to 2014/15

	2011/12 All modes	2012/13 All modes	2013/14 All modes	2014/15 Full-time	Part-time	All modes
All UK HE providers						
Female						
Postgraduate research	11190	12035	11550	10120	2390	12505
Postgraduate taught	132015	135990	136150	94245	43025	137270
..of which Postgraduate Certificate in Education	14490	15165	16100	14410	790	15205
First degree	221805	227130	237505	202945	22135	225080
Foundation degree	16390	15030	11500	6295	3835	10130
Other undergraduate	65050	59285	47565	20695	20535	41235
..of which Professional Graduate Certificate in Education	3925	3340	2755	1825	730	2555
Total female	446450	449470	444270	334300	91920	426220
Male						
Postgraduate research	12925	13865	13130	11895	2235	14130
Postgraduate taught	107965	100110	97020	69485	28175	97660
..of which Postgraduate Certificate in Education	5785	5885	6255	5840	265	6105
First degree	169085	176595	184095	155360	15085	170445
Foundation degree	10755	10205	7430	4065	2680	6745
Other undergraduate	39940	37580	31515	18210	11500	29705
..of which Professional Graduate Certificate in Education	1840	1570	1285	800	380	1180
Total male	340670	338355	333195	259010	59675	318685
All sexes						
Postgraduate research	24115	25900	24690	22015	4625	26640
Postgraduate taught	239975	236115	233220	163750	71210	234960
..of which Postgraduate Certificate in Education	20275	21055	22355	20255	1055	21310
First degree	390890	403770	421635	358355	37225	395580
Foundation degree	27145	25240	18930	10365	6515	16875
Other undergraduate	104990	96875	79085	38910	32040	70950
..of which Professional Graduate Certificate in Education	5760	4910	4040	2625	1110	3735
Total all sexes*	787120	787900	777555	593390	151615	745005

Source: Higher Education Statistics Agency Limited

In this table 0,1, 2 are rounded to 0. All other numbers are rounded up or down to the nearest multiple of 5.

* Students with a sex of 'other' are included in total figures but not in separate breakdowns.

20.8 Students in further [1] and higher [2] Education - time series

United Kingdom   Thousands

Further education students	2010/11	2011/12	2012/13	2013/14	2014/15
All					
England(4)	4,264.9	4,216.6	4,320.3	3,913.5	3,585.3
Wales(5)	212.7	211.3	197.5	188.8	168.1
Scotland	311.0	256.5	235.8	237.3	238.3
Northern Ireland	144.4	141.7	145.4	130.2	128.4
Males					
England(4)	1,941.2	1,940.9	1,985.9	1,793.2	1,629.8
Wales(5)	94.0	92.1	86.5	82.9	75.0
Scotland	144.8	121.0	113.1	115.6	116.6
Northern Ireland	72.2	71.1	73.9	66.7	65.6
Females					
England(4)	2,323.7	2,275.7	2,334.4	2,120.2	1,955.6
Wales(5)	118.7	119.3	111.1	105.9	93.1
Scotland	166.2	135.5	122.7	121.6	121.6
Northern Ireland	72.3	70.8	71.5	63.6	62.8

Higher education students	2010/11		2011/12		2012/13		2013/14		2014/15	
	Full-time	Part-time	Full-time	Part-time	Full-time	Part-time	Full-time	Part-time	Full-time	Part-time
All										
Postgraduate	310.5	282.5	309.7	261.8	297.0	242.7	305.4	237.0	305.4	234.7
of which										
PhD & equivalent	65.5	24.5	69.5	25.5	71.3	25.3	74.4	25.9	74.7	25.4
Masters and Others	245.0	257.9	240.2	236.3	225.6	217.3	231.1	211.1	229.7	207.5
First Degree	1,258.0	224.7	1,319.8	241.3	1,319.6	229.8	1,351.8	203.6	1,358.6	187.0
Other Undergraduate	170.5	413.1	151.1	378.5	123.6	301.4	92.5	286.9	122.6	216.9
Total	**1,739.0**	**920.3**	**1,780.6**	**881.6**	**1,740.1**	**773.8**	**1,749.7**	**727.5**	**1,786.6**	**638.5**
Males										
Postgraduate	155.5	115.9	148.8	108.2	139.3	100.0	142.3	96.9	140.7	94.7
of which										
PhD & equivalent	35.7	12.0	38.0	12.4	39.0	12.2	40.7	12.4	40.3	12.1
Masters and Others	119.8	103.9	110.8	95.8	100.3	87.8	101.6	84.5	100.0	82.1
First Degree	573.9	92.9	601.9	100.0	599.8	95.5	610.5	86.3	608.9	80.5
Other Undergraduate	70.7	154.0	63.8	142.3	54.4	114.5	42.2	114.3	57.7	84.7
Total	**800.1**	**362.8**	**814.5**	**350.5**	**793.5**	**310.1**	**795.0**	**297.6**	**807.4**	**260.0**
Females										
Postgraduate	155.0	166.5	160.9	153.6	157.6	142.7	163.1	140.1	164.6	139.9
of which										
PhD & equivalent	29.8	12.6	31.5	13.1	32.3	13.1	33.7	13.5	34.3	13.3
Masters and Others	125.2	154.0	129.4	140.5	125.3	129.6	129.4	126.7	129.7	125.4
First Degree	684.0	131.8	717.9	141.3	719.8	134.3	741.3	117.2	749.5	106.4
Other Undergraduate	99.8	259.2	87.3	236.2	69.2	186.9	50.3	172.6	64.9	132.1
Total	**938.9**	**557.5**	**966.1**	**531.1**	**946.6**	**463.8**	**954.7**	**429.9**	**979.0**	**378.4**

Source: Department for Education; Welsh Government; Scottish Funding Council; Northern Ireland Department for the Economy

1. Includes home and overseas students.

2. Figures for Further Education Colleges (FECs) in Wales, Scotland and Northern Ireland are based on whole year enrolments. Figures for FECs in England are based on headcounts. Figures for FECs include apprenticeships. There are further education students in both Higher Education Institutions (HEIs) and FECs, mainly in FECs.

3. Figures for HEIs are based on the HESA 'standard registration' count (enrolments). They include students at The Open University. There are higher education students in both HEIs and FECs, mainly in HEIs.

4. These are figures for FECs in England. They are based on learner participation data from the Individualised Learner Record. They cannot be split by mode of attendance. There are no figures for HEIs in England.

5. These figures are for funded learners in General Further Education Colleges (including Tertiary), Sixth Form Colleges, Special Colleges (Agricultural and Horticultural Colleges and Art and Design Colleges), Specialist Colleges and External Institutions. They are based on learner participation data from the Individualised Learner Record. They cannot be split by mode of attendance. From 2010/11, these figures include students undertaking work based learning in FECs in Wales .

6. The data field "gender" has changed to be consistent with the Managing Information across Partners (MIAP) common data definitions coding frame. Students of "indeterminate gender" are included in totals over all students. Indeterminate means unable to be classified as either male or female and is not related in any way to trans-gender.

7. Full-time includes sandwich. Part-time comprises both day and evening, including block release and open/distance learning. For Scotland, full-time covers programmes of at least 640 hours of planned notional hours. Part-time includes short full-time, block/day release, evenings/weekends, assessment of work based learning. For Northern Ireland from 2013/14 sandwich courses or short courses of less than 4 weeks full-time study are considered to be part-time rather than full-time.

20.9 Students in higher education [1] by level, mode of study [2], gender [3] and subject group, 2014/15

United Kingdom(4)(5)(6)(7) — Home and Overseas Students — Thousands

	PhD & equivalent(8) Full-time	PhD & equivalent(8) Part-time	Masters and Others(9) Full-time	Masters and Others(9) Part-time	Total Postgraduate Full-time	Total Postgraduate Part-time	First degree(10) Full-time	First degree(10) Part-time	Other Undergraduate(11) Full-time	Other Undergraduate(11) Part-time	Total Undergraduate Full-time	Total Undergraduate Part-time	Total higher education students Full-time	Total higher education students Part-time
All														
Medicine & Dentistry	5.5	2.3	4.2	8.3	9.7	10.6	44.9	0.1	0.4	0.2	45.4	0.3	55.1	10.9
Subjects Allied to Medicine	4.3	2.3	12.6	43.4	16.9	45.9	138.9	19.4	10.6	50.9	149.4	70.3	166.4	116.1
Biological Sciences	11.3	2.4	11.4	9.5	22.7	11.9	145.7	23.1	8.1	5.7	153.7	28.8	176.4	40.7
Vet. Science, Agriculture & related	0.9	0.1	1.4	2.4	2.4	2.5	15.0	0.5	5.2	3.5	20.2	4.0	22.5	6.6
Physical Sciences	10.3	0.7	6.4	2.4	16.7	3.2	65.7	5.8	1.3	1.6	67.0	7.4	83.7	10.6
Mathematical and Computing Sciences	5.8	0.9	11.0	5.2	16.9	6.1	92.3	15.8	8.7	4.2	101.1	20.0	117.9	26.1
Engineering & Technology	12.0	1.3	17.1	9.3	29.1	10.6	96.7	12.2	10.9	20.5	107.6	32.7	136.7	43.4
Architecture, Building & Planning	1.3	0.5	7.4	5.7	8.7	6.2	25.1	4.6	3.2	6.1	28.3	10.7	37.0	17.0
Social Sciences (inc Law)	7.3	3.0	35.1	22.3	42.6	25.4	189.4	24.9	13.9	14.2	203.3	39.1	245.9	64.5
Business & Administrative Studies	3.9	2.4	62.0	34.9	66.0	37.6	186.7	19.8	21.1	27.7	207.8	47.5	273.8	85.1
Mass Communications & Documentation	0.6	0.4	7.0	2.4	7.6	2.8	36.7	0.9	1.8	0.5	38.4	1.4	46.0	4.2
Languages	3.9	1.3	6.9	3.3	10.8	4.6	74.8	9.9	1.9	9.7	76.7	19.6	87.6	24.2
Historical and Philosophical Studies	3.8	1.9	5.5	5.1	9.3	7.0	53.8	12.0	0.5	4.0	54.3	16.1	63.6	23.0
Creative Arts & Design	1.9	1.4	12.7	5.6	14.6	7.0	139.7	5.5	20.7	4.3	160.4	9.8	175.1	16.9
Education(12)	1.7	4.3	28.9	46.0	31.2	51.2	50.3	10.2	8.6	25.4	58.8	35.6	90.0	86.7
Other subjects(13)	-	-	0.1	1.8	0.1	1.8	2.7	22.2	3.0	21.8	5.6	44.0	5.7	45.8
Unknown(14)	-	-	-	-	-	0.1	0.2	-	2.9	16.5	3.1	16.5	3.1	16.6
All subjects	74.7	25.4	229.7	207.5	305.4	234.6	1358.6	187.0	122.6	216.9	1481.2	403.8	1786.6	638.4
of which overseas students	37.9	5.1	138.8	22.5	176.9	27.8	207.0	6.0	10.3	15.2	217.3	21.0	394.2	48.9
Males														
Medicine & Dentistry	2.2	1.1	1.5	3.7	3.7	4.8	19.9	-	0.1	0.1	20.0	0.1	23.7	4.9
Subjects Allied to Medicine	1.8	0.8	3.1	10.5	4.9	11.3	27.3	4.1	2.5	8.0	29.8	12.0	34.7	23.3
Biological Sciences	4.2	0.9	4.0	3.1	8.3	3.9	58.9	7.0	5.0	2.6	63.9	9.7	72.1	13.6
Vet. Science, Agriculture & related	0.4	0.1	0.6	0.9	1.0	0.9	4.1	0.2	1.7	1.7	5.8	1.9	6.8	2.9
Physical Sciences	6.6	0.4	3.5	1.4	10.1	1.8	39.8	3.4	0.7	1.1	40.6	4.5	50.7	6.3
Mathematical and Computing Sciences	4.3	0.7	7.6	4.0	11.9	4.7	71.3	12.1	7.6	3.2	78.9	15.4	90.8	20.0
Engineering & Technology	9.0	1.1	12.8	7.5	21.8	8.6	81.4	11.1	9.8	19.0	91.1	30.1	113.0	38.7
Architecture, Building & Planning	0.7	0.4	4.1	3.6	4.8	4.0	15.9	3.7	2.3	5.3	18.2	9.0	23.0	12.9
Social Sciences (inc Law)	3.7	1.3	14.0	7.6	17.7	8.9	72.7	8.1	3.3	3.2	76.0	11.4	93.8	20.3
Business & Administrative Studies	2.1	1.4	29.5	18.3	31.7	19.9	95.2	10.3	9.0	11.7	104.1	22.0	135.9	41.9
Mass Communications & Documentation	0.3	0.2	2.0	0.8	2.3	1.0	15.7	0.5	1.0	0.2	16.8	0.7	19.1	1.7
Languages	1.5	0.5	2.0	1.0	3.5	1.5	21.4	2.8	0.9	4.0	22.3	6.8	25.7	8.3
Historical and Philosophical Studies	2.1	1.0	2.5	2.5	4.7	3.6	25.4	5.0	0.2	1.5	25.6	6.5	30.3	10.1
Creative Arts & Design	0.9	0.7	4.3	2.0	5.2	2.7	51.1	2.2	8.7	1.3	59.8	3.5	65.0	6.2
Education(12)	0.5	1.6	8.4	14.6	9.0	16.4	7.7	0.9	1.7	7.2	9.4	8.1	18.4	24.5
Other subjects(13)	-	-	-	0.6	-	0.6	1.0	8.9	1.7	8.0	2.8	16.9	2.8	17.5
Unknown(14)	-	-	-	-	-	-	0.1	-	1.4	6.7	1.6	6.7	1.6	6.7
All subjects	40.3	12.1	100.0	82.1	140.7	94.7	608.9	80.5	57.7	84.7	666.6	165.3	807.4	259.9
of which overseas students	21.2	2.8	63.1	12.0	84.4	14.8	99.0	3.4	5.4	6.9	104.4	10.3	188.8	25.2
Females														
Medicine & Dentistry	3.3	1.2	2.7	4.6	6.0	5.8	25.1	0.1	0.3	0.1	25.4	0.2	31.4	6.0
Subjects Allied to Medicine	2.5	1.5	9.5	32.9	12.0	34.6	111.6	15.3	8.0	42.9	119.6	58.2	131.6	92.8
Biological Sciences	7.1	1.5	7.3	6.5	14.4	8.0	86.7	16.0	3.1	3.1	89.9	19.1	104.3	27.1
Vet. Science, Agriculture & related	0.5	0.1	0.8	1.5	1.4	1.6	10.9	0.3	3.5	1.7	14.3	2.1	15.7	3.7
Physical Sciences	3.7	0.3	2.8	1.1	6.6	1.4	25.9	2.4	0.6	0.6	26.4	3.0	33.0	4.3
Mathematical and Computing Sciences	1.5	0.2	3.4	1.2	5.0	1.5	21.0	3.6	1.1	1.0	22.1	4.6	27.1	6.1
Engineering & Technology	3.0	0.3	4.3	1.8	7.3	2.0	15.4	1.1	1.1	1.5	16.5	2.6	23.8	4.6
Architecture, Building & Planning	0.6	0.2	3.4	2.1	3.9	2.3	9.2	0.9	0.9	0.8	10.1	1.8	14.0	4.0
Social Sciences (inc Law)	3.7	1.7	21.1	14.7	24.9	16.5	116.7	16.8	10.6	10.9	127.3	27.7	152.1	44.2
Business & Administrative Studies	1.8	1.0	32.4	16.5	34.3	17.8	91.5	9.4	12.1	16.0	103.6	25.5	137.9	43.2
Mass Communications & Documentation	0.4	0.2	4.9	1.6	5.3	1.7	20.9	0.5	0.7	0.2	21.7	0.7	27.0	2.5
Languages	2.4	0.8	4.9	2.3	7.3	3.0	53.4	7.1	1.1	5.7	54.5	12.8	61.8	15.9

20.9 Students in higher education [1] by level, mode of study [2], gender [3] and subject group, 2014/15

United Kingdom(4)(5)(6)(7)	Home and Overseas Students												Thousands	
	Postgraduate level						Undergraduate level						Total	
	PhD & equivalent(8)		Masters and Others(9)		Total Postgraduate		First degree(10)		Other Undergraduate(11)		Total Undergraduate		higher education students	
	Full-time	Part-time	Full-time	Part-time	Full-time	Part-time	Full-time	Part-time	Full-time	Part-time	Full-time	Part-time	Full-time	Part-time
Historical and Philosophical Studies	1.7	0.8	3.0	2.5	4.6	3.4	28.5	7.0	0.2	2.5	28.7	9.6	33.3	13.0
Creative Arts & Design	1.0	0.7	8.4	3.5	9.4	4.3	88.5	3.3	12.0	3.0	100.6	6.3	110.0	10.6
Education(12)	1.2	2.8	20.5	31.4	22.1	34.7	42.6	9.2	6.8	18.2	49.4	27.5	71.5	62.2
Other subjects(13)	-	-	0.1	1.2	0.1	1.2	1.6	13.2	1.2	13.8	2.9	27.0	2.9	28.2
Unknown(14)	-	-	-	-	-	0.1	0.1	-	1.4	9.8	1.5	9.8	1.5	9.9
All subjects	34.3	13.3	129.7	125.4	164.6	139.8	749.5	106.4	64.9	132.1	814.4	238.5	979.0	378.3
of which overseas students	16.7	2.4	75.7	10.5	92.5	13.0	108.0	2.6	4.9	8.3	112.9	10.7	205.4	23.7

Source: Department for Education; Welsh Government; Scottish Funding Council; Northern Ireland Department for the Economy

1. Figures for Higher Education Institutions (HEIs) are Higher Education Statistics Agency 'standard registration' counts. HEIs include Open University. Figures for Further Education Colleges are whole year enrolments at Level 4 or above. Skills Funding Agency (SFA) funded provision (e.g. Higher Apprenticeships, Trailblazer Apprenticeships) has been excluded to avoid double counting with other tables in the publication.

2. Full-time mode of study includes sandwich. Part-time comprises both day and evening, including block release and open/distance learning. In Scotland, full-time covers programmes of at least 480 hours of planned notional hours. Part-time includes short full-time, block/day release, evenings/weekends, assessment of work based learning, distance/locally based learning, college based private study, other open learning and flexible learning. In Wales, full-time learners are those with at least 450 guided contact hours in the academic year. In Northern Ireland from 2013/14 sandwich courses or short courses of less than 4 weeks full-time study are considered to be part-time rather than full-time.

3. The data field "gender" has changed to be consistent with the Managing Information across Partners (MIAP) common data definitions coding frame. Students of "indeterminate gender" are included in totals over all students. Indeterminate means unable to be classified as either male or female and is not related in any way to trans-gender.

4. Figures for Further Education Colleges in England count all students on postgraduate level courses as Masters and Others; and, all students on undergraduate other than first degree courses as part-time.

5. Figures for Further Education Colleges in Wales are counts of unique learners. As a learner may pursue more than one course, only one subject per learner has been selected (based on the most recently started course of the learner where applicable). Students have been assigned a level on the basis of learning programme type. For the purpose of this table, HE learners are those pursuing a (non-WBL) overarching HE learning programme. (It excludes learners pursuing HE level activities within an FE or WBL programme.)

6. Figures for Further Education Colleges in Scotland do not include students with under 25% attendance rate.

7. Figures for Further Education Colleges in Northern Ireland are regulated course enrolments rather than headcounts.

8. Defined as 'Doctorate' in Scotland.

9. For Scotland includes masters (research/taught) and postgraduate diploma/certificate.

10. For Scotland includes first degree honours/ordinary.

11. For Scotland includes 'SVQ or NVQ: Level 4 and Level 5,' 'Diploma (HNC/D level for diploma and degree holders),' and 'HNC/D or equivalent'.

12. Includes Initial Teacher Training (ITT) and In-Service Education and Training (INSET).

13. Includes Combined and general programmes and programmes not otherwise classified.

14. Includes data for Further Education Colleges that cannot be split by subject group.

20.10 Qualified teachers by type of school and gender - time series

United Kingdom	(i) Full-time teachers										Thousands
	2000/01	2011/12	2012/13	2013/14	2014/15(9)	2015/16					
						UK	of which:				
							England(10)	Wales	Scotland(11)(12)	Northern Ireland(13)	
All											
Public sector mainstream											
Nursery(1)(2) and Primary(3)	211.2	198.6	205.2	209.6	214.9	216.0	177.0	10.6	21.3	7.0	
Middle(4)	.	.	0.2	0.2	0.3	0.3	.	0.3	.	.	
Secondary(5)	225.7	218.8	222.9	220.2	218.6	212.9	174.4	9.9	20.6	8.1	
Non-maintained mainstream(6)	52.3	55.5	56.9	57.3	59.7	61.2	60.2	0.9	..	0.1	
All Special(7)	16.5	14.8	15.4	18.8	19.4	19.3	16.3	0.6	1.6	0.7	
All schools(8)	**505.7**	**487.7**	**500.6**	**506.1**	**512.9**	**509.7**	**428.0**	**22.3**	**43.5**	**15.9**	
Males											
Public sector mainstream											
Nursery(1)(2) and Primary(3)	32.1	30.2	31.9	33.2	34.6	35.5	30.3	2.0	2.0	1.3	
Middle(4)	.	.	0.1	0.1	0.1	0.1	.	0.1	.	.	
Secondary(5)	102.9	89.8	90.8	89.3	88.2	86.0	71.3	3.8	8.1	2.9	
Non-maintained mainstream(6)	21.3	22.3	22.8	23.0	24.0	24.4	24.0	0.4	..	..	
All Special(7)	5.0	4.1	4.2	5.4	5.6	5.5	4.7	0.2	0.4	0.1	
All schools(8)	**161.3**	**146.4**	**149.8**	**151.0**	**152.4**	**151.6**	**130.3**	**6.5**	**10.5**	**4.3**	
Females											
Public sector mainstream											
Nursery(1)(2) and Primary(3)	179.1	166.8	171.7	175.1	178.5	178.8	146.8	8.6	17.7	5.8	
Middle(4)	.	.	0.1	0.1	0.2	0.2	.	0.2	.	.	
Secondary(5)	122.8	128.8	131.8	130.7	130.3	126.8	103.0	6.1	12.5	5.2	
Non-maintained mainstream(6)	30.9	33.2	34.1	34.4	35.8	36.8	36.2	0.5	..	0.1	
All Special(7)	11.6	10.7	11.2	13.4	13.8	13.8	11.6	0.4	1.2	0.5	
All schools(8)	**344.4**	**339.5**	**349.0**	**353.7**	**358.5**	**356.4**	**297.6**	**15.8**	**31.4**	**11.6**	

	(ii) Full-time equivalent (FTE) of part-time teachers										Thousands
	2000/01	2011/12	2012/13	2013/14	2014/15	2015/16					
						UK	of which:				
							England(10)	Wales	Scotland(11)	Northern Ireland(13)	
All											
Public sector mainstream											
Nursery(1)(2) and Primary(3)	21.9	39.5	39.7	41.4	39.5	42.3	35.9	1.6	3.9	0.9	
Middle(4)	.	-	-	-	-	-	.	.	.	.	
Secondary(5)	16.7	27.3	27.4	28.5	26.9	28.4	23.8	1.1	2.6	0.8	
Non-maintained mainstream(6)	10.2	13.0	12.7	12.4	12.7	13.0	12.8	0.2	..	-	
All Special(7)	1.6	2.6	2.5	3.3	3.1	3.2	2.7	0.1	0.3	0.1	
All schools(8)	**50.4**	**82.3**	**82.4**	**85.7**	**82.2**	**86.9**	**75.2**	**3.0**	**6.8**	**1.8**	

Sources: Department for Education; Welsh Government; Scottish Government; Northern Ireland Department of Education

1. Figures for Scotland from 2005/06 include only centres providing pre-school education as a local authority centre or in partnership with the local authority. Figures are not directly comparable with previous years

2. Figures for full-time teachers in pre-school education centres in Scotland from 2005/06 are based on the total full-time equivalent (FTE) of General Teaching Council (GTC) of Scotland registered staff.

3. Figures for England include primary converter academies, primary sponsor-led academies and primary free schools from 2010/11.

4. In Wales, the Middle School for pupils of both primary and secondary school age was introduced in 2012/13.

5. Figures for England include secondary converter academies, secondary sponsor-led academies and secondary free schools from 2010/11.

6. Excludes Scotland from 2011/12 because the collection was discontinued in 2010.

7. Includes PRU figures for England.

8. Excludes Pupil Referral Units (PRUs).

9. An error was identified in the 2014/15 figures for Northern Ireland. Revised figures have been included here and will therefore differ from previously published data.

10. Figures for England were derived from the School Workforce Census from 2009/10. Prior to 2009/10 figures were derived from the 618g Survey and the Database of Teacher Records.

11. Figures for pre-school education centres for Scotland cannot be split by gender.

12. Nursery figures for Scotland from 2010/11 are not directly comparable with previously published figures, due to a change in the timing of the Pre-school Education Census from January to September.

13. Figures for Northern Ireland exclude temporary teachers i.e. teachers filling vacant posts, secondments or career breaks.

this page is intentionally blank

Chapter 21

Crime and Justice

Crime and Justice

There are differences in the legal and judicial systems of England and Wales, Scotland and Northern Ireland which make it impossible to provide tables covering the UK as a whole in this section. These differences concern the classification of offences, the meaning of certain terms used in the statistics, the effects of the several Criminal Justice Acts and recording practices.

Recorded crime statistics
(Table 21.3)

Crimes recorded by the police provide a measure of the amount of crime committed. For a variety of reasons, many offences are either not reported to the police or not recorded by them. The changes in the number of offences recorded do not necessarily provide an accurate reflection of changes in the amount of crime committed.

The recorded crime statistics include all indictable and triable-either-way offences together with a few summary offences which are closely linked to these offences. The revised rules changed the emphasis of measurement more towards one crime per victim, and also increased the coverage of offences.

In order to further improve the consistency of recorded crime statistics and to take a more victim-oriented approach to crime recording, the National Crime Recording Standard (NCRS) was introduced across all forces in England, Wales and Northern Ireland from 1 April 2002. Some police forces implemented the principles of NCRS in advance of its introduction across all forces. The NCRS had the effect of increasing the number of offences recorded by the police and data before and after 2002/03 are not directly comparable.

For a variety of reasons many offences are either not reported to the police or not recorded by them. The changes in the number of offences recorded do not necessarily provide an accurate reflection of changes in the amount of crime committed.

Similarly, the Scottish Crime Recording Standard (SCRS) was introduced by the eight Scottish police forces with effect from 1 April 2004. This means that no corroborative evidence is required initially to record a crime-related incident as a crime if the victim perceived it as a crime. Again, the introduction of this new recording standard was expected to increase the numbers of minor crimes recorded by the police, such as minor crimes of vandalism and minor thefts and offences of petty assault and breach of the peace. However, it was expected that the SCRS would not have much impact on the figures for the more serious crimes such as serious assault, sexual assault, robbery or housebreaking.

The Sexual Offences Act 2003 introduced in May 2004 altered the definition and coverage of sexual offences. In particular, it redefined indecent exposure as a sexual offence, which is likely to account for much of the increase in sexual offences.

The Sexual Offences (Scotland) Act 2009 introduced in 1 December 2010 repealed a number of common law crimes including rape, clandestine injury to women and sodomy and replaced them with new statutory sexual offences. The Act created a number of new "protective" offences, which criminalise sexual activity with children and mentally disordered persons. Protective offences are placed into categories concerning young children (under 13) and older (13-15 years). The new legislation may result in some increases in Group 2 crimes. For example, the offences of voyeurism or indecent communication towards an adult would previously have been classified as breach of the peace. It is likely that the effect will be to change the distribution of these crimes among the sub classifications. For example, some crimes previously categorised as lewd and libidinous practices will now be classified as sexual assault. The standard breakdown provided in response to information requests on sexual offences has had to be revised to accommodate these changes.

Offences committed before 1 December 2010:

Rape & attempted rape includes:

- Rape
- Assault with intent to rape

Indecent assault includes:

- Indecent assault

Lewd and indecent behaviour includes:

- Public indecency

'Other' includes:

- Incest
- Unnatural crimes
- Prostitution
- Procuration and other sexual offences

Offences committed on or after 1 December 2010:

Rape & attempted rape includes:

- Rape
- Attempted rape

Sexual assault includes:

- Contact sexual assault (13-15 years old or adult 16+)
- other sexually coercive conduction (adult 16+)
- Sexual offences against children under 13
- Sexual activity with children aged 13-15
- Other sexual offences involving children aged 13-15
- Lewd and libidinous practices

Prostitution

- Offences relating to prostitution

'Other' includes:

- Incest
- Unnatural crimes
- Public indecency
- Sexual exposure
- Procuration and other sexual offences

Further information is available from Crime in England and Wales.

Court proceedings and police cautions
(Tables 21.4 to 21.8, 21.12 to 21.16, 21.19 to 21.20

The statistical basis of the tables of court proceedings is broadly similar in England and Wales, Scotland and Northern Ireland; the tables show the number of persons found guilty, recording a person under the heading of the principal offence of which they were found guilty, excluding additional findings of guilt at the same proceedings. A person found guilty at a number of separate court proceedings is included more than once.

The statistics on offenders cautioned in England and Wales cover only those who, on admission of guilt, were given a formal caution by, or on the instructions of, a senior police officer as an alternative to prosecution. Written warnings by the police for motor offences and persons paying fixed penalties for certain motoring offences are excluded. Formal cautions are not issued in Scotland. There are no statistics on cautioning available for Northern Ireland.

The Crime and Disorder Act 1998 created provisions in relation to reprimands and final warnings, new offences and orders which have been implemented nationally since 1 June 2000. They replace the system of cautioning for offenders aged under 18. Reprimands can be given to first-time offenders for minor offences. Any further offending results in either a final warning or a charge.

For persons proceeded against in Scotland, the statistics relate to the High Court of Justiciary, the sheriff courts and the district courts. The High Court deals with serious solemn (that is, jury) cases and has unlimited sentencing power. Sheriff courts are limited to imprisonment of 3 years for solemn cases, or 3 months (6 months when specified in legislation for second or subsequent offences and 12 months for certain statutory offences) for summary (that is, non-jury) cases. District courts deal only with summary cases and are limited to 60 days imprisonment and level 4 fines. Stipendiary magistrates sit in Glasgow District Court and have the summary sentencing powers of a sheriff.

In England and Wales, indictable offences are offences which are:

• triable only on indictment. These offences are the most serious breaches of the criminal law and must be tried at the Crown Court. 'Indictable-only' offences include murder, manslaughter, rape and robbery
• triable either way. These offences may be tried at the Crown Court or a magistrates' court

The Criminal Justice Act 1991 led to the following main changes in the sentences available to the courts in England and Wales:

• introduction of combination orders
• introduction of the 'unit fine scheme' at magistrates' courts
• abolishing the sentence of detention in a young offender institution for 14-year-old boys and changing the minimum and maximum sentence lengths for 15 to 17-year-olds to 10 and 12 months respectively, and
• abolishing partly suspended sentences of imprisonment and restricting the use of a fully suspended sentence

(The Criminal Justice Act 1993 abolished the 'unit fine scheme' in magistrates' courts, which had been introduced under the Criminal Justice Act 1991.

A charging standard for assault was introduced in England and Wales on 31 August 1994 with the aim of promoting consistency between the police and prosecution on the appropriate level of charge to be brought.

The Criminal Justice and Public Order Act 1994 created several new offences in England and Wales, mainly in the area of public order, but also including male rape (there is no statutory offence of male rape in Scotland, although such a crime may be charged as serious assault). The Act also:

• extended the provisions of section 53 of the Children and Young Persons Act 1993 for 10 to 13-year-olds
• increased the maximum sentence length for 15 to 17-year-olds to 2 years
• increased the upper limit from £2,000 to £5,000 for offences of criminal damage proceeded against as if triable only summarily
• introduced provisions for the reduction of sentences for early guilty pleas, and
• increased the maximum sentence length for certain firearm offences

 Provisions within the Crime (Sentences) Act 1997 (as amended by the Powers of Criminal Courts Sentencing Act 2000) in England and Wales, and the Crime and Punishment (Scotland) Act 1997 in Scotland, included:

• an automatic life sentence for a second serious violent or sexual offence unless there are exceptional circumstances (this provision has not been enacted in Scotland)
• a minimum sentence of 7 years for an offender convicted for a third time of a class A drug trafficking offence unless the court considers this to be unjust in all the circumstances, and
• in England and Wales, the new section 38A of the Magistrates' Courts' Act 1980 extending the circumstances in which a magistrates' court may commit a person convicted of an offence triable-either-way to the Crown Court for sentence – it was implemented in conjunction with section 49 of the Criminal Procedure and Investigations Act 1996, which involves the magistrates' courts in asking defendants to indicate a plea before the mode of trial decision is taken and compels the court to sentence, or commit for sentence, any defendant who indicates a guilty plea.

Under the Criminal Justice and Court Service Act 2000 new terms were introduced for certain orders. Community rehabilitation order is the new name for a probation order. A community service order is now known as a community punishment order. Finally, the new term for a combination order is community punishment and rehabilitation order. In April 2000 the secure training order was replaced by the detention and training order. Section 53 of the Children and Young Persons Act 1993 was repealed on 25 August 2000 and its provisions were transferred to sections 90 to 92 of the Powers of Criminal Courts (Sentencing) Act 2000. Reparation and action plan orders were implemented nationally from 1 June 2000. The drug treatment and testing order was introduced in England, Scotland and Wales from October 2000. The referral order was introduced in England, Scotland and Wales from April 2000. Youth rehabilitation orders came into effect in November 2009 as part of the Criminal Justice and Immigration Act 2008. These changes are now reflected in Table 21.8.

Following the introduction of the Libra case management system during 2008, offenders at magistrates' courts can now be recorded as sex 'Not Stated'. In 2008 one per cent of offenders sentenced were recorded as sex 'Not Stated' as well as 'Male', 'Female', or 'Other'. Amendments to the data tables have been made to accommodate this new category.

The system of magistrates' courts and Crown courts in Northern Ireland operates in a similar way to that in England and Wales. A particularly significant statutory development, however, has been the Criminal Justice (NI) Order 1996 which introduced a new sentencing regime into Northern Ireland, largely replicating that which was introduced into England and Wales by the Criminal Justice Acts of 1991 and 1993. The order makes many changes to both community and custodial sentences, while introducing new orders such as the combination order, the custody probation order, and orders for release on licence of sexual offenders.

Abbreviations
(Tables 21.4a, 21.6a-c, 21.6d-f)

Every effort is made to ensure that the figures presented are accurate and complete. However, it is important to note that these data have been extracted from large administrative data systems generated by the police forces and court

As a consequence, care should be taken to ensure data collection processes and their inevitable limitations are taken into account when those data are used.

Abbreviation	Description
Total Proc Against	Total Proceeded Against
Proc Disc	Proceedings Discontinued
Proc Disc	Discharge Section 6 Magistrates' Courts Act 1980
Charge Wdrn	Charge Withdrawn
Charge Dism	Charge Dismissed
Comm For Trial	Committed for Trial
Comm For Sent	Committed for Sentence
Total For Sent	Total for Sentence
Abslt Disch	Absolute Discharge
Condl Disch	Conditional Discharge
CRO	Community Rehabilitation Order
YRO	Youth Rehabilitation Order
SO	Supervision Order
CPO	Community Punishment Order
ACO	Attendance Centre Order
CP & RO	Community Punishment Order and Rehabilitation Order
Curf Order	Curfew Order
Rep Order	Reparation Order
APO	Action Plan Order
DTTO	Drug Treatment and Test Order
Ref Order	Referral Order
Comm Order	Community Order
YRO	Youth Rehabilitation Order
SS	Suspended Sentence
DTO	Detention and Training Order
YOI	Young Offender Institution
Unsus Sent Impri	Unsuspended sentence of imprisonment
Imm Cust	Immediate Custody
ODW	Otherwise dealt with

21.1a Police officers in England and Wales, by police force area, as at 31 March 2016

England and Wales

Police force	All officers (full-time equivalent)			Officers available for duty[1] (full-time equivalent)		
	Male	Female	Total	Male	Female	Total
Avon & Somerset	1,936	756	2,692	1,890	681	2,571
Bedfordshire	742	340	1,083	718	312	1,030
Cambridgeshire	959	390	1,349	941	368	1,308
Cheshire	1,413	598	2,011	1,376	550	1,926
Cleveland	944	315	1,259	854	264	1,118
Cumbria	718	400	1,118	699	369	1,067
Derbyshire	1,246	520	1,766	1,209	476	1,685
Devon & Cornwall	2,108	852	2,959	2,071	829	2,901
Dorset	892	331	1,223	853	300	1,153
Durham	796	318	1,115	781	295	1,077
Essex	2,040	853	2,894	1,988	761	2,750
Gloucestershire	751	338	1,090	733	310	1,043
Greater Manchester	4,478	1,819	6,297	4,312	1,642	5,954
Hampshire	2,009	875	2,883	1,942	776	2,718
Hertfordshire	1,323	605	1,929	1,293	535	1,828
Humberside	1,096	486	1,582	1,077	445	1,522
Kent	2,311	872	3,182	2,268	822	3,090
Lancashire	2,018	842	2,860	1,975	774	2,749
Leicestershire	1,369	491	1,859	1,334	442	1,776
Lincolnshire	773	301	1,073	751	277	1,028
London, City of	538	164	702	531	149	680
Merseyside	2,572	983	3,554	2,513	887	3,400
Metropolitan Police	23,708	8,417	32,125	23,114	7,663	30,778
Norfolk	1,102	412	1,515	1,089	383	1,473
Northamptonshire	839	375	1,214	821	346	1,167
Northumbria	2,377	959	3,336	2,339	881	3,221
North Yorkshire	936	405	1,341	919	372	1,290
Nottinghamshire	1,419	555	1,973	1,399	511	1,910
South Yorkshire	1,749	746	2,494	1,699	686	2,385
Staffordshire	1,206	453	1,660	1,189	421	1,610
Suffolk	793	294	1,087	782	273	1,054
Surrey	1,299	639	1,938	1,261	574	1,835
Sussex	1,846	819	2,666	1,810	753	2,563
Thames Valley	2,923	1,321	4,244	2,873	1,211	4,084
Warwickshire	584	251	836	571	235	807
West Mercia	1,458	621	2,079	1,425	584	2,009
West Midlands	4,859	2,085	6,944	4,727	1,909	6,636
West Yorkshire	3,107	1,394	4,501	3,034	1,261	4,296
Wiltshire	662	357	1,019	639	321	959
Dyfed-Powys	805	344	1,149	788	315	1,103
Gwent	798	329	1,127	758	304	1,062
North Wales	992	465	1,458	974	443	1,418
South Wales	2,074	809	2,883	2,001	744	2,745
Total 43 forces	**88,569**	**35,498**	**124,066**	**86,323**	**32,456**	**118,779**
Central service secondments	245	51	296	245	51	296
British Transport Police	2,437	530	2,968	2,300	483	2,784
Total	**91,251**	**36,078**	**127,329**	**88,868**	**32,990**	**121,858**

Source: Home Office

Notes

1. Officers available for duty is the number of officers in post excluding long-term absentees. In previous publications, these figures were provided on a headcount basis.

21.1b Special constables[1] by police force area and gender, as at 31 March 2016

England and Wales

Headcount[1]

Police force	Total			Black and Minority Ethnic (BME)			Joiners			Leavers		
	Male	Female	Total	Male	Female	Total	Male	Female	Total	Male	Female	Total
Avon & Somerset	285	109	394	6	2	8	53	36	89	55	44	99
Bedfordshire	162	66	228	17	6	23	54	26	80	50	27	77
Cambridgeshire	184	74	258	7	2	9	30	8	38	34	13	47
Cheshire	283	138	421	5	4	9	79	37	116	47	22	69
Cleveland	47	25	72	2	2	4	9	8	17	7	2	9
Cumbria	75	33	108	2	1	3	15	4	19	24	6	30
Derbyshire	147	65	212	8	4	12	48	31	79	37	20	57
Devon & Cornwall	380	184	564	1	3	4	28	16	44	48	40	88
Dorset	132	66	198	2	0	2	28	18	46	45	22	67
Durham	66	26	92	0	0	0	9	4	13	17	13	30
Essex	266	106	372	10	3	13	69	45	114	64	32	96
Gloucestershire	94	38	132	3	0	3	20	10	30	11	2	13
Greater Manchester	612	253	865	77	19	96	227	106	333	123	48	171
Hampshire	257	95	352	5	7	12	19	10	29	68	28	96
Hertfordshire	192	66	258	14	4	18	28	15	43	70	18	88
Humberside	244	137	381	3	2	5	45	34	79	51	47	98
Kent	229	73	302	5	3	8	80	46	126	49	11	60
Lancashire	333	147	480	20	10	30	164	99	263	88	63	151
Leicestershire	214	81	295	34	4	38	88	40	128	54	30	84
Lincolnshire	137	58	195	0	1	1	24	12	36	29	30	59
London, City of	46	15	61	4	2	6	5	1	6	5	1	6
Merseyside	234	95	329	14	4	18	83	42	125	63	41	104
Metropolitan Police	2,239	1,032	3,271	756	280	1,036	442	251	693	610	339	949
Norfolk	180	71	251	3	1	4	35	25	60	38	28	66
Northamptonshire	510	212	722	27	11	38	399	171	570	118	44	162
Northumbria	158	50	208	1	0	1	33	15	48	62	21	83
North Yorkshire	108	76	184	1	0	1	32	31	63	31	17	48
Nottinghamshire	180	107	287	9	5	14	54	48	102	38	30	68
South Yorkshire	236	147	383	12	14	26	47	29	76	65	60	125
Staffordshire	211	81	292	7	1	8	41	32	73	58	37	95
Suffolk	175	80	255	7	0	7	46	31	77	30	26	56
Surrey	82	27	109	2	1	3	10	7	17	22	6	28
Sussex	276	111	387	7	3	10	88	46	134	80	55	135
Thames Valley	359	147	506	28	8	36	98	46	144	135	65	200
Warwickshire	132	46	178	12	5	17	23	6	29	63	35	98
West Mercia	215	105	320	6	4	10	58	34	92	48	26	74
West Midlands	243	60	303	52	13	65	7	4	11	43	24	67
West Yorkshire	649	381	1,030	70	33	103	222	147	369	98	77	175
Wiltshire	112	52	164	3	0	3	11	12	23	21	12	33
Dyfed-Powys	118	53	171	0	0	0	21	11	32	4	4	8
Gwent	81	45	126	1	1	2	8	5	13	16	8	24
North Wales	99	84	183	0	0	0	38	43	81	15	13	28
South Wales	70	27	97	2	1	3	31	15	46	16	1	17
Total of 43 forces	**11,052**	**4,944**	**15,996**	**1,245**	**464**	**1,709**	**2,949**	**1,657**	**4,606**	**2,650**	**1,488**	**4,138**
British Transport Police	224	59	283	35	2	37	107	36	143	67	10	77
Total	**11,276**	**5,003**	**16,279**	**1,280**	**466**	**1,746**	**3,056**	**1,693**	**4,749**	**2,717**	**1,498**	**4,215**

Source: Home Office

Notes

1. Special constable figures are provided on a headcount basis.

21.1c Police forces strength:[1] by country and sex

As at 31 March

Numbers

		2003	2004	2005	2006	2007	2008	2009	2010	2011	2012	2013	2014	2015	2016
Northern Ireland															
Regular police[2,3]															
Strength:															
Men	KERU	6,171	6,108	6,016	5,992	5,949	5,761	5,669	5,548	5,371	5238	5085	4988	4988	4952
Women	KERV	1,266	1,418	1,547	1,534	1,600	1,653	1,735	1,837	1,922	1907	1877	1882	1882	1932
Reserve[4]															
Strength:															
Men	KERW	1,983	1,824	1,431	1,424	1,212	1,119	930	774	597	333	313	278	278	235
Women	KERX	453	485	410	402	400	382	345	311	283	247	222	184	184	148

Source: Police Service of Northern Ireland

1. All figures are full-time equivalent strength figures that have been rounded to the nearest whole

2 Does not include officers on secondment.

3 Also includes student officers.

4 As at 31/03/12 No longer any FTR in PSNI, As at 31/03/12 Reserve figures only include Con PT (Formerly known as PTR)

21.1d Number of Police Officers (Full-time Equivalent) in Scotland, and by Local Policing Divisions, as at 31 March 2016

as at 31 March	Scotland
2016	17,317

Police Officer Distribution

The chart below outlines the distribution of officers across each of the 13 local policing divisions together with the available regional and national resources.

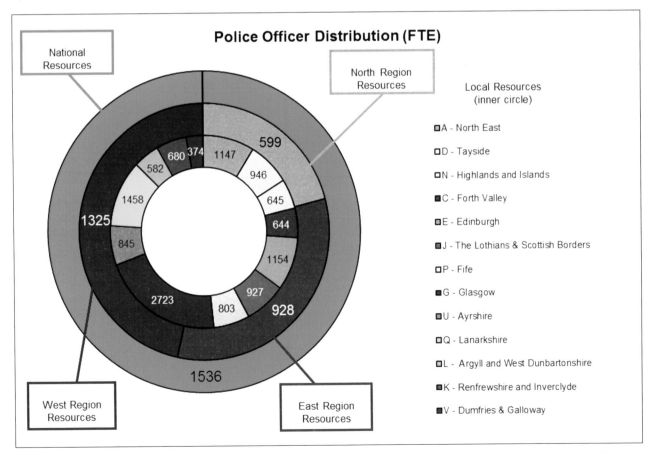

Sources: Police Scotland

21.2 Prison Population International Comparisons with other EU Countries

	Prison population total (no in penal institutions incl. Pre-trial detainees/remand prisoners)	Date	Estimated national population	Prison population rate (per 100,000 of national population)	Source of Prison Population Total
Northern Europe					
Denmark	3 408	1.9.2016	5.74M	59	NPA
Estonia	2 732	10.7.2017	1.32M	207	NPA
Finland	3 174	1.1.2017	5.5M	57	NPA
Iceland	124	1.9.2016	334,800	37	NPA
Ireland	3 552	31.8.2017	4.71 M	75	NPA
Latvia	4 301	1.1.2017	1.95 M	221	NPA
Lithuania	7 355	1.1.2016	2.9 M	254	C of E
Norway	3 874	28.9.2016	5.25 M	74	NPA
Sweden	5 245	1.1.2016	9.85 M	53	NPA
United Kingdom					
- England & Wales	86 294	1.9.2017	58.96 M	146	Ministry of Justice
- Northern Ireland	1 440	11.8.2017	1.87 M	77	NPA
- Scotland	7 480	28.7.2017	5.44 M	138	NPA
Faeroe Islands (Denmark)	10	average for 2015	48,935	19	Danish NPA
Guernsey (UK)	82	21.4.2017	65,700	125	Guernsey Prison Administration
Isle of Man (UK)	85	31.10.2016	88,000	85	Home Affairs Minister
Jersey (UK)	142	7.11.2016	104,100	136	Jersey Prison Administration
Southern Europe					
Albania	5 447	Apr-17	2.88 M	189	NPA
Andorra	41	1.1.2016	78,000	53	C of E
Bosnia & Hertzegovina					
- Federation	1 722	31.12.2014	2.35 M	73	C of E
- Republika Srpska	863	31.12.2016	1.3 M	66	Rep.Srpska Prison Administration
Croatia	3 228	30.9.2016	4.16 M	78	NPA
Cyprus	654	1.9.2015	847,900	77	C of E Annual Penal Statistics
Greece	9 789	1.6.2017	10.7 M	91	NPA
Italy	57 393	31.8.2017	60.45 M	95	Ministry of Justice
Kosovo/Kosova	1 849	Aug-16	1.75 M	106	U.S. State Dept. human rights report
Macedonia (FYR)	3 427	1.1.2016	2.07 M	166	NPA
Malta	569	31.12.2015	433,300	131	Home Affairs Minister
Montenegro	1 131	31.12.2015	622,700	182	United Nations Survey
Portugal	13 755	1.9.2017	10.29 M	134	NPA
San Marino	2	1.1.2016			C of E Annual Penal Statistics
		* most prisoners serve their sentences in Italian prisons and are not included in prison population for San Marino			
Serbia	10 065	March 2016	7.07 M	142	NPA
Slovenia	1 323	31.12.2016	2.07 M	64	NPA
Spain	60 240	11.8.2017	46.42 M	130	NPA
Gibraltar (UK)	56	12.12.2016	33,950	165	Government of Gibraltar
Western Europe					
Austria					NPA
Belgium	8 177	1.6.2016	8.75 M	93	Service Public Federal
France	70 018	1.7.2017	68.2 M	103	NPA
		* including French overseas departments and territories; excluding 11,695 persons not detained in penal institutions (écrouées non détenues)			
Germany	64139	31.3.2017	83 M	77	German Federal Statistical Office
Liechtenstein	10	1.1.2016	37,600	27	C of E
	* additional prisoners, serving more than two years (11 at November 2013), are held in Austrian & Swiss prisons in accordance with treaty agreements				
Luxembourg	705	1.9.2016	585,000	121	NPA
Monaco	28	1.1.2015	37,800	74	C of E
Netherlands	10 102	30.9.2016	17.04 M	59	NPA
Switzerland	6 912	7.9.2016	8.39 M	82	Swiss Federal Statistical Office
Europe/Asia					
Armenia	4 873	1.1.2016	3 M	162	C of E
Azerbaijan	23 311	2016	9.76 M	239	United Nations survey
Georgia	9 451	31.1.2017	3.72 M	254	National Statistical Office
Russian Federation	615 257	1.8.2017	144.6 M	425	NPA
Turkey	221 607	May-17	80.14 M	277	NPA
Central and Eastern Europe					
Belarus	29 776	31.12.2014	9.48 M	314	NPA
Bulgaria	9 028	Oct-14	7.21 M	125	U.S. State Dept. Human Rights Report
Czech Republic	22 574	30.8.2017	10.58 M	213	NPA
Hungary	18 146	8.11.2016	9.81 M	185	NPA
Moldova	7 868	1.7.2017	3.55 M	222	NPA
Poland	73 736	31.7.2017	37.91 M	195	NPA
Romania	26 529	29.8.2017	19.58 M	135	NPA
Slovakia	10 347	1.8.2017	5.43 M	191	NPA
Ukraine	60 771	1.9.2016	36.3 M	167	NPA
	* not including prisoners in Crimea, Sebastopol and those Donetsk & Luhansk areas that are not under the control of the Ukrainian authorities				

Source: International Centre for Prison Studies

C of E - Council of Europe
NPA - National Prison Administration

21.3 Police recorded crime by offence, year ending March 2006 to year ending December 2016 and percentage change between year ending December 2015 and year ending December 2016

England and Wales

Offence	Apr '05 to Mar '06	Apr '06 to Mar '07	Apr '07 to Mar '08	Apr '08 to Mar '09	Apr '09 to Mar '10	Apr '10 to Mar '11	Apr '11 to Mar '12	Apr '12 to Mar '13	Apr '13 to Mar '14	Apr '14 to Mar '15	Apr '15 to Mar '16	Jan '15 to Dec '15	Jan '16 to Dec '16	% change between years
VICTIM BASED CRIME	4,910,238	4,788,218	4,338,484	4,091,230	3,760,387	3,598,145	3,454,955	3,150,551	3,107,866	3,170,270	3,446,897	3,372,261	3,665,961	9
1 Murder [3]	..	..	..	..	..	..	..	..	..	..	..	..	..	..
4.1 Manslaughter [3]	..	..	..	..	..	..	..	..	..	..	..	..	..	..
4.1 Corporate manslaughter [3]	..	..	..	..	..	..	..	..	..	..	..	..	..	..
4.2 Infanticide [3]	..	..	..	..	..	..	..	..	..	..	..	..	..	..
Homicide [4,5,6]	764	758	775	664	620	639	553	558	533	539	574	576	697	21
2 Attempted murder [5]	920	633	621	574	591	523	483	412	501	565	684	694	740	7
4.3 Intentional destruction of viable unborn child	5	5	4	2	3	3	3	1	4	9	7	10	10	-
4.4 Causing death or serious injury by dangerous driving [7]	..	..	..	373	296	213	200	174	290	411	449	440	539	23
4.6 Causing death by careless driving when under the influence of drink or drugs	..	..	..	29	36	25	24	14	23	11	28	23	20	-
4.8 Causing death by careless or inconsiderate driving	..	..	..	35	188	172	179	139	136	158	133	137	125	-9
4.4/6/8 Causing death by dangerous or careless driving	432	459	422	..	..	..	..	..	..	..	..	..	..	..
5 More serious wounding or other act endangering life [8]	18,825	17,276	15,118	..	..	..	..	..	..	..	..	..	..	..
5A Wounding [8,9]	..	..	..	..	..	..	..	..	..	..	..	..	2	..
5B Use of substance or object to endanger life [8,9]	..	..	..	..	..	..	..	..	..	..	..	..	..	..
5C Possession of items to endanger life [8,9]	..	..	..	..	..	..	..	..	..	..	..	..	..	..
5D Assault with intent to cause serious harm [9]	..	..	..	..	..	..	..	17,006	17,929	20,556	23,028	22,284	24,839	11
5E Endangering life [9]	..	..	..	..	..	..	..	778	801	992	1,346	1,214	1,581	30
6 Endangering railway passengers [9]	646	484	402	320	231	257	214	..	..	..	..	..	..	..
7 Endangering life at sea [9]	13	5	10	8	6	4	6	..	..	..	..	..	..	..
8F Inflicting grievous bodily harm (GBH) without intent [10,11]	..	..	..	17,159	16,482	15,112	14,409	..	..	..	..	..	..	..
8H Racially or religiously aggravated inflicting GBH without intent [10,11]	..	..	..	384	224	188	169	..	..	..	..	..	1	..
37.1 Causing death by aggravated vehicle taking	24	18	18	14	5	14	8	8	4	8	6	11	9	-
4.7 Causing or allowing death or serious physical harm of child or vulnerable person [12]	5	3	..	7	3	5	6	8	22	16	23	26	29	-
4.9 Causing death by driving: unlicensed or disqualified or uninsured drivers	..	..	..	8	16	6	10	5	1	1	11	6	15	-
8A Other wounding [10]	516,523	481,822	430,818	374,255	355,962	328,463	301,223	290,956	300,653	348,388	402,343	389,497	425,869	9
8G Actual bodily harm (ABH) and other injury [10,11]	6,107	5,620	4,830	3,921	3,521	2,985	2,688	2,579	2,452	2,821	2,981	2,993	3,211	7
8D Racially or religiously aggravated other wounding [10]	..	..	..	..	..	..	..	..	..	..	..	..	..	..
8J Racially or religiously aggravated ABH or other injury [10,11]	..	..	..	..	..	..	..	..	..	..	1	..	..	..
8K Poisoning or female genital mutilation [10,11]	..	..	..	..	..	..	..	..	..	..	..	..	..	..
8N Assault with injury [11]	..	..	..	..	..	..	..	..	..	..	..	..	..	..
8P Racially or religiously aggravated assault with injury [11]	..	..	..	..	..	..	..	..	..	..	..	..	..	..
Violence with injury [13]	543,500	506,325	452,247	420,643	401,244	368,277	338,125	312,085	322,820	373,936	431,040	417,335	456,991	10
3 Threat or conspiracy to murder [13]	18,683	12,822	9,966	..	..	..	..	..	..	..	..	..	..	..
3A Conspiracy to murder [13]	..	..	..	56	45	36	36	28	30	40	48	45	54	-
3B Threats to kill [13]	..	..	..	9,448	9,523	9,480	7,643	7,347	8,471	12,878	17,276	16,398	20,749	27
8L Harassment [14,15,16]	54,644	55,493	52,107	48,363	52,959	51,173	48,141	54,532	61,211	81,584	155,425	132,155	202,755	53
8M Racially or religiously aggravated harassment [14,15]	2,548	2,657	2,424	2,395	2,370	1,971	1,625	1,500	1,445	1,873	1,788	1,901	1,773	-7
8Q Stalking [14]	..	..	..	..	..	..	..	..	..	2,879	4,154	3,765	4,613	23
11 Cruelty to and neglect of children [17]	5,045	4,917	5,287	6,204	6,611	6,087	6,081	6,370	8,000	9,167	12,805	11,442	14,112	23
11A Cruelty to children/young persons [17]	..	..	..	..	..	..	..	..	..	..	..	..	..	..
12 Abandoning a child under the age of two years [17]	49	23	19	23	9	6	12	..	..	..	..	..	..	..
13 Child abduction	919	696	595	567	560	548	532	513	565	816	1,038	1,020	1,088	7
14 Procuring illegal abortion	6	6	6	5	3	5	3	5	6	7	7	12	7	-
36 Kidnapping	2,799	2,367	1,991	2,035	1,860	1,717	1,516	1,388	1,728	2,187	2,999	2,737	3,582	31
104 Assault without injury on a constable	22,217	21,749	20,384	17,384	15,781	15,510	15,873	14,527	14,456	14,364	15,451	15,060	16,125	7
105A Assault without injury	183,555	202,701	198,653	197,035	203,098	205,975	202,509	198,390	211,257	272,882	343,168	327,761	387,829	18
105B Racially or religiously aggravated assault without injury	3,945	4,351	4,325	4,186	4,328	4,062	4,071	3,898	4,103	4,917	5,583	5,509	5,873	7
106 Modern Slavery [18]	..	..	..	..	..	..	..	..	..	..	882	565	1,721	205
Violence without injury	294,410	307,782	295,757	287,701	297,147	296,570	288,042	288,498	311,272	403,594	560,624	518,370	660,281	27
TOTAL VIOLENCE AGAINST THE PERSON	838,674	814,865	748,779	709,008	699,011	665,486	626,720	601,141	634,625	778,069	992,238	936,281	1,117,969	19

21.3 Police recorded crime by offence, year ending March 2006 to year ending December 2016 and percentage change between year ending December 2015 and year ending December 2016

England and Wales

Offence	Description	Apr '05 to Mar '06	Apr '06 to Mar '07	Apr '07 to Mar '08	Apr '08 to Mar '09	Apr '09 to Mar '10	Apr '10 to Mar '11	Apr '11 to Mar '12	Apr '12 to Mar '13	Apr '13 to Mar '14	Apr '14 to Mar '15	Apr '15 to Mar '16	Jan '15 to Dec '15	Jan '16 to Dec '16	% change between years
19A	Rape of a female [19, 20]	61	25	145	170										
19C	Rape of a female aged 16 or over [19]	8,725	8,222	7,610	7,768	9,027	9,469	9,773	9,646	12,307	18,315	22,523	21,637	25,304	17
19D	Rape of a female child under 16 [19]	3,153	2,853	2,422	2,537	2,908	2,877	2,777	2,803	3,407	4,461	5,248	5,282	5,557	5
19E	Rape of a female child under 13 [19]	1,388	1,524	1,487	1,658	1,967	2,243	2,212	2,372	2,835	3,517	4,185	4,121	4,257	3
19B	Rape of a male [19, 20]	22	18	10	22										
19F	Rape of a male aged 16 or over [19]	438	413	332	317	368	387	387	413	661	1,022	1,278	1,241	1,508	22
19G	Rape of a male child under 16 [19]	292	261	237	216	241	246	288	352	416	664	669	698	738	6
19H	Rape of a male child under 13 [19]	364	458	430	408	563	670	601	788	1,125	1,376	1,791	1,681	1,971	17
	Rape	**14,443**	**13,774**	**12,673**	**13,096**	**15,074**	**15,892**	**16,038**	**16,374**	**20,751**	**29,355**	**35,694**	**34,660**	**39,335**	**13**
16	Buggery [19, 20]	39	35	49	36										
17	Indecent assault on a male [19, 20]	347	76	209	158										
17A	Sexual assault on a male aged 13 and over [19]	1,428	1,450	1,323	1,161	1,208	1,285	1,261	1,400	1,957	2,905	3,454	3,389	3,976	17
17B	Sexual assault on a male child under 13 [19]	1,394	1,237	1,121	1,004	1,054	1,126	1,011	1,270	1,652	2,432	2,617	2,650	2,992	13
18	Gross indecency between males [19, 20]	20	12	17	14										
20	Indecent assault on a female [19, 20]	1,215	267	768	575										
20A	Sexual assault on a female aged 13 and over [19]	17,158	16,883	15,793	15,500	15,693	16,346	15,794	15,518	17,377	23,170	27,848	26,960	29,517	9
20B	Sexual assault on a female child under 13 [19]	4,647	4,245	3,984	3,665	4,148	4,298	3,991	4,177	5,129	6,290	7,384	7,318	7,696	5
21	Unlawful sexual intercourse with a girl under 13 [19]	138	67	33	51										
21	Sexual activity involving a child under 13 [19]	1,950	1,936	1,836	1,650	1,817	1,769	1,808	2,173	2,892	4,700	5,882	5,773	7,100	23
22	Unlawful sexual intercourse with a girl under 16 [19, 20]														
22B	Sexual activity involving a child under 16 [19]	3,283	3,208	3,123	3,318	3,992	4,039	3,971	4,468	5,881	8,645	11,338	10,850	12,588	16
22A	Causing sexual activity without consent [19, 21]	744	224	217	151	130	167	203	191	274	470	585	559	647	16
23	Incest or familial sexual offences [19]	966	1,344	1,125	1,041	1,111	803	637	509	491	625	771	745	835	12
25	Abduction of female [19, 20]	36	21	4	4										
70	Sexual activity with a person with a mental disorder [19]	139	163	127	131	124	130	101	115	134	213	244	245	285	16
71	Abuse of children through sexual exploitation [19, 22]	124	101	108	116	134	153	159	176	289	367	563	567	561	-1
72	Trafficking for sexual exploitation [18, 19]	33	43	57	52	58	66	59	70	123	184	27	111	16	-86
73	Abuse of position of trust of a sexual nature [19]	463	361	328	195	185	146	176	192	194	210	239	232	260	12
74	Gross indecency with a child [19, 20]	120	64	149	121										
88A	Sexual grooming [19, 23]	237	322	274	313	393	309	371	370	459	677	1,020	952	1,154	21
88B	Other miscellaneous sexual offences [19, 24, 25]	11,363	10,209	8,848											
88C	Other miscellaneous sexual offences [19, 25]				298	354	198	163	160	200	213	232	244	343	41
88D	Unnatural sexual offences [19, 25]				5	15	12	11	16	18	19	35	24	45	-
88E	Exposure and voyeurism [19, 25]				7,530	7,516	7,201	7,006	6,420	6,411	7,851	8,152	8,013	8,662	8
	Other sexual offences [19]	**45,844**	**42,268**	**39,493**	**37,089**	**37,932**	**38,048**	**36,722**	**37,225**	**43,481**	**58,971**	**70,391**	**68,632**	**76,677**	**12**
	TOTAL SEXUAL OFFENCES [19]	**60,287**	**56,042**	**52,166**	**50,185**	**53,006**	**53,940**	**52,760**	**53,599**	**64,232**	**88,326**	**106,085**	**103,292**	**116,012**	**12**
34A	Robbery of business property	8,760	9,454	9,173	9,350	8,182	7,729	6,770	6,120	5,789	5,399	5,428	5,462	5,567	2
34B	Robbery of personal property	89,438	91,922	75,600	70,780	66,923	68,460	67,918	59,035	52,039	44,744	45,682	45,231	50,257	11
	TOTAL ROBBERY	**98,198**	**101,376**	**84,773**	**80,130**	**75,105**	**76,189**	**74,688**	**65,155**	**57,828**	**50,143**	**51,110**	**50,693**	**55,824**	**10**
28	Burglary in a dwelling	298,355	290,454	279,125	282,977										
28A	Burglary in a dwelling					214,889	208,484	198,853	185,147	171,416	156,933	154,122	153,018	156,544	2
28B	Attempted burglary in a dwelling					44,706	42,298	40,287	37,386	36,361	35,023	35,435	35,225	37,354	6
28C	Distraction burglary in a dwelling					6,936	5,480	4,467	3,305	2,847	3,081	2,863	2,882	4,108	43
28D	Attempted distraction burglary in a dwelling					722	543	368	257	189	239	281	279	578	107
29	Aggravated burglary in a dwelling	2,162	1,806	1,571	1,454	1,353	1,360	1,337	1,181	1,175	1,281	1,697	1,580	2,075	31
	Domestic burglary	**300,517**	**292,260**	**280,696**	**284,431**	**268,606**	**258,165**	**245,312**	**227,276**	**211,988**	**196,557**	**194,398**	**192,984**	**200,659**	**4**
	of which: distraction burglary	11,552	12,750	10,058	9,092	7,658	6,023	4,835	3,562	3,036	3,320	3,144	3,161	4,686	48

21.3 Police recorded crime by offence, year ending March 2006 to year ending December 2016 and percentage change between year ending December 2015 and year ending December 2016

England and Wales

Offence	Offence	Apr '05 to Mar '06	Apr '06 to Mar '07	Apr '07 to Mar '08	Apr '08 to Mar '09	Apr '09 to Mar '10	Apr '10 to Mar '11	Apr '11 to Mar '12	Apr '12 to Mar '13	Apr '13 to Mar '14	Apr '14 to Mar '15	Apr '15 to Mar '16	Jan '15 to Dec '15	Jan '16 to Dec '16	% change between years
30	Burglary in a building other than a dwelling	344,195	329,473	302,799	296,970	..	..	..	..	..	..	..	..	..	..
30A	Burglary in a building other than a dwelling	..	..	..	..	236,019	230,868	223,153	202,440	200,570	185,394	177,874	178,754	174,891	-2
30B	Attempted burglary in a building other than a dwelling	..	..	..	..	35,868	33,515	32,473	29,959	30,549	28,709	28,551	28,501	28,475	0
31	Aggravated burglary in a building other than a dwelling	356	279	215	183	152	135	110	120	105	169	197	178	257	44
	Non-domestic burglary	344,551	329,752	303,014	297,153	272,039	264,518	255,736	232,519	231,224	214,272	206,622	207,433	203,623	-2
	Burglary	**645,068**	**622,012**	**583,710**	**581,584**	**540,645**	**522,683**	**501,048**	**469,795**	**443,212**	**410,829**	**401,020**	**400,417**	**404,282**	**1**
37.2	Aggravated vehicle taking [26]	10,943	10,920	10,334	9,730	8,000	6,954	6,253	5,652	5,255	5,417	5,701	5,510	5,765	5
45	Theft from a vehicle	507,239	502,651	432,412	396,976	339,170	313,467	300,377	285,047	276,366	235,869	238,842	237,515	247,649	4
48	Theft or unauthorised taking of a motor vehicle	203,239	182,464	159,704	137,508	109,684	99,208	85,803	74,168	70,053	70,218	76,170	74,556	87,103	17
126	Vehicle interference [27]	71,400	68,980	54,003	47,639	38,019	29,987	25,009	22,492	20,367	38,045	45,554	43,715	48,854	12
	Vehicle offences	**792,821**	**765,015**	**656,453**	**591,853**	**494,873**	**449,616**	**417,442**	**387,359**	**372,041**	**349,549**	**366,267**	**361,296**	**389,371**	**8**
39	Theft from the person	123,867	114,852	101,660	89,652	92,247	92,902	100,588	109,757	98,282	78,423	83,136	81,434	86,548	6
	Theft from the person	**123,867**	**114,852**	**101,660**	**89,652**	**92,247**	**92,902**	**100,588**	**109,757**	**98,282**	**78,423**	**83,136**	**81,434**	**86,548**	**6**
44	Theft or unauthorised taking of a pedal cycle	113,192	110,526	104,000	104,169	109,847	108,962	115,902	97,286	97,686	93,321	86,517	87,587	90,910	4
	Bicycle theft	**113,192**	**110,526**	**104,000**	**104,169**	**109,847**	**108,962**	**115,902**	**97,286**	**97,686**	**93,321**	**86,517**	**87,587**	**90,910**	**4**
46	Shoplifting	295,999	294,282	290,653	320,739	307,823	305,896	308,326	300,623	321,065	326,041	336,317	332,891	358,235	8
	Shoplifting	**295,999**	**294,282**	**290,653**	**320,739**	**307,823**	**305,896**	**308,326**	**300,623**	**321,065**	**326,041**	**336,317**	**332,891**	**358,235**	**8**
35	Blackmail [28]	1,645	2,481	1,201	1,363	1,450	1,491	1,369	1,497	2,134	3,502	5,894	5,068	7,283	44
40	Theft in a dwelling other than from an automatic machine or meter	54,757	54,471	51,336	51,220	53,338	54,798	54,518	52,384	50,513	50,801	51,179	50,821	51,508	1
41	Theft by an employee	17,048	16,323	15,864	15,467	13,169	12,141	11,589	10,446	10,320	10,749	10,657	10,840	10,152	-6
42	Theft of mail	9,351	4,740	3,051	3,724	3,098	2,792	2,447	2,878	2,163	1,999	2,356	2,339	2,565	10
43	Dishonest use of electricity	1,299	1,497	2,024	1,785	1,736	1,860	1,948	2,007	2,229	2,550	2,494	2,765	2,208	-20
47	Theft from automatic machine or meter [29]	42,049	33,721	11,932	7,651	7,753	6,215	6,692	6,394	4,950	4,215	3,943	4,062	3,676	-10
49	Other theft	554,368	536,603	526,949	472,325	436,244	481,585	491,559	419,685	389,024	359,115	343,719	349,147	341,059	-2
49A	Making off without payment [30]	87,767	82,261	73,895	80,048	70,397	66,505	61,351	50,833	51,550	59,394	64,544	63,094	72,282	15
	All other theft offences	768,284	732,097	686,252	633,583	587,185	627,387	631,473	546,124	512,883	492,325	484,786	488,136	490,733	1
	TOTAL THEFT OFFENCES	**2,739,231**	**2,638,784**	**2,422,728**	**2,321,580**	**2,132,620**	**2,107,446**	**2,074,779**	**1,900,944**	**1,845,169**	**1,750,488**	**1,758,043**	**1,751,761**	**1,820,079**	**4**
56	Arson [31]	45,731	43,100	39,327	..	..	..	..	..	..	..	..	..	..	..
56A	Arson endangering life [31]	..	..	..	3,629	3,623	3,325	3,100	2,588	2,574	2,806	3,273	3,230	3,386	5
56B	Arson not endangering life [31]	..	..	..	31,198	28,957	25,791	24,119	16,717	16,008	16,765	18,690	18,507	19,913	8
	Arson	**45,731**	**43,100**	**39,327**	**34,827**	**32,580**	**29,116**	**27,219**	**19,305**	**18,582**	**19,571**	**21,963**	**21,737**	**23,299**	**7**
58A	Criminal damage to a dwelling	297,579	288,285	256,804	235,424	198,623	172,916	155,982	131,157	121,525	117,967	125,347	123,884	129,751	5
58B	Criminal damage to a building other than a dwelling	161,436	160,207	131,146	109,440	88,687	75,677	67,329	57,631	52,599	50,557	52,093	51,566	53,033	3
58C	Criminal damage to a vehicle	468,143	483,237	425,632	389,719	336,927	289,045	259,871	222,770	217,994	214,746	227,154	223,379	230,681	3
58D	Other criminal damage	195,069	197,036	173,127	157,109	140,575	125,751	113,478	97,008	93,438	98,581	110,816	107,663	117,074	9
58E	Racially or religiously aggravated criminal damage to a dwelling [32]	1,742	1,543	1,150	999	849	639	499	..	..	..	..	..	..	..
58F	Racially or religiously aggravated criminal damage to a building other than a dwelling [32]	1,274	1,079	833	778	663	534	431	..	..	1	1	1	1	.
58G	Racially or religiously aggravated criminal damage to a vehicle [32]	1,899	1,711	1,338	1,304	1,135	869	788	..	..	1	1	1	1	.
58H	Racially or religiously aggravated other criminal damage [32]	975	953	681	727	606	537	411	..	..	3	..	3	2	.
58J	Racially or religiously aggravated criminal damage [32]	..	..	..	..	..	..	..	1,841	1,874	1,817	2,046	2,000	2,235	12
	Criminal damage	**1,128,117**	**1,134,051**	**990,711**	**895,500**	**768,065**	**665,968**	**598,789**	**510,407**	**487,430**	**483,673**	**517,458**	**508,497**	**532,778**	**5**
	TOTAL CRIMINAL DAMAGE AND ARSON	**1,173,848**	**1,177,151**	**1,030,038**	**930,327**	**800,645**	**695,084**	**626,008**	**529,712**	**506,012**	**503,244**	**539,421**	**530,234**	**556,077**	**5**

21.3 Police recorded crime by offence, year ending March 2006 to year ending December 2016 and percentage change between year ending December 2015 and year ending December 2016

England and Wales

Offence	Apr '05 to Mar '06	Apr '06 to Mar '07	Apr '07 to Mar '08	Apr '08 to Mar '09	Apr '09 to Mar '10	Apr '10 to Mar '11	Apr '11 to Mar '12	Apr '12 to Mar '13	Apr '13 to Mar '14	Apr '14 to Mar '15	Apr '15 to Mar '16	Jan '15 to Dec '15	Jan '16 to Dec '16	% change between years
OTHER CRIMES AGAINST SOCIETY	**515,453**	**534,159**	**542,656**	**539,153**	**504,649**	**480,330**	**448,626**	**402,617**	**398,679**	**403,429**	**440,919**	**428,785**	**498,658**	**16**
92A Trafficking in controlled drugs	25,276	26,550	28,323	29,885	33,223	32,336	31,316	29,746	29,348	27,345	25,807	26,287	24,638	-6
Trafficking of drugs	**25,276**	**26,550**	**28,323**	**29,885**	**33,223**	**32,336**	**31,316**	**29,746**	**29,348**	**27,345**	**25,807**	**26,287**	**24,638**	**-6**
92B Possession of controlled drugs 33														
92C Other drug offences	601	680	817	1,123	1,122	1,142	1,127	1,034	1,198	778	595	619	945	53
92D Possession of controlled drugs (excluding cannabis) 33	32,685	36,608	42,519	44,578	38,439	38,711	36,453	34,596	34,066	32,211	29,109	29,865	26,946	-10
92E Possession of cannabis 33	119,917	130,395	158,254	167,950	162,800	160,733	160,203	142,627	133,604	110,277	93,153	94,936	86,749	-9
Possession of drugs	**153,203**	**167,683**	**201,590**	**213,651**	**202,361**	**200,586**	**197,783**	**178,257**	**168,868**	**143,266**	**122,857**	**125,420**	**114,640**	**-9**
TOTAL DRUG OFFENCES	**178,479**	**194,233**	**229,913**	**243,536**	**235,584**	**232,922**	**229,099**	**208,003**	**198,216**	**170,611**	**148,664**	**151,707**	**139,278**	**-8**
8B Possession of weapons 34	35,590	34,689	32,513											
10A Possession of firearms with intent 34				1,973	1,587	1,385	1,151	998	1,077	1,287	1,523	1,502	1,912	27
10B Possession of firearms offences 35				4,460	4,070	3,650	3,402	3,052	2,929	3,046	3,244	3,073	3,567	16
10C Possession of other weapons 34				14,944	11,950	10,564	9,138	7,274	7,328	7,475	9,112	8,571	10,462	22
10D Possession of article with blade or point 34				13,985	10,885	10,474	9,762	8,425	9,050	9,871	11,494	11,059	13,105	19
81 Other firearms offences 36	4,106	4,239	4,560	293	253	254	229	160	237	188	244	247	276	12
90 Other knives offences	15	9	6	7	13	0	6	1	2	1	4	4	2	-
TOTAL POSSESSION OF WEAPONS OFFENCES	**39,711**	**38,937**	**37,079**	**35,662**	**28,758**	**26,327**	**23,688**	**19,910**	**20,623**	**21,868**	**25,621**	**24,456**	**29,324**	**20**
9A Public fear, alarm or distress 14,15	164,061	173,152	158,045	142,246	126,597	114,781	97,085	81,139	79,601	95,948	134,659	124,138	179,986	45
9B Racially or religiously aggravated public fear, alarm or distress 14,15	24,057	25,828	24,086	23,355	23,226	20,967	20,188	20,420	21,685	26,215	29,172	28,852	33,794	17
62 Treason 37	0	0	0	0	0	0	0							
62A Violent disorder 37								656	640	768	986	947	1,063	12
63 Treason felony 37	0	0	0	0	0	0	0							
64 Riot 37	7	4	2	3	0	2	3							
65 Violent disorder 37	2,457	1,742	1,180	1,022	859	751	696							
66 Other offences against the State or public order	31,999	35,935	35,067	37,663	37,572	36,580	32,886	29,990	32,474	36,114	39,430	38,313	44,586	16
TOTAL PUBLIC ORDER OFFENCES	**222,581**	**236,661**	**218,380**	**204,289**	**188,254**	**173,081**	**150,858**	**132,205**	**134,400**	**159,045**	**204,247**	**192,250**	**259,432**	**35**
15 Concealing an infant death close to birth	8	4	8	8	6	9	5	2	2	5	5	3	9	-
24 Exploitation of prostitution 19	153	190	184	173	148	153	110	120	124	154	173	185	200	8
26 Bigamy	101	61	74	64	60	44	31	39	40	46	71	61	74	21
27 Soliciting for prostitution 19	1,640	1,290	1,216	1,071	1,190	826	797	883	750	870	587	649	449	-31
33 Going equipped for stealing, etc.	4,382	4,253	3,781	3,791	3,647	4,129	3,765	3,473	3,472	3,049	2,663	2,755	2,651	-4
33A Making, supplying or possessing articles for use in fraud 38									2,927	2,451	2,624	2,634	2,360	-10
38 Profiting from or concealing proceeds of crime 38	1,548	1,961	2,382	2,505	2,609	2,344	1,779	1,427	1,485	1,501	1,592	1,588	1,710	8
53H Making or supplying articles for use in fraud 39			183	611	862	975	1,108	1,287						
53J Possession of articles for use in fraud 39			1,301	1,366	1,384	1,466	1,559	1,564						
54 Handling stolen goods	12,714	11,826	11,335	10,766	9,448	9,184	9,769	8,134	8,526	6,581	5,292	5,589	4,444	-20
59 Threat etc. to commit criminal damage	10,501	7,889	6,318	6,034	5,996	5,916	5,214	4,950	5,790	8,991	12,818	12,039	16,684	39
60 Forgery or use of drug prescription	693	593	440	446	343	298	361	379	416	423	395	380	334	-12
61 Other forgery	10,627	8,479	4,211	4,241	2,526	1,632	2,124	2,984	2,864	2,285	2,843	2,448	3,688	51
61A Possession of false documents			2,301	2,646	2,263	1,770	1,378	962	934	976	1,018	1,038	875	-16
67 Perjury	245	197	193	177	184	339	151	134	96	90	122	121	100	-17
68 Libel 40	1	1	0	1										
69 Offender Management Act offences 40				4	533	518	583	1,024	1,113	1,534	2,714	2,327	3,675	58
75 Betting, gaming and lotteries 40	6	13	13	22	21	14	12	10	11	19	35	31	27	-13
76 Aiding suicide	11	13	9	7	17	7	10	11						
78 Immigration offences 40	935	792	661	573	411	445	344							
79 Perverting the course of justice	12,712	11,114	9,131	8,396	7,997	6,890	5,698	4,947	5,368	6,295	6,380	6,390	6,376	0
80 Absconding from lawful custody	1,272	979	828	651	557	499	414	482	370	440	501	458	508	11

21.3 Police recorded crime by offence, year ending March 2006 to year ending December 2016 and percentage change between year ending December 2015 and year ending December 2016

England and Wales

Offence		Apr '05 to Mar '06	Apr '06 to Mar '07	Apr '07 to Mar '08	Apr '08 to Mar '09	Apr '09 to Mar '10	Apr '10 to Mar '11	Apr '11 to Mar '12	Apr '12 to Mar '13	Apr '13 to Mar '14	Apr '14 to Mar '15	Apr '15 to Mar '16	Jan '15 to Dec '15	Jan '16 to Dec '16	% change between years
82	Customs and Revenue offences [40]	49	27	10	13	10	3	5	..	..	..	..	..	..	..
83	Bail offences	177	83	25	3	4	6	3	2	3	7	191	56	734	1,211
84	Trade descriptions, etc [40]	1,360	1,353	1,321	1,143	809	486	263	..	..	..	..	..	..	..
85	Health and Safety offences [40]	8	9	8	15	6	2	8	..	..	..	..	..	..	..
86	Obscene publications, etc and protected sexual material	2,592	2,378	2,672	2,775	3,215	3,342	3,335	3,506	4,618	8,029	12,875	11,787	16,213	38
87	Protection from eviction [40]	75	69	81	71	81	73	68	..	..	..	..	..	..	..
89	Adulteration of food [40]	45	32	44	13	4	9	0	..	..	..	..	..	..	..
91	Public health offences [40,41]	128	50	44	115	488	398	289	..	..	..	..	..	..	..
94	Planning laws [40]	5	0	0	1	0	1	1	..	..	..	..	..	..	..
95	Disclosure, obstruction, false or misleading statements etc	368	266	425	506	426	348	363	294	359	308	229	254	220	-13
96	Wildlife crime [42]	..	..	..	..	..	..	..	..	..	34	83	75	72	-4
99	Other indictable or triable-either-way offences [18,40,43]	2,197	1,915	1,391	1,735	1,629	1,569	1,589	2,510	2,575	4,155	4,601	5,254	3,949	-25
802	Dangerous driving	5,923	5,353	4,725	4,240	3,941	3,475	3,239	3,092	3,152	3,276	4,077	3,804	4,601	21
814	Fraud, forgery associated with vehicle driver records	4,206	3,138	2,164	1,387	1,058	733	606	473	445	386	498	446	669	50
	TOTAL MISCELLANEOUS CRIMES AGAINST SOCIETY	**74,682**	**64,328**	**57,284**	**55,666**	**52,053**	**48,000**	**44,981**	**42,499**	**45,440**	**51,905**	**62,387**	**60,372**	**70,624**	**17**
	TOTAL RECORDED CRIME - ALL OFFENCES EXCLUDING FRAUD [44,45,46,47]	**5,425,691**	**5,322,377**	**4,881,140**	**4,630,383**	**4,265,036**	**4,078,475**	**3,903,581**	**3,553,168**	**3,506,545**	**3,573,699**	**3,887,816**	**3,801,046**	**4,164,619**	**10**
FRAUD OFFENCES [48]															
51	Fraud by company director [49]	626	101	162	815	85	207	45	103	..	..	..	..	2	..
52	False accounting	487	462	251	146	155	108	75	59	..	..	..	..	..	..
53A	Cheque and credit card fraud (pre Fraud Act 2006) [39]	87,860	59,011	..	..	..	..	..	..	..	..	..	..	..	..
53B	Preserved other fraud and repealed fraud offences (pre-Fraud Act 2006) [30,39]	40,415	45,593	9,984	3,494	3,666	3,342	3,799	3,027	..	..	..	..	2	..
53C	Fraud by false representation: cheque, plastic card and online bank accounts [29,39]	..	..	23,345	26,578	27,148	24,942	22,703	17,873	1	..	..	-1	..	..
53D	Fraud by false representation: other frauds [39]	..	..	34,544	38,884	39,626	42,460	44,719	40,325	5	..	..	..	..	..
53E	Fraud by failing to disclose information [39]	..	..	265	304	364	339	246	163	..	..	..	..	..	..
53F	Fraud by abuse of position [39]	..	..	675	926	1,160	1,033	1,170	927	1	..	..	..	..	..
53G	Obtaining services dishonestly [39]	..	..	1,880	1,152	1,042	..	..	..	..	..	..	..	..	..
55	Bankruptcy and insolvency offences	93	14	31	15	13	10	11	12	..	..	..	..	..	..
	TOTAL FRAUD OFFENCES RECORDED BY THE POLICE [39,47,48]	**129,481**	**105,181**	**71,137**	**72,314**	**73,259**	**72,441**	**72,768**	**62,489**	**7**	**..**	**..**	**-1**	**4**	**..**
	FRAUD OFFENCES RECORDED BY ACTION FRAUD [48,50]	..	..	..	..	..	46,658	117,402	211,221	230,367	220,691	224,178	250,496	12
	Fraud offences referred to NFIB by Cifas [50,51,52]	..	..	..	..	..	235,499	217,369	214,156	257,762	298,968	295,525	303,145	3
	Fraud offences referred to NFIB by Financial Fraud Action UK [50,52,53,54]	..	..	..	..	..	121,478	113,143	96,534	104,982	99,546	97,410	87,894	-10
	TOTAL FRAUD OFFENCES	**129,481**	**105,181**	**71,137**	**72,314**	**73,259**	**72,441**	**476,403**	**510,403**	**521,918**	**593,111**	**619,205**	**617,112**	**641,539**	**4**
	TOTAL RECORDED CRIME – ALL OFFENCES INCLUDING FRAUD [44,47]	**5,555,172**	**5,427,558**	**4,952,277**	**4,702,697**	**4,338,295**	**4,150,916**	**4,379,984**	**4,063,571**	**4,028,463**	**4,166,810**	**4,507,021**	**4,418,158**	**4,806,158**	**9**

Source: Police recorded crime, Home Office

Police recorded crime data are not designated as National Statistics.

NOTES TO ACCOMPANY TABLE 21.3

1. The National Crime Recording Standard (NCRS) was introduced in April 2002, although some forces adopted NCRS practices before the standard was formally introduced. Figures before and after that date are not directly comparable. The introduction of NCRS led to a rise in recording in year ending March 2003 and, particularly for violent crime, in the following years as forces continued to improve compliance with the new standard.

2. Includes the British Transport Police from year ending March 2003 onwards.

3. This is a total of all Homicide offences; Murder, Manslaughter, Corporate manslaughter and Infanticide

4. The homicide figure for year ending March 2003 includes 172 homicides attributed to Harold Shipman in previous years but coming to light in the official inquiry in 2002.

5. The homicide figure in year ending March 2006 of 764 includes 52 homicide victims of the 7 July London bombings, which also accounted for approximately one-quarter of the total of 920 attempted murders.

6. The homicide figure for year ending December 2016 includes 96 homicide victims of Hillsborough.

7. New offence of 'causing serious injury by dangerous driving' was added to this category in April 2013

8. Offence classifications 5A, 5B and 5C were introduced from 1 April 2008 and replaced classification 5. Classification 5A was influenced by a clarification in recording rules that had the effect of significantly increasing levels of recording in some forces. Classification 5A also included some other offences of endangering life as well as GBH with intent, though GBH with intent was the major part of this category.

9. Offence classifications 5D and 5E were introduced from 1 April 2012 and replaced classification 5A offences. Offence classification 5E was also introduced and replaced the remaining classification 5A offences, 5B, 5C, 6 and 7.

10. Offence classifications 8F, 8G, 8H, 8J and 8K were introduced from 1 April 2008 and had previously been recorded as part of classifications 8A or 8D.

11. Offence classification 8N was introduced from 1 April 2012 and replaced classifications 8F, 8G and 8K. Offence classification 8P was also introduced and replaced classifications 8H and 8J.

12. New offence of 'cause or allow a child or vulnerable adult to suffer serious physical harm' was added to this category in April 2013

13. Offence classifications 3A and 3B were introduced from 1 April 2008 and had previously been recorded as classification 3.

14. Prior to year ending March 2009, the police sent combined figures for harassment (8L, 8M) and public fear, alarm and distress (9A, 9B) offences. For the years ending March 2003 to March 2008, figures for these offence groups are estimated based upon the proportionate split between the offences in year ending March 2009. Stalking (8Q) was introduced as a separate crime classification in April 2014, following the introduction of the Protection of Freedoms Act 2012 section 111. Before this, stalking offences were included within harassment offences (8L).

15. Prior to year ending March 2009, the police sent combined figures for harassment (8L, 8M) and public fear, alarm and distress (9A, 9B) offences. For the years ending March 2003 to March 2008, figures for these offence groups are estimated based upon the proportionate split between the offences in year ending March 2009.

16. Changes in the Home Office Counting Rules (HOCR), implemented in April 2015, have resulted in the recording of two additional harassment offences (Disclosure of private sexual photographs and films with the intent to cause distress or anxiety' and 'Sending letters with intent to cause distress or anxiety'; the latter includes any form of electronic communication), not previously counted as notifiable offences under the headline category of violence without injury. There is no available back-series for these additional notifiable offences.

17. Offence classification 11A was introduced from 1 April 2012 and replaced classifications 11 and 12.

18. Modern Slavery (106) was introduced as a separate crime classification in April 2015. During April-July 2015 this classification included all of the offences that were previously recorded under category 72 (Trafficking for sexual exploitation) and some offences that were previously recorded under category 99 (Other indictable or triable-either-way offences). From 31 July 2015, a new set of Modern Slavery Act offences commenced, replacing all the offence codes previously listed under this classification.

19. The Sexual Offences Act 2003, introduced in May 2004, altered the definition and coverage of sexual offences.

20. Prior to year ending March 2010, a small number of offences continued to be recorded relating to offences repealed by the Sexual Offences Act 2003. While these may have been legitimately recorded for offences committed prior to May 2004 it is also possible that some may have been recorded in these old categories in error, so any changes based on small numbers should be interpreted with caution.

21. The increase in year ending March 2006 was accounted for by a large number of offences that were dealt with by the Norfolk Constabulary.

22. In April 2015 offence classification 71 was renamed 'Abuse of children through sexual exploitation'. This offence classification was previously named 'Abuse of children through prostitution and pornography'

23. The Sexual Grooming classification is currently restricted to those offences where the offender intentionally met the child or either the victim or the suspect travelled with the intention of meeting. From 1st April 2017, it will also include the criminal offence of anyone aged 18 or over intentionally communicating with a child under 16, where the person acts for a sexual purpose and the communication is sexual or intended to elicit a sexual response.

24. This offence consists solely of the former offence of 'Indecent Exposure' for years prior to year ending March 2005. This became the offence of 'Exposure' and was included within 'Other miscellaneous sexual offences' from May 2004.

25. Offence classification 88B was split into 88C–E with effect from year ending March 2009. Since that time offences of exposure have been recorded as classification 88E.

26. A change in the guidance within Home Office Counting Rules (HOCR) in April 2014 is likely to have led to offences that previously might have been recorded as theft from a vehicle now being recorded as vehicle interference when the motive of the offender was not clear.

27. Includes tampering with a motor vehicle.

28. The large increase in year ending March 2007 was due to the recording of threats made against shareholders of GlaxoSmithKline by animal rights activists.

29. Following a change in the implementation of the Fraud Act 2006, offences involving theft from an automatic machine using a plastic card are now regarded as false representation and recorded under classification 53C.

30. Offence classification 49A was introduced as a separate theft classification in year ending March 2014. Before this, it was recorded under the fraud offence classification 53B. Data for 49A are provided for all years following a special request to forces. In some cases, these have been estimated where forces were unable to provide data.

NOTES TO ACCOMPANY TABLE 21.3

31 Offence classifications 56A and 56B were introduced from 1 April 2008 and had previously been recorded as classification 56.

32 Offence classifications 58E-58H were amalgamated on 1 April 2012 to form classification 58J.

33 Possession of controlled drugs offences were split with effect from April 2004 into possession of cannabis and possession of drugs other than cannabis.

34 Offence classifications 10A, 10C and 10D were introduced from 1 April 2008 and had previously been recorded as classification 8B.

35 Offence classification 10B was introduced from 1 April 2008. Possession of firearms offences are those offences where the weapon has not been used during the commission of another offence.

36 These are offences under the Firearms Act 1968 and other Firearms Acts connected with licensing and certification of firearms. Such offences are not included in the firearms offences statistics.

37 Offence classifications 62-65 were amalgamated on 1 April 2012 to form classification 62A.

38 These offences were added to the series from 1 April 2003.

39 New offences were introduced under the Fraud Act 2006, which came into force on 15 January 2007.

40 Offence classifications 68, 75, 78, 82, 84, 85, 87, 89, 91 and 94 were included with classification 99 with effect from 1 April 2012.

41 The large increase in this offence from year ending March 2009 is mainly due to the recording of fly-tipping by some forces following advice that this offence is notifiable.

42 Wildlife crime (96) was introduced as a separate crime classification in April 2014. This saw a number of offences that were previously recorded under "Other notifiable offences" (99) brought together.

43 Due to the introduction of fly-tipping as an offence under "Other notifiable offences" (99) in April 2014, percentage changes may appear high in certain publications.

44 Some forces have revised their data and totals may therefore not agree with those previously published.

45 Following a system change at Norfolk constabulary in October 2015 a range of data reliability issues have been identified. At a national level the impact of this is small. The constabulary is expected to resolve these issues and revise data during 2016/17.

46 Following a system change at Suffolk constabulary in October 2015 a range of data reliability issues have been identified, including the fact that some of the data submitted by the force is known to be duplicated. For instance, around 3% of offences submitted by Suffolk for October to December are estimated to be duplicates. In particular, 20% of sexual offences recorded between October to December 2015 are estimated to be duplicates. At a national level the impact of this is small. The constabulary is expected to resolve these issues and provide revised data during 2016/17.

47 Data from some forces includes a very small number of crimes which have been erroneously recorded against an expired offence code (e.g. fraud offences). These erroneously recorded offences should be corrected to ensure they're recorded under the correct code (or cancelled) in time for the next quarter. Negative figures are due to offences which have been erroneously recorded in a previous quarter and subsequently cancelled.

48 Action Fraud have taken over the recording of fraud offences on behalf of individual police forces. This process began in April 2011 and was rolled out to all police forces by March 2013. Due to this change caution should be applied when comparing data over this transitional period and with earlier years. There were 7 cases in year ending March 2014 and 4 cases in year ending June 2016 where police forces recorded a fraud offence after the transfer of responsibility to Action Fraud. These cases may be revised in future quarters. See the User Guide for more details including information on transfer date to Action Fraud for each force.

49 The large increase in this offence in year ending March 2006 was due to one large-scale fraud recorded by the Cambridgeshire Constabulary. The increase in year ending March 2008 was due to a fraud recorded by North Yorkshire Police. The large increase in year ending March 2009 was due to large-scale frauds recorded by Gwent Police, Leicestershire Constabulary and the Metropolitan Police. The increase in year ending March 2011 was due to a large-scale fraud recorded by North Yorkshire Police.

50 It is possible that there may be some double or triple counting between Action Fraud, Cifas and FFA UK. Experts believe this duplication to be so small as to have an insignificant effect on crime trends, but there is currently no simple cross-referencing method within NFIB to detect the scale of it. Section 5.4 of the User Guide provides more information.

51 Cifas is a UK-wide fraud prevention service representing around 350 organisations from the public and private sectors. These organisations mainly share data on confirmed cases of fraud, particularly application, identity and first party frauds, via the Cifas National Fraud Database. Data supplied by Cifas to the National Fraud Intelligence Bureau (NFIB) are recorded in line with the Home Office Counting Rules (HOCR) for recorded crime.

52 Both sets of industry data from Cifas and FFA UK relate only to fraud affecting those organisations that are part of the respective membership networks. While membership of Cifas and FFA UK has remained fairly stable over the last few years, it is possible that coverage could change as new members join or previous members withdraw, which could impact on overall figures for fraud reported. Prior to year ending March 2012, fraud cases for these organisations were not sent to the NFIB.

53 Financial Fraud Action UK (FFA UK) is responsible for coordinating activities on fraud prevention in the UK payments industry. FFA UK collates information relating to cheque, plastic card and online bank accounts via its Fraud Intelligence Sharing System (FISS) database, and this is in turn provided to NFIB. FISS is an intelligence tool rather than a fraud reporting tool, and its main purpose is to share actionable intelligence about the criminals or entities relating to fraud
offences rather than count the numbers of victims of fraud. As a result, the number of cases presented in Table A4 is considerably less than the total number reported to FFA UK by its members. Comprehensive statistics on these fraud types are published twice yearly by FFA UK.

54 In July 2015 the company that was contracted to provide the Action Fraud call centre service went into administration. This led to an immediate downscaling of the call centre operation which is likely to have had had an effect on the volume of frauds recorded by Action Fraud during July, August and September 2015.

-   Indicates that data are not reported because the base number of offences is less than 50.

21.4 Persons[1] sentenced at all courts, by type of sentence and offence group, 12 months ending December 2006 to 2016 [2][3]

England and Wales — Persons sentenced

Year ending and type of sentence	Violence against the person	Sexual offences	Robbery	Theft Offences	Criminal damage and arson	Drug offences	Possession of weapons	Public order offences	Miscellaneous crimes against society	Fraud offences	All indictable offences	Summary non-motoring	Summary motoring	All summary offences	All offences
2006															
All Sentenced	**29,798**	**4,880**	**8,169**	**114,200**	**11,864**	**39,478**	**14,123**	**8,735**	**57,131**	**13,016**	**301,394**	**493,888**	**617,564**	**1,111,452**	**1,412,846**
Immediate custody	10,479	2,787	4,802	27,147	1,238	7,532	2,616	2,322	12,345	2,260	73,528	12,571	9,914	22,485	96,013
Suspended sentence	4,449	290	264	6,622	398	1,848	1,303	1,205	3,043	1,376	20,798	6,041	6,669	12,710	33,508
Community sentence	11,198	1,332	2,957	43,310	5,794	9,127	6,625	4,176	13,101	5,332	102,952	59,585	28,281	87,866	190,818
Fine[5]	999	164	13	13,465	1,306	13,271	1,505	475	17,994	1,411	50,603	354,941	548,556	903,497	954,100
Absolute discharge	53	17	7	729	88	334	81	20	838	32	2,199	3,692	5,858	9,550	11,749
Conditional discharge	1,229	139	26	19,013	2,302	6,532	1,757	371	4,297	2,349	38,015	41,996	7,340	49,336	87,351
Compensation	593	14	23	1,305	479	4	4	59	68	122	2,671	5,030	3,922	8,952	11,623
Otherwise dealt with[6]	798	137	77	2,609	259	830	232	107	5,445	134	10,628	10,032	7,024	17,056	27,684
Average custodial sentence (months)[7]	20	41	32	8	13	34	11	10	7	12	15	3	3	3	12
2007															
All Sentenced	**30,161**	**4,986**	**8,862**	**121,965**	**11,700**	**44,500**	**14,090**	**9,041**	**52,066**	**13,820**	**311,191**	**489,882**	**605,715**	**1,095,597**	**1,406,788**
Immediate custody	10,615	2,777	4,772	27,284	1,225	8,186	2,709	2,356	12,115	1,998	74,037	13,277	7,892	21,169	95,206
Suspended sentence	5,928	423	452	8,346	490	2,678	1,466	1,816	3,662	1,993	27,254	7,266	6,168	13,434	40,688
Community sentence	10,127	1,359	3,470	46,697	5,308	10,296	6,619	3,837	12,045	5,384	105,142	65,188	26,094	91,282	196,424
Fine[5]	1,004	130	33	14,036	1,135	14,190	1,243	414	14,782	1,485	48,452	342,011	543,354	885,365	933,817
Absolute discharge	58	11	4	815	89	379	70	24	738	28	2,216	3,609	5,161	8,770	10,986
Conditional discharge	1,145	157	30	20,980	2,424	7,825	1,721	372	4,627	2,625	41,906	45,934	6,171	52,105	94,011
Compensation	480	20	26	1,465	691	7	6	54	94	119	2,962	5,161	3,965	9,126	12,088
Otherwise dealt with[6]	804	109	75	2,342	338	939	256	168	4,003	188	9,222	7,436	6,910	14,346	23,568
Average custodial sentence (months)[7]	20	43	31	8	13	32	12	11	7	11	15	3	3	3	12
2008[4]															
All Sentenced	**29,147**	**5,049**	**8,495**	**127,484**	**9,006**	**52,909**	**14,576**	**8,559**	**46,300**	**13,416**	**314,941**	**492,451**	**546,545**	**1,038,996**	**1,353,937**
Immediate custody	10,897	2,952	5,095	29,324	1,062	9,488	3,374	2,382	12,306	2,178	79,058	14,089	6,378	20,467	99,525
Suspended sentence	5,943	406	444	8,376	407	2,958	1,813	1,908	3,951	2,249	28,455	7,696	5,000	12,696	41,151
Community sentence	9,553	1,360	2,832	47,146	3,982	12,273	6,661	3,450	10,725	4,801	102,783	65,687	21,702	87,389	190,172
Fine[5]	832	89	6	14,174	980	17,674	1,082	386	11,942	1,571	48,736	342,845	490,923	833,768	882,504
Absolute discharge	54	7	2	721	90	382	67	19	538	20	1,900	3,274	4,505	7,779	9,679
Conditional discharge	881	125	23	21,405	1,741	8,099	1,253	271	3,872	2,242	39,912	43,183	4,553	47,736	87,648
Compensation	337	7	13	1,204	492	2	1	19	81	109	2,265	4,402	3,232	7,634	9,899
Otherwise dealt with[6]	650	103	80	5,134	252	2,033	325	124	2,885	246	11,832	11,275	10,252	21,527	33,359
Average custodial sentence (months)[7]	21	45	33	8	15	33	13	11	8	13	16	3	3	3	13
2009															
All Sentenced	**30,493**	**5,028**	**8,664**	**128,137**	**7,274**	**56,656**	**15,054**	**16,852**	**43,749**	**14,685**	**326,592**	**513,321**	**558,365**	**1,071,686**	**1,398,278**
Immediate custody	11,530	2,940	5,155	28,424	944	9,426	3,462	5,147	10,583	2,654	80,265	14,698	5,268	19,966	100,231
Suspended sentence	6,385	402	476	8,676	368	3,119	2,449	2,586	4,084	2,586	31,131	8,970	5,056	14,026	45,157
Community sentence	9,937	1,388	2,915	48,290	3,317	13,657	6,785	5,938	10,246	5,522	107,995	67,820	20,162	87,982	195,977
Fine[5]	909	84	8	15,684	873	20,993	1,035	1,707	12,396	1,662	55,351	368,443	513,963	882,406	937,757
Absolute discharge	39	8	5	549	55	353	51	134	421	31	1,646	2,961	4,292	7,253	8,899
Conditional discharge	839	86	15	22,574	1,350	7,207	912	796	3,169	2,053	39,001	41,253	3,630	44,883	83,884
Compensation	280	6	9	1,071	201	0	0	18	50	97	1,732	3,543	2,313	5,856	7,588
Otherwise dealt with[6]	574	114	81	2,869	166	1,901	360	526	2,800	80	9,471	5,633	3,681	9,314	18,785
Average custodial sentence (months)[7]	21	49	34	9	20	32	13	7	8	12	16	3	3	3	14

21.4 Persons[1] sentenced at all courts, by type of sentence and offence group, 12 months ending December 2006 to 2016[2][3]

England and Wales

Persons sentenced

Year ending and type of sentence	Violence against the person	Sexual offences	Robbery	Theft Offences	Criminal damage and arson	Drug offences	Possession of weapons	Public order offences	Miscellaneous crimes against society	Fraud offences	All indictable offences	Summary non-motoring	Summary motoring	All summary offences	All offences
2010															
All Sentenced	**32,522**	**5,720**	**8,514**	**138,065**	**7,127**	**61,435**	**12,990**	**19,254**	**46,314**	**15,481**	**347,422**	**492,345**	**517,833**	**1,010,178**	**1,357,600**
Immediate custody	11,743	3,259	4,946	30,993	1,000	9,693	2,953	5,470	10,225	2,657	82,939	14,634	3,940	18,574	101,513
Suspended sentence	7,073	450	505	9,757	382	3,820	2,061	3,012	4,302	2,814	34,176	9,560	4,382	13,942	48,118
Community sentence	10,460	1,641	2,768	48,645	2,981	13,418	5,779	6,488	10,296	6,031	108,507	64,723	16,103	80,826	189,333
Fine[5]	952	106	4	16,848	772	23,354	999	2,161	12,434	1,807	59,437	343,650	483,234	826,884	886,321
Absolute discharge	41	7	4	588	56	425	49	179	465	21	1,835	2,909	4,068	6,977	8,812
Conditional discharge	1,023	127	13	24,585	1,410	8,526	864	938	3,400	1,917	42,803	44,597	3,033	47,630	90,433
Compensation	562	8	196	1,769	293	3	2	58	69	100	3,060	4,703	192	4,895	7,955
Otherwise dealt with[6]	668	122	78	4,880	233	2,196	283	948	5,123	134	14,665	7,569	2,881	10,450	25,115
Average custodial sentence (months)[7]	21	49	35	9	19	31	13	7	8	13	16	3	3	3	14
2011															
All Sentenced	**30,564**	**5,928**	**9,340**	**139,526**	**6,406**	**61,094**	**12,439**	**17,858**	**43,779**	**14,884**	**341,818**	**493,155**	**470,697**	**963,852**	**1,305,670**
Immediate custody	12,135	3,413	5,588	33,796	1,043	9,788	3,196	5,498	10,112	2,947	87,516	15,203	3,451	18,654	106,170
Suspended sentence	6,415	503	541	10,325	396	4,205	2,083	2,634	4,321	2,999	34,422	9,510	4,221	13,731	48,153
Community sentence	8,814	1,646	2,937	47,538	2,595	12,724	5,170	5,586	9,732	5,445	102,187	60,847	14,569	75,416	177,603
Fine[5]	1,140	120	4	16,995	715	23,317	920	2,149	11,351	1,580	58,291	351,816	439,729	791,545	849,836
Absolute discharge	42	8	1	572	48	428	46	157	486	17	1,805	2,721	3,626	6,347	8,152
Conditional discharge	990	89	12	24,139	1,161	8,345	755	877	3,161	1,683	41,212	42,356	2,731	45,087	86,299
Compensation	415	10	173	1,662	225	1	4	54	72	91	2,707	3,918	155	4,073	6,780
Otherwise dealt with[6]	613	139	84	4,499	223	2,286	265	903	4,544	122	13,678	6,784	2,215	8,999	22,677
Average custodial sentence (months)[7]	22	54	35	9	20	31	13	7	9	15	17	3	3	3	14
2012															
All Sentenced	**26,325**	**5,715**	**8,345**	**126,359**	**5,365**	**57,601**	**10,164**	**16,176**	**37,828**	**12,218**	**306,096**	**469,301**	**447,838**	**917,139**	**1,223,235**
Immediate custody	11,341	3,397	5,002	32,500	890	9,011	2,651	5,001	8,637	2,631	81,061	13,971	3,012	16,983	98,044
Suspended sentence	5,582	477	555	9,709	300	4,215	1,793	2,299	4,111	2,843	31,884	9,007	3,752	12,759	44,643
Community sentence	6,434	1,512	2,583	39,402	2,018	11,513	4,075	4,760	8,132	4,122	84,551	53,799	12,833	66,632	151,183
Fine[5]	1,305	101	4	15,911	674	21,344	783	2,243	10,135	1,171	53,671	342,433	420,724	763,157	816,828
Absolute discharge	59	8	2	530	47	407	33	157	337	23	1,603	2,592	3,301	5,893	7,496
Conditional discharge	929	92	17	22,263	998	8,816	576	838	2,797	1,210	38,536	38,980	2,350	41,330	79,866
Compensation	203	18	74	2,466	250	4	3	42	65	122	3,247	3,721	173	3,894	7,141
Otherwise dealt with[6]	472	110	108	3,578	188	2,291	250	836	3,614	96	11,543	4,798	1,693	6,491	18,034
Average custodial sentence (months)[7]	23	54	36	9	24	29	13	7	9	15	17	3	3	3	14
2013															
All Sentenced	**24,279**	**5,634**	**6,773**	**121,637**	**4,054**	**56,323**	**9,932**	**16,213**	**34,364**	**12,099**	**291,308**	**435,497**	**443,883**	**879,380**	**1,170,688**
Immediate custody	10,384	3,360	4,301	31,718	722	9,024	2,621	4,772	8,525	2,535	77,962	12,315	2,689	15,004	92,966
Suspended sentence	5,582	581	499	11,140	296	5,173	2,108	2,537	4,522	3,097	35,535	9,551	3,679	13,230	48,765
Community sentence	5,312	1,354	1,839	31,978	1,412	9,388	3,557	4,292	6,680	3,963	69,775	46,079	10,681	56,760	126,535
Fine[5]	1,376	125	30	16,500	503	20,712	823	2,828	9,124	1,166	53,187	320,480	419,737	740,217	793,404
Absolute discharge	60	5	1	580	19	346	33	116	352	13	1,525	2,368	3,107	5,475	7,000
Conditional discharge	874	91	19	21,629	783	9,396	488	963	2,377	1,089	37,709	36,191	1,943	38,134	75,843
Compensation	194	19	8	3,958	181	4	2	95	73	141	4,675	4,520	127	4,647	9,322
Otherwise dealt with[6]	497	99	76	4,134	138	2,280	300	610	2,711	95	10,940	3,993	1,920	5,913	16,853
Average custodial sentence (months)[7]	25	59	40	9	27	31	13	7	10	15	18	3	3	3	15

21.4 Persons[1] sentenced at all courts, by type of sentence and offence group, 12 months ending December 2006 to 2016[2][3]

England and Wales | | | | | | | | | | | | | | Persons sentenced

Year ending and type of sentence	Violence against the person	Sexual offences	Robbery	Theft Offences	Criminal damage and arson	Drug offences	Possession of weapons	Public order offences	Miscellaneous crimes against society	Fraud offences	All indictable offences	Summary non-motoring	Summary motoring	All summary offences	All offences
2014 All Sentenced	**26,502**	**6,233**	**5,582**	**116,158**	**2,469**	**51,297**	**9,987**	**17,058**	**31,709**	**13,338**	**280,333**	**457,409**	**471,462**	**928,871**	**1,209,204**
Immediate custody	11,131	3,687	3,686	30,067	619	8,756	2,655	4,820	8,054	2,298	75,773	12,933	2,607	15,540	91,313
Suspended sentence	6,492	721	440	11,948	263	5,525	2,321	3,036	4,835	3,359	38,940	10,370	3,669	14,039	52,979
Community sentence	5,296	1,497	1,319	25,413	737	7,154	3,310	4,023	5,755	4,426	58,930	44,016	9,692	53,708	112,638
Fine[5]	1,662	119	3	17,637	257	19,632	833	3,079	8,275	1,496	52,993	343,978	449,970	793,948	846,941
Absolute discharge	70	7	3	522	20	321	36	110	293	20	1,402	1,922	2,439	4,361	5,763
Conditional discharge	963	87	13	21,231	347	8,223	482	1,054	1,806	1,459	35,665	35,327	1,440	36,767	72,432
Compensation	151	5	7	2,494	71	0	0	44	46	93	2,911	3,242	76	3,318	6,229
Otherwise dealt with[6]	737	110	111	6,846	155	1,686	350	892	2,645	187	13,719	5,621	1,569	7,190	20,909
Average custodial sentence (months)[7]	23	62	41	9	25	32	13	7	10	16	18	3	3	3	16
2015 All Sentenced	**29,447**	**6,847**	**4,721**	**103,108**	**2,434**	**46,242**	**10,750**	**17,088**	**30,227**	**12,525**	**263,389**	**473,883**	**501,648**	**975,531**	**1,238,920**
Immediate custody	11,858	4,106	3,220	27,511	657	8,618	3,078	4,834	8,169	2,321	74,372	13,228	2,748	15,976	90,348
Suspended sentence	7,606	858	365	11,966	333	5,679	2,818	3,166	5,310	3,489	41,590	11,536	3,946	15,482	57,072
Community sentence	5,940	1,545	981	24,392	707	6,719	3,442	4,309	5,493	3,960	57,488	46,695	10,101	56,796	114,284
Fine[5]	2,030	104	3	15,138	203	16,445	706	2,993	7,106	1,333	46,061	358,362	479,598	837,960	884,021
Absolute discharge	80	10	3	950	12	430	41	202	410	23	2,161	4,533	2,248	6,781	8,942
Conditional discharge	1,166	81	14	18,382	321	7,255	442	1,004	1,676	1,234	31,575	33,010	1,443	34,453	66,028
Compensation	107	4	4	1,823	57	0	0	41	35	77	2,148	2,980	105	3,085	5,233
Otherwise dealt with[6]	660	139	131	2,946	144	1,096	223	539	2,028	88	7,994	3,539	1,459	4,998	12,992
Average custodial sentence (months)[7]	23	62	43	9	23	34	14	7	11	18	19	3	3	3	16

Source: Ministry of Justice Court Proceedings Database

. = nil

(1) Excludes other offenders, i.e. companies, public bodies, etc.

(2) Data relate to persons for whom these offences were the principal offences for which they were dealt with. When a defendant has been found guilty of two or more offences it is the offence for which the heaviest penalty is imposed. Where the same disposal is imposed for two or more offences, the offence selected is the offence for which the statutory maximum penalty is the most severe.

(3) Data are given on a principal disposal basis - i.e. reporting the most severe sentence for the principal offence.

(4) Excludes data for Cardiff magistrates' court for April, July and August 2008.

(5) Due to limitations in data supply, fine data from magistrates' courts has been omitted from our data since 2009 of values between £10,000 and £99,999.

(6) Including restriction orders, hospital orders, guardianship orders, police cells, and other disposals.

(7) Excludes life and other indeterminate sentences.

21.5 Persons cautioned for summary offences (excluding motoring) by offence, sex and age, 2015

Offence	10-11	12-14	15-17	18-20	21+	Total
104 Assaulting, resisting or obstructing a constable or designated officer in execution of duty	6	79	271	514	1615	2485
01: Male	6	37	149	326	944	1462
02: Female	0	42	121	188	668	1019
04: Not known	0	0	1	0	3	4
105 Common assault and battery	75	1144	1792	3353	25007	31371
01: Male	66	753	1143	2373	18399	22734
02: Female	8	376	628	961	6494	8467
04: Not known	1	15	21	19	114	170
107 Brothel Keeping	0	0	0	1	7	8
01: Male	0	0	0	0	1	1
02: Female	0	0	0	1	6	7
108 Cruelty to Animal	2	1	3	1	10	17
01: Male	1	0	3	1	10	15
02: Female	1	1	0	0	0	2
111A Offences under Dangerous Dogs Acts - summary	0	0	0	2	29	31
01: Male	0	0	0	2	12	14
02: Female	0	0	0	0	16	16
04: Not known	0	0	0	0	1	1
111B Other offences relating to dogs	0	0	0	0	3	3
01: Male	0	0	0	0	2	2
02: Female	0	0	0	0	1	1
112B Education Acts - Other	0	1	0	1	0	2
01: Male	0	1	0	1	0	2
115 Firearms Acts - summary offences	0	3	13	26	116	158
01: Male	0	3	13	26	114	156
02: Female	0	0	0	0	2	2
118 Night Poaching	0	0	1	1	4	6
01: Male	0	0	1	1	4	6
119 Day Poaching	0	0	1	0	13	14
01: Male	0	0	1	0	13	14
121A Offences under Hunting Act 2004	0	0	0	1	2	3
01: Male	0	0	0	1	2	3
122 Obstruction of highways, etc, other than by vehicle	0	0	0	0	2	2
01: Male	0	0	0	0	1	1
02: Female	0	0	0	0	1	1
123 Nuisance (other than by vehicle)	0	1	1	3	1	6
01: Male	0	1	1	3	1	6
125A Causing intentional harassment, alarm or distress - summary	3	30	89	118	843	1083
01: Male	3	25	74	92	659	853
02: Female	0	4	15	26	179	224
04: Not known	0	1	0	0	5	6
125B Causing fear or provocation of violence - summary	4	49	196	584	2316	3149
01: Male	2	37	161	496	1945	2641
02: Female	2	10	32	85	360	489
04: Not known	0	2	3	3	11	19
125C Causing harassment, alarm or distress - summary	3	139	321	315	1455	2233
01: Male	3	98	252	243	1116	1712
02: Female	0	40	69	71	333	513
04: Not known	0	1	0	1	6	8
125D Racially or religiously aggravated harassment, alarm or distress - summary	0	5	6	9	71	91
01: Male	0	4	4	7	56	71
02: Female	0	1	2	2	15	20
125F Public Order Act 1986 and associated acts - other offences	0	3	16	23	124	166
01: Male	0	3	15	21	116	155
02: Female	0	0	1	2	7	10
04: Not known					1	1
126 Interference with Motor Vehicles	0	12	12	18	32	74
01: Male	0	12	12	18	29	71
02: Female	0	0	0	0	2	2
04: Not known	0	0	0	0	1	1

21.5 Persons cautioned for summary offences (excluding motoring) by offence, sex and age, 2015

Offence	Ages					
	10-11	12-14	15-17	18-20	21+	Total
130 Theft of a motor vehicle (excl. aggravated vehicle taking) - summary (MOT)	2	53	184	124	207	570
01: Male	2	44	156	101	183	486
02: Female	0	7	25	22	24	78
04: Not known	0	2	3	1	0	6
137 Pedal cycle - Other offences	0	0	1	1	0	2
01: Male	0	0	1	1	0	2
137 Pedal cycle - Taking or riding a pedal cycle without consent	1	4	8	5	9	27
01: Male	1	1	7	4	9	22
02: Female	0	3	1	1	0	5
138 Offences involving impersonation, giving false or misleading information, failing to supply information, etc	0	0	0	1	7	8
01: Male	0	0	0	1	5	6
02: Female	0	0	0	0	2	2
140 Drunkenness, simple	0	0	1	5	76	82
01: Male	0	0	1	5	64	70
02: Female	0	0	0	0	12	12
141 Drunkenness, with aggravation - disorderly in a public place	0	21	255	482	2313	3071
01: Male	0	10	174	383	1793	2360
02: Female	0	11	80	98	515	704
04: Not known	0	0	1	1	5	7
141 Drunkenness, with aggravation - other	0	0	1	4	195	200
01: Male	0	0	0	0	41	41
02: Female	0	0	1	4	154	159
142B Remain on / enter premises in contravention of a closure notice or similar direction	0	11	36	98	249	394
01: Male	0	9	32	87	230	358
02: Female	0	2	4	11	19	36
143A Sale of alcohol to a person aged under 18	0	0	0	0	6	6
01: Male	0	0	0	0	6	6
143B Buying, attempting to buy or delivering alcohol to persons aged under 18	0	0	0	3	0	3
01: Male	0	0	0	2	0	2
02: Female	0	0	0	1	0	1
143E Other offences related to the sale of alcohol and licensed premises	0	0	0	4	62	66
01: Male	0	0	0	4	46	50
02: Female	0	0	0	0	14	14
04: Not known	0	0	0	0	2	2
149 Criminal or Malicious Damage Offence	61	819	1451	2009	8583	12923
01: Male	56	654	1197	1670	7026	10603
02: Female	4	144	240	324	1535	2247
04: Not known	1	21	14	15	22	73
151 Benefit fraud offences - summary	0	0	1	1	7	9
01: Male	0	0	0	1	4	5
02: Female	0	0	1	0	2	3
04: Not known	0	0	0	0	1	1
151-152 Other Social Security offences	0	0	0	0	2	2
01: Male	0	0	0	0	1	1
04: Not known	0	0	0	0	1	1
153-155 Offences against Military Law - Army, Navy and Air Force	0	0	0	0	8	8
01: Male	0	0	0	0	5	5
02: Female	0	0	0	0	3	3
160 Pedlars Act - Acting without certificate, refusal to produce certificate, etc	0	0	0	0	5	5
01: Male	0	0	0	0	5	5
162 Disorderly Behaviour	0	0	1	1	9	11
01: Male	0	0	0	1	5	6
02: Female	0	0	1	0	4	5

21.5 Persons cautioned for summary offences (excluding motoring) by offence, sex and age, 2015

Offence	Ages					
	10-11	12-14	15-17	18-20	21+	Total
166 Offence by Prostitute	**0**	**0**	**0**	**5**	**46**	**51**
01: Male	0	0	0	0	11	11
02: Female	0	0	0	5	34	39
04: Not known	0	0	0	0	1	1
167 Aiding, etc. Offence by Prostitute	**0**	**0**	**2**	**21**	**373**	**396**
01: Male	0	0	2	20	363	385
02: Female	0	0	0	0	4	4
04: Not known	0	0	0	1	6	7
168 Public Health Offence	**0**	**0**	**0**	**0**	**3**	**3**
01: Male	0	0	0	0	2	2
02: Female	0	0	0	0	1	1
169A Travelling by railway without paying correct fare, failing to show ticket, failing to give name and address, etc	**0**	**10**	**17**	**77**	**224**	**328**
01: Male	0	8	15	61	187	271
02: Female	0	2	2	16	37	57
169B Other railway offences	**0**	**3**	**3**	**12**	**104**	**122**
01: Male	0	3	3	11	73	90
02: Female	0	0	0	1	23	24
04: Not known	0	0	0	0	8	8
173 Stage Carriage or Public Service Vehicle Offence	**0**	**0**	**0**	**2**	**222**	**224**
01: Male	0	0	0	2	219	221
02: Female	0	0	0	0	3	3
175 Sexual Offences- Miscellaneous	**0**	**1**	**0**	**2**	**10**	**13**
01: Male	0	1	0	1	8	10
02: Female	0	0	0	1	1	2
04: Not known	0	0	0	0	1	1
182 Begging	**0**	**0**	**1**	**16**	**262**	**279**
01: Male	0	0	1	7	180	188
02: Female	0	0	0	9	81	90
04: Not known	0	0	0	0	1	1
183 Sleeping Out	**0**	**0**	**0**	**0**	**1**	**1**
01: Male	0	0	0	0	1	1
185 Being on enclosed premises for an unlawful purpose	**1**	**3**	**1**	**4**	**34**	**43**
01: Male	1	2	1	4	31	39
02: Female	0	1	0	0	3	4
193 Offences under the Drugs Act 2005 - summary	**0**	**0**	**3**	**3**	**16**	**22**
01: Male	0	0	3	3	16	22
194 Immigration Offence	**0**	**0**	**0**	**0**	**8**	**8**
01: Male	0	0	0	0	4	4
02: Female	0	0	0	0	4	4
195 Airports Act 1986 S.63	**0**	**0**	**0**	**0**	**2**	**2**
01: Male	0	0	0	0	2	2
195 Computer Misuse Act 1990 S.1	**0**	**0**	**0**	**2**	**14**	**16**
01: Male	0	0	0	0	5	5
02: Female	0	0	0	2	8	10
04: Not known	0	0	0	0	1	1
195 Copyright, Designs & Patents Act 1988	**0**	**0**	**0**	**0**	**1**	**1**
02: Female	0	0	0	0	1	1
195 Criminal Justice & Police Act 2001 s.42	**0**	**1**	**0**	**4**	**8**	**13**
01: Male	0	1	0	4	8	13
195 Criminal Justice & Public Order Act 1994 S.166 - Unauthorised person selling tickets for a football match	**0**	**0**	**0**	**0**	**8**	**8**
01: Male	0	0	0	0	8	8
195 Criminal Law Act 1967 S.5(2) - Causing wasteful employment of the police	**0**	**6**	**12**	**21**	**149**	**188**
01: Male	0	0	5	12	83	100
02: Female	0	6	7	9	65	87
04: Not known	0	0	0	0	1	1

21.5 Persons cautioned for summary offences (excluding motoring) by offence, sex and age, 2015

Offence	Ages					
	10-11	12-14	15-17	18-20	21+	Total
195 Criminal Law Act 1977 S.6 - Using or threatening violence for securing entry to premises	**0**	**2**	**6**	**6**	**44**	**58**
01: Male	0	2	4	5	39	50
02: Female	0	0	2	1	4	7
04: Not known	0	0	0	0	1	1
195 Malicious Communications Act - Sending letters etc. with intent to cause distress or anxiety	**1**	**15**	**30**	**54**	**448**	**548**
01: Male	1	9	20	38	366	434
02: Female	0	5	10	16	81	112
04: Not known	0	1	0	0	1	2
195 Offences by dealers in scrap metal and similar goods and in marine stores	**0**	**0**	**0**	**0**	**2**	**2**
01: Male	0	0	0	0	1	1
02: Female	0	0	0	0	1	1
195 Police Act 1996 S.90 - Impersonation of member of police force or special constable	**0**	**0**	**0**	**1**	**9**	**10**
01: Male	0	0	0	1	9	10
195 Protection from Harassment Act 1997 S.2 - Summary offence of harassment	**1**	**16**	**62**	**163**	**2144**	**2386**
01: Male	1	13	45	125	1673	1857
02: Female	0	3	17	35	464	519
04: Not known	0	0	0	3	7	10
196 Anti-social Behaviour Act 2003 S.32 - Contravention of direction by constable regarding dispersal of persons aged under 16 to their place of residence	**0**	**1**	**4**	**6**	**25**	**36**
01: Male	0	0	3	6	22	31
02: Female	0	1	1	0	3	5
196 Communications Act 2003 S.127 - Sending grossly offensive message/matter by electronic communications network	**0**	**16**	**35**	**58**	**468**	**577**
01: Male	0	14	28	48	369	459
02: Female	0	2	5	10	96	113
04: Not known	0	0	2	0	3	5
196 Firing an air weapon beyond premises	**0**	**0**	**1**	**0**	**2**	**3**
01: Male	0	0	1	0	2	3
196 Pursue course of conduct in breach of prohibition of harassment, which amounts to stalking	**0**	**0**	**0**	**1**	**32**	**33**
01: Male	0	0	0	1	26	27
02: Female	0	0	0	0	6	6
197 Betting or Gaming Offence	**0**	**0**	**1**	**12**	**50**	**63**
01: Male	0	0	1	12	47	60
02: Female	0	0	0	0	3	3
Other summary non-motoring offences	**0**	**18**	**77**	**63**	**192**	**350**
01: Male	0	14	68	55	155	292
02: Female	0	4	6	8	36	54
04: Not known	0	0	3	0	1	4
Grand Total	**160**	**2467**	**4916**	**8241**	**48289**	**64073**

Source: Ministry of Justice

CJS Outcomes by Offence 2006-2016: Pivot Table Analytical Tool for England and Wales

21.6a Offenders[1][2] found guilty at all courts by offence group, 2005 to 2015

England and Wales | | | | | | | | | | Number of offenders

Offence group	2005	2006	2007	2008[3]	2009	2010	2011[4]	2012	2013	2014	2015
Indictable offences											
Violence against the person	29,005	29,706	29,983	29,245	30,711	32,732	30,791	26,522	24,523	26,607	28,728
Sexual offences	4,775	4,850	5,005	5,042	5,042	5,733	5,958	5,728	5,665	6,251	6,885
Robbery	7,083	8,105	8,829	8,475	8,645	8,499	9,329	8,336	6,764	5,570	4,722
Theft Offences	120,410	116,725	124,683	130,498	131,116	140,912	141,969	128,943	124,110	118,292	105,244
Criminal damage and arson	42,070	42,232	43,977	42,320	40,457	39,558	36,671	32,199	29,384	27,841	27,923
Drug offences	39,091	39,582	44,565	52,943	56,831	61,979	61,657	58,125	57,012	51,814	46,810
Possession of weapons	14,732	14,709	14,709	14,980	15,388	13,378	12,616	10,447	10,139	10,176	10,961
Public order offences	8,808	8,695	9,042	8,519	17,347	19,591	17,998	16,167	16,267	17,306	17,190
Miscellaneous crimes against society	63,165	58,395	53,587	47,571	44,823	47,432	44,319	38,768	35,425	32,799	32,008
Fraud offences	12,960	12,934	13,874	13,336	14,771	15,651	15,036	12,446	12,327	13,574	12,676
Total indictable offenders	342,099	335,933	348,254	352,929	365,131	385,465	376,344	337,681	321,616	310,230	293,147
Summary offences											
Summary Non-Motoring	475,238	462,878	456,557	458,092	478,743	458,639	461,694	441,424	409,338	431,303	450,303
Summary motoring	667,087	622,495	611,093	552,197	564,563	523,371	475,542	452,455	448,450	476,137	505,664
Total summary offenders	1,142,325	1,085,373	1,067,650	1,010,289	1,043,306	982,010	937,236	893,879	857,788	907,440	955,967
Total offenders	**1,484,424**	**1,421,306**	**1,415,904**	**1,363,218**	**1,408,437**	**1,367,475**	**1,313,580**	**1,231,560**	**1,179,404**	**1,217,670**	**1,249,114**

Source: Ministry of Justice

Notes:

(1) The figures given in the table relate to defendants for whom these offences were the principal offences for which they were dealt with. When a defendant has been found guilty of two or more offences it is the offence for which the heaviest penalty is imposed. Where the same disposal is imposed for two or more offences, the offence selected is the offence for which the statutory maximum penalty is the most severe.

(2) Includes males, females, persons where sex "Not Stated" and other offenders, i.e. companies, public bodies, etc.

(3) Excludes convictions data for Cardiff magistrates' court for April, July, and August 2008.

(4) Due to improvements in quality assurance procedures, the number of convictions in the Crown Court in 2011 will differ from previously published figures.

21.6b Persons[1][2] found guilty at all courts or cautioned[3] for indictable offences per 100,000 population, by sex and age group, 2005 to 2015

England and Wales | | | | | | | Number of persons found guilty and/or cautioned per 100,000 population [7]

Year	All persons [4]	Males						Females					
		All ages	Aged 10-11	Aged 12-14	Aged 15-17	Aged 18-20	Aged 21 & over	All ages	Aged 10-11	Aged 12-14	Aged 15-17	Aged 18-20	Aged 21 & over
2005	814	1,427	320	1,684	4,489	4,707	1,104	234	27	371	780	639	187
2006	805	1,419	320	1,752	4,563	4,800	1,081	224	32	360	752	589	178
2007	826	1,454	324	1,812	4,752	4,949	1,100	230	26	360	787	576	185
2008 [5]	814	1,421	240	1,449	4,129	4,675	1,132	228	16	309	674	569	191
2009	1,146	1,909	350	2,014	5,681	6,464	1,500	411	87	1,018	1,538	1,088	304
2010	1,111	1,875	196	1,431	5,013	6,174	1,547	373	43	581	1,112	989	307
2011 [6]	1,061	1,806	145	1,223	4,479	5,593	1,537	338	23	366	873	851	295
2012	931	1,588	108	911	3,401	4,538	1,411	289	15	248	634	671	263
2013	869	1,479	68	696	2,797	3,896	1,362	270	12	184	500	563	256
2014	809	1,368	52	645	2,386	3,508	1,277	259	7	138	400	514	252
2015	730	1,235	44	573	2,000	3,031	1,171	229	5	125	325	421	226

Source: Ministry of Justice

Notes:

(1) The figures given in the table relate to defendants for whom these offences were the principal offences for which they were dealt with. When a defendant has been found guilty of two or more offences it is the offence for which the heaviest penalty is imposed. Where the same disposal is imposed for two or more offences, the offence selected is the offence for which the statutory maximum penalty is the most severe.

(2) Excludes companies.

(3) Motoring offences may attract written warnings, which are excluded from this table.

(4) Includes sex unknown/not stated.

(5) Excludes convictions data for Cardiff magistrates' court for April, July and August 2008.

(6) Due to improvements in quality assurance procedures, the number of convictions in the Crown Court in 2011 will differ from

(7) To calculate convictions per 100,000 population, the total number of convictions for a specific year are divided by the population of the year prior to the year of interest. Population figures come from the ONS mid-year population estimates (https://www.nomisweb.co.uk/). The population of the previous year is used due to population data available at the time of publication. Population figures used are based on population estimates for persons aged 10 and above.

21.7a Proceedings at the magistrates amd trials at the Crown Court by result, 2006 to 2015

England and Wales

All Defendants (thousands)

Offence Type	2006	2007	2008[9]	2009	2010	2011[10]	2012	2013	2014	2015
Indictable Only										
Number of offenders proceeded against at MC	33.3	35.0	34.7	36.9	36.7	35.1	31.0	30.7	29.0	26.4
Committed for trial at CC	26.9	28.2	29.5	31.8	31.5	29.7	26.5	27.3	26.5	24.2
Proceedings terminated early[4]	1.4	1.3	1.2	0.4	0.4	0.5	0.3	0.2	0.2	0.2
Tried at MC	4.9	5.4	4.0	4.8	4.8	4.9	4.2	3.2	2.4	2.1
Discharged at committal proceedings[5]	0.6	0.5	0.3	1.2	1.3	1.2	1.0	0.8	0.6	0.5
Dismissed (found not guilty after summary trial)	0.7	0.7	0.3	0.3	0.3	0.3	0.3	0.2	0.2	0.2
Found guilty at MC	3.6	4.2	3.3	3.3	3.2	3.5	2.9	2.2	1.6	1.4
Magistrates' court conviction trial rate[6]	72.5%	78.0%	83.7%	68.7%	67.0%	70.1%	69.6%	68.5%	68.0%	64.7%
For trial at CC[7]	19.8	22.0	22.8	22.8	22.9	22.1	20.6	18.8	18.6	18.3
Not Tried	0.3	0.3	0.3	0.3	0.4	0.3	0.2	0.2	0.2	0.3
Tried at CC	19.5	21.6	22.5	22.5	22.6	21.8	20.3	18.6	18.4	18.1
Acquitted	5.4	5.4	5.1	5.6	6.1	5.6	5.3	4.8	5.3	5.3
Found guilty at CC[10]	14.1	16.2	17.3	16.9	16.5	16.2	15.1	13.8	13.1	12.7
Crown court conviction trial rate[6]	72.4%	75.0%	77.1%	75.3%	73.2%	74.3%	74.0%	74.0%	71.3%	70.5%
All convictions	17.7	20.4	20.7	20.2	19.7	19.7	18.0	15.9	14.7	14.1
Conviction Ratio[8]	53.3%	58.5%	59.6%	54.7%	53.7%	56.0%	57.9%	51.9%	50.6%	53.3%
Triable Either Way Offences[8]										
Number of offenders proceeded against at MC	372.8	369.9	362.8	378.7	401.3	388.9	345.9	339.9	326.2	297.2
Committed for trial at CC	51.8	55.2	59.1	70.5	74.9	70.3	59.4	69.9	71.8	63.7
Proceedings terminated early[4]	62.1	54.4	48.2	47.7	50.7	48.5	41.8	37.4	34.8	31.2
Tried at MC	259.0	260.3	255.5	260.6	275.7	270.1	244.8	232.6	219.6	202.3
Discharged at committal proceedings[5]	7.0	5.7	4.2	3.8	3.3	2.6	2.2	0.8	0.0	0.0
Dismissed (found not guilty after summary trial)	8.0	7.0	5.0	4.2	4.5	4.1	4.3	4.2	4.9	4.8
Found guilty at MC	244.0	247.6	246.3	252.5	268.0	263.4	238.3	227.6	214.7	197.5
Magistrates' court conviction trial rate[6]	94.2%	95.1%	96.4%	96.9%	97.2%	97.5%	97.3%	97.9%	97.8%	97.6%
For trial at CC[7]	53.9	57.8	62.2	70.2	78.7	75.2	64.8	61.6	65.0	67.1
Not Tried	0.7	0.8	0.8	0.8	1.0	0.8	0.6	0.6	0.6	0.7
Tried at CC	53.2	56.9	61.4	69.4	77.7	74.3	64.1	61.0	64.4	66.4
Acquitted	11.7	11.7	11.5	12.9	14.8	13.5	11.5	10.0	10.5	11.2
Found guilty at CC[10]	41.4	45.2	49.9	56.5	62.9	60.8	52.7	51.0	53.9	55.2
Crown court conviction trial rate[6]	77.9%	79.5%	81.2%	81.4%	81.0%	81.8%	82.1%	83.6%	83.8%	83.1%
All convictions	285.4	292.9	296.2	309.0	330.9	324.2	291.0	278.7	268.6	252.7
Conviction Ratio[8]	76.6%	79.2%	81.7%	81.6%	82.5%	83.4%	84.1%	82.0%	82.4%	85.0%

21.7a Proceedings at the magistrates amd trials at the Crown Court by result, 2006 to 2015

England and Wales

All Defendants (thousands)

Offence Type	2006	2007	2008[9]	2009	2010	2011[10]	2012	2013	2014	2015
Summary non-motoring offences										
Number of offenders proceeded against at MC	612.0	599.3	593.3	619.2	607.1	606.5	581.9	546.1	565.9	590.6
Committed for trial at CC	0.6	0.8	0.7	0.7	0.5	0.5	0.3	0.7	0.6	0.5
Proceedings terminated early[4]	104.2	96.6	90.9	97.2	107.0	106.3	104.9	102.2	99.4	106.4
Tried at MC	507.1	502.0	501.7	521.2	499.5	499.7	476.6	443.2	465.9	483.7
Discharged at committal proceedings[5]	0.0	0.1	0.0	-	-	-	-	-	-	-
Dismissed (found not guilty after summary trial)	14.0	13.1	10.5	9.9	10.3	9.2	9.3	9.5	10.6	11.6
Found guilty at MC	493.2	488.7	491.2	511.3	489.2	490.5	467.3	433.7	455.3	472.1
Magistrates' court conviction trial rate[6]	97.2%	97.4%	97.9%	98.1%	97.9%	98.2%	98.0%	97.9%	97.7%	97.6%
For trial at CC[7]	2.6	2.9	3.0	3.5	4.4	3.8	3.0	2.8	2.9	3.2
Not Tried	0.0	0.0	0.0	0.0	0.0	0.0	0.0	0.0	0.0	0.0
Tried at CC	2.6	2.9	3.0	3.5	4.4	3.7	2.9	2.7	2.9	3.1
Acquitted	0.1	0.1	0.1	0.1	0.2	0.2	0.1	0.1	0.1	0.1
Found guilty at CC[10]	2.5	2.8	2.9	3.4	4.2	3.6	2.8	2.6	2.8	3.0
Crown court conviction trial rate[6]	96.8%	97.0%	97.0%	95.8%	96.1%	95.5%	95.9%	96.5%	95.4%	96.1%
All convictions	495.7	491.5	494.2	514.7	493.5	494.1	470.1	436.3	458.1	475.1
Conviction Ratio[8]	81.0%	82.0%	83.3%	83.1%	81.3%	81.5%	80.8%	79.9%	81.0%	80.4%
Summary motoring offences										
Number of offenders proceeded against at MC	761.1	728.4	649.2	659.6	608.1	549.6	525.8	524.7	546.7	577.9
Committed for trial at CC	0.2	0.2	0.1	0.1	0.1	0.0	0.0	0.1	0.1	0.0
Proceedings terminated early[4]	129.2	108.6	89.0	87.3	76.9	67.0	66.6	69.1	64.1	63.3
Tried at MC	631.8	619.5	560.1	572.3	531.2	482.5	459.2	455.4	482.6	514.6
Discharged at committal proceedings[5]	0.0	0.1	0.0	0.0	0.0	0.0	0.0	0.0	-	-
Dismissed (found not guilty after summary trial)	9.6	8.9	8.4	8.2	8.3	7.3	6.9	7.2	6.6	7.7
Found guilty at MC	622.1	610.5	551.7	564.1	522.9	475.2	452.3	448.3	476.0	506.9
Magistrates' court conviction trial rate[6]	98.5%	98.5%	98.5%	98.6%	98.4%	98.5%	98.5%	98.4%	98.6%	98.5%
For trial at CC[7]	0.4	0.6	0.5	0.5	0.5	0.4	0.3	0.3	0.3	0.3
Not Tried	-	-	0.0	-	0.0	-	-	0.0	-	0.0
Tried at CC	0.4	0.6	0.5	0.5	0.5	0.4	0.3	0.3	0.3	0.3
Acquitted	0.0	0.0	0.0	0.0	0.0	0.0	0.0	0.0	0.0	0.0
Found guilty at CC[10]	0.4	0.6	0.5	0.4	0.5	0.4	0.3	0.3	0.2	0.3
Crown court conviction trial rate[6]	97.7%	97.7%	98.2%	97.4%	97.6%	97.2%	97.1%	97.4%	96.5%	98.1%
All convictions	622.5	611.1	552.2	564.6	523.4	475.6	452.6	448.5	476.2	507.2
Conviction Ratio[8]	81.8%	83.9%	85.1%	85.6%	86.1%	86.5%	86.1%	85.5%	87.1%	87.8%

21.7a Proceedings at the magistrates amd trials at the Crown Court by result, 2006 to 2015

England and Wales

All Defendants (thousands)

Offence Type	2006	2007	2008[9]	2009	2010	2011[10]	2012	2013	2014	2015
All Offences										
Number of offenders proceeded against at MC	1779.2	1732.5	1640.0	1694.4	1653.2	1580.0	1484.6	1441.3	1467.8	1492.2
Committed for trial at CC	79.5	84.4	89.5	103.1	107.0	100.5	86.3	98.0	99.0	88.5
Proceedings terminated early[4]	296.9	260.9	229.3	232.5	235.0	222.2	213.6	208.9	198.5	201.0
Tried at MC	1402.8	1387.2	1321.2	1358.9	1311.2	1257.3	1184.8	1134.4	1170.4	1202.7
Discharged at committal proceedings[5]	7.7	6.5	4.6	5.1	4.6	3.8	3.2	1.6	0.6	0.5
Dismissed (found not guilty after summary trial)	32.3	29.7	24.1	22.6	23.3	20.9	20.8	21.1	22.3	24.2
Found guilty at MC	1362.8	1351.1	1292.5	1331.2	1283.3	1232.6	1160.8	1111.7	1147.6	1177.9
Magistrates' court conviction trial rate[6]	97.1%	97.4%	97.8%	98.0%	97.9%	98.0%	98.0%	98.0%	98.1%	97.9%
For trial at CC[7]	76.8	83.2	88.5	97.0	106.6	101.4	88.6	83.5	86.8	88.8
Not Tried	1.1	1.2	1.1	1.1	1.4	1.2	0.9	0.9	0.8	0.9
Tried at CC	75.7	82.0	87.4	95.8	105.1	100.2	87.7	82.6	85.9	87.9
Acquitted	17.2	17.2	16.8	18.6	21.0	19.3	16.9	14.9	15.9	16.7
Found guilty at CC[10]	58.5	64.8	70.7	77.2	84.1	80.9	70.8	67.7	70.1	71.2
Crown court conviction trial rate[6]	77.3%	79.0%	80.8%	80.6%	80.0%	80.7%	80.7%	81.9%	81.5%	81.0%
All convictions	1421.3	1415.9	1363.2	1408.4	1367.5	1313.6	1231.6	1179.4	1217.7	1249.1
Conviction Ratio[8]	79.9%	81.7%	83.1%	83.1%	82.7%	83.1%	83.0%	81.8%	83.0%	83.7%

Source: Ministry of Justice Court Proceedings Database

. = nil

(1) The figures given in the table relate to defendants for whom these offences were the principal offences for which they were dealt with. When a defendant has been found guilty of two or more offences it is the offence for which the heaviest penalty is imposed. Where the same disposal is imposed for two or more offences, the offence selected is the offence for which the statutory maximum penalty is the most severe.

(2) Includes males, females, persons where sex is unknown or not stated and other offenders, i.e. companies, public bodies, etc.

(3) Youth Courts are categorised as magistrates' courts in the data. This will impact the figures for indictable only cases at the magistrates' court which will include a high volume of juvenile cases.

(4) Includes proceedings discontinued under s.23(3) of the Prosecution of Offences Act 1985, charge withdrawn and cases "written off" (e.g. bench warrant unexecuted, adjourned sine die, defendant cannot be traced etc.).

(5) Under Sec. 6 of Magistrates' Court Act 1980

A magistrates' court inquiring into an offence as examining justices shall on consideration of the evidence -

   a) commit the accused for trial if it is of opinion that there is sufficient evidence to put him on trial by jury for any indictable offence;

   b) discharge him if it is not of that opinion and he is in custody for no other cause than the offence under inquiry;

Comparison with Crown Prosecution Service data suggests that these figures are overstated.

Committal hearings were abolished in 2013 for triable either way offences.

(6) Conviction trial rate is calculated as the number of offenders convicted as a proportion of the number tried, in a given year and court type.

(7) Excludes offenders that were committed for sentence from the magistrates' court.

(8) Conviction ratio is calculated as the number of offenders convicted as a proportion of the number prosecuted, in a given year.

(9) Excludes data for Cardiff magistrates' court for April, July, and August 2008.

(10) Due to improvements in quality assurance procedures, the number of convictions in the Crown Court in 2011 will differ from previously published figures.

21.7b Defendants[1][2] proceeded against at magistrates' courts by offence group, 2006 to 2015

England and Wales | | | | | | | | | | Defendants (thousands)

					Magistrates' courts				
Offence group	2006	2007	2008[3]	2009	2010	2011[4]	2012	2013	2014	2015
Indictable										
Violence against the person	49.5	46.2	45.1	49.2	50.6	44.7	37.0	36.9	39.5	39.5
Sexual offences	9.0	8.6	8.4	9.3	10.5	10.1	9.4	10.9	11.9	12.6
Robbery	13.2	14.0	13.1	13.7	13.7	14.4	12.3	10.9	9.0	7.2
Theft Offences	136.9	143.1	146.3	147.9	158.4	159.6	145.0	142.0	135.4	118.6
Criminal damage and arson	16.2	15.6	11.3	9.0	8.9	8.0	7.0	5.6	3.6	3.4
Drug offences	44.0	48.9	57.0	61.7	67.8	67.7	63.6	63.8	57.6	51.0
Possession of weapons	18.4	18.0	18.0	19.5	17.4	16.4	13.7	13.7	13.7	13.9
Public order offences	12.1	11.2	10.5	18.5	20.9	18.4	16.3	17.2	17.9	17.4
Miscellaneous crimes against society	90.8	81.9	71.7	68.2	70.2	66.1	56.9	53.1	49.4	44.6
Fraud offences	16.1	17.3	16.3	18.8	19.7	18.7	15.9	16.5	17.3	15.3
Total indictable defendants	406.1	404.9	397.5	415.6	438.0	424.0	377.0	370.6	355.2	323.6
Summary										
Summary non-motoring	612.0	599.3	593.3	619.2	607.1	606.5	581.9	546.1	565.9	590.6
Summary motoring	761.1	728.4	649.2	659.6	608.1	549.6	525.8	524.7	546.7	577.9
Total summary defendants	1373.1	1327.7	1242.6	1278.8	1215.2	1156.0	1107.6	1070.7	1112.6	1168.6
Total defendants	**1779.2**	**1732.5**	**1640.0**	**1694.4**	**1653.2**	**1580.0**	**1484.6**	**1441.3**	**1467.8**	**1492.2**

Source: Ministry of Justice Court Proceedings Database

21.7c Offenders[1][2] found guilty at all courts by offence group, 2006 to 2016

England and Wales | | | | | | | | | | Offenders (thousands)

Offence group	2006	2007	2008[3]	2009	2010	2011[4]	2012	2013	2014	2015
Indictable offences										
Violence against the person	29.7	30.0	29.2	30.7	32.7	30.8	26.5	24.5	26.9	29.7
Sexual offences	4.9	5.0	5.0	5.0	5.7	6.0	5.7	5.7	6.3	6.9
Robbery	8.1	8.8	8.5	8.6	8.5	9.3	8.3	6.8	5.6	4.7
Theft Offences	114.7	122.5	128.2	128.7	138.8	140.0	127.2	122.6	116.8	103.8
Criminal damage and arson	12.0	11.9	9.0	7.3	7.1	6.5	5.4	4.1	2.5	2.5
Drug offences	39.6	44.6	52.9	56.8	62.0	61.7	58.1	57.0	51.8	46.8
Possession of weapons	14.2	14.1	14.6	15.1	13.1	12.5	10.3	10.0	10.1	10.8
Public order offences	8.7	9.0	8.5	17.3	19.5	18.0	16.2	16.2	17.3	17.2
Miscellaneous crimes against society	58.4	53.6	47.6	44.8	47.4	44.3	38.7	35.3	32.6	31.7
Fraud offences	12.9	13.9	13.3	14.8	15.7	15.0	12.4	12.3	13.5	12.7
Total indictable offenders	303.1	313.3	316.9	329.2	350.6	343.9	308.9	294.6	283.3	266.8
Summary offences										
Summary Non-Motoring	495.7	491.5	494.2	514.7	493.5	494.1	470.1	436.3	458.1	475.1
Summary motoring	622.5	611.1	552.2	564.6	523.4	475.6	452.6	448.5	476.2	507.2
Total summary offenders	1118.2	1102.6	1046.3	1079.3	1016.8	969.7	922.6	884.8	934.4	982.3
Total offenders	**1421.3**	**1415.9**	**1363.2**	**1408.4**	**1367.5**	**1313.6**	**1231.6**	**1179.4**	**1217.7**	**1249.1**

Source: Ministry of Justice Court Proceedings Database

(1) The figures given in the table relate to defendants for whom these offences were the principal offences for which they were dealt with. When a defendant has been found guilty of two or more offences it is the offence for which the heaviest penalty is imposed. Where the same disposal is imposed for two or more offences, the offence selected is the offence for which the statutory maximum penalty is the most severe.

(2) Includes males, females, persons where sex is unknown or not stated and other offenders, i.e. companies, public bodies, etc.

(3) Excludes convictions data for Cardiff magistrates' court for April, July, and August 2008.

(4) Due to improvements in quality assurance procedures, the number of convictions in the Crown Court in 2011 will differ from previously published figures.

21.8 Persons[1] sentenced at all courts to immediate custody at all courts by length of sentence and average custodial sentence length, 2006 to 2015[2][3]

England and Wales

Number of persons

Type of offence and custody length	2006	2007	2008[4]	2009	2010	2011	2012	2013	2014	2015
All offences										
Up to and including 3 months	34,711	34,427	35,738	36,071	38,316	39,419	36,442	34,821	35,578	34,577
Over 3 months and up to and including 6 months	18,625	17,472	16,608	16,016	15,172	15,310	14,406	13,480	12,806	12,466
6 months	5,796	5,637	5,730	5,305	5,009	4,959	4,926	4,756	4,370	4,558
Over 6 months and less than 12 months	5,728	6,154	6,920	7,177	7,052	7,891	6,787	6,431	5,996	6,099
12 months	5,245	5,479	5,652	5,837	5,618	5,947	4,788	4,380	4,155	4,075
Over 12 months and up to and including 18 months	6,232	6,271	6,751	7,289	7,343	8,022	7,343	6,375	5,810	5,756
Over 18 months and up to and including 3 years	10,372	10,470	11,516	12,077	12,358	13,138	12,621	12,225	11,829	11,720
Over 3 years and less than 4 years	1,533	1,458	1,629	1,811	1,937	1,990	1,973	2,092	2,120	2,178
4 years	1,607	1,603	1,903	1,977	1,934	2,094	1,787	1,704	1,639	1,611
Over 4 years and up to and including 5 years	1,670	1,611	1,998	1,980	2,061	2,208	1,913	1,945	1,932	2,008
Over 5 years and up to and including 10 years	2,190	2,109	2,614	2,784	2,796	3,307	3,238	3,417	3,653	3,814
Over 10 years and less than life	309	316	405	485	514	671	661	936	983	1,117
Indeterminate sentence[5]	1,445	1,707	1,538	1,001	1,019	819	747	9	-	-
Life	550	492	523	421	384	395	412	395	442	369
Total sentenced to immediate custody	**96,013**	**95,206**	**99,525**	**100,231**	**101,513**	**106,170**	**98,044**	**92,966**	**91,313**	**90,348**
Average custodial sentence length (months)[6]	12.4	12.4	13.3	13.7	13.7	14.3	14.5	15.5	15.6	16.2
Indictable offences										
Up to and including 3 months	22,378	22,421	23,533	23,692	26,290	27,247	25,675	25,439	25,551	24,194
Over 3 months and up to and including 6 months	9,421	9,184	9,018	8,935	9,081	9,328	8,721	8,422	7,771	7,424
6 months	4,863	4,768	5,065	4,833	4,603	4,572	4,425	4,198	3,895	4,011
Over 6 months and less than 12 months	5,725	6,150	6,916	7,158	7,023	7,813	6,771	6,427	5,994	6,095
12 months	5,241	5,477	5,650	5,828	5,607	5,932	4,781	4,378	4,154	4,075
Over 12 months and up to and including 18 months	6,230	6,271	6,750	7,284	7,337	8,008	7,337	6,375	5,810	5,756
Over 18 months and up to and including 3 years	10,369	10,470	11,516	12,076	12,353	13,132	12,620	12,225	11,829	11,720
Over 3 years and less than 4 years	1,532	1,458	1,629	1,811	1,937	1,990	1,973	2,092	2,120	2,178
4 years	1,607	1,603	1,903	1,977	1,934	2,094	1,787	1,704	1,639	1,611
Over 4 years and up to and including 5 years	1,670	1,611	1,998	1,980	2,061	2,208	1,913	1,945	1,932	2,008
Over 5 years and up to and including 10 years	2,189	2,109	2,614	2,784	2,796	3,307	3,238	3,417	3,653	3,814
Over 10 years and less than life	309	316	405	485	514	671	661	936	983	1,117
Indeterminate sentence[5]	1,444	1,707	1,538	1,001	1,019	819	747	9	-	-
Life	550	492	523	421	384	395	412	395	442	369
Total sentenced to immediate custody	**73,528**	**74,037**	**79,058**	**80,265**	**82,939**	**87,516**	**81,061**	**77,962**	**75,773**	**74,372**
Average custodial sentence length (months)[6]	15.3	15.2	16.0	16.5	16.2	16.8	17.0	18.0	18.3	19.2

Source: Ministry of Justice Court Proceedings Database

. = nil

(1) Excludes other offenders, i.e. companies, public bodies, etc.

(2) Data relate to persons for whom these offences were the principal offences for which they were dealt with. When a defendant has been found guilty of two or more offences it is the offence for which the heaviest penalty is imposed. Where the same disposal is imposed for two or more offences, the offence selected is the offence for which the statutory maximum penalty is the most severe.

(3) Data are given on a principal disposal basis - i.e. reporting the most severe sentence for the principal offence.

(4) Excludes data for Cardiff magistrates' court for April, July and August 2008.

(5) Sentences of imprisonment for public protection were introduced by the Criminal Justice Act 2003, and abolished by the Legal Aid, Sentencing and Punishment of Offenders Act 2012.

(6) Excludes life and other indeterminate sentences.

21.9a Persons sentenced to life imprisonment by sex and age, 2006 to 2015

England and Wales | | | | | | | | | Number of persons

Sex and age	2006	2007	2008	2009	2010	2011	2012	2013	2014	2015
Males										
Aged 12-14	1	1	2	1	0	0	0	2	3	2
Aged 15-17	18	22	22	21	17	13	13	11	18	11
Aged 18-20	46	70	54	57	39	30	47	33	41	35
Aged 21 and over	469	378	417	322	308	328	320	320	360	304
All ages	534	471	495	401	364	371	380	366	422	352
Females										
Aged 12-14	0	0	0	0	0	0	0	0	0	1
Aged 15-17	0	3	1	1	2	2	1	0	0	0
Aged 18-20	2	3	2	1	2	5	1	0	1	3
Aged 21 and over	14	15	25	18	16	17	30	29	19	13
All ages	16	21	28	20	20	24	32	29	20	17
All persons										
Aged 12-14	1	1	2	1	0	0	0	2	3	3
Aged 15-17	18	25	23	22	19	15	14	11	18	11
Aged 18-20	48	73	56	58	41	35	48	33	42	38
Aged 21 and over	483	393	442	340	324	345	350	349	379	317
All ages	550	492	523	421	384	395	412	395	442	369

Source: Ministry of Justice

21.9b persons sentenced to determinate an indeterminate custodial sentences by age group, sex and type of sentence, 2010 to 2015

Sex and age	Year	Determinate Sentence	Extended sentence of imprisonment - EPP	Imprisonment for public protection - IPP	Life sentence	Total Immediate Custody
Male						
Aged Under 18	2010	3,877	10	41	17	3,945
	2011	3,864	26	28	13	3,931
	2012	2,819	6	30	13	2,868
	2013	2,196	0	0	13	2,209
	2014	1,716	0	0	21	1,737
	2015	1,672	0	0	13	1,685
Aged 18-20	2010	12,296	58	107	39	12,500
	2011	11,555	94	70	30	11,749
	2012	9,262	34	76	47	9,419
	2013	7,591	6	0	33	7,630
	2014	7,445	0	0	41	7,486
	2015	6,671	0	0	35	6,706
Aged 21 and over	2010	75,491	370	845	308	77,014
	2011	80,817	502	703	328	82,350
	2012	76,628	280	620	320	77,848
	2013	75,159	24	9	320	75,512
	2014	73,760	0	0	360	74,120
	2015	73,790	0	0	304	74,094
Female						
Aged Under 18	2010	256	0	0	2	258
	2011	266	1	1	2	270
	2012	181	0	0	1	182
	2013	117	0	0	0	117
	2014	106	0	0	0	106
	2015	71	0	0	1	72
Aged 18 - 20	2010	734	0	3	2	739
	2011	582	3	0	5	590
	2012	509	0	2	1	512
	2013	329	0	0	0	329
	2014	389	0	0	1	390
	2015	308	0	0	3	311
Aged 21 and over	2010	7,160	15	23	16	7,214
	2011	7,528	22	17	17	7,584
	2012	6,966	12	19	30	7,027
	2013	6,663	1	0	29	6,693
	2014	7,010	0	0	19	7,029
	2015	6,927	0	0	13	6,940
Sex not Stated						
Aged under 18	2010	26	0	0	0	26
	2011	31	0	0	0	31
	2012	41	0	0	0	41
	2013	27	0	0	0	27
	2014	17	0	0	0	17
	2015	29	0	0	0	29
Aged 18-20	2010	43	0	0	0	43
	2011	38	0	0	0	38
	2012	62	0	0	0	62
	2013	45	0	0	0	45
	2014	33	0	0	0	33
	2015	42	0	0	0	42

21.9b persons sentenced to determinate an indeterminate custodial sentences by age group, sex and type of sentence, 2010 to 2015

Sex and age	Year	Determinate Sentence	Extended sentence of imprisonment - EPP	Imprisonment for public protection - IPP	Life sentence	Total Immediate Custody
Aged 21 and over	2010	227	0	0	0	227
	2011	275	0	0	0	275
	2012	417	0	0	0	417
	2013	435	0	0	0	435
	2014	395	0	0	0	395
	2015	469	0	0	0	469
All Persons						
Aged Under 18	2010	4,159	10	41	19	4,229
	2011	4,161	27	29	15	4,232
	2012	3,041	6	30	14	3,091
	2013	2,340	0	0	13	2,353
	2014	1,839	0	0	21	1,860
	2015	1,772	0	0	14	1,786
Aged 18 - 20	2010	13,073	58	110	41	13,282
	2011	12,175	97	70	35	12,377
	2012	9,833	34	78	48	9,993
	2013	7,965	6	0	33	8,004
	2014	7,867	0	0	42	7,909
	2015	7,021	0	0	38	7,059
Aged 21 and over	2010	82,878	385	868	324	84,455
	2011	88,620	524	720	345	90,209
	2012	84,011	292	639	350	85,292
	2013	82,257	25	9	349	82,640
	2014	81,165	0	0	379	81,544
	2015	81,186	0	0	317	81,503
All Ages	2010	100,110	453	1,019	384	101,966
	2011	104,956	648	819	395	106,818
	2012	96,885	332	747	412	98,376
	2013	92,562	31	9	395	92,997
	2014	90,871	0	0	442	91,313
	2015	89,979	0	0	369	90,348

Source: Ministry of Justice

Criminal Justice System Statistics publication: Sentencing: Pivot Table Analytical Tool for England and Wales

a) The figures given relate to persons for whom these offences were the principal offences for which they were dealt with. When a defendant has been found guilty of two or more offences it is the offence for which the heaviest penalty is imposed. Where the same disposal is imposed for two or more offences, the offence selected is the offence for which the statutory maximum penalty is the most severe.

b) Every effort is made to ensure that the figures presented are accurate and complete. However, it is important to note that these data have been extracted from large administrative data systems generated by the courts. As a consequence, care should be taken to ensure data collection processes and their inevitable limitations are taken into account when those data are used.

21.10 First prison receptions[1] by type of first reception, sentence length, and sex

						Percentage change Oct-Dec 2014 to 2015	New data source			
	Oct-Dec 2014	Jan-Mar 2015	Apr-Jun 2015	Jul-Sep 2015	Oct-Dec 2015		Jan-Mar 2015	Apr-Jun 2015	Jul-Sep 2015	Oct-Dec 2015
All										
First receptions	25,087	25,555	24,790	24,291	23,595	-6%	24,514	23,683	22,958	22,567
Remand first receptions	-	-	-	-	-	-	13,507	13,136	12,617	12,595
Sentenced first receptions	-	-	-	-	-	-	10,963	10,499	10,298	9,919
Fine defaulter	-	-	-	-	-	-	140	123	113	86
Less than or equal to 6 months	-	-	-	-	-	-	6,763	6,377	6,384	6,173
Greater than 6 months to less than 12 months	-	-	-	-	-	-	1,185	1,055	1,023	1,002
12 months to less than 4 years	-	-	-	-	-	-	2,381	2,365	2,267	2,161
12 months to less than 2 years	-	-	-	-	-	-	1,288	1,245	1,243	1,126
2 years to less than 4 years	-	-	-	-	-	-	1,093	1,120	1,024	1,035
4 years or more (excluding indeterminate sentences)	-	-	-	-	-	-	475	545	500	469
4 years to less than 5 years	-	-	-	-	-	-	153	198	175	167
5 years to less than 7 years	-	-	-	-	-	-	161	185	171	152
7 years to less than 10 years	-	-	-	-	-	-	88	87	79	82
10 years to less than 14 years	-	-	-	-	-	-	44	48	39	32
14 years or more (excluding indeterminate sentences)	-	-	-	-	-	-	29	24	29	28
Extended determinate sentence	-	-	-	-	-	-	0	3	7	8
Indeterminate sentences	-	-	-	-	-	-	1	2	0	2
Sentence length not recorded	-	-	-	-	-	-	18	32	11	26
Civil non-criminal first receptions	-	-	-	-	-	-	**44**	**48**	**43**	**53**
Males										
First receptions	22,946	23,418	22,544	22,101	21,481	-6%	22,331	21,404	20,757	20,412
Remand first receptions	-	-	-	-	-	-	12,523	12,113	11,627	11,660
Sentenced first receptions	-	-	-	-	-	-	9,776	9,260	9,095	8,706
Fine defaulter	-	-	-	-	-	-	119	113	94	78
Less than or equal to 6 months	-	-	-	-	-	-	5,942	5,525	5,543	5,306

21.10 First prison receptions[1] by type of first reception, sentence length, and sex

	Oct-Dec 2014	Jan-Mar 2015	Apr-Jun 2015	Jul-Sep 2015	Oct-Dec 2015	Percentage change Oct-Dec 2014 to 2015	New data source Jan-Mar 2015	Apr-Jun 2015	Jul-Sep 2015	Oct-Dec 2015
Greater than 6 months to less than 12 months	-	-	-	-	-	-	1,062	932	937	889
12 months to less than 4 years	-	-	-	-	-	-	2,182	2,147	2,036	1,965
12 months to less than 2 years	-	-	-	-	-	-	1,167	1,121	1,114	1,014
2 years to less than 4 years	-	-	-	-	-	-	1,015	1,026	922	951
4 years or more (excluding indeterminate sentences)	-	-	-	-	-	-	454	510	474	441
4 years to less than 5 years	-	-	-	-	-	-	141	184	164	155
5 years to less than 7 years	-	-	-	-	-	-	155	175	160	146
7 years to less than 10 years	-	-	-	-	-	-	86	79	75	75
10 years to less than 14 years	-	-	-	-	-	-	44	46	39	31
14 years or more (excluding indeterminate sentences)	-	-	-	-	-	-	28	23	29	27
Extended determinate sentence	-	-	-	-	-	-	0	3	7	7
Indeterminate sentences	-	-	-	-	-	-	1	2	0	2
Sentence length not recorded	-	-	-	-	-	-	16	31	11	25
Civil non-criminal first receptions	-	-	-	-	-	-	**32**	**31**	**35**	**46**
Females										
First receptions	2,141	2,137	2,246	2,190	2,114	-1%	**2,183**	**2,279**	**2,201**	**2,155**
Remand first receptions	-	-	-	-	-	-	**984**	**1,023**	**990**	**935**
Sentenced first receptions	-	-	-	-	-	-	**1,187**	**1,239**	**1,203**	**1,213**
Fine defaulter	-	-	-	-	-	-	21	10	19	8
Less than or equal to 6 months	-	-	-	-	-	-	821	852	841	867
Greater than 6 months to less than 12 months	-	-	-	-	-	-	123	123	86	113
12 months to less than 4 years	-	-	-	-	-	-	199	218	231	196
12 months to less than 2 years	-	-	-	-	-	-	121	124	129	112
2 years to less than 4 years	-	-	-	-	-	-	78	94	102	84
4 years or more (excluding indeterminate sentences)	-	-	-	-	-	-	21	35	26	28
4 years to less than 5 years	-	-	-	-	-	-	12	14	11	12
5 years to less than 7 years	-	-	-	-	-	-	6	10	11	6
7 years to less than 10 years	-	-	-	-	-	-	2	8	4	7
10 years to less than 14 years	-	-	-	-	-	-	0	2	0	1

21.10 First prison receptions[1] by type of first reception, sentence length, and sex

	Oct-Dec 2014	Jan-Mar 2015	Apr-Jun 2015	Jul-Sep 2015	Oct-Dec 2015	Percentage change Oct-Dec 2014 to 2015	New data source Jan-Mar 2015	Apr-Jun 2015	Jul-Sep 2015	Oct-Dec 2015
14 years or more (excluding indeterminate sentences)	-	-	-	-	-	-	1	1	0	1
Extended determinate sentence	-	-	-	-	-	-	0	0	0	1
Indeterminate sentences	-	-	-	-	-	-	0	0	0	0
Sentence length not recorded	-	-	-	-	-	-	2	1	0	1
Civil non-criminal first receptions	-	-	-	-	-	-	12	17	8	7

Source: Ministry of Justice

(1) A first reception is a measure which counts a prisoners first movement into custody following a court hearing for a particular set of offences committed, and therefore gives the best indication of the number of new prisoners in the reporting period. A first reception has three categories:

i. **remand first reception**: this describes a prisoners first movement into custody where the prisoner spends at least one day on remand.

ii. **sentenced first reception**: this describes a prisoners first movement into custody where the prisoner has been sentenced at court, and thus spends no time on remand.

iii. **civil non-criminal first reception**: this describes a prisoners first movement into custody where the prisoner has only been committed to custody for a civil offence (e.g. contempt of court).

Due to improvements in IT systems, the 2015 prison releases data is now taken from a different source and, for statistical reporting purposes only, are produced using a different method. The 2015 figures from both the old and new systems have been presented in this release to aid comparison. Subsequent editions of the quarterly prison reception tables will only present data from the new data source.

21.11 Prison population under an immediate custodial sentence by offence group, age group and sex; 2007 to 2015, England and Wales

	30-Jun-07	30-Jun-08	30-Jun-09	30-Jun-09[1]	30-Jun-10	30-Jun-11	30-Jun-12	30-Jun-13	30-Jun-14	30-Jun-15
Males and females	**65,533**	**68,124**	**68,375**	**68,461**	**70,871**	**71,835**	**73,435**	**70,781**	**71,361**	**72,552**
Violence against the person	17,616	18,930	19,946	19,762	20,247	20,431	20,437	19,473	19,596	19,608
Sexual offences	7,336	7,616	7,972	8,176	9,304	9,850	10,473	10,540	11,192	12,230
Robbery	8,747	8,733	9,049	8,738	8,834	9,141	9,279	8,873	8,507	8,174
Burglary	7,920	7,935	7,884	7,403	6,857	7,102	7,345	7,073	7,141	..
Theft and handling	3,706	3,836	3,382	3,134	3,850	4,198	4,646	4,500	4,377	..
Fraud and forgery	1,738	2,020	1,875	1,923	1,544	1,376	1,454	1,320	1,352	1,471
Drug offences	10,613	10,982	10,696	10,420	11,064	10,621	10,682	10,175	10,306	10,323
Motoring offences	1,484	1,377	1,149	1,050	931	841	798	723	820	906
Other offences	5,991	6,439	6,117	6,186	7,353	7,755	7,826	7,625	7,644	7,626
Offence not recorded	383	256	304	1,669	887	520	495	479	426	462
Adults	**57,015**	**59,435**	**59,970**	**60,186**	**63,063**	**64,530**	**66,589**	**65,224**	**66,472**	**68,239**
Violence against the person	15,323	16,483	17,515	17,433	17,997	18,496	18,686	18,010	18,348	18,522
Sexual offences	6,986	7,242	7,597	7,822	8,841	9,396	10,044	10,187	10,867	11,897
Robbery	6,627	6,688	6,942	6,780	7,055	7,398	7,545	7,460	7,358	7,248
Burglary	6,808	6,770	6,711	6,329	5,808	6,052	6,379	6,316	6,527	..
Theft and handling	3,100	3,308	2,949	2,738	3,454	3,797	4,216	4,168	4,111	..
Fraud and forgery	1,688	1,973	1,828	1,881	1,513	1,352	1,425	1,298	1,337	1,445
Drug offences	9,951	10,144	9,926	9,695	10,382	10,002	10,124	9,670	9,699	9,702
Motoring offences	1,288	1,210	1,029	943	842	766	743	672	762	840
Other offences	4,931	5,404	5,215	5,221	6,403	6,813	6,984	7,011	7,062	7,189
Offence not recorded	313	212	258	1,344	768	458	443	432	401	437
18-20 year olds	**6,634**	**6,757**	**6,846**	**6,669**	**6,623**	**6,155**	**5,851**	**4,876**	**4,336**	**3,787**
Violence against the person	1,871	1,942	2,050	1,947	1,934	1,696	1,526	1,298	1,128	954
Sexual offences	277	300	298	281	406	406	382	326	291	291
Robbery	1,611	1,561	1,656	1,521	1,491	1,450	1,431	1,190	968	801
Burglary	828	846	922	816	848	846	815	676	556	..
Theft and handling	415	375	306	268	318	315	358	288	233	..
Fraud and forgery	40	43	46	41	28	22	29	21	13	22
Drug offences	588	727	685	641	618	560	524	471	575	573
Motoring offences	152	141	107	93	84	67	53	50	57	58
Other offences	800	788	734	760	784	745	690	518	491	355
Offence not recorded	51	35	42	301	112	48	43	38	24	24
15-17 year olds	**1,883**	**1,932**	**1,559**	**1,606**	**1,185**	**1,150**	**995**	**681**	**553**	**526**
Violence against the person	422	505	381	382	316	239	225	165	120	132
Sexual offences	73	74	77	73	57	48	47	27	34	42
Robbery	509	485	451	437	288	293	303	223	181	125
Burglary	283	319	251	258	201	204	151	81	58	..
Theft and handling	191	153	127	128	78	86	72	44	33	..
Fraud and forgery	10	4	1	1	3	2	0	1	2	4
Drug offences	74	111	86	84	64	59	34	34	32	48
Motoring offences	44	26	13	14	5	8	2	1	1	8
Other offences	259	247	168	205	166	197	152	96	91	82
Offence not recorded	19	9	4	24	7	14	9	9	1	1

	30-Jun-07	30-Jun-08	30-Jun-09	30-Jun-09[1]	30-Jun-10	30-Jun-11	30-Jun-12	30-Jun-13	30-Jun-14	30-Jun-15
Males	**62,188**	**64,600**	**64,993**	**65,047**	**67,450**	**68,424**	**69,976**	**67,587**	**68,163**	**69,310**
Violence against the person	16,929	18,159	19,108	18,913	19,349	19,520	19,488	18,568	18,694	18,695
Sexual offences	7,287	7,569	7,918	8,116	9,221	9,767	10,390	10,463	11,100	12,124
Robbery	8,437	8,437	8,715	8,406	8,562	8,840	8,951	8,551	8,210	7,867
Burglary	7,723	7,733	7,678	7,202	6,706	6,931	7,137	6,874	6,926	..
Theft and handling	3,332	3,373	2,963	2,741	3,412	3,747	4,141	4,034	3,852	..
Fraud and forgery	1,512	1,725	1,628	1,669	1,359	1,202	1,249	1,166	1,189	1,278
Drug offences	9,569	9,992	9,803	9,561	10,235	9,899	10,108	9,704	9,866	9,903
Motoring offences	1,453	1,356	1,130	1,034	910	824	778	701	794	890
Other offences	5,598	6,024	5,758	5,797	6,895	7,219	7,284	7,090	7,142	7,141
Offence not recorded	348	232	291	1,608	801	475	450	436	390	415
Adults	**54,007**	**56,270**	**56,882**	**57,088**	**59,951**	**61,394**	**63,374**	**62,181**	**63,397**	**65,129**
Violence against the person	14,755	15,830	16,792	16,707	17,223	17,673	17,832	17,162	17,493	17,647
Sexual offences	6,939	7,195	7,546	7,765	8,765	9,321	9,967	10,112	10,775	11,794
Robbery	6,383	6,448	6,663	6,507	6,828	7,143	7,254	7,165	7,081	6,964
Burglary	6,625	6,587	6,520	6,144	5,667	5,887	6,187	6,125	6,317	..
Theft and handling	2,754	2,880	2,559	2,371	3,039	3,365	3,734	3,719	3,598	..
Fraud and forgery	1,469	1,688	1,583	1,628	1,329	1,180	1,222	1,146	1,174	1,253
Drug offences	8,951	9,214	9,078	8,882	9,593	9,315	9,570	9,209	9,266	9,299
Motoring offences	1,259	1,191	1,010	927	822	749	723	651	738	825
Other offences	4,590	5,047	4,886	4,871	5,987	6,341	6,482	6,500	6,589	6,729
Offence not recorded	280	190	245	1,286	698	420	403	392	366	395
18-20 year olds	**6,354**	**6,454**	**6,593**	**6,398**	**6,337**	**5,896**	**5,623**	**4,733**	**4,213**	**3,655**
Violence against the person	1,772	1,843	1,949	1,840	1,820	1,615	1,439	1,244	1,081	916
Sexual offences	276	300	295	279	399	399	376	324	291	288
Robbery	1,558	1,517	1,611	1,473	1,451	1,408	1,396	1,165	948	778
Burglary	817	831	909	803	838	840	800	669	551	..
Theft and handling	392	346	281	245	296	296	335	271	221	..
Fraud and forgery	34	33	45	40	27	21	27	19	13	21

21.11 Prison population under an immediate custodial sentence by offence group, age group and sex; 2007 to 2015, England and Wales

	30-Jun-07	30-Jun-08	30-Jun-09	30-Jun-09[1]	30-Jun-10	30-Jun-11	30-Jun-12	30-Jun-13	30-Jun-14	30-Jun-15
Drug offences	546	672	643	598	579	525	506	461	568	556
Motoring offences	150	139	107	93	83	67	53	49	55	57
Other offences	758	739	711	729	746	684	652	495	462	330
Offence not recorded	51	34	42	298	98	41	39	36	23	19
15-17 year olds	**1,827**	**1,876**	**1,517**	**1,561**	**1,162**	**1,134**	**979**	**673**	**553**	**526**
Violence against the person	402	486	366	366	306	232	217	162	120	132
Sexual offences	73	74	77	72	57	47	47	27	34	42
Robbery	495	472	440	426	283	289	301	221	181	125
Burglary	281	315	248	255	201	204	150	80	58	..
Theft and handling	185	147	124	125	77	86	72	44	33	..
Fraud and forgery	9	4	1	1	3	1	0	1	2	4
Drug offences	71	106	82	81	63	59	32	34	32	48
Motoring offences	44	26	13	14	5	8	2	1	1	8
Other offences	250	238	161	197	162	194	150	95	91	82
Offence not recorded	17	8	4	24	5	14	8	8	1	1

	30-Jun-07	30-Jun-08	30-Jun-09	30-Jun-09[1]	30-Jun-10	30-Jun-11	30-Jun-12	30-Jun-13	30-Jun-14	30-Jun-15
Females	**3,345**	**3,524**	**3,382**	**3,414**	**3,421**	**3,411**	**3,459**	**3,194**	**3,198**	**3,242**
Violence against the person	687	771	839	849	898	911	949	905	902	913
Sexual offences	48	47	54	60	83	83	83	77	92	106
Robbery	310	295	334	332	272	301	328	322	297	307
Burglary	197	203	207	201	151	171	208	199	215	..
Theft and handling	374	462	418	393	438	451	505	466	525	..
Fraud and forgery	227	295	246	254	185	174	205	154	163	193
Drug offences	1,044	990	893	859	829	722	574	471	440	420
Motoring offences	31	22	19	16	21	17	20	22	26	16
Other offences	392	416	359	389	458	536	542	535	502	485
Offence not recorded	35	24	13	61	86	45	45	43	36	47
Adults	**3,009**	**3,164**	**3,088**	**3,098**	**3,112**	**3,136**	**3,215**	**3,043**	**3,075**	**3,110**
Violence against the person	568	653	723	726	774	823	854	848	855	875
Sexual offences	47	47	51	57	76	75	77	75	92	103
Robbery	244	239	279	273	227	255	291	295	277	284
Burglary	183	183	191	185	141	165	192	191	210	..
Theft and handling	346	428	391	367	415	432	482	449	513	..
Fraud and forgery	219	285	245	253	184	172	203	152	163	192
Drug offences	999	930	847	813	789	687	554	461	433	403
Motoring offences	29	20	19	16	20	17	20	21	24	15
Other offences	341	358	329	350	416	472	502	511	473	460
Offence not recorded	33	22	13	58	70	38	40	40	35	42
18-20 year olds	**280**	**303**	**253**	**271**	**286**	**259**	**228**	**143**	**123**	**132**
Violence against the person	99	99	101	107	114	81	87	54	47	38
Sexual offences	1	0	3	2	7	7	6	2	0	3
Robbery	54	43	45	48	40	42	35	25	20	23
Burglary	11	15	13	13	10	6	15	7	5	..
Theft and handling	23	29	25	23	22	19	23	17	12	..
Fraud and forgery	6	9	1	1	1	1	2	2	0	1
Drug offences	42	56	42	43	39	35	18	10	7	17
Motoring offences	2	2	0	0	1	0	0	1	2	1
Other offences	43	49	23	31	38	61	38	23	29	25
Offence not recorded	0	1	0	3	14	7	4	2	1	5
15-17 year olds	**56**	**57**	**42**	**45**	**23**	**16**	**16**	**8**	**0**	**0**
Violence against the person	20	19	15	16	10	7	8	3	0	0
Sexual offences	0	0	0	1	0	1	0	0	0	0
Robbery	13	13	10	11	5	4	2	2	0	0
Burglary	2	5	3	3	0	0	1	1	0	0
Theft and handling	6	6	3	3	1	0	0	0	0	0
Fraud and forgery	1	0	0	0	0	1	0	0	0	0
Drug offences	3	5	4	3	1	0	2	0	0	0
Motoring offences	0	0	0	0	0	0	0	0	0	0
Other offences	9	9	7	8	4	3	2	1	0	0
Offence not recorded	2	1	0	0	2	0	1	1	0	0

Source: Ministry of Justice

(1) Due to the introduction of a new prison IT system the 2010 prison population data is now taken from a different source. The 2009 figures from both the old and new systems have been presented to aid comparison.

On 30 June 2015 the classifications used to report the prison population by offence group transitioned over to the offence groups that the Office for National Statistics (ONS) introduced in 2013. These annual tables retain the figures on the old offence groups so comparisons can be made. Further information on these changes can be found in the "Statistical Notice and Consultation – Part 4" document which is published here: https://www.gov.uk/government/statistics/offender-management-statistics-quarterly-january-to-march-2015

21.12 Crimes recorded by the police, Scotland, 2006-07 to 2015-16

Number & Percentage

Crime group	2006-07	2007-08	2008-09	2009-10	2010-11	2011-12	2012-13	2013-14	2014-15	2015-16	% change 14-15 to 15-16
Total Crimes	419,257	385,509	377,433	338,124	323,247	314,188	273,053	270,397	256,350	246,243	-4
Non-sexual crimes of violence	14,099	12,874	12,612	11,228	11,438	9,533	7,530	6,785	6,357	6,775	7
Homicide etc.[3] (incl. causing death by driving)	159	142	134	106	122	121	91	106	105	81	-23
Attempted murder & serious assault[4]	7,345	6,711	6,472	5,621	5,493	4,693	3,643	3,268	3,166	4,007	27
Robbery	3,578	3,064	2,963	2,496	2,557	2,244	1,832	1,499	1,497	1,327	-11
Other violence	3,017	2,957	3,043	3,005	3,266	2,475	1,964	1,912	1,589	1,360	-14
Sexual crimes[5]	6,726	6,552	6,331	6,527	6,696	7,361	7,693	8,604	9,557	10,273	7
Rape & attempted rape	1,123	1,053	963	996	1,131	1,274	1,462	1,808	1,901	1,809	-5
Sexual assault	3,452	3,502	3,297	3,412	3,220	2,908	3,008	3,405	3,727	3,963	6
Crimes associated with prostitution	779	682	765	661	576	567	534	490	374	247	-34
Other sexual crimes	1,372	1,315	1,306	1,458	1,769	2,612	2,689	2,901	3,555	4,254	20
Crimes of dishonesty	183,760	166,718	167,812	153,256	155,870	154,337	135,899	137,324	126,857	115,789	-9
Housebreaking[6]	30,580	25,443	25,496	23,774	25,017	24,222	21,515	22,272	20,607	17,637	-14
Theft by opening a lockfast place (OLP)	7,422	6,378	6,952	5,074	4,059	3,529	3,239	3,218	2,879	2,193	-24
Theft from a motor vehicle by OLP	16,060	15,217	13,649	10,173	9,495	8,988	6,159	6,189	5,816	4,684	-19
Theft of a motor vehicle	15,000	12,105	11,551	9,304	8,716	7,060	5,731	5,976	5,423	5,028	-7
Shoplifting	28,750	29,186	32,048	30,332	29,660	29,758	26,449	27,693	27,364	28,424	4
Other theft	70,241	64,645	64,384	61,008	64,680	66,681	58,704	58,794	53,539	46,419	-13
Fraud	9,332	8,409	8,316	8,283	8,983	8,892	8,898	8,088	6,913	7,400	7
Other dishonesty	6,375	5,335	5,416	5,308	5,260	5,207	5,204	5,094	4,316	4,004	-7
Fire-raising, vandalism etc.	129,734	118,025	109,430	93,443	82,020	75,201	59,479	54,418	52,091	54,226	4
Fire-raising	4,976	4,635	4,651	4,244	3,966	3,755	3,066	2,549	2,351	2,595	10
Vandalism etc.	124,758	113,390	104,779	89,199	78,054	71,446	56,413	51,869	49,740	51,631	4
Other crimes	84,938	81,340	81,248	73,670	67,223	67,756	62,452	63,266	61,488	59,180	-4
Crimes against public justice	32,052	31,353	29,493	26,885	26,294	26,635	23,401	23,610	21,100	20,361	-4
Handling an offensive weapon	10,110	8,989	8,980	7,042	6,283	5,631	4,015	3,795	3,289	3,111	-5
Drugs	42,422	40,746	42,509	39,408	34,347	35,157	34,688	35,616	36,836	35,479	-4
Other	354	252	266	335	299	333	348	245	263	229	-13

Source: Recorded Crime in Scotland, Scottish Government

Notes:

3. Includes Murder, and Culpable homicide (common law), which includes Causing death by dangerous driving, Causing death by careless driving while under the influence of drink or drugs, Causing death by careless driving, Illegal driver involved in fatal accident and Corporate homicide.

4. For the definition of Serious assault and the distinction between Serious assault and Common assault please see Paragraph 7.13 within Annex 1 of Recorded Crime in Scotland

5. Implementation of the Sexual Offences (Scotland) Act on 1 December 2010 affected the comparability of the breakdown of Sexual crimes over time. For further information please see the 'Data Considerations' section under Sexual crimes within Chapter 3 of Recorded Crime in Scotland

6. Includes dwellings, non-dwellings and other premises. For a more detailed definition see Paragraph 7.15 within Annex 1 of Recorded Crime in Scotland.

21.13 People convicted by main crime/offence, 2006-07 to 2015-16, Scotland

Main crime or offence	2006-07	2007-08	2008-09	2009-10	2010-11	2011-12	2012-13	2013-14	2014-15	2015-16[1]	% change 2014-15 to 2015-16	All offences proved, 2015-16[2]
All crimes and offences	134,416	133,608	125,893	121,041	115,581	108,424	101,018	105,656	106,622	99,950	-6	134,362
All crimes	48,810	48,642	46,799	43,552	42,288	40,671	36,978	36,202	36,525	35,721	-2	48,118
Non-sexual crimes of violence	2,461	2,750	2,659	2,463	2,540	2,461	2,143	1,803	1,739	1,765	1	1,969
Homicide etc	121	136	116	118	117	111	115	93	80	84	5	91
Attempted murder and serious assault	1,496	1,732	1,709	1,511	1,419	1,365	1,285	1,043	1,049	1,112	6	1,204
Robbery	529	548	563	533	526	606	520	448	385	379	-2	436
Other non-sexual crimes of violence	315	334	271	301	478	379	223	219	225	190	-16	238
Sexual crimes	857	727	914	832	756	784	865	1,060	1,152	1,156	0	2,135
Rape and attempted rape	60	49	42	57	36	49	77	91	124	104	-16	178
Sexual assault	186	145	182	159	160	151	204	236	276	279	1	713
Crimes associated with prostitution	306	253	333	250	245	200	142	169	145	86	-41	90
Other sexual crimes	305	280	357	366	315	384	442	564	607	687	13	1,154
Crimes of dishonesty	18,382	17,728	17,429	15,951	15,613	14,772	13,250	12,579	12,538	11,580	-8	15,596
Housebreaking	2,025	1,867	1,860	1,604	1,540	1,498	1,365	1,037	982	853	-13	1,121
Theft by opening lockfast places	398	389	349	312	284	291	247	218	212	197	-7	284
Theft from a motor vehicle	408	447	387	297	270	250	200	143	112	100	-11	199
Theft of a motor vehicle	851	776	733	572	483	450	373	272	321	298	-7	570
Shoplifting	8,548	8,457	8,287	8,098	7,853	7,267	6,500	6,532	6,944	6,583	-5	8,400
Other theft	3,430	3,260	3,113	2,768	2,871	2,961	2,720	2,577	2,343	2,091	-11	2,820
Fraud	1,356	1,337	1,438	1,142	1,067	811	624	681	603	544	-10	965
Other dishonesty	1,366	1,195	1,262	1,158	1,245	1,244	1,221	1,119	1,021	914	-10	1,237
Fire-raising, vandalism, etc.	5,438	5,392	4,375	3,836	3,362	3,016	2,583	2,504	2,445	2,229	-9	2,808
Fire-raising	251	224	244	190	159	146	133	130	133	115	-14	142
Vandalism etc.	5,187	5,168	4,131	3,646	3,203	2,870	2,450	2,374	2,312	2,114	-9	2,666
Other crimes	21,672	22,045	21,422	20,470	20,017	19,638	18,137	18,256	18,651	18,991	2	25,610
Crimes against public justice	9,018	9,825	10,350	9,744	9,822	10,170	9,767	9,670	10,022	10,195	2	14,236
Handling offensive weapons	3,547	3,405	3,516	2,838	2,445	2,265	1,709	1,684	1,586	1,493	-6	1,855
Drugs	8,904	8,547	7,318	7,699	7,531	6,990	6,449	6,720	6,872	7,152	4	9,337
Other crime	203	268	238	189	219	213	212	182	171	151	-12	182
All offences	85,606	84,966	79,094	77,489	73,293	67,753	64,040	69,454	70,097	64,229	-8	86,244
Miscellaneous offences	40,492	39,610	34,165	31,508	29,187	29,470	28,587	29,169	31,131	31,660	2	44,503
Common assault	13,717	13,834	12,966	12,966	12,600	12,762	11,648	11,213	11,768	12,079	3	16,439
Breach of the peace etc.	18,104	17,494	16,003	14,077	12,114	12,544	12,961	13,731	15,588	16,298	5	23,205
Drunkenness and other disorderly conduct	3,363	3,432	898	705	624	309	220	306	250	148	-41	398
Urinating etc.	473	514	81	47	43	20	32	41	43	29	-33	70
Other miscellaneous	4,835	4,336	3,536	3,713	3,806	3,835	3,726	3,878	3,482	3,106	-11	4,391
Motor vehicle offences	45,114	45,356	44,929	45,981	44,106	38,283	35,453	40,285	38,966	32,569	-16	41,741
Dangerous and careless driving	3,774	3,967	3,696	3,405	3,167	2,858	2,811	3,574	3,414	3,572	5	4,130
Driving under the influence	8,066	7,820	7,222	6,232	5,351	5,287	4,735	4,091	3,681	3,539	-4	4,038
Speeding	13,395	14,156	13,589	14,357	12,955	12,381	12,034	14,125	14,008	12,365	-12	12,667
Unlawful use of motor vehicle	13,450	13,609	12,740	12,175	11,052	9,001	7,855	8,515	8,305	6,331	-24	11,233
Vehicle defect offences	1,707	1,414	1,483	1,662	1,723	1,504	1,243	1,611	1,580	1,534	-3	2,532
Seat belt offences	1,211	1,010	1,257	2,199	2,673	1,982	2,052	2,539	2,172	481	-78	595
Mobile phone offences	814	1,197	2,265	2,856	3,603	2,641	2,663	3,096	3,163	2,279	-28	2,389
Other motor vehicle offences	2,697	2,183	2,677	3,095	3,582	2,629	2,060	2,734	2,643	2,468	-7	4,157

Source: Criminal Proceedings in Scotland, Scottish Government

1. Figures for some categories dealt with by the high court - including homicide, rape and major drug cases - may be underestimated due to late recording of disposals - see annex notes B16 to B19 of Criminal Proceedings in Scotland
2. Number of individual offences relating to people with a charge proved, whether or not the main crime/offence involved.

21.14 People convicted by type of court, 2006-07 to 2015-16, Scotland

Number

Type of court	2006-07	2007-08	2008-09	2009-10	2010-11	2011-12	2012-13	2013-14	2014-15	2015-16
All court types	134,416	133,608	125,893	121,041	115,581	108,424	101,018	105,656	106,622	99,950
High court [1,2]	908	862	810	769	706	765	708	702	582	586
Sheriff solemn	4,685	5,195	4,533	4,223	4,022	4,141	4,292	4,180	4,757	4,988
Sheriff summary [3]	87,087	85,703	78,329	69,773	65,360	64,264	60,055	59,200	59,950	59,197
Justice of the Peace court [4]	41,736	41,848	42,221	46,276	45,493	39,254	35,963	41,574	41,333	35,179

Per cent

Type of court	2006-07	2007-08	2008-09	2009-10	2010-11	2011-12	2012-13	2013-14	2014-15	2015-16
All court types	100	100	100	100	100	100	100	100	100	100
High court [1,2]	1	1	1	1	1	1	1	1	1	1
Sheriff solemn	3	4	4	3	3	4	4	4	4	5
Sheriff summary [3]	65	64	62	58	57	59	59	56	56	59
Justice of the Peace court [4]	31	31	34	38	39	36	36	39	39	35

Index: 2006-07=100

Type of court	2006-07	2007-08	2008-09	2009-10	2010-11	2011-12	2012-13	2013-14	2014-15	2015-16
All court types	100	99	94	90	86	81	75	79	79	74
High court [1,2]	100	95	89	85	78	84	78	77	64	65
Sheriff solemn	100	111	97	90	86	88	92	89	102	106
Sheriff summary [3]	100	98	90	80	75	74	69	68	69	68
Justice of the Peace court [4]	100	100	101	111	109	94	86	100	99	84

Source: Criminal Proceedings in Scotland. Scottish Government

1. Includes cases remitted to the High court from the Sheriff court.
2. The figures for the most recent year, and to an extent earlier years, may be underestimated due to late recording of disposals. See annex notes B16 to B19.
3. Includes the stipendiary magistrates court in Glasgow.
4. Includes District courts up to 2009-10.

21.15 People convicted by main penalty, 2006-07 to 2015-16, Scotland

Number

Main penalty	2006-07	2007-08	2008-09	2009-10	2010-11	2011-12	2012-13	2013-14	2014-15	2015-16	% change 2014-15 to 2015-16
Total	134,416	133,608	125,893	121,041	115,581	108,424	101,018	105,656	106,622	99,950	-6
Custody	16,764	16,762	16,946	15,802	15,320	15,950	14,789	14,172	14,035	13,735	-2
Prison	13,234	13,378	13,709	12,760	12,810	13,356	12,727	12,402	12,327	12,023	-2
Young offenders institution	3,199	3,089	2,960	2,679	2,082	2,105	1,606	1,244	1,157	1,183	2
Supervised release order	135	178	206	179	230	267	265	286	324	350	8
Extended sentence	196	117	70	175	185	212	174	223	207	169	-18
Order for life-long restriction	-	-	1	9	13	10	17	17	20	10	-50
Community sentence	16,074	16,709	17,921	16,349	15,615	16,937	17,263	18,272	18,616	18,943	2
Community payback order	-	-	-	-	461	10,380	14,940	16,375	16,794	16,742	0
Restriction of liberty order	1,179	1,155	1,143	931	831	845	919	1,078	1,177	1,646	40
Drug treatment & testing order	865	822	885	807	806	642	607	589	528	486	-8
Community service order	5,285	5,601	5,784	5,471	5,306	2,642	479	141	68	40	-41
Probation and other community sentences[1]	8,745	9,131	10,109	9,140	8,211	2,428	318	89	49	29	-41
Financial penalty	84,820	83,344	73,991	72,491	67,576	59,320	53,429	57,795	56,792	49,918	-12
Fine	83,445	82,019	72,838	71,452	66,492	58,395	52,661	56,921	55,952	49,147	-12
Compensation order	1,375	1,325	1,153	1,039	1,084	925	768	874	840	771	-8
Other sentence	16,758	16,793	17,035	16,399	17,070	16,217	15,537	15,417	17,179	17,354	1
Admonition[2]	15,967	16,084	16,398	15,687	16,421	15,577	15,011	14,839	16,427	16,496	0
Absolute discharge, no order made	413	430	412	522	460	476	361	463	660	774	17
Remit to children's hearing	313	259	209	175	170	140	133	94	67	76	13
Insanity, hospital, guardianship order	65	20	16	15	19	24	32	21	25	8	-68
Average amount of penalty											
Custody (days)	232	249	263	282	278	290	285	296	289	292	
Fine (£)[3,4]	150	175	200	180	180	200	200	180	200	200	
Compensation order (£)[4,5]	150	150	180	180	190	200	200	200	200	200	

1. Includes supervised attendance orders, community reparation orders and anti-social behaviour orders.
2. Includes a small number of court cautions and dog-related disposals.
3. Excludes company fines.
4. Excludes a small number of large fines and calculated as the median.
5. As main or secondary penalty.

Percentage

Main penalty	2006-07	2007-08	2008-09	2009-10	2010-11	2011-12	2012-13	2013-14	2014-15	2015-16
Total										
Custody	12	13	13	13	13	15	15	13	13	14
Prison	10	10	11	11	11	12	13	12	12	12
Young offenders institution	2	2	2	2	2	2	2	1	1	1
Supervised release order	*	*	*	*	*	*	*	*	*	*
Extended sentence	*	*	*	*	*	*	*	*	*	*
Order for life-long restriction	-	-	*	*	*	*	*	*	*	*
Community sentence	12	13	14	14	14	16	17	17	17	19
Community payback order	-	-	-	-	*	10	15	15	16	17
Restriction of liberty order	1	1	1	1	1	1	1	1	1	2
Drug treatment & testing order	1	1	1	1	1	1	1	1	*	*
Community service order	4	4	5	5	5	2	*	*	*	*
Probation and other community sentences	7	7	8	8	7	2	*	*	*	*
Financial penalty	63	62	59	60	58	55	53	55	53	50
Fine	62	61	58	59	58	54	52	54	52	49
Compensation order	1	1	1	1	1	1	1	1	1	1
Other sentence	12	13	14	14	15	15	15	15	16	17
Admonition	12	12	13	13	14	14	15	14	15	17
Absolute discharge, no order made	*	*	*	*	*	*	*	*	1	1
Remit to children's hearing	*	*	*	*	*	*	*	*	*	*
Insanity, hospital, guardianship order	*	*	*	*	*	*	*	*	*	*

Source: Criminal Proceedings in Scotland, Scottish Government

*   Less than 0.5

21.16 People convicted by main penalty, gender and age, 2006-07 to 2015-16, Scotland

		2006-07	2007-08	2008-09	2009-10	2010-11	2011-12	2012-13	2013-14	2014-15	2015-16	% change 14-15 to 15-16
Total[1]		134,416	133,608	125,893	121,041	115,581	108,424	101,018	105,656	106,622	99,950	-6
Males[2]	Total	113,516	112,793	106,300	101,613	97,042	90,902	84,346	87,980	88,690	83,021	-6
	Under 21	25,639	24,526	20,536	17,328	15,145	13,135	10,358	9,187	8,639	8,422	-3
	21-30	40,406	41,224	38,899	37,316	35,177	32,761	30,337	30,703	30,172	28,135	-7
	31-40	25,854	25,146	24,755	24,149	23,564	22,467	21,567	22,836	23,764	22,097	-7
	41-100	21,617	21,897	22,110	22,820	23,156	22,539	22,084	25,254	26,115	24,367	-7
Females[2]	Total	20,602	20,565	19,581	19,424	18,531	17,437	16,557	17,590	17,927	16,929	-6
	Under 21	3,264	3,306	2,830	2,511	2,228	1,952	1,616	1,429	1,449	1,357	-6
	21-30	7,402	7,387	7,314	7,010	6,573	5,989	5,873	5,656	5,515	5,171	-6
	31-40	5,668	5,484	5,069	5,132	4,984	4,853	4,492	5,001	5,317	4,992	-6
	41-100	4,268	4,388	4,368	4,771	4,746	4,643	4,576	5,504	5,646	5,409	-4
Custody[1]		16,764	16,762	16,946	15,802	15,320	15,950	14,789	14,172	14,035	13,735	-2
Males[2]	Total	15,588	15,487	15,593	14,522	14,018	14,582	13,499	12,959	12,742	12,548	-2
	Under 21	3,070	2,987	2,858	2,601	2,014	2,050	1,588	1,238	1,139	1,191	5
	21-30	6,686	6,864	6,718	6,156	6,074	6,059	5,486	5,021	4,982	4,738	-5
	31-40	3,838	3,700	3,841	3,582	3,776	4,094	3,973	4,025	3,901	3,905	0
	41-100	1,994	1,936	2,176	2,183	2,154	2,379	2,452	2,675	2,720	2,714	0
Females[2]	Total	1,176	1,275	1,353	1,280	1,302	1,368	1,290	1,213	1,293	1,187	-8
	Under 21	200	182	182	175	168	160	116	83	84	71	-15
	21-30	592	615	682	581	588	620	599	491	483	401	-17
	31-40	258	312	325	295	324	349	345	395	488	459	-6
	41-100	126	166	164	229	222	239	230	244	238	256	8
Community sentence[1]		16,074	16,709	17,921	16,349	15,615	16,937	17,263	18,272	18,616	18,943	2
Males[2]	Total	13,564	13,886	14,954	13,483	12,977	14,090	14,395	15,245	15,533	15,872	2
	Under 21	4,486	4,471	4,607	3,640	3,446	3,292	2,743	2,635	2,529	2,500	-1
	21-30	4,878	4,935	5,303	5,036	4,696	5,249	5,590	5,674	5,776	5,773	0
	31-40	2,584	2,641	2,988	2,768	2,724	3,168	3,403	3,796	3,972	4,133	4
	41-100	1,616	1,839	2,056	2,039	2,111	2,381	2,659	3,140	3,256	3,466	6
Females[2]	Total	2,510	2,823	2,967	2,866	2,638	2,847	2,868	3,027	3,083	3,071	0
	Under 21	633	667	593	559	453	433	428	340	379	340	-10
	21-30	926	1,092	1,177	1,013	1,020	1,014	1,063	1,030	1,015	961	-5
	31-40	620	651	735	773	661	769	735	882	865	943	9
	41-100	331	413	462	521	504	631	642	775	824	827	0
Financial Penalty[1]		84,820	83,344	73,991	72,491	67,576	59,320	53,429	57,795	56,792	49,918	-12
Males[2]	Total	72,053	71,061	63,240	61,480	57,359	50,260	45,144	48,434	47,746	42,049	-12
	Under 21	14,646	13,597	9,886	8,462	7,071	5,365	4,061	3,697	3,344	3,038	-9
	21-30	25,214	25,792	23,102	22,258	20,360	17,798	15,812	16,478	15,558	13,885	-11
	31-40	16,655	16,147	15,074	14,942	14,085	12,261	11,185	12,005	12,459	10,740	-14
	41-100	15,538	15,525	15,178	15,818	15,843	14,836	14,086	16,254	16,385	14,386	-12
Females[2]	Total	12,490	12,047	10,739	11,007	10,210	8,983	8,174	9,282	9,042	7,869	-13
	Under 21	1,572	1,569	1,206	1,061	909	746	530	519	533	445	-17
	21-30	4,254	4,140	3,754	3,818	3,382	2,907	2,705	2,772	2,604	2,312	-11
	31-40	3,639	3,357	2,890	3,011	2,843	2,463	2,192	2,551	2,558	2,180	-15
	41-100	3,025	2,981	2,889	3,117	3,076	2,867	2,747	3,440	3,347	2,932	-12
Other sentence[1]		16,758	16,793	17,035	16,399	17,070	16,217	15,537	15,417	17,179	17,354	1
Males[2]	Total	12,311	12,359	12,513	12,128	12,688	11,970	11,308	11,342	12,669	12,552	-1
	Under 21	3,437	3,471	3,185	2,625	2,614	2,428	1,966	1,617	1,627	1,693	4
	21-30	3,628	3,633	3,776	3,866	4,047	3,655	3,449	3,530	3,856	3,739	-3
	31-40	2,777	2,658	2,852	2,857	2,979	2,944	3,006	3,010	3,432	3,319	-3
	41-100	2,469	2,597	2,700	2,780	3,048	2,943	2,887	3,185	3,754	3,801	1
Females[2]	Total	4,426	4,420	4,522	4,271	4,381	4,239	4,225	4,068	4,509	4,802	6
	Under 21	859	888	849	716	698	613	542	487	453	501	11
	21-30	1,630	1,540	1,701	1,598	1,583	1,448	1,506	1,363	1,413	1,497	6
	31-40	1,151	1,164	1,119	1,053	1,156	1,272	1,220	1,173	1,406	1,410	0
	41-100	786	828	853	904	944	906	957	1,045	1,237	1,394	13

Source: Criminal Proceedings in Scotland, Scottish Government

1. Includes a small number of cases for companies and where age and gender are unknown.
2. Gender totals exclude companies and where age and gender are unknown. The sum of gender totals may not equal disposal totals.

21.17a Average daily population in penal establishments by type of custody: 2004-05 to 2013-14

	2004-05	2005-06	2006-07	2007-08	2008-09	2009-10	2010-11	2011-12	2012-13	2013-14	% change over past year
Total	**6,776**	**6,856**	**7,187**	**7,376**	**7,827**	**7,964**	**7,854**	**8,179**	**8,057**	**7,894**	**-2**
Remand	1,223	1,250	1,572	1,561	1,679	1,522	1,474	1,601	1,469	1,474	*
Untried	1,036	1,032	1,329	1,306	1,415	1,170	1,112	1,238	1,155	1,163	1
Convicted awaiting sentence	188	218	243	255	264	352	362	363	314	311	-1
Young persons	261	285	361	355	334	305	262	258	198	167	-16
Adults	962	965	1,211	1,206	1,344	1,217	1,212	1,342	1,271	1,307	3
Sentenced	5,553	5,606	5,615	5,815	6,148	6,442	6,380	6,578	6,588	6,420	-3
Young persons (direct sentence)	545	607	621	658	658	690	576	533	473	383	-19
Adults (direct sentence)	4,599	4,553	4,433	4,516	4,879	5,120	5,111	5,332	5,392	5,334	-1
Fine defaulters	51	47	46	28	11	9	9	8	9	9	1
Recalls from supervision/licence	351	397	515	611	600	622	682	702	713	693	-3
Others	5	1	*	*	-	-	-	-	-	-	-
Sentenced by court martial	1	-	-	*	1	-	1	1	1	*	-
Civil prisoners	1	1	1	1	*	1	*	1	*	1	-
Men	**6,444**	**6,521**	**6,833**	**7,004**	**7,413**	**7,538**	**7,418**	**7,710**	**7,598**	**7,462**	**-2**
Remand	1,138	1,166	1,471	1,444	1,545	1,417	1,369	1,493	1,362	1,368	*
Untried	980	975	1,257	1,232	1,330	1,107	1,044	1,171	1,086	1,093	1
Convicted awaiting sentence	159	191	213	213	215	311	325	322	276	275	-1
Sentenced	5,305	5,355	5,362	5,560	5,868	6,121	6,049	6,217	6,236	6,094	-2
Young persons (direct sentence)	515	583	591	634	632	662	545	506	452	365	-19
Adults (direct sentence)	4,386	4,332	4,217	4,294	4,632	4,835	4,825	5,012	5,072	5,037	-1
Fine defaulters	47	44	43	26	10	8	9	8	9	9	*
Recalls from supervision/licence	350	395	511	604	593	615	670	690	702	683	-3
Others	5	1	*	*	-	-	-	-	-	-	-
Sentenced by court martial	1	-	-	*	1	-	1	1	1	*	-
Civil prisoners	1	*	*	1	*	1	*	*	*	*	-
Women	**332**	**335**	**354**	**372**	**414**	**426**	**436**	**469**	**459**	**432**	**-6**
Remand	85	84	101	117	133	105	105	108	107	106	-1
Untried	56	57	72	75	85	63	68	67	69	70	2
Convicted awaiting sentence	29	27	29	42	49	41	38	41	38	36	-5
Sentenced	247	251	253	256	280	321	331	361	353	326	-8
Young persons (direct sentence)	30	24	30	24	26	28	32	28	21	17	-18
Adults (direct sentence)	212	221	216	223	247	286	286	320	319	297	7
Fine defaulters	4	4	3	2	1	1	*	*	1	1	-
Recalls from supervision/licence	1	2	4	7	7	6	13	13	11	10	-
Others	*	*	-	-	-	-	-	-	-	-	-
Sentenced by court martial	-	-	-	-	-	-	-	-	*	*	-
Civil prisoners	*	*	*	*	*	*	*	*	*	*	-

- Nil
* Less than 0.5

Source: Scottish Government: Prison Statistics and Population Projections Scotland 2013-14

Due to an on-going technical issue, there have been delays in the Scottish Government processing prisons data for this table. Therefore, this table will not be updated until the next edition of Annual Abstract.

21.17b Average daily sentenced prison population by sentence length: 2004-05 to 2013-14

	2004-05	2005-06	2006-07	2007-08	2008-09	2009-10	2010-11	2011-12	2012-13	2013-14	% change over past year
Total	**5,551**	**5,605**	**5,614**	**5,814**	**6,147**	**6,441**	**6,378**	**6,576**	**6,587**	**6,419**	*-3*
Fine default	51	47	46	28	11	9	9	8	9	9	*1*
Less than 3 months	81	101	124	116	98	89	78	50	54	55	*2*
3 months - less than 6 months	450	442	444	426	402	350	347	383	355	364	*3*
6 months - less than 2 years	1,161	1,214	1,160	1,226	1,568	1,768	1,683	1,822	1,771	1,715	*-3*
2 years - less than 4 years	884	913	959	1,058	1,099	1,211	1,183	1,172	1,192	1,077	*-10*
4 years or over (excluding life)	1,957	1,841	1,701	1,653	1,642	1,630	1,596	1,599	1,619	1,597	*-1*
Life/Section 205/206 sentences	612	650	666	696	726	763	800	838	875	908	*4*
Persons recalled from supervision/licence	351	397	515	611	600	622	682	702	713	693	*-3*
Others	5	1	*	*	-	-	-	-	-	-	-
Young persons	**559**	**624**	**644**	**685**	**687**	**719**	**604**	**555**	**492**	**399**	*-19*
Fine default	5	5	4	2	1	1	1	1	1	1	-
Less than 3 months	9	14	13	13	11	8	6	3	3	3	*2*
3 months - less than 6 months	55	57	58	58	50	45	37	34	26	27	*5*
6 months - less than 2 years	212	241	241	244	268	307	242	246	200	170	*-15*
2 years - less than 4 years	118	142	136	175	165	182	164	137	129	91	*-29*
4 years or over (excluding life)	131	127	143	136	134	126	103	94	95	73	*-23*
Life/Section 205/206 sentences	19	26	30	31	30	22	23	19	21	18	*-11*
Persons recalled from supervision/licence	8	11	19	25	28	28	26	22	18	15	*-16*
Others	1	*	-	-	-	-	-	-	-	-	-
Adults	**4,992**	**4,981**	**4,970**	**5,129**	**5,460**	**5,722**	**5,775**	**6,021**	**6,096**	**6,021**	*-1*
Fine default	46	43	41	26	10	8	8	8	9	9	*
Less than 3 months	71	87	111	102	88	81	72	47	50	51	*2*
3 months - less than 6 months	395	386	386	367	352	305	310	349	329	337	*2*
6 months - less than 2 years	949	972	918	982	1,300	1,461	1,441	1,577	1,571	1,545	*-2*
2 years - less than 4 years	766	771	823	883	935	1,029	1,019	1,035	1,063	986	*-7*
4 years or over (excluding life)	1,826	1,713	1,558	1,517	1,509	1,504	1,492	1,506	1,524	1,524	*
Life/Section 205/206 sentences	592	623	637	664	696	741	776	819	854	890	*4*
Persons recalled from supervision/licence	343	385	496	586	572	594	656	681	695	678	*-2*
Others	4	1	*	*	-	-	-	-	-	-	-
Men	**5,304**	**5,355**	**5,362**	**5,558**	**5,867**	**6,120**	**6,048**	**6,215**	**6,235**	**6,094**	*-2*
Fine default	47	44	43	26	10	8	9	8	9	9	*
Less than 3 months	75	94	116	108	91	83	73	45	49	50	*3*
3 months - less than 6 months	421	415	419	402	375	324	319	352	331	339	*2*
6 months - less than 2 years	1,075	1,120	1,070	1,133	1,464	1,644	1,554	1,689	1,628	1,580	*-3*
2 years - less than 4 years	831	862	903	1,002	1,035	1,128	1,114	1,096	1,128	1,022	*-9*
4 years or over (excluding life)	1,905	1,791	1,651	1,605	1,593	1,580	1,537	1,528	1,548	1,538	*-1*
Life/Section 205/206 sentences	595	633	649	678	707	739	773	807	841	872	*4*
Persons recalled from supervision/licence	350	395	511	604	593	615	670	690	702	683	*-3*
Others	5	1	*	*	-	-	-	-	-	-	-
Women	**247**	**250**	**253**	**255**	**280**	**321**	**331**	**361**	**352**	**325**	*-8*
Fine default	4	4	3	2	1	1	*	*	1	1	-
Less than 3 months	6	7	8	8	7	7	5	5	5	4	*-15*
3 months - less than 6 months	30	27	25	24	28	26	28	31	24	25	*3*
6 months - less than 2 years	86	94	90	93	104	124	130	133	143	135	*-5*
2 years - less than 4 years	52	51	56	56	64	83	70	76	64	55	*-14*
4 years or over (excluding life)	52	49	49	48	49	50	59	71	71	59	*-17*
Life/Section 205/206 sentences	16	17	18	18	19	24	26	31	34	36	*5*
Persons recalled from supervision/licence	1	2	4	7	7	6	13	13	11	10	*-6*
Others	*	*	-	-	-	-	-	-	-	-	-

Note: Civil prisoners are excluded from this table.　　　　Source: Scottish Government Prison Statistics and Population Projections Scotland

Due to an on-going technical issue, there have been delays in the Scottish Government processing prisons data for this table. Therefore, this table will not be updated until the next edition of Annual Abstract.

21.17c Receptions to penal establishments by type of custody: 2004-05 to 2013-14

	2004-05	2005-06	2006-07	2007-08	2008-09	2009-10	2010-11	2011-12	2012-13	2013-14	% change over past year
Total	**38,348**	**38,747**	**43,504**	**40,448**	**38,986**	**36,518**	**35,990**	**37,003**	**33,837**	**33,626**	*-1*
Remand	18,539	19,105	22,811	22,136	22,303	20,637	21,022	21,658	19,171	19,323	*1*
Unruly certificate [1]	20	24	29	15	10	5	-				
Sentenced	19,653	19,489	20,429	18,227	16,566	15,821	14,942	15,333	14,652	14,294	*-2*
Young persons	2,673	2,935	2,982	2,762	2,447	2,324	1,862	1,804	1,411	1,191	*-16*
Direct sentenced	1,947	2,164	2,285	2,359	2,262	2,144	1,709	1,687	1,325	1,091	*-18*
Fine defaulters	726	771	697	403	185	180	153	117	86	100	*16*
Adults	16,710	16,207	16,980	15,053	13,698	13,057	12,560	13,038	12,788	12,631	*-1*
Direct sentenced	10,629	10,757	11,707	11,842	12,376	11,904	11,461	11,992	11,764	11,570	*-2*
Fine defaulters	6,081	5,450	5,273	3,211	1,322	1,153	1,099	1,046	1,024	1,061	*4*
Recalls from supervision/licence	270	347	467	412	421	440	520	491	453	472	*4*
Sentenced by court martial	6	-	-	2	1	-	2	-	1	-	*n/a*
Civil prisoners	6	4	4	11	4	12	22	12	13	9	*-31*
Legalised police cells [2]	124	125	231	57	102	43	2				
Men	**35,201**	**35,687**	**40,087**	**37,053**	**35,603**	**33,543**	**32,980**	**33,905**	**30,972**	**30,791**	*-1*
Remand	16,787	17,370	20,809	19,965	20,057	18,792	19,129	19,681	17,359	17,518	*1*
Unruly certificate [1]	19	24	26	14	10	5	-				
Sentenced	18,265	18,170	19,041	17,008	15,433	14,697	13,827	14,212	13,600	13,264	*-2*
Young persons	2,519	2,820	2,808	2,630	2,319	2,193	1,725	1,696	1,327	1,119	*-16*
Direct sentenced	1,826	2,076	2,155	2,245	2,143	2,019	1,576	1,587	1,250	1,024	*-18*
Fine defaulters	693	744	653	385	176	174	149	109	77	95	*23*
Adults	15,480	15,008	15,778	13,976	12,703	12,077	11,592	12,035	11,826	11,687	*-1*
Direct sentenced	9,898	10,011	10,904	11,012	11,470	11,008	10,568	11,048	10,873	10,689	*-2*
Fine defaulters	5,582	4,997	4,874	2,964	1,233	1,069	1,024	987	953	998	*5*
Recalls from supervision/licence	266	342	455	402	411	427	510	481	447	458	*2*
Sentenced by court martial	6	-	-	2	1	-	2	-	-	-	*n/a*
Civil prisoners	6	4	3	10	3	11	20	12	13	9	*-31*
Legalised police cells [2]	118	119	208	54	99	38	2				
Women	**3,147**	**3,060**	**3,417**	**3,395**	**3,383**	**2,975**	**3,010**	**3,098**	**2,865**	**2,835**	*-1*
Remand	1,752	1,735	2,002	2,171	2,246	1,845	1,893	1,977	1,812	1,805	***
Unruly certificate [1]	1	-	3	1	-	-	-				
Sentenced	1,388	1,319	1,388	1,219	1,133	1,124	1,115	1,121	1,052	1,030	*-2*
Young persons	154	115	174	132	128	131	137	108	84	72	*-14*
Direct sentenced	121	88	130	114	119	125	133	100	75	67	*-11*
Fine defaulters	33	27	44	18	9	6	4	8	9	5	*-44*
Adults	1,230	1,199	1,202	1,077	995	980	968	1,003	962	944	*-2*
Direct sentenced	731	746	803	830	906	896	893	944	891	881	*-1*
Fine defaulters	499	453	399	247	89	84	75	59	71	63	*-11*
Recalls from supervision/licence	4	5	12	10	10	13	10	10	6	14	*133*
Sentenced by court martial	-	-	-	-	-	-	-	-	1	-	*n/a*
Civil prisoners	-	-	1	1	1	1	2	-	-	-	*n/a*
Legalised police cells [2]	6	6	23	3	3	5					

Source: Scottish Government Prison Statistics and Population Projections Scotland

Notes: Receptions do not equate to persons received since someone receiving a custodial sentence after a period on remand, or several custodial sentences at different times or from different courts, will be counted more than once.

1. The legislation under which children may be remanded in custody on an unruly certificate was repealed in 2010.
2. Reporting on legalised police cells was discontinued in 2010-11 due to closures and very low volumes of usage of these facilities.

Due to an on-going technical issue, there have been delays in the Scottish Government processing prisons data for this table. Therefore, this table will not be updated until the next edition of Annual Abstract.

21.18 Scottish Prison Service Statement of Comprehensive Net Expenditure for the year ended 31 March 2015

	2014-15	2013-14
	£000	£000
Income		
Income from all sources	**(7,491)**	(7,518)
Expenditure		
Staff costs	**163,029**	150,176
Running costs	**115,513**	78,235
Other current expenditure	**31,539**	31,932
Total expenditure	**310,081**	260,343
Operating cost	**302,590**	252,825
Interest payable and similar charges	**11,181**	11,302
Net operating cost	**313,771**	264,127

Other Comprehensive Net Expenditure

	2014-15	2013-14
	£000	£000
Items that will not be reclassified to net operating costs:		
Net gain on revaluation of property, plant and equipment	**(45,176)**	(56,831)
Total comprehensive net expenditure	**268,595**	207,296

Source: Scottish Prison Service Annual Report & Accounts 2014-15

21.19 Number of recorded crimes in the 12 months to 28 February 2017 compared with the previous 12 months - Northern Ireland

Offence group	Number and percentage changes			
	Recorded crime			
	12 months to February 2016	12 months to February 2017[1,2]	change between years	% change between years[3]
VICTIM-BASED CRIME				
VIOLENCE AGAINST THE PERSON	35,530	33,466	-2,064	-5.8
Homicide	*21*	*16*	*-5*	-
Violence with injury	*14,949*	*14,019*	*-930*	*-6.2*
Violence without injury	*20,560*	*19,431*	*-1,129*	*-5.5*
SEXUAL OFFENCES	3,004	3,127	123	4.1
Rape	*770*	*814*	*44*	*5.7*
Other sexual offences	*2,234*	*2,313*	*79*	*3.5*
ROBBERY	757	657	-100	-13.2
Robbery of personal property	*563*	*521*	*-42*	*-7.5*
Robbery of business property	*194*	*136*	*-58*	*-29.9*
THEFT OFFENCES	34,695	31,014	-3,681	-10.6
Burglary	*8,978*	*7,185*	*-1,793*	*-20.0*
Domestic burglary	*5,985*	*4,774*	*-1,211*	*-20.2*
Non-domestic burglary	*2,993*	*2,411*	*-582*	*-19.4*
Theft from the person	*556*	*427*	*-129*	*-23.2*
Vehicle offences	*4,976*	*4,357*	*-619*	*-12.4*
Bicycle theft	*735*	*820*	*85*	*11.6*
Shoplifting	*6,847*	*6,147*	*-700*	*-10.2*
All other theft offences	*12,603*	*12,078*	*-525*	*-4.2*
CRIMINAL DAMAGE	20,605	19,436	-1,169	-5.7
OTHER CRIMES AGAINST SOCIETY				
DRUG OFFENCES	5,481	5,480	-1	0.0
Trafficking of drugs	*873*	*815*	*-58*	*-6.6*
Possession of drugs	*4,608*	*4,665*	*57*	*1.2*
POSSESSION OF WEAPONS OFFENCES	896	901	5	0.6
PUBLIC ORDER OFFENCES	1,432	1,266	-166	-11.6
MISCELLANEOUS CRIMES AGAINST SOCIETY	2,847	2,787	-60	-2.1
TOTAL RECORDED CRIME – ALL OFFENCES (excluding fraud)	**105,247**	**98,292**	**-6,955**	**-6.6**

Source: Police Service Northern Ireland

[1] Figures for the 12 months to 28 February 2017 are provisional and will be subject to change.
[2] Individual crime types may not add to Total Recorded Crime – All Offences as there will be some crimes yet to complete the validation process and be allocated to a crime classification.
[3] '-' indicates that for offences recorded a percentage change is not reported because the base number of offences is less than 50.

21.20 Northern Ireland Prison Receptions by Prisoner Type, Gender and Establishment

		2013	2014	2015	2014/15*	2015/16*
Remand	Maghaberry	2,236	2,194	2,100	2,122	2,170
	Hydebank Wood College Males	420	350	342	350	340
	Hydebank Wood College Females	209	192	191	182	215
	Total	2,865	2,736	2,633	2,654	2,725
Immediate Custody	Maghaberry	1,783	1,710	1,404	1,611	1,253
	Hydebank Wood College Males	258	195	151	185	143
	Hydebank Wood College Females	132	118	89	103	84
	Total	2,173	2,023	1,644	1,899	1,480
Fine Defaulter	Maghaberry	244	121	373	184	405
	Hydebank Wood College Males	33	11	30	19	35
	Hydebank Wood College Females	27	7	53	21	55
	Total	304	139	456	224	495
Non Criminal	Maghaberry	17	18	22	19	24
	Hydebank Wood College Males	1	1	1	1	1
	Hydebank Wood College Females	1	0	1	0	1
	Total	19	19	24	20	26
Males		4,992	4,600	4,423	4,491	4,371
Females		369	317	334	306	355
Establishment	Maghaberry	4,280	4,043	3,899	3,936	3,852
	Hydebank Wood College Males	712	557	524	555	519
	Hydebank Wood College Females	369	317	334	306	355
	Total	5,361	4,917	4,757	4,797	4,726

*Refers to the period 01 April to 31 March
Females includes Transgender persons

Source: Northern Ireland Population 2015

this page is intentionally blank

Transport and communications

Chapter 22

Transport and communication

Road data (Tables 22.4 & 22.5)

The Department for Transport has undertaken significant development work over the last few years to improve its traffic estimates and measurement of traffic flow on particular stretches of the road network. This work has previously been outlined in a number of publications (Road Traffic Statistics: 2001 SB(02)23, Traffic in Great Britain Q4 2002 Data SB(03)5 and Traffic in Great Britain Q1 2003 SB(03)6).

The main point to note is that figures for 1993 onwards have been calculated on a different basis from years prior to 1993. Therefore, figures prior to 1993 are not directly comparable with estimates for later years. Estimates on the new basis for 1993 and subsequent years were first published by the Department on 8 May 2003 in Traffic in Great Britain Q1 2003 SB(03)6. A summary of the main methodological changes to take place over the last couple of years appears below.
Traffic estimates are now disaggregated for roads in urban and rural areas rather than between built-up and non built-up roads. Built-up roads were defined as those with a speed limit of 40 mph or lower. This created difficulties in producing meaningful disaggregated traffic estimates because an increasing number of clearly rural roads were subject to a 40 mph speed limit for safety reasons. The urban/rural split of roads is largely determined by whether roads lie within the boundaries of urban areas with a population of 10,000 or more with adjustments in some cases for major roads at the boundary.

Traffic estimates are based on the results of many 12-hour manual counts in every year, which are grossed up to estimates of annual average daily flows using expansion factors based on data from automatic traffic counters on similar roads. These averages are needed so that traffic in off-peak times, at weekends and in the summer and winter months (when only special counts are undertaken) can be taken into account when assessing the traffic at each site. For this purpose roads are now sorted into 22 groupings (previously there were only seven) and this allows a better match of manual count sites with our automatic count sites. These groupings are based on a detailed analysis of the results from all the individual automatic count sites and take into account regional groupings, road category (that is, both the urban/rural classification of the road and the road class) and traffic flow levels. The groupings range from lightly trafficked, rural minor roads in holiday areas such as Cornwall and Devon, to major roads in central London.

With the increasing interest in sub-regional statistics, we have undertaken a detailed study of traffic counts on minor roads carried out in the last ten years. This has been done in conjunction with a Geographic Information System to enable us to establish general patterns of minor road traffic in each local authority. As a result of this, we have been able to produce more reliable estimate of traffic levels in each authority in our base year of 1999. This in turn has enabled us to produce better estimates of traffic levels back to 1993, as well as more reliable estimates for 1999 onwards.

The Department created a database for major roads based on a Geographic Information System and Ordnance Survey data. This was checked by local authorities and discussed with government regional offices and the Highways Agency to ensure that good local knowledge supplemented the available technical data.

Urban major and minor roads, from 1993 onwards, are defined as being within an urban area with a population of more than 10,000 people, based on the 2001 urban settlements. The definition for urban settlement can be found on the CLG web site at:
www.communities.gov.uk/planningandbuilding/planningbuilding/planningstatistics/urbanrural.

Rural major and minor roads, from 1993 onwards, are defined as being outside an urban settlement.

New vehicle registrations (Table 22.8)

Special concession group
Various revisions to the vehicle taxation system were introduced on 1 July 1995 and on 29 November 1995. Separate taxation classes for farmers' goods vehicles were abolished on 1 July 1995; after this date new vehicles of this type were registered as Heavy Goods Vehicles (HGVs). The total includes 5,900 vehicles registered between 1 January and 30 June in the (now abolished) agricultural and special machines group in classes which were not eligible to register in the special concession group. The old agricultural and special machines taxation group was abolished at end June 1995. The group includes agricultural and mowing machines, snow ploughs and gritting vehicles. Electric vehicles are also included in this group and are no longer exempt from Vehicle Excise Duty (VED). Steam propelled vehicles were added to this group from November 1995.

Other licensed vehicles
Includes three wheelers, pedestrian controlled vehicles, general haulage and showmen's tractors and recovery vehicles. Recovery vehicle tax class introduced January 1988.

Special vehicles group
The special vehicles group was created on 1 July 1995 and consists of various vehicle types over 3.5 tonnes gross weight but not required to pay VED as heavy goods vehicles. The group includes mobile cranes, work trucks, digging machines, road rollers and vehicles previously taxed as showman's goods and haulage. The figure shown for 1995 covers the period from 1 July to 31 December only.

National Travel Survey data (Tables 22.1 & 22.11)
The National Travel Survey (NTS) is designed to provide a databank of personal travel information for Great Britain. It has been conducted as a continuous survey since July 1988, following ad hoc surveys since the mid-1960s. The survey is designed to identify long-term trends and is not suitable for monitoring short-term trends.

In 2006, a weighting strategy was introduced to the NTS and applied retrospectively to data back to 1995. The weighting methodology adjusts for non-response bias and also adjusts for the drop-off in the number of trips recorded by respondents during the course of the travel week. All results now published for 1995 onwards are based on weighted data, and direct comparisons cannot be made to earlier years or previous publications.

During 2008, over 8,000 households provided details of their personal travel by filling in travel diaries over the course of a week. The drawn sample size from 2002 was nearly trebled compared with previous years following recommendations in a National Statistics Review of the NTS. This enables most results to be presented on a single year basis from 2002.

Travel included in the NTS covers all trips by British residents within Great Britain for personal reasons, including travel in the course of work.

A trip is defined as a one-way course of travel having a single main purpose. It is the basic unit of personal travel defined in the survey.

A round trip is split into two trips, with the first ending at a convenient point about half-way round as a notional stopping point for the outward destination and return origin.

A stage is that portion of a trip defined by the use of a specific method of transport or of a specific ticket (a new stage being defined if either the mode or ticket changes). The main mode of a trip is that used for the longest stage of the trip. With stages of equal length, the mode of the latest stage is used. Walks of less than 50 yards are excluded.

Travel details provided by respondents include trip purpose, method of travel, time of day and trip length. The households also provided personal information, such as their age, sex, working status, driving licence holding, and details of the cars available for their use.

Because estimates made from a sample survey depend on the particular sample chosen, they generally differ from the true values of the population. This is not usually a problem when considering large samples (such as all car trips in Great Britain), but it may give misleading information when considering data from small samples even after weighting.

The most recent editions of all NTS publications are available on the DfT website at: www.dft.gov.uk/transtat/personaltravel. Bulletins of key results are published annually. The most recent bulletin is National Travel Survey: 2016.

Households with regular use of cars (Table 22.11)

The mid-year estimates of the percentage of households with regular use of a car or van are based on combined data from the NTS, the Expenditure and Food Survey (previously the Family Expenditure Survey) and the General Household Survey. The method for calculating these figures was changed slightly in 2006, to incorporate weighted data from the NTS and the GHS. Figures since have also been revised to incorporate weighted data. Results by area type are based on weighted data from the NTS only.

Continuing Survey of Road Goods Transport (Tables 22.2, 22.17 & 22.18)

The estimates are derived from the Continuing Survey of Road Goods Transport (CSRGT). The samples are drawn from the computerised vehicle licence records held by the Driver and Vehicle Licensing Agency. Questionnaires are sent to the registered keepers of the sampled vehicles asking for a description of the vehicle and its activity during the survey week. The estimates are grossed to the vehicle population,, and at the overall national level have a 2 per cent margin of error (at 95 per cent confidence level). Further details and results are published in Road Freight Statistics, and previously in Transport of Goods by Road in Great Britain.

Methodological changes

A key component of National Statistics outputs is a programme of quality reviews carried out at least every five years to ensure that such statistics are fit for purpose and that their quality and value continue to improve. A quality review of the Department for Transport's road freight surveys, including the CSRGT, was carried out in 2003. A copy of the report can be accessed at: www.statistics.gov.uk/nsbase/methods_quality/quality_review/downloads/NSQR30FinalReport.doc

The quality review made a number of recommendations about the CSRGT. The main methodological recommendation was that, to improve the accuracy of survey estimates, the sample strata should be amended to reflect current trends in vehicle type, weight and legislative groups. These new strata are described more fully in Appendix C of the survey report. For practical and administrative reasons, changes were also made to the sample selection methodology (see Appendix B of the report). These changes have resulted in figures from 2004 not being fully comparable with those for 2003 and earlier years. Detailed comparisons should therefore be made with caution.

Railways: permanent way and rolling stock (Table 22.21)
1) Locomotives - locos owned by Northern Ireland Railways (NIR), does not include those from the Republic of Ireland Railway System.
2) Diesel electric etc rail motor vehicles - powered passenger carrying vehicles, includes diesel electric (DE) power cars and all Construcciones y Auxiliar de Ferocarriles (CAF) vehicles. (Note: only 16 of the CAF sets were delivered to NIR at the time.)
3) Loco hauled coaches - NIR owned De Dietrich plus Gatwick but not including gen van.
4) Rail car trailers - 80 class and 450 class trailers. Not CAF, they are all powered.
5) Rolling stock for maintenance and repair - a 'standalone' figure - may or may not be included in the above totals. Anything listed as 'repair' or 'workshop' in the motive power sheets is included. Also, those CAF vehicles not yet delivered at the time.
6) The information is a 'snapshot' taken from the motive power sheets at end of March, together with any other known information.

22.23 - 22.26
All data from Airline Statistics, Civil Aviation Authority

22.1 Average number of trips (trip rates) by purpose and main mode: England, 2015

Purpose	Walk	Bicycle	Car/ van driver	Car/ van passenger	Motorcycle	Other private transport[1]	Local bus	London Underground	Surface rail[2]	Other public transport[3]	All modes
						Trips per person per year					
Commuting	16	6	79	12	2	-	12	4	9	2	142
Business	2	-	22	2	*	-	1	1	2	-	31
Education / escort education	42	2	24	26	-	2	11	1	1	1	111
Shopping	37	2	81	37	-	1	16	-	1	2	177
Other escort	9	-	47	24	-	-	2	-	-	1	83
Personal business	18	1	39	22	-	1	6	1	1	2	89
Leisure[4]	33	5	89	81	-	2	13	2	5	6	237
Other including just walk	43	0	-	-	0	0	0	0	0	0	43
All purposes	200	17	381	204	3	7	61	9	20	13	914
Unweighted sample size: trips ('000s)	58	5	108	58	1	2	17	2	5	4	259

Source: National Travel Survey
Telephone: 020 7944 3097
Email: national.travelsurvey@dft.gsi.gov.uk

1 Mostly private hire bus (including school buses).
2 Surface rail includes London Overground.
3 Non-local bus, taxi / minicab and other public transport (air, ferries, light rail, trams).
4 Visit friends at home and elsewhere, entertainment, sport, holiday and day trip.

The figures in this table are National Statistics

The results presented in this table are weighted. The base (unweighted sample size) is shown in the table for information. Weights are applied to adjust for non-response to ensur the characteristics of the achieved sample match the population of Great Britain (1995-2012) or England (2013 onwards) and for the drop off in trip recording in diary data. The survey results are subject to sampling error.

22.2 Domestic freight transport: by mode: 2008-2014

	2008	2009	2010	2011	2012	2013	2014
(a) Goods moved						Billion tonne kilometres/percentage	
Coke and refined petroleum products							
Road [1]	5.5	4.3	5.9	5.8	7.1	5.3	5.5
Rail	1.1	1.1	1.0	1.3	0.9	0.0	0.0
Water	7.6	6.7	5.9	5.4	4.6	5.0	4.1
ow: coastwise	7.1	5.6	5.4	4.7	3.9	4.3	3.5
All modes	**14.2**	**12.1**	**12.8**	**12.4**	**12.5**	**10.3**	**9.6**
Coal and lignite							
Road [1]	1.7	1.2	1.5	0.7	1.0	1.0	1.1
Rail	7.2	5.5	6.1	6.4	7.6	9.0	8.5
Water	29.4	29.9	23.4	24.5	17.8	11.6	8.7
ow: coastwise	19.8	21.8	16.3	18.2	11.9	7.8	6.9
All modes	**38.3**	**36.6**	**31.0**	**31.6**	**26.4**	**21.5**	**18.3**
Other freight							
Road [1]	138.6	119.7	131.4	138.7	142.1	133.0	129.3
Rail	12.8	12.6	11.5	13.4	13.0	13.4	13.7
Water	12.7	11.9	12.6	13.1	13.1	12.5	14.2
All modes	**164.0**	**144.2**	**155.6**	**165.2**	**168.2**	**158.9**	**157.2**
All traffic							
Road [1]	145.8	125.2	138.9	145.2	150.1	139.2	135.9
Rail	21.1	19.2	18.6	21.0	21.4	22.4	22.1
Water	49.7	48.6	41.9	43.0	35.5	29.1	27.0
All modes	**216.5**	**192.9**	**199.3**	**209.2**	**207.1**	**190.7**	**185.1**
Percentage of all traffic							
Road [1]	67	65	70	69	73	73	73
Rail	10	10	9	10	10	12	12
Water	23	25	21	21	17	15	15
All modes	**100**	**100**	**100**	**100**	**100**	**100**	**100**
(b) Goods lifted						Million tonnes/percentage	
Coke and refined petroleum products							
Road [1]	69	53	67	66	82	59	59
Rail	6	6	5	5	7	0	0
Water	25	21	21	20	20	21	23
ow: coastwise	13	11	10	9	8	9	8
All modes	**100**	**80**	**93**	**92**	**109**	**80**	**82**
Coal and lignite							
Road [1]	21	13	12	9	10	9	13
Rail	42	36	37	42	48	53	42
Water	35	34	28	27	22	15	13
ow: coastwise	24	25	20	20	16	11	11
All modes	**98**	**83**	**77**	**78**	**81**	**77**	**68**
Other freight							
Road [1]	1,577	1,290	1,410	1,484	1,494	1,408	1,418
Rail	55	46	47	53	60	64	66
Water [3]	63	54	57	57	54	55	59
All modes	**1,695**	**1,390**	**1,513**	**1,594**	**1,609**	**1,527**	**1,543**
All traffic							
Road [1]	1,668	1,356	1,489	1,559	1,587	1,475	1,490
Rail	103	88	89	100	115	118	109
Water	123	110	106	104	96	91	95
All modes	**1,894**	**1,554**	**1,684**	**1,764**	**1,798**	**1,684**	**1,693**
Percentage of all traffic							
Road [1]	88	87	88	88	88	88	88
Rail	5	6	5	6	6	7	6
Water	6	7	6	6	5	5	6
All modes	**100**	**100**	**100**	**100**	**100**	**100**	**100**

1. Statistics for heavy goods vehicles only, those over 3.5 tonnes gross vehicle weight.

Sources: Road and water - DfT; Rail - ORR
Last updated: December 2015
Next update: December 2016
Telephone:
Road: 020 7944 5235
Rail: 020 7944 2419
Water: 020 7944 4892

22.3 Passenger transport, by mode: annual from 2002

Billion passenger kilometres/*percentage*

	Road																
Year	Buses and coaches	%	Cars, vans and taxis	%	Motor cycles	%	Pedal cycles	%	All Road	%	Rail[1]	%	Air (UK)[2]	%	All modes [3]	%
2002 ʳ	47	6	673	86	5	1	4	1	730	93	48	6	8	1.1	786	100
2003 ʳ	47	6	669	85	5	1	4	1	725	93	49	6	9	1.2	784	100
2004	41	5	673	86	6	1	4	1	724	92	50	6	10	1.2	784	100
2005	43	5	667	85	5	1	4	1	719	92	52	7	10	1.3	781	100
2006	41	5	672	85	6	1	5	1	723	92	55	7	10	1.3	788	100
2007	41	5	674	85	5	1	4	1	724	91	59	7	10	1.2	792	100
2008	43	5	666	84	6	1	5	1	720	91	61	8	9	1.1	789	100
2009	44	6	661	84	5	1	5	1	716	91	61	8	8	1.1	785	100
2010	45	6	644	83	5	1	5	1	699	91	65	8	8	1.0	771	100
2011	43	6	642	83	5	1	5	1	694	90	68	9	8	1.1	770	100
2012 ʳ	42	5	645	83	5	1	5	1	697	90	70	9	8	1.1	775	100
2013	40	5	641	83	5	1	5	1	691	90	72	9	8	1.1	771	100
2014 ʳ	40	5	654	83	5	1	6	1	704	89	75	10	8	1.1	788	100
2015 ᵖ,ᴿ	39	5	658	83	5	1	5	1	707	89	78	10	9	1.1	794	100

1. Financial years. National Rail (franchised operators only to 2008, franchised and non-franchised operators from 2009), urban metros and modern trams.
2. UK airlines, domestic passengers uplifted on scheduled and non-scheduled flights.
3. Excluding travel by water.
See notes and definitions for details of discontinuity in road passengers figures from 1993 and 1996 onwards.
R: ORR revised the passenger kilometres figure for 2015/16 in December 2016

Sources: Road - DfT Traffic Estimates, National Travel Survey; Rail - ORR; Air - CAA
Road: 020 7944 3097, Rail: 020 7944 2419, Air: 020 7944 2168
Email: publicationgeneral.enq@dft.gsi.gov.uk
The Rail and Air figures in this table are outside the scope of National Statistics

22.4 Motor vehicle traffic (vehicle kilometres) by road class in Great Britain, annual from 2002

Billion vehicle kilometres

		Major roads				Minor roads			
		'A' roads							
	Motorway [1]	Rural	Urban [2]	All 'A' roads	All major roads	Rural	Urban [2]	All minor roads	All roads
2002	92.6	136.4	82.2	218.6	311.2	63.9	108.6	172.5	483.7
2003	93.0	139.3	81.8	221.0	314.0	63.6	109.0	172.6	486.7
2004	96.6	141.3	82.8	224.1	320.7	64.9	108.3	173.3	493.9
2005	97.0	141.4	81.8	223.1	320.2	65.6	108.1	173.7	493.9
2006	99.5	143.6	82.5	226.1	325.5	67.9	107.6	175.5	501.1
2007	100.6	143.5	81.3	224.9	325.4	70.3	109.7	180.0	505.4
2008	100.1	142.8	80.1	222.8	323.0	70.3	107.3	177.6	500.6
2009	99.5	142.0	80.4	222.4	321.9	68.3	105.7	174.0	495.8
2010	98.2	139.8	79.7	219.5	317.7	68.1	102.1	170.2	487.9
2011	99.5	141.2	79.3	220.4	319.9	66.3	102.7	169.0	488.9
2012	100.4	140.4	78.1	218.5	319.0	64.6	103.5	168.1	487.1
2013	101.9	140.5	78.1	218.6	320.5	66.4	101.9	168.3	488.8
2014	104.3	143.5	79.4	222.9	327.2	70.1	104.2	174.4	501.5
2015	107.0	147.0	79.9	226.9	333.9	71.5	104.2	175.8	509.7

1 Includes trunk motorways and principal motorways
2 Urban roads: Major and minor roads within an urban area with a population of 10,000 or more. These are based on the 2001 urban settlements. The definition for 'urban settlement' is in 'Urban and rural area definitions: a user guide' which can be found on the Notes & definitions web page

The figures in this table are National Statistics.

Source: DfT National Road Traffic Survey
Telephone: 020 7944 3095
Email: roadtraff.stats@dft.gsi.gov.uk

22.5 Road lengths (kilometres) by road type in Great Britain, 2001-2015

Kilometres

Year	Motorways Trunk	Motorways Principal	Motorways Total	'A' roads Trunk	'A' roads Principal	'A' roads Total	All major roads	Minor roads 'B' road	Minor roads C' road	Minor roads U' road	Minor roads 'C' and 'U' roads	All minor roads	All roads
2001 [1]	3,431	45	3,476	11,369	35,285	46,654	**50,130**	30,196	84,742	225,901	310,643	**340,838**	**390,969**
2002	3,433	45	3,478	10,679	35,995	46,674	**50,152**	30,192	84,858	226,462	311,320	**341,512**	**391,664**
2003	3,432	46	3,478	9,615	37,038	46,653	**50,131**	30,188	84,976	227,048	312,024	**342,212**	**392,343**
2004 [2]	3,478	46	3,523	9,147	37,521	46,669	**50,192**	30,178	84,223	223,082	307,304	**337,482**	**387,674**
2005	3,471	48	3,518	8,708	38,019	46,727	**50,246**	30,189	84,459	223,183	307,642	**337,830**	**388,076**
2006 [2]	3,508	48	3,555	8,706	38,030	46,735	**50,291**	30,018	84,469	229,605	314,074	**344,092**	**394,383**
2007	3,518	41	3,559	8,670	38,073	46,743	**50,302**	30,265	84,423	229,889	314,312	**344,577**	**394,879**
2008	3,518	41	3,559	8,634	38,057	46,691	**50,249**	30,161	84,574	229,482	314,056	**344,217**	**394,467**
2009	3,519	41	3,560	8,596	38,173	46,770	**50,329**	30,141	84,813	229,145	313,958	**344,099**	**394,428**
2010	3,517	41	3,558	8,489	38,218	46,707	**50,265**	30,192	84,827	228,970	313,797	**343,989**	**394,253**
2011	3,529	41	3,570	8,508	38,225	46,734	**50,304**	30,208	84,831	228,953	313,784	**343,992**	**394,296**
2012	3,576	41	3,617	8,507	38,235	46,742	**50,359**	30,214	84,903	229,414	314,317	**344,531**	**394,890**
2013 [3]	3,600	41	3,641	8,505	38,245	46,749	**50,391**	30,217	:	:	314,853	**345,070**	**395,461**
2014 [3]	3,603	41	3,645	8,485	38,301	46,785	**50,430**	30,207	:	:	314,983	**345,190**	**395,620**
2015	3,612	41	3,654	8,478	38,298	46,776	**50,430**	30,286	84,362	230,626	314,988	**345,274**	**395,703**

Values may not sum to totals due to rounding
1. Figures for trunk and principal 'A' roads in England from 2001 onwards are affected by the detrunking programme.
2. New information from 2004 and from 2006 enabled better estimates of road lengths to be made - see Notes and definitions.
3. Minor roads figures in 2013, 2014 and 2016 have been derived differently, with 'C' and 'U' roads combined, as no R199b road length consultation with local authorities took place. See methodology note for further detail.

Symbols
: Value not available   . Not applicable
The figures in this table are National Statistics

Source: Department for Transport
Telephone: 020 7944 5032
Email: road.length@dft.gsi.gov.uk

22.6 Road traffic (vehicle kilometres) by vehicle type in Great Britain, annual from 2002

Billion vehicle kilometres

	Cars and taxis	Light Commercial Vehicles [1]	Heavy Goods Vehicles [2]	Other Vehicles Motorcycles	Other Vehicles Buses & Coaches	Other Vehicles Total [3]	All motor vehicles
2002	390.6	54.7	28.3	5.0	5.2	10.2	**483.7**
2003	390.0	57.4	28.4	5.6	5.3	10.9	**486.7**
2004	394.2	60.2	29.3	5.1	5.1	10.2	**493.9**
2005	392.7	61.8	28.9	5.3	5.1	10.4	**493.9**
2006	397.4	64.3	29.0	5.1	5.3	10.4	**501.1**
2007	397.9	67.4	29.3	5.5	5.4	10.9	**505.4**
2008	395.0	66.9	28.6	5.0	5.0	10.1	**500.6**
2009	394.0	65.5	26.2	5.1	5.0	10.1	**495.8**
2010	385.9	66.1	26.3	4.6	5.0	9.6	**487.9**
2011	387.4	66.6	25.6	4.6	4.7	9.3	**488.9**
2012	386.7	66.4	25.0	4.6	4.4	8.9	**487.1**
2013	386.2	68.5	25.2	4.3	4.5	8.8	**488.8**
2014	394.2	72.4	25.9	4.5	4.5	9.0	**501.5**
2015	398.6	75.5	26.8	4.5	4.3	8.8	**509.7**

1 Not exceeding 3,500 kgs gross vehicle weight, post 1982
2 Over 3,500 kgs gross vehicle weight, post 1982
3 Total of all other vehicles (i.e. motorcycles, buses, and coaches)
4 Data for 1993 onwards are not directly comparable with the figures for 1992 and earlier

The figures in this table are National Statistics.

Source: DfT National Road Traffic Survey
Telephone: 020 7944 3095
Email: roadtraff.stats@dft.gsi.gov.uk

22.7 Cars licensed by propulsion / fuel type, Great Britain, from 1994 to 2014

Great Britain   Thousands/*Percentages*

Year	Petrol	Diesel	Hybrid Electric	Gas[1]	Electric	Other[2]	Total
Total number of cars							
1994	19,620.9	1,576.2	0.0	1.8	0.1	0.2	21,199.2
1995	19,499.8	1,891.3	0.0	2.9	0.1	0.1	21,394.1
1996	20,051.6	2,181.6	0.0	4.1	0.1	0.1	22,237.5
1997	20,384.7	2,440.5	0.0	6.2	0.1	0.1	22,831.7
1998	20,590.5	2,692.9	0.0	9.6	0.2	0.1	23,293.3
1999	21,031.0	2,929.9	0.0	13.8	0.2	0.1	23,974.9
2000	21,232.6	3,152.7	-	20.0	0.2	-	24,405.5
2001	21,641.1	3,459.5	0.6	24.4	0.3	0.1	25,125.9
2002	21,839.5	3,912.4	0.9	28.8	0.3	0.1	25,781.9
2003	21,805.5	4,399.6	1.2	33.7	0.3	0.1	26,240.4
2004	21,976.6	5,010.6	2.8	37.6	0.4	0.1	27,028.1
2005	21,876.0	5,596.1	8.1	39.5	0.6	0.1	27,520.4
2006	21,465.8	6,083.3	16.6	42.4	0.8	0.2	27,609.2
2007	21,264.4	6,657.4	31.8	45.1	1.2	0.3	28,000.3
2008	20,899.1	7,163.5	46.7	49.6	1.3	0.4	28,160.7
2009	20,491.2	7,641.4	61.1	50.9	1.5	0.4	28,246.5
2010	20,083.1	8,202.7	82.1	51.0	1.5	0.5	28,420.9
2011	19,548.5	8,763.5	102.3	50.0	2.6	0.4	28,467.3
2012	19,158.8	9,385.1	125.3	48.7	4.1	0.4	28,722.5
2013	18,870.3	10,064.2	153.6	46.3	6.3	0.4	29,140.9
2014	18,632.6	10,730.9	188.1	43.2	16.2	0.4	29,611.5
Percentage of cars							
1994	92.6	7.4	0.0	-	-	-	100.0
1995	91.1	8.8	0.0	-	-	-	100.0
1996	90.2	9.8	0.0	-	-	-	100.0
1997	89.3	10.7	0.0	-	-	-	100.0
1998	88.4	11.6	0.0	-	-	-	100.0
1999	87.7	12.2	0.0	0.1	-	-	100.0
2000	87.0	12.9	-	0.1	-	-	100.0
2001	86.1	13.8	-	0.1	-	-	100.0
2002	84.7	15.2	-	0.1	-	-	100.0
2003	83.1	16.8	-	0.1	-	-	100.0
2004	81.3	18.5	-	0.1	-	-	100.0
2005	79.5	20.3	-	0.1	-	-	100.0
2006	77.7	22.0	0.1	0.2	-	-	100.0
2007	75.9	23.8	0.1	0.2	-	-	100.0
2008	74.2	25.4	0.2	0.2	-	-	100.0
2009	72.5	27.1	0.2	0.2	-	-	100.0
2010	70.7	28.9	0.3	0.2	-	-	100.0
2011	68.7	30.8	0.4	0.2	-	-	100.0
2012	66.7	32.7	0.4	0.2	-	-	100.0
2013	64.8	34.5	0.5	0.2	-	-	100.0
2014	62.9	36.2	0.6	0.1	0.1	-	100.0

1. Includes gas, gas bi-fuel, petrol/gas and gas-diesel
2. Includes new fuel technologies, fuel cells and steam.

Source: DVLA/DfT
Telephone: 020 7944 3077
Email : vehicles.stats@dft.gsi.gov.uk

22.8 Motor vehicles registered for the first time by tax class: Great Britain, annually 2000 to 2014

Great Britain Thousands

| Year | Private and light goods[1] | | Goods vehicles | Motor cycles, scooters and mopeds | Buses [2] | Special machines etc [5] | Other vehicles [3,4,5] | Total |
	Private cars[1]	Other vehicles[1]						
2000	2,430.0		50.0	183.0	8.0	24.0	176.0	2,871.0
2001	2,431.8	277.9	48.6	177.1	6.8	26.8	168.8	3,137.7
2002	2,528.8	286.8	44.9	162.2	7.8	.	199.0	3,229.0
2003	2,497.1	323.5	48.4	157.3	8.4	.	197.1	3,231.9
2004	2,437.4	347.3	48.0	133.7	8.3	.	210.7	3,185.4
2005	2,266.3	337.2	51.2	132.3	8.9	.	225.5	3,021.4
2006	2,160.7	338.4	47.9	131.9	7.6	.	227.1	2,913.6
2007	2,191.5	347.8	41.1	143.0	9.0	.	264.6	2,996.9
2008	1,891.9	296.4	47.0	138.4	8.3	.	290.2	2,672.2
2009	1,765.5	193.5	27.0	111.5	7.2	.	266.3	2,371.2
2010	1,765.3	229.3	27.0	97.1	6.4	.	292.7	2,417.8
2011	1,663.8	264.8	36.9	96.2	5.8	.	314.0	2,381.5
2012	1,784.1	244.4	38.0	96.6	7.8	.	299.0	2,469.8
2013	1,988.1	276.0	48.1	94.2	7.6	.	302.1	2,716.1
2014	2,180.8	324.9	33.4	103.6	7.0	.	324.1	2,973.7

Source: DVLA/DfT

1. Figures for 1969 to 1979 are estimated using the October 1982 tax classes. Figures for 1951 to 1969 refer to earlier classes. From 1980 onwards figures refer to the October 1990 taxation classes. Figures for 1969 and 1980 are given twice, once for the tax regime before and once for the tax regime afterwards.
2. Prior to 1995 this tax class was called 'Public Transport' and taxis and Hackney Carriages were included. Prior to 1969, tram cars were also included.
3. Includes crown and exempt vehicles, three wheelers, pedestrian controlled vehicles and showmen's goods vehicles.
4. Excludes vehicles officially registered by the armed forces.
5. Special Machines became part of the 'Crown and Exempt' taxation class with effect from January 2002.

Telephone: 020 7944 3077
Email : vehicles.stats@dft.gsi.gov.uk
Notes & definitions (https://www.gov.uk/government/publications/vehicles-statistics-guidance)

22.9a Practical car test[1] pass rates by gender, monthly, Great Britain: 2007/08 to 2015/16

Numbers / *Per cent*

| | Male tests | | | Female tests | | | Total tests[2] | | |
	Conducted	Passes	Pass rate (%)	Conducted	Passes	Pass rate (%)	Conducted	Passes	Pass rate (%)
Annually (financial years)									
2007/08	865,427	409,222	47.3	896,314	369,795	41.3	1,762,148	779,207	44.2
2008/09	849,757	413,014	48.6	888,917	374,466	42.1	1,738,992	787,618	45.3
2009/10	753,618	370,049	49.1	780,007	333,770	42.8	1,533,738	703,859	45.9
2010/11	772,551	383,417	49.6	833,040	360,639	43.3	1,605,599	744,058	46.3
2011/12	744,487	374,472	50.3	824,572	361,685	43.9	1,569,069	736,158	46.9
2012/13	682,699	345,599	50.6	753,774	331,653	44.0	1,436,481	677,255	47.1
2013/14	706,757	358,143	50.7	770,823	337,436	43.8	1,477,585	695,580	47.1
2014/15	733,161	370,343	50.5	799,341	348,367	43.6	1,532,504	718,711	46.9
2015/16	736,261	372,777	50.6	801,472	350,667	43.8	1,537,735	723,444	47.0

1 Includes test categories B and B1 Source: DVSA/DfT

2 Gender details about licence holders from other countries (such as Northern Ireland) are reliant upon information being captured accurately at the time of booking a test. In some cases, gender will not have been captured. Where gender has not been captured these candidates will only be recorded in total tests conducted. There will therefore be small anomalies where the gender totals do not match overall totals. Please note that all statistics are provisional until information for the whole financial year is published. Until that point, data for months / quarters from within the current financial year can be revised.

Telephone: 020 7944 3077
Email : vehicles.stats@dft.gsi.gov.uk
Notes & definitions (https://www.gov.uk/government/organisations/department-for-transport/series/driving-tests-and-instructors-statistics)

22.9b Practical motorcycle test[1] (Module 1) pass rates by gender, monthly, Great Britain, 2009/10 to 2015/16

Numbers / *Per cent*

	Male tests			Female tests			Total tests		
	Conducted	Passes	Pass rate (%)	Conducted	Passes	Pass rate (%)	Conducted	Passes	Pass rate (%)
Annually (financial years)									
2009/10[1]	44,165	28,123	63.7	6,655	2,765	41.5	50,823	30,891	60.8
2010/11	50,046	33,735	67.4	7,665	3,498	45.6	57,711	37,233	64.5
2011/12	52,726	38,325	72.7	6,868	3,706	54.0	59,594	42,031	70.5
2012/13	58,280	42,490	72.9	7,770	4,092	52.7	66,050	46,582	70.5
2013/14	41,299	29,366	71.1	4,964	2,458	49.5	46,263	31,824	68.8
2014/15	46,361	33,398	72.0	5,644	2,863	50.7	52,005	36,261	69.7
2015/16	49,784	36,744	73.8	5,986	3,043	50.8	55,770	39,787	71.3

1 All test data excludes mopeds.

Source: DVSA/DfT

2 The two-part modular motorcycle test was introduced on 27 April 2009. The figures for April 2009 only includes tests conducted between 27 and 30 April 2009. Please note that all statistics are provisional until information for the whole financial year is published. Until that point, data for months / quarters from within the current financial year can be revised.

Telephone: 020 7944 3077
Email : vehicles.stats@dft.gsi.gov.uk
Notes & definitions (https://www.gov.uk/government/organisations/department-for-transport/series/driving-tests-and-instructors-statistics)

22.9c Practical motorcycle test[1] (Module 2) pass rates by gender, Great Britain 2009/10 to 2015/16

Numbers / *Per cent*

	Male tests			Female tests			Total tests		
	Conducted	Passes	Pass rate (%)	Conducted	Passes	Pass rate (%)	Conducted	Passes	Pass rate (%)
Annually (financial years)									
2009/10[1]	34,550	24,122	69.8	3,363	2,352	69.9	37,914	26,474	69.8
2010/11	44,991	31,236	69.4	4,654	3,249	69.8	49,645	34,485	69.5
2011/12	52,619	36,367	69.1	5,292	3,559	67.3	57,911	39,926	68.9
2012/13	59,237	40,871	69.0	5,891	4,018	68.2	65,128	44,889	68.9
2013/14	40,052	28,110	70.2	3,423	2,343	68.4	43,475	30,453	70.0
2014/15	45,211	31,847	70.4	3,983	2,709	68.0	49,194	34,556	70.2
2015/16	48,972	35,001	71.5	4,212	2,924	69.4	53,184	37,925	71.3

1 All test data excludes mopeds.

Source: DVSA/DfT

2 The two-part modular motorcycle test was introduced on 27 April 2009. The figures for April 2009 only includes tests conducted between 27 and 30 April 2009. Please note that all statistics are provisional until information for the whole financial year is published. Until that point, data for months / quarters from within the current financial year can be revised.

Telephone: 020 7944 3077
Email : vehicles.stats@dft.gsi.gov.uk
Notes & definitions (https://www.gov.uk/government/organisations/department-for-transport/series/driving-tests-and-instructors-statistics)

22.9d Practical large goods vehicle (LGV) test[1] rates by gender, Great Britain 2007/08 to 2015/16

Numbers / *Per cent*

	Male tests			Female tests			Total tests		
	Conducted	Passes	Pass rate (%)	Conducted	Passes	Pass rate (%)	Conducted	Passes	Pass rate (%)
Annually (financial years)									
2007/08	66,445	30,693	46.2	4,305	2,077	48.2	70,766	32,779	46.3
2008/09	61,950	30,258	48.8	3,892	2,035	52.3	65,852	32,298	49.0
2009/10	43,119	22,058	51.2	3,305	1,816	54.9	46,426	23,876	51.4
2010/11	41,011	21,122	51.5	2,883	1,542	53.5	43,894	22,664	51.6
2011/12	43,525	22,762	52.3	3,024	1,639	54.2	46,549	24,401	52.4
2012/13	42,937	22,736	53.0	3,309	1,762	53.2	46,246	24,498	53.0
2013/14	44,993	24,296	54.0	3,290	1,928	58.6	48,283	26,224	54.3
2014/15	51,314	28,310	55.2	3,847	2,264	58.9	55,161	30,574	55.4
2015/16	65,295	36,113	55.3	4,938	2,887	58.5	70,233	39,000	55.5

1 Includes test categories C, C1, C+E, C1+E   Source: DVSA/DfT

Please note that all statistics are provisional until information for the whole financial year is published. Until that point, data for months / quarters from within the current financial year can be revised.

Telephone: 020 7944 3077
Email : vehicles.stats@dft.gsi.gov.uk
Notes & definitions (https://www.gov.uk/government/organisations/department-for-transport/series/driving-tests-and-instructors-statistics)

22.9e Practical passenger carrying vehicle (PCV) CPC test[1] rates by gender, Great Britain: 2008/09 to 2015/16

Numbers / *Per cent*

	Male tests			Female tests			Total tests		
	Conducted	Passes	Pass rate (%)	Conducted	Passes	Pass rate (%)	Conducted	Passes	Pass rate (%)
Annually (financial years)									
2008/09	1,089	763	70.1	123	92	74.8	1,212	855	70.5
2009/10	2,436	1,881	77.2	273	225	82.4	2,709	2,106	77.7
2010/11	2,280	1,892	83.0	265	230	86.8	2,545	2,122	83.4
2011/12	2,177	1,852	85.1	296	263	88.9	2,474	2,116	85.5
2012/13	2,626	2,254	85.8	309	259	83.8	2,935	2,513	85.6
2013/14	3,179	2,760	86.8	372	330	88.7	3,551	3,090	87.0
2014/15	2,720	2,364	86.9	325	291	89.5	3,046	2,656	87.2
2015/16	2,910	2,510	86.3	374	345	92.2	3,284	2,855	86.9

1 Includes all PCV CPC mod 4 tests   Source: DVSA/DfT

Please note that all statistics are provisional until information for the whole financial year is published. Until that point, data for months / quarters from within the current financial year can be revised.

Telephone: 020 7944 3077
Email : vehicles.stats@dft.gsi.gov.uk
Notes & definitions (https://www.gov.uk/government/organisations/department-for-transport/series/driving-tests-and-instructors-statistics)

22.10 Full car driving licence holders by age and gender: England, 1975/76 to 2015

	Percentage								Estimated licence holders (millions)	Unweighted sample size (individuals aged 17+)
	All aged 17+	17-20	21-29	30-39	40-49	50-59	60-69	70+		
All adults:										
1975/76	48	28	59	67	60	50	35	15	19.4	17,064
1985/86	57	33	63	74	71	60	47	27	24.3	19,835
1989/91	64	44	74	78	79	68	55	32	24.1	17,466
1992/94	67	48	75	82	80	74	59	33	25.4	16,401
1995/97[1]	69	44	74	82	82	76	64	39	26.3	16,716
1998/00	71	41	75	85	83	78	68	40	27.3	16,529
2002	71	32	67	83	83	81	70	45	27.6	13,836
2003	71	29	67	82	84	81	72	44	27.8	14,556
2004	70	27	65	82	83	81	73	46	27.8	14,228
2005	72	31	65	82	84	83	75	52	28.8	15,063
2006	72	35	67	82	84	82	76	51	29.3	14,815
2007	72	38	66	81	84	82	76	53	29.5	14,693
2008	73	36	64	83	84	83	78	53	30.0	14,290
2009	73	36	64	80	84	83	80	55	30.2	14,791
2010	73	33	63	81	85	83	80	57	30.6	14,118
2011	72	31	64	78	84	83	80	59	30.7	13,723
2012	73	36	64	78	85	82	80	59	31.1	14,578
2013	74	31	66	80	85	84	82	62	31.9	14,694
2014	73	29	63	79	85	83	81	62	31.8	13,964
2015	74	33	64	78	84	84	81	64	32.2	14,264
Males:										
1975/76	69	36	78	85	83	75	58	32	13.4	8,113
1985/86	74	37	73	86	87	81	72	51	15.1	9,367
1989/91	80	54	83	88	90	86	79	58	14.5	8,306
1992/94	82	55	83	90	89	88	82	59	14.8	7,652
1995/97[1]	82	51	81	90	89	89	83	65	14.9	7,934
1998/00	82	44	81	90	91	89	83	66	15.2	7,857
2002	80	34	72	89	89	89	85	68	15.2	6,586
2003	81	34	72	87	91	91	88	69	15.4	6,950
2004	80	29	69	87	89	90	87	72	15.3	6,723
2005	81	36	68	86	90	91	88	74	15.7	7,159
2006	81	37	71	87	88	90	90	77	15.9	7,078
2007	81	41	69	86	90	90	88	77	16.0	6,978
2008	81	36	67	88	90	91	90	75	16.2	6,818
2009	80	38	67	85	89	91	91	77	16.3	7,021
2010	80	34	66	86	90	89	90	78	16.4	6,769
2011	80	31	68	81	89	90	90	79	16.4	6,521
2012	80	40	67	81	88	89	90	80	16.6	6,981
2013	81	30	67	83	90	90	91	82	16.9	7,048
2014	80	34	66	82	91	89	90	80	17.0	6,630
2015	80	33	67	81	88	90	90	81	17.1	6,805
Females:										
1975/76	29	20	43	48	37	24	15	4	6.0	8,951
1985/86	41	29	54	62	56	41	24	11	9.2	10,468
1989/91	50	35	65	68	67	50	33	15	9.7	9,160
1992/94	55	42	69	74	71	59	38	16	10.8	8,749
1995/97[1]	58	36	68	74	74	63	46	22	11.4	8,781
1998/00	61	38	70	79	75	67	54	22	12.1	8,672
2002	61	30	62	77	77	74	55	28	12.5	7,250
2003	61	24	62	77	77	71	58	26	12.4	7,606
2004	61	24	61	77	77	71	60	28	12.5	7,505
2005	64	26	61	77	79	75	62	36	13.2	7,904
2006	64	32	62	78	80	74	64	32	13.4	7,737
2007	64	35	63	76	78	74	64	36	13.4	7,715
2008	65	35	61	78	80	76	67	37	13.8	7,472
2009	65	33	62	76	79	75	69	38	13.9	7,770
2010	66	32	60	77	80	77	70	41	14.2	7,349
2011	66	30	59	74	79	76	71	44	14.3	7,202
2012	66	31	62	75	81	75	71	43	14.5	7,597
2013	68	31	64	77	80	77	73	47	14.9	7,646
2014	67	25	61	75	80	78	73	47	14.8	7,334
2015	68	32	61	74	80	78	73	50	15.1	7,459

1 Figures prior to 1989 for Great Britain, rather than England only.
2 Figures prior to 1995 are based on unweighted data.
Notes & definitions: https://www.gov.uk/government/collections/national-travel-survey-statistics

Source: National Travel Survey
Telephone: 020 7944 3097
Email: national.travelsurvey@dft.gsi.gov.uk

The figures in this table are National Statistics
The results presented in this table are weighted. The base (unweighted sample size) is shown in the table for information.

Weights are applied to adjust for non-response to ensure the characteristics of the achieved sample match the population of Great Britain (1995-2012) or England (2013 onwards) and for the drop off in trip recording in diary data.
The survey results are subject to sampling error.

22.11a Household car availability: England, 2002 to 2015

Year	Percentage No car / van	One car / van	Two or more cars / vans	All households	Cars / vans per household	Cars / vans per adult (aged 17+)	Unweighted sample size (households)
2002	26	44	30	100	1.09	0.59	7,535
2003	26	42	31	100	1.11	0.60	7,853
2004	25	44	30	100	1.11	0.59	7,692
2005	25	43	33	100	1.16	0.61	8,065
2006	24	44	32	100	1.16	0.61	7,884
2007	25	43	33	100	1.16	0.61	7,879
2008	25	43	33	100	1.15	0.61	7,665
2009	25	43	32	100	1.15	0.60	7,858
2010	25	42	33	100	1.17	0.61	7,534
2011	25	43	32	100	1.15	0.60	7,289
2012	25	44	31	100	1.14	0.60	7,724
2013	25	43	32	100	1.15	0.60	7,820
2014	24	43	32	100	1.16	0.61	7,436
2015	25	42	33	100	1.18	0.62	7,563

The figures in this table are National Statistics

Weights are applied to adjust for non-response to ensure the characteristics of the achieved sample match the population of Great Britain (1995-2012) or England (2013 onwards) and for the drop off in trip recording in diary data.

The survey results are subject to sampling error.

Notes & definitions: https://www.gov.uk/government/collections/national-travel-survey-statistics

Source: National Travel Survey
Telephone: 020 7944 3097
Email: national.travelsurvey.dft.gsi.gov.uk

22.11b Household car ownership by region and Rural-Urban Classification: England, 2002/03 and 2014/15[1]

	Percentage No car / van		One car / van		Two or more cars / vans		Cars / vans per household		Unweighted sample size (households)	
	2002/03	2014/15	2002/03	2014/15	2002/03	2014/15	2002/03	2014/15	2002/03	2014/15
Region of residence:										
North East	37	29	44	42	20	29	0.86	1.06	847	825
North West	27	24	44	43	28	32	1.05	1.15	2,164	2,035
Yorkshire and The Humber	30	25	45	42	25	33	0.99	1.13	1,605	1,505
East Midlands	20	22	45	42	34	36	1.20	1.21	1,321	1,271
West Midlands	26	24	40	41	34	35	1.15	1.22	1,593	1,519
East of England	20	17	42	46	38	37	1.26	1.31	1,637	1,643
London	41	41	40	42	19	17	0.82	0.80	2,228	2,210
South East	18	18	43	42	39	40	1.30	1.34	2,332	2,480
South West	19	18	47	42	34	39	1.24	1.31	1,661	1,511
England excluding London	24	22	44	43	33	36	1.16	1.23	13,160	12,789
England	26	25	43	43	31	33	1.10	1.17	15,388	14,999
Rural-Urban Classification[2] of residence:										
Urban Conurbation	35	33	41	42	24	25	0.93	0.98	5,882	5,615
Urban City and Town	24	23	46	44	31	33	1.13	1.18	6,842	6,607
Rural Town and Fringe	17	14	42	44	41	42	1.32	1.39	1,440	1,450
Rural Village, Hamlet and Isolated Dwelling	7	6	39	35	53	59	1.63	1.77	1,224	1,327
All areas	26	25	43	43	31	33	1.10	1.17	15,388	14,999

Source: National Travel Survey
Telephone: 020 7944 3097
Email: national.travelsurvey@dft.gsi.gov.uk

1 Two survey years combined, e.g. 2014 and 2015. A survey year runs from mid-January to mid-January.

2 For more information on Rural-Urban Classifications see:

https://www.gov.uk/government/collections/rural-urban-definition

Notes & definitions: https://www.gov.uk/government/collections/national-travel-survey-statistics

The figures in this table are National Statistics

The results presented in this table are weighted. The base (unweighted sample size) is shown in the table for information.

Weights are applied to adjust for non-response to ensure the characteristics of the achieved sample match the population of Great Britain (1995-2012) or England (2013 onwards) and for the drop off in trip recording in diary data.

The survey results are subject to sampling error.

22.12 Vehicles licensed by taxation group: Northern Ireland 2011-2015[1]

Number at 31 December

Taxation Group (Taxation Classes)	2011		2012		2013		2014		2015	
	Number	%	Number	%	Number	%	Number	%	Number	%
Private Light Goods (10, 11, 23, 36, 39, 48, 49, 53, 59)	879,787	83.5	885,976	83.6	901,357	84.5	916,598	84.7	941,330	85.3
Motorcycles, Scooters & Mopeds (17, 18, 93)	25,196	2.4	23,560	2.2	22,745	2.1	22,151	2.0	20,848	1.9
General (HGV) Goods (1, 2, 45, 46)	23,084	2.2	22,114	2.1	22,052	2.1	21,868	2.0	20,065	1.8
Bus (34, 38)	3,015	0.3	3,094	0.3	3,315	0.3	3,262	0.3	3,283	0.3
Agricultural/Tractors (40 & 44)	18,555	1.8	19,775	1.9	20,784	1.9	21,963	2.0	22,338	2.0
Other (14-16, 19, 37, 47, 50, 55-58, 79, 81, 82, 91, 92)	2,159	0.2	2,154	0.2	2,200	0.2	2,426	0.2	2,579	0.2
Crown (60)	7,646	0.7	7,862	0.7	1,936	0.2	1,855	0.2	1,848	0.2
Exempt (>60 except 79, 81, 82, 91, 92, 93)	93,896	8.9	95,793	9.0	92,115	8.6	91,604	8.5	90,791	8.2
All Vehicles	**1,053,338**	**100.0**	**1,060,328**	**100.0**	**1,066,504**	**100.0**	**1,081,727**	**100.0**	**1,103,082**	**100.0**

Source: Driver and Vehicle Agency (DVA)

1 2015 PLG classification for Northern Ireland is based on the classification used for Great Britain by DfT i.e includes taxation classes 10, 11, 23, 36, 39, 48, 49, 53 & 59. Previously the categorisation of taxation groups for Northern Ireland differed to that used for Great Britain by DfT. In Private Light Goods, NI excluded 10, 23 and 53 and included 91 and 92.

22.13 Motor vehicles registered for the first time in NI by vehicle type: 2011-2015[1, 2]

Number

Vehicle Type	2011	2012	2013	2014	2015
Private Cars					
New cars	47,766	47,990	52,951	59,232	57,737
Used cars	30,129	31,601	34,814	21,448	1,137
All Private Cars	**77,895**	**79,591**	**87,765**	**80,680**	**58,874**
Buses					
New buses	:	:	:	:	251
Used buses	:	:	:	:	57
All Buses	**319**	**411**	**584**	**594**	**308**
Light Goods					
New Light Goods	:	:	:	:	6,954
Used Light Goods	:	:	:	:	324
All Light Goods	**8,984**	**8,609**	**9,573**	**9,079**	**7,278**
Heavy Goods					
New Heavy Goods	:	:	:	:	1,054
Used Heavy Goods	:	:	:	:	173
All Heavy Goods	**2,509**	**2,531**	**2,973**	**2,232**	**1,227**
Agricultural Vehicles[3]					
New Agricultural Vehicles	:	:	:	:	655
Used Agricultural Vehicles	:	:	:	:	162
All Agricultural Vehicles	**1,985**	**2,099**	**2,022**	**2,021**	**817**
Motorcycles[4]					
New Motorcycles	:	:	:	:	1,514
Used Motorcycles	:	:	:	:	140
All Motorcycles	**2,198**	**2,011**	**2,048**	**2,080**	**1,654**
Other Vehicles[5]					
New Other Vehicles	:	:	:	:	328
Used Other Vehicles	:	:	:	:	43
All Other Vehicles	**23**	**15**	**21**	**207**	**371**
New Vehicles	:	:	:	:	68,493
Used Vehicles	:	:	:	:	2,036
All Vehicles	**93,913**	**95,267**	**104,986**	**96,893**	**70,529**

Source: DVA

1 Prior to July 2014, any vehicle registered in NI for the first time, even if previously registered in GB, would have been counted as a first registration in NI. Since July 2014, only vehicles that have not previously been registered anywhere else in the UK are classed as NI first registrations, in line with the UK definition.

2 While figures for new vehicles are directly comparable, figures for used vehicles from July 2014 onwards are not directly comparable with previous figures due to the change in definition of a first registration

3 This category of vehicle body type has been changed to reflect the full coverage of agricultural vehicles (including tractors).

4 This category of vehicle body type also includes mopeds and scooters.

5 Prior to July 2014, this category of vehicle body type was classified as 'General Haulage and Special Types'. From July 2014 it is titled 'Other Vehicles' which brings the classification into line with the category presentation used by DfT. The category now includes special purpose vehicles, taxis, tricycles, not recorded and others.

22.14 Vehicle kilometres on local bus services by metropolitan area status and country: Great Britain, 2000/01 to 2015/16

Million

Year	Estimation method[1]	London	English metropolitan areas	English non-metropolitan areas	England	Scotland	Wales	Great Britain	England outside London
2000/01		371	654	1,134	2,158	369	126	2,653	1,788
2001/02		381	646	1,102	2,129	368	126	2,622	1,748
2002/03		404	630	1,088	2,122	374	123	2,619	1,718
2003/04		444	596	1,069	2,109	369	113	2,590	1,665
2004/05	Old	:	575	1,077	2,122	357	116	2,594	1,652
2004/05 r	New	470	592	1,061	2,122	359	130	2,611	1,652
2005/06 r		461	588	1,071	2,121	374	128	2,622	1,660
2006/07 r		465	591	1,066	2,122	384	124	2,630	1,657
2007/08 r		465	597	1,067	2,129	397	124	2,650	1,664
2008/09 r		474	589	1,076	2,139	386	126	2,651	1,665
2009/10 r		479	569	1,071	2,119	377	125	2,620	1,640
2010/11 r		481	567	1,072	2,120	346	125	2,591	1,639
2011/12 r		485	563	1,054	2,103	338	117	2,557	1,617
2012/13 r		486	553	1,049	2,088	327	116	2,531	1,602
2013/14 r		487	546	1,047	2,079	332	113	2,524	1,593
2014/15 r		485	531	1,040	2,056	330	106	2,493	1,571
2015/16		488	516	1,012	2,016	328	104	2,448	1,528

Source: DfT Public Service Vehicle Survey, Transport for London
Telephone: 020 7944 3094, Email: bus.statistics@dft.gsi.gov.uk

1 Break in the local bus series (outside London) due to changes in the estimation methodology from 2004/05.
2 Deregulation of the bus market took place in October 1986. For more information see the technical information
r Previously published figures have been revised. For details of the revisions (which include planned updates) please see the technical information .

Notes & Definitions: https://www.gov.uk/government/statistics/buses-statistics-guidance
The figures in this table are National Statistics

22.15 Local bus fares index (at current prices[2]) by metropolitan area status and country: Great Britain, annual from 2000

Index: March 2005=100

Year[1]	All items Retail Prices Index[3]	Local bus fares index							
		London	English metropolitan areas	English non-metropolitan areas	England	Scotland	Wales	Great Britain	England outside London
1995	77.4	71.1	61.8	61.8	63.9	70.2	63.5	64.6	61.8
1996	79.5	74.3	65.2	64.7	67.0	72.4	64.5	67.6	64.9
1997	81.6	77.0	69.0	67.9	70.2	77.8	67.2	71.1	68.4
1998	84.4	80.0	72.6	71.4	73.6	84.1	71.8	74.9	71.9
1999	86.1	83.3	75.8	74.9	77.0	87.5	75.3	78.3	75.3
2000	88.4	83.2	79.1	78.4	79.6	89.6	80.3	80.9	78.7
2001	90.4	83.9	83.3	82.7	82.9	92.2	84.7	84.1	82.9
2002	91.6	81.5	87.3	86.6	85.3	93.5	88.6	86.4	86.9
2003	94.4	81.8	90.3	90.8	88.0	96.1	91.6	89.2	90.6
2004	96.9	86.9	94.7	95.3	92.7	97.1	95.8	93.4	95.1
2005	100.0	100.0	100.0	100.0	100.0	100.0	100.0	100.0	100.0
2006	102.4	105.7	111.9	107.8	108.3	105.1	105.0	107.9	109.6
2007	107.3	116.6	113.6	102.0	110.2	111.4	111.5	110.4	106.9
2008	111.3	111.2	121.6	106.7	112.8	116.7	117.5	113.4	113.0
2009	110.9	120.0	136.5	113.9	122.5	126.5	125.3	123.1	123.2
2010	115.9	135.2	137.6	115.6	128.8	129.5	128.7	129.0	124.7
2011	122.0	144.5	146.4	119.4	135.7	132.2	130.1	135.2	130.3
2012	126.4	152.3	156.2	127.0	144.0	139.1	137.8	143.4	138.9
2013	130.6	159.4	161.3	134.3	150.8	145.1	147.2	150.1	145.4
2014	133.8	164.3	165.3	138.9	155.5	149.8	149.5	154.7	149.8
2015	135.0	168.8	171.4	143.8	160.6	153.2	155.8	159.7	155.3
2016	137.1	170.8	175.4	146.7	163.4	157.6	156.5	162.6	158.5

1 Index as at March.
2 Not adjusted for inflation.
3 These figures are not National Statistics

Source: DfT Fares Survey, Office for National Statistics
Telephone: 020 7944 3094
Email: bus.statistics@dft.gsi.gov.uk

Notes & Definitions: https://www.gov.uk/government/statistics/buses-statistics-guidance
The figures in this table are National Statistics except where indicated

22.16 Reported casualties by road user type and severity, Great Britain, 2005 - 2015

Number of casualties

	2005	2006	2007	2008	2009	2010	2011	2012	2013	2014	2015
Pedestrians											
Killed	671	675	646	572	500	405	453	420	398	446	408
KSI [1]	7,129	7,051	6,924	6,642	6,045	5,605	5,907	5,979	5,396	5,509	5,348
All severities	33,281	30,982	30,191	28,482	26,887	25,845	26,198	25,218	24,033	24,748	24,061
of which, children [2]											
Killed	63	71	57	57	37	26	33	20	26	29	25
KSI	2,134	2,025	1,899	1,784	1,660	1,646	1,602	1,545	1,358	1,379	1,283
All severities	11,250	10,131	9,527	8,648	7,983	7,929	7,807	6,999	6,396	6,481	6,317
Pedal cyclists											
Killed	148	146	136	115	104	111	107	118	109	113	100
KSI	2,360	2,442	2,564	2,565	2,710	2,771	3,192	3,340	3,252	3,514	3,339
All severities	16,561	16,196	16,195	16,297	17,064	17,185	19,215	19,091	19,438	21,287	18,844
of which, children											
Killed	20	31	13	12	14	7	6	13	6	6	6
KSI	527	503	522	417	458	398	398	324	282	279	278
All severities	4,286	3,765	3,633	3,306	3,204	2,828	2,881	2,198	1,958	2,005	1,929
Motorcyclists users [3]											
Killed	569	599	588	493	472	403	362	328	331	339	365
KSI	6,508	6,484	6,737	6,049	5,822	5,183	5,609	5,328	5,197	5,628	5,407
All severities	24,824	23,326	23,459	21,550	20,703	18,686	20,150	19,310	18,752	20,366	19,918
Car occupants											
Killed	1,675	1,612	1,432	1,257	1,059	835	883	801	785	797	754
KSI	14,617	14,254	12,967	11,968	11,112	9,749	9,225	9,033	8,426	8,832	8,642
All severities	178,302	171,000	161,433	149,188	143,412	133,205	124,924	119,708	109,787	115,530	111,707
Bus and coach occupants											
Killed	9	19	12	6	14	9	7	11	10	7	5
KSI	363	426	455	432	370	401	332	323	342	300	280
All severities	7,920	7,253	7,079	6,929	6,317	6,268	6,177	5,234	4,873	5,198	4,626
Van occupants											
Killed	54	52	58	43	36	34	34	33	37	33	32
KSI	587	564	494	445	417	359	340	363	371	400	417
All severities	6,048	5,914	5,340	4,913	4,743	4,494	4,499	4,533	4,426	4,915	4,750
HGV occupants											
Killed	55	39	52	23	14	28	28	29	21	14	31
KSI	395	383	363	240	189	212	195	198	168	176	193
All severities	2,843	2,530	2,476	1,930	1,519	1,578	1,415	1,339	1,296	1,353	1,203
All road users [4]											
Killed	3,201	3,172	2,946	2,538	2,222	1,850	1,901	1,754	1,713	1,775	1,730
KSI	32,155	31,845	30,720	28,572	26,912	24,510	25,023	24,793	23,370	24,582	23,874
All severities	271,017	258,404	247,780	230,905	222,146	208,648	203,950	195,723	183,670	194,477	186,189

1. Killed and seriously injured.

2. Casualties aged 0 -15.

3. Includes mopeds and scooters.

4. Includes other motor or non-motor vehicle users, and unknown road user type and casualty age.

The figures in this table are National Statistics

Source: DfT STATS19

Telephone: 020 7944 6595

Email: roadacc.stats@dft.gsi.gov.uk

22.17a Goods lifted[1] and goods moved[2] by mode of working[3]: by GB HGVs in the UK
UK activity of GB-registered heavy goods vehicles

	Million tonnes					Billion tonne kilometres				
	Goods lifted					Goods moved				
Year	Mainly public haulage	% of total	Mainly own account	% of total	All modes	Mainly public haulage	% of total	Mainly own account	% of total	All modes
2000	1,038	65	556	35	1,593	113	75	37	25	150
2001	1,052	67	529	33	1,581	115	77	35	23	149
2002	1,019	63	608	37	1,627	111	74	39	26	150
2003	1,053	64	590	36	1,643	114	75	37	25	152
2004	1,101	63	643	37	1,744	111	73	41	27	152
2005	1,079	62	667	38	1,746	110	72	43	28	153
2006	1,104	62	671	38	1,776	110	72	43	28	152
2007	1,116	61	706	39	1,822	113	72	45	28	157
2008	948	57	720	43	1,668	99	68	47	32	146
2009	690	51	666	49	1,356	77	62	48	38	125
2010	800	54	689	46	1,489	89	64	50	36	139
2011	789	51	770	49	1,559	86	60	59	40	145
2012	858	54	729	46	1,587	97	65	53	35	150
2013	810	55	665	45	1,475	92	66	48	34	139
2014	857	58	633	42	1,490	92	68	43	32	136

Source: Continuing Survey of Road Goods Transport (Great Britain)
Telephone: 020 7944 3903, Email: roadfreight.stats@dft.gsi.gov.uk

1. Goods lifted: the weight of goods carried, measured in tonnes.
2. Goods moved: the weight of goods carried multiplied by the distance hauled, measured in tonne kilometres.
3. Either public haulage operators, those who carry goods for other companies or individuals, or, own account operators, those who carry goods only for their own trade or business.

Note: discontinuities in the series (denoted by lines) are described in detail within the methodology note; comparisons across years where methodological changes have occurred should be treated with caution.
Methodology note: https://www.gov.uk/government/collections/road-freight-domestic-and-international-statistics
Notes & definitions: https://www.gov.uk/government/collections/road-freight-domestic-and-international-statistics

22.17b Goods moved[1] by type and weight[2] of vehicle: by GB HGVs in the UK
UK activity of GB-registered heavy goods vehicles

	Rigid vehicles					Articulated vehicles			Billion tonne kilometres
	Over 3.5t	Over 7.5t	Over 17t			Over 3.5t			All
Year	to 7.5t	to 17t	to 25t	Over 25t	All Rigids	to 33t	Over 33t	All Artics	vehicles
2000	5	11	5	15	36	14	100	114	150
2001	5	9	6	16	34	13	102	115	149
2002	5	7	6	17	36	10	104	114	150
2003	4	6	7	18	35	9	108	116	152
2004	4	5	7	19	36	7	109	116	152
2005	4	5	8	21	37	6	110	116	153
2006	4	3	8	20	36	6	111	117	152
2007	3	3	9	22	37	6	115	120	157
2008	3	2	8	20	33	5	108	113	146
2009	3	2	7	17	30	5	91	96	125
2010	3	2	7	18	31	4	104	108	139
2011	3	2	8	23	36	5	105	109	145
2012	3	2	8	22	35	4	111	115	150
2013	2	1	7	20	31	4	104	108	139
2014	2	1	7	20	31	3	101	105	136

Source: Continuing Survey of Road Goods Transport (Great Britain)
Telephone: 020 7944 3903, Email: roadfreight.stats.dft.gsi.gov.uk

1. Goods moved: the weight of goods carried multiplied by the distance hauled, measured in tonne kilometres.
2. Gross vehicle weight: the total weight of the vehicle plus its carrying capacity, from 3.5 to 44 tonnes.

Note: discontinuities in the series (denoted by lines) are described in detail within the methodology note; comparisons across years where methodological changes have occurred should be treated with caution.
Methodology note: https://www.gov.uk/government/collections/road-freight-domestic-and-international-statistics
Notes & definitions: https://www.gov.uk/government/collections/road-freight-domestic-and-international-statistics

22.17c Goods moved by commodity
UK activity of GB registered heavy goods vehicles

Billion tonne kilometres

Commodity	2004	2005	2006	2007	2008	2009	2010	2011	2012	2013[1]	2014
Products of agriculture, forestry, raw materials											
Agricultural products	12.8	11.9	11.5	12.3	11.7	10.1	10.7	11.8	13.1	11.5	12.4
Coal and lignite	1.2	1.5	1.4	1.5	1.7	1.2	1.5	0.7	1.0	1.0	1.1
Metal ore and other mining and quarrying	15.1	16.3	16.3	16.8	14.4	11.5	13.6	10.9	12.5	10.6	12.0
Subtotal	**29.1**	**29.6**	**29.2**	**30.6**	**27.9**	**22.8**	**25.8**	**23.5**	**26.6**	**23.0**	**25.5**
Food products, includ. beverages and tobacco											
Food products	30.3	29.9	30.7	32.8	31.2	32.2	34.3	33.7	38.2	35.8	30.3
Textile, leather and wood products											
Textiles and textile products; leather and leather products	2.0	1.9	2.2	2.2	1.6	2.0	2.0	1.5	1.4	2.4	1.9
Wood products	13.4	12.6	12.8	11.8	10.6	9.0	10.3	9.3	7.9	8.1	6.6
Subtotal	**15.4**	**14.5**	**15.0**	**14.0**	**12.3**	**11.0**	**12.3**	**10.8**	**9.3**	**10.5**	**8.5**
Metal, mineral and chemical products											
Coke and refined petroleum products	5.7	5.5	5.4	5.0	5.5	4.3	5.9	5.8	7.1	5.3	5.5
Chemical products	7.0	8.8	7.1	7.7	6.9	6.1	5.9	7.8	7.7	5.7	6.5
Glass, cement and other non-metallic mineral products	12.2	11.0	11.5	11.5	10.8	8.2	9.1	9.8	8.1	8.9	9.1
Metal products	7.3	7.3	6.7	8.2	5.7	4.9	5.0	5.1	7.2	4.5	4.7
Subtotal	**32.2**	**32.5**	**30.7**	**32.4**	**28.9**	**23.6**	**25.9**	**28.4**	**30.0**	**24.4**	**25.8**
Machinery and equipment, consumer durables											
Machinery and equipment	4.2	4.5	4.5	4.8	4.1	3.6	3.7	4.1	3.4	3.0	2.6
Transport equipment	4.7	4.7	4.7	4.5	4.4	3.3	3.8	3.7	4.3	2.5	3.9
Furniture	6.5	5.9	5.8	5.8	4.3	3.4	2.9	2.5	2.4	1.6	2.2
Subtotal	**15.4**	**15.2**	**15.1**	**15.1**	**12.8**	**10.3**	**10.4**	**10.2**	**10.2**	**7.1**	**8.7**
Other products											
Waste related products	5.5	6.4	6.4	7.4	6.3	4.6	5.6	9.3	9.0	8.9	9.3
Mail, parcels	4.3	4.1	4.2	3.6	3.8	3.0	3.9	5.8	4.3	3.1	3.8
Empty containers, pallets and other packaging	3.6	3.4	3.4	3.5	3.7	3.7	3.9	3.9	4.4	3.0	2.9
Household and office removals	0.1	0.2	0.2	0.1	0.1	0.0	0.1	1.0	1.6	2.4	2.6
Grouped goods	16.1	16.7	17.6	17.8	18.9	13.9	16.7	16.8	15.5	16.1	14.4
Unidentifiable goods	0.1	0.1	:	:	:	:	:	1.8	1.2	4.9	3.1
Other goods	:	:	:	:	:	:	:	:	0.0	0.0	1.0
Subtotal	**29.7**	**30.9**	**31.8**	**32.4**	**32.8**	**25.3**	**30.2**	**38.6**	**36.0**	**38.4**	**37.1**
All commodities	**152.1**	**152.6**	**152.4**	**157.3**	**145.8**	**125.2**	**138.9**	**145.2**	**150.1**	**139.2**	**135.9**

Source: Continuing Survey of Road Goods Transport (Great Britain)
Telephone: 020 7944 3903
Email: roadfreight.stats@dft.gsi.gov.uk

1. Commodity data from 2013 have been coded using a different coding frame, with classifications being retrospectively applied to earlier years. See the notes and definitions for more information.
':' = none recorded in the sample or not available due to small sample size
'~' = rounds to zero but different from a real zero

Note: discontinuities in the series (denoted by lines) are described in detail within the methodology note; comparisons across years where methodological changes have occurred should be treated with caution.
Methodology note: https://www.gov.uk/government/collections/road-freight-domestic-and-international-statistics
Notes & definitions: https://www.gov.uk/government/collections/road-freight-domestic-and-international-statistics

22.18a Goods lifted[1] by type and weight[2] of vehicle: by GB HGVs in the UK
UK activity of GB-registered heavy goods vehicles

Million tonnes

Year	Rigid vehicles					Articulated vehicles			All vehicles
	Over 3.5t to 7.5t	Over 7.5t to 17t	Over 17t to 25t	Over 25t	All Rigids	Over 3.5t to 33t	Over 33t	All artics	
2000	77	152	87	424	741	107	746	852	1,593
2001	80	123	86	443	733	97	751	848	1,581
2002	77	111	90	491	768	81	778	859	1,627
2003	70	89	100	506	765	69	809	878	1,643
2004	77	87	108	540	812	59	873	932	1,744
2005	70	70	110	562	812	51	883	934	1,746
2006	64	64	118	585	831	49	896	945	1,776
2007	54	52	127	614	848	49	926	975	1,822
2008	56	44	118	513	731	44	892	937	1,668
2009	56	37	102	377	572	38	746	785	1,356
2010	54	37	103	414	607	33	848	881	1,489
2011	55	36	108	479	677	39	844	883	1,559
2012	50	29	112	454	645	37	905	942	1,587
2013	44	25	97	448	614	37	824	861	1,475
2014	42	27	100	451	620	27	843	870	1,490

Source: Continuing Survey of Road Goods Transport (Great Britain)
Telephone: 020 7944 3903
Email: roadfreight.stats.dft.gsi.gov.uk

1. Goods lifted: the weight of goods carried, measured in tonnes.
2. Gross vehicle weight: the total weight of the vehicle plus its carrying capacity, from 3.5 to 44 tonnes.

Note: discontinuities in the series (denoted by lines) are described in detail within the methodology note; comparisons across years where methodological changes have occurred should be treated with caution.
Methodology note: https://www.gov.uk/government/collections/road-freight-domestic-and-international-statistics
Notes & definitions: https://www.gov.uk/government/collections/road-freight-domestic-and-international-statistics

22.18b Goods lifted by commodity
UK activity of GB registered heavy goods vehicles

Million tonnes

Commodity	2004	2005	2006	2007	2008	2009	2010	2011	2012	2013[1]	2014
Products of agriculture, forestry, raw materials											
Agricultural products	117	112	103	107	102	100	106	111	119	107	116
Coal and lignite	12	20	17	23	21	13	12	9	10	9	13
Metal ore and other mining and quarrying	381	394	390	398	335	234	270	232	236	234	229
Subtotal	**510**	**526**	**510**	**529**	**458**	**347**	**389**	**352**	**365**	**349**	**358**
Food products, includ. beverages and tobacco											
Food products	245	236	257	266	261	259	285	295	311	299	259
Textile, leather and wood products											
Textiles and textile products; leather and leather products	15	14	15	13	11	15	15	12	11	18	14
Wood products	103	95	89	92	89	71	74	67	59	58	51
Subtotal	**118**	**109**	**104**	**104**	**100**	**85**	**89**	**78**	**70**	**76**	**64**
Metal, mineral and chemical products											
Coke and refined petroleum products	68	69	66	69	69	53	67	66	82	59	59
Chemical products	53	64	55	56	53	46	44	63	57	41	49
Glass, cement and other non-metallic mineral products	187	170	177	173	173	121	140	136	121	119	141
Metal products	62	61	61	65	51	44	46	41	58	39	34
Subtotal	**369**	**364**	**360**	**363**	**346**	**264**	**296**	**306**	**318**	**257**	**284**
Machinery and equipment, consumer durables											
Machinery and equipment	38	44	46	48	40	39	39	40	32	24	20
Transport equipment	31	32	32	34	33	26	29	30	33	22	28
Furniture	43	40	41	40	29	26	22	16	16	12	17
Subtotal	**112**	**116**	**119**	**122**	**101**	**90**	**90**	**86**	**82**	**59**	**65**
Other products											
Waste related products	169	195	220	239	178	131	140	196	194	175	198
Mail, parcels	36	32	31	29	29	22	33	38	34	25	27
Empty containers, pallets and other packaging	41	39	37	41	40	36	37	40	39	29	30
Household and office removals	2	2	1	1	1	1	1	14	21	34	36
Grouped goods	140	128	135	129	152	121	128	143	145	136	130
Unidentifiable goods	2	1	:	:	:	:	:	12	8	36	28
Other goods	:	:	:	:	:	:	:	:	~	~	10
Subtotal	**389**	**396**	**426**	**439**	**401**	**310**	**340**	**442**	**441**	**434**	**460**
All commodities	**1,744**	**1,746**	**1,776**	**1,822**	**1,668**	**1,356**	**1,489**	**1,559**	**1,587**	**1,475**	**1,490**

Source: Continuing Survey of Road Goods Transport (Great Britain)
Telephone: 020 7944 3903
Email: roadfreight.stats@dft.gsi.gov.uk

1. Commodity data from 2013 have been coded using a different coding frame, with classifications being retrospectively applied to earlier years. See the notes and definitions for more information.
':' = none recorded in the sample or not available due to small sample size
'~' = rounds to zero but different from a real zero

Note: discontinuities in the series (denoted by lines) are described in detail within the methodology note; comparisons across years where methodological changes have occurred should be treated with caution.
Methodology note: https://www.gov.uk/government/collections/road-freight-domestic-and-international-statistics
Notes & definitions: https://www.gov.uk/government/collections/road-freight-domestic-and-international-statistics

22.19a Passenger journeys by sector - Great Britain

Great Britain annual data from 2002-03, Number of passenger journeys made (millions)

Financial year	Franchised long distance operators	Franchised London and South East operators	Franchised regional operators	Total franchised passenger journeys	Non franchised
2002-03	77.2	679.1	219.2	975.5	:
2003-04	81.5	690.0	240.2	1,011.7	:
2004-05	83.7	704.5	251.3	1,039.5	:
2005-06	89.5	719.7	267.3	1,076.5	:
2006-07	99.0	769.5	276.5	1,145.0	:
2007-08	103.9	828.4	285.8	1,218.1	:
2008-09	109.4	854.3	302.8	1,266.5	:
2009-10	111.6	842.2	304.0	1,257.9	1.4
2010-11	117.9	917.6	318.2	1,353.8	1.8
2011-12	125.3	993.8	340.9	1,460.0	1.5
2012-13	127.7	1,032.4	340.9	1,500.9	1.7
2013-14	129.0	1,106.9	350.5	1,586.5	1.9
2014-15	134.2	1,154.9	364.7	1,653.7	2.1

Source: LENNON ticketing and revenue database and Train Operating Companies (TOCs)

Symbols:(:) Data not available or Operator not in service **(r)** Data revised **(p)** Data are provisional

1. Data does not include Heathrow Express, Eurostar or light rail (inc. underground) services.
2. Data are provisional until the end of the financial year as train operators may revise data submitted to ORR.

More details on methodology can be found in the quality report relating to this dataset: http://orr.gov.uk/statistics/published-stats/statistical-releases

This dataset is used in the passenger rail usage statistical release. To view or download the statistical release: http://orr.gov.uk/statistics/published-stats/statistical-releases

For the latest information on data revisions, please see the revisions log: http://orr.gov.uk/statistics/code-of-practice/revisions-log

Passenger journeys on light rail and trams by system[1]: England

Million

Financial year	Docklands Light Railway	London Tramlink	Nottingham Express Transit	Midland Metro	Sheffield Supertram	Tyne and Wear Metro	Manchester Metrolink[2]	Blackpool Tramway	England
2000/01	38.4	15.0	:	5.4	11.1	32.5	17.2	4.1	123.6
2001/02	41.3	18.2	:	4.8	11.4	33.4	18.2	4.9	132.2
2002/03	45.7	18.7	:	4.9	11.5	36.6	18.8	4.5	140.7
2003/04	48.5	19.8	0.4	5.1	12.3	37.9	18.9	3.7	146.5
2004/05	50.1	22.0	8.5	5.0	12.8	36.8	19.7	3.9	158.7
2005/06	53.5	22.5	9.8	5.1	13.1	35.8	19.9	3.6	163.4
2006/07	63.9	24.6	10.1	4.9	14.0	37.9	19.8	3.4	178.6
2007/08	66.6	27.2	10.2	4.8	14.8	39.8	20.0	2.9	186.2
2008/09	67.8	27.2	9.8	4.7	15.0	40.6	21.1	2.3	188.6
2009/10	69.4	25.8	9.0	4.7	14.7	40.8	19.6	2.2	186.2
2010/11	78.3	27.9	9.7	4.8	15.0	39.9	19.2	1.6	196.5
2011/12	86.1	28.6	9.0	4.9	15.0	37.9	22.3	1.1	204.8
2012/13	100.0	30.1	7.4	4.8	14.4	37.0	25.0	3.7	222.5
2013/14	101.6	31.2	7.9	4.7	12.6	35.7	29.2	4.3	227.1
2014/15	110.2	30.7	8.1	4.4	11.5	38.1	31.2	4.1	238.2
2015/16	116.9	27.0	12.2	4.8	11.6	40.3	34.3	4.9	252.0

Source: DfT Light Rail and Tram Survey

Telephone: 020 7944 3094; Email: bus.statistics@dft.gsi.gov.uk

1 For further information on these systems including network and infrastructure changes that may affect the figures, please refer to the technical information.

2 Manchester Metrolink have revised their method for calculation of passenger boardings so the figures from 2010/11 are not directly comparable with previous years

Notes and Definitions: https://www.gov.uk/government/publications/light-rail-and-tram-statistics-guidance

The figures in this table are National Statistics

22.19b Passenger revenue by sector

Great Britain annual data from 2003-04 - passenger revenue by sector (£ millions)

Financial year	Franchised long distance operators	Franchised London and South East operators	Franchised regional operators	Total franchised passenger revenue	Non franchised
2003-04	1,384	1,932	585	3,901	:
2004-05	1,465	2,059	634	4,158	:
2005-06	1,609	2,197	687	4,493	:
2006-07	1,842	2,437	733	5,012	:
2007-08	2,036	2,717	801	5,555	:
2008-09	2,168	2,963	872	6,004	:
2009-10	2,216	3,046	916	6,179	36.7
2010-11	2,366	3,264	990	6,620	45.5
2011-12	2,533	3,602	1,094	7,229	43.9
2012-13	2,652	3,888	1,167	7,707	49.9
2013-14	2,779	4,180	1,244	8,203	54.4
2014-15	2,975	4,486	1,342	8,803	62.8

Source: LENNON Database and train operating companies

Data can be subject to revisions indicated by (R). For the latest information on data revisions, please see the revisions log: http://orr.gov.uk/statistics/code-of-practice/revisions-logs

This dataset is used in the passenger rail usage statistical release. To view or download the statistical release: http://orr.gov.uk/statistics/published-stats/statistical-releases

The quality report relating to this dataset can be found at http://orr.gov.uk/statistics/published-stats/statistical-releases

The quality report pulls together the key qualitative information on relevance, accuracy and reliability, timeliness and punctuality, accessibility and clarity and coherence and comparability. It also includes information on some additional quality principles on user needs and perceptions, confidentiality, transparency and security of data.

Passenger revenue at current prices[1] on light rail and trams by system[2]: England

£ million

Financial year	Docklands Light Railway	Croydon Tramlink	Nottingham Express Transit	Midland Metro	Sheffield Supertram	Tyne and Wear Metro	Manchester Metrolink	Blackpool Tramway	England
1999/00	21.0	:	:	2.5	6.8	23.3	17.0	4.3	74.8
2000/01	28.8	12.2	:	3.1	7.1	24.1	18.1	4.3	97.7
2001/02	32.2	12.9	:	3.9	7.6	25.0	20.1	4.7	106.5
2002/03	35.6	15.0	:	5.0	10.2	28.7	21.0	4.6	120.0
2003/04	37.2	16.1	:	5.2	9.2	31.4	20.9	3.9	124.0
2004/05	40.4	18.0	5.9	5.4	11.1	32.6	22.1	4.3	139.7
2005/06	46.1	18.8	7.3	5.9	10.4	34.4	22.6	4.4	150.0
2006/07	53.9	19.0	7.5	6.3	12.4	35.2	23.6	4.5	162.3
2007/08	63.1	20.9	7.9	6.3	13.7	37.3	22.4	4.0	175.5
2008/09	64.0	18.1	8.6	6.6	15.2	41.3	22.5	3.5	179.7
2009/10	74.9	16.2	7.9	6.5	15.0	40.8	23.4	3.0	187.7
2010/11	88.8	19.1	9.0	7.0	15.3	41.6	27.4	2.5	210.6
2011/12	105.3	21.2	8.4	7.4	15.4	42.2	33.7	1.7	235.3
2012/13	124.9	22.5	8.5	7.8	14.4	43.6	42.0	5.0	268.7
2013/14	133.1	23.5	8.3	7.9	13.9	45.2	51.8	6.1	289.8
2014/15	143.8	24.4	8.8	7.7	12.6	47.9	56.8	5.6	307.6

Source: DfT Light Rail and Tram Survey
Telephone: 020 7944 3094
Email: bus.statistics@dft.gsi.gov.uk

[1] These figures are not adjusted for inflation.

[2] For further information on these systems including infrastructure changes that may affect the figures, please refer to the technical information.

Notes and Definitions: https://www.gov.uk/government/publications/light-rail-and-tram-statistics-guidance

The figures in this table are National Statistics

22.19c Passenger kilometres by sector

Great Britain annual from 2002-03 -number of passenger kilometres travelled (billions)

Financial year	Franchised long distance operators	Franchised London and South East operators	Franchised regional operators	Total franchised passenger kilometres	Non franchised
1994-95	10.1	13.4	5.2	28.7	:
1995-96	10.5	13.8	5.8	30.0	:
1996-97	11.0	15.1	6.0	32.1	:
1997-98	12.3	16.1	6.3	34.7	:
1998-99	12.6	17.1	6.5	36.3	:
1999-00	13.2	18.4	6.9	38.5	:
2000-01	12.1	19.2	6.9	38.2	:
2001-02	12.9	19.3	7.0	39.1	:
2002-03	12.9	19.8	6.9	39.7	:
2003-04	13.3	20.1	7.5	40.9	:
2004-05	13.4	20.5	7.8	41.7	:
2005-06	14.2	20.7	8.2	43.1	:
2006-07	15.6	22.2	8.4	46.2	:
2007-08	16.5	23.5	8.9	48.9	:
2008-09	17.0	24.2	9.4	50.6	:
2009-10	17.6	23.8	9.7	51.1	0.3
2010-11	18.6	25.0	10.4	54.1	0.4
2011-12	19.2	26.4	11.1	56.7	0.4
2012-13	19.5	27.3	11.0	57.8	0.4
2013-14	19.7	28.6	11.4	59.7	0.5
2014-15	20.8	29.6	12.0	62.4	0.5

Source: Office of Rail and Road; LENNON Database and train operating companies

Data can be subject to revisions indicated by (R). For the latest information on data revisions, please see the revisions log: http://orr.gov.uk/statistics/code-of-practice/revisions-logs
Data are provisional (P) as train operating companies can revise their data.

This dataset is used in the passenger rail usage statistical release. To view or download the statistical release: http://orr.gov.uk/statistics/published-stats/statistical-releases

The quality report relating to this dataset can be found at http://orr.gov.uk/statistics/published-stats/statistical-releases
The quality report pulls together the key qualitative information on relevance, accuracy and reliability, timeliness and punctuality, accessibility and clarity and coherence and comparability. It also includes information on some additional quality principles on user needs and perceptions, confidentiality, transparency and security of data.

Passenger miles on light rail and trams by system[1]: England

Million

Financial year	Docklands Light Railway	London Tramlink	Nottingham Express Transit	Midland Metro	Sheffield Supertram	Tyne and Wear Metro	Manchester Metrolink[2]	Blackpool Tramway[3]	England
1999/00	106.9	:	:	31.0	47.3	142.9	78.3	8.1	414.6
2000/01	124.3	59.7	:	34.7	48.1	142.4	94.6	7.8	511.6
2001/02	128.5	61.5	:	31.1	49.7	148.1	100.2	9.3	528.5
2002/03	144.2	62.1	:	31.1	50.0	170.8	103.5	8.5	570.3
2003/04	146.3	65.2	1.2	33.3	53.5	176.4	105.0	7.0	588.0
2004/05	152.5	69.7	23.0	32.5	55.7	176.0	126.8	7.4	643.7
2005/06	160.0	72.7	25.9	33.5	57.0	173.4	128.0	6.9	657.4
2006/07	186.8	79.5	26.9	31.9	60.9	183.2	129.0	6.5	704.7
2007/08	202.8	87.9	27.3	31.4	64.4	194.4	130.5	5.4	744.1
2008/09	197.5	89.2	26.1	31.0	65.2	198.5	137.1	4.4	749.0
2009/10	226.5	83.5	23.6	30.8	64.0	203.2	128.1	4.1	763.8
2010/11	257.2	90.0	25.7	31.3	60.5	195.8	124.8	3.1	788.4
2011/12	283.0	92.2	24.9	31.7	60.3	188.8	141.9	2.1	824.9
2012/13	316.8	97.2	20.5	31.3	58.0	186.0	162.6	9.9	882.2
2013/14	333.6	100.9	22.2	30.5	50.7	183.5	188.3	12.7	922.4
2014/15	368.9	110.8	27.0	28.6	46.3	201.8	202.5	11.3	997.1

Source: DfT Light Rail and Tram Survey
Telephone: 020 7944 3094
Email: bus.statistics@dft.gsi.gov.uk

1 For further information on these systems including infrastructure changes that may affect the figures, please refer to the technical information.
2 Manchester Metrolink have revised their approach calculation of passenger boardings so the figure for 2010-11 is not directly comparable with previous years.
3 1983/84 to 1998/99 Blackpool Tramway data are imputed. The figures use passenger journeys data and an assumed average distance.
Notes and Definitions: https://www.gov.uk/government/publications/light-rail-and-tram-statistics-guidance

The figures in this table are National Statistics

22.19d Infrastructure on the railways

Great Britain

Year	Route open for traffic	Of which electrified	Route Open for Passenger & Freight Traffic	Route Open for Freight Traffic Only	Passenger Stations	Track kilometres
1988-89	16,599	4,376	14,309	2,290	2,470	:
1989-90	16,587	4,546	14,318	2,269	2,471	:
1990-91	16,584	4,912	14,317	2,267	2,488	:
1991-92	16,588	4,886	14,291	2,267	2,468	:
1992-93	16,528	4,910	14,317	2,211	2,468	:
1993-94	16,536	4,968	14,357	2,179	2,493	:
1994-95	16,542	4,970	14,359	2,183	2,489	:
1995-96	16,666	5,163	15,002	1,664	2,497	:
1996-97	16,666	5,176	15,034	1,632	2,498	:
1997-98	16,656	5,166	15,024	1,632	2,495	:
1998-99	16,659	5,166	15,038	1,621	2,499	:
1999-00	16,649	5,167	15,038	1,610	2,503	30,846
2000-01	16,652	5,167	15,042	1,610	2,508	30,846
2001-02	16,652	5,167	15,042	1,610	2,508	31,972
2002-03	16,670	5,167	15,042	1,610	2,508	31,766
2003-04	16,493	5,200	14,883	1,610	2,507	31,564
2004-05	16,116	5,200	14,328	1,788	2,508	31,482
2005-06	15,810	5,205	14,356	1,454	2,510	31,105
2006-07	15,795	5,250	14,353	1,442	2,520	31,063
2007-08	15,814	5,250	14,484	1,330	2,516	31,082
2008-09	15,814	5,250	14,494	1,320	2,516	31,119
2009-10	15,753	5,239	14,482	1,271	2,516	31,073
2010-11	15,777	5,262	14,506	1,271	2,532	31,108
2011-12	15,742	5,261	14,506	1,236	2,535	31,063
2012-13	15,753	5,265	14,504	1,249	2,532	31,075
2013-14	15,753	5,268	14,504	1,249	2,550	31,092
2014-15 (r)	15,760	5,272	14,506	1,254	2,552	31,120

Source: Network Rail

Symbols:

(:) Data not available

(r) Data revised

(p) Data are provisional

Prior to 2004-05 route length data and electrification data was collected using various systems and collected on a semi-annual basis. These systems, whilst often the most accurate measures available at the time, would not have provided as accurate a measure as the GEOGIS system and there is therefore a break in the time series between 2003-04 and 2004-05.

There is a break in the time series between 2006-07 and 2007-08 due to a new methodology where the route classification reference data was revamped. There is also a break in series between 1993-94 and 1994-95 for passenger stations data only.

More details on methodology can be found in the quality report relating to this dataset: http://orr.gov.uk/statistics/published-stats/statistical-releases

The quality report pulls together the key qualitative information on relevance, accuracy and reliability, timeliness and punctuality, accessibility and clarity and coherence and comparability. It also includes information on some additional quality principles on user needs and perceptions, confidentiality, transparency and security of data.

This dataset is used in the rail infrastructure, assets, and environment statistical release. To view or download the statistical release: http://orr.gov.uk/statistics/published-stats/statistical-releases

Revisions: The route open for freight traffic only has been revised for 2014-15. The data has changed from 1,256KM to 1,254KM. This is due to a calculation error from Network Rail in 2014-15. The route open for passenger and freight traffic has been updated to reflect this change (from 1,504KM in 2014-15 to 1,506KM in 2015-16)

Data can be subject to revisions indicated by (R). For the latest information on data revisions, please see the revisions log: http://orr.gov.uk/statistics/code-of-practice/revisions-log

22.19d Vehicle miles on light rail and trams by system[1]: England

Million

Financial year	Docklands Light Railway	London Tramlink	Nottingham Express Transit	Midland Metro	Sheffield Supertram	Tyne and Wear Metro	Manchester Metrolink	Blackpool Tramway	England
2000/01	1.8	1.3	:	1.2	1.5	2.9	2.7	0.8	12.2
2001/02	1.8	1.5	:	1.0	1.5	2.9	2.8	0.8	12.4
2002/03	2.0	1.5	:	1.1	1.6	3.9	2.9	0.7	13.7
2003/04	2.1	1.6	0.0	1.0	1.5	3.6	2.8	0.6	13.2
2004/05	2.0	1.5	0.6	1.0	1.5	3.5	2.8	0.5	13.5
2005/06	2.1	1.5	0.7	1.0	1.5	3.4	2.8	0.5	13.5
2006/07	2.7	1.6	0.7	1.0	1.5	3.6	2.3	0.6	14.1
2007/08	2.8	1.4	0.7	1.0	1.5	3.8	2.5	0.5	14.1
2008/09	2.5	1.4	0.7	1.0	1.5	3.5	2.4	0.5	13.5
2009/10	2.8	1.6	0.7	1.0	1.5	3.5	2.1	0.4	13.6
2010/11	2.9	1.6	0.7	1.0	1.5	3.5	2.3	0.3	13.9
2011/12	3.1	1.7	0.7	1.0	1.5	3.5	2.9	0.1	14.5
2012/13	3.6	1.8	0.7	1.0	1.5	3.4	3.6	0.5	16.1
2013/14	3.6	1.9	0.7	1.0	1.4	3.4	5.2	0.6	17.8
2014/15	3.6	2.0	0.8	1.0	1.4	3.5	5.6	0.5	18.4

Source: DfT Light Rail and Tram Survey
Telephone: 020 7944 3094, Email: bus.statistics@dft.gsi.gov.uk

1 For further information on these systems including infrastructure changes that may affect the figures, please refer to the technical information.
2 Figures for Manchester Metrolink represent total mileage of each tram 'set'. Where two sets are joined to form one train, the vehicle miles run will therefore be counted twice. Based on information supplied by the operator, this affects approximately 7% of services to 2012, around 12% in 12/13 and 20% in 13/14, meaning that figures for later years are not directly comparable with earlier ones (or with other systems). We estimate that the increasing use of double sets to form trains contributes around a third of the overall increase in vehicle mileage shown for this system

Notes and Definitions: https://www.gov.uk/government/publications/light-rail-and-tram-statistics-guidance
The figures in this table are National Statistics

22.19e Number of stations or stops on light rail and trams by system[1]: England

Financial year	Docklands Light Railway	Croydon Tramlink	Nottingham Express Transit	Midland Metro	Sheffield Supertram	Tyne and Wear Metro	Manchester Metrolink	Blackpool Tramway[2,3]	England
1995/96	28	.	.	.	45	46	26	62	207
1996/97	28	.	.	.	45	46	26	62	207
1997/98	29	.	.	.	46	46	26	62	209
1998/99	29	.	.	.	47	46	26	62	210
1999/00	34	.	.	23	47	46	36	62	248
2000/01	34	38	.	23	47	46	36	62	286
2001/02	34	38	.	23	48	58	36	62	299
2002/03	34	38	.	23	48	58	37	62	300
2003/04	34	38	23	23	48	58	37	62	323
2004/05	34	38	23	23	48	58	37	62	323
2005/06	38	39	23	23	48	59	37	62	329
2006/07	34	39	23	23	48	59	37	61	324
2007/08	39	38	23	23	48	60	37	61	329
2008/09	40	39	23	23	48	60	37	61	331
2009/10	40	39	23	23	48	60	37	59	329
2010/11	40	39	23	23	48	60	38	59	330
2011/12	45	39	23	23	48	60	42	31	311
2012/13	45	39	23	23	48	60	65	37	340
2013/14	45	39	23	23	48	60	77	37	352
2014/15	45	39	23	23	48	60	92	37	367

Source: DfT Light Rail and Tram Survey
Telephone: 020 7944 3094, Email: bus.statistics@dft.gsi.gov.uk

1 For further information on these systems including infrastructure changes that may affect the figures, please refer to the technical information.
2 The number of stops has been shown for one direction of the route (as is the case with the other systems). In publications prior to 2011/12 the figures shown covered both directions.
3 In 2012/13 Blackpool Tramway had 37 stops on the outward journey and 36 stops on the inward journey, as Fleetwood Ferry only had one platform.
Notes and Definitions (www.gov.uk/transport-statistics-notes-and-guidance-light-rail-and-tram-statistics)
The figures in this table are National Statistics

22.19f London Underground statistics, annual

	Passenger Journeys (millions)								Receipts (£ million)					Receipts per journey at 2015/16 prices[2]
	Ordinary[1]	Season ticket	All journeys	Passenger miles (millions)	Loaded train miles (millions)	Stations	Rail carriages	Route miles	Ordinary[1]	Season ticket	Traffic receipts	Traffic receipts at 2015/16 prices[2]	Receipts per journey (£)	
2000/01	486	484	970	4,642	40	274	3,954	254	610	519	1,129	1,574	1.16	1.62
2001/02	491	462	953	4,630	40	274	3,954	254	636	515	1,151	1,583	1.21	1.66
2002/03	495	446	942	4,578	41	274	3,954	254	628	510	1,138	1,525	1.21	1.62
2003/04	491	457	948	4,561	43	274	3,959	254	625	536	1,161	1,516	1.22	1.60
2004/05	486	490	976	4,726	43	274	3,959	254	663	578	1,241	1,572	1.27	1.61
2005/06	460	510	970	4,714	43	274	4,070	254	678	630	1,308	1,610	1.35	1.66
2006/07	519	521	1,040	4,938	43	273	4,070	254	782	635	1,417	1,694	1.36	1.63
2007/08	581	515	1,096	5,190	43	268	4,070	254	880	645	1,525	1,772	1.39	1.62
2008/09	616	473	1,089	5,372	44	270	4,070	254	962	654	1,615	1,828	1.48	1.68
2009/10	634	425	1,059	5,255	43	270	4,078	249	840	612	1,635	1,808	1.54	1.71
2010/11	660	447	1,107	5,515	43	270	4,134	249	1,087	672	1,759	1,889	1.59	1.71
2011/12	685	486	1,171	5,915	45	270	4,127	249	1,208	774	1,982	2,096	1.69	1.79
2012/13	723	506	1,229	6,275	47	270	4,180	249	1,293	833	2,125	2,207	1.73	1.80
2013/14	717	548	1,265	6,476	47	270	4,283	249	1,372	915	2,287	2,326	1.81	1.84
2014/15	747	558	1,305	6,740	50	270	4,281	250	1,400	1,011	2,410	2,415	1.85	1.85

1 Ordinary journeys include daily travelcards and those where concessionary fares apply.

2 Adjustment to values using the HM Treasury GDP Deflator (as at 31 March 2016). 'Other' income no longer available on the same basis as previously published.

The figures in this table are outside the scope of National Statistics

Source: Transport for London
Telephone: 020 7944 3094
Email: bus.statistics@dft.gsi.gov.uk

22.19g Glasgow Underground statistics, annual

Financial year	Passenger journeys (millions)	Passenger miles (millions)	Loaded train or tram miles [also referred to as vehicle miles] (millions)[1,r]	Stations or stops served	Passenger carriages or tramcars	Route miles open for passenger traffic	Passenger revenue at current prices (£ million)	Passenger revenue at 2015/16 prices (£ millions)
1999/00	14.7	29.2	0.7	15	41	6.8	10.0	14.2
2000/01	14.4	28.6	0.7	15	41	6.8	10.0	13.9
2001/02	13.8	27.4	0.7	15	41	6.8	10.1	13.9
2002/03	13.4	26.6	0.7	15	41	6.8	10.2	13.6
2003/04	13.3	26.5	0.6	15	41	6.8	10.3	13.5
2004/05	13.3	26.5	0.6	15	41	6.8	10.9	13.9
2005/06	13.2	26.2	0.6	15	41	6.5	11.2	13.8
2006/07	13.5	26.8	0.6	15	41	6.5	12.4	14.8
2007/08	14.5	28.8	0.6	15	41	6.5	12.9	15.0
2008/09	14.1	28.1	0.7	15	41	6.5	14.7	16.6
2009/10	13.1	26.0	0.6	15	41	6.5	14.1	15.6
2010/11	13.0	25.9	0.6	15	41	6.5	14.2	15.2
2011/12	12.9	25.6	0.7	15	41	6.5	14.3	15.1
2012/13	12.6	25.0	0.7	15	41	6.5	14.5	15.1
2013/14	12.7	25.3	0.7	15	41	6.5	16.0	16.2
2014/15	13.0	25.8	0.7	15	41	6.5	17.8	17.8

Source: DfT Light Rail and Tram Survey
Telephone: 020 7944 3094, Email: bus.statistics@dft.gsi.gov.uk

1 Loaded tram kilometers are only available as rolling stock totals, to calculate vehicle kilometres the figure provided by Glasgow is divided by 3, as all trams run with three carriages.

r Figures for 1982/83 to 2012/13 have been revised due to changes in the calculation, as advised by the operator.

Notes & Definitions: https://www.gov.uk/government/statistics/buses-statistics-guidance

The figures in this table are outside the scope of National Statistics

22.20a Freight moved

Great Britain annual data from 2003-04 - amount of freight moved on the rail network (billion net tonne kilometres)

Financial year	Coal	Metals	Construction	Oil and petroleum	International	Domestic intermodal	Other	Total (1)	Infrastructure (2)
2003-04	5.82	2.41	2.68	1.19	0.48	3.53	2.77	18.87	1.23
2004-05	6.66	2.59	2.86	1.22	0.54	3.96	2.53	20.35	1.29
2005-06	8.26	2.22	2.91	1.22	0.46	4.33	2.29	21.70	1.38
2006-07	8.56	2.04	2.70	1.53	0.44	4.72	1.89	21.88	1.36
2007-08	7.73	1.83	2.79	1.58	0.37	5.15	1.73	21.18	1.70
2008-09	7.91	1.53	2.70	1.52	0.42	5.17	1.38	20.63	1.55
2009-10	6.23	1.64	2.78	1.45	0.44	5.51	1.01	19.06	1.43
2010-11	5.46	2.23	3.19	1.32	0.42	5.68	0.94	19.23	1.54
2011-12	6.41	2.24	3.45	1.20	0.45	6.31	0.99	21.06	1.86
2012-13	7.50	1.81	3.05	1.21	0.43	6.30	1.16	21.46	1.73
2013-14	8.07	1.77	3.56	1.27	0.47	6.19	1.36	22.71	1.72
2014-15	6.50	1.82	3.93	1.21	0.60	6.49	1.67	22.21	1.69

Source: Network Rail

(1) Infrastructure data are not included in the total.
(2) This series excludes some possession trains used during engineering works.

Annual and quarterly data up to and including 1998-99 are only available to one decimal place so any discrepancies in the totals is due to rounding.

Data can be subject to revisions indicated by (R). For the latest information on data revisions, please see the revisions log: http://orr.gov.uk/statistics/code-of-practice/revisions-log

This dataset is used in the freight rail usage statistical release. To view or download the statistical release please see: http://orr.gov.uk/statistics/published-stats/statistical-releases

The quality report relating to this dataset can be found at http://orr.gov.uk/statistics/published-stats/statistical-releases

The quality report pulls together the key qualitative information on relevance, accuracy and reliability, timeliness and punctuality, accessibility and clarity and coherence and comparability. It also includes information on some additional quality principles on user needs and perceptions, confidentiality, transparency and security of data.

22.20b Freight lifted

Great Britain annual data from 2000-01 - mass of freight goods carried on the rail network (million tonnes)

Financial year	Coal	Other	Total
2000-01	35.3	60.3	95.6
2001-02	39.5	54.5	93.9
2002-03	34.0	53.0	87.0
2003-04	35.2	53.7	88.9
2004-05	44.1	56.8	100.9
2005-06	47.6	57.7	105.3
2006-07	48.7	59.5	108.2
2007-08	43.3	59.1	102.4
2008-09	46.6	56.1	102.7
2009-10	37.9	49.3	87.2
2010-11	38.8	51.1	89.9
2011-12	44.4	57.3	101.7
2012-13	52.0	61.1	113.1
2013-14	51.5	65.1	116.6
2014-15	43.5	67.0	110.5

Source: Freight Operating Companies

Annual and quarterly data up to and including 1998-99 are only available to one decimal place so any discrepancies in the totals is due to rounding.

Data can be subject to revisions indicated by (R). For the latest information on data revisions, please see the revisions log: http://orr.gov.uk/statistics/code-of-practice/revisions-log

This dataset is used in the freight rail usage statistical release. To view or download the statistical release please see: http://orr.gov.uk/statistics/published-stats/statistical-releases

The quality report relating to this dataset can be found at http://orr.gov.uk/statistics/published-stats/statistical-releases

The quality report pulls together the key qualitative information on relevance, accuracy and reliability, timeliness and punctuality, accessibility and clarity and coherence and comparability. It also includes information on some additional quality principles on user needs and perceptions, confidentiality, transparency and security of data.

22.21 Railways: permanent way and rolling stock
Northern Ireland
At end of year

Numbers

		2001	2002	2003	2004	2005	2006	2007	2008	2009/10	2010/11	2011/12	2012/13	2013/14	2014/15
Length of road open for traffic[1] (Km)	KNRA	334	334	334	299	299	299	299	299	299	299	299	299	299	299
Length of track open for traffic (Km)															
Total	KNRB	480	480	480	445	445	445	445	445	445	445	445	445	445	445
Running lines	KNRC	464	464	464	427	427	427	427	427	427	427	427	427	427	427
Sidings (as single track)	KNRD	16	16	16	18	18	18	18	18	18	18	18	18	18	18
Locomotives															
Diesel-electrics	KNRE	6	6	5	6	5	5	5	5	5	5	5	5	5	5
Passenger carrying vehicles															
Total	KNRF	106	100	100	102	124	125	128	130	130	130	130	156	150	150
Rail motor vehicles:															
Diesel-electric,etc	KNRG	29	28	28	28	70	85	84	84	84	84	84	110	134	134
Trailer carriages:															
Total locomotive hauled	KNRH	25	22	22	22	22	22	22	22	22	22	22	22	16	16
Ordinary coaches	KNRI	23	20	20	20	20	20	20	20	20	20	20	20	14	14
Restaurant cars	KNRJ	2	2	2	2	2	2	2	2	2	2	2	2	2	2
Rail car trailers	KNRK	52	50	50	52	32	18	22	24	24	24	24	10	0	0
Rolling stock for maintenance and repair	KNRT	18	18	39	46	48	48	48	48	48	48	48	50	47	47

1 The total length of railroad open for traffic irrespective of the number of tracks comprising the road.

Sources: Department for Regional Development;
Northern Ireland: 02890 540981

22.22 Operating statistics of railways
Northern Ireland

		Unit	2003	2004	2005/06	2006/07	2007/08	2008/09	2009/10	2010/11	2011/12	2012/13	2013/14	2014/15	2015/16
Maintenance of way and works															
Material used:															
Ballast	KNSA	Thousand m²	130.0	70.0	90.0	30.0	15.0	10.0	35.0	10.0	16.2	46.2	10.0	5.0	6.0
Rails	KNSB	Thousand tonnes	4.5	1.0	3.2	1.0	1.0	0.1	1.4	1.2	3.4	0.2	0.1	0.6	0.2
Sleepers	KNSC	Thousands	40.0	28.0	45.0	2.0	5.0	2.0	2.0	2.0	27.7	2.7	0.3	10.0	0.5
Track renewed	KNSD	Km	25.8	2.0	29.0	1.0	-	..	6.0	1.0	0.5	21.6	0.0	0.0	0.0
New Track laid	KPGD	Km	-	-	-	-	-	..	–	0.0	-	-	-	-	-
Engine kilometres															
Total[1]	KNSE	Thousand Km	4,170	4,110	4,618	4,677	5,108	5,047	4,899	5,088	5,082	5,258	5,760	5,904	6,037
Train kilometres:															
Total	KNSF	"	3,704	4,110	4,618	4,677	5,108	5,047	4,899	5,088	5,082	5,258	5,760	5,904	6,037
Coaching	KNSG	"	3,700	4,110	4,618	4,677	5,108	5,047	4,899	5,088	5,082	5,258	5,760	5,904	6,037
Freight	KNSH	"	4	-	-	-	-	-	-	-	-	-	-	-	-

Sources: Department for Regional Development;
Northern Ireland: 02890 540981

1 Including shunting, assisting, light, departmental, maintenance and repair.

22.23 Main Outputs of UK Airlines 1994 - 2015 in Tonne-kilometres Available and Used (a)

	Available Tonne-Kilometres						Tonne-Kilometres Used					
	Total (000 000)	Percentage growth on previous year	Scheduled services (000 000)	Percentage growth on previous year	Non-scheduled services (000 000)	Percentage growth on previous year	Total (000 000)	Percentage growth on previous year	Scheduled services (000 000)	Percentage growth on previous year	Non-scheduled services (000 000)	Percentage growth on previous year
1994	27 713	10.5	20 359	9.5	7 354	13.2	19 350	11.4	13 314	11.3	6 035	11.6
1995	29 901	7.9	22 016	8.1	7 885	7.2	21 306	10.1	14 890	11.8	6 416	6.3
1996	32 214	7.7	23 795	8.1	8 419	6.8	23 001	8.0	16 198	8.8	6 803	6.0
1997	35 571	10.4	26 507	11.4	9 064	7.7	25 091	9.1	17 914	10.6	7 176	5.5
1998	40 022	12.5	29 762	12.3	10 261	13.2	27 552	9.8	19 598	9.4	7 954	10.8
1999	41 911	4.7	31 856	7.0	10 055	-2.0	28 530	3.5	20 596	5.1	7 934	-0.3
2000	43 393	3.5	32 950	3.4	10 443	3.9	29 989	5.1	21 846	6.1	8 143	2.6
2001	42 374	-2.3	31 864	-3.3	10 510	0.6	28 118	-6.2	19 907	-8.9	8 211	0.8
2002	40 550	-4.3	30 433	-4.5	10 117	-3.7	27 913	-0.7	20 032	0.6	7 881	-4.0
2003	42 784	5.5	31 513	3.6	11 271	11.4	29 325	5.1	20 671	3.2	8 654	9.8
2004	43 904	2.6	32 442	2.9	11 462	1.7	29 923	2.0	20 963	1.4	8 960	3.5
2005	48 294	10.0	36 937	13.9	11 357	-0.9	29 494	-1.4	21 133	0.8	8 362	-6.7
2006	50 396	4.4	38 590	4.5	11 806	4.0	30 932	4.9	22 404	6.0	8 528	2.0
2007	54 190	7.5	40 979	6.2	13 211	11.9	32 863	6.2	23 557	5.1	9 306	9.1
2008	53 392	-1.5	41 316	0.8	12 076	-8.6	32 509	-1.1	24 107	2.3	8 402	-9.7
2009	49 150	-7.9	39 207	-5.1	9 944	-17.7	30 411	-6.5	23 427	-2.8	6 984	-16.9
2010	47 168	-4.0	38 059	-2.9	9 109	-8.4	29 915	-1.6	23 263	-0.7	6 651	-4.8
2011	50 120	6.3	41 043	7.8	9 078	-0.3	31 405	5.0	24 796	6.6	6 609	-0.6
2012	50 348	0.5	41 694	1.6	8 653	-4.7	31 621	0.7	25 251	1.8	6 370	-3.6
2013	50 111	-0.5	42 098	1.0	8 014	-7.4	31 704	0.3	25 684	1.7	6 019	-5.5
2014	50 543	0.9	43 737	3.9	6 806	-15.1	31 928	0.7	27 061	5.4	4 867	-19.2
2015	50 926	0.8	44 115	0.9	6 811	-	32 659	2.3	28 008	3.5	4 651	-4.4
Twelve month period to:												
Mar 2015	50 349		43 628		6 721		31 895		27 170		4 725	

Source: Civil Aviation Authority

(a) Excludes some charter operations performed by aircraft below 15 MTOM
(b) Excludes Small Airlines Public Transport Operations
(c) Excludes Air Europe Operations

22.24a Air Transport Movements(a) by Type and Nationality of Operator 2015

	Total	<------ Scheduled Services ------>			<-------- Charter Flights ------->		
		UK Operators	Other EU Operators	Other Overseas Operators	UK Operators	Other EU Operators	Other Overseas Operators
London Area Airports							
GATWICK	262 571	178 524	29 096	34 593	17 142	2 208	1 008
HEATHROW	472 060	261 676	96 390	111 592	872	1 486	44
LONDON CITY	79 251	45 141	27 635	6 474	-	1	-
LUTON	87 440	41 175	37 746	1 887	3 216	3 195	221
SOUTHEND	8 975	5 846	2 440	627	9	50	3
STANSTED	154 478	22 714	116 427	3 692	6 347	1 395	3 903
Total London Area Airports	1 064 775	555 076	309 734	158 865	27 586	8 335	5 179
Other UK Airports							
ABERDEEN	95 687	37 271	10 854	2 988	43 870	626	78
BARRA	947	947	-	-	-	-	-
BELFAST CITY (GEORGE BEST)	40 571	32 722	7 754	-	2	92	1
BELFAST INTERNATIONAL	36 273	29 712	315	489	3 451	2 268	38
BENBECULA	1 692	1 692	-	-	-	-	-
BIGGIN HILL	24	-	-	-	16	8	-
BIRMINGHAM	89 837	43 753	29 933	7 439	7 718	822	172
BLACKPOOL	6 554	-	1 046	-	5 508	-	-
BOURNEMOUTH	8 554	3 420	2 182	-	2 852	97	3
BRISTOL	54 741	33 696	15 538	-	5 162	345	-
CAMBRIDGE	373	-	245	-	61	67	-
CAMPBELTOWN	977	976	-	-	1	-	-
CARDIFF WALES	14 044	5 439	5 316	-	2 796	454	39
CITY OF DERRY (EGLINTON)	1 927	3	1 920	-	2	2	-
COVENTRY	676	-	-	-	499	177	-
DONCASTER SHEFFIELD	5 581	77	3 112	1	2 099	153	139
DUNDEE	1 174	1 114	-	-	38	22	-
DURHAM TEES VALLEY	3 920	1 898	1 970	-	10	42	-
EAST MIDLANDS INTERNATIONAL	56 378	16 294	14 571	445	11 394	11 783	1 891
EDINBURGH	107 211	69 174	26 896	5 093	4 200	1 844	4
EXETER	12 967	10 904	-	-	1 760	260	43
GLASGOW	80 322	56 299	14 767	3 680	4 543	524	509
GLOUCESTERSHIRE	1 210	-	1 207	-	1	2	-
HUMBERSIDE	10 911	1 940	2 035	-	5 262	1 672	2
INVERNESS	10 581	10 499	-	-	38	14	30
ISLAY	1 611	1 611	-	-	-	-	-
ISLES OF SCILLY (ST.MARYS)	10 585	10 585	-	-	-	-	-
KIRKWALL	10 701	10 566	-	-	131	-	4
LANDS END (ST JUST)	8 101	8 101	-	-	-	-	-
LEEDS BRADFORD	31 149	21 426	8 928	-	655	135	5
LERWICK (TINGWALL)	1 161	1 151	-	-	10	-	-
LIVERPOOL (JOHN LENNON)	32 882	20 480	12 204	2	94	81	21
LYDD	160	121	-	-	1	37	1
MANCHESTER	164 710	80 828	48 121	16 595	16 689	1 743	734
NEWCASTLE	42 070	24 599	9 453	1 250	5 860	371	537
NEWQUAY	5 976	5 753	218	-	2	3	-
NORWICH	22 898	5 899	2 517	-	11 506	1 223	1 753
OXFORD (KIDLINGTON)	6	-	-	-	2	4	-
PRESTWICK	4 264	4	4 120	2	6	42	90
SCATSTA	11 239	-	-	-	11 233	4	2
SHOREHAM	370	-	-	-	370	-	-
SOUTHAMPTON	34 249	33 738	345	-	60	104	2
STORNOWAY	6 284	6 275	-	-	5	4	-
SUMBURGH	11 057	6 895	-	90	4 023	49	-
TIREE	1 248	1 248	-	-	-	-	-
WICK JOHN O GROATS	2 203	1 893	-	-	304	6	-
Total Other UK Airports	1 046 056	599 003	225 567	38 074	152 234	25 080	6 098
Total All Reporting UK Airports	2 110 831	1 154 079	535 301	196 939	179 820	33 415	11 277
Non UK Reporting Airports							
ALDERNEY	5 802	5 795	-	-	7	-	-
GUERNSEY	23 608	21 982	119	-	904	602	1
ISLE OF MAN	19 081	11 684	6 816	-	532	48	1
Non UK Reporting Airports(Continued)							
JERSEY	25 453	22 787	747	14	1 197	702	6
Total Non UK Reporting Airports	73 944	62 248	7 682	14	2 640	1 352	8

Note
(a) Excludes Air Taxi operations

Source: Civil Aviation Authority

22.24b Air Passengers by Type and Nationality of Operator 2015

	Total Terminal and Transit Passengers	Scheduled Services						Charter Flights					
		UK Operators		Other EU Operators		Other Overseas Operators		UK Operators		Other EU Operators		Other Overseas Operators	
		Terminal	Transit	Terminal	Transit	Terminal	Transit	Terminal	Transit	Terminal	Transit	Terminal	Transit
London Area Airports													
GATWICK	40 269 087	26 499 644	3 731	3 850 213	381	5 805 486	1 568	3 609 370	1 749	326 725	1 199	168 630	391
HEATHROW	74 985 748	40 312 155	-	11 633 462	181	22 868 656	31 586	133 031	-	4 068	-	2 609	-
LONDON CITY	4 319 301	2 377 647	-	1 492 828	-	448 806	-	-	-	20	-	-	-
LUTON	12 263 505	5 829 648	315	5 769 569	468	206 885	-	422 215	7	30 728	107	3 536	27
SOUTHEND	900 648	795 806	14	89 738	-	8 743	-	546	-	5 705	-	96	-
STANSTED	22 519 178	2 698 322	2 141	18 892 372	1 631	318 587	-	570 856	206	23 041	103	10 265	1 654
Total London Area Airports	155 257 467	78 513 222	6 201	41 728 182	2 661	29 657 163	33 154	4 736 018	1 962	390 287	1 409	185 136	2 072
Other UK Airports													
ABERDEEN	3 469 525	1 774 513	20	762 307	170	105 396	-	759 949	7	54 802	-	12 361	-
BARRA	10 658	10 658	-	-	-	-	-	-	-	-	-	-	-
BELFAST CITY (GEORGE BEST)	2 692 713	2 072 032	-	610 399	-	-	-	97	-	10 107	-	78	-
BELFAST INTERNATIONAL	4 391 292	3 984 168	275	46 809	129	69 368	-	247 655	248	37 729	732	4 132	47
BENBECULA	32 146	32 125	21	-	-	-	-	-	-	-	-	-	-
BIGGIN HILL	644	-	-	-	-	-	-	352	-	292	-	-	-
BIRMINGHAM	10 187 122	3 784 304	1 192	3 409 068	921	1 359 433	165	1 516 929	223	90 047	883	20 278	3 679
BLACKPOOL	33 494	-	-	10 339	-	-	-	23 155	-	-	-	-	-
BOURNEMOUTH	706 776	160 079	1 077	367 816	-	-	-	173 237	237	3 890	29	411	-
BRISTOL	6 786 790	4 059 191	54	1 899 285	11	-	-	777 980	4 835	44 739	695	-	-
CAMBRIDGE	5 799	-	-	2 182	-	-	-	2 700	-	917	-	-	-
CAMPBELTOWN	8 511	8 252	223	-	-	-	-	36	-	-	-	-	-
CARDIFF WALES	1 160 506	256 366	1 134	376 777	60	-	-	465 361	464	53 501	465	6 378	-
CITY OF DERRY (EGLINTON)	284 485	29	3	284 209	-	-	-	170	-	74	-	-	-
DONCASTER SHEFFIELD	857 109	3 790	128	446 853	-	-	-	376 353	193	15 140	196	14 456	-
DUNDEE	21 973	20 110	31	-	-	-	-	1 470	-	362	-	-	-
DURHAM TEES VALLEY	140 902	30 599	439	105 723	90	-	-	642	-	3 409	-	-	-
EAST MIDLANDS INTERNATIONAL	4 450 862	1 410 437	1 172	2 239 608	1 160	-	-	781 092	795	13 238	1 516	1 844	-
EDINBURGH	11 114 587	6 709 166	721	3 398 925	302	755 321	-	217 259	178	32 344	-	371	-
EXETER	821 789	576 281	26	-	-	-	-	208 646	462	28 272	136	7 966	-
GLASGOW	8 714 307	5 309 482	1 057	1 665 278	257	772 835	1 644	897 413	-	58 721	347	5 802	1 471
GLOUCESTERSHIRE	12 267	-	-	12 243	14	-	-	2	-	8	-	-	-
HUMBERSIDE	222 107	33 800	465	121 869	-	-	-	40 512	14	24 645	438	364	-
INVERNESS	669 364	663 950	1 804	-	-	-	-	855	-	548	-	2 207	-
ISLAY	29 346	28 993	353	-	-	-	-	-	-	-	-	-	-
ISLES OF SCILLY (ST.MARYS)	94 718	94 718	-	-	-	-	-	-	-	-	-	-	-
KIRKWALL	160 234	149 298	9 898	-	-	-	-	30	812	-	-	196	-
LANDS END (ST JUST)	54 169	53 704	465	-	-	-	-	-	-	-	-	-	-
LEEDS BRADFORD	3 455 445	2 155 864	9 692	1 164 220	-	-	-	114 558	73	10 480	389	169	-
LERWICK (TINGWALL)	4 267	4 166	92	-	-	-	-	9	-	-	-	-	-
LIVERPOOL (JOHN LENNON)	4 301 495	2 374 112	1 809	1 908 285	3 738	-	185	3 996	-	7 415	-	1 955	-
LYDD	1 134	731	-	-	-	-	-	11	-	383	-	9	-
MANCHESTER	23 136 047	9 586 722	3 064	6 204 816	3 072	3 382 621	26 620	3 691 227	4 488	200 591	898	28 616	3 312
NEWCASTLE	4 562 853	2 560 046	2 667	798 329	172	262 240	-	898 533	166	34 083	-	6 617	-
NEWQUAY	251 987	238 860	1 709	10 934	-	-	-	37	-	447	-	-	-
NORWICH	459 664	110 217	-	142 194	-	-	-	106 063	-	80 227	-	20 963	-
OXFORD (KIDLINGTON)	166	-	-	-	-	-	-	44	-	122	-	-	-

22.24b Air Passengers by Type and Nationality of Operator 2015

	Total Terminal and Transit Passengers	Scheduled Services UK Operators Terminal	UK Operators Transit	Other EU Operators Terminal	Other EU Operators Transit	Other Overseas Operators Terminal	Other Overseas Operators Transit	Charter Flights UK Operators Terminal	UK Operators Transit	Other EU Operators Terminal	Other EU Operators Transit	Other Overseas Operators Terminal	Other Overseas Operators Transit
Other UK Airports (Continued)													
PRESTWICK	610 837	274	37	608 329	242	-	243	419	2	317	7	250	717
SCATSTA	253 526	-	-	-	-	-	-	253 500	-	17	-	9	-
SHOREHAM	490							490					
SOUTHAMPTON	1 789 470	1 755 173	13 832	8 916	-	-	-	4 392	-	7 151	-	6	-
STORNOWAY	127 282	124 485	2 298	-	-	-	-	165	-	334	-	-	-
SUMBURGH	271 994	170 832	232	-	-	348	-	97 294	1 636	1 652	-	-	-
TIREE	9 856	9 564	292	-	-	-	-	-	-	-	-	-	-
WICK JOHN O GROATS	25 484	21 759	-	-	-	-	-	2 250	1 332	143	-	-	-
Total Other UK Airports	96 396 192	50 338 850	56 282	26 605 713	10 338	6 707 562	28 857	11 664 883	16 165	816 147	6 731	135 438	9 226
Total All Reporting UK Airports	251 653 659	128 852 072	62 483	68 333 895	12 999	36 364 725	62 011	16 400 901	18 127	1 206 434	8 140	320 574	11 298
Non UK Reporting Airports													
ALDERNEY	59 843	59 754	-	-	-	-	-	89	-	-	-	-	-
GUERNSEY	891 616	851 201	33 643	5 070	82	-	-	514	28	987	88	3	-
ISLE OF MAN	781 601	678 540	1	97 843	743	-	-	2 546	-	1 891	-	37	-
JERSEY	1 554 390	1 470 444	21 674	40 042	100	298	-	974	102	20 080	22	654	-
Total Non UK Reporting Airports	3 287 450	3 059 939	55 318	142 955	925	298	-	4 123	130	22 958	110	694	-

Source: Civil Aviation Authority

22.25 Scheduled and Non-Scheduled Services: All Services 2015 (a)

Passenger Services

	Aircraft-Km (000)	Stage Flights	A/C Hours	(b) Number of Passengers Uplifted	Seat-Km Available (000)	Seat-Km Used (000)	As % of Avail	(b) Cargo Uplifted Tonnes	Tonne-Km Available (000)	Tonne-Kilometres Used Total (000)	Tonne-Kilometres Used Mail (000)	Tonne-Kilometres Used Freight (000)	Passenger (000)	As % of Avail
ACROPOLIS AVIATION LTD	352	136	506	906	6 711	2 896	43.2	-	4 239	266	-	-	266	6.3
AIRTANKER SERVICES LTD	4 499	731	5 814	60 154	1 345 287	908 766	67.6	3 849	183 547	120 759	-	35 945	84 814	65.8
ARAVCO LTD	148	50	192	157	2 373	512	21.6	-	239	39	-	-	39	16.3
AURIGNY AIR SERVICES	3 122	14 929	13 092	555 127	216 453	149 437	69.0	323	22 276	11 242	32	43	11 167	50.5
BA CITYFLYER LTD	22 695	32 805	47 377	1 933 155	2 026 334	1 459 539	72.0	1	202 496	120 841	-	-	120 841	59.7
BAE SYSTEMS (CORP AIR TVL) LTD	244	305	404	8 041	15 817	6 099	38.6	584	2 131	508	-	-	508	23.8
BLUE ISLANDS LIMITED	1 541	9 416	6 453	299 468	79 817	48 310	60.5	55	7 183	4 451	-	102	4 349	62.0
BMI REGIONAL	15 544	23 310	32 216	412 656	724 252	395 695	54.6	-	81 522	33 673	32	2	33 639	41.3
BRITISH AIRWAYS PLC	706 791	289 082	1 050 287	41 255 582	171 330 780	139 821 289	81.6	581 007	24 699 288	14 033 896	119 242	3 819 598	10 095 056	56.8
CELLO AVIATION LTD	833	755	1 609	9 354	103 984	85 883	82.6	-	12 011	8 501	-	-	8 501	70.8
EASTERN AIRWAYS	10 424	27 243	26 507	472 253	414 772	221 445	53.4	-	33 177	16 456	-	-	16 456	49.6
EASYJET AIRLINE COMPANY LTD	454 002	406 463	802 394	58 646 144	75 343 998	67 363 664	89.4	-	6 404 230	5 577 659	-	-	5 577 659	87.1
EXECUTIVE JET CHARTER LTD	123	72	169	236	1 510	426	28.2	-	128	38	-	-	38	29.7
FLYBE LTD	65 026	143 125	173 825	7 772 716	5 529 472	3 855 955	69.7	442	588 994	327 817	91	-	327 726	55.7
GAMA AVIATION (UK) LTD	262	129	344	543	3 731	1 315	35.2	-	302	120	-	-	120	39.7
HANGAR 8 AOC LTD	298	211	458	1 324	3 721	1 537	41.3	-	521	151	-	-	151	29.0
ISLES OF SCILLY SKYBUS	796	9 981	3 574	95 693	12 752	8 435	66.1	-	1 022	632	-	-	632	61.8
JET2.COM LTD	73 547	36 657	115 438	5 853 447	13 379 975	12 222 045	91.3	-	1 271 501	1 038 895	-	-	1 038 895	81.7
JOTA AVIATION LTD	258	443	648	3 211	24 645	15 803	64.1	-	2 394	1 322	-	-	1 322	55.2
LOGANAIR LTD	10 355	39 205	35 334	678 856	365 591	241 411	66.0	665	35 725	20 656	13	136	20 507	57.8
MONARCH AIRLINES	72 736	34 796	109 523	5 723 235	14 737 895	12 122 018	82.3	1 072	1 449 571	964 982	-	2 956	962 026	66.6
ORYX JET LTD	122	45	176	116	1 212	280	23.1	-	133	29	-	-	29	21.8
TAG AVIATION (UK) LTD	1 615	1 200	2 119	8 759	45 678	17 378	38.0	-	15 611	1 508	-	-	1 508	9.7
THOMAS COOK AIRLINES LTD	98 007	30 601	136 079	6 395 623	24 469 678	22 460 406	91.8	3 350	2 640 688	1 933 063	-	24 093	1 908 970	73.2
THOMSON AIRWAYS LTD	157 946	53 869	222 968	10 611 175	35 611 815	33 395 385	93.8	7 368	3 660 618	2 555 911	-	52 427	2 503 484	69.8
TITAN AIRWAYS LTD	7 530	4 187	11 914	135 107	1 418 845	1 031 076	72.7	339	121 062	87 840	179	-	87 661	72.6
TRIAIR (BERMUDA) LTD	108	34	151	96	1 298	552	42.5	-	239	60	-	-	60	25.1
VIRGIN ATLANTIC AIRWAYS LTD	150 228	27 147	195 653	5 768 327	48 409 574	37 039 418	76.5	197 127	8 012 750	4 868 684	-	1 395 036	3 473 648	60.8
Total Passenger Services	1 859 152	1 186 927	2 995 225	146 701 461	395 627 970	332 876 975	84.1	796 183	49 453 598	31 729 999	119 498	5 330 429	26 280 072	64.2

Cargo Services

	Aircraft-Km (000)	Stage Flights	A/C Hours	(b) Number of Passengers Uplifted	Seat-Km Available (000)	Seat-Km Used (000)	As % of Avail	(b) Cargo Uplifted Tonnes	Tonne-Km Available (000)	Tonne-Kilometres Used Total (000)	Tonne-Kilometres Used Mail (000)	Tonne-Kilometres Used Freight (000)	Passenger (000)	As % of Avail
AIRTANKER SERVICES LTD	9	8	15	-	-	-	..	7	319	22	-	22	-	6.9
ATLANTIC AIRLINES LTD	4 014	10 445	11 716	-	-	-	..	31 854	50 927	21 866	5 877	15 989	-	42.9
BRITISH AIRWAYS PLC	5 825	2 764	9 579	-	-	-	..	47 985	310 569	231 720	-	231 720	-	74.6
DHL AIR LTD	26 339	18 819	42 976	-	-	-	..	116 346	1 073 288	662 919	-	662 919	-	61.8
ISLES OF SCILLY SKYBUS	43	850	213	-	-	-	..	243	32	11	9	2	-	34.4
JET2.COM LTD	1 484	3 721	3 822	-	-	-	..	20 634	23 718	8 207	8 207	-	-	34.6
LOGANAIR LTD	-	-	-	-	-	-	..	1	-	-	-	-	-	..
TITAN AIRWAYS LTD	847	1 666	1 885	-	-	-	..	9 339	13 449	4 662	4 435	227	-	34.7
Total Cargo Services	38 561	38 273	70 207	-	-	-	..	226 410	1 472 302	929 407	18 528	910 879	-	63.1
Grand Total	1 897 713	1 225 200	3 065 432	146 701 461	395 627 970	332 876 975	84.1	1 022 592	50 925 900	32 659 406	138 026	6 241 308	26 280 072	64.1

(a) Excludes small airlines' public transport operations (see table 1.13)
(b) Excludes passengers and cargo uplifted on sub-charter operations

Source: Civil Aviation Authority

22.26a Aircraft Movements November 2015

	Total	Commercial Movements				Non-Commercial Movements						
		Air Transport Total	Of Which Air Taxi	Positioning Flights	Local Movements	Test and Training	Other Flights by Air Transport Operators	Aero Club	Private	Official	Military	Business Aviation
London Area Airports												
GATWICK	18 126	17 748	4	267	-	9	4	-	6	-	-	92
HEATHROW	37 153	36 973	4	105	-	6	10	-	-	6	6	47
LONDON CITY	6 921	6 848	371	42	-	12	-	-	-	-	-	19
LUTON	8 560	6 805	376	533	-	22	23	-	46	2	3	1 126
SOUTHEND	1 389	595	76	65	160	161	7	199	142	-	2	58
STANSTED	13 131	12 103	76	344	-	9	50	-	-	2	2	621
Total London Area Airports	85 280	81 072	907	1 356	160	219	94	199	194	10	13	1 963
METRO LONDON HELIPORT	692	125	125	133	98	-	100	-	200	4	4	28
Other UK Airports												
ABERDEEN	8 201	7 250	210	411	-	223	153	153	-	-	6	5
BARRA	76	76	-	-	-	-	-	-	-	-	-	-
BELFAST CITY (GEORGE BEST)	3 461	3 396	68	26	-	8	2	-	13	6	2	8
BELFAST INTERNATIONAL	4 109	3 043	170	99	290	12	3	69	14	-	527	52
BENBECULA	254	222	96	25	-	-	-	1	2	-	4	-
BIGGIN HILL	2 580	557	557	6	-	-	-	1 210	436	-	2	369
BIRMINGHAM	7 525	6 869	14	193	111	19	6	89	2	-	38	198
BLACKPOOL	1 530	617	79	4	12	74	-	514	249	-	4	56
BOURNEMOUTH	2 831	632	26	88	-	803	560	222	333	-	22	171
BRISTOL	4 430	3 805	102	54	-	53	2	313	200	-	3	-
CAMBRIDGE	989	24	-	7	126	12	-	529	101	4	36	150
CAMPBELTOWN	78	72	5	4	-	2	-	-	-	-	-	-
CARDIFF WALES	1 432	1 075	2	71	-	24	-	62	192	-	8	31
CARLISLE	530	30	30	8	8	-	-	371	78	-	4	11
CITY OF DERRY (EGLINTON)	255	170	1	8	-	22	1	30	20	-	2	-
COVENTRY	1 754	147	91	47	-	1 155	-	35	368	-	42	41
DONCASTER SHEFFIELD	764	434	25	39	-	102	-	47	100	-	8	-
DUNDEE	1 525	101	10	21	4	40	5	1 268	37	-	73	-
DURHAM TEES VALLEY	1 177	380	52	4	70	17	-	201	432	-	10	403
EAST MIDLANDS INTERNATIONAL	5 095	4 129	298	244	-	83	180	-	46	-	6	291
EDINBURGH	8 695	8 252	205	122	-	3	5	8	8	-	17	116
EXETER	1 928	908	115	47	133	260	35	222	188	2	10	33
GLASGOW	7 063	6 418	138	212	-	19	257	112	-	2	26	91
GLOUCESTERSHIRE	3 670	117	31	29	91	474	29	2 214	597	2	-	-
HAWARDEN	374	-	-	-	153	17	204	-	-	-	6	16
HUMBERSIDE	1 721	907	162	229	-	271	238	-	54	-	1	46
INVERNESS	2 159	1 102	314	144	25	207	16	510	106	2	-	-
ISLAY	144	124	10	14	-	-	-	-	6	-	12	-
ISLES OF SCILLY (ST.MARYS)	407	380	4	4	-	-	-	-	11	-	-	2
KIRKWALL	1 094	1 014	171	58	4	14	-	-	2	-	-	-
LANDS END (ST JUST)	410	328	2	4	11	51	-	2	10	4	8	1
LEEDS BRADFORD	2 204	1 806	50	116	-	20	14	126	111	2	-	-
LERWICK (TINGWALL)	224	138	76	78	5	-	2	-	1	2	27	89
LIVERPOOL (JOHN LENNON)	3 680	2 832	73	32	-	26	2	584	86	2	8	9
LYDD	884	21	15	22	-	2	-	411	321	90	4	300
MANCHESTER	12 421	11 811	21	285	4	4	13	-	-	-		

22.26a Aircraft Movements November 2015

	Total	Commercial Movements				Non-Commercial Movements						
		Air Transport Total	Of Which Air Taxi	Positioning Flights	Local Movements	Test and Training	Other Flights by Air Transport Operators	Aero Club	Private	Official	Military	Business Aviation
Other UK Airports(Continued)												
NEWCASTLE	3 700	2 878	51	132	-	2	2	-	462	154	58	12
NEWQUAY	895	335	60	13	-	113	-	-	177	-	219	38
NORWICH	2 603	1 935	212	363	4	101	26	79	90	-	5	-
OXFORD (KIDLINGTON)	2 584	32	32	291	5	1 418	18	169	494	-	-	157
PRESTWICK	1 297	210	9	53	-	320	-	238	130	-	346	-
SCATSTA	715	678	3	31	-	6	-	-	-	-	-	-
SHOREHAM	1 925	30	-	9	-	12	1	1 384	458	-	19	-
SOUTHAMPTON	2 763	2 446	4	125	-	35	155	-	-	-	2	-
STORNOWAY	798	661	153	44	8	73	-	-	8	-	4	-
SUMBURGH	1 344	1 161	236	105	18	60	-	-	-	-	-	-
SWANSEA	296	-	-	5	-	-	-	226	70	-	-	-
TIREE	135	129	4	5	-	-	-	-	1	-	-	-
WICK JOHN O GROATS	281	204	37	43	2	8	-	-	24	-	-	-
Total Other UK Airports	115 010	79 886	4 024	3 962	1 096	6 165	1 929	11 399	6 038	270	1 569	2 696
Total All Reporting UK Airports	200 982	161 083	5 056	5 451	1 354	6 384	2 123	11 598	6 432	284	1 586	4 687
Non UK Reporting Airports												
ALDERNEY	506	396	30	6	46	4	-	30	24	-	-	-
GUERNSEY	2 910	2 000	129	138	228	4	25	332	171	4	8	-
ISLE OF MAN	2 024	1 746	135	73	-	8	-	24	75	-	8	90
JERSEY	3 028	1 954	173	81	-	6	57	163	743	-	23	1
Total Non UK Reporting Airports	8 468	6 096	467	298	274	22	82	549	1 013	4	39	91

Source: Civil Aviation Authority

Note
Business Aviation was collected under a category in its own right with effect from June 2001 data. However, currently it is not possible for all airports to report using this category

22.26b Terminal and Transit Passengers 2015 Comparison with the Previous Year

	Terminal and Transit Passengers			Terminal Passengers			Transit Passengers		
	2015	2014	Percentage Change	2015	2014	Percentage Change	2015	2014	Percentage Change
London Area Airports									
GATWICK	40 269 087	38 103 667	6	40 260 068	38 093 930	6	9 019	9 737	-7
HEATHROW	74 985 748	73 405 330	2	74 953 981	73 371 096	2	31 767	34 234	-7
LONDON CITY	4 319 301	3 647 824	18	4 319 301	3 647 824	18	-	-	..
LUTON	12 263 505	10 484 938	17	12 262 581	10 481 501	17	924	3 437	-73
SOUTHEND	900 648	1 102 358	-18	900 634	1 102 260	-18	14	98	-86
STANSTED	22 519 178	19 965 093	13	22 513 443	19 958 047	13	5 735	7 046	-19
Total London Area Airports	155 257 467	146 709 210	6	155 210 008	146 654 658	6	47 459	54 552	-13
Other UK Airports									
ABERDEEN	3 469 525	3 723 662	-7	3 469 328	3 723 411	-7	197	251	-22
BARRA	10 658	10 521	1	10 658	10 521	1	-	-	..
BELFAST CITY (GEORGE BEST)	2 692 713	2 555 145	5	2 692 713	2 555 111	5	-	34	..
BELFAST INTERNATIONAL	4 391 292	4 033 954	9	4 389 861	4 031 685	9	1 431	2 269	-37
BENBECULA	32 146	31 213	3	32 125	31 190	3	21	23	-9
BIGGIN HILL	644	497	30	644	497	30	-	-	..
BIRMINGHAM	10 187 122	9 705 955	5	10 180 059	9 698 488	5	7 063	7 467	-5
BLACKPOOL	33 494	223 998	-85	33 494	223 998	-85	-	-	..
BOURNEMOUTH	706 776	661 584	7	705 433	660 374	7	1 343	1 210	11
BRISTOL	6 786 790	6 339 805	7	6 781 195	6 333 058	7	5 595	6 747	-17
CAMBRIDGE	5 799	20 663	-72	5 799	20 663	-72	-	-	..
CAMPBELTOWN	8 511	9 365	-9	8 288	9 331	-11	223	34	556
CARDIFF WALES	1 160 506	1 023 932	13	1 158 383	1 019 545	14	2 123	4 387	-52
CITY OF DERRY (EGLINTON)	284 485	350 257	-19	284 482	350 257	-19	3	-	..
DONCASTER SHEFFIELD	857 109	724 885	18	856 592	724 252	18	517	633	-18
DUNDEE	21 973	22 069	0	21 942	22 069	-1	31	-	..
DURHAM TEES VALLEY	140 902	142 379	-1	140 373	142 274	-1	529	105	404
EAST MIDLANDS INTERNATIONAL	4 450 862	4 510 544	-1	4 446 219	4 506 791	-1	4 643	3 753	24
EDINBURGH	11 114 587	10 160 004	9	11 113 386	10 158 906	9	1 201	1 098	9
EXETER	821 789	767 404	7	821 165	766 572	7	624	832	-25
GLASGOW	8 714 307	7 715 988	13	8 709 531	7 708 867	13	4 776	7 121	-33
GLOUCESTERSHIRE	12 267	15 172	-19	12 253	15 141	-19	14	31	-55
HUMBERSIDE	222 107	239 173	-7	221 190	237 329	-7	917	1 844	-50
INVERNESS	669 364	612 725	9	667 560	611 150	9	1 804	1 575	15
ISLAY	29 346	27 659	6	28 993	27 412	6	353	247	43
ISLES OF SCILLY (ST.MARYS)	94 718	90 944	4	94 718	90 944	4	-	-	..
KIRKWALL	160 234	161 347	-1	149 524	150 877	-1	10 710	10 470	2
LANDS END (ST JUST)	54 169	44 475	22	53 704	44 284	21	465	191	143
LEEDS BRADFORD	3 455 445	3 274 474	6	3 445 291	3 263 247	6	10 154	11 227	-10
LERWICK (TINGWALL)	4 267	3 739	14	4 175	3 591	16	92	148	-38
LIVERPOOL (JOHN LENNON)	4 301 495	3 986 654	8	4 295 763	3 984 023	8	5 732	2 631	118
LYDD	1 134	1 227	-8	1 134	1 227	-8	-	-	..
MANCHESTER	23 136 047	21 989 682	5	23 094 593	21 950 223	5	41 454	39 459	5
MANSTON (KENT INT)	-	12 508	..	-	12 385	..	-	123	..
NEWCASTLE	4 562 853	4 516 739	1	4 559 848	4 512 976	1	3 005	3 763	-20
NEWQUAY	251 987	221 047	14	250 278	219 167	14	1 709	1 880	-9
NORWICH	459 664	458 968	0	459 664	458 931	0	-	37	..

22.26b Terminal and Transit Passengers 2015 Comparison with the Previous Year

	Terminal and Transit Passengers			Terminal Passengers			Transit Passengers		
	2015	2014	Percentage Change	2015	2014	Percentage Change	2015	2014	Percentage Change
Other UK Airports(Continued)									
OXFORD (KIDLINGTON)	166	1 194	-86	166	1 194	-86	-	-	..
PRESTWICK	610 837	913 685	-33	609 589	912 399	-33	1 248	1 286	-3
SCATSTA	253 526	279 799	-9	253 526	279 799	-9	-	-	..
SHOREHAM	490	452	8	490	452	8	-	-	..
SOUTHAMPTON	1 789 470	1 831 700	-2	1 775 638	1 829 575	-3	13 832	2 125	551
STORNOWAY	127 282	129 481	-2	124 984	127 237	-2	2 298	2 244	2
SUMBURGH	271 994	264 521	3	270 126	262 626	3	1 868	1 895	-1
TIREE	9 856	9 322	6	9 564	9 026	6	292	296	-1
WICK JOHN O GROATS	25 484	28 145	-9	24 152	27 633	-13	1 332	512	160
Total Other UK Airports	96 396 192	91 848 656	5	96 268 593	91 730 708	5	127 599	117 948	8
Total All Reporting UK Airports	251 653 659	238 557 866	5	251 478 601	238 385 366	5	175 058	172 500	1
Non UK Reporting Airports									
ALDERNEY	59 843	61 317	-2	59 843	61 317	-2	-	-	..
GUERNSEY	891 616	894 602	0	857 775	860 213	0	33 841	34 389	-2
ISLE OF MAN	781 601	729 703	7	780 857	728 591	7	744	1 112	-33
JERSEY	1 554 390	1 495 707	4	1 532 492	1 474 279	4	21 898	21 428	2
Total Non UK Reporting Airports	3 287 450	3 181 329	3	3 230 967	3 124 400	3	56 483	56 929	-1

Source: Civil Aviation Authority

Notes

Please note that figures may change overtime as each new version is produced. Information relating to an airport that has ceased to handle regular traffic/closed will be excluded from this table completely. For data concerning historical years it is recommended that you use earlier produced versions of this table.

22.26c Freight by Type and Nationality of Operator August 2015 - Tonnes

	Total	Scheduled Services						Charter Flights					
		UK Operators		Other EU Operators		Other Overseas Operators		UK Operators		Other EU Operators		Other Overseas Operators	
		Set Down	Picked Up	Set Down	Picked Up	Set Down	Picked Up	Set Down	Picked Up	Set Down	Picked Up	Set Down	Picked Up
London Area Airports													
GATWICK	5 677	1 176	1 671	36	35	1 454	936	190	150	4	25	1	-
HEATHROW	122 540	26 099	28 500	914	836	31 859	31 565	-	-	1 433	1 326	8	-
LONDON CITY	2	-	-	-	1	-	-	-	-	-	-	-	-
LUTON	2 156	1	6	1	2	246	162	35	11	1 563	129	-	-
STANSTED	17 070	-	-	262	1	179	161	-	-	1 248	465	9 365	5 389
Total London Area Airports	147 445	27 276	30 177	1 214	874	33 738	32 825	225	161	4 248	1 944	9 374	5 389
Other UK Airports													
ABERDEEN	602	14	9	19	14	4	8	277	250	-	-	-	7
BARRA	2	2	-	-	-	-	-	-	-	-	-	-	-
BELFAST CITY (GEORGE BEST)	46	11	10	9	15	-	-	-	-	-	-	-	-
BELFAST INTERNATIONAL	2 502	1	5	3	3	1	1	16	10	1 517	959	-	-
BIRMINGHAM	502	-	-	3	3	207	279	3	1	-	-	-	-
BOURNEMOUTH	148	-	-	-	-	-	-	-	148	-	-	-	-
COVENTRY	201	-	-	-	-	-	-	115	85	-	-	-	-
DONCASTER SHEFFIELD	52	-	1	-	-	-	-	1	-	-	-	-	51
EAST MIDLANDS INTERNATIONAL	22 122	-	1	-	-	-	-	1 567	1 535	8 287	7 083	2 189	1 460
EDINBURGH	1 643	12	-	-	-	-	40	-	-	894	697	-	-
GLASGOW	1 292	13	24	3	4	302	863	1	-	-	-	33	50
HUMBERSIDE	10	-	1	-	-	-	-	2	5	-	1	-	-
ISLAY	24	11	13	-	-	-	-	-	-	-	-	-	-
ISLES OF SCILLY (ST.MARYS)	5	5	-	-	-	-	-	-	-	-	-	-	-
KIRKWALL	6	1	5	-	-	-	-	-	-	-	-	-	-
LANDS END (ST JUST)	5	-	5	-	-	-	-	-	-	-	-	-	-
LIVERPOOL (JOHN LENNON)	23	3	9	-	11	-	-	-	-	-	-	-	-
MANCHESTER	8 441	251	339	97	43	3 730	2 963	154	116	244	213	61	230
NEWCASTLE	272	-	-	1	-	61	180	-	-	-	-	14	15
NORWICH	34	-	-	-	-	-	-	15	19	-	-	-	-
PRESTWICK	1 089	-	-	630	271	-	-	-	-	-	-	19	169
SCATSTA	53	-	-	-	-	-	-	24	29	-	-	-	-
SOUTHAMPTON	18	3	10	-	-	-	-	-	-	3	3	-	-
STORNOWAY	6	5	1	-	-	-	-	-	-	-	-	-	-
SUMBURGH	39	22	1	-	-	-	-	9	7	-	-	-	-
TIREE	2	2	-	-	-	-	-	-	-	-	-	-	-
Total Other UK Airports	39 139	356	434	761	360	4 305	4 335	2 184	2 205	10 945	8 955	2 315	1 983

22.26c Freight by Type and Nationality of Operator August 2015 - Tonnes

	Total	Scheduled Services						Charter Flights					
		UK Operators		Other EU Operators		Other Overseas Operators		UK Operators		Other EU Operators		Other Overseas Operators	
		Set Down	Picked Up	Set Down	Picked Up	Set Down	Picked Up	Set Down	Picked Up	Set Down	Picked Up	Set Down	Picked Up
Non UK Reporting Airports													
ALDERNEY	10	7	3	-	-	-	-	-	-	-	-	-	-
GUERNSEY	160	13	9	-	-	-	-	74	-	63	1	-	-
ISLE OF MAN	31	10	3	-	-	-	-	19	-	-	-	-	-
JERSEY	226	12	4	-	-	-	-	143	8	38	20	-	-
Total Non UK Reporting Airports	428	42	19	-	-	-	-	236	9	102	21	-	-
Total All Reporting UK Airports	186 583	27 632	30 611	1 975	1 234	38 044	37 159	2 409	2 366	15 193	10 899	11 689	7 372

Source: Civil Aviation Authority

22.26d Mail by Type and Nationality of Operator 2015 - Tonnes

	Total	Scheduled Services						Charter Flights					
		UK Operators		Other EU Operators		Other Overseas Operators		UK Operators		Other EU Operators		Other Overseas Operators	
		Set Down	Picked Up	Set Down	Picked Up	Set Down	Picked Up	Set Down	Picked Up	Set Down	Picked Up	Set Down	Picked Up
London Area Airports													
GATWICK	5 522	234	998	684	1 758	453	1 367	1	26	-	-	-	-
HEATHROW	94 975	9 011	14 397	6 385	4 704	26 681	33 753	1	-	-	-	9	34
LONDON CITY	1 438	-	-	-	114	358	965	-	-	-	-	-	-
STANSTED	19 115	-	-	-	2	10	11	7 360	11 540	98	94	-	-
Total London Area Airports	121 050	9 245	15 395	7 069	6 577	27 502	36 097	7 363	11 566	98	94	9	34
Other UK Airports													
ABERDEEN	1 528	2	4	-	-	-	-	953	351	167	52	-	-
BELFAST INTERNATIONAL	16 771	-	-	-	-	-	-	9 945	6 747	74	5	-	-
BENBECULA	2	1	1	-	-	-	-	-	-	-	-	-	-
BIRMINGHAM	113	-	-	11	10	-	91	-	-	-	-	-	-
BOURNEMOUTH	7 275	-	-	19	28	-	-	3 264	3 757	75	132	-	-
BRISTOL	2	-	1	-	-	-	-	-	1	-	-	-	-
CARDIFF WALES	274	-	-	-	-	-	-	274	-	-	-	-	-
EAST MIDLANDS INTERNATIONAL	29 928	11	5	19	54	-	-	12 449	17 009	131	250	-	-
EDINBURGH	16 360	1 157	736	-	9	-	-	8 291	6 086	67	13	-	-
EXETER	3 532	-	-	-	-	-	-	1 947	1 585	-	-	-	-
GLASGOW	112	28	73	-	-	-	9	-	-	-	-	-	2
INVERNESS	4	-	-	-	-	-	-	2	-	1	-	-	-
ISLAY	69	43	26	-	-	-	-	-	-	-	-	-	-
ISLES OF SCILLY (ST.MARYS)	169	105	65	-	-	-	-	-	-	-	-	-	-
KIRKWALL	28	8	21	-	-	-	-	-	-	-	-	-	-
LANDS END (ST JUST)	163	58	105	-	-	-	-	-	-	-	-	-	-
MANCHESTER	3 765	11	1	1	9	9	3 733	2 320	2	212	-	-	-
NEWCASTLE	4 633	-	-	-	-	-	4	-	1 968	-	129	-	-
SOUTHAMPTON	10	10	-	-	-	-	-	-	-	-	-	-	-
STORNOWAY	1	1	-	-	-	-	-	-	-	-	-	-	-
TIREE	36	31	5	-	-	-	-	-	-	-	-	-	-
Total Other UK Airports	84 775	1 465	1 041	50	110	9	3 837	39 446	37 508	727	581	-	2
Total All Reporting UK Airports	205 824	10 709	16 436	7 119	6 688	27 511	39 934	46 809	49 074	825	675	9	36
Non UK Reporting Airports													
ALDERNEY	82	59	24	-	-	-	-	-	-	-	-	-	-
GUERNSEY	2 791	25	59	-	-	-	-	1 408	1 245	49	6	-	-
ISLE OF MAN	2 490	-	-	-	-	-	-	1 429	945	65	52	-	-
JERSEY	1 746	2	1	-	-	-	-	1 226	515	-	2	-	-
Total Non UK Reporting Airports	7 110	85	83	-	-	-	-	4 063	2 705	113	60	-	-

Source: Civil Aviation Authority

this page is intentionally blank

Government finance

Chapter 23

Government Finance

Public sector (Tables 23.1 to 23.3 and 23.6)

In Table 23.1 the term public sector describes the consolidation of central government, local government and public corporations. General government is the consolidated total of central government and local government. The table shows details of the key public sector finances' indicators, consistent with the European System of Accounts 2010 (ESA10), by sub-sector.

The concepts in Table 23.1 are consistent with the format for public finances in the Economic and Fiscal Strategy Report (EFSR), published by HM Treasury on 11 June 1998, and the Budget. The public sector current budget is equivalent to net saving in national accounts plus capital tax receipts. Net investment is gross capital formation, plus payments less receipts of investment grants, less depreciation. Net borrowing is net investment less current budget. Net borrowing differs from the net cash requirement (see below) in that it is measured on an accruals basis whereas the net cash requirement is mainly a cash measure which includes some financial transactions.

Table 23.2 shows the public sector key fiscal balances. The table shows the component detail of the public sector key fiscal balance by economic category. The tables are consistent with the Budget.

Table 23.3 shows public sector net debt. Public sector net debt consists of the public sector's financial liabilities at face value, minus its liquid assets – mainly foreign currency exchange reserves and bank deposits. General government gross debt (consolidated) in Table 23.3 is consistent with the definition of general government gross debt reported to the European Commission under the requirements of the Maastricht Treaty.

More information on the concepts in Table 23.1, 23.2 and 23.3 can be found in a guide to monthly public sector finance statistics, GSS Methodology Series No 12, the ONS First Releases Public Sector Finances and Financial Statistics Explanatory Handbook.

Table 23.6 shows the taxes and National Insurance contributions paid to central government, local government, and to the institutions of the European Union. The table is the same as Table 11.1 of the National Accounts Blue Book. More information on the data and concepts in the table can be found in Chapter 11 of the Blue Book.

Consolidated Fund and National Loans Fund (Tables 23.4, 23.5 and 23.7)

The central government embraces all bodies for whose activities a Minister of the Crown, or other responsible person, is accountable to Parliament. It includes, in addition to the ordinary government departments, a number of bodies administering public policy, but without the substantial degree of financial independence which characterises the public corporations. It also includes certain extra-budgetary funds and accounts controlled by departments.

The government's financial transactions are handled through a number of statutory funds or accounts. The most important of these is the Consolidated Fund, which is the government's main account with the Bank of England. Up to 31 March 1968 the Consolidated Fund was virtually synonymous with the term 'Exchequer', which was then the government's central cash account. From 1 April 1968 the National Loans Fund, with a separate account at the Bank of England, was set up by the National Loans Act 1968. The general effect of this Act was to remove from the Consolidated Fund most of the government's domestic lending and the whole of the government's borrowing transactions, and to provide for them to be brought to account in the National Loans Fund.

Revenue from taxation and miscellaneous receipts, including interest and dividends on loans made from votes, continue to be paid into the Consolidated Fund.

After meeting the ordinary expenditure on Supply Services and the Consolidated Fund Standing Services, the surplus or deficit of the Consolidated Fund (Table 23.4), is payable into or met by the National Loans Fund. Table 23.4 also provides a summary of the transactions of the National Loans Fund. The service of the National Debt, previously borne by the Consolidated Fund, is now met from the National Loans Fund which receives:

 • interest payable on loans to the nationalised industries, local authorities and other bodies, whether the loans were made before or after 1 April 1968 and

• the profits of the Issue Department of the Bank of England, mainly derived from interest on government securities, which were formerly paid into the Exchange Equalisation Account.

The net cost of servicing the National Debt after applying these interest receipts and similar items is a charge on the Consolidated Fund as part of the standing services. Details of National Loans Fund loans outstanding are shown in Table 23.5. Details of borrowing and repayments of debt, other than loans from the National Loans Fund, are shown in Table 23.7.

Income tax (Table 23.10, 23.11)

Following the introduction of Independent Taxation from 1990/91, the Married Couple's Allowance was introduced. It is payable in addition to the Personal Allowance and between 1990/91 and 1992/93 went to the husband unless the transfer condition was met. The condition was that the husband was unable to make full use of the allowance himself and, in that case, he could transfer only part or all of the Married Couple's Allowance to his wife. In 1993/94 all or half of the allowance could be transferred to the wife if the couple had agreed beforehand. The wife has the right to claim half the allowance. The Married Couple's Allowance, and allowances linked to it, were restricted to 20 per cent in 1994/95 and to 15 per cent from 1995/96. From 2000/01 only people born before 6 April 1935 are entitled to Married Couple's Allowance.

The age allowance replaces the single allowance, provided the taxpayer's income is below the limits shown in the table. From 1989/90, for incomes in excess of the limits, the allowance is reduced by £1 for each additional £2 of income until the ordinary limit is reached (before it was £2 for each £3 of additional income). The relief is due where the taxpayer is aged 65 or over in the year of assessment.

The additional Personal Allowance could be claimed by a single parent (or by a married man if his wife was totally incapacitated) who maintained a resident child at his or her own expense. Widow's Bereavement Allowance was due to a widow in the year of her husband's death and in the following year provided the widow had not remarried before the beginning of that year. Both the additional Personal Allowance and the Widow's Bereavement Allowance were abolished from April 2000.

The Blind Person's Allowance may be claimed by blind persons (in England and Wales, registered as blind by a local authority) and surplus Blind Person's Allowance may be transferred to a husband or wife. Relief on life assurance premiums is given by deduction from the premium payable. From 1984/85, it is confined to policies made before 14 March 1984.

From 1993/94 until 1998/99 a number of taxpayers with taxable income in excess of the lower rate limit only paid tax at the lower rate. This was because it was only their dividend income and (from 1996/97) their savings income which took their taxable income above the lower rate limit but below the basic rate limit, and such income was chargeable to tax at the lower rate and not the basic rate.

In 1999/2000 the 10 per cent starting rate replaced the lower rate and taxpayers with savings or dividend income at the basic rate of tax are taxed at 20 per cent and 10 per cent respectively. Before 1999/2000 these people would have been classified as lower rate taxpayers.

Rateable values (Table 23.12)

Major changes to local government finance in England and Wales took effect from 1 April 1990. These included the abolition of domestic rating (replaced by the Community Charge, then replaced in 1993 by the Council Tax), the revaluation of all non-domestic properties, and the introduction of the Uniform Business Rate. Also in 1990, a new classification scheme was introduced which has resulted in differences in coverage. Further differences are caused by legislative changes which have changed the treatment of certain types of property. There was little change in the total rateable value of non-domestic properties when all these properties were re-valued in April 1995. Rateable values for offices fell and there was a rise for all other property types shown in the table.

With effect from 1 April 2000, all non-domestic properties were re-valued. Overall there was an increase in rateable values of over 25 per cent compared with the last year of the 1995 list. The largest proportionate increase was for offices and cinemas, with all property types given in the table showing rises.

The latest revaluation affecting all non-domestic properties took effect from 1 April 2010. In this revaluation the overall increase in rateable values between 1 April of the first year of the new list and the same day on the last year of the 2005 list was 21 per cent. The largest proportionate increase was for offices and educational properties, with all property types in the table showing rises.

Local authority capital expenditure and receipts (Table 23.16)

Authorities finance capital spending in a number of ways, including use of their own revenue funds, borrowing or grants and contributions from elsewhere. Until 31 March 2004, the capital finance system laid down in Part 4 of the Local Government and Housing Act 1989 (the '1989 Act') provided the framework within which authorities were permitted to finance capital spending from sources other than revenue - that is by the use of borrowing, long-term credit or capital receipts.

Until 31 March 2004, capital spending could be financed by:

• revenue resources – either the General Fund Revenue Account, the Housing Revenue Account (HRA) or the Major Repairs Reserve – but an authority could not charge council tenants for spending on general services, or spending on council houses to local taxpayers

• borrowing or long-term credit as authorised by the credit approvals issued by central government. Credit approvals were normally accompanied by an element of Revenue Support Grant (RSG) covering most of the costs of borrowing

• grants received from central government

• contributions or grants from elsewhere – including the National Lottery and non-departmental public bodies (NDPBs) such as Sport England, English Heritage and Natural England, as well as private sector partners, capital receipts (that is, proceeds from the sale of land, buildings or other fixed assets) and sums set aside as Provision for Credit Liabilities (PCL). This required the use of a credit approval, unless the authority was debt-free

From 1 April 2004, capital spending can be financed in the same ways, except that central government no longer issues credit approvals to allow authorities to finance capital spending by borrowing. However, it continues to provide financial support in the usual way, via RSG or HRA subsidy, towards some capital spending financed by borrowing that is Supported Capital Expenditure (Revenue). Authorities are now free to finance capital spending by self-financed borrowing within limits of affordability set, having regard to the 2003 Act and the CIPFA Prudential Code. The concept of PCL has not been carried forward into the new system, although authorities that were debt-free and had a negative credit ceiling at the end of the old system could still spend amounts of PCL built up under the old rules.

Local authority financing for capital expenditure (Table 23.16, 23.17)

Capital spending by local authorities is mainly for buying, constructing or improving physical assets such as:
- buildings – schools, houses, libraries and museums, police and fire stations
- land – for development, roads, playing fields
- vehicles, plant and machinery – including street lighting and road signs

It also includes grants and advances made to the private sector or the rest of the public sector for capital purposes, such as advances to Registered Social Landlords Local authority capital expenditure more than doubled between 2001/02 and 2007/08.

The underlying trend in capital expenditure shows an increase of 8 per cent from 2008/09 to 2009/10. The exceptional event was the payment by the Greater London Authority (Transport for London) of £1.7 billion to Metronet in 2007/08.

New construction, conversion and renovation forms the major part of capital spending. The largest increases in capital expenditure in 2008/09 were in police (44 per cent), and education (22 per cent). Capital expenditure on transport increased by 14 per cent, allowing for the Greater London Authority's grant payment via TfL in respect of Metronet in 2007/08. Between 2004/05 and 2008/09 capital expenditure on transport had risen from 20 per cent to 24 per cent of the total, while capital expenditure on housing has fallen from 28 per cent to 25 per cent of the total.

The largest percentage increase in capital expenditure in 2009/10 was in transport (24 per cent). Capital expenditure on housing and police fell by 8 per cent and 11 per cent respectively. Between 2005/06 and 2009/10 capital expenditure on transport has risen from 21 per cent to 28 per cent of the total, while capital expenditure on housing has fallen from 27 per cent to 21 per cent of the total.

23.1 Sector analysis of key fiscal balances[1]
United Kingdom
Not seasonally adjusted

£ million[2]

		2008/09	2009/10	2010/11	2011/12	2012/13	2013/14	2014/15	2015/16
Surplus on current budget[3]									
Central Government	ANLV	−46 129	−100 728	−96 321	−85 935	−85 094	−68 665	−53 447	−36 523
Local government	NMMX	−7 676	−8 489	−5 877	−4 975	−4 760	−5 034	−6 113	−8 997
General Government	ANLW	−53 805	−109 217	−102 198	−90 910	−89 854	−73 699	−59 560	−45 520
Public corporations	IL6M	13 123	16 597	19 246	19 626	13 800	10 002	9 157	7 303
Public sector	ANMU	−39 905	−86 135	−74 978	−62 317	−72 638	−63 233	−48 655	−34 938
Net investment[4]									
Central government	-ANNS	48 073	55 263	42 653	27 241	39 669	33 819	35 357	33 918
Local government	-ANNT	−598	−2 329	−1 572	5 815	−3 002	−3 561	−4 200	−4 553
General Government	-ANNV	47 475	52 934	41 081	33 056	36 667	30 258	31 157	29 365
Public corporations	-JSH6	−5 855	−6 350	2 159	1 524	1 892	1 641	3 443	4 757
Public sector	-ANNW	41 622	46 581	43 245	34 589	38 584	31 910	34 623	34 136
Net borrowing[5]									
Central government	-NMFJ	94 202	155 991	138 974	113 176	124 763	102 484	88 804	70 441
Local government	-NMOE	7 078	6 160	4 305	10 790	1 758	1 473	1 913	4 444
General Government	-NNBK	101 280	162 151	143 279	123 966	126 521	103 957	90 717	74 885
Public corporations	-IL6E	−18 977	−22 945	−17 087	−18 102	−11 908	−8 361	−5 714	−2 546
Public sector	-ANNX	81 528	132 718	118 223	96 906	111 222	95 143	83 278	69 074
Net cash requirement									
Central government[6]	RUUX	163 909	197 488	132 069	108 644	94 596	79 811	83 659	57 348
Local government	ABEG	4 401	4 958	773	8 816	1 815	−3 207	271	1 827
General Government	RUUS	166 914	202 673	138 454	126 325	..	..	..	..
Public corporations	IL6F	17 466	−103 496	−117 821	−160 869	−102 959	−63 630	−5 372	−13 159
Public sector	RURQ	184 887	94 665	7 641	−54 661	−19 128	288	66 295	33 381
Public sector debt									
Public sector net debt	BKQK	2 177 693	2 293 106	2 310 550	2 236 659	2 265 491	2 032 132	1 849 595	1 889 110
Public sector net debt (£ billion)	RUTN	2 177.7	2 293.1	2 310.6	2 236.7	2 265.5	2 032.1	1 849.6	1 889.1
Public sector net debt as a percentage of GDP	RUTO	143.1	147.1	143.0	134.8	131.5	112.6	99.5	98.7
Excluding financial inte ventions									
Net debt	HF6W	769.9	1 004.3	1 149.9	1 242.6	1 352.7	1 459.0	1 546.3	1 600.4
Net debt as a % GDP	HF6X	50.6	64.4	71.2	74.9	78.5	80.9	83.2	83.7

1 Consistent with the latest Public Sector Finances data, compliant with the European System of Accounts 2010 (ESA10)
2 Unless otherwise stated.
3 Net saving *plus* capital taxes.
4 Gross capital formation *plus* payments *less* receipts of investment grants *less* depreciation.

5 Net investment *less* surplus on current budget. A version of General government net borrowing is reported to the European Commision under the requirements of the Maastricht Treaty.
6 Central government net cash requirement (own account).

Source: Office for National Statistics: 020 7014 2124

23.2 Public sector transactions and fiscal balances[1]
United Kingdom

£ million

		2008 /09	2009 /10	2010 /11	2011 /12	2012 /13	2013 /14	2014 /15	2015 /16
Current receipts									
Taxes on income and wealth	ANSO	211 350	188 883	201 886	202 328	198 674	201 943	211 323	220 119
Taxes on production	NMYE	170 275	172 397	194 293	207 193	211 838	223 913	232 161	241 123
Other current taxes[2]	MJBC	33 257	33 943	34 618	36 936	37 208	39 179	40 422	41 612
Taxes on capital	NMGI	26 552	2 431	2 722	2 955	3 150	4 417	3 879	4 720
Social contributions	ANBO	96 613	96 638	97 747	101 597	104 483	107 306	110 260	113 440
Gross operating surplus	ANBP	44 142	46 387	51 016	51 181	49 321	51 307	56 880	56 355
Interest and dividends from private sector and Rest of World	ANBQ	46 914	51 184	45 732	49 519	44 214	34 077	13 734	10 814
Rent and other current transfers[3]	ANBS	950	1 811	−136	−951	1 184	1 005	1 948	1 281
Total current receipts	ANBT	606 432	593 674	627 878	650 758	650 072	663 147	670 607	689 464
Current expenditure									
Current expenditure on goods and services[4]	GZSN	321 220	334 501	341 069	341 261	345 350	353 042	358 528	361 980
Subsidies	NMRL	8 404	10 083	8 512	7 878	9 143	9 374	10 501	11 999
Social benefit	ANLY	177 793	194 293	201 982	210 608	220 564	222 914	228 694	230 831
Net current grants abroad[5]	GZSI	−1 394	999	3 166	2 555	2 728	3 509	2 068	2 961
Other current grants	NNAI	25 548	28 711	27 345	25 981	23 490	22 094	20 769	20 330
Interest and dividends paid to private sector and Rest of World	ANLO	73 918	68 869	75 031	77 822	73 070	65 091	47 687	46 279
Total current expenditure	ANLT	616 516	649 173	670 420	679 510	689 095	692 056	684 798	689 575
Saving, gross plus capital taxes	ANSP	−10 084	−55 499	−42 542	−28 752	−39 023	−28 909	−14 191	−111
Depreciation	-ANNZ	−31 010	−32 887	−34 354	−35 812	−36 764	−37 886	−38 287	−39 454
Surplus on current budget	ANMU	−39 905	−86 135	−74 978	−62 317	−72 638	−63 233	−48 655	−34 938
Net investment									
Gross fixed capital formation[6]	ANSQ	56 561	60 847	59 480	54 497	52 467	55 691	54 945	55 937
Less depreciation	-ANNZ	−31 010	−32 887	−34 354	−35 812	−36 764	−37 886	−38 287	−39 454
Increase in inventories and valuables	ANSR	345	34	55	−38	5	159	61	−57
Capital grants to private sector and Rest of World	ANSS	39 757	16 768	14 462	12 239	20 080	11 078	12 677	12 852
Capital grants from private sector and Rest of World	-ANST	−27 013	−1 206	−827	−1 033	−1 451	−2 441	−2 135	−1 964
Total net investment	-ANNW	41 622	46 581	43 245	34 589	38 584	31 910	34 623	34 136
Net borrowing[7]	-ANNX	81 528	132 718	118 223	96 906	111 222	95 143	83 278	69 074
Financial transactions determining net cash requirement									
Net lending to private sector and Rest of World	ANSU	−9 557	−33 782	−56 144	−29 189	−48 936	−8 480	−567	−8 204
Net acquisition of UK company securities	ANSV	54 024	53 259	−28 571	−67 232	−53 510	−66 251	−14 271	−38 058
Accounts receivable/payable	ANSW	−2 060	23 412	−628	−772	1 591	−642	9 082	12 362
Adjustment for interest on gilts	ANSX	−4 885	1 817	−7 819	−2 291	−5 126	1 761	−1 396	−1 026
Other financial transactions[8]	ANSY	65 838	−82 760	−17 421	−52 083	−24 368	−21 243	−9 831	−767
Public sector net cash requirement	RURQ	184 887	94 665	7 641	−54 661	−19 128	288	66 295	33 381

1 See chapter text.
2 Includes domestic rates, council tax, community charge, motor vehicle duty paid by household and some licence fees.
3 ESA10 transactions D44, D45, D74, D75 and D72-D71: includes rent of land, oil royalties, other property income and fine .
4 Includes non-trading capital consumption.

5 Net of current grants received from abroad.
6 Including net acquisition of land.
7 Net investment *less* surplus on current budget.
8 Includes statistical discrepancy, finance leasing and similar borrowing, insurance technical reserves and some other minor adjustments.

Source: Office for National Statistics: 020 7014 2124

23.3 Public sector net debt[1]
United Kingdom

£ million

		2008 /09	2009 /10	2010 /11	2011 /12	2012 /13	2013 /14	2014 /15	2015 /16
Central government sterling gross debt:									
British government stock									
Conventional gilts	BKPK	426 107	608 511	697 968	788 568	..	..	..	..
Index linked gilts	BKPL	154 038	178 170	220 631	253 779	..	..	..	..
Total	BKPM	580 145	786 681	918 599	1 042 347	1 142 442	1 244 355	1 300 401	1 346 337
Sterling Treasury bills	BKPJ	43 748	62 866	63 174	69 933	56 370	56 453	65 011	77 915
National savings	ACUA	97 231	98 804	98 886	102 903	102 238	105 663	123 801	135 224
Tax instruments	ACRV	1 121	819	679	638	633	880	1 158	975
Other sterling debt[2]	BKSK	64 612	39 934	34 068	42 506	34 260	35 251	38 141	34 532
Central government sterling gross debt total	BKSL	786 857	989 104	1 115 406	1 258 327	1 335 943	1 442 602	1 528 712	1 595 183
Central government foreign currency gross debt:									
US$ bonds	BKPG	–	–	–	–	–	–	–	–
ECU bonds	EYSJ	–	–	–	–	..	..	..	..
ECU/Euro Treasury notes	EYSV	–	–	–	–	..	..	..	..
Other foreign currency debt	BKPH	–	–	–	–	..	..	..	..
Central government foreign currency gross debt total	BKPI	–	–	–	–	–	–	–	–
Central government gross debt total	BKPW	809 649	1 059 345	1 196 643	1 329 736	1 403 764	1 505 264	1 584 140	1 630 651
Local government gross debt total	EYKP	67 568	68 798	71 496	82 101	84 586	85 235	86 566	88 116
less									
Central government holdings of local government debt	-EYKZ	−50 508	−50 889	−52 848	−61 641	..	..	..	..
Local government holdings of central government debt	-EYLA	−2 960	−2 689	−2 076	−3 415	..	..	..	..
General government gross debt (consolidated)	BKPX	823 529	1 074 005	1 212 630	1 345 699	1 420 755	1 521 377	1 601 697	1 649 233
Public corporations gross debt	EYYD	62 580	63 166	63 708	68 055	71 411	72 778	77 098	80 626
less:									
Central government holdings of public corporations debt	-EYXY	−4 879	−5 617	−5 604	−5 839	..	..	..	..
Local government holdings of public corporations debt	-EYXZ	−107	−153	−155	−152	..	..	..	..
Public corporations holdings of central government debt	-BKPZ	−3 947	−3 352	−3 301	−4 383	..	..	..	..
Public corporations holdings of local government debt	-EYXV	−33	−63	−150	−110	..	..	..	..
Public sector gross debt (consolidated)	BKQA	2 854 230	2 920 886	2 940 728	2 926 703	2 859 892	2 510 829	2 244 061	2 238 310
Public sector liquid assets:									
Official reserves	AIPD	31 527	44 652	52 969	..	..	..	..	..
Central government deposits[3]	BKSM	5 242	4 351	5 783	6 672	6 034	8 280	7 274	5 566
Other central government	BKSN	39 075	48 143	21 204	45 634	31 813	45 572	27 344	20 336
Local government deposits[3]	BKSO	21 781	18 177	19 145	18 123	21 110	23 170	23 683	22 733
Other local government short term assets	BKQG	2 072	1 780	3 227	4 733	4 119	4 722	6 263	6 665
Public corporations deposits[3]	BKSP	3 831	5 011	4 470	5 712	6 809	6 960	7 093	6 759
Other public corporations short term assets	BKSQ	2 166	2 284	2 170	2 296	2 280	2 169	2 229	2 236
Public sector liquid assets total	BKQJ	676 013	640 232	634 808	684 580	616 744	520 460	436 308	391 954
Public sector net debt	BKQK	2 177 693	2 293 106	2 310 550	2 236 659	2 265 491	2 032 132	1 849 595	1 889 110
as percentage of GDP[4]	RUTO	*143.1*	*147.1*	*143.0*	*134.8*	*131.5*	*112.6*	*99.5*	*98.7*

1 See chapter text.
2 Including overdraft with Bank of England.
3 Bank and building society deposits.
4 Gross domestic product at market prices from 12 months centred on the end
  of the month.

Source: Office for National Statistics: 020 7014 2124

23.4a Central government surplus on current budget and net borrowing

£ million

						Current receipts				
	Taxes on production	of which	Taxes on income and wealth						Asset	Other	
				Income and capital gains	Other[2,3]	Other taxes	NICs[4]	Interest and dividends	Purchase Facility	receipts[5]	Total
	Total	VAT	Total	tax[1]							
dataset identifier	1	2	3	4	5	6	7	8	9	10	11
code	NMBY	NZGF	NMCU	LIBR	LIBP	LIQR	AIIH	LIQP	L6BD	LIQQ	ANBV
2003	149,460	77,343	148,082	116,509	31,573	9,511	71,540	7,570	0	12,911	399,074
2004	157,324	81,544	162,876	125,032	37,844	10,232	79,224	7,260	0	13,203	430,119
2005	160,882	83,425	182,434	135,867	46,567	10,869	84,459	6,953	0	13,930	459,527
2006	169,922	87,758	195,083	145,608	49,475	11,662	89,550	6,566	0	14,412	487,195
2007	178,597	92,025	206,856	157,087	49,769	12,666	93,210	7,789	0	14,803	513,921
2008	176,562	91,997	206,637	161,631	45,006	12,416	98,319	9,567	0	15,932	519,433
2009	165,687	79,862	191,287	152,553	38,734	11,788	94,445	8,851	0	16,737	488,795
2010	190,221	95,865	198,518	153,507	45,011	12,354	97,346	7,870	0	17,511	523,820
2011	205,821	111,437	205,814	159,070	46,744	14,492	101,441	8,019	0	18,377	553,964
2012	211,604	113,859	199,237	155,278	43,959	14,475	104,319	11,846	0	20,048	561,529
2013	221,196	118,234	204,453	160,697	43,756	16,436	106,085	26,746	18,609	21,318	596,234
2014	232,685	124,211	208,762	164,156	44,606	16,366	109,120	16,800	8,682	23,253	606,986
2015	240,044	129,177	217,813	172,795	45,018	17,330	114,067	17,447	8,685	22,921	629,622
2003/04	152,597	79,207	151,673	119,146	32,527	9,698	75,148	7,524	0	12,448	409,088
2004/05	157,740	81,864	169,171	128,714	40,457	10,325	80,923	6,887	0	13,496	438,542
2005/06	162,801	83,507	187,869	139,116	48,753	11,140	85,559	6,875	0	14,042	468,286
2006/07	172,712	90,008	199,556	150,325	49,231	11,924	90,916	6,596	0	14,481	496,185
2007/08	179,495	92,467	211,850	162,360	49,490	12,730	95,437	8,496	0	14,985	522,993
2008/09	170,708	87,791	199,606	158,691	40,915	12,197	96,613	9,498	0	16,264	504,886
2009/10	172,846	84,798	191,262	149,640	41,622	11,878	96,638	8,390	0	16,860	497,874
2010/11	194,716	99,523	202,787	156,851	45,936	12,348	97,747	7,961	0	17,805	533,364
2011/12	207,774	112,057	202,148	157,043	45,105	15,111	101,597	9,556	0	18,606	554,792
2012/13	212,649	114,428	200,407	156,222	44,185	14,716	104,483	16,638	6,428	20,481	569,374
2013/14	224,943	120,167	204,948	161,530	43,418	16,664	107,306	20,396	12,181	21,615	595,872
2014/15	233,486	124,846	213,794	169,181	44,613	16,585	110,260	19,217	10,739	23,226	616,568
2015/16	243,165	130,514	221,791	175,934	45,857	17,398	114,061	17,283	8,529	22,930	636,628
2008 Q1	43,994	23,010	70,996	58,197	12,799	3,180	27,222	2,601	0	3,853	151,846
2008 Q2	45,830	24,681	42,948	31,515	11,433	3,176	23,784	2,095	0	3,935	121,768
2008 Q3	44,070	22,938	51,410	40,021	11,389	3,156	23,597	2,367	0	4,073	128,673
2008 Q4	42,668	21,368	41,283	31,898	9,385	2,904	23,716	2,504	0	4,071	117,146
2009 Q1	38,140	18,804	63,965	55,257	8,708	2,961	25,516	2,532	0	4,185	137,299
2009 Q2	40,583	19,070	40,073	30,160	9,913	2,907	22,990	2,603	0	4,122	113,278
2009 Q3	42,790	20,649	47,049	36,786	10,263	3,105	22,535	1,714	0	4,183	121,376
2009 Q4	44,174	21,339	40,200	30,350	9,850	2,815	23,404	2,002	0	4,247	116,842
2010 Q1	45,299	23,740	63,940	52,344	11,596	3,051	27,709	2,071	0	4,308	146,378
2010 Q2	49,860	23,810	43,386	30,987	12,399	3,067	23,115	1,579	0	4,325	125,332
2010 Q3	47,178	24,090	49,856	38,451	11,405	3,247	22,983	2,242	0	4,406	129,912
2010 Q4	47,884	24,225	41,336	31,725	9,611	2,989	23,539	1,978	0	4,472	122,198
2011 Q1	49,794	27,398	68,209	55,688	12,521	3,045	28,110	2,162	0	4,602	155,922
2011 Q2	50,327	27,363	44,075	32,055	12,020	4,293	24,484	1,897	0	4,536	129,612
2011 Q3	52,989	28,427	50,450	38,637	11,813	3,808	24,326	2,112	0	4,597	138,282
2011 Q4	52,711	28,249	43,080	32,690	10,390	3,346	24,521	1,848	0	4,642	130,148
2012 Q1	51,747	28,018	64,543	53,661	10,882	3,664	28,266	3,699	0	4,831	156,750
2012 Q2	51,362	28,135	42,933	31,481	11,452	3,423	25,631	4,248	0	5,018	132,615
2012 Q3	53,336	28,030	50,002	38,314	11,688	3,853	25,201	1,944	0	5,085	139,421
2012 Q4	55,159	29,676	41,759	31,822	9,937	3,535	25,221	1,955	0	5,114	132,743
2013 Q1	52,792	28,587	65,713	54,605	11,108	3,905	28,430	8,491	6,428	5,264	164,595
2013 Q2	53,820	29,091	45,148	34,028	11,120	4,813	26,556	13,716	11,655	5,221	149,274
2013 Q3	56,871	30,064	49,918	38,765	11,153	3,971	25,239	2,740	526	5,280	144,019
2013 Q4	57,713	30,492	43,674	33,299	10,375	3,747	25,860	1,799	0	5,553	138,346
2014 Q1	56,539	30,520	66,208	55,438	10,770	4,133	29,651	2,141	0	5,561	164,233
2014 Q2	57,019	30,567	44,139	32,940	11,199	4,145	26,432	5,987	4,107	5,418	143,140
2014 Q3	58,581	30,592	52,371	40,891	11,480	4,289	26,279	2,743	525	5,671	149,934
2014 Q4	60,546	32,532	46,044	34,887	11,157	3,799	26,758	5,929	4,050	6,603	149,679
2015 Q1	57,340	31,155	71,240	60,463	10,777	4,352	30,791	4,558	2,057	5,534	173,815
2015 Q2	58,910	31,709	46,607	34,687	11,920	4,448	28,005	5,931	3,904	6,238	150,139
2015 Q3	61,219	32,694	53,660	41,953	11,707	4,468	27,401	2,727	411	5,478	154,953
2015 Q4	62,575	33,619	46,306	35,692	10,614	4,062	27,870	4,231	2,313	5,671	150,715
2016 Q1	60,461	32,492	75,218	63,602	11,616	4,420	30,785	4,394	1,901	5,543	180,821

Source: Office for National Statistics; HM Treasury

Relationship between columns 11=1+3+6+7+8+10

1. Includes capital gains tax paid by households. Includes income tax and capital gains tax paid by corporations.
2. Mainly comprises corporation tax and petroleum revenue tax.
3. Includes diverted profit tax
4. Formerly titled compulsory social contributions.
5. Consists largely of gross operating surplus, equates to depreciation for government. Also includes rent receipts.

23.4a Central government surplus on current budget and net borrowing

£ million

	Current expenditure				Saving, gross plus capital taxes	Depreciation	Current budget deficit	Net investment	Net borrowing
	Interest	Net Social Benefits	Other	Total					
dataset identifier	12	13	14	15	16	17	18	19	20
code	NMFX	GZSJ	LIQS	ANLP	ANPM	NSRN	-ANLV	-ANNS	-NMFJ
2003	22,050	117,683	263,138	402,871	-3,797	11,102	14,899	23,568	38,467
2004	23,621	126,449	281,285	431,355	-1,236	11,450	12,686	23,152	35,838
2005	26,451	130,527	300,667	457,645	1,882	12,125	10,243	27,761	38,004
2006	27,598	134,482	322,924	485,004	2,191	12,730	10,539	28,635	39,174
2007	31,700	143,582	332,595	507,877	6,044	13,150	7,106	30,791	37,897
2008	33,015	154,145	350,033	537,193	-17,760	14,155	31,915	44,268	76,183
2009	27,881	170,873	369,552	568,306	-79,511	14,804	94,315	51,863	146,178
2010	44,944	178,158	387,931	611,033	-87,213	15,515	102,728	43,645	146,373
2011	51,295	183,643	383,972	618,910	-64,946	16,417	81,363	37,300	118,663
2012	47,955	193,098	397,595	638,648	-77,119	17,135	94,254	35,544	129,798
2013	49,200	195,706	395,458	640,364	-44,130	17,497	61,627	30,802	92,429
2014	48,472	200,754	405,800	655,026	-48,040	17,843	65,883	36,258	102,141
2015	43,296	202,852	406,381	652,529	-22,907	18,220	41,127	37,908	79,035
2003/04	22,236	120,876	267,213	410,325	-1,237	10,795	12,032	22,620	34,652
2004/05	24,771	126,997	288,071	439,839	-1,297	11,707	13,004	24,986	37,990
2005/06	26,481	131,741	305,900	464,122	4,164	12,247	8,083	27,499	35,582
2006/07	28,761	135,745	323,004	487,510	8,675	12,804	4,129	30,385	34,514
2007/08	31,403	145,283	339,829	516,515	6,478	13,355	6,877	36,180	43,057
2008/09	31,704	159,241	352,995	543,940	-39,054	14,419	53,473	46,945	100,418
2009/10	31,750	172,792	376,790	581,332	-83,458	14,884	98,342	49,986	148,328
2010/11	46,784	178,825	388,213	613,822	-80,458	15,807	96,265	42,109	138,374
2011/12	49,837	186,180	389,154	625,171	-70,379	16,671	87,050	27,241	114,291
2012/13	48,983	194,778	392,749	636,510	-67,136	17,129	84,265	39,930	124,195
2013/14	48,797	196,144	400,846	645,787	-49,915	17,583	67,498	33,764	101,262
2014/15	45,371	202,079	404,847	652,297	-35,729	17,944	53,673	36,853	90,526
2015/16	45,127	203,681	405,044	653,852	-17,224	18,297	35,521	36,855	72,376
2008 Q1	7,146	34,851	87,828	129,825	22,021	3,441	-18,580	16,307	-2,273
2008 Q2	8,914	38,220	89,322	136,456	-14,688	3,515	18,203	7,212	25,415
2008 Q3	7,763	39,340	85,776	132,879	-4,206	3,579	7,785	9,531	17,316
2008 Q4	9,192	41,734	87,107	138,033	-20,887	3,620	24,507	11,218	35,725
2009 Q1	5,835	39,947	90,790	136,572	727	3,705	2,978	18,984	21,962
2009 Q2	7,931	42,077	95,467	145,475	-32,197	3,648	35,845	8,084	43,929
2009 Q3	4,394	43,141	91,436	138,971	-17,595	3,698	21,293	9,797	31,090
2009 Q4	9,721	45,708	91,859	147,288	-30,446	3,753	34,199	14,998	49,197
2010 Q1	9,704	41,866	98,028	149,598	-3,220	3,785	7,005	17,107	24,112
2010 Q2	12,305	43,631	98,314	154,250	-28,918	3,842	32,760	7,234	39,994
2010 Q3	10,140	44,979	94,759	149,878	-19,966	3,911	23,877	9,445	33,322
2010 Q4	12,795	47,682	96,830	157,307	-35,109	3,977	39,086	9,859	48,945
2011 Q1	11,544	42,533	98,310	152,387	3,535	4,077	542	15,571	16,113
2011 Q2	14,116	45,523	99,723	159,362	-29,750	4,065	33,815	5,887	39,702
2011 Q3	11,182	47,206	93,153	151,541	-13,259	4,118	17,377	7,336	24,713
2011 Q4	14,453	48,381	92,786	155,620	-25,472	4,157	29,629	8,506	38,135
2012 Q1	10,086	45,070	103,492	158,648	-1,898	4,331	6,229	5,512	11,741
2012 Q2	14,251	48,455	98,494	161,200	-28,585	4,226	32,811	16,174	48,985
2012 Q3	9,631	48,980	96,589	155,200	-15,779	4,270	20,049	6,381	26,430
2012 Q4	13,987	50,593	99,020	163,600	-30,857	4,308	35,165	7,477	42,642
2013 Q1	11,114	46,750	98,646	156,510	8,085	4,325	-3,760	9,898	6,138
2013 Q2	14,459	48,568	105,728	168,755	-19,481	4,363	23,844	5,541	29,385
2013 Q3	10,262	49,586	93,875	153,723	-9,704	4,400	14,104	7,303	21,407
2013 Q4	13,365	50,802	97,209	161,376	-23,030	4,409	27,439	8,060	35,499
2014 Q1	10,711	47,188	104,034	161,933	2,300	4,411	2,111	12,860	14,971
2014 Q2	13,940	50,044	105,023	169,007	-25,867	4,443	30,310	6,627	36,937
2014 Q3	11,011	51,263	97,216	159,490	-9,556	4,481	14,037	7,085	21,122
2014 Q4	12,810	52,259	99,527	164,596	-14,917	4,508	19,425	9,686	29,111
2015 Q1	7,610	48,513	103,081	159,204	14,611	4,512	-10,099	13,455	3,356
2015 Q2	13,431	50,400	103,578	167,409	-17,270	4,541	21,811	8,625	30,436
2015 Q3	10,499	51,337	98,927	160,763	-5,810	4,569	10,379	7,591	17,970
2015 Q4	11,756	52,602	100,795	165,153	-14,438	4,598	19,036	8,237	27,273
2016 Q1	9,441	49,342	101,744	160,527	20,294	4,589	-15,705	12,402	-3,303

Source: Office for National Statistics; HM Treasury

Relationship between columns 15=12+13+14 ; 18=(15-11)+17 ; 20=18+19

1. Includes capital gains tax paid by households. Includes income tax and capital gains tax paid by corporations.
2. Mainly comprises corporation tax and petroleum revenue tax.
3. Formerly titled compulsory social contributions.
4. Consists largely of gross operating surplus, equates to depreciation for government. Also includes rent receipts.

23.4b Central government surplus on current budget and net borrowing - monthly

£ million

Current receipts

| | Taxes on production | of which | Taxes on income and wealth | | | | | | Asset | Other | |
	Total	VAT	Total	Income and capital gains tax[1]	Other[2]	Other taxes	NICs[3]	Interest and dividends	Purchase Facility	receipts[4]	Total
dataset identifier code	NMBY	NZGF	NMCU	LIBR	LIBP	LIQR	AIIH	LIQP	L6BD	LIQQ	ANBV
2014 Jan	18,536	10,355	32,692	25,163	7,529	1,370	8,969	544	0	1,821	63,932
2014 Feb	18,221	9,919	17,124	15,462	1,662	1,379	9,490	495	0	1,782	48,491
2014 Mar	19,539	10,246	16,504	14,813	1,691	1,434	11,192	1,096	0	1,825	51,590
2014 Apr	18,585	10,226	16,792	11,470	5,322	1,329	8,853	4,697	4,107	1,759	52,015
2014 May	18,978	10,134	11,934	10,222	1,712	1,513	8,511	624	0	1,762	43,322
2014 Jun	19,138	10,207	12,972	11,248	1,724	1,417	9,068	654	0	1,756	45,005
2014 Jul	19,562	10,189	24,175	17,586	6,589	1,455	8,753	1,264	525	1,808	57,017
2014 Aug	19,075	10,058	13,970	12,341	1,629	1,582	8,774	707	0	1,885	45,993
2014 Sep	19,603	10,345	13,330	10,964	2,366	1,537	8,752	758	0	1,842	45,822
2014 Oct	20,218	10,789	18,604	11,121	7,483	1,463	8,534	4,930	4,050	1,788	55,537
2014 Nov	19,792	10,770	12,592	11,140	1,452	1,358	8,761	478	0	2,906	45,887
2014 Dec	20,281	10,973	16,190	12,626	3,564	1,341	9,463	508	0	1,781	49,564
2015 Jan	18,906	10,684	36,639	28,458	8,181	1,374	9,214	2,606	2,057	1,778	70,517
2015 Feb	18,774	10,305	18,297	16,558	1,739	1,412	9,982	612	0	1,786	50,863
2015 Mar	19,324	10,166	17,236	15,447	1,789	1,476	11,595	1,329	0	1,815	52,775
2015 Apr	19,267	10,601	18,038	11,776	6,262	1,401	9,148	4,596	3,904	1,856	54,306
2015 May	19,399	10,452	12,966	11,384	1,582	1,553	9,309	678	0	2,023	45,928
2015 Jun	19,889	10,656	13,318	11,525	1,793	1,634	9,392	650	0	2,189	47,072
2015 Jul	20,781	10,822	25,391	18,538	6,853	1,663	9,053	1,023	411	1,842	59,753
2015 Aug	19,803	10,945	13,506	12,165	1,341	1,620	9,198	571	0	1,799	46,497
2015 Sep	20,253	10,927	13,855	11,251	2,604	1,586	8,995	1,127	0	1,797	47,613
2015 Oct	20,890	11,222	19,036	11,636	7,400	1,661	9,014	2,882	2,313	1,815	55,298
2015 Nov	20,284	11,006	13,346	11,529	1,817	1,508	9,091	668	0	1,856	46,753
2015 Dec	21,095	11,391	16,168	12,530	3,638	1,457	9,609	675	0	1,881	50,885
2016 Jan	19,774	11,038	38,031	30,310	7,721	1,433	9,744	2,464	1,901	1,770	73,216
2016 Feb	20,364	10,924	18,898	17,254	1,644	1,500	9,944	574	0	1,828	53,108
2016 Mar	19,880	10,530	17,972	16,039	1,933	1,600	10,943	1,354	0	1,889	53,638
2016 Apr	20,254	10,866	17,823	11,988	5,835	1,456	9,916	4,493	3,808	1,975	55,917
2016 May	19,546	10,405	13,407	11,454	1,953	1,549	9,896	917	0	1,900	47,215
2016 Jun	20,350	10,844	14,212	12,249	1,963	1,614	10,438	524	0	1,906	49,044

Current expenditure

	Interest	Net Social Benefits	Other	Total	Saving, gross plus capital taxes	Depreciation	Current budget deficit	Net investment	Net borrowing
dataset identifier code	NMFX	GZSJ	LIQS	ANLP	ANPM	NSRN	-ANLV	-ANNS	-NMFJ
2014 Jan	3,691	16,402	32,461	52,554	11,378	1,491	-9,887	3,494	-6,393
2014 Feb	4,388	14,829	35,994	55,211	-6,720	1,491	8,211	3,779	11,990
2014 Mar	2,600	16,042	35,307	53,949	-2,359	1,429	3,788	5,502	9,290
2014 Apr	5,367	16,867	40,627	62,861	-10,846	1,481	12,327	2,504	14,831
2014 May	4,226	16,842	30,825	51,893	-8,571	1,481	10,052	2,070	12,122
2014 Jun	4,315	16,041	33,134	53,490	-8,485	1,481	9,966	2,104	12,070
2014 Jul	3,710	17,239	32,456	53,405	3,612	1,494	-2,118	2,865	747
2014 Aug	4,253	16,716	31,603	52,572	-6,579	1,494	8,073	1,803	9,876
2014 Sep	3,015	17,003	32,584	52,602	-6,780	1,493	8,273	2,402	10,675
2014 Oct	4,873	17,029	32,460	54,362	1,175	1,503	328	2,986	3,314
2014 Nov	4,191	18,063	31,769	54,023	-8,136	1,503	9,639	2,328	11,967
2014 Dec	3,713	17,304	34,776	55,793	-6,229	1,502	7,731	3,741	11,472
2015 Jan	2,864	16,661	32,552	52,077	18,440	1,507	-16,933	3,226	-13,707
2015 Feb	3,824	15,298	35,239	54,361	-3,498	1,507	5,005	3,058	8,063
2015 Mar	890	16,614	34,869	52,373	402	1,506	1,104	6,270	7,374
2015 Apr	4,989	17,041	37,980	60,010	-5,704	1,518	7,222	2,448	9,670
2015 May	3,939	16,809	31,902	52,650	-6,722	1,518	8,240	2,095	10,335
2015 Jun	4,456	16,701	33,990	55,147	-8,075	1,518	9,593	2,591	12,184
2015 Jul	4,026	17,440	33,496	54,962	4,791	1,528	-3,263	2,703	-560
2015 Aug	3,969	16,613	32,187	52,769	-6,272	1,528	7,800	1,980	9,780
2015 Sep	2,457	17,161	32,875	52,493	-4,880	1,529	6,409	2,111	8,520
2015 Oct	5,079	16,897	33,328	55,304	-6	1,539	1,545	3,143	4,688
2015 Nov	3,176	18,336	32,558	54,070	-7,317	1,539	8,856	3,217	12,073
2015 Dec	3,453	17,487	34,593	55,533	-4,648	1,539	6,187	1,884	8,071
2016 Jan	4,067	16,497	32,520	53,084	20,132	1,553	-18,579	3,272	-15,307
2016 Feb	4,388	15,903	33,002	53,293	-185	1,553	1,738	3,155	4,893
2016 Mar	943	16,546	35,372	52,861	777	1,552	775	5,319	6,094
2016 Apr	5,115	17,271	36,160	58,546	-2,629	1,630	4,259	4,590	8,849
2016 May	4,596	16,984	32,062	53,642	-6,427	1,630	8,057	1,908	9,965
2016 Jun	3,611	16,733	35,179	55,523	-6,479	1,630	8,109	2,943	11,052

Source: Office for National Statistics; HM Treasury

1 Includes capital gains tax paid by households. Includes income tax and capital gains tax paid by corporations.
2 Mainly comprises corporation tax and petroleum revenue tax.
3 Formerly titled compulsory social contributions.
4 Consists largely of gross operating surplus, equates to depreciation for government. Also includes rent receipts.

23.5 National Loans Fund: assets and liabilities

United Kingdom as at 31 March 2016

	Note	At 31 March 2016 £m	At 31 March 2015 £m
Assets			
Advances	6	**206,574**	232,899
Loans	7	**2,822**	2,652
Other assets	8	**94,806**	89,203
IMF Quota Subscription & Lending	9	**21,385**	11,775
Total assets		**325,587**	336,529
Liabilities			
Gilt-edged stock	10	**1,525,159**	1,479,177
National Savings and Investments products	11	**135,149**	123,889
Other debt:			
FLS Treasury Bills	12	**86,387**	77,885
Other	12	**51,477**	51,269
Liabilities to the IMF	9	**16,229**	8,839
Total liabilities		**1,814,401**	1,741,059
Net liabilities		**1,488,814**	1,404,530
Liability of the Consolidated Fund to the National Loans Fund		**1,488,814**	1,404,530

John Kingman
Accounting Officer
HM Treasury

Source: HM Treasury

23.6a Taxes paid by UK residents to general government and the European Union
Total economy sector S.1

£ million

			2008	2009	2010	2011	2012	2013	2014	2015
Generation of income										
Uses										
Taxes on production and imports		D.2								
Taxes on products and imports		D.21								
Value added tax (VAT)		D.211								
Paid to central government	NZGF		92 002	79 900	95 865	111 437	113 859	118 234	124 211	128 816
Total	QYRC	D.211	92 002	79 900	95 865	111 437	113 859	118 234	124 211	128 816
Taxes and duties on imports excluding VAT		D.212								
Paid to central government: import duties[1]	NMXZ	D.2121	–	–	–	–	–	–	–	–
Paid to EU: import duties	FJWE	D.2121	2 636	2 645	2 933	2 925	2 885	2 914	2 949	3 077
Total	QYRB	D.212	2 636	2 645	2 933	2 925	2 885	2 914	2 949	3 077
Taxes on products excluding VAT and import duties		D.214								
Paid to central government										
Customs and excise revenue										
Beer	GTAM		3 140	3 189	3 278	3 429	3 425	3 337	3 337	3 255
Wines, cider, perry and spirits	GTAN		5 533	5 728	6 075	6 439	6 775	7 063	7 246	7 395
Tobacco	GTAO		8 203	9 056	9 076	9 361	9 897	9 479	9 436	9 190
Hydrocarbon oils	GTAP		24 790	25 894	27 013	26 923	26 703	26 698	27 095	27 416
Car tax	GTAT		–	–	–	–	–	–	–	–
Betting, gaming and lottery	CJQY		989	1 013	1 092	1 206	1 207	1 538	1 708	2 053
Air passenger duty	CWAA		1 876	1 800	2 094	2 605	2 766	2 960	3 154	3 119
Insurance premium tax	CWAD		2 281	2 259	2 401	2 942	3 022	3 018	2 964	3 294
Landfill tax	BKOF		954	842	1 065	1 090	1 094	1 191	1 143	1 065
Other	ACDN		–	–	–	–	–	–	–	–
Fossil fuel levy	CIQY		–	–	–	–	–	–	–	–
Gas levy	GTAZ		–	–	–	–	–	–	–	–
Stamp duties	GTBC		9 499	7 141	9 098	8 831	8 918	11 542	14 069	13 791
Levies on exports (third country trade)	CUDF		–	–	–	–	–	–	–	–
Camelot payments to national lottery										
Distribution fund	LIYH		1 405	1 553	1 625	1 793	1 832	1 644	1 721	1 713
Purchase tax	EBDB		–	–	–	–	–	–	–	–
Hydro-benefit	LITN		–	–	–	–	–	–	–	–
Aggregates levy	MDUQ		334	275	290	290	264	282	342	354
Milk super levy	DFT3		–	–	–	–	–	–	–	–
Climate change levy	LSNT		717	693	666	675	624	1 098	1 506	1 740
Channel 4 funding formula	EG9G		–	–	–	–	–	–	–	–
Renewable energy obligations	EP89		996	1 099	1 243	1 423	1 842	2 391	2 931	3 691
Rail franchise premia	LITT		285	496	792	993	1 275	1 275	1 501	1 611
Other taxes and levies	GCSP		–	–	–	–	–	–	–	–
Vehicle registration tax	MVPC		134	122	123	120	125	138	151	169
Total paid to central government[6]	NMYB		61 136	61 160	65 931	68 120	69 769	73 604	78 304	79 856
Paid to the european union										
Sugar levy	GTBA		53	10	12	12	13	12	11	10
European coal and steel community levy	GTBB		–	–	–	–	–	–	–	–
Total paid to the european union	FJWG		53	10	12	12	13	12	11	10
Total taxes on products excluding VAT and import duties[6]	QYRA	D.214	61 189	61 170	65 943	68 132	69 782	73 616	78 315	79 866
Total taxes on products and imports	NZGW	D.21	155 827	143 715	164 741	182 494	186 526	194 764	205 475	211 759
Production taxes other than on products		D.29								
Paid to central government										
Consumer credit act fees	CUDB		328	435	480	480	480	480	480	480
National non-domestic rates	CUKY		20 607	21 361	21 509	22 444	23 514	24 386	24 826	25 268
Northern Ireland non-domestic rates	NSEZ		328	325	361	368	366	373	378	397
Levies paid to central government levy-funded bodies	LITK		459	746	569	576	600	585	630	648
London regional transport levy	GTBE		–	–	–	–	–	–	–	–
IBA levy	GTAL		–	–	–	–	–	–	–	–
Motor vehicle duties paid by businesses	EKED		885	908	937	931	940	977	946	1 112
Regulator fees	GCSQ		70	72	90	78	81	84	93	87
Northern Ireland driver vehicle agency	IY9N		4	4	4	4	4	4	4	4
Bank payroll tax: accrued receipts	JT2Q		–	–	3 413	–	–	–	–	–
Emissions trading scheme	M98G		–	31	157	288	288	316	504	552
Carbon reduction commitment	L8UA		–	–	–	–	346	606	569	535
Total	NMBX		22 681	23 882	27 520	25 169	26 619	27 811	28 430	29 083
Paid to local government										
Non-domestic rates[2]	DM9L		301	317	329	336	344	350	353	377
Crossrail business rates supplement	MHG4		–	–	168	228	233	217	218	224
Toal	NMYH		301	317	497	564	577	567	571	601
Total production taxes other than on products	NMYD	D.29	22 982	24 199	28 017	25 733	27 196	28 378	29 001	29 684
Total taxes on production and imports, paid		D.2								
Paid to central government	NMBY		175 819	164 942	189 316	204 726	210 247	219 649	230 945	237 755
Paid to local government	NMYH		301	317	497	564	577	567	571	601
Paid to the European Union	FJWB		2 689	2 655	2 945	2 937	2 898	2 926	2 960	3 087
Total	NZGX	D.2	178 809	167 914	192 758	208 227	213 722	223 142	234 476	241 443

23.6b

Taxes paid by UK residents to general government and the European Union

Total economy sector S.1

£ million

			2008	2009	2010	2011	2012	2013	2014	2015
Secondary distribution of income										
Uses										
Current taxes on income, wealth etc.		D.5								
Taxes on income		D.51								
Paid to central government										
Households income taxes	DRWH		154 833	143 640	150 056	154 074	149 466	155 214	158 872	166 291
Corporation tax	ACCD		46 672	35 458	41 206	42 263	39 857	39 438	40 635	44 064
Petroleum revenue tax	DBHA		2 663	1 047	1 349	1 775	2 106	1 296	568	−552
Windfall tax	EYNK		–	–	–	–	–	–	–	–
Other taxes on income	BMNX		8 190	10 387	5 041	6 594	7 308	7 129	6 804	8 350
Total	NMCU	D.51	212 358	190 532	197 652	204 706	198 737	203 077	206 879	218 153
Other current taxes		D.59								
Paid to central government										
Motor vehicle duty paid by households	CDDZ		4 639	4 722	4 903	4 889	4 933	5 124	5 029	4 787
Northern Ireland domestic rates	NSFA		329	355	335	391	416	409	404	385
Boat licences	NSNP		–	–	–	–	–	–	–	–
Fishing licences	NRQB		20	20	20	23	21	21	21	21
National non-domestic rates paid by Non-market sectors[3]	BMNY		1 354	1 423	1 481	1 637	1 709	1 731	1 752	1 767
Passport fees	E8A6		376	351	400	368	362	343	386	439
Television licence fee	DH7A		2 949	3 009	3 088	3 088	3 117	3 082	3 124	3 131
Northern Ireland driver vehicle agency	IY9O		15	14	12	12	12	12	12	12
Bank levy	KIH3		–	–	–	1 454	1 609	2 171	2 693	3 367
Total	NMCV		9 682	9 894	10 239	11 862	12 179	12 893	13 421	13 909
Paid to local government										
Domestic rates[2]	NMHK		122	131	146	157	164	170	176	194
Community charge	NMHL		–	–	–	–	–	–	–	–
Council tax	NMHM		24 252	24 916	25 429	25 715	26 045	27 051	27 933	28 723
Total	NMIS		24 374	25 047	25 575	25 872	26 209	27 221	28 109	28 917
Total	NVCM	D.59	34 056	34 941	35 814	37 734	38 388	40 114	41 530	42 826
Total current taxes on income, wealth etc		D.5								
Paid to central government	NMCP		222 040	200 426	207 891	216 568	210 916	215 970	220 300	232 062
Paid to local government	NMIS		24 374	25 047	25 575	25 872	26 209	27 221	28 109	28 917
Total	NMZL	D.5	246 414	225 473	233 466	242 440	237 125	243 191	248 409	260 979
Social contributions		D.61								
Actual social contributions										
Paid to central government										
(National insurance contributions)										
Employers' compulsory contributions	CEAN		57 080	54 411	55 887	58 174	60 600	61 912	63 844	66 169
Employees' compulsory contributions	GCSE		38 186	37 184	38 703	40 626	41 159	41 588	42 604	44 309
Self- and non-employed persons' Compulsory contributions	NMDE		3 053	2 850	2 756	2 641	2 560	2 585	2 672	3 122
Total	AIIH		98 319	94 445	97 346	101 441	104 319	106 085	109 120	113 600
Capital account		Part								
Changes in liabilities and net worth										
Other capital taxes		D.91								
Paid to central government										
Inheritance tax	GILF		3 130	2 305	2 592	2 856	3 041	3 293	3 702	4 365
Tax on other capital transfers	GILG		50	50	50	50	50	50	50	50
Tax on swiss bank accounts[4]	KW69		–	–	–	–	–	876	–	–
Development land tax and other	GCSV		–	–	–	–	–	–	–	–
Tax paid on local government equal pay settlements	C625		77	46	–	30	38	36	134	33
FSCS levies on private sector[5]	HZQ4		21 816	1 805	–	–	–	–	–	–
Total	NMGI	D.91	25 073	4 206	2 642	2 936	3 129	4 255	3 886	4 448
Total taxes and Compulsory social contributions										
Paid to central government	GCSS		521 251	464 019	497 195	525 671	528 611	545 959	564 251	587 865
Paid to local government	GCST		24 675	25 364	26 072	26 436	26 786	27 788	28 680	29 518
Paid to the European Union	FJWB		2 689	2 655	2 945	2 937	2 898	2 926	2 960	3 087
Total	GCSU		548 615	492 038	526 212	555 044	558 295	576 673	595 891	620 470

1 These taxes existed before the UKs entry into the EEC in 1973.
2 From 1990/1991 onwards these series only contain rates paid in Northern Ireland.
3 Up until 1995/96 these payments are included in national non-domestic rates under production taxes other than on products.
4 Tax liable from banking deposits of UK residents held in Swiss banks.
5 Financial Services Compensation Scheme.
6 Total taxes for D.214 will not necessarily equal the sum of its components

Source: Office for National Statistics, The Blue Book 2016

23.7 Central government
ESA 2010 sector S.1311

£ million

			2008	2009	2010	2011	2012	2013	2014	2015
Financial account		III.2								
Net acquisition of financial assets		F.A								
Monetary gold and special drawing rights		F.1								
Monetary gold	NARO	F.11	–	–	–	–	–	–	–	–
Special drawing rights	NARP	F.12	−24	8 522	18	333	111	43	−14	55
Total	NWXM	F.1	−24	8 522	18	333	111	43	−14	55
Currency and deposits		F.2								
Transferable deposits		F.22								
With UK monetary financial institutions	NART	F.22N1	17 989	7 554	−5 318	4 798	5 222	−3 186	1 026	−2 527
Of which: foreign currency deposits with UK MFIs[1]	NARV	F.22N12	−1 208	−782	28	1 737	−271	901	−1 117	−850
With rest of the world monetary financial institutions	NARX	F.22N9	2 913	540	423	140	935	142	463	2 997
Other deposits	RYWO	F.29	11 021	7 075	−9 754	7 583	−898	9 862	4 152	−8 782
Total	NARQ	F.2	31 923	15 169	−14 649	12 521	5 259	6 818	5 641	−8 312
Debt securities		F.3								
Short-term		F.31								
Issued by UK monetary financial institutions	NSUN	F.31N5	1 974	−2 144	−400	–	–	–	–	–
Money market instruments										
Issued by other UK residents	NSRI	F.31N6	–	882	1 349	3 336	−3 404	1 459	−1 137	−2 348
Issued by rest of the world	NASM	F.31N9	−1 029	471	466	315	−967	−2 314	363	908
Long-term		F.32								
Issued by UK monetary financial institutions and other UK residents	NASV	F.32N5-6	4 978	−5 236	–	–	1 152	−327	–	–
Issued by rest of the world	NASW	F.32N9	−1 085	−820	5 439	4 099	5 182	−2 863	5 566	17 529
Total	NARZ	F.3	4 838	−6 847	6 854	7 750	1 963	−4 045	4 792	16 089
Loans		F.4								
Long-term		F.42								
Secured on dwellings	NATM	F.422	–	–	−6 616	−9 162	−6 649	−6 500	−9 030	−17 678
Other loans by UK residents	NATR	F.424N1	6 445	3 751	8 707	5 513	16 889	6 140	12 407	14 296
Other loans by rest of the world	NATS	F.424N9	–	–	–	–	–	–	–	–
Total	NATB	F.4	6 445	3 751	2 091	−3 649	10 240	−360	3 377	−3 382
Equity and investment fund shares/units		F.5								
Equity		F.51								
Listed UK shares	NATY	F.511N1	11 546	40 574	−903	−1 242	1 832	−9 222	−5 559	−12 672
Unlisted UK shares	NATZ	F.512N1	−1 545	−277	482	–	7	−21 957	−2 375	−753
Other equity		F.519								
Other UK equity	NAUA	F.519N6	–	−4 421	–	–	–	−10	−40	−1
UK shares and bonds issued by other UK residents	NSOX	F.519N7	–	–	–	–	–	–	–	–
Shares and other equity issued by rest of the world	NAUD	F.519N9	179	300	77	337	178	1 497	285	93
Total	NATT	F.5	10 180	36 176	−344	−905	2 017	−29 692	−7 689	−13 333
Financial derivatives and employee stock options	MN5T	F.7	1 151	619	−317	−123	575	−33	−889	−977
Of which: financial derivatives	CFZG	F.71	1 151	619	−317	−123	575	−33	−889	−977
Other accounts receivable	NAUN	F.8	18 996	126	3 269	363	2 117	5 163	4 730	11 183
Total net acquisition of financial assets	NARM	F.A	73 509	57 516	−3 078	16 290	22 282	−22 106	9 948	1 323

1 Monetary financial institutions.

Source: Office for National Statistics, The Blue Book 2016

23.7

Central government
ESA 2010 sector S.1311

£ million

			2008	2009	2010	2011	2012	2013	2014	2015
Financial account		III.2								
Net acquisition of financial liabilities		F.L								
Special drawing rights	M98C	F.12	–	8 654	–	–	–	–	–	–
Currency and deposits		F.2								
Currency	NAUV	F.21	95	48	82	30	158	30	191	168
Other deposits	NAVC	F.29	21 013	8 236	–7 118	9 209	–2 348	–7 959	17 439	10 900
Total	NAUU	F.2	21 108	8 284	–7 036	9 239	–2 190	–7 929	17 630	11 068
Debt securities		F.3								
Short-term		F.31								
Issued by UK central government	NAVF	F.31N1	13 179	25 975	–2 077	14 454	–18 706	–14 315	25 809	19 721
Long-term		F.32								
UK central government securities	NAVT	F.32N11	95 850	195 725	170 951	121 587	129 283	103 137	64 402	58 475
Other UK central government bonds	NAVU	F.32N12	3 454	–1 459	900	3 239	4 590	2 999	199	–5 437
Bonds issued by UK MFIs[1] and other UK residents	MNR7	F.32N5-6	–	–	–5 416	–10 967	–5 296	–11 682	–3 738	–14 718
Total	NAVD	F.3	112 483	220 241	164 358	128 313	109 871	80 139	86 672	58 041
Loans		F.4								
Short-term		F.41								
By UK monetary financial institutions	NAWH	F.41N1	7 815	–28 068	–1 794	238	–601	848	–1 423	3 786
By rest of the world	NAWL	F.41N9	504	–1 731	–44	–208	911	–825	1 228	5 021
Long-term		F.42								
Finance leasing	NAWU	F.423	63	50	145	–	–	–	–	–
Other loans by UK residents	NAWV	F.424N1	–7	–18	–9	–9	193	194	41	–5
Other loans by rest of the world	NAWW	F.424N9	–59	–21	–561	–2 055	–256	293	797	448
Total	NAWF	F.4	8 316	–29 788	–2 263	–2 034	247	510	643	9 250
Insurance, pensions and standardised guarantee schemes		F.6								
Provisions for calls under standardised guarantees	MW4E	F.66	–	–	–	–	–	–	27	14
Total	DM53	F.6	–	–	–	–	–	–	27	14
Other accounts payable	NAXR	F.8	2 964	2 869	–10 781	–139	45 528	642	6 521	324
Total net acquisition of financial liabilities	NAUQ	F.L	144 871	210 260	144 278	135 379	153 456	73 362	111 493	78 697
Net lending(+) / net borrowing(-)		B.9								
Total net acquisition of financial assets	NARM	F.A	73 509	57 516	–3 078	16 290	22 282	–22 106	9 948	1 323
less total net acquisition of financial liabilities	NAUQ	F.L	144 871	210 260	144 278	135 379	153 456	73 362	111 493	78 697
Net lending(+) / borrowing(-) from the financial account	NZDX	B.9f	–71 362	–152 744	–147 356	–119 089	–131 174	–95 468	–101 545	–77 374
Statistical discrepancy between the financial and non-financial accounts	NZDW	dB.9	87	194	–176	–923	681	954	–310	–119
Net lending (+) / borrowing (-) from non-financial accounts	NMFJ	B.9n	–71 275	–152 550	–147 532	–120 012	–130 493	–94 514	–101 855	–77 493

1 Monetary financial institutions.

Source: Office for National Statistics, The Blue Book 2016

23.8 Central government net cash requirement on own account (receipts and outlays on a cash basis)

£ million

	Cash receipts								Cash outlays				
	HM Revenue and Customs[8]												
	Total paid over[1]	Income tax[2]	Corporation tax[10]	NICs[3]	V.A.T.[4]	Interest and dividends	Other receipts[5]	Total	Interest payments	Net acquisition of company securities[6]	Net departmental outlays[7]	Total	Own account NCR[9]
	1	2	3	4	5	6	7	8	9	10	11	12	13
dataset identifier code													
	MIZX	RURC	N445	ABLP	EYOO	RUUL	RUUM	RUUN	RUUO	ABIF	RUUP	RUUQ	M98S
2003	325,138	116,627	28,835	69,360	67,525	7,335	25,329	357,802	20,348	-39	379,418	399,727	41,925
2004	347,514	125,909	31,536	77,026	71,907	6,855	25,137	379,506	21,027	0	400,631	421,658	42,152
2005	372,567	135,213	38,282	83,612	73,012	6,549	26,341	405,457	22,434	0	421,021	443,455	37,998
2006	401,362	144,983	47,616	87,156	76,103	6,640	28,115	436,117	25,834	-347	448,131	473,618	37,501
2007	422,465	154,346	44,528	96,656	80,301	8,251	30,083	460,799	25,537	-2,340	470,169	493,366	32,567
2008	428,380	162,758	47,288	98,504	80,709	9,354	30,556	468,290	26,033	19,714	544,720	590,467	122,177
2009	384,875	153,101	36,236	95,053	68,637	6,666	31,282	422,823	29,304	41,809	548,810	619,923	197,100
2010	411,846	153,237	42,153	95,860	80,865	5,274	34,063	451,183	34,008	0	569,599	603,607	152,424
2011	434,438	157,066	43,236	101,033	95,208	5,757	42,235	482,430	43,923	0	557,494	601,417	118,987
2012	436,196	154,430	40,726	102,232	98,619	9,842	38,399	484,437	39,934	-14,287	565,919	591,566	107,129
2013	451,668	159,730	40,417	106,702	103,726	46,577	36,652	534,897	48,025	-6,584	567,570	609,011	74,114
2014	467,588	164,107	41,576	109,238	109,165	16,854	92,517	576,959	41,777	-5,207	635,158	671,728	94,769
2015	489,448	173,362	44,931	113,130	114,135	14,882	64,354	568,684	42,255	-16,949	631,187	656,493	87,809
2004 Q1	94,758	40,033	6,881	20,695	17,330	2,161	5,013	101,932	4,704	0	97,198	101,902	-30
2004 Q2	82,029	26,273	7,188	20,601	18,039	1,546	5,791	89,366	5,140	0	98,121	103,261	13,895
2004 Q3	87,673	32,619	8,142	18,585	17,707	1,549	7,474	96,696	5,192	0	98,424	103,616	6,920
2004 Q4	83,054	26,984	9,325	17,145	18,831	1,599	6,859	91,512	5,991	0	106,888	112,879	21,367
2005 Q1	103,161	43,699	9,367	21,767	18,449	1,939	4,950	110,050	5,487	0	99,835	105,322	-4,728
2005 Q2	86,274	30,011	7,887	20,941	17,342	1,469	6,592	94,335	5,568	0	105,729	111,297	16,962
2005 Q3	94,524	33,214	9,885	22,007	18,188	1,611	7,430	103,565	5,836	0	105,215	111,051	7,486
2005 Q4	88,608	28,289	11,143	18,897	19,033	1,530	7,369	97,507	5,543	0	110,242	115,785	18,278
2006 Q1	112,661	46,442	13,394	23,677	18,293	1,783	5,631	120,075	6,174	-347	107,430	113,257	-6,818
2006 Q2	91,224	31,700	8,012	22,211	18,021	1,497	6,459	99,180	5,298	0	117,434	122,732	23,552
2006 Q3	100,664	37,048	13,087	20,798	18,731	1,428	8,403	110,495	8,628	0	108,129	116,757	6,262
2006 Q4	96,813	29,793	13,123	20,470	21,058	1,932	7,622	106,367	5,734	0	115,138	120,872	14,505
2007 Q1	117,636	52,992	10,605	23,795	19,550	1,897	4,875	124,408	6,619	0	110,361	116,980	-7,428
2007 Q2	96,004	30,504	8,177	25,932	20,123	1,864	8,204	106,072	5,959	-2,340	121,026	124,645	18,573
2007 Q3	107,134	38,606	12,627	24,165	19,301	1,986	9,934	119,054	6,486	0	114,418	120,904	1,850
2007 Q4	101,691	32,244	13,119	22,764	21,327	2,504	7,070	111,265	6,473	0	124,364	130,837	19,572
2008 Q1	126,971	55,652	13,108	27,550	19,850	2,646	5,997	135,614	6,472	0	118,768	125,240	-10,374
2008 Q2	97,153	35,630	8,722	23,517	20,087	2,252	8,154	107,559	6,449	0	131,441	137,890	30,331
2008 Q3	108,990	40,772	12,955	24,801	21,235	2,266	9,143	120,399	6,566	-255	150,477	156,788	36,389
2008 Q4	95,266	30,704	12,503	22,636	19,537	2,190	7,262	104,718	6,546	19,969	144,034	170,549	65,831
2009 Q1	115,103	54,185	9,749	25,930	17,580	2,016	3,449	120,568	6,386	12,536	131,608	150,530	29,962
2009 Q2	85,699	32,649	6,569	22,727	16,102	1,892	9,626	97,217	8,534	-2,021	145,058	151,571	54,354
2009 Q3	93,410	37,031	8,256	23,574	16,847	1,357	9,721	104,488	7,577	0	133,158	140,735	36,247
2009 Q4	90,663	29,236	11,662	22,822	18,108	1,401	8,486	100,550	6,807	31,294	138,986	177,087	76,537
2010 Q1	112,559	48,458	10,146	26,393	19,103	1,551	4,493	118,603	9,271	0	139,909	149,180	30,577
2010 Q2	94,699	35,719	7,404	22,870	19,886	1,049	8,868	104,616	6,956	0	147,380	154,336	49,720
2010 Q3	107,569	38,793	11,525	23,950	20,564	1,370	11,557	120,496	10,782	0	136,851	147,633	27,137
2010 Q4	97,019	30,267	13,078	22,647	21,312	1,304	9,145	107,468	6,999	0	145,459	152,458	44,990
2011 Q1	120,293	52,311	11,038	27,081	21,737	1,836	9,019	131,148	11,840	0	135,142	146,982	15,834
2011 Q2	99,487	34,458	7,591	24,283	24,084	1,229	10,614	111,330	7,392	0	145,667	153,059	41,729
2011 Q3	110,502	38,849	11,846	25,861	23,984	1,506	13,346	125,354	17,071	0	137,097	154,168	28,814
2011 Q4	104,156	31,448	12,761	23,808	25,403	1,186	9,256	114,598	7,620	0	139,588	147,208	32,610
2012 Q1	123,458	50,524	10,937	27,665	24,821	3,331	6,142	132,931	12,421	-747	135,613	147,287	14,356
2012 Q2	100,129	34,290	7,529	24,669	24,469	3,583	11,978	115,690	7,542	-11,109	147,487	143,920	28,230
2012 Q3	109,251	38,709	10,099	25,873	24,524	1,462	10,843	121,556	12,622	-1,174	136,553	148,001	26,445
2012 Q4	103,358	30,907	12,161	24,025	24,805	1,466	9,436	114,260	7,349	-1,257	146,266	152,358	38,098
2013 Q1	124,619	52,049	10,693	27,470	26,772	13,219	14,153	151,991	13,618	-733	143,648	156,533	4,542
2013 Q2	105,685	36,960	7,485	27,227	24,915	13,088	7,493	126,266	7,110	-382	148,767	155,495	29,229
2013 Q3	114,459	39,123	10,530	26,916	25,681	14,898	8,414	137,771	20,372	-3,355	135,380	152,397	14,626
2013 Q4	106,905	31,598	11,709	25,089	26,358	5,372	6,592	118,869	6,925	-2,114	139,775	144,586	25,717
2014 Q1	129,451	53,123	10,603	28,459	27,488	4,136	51,055	184,642	13,707	-4,217	186,209	195,699	11,057
2014 Q2	109,055	36,578	8,358	26,589	26,961	5,319	11,695	126,069	7,044	-85	154,377	161,336	35,267
2014 Q3	118,047	41,060	10,416	28,124	26,883	1,725	12,207	131,979	14,039	-518	140,325	153,846	21,867
2014 Q4	111,035	33,346	12,199	26,066	27,833	5,674	17,560	134,269	6,987	-387	154,247	160,847	26,578
2015 Q1	138,508	57,683	12,031	29,629	29,478	4,087	16,646	159,241	13,714	-1,043	154,303	166,974	7,733
2015 Q2	113,942	38,285	9,459	28,415	27,058	5,156	10,234	129,332	7,255	-4,965	157,978	160,268	30,936
2015 Q3	121,984	42,789	10,833	28,587	28,603	2,080	17,614	141,678	14,081	-4,636	153,427	162,872	21,194
2015 Q4	115,014	34,605	12,608	26,499	28,996	3,559	19,860	138,433	7,205	-6,305	165,479	166,379	27,946
2016 Q1	143,924	59,832	11,508	30,202	31,091	4,018	17,103	165,045	13,687	-1,637	150,646	162,696	-2,349

Relationships between columns 1+6+7=8; 9+10+11=12; 12-8=13

Source: Office for National Statistics; HM Treasury

1 Comprises payments into the Consolidated Fund and all payovers of NICS excluding those for Northern Ireland.
2 Income tax includes capital gains tax and is gross of any tax credits treated by HM Revenue and Customs as tax deductions.
3 UK receipts net of personal pension rebates; gross of Statutory Maternity Pay and Statutory Sick Pay.
4 Payments into Consolidated Fund.
5 Including some elements of expenditure not separately identified.
6 Mainly comprises privatisation proceeds.
7 Net of certain receipts, and excluding on-lending to local authorities and public corporations.
8 A much more detailed breakdown of tax receipts is available from HM Revenue and Customs at www.hmrc.gov.uk/statistics/receipts.htm.
9 NCR = Net Cash Requirement. Without Northern Rock Asset Management & Bradford and Bingley.
10 Gross of tax credits

23.9 HM Revenue and Customs receipts

Amounts: £ million

Year	Total Paid Over [1]	Total HMRC receipts [2,3,10]	Total Income Tax [4]	Of which: PAYE Income Tax**	Of which: SA Income Tax**	Capital Gains Tax	Apprenticeship Levy	NICs	VAT	Total Corporation Tax [5]	Of which offshore** [6]	Bank Levy	Bank Surcharge	Bank payroll tax	Petroleum Revenue Tax	Fuel duties	IHT [7]	Shares	Stamp Duty Land Tax	Annual Tax on Enveloped Dwellings
	MIZX			BKMR	LISB	BKLO		ABLP	EYOO	N445				JT2R	ACCJ	ACDD	ACCH	BKST	BKSU	
2004-05	355,917	375,801	127,294	108,699	17,141	2,282		78,098	73,026	34,031	3,831				1,284	23,313	2,922	2,715	6,251	
2005-06	382,067	402,874	134,916	113,894	18,077	3,042		85,522	72,856	42,355	7,307				2,016	23,438	3,259	3,465	7,454	
2006-07	406,337	428,629	147,712	124,799	20,306	3,830		87,274	77,360	44,875	6,709				2,155	23,585	3,545	3,757	9,635	
2007-08	431,800	456,121	151,738	126,760	22,443	5,268		100,410	80,599	47,036	5,728				1,680	24,615	3,824	4,167	9,958	
2008-09	416,512	445,531	153,442	128,470	22,531	7,852		96,882	78,439	43,927	9,826				2,567	24,905	2,839	3,203	4,796	
2009-10	382,331	414,920	144,881	122,584	21,708	2,491		95,517	70,160	36,628	4,998				923	26,197	2,384	3,017	4,886	
2010-11	419,580	453,614	153,491	132,263	22,108	3,601		96,548	83,502	43,040	6,864			3,416	1,458	27,256	2,717	2,971	5,961	
2011-12	437,603	472,315	150,939	132,189	20,334	4,337		101,617	98,292	43,130	8,840	1,612		-2	2,032	26,800	2,903	2,794	6,125	
2012-13	437,357	473,777	152,030	132,433	20,550	3,927		102,037	100,572	40,482	4,412	1,595		0	1,737	26,571	3,105	2,234	6,907	
2013-14	456,500	493,646	156,898	134,686	20,854	3,908		107,690	104,718	40,327	3,556	2,200		0	1,118	26,881	3,402	3,108	9,273	100
2014-15	476,645	515,349	163,109	139,506	23,645	5,559		110,406	111,363	43,005	2,026	2,748		0	77	27,156	3,804	2,926	10,738	116
2015-16	494,864	533,686	168,451	145,652	24,327	7,060		113,701	115,415	44,410	713	3,392		0	-562	27,623	4,650	3,320	10,682	178
Apr-12	44,065	46,867	14,148	14,179	19	11		9,798	10,232	4,976	-	287		0	150	2,386	236	204	479	
May-12	30,304	33,410	10,166	10,912	-103	4		8,335	8,363	1,330	-	-		0	127	2,119	261	75	534	
Jun-12	25,760	28,927	9,956	10,264	-67	3		6,536	5,873	1,223	-	-		0	53	2,247	255	213	509	
Jul-12	46,840	50,799	17,464	11,290	6,146	4		9,699	10,058	6,947	-	526		0	101	2,212	288	189	666	
Aug-12	33,976	37,053	11,443	10,648	977	4		8,287	9,047	1,293	-	-		0	108	2,237	335	218	683	
Sep-12	28,435	30,989	9,794	10,318	28	2		7,887	5,420	1,859	1,573	-		0	533	2,260	235	166	588	
Oct-12	41,068	44,041	11,030	10,772	-12	9		8,259	10,248	7,890	-	366		0	126	2,220	282	174	624	
Nov-12	31,877	34,095	9,265	10,301	-67	4		7,890	8,756	1,389	-	-		0	141	2,324	256	231	611	
Dec-12	30,413	33,088	10,596	10,204	409	4		7,876	5,803	2,881	1,493	-		0	107	2,331	237	188	591	
Jan-13	57,228	62,301	23,578	11,103	10,685	2,971		9,926	11,210	7,903	-	416		0	75	2,008	221	159	623	
Feb-13	36,473	39,227	13,588	11,018	2,347	820		8,751	9,129	1,438	-	-		0	115	2,155	163	145	502	
Mar-13	30,918	32,982	11,002	11,426	189	90		8,793	6,434	1,351	1,346	-		0	101	2,072	337	271	496	
Apr-13	44,225	47,392	14,785	14,051	52	2		9,916	10,177	4,777	-	334		0	77	2,258	309	222	660	-
May-13	32,327	35,813	11,858	12,048	-132	3		8,528	8,263	1,322	-	-		0	91	2,267	293	323	646	-
Jun-13	29,133	32,422	10,309	10,405	-79	3		8,783	6,505	1,386	-	-		0	45	2,319	304	225	560	-
Jul-13	49,068	53,114	17,840	11,267	6,548	3		10,543	10,230	6,990	-	658		0	-1	2,187	339	304	886	-
Aug-13	35,214	36,969	10,947	10,338	862	2		8,254	9,192	1,385	-	-		0	80	2,317	266	207	803	-
Sep-13	30,177	33,250	10,329	10,371	12	3		8,119	6,259	2,155	1,306	-		0	410	2,260	251	191	817	2
Oct-13	42,906	45,812	10,931	10,537	-77	3		8,495	11,546	7,261	-	624		0	98	2,226	312	312	852	76
Nov-13	32,907	35,808	9,982	10,136	-81	2		8,219	9,056	1,324	-	-		0	84	2,347	270	249	781	6
Dec-13	31,092	34,243	10,679	10,366	414	2		8,375	5,756	3,124	1,229	-		0	121	2,282	259	256	960	8
Jan-14	58,102	61,513	22,539	11,488	10,673	3,006		10,246	11,139	7,478	-	584		0	-1	2,070	263	244	843	1
Feb-14	39,569	42,179	14,048	11,285	2,427	732		9,157	10,432	1,538	-	-		0	69	2,215	271	276	721	2
Mar-14	31,780	35,130	12,650	12,395	235	149		9,056	6,162	1,587	1,021	-		0	45	2,134	264	299	743	5
Apr-14	46,696	50,007	15,344	14,822	103	2		10,001	11,192	5,186	-	485		0	83	2,303	362	233	872	40
May-14	33,140	36,301	10,754	11,463	-128	5		8,212	9,426	1,589	-	-		0	70	2,231	296	363	828	51
Jun-14	29,219	32,759	10,467	10,859	-113	6		8,376	6,347	1,592	-	-		0	80	2,317	288	219	898	6
Jul-14	50,178	54,247	18,499	11,610	6,666	5		10,630	11,076	6,584	-	734		0	-52	2,245	324	235	1,091	3
Aug-14	37,064	39,576	11,903	10,868	1,349	2		8,726	9,975	1,587	-	-		0	-13	2,375	336	256	994	2

23.9 HM Revenue and Customs receipts

Amounts: £ million

Year	Total Paid Over [1]	Total HMRC receipts [2,3,10]	Total Income Tax [4]	Of which: PAYE Income Tax**	Of which: SA Income Tax**	Capital Gains Tax	Apprenticeship Levy	NICs	VAT	Total Corporation Tax [5]	Of which offshore** [6]	Bank Levy	Bank Surcharge	Bank payroll tax	Petroleum Revenue Tax	Fuel duties	IHT [7]	Shares	Stamp Duty Land Tax	Annual Tax on Enveloped Dwellings
	MIZX			BKMR	LISB	BKLO		ABLP	EYOO	N445				JT2R	ACCJ	ACDD	ACCH	BKST	BKSU	
Sep-14	30,805	33,649	10,647	10,900	48	3		8,768	5,834	2,238	840	-		0	82	2,238	343	151	1,074	2
Oct-14	43,878	46,840	11,511	10,865	-50	2		8,750	11,238	7,379	-	783		0	54	2,271	335	319	965	2
Nov-14	34,530	37,707	10,521	10,654	-84	4		8,467	9,991	1,351	-			0	66	2,374	309	192	893	2
Dec-14	32,627	36,662	11,310	10,844	495	-2		8,849	6,601	3,468	642			0	85	2,322	338	225	1,016	2
Jan-15	62,655	66,997	24,671	11,876	12,213	4,258		10,563	12,155	8,360	-	747		0	-201	2,064	273	247	717	1
Feb-15	41,295	42,912	14,170	11,699	2,819	1,101		9,414	10,238	1,686	-			0	39	2,297	306	236	666	1
Mar-15	34,558	37,690	13,311	13,046	326	172		9,652	7,291	1,984	543			0	-216	2,119	292	249	724	4
Apr-15	48,302	51,494	15,237	14,762	-90	2		11,122	10,921	6,099	-	587		0	19	2,300	379	274	792	77
May-15	34,275	37,624	11,521	12,162	-219	4		8,472	9,492	1,513	-			0	18	2,301	364	367	753	58
Jun-15	31,365	34,342	11,517	12,094	-51	2		8,821	6,462	1,788	-			0	-103	2,341	426	176	800	7
Jul-15	51,861	57,066	19,510	12,124	7,586	4		10,798	11,517	7,029	-	998		0	-136	2,322	445	280	1,075	5
Aug-15	37,655	39,677	11,872	11,584	629	2		8,877	10,020	1,356	-			0	-47	2,360	371	248	885	4
Sep-15	32,468	35,602	11,396	11,704	20	4		8,912	6,921	2,513	342			0	7	2,278	360	210	960	4
Oct-15	44,791	48,197	11,857	11,387	-72	21		8,933	11,883	7,398	-	964		0	20	2,324	444	270	902	8
Nov-15	36,285	39,951	11,171	11,394	-30	9		8,653	10,905	1,709	-			0	30	2,383	369	214	908	5
Dec-15	33,938	36,729	11,545	11,440	625	3		8,913	6,392	3,490	159			0	18	2,327	354	253	1,095	1
Jan-16	64,015	68,619	24,875	12,113	12,447	5,397		10,511	12,539	7,787	-	843		0	-80	2,140	315	298	804	2
Feb-16	44,779	45,938	15,278	12,307	3,150	1,371		9,726	10,876	1,860	-			0	-269	2,279	435	495	801	1
Mar-16	35,130	38,447	12,672	12,581	333	241		9,965	7,488	1,867	212			0	-39	2,267	388	238	906	5
Apr-16	48,485	52,063	16,216	15,627	-111	7		10,740	11,087	5,783	-	564	20	0	-15	2,366	417.2	246	1,172	88

Source: HM Revenue & Customs

1 Comprises of payments into the Consolidated Fund and all payovers of NICs excluding those of Northern Ireland

2 Total HMRC Receipts includes payments into the Consolidated Fund and all payovers of NICs including those of Northern Ireland. Receipts are gross of Tax Credits (Expenditure): this follows the changes generated by revisions to the European System of Accounts (ESA2010) and the Public Sector Finances Review.

3 Consistent with the OBR definition published in the supplementary fiscal table 2.8 i.e. on a cash basis.

4 Income tax is gross of tax credits and includes other smaller elements of income tax but excludes capital gains tax

5 Receipts are gross of tax credits. As of November 2014 Bank Levy receipts are shown seperately and as of April 2016 Bank Surcharge receipts are shown seperately, and are no longer included in the CT total. DPT receipts also included within this total and although these are different taxes, they have been combined as showing DPT separately could result in disclosing taxpayer information.

6 The majority of UK Oil & Gas companies payments are due in three instalments, (Jul, Oct and Jan): receipts are reported in a similar pattern following each instalment.

7 Excludes non cash elements which are shown in the table Inheritance Tax: Analysis of Receipts

8 From April 2013, includes receipts from Carbon Price Floor

9 From April 2011, the Child Benefit series has been revised to ensure consistency with HMRC Resource Accounts

10 Total of columns D, G to J, and L to AG

11 Monthly Data unavailable.

* Figures remain as provisional until they are aligned to the HMRC Annual Report and Trust Statement, which is published following the end of each financial year.
** Figures in italic are included with the relevant total for either income tax or corporation tax

Archived tables can be found here: https://www.gov.uk/government/collections/hm-revenue-customs-receipts

For any queries regarding this table, please email karen.mason@hmrc.gsi.gov.uk
Room 2/62, 100 Parliament Street, London, WC1A 2BQ

23.9 HM Revenue and Customs receipts

Amounts: £ million

Year	Tobacco duties	Spirits duties	Beer duties	Wines duties	Cider duties	Betting & Gaming	Air Passenger Duty	Insurance Premium Tax	Landfill Tax	Climate Change Levy[8]	Aggregates Levy	Swiss Capital Tax	Misc	Customs Duties	Child and Working Tax Credits	Corporation Tax Credits[11]	Child Benefit Payments[9]
	ACDE	ACDF	ACDG	ACDH	ACDI	ACDJ	ACDP	ACDO	DOLC	LSNS	MDUP			ADET			
2004-05	8,100	2,385	3,101	2,233	157	1,421	864	2,359	672	764	334		0	2,195	15,896	610	9,593
2005-06	7,959	2,309	3,076	2,308	168	1,421	905	2,343	733	744	326		1	2,258	17,332	669	9,770
2006-07	8,149	2,256	3,072	2,385	200	1,391	971	2,314	804	712	321		1	2,325	18,684	715	10,156
2007-08	8,094	2,374	3,067	2,641	220	1,481	1,994	2,306	877	688	339		1	2,456	20,030	918	10,603
2008-09	8,219	2,358	3,127	2,741	244	1,474	1,862	2,281	954	716	334		0	2,659	24,099	1,181	11,262
2009-10	8,813	2,570	3,182	2,949	311	1,439	1,856	2,259	842	695	275		0	2,646	27,601	1,147	11,824
2010-11	9,144	2,675	3,296	3,101	324	1,533	2,155	2,400	1,065	674	288		0	2,998	28,879	1,313	12,160
2011-12	9,551	2,889	3,463	3,356	329	1,633	2,607	2,941	1,090	676	290	0	0	2,912	29,830	1,399	12,177
2012-13	9,681	2,931	3,426	3,537	326	1,680	2,791	3,021	1,092	635	265	342	0	2,854	29,888	1,471	12,167
2013-14	9,531	3,056	3,346	3,713	340	2,098	3,013	3,014	1,189	1,068	285	466	0	2,901	29,710	1,582	11,438
2014-15	9,548	3,023	3,310	3,837	320	2,116	3,175	2,965	1,144	1,491	342	66	0	3,007	29,732	2,033	11,582
2015-16	9,485	3,147	3,271	3,973	296	2,666	3,077	3,293	919	1,763	356	32	0	3,089	28,539	2,334	11,681
Apr-12	1,818	352	386	381	36	147	213	133	186	54	33	0	0	220	2,378	n/a	943
May-12	136	115	238	217	22	154	223	574	45	139	18	0	0	216	2,881	n/a	1,180
Jun-12	600	202	336	284	35	105	231	8	11	2	12	0	0	231	2,401	n/a	949
Jul-12	759	202	286	259	28	163	246	157	219	55	39	0	0	231	2,766	n/a	1,042
Aug-12	1,054	184	287	291	31	188	284	627	57	108	19	0	0	268	2,666	n/a	1,059
Sep-12	680	228	308	282	31	118	272	16	38	2	12	0	0	261	2,220	n/a	987
Oct-12	979	222	251	261	23	127	246	189	184	44	37	0	0	252	2,527	n/a	1,009
Nov-12	769	365	289	355	27	164	260	561	60	82	19	0	0	278	2,418	n/a	996
Dec-12	622	430	318	427	29	124	195	12	68	2	14	0	0	234	2,532	n/a	1,027
Jan-13	1,052	217	293	291	24	147	237	163	153	48	36	342	0	209	2,351	n/a	1,016
Feb-13	566	151	205	236	20	150	119	562	66	97	16	0	0	232	2,302	n/a	895
Mar-13	648	263	230	252	21	95	263	20	6	3	11	0	0	225	2,446	n/a	1,064
Apr-13	1,725	387	283	370	33	161	242	171	198	57	30	0	0	217	2,394	n/a	886
May-13	201	125	267	229	24	212	217	544	53	117	18	0	0	213	2,655	n/a	1,003
Jun-13	560	192	310	287	33	112	227	11	13	2	12	0	0	224	2,450	n/a	968
Jul-13	724	206	271	276	30	226	289	212	183	185	36	258	0	238	2,932	n/a	989
Aug-13	880	211	319	323	40	206	302	568	98	135	26	147	0	263	2,412	n/a	1,010
Sep-13	822	228	285	310	34	125	308	8	43	4	14	0	0	274	2,348	n/a	861
Oct-13	964	237	255	287	22	198	273	216	168	102	40	35	0	279	2,539	n/a	1,034
Nov-13	858	391	286	378	28	191	265	532	89	162	21	10	0	278	2,275	n/a	943
Dec-13	530	419	298	455	30	137	216	21	39	10	14	8	0	246	2,729	n/a	965
Jan-14	1,001	224	328	291	23	222	239	158	242	107	40	0	0	225	2,373	n/a	986
Feb-14	625	161	208	236	22	188	222	545	53	183	20	5	0	251	2,286	n/a	883
Mar-14	640	276	235	272	22	121	213	28	12	6	13	4	0	194	2,317	n/a	911
Apr-14	1,751	271	257	371	28	191	232	184	184	115	35	58	0	228	2,654	n/a	1,023
May-14	229	178	300	255	28	220	255	512	53	201	21	0	0	224	2,453	n/a	980
Jun-14	576	218	333	302	33	136	267	30	16	2	16	1	0	234	2,442	n/a	904
Jul-14	667	241	289	298	29	210	270	209	224	153	47	1	0	237	2,882	n/a	1,006
Aug-14	933	218	295	324	33	196	301	544	64	241	25	1	0	256	2,286	n/a	1,007

23.9 HM Revenue and Customs receipts

Amounts: £ million

Year	Tobacco duties	Spirits duties	Beer duties	Wines duties	Cider duties	Betting & Gaming	Air Passenger Duty	Insurance Premium Tax	Landfill Tax	Climate Change Levy[8]	Aggregates Levy	Swiss Capital Tax	Misc	Customs Duties	Child and Working Tax Credits	Corporation Tax Credits[11]	Child Benefit Payments[9]
	ACDE	ACDF	ACDG	ACDH	ACDI	ACDJ	ACDP	ACDO	DOLC	LSNS	MDUP			ADET			
Sep-14	657	212	271	304	26	137	334	20	21	12	18	1	0	258	2,410	n/a	919
Oct-14	940	277	259	315	26	242	294	207	222	122	49	0	0	281	2,510	n/a	970
Nov-14	835	376	287	392	27	217	283	518	67	222	25	0	0	285	2,209	n/a	937
Dec-14	589	410	298	448	27	121	229	23	17	6	20	4	0	257	2,748	n/a	974
Jan-15	994	240	305	326	21	153	254	186	200	175	46	0	0	244	2,221	n/a	983
Feb-15	600	175	186	240	18	213	234	516	63	236	24	0	0	254	2,263	n/a	898
Mar-15	778	205	230	261	25	82	223	18	14	6	17	0	0	251	2,656	n/a	981
Apr-15	1,453	251	279	332	25	174	261	195	166	223	42	28	0	258	2,436	n/a	967
May-15	237	220	292	324	28	364	232	517	53	241	27	0	0	226	2,299	n/a	1,004
Jun-15	572	239	283	308	27	116	260	24	14	12	19	0	0	232	2,497	n/a	954
Jul-15	757	270	296	329	27	352	274	221	172	210	50	1	0	260	2,761	n/a	1,009
Aug-15	1,217	222	304	337	29	201	304	556	59	207	27	0	0	265	2,241	n/a	939
Sep-15	467	229	275	305	26	111	303	25	9	4	14	0	0	267	2,336	n/a	1,032
Oct-15	846	274	269	313	26	283	271	200	175	181	49	0	0	287	2,334	n/a	1,160
Nov-15	840	378	269	400	27	261	293	562	58	193	27	0	0	289	2,245	n/a	745
Dec-15	508	414	297	475	27	106	211	23	4	4	19	0	0	251	2,683	n/a	969
Jan-16	915	246	314	330	22	280	253	222	152	169	46	3	0	237	2,033	n/a	992
Feb-16	634	156	164	235	14	320	200	719	49	312	22	0	0	260	2,272	n/a	916
Mar-16	1,039	247	229	284	17	100	215	30	8	8	15	0	0	258	2,401	n/a	994
Apr-16	1,074	239	286	346	26	265	224	239	144	237	40	0	0	252	2,476	n/a	1,034

Source: HM Revenue & Customs

[1] Comprises of payments into the Consolidated Fund and all payovers of NICs excluding those of Northern Ireland

[2] Total HMRC Receipts includes payments into the Consolidated Fund and all payovers of NICs including those of Northern Ireland. Receipts are gross of Tax Credits (Expenditure): this follows the changes generated by revisions to the European System of Accounts (ESA2010) and the Public Sector Finances Review.

[3] Consistent with the OBR definition published in the supplementary fiscal table 2.8 i.e. on a cash basis.

[4] Income tax is gross of tax credits and includes other smaller elements of income tax but excludes capital gains tax

[5] Receipts are gross of tax credits. As of November 2014 Bank Levy receipts are shown seperately and as of April 2016 Bank Surcharge receipts are shown seperately, and are no longer included in the CT total. DPT receipts also included within this total and although these are different taxes, they have been combined as showing DPT separately could result in disclosing taxpayer information.

[6] The majority of UK Oil & Gas companies payments are due in three instalments, (Jul, Oct and Jan): receipts are reported in a similar pattern following each instalment.

[7] Excludes non cash elements which are shown in the table Inheritance Tax: Analysis of Receipts

[8] From April 2013, includes Receipts from Carbon Price Floor

[9] From April 2011, the Child Benefit series has been revised to ensure consistency with HMRC Resource Accounts

[10] Total of columns D, G to J, and L to AG

[11] Monthly Data unavailable.

* Figures remain as provisional until they are aligned to the HMRC Annual Report and Trust Statement, which is published following the end of each financial year.

** Figures in italic are included with the relevant total for either income tax or corporation tax

Archived tables can be found here: https://www.gov.uk/government/collections/hm-revenue-customs-receipts

For any queries regarding this table, please email karen.mason@hmrc.gsi.gov.uk
Room 2/62, 100 Parliament Street, London, WC1A 2BQ

23.10 INCOME TAX PERSONAL ALLOWANCES AND RELIEFS, 1990-91 TO 2016-17

| Financial years | Non-aged allowances | | | | | | Aged allowances | | | | Income limit (3) |
	Personal	Married couple's (1)	Blind person's (2)	Dividend	Savings Basic rate	Savings Higher rate	Personal 65-74	Personal 75+	Married couple's 65-74	Married couple's 75+	
1990-91	3,005	1,720	1,080	-	-	-	3,670	3,820	2,145	2,185	12,300
1991-92	3,295	1,720	1,080	-	-	-	4,020	4,180	2,355	2,395	13,500
1992-93	3,445	1,720	1,080	-	-	-	4,200	4,370	2,465	2,505	14,200
1993-94	3,445	1,720	1,080	-	-	-	4,200	4,370	2,465	2,505	14,200
1994-95	3,445	1,720 (4)	1,200	-	-	-	4,200	4,370	2,665 (4)	2,705 (4)	14,200
1995-96	3,525	1,720 (5)	1,200	-	-	-	4,630	4,800	2,995 (5)	3,035 (5)	14,600
1996-97	3,765	1,790 (5)	1,250	-	-	-	4,910	5,090	3,115 (5)	3,155 (5)	15,200
1997-98	4,045	1,830 (5)	1,280	-	-	-	5,220	5,400	3,185 (5)	3,225 (5)	15,600
1998-99	4,195	1,900 (5)	1,330	-	-	-	5,410	5,600	3,305 (5)	3,345 (5)	16,200
1999-00	4,335	1,970 (6)	1,380	-	-	-	5,720	5,980	5,125 (6)	5,195 (6)	16,800
2000-01	4,385	-	1,400	-	-	-	5,790	6,050	5,185 (6,7)	5,255 (6,7)	17,000
2001-02	4,535	-	1,450	-	-	-	5,990	6,260	5,365 (6,7)	5,435 (6,7)	17,600
2002-03	4,615	-	1,480	-	-	-	6,100	6,370	5,465 (6,7)	5,535 (6,7)	17,900
2003-04	4,615	-	1,510	-	-	-	6,610	6,720	5,565 (6,7)	5,635 (6,7)	18,300
2004-05	4,745	-	1,560	-	-	-	6,830	6,950	5,725 (6,7)	5,795 (6,7)	18,900
2005-06	4,895	-	1,610	-	-	-	7,090	7,220	5,905 (6,7)	5,975 (6,7)	19,500
2006-07	5,035	-	1,660	-	-	-	7,280	7,420	6,065 (6,7)	6,135 (6,7)	20,100
2007-08	5,225	-	1,730	-	-	-	7,550	7,690	6,285 (6,7)	6,365 (6,7)	20,900
2008-09	6,035	-	1,800	-	-	-	9,030	9,180	6,535 (6,7)	6,625 (6,7)	21,800
2009-10	6,475	-	1,890	-	-	-	9,490	9,640	-	6,965 (6,7)	22,900
2010-11	6,475 (8)	-	1,890	-	-	-	9,490	9,640	-	6,965 (6,7)	22,900
2011-12	7,475 (8)	-	1,980	-	-	-	9,940	10,090	-	7,295 (6,7)	24,000
2012-13	8,105 (8)	-	2,100	-	-	-	10,500	10,660	-	7,705 (6,7)	25,400
2013-14	9,440 (8)	-	2,160	-	-	-	10,500 (9)	10,660 (10)	-	7,915 (6,7)	26,100
2014-15	10,000 (8)	-	2,230	-	-	-	10,500 (9)	10,660 (10)	-	8,165 (6,7)	27,000
2015-16	10,600 (8)	-	2,290	-	-	-	-	10,660 (10)	-	8,355 (6,7)	27,700
2016-17	11,000 (8)	-	2,290	5,000 (11)	1,000 (12)	500 (12)	-	-	-	8,355 (6,7)	27,700

Source: HM Revenue & Customs - Table updated April 2016

(1) Given in addition to the personal allowance to married couples. The additional personal allowance and the widow's bereavement allowance have the same value as the married couple's allowance.
(2) Married couples where both spouses are blind get double the single amount.
(3) Where an individual's income exceeds the income limit, their aged personal allowance is reduced by £1 for every £2 above the income limit, potentially down to the non aged allowance level.
(4) Allowance available at a flat rate of 20%.
(5) Allowance available at a flat rate of 15%.
(6) Allowance available at a flat rate of 10%.
(7) At least one of the partners must have been born before 6 April 1935.
(8) The Personal Allowance reduces where an individuals income is above £100,000 - by £1 for every £2 of income above the £100,000 limit. This reduction applies irrespective of age or date of birth.
(9) Available to people born in the period 6 April 1938 to 5 April 1948.
(10) Available to people born on or before 5 April 1938.
(11) The Dividend Allowance, introduced for 2016-17, means that no tax is payable on the first £5,000 of dividend income, irrespective of the total amount of dividend and non-dividend income received.
(12) The Personal Savings Allowance, introduced for 2016-17, provides for an amount of savings income to be received tax-free. The upper bound for the tax-free allowance depends on the top marginal tax rate on an individual's total income; the threshold for higher rate taxpayers is half that for basic rate taxpayers and is set to £0 for additional rate taxpayers. The effect of the Personal Allowance, Starting Rate and Personal Savings Allowance for 2016-17 is that an individual with total taxable income of £17,000 will pay no tax on savings income.

23.11 RATES OF INCOME TAX: 2002-03 TO 2016-17

	2002-03 Bands of taxable income(1) £	Rate of tax %		2003-04 Bands of taxable income(1) £	Rate of tax %		2004-05 Bands of taxable income(1) £	Rate of tax %	
Starting rate	1-1,920	10		1-1,960	10		1-2,020.	10	
Basic rate	1,921-29,900	22	(5)	1,961-30,500	22	(5)	2,021-31,400	22	(5)
Higher rate	Over 29,900	40	(6)	Over 30,500	40	(6)	Over 31,400	40	(6)

	2005-06 Bands of taxable income(1) £	Rate of tax %		2006-07 Bands of taxable income(1) £	Rate of tax %		2007-08 Bands of taxable income(1) £	Rate of tax %	
Starting rate	1-2.090	10		1-2,150	10		1-2,230	10	
Basic rate	2,091-32,400	22	(5)	2,151-33,300	22	(5)	2,231-34,600	22 (5)	
Higher rate	Over 32,400	40	(6)	Over 33,300	40	(6)	Over 34,600	40 (6)	

	2008-09 Bands of taxable income(1) £	Rate of tax %		2009-10 Bands of taxable income(1) £	Rate of tax %		2010-11 Bands of taxable income(1) £	Rate of tax %	
Basic rate (7)	1-34,800	20	(8)	1-37,400	20	(8)	1-37,400	20	(8)
Higher rate	Over 34,800	40	(6)	Over 37,400	40	(6)	Over 37,400	40	(6)
Additional Rate	Not Applicable			Not Applicable			Over 150,000	50	(9)

	2011-12 Bands of taxable income(1) £	Rate of tax %		2012-13 Bands of taxable income(1) £	Rate of tax %		2013-14 Bands of taxable income(1) £	Rate of tax %	
Basic rate (7)	1-35,000	20	(8)	1-34,370	20	(8)	1-32,010	20	(8)
Higher rate	Over 35,000	40	(6)	Over 34,370	40	(6)	Over 32,010	40	(6)
Additional Rate	Over 150,000	50	(9)	Over 150,000	50	(9)	Over 150,000	45	(10)

	2014-15 Bands of taxable income(1) £	Rate of tax %		2015-16 Bands of taxable income(1) £	Rate of tax %		2016-17 Bands of taxable income(1) £	Rate of tax %	
Basic rate (7)	1-31,865	20	(8)	1-31,785	20	(8)	1-32,000	20	(11)
Higher rate	Over 31,865	40	(6)	Over 31,785	40	(6)	Over 32,000	40	(12)
Additional Rate	Over 150,000	45	(10)	Over 150,000	45	(10)	Over 150,000	45	(13)

Spurce: HM Revenue & Customs - Table updated April 2016

(1) Taxable income is defined as gross income for income tax purposes less any allowances and reliefs available at the taxpayer's marginal rate.

(2) Applies to the income of discretionary and accumulation trusts. Prior to 1993-94 trusts paid tax at the basic rate, with an additional rate of 10%.

(3) The basic rate of tax on gross dividend income is 20%.

(4) The basic rate of tax on gross dividends and savings income is 20%.

(5) The basic rate of tax on gross dividends is 10% and savings income is 20%.

(6) The higher rate of tax on gross dividends is 32.5%.

(7) From 2008-09 the starting rate is abolished for all non-savings income (e.g. employment, self-employed trading profits, pensions and property income), which is the first slice of income to be charged to income tax. The starting rate and the starting rate limit for savings is shown in the table below. Where taxable non-savings income does not fully occupy the starting rate limit the remainder of the starting rate limit is available for savings income.

(8) The basic rate of tax on gross dividends is 10%.

(9) The additional rate of tax on gross dividends is 42.5%.

(10) The additional rate of tax on gross dividends is 37.5%.

(11) The basic rate of tax on net dividends is 7.5%.

(12) The higher rate of tax on net dividends is 32.5%.

(13) The additional rate of tax on net dividends is 38.1%.

23.12 Number of rateable properties[1] and total rateable value[2] by property type 1[A] and country as at 31 March 2016

Coverage: England and Wales
Properties (counts), Value (£ thousands)

Property type 1[A]	England		Wales		England & Wales	
	Rateable properties[1]	Rateable value[2]	Rateable properties[1]	Rateable value[2]	Rateable properties[1]	Rateable value[2]
All properties	**1,845,400**	**57,669,278**	**111,100**	**2,462,501**	**1,956,490**	**60,131,779**
Commercial	**1,383,580**	**42,002,363**	**79,980**	**1,551,451**	**1,463,570**	**43,553,814**
Advertising rights	37,150	67,126	1,020	1,004	38,170	68,130
Holiday sites	6,100	198,102	1,460	27,017	7,560	225,119
Garages & petrol stations	37,320	1,092,032	3,040	51,093	40,360	1,143,125
Hotels etc.	53,900	1,543,738	5,620	57,562	59,530	1,601,301
Pubs & wine bars	52,870	1,579,373	4,390	84,837	57,260	1,664,210
Markets	1,380	35,102	-	1,545	1,480	36,648
Offices	361,350	13,500,244	16,600	282,328	377,950	13,782,571
Car parks	58,470	525,743	1,800	18,905	60,270	544,648
Restaurants & cafes	40,210	1,208,670	2,530	47,346	42,740	1,256,016
Showroom and premises	7,740	205,245	-	7,142	8,130	212,387
Hypermarket and premises	-	102,649	-	4,930	-	107,579
Superstore and premises	2,020	2,764,814	-	169,292	2,150	2,934,106
Other Shops	463,590	10,109,336	27,650	412,258	491,240	10,521,594
Shops[3]	473,410	13,182,043	28,170	593,622	501,580	13,775,665
Warehouses & stores[4]	217,300	8,213,003	12,220	360,552	229,520	8,573,555
Other commercial	44,110	857,185	3,040	25,640	47,150	882,825
Educational, training & cultural	**44,250**	**3,320,045**	**3,030**	**145,167**	**47,280**	**3,465,212**
Local authority schools & colleges	22,470	1,886,260	1,840	96,273	24,320	1,982,533
Libraries and museums	4,340	255,510	-	9,035	4,710	264,545
Private schools & colleges	3,560	422,000	-	3,833	3,630	425,833
Universities	870	466,136	-	26,961	950	493,096
Other educational, training and cultural	13,010	290,140	670	9,064	13,670	299,205
Utilities	**11,510**	**1,086,444**	**990**	**125,852**	**12,510**	**1,212,297**
Docks	-	66,239	-	5,169	-	71,407
Electricity companies	1,680	570,418	-	97,541	1,930	667,958
Bus stations, moorings etc.	1,910	52,471	-	1,052	1,940	53,523
Other utilities	7,870	397,317	700	22,091	8,580	419,408
Industrial	**236,870**	**6,060,556**	**15,700**	**394,639**	**252,570**	**6,455,195**
Factories, mills & workshops[5]	228,300	5,147,812	14,880	337,255	243,180	5,485,066
Quarries, mines etc.	5,050	462,925	-	24,694	5,490	487,619
Other industrial	3,520	449,819	-	32,690	3,890	482,510
Leisure	**84,280**	**1,658,329**	**5,270**	**82,916**	**89,550**	**1,741,245**
Community centres & halls	32,320	624,644	2,910	32,414	35,230	657,058
Sports centres & stadia	740	170,425	-	9,928	800	180,352
Sports grounds, golf courses etc	10,170	250,063	670	12,521	10,840	262,584
Cinemas, theatres etc.	2,370	211,235	-	11,960	2,580	223,195
Other leisure	38,690	401,962	1,420	16,093	40,100	418,055
Miscellaneous	**84,900**	**3,541,541**	**6,120**	**162,475**	**91,030**	**3,704,016**
Cemeteries and crematoria	2,490	30,375	-	1,528	2,720	31,903
Medical facilities	25,800	1,279,296	1,650	66,539	27,460	1,345,835
Local government offices[6]	1,800	176,395	-	15,405	1,920	191,801
Police stations & courts	2,120	384,706	-	19,099	2,380	403,805
Hostels & homes	1,300	22,254	-	2,298	1,640	24,552
Other properties	51,390	1,648,516	3,520	57,605	54,910	1,706,121

Source: VOA administrative data as at 31 March 2016

Table notes

Counts are rounded to the nearest ten with counts fewer than 500 but greater than 0 reported as negligible and denoted by '-'.

Total rateable values are rounded to the nearest £1000 with amounts smaller than £0.5million but larger than £0 reported as negligible and denoted by '-'.

Totals may not sum due to rounding.

Footnotes

[1] **Rateable property (also known as hereditament)** - A unit of property that is, or may become, liable to non-domestic rating and thus appears in a rating list

[2] **Rateable value** - The legal term for the notional annual rent of a rateable property assessed by the VOA. Every property has a rateable value that is based broadly on the annual rent that the property could have been let for on the open market at a particular date (this is 1 April 2003 for the 2005 lists and 1 April 2008 for the 2010 lists).

[3] **Shops** - This is the total of showrooms, hypermarket, superstore and premises including "other shops".

[4] **Warehouses & stores** - In tables CL4, CL5 and CL6 warehouses and stores are labelled as warehouses.

[5] **Factories, mills & workshops** - In tables CL4, CL5 and CL6 factories, mills and workshops are labelled as factories.

[6] **Local government offices** - Local government offices are shown in this table under the 'Miscellaneous' category but are included in the figures for property type 'Offices' in all other tables.

[A] **Property type 1** - This splits the properties up into 6 broad property types and 35 more detailed property types. These are categorised using primary description codes. There are 119 primary description codes and are more generic than SCat code and show the nature of the use of the rateable property.

23.13 Revenue expenditure of local authorities

£ million

	2013/14 outturn	2014/15 outturn	2015/16 outturn	2016/17 outturn	2017/18 budget
England					
Education services	35,881	34,477	34,976	34,211	33,343
Highways and Transport services	4,795	4,537	4,922	4,401	4,240
Social care services	21,480	22,587	21,779	22,224	23,651
Public Health services	2,508	2,737	3,321	3,496	3,410
Housing services (excluding HRA)	2,025	1,852	1,742	1,610	1,543
Cultural, environmental and planning services	9,176	8,915	8,695	8,438	8,332
of which:					
Cultural services	2,831	2,682	2,496	2,351	2,190
Environmental services	4,992	4,945	5,048	5,028	5,064
Planning and development services	1,353	1,288	1,151	1,059	1,078
Police services	10,920	10,889	10,951	11,094	11,145
Fire and rescue services	2,089	2,045	2,080	2,052	2,055
Central services	2,845	3,068	3,112	3,055	2,987
Other services	91	92	281	342	264
Total Service Expenditure	**91,809**	**91,199**	**91,859**	**90,923**	90,970
plus precepts, levies, trading accounts and adjustments					
Housing Benefits [1]	20,982	21,113	21,103	20,792	20,304
Parish Precepts	367	389	409	445	486
Levies [2]	56	48	56	58	69
Trading Account Adjustments and other adjustments[3]	-368	-345	-339	-332	-458
Total Net current expenditure	**112,885**	**112,404**	**113,089**	**111,886**	111,370
Capital financing [4]	4,468	4,528	4,463	4,193	4,261
Capital Expenditure charged to Revenue Account (CERA) [5]	2,778	3,010	1,320	1,265	1,785
Revenue expenditure	**96,419**	**95,943**	**95,437**	**94,134**	94,470
Government Grants	64,578	61,312	56,611	54,008	50,188
Local Services Support Grant (LSSG)	77	48	28	26	23
Revenue Support Grant	15,175	12,675	9,509	7,184	3,868
Police grant	7,565	7,784	7,421	7,387	7,293
Retained income from Business Rate Retention Scheme	10,719	11,331	11,867	11,555	14,665
Appropriations to(-) / from (+) revenue reserves	-2,379	-949	1,834	1,885	1,444
Other items [6]	130	284	390	605	541
Council tax requirement	**23,371**	**23,964**	**24,734**	**26,082**	27,631

1. Includes Housing benefits: subsidy limitation transfers from HRA and Contribution to the HRA re items shared by the whole community
2. Includes Integrated Transport Authority Levy, Waste Disposal Authority Levy, London Pensions Fund Authority Levy and Other levies

3. Includes External Trading Accounts, Internal Trading Accounts, Capital items accounted for in External Trading Accounts, Capital items accounted for in Internal Trading Accounts, Adjustments to net current expenditure and Appropriations to/from Accumulated Asbences Account
4. Includes provision for repayment of principal, leasing payments, external interest payments and HRA item 8 interest payments and receipts
5. Includes both Capital expenditure charged to the General Fund Revenue account and for Public Health

6 Other items includes 'Inter-authority transfers in respect of reorganisation' and 'Other Items' which is the net collection fund surpluses/deficits from the previous year

Sources: Communities and Local Government: 0303 444 1333
Scottish Government, Local Government Finance Statistics : 0131 244 7033
Welsh Government: 02920 825355

23.13 Revenue expenditure of local authorities

	2011/12 outturn	2012/13 outturn	2013/14 outturn	2014/15 outturn	2015/16 outturn	2016/17 outturn	2017/18 buget
Scotland							
Net revenue expenditure on general fund	12,775,358	12,861,163	11,716,206	11,899,127	11,994,014	11,874,970	11,902,094
Wales[7]							
Education	2576.0	2598.3	2640.6	2630.2	255.1	2576.9	2598.9
Social services	1440.3	1498.6	1564.7	1599.0	1639.0	1666.6	1728.7
Council fund housing [8]	965.4	1065.9	1098.2	1139.5	1141.2	1128.5	1141.3
Local environmental services	419.1	424.4	420.1	412.7	377.8	373.3	373.8
Roads and transport	316.3	310.2	307.1	302.2	286.5	283.3	280.5
Libraries, culture, heritage, sport and recreation	264.5	272.3	263.1	242.7	218.6	207.8	203.9
Planning, economic development and community development	134.0	119.2	124.8	110.1	80.6	80.9	84.9
Local tax collection	30.2	30.1	33.7	40.4	36.2	30.2	25.9
Debt financing costs: counties	325.6	328.0	333.8	337.4	338.3	320.5	310.2
Central administrative and other revenue expenditure: counties [9]	302.7	318.7	307.1	294.7	313.3	345.1	360.9
Total county and county borough council expenditure	6774.2	6965.7	7093.2	7108.7	6986.6	7013.3	7109.1
Total police expenditure	663.0	667.2	697.8	667.6	666.9	668.4	675.7
Total fire expenditure	149.0	149.7	149.3	148.4	144.8	147.6	150.5
Total national park expenditure	16.2	17.8	17.3	15.4	14.5	13.8	14.6
Gross revenue expenditure	7602.4	7800.4	7957.6	7940.1	7812.8	7843.0	7950.0
less specific and special government grants	1825.7	1963.1	1932.8	1981.1	1935.1	1904.0	1930.7
Net revenue expenditure	5776.7	5837.3	6024.8	5959.0	5877.7	5939.0	6019.3
Putting to (+)/drawing from (-) reserves	-21.6	-63.2	-66.2	-72.2	-84.5	-105.1	-103.3
Council tax reduction scheme	-	-	244.0	247.3	255.7	257.7	258.0
Budget requirement	5775.1	5774.1	6202.6	6134.1	6048.9	6091.7	6174.0
Plus discretionary non-domestic rate relief	3.1	3.2	3.5	3.5	3.6	3.5	3.6
less revenue support grant	3382.1	3257.0	3488.8	3363.5	3303.7	3261.3	3193.3
less police grant	245.7	228.5	240.1	236.2	221.9	218.0	211.2
less re-distributed non-domestic rates income	787.0	911.0	1032.0	1041.0	956.0	977.0	1059.0
Council tax requirement	1343.3	1380.9	1423.1	1497.0	1570.9	1638.8	1714.0
of which:							
Paid by council tax reduction scheme	195.5	243.1	244.0	247.3	255.7	257.7	258.0
Paid directly by council tax payers	1147.8	1137.8	1179.1	1249.7	1315.2	1381.0	1455.9

Sources: Communities and Local Government: 0303 444 1333
Scottish Government, Local Government Finance Statistics : 0131 244 7033
Welsh Government: 02920 825355

7 Includes police, fire and national park authorities. Service expenditure excludes that financed by sales, fees and charges, but includes that financed by specific and special government grants.
8 Includes housing benefit, and private sector housing costs such as provision for the homeless. Excludes council owned housing.
9 Includes capital expenditure charged to the revenue account. The figure is net of any interest expected to accrue on balances. Also includes coroners' and other courts, community councils, unallocated contingencies, costs of corporate management, democratic representation and management and central administration costs not allocated to services.

. Data not applicable.

23.14 Financing of revenue expenditure England and Wales

England and Wales
Years ending 31 March

£ million

		2006 /07	2007 /08	2008 /09	2009 /10	2010 /11	2011 /12	2012 /13	2013 /14	2014 /15[1]	2015 /16[1]	2016 /17
England[2]												
Revenue expenditure[3]												
Cash £m	KRTN	88,172	92,384	98,107	103,276	104,256	99,278	94,148	96,419	95942	95437	94,134
Government grants												
Cash £m	KRTO	49,093	51,657	53,007	57,755	57,657	56,237	46,765	64,578	61312	56611	54,008
Percentage of revenue expenditure	KRTP	56	56	54	56	55	57	50	67	64	59	57
Redistributed business rates[4]												
Cash £m	KRTQ	17,506	18,506	20,506	19,515	21,517	19,017	23,129	-	-	-	-
Percentage of revenue expenditure	KRTR	20	20	21	19	21	19	25	-	-	-	-
Retained income from rate retention												
Cash £m		-	-	-	-	-	-	-	10,719	11331	11867	11,555
Percentage of revenue expenditure		-	-	-	-	-	-	-	11	12	12	12
Council tax												
Cash £m	KRTS	22,453	23,608	24,759	25,633	26,254	26,451	26,715	23,371	23964	24734	26,082
Percentage of revenue expenditure	KRTT	25	26	25	25	25	27	28	24	25	26	28
Wales												
Gross revenue expenditure[5]	ZBXH	6,472	6,739	7,184	7,523	7,636	7,741	7,919	8026 [10]	8,003	7,813	7,843
General government grants[6]	ZBXI	3,169	3,287	3,335	3,428	3,525	3,628	3,485	3751 [10]	3,600	3,526	4,456
Specific government grants[7]	ZBXG	1,530	1,630	1,809	1,987	2,020	2,014	2,112	2064 [10]	2,109	1,935	1,904
Share of redistributed business rates	ZBXJ	730	791	868	894	935	787	911	1032 [10]	1,041	956	977
Council tax income[8]	ZBXK	1,071	1,131	1,188	1,240	1,295	1,343	1,381	1423 [10]	1,497	1,571	1,638
Other[9]	ZBXL	-27	-99	-16	-26	-139	-31	29	-244 [10]	-243	-175	-105

Sources: Communities and Local Government: 0303 444 1333;
Welsh Government 02920 825355

1. Budget estimates.
2 Produced on a non-Financial Reporting Standard 17 (FRS17) basis.
3 The sum of government grants, business rates and local taxes does not normally equal revenue expenditure because of the use of reserves.
4 1993-94 to 2003-04 includes City of London Offset.

5 Gross revenue expenditure is total local authority expenditure on services, plus capital charges, but net of any income from sales, fees, and charges and other non-grant sources. It includes expenditure funded by specific grants. The figures have been adjusted to account for FRS17 pension costs.

6 Includes all unhypothecated grants, namely revenue support grant, police grant, council tax reduction scheme grant, transitional grant and the adjustment to reverse the transfer.
7 Comprises specific and supplementary grants,excluding police grant.
8 This includes community council precepts, and income covered by charge/council tax benefit grant, but excludes council tax reduction scheme (2013-14).
9 Includes use of reserves and discretionary non-domestic rate relief.

10. In 2013-14, the education revenue outturn data collection was changed to be comparable with the revenue budget collection. Overall education expenditure is not comparable with previous years due to the movement of all Flying Start expenditure to Social Services. Gross revenue expenditure and income for Neath Port Talbot are not consistent with previous years due to errors in reporting.

23.15 Financing of capital expenditure

£ million

	2011-12	2012-13	2013-14	2014-15	2015-16	2016-17 (h)
					(P)	(F)
Central government grants (g)	7,170	8,481	7,483	8,520	9,329 (R)	9,001
EU structural funds grants	77	55	57	132	106	24
Grants and contributions from private developers and from leaseholders etc	747	693	750	727	962 (R)	1,421
Grants and contributions from NDPBs (a)	522	442	443	564	426 (R)	698
National lottery grants	121	67	49	53	48	83
Use of capital receipts	1,647	1,294	1,516	1,879	2,148 (R)	3,298
Revenue financing of capital expenditure	4,504	3,167	4,920	5,241	4,367 (R)	5,070
of which:						
Housing Revenue Account (CERA)	*324*	*466*	*578*	*686*	*924* (R)	*1,509*
Major Repairs Reserve	*1,160*	*1,259*	*1,491*	*1,526*	*1,683*	*1,595*
General Fund (CERA)	*3,020*	*1,442* (b)	*2,851*	*3,029*	*1,760* (R)	*1,965*
Capital expenditure financed by borrowing/credit	18,819	4,842	4,454	4,422	4,747 (R)	9,925
of which:						
SCE(R) Single Capital Pot(c)	338	88	70	-	-	-
SCE(R) Separate Programme Element(c)	74	30	8	-	-	-
Other borrowing & credit arrangements not supported by central government (d)	18,406 (e)	4,724	4,376	4,422	4,747 (R)	9,925
Total (i)	**33,606** (e)	**19,042**	**19,671**	**21,539**	**22,133** (R)	**29,519**
Flexible Use of Capital Receipts (f)	-	-	-	-	-	-83 (R)

Source: Department for Communities and Local Government

(a) Non-Departmental Public Bodies, organisations that are not government departments but which have a role in the processes of national government, such as the Sport England, English Heritage and Natural England.

(b) This reflects reallocation of expenditure by TfL as part of year end process of reconciling funding to its subsidiaries

(c) Supported capital expenditure (SCE) financed by borrowing that is attracting central government support has been discontinued as of March 31 2011. This may have a bearing on the financing of capital expenditure. A residue of schemes up to 2013-14 were financed through this form of borrowing from earlier years.

(d) The Prudential System, which came into effect on 1 April 2004, allows local authorities to raise finance for capital expenditure - without Government consent - where they can afford to service the debt without extra Government support.

(e) It is estimated that approximately £13 billion is associated with the financing of the HRA self-financing determination payment.

(f) Flexibility of Capital Receipts allows local authorities to use the receipts from the sale of capital assets for efficiency savings projects that would be recorded in the revenue account.

(g) Central government grants includes grants awarded by the GLA.

(h) Total provisional capital expenditure may differ from the expenditure total due to rounding error and exclusion of spend by virtue of 16 (2)(b) direction.

(i) Financing of capital expenditure forecast has not been adjusted. This means total forecast spend is approximately 20% lower than the resource total.

(R) Marked items have been revised due to minor revisions by six authorities

23.16a Capital receipts: all services: England 2014-15

£ thousand

Service Block	Sale & disposal of tangible fixed assets	Sale of intangible assets	Repayments of grants loans & financial assistance	Total Receipts
Pre-primary & Primary Education	34,105	0	95	34,200
Secondary Education	51,860	0	454	52,314
Special Education	14,676	0	0	14,676
Non-school funding	19,002	0	2,377	21,379
Total Education	**119,643**	**0**	**2,926**	**122,569**
Roads, Street Lights & Safety	13,516	0	117	13,633
Parking of Vehicles	19,030	0	0	19,030
Public Passenger Transport-Bus	808	0	0	808
Public Passenger Transport-Rail & Other	2,710	0	0	2,710
Airports	0	0	112	112
Local Authority Ports and Piers	0	0	0	0
Tolled Road bridges,tunnels,ferries, public transport companies	101	0	1,905	2,006
Total Transport	**36,165**	**0**	**2,134**	**38,299**
Social Services	**66,379**	**2,130**	**5,412**	**73,921**
Public Health	**522**	**0**	**0**	**522**
Total Housing	**1,350,633**	**28,776**	**25,865**	**1,405,274**
Culture and heritage	3,173	89	824	4,086
Recreation and sport	5,330	42	2,232	7,604
Open spaces	8,670	633	241	9,544
Tourism	981	0	0	981
Library Services	2,988	0	0	2,988
Total Culture and related services	**21,142**	**764**	**3,297**	**25,203**
Cemeteries, cremation and mortuary	2,439	0	0	2,439
Coast protection	104	0	133	237
Community safety	8	0	0	8
Community safety (CCTV)	0	0	0	0
Flood defence and land drainage	0	0	0	0
Agriculture and fisheries	27,193	0	0	27,193
Regulatory Services (Environmental health)	1,639	0	114	1,753
Regulatory Services (Trading standards)	6	0	0	6
Street cleaning not chargeable to highways	1,262	0	0	1,262
Waste collection	2,532	0	1,617	4,149
Waste disposal	347	0	0	347
Trade Waste	10	0	0	10
Recycling	60	0	0	60
Waste minimisation	0	0	0	0
Climate change costs	0	0	127	127
Total environmental services	**35,600**	**0**	**1,991**	**37,591**
Planning and development services	**146,485**	**0**	**17,267**	**163,752**
Police	**243,937**	**0**	**1,263**	**245,200**
Fire and rescue services	**22,635**	**153**	**0**	**22,788**
Central Services (including Court services)	**571,431**	**2,908**	**11,042**	**585,381**
Industrial and Commercial	247,177	85	711	247,973
Other Trading	14,586	0	240	14,826
Total Trading	**261,763**	**85**	**951**	**262,799**
Total All services	**2,876,335**	**34,816**	**72,148**	**2,983,299**

Source: Communities and Local Government Capital Outturn Return 2014-15 (COR) data

Please note that total expenditure on grants (total all services) and total expenditure (total all services) do not tally with the figures on our release because of the GLA adjustment. The GLA adjustment is done for the All England Total, but cannot be done for individual authorities. The GLA adjustment removes the double counting arising from grants paid from GLA to London boroughs and subsequently London boroughs expenditure using that grant.

23.16b Capital expenditure: all services: England 2014-15

Service Block	Acquisition of land & existing buildings	New construction conversion & renovation	Vehicles	Plant machinery & equipment	Intangible fixed assets	Total payments on fixed assets	Expenditure on grants	Expenditure on loans & other financial assistance	Total Expenditure
Pre-primary & Primary Education	17,971	1,946,177	3,155	89,604	766	2,057,673	164,264	235	2,222,172
Secondary Education	8,070	650,838	1,911	33,441	237	694,497	142,480	68	837,045
Special Education	6,637	239,735	502	5,954	280	253,108	10,410	0	263,518
Non-school funding	6,075	110,008	965	9,836	2,287	129,171	19,682	8,300	157,153
Total Education	**38,753**	**2,946,758**	**6,533**	**138,835**	**3,570**	**3,134,449**	**336,836**	**8,603**	**3,479,888**
Roads, Street Lights & Safety	22,346	3,305,035	14,950	29,280	8,827	3,380,438	70,281	3,652	3,454,371
Parking of Vehicles	11,819	44,055	674	6,803	393	63,744	485	0	64,229
Public Passenger Transport-Bus	5,736	120,295	3,817	45,277	1,973	177,098	39,745	0	216,843
Public Passenger Transport-Rail & Other	23,904	229,664	16,743	26,809	20,987	318,107	1,526,327	650,200	2,494,634
Airports	0	6,992	0	0	0	6,992	0	11,000	17,992
Local Authority Ports and Piers	2,080	8,560	24	1,637	0	12,301	0	1,760	14,061
Tolled Road bridges,tunnels,ferries, public transport companies	8,481	20,725	697	54	4	29,961	0	0	29,961
Total Transport	**74,366**	**3,735,326**	**36,905**	**109,860**	**32,184**	**3,988,641**	**1,636,838**	**666,612**	**6,292,091**
Social Services	**6,860**	**139,529**	**3,697**	**30,822**	**9,571**	**190,479**	**48,246**	**25,636**	**264,361**
Public Health	**0**	**2,466**	**210**	**163**	**86**	**2,925**	**4,246**	**0**	**7,171**
Total Housing	**338,069**	**3,286,964**	**3,312**	**44,792**	**3,476**	**3,676,613**	**1,046,038**	**81,708**	**4,804,359**
Culture and heritage	16,235	158,645	723	7,756	395	183,754	18,021	4,926	206,701
Recreation and sport	12,142	428,994	3,231	26,805	305	471,477	23,642	21,310	516,429
Open spaces	2,432	114,057	7,771	9,697	169	134,126	11,015	356	145,497
Tourism	10	27,209	12	453	3	27,687	1,667	0	29,354
Library Services	2,688	46,397	545	7,375	514	57,519	1,808	0	59,327
Total Culture and related services	**33,507**	**775,302**	**12,282**	**52,086**	**1,386**	**874,563**	**56,153**	**26,592**	**957,308**
Cemeteries, cremation and mortuary	3,305	24,502	201	4,194	21	32,223	104	0	32,327
Coast protection	3	52,994	92	742	1,159	54,990	3,546	1,440	59,976
Community safety	0	2,749	357	2,217	58	5,381	1,058	0	6,439
Community safety (CCTV)	63	2,138	26	4,775	0	7,002	23	0	7,025
Flood defence and land drainage	20	63,544	315	297	14	64,190	14,375	36	78,601
Agriculture and fisheries	3,794	6,193	0	46	0	10,033	91	0	10,124
Regulatory Services (Environmental health)	0	5,062	1,176	983	210	7,431	469	503	8,403
Regulatory Services (Trading standards)	0	499	468	697	0	1,664	33	0	1,697
Street cleaning not chargeable to highways	0	447	14,516	5,299	0	20,262	3	0	20,265
Waste collection	2,782	11,294	55,903	26,069	148	96,196	137	0	96,333
Waste disposal	5,439	116,318	5,916	12,027	239	139,939	6,972	22,821	169,732
Trade Waste	0	0	1,369	30	0	1,399	0	0	1,399
Recycling	15	104,250	8,125	9,533	42	121,965	2,478	0	124,443
Waste minimisation	0	35,263	0	733	0	35,996	22	0	36,018
Climate change costs	112	11,583	155	5,308	0	17,158	8,742	1,688	27,588
Total environmental services	**15,533**	**436,836**	**88,619**	**72,950**	**1,891**	**615,829**	**38,053**	**26,488**	**680,370**
Planning and development services	**191,499**	**554,437**	**9,692**	**31,810**	**8,929**	**796,367**	**287,973**	**268,887**	**1,353,227**
Police	**21,775**	**189,442**	**85,914**	**219,193**	**28,407**	**544,731**	**1,263**	**233**	**546,227**
Fire and rescue services	**4,372**	**100,503**	**47,582**	**33,670**	**6,064**	**192,191**	**86**	**0**	**192,277**
Central Services (including Court services)	**177,121**	**628,475**	**54,711**	**204,175**	**129,780**	**1,194,262**	**87,439**	**82,717**	**1,364,418**
Industrial and Commercial	114,852	103,426	555	5,402	191	224,426	3,375	16,850	244,651
Other Trading	4,706	42,731	14,780	1,671	268	64,156	2,445	3,865	70,466
Total Trading	**119,558**	**146,157**	**15,335**	**7,073**	**459**	**288,582**	**5,820**	**20,715**	**315,117**
Total All services	**1,021,413**	**12,942,195**	**364,792**	**945,429**	**225,803**	**15,499,632**	**3,548,991**	**1,208,191**	**20,256,814**

Source: Communities and Local Government Capital Outturn Return 2014-15 (COR) data

Please note that total expenditure on grants (total all services) and total expenditure (total all services) do not tally with the figures on our release because of the GLA adjustment. The GLA adjustment is done for the All England Total, but cannot be done for individual authorities. The GLA adjustment removes the double counting arising from grants paid from GLA to London boroughs and subsequently London boroughs expenditure using that grant.

23.17 Local authority capital expenditure by service

£ million

	1996-97	2010-11	2011-12	2012-13	2013-14	2014-15	2015-16	2015-16 over 2014-15 percentage change
Education	57.4	233.3	260.6	267.4	274.0	245.6	335.0	36
Social services	12.4	22.3	18.8	22.9	17.7	22.9	12.6	-45
Transport	113.2	210.9	206.9	231.5	175.1	168.1	119.7	-29
Housing	271.0	210.1	230.1	216.4	223.6	260.3	316.5	22
General administration	36.0	50.6	42.6	63.4	47.7	41.9	36.3	-13
Planning and development	39.3	73.9	94.7	109.2	123.7	103.3	92.7	-10
Other services	145.3	143.3	144.7	143.4	125.1	125.1	1,039.4	731
Law, order and protective services	18.6	53.2	37.9	33.9	53.7	48.0	57.3	19
Total expenditure	693.2	997.7	1,036.3	1,088.1	1,040.6	1,015.2	2,009.6	98
Total expenditure excluding HRA subsidy buyout							1,090.6	7

Source: Local authority revenue and capital outturn expenditure, Welsh Government

23.18 Service Analysis of Revenue Expenditure and Income, 2015-16 Scotland

£ thousands

	Gross Expenditure on Funding Basis	Total Income	Net Revenue Expenditure on Funding Basis
Education	**4,945,624**	**(209,836)**	**4,735,788**
Pre-primary education	384,833	(15,808)	369,025
Primary education	1,905,451	(71,575)	1,833,876
Secondary education	1,946,888	(82,137)	1,864,751
Special education	549,727	(15,728)	533,999
Community Learning	125,921	(17,007)	108,914
Other non-school funding	32,804	(7,581)	25,223
Cultural and related services	**690,792**	**(92,615)**	**598,177**
Museums and galleries	45,587	(3,662)	41,925
Other cultural and heritage services	72,945	(15,224)	57,721
Library service	114,145	(4,849)	109,296
Promotional Events	12,574	(1,064)	11,510
Other Tourism	14,074	(1,532)	12,542
Countryside recreation and management	27,085	(3,878)	23,207
Sport facilities	195,597	(34,823)	160,774
Community parks and open spaces	142,247	(15,862)	126,385
Other recreation and sport	66,538	(11,721)	54,817
Social work	**4,044,181**	**(874,836)**	**3,169,345**
Service Strategy	41,134	(4,778)	36,356
Children's Panel	945	(321)	624
Children and families	923,249	(23,175)	900,074
Older persons	1,783,171	(438,723)	1,344,448
Adults with physical or sensory disabilities	234,179	(30,451)	203,728
Adults with learning disabilities	714,372	(186,950)	527,422
Adults with mental health needs	165,627	(65,634)	99,993
Adults with other needs	73,399	(23,453)	49,946
Criminal justice social work services	108,105	(101,351)	6,754
Roads and transport[1]	**621,891**	**(203,591)**	**418,300**
Road construction	4,418	1,808	6,226
Winter maintenance	64,629	(2,771)	61,858
Maintenance & repairs	204,132	(50,404)	153,728
Road lighting	73,442	(5,611)	67,831
School crossing patrols	13,282	(135)	13,147
Other network and traffic management	63,315	(19,582)	43,733
Parking	33,893	(69,322)	(35,429)
Non-LA PT: Concessionary fares	9,249	(1,046)	8,203
Non-LA PT: Support to operators	90,565	(5,239)	85,326
Non-LA PT: Co-ordination	34,565	(40,113)	(5,548)
Local authority Transport	28,974	(9,772)	19,202
Road Bridges	1,427	(1,404)	23
Environmental services	**816,944**	**(132,809)**	**684,135**
Cemetery, cremation and mortuary services	37,757	(35,627)	2,130
Coast protection	1,356	(386)	970
Flood defence and land drainage	15,159	(1,096)	14,063
Environmental Health	100,252	(15,603)	84,649
Trading Standards	36,084	(1,752)	34,332
Waste Collection	231,234	(50,355)	180,879
Waste Disposal	292,667	(25,407)	267,260
Other waste management	102,435	(2,583)	99,852
Planning and Development Services	**424,310**	**(181,394)**	**242,916**
Planning: Building control	37,557	(41,209)	(3,652)
Planning: Development control	54,532	(34,009)	20,523
Planning: Policy	35,322	(6,839)	28,483
Planning: Environmental initiatives	24,528	(6,828)	17,700
Economic development	272,371	(92,509)	179,862

23.18 Service Analysis of Revenue Expenditure and Income, 2015-16 Scotland

£ thousands

	Gross Expenditure on Funding Basis	Total Income	Net Revenue Expenditure on Funding Basis
Central Services[2]	685,713	(217,646)	468,067
Council tax collection	57,528	(29,993)	27,535
Council tax reduction administration	33,224	(10,233)	22,991
Non-domestic rates collection	8,989	(2,201)	6,788
Housing benefit administration	36,696	(19,738)	16,958
Registration of births, deaths and marriages	13,667	(9,420)	4,247
Emergency Planning (non Police or Fire)	3,866	(167)	3,699
Licensing	19,547	(21,201)	(1,654)
Conducting Elections	8,739	(4,872)	3,867
Registration of electors	16,615	(2,875)	13,740
Council tax valuation	9,399	(291)	9,108
Non-domestic lands valuation	13,992	(936)	13,056
Local Land Charges	510	(17)	493
Non-road lighting	11,636	(4,175)	7,461
General grants, bequests and donations	7,178	(398)	6,780
Corporate and democratic core costs	154,533	(2,416)	152,117
Non-distributed costs	118,656	(2,516)	116,140
Other	170,938	(106,197)	64,741
Non-HRA Housing	2,398,253	(2,104,025)	294,228
Private sector housing renewal	89,304	(61,279)	28,025
Housing benefits: Rent allowances	1,122,995	(1,081,829)	41,166
Housing benefits: Rent rebate	675,372	(687,625)	(12,253)
Homelessness	193,671	(105,031)	88,640
Welfare Services	13,681	(870)	12,811
Administration of housing advances	157	(200)	(43)
Housing Support Services	136,416	(6,419)	129,997
Other non-HRA housing (excl admin of Housing Benefits)	166,657	(160,772)	5,885
Trading Services	46,778	(63,308)	(16,530)
General Fund Total	14,674,486	(4,080,060)	10,594,426
Housing Revenue Account	660,183	(1,150,011)	(489,828)
All Services (GF + HRA)	15,334,669	(5,230,071)	10,104,598

Source: Scottish Government, Local Financial Returns

1. Regional Transport Partnerships expenditure is apportioned to councils by population (NRS 2015 mid-year population estimates).

2. Expenditure on council tax and non-domestic valuation and registration of electors is apportioned to councils using the amount that the Valuation Joint Boards requisition from them.

23.19a Revenue Income by Source, 2011-12 to 2014-15 Scotland

£ millions

	2011-12	2012-13	2013-14[a]	2014-15
General Funding:	**12,483**	**12,543**	**11,724**	**11,923**
General Revenue Grant	7,790	7,782	7,225	7,167
Non-Domestic Rates	2,203	2,297	2,436	2,656
Council Tax[2]	2,301	2,319	1,978	2,022
Other Funding	189	145	85	78
Service Income:	**5,704**	**5,777**	**5,066**	**5,185**
Government Grants (excl GRG)	2,561	2,640	1,974	1,984
Other Grants, Reimbursements an	856	807	774	833
Customer and Client Receipts	2,287	2,330	2,317	2,368
Total Revenue Income	**18,188**	**18,320**	**16,790**	**17,108**

Source: Scottish Government Local Financial Returns (LFRs): LFR 00

a. Figures for 2013-14 and later are not comparable with prior years due to changes to the way that Police and Fire are funded following the formation of Police Scotland and the Scottish Fire and Rescue Service. See section 5.2 for more details.

2. Pre-2013-14 Council Tax figures are not comparable with later years as Council Tax Reduction (CTR) was introduced from 1 April 2013 to replace Council Tax Benefit (CTB), which was abolished by the UK Government as part of its welfare reform programme. Due to differences in the administration of the two schemes, Council Tax figures before 2013-14 include CTB, whereas figures from 2013-14 onwards do not include CTR.

23.19b Total Capital Expenditure and Financing, 2011-12 to 2014-15

£ thousands

	2011-12	2012-13	2013-14[a]	2014-15
Acquisition of land, leases, existing buildings or works	137,332	146,930	90,335	63,604
New construction, conversions & enhancement to existing buildings	2,142,293	2,037,385	1,967,310	1,948,992
Vehicles, machinery & equipment	194,836	197,022	189,509	174,443
Intangible assets	6,052	6,638	13,119	14,061
Total Gross Capital Expenditure	**2,480,513**	**2,387,975**	**2,260,273**	**2,201,100**
Revenue Expenditure funded from Capital Resources	181,021	161,349	199,728	199,002
Total Expenditure to be met from Capital Resources	**2,661,534**	**2,549,324**	**2,460,001**	**2,400,102**
Scottish Government General Capital Grant	565,541	450,088	438,163	680,491
Scottish Government Specific Capital Grants	234,365	217,281	180,549	203,444
Grants from Scottish Government Agencies and NDPBs	82,764	141,311	150,761	108,610
Other Grants and Contributions	85,714	124,311	142,077	107,731
Borrowing (advances from Loans fund)	1,261,468	1,165,387	1,105,526	829,701
Capital receipts used from asset sales/disposals	94,020	105,937	92,167	107,919
Capital Fund applied	21,653	36,867	24,798	34,595
Capital funded from current revenue	209,122	294,087	295,335	284,911
Assets acquired under credit arrangements (e.g. finance leases, PPP/PFI)	106,888	14,055	30,625	42,701
Total Financing	**2,661,534**	**2,549,324**	**2,460,001**	**2,400,102**

Source: Scottish Government Capital Returns (CR Final)

a. Following the Police and Fire Reform (Scotland) Act 2012 figures from 2013-14 onwards may not be comparable with previous years.

23.20 – Subjective Analysis of General Fund Revenue Expenditure and Income, Scotland 2015-16

£thousands

	Education Services	Culture and Related Services	Social Work Services	Roads and Transport	Environmental Services	Planning and Development Services	Central Services	Housing Services (Non-HRA)	Trading with the Public	Total General Fund Services	HRA Housing Services	Total Housing Services (GF + HRA)
EXPENDITURE												
Employee Costs												
Teachers	2,432,145									2,432,145	-	2,432,145
All other Employees	994,524	231,647	1,410,312	197,009	324,778	176,173	467,979	112,228	18,153	3,932,803	142,327	4,075,130
Total Employee Costs Before Statutory Adjustments	3,426,669	231,647	1,410,312	197,009	324,778	176,173	467,979	112,228	18,153	6,364,948	142,327	6,507,275
Reversal of pension costs calculated in accordance with the Code (i.e. IAS 19)	(208,808)	(45,501)	(270,058)	(47,579)	(63,664)	(40,587)	(85,337)	(22,429)	(7,434)	(791,397)	(36,101)	(827,498)
Contribution to pension fund calculated under statute	148,683	30,906	175,934	31,577	41,919	25,842	95,407	13,929	4,439	568,636	23,917	592,553
Statutory adjustment for short term accumulating absences	14,373	647	2,884	206	686	479	1,612	217	66	21,170	135	21,305
Statutory adjustment for equal pay	0	0	0	0	0	0	(9,481)	0	0	(9,481)	0	(9,481)
Total Employee Costs After Statutory Adjustments	3,380,917	217,699	1,319,072	181,213	303,719	161,907	470,180	103,945	15,224	6,153,876	130,278	6,284,154
Operating Costs												
Premises Related Costs	1,091,940	232,594	135,208	267,428	120,501	91,576	106,800	74,238	11,173	2,131,458	823,995	2,955,453
Transport Related Expenditure	167,704	21,597	52,562	78,565	82,229	5,295	20,374	1,851	11,934	442,111	3,873	445,984
Supplies and Services	451,409	116,451	148,714	212,617	181,520	71,915	151,679	66,467	12,806	1,413,578	171,650	1,585,228
Third Party Payments	285,476	253,155	2,220,260	299,746	186,397	107,347	89,214	279,103	7,837	3,728,535	46,341	3,774,876
Joint authorities - Requisitions Only				0			28,396			28,396		28,396
Other local authorities	14,053	15,519	9,686	46,037	927	2,583	374	166	0	89,345	20,906	110,251
Health authorities	7,869	0	111,990	228	5	0	0	259	0	120,351	0	120,351
All Other Third Party Payments	263,554	237,636	2,098,584	253,481	185,465	104,764	60,444	278,678	7,837	3,490,443	25,435	3,515,878
Total Operating Costs Before Statutory Adjustments	1,996,529	623,797	2,556,744	858,356	570,647	276,133	368,067	421,659	43,750	7,715,682	1,045,859	8,761,541
Reversal of Depreciation and Impairment of Non-Current Assets	(589,800)	(174,262)	(81,024)	(275,466)	(91,111)	(67,876)	(87,311)	(7,438)	(14,039)	(1,388,327)	(510,740)	(1,899,067)
Reversal of Impairment of assets in the surplus/deficit on the provision on services	(28,778)	(3,904)	(276)	(2,662)	1,127	(6,498)	(2,282)	852	(4)	(42,425)	(88,095)	(130,520)
Reversal of Amortisation and Impairment of Intangible Assets	(844)	(175)	(1,523)	(376)	(473)	(1,367)	(3,514)	(121)	0	(8,393)	(76)	(8,469)
Total Operating Costs After Statutory Adjustments	1,377,107	445,456	2,473,921	579,852	480,190	200,392	274,960	414,952	29,707	6,276,537	446,948	6,723,485
Transfer Payments												
School Children and students	21,877									21,877		21,877
Social Work Clients			61,784							61,784		61,784
Housing benefits								1,798,367		1,798,367		1,798,367
Debits resulting from soft loans to clients etc.	0	(5)	2	9	0	4	4	0	0	14	102	116
Integrated Joint Boards (net)	(20)	(72)	109	0	(25)	0	(5)	(18)	0	(31)	0	(31)
Other Transfer Payments	16,409	16,835	39,907	3,472	7,316	33,711	1,650	110,673	146	230,119	25,307	255,426
Total Transfer Payments Before Statutory Adjustments	38,266	16,758	101,802	3,481	7,291	33,715	1,649	1,909,022	146	2,112,130	25,409	2,137,539
Reversal of grants paid which are funded from capital under statute – consent to borrow	0	0	0	(21,439)	0	(1,670)	(1,492)	(33,886)	0	(58,487)	(2,140)	(60,627)
Total Transfer Payments After Statutory Adjustments	38,266	16,758	101,802	(17,958)	7,291	32,045	157	1,875,136	146	2,053,643	23,269	2,076,912
Support Services												
Total Support Services Before Statutory Adjustments	204,401	46,060	215,527	41,132	62,229	47,089	202,772	32,636	2,042	853,888	76,346	930,234
Statutory adjustments for Support Services	(17,654)	(5,028)	(13,894)	(3,813)	(7,031)	(3,574)	(8,679)	(1,798)	(300)	(61,771)	(1,330)	(63,101)
Total Support Services After Statutory Adjustments	186,747	41,032	201,633	37,319	55,198	43,515	194,093	30,838	1,742	792,117	75,016	867,133
Adjustment for Inter Account and Inter Authority Transfers												
Contributions from Other Local Authorities	(9,718)	(834)	(12,713)	(32,360)	(1,921)	(1,487)	(6,072)	(107)	0	(65,212)	(160)	(65,372)
Recharges (income from other accounts within the authority)	(27,695)	(29,319)	(39,534)	(82,299)	(27,533)	(12,062)	(218,651)	(26,511)	(41)	(463,645)	(15,168)	(478,813)
Requisitions adjustment	0	0	0	(43,876)	0	0	(28,954)	0	0	(72,830)	0	(72,830)
Total Adjustment for Inter Account and Inter Authority Transfers	(37,413)	(30,153)	(52,247)	(158,535)	(29,454)	(13,549)	(253,677)	(26,618)	(41)	(601,687)	(15,328)	(617,015)
Gross Expenditure Before Statutory Adjustments	5,628,452	888,109	4,232,138	941,443	935,491	519,561	786,790	2,448,927	64,050	16,444,961	1,274,613	17,719,574
Gross Expenditure on Funding Basis	4,945,624	690,792	4,044,181	621,891	816,944	424,310	685,713	2,398,253	46,778	14,674,486	660,183	15,334,669

23.20 – Subjective Analysis of General Fund Revenue Expenditure and Income, Scotland 2015-16

£thousands

	Education Services	Culture and Related Services	Social Work Services	Roads and Transport	Environmental Services	Planning and Development Services	Central Services	Housing Services (Non-HRA)	Trading with the Public	Total General Fund Services	HRA Housing Services	Total Services (GF + HRA)
INCOME												
Government Grants												
Ring-fenced Revenue Grants	(4,501)	-	-	-	-	-	-	0	-	(4,501)	0	(4,501)
General Capital Grant used to fund grants to third parties	0	(233)	0	(82)	0	(2,062)	(1,492)	(113,435)	0	(117,304)	(2,140)	(119,444)
Other Central Government Grants (excl GRG)	(42,829)	(5,228)	(85,098)	(4,358)	(1,878)	(16,241)	(30,410)	(1,721,213)	(88)	(1,907,343)	(4,413)	(1,911,756)
Total Government Grants	**(47,330)**	**(5,461)**	**(85,098)**	**(4,440)**	**(1,878)**	**(18,303)**	**(31,902)**	**(1,834,648)**	**(88)**	**(2,029,148)**	**(6,553)**	**(2,035,701)**
Other Grants reimbursements and Contributions												
Contributions from Health Authorities	-	-	(455,186)	-	-	-	-	-	-	(455,186)	-	(455,186)
All other grants, reimbursements and contributions	(40,029)	(18,326)	(70,473)	(12,322)	(7,106)	(28,409)	(23,066)	(109,738)	(143)	(309,612)	(2,738)	(312,350)
Total Other Grants reimbursements and Contributions	**(40,029)**	**(18,326)**	**(525,659)**	**(12,322)**	**(7,106)**	**(28,409)**	**(23,066)**	**(109,738)**	**(143)**	**(764,798)**	**(2,738)**	**(767,536)**
Customer and Client Receipts												
Income from charges to service users	(57,443)	(30,489)	(238,990)	(63,964)	(47,283)	(35,430)	(27,575)	(22,496)	(20,560)	(544,230)	(92,891)	(637,121)
Rent Income	(1,682)	(6,910)	(3,181)	(11,789)	(1,125)	(33,255)	(17,978)	(88,708)	(1,501)	(166,129)	(1,033,710)	(1,199,839)
Other Sales, Fees and Charges	(63,352)	(31,427)	(21,908)	(107,225)	(75,417)	(65,997)	(116,841)	(48,431)	(41,016)	(571,614)	(14,119)	(585,733)
Total Customer and Client Receipts	**(122,477)**	**(68,826)**	**(264,079)**	**(182,978)**	**(123,825)**	**(134,682)**	**(162,394)**	**(159,635)**	**(63,077)**	**(1,281,973)**	**(1,140,720)**	**(2,422,693)**
Other Income	**0**	**(2)**	**0**	**(3,851)**	**0**	**0**	**(284)**	**(4)**	**0**	**(4,141)**	**0**	**(4,141)**
Total Income	**(209,836)**	**(92,615)**	**(874,836)**	**(203,591)**	**(132,809)**	**(181,394)**	**(217,646)**	**(2,104,025)**	**(63,308)**	**(4,080,060)**	**(1,150,011)**	**(5,230,071)**
Net Revenue Expenditure Before Statutory Adjustments	5,418,616	795,494	3,357,302	737,852	802,682	338,167	569,144	344,902	742	12,364,901	124,602	12,489,503
Net Revenue Expenditure on Funding Basis	4,735,788	598,177	3,169,345	418,300	684,135	242,916	468,067	294,228	(16,530)	10,594,426	(489,828)	10,104,598

23.21 Local government current expenditure on services in Northern Ireland by, 2012-13 to 2016-17

					£ million
	2012-13 outturn	2013-14 outturn	2014-15 outturn	2015-16 outturn	2016-17 plans
Northern Ireland					
Economic affairs	23	21	27	23	24
of which: enterprise and economic development	23	21	27	23	24
Environment protection	178	180	186	190	189
Housing and community amenities	91	98	99	100	158
Health	50	52	52	53	45
Recreation, culture and religion	215	221	211	230	192
Total Northern Ireland	**557**	**571**	**575**	**596**	**608**
Debt interest [1]	515	547	775	761	722
Total local government current expenditure on services	**134,373**	**134,145**	**133,965**	**133,202**	**132,968**
Accounting adjustments	20,409	21,672	22,267	23,472	23,095
Total local government current expenditure	**154,782**	**155,817**	**156,232**	**156,674**	**156,063**

Source: HM Treasury Public Expenditure Statistical Analyses (PESA)

(1) Debt interest is not allocated to individual countries, so is only included in the total UK figures. It excludes all intra-public sector debt interest payments.

this page is intentionally blank

836

Agriculture

Chapter 24

Agriculture

Input and Output (Tables 24.1 and 24.2)

For both tables, output is net of VAT collected on the sale of non-edible products. Figures for total output include subsidies on products, that is, payments that have the purpose of influencing production, their prices or remuneration of the factors of production. Unspecified crops include turf, other minor crops and arable area payments for fodder maize. Eggs include the value of duck eggs and exports of eggs for hatching. Landlords' expenses are included within farm maintenance, miscellaneous expenditure and depreciation of buildings and works. Also included within 'Other farming costs' are livestock and crop costs, water costs, insurance premia, bank charges, professional fees, rates, and other farming costs.

Non-subsidy payments

Payments other than subsidies on products from which farmers can benefit as a consequence of engaging in agriculture. This includes:
• environment and countryside management schemes
• organic farming schemes
• support schemes for less favoured areas
• Single Payment Scheme
• animal disease compensation attributable to income
• other payments

Compensation of employees and interest charges

Total compensation of employees excludes the value of work done by farm labour on own account capital formation in buildings and work. 'Interest' relates to interest charges on loans for current farming purposes and buildings, less interest on money held on short-term deposit.

Rent

Rent paid (after deductions) is the rent paid on all tenanted land including 'conacre' land in Northern Ireland, less landlords' expenses and the benefit value of dwellings on that land. Rent received (after deductions) is the rent received by farming landowners from renting of land to other farmers, less landlords' expenses and the benefit value of dwellings on that land. Total net rent is the net rent flowing out of the agricultural sector paid to non-farming landowners, including that part of tenanted land in Northern Ireland.

Agricultural censuses and surveys (Tables 24.3 and 24.5 and 24.12)

Data in thse tables are sourced primarily from the June/July Surveys of Agriculture carried out in the four UK countries each year. The exceptions to this are the holder age data (sourced from the EU Farm Structure Survey) and land use data in Scotland (sourced from Single Application Form (SAF) subsidy data). Also, cattle data are sourced from the Cattle Tracing System (CTS) in England, Wales and Scotland (from 2013) and from the equivalent Animal and Public Health Administration (APHIS) system in Northern Ireland. Prior to 2013 Scottish cattle data was sourced from agricultural surveys.

From 2009 onwards, England data relate to "commercial" holdings only. The term "commercial" covers all English holdings which have more than 5 hectares of agricultural land, 1 hectare of orchards, 0.5 hectares of vegetables or 0.1 hectares of protected crops, or more than 10 cattle, 50 pigs, 20 sheep, 20 goats, or 1,000 poultry. These thresholds are specified in the EU Farm Structure Survey Regulation EC 1166/2008.

Estimated quantity of crops and grass harvested
(Table 24.4)

The estimated yield of sugar beet is obtained from production figures supplied by British Sugar plc in England and Wales. In Great Britain, potato yields are estimated in consultation with the Potato Council Limited.

Forestry
(Table 24.6)

Statistics for state forestry are from Forestry Commission and Forest Service management information systems. For private forestry in Great Britain, statistics on new planting and restocking are based on records of grant aid and estimates of planting undertaken without grant aid, and softwood production is estimated from a survey of the largest timber harvesting companies. Hardwood production is estimated from deliveries of roundwood to primary wood processors and others, based on surveys of the UK timber industry, data provided by trade associations and estimates provided by the Expert Group on Timber and Trade Statistics.

Fisheries
(Table 24.14)
Figures show the number of registered and licensed fishing vessels based on information provided by the Marine Management Organisation.

Estimated average household food consumption – 'Family Food' Expenditure and Food Survey
(Table 24.15)
In 2008 the Expenditure and Food Survey (EFS) was renamed as the Living Costs and Food Survey (LCFS) when it became part of the Integrated Household Survey (IHS). The Expenditure and Food Survey started in April 2001, having been preceded by the National Food Survey (NFS) and the Family Expenditure Survey (FES). Both surveys were brought into one to provide value for money without compromising data quality. The EFS was effectively a continuation of the FES extended to record quantities of purchases. This extension is now known as the Family Food Module of the LCFS. Estimates from the NFS prior to 2000 have been adjusted by aligning estimates for the year 2000 with corresponding estimates from the FES. From 2006 the survey moved onto a calendar year basis (from the previous financial year basis) in preparation for its integration to the Integrated Household Survey from January 2008.

The Living Costs and Food Survey is a voluntary sample survey of private households throughout the UK. The basic unit of the survey is the household which is defined as a group of people living at the same address and sharing common catering arrangements. The survey is continuous, interviews being spread evenly over the year to ensure that seasonal effects are covered. Each household member over the age of seven keeps a diary of all their expenditure over a two-week period. A simplified version of the diary is used by those aged between seven and 15. The diaries record expenditure and quantities of purchases of food and drink rather than consumption of food and drink. Items of food and drink are defined as either household or eating out and are recorded in the form the item was purchased not how it was consumed. 'Household' covers all food that is brought into the household. 'Eating out' covers all food that never enters the household, for example restaurant meals, school meals and snacks eaten away from home.

24.1 Production and income accounts (at current prices) [a]
United Kingdom

Contact: Helen Mason, Department for Environment,
Food and Rural Affairs, Room 201, Foss House, Kings
Pool, 1-2 Peasholme Green, York, YO1 7PX
Email: farmingaccounts@defra.gsi.gov.uk

£ million   Calendar years

	2004	2005	2006	2007	2008	2009	2010	2011	2012	2013	2014	2015
1 Output of cereals	1 707	1 434	1 507	1 949	3 180	2 312	2 267	3 230	3 201	3 375	3 459	2 971
of which: wheat	1 232	1 018	1 066	1 325	2 270	1 562	1 680	2 322	2 162	2 073	2 453	2 053
barley	433	380	384	555	817	675	521	809	920	1 136	900	828
oats	40	34	54	65	90	72	63	94	114	160	99	85
2 Output of industrial crops	683	679	597	702	1 010	913	1 051	1 524	1 356	1 183	1 160	1 053
of which: oilseed rape	257	261	310	426	631	485	674	1 110	986	744	684	711
protein crops	109	94	72	81	131	136	127	103	98	123	123	137
sugar beet	280	278	178	162	208	246	197	251	227	270	315	173
3 Output of forage plants	142	155	167	132	143	190	189	186	146	217	265	269
4 Output of vegetables and horticultural products	1 613	1 682	1 738	1 822	1 909	1 966	2 263	2 337	2 398	2 530	2 357	2 384
of which: fresh vegetables	834	912	1 001	1 054	1 090	1 088	1 266	1 224	1 255	1 340	1 191	1 235
plants and flowers	779	770	737	768	819	879	997	1 114	1 142	1 191	1 166	1 149
5 Output of potatoes (including seeds)	715	535	650	708	793	681	598	711	659	947	677	577
6 Output of fruit	318	390	377	459	535	570	585	604	573	602	622	690
7 Output of other crop products incl. seeds	238	271	252	189	335	383	439	475	644	581	648	513
Total crop output (sum 1-7)	**5 416**	**5 147**	**5 288**	**5 961**	**7 904**	**7 016**	**7 392**	**9 067**	**8 977**	**9 435**	**9 187**	**8 457**
8 Output of livestock	4 812	5 090	5 065	5 146	6 372	7 027	7 313	8 167	8 628	9 128	8 964	8 654
primarily for meat	4 154	4 296	4 362	4 430	5 502	5 843	6 106	6 902	7 244	7 738	7 468	7 396
of which: cattle	1 279	1 466	1 561	1 623	2 071	2 131	2 154	2 573	2 794	2 886	2 611	2 756
pigs	680	677	685	736	866	968	978	1 070	1 132	1 274	1 264	1 080
sheep	726	686	709	641	798	967	979	1 149	1 027	1 037	1 122	1 119
poultry	1 306	1 300	1 233	1 249	1 579	1 590	1 799	1 904	2 078	2 324	2 250	2 220
gross fixed capital formation	657	794	703	716	870	1 184	1 208	1 265	1 384	1 390	1 496	1 258
of which: cattle	337	545	419	410	577	750	714	631	856	917	925	687
pigs	8	6	8	5	6	8	8	8	8	6	5	4
sheep	176	112	146	153	125	238	295	413	317	272	332	290
poultry	136	131	131	149	162	188	191	213	203	195	234	278
9 Output of livestock products	3 038	3 010	2 918	3 286	4 019	3 711	3 973	4 387	4 486	5 072	5 369	4 455
of which: milk	2 610	2 592	2 497	2 823	3 447	3 123	3 329	3 738	3 767	4 271	4 594	3 691
eggs	378	349	362	410	520	531	561	559	662	718	679	681
Total livestock output (8+9)	**7 849**	**8 100**	**7 983**	**8 432**	**10 391**	**10 738**	**11 286**	**12 554**	**13 114**	**14 200**	**14 334**	**13 110**
10 Other agricultural activities	717	638	622	680	790	868	918	1 026	1 015	1 052	1 122	1 091
11 Inseparable non-agricultural activities	637	678	684	763	813	897	936	1 003	1 041	1 176	1 170	1 248
12 Output (at market prices) (sum 1 to 11)	14 619	14 563	14 577	15 836	19 897	19 519	20 532	23 649	24 146	25 864	25 813	23 906
13 Total subsidies (less taxes) on product	2 172	214	87	62	57	38	29	28	20	21	21	36
14 Gross output at basic prices (12+13)	**16 791**	**14 777**	**14 664**	**15 898**	**19 955**	**19 557**	**20 561**	**23 677**	**24 167**	**25 885**	**25 833**	**23 942**
Intermediate consumption												
15 Seeds	692	723	635	683	790	779	737	761	742	867	766	715
16 Energy	669	779	831	897	1 166	1 101	1 216	1 380	1 429	1 450	1 378	1 184
of which: electricity and fuels for heating	209	235	258	274	340	344	357	369	386	386	374	377
motor and machinery fuels	460	544	573	623	826	758	859	1 012	1 043	1 065	1 004	807
17 Fertilisers	734	785	791	792	1 455	1 176	1 339	1 589	1 523	1 511	1 462	1 393
18 Plant protection products	576	547	518	571	656	674	711	772	839	856	941	964
19 Veterinary expenses	279	280	284	302	338	364	405	401	420	447	457	454

24.1 Production and income accounts (at current prices) [a]

United Kingdom

Contact: Helen Mason, Department for Environment,
Food and Rural Affairs, Room 201, Foss House, Kings
Pool, 1-2 Peasholme Green, York, YO1 7PX

Email: farmingaccounts@defra.gsi.gov.uk

£ million | | | | | | | | | | | Calendar years |
| --- | --- | --- | --- | --- | --- | --- | --- | --- | --- | --- | --- | --- |
| | 2004 | 2005 | 2006 | 2007 | 2008 | 2009 | 2010 | 2011 | 2012 | 2013 | 2014 | 2015 |
| 20 Animal feed | 2 716 | 2 490 | 2 595 | 2 983 | 3 863 | 3 694 | 4 087 | 4 508 | 4 895 | 5 558 | 5 053 | 4 730 |
| of which: compounds | 1 450 | 1 318 | 1 426 | 1 702 | 2 186 | 2 088 | 2 255 | 2 622 | 2 876 | 3 290 | 2 999 | 2 845 |
| straights | 883 | 807 | 785 | 879 | 1 197 | 1 156 | 1 387 | 1 374 | 1 453 | 1 569 | 1 413 | 1 292 |
| feed produced & used on farm or purchased from other farms | 384 | 365 | 384 | 401 | 480 | 450 | 444 | 512 | 566 | 699 | 642 | 593 |
| 21 Total maintenance | 1 014 | 993 | 1 012 | 1 084 | 1 204 | 1 280 | 1 364 | 1 444 | 1 442 | 1 501 | 1 607 | 1 597 |
| of which: materials | 654 | 644 | 645 | 687 | 734 | 789 | 846 | 900 | 903 | 937 | 962 | 943 |
| buildings | 359 | 349 | 367 | 397 | 470 | 491 | 518 | 544 | 539 | 563 | 645 | 654 |
| 22 Agricultural services | 635 | 629 | 621 | 679 | 789 | 868 | 918 | 1 025 | 1 015 | 1 052 | 1 122 | 1 091 |
| 23 FISIM | 90 | 111 | 115 | 122 | 115 | 71 | 86 | 103 | 96 | 105 | 99 | 108 |
| 24 Other goods and services | 2 361 | 2 348 | 2 323 | 2 387 | 2 619 | 2 717 | 2 807 | 3 013 | 3 118 | 3 140 | 3 165 | 3 145 |
| 25 Total intermediate consumption (sum 15 to 24) | 9 766 | 9 686 | 9 723 | 10 501 | 12 996 | 12 725 | 13 669 | 14 998 | 15 520 | 16 488 | 16 051 | 15 380 |
| 26 Gross value added at market prices (12-25) | 4 853 | 4 878 | 4 853 | 5 334 | 6 902 | 6 795 | 6 863 | 8 651 | 8 626 | 9 376 | 9 761 | 8 526 |
| 27 Gross value added at basic prices (14-25) | 7 025 | 5 092 | 4 941 | 5 397 | 6 959 | 6 832 | 6 891 | 8 679 | 8 646 | 9 397 | 9 782 | 8 561 |
| 28 Total consumption of Fixed Capital | 2 712 | 2 915 | 2 962 | 3 023 | 3 427 | 3 521 | 3 534 | 3 877 | 4 008 | 3 985 | 4 067 | 3 950 |
| of which: equipment | 1 194 | 1 207 | 1 208 | 1 222 | 1 280 | 1 363 | 1 440 | 1 535 | 1 610 | 1 674 | 1 719 | 1 757 |
| buildings | 851 | 928 | 956 | 992 | 1 055 | 982 | 940 | 980 | 1 004 | 979 | 975 | 985 |
| livestock | 667 | 779 | 798 | 809 | 1 091 | 1 176 | 1 154 | 1 362 | 1 395 | 1 333 | 1 373 | 1 208 |
| cattle | 364 | 490 | 499 | 503 | 743 | 731 | 679 | 791 | 870 | 857 | 876 | 701 |
| pigs | 9 | 7 | 7 | 6 | 7 | 8 | 8 | 8 | 8 | 7 | 5 | 4 |
| sheep | 167 | 151 | 162 | 157 | 188 | 269 | 291 | 358 | 301 | 267 | 295 | 287 |
| poultry | 127 | 132 | 129 | 142 | 153 | 167 | 176 | 205 | 216 | 202 | 197 | 217 |
| 29 Net value added at market prices (26-28) | 2 142 | 1 963 | 1 892 | 2 312 | 3 475 | 3 273 | 3 329 | 4 775 | 4 618 | 5 391 | 5 694 | 4 575 |
| 30 Net value added at basic prices (27-28) | 4 314 | 2 177 | 1 979 | 2 374 | 3 532 | 3 311 | 3 357 | 4 802 | 4 638 | 5 411 | 5 715 | 4 611 |
| 31 Other taxes on production | - 95 | - 101 | - 99 | - 101 | - 102 | - 106 | - 112 | - 121 | - 121 | - 118 | - 99 | - 96 |
| 32 Other subsidies on production | 781 | 2 852 | 3 042 | 2 932 | 3 237 | 3 616 | 3 495 | 3 482 | 3 262 | 3 339 | 2 940 | 2 803 |
| 33 Net value added at factor cost (30+31+32) | 5 000 | 4 928 | 4 923 | 5 205 | 6 667 | 6 821 | 6 741 | 8 163 | 7 778 | 8 632 | 8 555 | 7 318 |
| 34 Compensation of employees | 1 894 | 1 944 | 1 973 | 2 004 | 2 065 | 2 165 | 2 226 | 2 341 | 2 353 | 2 403 | 2 406 | 2 502 |
| 35 Rent | 411 | 389 | 395 | 381 | 408 | 420 | 440 | 479 | 494 | 520 | 555 | 562 |
| 36 Interest | 391 | 403 | 372 | 417 | 349 | 220 | 230 | 295 | 310 | 332 | 399 | 419 |
| 37 Total Income from Farming (33-34-35-36) | 2 304 | 2 193 | 2 183 | 2 403 | 3 844 | 4 016 | 3 846 | 5 048 | 4 621 | 5 378 | 5 196 | 3 835 |

Table source: Defra

	2004	2005	2006	2007	2008	2009	2010	2011	2012	2013	2014	2015
GDP deflator (a) 2012 = 100	80.2	82.6	85.0	87.4	89.9	91.8	94.6	96.6	98.2	100	102	102.2
Total Income from Farming in real terms	*2 988*	*2 762*	*2 670*	*2 861*	*4 446*	*4 550*	*4 226*	*5 434*	*4 895*	*5 585*	*5 297*	*3 903*

Source: Department for Environment, Food and Rural Affairs

(a) GDP deflator is used to convert current prices into real term prices

24.2 Total factor productivity volume indices (2010=100)

	2004	2005	2006	2007	2008	2009	2010	2011	2012	2013	2014	2015
1 Output of cereals	101.8	96.6	96.3	89.2	116.7	102.4	100.0	105.0	92.6	92.6	118.8	120.4
wheat	100.6	96.7	96.4	86.8	113.7	93.6	100.0	104.2	88.2	75.9	109.7	109.1
rye	86.4	86.4	86.4	86.4	86.4	86.4	100.0	100.0	68.2	90.9	90.9	90.9
barley	113.6	103.6	97.9	100.4	132.4	141.2	100.0	110.7	111.3	154.3	153.5	164.5
oats and summer cereal mixtures	84.9	71.2	106.6	103.0	119.6	109.8	100.0	92.1	93.3	150.6	114.1	119.7
other cereals	79.9	80.8	80.8	67.9	77.5	120.2	100.0	99.5	93.3	106.0	105.1	89.3
2 Output of industrial crops	90.6	96.6	87.7	86.2	93.9	99.5	100.0	118.3	105.8	98.6	111.6	109.5
oil seeds	65.1	78.0	75.9	83.1	86.8	87.0	100.0	122.9	112.9	95.2	108.3	111.3
oilseed rape	65.1	76.8	76.4	85.2	88.5	87.5	100.0	123.7	114.6	95.4	110.3	114.0
other oil seeds	73.5	124.3	70.1	27.3	41.2	75.4	100.0	98.9	58.0	86.4	54.6	39.7
protein crops	119.2	125.9	102.5	71.1	93.0	117.2	100.0	76.0	55.5	68.9	81.8	124.5
sugar beet	138.5	133.1	113.4	103.2	117.1	129.6	100.0	130.3	111.7	129.2	142.6	95.3
other industrial crops	107.0	105.1	105.3	101.8	99.7	98.1	100.0	101.1	101.1	101.1	101.1	101.1
3 Output of forage plants	115.2	114.3	112.2	117.8	104.1	105.3	100.0	107.1	109.0	121.3	121.3	121.3
4 Output of vegetables and horticultural products	103.7	103.8	98.0	96.9	98.8	96.7	100.0	97.4	94.7	97.6	100.0	100.2
fresh vegetables	92.5	96.5	94.9	90.4	92.8	96.9	100.0	97.7	92.8	97.4	102.4	102.8
plants and flowers	119.1	113.6	101.9	106.1	107.2	96.4	100.0	97.2	96.7	97.7	97.3	97.4
5 Output of potatoes	138.5	126.7	119.3	115.7	124.9	126.6	100.0	116.4	90.7	112.8	109.7	94.1
6 Output of fruit	70.0	80.0	78.2	92.5	94.8	99.7	100.0	101.3	93.1	100.2	106.9	110.4
7 Output of other crop products	108.0	97.8	97.7	78.8	98.8	103.5	100.0	114.4	126.9	119.1	133.9	123.2
Total crop output (sum 1 - 7)	**100.7**	**99.9**	**95.5**	**93.6**	**105.9**	**101.9**	**100.0**	**105.5**	**95.6**	**97.9**	**110.4**	**109.5**
8 Output of livestock (meat)	98.4	102.4	99.9	100.6	99.6	96.7	100.0	106.0	102.8	102.9	102.7	105.6
cattle	89.4	101.7	97.5	99.8	98.1	95.4	100.0	111.9	102.0	98.0	96.3	100.2
pigs	95.6	95.0	94.8	99.8	98.7	95.3	100.0	106.4	108.6	111.9	115.8	119.9
sheep	113.3	115.0	115.4	114.8	111.7	108.1	100.0	105.9	101.2	103.3	108.3	110.2
poultry	102.3	101.2	98.0	94.7	95.7	92.7	100.0	99.5	102.2	105.5	102.5	104.4
other animals	100.0	100.0	100.1	100.0	100.0	100.0	100.0	100.0	100.0	100.0	100.0	100.0
9 Output of livestock products	101.7	101.9	100.6	98.3	97.0	96.2	100.0	101.3	98.9	100.2	107.3	109.9
milk	104.5	103.8	102.8	100.9	98.6	97.5	100.0	101.5	99.8	100.5	108.5	111.4
eggs	86.7	88.1	85.0	83.0	88.3	89.2	100.0	99.6	96.5	99.5	100.0	103.5
raw wool	131.0	134.4	121.3	112.5	107.7	99.0	100.0	105.3	110.4	97.4	99.8	101.2
other animal products	81.9	135.1	135.2	107.2	87.8	92.9	100.0	98.7	57.5	84.2	106.8	88.9
Total livestock output (8 + 9)	**99.8**	**102.2**	**100.3**	**99.7**	**98.6**	**96.5**	**100.0**	**104.1**	**101.2**	**101.8**	**104.6**	**107.4**
10 Inseparable non-agricultural activities	87.0	88.8	85.5	90.4	91.0	100.5	100.0	101.5	103.1	115.4	113.2	120.7
11 All outputs	**99.1**	**100.3**	**97.4**	**96.6**	**100.9**	**98.7**	**100.0**	**104.5**	**99.1**	**100.9**	**107.0**	**108.7**
12 Seeds	65.6	78.2	85.3	98.9	94.5	92.7	100.0	97.6	101.6	107.0	107.0	106.2
13 Energy	102.0	95.0	90.0	94.0	89.9	102.5	100.0	96.3	96.3	97.0	95.9	98.0
electricity and fuels for heating	109.5	104.2	94.9	94.0	94.0	100.5	100.0	94.5	93.8	87.4	80.7	82.4
motor and machinery fuels	98.8	91.1	87.8	94.0	88.2	103.4	100.0	96.9	97.2	100.9	102.2	104.4
14 Fertilisers	123.2	115.1	108.4	109.7	97.6	88.4	100.0	103.2	97.9	99.2	100.5	100.9
15 Plant protection products	88.3	81.2	74.9	81.3	91.5	92.3	100.0	108.1	117.9	124.9	130.6	134.2
16 Veterinary expenses	81.6	82.5	78.3	81.9	95.5	102.4	100.0	97.2	100.3	104.1	105.6	104.1
17 Animal feed	93.3	91.6	90.9	88.3	92.5	92.6	100.0	93.0	94.8	98.9	101.3	105.4
compounds	91.7	88.4	92.7	95.5	95.0	93.7	100.0	97.7	103.0	109.3	109.9	114.5
straights	96.2	97.3	87.9	76.3	88.2	90.9	100.0	85.3	81.6	82.1	87.4	90.8
18 Total maintenance	98.0	90.8	87.6	90.1	95.0	98.7	100.0	99.8	99.3	100.5	106.9	107.0
materials	104.2	96.3	91.3	93.7	94.7	97.4	100.0	101.4	100.2	102.2	103.1	101.1
buildings	88.3	82.3	81.9	84.4	95.6	100.8	100.0	97.2	97.8	97.6	112.9	116.6
19 FISIM	100.0	100.0	100.0	100.0	100.0	100.0	100.0	100.0	100.0	100.0	100.0	100.0
20 Other goods and services	108.7	104.3	100.0	101.3	99.7	103.3	100.0	102.7	97.6	98.5	96.8	99.3
21 Intermediate consumption (excl Agricultural services)	**97.4**	**94.8**	**92.2**	**94.2**	**94.9**	**96.3**	**100.0**	**98.5**	**98.3**	**101.0**	**102.5**	**104.7**
22 Consumption fixed capital (excluding livestock)	**101.2**	**100.2**	**99.2**	**98.9**	**99.6**	**100.6**	**100.0**	**102.2**	**104.0**	**105.9**	**107.3**	**108.8**
equipment	95.8	94.8	93.5	93.6	95.5	97.7	100.0	103.9	107.2	110.8	113.7	116.8
buildings	108.9	108.2	107.4	106.5	105.7	104.9	100.0	99.6	99.1	98.4	97.7	96.9
23 All Labour	**105.8**	**104.6**	**103.1**	**102.4**	**102.0**	**100.5**	**100.0**	**101.6**	**101.6**	**100.8**	**100.9**	**101.2**
Compensation of employees	106.9	105.3	102.0	101.2	102.0	100.7	100.0	102.4	102.4	101.7	101.8	102.1
Entrepreneurial workers (farm and specialist contractor)	105.3	104.3	103.7	103.0	102.0	100.3	100.0	101.2	101.2	100.3	100.5	100.7
24 Land	**99.9**	**100.0**	**101.6**	**100.7**	**100.5**	**100.5**	**100.0**	**99.6**	**99.7**	**100.1**	**100.0**	**99.5**
25 All Inputs and Entrepreneurial Labour	**100.9**	**99.2**	**97.3**	**97.9**	**98.2**	**98.5**	**100.0**	**100.1**	**100.1**	**101.4**	**102.3**	**103.6**
Total factor productivity (11 divided by26)	**98.2**	**101.1**	**100.1**	**98.7**	**102.8**	**100.2**	**100.0**	**104.4**	**99.0**	**99.5**	**104.5**	**105.0**
Partial factor productivity indicators												
Productivity by intermediate consumption (11 divided by 21)	101.8	105.9	105.6	102.6	106.4	102.5	100.0	106.1	100.8	99.9	104.3	103.8
Productivity by capital consumption (11 divided by 22)	98.0	100.1	98.2	97.7	101.3	98.1	100.0	102.2	95.3	95.3	99.7	99.9
Productivity by labour (11 divided by 23)	93.7	95.9	94.4	94.3	99.0	98.2	100.0	102.9	97.5	100.1	106.0	107.4
Productivity by land (11 divided by 24)	99.2	100.3	95.9	95.9	100.4	98.2	100.0	104.9	99.3	100.8	106.9	109.3

Source: Agriculture in the UK, Department for Environment, Food and Rural Affairs
Enquiries: David Fernall on +44 (0) 20 8026 6202
email: david.fernall@defra.gsi.gov.uk

24.3 Agricultural land use (a)

Thousand hectares | At June of each year

	2003	2004	2005	2006	2007	2008	2009	2010	2011	2012	2013	2014	2015
Utilised agricultural area (UAA) (b)	1764 4	1760 6	1761 4	1789 7	1773 7	1770 3	1732 5	1723 4	1717 2	1719 0	1725 9	1724 0	1714 7
UAA as a proportion of total UK area	72%	72%	72%	73%	73%	73%	71%	71%	70%	70%	71%	71%	70%
Total agricultural area	1846 5	1843 1	1848 6	1877 0	1869 2	1869 7	1829 7	1828 2	1826 3	1834 9	1844 9	1845 6	1842 8
Common rough grazing	123 6	123 7	123 6	124 1	123 8	123 8	123 7	122 8	119 9	120 0	119 8	119 9	119 9
Total area on agricultural holdings	1722 8	1719 4	1725 0	1752 9	1745 3	1745 9	1706 0	1705 4	1706 4	1714 9	1725 0	1725 7	1722 9
Total croppable area	639 5	642 3	631 3	619 7	621 5	607 0	609 2	601 5	610 6	625 8	631 0	627 8	605 9
Total crops	447 6	458 9	442 1	439 7	444 0	473 5	460 7	461 0	467 3	474 8	466 5	472 2	467 9
Arable crops (c)	430 1	441 3	425 1	423 1	427 1	456 5	443 7	444 1	449 7	457 6	450 2	455 9	450 5
Cereals	305 7	313 0	291 9	286 4	288 5	327 4	307 6	301 3	307 5	314 2	302 8	317 9	310 0
Oilseeds (includes linseed and borage)	49 2	52 8	56 4	60 5	68 7	62 1	60 0	68 6	74 2	78 5	75 2	69 1	67 0
Potatoes	14 5	14 8	13 7	14 0	14 0	14 4	14 4	13 8	14 6	14 9	13 9	14 1	12 9
Other crops	60 7	60 7	63 1	62 3	55 9	52 7	61 6	60 4	53 4	50 0	58 2	54 8	60 6
Horticultural crops	17 6	17 5	17 0	16 6	16 9	17 0	17 0	16 9	17 5	17 2	16 3	16 4	17 4
Uncropped arable land (d)(e)	71 8	58 9	69 9	66 3	59 9	19 4	24 4	17 4	15 6	15 3	25 5	16 0	21 4
Temporary grass under 5 years old	120 0	124 6	119 3	113 7	117 6	114 1	124 1	123 2	127 8	135 7	139 0	139 6	116 7
Total permanent grassland	1001 3	994 6	1006 5	1045 8	1028 4	1039 5	999 6	998 0	985 8	972 5	974 2	975 5	988 0
Grass over 5 years old	568 3	562 0	571 1	596 7	596 5	603 6	586 5	592 5	587 7	579 9	580 2	582 4	607 8
Sole right rough grazing (f)	432 9	432 6	435 4	449 1	431 9	435 9	413 1	405 5	398 1	392 6	394 0	393 0	380 1
Other land on agricultural holdings	82 1	82 5	87 2	87 4	95 4	99 4	97 2	105 9	110 0	116 6	119 8	122 4	129 0
Woodland	54 4	56 3	58 3	60 6	66 3	70 5	72 6	77 4	78 6	82 7	86 5	89 7	96 1
Land used for outdoor pigs	. .	. .	. .	. .	. .	. .	. .	1 0	9	7	9	8	9
All other non-agricultural land	27 6	26 2	28 9	26 8	29 1	28 9	24 6	27 4	30 5	33 2	32 4	31 8	32 0

Source: June Surveys/Census of Agriculture/SAF land data Scotland.
Enquiries: Amanda Lyons on +44 (0) 20 8026 6126
email: farming-statistics@defra.gsi.gov.uk

Please note that totals may not add up to the sum of components due to rounding. Totals may not agree across tables for the same reason.

#: The 2011 UK totals for other arable crops and glasshouse crops were revised in May 2012 to account for calculation changes in the Scotland and Northern Ireland figures. As a result some subtotals have also been revised.

(a) Figures for England from 2009 onwards relate to commercial holdings only. More information on commercial holdings can be found in the introduction section of this chapter.

(b) UAA includes all arable and horticultural crops, uncropped arable land, common rough grazing, temporary and permanent grassland and land used for outdoor pigs (it excludes woodland and other non-agricultural land).
(c) Includes crops grown on previous set-aside land for England for 2007.
(d) Includes uncropped set-aside land for 2007.
(e) Includes all arable land not in production, including land managed in Good Agricultural and Environmental Condition (GAEC12), wild bird cover and game cover. In the 2009 form guidance notes for England, bird cover and game strips were for the first time explicitly stated as belonging in this category, so the 2009 figure may have captured more of this land than in previous years.
(f) Also includes mountains, hills, heathland or moorland.

- means 'nil' or 'negligible' (less than half the last digit shown).
. . means 'not available' or 'not applicable'.

© Crown copyright 2017

24.4a Estimated quantity of crops and grass harvested

United Kingdom | Thousand tonnes

		2003	2004	2005	2006	2007	2008	2009	2010	2011	2012	2013	2014	2015
Wheat	BADO	14 288	15 473	14 863	14 755	13 221	17 227	14 076	14 878	15 257	13 261	11 921	16 606	16 444
Barley	BADP	6 370	5 816	5 495	5 239	5 079	6 144	6 668	5 252	5 494	5 522	7 092	6 911	7370
Oats	BADQ	749	627	528	728	712	784	744	685	613	627	964	820	799
Sugar Beet	BADR	9 168	9 042	8 687	7 400	6 733	7 641	8 457	6 527	8 504	7 291	8 432	9 310	6218
Potatoes	BADS	6 058	6 246	5 979	5 727	5 564	6 132	6 396	6 056	6 310	4 658	5 902	5 911	5 588

Source: Agriculture in the UK, Department for Environment, Food and Rural Affairs
Enquiries: Allan Howsam
email: allan.howsam@defra.gsi.gov.uk

24.4b Fruit: Home Production marketed for the calendar year in the UK

(Thousand tonnes)

CALENDAR YEAR	2003	2004	2005	2006	2007	2008	2009	2010	2011	2012	2013	2014	2015
ORCHARD FRUIT													
Dessert Apples -													
Cox's Orange Pippin	35	47	60	64	39	51	47	46	46	32	35	38	41
Gala	..	..	..	..	..	..	..	..	..	..	..	..	..
Braeburn	..	..	..	..	..	..	..	..	..	..	..	..	..
Other Dessert	..	..	..	..	..	..	..	..	..	..	..	..	..
Worcester Pearmain	2	3	3	2	2	2	2	2	2	2	2	2	2
Discovery	2	2	3	3	3	3	3	3	3	2	3	3	3
Early Season	1	2	2	2	2	2	2	2	2	2	2	2	3
Mid Season Desserts	7	7	8	8	7	7	7	7	7	6	7	8	8
Late Season Desserts	22	32	43	50	53	54	61	64	69	73	82	95	104
Total Dessert Apples :	**69**	**92**	**118**	**129**	**106**	**118**	**122**	**125**	**128**	**116**	**131**	**148**	**160**
Culinary Apples -													
Bramley's Seedling	73	77	99	110	135	123	106	109	111	86	84	97	89
Other Culinary	2	1	1	1	1	1	1	1	1	1	1	1	1
Total Culinary Apples :	**75**	**78**	**100**	**111**	**136**	**124**	**107**	**110**	**112**	**87**	**85**	**98**	**90**
Pears -													
Conference	27	21	20	25	18	17	17	27	27	21	18	22	23
Williams Bon Chretien	0	..	..	..	..	..	..	..	..	..	..	..	..
Comice	2	..	..	..	..	..	..	..	..	..	..	..	..
Others (b)	1	2	4	4	3	3	4	4	5	4	4	4	4
Total Pears :	**30**	**23**	**23**	**28**	**21**	**20**	**20**	**31**	**32**	**26**	**22**	**26**	**26**
Cider Apples & Perry Pears:	..	..	..	..	..	..	..	..	..	..	..	297	323
Plums -													
Victoria	7	8	7	7	7	1	6	6	6	2	6	6	5
Marjorie's Seedling	2	..	..	..	..	..	..	..	..	..	..	..	..
Pershore Yellow Egg	..	..	..	..	..	..	..	..	..	..	..	..	..
Damsons	1	..	..	..	..	..	..	..	..	..	..	..	..
Other Plums	5	5	6	6	6	1	7	7	7	3	7	6	6
Total Plums :	**15**	**14**	**13**	**13**	**13**	**3**	**13**	**13**	**13**	**6**	**12**	**12**	**11**
Cherries :	**1**	**1**	**1**	**1**	**1**	**1**	**1**	**1**	**2**	**2**	**3**	**4**	**5**
Others & Mixed :	**2**	**2**	**2**	**2**	**3**	**4**	**4**	**4**	**5**	**4**	**5**	**4**	**4**
TOTAL ORCHARD FRUIT :	**191**	**209**	**258**	**286**	**411**	**401**	**399**	**416**	**422**	**371**	**389**	**588**	**620**
Soft Fruit													
Strawberries	47	52	69	68	83	94	99	96	102	95	94	104	115
Raspberries	8	10	12	12	15	16	16	16	16	16	15	18	17
Blackcurrants	19	18	20	16	12	14	16	18	12	12	17	13	15
Other Soft Fruit:	5	5	5	6	8	8	9	9	8	8	8	8	9
TOTAL SOFT FRUIT:	**80**	**86**	**105**	**101**	**118**	**131**	**139**	**138**	**137**	**130**	**133**	**143**	**157**
TOTAL FRUIT :	**271**	**295**	**363**	**387**	**529**	**532**	**537**	**555**	**559**	**501**	**522**	**731**	**777**

Source: Basic Horticultural Statistics, Department for Environment, Food and Rural Affairs
Contact details: crops-statistics@defra.gsi.gov.uk

".." indicates data not available
© Crown Copyright, 2017

24.c Field Vegetables: Home production marketed for the calendar year in the UK

(Thousand Tonnes)

CALENDAR YEAR	2002	2003	2004	2005	2006	2007	2008	2009	2010	2011	2012	2013	2014	2015
Roots and Onions														
Beetroot	56	59	53	51	57	57	55	55	57	59	62	69	72	72
Carrots	718	602	676	710	712	727	711	695	768	685	674	729	755	731
Parsnips	102	92	77	72	84	86	90	86	90	87	83	83	85	84
Turnips and Swedes	104	97	97	103	115	101	106	109	113	102	84	99	97	104
Onions, Dry Bulb	283	374	341	414	359	304	349	355	364	313	374	355	374	394
Onions, Spring	11	16	14	24	24	20	15	14	14	15	14	14	14	14
Total :	1,275	1,239	1,259	1,374	1,351	1,294	1,327	1,314	1408	1260	1291	1349	1396	1399
Brassicas														
Brussels Sprouts	43	56	44	46	50	41	43	44	43	47	43	51	50	51
Cabbage, Spring	22	29	34	32	36	35	30	28	24	24	23	23	25	24
Cabbage, Summer and Autumn	44	41	44	77	61	56	56	62	61	60	49	56	56	54
Cabbage, Winter	178	159	143	157	158	126	149	146	162	151	151	141	150	153
Cauliflower	117	126	168	133	124	122	116	108	109	102	90	91	93	91
Broccoli	53	62	66	87	72	68	73	78	79	78	65	69	68	72
Total :	456	473	500	532	500	448	468	465	479	463	421	431	441	444
Legumes														
Beans, Broad (c)	10	12	10	10	10	10	9	12	12	11	12	14	13	15
Beans, Runner and Dwarf (a)	19	20	23	21	18	17	16	15	16	15	14	15	15	14
Beans	. .	. .	. .	. .	. .	. .	. .	. .	. .	. .	. .	. .	. .	. .
Peas, Green for Market	7	6	6	6	6	6	6	6	6	6	6	6	6	6
Peas, Green for Processing (b,c)	169	168	131	130	124	98	153	168	156	178	124	155	155	157
Pease, Green	. .	. .	. .	. .	. .	. .	. .	. .	. .	. .	. .	. .	. .	. .
Peas, Harvested Dry (c)	24	16	30	37	24	33	25	40	49	57	22	44	51	72
Total :	230	222	199	204	182	163	209	241	239	268	178	234	240	263
Others														
Asparagus	2	2	2	2	3	3	3	4	4	5	5	5	6	5
Celery	32	37	41	47	36	47	50	49	51	51	51	51	53	54
Courgette	. .	. .	. .	. .	. .	. .	. .	. .	. .	. .	. .	. .	. .	. .
Leeks	38	36	41	51	47	50	42	37	42	41	37	35	36	34
Lettuce	110	126	143	133	126	108	117	128	127	126	116	117	124	122
Baby leaf	. .	. .	. .	. .	. .	. .	. .	. .	. .	. .	. .	. .	. .	. .
Rhubarb (c)	19	18	21	19	17	16	16	20	21	20	22	24	30	25
Watercress	2	2	2	2	2	2	2	2	2	2	2	2	2	2
Others, field grown	104	104	110	124	116	113	116	144	141	128	118	123	128	123
Total :	307	325	360	378	348	339	346	384	388	373	352	356	378	364
TOTAL FIELD VEGETABLES :	2,268	2,260	2,318	2,488	2,382	2,244	2,349	2,405	2513	2362	2242	2370	2455	2471

Source: Basic Horticultural Statistics, Department for Environment, Food and Rural Affairs

Contact details: crops-statistics@defra.gsi.gov.uk

(a) Dwarf beans are sometimes called French beans
(b) Also known as vining peas
(c) Shelled weight
". ." indicates data not available

24.5 Crop areas and livestock numbers [a]

	2004	2005	2006	2007	2008	2009	2010	2011	2012	2013	2014	2015
Crop areas (thousand hectares)												
Total area of arable crops (b)	441 3	425 1	423 1	427 1	456 5	443 7	444 1	449 7	457 6	450 2	455 9	450 5
of which:												
of which:	199 0	186 7	183 6	183 0	208 0	177 5	193 9	196 9	199 2	161 5	193 6	183 2
wheat	100 7	93 8	88 1	89 8	103 2	114 3	92 1	97 0	100 2	121 3	108 0	110 1
barley	10 8	9 0	12 1	12 9	13 5	12 9	12 4	10 9	12 2	17 7	13 7	13 1
oats	2 5	2 4	2 5	2 7	2 7	2 8	2 9	2 7	2 6	2 4	2 6	3 5
rye, mixed corn and triticale	49 8	51 9	56 8	67 4	59 8	57 0	64 2	70 5	75 6	71 5	67 5	65 2
oilseed rape	2 9	4 5	3 6	1 3	1 6	2 8	4 4	3 6	2 9	3 4	1 5	1 5
linseed	14 8	13 7	14 0	14 0	14 4	14 4	13 8	14 6	14 9	13 9	14 1	12 9
potatoes	15 4	14 8	13 0	12 5	12 0	11 4	11 8	11 3	12 0	11 7	11 6	9 0
sugar beet (not for stockfeeding)	24 2	23 9	23 1	16 1	14 8	22 8	21 0	15 5	12 0	14 7	13 9	21 3
peas for harvesting dry and field beans	11 8	13 1	13 7	14 6	15 3	16 3	16 4	16 4	15 8	19 4	18 3	18 7
maize												
Total area of horticultural crops	17 5	17 0	16 6	16 9	17 0	17 0	16 9	17 5	17 2	16 3	16 4	17 4
of which:												
vegetables grown outdoors	12 5	12 1	11 9	12 1	12 2	12 5	12 1	12 9	12 3	11 6	11 6	12 3
orchard fruit (c)	2 4	2 3	2 3	2 3	2 4	2 2	2 4	2 4	2 4	2 3	2 3	2 6
soft fruit & wine grapes	9	9	1 0	1 0	1 0	1 0	1 0	1 0	9	1 0	9	1 0
outdoor plants and flowers	1 5	1 4	1 2	1 3	1 3	1 1	1 2	1 1	1 2	1 2	1 2	1 3
glasshouse crops	2	2	2	2	2	2	2	2	3	3	3	3
Livestock numbers (thousand head)												
Total cattle and calves (d)	1058 8	1077 0	1064 4	1037 0	1016 3	1008 2	1017 0	998 8	995 2	984 4	983 7	991 9
of which:												
cows in the dairy herd (e)	212 9	199 8	196 3	193 7	189 2	183 8	183 0	179 6	179 6	178 2	184 1	189 5
cows in the beef herd (f)	173 6	175 1	174 5	170 9	167 8	163 3	166 8	168 7	166 6	161 1	156 9	157 6
Total sheep and lambs	3581 7	3541 6	3472 2	3394 6	3313 1	3144 5	3108 4	3163 4	3221 5	3285 6	3374 3	3333 7
of which:												
breeding flock 1 year and over	1763 0	1693 5	1663 7	1606 4	1561 6	1463 6	1474 0	1486 8	1522 9	1556 1	1602 6	1602 4
lambs under one year old	1723 8	1748 8	1705 8	1685 5	1657 4	1589 2	1543 1	1599 0	1622 9	1638 1	1693 6	1652 8
Total pigs	515 9	486 2	493 3	483 4	471 4	454 0	446 0	444 1	448 1	488 5	481 5	473 9
of which:												
sows in pig and other sows for breeding	44 9	40 3	40 1	39 8	36 5	37 9	36 0	36 2	35 7	35 5	34 9	35 2
gilts in pig	6 6	6 7	6 7	5 7	5 5	4 8	6 7	7 0	6 9	6 6	5 7	5 6
Total poultry	18175 9	17390 9	17308 1	16766 7	16620 0	15275 3	16386 7	16255 1	16006 1	16260 9	16968 4	16757 9
of which:												
table fowl	11988 8	11147 5	11067 2	10979 4	10985 9	9875 4	10530 9	10246 1	10255 8	10457 6	11037 4	10705 6
laying flock (including pullets)	3781 1	4047 2	3825 7	3625 7	3525 3	3326 6	3749 7	3835 7	3664 6	3584 1	3714 6	3699 8
breeding flock	1012 5	856 1	927 3	1146 1	906 8	939 7	961 0	1025 3	998 7	1118 4	1125 8	1251 1
turkeys, ducks, geese and all other poultry	1393 5	1340 0	1487 9	1015 4	1201 9	1133 5	1145 1	1148 1	1087 0	1100 8	1090 7	1101 4

Source: Department for Education, Food and Rural Affairs
Enquiries: Amanda Lyons on +44 (0) 20 8026 6126
email: farming-statistics@defra.gsi.gov.uk

Please note that totals may not add up to the sum of components due to rounding. Totals may not agree across tables for the same reason.

#: The 2011 UK totals for other arable crops and glasshouse crops were revised in May 2012 to account for calculation changes in the Scotland and Northern Ireland figures. As a result some subtotals have also been revised.
(a) Figures for England from 2009 onwards relate to commercial holdings only. More information on commercial
(b) Includes arable crops grown on set-aside land in 2007 for England only.
(c) Includes non-commercial orchards.
(d) Cattle figures in this table are based on all agricultural holdings. Therefore these figures do not match the totals
(e) Dairy cows are defined as female dairy cows over 2 years old with offspring.
(f) Beef cows are defined as female beef cows over 2 years old with offspring.

- means 'nil' or 'negligible' (less than half the last digit shown).
. . means 'not available' or 'not applicable'.

24.6 Forestry

United Kingdom

		2005	2006	2007	2008	2009	2010	2011	2012	2013	2014	2015	2016
Woodland area[1] - (Thousand hectares)													
United Kingdom	C5OF	2825	2829	2837	2841	2841	3059	3067	3110	3125	3138	3154	3160
England [3]	C5OG	1119	1121	1124	1127	1128	1290	1292	1298	1298	1302	1304	1306
Wales [3]	C5OI	286	285	285	285	284	303	304	305	305	306	306	306
Scotland [3]	C5OH	1334	1337	1341	1342	1341	1378	1383	1403	1411	1419	1432	1436
Northern Ireland [4]	C5OJ	85	86	87	87	88	88	88	105	111	111	112	112
Forestry Commission/Forest Service	C5OK	838	832	827	821	814	868	869	874	874	870	871	864
Private Sector Woodland [2]	C5OL	1987	1997	2010	2020	2027	2191	2199	2236	2252	2268	2283	2296
Conifer	C5OM	1647	1642	1640	1635	1628	1603	1604	1617	1619	1608	1614	1615
Broadleaved [5]	C5ON	1178	1187	1197	1207	1213	1457	1463	1493	1508	1531	1540	1545

		2002 /03	2003 /04	2004 /05	2005 /06	2006 /07	2007 /08	2008 /09	2009 /10	2010 /11	2011 /12	2012 /13	2013 /14	2014 /15	2015 /16
New Planting[7] - (Thousand hectares)															
United Kingdom	C5OO	13.7	12.4	12.0	8.8	10.8	7.5	6.4	5.4	8.2	12.7	10.8	12.9	10.3	5.5
England	C5OP	5.9	4.6	5.3	3.7	3.2	2.6	2.5	2.3	2.5	2.6	2.6	3.3	2.4	0.7
Wales	C5OR	0.5	0.4	0.6	0.5	0.6	0.2	0.2	0.2	0.3	0.8	0.9	0.9	0.1	**0.1**
Scotland	C5OQ	6.7	6.8	5.7	4.0	6.6	4.2	3.4	2.7	5.1	9.0	7.0	8.3	7.6	4.6
Northern Ireland	C5OS	0.6	0.5	0.4	0.6	0.5	0.6	0.3	0.2	0.3	0.3	0.3	0.3	0.2	0.1
Forestry Commission/Forest Service/Natural Resources Wales[1]	C5OT	0.9	0.2	0.1	0.3	0.2	0.2	0.9	0.7	0.8	1.3	0.9	0.6	0.4	0.7
Private Sector Woodland [6]	C5OU	12.8	12.1	11.9	8.5	10.6	7.4	5.5	4.7	7.3	11.4	9.9	12.3	9.9	4.8
Conifer	C5OV	3.8	2.9	2.1	1.1	2.1	0.9	1.2	0.5	1.5	3.5	1.9	2.2	2.6	1.9
Broadleaved [5]	C5OW	9.9	9.4	9.9	7.7	8.7	6.7	5.2	4.9	6.6	9.2	8.9	10.7	7.7	3.6
Restocking[8],[9] - (Thousand hectares)															
United Kingdom	C5OX	14.5	14.9	16.1	15.9	19.0	18.9	16.1	15.1	14.0	12.3	13.1	15.8	17.6	13.6
England	C5OY	3.4	3.2	2.8	3.2	2.8	3.5	3.5	2.8	4.0	3.6	4.0	4.5	6.4	3.3
Wales	C5P2	1.9	1.8	1.8	2.8	3.0	2.3	2.2	2.1	2.1	2.0	2.0	2.3	1.9	1.8
Scotland	C5OZ	8.5	8.9	10.4	9.0	12.4	12.6	9.6	9.5	6.9	5.7	6.0	7.9	8.5	7.8
Northern Ireland	C5P3	0.7	1.1	1.0	0.9	0.8	0.5	0.8	0.7	1.0	1.0	1.2	1.2	0.8	0.7
Forestry Commission/Forest Service/Natural Resources Wales[1]	C5P4	9.1	9.9	10.6	10.4	11.0	10.4	9.2	7.1	10.0	8.9	9.3	10.9	11.0	11.0
Private Sector Woodland [6]	C5P5	5.3	5.0	5.5	5.5	8.0	8.5	6.9	8.0	4.1	3.3	3.8	4.9	6.6	2.7
Conifer	C5P6	12.0	12.1	13.0	12.5	15.3	14.8	12.1	11.5	10.3	9.0	9.7	11.6	10.7	10.0
Broadleaved [5]	C5P7	2.4	2.8	3.0	3.4	3.6	4.1	4.0	3.6	3.8	3.3	3.4	4.2	6.9	3.6

		2004	2005	2006	2007	2008	2009	2010	2011	2012	2013	2014	2015
Wood Production (volume - Thousand green tonnes)													
United Kingdom	C5P8	8650	8670	8680	9180	8670	8930	9760	10540	10627	11469	11963	11302
Softwood total	C5PA	8140	8080	8240	8740	8240	8390	9220	10000	10095	10940	11431	10774
Forestry Commission/Forest Service/Natural Resources Wales[8]	C5PB	5000	4680	4630	4690	4460	5220	4700	4950	4891	5163	4971	4820
Private Sector [10]	C5PC	3650	3990	4050	4480	4210	3720	5070	5600	5737	6307	6992	6482
Hardwood[11]	C5PD	510	590	440	440	430	540	540	540	532	529	532	528

Source: Forestry Commission, Natural Resources Wales, Forest Service, National Forest Inventory.

1. FC: Forestry Commission (England and Scotland), NRW: Natural Resources Wales, FS: Forest Service
   (Northern Ireland). NRW estimates only relate to woodland formerly owned/managed by FC Wales.
2. Private sector: all other woodland. Includes woodland previously owned/managed by the Countryside Council for Wales
   and the Environment Agency in Wales, other publicly owned woodland (e.g. owned by local authorities)
   and privately owned woodland.
3. Figures for England, Wales and Scotland are based on data obtained from the National Forest Inventory (NFI) and adjusted
   for new planting, but at present no adjustment is made for woodland recently converted to another land use.
   Further information on how the figures have been estimated is available in the Sources chapter.
4. Figures for Northern Ireland are obtained from the Northern Ireland Woodland Register.
5. Broadleaves include coppice and coppice with standards.
6. Private sector figures are based on areas for which grants were paid during the year. Estimate of areas planted without grant aid are also
   included (where possible), although private sector non grant-aided planting may be under-represented in the figures. Figures for grant-aided
   planting under Rural Development Contracts in Scotland relate to calendar years.
7. The planting season lies both sides of 31 March, and the weather can cause planting to be advanced or delayed.
8. Includes natural colonisation and natural regeneration.
9. Restocking by natural regeneration in non-clearfell areas may be under-represented in the above table
10. Private sector: removals from all other woodland (including some publicly owned woodland).
11. Most hardwood production in the UK comes from private sector woodland; the figures are estimates based on reported deliveries to wood processing industries and others.

24.7 Sales for food of agricultural produce and livestock

			2003	2004 (b)	2005	2006	2007	2008	2009	2010 (b)	2011	2012	2013	2014	2015
Milk:															
Utilised for liquid consumption	KCQO	Million litres	6 753	6 693	6 652	6 734	6 724	6 678	6 626	6 836	6 892	6 785	6 856	6 903	6 727
Utilised for manufacture	KCQP	"	7 140	6 724	6 490	6 266	6 085	5 840	5 699	6 112	6 260	6 015	6 223	7 093	7 464
Total available for domestic use	KCQQ	"	14 290	13 765	13 478	13 325	13 146	12 816	12 777	13 131	13 292	13 110	13 226	14 221	14 497
Hen eggs in shell	KCQR	Million dozens	730	773	772	742	720	754	751	826	821	797	829	839	866
Cattle and calves: (a)															
Cattle	KCQS	Thousands	2 194	2 250	2 276	2 208	2 155	1 956	1 946	2 063	2 090	1 930	1 892	1 934	1 906
Calves	KCQT	"	87	101	111	125	108	91	43	61	92	80	93	142	122
Total	KCQU	"	2 286	2 361	2 409	2 702	2 724	2 613	2 476	2 678	2 824	2 652	2 594	2 678	2 655
Sheep and lambs	KCQV	"	15 436	15 493	16 539	16 590	16 036	16 989	15 911	14 440	15 007	14 221	15 024	15 061	15 195
Pigs: (a)															
Clean pigs	MBGD	"	8 758	8 590	8 494	8 518	8 858	8 755	8 348	8 670	9 204	9 426	9 479	9 698	10 117
Sows and boars (d)	KCQZ	"	246	243	215	209	218	242	209	(c)	(c)	276	265	255	259
Total (d)	KCRA	"	9 003	8 833	8 709	8 727	9 076	8 997	8 557	(c)	(c)	9 702	9 743	9 953	10 376
Poultry (b)	KCRB	Millions	883	882	901	884	873	862	868	933	931	952	976	972	1 029

Source: Defra statistics, Agriculture in the UK and slaugher statistics: 01904 455096

(a) Measures of home-fed marketings, dressed carcase weights, production and value include animals raised and slaughtered in the UK, excluding any animals removed from the food chain.
(b) For comparability with other years, the figures for 2004 and 2010 have been adjusted from a 53-week to a 52-week basis where appropriate.
(c) This data is confidential

24.8 Number of livestock farmed organically

Thousand heads

	2006	2007	2008	2009	2010	2011	2012	2013	2014	2015
United Kingdom										
Total fully organic and in conversion										
Cattle	244.8	250.4	319.6	331.2	350.2	334.8	290.2	283.3	304.4	293.1
Sheep (a)	:	:	:	884.8	981.2	1 161.7	1 152.1	999.2	958.9	874.2
Pigs	32.9	50.4	71.2	49.4	47.4	52.6	34.6	30.2	28.3	30.0
Poultry	4 421.3	4 440.7	4 362.9	3 958.7	3 870.9	2 838.2	2 457.7	2 487.6	2 398.8	2 560.3
Other livestock (b)	4.9	4.0	4.8	3.4	4.5	5.0	4.2	4.1	5.7	4.4
England										
Total fully organic and in conversion										
Cattle	177.1	176.0	214.1	236.5	248.6	233.5	201.7	199.5	215.6	217.8
Sheep (a)	:	:	:	380.4	431.3	423.6	434.5	400.8	405.0	415.8
Pigs	32.3	49.0	57.1	46.5	42.1	47.9	29.5	26.5	25.8	22.2
Poultry	2 820.2	2 674.2	2 293.9	1 969.4	1 931.1	1 746.1	1 681.2	1 687.5	1 495.9	1 512.5
Other livestock (b)	3.6	2.2	2.7	1.6	2.0	1.3	3.6	3.4	3.1	3.9

(a) We are unable to provide full historical data for sheep as there are some inconsistencies in the historical data
(b) "Other livestock" includes goats, farmed deer, horses, camelids and any livestock not recorded elsewhere.
:   data not available

Source: Department for Environment, Food and Rural Affairs
Enquiries : Sarah Thompson
sarah.thompson@defra.gsi.gov.uk

24.9 Total number of organic producers and processors

Number

	2006	2007	2008	2009	2010	2011	2012	2013	2014	2015
United Kingdom	**7 043**	**7 631**	**7 896**	**7 567**	**7 287**	**6 929**	**6 487**	**6072**	**6002**	**6056**
England	5 005	5 516	5 474	5 278	5 131	4 897	4 592	4419	4454	4579
Wales	835	953	1 230	1 176	1 166	1 119	1 080	913	779	741
Scotland	911	860	889	820	737	679	611	551	576	539
Northern Ireland	292	302	303	293	253	234	204	189	193	197
North East	161	173	179	167	160	152	137	127	130	137
North West	332	367	367	333	315	301	273	253	246	277
Yorkshire & Humberside	319	356	330	308	302	278	262	240	238	257
East Midlands	446	487	449	422	408	383	366	351	346	329
West Midlands	520	556	555	507	494	476	442	426	424	438
Eastern	556	574	551	529	515	481	456	449	445	457
South East (Inc London)	939	1 042	1 041	1 024	984	975	950	957	1020	1083
South West	1 732	1 961	2 002	1 988	1 953	1 851	1 706	1616	1605	1601

Source: Department for Environment, Food and Rural Affairs

Enquiries : Sarah Thompson

sarah.thompson@defra.gsi.gov.uk

24.10a: Land area farmed organically

Thousand hectares

	2006	2007	2008	2009	2010	2011	2012	2013	2014	2015
In conversion land area										
North East	6.9	4.8	9.8	6.5	4.0	2.9	2.7	1.0	0.8	0.3
North West	1.8	3.3	3.8	3.4	2.4	1.4	1.1	0.9	0.6	0.3
Yorkshire & Humberside	3.4	4.1	3.8	2.7	0.9	0.7	0.6	0.5	0.6	0.5
East Midlands	2.1	3.1	3.7	3.1	1.0	0.5	0.6	0.7	0.9	0.7
West Midlands	4.0	5.7	8.2	5.7	2.1	1.8	1.4	0.8	1.2	1.0
Eastern	3.6	5.3	4.8	4.1	1.4	1.0	0.7	0.7	0.5	1.0
South East (inc. London)	13.2	14.6	10.4	7.3	4.3	3.7	3.1	3.0	1.9	0.7
South West	31.6	48.2	46.5	34.7	13.6	13.5	8.9	6.3	6.1	5.5
England	**66.5**	**89.0**	**91.1**	**67.6**	**29.8**	**25.4**	**19.2**	**14.0**	**12.5**	**10.0**
Wales	15.4	30.9	49.5	36.8	4.0	2.4	1.5	1.9	4.1	9.4
Scotland	35.2	34.8	6.2	12.0	12.6	5.1	8.0	8.4	3.0	1.0
Northern Ireland	4.0	3.2	2.3	3.0	4.4	4.0	3.6	0.1	0.2	0.3
United Kingdom	**121.1**	**157.9**	**149.1**	**119.4**	**50.8**	**36.9**	**32.2**	**24.4**	**19.7**	**20.6**
Fully organic land area										
North East	22.6	25.8	25.6	26.8	30.6	28.1	27.3	26.9	26.3	27.6
North West	19.4	20.4	21.2	19.8	20.0	16.4	15.5	14.0	13.6	13.8
Yorkshire & Humberside	9.0	9.6	10.9	11.9	13.8	12.5	9.9	10.2	10.1	10.2
East Midlands	12.5	13.2	12.2	14.4	16.3	15.2	15.5	14.1	13.7	13.5
West Midlands	26.3	28.2	29.7	32.0	35.4	28.9	30.6	30.8	29.3	28.3
Eastern	10.8	12.7	13.2	14.2	17.3	15.8	14.1	14.1	13.8	13.7
South East (inc. London)	35.8	42.5	47.2	51.6	54.1	51.4	46.5	48.1	45.6	45.0
South West	93.4	106.3	123.9	140.4	174.6	157.2	145.5	143.4	143.1	141.6
England	**229.9**	**258.7**	**284.0**	**311.2**	**362.0**	**325.6**	**304.8**	**301.7**	**295.7**	**293.7**
Wales	63.5	65.1	75.1	88.6	118.8	120.4	118.4	100.0	91.6	73.5
Scotland	200.1	193.1	225.1	209.3	176.3	164.8	143.7	140.0	132.9	125.3
Northern Ireland	5.1	7.3	10.1	10.3	10.4	8.3	6.6	9.3	8.8	8.2
United Kingdom	**498.6**	**524.3**	**594.4**	**619.3**	**667.6**	**619.1**	**573.4**	**550.9**	**529.0**	**500.8**
Total fully organic and in conversion land area										
North East	29.5	30.6	35.4	33.3	34.6	31.1	30.0	27.9	27.1	27.9
North West	21.2	23.7	25.0	23.2	22.4	17.8	16.6	14.9	14.2	14.1
Yorkshire & Humberside	12.4	13.7	14.7	14.6	14.6	13.2	10.5	10.7	10.8	10.7
East Midlands	14.5	16.3	16.0	17.6	17.3	15.7	16.1	14.8	14.6	14.3
West Midlands	30.3	33.9	37.9	37.7	37.5	30.7	31.9	31.6	30.5	29.4
Eastern	14.4	18.0	18.0	18.4	18.7	16.7	14.8	14.9	14.3	14.7
South East (inc. London)	49.0	57.1	57.6	58.9	58.4	55.1	49.6	51.1	47.5	45.7
South West	125.0	154.5	170.5	175.1	188.2	170.7	154.4	149.7	149.2	147.1
England	**296.4**	**347.8**	**375.1**	**378.8**	**391.8**	**351.0**	**323.9**	**315.6**	**308.1**	**303.7**
Wales	79.0	96.0	124.6	125.4	122.9	122.7	119.9	101.9	95.7	82.9
Scotland	235.3	227.9	231.3	221.3	188.9	169.9	151.7	148.4	135.8	126.3
Northern Ireland	9.1	10.5	12.5	13.3	14.8	12.3	10.1	9.4	9.0	8.5
United Kingdom	**619.8**	**682.2**	**743.5**	**738.7**	**718.3**	**656.0**	**605.7**	**575.3**	**548.6**	**521.4**

Source: Department for Environment, Food and Rural Affairs

Enquiries : Sarah Thompson

sarah.thompson@defra.gsi.gov.uk

24.10b Fully organic and in conversion land use

Thousand hectares

	2006	2007	2008	2009	2010	2011	2012	2013	2014	2015
England										
In-conversion area										
Cereals	8.4	9.0	8.4	5.3	1.6	1.0	1.1	1.1	0.8	0.8
Other crops	2.9	2.9	2.0	1.5	0.5	0.4	0.2	0.2	0.2	0.2
Fruit & nuts	0.2	0.4	0.4	0.3	0.2	0.2	0.1	0.1	0.1	0.0
Vegetables (including potatoes)	1.6	2.0	1.7	1.2	0.4	0.2	0.2	0.1	0.1	0.1
Herbaceous & ornamentals	0.1	0.1	0.5	0.5	0.9	0.4	0.3	0.5	0.4	0.1
Temporary pasture	19.1	28.6	27.8	16.0	6.4	5.2	5.0	3.4	2.7	2.7
Permanent pasture (inc rough grazing)	27.9	37.9	46.0	38.6	16.8	14.1	10.2	7.4	7.3	5.5
Woodland	3.5	4.8	2.2	1.7	1.6	1.6	0.8	0.6	0.5	0.4
Unutilised land	2.7	3.3	2.2	2.4	1.2	2.3	1.3	0.6	0.3	0.2
Total	**66.5**	**89.0**	**91.1**	**67.6**	**29.8**	**25.4**	**19.2**	**14.0**	**12.5**	**10.0**
Fully organic area										
Cereals	28.7	31.1	35.5	41.1	43.6	40.4	36.8	34.1	34.1	32.3
Other crops	5.3	6.0	5.7	6.4	7.2	6.6	5.7	5.4	5.1	4.9
Fruit & nuts	1.5	1.5	1.5	1.8	2.0	1.9	2.0	1.9	2.0	1.8
Vegetables (including potatoes)	10.8	11.4	13.4	13.2	13.2	11.9	9.5	9.0	7.6	8.5
Herbaceous & ornamentals	0.6	0.4	3.7	3.8	3.9	4.6	4.8	5.3	7.0	5.3
Temporary pasture	62.9	72.9	78.5	87.1	96.7	90.9	82.1	77.9	74.6	73.0
Permanent pasture (inc rough grazing)	114.2	127.0	139.0	148.2	182.6	159.0	152.9	155.9	154.4	155.4
Woodland	2.3	4.3	2.1	3.3	4.5	4.6	4.6	4.8	4.5	4.8
Unutilised land	3.7	4.1	4.6	6.3	8.3	5.6	6.3	7.3	6.5	7.6
Total	**229.9**	**258.7**	**284.0**	**311.2**	**362.0**	**325.6**	**304.8**	**301.7**	**295.7**	**293.7**
Total fully organic and in conversion land use										
Cereals	37.1	40.1	44.0	46.4	45.3	41.4	37.9	35.2	34.9	33.1
Other crops	8.2	8.9	7.6	7.9	7.8	7.0	6.0	5.6	5.3	5.1
Fruit & nuts	1.7	1.9	1.8	2.1	2.2	2.1	2.1	2.0	2.1	1.8
Vegetables (inc potatoes)	12.4	13.5	15.2	14.5	13.7	12.2	9.7	9.2	7.7	8.7
Herbaceous & ornamentals	0.7	0.5	4.2	4.3	4.8	5.0	5.1	5.8	7.4	5.4
Temporary pasture	82.0	101.5	106.3	103.1	103.1	96.1	87.1	81.2	77.3	75.7
Permanent pasture (inc rough grazing)	142.1	164.9	184.9	186.8	199.4	173.2	163.1	163.2	161.7	160.9
Woodland	5.8	9.1	4.3	4.9	6.1	6.2	5.4	5.4	5.0	5.2
Unutilised land	6.4	7.5	6.8	8.7	9.5	7.9	7.6	8.0	6.8	7.8
Total	**296.4**	**347.8**	**375.1**	**378.8**	**391.8**	**351.0**	**323.9**	**315.6**	**308.1**	**303.7**

Source: Department for Environment, Food and Rural Affairs

Enquiries : Sarah Thompson

sarah.thompson@defra.gsi.gov.uk

\# Revisions have been made to this data after an error in the way these categories were reported came to light. The revisions only affect these categories and the totals remain unchanged. More details can be found on the Metadata tab.

24.11 Wages in Agriculture: Minimum weekly rates of pay

Minimum weekly rates of pay in force in 2015 for workers working <u>standard weekly hours</u>

1 January to 30 September 2015					
Grade 6	**Grade 5**	**Grade 4**	**Grade 3**	**Grade 2**	**Grade 1**
£	**£**	**£**	**£**	**£**	**£**
366.60	339.30	320.19	298.74	271.44	242.19

Grade 1 - Initial Grade
Grade 2 - Standard Grade
Grade 3 - Lead Worker
Grade 4 - Craft Grade
Grade 5 - Supervisory Grade
Grade 6 - Farm Management Grade

Higher rates apply to Full Time and Part Time Flexible Workers.

Source: Department for Environment, Food and Rural Affairs

24.12 Number of people working on commercial agricultural holdings: 2010 - onwards [a]

Thousands

	2010	2011	2012	2013	2014	2015
Total labour force (incl. farmers and spouses)	**466**	**476**	**481**	**464**	**476**	**476**
Farmers, business partners, directors and spouses	**295**	**299**	**298**	**290**	**294**	**294**
Full time	134	140	141	138	140	142
Part time [b]	161	159	158	152	155	152
Regular employees, salaried managers and casual workers	**171**	**177**	**183**	**173**	**181**	**183**
Regular employees [c]	**115**	**115**	**116**	**112**	**115**	**115**
Full time	72	73	73	71	72	73
Part time [b]	42	42	44	41	43	43
Seasonal, casual or gang labour	**56**	**62**	**67**	**61**	**66**	**67**

Source: Department for Environment, Food and Rural Affairs

(a) Figures for England relate to commercial holdings only.
(b) Part-time is defined as working less than 39 hours per week (England & Wales), 38 hours per week (Scotland) and 30 hours per week (N. Ireland). (c) Not all UK countries collect separate estimates for salaried managers. These figures are included with regular employees.

24.13 Summary of UK fishing industry: 2006 to 2015

£ million (unless otherwise specified)

	2006	2007	2008	2009	2010	2011	2012	2013	2014	2015
Fleet size at end of year [a]										
(no. of vessels)	6,752	6,763	6,573	6,500	6,477	6,444	6,406	6,399	6,383	6,187
Employment										
(no. of fishermen)	12,934	12,871	12,614	12,212	12,703	12,405	12,445	12,235	11,845	12,107
Total landings by UK vessels [b]										
Quantity ('000 tonnes)	619.6	613.9	587.2	582.9	605.3	596.0	628.0	626.8 R	757.9 R	708.1
Value (£ million)	614.3	646.3	634.5	679.6	720.3	832.0 R	787.9 R	741.3 R	864.1 R	775.1
Imports										
Quantity ('000 tonnes)	753.3	747.9	781.7	720.6	703.8	720.2	754.5	739.4	721.9 R	680.8
Value (£ million) [c]	1,920.6	1,993.9	2,210.1	2,177.2	2,254.7	2,558.6	2,570.0	2,757.0	2,737.8 R	2673.0
Exports										
Quantity ('000 tonnes)	415.6	466.9	415.8	479.7	516.7	436.1	465.9	452.1	501.8 R	443.3
Value (£ million) [c]	942.2	982.0	1009.4	1166.1	1,345.7	1,463.9	1,343.9	1,460.3	1,566.3 R	1337.3
Total household consumption										
of fish ('000 tonnes) [d]	519	515	510	501	483	472	467	481	479	nd
Population ('000 persons) [j]	58,603	59,737	60,816	60,907	61,464	61,528	61,946	63,421	63,879	nd
Total consumer expenditure										
on fish (£ million)	3,410	3,599	3,650	3,711	3,742	3,866	3,998	4,271	4,309	nd
on food (£ million) [e]	74,193	77,716	67,635	70,143	72,587	73,744	77,523	81,291	80,669	nd
Fish as a % of food [e]	4.6%	4.6%	5.4%	5.3%	5.2%	5.2%	5.2%	5.3%	5.3%	nd
Landed Price Index [f]	134.4	136.2	141.1	141.7	152.2	163.7	153.9	146.9	142.7	150.2
Retail Price Index [g]	108.5	115.7	124.0	130.3	138.3	151.0	157.4	163.4	168.2	163.2
Consumer Price Index [h]	111.4	120.7	126.7	131.4	140.0	152.9	158.4	163.6	167.8	161.9
GDP for Fishing [i]										
Current price gross value added at basic prices (KK37)	465 R	481 R	468 R	472 R	582 R	489 R	506 R	529 R	615 R	604
Output index (chain volume measures) (L2KO) (2009=100)	92.7 R	99.5 R	94.6 R	96.8 R	100.0 R	100.5 R	100.3 R	100.0 R	113.5 R	112.2
GDP for Agriculture, Forestry and Fishing										
Current price gross value added at basic prices (KKD5)	8,123 R	8,658 R	9,859 R	8,337 R	10,332 R	9,858 R	9,973 R	11,093 R	10,998 R	10,796
Output index (chain volume measures) (L2KL) (2011=100)	100.4 R	96.7 R	103.4 R	97.1 R	96.5 R	107.1 R	99.3 R	100.0 R	113.9 R	115.1
GDP at Market Prices										
Current price GDP at market prices (KKP5) (£ billion)	1,311 R	1,378 R	1,414 R	1,382 R	1,415 R	1,452 R	1,496 R	1,552 R	1,624 R	1,661
Chain volume measures index (YBEZ) (2013=100)	96.0 R	98.5 R	97.9 R	93.6 R	95.4 R	96.9 R	98.1 R	100 R	103.1 R	105.4
Percentage contribution of GVA from fishing to GVA for agriculture, hunting, forestry and fishing										
Current prices (%)	5.7% R	5.6% R	4.7% R	5.7% R	5.6% R	5.0% R	5.1% R	4.8% R	5.6% R	5.6%

Source: Fisheries Administrations in the UK, H.M. Customs and Excise, Expenditure and Food Survey, Office for National Statistics

(a) The number of vessels includes those registered in the Channel Islands and Isle of Man.

(b) The quantity of landed fish is expressed in terms of liveweight. The figures relate to landings both into the UK and abroad.

(c) Imports are valued at cost, including insurance and freight terms whereas exports are valued at free on board terms.

(d) Figures for 2005 are based on financial year data.

(e) Including non-alcoholic beverages.

(f) The landed price index has been calculated on an annual basis with 2000 = 100.

(g) The fish component of the RPI which includes canned and processed fish. The index has been re-based such that 2000 = 100.

(h) The fish component of the CPI which includes canned and processed fish. The index has been re-based such that 2000 = 100.

(i) GDP for fishing includes landings abroad, according to the KK37 index.

(j) The population estimate has been updated to be consistent with the Living Costs and Food Survey figures, which provide the basis for the household consumption and consumers expenditure figures given in this table.

24.14 UK Fishing Fleet [1]

UK Fleet as of 1st January	2011	2012	2013	2014	2015
By Size					
Total	**6474**	**6428**	**6428**	**6420**	**6276**
10m and under	5042	5038	5048	5049	4926
10 - 12m	404	407	412	403	393
12 - 18m	499	486	480	479	475
18 - 24m	273	250	243	246	245
24 - 40m	199	190	191	190	183
40m and over	57	57	54	53	54
By Segment					
Drift and/or fixed netters	731	717	636	664	650
Dredgers	283	267	291	301	307
Demersal trawlers and/or demersal seiners	905	889	855	828	812
Vessels using pots and/or traps	2105	2011	1991	1994	1978
Vessels using hooks	519	574	565	496	552
Vessels using polyvalent active gears only	37	39	30	39	58
Vessels using polyvalent passive gears only	86	77	92	80	64
Vessels using active and passive gears	7	8	6	9	6
Purse seiners	40	41	37		3
Beam trawlers	83	96	93	83	73
Pelagic trawlers				37	33
Inactive during previous year	1678	1709	1832	1889	1740
Total UK Fleet	**6474**	**6428**	**6428**	**6420**	**6276**

Source: Marine Management Organisation

1 Includes Channel Islands and Isle of Man

2 An inactive vessel is defined as a registered vessel that has not undertaken fishing activity in the reference year

24.15 Estimated household food consumption[1]

Grammes per person per week

		Great Britain					United Kingdom		
		1997	1998	1999	2000		2003 /04	2004 /05	2005 /06
Liquid wholemilk[2] (ml)	KPQM	712	693	634	664	VQEW	585	484	460
Fully skimmed (ml)	KZBH	158	164	167	164	VQEX	154	158	159
Semi skimmed (ml)	KZBI	978	945	958	975	VQEZ	926	975	1008
Other milk and cream (ml)	KZBJ	248	243	248	278	VQFA	358	366	385
Cheese	KPQO	109	104	104	110	VQFB	113	110	116
Butter	KPQP	38	39	37	39	VQFC	35	35	38
Margarine	KPQQ	26	26	20	21	VQFD	12	11	20
Low and reduced fat spreads	KZBK	77	69	71	68	VQFE	71	68	55
All other oils and fats (ml for oils)	KPQR	62	62	58	58	VQFF	68	68	70
Eggs (number)	KPQS	2	2	2	2	VQFG	2	2	2
Preserves and honey	KPQT	41	38	33	33	VQFH	33	34	35
Sugar	KPQU	128	119	107	105	VQFI	102	99	94
Beef and veal	KPQV	110	109	110	124	VQFJ	119	123	120
Mutton and lamb	KPQW	56	59	57	55	VQFK	49	50	53
Pork	KPQX	75	76	69	68	VQFL	56	56	52
Bacon and ham, uncooked	KPQY	72	76	68	71	VQFM	70	70	68
Bacon and ham, cooked (including canned)	KPQZ	41	40	39	41	VQFN	47	43	44
Poultry uncooked	JZCH	221	218	201	214	VQFO	200	197	212
Cooked poultry (not purchased in cans)	KYBP	33	33	35	39	VQFQ	48	49	48
Other cooked and canned meats	KPRB	52	49	48	51	VQFR	60	58	56
Offals	KPRC	7	5	5	5	VQFS	7	5	5
Sausages, uncooked	KPRD	63	60	58	60	VQFT	70	67	64
Other meat products	KPRE	209	216	221	239	VQFU	335	330	323
Fish, fresh and processed (including shellfish)	KPRF	70	70	70	67				
Canned fish	KPRG	31	29	31	32				
Fish and fish products, frozen	KPRH	46	46	42	44				
Fish, fresh chilled or frozen						VQAI	45	42	45
Other fish and fish products						VQAJ	111	115	122
Potatoes (excluding processed)	KPRI	745	715	673	707	VQFY	600	570	587
Fresh green vegetables	KPRJ	251	246	245	240	VQAK	228	225	235
Other fresh vegetables	KPRK	497	486	500	492	VQAL	505	536	567
Frozen potato products	KYBQ	106	111	113	120				
Other frozen vegetables	KPRL	94	88	87	80				
Potato products not frozen	JZCF	90	89	86	82				
Canned beans	KPRM	122	118	112	114				
Other canned vegetables (excl. potatoes)	KPRN	104	99	92	97				
Other processed vegetables (excl. potatoes)	LQZH	52	54	59	54				
All processed vegetables						VQAM	611	597	608
Apples	KPRO	179	181	169	180	VQGN	171	173	179
Bananas	KPRP	195	198	202	206	VQGO	211	217	225
Oranges	KPRQ	62	63	50	54	VQGP	64	57	59
All other fresh fruit	KPRR	276	274	290	304	VQGS	343	358	392
Canned fruit	KPRS	44	37	38	38	VQGT	40	38	36
Dried fruit, nuts and fruit and nut products	KPRT	35	34	30	35	VQGU	40	46	51
Fruit juices (ml)	KPRU	277	304	284	303	VQGX	322	280	350
Flour	KPRV	54	55	56	67	VQGY	52	55	60
Bread	KPRW	746	742	717	720	VQGZ	728	695	701
Buns, scones and teacakes	KPRX	43	41	40	43	VQHA	44	47	46
Cakes and pastries	KPRY	93	88	87	89	VQHB	120	117	122
Biscuits	KPRZ	138	137	132	141	VQHC	163	165	165
Breakfast cereals	KPSA	135	136	134	143	VQHE	134	131	135
Oatmeal and oat products	KPSB	16	11	13	15	VQHF	12	14	19
Other cereals and cereal products	JZCG	293	270	284	291	VQHG	360	354	378
Tea	KPSC	36	35	32	34	VQHK	31	31	33
Instant coffee	KPSD	11	12	11	11	VQHL	13	13	13
Canned soups	KPSE	70	71	67	71	VQHM	77	76	82
Pickles and sauces	KPSF	92	96	91	107	VQHN	121	120	125

1 See chapter text.
2 Including also school and welfare milk (pre-2001-02)

24.15 Estimated household food consumption[1]

Grammes per person per week
United Kingdom

		2006	2007	2008	2009	2010	2011	2012	2013	2014	2015
Liquid wholemilk[2] (ml)	VQEW	477	420	410	412	352	355	297	285	263	312
Fully skimmed (ml)	VQEX	163	173	158	165	172	167	158	155	154	145
Semi skimmed (ml)	VQEZ	974	982	987	991	985	984	1051	996	1045	964
Other milk and cream (ml)	VQFA	395	397	392	427	389	398	394	410	387	407
Cheese	VQFB	116	119	111	116	118	118	114	118	111	112
Butter	VQFC	40	41	40	39	40	40	41	42	40	43
Margarine	VQFD	18	19	22	24	23	20	24	23	18	17
Low and reduced fat spreads	VQFE	57	53	51	48	49	46	43	38	39	35
All other oils and fats (ml for oils)	VQFF	69	68	72	71	71	63	71	67	61	67
Eggs (number)	VQFG	2	2	2	2	2	2	2	2	2	2
Preserves and honey	VQFH	34	33	34	35	36	33	32	31	31	31
Sugar	VQFI	92	92	93	90	90	93	91	91	78	75
Beef and veal	VQFJ	128	126	111	112	114	112	104	97	101	103
Mutton and lamb	VQFK	54	55	45	46	44	37	36	35	37	35
Pork	VQFL	55	54	55	54	53	56	55	51	57	50
Bacon and ham, uncooked	VQFM	66	64	63	68	70	69	68	64	62	60
Bacon and ham, cooked (including canned)	VQFN	45	45	45	43	43	43	40	39	40	39
Poultry uncooked	VQFO	207	208	207	205	201	206	214	203	206	198
Cooked poultry (not purchased in cans)	VQFQ	48	43	44	41	41	41	37	38	35	33
Other cooked and canned meats	VQFR	53	50	51	51	48	46	44	43	42	38
Offals	VQFS	5	5	5	6	5	7	6	5	5	4
Sausages, uncooked	VQFT	65	65	62	65	66	64	67	61	59	56
Other meat products	VQFU	315	316	311	309	331	318	317	313	311	314
Fish, fresh and processed (including shellfish)											
Canned fish											
Fish and fish products, frozen											
Fish, fresh chilled or frozen	VQAI	47	43	43	41	38	34	37	36	39	37
Other fish and fish products	VQAJ	123	122	118	117	113	113	108	110	105	110
Potatoes (excluding processed)	VQFY	565	537	535	514	501	496	478	439	431	429
Fresh green vegetables	VQAK	221	224	203	201	192	189	183	179	181	182
Other fresh vegetables	VQAL	566	566	557	552	565	550	551	569	564	576
Frozen potato products											
Other frozen vegetables											
Potato products not frozen											
Canned beans											
Other canned vegetables (excl. potatoes)											
Other processed vegetables (excl. potatoes)											
All processed vegetables	VQAM	601	594	599	597	592	601	597	597	574	592
Apples	VQGN	180	178	162	163	156	149	135	137	131	136
Bananas	VQGO	226	230	219	205	204	220	214	219	221	216
Oranges	VQGP	55	59	49	45	47	48	50	47	48	48
All other fresh fruit	VQGS	394	389	360	348	348	347	346	340	365	374
Canned fruit	VQGT	39	35	32	29	30	30	29	26	26	27
Dried fruit, nuts and fruit and nut products	VQGU	53	51	52	51	52	49	51	56	57	56
Fruit juices (ml)	VQGX	366	340	325	302	296	307	282	288	247	235
Flour	VQGY	54	54	63	58	58	71	73	57	52	60
Bread	VQGZ	692	677	659	656	634	621	615	607	555	544
Buns, scones and teacakes	VQHA	45	44	43	47	45	46	45	47	48	49
Cakes and pastries	VQHB	120	115	111	111	108	105	105	103	99	105
Biscuits	VQHC	165	163	170	169	162	164	160	165	162	164
Breakfast cereals	VQHE	135	130	130	133	133	132	128	127	126	126
Oatmeal and oat products	VQHF	17	19	20	21	21	20	22	24	23	23
Other cereals and cereal products	VQHG	378	387	386	393	402	395	392	398	411	417
Tea	VQHK	30	30	30	29	28	27	26	25	25	24
Instant coffee	VQHL	14	13	14	15	15	14	13	14	12	13
Canned soups	VQHM	79	79	76	78	76	75	85	79	70	71
Pickles and sauces	VQHN	128	129	130	132	131	131	129	130	128	126

Sources: Living Costs and Food Survey;
Department for Environment Food and Rural Affairs;
Office for National Statistics.
Contact: 020802 66129

familyfood@defra.gsi.gov.uk

Sources:

This index of sources gives the titles of official publications or other sources containing statistics allied to those in the tables of this Annual Abstract. These publications provide more detailed analyses than are shown in the Annual Abstract. This index includes publications to which reference should be made for short–term (monthly or quarterly) series.

Table number	Government department or other organisation

Chapter 1: Area

1.1	ONS Geography Codes; Office for National Statistics - Standard Area Measurement for UK Local Authority Districts (SAM 2015)

Chapter 2: Parliamentary elections

2.1	British Electoral Facts 1832-2012; Plymouth University for the Electoral Commission
2.2a	Chronology of British Parliamentary By-elections 1833-1987; British Electoral Facts 1832-2006;
	House of Commons Library, RP10/50 By-election results 2005-10; SN05833 By-elections since 2010 General Election
2.2b	British Parliamentary Election Results; House of Commons Library By-election results
2.3a	House of Commons Library Briefing Paper CBP7594, National Assembly for Wales Elections: 2016
2.3b	British Electoral Facts 1832-2006; House of Commons Library
2.4	British Electoral Facts 1832-2006; Electoral Office for Northern Ireland

Chapter 3 International Development

3.1	Department for International Development
3.2	Department for International Development
3.3	Department for International Development

Chapter 4 Labour Market

4.1	Labour Force Survey, Office for National Statistics
4.2	Labour Force Survey, Office for National Statistics
4.3	Labour Force Survey, Office for National Statistics
4.4	Labour Force Survey, Office for National Statistics
4.5a	Eurostat, OECD, National Statistical Offices. Labour market statistics
4.5b	Labour Disputes Inquiry, Office for National Statistics
4.6	Annual Civil Service Employment Survey, Office for National Statistics
4.7	Labour Force Survey, Office for National Statistics
4.8	Labour Force Survey, Office for National Statistics
4.9	Office for National Statistics
4.10	Labour Market Statistics,Office for National Statistics; Nomisweb
4.11a	Annual Survey of Hours and Earnings, Office for National Statistics
4.11b	Annual Survey of Hours and Earnings, Office for National Statistics
4.12a	Annual Survey of Hours and Earnings, Office for National Statistics
4.12b	Annual Survey of Hours and Earnings, Office for National Statistics
4.13	Office for National Statistics
4.14a	Monthly wages and salaries survey
4.14b	Monthly wages and salaries survey
4.14c	Monthly wages and salaries survey
4.14d	Monthly wages and salaries survey
4.15a	Annual Survey of Hours and Earnings, Office for National Statistics
4.15b	Annual Survey of Hours and Earnings, Office for National Statistics
4.16	Annual Survey of Hours and Earnings, Office for National Statistics
4.17	Certification Officer Annual Report 2015/16

Chapter 5 Social Protection

5.1	HM Revenue and Customs; Department for Work and Pensions
5.2	HM Revenue and Customs; National Insurance Fund Account Great Britain
5.3	HM Revenue and Customs
5.4	Department for Work and Pensions
5.5	Department for Work and Pensions
5.6	Department for Work and Pensions
5.7	Department for Work and Pensions Work and Pensions Longitudinal Study 100% data
5.8	Department for Work and Pensions (DWP); Work and Pensions Longitudinal Study (WPLS)
5.9a	HM Revenue and Customs

Table number	Government department or other organisation
9.16	Community Life Survey, Cabinet Office
9.17	International Passenger Survey, Office for National Statistics
9.18	Office for National Statistics
9.19	RAJAR

Chapter 10 Environment

10.1	Ricardo Energy & Environment, Office for National Statistics
10.2	Ricardo Energy & Environment, Office for National Statistics
10.3	Department of Energy and Climate Change
10.4	Ricardo Energy and Environment, Department for Business, Energy & Industrial Strategy, Office for National Statistics
10.5	Department of Energy and Climate Change
10.6	Department of Energy and Climate Change
10.7	Department of Energy and Climate Change
10.8	Department for Environment, Food and Rural Affairs; Food and Agriculture Organization of the United Nations; Eurostat; Kentish Cobnuts Association; British Geological Survey; HM Revenue & Customs; Office for National Statistics;
10.9	Met Office; National Hydrological Monitoring Programme, Centre for Ecology and Hydrology
10.10	Met Office
10.11	Environment Agency
10.12	Scottish Environment Protection Agency
10.13	Water PLCs; Environment Agency; National Hydrological Monitoring Programme, Centre for Ecology and Hydrology
10.14a	Office of Water Services (OFWAT)
10.14b	Office of Water Services (OFWAT)
10.15	Environment Agency
10.16	Environment Agency
10.17	Environment Agency
10.18	Office for National Statistics; Department of Energy and Climate Change
10.19a	Department for Environment, Food and Rural Affairs
10.19b	WasteDataFlow, Natural Resources Wales
10.19c	Scottish Environment Protection Agency
10.19d	Northern Ireland Environment Agency, NISRA, LPS
10.20a	Department for Environment Food and Rural affairs
10.20b	Department for Environment Food and Rural affairs; Office for National Statistics
10.20c	WasteDataFlow, Department for Environment, Food and Rural Affairs
10.20d	Department for Environment Food and Rural affairs
10.21	The Chartered Institute of Environmental Health
10.22	Office for National Statistics

Chapter 11 Housing

11.1a	Department for Communities and Local Government
11.1b	Welsh Assembly Government
11.1c	Scottish Government
11.1d	Continuous Household Survey
11.2	Department or Communities and Local Government; Welsh Assembly Government; Scottish Government; Department for Social Development (NI)
11.3	P2 returns from local authorities; National House Building Council (NHBC); Approved inspector data returns; Welsh Assembly Government; Scottish Government; Department of Finance and Personnel (DFPNI); District Council Building Control (NI)
11.4a	Department for Communities and Local Government
11.4b	Welsh Government
11.5	HM Courts and Tribunals Service CaseMan; Possession Claim OnLine (PCOL); Council of Mortgage Lenders (CML)
11.6	Compendium of Housing Finance Statistics; Housing Finance and CML website; Council of Mortgage Lenders
11.7	Department for Communities and Local Government
11.8	Welsh Government, Homelessness data collection
11.9	Scottish Government

Chapter 12 Banking and Finance

12.1a	Bank of England
12.1b	Bank of England
12.2a	UK Payments Administration Ltd
12.2b	UK Payments Administration Ltd
12.2c	UK Payments Administration Ltd
12.2d	UK Payments Administration Ltd
12.2e	UK Payments Administration Ltd
12.2f	UK Payments Administration Ltd
12.3a	Bank of England
12.3b	Bank of England
12.3c	Bank of England
12.3d	Bank of England
12.3e	Bank of England

Table number	Government department or other organisation
12.3f	Bank of England
12.3g	Bank of England
12.3h	Bank of England
12.4a	Bank of England
12.4b	Bank of England
12.4c	Bank of England
12.4d	Bank of England
12.5a	Bank of England
12.5b	Bank of England
12.6a	Bank of England
12.6b	Bank of England
12.7	Bank of England
12.8	Bank of England
12.9	Bank of England
12.10	Bank of England
12.11	Bank of England
12.12	Bank of England
12.13a	Office for National Statistics
12.13b	Office for National Statistics
12.14	Office for National Statistics
12.15a	Office for National Statistics
12.15b	Office for National Statistics
12.16a	Insolvency Service
12.16b	Accountant in Bankruptcy (AiB), Companies House
12.16c	Department for Enterprise, Trade and Investment, Northern Ireland (DETINI)
12.17a	Insolvency Service; Companies House
12.17b	Companies House
12.17c	Department for Enterprise, Trade and Investment Northern Ireland (DETINI); Companies House
12.18a	Bank of England
12.18b	Bank of England
12.18c	Bank of England
12.18d	Bank of England
12.19	Bank of England
12.20	Mergers and Acquisitions Surveys, Office for National Statistics

Chapter 13 Services

13.1a	Annual Business Survey (ABS), Office for National Statistics
13.1b	Annual Business Survey (ABS), Office for National Statistics
13.2	Office for National Statistics
13.3	Annual Business Survey (ABS), Office for National Statistics
13.4	Annual Business Survey (ABS), Office for National Statistics

Chapter 14 Defence

14.1	Defence Economics (Defence Expenditure Analysis) and Defence Resources, Ministry of Defence
14.2	Defence Statistics (Tri-Service), Ministry of Defence
14.3a	Navy Command, Ministry of Defence
14.3b	Army Org Branch, Ministry of Defence
14.3c	Navy Command; Army Org Branch; Air Command
14.3d	MOD Finance & Military Capability
14.4	Defence Statistics (Tri-Service), Ministry of Defence
14.5	Defence Statistics (Tri-Service), Ministry of Defence
14.6a	Defence Statistics (Tri-Service), Ministry of Defence
14.6b	Defence Statistics (Civilian), Ministry of Defence
14.6c	Defence Statistics (Civilian), Ministry of Defence
14.7a	MOD Defence Infrastructure Organisation, Ministry of Defence
14.7b	MOD Defence Infrastructure Organisation, Ministry of Defence
14.8a	Defence Statistics (Tri-Service), Ministry of Defence
14.8b	Defence Statistics (Tri-Service), Ministry of Defence
14.9a	Defence Statistics (Health), Ministry of Defence
14.9b	Defence Statistics (Health), Ministry of Defence
14.10a	UK Defence Statistics, Ministry of Defence
14.10b	UK Defence Statistics, ARCC Database, Ministry of Defence
14.10c	UK Defence Statistics, ARCC Database, Ministry of Defence
14.10d	HQ Surgeon General
14.11	Marine Management Organisation

Table number	Government department or other organisation

Chapter 18 Production

18.1	Annual Business Survey (ABS), Office for National Statistics
18.2	PRODCOM , Office for National Statistics
18.3	Office for National Statistics
18.4	Department for Business, Energy & Industrial Strategy
18.5	Department for Business, Energy & Industrial Strategy
18.6	Department for Business, Energy & Industrial Strategy
18.7	Department for Business, Energy & Industrial Strategy
18.8	Department for Business, Energy & Industrial Strategy
18.9	Department for Business, Energy & Industrial Strategy
18.10	Department for Business, Energy & Industrial Strategy
18.11	Department for Business, Energy & Industrial Strategy
18.12	Department for Business, Energy & Industrial Strategy
18.13	Department for Business, Energy & Industrial Strategy
18.14	International Steel Statistics Bureau
18.15	International Steel Statistics Bureau
18.16	International Steel Statistics Bureau
18.17	British Survey of Fertiliser Practice (Defra)
18.18a	Office for National Statistics, Department of Business, Innovation and Skills; Dept. of Enterprise, Trade & Investment (Northern Ireland), Crown Estate Commissioners
18.18b	Department of Enterprise, Trade & Investment (Northern Ireland); Department of Economic Development (Isle of Man), Company data (Guernsey and Jersey)
18.19a	Department for Business, Energy & Industrial Strategy
18.19b	Department for Business, Energy & Industrial Strategy
18.19c	Department for Business, Energy & Industrial Strategy
18.19d	Department for Business, Energy & Industrial Strategy
18.19e	Department for Business, Energy & Industrial Strategy
18.19f	Department for Business, Energy & Industrial Strategy
18.20	Office for National Statistics
18.21	Office for National Statistics
18.22	Office for National Statistics
18.23	Office for National Statistics
18.24	Her Majesty's Revenue and Customs
18.25	Her Majesty's Revenue and Customs

Chapter 19 National Accounts

19.1	Blue Book 2016, Office for National Statistics
19.2	Blue Book 2016, Office for National Statistics
19.3	Blue Book 2016, Office for National Statistics
19.4	Blue Book 2016, Office for National Statistics
19.5	Blue Book 2016, Office for National Statistics
19.6	Blue Book 2016, Office for National Statistics
19.7	Blue Book 2016, Office for National Statistics
19.8	Blue Book 2016, Office for National Statistics
19.9	Blue Book 2016, Office for National Statistics
19.10	Blue Book 2016, Office for National Statistics
19.11	Blue Book 2016, Office for National Statistics
19.12	Blue Book 2016, Office for National Statistics
19.13	Blue Book 2016, Office for National Statistics
19.14	Blue Book 2016, Office for National Statistics
19.15	Blue Book 2016, Office for National Statistics
19.16	Blue Book 2016, Office for National Statistics
19.17	Blue Book 2016, Office for National Statistics
19.18	Office for National Statistics
19.19	Blue Book 2016, Office for National Statistics
19.20	Blue Book 2016, Office for National Statistics
19.21	Blue Book 2016, Office for National Statistics
19.22	Blue Book 2016, Office for National Statistics

Chapter 20 Education

20.1	Department for Education; Welsh Government; Scottish Government; Northern Ireland Department of Education
20.2	Department for Education; Welsh Government; Scottish Government; Northern Ireland Department of Education
20.3	Department for Education; Welsh Government; Scottish Government; Northern Ireland Department of Education
20.4	School Census and School Level Annual School Census, Department for Education
20.5	Department for Education; Welsh Government; Scottish Government; Northern Ireland Department of Education
20.6	Higher Education Statistics Agency Limited
20.7	Higher Education Statistics Agency Limited
20.8	Department for Education; Welsh Government; Scottish Funding Council; Northern Ireland Department for the Economy